WILKINSON

ROAD TRAFFI
OFFENCES

WILKINSON'S
ROAD TRAFFIC OFFENCES

Twenty-fifth Edition

VOLUME 2

Prepared by KATHRYN SWIFT, LL.B.

General Editor
KEVIN McCORMAC, O.B.E., M.A.
of Gray's Inn, Barrister

SWEET & MAXWELL   THOMSON REUTERS

Published in 2011 by
Sweet & Maxwell
100 Avenue Road, London NW3 3PF
part of Thomson Reuters (Professional) UK Limited
(Registered in England & Wales, Company No 1679046.
Registered Office and address for service:
Aldgate House, 33 Aldgate High Street, London EC3N 1DL)

Tables typeset by Servis Filmsetting Ltd, Manchester

All other typesetting by Sweet & Maxwell Ltd, 100 Avenue Road, London, NW3 3PF
Printed and bound by CPI Group (UK) Ltd, Croydon, CR0 4YY

For further information on our products and services, visit
www.sweetandmaxwell.co.uk

No natural forests were destroyed to make this product; only farmed timber
was used and replanted.

A CIP catalogue record of this book is available from the British Library.

ISBN 9780414045774

Twenty-fifth Edition 2011

CONTENTS

TABLE OF CASES

TABLE OF STATUTES

*All entries are tabled to paragraph number. Paragraph numbers in **bold** type indicate where the entry is reproduced.*

TABLE OF STATUTORY INSTRUMENTS

*All entries are tabled to paragraph number. Paragraph numbers in **bold** type indicate where the entry is reproduced.*

TABLE OF EUROPEAN PROVISIONS

*All entries are tabled to paragraph number. Paragraph numbers in **bold** type indicate where the entry is reproduced.*

Treaties

Regulations

Directives

Decisions

EC Commission and Council Decisions

EEA Joint Committee Decisions

TABLE OF INTERNATIONAL CONVENTIONS AND AGREEMENTS

*All entries are tabled to paragraph number. Paragraph numbers in **bold** type indicate where the entry is reproduced.*

Section A

Statutes

Road Traffic Offenders Act 1988
  (1988 c.53)
    ss.1–9, 11–18, 20, 22, 24–30, 30A–30D, 31, 33, 34,
      34A–34G, 35, 35A, 35B, 36–40, 41A, 41B, 42–44,
      44A, 45, 45A, 46–49, 51–57, 57A, 58, 58A, 59, 61,
      61A, 62–77, 77A, 78–83, 84A, 85, 86, 89, 90,
      90A–90D, 90F, 91, 91ZA, 91ZB, 91A, 91B, 92–94,
      96, 97, 97A, 98, 99, Schs 1–4   A19.01
Road Traffic Regulation Act 1984
  (1984 c.27)
    ss.5–8, 11, 14, 16, 16A–16C, 17, 25, 28, 35, 35A, 35B,
      46, 47–49, 51, 52, 61, 64, 81–89, 96, 99, 104, 105,
      106A, 107–112, 115–117, 121A, 130, 136–138, 140,
      141A, 142, 144, Schs 6, 8, 10, 11   A13.01
Theft Act 1968
  (1968 c.60)
    ss.12, 12A, 25   A3.01
Town Police Clauses Act 1847
  (10 & 11 Vict. c.89)
    s.38   A1.01
Transport Act 1968
  (1968 c.73)
    ss.95–97, 97A, 97AA, 97B–97H, 98, 99, 99ZA–99ZF,
      99A–99C, 102, 102A–102C, 103   A4.01
Transport Act 1985
  (1985 c.67)
    ss.2, 11–13, 13A, 18, 19, 21–23, 23A, 30, 34–36, 38, 39,
      127, 137, Schs 1, 7   A16.01
Transport and Works Act 1992
  (1992 c.42)
    ss.58, 59   A23.01
Vehicle Excise and Registration Act 1994
  (1994 c.22)
    ss.1, 2, 5, 7, 9–12, 14–15, 15A, 16–18, 19A, 19B, 20, 23,
      24, 26, 27, 27A, 28, 28A, 29–31, 31A–31C, 32,
      32A, 33–35, 35A, 36–43, 43A, 43B, 43C, 44–46,
      46A, 47, 49–51, 51A, 52, 53, 55, 59, 60A, 61, 61B,
      62, 64, 67, Schs 1, 2, 2A, 4   A24.01

The Town Police Clauses Act 1847

(10 & 11 VICT. C.89)

An Act for consolidating in one Act certain provisions usually contained in Acts for regulating the police of towns.   **A1.01**

[22nd July 1847]

*   *   *

What vehicles to be deemed hackney carriages

38. Every wheeled carriage, whatever may be its form or construction, used in standing or plying for hire in any street within the prescribed distance, and every carriage standing upon any street within the prescribed distance, having thereon any numbered plate required by this or the special Act to be fixed upon a hackney carriage, or having thereon any plate resembling or intended to resemble any such plate as aforesaid, shall be deemed to be a hackney carriage within the meaning of this Act; and in all proceedings at law or otherwise the term *"hackney carriage"* shall be sufficient to describe any such carriage: **A1.02**

Provided always, that no stage coach used for the purpose of standing or plying for passengers to be carried for hire at separate fares, and duly licensed for that purpose, and having thereon the proper numbered plates required by law to be placed on such stage coaches, shall be deemed to be a hackney carriage within the meaning of this Act.

[The definition of "hackney carriage" in this Act is incorporated by reference into s.80 of the Local Government (Miscellaneous Provisions) Act 1976 (q.v.).]   **A1.03**

The Criminal Law Act 1967

(1967 c.58)

A2.01 *An Act to amend the law in England and Wales by abolishing the division of crimes into felonies and misdemeanours and to amend and simplify the law in respect of matters arising from or related to that division or the abolition of it … and for purposes connected therewith.*

[21st July 1967]

* * *

Trial of offences

A2.02   **6.**—(1) *[Plea on indictment; failure to plead.]*

(2) *[Alternative verdicts on indictment for murder.]*

(3) Where, on a person's trial on indictment for any offence except treason or murder, the jury find him not guilty of the offence specifically charged in the indictment, but the allegations in the indictment amount to or include (expressly or by implication) an allegation of another offence falling within the jurisdiction of the court of trial, the jury may find him guilty of that other offence or of an offence of which he could be found guilty on an indictment specifically charging that other offence.

[(3A) *[Common assault, etc. as an alternative verdict.]*]

[(3B) *[Common assault, etc. as an alternative verdict.]*]

(4) For purposes of subsection (3) above any allegation of an offence shall be taken as including an allegation of attempting to commit that offence; and where a person is charged on indictment with attempting to commit an offence or with any assault or other act preliminary to an offence, but not with the completed offence, then (subject to the discretion of the court to discharge the jury [or otherwise act] with a view to the preferment of an indictment for the completed offence) he may be convicted of the offence charged notwithstanding that he is shown to be guilty of the completed offence.

(5) Where a person arraigned on an indictment pleads not guilty of an offence charged in the indictment but guilty of some other offence of which he might be found guilty on that charge, and he is convicted on that plea of guilty without trial for the offence of which he has pleaded not guilty, then (whether or not the two offences are separately charged in distinct counts) his conviction of the one offence shall be an acquittal of the other.

(6) *[Abolition of proceedings by criminal information.]*

(7) Subsections (1) to (3) above shall apply to an indictment containing more than one count as if each count were a separate indictment.

A2.03   *[Section 6 is printed as amended by the Criminal Justice Act 2003 s.331 and Sch.36. para.41; the Domestic Violence, Crime and Victims Act 2004 s.11.*

Section 6(3) is expressly saved by the Road Traffic Offenders Act 1988 s.24(1).]

The Theft Act 1968

(1968 c.60)

An Act to revise the law of England and Wales as to theft and similar or associated offences ... **A3.01**

[26th July 1968]

* * *

Taking motor vehicle or other conveyance without authority

12.—(1) Subject to subsections (5) and (6) below, a person shall be guilty of **A3.02** an offence if, without having the consent of the owner or other lawful authority, he takes any conveyance for his own or another's use or, knowing that any conveyance has been taken without such authority, drives it or allows himself to be carried in or on it.

(2) A person guilty of an offence under subsection (1) above shall [be liable on summary conviction to a fine not exceeding level 5 on the standard scale, to imprisonment for a term not exceeding six months, or to both].

(3) [...]

(4) If on the trial of an indictment for theft the jury are not satisfied that the accused committed theft, but it is proved that the accused committed an offence under subsection (1) above, the jury may find him guilty of the offence under subsection (1) [and if he is found guilty of it, he shall be liable as he would have been liable under subsection (2) above on summary conviction].

[(4A) Proceedings for an offence under subsection (1) above (but not proceedings of a kind falling within subsection (4) above) in relation to a mechanically propelled vehicle—

  (a) shall not be commenced after the end of the period of three years beginning with the day on which the offence was committed; but

  (b) subject to that, may be commenced at any time within the period of six months beginning with the relevant day.]

[(4B) In subsection (4A)(b) above *"the relevant day"* means—

  (a) in the case of a prosecution for an offence under subsection (1) above by a public prosecutor, the day on which sufficient evidence to justify the proceedings came to the knowledge of any person responsible for deciding whether to commence any such prosecution;

  (b) in the case of a prosecution for an offence under subsection (1) above which is commenced by a person other than a public prosecutor after the discontinuance of a prosecution falling within paragraph (a) above which relates to the same facts, the day on which sufficient evidence to justify the proceedings came to the knowledge of the person who has decided to commence the prosecution or (if later) the discontinuance of the other prosecution;

  (c) in the case of any other prosecution for an offence under subsection

(1) above, the day on which sufficient evidence to justify the proceedings came to the knowledge of the person who has decided to commence the prosecution.]

[(4C) For the purposes of subsection (4A)(b) above a certificate of a person responsible for deciding whether to commence a prosecution of a kind mentioned in subsection (4B)(a) above as to the date on which such evidence as is mentioned in the certificate came to the knowledge of any person responsible for deciding whether to commence any such prosecution shall be conclusive evidence of that fact.]

(5) Subsection (1) above shall not apply in relation to pedal cycles; but, subject to subsection (6) below, a person who, without having the consent of the owner or other lawful authority, takes a pedal cycle for his own or another's use, or rides a pedal cycle knowing it to have been taken without such authority, shall on summary conviction be liable to a fine not exceeding [level 3 on the standard scale].

(6) A person does not commit an offence under this section by anything done in the belief that he has lawful authority to do it or that he would have the owner's consent if the owner knew of his doing it and the circumstances of it.

(7) For the purposes of this section —

    (a) *"conveyance"* means any conveyance constructed or adapted for the carriage of a person or persons whether by land, water or air, except that it does not include a conveyance constructed or adapted for use only under the control of a person not carried in or on it, and " *drive* " shall be construed accordingly; and

    (b) *"owner"*, in relation to a conveyance which is the subject of a hiring agreement or hire-purchase agreement, means the person in possession of the conveyance under that agreement.

A3.03   *[Section 12 is printed as amended by the Criminal Justice Act 1982 ss.38, 46; the Police and Criminal Evidence Act 1984 s.119(2) and Sch.7, Pt I; the Criminal Justice Act 1988 s.37(1); the Vehicles (Crime) Act 2001 Pt 3 s.37(1).*

If a magistrates' court grants bail to a person charged with or convicted of an offence under s.12 or s.12A of this Act, the prosecution (provided that objection was taken to the application for bail) may appeal to a judge of the Crown Court against the order granting bail under the Bail (Amendment) Act 1993 s.1 (not reproduced in this work).

The offence of taking a motor vehicle or other conveyance without authority, etc., contrary to s.12(1), is an offence which has been specified by the Motor Salvage Operators (Specified Offences) Order 2002 (SI 2002/1917; not reproduced in this work) as an offence which is relevant to whether an applicant for registration (or for the renewal of registration) as a motor salvage operator is a fit and proper person (under the Vehicles (Crime) Act 2001 s.3(3) and (4)(b)).

The provisions of s.12(4A), (4B) and (4C) do not apply to any offence committed before October 1, 2001; see s.37(2) of the Vehicles (Crime) Act 2001.

An offence under s.12(5) of taking or riding a pedal cycle without the owner's consent may be recorded in national police records; see the National Police Records (Recordable Offences) Regulations 2000 (SI 2000/1139; not reproduced in this work).

An offence under s.12 is prescribed for the purposes of s.103(4)(b) of the Crim-

inal Justice Act 2003 (categories of offences where propensity to commit offences of the kind with which a defendant is charged is an issue). See the Criminal Justice Act 2003 (Categories of Offences) Order 2004 (SI 2004/3346) Pt 1.]

[Aggravated vehicle-taking

12A.—(1) Subject to subsection (3) below, a person is guilty of aggravated   **A3.04**
taking of a vehicle if—

    (a) he commits an offence under section 12(1) above (in this section referred to as a "basic offence") in relation to a mechanically propelled vehicle; and

    (b) it is proved that, at any time after the vehicle was unlawfully taken (whether by him or another) and before it was recovered, the vehicle was driven, or injury or damage was caused, in one or more of the circumstances set out in paragraphs (a) to (d) of subsection (2) below.

(2) The circumstances referred to in subsection (1)(b) above are—

    (a) that the vehicle was driven dangerously on a road or other public place;

    (b) that, owing to the driving of the vehicle, an accident occurred by which injury was caused to any person;

    (c) that, owing to the driving of the vehicle, an accident occurred by which damage was caused to any property, other than the vehicle;

    (d) that damage was caused to the vehicle.

(3) A person is not guilty of an offence under this section if he proves that, as regards any such proven driving, injury or damage as is referred to in subsection (1)(b) above, either—

    (a) the driving, accident or damage referred to in subsection (2) above occurred before he committed the basic offence; or

    (b) he was neither in nor on nor in the immediate vicinity of the vehicle when that driving, accident or damage occurred.

(4) A person guilty of an offence under this section shall be liable on conviction on indictment to imprisonment for a term not exceeding two years or, if it is proved that, in circumstances falling within subsection (2)(b) above, the accident caused the death of the person concerned, [fourteen] years.

(5) If a person who is charged with an offence under this section is found not guilty of that offence but it is proved that he committed a basic offence, he may be convicted of the basic offence.

(6) If by virtue of subsection (5) above a person is convicted of a basic offence before the Crown Court, that court shall have the same powers and duties as a magistrates' court would have had on convicting him of such an offence.

(7) For the purposes of this section a vehicle is driven dangerously if—

    (a) it is driven in a way which falls far below what would be expected of a competent and careful driver; and

    (b) it would be obvious to a competent and careful driver that driving the vehicle in that way would be dangerous.

(8) For the purposes of this section a vehicle is recovered when it is restored to its owner or to other lawful possession or custody; and in this subsection *"owner"* has the same meaning as in section 12 above.]

A3.05   *[Section 12A was inserted by the Aggravated Vehicle-Taking Act 1992 s.1 and is printed as amended by the Criminal Justice Act 2003 s.285.*

As to bail, see the note to s.12 of this Act above.

The offence of aggravated vehicle-taking, contrary to s.12A, is an offence which has been specified by the Motor Salvage Operators (Specified Offences) Order 2002 (SI 2002/1917; not reproduced in this work) as an offence which is relevant to whether an applicant for registration (or for the renewal of registration) as a motor salvage operator is a fit and proper person (under the Vehicles (Crime) Act 2001 s.3(3) and (4)(b)).

An offence under s.12A is prescribed for the purposes of s.103(4)(b) of the Criminal Justice Act 2003 (categories of offences where propensity to commit offences of the kind with which a defendant is charged is an issue). See the Criminal Justice Act 2003 (Categories of Offences) Order 2004 (SI 2004/3346) Pt 1.

In accordance with s.65A(2)(j) of the Police and Criminal Evidence Act 1984, a s.12A offence involving an accident which caused a person's death is a qualifying offence as regards the taking of biometric data (fingerprints and non-intimate samples) (see Crime and Security Act 2010 s.7).]

*   *   *

Going equipped for stealing, etc.

A3.06   **25.**—(1) A person shall be guilty of an offence if, when not at his place of abode, he has with him any article for use in the course of or in connection with any [burglary or theft].

(2) A person guilty of an offence under this section shall on conviction on indictment be liable to a term of imprisonment for a term not exceeding three years.

(3) Where a person is charged with an offence under this section, proof that he had with him any article made or adapted for use in committing a [burglary or theft] shall be evidence that he had it with him for such use.

(4) [...]

(5) For the purposes of this section an offence under section 12(1) of this Act of taking a conveyance shall be treated as theft [...].

A3.07   *[Section 25 is printed as amended by the Serious Organised Crime and Police Act 2005 s.111 and Sch.7, para.17, and Sch.17, Pt 2; the Fraud Act 2006 s.14(1) and (3), Sch.1 para.8, and Sch.3.*

The offence of going equipped to steal or take a motor vehicle, contrary to s.25(1), is an offence which has also been specified by the Motor Salvage Operators (Specified Offences) Order 2002 (SI 2000/1917; not reproduced in this work) as an offence which is relevant to whether an applicant for registration (or for the renewal of registration) as a motor salvage operator is a fit and proper person (under the Vehicles (Crime) Act 2001 s.3(3) and (4)(b)).

An offence under s.25 is prescribed for the purposes of s.103(4)(b) of the Criminal Justice Act 2003 (categories of offences where propensity to commit offences of the kind with which a defendant is charged is an issue). See the Criminal Justice Act 2003 (Categories of Offences) Order 2004 (SI 2004/3346) Pt 1.]

The Transport Act 1968

(1968 c.73)

An Act to make further provision with respect to transport and related matters.　　**A4.01**

[25th October 1968]

ARRANGEMENT OF SECTIONS

* * *

PART VI

DRIVERS' HOURS

*   *   *

A4.02   *[Part VI of the Transport Act 1968 (the only Part of the Act reproduced in this work) does not apply to a person or vehicle in the service of a visiting force or headquarters (as defined); see the Visiting Forces and International Headquarters (Application of Law) Order 1999 (SI 1999/1736; not reproduced in this work) art.8(1)(a).]*

PART VI

DRIVERS' HOURS

Vehicles and drivers subject to control under Part VI

A4.03   95.—(1), (1A) *[Omitted.]*

(2) This Part of this Act applies to—

    (a) passenger vehicles, that is to say—

       (i) public service vehicles; and

       (ii) motor vehicles (other than public service vehicles) constructed or adapted to carry more than twelve passengers;

    (b) goods vehicles, that is to say—

       (i) heavy locomotives, light locomotives, motor tractors and any motor vehicle so constructed that a trailer may by partial superimposition be attached to the vehicle in such a manner as to cause a substantial part of the weight of the trailer to be borne by the vehicle; and

       (ii) motor vehicles (except those mentioned in paragraph (a) of this subsection) constructed or adapted to carry goods other than the effects of passengers.

    [(c) vehicles not falling within paragraph (a) and (b) of this subsection which—

       (i) are vehicles within the meaning given byArticle 4 of the Community Drivers' Hours Regulation; and

       (ii) are not referred to in Article 3 of that Regulation.]

(3) This Part of this Act applies to any such person as follows (in this Part of this Act referred to as *"a driver"*), that is to say—

    (a) a person who drives a vehicle to which this Part of this Act applies in the course of his employment (in this Part of this Act referred to as *"an employee-driver"*); and

    (b) a person who drives such a vehicle for the purposes of a trade or business carried on by him (in this Part of this Act referred to as *"an owner-driver"*);

and in this Part of this Act references to driving by any person are references to his driving as aforesaid.

A4.04   *[Section 95 is printed as amended by the Community Drivers' Hours and Recording Equipment (Amendment) Regulations 1998 (SI 1998/2006); the Community Drivers' Hours and Recording Equipment Regulations 2007 (SI 2007/1819).]*

Permitted driving time and periods of duty

96.—(1) Subject to the provisions of this section, a driver shall not on any   **A4.05** working day drive a vehicle or vehicles to which this Part of this Act applies for periods amounting in the aggregate to more than ten hours.

(2) Subject to the provisions of this section, if on any working day a driver has been on duty for a period of, or for periods amounting in the aggregate to, five and a half hours and—

    (a) there has not been during that period, or during or between any of those periods, an interval of not less than half an hour in which he was able to obtain rest and refreshment; and

    (b) the end of that period, or of the last of those periods, does not mark the end of that working day,

there shall at the end of that period, or of the last of those periods, be such an interval as aforesaid.

(3) Subject to the provisions of this section, the working day of a driver—

    (a) except where paragraph (b) or (c) of this subsection applies, shall not exceed eleven hours;

    (b) if during that day he is off duty for a period which is, or periods which taken together are, not less than the time by which his working day exceeds eleven hours, shall not exceed twelve and a half hours;

    (c) if during that day—

        (i) all the time when he is driving vehicles to which this Part of this Act applies is spent in driving one or more express carriages or contract carriages, and

        (ii) he is able for a period of not less than four hours to obtain rest and refreshment,

    shall not exceed fourteen hours.

(4) Subject to the provisions of this section, there shall be, between any two successive working days of a driver, an interval for rest which—

    (a) subject to paragraph (b) of this subsection, shall not be of less than eleven hours;

    (b) if during both those days all or the greater part of the time when he is driving vehicles to which this Part of this Act applies is spent in driving one or more passenger vehicles, may, on one occasion in each working week, be of less than eleven hours but not of less than nine and a half hours;

and for the purposes of this Part of this Act a period of time shall not be treated, in the case of an employee-driver, as not being an interval for rest by reason only that he may be called upon to report for duty if required.

(5) Subject to the provisions of this section a driver shall not be on duty in any working week for periods amounting in the aggregate to more than sixty hours.

(6) Subject to the provisions of this section, there shall be, in the case of each working week of a driver, a period of not less than twenty-four hours for which he is off duty, being a period either falling wholly in that week or beginning in that week and ending in the next week; but—

(a) where the requirements of the foregoing provisions of this subsection have been satisfied in the case of any week by reference to a period ending in the next week, no part of that period (except any part after the expiration of the first twenty-four hours of it) shall be taken into account for the purpose of satisfying those requirements in the case of the next week; and

(b) those requirements need not be satisfied in the case of any working week of a driver who on each working day falling wholly or partly in that week drives one or more stage carriages if that week is immediately preceded by a week in the case of which those requirements have been satisfied as respects that driver or during which he has not at any time been on duty.

(7) If in the case of the working week of any driver the following requirement is satisfied, that is to say, that, in each of the periods of twenty-four hours beginning at midnight which make up that week, the driver does not drive a vehicle to which this Part of this Act applies for a period of, or periods amounting in the aggregate to, more than four hours, the foregoing provisions of this section shall not apply to him in that week, except that the provisions of subsections (1), (2) and (3) shall nevertheless have effect in relation to the whole of any working day falling partly in that week and partly in a working week in the case of which that requirement is not satisfied.

(8) If on any working day a driver does not drive any vehicle to which this Part of this Act applies—

(a) subsections (2) and (3) of this section shall not apply to that day, and

(b) the period or periods of duty attributable to that day for the purposes of subsection (5) of this section shall, if amounting to more than eleven hours, be treated as amounting to eleven hours only.

(9) For the purposes of subsections (1) and (7) of this section no account shall be taken of any time spent driving a vehicle elsewhere than on a road if the vehicle is being so driven in the course of operations of agriculture or forestry.

(10) For the purposes of enabling drivers to deal with cases of emergency or otherwise to meet a special need, the [Secretary of State for Transport] may by regulations—

(a) create exemptions from all or any of the requirements of subsections (1) to (6) of this section in such cases and subject to such conditions as may be specified in the regulations;

(b) empower the traffic [commissioner] for any area, subject to the provisions of the regulations—

(i) to dispense with the observance of all or any of those requirements (either generally or in such circumstances or to such extent as the [commissioner thinks] fit) in any particular case for which provision is not made under paragraph (a) of this subsection;

(ii) to grant a certificate (which, for the purposes of any proceedings under this Part of this Act, shall be conclusive evidence of the facts therein stated) that any particular case falls or fell within any exemption created under the said paragraph (a);

and regulations under this subsection may enable any dispensation under paragraph (b)(i) of this subsection to be granted retrospectively and provide for a

document purporting to be a certificate granted by virtue of paragraph (b)(ii) of
this subsection to be accepted in evidence without further proof.

(11) If any of the requirements of [the domestic drivers' hours code] is
contravened in the case of any driver—

    (a) that driver; and

    (b) any other person (being that driver's employer or a person to whose
        orders that driver was subject) who caused or permitted the contraven-
        tion;

shall be liable on summary conviction to a fine not exceeding [level 4 on the standard scale]; but a person shall not be liable to be convicted under this subsection
if he proves to the court—

        (i) that the contravention was due to unavoidable delay in the
           completion of a journey arising out of circumstances which he
           could not reasonably have foreseen; or

        (ii) in the case of a person charged under paragraph (b) of this
           subsection, that the contravention was due to the fact that the
           driver had for any particular period or periods driven or been on
           duty otherwise than in the employment of that person or, as the
           case may be, otherwise than in the employment in which he is
           subject to the orders of that person, and that the person charged
           was not, and could not reasonably have become, aware of that
           fact.

[(11A) Where, in the case of a driver … of a motor vehicle, there is […] a
contravention of any requirement of [the applicable Community rules] as to period of driving, or distance driven, or periods on or off duty, then the offender and
[the offender's employer, and any other person to whose orders the offender was
subject,] shall be liable on summary conviction to a fine not exceeding [level 4 on
the standard scale].]

[(11B) But a person shall not be liable to be convicted under subsection (11A)
if—

    (a) he proves the matters specified in paragraph (i) of subsection (11); or

    (b) being charged as the offender's employer or a person to whose orders
        the offender was subject, he proves the matters specified in paragraph
        (ii) of that subsection [; or

    (c) being charged as mentioned in paragraph (b), he proves—

        (i) that at the time of the contravention he was complying with
           Article 10(1) (distance-related payments etc) and Article 10(2)
           (organisation of drivers' work etc) of the Community Drivers'
           Hours Regulation; and

        (ii) that he took all reasonable steps to avoid the contravention.]

[(11C) A person who—

    (a) is subject to the requirement imposed by Article 10(4) of the Com-
        munity Drivers' Hours Regulation (undertakings etc to ensure that
        contractually agreed transport time schedules respect that Regula-
        tion); and

    (b) fails to take all reasonable steps to comply with that requirement,
        shall be liable on summary conviction to a fine not exceeding level 4
        on the standard scale.]

[(11D) If a driver who is subject to the orders of more than one transport undertaking fails, without reasonable excuse, to provide each of them with sufficient information to enable them to avoid a contravention of Chapter 2 of the Community Drivers' Hours Regulation, he shall be liable on summary conviction to a fine not exceeding level 4 on the standard scale.]

(12) The [Secretary of State for Transport] may by order—

    (a) direct that subsection (1) of this section shall have effect with the substitution for the reference to ten hours of a reference to nine hours, either generally or with such exceptions as may be specified in the order;

    (b) direct that paragraph (a) of subsection (3) of this section shall have effect with the substitution for the reference to eleven hours of a reference to any shorter period, or remove, modify or add to the provisions of that subsection containing exceptions to the said paragraph (a);

    (c) remove, modify or add to any of the requirements of subsections (1), (4), (5) or (6) of this section or any of the exemptions provided for by subsections (7), (8) and (9) thereof;

and any order under this subsection may contain such transitional and supplementary provisions as the [Secretary of State for Transport] thinks necessary or expedient, including provisions amending any definition in section 103 of this Act which is relevant to any of the provisions affected by the order.

[(13) In this Part of this Act *"the domestic drivers' hours code"* means the provisions of subsections (1) to (6) of this section as for the time being in force (and, in particular, as modified, added to or substituted by or under any instrument in force under section 95(1) of this Act or subsection (10) or (12) of this section).]

A4.06 *[Section 96 is printed as amended by the Secretary of State for the Environment Order 1970 (SI 1970/1681); the European Communities Act 1972 s.4 and Sch.4, para.9(2); the Road Traffic (Drivers' Ages and Hours of Work) Act 1976 s.2(1); the Secretary of State for Transport Order 1976 (SI 1976/1775); the Transport Act 1978 s.10; the Minister of Transport Order 1979 (SI 1979/571); the Transfer of Functions (Transport) Order 1981 (SI 1981/238); the Criminal Justice Act 1982 ss.38 and 46(1); the Transport Act 1985 s.3 and Sch.2, Pt II, para.1(2); the Community Drivers' Hours and Recording Equipment Regulations 1986 (SI 1986/1457) reg.2; the Secretary of State for the Environment, Transport and the Regions Order 1997 (SI 1997/2971); the Secretaries of State for Transport, Local Government and the Regions and for Environment, Food and Rural Affairs Order 2001 (SI 2001/2568); the Transfer of Functions (Transport, Local Government and the Regions) Order 2002 (SI 2002/2626); the Community Drivers' Hours and Recording Equipment Regulations 2007 (SI 2007/1819); the Passenger and Goods Vehicles (Recording Equipment) (Downloading and Retention of Data) Regulations 2008 (SI 2008/198).*

For modifications of subs.(9), above, in relation to drivers engaged in quarrying operations or on building construction and civil engineering work, see the Drivers' Hours (Goods Vehicles) (Modifications) Order 1970 (SI 1970/257) below.

The text of s.96 as it applies to the drivers of passenger vehicles is modified by the Drivers' Hours (Passenger and Goods Vehicles) (Modifications) Order 1971

(SI 1971/818); and the text as so modified is set out as an appendix to SI 1971/818 below. The text of s.96 as it applies to the drivers of goods vehicles is modified by the Drivers' Hours (Goods Vehicles) (Modifications) Order 1986 (SI 1986/1459); and the text as so modified is set out as an appendix to SI 1986/1459 (q.v.).

Offences under s.96(11) and (11A) are fixed penalty offences for the purposes of Pt 3 of the Road Traffic Offenders Act 1988 (see the Fixed Penalty Offences Order 2009 (SI 2009/483) art.2). The amounts for the fixed penalty offences are prescribed by the Fixed Penalty Order 2000 (SI 2000/2792), as amended by the Fixed Penalty (Amendment) Order 2009 (SI 2009/488).

Section 95(1) of this Act, as amended, inter alia, empowers the Secretary of State to make regulations substituting, adapting, etc.,the provisions of this Part of this Act to take account of the operation of any Community provision.]

[Installation and use of recording equipment

97.—[(1) No person shall use, or cause or permit to be used, a vehicle to which this section applies—   **A4.07**

 [(a) unless there is in the vehicle recording equipment which—

   (i) has been installed in accordance with the Community Recording Equipment Regulation;

   (ii) complies with [the relevant Annexes] to that Regulation; and

   (iii) is being used as provided by [Articles 13 to 15] of that Regulation] [, or]

 [(b) in which there is recording equipment which has been repaired (whether before or after installation) otherwise than in accordance with the Community Recording Equipment Regulation;]

and any person who contravenes this subsection shall be liable on summary conviction to a fine not exceeding [level 5] on the standard scale.]

[(1A) A person shall not be liable to be convicted under subsection (1) of this section if he proves to the court that he neither knew nor ought to have known that the recording equipment had not been installed or repaired, as the case may be, in accordance with the Community Recording Equipment Regulation.]

(2) A person shall not be liable to be convicted under subsection (1)[(a)] of this section if he proves to the court that the vehicle in question was proceeding to a place where recording equipment which would comply with the requirements of [the relevant Annexes to] the Community Recording Equipment Regulation was to be installed in the vehicle in accordance with that Regulation.

(3) A person shall not be liable to be convicted under subsection (1)[(a)] of this section by reason of the recording equipment installed in the vehicle in question not being in working order if he proves to the court that—

 (a) it had not become reasonably practicable for the equipment to be repaired by an approved fitter or workshop; and

 (b) the requirements of [Article 16(2)] of the Community Recording Equipment Regulation were being complied with.

(4) A person shall not be liable to be convicted under subsection (1)[(a)] of this section by reason of any seal on the recording equipment installed in the vehicle in question not being intact if he proves to the court that—

    (a) the breaking or removal of the seal could not have been avoided;

    (b) it had not become reasonably practicable for the seal to be replaced by an approved fitter or workshop; and

    (c) in all other respects the equipment was being used as provided by [Articles 13 to 15] of the Community Recording Equipment Regulation.

[(4A) A person shall not be liable to be convicted under subsection (1)[(a)] of this section by reason of the driver card not being used with the recording equipment installed in the vehicle in question if he proves to the court that—

    (a) the driver card was damaged, malfunctioning, lost or stolen;

    (b) the requirements of Article 16(2) and, apart from the last paragraph thereof, Article 16(3) of the Community Recording Equipment Regulation were being complied with; and

    (c) in all other respects the recording equipment was being used as provided by Articles 13 to 15 of that Regulation.]

(5) For the purposes of this section recording equipment is used as provided by [Articles 13 to 15] of the Community Recording Equipment Regulation if, and only if, the circumstances of its use are such that each requirement of those Articles is complied with.

(6) This section applies at any time to any vehicle to which this Part of this Act applies if, at that time, Article 3 of the Community Recording Equipment Regulation requires recording equipment to be installed and used in that vehicle; and in this section and [sections 97B to 97G] of the Act any expression which is also used in that Regulation has the same meaning as in that Regulation.

(7) In this Part of this Act—

    ["the Community Recording Equipment Regulation" means Council Regulation (EEC) No.3821/85 [q.v.] on recording equipment in road transport as read with the Community Drivers' Hours and Recording Equipment Regulations 2007 [SI 2007/1819].]

    "recording equipment" means equipment for recording information as to the use of a vehicle.

    ["the relevant Annexes" to the Community Recording Equipment Regulation—

        (a) in the case of a vehicle put into service for the first time before 1st May 2006 means—

            (i) either Annex I or Annex IB to that Regulation; and

            (ii) Annex II to that Regulation; and

        (b) in the case of a vehicle put into service for the first time on or after that date means—

            (i) Annex IB to that Regulation; and

            (ii) Annex II to that Regulation.]]

A4.08   [Section 97 was substituted by the Passenger and Goods Vehicles (Recording Equipment) Regulations 1979 (SI 1979/1746) and is printed as subsequently amended by the Passenger and Goods Vehicles (Recording Equipment) (Amendment) Regulations 1984 (SI 1984/144) reg.2(2); the Criminal Justice Act 1982 ss.39(2), 46(1) and Sch.3; the Community Drivers' Hours and Recording Equipment Regulations 1986 (SI 1986/1457) reg.3; the Passenger and Goods Vehicles

(Recording Equipment) Regulations 1989 (SI 1989/2121); the Passenger and Goods Vehicles (Recording Equipment) Regulations 1996 (SI 1996/941); the Passenger and Goods Vehicles (Recording Equipment) Regulations 2005 (SI 2005/1904) reg.2; the Passenger and Goods Vehicles (Recording Equipment) (Fitting Date) Regulations 2006 (SI 2006/1117) reg.2; the Passenger and Goods Vehicles (Community Recording Equipment Regulation) Regulations 2006 (SI 2006/3276) reg.2; the Passenger and Goods Vehicles (Recording Equipment) (Downloading and Retention of Data) Regulations 2008 (SI 2008/198) reg.4; the Passenger and Goods Vehicles (Community Recording Equipment Regulation) Regulations 2010 (SI 2010/892) reg.3.

An offence under s.97(1) is a fixed penalty offence for the purposes of Pt 3 of the Road Traffic Offenders Act 1988 (see the Fixed Penalty Offences Order 2009 (SI 2009/483) art.2). The amount for the fixed penalty offence is prescribed by the Fixed Penalty Order 2000 (SI 2000/2792), as amended by the Fixed Penalty (Amendment) Order 2009 (SI 2009/488).]

[Provisions supplementary to section 97

97A. [...]   **A4.09**

[Forgery, etc., of seals on recording equipment

97AA.—(1) A person who, with intent to deceive, forges, alters or uses any seal on recording equipment installed in, or designed for installation in, a vehicle to which section 97 of this Act applies, shall be guilty of an offence.   **A4.10**

(2) A person guilty of an offence under subsection (1) above shall be liable—

    (a) on conviction on indictment, to imprisonment for a term not exceeding two years, or

    (b) on summary conviction, to a fine not exceeding the statutory maximum.

(3) In the application of this section to England and Wales a person *"forges"* a seal if he makes a false seal in order that it may be used as genuine.]

[Section 97AA was inserted by the Passenger and Goods Vehicles (Recording Equipment) Regulations 1989 (SI 1989/2121).]   **A4.11**

[Records, etc., produced by equipment may be used in evidence

97B.—(1) Where recording equipment is installed in a vehicle to which this Part of this Act applies, any record produced by means of the equipment shall, in any proceedings under this Part of this Act, be evidence ... of the matters appearing from the record.   **A4.12**

(2) Any entry made on a record sheet [or print out] by a [driver] for the purposes of [Article 15(2) or (5) or 16(2)] of the Community Recording Equipment Regulation shall, in any proceedings under this Part of this Act, be evidence ... of the matters appearing from that entry.]

[Section 97B was inserted by the Passenger and Goods Vehicles (Recording Equipment) Regulations 1979 (SI 1979/1746) and is printed as subsequently amended by the Community Drivers' Hours and Recording Equipment Regulations 1986 (SI 1986/1457) reg.3; the Passenger and Goods Vehicles (Recording Equipment) Regulations 2005 (SI 2005/1904) reg.3.   **A4.13**

Words relating exclusively and expressly to Scotland in s.97(1) and (2) have been omitted.]

[Delivery of record sheets and other documents

A4.14   97C.—(1) This section applies to the following documents—

(a) record sheets;

(b) manual records and printouts made in accordance with the Community Recording Equipment Regulation.

(2) If such a document relates to a person in his capacity as the driver of a vehicle to which section 97 applies, he must before the end of the delivery period deliver the document to the transport undertaking to whose orders he was subject in driving the vehicle.

(3) The delivery period is the period of 42 days starting on the day after the latest date to which the document relates.

(4) A person who without reasonable excuse fails to comply with subsection (2) is liable on summary conviction to a fine not exceeding level 4 on the standard scale.

(5) If a transport undertaking fails without reasonable excuse to secure that each driver subject to its orders complies with subsection (2), in respect of documents relating to him in his capacity as such a driver, it is liable on summary conviction to a fine not exceeding level 4 on the standard scale.

(6) If a person is subject to the orders of two or more transport undertakings in driving a vehicle during a period to which a document relates—

(a) subsection (2) has effect as if it were a requirement to deliver that document to the undertaking to whose orders he was first subject in driving the vehicle during that period;

(b) subsection (5), in relation to that document, applies only to the undertaking to whose orders he was first subject in driving the vehicle during that period.]

A4.15   *[Section 97C was inserted by the Passenger and Goods Vehicles (Recording Equipment) (Downloading and Retention of Data) Regulations 2008 (SI 2008/ 198) reg.2.]*

[Vehicle units: downloading data

A4.16   97D.—(1) This section applies where a transport undertaking is required by article 10 of the Community Drivers' Hours Regulation to ensure that data is downloaded from a vehicle unit in a vehicle.

(2) The undertaking must ensure that relevant data is downloaded from the unit not later than the end of the download period if—

(a) it controls the use of the vehicle throughout that period, and

(b) it uses the vehicle at some point during that period.

(3) The download period begins and ends as set out in the following table—

TABLE

Case	Download period begins	Download period ends
1. The undertaking has not previously downloaded data from the unit under this section	On the first day after the commencement of this section on which the undertaking— (a) controls the use of the vehicle, and (b) is required by article 10 to ensure that data is downloaded from the unit	On the earlier of— (a) the expiry of the period of 56 days starting on the first day of the download period; (b) any downloading of the data before the expiry of that period
2. The undertaking uses the vehicle during the period of 56 days starting on the day after the last downloading under this section	On the day after the last downloading under this section	
3. The undertaking does not use the vehicle during the period of 56 days starting on the day after the last downloading under this section	On the first day of the undertaking's use of the vehicle after the last downloading under this section	

(4) The undertaking must ensure that all relevant data is downloaded from the unit—

  (a) immediately before transferring control of the use of the vehicle to another person;

  (b) without delay upon permanently removing the unit from service in the vehicle;

  (c) without delay upon becoming aware that the unit is malfunctioning;

  (d) without delay in any circumstances such that the imminent erasure of the data by the unit, in the normal course of its operations, is reasonably foreseeable.

(5) But subsection (4)(c) does not apply if because of the malfunctioning of the unit it is impossible to download the data.

(6) For the purposes of this section "relevant data" means any data recorded by the vehicle unit in a vehicle, other than detailed speed data.

(7) For the purposes of this section and section 97E an undertaking controls the use of a vehicle during any period in which it may determine when, by whom and for what purpose the vehicle may be driven.

(8) In this section and sections 97E to 97G, "downloaded" is to be construed in accordance with the definition of "downloading" in Annex 1B to the Community Recording Equipment Regulation.

A4.17 *[Section 97D was inserted by the Passenger and Goods Vehicles (Recording Equipment) (Downloading and Retention of Data) Regulations 2008 (SI 2008/198) reg.2.]*

[Driver cards: downloading data

A4.18 **97E.**—(1) This section applies where a transport undertaking is required by article 10 of the Community Drivers' Hours Regulation to ensure that data is downloaded from a driver card issued to a driver.

(2) The undertaking must ensure that all data is downloaded from the card not later than the end of the download period.

(3) The download period begins and ends as set out in the following table—

TABLE

Case	Download period begins	Download period ends
1. The undertaking has not previously downloaded data from the card under this section	On the first day after the commencement of this section on which— (a) the driver drives for the undertaking, and (b) the undertaking is required by article 10 to ensure that data is downloaded from the card	On the earlier of— (a) the expiry of the period of 28 days starting on the first day of the download period; (b) any downloading of the data before the expiry of that period
2. The undertaking has previously downloaded data from the card under this section	On the first day on which the driver drives for the undertaking after the last downloading under this section	

(4) The undertaking must ensure that the data is downloaded from the card—

(a) immediately before the driver ceases to be employed by the undertaking as a driver, or otherwise to carry out work for the undertaking as a driver;

(b) without delay upon becoming aware that the card has been damaged or is malfunctioning;

(c) without delay in any circumstances such that the imminent erasure of the data, in the normal course of use of the card, is reasonably foreseeable;

(d) if it is not possible to do so other than by means of a vehicle unit installed in a vehicle, immediately before ceasing to control the use of that vehicle.

(5) But subsection (4)(b) does not apply if because of the damage to the card or its malfunctioning it is impossible to download the data.]

A4.19 *[Section 97E was inserted by the Passenger and Goods Vehicles (Recording*

Equipment) (Downloading and Retention of Data) Regulations 2008 (SI 2008/198) reg.2.]

[Downloading data: requirement imposed by an officer

97F.—(1) This section applies where—   **A4.20**

    (a) an officer has reason to believe that an offence under this Part of this Act or under the Traffic Acts has been committed in respect of the use of a vehicle, and

    (b) article 10(5) of the Community Drivers' Hours Regulation applies to a transport undertaking in respect of the vehicle unit in the vehicle or a driver card issued to a person who has driven the vehicle.

(2) The officer may, on production if so required of his authority, require the undertaking without delay—

    (a) download data from the vehicle unit or driver card;

    (b) to permit him to inspect or copy the downloaded data.

(3) In this section—

    (a) *"download"* is to be construed in accordance with the definition of *"downloading"* in Annex 1B to the Community Recording Equipment Regulation;

    (b) *"the Traffic Acts"* has the meaning given in section 192(1) of the Road Traffic Act 1988.]

[Section 97F was inserted by the Passenger and Goods Vehicles (Recording   **A4.21**
Equipment) (Downloading and Retention of Data) Regulations 2008 (SI 2008/198) reg.2.]

[Downloading data: requirement imposed by an officer

97G.—(1) A transport undertaking commits an offence if, without reasonable   **A4.22**
excuse, it fails to comply with section 97D or 97E, or with a requirement imposed under section 97F.

(2) A transport undertaking commits an offence if, without reasonable excuse, it fails to comply with any requirement imposed by article 10 of the Community Drivers' Hours Regulation in respect of the retention of data downloaded in accordance with section 97D to 97F.

(3) An offence under this section is punishable on summary conviction with a fine not exceeding level 5 on the standard scale.]

[Section 97G was inserted by the Passenger and Goods Vehicles (Recording   **A4.23**
Equipment) (Downloading and Retention of Data) Regulations 2008 (SI 2008/198) reg.2.]

[Access to downloaded data

97H.—(1) An officer may, on production if so required of his authority, require   **A4.24**
a person to make readily accessible to him, either on or from premises occupied or controlled by the person in question, that person's retained data.

(2) Any person who without reasonable excuse fails to comply with a requirement under subsection (1) is liable on summary conviction to a fine not exceeding level 5 on the standard scale.

(3) For the purposes of subsection (1), data is a person's "retained data" if he

is required by article 10 of the Community Drivers' Hours Regulation to retain it for at least 12 months following its recording.]

A4.25 *[Section 97H was inserted by the Passenger and Goods Vehicles (Recording Equipment) (Downloading and Retention of Data) Regulations 2008 (SI 2008/198) reg.2.]*

Written records

A4.26 **98.**—(1) *[Power to make regulations regarding keeping records and maintaining registers.]*

(2) *[Power to include supplementary and incidental provisions in regulations.]*

[(2A) The requirements of regulations made under this section shall not apply as respects the driving of a vehicle to which section 97 of this Act applies and [which is installed with recording equipment complying with the relevant Annexes (within the meaning of that section)].]

(3) *[Dispensations from requirements imposed by this section.]*

(4) Any person who contravenes any regulations made under this section [or any requirement as to [books, records or documents]] of [the applicable Community rules] shall be liable on summary conviction to a fine not exceeding [level 4 on the standard scale]; but the employer of an employee-driver shall not be liable to be convicted under this subsection by reason of contravening any such regulation whereby he is required to cause any records to be kept if he proves to the court that he has given proper instructions to his employees with respect to the keeping of the records and has from time to time taken reasonable steps to secure that those instructions are being carried out.

[(4A) A person shall not be liable to be convicted under subsection (4) of this section by reason of contravening any regulation made under this section if he proves to the court that, if the vehicle in question had been such a vehicle as is mentioned in subsection (2A) of this section, there would have been no contravention of the provisions of this Part of this Act so far as they relate to the use of such vehicles.]

(5) Any entry made by an employee-driver for the purposes of regulations under this section [or of [the applicable Community rules]] shall, in any proceedings under this Part of this Act, be admissible in evidence against his employer.

A4.27 *[Section 98 is printed as amended by the European Communities Act 1972 s.4, and Sch.4, para.9; the Road Traffic (Drivers' Ages and Hours of Work) Act 1976 s.2(1); the Passenger and Goods Vehicles (Recording Equipment) Regulations 1979 (SI 1979/1746); the Criminal Justice Act 1982 ss.38, 46(1); the Passenger and Goods Vehicles (Recording Equipment) Regulations 2005 (SI 2005/1904) reg.4.*

An offence under s.98(4) is a fixed penalty offence for the purposes of Pt 3 of the Road Traffic Offenders Act 1988 (see the Fixed Penalty Offences Order 2009 (SI 2009/483) art.2). The amount for the fixed penalty offence is prescribed by the Fixed Penalty Order 2000 (SI 2000/2792), as amended by the Fixed Penalty (Amendment) Order 2009 (SI 2009/488).

The Drivers' Hours (Goods Vehicles) (Keeping of Records) Regulations 1987 (SI 1987/1421) (q.v.) were made under s.98.]

Inspection of records and other documents

99.—(1) An officer may, on production if so required of his authority, require   **A4.28**
any person to produce, and permit him to inspect and copy—

      (a) any book or register which that person is required by regulations
under section 98 of this Act to carry or have in his possession for the
purpose of making in it any entry required by those regulations or
which is required under those regulations to be carried on any vehicle
of which that person is the driver;

      (b) any ..., book or register which that person is required by regulations
under section ... 98 of this Act to preserve;

    [(bb) [...]]

      (c) if that person is the owner of a vehicle to which this Part of this Act
applies, any other document of that person which the officer may reasonably require to inspect for the purpose of ascertaining whether the
provisions of this Part of this Act or of regulations made thereunder
have been complied with;

    [(d) [...]]

and that [...] book, register or document shall, if the officer so requires by notice
in writing served on that person, be produced at the office of the traffic [commis-
sioner] specified in the notice within such time (not being less than ten days)
from the service of the notice as may be so specified.

(2) An officer may, on production if so required of his authority—

    [(a) at any time, enter any vehicle to which this Part of this Act applies
and inspect that vehicle and any recording equipment installed in it
and inspect and copy any record sheet on the vehicle on which a record has been produced by means of the equipment or an entry has
been made;]

      (b) at any time which is reasonable having regard to the circumstances of
the case, enter any premises on which he has reason to believe that
such a vehicle is kept or that any such [record sheets], books, registers
or other documents as are mentioned in subsection (1) of this section
are to be found, and inspect any such vehicle, and inspect and copy
any such record [sheet], book, register, or document which he finds
there.

(3) For the purpose of exercising his powers under subsection (2)(a) and, in
respect of a document carried on, or by the driver of, a vehicle, under subsection
(1) (a) [...] of this section, an officer may detain the vehicle in question during
such time as is required for the exercise of that power.

(4) Any person who—

      (a) fails to comply with any requirement under subsection (1) of this sec-
tion; or

      (b) obstructs an officer in the exercise of his powers under subsection (2)
or (3) of this section,

shall be liable on summary conviction to a fine not exceeding [level 3 on the standard scale].

[(4A) A person shall not be liable to be convicted under subsection (4) of this
section by reason of failing to comply with any requirement under subsection

6(1)(a) or (b) of this section if he proves to the court that, if the vehicle in question had been such a vehicle as is mentioned in section 98(2A) of this Act, there would have been no contravention of the provisions of this Part of this Act so far as they relate to the use of such vehicles.]

(5) Any person who makes, or causes to be made, [...] any entry in a [book, register or document kept or carried] for the purposes of regulations under section 98 thereof [...] which he knows to be false or, with intent to deceive, alters or causes to be altered any such record or entry shall be liable—

(a) on summary conviction, to a fine not exceeding [the prescribed sum];
(b) on conviction on indictment, to imprisonment for a term not exceeding two years.

(6) If an officer has reason to believe that an offence under subsection (5) of this section has been committed in respect of any record or document inspected by him under this section, he may seize that record or document; and where a record or document is seized as aforesaid and within six months of the date on which it was seized no person has been charged since that date with an offence in relation to that record or document under that subsection and the record or document has not been returned to the person from whom it was taken, a magistrates' court shall, on an application made for the purpose by that person or by an officer, make such order respecting the disposal of the record or document and award such costs as the justice of the case may require.

(7) *[Applies to Scotland.]*

(8) [In this Part of this Act] *"officer"* means [an examiner appointed under section 66A of the Road Traffic Act 1988] and any person authorised for the purposes [of this Part] by the traffic [commissioner] for any area.

(9) The powers conferred by [this Part of this Act on an officer] shall be exercisable also by a police constable, who shall not, if wearing uniform, be required to produce any authority.

(10) In this section references to the inspection and copying of any record produced by means of [recording equipment installed] in a vehicle include references to the application to the record of any process for eliciting the information recorded thereby and to taking down the information elicited from it.

[(11) Subsections (1) to (7) and (10) do not apply in respect of vehicles to which section 97 of this Act applies.]

A4.29   *[Section 99 is printed as amended by the European Communities Act 1972 s.4 and Sch.4 para.9; the Road Traffic Act 1972 s.203(1) and Sch.7; the Road Traffic (Drivers' Ages and Hours of Work) Act 1976 s.2(1); the Interpretation Act 1978 s.17(2)(a); the Passenger and Goods Vehicles (Recording Equipment) Regulations 1979 (SI 1979/1746); the Magistrates' Courts Act 1980 s.32(2); the Criminal Justice Act 1982 ss.38, 46(1); the Transport Act 1985 s.3(5) and Sch.2 Pt II para.1(4); the Community Drivers' Hours and Recording Equipment Regulations 1986 (SI 1986/1457) reg.3; the Road Traffic Act 1991 s.48 and Sch.4 para.2; the Passenger and Goods Vehicles (Recording Equipment) Regulations 2005 (SI 2005/1904) reg.5.*

As to the "prescribed sum", see the Magistrates' Courts Act 1980 s.32(9) below.

An offence under s.99(4) is a fixed penalty offence for the purposes of Pt 3 of the Road Traffic Offenders Act 1988 (see the Fixed Penalty Offences Order 2009

(SI 2009/483) art.3), but only insofar as the offence relates to failing to comply with a requirement under s.99(1)(a) or obstructing an officer in the exercise of his powers under s.99(2)(a) or (3). The amount for the fixed penalty offence is prescribed by the Fixed Penalty Order 2000 (SI 2000/2792), as amended by the Fixed Penalty (Amendment) Order 2009 (SI 2009/488).]

[Inspection of records and other documents and data relating to recording equipment

99ZA.—(1) An officer may, on production if so required of his authority,   **A4.30** require any person to produce, and permit him to inspect, remove, retain and copy—

    (a) if that person is the owner of a vehicle to which section 97 applies, any document of that person which the officer may reasonably require to inspect for the purpose of ascertaining whether the provisions of this Part of this Act have been complied with;

    (b) any record sheet or hard copy of electronically stored data which that person is required by the Community Recording Equipment Regulation to retain or to be able to produce;

    (c) any book, register or other document required by the applicable Community Rules or which the officer may reasonably require to inspect for the purpose of ascertaining whether the requirements of the applicable Community rules have been complied with.

(2) An officer may, on production if so required of his authority, require any person—

    (a) to produce and permit him to inspect any driver card which that person is required by Article 15(7) of the Community Recording Equipment Regulation to be able to produce; and

    (b) to permit the officer to copy the data stored on the driver card (and to remove temporarily the driver card for the purpose of doing so) and to remove and retain the copy.

(3) If the officer so requires by notice in writing, anything that a person is required to produce under subsection (1) or (2) of this section shall, instead of being produced when the requirement under those subsections is imposed, be produced at an address specified in the notice, within such time (not being less than ten days) from the service of the notice as is so specified.

(4) Where a notice is served under subsection (3) of this section, the officer may exercise his powers under this section at the place specified in the notice.

(5) In this Part of this Act any reference to copying data stored on a driver card or on digital recording equipment includes a reference to making a hard copy or an electronic copy of the data (and any reference to copies of data shall be construed accordingly).

(6) In this Part of this Act—

    "digital recording equipment" means recording equipment that complies with Annex IB to the Community Recording Equipment Regulation;

    "driver card" has the meaning given in that Annex;

    "electronic copy" of data means a copy of data stored electronically together with the data's digital signature (within the meaning of that Annex);

"hard copy" in relation to data stored electronically means a printed out version of the data.]

A4.31   *[Section 99ZA is printed as inserted by the Passenger and Goods Vehicles (Recording Equipment) Regulations 2005 (SI 2005/1904) reg.6.]*

[Power of entry

A4.32   **99ZB.**—(1) An officer may, on production if so required of his authority, at any time enter any vehicle to which section 97 of this Act applies in order to inspect that vehicle and any recording equipment in or on it.

(2) Where any officer enters any vehicle under subsection (1) of this section he may—

     (a) inspect, remove, retain and copy any record sheet that he finds there on which a record has been produced by means of analogue recording equipment or on which an entry has been made;

     (b) inspect, remove, retain and copy any hard copy of data that he finds there which was stored on any digital recording equipment or on a driver card;

     (c) inspect, remove, retain and copy any other document that he finds there which the officer may reasonably require to inspect for the purpose of ascertaining whether the requirements of the applicable Community rules have been complied with;

     (d) inspect any driver card that he finds there, copy the data stored on it (using any digital recording equipment in or on the vehicle or temporarily removing the driver card for the purpose of copying the data) and remove and retain the copy;

     (e) copy data stored on any digital recording equipment that is in or on the vehicle and remove and retain that copy;

     (f) inspect any recording equipment that is in or on the vehicle and, if necessary for the purposes of the inspection, remove it from the vehicle;

     (g) retain the recording equipment as evidence if he finds that it has been interfered with;

     (h) inspect the vehicle for the purpose of ascertaining whether there is in or on the vehicle any device which is capable of interfering with the proper operation of any recording equipment in or on the vehicle;

     (i) inspect anything in or on the vehicle which he believes is such a device and, if necessary for the purpose of the inspection, remove it from the vehicle;

     (j) retain the device as evidence if he finds that it is capable of interfering with the proper operation of the recording equipment.

(3) Where any officer who is an examiner appointed under section 66A of the Road Traffic Act 1988, or any constable, enters any vehicle under subsection (1) of this section, he may, if he has reason to believe that—

     (a) any recording equipment in or on the vehicle has been interfered with so as to affect its proper operation, or

     (b) there is in or on the vehicle any device which is capable of interfering with the proper operation of any recording equipment in or on the vehicle, require the driver or operator of the vehicle to take it to an address specified by the officer or constable for the purposes of enabling an inspection of the recording equipment, the vehicle or any device in or on it to be carried out.

(4) An officer may, on production if so required of his authority, at any time which is reasonable having regard to the circumstances of the case, enter any premises on which he has reason to believe that—

    (a) a vehicle to which section 97 of this Act applies is kept;

    (b) any such document as is mentioned in section 99ZA(1) of this Act is to be found;

    (c) any driver card or copy of data previously stored on a driver card or on recording equipment is to be found; or

    (d) any digital recording equipment is to be found.

(5) Where any officer enters any premises under subsection (4) of this section he may—

    (a) inspect any vehicle which he finds there and to which section 97 of this Act applies;

    (b) inspect, remove, retain and copy any such document as is mentioned in section 99ZA(1) of this Act that he finds there;

    (c) make a copy of any such copy of data as is mentioned in subsection (4)(c) of this section that he finds there, and remove and retain the copies he makes;

    (d) inspect any driver card that he finds there, copy the data stored on it (using any digital recording equipment on the premises or temporarily removing the driver card for the purpose of copying the data) and remove and retain the copy;

    (e) copy data stored on any digital recording equipment that he finds there and remove and retain that copy;

    (f) inspect any recording equipment that he finds there and, if necessary for the purposes of inspection, remove it from the premises;

    (g) retain any such recording equipment as evidence if he finds that it has been interfered with;

    (h) inspect anything that he finds there which he believes is a device capable of interfering with the proper operation of any recording equipment and, if necessary for the purpose of the inspection, remove it from the premises;

    (i) retain any such device as evidence if he finds that it is capable of interfering with the proper operation of recording equipment.

(6) For the purposes of—

    (a) exercising any of his powers under this section in relation to a vehicle or anything found in or on a vehicle, or

    (b) exercising any of his powers under section 99ZA(1) or (2) of this Act in respect of a document or driver card carried by the driver of a vehicle,

an officer may detain the vehicle during such time as is required for the exercise of that power.

(7) If—

(a) at the time when a requirement is imposed under subsection (3) of this section the vehicle is more than five miles from the address specified by the officer or constable to which the vehicle is to be taken; and

(b) the Community Recording Equipment Regulation is found not to have been contravened in relation to the recording equipment, the vehicle or any device in or on it;

the relevant person must pay, in respect of loss occasioned, such amount as in default of agreement may be determined by a single arbitrator (in Scotland, arbiter) agreed upon by the parties or, in default of agreement, appointed by the Secretary of State.

(8) In subsection (7) of this section *"relevant person"* means—

(a) if the requirement was imposed by an examiner appointed under section 66A of the Road Traffic Act 1988, the Secretary of State, and

(b) if the requirement was imposed by a constable, the chief officer of police for the police area in which the requirement was imposed.

(9) In this Part of this Act *"analogue recording equipment"* means recording equipment that complies with Annex I to the Community Recording Equipment Regulation.]

A4.33 *[Section 99ZB is printed as inserted by the Passenger and Goods Vehicles (Recording Equipment) Regulations 2005 (SI 2005/1904) reg.6.]*

[Sections 99ZA and 99ZB: supplementary

A4.34 **99ZC.**—(1) Where an officer makes any hard copy of data stored on a driver card or on recording equipment under section 99ZA or 99ZB of this Act he may require a person to sign the hard copy (if necessary with manual corrections) to confirm that it is a true and complete record of his activities during the period covered by it.

(2) Any record sheet, book, register, other document or any electronic copy of data that is retained by an officer under section 99ZA or 99ZB of this Act may only be retained—

(a) for six months; and

(b) if it is required as evidence in any proceedings, any further period during which it is so required.

(3) In sections 99ZA and 99ZB of this Act references to the inspection and copying of any record produced by means of equipment in or on a vehicle include references to the application to the record of any process for eliciting the information recorded by it and to taking down the information elicited from it.]

A4.35 *[Section 99ZC is printed as inserted by the Passenger and Goods Vehicles (Recording Equipment) Regulations 2005 (SI 2005/1904) reg.6.]*

[Offence of failing to comply with requirements or obstructing an officer

A4.36 **99ZD.**—(1) A person commits an offence if he—

(a) fails without reasonable excuse to comply with any requirement imposed on him by an officer under any of sections 99ZA to 99ZC of this Act; or

(b) obstructs an officer in the exercise of his powers under section 99ZB or 99ZF of this Act.

(2) A person guilty of an offence under subsection (1) of this section is liable on summary conviction to a fine not exceeding level 5 on the standard scale.]

[Section 99ZD is printed as inserted by the Passenger and Goods Vehicles   **A4.37** *(Recording Equipment) Regulations 2005 (SI 2005/1904) reg.6.*

An offence under s.99ZD(1) is a fixed penalty offence for the purposes of Pt 3 of the Road Traffic Offenders Act 1988 (see the Fixed Penalty Offences Order 2009 (SI 2009/483) art.3), except where that offence is committed by failing to sign a hard copy of downloaded data when required to do so under s.99ZC(1) or obstructing an officer in the exercise of powers under s.99ZF. The amount for the fixed penalty offence is prescribed by the Fixed Penalty Order 2000 (SI 2000/ 2792), as amended by the Fixed Penalty (Amendment) Order 2009 (SI 2009/ 488).]

[Offences: false records and data, etc.

99ZE.—(1) A person commits an offence—   **A4.38**

    (a) if he makes, or causes or permits to be made, a relevant record or entry which he knows to be false;

    (b) if, with intent to deceive, he alters, or causes or permits to be altered, a relevant record or entry;

    (c) if he destroys or suppresses, or causes or permits to be destroyed or suppressed, a relevant record or entry; or

    (d) if he fails without reasonable excuse to make a relevant record or entry, or causes or permits such a failure.

(2) For the purposes of subsection (1) of this section a *"relevant record or entry"* is—

    (a) any record or entry required to be made by or for the purposes of the Community Recording Equipment Regulation or section 97 of this Act; or

    (b) any entry in a book, register or document kept or carried for the purposes of the applicable Community rules.

(3) A person commits an offence—

    (a) if he records or causes or permits to be recorded any data which he knows to be false on recording equipment or on a driver card;

    (b) if he records or causes or permits to be recorded any data which he knows to be false on any hard copy of data previously stored on re- cording equipment or on a driver card;

    (c) if, with intent to deceive, he alters, or causes or permits to be altered, any data stored on recording equipment or on a driver card or appear- ing on any copy of data previously so stored;

    (d) if, with intent to deceive, he produces anything falsely purporting to be a hard copy of data stored on recording equipment or on a driver card;

    (e) if he destroys or suppresses, or causes or permits to be destroyed or suppressed, any data stored in compliance with the requirements of the applicable Community rules on recording equipment or on a driver card; or

    (f) if he fails without reasonable excuse to record any data on recording equipment or on a driver card, or causes or permits such a failure.

(4) A person guilty of an offence under subsection (1) or (3) of this section consisting otherwise than in permitting an act or omission is liable—

    (a) on summary conviction, to a fine not exceeding the statutory maximum; or

    (b) on conviction on indictment, to imprisonment for a term not exceeding two years or to a fine, or to both.

(5) A person guilty of an offence under subsection (1) or (3) of this section consisting in permitting an act or omission is liable on summary conviction to a fine not exceeding level 5 on the standard scale.

(6) A person commits an offence if he produces, supplies or installs any device—

    (a) that is designed to interfere with the proper operation of any recording equipment, or

    (b) that is designed to enable the falsification, alteration, destruction or suppression of data stored in compliance with requirements of the applicable Community Rules on any recording equipment or driver's card.

(7) A person commits an offence if without reasonable excuse he provides information which would assist other persons in producing any such device.

(8) A person shall not be liable to be convicted under subsection (6) or (7) of this section if he proves to the court that he produced, supplied or installed the device, or provided information to assist a person in producing a device, for use in connection with the enforcement of the provisions of this Part of this Act.

(9) A person guilty of an offence under subsection (6) or (7) of this section is liable on summary conviction to a fine not exceeding level 5 on the standard scale.

(10) For the purposes of this section, a person shall be taken to permit an act or omission if he is, or ought reasonably to be, aware of the act or omission, or of it being a likelihood, and takes no steps to prevent it.]

A4.39   *[Section 99ZE is printed as inserted by the Passenger and Goods Vehicles (Recording Equipment) Regulations 2005 (SI 2005/1904) reg.6.]*

[Power to seize documents

A4.40   **99ZF.**—(1) If an officer has reason to believe that an offence under section 99ZE of this Act has been committed in respect of any document inspected by him under section 99ZA or 99ZB of this Act, he may seize that document.

(2) Where a document is so seized, a magistrates' court shall, on an application made for the purpose by that person or by an officer, make such order respecting the disposal of the document and award such costs as the justice of the case may require if—

    (a) within six months of the date on which it was seized no person has been charged since that date with an offence under section 99ZE of this Act in relation to that document; and

    (b) the document has not been returned to the person from whom it was taken.

(3) ....]

A4.41   *[Section 99ZF is printed as inserted by the Passenger and Goods Vehicles*

(Recording Equipment) Regulations 2005 (SI 2005/1904) reg.6. Section 99ZF(3) relates expressly and exclusively to Scotland and is omitted.]

[Power to prohibit driving of vehicle

99A.—(1) If—   **A4.42**

   (a) the driver of a UK vehicle obstructs an authorised person in the exercise of his powers under subsection (2) or (3) of section 99 [or under section 99ZB] of this Act or fails to comply with any requirement made by an authorised person under subsection (1) of [section 99 or under any of sections 99ZA to 99ZC of this Act],

   (b) it appears to an authorised person that, in relation to a UK vehicle or its driver, there has been a contravention of any of the provisions of—

      (i) sections 96 to 98 of this Act and any orders or regulations under those sections, or

      (ii) the applicable Community rules,

   or that there will be such a contravention if the vehicle is driven on a road, or

   (c) it appears to an authorised person that an offence under section 99(5) [or under section 99ZE] of this Act has been committed in respect of UK vehicle or its driver,

the authorised person may prohibit the driving of the vehicle on a road either for a specified period or without limitation of time.

(2) Where an authorised person prohibits the driving of a vehicle under this section, he may also direct the driver to remove the vehicle (and, if it is a motor vehicle drawing a trailer, also to remove the trailer) to such place and subject to such conditions as are specified in the direction; and the prohibition shall not apply to the removal of the vehicle in accordance with that direction.

(3) On imposing a prohibition under subsection (1) of this section, the authorised person shall give notice in writing of the prohibition to the driver of the vehicle, specifying the circumstances (as mentioned in paragraph (a), (b) or (c) of that subsection) in consequence of which the prohibition is imposed and stating whether it is imposed only for a specified period (and if so specifying the period) or without limitation of time.

(4) Any direction under subsection (2) of this section may be given—

    (a) in the notice under subsection (3) of this section, or

    (b) in a separate notice in writing given to the driver of the vehicle.

(5) In this section —

   "authorised person" means—

      (a) an examiner appointed by the Secretary of State under section 66A of the Road Traffic Act 1988, or

      (b) a constable authorised to act for the purposes of this section by or on behalf of a chief officer of police;

   "UK vehicle" means a vehicle registered under the Vehicle Excise and Registration Act 1994.]

[(6) Schedule 4 to the Road Safety Act 2006 makes provision about the immobilisation of vehicles the driving of which has been prohibited under subsection (1) of this section and about their removal and disposal.]

A4.43   *[Section 99A was inserted by the Transport Act 2000 s.266, and is printed as amended by the Passenger and Goods Vehicles (Recording Equipment) Regulations 2005 (SI 2005/1904) reg.7; the Road Safety Act 2006 s.12(1).*

The Road Safety (Immobilisation, Removal and Disposal of Vehicles) Regulations 2009 (SI 2009/493) [q.v.] apply with respect to any case where the driving has been prohibited under this section.]

[Duration and removal of prohibition

A4.44   **99B.**—(1) Subject to any exemption granted under subsection (2) of this section, a prohibition under subsection (1) of section 99A of this Act shall come into force as soon as notice of it has been given in accordance with subsection (3) of that section and shall continue in force—

     (a) until it is removed under subsection (3) of this section, or

     (b) in the case of a prohibition imposed for a specified period, until it is removed under that subsection or that period expires, whichever first occurs.

(2) Where notice of a prohibition has been given under section 99A(3) of this Act in respect of a vehicle, an exemption in writing for the use of the vehicle in such manner, subject to such conditions and for such purposes as may be specified in the exemption may be granted by any authorised person.

(3) A prohibition under section 99A(1) of this Act may be removed by any authorised person, if he is satisfied that appropriate action has been taken to remove or remedy the circumstances (as mentioned in paragraph (a), (b) or (c) of section 99A(1) of this Act) in consequence of which the prohibition was imposed; and on doing so the authorised person shall give notice in writing of the removal of the prohibition to the driver of the vehicle.

(4) In this section, *"authorised person"* has the same meaning as in section 99A of this Act.]

A4.45   *[Section 99B was inserted by the Transport Act 2000 s.266.]*

[Failure to comply with prohibition

A4.46   **99C.** Any person who—

     (a) drives a vehicle on a road in contravention of a prohibition imposed under section 99A(1) of this Act,

     (b) causes or permits a vehicle to be driven on a road in contravention of such a prohibition, or

     (c) refuses or fails to comply within a reasonable time with a direction given under section 99A(2) of this Act,

shall be guilty of an offence and liable on summary conviction to a fine not exceeding level 5 on the standard scale.]

A4.47   *[Section 99C was inserted by the Transport Act 2000 s.266.*

An offence under s.99C is a fixed penalty offence for the purposes of Pt 3 of the Road Traffic Offenders Act 1988 (see the Fixed Penalty Offences Order 2009 (SI 2009/483) art.2). The amount for the fixed penalty offence is prescribed by the Fixed Penalty Order 2000 (SI 2000/2792), as amended by the Fixed Penalty (Amendment) Order 2009 (SI 2009/488).]

* * *

Application to the Crown and exemption for police and [fire and rescue authority]

102.—(1) Subject to subsection (2) of this section, this Part of this Act shall apply to vehicles and persons in the public service of the Crown.   **A4.48**

(2) This Part of this Act shall not apply in the case of motor vehicles owned by the Secretary of State for Defence and used for naval, military or air force purposes or in the case of vehicles so used while being driven by persons for the time being subject to the orders of a member of the armed forces of the Crown.

[(3) Where an offence under this Part of this Act is alleged to have been committed in connection with a vehicle in the public service of the Crown, proceedings may be brought in respect of the offence against a person nominated for the purpose on behalf of the Crown; and, subject to subsection (3A) below, where any such offence is committed any person so nominated shall also be guilty of the offence as well as any person actually responsible for the offence (but without prejudice to proceedings against any person so responsible).]

[(3A) Where a person is convicted of an offence by virtue of subsection (3) above—

    (a) no order may be made on his conviction save an order imposing a fine,

    (b) payment of any fine imposed on him in respect of that offence may not be enforced against him, and

    (c) apart from the imposition of any such fine, the conviction shall be disregarded for all purposes other than any appeal (whether by way of case stated or otherwise).]

(4) This Part of this Act shall not apply in the case of motor vehicles while being used for police or [fire and rescue authority] purposes.

[Section 102 is printed as amended by the Road Traffic (Consequential Provisions) Act 1988 s.4 and Sch.3 para 6(6); the Fire and Rescue Services Act 2004 s.53 and Sch.1 para.25.]   **A4.49**

[Exclusion of application to tramcars and trolley vehicles

102A.—(1) This Part of this Act and section 255 of the Road Traffic Act 1960 in its application thereto shall not apply to tramcars or trolley vehicles operated under statutory powers.   **A4.50**

(2) In this section *"operated under statutory powers"* means, in relation to tramcars or trolley vehicles, that their use is authorised or regulated by special Act of Parliament or by an order having the force of an Act.

(3) Subsection (1) above shall have effect subject to any such Act or order as is mentioned in subsection (2) above, and any such Act or order may apply to tramcars or trolley vehicles to which it relates any of the provisions excluded by the said subsection (1).]

[Section 102A was inserted by the Road Traffic (Consequential Provisions) Act 1988 s.4 and Sch.3, para.6(7).]   **A4.51**

[Partnerships and other unincorporated associations

102B.—(1) Proceedings for an offence under this Part of this Act alleged to   **A4.52**

have been committed by a partnership must be brought in the name of the partnership (and not in that of any of the partners).

(2) Proceedings for an offence under this Part of this Act alleged to have been committed by an unincorporated association (other than a partnership) must be brought in the name of the association (and not in that of any of its members).

(3) Rules of court relating to the service of documents have effect as if the partnership or association were a body corporate.

(4) In proceedings for an offence under this Part of this Act brought against a partnership or an unincorporated association, the following provisions apply as they do in relation to a body corporate—

    (a) section 33 of the Criminal Justice Act 1925 and Schedule 3 to the Magistrates' Courts Act 1980;

    (b) *[applies to Scotland]*.

(5) A fine imposed on a partnership on its conviction for an offence under this Part of this Act must be paid out of the partnership assets.

(6) A fine imposed on an unincorporated association on its conviction for an offence under this Part of this Act must be paid out of the funds of the association.

(7) Subsections (1) and (2) do not affect any liability of a partner, officer or member under section 102C.]

A4.53   *[Section 102B was inserted by the Passenger and Goods Vehicles (Recording Equipment) (Downloading and Retention of Data) Regulations 2008 (SI 2008/198) reg.3.]*

[Offences by bodies corporate, etc.

A4.54   **102C.**—(1) If an offence under this Part of this Act committed by a body corporate is proved—

    (a) to have been committed with the consent or connivance of an officer of the body, or

    (b) to be attributable to any neglect on the part of an officer of the body, he, as well as the body corporate, is guilty of the offence.

(2) In subsection (1) a reference to an officer of a body includes a reference to—

    (a) a director, manager or secretary;

    (b) a person purporting to act as an officer of the body.

(3) If the affairs of a body corporate are managed by its members, subsection (1) applies in relation to the acts and defaults of a member in connection with his functions of management as if he were a director of the body.

(4) IIf an offence under this Part of this Act committed by a partnership is proved—

    (a) to have been committed with the consent or connivance of a partner, or

    (b) to be attributable to any neglect on the part of a partner, he, as well as the partnership, is guilty of the offence.

(5) In subsection (4) a reference to a partner includes a reference to a person purporting to act as a partner.

(6) If an offence under this Part of this Act committed by an unincorporated association (other than a partnership) is proved—

(a) to have been committed with the consent or connivance of an officer of the association, or

(b) to be attributable to any neglect on the part of an officer of the association, he, as well as the association, is guilty of the offence.

(7) In subsection (6) a reference to an officer of an association includes a reference to—

(a) a member of its governing body;

(b) a person purporting to act in the capacity of an officer of the association.]

[Section 102C was inserted by the Passenger and Goods Vehicles (Recording Equipment) (Downloading and Retention of Data) Regulations 2008 (SI 2008/ 198) reg.3.]   **A4.55**

Interpretation, supplementary provisions, etc., for Part VI

103.—(1) In this Part of this Act —   **A4.56**

"agriculture" has the meaning assigned by section 109(3) of the Agriculture Act 1947 *[see note below]* …;

[*"analogue recording equipment"* has the meaning given by section 99ZB(9) of this Act;]

[*"the Community Drivers' Hours Regulation"* means Regulation (EC) No.561/2006 *[q.v.]* of the European Parliament and of the Council as amended from time to time;]

[*"the applicable Community rules"* means any directly applicable Community provision for the time being in force about the driving of road vehicles [and includes the European Agreement concerning the Work of Crews of Vehicles engaged in International Road Transport of 1st July 1970, as amended, as applied by Article 2(3) of the Community Drivers' Hours Regulation];]

[*"the Community Recording Equipment Regulation"* has the meaning given by section 97(7) of this Act;]

[*"copying"* and *"copies"*, in relation to data stored on a driver card or digital recording equipment, is to be construed in accordance with section 99ZA(5) of this Act;]

[*"digital recording equipment"* has the meaning given by section 99ZA(6) of this Act;]

[*"the domestic drivers' hours code"* has the meaning given by section 96(13) of this Act;]

"driver", *"employee-driver"* and *"owner-driver"* have the meaning assigned by section 95(3) of this Act;

[*"driver card"* has the meaning given by section 99ZA(6) of this Act;]

[*"electronic copy"* of data has the meaning given by section 99ZA(6) of this Act;]

"employer", in relation to an employee-driver, means the employer of that driver in the employment by virtue of which that driver is an employee-driver;

[*"hard copy"* in relation to data stored electronically has the meaning given by section 99ZA(6) of this Act;]

* * *

[*"officer"* has the meaning given by section 99(8) of this Act;]

"prescribed" means prescribed by regulations made by the [Secretary of State for Transport];

[*"recording equipment"* has the meaning given by section 97(7) of this Act;]

[*"record sheet"* includes a temporary sheet attached to a record sheet in accordance with [Article 16(2) of the Community Recording Equipment Regulation;]]

[*"relevant Community provision"* means any Community provision for the time being in force about the driving of road vehicles, whether directly applicable or not;]

[*"transport undertaking"* has the meaning given in the Community Drivers' Hours Regulation;]

"working day" in relation to any driver, means—

    (a) any period during which he is on duty and which does not fall to be aggregated with any other such period by virtue of paragraph (b) of this definition; and

    (b) where a period during which he is on duty is not followed by an interval for rest of not less than eleven hours or (where permitted by virtue of section 96(4)(b) of this Act) of not less than nine and a half hours, the aggregate of that period and each successive such period until there is such an interval as aforesaid, together with any interval or intervals between periods so aggregated;

[*"working week"* means, subject to subsection (5) of this section, a week beginning at midnight between Sunday and Monday;]

and any expression not defined above which is also used in the [Road Traffic Act 1988] has the same meaning as in that Act.

(2) For the purposes of this Part of this Act a director of a company shall be deemed to be employed by it.

(3) In this Part of this Act references to a person driving a vehicle are references to his being at the driving controls of the vehicle for the purpose of controlling its movement, whether it is in motion or is stationary with the engine running.

(4) In this Part of this Act references to a driver on duty are references—

    (a) in the case of an employee-driver, to his being on duty (whether for the purpose of driving a vehicle to which this Part of this Act applies or for other purposes) in the employment by virtue of which he is an employee-driver, or in any other employment under the person who is his employer in the first-mentioned employment; and

    (b) in the case of an owner-driver, to his driving a vehicle to which this Part of this Act applies for the purposes of a trade or business carried on by him or being otherwise engaged in work for the purposes of that trade or business, being work in connection with such a vehicle or the load carried thereby.

(5) The traffic [commissioner] for any area may, on the application of an owner-driver or of the employer of an employee-driver, from time to time direct

that a week beginning at midnight between two days other than [Sunday and Monday] shall be, or be deemed to have been, a working week in relation to that owner-driver or employee-driver; but where by virtue of any such direction a new working week begins before the expiration of a previous working week then, without prejudice to the application of the provisions of this Part of this Act in relation to the new working week, those provisions shall continue to apply in relation to the previous working week until its expiration.

(6) In [section] 98(2)(e) of this Act *"a small goods vehicle"* means a goods vehicle which has a plated weight of the prescribed description not exceeding [3500 kilograms] or (not having a plated weight) has an unladen weight not exceeding [1525 kilograms]; but the [Secretary of State for Transport] may by regulations direct that the foregoing provisions of this subsection shall have effect, in relation to either or both of those sections—

(a) with the substitution for either of the weights there specified of such other weight as may be specified in the regulations;

(b) with the substitution for either of those weights or for any other weight for the time being specified as aforesaid of a weight expressed in terms of the metric system, being a weight which is equivalent to that for which it is substituted or does not differ from it by more than 5 per cent thereof.

[(7) An offence under this Part of this Act may be treated for the purpose of conferring jurisdiction on a court (but without prejudice to any jurisdiction it may have apart from this subsection) as having been committed in any of the following places, that is to say—

(a) the place where the person charged with the offence was driving when evidence of the offence first came to the attention of a constable or vehicle examiner;

(b) the place where that person resides or is believed to reside or be at the time when the proceedings are commenced; or

(c) the place where at that time that person or, in the case of an employee-driver, that person's employer or, in the case of an owner-driver, the person for whom he was driving, has his place or principal place of business or his operating centre for the vehicle in question.

In this subsection *"vehicle examiner"* means an officer within the meaning of section 99 of this Act.]

(8) The enactments specified in Schedule 11 to this Act shall have effect subject to the amendments there specified.

(9) Any order made under section 166(2) of this Act appointing a day for the purposes of any of the provisions of this Part of this Act may contain such transitional provisions as the [Secretary of State for Transport] thinks necessary or expedient as respects the application of any particular provision of this Part of this Act to a working week or working day falling partly before and partly after the date on which that provision comes into operation.

[Section 103 is printed as amended by the Road Traffic (Drivers' Ages and **A4.57** *Hours of Work) Act 1976 ss.2(1) and 3; the Interpretation Act 1978 s.17(2)(a); the Minister of Transport Order 1979 (SI 1979/571); the Passenger and Goods Vehicles (Recording Equipment) Regulations 1979 (SI 1979/1746); the Transfer of Functions (Transport) Order 1981 (SI 1981/238); the Road Traffic Acts 1960*

and 1972, Road Traffic Regulation Act 1967, and Transport Act 1968 (Metrication) Regulations 1981 (SI 1981/1373); the Transport Act 1985 ss.3(5) and 139(3), Sch.2, Pt II, para.1(5), Sch.8; the Community Drivers' Hours and Recording Equipment Regulations 1986 (SI 1986/1457) reg.3; the Drivers' Hours (Harmonisation with Community Rules) Regulations 1986 (SI 1986/1458) reg.3; the Secretary of State for the Environment, Transport and the Regions Order 1997 (SI 1997/2971); the Secretaries of State for Transport, Local Government and the Regions and for Environment, Food and Rural Affairs Order 2001 (SI 2001/2568); the Transfer of Functions (Transport, Local Government and the Regions) Order 2002 (SI 2002/2626); the Passenger and Goods Vehicles (Recording Equipment) Regulations 2005 (SI 2005/1904) reg.8; the Community Drivers' Hours and Recording Equipment Regulations 2007 (SI 2007/1819) reg.8; the Passenger and Goods Vehicles (Recording Equipment) (Downloading and Retention of Data) Regulations 2008 (SI 2008/198) reg.4.

In the definition of "agriculture", words relating expressly and exclusively to Scotland have been omitted. The term "agriculture" is defined in s.109(3) of the Agriculture Act 1947 as follows:

> *"agriculture"* includes horticulture, fruit growing, seed growing, dairy farming and live-stock breeding and keeping, the use of land as grazing land, meadow land, osier land, market gardens and nursery grounds, and the use of land for woodlands where that use is ancillary to the farming of land for other agricultural purposes, and *"agricultural"* shall be construed accordingly;

The definition of "working day" has been modified in its application to the drivers of passenger vehicles and goods vehicles; see further the Drivers' Hours (Passenger and Goods Vehicles) (Modifications) Order 1971 (SI 1971/818) and the Drivers' Hours (Goods Vehicles) (Modifications) Order 1986 (SI 1986/1459) below.

The amendments to subs.(6) effected by the Road Traffic Acts 1960 and 1972, Road Traffic Regulation Act 1967, and Transport Act 1968 (Metrication) Regulations (SI 1981/1373) (namely "3500 kilograms" for "3 tons" and "1525 kilograms" for "30 hundredweight") were expressed specifically to apply to s.98(2) of this Act.]

The Chronically Sick and Disabled Persons Act 1970

(1970 c.44)

An Act to make further provision with respect to the welfare of chronically sick and disabled persons; and for connected purposes.

A5.01

[29th May 1970]

*　　*　　*

Use of invalid carriages on highways

20.—(1) In the case of a vehicle which is an invalid carriage complying with the prescribed requirements and which is being used in accordance with the prescribed conditions—

A5.02

(a) no statutory provision prohibiting or restricting the use of footways shall prohibit or restrict the use of that vehicle on a footway;

(b) if the vehicle is mechanically propelled, it shall be treated for the purposes of the [Road Traffic Regulation Act [1984] and [the Road Traffic Act 1988[, except section 22A of that Act (causing danger to road users by interfering with motor vehicles, etc.),] and the Road Traffic Offenders Act 1988]] as not being a motor vehicle [and sections 1 to 4, [21, 34,] 163, 170 and 181 of the Road Traffic Act 1988 shall not apply to it]; and

(c) whether or not the vehicle is mechanically propelled, it shall be exempted from the requirements of [section 83 of the said Act of 1988].

(2) In this section —

"footway" means a way which is a footway, footpath or bridleway within the meaning of [the Highways Act 1980] [or a restricted byway within the meaning of Part 2 of the Countryside and Rights of Way Act 2000]…;

"invalid carriage" means a vehicle, whether mechanically propelled or not, constructed or adapted for use for the carriage of one person, being a person suffering from some physical defect or disability;

"prescribed" means prescribed by regulations made by the [Secretary of State for Transport];

"statutory provision" means a provision contained in, or having effect under, any enactment.

(3) *[Omitted.]*

[Section 20 is printed as amended by the Secretary of State for the Environment Order 1970 (SI 1970/1681); the Road Traffic Act 1972 s.203(1) and Sch.7; the Secretary of State for Transport Order 1976 (SI 1976/1775); the Minister of Transport Order 1979 (SI 1979/571); the Highways Act 1980 s.343(2) and Sch.24, para.19; the Transfer of Functions (Transport) Order 1981 (SI 1981/

A5.03

238); the Road Traffic Regulation Act 1984 s.146(a) and Sch.13, para.10; the Road Traffic (Consequential Provisions) Act 1988 s.4 and Sch.3 para.7; the Road Traffic Act 1991 s.48 and Sch.4, para.3(a) and (b); the Secretary of State for the Environment, Transport and the Regions Order 1997 (SI 1997/2971); the Countryside and Rights of Way Act 2000 ss.67 and 103(2) and Sch.7 para.3; the Secretaries of State for Transport, Local Government and the Regions and for Environment, Food and Rural Affairs Order 2001 (SI 2001/2568); the Transfer of Functions (Transport, Local Government and the Regions) Order 2002 (SI 2002/2626); the Restricted Byways (Application and Consequential Amendment of Provisions) Regulations 2006 (SI 2006/1177) Sch., Pt I.

Words relating expressly and exclusively to Scotland have been omitted from the definition of "footway".

The Use of Invalid Carriages on Highways Regulations 1988 (SI 1988/2268) (q.v.) have been made under this section.]

Badges for display on motor vehicles used by disabled persons

A5.04   **21.**—(1)–(4) *[Omitted.]*

[(4A) A badge issued under this section may be displayed only in such circumstances and in such manner as may be prescribed.]

[(4B) A person who drives a motor vehicle on a road (within the meaning of the Road Traffic Act 1988) at a time when a badge [purporting to be] of a form prescribed under this section is displayed on the vehicle is guilty of an offence unless the badge is issued under this section and displayed in accordance with regulations made under it.]

[(4BA) Where it appears to a constable or enforcement officer that there is displayed on any motor vehicle a badge purporting to be of a form prescribed under this section, he may require any person who—

  (a) is in the vehicle, or

  (b) appears to have been in, or to be about to get into, the vehicle,

to produce the badge for inspection.]

[(4BB) In subsection (4BA) *"enforcement officer"* means—

  (a) a traffic warden;

  (b) a civil enforcement officer (within the meaning of section 76 of the Traffic Management Act 2004);

  (c) a parking attendant (within the meaning of section 63A of the Road Traffic Regulation Act 1984).]

[(4BC) The power conferred on an enforcement officer by subsection (4BA) is exercisable only for purposes connected with the discharge of his functions in relation to a stationary vehicle.]

[(4BD) A person who without reasonable excuse fails to produce a badge when required to do so under subsection (4BA) shall be guilty of an offence.]

[(4C) A person guilty of an offence under subsection (4B) [or (4BD)] above shall be liable on summary conviction to a fine not exceeding level 3 on the standard scale.]

(5)–(7E) *[Omitted.]*

(8) The local authorities for the purposes of this section shall be the common council of the City of London, the council of a county … [or metropolitan district]

in England ... or of a London borough [, the council of a Welsh county or county borough] ...; and in this section *"motor vehicle"* has the same meaning as in the Road Traffic Regulation Act [1984].

(9) *[Omitted.]*

[Section 21 is printed as amended by the Local Government Act 1972 s.272(1) **A5.05** *and Sch.30; the Road Traffic Regulation Act 1984 s.146(a) and Sch.13, para.11; the Local Government Act 1985 s.8 and Sch.5 Pt I para.1; the Road Traffic Act 1991 s.35(1) and (4); the Local Government (Wales) Act 1994 s.22(4) and Sch.10, para.8 (see also ibid. s.66(8) and Sch.18); the Traffic Management Act 2004 s.94.*

Words relating expressly and exclusively to Scotland have been omitted from subs.(8) above.

The Disabled Persons (Badges for Motor Vehicles) (England) Regulations 2000 (SI 2000/682 below) and the Disabled Persons (Badges for Motor Vehicles) (Wales) Regulations 2000 (SI 2000/1786) have been made under this section and the Local Authorities' Traffic Orders (Exemptions for Disabled Persons) (England) Regulations 2000 (SI 2000/683) and the Local Authorities' Traffic Orders (Exemptions for Disabled Persons) (Wales) Regulations 2000 (SI 2000/1785) have been made in part under this section.]

[Recognition of badges issued outside Great Britain

21A.—(1) For the purposes of this section and section 21B, a *"recognised* **A5.06** *badge"* means—

    (a) a badge issued under section 14 of the Chronically Sick and Disabled Persons (Northern Ireland) Act 1978, or any provision replacing that section, as from time to time amended, or

    (b) a badge issued under provisions of the law of any jurisdiction outside the United Kingdom that are specified in regulations made by the appropriate national authority.

(2) In exercising the power under subsection (1)(b), the appropriate national authority may specify a provision only if it appears to the authority that badges issued under the provision are issued by reference to persons who are, or include, disabled persons.

(3) A recognised badge may be displayed on a motor vehicle only in such circumstances and in such manner as may be prescribed by regulations made by the appropriate national authority.

(4) A person who drives a motor vehicle on a road (within the meaning of the Road Traffic Act 1988) at a time when a badge purporting to be a recognised badge is displayed on the vehicle is guilty of an offence unless the badge is a recognised badge and is displayed in accordance with regulations made under subsection (3).

(5) A person guilty of an offence under subsection (4) shall be liable on summary conviction to a fine not exceeding level 3 on the standard scale.

(6) Where it appears to a constable or enforcement officer that there is displayed on any motor vehicle a badge purporting to be a recognised badge, he may require any person who—

    (a) is in the vehicle, or

(b) appears to have been in, or to be about to get into, the vehicle,

to produce the badge for inspection.

(7) The power conferred on an enforcement officer by subsection (6) is exercisable only for purposes connected with the discharge of his functions in relation to a stationary vehicle.

(8) A person who without reasonable excuse fails to produce a badge when required to do so under subsection (6) shall be guilty of an offence and liable on summary conviction to a fine not exceeding level 3 on the standard scale.

(9) In this section *"enforcement officer"* has the meaning given by section 21(4BB).]

A5.07   *[Section 21A is printed as inserted by the Disability Discrimination Act 2005 s.9.]*

[Recognised badges treated as badges under section 21 for certain purposes

A5.08   **21B.**—(1) The concessions mentioned in subsection (2) shall apply in respect of vehicles lawfully displaying a recognised badge as they apply in respect of vehicles lawfully displaying a badge issued under section 21.

(2) The concessions are—

     (a) any exemption from an order under the Road Traffic Regulation Act 1984 given by reference to vehicles lawfully displaying a badge issued under section 21;

     (b) any provision made in an order under that Act for the use of a parking place by such vehicles.

(3) The appropriate national authority may by regulations provide that recognised badges are to be treated, for purposes specified in the regulations, as if they were badges issued under section 21.]

A5.09   *[Section 21B is printed as inserted by the Disability Discrimination Act 2005 s.9.]*

[Sections 21A and 21B: regulations and interpretation

A5.10   **21C.**—(1) Any power to make regulations under section 21A or 21B—

     (a) is exercisable by statutory instrument, and

     (b) includes power—

         (i) to make different provision for different cases, and

         (ii) to make incidental, supplementary, transitional or consequential provision.

(2) A statutory instrument containing regulations made under section 21A or 21B by the Secretary of State is subject to annulment in pursuance of a resolution of either House of Parliament.

(3) In sections 21A and 21B, *"appropriate national authority"* means—

     (a) in relation to England, the Secretary of State;

     (b) in relation to Wales, the National Assembly for Wales.]

A5.11   *[Section 21C is printed as inserted by the Disability Discrimination Act 2005 s.9.]*

The Road Traffic (Foreign Vehicles) Act 1972

(1972 c.27)

An Act to make provision, in relation to foreign goods vehicles and foreign public service vehicles, for securing the observance of certain statutory provisions relating to road traffic; and for purposes connected with those matters.   **A6.01**

[11th May 1972]

ARRANGEMENT OF SECTIONS

[Visiting forces and headquarters (as defined), members of such forces or headquarters, and persons employed by such forces are exempt from the operation of the 1972 Act to the extent that, by virtue of any rule of law whereby enactments do not bind the Crown, such forces, headquarters, members or persons would have been so exempt if the forces or headquarters had been part of the home forces; see the Visiting Forces and International Headquarters (Application of Law) Order 1999 (SI 1999/1736; not reproduced in this work) art.12(1) and Sch.5.]   **A6.02**

Power in certain cases to prohibit driving of foreign vehicle

1.—(1) The provisions of this section shall have effect with respect to any foreign goods vehicle or foreign public service vehicle where—   **A6.03**

    (a) an examiner [or an authorised inspector] exercises, in relation to the vehicle or its driver, any functions of the examiner [or authorised inspector] under an enactment [or instrument] specified in the first column of Schedule 1 to this Act, or [any functions of the authorised inspecting officer under a Community instrument specified in that column, or]

    (b) an authorised person exercises, in relation to the vehicle, any functions of that person under [sections 78 and 79 of the Road Traffic Act 1988] (weighing of motor vehicles).

(2) If in any such case as is mentioned in subsection (1)(a) of this section—

   (a) the driver obstructs the examiner [or authorised inspector] in the exercise of his functions under the enactment [or instrument] in question, or refuses, neglects or otherwise fails to comply with any requirement made by the examiner [or authorised inspector] under that enactment [or instrument], or

   (b) it appears to the examiner [or authorised inspector] that, in relation to the vehicle or its driver, there has been a contravention of any of the enactments or instruments specified in the first column of Schedule 2 to this Act, or that there will be such a contravention if the vehicle is driven on a road,

the examiner [or authorised inspector] may prohibit the driving of the vehicle on a road, either absolutely or for a specified purpose, and either for a specified period or without any limitation of time.

(3) If in any such case as is mentioned in subsection (1)(b) of this section—

   (a) the driver obstructs the authorised person in the exercise of his functions under [the said sections 78 and 79], or refuses, neglects or otherwise fails to comply with any requirement made by the authorised person under [those sections], or

   (b) it appears to the authorised person that any limit of weight applicable to the vehicle by virtue of regulations made under [section 41 of the Road Traffic Act 1988] has been exceeded, or will be exceeded if the vehicle is driven on a road,

the authorised person may prohibit the driving of the vehicle on a road, either absolutely or for a specified purpose.

(4) Where an examiner [or an authorised inspector] or an authorised person prohibits the driving of a vehicle under this section, he may also direct the driver to remove the vehicle (and, if it is a motor vehicle drawing a trailer, also to remove the trailer) to such place and subject to such conditions as are specified in the direction; and the prohibition shall not apply to the removal of the vehicle in accordance with that direction.

(5) Where a prohibition is imposed under subsection (2) or subsection (3) of this section, the examiner [or authorised inspector] or authorised person shall forthwith give notice in writing of the prohibition to the driver of the vehicle, specifying the circumstances (as mentioned in paragraph (a) or paragraph (b) of either of those subsections) in consequence of which the prohibition is imposed, and—

   (a) stating whether the prohibition is on all driving of the vehicle or only on driving it for a specified purpose (and, if the latter, specifying the purpose), and

   (b) where the prohibition is imposed under subsection (2) of this section, also stating whether it is imposed only for a specified period (and, if so, specifying the period) or without limitation of time;

and any direction under subsection (4) of this section may be given either in that notice or in a separate notice in writing given to the driver of the vehicle.

[(6) In the case of a goods vehicle—

   (a) a prohibition under subsection (2)(b) above, by reference to a supposed contravention of [section 40A of the Road Traffic Act 1988 (using vehicle in dangerous condition, etc.) or regulations under section 41 of that Act (construction, weight, equipment, etc., of motor vehicles and trailers),] may be imposed with a direction making it irremovable unless and until the vehicle has been inspected at an official testing station;

  (b) a prohibition imposed under subsection (3) above may be against driving the vehicle on a road until the weight has been reduced and official notification has been given to whoever is for the time being in charge of the vehicle that it is permitted to proceed.]

[(7) Official notification for the purposes of subsection (6)(b) above must be in writing and be given by an authorised person and may be withheld until the vehicle has been weighed or re-weighed in order to satisfy the person giving the notification that the weight has been sufficiently reduced.]

[Section 1 is printed as amended by the Transport Act 1978 s.9(1) and Sch.3,   **A6.04**
para.8; the Transport Act 1982 s.10(4); the Road Transport (International Passenger Services) Regulations 1984 (SI 1984/748) reg.22; the Road Traffic Act 1991 s.4 and Sch.4, para.6; the Public Service Vehicles (Community Licences) Regulations 1999 (SI 1999/1322) reg.13(1).

The references to "authorised inspector" in this section were inserted by the Transport Act 1982 s.10(4), and will take effect from a date to be announced. Until such date, the text of s.1 should be read as if such references were omitted.

For the powers of the Secretary of State for Transport to give information in relation to tests and inspections of commercial motor vehicles and their trailers carried out under s.1 to competent authorities in other EU Member States and in Northern Ireland and Gibraltar in compliance with Directive 2000/30/EC (O.J. No.L203, August 10, 2000, p.1), see the Road Vehicles (Testing) (Disclosure of Information) (Great Britain) Regulations 2002 (SI 2002/2426).

The Road Safety (Immobilisation, Removal and Disposal of Vehicles) Regulations 2009 (SI 2009/493) [q.v.] apply with respect to any case where the driving has been prohibited under this section.]

Provisions supplementary to section 1

2.—(1) Subject to any exemption granted under subsection (2) of this section,   **A6.05** a prohibition under section 1 of this Act shall come into force as soon as notice of it has been given in accordance with subsection (5) of that section, and shall continue in force until it is removed under the following provisions of this section (or, in the case of a prohibition imposed only for a specified period, shall continue in force until either it is removed under this section or that period expires, whichever first occurs).

(2) Where notice of a prohibition has been given under subsection (5) of section 1 of this Act in respect of a vehicle, an exemption in writing for the use of the vehicle in such manner, subject to such conditions and for such purpose as may be specified in the exemption may be granted—

  (a) in the case of a prohibition under subsection (2) of that section, by any examiner [or authorised inspector], or

  (b) in the case of a prohibition under subsection (3) of that section, by any authorised person.

(3) A prohibition under subsection (2) of section 1 of this Act may be removed by any examiner [or authorised inspector], and a prohibition under subsection (3) of that section may be removed by any authorised person, if he is satisfied that appropriate action has been taken to remove or remedy the circumstances (as mentioned in paragraph (a) or paragraph (b) of either of those subsections) in consequence of which the prohibition was imposed; and on doing so the examiner [or authorised inspector] or authorised person shall forthwith give notice in writing of the removal of the prohibition to the driver of the vehicle.

[(3A) If the prohibition under section 1 of this Act has been imposed with a direction under subsection (6)(a) of that section, the prohibition shall not then be removed under subsection (3) above unless and until the vehicle has been inspected at an official testing station.]

[(3B) In the case of vehicles brought to an official testing station for inspection with a view to removal of a prohibition, [section [72A] of the Road Traffic Act 1988] (fees for inspection) applies.]

(4) In the exercise of his functions under section 1 of this Act or under this section an examiner [or an authorised inspector] shall act in accordance with any general directions given by the Secretary of State; and (without prejudice to the preceding provisions of this subsection) an examiner [or an authorised inspector], in exercising his functions under subsection (2) of this section, shall act in accordance with any directions given by the Secretary of State with respect to the exercise of those functions in any particular case.

A6.06 *[Section 2 is printed as amended by the Transport Act 1978 s.9(1) and Sch.3, para.9; the Transport Act 1982 s.10(4); the Road Traffic (Consequential Provisions) Act 1988 s.4 and Sch.3, para.9(2); the Road Traffic Act 1991 s.48 and Sch.4, para.7.*

The references to "authorised inspector" were inserted by the Transport Act 1982 s.10(4), and will take effect from a date to be announced. Until such date, the text of s.2 should be read as if such references were omitted.]

Enforcement provisions

A6.07 **3.**—(1) Any person who—

(a) drives a vehicle on a road in contravention of a prohibition imposed under section 1 of this Act, or

(b) causes or permits a vehicle to be driven on a road in contravention of such a prohibition, or

(c) refuses, neglects or otherwise fails to comply within a reasonable time with a direction given under subsection (4) of that section,

shall be guilty of an offence and shall be liable on summary conviction to a fine not exceeding [level 5 on the standard scale].

(2) [...]

(3) Where a constable in uniform has reasonable cause to suspect the driver of a vehicle of having committed an offence under subsection (1) of this section, the constable may detain the vehicle, and for that purpose may give a direction, specifying an appropriate person and directing the vehicle to be removed by that person to such place and subject to such conditions as are specified in the direction; and the prohibition shall not apply to the removal of the vehicle in accordance with that direction.

(4) Where under subsection (3) of this section a constable—

    (a) detains a motor vehicle drawing a trailer, or

    (b) detains a trailer drawn by a motor vehicle,

then, for the purpose of securing the removal of the trailer, he may also (in a case falling within paragraph (a) of this subsection) detain the trailer or (in a case falling within paragraph (b) of this subsection) detain the motor vehicle; and a direction under subsection (3) of this section may require both the motor vehicle and the trailer to be removed to the place specified in the direction.

(5) A vehicle which, in accordance with a direction given under subsection (3) of this section, is removed to a place specified in the direction shall be detained in that place, or in any other place to which it is removed in accordance with a further direction given under that subsection, until a constable (or, if that place is in the occupation of the Secretary of State, the Secretary of State) authorises the vehicle to be released on being satisfied—

    (a) that the prohibition (if any) imposed in respect of the vehicle under section 1 of this Act has been removed, or that no such prohibition was imposed, or

    (b) that appropriate arrangements have been made for removing or remedying the circumstances in consequence of which any such prohibition was imposed, or

    (c) that the vehicle will be taken forthwith to a place from which it will be taken out of Great Britain, or

    (d) in the case of a vehicle detained under subsection (4) of this section, that (in the case of a motor vehicle) the purpose for which it was detained has been fulfilled or (in the case of a trailer) it is no longer necessary to detain it for the purpose of safe-guarding the trailer or its load.

(6) Any person who—

    (a) drives a vehicle in accordance with a direction given under this section, or

    (b) is in charge of a place at which a vehicle is detained under subsection (5) of this section,

shall not be liable for any damage to, or loss in respect of, the vehicle or its load unless it is shown that he did not take reasonable care of the vehicle while driving it or, as the case may be, did not, while the vehicle was detained in that place, take reasonable care of the vehicle or (if the vehicle was detained there with its load) did not take reasonable care of its load.

(7) In this section *"appropriate person"* —

    (a) in relation to a direction to remove a motor vehicle, other than a motor vehicle drawing a trailer, means a person licensed to drive vehicles of the class to which the vehicle belongs, and

    (b) in relation to a direction to remove a trailer, or to remove a motor vehicle drawing a trailer, means a person licensed to drive vehicles of a class which, when the direction is complied with, will include the motor vehicle drawing the trailer in accordance with that direction.

[(8) Schedule 4 to the Road Safety Act 2006 makes provision about the immobilisation of vehicles the driving of which has been prohibited under section 1 of this Act and about their removal and disposal.]

A6.08   *[Section 3 is printed as amended by the Criminal Justice Act 1982 ss.37, 39(2), 46, and Sch.3; the Police and Criminal Evidence Act 1984 s.119(2) and Sch.7; the Road Safety Act 2006 s.12(2).*

An offence under s.3(1) is a fixed penalty offence for the purposes of Pt 3 of the Road Traffic Offenders Act 1988 (see the Fixed Penalty Offences Order 2009 (SI 2009/483) art.2). The amount for the fixed penalty offence is prescribed by the Fixed Penalty Order 2000 (SI 2000/2792), as amended by the Fixed Penalty (Amendment) Order 2009 (SI 2009/488).]

Production of certain documents

A6.09   **4.**—(1) Subsection (3) of this section shall have effect in relation to a vehicle where it appears to an examiner that the vehicle—

    (a) is a foreign goods vehicle within the meaning of regulations for the time being in force under [section 57(6) of the Goods Vehicles (Licensing of Operators) Act 1995] (which enables certain provisions of that Act to be modified in their application to vehicles brought temporarily into Great Britain), and

    (b) is being used, or has been brought into Great Britain for the purpose of being used, in such circumstances as, by virtue of [section 2(1)] of that Act as modified by the regulations, to require a document of a description specified in the regulations to be carried on it.

(2) The next following subsection shall also have effect in relation to a vehicle where it appears to an examiner that the vehicle—

    (a) is a foreign public service vehicle, and

    (b) is being used, or has been brought into Great Britain for the purpose of being used, in such circumstances as, by virtue of [section 12(1) of the Public Passenger Vehicles Act 1981 as modified by regulations for the time being in force under section 60(1)(m) of that Act] (which enables certain provisions of that Act to be modified in their application to public service vehicles [registered outside Great Britain]), to require a document of a description specified in the regulations to be carried on it.

(3) In the circumstances mentioned in subsection (1) or subsection (2) of this section, the examiner, on production if so required of his authority,—

    (a) may require the driver of the vehicle to produce a document of the description in question and to permit the examiner to inspect and copy it, and

    (b) may detain the vehicle for such time as is requisite for the purpose of inspecting and copying the document;

and, if the driver refuses or fails to comply with any such requirement (including any case where he does so by reason that no such document is carried on the vehicle), the examiner may prohibit the driving of the vehicle on a road, either absolutely or for a specified purpose, and either for a specified period or without limitation of time.

(4) In subsections (4) and (5) of section 1 and in section 2 and 3 of this Act any reference to a prohibition imposed under section 1, or under subsection (2) of section 1, of this Act shall be construed as including a reference to a prohibition imposed under this section; and, in relation to a prohibition imposed under this

section, so much of section 1(5) or of section 2(3) of this Act as relates to the circumstances in consequence of which the prohibition was imposed shall be read subject to the appropriate modifications.

[Section 4 is printed as amended by the Transport Act 1980 s.43(1) and Sch.5, **A6.10**
Pt II; the Public Passenger Vehicles Act 1981 s.88(2) and Sch.7, para.16; the
Goods Vehicles (Licensing of Operators) Act 1995 s.60(1) and Sch.7, para.5(1).]

5., 6. [...]   **A6.11**

Interpretation and transitional provisions

7.—(1) In this Act, except in so far as the context otherwise requires, the fol-   **A6.12**
lowing expressions have the meanings hereby assigned to them respectively, that
is to say—

  "authorised person" means a person (whether an examiner or not) autho-
    rised to exercise the powers of [section 78 of the Road Traffic Act
    1988] with respect to the weighing of motor vehicles and trailers;
  "drivers" —
    (a) in relation to a motor vehicle, includes any person who is in
      charge of the vehicle and, if a separate person acts as steers-
      man, includes that person as well as any other person in charge
      of the vehicle or engaged in the driving of it, and
    (b) in relation to a trailer, means any person who (in accordance
      with the preceding paragraph) is the driver of the motor vehi-
      cle by which the trailer is drawn;
  "examiner" means [an examiner appointed under section 66A of the Road
    Traffic Act 1988, or a constable authorised to act for the purposes of
    this Act by or on behalf of a chief officer of police];
  "foreign goods vehicle" (except in section 4 of this Act) means a goods ve-
    hicle which has been brought into Great Britain and which, if a motor
    vehicle, is not registered in the United Kingdom or, if a trailer, is
    drawn by a motor vehicle not registered in the United Kingdom which
    has been brought into Great Britain;
  "foreign public service vehicle" means a public service vehicle which has
    been brought into Great Britain and is not registered in the United
    Kingdom;
  "goods vehicle" means a motor vehicle constructed or adapted for use for
    the carriage or haulage of goods or burden of any description, or a
    trailer so constructed or adapted;
  [*"official testing station"* means a station maintained by the Secretary of
    State under [section [72A] of the Road Traffic Act 1988] [or premises
    designated by him under section 10(12) of the Transport Act 1982];]
  "public service vehicle" shall be construed in accordance with [the Public
    Passenger Vehicles Act 1981];
  "road" means any highway and any other road to which the public has ac-
    cess, and includes bridges over which a road passes.

[(1A) References in any provision of this Act to an authorised inspector are
references to a person authorised by the Secretary of State under section 8 of the
Transport Act 1982 to exercise the function to which that provision relates.]

(2) In this Act any reference to driving a vehicle shall, in relation to a trailer, be construed as a reference to driving the motor vehicle by which the trailer is drawn.

(3) In this Act any reference to a motor vehicle drawing a trailer, or to a motor vehicle by which a trailer is drawn, shall be construed as a reference to a motor vehicle to which a trailer is attached for the purpose of being drawn by it; and where, for the purpose of being drawn by a motor vehicle, two or more trailers (one of which is attached to the motor vehicle) are attached to each other, the motor vehicle shall for the purposes of this Act be treated as drawing each of those trailers.

(4) For the purposes of this Act a motor vehicle which does not for the time being have exhibited on it a licence or trade plates [issued under the Vehicle Excise and Registration Act 1994 shall] be presumed, unless the contrary is proved, not to be registered in the United Kingdom.

(5) Where, in accordance with subsection (4) of this section, a motor vehicle is presumed not to be registered in the United Kingdom, but is subsequently proved to have been so registered, anything which—

    (a) has been done in relation to the vehicle, or in relation to a trailer drawn by it, by a person relying in good faith on that presumption and purporting to act by virtue of any provision of this Act, and

    (b) would have been lawfully done by virtue of that provision if the vehicle had not been registered in the United Kingdom,

shall be treated as having been lawfully done by virtue of that provision.

(6) Any reference in any provision of this Act to regulations made under an enactment specified in that provision shall be construed as including a reference to any regulations which, by virtue of that or any other enactment, have effect, or are to be treated, as if made under the enactment so specified.

(7) [...]

A6.13   *[Section 7 is printed as amended by the Road Traffic Act 1974 s.24(3) and Sch.7; the Transport Act 1978 s.9(1) and Sch.3, para.10; the Transport Act 1980 s.43(1) and Sch.5, Pt II; the Public Passenger Vehicles Act 1981 s.88(2) and Sch.7, para.17; the Transport Act 1982 s.74(1) and Sch.5, para.17(2); the Road Traffic (Consequential Provisions) Act 1988 s.4 and Sch.3, para.9(3); the Road Traffic Act 1991 s.48 and Sch.4, para.8(a) and (b); the Vehicle Excise and Registration Act 1994 s.63 and Sch.3, para.5.*

The reference in the definition of "official testing station" to premises designated under s.10(2) of the Transport Act 1982 and s.7(1A) above were inserted by ibid. s.74(1) and Sch.5, para.17(2), with effect from a date to be announced. Until such date, the text of s.7 should be read as if that reference and s.7(1A) were omitted.]

Short title, commencement and extent

A6.14   **8.** *[Omitted.]*

Section 1   SCHEDULE 1

[PROVISIONS] CONFERRING FUNCTIONS ON EXAMINERS

Provisions   *Function conferred*   **A6.15**

*   *   *

[Section 99 [and sections 99ZA to 99ZC] of the Transport Act 1968.]	[To inspect and copy record sheets, books, registers and other documents required to be carried on goods vehicles and public service vehicles, to inspect [driver cards and] recording equipment [and to copy data recorded on such cards or equipment or to inspect] and copy record sheets on which records have been produced by such equipment or entries have been made.]
[Section 67 of the Road Traffic Act 1988.]	To test the condition of motor vehicles on roads.
[Section 68 of the Road Traffic Act 1988.]	To inspect … vehicles to secure proper maintenance.
[Regulation 16 of the Road Transport (International Passenger Services) Regulations 1984.]	[To require the production of, and to inspect, copy and mark, documents required to be kept or carried on certain passenger vehicles.]
[Article 3 A (3) of Council Regulation (EEC) No.684/92 of 16 March 1992 on common rules for the international carriage of passengers by coach and bus [*q.v.*], as amended by Council Regulation (E.C.) No.11/98 of 11 December 1997.]	[To require the production of a certain document which is required to be kept on board certain passenger vehicles.]
[Article 5(4) of Council Regulation (EEC) No.881/92 of 26th March 1992 on access to the market in the carriage of goods by road within the Community to or from the territory of a Member State or passing across the territory of one or more Member States [*q.v.*].	[To require the production of a certified copy of a Community authorisation which is required to be kept on board certain goods vehicles.]
[Regulation 7 of the Road Transport (Passenger Vehicles Cabotage) Regulations 1999 [*SI 1999/3413, q.v.*].	[To require the production of certain documents which are required to be kept on board certain passenger vehicles.]

[Schedule 1 is printed as amended by the Passenger and Goods Vehicles (Re-   **A6.16**
cording Equipment) Regulations 1979 (SI 1979/1746) reg.3; the Transport Act
1980 s.43(1) and Sch.5 Pt II; the Public Passenger Vehicles Act 1981 s.88(2) and
Sch.7, para.18; the Road Transport (International Passenger Services) Regula-
tions 1984 (SI 1984/748) reg.22; the Road Traffic (Consequential Provisions)
Act 1988 s.4 and Sch.3, para.9(4); the Road Traffic Act 1991 s.83 and Sch.8; the
Public Service Vehicles (Community Licences) Regulations 1999 (SI 1999/1322)
reg.13(2) below; the Road Transport (Passenger Vehicles Cabotage) Regula-
tions 1999 (SI 1999/3413) reg.10(1)(a) below; the Goods Vehicles (Community
Authorisations) (Modification of the Road Traffic (Foreign Vehicles) Act 1972)
Regulations 2002 (SI 2002/1415) reg.2(2); the Passenger and Goods Vehicles
(Recording Equipment) Regulations 2005 (SI 2005/1904) reg.9.]

Section 1　　　　　　　　SCHEDULE 2

PROVISIONS RELATING TO VEHICLES AND THEIR DRIVERS

A6.17

Provisions	*Effect*
[Section 2 of the Goods Vehicles (Licensing of Operators) Act 1995.]	To require users of certain goods vehicles to hold operators' licences unless exempted from doing so.
Regulations under [section 57(2)(d) of the Goods Vehicles (Licensing of Operators) Act 1995].	To require goods vehicles to be identified by plates, marks etc.
Sections 96 to 98 of the Transport Act 1968 and regulations and orders made under those sections [and [the applicable Community rules] within the meaning of Part VI of that Act].	To limit driving time and periods of duty of drivers of goods and public service vehicles and to require the installation of recording equipment in, and the keeping of records on, such vehicles.
Any order under section 100 of the Transport Act 1968.	To give effect to international agreements relating to vehicles used on international journeys.
[Regulations under section 41 of the Road Traffic Act 1988.]	To regulate the construction, weight, equipment and use of motor vehicles and trailers on roads.
Sections 68 to 73 and 76 to 79 of the Road Traffic Act 1972 and regulations made under those sections.	*To require vehicles to carry front and rear lamps, headlamps and reflectors, to regulate their position, character and use and to make special provision for vehicles carrying overhanging or projecting loads and vehicles towing and being towed.*
[Regulation 19 of the Road Transport (International Passenger Services) Regulations 1984.]	[To impose penalties for contravention of certain requirements relating to international passenger services.]
[Regulations 3 and 7 of the Goods Vehicles (Community Authorisations) Regulations 1992 [*SI 1992/3077, q.v.*].]	[To impose a penalty for contravention of certain requirements relating to the use of goods vehicles.]
[Section 40A of the Road Traffic Act 1988.]	[To create offence of using motor vehicle or trailer in dangerous condition etc.]
[Regulations 3 and 7 of the Public Service Vehicles (Community Licences) Regulations 1999 [*SI 1999/1322, q.v.*].]	[To impose a penalty for contravention of certain requirements relating to international passenger services.]
[Regulations 3, 4 and 7 of the Road Transport (Passenger Vehicles Cabotage) Regulations 1999 [*SI 1999/3413, q.v.*].]	[To impose penalties for contravention of certain requirements relating to national passenger services by a carrier registered in a foreign member State.]

A6.18　　*[Schedule 2 is printed as amended by the European Communities Act 1972 s.4(1) and Sch.4, para.9(4); the Road Traffic (Drivers' Ages and Hours of Work) Act 1976 s.2(3); the Road Transport (International Passenger Services) Regulations 1984 (SI 1984/748) reg.22; the Road Traffic (Consequential Provisions) Act 1988 ss.3(1) and 4, Sch.1, Pt I, and Sch.3, para.9(5); the Road Traffic Act 1991 s.48 and Sch.4, para.9; the Goods Vehicles (Licensing of Operators) Act 1995 s.60(1) and Sch.7, para.6; the Public Service Vehicles (Community Licences) Regulations 1999 (SI 1999/1322) reg.13(3) below; the Road Transport (Passenger Vehicles Cabotage) Regulations 1999 (SI 1999/3413) reg.10(1)(b) below; the Goods Vehicles (Community Authorisations) (Modification of the*

Road Traffic (Foreign Vehicles) Act 1972) Regulations 2002 (SI 2002/1415) reg.2(2).

The words printed in italics have lapsed.]

The International Road Haulage Permits Act 1975

(1975 c.46)

A7.01 *An Act to make further provision with respect to the forgery, carriage and production of licences, permits, authorisations and other documents relating to the international carriage of goods by road; and for purposes connected therewith.*

[1st August 1975]

Carriage on United Kingdom vehicles, and production, of international road haulage permits

A7.02 1.—(1) The Secretary of State may by regulations made by statutory instrument provide that—

    (a) a goods vehicle registered in the United Kingdom, or

    (b) a trailer drawn by a vehicle registered in the United Kingdom, or

    (c) an unattached trailer which is for the time being in the United Kingdom,

may not be used on a journey to which the regulations apply, being a journey—

    (i) for or in connection with the carriage or haulage of goods either for hire or reward or for or in connection with any trade or business carried on by the user of the vehicle, and

    (ii) either between a place in the United Kingdom and a place outside the United Kingdom or, if the journey passes through any part of the United Kingdom, between places both of which are outside the United Kingdom,

unless a document of a description specified in the regulations is carried on the vehicle or, in the case of a trailer, is carried either on the vehicle drawing it or by a person in charge of it.

(2) If it appears to an examiner that a goods vehicle registered in the United Kingdom or a trailer is being used in such circumstances that, by virtue of regulations under subsection (1) above, a document of a description specified in the regulations is required to be carried as mentioned in that subsection he may, on production if so required of his authority,—

    (a) require the driver of the goods vehicle concerned or, in the case of a trailer, the driver of the vehicle drawing it or the person in charge of it to produce a document of the description in question and to permit the examiner to inspect and copy it,

    (b) detain the goods vehicle or trailer concerned for such time as is requisite for the purpose of inspecting and copying the document,

    (c) at any time which is reasonable having regard to the circumstances of the case enter any premises on which he has reason to believe that there is kept a vehicle (whether a goods vehicle or a trailer) which is being used on a journey to which regulations under subsection (1) above apply, and

(d) at any time which is reasonable having regard to the circumstances of the case enter any premises in which he has reason to believe that any document of a description specified in regulations under subsection (1) above is to be found and inspect and copy any such document which he finds there.

(3) If, without reasonable excuse, any person uses a goods vehicle or trailer in contravention of regulations under subsection (1) above he shall be liable on summary conviction to a fine not exceeding [level 4 on the standard scale].

(4) If the driver of a goods vehicle which is being used in such circumstances as are specified in subsection (2) above or the person in charge of, or the driver of a vehicle drawing, a trailer which is being so used—

(a) without reasonable excuse refuses or fails to comply with a requirement under subsection (2) above, or

(b) wilfully obstructs an examiner in the exercise of his powers under that subsection,

he shall be liable on summary conviction to a fine not exceeding [level 3 on the standard scale].

(5) If any person (other than a person specified in subsection (4) above) wilfully obstructs an examiner in the exercise of his powers under paragraph (d) of subsection (2) above, he shall be liable on summary conviction to a fine not exceeding [level 3 on the standard scale].

(6) For the purposes of this section a motor vehicle which for the time being has exhibited on it a licence or trade plates [issued under the Vehicle Excise and Registration Act 1994 shall] be presumed, unless the contrary is proved, to be registered in the United Kingdom.

(7) [Need for consultation before regulations made.]

(8) Any reference in this section to a person using a vehicle (whether a goods vehicle or a trailer) shall be construed as if this section were included in [the Goods Vehicles (Licensing of Operators) Act 1995] …

(9) In this section —

"examiner" means an examiner appointed under … [… [section 66A] of the Road Traffic Act 1988] …;

"goods vehicle" means a motor vehicle constructed or adapted for use for the carriage of goods or burden of any description;

"trailer" means a trailer so constructed or adapted;

and for the purposes of this subsection "motor vehicle" and "trailer" have the same meaning as [in the Road Traffic Act 1988] …

[Section 1 is printed as amended by the Criminal Justice Act 1982 ss.37, 38 **A7.03** and 46; the Road Traffic (Consequential Provisions) Act 1988 s.4 and Sch.3, para.13; the Road Traffic Act 1991 ss.48, 83, Sch.4, para.10, and Sch.8; the Vehicle Excise and Registration Act 1994 s.63 and Sch.3, para.8; the Goods Vehicles (Licensing of Operators) Act 1995 s.60(1) and Sch.7, para.7.

References to Northern Ireland legislation have been omitted from the text of s.1(8) and (9).]

Power to prohibit vehicle or trailer being taken out of the United Kingdom

2.—(1) If it appears to an examiner:—   **A7.04**

(a) that a goods vehicle or a trailer is being used in such circumstances as are specified in subsection (2) of section 1 above, and

(b) that, without reasonable excuse, the driver of the goods vehicle or, as the case may require, the person in charge of, or the driver of a vehicle drawing, the trailer has refused or failed to comply with a requirement under that subsection,

the examiner may prohibit the removal of the goods vehicle or trailer out of the United Kingdom, either absolutely or for a specified purpose, and either for a specified period or without limitation of time.

(2) Where an examiner prohibits the removal of a goods vehicle or trailer out of the United Kingdom under subsection (1) above, he shall forthwith give notice in writing of the prohibition to the driver of the goods vehicle or, as the case may require, to the person in charge of, or the driver of the vehicle drawing, the trailer, specifying—

(a) the circumstances in consequence of which the prohibition is imposed,

(b) whether the prohibition applies absolutely or for a specified purpose, and

(c) whether the prohibition is for a specified period or without limit of time,

and the prohibition under subsection (1) above shall come into force as soon as notice thereof is given under this subsection.

(3) Where an examiner is satisfied, with respect to a goods vehicle or trailer to which a prohibition under subsection (1) above relates,—

(a) that the goods vehicle or trailer is being used on a journey to which regulations under section 1(1) above do not apply, or

(b) that there is carried on the goods vehicle or, in the case of a trailer, on the vehicle drawing it or by a person in charge of it a document of a description specified in those regulations,

he may remove the prohibition and, where he does so, shall forthwith give notice in writing of the removal of the prohibition to the driver of the goods vehicle or, as the case may require, to the person in charge of, or the driver of the vehicle drawing, the trailer and the prohibition shall cease to have effect on the giving of that notice.

(4) Unless the person to whom a notice is given under subsection (2) or subsection (3) above is the person using the vehicle concerned, as soon as practicable after such a notice has been given, the examiner who gave it shall take steps to bring the contents of the notice to the attention of the person using the vehicle.

(5) In the exercise of his functions under this section, an examiner shall act in accordance with any general directions given by the Secretary of State.

(6) Any person who, without reasonable excuse,—

(a) removes a goods vehicle or trailer out of the United Kingdom in contravention of a prohibition under subsection (1) above, or

(b) causes or permits a goods vehicle or trailer to be removed out of the United Kingdom in contravention of such a prohibition,

shall be guilty of an offence and liable on summary conviction to a fine not exceeding [level 4 on the standard scale].

(7) Subsections (8) and (9) of section 1 above shall apply in relation to this section as they apply in relation to that.

[Section 2 is printed as amended by the Criminal Justice Act 1982 ss.37, 38 and 46.]   **A7.05**

3. [...]   **A7.06**

[Section 3 was repealed by the Goods Vehicles (Licensing of Operators) Act 1995.]

4–5. *[Omitted.]*   **A7.07**

The Local Government (Miscellaneous Provisions) Act 1976

(1976 c.57)

A8.01 *An Act to make amendments for England and Wales of provisions of the law which relates to local authorities or highways and is commonly amended by local Acts ...*

[15th November 1976]

ARRANGEMENT OF SECTIONS

PART I

GENERAL

*   *   *

Supplemental

PART I

GENERAL

* * *

Supplemental

Interpretation, etc., of Part I

44.—(1), (1ZA), (1A), (1B), (2) *[Omitted.]*   **A8.02**

(3) When an offence under this Part of this Act (including an offence under byelaws made by virtue of section 12 of this Act) which has been committed by a body corporate is proved to have been committed with the consent or connivance of, or to be attributable to any neglect on the part of, any director, manager, secretary or other similar officer of the body corporate or any person who was purporting to act in any such capacity, he as well as the body corporate shall be guilty of that offence and be liable to be proceeded against and punished accordingly.

Where the affairs of a body corporate are managed by its members the preceding provisions of this subsection shall apply in relation to the acts and defaults of a member in connection with his functions of management as if he were a director of the body corporate.

(4)–(6) *[Omitted.]*

*[Section 43 is printed as amended by the Postal Services Act 2000 (Consequen-   **A8.03** tial Modifications No.1) Order 2001 (SI 2001/1149; not reproduced in this work) art.3(1) and Sch.1.*

Section 44(3) is expressly applied to offences under Pt II of this Act by s.72(2).]

PART II

HACKNEY CARRIAGES AND PRIVATE HIRE VEHICLES

Application of Part II

45.—(1) The provisions of this Part of this Act, except this section, shall come   **A8.04** into force in accordance with the following provisions of this section.

(2) If the Act of 1847 is in force in the area of a district council, the council may resolve that the provisions of this Part of this Act, other than this section, are

to apply to the relevant area; and if the council do so resolve those provisions shall come into force in the relevant area on the day specified in that behalf in the resolution (which must not be before the expiration of the period of one month beginning with the day on which the resolution is passed).

In this subsection *"the relevant area"*, in relation to a council, means—

    (a) if the Act of 1847 is in force throughout the area of the council, that area; and

    (b) if the Act of 1847 is in force for part only of the area of the council, that part of that area.

(3) A council shall not pass a resolution in pursuance of the foregoing subsection unless they have—

    (a) published in two consecutive weeks, in a local newspaper circulating in their area, notice of their intention to pass the resolution; and

    (b) served a copy of the notice, not later than the date on which it is first published in pursuance of the foregoing paragraph, on the council of each parish or community which would be affected by the resolution or, in the case of such a parish which has no parish council, on the chairman of the parish meeting.

(4) If after a council has passed a resolution in pursuance of subsection (2) of this section the Act of 1847 comes into force for any part of the area of the council for which it was not in force when the council passed the resolution, the council may pass a resolution in accordance with the foregoing provisions of this section in respect of that part as if that part were included in the relevant area for the purposes of subsection (2) of this section.

Vehicle drivers' and operators' licences

A8.05   **46.**—(1) Except as authorised by this Part of this Act —

    (a) no person being the proprietor of any vehicle, not being a hackney carriage [or London cab] in respect of which a vehicle licence is in force, shall use or permit the same to be used in a controlled district as a private hire vehicle without having for such a vehicle a current licence under section 48 of this Act;

    (b) no person shall in a controlled district act as driver of any private hire vehicle without having a current licence under section 51 of this Act;

    (c) no person being the proprietor of a private hire vehicle licensed under this Part of this Act shall employ as the driver thereof for the purpose of any hiring any person who does not have a current licence under the said section 51;

    (d) no person shall in a controlled district operate any vehicle as a private hire vehicle without having a current licence under section 55 of this Act;

    (e) no person licensed under the said section 55 shall in a controlled district operate any vehicle as a private hire vehicle—

        (i) if for the vehicle a current licence under the said section 48 is not in force, or

        (ii) if the driver does not have a current licence under the said section 51.

(2) If any person knowingly contravenes the provisions of this section he shall be guilty of an offence.

[Section 46 is printed as amended by the Transport Act 1985 s.139(2) and Sch.7, para.17(1).]   **A8.06**

Licensing of hackney carriages

47. *[Omitted.]*   **A8.07**

Licensing of private hire vehicles

48.—(1)–(4) *[Omitted.]*   **A8.08**

(5) Where a district council grant under this section a vehicle licence in respect of a private hire vehicle they shall issue a plate or disc identifying that vehicle as a private hire vehicle in respect of which a vehicle licence has been granted.

(6) (a) Subject to the provisions of this Part of this Act, no person shall use or permit to be used in a controlled district as a private hire vehicle a vehicle in respect of which a licence has been granted under this section unless the plate or disc issued in accordance with subsection (5) of this section is exhibited on the vehicle in such manner as the district council shall prescribe by condition attached to the grant of the licence.

(b) If any person without reasonable excuse contravenes the provisions of this subsection he shall be guilty of an offence.

(7) *[Omitted.]*

[Section 48 has been applied to applications for vehicle licences made at any time before April 1, 2000 to the council of a "wholly excluded district" (i.e. a district the whole of which ceased on that date to be within the metropolitan police district) or the council of a "partially excluded district" (i.e. a district part of which ceased on that date to be within the metropolitan police district) to which Pt II of this Act did not apply before March 13, 2000, see art.4(3) of the Greater London Authority Act 1999 (Hackney Carriages and Private Hire Vehicles) (Transitional and Consequential Provisions) Order 2000 (SI 2000/412; not reproduced in this work).   **A8.09**

For prescribed provisions relating to vehicles licensed under this section, see the Local Services (Operation by Licensed Hire Cars) Regulations 2009 (SI 2009/2863) reg.4.]

Transfer of hackney carriages and private hire vehicles

49.—(1) If the proprietor of a hackney carriage or of a private hire vehicle in respect of which a vehicle licence has been granted by a district council transfers his interest in the hackney carriage or private hire vehicle to a person other than the proprietor whose name is specified in the licence, he shall within fourteen days after such transfer give notice in writing thereof to the district council specifying the name and address of the person to whom the hackney carriage or private hire vehicle has been transferred.   **A8.10**

(2) If a proprietor without reasonable excuse fails to give notice to a district council as provided by subsection (1) of this section he shall be guilty of an offence.

Provisions as to proprietors

A8.11   **50.**—(1) Without prejudice to the provisions of section 68 of this Act, the proprietor of any hackney carriage or of any private hire vehicle licensed by a district council shall present such hackney carriage or private hire vehicle for inspection and testing by or on behalf of the council within such period and at such place within the area of the council as they may by notice reasonably require:

Provided that a district council shall not under the provisions of this subsection require a proprietor to present the same hackney carriage or private hire vehicle for inspection and testing on more than three separate occasions during any one period of twelve months.

(2) The proprietor of any hackney carriage or private hire vehicle—

    (a) licensed by a district council under the Act of 1847 or under this Part of this Act; or

    (b) in respect of which an application for a licence has been made to a district council under the Act of 1847 or under this Part of this Act;

shall, within such period as the district council may by notice reasonably require, state in writing the address of every place where such hackney carriage or private hire vehicle is kept when not in use, and shall if the district council so require afford to them such facilities as may be reasonably necessary to enable them to cause such hackney carriage or private hire vehicle to be inspected and tested there.

(3) Without prejudice to the provisions of [section 170 of the Act of 1988], the proprietor of a hackney carriage or of a private hire vehicle licensed by a district council shall report to them as soon as reasonably practicable, and in any case within seventy-two hours of the occurrence thereof, any accident to such hackney carriage or private hire vehicle causing damage materially affecting the safety, performance or appearance of the hackney carriage or private hire vehicle or the comfort or convenience of persons carried therein.

(4) The proprietor of any hackney carriage or of any private hire vehicle licensed by a district council shall at the request of any authorised officer of the council produce for inspection the vehicle licence for such hackney carriage or private hire vehicle and the certificate of the policy of insurance or security required by [Part VI of the Act of 1988] in respect of such hackney carriage or private hire vehicle.

(5) If any person without reasonable excuse contravenes the provisions of this section, he shall be guilty of an offence.

A8.12   *[Section 50 is printed as amended by the Road Traffic (Consequential Provisions) Act 1988 s.4 and Sch.3, para.16(2).]*

Licensing of drivers of private hire vehicles

A8.13   **51.** *[Omitted.]*

Appeals in respect of drivers' licences

A8.14   **52.** *[Omitted.]*

Drivers' licences for hackney carriages and private hire vehicles

A8.15   **53.**—(1)

(a) Every licence granted by a district council under the provisions of this Part of this Act to any person to drive a private hire vehicle shall remain in force for three years from the date of such licence or for such lesser period as the district council may specify in such licence.

(b) Notwithstanding the provisions of the Public Health Act 1875 and the Town Police Clauses Act 1889, every licence granted by a district council under the provisions of the Act of 1847 to any person to drive a hackney carriage shall remain in force for three years from the date of such licence or for such lesser period as they may specify in such licence.

(2) Notwithstanding the provisions of the Act of 1847, a district council may demand and recover for the grant to any person of a licence to drive a hackney carriage, or a private hire vehicle, as the case may be, such a fee as they consider reasonable with a view to recovering the costs of issue and administration and may remit the whole or part of the fee in respect of a private hire vehicle in any case in which they think it appropriate to do so.

(3) The driver of any hackney carriage or of any private hire vehicle licensed by a district council shall at the request of any authorised officer of the council or of any constable produce for inspection his driver's licence either forthwith or—

(a) in the case of a request by an authorised officer, at the principal offices of the council before the expiration of the period of five days beginning with the day following that on which the request is made;

(b) in the case of a request by a constable, before the expiration of the period aforesaid at any police station which is within the area of the council and is nominated by the driver when the request is made.

(4) If any person without reasonable excuse contravenes the provisions of this section, he shall be guilty of an offence.

Issue of drivers' badges

54.—(1) When granting a driver's licence under section 51 of this Act a district council shall issue a driver's badge in such a form as may from time to time be prescribed by them.   **A8.16**

(2) (a) A driver shall at all times when acting in accordance with the driver's licence granted to him wear such badge in such position and manner as to be plainly and distinctly visible.

(b) If any person without reasonable excuse contravenes the provisions of this subsection, he shall be guilty of an offence.

Licensing of operators of private hire vehicles

55. *[Omitted.]*   **A8.17**

Operators of private hire vehicles

56.—(1) For the purposes of this Part of this Act every contract for the hire of a private hire vehicle licensed under this Part of this Act shall be deemed to be made with the operator who accepted the booking for that vehicle whether or not he himself provided the vehicle.   **A8.18**

(2) Every person to whom a licence in force under section 55 of this Act has

been granted by a district council shall keep a record in such form as the council may, by condition attached to the grant of the licence, prescribe and shall enter therein, before the commencement of each journey, such particulars of every booking of a private hire vehicle invited or accepted by him, whether by accepting the same from the hirer or by undertaking it at the request of another operator, as the district council may by condition prescribe and shall produce such record on request to any authorised officer of the council or to any constable for inspection.

(3) Every person to whom a licence in force under section 55 of this Act has been granted by a district council shall keep such records as the council may, by condition attached to the grant of the licence, prescribe of the particulars of any private hire vehicle operated by him and shall produce the same on request to any authorised officer of the council or to any constable for inspection.

(4) A person to whom a licence in force under section 55 of this Act has been granted by a district council shall produce the licence on request to any authorised officer of the council or any constable for inspection.

(5) If any person without reasonable excuse contravenes the provisions of this section, he shall be guilty of an offence.

Power to require applicants to submit information

A8.19   57.—(1) A district council may require any applicant for a licence under the Act of 1847 or under this Part of this Act to submit to them such information as they may reasonably consider necessary to enable them to determine whether the licence should be granted and whether conditions should be attached to any such licence.

(2) Without prejudice to the generality of the foregoing subsection —

(a) a district council may require an applicant for a driver's licence in respect of a hackney carriage or a private hire vehicle—

(i) to produce a certificate signed by a registered medical practitioner to the effect that he is physically fit to be the driver of a hackney carriage or a private hire vehicle; and

(ii) whether or not such a certificate has been produced, to submit to examination by a registered medical practitioner selected by the district council as to his physical fitness to be the driver of a hackney carriage or a private hire vehicle;

(b) a district council may require an applicant for an operator's licence to submit to them such information as to—

(i) the name and address of the applicant;

(ii) the address or addresses whether within the area of the council or not from which he intends to carry on business in connection with private hire vehicles licensed under this Part of this Act;

(iii) any trade or business activities he has carried on before making the application;

(iv) any previous application he has made for an operator's licence;

(v) the revocation or suspension of any operator's licence previously held by him;

(vi) any convictions recorded against the applicant;

as they may reasonably consider necessary to enable them to determine whether to grant such licence;

    (c) in addition to the information specified in paragraph (b) of this subsection, a district council may require an applicant for an operator's licence to submit to them—

        (i) if the applicant is or has been a director or secretary of a company, information as to any convictions recorded against that company at any relevant time; any trade or business activities carried on by that company; any previous application made by that company for an operator's licence; and any revocation or suspension of an operator's licence previously held by that company;

        (ii) if the applicant is a company, information as to any convictions recorded against a director or secretary of that company; any trade or business activities carried on by any such director or secretary; any previous application made by any such director or secretary for an operator's licence; and any revocation or suspension of an operator's licence previously held by such director or secretary;

        (iii) if the applicant proposes to operate the vehicle in partnership with any other person, information as to any convictions recorded against that person; any trade or business activities carried on by that person; any previous application made by that person for an operator's licence; and any revocation or suspension of an operator's licence previously held by him.

(3) If any person knowingly or recklessly makes a false statement or omits any material particular in giving information under this section, he shall be guilty of an offence.

Return of identification plate or disc on revocation or expiry of licence, etc.

58.—(1) On—   A8.20

    (a) the revocation or expiry of a vehicle licence in relation to a hackney carriage or private hire vehicle; or

    (b) the suspension of a licence under section 68 of this Act;

a district council may by notice require the proprietor of that hackney carriage or private hire vehicle licensed by them to return to them within seven days after the service on him of that notice the plate or disc which—

    (a) in the case of a hackney carriage, is required to be affixed to the carriage as mentioned in section 38 of the Act of 1847; and

    (b) in the case of a private hire vehicle, was issued for the vehicle under section 48(5) of this Act.

(2) If any proprietor fails without reasonable excuse to comply with the terms of a notice under subsection (1) of this section —

    (a) he shall be guilty of an offence and liable on summary conviction to a fine not exceeding [level 3 on the standard scale] and to a daily fine not exceeding ten pounds; and

    (b) any authorised officer of the council or constable shall be entitled to remove and retain the said plate or disc from the said hackney carriage or private hire vehicle.

A8.21   *[Section 58 is printed as amended by the Criminal Justice Act 1982 ss.38 and 46.]*

Qualifications for drivers of hackney carriages

A8.22   **59.** *[Omitted.]*

Suspension and revocation of vehicle licences

A8.23   **60.** *[Omitted.]*

Suspension and revocation of drivers' licences

A8.24   **61.**—(1) *[Omitted.]*

     (2) (a) Where a district council suspend, revoke or refuse to renew any licence under this section they shall give to the driver notice of the grounds on which the licence has been suspended or revoked or on which they have refused to renew such licence within fourteen days of such suspension, revocation or refusal and the driver shall on demand return to the district council the driver's badge issued to him in accordance with section 54 of this Act.

        (b) If any person without reasonable excuse contravenes the provisions of this section he shall be guilty of an offence and liable on summary conviction to a fine not exceeding [level 1 on the standard scale].

[(2A) Subject to subsection (2B) of this section, a suspension or revocation of the licence of a driver under this section takes effect at the end of the period of 21 days beginning with the day on which notice is given to the driver under subsection (2)(a) of this section.]

[(2B) If it appears that the interests of public safety require the suspension or revocation of the licence to have immediate effect, and the notice given to the driver under subsection (2)(a) of this section includes a statement that that is so and an explanation why, the suspension or revocation takes effect when the notice is given to the driver.]

     (3) *[Omitted.]*

A8.25   *[Section 61 is printed as amended by the Criminal Justice Act 1982 ss.38 and 46; the Road Safety Act 2006 s.52(2).]*

Suspension and revocation of operators' licences

A8.26   **62.** *[Omitted.]*

Stands for hackney carriages

A8.27   **63.** *[Omitted.]*

Prohibition of other vehicles on hackney carriage stands

A8.28   **64.**—(1) No person shall cause or permit any vehicle other than a hackney carriage to wait on any stand for hackney carriages during any period for which that stand has been appointed, or is deemed to have been appointed, by a district council under the provisions of section 63 of this Act.

(2) Notice of the prohibition in this section shall be indicated by such traffic signs as may be prescribed or authorised for the purpose by the Secretary of State in pursuance of his powers under [section 64 of the Road Traffic Regulation Act 1984].

(3) If any person without reasonable excuse contravenes the provisions of this section, he shall be guilty of an offence.

(4) In any proceedings under this section against the driver of a public service vehicle it shall be a defence to show that, by reason of obstruction to traffic or for other compelling reason, he caused his vehicle to wait on a stand or part thereof and that he caused or permitted his vehicle so to wait only for so long as was reasonably necessary for the taking up or setting down of passengers.

[Section 64 is printed as amended by the Road Traffic Regulation Act 1984   **A8.29**
s.146(a) and Sch.13, para.36.]

Fixing of fares for hackney carriages

65. *[Omitted.]*   **A8.30**

Fares for long journeys

66. *[Omitted.]*   **A8.31**

Hackney carriages used for private hire

67. *[Omitted.]*   **A8.32**

Fitness of hackney carriages and private hire vehicles

68. Any authorised officer of the council in question or any constable shall   **A8.33**
have power at all reasonable times to inspect and test, for the purpose of ascertaining its fitness, any hackney carriage or private hire vehicle licensed by a district council, or any taximeter affixed to such a vehicle, and if he is not satisfied as to the fitness of the hackney carriage or private hire vehicle or as to the accuracy of its taximeter he may by notice in writing require the proprietor of the hackney carriage or private hire vehicle to make it or its taximeter available for further inspection and testing at such reasonable time and place as may be specified in the notice and suspend the vehicle licence until such time as such authorised officer or constable is so satisfied:

Provided that, if the authorised officer or constable is not so satisfied before the expiration of a period of two months, the said licence shall, by virtue of this section, be deemed to have been revoked and subsections (2) and (3) of section 60 of this Act shall apply with any necessary modifications.

Prolongation of journeys

69. *[Omitted.]*   **A8.34**

Fees for vehicle and operators' licences

70. *[Omitted.]*   **A8.35**

Taximeters

71. *[Omitted.]*   **A8.36**

Offences due to fault of other person

A8.37   72.—(1) Where an offence by any person under this Part of this Act is due to the act or default of another person, then, whether proceedings are taken against the first-mentioned person or not, that other person may be charged with and convicted of that offence, and shall be liable on conviction to the same punishment as might have been imposed on the first-mentioned person if he had been convicted of the offence.

(2) Section 44(3) of this Act shall apply to an offence under this Part of this Act as it applies to an offence under Part I of this Act.

Obstruction of authorised officers

A8.38   73.—(1) Any person who—

(a) wilfully obstructs an authorised officer or constable acting in pursuance of this Part of this Act or the Act of 1847; or

(b) without reasonable excuse fails to comply with any requirement properly made to him by such officer or constable under this Part of this Act; or

(c) without reasonable cause fails to give such an officer or constable so acting any other assistance or information which he may reasonably require of such person for the purpose of the performance of his functions under this Part of this Act or the Act of 1847;

shall be guilty of an offence.

(2) If any person, in giving any such information as is mentioned in the preceding subsection, makes any statement which he knows to be false, he shall be guilty of an offence.

Saving for certain businesses

A8.39   74. Where any provision of this Part of this Act coming into operation on [the relevant day] requires the licensing of a person carrying on any business, or of any vehicle used by a person in connection with any business, it shall be lawful for any person who—

(a) immediately before that day was carrying on that business; and

(b) had before that day duly applied for the licence required by that provision;

to continue to carry on that business until he is informed of the decision with regard to his application and, if the decision is adverse, during such further time as is provided under section 77 of this Act.

[In this section *"the relevant day"* means—

(a) in relation to a district the whole or part of which ceased to be within the metropolitan police district by virtue of the coming into force of section 323 of the Greater London Authority Act 1999 (alteration of the metropolitan police district), 1st April 2000;

(b) in any other case, a day fixed by resolution under section 45 of this Act.]

A8.40   *[Section 74 has been amended by art.7(1) and (2) of the Greater London Authority Act 1999 (Hackney Carriages and Private Hire Vehicles) (Transitional and Consequential Provisions) Order 2000 (SI 2000/412; not reproduced in this work).]*

Saving for certain vehicles, etc.

75.—(1) Nothing in this Part of this Act shall— **A8.41**

    (a) apply to a vehicle used for bringing passengers or goods within a controlled district in pursuance of a contract for the hire of the vehicle made outside the district if the vehicle is not made available for hire within the district;

    (b) [...];

    (c) apply to a vehicle while it is being used in connection with a funeral or a vehicle used wholly or mainly, by a person carrying on the business of a funeral director, for the purpose of funerals;

  [(cc) apply to a vehicle while it is being used in connection with a wedding;]

    (d) require the display of any plate, disc or notice in or on any private hire vehicle licensed by a council under this Part of this Act during such period that such vehicle is used for carrying passengers for hire or reward—

        (i) ...

        (ii) under a contract for the hire of the vehicle for a period of not less than 24 hours.

(2) Paragraphs (a), (b) and (c) of section 46(1) of this Act shall not apply to the use or driving of a vehicle or to the employment of a driver of a vehicle while the vehicle is used as a private hire vehicle in a controlled district if a licence issued under section 48 of this Act by the council whose area consists of or includes another controlled district is then in force for the vehicle and a driver's licence issued by such a council is then in force for the driver of the vehicle.

(2A) *[Applies to Scotland.]*

[(2B) Paragraphs (a), (b) and (c) of section 46(1) of this Act shall not apply to the use or driving of a vehicle, or to the employment of a driver of a vehicle, if—

    (a) a London PHV licence issued under section 7 of the Private Hire Vehicles (London) Act 1998 is in force in relation to that vehicle; and

    (b) the driver of the vehicle holds a London PHV driver's licence issued under section 13 of that Act.]

(3) Where a licence under section 48 of this Act is in force for a vehicle, the council which issued the licence may, by a notice in writing given to the proprietor of the vehicle, provide that paragraph (a) of subsection (6) of that section shall not apply to the vehicle on any occasion specified in the notice or shall not so apply while the notice is carried in the vehicle; and on any occasion on which by virtue of this subsection that paragraph does not apply to a vehicle section 54(2)(a) of this Act shall not apply to the driver of the vehicle.

    [Section 75 is printed as amended by the Transport Act 1985 s.139(2) and **A8.42** *Sch.7, para.17(2); the Private Hire Vehicles (London) Act 1998 ss.39(1), 40(2) and Sch.1, para.1; the Road Safety Act 2006 s.53, s.59 and Sch.7(1).]*

Penalties

76. Any person who commits an offence against any of the provisions of this **A8.43**

Part of this Act in respect of which no penalty is expressly provided shall be liable on summary conviction to a fine not exceeding [level 3 on the standard scale].

A8.44   *[Section 76 is printed as amended by the Criminal Justice Act 1982 ss.38 and 46.]*

Appeals (against decisions of district councils)

A8.45   **77.** *[Omitted.]*

Application of provisions of Act of 1936

A8.46   **78.** *[Omitted.]*

Authentication of licences

A8.47   **79.** *[Omitted.]*

Interpretation of Part II

A8.48   **80.**—(1) In this Part of this Act, unless the subject or context otherwise requires—

"*the Act of 1847*" means the provisions of the Town Police Clauses Act 1847 with respect to hackney carriages;

"*the Act of 1936*" means the Public Health Act 1936;

*   *   *

"*authorised officer*" means any officer of a district council authorised in writing by the council for the purposes of this Part of this Act;

"*contravene*" includes fail to comply;

["*controlled district*" means any area for which this Part of this Act is in force by virtue of—

(a) a resolution passed by a district council under section 45 of this Act; or

(b) section 255(4) of the Greater London Authority Act 1999;]

"*daily fine*" means a fine for each day during which an offence continues after conviction thereof;

"*the district*", in relation to a district council in whose area the provisions of this Part of this Act are in force, means—

(a) if those provisions are in force throughout the area of the council, that area; and

(b) if those provisions are in force for part only of the area of the council, that part of that area;

"*driver's badge*" means, in relation to the driver of a hackney carriage, any badge issued by a district council under byelaws made under section 68 of the Act of 1847 and, in relation to the driver of a private hire vehicle, any badge issued by a district council under section 54 of this Act;

"*driver's licence*" means, in relation to the driver of a hackney carriage, a licence under section 46 of the Act of 1847 and, in relation to the driver of a private hire vehicle, a licence under section 51 of this Act;

"hackney carriage" has the same meaning as in the Act of 1847 [*q.v.*];

"hackney carriage byelaws" means the byelaws for the time being in force in the controlled district in question relating to hackney carriages;

[*"London cab"* means a vehicle which is a hackney carriage within the meaning of the Metropolitan Public Carriage Act 1869;]

"operate" means in the course of business to make provision for the invitation or acceptance of bookings for a private hire vehicle;

"operator's licence" means a licence under section 55 of this Act;

"private hire vehicle" means a motor vehicle constructed or adapted to seat [fewer than nine passengers], other than a hackney carriage or public service vehicle [or a London cab] [or tramcar], which is provided for hire with the services of a driver for the purpose of carrying passengers;

"proprietor" includes a part-proprietor and, in relation to a vehicle which is the subject of a hiring agreement or hire-purchase agreement, means the person in possession of the vehicle under that agreement;

"public service vehicle" has the same meaning as in [the Public Passenger Vehicles Act 1981];

"taximeter" means any device for calculating the fare to be charged in respect of any journey in a hackney carriage or private hire vehicle by reference to the distance travelled or time elapsed since the start of the journey, or a combination of both; and

"vehicle licence" means in relation to a hackney carriage a licence under sections 37 to 45 of the Act of 1847 [in relation to a London cab a licence under section 6 of the Metropolitan Public Carriage Act 1869] and in relation to a private hire vehicle means a licence under section 48 of this Act.

(2) In this Part of this Act references to a licence, in connection with a controlled district, are references to a licence issued by the council whose area consists of or includes that district, and *"licensed"* shall be construed accordingly.

(3) Except where the context otherwise requires, any reference in this Part of this Act to any enactment shall be construed as a reference to that enactment as applied, extended, amended or varied by, or by virtue of, any subsequent enactment including this Act.

[(4) In this Part of this Act, except where the context otherwise requires, references to a district council shall, in relation to Wales, be construed as references to a county council or county borough council.]

[Section 80 is printed as amended by the Transport Act 1980 s.43(1) and Sch.5, Pt II; the Public Passenger Vehicles Act 1981 s.88(2) and Sch.7, para.20; the Transport Act 1985 s.139(2) and Sch.7, para.17(3); the Road Traffic (Consequential Provisions) Act 1988 s.3(1) and Sch.1, Pt I; the Transport and Works Act 1992 s.62(3); the Local Government Reorganisation (Wales) (Consequential Amendments No.3) Order 1996 (SI 1996/3071; not reproduced in this work); the Greater London Authority Act 1999 (Hackney Carriages and Private Hire Vehicles) (Transitional and Consequential Provisions) Order 2000 (SI 2000/412; not reproduced in this work) art.7(1) and (3).] **A8.49**

The Magistrates' Courts Act 1980

(1980 c.43)

A9.01 *An Act to consolidate certain enactments relating to the jurisdiction of, and the practice and procedure before, magistrates' courts ...*

[1st August 1980]

* * *

Non-appearance of accused: general provisions

A9.02 **11.**—(1) Subject to the provisions of this Act, where at the time and place appointed for the trial or adjourned trial of an information the prosecutor appears but the accused does not, [—

    (a) if the accused is under 18 years of age, the court may proceed in his absence; and

    (b) if the accused has attained the age of 18 years, the court shall proceed in his absence unless it appears to the court to be contrary to the interests of justice to do so.

This is subject to subsections (2), (2A), (3) and (4).]

(2) Where a summons has been issued, the court shall not begin to try the information in the absence of the accused unless either it is proved to the satisfaction of the court, on oath or in such other manner as may be prescribed, that the summons was served on the accused within what appears to the court to be a reasonable time before the trial or adjourned trial or the accused has appeared on a previous occasion to answer the information.

[(2A) The court shall not proceed in the absence of the accused if it considers that there is an acceptable reason for his failure to appear.]

(3) [In proceedings to which this subsection applies, the court] shall not in a person's absence sentence him to imprisonment or detention in a detention centre or make [a [detention and training order] or] an order under [paragraph 8(2)(a) or (b) of Schedule 12 to the Criminal Justice Act 2003] that a suspended sentence passed on him shall take effect.

[(3A) But where a sentence or order of a kind mentioned in subsection (3) is imposed or given in the absence of the offender, the offender must be brought before the court before being taken to a prison or other institution to begin serving his sentence (and the sentence or order is not to be regarded as taking effect until he is brought before the court).]

(4) A magistrates' court shall not in a person's absence impose any disqualification on him, except on resumption of the hearing after an adjournment under section 10(3) above; and where a trial is adjourned in pursuance of this subsection the notice required by section 10(2) above shall include notice of the reason for the adjournment.

[(5) Subsections (3) and (4) apply to—

    (a) proceedings instituted by an information, where a summons has been issued; and

(b) proceedings instituted by a written charge.

(6) Nothing in this section requires the court to enquire into the reasons for the accused's failure to appear before deciding whether to proceed in his absence.

(7) The court shall state in open court its reasons for not proceeding under this section in the absence of an accused who has attained the age of 18 years; and the court shall cause those reasons to be entered in its register of proceedings.]

[Section 11 is printed as amended by the Criminal Justice and Public Order **A9.03**
Act 1994 s.168(2) and Sch.10, para.39; the Crime and Disorder Act 1998 ss.119, 121(2) and Sch.8, para.39; the Powers of Criminal Courts (Sentencing) Act 2000 s.165(1) and Sch.9, para.61; the Criminal Justice Act 2003 s.304 and Sch.32, para.26; the Criminal Justice and Immigration Act 2008 s.54.

References in any enactment to a "detention centre" (as in s.11(3) above) are treated as if they are references to a young offender institution; see the Criminal Justice Act 1988 s.123(6) and Sch.8, para.1.

With effect from a date to be announced under the Criminal Justice and Court Services Act 2000 s.80(2), the words "or detention in a detention centre" in s.11(3) will be repealed by the 2000 Act s.74 and Sch.7, paras 58 and 59 (and see also ibid. s.75 and Sch.8).]

[Non-appearance of accused: plea of guilty

12.—(1) This section shall apply where—   **A9.04**

    (a) a summons has been issued requiring a person to appear before a magistrates' court, other than a youth court, to answer to an information for a summary offence, not being—

        (i) [...]

        (ii) an offence specified in an order made by the Secretary of State by statutory instrument; and

    (b) the [designated officer for] the court is notified by or on behalf of the prosecutor that the documents mentioned in subsection (3) below have been served upon the accused with the summons.

(2) The reference in subsection (1)(a) above to the issue of a summons requiring a person to appear before a magistrates' court other than a youth court includes a reference to the issue of a summons requiring a person who has attained the age of 16 at the time when it is issued to appear before a youth court.

(3) The documents referred to in subsection (1)(b) above are—

    (a) a notice containing such statement of the effect of this section as may be prescribed;

    [(b) either of the following, namely—

        (i) a concise statement of such facts relating to the charge will be placed before the court by the prosecutor if the accused pleads guilty without appearing before the court, or

        (ii) a copy of such written statement or statements complying with subsections (2)(a) and (b) and (3) of section 9 of the Criminal Justice Act 1967 (proof by written statement) as will be so placed in those circumstances; and]

    (c) if any information relating to the accused will or may, in those circumstances be placed before the court by or on behalf of the prosecutor, a notice containing or describing that information.

(4) Where the [designated officer for] the court receives a notification in writing purporting to be given by the accused or by a legal representative acting on his behalf that the accused desires to plead guilty without appearing before the court—

> (a) the [designated officer for] the court shall inform the prosecutor of the receipt of the notification; and
>
> (b) the following provisions of this section shall apply.

(5) If at the time and place appointed for the trial or adjourned trial of the information—

> (a) the accused does not appear; and
>
> (b) it is proved to the satisfaction of the court, on oath or in such manner as may be prescribed, that the documents mentioned in subsection (3) above have been served upon the accused with the summons,

the court may, subject to section 11(3) and (4) above and subsections (6) to (8) below, proceed to hear and dispose of the case in the absence of the accused, whether or not the prosecutor is also absent, in like manner as if both parties had appeared and the accused had pleaded guilty.

(6) If at any time before the hearing the [designated officer for] the court receives an indication in writing purporting to be given by or on behalf of the accused that he wishes to withdraw the notification—

> (a) the [designated officer for] the court shall inform the prosecutor of the withdrawal; and
>
> (b) the court shall deal with the information as if the notification had not been given.

(7) Before accepting the plea of guilty and convicting the accused under subsection (5) above, the court shall cause the following to be read out before the court by the clerk of the court, namely—

> [(a) in a cause where a statement of facts as mentioned in subsection (3)(b)(i) above was served on the accused with the summons, that statement;]
>
> [(aa) in a case where a statement or statements as mentioned in subsection (3)(b)(ii) above was served on the accused with the summons and the court does not otherwise direct, that statement or those statements;]
>
> (b) any information contained in a notice so served, and information described in such a notice and produced by or on behalf of the prosecutor;
>
> (c) the notification under subsection (4) above; and
>
> (d) any submission received with the notification which the accused wishes to be brought to the attention of the court with a view to mitigation of sentence.

[(7A) Where the court gives a direction under subsection (7)(aa) above the court shall cause an account to be given orally before the court by the clerk of the court of so much of any statement as is not read aloud.]

[(7B) Whether or not a direction under paragraph (aa) of subsection (7) above is given in relation to any statement served as mentioned in that paragraph the court need not cause to be read out the declaration required by section 9(2)(b) of the Criminal Justice Act 1967.]

(8) If the court proceeds under subsection (5) above to hear and dispose of the case in the absence of the accused, the court shall not permit—

(a) any other statement with respect to any facts relating to the offence charged; or

(b) any other information relating to the accused,

to be made or placed before the court by or on behalf of the prosecutor except on a resumption of the trial after an adjournment under section 10(3) above.

(9) If the court decides not to proceed under subsection (5) above to hear and dispose of the case in the absence of the accused, it shall adjourn or further adjourn the trial for the purpose of dealing with the information as if the notification under subsection (4) above had not been given.

(10) In relation to an adjournment on the occasion of the accused's conviction in his absence under subsection (5) above or to an adjournment required by subsection (9) above, the notice required by section 10(2) above shall include notice of the reason for the adjournment.

(11) No notice shall be required by section 10(2) above in relation to an adjournment—

(a) which is for not more than 4 weeks; and

(b) the purpose of which is to enable the court to proceed under subsection (5) above at a later time.

(12) No order shall be made under subsection (1) above unless a draft of the order has been laid before and approved by the resolution of each House of Parliament.

(13) Any such document as is mentioned in subsection (3) above may be served in Scotland with a summons which is so served under the Summary Jurisdiction (Process) Act 1881.]

[Section 12 is printed as substituted by the Criminal Justice and Public Order **A9.05**
Act 1994 s.45 and Sch.5, para.1; the Magistrates' Courts (Procedure) Act 1998 s.45 and Sch.5, para.1; and the Access to Justice Act 1999 s.90(1) and Sch.13 (paras 95 and 97); the Criminal Justice Act 2003 s.308 and Sch.37, Pt 12; the Courts Act 2003 s.109(1) and Sch.8, para.203.

Reference is made in s.12 to the Criminal Justice Act 1967 s.9(2)(a), (b) and (3), which is not reproduced in this work; s.9(2)(a) requires the statement to be signed; s.9(2)(b) requires the statement to contain a declaration that it is true; and s.9(3) requires a statement made by a person under 18 years to give his age, a statement made by a person who cannot read it to be accompanied by a declaration that it has been read out before it was signed, and a statement referring to an exhibit to be accompanied by such (when served) or by information as to its availability for inspection.]

[Application of section 12 where accused appears

12A.—(1) Where the [designated officer for] the court has received such a **A9.06**
notification as is mentioned in subsection (4) of section 12 above but the accused nevertheless appears before the court at the time and place appointed for the trial or adjourned trial, the court may, if he consents, proceed under subsection (5) of that section as if he were absent.

(2) Where the [designated officer for] the court has not received such a notification and the accused appears before the court at that time and place and informs the court that he desires to plead guilty, the court may, if he consents, proceed under section 12(5) above as if he were absent and the [designated officer] had received such a notification.

(3) For the purposes of subsections (1) and (2) above, subsections (6) to (11) of section 12 above shall apply with the modifications mentioned in subsection (4) or, as the case may be, subsection (5) below.

(4) The modifications for the purposes of subsection (1) above are that—

(a) before accepting the plea of guilty and convicting the accused under subsection (5) of section 12 above, the court shall afford the accused an opportunity to make an oral submission with a view to mitigation of sentence; and

(b) where he makes such a submission, subsection (7)(d) of that section shall not apply.

(5) The modifications for the purposes of subsection (2) above are that—

(a) subsection (6) of section 12 above shall apply as if any reference to the notification under subsection (4) of that section were a reference to the consent under subsection (2) above;

(b) subsection (7)(c) and (d) of that section shall not apply; and

(c) before accepting the plea of guilty and convicting the accused under subsection (5) of that section, the court shall afford the accused an opportunity to make an oral submission with a view to mitigation of sentence.]

A9.07   *[Section 12A was inserted by the Criminal Justice and Public Order Act 1994 s.45 and Sch.5, para.2; the Courts Act 2003 s.109(1) and Sch.8, para.204.]*

Non-appearance of accused: issue of warrant

A9.08   13.—(1) Subject to the provisions of this section, where the court, instead of proceeding in the absence of the accused, adjourns or further adjourns the trial, the court may … issue a warrant for his arrest.

(2) Where a summons has been issued, the court shall not issue a warrant under this section [unless the condition in subsection (2A) below or that in subsection (2B) below is fulfilled].

[(2A) The condition in this subsection is that it is proved to the satisfaction of the court, on oath or in such other manner as may be prescribed, that the summons was served on the accused within what appears to the court to be a reasonable time before the trial or adjourned trial.]

[(2B) The condition in this subsection is that—

(a) the adjournment now being made is a second or subsequent adjournment of the trial,

(b) the accused was present on the last (or only) occasion when the trial was adjourned, and

(c) on that occasion the court determined the time for the hearing at which the adjournment is now being made.]

[(3) A warrant for the arrest of any person who has attained the age of 18 shall not be issued under this section unless—

(a) [...] the offence to which the warrant relates is punishable with imprisonment, or

(b) the court, having convicted the accused, proposes to impose a disqualification on him.]

[(3A) A warrant for the arrest of any person who has not attained the age of 18 shall not be issued under this section unless—

[(a) the offence to which the warrant relates is punishable, in the case of a person who has attained the age of 18, with imprisonment, or]

(b) the court, having convicted the accused, proposes to impose a disqualification on him.]

[(4) This section shall not apply to an adjournment on the occasion of the accused's conviction in his absence under subsection (5) of section 12 above or to an adjournment required by subsection (9) of that section.]

(5) [...]

[Section 13 is printed as amended by the Criminal Justice Act 1991 s.68 and Sch.8, para.6(1)(a); the Criminal Justice and Public Order Act 1994 s.45 and Sch.5, para.3(2) and (3); the Criminal Procedure and Investigations Act 1996 s.48(1)–(3); the Magistrates' Courts (Procedure) Act 1998 s.3; the Criminal Justice Act 2003 s.31 and Sch.37, Pt 12; the Criminal Justice and Immigration Act 2008 s.54(7).]   **A9.09**

* * *

Penalties on summary conviction for offences triable either way

32.—(1) *[Omitted.]*   **A9.10**

(2) For any offence triable either way which is not listed in Schedule 1 to this Act, being an offence under a relevant enactment, the maximum fine which may be imposed on summary conviction shall by virtue of this subsection be the prescribed sum unless the offence is one for which by virtue of an enactment other than this subsection a larger fine may be imposed on summary conviction.

(3)–(8) *[Omitted.]*

(9) In this section —

"fine" includes a pecuniary penalty but does not include a pecuniary forfeiture or pecuniary compensation;

"the prescribed sum" means [£5,000] or such sum as is for the time being substituted in this definition by an order in force under section 143(1) below;

"relevant enactment" means an enactment contained in the Criminal Law Act 1977 or in any Act passed before, or in the same Session as, that Act.

[Section 32 is printed as amended by the Criminal Justice Act 1991 s.17(2)(c).   **A9.11**
The definition of the "prescribed sum" in this section has been incorporated by reference into the Interpretation Act 1978 Sch.1.

None of the offences listed in Sch.1 to this Act (to which s.32(2) refers) is a road traffic offence.]

* * *

"Magistrates' court"

A9.12   148.—(1) In this Act the expression *"magistrates' court"* means any justice or justices of the peace acting under any enactment or by virtue of his or their commission or under the common law.

(2) *[Omitted.]*

A9.13   *[The definition in subs.(1) is incorporated by reference into the Public Passenger Vehicles Act 1981 s.82 below.]*

The Highways Act 1980

(1980 c.66)

*An Act to consolidate the Highways Acts 1959 to 1971 and related enactments,
with amendments to give effect to recommendations of the Law Commission.*

[13th November 1980]

A10.01

*   *   *

Penalty for wilful obstruction

137.—(1) If a person, without lawful authority or excuse, in any way wilfully
obstructs the free passage along a highway he is guilty of an offence and liable to
a fine not exceeding [level 3 on the standard scale].

A10.02

(2) [...]

*[Section 137 is printed as amended by the Criminal Justice Act 1982 ss.38,
46(1); the Police and Criminal Evidence Act 1984 s.119(2) and Sch.7, Pt I.*

A10.03

*As to the application of the fixed penalty procedure to offences under s.137,
see the Road Traffic Offenders Act 1988 Sch.3 below. Offences under s.137(1)
have been designated as fixed penalty parking offences by the Schedule to the
Fixed Penalty Order 2000 (SI 2000/2792).*

*Section 1 of the Highways (Obstruction by Body Corporate) Act 2004 applies
s.137 to s.314 of the Highways Act 1980 (Offences by body corporate) with effect
from January 15, 2005.]*

[Power to order offender to remove obstruction

137ZA.—(1) Where a person is convicted of an offence under section 137
above in respect of the obstruction of a highway and it appears to the court that—

A10.04

    (a) the obstruction is continuing, and

    (b) it is in that person's power to remove the cause of the obstruction,

the court may, in addition to or instead of imposing any punishment, order him to
take, within such reasonable period as may be fixed by the order, such steps as
may be specified in the order for removing the cause of the obstruction.

(2) The time fixed by an order under subsection (1) above may be extended or
further extended by order of the court on an application made before the end of
the time as originally fixed or as extended under this subsection, as the case may
be.

(3) If a person fails without reasonable excuse to comply with an order under
subsection (1) above, he is guilty of an offence and liable to a fine not exceeding
level 5 on the standard scale; and if the offence is continued after conviction he is
guilty of a further offence and liable to a fine not exceeding one-twentieth of that
level for each day on which the offence is so continued.

(4) Where, after a person is convicted of an offence under subsection (3)
above, the highway authority for the highway concerned exercise any power to
remove the cause of the obstruction, they may recover from that person the

amount of any expenses reasonably incurred by them in, or in connection with, doing so.

(5) A person against whom an order is made under subsection (1) above is not liable under section 137 above in respect of the obstruction concerned—

(a) during the period fixed under that subsection or any extension under subsection (2) above, or

(b) during any period fixed under section 311(1) below by a court before whom he is convicted of an offence under subsection (3) above in respect of the order.]

A10.05   *[Section 137ZA was inserted by the Countryside and Rights of Way Act 2000 ss.64(1) and 103(2). The provisions of s.137ZA do not apply to any offence under s.137 of the 1980 Act which was committed before January 30, 2001; see the 2000 Act s.64(2).*

Section 314 of the Highways Act 1980 (Offences by body corporate) applies to any offence under s.137ZA(3) above committed after January 15, 2005, including an offence committed in respect of an order made before that date (see the Highways (Obstruction by Body Corporate) Act 2004 s.1(2)).]

*   *   *

Further provision as to interpretation

A10.06   **329.**—(1) In this Act, except where the context otherwise requires—

*   *   *

"*bridge*" does not include a culvert, but, save as aforesaid, means a bridge or viaduct which is part of a highway, and includes the abutments and any other part of a bridge but not the highway carried thereby;

"*bridleway*" means a highway over which the public have the following, but no other, rights of way, that is to say, a right of way on foot and a right of way on horseback or leading a horse, with or without a right to drive animals of any description along the highway;

*   *   *

"*carriageway*" means a way constituting or comprised in a highway, being a way (other than a cycle track) over which the public have a right of way for the passage of vehicles;

*   *   *

"*cycle track*" means a way constituting or comprised in a highway, being a way over which the public have the following, but no other, rights of way, that is to say, a right of way on pedal cycles [(other than pedal cycles which are motor vehicles within the meaning of [the Road Traffic Act 1988])] with or without a right of way on foot;

*   *   *

"*footpath*" means a highway over which the public have a right of way on foot only, not being a footway;

"footway" means a way comprised in a highway which also comprises a carriageway, being a way over which the public have a right of way on foot only;

*   *   *

"the Minister", subject to subsection (5) below, means as respects England, the [Secretary of State for Transport] and as respects Wales, the Secretary of State; and in section 258 of, and paragraphs 7, 8(1) and (3), 14, 15(1) and (3), 18(2), 19 and 21 of Schedule 1 to, this Act, references to the Minister and the Secretary of State acting jointly are to be construed, as respects Wales, as references to the Secretary of State acting alone;

*   *   *

"proposed highway" means land on which, in accordance with plans made by a highway authority, that authority are for the time being constructing or intending to construct a highway shown in the plans;

*   *   *

[*"restricted byway"* has the same meaning as in Part II of the Countryside and Rights of Way Act 2000;]

*   *   *

"special road" means a highway, or a proposed highway, which is a special road in accordance with section 16 above [or by virtue of an order granting development consent under the Planning Act 2008];

*   *   *

"statutory undertakers" means persons authorised by any enactment to carry on any of the following undertakings:—

    (a) a railway, tramway, road transport, water transport, canal, inland navigation, dock, harbour, pier or lighthouse undertaking, or

    (b) an undertaking for the supply of … or hydraulic power,

and "statutory undertaking" is to be construed accordingly;

[*"street"* has the same meaning as in Part III of the New Roads and Street Works Act 1991;]

*   *   *

"trunk road" means a highway, or a proposed highway, which is a trunk road by virtue of section 10(1) or section 19 above or by virtue of an order or direction under section 10 above [or an order granting development consent under the Planning Act 2008] or under any other enactment;

*   *   *

(2)–(5) *[Omitted.]*

[Only selected definitions from s.329(1) are set out above.]   **A10.07**

The definition of "cycle track" is printed as amended by the Cycle Tracks Act 1984, s.1(1) and the Road Traffic (Consequential Provisions) Act 1988 s.4 and Sch.3, para.21(2).

The definition of "the Minister" is printed as amended by the Transfer of Functions (Transport) Order 1981 (SI 1981/238); the Secretary of State for the Environment, Transport and the Regions Order 1997 (SI 1997/2971); the Secretaries of State for the Transport, Local Government and the Regions and for Environment, Food and Rural Affairs Order 2001 (SI 2001/2568); the Transfer of Functions (Transport, Local Government and the Regions) Order 2002 (SI 2002/2626).

The definition of "restricted byway" was inserted by the Countryside and Rights of Way Act 2000 Sch.5, para.16.

The definition of "special road" is printed as amended by the Planning Act 2008 s.36 and Sch.2, para.29.

The definition of "statutory undertakers" is printed as amended by the Gas Act 1986 s.67(4) and Sch.9, Pt I; by the Gas Act 1995 s.16(1) and Sch.4, para.2(1)(xxix), a public gas transporter is deemed to be a statutory undertaker for the purpose of the Highways Act 1980. The definition has also been amended by the Water Act 1989 s.190(3) and Sch.27, Pt I; by ibid. s.190(1) and Sch.25, para.1(1) and (2)(xxv), the National Rivers Authority, every water undertaker and every sewerage undertaker is deemed to be a statutory undertaker, and its undertaking a statutory undertaking, for the purposes of the Highways Act 1980. The definition was further amended by the Electricity Act 1989 s.112(4) and Sch.18; by ibid. ss.3(7) and 112(1) and Sch.16, paras 2(4)(d) and 38, a person who holds a licence under s.6 of the Act (licence authorising supply of electricity) and who is entitled to exercise any power conferred by para.1 of Sch.4 to the Electricity Act 1989 (street works, etc.) is deemed to be a statutory undertaker, and his undertaking a statutory undertaking, for the purposes of the Highways Act 1980.

The definition of "street" is printed as substituted by the New Roads and Street Works Act 1991 s.168(1) and Sch.8, Pt I, para.15(1) and (2).

That term is defined for the purposes of Pt III of the 1991 Act by s.48 which, so far as material, reads as follows:

    (1) In this Part a "*street*" means the whole or any part of the following, irrespective of whether it is a thoroughfare—

        (a) any highway, road, lane, footway, alley or passage,

        (b) any square or court, and

        (c) any land laid out as a way whether it is for the time being formed as a way or not.

    Where a street passes over a bridge or through a tunnel, references in this Part to the street include that bridge or tunnel.

    (2) The provisions of this Part apply to a street which is not a maintainable highway subject to such exceptions and adaptations as may be prescribed.

    (3) *[Meaning of "street works".]*

   (3A) *["Street works" for the purposes of subs.(3).]*

    (4) *[Meaning of "undertaker".]*

    (5) *[Meaning of references to the undertaker in relation to apparatus in a street.]*

Section 10 of this Act (to which reference is made in the definition of "trunk road" in s.329(1)) provides that all highways which were trunk roads under the earlier legislation should continue to be trunk roads and s.19 provides that a special road to be provided under a scheme will (unless otherwise provided in the scheme) become a trunk road.

The definition of "trunk road" is printed as amended by the Planning Act 2008 s.36 and Sch.2, para.29.

Section 329(5) relates to functions in relation to part of a particular road (as to which, see further the Transfer of Functions (Transport) Order 1981 (SI 1981/ 238) art.3(1)) and the National Assembly for Wales (Transfer of Functions) Order 1999 (SI 1999/672; not reproduced in this work) art.2 and Sch.1.]

*   *   *

SCHEDULE 4

CLASSES OF TRAFFIC FOR PURPOSES OF SPECIAL ROADS

Class I: **A10.08**

Heavy and light locomotives, motor tractors, heavy motor cars, motor cars and motor cycles whereof the cylinder capacity of the engine is not less than 50 cubic centimetres, and trailers drawn thereby, which comply with general regulations as to construction and use made, or having effect as if made, under [s.41 of the Road Traffic Act 1988] and in the case of which the following conditions are satisfied:—

   (i) that the whole weight of the vehicle is transmitted to the road surface by means of wheels;

   (ii) that all wheels of the vehicle are equipped with pneumatic tyres;

   (iii) that the vehicle is not controlled by a pedestrian;

   (iv) that the vehicle is not a vehicle chargeable with duty under [paragraph 4(3) of Schedule 1 to the Vehicle Excise and Registration Act 1994]; and

   (v) in the case of a motor vehicle, that it is so constructed as to be capable of attaining a speed of 25 miles per hour on the level under its own power, when unladen and not drawing a trailer.

Class II:

Motor vehicles and trailers the use of which for or in connection with the conveyance of abnormal indivisible loads is authorised by order made, or having effect as if made, by the Minister under [section 44(1) of the Road Traffic Act 1988].

Motor vehicles and trailers constructed for naval, military, air force or other defence purposes, the use of which is authorised by order made, or having effect as if made, by the Minister under [section 44(1) of the Road Traffic Act 1988].

Motor vehicles and trailers, to which any of the following Articles of the Motor Vehicles (Authorisation of Special Types) General Order 1973, namely Article 16 (which relates to vehicles for moving excavated material), Article 17 (which relates inter alia to vehicles constructed for use outside the United Kingdom) and Article 21 (which relates to engineering plant) relate and which are authorised to be used by any of those Articles of the said order or by any other [order made, or having effect as if made, under section 44(1) of the Road Traffic Act 1988], the said motor vehicles being vehicles in respect of which the following condition is satisfied, that is to say, that the vehicle is so constructed as to be capable of attaining a speed of 25 miles per hour on the level under its own power, when unladen and not drawing a trailer.

Class III:

Motor vehicles controlled by pedestrians.

Class IV:

All motor vehicles (other than invalid carriages and motor cycles whereof the cylinder capacity of the engine is less than 50 cubic centimetres) not comprised in Class I, Class II or Class III.

Class V:

Vehicles drawn by animals.

Class VI:

Vehicles (other than pedal cycles, perambulators, push-chairs and other forms of baby carriages) drawn or propelled by pedestrians.

Class VII:

Pedal cycles.

Class VIII:

Animals ridden, led or driven.

Class IX:

Pedestrians, perambulators, push-chairs and other forms of baby carriages and dogs held on a lead.

Class X:

Motor cycles whereof the cylinder capacity of the engine is less than 50 cubic centimetres.

Class XI:

Invalid carriages.

In this Schedule any expression defined for the purposes of [the Road Traffic Act 1988] has the same meaning as in that Act and the expression *"abnormal indivisible load"* has the same meaning as in the Motor Vehicles (Authorisation of Special Types) General Order 1973.

A10.09   *[Schedule 4 is printed as amended by the Road Traffic (Consequential Provisions) Act 1988 s.4 and Sch.3, para.21(3); the Vehicle Excise and Registration Act 1994 s.64 and Sch.4, para.4.*

Schedule 4 refers to the Motor Vehicles (Authorisation of Special Types) General Order 1973 (SI 1973/1101). Reference should now be made to the Road Vehicles (Authorisation of Special Types) (General) Order 2003 (SI 2003/1998) (q.v.).

For the Vehicle Excise and Registration Act 1994 Sch.1, para.4(3), and the Road Traffic Act 1988 s.44(1), see below.]

The Public Passenger Vehicles Act 1981

(1981 c.14)

A11.01 *An Act to consolidate certain enactments relating to public passenger vehicles.*

[15th April 1981]

ARRANGEMENT OF SECTIONS

PART I

PRELIMINARY

Definition and classification of public service vehicles

*   *   *

Schedule 2 —Definition of certain PSVs used without PSV operators' licences

Schedule 3 —Supplementary provision as to qualifications for PSV operator's licence

*   *   *

A11.02

[Visiting forces and headquarters (as defined), members of such forces or headquarters, and persons employed by such forces are exempt from the operation of the 1981 Act to the extent that, by virtue of any rule of law whereby enactments do not bind the Crown, such forces, headquarters, members or persons would have been so exempt if the forces or headquarters had been part of the home forces; see the Visiting Forces and International Headquarters (Application of Law) Order 1999 (SI 1999/1736; not reproduced in this work) art.12(1) and Sch.5.]

Part I

Preliminary

Definition and classification of public service vehicles

Definition of "public service vehicle"

A11.03

1.—(1) Subject to the provisions of this section, in this Act *"public service vehicle"* means a motor vehicle (other than a tramcar) which—

    (a) being a vehicle adapted to carry more than eight passengers, is used for carrying passengers for hire or reward; or

    (b) being a vehicle not so adapted, is used for carrying passengers for hire or reward at separate fares in the course of a business of carrying passengers.

(2) For the purposes of subsection (1) above a vehicle "is used" as mentioned in paragraph (a) or (b) of that subsection if it is being so used or if it has been used as mentioned in that paragraph and that use has not been permanently discontinued.

(3) A vehicle carrying passengers at separate fares in the course of a business of carrying passengers, but doing so in circumstances in which the conditions set out in Part I, … or III of Schedule 1 to this Act are fulfilled, shall be treated as not being a public service vehicle unless it is adapted to carry more than eight passengers.

(4) For the purposes of this section a journey made by a vehicle in the course of which one or more passengers are carried at separate fares shall not be treated as made in the course of a business of carrying passengers if—

    (a) the fare or aggregate of the fares paid in respect of the journey does not exceed the amount of the running costs of the vehicle for the journey; and

    (b) the arrangements for the payment of fares by the passenger or passengers so carried were made before the journey began;

and for the purposes of paragraph (a) above the running costs of a vehicle for a journey shall be taken to include an appropriate amount in respect of depreciation and general wear.

(5) For the purposes of this section, ... and Schedule 1 to this Act —

    (a) a vehicle is to be treated as carrying passengers for hire or reward if payment is made for, or for matters which include, the carrying of passengers, irrespective of the person to whom the payment is made and, in the case of a transaction effected by or on behalf of a member of any association of persons (whether incorporated or not) on the one hand and the association or another member thereof on the other hand, notwithstanding any rule of law as to such transactions;

    (b) a payment made for the carrying of a passenger shall be treated as a fare notwithstanding that it is made in consideration of other matters in addition to the journey and irrespective of the person by or to whom it is made;

    (c) a payment shall be treated as made for the carrying of a passenger if made in consideration of a person's being given a right to be carried, whether for one or more journeys and whether or not the right is exercised.

(6) Where a fare is paid for the carriage of a passenger on a journey by air, no part of that fare shall be treated for the purposes of subsection (5) above as paid in consideration of the carriage of the passenger by road by reason of the fact that, in case of mechanical failure, bad weather or other circumstances outside the operator's control, part of that journey may be made by road.

[Section 1 is printed as amended by the Transport Act 1985 s.139(3) and Sch.8.]   **A11.04**

2. [...]   **A11.05**

*   *   *

PART II

GENERAL PROVISIONS RELATING TO PUBLIC SERVICE VEHICLES

Fitness of public service vehicles

Certificate of initial fitness (or equivalent) required for use as public service vehicles

6.—(1) [Subject to subsection (1ZA) below,] a public service vehicle adapted   **A11.06** to carry more than eight passengers shall not be used on a road unless—

    (a) [an examiner appointed under section 66A of the Road Traffic Act 1988] [or an authorised inspector] has issued a certificate (in this Act referred to as a *"certificate of initial fitness"*) that the prescribed conditions as to fitness are fulfilled in respect of the vehicle; or

    (b) a certificate under section 10 of this Act has been issued in respect of the vehicle; or

    [(c)] one of the following certificates has effect with respect to the vehicle—

        (i) an EC certificate of conformity;

        (ii) a national small series certificate of conformity;

(iii) an individual approval certificate.]

[(1ZA) In the case of a public service vehicle to which subsection (1ZB) below applies, subsection (1) above has effect as if paragraphs (a) and (b) of that subsection were omitted.

(1ZB) This subsection applies to any public service vehicle which, by virtue of regulation 6 of the Approval Regulations, may not—

(a) be granted a first licence under section 21 of the Vehicle Excise and Registration Act 1994, or

(b) be registered before the issue of a first licence under that section,

unless one of the certificates mentioned in paragraph (d) of subsection (1) above has effect with respect to the vehicle.]

[(1A) *[Omitted.]*]

(2) Subject to section 68(3) of this Act, if a vehicle is used in contravention of subsection (1) above, the operator of the vehicle shall be liable on summary conviction to a fine not exceeding [level 4 on the standard scale].

[(3) In this section—

"*Approval Regulations*" means the Road Vehicles (Approval) Regulations 2009;

"*EC certificate of conformity*", "*national small series certificate of conformity*" and "*individual approval certificate*" have the meaning given by regulation 3(1) of the Approval Regulations.]

A11.07 *[Section 6 is printed as amended by the Criminal Justice Act 1982 ss.37 and 46; the Road Traffic (Consequential Provisions) Act 1988 s.4 and Sch.3, para.22; the Road Traffic Act 1991 s.48 and Sch.4, para.14; the Road Vehicles (Approval) (Consequential Amendments) Regulations 2009 (SI 2009/818) reg.2.*

The words "or an authorised inspector" in s.6(1)(a) printed inside square brackets were added by the Transport Act 1982 s.10(3), as amended by the Road Traffic Act 1991 s.48 and Sch.4, para.19(1) and (2), and will take effect from a date to be announced.

The application of ss.6, 12, 18 and 22 of this Act to certain vehicles is excluded (and in some cases a modified version of s.12 is applied) by the Road Transport (International Passenger Services) Regulations 1984 (SI 1984/748) regs 4–12 (inclusive) (q.v.).]

Certifying officers and public service vehicle examiners

A11.08 7. […]

Powers of, and facilities for, inspection of public service vehicles

A11.09 8.—(1), (1A), (2) […]

(3) The Secretary of State may—

(a) provide and maintain stations where inspections of public service vehicles … may be carried out;

(b) designate premises as stations where such inspections may be carried out; and

(c) provide and maintain apparatus for the carrying out of such inspections;

and in this Act *"official PSV testing station"* means a station provided, or any premises for the time being designated, under this subsection.

[Section 8 is printed as amended by the Road Traffic Act 1991 ss.11, 83 and Sch.8.]   **A11.10**

Power to prohibit driving of unfit public service vehicles

9. [...]   **A11.11**

Extensions of sections 8 and 9 to certain passenger vehicles other than public service vehicles

9A.—(1) Section 8 of this Act shall apply ... to any motor vehicle (other than a tramcar) which is adapted to carry more than eight passengers but is not a public service vehicle as it applies to a public service vehicle.   **A11.12**

(2) [...]

[Section 9A was inserted by the Transport Act 1985 s.33, and is printed as amended by the Road Traffic Act 1991 s.83 and Sch.8.]   **A11.13**

Approval of type vehicle and effect thereof

10. *[Omitted.]*   **A11.14**

Modification of section 6 in relation to experimental vehicles

11.—(1) Where it appears to the Secretary of State expedient to do so for the purpose of the making of tests or trials of a vehicle or its equipment, he may by order made in respect of that vehicle for the purposes of section 6 of this Act dispense with such of the prescribed conditions as to fitness referred to in subsection (1)(a) of that section as are specified in the order.   **A11.15**

(2) While such an order is in force in respect of a vehicle, section 6 of this Act shall have effect in relation to the vehicle as if the prescribed conditions as to fitness referred to in subsection (1)(a) of that section did not include such of those conditions as are dispensed with by the order.

(3) An order under this section shall specify the period for which it is to continue in force, and may contain, or authorise the imposition of, requirements, restrictions or prohibitions relating to the construction, equipment or use of the vehicle to which the order relates.

(4) Where an order under this section in respect of a vehicle is revoked or otherwise ceases to have effect, any certificate of initial fitness issued under section 6 of this Act in respect of the vehicle while the order was in force shall, for the purposes of that section as regards any use of the vehicle after the order has ceased to have effect, be deemed never to have been issued.

Public service vehicle operators' licences

PSV operators' licences

12.—[(1) A public vehicle shall not be used on a road for carrying passengers for hire or reward except under a PSV operator's licence granted in accordance with the following provision of this Part of this Act.]   **A11.16**

(2)–(4) *[Omitted.]*

(5) Subject to section 68(3) of this Act, if a vehicle is used in contravention of subsection (1) above, the operator of the vehicle shall be liable on summary conviction to a fine not exceeding [level 4 on the standard scale].

A11.17   *[Section 12 is printed as amended by the Criminal Justice Act 1982 ss.37 and 46; the Transport Act 1985 s.1(3) and Sch.1, para.4.*

For s.68(3) of this Act, see below.

An offence under s.12(5) is a fixed penalty offence for the purposes of Pt 3 of the Road Traffic Offenders Act 1988 (see the Fixed Penalty Offences Order 2009 (SI 2009/483) art.2). The amount for the fixed penalty offence is prescribed by the Fixed Penalty Order 2000 (SI 2000/2792), as amended by the Fixed Penalty (Amendment) Order 2009 (SI 2009/488).

The application of this section to certain vehicles is excluded (or a modified version of the section is applied); see further the notes to s.6 of this Act.]

[Detention of certain PSVs used without PSV operators' licences

A11.18   **12A.** Schedule 2A (which relates to the detention, removal and disposal of PSVs which are adapted to carry more than 8 passengers and in respect of which it appears that section 12(1) is contravened) shall have effect.]

A11.19   *[Section 12A is printed as inserted by the Local Transport Act 2008 s.47.]*

*   *   *

Conditions attached to licences

A11.20   **16.**—(1) [Subject to subsection (1A) below and section 12(7) of the Transport Act 1985] [a traffic commissioner] on granting a PSV operator's licence shall attach to it one or more conditions specifying the maximum number of vehicles (being vehicles having their operating centre in the area of [that commissioner]) which the holder of the licence may at any one time use under the licence.

[(1A) In the case of a restricted licence, the number specified as the maximum in any condition imposed under subsection (1) above shall not, except in any prescribed case or class of case, exceed two.]

(2) Conditions attached under subsection (1) above to a PSV operator's licence may specify different maximum numbers for different descriptions of vehicle.

(3) [A traffic commissioner] may (whether at the time when the licence is granted or at any time thereafter) attach to a PSV operator's licence granted by [him] such conditions or additional conditions as [he thinks] fit for restricting or regulating the use of vehicles under the licence, being conditions of any prescribed description.

(4) Without prejudice to the generality of the power to prescribe descriptions of conditions for the purposes of subsection (3) above, the descriptions which may be so prescribed include conditions for regulating the places at which vehicles being used under a PSV operator's licence may stop to take up or set down passengers.

(5), (6) *[Variation of operator's licence by traffic commissioner.]*

(6A), (6B) *[Consideration by traffic commissioner of undertakings given for purposes of s.16(6).]*

(7) Subject to section 68(3) of this Act, if a condition attached to a PSV

operator's licence is contravened, the holder of the licence shall be liable on summary conviction to a fine not exceeding [level 3 on the standard scale].

(8) Compliance with any condition attached to a PSV operator's licence ... [(other than a condition so attached under subsection (1A) above)] may be temporarily dispensed with by the traffic [commissioner] by whom the licence was granted if [he is] satisfied that compliance with the condition would be unduly onerous by reason of circumstances not foreseen when the condition was attached or, if the condition has been altered, when it was last altered.

(9) It is hereby declared that the conditions attached under subsection (1) [or (1A)] above to a PSV operator's licence granted by the traffic [commissioner] for any area do not affect the use by the holder of the licence of a vehicle—

    (a) under a PSV operator's licence granted to him by the traffic [commissioner] for another area; or

    (b) in circumstances such that another person falls to be treated as the operator of the vehicle (for example, by virtue of regulations under section 81(l)(a) of this Act).

[Section 16 is printed as amended by the Criminal Justice Act 1982 ss.37 and **A11.21** *46; the Transport Act 1985 ss.3(5), 24(1), 139(2) and (3), Sch.2, Pt II, para.4(7), Sch.7, para.21(4), and Sch.8.*

For ss.68(3) and 81(1)(a) of this Act, see below.

The Public Service Vehicles (Operators' Licences) Regulations 1995 (SI 1995/ 2908) below were in part made under this section.]

[Conditions as to matters required to be notified

16A.—(1) On issuing a standard licence, a traffic commissioner shall attach to **A11.22** it the following conditions, namely—

    (a) a condition requiring the licence-holder to inform the commissioner of any event which could affect the fulfilment by the licence-holder of any of the requirements of section 14(1) of this Act, and to do so within 28 days of the event; and

    (b) a condition requiring the licence-holder to inform the commissioner of any event which could affect the fulfilment by a relevant transport manager of the requirements mentioned in section 14(1)(a) or (c) of this Act, and to do so within 28 days of the event coming to the licence-holder's knowledge.

(2) In subsection (1)(b) above the reference to a *"relevant transport manager"* is a reference to any transport manager employed by the licence-holder who is relied on by the licence-holder to fulfil the requirements of section 14(1)(c) of this Act.

(3) Any person who contravenes any condition attached under this section to a licence of which he is the holder is guilty of an offence and liable on summary conviction to a fine not exceeding level 4 on the standard scale.]

[Section 16A was inserted by the Public Service Vehicles Operators (Qualifica- **A11.23** *tions) Regulations 1999 (SI 1999/2431; not reproduced in this work).*

The requirements in s.14(1) (to which reference is made in the text of s.16A) are: (a) the requirement to be of good repute; (b) the requirement to be of appropriate financial standing; and (c) the requirement as to professional competence.]

Revocation, suspension, etc., of licences

A11.24   **17.** *[Omitted.]*

[Assessors to assist traffic commissioners

A11.25   **17A.** *[Omitted.]*]

Duty to exhibit operator's disc

A11.26   **18.**—(1) Where a vehicle is being used in circumstances such that a PSV operator's licence is required, there shall be fixed and exhibited on the vehicle in the prescribed manner an operator's disc issued under this section showing particulars of the operator of the vehicle and of the PSV operator's licence under which the vehicle is being used.

[(2) A traffic commissioner on granting a PSV operator's licence shall supply the person to whom the licence is granted—

    (a) with a number of operators' discs equal to the maximum number of vehicles that he may use under the licence in accordance with the condition or conditions attached to the licence under section 16(1) of this Act; or

    (b) with such lesser number of operators' discs as he may request.]

[(2A) Where, in the case of any PSV operator's licence, the maximum number referred to in subsection (2)(a) above is increased on the variation of one or more of the conditions there referred to, the traffic commissioner on making the variation shall supply the holder of the licence

    (a) with such number of additional operators' discs as will bring the total number of operators' discs held by him in respect of the licence to that maximum number, or

    (b) with such lesser number of additional operators' discs as he may request.]

[(2B) Where the number of operators' discs currently held in respect of a PSV operator's licence is less than the maximum number referred to in subsection (2)(a) above, the traffic commissioner by whom the licence was granted shall on the application of the holder of the licence supply him with such number of additional operators' discs as is mentioned in subsection (2A)(a) or (b) above.]

[(2C) Where, in accordance with regulations under subsection (3)(aa) below, all the operators' discs held in respect of a PSV operator's licence expire at the same time, the traffic commissioner by whom the licence was granted shall supply the holder of the licence with a number of new operators' discs equal to the number of discs that have expired.]

(3) Regulations may make provision—

    (a) as to the form of operators' discs and the particulars to be shown on them;

    [(aa) as to the expiry of operators' discs;]

    (b) with respect to the custody and production of operators' discs;

    (c) for the issue of new operators' discs in place of those lost, destroyed or defaced;

    (d) for the return of operators' discs [on their expiry or otherwise ceasing to have effect] on the revocation or [termination] of a PSV operator's licence or in the event of a variation of one or more conditions attached to a licence under section 16(1) of this Act having the effect of reducing the maximum number of vehicles which may be used under the licence[;]

[(e) for the voluntary return of operators' discs by the holder of a PSV operator's licence.]

(4) Subject to section 68(3) of this Act, if a vehicle is used in contravention of subsection (1) above, the operator of the vehicle shall be liable on summary conviction to a fine not exceeding [level 3 on the standard scale].

[Section 18 is printed as amended by the Criminal Justice Act 1982 ss.37 and 46; the Transport Act 1985 ss.3(5), 24(2), and Sch.2, Pt II, para.4(9); the Deregulation and Contracting Out Act 1994 ss.63 and 68 and Sch.14, para.6.   **A11.27**

The Public Service Vehicles (Operators' Licences) Regulations 1995 (SI 1995/ 2908) below were in part made under this section.

For s.68(3) of this Act, see below.

The application of this section to certain vehicles is excluded; see further the notes to s.6 of this Act.

The text of s.18(1) in its application to an operator who is a partnership is modified by the Operation of Public Service Vehicles (Partnership) Regulations 1986 (SI 1986/1628) Sch., Pt I (not reproduced in this work) so that the firm's name is disclosed on the disc.]

Duty to inform traffic commissioners of relevant convictions, etc.

19.—(1) A person who has applied for a PSV operator's licence shall forth-   **A11.28** with notify the traffic [commissioner] to whom the application was made if, in the interval between the making of the application and the date on which it is disposed of, a relevant conviction occurs of the applicant, or any employee or agent of his, or of any person proposed to be engaged as transport manager whose repute and competence are relied on in connection with the application.

(2) It shall be the duty of the holder of a PSV operator's licence to give notice in writing to the traffic [commissioner] by whom the licence was granted of—

(a) any relevant conviction of the holder; and

(b) any relevant conviction of any officer, employee or agent of the holder for an offence committed in the course of the holder's road passenger transport business,

and to do so within 28 days of the conviction in the case of a conviction of the holder or his transport manager and within 28 days of the conviction coming to the holder's knowledge in any other case.

[(2A) For the purposes of subsections (1) and (2) above the issue to a person of a fixed penalty notice or conditional offer under Part 3 of the Road Traffic Offenders Act 1988 in respect of an offence prescribed for the purposes of this Act is to be treated as if it were a relevant conviction of him.]

(3) It shall be the duty of the holder of a PSV operator's licence within 28 days of the occurrence of—

(a) the bankruptcy or liquidation of the holder, or the sequestration of his estate [or [the entry into administration of] the holder] or the appointment of a receiver, manager or trustee of his road passenger transport business; or

(b) any change in the identity of the transport manager of the holder's road passenger transport business,

to give notice in writing of that event to the traffic [commissioner] by whom the licence was granted.

(4) [A traffic commissioner] on granting or varying a PSV operator's licence, or at any time thereafter, may require the holder of the licence to inform [him] forthwith or within a time specified by [him] of any material change specified by [him] in any of [the holder's] circumstances which were relevant to the grant or variation of the licence.

(5) Subject to section 68(1) of this Act, a person who fails to comply with subsection (1), (2) or (3) above or with any requirement under subsection (4) above shall be liable on summary conviction to a fine not exceeding [level 3 on the standard scale].

A11.29   *[Section 19 is printed as amended by the Criminal Justice Act 1982 ss.37 and 46; the Insolvency Act 1985 s.235(1) and Sch.8, para.34; the Transport Act 1985 s.3(5) and Sch.2, Pt II, para.4(10); the Insolvency Act 1986 s.439(2) and Sch.14; the Enterprise Act 2002 (Insolvency) Order 2003 (SI 2003/2096) art.4; the Road Safety Act 2006 s.7(2).*

For s.68(1) of this Act, see below.

The text of s.19(1), (2) and (3) in its application to an operator which is a partnership is modified by the Operation of Public Service Vehicles (Partnership) Regulations 1986 (SI 1986/1628) Sch., Pt I (not reproduced in this work) so as (inter alia) to require a relevant conviction of any partner, employee or agent to be notified under subs.(1) and subs.(2) and so as to require dissolution of the partnership to be given under subs.(3).]

Duty to give traffic commissioners information about vehicles

A11.30   **20.**—(1) It shall be the duty of the holder of a PSV operator's licence, on the happening to any public service vehicle owned by him of any failure or damage of a nature calculated to affect the safety of occupants of the public service vehicle or of persons using the road, to report the matter as soon as is practicable to the [Secretary of State].

(2) It shall be the duty of the holder of a PSV operator's licence, on any alteration otherwise than by replacement of parts being made in the structure or fixed equipment of any public service vehicle owned by him, to give notice of the alteration as soon as is practicable to the [Secretary of State].

(3) The traffic [commissioner] by whom a PSV operator's licence was granted may—

(a) require the holder of the licence to supply [him] forthwith or within a specified time with such information as [he] may reasonably require about the public service vehicles owned by [the holder] and normally kept at an operating centre within the area of [that commissioner], and to keep up to date information supplied by [the holder] under this paragraph; or

(b) require the holder or former holder of the licence to supply [him] forthwith or within a specified time with such information as [he]

> may reasonably require about the public service vehicles owned by [the holder or former holder] at any material time specified by [him] which were at that time normally kept at an operating centre within the area of [that commissioner].

In this subsection *"material time"* means a time when the PSV operator's licence in question was in force.

(4) Subject to section 68(1) of this Act, a person who fails to comply with the provisions of subsection (1) or (2) above or with any requirement under subsection (3) above shall be liable on summary conviction to a fine not exceeding [level 3 on the standard scale].

(5) A person who in purporting to comply with any requirement under subsection (3) above supplies any information which he knows to be false or does not believe to be true shall be liable on summary conviction to a fine not exceeding [level 4 on the standard scale].

(6) [...]

[Section 20 is printed as amended by the Criminal Justice Act 1982 ss.37 and   **A11.31**
46; the Transport Act 1985 ss.3(5) and 29, Sch.2, Pt II, para.4(11); the Road Traffic Act 1991 s.83 and Sch.8.

Section 20 has also been prospectively amended with effect from a date to be announced by the Transport Act 1982 s.10, and the Road Traffic Act 1991 s.48 and Sch.4, para.19.

For s.68(1) of this Act, see below.]

Certificates of qualification

21. *[Omitted.]*   **A11.32**

Drivers' licences

Drivers' licences

22. [...]   **A11.33**

Appeals to courts of summary jurisdiction in connection with drivers' licences

23. [...]   **A11.34**

Northern Ireland drivers' licences

23A. [...]   **A11.35**

Regulation of conduct, etc., of drivers, inspectors, conductors and passengers

Regulation of conduct of drivers, inspectors and conductors

24.—(1) Regulations may make provision for regulating the conduct, when   **A11.36**
acting as such, of—

    (a) ... drivers of public service vehicles, and

    (b) inspectors and conductors of such vehicles [, and]

    [(c) drivers, inspectors and conductors of tramcars.]

(2) Subject to section 68(1) of this Act, if a person to whom regulations having effect by virtue of this section apply contravenes, or fails to comply with, any

of the provisions of the regulations, he shall be liable on summary conviction to a fine not exceeding [level 2 on the standard scale] and, in the case of an offence by a person acting as driver [of a public service vehicle], the court by which he is convicted may, if it thinks fit, cause particulars of the conviction to be endorsed upon [counterpart of] the licence granted to that person under [Part III of the Road Traffic Act 1988] [or, as the case may be, the counterpart (if any) of his Community licence (within the meaning of that Part)] [or, if he is not the holder of a licence (within the meaning of Part 3 of the Road Traffic Act 1988), on his driving record (within the meaning of section 97A of the Road Traffic Offenders Act 1988)].

(3) The person who has the custody of [any counterpart of a licence which is to be endorsed under subsection (2) above] shall, if so required by the convicting court, produce [it and the licence] within a reasonable time for the purpose of endorsement, and, subject to section 68(1) of this Act, if he fails to do so, shall be liable on summary conviction to a fine not exceeding [level 3 on the standard scale].

(4) In this section and in section 25 of this Act *"inspector"*, in relation to a public service vehicle, means a person authorised to act as an inspector by the holder of the PSV operator's licence under which the vehicle is being used.

[(5) Notwithstanding section 1(1) of this Act, in this section and in sections 25 and 26 of this Act *"public service vehicle"* shall be construed as meaning a public service vehicle being used on a road for carrying passengers for hire or reward.]

A11.37 *[Section 24 is printed as amended by the Criminal Justice Act 1982 ss.37 and 46; the Road Traffic (Driver Licensing and Information Systems) Act 1989 ss.7, 16, 24(2) and (4), Sch.3, para.2(a), (b) and (c), and Sch.6; the Driving Licences (Community Driving Licence) Regulations 1990 (SI 1990/144); the Transport and Works Act 1992 s.61(1), (2)(a) and (b); the Driving Licences (Community Driving Licence) Regulations 1996 (SI 1996/1974) reg.5 and Sch.4 (not reproduced in this work); the Road Safety Act 2006 s.9 and Sch.2, para.1.*

With effect from a day to be appointed, in relation to endorsement (all drivers), s.24 will be amended by the Road Safety Act 2006 s.10 and Sch.3, para.1, s.59 and Sch.7(4):

1. *in s.24(2), the words "send notice of the particulars of the conviction to the Secretary of State requiring the Secretary of State to endorse them on the person's driving record (within the meaning of section 97A of the Road Traffic Offenders Act 1988)" will be substituted for the words from "cause particulars" to the end;*

2. *s.24(3) shall be omitted.*

For the provisions relating to the commencement of ss.9 and 10 of and Schs 2 and 3 to the Road Safety Act 2006, see ibid. s.61(8) below.

For s.68(1) of this Act, see below.

The Public Service Vehicles (Conduct of Drivers, Inspectors, Conductors and Passengers) Regulations 1990 (SI 1990/1020) (q.v.) were made in part under this section.]

Regulation of conduct of passengers

A11.38 25.—(1) *[Regulation-making power.]*

(2) [...]

(3) Subject to section 68(1) of this Act, if a person contravenes, or fails to comply with, a provision of regulations having effect by virtue of this section, he shall be liable on summary conviction to a fine not exceeding [level 3 on the standard scale].

(4) *[Applies to Scotland.]*

[Section 25 is printed as amended (so far as relevant to this work) by the Criminal Justice Act 1982 ss.37 and 46; the Police and Criminal Evidence Act 1984 s.119(2) and Sch.7, Pt I. **A11.39**

The Public Service Vehicles (Conduct of Drivers, Inspectors, Conductors and Passengers) Regulations 1990 (SI 1990/1020) (q.v.) have effect in part as if made under this section.

For s.68(1) of this Act, see below.]

Control of number of passengers

26.—(1) *[Regulation-making power.]*   **A11.40**

(2) Subject to section 68(1) and (3) of this Act, if a person contravenes, or fails to comply with, a provision of regulations having effect by virtue of this section, he shall be liable on summary conviction to a fine not exceeding [level 2 on the standard scale].

[Section 26 is printed as amended by the Criminal Justice Act 1982 ss.37, 39(1), 46, and Sch.2. **A11.41**

For s.68(1) and (3) of this Act, see below.

The Public Service Vehicles (Carrying Capacity) Regulations 1984 (SI 1984/1406) (not reproduced in this work) were made in part under this section.]

* * *

PART IV

MODIFICATION OF REQUIREMENTS OF PART II IN RELATION TO CERTAIN VEHICLES AND AREAS

Fare-paying passengers on school buses

Fare-paying passengers on school buses

46.—(1) Subject to subsection (2) below, a local education authority may—   **A11.42**

   (a) use a school bus, when it is being used to provide free school transport, to carry as fare-paying passengers persons other than those for whom the free school transport is provided;

   (b) use a school bus belonging to the authority, when it is not being used to provide free school transport, to provide a local ... service;

and sections 6, 8, 9, [and 12(1)] of this Act shall not apply to a school bus belonging to a local education authority in the course of its use by the authority in accordance with this subsection.

(2) Subsection (1) above does not affect the duties of a local education authority in relation to the provision of free school transport or authorise a local education authority to make any charge for the carriage of a pupil on a journey which

he is required to make in the course of his education at a school maintained by such an authority.

(3) In this section —

[*"free school transport"* means transport provided by a local education authority free of charge—

(a) in pursuance of arrangements under [section 508B(1), section 508C(1), section 508F(1),] section 509(1) or (1A) or section 509AA(7)(b) or (9)(a) of the Education Act 1996, [...]

[(aa) in pursuance of arrangements made by the authority in pursuance of a scheme made by them under Schedule 35C to that Act (school travel schemes), or]

(b) otherwise, in the exercise of any function of the authority,

for the purpose of facilitating the attendance of persons receiving education or training at any premises;]

*   *   *

"school bus", in relation to a local education authority, means a motor vehicle which is used by that authority to provide free school transport.

(4) *[Applies to Scotland.]*

A11.43   *[Section 46 is printed as amended by the Transport Act 1985 ss.1(3) and 139(3), Sch.1, para.6, and Sch.8; the Road Traffic (Driver Licensing and Information Systems) Act 1989 s.7 and Sch.3, para.3; the Further and Higher Education Act 1992 s.93(1) and Sch.8, para.90; the Education Act 2002 s.215(1) and Sch.21, para.4; the Education and Inspections Act 2006 s.85 and Sch.10, para.1(b).]*

*   *   *

PART V

MISCELLANEOUS AND SUPPLEMENTARY

*   *   *

General power to make regulations for purposes of Act

A11.44   **60.**—(1)–(1A) *[Omitted.]*

(2) In this Act *"prescribed"* means prescribed by regulations and *"regulations"* means regulations made [by the Secretary of State].

(3) [...]

A11.45   *[Section 60 is printed as amended by the Transport Act 1985 s.134(2)(c) and (d).*

The Community Bus Regulations 1986 (SI 1986/1245; not reproduced in this work), the Minibus and Other Section 19 Permit Buses Regulations 1987 (SI 1987/1230; not reproduced in this work), the Public Service Vehicles (Conduct of Drivers, Inspectors, Conductors and Passengers) Regulations 1990 (SI 1990/1020) (q.v.), the Public Service Vehicles (Operators' Licences) Regulations 1995 (SI 1995/2908) (q.v.), the Public Service Vehicles (Operators' Licences) (Fees) Regulations 1995 (SI 1995/2909; not reproduced in this work), the Public Ser-

vice Vehicles (Traffic Regulation Conditions) (England and Wales) Regulations 2004 (SI 2004/2682; not reproduced in this work), the Community Bus Regulations 2009 (SI 2009/366; not reproduced in this work) and the Section 19 Permit Regulations 2009 (SI 2009/365; not reproduced in this work) were made in part under this section.]

*   *   *

Provisions relating to offences and legal proceedings

Forgery and misuse of documents

65.—(1) This section applies to the following documents and other things, namely—

    (a) a licence under Part II ... of this Act;

    (b) a certificate of initial fitness under section 6 of this Act;

  [(bb) a notice removing a prohibition under section 9 of this Act;]

    (c) a certificate under section 10 of this Act that a vehicle conforms to a type vehicle;

    (d) an operator's disc under section 18 of this Act;

    (e) a certificate under section 21 of this Act as to the repute, financial standing or professional competence of any person;

  [(ea) a control document issued under Article 6 of Council Regulation (EC) No.12/98 of 11 December 1997;]

    (f) [...]

(2) A person who, with intent to deceive—

    (a) forges or alters, or uses or lends to, or allows to be used by, any other person, a document or other thing to which this section applies; or

    (b) makes or has in his possession any document or other thing so closely resembling a document or other thing to which this section applies as to be calculated to deceive,

shall be liable—

       (i) on conviction on indictment, to imprisonment for a term not exceeding two years;

      (ii) on summary conviction, to a fine not exceeding the statutory maximum.

(3) In the application of this section to England and Wales—

    [*"forges"* means makes a false document or other thing in order that it may be used as genuine]; ...

(4) [...]

[Section 65 is printed as amended by the Forgery and Counterfeiting Act 1981 s.12; the Transport Act 1985 s.139(3) and Sch.8; the Road Traffic Act 1991 s.83 and Sch.8; the Statute Law (Repeals) Act 1993 s.1(1) and Sch.1, Pt XIV, group 2; the Road Transport (Passenger Vehicles Cabotage) Regulations 1999 (SI 1999/ 3413) reg.10(2) and (3).

As to references in ss.65(1)(a) and 66(a) to a licence under any Part of this Act, see the Road Transport (International Passenger Services) Regulations 1984 (SI 1984/748) reg.21 below.]

A11.46

A11.47

False statements to obtain licence, etc.

A11.48   **66.** A person who knowingly makes a false statement for the purpose of—

    (a) obtaining the grant of a licence under Part II … of this Act to himself or any other person, obtaining the variation of such licence, preventing the grant or variation of any such licence or procuring the imposition of a condition or limitation in relation to any such licence;

    (b) obtaining the issue of a certificate of initial fitness under section 6 of this Act;

    (c) obtaining the issue of a certificate under section 10 of this Act that a vehicle conforms to a type vehicle;

    (d) obtaining the issue of an operator's disc under section 18 of this Act; …

    (e) obtaining the issue of a certificate under section 21 of this Act as to the repute, financial standing or professional competence of any person; [or]

    [(f) obtaining the issue of a control document under Article 6 of Council Regulation (EC) No.12/98 of 11 December 1997;]

shall be liable on summary conviction to a fine not exceeding [level 4 on the standard scale].

A11.49   *[Section 66 is printed as amended by the Criminal Justice Act 1982 ss.37 and 46; the Transport Act 1985 s.139(3) and Sch.8; the Road Transport (Passenger Vehicles Cabotage) Regulations 1999 (SI 1999/3413) reg.10(2) and (4).*

See further the note to s.65.]

Issue of false documents

A11.50   **66A.** *[Omitted.]*

Penalty for breach of regulations

A11.51   **67.** Subject to section 68(1) of this Act, if a person acts in contravention of, or fails to comply with, any regulations made by the Secretary of State under this Act … and contravention thereof, or failure to comply therewith, is not made an offence under any other provision of this Act, he shall for each offence be liable on summary conviction to a fine not exceeding [level 2 on the standard scale].

A11.52   *[Section 67 is printed as amended by the Criminal Justice Act 1982 ss.37 and 46; the Transport Act 1985 s.139(3) and Sch.8.]*

Defences available to persons charged with certain offences

A11.53   **68.**—(1) It shall be a defence for a person charged with an offence under any of the provisions of this Act mentioned in subsection (2) below to prove that there was a reasonable excuse for the act or omission in respect of which he is charged.

    (2) The provisions referred to in subsection (1) above are—

    (a) sections 19(5), 20(4), 24(2) and (3), 25(3), 26(2), … 67 and 70(3); …

    (b) […]

    (3) It shall be a defence for a person charged with an offence under any of the provisions of this Act mentioned in subsection (4) below to prove that he took all

reasonable precautions and exercised all due diligence to avoid the commission of any offence under that provision.

(4) The provisions referred to in subsection (3) above are—

    (a) sections 6(2), ... 12(5), 16(7), 18(4), 26(2), [and 27(2)] ; ...

    (b) [...]

[Section 68 is printed as amended by the Transport Act 1985 ss.1(3) and 139(3), Sch.1, para.11, and Sch.8; the Road Traffic (Driver Licensing and Information Systems) Act 1989 s.16 and Sch.6; the Road Traffic Act 1991 s.83 and Sch.8.]   **A11.54**

Restriction on institution in England and Wales of proceedings under Part II

69.—(1) Subject to the provisions of this section proceedings for an offence under Part II ... of this Act shall not, in England and Wales, be instituted except by or on behalf of the Director of Public Prosecutions or by a person authorised in that behalf by [a traffic commissioner], a chief officer of police, or the council of a county or district.   **A11.55**

(2) Subsection (1) above shall not apply to proceedings for the breach of regulations having effect by virtue of section 25 or 26 of this Act.

(3) [...]

[Section 69 is printed as amended by the Transport Act 1985 ss.3(5) and 139(3), Sch.2, Pt II, para.4(19), and Sch.8; the Statute Law (Repeals) Act 2004 s.1(1) and Sch.1, Pt 14.]   **A11.56**

Duty to give information as to identity of driver in certain cases

70.—(1) Where the driver of a vehicle is alleged to be guilty of an offence under Part II ... of this Act —   **A11.57**

    (a) the person keeping the vehicle shall give such information as to the identity of the driver as he may be required to give by or on behalf of a chief officer of police, and

    (b) any other person shall if required as aforesaid give any information which it is in his power to give and may lead to the identification of the driver.

(2) A person who fails to comply with the requirement of paragraph (a) of subsection (1) above shall, unless he shows to the satisfaction of the court that he did not know and could not with reasonable diligence ascertain who the driver of the vehicle was, be liable on summary conviction to a fine not exceeding [level 3 on the standard scale].

(3) Subject to section 68(1) of this Act, a person who fails to comply with the requirement of paragraph (b) of subsection (1) above shall be liable on summary conviction to a fine not exceeding [level 3 on the standard scale].

[Section 70 is printed as amended by the Criminal Justice Act 1982 s.38(1), (6) and (8) (it being assumed that the s.70 offence, being a re-enactment of an offence in the Road Traffic Act 1960, was a summary offence created not later than July 29, 1977 and hence within the scope of s.38(1) of the 1982 Act); the Transport Act 1985 s.139(3) and Sch.8.]   **A11.58**

* * *

Evidence by certificate

A11.59   **71.**—(1) In any proceedings in England or Wales for an offence under Part II ... of this Act a certificate in the prescribed form, purporting to be signed by a constable and certifying that the person specified in the certificate stated to the constable—

(a) that a particular motor vehicle was being driven or used by, or belonged to, that person on a particular occasion; or

(b) that a particular motor vehicle on a particular occasion was used by or belonged to a firm in which that person also stated that he was at the time of the statement a partner; or

(c) that a particular motor vehicle on a particular occasion was used by or belonged to a company of which that person also stated that he was at the time of the statement a director, officer or employee,

shall be admissible as evidence for the purpose of determining by whom the vehicle was being driven or used or to whom it belonged, as the case may be, on that occasion.

(2) Nothing in subsection (1) above shall be deemed to make a certificate admissible as evidence in proceedings for an offence except in a case where and to the like extent to which oral evidence to the like effect would have been admissible in those proceedings.

(3) Nothing in subsection (1) above shall be deemed to make a certificate admissible as evidence in proceedings for an offence—

(a) unless a copy thereof has, not less than seven days before the hearing or trial, been served in the prescribed manner on the person charged with the offence; or

(b) if that person, not later than three days before the hearing or trial or within such further time as the court may in special circumstances allow, serves a notice in the prescribed form and manner on the prosecutor requiring attendance at the trial of the person who signed the certificate.

(4) In this section *"prescribed"* means prescribed by rules made by the Secretary of State by statutory instrument.

A11.60   *[Section 71 is printed as amended by the Transport Act 1985 s.139(3) and Sch.8.]*

Proof in summary proceedings of identity of driver of vehicle

A11.61   **72.** Where on a summary trial in England or Wales of an information for an offence under Part II ... of this Act —

(a) it is proved to the satisfaction of the court, on oath or in a manner prescribed by rules made under [section 144 of the Magistrates' Courts Act 1980], that a requirement under subsection (1) of section 70 of this Act to give information as to the identity of the driver of a particular vehicle on the particular occasion to which the information relates has been served on the accused by post; and

(b) a statement in writing is produced to the court purporting to be signed by the accused that the accused was the driver of that vehicle on that occasion,

the court may accept that statement as evidence that the accused was the driver of that vehicle on the occasion.

[Section 72 is printed as amended by the Magistrates' Courts Act 1980   **A11.62**
s.154(2) and Sch.8, para.5 (which came into operation after this Act had received the royal assent but before this Act came into operation); the Transport Act 1985 s.139(3) and Sch.8.]

Time within which summary proceedings for certain offences may be commenced

73. Summary proceedings for an offence under section 65 or 66 of this Act   **A11.63**
may be brought within a period of six months from the date on which evidence sufficient in the opinion of the prosecutor to warrant the proceedings came to his knowledge; but no such proceedings shall be brought by virtue of this section more than three years after the commission of the offence.

For the purposes of this section a certificate by or on behalf of the prosecutor and stating the date on which such evidence as aforesaid came to his knowledge shall be conclusive evidence of that fact; and a certificate stating that matter and purporting to be so signed shall be deemed to be so signed unless the contrary is proved.

Offences by companies

74.—(1) Where an offence under Part II ... of this Act committed by a company   **A11.64**
is proved to have been committed with the consent or connivance of, or to be attributable to any neglect on the part of, any director, manager, secretary or other similar officer of the company, or any person who was purporting to act in any such capacity, he, as well as the company, shall be guilty of that offence and be liable to be proceeded against and punished accordingly.

(2) Where the affairs of a company are managed by its members, subsection (1) above shall apply in relation to the acts and defaults of a member in connection with his functions of management as if he were a director of the company.

[Section 74 is printed as amended by the Transport Act 1985 s.139(3) and   **A11.65**
Sch.8.]

*   *   *

Vehicles excluded from regulation as private hire vehicles

79. At any time when a vehicle would apart from section [1(4)] of this Act be a   **A11.66**
public service vehicle, it shall continue to be treated as such for the purposes only of provisions contained in a local Act,... or in Part II of the Local Government (Miscellaneous Provisions) Act 1976, which regulate the use of private hire vehicles provided for hire with the services of a driver for the purpose of carrying passengers and exclude public service vehicles from the scope of that regulation.

[Section 79 is printed as amended by the Transport Act 1985 s.139(2) and   **A11.67**
Sch.7, para.21(10); the Transport Act 2000 s.265(1).

Words relating exclusively to Scotland in s.79 have been omitted.]

[Small PSVs subject to regulation as private hire vehicles

A11.68   **79A.**—(1) If a small bus is being provided for hire with the services of a driver for the purpose of carrying passengers otherwise than at separate fares, it is not to be regarded as a public service vehicle for the purpose of—

         (a) Part II of the Local Government (Miscellaneous Provisions) Act 1976, or

         (b) any local Act applying in any area in England and Wales which regulates the use of private hire vehicles provided for hire with the services of a driver for the purpose of carrying passengers and excludes public service vehicles from the scope of that regulation.

(2) If a small bus is being made available with a driver to the public for hire for the purpose of carrying passengers otherwise than at separate fares, it is not to be regarded as a public service vehicle for the purpose of the Private Hire Vehicles (London) Act 1998.

(3) But subsection (1) or (2) does not apply where the vehicle is being so provided or made available in the course of a business of carrying passengers by motor vehicles all but a small part of which involves the operation of large buses.

(4) In this section—

         "small bus" means a public service vehicle within paragraph (b) of subsection (1) of section 1 of this Act; and

         "large buses", means public service vehicles within paragraph (a) of that subsection.]

A11.69   *[Section 79A was inserted by the Transport Act 2000 s.265(2).]*

*   *   *

Interpretation of references to the operator of a vehicle or service

A11.70   **81.**—(1) For the purposes of this Act —

         (a) regulations may make provision as to the person who is to be regarded as the operator of a vehicle which is made available by one holder of a PSV operator's licence to another under a hiring arrangement; and

         (b) where regulations under paragraph (a) above do not apply, the operator of a vehicle is—

            (i) the driver, if he owns the vehicle; and

            (ii) in any other case, the person for whom the driver works (whether under a contract of employment or any other description of contract personally to do work).

(2) [...]

A11.71   *[Section 81 is printed as amended by the Transport Act 1985 s.1(3) and Sch.1, para.12.]*

General interpretation provisions

A11.72   **82.**—(1) In this Act, unless the context otherwise requires—

         "certificate of initial fitness" has the meaning given by section 6;

* * *

"company" means a body corporate;

* * *

"contravention", in relation to any condition or provision, includes a failure to comply with the condition or provision, and *"contravene"* shall be construed accordingly;

"director", in relation to a company, includes any person who occupies the position of a director, by whatever name called;

"driver", where a separate person acts as steersman of a motor vehicle, includes that person as well as any other person engaged in the driving of the vehicle, and *"drive"* shall be construed accordingly;

* * *

"fares" include sums payable in respect of a contract ticket or a season ticket;

"international operation" means a passenger transport operation starting or terminating in the United Kingdom and involving an international journey by the vehicle concerned, whether or not any driver leaves or enters the United Kingdom with that vehicle;

"local authority" means—

>   (a) in relation to England and Wales, any local authority within the meaning of the Local Government Act 1972;
>
>   (b) *[applies to Scotland.]*

[*"local service"* has the same meaning as in the Transport Act 1985;]

"magistrates' court" [has the same meaning] as in the Magistrates' Courts Act 1980;

"modification" includes addition, omission and alteration, and related expressions shall be construed accordingly;

"motor vehicle" means a mechanically propelled vehicle intended or adapted for use on roads;

"national operation" means a passenger transport operation wholly within the United Kingdom;

"official PSV testing station" has the meaning given by section 8(3);

"operating centre", in relation to a vehicle, means the base or centre at which the vehicle is normally kept;

"operator" has the meaning given by section 81;

"owner", in relation to a vehicle which is the subject of an agreement for hire, hire-purchase, conditional sale or loan, means the person in possession of the vehicle under that agreement, and references to owning a vehicle shall be construed accordingly;

"prescribed" has the meaning given by section 60(2);

[*"prescribed testing authority"* means such person authorised by the Secretary of State under section 8 of the Transport Act 1982 to carry on a vehicle testing business within the meaning of Part II of that Act as may be prescribed;]

"PSV operator's licence" means a PSV operator's licence granted under the provisions of Part II of this Act;

"public service vehicle" has the meaning given by section 1;

"relevant conviction" means a conviction (other than a spent conviction) of any offence prescribed for the purposes of this Act, or an offence under the law of Northern Ireland, or of a country or territory outside the United Kingdom, corresponding to an offence so prescribed;

"restricted licence" means such a PSV operator's licence as is mentioned in section 13(3);

"road" means any highway and any other road to which the public has access, and includes bridges over which a road passes;

*   *   *

"standard licence" means a PSV operator's licence which is not a restricted licence;

"statutory provision" means a provision contained in an Act or in subordinate legislation within the meaning of the Interpretation Act 1978;

[*"traffic commissioner"* means the person appointed to be the commissioner for a traffic area constituted for the purposes of this Act;]

"tramcar" includes any carriage used on any road by virtue of an order made under the Light Railways Act 1896;

"transport manager", in relation to a business, means an individual who, either alone or jointly with one or more other persons, has continuous and effective responsibility for the management of the road passenger transport operations of the business;

*   *   *

[(1A) References in any provision of this Act to an authorised inspector are references to an authorised inspector under section 8 of the Transport Act 1982 and, where the function to which that provision relates is one of those specified in section 9 of that Act (testing and surveillance functions), are limited to an authorised inspector authorised under section 8 to exercise that function.]

(2) Any reference in this Act to a Community instrument or to a particular provision of such an instrument—

    (a) is a reference to that instrument or provision as amended from time to time, and

    (b) if that instrument or provision is replaced, with or without modification, shall be construed as a reference to the instrument or provision replacing it.

[(3) In this Act —

    (a) any reference to a county shall be construed in relation to Wales as including a reference to a county borough;

    (b) any reference to a county council shall be construed in relation to Wales as including a reference to a county borough council; and

    (c) section 17(4) and (5) of the Local Government (Wales) Act 1994 (references to counties and districts to be construed generally in relation to Wales as references to counties and county boroughs) shall not apply.]

[Section 82 is printed as amended by the Transport Act 1982 s.74(1) and Sch.5, **A11.73**
para.23; the Transport Act 1985 ss.1(3), 3(5) and 139(3), Sch.1, para.13, Sch.2,
Pt II, para.4(20), and Sch.8; the Road Traffic Act 1991 s.83 and Sch.8; the Local
Government (Wales) Act 1994 s.22(1) and Sch.7, para.36; the Access to Justice
Act 1999 s.76(2) and Sch.10, paras 33 and 37.

The definition of "prescribed testing authority" (in s.82(1)) and s.82(1A),
which were inserted by the Transport Act 1982 s.74(1) and Sch.5, para.23) will
take effect from a date or dates to be announced.

The term "local authority" is defined for the purposes of the Local Govern-
ment Act 1972 by ibid. s.270(1) (as amended by the Local Government Act 1985
s.102(2) and Sch.17; the Local Government (Wales) Act 1994 s.1(5)) as "a county
council, ... a district council, a London borough council or a parish [council but,
in relation to Wales, means a county council, county borough council or com-
munity council]".]

Construction of references in other Acts, etc., to public service vehicles, licensing authorities, etc.

83.—(1) A provision of an Act other than this Act or of an instrument having **A11.74**
effect under an enactment not repealed by this Act which (however expressed)
defines *"public service vehicle"* ... by reference to the Road Traffic Act 1930 or
the Road Traffic Act 1960 shall have effect as if it provided that that expression
should be construed in like manner as if it were contained in this Act.

(2) [...]

[Section 83 is printed as amended by the Transport Act 1985 ss.1(3) and **A11.75**
139(3), Sch.1, para.14, and Sch.8.]

*   *   *

SCHEDULE 1

PUBLIC SERVICE VEHICLES: CONDITIONS AFFECTING STATUS FOR CLASSIFICATION

PART I

SHARING OF TAXIS AND HIRE-CARS

1. The making of the agreement for the payment of separate fares must not have been **A11.76**
initiated by the driver or by the owner of the vehicle, by any person who has made the vehicle available under any arrangement, or by any person who receives any remuneration in
respect of the arrangements for the journey.

2.—(1) The journey must be made without previous advertisement to the public of facil- **A11.77**
ities for its being made by passengers to be carried at separate fares, except where the local
authorities concerned have approved the arrangements under which the journey is made as
designed to meet the social and welfare needs of one or more communities, and their approvals remain in force.

(2) In relation to a journey the local authorities concerned for the purposes of this
paragraph are those in whose area any part of the journey is to be made; and in this sub-
paragraph *"local authority"* means—

    (a) in relation to England and Wales, [the council of a county, metropolitan district
       or London borough and the Common Council of the City of London];

    (b) *[applies to Scotland.]*

3. [...]   **A11.78**

PART II

PARTIES OF OVERSEAS VISITORS

A11.79   4. [...]

PART III

ALTERNATIVE CONDITIONS AFFECTING STATUS FOR CLASSIFICATION

A11.80   5. Arrangements for the bringing together of all the passengers for the purpose of making the journey must have been made otherwise than by, or by a person acting on behalf of—

(a) the holder of the PSV operator's licence under which the vehicle is to be used, if such a licence is in force,

(b) the driver or the owner of the vehicle or any person who has made the vehicle available under any arrangement, if no such licence is in force,

and otherwise than by any person who receives any remuneration in respect of the arrangements.

A11.81   6. The journey must be made without previous advertisement to the public of the arrangements therefor.

7. All passengers must, in the case of a journey to a particular destination, be carried to, or to the vicinity of, that destination, or, in the case of a tour, be carried for the greater part of the journey.

8. No differentiation of fares for the journey on the basis of distance or of time must be made.

PART IV

SUPPLEMENTARY

A11.82   9. For the purposes of paragraphs 2 and 6 above no account shall be taken of any such advertisement as follows, that is to say—

(a) a notice displayed or announcement made—

(i) at or in any place of worship for the information of persons attending that place of worship;

(ii) at or in any place of work for the information of persons who work there; or

(iii) by any club or other voluntary association at or in any premises occupied or used by the club or association;

(b) a notice contained in any periodical published for the information of, and circulating wholly or mainly among—

(i) persons who attend or might reasonably be expected to attend a particular place of worship or a place of worship in a particular place; or

(ii) persons who work at a particular place of work or at any of two or more particular places of work; or

(iii) the members of a club or other voluntary association.

A11.83   [*Schedule 1 is printed as amended by the Local Government Act 1985 s.8(1) and Sch.5, para.3(7); the Transport Act 1985 s.139(2) and (3), Sch.7, para.21(12), and Sch.8.*]

SCHEDULE 2

TRAFFIC COMMISSIONERS

A11.84   *[Omitted.]*

[SCHEDULE 2A

DETENTION OF CERTAIN PSVS USED WITHOUT PSV OPERATORS' LICENCES

Interpretation

1.—(1) In this Schedule—   **A11.85**

"*authorised person*" means—

(a) an examiner appointed by the Secretary of State under section 66A of the Road Traffic Act 1988, or

(b) a person acting under the direction of such an examiner;

"*contents*" , in relation to a vehicle, means any goods carried by that vehicle which are not personal effects;

"*immobilisation device*" , means any device or appliance which is an immobilisation device for the purposes of section 104 of the Road Traffic Regulation Act 1984;

"*operator*" , in relation to a public service vehicle, means—

(a) the driver, if he owns the vehicle, or

(b) in any other case, the person for whom the driver works (whether under a contract of employment or any other description of contract personally to do the work),

but this is subject to any regulations that may be made under subparagraph (2)(a) below;

"*personal effects*" means—

(a) any personal effects of any individual, and

(b) any articles being carried by a vehicle for the purpose of their delivery from one person to another.

(2) Regulations may make provision for any purpose of this Schedule or regulations under it as to—

(a) the person who is to be regarded as the "operator" of a public service vehicle in such circumstances as may be specified or described in the regulations;

(b) the meaning of "owner" as regards a public service vehicle.

(3) Regulations made by virtue of sub-paragraph (2)(b) above may, in particular, provide that the owner of a motor vehicle at a particular time is to be taken to be any person in whose name the vehicle is then registered by virtue of the Vehicle Excise and Registration Act 1994.

Detention of property

2.—(1) Regulations may provide that where an authorised person has reason to believe   **A11.86** that a public service vehicle adapted to carry more than 8 passengers is being, or has been, used on a road in contravention of section 12(1) of this Act, the person may detain the vehicle and its contents.

(2) Regulations made by virtue of sub-paragraph (1) above may not authorise a person other than a constable in uniform to stop a vehicle on any road.

The vehicle and any other property detained, the passengers, and any personal effects

3.—(1) Regulations may, in connection with the detaining of a vehicle by virtue of   **A11.87** paragraph 2 above, make provision with respect to any of the following—

(a) the vehicle;

(b) any other property detained or to be detained by virtue of paragraph 2 above;

(c) any passengers who have been travelling on the vehicle;

(d) any personal effects remaining on the vehicle.

(2) Regulations under this paragraph must include provision requiring passengers who have been travelling on the vehicle to be transported in safety to their destination or to a suitable place from which to continue their journey.

Immobilisation of vehicle

A11.88 4.—(1) Regulations may provide that, before a vehicle is removed by virtue of paragraph 6 below, an authorised person may—

(a) fix an immobilisation device to the vehicle in the place where the vehicle has been detained, or

(b) move the vehicle, or require it to be moved, to a more convenient place and fix an immobilisation device to the vehicle in that other place.

(2) Regulations may also provide—

(a) that, on any occasion when an immobilisation device is fixed to a vehicle, the person fixing the device must also fix to the vehicle an immobilisation notice (see sub-paragraph (3) below);

(b) that a vehicle to which an immobilisation device has been fixed may only be released from the device by or under the direction of an authorised person; and

(c) that an immobilisation notice must not be removed or interfered with except by or on the authority of an authorised person.

(3) In this paragraph *"immobilisation notice"* means a notice—

(a) indicating that an immobilisation device has been fixed to the vehicle,

(b) warning that no attempt should be made to drive the vehicle or otherwise put it in motion, and

(c) giving such other information as may be prescribed.

Offences relating to immobilisation

A11.89 5.—(1) Regulations may provide that a person—

(a) who removes or attempts to remove an immobilisation device fixed to a vehicle under regulations made by virtue of paragraph 4(1) above, but

(b) who is not authorised to do so in accordance with paragraph 4(2)(b) above, is guilty of an offence and liable on summary conviction to a fine not exceeding level 3 on the standard scale.

(2) Regulations may provide that a person who removes or interferes with an immobilisation notice in contravention of regulations made by virtue of paragraph 4(2)(c) above is guilty of an offence and liable on summary conviction to a fine not exceeding level 2 on the standard scale.

Removal and delivery of property into custody of nominated custodian

A11.90 6. *[Omitted.]*

Informing persons that their property has been detained etc

7. *[Omitted.]*

Return of vehicle

A11.91 8. *[Omitted.]*

Application to traffic commissioner for return of vehicle

9. *[Omitted.]*

Hearings by traffic commissioner

A11.92 10. *[Omitted.]*

Consequences of the traffic commissioner's determination

11. *[Omitted.]*

Appeal to Transport Tribunal from traffic commissioner

A11.93 12. *[Omitted.]*

Sale or destruction of vehicle where no application made under paragraph 9

13. *[Omitted.]*

Return or disposal of contents and personal effects

14. *[Omitted.]*   **A11.94**

Custody of property

15. *[Omitted.]*

Proceeds of sale

16. *[Omitted.]*   **A11.95**

Disputes

17. *[Omitted.]*

Obstruction of authorised person

18. Regulations may provide that a person who intentionally obstructs an authorised   **A11.96** person in the exercise of the powers of such a person under regulations made by virtue of this Schedule is guilty of an offence and liable on summary conviction to a fine not exceeding level 3 on the standard scale.

Offences as to securing possession of property

19.—(1) Regulations may provide that a person is guilty of an offence if—   **A11.97**

  (a) the person makes a declaration with a view to securing the return of a vehicle under regulations made by virtue of paragraph 11 above;

  (b) the declaration is that the vehicle was not being, or had not been, used in contravention of section 12(1) of this Act; and

  (c) the declaration is, to the person's knowledge, either false or in any material respect misleading.

(2) Regulations may provide that a person guilty of such an offence is liable—

  (a) on summary conviction, to a fine not exceeding the statutory maximum; and

  (b) on conviction on indictment, to imprisonment for a term not exceeding two years or to a fine or to both.]

[Schedule 2A is printed as inserted by the Local Transport Act 2008 s.47 and   **A11.98** *Sch.3.]*

Section 14(2) and 17(6)   SCHEDULE 3

Supplementary Provision as to Qualifications for PSV Operator's Licence

Good repute

1.—(1) In determining whether an individual is of good repute, [a traffic commissioner]   **A11.99** shall have regard to all the relevant evidence and in particular to—

  (a) relevant convictions of his and of his employees and agents;

[(aa) relevant fixed penalty notices issued to him and to his employees and agents; and]

  (b) such other information as the [commissioner] may have as to his previous conduct, in whatever capacity, in relation to the operation of vehicles of any description in the course of a business.

(2) In determining whether a company is of good repute, [a traffic commissioner] shall have regard to all the relevant evidence and in particular to—

  (a) relevant convictions of the company and its officers, employees and agents; and

[(aa) relevant fixed penalty notices issued to the company's officers, employees and agents;]

(b) such other information as the [commissioner] may have as to previous conduct of—

  (i) the company's officers, employees and agents in relation to the operation of vehicles of any description in the course of any business carried on by the company; and

  (ii) each of the company's directors, in whatever capacity, in relation to the operation of vehicles of any description in the course of any other business.

[(2A) In sub-paragraphs (1)(aa) and (2)(aa) above *"relevant fixed penalty notice"* means a fixed penalty notice or conditional offer issued under Part 3 of the Road Traffic Offenders Act 1988 in respect of an offence prescribed for the purposes of this Act.]

[(3) A traffic commissioner shall determine that an individual is not of good repute if he has—

(a) more than one conviction of a serious offence; or

(b) been convicted of road transport offences.]

[(4) For the purposes of sub-paragraph (3)(a) above a *"serious offence"* is—

(a) an offence under the law in force in any part of the United Kingdom for which a sentence of imprisonment for a term exceeding three months, a fine exceeding level 4 on the standard scale or [a community order requiring the offender to perform unpaid work for more than sixty hours] was imposed; and

(b) any corresponding offence under the law of a country or territory outside the United Kingdom for which a corresponding punishment was imposed.]

[(5) For the purposes of sub-paragraph (3)(b) above a *road transport offence* is—

(a) an offence under the law of any part of the United Kingdom relating to road transport including in particular—

  (i) an offence relating to drivers' hours of work or rest periods, the weights or dimensions of commercial vehicles, road or vehicle safety or the protection of the environment; and

  (ii) any other offence concerning professional liability; or

(b) any corresponding offence under the law of a country or territory outside the United Kingdom.]

[(6) In sub-paragraph (4)(a) above *"a sentence of imprisonment"* includes any form of custodial sentence or order other than one under the enactments relating to mental health and [a *"community order"* means an order under section 177 of the Criminal Justice Act 2003, a community punishment order made before the commencement of that section or a community service order under the Community Service by Offenders (Scotland) Act 1978 [or a service community order or overseas community order under the Armed Forces Act 2006]].

[(7) In sub-paragraphs (4)(a) and (5)(a) above references to an offence under the law in force in any part of the United Kingdom include a reference to [an offence under section 42 of the Armed Forces Act 2006].]

[(8) For the purposes of sub-paragraph (3) above spent convictions shall be disregarded; and a traffic commissioner may also disregard an offence if such time as he considers appropriate has elapsed since the date of the conviction.]

[(9) Sub-paragraph (3) above is without prejudice to the power of a traffic commissioner to determine that an individual is not of good repute for reasons other than convictions of the kind there mentioned.]

[(10) In this paragraph references to an individual include references to a transport manager as well as to an individual who is an applicant for, or the holder of, a PSV operator's licence.]

Appropriate financial standing

A11.100   2. *[Omitted.]*

Professional competence

3–7. *[Omitted.]*   **A11.101**

Persons engaged in road passenger transport before 1st January 1978

8–10. *[Omitted.]*   **A11.102**

[Schedule 3 is printed as amended by the Transport Act 1985 s.3(5) and Sch.2,   **A11.103**
Pt II, para.4(21)(a); the Public Service Vehicle Operators (Qualifications)
Regulations 1990 (SI 1990/1851); the Public Service Vehicle Operators
(Qualifications) Regulations 1999 (SI 1999/2431); and the Powers of Criminal
Courts (Sentencing) Act 2000 s.165(1) and Sch.9, para.81; by the Criminal
Justice Act 2003 s.304 and Sch.32, para.32; the Road Safety Act 2006 s.7(1) and
(3)–(5); the Armed Forces Act 2006 s.378 and Sch.16, para.90.

Provisions from para.1 are incorporated by reference into the Public Service
Vehicles (Operators' Licences) Regulations 1995 (SI 1995/2908) Schedule
below.]

The Criminal Attempts Act 1981

(1981 c.47)

A12.01 *An Act to amend the law of England and Wales ... and ... to make provision against unauthorised interference with vehicles ...*

[27th July 1981]

*   *   *

PART II

SUSPECTED PERSONS, ETC.

*   *   *

Interference with vehicles

A12.02   **9.**—(1) A person is guilty of the offence of vehicle interference if he interferes with a motor vehicle or trailer or with anything carried in or on a motor vehicle or trailer with the intention that an offence specified in subsection (2) below shall be committed by himself or some other person.

(2) The offences mentioned in subsection (1) above are—

    (a) theft of the motor vehicle or trailer or part of it;

    (b) theft of anything carried in or on the motor vehicle or trailer; and

    (c) an offence under section 12(1) of the Theft Act 1968 (taking and driving away without consent);

and, if it is shown that a person accused of an offence under this section intended that one of those offences should be committed, it is immaterial that it cannot be shown which it was.

(3) A person guilty of an offence under this section shall be liable on summary conviction to imprisonment for a term not exceeding three months or to a fine not exceeding [level 4 in the standard scale] or to both.

(4) [...]

(5) In this section *"motor vehicle"* and *"trailer"* have the meanings assigned to them by [section 185(1) of the Road Traffic Act 1988 [*q.v.*]].

A12.03   *[Section 9 is printed as amended by the Criminal Justice Act 1982 s.46(1); the Police and Criminal Evidence Act 1984 s.119(2) and Sch.7, Pt I; the Road Traffic (Consequential Provisions) Act 1988 s.4 and Sch.3, para.23.*

In s.9(3) above, the words "51 weeks" will be substituted for the words "three months" by the Criminal Justice Act 2003 s.280(2) and Sch.26, para.28 with effect from a day to be appointed.

The offence of interference with a motor vehicle, contrary to s.9, is an offence which has been specified by the Motor Salvage Operators (Specified Offences) Order 2002 (SI 2002/1917; not reproduced in this work) as an offence which is relevant to whether an applicant for registration (or for the renewal of registra-

tion) as a motor salvage operator is a fit and proper person (under the Vehicles (Crime) Act 2001 s.3(3) and (4)(b)).]

The Road Traffic Regulation Act 1984

(1984 c.27)

A13.01 *An Act to consolidate the Road Traffic Regulation Act 1967 and certain related enactments, with amendments to give effect to recommendations of the Law Commission and the Scottish Law Commission.*

[26th June 1984]

ARRANGEMENT OF SECTIONS

*   *   *

PART VI
Speed Limits

*   *   *

PART VIII
Control and Enforcement
Removal or immobilisation of vehicles

*   *   *

*   *   *

*   *   *

Enforcement of excess parking charges

PART IX
Further Provisions as to Enforcement
General provisions

*   *   *

*   *   *

PART X
GENERAL AND SUPPLEMENTARY PROVISIONS

*   *   *

*   *   *

SCHEDULES

*   *   *

[All the functions of a Minister of the Crown under the Road Traffic Regula-   **A13.02**
tion Act 1984 exercisable in relation to Wales (except where otherwise indicated
in notes below) have been transferred to the National Assembly for Wales by the
National Assembly for Wales (Transfer of Functions) Order 1999 (SI 1999/672;
not reproduced in this work) art.2 and Sch.1. See also the National Assembly for
Wales (Transfer of Functions) Order 2004 (SI 2004/3044) art.2 and Sch.1 as
regards the transfer of functions under ss.99–103 of this Act to the National As-
sembly for Wales.

All proceedings under this Act (except those under ss.35A(2), 43(5) and (12),
47(3), 52(1), 108(3), 115(1) and (2), 116(1) and 129(3)) are specified by the
Prosecution of Offences Act 1985 (Specified Proceedings) Order 1999 (SI 1999/
904) below as being proceedings the conduct of which the Director of Public
Prosecutions is not required to take over from the police under the Prosecution
of Offences Act 1985 s.3(3)(a).]

PART I

GENERAL PROVISIONS FOR TRAFFIC REGULATION

Outside Greater London

*   *   *

Contravention of traffic regulation order

A13.03   **5.**—(1) A person who contravenes a traffic regulation order, or who uses a vehicle, or causes or permits a vehicle to be used in contravention of a traffic regulation order, shall be guilty of an offence.

(2) [...]

A13.04   *[Subsection (2) was repealed by the New Roads and Street Works Act 1991 s.168(2) and Sch.9.*

The term "traffic regulation order" is defined as an order under s.1 of this Act by ibid. s.1(1).

For the mode of trial of and punishment for offences under s.5, see the Road Traffic Offenders Act 1988 Sch.2, Pt I below.]

In Greater London

Orders similar to traffic regulation orders

A13.05   **6.**—(1) [The traffic authority for a road in Greater London may make an order under this section for controlling or regulating vehicular and other traffic (including pedestrians).

Provision may, in particular, be made—]

(a) for any of the purposes, or with respect to any of the matters, mentioned in Schedule 1 to this Act, and

(b) for any other purpose which is a purpose mentioned in any of paragraphs [(a) to (g)] of section 1(1) of this Act.

(2) *[Power to make orders in respect of roads for which the Secretary of State is responsible.]*

(3) Any order under this section may be made so as to apply—

[(a) to the whole area of a local authority, or to particular parts of that area, or to particular places or streets or parts of streets in that area;]

(b) throughout the day, or during particular periods;

(c) on special occasions only, or at special times only;

(d) to traffic of any class;

(e) subject to such exceptions as may be specified in the order or determined in a manner provided for by it.

(4) [...]

(5) No order under this section shall contain any provision for regulating the speed of vehicles on roads.

(6) In this section, in section 7 of this Act and in Schedule 1 to this Act *"street"* includes any highway, any bridge carrying a highway and any lane, mews, footway, square, court, alley or passage whether a thoroughfare or not ...

[Section 6 is printed as amended by the Local Government Act 1985 s.8(1) and **A13.06**
Sch.5, para.4(3); the New Roads and Street Works Act 1991 s.168(1) and (2),
Sch.8, para.21, and Sch.9; the Environment Act 1995 s.120(1) and Sch.22,
para.36(2).

As to the application of s.6 to tramcars and trolley vehicles (other than duo-
buses), see the Tramcars and Trolley Vehicles (Modification of Enactments)
Regulations 1992 (SI 1992/1217) (q.v.) regs 3, 5 and 11.

Sections 6–8 of this Act do not apply to any person or vehicle in the service of
a visiting force or headquarters (as defined); see the Visiting Forces and
International Headquarters (Application of Law) Order 1999 (SI 1999/1736; not
reproduced in this work) art.8(1) and (2)(a).

In accordance with art.5 of the Transport for London (Consequential Provi-
sions) Order 2003 (SI 2003/1615), in red route traffic orders made by the Traffic
Director of London under s.6, any reference to a bus service provided under an
agreement with London Regional Transport shall be treated as a reference to a
bus service provided under an agreement with Transport for London or a subsid-
iary of Transport for London.]

Supplementary provisions as to orders under section 6

7.—(1) Any order under section 6 of this Act may make provision for identify-   **A13.07**
ing any part of any road to which, or any time at which or period during which,
any provision contained in the order is for the time being to apply by means of a
traffic sign of a type or character specified in the order (being a type prescribed or
character authorised under section 64 of this Act) and for the time being lawfully
in place; and, for the purposes of any order so made, any such traffic sign placed
on or near a street shall be deemed to be lawfully in place unless the contrary is
proved.

(2) Any such order which imposes any restriction on the use by vehicles of
streets in Greater London, or the waiting of vehicles in such streets, may include
provision with respect to the issue and display of certificates or other means of
identification of vehicles which are excepted from the restriction, whether generally or in particular circumstances or at particular times.

(3) Any such order may also include provision with respect to the issue,
display and operation of devices … for indicating the time at which a vehicle arrived at, and the time at which it ought to leave, any place in a street in which
waiting is restricted by the order, or one or other of those times, and for treating
the indications given by any such device as evidence of such facts and for such
purposes as may be prescribed by the order.

(4) Any such order may provide for the suspension or modification, so long as
the order remains in force, of any provisions of any Acts (whether public general
or local or private, and including provisions contained in this Act), byelaws or
regulations dealing with the same subject matter as the order, or of any Acts
conferring power to make byelaws or regulations dealing with the same subject
matter, so far as such provisions apply to any place or street to which the order
applies.

(5) *[Prohibition on appeals against decisions relating to road service licences*
in certain circumstances.]

(6) *[Duty to consult before making order under s.6 .]*

(7) *[Definition for purposes of s.7(5) .]*

A13.08   *[Section 7 is printed as amended by the Deregulation (Parking Equipment) Order 1996 (SI 1996/1553) art.2(1)(a) and Sch.*

As to visiting forces, etc.,see the note to s.6 above.]

Contravention of order under section 6

A13.09   **8.**—(1) Any person who acts in contravention of, or fails to comply with, an order under section 6 of this Act shall be guilty of an offence.

[(1A) [...]]

(2) [...]

A13.10   *[Section 8 is printed as amended by the New Roads and Street Works Act 1991 s.168(2) and Sch.9; the Traffic Management Act 2004 s.98 and Sch.12.*

With regard to "designated London boroughs" under the Road Traffic Act 1991, the whole of Greater London is a civil enforcement area for parking contraventions within para.2 of Sch.7 to the Traffic Management Act 2004 (see the 2004 Act s.74 and Sch.8, para.1). The whole of London will also be a civil enforcement area for bus lane contraventions (see the 2004 Act Sch.8, para.4, when in force). A London local authority or Transport for London may declare its own area to be a civil enforcement area for moving traffic contraventions, and the Secretary of State may make an order, on the application of a London local authority, designating all or part of that authority's area to be a civil enforcement area for parking contraventions within Sch.7, para.3 of the Traffic Management Act 2004. For a listing of designated London boroughs under the 1991 Act, see the note to this section in the twenty-first edition of this work. The Transport for London (Consequential Provisions) Order 2005 (SI 2005/56) modifies provisions of the London Local Authorities Acts 1995 and 2000 relating to parking so as to apply them to Transport for London as well as London borough councils.

For the mode of trial of and punishment for offences under s.8, see the Road Traffic Offenders Act 1988 Sch.2, Pt I.

As to visiting forces, etc., see the notes to s.6 above.]

Experimental traffic schemes

Experimental traffic orders

A13.11   **9.** *[Omitted.]*

Supplementary provisions as to experimental traffic orders

A13.12   **10.** *[Omitted.]*

Contravention of experimental traffic order

A13.13   **11.**—[(1)] Any person who acts in contravention of, or fails to comply with, an experimental traffic order shall be guilty of an offence.

[(2) [...]]

A13.14   *[Section 11 is printed as amended by the Traffic Management Act 2004 s.98 and Sch.12.*

For the mode of trial of and punishment for offences under s.11, see the Road Traffic Offenders Act 1988 Sch.2, Pt I.]

Experimental traffic schemes in Greater London

12. [...]

Contravention of regulations under section 12

13. [...]

Temporary suspension

Temporary suspension of provisions under section 6 or 9 order

13A. *[Omitted.]*

PART II

TRAFFIC REGULATION IN SPECIAL CASES

[Temporary prohibition or restriction on roads

14.—(1) If the traffic authority for a road are satisfied that traffic on the road should be restricted or prohibited—

    (a) because works are being or are proposed to be executed on or near the road; or

    (b) because of the likelihood of danger to the public, or of serious damage to the road, which is not attributable to such works; or

    (c) for the purpose of enabling the duty imposed by section 89(1)(a) or (2) of the Environmental Protection Act 1990 (litter clearing and cleaning) to be discharged,

the authority may by order restrict or prohibit temporarily the use of that road, or of any part of it, by vehicles, or vehicles of any class, or by pedestrians, to such extent and subject to such conditions or exceptions as they may consider necessary.

    [(1A) *[Applies to Scotland.]*]

    (2) The traffic authority for a road may at any time by notice restrict or prohibit temporarily the use of the road, or of any part of it, by vehicles, or vehicles of any class, or by pedestrians, where it appears to them that it is—

    (a) necessary or expedient for the reason mentioned in paragraph (a) or the purpose mentioned in paragraph (c) of subsection (1) above; or

    (b) necessary for the reason mentioned in paragraph (b) of that subsection,

that the restriction or prohibition should come into force without delay.

    (3) When considering the making of an order or the issue of a notice under the foregoing provisions an authority shall have regard to the existence of alternative routes suitable for the traffic which will be affected by the order or notice.

    (4) The provision that may be made by an order or notice under the foregoing provisions is—

    (a) any such provision as is mentioned in section 2(1), (2) or (3) or 4(1) of this Act; or

    (b) any provision restricting the speed of vehicles;

but no such order or notice shall be made or issued with respect to any road which would have the effect of preventing at any time access for pedestrians to any premises situated on or adjacent to the road, or to any other premises accessible for pedestrians from, and only from, the road.

(5) Where any such order or notice is made or issued by an authority (in this subsection referred to as the *"initiating authority"*) any such provision as is mentioned in subsection (4) above may be made as respects any alternative road—

    (a) if that authority is the traffic authority for the alternative road, by an order made by the initiating authority or by that notice;

    (b) if the initiating authority is not the traffic authority for the alternative road, by an order made by the initiating authority with the consent of the traffic authority for the alternative road.

(6) Section 3(1) and (2) of this Act shall apply to the provisions that may be made under subsection (5) above as they apply to the provisions of a traffic regulation order.

(7) An order or notice made or issued under this section may—

    (a) suspend any statutory provision to which this subsection applies; or

    (b) for either of the reasons or for the purpose mentioned in subsection (1) above suspend any such provision without imposing any such restriction or prohibition as is mentioned in subsection (1) or (2) above.

(8) Subsection (7) above applies to—

    (a) any statutory provision of a description which could have been contained in an order or notice under this section;

    (b) an order under section 32(1)(b), 35, 45, 46 or 49 of this Act or any such order as is mentioned in paragraph 11(1) of Schedule 10 to this Act; and

    (c) an order under section 6 of this Act so far as it designates any parking places in Greater London.

(9) In this section *"alternative road"*, in relation to a road as respects which an order is made under subsection (1) or a notice is issued under subsection (2) above, means a road which—

    (a) provides an alternative route for traffic diverted from the first-mentioned road or from any other alternative road; or

    (b) is capable of providing such an alternative route apart from any statutory provision authorised by subsection (7) above to be suspended by an order made or notice issued by virtue of subsection (5) above.]

A13.19   *[Section 14 (and also s.15) was substituted by the Road Traffic (Temporary Restrictions) Act 1991 s.1(1) and Sch.1.*

As to the application of s.14 to tramcars and trolley vehicles (other than duobuses), see the Tramcars and Trolley Vehicles (Modification of Enactments) Regulations 1992 (SI 1992/1217) (q.v.) regs 4 and 6 (for transitional provisions, see ibid., regs 15 and 16). As to the application of s.14 to trams, see also the Leeds Supertram Act 1993 (c.xv) s.4(4).

As to the transfer of functions of a Minister of the Crown under s.14(1), (2), (3) and (5) which are exercisable in Scotland in relation to the imposition of speed limits to the Scottish Ministers, see the Scotland Act 1998 (Transfer of Functions to the Scottish Ministers etc.) Order 1999 (SI 1999/1750; not reproduced in this work) art.2 and Sch.1.

As to the transfer of functions of a Minister of the Crown under s.14 which are exercisable by virtue of s.22C of the Road Traffic Regulation Act 1984 (terrorism) to the Scottish Ministers, see the Scotland Act 1998 (Transfer of Functions to the Scottish Ministers, etc.) Order 2005 (SI 2005/849) (S.2) art.2 and Sch.]

Duration of orders and notices under section 14

15. *[Omitted.]* A13.20

Supplementary provisions as to orders and notices under section 14

16.—(1) A person who contravenes, or who uses or permits the use of a vehicle in contravention of, a restriction or prohibition imposed under section 14 of this Act shall be guilty of an offence. A13.21

(2), (2A) *[Regulation-making power.]*

(3), (4) [...]

[Subsections (3) and (4) were repealed by the New Roads and Street Works Act 1991 s.168(2) and Sch.9. A13.22

The Road Traffic (Temporary Restrictions) Procedure Regulations 1992 (SI 1992/1215) (not reproduced in this work) have been made under this section.

As to notice of intended prosecution of certain offences under s.16(1), see the Road Traffic Offenders Act 1988 Sch.1, para.1A below.

For the mode of trial of and punishment for offences under s.16, see the Road Traffic Offenders Act 1988 Sch.2, Pt I.

As to the transfer of functions of a Minister of the Crown under s.16(2) and (2A) which are exercisable in Scotland in relation to the imposition of speed limits to the Scottish Ministers, see the Scotland Act 1998 (Transfer of Functions to the Scottish Ministers etc.) Order 1999 (SI 1999/1750; not reproduced in this work) art.2 and Sch.1.]

[Prohibition or restriction on roads in connection with certain events

16A.—(1) In this section *"relevant event"* means any sporting event, social event or entertainment which is held on a road. A13.23

(2) If the traffic authority for a road are satisfied that traffic on the road should be restricted or prohibited for the purpose of—

(a) facilitating the holding of a relevant event,

(b) enabling members of the public to watch a relevant event, or

(c) reducing the disruption to traffic likely to be caused by a relevant event,

the authority may by order restrict or prohibit temporarily the use of that road, or any part of it, by vehicles of any class or by pedestrians, to such extent and subject to such conditions or exceptions as they may consider necessary or expedient.

(3) Before making an order under this section the authority shall satisfy themselves that it is not reasonably practicable for the event to be held otherwise than on a road.

(4) An order under this section —

(a) may not be made in relation to any race or trial falling within subsection (1) of section 12 of the Road Traffic Act 1988 (motor racing on public ways);

    (b) may not be made in relation to any competition or trial falling within subsection (1) of section 13 of that Act (regulation of motoring events on public ways) unless the competition or trial is authorised by or under regulations under that section; and

    (c) may not be made in relation to any race or trial falling within subsection (1) of section 31 of that Act (regulation of cycle racing on public ways) unless the race or trial is authorised by or under regulations made under that section.

(5) An order under this section may relate to the road on which the relevant event is to be held or to any other road.

(6) In the case of a road for which the Secretary of State is the traffic authority, the power to make an order under this section is also exercisable, with his consent, by the local traffic authority or by any local traffic authority which is the traffic authority for any other road to which the order relates.

(7) In the case of a road for which a local traffic authority is the traffic authority, the power to make an order under this section is also exercisable, with the consent of that local traffic authority, by a local traffic authority which is the traffic authority for any other road to which the order relates.

(8) When considering the making of an order under this section, an authority shall have regard to the safety and convenience of alternative routes suitable for the traffic which will be affected by the order.

(9) The provision that may be made by an order under this section is—

    (a) any such provision as is mentioned in section 2(1), (2) or (3) or 4(1) of this Act;

    (b) any provision restricting the speed of vehicles; or

    (c) any provision restricting or prohibiting—

        (i) the riding of horses, or

        (ii) the leading or driving of horses, cattle, sheep or other animals,

but no such order shall be made with respect to any road which would have the effect of preventing at any time access for pedestrians to any premises situated on or adjacent to the road, or to any other premises accessible for pedestrians from, and only from, the road.

(10) An order under this section may—

    (a) suspend any statutory provision to which this subsection applies; or

    (b) for any of the purposes mentioned in subsection (2) above, suspend any such provision without imposing any such restriction or prohibition as is mentioned in that subsection.

(11) Subsection (10) above applies to—

    (a) any statutory provision of a description which could have been contained in an order under this section;

    (b) an order under section 32(1)(b), 35, 45, 46 or 49 of this Act or any such order as is mentioned in paragraph 11(1) of Schedule 10 to this Act; and

    (c) an order under section 6 of this Act so far as it designates any parking places in Greater London.]

[Section 16A was inserted by the Road Traffic Regulation (Special Events) Act   **A13.24**
1994 s.1(1).

For modifications to s.16A, which apply in Greater London, see the London Local Authorities and Transport for London Act 2008 s.12 (Prohibition or restriction on roads in connection with filming).]

[Restrictions on orders under section 16A

16B.—(1) An order under section 16A of this Act shall not continue in force   **A13.25**
for a period of more than three days beginning with the day on which it comes into force unless—

    (a) the order is made by the Secretary of State as the traffic authority for the road concerned; or

    (b) before the order is made, he has agreed that it should continue in force for a longer period.

(2) Where an order under section 16A of this Act has not ceased to be in force and the relevant event to which it relates has not ended, the Secretary of State may, subject to subsections (4) and (5) below, from time to time direct that the order shall continue in force for a further period not exceeding three days beginning with the day on which it would otherwise cease to be in force.

(3) A direction under subsection (2) above may relate to all the roads to which the order under section 16A of this Act relates or only to specified roads.

(4) Where an order under section 16A of this Act relates only to roads for which the Secretary of State is not himself the traffic authority, he shall not give a direction under subsection (2) above except at the request of the traffic authority for any road to which the order relates.

(5) Where an order under section 16A of this Act relates to any road for which the Secretary of State is not himself the traffic authority, he shall not give a direction under subsection (2) above affecting that road except with the consent of the traffic authority for that road.

(6) Where an order has been made under section 16A of this Act in any calendar year, no further order may be made under that section in that year so as to affect any length of road affected by the previous order, unless the further order—

    (a) is made by the Secretary of State as the traffic authority for the road concerned; or

    (b) is made with his consent.

(7) For the purposes of subsection (6) above, a length of road is affected by an order under section 16A of this Act if the order contains provisions—

    (a) prohibiting or restricting traffic on that length of road; or

    (b) suspending any statutory provision applying to traffic on that length of road.]

[Section 16B was inserted by the Road Traffic Regulation (Special Events) Act   **A13.26**
1994 s.1(1).

For modifications to s.16B, which apply in Greater London, see the London Local Authorities and Transport for London Act 2008 s.13 (Restrictions on orders and notices).]

[Supplementary provisions as to orders under section 16A

16C.—(1) A person who contravenes, or who uses or permits the use of a   **A13.27**

vehicle in contravention of, a restriction or prohibition imposed by an order under section 16A of this Act shall be guilty of an offence.

(2), (3) *[Regulations as to procedure for making orders under s.16A.]*]

A13.28 *[Section 16C was inserted by the Road Traffic Regulation (Special Events) Act 1994 s.1(1).]*

Traffic regulation on special roads

A13.29 **17.**—[(1) A special road shall not be used except by traffic of a class authorised to do so—

    (a) in England and Wales, by a scheme made, or having effect as if made, under section 16 of the Highways Act 1980 or by virtue of paragraph 3 of Schedule 23 to that Act, or

    (b) *[applies to Scotland.]*]

(2) The Secretary of State may make regulations with respect to the use of special roads. [Such regulations may, in particular—

    (a) regulate the manner in which and the conditions subject to which special roads may be used by traffic authorised to do so;]

    (b) authorise, or enable such authority as may be specified in the regulations to authorise, the use of special roads on occasion or in an emergency or for the purpose of crossing, or for the purpose of securing access to premises abutting on or adjacent to the roads, by traffic other than that described in paragraph (a) above;…

    (c) relax, or enable any authority so specified to relax, any prohibition or restriction imposed by the regulations.

    [(d) include provisions having effect in such places, at such times, in such manner or in such circumstances as may for the time being be indicated by traffic signs in accordance with the regulations.]

(3) Regulations made under subsection (2) above may make provision with respect to special roads generally, or may make different provision with respect to special roads provided for the use of different classes of traffic, or may make provision with respect to any particular special road.

[(3A) *[Applies to Scotland.]*]

(4) If a person uses a special road in contravention of this section or of regulations under subsection (2) above, he shall be guilty of an offence.

[(5) The provisions of this section and of any regulations under subsection (2) above do not apply in relation to a road, or part of a road, until the date declared by the traffic authority, by notice published in the prescribed manner, to be the date on which the road or part is open for use as a special road.

This does not prevent the making of regulations under subsection (2) above before that date, so as to come into force in relation to that road or part on that date.]

(6) In this section *"use"*, in relation to a road, includes crossing …

A13.30 *[Section 17 is printed as amended by the New Roads and Street Works Act 1991 s.168(1) and (2), Sch.8, Pt II, para.28(1)–(5), and Sch.9; the Road Traffic Act 1991 ss.48, 83, Sch.4, para.25, and Sch.8.*

Words in s.17(1) relating expressly and exclusively to Scotland have been omitted.

The Motorways Traffic (England and Wales) Regulations 1982 (SI 1982/1163) (q.v.) have effect as if made under this section.

As to notice of intended prosecution of certain offences under s.17(4), see the Road Traffic Offenders Act 1988 Sch.1, para.1A below.

For the application of the fixed penalty procedure to offences under subs.(4), see the Road Traffic Offenders Act 1988 Pt III and Sch.3 below.

As to the admissibility of evidence of speeding in respect of offences under s.17(4), see s.20 of the Road Traffic Offenders Act 1988.

As exceptions to the transfer of functions to the National Assembly for Wales of functions of a Minister of the Crown exercisable in relation to Wales (see the note at § A13.02 above), the functions under s.17(2) and (3) with respect to special roads generally have been expressly excluded from that transfer; see the National Assembly for Wales (Transfer of Functions) Order 1999 (SI 1999/672; not reproduced in this work) art.2 and Sch.1.

As to the transfer of the function of the Secretary of State under s.17(2) and (5) which is exercisable in Scotland in relation to the making of regulations with respect to any particular special road to the Scottish Ministers, see the Scotland Act 1998 (Transfer of Functions to the Scottish Ministers etc.) Order 1999 (SI 1999/1750; not reproduced in this work) art.2 and Sch.1. As to the exercise of other functions under s.17(2) only after consultation with the Scottish Ministers, see SI 1999/1750 art.4 and Sch.3.]

Further provisions as to special roads

17A. *[Omitted.]* **A13.31**

* * *

PART III

CROSSINGS AND PLAYGROUNDS

Pedestrian crossings

Powers of local authorities with respect to pedestrian crossings on roads other than trunk roads

23. *[Omitted.]* **A13.32**

Pedestrian crossings on trunk roads

24. *[Omitted.]* **A13.33**

Pedestrian crossing regulations

25.—(1) The Secretary of State may make regulations with respect to the pre- **A13.34** cedence of vehicles and pedestrians respectively, and generally with respect to the movement of traffic (including pedestrians), at and in the vicinity of crossings.

(2)–(4) *[Omitted.]*

(5) A person who contravenes any regulations made under this section shall be guilty of an offence.

(6) In this section *"crossing"* means a crossing for pedestrians established—

    (a) by a local authority under section 23 of this Act, or

    (b) by the Secretary of State in the discharge of the duty imposed on him by section 24 of this Act, and (in either case) indicated in accordance with the regulations having effect as respects that crossing; and, for the purposes of a prosecution for a contravention of the provisions of a regulation having effect as respects a crossing, the crossing shall be deemed to be so established and indicated unless the contrary is proved.

A13.35 *[The Zebra, Pelican and Puffin Crossings and General Directions 1997 (SI 1997/2400) (q.v.) have been made in part under this section.*

See also para.9(2) of Sch.10 to this Act below.

For the application of the fixed penalty procedure to offences under subs.(5) (except offences in respect of moving motor vehicles), see the Road Traffic Offenders Act 1988 Pt III, and Sch.3 below.

As an exception to the transfer of functions to the National Assembly for Wales of functions of a Minister of the Crown exercisable in relation to Wales (see the note at § A13.02 above), the functions under s.25 (other than s.25(4) together with the other provisions of s.25 so far as relating thereto) have been expressly excluded from that transfer; see the National Assembly for Wales (Transfer of Functions) Order 1999 (SI 1999/672; not reproduced in this work) art.2 and Sch.1.

As to the exercise of functions of the Secretary of State under s.25(1) which are exercisable in relation to Scotland only after consultation with the Scottish Ministers, see the Scotland Act 1998 (Transfer of Functions to the Scottish Ministers etc.) Order 1999 (SI 1999/1750; not reproduced in this work) art.4 and Sch.3.]

School crossings

Arrangements for school crossing patrols

A13.36 **26.** *[Omitted.]*

27. [...]

Stopping of vehicles at school crossings

A13.37 **28.**—(1) When ... a vehicle is approaching a place in a road where [a person is] crossing or seeking to cross the road, a school crossing patrol wearing a uniform approved by the Secretary of State shall have power, by exhibiting a prescribed sign, to require the person driving or propelling the vehicle to stop it.

(2) When a person has been required under subsection (1) above to stop a vehicle—

(a) he shall cause the vehicle to stop before reaching the place where the [person is] crossing or seeking to cross and so as not to stop or impede [his] crossing, and

(b) the vehicle shall not be put in motion again so as to reach the place in question so long as the sign continues to be exhibited.

(3) A person who fails to comply with paragraph (a) of subsection (2) above, or who causes a vehicle to be put in motion in contravention of paragraph (b) of that subsection, shall be guilty of an offence.

(4) In this section —

(a) *"prescribed sign"* means a sign of a size, colour and type prescribed by regulations made by the Secretary of State or, if authorisation is given by the Secretary of State for the use of signs of a description not so prescribed, a sign of that description;

(b) *"school crossing patrol"* means a person authorised to patrol in accordance with arrangements under section 26 of this Act;

and regulations under paragraph (a) above may provide for the attachment of reflectors to signs or for the illumination of signs.

(5) For the purposes of this section —

(a) where it is proved that a sign was exhibited by a school crossing patrol, it shall be presumed, unless the contrary is proved, to be of a size, colour and type prescribed, or of a description authorised, under subsection (4)(b) above, and, if it was exhibited in circumstances in which it was required by the regulations to be illuminated, to have been illuminated in the prescribed manner; [and]

(b) where it is proved that a school crossing patrol was wearing a uniform, the uniform shall be presumed, unless the contrary is proved, to be a uniform approved by the Secretary of State; ...

[Section 28 is printed as amended by the Transport Act 2000 s.270(1) and (3); **A13.38**
and s.274 and Sch.31, Pt V(2).

The Traffic Signs (Welsh and English Language Provisions) Regulations and General Directions 1985 (SI 1985/713) below and the School Crossing Patrol Sign (England and Wales) Regulations 2006 (SI 2006/2215); not reproduced in this work) were made in part under this section. SI 2006/2215 prescribes, as respects England and Wales, the size, colour and type of the sign which a school crossing patrol may exhibit for the purpose of stopping a vehicle in accordance with s.28(1) above.

As an exception to the transfer of functions to the National Assembly for Wales of functions of a Minister of the Crown exercisable in relation to Wales (see the note at § A13.02 above), the functions under s.28 have been expressly excluded from that transfer; see the National Assembly for Wales (Transfer of Functions) Order 1999 (SI 1999/672; not reproduced in this work) art.2 and Sch.1.

As to the transfer of the function of the Secretary of State under s.28(4)(a) which is exercisable in Scotland of authorising the use of signs of a description not prescribed by regulations under s.28(4)(a) to the Scottish Ministers, see the Scotland Act 1998 (Transfer of Functions to the Scottish Ministers etc.) Order 1999 (SI 1999/1750; not reproduced in this work) art.2 and Sch.1.]

*   *   *

PART IV

PARKING PLACES

Provision of off-street parking, and parking on roads without payment

Power of local authorities to provide parking places

32. *[Omitted.]*   **A13.39**

Additional powers of local authorities in connection with off-street parking places

33. *[Omitted.]*   **A13.40**

Provision of access to premises through off-street parking places

A13.41   **34.** *[Omitted.]*

Provision as to use of parking places provided under section 32 or section 33

A13.42   **35.**—(1) As respects any parking place—

> (a) provided by a local authority under section 32 of this Act, or
>
> (b) provided under any letting or arrangements made by a local authority under section 33(4) of this Act,

the local authority, subject to Parts I to III of Schedule 9 to this Act, may by order make provisions as to—

>> (i) the use of the parking place, and in particular the vehicles or class of vehicles which may be entitled to use it,
>>
>> (ii) the conditions on which it may be used,
>>
>> (iii) the charges to be paid in connection with its use (where it is an off-street one), and
>>
>> (iv) the removal from it of a vehicle left there in contravention of the order and the safe custody of the vehicle,

[and the power under paragraph (iii) to make provision as to the payment of charges shall include power to make provision requiring those charges, or any part of them, to be paid by means of the hire or purchase in advance, or the use, of parking devices in accordance with the order].

(2) Where under section 34 of this Act a means of access to any premises has been provided by a local authority through an off-street parking place, then, subject to Parts I to III of Schedule 9 to this Act and to the provisions of any agreement made by the local authority under subsection (3) of section 34 and to any rights granted by them under that subsection, the authority may by an order under subsection (1) above make provision as to the use of the parking place as the means of access and, in particular, as to the vehicles or class of vehicles which may be entitled to use the means of access and as to the conditions on which the means of access may be used.

(3) An order under subsection (1) above may provide for a specified apparatus or device to be used—

> (a) as a means to indicate—
>
>> (i) the time at which a vehicle arrived at, and the time at which it ought to leave, a parking place or one or other of those times, or
>>
>> (ii) the charges paid or payable in respect of a vehicle in an off-street parking place; or
>
> (b) as a means to collect any such charges,

and may make provision regulating the use of any such apparatus or device …

[(3A) An order under subsection (1) above may also provide—

> (a) for regulating the issue, use and surrender of parking devices;
>
> (b) for requiring vehicles to display parking devices when left in any parking place in respect of which the parking devices may be used;
>
> (c) without prejudice to the generality of paragraph (b) above, for regulating the manner in which parking devices are to be displayed or operated;

    (d) for prescribing the use, and the manner of use, of apparatus ... designed to be used in connection with parking devices;

    (e) for treating—

        (i) the indication given by a parking device, or

        (ii) the display or the failure to display a parking device on or in any vehicle left in any parking place,

      as evidence (and, in Scotland, as sufficient evidence) of such facts as may be provided by the order;

    (f) for the refund, in such circumstances and in such manner as may be prescribed in the order, of the whole or part of the amount of any charge paid in advance in respect of a parking device;

    (g) for the payment of a deposit in respect of the issue of a parking device and for the repayment of the whole or any part of any such deposit.]

[(3B) In this section and in section 35A below *"parking device"* means either a card, disc, token, meter, permit, stamp or other similar device, whether used in a vehicle or not ... which being used either by itself, or in conjunction with any such apparatus as is referred to in subsection (3A)(d) above—

    (a) indicates, or causes to be indicated, the payment of a charge, and—

        (i) the period in respect of which it has been paid and the time of the beginning or end of the period, or

        (ii) whether or not the period for which it has been paid or any further period has elapsed, or

        (iii) the period for which the vehicle in relation to which the parking device is used is permitted to park in the parking place, and the time of the beginning or end of the period, or

        (iv) whether or not the period for which the vehicle in relation to which the parking device is used is permitted to park in the parking place or any further period has elapsed; or

    (b) operates apparatus controlling the entry of vehicles to or their exit from the parking place, or enables that apparatus to be operated;

or any other device of any such description as may from time to time be prescribed for the purposes of this section and section 35A below by order made by the Secretary of State ...]

[(3C) An order under subsection (3B) above which revokes or amends a previous order under that subsection may make such saving and transitional provision as appears to the Secretary of State to be necessary or expedient.]

[(3D) The power to make orders under subsection (3B) above is exercisable by statutory instrument which shall be subject to annulment in pursuance of a resolution of either House of Parliament.]

(4)–(9) [...]

[Section 35 is printed as amended by the Road Traffic (Consequential Provisions) Act 1988 s.3 and Sch.1; the Parking Act 1989 s.1; the Road Traffic Act 1991 ss.44(2), 83 and Sch.8; the Deregulation (Parking Equipment) Order 1996 (SI 1996/1553) art.2(1)(a) and Sch. (not reproduced in this work).   **A13.43**

The amendments effected by the Parking Act 1989 s.1, are stated by s.1(5) not to affect the validity of orders under subs.(1) above which were made before May 16, 1990.]

[Offences and proceedings in connection with parking places provided under section 32 or section 33

A13.44

35A.—(1) In the event of any contravention of, or non-compliance with, a provision of an order under section 35(1) above, the person responsible shall be guilty of an offence.

(2) A person who, with intent to defraud—

    (a) interferes with any such apparatus or device mentioned in section 35(3) above as is by an order under section 35(1) above to be used for the collection of charges at an off-street parking place, or operates or attempts to operate it by the insertion of objects other than current coins or bank notes of the appropriate denomination, or the appropriate credit or debit cards, or

    (b) interferes with any such apparatus as is mentioned in section 35(3A)(d) above or with a parking device, or operates or attempts to operate any such apparatus or any parking device otherwise than in the manner prescribed, or

    (c) displays a parking device otherwise than in the manner prescribed,

shall be guilty of an offence.

(3) An order under section 35(1) above may include provision—

    (a) for determining the person responsible for any contravention of or non-compliance with the order;

    (b) for treating—

        (i) the indications given by any such apparatus or device as is mentioned in section 35(3) above used in pursuance of the order, or

        (ii) the indications given by any such apparatus as is mentioned in section 35(3A)(d) above used in pursuance of the order, or any tickets issued by it, or the absence of any such ticket from a vehicle left in a parking place,

    as evidence … of such facts and for such purposes as may be provided by the order;

    (c) for applying with any appropriate adaptations any of the provisions of subsections (4) to (6) of section 47 of this Act.

(4) […]

(5) While a vehicle is within a parking place, it shall not be lawful for the driver or conductor of the vehicle, or for any person employed in connection with it, to ply for hire or accept passengers for hire; and if a person acts in contravention of this subsection he shall be guilty of an offence.

(6) In this section —

    "credit card" means a card or similar thing issued by any person, use of which enables the holder to defer the payment by him of the charge for parking a vehicle; and

    "debit card" means a card or similar thing issued by any person, use of which by the holder causes the charge for parking a vehicle to be paid by the electronic transfer of funds from any current account of his at a bank or other institution providing banking services.]

[Section 35A was inserted by the Parking Act 1989 s.2, and is printed as **A13.45**
subsequently amended by the Deregulation (Parking Equipment) Order 1996 (SI
1996/1553) art.2(1)(a) and Sch. (not reproduced in this work).

Words in s.35A(3)(b) relating specifically and exclusively to Scotland have
been omitted.

As to the conduct of proceedings under s.35A(2), see the note at § A13.02
above.

For the application of the fixed penalty procedure to offences under subs.(1),
see the Road Traffic Offenders Act 1988 Pt III and Sch.3 below.]

[Display of information

35B.—(1) The Secretary of State may make regulations requiring local authori- **A13.46**
ties to display at off-street parking places provided by them under section 32
above such information about parking there as is specified in the regulations.

(2) Regulations under this section may also—
- (a) require the display of any orders under section 35(1) above relating to the parking place;
- (b) specify the manner in which the information and orders are to be displayed;
- (c) exempt local authorities, in specified circumstances or subject to specified conditions, from the requirement to display information and orders, or to display them in the specified manner; and
- (d) provide, in relation to a parking place at which a local authority fails to comply with the regulations or with any specified provision of the regulations, that, except in any specified circumstances, any order under section 35(1) above shall be of no effect in its application to that parking place in so far as it requires the payment of any charge in connection with use of the parking place—
  - (i) while the failure to comply continues, and
  - (ii) as respects vehicles parked there when the failure to comply was remedied, during a specified period thereafter.

(3) Regulations under this section may make different provision for different
circumstances and for different descriptions of parking place, and may exempt
specified descriptions of parking place from any provision of the regulations.

(4) In any proceedings for contravention of, or non-compliance with, an order
under section 35(1) above relating to an off-street parking place, it shall be assumed, unless the contrary is shown, that any relevant regulations under this section were complied with at all material times.]

[Section 35B was inserted by the Parking Act 1989, s.3.]   **A13.47**

Variation of charges at off-street parking places by notice

35C. *[Omitted.]*   **A13.48**

*   *   *

Parking on highways for payment

Designation of paying parking places on highways

45. *[Omitted.]*   **A13.49**

Charges at, and regulation of, designated parking places

A13.50   **46.**—(1) Subject to Parts I to III of Schedule 9 to this Act the authority by whom a designation order is made [with respect to any parking place outside Greater London[, and not in a civil enforcement area for parking contraventions]] shall by order prescribe any charges to be paid for vehicles left in a parking place designated by the order; and any such charge may be prescribed either—

> (a) as an amount (in this Act referred to as an *"initial charge"*) payable in respect of an initial period and an amount (in this Act referred to as an *"excess charge"*) payable, in addition to an initial charge, in respect of any excess over an initial period, or
>
> (b) as an amount payable regardless of the period for which a vehicle is left.

[(1A) *[Prescription of charges by order.]*]

(2) The authority by whom a designation order is made may, subject to Parts I to III of Schedule 9 to this Act, by order make such provision as may appear to that authority to be necessary or expedient for regulating or restricting the use of any parking place designated by the order, or otherwise for or in connection with the operation of such a parking place, and in particular (but without prejudice to the generality of the foregoing words) provision—

> (a) for regulating the time at which and the method by which any charge is to be paid and for requiring the use of apparatus (in this Act referred to as a *"parking meter"*) …, being apparatus designed either—
>
>> (i) to indicate whether any charge has been paid and whether the period for which it has been paid or any further period has elapsed, or
>>
>> (ii) to indicate the time and to issue tickets indicating the payment of a charge and the period in respect of which it has been paid;
>
> (b) for treating the indications given by a parking meter or any ticket issued by it, or the absence of any such ticket from a vehicle left in a parking place, as evidence (and, in Scotland, sufficient evidence) of such facts as may be provided by the order;
>
> [(c) for prohibiting the insertion in a parking meter of coins or bank notes additional to those inserted by way of payment of any charge, or for prohibiting the insertion or re-insertion in a parking meter of a credit or debit card additional to the original insertion of such a card.]

(d)–(k) *[Omitted.]*

(3) *[Periodical inspection of parking meters.]*

(4) *[Periodical inspection of apparatus.]*

[(5) In this section and in section 47 below, *"credit card"* and *"debit card"* have the meanings given by section 35A(6) above.]

[(6) In this section "civil enforcement area for parking contraventions" has the same meaning as in Part 6 of the Traffic Management Act 2004.]

A13.51   *[Section 46 is printed as amended by the Parking Act 1989 s.4 and Sch., para.2; the Road Traffic Act 1991 s.64(1) and (2); the Deregulation (Parking Equipment) Order 1996 (SI 1996/1553) art.2(1)(a) and Sch. (not reproduced in this work); the Traffic Management Act 2004 s.91 and Sch.11, para.1.]*

Variation of charges at designated parking places by notice

46A. *[Omitted.]*   **A13.52**

Offences relating to designated parking places

47.—(1) A person who—   **A13.53**

(a) being the driver of a vehicle, leaves the vehicle in a designated parking place otherwise than as authorised by or under an order relating to the parking place, or leaves the vehicle in a designated parking place for longer after the excess charge has been incurred than the time so authorised, or fails duly to pay any charge payable under section 45 of this Act, or contravenes or fails to comply with any provision of an order relating to the parking place as to the manner in which vehicles shall stand in, or be driven in or out of, the parking place, or

(b) whether being the driver of a vehicle or not, otherwise contravenes or fails to comply with any order relating to designated parking places,

shall, subject to section 48 of this Act, be guilty of an offence […].

(2) In relation to an offence under paragraph (a) of subsection (1) above of leaving a vehicle for longer after the excess charge has been incurred than the time authorised by an order relating to the parking place, or failing duly to pay any charge payable under section 45 of this Act, the reference in that paragraph to the driver of a vehicle shall be construed as a reference to the person driving the vehicle at the time when it was left in the parking place.

(3) A person who, with intent to defraud, interferes with a parking meter, or operates or attempts to operate a parking meter by the insertion of objects other than current coins [or bank notes of the appropriate denomination, or the appropriate credit or debit cards], shall be guilty of an offence.

(4) Where, in any proceedings in England or Wales for an offence under this section of failing to pay any charge, it is proved that the amount which has become due, or any part of that amount, has not been duly paid, the court shall order the payment of the sum not paid; and any sum ordered to be paid by virtue of this subsection shall be recoverable as a penalty.

(5) […]

(6) Where in any proceedings for an offence under this section of failing to pay an excess charge it is not proved that the excess charge had become due, but it is proved that an initial charge has not been paid, the defendant may be convicted of an offence under this section of failing to pay an initial charge.

(7) […]

[Section 47 is printed as amended by the Road Traffic (Consequential Provisions) Act 1988 s.3 and Sch.1; the Parking Act 1989 s.4 and Sch., para.3; the Road Traffic Act 1991 s.65(1); the Deregulation (Parking Equipment) Order 1996 (SI 1996/1553) art.2(1)(a) and Sch. (not reproduced in this work); the Traffic Management Act 2004 s.98 and Sch.12.   **A13.54**

As to the conduct of proceedings under s.47(3), see the note at § A13.02 above.

For the application of the fixed penalty procedure to offences under s.47(1), see the Road Traffic Offenders Act 1988 Pt III and Sch.3 below.]

Acceptance of payment as bar to proceedings under section 47

48.—(1) Where a parking meter relating to the space in which a vehicle is left   **A13.55**

in a designated parking place indicates that the period for which payment was made for the vehicle by an initial charge has expired, but the authority by whom the parking place is controlled are satisfied that the initial charge was not paid, acceptance by the authority of payment of the excess charge shall be a bar to proceedings for an offence under section 47(1)(a) of this Act of failing to pay the initial charge.

(2) Where in the case of any vehicle—

    (a) an authorisation by way of such a certificate, other means of identification or device as is referred to in section 4(2), 4(3), 7(2) or 7(3) of this Act, or such a permit or token as is referred to in section 46(2)(i) of this Act, has been issued with respect to the vehicle, and

    (b) the authority by whom a designated parking place is controlled are satisfied that, in accordance with the terms on which the authorisation was issued, a charge has become payable and has not been paid in respect of any period for which the vehicle has been left in that parking place,

acceptance by that authority of payment of the amount of that charge shall be a bar to proceedings for an offence under section 47(1)(a) of this Act of failing duly to pay the charge.

Supplementary provisions as to designation orders and designated parking places

A13.56   49.—(1) Where under a designation order vehicles may not be left at all times in the designated parking place—

    (a) the parking place shall for the purposes of sections 46 and 47 of this Act be treated, as respects any time during which vehicles may not be left there in pursuance of the order, as if it were not designated by the order; and

    (b) any vehicle left in the parking place which remains there at the beginning of a period during which vehicles may be left there in pursuance of the order shall, for the purposes of those sections, be treated as if it had been left there at the beginning of that period, but without prejudice to any rights or liabilities in respect of anything done or omitted at any time before the beginning, or after the end, of that period.

(2) [Revocation of designation as a parking place.]

(3) [...]

(4) Subject to Parts I to III of Schedule 9 to this Act, the authority by whom a parking place is designated under section 45 of this Act may by order empower the local authority, the chief officer of police or any other person specified by or under the order to provide for the moving, in case of emergency, of vehicles left in the parking place; to suspend the use of the parking place or any part of it on such occasions or in such circumstances as may be determined by or under the order; and to provide for the temporary removal of any parking meters installed at the parking place.

[(4A) A constable, or a person acting under the instructions (whether general or specific) of the chief officer of police, may suspend the use of a parking place designated under section 45 of this Act for not more than 7 days in order to prevent or mitigate congestion or obstruction of traffic, or danger to or from traffic, in consequence of extraordinary circumstances.]

(5) *[Acquisition of parking meters, etc.]*

(6) *[Exercise of powers by order.]*

[Section 49 is printed as amended by the Road Traffic Act 1991 s.48 and Sch.4, **A13.57**
para.27; the Local Government (Wales) Act 1994 s.22(1) and Sch.7, para.38(4).]

50. [...]   **A13.58**

[Parking devices for designated parking places

51.—(1) Any power of a local authority to make charges under section 45 of   **A13.59**
this Act for vehicles left in a designated parking place shall include power to
require those charges, or any part of them, to be paid by means of the hire or
purchase in advance, or the use, of parking devices in accordance with any relevant provision of an order under section 46 of this Act.

(2) Any power of a local authority to make orders under section 46(2) of this
Act shall include power by any such order to make provision—

    (a) for regulating the issue, use and surrender of parking devices;

    (b) for requiring vehicles to display parking devices when left in any
        parking place in respect of which the parking devices may be used;

    (c) without prejudice to the generality of paragraph (b) above, for regulat-
        ing the manner in which parking devices are to be displayed or oper-
        ated;

    (d) for prescribing the use, and the manner of use, of apparatus ...
        designed to be used in connection with parking devices;

    (e) for treating—

        (i) the indications given by a parking device; or

        (ii) the display or the failure to display a parking device on or in any
            vehicle left in any parking place,

        as evidence ... of such facts as may be provided by the order;

    (f) for the refund, in such circumstances and in such manner as may be
        prescribed in the order, of the whole or part of the amount of any
        charge paid in advance in respect of a parking device;

    (g) for the payment of a deposit in respect of the issue of a parking device
        and for the repayment of the whole or part of any such deposit.

(3) For the purposes of subsection (2) above—

    (a) the references to parking meters in section 46(2)(b) and (c) of this Act
        shall include references to the apparatus referred to in subsection
        (2)(d) above; and

    (b) the reference in section 46(2)(c) of this Act to the insertion in a park-
        ing meter of coins [or banknotes] additional to those inserted by way
        of payment of any charge [or to the insertion or re-insertion in a park-
        ing meter of a credit or debit card additional to the original insertion
        of such a card] shall include (so far as is appropriate) a reference to
        insertions or re-insertions in any such apparatus of parking devices
        additional to the original insertion of those devices.

(4) [In this section and in section 52 below *"parking device"* means either] a
card, disc, token, meter, permit, stamp or other similar device, whether used in a
vehicle or not ... which, being used either by itself, or in conjunction with any

such apparatus as is referred to in subsection (2)(d) above, indicates, or causes to be indicated, the payment of a charge, and—

    (a) the period in respect of which it has been paid and the time of the beginning or end of the period; or

    (b) whether [or not] the period for which it has been paid or any further period has elapsed [; or]

    [(c) the period for which the vehicle in relation to which the parking device is used is permitted to park in the parking place, and the time of the beginning or end of the period; or]

    [(d) whether or not the period for which the vehicle in relation to which the parking device is used is permitted to park in the parking place or any further period has elapsed;]

[or any other device of any such description as may from time to time be prescribed for the purposes of this section and section 52 below by order made by the Secretary of State ...]

    (4A) *[Saving and transitional provisions in orders.]*

    (4B) *[Exercise of order-making power.]*

    (5), (6) [...]

A13.60   *[Section 51 is printed as substituted by the Road Traffic Regulation (Parking) Act 1986 s.2(1), and as subsequently amended by the Parking Act 1989, s.4 and Schedule, para.4; the Road Traffic Act 1991 s.48 and Sch.4, para.28; the Deregulation (Parking Equipment) Order 1996 (SI 1996/1553) art.2(1)(a) and Sch. (not reproduced in this work).*

    Words relating specifically and exclusively to Scotland have been omitted from s.51(2)(e).]

Offences and proceedings in connection with parking devices and associated apparatus

A13.61   **52.**—(1) A person who, with intent to defraud,—

    (a) interferes with any apparatus referred to in section 51(2)(d) of this Act or with a parking device, or operates or attempts to operate any such apparatus or any parking device otherwise than in the manner prescribed, or

    (b) displays a parking device otherwise than in the manner prescribed, shall be guilty of an offence.

    (2) [...]

    (3) In section 48(1) of this Act the reference to a parking meter relating to the space in which a vehicle is left in a designated parking place shall include references to—

    (a) any such apparatus as is referred to in section 51(2)(d) of this Act which relates to the space in which a vehicle is so left, and

    (b) to a parking device used in respect of a vehicle left in a space in a designated parking place.

A13.62   *[Section 52 is printed as amended by the Road Traffic (Consequential Provisions) Act 1988 s.3 and Sch.1; the Deregulation (Parking Equipment) Order 1996 (SI 1996/1553) art.2(1)(a) and Sch. (not reproduced in this work).*

As to the conduct of the proceedings under s.52(1), see the note at § A13.02 above.]

*   *   *

Special parking provisions

Loading areas

61.—(1) If it appears to [the council of a county, metropolitan district or   **A13.63**
London borough or the Common Council of the City of London] that any land in
their area which is not part of a highway has been set apart by the occupier of the
land for use as a place where vehicles may be driven and parked for the purpose
of being loaded or unloaded in connection with a trade or business carried on or
in the vicinity of the land, the council may, subject to Part III of Schedule 9 to
this Act, by an order made with the consent of the owner and the occupier of the
land—

>   (a) designate the land as an area to which the following provisions of this
>   section apply (in this section referred to as a *"loading area"*), and
>   (b) specify the trade or business in question.

(2) A council which has made an order in pursuance of subsection (1) above—

>   (a) may vary the order by a subsequent order made with the consent of
>   the owner and the occupier of the land to which the order relates;
>   (b) may revoke the order by a subsequent order made with the consent of
>   the owner and the occupier of the loading area in question; and
>   (c) shall revoke the order by a subsequent order if requested in writing to
>   do so by the owner and the occupier of the loading area in question.

(3) An order in pursuance of subsection (1) or (2)(a) above may contain provisions prohibiting the parking, in the loading area to which the order relates, of
vehicles of such kinds as are specified in the order, except authorised vehicles, at
all times or at times so specified, and may make different provision in pursuance
of the preceding provisions of this subsection for different parts of the area; and
in this subsection *"authorised vehicle"*, in relation to a loading area, means a
goods vehicle (as defined by [section 192(1) of the Road Traffic Act 1988]) which
is in the area for the purpose of being loaded or unloaded in connection with the
trade or business specified in the order designating the area.

(4) Where an order has been made by a council in pursuance of subsection (1)
above and, by virtue of paragraph 22(1)(e) of Schedule 9 to this Act, traffic signs
are required to be placed on the loading area to which the order relates, a person
authorised in that behalf by the council may enter on the loading area for the
purpose of placing any such traffic signs and for the purpose of maintaining or
removing the signs.

(5) A person who, without reasonable excuse, causes a vehicle to be in any
part of a loading area at a time when the parking of it there is prohibited by an order made in pursuance of subsection (1) above shall be guilty of an offence.

(6) References in subsections (2) to (5) above to an order made in pursuance
of subsection (1) above include, in the case of such an order which has been
varied in pursuance of subsection (2)(a) of this section, references to the order as
so varied.

(7) Subsections (3) to (5) of section 44 of the Local Government (Miscellaneous Provisions) Act 1976 (which contain ancillary provisions for the purposes of Part I of that Act) shall have effect as if this section were included in that Part of that Act.

(8) In this section *"owner"*, in relation to any land, means a person who, either on his own account or as agent or trustee for another person, is receiving the rackrent of the land or would be entitled to receive it if the land were let at a rackrent; and any reference to a traffic sign, in relation to any land which is not a road, includes a reference to any object, device, line or mark which would be a traffic sign (as defined by section 64 of this Act) if the land were a road.

A13.64   *[Section 61 is printed as amended by the Local Government Act 1985 s.8(1) and Sch.5, Pt I, para.4(25); the Road Traffic (Consequential Provisions) Act 1988 s.4 and Sch.3, para.25(2).]*

*   *   *

PART V

TRAFFIC SIGNS

General provisions as to traffic signs

A13.65   **64.**—(1) In this Act *"traffic sign"* means any object or device (whether fixed or portable) for conveying, to traffic on roads or any specified class of traffic, warnings, information, requirements, restrictions or prohibitions of any description—

> (a) specified by regulations made by the Ministers acting jointly, or
>
> (b) authorised by the Secretary of State,

and any line or mark on a road for so conveying such warnings, information, requirements, restrictions or prohibitions.

(2) Traffic signs shall be of the size, colour and type prescribed by regulations made as mentioned in subsection (1)(a) above except where the Secretary of State authorises the erection or retention of a sign of another character; and for the purposes of this subsection illumination, whether by lighting or by the use of reflectors or reflecting material, or the absence of such illumination, shall be part of the type or character of a sign.

(3) Regulations under this section may be made so as to apply either generally or in such circumstances only as may be specified in the regulations.

(4) Except as provided by this Act, no traffic sign shall be placed on or near a road except—

> (a) a notice in respect of the use of a bridge;
>
> (b) a traffic sign placed, in pursuance of powers conferred by a special Act of Parliament or order having the force of an Act, by the owners or operators of a tramway, light railway or trolley vehicle undertaking, a dock undertaking or a harbour undertaking; or
>
> (c) a traffic sign placed on any land—
>
>> (i) by a person authorised under the following provisions of this Act to place the sign on a [road], and
>>
>> (ii) for a purpose for which he is authorised to place it on a [road].

(5) Regulations under this section, or any authorisation under subsection (2) above, may provide that [section 36 of the Road Traffic Act 1988] (drivers to comply with traffic directions) shall apply to signs of a type specified in that behalf by the regulations or, as the case may be, to the sign to which the authorisation relates.

(6) References in any enactment (including any enactment contained in this Act) to the erection or placing of traffic signs shall include references to the display of traffic signs in any manner, whether or not involving fixing or placing.

[Section 64 is printed as amended by the Road Traffic (Consequential Provisions) Act 1988 s.4 and Sch.3, para.25(3); the New Roads and Street Works Act 1991 s.168(1) and Sch.8, Pt II, para.47.

As an exception to the transfer of functions to the National Assembly for Wales of functions of a Minister of the Crown exercisable in relation to Wales (see the note at § A13.02 above), the functions under s.64 (other than so far as s.64 confers the power to (i) prescribe a variant of any sign of a type prescribed by "the Ministers" and carrying words in English, being a variant identical with a sign of that type except for the substitution or addition of words in Welsh (and any increase in size needed to accommodate the substituted or added words); and (ii) authorise signs not otherwise prescribed) have been expressly excluded from that transfer; see the National Assembly for Wales (Transfer of Functions) Order 1999 (SI 1999/672; not reproduced in this work) art.2 and Sch.1.

As to the transfer of functions of the Secretary of State under s.64(1)(b) and (2) which are exercisable in relation to Scotland to the Scottish Ministers, see the Scotland Act 1998 (Transfer of Functions to the Scottish Ministers etc.) Order 1999 (SI 1999/1750; not reproduced in this work) art.2 and Sch.1. As to the exercise of functions of the Secretary of State under s.64(1)(a) which are exercisable in relation to Scotland only after consultation with the Scottish Ministers, see SI 1999/1750 art.4 and Sch.3.

The functions under s.64 which are exercisable jointly by the Secretaries of State charged with general responsibility under this Act in relation to England, Wales and Scotland, respectively, have been transferred to the Secretary of State with effect from December 27, 1999; see the Transfer of Functions (Road Traffic) Order 1999 (SI 1999/3143; not reproduced in this work).

The Traffic Signs (Welsh and English Language Provisions) Regulations and General Directions 1985 (SI 1985/713) (q.v.), the Zebra, Pelican and Puffin Crossings Regulations and General Directions 1997 (SI 1997/2400) (q.v.), the Traffic Signs (Temporary Obstructions) Regulations 1997 (SI 1997/3053) (q.v.), and the Traffic Signs Regulations and General Directions 2002 (SI 2002/3113) (q.v.) were made in part under this section.]

A13.66

*   *   *

PART VI

SPEED LIMITS

General speed limit for restricted roads

81.—(1) It shall not be lawful for a person to drive a motor vehicle on a restricted road at a speed exceeding 30 miles per hour.

A13.67

(2) The Ministers acting jointly may by order made by statutory instrument and approved by a resolution of each House of Parliament increase or reduce the rate of speed fixed by subsection (1) above, either as originally enacted or as varied under this subsection.

A13.68   *[Provision is made for the application of s.81 to directions in orders made under the Road Traffic Act 1934 s.1, by Sch.10, para.14, to this Act (q.v.).*

As an exception to the transfer of functions to the National Assembly for Wales of functions of a Minister of the Crown exercisable in relation to Wales (see the note at § A13.02 above), the functions under s.81 have been expressly excluded from that transfer; see the National Assembly for Wales (Transfer of Functions) Order 1999 (SI 1999/672; not reproduced in this work) art.2 and Sch.1. The functions of the Ministers under s.81(2) are, however, exercisable only after consultation with the National Assembly; see SI 1999/672 art.5(1) and Sch.2.

As to the exercise of functions of the Ministers under s.81(2) which are exercisable in relation to Scotland only after consultation with the Scottish Ministers, see the Scotland Act 1998 (Transfer of Functions to the Scottish Ministers etc.) Order 1999 (SI 1999/1750; not reproduced in this work) art.4 and Sch.3.

The functions under s.81(2) which are exercisable jointly by the Secretaries of State charged with general responsibility under this Act in relation to England, Wales and Scotland, respectively, have been transferred to the Secretary of State with effect from December 27, 1999; see the Transfer of Functions (Road Traffic) Order 1999 (SI 1999/3143; not reproduced in this work).]

What roads are restricted roads

A13.69   **82.**—(1) Subject to the provisions of this section and of section 84(3) of this Act, a road is a restricted road for the purposes of section 81 of this Act [if—

      (a) in England and Wales, there is provided on it a system of street lighting furnished by means of lamps placed not more than 200 yards apart;

      (b) *[applies to Scotland.]*]

    (2) [The traffic authority for a road may direct]

      (a) that [the road] which is a restricted road for the purposes of section 81 of this Act shall cease to be a restricted road for those purposes, or

      (b) that [the road] which is not a restricted road for those purposes shall become a restricted road for those purposes.

[(3) A special road is not a restricted road for the purposes of section 81 on or after the date declared by the traffic authority, by notice published in the prescribed manner, to be the date on which the special road, or the relevant part of the special road, is open for use as a special road.]

A13.70   *[Section 82 is printed as amended by the New Roads and Street Works Act 1991 s.168(1) and Sch.8, Pt II, para.59(1)–(4).*

As to the transfer of functions of a Minister of the Crown under s.82(1)(b), (2) and (3) which are exercisable in relation to Scotland to the Scottish Ministers, see the Scotland Act 1998 (Transfer of Functions to the Scottish Ministers etc.) Order 1999 (SI 1999/1750; not reproduced in this work) art.2 and Sch.1.

Certain roads may be deemed to be roads subject to a direction under s.82(2)(a) by Sch.10, para.16, to this Act (q.v.).]

Provisions as to directions under section 82(2)

83.—(1) [A direction under section 82(2) by the Secretary of State shall be given] by means of an order made by the Secretary of State after giving public notice of his intention to make an order.   **A13.71**

[(2) A direction under section 82(2) by a local traffic authority shall be given by means of an order made by the authority.]

(3) Section 68(1)(c) of this Act shall apply to any order made under subsection (2) above.

[Section 83 is printed as amended by the New Roads and Street Works Act   **A13.72** *1991 s.168(1) and Sch.8, Pt II, para.60(1)–(3).*

As to the transfer of functions of the Secretary of State under s.83(1) which are exercisable in relation to Scotland to the Scottish Ministers, see the Scotland Act 1998 (Transfer of Functions to the Scottish Ministers etc.) Order 1999 (SI 1999/ 1750; not reproduced in this work) art.2 and Sch.1.]

Speed limits on roads other than restricted roads

84.—[(1) An order made under this subsection as respects any road may pro-   **A13.73** hibit—

    (a) the driving of motor vehicles on that road at a speed exceeding that specified in the order,

    (b) the driving of motor vehicles on that road at a speed exceeding that specified in the order during periods specified in the order, or

    (c) the driving of motor vehicles on that road at a speed exceeding the speed for the time being indicated by traffic signs in accordance with the order.]

[(1A) An order made by virtue of subsection (1)(c) above may—

    (a) make provision restricting the speeds that may be indicated by traffic signs or the periods during which the indications may be given, and

    (b) provide for the indications to be given only in such circumstances as may be determined by or under the order;

but any such order must comply with regulations made under subsection (1B) below, except where the Secretary of State authorises otherwise in a particular case.]

[(1B) The Secretary of State may make regulations governing the provision which may be made by orders of local authorities under subsection (1)(c) above, and any such regulations may in particular—

    (a) prescribe the circumstances in which speed limits may have effect by virtue of an order,

    (b) prescribe the speed limits which may be specified in an order, and

    (c) make transitional provision and different provision for different cases.]

[(2) The power to make an order under subsection (1) is exercisable by the traffic authority, who shall before exercising it in any case give public notice of their intention to do so.]

(3) While an order [made by virtue of subsection (1)(a)] above is in force as respects a road, that road shall not be a restricted road for the purposes of section 81 of this Act.

(4) This section does not apply to any part of a special road which is open for use as a special road.

(5) Section 68(1)(c) of this Act shall apply to any order made under subsection (1) above.

[(6) Any reference in a local Act to roads subject to a speed limit shall, unless the contrary intention appears, be treated as not including a reference to roads subject to a speed limit imposed only by virtue of subsection (1)(b) or (c) above.]

A13.74 *[Section 84 is printed as amended by the New Roads and Street Works Act 1991 s.168(1) and Sch.8, Pt II, para.61; the Road Traffic Act 1991 s.45(1)–(4).*

Orders made before July 1, 1992 under s.84 do not apply to tramcars or trolley vehicles (other than duobuses): the Tramcars and Trolley Vehicles (Modification of Enactments) Regulations 1992 (SI 1992/1217) reg.15 (q.v.). The application of such orders to duobuses is regulated by ibid. reg.16 (q.v.).

Certain speed limits which were in force before November 1, 1962 are deemed by Sch.10, para.15, to this Act (q.v.) to have been imposed by orders under s.84(1).

The consent of the Secretary of State (under para.13 or 14 of Sch.9 to this Act) to the making of orders under s.84(1) which contain provisions applying a speed limit of 20 miles per hour to any road was dispensed with after June 16, 1999 by the Road Traffic Regulation Act 1984 (Amendment) Order 1999 (SI 1999/1608; not reproduced in this work).

As to the transfer of functions of the Secretary of State under s.84(1), (1A) and (1B) which are exercisable in relation to Scotland to the Scottish Ministers, see the Scotland Act 1998 (Transfer of Functions to the Scottish Ministers etc.) Order 1999 (SI 1999/1750; not reproduced in this work) art.2 and Sch.1.]

Traffic signs for indicating speed restrictions

A13.75 **85.**—(1) For the purpose of securing that adequate guidance is given to drivers of motor vehicles as to whether any, and if so what, limit of speed is to be observed on any road, it shall be the duty of the Secretary of State, [in the case of a road for which he is the traffic authority, to] erect and maintain … traffic signs in such positions as may be requisite for that purpose.

(2) [In the case of any other road, it is the duty of the local traffic authority—]

    (a) to erect and maintain … traffic signs in such positions as may be requisite in order to give effect to general or other directions given by the Secretary of State for the purpose mentioned in subsection (1) above, and

    (b) to alter or remove traffic signs as may be requisite in order to give effect to such directions, either in consequence of the making of an order by the Secretary of State or otherwise.

(3) If a [local traffic authority] makes default in executing any works required for the performance of the duty imposed on them by subsection (2) above, the Secretary of State may himself execute the works; and the expense incurred by him in doing so shall be recoverable by him from the local authority and, in England or Wales, shall be so recoverable summarily as a civil debt.

(4) [Where no such system of street or carriageway lighting as is mentioned in section 82(1) is provided on a road], but a limit of speed is to be observed on the road, a person shall not be convicted of driving a motor vehicle on the road at a speed exceeding the limit unless the limit is indicated by means of such traffic signs as are mentioned in subsection (1) or subsection (2) above.

(5) In any proceedings for a contravention of section 81 of this Act, where the proceedings relate to driving on a road provided with [such a system of street or carriageway lighting], evidence of the absence of traffic signs displayed in pursuance of this section to indicate that the road is not a restricted road for the purposes of that section shall be evidence that the road is a restricted road for those purposes.

(6) Where by regulations made under section 17(2) of this Act a limit of speed is to be observed then, if it is to be observed—

    (a) on all special roads, or

    (b) on all special roads provided for the use of particular classes of traffic, or

    (c) on all special roads other than special roads of such description as may be specified in the regulations, or

    (d) as mentioned in paragraph (a), (b) or (c) above except for such lengths of special road as may be so specified,

this section shall not apply in relation to that limit (but without prejudice to its application in relation to any lower limit of maximum speed or, as the case may be, any higher limit of minimum speed, required by any such regulations to be observed on any specified length of any specified special road).

(7) The power to give general directions under subsection (2) above shall be exercisable by statutory instrument.

[Section 85 is printed as amended by the New Roads and Street Works Act **A13.76**
1991 s.168(1) and Sch.8, Pt II, para.62(1)–(6); the Road Traffic Act 1991 ss.48, 83, Sch.4, para.30, and Sch.8.

As an exception to the transfer of functions to the National Assembly for Wales of functions of a Minister of the Crown exercisable in relation to Wales (see the note at § A13.02 above), the function under s.85(2) (so far as it relates to the giving of general directions) has been expressly excluded from that transfer; see the National Assembly for Wales (Transfer of Functions) Order 1999 (SI 1999/672; not reproduced in this work) art.2 and Sch.1.

As to the transfer of functions of the Secretary of State under s.85(1) and (3) which are exercisable in relation to Scotland to the Scottish Ministers, and the function under s.85(2) of giving directions other than general directions, see the Scotland Act 1998 (Transfer of Functions to the Scottish Ministers etc.) Order 1999 (SI 1999/1750; not reproduced in this work) art.2 and Sch.1. As to the exercise of function of the Secretary of State of giving general directions with respect to traffic signs to indicate speed limits under s.85(2)(a) which are exercisable in relation to Scotland only after consultation with the Scottish Ministers, see SI 1999/1750 art.4 and Sch.3.]

Speed limits for particular classes of vehicles

86.—(1) It shall not be lawful for a person to drive a motor vehicle of any class   **A13.77**
on a road at a speed greater than the speed specified in Schedule 6 to this Act as the maximum speed in relation to a vehicle of that class.

    (2), (3) *[Omitted.]*

    (4) *[…]*

    (5), (6) *[Omitted.]*

A13.78   *[Subsection (4) was repealed by the New Roads and Street Works Act 1991 s.168(1) and (2), Sch.8, Pt II, para.63, and Sch.9.*

As an exception to the transfer of functions to the National Assembly for Wales of functions of a Minister of the Crown exercisable in relation to Wales (see the note at § A13.02 above), the functions under s.86 have been expressly excluded from that transfer; see the National Assembly for Wales (Transfer of Functions) Order 1999 (SI 1999/672; not reproduced in this work) art.2 and Sch.1.

As to the exercise of functions of a Minister of the Crown under s.86(2) which are exercisable in relation to Scotland only after consultation with the Scottish Ministers, see the Scotland Act 1998 (Transfer of Functions to the Scottish Ministers etc.) Order 1999 (SI 1999/1750; not reproduced in this work) art.4 and Sch.3.]

Exemption of [fire and rescue authority], ambulance and police vehicles for speed limits

A13.79   **87.**—[(1)] No statutory provisions imposing a speed limit on motor vehicles shall apply to any vehicle on an occasion when it is being used for [fire and rescue authority], ambulance or police purposes, if the observance of that provision would be likely to hinder the use of the vehicle for the purpose for which it is being used on that occasion.

[(2) Subsection (1) above applies in relation to a vehicle being used—

    (a) for Serious Organised Crime Agency purposes, or

    (b) for training persons to drive vehicles for use for Serious Organised Crime Agency purposes,

as it applies in relation to a vehicle being used for police purposes.]

[(3) But (except where it is being used for training the person by whom it is being driven) subsection (1) above does not apply in relation to a vehicle by virtue of subsection (2) above unless it is being driven by a person who has been trained in driving vehicles at high speeds.]

A13.80   *[Section 87 is printed as amended by the Fire and Rescue Services Act 2004 s.53 and Sch.1, para.55; the Serious Organised Crime and Police Act 2005 s.59 and Sch.4, para.42.*

With effect from a day to be appointed, s.87 will be substituted by the Road Safety Act 2006 s.19 as follows:

[Exemptions from speed limits

    87.—(1) No statutory provision imposing a speed limit on motor vehicles shall apply to any vehicle on an occasion when—

        (a) it is being used for fire and rescue authority purposes or for or in connection with the exercise of any function of a relevant authority as defined in section 6 of the Fire (Scotland) Act 2005, for ambulance purposes or for police or Serious Organised Crime Agency purposes,

        (b) it is being used for other prescribed purposes in such circumstances as may be prescribed, or

        (c) it is being used for training persons to drive vehicles for use for any of the purposes mentioned in paragraph (a) or (b) above,

if the observance of that provision would be likely to hinder the use of the vehicle for the purpose for which it is being used on that occasion.

(2) Subsection (1) above does not apply unless the vehicle is being driven by a person who—

- (a) has satisfactorily completed a course of training in the driving of vehicles at high speed provided in accordance with regulations under this section, or
- (b) is driving the vehicle as part of such a course.

(3) The Secretary of State may by regulations make provision about courses of training in the driving of vehicles at high speed.

(4) The regulations may include—

- (a) provision about the nature of courses,
- (b) provision for the approval by the Secretary of State of persons providing courses or giving instruction on courses and the withdrawal of approvals (including provision for appeals against refusal and withdrawal of approvals),
- (c) provision specifying the maximum fees that a person may be required to pay for a course,
- (d) provision for the training or assessment, or the supervision of the training or assessment, of persons providing courses or giving instruction on courses,
- (e) provision for the evidencing of the successful completion of courses,
- (f) provision authorising the Secretary of State to make available information about persons providing courses or giving instruction on courses, and
- (g) provision treating courses of training in the driving of vehicles at high speed which have been completed before the coming into force of the regulations as if they had been provided in accordance with the regulations.

(5) The regulations may include provision for the charging of reasonable fees in respect of any function conferred or imposed on the Secretary of State by the regulations.

(6) The regulations may make different provision—

- (a) for different classes of vehicle,
- (b) for different descriptions of persons, or
- (c) otherwise for different circumstances.]/

Temporary speed limits

88.—(1) Where it appears to the Secretary of State desirable to do so in the interests of safety or for the purpose of facilitating the movement of traffic, he may, after giving public notice of his intention to do so, by order prohibit, for a period not exceeding 18 months, the driving of motor vehicles—   **A13.81**

- (a) on all roads, or on all roads in any area specified in the order, or on all roads of any class so specified, or on all roads other than roads of any class so specified, or on any road so specified, at a speed greater than that specified in the order, or
- (b) on any road specified in the order, at a speed less than the speed specified in the order, subject to such exceptions as may be so specified.

(2) Any prohibition imposed by an order under subsection (1) above may be so imposed either generally, or at times, on days or during periods specified in the

order; but the provisions of any such order shall not, except in so far as may be provided by the order, affect the provisions of sections 81 to 84 of this Act.

(3) For the purposes of an order under subsection (1)(a) above, roads may be classified by reference to any circumstances appearing to the Secretary of State to be suitable for the purpose, including their character, the nature of the traffic to which they are suited or the traffic signs provided on them.

(4) The provisions of any order under subsection (1) above may be continued, either indefinitely or for a specified period, by an order of the Secretary of State made by statutory instrument, which shall be subject to annulment in pursuance of a resolution of either House of Parliament.

(5) Where by virtue of an order under this section a speed limit is to be observed, then—

    (a) if it is to be observed on all roads, on all roads of any class specified in the order or on all roads other than roads of any class so specified, section 85 of this Act shall not apply in relation to that limit;

    (b) if it is to be observed on all roads in any area and, at all points where roads lead into the area, is indicated as respects the area as a whole by means of such traffic signs as are mentioned in subsection (1) or subsection (2) of section 85 of this Act, the limit shall, for the purposes of subsection (4) of that section, be taken as so indicated with respect to all roads in the area.

(6) This section does not apply to any part of a special road which is open for use as a special road.

(7) If a person drives a motor vehicle on a road in contravention of an order under subsection (1)(b) above, he shall be guilty of an offence; but a person shall not be liable to be convicted of so driving solely on the evidence of one witness to the effect that, in the opinion of the witness, he was driving the vehicle at a speed less than that specified in the order.

A13.82 *[As to the admissibility of evidence of speeding in respect of offences under s.88(7), see s.20 of the Road Traffic Offenders Act 1988 below.*

As an exception to the transfer of functions to the National Assembly for Wales of functions of a Minister of the Crown exercisable in relation to Wales (see the note at § A13.02 above), the functions under s.88 have been expressly excluded from that transfer; see the National Assembly for Wales (Transfer of Functions) Order 1999 (SI 1999/672; not reproduced in this work) art.2 and Sch.1.

As to the exercise of functions of the Secretary of State under s.88(1) and (4) which are exercisable in relation to Scotland only after consultation with the Scottish Ministers, see the Scotland Act 1998 (Transfer of Functions to the Scottish Ministers etc.) Order 1999 (SI 1999/1750; not reproduced in this work) art.4 and Sch.3.

As to notice of intended prosecution of offences under s.88(7), see the Road Traffic Offenders Act 1988 Sch.1, para.1A below.

For the application of the fixed penalty procedure to offences under subs.(7), see the Road Traffic Offenders Act 1988 Pt III and Sch.3 below.]

Speeding offences generally

A13.83 **89.**—(1) A person who drives a motor vehicle on a road at a speed exceeding a limit imposed by or under any enactment to which this section applies shall be guilty of an offence.

(2) A person prosecuted for such an offence shall not be liable to be convicted solely on the evidence of one witness to the effect that, in the opinion of the witness, the person prosecuted was driving the vehicle at a speed exceeding a specified limit.

(3) The enactments to which this section applies are—

    (a) any enactment contained in this Act except section 17(2);

    (b) section 2 of the Parks Regulation (Amendment) Act 1926; and

    (c) any enactment not contained in this Act, but passed after 1st September 1960, whether before or after the passing of this Act.

(4) If a person who employs other persons to drive motor vehicles on roads publishes or issues any time-table or schedule, or gives any directions, under which any journey, or any stage or part of any journey, is to be completed within some specified time, and it is not practicable in the circumstances of the case for that journey (or that stage or part of it) to be completed in the specified time without the commission of such an offence as is mentioned in subsection (1) above, the publication or issue of the time-table or schedule, or the giving of the directions, may be produced as prima facie evidence that the employer procured or (as the case may be) incited the persons employed by him to drive the vehicles to commit such an offence.

[As to the admissibility of evidence of speeding in respect of offences under   **A13.84**
s.89(1), see s.20 of the Road Traffic Offenders Act 1988 below.

    As to notice of intended prosecution of offences under s.89(1), see the Road Traffic Offenders Act 1988 Sch.1, para.1A below.

    For the application of the fixed penalty procedure to offences under subs.(1), see the Road Traffic Offenders Act 1988 Pt III and Sch.3 below.]

90., 91. [...]   **A13.85**

         *   *   *

PART VIII

CONTROL AND ENFORCEMENT

         *   *   *

Appointment of traffic wardens

95. *[Omitted.]*   **A13.86**

Appointment of traffic wardens

96.—(1) An order under section 95(5) of this Act may provide that, for the   **A13.87** purposes of any functions which traffic wardens are authorised by the order to discharge, but subject to the provisions of subsection (3) below, references to a constable or police constable in all or any of the enactments specified in subsection (2) below shall include references to a traffic warden.

(2) The enactments referred to in subsection (1) above are—

    (a) section 52 of the Metropolitan Police Act 1839, so far as it relates to the giving by the commissioner of directions to constables for preventing obstructions;

   (b) section 22 of the local Act of the second and third year of the reign of Queen Victoria, chapter 94, so far as it makes similar provision with respect to the City of London;

  (bb) in this Act —

     (i) section 100(3) (which relates to the interim disposal of vehicles removed under section 99); and

    (ii) sections 104 and 105 (which relate to the immobilisation of illegally parked vehicles);

   (c) in the Road Traffic Act 1988 —

     (i) sections 35(1), 36 and 37 (which relate to compliance with traffic directions given by police constables);

  [(ia) section 67(3) (which relates to the power of a constable in uniform to stop vehicles for testing);]

    (ii) section 163 (which relates to the power of a constable to stop vehicles);

   (iii) section 164(1), (2) and (6) (which relate to the power of a constable to require the production of a driving licence in certain circumstances); and

   (iv) sections 165 and 169 (which relate to the powers of constables to obtain names and addresses of drivers and others and to require production of evidence of insurance or security and test certificates);

    and

   (d) section 11 of the Road Traffic Offenders Act 1988.

(3) Any power of a constable for the purposes of the following provisions of the Road Traffic Act 1988, namely, sections 164(1), (2) and (6) and 165, shall be exercisable by a traffic warden under an order made by virtue of subsection (1) above only where—

   (a) the traffic warden is assisting a constable, or

   (b) the traffic warden has reasonable cause to believe that an offence has been committed of a description specified in relation to the section in question for the purposes of this paragraph by the order, and, in the case of a power for the purposes of section 165 of the Road Traffic Act 1988, the order authorises the use of that power in relation to that offence, ...

   (c) [...]

[(4) Where an order has been made pursuant to subsection (2)(bb)(i) above, in section 100(3) of this Act the words *"chief officer of the police force to which the constable belongs"* shall be deemed to include a reference to a chief officer of police under whose direction a traffic warden acts.

(5) Any order made under section 95(5) of this Act may make different provision for different cases or classes of case, or in respect of different areas.]

A13.88   *[Section 96 is printed as amended by the Road Traffic Act 1991 Sch.4, para.31(3); the Police Reform Act 2002 ss.44(1), (2), (3)(a), 107 and Sch.8.]*

Supplementary provisions as to traffic wardens

A13.89   97. *[Omitted.]*

98. [...]

Removal or immobilisation of vehicles

Removal of vehicles illegally, obstructively or dangerously parked, or abandoned or broken down

99.—(1), (2) *[Power to make regulations for removal of vehicles.]*   **A13.90**

(3) *[Notice to occupier of land where vehicle is.]*

(4) [. . .]

(5) In this section *"vehicle"* means any vehicle, whether or not it is in a fit state for use on roads, and includes any chassis or body, with or without wheels, appearing to have formed part of such a vehicle, and any load carried by, and anything attached to, such a vehicle.

[(6) *[Interpretation of s.99.]]*

[Section 99(6) (not reproduced) was inserted by the Road Traffic Act 1991   **A13.91**
s.48 and Sch.4, para.32.

Section 99(4) (not reproduced) was omitted by the Clean Neighbourhoods and Environment Act 2005 s.15 and Sch.4, Pt 1. For transitional provisions with regard to s.99 as amended by the 2005 Act, see the Clean Neighbourhoods and Environment Act 2005 (Commencement No.2, Transitional Provisions and Savings) (England and Wales) Order 2005 (SI 2005/2896).

The definition in s.99(5) has been incorporated by reference into the Removal and Disposal of Vehicles (Loading Areas) Regulations 1986 (SI 1986/184) reg.2 (q.v.), and the Removal and Disposal of Vehicles Regulations 1986 (SI 1986/183) reg.2 (q.v.).

For the powers of civilians designated or accredited by a chief officer of police to remove abandoned vehicles, see the Police Reform Act 2002 ss.38, 41 and Sch.4, para.10, Sch.5, para.7; not reproduced in this work.

For the power to make regulations under this section in relation to the removal of vehicles by traffic officers, see the Traffic Management Act 2004 s.9; not reproduced in this work.

As an exception to the transfer of functions to the National Assembly for Wales of functions of a Minister of the Crown exercisable in relation to Wales (see the note at § A13.02 above), the functions under s.99 have been expressly excluded from that transfer; see the National Assembly for Wales (Transfer of Functions) Order 1999 (SI 1999/672; not reproduced in this work) art.2 and Sch.1.]

Interim disposal of vehicles removed under section 99

100. *[Omitted.]*   **A13.92**

Ultimate disposal of vehicles abandoned and removable under this Act

101. *[Omitted.]*   **A13.93**

Right of owner to recover vehicle or proceeds of sale

101A. *[Omitted.]*

Representations and appeals

101B. *[Omitted.]*   **A13.94**

Charges for removal, storage and disposal of vehicles

102. *[Omitted.]*

Supplementary provisions as to removal of vehicles

A13.95   103. *[Omitted.]*

Immobilisation of vehicles illegally parked

A13.96   104.—(1) Subject to sections 105 and 106 of this Act, where a constable finds on a road a vehicle which has been permitted to remain at rest there in contravention of any prohibition or restriction imposed by or under any enactment, he may—

> (a) fix an immobilisation device to the vehicle while it remains in the place in which he finds it; or
>
> (b) move it from that place to another place on the same or another road and fix an immobilisation device to it in that other place

or authorise another person to take under his direction any action he could himself take by virtue of paragraph (a) or (b) above.

(2) On any occasion when an immobilisation device is fixed to a vehicle in accordance with this section the constable or other person fixing the device shall also affix to the vehicle a notice—

> (a) indicating that such a device has been fixed to the vehicle and warning that no attempt should be made to drive it or otherwise put it in motion until it has been released from that device;
>
> (b) specifying the steps to be taken in order to secure its release; and
>
> (c) giving such other information as may be prescribed.

(3) A vehicle to which an immobilisation device has been fixed in accordance with this section may only be released from that device by or under the direction of a [person authorised to give such a direction by the chief officer of police within whose area the vehicle in question was found].

(4) Subject to subsection (3) above, a vehicle to which an immobilisation device has been fixed in accordance with this section shall be released from that device on payment in any manner specified in the notice affixed to the vehicle under subsection (2) above of such charge in respect of the release as may be prescribed.

(5) A notice affixed to a vehicle under this section shall not be removed or interfered with except by or under the authority of the person in charge of the vehicle or the person by whom it was put in the place where it was found by the constable; and any person contravening this subsection shall be guilty of an offence.

(6) Any person who, without being authorised to do so in accordance with this section, removes or attempts to remove an immobilisation device fixed to a vehicle in accordance with this section shall be guilty of an offence.

(7) Where a vehicle is moved in accordance with this section before an immobilisation device is fixed to it, any power of removal under regulations for the time being in force under section 99 of this Act which was exercisable in relation to that vehicle immediately before it was so moved shall continue to be exercisable in relation to that vehicle while it remains in the place to which it was so moved.

(8) In relation to any vehicle which is removed in pursuance of any such regulations or under section 3 of the Refuse Disposal (Amenity) Act 1978 (duty of local authority to remove abandoned vehicles) from a place to which it was moved in accordance with this section, references in the definition of "person responsible" in section 102(8) of this Act and section 5 of the said Act of 1978 mentioned above (recovery from person responsible of charges and expenses in respect of vehicles removed) to the place from which the vehicle was removed shall be read as references to the place in which it was immediately before it was moved in accordance with this section.

(9) In this section *"immobilisation device"* means any device or appliance designed or adapted to be fixed to a vehicle for the purpose of preventing it from being driven or otherwise put in motion, being a device or appliance of a type approved by the Secretary of State for use for that purpose in accordance with this section.

(10) [...]

(11), (12) *[Omitted.]*

[(12A) For the purposes of this section, the suspension under section 13A or 49 of this Act of the use of a parking place is a restriction imposed under this Act.]

[Section 104 is printed as amended by the Road Traffic Act 1991 ss.48, 83, **A13.97** *Sch.4, paras 34(1) and (2), 35, and Sch.8.*

Section 106 (to which s.104 is subject) states that ss.104 and 105 only extend to such areas as the Secretary of State specifies. The only known orders having effect under s.106 are the Immobilisation of Vehicles Illegally Parked (London Boroughs of Camden, Kensington and Chelsea, and Westminster, and the City of London) Order 1986 (SI 1986/1225) and the Immobilisation of Vehicles Illegally Parked (London Borough of Hammersmith and Fulham) Order 1989 (SI 1989/1746; not reproduced in this work). However, ss.104–106 of this Act have been applied to Crown roads in the royal parks (Hyde Park, Kensington Gardens, Regent's Park, St James's Park and Green Park in Greater London) as they apply in relation to other roads to which the public has access; Crown Roads (Royal Parks) (Application of Road Traffic Enactments) Order 1987 (SI 1987/363) art.5 (not reproduced in this work).

The following immobilisation devices have been approved:

the "Wheelok 'P'"	Immobilisation Devices (Approval) Order 1983
the "Bulldog Model 11 T"	Immobilisation Devices (Approval) Order 1983
the "Wheelok Model P II"	Immobilisation Devices (Approval) Order 1986
the "Claw"	Immobilisation Devices (Approval) Order 1987
the "Prest On"	Immobilisation Device Approval 1993
the TMP "Professional" Wheel Clamp	Immobilisation Device Approval 1997
the TMP "Secura" Wheel Clamp	Immobilisation Device Approval 1998

the TMP "HGV" Wheel Clamp	*Immobilisation Device (No.2) Approval 1998*
the TMP "Triangle" Wheel Clamp	*Immobilisation Device Approval 2005*
the LCC "Yellow Triangle" Wheel Clamp	*Immobilisation Device (No.2) Approval 2005*

Neither the orders nor the approvals are published as statutory instruments. The 1983 order was dated April 22, 1983; the 1986 order was dated June 30, 1986; the 1987 order was dated November 2, 1987; the 1993 approval was dated October 2, 1993; the 1997 approval was dated January 29, 1997; the 1998 approval and the 1998 (No.2) approval were both dated November 5, 1998; the 2005 approval was dated April 1, 2005; the 2005 (No.2) approval was dated June 1, 2005.

As an exception to the transfer of functions to the National Assembly for Wales of functions of a Minister of the Crown exercisable in relation to Wales (see the note at § A13.02 above), the functions under s.104 have been expressly excluded from that transfer; see the National Assembly for Wales (Transfer of Functions) Order 1999 (SI 1999/672; not reproduced in this work) art.2 and Sch.1.

The Vehicles (Charges for Release from Immobilisation Devices) Regulations 1992 (SI 1992/386; not reproduced in this work) prescribe the charge for release from an immobilisation device under s.104(4).]

Exemptions from section 104

A13.98   **105.**—(1) Subject to the following provisions of this section, section 104(1) of this Act shall not apply in relation to a vehicle found by a constable in the circumstances mentioned in that subsection if [...]—

    (a) a current disabled person's badge is displayed on the vehicle; or

   [(aa) a current recognised badge (within the meaning given by section 21A of Chronically Sick and Disabled Persons Act 1970) is displayed on the vehicle; or]

    (b) the vehicle is in a meter bay within a parking place designated by a designation order.

(2) The exemption under subsection (1)(b) above shall not apply in the case of any vehicle [found otherwise than in Greater London] if—

    (a) the meter bay in which it was found was not authorised for use as such at the time when it was left there (referred to below in this section as the time of parking); or

    (b) an initial charge was not duly paid at the time of parking; or

    (c) there has been since that time any contravention in relation to the relevant parking meter of any provision made by virtue of section 46(2)(c) of this Act; or

    (d) more than two hours have elapsed since the end of any period for which an initial charge was duly paid at the time of parking or (as the case may be) since the end of any unexpired time in respect of another vehicle available on the relevant parking meter at the time of parking.

   [(2A) The exemption under subsection (1)(b) above shall not apply in the case of any vehicle found in Greater London if the meter bay in which it was found was not authorised for use as such at the time when it was left there.]

(3) For the purposes of [subsections (2)(a) and (2A)] above, a meter bay in a parking place designated by a designation order is not authorised for use as such at any time when—

    (a) by virtue of section 49(1)(a) of this Act the parking place is treated for the purposes of sections 46 and 47 of this Act as if it were not designated by that order; or

    (b) the use of the parking place or of any part of it that consists of or includes that particular meter bay is suspended ...

(4) In relation to any vehicle found in a meter bay within a parking place designated by a designation order, references in subsection (2) above to an initial charge are references to an initial charge payable in respect of that vehicle under section 45 or 50 of this Act.

(5) In any case where section 104(1) of this Act would apply in relation to a vehicle but for subsection (1)(a) above, the person guilty of contravening the prohibition or restriction mentioned in section 104(1) is also guilty of an offence under this subsection if the conditions mentioned in subsection (6) below are met.

(6) Those conditions are that at the time when the contravention occurred—

    (a) the vehicle was not being used [in accordance with regulations under] section 21 of the Chronically Sick and Disabled Persons Act 1970 (badges for display on motor vehicles used by disabled persons); and

    (b) he was not using the vehicle in circumstances falling within section [117(1)(b)] of this Act.

[(6A) In any case where section 104(1) of this Act would apply in relation to a vehicle but for subsection (1)(aa) above, the person guilty of contravening the prohibition or restriction mentioned in section 104(1) is also guilty of an offence under this subsection if the conditions mentioned in subsection (6B) below are met.]

[(6B) Those conditions are that at the time when the contravention occurred—

    (a) the vehicle was not being used in accordance with regulations under section 21A of the Chronically Sick and Disabled Persons Act 1970 (display of non-GB badges); and

    (b) he was not using the vehicle in circumstances falling within section 117(1A)(b) of this Act.]

(7) In this section, *"meter bay"* means a parking space equipped with a parking meter; and the references in subsection (2) above to the relevant parking meter are references to the parking meter relating to the meter bay in which the vehicle in question was found.

[Section 105 is printed as amended by the Road Traffic Act 1991 ss.48, 81, 83, **A13.99**
Sch.4, para.36(1)–(3), Sch.7, para.6, and Sch.8; the Disability Discrimination Act 2005 Sch.1, Pt 2, para.43 and Sch.2.

As an exception to the transfer of functions to the National Assembly for Wales of functions of a Minister of the Crown exercisable in relation to Wales (see the note at § A13.02 above), the functions under s.105 have been expressly excluded from that transfer; see the National Assembly for Wales (Transfer of Functions) Order 1999 (SI 1999/672; not reproduced in this work) art.2 and Sch.1.]

A13.100   **106.** *[Initial experimental period for immobilisation of vehicles.]*

[Immobilisation of vehicles in London

A13.101   **106A.**—(1) Sections 104 and 105 of this Act shall extend throughout Greater London if the Secretary of State makes an order to that effect.

(2) If such an order is made, section 106 of this Act shall cease to apply in relation to Greater London when the order comes into force.

(3) *[Amends s.106 before any order under subs.(2) above takes effect.]*

(4) *[Orders to be made by statutory instruments.]*]

A13.102   *[Section 106A was inserted by the Road Traffic Act 1991 s.75.]*

Enforcement of excess parking charges

Liability of vehicle owner in respect of excess parking charge

A13.103   **107.**—(1) This section applies where—

(a) an excess charge has been incurred in pursuance of an order under sections 45 and 46 of this Act;

(b) notice of the incurring of the excess charge has been given or affixed as provided in the order; and

(c) the excess charge has not been duly paid in accordance with the order;

and in the following provisions of this Part of this Act *"the excess charge offence"* means the offence under section 47 of this Act of failing duly to pay the excess charge.

(2) Subject to the following provisions of this section —

(a) for the purposes of the institution of proceedings in respect of the excess charge offence against any person as being the owner of the vehicle at the relevant time, and

(b) in any proceedings in respect of the excess charge offence brought against any person as being the owner of the vehicle at the relevant time,

it shall be conclusively presumed (notwithstanding that that person may not be an individual) that he was the driver of the vehicle at the time and, accordingly, that acts or omissions of the driver of the vehicle at that time were his acts or omissions.

(3) Subsection (2) above shall not apply in relation to any person unless, within the period of 6 months beginning on the day on which the notice of the incurring of the excess charge was given or affixed as mentioned in subsection (1)(b) above, a notice under section 108 of this Act has been served on him—

(a) by or on behalf of the authority which is the local authority for the purposes of sections 45 and 46 of this Act in relation to the parking place concerned, or

(b) by or on behalf of the chief officer of police.

(4) If the person on whom a notice under section 108 of this Act is served in accordance with subsection (3) above was not the owner of the vehicle at the relevant time, subsection (2) above shall not apply in relation to him if he furnishes a statutory statement of ownership to that effect in compliance with the notice.

(5) The presumption in subsection (2) above shall not apply in any proceedings brought against any person as being the owner of the vehicle at the relevant time if, in those proceedings, it is proved—

    (a) that at the relevant time the vehicle was in the possession of some other person without the consent of the accused, or

    (b) that the accused was not the owner of the vehicle at the relevant time and that he has a reasonable excuse for failing to comply with the notice under section 108 of this Act served on him in accordance with subsection (3) above.

Notice in respect of excess parking

108.—(1) A notice under this section shall be in the prescribed form, shall give **A13.104** particulars of the excess charge and shall provide that, unless the excess charge is paid before the expiry of the appropriate period, the person on whom the notice is served—

    (a) is required, before the expiry of that period, to furnish to the authority or chief officer of police by or on behalf of whom the notice was served a statutory statement of ownership (as defined in Part I of Schedule 8 to this Act), and

    (b) is invited, before the expiry of that period, to furnish to that authority or chief officer of police a statutory statement of facts (as defined in Part II of that Schedule).

(2) If, in any case where—

    (a) a notice under this section has been served on any person, and

    (b) the excess charge specified in the notice is not paid within the appropriate period,

the person so served fails without reasonable excuse to comply with the notice by furnishing a statutory statement of ownership he shall be guilty of an offence.

(3) If, in compliance with or in response to a notice under this section, any person furnishes a statement which is false in a material particular, and does so recklessly or knowing it to be false in that particular, he shall be guilty of an offence.

(4) Where a notice under this section has been served on any person in respect of any excess charge—

    (a) payment of the charge by any person before the date on which proceedings are begun for the excess charge offence, or, as the case may be, for an offence under subsection (2) above in respect of a failure to comply with the notice, shall discharge the liability of that or any other person (under this or any other enactment) for the excess charge offence or, as the case may be, for the offence under subsection (2) above;

    (b) conviction of any person of the excess charge offence shall discharge the liability of any other person (under this or any other enactment) for that offence and the liability of any person for an offence under subsection (2) above in respect of a failure to comply with the notice; and

    (c) conviction of the person so served of an offence under subsection (2) above in respect of a failure to comply with the notice shall discharge the liability of any person for the excess charge offence;

but, except as provided by this subsection, nothing in section 107 of this Act or this section shall affect the liability of any person for the excess charge offence.

A13.105   *[As to the conduct of proceedings under s.108(3), see the note at § A13.02 above.]*

Modifications of sections 107 and 108 in relation to hired vehicles

A13.106   109.—(1) This section shall apply where—

    (a) a notice under section 108 of this Act has been served on a vehicle-hire firm, and

    (b) at the relevant time the vehicle in respect of which the notice was served was let to another person by the vehicle-hire firm under a hiring agreement to which this section applies.

(2) Where this section applies, it shall be a sufficient compliance with the notice served on the vehicle-hire firm if the firm furnishes to the chief officer of police or local authority by or on behalf of whom the notice was served a statement in the prescribed form, signed by or on behalf of the vehicle-hire firm, stating that at the relevant time the vehicle concerned was hired under a hiring agreement to which this section applies, together with—

    (a) a copy of that hiring agreement, and

    (b) a copy of a statement of liability in the prescribed form, signed by the hirer under that hiring agreement;

and accordingly, in relation to the vehicle-hire firm on whom the notice was served, the reference in section 108(2) of this Act to a statutory statement of ownership shall be construed as a reference to a statement under this subsection together with the documents specified in paragraphs (a) and (b) above.

(3) If, in a case where this section applies, the vehicle-hire firm has complied with the notice served on the firm by furnishing the statement and copies of the documents specified in subsection (2) above, then sections 107 and 108 of this Act shall have effect as if in those provisions—

    (a) any reference to the owner of the vehicle were a reference to the hirer under the hiring agreement, and

    (b) any reference to a statutory statement of ownership were a reference to a statutory statement of hiring.

(4) Where, in compliance with a notice under section 108 of this Act, a vehicle-hire firm has furnished copies of a hiring agreement and statement of liability as mentioned in subsection (2) above, a person authorised in that behalf by the chief officer of police or local authority to whom the documents are furnished may, at any reasonable time within 6 months after service of that notice, and on production of his authority, require the production by the firm of the originals of those documents; and if, without reasonable excuse, a vehicle-hire firm fails to produce the original of a document when required to do so under this subsection, the firm shall be treated as not having complied with the notice under section 108 of this Act.

(5) This section applies to a hiring agreement, under the terms of which the vehicle concerned is let to the hirer for a fixed period of less than 6 months

(whether or not that period is capable of extension by agreement between the parties or otherwise); and any reference in this section to the currency of the hiring agreement includes a reference to any period during which, with the consent of the vehicle-hire firm, the hirer continues in possession of the vehicle as hirer, after the expiry of the fixed period specified in the agreement, but otherwise on terms and conditions specified in it.

(6) In this section *"statement of liability"* means a statement made by the hirer under a hiring agreement to which this section applies to the effect that the hirer acknowledges that he will be liable, as the owner of the vehicle, in respect of any excess charge which, during the currency of the hiring agreement, may be incurred with respect to the vehicle in pursuance of an order under sections 45 and 46 of this Act.

(7) In this section —

    "hiring agreement" refers only to an agreement which contains such particulars as may be prescribed and does not include a hire-purchase agreement within the meaning of the Consumer Credit Act 1974, and

    "vehicle-hire firm" means any person engaged in hiring vehicles in the course of a business.

[The term "hire-purchase agreement" (see s.109(7) above) is defined by the Consumer Credit Act 1974 s.189(1), as follows: **A13.107**

    "hire-purchase agreement" means an agreement, other than a conditional sale agreement, under which—

    (a) goods are bailed ... in return for periodical payments by the person to whom they are bailed ..., and

    (b) the property in the goods will pass to that person if the terms of the agreement are complied with and one or more of the following occurs—

      (i) the exercise of an option to purchase by that person,

      (ii) the doing of any other specified act by any party to the agreement,

      (iii) the happening of any other specified event;

The following definition appears in ibid. s.189(1):

    "conditional sale agreement" means an agreement for the sale of goods or land under which the purchase price or part of it is payable by instalments, and the property in the goods or land is to remain in the seller (notwithstanding that the buyer is to be in possession of the goods or land) until such conditions as to the payment of instalments or otherwise as may be specified in the agreement are fulfilled;]

Time for bringing, and evidence in, proceedings for certain offences

110.—(1) Proceedings in England and Wales for an offence under section 108(3) of this Act may be brought within a period of six months from the date on which evidence sufficient in the opinion of the prosecutor to warrant the proceedings came to his knowledge; but no such proceedings shall be brought by virtue of this section more than 3 years after the commission of the offence. **A13.108**

(2) *[Applies to Scotland.]*

(3) For the purposes of subsections (1) and (2) above a certificate signed by or

on behalf of the prosecutor or, as the case may be, the Lord Advocate or the local authority, and stating the date on which evidence such as is mentioned in the subsection in question came to his or their knowledge, shall be conclusive evidence of that fact; and a certificate stating that matter and purporting to be so signed shall be deemed to be so signed unless the contrary is proved.

(4) Where any person is charged with the offence of failing to pay an excess charge, and the prosecutor produces to the court any of the statutory statements in Schedule 8 to this Act or a copy of a statement of liability (within the meaning of section 109 of this Act) purporting—

>   (a) to have been furnished in compliance with or in response to a notice under section 108 of this Act, and

>   (b) to have been signed by the accused,

the statement shall be presumed, unless the contrary is proved, to have been signed by the accused and shall be evidence … in the proceedings of any facts stated in it tending to show that the accused was the owner, the hirer or the driver of the vehicle concerned at a particular time.

A13.109   *[Words relating exclusively and expressly to Scotland have been omitted from s.110(4).]*

Supplementary provisions as to excess charges

A13.110   **111.**—(1) The provisions of Schedule 8 to this Act shall have effect for the purposes of sections 107 to 109 of this Act (in this section referred to as *"the specified sections"*).

(2) In the specified sections—

>   *"appropriate period"*, in relation to a notice under section 108 of this Act, means the period of 14 days from the date on which the notice is served, or such longer period as may be specified in the notice or as may be allowed by the chief officer of police or authority by or on behalf of whom the notice is served;

>   *"driver"*, in relation to an excess charge and in relation to an offence of failing duly to pay such a charge, means the person driving the vehicle at the time when it is alleged to have been left in the parking place concerned;

>   *"relevant time"*, in relation to an excess charge, means the time when the vehicle was left in the parking place concerned, notwithstanding that the period in respect of which the excess charge was incurred did not begin at that time.

(3) For the purposes of the specified sections the owner of a vehicle shall be taken to be the person by whom the vehicle is kept; and for the purpose of determining, in the course of any proceedings brought by virtue of the specified sections, who was the owner of the vehicle at any time, it shall be presumed that the owner was the person who was the registered keeper of the vehicle at that time.

(4) Notwithstanding the presumption in subsection (3) above, it shall be open to the defence in any proceedings to prove that the person who was the registered keeper of a vehicle at a particular time was not the person by whom the vehicle was kept at that time, and it shall be open to the prosecution to prove that the vehicle was kept by some other person at that time.

(5) A notice under section 108 of this Act may be served on any person—

    (a) by delivering it to him or by leaving it at his proper address, or

    (b) by sending it to him by post;

and, where the person on whom such a notice is to be served is a body corporate, it shall be duly served if it is served on the secretary or clerk of that body.

(6) For the purposes of subsection (5) above and of section 7 of the Interpretation Act 1978 (references to service by post) in its application to that subsection, the proper address of any person on whom such a notice is to be served—

    (a) shall, in the case of the secretary or clerk of a body corporate, be that of the registered or principal office of that body or the registered address of the person who is the registered keeper of the vehicle concerned at the time of service, and

    (b) shall in any other case be the last known address of the person to be served.

(7) References in this section to the person who was or is the registered keeper of a vehicle at any time are references to the person in whose name the vehicle was or is at that time registered under [the Vehicle Excise and Registration Act 1994]; and, in relation to any such person, the reference in subsection (6)(a) above to that person's registered address is a reference to the address recorded in the record kept under that Act with respect to that vehicle as being that person's address.

(8) For the purposes of sections 1(2) and 2(1) of the Magistrates' Courts Act 1980 (power to issue summons or warrant and jurisdiction to try offences), any offence under subsection (2) of section 108 of this Act shall be treated as committed at any address which at the time of service of the notice under that section to which the offence relates was the accused's proper address (in accordance with subsection (6) above) for the service of any such notice as well as at the address to which any statutory statement furnished in response to that notice is required to be returned in accordance with the notice.

[Section 111 is printed as amended by the Vehicle Excise and Registration Act **A13.111**
1994 s.63 and Sch.3, para.18(1).]

PART IX

FURTHER PROVISIONS AS TO ENFORCEMENT

General provisions

Information as to identity of driver or rider

112.—(1) This section applies to any offence under any of the foregoing provisions of this Act except—   **A13.112**

    (a) sections 43, 52, 88(7), 104, 105 and 108;

    (b) the provisions of subsection (2) or (3) of section 108 as modified by subsections (2) and (3) of section 109; and

    (c) section [35A(5)] in its application to England and Wales.

(2) Where the driver of a vehicle is alleged to be guilty of an offence to which this section applies—

    (a) the person keeping the vehicle shall give such information as to the identity of the driver as he may be required to give—

      (i) by or on behalf of a chief officer of police, or

      (ii) in the case of an offence under section [35A(1)] or against section 47 of this Act, by or on behalf of a chief officer of police or, in writing, by or on behalf of the local authority for the parking place in question; and

   (b) any other person shall, if required as mentioned in paragraph (a) above, give any information which it is in his power to give and which may lead to the identification of the driver.

(3) In subsection (2) above, references to the driver of a vehicle include references to a person riding a bicycle or tricycle (not being a motor vehicle); and—

   (a) [...]

   (b) in relation to an offence under section 61(5) of this Act, subsection (2)(a) above shall have effect as if, for subparagraphs (i) and (ii), there were substituted the words "by a notice in writing given to him by a local authority in whose area the loading area in question is situated",

and in subsection (2)(a) above, as modified by paragraph (b) of this subsection, *"local authority"* means any of the following, that is to say, a county council, ... a district council, a London borough council and the Common Council of the City of London.

(4) Except as provided by subsection (5) below, a person who fails to comply with the requirements of subsection (2)(a) above shall be guilty of an offence unless he shows to the satisfaction of the court that he did not know, and could not with reasonable diligence have ascertained, who was the driver of the vehicle or, as the case may be, the rider of the bicycle or tricycle; and a person who fails to comply with the requirements of subsection (2)(b) above shall be guilty of an offence.

(5) *[Applies to Scotland.]*

A13.113   *[Section 112 is printed as amended by the Local Government Act 1985 s.102(2) and Sch.17; the Parking Act 1989 s.4 and Sch., para.6.]*

A13.114   **113.** [...]

           114. [...]

Mishandling of parking documents and related offences

A13.115   **115.**—[(1) A person shall be guilty of an offence who, with intent to deceive—

   (a) uses, or lends to, or allows to be used by, any other person,—

      (i) any parking device or apparatus designed to be used in connection with parking devices;

      (ii) any ticket issued by a parking meter, parking device or apparatus designed to be used in connection with parking devices;

      (iii) any authorisation by way of such a certificate, other means of identification or device as is referred to in any of sections 4(2), 4(3), 7(2) and 7(3) of this Act; or

      (iv) any such permit or token as is referred to in section 46(2)(i) of this Act;

   (b) makes or has in his possession anything so closely resembling any such thing as is mentioned in paragraph (a) above as to be calculated to deceive; or

(c) *[applies to Scotland.]]*

(2) A person who knowingly makes a false statement for the purpose of procuring the grant or issue to himself or any other person of any such authorisation as is mentioned in subsection (1) above shall be guilty of an offence.

(2A) [...]

(3) *[Applies to Scotland.]*

[Section 115 is printed as amended by the Road Traffic Regulation (Parking) **A13.116** *Act 1986 s.2(2); the Deregulation (Parking Equipment) Order 1996 (SI 1996/ 1553) art.2(1)(a) and Sch. (not reproduced in this work).*

As to the conduct of proceedings under s.115(1) and (2), see the note to this Act at § A13.02 above.]

Provisions supplementary to section 115

116.—(1) If any person authorised in that behalf by or under a designation or- **A13.117** der has reasonable cause to believe that a document or article carried on a vehicle, or by the driver or person in charge of a vehicle, is a document or article in relation to which an offence has been committed under subsection (1) of section 115 of this Act (so far as that subsection relates to such authorisations as are referred to in it) or under subsection (2) of that section, he may detain that document or article, and may for that purpose require the driver or person in charge of the vehicle to deliver up the document or article; and if the driver or person in charge of the vehicle fails to comply with that requirement, he shall be guilty of an offence.

(2) When a document or article has been detained under subsection (1) above and—

    (a) at any time after the expiry of 6 months from the date when that detention began no person has been charged since that date with an offence in relation to the document or article under subsection (1) or (2) of section 115 of this Act, and

    (b) the document or article has not been returned to the person to whom the authorisation in question was issued or to the person who at that date was the driver or person in charge of the vehicle,

then, on an application made for the purpose to a magistrates' court ..., the court shall make such order respecting disposal of the document or article and award such costs ... as the justice of the case may require.

(3) Any of the following, but no other, persons shall be entitled to make an application under subsection (2) above with respect to a document or article, that is to say—

    (a) the person to whom the authorisation was issued;

    (b) the person who, at the date when the detention of the document or article began, was the driver or person in charge of the vehicle; and

    (c) the person for the time being having possession of the document or article.

[Words relating exclusively and expressly to Scotland in s.116(2) have been **A13.118** *omitted.*

As to the conduct of proceedings under s.116(1), see the note at § A13.02 above.]

Wrongful use of disabled person's badge

A13.119   117.—[(1) A person who at any time acts in contravention of, or fails to comply with, any provision of an order under this Act relating to the parking of motor vehicles is also guilty of an offence under [this subsection] if at that time—

    (a) there was displayed on the motor vehicle in question a badge [purporting to be] of a form prescribed under section 21 of the Chronically Sick and Disabled Persons Act 1970, and

    (b) he was using the vehicle in circumstances where a disabled person's concession would be available to a disabled person's vehicle,

but he shall not be guilty of an offence under [this subsection] if the badge was issued under that section and displayed in accordance with regulations made under it.]

[(1A) A person who at any time acts in contravention of, or fails to comply with, any provision of an order under this Act relating to the parking of motor vehicles is also guilty of an offence under this subsection if at that time—

    (a) there was displayed on the motor vehicle in question a badge purporting to be a recognised badge, and

    (b) he was using the vehicle in circumstances where a concession would, by virtue of section 21B of the Chronically Sick and Disabled Persons Act 1970, be available to a vehicle lawfully displaying a recognised badge,

but he shall not be guilty of an offence under this subsection if the badge was a recognised badge and displayed in accordance with regulations made under section 21A of that Act.]

    (2) [...]

    (3) In this section —

*   *   *

    "disabled person's concession" means—

      (a) an exemption from an order under this Act given by reference to disabled persons' vehicles; or

      (b) a provision made in any order under this Act for the use of a parking place by disabled persons' vehicles.

    [*"recognised badge"* has the meaning given in section 21A of the Chronically Sick and Disabled Persons Act 1970.]

A13.120   *[Section 117 is printed as amended by the Road Traffic Act 1991 ss.35(6), 83, and Sch.8; the Traffic Management Act 2004 s.94(5); the Disability Discrimination Act 2005 Sch.1, Pt 2, para.44.*

    Disabled persons' badges are in the form prescribed in the Schedule to the Disabled Persons (Badges for Motor Vehicles) (England) Regulations 2000 (SI 2000/682; not reproduced in this work) and in the Schedule to the Disabled Persons (Badges for Motor Vehicles) (Wales) Regulations 2000 (SI 2000/1786; not reproduced in this work) which were made under the Chronically Sick and Disabled Persons Act 1970 s.21 (q.v.).]

118. [...]

119. *[Applies to Scotland.]*

120., 121. [...]

PART X

GENERAL AND SUPPLEMENTARY PROVISIONS

*   *   *

[Traffic authorities

121A.—(1) The Secretary of State is the traffic authority—
>   for every highway in England and Wales for which he is the highway authority within the meaning of the Highways Act 1980, and

[(1A) Transport for London is the traffic authority for every GLA road.]

[(1AA) *[Applies to Scotland.]*

(2) In Greater London, the council of the London borough or the Common Council of the City of London are the traffic authority for all roads in the borough or, as the case may be, in the City [which are not GLA roads and] for which the Secretary of State is not the traffic authority.

(3) In England and Wales outside Greater London, the council of the county or metropolitan district are the traffic authority for all roads in the county or, as the case may be, the district for which the Secretary of State is not the traffic authority.

(4) [...]

(5) In this Act *"local traffic authority"* means a traffic authority other than
>   [(a) in relation to England and Wales,] the Secretary of State[; or]
>   [(b) *[applies to Scotland.]*

[Section 121A was inserted by the New Roads and Street Works Act 1991
s.168(1) and Sch.8, Pt II, para.70; the Greater London Authority Act 1999 s.271 (which, inter alia, inserted s.121(1A)).

Section 121A is printed as amended by the Scotland Act 1998 (Consequential Modifications) Order 2001 (SI 2001/1400) art.2 and Sch., para.1.

Section 121A(1A) as inserted by the Scotland Act 1998 (Consequential Modifications) (No.2) Order 1999 (SI 1999/1820) has been repealed by the Scotland Act 1998 (Consequential Modifications) Order 2001 (SI 2001/1400) art.2 and Schedule, para.1(1) and (4). The text of s.121A(1A) printed above is not affected.]

London borough council exercising powers so as to affect another traffic authority's roads

121B. *[Omitted.]*

Functions of GLA under this Act to be exercised by the Mayor

121C. *[Omitted.]*

*   *   *

Application of Act to Crown

A13.126   **130.**—(1) Subject to the provisions of this section and section 132 of this Act, the provisions of this Act specified in subsection (2) below shall apply to vehicles and persons in the public service of the Crown.

(2) The provisions referred to in subsection (1) above are—

     (a) sections 1 to 5, 9 [to 16C], 21 to 26, 38, 42, 45 to 51, 52 ... (3), 58 to 60, 62 to 67, 69 to 71, [76 to 90], 99, 100, 104, 105, 125 and 126;

     (b) except in relation to vehicles and persons in the armed forces of the Crown when on duty, sections 6 to 8; and

     (c) ...

(3) In relation to vehicles used for naval, military or air force purposes, while being driven by persons for the time being subject to the orders of a member of the armed forces of the Crown, the Secretary of State may by regulations vary the provisions of any statutory provision imposing a speed limit on motor vehicles; but regulations under this subsection may provide that any variation made by the regulations shall have effect subject to such conditions as may be specified in the regulations.

(4) [...]

(5) [...]

A13.127   *[Section 130 is printed as amended by the Road Traffic (Consequential Provisions) Act 1988 s.3(1) and Sch.1, Pt I; the New Roads and Street Works Act 1991 s.168(1) and Sch.8, Pt II, para.74; the Road Traffic Regulation (Special Events) Act 1994 s.3(1) and Sch., para.3; the Deregulation (Parking Equipment) Order 1996 (SI 1996/1553) art.2(1)(a) and Schedule (not reproduced in this work).*

Section 132 of this Act (to which this section is subject) makes special provision regarding certain Crown roads.

As to the effect of s.130(3) in relation to vehicles used for the purposes of a visiting force or headquarters (as defined), when being driven by a person subject to the orders of a member of such a force or headquarters, see the Visiting Forces and International Headquarters (Application of Law) Order 1999 (SI 1999/1736; not reproduced in this work) art.8(3).

As an exception to the transfer of functions to the National Assembly for Wales of functions of a Minister of the Crown exercisable in relation to Wales (see the note at § A13.02 above), the functions under s.130 have been expressly excluded from that transfer; see the National Assembly for Wales (Transfer of Functions) Order 1999 (SI 1999/672; not reproduced in this work) art.2 and Sch.1.]

*   *   *

Meaning of "motor vehicle" and other expressions relating to vehicles

A13.128   **136.**—(1) In this Act, subject to section 20 of the Chronically Sick and Disabled Persons Act 1970 (which makes special provision with respect to invalid carriages), *"motor vehicle"* means a mechanically propelled vehicle intended or adapted for use on roads and *"trailer"* means a vehicle drawn by a motor vehicle.

(2) In this Act *"motor car"* means a mechanically propelled vehicle, not be-

ing a motor cycle or an invalid carriage, which is constructed itself to carry a load or passengers and of which the weight unladen—

  (a) if it is constructed solely for the carriage of passengers and their effects, is adapted to carry not more than 7 passengers exclusive of the driver, and is fitted with tyres of such type as may be specified in regulations made by the Secretary of State, does not exceed 3050 kilograms;

  (b) if it is constructed or adapted for use for the conveyance of goods or burden of any description, does not exceed 3050 kilograms (or 3500 kilograms if the vehicle carries a container or containers for holding, for the purposes of its propulsion, any fuel which is wholly gaseous at 17.5 degrees Celsius under a pressure of 1.013 bar or plant and materials for producing such fuel); or

  (c) in a case falling within neither of the foregoing paragraphs, does not exceed 2540 kilograms.

(3) In this Act *"heavy motor car"* means a mechanically propelled vehicle, not being a motor car, which is constructed itself to carry a load or passengers and of which the weight unladen exceeds 2540 kilograms.

(4) In this Act (except for the purposes of [sections 57 and 63]) *"motor cycle"* means a mechanically propelled vehicle (not being an invalid carriage) with fewer than 4 wheels, of which the weight unladen does not exceed 410 kilograms.

(5) In this Act *"invalid carriage"* means a mechanically propelled vehicle of which the weight unladen does not exceed 254 kilograms and which is specially designed and constructed, and not merely adapted, for the use of a person suffering from some physical default or disability and is used solely by such a person.

(6) In this Act *"motor tractor"* means a mechanically propelled vehicle which is not constructed itself to carry a load, other than excepted articles, and of which the weight unladen does not exceed 7370 kilograms.

(7) In this Act *"light locomotive"* and *"heavy locomotive"* mean a mechanically propelled vehicle which is not constructed itself to carry a load, other than excepted articles, and of which the weight unladen—

  (a) in the case of a light locomotive, exceeds 7370 but does not exceed 11690 kilograms, and

  (b) in the case of a heavy locomotive, exceeds 11690 kilograms.

(8) In subsections (6) and (7) above *"excepted articles"* means any of the following, that is to say, water, fuel, accumulators and other equipment used for the purpose of propulsion, loose tools and loose equipment.

[Section 136 is printed as amended by the Transport Act 2000 s.271(1) and (3).   **A13.129**

As an exception to the transfer of functions to the National Assembly for Wales of functions of a Minister of the Crown exercisable in relation to Wales (see the note at § A13.02 above), the functions under s.136 have been expressly excluded from that transfer; see the National Assembly for Wales (Transfer of Functions) Order 1999 (SI 1999/672; not reproduced in this work) art.2 and Sch.1.]

Supplementary provisions relating to section 136

137.—(1) A side-car attached to a motor vehicle shall, if it complies with such   **A13.130** conditions as may be specified in regulations made by the Secretary of State, be regarded as forming part of the vehicle to which it is attached and not as being a trailer.

(2) For the purposes of section 136 of this Act, in a case where a motor vehicle is so constructed that a trailer may by partial superimposition be attached to the vehicle in such a manner as to cause a substantial part of the weight of the trailer to be borne by the vehicle, that vehicle shall be deemed to be a vehicle itself constructed to carry a load.

(3) For the purposes of that section, in the case of a motor vehicle fitted with a crane, dynamo, welding plant or other special appliance or apparatus which is a permanent or essentially permanent fixture, the appliance or apparatus shall not be deemed to constitute a load or goods or burden of any description, but shall be deemed to form part of the vehicle.

(4) The Secretary of State may by regulations vary any of the maximum or minimum weights specified in section 136 of this Act; and such regulations may have effect—

    (a) either generally or in the case of vehicles of any class specified in the regulations, and

    (b) either for the purposes of this Act and of all regulations made under it or for such of those purposes as may be so specified.

(5) Nothing in section 86 of this Act shall be construed as limiting the powers conferred by subsection (4) above.

A13.131　　*[As an exception to the transfer of functions to the National Assembly for Wales of functions of a Minister of the Crown exercisable in relation to Wales (see the note at § A13.02 above), the functions under s.137 have been expressly excluded from that transfer; see the National Assembly for Wales (Transfer of Functions) Order 1999 (SI 1999/672; not reproduced in this work) art.2 and Sch.1.]*

Meaning of "heavy commercial vehicle"

A13.132　　138.—(1) Subject to subsections (4) to (7) below, in this Act *"heavy commercial vehicle"* means any goods vehicle which has an operating weight exceeding 7.5 tonnes.

(2) The operating weight of a goods vehicle for the purposes of this section is—

    (a) in the case of a motor vehicle not drawing a trailer, or in the case of a trailer, its maximum laden weight;

    (b) in the case of an articulated vehicle, its maximum laden weight (if it has one) and otherwise the aggregate maximum laden weight of all the individual vehicles forming part of that articulated vehicle; and

    (c) in the case of a motor vehicle (other than an articulated vehicle) drawing one or more trailers, the aggregate maximum laden weight of the motor vehicle and the trailer or trailers attached to it.

(3) In this section —

"articulated vehicle" means a motor vehicle with a trailer so attached to it as to be partially superimposed upon it;

"goods vehicle" means a motor vehicle constructed or adapted for use for the carriage of goods or burden of any description, or a trailer so constructed or adapted;

"trailer" means any vehicle other than a motor vehicle;

and references to the maximum laden weight of a vehicle are references to the total laden weight which must not be exceeded in the case of that vehicle if it is to be used in Great Britain without contravening any regulations for the time being in force under [section 41 of the Road Traffic Act 1988] (construction and use regulations).

(4) The Secretary of State may by regulations amend subsections (1) and (2) above (whether as originally enacted or as previously amended under this subsection)—

    (a) by substituting weights of a different description for any of the weights there mentioned, or

    (b) in the case of subsection (1) above, by substituting a weight of a different description or amount, or a weight different both in description and amount, for the weight there mentioned.

(5) Different regulations may be made under subsection (4) above for the purposes of different provisions of this Act and as respects different classes of vehicles or as respects the same class of vehicles in different circumstances and as respects different times of the day or night and as respects roads in different localities.

(6) Regulations made under subsection (4) above shall not so amend subsection (1) above that there is any case in which a goods vehicle whose operating weight (ascertained in accordance with subsection (2) above as originally enacted) does not exceed 7.5 tonnes is a heavy commercial vehicle for any of the purposes of this Act.

(7), (8) [...]

[Section 138 is printed as amended by the Road Traffic (Consequential Provisions) Act 1988 s.4 and Sch.3, para.25(8) and by the Statute Law (Repeals) Act 1993 s.1(1) and Sch. 1, Pt XV, group 1.   **A13.133**

As an exception to the transfer of functions to the National Assembly for Wales of functions of a Minister of the Crown exercisable in relation to Wales (see the note at § A13.02 above), the functions under s.138 have been expressly excluded from that transfer; see the National Assembly for Wales (Transfer of Functions) Order 1999 (SI 1999/672; not reproduced in this work) art.2 and Sch.1.]

Hovercraft

139. *[Omitted.]*   **A13.134**

Certain vehicles not to be treated as motor vehicles

140.—(1) For the purposes of this Act —   **A13.135**

    (a) a mechanically propelled vehicle which is an implement for cutting grass, is controlled by a pedestrian and is not capable of being used or adapted for any other purpose;

    (b) any other mechanically propelled vehicle controlled by a pedestrian which may be specified by regulations made by the Secretary of State for the purposes of this section and of [section 189 of the Road Traffic Act 1988]; and

    (c) an electrically assisted pedal cycle of such class as may be prescribed by regulations so made, shall be treated as not being a motor vehicle.

(2) In this section *"controlled by a pedestrian"* means that the vehicle either—

      (a) is constructed or adapted for use only under such control, or

      (b) is constructed or adapted for use either under such control or under the control of a person carried on it, but is not for the time being in use under, or proceeding under, the control of a person carried on it.

A13.136   *[Section 140 is printed as amended by the Road Traffic (Consequential Provisions) Act 1988 s.4 and Sch.3, para.25(9).*

As an exception to the transfer of functions to the National Assembly for Wales of functions of a Minister of the Crown exercisable in relation to Wales (see the note at § A13.02 above), the functions under s.140 have been expressly excluded from that transfer; see the National Assembly for Wales (Transfer of Functions) Order 1999 (SI 1999/672; not reproduced in this work) art.2 and Sch.1.]

A13.137   **141. [...]**

[Tramcars and trolley vehicles: regulations

A13.138   **141A.**—(1) The Secretary of State may by regulations provide that such of the provisions mentioned in subsection (2) below as are specified in the regulations shall not apply, or shall apply with modifications—

      (a) to all tramcars or to tramcars of any specified class, or

      (b) to all trolley vehicles or to trolley vehicles of any specified class.

(2) The provisions referred to in subsection (1) above are the provisions of sections 1 to 14, [16A to 16C,] 18 and 81 to 89 of this Act.

(3) Regulations under this section —

      (a) may make different provision for different cases,

      (b) may include such transitional provisions as appear to the Secretary of State to be necessary or expedient, and

      (c) may make such amendments to any special Act as appear to the Secretary of State to be necessary or expedient in consequence of the regulations or in consequence of the application to any tramcars or trolley vehicles of any of the provisions mentioned in subsection (2) above.

(4) In this section —

    "special Act" means a local Act of Parliament passed before the commencement of this section which authorises or regulates the use of tramcars or trolley vehicles;

    "tramcar" includes any carriage used on any road by virtue of an order under the Light Railways Act 1896; and

    "trolley vehicle" means a mechanically propelled vehicle adapted for use on roads without rails under power transmitted to it from some external source (whether or not there is in addition a source of power on board the vehicle).]

A13.139   *[Section 141A was inserted by the Road Traffic Act 1991, s.46(1), and is printed as subsequently amended by the Road Traffic Regulation (Special Events) Act 1994 s.3(1) and Sch., para.4.*

As an exception to the transfer of functions to the National Assembly for Wales of functions of a Minister of the Crown exercisable in relation to Wales (see the note at § A13.02 above), the functions under s.141A have been expressly excluded from that transfer; see the National Assembly for Wales (Transfer of Functions) Order 1999 (SI 1999/672; not reproduced in this work) art.2 and Sch.1.]

General interpretation of Act

142.—(1) In this Act, except where the context otherwise requires, the follow-   **A13.140**
ing expressions have the meanings hereby assigned to them respectively, that is
to say—

> *"bridge authority"* means the authority or person responsible for the main-
> tenance of a bridge;

> *"bridleway"* means a way over which the public have the following, but no
> other, rights of way, that is to say, a right of way on foot and a right
> of way on horseback or leading a horse, with or without a right to
> drive animals of any description along the way;

> [*"credit card"* and *"debit card"* have the meanings given by section
> 35A(6) [*q.v.*] of this Act;]

> *"designation order"* means an order under section 45 of this Act (includ-
> ing any order so made by virtue of section 50(1) of this Act) and
> *"designated parking place"* means a parking place designated by a
> designation order;

> *"disabled person's badge"* means any badge issued, or having effect as if
> issued, under any regulations for the time being in force under sec-
> tion 21 of the Chronically Sick and Disabled Persons Act 1970;

> *"disabled person's vehicle"* means a vehicle lawfully displaying a disabled
> person's badge;

> *"driver"* where a separate person acts as steersman of a motor vehicle,
> includes that person as well as any other person engaged in the driv-
> ing of the vehicle, and *"drive"* and *"driving"* shall be construed ac-
> cordingly;

> *"excess charge"* has the meaning assigned to it by section 46(1) of this Act
> [*q.v.*];

> *"experimental traffic order"* has the meaning assigned to it by section 9(1)
> of this Act;

> except in section 71(2) of this Act, *"footpath"* means a way over which the
> public has a right of way on foot only;

> [*"GLA road"* (subject to section (4) below) has the same meaning as in the
> Highways Act 1980 (see sections 329(1) and 14D(1) of that Act);]

> [*"GLA side road"* shall be construed in accordance with section 124A(9)
> of this Act;]

*   *   *

> *"initial charge"* has the meaning assigned to it by section 46(1) of this Act
> [*q.v.*];

*   *   *

> *"magistrates' court"* [has the same meaning] as in the Magistrates' Courts
> Act 1980 [*q.v.*];

"the Ministers" means the Secretaries of State charged with general responsibility under this Act in relation to England, Wales and Scotland respectively;

[*"off-street parking accommodation"* means parking accommodation for motor vehicles off the highway ...;]

subject to section 111(3) and (4) of, and paragraph 11(2) and (3) of Schedule 12 to, this Act, *"owner"*, in relation to a vehicle which is subject to a hiring agreement or hire-purchase agreement, means the person in possession of the vehicle under that agreement;

"parking device" has the meaning assigned to it by [section 35(3B) [*q.v.*] or, as the case may be,] section 51(4) [*q.v.*] of this Act;

"parking meter" has the meaning assigned to it by section 46(2)(a) of this Act [*q.v.*];

"prescribed" means prescribed by regulations made by the Secretary of State;

"public service vehicle" [has the same meaning] as in the Public Passenger Vehicles Act 1981 [*q.v.*];

[*"restricted byway"* has the same meaning as in Part 2 of the Countryside and Rights of Way Act 2000;]

[*"road"* —

    (a) in England and Wales, means any length of highway or of any other road to which the public has access, and includes bridges over which a road passes, and

    (b) *[applies to Scotland.]*;]

[*"special road"*, in England and Wales, has the same meaning as in the Highways Act 1980 ...;]

"statutory", in relation to any prohibition, restriction, requirement or provision, means contained in, or having effect under, any enactment (including any enactment contained in this Act) ;

"street parking place" and *"off-street parking place"* refer respectively to parking places on land which does, and on land which does not, form part of a road;

[*"traffic authority"* and *"local traffic authority"* have the meanings given by section 121A of this Act;]

"traffic sign" has the meaning assigned to it by section 64(1) of this Act [*q.v.*]; and

"traffic regulation order" has the meaning assigned to it by section 1 of this Act.

[*"trunk road"* has the same meaning as in the Highways Act 1980 (see section 329(1) of that Act) [*q.v.*]]

[(1A) In this Act —

    (a) any reference to a county shall be construed in relation to Wales as including a reference to a county borough;

    (b) any reference to a county council shall be construed in relation to Wales as including a reference to a county borough council; and

    (c) section 17(4) and (5) of the Local Government (Wales) Act 1994 (references to counties and districts to be construed generally in relation to Wales as references to counties and county boroughs) shall not apply.]

(2) Any reference in this Act to a tricycle shall be construed as including a reference to a cycle which is not a motor vehicle and has 4 or more wheels.

(3) References in this Act to a class of vehicles or traffic (other than the references in section 17) shall be construed as references to a class defined or described by reference to any characteristics of the vehicles or traffic or to any other circumstances whatsoever.

[(4) Any reference in this Act to a GLA road includes a reference to a GLA side road.]

[Section 142 is printed as amended by the Roads (Scotland) Act 1984 s.156(1) **A13.141** *and (3), Sch.9, para.93(44), and Sch.11; the Local Government Act 1985 ss.8(1) and 102(2), Sch.5, para.4(37), and Sch.17; the Transport Act 1985 s.1(3) and Sch.1, para.15(4); the Parking Act 1989 s.4 and Sch., para.8; the New Roads and Street Works Act 1991 s.168(1) and Sch.8, Pt II, para.78; the Local Government (Wales) Act 1994 s.22(1) and Sch.7, para.38(10); the Access to Justice Act 1999 s.76(2) and Sch.10, para.38; the Greater London Authority Act 1999 s.294(1), (3) and (4); the Restricted Byways (Application and Consequential Amendment of Provisions) Regulations 2006 (SI 2006/1177) Sch.*

Words relating expressly and exclusively to Scotland have been omitted from the definitions.]

Saving for law of nuisance

143. *[Omitted.]*   **A13.142**

Transitional provisions and savings

144.—(1) The transitional provisions and savings in Schedule 10 to this Act   **A13.143** shall have effect.

(2) The enactment in this Act of the provisions specified in the first column of Schedule 11 to this Act (being re-enactments, with or without modifications, of provisions contained in the instruments specified in the corresponding entries in the second column of that Schedule, which were instruments made in the exercise of powers conferred by Acts of Parliament) shall be without prejudice to the validity of those re-enacted provisions; and any question as to their validity shall be determined as if the re-enacted provisions were contained in instruments made in the exercise of those powers.

*   *   *

Section 86   SCHEDULE 6

SPEED LIMITS FOR VEHICLES OF CERTAIN CLASSES

PART I

VEHICLES FITTED WITH PNEUMATIC TYRES ON ALL WHEELS

(see application provisions below the following Table)   **A13.144**

TABLE

1	2	3		
Item No	Class of Vehicle	Maximum speed (in miles per hour) while vehicle is being driven on:		
		(a) Motorway	(b) Dual carriageway road not being a motorway	(c) Other road
1	A passenger vehicle, motor caravan or dual-purpose vehicle not drawing a trailer being a vehicle with an unladen weight exceeding 3.05 tonnes or adapted to carry more than 8 passengers:			
	(i) if not exceeding 12 metres in overall length	70	60	50
	(ii) if exceeding 12 metres in overall length	60	60	50
2	An invalid carriage	not applicable	20	20
3	A passenger vehicle, motor caravan, car-derived van or dual-purpose vehicle drawing one trailer	[60]	[60]	50
4	A passenger vehicle, motor caravan, car-derived van or dual-purpose vehicle drawing more than one trailer	40	20	20
5	(1) A goods vehicle having a maximum laden weight not exceeding 7.5 tonnes and which is not— (a) an articulated vehicle, or (b) drawing a trailer, or (c) a car-derived van	70	60	50
	(2) A goods vehicle which is— (a) (i) an articulated vehicle having a maximum laden weight not exceeding 7.5 tonnes, or (ii) a motor vehicle, other than a car-derived van, which is drawing one trailer where the aggregate maximum laden weight of the motor vehicle and the trailer does not exceed 7.5 tonnes	60	[60]	50

1	2	3		
Item No	Class of Vehicle	Maximum speed (in miles per hour) while vehicle is being driven on:		
		(a) Motorway	(b) Dual car-riageway road not being a motorway	(c) Other road
	(b) (i) an articulated vehicle having a maximum laden weight exceeding 7.5 tonnes, (ii) a motor vehicle having a maximum laden weight exceeding 7.5 tonnes and not drawing a trailer, or (iii) a motor vehicle drawing one trailer where the aggregate maximum laden weight of the motor vehicle and the trailer exceeds 7.5 tonnes	60	50	40
	(c) a motor vehicle, other than a car-derived van, drawing more than one trailer	40	20	20
6	A motor tractor (other than an industrial tractor), a light locomotive or a heavy locomotive—			
	(a) if the provisions about springs and wings as specified in paragraph 3 of Part IV of this Schedule are complied with and the vehicle is not drawing a trailer, or if those provisions are complied with and the vehicle is drawing one trailer which also complies with those provisions	40	30	30
	(b) in any other case	20	20	20
7	A works truck	18	18	18
8	An industrial tractor	not applicable	18	18
[9	An agricultural motor vehicle	40	40	40]

Application

This Part applies only to motor vehicles, not being track-laying vehicles, every wheel of which is fitted with a pneumatic tyre and to such vehicles drawing one or more trailers, not being track-laying vehicles, every wheel of which is fitted with a pneumatic tyre.   **A13.145**

[*Schedule 6, Pt I, is printed as amended by the Motor Vehicles (Variation of Speed Limits) Regulations 1986 (SI 1986/1175; not reproduced in this work).*   **A13.146**

As an exception to the transfer of functions to the National Assembly for Wales of functions of a Minister of the Crown exercisable in relation to Wales (see the

note at § A13.02 above), the functions under Sch.6 as a whole have been expressly
excluded from that transfer; see the National Assembly for Wales (Transfer of
Functions) Order 1999 (SI 1999/672; not reproduced in this work) art.2 and
Sch.1.]

PART II

VEHICLES (OTHER THAN TRACK-LAYING VEHICLES) NOT FITTED WITH PNEUMATIC TYRES ON ALL
WHEELS

A13.147   (see application provisions below the following Table)

TABLE

1	2	3
Item No	*Class of Vehicle*	*Maximum speed (in miles per hour) while vehicle is being driven on a road*
1	A motor vehicle, or in the case of a motor vehicle drawing one or more trailers, the combination, where— (a) every wheel is fitted with a resilient tyre, or (b) at least one wheel is fitted with a resilient tyre and every wheel which is not fitted with a resilient tyre is fitted with a pneumatic tyre	20
2	A motor vehicle, or in the case of a motor vehicle drawing one or more trailers, the combination, where any wheel is not fitted with either a pneumatic tyre or a resilient tyre	5

Application

A13.148   This Part does not apply to—

    (a) a motor vehicle which is a track-laying vehicle; or

    (b) a motor vehicle which is not a track-laying vehicle but which is drawing one or more trailers any one of which is a track-laying vehicle.

A13.149   *[See the note to Pt I of this Schedule.]*

PART III

TRACK-LAYING VEHICLES

A13.150   (see application provisions below the following Table)

TABLE

1	2	3
Item No	*Class of Vehicle*	*Maximum speed (in miles per hour) while vehicle is being driven on a road*
1	A motor vehicle, being a track-laying vehicle which is fitted with— (a) springs between its frame and its weight-carrying rollers, and (b) resilient material between the run of its weight-carrying rollers and the surface of the road, and which is not drawing a trailer	20
2	A vehicle specified in item 1 above drawing one or more trailers each one of which is either— (a) a track-laying vehicle fitted with springs and resilient material as mentioned in that item, or (b) not a track-laying vehicle and each wheel of which is fitted with either a pneumatic tyre or a resilient tyre	20
3	A vehicle specified in item 1 above drawing one or more trailers any one of which is either— (a) a track-laying vehicle not fitted with springs and resilient material as mentioned in that item, or (b) not a track-laying vehicle and at least one wheel of which is not fitted with either a pneumatic tyre or a resilient tyre	5
4	A motor vehicle being a track-laying vehicle which is not fitted with springs and resilient material as mentioned in item 1 above, whether drawing a trailer or not	5
5	A motor vehicle not being a track-laying vehicle, which is drawing one or more trailers any one or more of which is a track-laying vehicle— (a) if every wheel of the motor vehicle and of any non-track-laying trailer is fitted with a pneumatic tyre or with a resilient tyre, and every trailer which is a track-laying vehicle is fitted with springs and resilient material as mentioned in item 1 (b) in any other case	20 5

Application

This Part applies to—

    (a) a motor vehicle which is a track-laying vehicle, and

    (b) a motor vehicle of any description which is drawing one or more trailers any one or more of which is a track-laying vehicle.

[See the note to Pt II of this Schedule.]

A13.151

A13.152

PART IV

APPLICATION AND INTERPRETATION

A13.153   **1.** This Schedule does not apply to a vehicle which is being used for the purpose of experiments or trials under section 6 of the Road Improvement Act 1925 or section 283 of the Highways Act 1980.

A13.154   **2.** In this Schedule —

> [*"agricultural motor vehicle"*,] *"articulated vehicle"*, *"dual-purpose vehicle"*, *"industrial tractor"*, *"passenger vehicle"*, *"pneumatic tyre"*, *"track-laying"*, *"wheel"* and *"works truck"* have the same meanings as are respectively given to those expressions in [Regulation 3(2) of the Road Vehicles (Construction and Use) Regulations 1986] [*SI 1986/1078 (q.v.)*];

> *"car-derived van"* means a goods vehicle which is constructed or adapted as a derivative of a passenger vehicle and which has a maximum laden weight not exceeding 2 tonnes;

> *"construction and use requirements"* has the same meaning as in [section 41(7) of the Road Traffic Act 1988];

> *"dual-carriageway road"* means a road part of which consists of a central reservation to separate a carriageway to be used by vehicles proceeding in one direction from a carriageway to be used by vehicles proceeding in the opposite direction;

> *"goods vehicle"* has the same meaning as in [section 192(1) of the Road Traffic Act 1988];

> *"maximum laden weight"* in relation to a vehicle or a combination of vehicles means—

>> (a) in the case of a vehicle, or combination of vehicles, in respect of which a gross weight not to be exceeded in Great Britain is specified in construction and use requirements, that weight;

>> (b) in the case of any vehicle, or combination of vehicles, in respect of which no such weight is specified in construction and use requirements, the weight which the vehicle, or combination of vehicles, is designed or adapted not to exceed when in normal use and travelling on a road laden;

> *"motor caravan"* has the same meaning as in [Regulation 2(1) of the Motor Vehicles (Type Approval) (Great Britain) Regulations 1984] [*SI 1984/981*];

> *"motorway"* has the same meaning as in Regulation 3(1) of the Motorways Traffic (England and Wales) Regulations 1982 [*SI 1982/1163 (q.v.)*], as regards England and Wales …; and

> *"resilient tyre"* means a tyre, not being a pneumatic tyre, which is soft or elastic.

A13.155   **3.** The specification as regards springs and wings mentioned in item 6 of Part I of this Schedule is that the vehicle—

> (i) is equipped with suitable and sufficient springs between each wheel and the frame of the vehicle, and

> (ii) unless adequate protection is afforded by the body of the vehicle, is provided with wings or other similar fittings to catch, so far as practicable, mud or water thrown up by the rotation of the wheels.

A13.156   **4.** A vehicle falling in two or more classes specified in Part I, II or III of this Schedule shall be treated as falling within the class for which the lower or lowest speed limit is specified.

A13.157   *[Schedule 6, Pt IV, is printed as amended by the Interpretation Act 1978 ss.17(2)(a) and 23; the Motor Vehicles (Variation of Speed Limits) Regulations*

1986 (SI 1986/1175; not reproduced in this work); the Road Traffic (Consequential Provisions) Act 1988 s.4 and Sch.3, para.25(10).

Words in the definition of "motorway" relating expressly and exclusively to Scotland have been omitted.

See also s.144(2) above and the note to Pt I of this Schedule.]

SCHEDULE 7

[...]   A13.158

Section 111   ### SCHEDULE 8

STATUTORY STATEMENTS (EXCESS CHARGES)

PART I

STATUTORY STATEMENT OF OWNERSHIP OR HIRING

1. For the purposes of the specified sections, a statutory statement of ownership is a   A13.159
statement in the prescribed form, signed by the person furnishing it and stating—

(a) whether he was the owner of the vehicle at the relevant time; and

(b) if he was not the owner of the vehicle at the relevant time, whether he ceased to be the owner before, or became the owner after, the relevant time, and, if the information is in his possession, the name and address of the person to whom, and the date on which, he disposed of the vehicle or, as the case may be, the name and address of the person from whom, and the date on which, he acquired it.

2. For the purposes of the specified sections, a statutory statement of hiring is a state-   A13.160
ment in the prescribed form, signed by the person furnishing it, being the person by whom a statement of liability was signed and stating—

(a) where at the relevant time the vehicle was let to him under the hiring agreement to which the statement of liability refers; and

(b) if it was not, the date on which he returned the vehicle to the possession of the vehicle-hire firm concerned.

PART II

STATUTORY STATEMENT OF FACTS

[**3.** For the purposes of the specified sections, a statutory statement of facts is a statement   A13.161
which is in the prescribed form and which either—

(a) states that the person furnishing it was the driver of the vehicle at the relevant time and is signed by him; or

(b) states that the person was not the driver of the vehicle at the relevant time, states the name and address at the time the statement is furnished of the person who was the driver of the vehicle at the relevant time and is signed both by the person furnishing it and by the person stated to be the driver of the vehicle at the relevant time.]

*[Paragraph 3 of Sch.8 is printed as substituted by the Statute Law (Repeals)   A13.162
Act 2004 s.1(2) and Sch.2, para.16.]*

PART III

INTERPRETATION

4. In this Schedule *"the specified sections"* has the meaning assigned to it by subsection   A13.163
(1) of section 111 of this Act.

5. Subsections (2) to (4) of that section shall have effect for the purposes of Parts I and II of this Schedule as they have effect for the purposes of the specified sections.

6. In paragraph 2 above *"statement of liability"*, *"hiring agreement"* and *"vehicle-hire firm"* have the same meanings as in section 109 of this Act.

SCHEDULE 9

SPECIAL PROVISIONS AS TO CERTAIN ORDERS

A13.164   *[Omitted.]*

SCHEDULE 10

TRANSITIONAL PROVISIONS AND SAVINGS

*   *   *

Pedestrian crossings

A13.165   **9.**—(1) *[Omitted.]*

(2) Section 25(6) of this Act shall apply in relation to a crossing established, or having effect as if established—

     (a) by a local authority under section 21 of the 1967 Act (whether as that section had effect at any time before the commencement of the said Act of 1980 or as it had effect by virtue of that Act), or

     (b) by a Minister under section 22 of the 1967 Act,

as it applies in relation to a crossing established by a local authority under section 23 or by the Secretary of State under section 24 of this Act.

*   *   *

Speed limits

A13.166   **14.**—(1) A direction in an order made under section 1 of the Road Traffic Act 1934 that a length of road is to be deemed to be, or not to be, a road in a built-up area, if—

     (a) by virtue of paragraph 10 of Schedule 8 to the 1967 Act it had effect as a direction that that length of road was to become, or (as the case may be) was to cease to be, a restricted road for the purposes of section 71 of that Act, and

     (b) the direction continues so to have effect immediately before the commencement of this Act,

shall have the like effect for the purposes of section 81 of this Act [*q.v.*].

(2) Any reference in any provision of an Act, or of any instrument (other than such an order as is mentioned in sub-paragraph (1) above) made under an enactment repealed by the Road Traffic Act 1960, to a road in a built-up area, if the provision is in force immediately before the commencement of this Act, shall be construed as a reference to a restricted road for the purposes of section 81 of this Act.

A13.167   **15.** Any limit of speed which was in force on 1st November 1962 by virtue of any direction, order or regulation given or made by an authority under section 19(2), 26 or 34 of the Road Traffic Act 1960, if—

     (a) by virtue of paragraph 12 of Schedule 8 to the 1967 Act it was deemed to have been imposed by an order made by that authority under section 74(1) of the 1967 Act, and

     (b) it continues to be in force immediately before the commencement of this Act,

shall be deemed to have been imposed by an order made by that authority under section 84(1) of this Act and may be revoked or varied accordingly.

A13.168   **16.**—(1) This paragraph applies to any road which—

     (a) would have become a restricted road for the purposes of section 71 of the 1967 Act on 1st November 1982 as a result of the repeal of section 72(2) of the 1967 Act by section 61 of the Transport Act 1982; but

(b) by reason of section 61(2) of that Act was taken to have ceased to be a restricted road before that day by virtue of a direction duly given under section 72(3) of the 1967 Act and still in force at the beginning of that day; and

(c) did not become a restricted road at any time between the beginning of that day and the commencement of this Act.

(2) At the commencement of this Act, any road to which this paragraph applies shall be treated as if it were the subject of a direction duly given under section 82(2)(a) of this Act [*q.v.*].

(3) Nothing in sub-paragraph (2) above prevents a direction under section 82(2)(b) of this Act being given in respect of any road to which this paragraph applies.

*   *   *

Statutory statement of facts

20. [...]   **A13.169**

[Paragraph 20 of Sch.10 was repealed by the Statute Law (Repeals) Act 2004 s.1(1) and Sch.1, Pt 14.]

SCHEDULE 11

PROVISIONS OF THIS ACT AND INSTRUMENTS REFERRED TO IN SECTION 144(2)

A13.170

	Provisions of Act	*Instruments*
1.	Sections 99 to 102 and 103(3).	The Removal and Disposal of Vehicles (Alteration of Enactments) Order 1967 (S.I. 1967 No.1900).
2.	Schedule 6.	The Motor Vehicles (Variation of Speed Limits) Regulations 1984 (S.I. 1984 No.325).

The Police and Criminal Evidence Act 1984

(1984 c.60)

A14.01 *An Act to make further provision in relation to the powers and duties of the police ...*

[31st October 1984]

ARRANGEMENT OF SECTIONS

PART I

POWERS TO STOP AND SEARCH

Power of constable to stop and search persons, vehicles, etc.

A14.02   **1.**—(1) A constable may exercise any power conferred by this section —

(a) in any place to which at the time when he proposes to exercise the power the public or any section of the public has access, on payment or otherwise, as of right or by virtue of express or implied permission; or

(b) in any other place to which people have ready access at the time when he proposes to exercise the power but which is not a dwelling.

(2) Subject to subsections (3) to (5) below, a constable—

(a) may search—

(i) any person or vehicle;

(ii) anything which is in or on a vehicle,

for stolen or prohibited articles[, any article to which subsection (8A) below applies or any firework to which subsection (8B) below applies]; and

(b) may detain a person or vehicle for the purpose of such a search.

(3) This section does not give a constable power to search a person or vehicle or anything in or on a vehicle unless he has reasonable grounds for suspecting that he will find stolen or prohibited articles[, any article to which subsection (8A) below applies or any firework to which subsection (8B) below applies].

(4) *[Omitted.]*

(5) If a vehicle is in a garden or yard occupied with and used for the purposes of a dwelling or on other land so occupied and used, a constable may not search the vehicle or anything in or on it in the exercise of the power conferred by this section unless he has reasonable grounds for believing—

(a) that the person in charge of the vehicle does not reside in the dwelling; and

(b) that the vehicle is not in the place in question with the express or implied permission of a person who resides in the dwelling.

(6) If in the course of such a search a constable discovers an article which he has reasonable grounds for suspecting to be a stolen or prohibited article[, an article to which subsection (8A) below applies or a firework to which subsection (8B) below applies], he may seize it.

(7) An article is prohibited for the purposes of this Part of this Act if it is—

(a) an offensive weapon; or

(b) an article—

(i) made or adapted for use in the course of or in connection with an offence to which this sub-paragraph applies; or

(ii) intended by the person having it with him for such use by him or by some other person.

(8) The offences to which subsection (7)(b)(i) above applies are—

(a) burglary;

(b) theft;

(c) offences under section 12 of the Theft Act 1968 (taking motor vehicle or other conveyance without authority); [...]

[(d) fraud (contrary to section 1 of the Fraud Act 2006)] [; and

(e) offences under section 1 of the Criminal Damage Act 1971 (destroying or damaging property).]

[(8A) *[Applies to offence of having article with blade or point in public place.]*]

[(8B) *[Applies to a contravention of a prohibition imposed by fireworks regulations.]*]

[(8C) *[Defines "fireworks" and "fireworks regulations".]*]

(9) In this Part of this Act *"offensive weapon"* means any article—

(a) made or adapted for use for causing injury to persons; or

(b) intended by the person having it with him for such use by him or by some other person.

[Section 1 is printed as amended by the Criminal Justice Act 1988 s.140(1); **A14.03** *the Criminal Justice Act 2003 ss.1(2) and 332, and Sch.37, Pt 1; the Serious Organised Crime and Police Act 2005 s.115; the Fraud Act 2006 s.14(1) and Sch.1, para.21.*

Guidance on the exercise of powers requiring reasonable grounds of suspicion (e.g. as in s.1(3)) is given in the code of practice for the exercise by police officers of statutory powers to stop and search (Code A (2011) under this Act), paras 2.2–2.11. These paragraphs read as follows (they are reproduced by kind permission of the Controller of HMSO):

2.2   Reasonable grounds for suspicion depend on the circumstances in each case. There must be an objective basis for that suspicion based on facts, information, and/or intelligence which are relevant to the likelihood of finding an article of a certain kind or, in the case of searches under section 43 of the Terrorism Act 2000, to the likelihood that the person is a terrorist. Reasonable suspicion can never be supported on the basis of personal factors. It must rely on intelligence or information about, or some specific behaviour by, the person concerned. For example, unless the police have a description of a suspect, a person's physical appearance (including any of the "protected characteristics" set out in the Equality Act 2010 ...), or the fact that the person is known to have a previous conviction, cannot be used alone or in combination with each other, or in combination with any other factor, as the reason for searching that person. Reasonable suspicion cannot be based on generalisations or stereotypical images of certain groups or categories of people as more likely to be involved in criminal activity.

2.3   Reasonable suspicion may also exist without specific information or intelligence and on the basis of the behaviour of a person. For example, if an officer encounters someone on the street at night who is obviously trying to hide something, the officer may (depending on the other surrounding circumstances) base such suspicion on the fact that this kind of behaviour is often linked to stolen or prohibited articles being carried. Similarly, for the purposes of section 43 of the Terrorism Act 2000, suspicion that a person is a terrorist may arise from the person's behaviour at or near a location which has been identified as a potential target for terrorists.

2.4   However, reasonable suspicion should normally be linked to accurate and current intelligence or information, such as information describing an article being carried, a suspected offender, or a person who has been seen carrying a type of article known to have been stolen recently from premises in the area. Searches based on accurate and current intelligence or information are more likely to be effective. Targeting searches in a particular area at specified crime problems increases their effectiveness and minimises inconvenience to law-abiding members of the public. It also helps in justifying the use of searches both to those who are searched and to the public. This does not however prevent stop and search powers being exercised in other locations where such powers may be exercised and reasonable suspicion exists.

2.5   Searches are more likely to be effective, legitimate, and secure public confidence when reasonable suspicion is based on a range of factors. The overall use of these powers is more likely to be effective when up to date and accurate intelligence or information is communicated to officers and they are well-informed about local crime patterns.

2.6   Where there is reliable information or intelligence that members of a group or gang habitually carry knives unlawfully or weapons or controlled drugs, and wear a distinctive item of clothing or other means of identification to indicate their membership of the group or gang, that distinctive item of clothing or other means of identification may provide reasonable grounds to stop and search a person. ...

2.7   A police officer may have reasonable grounds to suspect that a person is in innocent possession of a stolen or prohibited article or other item for which he or she is empowered to search. In that case the officer may stop and search the person even though there would be no power of arrest.

2.8   Under section 43(1) of the Terrorism Act 2000 a constable may stop and search a person whom the officer reasonably suspects to be a terrorist to discover whether the person is in possession of anything which may constitute evidence that the person is a terrorist. These searches may only be carried out by an officer of the same sex as the person searched (see Annex F). An authorisation under section 44(1) of the Terrorism Act 2000 allows vehicles to be stopped and searched by a constable in uniform who reasonably suspects that articles which could be used in connection with terrorism will be found in the vehicle or in anything in or on that vehicle. ...

2.9   An officer who has reasonable grounds for suspicion may detain the person concerned in order to carry out a search. Before carrying out a search the officer may ask questions about the person's behaviour or presence in circumstances which gave rise to the suspicion. As a result of questioning the detained person, the reasonable grounds for suspicion necessary to detain that person may be confirmed or, because of a satisfactory explanation, be eliminated. ... Questioning may also reveal reasonable grounds to suspect the possession of a different kind of unlawful article from that originally suspected. Reasonable grounds for suspicion however cannot be provided retrospectively by such questioning during a person's detention or by refusal to answer any questions put.

2.10   If, as a result of questioning before a search, or other circumstances which come to the attention of the officer, there cease to be reasonable grounds for suspecting that an article is being carried of a kind for which there is a power to stop and search, no search may take place. ... In the absence of any other lawful power to detain, the person is free to leave at will and must be so informed

2.11   There is no power to stop or detain a person in order to find grounds for a search. Police officers have many encounters with members of the public which do not involve detaining people against their will. If reasonable grounds for suspicion emerge during such an encounter, the officer may search the person, even though no grounds existed when the encounter began. If an officer is detaining someone for the purpose of a search, he or she should inform the person as soon as detention begins.

The notes to the above paragraphs in Code A are not reproduced.]

Provisions relating to search under section 1 and other powers

2.—(1) A constable who detains a person or vehicle in the exercise—   **A14.04**

    (a) of the power conferred by section 1 above; or

    (b) of any other power—

        (i) to search a person without first arresting him; or

        (ii) to search section 1 of the Arbitration Act 1996 a section 2 vehicle without making an arrest,

need not conduct a search if it appears to him subsequently—

        (i) that no search is required; or

        (ii) that a search is impracticable.

(2) If a constable contemplates a search, other than a search of an unattended vehicle, in the exercise—

    (a) of the power conferred by section 1 above; or

    (b) of any other power, except the power conferred by section 6 below and the power conferred by section 27(2) of the Aviation Security Act 1982 —

        (i) to search a person without first arresting him; or

        (ii) to search a vehicle without making an arrest,

it shall be his duty, subject to subsection (4) below, to take reasonable steps before he commences the search to bring to the attention of the appropriate person—

        (i) if the constable is not in uniform, documentary evidence that he is a constable; and

      (ii) whether he is in uniform or not, the matters specified in subsection (3) below;

and the constable shall not commence the search until he has performed that duty.

    (3) The matters referred to in subsection (2)(ii) above are—

      (a) the constable's name and the name of the police station to which he is attached;

      (b) the object of the proposed search;

      (c) the constable's grounds for proposing to make it; and

      (d) the effect of section 3(7) or (8) below, as may be appropriate.

    (4) A constable need not bring the effect of section 3(7) or (8) below to the attention of the appropriate person if it appears to the constable that it will not be practicable to make the record in section 3(1) below.

    (5) In this section *"the appropriate person"* means—

      (a) if the constable proposes to search a person, that person; and

      (b) if he proposes to search a vehicle, or anything in or on a vehicle, the person in charge of the vehicle.

    (6) On completing a search of an unattended vehicle or anything in or on such a vehicle in the exercise of any such power as is mentioned in subsection (2) above a constable shall leave a notice—

      (a) stating that he has searched it;

      (b) giving the name of the police station to which he is attached;

      (c) stating that an application for compensation for any damage caused by the search may be made to that police station; and

      (d) stating the effect of section 3(8) below.

    (7) The constable shall leave the notice inside the vehicle unless it is not reasonably practicable to do so without damaging the vehicle.

    (8) The time for which a person or vehicle may be detained for the purposes of such a search is such time as is reasonably required to permit a search to be carried out either at the place where the person or vehicle was first detained or nearby.

    (9) Neither the power conferred by section 1 above nor any other power to detain and search a person without first arresting him or to detain and search a vehicle without making an arrest is to be construed—

      (a) as authorising a constable to require a person to remove any of his clothing in public other than an outer coat, jacket or gloves; or

      (b) as authorising a constable not in uniform to stop a vehicle.

    (10) This section and section 1 above apply to vessels, aircraft and hovercraft as they apply to vehicles.

A14.05   *[Section 2 is modified by the Serious Organised Crime and Police Act 2005 (Application and Modification of Certain Enactments to Designated Staff of SOCA) Order 2006 (SI 2006/987) Pt 2, Sch.2 to confer powers on the police (as well as constables) to enable powers under s.2 to be exercised by designated members of the staff of the Serious Organised Crime Agency (see s.43 of the Serious Organised Crime and Police Act 2005).]*

Duty to make records concerning searches

3.—(1) Where a constable has carried out a search in the exercise of any such power as is mentioned in section 2(1) above, other than a search—   **A14.06**

    (a) under section 6 below; or

    (b) under section 27(2) of the Aviation Security Act 1982,

[a record of the search shall be made] in writing unless it is not practicable to do so.

  (2) *[Omitted.]*

  (3)–(5) *[Repealed.]*

  (6), (6A) *[Omitted.]*

  (7) [If a record of a search of a person has been made under this section,] the person who was searched shall be entitled to a copy of the record if he asks for one before the end of the period specified in subsection (9) below.

  (8) If—

    (a) the owner of a vehicle which has been searched or the person who was in charge of the vehicle at the time when it was searched asks for a copy of the record of the search before the end of the period specified in subsection (9) below; and

    [(b) a record of the search of the vehicle has been made under this section,]

the person who made the request shall be entitled to a copy.

  (9) The period mentioned in subsections (7) and (8) above is the period of [3 months] beginning with the date on which the search was made.

  (10) The requirements imposed by this section with regard to records of searches of vehicles shall apply also to records of searches of vessels, aircraft and hovercraft.

[Section 3 is printed as amended by the Crime and Security Act 2010 s.1.]   **A14.07**

Road checks

4.—(1) This section shall have effect in relation to the conduct of road checks by police officers for the purpose of ascertaining whether a vehicle is carrying—   **A14.08**

    (a) a person who has committed an offence other than a road traffic offence or a [vehicle] excise offence;

    (b) a person who is a witness to such an offence;

    (c) a person intending to commit such an offence; or

    (d) a person who is unlawfully at large.

  (2) For the purposes of this section a road check consists of the exercise in a locality of the power conferred by [section 163 of the Road Traffic Act 1988] in such a way as to stop during the period for which its exercise in that way in that locality continues all vehicles or vehicles selected by any criterion.

  (3) Subject to subsection (5) below, there may only be such a road check if a police officer of the rank of superintendent or above authorises it in writing.

  (4) An officer may only authorise a road check under subsection (3) above—

    (a) for the purpose specified in subsection (1)(a) above, if he has reasonable grounds—

> (i) for believing that the offence is [an indictable offence]; and
> (ii) for suspecting that the person is, or is about to be, in the locality in which vehicles would be stopped if the road check were authorised;
>
> (b) for the purpose specified in subsection (1)(b) above, if he has reasonable grounds for believing that the offence is [an indictable offence];
> (c) for the purpose specified in subsection (1)(c) above, if he has reasonable grounds—
> > (i) for believing that the offence would be [an indictable offence]; and
> > (ii) for suspecting that the person is, or is about to be, in the locality in which vehicles would be stopped if the road check were authorised;
> (d) for the purpose specified in subsection (1)(d) above, if he has reasonable grounds for suspecting that the person is, or is about to be, in that locality.

(5) An officer below the rank of superintendent may authorise such a road check if it appears to him that it is required as a matter of urgency for one of the purposes specified in subsection (1) above.

(6) If an authorisation is given under subsection (5) above, it shall be the duty of the officer who gives it—

> (a) to make a written record of the time at which he gives it; and
> (b) to cause an officer of the rank of superintendent or above to be informed that it has been given.

(7) The duties imposed by subsection (6) above shall be performed as soon as it is practicable to do so.

(8) An officer to whom a report is made under subsection (6) above may, in writing, authorise the road check to continue.

(9) If such an officer considers that the road check should not continue, he shall record in writing—

> (a) the fact that it took place; and
> (b) the purpose for which it took place.

(10) An officer giving an authorisation under this section shall specify the locality in which vehicles are to be stopped.

(11) An officer giving an authorisation under this section, other than an authorisation under subsection (5) above—

> (a) shall specify a period, not exceeding seven days, during which the road check may continue; and
> (b) may direct that the road check—
> > (i) shall be continuous; or
> > (ii) shall be conducted at specified times,
> > during that period.

(12) If it appears to an officer of the rank of superintendent or above that a road check ought to continue beyond the period for which it has been authorised he may, from time to time, in writing specify a further period, not exceeding seven days, during which it may continue.

(13) Every written authorisation shall specify—

    (a) the name of the officer giving it;

    (b) the purpose of the road check; and

    (c) the locality in which vehicles are to be stopped.

(14) The duties to specify the purposes of a road check imposed by subsections (9) and (13) above include duties to specify any relevant [indictable offence].

(15) Where a vehicle is stopped in a road check, the person in charge of the vehicle at the time when it is stopped shall be entitled to obtain a written statement of the purpose of the road check if he applies for such a statement not later than the end of the period of twelve months from the day on which the vehicle was stopped.

(16) Nothing in this section affects the exercise by police officers of any power to stop vehicles for purposes other than those specified in subsection (1) above.

[Section 4 is printed as amended by the Road Traffic (Consequential Provisions) Act 1988 s.4 and Sch.3, para.27(1); the Vehicle Excise and Registration Act 1994 s.63 and Sch.3, para.19; the Serious Organised Crime and Police Act 2005 s.111 and Sch.7, para.43(2)(a) and (b).   **A14.09**

Section 4 is omitted by the Serious Organised Crime and Police Act 2005 (Application and Modification of Certain Enactments to Designated Staff of SOCA) Order 2006 (SI 2006/987) Pt 2, Sch.2 in relation to powers conferred on designated members of the staff of the Serious Organised Crime Agency (see § A14.05 above).]

*   *   *

Statutory undertakers, etc.

6.—(1) A constable employed by statutory undertakers may stop, detain and search any vehicle before it leaves a goods area included in the premises of the statutory undertakers.   **A14.10**

[(1A) Without prejudice to any powers under subsection (1) above, a constable employed [by the [British Transport Police Authority]] may stop, detain and search any vehicle before it leaves a goods area which is included in the premises of any successor of the British Railways Board and is used wholly or mainly for the purposes of a relevant undertaking.]

(2) In this section *"goods area"* means any area used wholly or mainly for the storage or handling of goods[; and *"successor of the British Railways Board"* and *"relevant undertaking"* have the same meaning as in the Railways Act 1993 (Consequential Modifications) Order 1999].

(3), (4) [. . .]

[Section 6 is printed as amended by the Railways Act 1993 (Consequential   **A14.11**
Modifications) (No.2) Order 1999 (SI 1999/1998; not reproduced in this work) art.5; the Transport Act 2000 s.217 and Sch.8, para.5; the British Transport Police (Transitional and Consequential Provisions) Order 2004 (SI 2004/1573) art.12(e) (the amendment in SI 2004/1573 contains a drafting error by reference to a substitution of words in subs.(1) which do not exist—the substitution has been made editorially in subs.(1A)). The definitions to which reference is made in s.6(2) may be found in SI 1999/1998 art.2(1).

The application to s.6(1) of the code of practice for the exercise by police offic-
ers of statutory powers of stop and search is expressly excluded by Code A (2008)
under this Act (see introductory paragraphs of Code A with the heading
"General").]

Part I—supplementary

A14.12   7.—(1), (2) *[Omitted.]*

(3) In this Part of this Act *"statutory undertakers"* means persons authorised
by any enactment to carry on any railway, light railway, road transport, water
transport, canal, inland navigation, dock or harbour undertaking.

*   *   *

PART III

ARREST

[Arrest without warrant: constables

A14.13   24.—(1) A constable may arrest without a warrant—

(a) anyone who is about to commit an offence;

(b) anyone who is in the act of committing an offence;

(c) anyone whom he has reasonable grounds for suspecting to be about to
commit an offence;

(d) anyone whom he has reasonable grounds for suspecting to be committing an offence.

(2) If a constable has reasonable grounds for suspecting that an offence has
been committed, he may arrest without a warrant anyone whom he has reasonable grounds to suspect of being guilty of it.

(3) If an offence has been committed, a constable may arrest without a warrant—

(a) anyone who is guilty of the offence;

(b) anyone whom he has reasonable grounds for suspecting to be guilty
of it.

(4) But the power of summary arrest conferred by subsection (1), (2) or (3) is
exercisable only if the constable has reasonable grounds for believing that for
any of the reasons mentioned in subsection (5) it is necessary to arrest the person
in question.

(a) anyone who is in the act of committing an arrestable offence;

(b) anyone whom he has reasonable grounds for suspecting to be committing such an offence.

(5) The reasons are—

(a) to enable the name of the person in question to be ascertained (in the
case where the constable does not know, and cannot readily ascertain,
the person's name, or has reasonable grounds for doubting whether a
name given by the person as his name is his real name);

(b) correspondingly as regards the person's address;

(c) to prevent the person in question—

    (i) causing physical injury to himself or any other person;

    (ii) suffering physical injury;

    (iii) causing loss of or damage to property;

    (iv) committing an offence against public decency (subject to subsection (6)); or

    (v) causing an unlawful obstruction of the highway;

(d) to protect a child or other vulnerable person from the person in question;

(e) to allow the prompt and effective investigation of the offence or of the conduct of the person in question;

(f) to prevent any prosecution for the offence from being hindered by the disappearance of the person in question.

(6) Subsection (5)(c)(iv) applies only where members of the public going about their normal business cannot reasonably be expected to avoid the person in question.]

[Section 24 is printed as substituted by the Serious Organised Crime and Police Act 2005 s.110.   **A14.14**

Section 24 has effect in relation to any offence whenever committed (Serious Organised Crime and Police Act 2005 s.110(4)).

For the code of practice for the statutory power of arrest by police officers, Code G, see http://www.homeoffice.gov.uk/police/powers/pace-codes/ *[accessed March 2, 2011], where the latest versions of the PACE Codes of Practice are available. Code G applies to any arrest made by a police officer after midnight on December 31, 2005.]*

[Arrest without warrant: other persons

    24A.—(1) A person other than a constable may arrest without a warrant—   **A14.15**

(a) anyone who is in the act of committing an indictable offence;

(b) anyone whom he has reasonable grounds for suspecting to be committing an indictable offence

(2) Where an indictable offence has been committed, a person other than a constable may arrest without a warrant—

(a) anyone who is guilty of the offence;

(b) anyone whom he has reasonable grounds for suspecting to be guilty of it.

(3) But the power of summary arrest conferred by subsection (1) or (2) is exercisable only if—

(a) the person making the arrest has reasonable grounds for believing that for any of the reasons mentioned in subsection (4) it is necessary to arrest the person in question; and

(b) it appears to the person making the arrest that it is not reasonably practicable for a constable to make it instead.

(4) The reasons are to prevent the person in question—

(a) causing physical injury to himself or any other person;

(b) suffering physical injury;

(c) causing loss of or damage to property; or

(d) making off before a constable can assume responsibility for him.]

[(5) This section does not apply in relation to an offence under Part 3 or 3A of the Public Order Act 1986.]

A14.16   *[Section 24A is printed as substituted by the Serious Organised Crime and Police Act 2005 s.110 and as amended by the Racial and Religious Hatred Act 2006 s.2.*

Section 24A has effect in relation to any offence whenever committed (Serious Organised Crime and Police Act 2005 s.110(4)).]

General arrest conditions

A14.17   **25.—**   [. . .]

A14.18   *[Section 25 was revoked by the Serious Organised Crime and Police Act 2005 s.110(2) and Sch.17, Pt 2.]*

Repeal of statutory powers of arrest without warrant or order

A14.19   **26.—**(1) Subject to subsection (2) below, so much of any Act (including a local Act) passed before this Act as enables a constable—

     (a) to arrest a person for an offence without a warrant; or

     (b) to arrest a person otherwise than for an offence without a warrant or an order of a court,

shall cease to have effect.

(2) Nothing in subsection (1) above affects the enactments specified in Schedule 2 to this Act.

A14.20   *[The enactments originally listed in Sch.2 to this Act included ss.5(5), 7 and 10 of the Road Traffic Act 1972; reference to these provisions in Sch.2 was repealed by the Road Traffic (Consequential Provisions) Act 1988 s.3(1) and Sch.1, Pt I.]*

*   *   *

Arrest for further offence

A14.21   **31.** Where—

     (a) a person—

        (i) has been arrested for an offence; and

        (ii) is at a police station in consequence of that arrest; and

     (b) it appears to a constable that, if he were released from that arrest, he would be liable to arrest for some other offence,

   he shall be arrested for that other offence.

*   *   *

PART IV

DETENTION

Detention—conditions and duration

Limitations on police detention

A14.22   **34.—**(1) A person arrested for an offence shall not be kept in police detention except in accordance with the provisions of this Part of this Act.

(2) Subject to subsection (3) below, if at any time a custody officer—

    (a) becomes aware, in relation to any person in police detention, that the grounds for the detention of that person have ceased to apply; and

    (b) is not aware of any other grounds on which the continued detention of that person could be justified under the provisions of this Part of this Act,

it shall be the duty of the custody officer, subject to subsection (4) below, to order his immediate release from custody.

(3) No person in police detention shall be released except on the authority of a custody officer at the police station where his detention was authorised or, if it was authorised at more than one station, a custody officer at the station where it was last authorised.

(4) A person who appears to the custody officer to have been unlawfully at large when he was arrested is not to be released under subsection (2) above.

(5) A person whose release is ordered under subsection (2) above shall be released without bail unless it appears to the custody officer—

    (a) that there is need for further investigation of any matter in connection with which he was detained at any time during the period of his detention; or

    [(b) that, in respect of any such matter, proceedings may be taken against him or he may be reprimanded or warned under section 65 of the Crime and Disorder Act 1998,]

and, if it so appears, he shall be released on bail.

(6) For the purposes of this Part of this Act a person arrested under [section 6D of the Road Traffic Act 1988] [or section 30(2) of the Transport and Works Act 1992 (c.42)] is arrested for an offence.

    [(7) For the purposes of this Part a person who—

    (a) attends a police station to answer bail granted under section 30A,

    (b) returns to a police station to answer bail granted under this Part, or

    (c) is arrested under section 30D or 46A,

is to be treated as arrested for an offence and that offence is the offence in connection with which he was granted bail.]

[Section 34 is printed as amended by the Road Traffic (Consequential Provisions) Act 1988 s.4 and Sch.3, para.27(2); the Criminal Justice and Public Order Act 1994 s.29(1) and (3); the Criminal Justice and Court Services Act 2000 s.56(2); the Police Reform Act 2002 s.53(1); the Railways and Transport Safety Act 2003 s.107 and Sch.7, para.12; the Criminal Justice Act 2003 s.12 and Sch.1, para.5.   **A14.23**

The Crime and Disorder Act 1998 s.65 (to which reference is made in s.34(5)(b) above) provides for reprimands and warnings to be given to offenders under the age of 18.]

Designated police stations

35.—(1) The chief officer of police for each police area shall designate the police stations in his area which, subject to [sections 30(3) and (5), 30A(5) and 30D(2)], are to be the stations in that area to be used for the purpose of detaining arrested persons.   **A14.24**

(2) *[Omitted.]*

[(2A) The Chief Constable of the British Transport Police Force may designate police stations which (in addition to those designated under subsection (1) above) may be used for the purpose of detaining arrested persons.]

(3) *[Omitted.]*

(4) In this Act *"designated police station"* means a police station for the time being designated under this section.

A14.25   *[Section 35 is printed as amended by the Anti-terrorism, Crime and Security Act 2001 ss.101 and 127(2)(f) and Sch.7, paras 11 and 12; the Criminal Justice Act 2003 s.12 and Sch.1, para.6.]*

Custody officers at police stations

A14.26   36.—(1) One or more custody officers shall be appointed for each designated police station.

(2) A custody officer for [a police station designated under section 35(1) above] shall be appointed—

    (a) by the chief officer of police for the area in which the designated police station is situated; or

    (b) by such other police officer as the chief officer of police for that area may direct.

[(2A) A custody officer for a police station designated under section 35(2A) above shall be appointed—

    (a) by the Chief Constable of the British Transport Police; or

    (b) by such member of that Force as that Chief Constable may direct.]

[(3) No officer may be appointed as a custody officer unless the officer is of least the rank of sergeant.]

(4) An officer of any rank may perform the functions of a custody officer at a designated police station if a custody officer is not readily available to perform them.

(5) Subject to the following provisions of this section and to section 39(2) below, none of the functions of a custody officer in relation to a person shall be performed by [an officer] who at the time when the function falls to be performed is involved in the investigation of an offence for which that person is in police detention at that time.

(6) Nothing in subsection (5) above is to be taken to prevent a custody officer—

    (a) performing any function assigned to custody officers—

        (i) by this Act; or

        (ii) by a code of practice issued under this Act;

    (b) carrying out the duty imposed on custody officers by section 39 below;

    (c) doing anything in connection with the identification of a suspect; or

    (d) doing anything under [sections 7 and 8 of the Road Traffic Act 1988].

(7) Where an arrested person is taken to a police station which is not a designated police station, the functions in relation to him which at a designated police station would be the functions of a custody officer shall be performed—

    (a) by an officer who is not involved in the investigation of an offence for which he is in police detention, if [such an officer] is readily available; and

    (b) if no [such officer] is readily available, by the officer who took him to the station or any other officer.

[(7A) Subject to subsection (7B), subsection (7) applies where a person attends a police station which is not a designated station to answer to bail granted under section 30A as it applies where a person is taken to such a station.]

[(7B) Where subsection (7) applies because of subsection (7A), the reference in subsection (7)(b) to the officer who took him to the station is to be read as a reference to the officer who granted him bail.]

(8) References to a custody officer in [section 34 above or in] the following provisions of this Act include references to [an officer] other than a custody officer who is performing the functions of a custody officer by virtue of subsection (4) or (7) above.

(9) Where by virtue of subsection (7) above an officer of a force maintained by a police authority who took an arrested person to a police station is to perform the functions of a custody officer in relation to him, the officer shall inform an officer who—

    (a) is attached to a designated police station; and

    (b) is of at least the rank of inspector,

that he is to do so.

(10) The duty imposed by subsection (9) above shall be performed as soon as it is practicable to perform it.

[Section 36 is printed as amended by the Road Traffic (Consequential Provisions) Act 1988 s.4 and Sch.3, para.27(3); the Anti-Terrorism, Crime and Security Act 2001 ss.101, 127(2)(f) and Sch.7, paras 11 and 13(1)–(3); the Criminal Justice Act 2003 s.12 and Sch.1, para.7; the Serious Organised Crime and Police Act 2005 s.121(5)(a); the Policing and Crime Act 2009 s.112 and Sch.7, Pt 13, para.123(3) and Sch.8, Pt 13.]   **A14.27**

Duties of custody officer before charge

37.—(1) Where—   **A14.28**

    (a) a person is arrested for an offence—

        (i) without a warrant; or

        (ii) under a warrant not endorsed for bail, …

the custody officer at each police station where he is detained after his arrest shall determine whether he has before him sufficient evidence to charge that person with the offence for which he was arrested and may detain him at the police station for such period as is necessary to enable him to do so.

(2) If the custody officer determines that he does not have such evidence before him, the person arrested shall be released either on bail or without bail, unless the custody officer has reasonable grounds for believing that his detention without being charged is necessary to secure or preserve evidence relating to an offence for which he is under arrest or to obtain evidence by questioning him.

(3) If the custody officer has reasonable grounds for so believing, he may authorise the person arrested to be kept in police detention.

(4)–(6) *[Written record of grounds for detention.]*

(7) Subject to section 41(7) below, if the custody officer determines that he has before him sufficient evidence to charge the person arrested with the offence for which he was arrested, the person arrested—

[(a) shall be—

(i) released without charge and on bail, or

(ii) kept in police detention,

for the purpose of enabling the Director of Public Prosecutions to make a decision under section 37B below,]

(b) shall be released without charge and on bail but not for that purpose,

(c) shall be released without charge and without bail, or

(d) shall be charged.]

[(7A) The decision as to how a person is to be dealt with under subsection (7) above shall be that of the custody officer.]

[(7B) Where a person is [dealt with under subsection (7)(a)] above, it shall be the duty of the custody officer to inform him that he is being released[, or (as the case may be) detained,] to enable the Director of Public Prosecutions to make a decision under section 37B below.]

(8) Where—

(a) a person is released under subsection (7)(b) [or (c)] above; and

(b) at the time of his release a decision whether he should be prosecuted for the offence for which he was arrested has not been taken,

it shall be the duty of the custody officer so to inform him.

[(8A) [Duty with regard to testing for presence of Class A drug]]

[(8B) [Requirements as to detention of a person for testing for the presence of Class A drug]]

(9) If the person arrested is not in a fit state to be dealt with under subsection (7) above, he may be kept in police detention until he is.

(10) [Duty under s.37(1) to be performed as soon as practicable.]

(11)–(14) […]

(15) [Definitions.]

A14.29   [Section 37 is printed as amended by the Criminal Justice Act 1991 s.101(2) and Sch.13; the Criminal Justice and Public Order Act 1994 s.29(1) and (4)(a), s.168(3) and Sch.11; the Criminal Justice Act 2003 s.28 and Sch.2, para.2; the Drugs Act 2005 s.23 and Sch.1, para.2; the Police and Justice Act 2006 s.11, s.52 and Sch.14, para.9.

Section 37 (including any provision of that section as applied by s.40(8) of the 1984 Act (review of police detention)) will have effect subject to certain modifications in the case of a retrial for serious offences, see the Criminal Justice Act 2003 s.87(6).]

[Guidance

A14.30   37A. [Omitted.]]

[Consultation with the Director of Public Prosecutions

A14.31   37B. [Omitted.]]

[Breach of bail following release under section 37(7)(a)

A14.32   37C. [Omitted.]]

[**Release under section 37(7)(a): further provision**

37D. *[Omitted.]*]   A14.33

Duties of custody officer after charge

38. *[Omitted.]*   A14.34

Responsibilities in relation to persons detained

39.—(1) Subject to subsections (2) and (4) below, it shall be the duty of the   A14.35
custody officer at a police station to ensure—
- (a) that all persons in police detention at that station are treated in accordance with this Act and any code of practice issued under it and relating to the treatment of persons in police detention; and
- (b) that all matters relating to such persons which are required by this Act or by such codes of practice to be recorded are recorded in the custody records relating to such persons.

(2) If the custody officer, in accordance with any code of practice issued under this Act, transfers or permits the transfer of a person in police detention—
- (a) to the custody of a police officer investigating an offence for which that person is in police detention; or
- (b) to the custody of an officer who has charge of that person outside the police station,

the custody officer shall cease in relation to that person to be subject to the duty inposed on him by subsection (1)(a) above; and it shall be the duty of the officer to whom the transfer is made to ensure that he is treated in accordance with the provisions of this Act and of any such codes of practice as are mentioned in subsection (1) above.

(3) If the person detained is subsequently returned to the custody of the custody officer, it shall be the duty of the officer investigating the offence to report to the custody officer as to the manner in which this section and the codes of practice have been complied with while that person was in his custody.

(4) If an arrested juvenile is [moved to local authority accommodation] under section 38(6) above, the custody officer shall cease in relation to that person to be subject to the duty imposed on him by subsection (1) above.

(5) [...]

(6) Where—
- (a) an officer of higher rank than the custody officer gives directions relating to a person in police detention; and
- (b) the directions are at variance—
  - (i) with any decision made or action taken by the custody officer in the performance of a duty imposed on him under this Part of this Act; or
  - (ii) with any decision or action which would but for the directions have been made or taken by him in the performance of such a duty,

the custody officer shall refer the matter at once to an officer of the rank of superintendent or above who is responsible for the police station for which the custody officer is acting as custody officer.

A14.36　　*[Section 39 is printed as amended by the Children Act 1989 s.108(5) and (7), Sch.13 para.54, and Sch.15; the Policing and Crime Act 2009 s.112 and Sch.7, Pt 13, para.123(4) and Sch.8, Pt 13.]*

Review of police detention

A14.37　　**40.** *[Omitted.]*

[Use of telephone for review under s.40

A14.38　　**40A.** *[Omitted.]]*

Limits on period of detention without charge

A14.39　　**41.**—(1) Subject to the following provisions of this section and to sections 42 and 43 below, a person shall not be kept in police detention for more than 24 hours without being charged.

(2) The time from which the period of detention of a person is to be calculated (in this Act referred to as *"the relevant time"*) —

(a) in the case of a person to whom this paragraph applies, shall be—

(i) the time at which that person arrives at the relevant police station, or

(ii) the time 24 hours after the time of that person's arrest,

whichever is the earlier;

(b) in the case of a person arrested outside England and Wales, shall be—

(i) the time at which that person arrives at the first police station to which he is taken in the police area in England and Wales in which the offence for which he was arrested is being investigated; or

(ii) the time 24 hours after the time of that person's entry into England and Wales,

whichever is the earlier;

(c) in the case of a person who—

(i) attends voluntarily at a police station; or

(ii) accompanies a constable to a police station without having been arrested,

and is arrested at the police station, the time of his arrest;

[(ca) in the case of a person who attends a police station to answer bail granted under section 30A, the time when he arrives at the police station;]

(d) in any other case, except where subsection (5) below applies, shall be the time at which the person arrested arrives at the first police station to which he is taken after his arrest.

(3) Subsection (2)(a) above applies to a person if—

(a) his arrest is sought in one police area in England and Wales;

(b) he is arrested in another police area; and

(c) he is not questioned in the area in which he is arrested in order to obtain evidence in relation to an offence for which he is arrested;

and in sub-paragraph (i) of that paragraph *"the relevant police station"* means the first police station to which he is taken in the police area in which his arrest was sought.

(4) Subsection (2) above shall have effect in relation to a person arrested under section 31 above as if every reference in it to his arrest or his being arrested were a reference to his arrest or his being arrested for the offence for which he was originally arrested.

(5) If—

    (a) a person is in police detention in a police area in England and Wales (*"the first area"*); and

    (b) his arrest for an offence is sought in some other police area in England and Wales (*"the second area"*); and

    (c) he is taken to the second area for the purposes of investigating that offence, without being questioned in the first area in order to obtain evidence in relation to it,

the relevant time shall be—

    (i) the time 24 hours after he leaves the place where he is detained in the first area; or

    (ii) the time at which he arrives at the first police station to which he is taken in the second area,

whichever is the earlier.

(6) When a person who is in police detention is removed to hospital because he is in need of medical treatment, any time during which he is being questioned in hospital or on the way there or back by a police officer for the purpose of obtaining evidence relating to an offence shall be included in any period which falls to be calculated for the purposes of this Part of this Act, but any other time while he is in hospital or on his way back shall not be so included.

(7) Subject to subsection (8) below, a person who at the expiry of 24 hours after the relevant time is in police detention and has not been charged shall be released at that time either on bail or without bail.

(8) Subsection (7) above does not apply to a person whose detention for more than 24 hours after the relevant time has been authorised or is otherwise permitted in accordance with section 42 or 43 below.

(9) A person released under subsection (7) above shall not be re-arrested without a warrant for the offence for which he was previously arrested unless new evidence justifying a further arrest has come to light since his release [; but this subsection does not prevent an arrest under section 46A below].

[Section 41 is printed as amended by the Criminal Justice and Public Order Act 1994, s.29(1) and (4)(b); the Criminal Justice Act 2003 s.12 and Sch.1, para.8.]   **A14.40**

*   *   *

[Power of arrest for failure to answer police bail

46A. *[Omitted.]*]   **A14.41**

PART V

QUESTIONING AND TREATMENT OF PERSONS BY POLICE

*   *   *

Right to have someone informed when arrested

A14.42
56.—(1) Where a person has been arrested and is being held in custody in a police station or other premises, he shall be entitled, if he so requests, to have one friend or relative or other person who is known to him or who is likely to take an interest in his welfare told, as soon as is practicable except to the extent that delay is permitted by this section, that he has been arrested and is being detained there.

(2) Delay is only permitted—

(a) in the case of a person who is in police detention for [an indictable offence]; and

(b) if an officer of at least the rank of [inspector] authorises it.

(3) In any case the person in custody must be permitted to exercise the right conferred by subsection (1) above within 36 hours from the relevant time, as defined in section 41(2) above.

(4) An officer may give an authorisation under subsection (2) above orally or in writing but, if he gives it orally, he shall confirm it in writing as soon as is practicable.

(5) [Subject to subsection (5A) below] an officer may only authorise delay where he has reasonable grounds for believing that telling the named person of the arrest—

(a) will lead to interference with or harm to evidence connected with [an indictable offence] or interference with or physical injury to other persons; or

(b) will lead to the alerting of other persons suspected of having committed such an offence but not yet arrested for it; or

(c) will hinder the recovery of any property obtained as a result of such an offence.

[(5A) *[Applies to drug trafficking offences.]*]

(6) If a delay is authorised—

(a) the detained person shall be told the reason for it; and

(b) the reason shall be noted on his custody record.

(7) The duties imposed by subsection (6) above shall be performed as soon as is practicable.

(8) The rights conferred by this section on a person detained at a police station or other premises are exercisable whenever he is transferred from one place to another; and this section applies to each subsequent occasion on which they are exercisable as it applies to the first such occasion.

(9) There may be no further delay in permitting the exercise of the right conferred by subsection (1) above once the reason for authorising delay ceases to subsist.

(10) *[Applies to terrorism provisions.]*

(11) *[Omitted.]*

[Section 56 is printed as amended by the Drug Trafficking Offences Act 1986 **A14.43**
s.32(1); Terrorism Act 2000 s.125 and Sch.15, para.5(1) and (5); the Criminal
Justice and Police Act 2001 ss.74 and 138(2); the Serious Organised Crime and
Police Act 2005 s.111 and Sch.7, para.43(9).]

Additional rights of children and young persons

57. *[Amends the Children and Young Persons Act 1933, s.34.]*   **A14.44**

Access to legal advice

58.—(1) A person arrested and held in custody in a police station or other   **A14.45**
premises shall be entitled, if he so requests, to consult a solicitor privately at any
time.

(2) Subject to subsection (3) below, a request under subsection (1) above and
the time at which it was made shall be recorded in the custody record.

(3) Such a request need not be recorded in the custody record of a person who
makes it at a time while he is at a court after being charged with an offence.

(4) If a person makes such a request, he must be permitted to consult a solicitor as soon as is practicable except to the extent that delay is permitted by this
section.

(5) In any case he must be permitted to consult a solicitor within 36 hours
from the relevant time, as defined in section 41(2) above.

(6) Delay in compliance with a request is only permitted—

    (a) in the case of a person who is in police detention for [an indictable of-
        fence]; and

    (b) if an officer of at least the rank of superintendent authorises it.

(7) An officer may give an authorisation under subsection (6) above orally or
in writing, but, if he gives it orally, he shall confirm it in writing as soon as is
practicable.

(8) [Subject to subsection (8A) below] an officer may only authorise delay
where he has reasonable grounds for believing that the exercise of the right
conferred by subsection (1) above at the time when the person detained desires to
exercise it—

    (a) will lead to interference with or harm to evidence connected with [an
        indictable offence] or interference with or physical injury to other
        persons; or

    (b) will lead to the alerting of other persons suspected of having commit-
        ted such an offence but not yet arrested for it; or

    (c) will hinder the recovery of any property obtained as a result of such
        an offence.

[(8A) *[Applies to drug trafficking offences.]*]

(9) If delay is authorised—

    (a) the detained person shall be told the reason for it; and

    (b) the reason shall be noted on his custody record.

(10) The duties imposed by subsection (9) above shall be performed as soon
as is practicable.

(11) There may be no further delay in permitting the exercise of the right

conferred by subsection (1) above once the reason for authorising delay ceases to subsist.

[(12) Nothing in this section applies to a person arrested or detained under the terrorism provisions.]

A14.46   *[Section 58 is printed as amended by the Drug Trafficking Offences Act 1986 s.32(2); the Terrorism Act 2000 s.125(1) and Sch.5, para.5(1) and (6); the Serious Organised Crime and Police Act 2005 s.111 and Sch.7, para.43(10).]*

*   *   *

PART VIII

EVIDENCE IN CRIMINAL PROCEEDINGS—GENERAL

*   *   *

Miscellaneous

Exclusion of unfair evidence

A14.47   78.—(1) In any proceedings the court may refuse to allow evidence on which the prosecution proposes to rely to be given if it appears to the court that, having regard to all the circumstances, including the circumstances in which the evidence was obtained, the admission of the evidence would have such an adverse effect on the fairness of the proceedings that the court ought not to admit it.

(2) Nothing in this section shall prejudice any rule of law requiring a court to exclude evidence.

[(3) This section shall not apply in the case of proceedings before a magistrates' court inquiring into an offence as examining justices.]

A14.48   *[Section 78 is printed as amended by the Criminal Procedure and Investigations Act 1996 s.47 and Sch.1, para.26.*

With effect from a day to be appointed, subs.(3) of s.78 will be revoked by the Criminal Justice Act 2003 s.41 and Sch.3, para.56(5) and Sch.37, Pt 4.]

Time for taking accused's evidence

A14.49   79. If at the trial of any person for an offence—

(a) the defence intends to call two or more witnesses to the facts of the case; and

(b) those witnesses include the accused,

the accused shall be called before the other witness or witnesses unless the court in its discretion otherwise directs.

*   *   *

Part VIII Supplementary

Part VIII—interpretation

A14.50   82.—(1) In this Part of this Act —

"Confession" includes any statement wholly or partly adverse to the person

who made it, whether made to a person in authority or not and whether made in words or otherwise;

[...]

"proceedings" means criminal proceedings, including [service proceedings]; and

"Service court" means [the Court Martial or the Service Civilian Court].

[(1A) In subsection (1) *"service proceedings"* means proceedings before a court (other than a civilian court) in respect of a service offence; and *"service offence"* and *"civilian court"* here have the same meanings as in the Armed Forces Act 2006.]

(2) [...]

(3) Nothing in this Part of this Act shall prejudice any power of a court to exclude evidence (whether by preventing questions from being put or otherwise) at its discretion.

[Section 82 is printed as amended by the Armed Forces Act 1996 ss.5, 35, **A14.51** *Sch.6, paras 14, 104, 105 and 107 and Sch.7, Pt I; the Youth Justice and Criminal Evidence Act 1999 s.67(3) and Sch.6; the Armed Forces Act 2001 Sch.7(1), para.1; the Armed Forces Act 2006 s.378 and Sch.16, para.104, Sch.17.]*

PART XI

MISCELLANEOUS AND SUPPLEMENTARY

*   *   *

Meaning of "serious arrestable offence"

116. [. . .]   **A14.52**

[Section 116 was revoked by the Serious Organised Crime and Police Act **A14.53** *2005 s.111, Sch.7, para.43(12) and Sch.17, Pt 2, with effect from January 1, 2006.]*

*   *   *

SCHEDULE 1A

SPECIFIC OFFENCES WHICH ARE ARRESTABLE OFFENCES

[. . .]   **A14.54**

[Schedule 1A was revoked by the Serious Organised Crime and Police Act 2005 s.111, Sch.7, para.24(3) and Sch.17, Pt 2, with effect from January 1, 2006.]

SCHEDULE 5

SERIOUS ARRESTABLE OFFENCES

PART II

[. . .]

[Schedule 5 was revoked by the Serious Organised Crime and Police Act 2005 **A14.55** *s.111, Sch.7, para.43(14) and Sch.17, Pt 2, with effect from January 1, 2006.]*

The Prosecution of Offences Act 1985

(1985 c.23)

A15.01 *An Act to provide for the establishment of a Crown Prosecution Service for England and Wales; to make provision as to costs in criminal cases ...*

[23rd May 1985]

ARRANGEMENT OF SECTIONS

*   *   *

PART I
THE CROWN PROSECUTION SERVICE
Constitution and functions of Service

Section

*   *   *

*   *   *

PART II
COSTS IN CRIMINAL CASES
Award of costs out of central funds

Award of costs against accused
Other awards
Supplemental

*   *   *

*   *   *

PART I

THE CROWN PROSECUTION SERVICE

Constitution and functions of Service

*   *   *

Functions of the Director

A15.02   **3.**—(1), (2) *[Omitted.]*

(3) In this section—

2/212

* * *

"police force" means any police force maintained by a police authority under [the Police Act 1996] ... and any other body of constables for the time being specified by order made by the Secretary of State for the purposes of this section;

* * *

A15.03

[The definition of "police force" in subs.(3) is incorporated by reference into s.17 (q.v.).

The definition is printed as amended by the Police Act 1996 s.103 and Sch.7, para.39; the Police Act 1997 s.134(1) and Sch.9, para.48; the Serious Organised Crime and Police Act 2005 s.59 and Sch.4, para.47.]

* * *

PART II

COSTS IN CRIMINAL CASES

Award of costs out of central funds

Defence costs

A15.04

16.—(1) Where—

    (a) an information laid before a justice of the peace for any area, charging any person with an offence, is not proceeded with;

    (b) a magistrates' court inquiring into an indictable offence as examining justices determines not to commit the accused for trial;

    (c) a magistrates' court dealing summarily with an offence dismisses the information;

that court or, in a case falling within paragraph (a) above, a magistrates' court for that area, may make an order in favour of the accused for a payment to be made out of central funds in respect of his costs (a "defendant's costs order").

    (2) Where—

    (a) any person is not tried for an offence for which he has been indicted or [sent] for trial; or

    [(aa) *[Relates to complex cases of serious fraud.]*]

    (b) any person is tried on indictment and acquitted on any count in the indictment;

the Crown Court may make a defendant's costs order in favour of the accused.

    (3) Where a person convicted of an offence by a magistrates' court appeals to the Crown Court under section 108 of the Magistrates' Courts Act 1980 (right of appeal against conviction of sentence), and, in consequence of the decision on appeal—

    (a) his conviction is set aside; or

    (b) a less severe punishment is awarded;

the Crown Court may make a defendant's costs order in favour of the accused.

    (4) Where the Court of Appeal—

    (a) allows an appeal under Part I of the Criminal Appeal Act 1968
       against—

       (i) conviction;

       (ii) a verdict of not guilty by reason of insanity; or

      [(iii) a finding under the Criminal Procedure (Insanity) Act 1964 that
         the appellant is under a disability, or that he did the act or made
         the omission charged against him;] or

   [(aa) directs under section 8(1B) of the Criminal Appeal Act 1968 the entry
      of a judgment and verdict of acquittal;]

    (b) on an appeal under that Part against conviction—

       (i) substitutes a verdict of guilty of another offence;

       (ii) in a case where a special verdict has been found, orders a differ-
         ent conclusion on the effect of that verdict to be recorded; or

       (iii) is of the opinion that the case falls within paragraph (a) or (b) of
         section 6(1) of that Act (cases where the court substitutes a find-
         ing of insanity or unfitness to plead); ...

    (c) on an appeal under that Part against sentence, exercises its power
      under section 11(3) of that Act (powers where the court considers that
      the appellant should be sentenced differently for an offence for which
      he was dealt with by the court below);

   [(d) allows, to any extent, an appeal under section 16A of that Act (appeal
      against order made in cases or unfitness to plead);]

the court may make a defendant's costs order in favour of the accused.

  [(4A) *[Relates to complex cases of serious fraud.]*]

  (5) Where—

    (a) any proceedings in a criminal cause or matter are determined before a
      Divisional Court of the Queen's Bench Division;

    (b) the [Supreme Court] determines an appeal, or application for leave to
      appeal, from such a Divisional Court in a criminal cause or matter;

    (c) the Court of Appeal determines an application for leave to appeal to
      the [Supreme Court] under Part II of the Criminal Appeal Act 1968;
      or

    (d) the [Supreme Court] determines an appeal, or application for leave to
      appeal, under Part II of that Act;

the court may make a defendant's costs order in favour of the accused.

  (6) A defendant's costs order shall, subject to the following provisions of this
section, be for the payment out of central funds, to the person in whose favour the
order is made, of such amount as the court considers reasonably sufficient to
compensate him for any expenses properly incurred by him in the proceedings.

  (7) Where a court makes a defendant's costs order but is of the opinion that
there are circumstances which make it inappropriate that the person in whose favour the order is made should recover the full amount mentioned in subsection
(6) above, the court shall—

    (a) assess what amount would, in its opinion, be just and reasonable; and

    (b) specify that amount in the order.

  (8) [...]

(9) Subject to subsection (7) above, the amount to be paid out of central funds in pursuance of a defendant's costs order shall—

    (a) be specified in the order, in any case where the court considers it appropriate for the amount to be so specified and the person in whose favour the order is made agrees the amount; and

    (b) in any other case, be determined in accordance with regulations made by the Lord Chancellor for the purposes of this section.

(10) Subsection (6) above shall have effect, in relation to any case falling within subsection (1)(a) or (2)(a) above, as if for the words "in the proceedings" there were substituted the words "in or about the defence".

(11) Where a person ordered to be retried is acquitted at his retrial, the costs which may be ordered to be paid out of central funds under this section shall include—

    (a) any costs which, at the original trial, could have been ordered to be so paid under this section if he had been acquitted; and

    (b) if no order was made under this section in respect of his expenses on appeal, any sums for the payment of which such an order could have been made.

(12) *[Meaning of "relevant transfer provision".]*

[Section 16 is printed as amended by the Criminal Justice Act 1988 s.170(1) **A15.05** *and Sch.15, para.103; the Legal Aid Act 1988 s.45(2) and Sch.6; the Criminal Procedure (Insanity and Unfitness to Plead) Act 1991 s.7 and Sch.3, para.7; the Criminal Justice Act 2003 s.41 and Sch.3, para.57(3)(b)(i); the Domestic Violence, Crime and Victims Act 2004 s.58, Sch.10, para.25 and Sch.11; the Constitutional Reform Act 2005 s.40 and Sch.9, para.41.*

With effect from a day (or days) to be appointed, the following amendments will be made to s.16 by the Criminal Justice Act 2003 s.41 and Sch.3, para.57 and Sch.37, Pt 4:

    1. *in s.16(1), para.(b) will be revoked;*

    2. *in s.16(2), para.(aa) will be revoked;*

    3. *s.16(12) will be revoked.]*

Prosecution costs

17.—(1) Subject to subsection (2) below, the court may—   **A15.06**

    (a) in any proceedings in respect of an indictable offence; and

    (b) in any proceedings before a Divisional Court of the Queen's Bench Division or the [Supreme Court] in respect of a summary offence;

order the payment out of central funds of such amount as the court considers reasonably sufficient to compensate the prosecutor for any expenses properly incurred by him in the proceedings.

(2) No order under this section may be made in favour of—

    (a) a public authority; or

    (b) a person acting—

        (i) on behalf of a public authority; or

        (ii) in his capacity as an official appointed by such an authority.

(3) Where a court makes an order under this section but is of the opinion that

there are circumstances which make it inappropriate that the prosecution should recover the full amount mentioned in subsection (1) above, the court shall—

    (a) assess what amount would, in its opinion, be just and reasonable; and

    (b) specify that amount in the order.

(4) Subject to subsection (3) above, the amount to be paid out of central funds in pursuance of an order under this section shall—

    (a) be specified in the order, in any case where the court considers it appropriate for the amount to be so specified and the prosecutor agrees the amount; and

    (b) in any other case be determined in accordance with regulations made by the Lord Chancellor for the purposes of this section.

(5) Where the conduct of proceedings to which subsection (1) above applies is taken over by the Crown Prosecution Service, that subsection shall have effect as if it referred to the prosecutor who had the conduct of the proceedings before the intervention of the Service and to expenses incurred by him up to the time of intervention.

(6) In this section *"public authority"* means—

    (a) a police force within the meaning of section 3 of this Act;

    (b) the Crown Prosecution Service or any other government department;

    (c) a local authority or other authority or body constituted for purposes of—

        (i) the public service or of local government; or

        (ii) carrying on under national ownership any industry or undertaking or part of an industry or undertaking; or

    (d) any other authority or body whose members are appointed by Her Majesty or by any Minister of the Crown or government department or whose revenues consist wholly or mainly of money provided by Parliament.

A15.07   *[Section 17 is printed as amended by the Constitutional Reform Act 2005 s.40 and Sch.9, para.41.]*

Award of costs against accused

Award of costs against accused

A15.08   **18.**—(1) Where—

    (a) any person is convicted of an offence before a magistrates' court;

    (b) the Crown Court dismisses an appeal against such a conviction or against the sentence imposed on that conviction; or

    (c) any person is convicted of an offence before the Crown Court;

the court may make such order as to the costs to be paid by the accused to the prosecutor as it considers just and reasonable.

(2) Where the Court of Appeal dismisses—

    (a) an appeal or application for leave to appeal under Part I of the Criminal Appeal Act 1968; or

    (b) an application by the accused for leave to appeal to the [Supreme Court] under Part II of this Act;

    [(c) *[relates to complex cases of serious fraud]*] [or

    (d) an appeal or application for leave to appeal under section 35(1) of the Criminal Procedure and Investigations Act 1996] it may make such order as to the costs to be paid by the accused, to such person as may be named in the order, as it considers just and reasonable.

[(2A) Where the Court of Appeal reverses or varies a ruling on an appeal under Part 9 of the Criminal Justice Act 2003, it may make such order as to the costs to be paid by the accused, to such person as may be named in the order, as it considers just and reasonable.]

(3) The amount to be paid by the accused in pursuance of an order under this section shall be specified in the order.

(4) Where any person is convicted of an offence before a magistrates' court and—

> (a) under the conviction the court orders payment of any sum as a fine, penalty, forfeiture or compensation; and
>
> (b) the sum so ordered to be paid does not exceed £5;

the court shall not order the accused to pay any costs under this section unless in the particular circumstances of the case it considers it right to do so.

(5) Where any person under [the age of eighteen] is convicted of an offence before a magistrates' court, the amount of any costs ordered to be paid by the accused under this section shall not exceed the amount of any fine imposed on him.

(6) Costs ordered to be paid under subsection (2) [or (2A)] above may include the reasonable costs of any transcript of a record of proceedings made in accordance with rules of court made for the purposes of section 32 of the Criminal Appeal Act 1968.

[Section 18 is printed as amended by the Criminal Justice and Public Order Act 1994 s.168(1) and Sch.9, para.26; the Criminal Justice Act 2003 s.69 and s.312(3); the Constitutional Reform Act 2005 s.40 and Sch.9, para.41.]   **A15.09**

Other awards

Provisions for orders as to costs in other circumstances

19.—(1)–(3A) *[Regulation-making powers.]*   **A15.10**

(4) The Court of Appeal may order the payment out of central funds of such sums as appear to it to be reasonably sufficient to compensate an appellant who is not in custody and who appears before it on, or in connection with, his appeal under Part I of the Criminal Appeal Act 1968.

(5) *[Regulation-making powers.]*

Costs against legal representatives, etc.

19A. *[Omitted.]*   **A15.11**

[Provision for award of costs against third parties

19B. *[Omitted.]]*

Supplemental

Regulations

20. *[Omitted.]*   **A15.12**

Interpretation, etc.

21.—(1) In this Part —   **A15.13**

[*"accused"* and *"appellant"*, in a case where section 44A of the Criminal Appeal Act 1968 (death of convicted person) applies, include the person approved under that section;]

"defendant's costs order" has the meaning given in section 16 of this Act;

*   *   *

[*"legally assisted person"*, in relation to any proceedings, means a person to whom [a right to representation funded by the Legal Services Commission as part of the Criminal Defence Service] has been granted for the purposes of the proceedings;]

"proceedings" includes—

    (a) proceedings in any court below; and

    (b) in relation to the determination of an appeal by any court, any application made to that court for leave to bring the appeal; and

"witness" means any person properly attending to give evidence, whether or not he gives evidence or is called at the instance of one of the parties or of the court, but does not include a person attending as a witness to character only unless the court has certified that the interests of justice required his attendance.

(2) Except as provided by or under this Part no costs shall be allowed on the hearing or determination of, or of any proceedings preliminary or incidental to, an appeal to the Court of Appeal under Part I of the Criminal Appeal Act 1968.

(3) Subject to rules of court made under section 53(1) of the Supreme Court Act 1981 (power by rules to distribute business of Court of Appeal between its civil and criminal divisions), the jurisdiction of the Court of Appeal under this Part, or under regulations made under this Part, shall be exercised by the criminal division of that Court; and references in this Part to the Court of Appeal shall be construed as references to that division.

(4) For the purposes of sections 16 and 17 of this Act, the costs of any party to proceedings shall be taken to include the expense of compensating any witness for the expense, trouble or loss of time, properly incurred in or incidental to his attendance.

[(4A) Where one party to any proceedings is a legally assisted person then—

    (a) for the purposes of sections 16 and 17 of this Act, his costs shall be taken not to include [the cost of representation funded for him by the Legal Services Commission as part of the Criminal Defence Service;] and

    (b) for the purposes of sections 18 [[to 19B] of this Act, his costs shall be taken to include the cost of representation funded for him by the Legal Services Commission as part of the Criminal Defence Service].]

(5) Where, in any proceedings in a criminal cause or matter or in either of the cases mentioned in subsection (6) below, an interpreter is required because of the accused's lack of English, the expenses properly incurred on his employment shall not be treated as costs of any party to the proceedings.

(6) The cases are—

    (a) where an information charging the accused with an offence is laid before a justice of the peace … but not proceeded with and the expenses are incurred on the employment of the interpreter for the proceedings on the information; and

(b) where the accused is [sent] for trial but not tried and the expenses are incurred on the employment of the interpreter for the proceedings in the Crown Court.

[Section 21 is printed as amended by the Legal Aid Act 1988 s.45(2) and (4), Sch.5, paras 14 and 15, and Sch.6; the Criminal Appeal Act 1995 s.29(1) and Sch.2, para.15; the Access to Justice Act 1999 s.106 and Sch.15, Pt 5(3); and also s.24 and Sch.4, paras 27 and 30; the Courts Act 2003 s.109(1) and Sch.8, para.289; the Criminal Justice Act 2003 s.41 and Sch.3, para.57(4). **A15.14**

In s.21(4A)(a), the word "include" has been retained editorially although it was formally repealed by the Access to Justice Act 1999 s.24 and Sch.4, paras 27 and 30(1) and (3)(a).]

The Transport Act 1985

(1985 c.67)

A16.01 *An Act to amend the law relating to road passenger transport ...*

[30th October 1985]

* * *

PART II
Regulation of Road Passenger Transport in London
London local service licences

Section

* * *

* * *

PART VI
Miscellaneous and General

Section

* * *

Provisions supplementary to Parts I and II

* * *

* * *

General supplementary provisions

* * *

* * *

SCHEDULES

* * *

PART I

GENERAL PROVISIONS RELATING TO ROAD PASSENGER TRANSPORT

*   *   *

Meaning of "local service"

Local services

A16.02   **2.**—(1) In this Act *"local service"* means a service, using one or more public service vehicles, for the carriage of passengers by road at separate fares other than one—

    (a) which is excluded by subsection (4) below; or

    (b) in relation to which (except in an emergency) one or both of the conditions mentioned in subsection (2) below are met with respect to every passenger using the service.

   (2) The conditions are that—

    (a) the place where he is set down is fifteen miles or more, measured in a straight line, from the place where he was taken up;

    (b) some point on the route between those places is fifteen miles or more, measured in a straight line, from either of those places.

   (3) Where a service consists of one or more parts with respect to which one or both of the conditions are met, and one or more parts with respect to which neither of them is met, each of those parts shall be treated as a separate service for the purposes of subsection (1) above.

   (4) A service shall not be regarded for the purposes of this Act as a local service if—

    (a) the conditions set out in Part III of Schedule 1 to the 1981 Act (trips organised privately by persons acting independently of vehicle operators, etc.) are met in respect of each journey made by the vehicles used in providing the service; or

    (b) every vehicle used in providing the service is so used under a permit granted under section 19 of this Act.

   (5) Subsections (5)(b), (c) and (6) of section 1 of the 1981 Act (meaning of "fares") shall apply for the purposes of this section.

*   *   *

Taxis and hire cars

*   *   *

Advance booking of taxis and hire cars at separate fares

A16.03   **11.**—(1) Where the conditions mentioned in subsection (2) below are met, a licensed taxi or licensed hire car may be used for the carriage of passengers for hire or reward at separate fares without thereby—

    (a) becoming a public service vehicle for the purposes of the 1981 Act or any related enactment; or

(b) ceasing (otherwise than by virtue of any provision made under section 13 of this Act) to be subject to the taxi code or (as the case may be) the hire car code.

(2) The conditions are that—

(a) all the passengers carried on the occasion in question booked their journeys in advance; and

(b) each of them consented, when booking his journey, to sharing the use of the vehicle on that occasion with others on the basis that a separate fare would be payable by each passenger for his own journey on that occasion.

Use of taxis [or hire cars] in providing local services

12.—(1) Where the holder of a taxi licence [or a private hire vehicle licence]— **A16.04**

(a) applies to the appropriate traffic commissioner for a restricted PSV operator's licence to be granted to him under Part II of the 1981 Act; and

(b) states in his application that he proposes to use one or more licensed taxis to provide a local service;

section 14 of the 1981 Act (conditions to be met before grant of PSV operator's licence) shall not apply and the commissioner shall grant the application.

(2) In this section *"special licence"* means a restricted PSV operator's licence granted by virtue of this section.

(3) [...]

(4) Without prejudice to his powers to attach other conditions under section 16 of the 1981 Act, any traffic commissioner granting a special licence shall attach to it, under that section, the conditions mentioned in subsection (5) below.

(5) The conditions are—

(a) that every vehicle used under the licence shall be one for which the holder of the licence has a taxi licence [or a private hire vehicle licence]; and

(b) that no vehicle shall be used under the licence otherwise than for the purpose of providing a local service with one or more stopping places within the area of the authority which granted [the relevant licence for that vehicle].

(6) In subsection (5)(b) above *"local service"* does not include an excursion or tour.

(7) The maximum number of vehicles which the holder of a special licence may at any one time use under the licence shall be the number of vehicles for which (for the time being) he holds [relevant licences]; and a condition to that effect shall be attached to every special licence under section 16(1) of the 1981 Act.

(8) Section 1(2) of the 1981 Act (vehicle used as public service vehicle to be treated as such until that use is permanently discontinued) shall not apply to any use of a licensed taxi [or a licensed hire car] for the provision of a local service under a special licence.

(9) At any time when a licensed taxi [or a licensed hire car] is being so used it shall carry such documents, plates and marks, in such manner as may be prescribed.

(10) [At any time when a licensed taxi or a licensed hire car is being so used the prescribed provisions of the taxi code or, as the case may be, the hire car code shall apply in relation to it;] and any such provision may be so applied subject to such modifications as may be prescribed.

[(10A) In subsections (9) and (10) *"prescribed"* means prescribed by the appropriate authority.]

(11) For the purposes of section 12(3) of the 1981 Act (which provides that where two or more PSV operators' licences are held they must be granted by traffic commissioners for different traffic areas), special licences shall be disregarded.

(12) A person may hold more than one special licence but shall not at the same time hold more than one such licence granted by the traffic commissioner for a particular traffic area.

(13) The following provisions shall not apply in relation to special licences or (as the case may be) the use of vehicles under such licences—

> (a) sections 16(1A) and (2), 17(3)(d), 18 to 20 … and 26 of the 1981 Act; and
>
> (b) section 26(5) and (6) of this Act;

and for the purposes of section 12 of that Act this section shall be treated as if it were in Part II of that Act.

A16.05   *[Section 12 is printed as amended by the Road Traffic (Driver Licensing and Information Systems) Act 1989 s.16 and Sch.6; the Deregulation and Contracting Out Act 1994 s.68 and Sch.14, para.8; the Local Transport Act 2008 s.53.*

The text of s.12(12) in its application to the holder of a special licence who is in a partnership is modified by the Operation of Public Service Vehicles (Partnership) Regulations 1986 (SI 1986/1628) Sch., Pt 2 (not reproduced in this work).

The Local Services (Operation by Licensed Hire Cars) Regulations 2009 (SI 2009/2863) apply in relation to a vehicle which is a licensed hire car for the purposes of this section at any time when that vehicle is being used to provide a local service under a special licence (reg.3).]

Provisions supplementary to sections 10 to 12

A16.06   **13.**—(1), (2) *[Power to make orders modifying taxi code and hire car code.]*

(3) In this section, and in sections 10 to 12 of this Act —

> [*"the appropriate authority"* means—
>
> > (a) in relation to—
> >
> > > (i) a taxi licensed under section 37 of the Town Police Clauses Act 1847 or any similar enactment which applies outside the London taxi area,
> > >
> > > (ii) a licensed hire car licensed under section 48 of the Local Government (Miscellaneous Provisions) Act 1976, or
> > >
> > > (iii) *[applies to Scotland]*,
> >
> > the Secretary of State;
> >
> > (b) in relation to—
> >
> > > (i) a taxi licensed under section 6 of the Metropolitan Public Carriage Act 1869, or

(ii) a licensed hire car licensed under section 7 of the Private Hire Vehicles (London) Act 1998,

Transport for London;]

"licensed taxi" means—

    (a) in England and Wales, a vehicle licensed under—

        (i) section 37 of the Town Police Clauses Act 1847; or

        (ii) section 6 of the Metropolitan Public Carriage Act 1869; or under any similar enactment; and

    (b) *[applies to Scotland.]*

"London taxi area" means the area to which the Metropolitan Public Carriage Act 1869 applies;

[*"licensed hire car"* means—

    (a) in England and Wales—

        (i) for the purposes of section 11 of this Act, a vehicle licensed under section 48 of the Local Government (Miscellaneous Provisions) Act 1976 or section 7 of the Private Hire Vehicles (London) Act 1998,

        (ii) for the purposes of section 12 of this Act, a vehicle licensed under s ection 48 of the Local Government (Miscellaneous Provisions) Act 1976;

    (b) *[applies to Scotland]*;]

"hire car code", in relation to a licensed hire car used as mentioned in section 11 [or 12] of this Act, means those provisions made by or under any enactment which would apply if it were hired by a single passenger for his exclusive use;

"related enactment", in relation to the 1981 Act, means any statutory provision (whenever passed or made) relating to public service vehicles in which public service vehicle is defined directly or indirectly by reference to the provisions of the 1981 Act;

"taxi code", in relation to any licensed taxi used as mentioned in section 10, 11 or 12 of this Act, means—

    (a) in England and Wales, those provisions made by or under any enactment which would apply if the vehicle were plying for hire and were hired by a single passenger for his exclusive use; and

    (b) *[applies to Scotland.]*

"taxi licence" means a licence under section 6 of the Metropolitan Public Carriage Act 1869, section 37 of the Town Police Clauses Act 1847 or any similar enactment, or a taxi licence under section 10 of the Civic Government (Scotland) Act 1982.

[*"relevant licence"* means—

    (a) in relation to a licensed taxi, a taxi licence, and

    (b) in relation to a licensed hire car, a private hire vehicle licence;

"private hire vehicle licence" means—

    (a) in England and Wales, a licence under section 48 of the Local Government (Miscellaneous Provisions) Act 1976;

    (b) *[applies to Scotland].*]

(4) *[Scope of orders under s.13(1).]*

A16.07   *[Section 13 is printed as amended by the Private Hire Vehicles (London) Act 1998 ss.39(1), 40(2) and Sch.1, para.4; the Local Transport Act 2008 s.54.]*

[Application of sections 10 to 13 to London

A16.08   **13A.**—(1) Transport for London may by order provide that section 12 of this Act is to apply to vehicles licensed under section 7 of the Private Hire Vehicles (London) Act 1998 as it applies to vehicles licensed under section 48 of the Local Government (Miscellaneous Provisions) Act 1976.

(2) An order under subsection (1) of this section may amend the definitions of *"licensed hire car"* and *"private hire vehicle licence"* in section 13 of this Act accordingly.

(3) Transport for London must consult such representative organisations as it thinks fit before making—

     (a) regulations under section 12(9) or (10) of this Act;

     (b) an order under section 13(1) of this Act or subsection (1) of this section.

(4) Any power of Transport for London to make—

     (a) regulations under section 12(9) or (10) of this Act, or

     (b) an order under section 13(1) of this Act, includes a power to vary or revoke any previous such regulations or order (as the case may be).

(5) Subsection (4) applies notwithstanding that the previous regulations were made, or the previous order was made, by the Secretary of State by statutory instrument.

(6) Transport for London must print and publish—

     (a) any regulations made by it under section 12(9) or (10) of this Act;

     (b) any order made by it under section 13(1) of this Act or subsection (1) of this section.

(7) Transport for London may charge a fee for the sale of copies of any regulations, or any order, printed under subsection (6).]

A16.09   *[Section 13A is printed as inserted by the Local Transport Act 2008 s.54(8).]*

            *   *   *

Modification of PSV requirements in relation to vehicles used for certain purposes

Exemption from PSV operator and driver licensing requirements of vehicles used under permits

A16.10   **18.**—[(1)] [Section 12(1)] of the 1981 Act (licensing of operators ... in relation to the use of public service vehicles for the carriage of passengers) shall not apply—

     (a) to the use of any vehicle under a permit granted under section 19 of this Act, if and so long as the requirements under subsection (2) of that section are met; [or]

     (b) to the use of any vehicle under a permit granted under section 22 of this Act; ...]

(c) [...]

[(2) Where a holder of a licence under Part III of the Road Traffic Act 1988 was first granted a licence under that Part before 1st January 1997, he may drive any small bus at a time when it is being used as mentioned in paragraph (a) or (b) of subsection (1) above, notwithstanding that his licence under that Part does not authorise him to drive a small bus when it is being so used.

(3) Where—

(a) a holder of a licence under Part III of the Road Traffic Act 1988 was first granted a licence under that Part on or after 1st January 1997, or

(b) a Community licence holder is authorised by virtue of section 99A(1) of that Act to drive in Great Britain a motor vehicle of any class,

he may drive any small bus to which subsection (4) below applies at a time when it is being used as mentioned in paragraph (a) or (b) of subsection (1) above, notwithstanding that he is not authorised by his licence under that Part or by virtue of that section (as the case may be) to drive such a bus.

(4) This subsection applies to any small bus which, when laden with the heaviest load which it is constructed to carry, weighs—

(a) not more than 3.5 tonnes, excluding any part of that weight which is attributable to specialised equipment intended for the carriage of disabled passengers, and

(b) not more than 4.25 tonnes otherwise.

(5) In this section —

"Community licence" has the same meaning as in Part III of the Road Traffic Act 1988,

and

"small bus" has the same meaning as in sections 19 to 21 of this Act.]

[Section 18 is printed as amended by the Road Traffic (Driver Licensing and **A16.11**
Information Systems) Act 1989 ss.7, 16, Sch.3, para.4(a)–(c), and Sch.6; the
Driving Licences (Community Driving Licence) Regulations 1996 (SI 1996/1974)
reg.4 and Sch.3, para.1 (not reproduced in this work).]

[Permits in relation to use of public service vehicles by educational and other bodies]

19.—(1) In this section and sections 20 and 21 of this Act —   **A16.12**

"bus" means a vehicle which is adapted to carry more than eight passengers;

"large bus" means a vehicle which is adapted to carry more than sixteen passengers;

"small bus" means a vehicle which is adapted to carry more than eight but not more than sixteen passengers; and

"permit" means a permit granted under this section in relation to the use of [a public service vehicle] for carrying passengers for hire or reward.

(2) The requirements that must be met in relation to the use of [a public service vehicle] under a permit for the exemption under [section 18(1)(a)] of this Act to apply are that the [vehicle]—

(a) is being used by a body to whom a permit has been granted under this section;

(b) is not being used for the carriage of members of the general public nor with a view to profit nor incidentally to an activity which is itself carried on with a view to profit;

(c) is being used in every respect in accordance with any conditions attached to the permit; and

(d) is not being used in contravention of any provision of regulations made under section 21 of this Act.

(3) A permit in relation to the use of [a public service vehicle other than a large bus] may be granted by a body designated by an order under subsection (7) below either to itself or to any other body to whom, in accordance with the order, it is entitled to grant a permit.

(4) A permit in relation to the use of [a public service vehicle other than a large bus] may be granted by a traffic commissioner to any body appearing to him to be eligible in accordance with subsection (8) below and to be carrying on in his area an activity which makes it so eligible.

(5) A permit in relation to the use of a large bus may be granted by a traffic commissioner to any body which assists and co-ordinates the activities of bodies within his area which appear to him to be concerned with—

(a) education;

(b) religion;

(c) social welfare; or

(d) other activities of benefit to the community.

(6) A traffic commissioner shall not grant a permit in relation to the use of a large bus unless satisfied that there will be adequate facilities or arrangements for maintaining any bus used under the permit in a fit and serviceable condition.

(7) The Secretary of State may by order designate for the purpose of this section bodies appearing to him to be eligible in accordance with subsection (8) below and, with respect to any body designated by it, any such order—

(a) shall specify the classes of body to whom the designated body may grant permits;

(b) may impose restrictions with respect to the grant of permits by the designated body and, in particular, may provide that no permit may be granted, either generally or in such cases as may be specified in the order, unless there are attached to the permit such conditions as may be so specified; and

(c) may require the body to make returns [and keep records] with regard to the permits granted[, varied or revoked] by it.

(8) A body is eligible in accordance with this subsection if it is concerned with—

(a) education;

(b) religion;

(c) social welfare;

(d) recreation; or

(e) other activities of benefit to the community.

(9) A body may hold more than one permit but may not use more than one [vehicle] at any one time under the same permit.

[Section 19 is printed as amended by the Local Transport Act 2008 s.57. **A16.13**

The functions of the Secretary of State exercisable under s.19(7) in relation to Wales have been transferred to the National Assembly for Wales by the National Assembly for Wales (Transfer of Functions) Order 1999 (SI 1999/672; not reproduced in this work) art.2 and Sch.1.

As to the transfer of functions of the Secretary of State under s.19(7) which are exercisable in relation to Scotland to the Scottish Ministers, see the Scotland Act 1998 (Transfer of Functions to the Scottish Ministers etc.) Order 1999 (SI 1999/ 1750; not reproduced in this work) art.2 and Sch.1.

For the bodies designated for the purposes of s.19(7), see the Section 19 Minibus (Designated Bodies) Order 1987 (SI 1987/1229), as amended (not reproduced in this work).]

Further provision with respect to permits under section 19

20. *[Omitted.]* **A16.14**

Permits under section 19: regulations

21.—(1) Regulations may prescribe— **A16.15**

    (a) the conditions to be fulfilled by any person driving a bus while it is being used under a permit;

    (b) the conditions as to fitness which are to be fulfilled by any small bus used under a permit;

    (c) the form of permits; and

    (d) the documents, plates and marks to be carried by any bus while it is being used under a permit and the manner and position in which they are to be carried.

(2) Where regulations are made by virtue of subsection (1)(b) above, section 6 of the 1981 Act (certificate of initial fitness for public service vehicles) shall not apply in relation to any small bus subject to the regulations.

(3) Regulations under this section may contain such transitional provisions as the Secretary of State thinks fit.

[The Section 19 Permit Regulations 2009 (SI 2009/365; not reproduced in this **A16.16** *work) have been made in part under s.21.]*

Community bus permits

22.—(1) In this section and section 23 of this Act — **A16.17**

    "community bus service" means a local service provided—

        (a) by a body concerned for the social and welfare needs of one or more communities;

        (b) without a view to profit, either on the part of that body or of anyone else; and

        (c) by means of a vehicle adapted to carry more than eight [...]; and

    "community bus permit" means a permit granted under this section in relation to the use of a public service vehicle—

        (a) in providing a community bus service; or

        (b) in providing a community bus service and (other than in the course of a local service) carrying passengers for hire or reward where the carriage of those passengers will directly assist the provision of the community bus service by providing financial support for it.

(2)–(4) *[Omitted.]*

A16.18 *[Section 22 is printed as amended by the Local Transport Act 2008 s.59(2) and s.141 and Sch.7(3).]*

Further provisions with respect to community bus permits

A16.19 **23.**—(1)–(4) *[Omitted.]*

(5) Subject to section 68(3) of the 1981 Act (as applied by section 127(4) of this Act), if a condition attached to a community bus permit is contravened, the holder of the permit shall be liable on summary conviction to a fine not exceeding level 3 on the standard scale.

(6), (7) [...]

A16.20 *[The Community Bus Regulations 2009 (SI 2009/366; not reproduced in this work) have been made in part under s.23.]*

[Power to limit permits under section 19 or 22 to 5 years

A16.21 **23A.**—(1) Regulations may provide that any permit granted under section 19 or 22 of this Act on or after a date specified in the regulations is to be for such period not exceeding 5 years as may be identified in the permit by the person granting it.

(2) Nothing in subsection (1) above or any regulations made by virtue of that subsection prevents the grant of subsequent permits under section 19 or 22 of this Act to any person for further such periods.]

A16.22 *[Section 23A is printed as inserted by the Local Transport Act 2008 s.60(1).]*

* * *

Further amendments with respect to PSV operators' licences

* * *

Plying for hire by large public service vehicles

A16.23 **30.**—(1) A public service vehicle which is adapted to carry more than eight passengers shall not be used on a road in plying for hire as a whole.

(2) Subject to section 68(3) of the 1981 Act (as applied by section 127(4) of this Act), if a vehicle is used in contravention of subsection (1) above, the operator of the vehicle shall be liable on summary conviction to a fine not exceeding level 3 on the standard scale.

* * *

PART II

REGULATION OF ROAD PASSENGER TRANSPORT IN LONDON

A16.24 *[Part 2 of this Act (ss.34–46) has been prospectively repealed by the Greater*

London Authority Act 1999 s.423 and Sch.34, Pt 2. At March 1, 2011, no date had been announced for its repeal, but art.3(3) of the Regulation of Bus Services in Greater London (Transitional Provisions) Order 2000 (SI 2000/1462; not reproduced in this work) states that it will be repealed immediately after the end of the transitional period (as defined). By art.2 of SI 2000/1462, the "transitional period" is defined as the period which begins with July 3, 2000 and ends with the last day on which a London local service licence granted under the 1985 Act ceases to be in force.]

London local service licences

London local services

34.—(1) In this Act *"London local service"* means (subject to subsection (3) below) a local service with one or more stopping places in London.   **A16.25**

(2) In this Part of this Act —

    (a) *"bus service"* means a local service other than an excursion or tour; and

    (b) *"London bus service"* means a London local service other than an excursion or tour.

(3) Where a local service is or is to be provided both inside and outside London, any part of the service which is or is to be provided outside London shall be treated as a separate service for the purposes of this Act if there is any stopping place for that part of the service outside London.

[As to the prospective repeal of all the provisions in Pt 2 of this Act, see the note at § A16.24 above.]   **A16.26**

London local service licences

35.—(1) Subject to subsection (2) below and to section 36 of this Act, a London local service shall not be provided except under a London local service licence granted in accordance with the following provisions of this Part of this Act.   **A16.27**

(2) A London local service licence is not required for the provision by any person under an agreement with the Railways Board[, or the Director of Passenger Rail Franchising, of any service secured by the Board or, as the case may be, the Director of Rail Franchising under section 4A of the 1962 Act (provision of road passenger transport services)].

(3) The traffic commissioner for the Metropolitan Traffic Area (referred to below in this Part of this Act as the metropolitan traffic commissioner) shall be responsible for granting London local service licences.

(4) Subject to subsection (5) below and to section 38(4) of this Act, a London local service licence shall be of no effect at any time at which the holder does not also hold—

    (a) a PSV operator's licence granted by the metropolitan traffic commissioner or by the traffic commissioner for any other traffic area …; or

    (b) a permit under section 22 of this Act.

(5) Subsection (4) above does not apply to a London local service licence held by a local education authority.

(6) Subject to section 68(3) of the 1981 Act (as applied by section 127(4) of this Act), if a London local service is provided in contravention of subsection (1) above, the operator of the service shall be liable on summary conviction to a fine not exceeding level 3 on the standard scale.

A16.28   *[Section 35 is printed as amended by the Railways Act 1993 (Consequential Modifications) (No.2) Order 1994 (SI 1994/1649; not reproduced in this work); the Statute Law (Repeals) Act 1995 s.1(1) and Sch.1, Pt 5, group 2.*

As to the prospective repeal of all the provisions in Pt 2 of this Act, see the note at § A16.24 above.

Pending the repeal of Pt 2, s.35 has effect (after July 2, 2000) as if subss.(1)– (2) and (6) were omitted; see the Regulation of Bus Services in Greater London (Transitional Provisions) Order 2000 (SI 2000/1462; not reproduced in this work) art.3(1)(a).

See further s.39(4) of this Act below.]

London bus services under the control of London Regional Transport

A16.29   **36.**—(1) A London local service licence is not required for the provision of a London bus service—

      (a) by London Regional Transport or any subsidiary of theirs; or

      (b) by any other person in pursuance of any agreement entered into by London Regional Transport by virtue of [section 3(2) or (2A)(a)] of the London Regional Transport Act 1984 (referred to below in this section as the 1984 Act).

   (2)–(7) *[Omitted.]*

A16.30   *[Section 36 is printed as amended by the London Regional Transport Act 1996 s.4(2)(c).*

As to the prospective repeal of all the provisions in Pt 2 of this Act, see the note at § A16.24 above.

Pending the repeal of Pt 2 as a whole, Pt 2 has effect (after July 2, 2000) as if s.36 were omitted; see the Regulation of Bus Services in Greater London (Transitional Provisions) Order 2000 (SI 2000/1462; not reproduced in this work) art.3(1)(b).]

Grant of licences

A16.31   **37.** *[Omitted.]*

Conditions attached to licences

A16.32   **38.**—(1)–(6) *[Omitted.]*

(7) Subject to s.68(3) of the 1981 Act (as applied by s.127(4) of this Act), if a condition attached under this section to a London local service licence is contravened, the holder of the licence shall be liable on summary conviction to a fine not exceeding level 3 on the standard scale.

A16.33   *[As to the prospective repeal of all the provisions in Pt II of this Act, see the note at § A16.24 above.]*

Grant of licences for certain excursions or tours

A16.34   **39.**—(1) This section applies where, in the case of any application for a London local service licence, the metropolitan traffic commissioner is satisfied that the service which the applicant proposes to provide under the licence ("the proposed service") would be an excursion or tour and is also satisfied either—

    (a) that the proposed service would not compete directly with any autho-rised London bus service; or

    (b) that the proposed service would operate only to enable passengers to attend special events.

(2) In subsection (1)(a) above, *"authorised London bus service"* means—

    (a) any London bus service for which a London local service licence has been granted; and

    (b) any London bus service which, by virtue of section 36(1) of this Act, does not require a London local service licence.

(3) In any case to which this section applies, sections 35, 37 and 38 of this Act shall apply subject to the modifications provided by the following provisions of this section.

(4) Section 35(4) of this Act shall not prevent a London local service licence granted in pursuance of this section from having effect for the purposes of the provision of a service by means of a vehicle whose operator holds any such licence or permit as is there mentioned …

(5)–(10) *[Omitted.]*

[Section 39 is printed as amended by the Statute Law (Repeals) Act 1995 s.1(1)   **A16.35** *and Sch.1, Pt 5, group 2.*

    As to the prospective repeal of all the provisions in Pt 2 of this Act, see the note at § A16.24 above.]

*   *   *

Part VI

Miscellaneous and General

*   *   *

Provisions supplementary to Parts I and II

*   *   *

Offences and legal proceedings

127.—(1) Section 65 of the 1981 Act (forgery and misuse of documents) shall   **A16.36** apply to the following documents, namely—

    (a) a permit under section 19 or 22 of this Act; and

    (b) a London local service licence.

(2) Section 66 of that Act (false statements to obtain licence, etc.) shall apply in relation to a false statement for the purpose of obtaining the grant of any such permit or licence as it applies in relation to a false statement for the purposes there mentioned.

(3) Section 67 of that Act (penalty for breach of regulations under that Act) shall have effect as if Parts I and II of this Act were contained in that Act.

(4) The defence provided by section 68(3) of that Act (that the person charged took all reasonable precautions and exercised all due diligence to avoid the commission of an offence under certain provisions of that Act) shall apply in relation to an offence under any of the following provisions of this Act, that is to say, sections 23(5), 30(2), 35(6) and 37(7).

(5) The provisions of that Act mentioned in subsection (6) below shall apply in relation to an offence, or (as the case may be) in relation to proceedings for an offence, under Part I or II of this Act as they apply in relation to an offence, or in relation to proceedings for an offence, under Part II of that Act.

(6) Those provisions are—

> section 69 (restrictions on institution in England or Wales of proceedings for an offence under Part II);
>
> section 70 (duty to give information as to identity of driver in certain cases);
>
> section 71 (evidence of certificate in proceedings in England or Wales for an offence under Part II);
>
> section 72 (proof in summary proceedings in England and Wales of identity of driver of vehicle); and
>
> section 74 (offences under Part II committed by companies).

(7) *[Applies to Scotland.]*

General supplementary provisions

*   *   *

Interpretation

A16.37   137.—(1) In this Act, unless the context otherwise requires—

> *"the 1962 Act"* means the Transport Act 1962;
>
> *"the 1972 Act"* means the Local Government Act 1972;
>
> *"the 1968 Act"* means the Transport Act 1968;
>
> *"the 1981 Act"* means the Public Passenger Vehicles Act 1981;
>
> *"body"* means a body of persons, whether corporate or unincorporate;

*   *   *

> *"excursion or tour"* means a service for the carriage of passengers by road at separate fares on which the passengers travel together on a journey, with or without breaks, from one or more places to one or more other places and back;

*   *   *

> *"local service"* has the meaning given by section 2 of this Act;
>
> *"London"* means the administrative area of Greater London as for the time being constituted;
>
> *"London local service"* has the meaning given by section 34(1) of this Act;

*   *   *

> *"prescribed"* means prescribed by regulations;

* * *

"regulations" means regulations made by the Secretary of State;

* * *

"social services functions" means functions which are social services functions for the purposes of the Local Authority Social Services Act 1970;

* * *

"stopping place" means, in relation to any service or part of a service, a point at which passengers are (or, in the case of a proposed service, are proposed to be) taken up or set down in the course of that service or part;

* * *

"traffic area" means a traffic area constituted for the purposes of the 1981 Act, and section 80 of that Act shall apply to references in this Act to the Metropolitan Traffic Area;

* * *

and the expressions listed in subsection (2) below have the same meaning as in the 1981 Act.

(2) Those expressions are—

"company";
"contravention";
"fares";
"modification";
"operator" (in references to the operator of a vehicle);
"operating centre";
"PSV operator's licence";
"public service vehicle";
"road";
"statutory provision"; and
"traffic commissioner".

[(2A) In this Act —

(a) any reference to a county shall be construed in relation to Wales as including a reference to a county borough;

(b) any reference to a county council shall be construed in relation to Wales as including a reference to a county borough council; and

(c) section 17(4) and (5) of the Local Government (Wales) Act 1994 (references to counties and districts to be construed generally in relation to Wales as references to counties and county boroughs) shall not apply.]

(3) References in this Act to a vehicle's being used for carrying passengers for hire or reward shall be read in accordance with section 1(5) of the 1981 Act.

(4)–(6) *[Omitted.]*

(7) For the purposes of this Act the operator of a passenger transport service

of any description is the person, or each of the persons, providing the service; and for those purposes the operator of a vehicle being used on a road for the carriage of passengers for hire or reward at separate fares shall be taken to be providing the service by means of the vehicle unless he proves that the service is or forms part of a service provided not by himself but by one or more other persons.

(8) *[Omitted.]*

A16.38   *[Section 137 is printed as amended by the New Roads and Street Works Act 1991 s.168(1) and (2), Sch.8, Pt 4, para.117(1) and (3), and Sch.9; the Statute Law (Repeals) Act 1993 s.1(1) and Sch.1, Pt 14, group 2; the Local Government (Wales) Act 1994 s.22(1) and Sch.7, para.39(10).*

Only selected definitions in s.137(1) are reproduced.

The Public Service Vehicles (Conduct of Drivers, Inspectors, Conductors and Passengers) Regulations 1990 (SI 1990/1020) (q.v.) were made in part under s.137.]

*　　*　　*

SCHEDULE 1

AMENDMENTS CONSEQUENTIAL ON THE ABOLITION OF ROAD SERVICE LICENSING

*　　*　　*

A16.39   16.—(1) Subject to any provision made by or under this Act, in any enactment or instrument passed or made before the commencement of section 1 of this Act —

(a) any reference to a stage carriage service shall be construed as a reference to a local service;

(b) any reference to an express carriage service shall be construed as a reference to any service for the carriage of passengers for hire or reward at separate fares which is neither a local service nor one provided by a vehicle to which sub-paragraph (2) below applies;

(c) any reference to a stage carriage shall be construed as a reference to a public service vehicle being used in the provision of a local service;

(d) any reference to any express carriage shall be construed as a reference to a public service vehicle being used to carry passengers for hire or reward at separate fares other than one being used in the provision of a local service; and

(e) any reference to a contract shall be construed as a reference to a public service vehicle being used to carry passengers for hire or reward otherwise than at separate fares.

(2) When used in circumstances in which the conditions set out in Part III of Schedule I to the 1981 Act are fulfilled, a public service vehicle carrying passengers at separate fares shall be treated, for the purposes of any enactment or instrument to which paragraph (d) or (e) of sub-paragraph (1) above applies, as being used to carry passengers otherwise than at separate fares.

A16.40   *[Although s.1(3) of the Act was brought into operation on January 6, 1986 (see the Transport Act 1985 (Commencement No.1) Order 1985 (SI 1985/1887) art.3(1) and Sch.) for limited purposes ("to the extent necessary for the bringing into force of the provisions of Sch.1 brought into force by this Order"), it is thought that "commencement" of s.1 (see para.16(1) above) is the date when that section was brought fully into operation (i.e. October 26, 1986) (see the Transport Act 1985 (Commencement) (No.6) Order 1986 (SI 1986/1794)).]*

* * *

SCHEDULE 7

Minor and Consequential Amendments

General

1. In England and Wales, the provisions made by or under any enactment which apply **A16.41**
to motor vehicles used—

    (a) to carry passengers under a contract express or implied for the use of the vehicle
        as a whole at or for a fixed or agreed rate or sum; and

    (b) to ply for hire for such use;

shall apply to motor vehicles adapted to carry less than nine passengers as they apply to
motor vehicles adapted to carry less than eight passengers.

The Criminal Justice Act 1988

(1988 c.33)

A17.01 *An Act ... to amend the law with regard to the jurisdiction and powers of criminal courts ... and for connected purposes.*

[29th July 1988]

*   *   *

PART IV

REVIEWS OF SENTENCING

Scope of Part IV

A17.02   **35.**—(1) A case to which this Part of this Act applies may be referred to the Court of Appeal under section 36 below.

(2) Subject to Rules of Court, the jurisdiction of the Court of Appeal under section 36 below shall be exercised by the criminal division of the Court, and references to the Court of Appeal in this Part of this Act shall be construed as references to that division.

(3) This Part of this Act applies to any case[—

    (a) of a description specified in an order under this section; or

    (b) in which sentence is passed on a person—

        (i) for an offence triable only on indictment; or

        (ii) for an offence of a description specified in an order under this section]

(4) The Secretary of State may by order made by statutory instrument provide that this Part of this Act shall apply to any case [of a description specified in the order or to any case] in which sentence is passed on a person for an offence triable either way of a description specified in the order.

(5) A statutory instrument containing an order under this section shall be subject to annulment in pursuance of a resolution of either House of Parliament.

(6) In this Part of this Act *"sentence"* has the same meaning as in the Criminal Appeal Act 1968, except that it does not include an interim hospital order under Part III of the Mental Health Act 1983, and "sentencing" shall be construed accordingly.

(7)–(11) *[Apply to Northern Ireland.]*

A17.03   *[Section 35 is printed as amended by the Criminal Justice and Public Order Act 1994 s.168(1) and Sch.9, para.34.*

The term "sentence" is defined in s.50 of the Criminal Appeal Act 1968 for the purposes of that Act.]

Reviews of sentencing

A17.04   **36.**—(1) If it appears to the Attorney General—

    (a) that the sentencing of a person in a proceeding in the Crown Court has been unduly lenient; and

    (b) that the case is one to which this Part of this Act applies,

he may, with the leave of the Court of Appeal, refer the case to them for them to review the sentencing of that person; and on such a reference the Court of Appeal may—

      (i) quash any sentence passed on him in the proceeding; and

      (ii) in place of it pass such sentence as they think appropriate for the case and as the court below had power to pass when dealing with him.

(2) Without prejudice to the generality of subsection (1) above, the condition specified in paragraph (a) of that subsection may be satisfied if it appears to the Attorney General that the judge

    [(a) erred in law as to his powers of sentencing; or

    (b) failed to impose a sentence required by—

      (i) section 51A(2) of the Firearms Act 1968;

      (ii) section 110(2) or 111(2) of the Powers of Criminal Courts (Sentencing) Act 2000; [...]

      (iii) [section 225(2) or 226(2)] of the Criminal Justice Act 2003;]

      [(iv) under section 29(4) or (6) of the Violent Crime Reduction Act 2006.]

(3) For the purposes of this Part of this Act any two or more sentences are to be treated as passed in the same proceeding if they would be so treated for the purposes of section [11] of the Criminal Appeal Act 1968.

    [(3A) *[Review of minimum term of mandatory life sentence].*]

(4) No judge shall sit as a member of the Court of Appeal on the hearing of, or shall determine any application in proceedings incidental or preliminary to, a reference under this section of a sentence passed by himself.

(5) Where the Court of Appeal have concluded their review of a case referred to them under this section the Attorney General or the person to whose sentencing the reference relates may refer a point of law involved in any sentence passed on that person in the proceeding to [the Supreme Court for its opinion], and [the Supreme Court shall consider the point and give its opinion] on it accordingly, and either remit the case to the Court of Appeal to be dealt with or [itself deal with the case].

(6) A reference under subsection (5) above shall be made only with the leave of the Court of Appeal or [the Supreme Court]; and leave shall not be granted unless it is certified by the Court of Appeal that the point of law is of general public importance and it appears to the Court of Appeal or [the Supreme Court] (as the case may be) that the point is one which ought to be considered by [the Supreme Court].

(7) For the purpose of dealing with a case under this section the [Supreme Court] may exercise any powers of the Court of Appeal.

(8) The supplementary provisions contained in Schedule 3 to this Act shall have effect.

(9) *[Applies to Northern Ireland.]*

A17.05   *[Section 36 is printed as amended by the Crime (Sentences) Act 1997 s.55(1) and Sch.4, para.13; the Powers of Criminal Courts (Sentencing) Act 2000 s.165(1) and Sch.9, para.102; the Criminal Justice Act 2003 s.272(1), s.304 and Sch.32, para.46, s.331 and Sch.36, para.96(a); the Constitutional Reform Act 2005 s.40; the Violent Crime Reduction Act 2006 s.49, Sch.1, para.3(2) and s.65, Sch.5; the Criminal Justice and Immigration Act 2008 s.148 and Sch.26(2), para.23.]*

PART V

JURISDICTION, IMPRISONMENT, FINES, ETC.

Jurisdiction

*   *   *

Power to join in indictment count for common assault, etc.

A17.06   **40.**—(1) A count charging a person with a summary offence to which this section applies may be included in an indictment if the charge—

    (a) is founded on the same facts or evidence as a count charging an indictable offence; or

    (b) is part of a series of offences of the same or similar character as an indictable offence which is also charged,

but only if (in either case) the facts or evidence relating to the offence were disclosed [to a magistrates' court inquiring into the offence as examining justices] [or are disclosed by material which, in pursuance of regulations made under paragraph 1 of Schedule 3 to the Crime and Disorder Act 1998 (procedure where person sent for trial under section 51 [or 51A]), has been served on the person charged].

(2) Where a count charging an offence to which this section applies is included in an indictment, the offence shall be tried in the same manner as if it were an indictable offence; but the Crown Court may only deal with the offender in respect of it in a manner in which a magistrates' court could have dealt with him.

(3) The offences to which this section applies are—

    (a) common assault;

    [(aa) an offence under section 90(1) of the Criminal Justice Act 1991 (assaulting a prisoner custody officer);]

    [(ab) an offence under section 13(1) of the Criminal Justice and Public Order Act 1994 (assaulting a secure training custody officer);]

    (b) an offence under section 12(1) of the Theft Act 1968 (taking motor vehicle or other conveyance without authority, etc.);

    (c) an offence under [section 103(1)(b) of the Road Traffic Act 1988] (driving a motor vehicle while disqualified);

    (d) an offence mentioned in the first column of Schedule 2 to the Magistrates' Courts Act 1980 (criminal damage, etc.) which would otherwise be triable only summarily by virtue of section 22(2) of that Act; and

    (e) any summary offence specified under subsection (4) below.

(4) The Secretary of State may by order made by statutory instrument specify for the purposes of this section any summary offence which is punishable with imprisonment or involves obligatory or discretionary disqualification from driving.

(5) *[Statutory instruments subject to negative resolution procedure.]*

[Section 40 is printed as amended by the Road Traffic (Consequential Provisions) Act 1988 s.4 and Sch.3, para.39; the Criminal Justice and Public Order Act 1994 s.168(1) and Sch.9, para.35; the Crime and Disorder Act 1998 s.119 and Sch.8, para.66; and the Criminal Justice Act 2003 s.41 and Sch.3, para.60(7)(b).   **A17.07**

The words "to a magistrates' court inquiring into the offence as examining justices" within square brackets in s.40(1) were inserted in place of the words "in an examination or deposition taken before a justice in the presence of the person charged" on March 8, 1997 by the Criminal Procedure and Investigations Act 1996 s.47 and Sch.1, para.34, in relation to any alleged offence in relation to which Pt 1 of the 1996 Act applies; see the Criminal Procedure and Investigations Act 1996 (Commencement) (Section 65 and Schedules 1 and 2) Order 1997 (SI 1997/683). With effect from a day (or days) to be appointed, these words will be revoked by the Criminal Justice Act 2003 s.41 and Sch.3, para.60(7)(a) and Sch.37, Pt 4.]

Power of Crown Court to deal with summary offence where person committed for either-way offence

41.—(1) Where a magistrates' court commits a person to the Crown Court for   **A17.08**
trial on indictment for an offence triable either way or a number of such offences, it may also commit him for trial for any summary offence with which he is charged and which—

    (a) is punishable with imprisonment or involves obligatory or discretionary disqualification from driving; and

    (b) arises out of circumstances which appear to the court to be the same as or connected with those giving rise to the offence, or one of the offences, triable either way,

whether or not evidence relating to that summary offence appears on the depositions or written statements in the case; and the trial of the information charging the summary offence shall then be treated as if the magistrates' court had adjourned it under section 10 of the Magistrates' Courts Act 1980 and had not fixed the time and place for its resumption.

(2) Where a magistrates' court commits a person to the Crown Court for trial on indictment for a number of offences triable either way and exercises the power conferred by subsection (1) above in respect of a summary offence, the magistrates' court shall give the Crown Court and the person who is committed for trial a notice stating which of the offences triable either way appears to the court to arise out of circumstances which are the same as or connected with those giving rise to the summary offence.

(3) A magistrates' court's decision to exercise the power conferred by subsection (1) above shall not be subject to appeal or liable to be questioned in any court.

(4) The committal of a person under this section in respect of an offence to

which section 40 above applies shall not preclude the exercise in relation to the offence of the power conferred by that section; but where he is tried on indictment for such an offence, the functions of the Crown Court under this section in relation to the offence shall cease.

(5) If he is convicted on the indictment, the Crown Court shall consider whether the conditions specified in subsection (1) above were satisfied.

(6) If it considers that they were satisfied, it shall state to him the substance of the summary offence and ask him whether he pleads guilty or not guilty.

(7) If he pleads guilty, the Crown Court shall convict him, but may deal with him in respect of that offence only in a manner in which a magistrates' court could have dealt with him.

[(8) If he does not plead guilty, the Crown Court may try him for the offence, but may deal with him only in a manner in which a magistrates' court could have dealt with him.]

(9) [...]

(10) The Crown Court shall inform the [designated officer for] the magistrates' court of the outcome of any proceedings under this section.

(11) Where the Court of Appeal allows an appeal against conviction of an offence triable either way which arose out of circumstances which were the same as or connected with those giving rise to a summary offence of which the appellant was convicted under this section —

> (a) it shall set aside his conviction of the summary offence and give the [designated officer for] the magistrates' court notice that it has done so; and
>
> (b) it may direct that no further proceedings in relation to the offence are to be undertaken;

and the proceedings before the Crown Court in relation to the offence shall thereafter be disregarded for all purposes.

(12) A notice under subsection (11) above shall include particulars of any direction given under paragraph (b) of that subsection in relation to the offence.

(13) [...]

A17.09   *[Section 41 is printed as amended by the Access to Justice Act 1999 s.90(1), Sch.13, paras 136 and 137, s.106 and Sch.15, Pt V(7); the Courts Act 2003 s.109(1) and (3), Sch.8, para.303 and Sch.10.*

The following new subsection is prospectively inserted after subs.(4) by the Domestic Violence, Crime and Victims Act 2004 s.58(1) and Sch.10, para.28:

> [(4A) The committal of a person under this section in respect of an offence to which section 40 above applies shall not prevent him being found guilty of that offence under section 6(3) of the Criminal Law Act 1967 (alternative verdicts on trial on indictment); but where he is convicted under that provision of such an offence, the functions of the Crown Court under this section in relation to the offence shall cease.]

With effect from a day to be appointed, s.41 will be revoked by the Criminal Justice Act 2003 s.41 and Sch.3, para.60(8) and Sch.37, Pt 4.]

*   *   *

Section 36   SCHEDULE 3

REVIEWS OF SENTENCING—SUPPLEMENTARY

A17.10   1. Notice of an application for leave to refer a case to the Court of Appeal under section

36 above shall be given within 28 days from the day on which the sentence, or the last of the sentences, in the case was passed.

2. If the registrar of criminal appeals is given notice of a reference or application to the Court of Appeal under section 36 above, he shall—   **A17.11**

    (a) take all necessary steps for obtaining a hearing of the reference or application; and

    (b) obtain and lay before the Court in proper form all documents, exhibits and other things which appear necessary for the proper determination of the reference or application.

3. Rules of court may enable a person to whose sentencing such a reference or application relates to obtain from the registrar any documents or things, including copies or reproductions of documents, required for the reference or application and may authorise the registrar to make charges for them in accordance with scales and rates fixed from time to time by the Treasury.   **A17.12**

4. An application to the Court of Appeal for leave to refer a case to the [Supreme Court] under section 36(5) above shall be made within the period of 14 days beginning with the date on which the Court of Appeal conclude their review of the case; and an application to the [Supreme Court] for leave shall be made within the period of 14 days beginning with the date on which the Court of Appeal conclude their review or refuse leave to refer the case to the [Supreme Court].   **A17.13**

[Paragraph 4 is printed as amended by the Constitutional Reform Act 2005 s.40 and Sch.9, para.48.]   **A17.14**

5. The time during which a person whose case has been referred for review under section 36 above is in custody pending its review and pending any reference to the [Supreme Court] under subsection (5) of that section shall be reckoned as part of the term of any sentence to which he is for the time being subject.   **A17.15**

[Paragraph 5 is printed as amended by the Constitutional Reform Act 2005 s.40 and Sch.9, para.48.]   **A17.16**

6. Except as provided by paragraphs 7 and 8 below, a person whose sentencing is the subject of a reference to the Court of Appeal under section 36 above shall be entitled to be present, if he wishes it, on the hearing of the reference, although he may be in custody.   **A17.17**

7. A person in custody shall not be entitled to be present—   **A17.18**

    (a) on an application by the Attorney General for leave to refer a case; or

    (b) on any proceedings preliminary or incidental to a reference,

unless the Court of Appeal give him leave to be present.

8. The power of the Court of Appeal to pass sentence on a person may be exercised although he is not present.   **A17.19**

9. A person whose sentencing is the subject of a reference to the [Supreme Court] under section 36(5) above and who is detained pending the hearing of that reference shall not be entitled to be present on the hearing of the reference or of any proceeding preliminary or incidental thereto except where an order of the [Supreme Court] authorises him to be present, or where the [Supreme Court] or the Court of Appeal, as the case may be, give him leave to be present.   **A17.20**

[Paragraph 9 is printed as amended by the Constitutional Reform Act 2005 s.40 and Sch.9, para.48.]   **A17.21**

10. The term of any sentence passed by the Court of Appeal or [Supreme Court] under section 36 above shall, unless they otherwise direct, begin to run from the time when it would have begun to run if passed in the proceeding in relation to which the reference was made.   **A17.22**

[Paragraph 10 is printed as amended by the Constitutional Reform Act 2005 s.40 and Sch.9, para.48.]   **A17.23**

11. When on a reference to the Court of Appeal under section 36 above or a reference to   **A17.24**

the [Supreme Court] under subsection (5) of that section the person whose sentencing is the subject of the reference appears by counsel for the purpose of presenting any argument to [the Court of Appeal or the Supreme Court], he shall be entitled to his costs, that is to say to the payment out of central funds of such funds as are reasonably sufficient to compensate him for expenses properly incurred by him for the purpose of being represented on the reference; and any amount recoverable under this paragraph shall be ascertained, as soon as practicable, by the registrar of criminal appeals or, as the case may be, [under Supreme Court Rules].

A17.25   *[Paragraph 11 is printed as amended by the Constitutional Reform Act 2005 s.40 and Sch.9, para.48.]*

A17.26   **12.** *[Applies to Northern Ireland.]*

The Road Traffic Act 1988

(1988 c.52)

An Act to consolidate certain enactments relating to road traffic with amendments to give effect to recommendations of the Law Commission and the Scottish Law Commission.   A18.01

[15th November 1988]

ARRANGEMENT OF SECTIONS
PART I
PRINCIPAL ROAD SAFETY PROVISIONS
Driving offences

*   *   *

PART II
CONSTRUCTION AND USE OF VEHICLES AND EQUIPMENT
Using vehicle in dangerous condition

PART III

LICENSING OF DRIVERS OF VEHICLES

Requirement to hold licence

* * *

PART V
DRIVING INSTRUCTION
Instructors to be registered or licensed

Registration

* * *

* * *

Licences

* * *

Appeals

* * *

Examinations and tests

Disabled persons: emergency control certificates, etc.

* * *

General and supplemental

* * *

PART 1

PRINCIPAL ROAD SAFETY PROVISIONS

Driving offences

[Causing death by dangerous driving

1. A person who causes the death of another person by driving a mechanically propelled vehicle dangerously on a road or other public place is guilty of an offence.]   **A18.02**

[Section 1 is printed as substituted by the Road Traffic Act 1991 s.1.   **A18.03**

The offence under s.1 is expressly excluded from the application of the Criminal Justice Act 1982 s.32 (early release of prisoners); see Pt II of Sch.1 to that Act, as amended by the Road Traffic (Consequential Provisions) Act 1988 s.4 and Sch.3, para.24.

As to alternative charges to a charge under s.1, see the Road Traffic Offenders Act 1988 s.24(1) below.

The offence under s.1 being punishable by a term of imprisonment, if a magistrates' court grants bail to a person charged with or convicted of an offence under this section, the prosecution may appeal to a judge of the Crown Court against the order granting bail under the Bail (Amendment) Act 1993 s.1 (as amended; not reproduced in this work).

Subject to (in particular) the Criminal Justice Act 2003 s.152 (general restrictions on imposing discretionary custodial sentences) and s.153 (length of discretionary custodial sentences), where a person aged at least 14 but under 18 is convicted of an offence under this section and the court is of the opinion that none of the other methods in which the case may legally be dealt with is suitable, it may sentence the offender to be detained for such period (not exceeding the maximum term of imprisonment with which the offence is punishable in the case of a person aged 21 or over) as may be specified, and that person will be detained in such place and under such conditions as the Secretary of State may direct or arrange; see the Powers of Criminal Courts Sentencing Act 2000 ss.91(3), (4) and 92(1).]

[Dangerous driving

A18.04   **2.** A person who drives a mechanically propelled vehicle dangerously on a road or other public place is guilty of an offence.]

A18.05   *[Section 2 is printed as substituted by the Road Traffic Act 1991 s.1.*

As to alternative charges to a charge under s.2, see the Road Traffic Offenders Act 1988 s.24(1) below.]

[Meaning of dangerous driving

A18.06   **2A.**—(1) For the purposes of sections 1 and 2 above a person is to be regarded as driving dangerously if (and, subject to subsection (2) below, only if)—

> (a) the way he drives falls far below what would be expected of a competent and careful driver, and
>
> (b) it would be obvious to a competent and careful driver that driving in that way would be dangerous.

(2) A person is also to be regarded as driving dangerously for the purposes of sections 1 and 2 above if it would be obvious to a competent and careful driver that driving the vehicle in its current state would be dangerous.

(3) In subsections (1) and (2) above *"dangerous"* refers to danger either of injury to any person or of serious damage to property; and in determining for the purposes of those subsections what would be expected of, or obvious to, a competent and careful driver in a particular case, regard shall be had not only to the circumstances of which he could be expected to be aware but also to any circumstances shown to have been within the knowledge of the accused.

(4) In determining for the purposes of subsection (2) above the state of a vehicle, regard may be had to anything attached to or carried on or in it and to the manner in which it is attached or carried.]

A18.07   *[Section 2A was inserted by the Road Traffic Act 1991 s.1.]*

[Causing death by careless, or inconsiderate, driving

A18.08   **2B.** A person who causes the death of another person by driving a mechanically propelled vehicle on a road or other public place without due care and attention, or without reasonable consideration for other persons using the road or place, is guilty of an offence.]

A18.09   *[Section 2B is printed as inserted by the Road Safety Act 2006 s.20(1).]*

[Careless, and inconsiderate, driving

A18.10   **3.** If a person drives a mechanically propelled vehicle on a road or other public place without due care and attention, or without reasonable consideration for other persons using the road or place, he is guilty of an offence.]

A18.11   *[Section 3 is printed as substituted by the Road Traffic Act 1991 s.2.]*

[Meaning of careless, or inconsiderate, driving

A18.12   **3ZA.**—(1) This section has effect for the purposes of sections 2B and 3 above and section 3A below.

(2) A person is to be regarded as driving without due care and attention if (and only if) the way he drives falls below what would be expected of a competent and careful driver.

(3) In determining for the purposes of subsection (2) above what would be expected of a careful and competent driver in a particular case, regard shall be had not only to the circumstances of which he could be expected to be aware but also to any circumstances shown to have been within the knowledge of the accused.

(4) A person is to be regarded as driving without reasonable consideration for other persons only if those persons are inconvenienced by his driving.]

[Section 3ZA is printed as inserted by the Road Safety Act 2006 s.30.]   **A18.13**

[Causing death by driving: unlicensed, disqualified or uninsured drivers

3ZB. A person is guilty of an offence under this section if he causes the death   **A18.14**
of another person by driving a motor vehicle on a road and, at the time when he is driving, the circumstances are such that he is committing an offence under—

    (a) section 87(1) of this Act (driving otherwise than in accordance with a licence),

    (b) section 103(1)(b) of this Act (driving while disqualified), or

    (c) section 143 of this Act (using motor vehicle while uninsured or unsecured against third party risks).]

[Section 3ZB is printed as inserted by the Road Safety Act 2006 s.21(1).]   **A18.15**

[Causing death by careless driving when under the influence of drink or drugs

3A.—(1) If a person causes the death of another person by driving a mechani-   **A18.16**
cally propelled vehicle on a road or other public place without due care and attention, or without reasonable consideration for other persons using the road or place, and—

    (a) he is, at the time when he is driving, unfit to drive through drink or drugs, or

    (b) he has consumed so much alcohol that the proportion of it in his breath, blood or urine at that time exceeds the prescribed limit, or

    (c) he is, within 18 hours after that time, required to provide a specimen in pursuance of section 7 of this Act, but without reasonable excuse fails to provide it, [or

    (d) he is required by a constable to give his permission for a laboratory test of a specimen of blood taken from him under section 7A of this Act, but without reasonable excuse fails to do so,]

he is guilty of an offence.

(2) For the purposes of this section a person shall be taken to be unfit to drive at any time when his ability to drive properly is impaired.

(3) Subsection (1)(b)[, (c) and (d)] above shall not apply in relation to a person driving a mechanically propelled vehicle other than a motor vehicle.]

[Section 3A was inserted by the Road Traffic Act 1991 s.3 and is printed as   **A18.17**
amended by the Road Safety Act 2006 s.31(2) and (3).

*As to alternative charges to a charge under s.3A, see the Road Traffic Offend-
ers Act 1988 s.24(1) below.*

*Subject to (in particular) the Criminal Justice Act 2003 s.152 (general restric-
tions on imposing discretionary custodial sentences) and s.153 (length of*

discretionary custodial sentences), where a person aged at least 14 but under 18 is convicted of an offence under this section and the court is of the opinion that none of the other methods in which the case may legally be dealt with is suitable, it may sentence the offender to be detained for such period (not exceeding the maximum term of imprisonment with which the offence is punishable in the case of a person aged 21 or over) as may be specified, and that person will be detained in such place and under such conditions as the Secretary of State may direct or arrange; see the Powers of Criminal Courts Sentencing Act 2000 ss.91(3), (4) and 92(1).

Offences under s.3A committed on or after January 31, 2002, and any persons committing such offences, are prescribed for the purposes of the Road Traffic Offenders Act 1988 s.36(1), by the Driving Licences (Disqualification until Test Passed) (Prescribed Offence) Order 2001 (SI 2001/4051) below.]

Motor vehicles: drink and drugs

Driving, or being in charge, when under influence of drink or drugs

A18.18   **4.**—(1) A person who, when driving or attempting to drive a [mechanically propelled vehicle] on a road or other public place, is unfit to drive through drink or drugs is guilty of an offence.

(2) Without prejudice to subsection (1) above, a person who, when in charge of a [mechanically propelled vehicle] which is on a road or other public place, is unfit to drive through drink or drugs is guilty of an offence.

(3) For the purposes of subsection (2) above, a person shall be deemed not to have been in charge of a [mechanically propelled vehicle] if he proves that at the material time the circumstances were such that there was no likelihood of his driving it so long as he remained unfit to drive through drink or drugs.

(4) The court may, in determining whether there was such a likelihood as is mentioned in subsection (3) above, disregard any injury to him and any damage to the vehicle.

(5) For the purposes of this section, a person shall be taken to be unfit to drive if his ability to drive properly is for the time being impaired.

(6) [...]

(7) [...]

(8) [...]

A18.19   *[Section 4 is printed as amended by the Road Traffic Act 1991, s.4; the Serious Organised Crime and Police Act 2005 s.111 and Sch.7, para.27(2) and Sch.17, Pt 2.*

As to alternative charges to a charge under s.4(1), see the Road Traffic Offenders Act 1988 s.24(1) below.

As to the application of ss.4–11 to tramcars and other guided vehicles, see s.192A below.

The code of practice for the identification of persons by police officers does not affect any procedure under ss.4–11 of this Act; see para.2.17(i) of Code D (2011) under the Police and Criminal Evidence Act 1984.]

Driving or being in charge of a motor vehicle with alcohol concentration above prescribed limit

A18.20   **5.**—(1) If a person—

(a) drives or attempts to drive a motor vehicle on a road or other public place, or

(b) is in charge of a motor vehicle on a road or other public place,

after consuming so much alcohol that the proportion of it in his breath, blood or urine exceeds the prescribed limit he is guilty of an offence.

(2) It is a defence for a person charged with an offence under subsection (1)(b) above to prove that at the time he is alleged to have committed the offence the circumstances were such that there was no likelihood of his driving the vehicle whilst the proportion of alcohol in his breath, blood or urine remained likely to exceed the prescribed limit.

(3) The court may, in determining whether there was such a likelihood as is mentioned in subsection (2) above, disregard any injury to him and any damage to the vehicle.

[As to alternative charges to a charge under s.5(1), see the Road Traffic Of-   **A18.21**
fenders Act 1988 s.24(1) below.

See also the notes to s.4 above.]

[Power to administer preliminary tests

6.—(1) If any of subsections (2) to (5) applies a constable may require a person   **A18.22** to co-operate with any one or more preliminary tests administered to the person by that constable or another constable.

(2) This subsection applies if a constable reasonably suspects that the person—

    (a) is driving, is attempting to drive or is in charge of a motor vehicle on a road or other public place, and

    (b) has alcohol or a drug in his body or is under the influence of a drug.

(3) This subsection applies if a constable reasonably suspects that the person—

    (a) has been driving, attempting to drive or in charge of a motor vehicle on a road or other public place while having alcohol or a drug in his body or while unfit to drive because of a drug, and

    (b) still has alcohol or a drug in his body or is still under the influence of a drug.

(4) This subsection applies if a constable reasonably suspects that the person—

    (a) is or has been driving, attempting to drive or in charge of a motor vehicle on a road or other public place, and

    (b) has committed a traffic offence while the vehicle was in motion.

(5) This subsection applies if—

    (a) an accident occurs owing to the presence of a motor vehicle on a road or other public place, and

    (b) a constable reasonably believes that the person was driving, attempting to drive or in charge of the vehicle at the time of the accident.

(6) A person commits an offence if without reasonable excuse he fails to co-operate with a preliminary test in pursuance of a requirement imposed under this section.

(7) A constable may administer a preliminary test by virtue of any of subsections (2) to (4) only if he is in uniform.

(8) In this section—

(a) a reference to a preliminary test is to any of the tests described in sections 6A to 6C, and

(b) *"traffic offence"* means an offence under—

    (i) a provision of Part II of the Public Passenger Vehicles Act 1981 (c.14),

    (ii) a provision of the Road Traffic Regulation Act 1984 (c.27),

    (iii) a provision of the Road Traffic Offenders Act 1988 (c.53) other than a provision of Part III, or

    (iv) a provision of this Act other than a provision of Part V.]

A18.23   *[Section 6 is printed as substituted by the Railways and Transport Safety Act 2003 s.107 and Sch.7, para.1.]*

[Preliminary breath test

A18.24   **6A.**—(1) A preliminary breath test is a procedure whereby the person to whom the test is administered provides a specimen of breath to be used for the purpose of obtaining, by means of a device of a type approved by the Secretary of State, an indication whether the proportion of alcohol in the person's breath or blood is likely to exceed the prescribed limit.

(2) A preliminary breath test administered in reliance on section 6(2) to (4) may be administered only at or near the place where the requirement to co-operate with the test is imposed.

(3) A preliminary breath test administered in reliance on section 6(5) may be administered—

    (a) at or near the place where the requirement to co-operate with the test is imposed, or

    (b) if the constable who imposes the requirement thinks it expedient, at a police station specified by him.]

A18.25   *[Section 6A is printed as inserted by the Railways and Transport Safety Act 2003 s.107 and Sch.7, para.1. The following devices have been approved for use in England, Wales and Scotland under s.6A(1):*

Intoximeter Alco-Sensor FST	(see the Preliminary Breath Test Device Approval 2005, effective July 18, 2005)
Draeger Alcotest 6510	(see the Preliminary Breath Test Device Approval 2005, effective July 18, 2005)
Draeger Alcotest 6810 GB	(see the Preliminary Breath Test Device Approval 2008, effective April 30, 2008)
Lion Alcometer 500 B	(see the Preliminary Breath Test Device Approval 2008, effective April 30, 2008)
Envitec AlcoQuant 6020	(see the Preliminary Breath Test Device Approval 2008, effective April 30, 2008)*]

[Preliminary impairment test

A18.26   **6B.**—(1) A preliminary impairment test is a procedure whereby the constable administering the test—

    (a) observes the person to whom the test is administered in his performance of tasks specified by the constable, and

(b) makes such other observations of the person's physical state as the constable thinks expedient.

(2) The Secretary of State shall issue (and may from time to time revise) a code of practice about—

(a) the kind of task that may be specified for the purpose of a preliminary impairment test,

(b) the kind of observation of physical state that may be made in the course of a preliminary impairment test,

(c) the manner in which a preliminary impairment test should be administered, and

(d) the inferences that may be drawn from observations made in the course of a preliminary impairment test.

(3) In issuing or revising the code of practice the Secretary of State shall aim to ensure that a preliminary impairment test is designed to indicate—

(a) whether a person is unfit to drive, and

(b) if he is, whether or not his unfitness is likely to be due to drink or drugs.

(4) A preliminary impairment test may be administered—

(a) at or near the place where the requirement to co-operate with the test is imposed, or

(b) if the constable who imposes the requirement thinks it expedient, at a police station specified by him.

(5) A constable administering a preliminary impairment test shall have regard to the code of practice under this section.

(6) A constable may administer a preliminary impairment test only if he is approved for that purpose by the chief officer of the police force to which he belongs.

(7) A code of practice under this section may include provision about—

(a) the giving of approval under subsection (6), and

(b) in particular, the kind of training that a constable should have undergone, or the kind of qualification that a constable should possess, before being approved under that subsection.]

[Section 6B is printed as inserted by the Railways and Transport Safety Act **A18.27**
2003 s.107 and Sch.7, para.1.

The Secretary of State has issued a Code of Practice for Preliminary Impairment Tests under the power contained in s.6B(2) above. The Code is for the use of police officers trained and authorised to carry out preliminary impairment tests.]

[Preliminary drug test

6C.—(1) A preliminary drug test is a procedure by which a specimen of sweat **A18.28**
or saliva is—

(a) obtained, and

(b) used for the purpose of obtaining, by means of a device of a type approved by the Secretary of State, an indication whether the person to whom the test is administered has a drug in his body.

(2) A preliminary drug test may be administered—

    (a) at or near the place where the requirement to co-operate with the test is imposed, or

    (b) if the constable who imposes the requirement thinks it expedient, at a police station specified by him.]

A18.29   *[Section 6C is printed as inserted by the Railways and Transport Safety Act 2003 s.107 and Sch.7, para.1.]*

[Arrest

A18.30   **6D.**—(1) A constable may arrest a person without warrant if as a result of a preliminary breath test the constable reasonably suspects that the proportion of alcohol in the person's breath or blood exceeds the prescribed limit.

[(1A) The fact that specimens of breath have been provided under section 7 of this Act by the person concerned does not prevent subsection (1) above having effect if the constable who imposed on him the requirement to provide the specimens has reasonable cause to believe that the device used to analyse the specimens has not produced a reliable indication of the proportion of alcohol in the breath of the person.]

(2) A constable may arrest a person without warrant if—

    (a) the person fails to co-operate with a preliminary test in pursuance of a requirement imposed under section 6, and

    (b) the constable reasonably suspects that the person has alcohol or a drug in his body or is under the influence of a drug.

[(2A) A person arrested under this section may, instead of being taken to a police station, be detained at or near the place where the preliminary test was, or would have been, administered, with a view to imposing on him there a requirement under section 7 of this Act.]

(3) A person may not be arrested under this section while at a hospital as a patient.]

A18.31   *[Section 6D is printed as inserted by the Railways and Transport Safety Act 2003 s.107 and Sch.7, para.1; the Serious Organised Crime and Police Act 2005 s.154(1)–(3).]*

[Power of entry

A18.32   **6E.**—(1) A constable may enter any place (using reasonable force if necessary) for the purpose of—

    (a) imposing a requirement by virtue of section 6(5) following an accident in a case where the constable reasonably suspects that the accident involved injury of any person, or

    (b) arresting a person under section 6D following an accident in a case where the constable reasonably suspects that the accident involved injury of any person.

(2) This section—

    (a) does not extend to Scotland, and

    (b) is without prejudice to any rule of law or enactment about the right of a constable in Scotland to enter any place.]

A18.33   *[Section 6E is printed as inserted by the Railways and Transport Safety Act 2003 s.107 and Sch.7, para.1.]*

Provision of specimens for analysis

7.—(1) In the course of an investigation into whether a person has committed   **A18.34** an offence under [section 3A, 4] or 5 of this Act a constable may, subject to the following provisions of this section and section 9 of this Act, require him—

    (a) to provide two specimens of breath for analysis by means of a device of a type approved by the Secretary of State, or

    (b) to provide a specimen of blood or urine for a laboratory test.

[(2) A requirement under this section to provide specimens of breath can only be made—

    (a) at a police station,

    (b) at a hospital, or

    (c) at or near a place where a relevant breath test has been administered to the person concerned or would have been so administered but for his failure to co-operate with it.

(2A) For the purposes of this section "a relevant breath test" is a procedure involving the provision by the person concerned of a specimen of breath to be used for the purpose of obtaining an indication whether the proportion of alcohol in his breath or blood is likely to exceed the prescribed limit.

(2B) A requirement under this section to provide specimens of breath may not be made at or near a place mentioned in subsection (2)(c) above unless the constable making it—

    (a) is in uniform, or

    (b) has imposed a requirement on the person concerned to co-operate with a relevant breath test in circumstances in which section 6(5) of this Act applies.

(2C) Where a constable has imposed a requirement on the person concerned to co-operate with a relevant breath test at any place, he is entitled to remain at or near that place in order to impose on him there a requirement under this section.

(2D) If a requirement under subsection (1)(a) above has been made at a place other than at a police station, such a requirement may subsequently be made at a police station if (but only if)—

    (a) a device or a reliable device of the type mentioned in subsection (1)(a) above was not available at that place or it was for any other reason not practicable to use such a device there, or

    (b) the constable who made the previous requirement has reasonable cause to believe that the device used there has not produced a reliable indication of the proportion of alcohol in the breath of the person concerned.]

(3) A requirement under this section to provide a specimen of blood or urine can only be made at a police station or at a hospital; and it cannot be made at a police station unless—

    (a) the constable making the requirement has reasonable cause to believe that for medical reasons a specimen of breath cannot be provided or should not be required, or

    (b) [specimens of breath have not been provided elsewhere and] at the time the requirement is made a device or a reliable device of the type mentioned in subsection (1)(a) above is not available at the police station or it is then for any other reason not practicable to use such a device there, or

[(bb) a device of the type mentioned in subsection (1)(a) above has been used [(at the police station or elsewhere)] but the constable who required the specimens of breath has reasonable cause to believe that the device has not produced a reliable indication of the proportion of alcohol in the breath of the person concerned, or]

[(bc) as a result of the administration of a preliminary drug test, the constable making the requirement has reasonable cause to believe that the person required to provide a specimen of blood or urine has a drug in his body, or]

(c) the suspected offence is one under [section 3A, 4] of this Act and the constable making the requirement has been advised by a medical practitioner that the condition of the person required to provide the specimen might be due to some drug;

but may then be made notwithstanding that the person required to provide the specimen has already provided or been required to provide two specimens of breath.

(4) If the provision of a specimen other than a specimen of breath may be required in pursuance of this section the question whether it is to be a specimen of blood or a specimen of urine [and, in the case of a specimen of blood, the question who is to be asked to take it shall be decided (subject to subsection (4A)) by the constable making the requirement].

[(4A) Where a constable decides for the purposes of subsection (4) to require the provision of a specimen of blood, there shall be no requirement to provide such a specimen if—

(a) the medical practitioner who is asked to take the specimen is of the opinion that, for medical reasons, it cannot or should not be taken; or

(b) the registered health care professional who is asked to take it is of that opinion and there is no contrary opinion from a medical practitioner;

and, where by virtue of this subsection there can be no requirement to provide a specimen of blood, the constable may require a specimen of urine instead.]

(5) A specimen of urine shall be provided within one hour of the requirement for its provision being made and after the provision of a previous specimen of urine.

(6) A person who, without reasonable excuse, fails to provide a specimen when required to do so in pursuance of this section is guilty of an offence.

(7) A constable must, on requiring any person to provide a specimen in pursuance of this section, warn him that a failure to provide it may render him liable to prosecution.

A18.35   *[Section 7 is printed as amended by the Road Traffic Act 1991 s.48 and Sch.4, para.42(a) and (b); the Criminal Procedure and Investigations Act 1996 s.63(1); the Police Reform Act 2002 s.55(1) and (2); the Railways and Transport Safety Act 2003 s.107 and Sch.7, para.2; the Serious Organised Crime and Police Act 2005 s.154(4)–(6).*

In s.7, s.7(3)(bb) applies only where it is proposed to make a requirement mentioned in s.7(3) after the day appointed under s.63(4) of the Criminal Proce-

dure and Investigations Act 1996; see ibid. s.63(3). The Criminal Procedure and Investigations Act 1996 (Appointed Day No.3) Order 1997 (SI 1997/682) designated April 1, 1997 as the appointed day for the purposes of s.63(4) of the 1996 Act.

The breath analysis devices approved under s.7(1)(a) are:

Camic Datamaster[1]	effective March 1, 1998 (see the Breath Analysis Devices Approval 1998, dated February 2, 1998) effective July 1, 2005 (see the Breath Analysis Devices Approval, dated June 2005)
Lion Intoxilyzer 6000UK[2]	effective March 1, 1998 (see the Breath Analysis Devices Approval 1998, dated February 2, 1998)
Intoximeter EC/IR[3]	effective March 1, 1998 (see the Breath Analysis Devices (No.2) Approval 1998, dated February 25, 1998) effective July 1, 2005 (see the Breath Analysis Devices Approval, dated June 2005)
Lion Intoxilyzer 6000 UK[4]	effective June 1, 1998 (see the Breath Analysis Devices (No.3) Approval 1998, dated May 22, 1998)
Lion Intoxilyzer 6000 UK[5]	effective November 2, 1999 (see the Breath Analysis Devices Approval 1999, dated October 25, 1999) effective July 1, 2005 (see the Breath Analysis Devices Approval, dated June 2005)

[1] comprising the Camic Datamaster, the Camic gas system and software version 31-10-95

[2] comprising the Lion Intoxilyzer 6000UK, the Lion Intoxilyzer 6000UK gas delivery system type A or type C and software version 2.33

[3] comprising the Lion Intoximeter EC/IR, the Lion Intoximeter EC/IR gas delivery system and software version EC/IR-UK 5.23

[4] comprising the Lion Intoxilyzer 6000UK, the Lion Intoxilyzer 6000UK gas delivery system type B and software version 2.33

[5] comprising the Lion Intoxilyzer 6000UK, the Lion Intoxilyzer 6000UK gas delivery system type A, B and C and software version 2.33 or 2.34

In the code of practice for the detention, treatment and questioning of persons by police officers it is stated that procedures under s.7 of this Act do not constitute interviewing for the purpose of the code; see para.11.1A of Code C (2008) under the Police and Criminal Evidence Act 1984.

See also the notes to s.4 above.]

[Specimens of blood taken from persons incapable of consenting

7A.—(1) A constable may make a request to a medical practitioner for him to take a specimen of blood from a person (*"the person concerned"*) irrespective of whether that person consents if —   **A18.36**

    (a) that person is a person from whom the constable would (in the absence of any incapacity of that person and of any objection under section 9) be entitled under section 7 to require the provision of a specimen of blood for a laboratory test;

(b) it appears to that constable that that person has been involved in an accident that constitutes or is comprised in the matter that is under investigation or the circumstances of that matter;

(c) it appears to that constable that that person is or may be incapable (whether or not he has purported to do so) of giving a valid consent to the taking of a specimen of blood; and

(d) it appears to that constable that that person's incapacity is attributable to medical reasons.

(2) A request under this section —

(a) shall not be made to a medical practitioner who for the time being has any responsibility (apart from the request) for the clinical care of the person concerned; and

(b) shall not be made to a medical practitioner other than a police medical practitioner unless—

(i) it is not reasonably practicable for the request to made to a police medical practitioner; or

(ii) it is not reasonably practicable for such a medical practitioner (assuming him to be willing to do so) to take the specimen.

(3) It shall be lawful for a medical practitioner to whom a request is made under this section, if he thinks fit—

(a) to take a specimen of blood from the person concerned irrespective of whether that person consents; and

(b) to provide the sample to a constable.

(4) If a specimen is taken in pursuance of a request under this section, the specimen shall not be subjected to a laboratory test unless the person from whom it was taken—

(a) has been informed that it was taken; and

(b) has been required by a constable to give his permission for a laboratory test of the specimen; and

(c) has given his permission.

(5) A constable must, on requiring a person to give his permission for the purposes of this section for a laboratory test of a specimen, warn that person that a failure to give the permission may render him liable to prosecution.

(6) A person who, without reasonable excuse, fails to give his permission for a laboratory test of a specimen of blood taken from him under this section is guilty of an offence.

(7) In this section *"police medical practitioner"* means a medical practitioner who is engaged under any agreement to provide medical services for purposes connected with the activities of a police force.]

A18.37　　*[Section 7A is printed as inserted by the Police Reform Act 2002 s.56.]*

Choice of specimens of breath

A18.38　　**8.**—(1) Subject to subsection (2) below, of any two specimens of breath provided by any person in pursuance of section 7 of this Act that with the lower proportion of alcohol in the breath shall be used and the other shall be disregarded.

(2) If the specimen with the lower proportion of alcohol contains no more than 50 microgrammes of alcohol in 100 millilitres of breath, the person who provided it may claim that it should be replaced by such specimen as may be required under section 7(4) of this Act and, if he then provides such a specimen, neither specimen of breath shall be used.

[(2A) If the person who makes a claim under subsection (2) above was required to provide specimens of breath under section 7 of this Act at or near a place mentioned in subsection (2)(c) of that section, a constable may arrest him without warrant.]

(3) The Secretary of State may by regulations substitute another proportion of alcohol in the breath for that specified in subsection (2) above.

[Section 8 is printed as amended by the Serious Organised Crime and Police   **A18.39**
Act 2005 s.154(7).

See also the notes to s.4 above.]

Protection for hospital patients

9.—(1) While a person is at a hospital as a patient he shall not be required [to   **A18.40** co-operate with a preliminary test] or to provide a specimen [under section 7 of this Act] unless the medical practitioner in immediate charge of his case has been notified of the proposal to make the requirement; and—

    (a) if the requirement is then made, [it shall be for co-operation with a test administered, or for the provision of a specimen, at the hospital], but

    (b) if the medical practitioner objects on the ground specified in subsection (2) below, the requirement shall not be made.

[(1A) While a person is at a hospital as a patient, no specimen of blood shall be taken from him under section 7A of this Act and he shall not be required to give his permission for a laboratory test of a specimen taken under that section unless the medical practitioner in immediate charge of his case—

    (a) has been notified of the proposal to take the specimen or to make the requirement; and

    (b) has not objected on the ground specified in subsection (2).

(2) The ground on which the medical practitioner may object is—

    (a) in a case falling within subsection (1), that the requirement or the provision of the specimen or (if one is required) the warning required by section 7(7) of this Act would be prejudicial to the proper care and treatment of the patient; and

    (b) in a case falling within subsection (1A), that the taking of the specimen, the requirement or the warning required by section 7A(5) of this Act would be so prejudicial.]

[Section 9 is printed as amended by the Police Reform Act 2002 s.56(2); the   **A18.41** *Railways and Transport Safety Act 2003 s.107 and Sch.7, para.3; the Serious Organised Crime and Police Act 2005 s.154(8).*

See also the notes to s.4 above.]

Detention of persons affected by alcohol or a drug

10.—(1) Subject to subsections (2) and (3) below, a person required [under   **A18.42**

section 7 or 7A] to provide a specimen of breath, blood or urine may afterwards be detained at a police station [(or, if the specimen was provided otherwise than at a police station, arrested and taken to and detained at a police station) if a constable has reasonable grounds for believing] that, were that person then driving or attempting to drive a [mechanically propelled vehicle] on a road, he would [commit] an offence under section 4 or 5 of this Act.

(2) [Subsection (1) above does not apply to the person if it ought reasonably to appear to the] constable that there is no likelihood of his driving or attempting to drive a [mechanically propelled vehicle] whilst his ability to drive properly is impaired or whilst the proportion of alcohol in his breath, blood or urine exceeds the prescribed limit.

[(2A) A person who is at a hospital as a patient shall not be arrested and taken from there to a police station in pursuance of this section if it would be prejudicial to his proper care and treatment as a patient.]

(3) A constable must consult a medical practitioner on any question arising under this section whether a person's ability to drive properly is or might be impaired through drugs and must act on the medical practitioner's advice.

A18.43 *[Section 10 is printed as amended by the Road Traffic Act 1991 s.48 and Sch.4, para.43; the Railways and Transport Safety Act 2003 s.107 and Sch.7, para.4; the Serious Organised Crime and Police Act 2005 s.154(9)–(12).*

See also the notes to s.4 above.]

Interpretation of sections [3A] to 10

A18.44 11.—(1) The following provisions apply for the interpretation of sections [3A] to 10 of this Act.

(2) In those sections—

[...]

"drug" includes any intoxicant other than alcohol,

"fail" includes refuse,

"hospital" means an institution which provides medical or surgical treatment for in-patients or out-patients,

"the prescribed limit" means, as the case may require—

(a) 35 microgrammes of alcohol in 100 millilitres of breath,

(b) 80 milligrammes of alcohol in 100 millilitres of blood, or

(c) 107 milligrammes of alcohol in 100 millilitres of urine, or such other proportion as may be prescribed by regulations made by the Secretary of State.

[*"registered health care professional"* means a person (other than a medical practitioner) who is—

(a) a registered nurse; or

(b) a registered member of a health care profession which is designated for the purposes of this paragraph by an order made by the Secretary of State.]

[(2A) A health care profession is any profession mentioned in section 60(2) of the Health Act 1999 (c.8) other than the profession of practising medicine and the profession of nursing.]

[(2B) An order under subsection (2) shall be made by statutory instrument;

and any such statutory instrument shall be subject to annulment in pursuance of a resolution of either House of Parliament.]

(3) [A person does not co-operate with a preliminary test or provide a specimen of breath for analysis unless his co-operation or the specimen]—

(a) is sufficient to enable the test or the analysis to be carried out, and

(b) is provided in such a way as to enable the objective of the test or analysis to be satisfactorily achieved.

[(4) A person provides a specimen of blood if and only if—

(a) he consents to the taking of such a specimen from him; and

(b) the specimen is taken from him by a medical practitioner or, if it is taken in a police station, either by a medical practitioner or by a registered health care professional.]

[Section 11 is printed as amended by the Road Traffic Act 1991 s.48 and Sch.4, **A18.45** *para.44; the Police Reform Act 2002 s.55(3)–(5); the Railways and Transport Safety Act 2003 s.107 Sch.7, para.5 and Sch.8.*

The devices which have been approved for use in England and Wales under s.11(2) are:

Alcotest 80	(see the Breath Test Device (Approval) (No.1) Order 1968)
Alcotest 80A	(see the Breath Test Device (Approval) (No.1) Order 1975)
Alcolyser	(see the Breath Test Device (Approval) (No.1) Order 1979)
Alcolmeter	(see the Breath Test Device (Approval) (No.2) Order 1979)
Alert	(see the Breath Test Device (Approval) (No.1) Order 1980)
Lion Alcometer S–L2A	(see the Breath Test Device (Approval) Order 1987)
Draeger Alcotest 7410	(see the Breath Test Device (Approval) 1993)
Lion Alcolmeter SL–400 (UK) (INDICATING DISPLAY FORM)	(see the Breath Test Device (No.2) (Approval) 1993)
Lion Alcolmeter SL–400A (INDICATING DISPLAY FORM)	(see the Breath Test Device (Approval) 1997)
Alcosensor IV UK	(see the Breath Test Device Approval 1999 (effective October 15, 1999))
Lion Alcolmeter SL–400A	(see the Breath Test Device (Approval) 2000)

(INDICATING DISPLAY FORM) software version 3.31	
Alcolmeter SL–400B	(see the Breath Test Device Approval 2002, effective December 12, 2002)
Lion Alcolmeter SL–400AM	(see the Breath Test Approval 2003, effective July 15, 2003)
Lion Alcolmeter 500	(see the Breath Test Device Approval 2004, effective January 15, 2004)
Alcolmeter 400A (digital display form)	(see the Breath Test Device Approval (No.3) 2004, effective February 25, 2004))

See further the notes to s.4 above.]

Motor racing and motoring events on public ways

Motor racing on public ways

A18.46 **12.**—(1) A person who promotes or takes part in a race or trial of speed between motor vehicles on a public way is guilty of an offence.

(2) In this section *"public way"* means, in England and Wales, a [highway] …

A18.47 *[Section 12 is printed as amended by the Road Traffic Act 1991 s.48 and Sch.4, para.45.*

Words relating exclusively and expressly to Scotland have been omitted from s.12(2).]

Regulation of motoring events on public ways

A18.48 **13.**—(1) A person who promotes or takes part in a competition or trial (other than a race or trial of speed) involving the use of motor vehicles on a public way is guilty of an offence unless the competition or trial—

    (a) is authorised, and

    (b) is conducted in accordance with any conditions imposed,

by or under regulations under this section.

(2) The Secretary of State may by regulations authorise, or provide for authorising, the holding of competitions or trials (other than races or trials of speed) involving the use of motor vehicles on public ways either—

    (a) generally, or

    (b) as regards any area, or as regards any class or description of competition or trial or any particular competition or trial,

subject to such conditions, including conditions requiring the payment of fees, as may be imposed by or under the regulations.

(3) Regulations under this section may—

    (a) prescribe the procedure to be followed, and the particulars to be given, in connection with applications for authorisation under the regulations, and

(b) make different provision for different classes or descriptions of competition or trial.

(4) In this section *"public way"* means, in England and Wales, a [highway] …

A18.49
[Section 13 is printed as amended by the Road Traffic Act 1991 s.48 and Sch.4, para.46.

The functions of the Secretary of State exercisable under s.13(2) in relation to Wales have been transferred to the National Assembly for Wales by the National Assembly for Wales (Transfer of Functions) Order 1999 (SI 1999/672; not reproduced in this work) art.2 and Sch.1.

As to the transfer of functions of the Secretary of State under s.13(2) which are exercisable in relation to Scotland to the Scottish Ministers, see the Scotland Act 1998 (Transfer of Functions to the Scottish Ministers etc.) Order 1999 (SI 1999/ 1750; not reproduced in this work) art.2 and Sch.1.

Words relating exclusively and expressly to Scotland have been omitted from s.13(4).]

[Disapplication of sections 1 to 3 for authorised motoring events

13A.—(1) A person shall not be guilty of an offence under sections 1, 2 or 3 of this Act by virtue of driving a vehicle in a public place other than a road if he shows that he was driving in accordance with an authorisation for a motoring event given under regulations made by the Secretary of State.   **A18.50**

(2) Regulations under this section may in particular—

(a) prescribe the persons by whom, and limit the circumstances in which and the places in respect of which, authorisations may be given under the regulations;

(b) specify conditions which must be included among those incorporated in authorisations;

(c) provide for authorisations to cease to have effect in prescribed circumstances;

(d) provide for the procedure to be followed, the particulars to be given, and the amount (or the persons who are to determine the amount) of any fees to be paid, in connection with applications for authorisations;

(e) make different provisions for different cases.]

[Section 13A was inserted by the Road Traffic Act 1991 s.5.   **A18.51**

The functions of the Secretary of State exercisable under s.13A in relation for Wales have been transferred to the National Assembly for Wales by the National Assembly for Wales (Transfer of Functions) Order 1999 (SI 1999/672; not reproduced in this work) art.2 and Sch.1.

As to the transfer of functions of the Secretary of State under s.13A(1) which are exercisable in relation to Scotland to the Scottish Ministers, see the Scotland Act 1998 (Transfer of Functions to the Scottish Ministers etc.) Order 1999 (SI 1999/1750; not reproduced in this work) art.2 and Sch.1.

The bodies which may authorise off-road events under s.13A are specified in the Motor Vehicles (Off Road Events) Regulations 1995 (SI 1995/1371) (not reproduced in this work).]

Protective measures: seat belts, helmets, etc.

Seat belts: adults

A18.52   **14.**—(1) The Secretary of State may make regulations requiring, subject to such exceptions as may be prescribed, persons who are driving or riding in motor vehicles on a road to wear seat belts of such description as may be prescribed.

(2) Regulations under this section —

(a) may make different provision in relation to different classes of vehicles, different descriptions of persons and different circumstances,

[(aa) may, for the purpose of implementing the seat belt Directive, authorise the wearing of a seat belt approved under the law of a member State other than the United Kingdom,]

(b) shall include exceptions for—

[(i) the driver of or a passenger in a motor vehicle constructed or adapted for carrying goods, while on a journey which does not exceed the prescribed distance and which is undertaken for the purpose of delivering or collecting any thing,]

(ii) the drivers of vehicles while performing a manoeuvre which includes reversing,

(iii) any person holding a valid certificate signed by a medical practitioner to the effect that it is inadvisable on medical grounds for him to wear a seat belt,

[(bb) shall, for the purpose of implementing the seat belt Directive, include an exception for any person holding a certificate to the like effect as that mentioned in paragraph (b)(iii) above which was issued in a member State other than the United Kingdom and which, under the law of that State, is valid for purposes corresponding to those of this section,]

(c) may make any prescribed exceptions subject to such conditions as may be prescribed, and

(d) may prescribe cases in which a fee of a prescribed amount may be charged on an application for any certificate required as a condition of any prescribed exception.

(3) A person who drives or rides in a motor vehicle in contravention of regulations under this section is guilty of an offence; but, notwithstanding any enactment or rule of law, no person other than the person actually committing the contravention is guilty of an offence by reason of the contravention.

(4) If the holder of any such certificate as is referred to in subsection (2)(b) [or (bb)] above is informed by a constable that he may be prosecuted for any offence under subsection (3) above, he is not in proceedings for that offence entitled to rely on the exception afforded to him by the certificate unless—

(a) it is produced to the constable at the time he is so informed, or

(b) it is produced—

(i) within seven days after the date on which he is so informed, or

(ii) as soon as is reasonably practicable,

at such police station as he may have specified to the constable, or

(c) where it is not produced at such police station, it is not reasonably practicable for it to be produced there before the day on which the proceedings are commenced.

(5) For the purposes of subsection (4) above, the laying of the information ... shall be treated as the commencement of the proceedings.

(6) Regulations under this section requiring the wearing of seat belts by persons riding in motor vehicles shall not apply to children under the age of fourteen years.

[(7) In this section, *"the seat belt Directive"* means the Directive of the Council of the European Communities, dated 16th December 1991, (No.91/671/EEC) on the approximation of the laws of the member States relating to compulsory use of safety belts in vehicles of less than 3.5 tonnes [*O.J. No.L373, December 31, 1991, p.26*].]

[Section 14 is printed as amended by the Road Traffic Act 1991 s.48 and Sch.4, para.47; the Road Traffic Act 1988 (Amendment) Regulations 1992 (SI 1992/3105; not reproduced in this work) reg.2; the Railways and Transport Safety Act 2003 s.110.   **A18.53**

Words relating exclusively and expressly to Scotland have been omitted from s.14(5).

Directive 91/671/EEC (O.J. No.L373, December 31, 1991, p.26) "the seat belt Directive", referred to in s.14(7) has been amended by Directive 2003/20/EC (O.J. No.L115, May 9, 2003, p.63). The title of the Directive has been replaced by the following: "Council Directive of 16 December 1991 relating to the compulsory use of safety belts and child-restraint systems in vehicles".

The fixed penalty procedure applies to offences under s.14; see the Road Traffic Offenders Act 1988 Sch.3.

The Motor Vehicles (Wearing of Seat Belts) Regulations 1993 (SI 1993/176) (q.v.) have been made (in part) under s.14.]

Restriction on carrying children not wearing seat belts in motor vehicles

15.—(1) Except as provided by regulations, where a child under the age of fourteen years is in the front of a motor vehicle, a person must not without reasonable excuse drive the vehicle on a road unless the child is wearing a seat belt in conformity with regulations.   **A18.54**

[(1A) Where—

    (a) a child is in the front of a motor vehicle other than a bus,

    (b) the child is in a rear-facing child restraining device, and

    (c) the passenger seat where the child is placed is protected by a front air bag,

a person must not without reasonable excuse drive the vehicle on a road unless the air bag is deactivated.]

(2) It is an offence for a person to drive a motor vehicle in contravention of subsection (1) [or (1A)] above.

[(3) Except as provided by regulations, where—

    (a) a child under the age of three years is in the rear of a motor vehicle, or

    (b) a child of or over that age but under the age of fourteen years is in the rear of a motor vehicle and any seat belt is fitted in the rear of that vehicle, a person must not without reasonable excuse drive the vehicle on a road unless the child is wearing a seat belt in conformity with regulations.]

[(3A) Except as provided by regulations, where—

(a) a child who is under the age of 12 years and less than 150 centimetres in height is in the rear of a passenger car,

(b) no seat belt is fitted in the rear of the passenger car, and

(c) a seat in the front of the passenger car is provided with a seat belt but is not occupied by any person,

a person must not without reasonable excuse drive the passenger car on a road.]

(4) It is an offence for a person to drive a motor vehicle in contravention of subsection (3) [or (3A)] above.

(5) Provision may be made by regulations—

(a) excepting from the prohibition in subsection (1) [, (3) or (3A)] above children of any prescribed description, vehicles of a prescribed class or the driving of vehicles in such circumstances as may be prescribed,

(b) defining in relation to any class of vehicle what part of the vehicle is to be regarded as the front of the vehicle for the purposes of subsection (1) [or (3A)] above or as the rear of the vehicle for the purposes of subsection (3) [or (3A)] above,

(c) prescribing for the purposes of subsection (1) or (3) above the descriptions of seat belt to be worn by children of any prescribed description and the manner in which such seat belt is to be fixed and used.

[(5A) Without prejudice to the generality of subsection (5) above, regulations made by virtue of paragraph (c) of that subsection may, for the purpose of implementing the seat belt Directive,—

(a) make different provision in relation to different vehicles and different circumstances,

(b) authorise the wearing of a seat belt approved under the law of any member State other than the United Kingdom.]

[(6) Regulations made for the purposes of subsection (3) or (3A) above—

(a) shall include an exemption for any child holding a valid certificate signed by a medical practitioner to the effect that it is inadvisable on medical grounds for him to wear a seat belt, and

(b) shall, for the purpose of implementing the seat belt Directive, include an exemption for any child holding a certificate to the like effect which was issued in any member State other than the United Kingdom and which, under the law of that State, is valid for purposes corresponding to those of this section,

but such regulations may, for the purpose of implementing that Directive, make either of those exemptions subject to such conditions as may be prescribed.]

(7) If the driver of a motor vehicle is informed by a constable that he may be prosecuted for an offence under subsection (4) above, he is not in proceedings for that offence entitled to rely on an exception afforded to a child by a certificate referred to in subsection (6) above unless—

(a) it is produced to the constable at the time he is so informed, or

(b) it is produced—

    (i) within seven days after the date on which he is so informed, or

    (ii) as soon as is reasonably practicable,

at such police station as he may have specified to the constable, or

  (c) where it is not produced at such police station, it is not reasonably practicable for it to be produced there before the day on which the proceedings are commenced.

(8) For the purposes of subsection (7) above, the laying of the information ... shall be treated as the commencement of the proceedings.

(9) In this section —

  [*"bus"* means a motor vehicle that—

    (a) has at least four wheels,

    (b) is constructed or adapted for the carriage of passengers,

    (c) has more than eight seats in addition to the driver's seat, and

    (d) has a maximum design speed exceeding 25 kilometres per hour;]

  [*"maximum laden weight"* has the meaning given by Part IV of Schedule 6 to the Road Traffic Regulation Act 1984 [*q.v.*],]

  [*"passenger car"* means a motor vehicle which—

    (a) is constructed or adapted for use for the carriage of passengers and is not a goods vehicle,

    (b) has no more than eight seats in addition to the driver's seat,

    (c) has four or more wheels,

    (d) has a maximum design speed exceeding 25 kilometres per hour, and

    (e) has a maximum laden weight not exceeding 3.5 tonnes,]

  "regulations" means regulations made by the Secretary of State under this section, ...

  "seat belt" includes any description of restraining device for a child and any reference to wearing a seat belt is to be construed accordingly;

  [*"the seat belt Directive"* has the same meaning as in section 14.]

[(9A) The reference in subsection (1) above to the air bag being deactivated includes a reference to the case where the air bag is designed or adapted in such a way that it cannot inflate enough to pose a risk of injury to a child travelling in a rear-facing child restraining device in the seat in question.]

(10) [...]

[Section 15 is printed as amended by the Road Traffic Act 1991 s.83 and Sch.8;   **A18.55** *the Road Traffic Act 1988 (Amendment) Regulations 1992 (SI 1992/3105; not reproduced in this work) reg.3; the Motor Vehicles (Wearing of Seat Belts) (Amendment) Regulations 2006 (SI 2006/1892) reg.3.*

Words relating exclusively and expressly to Scotland have been omitted from s.15(8).

The fixed penalty procedure applies to offences under s.15(2) and s.15(4); see the Road Traffic Offenders Act 1988 Sch.3.

The Motor Vehicles (Wearing of Seat Belts by Children in Front Seats) Regulations 1993 (SI 1993/31) (q.v.) were made under s.15 and the Motor Vehicles (Wearing of Seat Belts) Regulations 1993 (SI 1993/176) (q.v.) were made in part under s.15.]

[Safety equipment for children in motor vehicles

A18.56   **15A.**—(1), (2) *[Power to make regulations prescribing types of equipment recommended as conducive to safety.]*

(3) Except in such circumstances as may be prescribed, if a person sells, or offers for sale, equipment of any description for which a type is prescribed under this section as equipment which is so conducive and that equipment—

     (a) is not of a type so prescribed, or

     (b) is sold or offered for sale in contravention of regulations under this section,

he is, subject to subsection (5) below, guilty of an offence.

(4) Except in such circumstances as may be prescribed, if a person sells, or offers for sale, equipment of any description for which a type is prescribed under this section as equipment conducive to the safety in the event of accident—

     (a) of children not of a class prescribed in relation to equipment of that type, or

     (b) of children in motor vehicles not of a class prescribed in relation to equipment of that type,

he is, subject to subsection (5) below, guilty of an offence.

(5) A person shall not be convicted of an offence under this section in respect of the sale or offer for sale of equipment if he proves that it was sold or, as the case may be, offered for sale for export from Great Britain.

(6) The provisions of Schedule 1 to this Act shall have effect in relation to contraventions of this section.

(7) Regulations under this section may make different provision in relation to different circumstances.

(8) This section applies to equipment of any description for use in a motor vehicle consisting of—

     (a) a restraining device for a child or for a carry-cot, or

     (b) equipment designed for use by a child in conjunction with any description of restraining device.

(9) References in this section to selling or offering for sale include respectively references to letting on hire and offering to let on hire.]

A18.57   *[Section 15A was inserted by the Motor Vehicles (Safety Equipment for Children) Act 1991 s.1.]*

[Requirement to notify bus passengers to wear seat belts

A18.58   **15B.**—(1) Subject to subsection (6) below, the operator of a bus in which any of the passenger seats are equipped with seat belts shall take all reasonable steps to ensure that every passenger is notified that he is required to wear a seat belt at all times when—

     (a) he is in a seat equipped with a seat belt, and

     (b) the bus is in motion.

(2) For the purposes of subsection (1) above, a passenger may be notified only by one or more of the following means—

     (a) an official announcement, or an audio-visual presentation, made when the passenger joins the bus or within a reasonable time of his doing so;

(b) a sign prominently displayed at each passenger seat equipped with a seat belt.

In paragraph (a) above, *"official announcement"* means an announcement by the driver of the bus, by a conductor or courier or by a person who is a group leader in relation to any group of persons who are passengers on the bus.

(3) For the purposes of subsection (2)(b) above, a sign that takes the form of a pictorial symbol must be in the form shown in Schedule 2A, depicting a white figure on a blue background.

(4) An operator who fails to comply with subsection (1) above is guilty of an offence.

(5) Where an offence under subsection (4) above which has been committed by a body corporate is proved to have been committed with the consent or connivance of, or to be attributable to any neglect on the part of, a director, manager, secretary or other similar officer of the body corporate, or any person who was purporting to act in such a capacity, he as well as the body corporate shall be guilty of the offence and shall be liable to be proceeded against and punished accordingly.

(6) Subsection (1) above does not apply in relation to a bus—

(a) which is being used to provide a local service (within the meaning of the Transport Act 1985) in a built-up area, or

(b) which is constructed or adapted for the carriage of standing passengers and on which the operator permits standing.

For the purposes of paragraph (a) above, a local service is provided in a built-up area if the entire route used by that service consists of restricted roads.

(7) In this section—

"bus" has the same meaning as in section 15;

"operator", in relation to a bus, means—

(a) the owner of the bus, or

(b) if the bus is in the possession of any other person under an agreement for hire, hire-purchase, conditional sale, loan or otherwise, that person;

"passenger seat", in relation to a bus, means any seat other than the driver's seat;

"restricted road" means a road that is restricted for the purposes of section 81 of the Road Traffic Regulation Act 1984 (ignoring any direction under section 82(2)(b) of that Act) or would be so restricted but for a direction under section 82(2)(a) or an order under section 84(1) of that Act.]

[Section 15B is printed as inserted by the Motor Vehicles (Wearing of Seat Belts) (Amendment) Regulations 2006 (SI 2006/1892) reg.4.]   **A18.59**

Wearing of protective headgear

16.—(1) The Secretary of State may make regulations requiring, subject to such exceptions as may be specified in the regulations, persons driving or riding (otherwise than in side-cars) on motor cycles of any class specified in the regulations to wear protective headgear of such description as may be so specified.   **A18.60**

(2) A requirement imposed by regulations under this section shall not apply to any follower of the Sikh religion while he is wearing a turban.

(3) Regulations under this section may make different provision in relation to different circumstances.

(4) A person who drives or rides on a motor cycle in contravention of regulations under this section is guilty of an offence; but notwithstanding any enactment or rule of law no person other than the person actually committing the contravention is guilty of an offence by reason of the contravention unless the person actually committing the contravention is a child under the age of sixteen years.

A18.61   *[The fixed penalty procedure applies to offences under s.16; see the Road Traffic Offenders Act 1988 Sch.3.*

The Motor Cycles (Protective Helmets) Regulations 1998 (SI 1998/1807) (q.v.) have effect as if made in part under s.16.]

Protective helmets for motor cyclists

A18.62   **17.**—(1) The Secretary of State may make regulations prescribing (by reference to shape, construction or any other quality) types of helmet recommended as affording protection to persons on or in motor cycles, or motor cycles of different classes, from injury in the event of accident.

(2) If a person sells, or offers for sale, a helmet as a helmet for affording such protection and the helmet is neither—

> (a) of a type prescribed under this section, nor
>
> (b) of a type authorised under regulations made under this section and sold or offered for sale subject to any conditions specified in the authorisation,

subject to subsection (3) below, he is guilty of an offence.

(3) A person shall not be convicted of an offence under this section in respect of the sale or offer for sale of a helmet if he proves that it was sold or, as the case may be, offered for sale for export from Great Britain.

(4) The provisions of Schedule 1 to this Act shall have effect in relation to contraventions of this section.

(5) In this section and that Schedule *"helmet"* includes any head-dress, and references in this section to selling or offering for sale include respectively references to letting on hire and offering to let on hire.

A18.63   *[As to the institution of proceedings under s.17, see the Road Traffic Offenders Act 1988 s.4(1) below.*

Proceedings under s.17(2) are specified by the Prosecution of Offences Act 1985 (Specified Proceedings) Order 1999 (SI 1999/904) below as being proceedings the conduct of which the Director of Public Prosecutions is not required to take over from the police under the Prosecution of Offences Act 1985 s.3(3)(a).

The Motor Cycles (Protective Helmets) Regulations 1998 (SI 1998/1807) (q.v.) have effect as if made in part under this section.]

Authorisation of head-worn appliances for use on motor cycles

A18.64   **18.**—(1) The Secretary of State may make regulations prescribing (by reference to shape, construction or any other quality) types of appliance of any description to which this section applies as authorised for use by persons driving or riding (otherwise than in side-cars) on motor cycles of any class specified in the regulations.

(2) Regulations under this section —

    (a) may impose restrictions or requirements with respect to the circumstances in which appliances of any type prescribed by the regulations may be used, and

    (b) may make different provision in relation to different circumstances.

(3) If a person driving or riding on a motor cycle on a road uses an appliance of any description for which a type is prescribed under this section and that appliance—

    (a) is not of a type so prescribed, or

    (b) is otherwise used in contravention of regulations under this section,

he is guilty of an offence.

(4) If a person sells, or offers for sale, an appliance of any such description as authorised for use by persons on or in motor cycles, or motor cycles of any class, and that appliance is not of a type prescribed under this section as authorised for such use, he is, subject to subsection (5) below, guilty of an offence.

(5) A person shall not be convicted of an offence under this section in respect of the sale or offer for sale of an appliance if he proves that it was sold or, as the case may be, offered for sale for export from Great Britain.

(6) The provisions of Schedule 1 to this Act shall have effect in relation to contraventions of subsection (4) above.

(7) This section applies to appliances of any description designed or adapted for use—

    (a) with any headgear, or

    (b) by being attached to or placed upon the head,

(as, for example, eye protectors or earphones).

(8) References in this section to selling or offering for sale include respectively references to letting on hire and offering to let on hire.

[As to the institution of proceedings under s.18, see the Road Traffic Offenders **A18.65**
Act 1988 s.4(1).

Proceedings under s.18(3) are specified by the Prosecution of Offences Act 1985 (Specified Proceedings) Order 1999 (SI 1999/904) below as being proceedings the conduct of which the Director of Public Prosecutions is not required to take over from the police under the Prosecution of Offences Act 1985 s.3(3)(a).

The fixed penalty procedure applies to offences under s.18; see the Road Traffic Offenders Act 1988 Sch.3 below. Offences under s.18 have been designated as fixed penalty offences by the Fixed Penalty Offences Order 2004 (SI 2004/2922).

The Motor Cycle (Eye Protectors) Regulations 1999 (SI 1999/535) (q.v.) have been made under s.18.]

Stopping on verges, etc., or in dangerous positions, etc.

Prohibition of parking of HGVs on verges, central reservations and footways

19.—(1) Subject to subsection (2) below, a person who parks a heavy com-   **A18.66**
mercial vehicle (as defined in section 20 of this Act) wholly or partly—

    (a) on the verge of a road, or

    (b) on any land situated between two carriageways and which is not a footway, or

    (c) on a footway,

is guilty of an offence.

(2) A person shall not be convicted of an offence under this section in respect of a vehicle if he proves to the satisfaction of the court—

    (a) that it was parked in accordance with permission given by a constable in uniform, or

    (b) that it was parked in contravention of this section for the purpose of saving life or extinguishing fire or meeting any other like emergency, or

    (c) that it was parked in contravention of this section but the conditions specified in subsection (3) below were satisfied.

(3) The conditions mentioned in subsection (2)(c) above are—

    (a) that the vehicle was parked on the verge of a road or on a footway for the purpose of loading or unloading, and

    (b) that the loading or unloading of the vehicle could not have been satisfactorily performed if it had not been parked on the footway or verge, and

    (c) that the vehicle was not left unattended at any time while it was so parked.

(4) In this section *"carriageway"* and *"footway"*, in relation to England and Wales, have the same meanings as in the Highways Act 1980.

A18.67   *[As to the possible disapplication of s.19, see Sch.3, para.2(4), to the Road Traffic Act 1991 below.*

    The fixed penalty procedure applies to offences under s.19; see the Road Traffic Offenders Act 1988 Sch.3 below. Offences under s.19 have been designated as fixed penalty parking offences by the Fixed Penalty Order 2000 (SI 2000/2792).

    The terms "carriageway" and "footway" are defined in s.329(1) of the Highways Act 1980 (q.v.).]

A18.68   19A. [...]

Definition of "heavy commercial vehicle" for the purposes of section 19

A18.69   20.—(1) In section 19 of this Act, *"heavy commercial vehicle"* means any goods vehicle which has an operating weight exceeding 7.5 tonnes.

(2) The operating weight of a goods vehicle for the purposes of this section is—

    (a) in the case of a motor vehicle not drawing a trailer or in the case of a trailer, its maximum laden weight,

    (b) in the case of an articulated vehicle, its maximum laden weight (if it has one) and otherwise the aggregate maximum laden weight of all the individual vehicles forming part of that articulated vehicle, and

    (c) in the case of a motor vehicle (other than an articulated vehicle) drawing one or more trailers, the aggregate maximum laden weight of the motor vehicle and the trailer or trailers attached to it.

(3) In this section *"articulated vehicle"* means a motor vehicle with a trailer so attached to it as to be partially superimposed upon it; and references to the maximum laden weight of a vehicle are references to the total laden weight which must not be exceeded in the case of that vehicle if it is to be used in Great Britain without contravening any regulations for the time being in force under section 41 of this Act.

(4) In this section, and in the definition of *"goods vehicle"* in section 192 of this Act as it applies for the purposes of this section, *"trailer"* means any vehicle other than a motor vehicle.

(5) The Secretary of State may by regulations amend subsections (1) and (2) above (whether as originally enacted or as previously amended under this subsection) —

(a) by substituting weights of a different description for any of the weights there mentioned, or

(b) in the case of subsection (1) above, by substituting a weight of a different description or amount, or a weight different both in description and amount, for the weight there mentioned.

(6) Different regulations may be made under subsection (5) above as respects different classes of vehicles or as respects the same class of vehicles in different circumstances and as respects different times of the day or night and as respects different localities.

(7) Regulations under subsection (5) above shall not so amend subsection (1) above that there is any case in which a goods vehicle whose operating weight (ascertained in accordance with subsection (2) above as originally enacted) does not exceed 7.5 tonnes is a heavy commercial vehicle for any of the purposes of section 19 of this Act.

Prohibition of driving or parking on cycle tracks

21.—(1) Subject to the provisions of this section, any person who without lawful authority, drives or parks a [mechanically propelled] wholly or partly on a cycle track is guilty of an offence. **A18.70**

(2) A person shall not be convicted of an offence under subsection (1) above with respect to a vehicle if he proves to the satisfaction of the court—

(a) that the vehicle was driven or (as the case may be) parked in contravention of that subsection for the purpose of saving life, or extinguishing fire or meeting any other like emergency, or

(b) that the vehicle was owned or operated by a highway authority or by a person discharging functions on behalf of a highway authority and was driven or (as the case may be) parked in contravention of that subsection in connection with the carrying out by or on behalf of that authority of any of the following, that is, the cleansing, maintenance or improvement of, or the maintenance or alteration of any structure or other work situated in, the cycle track or its verges[, or the preventing or removing of obstructions to the cycle track or the preventing or abating in any other way of nuisances or other interferences with the cycle track,], or

(c) that the vehicle was owned or operated by statutory undertakers and was driven or (as the case may be) parked in contravention of that subsection in connection with the carrying out by those undertakers of any works in relation to any apparatus belonging to or used by them for the purpose of their undertaking.

(3) In this section —

(a) *"cycle track"* and other expressions used in this section and in the Highways Act 1980 have the same meaning as in that Act,

[(aa) in subsection (1) *"mechanically propelled vehicle"* does not include a vehicle falling within paragraph (a), (b) or (c) of section 189(1) of this Act.]

(b) in subsection (2)(c) above *"statutory undertakers"* means any body who are statutory undertakers within the meaning of the Highways Act 1980, any sewerage authority within the meaning of that Act or the operator of [an electronic communications code network], and in relation to any such sewerage authority *"apparatus"* includes sewers or sewerage disposal works.

(4) This section does not extend to Scotland.

A18.71   *[Section 21 is printed as amended by the Countryside and Rights of Way Act 2000 ss.67, 70(4) and 103(2) and Sch.7, para.4(1)–(3); the Communications Act 2003 s.406 and Sch.17, para.95.*

For the definition of "an electronic communications code network", see the Communications Act 2003 Sch.17, para.1(1).

The terms "cycle track" and "statutory undertakers" are defined in s.329(1) of the Highways Act 1980 (q.v.). The definition of "sewerage authority" which was formerly included in the Highways Act 1980 s.329(1), was repealed by the Water Act 1989.

A public gas transporter is deemed by the Gas Act 1995 s.16(1) and Sch.4, para.2(1)(xxxvii), to be a statutory undertaker for the purposes of s.21.]

Leaving vehicles in dangerous positions

A18.72   **22.** If a person in charge of a vehicle causes or permits the vehicle or a trailer drawn by it to remain at rest on a road in such a position or in such condition or in such circumstances as to [involve a danger of injury] to other persons using the road, he is guilty of an offence.

A18.73   *[Section 22 is printed as amended by the Road Traffic Act 1991 s.48 and Sch.4, para.48.*

The fixed penalty procedure applies to offences under s.22; see the Road Traffic Offenders Act 1988 Sch.3 below.]

[Causing danger to other road-users

A18.74   **22A.**—(1) A person is guilty of an offence if he intentionally and without lawful authority or reasonable cause—

(a) causes anything to be on or over a road, or

(b) interferes with a motor vehicle, trailer or cycle, or

(c) interferes (directly or indirectly) with traffic equipment,

in such circumstances that it would be obvious to a reasonable person that to do so would be dangerous.

(2) In subsection (1) above *"dangerous"* refers to danger either of injury to

any person while on or near a road, or of serious damage to property on or near a road; and in determining for the purposes of that subsection what would be obvious to a reasonable person in a particular case, regard shall be had not only to the circumstances of which he could be expected to be aware but also to any circumstances shown to have been within the knowledge of the accused.

(3) In subsection (1) above *"traffic equipment"* means—

(a) anything lawfully placed on or near a road by a highway authority;

(b) a traffic sign lawfully placed on or near a road by a person other than a highway authority;

(c) any fence, barrier or light lawfully placed on or near a road—

(i) in pursuance of section 174 of the Highways Act 1980, ... or section 65 of the New Roads and Street Works Act 1991 (which provide for guarding, lighting and signing in streets where works are undertaken), or

(ii) by a constable or a person acting under the instructions (whether general or specific) of a chief officer of police.

(4) For the purposes of subsection (3) above anything placed on or near a road shall unless the contrary is proved be deemed to have been lawfully placed there.

(5) In this section *"road"* does not include a footpath or bridleway.

(6) This section does not extend to Scotland.]

[Section 22A was inserted by the Road Traffic Act 1991 s.6, and is printed as **A18.75**
amended by the New Roads and Street Works Act 1991 s.168(1) and Sch.8, Pt 4, para.121(1) and (2).

The offence under s.22A being punishable on indictment by a term of imprisonment, if a magistrates' court grants bail to a person charged with or convicted of an offence under this section, the prosecution may appeal to a judge of the Crown Court against the order granting bail under the Bail (Amendment) Act 1993 s.1 (not reproduced in this work).]

Other restrictions in interests of safety

Restriction of carriage of persons on motor cycles

23.—(1) Not more than one person in addition to the driver may be carried on **A18.76** a [motor bicycle].

(2) No person in addition to the driver may be carried on a [motor bicycle] otherwise than sitting astride the motor cycle and on a proper seat securely fixed to the motor cycle behind the driver's seat.

(3) If a person is carried on a motor cycle in contravention of this section, the driver of the motor cycle is guilty of an offence.

[Section 23 is printed as amended by the Road Traffic (Driver Licensing and **A18.77**
Information Systems) Act 1989 s.7 and Sch.3, para.6.

The fixed penalty procedure applies to offences under s.23; see the Road Traffic Offenders Act 1988 Sch.3 below.]

Restriction of carriage of persons on bicycles

24.—(1) Not more than one person may be carried on a road on a bicycle not **A18.78** propelled by mechanical power unless it is constructed or adapted for the carriage of more than one person.

(2) In this section —

    (a) references to a person carried on a bicycle include references to a person riding the bicycle, and

    (b) *"road"* includes bridleway.

(3) If a person is carried on a bicycle in contravention of subsection (1) above, each of the persons carried is guilty of an offence.

A18.79   *[For the application of the fixed penalty procedure to carrying more than one person on a pedal cycle contrary to s.24, see the Road Traffic Offences Act 1988 Pt 3 and Sch.3.*

    Proceedings under s.24(3) are specified by the Prosecution of Offences Act 1985 (Specified Proceedings) Order 1999 (SI 1999/904) below as being proceedings the conduct of which the Director of Public Prosecutions is not required to take over from the police under the Prosecution of Offences Act 1985 s.3(3)(a).]

Tampering with motor vehicles

A18.80   **25.** If, while a motor vehicle is on a road or on a parking place provided by a local authority, a person—

    (a) gets on to the vehicle, or

    (b) tampers with the brake or other part of its mechanism,

without lawful authority or reasonable cause he is guilty of an offence.

A18.81   *[Offences under s.25 and any other offences of which persons may have been convicted in the same proceedings may be recorded in national police records; see the National Police Records (Recordable Offences) Regulations 2000 (SI 2000/1139) (not reproduced in this work).*

    An offence under s.25 is an offence which has been specified by the Motor Salvage Operators (Specified Offences) Order 2002 (SI 2002/1917; not reproduced in this work) as an offence which is relevant to whether an applicant for registration (or for the renewal of registration) as a motor salvage operator is a fit and proper person (under the Vehicles (Crime) Act 2001 s.3(3) and (4)(b)).]

Holding or getting on to vehicle in order to be towed or carried

A18.82   **26.**—(1) If, for the purpose of being carried, a person without lawful authority or reasonable cause takes or retains hold of, or gets on to, a motor vehicle or trailer while in motion on a road he is guilty of an offence.

(2) If, for the purpose of being drawn, a person takes or retains hold of a motor vehicle or trailer while in motion on a road he is guilty of an offence.

A18.83   *[Proceedings under s.26(1) and (2) are specified by the Prosecution of Offences Act 1985 (Specified Proceedings) Order 1999 (SI 1999/904) below as being proceedings the conduct of which the Director of Public Prosecutions is not required to take over from the police under the Prosecution of Offences Act 1985 s.3(3)(a).]*

Control of dogs on roads

A18.84   **27.**—(1) A person who causes or permits a dog to be on a designated road without the dog being held on a lead is guilty of an offence.

(2) In this section *"designated road"* means a length of road specified by an

order in that behalf of the local authority in whose area the length of road is situated.

(3) The powers which under subsection (2) above are exercisable by a local authority in England and Wales are, in the case of a road part of the width of which is in the area of one local authority and part in the area of another, exercisable by either authority with the consent of the other.

(4) An order under this section may provide that subsection (1) above shall apply subject to such limitations or exceptions as may be specified in the order, and (without prejudice to the generality of this subsection) subsection (1) above does not apply to dogs proved—

> (a) to be kept for driving or tending sheep or cattle in the course of a trade or business, or
>
> (b) to have been at the material time in use under proper control for sporting purposes.

(5) An order under this section shall not be made except after consultation with the chief officer of police.

(6) The Secretary of State may make regulations—

> (a) prescribing the procedure to be followed in connection with the making of orders under this section, and
>
> (b) requiring the authority making such an order to publish in such manner as may be prescribed by the regulations notice of the making and effect of the order.

(7) In this section *"local authority"* means—

> (a) in relation to England and Wales, the council of a county, metropolitan district or London borough or the Common Council of the City of London, and
>
> (b) *[applies to Scotland.]*

(8) The power conferred by this section to make an order includes power, exercisable in like manner and subject to the like conditions, to vary or revoke it.

[The functions of the Secretary of State exercisable under s.27(6) in relation to Wales have been transferred to the National Assembly for Wales by the National Assembly for Wales (Transfer of Functions) Order 1999 (SI 1999/672; not reproduced in this work) art.2 and Sch.1. **A18.85**

As to the transfer of functions of the Secretary of State under s.17(6), (2) which are exercisable in relation to Scotland to the Scottish Ministers, see the Scotland Act 1998 (Transfer of Functions to the Scottish Ministers etc.) Order 1999 (SI 1999/1750; not reproduced in this work) art.2 and Sch.1.

As to the institution of proceedings under s.27, see the Road Traffic Offenders Act 1988 s.4(2) below.]

Cycling offences and cycle racing

[Dangerous cycling

28.—(1) A person who rides a cycle on a road dangerously is guilty of an offence. **A18.86**

(2) For the purposes of subsection (1) above a person is to be regarded as riding dangerously if (and only if)—

(a) the way he rides falls far below what would be expected of a competent and careful cyclist, and

(b) it would be obvious to a competent and careful cyclist that riding in that way would be dangerous.

(3) In subsection (2) above *"dangerous"* refers to danger either of injury to any person or of serious damage to property; and in determining for the purposes of that subsection what would be obvious to a competent and careful cyclist in a particular case, regard shall be had not only to the circumstances of which he could be expected to be aware but also to any circumstances shown to have been within the knowledge of the accused.]

A18.87   *[Section 28 is printed as substituted by the Road Traffic Act 1991 s.7.*

As to alternative charges to a charge under s.28, see the Road Traffic Offenders Act 1988 s.24(1) below.]

Careless, and inconsiderate, cycling

A18.88   **29.** If a person rides a cycle on a road without due care and attention, or without reasonable consideration for other persons using the road, he is guilty of an offence.

[...]

A18.89   *[Section 29 is printed as amended by the Road Traffic Act 1991 s.83 and Sch.8.*

Proceedings under s.29 are specified by the Prosecution of Offences Act 1985 (Specified Proceedings) Order 1999 (SI 1999/904) below as being proceedings the conduct of which the Director of Public Prosecutions is not required to take over from the police under the Prosecution of Offences Act 1985 s.3(3)(a).]

Cycling when under influence of drink or drugs

A18.90   **30.**—(1) A person who, when riding a cycle on a road or other public place, is unfit to ride through drink or drugs (that is to say, is under the influence of drink or a drug to such an extent as to be incapable of having proper control of the cycle) is guilty of an offence.

(2) *[Applies to Scotland.]*

(3) [...]

A18.91   *[Section 30 is printed as amended by the Road Traffic Act 1991 s.83 and Sch.8.]*

Regulation of cycle racing on public ways

A18.92   **31.**—(1) A person who promotes or takes part in a race or trial of speed on a public way between cycles is guilty of an offence, unless the race or trial—

(a) is authorised, and

(b) is conducted in accordance with any conditions imposed,

by or under regulations under this section.

(2) The Secretary of State may by regulations authorise, or provide for authorising, for the purposes of subsection (1) above, the holding on a public way other than a bridleway—

(a) of races or trials of speed of any class or description, or

(b) of a particular race or trial of speed,

in such cases as may be prescribed and subject to such conditions as may be imposed by or under the regulations.

(3) Regulations under this section may—

   (a) prescribe the procedure to be followed, and the particulars to be given, in connection with applications for authorisation under the regulations, and

   (b) make different provision for different classes or descriptions of race or trial.

(4) Without prejudice to any other powers exercisable in that behalf, the chief officer of police may give directions with respect to the movement of, or the route to be followed by, vehicular traffic during any period, being directions which it is necessary or expedient to give in relation to that period to prevent or mitigate—

   (a) congestion or obstruction of traffic, or

   (b) danger to or from traffic,

in consequence of the holding of a race or trial of speed authorised by or under regulations under this section.

(5) Directions under subsection (4) above may include a direction that any road or part of a road specified in the direction shall be closed during the period to vehicles or to vehicles of a class so specified.

[(6) In this section *"public way"* means, in England and Wales, a highway … but does not include a footpath.]

[Section 31 is printed as amended by the Road Traffic Act 1991 s.48 and Sch.4, para.49.   **A18.93**

Words relating expressly and exclusively to Scotland have been omitted from s.31(6).

The functions of the Secretary of State exercisable under s.31(2) in relation to Wales have been transferred to the National Assembly for Wales by the National Assembly for Wales (Transfer of Functions) Order 1999 (SI 1999/672; not reproduced in this work) art.2 and Sch.1.

As to the transfer of functions of the Secretary of State under s.31(2) which are exercisable in relation to Scotland to the Scottish Ministers, see the Scotland Act 1998 (Transfer of Functions to the Scottish Ministers etc.) Order 1999 (SI 1999/ 1750; not reproduced in this work) art.2 and Sch.1.

Proceedings under s.31(1) are specified by the Prosecution of Offences Act 1985 (Specified Proceedings) Order 1999 (SI 1999/904) below as being proceedings the conduct of which the Director of Public Prosecutions is not required to take over from the police under the Prosecution of Offences Act 1985 s.3(3)(a).]

Electrically assisted pedal cycles

32.—(1) An electrically assisted pedal cycle of a class specified in regulations   **A18.94** made for the purposes of section 189 of this Act and section 140 of the Road Traffic Regulation Act 1984 shall not be driven on a road by a person under the age of fourteen.

(2) A person who—

   (a) drives such a pedal cycle, or

   (b) knowing or suspecting that another person is under the age of fourteen, causes or permits him to drive such a pedal cycle,

in contravention of subsection (1) above is guilty of an offence.

Use of motor vehicles away from roads

Control of use of footpaths [bridleways and restricted byways] for motor vehicle trials

A18.95

33.—(1) A person must not promote or take part in a trial of any description between motor vehicles on a footpath [bridleway or restricted byway] unless the holding of the trial has been authorised under this section by the local authority.

(2) A local authority shall not give an authorisation under this section unless satisfied that consent in writing to the use of any length of footpath [bridleway or restricted byway] for the purposes of the trial has been given by the owner and by the occupier of the land over which that length of footpath [bridleway or restricted byway] runs, and any such authorisation may be given subject to compliance with such conditions as the authority think fit.

(3) A person who—

    (a) contravenes subsection (1) above, or

    (b) fails to comply with any conditions subject to which an authorisation under this section has been granted,

is guilty of an offence.

(4) The holding of a trial authorised under this section is not affected by any statutory provision prohibiting or restricting the use of footpaths or bridleways or a specified footpath [bridleway or restricted byway]; but this section does not prejudice any right or remedy of a person as having any interest in land.

(5) In this section *"local authority"* —

    (a) in relation to England and Wales, means the council of a county, metropolitan district or London borough, and

    (b) *[applies to Scotland.]*

[(6) In this section *"restricted byway"* means a way over which the public have restricted byway rights within the meaning of Part 2 of the Countryside and Rights of Way Act 2000, with or without a right to drive animals of any description along the way, but no other rights of way.]

A18.96   *[Section 33 is printed as amended by the Restricted Byways (Application and Consequential Amendment of Provisions) Regulations 2006 (SI 2006/1177) Sch.]*

[Prohibition of driving mechanically propelled vehicles elsewhere than on roads.

A18.97

34.—(1) Subject to the provisions of this section, if without lawful authority a person drives a mechanically propelled vehicle—

    (a) on to or upon any common land, moorland or land of any other description, not being land forming part of a road, or

    (b) on any road being a footpath, bridleway or restricted byway,

he is guilty of an offence.

(2) For the purposes of subsection (1)(b) above, a way shown in a definitive map and statement as a footpath, bridleway or restricted byway is, without prejudice to section 56(1) of the Wildlife and Countryside Act 1981, to be taken to be a way of the kind shown, unless [...] the contrary is proved.

[(2A) It is not an offence under this section for a person with an interest in land, or a visitor to any land, to drive a mechanically propelled vehicle on a road if, immediately before the commencement of section 47(2) of the Countryside and Rights of Way Act 2000, the road was—

    (a) shown in a definitive map and statement as a road used as a public path, and

    (b) in use for obtaining access to the land by the driving of mechanically propelled vehicles by a person with an interest in the land or by visitors to the land.]

(3) It is not an offence under this section to drive a mechanically propelled vehicle on any land within fifteen yards of a road, being a road on which a motor vehicle may lawfully be driven, for the purpose only of parking the vehicle on that land.

(4) A person shall not be convicted of an offence under this section with respect to a vehicle if he proves to the satisfaction of the court that it was driven in contravention of this section for the purpose of saving life or extinguishing fire or meeting any other like emergency.

(5) [Saving for s.193 of the Law of Property Act 1925 and byelaws and law of trespass.]

(6) Subsection (2) above [does] not extend to Scotland.

(7) In this section—

    "definitive map and statement" has the same meaning as in Part III of the Wildlife and Countryside Act 1981;

    ["interest", in relation to land, includes any estate in land and any right over land (whether exercisable by virtue of the ownership of an estate or interest in the land or by virtue of a licence or agreement) and, in particular, includes rights of common and sporting rights;]

    "mechanically propelled vehicle" does not include a vehicle falling within paragraph (a), (b) or (c) of section 189(1) of this Act; and

    "restricted byway" means a way over which the public have restricted byway rights within the meaning of Part II of the Countryside and Rights of Way Act 2000, with or without a right to drive animals of any description along the way, but no other rights of way.]

  [(8) A person—

    (a) entering any land in exercise of rights conferred by virtue of section 2(1) of the Countryside and Rights of Way Act 2000, or

    (b) entering any land which is treated by section 15(1) of that Act as being accessible to the public apart from that Act,

is not for the purposes of subsection (2A) a visitor to the land.]

[Section 34 is printed as substituted by the Countryside and Rights of Way Act **A18.98** *2000 ss.67 and 103(2) and Sch.7, para.5; the Natural Environment and Rural Communities Act 2006 ss.70 and 105(2) and Sch.12.*

The fixed penalty procedure applies to offences under s.34; see the Road Traffic Offenders Act 1988 Sch.3 below.]

Directions to traffic and to pedestrians and traffic signs

Drivers to comply with traffic directions

35.—(1) Where a constable is for the time being engaged in the regulation of   **A18.99** traffic in a road, a person driving or propelling a vehicle who neglects or refuses—

> (a) to stop the vehicle, or
>
> (b) to make it proceed in, or kept to, a particular line of traffic,

when directed to do so by the constable [or traffic officer] in the execution of his duty [or the traffic officer (as the case may be)] is guilty of an offence.

(2) Where—

> (a) a traffic survey of any description is being carried out on or in the vicinity of a road, and
>
> (b) a constable [or traffic officer] gives to a person driving or propelling a vehicle a direction—
>
>> (i) to stop the vehicle,
>>
>> (ii) to make it proceed in, or keep to, a particular line of traffic, or
>>
>> (iii) to proceed to a particular point on or near the road on which the vehicle is being driven or propelled,
>
> being a direction given for the purposes of the survey (but not a direction requiring any person to provide any information for the purposes of a traffic survey),

the person is guilty of an offence if he neglects or refuses to comply with the direction.

(3) The power to give such a direction as is referred to in subsection (2) above for the purposes of a traffic survey shall be so exercised as not to cause any unreasonable delay to a person who indicates that he is unwilling to provide any information for the purposes of the survey.

A18.100   *[Section 35 is printed as amended by the Traffic Management Act 2004 s.6(2) (amendments in square brackets apply to England only).*

The fixed penalty procedure applies to offences under s.35; see the Road Traffic Offenders Act 1988 Sch.3 below.

Section 35 shall have effect in relation to the exercise of powers by designated or accredited persons to stop vehicles and direct traffic, see the Police Reform Act 2002 Sch.4, para.12 and Sch.5, para.9; not reproduced in this work.]

Drivers to comply with traffic signs

A18.101   36.—(1) Where a traffic sign, being a sign—

> (a) of the prescribed size, colour and type, or
>
> (b) of another character authorised by the Secretary of State under the provisions in that behalf of the Road Traffic Regulation Act 1984,

has been lawfully placed on or near a road, a person driving or propelling a vehicle who fails to comply with the indication given by the sign is guilty of an offence.

(2) A traffic sign shall not be treated for the purposes of this section as having been lawfully placed unless either—

> (a) the indication given by the sign is an indication of a statutory prohibition, restriction or requirement, or
>
> (b) it is expressly provided by or under any provision of the Traffic Acts that this section shall apply to the sign or to signs of a type of which the sign is one;

and, where the indication mentioned in paragraph (a) of this subsection is of the general nature only of the prohibition, restriction or requirement to which the sign relates, a person shall not be convicted of failure to comply with the indication unless he has failed to comply with the prohibition, restriction or requirement to which the sign relates.

(3) For the purposes of this section a traffic sign placed on or near a road shall be deemed—

    (a) to be of the prescribed size, colour and type, or of another character authorised by the Secretary of State under the provisions in that behalf of the Road Traffic Regulation Act 1984, and

    (b) (subject to subsection (2) above) to have been lawfully so placed,

unless the contrary is proved.

(4) Where a traffic survey of any description is being carried out on or in the vicinity of a road, this section applies to a traffic sign by which a direction is given—

    (a) to stop a vehicle,

    (b) to make it proceed in, or keep to, a particular line of traffic, or

    (c) to proceed to a particular point on or near the road on which the vehicle is being driven or propelled,

being a direction given for the purposes of the survey (but not a direction requiring any person to provide any information for the purposes of the survey).

(5) Regulations made by the [Secretary of State for Transport], the Secretary of State for Wales and the Secretary of State for Scotland acting jointly may specify any traffic sign for the purposes of column 5 of the entry in Schedule 2 to the Road Traffic Offenders Act 1988 relating to offences under this section (offences committed by failing to comply with certain signs involve discretionary disqualification).

[Section 36 is printed as amended by the Secretary of State for the Environment, Transport and the Regions Order 1997 (SI 1997/2971); the Secretaries of State for Transport, Local Government and the Regions and for Environment, Food and Rural Affairs Order 2001 (SI 2001/2568); the Transfer of Functions (Transport, Local Government and the Regions) Order 2002 (SI 2002/2626).

A18.102

The functions of the Secretary of State for Transport exercisable under s.36(5) in relation to Wales (so far as exercisable by the Secretary of State for Wales, but only to the extent that functions are exercisable by the National Assembly for Wales under s.64 of the Road Traffic Regulation Act 1984 above) have been transferred to the National Assembly by the National Assembly for Wales (Transfer of Functions) Order 1999 (SI 1999/672; not reproduced in this work) art.2 and Sch.1.

As to the exercise of functions of the Secretary of State for Transport under s.36(5) which are exercisable in relation to Scotland only after consultation with the Scottish Ministers, see the Scotland Act 1998 (Transfer of Functions to the Scottish Ministers etc.) Order 1999 (SI 1999/1750; not reproduced in this work) art.4 and Sch.3.

Every function of the Secretary of State for Transport, the Secretary of State for Scotland and the Secretary of State for Wales under s.36(5) has been transferred to the Secretary of State with effect from December 27, 1999; see the Transfer of Functions (Road Traffic) Order 1999 (SI 1999/3143; not reproduced in this work).

The fixed penalty procedure applies to offences under s.36; see the Road Traffic Offenders Act 1988 Sch.3 below.

As to the admissibility of evidence of speeding in respect of offences under s.36(1), see the Road Traffic Offenders Act 1988 s.20 below.

The traffic signs to which this section are applied are prescribed by the Traffic Signs (Temporary Obstructions) Regulations 1997 (SI 1997/3053) reg.4 (q.v.) and the Traffic Signs Regulations and General Directions 2002 (SI 2002/3113) reg.10(1) (q.v.).]

Directions to pedestrians

A18.103   **37.** Where a constable in uniform [or traffic officer] is for the time being engaged in the regulation of vehicular traffic in a road, a person on foot who proceeds across or along the carriageway in contravention of a direction to stop given by the constable in the execution of his duty [or the traffic officer (as the case may be)], either to persons on foot or to persons on foot and other traffic, is guilty of an offence.

A18.104   *[Section 37 is printed as amended by the Traffic Management Act 2004 s.6(3) (amendments in square brackets apply to England only).*

Section 37 shall have effect in relation to the exercise of powers by designated or accredited persons to stop vehicles and direct traffic, see the Police Reform Act 2002 Sch.4, para.12 and Sch.5, para.9; not reproduced in this work.]

Promotion of road safety

The Highway Code

A18.105   **38.**—(1) The Highway Code shall continue to have effect, subject however to revision in accordance with the following provisions of this section.

(2)–(6) *[Revision and publication of the Highway Code.]*

(7) A failure on the part of a person to observe a provision of the Highway Code shall not of itself render that person liable to criminal proceedings of any kind but any such failure may in any proceedings (whether civil or criminal, and including proceedings for an offence under the Traffic Acts, the Public Passenger Vehicles Act 1981 [*q.v.*] or sections 18 to 23 of the Transport Act 1985 [*q.v.*]) be relied upon by any party to the proceedings as tending to establish or negative any liability which is in question in those proceedings.

(8) In this section *"the Highway Code"* means the code comprising directions for the guidance of persons using roads issued under section 45 of the Road Traffic Act 1930, as from time to time revised under this section or under any previous enactment.

(9) *[Further provision as to the revision of the Highway Code.]*

Powers of Secretary of State and local authorities as to giving road safety information and training

A18.106   **39.** *[Omitted.]*

Powers of Secretary of State to subsidise bodies other than local authorities for giving road safety information and training

A18.107   **40.** *[Omitted.]*

PART II

CONSTRUCTION AND USE OF VEHICLES AND EQUIPMENT

[Using vehicle in dangerous condition]

[Using vehicle in dangerous condition, etc.

40A. A person is guilty of an offence if he uses, or causes or permits another to **A18.108**
use, a motor vehicle or trailer on a road when—

(a) the condition of the motor vehicle or trailer, or of its accessories or
   equipment, or

(b) the purpose for which it is used, or

(c) the number of passengers carried by it, or the manner in which they
   are carried, or

(d) the weight, position or distribution of its load, or the manner in which
   it is secured,

is such that the use of the motor vehicle or trailer involves a danger of injury to
any person.]

[Section 40A and the italicised heading preceding it were inserted by the Road **A18.109**
Traffic Act 1991 s.8(1).

Section 40A does not apply to tramcars nor to trolley vehicles (other than duo-
buses): Tramcars and Trolley Vehicles (Modification of Enactments) Regula-
tions 1992 (SI 1992/1217) regs 7, 9 and 11 (q.v.).]

General regulation of construction, use, etc.

Regulation of construction, weight, equipment and use of vehicles

41.—(1) The Secretary of State may make regulations generally as to the use **A18.110**
of motor vehicles and trailers on roads, their construction and equipment and the
conditions under which they may be so used.
Subsections (2) to (4) below do not affect the generality of this subsection.

(2) *[Particular provisions which may be included in regulations.]*

(3) *[Provisions as to goods vehicles which may be included in regulations.]*

(4) *[Provisions as to lighting equipment and reflectors which may be included*
in regulations.]

[(4A) *[Provisions as to speed limiters which may be included in regulations.]]*

(5) *[Power to make different regulations for different classes of vehicles, etc.]*

(6) In framing regulations under this section prescribing a weight of any description which is not to be exceeded in the case of goods vehicles of a class for
which a certificate of conformity or Minister's approval certificate may be issued
under section 57 or 58 of this Act the Secretary of State must have regard to the
design weight of the like description determined by virtue of section 54 of this
Act for vehicles of that class and must secure that the first-mentioned weight does
not exceed the design weight.

(7) In this Part of this Act —

"construction and use requirements" means requirements, whether

applicable generally or at specified times or in specified circumstances, imposed under this section,

"*plated particulars*" means such particulars as are required to be marked on a goods vehicle in pursuance of regulations under this section by means of a plate,

"*plated weights*" means such weights as are required to be so marked.

A18.111   *[With effect from a day to be appointed, a new para.(ba) will be inserted into s.41(2) (not reproduced) and a new subs.(2A) will be inserted after s.41(2) by the Road Safety Act 2006 s.56(1)–(4). The new s.41(2A) relates to provisions which may be included with respect to the modification of motor vehicles to enable them to be propelled using fuel stored under pressure and will not be reproduced in the main work.*

With effect from a day to be appointed, a new para.(m) will be inserted at the end of s.41(2) (not reproduced) by the Road Safety Act 2006 s.18(1)(a) and the following text will be inserted in s.41(7) by the Road Safety Act 2006 s.18(1)(b):

["*speed assessment equipment detection device*" means a device the purpose, or one of the purposes, of which is to detect, or interfere with the operation of, equipment used to assess the speed of motor vehicles.]

The regulations which have effect as if made under s.41 include the Minibus (Conditions of Fitness, Equipment and Use) Regulations 1977 (SI 1977/2103), the Community Bus Regulations 1978 (SI 1978/1313), the Public Service Vehicles (Conditions of Fitness, Equipment, Use and Certification) Regulations 1981 (SI 1981/257) (q.v.), the Road Transport (International Passenger Services) Regulations 1984 (SI 1984/748) (q.v.), and the Road Vehicles (Construction and Use) Regulations 1986 (SI 1986/1078) (q.v.). The Road Vehicles Lighting Regulations 1989 (SI 1989/1796) (q.v.) have been made under this section (read together with s.43), as have the Road Vehicle (Authorised Weight) Regulations 1998 (SI 1998/ 3111) (q.v.).

Regulations made under s.41 before July 1, 1988 apply to trolley vehicles as if s.193 of and Sch.4 to the Road Traffic Act 1988 (the combined effect of which excluded the application of specified statutory provisions to certain vehicles, including trolley vehicles) and the corresponding earlier enactments had never been passed: Tramcars and Trolley Vehicles (Modification of Enactments) Regulations 1992 (SI 1992/1217) reg.17 (q.v.).]

[Breach of requirement as to brakes, steering-gear or tyres

A18.112   **41A.** A person who—

(a) contravenes or fails to comply with a construction and use requirement as to brakes, steering-gear or tyres, or

(b) uses on a road a motor vehicle or trailer which does not comply with such a requirement, or causes or permits a motor vehicle or trailer to be so used,

is guilty of an offence.]

A18.113   *[Section 41A was inserted by the Road Traffic Act 1991 s.8(2).]*

[Breach of requirement as to weight: goods and passenger vehicles

A18.114   **41B.**—(1) A person who—

    (a) contravenes or fails to comply with a construction and use requirement as to any description of weight applicable to—

        (i) a goods vehicle, or

        (ii) a motor vehicle or trailer adapted to carry more than eight passengers, or

    (b) uses on a road a vehicle which does not comply with such a requirement, or causes or permits a vehicle to be so used,

is guilty of an offence.

(2) In any proceedings for an offence under this section in which there is alleged a contravention of or failure to comply with a construction and use requirement as to any description of weight applicable to a goods vehicle, it shall be a defence to prove either—

    (a) that at the time when the vehicle was being used on the road—

        (i) it was proceeding to a weighbridge which was the nearest available one to the place where the loading of the vehicle was completed for the purpose of being weighed, or

        (ii) it was proceeding from a weighbridge after being weighed to the nearest point at which it was reasonably practicable to reduce the weight to the relevant limit, without causing an obstruction on any road, or

    (b) in a case where the limit of that weight was not exceeded by more than 5 per cent—

        (i) that that limit was not exceeded at the time when the loading of the vehicle was originally completed, and

        (ii) that since that time no person has made any addition to the load.]

[Section 41B was inserted by the Road Traffic Act 1991 s.8(2).]   **A18.115**

[Breach of requirement as to speed assessment equipment detection devices

41C. A person who—   **A18.116**

    (a) contravenes or fails to comply with a construction or use requirement as to speed assessment equipment detection devices, or

    (b) uses on a road a motor vehicle or trailer which does not comply with such a requirement, or causes or permits a motor vehicle or trailer to be so used,

is guilty of an offence.]

[Section 41C is prospectively inserted after s.41B by the Road Safety Act 2006   **A18.117** *s.18(2).]*

[Breach of requirements as to control of vehicle, mobile telephones etc.

41D. A person who contravenes or fails to comply with a construction and use   **A18.118** requirement—

    (a) as to not driving a motor vehicle in a position which does not give proper control or a full view of the road and traffic ahead, or not causing or permitting the driving of a motor vehicle by another person in such a position, or

    (b) as to not driving or supervising the driving of a motor vehicle while using a hand-held mobile telephone or other hand-held interactive communication device, or not causing or permitting the driving of a motor vehicle by another person using such a telephone or other device,

is guilty of an offence.]

A18.119 *[Section 41D is printed as inserted by the Road Safety Act 2006 s.26(1).]*

[Breach of other construction and use requirements

A18.120 42. A person who—

(a) contravenes or fails to comply with any construction or use requirement other than one within section 41A(a) or 41B(1)(a) [or 41D] of this Act, or

(b) uses on a road a motor vehicle or trailer which does not comply with such a requirement, or causes or permits a motor vehicle or trailer to be so used,

is guilty of an offence.]

A18.121 *[Section 42 is printed as substituted by the Road Traffic Act 1991 s.8(2) and as subsequently amended by the Road Safety Act 2006 s.26(2).*

With effect from a day (or days) to be appointed, in s.42(a), ", 41B(1)(a), 41C(a)" will be substituted for "or 41B(1)(a)" by the Road Safety Act 2006 s.18(3).

The fixed penalty procedure applies to offences under s.42; see the Road Traffic Offenders Act 1988 Sch.3 below. Offences under s.42 which consist of causing an unnecessary obstruction of a road in breach of reg.103 of the Road Vehicles (Construction and Use) Regulations 1986 (SI 1986/1087) (q.v.) have been designated as fixed penalty parking offences by the Schedule to the Fixed Penalty Order 2000 (SI 2000/2792). Emission offences and stationary idling offences (as defined) under this section have been designated as fixed penalty offences under the Road Traffic (Vehicle Emissions) (Fixed Penalty) (England) Regulations 2002 (SI 2002/1808) reg.7; the Road Traffic (Vehicle Emissions) (Fixed Penalty) (Scotland) Regulations 2003 (SI 2003/212) reg.7; and the Road Traffic (Vehicle Emissions) (Fixed Penalty) (Wales) Regulations 2003 (SI 2003/ 300 (W.42)) reg.7.

Proceedings under s.42(b) are specified by the Prosecution of Offences Act 1985 (Specified Proceedings) Order 1999 (SI 1999/904) below as being proceedings the conduct of which the Director of Public Prosecutions is not required to take over from the police under the Prosecution of Offences Act 1985 s.3(3)(a).]

Temporary exemption (contained in regulations) from application of regulations under section 41

A18.122 43. *[Omitted.]*

Authorisation of use on roads of special vehicles not complying with regulations under section 41

A18.123 44.—(1) The Secretary of State may by order authorise, subject to such restrictions and conditions as may be specified by or under the order, the use on roads—

(a) of special motor vehicles or trailers, or special types of motor vehicles or trailers, which are constructed either for special purposes or for tests or trials,

(b) of vehicles or trailers, or types of vehicles or trailers, constructed for use outside the United Kingdom,

(c) of new or improved types of motor vehicles or trailers, whether wheeled or wheelless, or of motor vehicles or trailers equipped with new or improved equipment or types of equipment, and

(d) of vehicles or trailers carrying loads of exceptional dimensions,

[and sections 40A to 42 of this Act shall not apply in relation to] the use of such vehicles, trailers, or types in accordance with the order.

(2) The Secretary of State may by order make provision for securing that, subject to such restrictions and conditions as may be specified by or under the order, regulations under section 41 of this Act shall have effect in their application to such vehicles, trailers and types of vehicles and trailers as are mentioned in subsection (1) above subject to such modifications or exceptions as may be specified in the order.

(3) The powers conferred by this section on the Secretary of State to make orders shall be exercisable by statutory instrument except in the case of orders applying only to specified vehicles or to vehicles of specified persons, but in that excepted case (as in others) the order may be varied or revoked by subsequent order of the Secretary of State.

[Section 44 is printed as amended by the Road Traffic Act 1991 s.48 and Sch.4, **A18.124** *para.51.*

The orders made by statutory instrument which have effect as if made under s.44 include the Road Vehicles (Authorisation of Special Types) (General) Order 2003 (SI 2003/1998) (q.v.).]

Tests of vehicles other than goods vehicles to which section 49 applies

Tests of satisfactory condition of vehicles

45.—(1) This section applies to motor vehicles other than goods vehicles which **A18.125** are required by regulations under section 49 of this Act to be submitted for a vehicle test under that section and has effect for the purpose of ascertaining whether the [following requirements are complied with, namely—

(a) the prescribed statutory requirements relating to the construction and condition of motor vehicles or their accessories or equipment, and

(b) the requirement that the condition of motor vehicles should not be such that their use on a road would involve a danger of injury to any person.]

(2) The Secretary of State may by regulations make provision—

(a) for the examination of vehicles submitted for examination under this section, and

(b) for the issue, where it is found on such an examination that the requirements mentioned in subsection (1) above are complied with, of a certificate (in this Act referred to as a *"test certificate"*) that at the date of the examination the requirements were complied with in relation to the vehicle.

(3) *[Examinations to be carried out by authorised examiners and others.]*

(4) *[Refusal of test certificate.]*

(5) *[Appeal against refusal of test certificate.]*

(6) *[Examination stations and equipment.]*

[(6A) *[Courses of instruction relating to examinations under s.45 .]*]

(6B) The Secretary of State shall maintain, or cause to be maintained, records containing such particulars as he thinks fit of—

  (a) vehicles submitted for examination under this section, and

  (b) the carrying out of and the results of the examinations.]

(7) *[Power to make regulations.]*

(8) In its application to vehicles in which recording equipment is required by Article 3 of the Community Recording Equipment Regulation to be installed and used, this section shall have effect as if any reference to prescribed statutory requirements relating to the construction and condition of motor vehicles or their accessories or equipment included a reference to the prescribed requirements of so much of that Regulation as relates to the installation of recording equipment and the seals to be fixed to such equipment.

A18.126　　　*[Section 45 is printed as amended by the Road Traffic Act 1991 s.48 and Sch.4, para.51; the Road Traffic (Vehicle Testing) Act 1999 s.1(3).*

　　　The Motor Vehicles (Tests) Regulations 1981 (SI 1981/1694) have effect as if made in part under s.45.]

[Regulations under section 45 of Road Traffic Act 1988]

A18.127　　　**46.** *[Omitted.]*

[Use of records of vehicle examinations, etc.]

A18.128　　　**46A.** *[Omitted.]*

[Evidence from records of vehicle examinations

A18.129　　　**46B.**—(1) A statement to which this section applies is admissible in any proceedings as evidence … of any fact stated in it with respect to—

  (a) the issue of a test certificate in respect of a vehicle, and

  (b) the date of issue of such a certificate,

to the same extent as oral evidence of that fact is admissible in the proceedings.

(2) This section applies to a statement contained in a document purporting to be—

  (a) a part of the records maintained under s.45(6B) of this Act,

  (b) a copy of a document forming part of those records, or

  (c) a note of any information contained in those records,

and to be authenticated by a person authorised to do so by the Secretary of State.

(3) In this section as it has effect in England and Wales—

　　"document" means anything in which information of any description is recorded;

　　"copy", in relation to a document, means anything onto which information recorded in the document has been copied, by whatever means and whether directly or indirectly; and

"statement" means any representation of fact, however made.

(4) *[Applies to Scotland.]*

(5) Nothing in subsection (4) above limits to civil proceedings the reference to proceedings in subsection (1) above.]

[Section 46B is printed as inserted by the Road Traffic (Vehicle Testing) Act **A18.130**
1999 s.4.

The words omitted from s.46B(1) relate exclusively to Scotland.]

Obligatory test certificates

47.—(1) A person who uses on a road at any time, or causes or permits to be so **A18.131**
used, a motor vehicle to which this section applies, and as respects which no test certificate has been issued within the appropriate period before that time, is guilty of an offence.

In this section and section 48 of this Act, the *"appropriate period"* means a period of twelve months or such shorter period as may be prescribed.

(2) Subject to subsections (3) and (5) below, the motor vehicles to which this section applies at any time are—

    (a) those first registered [under the Vehicle Excise and Registration Act 1994 or any corresponding earlier legislation], not less than three years before that time, and

    (b) those which, having a date of manufacture not less than three years before that time, have been used on roads (whether in Great Britain or elsewhere) before being [so registered],

being, in either case, motor vehicles other than goods vehicles which are required by regulations under section 49 of this Act to be submitted for a goods vehicle test.

(3) As respects a vehicle being—

    (a) a motor vehicle used for the carriage of passengers and with more than eight seats, excluding the driver's seat, or

    (b) a taxi (as defined in section 64(3) of the Transport Act 1980), being a vehicle licensed to ply for hire, or

    (c) an ambulance, that is to say, a motor vehicle which is constructed or adapted, and primarily used, for the carriage of persons to a place where they will receive, or from a place where they have received, medical or dental treatment, and which, by reason of design, marking or equipment is readily identifiable as a vehicle so constructed or adapted,

subsection (2)(a) above shall have effect as if for the period there mentioned there were substituted a period of one year.

[(4) For the purposes of subsection (2)(b) above there shall be disregarded—

    (a) the use of a vehicle before it is sold or supplied by retail, and

    (b) the use of a vehicle to which a motor dealer has assigned a mark under [section 24 of the Vehicle Excise and Registration Act 1994] before it is registered by the Secretary of State under [section 21(2)] of that Act.]

(5) This section does not apply to vehicles of such classes as may be prescribed.

(6) The Secretary of State may by regulations exempt from subsection (1) above the use of vehicles for such purposes as may be prescribed.

(7) The Secretary of State may by regulations exempt from subsection (1) above the use of vehicles in any such area as may be prescribed.

(8) For the purposes of this section the date of manufacture of a vehicle shall be taken to be the last day of the year during which its final assembly is completed, except where after that day modifications are made to the vehicle before it is sold or supplied by retail, and in that excepted case shall be taken to be the last day of the year during which the modifications are completed.

(9) The Secretary of State may by order made by statutory instrument direct that subsection (2) above shall have effect with the substitution, for three years (in both places), of such other period (not being more than ten years) as may be specified in the order.

An order under this subsection shall not have effect unless approved by resolution of each House of Parliament.

A18.132　　　*[Section 47 is printed as amended by the Finance Act 1994 s.5 and Sch.2, paras 25 and 29; Vehicle Excise and Registration Act 1994 s.63 and Sch.3, para.24.*

The fixed penalty procedure applies to offences under s.47; see the Road Traffic Offenders Act 1988 Sch.3 below. Offences under s.47 have been designated as fixed penalty offences by the Fixed Penalty Offences Order 2003 (SI 2003/1253).

Proceedings under s.47(1) are specified by the Prosecution of Offences Act 1985 (Specified Proceedings) Order 1999 (SI 1999/904) below as being proceedings the conduct of which the Director of Public Prosecutions is not required to take over from the police under the Prosecution of Offences Act 1985 s.3(3)(a).

The Motor Vehicles (Tests) Regulations 1981 (SI 1981/1694) have effect as if made in part under s.47.

For the conditions that must be met where an application is made for a vehicle licence under the Vehicle Excise and Registration Act 1994 for a vehicle to which s.47 applies, in order that the Secretary of State may be satisfied that (if one is required) an effective test certificate is in force for the vehicle, see the Motor Vehicles (Evidence of Test Certificates) Regulations 2004 (SI 2004/1896) reg.3.]

Supplementary provisions about test certificates

A18.133　　　**48.**—(1) *[Regulations changing length of appropriate period and period under s.47(2).]*

[(1A) A test certificate issued in respect of a vehicle within the period of one month ending immediately before the date on which section 47 of this Act first applies to the vehicle shall be treated for the purposes of that section as if issued at the end of that period.]

(2) Where—

    (a) within the appropriate period after a test certificate is issued or treated for the purposes of section 47 of this Act as issued, but

    (b) not earlier than one month before the end of that period,

a further test certificate is issued as respects the same vehicle, the further certificate shall be treated for the purposes of that section as if issued at the end of the appropriate period.

(3) Where the particulars contained in a test certificate in accordance with regulations made under section 45 of this Act include a date of expiry falling later, but not more than one month later, than the end of the appropriate period after the date on which it is issued—

    (a) the certificate shall be deemed to have been issued in respect of the same vehicle as an earlier test certificate, and

    (b) the date on which it was issued shall be deemed to have been a date falling within the last month of the appropriate period after the date on which that earlier certificate was issued or treated for the purposes of section 47 of this Act as issued;

and any date of expiry contained in a test certificate shall be deemed to have been entered in accordance with regulations under section 45 of this Act unless the contrary is proved.

(4) The Secretary of State may by regulations make provision for the issue, in such circumstances as may be prescribed, of a certificate of temporary exemption in respect of a public service vehicle adapted to carry more than eight passengers, exempting that vehicle from the provisions of section 47(1) of this Act for such period as may be specified in the certificate.

(5) In relation to any public service vehicle so adapted—

    (a) subsections [(1A),] (2) and (3) above shall have effect as if for "one month" (in [each place]) there were substituted "two months", and

    (b) subsection (3) above shall have effect as if for "last month" there were substituted "last two months".

(6) [...]

[Section 48 is printed as amended by the Road Traffic Act 1991 s.48 and Sch.4, **A18.134** *para.54(1) and (3); the Deregulation (Motor Vehicle Tests) Order 1996 (SI 1996/ 1700; not reproduced in this work) art.2.*

The term "public service vehicle" is defined in s.1 of the Public Passenger Vehicles Act 1981 (q.v.).]

Tests of certain classes of goods vehicles

Tests of satisfactory condition of goods vehicles and determination of plated weights, etc.

49.—(1) The Secretary of State may by regulations make provision for the ex- **A18.135** amination of goods vehicles of any prescribed class—

    (a) for the purpose of selecting or otherwise determining plated weights or other plated particulars for goods vehicles of that class, or

    (b) for the purpose of ascertaining whether any prescribed construction and use requirements (whether relating to plated particulars or not) are complied with in the case of goods vehicles of that class, [or

    (c) for the purpose of ascertaining whether the condition of the vehicle is such that its use on a road would involve a danger of injury to any person,

or for any of these purposes.]

(2) In particular the regulations may make provision—

    (a) for the determination, according to criteria or by methods prescribed by or determined under the regulations, of the plated particulars for a goods vehicle (including its plated weights), on an examination of the vehicle for the purpose, and for the issue on such an examination, except as provided by regulations made by virtue of paragraph (c) of this subsection, of a certificate (in this Act referred to as a *"plating certificate"*) specifying those particulars,

(b) for the issue, for a goods vehicle which has been found on examination for the purpose to comply with the prescribed construction and use requirements [and the requirement that the condition of the vehicle is not such that its use on a road would involve a danger of injury to any person], of a certificate (in this Act referred to as a *"goods vehicle test certificate"*) stating that the vehicle has been found so to comply, and

(c) for the refusal of a goods vehicle test certificate for a goods vehicle which is so found not to comply with those requirements and for requiring a written notification to be given—

    (i) of any such refusal, and

    (ii) of the grounds of the refusal,

and for the refusal of a plating certificate where a goods vehicle test certificate is refused.

(3) References in subsections (1) and (2) above to construction and use requirements shall be construed—

(a) in relation to an examination of a vehicle solely for the purpose of ascertaining whether it complies with any such requirements, as references to such of those requirements as are applicable to the vehicle at the time of the test, and

(b) in relation to an examination of a vehicle both for that purpose and for the purpose of determining its plated particulars, as references to such of those requirements as will be applicable to the vehicle if a plating certificate is issued for it.

(4) In this Part of this Act —

"examination for plating" means an examination under regulations under this section for the purpose of determining plated particulars for a goods vehicle, and

"goods vehicle test" means an examination under regulations under this section for the purpose of ascertaining whether any prescribed construction and use requirements [, or the requirement that the condition of the vehicle is not such that its use on a road would involve a danger of injury to any person,] are complied with in the case of a goods vehicle.

(5) In its application to vehicles in which recording equipment is required by Article 3 of the Community Recording Equipment Regulation to be installed and used, this section shall have effect as if any reference to prescribed construction and use requirements included a reference to prescribed requirements of so much of that Regulation as relates to the installation of recording equipment and the seals to be fixed to such equipment.

A18.136   *[Section 49 is printed as amended by the Road Traffic Act 1991 s.48 and Sch.4, para.54(1)–(4).*

With effect from a day to be appointed, the following new subsection will be inserted after s.49(3) by the Road Safety Act 2006 s.48(1):

[(3A) The Secretary of State must maintain, or cause to be maintained, records containing such particulars as he thinks fit of—

    (a) goods vehicles submitted for examination under this section, and

    (b) the carrying out of and the results of the examinations.]

The Goods Vehicles (Plating and Testing) Regulations 1988 (SI 1988/1478) (q.v.) have effect as if made in part under s.49.]

[Use of records of goods vehicle examinations, etc.

49A.—(1) This section applies to—   A18.137

    (a) the records maintained by the Secretary of State (or caused by him to be maintained) under section 49(3A) of this Act, and

    (b) the records maintained by the Secretary of State in connection with any functions exercisable by him under or by virtue of the Vehicle Excise and Registration Act 1994.

(2) The Secretary of State may use the information contained in records falling within either paragraph of subsection (1) above—

    (a) to check the accuracy of the records falling within the other paragraph of that subsection, and

    (b) where appropriate, to amend or supplement information contained in those records.

(3) The Secretary of State may also use the information contained in records falling within paragraph (b) of that subsection for the purpose of promoting compliance with section 53 of this Act.

(4) This section does not limit any powers of the Secretary of State apart from this section.]

[Section 49A is prospectively inserted after s.49 by the Road Safety Act 2006   A18.138 s.48(2).]

Appeals against determinations under section 49

50. *[Omitted.]*   A18.139

Particular aspects of regulations under section 49

51.—(1) Without prejudice to the generality of subsection (1) of section 49 of   A18.140 this Act, regulations under that section may—

    (a)–(b) *[Omitted.]*

    (c) prescribe the conditions subject to which vehicles will be accepted for such examination and, without prejudice to that—

        (i) authorise any person by whom an examination of the vehicle under the regulations or section 50 of this Act is carried out to drive the vehicle, whether on a road or elsewhere, and

        (ii) require that a driver of a vehicle examined under those regulations or that section is, except so far as permitted to be absent by the person carrying out the examination, present throughout the whole of the examination and drives the vehicle when directed to do so, and operates the controls in accordance with any directions given to him, by that person,

(d) *[Omitted.]*

(2) Regulations under section 49 of this Act may provide that a person who contravenes or fails to comply with a requirement of regulations imposed by virtue of subsection (1)(c)(ii) above is guilty of an offence.

(3) In this section any reference to the driving of a vehicle is, in relation to a trailer, a reference to the driving of the vehicle by which the trailer is drawn.

Supplementary provisions about tests, etc., of goods vehicles

A18.141   **52.** *[Omitted.]*

Obligatory goods vehicle test certificates

A18.142   **53.**—(1) If any person at any time on or after the relevant date—

    (a) uses on a road a goods vehicle of a class required by regulations under section 49 of this Act to have been submitted for examination for plating, or

    (b) causes or permits to be used on a road a goods vehicle of such a class,

and at that time there is no plating certificate in force for the vehicle, he is guilty of an offence.

In this subsection *"relevant date"*, in relation to any goods vehicle, means the date by which it is required by the regulations to be submitted for examination for plating.

(2) If any person at any time on or after the relevant date—

    (a) uses on a road a goods vehicle of a class required by regulations under section 49 of this Act to have been submitted for a goods vehicle test, or

    (b) causes or permits to be used on a road a goods vehicle of such a class,

and at that time there is no goods vehicle test certificate in force for the vehicle, he is guilty of an offence.

In this subsection *"relevant date"*, in relation to any goods vehicle, means the date by which it is required by the regulations to be submitted for its goods vehicle test.

(3) Any person who—

    (a) uses a goods vehicle on a road, or

    (b) causes or permits a goods vehicle to be so used,

when an alteration has been made to the vehicle or its equipment which is required by regulations under section 49 of this Act to be, but has not been, notified to the Secretary of State [or the prescribed testing authority] is guilty of an offence.

(4) In any proceedings for an offence under subsection (3) above, it shall be a defence to prove that the alteration was not specified in the relevant plating certificate in accordance with regulations under section 49 of this Act.

(5) The Secretary of State may by regulations—

    (a) exempt from all or any of the preceding provisions of this section the use of goods vehicles for such purposes or in such an area as may be prescribed and

(b) make provision for the issue in respect of a vehicle in such circumstances as may be prescribed of a certificate of temporary exemption exempting that vehicle from the provisions of subsection (1) or (2) above for such period as may be specified in the certificate.

[Section 53 is printed as prospectively amended by the Transport Act 1982 **A18.143** *s.10(7)(b) (as itself amended by the Road Traffic (Consequential Provisions) Act 1988 s.4 and Sch.2, Pt 1, para.4(4)(b)). The words printed within square brackets in subs.(3) will come into force on a date to be announced; see the Transport Act 1982 s.76(2).*

The Goods Vehicles (Plating and Testing) Regulations 1988 (SI 1988/1478) (q.v.) have effect as if made in part under s.53. As to notifiable alterations, see reg.30; and as to exemptions, see reg.44.

The Goods Vehicles (Production of Test Certificates) Regulations 2004 (SI 2004/2577) reg.3 prescribes that one of three requirements must be met where an application is made for a licence under the Vehicle Excise and Registration Act 1994 for a vehicle to which s.53(2) applies.]

Approval of design, construction, equipment and marking of vehicles

Type approval requirements

54.—(1) Without prejudice to section 41 of this Act, the Secretary of State **A18.144** may by regulations prescribe requirements (in this Part of this Act referred to as *"type approval requirements"*) —

(a) with respect to the design, construction, equipment and marking of vehicles of any class, being requirements which are applicable before, whether or not they are applicable after, vehicles of that class are used on a road,

(b) with respect to the design, construction, equipment and marking of vehicle parts of any class, being requirements which are applicable before, whether or not they are applicable after, vehicle parts of that class are fitted to a vehicle used on a road.

(2) Regulations under this section may provide for the determination, according to criteria or by methods prescribed by or determined under the regulations, of weights of any description which in the opinion of the Secretary of State should not be exceeded in the case of vehicles of any class.

(3) In this Part of this Act references to design weights shall be construed as references to weights determined by virtue of subsection (2) above.

(4) Subject to subsection (5) below, the following provisions of this Act to the end of section 60 apply in relation to parts of vehicles as they apply in relation to vehicles and, accordingly, any reference in those provisions to a vehicle, other than a reference to a goods vehicle, is to be read as including a reference to a vehicle part.

(5) Any provision which relates solely to goods vehicles or design weights does not apply in relation to parts of vehicles, but particular exclusions in those provisions do not affect the generality of this exclusion.

(6) In this Part of this Act, *"the relevant aspects of design, construction, equipment and marking"*, in relation to any vehicle, means those aspects of design, construction, equipment and marking which are subject to the type approval

requirements or which were used as criteria in determining design weights for that vehicle.

A18.145   *[The Motor Vehicles (Type Approval for Goods Vehicles) (Great Britain) Regulations 1982 (SI 1982/1271), the Motor Vehicles (Type Approval) (Great Britain) Regulations 1984 (SI 1984/981), the Motor Vehicles (Approval) Regulations 2001 (SI 2001/25) and the Motor Cycles Etc. (Single Vehicle Approval) Regulations 2003 (SI 2003/1959) have effect as if made in part under s.54.]*

Type approval certificates

A18.146   **55.**—(1) Where the Secretary of State is satisfied on application made to him by the manufacturer of a vehicle of a class to which regulations under section 54 of this Act apply and after examination of the vehicle—

    (a) that the vehicle complies with the relevant type approval requirements, and

    (b) that adequate arrangements have been made to secure that other vehicles purporting to conform with that vehicle in the relevant aspects of design, construction, equipment and marking will so conform in all respects or with such variations as may be permitted,

he may approve that vehicle as a type vehicle.

(2) Where the Secretary of State approves a vehicle as a type vehicle he must issue a certificate (in this Part of this Act referred to as a *"type approval certificate"*) stating that the vehicle complies with the relevant type approval requirements and specifying—

    (a) the permitted variations from the type vehicle, and

    (b) the design weights for vehicles so conforming in all respects and for vehicles so conforming with any such variations.

(3) In the following provisions of this section and in sections 56 to 59 of this Act *"conform"* means conform in all respects or with any permitted variation.

(4) Subject to subsection (6) below, a type approval certificate may be issued for a type vehicle where the Secretary of State is satisfied that one or more, but not all, of the relevant type approval requirements are complied with in the case of that vehicle.

(5) A further type approval certificate may be issued by virtue of subsection (4) above on the application of any person—

    (a) who manufactures any part of the vehicle, or

    (b) by whom the vehicle is finally assembled;

and references in the following provisions of this section and in sections 56 to 59 of this Act to a manufacturer shall be construed accordingly.

(6) The first type approval certificate issued for a type vehicle by virtue of subsection (4) above must specify the design weights for conforming vehicles, and accordingly—

    (a) so much of subsection (2) above or section 57(1) to (3) of this Act as requires the Secretary of State or a manufacturer to specify in any certificate under this or that section the design weights or plated weights for a vehicle or as requires the Secretary of State [or the prescribed testing authority] or a manufacturer to mark or secure the marking of the plated weights on a vehicle does not apply to a subsequent type approval certificate issued by virtue of subsection (4) above or to the certificates of conformity issued in consequence of such a type approval certificate, and

    (b) so much of section 58(2) of this Act as requires the Secretary of State to specify in any certificate issued by him the design weights and plated weights for a vehicle or to secure that the plated weights are marked on a vehicle does not apply to a Minister's approval certificate issued by virtue of subsection (4) above.

(7) Subsection (6) above does not apply in relation to vehicle parts.

(8) Where the Secretary of State determines on an application under this section not to issue a type approval certificate in respect of a vehicle, he must give to the applicant a written notification of the determination, stating the grounds on which it is based.

[Section 55 is printed as prospectively amended by the Transport Act 1982   **A18.147**
s.17(1)(a) (as itself amended by the Road Traffic (Consequential Provisions) Act 1988 s.4 and Sch.2, Pt 1, para.6(1)(b)). The words printed within square brackets in subs.(6) will come into force on a date to be announced; see the Transport Act 1982 s.76(2).

As to the application of s.55 to parts of vehicles, see s.54(4) and (5) above.]

Conditions of, and cancellation or suspension of, type approval certificates

56. *[Omitted.]*   **A18.148**

Certificates of conformity

57.—(1) The manufacturer of a type vehicle in respect of which a type approval certificate is in force may issue, in respect of each vehicle manufactured by him which conforms with the type vehicle in such of the relevant aspects of design, construction, equipment and marking as are mentioned in the type approval certificate, a certificate ...—   **A18.149**

    (a) stating that it does so conform, and

    (b) specifying the design weights for the vehicle,

and must in the case of goods vehicles of such classes as may be prescribed specify in the certificate one or more of the plated weights for the vehicle.

[(1A) In this Part of this Act (except in the expression *"EC certificate of conformity"* and in the definition of that expression in section 85 of this Act) *"certificate of conformity"* means a certificate issued under subsection (1) above.]

(2) *[Specification of plated weights in certificate of conformity.]*

(3) *[Marking of plated weights by means of plate.]*

(4) Any certificate of conformity issued in consequence of any type approval certificate issued by virtue of section 55(4) of this Act shall relate only to the requirement or requirements to which that type approval certificate relates.

(5) *[Inapplicability of subss.(2) and (3) to vehicle parts.]*

[Section 57 is printed as amended by the Motor Vehicles (EC Type Approval)   **A18.150**
Regulations 1992 (SI 1992/3107).

As to the application of s.57 to parts of vehicles, see s.54(4) and (5) above.

As to the terms "conform" and "manufacturer", see s.55(3) and (5) above; as to the term "goods vehicle", see s.62(3) below.]

Minister's approval certificates

A18.151

58.—(1) Where the Secretary of State is satisfied, on application made to him by any person in respect of a vehicle of a class to which regulations under section 54 of this Act apply and after examination of the vehicle, that—

    (a) the vehicle complies with the relevant type approval requirements, and

    (b) in the case of a goods vehicle, the Secretary of State has sufficient information to enable the plated weights to be ascertained for the vehicle,

he may issue a certificate (in this Part of this Act referred to as a *"Minister's approval certificate"*).

(2) *[Content of Minister's approval certificate.]*

(3) Where by virtue of section 57(4) of this Act a certificate of conformity issued in respect of a vehicle relates to one or more, but not all, of the relevant type approval requirements, the Secretary of State may issue in respect of that vehicle a Minister's approval certificate relating to one or more of the other relevant type approval requirements.

(4)–(6) *[Issue of Minister's approval certificate in respect of another vehicle without examination.]*

(7) *[Notice of refusal of Minister's approval certificate.]*

A18.152

[As to the application of s.58 to parts of vehicles, see s.54(4) and (5) above. As to the term "goods vehicle", see s.62(3) below.]

Supplementary provisions as to certificates of conformity and Minister's approval certificates

A18.153

59.—(1) The Secretary of State may by regulations require the prescribed alterations—

    (a) in any of the relevant aspects of design, construction, equipment or marking, or

    (b) in any such aspect which affects the plated weight,

made to any vehicle for which a certificate of conformity or a Minister's approval certificate is issued shall, subject to any exemption granted under subsection (2) below, be notified to the Secretary of State [or the prescribed testing authority].

(2) The Secretary of State may by notice in writing given to the manufacturer of vehicles or to the owner of a vehicle for which a Minister's approval certificate is issued—

    (a) direct that any specified alteration in any of the aspects mentioned in subsection (1) above to a vehicle to which the direction relates shall be notified to the Secretary of State [or the prescribed testing authority],

    (b) exempt a vehicle to which the notice relates from all or any of the requirements of regulations under subsection (1) above, subject to compliance with any conditions specified in the notice.

(3) *[Regulation-making power.]*

(4) A certificate of conformity or a Minister's approval certificate specifying any plated weights shall be treated for the purposes of the provisions of this Part

of this Act and any regulations made under them relating to plating certificates (except section 50(1) and (2) of this Act) as a plating certificate.

This subsection does not apply in relation to vehicle parts.

[Section 59 is printed as prospectively amended by the Transport Act 1982 s.10(7) (as itself amended by the Road Traffic (Consequential Provisions) Act 1988, s.4 and Sch.2, Pt 1, para.4(4)(d)). The words printed within square brackets in subs.(1) and (2) will come into force on a date to be announced; see the Transport Act 1982 s.76(2).

As to the application of s.59(1) and (2) to parts of vehicles, see s.54(4) and (5) above.

The Motor Vehicles (Type Approval for Goods Vehicles) (Great Britain) Regulations 1982 (SI 1982/1271) have effect as if made in part under s.59(1). As to the requirement to notify prescribed alterations, see reg.10.]

A18.154

Appeals against determinations under sections 54 to 59

60. *[Omitted.]*   **A18.155**

Regulations for the purposes of sections 54 to 60

61.—(1)–(3) *[Omitted.]*   **A18.156**

(4) Where regulations under this section impose the like requirement as may be imposed by regulations made by virtue of section 51(1)(c)(ii) of this Act, the regulations may provide that a person who contravenes or fails to comply with a requirement so imposed is guilty of an offence.

(5) [...]

[Section 61 is printed as amended by the Road Traffic Act 1991 s.83 and Sch.8.
The Motor Vehicles (Type Approval for Goods Vehicles) (Great Britain) Regulations 1982 (SI 1982/1271), the Motor Vehicles (Type Approval) (Great Britain) Regulations 1984 (SI 1984/981), the Motor Vehicles (Approval) Regulations 2001 (SI 2001/25) and the Motor Cycles Etc. (Single Vehicle Approval) Regulations 2003 (SI 2003/1959) have effect as if made in part under s.61(1).]

A18.157

Other supplementary provisions

62.—(1) *[Provision of stations for examination of vehicles.]*   **A18.158**

(2) *[Power to make regulations as to recognition of foreign type approval certificates, etc.]*

(3) Except in the case of vehicles of such class as may be prescribed, in sections 57, 58 and 61 of this Act *"goods vehicle"* includes a vehicle which is a chassis for, or will otherwise form part of, a vehicle which when completed will be a goods vehicle.

Obligatory type approval certificates, certificates of conformity and Minister's approval certificates

63.—(1) If—   **A18.159**

    (a) any person at any time on or after the day appointed by regulations made by the Secretary of State in relation to vehicles or vehicle parts of a prescribed class, being vehicles or vehicle parts to which type approval requirements prescribed by those regulations apply—

(i) uses on a road, or

(ii) causes or permits to be so used,

a vehicle of that class or a vehicle to which is fitted a vehicle part of that class, and

(b) it does not appear from one or more certificates then in force under sections 54 to 58 of this Act that the vehicle or vehicle part complies with those requirements,

he is guilty of an offence.

Different days may be appointed under this subsection in relation to different classes of vehicles or vehicle parts.

[(1A) For the purposes of subsection (1) above a vehicle shall be taken to comply with all relevant type approval requirements if an EC certificate of conformity has effect with respect to the vehicle.]

(2) If a plating certificate—

(a) has been issued for a goods vehicle to which section 53(1) of this Act or subsection (1) above applies, but

(b) does not specify a maximum laden weight for the vehicle together with any trailer which may be drawn by it,

any person who on or after the relevant date within the meaning of section 53(1) of this Act or, as the case may be, the day appointed under subsection (1) above uses the vehicle on a road for drawing a trailer, or causes or permits it to be so used, is guilty of an offence.

(3) Any person who—

(a) uses a vehicle on a road, or

(b) causes or permits a vehicle to be so used,

when an alteration has been made to the vehicle or its equipment which is required by regulations or directions under section 59 of this Act to be, but has not been, notified to the Secretary of State [or the prescribed testing authority] is guilty of an offence.

(4) In any proceedings for an offence under subsection (3) above, it shall be a defence to prove that the regulations were not or, as the case may be, the alteration was not, specified in the relevant certificate of conformity or Minister's approval certificate in accordance with regulations under section 59(3) of this Act.

[(5) The Secretary of State may make provision for securing that, subject to such restrictions and conditions as may be specified by or under the instrument by which the provision is made—

(a) the use of vehicles is exempted from all or any of the preceding provisions of this section for purposes specified in the instrument or in such an area as is so specified,

(b) goods vehicles are exempted from the provisions of subsection (2) above, and

(c) there are issued in respect of vehicles or vehicle parts, in such circumstances as may be specified in the instrument, certificates of temporary exemption exempting the vehicles or vehicle parts from the provisions of subsection (1) above for such period as may be provided in the certificate.]

[(6) Subject to subsection (7) below, the power conferred by subsection (5) above is exercisable by regulations.]

[(7) That power is exercisable by order in relation to—

(a) specified vehicles, or

(b) vehicles of specified persons;

and an order under this subsection may be varied or revoked by a subsequent order of the Secretary of State.]

[Section 63 is printed as amended by the Motor Vehicles (EC Type Approval) **A18.160** *Regulations 1992 (SI 1992/3107); the Transport Act 2000 s.264 (with effect from February 1, 2001; see the Transport Act 2001 (Commencement No.3) Order 2001 (SI 2001/57; not reproduced in this work) (the subsequent amendment of SI 2001/57 by the Transport Act 2000 (Commencement No.3) (Amendment) Order 2001 (SI 2001/115; not reproduced in this work) does not affect the amendment of s.63); and as prospectively amended by the Transport Act 1982 s.10(7)(c) (as itself amended by the Road Traffic (Consequential Provisions) Act 1988 s.4 and Sch.2, Pt 1, para.4(4)(c)). The words printed within square brackets in subs.(3) will come into force on a date to be announced; see the Transport Act 1982 s.76(2).*

As to the disapplication of s.63(1) in respect of the use of certain vehicles, see the Motor Vehicles (Approval) Regulations 2001 (SI 2001/25) reg.14(8).

The Motor Vehicles (Type Approval) (Great Britain) Regulations 1984 (SI 1984/981), the Motor Vehicles (Approval) Regulations 2001 (SI 2001/25) and the Motor Cycles Etc. (Single Vehicle Approval) Regulations 2003 (SI 2003/1959) have effect as if made in part under s.63(1).]

[Alteration of plated weights for goods vehicles without examination

[63A].—(1) *[Regulation-making power.]*   **A18.161**

(2) *[Appeal against determination under regulations under this section.]*

(3) *[Amplification of regulation-making power.]*

(4) In this section *"approval certificate"* means a plating certificate and any certificate of conformity or Minister's approval certificate specifying any plated weights.

(5) Any certificate issued in respect of a goods vehicle under regulations made under this section in replacement of an approval certificate of any description mentioned in subsection (4) above—

(a) shall be in the form appropriate for an approval certificate of that description;

(b) shall be identical in content with the certificate it replaces, save for any alterations in the plated weights authorised by the regulations; and

(c) shall be treated for the purposes of this Part of this Act (including this section) and any regulations made under any provision of this Part of this Act as if it were the same certificate as the certificate it replaces;

and any plate so issued in replacement of a plate fixed to the vehicle under [section 57 or 58] of this Act shall, when fixed to the vehicle, be treated as so fixed under that section.]

[Section 63A was inserted by the Transport Act 1982 s.18, and is printed as   **A18.162**

amended by the Road Traffic (Consequential Provisions) Act 1988 s.4 and Sch.2,
Pt 1, para.7.]

Using goods vehicle with unauthorised weights as well as authorised weights marked on it

A18.163   **64.**—(1) If there is fixed to a goods vehicle a plate containing plated weights of any description—

(a) determined for that vehicle by virtue of sections 49 to 52 of this Act, or

(b) specified in a certificate for that vehicle under section 57(1) or (2) or 58(2) or (5) of this Act,

the vehicle shall not, while it is used on a road, be marked with any other weights, except other plated weights, other weights required or authorised to be marked on the vehicle by regulations under section 41 of this Act or weights so authorised for the purposes of this section by regulations made by the Secretary of State and marked in the prescribed manner.

(2) In the event of a contravention of or failure to comply with this section the owner of the vehicle is guilty of an offence.

[Failure to hold EC certificate of conformity for unregistered light motor cycle or tractor

A18.164   **64A.**—(1) Subject to subsections (2) to (5) below, if a person uses on a road ... [a vehicle to which the motorcycle type approval Directive [or tractor type approval Directive] applies]—

(a) which has not been registered—

(i) under [section 21 of the Vehicle Excise and Registration Act 1994], or

(ii) under the law of [an EEA State] other than the United Kingdom, and

(b) in respect of which no EC certificate of conformity has effect,

he is guilty of an offence.

(2) [...]

[(2A) A person shall not be convicted of an offence under this section in respect of the use of a vehicle to which the motorcycle type approval Directive applies if he proves that the vehicle was one in respect of which the grant of a licence or nil licence under the Vehicle Excise and Registration Act 1994 was not prohibited by regulation 16 of the Motor Cycles Etc. (EC Type Approval) Regulations 1999 [*SI 1999/2920*].]

(3) This section does not apply in relation to a vehicle in respect of which a Minister's approval certificate issued under section 58(1) of this Act or a Department's approval certificate issued under Article 31A(4) of the Road Traffic (Northern Ireland) Order 1981 has effect.

(4) This section does not apply to the use of a vehicle under a trade licence (within the meaning of [the Vehicle Excise and Registration Act 1994]) in accordance with regulations made under [section 12(2)] of that Act.

(5) This section does not apply in relation to a vehicle brought temporarily into Great Britain by a person resident outside the United Kingdom.]

(6) [...]

[Section 64A was inserted by the Motor Vehicles (EC Type Approval) Regula-   **A18.165**
tions 1992 (SI 1992/3107) and is printed as amended by the Interpretation Act
1978 ss.17(2)(a) and 23; the Vehicle Excise and Registration Act 1994 s.63 and
Sch.3, para.24(3); the Motor Cycles Etc. (EC Type Approval) Regulations 1999
(SI 1999/2920); the Tractor etc. (EC Type-Approval) Regulations 2005 (SI 2005/
390); the Road Vehicles (Approval) (Consequential Amendments) Regulations
2009 (SI 2009/818) reg.3.

As to the EEA Agreement and the EEA states, see introductory note to Section
C, below.]

Vehicles and parts not to be sold without required certificate of conformity or Minister's approval certificate

65.—(1) If—   **A18.166**

    (a) any person at any time on or after the day appointed by regulations
       under section 63(1) of this Act supplies a vehicle or vehicle part of a
       class to which those regulations apply, and

    (b) it does not appear from one or more certificates in force at that time
       under sections 54 to 58 of this Act that the vehicle or vehicle part
       complies with all the relevant type approval requirements prescribed
       by those regulations,

he is guilty of an offence.

[(1A) For the purposes of subsection (1) above a vehicle shall be taken to
comply with all relevant type approval requirements if an EC certificate of
conformity has effect with respect to the vehicle.]

(2) In this section references to supply include—

    (a) sell,

    (b) offer to sell or supply, and

    (c) expose for sale.

(3) A person shall not be convicted of an offence under this section in respect
of the supply of a vehicle or vehicle part if he proves—

    (a) that it was supplied for export from Great Britain,

    (b) that he had reasonable cause to believe that it would not be used on a
       road in Great Britain or, in the case of a vehicle part, that it would not
       be fitted to a vehicle used on a road in Great Britain or would not be
       so used or fitted until it had been certified under sections 54 to 58 of
       this Act, or

    (c) that he had reasonable cause to believe that it would only be used for
       purposes or in any area prescribed by the Secretary of State under
       section 63(5) of this Act or, in the case of a goods vehicle, under sec-
       tion 53(5) of this Act.

(4) Nothing in subsection (1) above shall affect the validity of a contract or
any rights arising under or in relation to a contract.

[Section 65 is printed as amended by the Motor Vehicles (EC Type Approval)   **A18.167**
Regulations 1992 (SI 1992/3107).]

[Motor cycles not to be sold without EC certificate of conformity

65A.—(1) Subject to subsections (3) to (6) below, any person who supplies ...   **A18.168**
[a vehicle to which the motorcycle type approval Directive applies]—

    (a) which has not been registered—

        (i) under [section 21 of the Vehicle Excise and Registration Act 1994], or

        (ii) under the law of [an EEA State] other than the United Kingdom, and

    (b) in respect of which no EC certificate of conformity has effect,

is guilty of an offence.

    (2) In this section references to supply include—

    (a) sell,

    (b) offer to sell or supply, and

    (c) expose for sale.

    (3) [...]

[(3A) A person shall not be convicted of an offence under this section in respect of the supply of a vehicle [...] if he proves that the vehicle was one in respect of which the grant of a licence or nil licence under the Vehicle Excise and Registration Act 1994 was not prohibited by regulation 16 of the Motor Cycles Etc. (EC Type Approval) Regulations 1999 [*SI 1999/2920*].]

    (4) A person shall not be convicted of an offence under this section in respect of the supply of a vehicle if he proves—

    (a) that it was supplied for export from the United Kingdom to a country which is not [an EEA State], or

    (b) that he had reasonable cause to believe—

        (i) that it would not be used on a road in the United Kingdom or any other [EEA State], or

        (ii) that it would not be so used until an EC certificate of conformity had been issued in respect of it.

    (5) This section does not apply in relation to the supply of a vehicle—

    (a) to the Crown for naval, military or air force purposes,

    (b) for the purposes of the military forces of any country outside the United Kingdom,

    (c) to any public authority in the United Kingdom or any other member State for the purposes of civil defence within the meaning of the Civil Defence Act 1948,

    (d) to a police authority for police purposes, or

    (e) to any public authority in a member State outside the United Kingdom which has responsibilities for maintaining public order.

    (6) This section does not apply in relation to a vehicle in respect of which a Minister's approval certificate issued under section 58(1) of this Act or a Department's approval certificate issued under Article 31A(4) of the Road Traffic (Northern Ireland) Order 1981 has effect.

    (7) Nothing in subsection (1) above shall affect the validity of a contract or any rights arising under or in relation to a contract.]

    (8) [...]]

A18.169   *[Section 65A was inserted by the Motor Vehicles (EC Type Approval) Regulations 1992 (SI 1992/3107) and is printed as amended by the Interpretation Act*

1978 ss.17(2)(a) and 23; the Vehicle Excise and Registration Act 1994 s.63 and Sch.3, para.24(4); the Motor Cycles Etc. (EC Type Approval) Regulations 1999 (SI 1999/2920); the Road Vehicles (Approval) (Consequential Amendments) Regulations 2009 (SI 2009/818) reg.3.

As to the EEA Agreement and the EEA states, see introductory note to Section C, below]

Conditions for grant of excise licence

Regulations prohibiting the grant of excise licences for certain vehicles except on compliance with certain conditions

66. *[Omitted.]*   **A18.170**

[Vehicle examiners]

[Appointment of examiners

66A.—(1) The Secretary of State shall appoint such examiners as he considers **A18.171** necessary for the purpose of carrying out the functions conferred on them by this Part of this Act, [the Goods Vehicles (Licensing of Operators) Act 1995,] the Public Passenger Vehicles Act 1981, the Transport Act 1968 and any other enactment.

(2) An examiner appointed under this section shall act under the general directions of the Secretary of State.

(3) In this Part of this Act *"vehicle examiner"* means an examiner appointed under this section.]

[Section 66A (and the italicised heading preceding it) was inserted by the **A18.172** *Road Traffic Act 1991 s.9(1), and is printed as amended by the Goods Vehicles (Licensing of Operators) Act 1995 s.60(1) and Sch.7, para.11.*

Examiners appointed under s.66A(1) (together with police constables) are also authorised inspecting officers for the purposes of Regulation (EEC) 684/92 and Regulation (EC) 12/98 (see the Road Transport (Passenger Vehicles Cabotage) Regulations 1999 (SI 1999/3413) reg.8 below). With effect from December 4, 2011, Regulation (EEC) 684/92 and Regulation (EEC) 12/98 were repealed by European and Council Regulation (EC) 1073/2009 of October 21, 2009 on common rules for access to the international market for coach and bus services, and amending Regulation (EC) 561/2006 (O.J. No.L300, November 14, 2009, p.88) art.30. References to the repealed Regulations shall be construed as references to Regulation (EC) 1073/2009 and shall be read in accordance with the correlation table set out in ibid. Annex III.]

Testing vehicles on roads

Testing of condition of vehicles on roads

67.—(1) An authorised examiner may test a motor vehicle on a road for the **A18.173** purpose of—

[(a) ascertaining whether the following requirements, namely—

(i) the construction and use requirements, and

(ii) the requirement that the condition of the vehicle is not such that its use on a road would involve a danger of injury to any person, are complied with as respects the vehicle;]

    (b) bringing to the notice of the driver any failure to comply with those requirements.

[(2) For the purpose of testing a vehicle under this section the examiner—

    (a) may require the driver to comply with his reasonable instructions, and

    (b) may drive the vehicle.]

(3) A vehicle shall not be required to stop for a test except by a constable in uniform.

(4) The following persons may act as authorised examiners for the purposes of this section —

    (a) [...]

    (b) a person appointed as an examiner under section [66A] of this Act,

    (c) a person appointed to examine and inspect public carriages for the purposes of the Metropolitan Public Carriage Act 1869,

    (d) a person appointed to act for the purposes of this section by the Secretary of State,

    (e) a constable authorised so to act by or [on behalf of a] chief officer of police, and

    (f) a person appointed by the police authority for a police area to act, under the directions of the chief officer of police, for the purposes of this section.

(5) A person mentioned in subsection (4)(a) to (d) and (f) must produce his authority to act for the purposes of this section if required to do so.

(6) On the examiner proceeding to test a vehicle under this section, the driver may, unless the test is required under subsection (7) or (8) below to be carried out forthwith, elect that the test shall be deferred to a time, and carried out at a place, fixed in accordance with Schedule 2 to this Act, and the provisions of that Schedule shall apply accordingly.

(7) Where it appears to a constable that, by reason of an accident having occurred owing to the presence of the vehicle on a road, it is requisite that a test should be carried out forthwith, he may require it to be so carried out and, if he is not to carry it out himself, may require that the vehicle shall not be taken away until the test has been carried out.

(8) Where in the opinion of a constable the vehicle is apparently so defective that it ought not to be allowed to proceed without a test being carried out, he may require the test to be carried out forthwith.

(9) If a person obstructs an authorised examiner acting under this section, or fails to comply with a requirement of this section or Schedule 2 to this Act, he is guilty of an offence.

(10) In this section and in Schedule 2 to this Act —

    (a) *"test"* includes "inspect" or "inspection", as the case may require, and

    (b) references to a vehicle include references to a trailer drawn by it.

A18.174   *[Section 67 is printed as amended by the Road Traffic Act 1991 ss.10(1)–(5), 83 and Sch.8.*

For the powers of civilians designated or accredited by a chief officer of police to stop a vehicle under subs.(1), above, see the Police Reform Act 2002 ss.38, 41 and Sch.4, para.11, Sch.5, para.8; not reproduced in this work.

For the powers of the Secretary of State for Transport to give information in relation to tests and inspections of commercial motor vehicles and their trailers carried out under s.67 to competent authorities in other EU Member States and in Northern Ireland and Gibraltar in compliance with Directive 2000/30/EC (O.J. No.L203, August 10, 2000, p.1), see the Road Vehicles (Testing) (Disclosure of Information) (Great Britain) Regulations 2002 (SI 2002/2426).]

[Inspection of public passenger vehicles and goods vehicles]

[Inspection of public passenger vehicles and goods vehicles

68.—(1) A vehicle examiner—   **A18.175**

   (a) may at any time, on production if so required of his authority, inspect any vehicle to which this section applies and for that purpose detain the vehicle during such time as is required for the inspection, and

   (b) may at any time which is reasonable having regard to the circumstances of the case enter any premises on which he has reason to believe that such a vehicle is kept.

(2) The power conferred by subsection (1) above to inspect a vehicle includes power to test it and to drive it for the purpose of testing it.

(3) A person who intentionally obstructs an examiner in the exercise of his powers under subsection (1) above is guilty of an offence.

(4) A vehicle examiner or a constable in uniform may at any time require any person in charge of a vehicle to which this section applies and which is stationary on a road to proceed with the vehicle for the purpose of having it inspected under this section to any place where an inspection can be suitably carried out (not being more than five miles from the place where the requirement is made).

(5) A person in charge of a vehicle who refuses or neglects to comply with a requirement made under subsection (4) above is guilty of an offence.

(6) This section applies to—

   (a) goods vehicles,

   (b) public service vehicles, and

   (c) motor vehicles which are not public service vehicles but are adapted to carry more than eight passengers;

but subsection (1)(b) above shall not apply in relation to vehicles within paragraph (c) above or in relation to vehicles used to carry passengers for hire or reward only under permits granted under section 19 or 22 of the Transport Act 1985 (use of vehicles by educational and other bodies or in providing community bus services).]

[Section 68 (and the heading preceding it) is printed as substituted by the   **A18.176** *Road Traffic Act 1991 s.11. Section 68 has been prospectively amended (from a date to be announced) by the Transport Act 1982 s.10(6), as amended by the Road Traffic (Consequential Provisions) Act 1988 s.4 and Sch.2, Pt I, para.4; the Road Traffic Act 1991 s.48 and Sch.4, para.19(3).*

Section 68 does not apply to tramcars: Tramcars and Trolley Vehicles (Modification of Enactments) Regulations 1992 (SI 1992/1217) reg.7 (q.v.).

Section 68 applies to trolley vehicles (other than duobuses) as if s.68(4) were omitted; see SI 1992/1217 regs 10 and 11 (q.v.).

Sections 68–74 of this Act do not apply to any person or vehicle in the service of a visiting force or headquarters (as defined); see the Visiting Forces and International Headquarters (Application of Law) Order 1999 (SI 1999/1736; not reproduced in this work) art.8(1) and (2)(b).

For the powers of the Secretary of State for Transport to give information in relation to tests and inspections of commercial motor vehicles and their trailers carried out under s.68 to competent authorities in other EU Member States and in Northern Ireland and Gibraltar in compliance with Directive 2000/30/EC (O.J. No.L203, August 10, 2000, p.1), see the Road Vehicles (Testing) (Disclosure of Information) (Great Britain) Regulations 2002 (SI 2002/2426).]

[Prohibition of unfit vehicles]

[Power to prohibit driving of unfit vehicles

A18.177   **69.**—(1) If on any inspection of a vehicle under section 41, 45, 49, 61, 67, 68 or 77 of this Act it appears to a vehicle examiner that owing to any defects in the vehicle it is, or is likely to become, unfit for service, he may prohibit the driving of the vehicle on a road—

    (a) absolutely, or

    (b) for one or more specified purposes, or

    (c) except for one or more specified purposes.

(2) If on any inspection of a vehicle under any of the enactments mentioned in subsection (1) above it appears to an authorised constable that owing to any defects in the vehicle driving it (or driving it for any particular purpose or purposes or for any except one or more particular purposes) would involve a danger of injury to any person, he may prohibit the driving of the vehicle on a road—

    (a) absolutely, or

    (b) for one or more specified purposes, or

    (c) except for one or more specified purposes.

(3) A prohibition under this section shall come into force as soon as the notice under subsection (6) below has been given if—

    (a) it is imposed by an authorised constable, or

    (b) in the opinion of the vehicle examiner imposing it the defects in the vehicle in question are such that driving it, or driving it for any purpose within the prohibition, would involve a danger of injury to any person.

(4) Except where subsection (3) applies, a prohibition under this section shall (unless previously removed under section 72 of this Act) come into force at such time not later than ten days from the date of the inspection as seems appropriate to the vehicle examiner imposing the prohibition, having regard to all the circumstances.

(5) A prohibition under this section shall continue in force until it is removed under section 72 of this Act.

(6) A person imposing a prohibition under this section shall forthwith give no-

tice in writing of the prohibition to the person in charge of the vehicle at the time of the inspection—

    (a) specifying the defects which occasioned the prohibition;

    (b) stating whether the prohibition is on all driving of the vehicle or driving it for one or more specified purposes or driving it except for one or more specified purposes (and, where applicable, specifying the purpose or purposes in question); and

    (c) stating whether the prohibition is to come into force immediately or at the end of a specified period.

(7) Where a notice has been given under subsection (6) above, any vehicle examiner or authorised constable may grant an exemption in writing for the use of the vehicle in such manner, subject to such conditions and for such purpose as may be specified in the exemption.

(8) Where such a notice has been given, any vehicle examiner or authorised constable may by endorsement on the notice vary its terms and, in particular, alter the time at which the prohibition is to come into force or suspend it if it has come into force.

(9) In this section *"authorised constable"* means a constable authorised to act for the purposes of this section by or on behalf of a chief officer of police.]

[Section 69 (and the heading preceding it) is printed as substituted by the **A18.178** *Road Traffic Act 1991 s.12. Section 69 has been prospectively amended (from a date to be announced) by the Transport Act 1982 s.10(3), as substituted by the Road Traffic Act 1991 s.48 and Sch.4, para.19(2).*

Section 69 does not apply to tramcars: Tramcars and Trolley Vehicles (Modification of Enactments) Regulations 1992 (SI 1992/1217) reg.7 (q.v.).

The Road Safety (Immobilisation, Removal and Disposal of Vehicles) Regulations 2009 (SI 2009/493) [q.v.] apply with respect to any case where the driving has been prohibited under this section.

As to visiting forces, etc., see the notes to s.68 above.]

[Prohibitions conditional on inspection, etc.

69A.—(1) Where it appears to the person imposing a prohibition under section   **A18.179** 69 of this Act that the vehicle is adapted to carry more than eight passengers, or is a public service vehicle not so adapted, the prohibition may be imposed with a direction making it irremovable unless and until the vehicle has been inspected at an official PSV testing station within the meaning of the Public Passenger Vehicles Act 1981.

(2) Where it appears to that person that the vehicle is of a class to which regulations under section 49 of this Act apply, the prohibition may be imposed with a direction making it irremovable unless and until the vehicle has been inspected at an official testing station.

(3) Where it appears to that person that the vehicle is one to which section 47 of this Act applies, or would apply if the vehicle had been registered under [the Vehicle Excise and Registration Act 1994] more than three years earlier, the prohibition may be imposed with a direction making it irremovable unless and until the vehicle has been inspected, and a test certificate issued, under section 45 of this Act.

(4) In any other case, the prohibition may be imposed with a direction making

it irremovable unless and until the vehicle has been inspected in accordance with regulations under section 72 of this Act by a vehicle examiner or authorised constable (within the meaning of section 69 of this Act).]

A18.180   *[Section 69A was inserted by the Road Traffic Act 1991 s.12, and is printed as amended by the Vehicle Excise and Registration Act 1994 s.63 and Sch.3, para.24(1).*

Section 69A does not apply to tramcars: Tramcars and Trolley Vehicles (Modification of Enactments) Regulations 1992 (SI 1992/1217) reg.7 (q.v.).

Prohibitions imposed under s.69A may be removed in accordance with the Road Vehicles (Prohibition) Regulations 1992 (SI 1992/1285) (q.v.).

As to visiting forces, etc., see the notes to s.68 above.]

Power to prohibit driving of overloaded goods vehicles

A18.181   **70.**—(1) Subsections (2) and (3) below apply where a goods vehicle[, or a motor vehicle adapted to carry more than eight passengers,] has been weighed in pursuance of a requirement imposed under section 78 of this Act and it appears to—

     (a) [a vehicle examiner],

     (b) a person authorised with the consent of the Secretary of State to act for the purposes of this subsection by—

         (i) a highway authority other than the Secretary of State, or

         (ii) a local roads authority in Scotland, or

     (c) a constable authorised to act for those purposes by or on behalf of a chief officer of police,

that the limit imposed by construction and use requirements with respect to any description of weight which is applicable to that vehicle has been exceeded or would be exceeded if it were used on a road [or that by reason of excessive overall weight or excessive axle weight on any axle driving the vehicle would involve a danger of injury to any person].

(2) The person to whom it so appears may, whether or not a notice is given under section [69(6)] of this Act, give notice in writing to the person in charge of the vehicle prohibiting the driving of the vehicle on a road until—

     (a) that weight is reduced to that limit [or, as the case may be, so that it is no longer excessive], and

     (b) official notification has been given to whoever is for the time being in charge of the vehicle that it is permitted to proceed.

(3) The person to whom it so appears may also by direction in writing require the person in charge of the vehicle to remove it (and, if it is a motor vehicle drawing a trailer, also remove the trailer) to such place and subject to such conditions as are specified in the direction; and the prohibition shall not apply to the removal of the vehicle or trailer in accordance with that direction.

(4) Official notification for the purposes of subsection (2) above—

     (a) must be in writing and be given by [a vehicle examiner], a person authorised as mentioned in subsection (1) above or a constable authorised as so mentioned, and

     (b) may be withheld until the vehicle has been weighed or reweighed in order to satisfy the person giving the notification that the weight has been sufficiently reduced.

(5) Nothing in this section shall be construed as limiting the power of the Secretary of State to make regulations under section 71(2) of this Act.

[Section 70 is printed as amended by the Road Traffic Act 1991 s.13(1), (2)(a)–(c), (3)(a) and (b), and (4). **A18.182**

Section 70 does not apply to tramcars: Tramcars and Trolley Vehicles (Modification of Enactments) Regulations 1992 (SI 1992/1217) reg.7 (q.v.).

The Road Safety (Immobilisation, Removal and Disposal of Vehicles) Regulations 2009 (SI 2009/493) [q.v.] apply with respect to any case where the driving has been prohibited under this section.

As to visiting forces, etc., see the notes to s.68 above.]

[Unfit and overloaded vehicles: offences

71.—(1) A person who—   **A18.183**
    (a) drives a vehicle in contravention of a prohibition under section 69 or 70 of this Act, or
    (b) causes or permits a vehicle to be driven in contravention of such a prohibition, or
    (c) fails to comply within a reasonable time with a direction under section 70(3) of this Act,

is guilty of an offence.

(2) The Secretary of State may by regulations provide for exceptions from subsection (1) above.]

[Section 71 is printed as substituted by the Road Traffic Act 1991 s.14. **A18.184**

An offence under s.71(1) is a fixed penalty offence for the purposes of Pt 3 of the Road Traffic Offenders Act 1988 (see the Fixed Penalty Offences Order 2009 (SI 2009/483) art.2). The amount for the fixed penalty offence is prescribed by the Fixed Penalty Order 2000 (SI 2000/2792), as amended by the Fixed Penalty (Amendment) Order 2009 (SI 2009/488).

Section 71 does not apply to tramcars: Tramcars and Trolley Vehicles (Modification of Enactments) Regulations 1992 (SI 1992/1217) reg.7 (q.v.).

As to visiting forces, etc., see the notes to s.68 above.

The Road Vehicles (Prohibition) Regulations 1992 (SI 1992/1285) which set out exemptions from s.71(1) were made (in part) under s.71(2).]

Removal of prohibitions

72. *[Omitted.]*   **A18.185**

Power to establish official testing stations

72A. *[Omitted.]*   **A18.186**

Provisions supplementary to sections 69 to 72

73.—[(1), (1ZA), (1A), (1B) *[Action on giving notice under s.69(6) or s.70(2)].]*   **A18.187**
  [(1C) *[Action on giving notice under s.72(7)].]*
  (2) [...]
  (3) Any reference in sections 69 to 72 of this Act to the driving of a vehicle is,

in relation to a trailer, a reference to the driving of the vehicle by which the trailer is drawn.

(4) *[Definitions for purposes of ss.72, 73.]*

[(5) Schedule 4 to the Road Safety Act 2006 makes provision about the immobilisation of vehicles the driving of which has been prohibited under section 69 or 70 of this Act and about their removal and disposal.]

A18.188   *[Section 73 is printed as amended by the Road Safety Act 2006 s.12(3). As to visiting forces, etc., see the notes to s.68 above.]*

Miscellaneous provisions about vehicles and vehicle parts

Operator's duty to inspect, and keep records of inspections of, goods vehicles

A18.189   74.—(1) The Secretary of State may make regulations requiring the operator for the time being of a goods vehicle to which the regulations apply to secure—

(a) the carrying out by a suitably qualified person (including the operator if so qualified) of an inspection of the vehicle for the purpose of ascertaining whether [the following requirements are complied with, namely—

    (i)] the construction and use requirements with respect to any prescribed matters, being requirements applicable to the vehicle, [and

    (ii) the requirement that the condition of the vehicle is not such that its use on a road would involve a danger of injury to any person], and

(b) the making and authentication of records of such matters relating to any such inspection as may be prescribed, including records of the action taken to remedy any defects discovered on the inspection,

and providing for the preservation of such records for a prescribed period not exceeding fifteen months and their custody and production during that period.

(2) Regulations under this section may—

(a) apply to all goods vehicles or to goods vehicles of such classes as may be prescribed,

(b) require the inspection of goods vehicles under the regulations to be carried out at such times, or before the happening of such events, as may be prescribed, and

(c) make different provision for different cases.

(3) Any person who contravenes or fails to comply with any provision of regulations under this section is guilty of an offence.

(4) In this section *"the operator"*, in relation to a goods vehicle, means the person to whom it belongs or the hirer of it under a hire purchase agreement; but, if he has let it on hire (otherwise than by way of hire-purchase) or lent it to any other person, it means a person of a class prescribed by regulations under this section in relation to any particular class of goods vehicles or, subject to any such regulations, that other person.

A18.190   *[Section 74 is printed as amended by the Road Traffic Act 1991 s.48 and Sch.4, para.57.*

As to visiting forces, etc., see the notes to s.68 above.]

Vehicles not to be sold in unroadworthy condition or altered so as to be unroadworthy

75.—(1) Subject to the provisions of this section no person shall supply a motor vehicle or trailer in an unroadworthy condition.   **A18.191**

(2) In this section references to supply include—

    (a) sell,

    (b) offer to sell or supply, and

    (c) expose for sale.

(3) For the purposes of subsection (1) above a motor vehicle or trailer is in an unroadworthy condition if—

    (a) it is in such a condition that the use of it on a road in that condition would be unlawful by virtue of any provision made by regulations under section 41 of this Act as respects—

        (i) brakes, steering gear or tyres, or

        (ii) the construction, weight or equipment of vehicles, or

        (iii) [...]

    [(b) it is in such a condition that its use on a road would involve a danger of injury to any person.]

(4) Subject to the provisions of this section no person shall alter a motor vehicle or trailer so as to render its condition such that the use of it on a road in that condition

    [(a) would be unlawful by virtue of any provision made as respects the construction, weight or equipment of vehicles by regulations under section 41]

    [or

    (b) would involve a danger of injury to any person.]

(5) A person who supplies or alters a motor vehicle or trailer in contravention of this section, or causes or permits it to be so supplied or altered, is guilty of an offence.

(6) A person shall not be convicted of an offence under this section in respect of the supply or alteration of a motor vehicle or trailer if he proves—

    (a) that it was supplied or altered, as the case may be, for export from Great Britain, or

    (b) that he had reasonable cause to believe that the vehicle or trailer would not be used on a road in Great Britain, or would not be so used until it had been put into a condition in which it might lawfully be so used,

    ...

    (c) [...]

[(6A) Paragraph (b) of subsection (6) above shall not apply in relation to a person who, in the course of a trade or business—

    (a) exposes a vehicle or trailer for sale, unless he also proves that he took all reasonable steps to ensure that any prospective purchaser would be aware that its use in its current condition on a road in Great Britain would be unlawful, or

(b) offers to sell a vehicle or trailer, unless he also proves that he took all reasonable steps to ensure that the person to whom the offer was made was aware of that fact.]

(7) Nothing in the preceding provisions of this section shall affect the validity of a contract or any rights arising under a contract.

(8) [...]

A18.192   *[Section 75 is printed as amended by the Road Traffic Act 1991 ss.16(1)–(5), 83 and Sch.8.*

Section 75 does not apply to tramcars: Tramcars and Trolley Vehicles (Modification of Enactments) Regulations 1992 (SI 1992/1217) reg.7 (q.v.).]

Fitting and supply of defective or unsuitable vehicle parts

A18.193   **76.**—(1) If any person—

(a) fits a vehicle part to a vehicle, or

(b) causes or permits a vehicle part to be fitted to a vehicle,

in such circumstances that the use of the vehicle on a road would, by reason of that part being fitted to the vehicle [involve a danger of injury to any person or], constitute a contravention of or failure to comply with any of the construction and use requirements, he is guilty of an offence.

(2) A person shall not be convicted of an offence under subsection (1) above if he proves—

(a) that the vehicle to which the part was fitted was to be exported from Great Britain, or

(b) that he had reasonable cause to believe that that vehicle—

(i) would not be used on a road in Great Britain, or

(ii) that it would not be so used until it had been put into a condition in which its use [and would not involve a danger of injury to any person] would not constitute a contravention of or a failure to comply with any of the construction and use requirements.

(3) If a person—

(a) supplies a vehicle part or causes or permits a vehicle part to be supplied, and

(b) has reasonable cause to believe that the part is to be fitted to a motor vehicle, or to a vehicle of a particular class, or to a particular vehicle,

he is guilty of an offence if that part could not be fitted to a motor vehicle or, as the case may require, to a vehicle of that class or of a class to which the particular vehicle belongs, except in such circumstances that the use of the vehicle on a road would, by reason of that part being fitted to the vehicle, constitute a contravention of or failure to comply with any of the construction and use requirements [or involve a danger of injury to any person].

(4) In this section references to supply include—

(a) sell, and

(b) offer to sell or supply.

(5) A person shall not be convicted of an offence under subsection (3) above in respect of the supply of a vehicle part if he proves—

(a) that the part was supplied for export from Great Britain, or

(b) that he had reasonable cause to believe that—

    (i) it would not be fitted to a vehicle used on a road in Great Britain, or

    (ii) it would not be so fitted until it had been put into such a condition that it could be fitted otherwise than in such circumstances that the use of the vehicle on a road would, by reason of that part being fitted to the vehicle, constitute a contravention of or failure to comply with any of the construction and use requirements [or involve a danger of injury to any person].

(6) An authorised examiner may at any reasonable hour enter premises where, in the course of a business, vehicle parts are fitted to vehicles or are supplied and test and inspect any vehicle or vehicle part found on those premises for the purpose of ascertaining whether—

(a) a vehicle part has been fitted to the vehicle in such circumstances that the use of the vehicle on a road would, by reason of that part being fitted to the vehicle, constitute a contravention of or failure to comply with any of the construction and use requirements [or involve a danger of injury to any person], or

(b) the vehicle part could not be supplied for fitting to a vehicle used on roads in Great Britain without the commission of an offence under subsection (3) above.

(7) For the purpose of testing a motor vehicle and any trailer drawn by it the authorised examiner may drive it and for the purpose of testing a trailer may draw it with a motor vehicle.

(8) Any person who obstructs an authorised examiner acting under subsection (6) or (7) above is guilty of an offence.

(9) In subsections (6) to (8) above *"authorised examiner"* means a person who may act as an authorised examiner for the purposes of section 67 of this Act; and any such person, other than a constable in uniform, shall produce his authority to act for the purpose of subsections (6) and (7) above if required to do so.

(10) Nothing in this section shall affect the validity of a contract or of any rights arising under a contract.

[Section 76 is printed as amended by the Road Traffic Act 1991 s.48 and Sch.4, para.58(1)–(4).   **A18.194**

Section 76 does not apply to tramcars: Tramcars and Trolley Vehicles (Modification of Enactments) Regulations 1992 (SI 1992/1217) reg.7 (q.v.).]

Testing condition of used vehicles at sale rooms, etc.

77.—(1) An authorised examiner may at any reasonable hour enter premises   **A18.195**
where used motor vehicles or trailers are supplied in the course of a business and test and inspect any used motor vehicle or trailer found on the premises for the purpose of ascertaining whether it is in an unroadworthy condition for the purposes of section 75(1) of this Act.

(2) In this section (except paragraph (d) below) references to supply include—

(a) sell,

(b) offer for sale or supply,

(c) expose for sale, and

(d) otherwise keep for sale or supply.

(3) An authorised examiner may at any reasonable hour enter premises where vehicles or vehicle parts of a class prescribed for the purposes of section 63 of this Act are supplied in the course of a business and test and inspect any such vehicle or vehicle part for the purpose of ascertaining whether the vehicle or vehicle part complies with the type approval requirements applicable to a vehicle or vehicle part of that class.

(4) For the purpose of testing a motor vehicle and any trailer drawn by it the authorised examiner may drive it and for the purpose of testing a trailer may draw it with a motor vehicle.

(5) A person who obstructs an authorised examiner acting under this section is guilty of an offence.

(6) In this section *"authorised examiner"* means a person who may act as an authorised examiner for the purposes of section 67 of this Act; and any such person, other than a constable in uniform, shall produce his authority to act for the purposes of that section if required to do so.

(7) A motor vehicle or trailer shall be treated for the purposes of this section as used if, but only if, it has previously been sold or supplied by retail.

A18.196   *[Section 77 does not apply to tramcars or to trolley vehicles (other than duo-buses): Tramcars and Trolley Vehicles (Modification of Enactments) Regulations 1992 (SI 1992/1217) regs 7, 9 and 11 (q.v.).]*

Weighing of motor vehicles

A18.197   **78.**—(1) Subject to any regulations made by the Secretary of State, an authorised person may, on production of his authority, require the person in charge of a motor vehicle—

    (a) to allow the vehicle or any trailer drawn by it to be weighed, either laden or unladen, and the weight transmitted to the road by any parts of the vehicle or trailer in contact with the road to be tested, and

    (b) for that purpose, to proceed to a weighbridge or other machine for weighing vehicles.

(2) For the purpose of enabling a vehicle or a trailer drawn by it to be weighed or a weight to be tested in accordance with regulations under subsection (1) above, an authorised person may require the person in charge of the vehicle to drive the vehicle or to do any other thing in relation to the vehicle or its load or the trailer or its load which is reasonably required to be done for that purpose.

(3) If a person in charge of a motor vehicle—

    (a) refuses or neglects to comply with any requirement under subsection (1) or (2) above, or

    (b) obstructs an authorised person in the exercise of his functions under this section,

he is guilty of an offence.

(4) An authorised person may not require the person in charge of the motor vehicle to unload the vehicle or trailer, or to cause or allow it to be unloaded, for the purpose of its being weighed unladen.

(5) *[Regulation-making power.]*

(6) If—

(a) at the time when the requirement is made the vehicle is more than five miles from the weighbridge or other machine, and

(b) the weight is found to be within the limits authorised by law,

the highway authority (in Scotland, roads authority) on whose behalf the requirement is made must pay, in respect of loss occasioned, such amount as in default of agreement may be determined by a single arbitrator (in Scotland, arbiter) agreed upon by the parties or, in default of agreement, appointed by the Secretary of State.

(7) The Secretary of State may by order designate areas in Great Britain where subsection (6) above is to have effect, in such cases as may be specified by the order, with the substitution for five miles of a greater distance so specified.

An order under this subsection shall be made by statutory instrument subject to annulment by a resolution of either House of Parliament.

(8) In this section —

(a) *"road"* includes any land which forms part of a harbour or which is adjacent to a harbour and is occupied wholly or partly for the purposes of harbour operations,

(b) *"authorised person"* means a person authorised by a highway authority (in Scotland, a roads authority) or a constable authorised on behalf of such an authority by a police authority or a chief officer of police,

and in this subsection *"harbour"* and *"harbour operations"* have the meanings given to them by section 57(1) of the Harbours Act 1964.

[Section 78 does not apply to tramcars or to trolley vehicles (other than duo-buses): Tramcars and Trolley Vehicles (Modification of Enactments) Regulations 1992 (SI 1992/1217) regs 7, 9 and 11 (q.v.).]   **A18.198**

Further provisions relating to weighing of motor vehicles

79.—(1) Where a motor vehicle or trailer is weighed under section 78 of this   **A18.199**
Act, a certificate of weight must be given to the person in charge of the vehicle, and the certificate so given shall exempt the motor vehicle and the trailer, if any, from being weighed so long as it is during the continuance of the same journey carrying the same load.

(2) On production of his authority—

(a) [...]

(b) an examiner appointed under section [66A] of this Act, or

(c) any of the Secretary of State's officers authorised by him in that behalf,

may at any time exercise with respect to the weighing of [goods vehicles, public service vehicles, and vehicles which are not public service vehicles but are adapted to carry more than eight passengers] all such powers with respect to the weighing of motor vehicles and trailers as are exercisable under section 78 of this Act by a constable authorised as mentioned in subsection (8) of that section.

(3) The provisions of section 78 of this Act shall apply accordingly in relation to [such vehicles]—

(a) as if references to a constable so authorised included references to such [an] examiner or officer of the Secretary of State, and

(b) as if the reference in subsection (6) to the authority on whose behalf the requirement is made were a reference to the Secretary of State, and

(c) as if the reference in that subsection to the Secretary of State were a reference, in relation to England and Wales, to the Lord Chief Justice of England and, in relation to Scotland, to the Lord President of the Court of Session.

(4) A certificate in the prescribed form which—

(a) purports to be signed by an authorised person (within the meaning of section 78 of this Act) or by a person exercising powers by virtue of subsection (2) above, and

(b) states, in relation to a vehicle identified in the certificate, any weight determined in relation to that vehicle on the occasion of its being brought to a weighbridge or other machine in pursuance of a requirement under section 78(1) of this Act,

shall be evidence … of the matter so stated.

(5) If, for the purposes of or in connection with the determination of any weight in relation to a vehicle which is brought to a weighbridge or other machine as mentioned in section 78(1) of this Act, an authorised person (within the meaning of that section) or a person exercising powers by virtue of subsection (2) above—

(a) drives a vehicle or does any other thing in relation to a vehicle or its load or a trailer or its load, or

(b) requires the driver of a vehicle to drive it in a particular manner or to a particular place or to do any other thing in relation to a vehicle or its load or a trailer or its load,

neither he nor any person complying with such a requirement shall be liable for any damage to or loss in respect of the vehicle or its load or the trailer or its load unless it is shown that he acted without reasonable care.

A18.200   *[Section 79 is printed as amended by the Road Traffic Act 1991 ss.48 and 83, Sch.4, para.59(1)–(3) and Sch.8.*

Words relating exclusively to Scotland have been omitted from s.79(4).

Section 79 does not apply to tramcars or to trolley vehicles (other than duo-buses): Tramcars and Trolley Vehicles (Modification of Enactments) Regulations 1992 (SI 1992/1217) regs 7, 9 and 11 (q.v.).]

Approval marks

A18.201   80.—(1) Where any international agreement to which the United Kingdom is a party or a Community obligation provides—

(a) for markings to be applied—

(i) to motor vehicle parts of any description to indicate conformity with a type approved by any country, or

(ii) to a motor vehicle to indicate that the vehicle is fitted with motor vehicle parts of any description and either that the parts conform with a type approved by any country or that the vehicle is such that as so fitted it conforms with a type so approved, and

(b) for motor vehicle parts or, as the case may be, motor vehicles, bearing those markings to be recognised as complying with the requirements imposed by the law of another country, the Secretary of State may by regulations designate the markings as approval marks […].

(2) Any person who, without being authorised by the competent authority to apply any approval mark, applies that mark or a mark so nearly resembling it as to be calculated to deceive is guilty of an offence under the Trade Descriptions Act 1968 […].

(3) The conditions subject to which approval of any type may be given on behalf of the United Kingdom or the use of approval marks indicating conformity with a type approved by the United Kingdom may be authorised may include such conditions as to testing or inspection and the payment of fees as the Secretary of State may impose.

(4) In this section—

   "motor vehicle" means a mechanically propelled vehicle or a vehicle designed or adapted for towing by a mechanically propelled vehicle,

   "motor vehicle part" means any article made or adapted for use as part of a mechanically propelled vehicle or a vehicle drawn by a mechanically propelled vehicle, or for use as part of the equipment of any such vehicle, shall be treated as including any equipment for the protection of drivers or passengers in or on a motor vehicle notwithstanding that it does not form part of, or of the equipment of, that vehicle, and

   "the competent authority" means—

      (a) as respects any approval marks indicating conformity with a type approved by the United Kingdom, the Secretary of State, and

      (b) as respects any approval marks indicating conformity with a type approved by any other country, the authority having power under the law of that country to authorise the use of that mark.

[Section 80 is printed as amended by the Consumer Protection from Unfair **A18.202** *Trading Regulations 2008 (SI 2008/1277) Sch.2, para.46 and Sch.4(1).*

The Motor Vehicles (Designation of Approval Marks) Regulations 1979 (SI 1979/1088) have effect as if made under s.80.]

Pedal cycles and horse-drawn vehicles

Regulation of brakes, bells, etc.,on pedal cycles

81.—(1)–(4) *[Regulation-making powers.]*   **A18.203**

(5) Regulations under this section as to the use on roads of cycles may prohibit the sale or supply, or the offer of a sale or supply, of a cycle for delivery in such a condition that the use of it on a road in that condition would be a contravention of the regulations, but no provision made by virtue of this subsection shall affect the validity of any contract or any rights arising under a contract.

(6) If a person sells or supplies or offers to sell or supply a cycle in contravention of any prohibition imposed by regulations made by virtue of subsection (5) above, he is guilty of an offence, unless he proves—

      (a) that it was sold, supplied or offered for export from Great Britain, or

      (b) that he had reasonable cause to believe that it would not be used on a road in Great Britain, or would not be so used until it had been put into a condition in which it might lawfully be so used.

A18.204   *[The Pedal Cycles (Construction and Use) Regulations 1983 (SI 1983/1176) (not reproduced in this work) have effect as if made under s.81.]*

Regulation of brakes on horse-drawn vehicles

A18.205   **82.** *[Omitted.]*

Miscellaneous

Offences to do with reflectors and tail lamps

A18.206   **83.** A person who sells, or offers or exposes for sale, any appliance adapted for use as a reflector or tail lamp to be carried on a vehicle in accordance with the provisions of this Act or of any regulations made under it, not being an appliance which complies with the construction and use requirements applicable to a class of vehicles for which the appliance is adapted, is guilty of an offence.

A18.207   *[Section 83 does not apply to tramcars: Tramcars and Trolley Vehicles (Modification of Enactments) Regulations 1992 (SI 1992/1217) reg.7 (q.v.).]*

Appointment of officials and destination of fees

A18.208   **84.** *[Omitted.]*

Interpretation of Part II

A18.209   **85.**—[(1)] In this Part of this Act —

[*"EC certificate of conformity"* means—

(a) in the case of a light passenger vehicle, a certificate of conformity issued by a manufacturer under—

(i) regulation 4 of the Motor Vehicles (EC Type Approval) Regulations 1992 [*SI 1992/3107*],

(ii) regulation 5 of the Motor Vehicles (EC Type Approval) Regulations 1998 [*SI 1998/2051*],

(iii) regulation 15(1) or 20(4) of the Road Vehicles (Approval) Regulations 2009 [*SI 2009/717*], or

(iv) any provision of the law of a member State other than the United Kingdom giving effect to Article 6 of the light passenger vehicle type approval Directive or Article 18 of the road vehicles type approval Directive;

(b) in the case of a vehicle to which the motorcycle type approval Directive applies, a certificate of conformity—

(i) issued by a manufacturer under regulation 8(1) of the Motor Cycles Etc (EC Type Approval) Regulations 1999 (whether before, on or after 9th November 2003), or

(ii) issued by a manufacturer under any provision of the law of an EEA State other than the United Kingdom giving effect to Article 7(1) of the motorcycle type

approval Directive or to Article 7(1) of Council
Directive 92/61/EEC of 30th June 1992 relating to
the type approval of two- or three-wheeled motor
vehicles;

(c) in the case of a vehicle to which the tractor type approval
Directive applies, a certificate of conformity issued by a
manufacturer under—

    (i) regulation 6 of the Tractor etc (EC Type-Approval)
Regulations 2005, or

    (ii) any provision of the law of an EEA State other than
the United Kingdom effect to Article 6(1) of the tractor type approval Directive;

(d) in the case of any other vehicle, a certificate of conformity issued by a manufacturer under—

    (i) regulation 15(1) of the Road Vehicles (Approval)
Regulations 2009, or

    (ii) any provision of the law of a member State other than
the United Kingdom giving effect to Article 18 of the
road vehicles type approval Directive;]

[*"the Community Recording Equipment Regulation"* means Council
Regulation (EEC) No.3821/85 on recording equipment in road
transport as read with the Community Drivers' Hours and Recording
Equipment Regulations 2007.]

[*"EEA Agreement"* means the Agreement on the European Economic Area
signed at Oporto on 2nd May 1992 as adjusted by the Protocol signed
at Brussels on 17th March 1993 [*Cm. 2073 and Cm. 2183*] ;]

[*"EEA State"* means a State which is a contracting Party to the EEA
Agreement.]

[*"light passenger vehicle"* means any motor vehicle which—

(a) has at least four wheels,

(b) [...]

(c) is constructed or adapted for use for the carriage of passengers
and is not a goods vehicle,

(d) has no more than eight seats in addition to the driver's seat,
and

(e) has a maximum design speed exceeding 25 kilometres per
hour,

but does not include a quadricycle within the meaning of Article 1(3)
of the motorcycle type approval Directive [...],]

[*"the light passenger vehicle type approval Directive"* means Council
Directive 70/156/EEC of 6th February 1970 on the approximation of
the laws of the member States relating to the type approval of motor
vehicles and their trailers as amended by Council Directive 87/403/
EEC of 25th June 1987 and Council Directive 92/53/EEC of 18th
June 1992,]

[*"the motorcycle type approval Directive"* means Directive 2002/24/EC of
the European Parliament and of the Council of 18th March 2002 re-

lating to the type approval of two or three-wheel motor vehicles and repealing Council Directive 92/61/EEC, as corrected by a Corrigendum of 22nd February 2003;]

"*official testing station*" means a testing station maintained by the Secretary of State under section [72A] of this Act [or premises designated by him under section 10(12) of the Transport Act 1982],

"*prescribed*" means prescribed by regulations made by the Secretary of State,

["*prescribed testing authority*" means such approved testing authority as may be prescribed,]

["*public service vehicle*" has the same meaning as in the Public Passenger Vehicles Act 1981 [*q.v.*],]

["*the road vehicles type approval Directive*" means Directive 2007/46/EC of the European Parliament and of the Council of 5th September 2007 establishing a framework for the approval of motor vehicles and their trailers and of systems, components and separate technical units intended for such vehicles,]

"*sold or supplied by retail*" means sold or supplied otherwise than to a person acquiring solely for the purpose of resale or of re-supply for a valuable consideration,

"*tail lamp*" means, in relation to a vehicle, any lamp carried attached to the vehicle for the purpose of showing a red light to the rear in accordance with regulations under section 41 of this Act,

["*the tractor type approval Directive*" means Directive 2003/37/EC of the European Parliament and of the Council of 26th May 2003 on type-approval of agricultural or forestry tractors, their trailers and interchangeable towed machinery, together with their systems, components and separate technical units,]

"*traffic area*" has the same meaning as in the Public Passenger Vehicles Act 1981, and

"*vehicle part*" means any article which is a motor vehicle part, within the meaning of section 80 of this Act, and any other article which is made or adapted for use as part of, or as part of the equipment of, a vehicle which is intended or adapted to be used on roads but which is not a motor vehicle within the meaning of that section.

[(2) References in any provision of this Part of this Act to an authorised inspector are references to a person authorised by the Secretary of State under section 8 of the Transport Act 1982 to exercise the function to which that provision relates.]

A18.210   *[Section 85 is printed as amended by the Interpretation Act 1978 ss.17(2)(a) and 23; the Road Traffic Act 1991 s.48 and Sch.4, para.61; the Motor Vehicles (EC Type Approval) Regulations 1992 (SI 1992/3107); the Goods Vehicles (Licensing of Operators) Act 1995 s.60(1) and Sch.7, para.13 (see also s.60(2) and Sch.8, Pt 1); the Passenger and Goods Vehicles (Recording Equipment) Regulations 1996 (SI 1996/941) reg.3; the Motor Cycles Etc. (EC Type Approval) Regulations 1999 (SI 1999/2920); the Motor Cycles Etc. (EC Type Approval) (Amendment) Regulations 2003 (SI 2003/1099) reg.3; the Fire and Rescue Ser-*

vices Act 2004 s.53, Sch.1, para.69; the Passenger and Goods Vehicles (Community Recording Equipment Regulation) Regulations 2006 (SI 2006/3276) reg.2; the Road Vehicles (Approval) (Consequential Amendments) Regulations 2009 (SI 2009/818) reg.3; the Passenger and Goods Vehicles (Community Recording Equipment Regulation) Regulations 2010 (SI 2010/892) reg.3; and as prospectively amended by the Road Traffic (Consequential Provisions) Act 1988 s.4 and Sch.2, Pt 1, para.17(a)–(c).

The words printed within square brackets at the end of the definition of "official testing station", the definition of "prescribed testing station" and the text of s.85(2) will come into force on a date to be announced; see the Road Traffic (Consequential Provisions) Act 1988 s.8(3). The text of s.85 as enacted has prospectively been designated as s.85(1) (although no such textual amendment has been formally effected) following the prospective addition of s.85(2).

Section 8 of the Transport Act 1982 (which has not yet been brought into force) will make provision for private-sector plating and testing by "authorised inspectors".

As to the EEA Agreement and the EEA states, see the introductory note to Section C, below.]

Index to Part II

86. The expressions listed in the left-hand column below are respectively defined or (as the case may be) fall to be construed in accordance with the provisions of this Part of this Act listed in the right-hand column in relation to those expressions.   **A18.211**

Expression	Relevant provision
Certificate of conformity	[Section 57(1A)]
Community Recording Equipment Regulation	Section 85
Construction and use requirements	Section 41(7)
Design weights	Section 54(3)
[EC certificate of conformity	Section 85]
Examination for plating	Section 49(4)
…	
Goods vehicle test	Section 49(4)
Goods vehicle test certificate	Section 49(2)(b)
…	
[Light passenger vehicle	Section 85]
[Light passenger vehicle type approval Directive	Section 85]
Minister's approval certificate	Section 58(1)
[Motorcycle type Directive	Section 85]
Official testing station	Section 85
Plating certificate	Section 49(2)(a)
Plated particulars	Section 41(7)
Plated weights	Section 41(7)

Expression	Relevant provision
Prescribed	Section 85
[Public service vehicle	Section 85]
Relevant aspects of design, construction, equipment and marking	Section 54(6)
[Road vehicles type approval Directive	Section 85]
Sold or supplied by retail	Section 85
Tail lamp	Section 85
Test certificate	Section 45(2)
[Tractor type approval Directive	Section 85]
Traffic area	Section 85
Type approval certificate	Section 55(2)
Type approval requirements	Section 54(1)
[Vehicle examiner	Section 66A]
Vehicle part	Section 85

A18.212   *[Section 86 is printed as amended by the Road Traffic Act 1991 ss.48 and 83, Sch.4, para.62, and Sch.8; the Motor Vehicles (EC Type Approval) Regulations 1992 (SI 1992/3107); the Goods Vehicles (Licensing of Operators) Act 1995 s.60(1) and Sch.7, para.14 (see also s.60(2) and Sch.8, Pt 1); the Road Vehicles (Approval) (Consequential Amendments) Regulations 2009 (SI 2009/818) reg.3.]*

PART III

LICENSING OF DRIVERS OF VEHICLES

A18.213   *[The Secretary of State is empowered to make any information held by him (in any form) for the purposes of Pt 3 of this Act available to the Police Information Technology Organisation (PITO) for use by constables; see the Criminal Justice and Court Services Act 2000 s.71(1) and (4). The purposes for which constables (and also employees of police authorities) may be given access to information made available to the PITO are set out in the Motor Vehicles (Access to Driver Licensing Records) Regulations 2001 (SI 2001/3343) below.*

     With effect from April 1, 2007, the National Policing Improvement Agency (NPIA) replaced PITO and took on significant areas of its operations (see the Police and Justice Act 2006 s.1 and www.npia.police.uk [accessed March 2, 2011]).]

Requirement to hold licence

Drivers of motor vehicles to have driving licences

A18.214   **87.**—(1) It is an offence for a person to drive on a road a motor vehicle of any class [otherwise than in accordance with] a licence authorising him to drive a motor vehicle of that class.

     (2) It is an offence for a person to cause or permit another person to drive on a road a motor vehicle of any class [otherwise than in accordance with a licence authorising that other person] to drive a motor vehicle of that class.

[(3) [...]]

[Section 87 is printed as amended by the Road Traffic (Driver Licensing and **A18.215**
*Information Systems) Act 1989, ss.7 and 16, Sch.3, para.7, and Sch.6; the Road
Traffic Act 1991 s.17(1) and (2).*

*The following subsections were added to s.87 as it applies to tramcars by the
Tramcars and Trolley Vehicles (Modification of Enactments) Regulations 1992
(SI 1992/1217) reg.8:*

[(3) A licence authorising a person to drive a motor vehicle in category B within the
meaning of the Motor Vehicles (Driving Licences) Regulations 1987 [*SI 1987/1378, as
amended; see now SI 1999/2864*], shall be regarded as authorising that person to drive a
tramcar.]

[(4) Notwithstanding subsection (1) above, a person may drive or cause or permit another person to drive a tramcar if the driver was employed on duties which required the
driving of tramcars on a road at any time during the one year period ending immediately
before 1st July 1992.]

*Proceedings under s.87(2) are specified by the Prosecution of Offences Act
1985 (Specified Proceedings) Order 1999 (SI 1999/904) below as being proceedings the conduct of which the Director of Public Prosecutions is not required to
take over from the police under the Prosecution of Offences Act 1985, s.3(3)(a).*

*The fixed penalty procedure applies to offences under s.87(1); see the Road
Traffic Offenders Act 1988 Sch.3 below.]*

Exceptions

88.—(1) Notwithstanding section 87 of this Act, a person may drive or cause   **A18.216**
or permit another person to drive a vehicle of any class [at any time] if—
  [(a) the driver has held—
    (i) a licence under this Part of this Act to drive vehicles of that or a
    corresponding class, or
    [(ia) a Community licence to drive vehicles of that or a corresponding
    class, or]
    (ii) a Northern Ireland licence to drive vehicles of that or a corre-
    sponding class, or
    (iii) a British external licence or British Forces licence to drive
    vehicles of that or a corresponding class, or
    (iv) an exchangeable licence to drive vehicles of that or a correspond-
    ing class, and]
  [(b) either—
    (i) a qualifying application by the driver for the grant of a licence to
    drive vehicles of that class for a period which includes that time
    has been received by the Secretary of State, or]
    [(ii) a licence to drive vehicles of that class granted to him has been
    revoked or surrendered in pursuance of section 99(2A), (3) or (4)
    of this Act otherwise than by reason of a current disqualification
    or of its having been granted in error and he has complied with
    any requirements imposed on him under section 99(7B) of this
    Act, and]
  (c) any conditions which by virtue of section 97(3) or 98(2) of this Act

apply to the driving under the authority of the licence of vehicles of that class are complied with.

[(1A) An application for the grant of a licence to drive vehicles of any class is a qualifying application for the purposes of subsection (1)(b)(i) above if—

（a）the requirements of paragraphs (a), (b) so far as it relates to initial evidence and (c) of section 97(1) of this Act [*q.v.*] have been satisfied;

（b）the applicant—

    (i) is not subject to a current disqualification which is relevant to the licence he applies for, and

    (ii) is not prevented from obtaining it by section 89 of this Act [*q.v.*] [or [section 4 of or paragraph 6 or 9] of Schedule 1 to the Road Traffic (New Drivers) Act 1995]; and

（c）the declaration made in pursuance of section 92(1) of this Act [*q.v.*] indicates that he is not suffering from a relevant disability.]

[(1B) A disqualification is relevant to a licence for which a person makes an application if—

（a）in the case of an application made by virtue of any provision of subsection (1)(a) above, the disqualification subsists under or by virtue of any provision of the Road Traffic Acts and relates to vehicles of the class to which his application relates;

[(aa) in the case of an application made by virtue of subsection (1)(a)(ia) above, the disqualification subsists under or by virtue of any provision of the law of an EEA State (other than the United Kingdom) and relates to vehicles of the class, or of a class corresponding to the class, to which his application relates;]

（b）in the case of an application made by virtue of subsection (1)(a)(ii) above, the disqualification subsists under or by virtue of any provision of the law of Northern Ireland and relates to vehicles of the class, or of a class corresponding to the class, to which his application relates;

（c）in the case of an application made by virtue of subsection (1)(a)(iii) above, the disqualification subsists under or by virtue of any provision of the relevant external law or, as the case may be, is a disqualification for holding or obtaining a British Forces licence and relates to vehicles of the class, or of a class corresponding to the class, to which his application relates; and

（d）in the case of an application made by virtue of subsection (1)(a)(iv) above, the disqualification subsists under or by virtue of any provision of the law of the … country or territory under which the licence which he held was granted and relates to vehicles of the class, or of a class corresponding to the class, to which his application relates;

but a disqualification which does not prevent the person disqualified from obtaining a provisional licence or, as the case may be, a licence corresponding to a provisional licence is relevant to a full licence but not to a provisional licence.]

(2) The benefit of subsection (1) above does not extend—

（a）beyond the date when a licence is granted in pursuance of the application mentioned in subsection (1)(b) above or (as the case may be) in pursuance of section 99(7) [or (7A)] of this Act in consequence of the revocation or surrender so mentioned, or

(b) in a case where a licence is not in fact so granted, beyond the expiration of the period of one year or such shorter period as may be prescribed, beginning on the date of the application or (as the case may be) the revocation or surrender mentioned in subsection (1)(b) above[, or]

[(c) in a case where a licence is refused under section 92(3) of this Act [*q.v.*], beyond the day on which the applicant receives notice of the refusal.]

(3) The Secretary of State may by regulations provide that subsection (1) above shall also apply (where the requirements of that subsection are otherwise met) in the case of a person who has not previously held a licence to drive vehicles of the relevant class.

(4) Regulations made by virtue of subsection (3) above shall, if not previously revoked, expire at the end of the period of one year beginning with the day on which they came into operation.

(5) Regulations may provide that a person who becomes resident in Great Britain shall, during the prescribed period after he becomes so resident, be treated for the purposes of section 87 of this Act as the holder of a licence authorising him to drive motor vehicles of the prescribed classes if—

(a) he satisfies the prescribed conditions, and

(b) he is the holder of a permit of the prescribed description authorising him to drive vehicles under the law of a country outside the United Kingdom.

(6) Regulations made by virtue of subsection (5) above may provide for the application of any enactment relating to licences[, counterparts of licences] or licence holders, with or without modifications, in relation to any such permit and its holder respectively.

(7) Notwithstanding section 87 of this Act—

(a) a person who is not a holder of a licence may act as steersman of a motor vehicle, being a vehicle on which a speed limit of five miles per hour or less is imposed by or under section 86 of the Road Traffic Regulation Act 1984 [*q.v.*], under the orders of another person engaged in the driving of the vehicle who

[(i) is licensed in that behalf in accordance with the requirements of this Part and Part IV of this Act, or]

[(ii) is authorised by virtue of section 99A(1) of this Act to drive in Great Britain such a motor vehicle,]

and

(b) a person may cause or permit another person who is not the holder of a licence so to act.

[(8) In this Part of this Act —

"*British external licence*" means a licence granted in the Isle of Man or any of the Channel Islands under the relevant external law;

"*British Forces licence*" means a licence granted in the Federal Republic of Germany by the British authorities to members of the British

Forces or of the civilian components of those Forces or their dependants; and

"*relevant external law*" means the law for the time being in force in the Isle of Man or any of the Channel Islands which corresponds to this Part of this Act.]

A18.217   *[Section 88 is printed as amended by the Road Traffic (Driver Licensing and Information Systems) Act 1989 s.3(2)–(5); the Driving Licences (Community Driving Licence) Regulations 1990 (SI 1990/144); the Road Traffic (New Drivers) Act 1995 s.10(4) and Sch.2, paras 1 and 2; the Driving Licences (Community Driving Licence) Regulations 1996 (SI 1996/1974) reg.2 and Sch.1, para.1 (not reproduced in this work) (SI 1996/1974 is stated to give effect to Directive 91/439/EEC (O.J. No.L237, August 24, 1991, p.1) on driving licences); the Driving Licences (Community Driving Licence) Regulations 1998 (SI 1998/ 1420), regs 2 and 3 (not reproduced in this work) (SI 1998/1420 is stated to give effect to Directive 96/47/EC (O.J. No.L235, September 17, 1996, p.1) and Directive 97/26/EC (O.J. No.L150, June 7, 1997, p.41), both of which amended Directive 91/439/EC); the Crime (International Co-operation) Act 2003 s.91 and Sch.5, para.18(a); the Road Safety Act 2006 s.58(1).*

In s.88(1B)(a), the words "or Chapter 1 of Part 3 of the Crime (International Co-operation) Act 2003" will be inserted after the words "Road Traffic Acts" by the Crime (International Co-operation) Act 2003 s.91 and Sch.5, para.18(b), with effect from a day to be appointed.

With effect from a day to be appointed, after s.88(2), the following new subsection will be inserted by the Road Safety Act 2006 s.13(1):

[(2A) Subsection (1) above does not apply by virtue of an application mentioned in paragraph (b) of that subsection having been received by the Secretary of State if—

    (a) the application was made as a result of, or in anticipation of, the expiry of a disqualification relevant to the licence applied for,

    (b) either the nature of the disqualification or its imposition within a particular period after an earlier disqualification amounted to circumstances prescribed under subsection (4) of section 94 of this Act (disqualification: high risk offenders), and

    (c) the Secretary of State has notified the applicant that, because of that, he will be subject to a requirement under paragraph (a) or (b) of subsection (5) of that section.]

The amendment does not apply where the conviction in respect of which the disqualification was ordered was imposed before the coming into force of s.13(1) of the 2006 Act.

With effect from a day to be appointed, in s.88(6) and in relation to endorsement (all drivers), the words ", counterparts of licences" will be omitted by the Road Safety Act 2006 s.10 and Sch.3, para.3, Sch.7(4).

The Motor Vehicles (Driving Licences) Regulations 1999 (SI 1999/2864) (q.v.) were made in part under s.88(5) and (6).

As to orders made under ss.88(8) and 89(2)(b), see the notes to s.89 below.

As to the term "Great Britain" in s.88(5), see the Driving Licences (Community Driving Licence) Regulations 1982 (SI 1982/1555) reg.4(1).]

Tests

Tests of competence to drive

89.—(1) A licence authorising the driving of motor vehicles of any class shall **A18.218** not be granted to any person unless he [meets the relevant residence requirement and satisfies the Secretary of State]—

[(a) that at some time during the period of two years ending with the date the application is made but not earlier than the appointed day he has passed—

    (i) the test of competence to drive prescribed by virtue of subsection (3) below, or

    (ii) a Northern Ireland test of competence to drive which corresponds to such a test, or

    (iii) a test of competence which under subsection (6) below is a sufficient test;

    […]

(b) that at some time not earlier than the appointed day he has held—

    (i) a full licence authorising the driving of vehicles of that class, or

    (ii) a full Northern Ireland licence authorising the driving of vehicles of that or a corresponding class;

or that, if it is available to him, he satisfies the alternative requirement of section 89A of this Act [*q.v.*]; or

(c) that at some time during the period of two years ending with the date the application is made he has passed a test of competence to drive vehicles of that or a corresponding class … for the purpose of obtaining a British Forces licence; or

(d) that at some time not earlier than the appointed day he has held a full British external licence or a full British Forces licence to drive vehicles of that or a corresponding class […]; or

(e) that at some time during the period of two years ending with the date the application is made he has passed a test of competence to drive vehicles of that or a corresponding class conducted under the law … of Gibraltar …; or]

[(ea) that either at the time of the application for the licence he holds a Community licence authorising the driving of vehicles of that or a corresponding class or at some time he has held such a Community licence; or]

[(f) that, at the time of the application for the licence, he holds an exchangeable licence authorising the driving of vehicles of that or a corresponding class.]

This subsection is subject to the provisions of this Part of this Act as to provisional licences and to the provisions of any regulations made by virtue of section 105(2)(f) of this Act.

[(1A) An applicant meets the relevant residence requirement referred to in subsection (1) above if on the date the application for the licence is made—

(a) in a case where he satisfies the Secretary of State in respect of paragraph (ea) of that subsection, he is normally resident in the United

Kingdom or has been attending a course of study in the United Kingdom during the period of six months ending on that date;

(b) in a case where he satisfies the Secretary of State in respect of paragraph (f) of that subsection, he is normally resident in Great Britain but has not been so resident for more than the prescribed period; and

(c) in any other case, he is normally resident in Great Britain.]

[(2) For the purposes of subsection (1) above—

[(a) a licence which has been revoked under section 99(3) of this Act or under any corresponding provision of—

(i) the law of Northern Ireland,

(ii) the relevant external law, or

(iii) the law of an EEA State other than the United Kingdom,

as a licence granted in error shall be disregarded for the purposes of paragraph (b), (d) or (ea) (as the case may be) of that subsection;]

(b) [...]

(c) a British external licence to drive any class of goods vehicle or any class of passenger-carrying vehicle is to be disregarded for the purposes of paragraph (d) of that subsection unless the Secretary of State, by order made by statutory instrument, designates the relevant external law under which it is granted as one which makes satisfactory provision for the granting of such licences.]

[(2A) *[Approved training course for motor cyclists.]*]

(3)–[(5ZA)], (5A) *[Regulation-making powers.]*

(6) For the purposes of subsection [(1)(a)(iii) above or section 89A(2)(b)(iii) below], a test of competence shall be sufficient for the granting of a licence authorising the driving of—

(a) vehicles of any class, if at the time the test was passed it authorised the granting of a licence to drive vehicles of that class,

(b) vehicles of [all] classes which are designated by regulations as a group for the purposes of subsection (1)(a) above, if at the time the test was passed it authorised the granting of a licence to drive vehicles of any class included in the group, [and]

[(c) vehicles of all classes included in another such group, if a person passing the test is treated by virtue of regulations made for the purposes of this paragraph as competent also to drive vehicles of a class included in that other group.]

(7) If vehicles of any classes are designated by regulations as a group for the purposes of subsection (1)(b) above, a licence authorising the driving of vehicles of a class included in the group shall be deemed for the purposes of subsection [(1)(b)(i) above or section 89A(4)(a) below to authorise the driving of—

(a) vehicles of all classes included in the group [(except where regulations otherwise provide)], and

(b) vehicles of all classes included in another such group, if a person holding the licence is treated by virtue of regulations as competent also to drive vehicles of a class included in that other group.]

The reference in this subsection to a licence does not include a licence which has been revoked in pursuance of section 99(3) of this Act.

(8) For the purposes of this section and section 88(1) of this Act, an exchangeable licence issued in respect of a … country or territory shall not be treated as authorising a person to drive a vehicle of any [class] if—

(a) the licence is not for the time being valid for that purpose, or

(b) it was issued in respect of that [class] for a purpose corresponding to that mentioned in section 97(2) of this Act.

[(9) A test of competence falling within paragraphs (a)(ii), (c) or (e) of subsection (1) above shall be sufficient for the granting of a licence authorising the driving of—

(a) vehicles of all classes designated by regulations as a group for the purposes of subsection (1)(a) above, if [(except where regulations otherwise provide)] at the time the test was passed it authorised the granting of a licence to drive vehicles of any class included in the group, or of any class corresponding to a class included in the group, and

(b) vehicles of all classes included in another such group, if a person passing a test of competence authorising the granting of a licence to drive vehicles of a class included in the group mentioned in paragraph (a) above is treated by virtue of regulations as competent also to drive vehicles of a class included in that other group.]

[(10) A full Northern Ireland licence, a full British external licence, a full British Forces licence [, a Community licence] or an exchangeable licence shall be treated for the purposes of paragraphs (b)(ii), (d) [, (ea)] or (f) (as the case may be) of subsection (1) above as authorising the driving of—

(a) [(except where regulations otherwise provide)] vehicles of all classes designated by regulations as a group for the purposes of subsection (1)(b) above, if the licence authorises the driving of vehicles of any class included in the group, or any class corresponding to a class included in the group, and

(b) vehicles of all classes included in another such group, if by virtue of regulations a person holding a licence authorising him to drive vehicles of any class included in the group mentioned in paragraph (a) above is treated as competent also to drive vehicles of a class included in that other group.]

[(11) … in this section and section 89A *"the appointed day"* means the day appointed for the coming into force of section 1 of the Road Traffic (Driver Licensing and Information Systems) Act 1989.]

[Section 89 is printed as amended by the Road Traffic (Driver Licensing and Information Systems) Act 1989 ss.4(2) and (3) and 7, and Sch.3, para.8(b)–(e); the Driving Licences (Community Driving Licence) Regulations 1996 (SI 1996/1974) reg.2 and Sch.1, para.2 (not reproduced in this work); the Road Safety Act 2006 ss.36, 59 and Sch.7(9). **A18.219**

With effect from a date to be announced under the Transport Act 2000 s.275, the following words will be substituted at the beginning of s.89(6) for the word "for" by the Transport Act 2000 s.260 and Sch.29, paras 1 and 2:

[Subject to regulations under section 99ZA of this Act, for]

Section 260 of the 2000 Act, together with Sch.29, paras 1 and 2 thereto, was brought into force on February 1, 2001 by the Transport Act 2000 (Commencement No.3) Order 2001 (SI 2001/57; not reproduced in this work), but SI 2001/57 was itself amended by the Transport Act 2000 (Commencement No.3) (Amendment) Order 2001 (SI 2001/115; not reproduced in this work) so as to delete reference to (inter alia) s.260 and Sch.29, paras 1 and 2, from SI 2001/57.

Also with effect from a date (or dates) to be announced, s.89(2A) and (5A) will be repealed by the Transport Act 2000 s.274 and Sch.31, Pt V(1).

With effect from a day to be appointed, in s.89(1), the words "that he has, at such time or within such period as is prescribed, passed" will be substituted for the words in para.(a) before sub-para.(i) and also for the words from "that" to "passed" in paras (c) and (e) by the Road Safety Act 2006 s.38(1).

The Motor Vehicles (Driving Licences) Regulations 1999 (SI 1999/2864) (q.v.) were made in part under s.89(1A), (2A), (3), (4), (5), (5A), (6), (7), (9) and (10); see, in particular, reg.4.

The laws for the time being in force in (i) the Isle of Man; (ii) Jersey; and (iii) Guernsey (which each corresponds to Pt 3 of this Act) have been designated by the Driving Licences (Designation of Relevant External Law) Order 1996 (SI 1996/3206; not reproduced in this work) and the Driving Licences (Designation of Relevant External Law) Order 2002 (SI 2002/2590; not reproduced in this work) as making satisfactory provision for the granting of licences to drive all classes of (a) goods vehicles and (b) passenger carrying vehicles.]

[The alternative requirements to those in section 89

A18.220

89A.—(1) The alternative requirements referred to in section 89(1) of this Act are the following.

(2) The requirement which is alternative to that specified in section 89(1)(a) on an application by a person for a licence authorising the driving of motor vehicles of any class other than any class of goods vehicle or passenger-carrying vehicle prescribed for the purposes of subsection (3) below—

    (a) is available to that person if the application is made within the period of ten years beginning with the appointed day, and

    (b) is that at some time before the appointed day and during the period of ten years ending with the date the application is made he has passed—

        (i) the test of competence to drive prescribed by virtue of section 89(3) of this Act or a test of competence to drive which corresponds to such a test, or

        (ii) a Northern Ireland test of competence to drive which corresponds to any test falling within (i) above, or

        (iii) a test of competence which under section 89(6) of this Act is a sufficient test or a test of competence to drive which corresponds to such a test.

(3) The requirement which is alternative to that specified in section 89(1)(a) on an application by a person for a licence authorising the driving of any class of goods vehicle or passenger-carrying vehicle prescribed for the purposes of this subsection—

    (a) is available to that person if the application is made within the period of five years beginning with the appointed day, and

    (b) is that at some time before the appointed day and during the period of five years ending with the date the application is made he has passed—

        (i) a test of competence to drive a heavy goods vehicle or public service vehicle of a class corresponding to the class of vehicle to which his application relates, or

        (ii) a corresponding Northern Ireland test of competence to drive a heavy goods vehicle or public service vehicle of a class which corresponds to the class of goods vehicle or passenger-carrying vehicle to which his application relates.

(4) The requirement which is alternative to that specified in section 89(1)(b) on an application by a person for a licence authorising the driving of motor vehicles of any class other than any class of goods vehicle or passenger-carrying vehicle prescribed for the purposes of subsection (5) below is that at some time before the appointed day but not earlier than 1st January 1976 he has held—

    (a) a full licence authorising the driving of vehicles of a class corresponding to the class of motor vehicle to which his application relates, or

    (b) a full Northern Ireland licence authorising the driving of vehicles of a class corresponding to the class of motor vehicle to which his application relates.

(5) The requirement which is alternative to that specified in section 89(1)(b) on an application by a person for a licence authorising the driving of any class of goods vehicle or passenger-carrying vehicle prescribed for the purposes of this subsection is that at some time before the appointed day but not earlier than the beginning of the period of five years ending with the appointed day he has held—

    (a) a full heavy goods vehicle or a public service vehicle driver's licence authorising the driving of vehicles of a class corresponding to the class of vehicle to which his application relates, or

    (b) a full Northern Ireland licence to drive heavy goods vehicles of a class corresponding to the class of vehicle to which his application relates or a Northern Ireland licence to drive public service vehicles of a class corresponding to the class of vehicle to which his application relates.

(6) The requirement which is alternative to that specified in section 89(1)(d) on an application by a person for a licence authorising the driving of motor vehicles of any class—

    (a) is available to that person if the application is made within the period of ten years beginning with the appointed day, and

    (b) is that at some time before the appointed day and during the period of ten years ending with the date the application is made he has held a full British external licence or a full British Forces licence to drive vehicles of that or a corresponding class.

(7) In this section *"heavy goods vehicle"* and *"public service vehicle"* have the same meaning as they had for the purposes of Part IV of this Act or section 22 of the Public Passenger Vehicles Act 1981 before their repeal by section 1 of the Road Traffic (Driver Licensing and Information Systems) Act 1989.]

A18.221 *[Section 89A was inserted by the Road Traffic (Driver Licensing and Information Systems) Act 1989 s.4(4).*

Section 89A(2), (3) and (6) will be repealed with effect from a day to be appointed by the Road Safety Act 2006 s.59 and Sch.7(19), Spent Enactments.

The term "heavy goods vehicle" was defined for the purposes of Pt 4 of this Act before its repeal by s.1 of the Road Traffic (Driver Licensing and Information Systems) Act 1989 by s.120 as "(a) an articulated goods vehicle, or (b) a large goods vehicle, that is to say, a motor vehicle (not being an articulated goods vehicle) which is constructed or adapted to carry or to haul goods and the permissible maximum weight of which exceeds 7.5 tonnes".

The term "public service vehicle" was defined for the purposes of s.22 of the Public Passenger Vehicles Act 1981 before its repeal by s.1 of the Road Traffic (Driver Licensing and Information Systems) Act 1989 by s.22(1) of the 1981 Act as "a public service vehicle being used on a road for carrying passengers for hire or reward".

As to the prescription of classes of motor vehicle for the purposes of s.89A(5), see the Motor Vehicles (Driving Licences) Regulations 1999 (SI 1999/2864), regs 49 and 52 below.]

Review of conduct of test by magistrates' court

A18.222 **90.** *[Omitted.]*

Repayment of test fees

A18.223 **91.** *[Omitted.]*

Physical fitness

Requirements as to physical fitness of drivers

A18.224 **92.**—(1) An application for the grant of a licence must include a declaration by the applicant, in such form as the Secretary of State may require, stating whether he is suffering or has at any time (or, if a period is prescribed for the purposes of this subsection, has during that period) suffered from any relevant disability or any prospective disability.

(2) In this Part of this Act—

"*disability*" includes disease [and the persistent misuse of drugs or alcohol, whether or not such misuse amounts to dependency];

"*relevant disability*" in relation to any person means—

(a) any prescribed disability, and

(b) any other disability likely to cause the driving of a vehicle by him in pursuance of a licence to be a source of danger to the public, and

"*prospective disability*" in relation to any person means any other disability which—

(a) at the time of the application for the grant of a licence or, as the case may be, the material time for the purposes of the provision in which the expression is used, is not of such a kind that it is a relevant disability, but

(b) by virtue of the intermittent or progressive nature of the disability or otherwise, may become a relevant disability in course of time.

(3) If it appears from the applicant's declaration, or if on inquiry the Secretary of State is satisfied from other information, that the applicant is suffering from a relevant disability, the Secretary of State must, subject to the following provisions of this section, refuse to grant the licence.

(4) The Secretary of State must not by virtue of subsection (3) above refuse to grant a licence—

(a) on account of any relevant disability which is prescribed for the purposes of this paragraph, if the applicant has at any time passed a relevant test and it does not appear to the Secretary of State that the disability has arisen or become more acute since that time or was, for whatever reason, not disclosed to the Secretary of State at that time,

(b) on account of any relevant disability which is prescribed for the purposes of this paragraph, if the applicant satisfies such conditions as may be prescribed with a view to authorising the grant of a licence to a person in whose case the disability is appropriately controlled,

(c) on account of any relevant disability which is prescribed for the purposes of this paragraph, if the application is for a provisional licence.

(5) Where as a result of a test of competence to drive [or of information obtained under the relevant powers] the Secretary of State is satisfied that the person who took the test [or in relation to whom the information was obtained] is suffering from a disability such that there is likely to be a danger to the public—

(a) if he drives any vehicle, …

(b) if he drives a vehicle other than a vehicle of a particular [class], [or]

[(c) if he drives a vehicle except in accordance with particular conditions,]

the Secretary of State must serve notice in writing to that effect on that person and must include in the notice a description of the disability.

(6) Where a notice is served in pursuance of subsection (5)(a) above, then—

(a) if the disability is not prescribed under subsection (2) above, it shall be deemed to be so prescribed in relation to the person [on whom the notice is served], and

(b) if the disability is prescribed for the purposes of subsection (4)(c) above it shall be deemed not to be so prescribed in relation to him.

[(7) Where a notice is served in pursuance of subsection (5)(b) above, the Secretary of State may—

(a) if the person on whom the notice is served is an applicant for a licence, grant him a licence limited to vehicles of the particular class specified in the notice, or

(b) if he held a licence which is revoked by the Secretary of State and he complies with subsection (7ZB) below, grant him a licence limited to vehicles of that class,

and, if the Secretary of State so directs in the notice, his entitlement to drive other classes of vehicle by virtue of section 98(2) of this Act shall be limited as specified in the notice.]

[(7ZA) Where a notice is served in pursuance of subsection (5)(c) above, the Secretary of State may—

> (a) if the person on whom the notice is served is an applicant for a licence, grant him a licence authorising him to drive vehicles subject to the particular conditions specified in the notice, or
>
> (b) if he held a licence which is revoked by the Secretary of State and he complies with subsection (7ZB) below, grant him a licence authorising him to drive vehicles subject to those conditions,

and, if the Secretary of State so directs in the notice, any entitlement which the person has to drive vehicles by virtue of section 98(2) of this Act shall be subject to conditions as specified in the notice.]

[(7ZB) A person complies with this subsection if—

> (a) he surrenders the existing licence and its counterpart, and
>
> (b) where the Secretary of State so requires, he provides his name, address, sex and date and place of birth and a photograph which is a current likeness of him.]

[(7A) If he considers it appropriate to do so, the Secretary of State may, after serving a notice under any of the paragraphs of subsection (5) above, serve a further notice under that paragraph or a notive under another of those paragraphs; and on his serving the later notice the notice previously served shall cease to have effect and any licence previously granted in accordance with it shall be revoked by the later notice.]

[(7B) In subsection (5) above the references to a test of competence to drive and to information obtained under the relevant powers are references respectively to a test of competence prescribed for the purposes of section 89 or so much of such a test as is required to be taken in pursuance of section 94(5)(c) of this Act and to information obtained in pursuance of section 94(5)(a) or (b) of this Act.]

[(7C) A person whose licence is revoked by virtue of subsection (7A) above must deliver the licence [and its counterpart] to the Secretary of State forthwith after the revocation and a person who, without reasonable excuse, fails to do so is guilty of an offence.]

[(7D) In subsection (7B) above the references to section 94 of this Act include references to that section as applied by section 99D [or 109C] of this Act.]

(8) In this section *"relevant test"*, in relation to an application for a licence, means any such test of competence as is mentioned in section 89 of this Act or a test as to fitness or ability in pursuance of section 100 of the Road Traffic Act 1960 as originally enacted, being a test authorising the grant of a licence in respect of vehicles of the classes to which the application relates.

(9) Without prejudice to subsection (8) above, for the purposes of subsection (4)(a) above—

> [(a) an applicant shall be treated as having passed a relevant test if, and on the day on which, he passed a test of competence to drive which—
>
> > (i) under a provision of the law of Northern Ireland or a relevant external law corresponding to subsections (3) and (4) or (6) of section 89 of this Act, either is prescribed in relation to vehicles of classes corresponding to the classes to which the application relates or is sufficient under that law for the granting of a licence authorising the driving of vehicles of those classes, or

(ii) is sufficient for the granting of a British Forces licence authorising the driving of vehicles of those classes, and]

(b) in the case of an applicant who is treated as having passed a relevant test by virtue of paragraph (a) above, disclosure of a disability to [his licensing authority] shall be treated as disclosure to the Secretary of State.

[(10) A person who holds a licence authorising him to drive a motor vehicle of any class and who drives a motor vehicle of that class on a road is guilty of an offence if the declaration included in accordance with subsection (1) above in the application on which the licence was granted was one which he knew to be false.]

[Section 92 is printed as amended by the Road Traffic (Driver Licensing and **A18.225** *Information Systems) Act 1989 ss.5(2)(a)–(c), (3)(a) and (b), (4) and (5)(a) and (b), and 16 and Sch.6; the Driving Licences (Community Driving Licence) Regulations 1990 (SI 1990/144); the Road Traffic Act 1991 s.18(1); the Driving Licences (Community Driving Licence) Regulations 1996 (SI 1996/1974) reg.2 and Sch.1, para.3 (not reproduced in this work); the Driving Licences (Community Driving Licence) Regulations 1998 (SI 1998/1420) regs 2 and 4 (not reproduced in this work); the Crime (International Co-operation) Act 2003 s.91 and Sch.5, para.19.*

With effect from a day to be appointed and in relation to endorsement (all drivers), the words "and its counterpart" will be omitted in s.92(7ZB)(a) and (7C) by the Road Safety Act 2006 s.10 and Sch.3, para.4, s.59 and Sch.7(4).

The Motor Vehicles (Driving Licences) Regulations 1999 (SI 1999/2864) (q.v.) were made in part under s.92(2) and (4); see, in particular, regs 71–73.

In relation to s.92(4)(a), see further the Road Traffic (Consequential Provisions) Act 1988 s.5 and Sch.4, para.7(1).

As to the prescription of diabetes requiring insulin treatment for the purposes of s.92(4)(b), see the Motor Vehicles (Driving Licences) Regulations 1999 (SI 1999/2864) reg.73(6) below.]

Revocation of licence because of disability or prospective disability

93. *[Omitted.]*   **A18.226**

Provision of information, etc., relating to disabilities

94.—(1) If at any time during the period for which his licence remains in force,   **A18.227**
a licence holder becomes aware—

(a) that he is suffering from a relevant or prospective disability which he has not previously disclosed to the Secretary of State, or

(b) that a relevant or prospective disability from which he has at any time suffered (and which has been previously so disclosed) has become more acute since the licence was granted,

the licence holder must forthwith notify the Secretary of State in writing of the nature and extent of his disability.

(2) The licence holder is not required to notify the Secretary of State under subsection (1) above if—

(a) the disability is one from which he has not previously suffered, and

(b) he has reasonable grounds for believing that the duration of the disability will not extend beyond the period of three months beginning with the date on which he first becomes aware that he suffers from it.

(3) A person who fails without reasonable excuse to notify the Secretary of State as required by subsection (1) above is guilty of an offence.

[(3A) A person who holds a licence authorising him to drive a motor vehicle of any class and who drives a motor vehicle of that class on a road is guilty of an offence if at any earlier time while the licence was in force he was required by subsection (1) above to notify the Secretary of State but has failed without reasonable excuse to do so.]

(4) If [the prescribed circumstances obtain in relation to a person who is an applicant for, or the holder of, a licence or if] the Secretary of State has reasonable grounds for believing that a person who is an applicant for, or the holder of, a licence may be suffering from a relevant or prospective disability, subsection (5) below applies for the purpose of enabling the Secretary of State to satisfy himself whether or not [that person may be suffering from that or any other relevant or prospective disability].

(5) The Secretary of State may by notice in writing served on the applicant or holder—

　(a) require him to provide the Secretary of State, within such reasonable time as may be specified in the notice, with such an authorisation as is mentioned in subsection (6) below, or

　(b) require him, as soon as practicable, to arrange to submit himself for examination—

　　(i) by such registered medical practitioner or practitioners as may be nominated by the Secretary of State, or

　　(ii) with respect to a disability of a prescribed description, by such officer of the Secretary of State as may be so nominated,

　　for the purpose of determining whether or not he suffers or has at any time suffered from a relevant or prospective disability, or

　(c) except where the application is for, or the licence held is, a provisional licence, require him to submit himself for [such a test of competence to drive as the Secretary of State directs in the notice], being a test authorising the grant of a licence in respect of vehicles—

　　(i) of all or any of the classes to which the application relates, or

　　(ii) which he is authorised to drive (otherwise than by virtue of section 98(2) of this Act) by the licence which he holds,

　　as the case may be.

(6) The authorisation referred to in subsection (5)(a) above—

　(a) shall be in such form and contain such particulars as may be specified in the notice by which it is required to be provided, and

　(b) shall authorise any registered medical practitioner who may at any time have given medical advice or attention to the applicant or licence holder concerned to release to the Secretary of State any information which he may have, or which may be available to him, with respect to the question whether, and if so to what extent, the applicant or licence holder concerned may be suffering, or may at any time have suffered, from a relevant or prospective disability.

(7) If he considers it appropriate to do so in the case of any applicant or licence holder, the Secretary of State—

(a) may include in a single notice under subsection (5) above requirements under more than one paragraph of that subsection, and

(b) may at any time after the service of a notice under that subsection serve a further notice or notices under that subsection.

(8) If any person on whom a notice is served under subsection (5) above—

(a) fails without reasonable excuse to comply with a requirement contained in the notice, or

(b) fails any test of competence which he is required to take as mentioned in paragraph (c) of that subsection,

the Secretary of State may exercise his powers under sections 92 and 93 of this Act as if he were satisfied that the applicant or licence holder concerned is suffering from a relevant disability which is not prescribed for the purposes of any paragraph of section 92(4) of this Act or, if the Secretary of State so determines, as if he were satisfied that the applicant or licence holder concerned is suffering from a prospective disability.

(9) *[Secretary of State to defray expenses, etc., under subs.(5) .]*

[Section 94 is printed as amended by the Road Traffic (Driver Licensing and   **A18.228**
Information Systems) Act 1989 s.5(7) and (8); the Road Traffic Act 1991 s.18(2).

The circumstances prescribed under s.94(4) for the purposes of s.94(5) are set out in regs 74 and 75 of the Motor Vehicles (Driving Licences) Regulations 1999 (SI 1999/2864) (q.v.).

As to the application of s.94 to Community licence holders who are normally resident in Great Britain, see s.99D below.]

[Driving after refusal or revocation of licence

94A.—(1) A person who drives a motor vehicle of any class on a road   **A18.229** otherwise than in accordance with a licence authorising him to drive a motor vehicle of that class is guilty of an offence if—

[(a) at any earlier time the Secretary of State—

(i) has in accordance with section 92(3) of this Act refused to grant such a licence,

(ii) has under [section 93] of this Act revoked such a licence, or

(iii) has served notice on that person in pursuance of section 99C(1) or (2) [or 109B] of this Act requiring him to deliver to the Secretary of State a Community licence [or Northern Ireland licence] authorising him to drive a motor vehicle of that or a corresponding class, and]

[(b) since that earlier time he has not been granted—

(i) a licence under this Part of this Act, or

(ii) a Community licence [or Northern Ireland licence],

authorising him to drive a motor vehicle of that or a corresponding class.]

(2) Section 88 of this Act shall apply in relation to subsection (1) above as it applies in relation to section 87.]

A18.230   *[Section 94A was inserted by the Road Traffic Act 1991 s.18(3) and is printed as amended by the Driving Licences (Community Driving Licence) Regulations 1996 (SI 1996/1974) reg.2 and Sch.1, para.5 (not reproduced in this work); the Crime (International Co-operation) Act 2003 s.91 and Sch.5, para.20.]*

Notification of refusal of insurance on grounds of health

A18.231   **95.**—(1) If an authorised insurer refuses to issue to any person such a policy of insurance as complies with the requirements of Part VI of this Act on the ground that the state of health of that person is not satisfactory, or on grounds which include that ground, the insurer shall as soon as practicable notify the Secretary of State of that refusal and of the full name, address, sex and date of birth of that person as disclosed by him to the insurer.

(2) *"Authorised insurer"* means an insurer who is a member of the Motor Insurers Bureau (a company limited by guarantee and incorporated under the Companies Act 1929 on 14th June 1946).

(3) *"Insurer"* means—

     (a) a person who has permission under Part 4 of the Financial Services and Markets Act 2000 to effect or carry out relevant contracts of insurance, or

     (b) an EEA firm of the kind mentioned in paragraph 5(d) of Schedule 3 to that Act, which has permission under paragraph 15 of that Schedule (as a result of qualifying for authorisation under paragraph 12 of that Schedule) to effect or carry out relevant contracts of insurance.

(4) A contract is a relevant contract of insurance if the risk insured against relates to—

     (a) the insured sustaining accidental injury or death as a result of travelling as a passenger;

     (b) land vehicles;

     (c) goods in transit; or

     (d) motor vehicle liability.

(5) This section must be read with—

     (a) section 22 of the Financial Services and Markets Act 2000;

     (b) any order for the time being in force under that section; and

     (c) Schedule 2 to that Act.]

A18.232   *[Section 95 is printed as amended by the Financial Services and Markets Act 2000 (Consequential Amendments and Repeals) Order 2001 (SI 2001/3649; not reproduced in this work) art.312.*

An EEA firm of the kind mentioned in para.5(d) of Sch.3 to the Financial Services and Markets Act 2000 (see s.95(3)(b) above) is an undertaking pursuing the activity of the business of assurance within the meaning of what is now art.1 of Council Directive 2002/83/EC (O.J. No.L345, December 19, 2002, p.1) concerning life assurance, which has received authorisation under art.4 from the authorities of its home Member State, or of Council Directive 73/239/EEC (O.J. No.L228, August 8, 1973, p.3), as amended by Council Directive 93/49/EEC (O.J. L228, August 11, 1992, p.1), on the co-ordination of laws, regulations and administrative provisions relating to the taking up and pursuit of direct insurance business other than life assurance, which has received authorisation under

art.6 from the competent authorities of its home Member State. Section 22 of the
2000 Act (as supplemented by Sch.2) specifies kinds of regulated activity for the
purposes of that Act.]

Driving with uncorrected defective eyesight

96.—(1) If a person drives a motor vehicle on a road while his eyesight is such   **A18.233**
(whether through a defect which cannot be or one which is not for the time being
sufficiently corrected) that he cannot comply with any requirement as to eyesight
prescribed under this Part of this Act for the purposes of tests of competence to
drive, he is guilty of an offence.

(2) A constable having reason to suspect that a person driving a motor vehicle
may be guilty of an offence under subsection (1) above may require him to submit
to a test for the purpose of ascertaining whether, using no other means of correction than he used at the time of driving, he can comply with the requirement
concerned.

(3) If that person refuses to submit to the test he is guilty of an offence.

Granting of licences, their form and duration

Grant of licences

97.—(1) Subject to [the following provisions of this section] and section 92 of   **A18.234**
this Act [and, in the case of licences to drive large goods vehicles or passenger-
carrying vehicles, to Part IV of this Act], the Secretary of State must … grant a
licence to a person who—

    (a) makes an application for it in such manner and containing such
        particulars as the Secretary of State may specify [and pays the fee (if
        any) which is prescribed],

    (b) provides the Secretary of State with such evidence or further evidence
        in support of the application as the Secretary of State may require,

   [(c) surrenders to the Secretary of State—

        (i) any previous licence granted to him after 1st January 1976 and
            its counterpart,

     [(ia) any Northern Ireland licence held by him together with its
            Northern Ireland counterpart and its counterpart (if any) issued
            to him under this Part of this Act,]

        (ii) any Community licence and its counterpart (if any) issued to
            him, and

       (iii) any British external licence or British Forces licence or exchange-
            able licence held by him,

        or provides the Secretary of State with an explanation for not sur-
        rendering them which the Secretary of State considers adequate,]

    (d) is not[, in accordance with section 88(1B) of this Act, subject to a
        current disqualification which is relevant to the licence he applies for]
        and is not prevented from obtaining it by the provisions of section 89
        of this Act [or [section 4 of or paragraph 6 or 9] of Schedule 1 to the
        Road Traffic (New Drivers) Act 1995].

  [(1A) Where any licence to be granted to an applicant would be in the form of a photocard, the Secretary of State may under subsection (1)(a) and (b) above in particular require him to provide a photograph which is a current likeness of him.]

[(1AA) Where a licence under this Part of this Act is granted to a person who surrenders under sub-paragraph (ia) of subsection (1)(c) above his Northern Ireland licence together with the counterparts mentioned in that sub-paragraph to the Secretary of State—

    (a) that person ceases to be authorised by virtue of section 109(1) of this Act to drive in Great Britain a motor vehicle of any class, and

    (b) the Secretary of State must send the Northern Ireland licence and its Northern Ireland counterpart to the licensing authority in Northern Ireland together with particulars of the class of motor vehicles to which the licence granted under this Part of this Act relates.]

(2) If the application for the licence states that it is made for the purpose of enabling the applicant to drive a motor vehicle with a view to passing a test of competence to drive, any licence granted in pursuance of the application shall be a provisional licence for that purpose, and nothing in section 89 of this Act shall apply to such a licence.

(3) A provisional licence—

    (a) shall be granted subject to prescribed conditions,

    (b) shall, in any cases prescribed for the purposes of this paragraph, be restricted so as to authorise only the driving of vehicles of the classes so prescribed,

    (c) may, in the case of a person appearing to the Secretary of State to be suffering from a relevant disability or a prospective disability, be restricted so as to authorise only the driving of vehicles of a particular construction or design specified in the licence, …

    [(d) shall not authorise a person under the age of 21 years, before he has passed a test of competence to drive a motor bicycle,—

        (i) to drive a motor bicycle without a side-car unless it is a learner motor bicycle (as defined in subsection (5) below) or its first use (as defined in regulations) occurred before 1st January 1982 and the cylinder capacity of its engine does not exceed 125 cubic centimetres, or

        (ii) to drive a motor bicycle with a side-car unless its power to weight ratio is less than or equal to 0.16 kilowatts per kilogram,]

    [(e) except as provided under subsection (3B) below, shall not authorise a person, before he has passed a test of competence to drive, to drive on a road a motor [bicycle] [or moped] except where he has successfully completed an approved training course for motor cyclists or is undergoing training on such a course and is driving the motor [bicycle] [or moped] on the road as part of the training.]

[(3A) [Regulation-making power.]]

[(3B) [Power to grant exemptions from s.97(3)(e) by regulation.]]

(4) Regulations may authorise or require the Secretary of State to refuse a provisional licence authorising the driving of a motor [bicycle] [or moped] of a prescribed class if the applicant has held such a provisional licence and the licence applied for would come into force within the prescribed period—

(a) beginning at the end of the period for which the previous licence authorised (or would, if not surrendered or revoked, have authorised) the driving of such a motor [bicycle] [or moped], or

(b) beginning at such other time as may be prescribed.

(5) A learner motor [bicycle] is a motor [bicycle] which either is propelled by electric power or has the following characteristics—

(a) the cylinder capacity of its engine does not exceed 125 cubic centimetres,

[(b) the maximum net power output of its engine does not exceed eleven kilowatts.]

(c) [...]

[(6) In this section —

"*maximum net power output*", in relation to an engine, means the maximum net power output measured under full engine load, and

"*power to weight ratio*", in relation to a motor bicycle with a side-car, means the ratio of the maximum net power output of the engine of the motor bicycle to the weight of the combination with—

(a) a full supply of fuel in the tank,

(b) an adequate supply of other liquids needed for its propulsion, and

(c) no load other than its normal equipment, including loose tools.]

(7) [...]

[Section 97 is printed as amended by the Road Traffic (Driver Licensing and Information Systems) Act 1989 ss.6, 7 and 16, Sch.3, para.9, and Sch.6; the Road Traffic Act 1991 s.17(3); the Road Traffic (New Drivers) Act 1995 s.10(4) and Sch.2, paras 1 and 2; the Driving Licences (Community Driving Licence) Regulations 1996 (SI 1996/1974) reg.2 and Sch.1, para.6 (not reproduced in this work); the Driving Licences (Community Driving Licence) Regulations 1998 (SI 1998/1420) regs 2 and 6 (not reproduced in this work); the Crime (International Co-operation) Act 2003 s.78(2)(a) and (b), s.91 and Sch.5, para.21.

With effect from a date to be announced under the Transport Act 2000 s.275, the following words will be substituted for the words "[the following provisions of this section]" at the beginning of s.97(1) by the Transport Act 2000 s.260 and Sch.29, paras 1 and 3:

[subsection (2) below, section 92 of this Act and regulations under section 99ZA of this Act]

Section 260 of the 2000 Act, together with Sch.29, paras 1 and 3 thereto, was brought into force on February 1, 2001 by the Transport Act 2000 (Commencement No.3) Order 2001 (SI 2001/57; not reproduced in this work), but SI 2001/57 itself was amended by the Transport Act 2000 (Commencement No.3) (Amendment) Order 2001 (SI 2001/115; not reproduced in this work) so as to delete reference to (inter alia) s.260 and Sch.29, paras 1 and 3, from SI 2001/57.

Also with effect from a date (or dates) to be announced, ss.97(3)(e) and s.97(3A) and (3B) will be repealed by the Transport Act 2000 s.274 and Sch.31, Pt V(1).

With effect from a day to be appointed, the following new subsection will be

A18.235

inserted after s.97(1) by the Road Safety Act 2006 s.38(2):

[(1ZA) Regulations may provide that in prescribed circumstances a licence granted by the Secretary of State may be granted subject to prescribed conditions having effect—

  (a) for a prescribed period, or

  (b) until the happening of a prescribed event.]

With effect from a day to be appointed and in relation to endorsement (all drivers), the following amendments will be made to s.97 by the Road Safety Act 2006 s.10 and Sch.3, para.6, s.59 and Sch.7(4):

  1. *in s.97(1)(c)(i), the words "and its counterpart" will be omitted;*

  2. *in s.97(1)(c)(ia), the words from "together" to the end will be omitted;*

  3. *in s.97(1)(c)(ii), the words "and its counterpart (if any) issued to him" will be omitted;*

  4. *in s.97(1AA), the words "together with the counterparts mentioned in that sub-paragraph" and the words "and its Northern Ireland counterpart" will be omitted.*

As to the possible exemption for a holder of a full licence for a category A vehicle from the restriction imposed by s.97(3)(e) on driving a vehicle of another class included in category A, see the Motor Vehicle (Driving Licences) Regulations 1999 (SI 1999/2864) reg.69(2B) and (2C) below.

The fixed penalty procedure applies to offences under s.97; see the Road Traffic Offenders Act 1988 Sch.3.

Neither s.97(3) nor s.98(3) (in so far as they prevent such licence as is there mentioned from authorising any person to drive certain motor cycles) applies in the case of motor cycles in the service of a visiting force (as defined); see the Visiting Forces and International Headquarters (Application of Law) Order 1999 (SI 1999/1736; not reproduced in this work) art.8(4).

The Motor Vehicles (Driving Licences) Regulations 1999 (SI 1999/2864) (q.v.) were made in part under s.97(1), (1A), (3), (3A), (3B) and (4); see, in particular, reg.3(5) and (6).]

Form of licence

A18.236   98.—[(1) A licence shall be in the form of a photocard of a description specified by the Secretary of State or such other form as he may specify and—

  (a) the licence shall state whether, apart from subsection (2) below, it authorises its holder to drive motor vehicles of all classes or of certain classes only and, in the latter case, specify those classes,

  (b) the licence shall specify (in such manner as the Secretary of State may determine) the restrictions on the driving of vehicles of any class in pursuance of the licence to which its holder is subject by virtue of section 101 of this Act and any conditions on the driving of vehicles of any class in pursuance of the licence to which its holder is subject by virtue of section 92(7ZA) of this Act, and

  (c) in the case of a provisional licence, the licence or its counterpart shall specify (in such manner as the Secretary of State may determine) the conditions subject to which it is granted.]

[(1A) The Secretary of State may specify different descriptions of photocards, and different forms of licences not in the form of a photocard, for different cases and may determine the form of licence to be granted in any case.]

(2) Subject to subsections (3)[, (4) and (4A)] below, a [person who holds a licence which] authorises its holder to drive motor vehicles of certain classes only (not being—

[(a) a provisional licence, or]

[(b) any other prescribed description of licence)]

[may] drive motor vehicles of all other classes subject to the same conditions as if he were authorised by a provisional licence to drive motor vehicles of those other classes.

(3) [Subsection (2) above does not] authorise a person to drive—

(a) a vehicle of a class for the driving of which he could not, by reason of the provisions of section 101 of this Act, lawfully hold a licence, or

(b) unless [he has either passed a test of competence to drive a motor bicycle or attained the age of 21 years, a motor bicycle] which, by virtue of section 97(3)(d) of this Act, a provisional licence would not authorise him to drive before he had passed that test [or attained that age (as the case may be)][; or]

[(c) unless he has passed a test of competence to drive a motor bicycle [or moped] on a road in circumstances in which, by virtue of section 97(3)(e) of this Act, a provisional licence would not authorise him to drive it before he had passed that test.]

(4) In such cases [or as respects such classes of vehicles] as the Secretary of State may prescribe, the provisions of subsections (2) and (3) above shall not apply or shall apply subject to such limitations as he may prescribe.

[(4A) [Subsection (2) above does not] authorise a person on whom a notice under section 92(5)(b) of this Act [q.v.] has been served to drive motor vehicles otherwise than in accordance with the limits specified in the notice.]

(5) […]

[Section 98 is printed as amended by the Road Traffic (Driver Licensing and Information Systems) Act 1989 ss.5(10)(a) and (b) and 7 and Sch.3, para.11; the Driving Licences (Community Driving Licence) Regulations 1990 (SI 1990/144); the Road Traffic Act 1991 s.17(3); the Driving Licences (Community Driving Licence) Regulations 1996 (SI 1996/1974) reg.2 and Sch.1, para.7 (not reproduced in this work); the Driving Licences (Community Driving Licence) Regulations 1998 (SI 1998/1420) regs.2 and 7 (not reproduced in this work).

With effect from a date to be announced under the Transport Act 2000 s.275, the following words will be substituted for the word "below" in s.98(2) by the Transport Act 2000 s.260 and Sch.29, paras 1 and 4:

[and to regulations under section 99ZA of this Act]

Section 260 of the 2000 Act, together with Sch.29, paras 1 and 4 thereto, was brought into force on February 1, 2001 by the Transport Act 2000 (Commencement No.3) Order 2001 (SI 2001/57; not reproduced in this work), but SI 2001/57 itself was amended by the Transport Act 2000 (Commencement No.3) (Amendment) Order 2001 (SI 2001/115; not reproduced in this work) so as to delete reference to (inter alia) s.260 and Sch.29, paras 1 and 4, from SI 2001/57.

Also with effect from a date (or dates) to be announced, s.97(3)(c), and the

A18.237

word "[or]" preceding it, will be repealed by the Transport Act 2000 s.274 and Sch.31, Pt V(1).

With effect from a day to be appointed, in s.98(1)(c), the words "in the case of a provisional licence" will be omitted and the words "any conditions" will be substituted for the words "the conditions" by the Road Safety Act 2006 ss.38(3), 59 and Sch.7(11) and, in relation to endorsement (all drivers), the words "or its counterpart" will be omitted by ibid. s.10 and Sch.3, para.7, s.59 and Sch.7(4).

As to the application of s.98(3) to visiting forces, etc. see the notes to s.97 above.

The Motor Vehicles (Driving Licences) Regulations 1999 (SI 1999/2864) (q.v.) were made in part under s.98(2) and (4); see, in particular, regs 19 and 69.]

[Compulsory surrender of old-form licences

A18.238   **98A.**—(1) The Secretary of State may by order require the holders of licences of a specified description, or any specified description of the holders of such licences, to surrender the licences and their counterparts to the Secretary of State.

(2) An order under this section may specify as the description of licences to be surrendered—

    (a) licences which are not in the form of a photocard, or

    (b) licences in the form of a photocard of a description no longer specified by the Secretary of State as a form in which licences are granted.

(3) An order under this section must specify the date by which the licences to which it relates (and their counterparts) are to be surrendered; and may specify different dates in relation to different descriptions of licence holders.

(4) An order under this section must include provision for the grant of a new licence to every holder of a licence surrendered (with its counterpart) in pursuance of the order who—

    (a) pays such fee (if any) as is specified by the order, and

    (b) provides the Secretary of State with such evidence or further evidence as the Secretary of State may require (which may include a photograph which is a current likeness of him).

(5) A replacement licence granted pursuant to provision made by virtue of subsection (4) above expires on the date on which the surrendered licence would have expired had it not been surrendered (but subject to subsection (6) below).

(6) Where the period for which the surrendered licence was granted was based on an error with respect to the licence holder's date of birth such that (if the error had not been made) that licence would have been expressed to expire on a different date, the replacement licence expires on that different date.

(7) A person who, without reasonable excuse, fails to comply with any requirement to surrender a licence and its counterpart imposed by an order under this section is guilty of an offence.

(8) An order under this section may—

    (a) make different provision for different cases, and

    (b) contain such incidental and supplementary provisions as the Secretary of State considers appropriate.

(9) The power to make an order under this section is exercisable by statutory instrument.

(10) Before making an order under this section the Secretary of State must consult with such representative organisations as he thinks fit.

(11) A statutory instrument containing an order under this section is subject to annulment in pursuance of a resolution of either House of Parliament.]

[Section 98A is prospectively inserted by the Road Safety Act 2006 s.39(1).   **A18.239**

With effect from a day to be appointed and in relation to endorsement (all drivers), the following amendments will be made to s.98A, when in force, by the Road Safety Act 2006 s.10 and Sch.3, para.8, s.59 and Sch.7(4):

1. *in s.98A(1), the words "and their counterparts" will be omitted;*

2. *in s.98A(3), the words "(and their counterparts)" will be omitted;*

3. *in s.98A(4), the words "(with its counterpart)" will be omitted;*

4. *in s.98(7), the words "and its counterpart" will be omitted.]*

Duration of licences

99.—(1) [In so far as a licence authorises its holder to drive motor vehicles of   **A18.240** classes other than any prescribed class of goods vehicle or any prescribed class of passenger-carrying vehicle, it] shall, unless previously revoked or surrendered, remain in force, subject to subsection (2) below—

    (a) except in a case falling within paragraph (b) or (c) of this subsection, for the period ending on the seventieth anniversary of the applicant's date of birth or for a period of three years, whichever is the longer,

    (b) except in a case falling within paragraph (c) of this subsection, if the Secretary of State so determines in the case of a licence to be granted to a person appearing to him to be suffering from a relevant or prospective disability, for such period of not more than three years and not less than one year as the Secretary of State may determine, and

    (c) in the case of a licence granted in exchange for a subsisting licence and in pursuance of an application requesting a licence for the period authorised by this paragraph, for a period equal to the remainder of that for which the subsisting licence was granted,

and any such period shall begin with the date on which the licence in question is expressed to come into force.

[(1A) In so far as a licence authorises its holder to drive any prescribed class of goods vehicle or passenger-carrying vehicle, it shall, unless previously revoked, suspended or surrendered, remain in force—

    (a) except in a case falling within paragraph (c) or (d) of this subsection—

      (i) for the period ending on the forty-fifth anniversary of the applicant's date of birth or for a period of five years, whichever is the longer, or

      (ii) where the applicant's age at the date on which the licence is to come into force will exceed forty-five but not sixty-five years, for the period ending on the sixty-sixth anniversary of the applicant's date of birth or for a period of five years, whichever is the shorter,

    (b) except in a case falling within paragraph (d) of this subsection, where the applicant's age at that date will exceed sixty-five years, for a period of one year,

(c) except in a case falling within paragraph (b) or (d) of this subsection, if the Secretary of State so determines in the case of a licence to be granted to a person appearing to him to be suffering from a relevant or prospective disability, for such period of not more than three years and not less than one year as the Secretary of State may determine, and

(d) in the case of a licence granted in exchange for a subsisting licence and in pursuance of an application requesting a licence for the period authorised by this paragraph, for a period equal to the remainder of that for which the subsisting licence was granted,

and any such period shall begin with the date on which the licence in question is expressed to come into force.]

(2) To the extent that a provisional licence authorises the driving of a motor [bicycle] [or moped] of a prescribed class it shall, unless previously surrendered or revoked, remain in force—

(a) for such period as may be prescribed, or

(b) if the licence is granted to the holder of a previous licence which was surrendered, revoked or treated as being revoked—

   (i) for the remainder of the period for which the previous licence would have authorised the driving of such a motor [bicycle] [or moped], or

   (ii) in such circumstances as may be prescribed, for a period equal to that remainder at the time of surrender or revocation.

[(2A) Where, in accordance with the preceding provisions of this section, a licence in the form of a photocard remains in force for a period of more than ten years, the holder of the licence must surrender it and its counterpart to the Secretary of State not later than the end of the period of ten years beginning with—

(a) the date shown on the licence as the date of issue, or

(b) if the licence was granted by way of renewal or replacement of a licence bearing the same photograph, the date shown on the earliest licence bearing that photograph as the date of issue of that licence.]

(3) Where it appears to the Secretary of State—

[(a) that a licence granted by him to any person was granted in error or with an error or omission in the particulars specified in the licence, or

(aa) that the counterpart of a licence granted by him to any person is required to be endorsed in pursuance of any enactment or was issued with an error or omission in the particulars specified in the counterpart or required to be so endorsed on it, or]

(b) that the particulars specified in a licence granted by him to any person [or in its counterpart] do not comply with any requirement imposed since the licence was granted by any provision made by or having effect under any enactment,

the Secretary of State may serve notice in writing on that person revoking the licence and requiring him to surrender the licence [and its counterpart] forthwith to the Secretary of State [and it shall be the duty of that person to comply with the requirement].

[(3A) Where—

(a) the Secretary of State is sent under a provision of Northern Ireland law corresponding to section 97(1AA) of this Act a licence granted under this Part of this Act to a person to drive a motor vehicle of any class, and

(b) the Secretary of State is satisfied that a Northern Ireland licence to drive a motor vehicle of that or a corresponding class has been granted to that person,

the Secretary of State must serve notice in writing on that person revoking the licence granted under this Part of this Act.]

(4) Where the name or address of the licence holder as specified in a licence ceases to be correct, its holder must forthwith surrender the licence [and its counterpart] to the Secretary of State ...

(5) A person who [without reasonable excuse] fails to comply with the duty under subsection [(2A),] [(3) or] (4) above is guilty of an offence.

(6) Where a person who has a duty under this section to surrender his licence [and its counterpart] is not in possession of [them] in consequence of the fact that he has surrendered it to a constable or authorised person (within the meaning of Part III of the Road Traffic Offenders Act 1988) on receiving a fixed penalty notice given to him under section 54 of that Act, he does not fail to comply with the duty if he surrenders the licence [and its counterpart] to the Secretary of State immediately on [their] return.

[(7) On the surrender of a licence and its counterpart by a person in pursuance of subsection (2A), (3) and (4) above, the Secretary of State must (subject to the following provisions of this section) grant a new licence to that person [...].]

[(7ZA) The Secretary of State is not required by subsection (7) above to grant a new licence on the surrender of a licence and its counterpart by a person in pursuance of subsection (2A) above unless the person has paid the fee (if any) which is prescribed; but any other licence under that subsection is to be granted free of charge.]

[(7A) Where the surrendered licence was revoked because it was granted in error or in consequence of an error or omission appearing to the Secretary of State to be attributable to the fault of the licence holder or in consequence of a current disqualification, subsection (7) shall not apply but the Secretary of State may, if the person is not currently disqualified, grant a new licence to that person on payment of that fee (if any) which is prescribed.]

[(7B) The Secretary of State may require a person to provide—

(a) evidence of his name, address, sex and date and place of birth, and

(b) a photograph which is a current likeness of him,

before granting a new licence to him under subsection (7) or (7A) above.]

[(8) A replacement licence granted pursuant to subsection (7) or (7A) above shall expire on the date on which the surrendered licence would have expired had it not been surrendered except that, where the period for which the surrendered licence was granted was based on an error with respect to the licence holder's date of birth such that (if that error had not been made) that licence would have been expressed to expire on a different date, the replacement licence shall expire on that different date.]

[*Section 99 is printed as amended by the Road Traffic (Driver Licensing and* **A18.241**

Information Systems) Act 1989 ss.2(2) and 7 and Sch.3, para.12; the Driving Licences (Community Driving Licence) Regulations 1990 (SI 1990/144); Driving Licences (Community Driving Licence) Regulations 1996 (SI 1996/1974) reg.2 and Sch.1, para.8 (not reproduced in this work); the Driving Licences (Community Driving Licence) Regulations 1998 (SI 1998/1420) regs 2 and 8 (not reproduced in this work); the Crime (International Co-operation) Act 2003 s.78(3); and the Road Safety Act 2006 s.40(1) and (2), Sch.7(12).

In relation to endorsement (all drivers), the following amendments will be made to s.99 by the Road Safety Act 2006 s.10 and Sch.3, para.9, s.59 and Sch.7(4), with effect from a day to be appointed:

1. *in s.99(2A), the words "and its counterpart" will be omitted;*
2. *in s.99(3), para.(aa) will be omitted and in para.(b) the words "or in its counterpart" and the words "and its counterpart" will be omitted;*
3. *in s.99(4), the words "and its counterpart" will be omitted;*
4. *in s.99(6), the words "and its counterpart" will be omitted in both places, the word "it" will be substituted in both places for the word "them", and the word "its" will be substituted for the word "their";*
5. *in s.99(7), the words "and its conterpart" will be omitted;*
6. *in s.99(7ZA), the words "and its counterpart" will be omitted.*

The Motor Vehicles (Driving Licences) Regulations 1999 (SI 1999/2864) (q.v.) were made in part under s.99(1) and (1A); see, in particular, regs 15 and 49(2).]

[Driver training]

[Compulsory driver training courses

A18.242   99ZA. Regulations may make provision about training in the driving of motor vehicles by means of courses provided in accordance with the regulations (*"driver training courses"*).]

A18.243   *[Section 99ZA is printed as inserted by the Transport Act 2000 s.257.*

Sections 99ZB and 99ZC (noted below) are also inserted by the Transport Act 2000, s.257; they specify certain matters which may be included in regulations made under s.99ZA.]

[Requirements to complete training courses]

A18.244   **99ZB.** *[Omitted.]*

[Driver training courses: supplementary]

A18.245   **99ZC.** *[Omitted.]*

[Community licence holders]

[Authorisation to drive in Great Britain

A18.246   99A.—(1) A Community licence holder may drive, and a person may cause or permit a Community licence holder to drive, in Great Britain, a motor vehicle of any class which—

(a) he is authorised by his Community licence to drive, and
(b) he is not disqualified for holding or obtaining a licence under this Part of this Act to drive,

notwithstanding that he is not the holder of a licence under this Part of this Act.

(2) Subsections (3) and (4) below apply to a Community licence holder who is normally resident in Great Britain.

(3) In a case where the Community licence holder is authorised by his Community licence to drive motor vehicles of classes other than any prescribed class of goods vehicle or any prescribed class of passenger-carrying vehicle, he shall cease to be authorised by virtue of subsection (1) above to drive in Great Britain any such classes of motor vehicle from—

    (a) the date on which he attains the age of seventy years, or

    (b) the expiry of the period of three years beginning with the relevant date,

whichever is the later.

(4) In a case where the Community licence holder is authorised by his Community licence to drive any prescribed class of goods vehicle or any prescribed class of passenger-carrying vehicle, he shall cease to be authorised by virtue of subsection (1) above to drive in Great Britain any such class of vehicle from—

    [(a) except in a case falling within paragraph (b) or (c) of this subsection—

        (i) the date on which he attains the age of 45 years, or

        (ii) the expiry of the period of five years beginning with the relevant date, whichever is the later,]

    (b) where his age at the relevant date exceeds forty-five but not sixty-five years—

        (i) the date on which he attains the age of sixty-six years, or

        (ii) the expiry of the period of five years beginning with the relevant date,

    whichever is the earlier, and

    (c) where his age at the relevant date exceeds sixty-five years, the expiry of the period of one year beginning with that date.

(5) A Community licence holder—

    (a) to whom a counterpart of his Community licence is issued under section 99B of this Act, and

    (b) who is authorised by virtue of subsection (1) above to drive in Great Britain motor vehicles of certain classes only,

may drive, in Great Britain, motor vehicles of all other classes subject to the same conditions as if he were authorised by a provisional licence to drive motor vehicles of those other classes.

(6) Subsections (3) and (4) of section 98 of this Act shall apply in relation to subsection (5) above as they apply in relation to subsection (2) of that section.

(7) For the purposes of this Part and Part IV of this Act a Community licence shall not be treated as authorising a person to drive a vehicle of any class if it is not for the time being valid for that purpose in the EEA State in respect of which it was issued.

(8) In this section *"relevant date"*, in relation to a Community licence holder who is normally resident in Great Britain, means—

    (a) in the case where he first became so resident on or before 1 January 1997, that date; and

(b) in any other case, the date on which he first became so resident.]

A18.247 *[Section 99A (and the heading preceding it) was inserted by the Driving Licences (Community Driving Licence) Regulations 1996 (SI 1996/1974) reg.2 and Sch.1, para.9 (not reproduced in this work); the Driving Licences (Community Driving Licence) Regulations 1998 (SI 1998/1420) regs 2 and 9 (not reproduced in this work).*

With effect from a day to be appointed and in relation to endorsement (all drivers), subss.(5) and (6) of s.99A will be omitted by the Road Safety Act 2006 s.10 and Sch.3, para.10, s.59 and Sch.7(4).

The Motor Vehicles (Driving Licences) Regulations 1999 (SI 1999/2864) below were made in part under s.99A(3), (4) and (6). Attention is drawn in particular to reg.4 of SI 1999/2864 in connection with s.99A.]

[Information about resident Community licence holders

A18.248 **99B.**—(1) A Community licence holder who—

    (a) is normally resident in Great Britain, and

    (b) is authorised by his Community licence to drive medium-sized or large goods vehicles or passenger-carrying vehicles of any class,

shall, on or before the expiry of the period of twelve months beginning with the relevant date, deliver his Community licence to the Secretary of State and provide him with the information specified in, or required under, subsection (4) below.

(2) Subsection (1) above shall not apply to a Community licence holder from whom the Secretary of State has received a qualifying application (within the meaning of section 88(1A) of this Act) for the grant of a licence under this Part of this Act.

(3) The Secretary of State may issue to any Community licence holder who—

    (a) is normally resident in Great Britain, and

    (b) has delivered his Community licence to the Secretary of State, and provided him with the information specified in, or required under, subsection (4) below (whether or not in pursuance of this section),

a document (referred to in this Part of this Act in relation to a Community licence as a *"counterpart"*) in such form and containing such information as the Secretary of State may determine but designed for the endorsement of particulars relating to the Community licence.

(4) The information referred to in subsections (1) and (3) above is—

    (a) the name and address in Great Britain of the Community licence holder;

    (b) his date of birth;

    (c) the classes of vehicle which he is authorised by his Community licence to drive;

    (d) the period of validity of the Community licence in the EEA State in respect of which it was issued;

    (e) whether the licence was granted in exchange for a licence issued by a state other than an EEA State; and

    (f) such other information as the Secretary of State may require for the purposes of the proper exercise of any of his functions under this Part or Part IV of this Act.

(5) The Secretary of State—

    (a) may endorse a Community licence delivered to him (whether or not in pursuance of this section) in such manner as he may determine with any part of the information specified in, or required under, subsection (4) above or with information providing a means of ascertaining that information or any part of it; and

    (b) must return the Community licence to the holder.

(6) Where it appears to the Secretary of State that a counterpart of a Community licence—

    (a) is required to be endorsed in pursuance of any enactment or was issued with an error or omission in the information contained in it or in the particulars required to be endorsed on it, or

    (b) does not comply with any requirement imposed since it was issued by any provision made by, or having effect under, any enactment,

the Secretary of State may serve notice in writing on the Community licence holder requiring him to surrender the counterpart immediately to the Secretary of State and it shall be the duty of the Community licence holder to comply with any such requirement.

(7) Where the name or address of a Community licence holder as specified in the counterpart of his Community licence issued to him under this section ceases to be correct, the Community licence holder must surrender the counterpart and, in the case of a change of name, deliver his Community licence immediately to the Secretary of State and provide him with particulars of the alterations falling to be made in the name or address.

(8) On the surrender of a counterpart of a Community licence by any person in pursuance of subsection (6) or (7) above, the Secretary of State must issue to that person a new counterpart of the Community licence.

(9) On the delivery of a Community licence by any person in pursuance of subsection (7) above, the Secretary of State may endorse the Community licence with the correct name and must return the Community licence to that person.

(10) Where a Community licence holder has not complied with subsection (1) above, the Secretary of State may serve notice in writing on the holder requiring him to deliver his Community licence to the Secretary of State and to provide him with the information specified in, or required under, subsection (4) above within such period (not being less than 28 days from the date of service of the notice) as is specified in the notice.

(11) A person who drives a motor vehicle on a road is guilty of an offence if he fails without reasonable excuse—

    (a) to comply with a requirement contained in a notice served on him in pursuance of subsection (10) above, or

    (b) to comply with a requirement imposed under subsection (6) or (7) above.

(12) Where a Community licence holder who is required under subsection (6) or (7) above to surrender the counterpart of his Community licence or to deliver his Community licence is not in possession of it in consequence of the fact that he has surrendered it to a constable or authorised person (within the meaning of Part III of the Road Traffic Offenders Act 1988) on receiving a fixed penalty no-

tice given to him under section 54 of that Act, he does not fail to comply with that requirement if he surrenders the counterpart or delivers the Community licence immediately on its return.

(13) In England and Wales, proceedings for an offence by virtue of subsection (11)(a) above shall not be instituted except by the Secretary of State or by a constable acting with the approval of the Secretary of State.

(14) In this section *"relevant date"* has the meaning given by section 99A(8) of this Act.]

A18.249   *[Section 99B was inserted by the Driving Licences (Community Driving Licence) Regulations 1996 (SI 1996/1974) reg.2 and Sch.1, para.10 (not reproduced in this work).*

With effect from a day (or days) to be appointed and in relation to endorsement (all drivers), the following amendments will be made to s.99B by the Road Safety Act 2006 s.10 and Sch.3, para.11, s.59 and Sch.7(4):

1. *s.99B(3) will be omitted;*
2. *in s.99B(4), the words "subsection (1)" will be substituted for "subsections (1) and (3)";*
3. *in s.99B(5), the words "the driving record of a person who delivers to him a Community licence (whether or not in pursuance of this section)" will be substituted for the words "a Community licence delivered to him (whether or not in pursuance of this section) in such manner as he may determine";*
4. *s.99B(6) will be omitted;*
5. *for s.99B(7), the following text will be substituted:*

   [(7) Where the name of a Community licence holder as specified in his Community licence ceases to be correct, he must deliver his Community licence immediately to the Secretary of State and provide him with particulars of the alterations falling to be made in the name on it.]

6. *s.99B(8) will be omitted;*
7. *in s.99B(9), the words "and that person's driving record" will be inserted after "endorse the Community licence";*
8. *in s.99B(11)(b), "(6) or" will be omitted;*
9. *s.99B(12) will be omitted.]*

[Revocation of authorisation conferred by Community licence because of disability or prospective disability

A18.250   99C.—(1) If the Secretary of State is at any time satisfied on inquiry—

   (a) that a Community licence holder who is normally resident in Great Britain at that time is suffering from a relevant disability, and

   (b) that the Secretary of State would be required by virtue of section 92(3) of this Act to refuse an application made by him at that time for a licence authorising him to drive a vehicle of the class in respect of which his Community licence was issued or a class corresponding to that class,

the Secretary of State may serve notice in writing requiring the Community licence holder to deliver the Community licence and its counterpart (if any) immediately to the Secretary of State.

(2) If the Secretary of State is at any time satisfied on inquiry that a Community licence holder who is normally resident in Great Britain at that time is suffering from a prospective disability, the Secretary of State may—

    (a) serve notice in writing requiring the Community licence holder to deliver the Community licence and its counterpart (if any) immediately to the Secretary of State, and

    (b) on receipt of the Community licence and its counterpart (if any) grant to the Community licence holder, free of charge, a licence for a period determined by the Secretary of State under section 99(1)(b) of this Act.

(3) Where, in relation to a Community licence holder who is normally resident in Great Britain, the Secretary of State is at any time under a duty to serve notice on him in pursuance of section 92(5) of this Act, the Secretary of State may include in that notice a requirement that the Community licence holder deliver the Community licence and its counterpart (if any) immediately to the Secretary of State.

(4) A person who—

    (a) is required under, or by virtue of, any of subsections (1) to (3) above to deliver his Community licence and its counterpart (if any) to the Secretary of State, but

    (b) without reasonable excuse, fails to do so,

is guilty of an offence.

(5) Where a Community licence holder to whom a counterpart of his Community licence is issued under section 99B of this Act —

    (a) is required under, or by virtue of, any of subsections (1) to (3) above to deliver his Community licence and its counterpart to the Secretary of State, and

    (b) is not in possession of them in consequence of the fact that he has surrendered them to a constable or authorised person (within the meaning of Part III of the Road Traffic Offenders Act 1988) on receiving a fixed penalty notice given to him under section 54 of that Act,

he does not fail to comply with any such requirement if he delivers the Community licence and its counterpart to the Secretary of State immediately on their return.

(6) Where a Community licence holder is served with a notice in pursuance of any of subsections (1) to (3) above, he shall cease to be authorised by virtue of section 99A(1) of this Act to drive in Great Britain a motor vehicle of any class from such date as may be specified in the notice, not being earlier than the date of service of the notice.]

[Section 99C was inserted by the Driving Licences (Community Driving **A18.251**
Licence) Regulations 1996 (SI 1996/1974) reg.2 and Sch.1, para.11 (not reproduced in this work).

With effect from a day (days) to be appointed and in relation to endorsement (all drivers), the following amendments will be made to s.99C by the Road Safety Act 2006 s.10 and Sch.3, para.12, s.59 and Sch.7(4):

    1. in s.99C(1)–(4), the words "and its counterpart (if any)" will be omitted in each place;

2. *s.99C(5) will be omitted.]*

[Information relating to disabilities, etc.

A18.252   **99D.** Section 94 of this Act shall apply to a Community licence holder who is normally resident in Great Britain as if—

    (a) in subsection (1), for the words from the beginning to "aware" there were substituted "If a Community licence holder who is authorised by virtue of section 99A(1) of this Act to drive in Great Britain a motor vehicle of any class, is aware immediately before the relevant date (as defined by section 99A(8) of this Act), or becomes aware on or after that date",

    (b) for subsection (3A) there were substituted—

"(3A) A person who is authorised by virtue of section 99A(1) of this Act to drive in Great Britain a motor vehicle of any class and who drives on a road a motor vehicle of that class is guilty of an offence if at any earlier time while he was so authorised he was required by subsection (1) above to notify the Secretary of State but has failed without reasonable excuse to do so,"

    (c) in subsection (4), the words "an applicant for, or", in both places where they occur, were omitted,

    (d) in subsection (5), the words "applicant or" and the words from the beginning of paragraph (c) to "provisional licence" were omitted,

    (e) in subsection (6)(b), the words "applicant or", in both places where they occur, were omitted,

    (f) in subsection (7), the words "applicant or" were omitted, and

    (g) in subsection (8) —

      (i) for "93" there were substituted "99C", and

      (ii) the words "applicant or", in both places where they occur, were omitted.]

A18.253   *[Section 99D was inserted by the Driving Licences (Community Driving Licence) Regulations 1996 (SI 1996/1974) reg.2 and Sch.1, para.12 (not reproduced in this work).]*

[Return of Community licences delivered to Secretary of State

A18.254   **99E.** *[Omitted.]*]

Appeals

Appeals relating to licences

A18.255   **100.**—(1) A person who is aggrieved by the Secretary of State's—

    (a) refusal to grant or revocation of a licence in pursuance of section 92 or 93 of this Act, or

    (b) determination under section 99(1)(b) of this Act to grant a licence for three years or less, or

    (c) revocation of a licence in pursuance of section 99(3) [or (3A)] of this Act,

or by a notice served on him in pursuance of section 92(5) [, 99C or 109B] of this

Act may, after giving to the Secretary of State notice of his intention to do so, appeal to a magistrates' court …

(2) On any such appeal the court … may make such order as it or he thinks fit and the order shall be binding on the Secretary of State.

(3) It is hereby declared that, without prejudice to section 90 of this Act, in any proceedings under this section the court … is not entitled to entertain any question as to whether the appellant passed a test of competence to drive if he was declared by the person who conducted it to have failed it.

[Section 100 is printed as amended by the Driving Licences (Community Driving Licence) Regulations 1996 (SI 1996/1974) reg.2 and Sch.1, para.14 (not reproduced in this work); the Crime (International Co-operation) Act 2003 s.91 and Sch.5, para.22; the Courts Act 2003 s.109(1) and (3), Sch.8, para.307 and Sch.10. **A18.256**

Words relating exclusively and expressly to Scotland have been omitted from s.100.]

Disqualification (otherwise than on conviction)

Disqualification of persons under age

101.—(1) A person is disqualified for holding or obtaining a licence to drive a **A18.257** motor vehicle of a class specified in the following Table if he is under the age specified in relation to it in the second column of the Table.

[TABLE

	Class of motor vehicle	Age (in years)
1.	Invalid carriage	16
2.	Moped	16
3.	Motor bicycle	17
4.	Agricultural or forestry tractor	17
5.	Small vehicle	17
6.	Medium-sized goods vehicle	18
7.	Other motor vehicle	21]

(2) The Secretary of State may by regulations provide that subsection (1) above shall have effect as if for the classes of vehicles and the ages specified in the Table in that subsection there were substituted different classes of vehicles and ages or different classes of vehicles or different ages.

(3) Subject to subsection (4) below, the regulations may—

(a) apply to persons of a class specified in or under the regulations,

(b) apply in circumstances so specified,

(c) impose conditions or create exemptions or provide for the imposition of conditions or the creation of exemptions,

(d) contain such transitional and supplemental provisions (including provisions amending section 108, 120 or 183(5) of this Act) as the Secretary of State considers necessary or expedient.

(4) For the purpose of defining the class of persons to whom, the class of

vehicles to which, the circumstances in which or the conditions subject to which regulations made by virtue of subsection (2) above are to apply where an approved training scheme for drivers is in force, it is sufficient for the regulations to refer to a document which embodies the terms (or any of the terms) of the scheme or to a document which is in force in pursuance of the scheme.

(5) In subsection (4) above—

"*approved*" means approved for the time being by the Secretary of State for the purpose of the regulations,

"*training scheme for drivers*" means a scheme for training persons to drive vehicles of a class in relation to which the age which is in force under this section (but apart from any such scheme) is 21 years,

but no approved training scheme for drivers shall be amended without the approval of the Secretary of State.

A18.258   *[Section 101 is printed as amended by the Driving Licences (Community Driving Licence) Regulations 1996 reg.2 and Sch.1, para.15 (not reproduced in this work).*

The Motor Vehicles (Driving Licences) Regulations 1999 (SI 1999/2864) (q.v.) were made in part under s.101(2) and (3); see, in particular, ibid., reg.9.

Section 101 (in so far as it prohibits persons aged under 21 years from holding or obtaining licences to drive motor vehicles or persons under 18 years from holding or obtaining licences to drive medium-sized goods vehicles, but subject to any regulations under s.101(2)) does not apply to vehicles in the service of a visiting force (as defined); see the Visiting Forces and International Headquarters (Application of Law) Order 1999 (SI 1999/1736; not reproduced in this work) art.8(5).]

Disqualification to prevent duplication of licences

A18.259   **102.**—[(1)] A person is disqualified for obtaining a licence authorising him to drive a motor vehicle of any class so long as he is the holder of another licence authorising him to drive a motor vehicle of that class, whether the licence is suspended or not.

[(2) A person is also disqualified for holding or obtaining a licence authorising him to drive a motor vehicle of any class so long as he is authorised by virtue of section 109(1) of this Act to drive a motor vehicle of that or a corresponding class.]

A18.260   *[Section 102 is printed as amended by the Crime (International Co-operation) Act 2003 s.78(4).]*

[Disqualification if disqualified in Northern Ireland etc.]

Disqualification while disqualified in Northern Ireland, Isle of Man, Channel Islands or Gibraltar

A18.261   [**102A.**—(1) A person is disqualified for holding or obtaining a licence to drive a motor vehicle of any class so long as he is subject to a relevant disqualification imposed outside Great Britain.

(2) For the purposes of this section a person is subject to a relevant disqualification imposed outside Great Britain if, in respect of any offence—

(a) a court in Northern Ireland disqualifies him for holding or obtaining a Northern Ireland licence,

(b) a court in the Isle of Man or any of the Channel Islands disqualifies him for holding or obtaining a British external licence, or

(c) a court in Gibraltar disqualifies him for holding or obtaining a licence to drive a motor vehicle granted under the law of Gibraltar.

(3) A certificate signed by the Secretary of State which states, in respect of a person, any matter relating to the question whether he is subject to a relevant disqualification imposed outside Great Britain shall be evidence (in Scotland, sufficient evidence) of the matter so stated.

(4) A certificate stating that matter and purporting to be so signed shall be deemed to be so signed unless the contrary is proved.]

[Section 102A is printed as inserted by the Crime (International Co-operation) **A18.262**
Act 2003 s.76 (which also inserted the heading preceding s.102A).

For corresponding provisions, see the Road Traffic (Driving Disqualifications) (Northern Ireland) Order 2003 (SI 2003/2903 (NI 16)), which amends, inter alia, the Road Traffic (Northern Ireland) Order 1981 (SR 1981/154 (NI 1)).]

[Effects of disqualification]

[Obtaining licence, or driving, while disqualified

103.—(1) A person is guilty of an offence if, while disqualified for holding or   **A18.263**
obtaining a licence, he—

(a) obtains a licence, or

(b) drives a motor vehicle on a road.

(2) A licence obtained by a person who is disqualified is of no effect (or, where the disqualification relates only to vehicles of a particular class, is of no effect in relation to vehicles of that class).

(3) [...]

(4) [Subsection (1) above does] not apply in relation to disqualification by virtue of section 101 of this Act.

(5) [Subsection (1)(b) above does] not apply in relation to disqualification by virtue of section 102 of this Act.

(6) In the application of [subsection (1)] above to a person whose disqualification is limited to the driving of motor vehicles of a particular class by virtue of—

(a) section 102 [117 or 117A] of this Act, or

(b) subsection (9) of section 36 of the Road Traffic Offenders Act 1988 (disqualification until test is passed),

the references to disqualification for holding or obtaining a licence and driving motor vehicles are references to disqualification for holding or obtaining a licence to drive and driving motor vehicles of that class.]

[Section 103 is printed as substituted by the Road Traffic Act 1991 s.19 (which   **A18.264**
also inserted the heading preceding s.103), and as subsequently amended by the Driving Licences (Community Driving Licence) Regulations 1996 (SI 1996/1974) reg.2 and Sch.1, para.16 (not reproduced in this work); the Police Reform Act 2002 s.107, Sch.7, para.11(1)–(5) and Sch.8 (in relation to England and Wales only).]

Miscellaneous

Conduct of proceedings in certain courts by or against the Secretary of State.

A18.265   **104.** *[Omitted.]*

Regulations under this Part and the Road Traffic Offenders Act 1988

A18.266   **105.** *[Omitted.]*

Destination of fees for licences, etc.

A18.267   **106.** *[Omitted.]*

Service of notices under sections 92, 93 and 99(3)

A18.268   **107.** *[Omitted.]*

Interpretation

A18.269   **108.**—(1) In this Part of this Act —

[*"agricultural or forestry tractor"* means a motor vehicle which—

(a) has two or more axles,

(b) is constructed for use as a tractor for work off the road in connection with agriculture or forestry, and

(c) is primarily used as such,]

"articulated goods vehicle" means a motor vehicle which is so constructed that a trailer designed to carry goods may by partial superimposition be attached to it in such manner as to cause a substantial part of the weight of the trailer to be borne by the motor vehicle, and *"articulated goods vehicle combination"* means an articulated goods vehicle with a trailer so attached,

[*"British external licence"* and *"British Forces licence"* have the meanings given by section 88(8) [*q.v.*] of this Act,]

"Community licence" means a document issued in respect of [an EEA State] other than the United Kingdom by an authority of that or [another EEA State] (including the United Kingdom) authorising the holder to drive a motor vehicle, not being—

(a) a document containing a statement to the effect that that or a previous document was issued in exchange for a document issued in respect of a State other than [an EEA State], or

(b) a document in any of the forms for an international driving permit annexed to the Paris Convention on Motor Traffic of 1926 [*Cd. 3510*], the Geneva Convention on Road Traffic of 1949 [*Cmd. 578*] or the Vienna Convention on Road Traffic of 1968 [*Cmnd. 4032*], [or]

[(c) a document issued for a purpose corresponding to that mentioned in section 97(2) of this Act,]

[*"counterpart"* —

(a) in relation to a licence under this Part of this Act, means a document in such form as the Secretary of State may determine, issued with the licence, containing such information as he determines and designed for the endorsement of particulars relating to the licence, [...]

[(aa) in relation to a Northern Ireland licence, has the meaning given by section 109A of this Act (except in the definition of "Northern Ireland counterpart" below), and]

(b) in relation to a Community licence, has the meaning given by section 99B of this Act,]

"disability" has the meaning given by section 92 of this Act,

"disqualified" means disqualified for holding or obtaining a licence [(or, in cases where the disqualification is limited, a licence to drive motor vehicles of the class to which the disqualification relates)], and "disqualification" is to be interpreted accordingly,

[*"EEA Agreement"* means the Agreement on the European Economic Area signed at Oporto on 2nd May 1992 as adjusted by the Protocol signed at Brussels on 17th March 1993,]

[*"EEA State"* means a State which is a Contracting Party to the EEA Agreement,]

[*"exchangeable licence"* means a document authorising a person to drive a motor vehicle (not being a document mentioned in paragraph (b) of the definition of "Community licence")—

(a) issued in respect of Gibraltar by an authority of Gibraltar,

(b) issued in respect of a country or territory which is designed without restriction by an order under subsection (2)(a) below by an authority of that country or territory, or

(c) issued in respect of a country or territory which is designated by a restricted order under subsection (2)(b) below by an authority of that country or territory, being a document which is a licence of a description specified in that order,

and a licence of a description so specified as to which provision is made as mentioned in subsection (2B) below is only an exchangeable licence to the extent that it authorises its holder to drive vehicles of a class specified in the order,]

[*"full licence"* means a licence other than a provisional licence,]

[*"large goods vehicle"* has the meaning given by section 121(1) of this Act,]

"licence" [(except where the context otherwise requires)] means a licence to drive a motor vehicle granted under this Part of this Act ...,

"maximum gross weight", in relation to a motor vehicle or trailer, means the weight of the vehicle laden with the heaviest load which it is constructed or adapted to carry,

"maximum train weight", in relation to an articulated goods vehicle combination, means the weight of the combination laden with the heaviest load which it is constructed or adapted to carry,

[*"medium-sized goods vehicle"* means a motor vehicle—

(a) which is constructed or adapted to carry or to haul goods,

    (b) which is not adapted to carry more than nine persons inclusive of the driver, and

    (c) the permissible maximum weight of which exceeds 3.5 but not 7.5 tonnes,

and includes a combination of such a motor vehicle and a trailer where the relevant maximum weight of the trailer does not exceed 750 kilograms,]

["*moped*" means a motor vehicle which has fewer than four wheels and—

    (a) in the case of a vehicle the first use (as defined in regulations made for the purpose of section 97(3)(d) of this Act) of which occurred before 1st August 1977, has a cylinder capacity not exceeding 50 cubic centimetres and is equipped with pedals by means of which the vehicle is capable of being propelled, and

    (b) in any other case, has a maximum design speed not exceeding 50 kilometres per hour and, if propelled by an internal combustion engine, has a cylinder capacity not exceeding 50 cubic centimetres,]

["*motor bicycle*" means a motor vehicle which—

    (a) has two wheels, and

    (b) has a maximum design speed exceeding [45 kilometres per hour] and, if powered by an internal combustion engine, has a cylinder capacity exceeding 50 cubic centimetres,

and includes a combination of such a motor vehicle and a side-car,]

["*Northern Ireland driving licence*" or "*Northern Ireland licence*" means a licence to drive a motor vehicle granted under the law of Northern Ireland [and "*Northern Ireland counterpart*" means the document issued with the Northern Ireland licence as a counterpart under the law of Northern Ireland],]

["*passenger-carrying vehicle*" has the meaning given by section 121(1) of this Act,]

"*permissible maximum weight*", in relation to a goods vehicle (of whatever description), means—

    (a) in the case of a motor vehicle which neither is an articulated goods vehicle nor is drawing a trailer, the relevant maximum weight of the vehicle,

    (b) in the case of an articulated goods vehicle—

        (i) when drawing only a semi-trailer, the relevant maximum train weight of the articulated goods vehicle combination,

        (ii) when drawing a trailer as well as a semi-trailer, the aggregate of the relevant maximum train weight of the articulated goods vehicle combination and the relevant maximum weight of the trailer,

        (iii) when drawing a trailer but not a semi-trailer, the aggregate of the relevant maximum weight of the articulated goods vehicle and the relevant maximum weight of the trailer,

    (iv) when drawing neither a semi-trailer nor a trailer, the relevant maximum weight of the vehicle,

   (c) in the case of a motor vehicle (not being an articulated goods vehicle) which is drawing a trailer, the aggregate of the relevant maximum weight of the motor vehicle and the relevant maximum weight of the trailer,

"prescribed" means prescribed by regulations,

"prospective disability" has the meaning given by section 92 of this Act,

"provisional licence" means a licence granted by virtue of section 97(2) of this Act,

"regulations" means regulations made under section 105 of this Act,

"relevant disability" has the meaning given by section 92 of this Act,

[*"relevant external law"* has the meaning given by section 88(8) [*q.v.*] of this Act,]

"relevant maximum weight", in relation to a motor vehicle or trailer, means—

   (a) in the case of a vehicle to which regulations under section 49 of this Act apply which is required by regulations under section 41 of this Act to have a maximum gross weight for the vehicle marked on a plate issued by the Secretary of State under regulations under section 41, the maximum gross weight so marked on the vehicle,

   (b) in the case of a vehicle which is required by regulations under section 41 of this Act to have a maximum gross weight for the vehicle marked on the vehicle and does not also have a maximum gross weight marked on it as mentioned in paragraph (a) above, the maximum gross weight marked on the vehicle,

   (c) in the case of a vehicle on which a maximum gross weight is marked by the same means as would be required by regulations under section 41 of this Act if those regulations applied to the vehicle, the maximum gross weight so marked on the vehicle,

   (d) in the case of a vehicle on which a maximum gross weight is not marked as mentioned in paragraph (a), (b) or (c) above, the notional maximum gross weight of the vehicle, that is to say, such weight as is produced by multiplying the unladen weight of the vehicle by the number prescribed by the Secretary of State for the class of vehicle into which that vehicle falls,

"relevant maximum train weight", in relation to an articulated goods vehicle combination, means—

   (a) in the case of an articulated goods vehicle to which regulations under section 49 of this Act apply which is required by regulations under section 41 of this Act to have a maximum train weight for the combination marked on a plate issued by the Secretary of State under regulations under section 41, the maximum train weight so marked on the motor vehicle,

(b) in the case of an articulated goods vehicle which is required by regulations under section 41 of this Act to have a maximum train weight for the combination marked on the vehicle and does not also have a maximum train weight marked on it as mentioned in paragraph (a) above, the maximum train weight marked on the motor vehicle,

(c) in the case of an articulated goods vehicle on which a maximum train weight is marked by the same means as would be required by regulations under section 41 of this Act if those regulations applied to the vehicle, the maximum train weight so marked on the motor vehicle,

(d) in the case of an articulated goods vehicle on which a maximum train weight is not marked as mentioned in paragraph (a), (b) or (c) above, the notional maximum gross weight of the combination, that is to say, such weight as is produced by multiplying the sum of the unladen weights of the motor vehicle and the semi-trailer by the number prescribed by the Secretary of State for the class of articulated goods vehicle combination into which that combination falls,

"*semi-trailer*", in relation to an articulated goods vehicle, means a trailer attached to it in the manner described in the definition of articulated goods vehicle,

*   *   *

[*"small vehicle"* means a motor vehicle (other than an invalid carriage, moped or motor bicycle) which—

(a) is not constructed or adapted to carry more than nine persons inclusive of the driver, and

(b) has a maximum gross weight not exceeding 3.5 tonnes,

and includes a combination of such a motor vehicle and a trailer,]

*   *   *

"*test of competence to drive*" means such a test conducted under section 89 of this Act.

[*"approved training course for motor cyclists"* and, in relation to such a course, *"prescribed certificate of completion"* mean respectively any course of training approved under, and the certificate of completion prescribed in, regulations under section 97(3A) of this Act.]

(2), (2A), (2B), (3) *[Power to make orders designating countries, etc. for purposes of the definition of "exchangeable licences" in subs.(1).]*

A18.270   *[Section 108 is printed as amended by the Road Traffic (Driver Licensing and Information Systems) Act 1989 s.7 and Sch.3, para.15(a)–(e) and (f); the Driving Licences (Community Driving Licence) Regulations 1996 (SI 1996/1974) reg.2 and Sch.1, para.19 (not reproduced in this work); the Deregulation (Exchangeable Driving Licences) Order 1998 (SI 1998/1917 art.2 (not reproduced in this work); the Driving Licences (Community Driving Licence) Regulations 1998 (SI 1998/1420) regs 2 and 11 (not reproduced in this work); the Crime (International Co-operation) Act 2003 s.91, Sch.5, para.25 and Sch.6.*

With effect from a day to be appointed and in relation to endorsement (all drivers), the definition of "counterpart" will be omitted by the Road Safety Act 2006 s.10 and Sch.3, para.14, s.59 and Sch.7(4).

The following orders have effect as if made under s.108(2): the Driving Licences (Exchangeable Licences) Order 1984 (SI 1984/672), taking effect on June 1, 1984; the Driving Licences (Exchangeable Licences) Order 1985 (SI 1985/65), taking effect on February 2, 1985; the Driving Licences (Exchangeable Licences) (No.2) Order 1985 (SI 1985/1461), taking effect on November 1, 1985; the Driving Licences (Exchangeable Licences) Order 1999 (SI 1999/1641), taking effect on July 2, 1999; the Driving Licences (Exchangeable Licences) (Amendment) Order 2002 (SI 2002/1593), taking effect on June 21, 2002; the Driving Licences (Exchangeable Licences) Order 2002 (SI 2002/2379), taking effect from September 20, 2002; the Driving Licences (Exchangeable Licences) Order 2004 (SI 2004/301), taking effect from February 26, 2004, the Driving Licences (Exchangeable Licences) Order 2007 (SI 2007/95), taking effect from January 31, 2007, the Driving Licences (Exchangeable Licences) (Amendment) Order 2007 (SI 2007/96) (removing Kenya from the list of designated countries), taking effect January 31, 2007, in respect of driving licences issued in the countries specified and granted to persons who had passed a driving test in vehicles with automatic transmission.

As a result of these orders the following countries have been designated for the purposes of s.108(2):

Australia	*SI 1984/672*
Austria	*SI 1985/1461*
Barbados	*SI 1985/65*
British Virgin Islands	*SI 1985/65*
Canada (Provinces and Territories of)	*SI 1999/1641*
Cyprus	*SI 1985/65*
Falkland Islands	*SI 2004/301*
Faroe Islands	*SI 2007/95*
Finland	*SI 1985/65*
Hong Kong	*SI 1984/672*
Japan	*SI 1985/1461*
Korea	*SI 2002/2379*
Malta	*SI 1985/65*
Monaco	*SI 2002/2379*
New Zealand	*SI 1984/672*
Norway	*SI 1984/672*
Singapore	*SI 1984/672*
South Africa	*SI 1999/1641*
Sweden	*SI 1984/672*
Switzerland	*SI 1984/672*
Zimbabwe	*SI 1985/65.*

The Motor Vehicles (Driving Licences) Regulations 1999 (SI 1999/2864) below were made in part under s.108(1).

As to the European Economic Area, see the introductory note to Section C, below.]

Provisions as to Northern Ireland drivers' licences

A18.271 **109.**—(1) The holder of a [Northern Ireland driving licence] may drive, and a person may cause or permit the holder of such a licence to drive, in Great Britain [in accordance with that licence], a motor vehicle of any class which he is authorised by that licence to drive, and which he is not disqualified from driving under this Part [or Part IV] of this Act, notwithstanding that he is not the holder of a licence under this Part of this Act.

(2) Any driver holding a [Northern Ireland driving licence] shall be under the like obligation to produce such a licence [and its counterpart as if they had respectively been a licence granted under this Part of this Act and the counterpart to such a licence;] and the provisions—

(a) of this Act, [...]

as to the production of licences [and counterparts of licences] granted under this Part of this Act shall apply accordingly.

[...]

A18.272 *[Section 109 is printed as amended by the Road Traffic (Driver Licensing and Information Systems) Act 1989 s.7 and Sch.3, para.16; the Driving Licences (Community Driving Licence) Regulations 1990 (SI 1990/144); the Crime (International Co-operation) Act 2003 s.91, Sch.5, para.26 and Sch.6.*

With effect from a day to be appointed and in relation to endorsement (all drivers), s.109(2) will be substituted by the Road Safety Act 2006 s.10 and Sch.3, para.15 as follows:

[(2) For the purposes of this Act, any driver holding a Northern Ireland licence shall be under the same obligation to produce such a licence as if it had been a licence granted under this Part of this Act, and the provisions of this Act as to the production of licences granted under this Part of this Act shall apply accordingly.]*

[Counterparts issued to Northern Ireland licence holders

A18.273 **109A.**—(1) The Secretary of State may issue to any Northern Ireland licence holder who—

(a) has delivered his Northern Ireland licence to the Secretary of State, and

(b) has provided him with the information specified in, or required under, subsection (3) below (whether or not in pursuance of this section),

a document (referred to in this Part of this Act in relation to a Northern Ireland licence as a "counterpart").

(2) The counterpart must—

(a) be in such form, and

(b) contain such information,

designed for the endorsement of particulars relating to the Northern Ireland licence as the Secretary of State may determine.

(3) The information referred to in subsection (1) above is—

(a) the name and address (whether in Great Britain or Northern Ireland) of the Northern Ireland licence holder;

(b) his date of birth;

(c) the classes of vehicle which he is authorised by his Northern Ireland licence to drive;

(d) the period of validity of the licence;

(e) whether it was granted in exchange for a licence issued by a state other than an EEA State; and

(f) such other information as the Secretary of State may require for the purposes of the proper exercise of any of his functions under this Part or Part 4 of this Act.

(4) The Secretary of State—

(a) may endorse a Northern Ireland licence delivered to him (whether or not in pursuance of this section) in such manner as he may determine—

(i) with any part of the information specified in, or required under, subsection (3) above; or

(ii) with information providing a means of ascertaining that information or any part of it; and

(b) must return the Northern Ireland licence to the holder.

(5) Subsections (6) to (9), (11) (with the omission of paragraph (a)) and (12) of section 99B of this Act apply for the purposes of this section as if the references to a Community licence were references to a Northern Ireland licence.]

[Section 109A is printed as inserted by the Crime (International Co-operation) Act 2003, s.77(1). **A18.274**

For corresponding provisions, see the Road Traffic (Driving Disqualifications) (Northern Ireland) Order 2003 (SI 2003/2903 (NI 16)), which amends, inter alia, the Road Traffic (Northern Ireland) Order 1981 (SR 1981/154 (NI 1))

With effect from a day (or days) to be appointed and in relation to endorsement (all drivers), the following amendments will be made to s.109A by the Road Safety Act 2006 s.10 and Sch.3, para.16:

1. *for s.109A(1) and (2) the following text will be substituted:*

[(1) The Secretary of State may endorse the driving record of a Northern Ireland licence holder who delivers to him a Northern Ireland licence together with the information specified in, or required under, subsection (3) below with any part of that information.]

2. *for s.109A(4) and (5) the following text will be substituted:*

[(4) Where the name of a Northern Ireland licence holder as specified in his Northern Ireland licence ceases to be correct, he may deliver his Northern Ireland licence immediately to the Secretary of State and provide him with particulars of the alterations falling to be made in the name on it.

(5) On the delivery of a Northern Ireland licence by any person in pursuance of subsection (4) above, the Secretary of State may endorse the Northern Ireland licence and that person's driving record with the correct name and must return the Northern Ireland licence to that person.]

3. *in the heading, the words* "**Information about**" *will be substituted for the words* "**Counterparts issued to**".*]*

[Revocation of authorisation conferred by Northern Ireland licence because of disability or prospective disability

109B.—(1) If the Secretary of State is at any time satisfied on inquiry— **A18.275**

(a) that a Northern Ireland licence holder is suffering from a relevant disability, and

(b) that he would be required by virtue of section 92(3) of this Act to refuse an application made by the holder at that time for a licence authorising him to drive a vehicle of the class in respect of which his Northern Ireland licence was issued or a class corresponding to that class,

he may serve notice in writing requiring the licence holder to deliver immediately to the Secretary of State his Northern Ireland licence together with its Northern Ireland counterpart and its counterpart (if any) issued to him under this Part of this Act ("the relevant counterparts").

(2) If the Secretary of State is satisfied on inquiry that a Northern Ireland licence holder is suffering from a prospective disability, he may—

(a) serve notice in writing on the Northern Ireland licence holder requiring him to deliver immediately to the Secretary of State his Northern Ireland licence together with the relevant counterparts, and

(b) on receipt of the Northern Ireland licence and those counterparts and of an application made for the purposes of this subsection, grant to the Northern Ireland licence holder, free of charge, a licence for a period determined by the Secretary of State under section 99(1)(b) of this Act.

(3) The Secretary of State may require a person to provide—

(a) evidence of his name, address, sex and date and place of birth, and

(b) a photograph which is a current likeness of him,

before granting a licence to him on an application for the purposes of subsection (2) above.

(4) A person who—

(a) is required under, or by virtue of, this section to deliver to the Secretary of State his Northern Ireland licence and the relevant counterparts, but

(b) without reasonable excuse, fails to do so,

is guilty of an offence.

(5) Where a Northern Ireland licence holder to whom a counterpart is issued under section 109A of this Act—

(a) is required under, or by virtue of, this section to deliver his Northern Ireland licence and that counterpart to the Secretary of State, and

(b) is not in possession of them in consequence of the fact that he has surrendered them to a constable or authorised person (within the meaning of Part 3 of the Road Traffic Offenders Act 1988) on receiving a fixed penalty notice given to him under section 54 of that Act,

he does not fail to comply with any such requirement if he delivers them to the Secretary of State immediately on their return.

(6) Where a Northern Ireland licence holder is served with a notice in pursuance of this section, he shall cease to be authorised by virtue of section 109(1) of this Act to drive in Great Britain a motor vehicle of any class from such date as may be specified in the notice, not being earlier than the date of service of the notice.

(7) Where a Northern Ireland licence is delivered to the Secretary of State in pursuance of this section, he must—

    (a) send the licence and its Northern Ireland counterpart to the licensing authority in Northern Ireland, and

    (b) explain to them his reasons for so doing.]

[Section 109B is printed as inserted by the Crime (International Co-operation)   **A18.276**
Act 2003 s.79(2).

For corresponding provisions, see the Road Traffic (Driving Disqualifications) (Northern Ireland) Order 2003 (SI 2003/2903 (NI 16)), which amends, inter alia, the Road Traffic (Northern Ireland) Order 1981 (SR 1981/154 (NI 1)).

With effect from a day (or days) to be appointed and in relation to endorsement (all drivers), the following amendments will be made to s.109B by the Road Safety Act 2006 s.10 and Sch.3, para.17, s.59 and Sch.7(4):

    1. *in s.109B(1), the words from "together" to the end will be omitted;*

    2. *in s.109B(2), the words "together with the relevant counterparts" will be omitted in para.(a), and, in para.(b), the words "and those counterparts" will be omitted;*

    3. *in s.109B(4), the words "and the relevant counterparts" will be omitted;*

    4. *s.109B(5) will be omitted.]*

[Information relating to disabilities, etc.

109C. *[Omitted.]*]   **A18.277**

PART IV

LICENSING OF DRIVERS OF LARGE GOODS VEHICLES AND PASSENGER-CARRYING VEHICLES

Licensing of drivers of large goods vehicles and passenger-carrying vehicles

110.—(1) Licences under Part III of this Act to drive motor vehicles of classes   **A18.278**
which include large goods vehicles or passenger-carrying vehicles or large goods vehicles or passenger-carrying vehicles of any class shall be granted by the Secretary of State in accordance with this Part of this Act and shall, in so far as they authorise the driving of large goods vehicles or passenger-carrying vehicles, be otherwise subject to this Part of this Act in addition to Part III of this Act.

(2) In this Part of this Act —

    [*"Community licence"* has the same meaning as in Part III of this Act;]

    [*"LGV Community licence"* means a Community licence in so far as it authorises a person to drive large goods vehicles of any class;]

    "large goods vehicle driver's licence" means a licence under Part III of this Act in so far as it authorises a person to drive large goods vehicles of any class; and

    [*"PCV Community licence"* means a Community licence in so far as it authorises a person to drive passenger-carrying vehicles of any class;]

    "passenger-carrying vehicle driver's licence" means a licence under Part

III of this Act in so far as it authorises a person to drive passenger-carrying vehicles of any class.

A18.279   *[Section 110 is printed as substituted by the Road Traffic (Driver Licensing and Information Systems) Act 1989 s.2 and Sch.2; the Driving Licences (Community Driving Licence) Regulations 1996 (SI 1996/1974) reg.2 and Sch.1, para.20 (not reproduced in this work).]*

Functions of traffic commissioners

A18.280   **111.**—(1) The traffic commissioner for any area constituted for the purposes of the Public Passenger Vehicles Act 1981 shall exercise the functions conferred by the following provisions of this Part of this Act relating to the conduct of

     [(a) applicants for and holders of large goods vehicle and passenger-carrying vehicle drivers' licences, and]

     [(b) holders of LGV Community licences and PCV Community licences.]

(2) Traffic commissioners shall, in the exercise of those functions, act in accordance with directions given by the Secretary of State; but such directions shall be general directions not relating to the exercise of functions in a particular case.

A18.281   *[Section 111 is printed as substituted by the Road Traffic (Driver Licensing and Information Systems) Act 1989 s.2 and Sch.2; the Driving Licences (Community Driving Licence) Regulations 1996 (SI 1996/1974) reg.2 and Sch.1, para.21 (not reproduced in this work).]*

Grant of licences: fitness as regards conduct

A18.282   **112.** The Secretary of State shall not grant to an applicant a large goods vehicle driver's licence or a passenger-carrying vehicle driver's licence unless he is satisfied, having regard to his conduct, that he is a fit person to hold the licence applied for.

A18.283   *[Section 112 is printed as substituted by the Road Traffic (Driver Licensing and Information Systems) Act 1989 s.2 and Sch.2.]*

Grant of licences: referral of matters of conduct to traffic commissioners

A18.284   **113.**—(1) Any question arising under section 112 of this Act relating to the conduct of an applicant for a licence may be referred by the Secretary of State to the traffic commissioner for the area in which the applicant resides.

(2) On any reference under subsection (1) above, the traffic commissioner shall determine whether the applicant for the licence is or is not, having regard to his conduct, a fit person to hold a licence to drive large goods vehicles or passenger-carrying vehicles, as the case may be.

(3) A traffic commissioner to whom a reference has been made under this section may require the applicant for the licence to furnish the commissioner with such information as he may require and may, by notice to the applicant, require him to attend before the commissioner at the time and place specified by the commissioner to furnish the information and to answer such questions (if any) relating to his application as the commissioner may put to him.

(4) If the applicant fails without reasonable excuse to furnish information to or attend before or answer questions properly put by a commissioner when required to do so under subsection (3) above, the commissioner may decline to

proceed further with the application and, if he does so, the commissioner shall notify the Secretary of State of that fact and the Secretary of State shall refuse to grant the licence.

(5) The traffic commissioner to whom a reference has been made under this section shall, unless he has declined to proceed further with the application, notify the Secretary of State and the applicant of his determination in the matter and the decision of the commissioner shall be binding on the Secretary of State.

[Section 113 is printed as substituted by the Road Traffic (Driver Licensing and Information Systems) Act 1989 s.2 and Sch.2.]   **A18.285**

Conditions of certain licences

114.—(1) [The following licences, that is to say—   **A18.286**

    (a) a large goods vehicle or passenger-carrying vehicle driver's licence issued as a provisional licence,

    (b) a full large goods vehicle or passenger-carrying vehicle driver's licence granted to a person under the age of 21, and

    (c) a LGV Community licence held by a person under the age of 21 who is normally resident in Great Britain,]

shall be subject to the prescribed conditions, and if the holder of the licence fails, without reasonable excuse, to comply with any of the conditions he is guilty of an offence.

(2) It is an offence for a person knowingly to cause or permit another person who is under the age of 21 to drive a large goods vehicle of any class or a passenger-carrying vehicle of any class in contravention of the prescribed conditions to which that other person's licence is subject.

[Section 114 is printed as substituted by the Road Traffic (Driver Licensing and Information Systems) Act 1989 s.2 and Sch.2; the Driving Licences (Community Driving Licence) Regulations 1996 (SI 1996/1974) reg.2 and Sch.1, para.22 (not reproduced in this work).   **A18.287**

The Motor Vehicles (Driving Licences) Regulations 1999 (SI 1999/2864) (q.v.) were made in part under s.114(1); see, in particular, ibid. reg.54.]

Revocation or suspension of licences

115.—(1) A large goods vehicle or passenger-carrying vehicle driver's   **A18.288**
licence—

    (a) must be revoked if there come into existence, in relation to its holder, such circumstances relating to his conduct as may be prescribed;

    (b) must be revoked or suspended if his conduct is such as to make him unfit to hold such a licence;

and where the licence is suspended under paragraph (b) above it shall during the time of suspension be of no effect.

(2) Where it appears that the conduct of the holder of a licence falls within both paragraph (a) and paragraph (b) of subsection (1) above, proceedings shall be taken or continued under paragraph (a) and not under paragraph (b) and accordingly the power to suspend the licence, rather than revoke it, shall not be available.

(3) Regulations made for the purposes of [this section [or any of sections 115A, 117 or 117A] of this Act]—

    (a) may make different provision for large goods vehicles and for
        passenger-carrying vehicles and for different descriptions of persons;
        and

    (b) shall provide for the determination of the cases in which,

        [(i) under section 117 of this Act, a person whose licence has been
           revoked, or]

        [(ii) under section 117A of this Act, a person on whom a notice is
           served in pursuance of section 115A(1)(a) of this Act,]

        is to be disqualified indefinitely or for a period and, if for a period, for
        the determination of the period.

A18.289　　*[Section 115 is printed as substituted by the Road Traffic (Driver Licensing
and Information Systems) Act 1989 s.2 and Sch.2, and as amended by the Road
Traffic Act 1991 s.48 and Sch.4, para.64; the Driving Licences (Community
Driving Licence) Regulations 1996 (SI 1996/1974) reg.2 and Sch.1, para.23 (not
reproduced in this work).*

   *The Motor Vehicles (Driving Licences) Regulations 1999 (SI 1999/2864) (q.v.)
were made in part under s.115(1) and (3).*

   *The prescribed circumstances to which reference is made in s.115(1)(a), are
set out in SI 1999/2864, reg.55(1) below; and see also ibid. reg.55(2) and (3).]*

[Community licence holders: cessation of authorisation, etc.

A18.290　　**115A.**—(1) Where, in relation to a holder of a LGV Community licence or
PCV Community licence who is normally resident in Great Britain—

    (a) there exist immediately before the relevant date, or there come into
        existence on or after that date, such circumstances relating to his
        conduct as may be prescribed; or

    (b) his conduct is such as to make him unfit to be authorised by virtue of
        section 99A(1) of this Act to drive in Great Britain a large goods ve-
        hicle or passenger-carrying vehicle (as the case may be),

the Secretary of State must serve notice on the holder requiring him to deliver the
Community licence and its counterpart (if any) immediately to the Secretary of
State and it shall be the duty of the holder to comply with that requirement.

   (2) Where a notice is served in pursuance of subsection (1)(a) or (b) above on
the holder of a LGV Community licence or a PCV Community licence, he shall
cease to be authorised by virtue of section 99A(1) of this Act to drive in Great
Britain a large goods vehicle or passenger-carrying vehicle (as the case may be)
from such date as is specified in the notice, not being earlier than the date of service of the notice.

   (3) Where it appears to the Secretary of State that the conduct of a Community
licence holder falls within both paragraph (a) and paragraph (b) of subsection (1)
above, the Secretary of State must serve notice on the holder in pursuance of the
former paragraph only.

   (4) Any Community licence holder who fails without reasonable excuse to
comply with his duty under subsection (1) above is guilty of an offence.

   (5) In this section *"relevant date"*, in relation to a Community licence holder
who is normally resident in Great Britain, has the same meaning as in section
99A(8) of this Act.]

[Section 115A was inserted by the Driving Licences (Community Driving **A18.291**
Licence) Regulations 1996 (SI 1996/1974) reg.2 and Sch.1, para.24 (not
reproduced in this work).

The prescribed circumstances to which reference is made in s.115(1)(a), are
set out in the Motor Vehicles (Driving Licences) Regulations 1999 (SI 1999/
2864), reg.55(2) below; and see also ibid. reg.55(3) and (4).

With effect from a day to be appointed and in relation to endorsement (all
drivers), in s.115A(1), the words "and its counterpart (if any)" will be omitted by
the Road Safety Act 2006 s.10 and Sch.3, para.18, s.59 and Sch.7(4).]

Revocation or suspension of licences: referral of matters of conduct to traffic commissioners

116.—[(1) Any question arising—   **A18.292**

  (a) under section 116(1)(b) of this Act as to whether a person is or is not, by reason of his conduct, fit to hold a large goods vehicle or passenger-carrying vehicle driver's licence, as the case may be, or

  (b) under section 115A(1)(b) of this Act as to whether the holder of a LGV Community licence or PCV Community licence is or is not, by reason of his conduct, fit to be authorised by virtue of section 99A(1) of this Act to drive in Great Britain a large goods vehicle or passenger-carrying vehicle (as the case may be),

may be referred by the Secretary of State to the traffic commissioner for the area in which the holder of the licence resides.]

(2) Where, on any reference under [subsection (1)(a)] above, the traffic commissioner determines that the holder of the licence is not fit to hold a large goods vehicle or passenger-carrying vehicle driver's licence, as the case may be, he shall also determine whether the conduct of the holder of the licence is such as to require the revocation of his licence or only its suspension; and, if the former, whether the holder of the licence should be disqualified under section 117(2)(a) of this Act (and, if so, for what period) or under section 117(2)(b) of this Act.

[(2A) Where, on any reference under subsection (1)(b) above, the traffic commissioner determines that a Community licence holder is not fit to be authorised by virtue of section 99A(1) of this Act to drive in Great Britain a large goods vehicle or passenger-carrying vehicle (as the case may be), he shall also determine whether the Community licence holder—

  (a) should be disqualified under section 117A(2)(a) of this Act (and, if so, for what period) or under section 117A(2)(b) of this Act, or

  (b) should be granted, free of charge, a large goods vehicle or passenger-carrying vehicle driver's licence (and, if so, from what date it shall take effect).]

(3) A traffic commissioner to whom a reference has been made under subsection (1) above may require the holder of the licence to furnish the commissioner with such information as he may require and may, by notice to the holder, require him to attend before the commissioner at the time and place specified by the commissioner to furnish the information and to answer such questions (if any) relating to the subject matter of the reference as the commissioner may put to him.

(4) If the holder of the licence fails without reasonable excuse to furnish information to or to attend before or answer questions properly put by a commissioner

when required to do so under subsection (3) above, the commissioner may notify the failure to the Secretary of State and, if the commissioner does so,

> [(a) in a case where the licence in question is a LGV Community licence or a PCV Community licence, the holder shall cease to be authorised by virtue of section 99A(1) of this Act to drive in Great Britain a large goods or passenger-carrying vehicle (as the case may be) from such date as is specified in a notice served on the holder by the Secretary of State; and]

> [(b) in any other case, revoke the licence or suspend it for such period as he thinks fit.]

(5) Except where he has given such a notification as is mentioned in subsection (4) above, the traffic commissioner to whom a reference has been made under subsection (1) above shall notify his determination in the matter to the Secretary of State and the holder of the licence and the decision of the commissioner shall be binding on the Secretary of State.

(6) Where the Secretary of State, without making such a reference, determines to revoke or suspend a person's licence under section 115(1) of this Act he shall notify his determination in the matter to the holder of the licence and, where he suspends it, to the traffic commissioner for the area in which the holder of the licence resides.

A18.293   *[Section 116 is printed as substituted by the Road Traffic (Driver Licensing and Information Systems) Act 1989 s.2 and Sch.2; the Driving Licences (Community Driving Licence) Regulations 1996 (SI 1996/1974) reg.2 and Sch.1, para.25 (not reproduced in this work).]*

Disqualification on revocation of licence

A18.294   **117.**—(1) Where in pursuance of section 115(1)(a) of this Act the Secretary of State revokes a person's large goods vehicle or passenger-carrying vehicle driver's licence, the Secretary of State must, in accordance with the regulations made [in pursuance of section 115(3)], order that person to be disqualified indefinitely or for the period determined in accordance with the regulations.

(2) Where in pursuance of section 115(1)(b) of this Act the Secretary of State revokes a person's large goods vehicle or passenger-carrying vehicle driver's licence, the Secretary of State may—

> (a) order the holder to be disqualified indefinitely or for such period as the Secretary of State thinks fit, or

> (b) except where the licence is a provisional licence, if it appears to the Secretary of State that, owing to the conduct of the holder of the licence, it is expedient to require him to comply with the prescribed conditions applicable to provisional licences under Part III of this Act until he passes the prescribed test of competence to drive large goods vehicles or passenger-carrying vehicles of any class, order him to be disqualified for holding or obtaining a full licence until he passes such a test.

[(2A) *[Regulations applying subss.(1) and (2) where licence is treated as revoked under s.37(1) of the Road Traffic Offenders Act 1988.]*]

(3) If, while the holder of a large goods vehicle or passenger-carrying vehicle driver's licence is disqualified under subsection (1) above, the circumstances

prescribed for the purposes of section 115(1)(a) of this Act cease to exist in his case, the Secretary of State must, on an application made to him for the purpose, remove the disqualification.

(4) Where the holder of a large goods vehicle or passenger-carrying vehicle driver's licence is disqualified under subsection (2)(a) above, the Secretary of State may, in such circumstances as may be prescribed, remove the disqualification.

(5) Where the holder of a full licence is disqualified under subsection (2)(b) above, the Secretary of State must not afterwards grant him a full licence to drive a large goods vehicle or passenger-carrying vehicle of any class unless satisfied that he has since the disqualification passed the prescribed test of competence to drive vehicles of that class, and until he passes that test any full licence obtained by him shall be of no effect.

(6) So long as the disqualification under subsection (1) or (2)(a) above of the holder of a large goods vehicle or passenger-carrying vehicle driver's licence continues in force, a large goods vehicle or passenger-carrying vehicle driver's licence must not be granted to him and any such licence obtained by him shall be of no effect.

(7) In this section *"disqualified"*—

    (a) in a case of revocation on the ground of the conduct of the holder of the licence as a driver, means disqualified for holding or obtaining a licence under Part III of this Act to drive large goods vehicles of the prescribed classes and passenger-carrying vehicles of the prescribed classes; and

    (b) in a case of revocation of a passenger-carrying vehicle driver's licence on the ground of the conduct of the holder otherwise than as a driver, means disqualified for holding or obtaining a licence under Part III of this Act to drive passenger-carrying vehicles of the prescribed classes.

[Section 117 is printed as substituted by the Road Traffic (Driver Licensing and Information Systems) Act 1989 s.2 and Sch.2, and as amended by the Road Traffic Act 1991 s.48 and Sch.4, para.65(1)–(3).   **A18.295**

The Motor Vehicles (Driving Licences) Regulations 1999 (SI 1999/2864) (q.v.) were made in part under s.117(2A); see, in particular, reg.57.]

[Community licences: disqualification, etc.

117A.—(1) Where a notice is served on a Community licence holder in pursu-   **A18.296** ance of section 115A(1)(a) of this Act, the Secretary of State must, in accordance with the regulations made in pursuance of section 115(3), order that person to be disqualified indefinitely or for the period determined in accordance with the regulations.

(2) Where a notice is served on a Community licence holder in pursuance of section 115A(1)(b) of this Act, the Secretary of State may—

    (a) order that person to be disqualified indefinitely or for such period as the Secretary of State thinks fit,

    (b) if it appears to the Secretary of State that, owing to the conduct of the Community licence holder, it is expedient to require him to comply with the prescribed conditions applicable to provisional licences under Part III of this Act until he passes the prescribed test of competence to drive large goods vehicles or passenger-carrying vehicles of any class, order him to be disqualified for holding or obtaining a full licence until he passes such a test, or

(c) on receipt of the Community licence and its counterpart (if any), grant to the Community licence holder[, on payment of such fee (if any) as may be prescribed,] a large goods vehicle or passenger-carrying vehicle driver's licence which shall take effect from such date as the Secretary of State may determine.

[(3) Where, in pursuance of subsection (1) or (2) above, the Secretary of State orders a Community licence holder to be disqualified the Secretary of State must, on receipt of the Community licence and its counterpart (if any), grant to the Community licence holder[, on payment of such fee (if any) as may be prescribed,] a licence authorising the driving of the classes of vehicle which are unaffected by the disqualification.]

[(3A) The Secretary of State may require a person to provide—

(a) evidence of his name, address, sex and date and place of birth, and

(b) a photograph which is a current likeness of him,

before issuing a licence to him under subsection (3) above.]

(4) If, while the holder of a LGV Community licence or a PCV Community licence is disqualified under subsection (1) above, the circumstances prescribed for the purposes of section 115A(1)(a) of this Act cease to exist in his case, the Secretary of State must, on an application made to him for the purpose, remove the disqualification.

(5) Where the holder of a LGV Community licence or a PCV Community licence is disqualified under subsection (2)(a) above, the Secretary of State may, in such circumstances as may be prescribed, remove the disqualification.

(6) In this section *"disqualified"*—

(a) in a case where notice is served in pursuance of section 115A(1) of this Act on a Community licence holder on the ground of his conduct as a driver, means disqualified for holding or obtaining a licence under Part III of this Act to drive large goods vehicles of the prescribed classes and passenger-carrying vehicles of the prescribed classes; and

(b) in a case where notice is served in pursuance of section 115A(1) of this Act on a holder of a PCV Community licence on the ground of his conduct otherwise than as a driver, means disqualified for holding or obtaining a licence under Part III of this Act to drive passenger-carrying vehicles of the prescribed classes.]

A18.297 *[Section 117A was inserted by the Driving Licences (Community Driving Licence) Regulations 1996 (SI 1996/1974) reg.2 and Sch.1, para.26 (not reproduced in this work). It is printed as substituted by the Driving Licences (Community Driving Licence) Regulations 1998 (SI 1998/1420) regs 2 and 12 (not reproduced in this work) and as amended by the Road Safety Act 2006 s.40(2).*

With effect from a day to be appointed and in relation to endorsement (all drivers), the words "and its counterpart (if any)" will be omitted in both places in s.117A by the Road Safety Act 2006 s.10 and Sch.3, para.19, s.59 and Sch.7(4).]

Revoked or suspended licences: surrender, return and endorsement

A18.298 **118.**—(1) Where, in pursuance of section 115 of this Act, the Secretary of

State revokes a licence, he must serve notice on the holder of the licence [and its counterpart] requiring him to deliver the licence forthwith to the Secretary of State, and it shall be the duty of the holder of the licence to comply with the requirement.

(2) Where, in pursuance of section 115 of this Act, the Secretary of State suspends a licence, then—

(a) where he does so without making any reference under section 116 of this Act to a traffic commissioner, the Secretary of State must serve notice on the holder of the licence requiring him to deliver the licence forthwith to the traffic commissioner for the area in which the holder of the licence [and its counterpart] resides;

(b) where he does so in pursuance of a determination of a traffic commissioner on such a reference, the traffic commissioner must, if the [licence and its counterpart have] not previously been delivered to him, serve notice on the holder of the licence requiring him to deliver [them] forthwith to the commissioner;

and it shall be the duty of the holder of the licence to comply with the requirement.

(3) Any holder of a licence who fails without reasonable excuse to comply with his duty under subsection (1) or (2) above is guilty of an offence.

(4) On the delivery of a licence [and its counterpart] by a person to the Secretary of State in pursuance of subsection (1) above, the Secretary of State must issue to him, on payment of such fee (if any) as may be prescribed, a licence authorising the driving of the classes of vehicles which are unaffected by the revocation.

[(4A) The Secretary of State may require a person to provide—

(a) evidence of his name, address, sex and date and place of birth, and

(b) a photograph which is a current likeness of him,

before issuing a licence to him under subsection (4) above.]

[(5) On the delivery of a suspended licence and its counterpart to a traffic commissioner, the traffic commissioner must endorse the counterpart of the licence with particulars of the suspension and return the licence and its counterpart to the holder.]

[Section 118 is printed as substituted by the Road Traffic (Driver Licensing **A18.299** *and Information Systems) Act 1989 s.2 and Sch.2, and as subsequently amended by the Driving Licences (Community Driving Licence) Regulations 1990 (SI 1990/144); the Driving Licences (Community Driving Licence) Regulations 1998 (SI 1998/1420), regs 2 and 12 (not reproduced in this work).*

The Motor Vehicles (Driving Licences) Regulations 1999 (SI 1999/2864) (q.v.) were made in part under s.118(4).

With effect from a day (or days) to be appointed and in relation to endorsement (all drivers), the following amendments will be made to s.118 by the Road Safety Act 2006 s.10 and Sch.3, para.20, s.59 and Sch.7(4):

1. *in s.118(1), the words "and its counterpart" will be omitted;*

2. *the following text will be substituted for s.118(2):*

[(2) Where, in pursuance of section 115 of this Act, the Secretary of State suspends a licence, he must (unless the holder of the licence has already delivered his licence to a traffic commissioner on a reference under section 116 of this Act) serve notice on the holder of the licence requiring him to deliver the licence forthwith to the Secretary of State at the address specified in the notice, and it shall be the duty of the holder of the licence to comply with the requirement.

(2A) On the delivery of the licence or, where the licence has already been delivered to a traffic commissioner, on suspending the licence, the Secretary of State must endorse the particulars of the suspension on the licence holder's driving record.

(2B) The Secretary of State or, as the case may be, the traffic commissioner, must then return the licence to the holder.]

3. *in s.118(4), the words "and its counterpart" will be omitted;*

4. *s.118(5) will be omitted.]*

Appeals to magistrates' court

A18.300   **119.**—(1) A person who, being the holder of, or an applicant for, a large goods vehicle or passenger-carrying vehicle driver's licence [or the holder of a LGV Community licence or a PCV Community licence], is aggrieved by the Secretary of State's—

    (a) refusal or failure to grant such a licence in pursuance of section 112 or 113(4) of this Act,

    (b) suspension or revocation of such a licence in pursuance of section 115 or 116(4) of this Act, or

    (c) ordering of disqualification under section 117(2) [or 117A(2)] of this Act,

[or by a notice served on him in pursuance of section 115A(1) or 116(4) of this Act] may, after giving to the Secretary of State and any traffic commissioner to whom the matter was referred notice of his intention to do so, appeal to a magistrates' court …

(2) On any appeal under [subsection (1) above (except paragraph (c) of that subsection)] the Secretary of State and, if the matter was referred to a traffic commissioner, the commissioner shall be respondent.

(3) On any appeal under subsection (1) above the court … may make such order as it thinks fit and the order shall be binding on the Secretary of State.

A18.301   *[Section 119 is printed as substituted by the Road Traffic (Driver Licensing and Information Systems) Act 1989 s.2 and Sch.2; the Driving Licences (Community Driving Licence) Regulations 1996 (SI 1996/1974), reg.2 and Sch.1, para.27 (not reproduced in this work); the Courts Act 2003 s.109(1) and (3), Sch.8, para.308 and Sch.10.*

Words in s.119 relating expressly and exclusively to Scotland have been omitted.]

Regulations

A18.302   **120.**—(1) The Secretary of State may make regulations for any purpose for which regulations may be made under this Part of this Act and for prescribing anything which may be prescribed under this Part of this Act and generally for the purpose of carrying the provisions of this Part of this Act into effect.

(2) Regulations under this section may in particular require applicants for tests of competence under Part III of this Act to drive large goods vehicles or

passenger-carrying vehicles or for large goods vehicle or passenger-carrying vehicle driver's licences (whether full or provisional) to have such qualifications, experience and knowledge as may be prescribed and, in particular, where they are to be authorised to drive large goods vehicles or passenger-carrying vehicles of any class at an age below the normal minimum age for driving vehicles of that class, to fulfil such requirements with respect to participation in an approved training scheme for drivers as may be prescribed.

(3) In subsection (2) above—

　　"approved training scheme for drivers" means a training scheme for drivers (as defined in section 101(5) of this Act [*q.v.*]) approved for the time being by the Secretary of State for the purposes of regulations under that section; and

　　"normal minimum age for driving", in relation to the driving of vehicles of any class, means the age which is in force under section 101 of this Act (but apart from any approved training scheme for drivers) in relation to that class of vehicle.

(4) Regulations under this section may make different provision as respects different classes of vehicles or as respects the same class of vehicles in different circumstances.

(5) Regulations under this section may provide that a person who contravenes or fails to comply with any specified provision of the regulations is guilty of an offence.

(6) The Secretary of State may by regulations provide that this Part of this Act shall not apply to large goods vehicles or passenger-carrying vehicles of such classes as may be prescribed either generally or in such circumstances as may be prescribed.

[Section 120 is printed as substituted by the Road Traffic (Driver Licensing and Information Systems) Act 1989 s.2 and Sch.2.　　**A18.303**

The Motor Vehicles (Driving Licences) Regulations 1999 (SI 1999/2864) (q.v.) were made in part under s.120.]

Interpretation

121.—(1) In this Part of this Act—　　**A18.304**

　　[*"conduct"* means—

　　　　(a) in relation to an applicant for or the holder of a large goods vehicle driver's licence or the holder of a LGV Community licence, his conduct as a driver of a motor vehicle, and

　　　　(b) in relation to an applicant for or the holder of a passenger-carrying vehicle driver's licence or the holder of a PCV Community licence, his conduct both as a driver of a motor vehicle and in any other respect relevant to his holding a passenger-carrying vehicle driver's licence or (as the case may be) his authorisation by virtue of section 99A(1) of this Act to drive in Great Britain a passenger-carrying vehicle of any class,

　　including, in either case, such conduct in Northern Ireland;]

　　[*"counterpart"*, in relation to a licence to drive under Part III of this Act [or a Community licence], has the same meaning as in that Part;]

"*full licence*" means a large goods vehicle or passenger-carrying vehicle driver's licence other than a provisional licence;

["*large goods vehicle*" means a motor vehicle (not being a medium-sized goods vehicle within the meaning of Part III of this Act) which is constructed or adapted to carry or to haul goods and the permissible maximum weight of which exceeds 7.5 tonnes;]

"*passenger-carrying vehicle*" means—

    (a) a large passenger-carrying vehicle, that is to say, a vehicle used for carrying passengers which is constructed or adapted to carry more than 16 passengers, or

    (b) a small passenger-carrying vehicle, that is to say, a vehicle used for carrying passengers for hire or reward which is constructed or adapted to carry more than 8 but not more than 16 passengers;

[and includes a combination of such a motor vehicle and a trailer];

"*notice*" means notice in writing and "notify" shall be construed accordingly;

"*prescribed*" means, unless the context requires otherwise, prescribed by regulations under section 120 of this Act;

"*provisional licence*" means a licence granted by virtue of section 97(2) of this Act [*q.v.*]; [and

"*permissible maximum weight*" has the same meaning as in Part III of this Act.]

A18.305   *[Section 121 is printed as substituted by the Road Traffic (Driver Licensing and Information Systems) Act 1989 s.2 and Sch.2 (as so substituted, although text is designated s.121(1), there are no other subsections) and is printed as amended by the Driving Licences (Community Driving Licence) Regulations 1990 (SI 1990/144); the Driving Licences (Community Driving Licence) Regulations 1996 (SI 1996/1974) reg.2 and Sch.1, para.28 (not reproduced in this work).*

    With effect from a day to be appointed and in relation to endorsement (all drivers), the definition of "counterpart" will be omitted by the Road Safety Act 2006 s.10 and Sch.3, para.21, s.59 and Sch.7(4).

    The Motor Vehicles (Driving Licences) Regulations 1999 (SI 1999/2864) (q.v.) were made in part under s.121.]

Provisions as to Northern Ireland licences

A18.306   122. *[Omitted.]*

PART V

DRIVING INSTRUCTION

A18.307   *[Part 5 of this Act (ss.123–142) does not apply to any person or vehicle in the service of a visiting force or headquarters (as defined); see the Visiting Forces and International Headquarters (Application of Law) Order 1999 (SI 1999/1736; not reproduced in this work) art.8(1) and (2)(b).]*

Instructors to be registered or licensed

Driving instruction for payment to be given only by registered or licensed persons

123.—(1) No paid instruction in the driving of a motor car shall be given un- **A18.308**
less—

    (a) the name of the person giving the instruction is in the register of approved instructors established in pursuance of section 23 of the Road Traffic Act 1962 (in this Part of this Act referred to as "the register"), or

    (b) the person giving the instruction is the holder of a current licence granted under this Part of this Act authorising him to give such instruction.

(2) No paid instruction in the driving of a motor car shall be given unless there is fixed to and exhibited on that motor car in such manner as may be prescribed by regulations either—

    (a) a certificate in such form as may be so prescribed that the name of the person giving the instruction is in the register, or

    (b) a current licence granted under this Part of this Act authorising the person giving the instruction to give such instruction.

(3) For the purposes of subsections (1) and (2) above, instruction is paid instruction if payment of money or money's worth is, or is to be, made by or in respect of the person to whom the instruction is given for the giving of the instruction and for the purposes of this subsection instruction which is given—

    (a) free of charge to a person who is not the holder of a current licence to drive a motor vehicle granted under Part III of this Act (other than a provisional licence),

    (b) by, or in pursuance of arrangements made by, a person carrying on business in the supply of motor cars, and

    (c) in connection with the supply of a motor car in the course of that business,

shall be deemed to be given for payment of money by the person to whom the instruction is given.

(4) Where instruction is given in contravention of subsection (1) above—

    (a) the person by whom it is given, and

    (b) if that person is employed by another to give that instruction, that other, as well as that person,

is guilty of an offence.

(5) In proceedings against a person for an offence under subsection (4) above it shall be a defence for him to prove that he did not know, and had no reasonable cause to believe, that his name or, as the case may be, that of the person employed by him, was not in the register at the material time.

(6) If instruction is given in contravention of subsection (2) above, the person by whom it is given is guilty of an offence.

(7) Any reference in this Part of this Act to a current licence [or certificate] is a reference to a licence [or certificate] which has not expired and has not been cancelled, revoked or suspended.

[(8) In this Part of this Act —

> *"paid instruction"*, in relation to instruction in the driving of a motor car, shall be construed in accordance with subsection (3) above; and

> *"provisional licence"* has the same meaning as in Part III of this Act.]

A18.309   *[Section 123 is printed as amended by the Road Traffic (Driving Instruction by Disabled Persons) Act 1993 s.6 and Sch., paras 1 and 2.*

The register is now maintained under s.125 of this Act.

See further the Motor Cars (Driving Instruction) Regulations 2005 (SI 2005/1902) (not reproduced in this work) which were made in part under this section.

With effect from a day to be appointed, s.123 (as it has effect without the substitution of that section by the Road Safety Act 2006 s.42 and Sch.6, para.2, see below) will be amended as follows by the Driving Instruction (Suspension and Exemption Powers) Act 2009 s.4(1) and Sch.1, para.2:

> 1. *in s.123(1)(a), the words "and the registration is not suspended" will be inserted after "'register')"*
> 2. *in s.123(5), the words ", or (as the case may be) that the registration was at that time suspended" will be inserted the word "time".*

The inserted words will be repealed by s.4(2) of and Sch.2 to the Driving Instruction (Suspension and Exemption Powers) Act 2009 when those provisions are brought into force.

With effect from a day to be appointed, s.123 and the heading before it will be substituted by the Road Safety Act 2006 s.42 and Sch.6, para.2 as follows:

[Instructors and instruction businesses to be registered]

[Requirement of registration

123.—(1) A person—

> (a) must not give paid driving instruction of any prescribed description unless he is registered in respect of the giving of that description of driving instruction, and
> (b) must not carry on business in the provision of paid driving instruction of any prescribed description unless he is registered in respect of the carrying on of business in the provision of that description of driving instruction.

(2) A person—

> (a) must not give paid driving instruction of any prescribed description unless prescribed requirements as to the displaying of evidence that he is registered in respect of the giving of that description of driving instruction are complied with, and
> (b) must not carry on business in the provision of paid driving instruction of any prescribed description unless prescribed requirements as to the displaying of evidence that he is registered in respect of the carrying on of business in the provision of that description of driving instruction are complied with.

(3) In this Part of this Act *"driving instruction"* means instruction in relation to the driving of a motor vehicle.

(4) Regulations under this Part which prescribe a description of driving instruction may do so by reference to—

> (a) the class of motor vehicle to which the instruction relates,

(b) the description of persons to whom the instruction is given or provided, or

(c) the nature of the instruction or where or how it is given or provided.

(5) For the purposes of this Part of this Act instruction is paid instruction if payment of money or money's worth is, or is to be, made for the instruction by or in respect of the person to whom the instruction is given or provided.

(6) Regulations may prescribe circumstances in which instruction provided free of charge shall be deemed to be given for payment of money by or in respect of the person to whom the instruction is given or provided.

(7) For the purposes of this Part of this Act a person is "registered" if his name is in the register together with—

(a) an indication as to whether he is registered in respect of the giving of driving instruction or the carrying on of business in the provision of driving instruction (or both),

(b) an indication as to the description of driving instruction in respect of which he is registered, and

(c) such other particulars as may be prescribed,

and "registration" shall be construed accordingly.

(8) In this Part of this Act "*the register*" means the register established for the purposes of this Part of this Act under section 125 of this Act.]

[With effect from a day to be appointed, s.123 (as substituted) will be amended by the Driving Instruction (Suspension and Exemption Powers) Act 2009 s.1(2). In s.123(a) and (b), the words "and the registration is not suspended" will be inserted after the words "of driving instruction".]

[Paid driving instruction: offences

123A.—(1) If driving instruction is given in contravention of section 123(1)(a) of this Act—

(a) the person by whom it is given,

(b) if that person is employed by another to give that instruction, that other (as well as that person), and

(c) if that person is a franchisee under a driving instruction franchise, the franchisor under the driving instruction franchise (as well as that person),

is guilty of an offence.

(2) If a person contravenes section 123(1)(b) of this Act he is guilty of an offence.

(3) In proceedings against a person for an offence under subsection (1) or (2) above it shall be a defence for him to prove that he did not know, and had no reasonable cause to believe, that—

(a) in a case within paragraph (a) of subsection (1) above, or within subsection (2) above, he,

(b) in a case within paragraph (b) of subsection (1) above, the person employed by him, or

(c) in a case within paragraph (c) of that subsection, the person who was the franchisee under the driving instruction franchise,

was not at the material time registered in respect of the description of driving instruction in question.

(4) If a person contravenes section 123(2) of this Act he is guilty of an offence.]

[With effect from a day to be appointed, s.123A (as substituted) will be amended by the Driving Instruction (Suspension and Exemption Powers) Act 2009 s.1(3). In s.123A(3), the words ", or (as the case may be) that the registration was at that time suspended" will be inserted after the word "question".]]

Exemption of police instructors from prohibition imposed by section 123

A18.310   **124.**—(1) Section 123(1) and (2) of this Act does not apply to the giving of instruction by a police instructor in pursuance of arrangements made by a chief officer of police or, under the authority of a chief officer of police, in pursuance of arrangements made by a local authority.

[(1A) Section 123(1) and (2) also does not apply to the giving of instruction by a SOCA instructor in pursuance of arrangements made by the Director General of the Serious Organised Crime Agency.

In this subsection *"SOCA instructor"* means a member of the staff of the Serious Organised Crime Agency whose duties consist of or include the giving instruction in the driving of motor cars to other members of the Agency's staff.]

(2) In this section —

[…]

"police instructor" means a person who is—

     (a) a member of a police force whose duties consist of or include, or have consisted of or included; the giving of instruction in the driving of motor cars to persons being members of a police force, or

     (b) a civilian employed by a police authority for the purpose of giving such instruction to such persons, and

"local authority" means—

     (a) in relation to England and Wales, the council of a county, metropolitan district, or London borough or the Common Council of the City of London,

     (b) *[applies to Scotland.]*

(3) […]

A18.311   *[Section 124 is printed as amended by the Police Act 1997 s.134(1) and Sch.9, para.58; the Greater London Authority Act 1999 s.325 and Sch.27, para.60 (see also ibid. s.423 and Sch.34, Pt 7); and the Serious Organised Crime and Police Act 2005 s.59 and Sch.4, para.53 and s.174 and Sch.17, Pt 2.*

With effect from a day to be appointed, s.124 will be substituted by the Road Safety Act 2006 s.42 and Sch.6, para.3 as follows:

[Exemption from prohibitions imposed by section 123

124.—(1) Regulations may prescribe circumstances in which section 123 of this Act shall not apply in relation to driving instruction, or driving instruction of a prescribed description.

(2) The regulations may, in particular, make provision for section 123(1)(a) and (2)(a) of this Act not to apply in prescribed circumstances for the purpose of enabling persons to acquire experience in giving driving instruction.]

[With effect from a day to be appointed, s.124 (as substituted) will be amended by

the insertion of the following text (see Driving Instruction (Suspension and Exemption Powers) Act 2009 s.3):

[(3) Circumstances prescribed by virtue of this section may, in particular, consist of, or include, the exercise (whether in individual cases or otherwise) of a discretion by the Registrar or another person.

[(4) Regulations prescribing circumstances of the kind mentioned in subsection (3) may, in particular, make provision about—

> (a) the procedure to be followed in relation to any decision resulting from the exercise of the discretion,
>
> (b) the review or revocation of such a decision,
>
> (c) an appeal against such a decision,
>
> (d) the time when such a decision has effect,
>
> (e) the suspension of an exemption in connection with the making of such a decision (including provision corresponding to that made by, or capable of being made under, section 128ZB).

[(5) Regulations made by virtue of this section may, in particular, make provision for the payment of fees.]*]*

Registration

The register of approved instructors

125. *[Omitted.]*   **A18.312**

[With effect from a day to be appointed, s.125 will be substituted by the Road   **A18.313**
Safety Act 2006 s.42 and Sch.6, para.4.]

[Conditions of registration

125ZA. *[New s.125ZA is prospectively inserted by the Road Safety Act 2006*   **A18.314**
s.42 and Sch.6, para.5. When in force, it will not be reproduced in this work.]]

[Registration of disabled persons

125A.—(1)–(7) *[Omitted.]*   **A18.315**

(8) In this Part of this Act —

> *"appropriate motor car"* means, subject to section 125B(2) of this Act, a motor car equipped with automatic transmission;
>
> *"disability"* means a want of physical ability affecting the driving of motor cars; and
>
>> (i) *"relevant disability"*, in relation to a person, means any disability which is prescribed in regulations or any other disability likely to cause the driving of a motor car by him to be a source of danger to the public; and
>>
>> (ii) *"prospective disability"*, in relation to a person, means any other disability which, at the material time, is not of such a kind that it is a relevant disability but, by virtue of the intermittent or progressive nature of the disability or otherwise, may become a relevant disability in course of time;
>
> *"disabled person's limited driving licence"* means a licence of one of the following kinds, that is to say—

(a) a licence to drive a motor car granted under Part III of this Act (not being a provisional licence) which is limited, by virtue of a notice served under section 92(5)(b) of this Act, to an appropriate motor car; ...

(b) a licence to drive a motor car granted under the law in force in Northern Ireland (not being a licence corresponding to a provisional licence) which is similarly limited by virtue of any corresponding provision of that law; [and]

[(c) a Community licence authorising the driver of a motor car which is similarly limited by virtue of any corresponding provision of the law under which it was issued and a counterpart of that licence;]

"emergency control assessment" and *"emergency control certificate"* mean an assessment and a certificate under section 133A of this Act;

"modifications", in relation to a motor car, includes equipment; and

"registered disabled instructor" means a person whose name is in the register with an indication that he is disabled;

and any reference, in relation to a person, to the class of motor car covered by his disabled person's limited driving licence is a reference to the class of motor car specified in the notice served on him under section 92(5)(b) of this Act but disregarding any modifications specified in the notice.

A18.316   *[Section 125A was inserted by the Road Traffic (Driving Instruction by Disabled Persons) Act 1993 s.1 and is printed as subsequently amended by the Motor Cars (Driving Instruction) (Admission of Community Licence Holders) Regulations 1999 (SI 1999/357; not reproduced in this work).*

Section 125A(1)–(7) (not reproduced) will be amended, with effect from a day to be appointed, by the Road Safety Act 2006 s.42 and Sch.6, para.6(1)–(3), s.59 and Sch.7(4).

With effect from a day to be appointed, s.125A(8) will be amended by the Road Safety Act 2006 s.42 and Sch.6, para.6(4) as follows:

1. *the following text will be substituted for the definition of "appropriate motor car":*

   [" *appropriate motor vehicle*" means, subject to section 125B(2) of this Act, a motor vehicle equipped with automatic transmission;]

2. *in the definition of "disability", the words ", in respect of motor vehicles of any description, means a want of physical ability affecting the driving of motor vehicles of that description" will be substituted for the words "means a want of physical ability affecting the driving of motor cars";*

3. *in the definition of "relevant disability", the words "vehicle of the description in question" will be substituted for the word "car";*

4. *in the definition of "disabled person's limited driving licence", the word "vehicle" will be substituted in each place for the word "car";*

5. *in the definition of "modifications", the word "vehicle" will be substituted for the word "car";*

6. *in the definition of "registered disabled instructor", the words*

"registered as a disabled instructor in respect of instruction in the driving of a motor vehicle of a prescribed description given in a motor vehicle of that description" will be substituted for the words "whose name is in the register with an indication that he is disabled";

7. *in the words following the definition of "registered disabled instructor", the word "vehicle" will be substituted for the word "car", in both places.*

With effect from a day to be appointed and in relation to endorsement (all drivers), in s.125A(8)(c) (definition of "disabled person's limited driving licence") the words "and a counterpart of that licence" will be omitted by the Road Safety Act 2006 s.10 and Sch.3, para.23, Sch.7(4).]

Provisions supplementary to section 125A

125B. *[Omitted.]*   A18.317

Duration of registration

126. *[Omitted.]*   A18.318
[With effect from a day to be appointed, s.126 will be substituted by the Road Safety Act 2006 s.42 and Sch.6, para.8.]

Extension of duration of registration

127. *[Omitted.]*   A18.319

Removal of names from register

128. *[Omitted.]*   A18.320
[With effect from a day to be appointed, s.128 will be substituted by the Road Safety Act 2006 s.42 and Sch.6, para.10.]

[Suspension of registration by Registrar

128ZA. *[New s.128ZA is prospectively inserted by the Driving Instruction (Suspension and Exemption Powers) Act 2009 s.1(1). When in force, it will not be reproduced in this work.]]*   A18.321

[Compensation in respect of suspension

128ZB. *[New s.128ZB is prospectively inserted by the Driving Instruction (Suspension and Exemption Powers) Act 2009 s.1(1). When in force, it will not be reproduced in this work.]]*   A18.322

[Power to give directions as to further applications

128A. *[New s.128A is prospectively inserted by the Road Safety Act 2006 s.42 and Sch.6, para.11. When in force, it will not be reproduced in this work.]]*   A18.323

Licences

Licences for giving instruction so as to obtain practical experience

129.—[(1) A licence under this section is granted for the purpose of enabling a person to acquire practical experience in giving instruction in driving motor cars with a view to undergoing [either—   A18.324

(a) such part of the examination referred to in section 125(3)(a) of this Act, or

(b) such part of any examination prescribed for the purposes of section 125A(6)(a) of this Act,]

as consists of a practical test of ability and fitness to instruct.]

(2) *[Application for licence.]*

(3) *[Refusal of licence.]*

(4) *[Notice of decision.]*

(5) *[Form of licence, and conditions.]*

(5A) *[Conditions on licence of disabled instructor.]*

(5B) *[Definition of "authorised motor car" in s.129(5A) .]*

(6) *[Renewal of licence.]*

(7)–(8) *[Notice of refusal of licence.]*

A18.325　　*[Section 129 is printed as amended by the Road Traffic (Driving Instruction by Disabled Persons) Act 1993 s.2(1).*

With effect from a day to be appointed, s.129 (as it has effect without its omission by the Road Safety Act 2006 s.42 and Sch.6, para.12, see below) will be amended by the Driving Instruction (Suspension and Exemption Powers) Act 2009 s.4(1) and Sch.1, para.6. The 2009 Act inserts a new subs.(9), which applies in relation to suspension of a person's licence in connection with an application for a new licence. The new subsection will not be reproduced above. It will be repealed by s.4(2) of and Sch.2 to the 2009 Act when those provisions are brought into force.

With effect from a day to be appointed, s.129 will be omitted by the Road Safety Act 2006 s.42 and Sch.6, para.12, s.59 and Sch.7(14).]

Revocation of licences

A18.326　　130. *[Omitted.]*

A18.327　　*[With effect from a day to be appointed, s.130 will be omitted by the Road Safety Act 2006 s.42 and Sch.6, para.12, s.59 and Sch.7(14).]*

Appeals

Appeals against decisions of the Registrar

A18.328　　131. *[Omitted.]*

[With effect from a day to be appointed, s.131, and the italic heading before it, will be repealed by the Driving Instruction (Suspension and Exemption Powers) Act 2009 s.4(2) and Sch.2.]

[Compensation in respect of suspension

A18.329　　131A. *[New s.131A is prospectively inserted by the Driving Instruction (Suspension and Exemption Powers) Act 2009 s.4(1). When in force, it will not be reproduced in this work.]]*

Examinations and tests

Examinations and tests of ability to give driving instruction

A18.330　　132. *[Omitted.]*

[With effect from a day to be appointed, s.132 will be substituted by the Road Safety Act 2006 s.42 and Sch.6, para.14.

The heading before s.132 will be substituted by the words "Examinations and training" by ibid. s.42 and Sch.6, para.14.]

Review of examinations

133.—(1) On the application of a person who has [undergone a relevant exam- **A18.331** ination, or a part of such an examination]—

    (a) [a magistrates' court], or

    (b) *[applies to Scotland]*,

may determine whether the [examination or part was properly conducted].

(2) If it appears to the court ... that [the examination or part was not properly] conducted, the court ... may order that any fee payable by the applicant in respect of [the examination or part] shall not be paid or, if it has been paid, shall be repaid.

(3) No appeal shall lie under section 131 of this Act in respect of any matter in respect of which an application may be made to a magistrates' court ... under subsection (1) above.

[(4) In this section *"a relevant examination"* means—

    (a) an examination of ability to give instruction in the driving of motor cars,

    (b) a test of continued ability and fitness to give instruction in the driving of motor cars (or appropriate motor cars), or

    (c) an emergency control assessment.]

*[Section 133 is printed as amended by the Transport Act 2000 s.260 and **A18.332** Sch.29, paras 1 and 11; the Courts Act 2003 s.109(1) and Sch.8, para.309.*

Words relating exclusively to Scotland have been omitted from s.133.

With effect from a day to be appointed, s.133 will be substituted by the Road Safety Act 2006 s.42 and Sch.2, para.14 as follows:

[Review of examinations etc.

133.—(1) On the application of a person who has undergone a relevant instructor examination, or a part of a relevant instructor examination—

    (a) a magistrates' court, or

    (b) *[applies to Scotland]*,

may determine whether the examination, or the part of the examination, was properly conducted.

(2) In this Part of this Act *"relevant instructor examination"* means—

    (a) an examination of ability and fitness referred to in section 125ZA(2)(a) or 125A(6)(a) of this Act,

    (b) an examination of continued ability and fitness referred to in section 125ZA(4)(a) or 125A(7A)(a) of this Act, or

    (c) an emergency control assessment under section 133A of this Act.

(3) If it appears to the court ... that it was not properly conducted, the court ... may—

    (a) (except in the case of an emergency control assessment) order that the applicant shall be eligible to submit himself for another examination before the end of the period prescribed under section 132(2)(d) of this Act, and

(b) (in any case) order that any fee payable by the applicant in respect of the examination shall not be paid or, if it has been paid, shall be repaid.

(4) No appeal shall lie under section 131 of this Act in respect of any matter in respect of which an application may be made to a magistrates' court ... under subsection (1) above.]

[Words omitted in s.133 as substituted apply exclusively to Scotland.]]

[Training

A18.333 **133ZA.** *[New s.133ZA is prospectively inserted by the Road Safety Act 2006 s.42 and Sch.6, para.14. When in force, it will not be reproduced in this work.]]*

[Disabled persons: emergency control certificates, etc.]

[Assessment of disabled person's ability to control a motor car in an emergency

A18.334 **133A.**—(1) This section applies to any person who, by or under any provision of this Part of this Act, —

(a) is authorised to apply to undergo an emergency control assessment, or

(b) is required by the Registrar to submit himself for an emergency control assessment.

(2) An emergency control assessment is an assessment of whether the person being assessed would be able either—

(a) to take control of a motor car of a class covered by his disabled person's limited driving licence without any modifications, or

(b) to take control of a motor car of a class covered by his disabled person's limited driving licence only with appropriate modifications of such a motor car,

if an emergency arose while he was giving, in such a motor car, instruction in the driving of an appropriate motor car.

(3) Where a person is authorised to apply to undergo an emergency control assessment, for the application to be duly made, it must be made to the Secretary of State and must include—

(a) a declaration by the person making the application, in such form as the Secretary of State may require, stating every relevant disability or prospective disability from which the person is suffering or has at any time (or, if a period is prescribed by regulations, has during that period) suffered; and

(b) such other particulars as the Secretary of State may require.

(4) Where a person is required to submit himself for an emergency control assessment he must furnish to the Secretary of State such particulars as the Secretary of State may require.

[(4A) *[Regulation-making power.]*]

(5) An emergency control assessment—

(a) shall be conducted by a person appointed by the Secretary of State (in this section referred to as *"the assessor"*); and

(b) shall consist of such practical tests and other means of assessment as the Secretary of State may determine.

(6) On completing an emergency control assessment of a person, the assessor shall grant him an emergency control certificate if he is satisfied either—

    (a) that, in the circumstances mentioned in subsection (2) above, that person would be able to take control of a motor car of a class covered by his disabled person's limited driving licence without any modifications, or

    (b) that, in the circumstances mentioned in subsection (2) above, that person would be able to take control of a motor car of a class covered by his disabled person's limited driving licence only with appropriate modifications of such a motor car;

but if the assessor is not so satisfied, he shall refuse to grant a certificate to that person.

(7) An emergency control certificate granted to any person—

    (a) shall specify the class of motor car covered by his disabled person's limited driving licence in relation to which the assessor is satisfied as mentioned in subsection (6)(a) or (b) above, specifying, in a case falling within paragraph (b), the modifications that are appropriate; and

    (b) may include a recommendation that that person should undergo a further emergency control assessment after the end of such period as is specified in the certificate;

and shall otherwise be in such form as the Secretary of State may determine.

(8) Different modifications for different classes of motor car may be specified under subsection (7)(a) above.

(9) The assessor who has assessed any person under this section—

    (a) if he grants an emergency control certificate, shall—

        (i) give or send the certificate to that person, and

        (ii) send a copy of the certificate to the Registrar; and

    (b) if he refuses to grant such a certificate, shall—

        (i) give notice in writing to that person of his decision and of the reasons for it, and

        (ii) send a copy of the notice to the Registrar.]

[Section 133A was inserted by the Road Traffic (Driving Instruction by Disabled Persons) Act 1993 s.3; and it is printed as amended by the Transport Act 2000 s.260 and Sch.29, paras 1 and 10 (which inserted s.133A(4A) above).   **A18.335**

With effect from a day to be appointed, s.133A will be amended by the Road Safety Act 2006 s.42 and Sch.6, para.15 so that the word "vehicle" will be substituted in each place for the word "car".]

Further assessments

133B. *[Omitted.]*   **A18.336**

[Duty to disclose further disability

133C.—(1) This section applies to—   **A18.337**

    (a) registered disabled instructors, and

(b) persons who hold licences under section 129 of this Act granted by virtue of subsection (2)(b) of that section.

(2) If at any time a person to whom this section applies becomes aware—

(a) that he is suffering from a relevant or prospective disability which he has not previously disclosed to the Secretary of State under section 125A(3) or 133A(3) or (4) of this Act, or

(b) that a relevant or prospective disability from which he has at any time suffered (and which has been previously so disclosed) has become more acute since his current emergency control certificate was granted,

he must forthwith notify the Registrar in writing of the nature and extent of his disability.

(3) Subsection (2) above does not require a person to notify the Registrar if—

(a) the disability is one from which he has not previously suffered, and

(b) he has reasonable grounds for believing that the duration of the disability will not extend beyond the period of three months beginning with the date on which he first becomes aware that he suffers from it.

(4) A person who fails without reasonable excuse to notify the Registrar as required by subsection (2) above is guilty of an offence.]

A18.338   [Section 133C was inserted by the Road Traffic (Driving Instruction by Disabled Persons) Act 1993 s.4.

With effect from a day to be appointed, s.133C will be amended by the Road Safety Act 2006 s.42 and Sch.6, para.17, s.59 and Sch.7(14) as follows:

1. s.133C(1) will be omitted;

2. in s.133C(2), the words "registered disabled instructor" will be substituted for the words "person to whom this section applies".]

[Offences relating to giving by disabled person of paid driving instruction

A18.339   133D.—(1) This section applies to—

(a) registered disabled instructors, and

(b) persons who hold licences under section 129 of this Act granted by virtue of subsection (2)(b) of that section.

(2) No person to whom this section applies shall give paid instruction in the driving of a motor car unless he is the holder of a current emergency control certificate.

(3) No person to whom this section applies shall give, in any unauthorised motor car, paid instruction in the driving of a motor car.

(4) Where instruction is given in contravention of this section —

(a) the person by whom it is given, and

(b) if that person is employed by another to give that instruction, that other, as well as that person,

is guilty of an offence.

(5) In subsection (3) above "unauthorised motor car", in relation to any person, means a motor car other than one which falls within the class of motor car specified in his current emergency control certificate and, where modifications are specified in that certificate, is modified in accordance with the specification.]

[Section 133D was inserted by the Road Traffic (Driving Instruction by Dis- **A18.340**
abled Persons) Act 1993 s.5.

With effect from a day to be appointed, s.133C will be amended by the Road
Safety Act 2006 s.42 and Sch.6, para.18, s.59 and Sch.7(14) as follows:

1. *s.133D(1) will be omitted;*
2. *the word "vehicle" will be substituted for the word "car" in each place;*
3. *in s.133D(2) and (3), the words "registered disabled instructor" will*
   be substituted for the words "person to whom this section applies";
4. *s.133D(4) will be substituted as follows:*

> [(4) Where a registered disabled instructor gives instruction in contravention
> of this section—
>
> > (a) the instructor,
> > (b) if the instructor is employed by another person to give that instruction,
> > that other person (as well as the instructor), and
> > (c) if the instructor is a franchisee under a driving instruction franchise, the
> > franchisor (as well as the instructor),
>
> is guilty of an offence.]*]*

General and supplemental

Power to alter conditions for entry or retention in, and removal from, register and for grant or revocation of licences

134. *[Omitted.]*   **A18.341**

[With effect from a day to be appointed, s.134 will be substituted by the Road   **A18.342**
Safety Act 2006 s.42 and Sch.6, para.19.]

Power to prescribe form of certificate of registration, etc.

135.—(1) Regulations may prescribe all or any of the following—   **A18.343**

(a) a form of certificate for issue to persons whose names are in the register as evidence of their names being in the register,

(b) a form of badge for use by such persons, and

(c) an official title for such use.

(2) If a person whose name is not in the register—

(a) takes or uses a title prescribed under this section, or

(b) wears or displays a badge or certificate so prescribed, or

(c) takes or uses any name, title, addition or description implying that his
name is in the register,

he is guilty of an offence unless he proves that he did not know, and had no reasonable cause to believe, that his name was not in the register at the material
time.

(3) If a person carrying on business in the provision of instruction in the driving of motor vehicles—

(a) uses a title or description so prescribed in relation to any person
employed by him whose name is not in the register, or

(b) issues any advertisement or invitation calculated to mislead with respect to the extent to which persons whose names are in the register
are employed by him,

he is guilty of an offence unless he proves that he did not know, and had no reasonable cause to believe, that the name or names in question were not in the register at the material time.

A18.344   *[The Motor Cars (Driving Instruction) Regulations 2005 (SI 2005/1902) (not reproduced in this work) were made in part under this section.*

With effect from a day to be appointed, s.135 will be substituted by the Road Safety Act 2006 s.42 and Sch.6, para.20 as follows:

[Evidence of registration

135.—(1) Regulations may prescribe—

> (a) certificates or other items that may be issued to registered persons to be displayed as evidence of their registration, and
>
> (b) a title or other description which may be used as such evidence.

(2) If at any time a person who is not registered—

> (a) displays a certificate or other item prescribed under subsection (1)(a) above,
>
> (b) uses a title or other description prescribed under subsection (1)(b) above, or
>
> (c) uses a title or other description implying that he is registered,

he is guilty of a offence unless he proves that he did not know, and did not have reasonable cause to believe, that he was not registered at that time.

(3) If a person carrying on business in the provision of driving instruction at any time—

> (a) uses a title or other description prescribed under subsection (1)(b) above in relation to any relevant person who is not appropriately registered, or
>
> (b) issues any advertisement or invitation calculated to mislead with respect to the extent to which relevant persons are appropriately registered,

he is guilty of an offence unless he proves that he did not know, and did not have reasonable cause to believe, that the relevant person was, or relevant persons were, not appropriately registered at that time.

(4) For the purposes of subsection (3) above—

> (a) a relevant person is a person who is employed by the person carrying on business to give driving instruction, or is a franchisee giving driving instruction under a driving instruction franchise under which that person is the franchisor, and
>
> (b) a relevant person is appropriately registered if he is registered in respect of the giving of the description of driving instruction which he is employed to give or which is given by him under the driving instruction franchise.]*

Surrender of certificates and licences

A18.345   **136.** Where—

> (a) the name of a person to whom a certificate prescribed under section 135 of this Act has been issued is removed from the register in pursuance of this Part of this Act, or
>
> (b) a licence granted under this Part of this Act to a person expires or is revoked,

that person must, if so required by the Registrar by notice in writing, surrender the certificate or licence, as the case may be, to the Registrar within the period of fourteen days beginning with that on which the notice is given and, if he fails to do so, he is guilty of an offence.

[With effect from a day to be appointed, s.136 will be amended by the Road Safety Act 2006 s.42 and Sch.6, para.21 as follows: **A18.346**

1. *paras (a) and (b) will be substituted by the words "the registration of a person to whom a certificate or other item prescribed under section 135(1)(a) of this Act has been issued is terminated";*
2. *the words "other item" will be substituted for the words "licence, as the case may be,";*
3. *in the heading the word "**etc.**" will be substituted for the words "**and licences**".]*

Production of certificates and licences to constables and authorised persons

137.—(1) A person to whom a certificate prescribed under section 135 of this   **A18.347** Act is issued, or to whom a licence under this Part of this Act is granted, must, on being so required by a constable or any person authorised in writing by the Secretary of State in that behalf, produce the certificate or licence for examination.

(2) Where—

(a) the name of a person is removed from the register, or
(b) a licence granted under this Part of this Act to a person expires or is revoked,

then, if that person fails to satisfy an obligation imposed on him by section 136 of this Act, a constable or a person authorised in writing by the Secretary of State in that behalf may require him to produce any such certificate issued to him or the licence, and upon its being produced may seize it and deliver it to the Registrar.

(3) A person who is required under subsection (1) or (2) above to produce a document and fails to do so is, subject to subsection (4) below, guilty of an offence.

(4) In proceedings against any person for an offence under subsection (3) above, it shall be a defence for him to show that—

(a) within seven days beginning with the day following that on which the production of the document was so required, it was produced—

(i) where the requirement was made by a constable, at a police station specified at the time the production was required by the person required to produce the document,
(ii) where the requirement was made by a person other than a constable, at a place specified at that time by that person, or

(b) the document was produced at that police station or, as the case may be, place as soon as was reasonably practicable, or

(c) it was not reasonably practicable for it to be produced at that police station or, as the case may be, place before the day on which the proceedings were commenced,

and for the purposes of this subsection the laying of the information … shall be treated as the commencement of the proceedings.

[Words relating exclusively and expressly to Scotland have been omitted from **A18.348** *s.137.*

With effect from a day to be appointed, s.137 will be amended by the Road Safety Act 2006 s.42 and Sch.6, para.22, s.59 and Sch.7(14) as follows:

1. *in s.137(1), the words "or other item" will be inserted after "a certificate", the words ", or to whom a licence under this Part of this Act is granted" will be omitted, and the words "or other item" will be substituted for "or licence";*

2. *in s.137(2), the text below will be substituted for the words before "constable":*

   [Where—

   (a) a person's registration is terminated, and

   (b) he fails to satisfy an obligation imposed on him by section 136 of this Act,

   a]

3. *and the words "or other item issued to him" will be substituted for the words "issued to him or the licence";*

4. *in s.137(3) the words "certificate or other item" will be substituted, in each place, for the word "document";*

5. *in the heading, the word "**etc.**" will be substituted for the words "**and licences**".]*

Offences by corporations

A18.349   **138.** Where a body corporate is guilty of an offence under this Part of this Act and the offence is proved to have been committed with the consent or connivance of, or to be attributable to neglect on the part of, a director, manager, secretary or other similar officer of the body corporate, or a person who was purporting to act in any such capacity, he, as well as the body corporate, is guilty of that offence and liable to be proceeded against and punished accordingly.

Service of notices

A18.350   **139.** *[Omitted.]*

Receipts

A18.351   **140.** *[Omitted.]*

Regulations

A18.352   **141.** *[Omitted.]*

[Meaning of "motor car"

A18.353   **141A.**—(1) Notwithstanding section 185(1) of this Act, in this Part of this Act *"motor car"* means a motor vehicle (other than an invalid carriage or motor cycle)—

    (a) which is not constructed or adapted to carry more than nine persons inclusive of the driver, and

    (b) which has a maximum gross weight not exceeding 3.5 tonnes.

(2) In subsection (1) above *"maximum gross weight"* has the same meaning as in Part III of this Act.]

[Section 141A was inserted by the Driving Licences (Community Driving   **A18.354**
Licence) Regulations 1996 (SI 1996/1974) reg.2 and Sch.1, para.29 (not
reproduced in this work).

With effect from a day to be appointed, s.141A will be substituted as follows by
the Road Safety Act 2006 s.42 and Sch.6, para.25:

[Interpretation of Part 5

141A.—(1) For the purposes of this Part of this Act persons may carry on business in
the provision of driving instruction in any way, including in particular—

    (a) by giving instruction themselves,

    (b) by arranging for the giving of driving instruction by their employees,
    or

    (c) by arranging for the giving of driving instruction by persons who are
      franchisees under driving instruction franchises under which they are
      the franchisor.

(2) In this Part of this Act *"driving instruction franchise"* means an agreement under
which one party (the "franchisor") grants to another party (a "franchisee") rights
consisting of or including the right to use a particular trading name, style or design in
the carrying on of business in the giving of driving instruction.

(3) In this Part of this Act references to "the franchisor" and "a franchisee", in relation to a driving instruction franchise, shall be construed accordingly.

(4) In this Part of this Act *"current"*, in relation to a licence or certificate, means one
which has not expired and has not been cancelled, revoked or suspended.

(5) In this Part of this Act—

    (a) *"Community licence"* and *"counterpart"*, in relation to a Community licence,
    and

    (b) *"provisional licence"*,

have the same meanings as in Part 3 of this Act.]

[With effect from a day to be appointed and in relation to endorsement (all drivers),
in s.141A(5), as substituted, the words "and "counterpart", in relation to a Community
licence" will be omitted by the Road Safety Act 2006 s.10 and Sch.3, para.24, s.59 and
Sch.7(4).]]

Index to Part V

142. The expressions listed in the left-hand column below are respectively   **A18.355**
defined or (as the case may be) fall to be construed in accordance with the provisions of this Part of this Act listed in the right-hand column in relation to those
expressions.

Expression	Relevant provision
[*Appropriate motor car*	Section 125A(8)]
[*"Community licence" and "counterpart" in*	Section 125(10)]
relation thereto	
Current licence	Section 123(7)]
[*Disability, prospective disability and relevant*	Section 125A(8)]
disability	

Expression	Relevant provision
[Disabled person's limited driving licence	Section 125A(8)]
[Emergency control assessment and emergency control certificate	Section 125A(8)]
[Paid instruction	Section 123(8)]
[Provisional licence	Section 123(8)]
The register	Section 123]
[Registered disabled instructor	Section 125A(8)]
The Registrar	Section 125(2)]
Regulations	Section 141]

A18.356   [Section 142 is printed as amended by the Road Traffic (Driving Instruction by Disabled Persons) Act 1993 s.6 and Sch., paras 1 and 8, and is printed as subsequently amended by the Motor Cars (Driving Instruction) (Admission of Community Licence Holders) Regulations 1999 (SI 1999/357; not reproduced in this work).

Section 125(2) is not reproduced in this work; in that provision, "the registrar" is defined as the officer of the Secretary of State by whom, on behalf of the Secretary of State, the register of approved instructors is compiled and maintained. Section 125(10) (similarly, not reproduced in this work) was inserted by SI 1999/357 and defines "Community licence" and "counterpart" as in Pt 3 of this Act.

With effect from a day to be appointed, s.142 will be substituted as follows by the Road Safety Act 2006 s.42 and Sch.6, para.26:

[Index to Part 5

142. The expressions listed in the left-hand column below are respectively defined or (as the case may be) fall to be construed in accordance with the provisions of this Part of this Act listed in the right-hand column in relation to those expressions.

Expression	Relevant provision
Appropriate motor vehicle	Section 125A(8)
Carry on business in the provision of driving instruction	Section 141A(1)
Community licence and counterpart	Section 141A(5)
Current (in relation to a licence or certificate)	Section 141A(4)
Disability, prospective disability and relevant disability	Section 125A(8)
Disabled person's limited driving licence	Section 125A(8)
Driving instruction	Section 123(3)
Driving instruction franchise (and franchisor and franchisee)	Section 141A(2) and (3)
Emergency control assessment and emergency control certificate	Section 125A(8)
Modifications, in relation to a motor vehicle	Section 125A(8)
Paid instruction	Section 123(5) and (6)
Provisional licence	Section 141A(5)
Registered and registration	Section 123(7)
The register	Section 123(8)
Registered disabled instructor	Section 125A(8)

Expression	Relevant provision
The Registrar	Section 125(2)
Regulations	Section 141
Relevant instructor examination	Section 133(2)]

[With effect from a day to be appointed and in relation to endorsement (all drivers), in s.142, as substituted, the words "and counterpart" will be omitted by the Road Safety Act 2006 s.10 and Sch.3, para.25, s.59 and Sch.7(4).

With effect from a day to be appointed, s.142, as substituted, will be amended by the Driving Instruction (Suspension and Exemption Powers) Act 2009 s.1(4). In the entry in the table for "Registered and registration", the words "Sections 123(7) and 128ZA(7)" will be substituted for "Section 123(7)".]]

PART VI

THIRD-PARTY LIABILITIES

[Part 6 of this Act (ss.143–162) does not apply to any person or vehicle in the service of a visiting force or headquarters (as defined); see the Visiting Forces and International Headquarters (Application of Law) Order 1999 (SI 1999/1736; not reproduced in this work) art.8(1) and (2)(b).]   **A18.357**

Compulsory insurance or security against third-party risks

Users of motor vehicles to be insured or secured against third-party risks

143.—(1) Subject to the provisions of this Part of this Act —   **A18.358**

    (a) a person must not use a motor vehicle on a road [or other public place] unless there is in force in relation to the use of the vehicle by that person such a policy of insurance or such a security in respect of third-party risks as complies with the requirements of this Part of this Act, and

    (b) a person must not cause or permit any other person to use a motor vehicle on a road [or other public place] unless there is in force in relation to the use of the vehicle by that other person such a policy of insurance or such a security in respect of third-party risks as complies with the requirements of this Part of this Act.

(2) If a person acts in contravention of subsection (1) above he is guilty of an offence.

(3) A person charged with using a motor vehicle in contravention of this section shall not be convicted if he proves—

    (a) that the vehicle did not belong to him and was not in his possession under a contract of hiring or of loan,

    (b) that he was using the vehicle in the course of his employment, and

    (c) that he neither knew nor had reason to believe that there was not in force in relation to the vehicle such a policy of insurance or security as is mentioned in subsection (1) above.

(4) This Part of this Act does not apply to invalid carriages.

A18.359   *[Section 143 is printed as amended by the Motor Vehicles (Compulsory Insur-*
ance) Regulations 2000 (SI 2000/726; not reproduced in this work).

In the explanatory note accompanying SI 2000/726 it is stated that the regula-
tions were made for the purpose of complying with Directive 72/166/EEC (O.J.
No.L103, May 2, 1972, p.2), as modified by Directive 84/5/EEC (O.J. No.L8,
January 11, 1984, p.17), and Directive 90/232/EEC (O.J. No.L129, May 19,
1990, p.33), following the decision of the House of Lords in Cutter v Eagle Star
Insurance Co. Ltd; Clarke v Kato [1998] 4 All E.R. 417.

Proceedings under s.143 are specified by the Prosecution of Offences Act
1985 (Specified Proceedings) Order 1999 (SI 1999/904) below as being proceed-
ings the conduct of which the Director of Public Prosecutions is not required to
take over from the police under the Prosecution of Offences Act 1985 s.3(3)(a).

The fixed penalty procedure applies to offences under s.143; see the Road
Traffic Offenders Act 1988 Sch.3 below. Offences under s.143 have been
designated as fixed penalty offences by the Fixed Penalty Offences Order 2003
(SI 2003/1253).]

Exceptions from requirement of third-party insurance or security

A18.360   144.—(1) Section 143 of this Act does not apply to a vehicle owned by a person
who has deposited and keeps deposited with the Accountant General of the
[Senior Courts] the sum of [£500,000], at a time when the vehicle is being driven
under the owner's control.

[(1A), (1B) *[Power to alter the sum in s.144(1) by order.]*]

(2) Section 143 does not apply—

(a) to a vehicle owned—

(i) by the council of a county or county district in England and
Wales, [the Broads Authority,] the Common Council of the City
of London, the council of a London borough, [a National Park
authority], the Inner London Education Authority, [the London
Fire and Emergency Planning Authority] [an authority established for an area in England by an order under section 207 of
the Local Government and Public Involvement in Health Act
2007 (joint waste authorities)][, a joint authority (other than a
police authority) established by Part 4 of the Local Government
Act 1985, an economic prosperity board established under section 88 of the Local Democracy, Economic Development and
Construction Act 2009 or a combined authority established under
section 103 of that Act,]

(ii) by a [council constituted under section 2 of the Local Government, etc. (Scotland) Act 1994] in Scotland, or

(iii) by a joint board or committee in England or Wales, or joint committee in Scotland, which is so constituted as to include among
its members representatives of any such council,

at a time when the vehicle is being driven under the owner's control,

(b) to a vehicle owned by a police authority ..., at a time when it is being
driven under the owner's control, or to a vehicle at a time when it is
being driven for police purposes by or under the direction of a constable, or by a person employed by a police authority, ... or

[(ba) [...]]

(c) to a vehicle at a time when it is being driven on a journey to or from any place undertaken for salvage purposes pursuant to Part IX of the [Merchant Shipping Act 1995],

(d) [...],

[(da) to a vehicle owned by a health service body, as defined in section 60(7) of the National Health Service and Community Care Act 1990 [by a Primary Care Trust established under [section 18 of the National Health Service Act 2006]] [or by a Local Health Board established under section 11 of the National Health Service (Wales) Act 2006], [or by the [Commission for Healthcare Audit and Inspection]], at a time when the vehicle is being driven under the owner's control,]

[(db) to an ambulance owned by a National Health Service trust established under [section 25 of the National Health Service Act 2006, section 18 of the National Health Service (Wales) Act 2006] or the National Health Service (Scotland) Act 1978, at a time when a vehicle is being driven under the owner's control,]

[(dc) to an ambulance owned by an NHS foundation trust, at a time when the vehicle is being driven under the owner's control,]

(e) to a vehicle which is made available by the Secretary of State [or the Welsh Ministers] to any person, body or local authority in pursuance of [section 12 or 80 of the National Health Service Act 2006, or section 10 or 38 of the National Health Service (Wales) Act 2006] at a time when it is being used in accordance with the terms on which it is so made available,

(f) to a vehicle which is made available by the Secretary of State to any local authority, education authority or voluntary organisation in Scotland in pursuance of section 15 or 16 of the National Health Service (Scotland) Act 1978 at a time when it is being used in accordance with the terms on which it is so made available,

[(g) to a vehicle owned by [the Care Quality Commission], at a time when the vehicle is being driven under the owner's control.]

[Section 144 is printed as amended by the Norfolk and Suffolk Broads Act **A18.361** *1988 (c.iv); the Road Traffic (Consequential Provisions) Act 1988 s.4 and Sch.3, para.36; the National Health Service and Community Care Act 1990 s.60(2) and Sch.8; the Road Traffic Act 1991 s.20(1)–(3); the Local Government, etc. (Scotland) Act 1994 s.180(1) and Sch.13, para.159(8); the Environment Act 1995 s.78 and Sch.10, para.29; the Merchant Shipping Act 1995 ss.314(2), 316(2) and Sch.13, para.85; the Police Act 1997 s.134(1) and Sch.9, para.59; the Health Act 1999 (Supplementary and Consequential Provisions) Order 1999 (SI 1999/2795; not reproduced in this work) art.4; the Greater London Authority Act 1999 ss.325, 328, 423 and Schs 27 (para.61), 29 (para.54) (and see also the Greater London Authority Act 1999 (Commencement No.5 and Appointment of Reconstitution Day) Order 2000, SI 2000/1094; not reproduced in this work), and 34 (Pt 7); the Health Act 1999 (Supplementary, Consequential, etc., Provisions) Order 2000 (SI 2000/90; not reproduced in this work) art.3(1) and Sch.1, para.23; the National Health Service Reform and Health Care Professions Act 2002 ss.6(2), 42 and Sch.5, para.29; the Health and Social Care (Community Health and Stan-*

dards) Act 2003 (Commission for Healthcare Audit and Inspection and Commis-
sion for Social Care Inspection) (Consequential Provisions) Order 2004 (SI
2004/2987); the Serious Organised Crime and Police Act 2005 s.59 and Sch.4,
para.54, and Sch.17, Pt 2; and the National Health Service (Consequential Pro-
visions) Act 2006 s.2 and Sch.1, para.122; the Local Government and Public
Involvement in Health Act 2007 s.209 and Sch.13, para.45; the Constitutional
Reform Act 2005 s.59 and Sch.11, para.4; the Armed Forces Act 2006 s.378 and
Sch.17; the Health and Social Care Act 2008 s.95 and Sch.5(3), para.61(a) and
(b); the Local Democracy, Economic Development and Construction Act 2009
s.119 and Sch.6, para.80.

As to the inclusion of the Local Government Residuary Body for England
among the bodies specified in s.144(2), see the Local Government Residuary
Body (England) Order 1995 (SI 1995/401; not reproduced in this work).

The depositing of money for the purposes of s.144(1) with the Accountant Gen-
eral is governed by the Motor Vehicles (Third-Party Risks Deposits) Regulations
1992 (SI 1992/1284) (not reproduced in this work).]

[Offence of keeping vehicle which does not meet insurance requirements

A18.362   **144A.**—(1) If a motor vehicle registered under the Vehicle Excise and Registration Act 1994 does not meet the insurance requirements, the person in whose name the vehicle is registered is guilty of an offence.

(2) For the purposes of this section a vehicle meets the insurance requirements if—

     (a) it is covered by a such a policy of insurance or such a security in respect of third party risks as complies with the requirements of this Part of this Act, and

     (b) either of the following conditions is satisfied.

(3) The first condition is that the policy or security, or the certificate of insurance or security which relates to it, identifies the vehicle by its registration mark as a vehicle which is covered by the policy or security.

(4) The second condition is that the vehicle is covered by the policy or security because—

     (a) the policy or security covers any vehicle, or any vehicle of a particular description, the owner of which is a person named in the policy or security or in the certificate of insurance or security which relates to it, and

     (b) the vehicle is owned by that person.

(5) For the purposes of this section a vehicle is covered by a policy of insurance or security if the policy of insurance or security is in force in relation to the use of the vehicle.]

A18.363   *[Section 144A is printed as inserted after s.144 by the Road Safety Act 2006 s.22(1).]*

[Exceptions to section 144A offence

A18.364   **144B.**—(1) A person ("the registered keeper") in whose name a vehicle which does not meet the insurance requirements is registered at any particular time ("the relevant time") does not commit an offence under section 144A of this Act at that time if any of the following conditions are satisfied.

(2) The first condition is that at the relevant time the vehicle is owned as described—

(a) in subsection (1) of section 144 of this Act, or

(b) in paragraph (a), (b), (da), (db), (dc) or (g) of subsection (2) of that section,

(whether or not at the relevant time it is being driven as described in that provision).

(3) The second condition is that at the relevant time the vehicle is owned with the intention that it should be used as described in paragraph (c), (d), (e) or (f) of section 144(2) of this Act.

(4) The third condition is that the registered keeper—

(a) is not at the relevant time the person keeping the vehicle, and

(b) if previously he was the person keeping the vehicle, he has by the relevant time complied with any requirements under subsection (7)(a) below that he is required to have complied with by the relevant or any earlier time.

(5) The fourth condition is that—

(a) the registered keeper is at the relevant time the person keeping the vehicle,

(b) at the relevant time the vehicle is not used on a road or other public place, and

(c) the registered keeper has by the relevant time complied with any requirements under subsection (7)(a) below that he is required to have complied with by the relevant or any earlier time.

(6) The fifth condition is that—

(a) the vehicle has been stolen before the relevant time,

(b) the vehicle has not been recovered by the relevant time, and

(c) any requirements under subsection (7)(b) below that, in connection with the theft, are required to have been complied with by the relevant or any earlier time have been complied with by the relevant time.

[(6A) The sixth condition is that—

(a) the registered keeper is at the relevant time the person keeping the vehicle,

(b) neither a licence nor a nil licence under the Vehicle Excise and Registration Act 1994 was in force for the vehicle on 31st January 1998,

(c) neither a licence nor a nil licence has been taken out for the vehicle for a period starting after that date, and

(d) the vehicle has not been used or kept on a public road after that date.]

(7) Regulations may make provision—

(a) for the purposes of subsection (4)(b) and (5)(c) above, requiring a person in whose name a vehicle is registered to furnish such particulars and make such declarations as may be prescribed, and to do so at such times and in such manner as may be prescribed, and

(b) for the purposes of subsection (6)(c) above, as to the persons to whom, the times at which and the manner in which the theft of a vehicle is to be notified.

(8) Regulations may make provision amending this section for the purpose of providing for further exceptions to section 144A of this Act (or varying or revoking any such further exceptions).

(9) A person accused of an offence under section 144A of this Act is not entitled to the benefit of an exception conferred by or under this section unless evidence is adduced that is sufficient to raise an issue with respect to that exception; but where evidence is so adduced it is for the prosecution to prove beyond reasonable doubt that the exception does not apply.]

A18.365 *[Section 144B is printed as inserted after s.144A by the Road Safety Act 2006 s.22(1) and as amended by the Motor Vehicles (Insurance Requirements) Regulations 2011 (SI 2011/20) reg.5.]*

[Fixed penalty notices

A18.366   **144C.**—(1) Where on any occasion the Secretary of State has reason to believe that a person has committed an offence under section 144A of this Act, the Secretary of State may give the person a notice offering him the opportunity of discharging any liability to conviction for that offence by payment of a fixed penalty to the Secretary of State.

(2) Where a person is given a notice under this section in respect of an offence under section 144A of this Act—

    (a) no proceedings may be instituted for that offence before the end of the period of 21 days following the date of the notice, and

    (b) he may not be convicted of that offence if he pays the fixed penalty before the end of that period.

(3) A notice under this section must give such particulars of the circumstances alleged to constitute the offence as are necessary for giving reasonable information of the offence.

(4) A notice under this section must also state—

    (a) the period during which, by virtue of subsection (2) above, proceedings will not be taken for the offence,

    (b) the amount of the fixed penalty, and

    (c) the person to whom and the address at which the fixed penalty may be paid.

(5) Without prejudice to payment by any other method, payment of the fixed penalty may be made by pre-paying and posting a letter containing the amount of the penalty (in cash or otherwise) to the person mentioned in subsection (4)(c) above at the address so mentioned.

(6) Where a letter is sent in accordance with subsection (5) above payment is to be regarded as having been made at the time at which that letter would be delivered in the ordinary course of post.

(7) Regulations may make provision as to any matter incidental to the operation of this section, and in particular—

    (a) as to the form of a notice under this section,

    (b) as to the information to be provided in such a notice by virtue of this section, and

    (c) as to any further information to be provided in a such notice.

(8) The fixed penalty payable under this section is, subject to subsection (9) below, £100.

(9) Regulations may substitute a different amount for the amount for the time being specified in subsection (8) above.

(10) Regulations may make provision for treating a fixed penalty payable under this section as having been paid if a lesser amount is paid before the end of a prescribed period.

(11) In any proceedings a certificate which—

    (a) purports to be signed by or on behalf of the Secretary of State,and

    (b) states that payment of a fixed penalty was or was not receivedby a date specified in the certificate,

is evidence of the facts stated.]

[Section 144C is printed as inserted after s.144B by the Road Safety Act 2006 s.22(1).]   **A18.367**

[Section 144A offence: supplementary

144D.—(1) Schedule 2A makes provision about the immobilisation of vehicles as regards which it appears that an offence under section 144A of this Act is being committed and about their removal and disposal.   **A18.368**

(2) A person authorised by the Secretary of State for the purposes of this subsection may on behalf of the Secretary of State conduct and appear in any proceedings by or against the Secretary of State in connection with the enforcement of an offence under section 144A of this Act or under regulations made under section 160 of this Act by virtue of Schedule 2A to this Act—

    (a) in England and Wales, in a magistrates' court, and

    (b) *[applies to Scotland].*]

[Section 144D is printed as inserted after s.144C by the Road Safety Act 2006 s.22(1).]   **A18.369**

Requirements in respect of policies of insurance

145.—(1) In order to comply with the requirements of this Part of this Act, a policy of insurance must satisfy the following conditions.   **A18.370**

(2) The policy must be issued by an authorised insurer.

(3) Subject to subsection (4) below, the policy—

    (a) must insure such person, persons or classes of persons as may be specified in the policy in respect of any liability which may be incurred by him or them in respect of the death of or bodily injury to any person or damage to property caused by, or arising out of, the use of the vehicle on a road [or other public place] in Great Britain, and

  [(aa) must, in the case of a vehicle normally based in the territory of another member State, insure him or them in respect of any civil liability which may be incurred by him or them as a result of an event related to the use of the vehicle in Great Britain if,—

    (i) according to the law of that territory, he or they would be required to be insured in respect of a civil liability which would arise under that law as a result of that event if the place where the vehicle was used when the event occurred were in that territory, and

    (ii) the cover required by that law would be higher than that required by paragraph (a) above, and]

(b) must[, in the case of a vehicle normally based in Great Britain,] insure him or them in respect of any liability which may be incurred by him or them in respect of the use of the vehicle and of any trailer, whether or not coupled, in the territory other than Great Britain and Gibraltar of each of the member States of the Communities according to

　　[(i) the law on compulsory insurance against civil liability in respect of the use of vehicles of the State in whose territory the event giving rise to the liability occurred; or

　　(ii) if it would give higher cover, the law which would be applicable under this Part of this Act if the place where the vehicle was used when that event occurred were in Great Britain; and]

(c) must also insure him or them in respect of any liability which may be incurred by him or them under the provisions of this Part of this Act relating to payment for emergency treatment.

(4) The policy shall not, by virtue of subsection (3)(a) above, be required—

(a) to cover liability in respect of the death, arising out of and in the course of his employment, of a person in the employment of a person insured by the policy or of bodily injury sustained by such a person arising out of and in the course of his employment, or

(b) to provide insurance of more than [£1,000,000] in respect of all such liabilities as may be incurred in respect of damage to property caused by, or arising out of, any one accident involving the vehicle, or

(c) to cover liability in respect of damage to the vehicle, or

(d) to cover liability in respect of damage to goods carried for hire or reward in or on the vehicle or in or on any trailer (whether or not coupled) drawn by the vehicle, or

(e) to cover any liability of a person in respect of damage to property in his custody or under his control, or

(f) to cover any contractual liability.

[(4A) In the case of a person—

(a) carried in or upon a vehicle, or

(b) entering or getting on to, or alighting from, a vehicle,

the provisions of paragraph (a) of subsection (4) above do not apply unless cover in respect of the liability referred to in that paragraph is in fact provided pursuant to a requirement of the Employers' Liability (Compulsory Insurance) Act 1969.]

[(5) *"Authorised insurer"* has the same meaning as in section 95.]

(6) If any person or body of persons ceases to be a member of the Motor Insurers' Bureau, that person or body shall not by virtue of that cease to be treated as an authorised insurer for the purposes of this Part of this Act […]—

(a) in relation to any policy issued by the insurer before ceasing to be such a member, or

(b) in relation to any obligation (whether arising before or after the insurer ceased to be such a member) which the insurer may be called upon to meet under or in consequence of any such policy or under section 157 of this Act […] by virtue of making a payment in pursuance of such an obligation.

A18.371　　*[Section 145 is printed as amended by the Motor Vehicles (Compulsory Insur-*

ance) Regulations 1992 (SI 1992/3036; not reproduced in this work); the Road Traffic (NHS Charges) Act 1999 (except in relation to military hospitals), s.18(1)(a) and (b); the Road Traffic (NHS Charges) Act 1999 (Commencement No.1) Order 1999 (SI 1999/1075; not reproduced in this work); the Motor Vehicles (Compulsory Insurance) Regulations 2000 (SI 2000/726; not reproduced in this work); the Financial Services and Markets Act 2000 (Consequential Amendments and Repeals) Order 2001 (SI 2001/3649; not reproduced in this work) art.313; the Health and Social Care (Community Health and Standards) Act 2003 s.196 and Sch.14, para.1; the Motor Vehicles (Compulsory Insurance) Regulations 2007 (SI 2007/1426).

As to the implementation of EC law by SI 2000/726, see the notes to s.143 above.

As to s.145(2), see the Motor Vehicles (Compulsory Insurance) (No.2) Regulations 1973 (SI 1973/2143) reg.8, as amended, not reproduced in this work.]

Requirements in respect of securities

146. *[Omitted.]*   **A18.372**

Issue and surrender of certificates of insurance and of security

147.—(1) A policy of insurance shall be of no effect for the purposes of this   **A18.373** Part of this Act unless and until there is delivered by the insurer to the person by whom the policy is effected a certificate (in this Part of this Act referred to as a *"certificate of insurance"*) in the prescribed form and containing such particulars of any conditions subject to which the policy is issued and of any other matters as may be prescribed.

[(1A) A certificate of insurance is to be treated for the purposes of this Part of this Act as having been delivered under subsection (1) above to the person by whom the policy is effected if—

     (a) it is transmitted electronically by the insurer to the person in accordance with subsection (1B) below, or

     (b) it is made available by the insurer to the person on a website in accordance with subsection (1C) below.

(1B) A certificate is transmitted electronically by an insurer to a person in accordance with this subsection if—

     (a) on effecting the policy to which the certificate relates, the person agreed to its electronic transmission for the purposes of subsection (1) above, and

     (b) the certificate is transmitted by the insurer to an electronic address specified by the person for this purpose.

(1C) A certificate is made available by an insurer to a person on a website in accordance with this subsection if—

     (a) on effecting the policy to which the certificate relates, the person agreed to its electronic transmission for the purposes of subsection (1) above, and

     (b) the insurer makes the certificate available to the person by placing an electronic copy of it on a website, and

     (c) the person is notified by the insurer, in a manner agreed by the person, of—

(i) the certificate's presence on the website,

(ii) the address of the website,

(iii) the place on the website where he may access the certificate, and

(iv) how he may access the certificate.

(1D) Where a certificate made available on a website is treated by virtue of subsection (1A)(b) above as having been delivered by an insurer to a person, the insurer must ensure that the certificate remains continuously accessible to the person on the website until the expiry of the last day on which the policy to which it relates has effect.

(1E) For the purposes of subsection (1D) above, a certificate is to be treated as remaining continuously accessible to a person on a website, despite its being temporarily inaccessible to him on the website, if the insurer has taken all reasonable steps to make it continuously accessible to him on the website (including steps to remedy any temporary inaccessibility).]

(2) *[Certificate of security.]*

(3) Different forms and different particulars may be prescribed for the purposes of subsection (1) or (2) above in relation to different cases or circumstances.

(4) Where a certificate has been delivered under this section[, otherwise than as described in subsection (1A)(a) or (b) above,] and the policy or security to which it relates is cancelled by mutual consent or by virtue of any provision in the policy or security, the person to whom the certificate was delivered must, within seven days from the taking effect of the cancellation—

(a) surrender the certificate to the person by whom the policy was issued or the security was given, or

(b) if the certificate has been lost or destroyed, make a statutory declaration to that effect.

[(4A) Where subsection (4) above applies in respect of a certificate of insurance that has not been lost or destroyed, the person to whom the certificate was delivered—

(a) may, instead of surrendering the certificate under subsection (4)(a) above, transmit to the insurer, by means of an electronic communication to an electronic address specified by the insurer, a statement confirming that the policy to which the certificate relates has ceased to have effect, and

(b) if he does so, is to be treated as having surrendered the certificate.

(4B) Where subsection (4) above applies in respect of a certificate of insurance that has been lost or destroyed, the person to whom the certificate was delivered—

(a) may, instead of making a statutory declaration as described in subsection (4)(b) above, transmit to the insurer, by means of an electronic communication to an electronic address specified by the insurer, a statement confirming that the certificate has been lost or (as applicable) destroyed, and

(b) if he does so, is to be treated as having made a statutory declaration as described in subsection (4)(b) above.

(4C) Subsection (4D) below applies where—

(a) a certificate of insurance is treated, by virtue of subsection (1A) above, as having been delivered to a person under this section, and

    (b) the policy to which it relates is cancelled by mutual consent or by virtue of any provision in the policy.

(4D) The person must, within seven days from the taking effect of the cancellation, either—

    (a) transmit to the insurer, by means of an electronic communication to an electronic address specified by the insurer, a statement confirming that the policy to which the certificate relates has ceased to have effect, or

    (b) deliver to the insurer a legible printed copy of the certificate endorsed with a statement made and signed by him to that effect.

(4E) A person who transmits a statement or delivers a copy of a certificate as described in paragraph (a) or (b) of subsection (4D) above is to be treated as having surrendered the certificate in question.

(4F) In this section, *"electronic communication"* has the meaning given in the Electronic Communications Act 2000.]

(5) A person who fails to comply with subsection (4) [or (4D)] above is guilty of an offence.

[Section 147 is printed as amended by the Motor Vehicles (Electronic Com- **A18.374**
munication of Certificates of Insurance) Order 2010 (SI 2010/1117) art.3.

As to s.147(1), see the Motor Vehicles (Compulsory Insurance) (No.2) Regulations 1973 (SI 1973/2143) reg.8, as amended, not reproduced in this work.

As to the prescribed forms of certificates under s.147(3) and provisions relating to the forms and completion of certificates, see the Motor Vehicles (Third Party Risks) Regulations 1972 (SI 1972/1217) Schedule below.]

Avoidance of certain exceptions to policies or securities

148.—(1) Where a certificate of insurance or certificate of security has been **A18.375** delivered under section 147 of this Act to the person by whom a policy has been effected or to whom a security has been given, so much of the policy or security as purports to restrict—

    (a) the insurance of the persons insured by the policy, or

    (b) the operation of the security,

(as the case may be) by reference to any of the matters mentioned in subsection (2) below shall, as respects such liabilities as are required to be covered by a policy under section 145 of this Act, be of no effect.

(2) Those matters are—

    (a) the age or physical or mental condition of persons driving the vehicle,

    (b) the condition of the vehicle,

    (c) the number of persons that the vehicle carries,

    (d) the weight or physical characteristics of the goods that the vehicle carries,

    (e) the time at which or the areas within which the vehicle is used,

    (f) the horsepower or cylinder capacity or value of the vehicle,

    (g) the carrying on the vehicle of any particular apparatus, or

    (h) the carrying on the vehicle of any particular means of identification other than any means of identification required to be carried by or under [the Vehicle Excise and Registration Act 1994].

(3) Nothing in subsection (1) above requires an insurer or the giver of a security to pay any sum in respect of the liability of any person otherwise than in or towards the discharge of that liability.

(4) Any sum paid by an insurer or the giver of a security in or towards the discharge of any liability of any person which is covered by the policy or security by virtue only of subsection (1) above is recoverable by the insurer or giver of the security from that person.

(5) A condition in a policy or security issued or given for the purposes of this Part of this Act providing—

    (a) that no liability shall arise under the policy or security, or

    (b) that any liability so arising shall cease,

in the event of some specified thing being done or omitted to be done after the happening of the event giving rise to a claim under the policy or security, shall be of no effect in connection with such liabilities as are required to be covered by a policy under section 145 of this Act.

(6) Nothing in subsection (5) above shall be taken to render void any provision in a policy or security requiring the person insured or secured to pay to the insurer or the giver of the security any sums which the latter may have become liable to pay under the policy or security and which have been applied to the satisfaction of the claims of third parties.

(7) Notwithstanding anything in any enactment, a person issuing a policy of insurance under section 145 of this Act shall be liable to indemnify the persons or classes of persons specified in the policy in respect of any liability which the policy purports to cover in the case of those persons or classes of persons.

A18.376   *[Section 148 is printed as amended by the Vehicle Excise and Registration Act 1994 s.63 and Sch.3, para.24(1).]*

Avoidance of certain agreements as to liability towards passengers

A18.377   **149.**—(1) This section applies where a person uses a motor vehicle in circumstances such that under section 143 of this Act there is required to be in force in relation to his use of it such a policy of insurance or such a security in respect of third-party risks as complies with the requirements of this Part of this Act.

(2) If any other person is carried in or upon the vehicle while the user is so using it, any antecedent agreement or understanding between them (whether intended to be legally binding or not) shall be of no effect so far as it purports or might be held—

    (a) to negative or restrict any such liability of the user in respect of persons carried in or upon the vehicle as is required by section 145 of this Act to be covered by a policy of insurance, or

    (b) to impose any conditions with respect to the enforcement of any such liability of the user.

(3) The fact that a person so carried has willingly accepted as his the risk of negligence on the part of the user shall not be treated as negativing any such liability of the user.

(4) For the purposes of this section —

    (a) references to a person being carried in or upon a vehicle include references to a person entering or getting on to, or alighting from, the vehicle, and

(b) the reference to an antecedent agreement is to one made at any time before the liability arose.

Insurance or security in respect of private use of vehicle to cover use under car-sharing arrangements

150.—(1) To the extent that a policy or security issued or given for the   **A18.378** purposes of this Part of this Act —

   (a) restricts the insurance of the persons insured by the policy or the operation of the security (as the case may be) to use of the vehicle for specified purposes (for example, social, domestic and pleasure purposes) of a non-commercial character, or

   (b) excludes from that insurance or the operation of the security (as the case may be)—

      (i) use of the vehicle for hire or reward, or

      (ii) business or commercial use of the vehicle, or

      (iii) use of the vehicle for specified purposes of a business or commercial character,

then, for the purposes of that policy or security so far as it relates to such liabilities as are required to be covered by a policy under section 145 of this Act, the use of a vehicle on a journey in the course of which one or more passengers are carried at separate fares shall, if the conditions specified in subsection (2) below are satisfied, be treated as falling within that restriction or as not falling within that exclusion (as the case may be).

(2) The conditions referred to in subsection (1) above are—

   (a) the vehicle is not adapted to carry more than eight passengers and is not a motor cycle,

   (b) the fare or aggregate of the fares paid in respect of the journey does not exceed the amount of the running costs of the vehicle for the journey (which for the purposes of this paragraph shall be taken to include an appropriate amount in respect of depreciation and general wear), and

   (c) the arrangements for the payment of fares by the passenger or passengers carried at separate fares were made before the journey began.

(3) Subsections (1) and (2) above apply however the restrictions or exclusions described in subsection (1) are framed or worded.

(4) In subsections (1) and (2) above *"fare"* and *"separate fares"* have the same meaning as in section 1(4) of the Public Passenger Vehicles Act 1981 [*q.v.*].

Duty of insurers or persons giving security to satisfy judgment against persons insured or secured against third-party risks

151. *[Omitted.]*   **A18.379**

Exceptions to section 151

152. *[Omitted.]*   **A18.380**

Bankruptcy, etc., of insured or secured persons not to affect claims by third parties

153. *[Omitted.]*   **A18.381**

Duty to give information as to insurance or security where claim made

A18.382   **154.**—(1) A person against whom a claim is made in respect of any such liability as is required to be covered by a policy of insurance under section 145 of this Act must, on demand by or on behalf of the person making the claim—

    (a) state whether or not, in respect of that liability—

        (i) he was insured by a policy having effect for the purposes of this Part of this Act or had in force a security having effect for those purposes, or

        (ii) he would have been so insured or would have had in force such a security if the insurer or, as the case may be, the giver of the security had not avoided or cancelled the policy or security, and

    (b) if he was or would have been so insured, or had or would have had in force such a security—

        (i) give such particulars with respect to that policy or security as were specified in any certificate of insurance or security delivered in respect of that policy or security, as the case may be, under section 147 of this Act, or

        (ii) where no such certificate was delivered under that section, give the following particulars, that is to say, the registration mark or other identifying particulars of the vehicle concerned, the number or other identifying particulars of the insurance policy issued in respect of the vehicle, the name of the insurer and the period of the insurance cover.

(2) If without reasonable excuse, a person fails to comply with the provisions of subsection (1) above, or wilfully makes a false statement in reply to any such demand as is referred to in that subsection, he is guilty of an offence.

Deposits

A18.383   **155.** *[Omitted.]*

Power to require evidence of insurance or security on application for vehicle excise licence

A18.384   **156.** *[Omitted.]*

Payments for treatment of traffic casualties

Payment for hospital treatment of traffic casualties

A18.385   **157.**—(1) Subject to subsection (2) below, where—

    (a) a payment, other than a payment under section 158 of this Act, is made (whether or not with an admission of liability) in respect of the death of, or bodily injury to, any person arising out of the use of a motor vehicle on a road or in a place to which the public have a right of access, and

    (b) the payment is made—

        (i) by an authorised insurer, the payment being made under or in consequence of a policy issued under section 145 of this Act, or

    (ii) by the owner of a vehicle in relation to the use of which a security under this Part of this Act is in force, or

    (iii) by the owner of a vehicle who has made a deposit under this Part of this Act, and

  (c) the person who has so died or been bodily injured has to the knowledge of the insurer or owner, as the case may be, received treatment at a hospital, whether as an in-patient or as an out-patient, in respect of the injury so arising,

the insurer or owner must pay the expenses reasonably incurred by the hospital in affording the treatment, after deducting from the expenses any moneys actually received in payment of a specific charge for the treatment, not being moneys received under any contributory scheme.

  (2) The amount to be paid shall not exceed [£2,949.00] for each person treated as an in-patient or [£295.00] for each person treated as an out-patient.

  (3) For the purposes of this section *"expenses reasonably incurred"* means—

  (a) in relation to a person who receives treatment at a hospital as an in-patient, an amount for each day he is maintained in the hospital representing the average daily cost, for each in-patient, of the maintenance of the hospital and the staff of the hospital and the maintenance and treatment of the in-patients in the hospital, and

  (b) in relation to a person who receives treatment at a hospital as an out-patient, reasonable expenses actually incurred.

[Section 157 is printed as amended by the Road Traffic Accidents (Payments for Treatment) Order 1995 (SI 1995/889) (not reproduced in this work) and the sums set out above in s.157(2) relate to treatment given after April 16, 1995 and examinations made after that date of persons who die or suffer bodily injury.]   **A18.386**

Payment for emergency treatment of traffic casualties

158.—(1) Subsection (2) below applies where—   **A18.387**

  (a) medical or surgical treatment or examination is immediately required as a result of bodily injury (including fatal injury) to a person caused by, or arising out of, the use of a motor vehicle on a road, and

  (b) the treatment or examination so required (in this Part of this Act referred to as *"emergency treatment"*) is effected by a legally qualified medical practitioner.

  (2) The person who was using the vehicle at the time of the event out of which the bodily injury arose must, on a claim being made in accordance with the provisions of section 159 of this Act, pay to the practitioner (or, where emergency treatment is effected by more than one practitioner, to the practitioner by whom it is first effected)—

  (a) a fee of [£21.30] in respect of each person in whose case the emergency treatment is effected by him, and

  (b) a sum, in respect of any distance in excess of two miles which he must cover in order—

    (i) to proceed from the place from which he is summoned to the place where the emergency treatment is carried out by him, and

    (ii) to return to the first mentioned place,

equal to [41 pence] for every complete mile and additional part of a mile of that distance.

(3) Where emergency treatment is first effected in a hospital, the provisions of subsections (1) and (2) above with respect to payment of a fee shall, so far as applicable, but subject (as regards the recipient of a payment) to the provisions of section 159 of this Act, have effect with the substitution of references to the hospital for references to a legally qualified medical practitioner.

(4) Liability incurred under this section by the person using a vehicle shall, where the event out of which it arose was caused by the wrongful act of another person, be treated for the purposes of any claim to recover damage by reason of that wrongful act as damage sustained by the person using the vehicle.

A18.388   *[Section 158 is printed as amended by the Road Traffic Accidents (Payments for Treatment) Order 1995 (SI 1995/889) (not reproduced in this work) and the sums set out above in s.158(2) relate to treatment given after April 16, 1995 and examinations made after that date of persons who die or suffer bodily injury.]*

Supplementary provisions as to payments for treatment

A18.389   **159.**—(1) A payment falling to be made under section 157 or 158 of this Act in respect of treatment in a hospital must be made [to the hospital].

(2) A claim for a payment under section 158 of this Act may be made at the time when the emergency treatment is effected, by oral request to the person who was using the vehicle, and if not so made must be made by request in writing served on him within seven days from the day on which the emergency treatment was effected.

(3) Any such request in writing—

    (a) must be signed by the claimant or, in the case of a hospital, by an executive officer of [the hospital claiming the payment],

    (b) must state the name and address of the claimant, the circumstances in which the emergency treatment was effected, and that it was first effected by the claimant or, in the case of a hospital, in the hospital, and

    (c) may be served by delivering it to the person who was using the vehicle or by sending it in a prepaid registered letter, or the recorded delivery service, addressed to him at his usual or last known address.

(4) A payment made under section 158 of this Act shall operate as a discharge, to the extent of the amount paid, of any liability of the person who was using the vehicle, or of any other person, to pay any sum in respect of the expenses or remuneration of the practitioner or hospital concerned of or for effecting the emergency treatment.

(5) A chief officer of police must, if so requested by a person who alleges that he is entitled to claim a payment under section 158 of this Act, provide that person with any information at the disposal of the chief officer—

    (a) as to the identification marks of any motor vehicle which that person alleges to be a vehicle out of the use of which the bodily injury arose, and

    (b) as to the identity and address of the person who was using the vehicle at the time of the event out of which it arose.

A18.390   *[Section 159 is printed as amended by the Health Authorities Act 1995 s.2(1)* *and (3) and Sch.1, para.117; the Road Traffic (NHS Charges) Act 1999 (except in relation to military hospitals) s.18(2)(a) and (b); the Road Traffic (NHS Charges) Act 1999 (Commencement No.1) Order 1999 (SI 1999/1075; not reproduced in this work).*

The functions of the Secretary of State exercisable under s.159 in relation to Wales have been transferred to the National Assembly for Wales by the National Assembly for Wales (Transfer of Functions) Order 1999 (SI 1999/672; not reproduced in this work) art.2 and Sch.1.]

General

[Disclosure of information

159A.—(1) Regulations may make provision for and in connection with requir-   **A18.391**
ing MIIC to make information available to any prescribed person for the purposes of the exercise of any of that person's functions in connection with the enforcement of an offence under this Part of this Act or under regulations made under section 160 of this Act.

(2) In this section—

"*MIIC*" means the Motor Insurers' Information Centre (a company limited by guarantee and incorporated under the Companies Act 1985 on 8th December 1998), and

"*information*" means information held in any form.]

[Section 159A is printed as inserted before s.160 by the Road Safety Act 2006   **A18.392**
s.22(2).]

Regulations

160. *[Omitted.]*   **A18.393**

Interpretation

161.—(1) In this Part of this Act —   **A18.394**

["*hospital*" means any institution which provides medical or surgical treatment for in-patients, other than—

    (a) a health service hospital within the meaning of [the National Health Service Act 2006 or the National Health Service (Wales) Act 2006] or the National Health Service (Scotland) Act 1978,

    (b) [...]

    (c) any institution carried on for profit,]

"*policy of insurance*" includes a covering note,

"*salvage*" means the preservation of a vessel which is wrecked, stranded or in distress, or the lives of persons belonging to, or the cargo or apparel of, such a vessel, and

"*under the owner's control*" means, in relation to a vehicle, that it is being driven by the owner or by a servant of the owner in the course of his employment or is otherwise subject to the control of the owner.

(2) In any provision of this Part of this Act relating to the surrender, or the loss or destruction, of a certificate of insurance or certificate of security, references to such a certificate—

(a) shall, in relation to policies or securities under which more than one certificate is issued, be construed as references to all certificates, and

(b) shall, where any copy has been issued of any certificate, be construed as including a reference to that copy.

(3) In this Part of this Act, any reference to an accident includes a reference to two or more causally related accidents.

A18.395   *[Section 161 is printed as amended by the Road Traffic (NHS Charges) Act 1999 (except in relation to military hospitals) s.18(3)(a); the Road Traffic (NHS Charges) Act 1999 (Commencement No.1) Order 1999 (SI 1999/1075; not reproduced in this work); the Health and Social Care (Community Health and Standards) Act 2003 s.169(2) and Sch.14, para.1.]*

Index to Part VI

A18.396   **162.** The expressions listed in the left-hand column below are respectively defined or (as the case may be) fall to be construed in accordance with the provisions of this Part of this Act listed in the right-hand column in relation to those expressions.

Expression	Relevant provision
Accident	Section 161(3)
[Authorised insurer	Section 145(5)]
Certificate of insurance	Sections 147(1) and 161(2)
Certificate of security	Sections 147(2) and 161(2)
Hospital	Section 161(1)
Policy of insurance	Section 161(1)
Prescribed	Section 160(1)
Regulations	Section 160(1)
Salvage	Section 161(1)
Under the owner's control	Section 161(1)

A18.397   *[Section 162 is printed as amended by the Financial Services and Markets Act 2000 (Consequential Amendments and Repeals) Order 2001 (SI 2001/3649) art.314.]*

PART VII

MISCELLANEOUS AND GENERAL

[Requirement for approval of persons to assist at tests]

[Approved test assistants

A18.398   **162A.**—(1) The Secretary of State may make regulations permitting any person wishing to be accompanied at a relevant test by another person (a "test assistant") to be so accompanied if—

(a) he submits himself for the relevant test in any circumstances in which the Secretary of State considers it appropriate that he should be entitled to be so accompanied, and

(b) the test assistant is approved in accordance with regulations under this section to accompany people at relevant tests in such circumstances in order to assist them in undergoing the relevant tests.

(2) The circumstances in which the Secretary of State considers it appropriate that a person should be entitled to be accompanied by a test assistant at a relevant test may include, for example, circumstances in which he is likely to have difficulty in hearing, understanding or responding to instructions or questions in the course of the relevant test without assistance.

(3) The regulations may make provision in relation to the approval of test assistants and may, in particular, include provision—

(a) in relation to the making of applications for approval,

(b) for the payment in respect of applications for approval, or of approvals, (or both) of fees of such amounts as are prescribed,

(c) in relation to the period for which an approval is to have effect and withdrawing approval,

(d) authorising the imposition of conditions on an approval,

(e) for an appeal to lie to the Transport Tribunal against a refusal of an application for approval, the imposition of conditions on an approval or the withdrawal of approval,

(f) prescribing circumstances in which an approved test assistant may not act as such,

(g) as to the evidencing by persons of their status as approved test assistants, and

(h) authorising the Secretary of State to make available (with or without charge) information about approved test assistants.

(4) The regulations may make different provision in relation to different cases.

(5) The following are relevant tests—

(a) tests of competence to drive a motor vehicle prescribed by virtue of section 89(3) of this Act or section 36(5) of the Road Traffic Offenders Act 1988,

(b) examinations of ability and fitness (or continued ability and fitness) to give driving instruction for which provision is made by virtue of section 132 of this Act, and

(c) emergency control assessments under section 133A of this Act.]

[Section 162A and the heading above it are printed as inserted by the Road Safety Act 2006 s.43.]   **A18.399**

Powers of constables and other authorised persons

Power of police to stop vehicles

163.—(1) A person driving a [mechanically propelled vehicle] on a road must   **A18.400** stop the vehicle on being required to do so by a constable in uniform [or a traffic officer].

(2) A person riding a cycle on a road must stop the cycle on being required to do so by a constable in uniform.

(3) If a person fails to comply with this section he is guilty of an offence.

[(4) [...]]

A18.401   *[Section 163 is printed as amended by the Road Traffic Act 1991 s.48 and Sch.4, para.67; the Police Reform Act 2002 s.49(1); the Traffic Management Act 2004 s.6(4); the Serious Organised Crime and Police Act 2005 s.111 and Sch.7, para.27(3), and Sch.17, Pt 2.*

For the exercise of the power to require a vehicle to stop for the purpose of a road check by a designated community support officer, see the Police Reform Act 2002 s.44 and Sch.4, para.13; not reproduced in this work.

The power of a constable in uniform under s.163(2) above may be exercised by community support officers and accredited persons in relation to a person reasonably believed to have committed an offence under s.72 of the Highway Act 1835 (riding on a footway) by cycling (see the Police Reform Act 2002 Sch.4, para.11A, Sch.5, para.8A).]

Power of constables to require production of driving licence and in certain cases statement of date of birth

A18.402   **164.**—(1) Any of the following persons—

    (a) a person driving a motor vehicle on a road,

    (b) a person whom a constable [or vehicle examiner] has reasonable cause to believe to have been the driver of a motor vehicle at a time when an accident occurred owing to its presence on a road,

    (c) a person whom a constable [or vehicle examiner] has reasonable cause to believe to have committed an offence in relation to the use of a motor vehicle on a road, or

    (d) a person—

        (i) who supervises the holder of a provisional licence while the holder is driving a motor vehicle on a road, or

        (ii) whom a constable [or vehicle examiner] has reasonable cause to believe was supervising the holder of a provisional licence while driving, at a time when an accident occurred owing to the presence of the vehicle on a road or at a time when an offence is suspected of having been committed by the holder of the provisional licence in relation to the use of the vehicle on a road,

must, on being so required by a constable [or vehicle examiner], produce his licence [and its counterpart] for examination, so as to enable the constable [or vehicle examiner] to ascertain the name and address of the holder of the licence, the date of issue, and the authority by which [they were] issued.

(2) [A person required by a constable under subsection (1) above to produce his licence] must in prescribed circumstances, on being so required by the constable, state his date of birth.

(3) If—

    [(a) the Secretary of State has—

        (i) revoked a licence under [92,] section 93 or 99 of this Act, or

        (ii) revoked or suspended a large goods vehicle driver's licence or a passenger-carrying vehicle driver's licence under section 115 of this Act, and] [or

      [(iii) served notice requiring the delivery of a licence to him in pursuance of section 99C[, 109B] or 115A of this Act, and

(b) the holder of the licence fails to deliver it [and its counterpart] to the Secretary of State [or the traffic commissioner, as the case may be] in pursuance of [section 92,] 93, 99, [99C[, 109B], 115A or 118] (as the case may be)],

a constable [or vehicle examiner] may require him to [produce the licence and its counterpart], and upon [their] being produced may seize [them] and deliver [them] to the Secretary of State.

(4) Where a constable has reasonable cause to believe that the holder of a licence, or any other person, has knowingly made a false statement for the purpose of obtaining the grant of the licence, the constable may require the holder of the licence to produce it [and its counterpart] to him.

[(4A) Where a constable to whom a provisional licence has been produced by a person driving a motor bicycle has reasonable cause to believe that the holder was not driving it as part of the training being provided on a training course for motor cyclists, the constable may require him to produce the prescribed certificate of completion of a training course for motor cyclists.]

(5) Where a person has been required under [section 26 or 27 of the Road Traffic Offenders Act 1988[, section 40B of the Child Support Act 1991] [, section 40 of the Crime (Sentences) Act 1997, section 146 or 147 of the Powers of Criminal Courts (Sentencing) Act 2000] or section 223A or 436A of the Criminal Procedure (Scotland) Act 1975] to produce a licence [and its counterpart] to the court and fails to do so, a constable may require him to produce [them] and, upon [their] being produced, may seize [them] and deliver [them] to the court.

(6) If a person required under the preceding provisions of this section to produce a licence [and its counterpart] or state his date of birth [or to produce his certificate of completion of a training course for motor cyclists] ... fails to do so he is, subject to subsections (7) [to (8A)] below, guilty of an offence.

(7) Subsection (6) above does not apply where a person required on any occasion under the preceding provisions of this section to produce a licence [and its counterpart]—

    (a) produces on that occasion a current receipt for the licence [and its counterpart] issued under section 56 of the Road Traffic Offenders Act 1988 [*q.v.*] and, if required to do so, produces the licence [and its counterpart] in person immediately on [their] return at a police station that was specified on that occasion, or

    (b) within seven days after that occasion produces such a receipt in person at a police station that was specified by him on that occasion and, if required to do so, produces the licence [and its counterpart] in person immediately on [their] return at that police station.

(8) In proceedings against any person for the offence of failing to produce a licence [and its counterpart] it shall be a defence for him to show that—

    (a) within seven days after the production of his licence [and its counterpart] was required he produced [them] in person at a police station that was specified by him at the time [their] production was required, or

    (b) he produced [them] in person there as soon as was reasonably practicable, or

    (c) it was not reasonably practicable for him to produce [them] there before the day on which the proceedings were commenced, and for the purposes of this subsection the laying of the information … shall be treated as the commencement of the proceedings.

[(8A) Subsection (8) above shall apply in relation to a certificate of completion of a training course for motor cyclists as it applies in relation to a licence.]

(9) Where in accordance with this section a person has stated his date of birth to a constable, the Secretary of State may serve on that person a notice in writing requiring him to provide the Secretary of State—

> (a) with such evidence in that person's possession or obtainable by him as the Secretary of State may specify for the purpose of verifying that date, and
>
> (b) if his name differs from his name at the time of his birth, with a statement in writing specifying his name at that time,

and a person who knowingly fails to comply with a notice under this subsection is guilty of an offence.

(10) A notice authorised to be served on any person by subsection (9) above may be served on him by delivering it to him or by leaving it at his proper address or by sending it to him by post; and for the purposes of this subsection and section 7 of the Interpretation Act 1978 in its application to this subsection the proper address of any person shall be his latest address as known to the person giving the notice.

[(11) In this section —

> "licence" means a licence[, a Northern Ireland licence] under Part III of this Act or a [Northern Ireland] Community licence,
>
> "vehicle examiner" means an examiner appointed under section 66A of this Act;

and "Community licence", "counterpart", "provisional licence", "training course for motor cyclists" and, in relation to such a course, "the prescribed certificate of completion" have the same meanings as in Part III of this Act.]

A18.403   *[Section 164 is printed as amended by the Road Traffic (Driver Licensing and Information Systems) Act 1989 s.7 and Sch.3, para.18(a)–(d); the Driving Licences (Community Driving Licence) Regulations 1990 (SI 1990/144); the Road Traffic Act 1991 ss.48, 83, Sch.4, para.68(1)–(8) and Sch.8; the Driving Licences (Community Driving Licence) Regulations 1996 (SI 1996/1974) reg.2 and Sch.1, para.30 (not reproduced in this work); the Driving Licences (Community Driving Licence) Regulations 1998 (SI 1998/1420) regs 2 and 14 (not reproduced in this work); the Powers of Criminal Courts (Sentencing) Act 2000 s.165(1) and Sch.9, para.117; the Child Support, Pensions and Social Security Act 2000 s.16(4); the Crime (International Co-operation) Act 2003 s.91 and Sch.5, para.27(a)(ii), (iii) (part), (b).*

With effect from a date to be announced under the Transport Act 2000 s.275, the following amendments will be made to s.164 by the Transport Act 2000 s.260 and Sch.29, paras 1 and 5:

> 1. *the following text will be substituted for s.164(4A) (Transport Act 2000 Sch.29, paras 1 and 5(1) and (2)) —*

>> [(4A) If regulations make provision for the evidencing of the successful completion of driver training courses or a person's being within the exemption specified in subsection (2), or any exemption provided by virtue of subsection

(3), of section 99ZA of this Act, a person driving on a road a motor vehicle which he—

    (a) is not authorised so to drive without having successfully completed such a course, or

    (b) would not be authorised so to drive apart from the exemption,

may be required by a constable to produce prescribed evidence of the successful completion by him of such a course or of his being within the exemption.]

2. *the following words will be substituted in s.164(6) for the words "his certificate of completion of a training course for motor cyclists" (Transport Act 2000 Sch.29, paras 1 and 5(1) and (3))—*

[prescribed evidence of the successful completion by him of a driver training course or of his being within an exemption]

3. *the following words will be substituted in s.164(8A) for the words "a certificate of completion of a training course for motor cyclists" (Transport Act 2000 Sch.29, paras 1 and 5(1) and (4))—*

[prescribed evidence of the successful completion of a driver training course or of being within an exemption]

and

4. *in s.164(11), the words ""counterpart" and "provisional licence"" will be substituted for the words from ""counterpart,"" to ""completion"" (Transport Act 2000 Sch.29, paras 1 and 5(1) and (5)).*

With effect from a day (or days) to be appointed, in s.164(3)(a), the words "a person is required to deliver his licence and its counterpart to the Secretary of State under section 63 of the Crime (International Co-operation) Act 2003 or" will be inserted before the words "Secretary of State" by the Crime (International Co-operation) Act 2003 s.91 and Sch.5, para.27(a)(i); in s.164(3)(b), the words "or section 63 of the Crime (International Co-operation) Act 2003" will be inserted after the words "or 118" by ibid. s.91 and Sch.5, para.27(a)(iii).

With effect from a day to be appointed, the Criminal Justice Act 2003 s.304 and Sch.32, para.51 will substitute the words "section 301 of the Criminal Justice Act 2003" for the words "section 40 of the Crime (Sentences) Act 1997" in subs.(5) of s.164.

With effect from a day (or days) to be appointed and in relation to endorsement (all drivers), the following amendments will be made to s.164 by the Road Safety Act 2006 s.10 and Sch.3, para.26, s.59 and Sch.7(4):

1. *the words "and its counterpart" will be omitted in each place;*

2. *in s.164(1), the words "it was" will be substituted for the words "they were";*

3. *in s.164(3), the word "its" will be substituted for the word "their", and the word "it" will be substituted for the word "them", in both places;*

4. *in s.164(5), the word "it" will be substituted for the word "them", in each place, and the word "its" will be substituted for the word "their";*

5. *in s.164(7), the word "its" will be substituted for the word "their", in both places;*

6. *in s.164(8), the word "it" will be substituted for the word "them", in each place, and the word "its" will be substituted for the word "their";*

7. *in s.164(11), the reference to "counterpart" will be omitted.*

Words in s.164(8) relating exclusively and expressly to Scotland have been omitted.

With effect from a day to be appointed, the words ", section 40B of the Child Support Act 1991" in s.164(5) will be omitted by the Welfare Reform Act 2009 s.58 and Sch.7(4), para.1.

The circumstances in which a police constable may require a person to state his date of birth are prescribed in the Motor Vehicles (Driving Licences) Regulations 1999 (SI 1999/2864) reg.83 (q.v.).

As to the application of s.164(1), (6) and (8) to domestic driving permits, Convention driving permits, British Forces (BFG) driving licences and to the holders of such licences and permits, see the Motor Vehicles (Driving Licences) Regulations 1999 (SI 1999/2864) reg.80, below; and see also the Motor Vehicles (International Circulation) Order 1975 (SI 1975/1208) Sch.3, para.5(1) and (2)(a), below.

Proceedings under s.164(6) and (9) are specified by the Prosecution of Offences Act 1985 (Specified Proceedings) Order 1999 (SI 1999/904) below as being proceedings the conduct of which the Director of Public Prosecutions is not required to take over from the police under the Prosecution of Offences Act 1985 s.3(3)(a).

Reference is made in s.164(5) above (and also in s.27(3) of the Road Traffic Offenders Act 1988) to s.40B of the Child Support Act 1991. The latter section, together with s.39A of the 1991 Act, was inserted into the 1991 Act by the Child Support, Pensions and Social Security Act 2000 s.16(1) and (3). Sections 39A and 40B of the 1991 Act read as follows:

Commitment to prison and disqualification from driving

39A.—(1) Where the [Commission] has sought—

(a) in England and Wales to levy an amount by distress under this Act; or

(b) to recover an amount by virtue of section 36 or 38,

and that amount, or any portion of it, remains unpaid [it] may apply to the court under this section.

(2) An application under this section is for whichever the court considers appropriate in all the circumstances of—

(a) the issue of a warrant committing the liable person to prison; or

(b) an order for him to be disqualified from holding or obtaining a driving licence.

(3) On any such application the court shall (in the presence of the liable person) inquire as to—

(a) whether he needs a driving licence to earn his living;

(b) his means; and

(c) whether there has been wilful refusal or culpable neglect on his part.

(4) The [Commission] may make representations to the court as to whether [it] thinks it more appropriate to commit the liable person to prison or to disqualify him from holding or obtaining a driving licence; and the liable person may reply to those representations.

(5) In this section and section 40B, *"driving licence"* means a licence to drive a motor vehicle granted under Part III of the Road Traffic Act 1988.

(6) In this section *"the court"* means—

(a) in England and Wales, a magistrates' court;

(b) *[applies to Scotland]*.

[Section 39A is printed as amended by the Child Maintenance and Other Payments Act 2008 s.13 and Sch.3, para.41.

In s.39A(1)(a), with effect from a day to be appointed, the words "recover an amount by virtue of section 35(1)" will be substituted for the words "levy an amount by distress under this Act" by the Tribunals, Courts and Enforcement Act 2007 s.62(3) and Sch.13, para.95.

With effect from a day to be appointed, s.39A of the Child Support Act 1991 will be repealed (see the Child Maintenance and Other Payments Act 2008 s.58 and Sch.8).]

Disqualification from driving: further provision

40B.—(1) If, but only if, the court is of the opinion that there has been wilful refusal or culpable neglect on the part of the liable person, it may—

(a) order him to be disqualified, for such period specified in the order but not exceeding two years as it thinks fit, from holding or obtaining a driving licence (a *"disqualification order"*); or

(b) make a disqualification order but suspend its operation until such time and on such conditions (if any) as it thinks just.

(2) The court may not take action under both section 40 and this section.

(3) A disqualification order must state the amount in respect of which it is made, which to be the aggregate of—

(a) the amount mentioned in section 35(1), or so much of it as remains outstanding; and

(b) an amount (determined in accordance with regulations made by the Secretary of State) in respect of the costs of the application under section 39A.

(4) A court which makes a disqualification order shall require the person to whom it relates to produce any driving licence held by him, and its counterpart (within the meaning of section 108(1) of the Road Traffic Act 1988).

(5) On an application by the [Commission] of the liable person, the court—

(a) may make an order substituting a shorter period of disqualification, or make an order revoking the disqualification order, if part of the amount referred to in subsection (3) (the *"amount due"*) is paid to any person authorised to receive it; and

(b) must make an order revoking the disqualification order if all of the amount is so paid.

(6) The [Commission] may make representations to the court as to the amount which should be paid before it would be appropriate to make an order revoking the disqualification order under subsection (5)(a), and the person liable may reply to those representations.

(7) The [Commission] may make a further application under section 39A if the amount due has not been paid in full when the period of disqualification specified in the disqualification order expires.

(8) Where a court—

(a) makes a disqualification order;

(b) makes an order under subsection (5); or

(c) allows an appeal against a disqualification order,

it shall send notice of that fact to the [Commission]; and the notice shall contain such particulars and be sent in such manner and to such address as the [Commission] may determine.

(9) Where a court makes a disqualification order, it shall also send [any driving] licence and its counterpart, on their being produced to the court, to the [Commission] at such address as [it] may determine.

(10) Section 80 of the Magistrates' Courts Act 1980 (application of money found on defaulter) shall apply in relation to a disqualification order under this section in relation to a liable person as it applies in relation to the enforcement of a sum mentioned in subsection (1) of that section.

(11) The Secretary of State may by regulations make provision in relation to disqualification orders corresponding to the provision he may make under section 40(11).

(12) *[Applies to Scotland]*.

[Section 40B is printed as amended by the Road Safety Act 2006 s.9 and Sch.2, para.33, s.59 and Sch.78(4); the Child Maintenance and Other Payments Act 2008 s.13 and Sch.3, para.42.

In relation to endorsement (all drivers), s.40B, as amended above, will be further amended by the Road Safety Act 2006 s.10 and Sch.3, para.65, s.59 and Sch.7, Pt 4 so that in subs.(4) the words from "and" to the end will be omitted and in subs.(9) the words "and its counterpart" will be omitted and the word "its" will be substituted for the word "their".

With effect from a day to be appointed, s.40B(3)(a) will be substituted by the Tribunals, Courts and Enforcement Act 2007 s.62(3) and Sch.13, para.97 as follows:

[(a) the amount outstanding, as defined by paragraph 50(3) of Schedule 12 to the Tribunals, Courts and Enforcement Act 2007 (taking control of goods); and].

With effect from a day to be appointed, the following amendments will be made to s.40B by the Child Maintenance and Other Payments Act 2008 s.30(1) and (2), s.57 and Sch.7, para.1(15–18) and s.58 and Sch.8:

1. for the heading and s.40B(1), the following text will be substituted:

[Disqualification for holding or obtaining driving licence

40B.—(A1) The Commission may apply to the court for an order disqualifying a person for holding or obtaining a driving licence where—

(a) it has sought to recover an amount from the person by means of taking enforcement action by virtue of section 35 or 38, or by means of a third party debt order or a charging order by virtue of section 36;

(b) the whole or any part of the amount remains unpaid; and

(c) the Commission is of the opinion that there has been wilful refusal or culpable neglect on the part of the person from whom it has sought to recover the amount ("the liable person").

(A2) Disqualification by an order under subsection (A1) (a "disqualification order") shall be for such period not exceeding two years as the court may specify in the order.

(A3) For the purposes of subsection (A1)(a), the Commission is to be taken to have sought to recover an amount by means of a charging order if an interim charging order has been made, whether or not any further steps have been taken to recover the amount.

(A4) On an application under subsection (A1) the court shall (in the presence of the liable person) inquire as to—

    (a) whether the liable person needs a driving licence to earn a living;

    (b) the liable person's means; and

    (c) whether there has been wilful refusal or culpable neglect on the part of the liable person.

(A5) On an application under subsection (A1) the court shall not question—

    (a) the liability order by reference to which the Commission acted as mentioned in paragraph (a) of that subsection; or

    (b) the maintenance calculation by reference to which that liability order was made.

(1) If, but only if, the court is of the opinion that there has been wilful refusal or culpable neglect on the part of the liable person, it may—

    (a) make a disqualification order against the liable person; or

    (b) make such an order but suspend its operation until such time and on such conditions (if any) as it thinks just.

    2. *in s.40B(3)(a), the words "sought to be recovered as mentioned in subsection (A1)(a)" will be substituted for the words "mentioned in section 35(1)";*

    3. *in s.40(3)(b), the words "this section" will be substituted for "section 39A";*

    4. *in s.40B(7), the words "this section" will be substituted for the words "section 39A";*

    5. *for s.40B(10), the following text will be substituted:*

[(10) On making a disqualification order, the court may order the liable person to be searched.

(10A) Any money found on such a search shall, unless the court otherwise directs, be applied towards payment of the amount due; and the balance (if any) shall be returned to the person searched.

(10B) The court shall not allow the application under subsection (10A) of money found on a search under subsection (10) if it is satisfied that the money does not belong to the person searched.

(10C) The court may exercise the powers conferred on it by subsection (5) without the need for an application where money found on a search under subsection (10) is applied towards payment of the amount due.]

    6. *after s.40B(12) (not reproduced) the following new subsection will be inserted:*

[(13) In this section—

    "court" (except for the purposes of subsection (8)(c)) means—

        (a) in England and Wales, a magistrates' court;

        (b) *[applies to Scotland]*;

    "driving licence" means a licence to drive a motor vehicle granted under Part 3 of the Road Traffic Act 1988.]

With effect from a day to be appointed, s.40B will be omitted by the Welfare Reform Act 2009 s.51 and Sch.5, para.8 and s.58 and Sch.7(4), para.1.]

Power of constables to obtain names and addresses of drivers and others, and to require production of evidence of insurance or security and test certificates

165.—(1) Any of the following persons—

(a) a person driving a motor vehicle (other than an invalid carriage) on a road, or

(b) a person whom a constable [or vehicle examiner] has reasonable cause to believe to have been the driver of a motor vehicle (other than an invalid carriage) at a time when an accident occurred owing to its presence on a road [or other public place], or

(c) a person whom a constable [or vehicle examiner] has reasonable cause to believe to have committed an offence in relation to the use on a road of a motor vehicle (other than an invalid carriage),

must, on being so required by a constable [or vehicle examiner], give his name and address and the name and address of the owner of the vehicle and produce the following documents for examination.

(2) Those documents are—

(a) the relevant certificate of insurance or certificate of security (within the meaning of Part VI of this Act), or such other evidence that the vehicle is not or was not being driven in contravention of section 143 of this Act as may be prescribed by regulations made by the Secretary of State,

(b) in relation to a vehicle to which section 47 of this Act applies, a test certificate issued in respect of the vehicle as mentioned in subsection (1) of that section, and

(c) in relation to a goods vehicle the use of which on a road without a plating certificate or goods vehicle test certificate is an offence under section 53(1) or (2) of this Act, any such certificate issued in respect of that vehicle or any trailer drawn by it.

[(2A) Subsections (2B) and (2C) below apply where a certificate of insurance is treated as having been delivered to a person under section 147(1) of this Act by virtue of section 147(1A) of this Act.

(2B) In the case of a certificate transmitted to a person as described in section 147(1A)(a) of this Act, the person is to be treated for the purposes of this section as producing the relevant certificate of insurance if—

(a) using electronic equipment provided by him or made available to him by the constable or examiner, he provides the constable or examiner with electronic access to a copy of the certificate, or

(b) he produces a legible printed copy of the certificate.

(2C) In the case of a certificate made available to a person as described in section 147(1A)(b) of this Act, the person is to be treated for the purposes of this section as producing the relevant certificate of insurance if—

(a) using electronic equipment provided by him or made available to him by the constable or examiner, he provides the constable or examiner with electronic access on the website in question to a copy of the certificate, or

(b) he produces a legible printed copy of the certificate.

(2D) Nothing in subsection (2B) or (2C) above requires a constable or examiner to provide a person with electronic equipment for the purpose of compliance with a requirement imposed on the person by this section.]

(3) Subject to subsection (4) below, a person who fails to comply with a requirement under subsection (1) above is guilty of an offence.

(4) A person shall not be convicted of an offence under [subsection (3)] above by reason only of failure to produce any certificate or other evidence ... if in proceedings against him for the offence he shows that—

    (a) within seven days after the date on which the production of the certificate or other evidence was required it was produced at a police station that was specified by him at the time when its production was required, or

    (b) it was produced there as soon as was reasonably practicable, or

    (c) it was not reasonably practicable for it to be produced there before the day on which the proceedings were commenced,

and for the purposes of this subsection the laying of the information ... shall be treated as the commencement of the proceedings.

(5) A person—

    (a) who supervises the holder of a provisional licence granted under Part III of this Act while the holder is driving on a road a motor vehicle (other than an invalid carriage), or

    (b) whom a constable [or vehicle examiner] has reasonable cause to believe was supervising the holder of such a licence while driving, at a time when an accident occurred owing to the presence of the vehicle on a road or at a time when an offence is suspected of having been committed by the holder of the provisional licence in relation to the use of the vehicle on a road,

must, on being so required by a constable [or vehicle examiner], give his name and address and the name and address of the owner of the vehicle.

(6) A person who fails to comply with a requirement under subsection (5) above is guilty of an offence.

(7) In this section *"owner"*, in relation to a vehicle which is the subject of a hiring agreement, includes each party to the agreement [and *"vehicle examiner"* means an examiner appointed under section 66A of this Act] .

[Section 165 is printed as amended by the Road Traffic (Driver Licensing and **A18.405** *Information Systems) Act 1989 s.7 and Sch.3, para.19; the Road Traffic Act 1991 ss.48, 83, Sch.4, para.69(1)–(4) and Sch.8; the Motor Vehicles (Compulsory Insurance) Regulations 2000 (SI 2000/726; not reproduced in this work; as to SI 2000/726, see further the notes to s.143 of this Act); the Motor Vehicles (Electronic Communication of Certificates of Insurance) Order 2010 (SI 2010/1117) art.6.*

Words in s.165(4) relating exclusively and expressly to Scotland have been omitted.

Proceedings under s.165(3) and (6) are specified by the Prosecution of Offences Act 1985 (Specified Proceedings) Order 1999 (SI 1999/904) below as being proceedings the conduct of which the Director of Public Prosecutions is not required to take over from the police under the Prosecution of Offences Act 1985 s.3(3)(a).

Section 165 does not apply to any person or vehicle in the service of a visiting force or headquarters (as defined); see the Visiting Forces and International Headquarters (Application of Law) Order 1999 (SI 1999/1736; not reproduced in this work) art.8(1) and (2)(b).

The requirements under this section to produce test certificates and to give names and addresses, are expressly applied to persons in connection with vehicles to which s.47 of this Act applies, notwithstanding that such persons (or the drivers) are or were at any material time persons in the service of a visiting force or headquarters; see SI 1999/1736 art.8(6).

The requirement under s.165(1) to produce any certificate mentioned in s.165(2)(c) applies to any person in connection with a goods vehicle so mentioned, notwithstanding that such person (or the driver) is or was at any material time a person in the service of a visiting force or headquarters; see the Visiting Forces and International Headquarters (Application of Law) Order 1999 (SI 1999/1736; not reproduced in this work) art.8(7).]

[Power to seize vehicles driven without licence or insurance

A18.406   **165A.**—(1) Subsection (5) applies if any of the following conditions is satisfied.

(2) The first condition is that—

    (a) a constable in uniform requires, under section 164, a person to produce his licence and its counterpart for examination,

    (b) the person fails to produce them, and

    (c) the constable has reasonable grounds for believing that a motor vehicle is or was being driven by the person in contravention of section 87(1).

(3) The second condition is that—

    (a) a constable in uniform requires, under section 165, a person to produce evidence that a motor vehicle is not or was not being driven in contravention of section 143,

    (b) the person fails to produce such evidence, and

    (c) the constable has reasonable grounds for believing that the vehicle is or was being so driven.

(4) The third condition is that—

    (a) a constable in uniform requires, under section 163, a person driving a motor vehicle to stop the vehicle,

    (b) the person fails to stop the vehicle, or to stop the vehicle long enough, for the constable to make such lawful enquiries as he considers appropriate, and

    (c) the constable has reasonable grounds for believing that the vehicle is or was being driven in contravention of section 87(1) or 143.

(5) Where this subsection applies, the constable may—

    (a) seize the vehicle in accordance with subsections (6) and (7) and remove it;

    (b) enter, for the purpose of exercising a power falling within paragraph (a), any premises (other than a private dwelling house) on which he has reasonable grounds for believing the vehicle to be;

    (c) use reasonable force, if necessary, in the exercise of any power conferred by paragraph (a) or (b).

(6) Before seizing the motor vehicle, the constable must warn the person by whom it appears that the vehicle is or was being driven in contravention of section 87(1) or 143 that he will seize it—

(a) in a section 87(1) case, if the person does not produce his licence and its counterpart immediately;

(b) in a section 143 case, if the person does not provide him immediately with evidence that the vehicle is not or was not being driven in contravention of that section.

But the constable is not required to give such a warning if the circumstances make it impracticable for him to do so.

(7) If the constable is unable to seize the vehicle immediately because the person driving the vehicle has failed to stop as requested or has driven off, he may seize it at any time within the period of 24 hours beginning with the time at which the condition in question is first satisfied.

(8) The powers conferred on a constable by this section are exercisable only at a time when regulations under section 165B are in force.

(9) In this section—

(a) a reference to a motor vehicle does not include an invalid carriage;

(b) a reference to evidence that a motor vehicle is not or was not being driven in contravention of section 143 is a reference to a document or other evidence within section 165(2)(a);

(c) *"counterpart"* and *"licence"* have the same meanings as in section 164;

(d) *"private dwelling house"* does not include any garage or other structure occupied with the dwelling house, or any land appurtenant to the dwelling house.]

[Section 165A is printed as inserted by the Serious Organised Crime and Po-   **A18.407**
lice Act 2005 s.152.

For provisions as to the removal and detention of vehicles seized under s.165A, see the Road Traffic Act 1988 (Retention and Disposal of Seized Vehicles) Regulations 2005 (SI 2005/1606) below. See also the Disclosure of Vehicle Insurance Information Regulations 2005 (SI 2005/2833) (not reproduced in this work) for provisions on the disclosure of information with regard to the insurance status of vehicles.]

[Retention etc. of vehicles seized under section 165A

165B.—(1) The Secretary of State may by regulations make provision as to—   **A18.408**

(a) the removal and retention of motor vehicles seized under section 165A; and

(b) the release or disposal of such motor vehicles.

(2) Regulations under subsection (1) may, in particular, make provision—

(a) for the giving of notice of the seizure of a motor vehicle under section 165A to a person who is the registered keeper, the owner or the driver of that vehicle;

(b) for the procedure by which a person who claims to be the registered keeper or the owner of a motor vehicle seized under section 165A may seek to have it released;

(c) for requiring the payment, by the registered keeper, owner or driver of the vehicle, of fees, charges or costs in relation to the removal and retention of such a motor vehicle and to any application for its release;

(d) as to the circumstances in which a motor vehicle seized under section 165A may be disposed of;

(e) as to the destination—

　(i) of any fees or charges payable in accordance with the regulations;

　(ii) of the proceeds (if any) arising from the disposal of a motor vehicle seized under section 165A;

(f) for the delivery to a local authority, in circumstances prescribed by or determined in accordance with the regulations, of any motor vehicle seized under section 165A.

(3) Regulations under subsection (1) must provide that a person who would otherwise be liable to pay any fee or charge under the regulations is not liable to pay it if—

(a) he was not driving the motor vehicle at the time in question, and

(b) he did not know that the vehicle was being driven at that time, had not consented to its being driven and could not, by the taking of reasonable steps, have prevented it from being driven.

(4) Regulations under subsection (1) may make different provision for different cases.

(5) In this section—

"local authority"—

(a) in relation to England, means—

　(i) a county council,

　(ii) the council of a district comprised in an area for which there is no county council,

　(iii) a London borough council,

　(iv) the Common Council of the City of London, or

　(v) Transport for London;

(b) in relation to Wales, means the council of a county or county borough; and

(c) in relation to Scotland, means a council constituted under section 2 of the Local Government etc. (Scotland) Act 1994;

"registered keeper", in relation to a motor vehicle, means the person in whose name the vehicle is registered under the Vehicle Excise and Registration Act 1994.]

A18.409　*[Section 165B is printed as inserted by the Serious Organised Crime and Police Act 2005 s.152.]*

[Powers of certain officers as respects goods vehicles and passenger-carrying vehicles

A18.410　166. [A person authorised for the purpose by a traffic commissioner appointed under the Public Passenger Vehicles Act 1981,] may, on production if so required of his authority, exercise in the case of goods vehicles or passenger-carrying vehicles of any prescribed class all such powers as are, under section 164(1) or (3) or 165 of this Act [*q.v.*], exercisable by a constable.]

A18.411　*[Section 166 is printed as substituted by the Road Traffic (Driver Licensing* *and Information Systems) Act 1989 s.7 and Sch.3, para.20, and as subsequently amended by the Road Traffic Act 1991 s.48 and Sch.4, para.70.]*

Power of arrest in Scotland for reckless or careless driving or cycling

167. *[Omitted.]*   **A18.412**

Duty to give name and address

Failure to give, or giving false, name and address in case of reckless or careless or inconsiderate driving or cycling

168. Any of the following persons—   **A18.413**

     (a) the driver of a [mechanically propelled vehicle] who is alleged to have committed an offence under section 2 or 3 of this Act, or

     (b) the rider of a cycle who is alleged to have committed an offence under section 28 or 29 of this Act,

who refuses, on being so required by any person having reasonable ground for so requiring, to give his name or address, or gives a false name or address, is guilty of an offence.

[Section 168 is printed as amended by the Road Traffic Act 1991 s.48 and   **A18.414**
Sch.4, para.71.

Proceedings under s.168 are specified by the Prosecution of Offences Act 1985 (Specified Proceedings) Order 1999 (SI 1999/904) below as being proceedings the conduct of which the Director of Public Prosecutions is not required to take over from the police under the Prosecution of Offences Act 1985 s.3(3)(a).]

Pedestrian contravening constable's direction to stop to give name and address

169. A constable may require a person committing an offence under section 37   **A18.415**
of this Act to give his name and address, and if that person fails to do so he is guilty of an offence.

Duties in case of accident

Duty of driver to stop, report accident and give information or documents

170.—(1) This section applies in a case where, owing to the presence of a   **A18.416**
[mechanically propelled vehicle] on a road [or other public place], an accident occurs by which—

     (a) personal injury is caused to a person other than the driver of that [mechanically propelled vehicle], or

     (b) damage is caused—

         (i) to a vehicle other than that [mechanically propelled vehicle] or a trailer drawn by that [mechanically propelled vehicle], or

        (ii) to an animal other than an animal in or on that [mechanically propelled vehicle] or a trailer drawn by that [mechanically propelled vehicle], or

       (iii) to any other property constructed on, fixed to, growing in or otherwise forming part of the land on which the road [or place] in question is situated or land adjacent to such land.

(2) The driver of the [mechanically propelled vehicle] must stop and, if required to do so by any person having reasonable grounds for so requiring, give his name and address and also the name and address of the owner and the identification marks of the vehicle.

(3) If for any reason the driver of the [mechanically propelled vehicle] does not give his name and address under subsection (2) above, he must report the accident.

(4) A person who fails to comply with subsection (2) or (3) above is guilty of an offence.

(5) If, in a case where this section applies by virtue of subsection (1)(a) above, the driver of [a motor vehicle] does not at the time of the accident produce such a certificate of insurance or security, or other evidence, as is mentioned in section 165(2)(a) of this Act —

    (a) to a constable, or

    (b) to some person who, having reasonable grounds for so doing, has required him to produce it,

the driver must report the accident and produce such a certificate or other evidence.

This subsection does not apply to the driver of an invalid carriage.

(6) To comply with a duty under this section to report an accident or to produce such a certificate of insurance or security, or other evidence, as is mentioned in section 165(2)(a) of this Act, the driver—

    (a) must do so at a police station or to a constable, and

    (b) must do so as soon as is reasonably practicable and, in any case, within twenty-four hours of the occurrence of the accident.

(7) A person who fails to comply with a duty under subsection (5) above is guilty of an offence, but he shall not be convicted by reason only of a failure to produce a certificate or other evidence if, within [seven] days after the occurrence of the accident, the certificate or other evidence is produced at a police station that was specified by him at the time when the accident was reported.

(8) In this section *"animal"* means horse, cattle, ass, mule, sheep, pig, goat or dog.

A18.417   *[Section 170 is printed as amended by the Road Traffic Act 1991 s.48 and Sch.4, para.72(1)–(4); the Motor Vehicles (Compulsory Insurance) Regulations 2000 (SI 2000/726; not reproduced in this work; as to SI 2000/726, see further the notes to s.143 of this Act).*

The provisions of s.170(5)–(7) do not apply to any person or vehicle in the service of a visiting force or headquarters (as defined); see the Visiting Forces and International Headquarters (Application of Law) Order 1999 (SI 1999/1736; not reproduced in this work) art.8(1) and (2)(b).]

Other duties to give information or documents

Duty of owner of motor vehicle to give information for verifying compliance with requirement of compulsory insurance or security

A18.418   171.—(1) For the purpose of determining whether a motor vehicle was or was not being driven in contravention of section 143 of this Act on any occasion when the driver was required under section 165(1) or 170 of this Act to produce such a certificate of insurance or security, or other evidence, as is mentioned in section 165(2)(a) of this Act, the owner of the vehicle must give such information as he may be required, by or on behalf of a chief officer of police, to give.

(2) A person who fails to comply with the requirement of subsection (1) above is guilty of an offence.

(3) In this section *"owner"*, in relation to a vehicle which is the subject of a hiring agreement, includes each party to the agreement.

[Section 171 does not apply to any person or vehicle in the service of a visiting **A18.419** *force or headquarters (as defined); see the Visiting Forces and International Headquarters (Application of Law) Order 1999 (SI 1999/1736; not reproduced in this work) art.8(1) and (2)(b).]*

[Duty to give information as to identity of driver, etc., in certain circumstances

172.—(1) This section applies—　　　　　　　　　　　　　　　　　　**A18.420**

    (a) to any offence under the preceding provisions of this Act except—

        (i) an offence under Part V, or

        (ii) an offence under section 13, 16, 51(2), 61(4), 67(9), 68(4), 96 or 120,

    and to an offence under section 178 of this Act,

    (b) to any offence under sections 25, 26 or 27 of the Road Traffic Offenders Act 1988,

    (c) to any offence against any other enactment relating to the use of vehicles on roads, [...] and

    (d) to manslaughter ... by the driver of a motor vehicle.

(2) Where the driver of a vehicle is alleged to be guilty of an offence to which this section applies—

    (a) the person keeping the vehicle shall give such information as to the identity of the driver as he may be required to give by or on behalf of a chief officer of police, and

    (b) any other person shall if required as stated above give any information which it is in his power to give and may lead to identification of the driver.

(3) Subject to the following provisions, a person who fails to comply with a requirement under subsection (2) above shall be guilty of an offence.

(4) A person shall not be guilty of an offence by virtue of paragraph (a) of subsection (2) above if he shows that he did not know and could not with reasonable diligence have ascertained who the driver of the vehicle was.

(5) Where a body corporate is guilty of an offence under this section and the offence is proved to have been committed with the consent or connivance of, or to be attributable to neglect on the part of, a director, manager, secretary or other similar officer of the body corporate, or a person who was purporting to act in any such capacity, he, as well as the body corporate, is guilty of that offence and liable to be proceeded against and punished accordingly.

(6) Where the alleged offender is a body corporate ... or the proceedings are brought against him by virtue of subsection (5) above or subsection (11) below,

subsection (4) above shall not apply unless, in addition to the matters there mentioned, the alleged offender shows that no record was kept of the persons who drove the vehicle and that the failure to keep a record was reasonable.

(7) A requirement under subsection (2) may be made by written notice served by post; and where it is so made—

(a) it shall have effect as a requirement to give the information within the period of 28 days beginning with the day on which the notice is served, and

(b) the person on whom the notice is served shall not be guilty of an offence under this section if he shows either that he gave the information as soon as reasonably practicable after the end of that period or that it has not been reasonably practicable for him to give it.

(8) Where the person on whom a notice under subsection (7) above is to be served is a body corporate, the notice is duly served if it is served on the secretary or clerk of that body.

(9) For the purposes of section 7 of the Interpretation Act 1978 as it applies for the purposes of this section the proper address of any person in relation to the service on him of a notice under subsection (7) above is—

(a) in the case of the secretary or clerk of a body corporate, that of the registered or principal office of that body or (if the body corporate is the registered keeper of the vehicle concerned) the registered address, and

(b) in any other case, his last known address at the time of service.

(10) In this section —

"registered address", in relation to the registered keeper of a vehicle, means the address recorded in the record kept under [the Vehicle Excise and Registration Act 1994] with respect to that vehicle as being that person's address, and

"registered keeper", in relation to a vehicle, means the person in whose name the vehicle is registered under that Act;

and references to the driver of a vehicle include references to the rider of a cycle.

(11) *[Offences committed in Scotland.]*]

A18.421   *[Section 172 is printed as substituted by the Road Traffic Act 1991 s.21, and as subsequently amended by the Vehicle Excise and Registration Act 1994 s.63 and Sch.3, para.24(1); the Statute Law (Repeals) Act 2004 s.1(1) and Sch.1, Pt 14.*

Words relating expressly and exclusively to Scotland have been omitted from s.172(1)(d) and (6).

The fixed penalty procedure applies to offences under s.172; see the Road Traffic Offenders Act 1988 Sch.3 below. Offences under s.172 have been designated as fixed penalty offences by the Fixed Penalty Offences Order 2003 (SI 2003/1253).

Proceedings under s.172(3) are specified by the Prosecution of Offences Act 1985 (Specified Proceedings) Order 1999 (SI 1999/904) below as being proceedings the conduct of which the Director of Public Prosecutions is not required to take over from the police under the Prosecution of Offences Act 1985 s.3(3)(a).]

Forgery, false statements, etc.

Forgery of documents, etc.

173.—(1) A person who, with intent to deceive—

A18.422

    (a) forges, alters or uses a document or other thing to which this section applies, or

    (b) lends to, or allows to be used by, any other person a document or other thing to which this section applies, or

    (c) makes or has in his possession any document or other thing so closely resembling a document or other thing to which this section applies as to be calculated to deceive,

is guilty of an offence.

    (2) This section applies to the following documents and other things—

    (a) any licence under any Part of this Act [or, in the case of a licence to drive, any counterpart of such a licence],

    [(aa) any counterpart of a [Northern Ireland licence or] Community licence,]

    (b) any test certificate, goods vehicle test certificate, plating certificate, certificate of conformity or Minister's approval certificate (within the meaning of Part II of this Act),

    (c) any certificate required as a condition of any exception prescribed under section 14 of this Act,

    [(cc) any seal required by regulations made under section 41 of this Act with respect to speed limiters,]

    (d) [any plate containing particulars required to be marked on a vehicle by regulations under section 41 of this Act] or containing other particulars required to be marked on a goods vehicle by section 54 to 58 of this Act or regulations under those sections,

    [(dd) any document evidencing the appointment of an examiner under section 66A of this Act,]

    (e) any records required to be kept by virtue of section 74 of this Act,

    (f) any document which, in pursuance of section 89(3) ... of this Act, is issued as evidence of the result of a test of competence to drive,

    [(ff) any document evidencing the successful completion of a driver training course provided in accordance with regulations under section 99ZA of this Act,]

    (g) any [certificate under section 133A or any] badge or certificate prescribed by regulations made by virtue of section 135 of this Act,

    (h) any certificate of insurance or certificate of security under Part VI of this Act,

    (j) any document produced as evidence of insurance in pursuance of Regulation 6 of the Motor Vehicles (Compulsory Insurance) (No.2) Regulations 1973 [*SI 1973/2143; not reproduced in this work*],

    (k) any document issued under regulations made by the Secretary of State in pursuance of his power under section 165(2)(a) of this Act to prescribe evidence which may be produced in lieu of a certificate of insurance or a certificate of security, ...

(l) any international road haulage permit[, and]

[(m) [a certificate of the kind referred to in section 34B(1) of the Road Traffic Offenders Act 1988.]]

(3) In the application of this section to England and Wales *"forges"* means makes a false document or other thing in order that it may be used as genuine.

[(4) In this section *"counterpart"*[, *"Community licence"* and *"Northern Ireland licence"*] have the same meanings as in Part III of this Act.]]

A18.423   *[Section 173 is printed as amended by the Road Traffic (Driver Licensing and Information Systems) Act 1989 s.7 and Sch.3, para.22; the Driving Licences (Community Driving Licence) Regulations 1990 (SI 1990/144); the Road Traffic Act 1991 ss.48, 83, Sch.4, para.73(1)–(6), and Sch.8; the Road Traffic (Driving Instruction by Disabled Persons) Act 1993 s.6 and Sch., paras 1 and 9; the Driving Licences (Community Driving Licence) Regulations 1996 (SI 1996/1974) reg.2 and Sch.1, para.32 (not reproduced in this work); the Crime (International Co-operation) Act 2003 s.91 and Sch.5, para.29; the Road Safety Act 2006 s.41(4).*

With effect from a day to be appointed, the following amendments will be made to s.173:

1. *in s.173(2), for para.(g), the following text will be substituted for the Road Safety Act 2006 s.42 and Sch.6, para.27:*

   [(g) any document evidencing the passing of an examination (or part of an examination) required by regulations under section 132 of this Act or the successful completion of training provided in accordance with regulations under section 133ZA of this Act,

   (ga) any certificate under section 133A of this Act,

   (gb) any certificate or other item prescribed under section 135(1)(a) of this Act,]

2. *in s.173(2), the word "and" will be omitted after para.(l) by the Road Safety Act 2006 s.59 and Sch.7(10), and the following text will be inserted by ibid. s.37(8):*

   [and

   (n) any document produced as evidence of the passing of an appropriate driving test within the meaning of section 36 of that Act.]

With effect from a day to be appointed and in relation to endorsement (all drivers), the following amendments will be made to s.173 by the Road Safety Act 2006 s.10 and Sch.3, para.28, s.59 and Sch.7(4):

1. *in s.173(2), the words from "or" to the end will be omitted in para.(a), and para.(aa) will be omitted;*

2. *in s.173(4), the word "counterpart" will be omitted.*

As to the application of s.173 to domestic driving permits, Convention driving permits, British Forces (BFG) driving licences and to the holders of such licences and permits, see the Motor Vehicles (Driving Licences) Regulations 1999 (SI 1999/2864) reg.80 below; and see also the Motor Vehicles (International Circulation) Order 1975 (SI 1975/1208) Sch.3, para.5(1) and (2)(c) below.]

False statements and withholding material information

A18.424   174.—(1) A person who knowingly makes a false statement for the purpose—

(a) of obtaining the grant of a licence under any Part of this Act to himself or any other person, or

(b) of preventing the grant of any such licence, or

(c) of procuring the imposition of a condition or limitation in relation to any such licence, or

(ca) of obtaining a document evidencing the successful completion of a driver training course provided in accordance with regulations under section 99ZA of this Act, or]

(d) of securing the entry or retention of the name of any person in the register of approved instructors maintained under Part V of this Act, or

[(dd) of obtaining the grant to any person of a certificate under section 133A of this Act, or]

(e) of obtaining the grant of an international road haulage permit to himself or any other person,

is guilty of an offence.

(2) A person who, in supplying information or producing documents for the purposes either of sections 53 to 60 and 63 of this Act or of regulations made under section 49 to 51, 61, 62 and 66(3) of this Act —

(a) makes a statement which he knows to be false in a material particular or recklessly makes a statement which is false in a material particular, or

(b) produces, provides, sends or otherwise makes use of a document which he knows to be false in a material particular or recklessly produces, provides, sends or otherwise makes use of a document which is false in a material particular,

is guilty of an offence.

(3) A person who—

(a) knowingly produces false evidence for the purposes of regulations under section 66(1) of this Act, or

(b) knowingly makes a false statement in a declaration required to be made by the regulations,

is guilty of an offence.

(4) A person who—

(a) wilfully makes a false entry in any record required to be made or kept by regulations under section 74 of this Act, or

(b) with intent to deceive, makes use of any such entry which he knows to be false,

is guilty of an offence.

(5) A person who makes a false statement or withholds any material information for the purpose of obtaining the issue—

(a) of a certificate of insurance or certificate of security under Part VI of this Act, or

(b) of any document issued under regulations made by the Secretary of State in pursuance of his power under section 165(2)(a) of this Act to prescribe evidence which may be produced in lieu of a certificate of insurance or a certificate of security, is guilty of an offence.

A18.425   *[Section 174 is printed as amended by the Road Traffic (Driving Instruction by Disabled Persons) Act 1993, s.6 and Schedule, paras 1 and 10; the Road Safety Act 2006 s.41(5).*

With effect from a day to be appointed, the following new paragraph will be inserted after s.174(1)(d) by the Road Safety Act 2006 s.42 and Sch.6, para.28:

> [(da) of obtaining a document evidencing the passing of an examination (or part of an examination) required by regulations under section 132 of this Act or the successful completion of training provided in accordance with regulations under section 133ZA of this Act, or]

As to the application of s.174 to Convention driving permits, see the Motor Vehicles (International Circulation) Order 1975 (SI 1975/1208) art.1(9) below.]

Issue of false documents

A18.426   **175.** If a person issues—

(a) any such document as is referred to in section 174(5)(a) or (b) of this Act, or

(b) a test certificate or certificate of conformity (within the meaning of Part II of this Act),

and the document or certificate so issued is to his knowledge false in a material particular, he is guilty of an offence.

Power to seize articles in respect of which offences under sections 173 to 175 may have been committed

A18.427   **176.**—(1) If a constable has reasonable cause to believe that a document produced to him—

(a) in pursuance of section 137 of this Act, or

(b) in pursuance of any of the preceding provisions of this Part of this Act,

is a document in relation to which an offence has been committed under section 173, 174 or 175 of this Act or under section 115 of the Road Traffic Regulation Act 1984 [*q.v.*], he may seize the document.

[(1A) Where a licence to drive or a counterpart of any such licence or of any Northern Ireland licence or Community licence may be seized by a constable under subsection (1) above, he may also seize the counterpart, the licence to drive or the Northern Ireland licence or Community licence (as the case may be) produced with it.]

(2) When a document is seized under subsection (1) above, the person from whom it was taken shall, unless—

(a) the document has been previously returned to him, or

(b) he has been previously charged with an offence under any of those sections,

be summoned before a magistrates' court ... to account for his possession of the document.

(3) The court ... must make such order respecting the disposal of the document and award such costs as the justice of the case may require.

[(3A) An order under subsection (3) above respecting the disposal of any such licence or Community licence to drive or a counterpart of any such licence or of a Northern Ireland licence or Community licence may include an order respecting the disposal of any document seized under subsection (1A) above.]

(4) If a constable, [an examiner appointed under section 66A] of this Act has reasonable cause to believe that a document or plate carried on a motor vehicle or by the driver of the vehicle is a document or plate to which this subsection applies, he may seize it.

For the purposes of this subsection the power to seize includes power to detach from a vehicle.

(5) Subsection (4) above applies to a document or plate in relation to which an offence has been committed under sections 173, 174 or 175 of this Act in so far as they apply—

  (a) to documents evidencing the appointment of examiners [under section 66A] of this Act, or

  (b) to goods vehicle test certificates, plating certificates, certificates of conformity or Minister's approval certificates (within the meaning of Part II of this Act), or

  (c) to plates containing plated particulars (within the meaning of that Part) or containing other particulars required to be marked on goods vehicles by sections 54 to 58 of this Act or regulations made under them, or

  (d) to records required to be kept by virtue of section 74 of this Act, or

  (e) to international road haulage permits.

(6) When a document or plate is seized under subsection (4) above, either the driver or owner of the vehicle shall, if the document or plate is still detained and neither of them has previously been charged with an offence in relation to the document or plate under section 173, 174 or 175 of this Act, be summoned before a magistrates' court ... to account for his possession of, or the presence on the vehicle of, the document or plate.

(7) The court ... must make such order respecting the disposal of the document or plate and award such costs as the justice of the case may require.

[(8) In this section *"counterpart"*[, *"Community licence"* and *"Northern Ireland licence"*] have the same meanings as in Part III of this Act.]

[Section 176 is printed as amended by the Road Traffic Act 1991 s.48 and   **A18.428**
Sch.4, para.74(1)–(3); the Driving Licences (Community Driving Licence) Regulations 1990 (SI 1990/144); the Driving Licences (Community Driving Licence) Regulations 1996 (SI 1996/1974) reg.2 and Sch.1, para.33; the Crime (International Co-operation) Act 2003 s.91 and Sch.5, para.30.

With effect from a day to be appointed and in relation to endorsement (all drivers), s.176(1A), (3A) and (8) will be omitted by the Road Safety Act 2006 s.10 and Sch.3, para.29, s.59 and Sch.7(4).

Words relating exclusively and expressly to Scotland have been omitted from s.176(2), (3), (6) and (7).]

Impersonation of authorised examiner, etc.

177. A person is guilty of an offence if, with intent to deceive, he falsely   **A18.429**
represents himself—

      (a) to be, or to be employed by, a person authorised in accordance with regulations made under section 41 of this Act with respect to the checking and sealing of speed limiters, or

      (b) to be a person entitled under section 45 of this Act to carry out examinations of vehicles under that section.]

A18.430   *[Section 177 is printed as amended by the Road Traffic Act 1991 s.48 and Sch.4, para.75; the Road Traffic (Vehicle Testing) Act 1999 s.7(1) and Sch., para.3(1).]*

Offences in Scotland

Taking motor vehicle without authority, etc.

A18.431   **178.** *[Omitted.]*

Inquiries

General power to hold inquiries

    179. *[Omitted.]*

General provisions as to inquiries

A18.432   **180.** *[Omitted.]*

General provisions as to accident inquiries

A18.433   **181.** *[Omitted.]*

Special provisions as to accident inquiries in Greater London

A18.434   **182.** *[Omitted.]*

Application to the Crown

Application to the Crown

A18.435   **183.**—(1) Subject to the provisions of this section —

      (a) Part I of this Act,

      (b) Part II of this Act, except sections 68 to 74 and 77,

      (c) Part III of this Act ...,

      (d) Part IV of this Act, and

      (e) in this Part, sections 163, 164, 168, 169, 170(1) to (4), 177, 178, 181 and 182,

apply to vehicles and persons in the public service of the Crown.

    (2) Sections 49 to 63 and [sections 64A, 65 and 65A] of this Act apply—

      (a) to vehicles in the public service of the Crown only if they are registered or liable to be registered under [the Vehicle Excise and Registration Act 1994], and

      (b) to trailers in the public service of the Crown only while drawn by vehicles (whether or not in the public service of the Crown) which are required to be so registered.

(3) Where those sections so apply they do so subject to the following modifications—

    (a) examinations of such vehicles in pursuance of regulations under section 49 or 61(2)(a) of this Act may be made by or under the directions of examiners authorised by the Secretary of State for the purpose instead of by or under the directions of examiners appointed under section [66A of this Act], …

    (b) […]

(4) Neither section 97(3) nor section 98(3) of this Act, in so far as they prevent such a licence as is there mentioned from authorising a person to drive certain [motor bicycles] [and mopeds], applies—

    (a) in the case of [motor bicycles] [and mopeds] owned by the Secretary of State for Defence and used for naval, military or air force purposes, or

    (b) in the case of [motor bicycles] [and mopeds] so used while being ridden by persons for the time being subject to the orders of a member of the armed forces of the Crown.

(5) Subject to regulations made under subsection (2) of section 101 of this Act, that section (in so far as it prohibits persons under 21 from holding or obtaining a licence to drive motor vehicles or persons under 18 from holding or obtaining a licence to drive medium-sized goods vehicles) does not apply—

    (a) in the case of motor vehicles owned by the Secretary of State for Defence and used for naval, military or air force purposes, or

    (b) in the case of vehicles so used while being driven by persons for the time being subject to the orders of a member of the armed forces of the Crown.

[(6) The functions under Part IV of this Act of traffic commissioners in relation to licences issued to persons [subject to service law (within the meaning of the Armed Forces Act 2006)] to drive large goods vehicles or passenger-carrying vehicles in the public service of the Crown shall be exercised by the prescribed authority.]

(7) Section 165 of this Act, in so far as it provides for the production of test certificates and the giving of names and addresses, applies to a person in connection with a vehicle to which section 47 of this Act applies notwithstanding that he or the driver is or was at any material time in the public service of the Crown.

(8) Subsection (1) of section 165 of this Act, in so far as it provides for the production of any certificate mentioned in subsection (2)(c) of that section, applies to a person in connection with a goods vehicle so mentioned notwithstanding that he or the driver is or was at any material time in the public service of the Crown.

[Section 183 is printed as amended by the Road Traffic (Driver Licensing and **A18.436** *Information Systems) Act 1989 s.7 and Sch.3, para.23; the Road Traffic Act 1991 ss.48, 83, Sch.4, para.77, and Sch.8; the Motor Vehicles (EC Type Approval) Regulations 1992 (SI 1992/3107); the Vehicle Excise and Registration Act 1994 s.63 and Sch.3, para.24(1); the Driving Licences (Community Driving Licence) Regulations 1996 (SI 1996/1974) reg.2 and Sch.1, para.34 (not reproduced in this work); the Driving Licences (Community Driving Licence) Regulations 1998 (SI 1998/1420) regs 2 and 15 (not reproduced in this work); the Police Reform*

Act 2002 s.107, Sch.7, para.12 and Sch.8 (with respect to England and Wales only); the Armed Forces Act 2006 s.378 and Sch.16, para.116.

With effect from a date to be announced under the Road Traffic (Consequential Provisions) Act 1988 s.8(3), ibid. s.4 and Sch.2, Pt I, para.18, will effect the following amendments to s.183:

    1. *in s.183(2), for "63" there will be substituted "63A";*

    2. *the following words will be inserted at the end of s.183(3)(a) —*

[or of authorised inspectors under section 8 of the Transport Act 1982]

    and

    3. *s.183(3)(b) will be omitted.*

With effect from a day to be appointed, the following new paragraph will be inserted after s.183(6) by the Road Safety Act 2006 s.42 and Sch.6, para.29:

[(6A) The Secretary of State may by regulations provide that Part 5 of this Act is to apply in relation to persons in the public service of the Crown but subject to any prescribed omissions, additions or other modifications.]

The Motor Vehicles (Driving Licences) Regulations 1999 (SI 1999/2864) (q.v.) were made in part under s.183(6).]

Application of sections 5 to 10 to persons subject to service discipline

A18.437   184.—(1) Sections 5 to 10 of this Act, in their application to [persons subject to service law and civilians subject to service discipline], apply outside as well as within Great Britain and have effect as if—

    (a) references to proceedings for an offence under any enactment included references to proceedings for [an offence under section 42 of the Armed Forces Act 2006 as respects which the corresponding offence under the law of England and Wales is that offence],

    (b) references to the court included a reference to any [officer] before whom the proceedings take place,

    (c) references to a constable included references to a member of the provost staff,

    (d) references to a police station included references to a naval, military or air force unit or establishment,

    (e) references to a hospital included references to a naval, military or air force unit or establishment at which medical or surgical treatment is provided for [persons subject to service law or civilians subject to service discipline], ...

    (f) [in section 6 a reference to a traffic offence] included a reference to an offence under section 42 of the Armed Forces Act 2006 as respects which the corresponding offence under the law of England and Wales is a traffic offence within the meaning of section 6, and

    [(g) in section 6E as it applies by virtue of paragraph (c) above, subsection (2) were omitted and the reference in subsection (1) to any place were to—

        (i) service living accommodation (as defined by section 96 of the Armed Forces Act 2006), or

        (ii) premises occupied as a residence (alone or with other persons)

by the person on whom the requirement is to be imposed or the
person to be arrested.]

[(2) A member of the provost staff may arrest [without warrant a person who
is subject to service law or is a civilian subject to service discipline] if he has reasonable cause to suspect that that person is or has been committing an offence
under section 4.]

[(2A) The power conferred by subsection (2) is exercisable outside as well as
within Great Britain.]

[(3) In this section —

"*civilian subject to service discipline*" has the same meaning as in the
Armed Forces Act 2006;

"*corresponding offence under the law of England and Wales*", in relation
to an offence under section 42 of that Act, has the meaning given by
that section;

"*member of the provost staff*" means—

(a) anyone who is, or by reason of section 375(5) of that Act is to
be treated as, a service policeman for the purposes of that Act;
or

(b) a person lawfully exercising authority on behalf of a provost
officer (within the meaning of that Act);

"*subject to service law*" has the same meaning as in that Act.]

[Section 184 is printed as amended the Railways and Transport Safety Act   **A18.438**
2003 s.107 and Sch.7, para.6; the Serious Organised Crime and Police Act 2005
s.111 and Sch.7, para.59; the Armed Forces Act 2006 s.378 and Sch.16, para.117
and Sch.17(4).]

Interpretation

Meaning of "motor vehicle" and other expressions relating to vehicles

185.—(1) In this Act —   **A18.439**

"*heavy locomotive*" means a mechanically propelled vehicle which is not
constructed itself to carry a load other than any of the excepted
articles and the weight of which unladen exceeds 11690 kilograms,

"*heavy motor car*" means a mechanically propelled vehicle, not being a
motor car, which is constructed itself to carry a load or passengers
and the weight of which unladen exceeds 2540 kilograms,

"*invalid carriage*" means a mechanically propelled vehicle the weight of
which unladen does not exceed 254 kilograms and which is specially
designed and constructed, and not merely adapted, for the use of a
person suffering from some physical defect or disability and is used
solely by such a person,

"*light locomotive*" means a mechanically propelled vehicle which is not
constructed itself to carry a load other than any of the excepted
articles and the weight of which unladen does not exceed 11690
kilograms but does exceed 7370 kilograms,

"*motor car*" means a mechanically propelled vehicle, not being a motor
cycle or an invalid carriage, which is constructed itself to carry a load
or passengers and the weight of which unladen—

(a) if it is constructed solely for the carriage of passengers and their effects, is adapted to carry not more than seven passengers exclusive of the driver and is fitted with tyres of such type as may be specified in regulations made by the Secretary of State, does not exceed 3050 kilograms,

(b) if it is constructed or adapted for use for the conveyance of goods or burden of any description, does not exceed 3050 kilograms, or 3500 kilograms if the vehicle carries a container or containers for holding for the purposes of its propulsion any fuel which is wholly gaseous at 17.5 degrees Celsius under a pressure of 1.013 bar or plant and materials for producing such fuel,

(c) does not exceed 2540 kilograms in a case not falling within sub-paragraph (a) or (b) above,

"motor cycle" means a mechanically propelled vehicle, not being an invalid carriage, with less than four wheels and the weight of which unladen does not exceed 410 kilograms,

"motor tractor" means a mechanically propelled vehicle which is not constructed itself to carry a load, other than the excepted articles, and the weight of which unladen does not exceed 7370 kilograms,

"motor vehicle" means, subject to section 20 of the Chronically Sick and Disabled Persons Act 1970 (which makes special provision about invalid carriages, within the meaning of that Act), a mechanically propelled vehicle intended or adapted for use on roads, and

"trailer" means a vehicle drawn by a motor vehicle

(2) In subsection (1) *"excepted articles"* means any of the following: water, fuel, accumulators and other equipment used for the purpose of propulsion, loose tools and loose equipment.

Supplementary provisions about those expressions

A18.440   **186.**—(1) For the purposes of section 185 of this Act, a side-car attached to a motor vehicle, if it complies with such conditions as may be specified in regulations made by the Secretary of State, is to be regarded as forming part of the vehicle to which it is attached and as not being a trailer.

(2) For the purposes of section 185 of this Act, in a case where a motor vehicle is so constructed that a trailer may by partial super-imposition be attached to the vehicle in such a manner as to cause a substantial part of the weight of the trailer to be borne by the vehicle, that vehicle is to be deemed to be a vehicle itself constructed to carry a load.

(3) For the purposes of section 185 of this Act, in the case of a motor vehicle fitted with a crane, dynamo, welding plant or other special appliance or apparatus which is a permanent or essentially permanent fixture, that appliance or apparatus is not to be deemed to constitute a load or goods or burden of any description, but is to be deemed to form part of the vehicle.

(4)–(6) *[Power to vary maximum and minimum weights under s.185 by regulations.]*

Articulated vehicles

A18.441   **187.**—(1) Unless it falls within subsection (2) below, a vehicle so constructed that it can be divided into two parts both of which are vehicles and one of which is a motor vehicle shall (when not so divided) be treated for the purposes of the enactments mentioned in subsection (3) below as that motor vehicle with the other part attached as a trailer.

(2) A passenger vehicle so constructed that—

    (a) it can be divided into two parts, both of which are vehicles and one of which is a motor vehicle, but cannot be so divided without the use of facilities normally available only at a workshop, and

    (b) passengers carried by it when not so divided can at all times pass from either part to the other,

shall (when not so divided) be treated for the purposes of the enactments mentioned in subsection (3) below as a single motor vehicle.

(3) The enactments referred to in subsection (1) and (2) above are the Road Traffic Act 1960, Parts I and II of the Public Passenger Vehicles Act 1981, and the Traffic Acts.

(4) In this section *"passenger vehicle"* means a vehicle constructed or adapted for use solely or principally for the carriage of passengers.

Hover vehicles

188.—(1) For the purposes of the Road Traffic Acts, a hovercraft within the meaning of the Hovercraft Act 1968 (in this section referred to as a hover vehicle)—   **A18.442**

    (a) is a motor vehicle, whether or not it is intended or adapted for use on roads, but

    (b) apart from that is to be treated, subject to subsection (2) below, as not being a vehicle of any of the classes defined in section 185 of this Act.

(2) *[Regulations as to application of provisions of this Act to hover vehicles.]*

Certain vehicles not to be treated as motor vehicles

189.—(1) For the purposes of the Road Traffic Acts—   **A18.443**

    (a) a mechanically propelled vehicle being an implement for cutting grass which is controlled by a pedestrian and is not capable of being used or adapted for any other purpose,

    (b) any other mechanically propelled vehicle controlled by a pedestrian which may be specified by regulations made by the Secretary of State for the purposes of this section and section 140 of the Road Traffic Regulation Act 1984 [*q.v.*], and

    (c) an electrically assisted pedal cycle of such a class as may be prescribed by regulations so made,

is to be treated as not being a motor vehicle.

(2) In subsection (1) above *"controlled by a pedestrian"* means that the vehicle either—

    (a) is constructed or adapted for use only under such control, or

    (b) is constructed or adapted for use either under such control or under the control of a person carried on it, but is not for the time being in use under, or proceeding under, the control of a person carried on it.

A18.444   *[The Electrically Assisted Pedal Cycles Regulations 1983 (SI 1983/1168) have effect as if made under s.189(1)(c).]*

Method of calculating weight of motor vehicles and trailers

A18.445   **190.**—(1) This section applies for the purposes of the Traffic Acts and of any other enactments relating to the use of motor vehicles or trailers on roads.

(2) The weight unladen of a vehicle or trailer shall be taken to be the weight of the vehicle or trailer—

     (a) inclusive of the body and all parts (the heavier being taken where alternative bodies or parts are used) which are necessary to or ordinarily used with the vehicle or trailer when working on a road, but

     (b) exclusive of the weight of water, fuel or accumulators used for the purpose of the supply of power for the propulsion of the vehicle or, as the case may be, of any vehicle by which the trailer is drawn, and of loose tools and loose equipment.

A18.446   *[Section 190 does not apply to tramcars: Tramcars and Trolley Vehicles (Modification of Enactments) Regulations 1992 (SI 1992/1217) reg.7.]*

Interpretation of statutory references to carriages

A18.447   **191.** A motor vehicle or trailer—

     (a) is to be deemed to be a carriage within the meaning of any Act of Parliament, whether a public general Act or a local Act, and of any rule, regulation or byelaw made under any Act of Parliament, and

     (b) if used as a carriage of any particular class shall for the purpose of any enactment relating to carriages of any particular class be deemed to be a carriage of that class.

A18.448   *[Section 191 does not apply to tramcars: Tramcars and Trolley Vehicles (Modification of Enactments) Regulations 1992 (SI 1992/1217) reg.7.]*

General interpretation of Act

A18.449   **192.**—(1) In this Act —

     [*"approved testing authority"* means a person authorised by the Secretary of State under section 8 of the Transport Act 1982 to carry on a vehicle testing business within the meaning of Part II of that Act,]

     "bridleway" means a way over which the public have the following, but no other, rights of way: a right of way on foot and a right of way on horseback or leading a horse, with or without a right to drive animals of any description along the way,

     "carriage of goods" includes the haulage of goods,

     "cycle" means a bicycle, a tricycle, or a cycle having four or more wheels, not being in any case a motor vehicle,

     "driver", where a separate person acts as a steersman of a motor vehicle, includes (except for the purposes of section 1 of this Act) that person as well as any other person engaged in the driving of the vehicle, and *"drive"* is to be interpreted accordingly,

"footpath", in relation to England and Wales, means a way over which the public have a right of way on foot only,

"goods" includes goods or burden of any description,

"goods vehicle" means a motor vehicle constructed or adapted for use for the carriage of goods, or a trailer so constructed or adapted,

[*"highway authority"*, in England and Wales, means—

    (a) in relation to a road for which he is the highway authority within the meaning of the Highways Act 1980, the Secretary of State, and

    (b) in relation to any other road, the council of the county, metropolitan district or London borough, or the Common Council of the City of London, as the case may be;]

"international road haulage permit" means a licence, permit, authorisation or other document issued in pursuance of a Community instrument relating to the carriage of goods by road between member States or an international agreement to which the United Kingdom is a party and which relates to the international carriage of goods by road,

"owner", in relation to a vehicle which is the subject of a hiring agreement or hire-purchase agreement, means the person in possession of the vehicle under that agreement,

*   *   *

"prescribed" means prescribed by regulations made by the Secretary of State,

"road",

    [(a)] in relation to England and Wales, means any highway and any other road to which the public has access, and includes bridges over which a road passes, [and]

    [(b) *[applies to Scotland]*,]

"the Road Traffic Acts" means the Road Traffic Offenders Act 1988, the Road Traffic (Consequential Provisions) Act 1988 (so far as it reproduces the effect of provisions repealed by that Act) and this Act,

"statutory", in relation to any prohibition, restriction, requirement or provision, means contained in, or having effect under, an enactment (including any enactment contained in this Act),

"the Traffic Acts" means the Road Traffic Acts and the Road Traffic Regulation Act 1984 [*q.v.*],

"traffic sign" has the meaning given by section 64(1) of the Road Traffic Regulation Act 1984 [*q.v.*],

"tramcar" includes any carriage used on any road by virtue of an order under the Light Railways Act 1896, and

"trolley vehicle" means a mechanically propelled vehicle adapted for use on roads without rails [under] power transmitted to it from some external source [(whether or not there is in addition a source of power on board the vehicle)].

[(1A) In this Act—

    (a) any reference to a county shall be construed in relation to Wales as including a reference to a county borough; and

(b) section 17(4) and (5) of the Local Government (Wales) Act 1994 (references to counties and districts to be construed generally in relation to Wales as references to counties and county boroughs) shall not apply.]

(2) *[Applies to Scotland.]*

(3) References in this Act to a class of vehicles are to be interpreted as references to a class defined or described by reference to any characteristics of the vehicles or to any other circumstances whatsoever [and accordingly as authorising the use of "category" to indicate a class of vehicles, however defined or described].

A18.450   *[Section 192 is printed as amended by the Road Traffic (Driver Licensing and Information Systems) Act 1989 s.7 and Sch.3, para.24; the Road Traffic Act 1991 s.48 and Sch.4, para.78(1)–(3); the New Roads and Street Works Act 1991 s.168(1) and Sch.8, Pt 4, para.121(1) and (4); the Local Government (Wales) Act 1994 s.22(1) and Sch.7, para.40(1); the Access to Justice Act 1999 s.106 and Sch.15, Pt 5(1).*

In s.192(1), the definition of "approved testing authority" has been prospectively inserted by the Road Traffic (Consequential Provisions) Act 1988 s.4 and Sch.2, Pt 1, para.19. That definition will be brought into force on a date to be announced; see ibid. s.8(3). Until such date, the text of s.192(1) should be read as if that definition were omitted.

The Motor Vehicles (Driving Licences) Regulations 1999 (SI 1999/2864) (q.v.) were made in part under s.192(1).]

[Tramcars and other guided vehicles: drink and drugs

A18.451   **192A.**—(1) Sections 4 to 11 of this Act shall not apply (to the extent that apart from this subsection they would) to vehicles on any transport system to which Chapter I of Part II of the Transport and Works Act 1992 (offences involving drink or drugs on railways, tramways and certain other guided transport systems) applies.

(2) Subject to subsection (1) above, the Secretary of State may by regulations provide that sections 4 to 11 of this Act shall apply to vehicles on a system of guided transport specified in the regulations with such modifications as he considers necessary or expedient.

(3) Regulations under subsection (2) above may make different provision for different cases.

(4) In this section —

     "guided transport" means transport by vehicles guided by means external to the vehicles (whether or not the vehicles are also capable of being operated in some other way), and

     "vehicle" includes mobile traction unit.]

A18.452   *[Section 192A was inserted by the Transport and Works Act 1992 s.39.]*

A18.453   **193.** […]

     [Section 193 was repealed by the Road Traffic Act 1991 s.83 and Sch.8.]

[Tramcars and trolley vehicles

A18.454   **193A.**—(1) The Secretary of State may by regulations provide that such of the provisions mentioned in subsection (2) below as are specified in the regulations shall not apply, or shall apply with modifications—

  (a) to all tramcars or to tramcars of any specified class, or

  (b) to all trolley vehicles or to trolley vehicles of any specified class.

(2) The provisions referred to in subsection (1) above are the provisions of—

  (a) sections 12, 40A to 42, 47, 48, 66, 68 to 73, 75 to 79, 83, 87 to 109, 143 to 165, 168, 170, 171, 178, 190 and 191 of this Act, and

  (b) sections 1, 2, 7, 8, 22, 25 to 29, 31, 32, 34 to 48, [[91ZA to] 91B,] 96 and 97 of the Road Traffic Offenders Act 1988 (provisions requiring warning of prosecution, etc., and provisions connected with the licensing of drivers).

(3) Regulations under this section —

  (a) may make different provision for different cases,

  (b) may include such transitional provisions as appear to the Secretary of State to be necessary or expedient, and

  (c) may make such amendments to any special Act as appear to the Secretary of State to be necessary or expedient in consequence of the regulations or in consequence of the application to any tramcars or trolley vehicles of any of the provisions mentioned in subsection (2) above.

(4) In this section *"special Act"* means a local Act of Parliament passed before the commencement of this section which authorises or regulates the use of tramcars or trolley vehicles.]

[Section 193A was inserted by the Road Traffic Act 1991 s.46(2); the Driving **A18.455** *Licences (Community Driving Licence) Regulations 1996 (SI 1996/1974) reg.2 and Sch.1, para.35 (not reproduced in this work); the Crime (International Co-operation) Act 2003 s.91 and Sch.5, para.31.]*

General index

194. The expressions listed in the left-hand column below are respectively **A18.456** defined or (as the case may be) fall to be construed in accordance with the provisions of this Act listed in the right-hand column in relation to those expressions.

Expression	Relevant provision
Bridleway	Section 192
Carriage of goods	Section 192
Carriageway	Section 192
Cycle	Section 192
Drive	Section 192
Driver	Section 192
Footpath	Section 192
Footway	Section 192
Goods	Section 192
Goods vehicle	Section 192
Goods vehicle test certificate	Section 49(2)(b)

Expression	Relevant provision
Heavy locomotive	Section 185
Heavy motor car	Section 185
Highway authority	Section 192
International road haulage permit	Section 192
Invalid carriage	Section 185
Light locomotive	Section 185
Local roads authority	Section 192
Motor car	Section 185
Motor cycle	Section 185
Motor tractor	Section 185
Motor vehicle	Section 185, 186(1), 187, 188, 189
Owner	Section 192
Plating certificate	Section 49(2)(a)
Prescribed	Section 192
Public road	Section 192
Road	Section 192
Roads authority	Section 192
Road Traffic Acts	Section 192
Special road	Section 192
Statutory	Section 192
Test certificate	Section 45(2)
Traffic Acts	Section 192
Traffic sign	Section 192
Trailer	Section 185
Tramcar	Section 192
Trolley vehicle	Section 192
Trunk road	Section 192
Unladen weight	Section 190

A18.457   *[With effect from a date to be announced under the Transport Act 2000 s.275, the following entries will be inserted into the appropriate place in s.194 by the Transport Act 2000 s.260 and Sch.29, paras 1 and 6:*

    [*Driver training course*   Section 99ZA]

    Section 260 of the 2000 Act, together with Sch.29, paras 1 and 6 thereto, was brought into force on February 1, 2001 by the Transport Act 2000 (Commencement No.3) Order 2001 (SI 2001/57; not reproduced in this work), but SI 2001/57 was itself amended by the Transport Act 2000 (Commencement No.3) (Amendment) Order 2001 (SI 2001/115; not reproduced in this work) so as to delete reference to (inter alia) s.260 and Sch.29, paras 1 and 6, from SI 2001/57.]

Supplementary

Provisions as to regulations

A18.458   **195.** *[Omitted.]*

Provision, etc., of weighbridges

196. *[Omitted.]*   A18.459

Short title, commencement and extent

197.—(1) This Act may be cited as the Road Traffic Act 1988.   A18.460

(2) This Act shall come into force, *subject to the transitory provisions in Schedule 5 to the Road Traffic (Consequential Provisions) Act 1988*, at the end of the period of six months beginning with the day on which it is passed.

(3) This Act, except section 80 and except as provided by section 184, does not extend to Northern Ireland.

[The words printed in italics in s.197(2) have lapsed.]   A18.461

Sections 17 and 18   SCHEDULE 1

SUPPLEMENTARY PROVISIONS IN CONNECTION WITH PROCEEDINGS FOR OFFENCES UNDER SECTIONS
[15A,] 17 AND 18(4)

[The heading to Sch.1 is printed as amended by the Motor Vehicles (Safety   A18.462
Equipment for Children) Act 1991 s.2(1).]

Proceedings in England and Wales

1.—(1) A person against whom proceedings are brought in England and Wales for an   A18.463
offence under section [15A,] 17 or 18(4) of this Act is, upon information duly laid by him and on giving the prosecution not less than three clear days' notice of his intention, entitled to have any person to whose act or default he alleges that the contravention of that section was due brought before the court in the proceedings.

(2) If, after the contravention has been proved, the original accused proves that the contravention was due to the act or default of that other person—

(a) that other person may be convicted of the offence, and

(b) if the original accused further proves that he has used all due diligence to secure that section 17 or, as the case may be, 18(4) was complied with, he shall be acquitted of the offence.

(3) Where an accused seeks to avail himself of the provisions of sub-paragraphs (1) and (2) above—

(a) the prosecution, as well as the person whom the accused charges with the offence, has the right to cross-examine him, if he gives evidence, and any witness called by him in support of his pleas, and to call rebutting evidence, and

(b) the court may make such order as it thinks fit for the payment of costs by any party to the proceedings to any other party to the proceedings.

[Paragraph 1 of Sch.1 is printed as amended by the Motor Vehicles (Safety   A18.464
Equipment for Children) Act 1991 s.2(1).]

2.—(1) Where—   A18.465

(a) it appears that an offence under section [15A,] 17 or 18(4) of this Act has been committed in respect of which proceedings might be taken in England and Wales against some person (referred to below in this paragraph as *"the original offender"*), and

(b) a person proposing to take proceedings in respect of the offence is reasonably satisfied—

(i) that the offence of which complaint is made was due to an act or default of some other person, being an act or default which took place in England and Wales, and

    (ii) that the original offender could establish a defence under paragraph 1 of this Schedule,

the proceedings may be taken against that other person without proceedings first being taken against the original offender.

(2) In any such proceedings the accused may be charged with, and on proof that the contravention was due to his act or default be convicted of, the offence with which the original offender might have been charged.

A18.466   *[Paragraph 2 of Sch.1 is printed as amended by the Motor Vehicles (Safety Equipment for Children) Act 1991 s.2(1).]*

A18.467   3.—(1) Where proceedings are brought in England and Wales against a person (referred to below in this paragraph as *"the accused"*) in respect of a contravention of section 17 or 18(4) of this Act and it is proved—

    (a) that the contravention was due to the act or default of some other person, being an act or default which took place in Scotland, and

    (b) that the accused used all due diligence to secure compliance with that section,

the accused shall, subject to the provisions of this paragraph, be acquitted of the offence.

(2) The accused is not entitled to be acquitted under this paragraph unless within seven days from the date of the service of the summons on him—

    (a) he has given notice in writing to the prosecution of his intention to rely upon the provisions of this paragraph, specifying the name and address of the person to whose act or default he alleges that the contravention was due, and

    (b) he has sent a like notice to that person.

(3) The person specified in a notice served under this paragraph is entitled to appear at the hearing and give evidence and the court may, if it thinks fit, adjourn the hearing to enable him to do so.

(4) Where it is proved that the contravention of section 17 or 18(4) of this Act was due to the act or default of some person other than the accused, being an act or default which took place in Scotland, the court must (whether or not the accused is acquitted) cause notice of the proceedings to be sent to the Secretary of State.

A18.468   *[Paragraph 3 of Sch.1 is printed as amended by the Motor Vehicles (Safety Equipment for Children) Act 1991 s.2(1).]*

Proceedings in Scotland

A18.469   4. *[Omitted.]*

Proceedings in Great Britain

A18.470   5.—[(1A) Subject to the provisions of this paragraph, in any proceedings (whether in England and Wales or Scotland) for an offence under section 15A of this Act it shall be a defence for the accused to prove—

    (a) if the offence is under subsection (3)(a) of that section—

      (i) that he purchased the equipment in question as being of a type which could be lawfully sold or offered for sale as conducive to the safety in the event of accident of prescribed classes of children in prescribed classes of motor vehicles and with a written warranty to that effect;

      (ii) that he had no reason to believe at the time of the commission of the alleged offence that it was not of such a type; and

      (iii) that it was then in the same state as when he purchased it;

    (b) if the offence is under subsection (3)(b) of that section, he provided information in relation to the equipment and it is alleged that it did not include appropriate information or included or consisted of inappropriate information—

      (i) that the information provided by him was information which had been provided to him with a written warranty to the effect that it was the information required to be provided by him under section 15A of this Act; and

(ii) that he had no reason to believe at the time of the commission of the alleged offence that the information provided by him was not the information required to be provided under that section; or

(c) if the offence is under subsection (3)(b) of that section, he provided information in relation to the equipment and it is alleged that it was not provided in the manner required under that section—

(i) that the information provided by him had been provided to him either with a written warranty to the effect that it was provided to him in the manner in which it was required to be provided by him under that section or with instructions as to the manner in which the information should be provided by him and with a written warranty to the effect that provision in that manner would comply with regulations under that section;

(ii) that he had no reason to believe at the time of the commission of the alleged offence that he was not providing the information in the manner required under that section; and

(iii) that the information was then in the same state as when it was provided to him or, as the case may be, that it was provided by him in accordance with the instructions given to him.]

(1) Subject to the provisions of this paragraph, in any proceedings (whether in England and Wales or Scotland) for an offence under section 17 or 18(4) of this Act it shall be a defence for the accused to prove—

(a) that he purchased the helmet or appliance in question as being of a type which—

(i) in the case of section 17, could be lawfully sold or offered for sale under that section, and

(ii) in the case of section 18(4), could be lawfully sold or offered for sale under section 18 as authorised for use in the manner in question,

and with a written warranty to that effect, and

(b) that he had no reason to believe at the time of the commission of the alleged offence that it was not of such a type, and

(c) that it was then in the same state as when he purchased it.

(2) A warranty is only a defence in any such proceedings if—

(a) the accused—

(i) has, not later than three clear days before the date of the hearing, sent to the prosecutor a copy of the warranty with a notice stating that he intends to rely on it and specifying the name and address of the person from whom he received it, and

(ii) has also sent a like notice of his intention to that person, and

(b) in the case of a warranty given by a person outside the United Kingdom, the accused proves that he had taken reasonable steps to ascertain, and did in fact believe in, the accuracy of the statement contained in the warranty.

(3) Where the accused is a servant of the person who purchased the [equipment, helmet or appliance in question under a warranty, or to whom the information in question was provided] under a warranty, he is entitled to rely on the provisions of this paragraph in the same way as his employer would have been entitled to do if he had been the accused.

(4) The person by whom the warranty is alleged to have been given is entitled to appear at the hearing and to give evidence and the court may, if it thinks fit, adjourn the hearing to enable him to do so.

[Paragraph 5 of Sch.1 is printed as amended by the Motor Vehicles (Safety Equipment for Children) Act 1991 s.2(2) and (3).]   **A18.471**

[6.—(1) An accused who in any proceedings for an offence under section 15A, 17 or 18(4) of this Act wilfully applies to equipment, information, a helmet or, as the case may be, an appliance a warranty not given in relation to it is guilty of an offence.   **A18.472**

(2) A person who, in respect of equipment, a helmet or an appliance sold by him, or information provided by him, being equipment, a helmet, an appliance or information in respect of which a warranty might be pleaded under paragraph 5 of this Schedule, gives to the purchaser a false warranty in writing, is guilty of an offence, unless he proves that when he gave the warranty he had reason to believe that the statements of description contained in it were accurate.

(3) Where the accused in a prosecution for an offence under section 15A, 17 or 18(4) of this Act relies successfully on a warranty given to him or his employer, any proceedings under sub-paragraph (2) above in respect of the warranty may, at the option of the prosecutor, be taken before a court having jurisdiction in the place—

    (a) where the equipment, helmet or appliance, or any of the equipment, helmets or appliances, to which the warranty relates was procured;

    (b) where the information, or any of it, to which the warranty relates was provided; or

    (c) where the warranty was given.]

A18.473   *[Paragraph 6 of Sch.1 is printed as substituted by the Motor Vehicles (Safety Equipment for Children) Act 1991 s.2(4).]*

A18.474   [7. In this Schedule, *"equipment"* means equipment to which section 15A of this Act applies and *"appliance"* means an appliance to which section 18 of this Act applies.]

A18.475   *[Paragraph 7 of Sch.1 is printed as substituted by the Motor Vehicles (Safety Equipment for Children) Act 1991 s.2(4).]*

Section 67   SCHEDULE 2

DEFERRED TESTS OF CONDITION OF VEHICLES

A18.476   1. Where the driver is the owner of the vehicle, he may at the time of electing that the test shall be deferred—

    (a) specify a period of seven days within which the deferred test is to take place, being a period falling within the next thirty days, disregarding any day on which the vehicle is outside Great Britain, and

    (b) require that the deferred test shall take place on premises then specified by him where the test can conveniently be carried out or that it shall take place in such area in England ..., being a county district or Greater London [in such county or county borough in Wales], or such area in Scotland, being [the area of a council constituted under section 2 of the Local Government, etc. (Scotland) Act 1994], as he may specify at that time.

A18.477   *[Paragraph 1 of Sch.2 is printed as amended by the Local Government (Wales) Act 1994 ss.22(1) and 66(8), Sch.7, para.40(2), and Sch.18; the Local Government, etc. (Scotland) Act 1994 s.180(1) and Sch.13, para.159(9).]*

A18.478   2. When the driver is not the owner of the vehicle he shall inform the examiner of the name and address of the owner of the vehicle and the owner shall be afforded an opportunity of specifying such a period, and such premises or area.

A18.479   3.—(1) Where under the preceding provisions of this Schedule a period has been specified within which the deferred test is to be carried out, the time for carrying it out shall be such time within that period as may be notified, being a time not earlier than two days after the giving of the notification.

(2) Where no such period has been specified, the time for the carrying out of the deferred test shall be such time as may be notified, being a time not earlier than seven days after the giving of the notification.

(3) Where premises have been specified under the preceding provisions of this Schedule for the carrying out of the deferred test, and the test can conveniently be carried out on those premises, it must be carried out there.

(4) Where sub-paragraph (3) above does not apply, the place for carrying out the

deferred test shall be such place as may be notified with the notification of the time for the carrying out of the test, and where an area has been so specified the place shall be a place in that area.

(5) Notwithstanding the preceding provisions of this paragraph, the time and place for the carrying out of the deferred test may be varied by agreement between an authorised examiner and the owner of the vehicle.

(6) In this paragraph —

"*notified*" means notified in writing to the owner of the vehicle on behalf of the Secretary of State, and

"*notification*" shall be construed accordingly,

and any notification under this paragraph may be given by post.

4. The owner of the vehicle must produce it, or secure its production, at the time and place fixed for the carrying out of the deferred test.　　　　**A18.480**

5.—(1) References in this Schedule to the owner of a vehicle are references to the owner of the vehicle at the time at which the election is made under section 67(6) of this Act that the test should be deferred.　　　　**A18.481**

(2) For the purposes of this Schedule —

    (a) subject to sub-paragraph (b) below, if at the time at which that election is made the vehicle is in the possession of a person under a hire-purchase agreement or hiring agreement, that person shall be deemed to be the owner of the vehicle to the exclusion of any other person,

    (b) if at that time the vehicle is being used under an international circulation permit, the person to whom the permit was issued shall be deemed to be the owner of the vehicle to the exclusion of any other person.

Section 15B　　　　　　[SCHEDULE 2A

APPEALS UNDER SECTION 131 AGAINST DECISIONS OF THE REGISTRAR

FORM OF SEAT BELT SYMBOL FOR BUSES　　　　**A18.482**

[Schedule 2A is printed as inserted by the Motor Vehicles (Wearing of Seat-belts) (Amendment) Regulations 2006 (SI 2006/1892) reg.5.]　　　　**A18.483**

[The Schedule set out below was inserted after Sch.2 by the Road Safety Act 2006 s.22(3) and Sch.5. The numbering of the Schedule as Sch.2A appears to be in error following the insertion of Sch.2A, Form of Seat Belt Symbol for Buses, by SI 2006/1892, see § A18.482 above.　　　　**A18.484**

Words omitted from the Schedule relate to Scotland.]

Section 144D   [SCHEDULE 2A

OFFENCE OF KEEPING VEHICLE WHICH DOES NOT MEET INSURANCE REQUIREMENTS: IMMOBILISA-
TION, REMOVAL AND DISPOSAL OF VEHICLES

Immobilisation

A18.485 **1.**—(1) Regulations may make provision with respect to any case where an authorised person has reason to believe that, on or after such date as may be prescribed, an offence under section 144A of this Act is being committed as regards a vehicle which is stationary on a road or other public place.

(2) The regulations may provide that the authorised person or a person acting under his direction may—

(a) fix an immobilisation device to the vehicle while it remains in the place where it is stationary, or

(b) move it from that place to another place on the same or another road or public place and fix an immobilisation device to it in that other place.

(3) The regulations may provide that on any occasion when an immobilisation device is fixed to a vehicle in accordance with the regulations the person fixing the device must also fix to the vehicle a notice—

(a) indicating that the device has been fixed to the vehicle and warning that no attempt should be made to drive it or otherwise put it in motion until it has been released from the device,

(b) specifying the steps to be taken to secure its release, and

(c) giving such other information as may be prescribed.

(4) The regulations may provide that a vehicle to which an immobilisation device has been fixed in accordance with the regulations—

(a) may only be released from the device by or under the direction of an authorised person, but

(b) subject to that, must be released from the device if the first and second requirements specified below are met.

(5) The first requirement is that such charge in respect of the release as may be prescribed is paid in any manner specified in the immobilisation notice.

(6) The second requirement is that, in accordance with instructions specified in the immobilisation notice, there is produced such evidence as may be prescribed establishing—

(a) that any person who proposes to drive the vehicle away will not in doing so be guilty of an offence under section 143 of this Act, and

(b) that the person in whose name the vehicle is registered under the Vehicle Excise and Registration Act 1994 is not guilty of an offence under section 144A of this Act as regards the vehicle.

(7) The regulations may provide that they do not apply in relation to a vehicle if—

(a) a current disabled person's badge is displayed on the vehicle, or

(b) such other conditions as may be prescribed are fulfilled, and *"disabled person's badge"* means a badge issued, or having effect as if issued, under any regulations for the time being in force under section 21 of the Chronically Sick and Disabled Persons Act 1970.

(8) The regulations may provide that an immobilisation notice is not to be removed or interfered with except by or on the authority of a person falling within a prescribed description.

Offences connected with immobilisation

A18.486 **2.**—(1) The regulations may provide that a person contravening provision made under paragraph 1(8) above is guilty of an offence.

(2) The regulations may provide that a person who, without being authorised to do so in accordance with provision made under paragraph 1 above, removes or attempts to remove an immobilisation device fixed to a vehicle in accordance with the regulations is guilty of an offence.

(3) The regulations may provide that where they would apply in relation to a vehicle but for provision made under paragraph 1(7)(a) above and the vehicle was not, at the time it was stationary, being used—

(a) in accordance with regulations under section 21 of the Chronically Sick and Disabled Persons Act 1970, and

(b) in circumstances falling within section 117(1)(b) of the Road Traffic Regulation Act 1984 (use where a disabled person's concession would be available),

the person in charge of the vehicle at that time is guilty of an offence.

(4) The regulations may provide that where—

(a) a person makes a declaration with a view to securing the release of a vehicle from an immobilisation device purported to have been fixed in accordance with the regulations,

(b) the declaration is that no offence under section 144A of this Act is or was being committed as regards the vehicle, and

(c) the declaration is to the person's knowledge either false or in any material respect misleading,

he is guilty of an offence.

Removal and disposal of vehicles

3.—(1) The regulations may make provision with respect to any case where— **A18.487**

(a) an authorised person has reason to believe that an offence under section 144A of this Act is being committed as regards a vehicle which is stationary on a road or other public place, and such conditions as may be prescribed are fulfilled, or

(b) an authorised person has reason to believe that such an offence was being committed as regards a vehicle at a time when an immobilisation device which is fixed to the vehicle was fixed to it in accordance with the regulations, and such conditions as may be prescribed are fulfilled.

(2) The regulations may provide that the authorised person, or a person acting under his direction, may remove the vehicle and deliver it into the custody of a person—

(a) who is identified in accordance with prescribed rules, and

(b) who agrees to accept delivery in accordance with arrangements agreed between that person and the Secretary of State,

and the arrangements may include provision as to the payment of a sum to the person into whose custody the vehicle is delivered.

(3) The regulations may provide that the person into whose custody the vehicle is delivered may dispose of it, and may in particular make provision as to—

(a) the time at which the vehicle may be disposed of, and

(b) the manner in which it may be disposed of.

(4) The regulations may make provision allowing a person to take possession of the vehicle if—

(a) he claims it before it is disposed of, and

(b) any prescribed conditions are fulfilled.

(5) The regulations may provide for a sum of an amount arrived at under prescribed rules to be paid to a person if—

(a) he claims after the vehicle's disposal to be or to have been its owner,

(b) the claim is made within a prescribed time of the disposal, and

(c) any other prescribed conditions are fulfilled.

(6) The regulations may provide that—

(a) the Secretary of State, or

(b) a person into whose custody the vehicle is delivered under the regulations,

may recover from the vehicle's owner (whether or not a claim is made under provision made under sub-paragraph (4) or (5) above) such charges as may be prescribed in respect of all or any of the following, namely its release, removal, custody and disposal; and *"owner"* means the person who was the owner when the vehicle was removed.

(7) The conditions prescribed under sub-paragraph (4) above may include conditions as to—

(a) satisfying the person with custody that the claimant is the vehicle's owner,

(b) the payment of prescribed charges in respect of the vehicle's release, removal and custody,

(c) the production of such evidence as may be prescribed establishing that in driving the vehicle away the claimant will not be guilty of an offence under section 143 of this Act, and

(d) the production of such evidence as may be prescribed establishing that the person in whose name the vehicle is registered under the Vehicle Excise and Registration Act 1994 is not guilty of an offence under section 144A of this Act as regards the vehicle.

(8) The regulations may in particular include provision for purposes corresponding to those of sections 101 and 102 of the Road Traffic Regulation Act 1984 (disposal and charges) subject to such additions, omissions or other modifications as the Secretary of State thinks fit.

Offences as to securing possession of vehicles

A18.488   **4.** The regulations may provide that where—

(a) a person makes a declaration with a view to securing possession of a vehicle purported to have been delivered into the custody of a person in accordance with provision made under paragraph 3 above,

(b) the declaration is that no offence under section 144A of this Act is or was being committed as regards the vehicle, and

(c) the declaration is to the person's knowledge either false or in any material respect misleading,

he is guilty of an offence.

Disputes

A18.489   **5.** The regulations may make provision about the proceedings to be followed where a dispute occurs as a result of the regulations, and may in particular make provision—

(a) for an application to be made to a magistrates' court ..., or

(b) for a court to order a sum to be paid by the Secretary of State.

Authorised persons

A18.490   **6.** As regards anything falling to be done under the regulations (such as receiving payment of a charge or other sum) the regulations may provide that it may be done—

(a) by an authorised person, or

(b) by an authorised person or a person acting under his direction.

Application of Road Traffic Offenders Act 1988

A18.491   **7.** The regulations may make provision for the application of any or all of sections 1, 6, 11 and 12(1) of the Road Traffic Offenders Act 1988 to an offence for which provision is made by the regulations.

Interpretation

A18.492   **8.**—(1) The regulations may make provision as to the meaning for the purposes of the regulations of "owner" as regards a vehicle.

(2) In particular, the regulations may provide that for the purposes of the regulations the owner of a vehicle is taken to be the person in whose name it is then registered under the Vehicle Excise and Registration Act 1994.

9.—(1) The regulations may make provision as to the meaning in the regulations of "authorised person".

(2) In particular, the regulations may provide that—

   (a) references to an authorised person are to a person authorised by the Secretary of State for the purposes of the regulations,

   (b) an authorised person may be a local authority or an employee of a local authority or a member of a police force or some other person, and

   (c) different persons may be authorised for the purposes of different provisions of the regulations.

10. In this Schedule—

   (a) references to an immobilisation device are to a device or appliance which is an immobilisation device for the purposes of section 104 of the Road Traffic Regulation Act 1984 (immobilisation of vehicles illegally parked), and

   (b) references to an immobilisation notice are to a notice fixed to a vehicle in accordance with the regulations.]

A18.493

A18.494

Section 131   SCHEDULE 3

APPEALS UNDER SECTION 131 AGAINST DECISIONS OF THE REGISTRAR
[Repealed by the Transport Act 2000 s.274 and Sch.31, Pt 5(1).]   **A18.495**

SCHEDULE 4

PROVISIONS NOT APPLICABLE TO TRAMCARS, ETC.
[Repealed by the Road Traffic Act 1991 s.83 and Sch.8.]   **A18.496**

The Road Traffic Offenders Act 1988

(1988 c.53)

A19.01 *An Act to consolidate certain enactments relating to the prosecution and punishment (including the punishment without conviction) of road traffic offences with amendments to give effect to recommendations of the Law Commission and the Scottish Law Commission.*

[15th November 1988]

ARRANGEMENT OF SECTIONS
PART I
TRIAL
Introductory

Verdict

*   *   *

PART II

SENTENCE

Introductory

*   *   *

Fine and imprisonment

Disqualification

*   *   *

PART 3A
FINANCIAL PENALTY DEPOSITS

PART IV
MISCELLANEOUS AND GENERAL

*   *   *

PART I

TRIAL

Introductory

Requirement of warning, etc., of prosecutions for certain offences

A19.02   **1.**—(1) Subject to section 2 of this Act, [a person shall not be convicted of an offence to which this section applies unless]—

     (a) he was warned at the time the offence was committed that the question of prosecuting him for some one or other of the offences to which this section applies would be taken into consideration, or

     (b) within fourteen days of the commission of the offence a summons … for the offence was served on him, or

     (c) within fourteen days of the commission of the offence a notice of the intended prosecution specifying the nature of the alleged offence and the time and place where it is alleged to have been committed, was—

        (i) in the case of an offence under section 28 or 29 of the Road Traffic Act 1988 (cycling offences), served on him,

        (ii) in the case of any other offence, served on him or on the person, if any, registered as the keeper of the vehicle at the time of the commission of the offence.

[(1A) A notice required by this section to be served on any person may be served on that person—

     (a) by delivering it to him;

     (b) by addressing it to him and leaving it at his last known address; or

     (c) by sending it by registered post, recorded delivery service or first class post addressed to him at his last known address.]

(2) A notice shall be deemed for the purposes of subsection (1)(c) above to

have been served on a person if it was sent by registered post or recorded delivery service addressed to him at his last known address, notwithstanding that the notice was returned as undelivered or was for any other reason not received by him.

(3) The requirement of subsection (1) above shall in every case be deemed to have been complied with unless and until the contrary is proved.

(4) Schedule 1 to this Act shows the offences to which this section applies.

[Section 1 is printed as amended by the Road Traffic Act 1991 s.48 and Sch.4, **A19.03** *para.80; the Criminal Justice and Public Order Act 1994 s.168(1) and Sch.9, para.6(3).*

Words in s.1(1)(b) relating exclusively and expressly to Scotland have been omitted.

In note 16B to the code of practice for the detention, treatment and questioning of persons by police officers (Code C (2008) under the Police and Criminal Evidence Act 1984) it is stated that the giving of a warning or the service of a notice of intended prosecution under s.1 of this Act does not amount to informing a detainee that he may be prosecuted for an offence and so does not preclude further questioning in relation to that offence; in this context, see also para.16.5 of that code.]

Requirement of warning, etc.: supplementary

2.—(1) The requirement of section 1(1) of this Act does not apply in relation **A19.04** to an offence if, at the time of the offence or immediately after it, an accident occurs owing to the presence on a road of the vehicle in respect of which the offence was committed.

(2) The requirement of section 1(1) of this Act does not apply in relation to an offence in respect of which—

    (a) a fixed penalty notice (within the meaning of Part III of this Act) has been given or fixed under any provision of that Part, or

    (b) a notice has been given under section 54(4) of this Act.

(3) Failure to comply with the requirement of section 1(1) of this Act is not a bar to the conviction of the accused in a case where the court is satisfied—

    (a) that neither the name and address of the accused nor the name and address of the registered keeper, if any, could with reasonable diligence have been ascertained in time for a summons or, as the case may be, a complaint to be served or for a notice to be served or sent in compliance with the requirement, or

    (b) that the accused by his own conduct contributed to the failure.

[(4) Failure to comply with the requirement of section 1(1) of this Act in relation to an offence is not a bar to the conviction of a person of that offence by virtue of the provisions of—

    (a) section 24 of this Act, or

    (b) any of the enactments mentioned in section 24(6);

but a person is not to be convicted of an offence by virtue of any of those provisions if section 1 applies to the offence with which he was charged and the requirement of section 1(1) was not satisfied in relation to the offence charged.]

[Section 2 is printed as amended by the Road Traffic Act 1991 s.4 and Sch.4, **A19.05** *para.81. See also the notes to s.1 of this Act.]*

Restriction on institution of proceedings for certain offences

A19.06   3.—(1) […]

(2) In England and Wales, proceedings for an offence under section 94(3) of the Road Traffic Act 1988 (notice about relevant or prospective disability) shall not be instituted except by the Secretary of State or by a constable acting with the approval of the Secretary of State.

[(2A) In subsection (2) above the reference to section 94(3) of the Road Traffic Act 1988 includes a reference to that section as applied by section 99D [or 109C] of that Act.]

A19.07   *[Section 3 is printed as amended by the Road Traffic (Driver Licensing and Information Systems) Act 1989 s.16 and Sch.6; the Driving Licences (Community Driving Licence) Regulations 1996 (SI 1996/1974) reg.3 and Sch.2, para.1 (not reproduced in this work); the Crime (International Co-operation) Act 2003 s.91 and Sch.5, para.33.]*

Offences for which local authorities in England and Wales may institute proceedings

A19.08   4.—(1) The council of a county, metropolitan district or London borough or the Common Council of the City of London may institute proceedings for an offence under section [15A of the Road Traffic Act 1988 (safety equipment for children in motor vehicles) or under section 17 or 18 of that Act] (helmets and other head-worn appliances for motor cyclists).

(2) The council of a county, metropolitan district or London borough or the Common Council of the City of London may institute proceedings for an offence under section 27 of that Act (dogs on roads) relating to a road in their area.

(3) The council of a county, district or London borough or the Common Council of the City of London may institute proceedings for offences under section [35A(1), (2) or (5)] of the Road Traffic Regulation Act 1984 which are committed in connection with parking places provided by the council, or provided under any letting arrangements made by the council under section 33(4) of that Act.

(4) The council of a county, metropolitan district or London borough or the Common Council of the City of London may institute proceedings for an offence under section 47 or 52 of the Road Traffic Regulation Act 1984 in connection with a designated parking place controlled by the council.

(5) In England, the council of a county or metropolitan district and, in Wales, the council of a county [or county borough] may institute proceedings for an offence under section 53 of the Road Traffic Regulation Act 1984 in connection with a designated parking place in the council's area …

(6) In this section *"parking place"* means a place where vehicles, or vehicles of any class, may wait and *"designated parking place"* has the same meaning as in the Road Traffic Regulation Act 1984.

(7) This section extends to England and Wales only.

[(8) In relation to Wales, any reference in subsections (1) to (4) above to a county shall be read as including a reference to a county borough.]

A19.09   *[Section 4 is printed as amended by the Parking Act 1989 s.4 and Schedule, para.10; the Motor Vehicles (Safety Equipment for Children) Act 1991 s.3(1);*

the Local Government (Wales) Act 1994 ss.22(1) and 66(8), Sch.7, para.41, and Sch.18.

The term "designated parking place" is defined in the Road Traffic Regulation Act 1984 s.142(1) (q.v.).]

Exemption from Licensing Act offence

5. A person liable to be charged with an offence under [section 3A, 4], 5, 7 or **A19.10** 30 of the Road Traffic Act 1988 (drink and drugs) is not liable to be charged under section 12 of the Licensing Act 1872 with the offence of being drunk while in charge, on a highway or other public place, of a carriage.

[Section 5 is printed as amended by the Road Traffic Act 1991 s.48 and Sch.4, para.82.]

Time within which summary proceedings for certain offences must be commenced

6.—(1) Subject to subsection (2) below, summary proceedings for an offence **A19.11** to which this section applies may be brought within a period of six months from the date on which evidence sufficient in the opinion of the prosecutor to warrant the proceedings came to his knowledge.

(2) No such proceedings shall be brought by virtue of this section more than three years after the commission of the offence.

(3) For the purposes of this section, a certificate signed by or on behalf of the prosecutor and stating the date on which evidence sufficient in his opinion to warrant the proceedings came to his knowledge shall be conclusive evidence of that fact.

(4) A certificate stating that matter and purporting to be so signed shall be deemed to be so signed unless the contrary is proved.

(5) *[Applies to Scotland.]*

(6) Schedule 1 to this Act shows the offences to which this section applies.

[The application of s.6 has been extended to offences under the Goods Vehicles **A19.12** *(Licensing of Operators) Act 1995 ss. 9(3)(a) and (b), 38 and 39 by ibid. s.51 below; but Sch.1 to this Act has not been amended to give effect to this amendment.]*

Duty of accused to provide licence

7.—[(1)] A person who is prosecuted for an offence involving [obligatory or **A19.13** discretionary endorsement] and who is the holder of a licence must—

   (a) cause it to be delivered to the [proper officer] of the court not later than the day before the date appointed for the hearing, or

   (b) post it, at such a time that in the ordinary course of post it would be delivered not later than that day, in a letter duly addressed to the clerk and either registered or sent by the recorded delivery service, or

   (c) have it with him at the hearing [and the foregoing obligations imposed on him as respects the licence also apply as respects the counterpart to the licence].

[(2) In subsection (1) above *"proper officer"* means—

   (a) in relation to a magistrates' court in England and Wales, the [designated officer] for the court, and

(b) in relation to any other court, the clerk of the court.]

A19.14   *[Section 7 is printed as amended by the Driving Licences (Community Driving Licence) Regulations 1990 (SI 1990/144); the Road Traffic Act 1991 s.48 and Sch.4, para.83; the Access to Justice Act 1999 s.90(1) and Sch.13, paras 140 and 141; the Courts Act 2003 s.109(1) and Sch.8, para.310.*

With effect from a day to be appointed and in relation to endorsement (all drivers), in s.7(1) the words from "and the foregoing" to the end will be omitted by the Road Safety Act 2006 s.10 and Sch.3, para.31, s.59 and Sch.7(4).

As to the application of s.7 to domestic driving permits, Convention driving permits and British Forces (BFG) driving licences and to the holders of such licences and permits, see the Motor Vehicles (Driving Licences) Regulations 1999 (SI 1999/2864) reg.80, below. As to the application of s.7 to Community licences, see s.91A(1) below.]

Duty to include date of birth and sex in written plea of guilty

A19.15   **8.** A person who—

(a) gives a notification [to [the designated officer for a magistrates' court] in pursuance of section 12(4)] of the Magistrates' Courts Act 1980 (written pleas of guilty), or

(b) *[applies to Scotland.]*

in respect of an offence involving obligatory or discretionary disqualification or of such other offence as may be prescribed by regulations under section 105 of the Road Traffic Act 1988, must include in the notification or intimation a statement of the date of birth and sex of the accused.

A19.16   *[Section 8 is printed as amended by the Magistrates' Courts (Procedure) Act 1998 s.4(1)(a); the Access to Justice Act 1999 s.90(1) and Sch.13, paras 140 and 142; the Courts Act 2003 s.109(1) and Sch.8, para.311.]*

Trial

Mode of trial

A19.17   **9.** An offence against a provision of the Traffic Acts specified in column 1 of Part I of Schedule 2 to this Act or regulations made under such a provision (the general nature of which offence is indicated in column 2) shall be punishable as shown against the offence in column 3 (that is, on summary conviction or on indictment or in either one way or the other).

Jurisdiction of district court in Scotland

A19.18   **10.** *[Omitted.]*

Evidence by certificate as to driver, user or owner

A19.19   **11.**—(1) In any proceedings in England and Wales for an offence to which this section applies, a certificate in the prescribed form, purporting to be signed by a constable and certifying that a person specified in the certificate stated to the constable—

(a) that a particular [mechanically propelled vehicle] was being driven or used by, or belonged to, that person on a particular occasion, or

(b) that a particular [mechanically propelled vehicle] on a particular occasion was used by, or belonged to, a firm and that he was, at the time of the statement, a partner in that firm, or

(c) that a particular [mechanically propelled vehicle] on a particular occasion was used by, or belonged to, a corporation and that he was, at the time of the statement, a director, officer or employee of that corporation,

shall be admissible as evidence for the purpose of determining by whom the vehicle was being driven or used, or to whom it belonged, as the case may be, on that occasion.

(2) Nothing in subsection (1) above makes a certificate admissible as evidence in proceedings for an offence except in a case where and to the like extent to which oral evidence to the like effect would have been admissible in those proceedings.

(3) Nothing in subsection (1) above makes a certificate admissible as evidence in proceedings for an offence—

(a) unless a copy of it has, not less than seven days before the hearing or trial, been served in the prescribed manner on the person charged with the offence, or

(b) if that person, not later than three days before the hearing or trial or within such further time as the court may in special circumstances allow, serves a notice in the prescribed form and manner on the prosecutor requiring attendance at the trial of the person who signed the certificate.

[(3A) Where the proceedings mentioned in subsection (1) above are proceedings before a magistrates' court inquiring into an offence as examining justices this section shall have effect with the omission of—

(a) subsection (2), and

(b) in subsection (3), paragraph (b) and the word "or" immediately preceding it.]

(4) In this section *"prescribed"* means prescribed by rules made by the Secretary of State by statutory instrument.

(5) Schedule 1 to this Act shows the offences to which this section applies.

[Section 11 is printed as amended by the Road Traffic Act 1991 s.48 and Sch.4, **A19.20** *para.84; the Criminal Procedure and Investigations Act 1996 s.47 and Sch.1, para.35.*

Section 11(3A) applies in relation to any alleged offence in relation to which Pt 1 of the 1996 Act applies (see the Criminal Procedure and Investigations Act 1996 (Commencement) (Section 65 and Schedules 1 and 2) Order 1997 (SI 1997/683); not reproduced in this work).

With effect from a day to be appointed, subs.(3A) of s.11 will be revoked by the Criminal Justice Act 2003 s.41 and Sch.3, para.61(2) and Sch.37, Pt 4.

The Evidence by Certificate Rules 1961 (SI 1962/248; not reproduced in this work) have effect as if made under s.11.]

Proof, in summary proceedings, of identity of driver of vehicle

12.—(1) Where on the summary trial in England and Wales of an information **A19.21** for an offence to which this subsection applies—

(a) it is proved to the satisfaction of the court, on oath or in manner prescribed by [Criminal Procedure Rules], that a requirement under section 172(2) of the Road Traffic Act 1988 [*q.v.*] to give information as to the identity of the driver of a particular vehicle on the particular occasion to which the information relates has been served on the accused by post, and

(b) a statement in writing is produced to the court purporting to be signed by the accused that the accused was the driver of that vehicle on that occasion,

the court may accept that statement as evidence that the accused was the driver of that vehicle on that occasion.

(2) Schedule 1 to this Act shows the offences to which subsection (1) above applies.

(3) Where on the summary trial in England and Wales of an information for an offence to which section 112 of the Road Traffic Regulation Act 1984 [*q.v.*] applies—

(a) it is proved to the satisfaction of the court, on oath or in manner prescribed by [Criminal Procedure Rules], that a requirement under section 112(2) of the Road Traffic Regulation Act 1984 to give information as to the identity of the driver of a particular vehicle on the particular occasion to which the information relates has been served on the accused by post, and

(b) a statement in writing is produced to the court purporting to be signed by the accused that the accused was the driver of that vehicle on that occasion,

the court may accept that statement as evidence that the accused was the driver of that vehicle on that occasion.

(4) *[Applies to Scotland.]*

A19.22   *[Section 12 has been amended by the Road Traffic Act 1991 s.48 and Sch.4, para.85 (which inserted s.12(4)); the Courts Act 2003 (Consequential Amendments) Order 2004 (SI 2004/2035) art.30.*

The amendment made by SI 2004/2035 in s.12(1)(a) and (3)(a) shall not affect the general operation of the Road Traffic Offenders Act 1988 in so far as it relates to rules of court other than Criminal Procedure Rules during the period between the coming into force of the Order and the coming into force of the first Criminal Procedure Rules made under the Courts Act 2003 s.69 (see art.2(2) of the 2004 Order).]

Admissibility of records as evidence

A19.23   13.—(1) This section applies to a statement contained in a document purporting to be—

(a) a part of the records maintained by the Secretary of State in connection with any functions exercisable by him by virtue of Part III of the Road Traffic Act 1988 or a part of any other records maintained by the Secretary of State with respect to vehicles [or of any records maintained with respect to vehicles by an approved testing authority in connection with the exercise by that authority of any functions conferred on such authorities, or on that authority as such an authority, by or under any enactment], or

(b) a copy of a document forming part of those records, or

(c) a note of any information contained in those records,

and to be authenticated by a person authorised in that behalf by the Secretary of State [or (as the case may be) the approved testing authority].

(2) A statement to which this section applies shall be admissible in any proceedings as evidence … of any fact stated in it to the same extent as oral evidence of that fact is admissible in those proceedings.

[(3) In the preceding subsections, except in Scotland—

"*copy*", in relation to a document, means anything onto which information recorded in the document has been copied, by whatever means and whether directly or indirectly;

"*document*" means anything in which information of any description is recorded; and

"*statement*" means any representation of fact, however made.]

[(3A) In any case where—

(a) a person is convicted by a magistrates' court of a summary offence under the Traffic Acts or the Road Traffic (Driver Licensing and Information Systems) Act 1989,

(b) a statement to which this section applies is produced to the court in the proceedings,

(c) the statement specifies an alleged previous conviction of the accused of an offence involving obligatory endorsment or an order made on the conviction, and

(d) the accused is not present in the person before the court when the statement is produced,

the court may take account of the previous conviction or order as if the accused had appeared and admitted it.

(3B) Section 104 of the Magistrates' Courts Act 1980 (under which the previous convictions may be adduced in the absence of the accused after giving him seven days' notice of them) does not limit the effect of subsection (3A) above.]

(4) In any case where—

(a) a statement to which this section applies is produced to a magistrates' court in any proceedings for an offence involving obligatory or discretionary disqualification [other than a summary offence under any of the enactments mentioned in subsection (3A) above],

(b) the statement specifies an alleged previous conviction of an accused person of any such offence or any order made on the conviction,

(c) it is proved to the satisfaction of the court, on oath or in such manner as may be prescribed by [Criminal Procedure Rules], that not less than seven days before the statement is so produced a notice was served on the accused, in such form and manner as may be so prescribed, specifying the previous conviction or order and stating that it is proposed to bring it to the notice of the court in the event of or, as the case may be, in view of his conviction, and

(d) the accused is not present in person before the court when the statement is so produced,

the court may take account of the previous conviction or order as if the accused had appeared and admitted it.

(5) Nothing in the preceding provisions of this section enables evidence to be given in respect of any matter other than a matter of a description prescribed by regulations made by the Secretary of State.

(6) *[Regulation-making power.]*

[(7) Where the proceedings mentioned in subsection (2) above are proceedings before a magistrates' court inquiring into an offence as examining justices this section shall have effect as if—

(a) in subsection (2) the words "to the same extent as oral evidence of that fact is admissible in those proceedings" were omitted;

(b) in subsection (4) the word "and" were inserted at the end of paragraph (a);

(c) in subsection (4), paragraphs (c) and (d) and the words "as if the accused had appeared and admitted it" were omitted.]

A19.24   *[Section 13 is printed as prospectively amended by the Road Traffic (Consequential Provisions) Act 1988 s.4 and Sch.2, Pt 1, para.20; and as amended by the Civil Evidence Act 1995 s.15(1) and Sch.1, para.15; the Criminal Procedure and Investigations Act 1996 s.47 and Sch.1, para.36; the Magistrates' Court (Procedure) Act 1998 s.2(1) and (2); the Courts Act 2003 (Consequential Amendments) Order 2004 (SI 2004/2035) art.31.*

The amendment made by SI 2004/2035 in s.13(4)(c) shall not affect the general operation of the Road Traffic Offenders Act 1988 in so far as it relates to rules of court other than Criminal Procedure Rules during the period between the coming into force of the Order and the coming into force of the first Criminal Procedure Rules made under the Courts Act 2003 s.69 (see art.2(2) of the 2004 Order).

Section 13(3A) (which applies to Scotland) was inserted by the Civil Evidence Act 1995 s.15(1) and Sch.1, para.15. Two new subsections were later inserted by the Magistrates' Courts (Procedure) Act 1998 s.2(1); these were designated as s.13(3A) and (3B), with the consequence that there are two subsections designated as s.3(3A).

Section 13(7), which was inserted by the Criminal Procedure and Investigations Act 1996 s.47 and Sch.1, para.36, applies in relation to any alleged offence in relation to which Pt 1 of the 1996 Act applies (see the Criminal Procedure and Investigations Act 1996 (Commencement) (Section 65 and Schedules 1 and 2) Order 1997 (SI 1997/683); not reproduced in this work). With effect from a day to be appointed, subs.(7) will be revoked by the Criminal Justice Act 2003 s.41 and Sch.3, para.61(3) and Sch.37, Pt 4.

Words in s.13(2) which relate exclusively and expressly to Scotland have been omitted.

With regard to the application of s.13 to records maintained for the purposes of the Motor Vehicles (International Circulation) Order 1975 (SI 1975/1208) art.1, see ibid. art.1(10) below.]

Use of records kept by operators of goods vehicles

A19.25   14. In any proceedings [for an offence under section 40A of the Road Traffic Act 1988 or] for a contravention of or failure to comply with construction and use requirements (within the meaning of Part II of the Road Traffic Act 1988) or regulations under section 74 of that Act [*q.v.*], any record purporting to be made and authenticated in accordance with regulations under that section shall be evidence ... of the matters stated in the record and of its due authentication.

[Section 14 is printed as amended by the Road Traffic Act 1991 s.48 and Sch.4,   **A19.26**
para.86.

Words in s.14 which relate exclusively and expressly to Scotland have been omitted.

As to the meaning of the term "construction and use requirements" in Pt 2 of the Road Traffic Act 1988, see ibid. s.41(7) above.]

Use of specimens in proceedings for an offence under section 4 or 5 of the Road Traffic Act

15.—(1) This section and section 16 of this Act apply in respect of proceedings for an offence under [section 3A, 4 or 5 of the Road Traffic Act 1988 (driving offences connected with drink or drugs)] [*q.v.*]; and expressions used in this section and section 16 of this Act have the same meaning as in [sections 3A to 10] of that Act.   **A19.27**

(2) Evidence of the proportion of alcohol or any drug in a specimen of breath, blood or urine provided by [or taken from] the accused shall, in all cases [(including cases where the specimen was not provided [or taken] in connection with the alleged offence)], be taken into account and, subject to subsection (3) below, it shall be assumed that the proportion of alcohol in the accused's breath, blood or urine at the time of the alleged offence was not less than in the specimen.

[(3) That assumption shall not be made if the accused proves—

  (a) that he consumed alcohol before he provided the specimen [or had it taken from him] and—

    (i) in relation to an offence under section 3A, after the time of the alleged offence, and

    (ii) otherwise, after he had ceased to drive, attempt to drive or be in charge of a vehicle on a road or other public place, and

  (b) that had he not done so the proportion of alcohol in his breath, blood or urine would not have exceeded the prescribed limit and, if it is alleged that he was unfit to drive through drink, would not have been such as to impair his ability to drive properly.]

(4) A specimen of blood shall be disregarded [unless—

  (a) it was taken from the accused with his consent and either—

    (i) in a police station by a medical practitioner or a registered health care professional; or

    (ii) elsewhere by a medical practitioner; or

  (b) it was taken from the accused by a medical practitioner under section 7A of the Road Traffic Act 1988 and the accused subsequently gave his permission for a laboratory test of the specimen.]

(5) Where, at the time a specimen of blood or urine was provided by the accused, he asked to be provided with such a specimen, evidence of the proportion of alcohol or any drug found in the specimen is not admissible on behalf of the prosecution unless—

  (a) the specimen in which the alcohol or drug was found is one of two parts into which the specimen provided by the accused was divided at the time it was provided, and

(b) the other part was supplied to the accused.

[(5A) Where a specimen of blood was taken from the accused under section 7A of the Road Traffic Act 1988, evidence of the proportion of alcohol or any drug found in the specimen is not admissible on behalf of the prosecution unless—

    (a) the specimen in which the alcohol or drug was found is one of two parts into which the specimen taken from the accused was divided at the time it was taken; and

    (b) any request to be supplied with the other part which was made by the accused at the time when he gave his permission for a laboratory test of the specimen was complied with.]

A19.28　　*[Section 15 is printed as amended by the Road Traffic Act 1991 s.48 and Sch.4, para.87(1)–(4); the Police Reform Act 2002 s.57(1)–(4).*

The code of practice for the identification of persons by police officers does not affect any procedure under s.15 or s.16 of this Act; see para.2.17(i) of Code D (2011) under the Police and Criminal Evidence Act 1984.]

Documentary evidence as to specimens in such proceedings

A19.29　　**16.**—(1) Evidence of the proportion of alcohol or a drug in a specimen of breath, blood or urine may, subject to subsections (3) and (4) below and to section 15(5) [and (5A)] of this Act, be given by the production of a document or documents purporting to be whichever of the following is appropriate, that is to say—

    (a) a statement automatically produced by the device by which the proportion of alcohol in a specimen of breath was measured and a certificate signed by a constable (which may but need not be contained in the same document as the statement) that the statement relates to a specimen provided by the accused at the date and time shown in the statement, and

    (b) a certificate signed by an authorised analyst as to the proportion of alcohol or any drug found in a specimen of blood or urine identified in the certificate.

(2) Subject to subsections (3) and (4) below, evidence that a specimen of blood was taken from the accused with his consent by a medical practitioner [or a registered health care professional] may be given by the production of a document purporting to certify that fact and to be signed by a medical practitioner [or a registered health care professional].

(3) Subject to subsection (4) below—

    (a) a document purporting to be such a statement or such a certificate (or both such a statement and such a certificate) as is mentioned in subsection (1)(a) above is admissible in evidence on behalf of the prosecution in pursuance of this section only if a copy of it either has been handed to the accused when the document was produced or has been served on him not later than seven days before the hearing, and

    (b) any other document is so admissible only if a copy of it has been served on the accused not later than seven days before the hearing.

(4) A document purporting to be a certificate (or so much of a document as

purports to be a certificate) is not so admissible if the accused, not later than three days before the hearing or within such further time as the court may in special circumstances allow, has served notice on the prosecutor requiring the attendance at the hearing of the person by whom the document purports to be signed.

(5) *[Applies to Scotland.]*

(6) A copy of a certificate required by this section to be served on the accused or a notice required by this section to be served on the prosecutor may be served personally or sent by registered post or recorded delivery service.

[(6A) Where the proceedings mentioned in section 15(1) of this Act are proceedings before a magistrates' court inquiring into an offence as examining justices this section shall have effect with the omission of subsection (4).]

(7) In this section *"authorised analyst"* means—

    (a) any person possessing the qualifications prescribed by regulations made under [section 27 of the Food Safety Act 1990] as qualifying persons for appointment as public analysts under those Acts, and

    (b) any other person authorised by the Secretary of State to make analyses for the purposes of this section.

[Section 16 is printed as amended by the Food Safety Act 1990 s.59(1) and Sch.3, para.38; the Criminal Procedure and Investigations Act 1996 s.47 and Sch.1, para.37; the Police Reform Act 2002 s.57(5) and (6).   **A19.30**

Section 16(6A), which was inserted by the Criminal Procedure and Investigations Act 1996 s.47 and Sch.1, para.37, applies in relation to any alleged offence in relation to which Pt 1 of the 1996 Act applies (see the Criminal Procedure and Investigations Act 1996 (Commencement) (Section 65 and Schedules 1 and 2) Order 1997 (SI 1997/683); not reproduced in this work). With effect from a day to be appointed, subs.(6A) will be revoked by the Criminal Justice Act 2003 s.41 and Sch.3, para.61(4) and Sch.37, Pt 4.

See also the notes to s.15 of this Act.]

Provisions as to proceedings for certain offences in connection with the construction and use of vehicles and equipment

17.—(1) If in any proceedings for an offence under [section 40A, 41A, 41B or   **A19.31** 42 of the Road Traffic Act 1988 (using vehicle in dangerous condition or contravention] of construction and use regulations) [*q.v.*] —

    (a) any question arises as to weight of any description specified in the plating certificate for a goods vehicle, and

    (b) a weight of that description is marked on the vehicle,

it shall be assumed, unless the contrary is proved, that the weight marked on the vehicle is the weight so specified.

(2) If, in any proceedings for an offence—

    (a) under Part II of the Road Traffic Act 1988, except sections 47 and 75, or

    (b) under section 174(2) or (5) (false statement and deception) of that Act,

any question arises as to the date of manufacture of a vehicle, a date purporting to be such a date and marked on the vehicle in pursuance of regulations under that Part of that Act shall be evidence … that the vehicle was manufactured on the date so marked.

(3) If in any proceedings for the offence of driving a ... vehicle on a road, or causing or permitting a ... vehicle to be so driven, in contravention of a prohibition under section 70(2) of the Road Traffic Act 1988 any question arises whether a weight of any description has been reduced to a limit imposed by construction and use requirements[, or so that it has ceased to be excessive,] the burden of proof shall lie on the accused.

(4) *[Applies to Scotland.]*

A19.32   *[Section 17 is printed as amended by the Road Traffic Act 1991 ss.48, 83, Sch.4, para.88(1)–(3), and Sch.8.*

Words in s.17(2) relating exclusively and expressly to Scotland have been omitted.]

Evidence by certificate as to registration of driving instructors and licences to give instruction

A19.33   **18.**—(1) A certificate signed by the Registrar and stating that, on any date—

     (a) a person's name was, or was not, in the register,

     (b) the entry of a person's name was made in the register or a person's name was removed from it,

     (c) a person was, or was not, the holder of a current licence under section 129 of the Road Traffic Act 1988 [*q.v.*], or

     (d) a licence under that section granted to a person came into force or ceased to be in force,

shall be evidence of the facts stated in the certificate in pursuance of this section.

(2) A certificate so stating and purporting to be signed by the Registrar shall be deemed to be so signed unless the contrary is proved.

(3) In this section *"current licence"*, *"Registrar"* and *"register"* have the same meanings as in Part V of the Road Traffic Act 1988.

A19.34   *[For the definitions of "current licence", "Registrar", and "register", see s.142 of the Road Traffic Act 1988 above.*

With effect from a day to be appointed, s.18 will be amended as follows by the Road Safety Act 2006 s.42 and Sch.6, para.32:

     1. *in s.18(1), for paras (a)–(d) the following text will be substituted:*

         [(a) a person was, or was not, registered,

         (b) a person became registered or a person's registration was terminated, or

         (c) a person was, or was not, exempt from the prohibitions imposed by section 123 of the Road Traffic Act 1988 (requirement of registration) by virtue of provision made by regulations under section 124 of that Act,]

     2. *in s.18(3), the words ""Registrar", "registered" and "registration""" will be substituted for the words from "current" to "register";*

     3. *in the heading the words* **"etc. of driving instructors etc."** *will be substituted for the words* **"of driving instructors and licences to give instruction"**.

With effect from a day to be appointed, s.18(1) (as it has effect without the substitution of paras (a) to (d) of that subsection by the Road Safety Act 2006 s.42 and Sch.6, para.32, see above) will be amended by the Driving Instruction (Suspension and Exemption Powers) Act 2009 s.4(1) and Sch.1, para.4. After s.18(1)(b), the following new paragraph will be inserted:

[(ba) a person's registration was, or was not, suspended,]

The inserted paragraph will be repealed with effect from a day to be appointed when s.4(2) of and Sch.2 to the 2009 Act are brought into force.

With effect from a day to be appointed, s.18(1) (as it has effect with the substitution of paras (a) to (d) of that subsection by the Road Safety Act 2006 s.42 and Sch.6, para.32, when in force, see above) will be amended by the Driving Instruction (Suspension and Exemption Powers) Act 2009 s.1(5). After s.18(1)(b) and before the word "or" at the end of the paragraph, the following new paragraph will be inserted:

[(ba) a person's registration was, or was not, suspended,]]

Evidence of disqualification in Scotland

19. *[Omitted.]*   A19.35

[Speeding offences, etc.: admissibility of certain evidence

20.—(1) Evidence ... of a fact relevant to proceedings for an offence to which   A19.36
this section applies may be given by the production of—

(a) a record produced by a prescribed device, and

(b) (in the same or another document) a certificate as to the circumstances in which the record was produced signed by a constable or by a person authorised by or on behalf of the chief officer of police for the police area in which the offence is alleged to have been committed;

but subject to the following provisions of this section.

(2) This section applies to—

(a) an offence under section 16 of the Road Traffic Regulation Act 1984 consisting in the contravention of a restriction on the speed of vehicles imposed under section 14 of that Act;

(b) an offence under subsection (4) of section 17 of that Act consisting in the contravention of a restriction on the speed of vehicles imposed under that section;

(c) an offence under section 88(7) of that Act (temporary minimum speed limits);

(d) an offence under section 89(1) of that Act (speeding offences generally);

(e) an offence under section 36(1) of the Road Traffic Act 1988 consisting in the failure to comply with an indication given by a light signal that vehicular traffic is not to proceed.

[(f) an offence under Part I or II of the Road Traffic Regulation Act 1984 of contravening or failing to comply with an order or regulations made under either of those Parts relating to the use of an area of road which is described as a bus lane or a route for use by buses only.]

[(g) an offence under section 29(1) of the Vehicle Excise and Registration Act 1994 [*q.v.*] (using or keeping an unlicensed vehicle on a public road).]

(3) The Secretary of State may by order amend subsection (2) above by making additions to or deletions from the list of offences for the time being set out there; and an order under this subsection may make such transitional provision as appears to him to be necessary or expedient.

(4) A record produced or measurement made by a prescribed device shall not be admissible as evidence of a fact relevant to proceedings for an offence to which this section applies unless—

> (a) the device is of a type approved by the Secretary of State, and
>
> (b) any conditions subject to which the approval was given are satisfied.

(5) Any approval given by the Secretary of State for the purposes of this section may be given subject to conditions as to the purposes for which, and the manner and other circumstances in which, any device of the type concerned is to be used.

(6) In proceedings for an offence to which this section applies, evidence ...—

> (a) of a measurement made by a device, or of the circumstances in which it was made, or
>
> (b) that a device was of a type approved for the purposes of this section, or that any conditions subject to which an approval was given were satisfied,

may be given by the production of a document which is signed as mentioned in subsection (1) above and which, as the case may be, gives particulars of the measurement or of the circumstances in which it was made, or states that the device was of such a type or that, to the best of the knowledge and belief of the person making the statement, all such conditions were satisfied.

(7) For the purposes of this section a document purporting to be a record of the kind mentioned in subsection (1) above, or to be a certificate or other document signed as mentioned in that subsection or in subsection (6) above, shall be deemed to be such a record, or to be so signed, unless the contrary is proved.

(8) Nothing in subsection (1) or (6) above makes a document admissible as evidence in proceedings for an offence unless a copy of it has, not less than seven days before the hearing or trial, been served on the person charged with the offence; and nothing in those subsections makes a document admissible as evidence of anything other than the matters shown on a record produced by a prescribed device if that person, not less than three days before the hearing or trial or within such further time as the court may in special circumstances allow, serves a notice on the prosecutor requiring attendance at the hearing or trial of the person who signed the document.

(8A) *[Applies to Scotland.]*

[(8A) Where the proceedings for an offence to which this section applies are proceedings before a magistrates' court inquiring into an offence as examining justices this section shall have effect as if in subsection (8) the words from "and nothing" to the end of the subsection were omitted.]

(9) In this section *"prescribed device"* means a device of a description specified in an order made by the Secretary of State.

(10) *[Orders under s.20(3) and (9) to be statutory instruments.]*]

A19.37   *[Section 20 is printed as substituted by the Road Traffic Act 1991 s.23, and as subsequently amended by the Criminal Justice (Scotland) Act 1995 s.117(1) and*

Sch.6, para.172; the Criminal Procedure and Investigations Act 1996 s.47 and Sch.1, para.38; the Road Traffic Offenders (Additional Offences and Prescribed Devices) Order 1997 (SI 1997/384; not reproduced in this work); the Road Traffic Offenders (Additional Offences and Prescribed Devices) Order 2001 (SI 2001/1814) art.3 below.

Section 20(8A) was inserted after s.20(8) (with effect from March 31, 1996) by the Criminal Justice (Scotland) Act 1995 s.117(1) and Sch.6, para.172 (see the Criminal Justice (Scotland) Act 1995 (Commencement No.2, Transitional Provisions and Savings) Order 1996 (SI 1996/517; not reproduced in this work).

The text of s.20(8A) reproduced above (as so numbered) was inserted after s.20(8) by the Criminal Procedure and Investigations Act 1996 s.47 and Sch.1, para.38, with effect from March 8, 1997 in relation to any alleged offence in relation to which Pt 1 of the 1996 Act applies (see the Criminal Procedure and Investigations Act 1996 (Commencement) (Section 65 and Schedules 1 and 2) Order 1997 (SI 1997/683); not reproduced in this work). With effect from a day to be appointed, subs.(8A) of s.20 will be revoked by the Criminal Justice Act 2003 s.41 and Sch.3, para.61(5) and Sch.37, Pt 4.

Words relating expressly and exclusively to Scotland in s.20(1) and (6) have been omitted.

The Road Traffic Offenders (Prescribed Devices) Order 1992 (SI 1992/1209; not reproduced in this work) (prescribing devices designed or adapted for measuring by radar the speed of motor vehicles), the Road Traffic Offenders (Prescribed Devices) (No.2) Order 1992 (SI 1992/2843; not reproduced in this work) (prescribing devices designed or adapted for recording by photographic or other image recording means the position of motor vehicles in relation to light signals), the Road Traffic Offenders (Prescribed Devices) Order 1993 (SI 1993/1698; not reproduced in this work) (prescribing (i) devices designed or adapted for recording a measurement of the speed of motor vehicles activated by means of sensors or cables on or near the surface of the highway; and (ii) devices designed or adapted for recording a measurement of the speed of motor vehicles activated by means of a light beam or beams), the Road Traffic Offenders (Additional Offences and Prescribed Devices) Order 1997 (SI 1997/384; not reproduced in this work) (prescribing a camera designed or adapted to record the presence of a vehicle on an area of road which is a bus lane or a route for use by buses only), the Road Traffic (Prescribed Devices) Order 1999 (SI 1999/162; not reproduced in this work) (prescribing a device designed or adapted for recording a measurement of the speed of motor vehicles by (i) capturing by unattended cameras images of the motor vehicle at each of two predetermined points on the road; (ii) digitally recording each image and the time at which it is captured; and (iii) calculating the average speed of the motor vehicle over the distance between the two positions by reference to the times at which each image is captured), and the Road Traffic Offenders (Prescribed Devices) Order 2008 (SI 2008/1332; not reproduced in this work) (permitting the use of devices that record the time it takes for a vehicle to travel between two points on a road by manual activation and which are capable of measuring the distance between those two points by means of the odometer pulses of the vehicle to which they are fitted) have been made under s.20.

The following radar speed measuring devices were approved by the Home Secretary under the former provision and have continuing effect as if given for the purposes of s.20(4): Road Traffic Act 1991 (Commencement No.4 and Transitional Provisions) Order 1992 (SI 1992/1286) (not reproduced in this work) (and see also the Radar Speed Measuring Devices Revocation of Approval dated July 31, 1997 and the Radar Speed Measuring Devices Revocation of Approval, effective June 1, 2005):

Device	Date of approval	Effective date for use
Kustom HR4	July 1, 1986	July 31, 1986
Kustom HR8	July 1, 1986	July 31, 1986
Kustom Falcon	December 22, 1986	January 1, 1986
Kustom Roadrunner	December 22, 1986	January 1, 1987
Muniquip K-GP	October 12, 1989	November 8, 1989

The following devices have been approved by the Home Secretary under the above provisions:

Radar	Date of approval	Extent of approval	Effective date for use
Gatsometer BV Type 24+AUS[1]	June 24, 1992	s.20(2)(a)–(d)	July 1, 1992
Serco Speed Enforcement System Type 1[2]	May 22, 1995	s.20(2)(a)–(b)	May 24, 1995
Kustom Cordless Falcon	September 15, 1997	s.20(2)(a)–(d)	October 31, 1997
Speedar SR1 Speed Measuring Device	January 20, 1998	s.20(2)(a)–(d)	February 10, 1998
Speedar SR1 Speed Measuring Device	January 2005	s.20(2)(a)–(d)	January 2005
Highways Agency Digital Enforcement Camera (HADECS)[3]	November 2, 2006	s.20(2)(a)–(d)	November 2, 2006
Gatsometer Type 24-IDC	April 1, 2008	s.20(2)(a)–(d)	March 31, 2008

Radar	Date of approval	Extent of approval	Effective date for use
Highways Agency Digital Enforcement Camera System[4]	June 26, 2008	s.20(2)(a)–(d)	July 1, 2008

[1] the Radar Speed Measuring Device Conditional Approval 2000 dated November 8, 2000 (not reproduced in this work), limits the approval of the Gatsometer BV Type 24+AUS to the detection of speeding offences of 30 mph or above

[2] approved when operating singly on a gantry and on range 1 or 2 settings with either Techspan Systems Controlled Motorway Indicator Type 450EE or Securite et Signalisation (SES) Controlled Motorway Indicator Type 450EE

[3] approved when operated with Variable Messages Signs Ltd Advanced Motorway Indicator Type 450 EE or Colas Advanced Motorway Indicator Type 450 EE

[4] approved when operated with Variable Message Signs Ltd Advanced Motorway Indicator Type 450 EE or Colas Advanced Motorway Indicator Type 450 EE

Light signals	Date of approval	Extent of approval	Effective date for use
Gatsometer BV Type 36	December 17, 1992	s.20(2)(e)	January 1, 1993
Traffiphot IIIG Red light Monitor	December 17, 1992	s.20(2)(e)	January 1, 1993
Interface[5]	July 7, 1999	s.20(2)(e)	July 17, 1999
Redguard	May 15, 2003	s.20(2)(e)	May 20, 2003
Level Crossing Camera[6]	October 2003	s.20(2)(e)	November 1, 2003
Redspeed	November 2004	s.20(2)(e)	November 3, 2004
Redguard	November 2004	s.20(2)(e)	November 3, 2004

[5] for railway level crossing signals; when manufactured by Peek Traffic Ltd for use only with CE approved version of Traffiphot IIIG Red Light Monitor; when manufactured by B.I.C. Electronics Ltd for use only with CE approved version of Gatsometer BV Type 36

[6] approved for use only with the CE approved version of the Traffiphot IIIG Red Light Monitor

Road sensors	Date of approval	Extent of approval	Effective date for use
micro Mercury Speed Measuring System 90500	July 25, 1993	s.20(2)(a)–(d)	August 9, 1993
micro Mercury Vision System 92600	July 25, 1993	s.20(2)(a)–(d)	August 9, 1993
Speedmaster DS2	July 25, 1993	s.20(2)(a)–(d)	August 9, 1993
Autovision 2[7]	July 25, 1993	s.20(2)(a)–(d)	August 9, 1993
Truvelo M4 Squared Speed Measuring Device	July 25, 1993	s.20(2)(a)–(d)	August 9, 1993
Speedman Enforcement System	July 25, 1993	s.20(2)(a)–(d)	August 9, 1993
Traffiphot "S" Speed Detection Device	February 27, 1994	s.20(2)(a)–(d)	March 11, 1994
Truvelo Combi S Speed Camera System[8]	May 29, 1997	s.20(2)(a)–(d)	June 23, 1997
Truvelo Combi S-mc Speed Camera System[9]	April 8, 1999	s.20(2)(a)–(d)	April 15, 1999
Speedmaster DS3	May 14, 1999	s.20(2)(a)–(d)	May 24, 1999
Autovision 3 (AV3)[10]	May 14, 1999	s.20(2)(a)–(d)	May 24, 1999
Leica XV2 Speed Laser	February 7, 2001	s.20(2)(a)–(d)	February 12, 2001
SpeedCurb	May 15, 2003	s.20(a)–(d)	May 20, 2003
Redspeed	May 15, 2003	s.20(a)–(d)	May 20, 2003
SpeedCurb	November 2004	s.20(a)–(d)	November 3, 2004
Redspeed	November 2004	s.20(a)–(d)	November 3, 2004

[7] subject to the condition that it is used in conjunction with the Speedmaster DS2

[8] comprising the M4 Squared MPC Speedmaster and the Robot DCE camera, subject to the condition tht a magenta filter is used when photographing the front of a vehicle

[9] comprising the M4 Squared MPC Speedmeter, the Robot DCE camera and a memory card facility, provided that a magenta filter is used when photographing the front of a vehicle

[10] when used with Speedmaster DS3

Light beams	Date of approval	Extent of approval	Effective date for use
LTI 20.20 TS/M Speed Measuring Device	October 16, 1993	s.20(2)(a)–(d)	November 1, 1993
Kustom Prolaser II Speed Measuring Device	August 26, 1995	s.20(2)(a)–(d)	September 18, 1995
LTI 20.20 TS/M "Speedscope" Speed Measuring Device	March 20, 1996	s.20(2)(a)–(d)	April 1, 1996
LASTEC Local Video System[11]	January 20, 1998	s.20(2)(a)–(d)	February 10, 1998
LaserCam Digital Camera System[11]	February 9, 1998	s.20(2)(a)–(d)	February 26, 1998
RIEGL LR 90–235/ P	September 28, 1998	s.20(2)(a)–(d)	October 16, 1998
Cleartone Stealth Speedlaser	April 25, 1999	s.20(2)(a)–(d)	May 5, 1999
Laser Data Interface (LDI)[12]	May 14, 1999	s.20(2)(a)–(d)	May 24, 1999
Autovision 3 (AV3)[13]	May 14, 1999	s.20(2)(a)–(d)	May 24, 1999
Unipar Urban Speed Ace	May 17, 1999	s.20(2)(a)–(d)	May 28, 1999
LTI 20.20 Ultralyte 100	July 7, 1999	s.20(2)(a)–(d)	July 15, 1999
Jenoptik LaserPatrol Speedlaser	October 6, 1999	s.20(2)(a)–(d)	October 15, 1999
Leica XV2 Speed Laser	February, 2001	s.20(2)(a)–(d)	February 12, 2001

Light beams	Date of approval	Extent of approval	Effective date for use
ProLaser III			
Handheld Speedmeter	October, 2002	s.20(2)(a)–(d)	October 21, 2002
Autovision (AV3)[14]	February 6, 2003	s.20(2)(a)–(d)	February 17, 2003
LaserCam NT	April 3, 2003	s.20(2)(a)–(d)	April 14, 2003
LaserCam NT			
Speedmeter	February 16, 2004	s.20(2)(a)–(d)	February 14, 2004
Unipar SL 700	March 2005	s.20(2)(a)–(d)	April 1, 2005
LASTEC Local Video System	September 2005	s.20(2)(a)–(d)	September 15, 2005
Lastec Concept			
DVD system[15]	March 28, 2007	s.20(2)(a)–(d)	April 1, 2007
LTI.20.20 Ultralyte 1000	December 6, 2007	s.20(2)(a)–(d)	November 30, 2007
Truvelo Prolaser III			
Camcorder[16]	December 13, 2007	s.20(2)(a)–(d)	November 30, 2007

[11] when used in conjunction with either the LTI 20.20 TS/M speed measuring device or with the LTI 20.20 TS/M "Speedscope" speed measuring device

[12] when used with both the Kustom ProLaser II speed measuring device and Autovision 3 (AV3)

[13] when used with both the Kustom ProLaser II speed measuring device and the Laser date Interface (LDI)

[14] approved when used in conjunction with the ProLaser III Hand Held Speedmeter device

[15] approved when used in conjunction with either the LTI.20.20 Ultralyte 100 speed measuring device or the LTI.20.20 TS/M "Speedscope" speed measuring device

[16] approved for use as an optional attachment to the approved hand-held Prolaser III Laser speedmeter when tripod mounted only and separately powered

Distance over time speed measurement	Date of approval	Extent of approval	Effective date for use
Speed Violation			
Detection			
Deterrent			
(SVDD)	March 19, 1999	s.20(2)(a)–(d)	April 1, 1999

Bus lane enforcement camera	Date of approval	Extent of approval	Effective date for use
JAI BUSTER 2001[17]	October 29, 1997	s.20(2)(f)	December 5, 1997
Peek Guardian Freelane	August 25, 1998	s.20(2)(f)	September 7, 1998

Peek Guardian
    Freelane
    MKII
	September 22, 2000	s.20(2)(f)	October 3, 2000

[17] approved when operation with the TM1/B Transponder and Odometer and the London Transport Buses Locational Microwave Beacon

Odometer pulses	Date of approval	Extent of approval	Effective date for use
Puma SE6 Speedmeter[18]	June 30, 2008	s.20(2)(a)–(d)	June 30, 2008

[18] approved provided the device is operated by a trained operator, certified as such by the Chief Constable]

Proceedings in which evidence of one witness sufficient in Scotland

    21. *[Omitted.]*   **A19.38**

Notification of disability

    22.—(1) If in any proceedings for an offence committed in respect of a motor   **A19.39** vehicle it appears to the court that the accused may be suffering from any relevant disability or prospective disability (within the meaning of Part III of the Road Traffic Act 1988) the court must notify the Secretary of State.

    (2) A notice sent by a court to the Secretary of State in pursuance of this section must be sent in such manner and to such address and contain such particulars as the Secretary of State may determine.

    [As to the meaning of the terms "relevant disability" and "prospective disabil-   **A19.40** *ity" in Pt 3 of the Road Traffic Act 1988, see ibid. s.92(2) above.]*

Verdict

Alternative verdicts in Scotland

    23. *[Omitted.]*   **A19.41**

[Alternative verdicts: general

    24.—[(A1) Where—   **A19.42**
        (a) a person charged with manslaughter in connection with the driving of a mechanically propelled vehicle by him is found not guilty of that offence, but

(b) the allegations in the indictment amount to or include an allegation of any of the relevant offences,

he may be convicted of that offence.]

[(A2) For the purposes of subsection (A1) above the following are the relevant offences—

(a) an offence under section 1 of the Road Traffic Act 1988 (causing death by dangerous driving),

(b) an offence under section 2 of that Act (dangerous driving),

(c) an offence under section 3A of that Act (causing death by careless driving when under influence of drink or drugs), and

(d) an offence under section 35 of the Offences against the Person Act 1861 (furious driving).]

(1) Where—

(a) a person charged with an offence under a provision of the Road Traffic Act 1988 specified in the first column of the Table below (where the general nature of the offences is also indicated) is found not guilty of that offence, but

(b) the allegations in the indictment or information ... amount to or include an allegation of an offence under one or more of the provisions specified in the corresponding entry in the second column,

he may be convicted of that offence or of one or more of those offences.

Offence charged	Alternative
Section 1 (causing death by dangerous driving)	Section 2 (dangerous driving) [Section 2B (causing death by careless, or inconsiderate, driving)] Section 3 (careless, and inconsiderate, driving)
Section 2 (dangerous driving)	Section 3 (careless, and inconsiderate, driving)
[Section 2B (causing death by careless, or inconsiderate, driving)	Section 3 (careless, and inconsiderate, driving)]
Section 3A (causing death by careless driving when under influence of drink or drugs)	[Section 2B (causing death by careless, or inconsiderate driving)] Section 3 (careless, and inconsiderate, driving) Section 4(1) (driving when unfit to drive through drink or drugs) Section 5(1)(a) (driving with excess alcohol in breath, blood or urine) Section 7(6) (failing to provide specimen)
Section 4(1) (driving or attempting to drive when unfit to drive through drink or drugs)	[Section 7A(6) (failing to give permission for laboratory test)] Section 4(2) (being in charge of a vehicle when unfit to drive through drink or drugs)

Offence charged	Alternative
Section 5(1)(a) (driving or attempting to drive with excess alcohol in breath, blood or urine)	Section 5(1)(b) (being in charge of a vehicle with excess alcohol in breath, blood or urine)
Section 28 (dangerous cycling)	Section 29 (careless, and inconsiderate, cycling)

(2) Where the offence with which a person is charged is an offence under section 3A of the Road Traffic Act 1988, subsection (1) above shall not authorise his conviction of any offence of attempting to drive.

(3) Where a person is charged with having committed an offence under section 4(1) or 5(1)(a) of the Road Traffic Act 1988 by driving a vehicle, he may be convicted of having committed an offence under the provision in question by attempting to drive.

(4) Where by virtue of this section a person is convicted before the Crown Court of an offence triable only summarily, the court shall have the same powers and duties as a magistrates' court would have had on convicting him of that offence.

(5) *[Convictions and penalties in Scotland.]*

(6) This section has effect without prejudice to section 6(3) of the Criminal Law Act 1967 (alternative verdicts on trial on indictment), [sections 295, 138(4), 256 and 293 of and Schedule 3 to the Criminal Procedure (Scotland) Act 1995] and section 23 of this Act.]

[Section 24 is printed as substituted by the Road Traffic Act 1991 s.24; and as subsequently amended by the Criminal Procedure (Consequential Provisions) (Scotland) Act 1995 s.5 and Sch.4, para.71(1) and (3); the Road Safety Act 2006 s.20, s.31(4) and s.33.   **A19.43**

Words relating expressly and exclusively to Scotland in s.24(1) have been omitted.]

After conviction

Information as to date of birth and sex

25.—(1) If on convicting a person of an offence involving obligatory or discretionary disqualification or of such other offence as may be prescribed by regulations under section 105 of the Road Traffic Act 1988 the court does not know his date of birth, the court must order him to give that date to the court in writing.   **A19.44**

(2) If a court convicting a person of such an offence in a case where—

    (a) notification has been given [to [the designated officer for a magistrates' court] in pursuance of section 12(4)] of the Magistrates' Courts Act 1980 (written pleas of guilty) ..., and

    (b) the notification or intimation did not include a statement of the person's sex,

does not know the person's sex, the court must order the person to give that information to the court in writing.

(3) A person who knowingly fails to comply with an order under subsection (1) or (2) above is guilty of an offence.

(4) Nothing in [section 7 of the Powers of Criminal Courts (Sentencing) Act 2000] (where magistrates' court commits a person to the Crown Court to be dealt with, certain powers and duties transferred to that court) applies to any duty imposed upon a magistrates' court by subsection (1) or (2) above.

(5) Where a person has given his date of birth in accordance with this section or section 8 of this Act, the Secretary of State may serve on that person a notice in writing requiring him to provide the Secretary of State—

(a) with such evidence in that person's possession or obtainable by him as the Secretary of State may specify for the purpose of verifying that date, and

(b) if his name differs from his name at the time of his birth, with a statement in writing specifying his name at that time.

(6) A person who knowingly fails to comply with a notice under subsection (5) above is guilty of an offence.

(7) A notice to be served on any person under subsection (5) above may be served on him by delivering it to him or by leaving it at his proper address or by sending it to him by post; and for the purposes of this subsection and section 7 of the Interpretation Act 1978 in its application to this subsection the proper address of any person shall be his latest address as known to the person serving the notice.

A19.45   *[Section 25 is printed as amended by the Magistrates' Courts (Procedure) Act 1998 s.4(1)(a); the Powers of Criminal Courts (Sentencing) Act 2000 s.165(1) and Sch.9, para.118; the Access to Justice Act 1999 s.90(1) and Sch.13, paras 140 and 142; the Courts Act 2003 s.109(1) and Sch.8, para.311.*

Words in s.25(2) relating exclusively and expressly to Scotland have been omitted.]

[Interim disqualification

A19.46   26.—(1) Where a magistrates' court—

(a) commits an offender to the Crown Court under [section 6 of the Powers of Criminal Courts (Sentencing) Act 2000 or any enactment mentioned in subsection (4) of that section] applies, or

(b) remits an offender to another magistrates' court under [section 10 of that Act],

to be dealt with for an offence involving obligatory or discretionary disqualification, it may order him to be disqualified until he has been dealt with in respect of the offence.

(2) Where a court in England and Wales—

(a) defers passing sentence on an offender under [section 1 of that Act] in respect of an offence involving obligatory or discretionary disqualification, or

(b) adjourns after convicting an offender of such an offence but before dealing with him for the offence,

it may order the offender to be disqualified until he has been dealt with in respect of the offence.

(3) *[Applies to Scotland.]*

(4) Subject to subsection (5) below, an order under this section shall cease to have effect at the end of the period of six months beginning with the day on which it is made, if it has not ceased to have effect before that time.

(5) *[Applies to Scotland.]*

(6) Where a court orders a person to be disqualified under this section (*"the first order"*), no court shall make a further order under this section in respect of the same offence or any offence in respect of which an order could have been made under this section at the time the first order was made.

(7) Where a court makes an order under this section in respect of any person it must—

    (a) require him to produce to the court any licence held by him and its counterpart, and

    (b) retain the licence and counterpart until it deals with him or (as the case may be) cause them to be sent to the [proper officer] of the court which is to deal with him.

[(7A) In subsection (7) above *"proper officer"* means—

    (a) in relation to a magistrates' court in England and Wales, the [designated officer] for the court, and

    (b) in relation to any other court, the clerk of the court.]

(8) If the holder of the licence has not caused it and its counterpart to be delivered, or has not posted them, in accordance with section 7 of this Act and does not produce the licence and counterpart as required under subsection (7) above, then he is guilty of an offence.

(9) Subsection (8) above does not apply to a person who—

    (a) satisfies the court that he has applied for a new licence and has not received it, or

    (b) surrenders to the court a current receipt for his licence and its counterpart issued under section 56 of this Act, and produces the licence and counterpart to the court immediately on their return.

(10) Where a court makes an order under this section in respect of any person, sections 44(1)[, 47(2) [, 91ZA(7) and 91A(5)] of this Act] and section 109(3) of the Road Traffic Act 1988 (Northern Ireland drivers' licences) shall not apply in relation to the order, but—

    (a) the court must send notice of the order to the Secretary of State, and

    (b) if the court which deals with the offender determines not to order him to be disqualified under section 34 or 35 of this Act, it must send notice of the determination to the Secretary of State.

(11) A notice sent by a court to the Secretary of State in pursuance of subsection (10) above must be sent in such manner and to such address and contain such particulars as the Secretary of State may determine.

(12) Where on any occasion a court deals with an offender—

    (a) for an offence in respect of which an order was made under this section, or

    (b) for two or more offences in respect of any of which such an order was made,

any period of disqualification which is on that occasion imposed under section 34 or 35 of this Act shall be treated as reduced by any period during which he was disqualified by reason only of an order made under this section in respect of any of those offences.

(13) Any reference in this or any other Act (including any Act passed after

this Act) to the length of a period of disqualification shall, unless the context otherwise requires, be construed as a reference to its length before any reduction under this section.

(14) In relation to licences which came into force before 1st June 1990, the references in this section to counterparts of licences shall be disregarded.]

A19.47   *[Section 26 is printed as substituted by the Road Traffic Act 1991 s.25, and as subsequently amended by the Driving Licences (Community Driving Licence) Regulations 1996 (SI 1996/1974) reg.3 and Sch.1, para.2 (not reproduced in this work); the Powers of Criminal Courts (Sentencing) Act 2000 s.165(1) and Sch.9, para.119; the Access to Justice Act 1999 s.90(1) and Sch.13, paras 140 and 143; the Crime (International Co-operation) Act 2003 s.91 and Sch.5, para.34; the Courts Act 2003 s.109(1) and Sch.8, para.312.*

With effect from a day to be appointed and in relation to endorsement (all drivers), the following amendments will be made to s.26 by the Road Safety Act 2006 s.10 and Sch.3, para.32, s.59 and Sch.7(4):

1. *in s.26(7), the words "and its counterpart" will be omitted in para.(a), and, in para.(b), the words "and counterpart" will be omitted and the word "it" will be substituted for the word "them";*

2. *in s.26(8), the words "and its counterpart" and the words "and counterpart" will be omitted, and the word "it" will be substituted for "them";*

3. *in s.26(9), the words "and its counterpart" and the words "and counterpart" will be omitted, and the word "its" will be substituted for "their";*

4. *s.26(14) will be omitted.*

As to the application of s.26(7), (8) and (9)(b) to Community licences, see s.91A(1) below. As to references in s.26(9)(a) to a new licence, see further s.91A(2) below.]

PART II

SENTENCE

Introductory

Production of licence

A19.48   **27.**—(1) Where a person who is the holder of a licence is convicted of an offence involving obligatory [or discretionary disqualification, and a court proposes to make an order disqualifying him or an order under section 44 of this Act, the court must, unless it has already received them,] require the licence [and its counterpart] to be produced to it.

(2) [...]

(3) If the holder of the licence has not caused it [and its counterpart] to be delivered, or posted it, in accordance with section 7 of this Act and does not produce it [and its counterpart] as required [under this section or [section 40 of the Crime (Sentences) Act 1997, section 146 or 147 of the Powers of Criminal Courts (Sentencing) Act 2000], or section 223A or 436A of the Criminal Procedure (Scotland) Act 1975][, or if the holder of the licence does not produce it and its

counterpart as required by section 40B of the Child Support Act 1991, then,] unless he satisfies the court that he has applied for a new licence and has not received it—

    (a) he is guilty of an offence, and

    (b) the licence shall be suspended from the time when its production was required until it [and its counterpart] is produced to the court and shall, while suspended, be of no effect.

(4) Subsection (3) above does not apply where the holder of the licence—

    (a) has caused a current receipt for the licence [and its counterpart] issued under section 56 of this Act to be delivered to the [proper officer] of the court not later than the day before the date appointed for the hearing, or

    (b) has posted such a receipt, at such time that in the ordinary course of post it would be delivered not later than that day, in a letter duly addressed to the [proper officer] and either registered or sent by the recorded delivery service, or

    (c) surrenders such a receipt to the court at the hearing,

and produces the licence [and its counterpart] to the court immediately on [their] return.

[(5) In subsection (4) above *"proper officer"* means—

    (a) in relation to a magistrates' court in England and Wales, the [designated officer] for the court, and

    (b) in relation to any other court, the clerk of the court.]

[Section 27 is printed as amended by the Driving Licences (Community Driving Licence) Regulations 1990 (SI 1990/144); the Road Traffic Act 1991 s.48 and Sch.4, para.91(1)–(4) (see also s.83 and Sch.8); the Powers of Criminal Courts (Sentencing) Act 2000 s.165(1) and Sch.9, para.120; the Child Support, Pensions and Social Security Act 2000 s.16(5); the Access to Justice Act 1999 s.90(1) and Sch.13, paras 140 and 144; the Courts Act 2003 s.109(1) and Sch.8, para.313.   **A19.49**

With effect from a day to be appointed, in s.27(3), the words "section 301 of the Criminal Justice Act 2003" will be substituted for the words "section 40 of the Crime (Sentences) Act 1997" by the Criminal Justice Act 2003 s.304 and Sch.32, para.53.

With effect from a day to be appointed and in relation to endorsement (all drivers), the following amendments will be made to s.27 by the Road Safety Act 2006 s.10 and Sch.3, para.33, s.59 and Sch.7(4):

    1. *the words "and its counterpart" will be omitted in each place;*

    2. *in s.27(1), the word "it" will be substituted for the word "them";*

    3. *in s.27(3)(b), the words "is produced" will be substituted for the words "are produced";*

    4. *in s.27(4), the word "its", will be substituted for the word "their".*

With effect from a day to be appointed, in s.27(3), the words from ", or if the holder" to "Child Support Act 1991, then," will be omitted by the Welfare Reform Act 2009 s.58 and Sch.7(4), para.1.

Section 27(4) has been repealed in so far as it extends to Scotland by the Statute Law (Repeals) Act 2004 s.1(1) and Sch.1, Pt 14.

As to the application of s.27(1) and (3) to domestic driving permits, Conven-

tion driving permits, British Forces (BFG) driving licences and to the holders of such licences and permits, see the Motor Vehicles (Driving Licences) Regulations 1999 (SI 1999/2864) reg.80 below. As to the application of s.7 to Community licences, see s.91A(1) below.

As to the Child Support Act 1991 s.40B (to which reference is made in s.27(3) above), see the notes to s.164 of the Road Traffic Act 1988 above.]

[Penalty points to be attributed to an offence

A19.50   **28.**—(1) Where a person is convicted of an offence involving obligatory endorsement, then, subject to the following provisions of this section, the number of penalty points to be attributed to the offence is—

> (a) the number shown in relation to the offence in the last column of Part I or Part II of Schedule 2 to this Act, or
>
> (b) where a range of numbers is shown, a number within that range.

(2) Where a person is convicted of an offence committed by aiding, abetting, counselling or procuring, or inciting to the commission of, an offence involving obligatory disqualification, then, subject to the following provisions of this section, the number of penalty points to be attributed to the offence is ten.

[(3) For the purposes of sections 57(5)[, 57A(6), 77(5) and 77A(8)] of this Act, the number of penalty points to be attributed to an offence is—

> (a) where both a range of numbers and a number followed by the words "(fixed penalty)" is shown in the last column of Part 1 of Schedule 2 to this Act in relation to the offence, that number,
>
> (b) where a range of numbers followed by the words "or appropriate penalty points (fixed penalty)" is shown there in relation to the offence, the appropriate number of penalty points for the offence, and
>
> (c) where only a range of numbers is shown there in relation to the offence, the lowest number in the range.

(3A) For the purposes of subsection (3)(b) above the appropriate number of penalty points for an offence is such number of penalty points as the Secretary of State may by order made by statutory instrument prescribe.

(3B) An order made under subsection (3A) above in relation to an offence may make provision for the appropriate number of penalty points for the offence to be different depending on the circumstances, including (in particular)—

> (a) the nature of the contravention or failure constituting the offence,
>
> (b) how serious it is,
>
> (c) the area, or sort of place, where it takes place, and
>
> (d) whether the offender appears to have committed any offence or offences of a description specified in the order during a period so specified.]

(4) Where a person is convicted (whether on the same occasion or not) of two or more offences committed on the same occasion and involving obligatory endorsement, the total number of penalty points to be attributed to them is the number or highest number that would be attributed on a conviction of one of them (so that if the convictions are on different occasions the number of penalty points to be attributed to the offences on the later occasion or occasions shall be restricted accordingly).

(5) In a case where (apart from this subsection) subsection (4) above would apply to two or more offences, the court may if it thinks fit determine that that subsection shall not apply to the offences (or, where three or more offences are concerned, to any one or more of them).

(6) Where a court makes such a determination it shall state its reasons in open court and, if it is a magistrates' court ... shall cause them to be entered in the register ... of its proceedings.

(7)–(9) *[Alteration of numbers relating to offences in Sch.2 by statutory instrument.]]*

[Section 28 is printed as substituted by the Road Traffic Act 1991 s.27 and as   **A19.51**
amended by the Road Safety Act 2006 s.4 and s.9 and Sch.2, para.3.

In relation to endorsement (all drivers), s.28(3) (as amended by the Road Safety Act 2006 Sch.2) will be amended so that "57A(6)" will be substituted for "57(5), 57A(6), 77(5)" by the Road Safety Act 2006 s.10 and Sch.3, para.34.

For the provisions as regards the commencement of ss.9 and 10 of and Schs 2 and 3 to the Road Safety Act 2006, see s.61(8) below.

Words relating expressly and exclusively to Scotland in s.28(6) have been omitted.]

[Penalty points to be taken into account on conviction

29.—(1) Where a person is convicted of an offence involving obligatory   **A19.52**
endorsement, the penalty points to be taken into account on that occasion are (subject to subsection (2) below)—

    (a) any that are to be attributed to the offence or offences of which he is convicted, disregarding any offence in respect of which an order under section 34 of this Act is made, and

    (b) any that were on a previous occasion ordered to be endorsed on the counterpart of any licence held by him [or on his driving record] , unless the offender has since that occasion and before the conviction been disqualified under section 35 of this Act.

(2) If any of the offences was committed more than three years before another, the penalty points in respect of that offence shall not be added to those in respect of the other.

(3) In relation to licences which came into force before 1st June 1990, the reference in subsection (1) above to the counterpart of a licence shall be construed as a reference to the licence itself.]

[Section 29 is printed as substituted by the Road Traffic Act 1991 s.28 and as   **A19.53**
amended by the Road Safety Act 2006 s.9 and Sch.2, para.4.

With effect from a day to be appointed, a new subs.(2A) will be inserted after s.29(2) by the Road Safety Act 2006 s.34(2) as follows:

    [(2A) Subsection (1)(b) above has effect subject to section 30A(4) of this Act.]

In relation to endorsement (all drivers), s.29(1)(b) (as amended by the Road Safety Act 2006 Sch.2) will be further amended so that the words "the counterpart of any licence held by him or on" are omitted, and s.29(3) is omitted by the Road Safety Act 2006 s.10 and Sch.3, para.35, s.59 and Sch.7(4).

For the provisions as regards the commencement of ss.9 and 10 of and Schs 2 and 3 to the Road Safety Act 2006, see s.61(8) below.

As to the application of s.29(1) to Community licences, see s.91A(1) below.]

Penalty points: modification where fixed penalty also in question

A19.54   **30.**—(1) Sections 28 and 29 of this Act shall have effect subject to this section in any case where—

> (a) a person is convicted of an offence involving [obligatory endorsement], and
>
> (b) the court is satisfied that [the counterpart of] his licence [or his driving record] has been or is liable to be endorsed under section 57[, 57A, 77 or 77A] of this Act in respect of an offence (referred to in this section as the *"connected offence"*) committed on the same occasion as the offence of which he is convicted.

    (2) … the number of penalty points to be attributed to the offence of which he is convicted is—

> (a) the number of penalty points to be attributed to that offence under section [28] of this Act apart from this section, less
>
> (b) the number of penalty points required to be endorsed on [the counterpart of] his licence [or on his driving record] under section 57[, 57A, 77 or 77A] of this Act in respect of the connected offence [(except so far as they have already been deducted by virtue of this paragraph].

    (3) […]

A19.55   *[Section 30 is printed as amended by the Driving Licences (Community Driving Licence) Regulations 1990 (SI 1990/144); the Road Traffic Act 1991 s.48 and Sch.4, para.92(1)–(4) (see also s.83 and Sch.8); the Road Safety Act 2006 s.9 and Sch.2, para.5.*

As to the application of s.30 to Community licences, see s.91A(1) below.

Section 30 has been repealed in so far as it extends so Scotland by the Statute Law (Repeals) Act 2004, s.1(1) and Sch.1, Pt 14.

In relation to endorsement (all drivers), s.30 (as amended by the Road Safety Act 2006 Sch.2) will be further amended, with effect from a day to be appointed, so that:

> 1. *in s.30(1)(b) the words "the counterpart of his licence or" are omitted, and "57A" is substituted for "57, 57A, 77 by the Road Safety Act 2006 s.10 and Sch.3, para.36(2), s.59 and Sch.7(4);*
>
> 2. *in s.30(2)(b), the words "on the counterpart of his licence or" are omitted, and "57A" is substituted for "57, 57A, 77" by the Road Safety Act 2006 s.10 and Sch.3, para.36(3), s.59 and Sch.7(4).*

For the provisions as regards the commencement of ss.9 and 10 of and Schs 2 and 3 to the Road Safety Act 2006, see s.61(8) below.]

[Reduced penalty points for attendance on course

A19.56   **30A.**—(1) This section applies where—

> (a) a person is convicted of a specified offence by or before a court,
>
> (b) penalty points are to be attributed to the offence and the court does not order him to be disqualified, and
>
> (c) at least seven but no more than eleven penalty points are to be taken into account on the occasion of the conviction.

(2) In this section *"specified offence"* means—

    (a) an offence under section 3 of the Road Traffic Act 1988 (careless, and inconsiderate, driving),

    (b) an offence under section 36 of that Act (failing to comply with traffic signs),

    (c) an offence under section 17(4) of the Road Traffic Regulation Act 1984 (use of special road contrary to scheme or regulations), or

    (d) an offence under section 89(1) of that Act (exceeding speed limit).

(3) But the Secretary of State may by regulations amend subsection (2) above by adding other offences or removing offences.

(4) Where this section applies, the court may make an order that three of the penalty points attributed to the offence (or all of them if three or fewer are so attributed) shall not be taken into account under section 29(1)(b) of this Act on the occasion of any conviction of an offence after the end of the period of twelve months beginning with the date of the order if, by the relevant date, the offender completes an approved course specified in the order.

(5) In subsection (4) above—

    "an approved course" means a course approved by the appropriate national authority for the purposes of this section in relation to the description of offence of which the offender is convicted, and

    "the relevant date" means such date, no later than ten months after the day on which the order is made, as is specified in the order.

(6) A court shall not make an order under this section in the case of an offender convicted of an offence if—

    (a) the offender has, during the period of three years ending with the date on which the offence was committed, committed a specified offence and successfully completed an approved course pursuant to an order made under this section or section 34A of this Act on conviction of that offence, or

    (b) the offence was committed during his probationary period.

(7) A court shall not make an order under this section in the case of an offender unless—

    (a) the court is satisfied that a place on the course specified in the order will be available for the offender,

    (b) the offender appears to the court to be of or over the age of 17,

    (c) the court has informed the offender (orally or in writing and in ordinary language) of the effect of the order and of the amount of the fees which he is required to pay for the course and when he must pay them, and

    (d) the offender has agreed that the order should be made.]

[Section 30A is prospectively inserted after s.30 by the Road Safety Act 2006   **A19.57**
s.34(3).]

[Certificates of completion of courses

30B.—(1) An offender shall be regarded for the purposes of section 30A of   **A19.58** this Act as having completed a course satisfactorily if (and only if) a certificate that he has done so is received by the proper officer of the supervising court.

(2) A course provider must give a certificate under subsection (1) above to the offender not later than fourteen days after the date specified in the order as the latest date for the completion of the course unless the offender—

    (a) fails to make due payment of fees for the course,

    (b) fails to attend the course in accordance with the course provider's reasonable instructions, or

    (c) fails to comply with any other reasonable requirement of the course provider.

(3) A certificate under subsection (1) above is to be given by the course provider and shall be in such form, and contain such particulars, as may be prescribed by, or determined in accordance with, regulations made by the appropriate national authority.

(4) Where a course provider decides not to give a certificate under subsection (1) above to the offender, he shall give written notice of the decision to the offender as soon as possible, and in any event not later than fourteen days after the date specified in the order as the latest date for completion of the course.

(5) An offender to whom a notice is given under subsection (4) above may, within such period as may be prescribed by rules of court, apply to the supervising court, or (if the supervising court is not the Crown Court, the High Court of Justiciary or the relevant local court) to either the supervising court or the relevant local court, for a declaration that the course provider's decision not to give a certificate under subsection (1) above was contrary to subsection (2) above.

(6) If the court grants the application, section 30A of this Act shall have effect as if the certificate had been duly received by the proper officer of the supervising court.

(7) If fourteen days after the date specified in the order as the latest date for completion of the course the course provider has given neither the certificate under subsection (1) above nor a notice under subsection (4) above, the offender may, within such period as may be prescribed by rules of court, apply to the supervising court, or (if the supervising court is not the Crown Court, the High Court of Justiciary or the relevant local court) to either the supervising court or the relevant local court, for a declaration that the course provider is in default.

(8) If the court grants the application, section 30A of this Act shall have effect as if the certificate had been duly received by the proper officer of the supervising court.

(9) A notice under subsection (4) above shall specify the ground on which it is given; and the appropriate national authority may by regulations make provision as to the form of notices under that subsection and as to the circumstances in which they are to be treated as given.

(10) Where the proper office of a court receives a certificate under subsection (1) above, or a court grants an application under subsection (5) or (7) above, the proper officer or court must send notice of that fact to the Secretary of State; and the notice must be sent in such manner and to such address, and must contain such particulars, as the Secretary of State may determine.]

A19.59   *[Section 30B is prospectively inserted after s.30A (when in force) by the Road Safety Act 2006 s.34(3).]*

[Approval of courses

A19.60   **30C.**—(1) If an application is made to the appropriate national authority for the approval of a course for the purposes of section 30A of this Act, the appropriate national authority must decide whether to grant or refuse he application.

(2) In reaching that decision the appropriate national authority must have regard to—

    (a) the nature of the course, and

    (b) whether the course provider is an appropriate person to provide the course and administer its provision efficiently and effectively,

and may take into account any recommendations made by any persons appointed to consider the application.

(3) A course may be approved subject to conditions specified by the appropriate national authority.

(4) An approval of a course is for the period specified by the appropriate national authority (which must not exceed seven years), subject to withdrawal of approval.

(5) Regulations made by the appropriate national authority may make provision in relation to the approval of courses and may, in particular, include provision—

    (a) in relation to the making of applications for approval,

    (b) for the payment in respect of applications for approval, or of approvals, (or of both) of fees of such amounts as are prescribed by the regulations,

    (c) specifying the maximum fees that a person may be required to pay for a course and by when they are to be paid,

    (d) for the monitoring of courses and course providers,

    (e) in relation to withdrawing approval,

    (f) for an appeal to lie to the Transport Tribunal against a refusal of an application for approval, the imposition of conditions on the grant of such an application or the withdrawal of approval, and

    (g) authorising the appropriate national authority to make available (with or without charge) information about courses and course providers.]

[Section 30C is prospectively inserted after s.30B (when in force) by the Road Safety Act 2006 s.34(3).]   **A19.61**

[Provisions supplementary to sections 30A to 30C

30D.—(1) The appropriate national authority may issue guidance to course providers, or to any category of course provider, as to the conduct of courses approved for the purposes of section 30A of this Act; and—   **A19.62**

    (a) course providers shall have regard to any guidance given to them under this subsection, and

    (b) in determining for the purposes of section 30B of this Act whether any instructions or requirements of a course provider were reasonable, a court shall have regard to any guidance given to him under this subsection.

(2) The Secretary of State may by regulations make provision—

    (a) amending section 30A(1)(c) of this Act by substituting for the lower number of penalty points for the time being specified there a different number of penalty points, or

(b) amending section 30A(6)(a) of this Act by substituting for the period for the time being specified there a different period.

(3) In sections 30A to 30C of this Act and this section—

"appropriate national authority" means (as respects Wales) the National Assembly for Wales and (otherwise) the Secretary of State;

"course provider", in relation to a course, means the person by whom it is, or is to be, provided;

"probationary period" has the meaning given in section 1 of the Road Traffic (New Drivers) Act 1995;

"proper officer" means —

(a) in relation to a magistrates' court in England and Wales, the designated officer for the court, and

(b) otherwise, the clerk of the court;

"relevant local court" , in relation to an order made under section 30A of this Act in the case of an offender, means—

(a) in England and Wales, a magistrates' court acting for the local justice area in which the offender resides, and

(b) *[applies to Scotland]*; and

"supervising court", in relation to an order under section 30A of this Act, means—

(a) in England and Wales, if the Crown Court made the order the Crown Court and otherwise a magistrates' court acting for the same local justice area as the court which made the order, and

(b) *[applies to Scotland]*.

(4) Any power to make regulations under section 30A, 30B or 30C of this Act or this section includes power to make different provision for different cases, and to make such incidental or supplementary provision as appears to the appropriate national authority to be necessary or appropriate.

(5) Any power to make regulations under section 30A, 30B or 30C of this Act or this section shall be exercisable by statutory instrument.

(6) No regulations shall be made under section 30A of this Act or this section unless a draft of the regulations has been laid before, and approved by a resolution of, each House of Parliament.

(7) A statutory instrument containing regulations made under section 30B or 30C of this Act by the Secretary of State shall be subject to annulment in pursuance of a resolution of either House of Parliament.]

A19.63 *[Section 30D is prospectively inserted after s.30C (when in force) by the Road Safety Act 2006 s.34(3).]*

Court may take particulars endorsed [...] into consideration

A19.64 **31.**—[(1) Where a person is convicted of an offence involving obligatory or discretionary disqualification—

(a) any existing endorsement on the counterpart of his licence or on his driving record is prima facie evidence of the matters endorsed, and

(b) the court may, in determining what order to make in pursuance of the conviction, take those matters into consideration.]

(2) *[Applies to Scotland.]*

[Section 31 is printed as amended by the Driving Licences (Community Driv- **A19.65**
ing Licence) Regulations 1990 (SI 1990/144); the Road Traffic Act 1991 s.48 and
Sch.4, para.93; the Road Safety Act 2006 s.9 and Sch.2, para.6.

As to the application of s.31 to Community licences, see s.91A(1) below.

With effect from a day to be appointed, s.31(1) (as amended by the Road Safety
Act 2006, Sch.2) will be further amended so that the words "the counterpart of
his licence or on" are omitted by the Road Safety Act 2006 s.10 and Sch.3,
para.37, s.59 and Sch.7(4).

For the provisions as regards the commencement of ss.9 and 10 of and Schs 2
and 3 to the Road Safety Act 2006, see s.61(8) below.]

In Scotland, court may take extract from licensing records into account

32. *[Omitted.]*

Fine and imprisonment

Fine and imprisonment

33.—(1) Where a person is convicted of an offence against a provision of the **A19.66**
Traffic Acts specified in column 1 of Part I of Schedule 2 to this Act or regulations made under any such provision, the maximum punishment by way of fine or
imprisonment which may be imposed on him is that shown in column 4 against
the offence and (where appropriate) the circumstances or the mode of trial there
specified.

(2) Any reference in column 4 of that Part to a period of years or months is to
be construed as a reference to a term of imprisonment of that duration.

Forfeiture of vehicles: Scotland

33A. *[Omitted.]* **A19.67**

Disqualification

Disqualification for certain offences

34.—(1) Where a person is convicted of an offence involving obligatory **A19.68**
disqualification, the court must order him to be disqualified for such period not
less than twelve months as the court thinks fit unless the court for special reasons
thinks fit to order him to be disqualified for a shorter period or not to order him to
be disqualified.

[(1A) Where a person is convicted of an offence under section 12A of the
Theft Act 1968 (aggravated vehicle-taking), the fact that he did not drive the vehicle in question at any particular time or at all shall not be regarded as a special
reason for the purposes of subsection (1) above.]

[(2) Where a person is convicted of an offence involving discretionary
disqualification, and either—

    (a) the penalty points to be taken into account on that occasion number
         fewer than twelve, or

    (b) the offence is not one involving obligatory endorsement, the court may order him to be disqualified for such period as the court thinks fit.]

(3) Where a person convicted of an offence under any of the following provisions of the Road Traffic Act 1988, that is—

    (a) section 4(1) (driving or attempting to drive while unfit),

   [(aa) section 3A (causing death by careless driving when under the influence of drink or drugs),]

    (b) section 5(1)(a) (driving or attempting to drive with excess alcohol),

    (c) section 7(6) (failing to provide a specimen) where that is an offence involving obligatory disqualification,

   [(d) section 7A(6) (failing to allow a specimen to be subjected to laboratory test) where that is an offence involving obligatory disqualification;]

has within the ten years immediately preceding the commission of the offence been convicted of any such offence, subsection (1) above shall apply in relation to him as if the reference to twelve months were a reference to three years.

[(4) Subject to subsection (3) above, subsection (1) above shall apply as if the reference to twelve months were a reference to two years—

    (a) in relation to a person convicted of—

      (i) manslaughter ... or

      (ii) an offence under section 1 of the Road Traffic Act 1988 (causing death by dangerous driving), or

      (iii) an offence under section 3A of that Act (causing death by careless driving while under the influence of drink or drugs), and

    (b) in relation to a person on whom more than one disqualification for a fixed period of 56 days or more has been imposed within the three years immediately preceding the commission of the offence.]

[(4A) For the purposes of subsection (4)(b) above there shall be disregarded any disqualification imposed under section 26 of this Act or [section 147 of the Powers of Criminal Courts (Sentencing) Act 2000] or section 223A or 436A of the Criminal Procedure (Scotland) Act 1975 (offences committed by using vehicles) and any disqualification imposed in respect of an offence of stealing a motor vehicle, an offence under section 12 or 25 of the Theft Act 1968, an offence under section 178 of the Road Traffic Act 1988, or an attempt to commit such an offence.]

[(4B) Where a person convicted of an offence under section 40A of the Road Traffic Act 1988 (using vehicle in dangerous condition, etc.) has within the three years immediately preceding the commission of the offence been convicted of any such offence, subsection (1) above shall apply in relation to him as if the reference to twelve months were a reference to six months.]

(5) The preceding provisions of this section shall apply in relation to a conviction of an offence committed by aiding, abetting, counselling or procuring, or inciting to the commission of, an offence involving obligatory disqualification as if the offence were an offence involving discretionary disqualification.

   [(5A) *[Applies to Scotland.]*]

(6) This section is subject to section 48 of this Act.

A19.69   *[Section 34 is printed as amended by the Road Traffic Act 1991 s.29(1)–(4);*

the Aggravated Vehicle-Taking Act 1992 s.3(2); the Powers of Criminal Courts (Sentencing) Act 2000 s.165(1) and Sch.9, para.121; the Police Reform Act 2002 ss.56(3), 107 and Sch.8; the Road Safety Act 2006 s.25(2).

With effect from a day to be appointed the following text will be inserted after s.34(4A) by the Coroners and Justice Act 2009 s.177 and Sch.21, Pt 9, para.90(2):

[(4AA) For the purposes of subsection (4)(b), a disqualification is to be disregarded if the period of disqualification would have been less than 56 days but for an extension period added pursuant to—

  (a) section 35A or 35C,

  (b) section 248D of the Criminal Procedure (Scotland) Act 1995, or

  (c) section 147A of the Powers of Criminal Courts (Sentencing) Act 2000.]

Words in s.34(4) relating expressly and exclusively to Scotland have been omitted.]

[Reduced disqualification period for attendance on courses

34A.—(1) This section applies where—   **A19.70**

  (a) a person is convicted of an offence under section 3A (causing death by careless driving when under influence of drink or drugs), 4 (driving or being in charge when under influence of drink or drugs), 5 (driving or being in charge with excess alcohol) or 7 (failing to provide a specimen) of the Road Traffic Act 1988, and

  (b) the court makes an order under section 34 of this Act disqualifying him for a period of not less than twelve months.

(2) Where this section applies, the court may make an order that the period of disqualification imposed under section 34 shall be reduced if, by a date specified in the order under this section, the offender satisfactorily completes a course approved by the Secretary of State for the purposes of this section and specified in the order.

(3) The reduction made by an order under this section in a period of disqualification imposed under section 34 shall be a period specified in the order of not less than three months and not more than one quarter of the unreduced period (and accordingly where the period imposed under section 34 is twelve months, the reduced period shall be nine months).

(4) The court shall not make an order under this section unless—

  (a) it is satisfied that a place on the course specified in the order will be available for the offender,

  (b) the offender appears to the court to be of or over the age of 17,

  (c) the court has explained the effect of the order to the offender in ordinary language, and has informed him of the amount of the fees for the course and of the requirement that he must pay them before beginning the course, and

  (d) the offender has agreed that the order should be made.

(5) The date specified in an order under this section as the latest date for completion of a course must be at least two months before the last day of the period of disqualification as reduced by the order.

(6) An order under this section shall name the petty sessions area … in which the offender resides or will reside.]

A19.71   *[Section 34A was inserted by the Road Traffic Act 1991 s.30.*

Words in s.34A(6) relating expressly and exclusively to Scotland have been omitted.

The functions of the Secretary of State exercisable under s.34A in relation to Wales have been transferred to the National Assembly for Wales by the National Assembly for Wales (Transfer of Functions) Order 1999 (SI 1999/672; not reproduced in this work) art.2 and Sch.1.]

[Certificates of completion of courses

A19.72   **34B.**—(1) An offender shall be regarded for the purposes of section 34A of this Act as having completed a course satisfactorily if (and only if) a certificate that he has done so is received by the [proper officer] of the supervising court before the end of the period of disqualification imposed under section 34.

(2) If the certificate referred to in subsection (1) above is received by the [proper officer] of the supervising court before the end of the period of disqualification imposed under section 34 but after the end of the period as it would have been reduced by the order, the order shall have effect as if the reduced period ended with the day on which the certificate is received by the [proper officer].

(3) The certificate referred to in subsection (1) above shall be a certificate in such form, containing such particulars, and given by such person, as may be prescribed by, or determined in accordance with, regulations made by the Secretary of State.

(4) A course organiser shall give the certificate mentioned in subsection (1) above to the offender not later than fourteen days after the date specified in the order as the latest date for completion of the course, unless the offender fails to make due payment of the fees for the course, fails to attend the course in accordance with the organiser's reasonable instructions, or fails to comply with any other reasonable requirements of the organiser.

(5) Where a course organiser decides not to give the certificate mentioned in subsection (1) above, he shall give written notice of his decision to the offender as soon as possible, and in any event not later than fourteen days after the date specified in the order as the latest date for completion of the course.

(6) An offender to whom a notice is given under subsection (5) above may, within such period as may be prescribed by rules of court, apply to the supervising court for a declaration that the course organiser's decision not to give a certificate was contrary to subsection (4) above; and if the court grants the application section 34A of this Act shall have effect as if the certificate had been duly received by the [proper officer] of the court.

(7) If fourteen days after the date specified in the order as the latest date for completion of the course the course organiser has given neither the certificate mentioned in subsection (1) above nor a notice under subsection (5) above, the offender may, within such period as may be prescribed by rules of court, apply to the supervising court for a declaration that the course organiser is in default; and if the court grants the application section 34A of this Act shall have effect as if the certificate had been duly received by the [proper officer] of the court.

(8) A notice under subsection (5) above shall specify the ground on which it is given, and the Secretary of State may by regulations make provision as to the form of notices under that subsection and as to the circumstances in which they are to be treated as given.

(9) Where the [proper officer of a court] receives a certificate of the kind referred to in subsection (1) above, or a court grants an application under subsection (6) or (7) above, the [officer or] court must send notice of that fact to the Secretary of State; and the notice must be sent in such manner and to such address, and must contain such particulars, as the Secretary of State may determine.]

[Section 34B was inserted by the Road Traffic Act 1991 s.30, and is printed as   **A19.73**
amended by the Access to Justice Act 1999 s.90(1) and Sch.13, paras 140 and 145.

The functions of the Secretary of State exercisable under s.34B (except s.34B(9)) in relation to Wales have been transferred to the National Assembly for Wales by the National Assembly for Wales (Transfer of Functions) Order 1999 (SI 1999/672; not reproduced in this work) art.2 and Sch.1.

The Road Traffic (Courses for Drink-Drive Offenders) Regulations 1992 (SI 1992/3013; not reproduced in this work) have been made under this section and s.34C.]

[Provisions supplementary to sections 34A and 34B

34C.—(1) The Secretary of State may issue guidance to course organisers, or   **A19.74**
to any category of course organiser as to the conduct of courses approved for the purposes of section 34A of this Act; and—

   (a) course organisers shall have regard to any guidance given to them under this subsection, and

   (b) in determining for the purposes of section 34B(6) whether any instructions or requirements of an organiser were reasonable, a court shall have regard to any guidance given to him under this subsection.

(2) In sections 34A and 34B and this section—

"course organiser", in relation to a course, means the person who, in accordance with regulations made by the Secretary of State, is responsible for giving the certificates mentioned in section 34B(1) in respect of the completion of the course;

[*"proper officer"* means—

   (a) in relation to a magistrates' court in England and Wales, the justices' chief executive for the court, and

   (b) *[applies to Scotland]*;]

"supervising court", in relation to an order under section 34A, means—

   (a) in England and Wales, a magistrates' court acting for the petty sessions area named in the order as the area where the offender resides or will reside;

   (b) *[applies to Scotland.]*

*   *   *

(3) *[Exercise of power to make regulations.]*]

[Section 34C was inserted by the Road Traffic Act 1991 s.30 and is printed as   **A19.75**
amended by the Access to Justice Act 1999 s.106 and Sch.15, Pt 5(1); and also (with effect from April 1, 2003) by the 1999 Act ss.90(1) and 106, Schs 13 (paras 140 and 146) and 15 (Pt 5(7)) by the insertion of the definition of "proper officer" and the deletion of words at the end of s.34C(2) (see the Access to Justice

Act 1999 (Commencement No.7, Transitional Provisions and Savings) Order 2001 (SI 2001/916; not reproduced in this work) arts 1(2) and 2(a)(ii) and (c)(ii)).

As regards the requirement in subs.(1)(b) above for the court to have regard to any guidance given to course organisers, the Department of Transport has published "A Guide to the Operation of Approved Courses for Drink-drive Offenders", which is available via the Road Safety and Driver and Rider Safety links at www.dft.gov.uk/dsa/category.asp?cat=773 [accessed March 2, 2011].

The functions of the Secretary of State exercisable under s.34C in relation to Wales have been transferred to the National Assembly for Wales by the National Assembly for Wales (Transfer of Functions) Order 1999 (SI 1999/672; not reproduced in this work), art.2 and Sch.1.

See further the note to s.34B above.]

A19.76   *[With effect from a day or days to be appointed, ss.34A–34C will be substituted by the following text (Road Safety Act 2006 s.35):*

[Reduced disqualification for attendance on courses

34A.—(1) This section applies where—

   (a) a person is convicted of a relevant drink offence or a specified offence by or before a court, and

   (b) the court makes an order under section 34 of this Act disqualifying him for a period of not less than twelve months.

(2) In this section *"relevant drink offence"* means—

   (a) an offence under paragraph (a) of subsection (1) of section 3A of the Road Traffic Act 1988 (causing death by careless driving when unfit to drive through drink) committed when unfit to drive through drink,

   (b) an offence under paragraph (b) of that subsection (causing death by careless driving with excess alcohol),

   (c) an offence under paragraph (c) of that subsection (failing to provide a specimen) where the specimen is required in connection with drink or consumption of alcohol,

   (d) an offence under section 4 of that Act (driving or being in charge when under influence of drink) committed by reason of unfitness through drink,

   (e) an offence under section 5(1) of that Act (driving or being in charge with excess alcohol),

   (f) an offence under section 7(6) of that Act (failing to provide a specimen) committed in the course of an investigation into an offence within any of the preceding paragraphs, or

   (g) an offence under section 7A(6) of that Act (failing to allow a specimen to be subjected to a laboratory test) in the course of an investigation into an offence within any of the preceding paragraphs.

(3) In this section *"specified offence"* means—

   (a) an offence under section 3 of the Road Traffic Act 1988 (careless, and inconsiderate, driving),

   (b) an offence under section 36 of that Act (failing to comply with traffic signs),

   (c) an offence under section 17(4) of the Road Traffic Regulation Act 1984 (use of special road contrary to scheme or regulations), or

   (d) an offence under section 89(1) of that Act (exceeding speed limit).

(4) But the Secretary of State may by regulations amend subsection (3) above by adding other offences or removing offences.

(5) Where this section applies, the court may make an order that the period of disqualification imposed under section 34 of this Act ("the unreduced period") shall be reduced if, by the relevant date, the offender satisfactorily completes an approved course specified in the order.

(6) In subsection (5) above—

"*an approved course*" means a course approved by the appropriate national authority for the purposes of this section in relation to the description of offence of which the offender is convicted, and

"*the relevant date*" means such date, at least two months before the last day of the period of disqualification as reduced by the order, as is specified in the order.

(7) The reduction made in a period of disqualification by an order under this section is a period specified in the order of—

(a) not less than three months, and

(b) not more than one quarter of the unreduced period,

(and, accordingly, where the unreduced period is twelve months, the reduced period is nine months).

(8) A court shall not make an order under this section in the case of an offender convicted of a specified offence if—

(a) the offender has, during the period of three years ending with the date on which the offence was committed, committed a specified offence and successfully completed an approved course pursuant to an order made under this section or section 30A of this Act on conviction of that offence, or

(b) the specified offence was committed during his probationary period.

(9) A court shall not make an order under this section in the case of an offender unless—

(a) the court is satisfied that a place on the course specified in the order will be available for the offender,

(b) the offender appears to the court to be of or over the age of 17,

(c) the court has informed the offender (orally or in writing and in ordinary language) of the effect of the order and of the amount of the fees which he is required to pay for the course and when he must pay them, and

(d) the offender has agreed that the order should be made.]

[With effect from a day to be appointed, s.34A, as substituted, will be amended by the Coroners and Justice Act 2009 s.177 and Sch.21, Pt 9, para.90(3) as follows:

1. *in s.34A(1)(b), the words "(disregarding any extension period added pursuant to section 35A or 35C)" will be inserted after the word "months";*

2. *in s.34A(5), the words "(disregarding any extension period added pursuant to section 35A or 35C)" will be inserted after the words "of this Act";*

3. *in s.35A(6), the words "(but including any extension period added pursuant to section 35A or 35C)" will be inserted after the word "order", in the first place that it occurs;*

4. *after s.34A(7), the following new subsection will be inserted:*

[(7A) "*The reduced period*" is the period of disqualification imposed under section 34 of this Act (disregarding any extension period added pursuant to section 35A or 35C) as reduced by an order under this section.]

For transitory provisions in relation to the bringing into force of s.35 of the Road Safety Act 2006 and the amendments in the 2009 Act, see the 2009 Act s.177 and Sch.22, Pt 4, paras 30 and 31. Paragraph 31 of Sch.22 amends s.34A during the transitory period arising after the coming into force of that paragraph and ending with the coming into force of s.35 of the 2006 Act.]

[Certificates of completion of courses

34B.—(1) An offender shall be regarded for the purposes of section 34A of this Act as having completed a course satisfactorily if (and only if) a certificate that he has done so is received by the proper officer of the supervising court before the end of the unreduced period.

(2) If a certificate under subsection (1) above is so received before the end of the unreduced period but after the end of the period which would (apart from this subsection) be the reduced period, the reduced period is to be taken to end with the day on which the certificate is so received.

(3) A certificate under subsection (1) above is to be given by the course provider and shall be in such form, and contain such particulars, as may be prescribed by, or determined in accordance with, regulations made by the appropriate national authority.

(4) A course provider must give a certificate under subsection (1) above to the offender not later than fourteen days after the date specified in the order as the latest date for the completion of the course unless the offender—

    (a) fails to make due payment of fees for the course,

    (b) fails to attend the course in accordance with the course provider's reasonable instructions, or

    (c) fails to comply with any other reasonable requirement of the course provider.

(5) Where a course provider decides not to give a certificate under subsection (1) above to the offender, he shall give written notice of the decision to the offender as soon as possible, and in any event not later than fourteen days after the date specified in the order as the latest date for completion of the course.

(6) An offender to whom a notice is given under subsection (5) above may, within such period as may be prescribed by rules of court, apply to the supervising court, or (if the supervising court is not the Crown Court, the High Court of Justiciary or the relevant local court) to either the supervising court or the relevant local court, for a declaration that the course provider's decision not to give a certificate under subsection (1) above was contrary to subsection (4) above.

(7) If the court grants the application, section 34A of this Act shall have effect as if the certificate had been duly received by the proper officer of the supervising court.

(8) If fourteen days after the date specified in the order as the latest date for completion of the course the course provider has given neither a certificate under subsection (1) above nor a notice under subsection (5) above, the offender may, within such period as may be prescribed by rules of court, apply to the supervising court, or (if the supervising court is not the Crown Court, the High Court of Justiciary or the relevant local court) to either the supervising court or the relevant local court, for a declaration that the course provider is in default.

(9) If the court grants the application, section 34A of this Act shall have effect as if the certificate had been duly received by the proper officer of the supervising court.

(10) A notice under subsection (5) above shall specify the ground on which it is given; and the appropriate national authority may by regulations make provision as to the form of notices under that subsection and as to the circumstances in which they are to be treated as given.

(11) Where the proper officer of a court receives a certificate under subsection (1) above, or a court grants an application under subsection (6) or (8) above, the proper officer or court must send notice of that fact to the Secretary of State; and the notice must be sent in such manner of State may determine.]

[With effect from a day to be appointed, s.34B, as substituted, will be amended by the Coroners and Justice Act 2009 s.177 and Sch.21, Pt 9, para.90(3) as follows:

1. *in s.34B(1), the words "total unreduced period of disqualification" will be substituted for the words "unreduced period";*

2. *in s.34B(2), the words "total unreduced period of disqualification" will be substituted for the words "unreduced period", and the words "the total reduced period of disqualification" will be substituted for the words "reduced period", in both places that they occur;*

3. *after s.34B(11), the following new subsection will be added:*

[(12) For the purposes of this section—

"the total reduced period of disqualification" means the period of disqualification imposed under section 34 (including any extension period added to that period pursuant to section 35A or 35C), as reduced by an order under section 34A;

"the total unreduced period of disqualification" means the period of disqualification imposed under section 34 (including any such extension period), disregarding any reduction by such an order.]

For transitory provisions in relation to the bringing into force of s.35 of the Road Safety Act 2006 and the amendments in the 2009 Act, see the 2009 Act s.177 and Sch.22, Pt 4, paras 30 and 32. Paragraph 32 of Sch.22 amends s.34B during the transitory period arising after the coming into force of that paragraph and ending with the coming into force of s.35 of the 2006 Act.]

[Approval of courses

34BA.—(1) If an application is made to the appropriate national authority for the approval of a course for the purposes of section 34A of this Act, the appropriate national authority must decide whether to grant or refuse the application.

(2) In reaching that decision the appropriate national authority must have regard to—

    (a) the nature of the course, and

    (b) whether the course provider is an appropriate person to provide the course and administer its provision efficiently and effectively,

and may take into account any recommendations made by any persons appointed to consider the application.

(3) A course may be approved subject to conditions specified by the appropriate national authority.

(4) An approval of a course is for the period specified by the appropriate national authority (which must not exceed seven years), subject to withdrawal of approval.

(5) Regulations made by the appropriate national authority may make provision in relation to the approval of courses and may, in particular, include provision—

     (a) in relation to the making of applications for approval,

     (b) for the payment in respect of applications for approval, or of approvals, (or of both) of fees of such amounts as are prescribed by the regulations,

     (c) specifying the maximum fees that a person may be required to pay for a course and by when they are to be paid,

     (d) for the monitoring of courses and course providers,

     (e) in relation to withdrawing approval,

     (f) for an appeal to lie to the Transport Tribunal against a refusal of an application for approval, the imposition of conditions on the grant of such an application or the withdrawal of approval, and

     (g) authorising the appropriate national authority to make available (with or without charge) information about courses and course providers.]

[Provisions supplementary to sections 34A to 34BA

34C.—(1) The appropriate national authority may issue guidance to course providers, or to any category of course provider, as to the conduct of courses approved for the purposes of section 34A of this Act; and—

     (a) course providers shall have regard to any guidance given to them under this subsection, and

     (b) in determining for the purposes of section 34B of this Act whether any instructions or requirements of a course provider were reasonable, a court shall have regard to any guidance given to him under this subsection.

(2) The Secretary of State may by regulations make provision—

     (a) amending section 34A(1)(b) of this Act by substituting for the period for the time being specified there a different period,

     (b) amending section 34A(7) of this Act by substituting for the period for the time being specified there a different period, or by substituting for the fraction of the unreduced period for the time being specified there a different fraction of that period, (or by doing both), or

     (c) amending section 34A(8)(a) of this Act by substituting for the period for the time being specified there a different period.

(3) In sections 34A to 34BA of this Act and this section—

     "appropriate national authority" means (as respects Wales) the National Assembly for Wales and (otherwise) the Secretary of State;

     "course provider", in relation to a course, means the person by whom it is, or is to be, provided;

     "probationary period" has the meaning given in section 1 of the Road Traffic (New Drivers) Act 1995;

     "proper officer" means —

          (a) in relation to a magistrates' court in England and Wales, the designated officer for the court, and

          (b) otherwise, the clerk of the court;

     "relevant local court", in relation to an order under section 34A of this Act in the case of an offender, means—

          (a) in England and Wales, a magistrates' court acting for the local justice area in which the offender resides, and

(b) *[applies to Scotland]*; and

"*supervising court*", in relation to an order under section 34A of this Act, means—

       (a) in England and Wales, if the Crown Court made the order the Crown Court and otherwise a magistrates' court acting for the same local justice area as the court which made the order, and

       (b) *[applies to Scotland]*.

(4) Any power to make regulations under section 34A, 34B or 34BA of this Act or this section includes power to make different provision for different cases, and to make such incidental or supplementary provision as appears necessary or appropriate.

(5) Any power to make regulations under section 34A, 34B or 34BA of this Act or this section shall be exercisable by statutory instrument.

(6) No regulations shall be made under section 34A of this Act or this section unless a draft of the regulations has been laid before, and approved by a resolution of, each House of Parliament.

(7) A statutory instrument containing regulations made under section 34B or 34BA of this Act by the Secretary of State shall be subject to annulment in pursuance of a resolution of either House of Parliament.]*/*

[Reduced disqualification period: alcohol ignition interlock programme orders

34D.—(1) This section applies where—
                                                 A19.77

    (a) a person is convicted of a relevant drink offence by or before a court,

    (b) he has committed another relevant drink offence at any time during the period of ten years ending with the date of the conviction,

    (c) the court makes an order under section 34 of this Act but does not make an order under section 34A of this Act, and

    (d) the period stated by the court as that for which, apart from this section, he would be disqualified ("the unreduced period") is not less than two years.

(2) In this section "*relevant drink offence*" means—

    (a) an offence under paragraph (a) of subsection (1) of section 3A of the Road Traffic Act 1988 (causing death by careless driving when unfit to drive through drink) committed when unfit to drive through drink,

    (b) an offence under paragraph (b) of that subsection (causing death by careless driving with excess alcohol),

    (c) an offence under paragraph (c) of that subsection (failing to provide a specimen) where the specimen is required in connection with drink or consumption of alcohol,

    (d) an offence under section 4 of that Act (driving or being in charge when under influence of drink) committed by reason of unfitness through drink,

    (e) an offence under section 5(1) of that Act (driving or being in charge with excess alcohol),

    (f) an offence under section 7(6) of that Act (failing to provide a specimen) committed in the course of an investigation into an offence within any of the preceding paragraphs, or

    (g) an offence under section 7A(6) of that Act (failing to allow a specimen to be subjected to a laboratory test) in the course of an investigation into an offence within any of the preceding paragraphs.

(3) Where this section applies, the court may specify a lesser period of disqualification ("the reduced period") if it also makes an order (an "alcohol ignition interlock programme order") requiring the offender to comply with the alcohol ignition interlock conditions.

(4) The difference between the unreduced period and the reduced period shall be a period specified in the order of—

    (a) not less than 12 months, and

    (b) not more than one half of the unreduced period.

(5) If the offender contravenes the alcohol ignition interlock conditions, a further order under section 34 disqualifying him for the rest of the unreduced period is to be treated as having been made by the court immediately before the contravention.

(6) "The alcohol ignition interlock conditions" are that the offender—

    (a) must participate fully in an approved alcohol ignition interlock programme specified in the order during such part of the unreduced period as is so specified, and

    (b) during the part of that period following the reduced period, must not drive a motor vehicle unless it is fitted with an alcohol ignition interlock in good working order and must not drive a motor vehicle which is so fitted when not using the alcohol ignition interlock properly.

(7) A court shall not make an alcohol ignition interlock programme order in the case of an offender unless—

    (a) the court is satisfied that a place on the approved alcohol ignition interlock programme specified in the order will be available for the offender,

    (b) the offender appears to the court to be of or over the age of 17,

    (c) the court has informed the offender (orally or in writing and in ordinary language) of the effect of the order and the amount of the fees which he is required to pay for the programme and when he must pay them, and

    (d) the offender has agreed that the order should be made.

(8) For the purposes of this section an "approved alcohol ignition interlock programme" is a programme approved by the appropriate national authority and involving the provision of an alcohol ignition interlock for use by the offender, training in its use and other education and counselling relating to the consumption of alcohol and driving.

(9) For the purposes of this section *"alcohol ignition interlock"* means a device—

    (a) of a type approved by the Secretary of State, and

    (b) designed to be fitted to a motor vehicle with the purpose of preventing the driving of the vehicle by a person who does not, both before starting driving the vehicle and at regular intervals while driving it, provide specimens of breath in which the proportion of alcohol is likely not to exceed the limit specified in subsection (10) below.

(10) That limit is 9 microgrammes of alcohol in 100 millilitres of breath or such other proportion of alcohol to breath as the Secretary of State may by regulations prescribe.

(11) For the purposes of this section an offender uses an alcohol ignition interlock properly if (and only if) he is complying with all the instructions given to him about its use as part of the approved alcohol ignition interlock programme.

(12) Where an alcohol ignition interlock is fitted to a motor vehicle as part of an approved alcohol ignition interlock programme relating to an offender, a person commits an offence if—

> (a) he interferes with the alcohol ignition interlock with intent to cause it not to function or not to function properly, or
>
> (b) he is a person other than the offender and provides or attempts to provide a specimen of breath for the purposes of the alcohol ignition interlock with intent to enable the driving (or continued driving) of the vehicle by the offender.]

[Section 34D is prospectively inserted after s.34C by the Road Safety Act 2006 **A19.78** *s.15(1).*

With effect from a day to be appointed, s.34D, as inserted, will be amended by the Coroners and Justice Act 2009 s.177 and Sch.21, Pt 9, para.90(5) as follows:

> 1. *in s.34D(1)(d), the words "and disregarding any extension period added pursuant to section 35A or 35C" will be inserted after the word "section";*
>
> 2. *in s.34D(3), the words "as the period of disqualification under section 34 (disregarding any extension period added pursuant to section 35A or 35C)" will be inserted after the word "specify";*
>
> 3. *after s.34D(5), the following text will be inserted:*

[(5A) An appropriate extension period (within the meaning of section 35A or 35C) is not to be added to the further order referred to in subsection (5).]

> 4. *in s.34D(6)(a), the words "total unreduced period of disqualification" will be substituted for the words "unreduced period", and in s.34D(6)(b), the words "total reduced period of disqualification" will be substituted for the words "reduced period";*
>
> 5. *after s.34D(6), the following text will be inserted:*

[(6A) In subsection (6)—

> *"the total reduced period of disqualification"* means the period of disqualification imposed under section 34 (including any extension period added to that period pursuant to section 35A or 35C), as reduced by an order under this section;
>
> *"the total unreduced period of disqualification"* means the period of disqualification imposed under section 34 (including any such extension period), disregarding any reduction by such an order.]

Section 16 of the Road Safety Act 2006 provides for an experimental period for alcohol ignition interlocks as introduced by ibid. s.15. Reference should be made to s.16(3) for the definition of "the experimental period" in respect of orders made under s.34D, when in force.]

[Certificates of failing fully to participate

34E.—(1) An offender shall be regarded for the purposes of section 34D of　**A19.79**

this Act as not fully participating in an approved alcohol ignition interlock programme if (and only if) a certificate that that is so is received by the proper officer of the supervising court.

(2) A certificate under subsection (1) above may be given if (and only if) the offender has failed—

(a) to make due payment of fees for the programme,

(b) to attend for training, education or counselling forming part of the programme in accordance with the programme provider's reasonable instructions,

(c) to attend at a place specified by the programme provider for the monitoring and maintenance of the alcohol ignition interlock, at a time specified by the programme provider or a person with whom the programme provider has made arrangements for its monitoring and maintenance, or

(d) to comply with any other reasonable requirement of the programme provider.

(3) A certificate under subsection (1) above is to be given by the programme provider and shall be in such form, and contain such particulars, as may be prescribed by, or determined in accordance with, regulations made by the appropriate national authority.

(4) Where a programme provider decides to give a certificate under subsection (1) above, he shall give written notice of the decision to the offender as soon as possible.

(5) An offender to whom a notice is given under subsection (4) above may, within such period as may be prescribed by rules of court, apply to the supervising court, or (if the supervising court is not the Crown Court, the High Court of Justiciary or the relevant local court) to either the supervising court or the relevant local court, for a declaration that the programme provider has given the certificate under subsection (1) above in contravention of subsection (2) above.

(6) If the court grants the application, section 34D of this Act shall have effect as if the certificate had not been duly received by the proper officer of the supervising court.

(7) A notice under subsection (4) above shall specify the ground on which it is given; and the appropriate national authority may by regulations make provision as to the form of notices under that subsection and as to the circumstances in which they are to be treated as given.

(8) Where the proper office of a court receives a certificate under subsection (1) above, or a court grants an application under subsection (5) above, the proper officer or court must send notice of that fact to the Secretary of State; and the notice must be sent in such manner and to such address, and must contain such particulars, as the Secretary of State may determine.]

A19.80   *[Section 34E is prospectively inserted by the Road Safety Act 2006 s.15(1).*

Section 16 of the Road Safety Act 2006 provides for an experimental period for alcohol ignition interlocks as introduced by ibid. s.15.]

[Approval of programmes

A19.81   34F.—(1) If an application is made to the appropriate national authority for the approval of a programme for the purposes of section 34D of this Act, the appropriate national authority must decide whether to grant or refuse the application.

(2) In reaching that decision the appropriate national authority must have regard to—

    (a) the nature of the programme, and

    (b) whether the programme provider is an appropriate person to provide the programme and administer its provision efficiently and effectively,

and may take into account any recommendations made by any persons appointed to consider the application.

(3) A programme may be approved subject to conditions specified by the appropriate national authority.

(4) An approval of a programme is for the period specified by the appropriate national authority (which must not exceed seven years), subject to withdrawal of approval.

(5) Regulations made by the appropriate national authority may make provision in relation to the approval of programmes and may, in particular, include provision—

    (a) in relation to the making of applications for approval,

    (b) for the payment in respect of applications for approval, or of approvals, (or of both) of fees of such amounts as are prescribed by the regulations,

    (c) specifying the maximum fees that a person may be required to pay for a programme and by when they are to be paid,

    (d) for the monitoring of programmes and programme providers,

    (e) in relation to withdrawing approval,

    (f) for an appeal to lie to the Transport Tribunal against a refusal of an application for approval, the imposition of conditions on the grant of such an application or the withdrawal of approval, and

    (g) authorising the appropriate national authority to make available (with or without charge) information about programmes and programme providers.]

[Section 34F is prospectively inserted by the Road Safety Act 2006 s.15(1).   **A19.82**
Section 16 of the Road Safety Act 2006 provides for an experimental period for alcohol ignition interlocks as introduced by ibid. s.15.]

[Provisions supplementary to sections 34D to 34F

34G.—(1) The appropriate national authority may issue guidance to programme providers, or to any category of programme provider, as to the conduct of programmes approved for the purposes of section 34D of this Act; and—   **A19.83**

    (a) programme providers shall have regard to any guidance given to them under this subsection, and

    (b) in determining for the purposes of section 34E of this Act whether any instructions or requirements of a programme provider were reasonable, a court shall have regard to any guidance given to him under this subsection.

(2) The Secretary of State may by regulations make provision—

(a) amending section 34D(1)(b) of this Act by substituting for the period for the time being specified there a different period,

(b) amending section 34D(1)(d) of this Act by substituting for the period for the time being specified there a different period, or

(c) amending section 34D(4) of this Act by substituting for the period for the time being specified there a different period, or by

substituting for the fraction of the unreduced period for the time being specified there a different fraction of that period, (or by doing both).

(3) In sections 34D to 34F of this Act and this section—

"*appropriate national authority*" means (as respects Wales) the National Assembly for Wales and (otherwise) the Secretary of State;

"*contravention*" includes failure to comply;

"*programme provider*", in relation to an alcohol ignition interlock programme, means the person by whom it is, or is to be, provided;

"*proper officer*" means—

(a) in relation to a magistrates' court in England and Wales, the designated officer for the court, and

(b) otherwise, the clerk of the court;

"*relevant local court*", in relation to an alcohol ignition interlock programme order in the case of an offender, means—

(a) in England and Wales, a magistrates' court acting for the local justice area in which the offender resides, and

(b) *[applies to Scotland]*; and

"*supervising court*", in relation to an alcohol ignition interlock programme order, means—

(a) in England and Wales, if the Crown Court made the order the Crown Court and otherwise a magistrates' court acting for the same local justice area as the court which made the order, and

(b) *[applies to Scotland]*.

(4) Any power to make regulations under section 34D, 34E or 34F of this Act or this section includes power to make different provision for different cases, and to make such incidental or supplementary provision as appears to the appropriate national authority to be necessary or appropriate.

(5) Any power to make regulations under section 34D, 34E or 34F of this Act or this section shall be exercisable by statutory instrument.

(6) A statutory instrument containing regulations made under section 34D, 34E or 34F of this Act by the Secretary of State shall be subject to annulment in pursuance of a resolution of either House of Parliament.

(7) No regulations shall be made under this section unless a draft of the regulations has been laid before, and approved by a resolution of, each House of Parliament.]

A19.84   *[Section 34G is prospectively inserted by the Road Safety Act 2006 s.15(1).*

Section 16 of the Road Safety Act 2006 provides for an experimental period for alcohol ignition interlocks as introduced by ibid. s.15.]

Disqualification for repeated offences

A19.85   35.—(1) Where—

(a) a person is convicted of an offence [to which this subsection applies], and

(b) the penalty points to be taken into account on that occasion number twelve or more,

the court must order him to be disqualified for not less than the minimum period unless the court is satisfied, having regard to all the circumstances, that there are grounds for mitigating the normal consequences of the conviction and thinks fit to order him to be disqualified for a shorter period or not to order him to be disqualified.

[(1A) Subsection (1) above applies to—

(a) an offence involving discretionary disqualification and obligatory endorsement, and

(b) an offence involving obligatory disqualification in respect of which no order is made under section 34 of this Act.]

(2) The minimum period referred to in subsection (1) above is—

(a) six months if no previous disqualification imposed on the offender is to be taken into account, and

(b) one year if one, and two years if more than one, such disqualification is to be taken into account;

and a previous disqualification imposed on an offender is to be taken into account if it [was for a fixed period of 56 days or more and was imposed] within the three years immediately preceding the commission of the latest offence in respect of which penalty points are taken into account under section 29 of this Act.

(3) Where an offender is convicted on the same occasion of more than one offence [to which subsection (1) above applies]—

(a) not more than one disqualification shall be imposed on him under subsection (1) above,

(b) in determining the period of the disqualification the court must take into account all the offences, and

(c) for the purposes of any appeal any disqualification imposed under subsection (1) above shall be treated as an order made on the conviction of each of the offences.

(4) No account is to be taken under subsection (1) above of any of the following circumstances—

(a) any circumstances that are alleged to make the offence or any of the offences not a serious one,

(b) hardship, other than exceptional hardship, or

(c) any circumstances which, within the three years immediately preceding the conviction, have been taken into account under that subsection in ordering the offender to be disqualified for a shorter period or not ordering him to be disqualified.

(5) References in this section to disqualification do not include a disqualification imposed under section 26 of this Act or [section 147 of the Powers of Criminal Courts (Sentencing) Act 2000] [or section 223A or 436A of the Criminal Procedure (Scotland) Act 1975 (offences committed by using vehicles) or a disqualification imposed in respect of an offence of stealing a motor vehicle, an offence under section 12 or 25 of the Theft Act 1968, an offence under section 178 of the Road Traffic Act 1988, or an attempt to commit such an offence].

[(5A) The preceding provisions of this section shall apply in relation to a conviction of an offence committed by aiding, abetting, counselling, procuring, or inciting to the commission of, an offence involving obligatory disqualification as if the offence were an offence involving discretionary disqualification.]

(6) *[Applies to Scotland.]*

(7) This section is subject to section 48 of this Act.

A19.86 *[Section 35 is printed as amended by the Road Traffic Act 1991 s.48 and Sch.4, para.95(1)–(7); the Powers of Criminal Courts (Sentencing) Act 2000 s.165(1) and Sch.9, para.122.*

With effect from a day to be appointed, the following amendments will be made to s.35 by the Coroners and Justice Act 2009 s.177 and Sch.21, Pt 9, para.90(6):

1. *in s.35(2), the words ", subject to subsection (2A)," will be inserted in the words following para.(b), after "offender is";*

2. *after s.35(2), the following text will be inserted:*

[(2A) A previous disqualification imposed on an offender for a fixed period is not to be taken into account for the purposes of subsection (2) if that period would have been less than 56 days but for an extension period added pursuant to—

   (a) section 35A or 35C,

   (b) section 248D of the Criminal Procedure (Scotland) Act 1995, or

   (c) section 147A of the Powers of Criminal Courts (Sentencing) Act 2000.]*]*

[Extension of disqualification where custodial sentence also imposed

A19.87 **35A.**—(1) This section applies where a person is convicted in England and Wales of an offence for which the court—

   (a) imposes a custodial sentence, and

   (b) orders the person to be disqualified under section 34 or 35.

(2) The order under section 34 or 35 must provide for the person to be disqualified for the appropriate extension period, in addition to the discretionary disqualification period.

(3) The discretionary disqualification period is the period for which, in the absence of this section, the court would have disqualified the person under section 34 or 35.

(4) The appropriate extension period is—

   (a) where an order under section 82A(2) of the Powers of Criminal Courts (Sentencing) Act 2000 (life sentence: determination of tariffs) is made in relation to the custodial sentence, a period equal to the part of the sentence specified in that order;

   (b) in the case of a detention and training order under section 100 of that Act (offenders under 18: detention and training orders), a period equal to half the term of that order;

   (c) in the case of a detention and training order under section 100 of that Act (offenders under 18: detention and training orders), a period equal to half the term of that order;

   (d) where an order under section 183 of that Act (intermittent custody orders) is made in relation to the custodial sentence, a period equal to the number of custodial days specified pursuant to section 183(1)(a) of that Act less any relevant discount;

(e) where section 227 of that Act (extended sentence for certain violent or sexual offences: persons 18 or over) applies in relation to the custodial sentence, a period equal to half the term imposed pursuant to section 227(2C)(a) of that Act calculated after that term has been reduced by any relevant discount;

(f) where section 228 of that Act (extended sentence for certain violent or sexual offences: persons under 18) applies in relation to the custodial sentence, a period equal to half the term imposed pursuant to section 228(2B)(a) of that Act calculated after that term has been reduced by any relevant discount;

(g) where an order under section 269(2) of that Act (determination of minimum term in relation to mandatory life sentence: early release) is made in relation to the custodial sentence, a period equal to the part of the sentence specified in that order;

(h) in any other case, a period equal to half the custodial sentence imposed calculated after that sentence has been reduced by any relevant discount.

(5) If a period determined under subsection (4) includes a fraction of a day, that period is to be rounded up to the nearest number of whole days.

(6) The *"relevant discount"* is the total number of days to count as time served by virtue of a direction under—

(a) section 240 of the Criminal Justice Act 2003 (crediting periods of remand in custody), or

(b) section 240A of that Act (crediting periods of remand on bail).

(7) This section does not apply where—

(a) the custodial sentence was a suspended sentence,

(b) the court has made an order under section 269(4) of the Criminal Justice Act 2003 (determination of minimum term in relation to mandatory life sentence: no early release) in relation to the custodial sentence, or

(c) the court has made an order under section 82A(4) of the Powers of Criminal Courts (Sentencing) Act 2000 (determination of minimum term in relation to discretionary life sentence: no early release) in relation to the custodial sentence.

(8) Subsection (9) applies where an amending order provides that the proportion of a prisoner's sentence referred to in section 244(3)(a) or 247(2) of the Criminal Justice Act 2003 (release of prisoners in certain circumstances) is to be read as a reference to another proportion ("the new proportion").

(9) The Secretary of State may by order—

(a) if the amending order makes provision in respect of section 244(3)(a) of that Act, provide that the proportion specified in subsection (4)(h) of this section is to be read, in the case of a custodial sentence to which the amending order applies, as a reference to the new proportion;

(b) if the amending order makes provision in respect of section 247(2) of that Act, provide that the proportion specified in subsection (4)(e) and (f) of this section is to be read, in the case of a custodial sentence to which the amending order applies, as a reference to the new proportion.

(10) An order under subsection (9) is to be made by statutory instrument and a draft of the statutory instrument containing the order must be laid before, and approved by a resolution of, each House of Parliament.

(11) In this section—

"*amending order*" means an order under section 267 of the Criminal Justice Act 2003 (alteration by order of relevant proportion of sentence);

"*custodial sentence*" has the meaning given by section 76 of the Powers of Criminal Courts (Sentencing) Act 2000;

"*suspended sentence*" has the meaning given by section 189 of the Criminal Justice Act 2003.]

A19.88   *[Section 35A is prospectively inserted by the Coroners and Justice Act 2009 s.137 and Sch.16, para.2.*

Paragraph 2 of Sch.16 to the Coroners and Justice Act 2009 does not apply in relation to, or have effect by reference to, offences committed wholly or partly before the commencement of that paragraph (see the Coroners and Justice Act 2009 s.177 and Sch.22, Pt 4, para.29).]

[Effect of custodial sentence in other cases

A19.89   **35B.**—(1) This section applies where a person is convicted in England and Wales of an offence for which a court proposes to order the person to be disqualified under section 34 or 35 and—

(a) the court proposes to impose on the person a custodial sentence (other than a suspended sentence) for another offence, or

(b) at the time of sentencing for the offence, a custodial sentence imposed on the person on an earlier occasion has not expired.

(2) In determining the period for which the person is to be disqualified under section 34 or 35, the court must have regard to the consideration in subsection (3) if and to the extent that it is appropriate to do so.

(3) The consideration is the diminished effect of disqualification as a distinct punishment if the person who is disqualified is also detained in pursuance of a custodial sentence.

(4) If the court proposes to order the person to be disqualified under section 34 or 35 and to impose a custodial sentence for the same offence, the court may not in relation to that disqualification take that custodial sentence into account for the purposes of subsection (2).

(5) In this section "*custodial sentence*" and "*suspended sentence*" have the same meaning as in section 35A.]

A19.90   *[Section 35B is prospectively inserted by the Coroners and Justice Act 2009 s.137 and Sch.16, para.2.*

Paragraph 2 of Sch.16 to the Coroners and Justice Act 2009 does not apply in relation to, or have effect by reference to, offences committed wholly or partly before the commencement of that paragraph (see the Coroners and Justice Act 2009 s.177 and Sch.22, Pt 4, para.29).]

[Disqualification until test is passed

36.—(1) Where this subsection applies to a person the court must order him to   **A19.91**
be disqualified until he passes the appropriate driving test.

(2) Subsection (1) above applies to a person who is disqualified under section 34 of this Act on conviction of—

    (a) manslaughter ... by the driver of a motor vehicle, or

    (b) an offence under section 1 (causing death by dangerous driving) or section 2 (dangerous driving) of the Road Traffic Act 1988.

(3) Subsection (1) above also applies—

    (a) to a person who is disqualified under section 34 or 35 of this Act in such circumstances or for such period as the Secretary of State may by order prescribe, or

    (b) to such other persons convicted of such offences involving obligatory endorsement as may be so prescribed.

(4) Where a person to whom subsection (1) above does not apply is convicted of an offence involving obligatory endorsement, the court may order him to be disqualified until he passes the appropriate driving test (whether or not he has previously passed any test).

(5) In this section —

    "appropriate driving test" means—

        (a) an extended driving test, where a person is convicted of an offence involving obligatory disqualification or is disqualified under section 35 of this Act,

        (b) a test of competence to drive, other than an extended driving test, in any other case,

    "extended driving test" means a test of competence to drive prescribed for the purposes of this section, and

    "test of competence to drive" means a test prescribed by virtue of section 89(3) of the Road Traffic Act 1988.

(6) In determining whether to make an order under subsection (4) above, the court shall have regard to the safety of road users.

(7) Where a person is disqualified until he passes the extended driving test—

    (a) any earlier order under this section shall cease to have effect, and

    (b) a court shall not make a further order under this section while he is so disqualified.

(8) Subject to subsection (9) below, a disqualification by virtue of an order under this section shall be deemed to have expired on production to the Secretary of State of evidence, in such form as may be prescribed by regulations under section 105 of the Road Traffic Act 1988, that the person disqualified has passed the test in question since the order was made.

(9) A disqualification shall be deemed to have expired only in relation to vehicles of such classes as may be prescribed in relation to the test passed by regulations under that section.

(10) Where there is issued to a person a licence on the counterpart of which are endorsed particulars of a disqualification under this section, there shall also be endorsed the particulars of any test of competence to drive that he has passed since the order of disqualification was made.

[(10A) Where a person's driving record is endorsed with particulars of a disqualification under this section, it shall also be endorsed with the particulars of any test of competence to drive that he has passed since the order of disqualification was made.]

(11) For the purposes of an order under this section, a person shall be treated as having passed a test of competence to drive other than an extended driving test if he passes a corresponding test conducted—

  (a) under the law of Northern Ireland, the Isle of Man, any of the Channel Islands, another [EEA State], Gibraltar or a designated country or territory …, or

  (b) for the purposes of obtaining a British Forces licence (as defined by section 88(8) of [the Road Traffic Act 1988]);

and accordingly subsections (8) to (10) above shall apply in relation to such a test as they apply in relation to a test prescribed by virtue of section 89(3) of that Act.

[(11A) For the purposes of subsection (11) above *"designated country or territory"* means a country or territory designated by order under section 108(2) of the Road Traffic Act 1988 but a test conducted under the law of such a country or territory shall not be regarded as a corresponding test unless a person passing such a test would be entitled to an exchangeable licence as defined in section 108(1) of that Act.]

(12) This section is subject to section 48 of this Act.

(13) *[Orders under s.36(3) to be statutory instruments.]*

(14) The Secretary of State shall not make an order under subsection (3) above after the end of 2001 if he has not previously made such an order.]

A19.92 *[Section 36 is printed as substituted by the Road Traffic Act 1991 s.32, and as subsequently amended by the Driving Licences (Community Driving Licence) Regulations 1996 (SI 1996/1974) reg.3 and Sch.2, para.3 (not reproduced in this work); the Deregulation (Exchangeable Driving Licences) Order 1998 (SI 1998/ 1917) art.3 (not reproduced in this work); the Road Safety Act 2006 s.9 and Sch.2, para.7.*

 With effect from a day (or days) to be appointed, s.36 will be amended as follows:

  1. *in s.36(3), the words "for such period, in such circumstances or for such period and in such circumstances" will be substituted for the words "in such circumstances or for such period"; the word "specify" will be substituted for the word "prescribe"; and the words "the Secretary of State may by order specify" will be substituted for the words "may be so prescribed" by the Road Safety Act 2006 s.37(2);*

  2. *in s.36(5), the following text will be substituted for the definition of "appropriate driving test" by the Road Safety Act 2006 s.37(3):*

   ["appropriate driving test" means —

    (a) *in such circumstances as the Secretary of State may prescribe, an extended driving test, and*

(b) otherwise, a test of competence to drive which is not an extended driving test,]

and the words "by regulations made by the Secretary of State" will be inserted after the word "section" in the definition of "extended driving test" (ibid.);

3. *in s.36(8), the words "made by the Secretary of State" will be substituted for the words "under section 105 of the Road Traffic Act 1988" by the Road Safety Act 2006 s.37(4);*

4. *in s.36(9), the words "made by the Secretary of State" will be substituted for the words "under that section" by the Road Safety Act 2006 s.37(5);*

5. *after s.36(13), the following new subsection will be inserted by the Road Safety Act 2006 s.37(6):*

[(13A) Before making an order under subsection (3) above the Secretary of State must consult with such representative organisations as he thinks fit.]

6. *s.36(14) will be omitted by the Road Safety Act 2006 s.37(7), s.59 and Sch.7(10).*

With effect from a day to be appointed and in relation to endorsement (all drivers), s.36 (as amended above) will be further amended by the Road Safety Act 2006 s.10 and Sch.3, para.39, s.59 and Sch.7(4) so that s.36(10) is omitted.

For the provisions as regards the commencement of ss.9 and 10 of and Schs 2 and 3 to the Road Safety Act 2006, see s.61(8) below.

Words in s.36(2)(a) relating expressly and exclusively to Scotland have been omitted.

Offences under the Road Traffic Act 1988 s.3A (causing death by dangerous driving when under the influence of drink or drugs) committed on or after January 31, 2002, and any persons committing such offences, are prescribed for the purposes of s.36(1) by the Driving Licences (Disqualification until Test Passed) (Prescribed Offence) Order 2001 (SI 2001/4051) below.

As to the European Economic Area (EEA), see the introductory note to Section C below.]

Effect of order of disqualification

37.—(1) Where the holder of a licence is disqualified by an order of a court, the licence shall be treated as being revoked with effect from the beginning of the period of disqualification.   **A19.93**

[(1A) Where—
    (a) the disqualification is for a fixed period shorter than 56 days in respect of an offence involving obligatory endorsement, or
    (b) the order is made under section 26 of this Act,
subsection (1) above shall not prevent the licence from again having effect at the end of the period of disqualification.]

(2) Where the holder of the licence appeals against the order and the disqualification is suspended under section 39 of this Act, the period of disqualification shall be treated for the purpose of subsection (1) above as beginning on the day on which the disqualification ceases to be suspended.

(3) Notwithstanding anything in Part III of the Road Traffic Act 1988, a person disqualified by an order of a court under section [36] of this Act is (unless he is also disqualified otherwise than by virtue of such an order) entitled to obtain and to hold a provisional licence and to drive a motor vehicle in accordance with the conditions subject to which the provisional licence is granted.

A19.94   *[Section 37 is printed as amended by the Road Traffic Act 1991 ss.33, 48 and Sch.4, para.96.*

With effect from a day to be appointed, the following amendments will be made to s.37 by the Coroners and Justice Act 2009 s.177 and Sch.21, Pt 9, para.90(7):

1. *in s.37(1A)(a), the words "(disregarding any extension period)" will be inserted after the words "56 days";*

2. *in s.37(1A), the words "(including any extension period)" will be inserted after the words "period of disqualification";*

3. *after s.37(1A), the following text will be inserted:*

[(1B) In subsection (1A) *"extension period"* means an extension period added pursuant to—

    (a) section 35A or 35C,

    (b) section 248D of the Criminal Procedure (Scotland) Act 1995, or

    (c) section 147A of the Powers of Criminal Courts (Sentencing) Act 2000.] *]*

Appeal against disqualification

A19.95   **38.**—(1) A person disqualified by an order of a magistrates' court under section 34 or 35 of this Act may appeal against the order in the same manner as against a conviction.

(2) *[Applies to Scotland.]*

Suspension of disqualification pending appeal

A19.96   **39.**—(1) Any court in England and Wales (whether a magistrates' court or another) which makes an order disqualifying a person may, if it thinks fit, suspend the disqualification pending an appeal against the order.

(2) *[Applies to Scotland.]*

(3) Where a court exercises its power under subsection (1) or (2) above, it must send notice of the suspension to the Secretary of State.

(4) The notice must be sent in such manner and to such address and must contain such particulars as the Secretary of State may determine.

Power of appellate courts in England and Wales to suspend disqualification

A19.97   **40.**—(1) This section applies where a person has been convicted by or before a court in England and Wales of an offence involving obligatory or discretionary disqualification and has been ordered to be disqualified; and in the following provisions of this section —

    (a) any reference to a person ordered to be disqualified is to be construed as a reference to a person so convicted and so ordered to be disqualified, and

    (b) any reference to his sentence includes a reference to the order of disqualification and to any other order made on his conviction and, accordingly, any reference to an appeal against his sentence includes a reference to an appeal against any order forming part of his sentence.

(2) Where a person ordered to be disqualified—

    (a) appeals to the Crown Court, or

    (b) appeals or applies for leave to appeal to the Court of Appeal,

against his conviction or his sentence, the Crown Court or, as the case may require, the Court of Appeal may, if it thinks fit, suspend the disqualification.

(3) Where a person ordered to be disqualified has appealed or applied for leave to appeal to the [Supreme Court]—

    (a) under section 1 of the Administration of Justice Act 1960 from any decision of a Divisional Court of the Queen's Bench Division which is material to his conviction or sentence, or

    (b) under section 33 of the Criminal Appeal Act 1968 from any decision of the Court of Appeal which is material to his conviction or sentence,

the Divisional Court or, as the case may require, the Court of Appeal may, if it thinks fit, suspend the disqualification.

(4) Where a person ordered to be disqualified makes an application in respect of the decision of the court in question under section 111 of the Magistrates' Courts Act 1980 (statement of case by magistrates' court) or section 28 of the Supreme Court Act 1981 (statement of case by Crown Court) the High Court may, if it thinks fit, suspend the disqualification.

(5) Where a person ordered to be disqualified—

    (a) applies to the High Court for an order of certiorari to remove into the High Court any proceedings of a magistrates' court or of the Crown Court, being proceedings in or in consequence of which he was convicted or his sentence was passed, or

    (b) applies to the High Court for leave to make such an application,

the High Court may, if it thinks fit, suspend the disqualification.

(6) Any power of a court under the preceding provisions of this section to suspend the disqualification of any person is a power to do so on such terms as the court thinks fit.

(7) Where, by virtue of this section, a court suspends the disqualification of any person, it must send notice of the suspension to the Secretary of State.

(8) The notice must be sent in such manner and to such address and must contain such particulars as the Secretary of State may determine.

[Section 40 is printed as amended by the Constitutional Reform Act 2005 s.40   **A19.98**
and Sch.9, para.50.]

Power of High Court of Justiciary to suspend disqualification

   41. *[Omitted.]*   **A19.99**

[Suspension of disqualification pending determination of applications under section 34B

   41A.—(1) Where a person makes an application to a court under section 34B   **A19.100**
of this Act, the court may suspend the disqualification to which the application relates pending the determination of the application.

(2) Where a court exercises its power under subsection (1) above it must send notice of the suspension to the Secretary of State.

(3) The notice must be sent in such manner and to such address, and must contain such particulars, as the Secretary of State may determine.]

A19.101   *[Section 41A was inserted by the Road Traffic Act 1991 s.48 and Sch.4, para.97.]*

[Suspension of certificate pending determination of applications under section 34E

A19.102   **41B.**—(1) Where a person given a certificate under subsection (1) of section 34E of this Act makes an application to a court under subsection (5) of that section, the court may suspend the effect of the certificate pending the determination of the application.

(2) Where a court exercises its power under subsection (1) above it must send notice of the suspension to the Secretary of State.

(3) The notice must be sent in such manner and to such address and must contain such particulars, as the Secretary of State may determine.]

A19.103   *[Section 41B is prospectively inserted after s.41A by the Road Safety Act 2006 s.15(2).]*

Removal of disqualification

A19.104   **42.**—(1) Subject to the provisions of this section, a person who by an order of a court is disqualified may apply to the court by which the order was made to remove the disqualification.

(2) On any such application the court may, as it thinks proper having regard to—

    (a) the character of the person disqualified and his conduct subsequent to the order,

    (b) the nature of the offence, and

    (c) any other circumstances of the case,

either by order remove the disqualification as from such date as may be specified in the order or refuse the application.

(3) No application shall be made under subsection (1) above for the removal of a disqualification before the expiration of whichever is relevant of the following periods from the date of the order by which the disqualification was imposed, that is—

    (a) two years, if the disqualification is for less than four years,

    (b) one half of the period of disqualification, if it is for less than ten years but not less than four years,

    (c) five years in any other case;

and in determining the expiration of the period after which under this subsection a person may apply for the removal of a disqualification, any time after the conviction during which the disqualification was suspended or he was not disqualified shall be disregarded.

(4) Where an application under subsection (1) above is refused, a further application under that subsection shall not be entertained if made within three months after the date of the refusal.

(5) If under this section a court orders a disqualification to be removed, the court—

[(a) must—

    (i) if particulars of the disqualification were previously endorsed on the counterpart of any licence previously held by the applicant, cause particulars of the order to be endorsed on that counterpart, and

    (ii) if particulars of the disqualification were previously endorsed on the driving record of the applicant, send notice of the order to the Secretary of State,]

(b) may in any case order the applicant to pay the whole or any part of the costs of the application.

[(5A) Subsection [(5)(a)(i)] above shall apply only where the disqualification was imposed in respect of an offence involving obligatory endorsement; and in any other case the court must send notice of the order made under this section to the Secretary of State.]

[(5AA) If the disqualification was imposed in respect of an offence involving obligatory endorsement, the Secretary of State must, on receiving notice of an order under subsection (5)(a)(ii) above, make any necessary adjustments to the endorsements on the person's driving record to reflect the order.]

[(5B) A notice under subsection [(5)(a)(ii) or] (5A) above must be sent in such manner and to such address, and must contain such particulars, as the Secretary of State may determine.]

(6) The preceding provisions of this section shall not apply where the disqualification was imposed by order under section 36(1) of this Act.

[Section 42 is printed as amended by the Driving Licences (Community Driving Licence) Regulations 1990 (SI 1990/144); the Road Traffic Act 1991 s.48 and Sch.4, para.98; the Road Safety Act 2006 s.9 and Sch.2, para.8. **A19.105**

With effect from a day to be appointed and in relation to endorsement (all drivers), s.42 will be amended by the Road Safety Act 2006 s.10 and Sch.3, para.40, s.59 and Sch.7(4) as follows:

    1. in s.42(5), para.(a) will be substituted as follows:

        [(a) must send notice of the order to the Secretary of State,];

    2. s.42(5A) will be omitted;

    3. in s.42(5AA), "(5)(a)" will be substituted for "(5)(a)(ii)";

    4. in s.42(5B), "(5)(a)" will be substituted for "(5)(a)(ii) or (5A)".

For the provisions as regards the commencement of ss.9 and 10 of and Schs 2 and 3 to the Road Safety Act 2006, see s.61(8) below.

With effect from a day to be appointed, the following amendments will be made to s.42 by the Coroners and Justice Act 2009 s.177 and Sch.21, Pt 9, para.90(8):

    1. in s.42(3), the words "the relevant date" will be substituted for the words "the date of the order by which the disqualification was imposed", the words "(disregarding any extension period)" will be inserted after the words "four years", and in para.(b), the words "period of disqualification (disregarding any extension period), if the disqualification is (disregarding any extension period)" will be substituted for the words "period of disqualification, if it is";

2. *after s.42(3), the following text will be inserted:*

[(3A) In subsection (3) *"the relevant date"* means—
    (a) the date of the order imposing the disqualification in question, or
    (b) if the period of the disqualification is extended by an extension period, the date in paragraph (a) postponed by a period equal to that extension period.]

3. *after s.42(3A), as inserted, the following subsection will be inserted:*

[(3B) *"Extension period"* means an extension period added pursuant to—
    (a) section 35A or 35C,
    (b) section 248D of the Criminal Procedure (Scotland) Act 1995, or
    (c) section 147A of the Powers of Criminal Courts (Sentencing) Act 2000.]

As to the application of s.42(5) to domestic driving permits, Convention driving permits, British Forces (BFG) driving licences and to the holders of such licences and permits, see the Motor Vehicles (Driving Licences) Regulations 1999 (SI 1999/2864), reg.80. As to the application of s.42 to Community licences, see s.91A(1) below.]

Rule for determining end of period of disqualification

A19.106   43. In determining the expiration of the period for which a person is disqualified by an order of a court made in consequence of a conviction, any time after the conviction during which the disqualification was suspended or he was not disqualified shall be disregarded.

Endorsement

[Orders for endorsement]

A19.107   44.—(1) Where a person is convicted of an offence involving obligatory endorsement, the court must order there to be endorsed on [the counterpart of] any licence held by him particulars of the conviction and also—
    (a) if the court orders him to be disqualified, particulars of the disqualification, or
    (b) if the court does not order him to be disqualified—
      (i) particulars of the offence, including the date when it was committed, and
      (ii) the penalty points to be attributed to the offence.

(2) Where the court does not order the person convicted to be disqualified, it need not make an order under subsection (1) above if for special reasons it thinks fit not to do so.

(3) *[Applies to Scotland.]*

[(3A) Where a person who is not the holder of a licence is convicted of an offence involving obligatory endorsement, subsection (1) above applies as if the reference to the counterpart of any licence held by him were a reference to his driving record.]

(4) This section is subject to section 48 of this Act.

[Section 44 is printed as amended by the Driving Licences (Community Driving Licence) Regulations 1990 (SI 1990/144); the Road Safety Act 2006 s.9. **A19.108**

With effect from a day to be appointed and in relation to endorsement (all drivers), s.44 will be amended by the Road Safety Act 2006 s.10, s.59 and Sch.7(4) as follows:

1. *in s.44(1), the words "his driving record" will be substituted for the words "the counterpart of any licence held by him";*
2. *s.44(3A) will be omitted.*

For the provisions relating to the commencement of ss.9 and 10 of the 2006 Act, see ibid. s.61(8) below.

As to the application of s.44(1) to Community licences, see s.91A(1) below.]

[Endorsement of driving record in accordance with order

44A.—(1) Where the court orders the endorsement of a person's driving record with any particulars or penalty points it must send notice of the order to the Secretary of State. **A19.109**

(2) On receiving the notice, the Secretary of State must endorse those particulars or penalty points on the person's driving record.

(3) A notice sent by the court to the Secretary of State in pursuance of this section must be sent in such manner and to such address and contain such particulars as the Secretary of State may require.]

[Section 44A is printed as inserted by the Road Safety Act 2006 s.9(3) (unlicensed and foreign drivers).] **A19.110**

Effect of endorsement [of counterparts]

45.—(1) An order that any particulars or penalty points are to be endorsed on [the counterpart of] any licence held by the person convicted shall […] operate as an order that [the counterpart of] any licence he may then hold or may subsequently obtain is to be so endorsed until he becomes entitled under subsection (4) below to have a licence issued to him [with its counterpart] free from the particulars or penalty points. **A19.111**

(2) On the issue of a new licence to a person, any particulars or penalty points ordered to be endorsed on [the counterpart of] any licence held by him shall be entered on [the counterpart of] the licence unless he has become entitled under subsection (4) below to have a licence issued to him free from those particulars or penalty points.

(3) […]

(4) [A person the counterpart of whose licence has been ordered to be endorsed is entitled to have issued to him with effect from the end of the period for which the endorsement remains effective a new licence with a counterpart free from the endorsement if] he applies for a new licence in pursuance of section 97(1) of the Road Traffic Act 1988, surrenders any subsisting licence [and its counterpart], pays the fee prescribed by regulations under Part III of that Act and satisfies the other requirements of section 97(1).

(5) An endorsement ordered on a person's conviction of an offence remains effective (subject to subsections (6) and (7) below)—

(a) if an order is made for the disqualification of the offender, until four years have elapsed since the conviction, and

(b) if no such order is made, until either—

    (i) four years have elapsed since the commission of the offence, or

    [(ii) an order is made for the disqualification of the offender under section 35 of this Act].

(6) Where the offence was one under section 1 or 2 of [the Road Traffic Act 1988] (causing death by [dangerous] driving and [dangerous] driving), the endorsement remains in any case effective until four years have elapsed since the conviction.

(7) Where the offence was one—

    [(a) [under] section 3A, 4(1) or 5(1)(a) of that Act (driving offences connected with drink or drugs),

    (b) under section 7(6) of that Act (failing to provide specimen) involving obligatory disqualification, [or

    (c) under section 7A(6) of that Act (failing to allow a specimen to be subjected to laboratory test),]

the endorsement remains effective until eleven years have elapsed since the conviction.

A19.112   *[Section 45 is printed as amended by the Road Traffic (Driver Licensing and Information Systems) Act 1989 ss.7 and 16 and Sch.3, para.25(a) and (b); the Driving Licences (Community Driving Licence) Regulations 1990 (SI 1990/144); the Road Traffic Act 1991 s.48 and Sch.4, para.99(1)–(4); the Road Safety Act 2006 ss.9, 14, 58(3), 59 and Sch.2, para.9 and Sch.7(3) and (5).*

With effect from a day to be appointed and in relation to endorsement (all drivers), s.45 (as amended above) will be omitted by the Road Safety Act 2006 s.10 and Sch.3, para.41, s.59 and Sch.7(4).

For the provisions relating to the commencement of ss.9 and 10 of and Schs 2 and 3 to the 2006 Act, see ibid. s.61(8) below.]

[Effect of endorsement of driving records

A19.113   45A.—(1) An order that any particulars or penalty points are to be endorsed on a person's driving record shall operate as an order that his driving record is to be so endorsed until the end of the period for which the endorsement remains effective.

(2) At the end of the period for which the endorsement remains effective the Secretary of State must remove the endorsement from the person's driving record.

(3) On the issue of a new licence to a person, any particulars ordered to be endorsed on his driving record shall be entered on the counterpart of the licence unless he has become entitled under subsection (4) below to have a licence issued to him with its counterpart free from those particulars or penalty points.

(4) A person the counterpart of whose licence has been endorsed under subsection (3) above is entitled to have issued to him with effect from the end of the period for which the endorsement remains effective a new licence with a counterpart free from the endorsement if he applies for a new licence in pursuance of section 97(1) of the Road Traffic Act 1988, surrenders any subsisting licence and its counterpart, pays the fee prescribed by regulations under Part 3 of that Act and satisfies the other requirements of section 97(1).

(5) The period for which an endorsement remains effective is determined in accordance with section 45(5) to (7) of this Act.]

[Section 45A is printed as inserted by the Road Safety Act 2006 s.9 and Sch.2, **A19.114**
para.10.

Section 45A, as inserted, will be amended with effect from a day to be ap-
pointed and in relation to endorsement (all drivers) by the Road Safety Act 2006
s.10 and Sch.3, para.42, so as to substitute the following text:

[(3) An endorsement ordered on a person's conviction of an offence remains effective (subject to subsections (4) and (5) below)—

  (a) if an order is made for the disqualification of the offender, until four
      years have elapsed since the conviction, and

  (b) if no such order is made, until either—

      (i) four years have elapsed since the commission of the offence, or

      (ii) an order is made for the disqualification of the offender under section
           35 of this Act.

(4) Where the offence was one under section 1 or 2 of the Road Traffic Act 1988
(causing death by dangerous driving and dangerous driving), the endorsement remains
in any case effective until four years have elapsed since the conviction.

(5) Where the offence was one—

  (a) under section 3A, 4(1) or 5(1)(a) of that Act (driving offences connected
      with drink or drugs),

  (b) under section 7(6) of that Act (failing to provide specimen) involving
      obligatory disqualification, or

  (c) under section 7A(6) of that Act (failing to allow a specimen to be
      subjected to laboratory test),

the endorsement remains effective until eleven years have elapsed since the
conviction.]

For the provisions relating to the commencement of ss.9 and 10 of and Schs 2
and 3 to the 2006 Act, see ibid. s.61(8) below.]

General

Combination of disqualification and endorsement with probation orders and orders for discharge

46.—(1) Notwithstanding anything in [section 14(3) of the Powers of Criminal   **A19.115**
Courts (Sentencing) Act 2000] (conviction of offender ... discharged to be
disregarded for the purposes of enactments relating to disqualification), a court in
England and Wales which on convicting a person of an offence involving obligatory or discretionary disqualification makes—

  (a) [...]

  (b) an order discharging him absolutely or conditionally,

may on that occasion also exercise any power conferred, and must also discharge
any duty imposed, on the court by sections 34, 35, 36[, 44 or 44A] of this Act.

(2) A conviction—

  (a) in respect of which a court in England and Wales has ordered a person
      to be disqualified, or

  (b) of which particulars have been endorsed on [the counterpart of] any
      licence held by him [or on his driving record],

is to be taken into account, notwithstanding anything in [section 14(1) of the
Powers of Criminal Courts (Sentencing) Act 2000] (conviction of offender ...

discharged to be disregarded for the purpose of subsequent proceedings), in determining his liability to punishment or disqualification for any offence involving obligatory or discretionary disqualification committed subsequently.

(3) *[Applies to Scotland.]*

A19.116 *[Section 46 is printed as amended by the Driving Licences (Community Driving Licence) Regulations 1990 (SI 1990/144); the Criminal Justice Act 1991 s.100 and Sch.11, para.38(1) and (2) (see also s.101(2) and Sch.13); the Powers of Criminal Courts (Sentencing) Act 2000 s.165(1) and Sch.9, para.123; the Criminal Justice Act 2003 s.304, Sch.32, para.54 and Sch.37, Pt 7; the Road Safety Act 2006 s.9 and Sch.2, para.11.*

With effect from a day to be appointed and in relation to endorsement (all drivers), s.46(2)(b) will be amended by the Road Safety Act 2006 s.10 and Sch.3, para.43, s.59 and Sch.7(4) so that the words "the counterpart of any licence held by him or on" will be omitted.

As to the application of s.46(2) to Community licences, see s.91A(1) below.]

Supplementary provisions as to disqualifications and endorsements

A19.117 47.—(1) In any case where a court exercises its power under section 34, 35 or 44 of this Act not to order any disqualification or endorsement or to order disqualification for a shorter period than would otherwise be required, it must state the grounds for doing so in open court and, if it is a magistrates' court …, must cause them to be entered in the register … of its proceedings.

(2) Where a court orders the endorsement of [the counterpart of] any licence held by a person it may[, and where a court orders the holder of a licence to be disqualified for a period of 56 days or more it must,] send the [licence and its counterpart, on their] being produced to the court, to the Secretary of State; and if the court orders the endorsement but does not send the licence [and its counterpart] to the Secretary of State it must send him notice of the endorsement.

[(2A) Subsection (2) above is subject to section 2(2) of and paragraph 7(2) of Schedule 1 to the Road Traffic (New Drivers) Act 1995 [*q.v.*] (obligation of court to send licence and its counterpart to the Secretary of State).]

(3) Where on an appeal against [an order for the endorsement of a licence [or a driving record] or the disqualification of a person] the appeal is allowed, the court by which the appeal is allowed must send notice of that fact to the Secretary of State.

[(3A) On receiving such a notice in relation to a person who is not the holder of a licence, the Secretary of State must make any necessary adjustments to the endorsements on the person's driving record to reflect the outcome of the appeal.]

(4) A notice sent by a court to the Secretary of State in pursuance of this section must be sent in such manner and to such address and contain such particulars as the Secretary of State may determine, and a licence [and the counterpart of a licence] so sent in pursuance of this section must be sent to such address as the Secretary of State may determine.

A19.118 *[Section 47 is printed as amended by the Driving Licences (Community Driving Licence) Regulations 1990 (SI 1990/144); the Road Traffic Act 1991 s.48 and Sch.4, para.100(1)–(3); and the Road Traffic (New Drivers) Act 1995 s.10(4) and Sch.2, paras 3 and 4; the Road Safety Act 2006 s.9 and Sch.2, para.12.*

Words relating exclusively and expressly to Scotland have been omitted from s.47(1).

As to the application of s.47 to domestic driving permits, Convention driving permits, British Forces (BFG) driving licences and to the holders of such licences and permits, see the Motor Vehicles (Driving Licences) Regulations 1999 (SI 1999/2864) reg.80 below. As to the application of s.47(3) to Community licences, see s.91A(1) below.

With effect from a day to be appointed and in relation to endorsement (all drivers), the following amendments will be made to s.47 by the Road Safety Act 2006 s.10 and Sch.3, para.44, s.59 and Sch.7(4):

    1. *s.47(2) will be substituted as follows:*

> [(2) Where a court orders the endorsement of a person's driving record it may, and where a court orders a person to be disqualified for a period of 56 days or more it must, send any licence of the person that is produced to the court, to the Secretary of State.]

    2. *in s.47(2A), the words "and its counterpart" will be omitted;*

    3. *in s.47(3), the words "a licence or" will be omitted;*

    4. *in s.47(3A), the words "in relation to a person who is not the holder of a licence," will be omitted;*

    5. *in s.47(4), the words "and the counterpart of a licence" will be omitted.*

For the provisions relating to the commencement of ss.9 and 10 of and Schs 2 and 3 to the Road Safety Act 2006, see ibid. s.61(8) below.

With effect from a day to be appointed, the following amendments will be made to s.47 by the Coroners and Justice Act 2009 s.177 and Sch.21, Pt 9, para.90(9):

    1. *in s.47(2), as prospectively substituted by the Road Safety Act 2006 Sch.3, para.44(2) above, the words "(disregarding any extension period)" will be inserted after the words "or more";*

    2. *after s.47(2), the following text will be inserted:*

> [(2ZA) In subsection (2) *"extension period"* means an extension period added pursuant to—
>
>   (a) section 35A or 35C,
>
>   (b) section 248D of the Criminal Procedure (Scotland) Act 1995, or
>
>   (c) section 147A of the Powers of Criminal Courts (Sentencing) Act 2000.]

For transitory provisions in relation to the bringing into force of para.44(2) of Sch.3 to the Road Safety Act 2006 and the amendments in the 2009 Act, see the 2009 Act s.177 andSch.22, Pt 4, paras 30 and 33. Paragraph 33 of Sch.22 amends s.47(2) during the transitory period arising after the coming into force of that paragraph and ending with the coming into force of para.44(2) of Sch.3 to the 2006 Act.]

[Exemption from disqualification and endorsement for certain construction and use offences

48.—(1) Where a person is convicted of an offence under section 40A of the Road Traffic Act 1988 (using vehicle in dangerous condition, etc.) the court must not— **A19.119**

    (a) order him to be disqualified, or

    (b) order any particulars or penalty points to be endorsed on the counterpart of any licence held by him [or on his driving record], if he proves that he did not know, and had no reasonable cause to suspect, that the use of the vehicle involved a danger of injury to any person.

(2) Where a person is convicted of an offence under section 41A of the Road Traffic Act 1988 (breach of requirement as to brakes, steering-gear or tyres) the court must not—

(a) order him to be disqualified, or

(b) order any particulars or penalty points to be endorsed on the counter-part of any licence held by him [or on his driving record],

if he proves that he did not know, and had no reasonable cause to suspect, that the facts of the case were such that the offence would be committed.

(3) In relation to licences which came into force before 1st June 1990, the references in subsections (1) and (2) above to the counterpart of a licence shall be construed as references to the licence itself.]

A19.120   *[Section 48 is printed as substituted by the Road Traffic Act 1991 s.48 and Sch.4, para.101; the Road Safety Act 2006 s.9 and Sch.2, para.13.*

With effect from a day to be appointed and in relation to endorsement (all drivers), the following amendments will be made to s.48 by the Road Safety Act 2006 s.10 and Sch.3, para.45, s.59 and Sch.7(4):

     1. *in s.48(1) and (2), the words "the counterpart of any licence held by him or on" will be omitted;*

     2. *s.48(3) will be omitted.*

For the provisions relating to the commencement of ss.9 and 10 of and Schs 2 and 3 to the Road Safety Act 2006, see ibid. s.61(8) below.

As to the application of s.48(1) and (2) to Community licences, see s.91A(1) below.]

Offender escaping consequences of endorsable offence by deception

A19.121   **49.**—(1) This section applies where in dealing with a person convicted of an offence involving obligatory endorsement a court was deceived regarding any circumstances that were or might have been taken into account in deciding whether or for how long to disqualify him.

(2) If—

(a) the deception constituted or was due to an offence committed by that person, and

(b) he is convicted of that offence,

the court by or before which he is convicted shall have the same powers and duties regarding an order for disqualification as had the court which dealt with him for the offence involving obligatory endorsement but must, in dealing with him, take into account any order made on his conviction of the offence involving obligatory endorsement.

Powers of district court in Scotland

A19.122   **50.** *[Omitted.]*

PART III

FIXED PENALTIES

A19.123   *[As to the application of the provisions of Pt 3 (ss.51–90), other than ss.75(12),*

76(8) and 77(9), to Community licences where the licence holder has been issued with a counterpart, see s.91A(3) below.]

Introductory

Fixed penalty offences

51.—(1) Any offence in respect of a vehicle under an enactment specified in column 1 of Schedule 3 to this Act is a fixed penalty offence for the purposes of this Part of this Act, but subject to subsection (2) below and to any limitation or exception shown against the enactment in column 2 (where the general nature of the offence is also indicated).   **A19.124**

(2) An offence under an enactment so specified is not a fixed penalty offence for those purposes if it is committed by causing or permitting a vehicle to be used by another person in contravention of any provision made or restriction or prohibition imposed by or under any enactment.

(3) *[Power to vary fixed penalty offences by order.]*

[Proceedings under s.51(1) are specified by the Prosecution of Offences Act 1985 (Specified Proceedings) Order 1999 (SI 1999/904) below as being proceedings the conduct of which the Director of Public Prosecutions is not required to take over from the police under the Prosecution of Offences Act 1985 s.3(3)(a).]   **A19.125**

Fixed penalty notices

52.—(1) In this Part of this Act *"fixed penalty notice"* means a notice offering the opportunity of the discharge of any liability to conviction of the offence to which the notice relates by payment of a fixed penalty in accordance with this Part of this Act.   **A19.126**

(2) A fixed penalty notice must give such particulars of the circumstances alleged to constitute the offence to which it relates as are necessary for giving reasonable information about the alleged offence.

(3) A fixed penalty notice must state—

(a) the period during which, by virtue of section 78(1) of this Act, proceedings cannot be brought against any person for the offence to which the notice relates, being the period of twenty-one days following the date of the notice or such longer period (if any) as may be specified in the notice (referred to in this Part of this Act as the *"suspended enforcement period"*),

(b) the amount of the fixed penalty, and

(c) [the person to] whom and the address at which the fixed penalty may be paid.

(4) [...]

[Section 52 is printed as amended by the Access to Justice Act 1999 s.90(1) and Sch.13, paras 140 and 147; the Statute Law (Repeals) Act 2004 s.1(1) and Sch.1, Pt 14; the Courts Act 2003 s.109(1) and Sch.8, para.314; the Road Safety Act 2006 s.5 and Sch.1, para.1.   **A19.127**

Words relating exclusively and expressly to Scotland have been omitted from s.52(3)(c).]

[Amount of fixed penalty

53.—(1) The fixed penalty for an offence is—   **A19.128**

(a) such amount as the Secretary of State may by order prescribe, or

(b) one half of the maximum amount of the fine to which a person committing that offence would be liable on summary conviction,

whichever is the less.

[(2) Any order made under subsection (1)(a) above in relation to an offence may make provision for the fixed penalty for the offence to be different depending on the circumstances, including (in particular)—

(a) the nature of the contravention or failure constituting the offence,

(b) how serious it is,

(c) the area, or sort of place, where it takes place, and

(d) whether the offender appears to have committed any offence or offences of a description specified in the order during a period so specified.]

A19.129   *[Section 53 is printed as substituted by the Road Traffic Act 1991 s.48 and Sch.4, para.102 and as subsequently amended by the Road Safety Act 2006 s.3(2).].*

Giving notices to suspected offenders

Notices on the spot [etc.]

A19.130   **54.**—(1) This section applies where [in England and Wales] on any occasion a constable in uniform[, or a vehicle examiner who produces his authority] has reason to believe that a person he finds is committing or has on that occasion committed a fixed penalty offence.

(2) Subject to [the following provisions of this section, the constable [or vehicle examiner] may give him a fixed penalty notice in respect of the offence.

(3) Where the offence appears to the constable [or vehicle examiner] to involve obligatory endorsement[, and the person is the holder of a licence,] the constable [or vehicle examiner] may only give him a fixed penalty notice under subsection (2) above in respect of the offence if—

(a) he produces his licence [and its counterpart] for inspection by the constable [or vehicle examiner],

(b) the constable [or vehicle examiner] is satisfied, on inspecting the licence [and its counterpart], that he would not be liable to be disqualified under section 35 of this Act if he were convicted of that offence, and

(c) he surrenders his licence [and its counterpart] to the constable [or vehicle examiner] to be retained and dealt with in accordance with this Part of this Act.

(4) Where—

(a) the offence appears to the constable [or vehicle examiner] to involve obligatory endorsement,

[(aa) the person concerned is the holder of a licence, and]

(b) [he] does not produce his licence [and its counterpart] for inspection by the constable [or vehicle examiner],

the constable [or vehicle examiner] may give him a notice stating that if [he delivers] the notice together with his licence in [accordance with subsection (4A) below] and the requirements of subsection (5)(a) and (b) below are met he will then be given a fixed penalty notice in respect of the offence.

[(4A) Delivery must—

    (a) if the notice is given by a constable, be made in person, within seven days after the notice is given, to a constable or authorised person at the police station specified in the notice (being a police station chosen by the person concerned), or

    (b) if the notice is given by a vehicle examiner, be made (either by post or in person), within fourteen days after the notice is given, to the Secretary of State at the place specified in the notice.]

(5) If a person to whom a notice has been given under subsection (4) above [delievers] the notice together with his licence [and its counterpart] in [accordance with subsection (4A) above] and the following requirements are met, that is—

    (a) the [person to whom the notice under subsection (4) above is delivered] is satisfied, on inspecting the licence [and its counterpart], that he would not be liable to be disqualified under section 35 of this Act if he were convicted of the offence, and

    (b) [...] his licence [and its counterpart] [are delivered] to be retained and dealt with in accordance with this Part of this Act,

the [person to whom the notice under subsection (4) above is delivered] must give him a fixed penalty notice in respect of the offence to which the notice under subsection (4) above relates.

[(5A) Where the offence appears to the constable or vehicle examiner to involve obligatory endorsement, and the person is not the holder of a licence, the constable or vehicle examiner may only give him a fixed penalty notice under subsection (2) above in respect of the offence if the constable or vehicle examiner is satisfied, on accessing information held on his driving record, that he would not be liable to be disqualified under section 35 of this Act if he were convicted of that offence.

(5B) Subsection (5C) below applies where—

    (a) the offence appears to the constable or vehicle examiner to involve obligatory endorsement,

    (b) the person concerned is not the holder of a licence, and

    (c) the constable or vehicle examiner is unable to satisfy himself, by accessing information held on his driving record, that he would not be liable to be disqualified under section 35 of this Act if he were convicted of that offence.

(5C) Where this subsection applies, the constable or vehicle examiner may give the person a notice stating that if—

    (a) he delivers the notice in accordance with subsection (5D) below, and

    (b) the person to whom it is delivered is satisfied, on accessing information held on his driving record, that he would not be liable to be disqualified under section 35 of this Act if he were convicted of that offence,

he will then be given a fixed penalty notice in respect of the offence.

(5D) Delivery must—

(a) if the notice is given by a constable, be made in person, within seven days after the notice is given, to a constable or authorised person at the police station specified in the notice (being a police station chosen by the person concerned), or

(b) if the notice is given by a vehicle examiner, be made (either by post or in person), within fourteen days after the notice is given, to the Secretary of State at the place specified in the notice.

(5E) If a person to whom a notice has been given under subsection (5C) above delivers the notice in accordance with subsection (5D) above, and the person to whom it is delivered is satisfied, on accessing information held on his driving record, that he would not be liable to be disqualified under section 35 of this Act if he were convicted of the offence, that person must give him a fixed penalty notice in respect of the offence to which the notice under subsection (5C) relates.]

(6) A notice under subsection (4) [or (5C)] above shall give such particulars of the circumstances alleged to constitute the offence to which it relates as are necessary for giving reasonable information about the alleged offence.

(7) A licence [and the counterpart of a licence] surrendered [or delivered] in accordance with this section must be sent to the fixed penalty clerk [if the fixed penalty notice was given by a constable or authorised person].

(8) [...]

(9) In this Part of this Act *"authorised person"*, in relation to a fixed penalty notice given at a police station, means a person authorised for the purposes of this section by or on behalf of the chief officer of police for the area in which the police station is situated [or a person authorised for those purposes by or on behalf of the chief constable of the British Transport Police].

[(10) In determining for the purposes of [this section] whether a person convicted of an offence would be liable to disqualification under section 35, it shall be assumed, in the case of an offence in relation to which a range of numbers is shown in the last column of Part I of Schedule 2 to this Act, that the number of penalty points to be attributed to the offence would be the lowest in the range.]

A19.131   *[Section 54 is printed as amended by the Driving Licences (Community Driving Licence) Regulations 1990 (SI 1990/144); the Road Traffic Act 1991 ss.48, 83, Sch.4, para.103(1)–(3), and Sch.8; the Police Reform Act 2002 s.76(1) and (2) (with respect to England and Wales only); the Road Safety Act 2006 s.5 and Sch.1, para.3, s.9, s.59 and Sch.7(2), s.9 and Sch.2, para.14.*

With effect from a day (or days) to be appointed and in relation to endorsement (all drivers), s.54 will be amended as follows:

1. *the following text will be substituted for s.54(3)–(5E) by the Road Safety Act 2006 s.10(4):*

[(3) Where the offence appears to the constable or vehicle examiner to involve obligatory endorsement, the constable or vehicle examiner may only give him a fixed penalty notice under subsection (2) above in respect of the offence if—

(a) the constable or vehicle examiner is satisfied, on accessing information held on his driving record, that he would not be liable to be disqualified under section 35 of this Act if he were convicted of that offence, and

(b) in the case of a person who is the holder of a licence, he produces it for inspection by the constable or vehicle examiner and surrenders it to him to be retained and dealt with in accordance with this Part of this Act.

(4) Where the offence appears to the constable or vehicle examiner to involve obligatory endorsement, subsection (5) below applies if—

(a) the constable or vehicle examiner is unable to satisfy himself, by accessing information held on his driving record, that he would not be liable to be disqualified under section 35 of this Act if he were convicted of that offence, or

(b) in the case of a person who is the holder of a licence, he does not produce it for inspection by the constable or vehicle examiner.

(5) Where this subsection applies, the constable or vehicle examiner may give the person a notice stating that if—

(a) he delivers the notice and (if he is the holder of a licence) his licence in accordance with subsection (5A) below, and

(b) the requirements of subsection (5B) below are met,

he will then be given a fixed penalty notice in respect of the offence.

(5A) Delivery must—

(a) if the notice is given by a constable, be made in person, within seven days after the notice is given, to a constable or authorised person at the police station specified in the notice (being a police station chosen by the person concerned), or

(b) if the notice is given by a vehicle examiner, be made (either by post or in person), within fourteen days after the notice is given, to the Secretary of State at the place specified in the notice.

(5B) If a person to whom a notice has been given under subsection (5) above delivers the notice and (if he is the holder of a licence) his licence in accordance with subsection (5A) above, and the following requirements are met, that is—

(a) the person to whom the notice is delivered is satisfied, on accessing information held on his driving record, that he would not be liable to be disqualified under section 35 of this Act if he were convicted of the offence, and

(b) if he is the holder of a licence, it is delivered to be retained and dealt with in accordance with this Part of this Act,

the person to whom the notice is delivered must give him a fixed penalty notice in respect of the offence to which the notice under subsection (5) above relates.]

2. *in s.54(6), "(5)" will be substituted for "(4) or (5C)" by the Road Safety Act 2006 s.10(5);*

3. *in s.54(7), the words "and a counterpart of a licence" will be omitted by the Road Safety Act 2006 s.10(6), s.59 and Sch.7(4).*

For the provisions relating to the commencement of ss.9 and 10 of and Schs 2 and 3 to the 2006 Act, see ibid. s.61(8) below.

For the power of civilians designated or accredited by a chief officer of police to give a person a fixed penalty notice under this section for an offence under s.72 of the Highway Act 1835 (riding on a footway), see the Police Reform Act 2002 ss.38, 41 and Sch.4, para.2(b), Sch.5, para.1(2); not reproduced in this work.]

Effect of fixed penalty notice given under section 54

55.—(1) This section applies where a fixed penalty notice relating to an   **A19.132**

offence has been given to any person under section 54 of this Act, and references in this section to the recipient are to the person to whom the notice was given.

(2) No proceedings shall be brought against the recipient for the offence to which the fixed penalty notice relates unless before the end of the suspended enforcement period he has given notice requesting a hearing in respect of that offence in the manner specified in the fixed penalty notice.

(3) Where—

    (a) the recipient has not given notice requesting a hearing in respect of the offence to which the fixed penalty notice relates in the manner so specified, and

    (b) the fixed penalty has not been paid in accordance with this Part of this Act before the end of the suspended enforcement period,

a sum equal to the fixed penalty plus one-half of the amount of that penalty may be registered under section 71 of this Act for enforcement against the recipient as a fine.

Licence receipts

A19.133   **56.**—(1) A [person] to whom a person surrenders [or delivers] his licence [and its counterpart] on receiving a fixed penalty notice given to him under section 54 of this Act must issue a receipt for the licence [and its counterpart] under this section.

(2) [Where the duty in section 54(7) of this Act applies, the] fixed penalty clerk may, on the application of a person who has surrendered [or delivered] his licence [and its counterpart] in those circumstances, issue a new receipt for [them].

(3) A receipt issued under this section ceases to have effect—

    (a) if issued [under subsection (1) above], on the expiration of the period of one month beginning with the date of issue or such longer period as may be prescribed, and

    (b) if issued [under subsection (2) above], on such date as he may specify in the receipt,

or, if earlier, on the return of the licence [and its counterpart] to the licence holder.

A19.134   *[Section 56 is printed as amended by the Driving Licences (Community Driving Licence) Regulations 1990 (SI 1990/144); the Road Safety Act 2006 s.5 and Sch.1, para.4.*

With effect from a day to be appointed and in relation to endorsement (all drivers), the following amendments will be made to s.56 by the Road Safety Act 2006 s.10 and Sch.3, para.46, s.59 and Sch.7(4):

    1. *the words "and its counterpart" will be omitted in each place;*

    2. *s.56(2) the word "it" will be substituted for the word "them".]*

Endorsement of [counterparts] without hearings

A19.135   **57.**—(1) Subject to subsection (2) below, where a person [who is the holder of a licence] (referred to in this section as "the licence holder") [has been given a fixed penalty notice under section 54 of this Act in respect of an offence involving obligatory endorsement,] [the counterpart of] his licence may be endorsed in accordance with this section without any order of a court.

(2) [The counterpart of] a person's licence may not be endorsed under this section if at the end of the suspended enforcement period—

    (a) he has given notice, in the manner specified in the fixed penalty notice, requesting a hearing in respect of the offence to which the fixed penalty notice relates, and

    (b) the fixed penalty has not been paid in accordance with this Part of this Act.

(3) On the payment of the fixed penalty before the end of the suspended enforcement period, the [person to whom it is paid] must endorse the relevant particulars on the [the counterpart of] licence and return it [together with the licence] to the licence holder.

(4) Where any sum determined by reference to the fixed penalty is registered under section 71 of this Act for enforcement against the licence holder as a fine, the [person to whom the fixed penalty is required to be paid] must endorse the relevant particulars on the [counterpart of the] licence and return it [together with the licence] to the licence holder—

    (a) if he is himself [the person] who registers that sum, on the registration of that sum, and

    (b) in any other case, on being notified of the registration by [the person] who registers that sum.

(5) References in this section to the relevant particulars are to—

    (a) particulars of the offence, including the date when it was committed, and

    (b) the number of penalty points to be attributed to the offence.

(6) [Where the endorsement of] [the counterpart of] a person's licence under this section [is made by the fixed penalty clerk] the fixed penalty clerk must send notice of the endorsement and of the particulars endorsed to the Secretary of State.

[(7) Subsections (3) and (4) above are subject to section 2(4)(a) of and paragraph 7(4)(a) of Schedule 1 to the Road Traffic (New Drivers) Act 1995 [*q.v.*]; and the fixed penalty clerk need not comply with subsection (6) above in a case where he sends a person's licence and its counterpart to the Secretary of State under section 2(4)(b) of or paragraph 7(4)(b) of Schedule 1 to that Act.]

[Section 57 is printed as amended by the Driving Licences (Community Driving Licence) Regulations 1990 (SI 1990/144); the Road Traffic (New Drivers) Act 1995 s.10(4) and Sch.2, paras 3 and 5; the Road Safety Act 2006 s.5 and Sch.1, para.5(2), and s.9 and Sch.2, para.15.   **A19.136**

With effect from a day to be appointed and in relation to endorsement (all drivers), s.57 will be omitted by the Road Safety Act 2006 s.10(7), s.59 and Sch.7(4).]

[Endorsement of driving records without hearings

57A.—(1) Subject to subsection (2) below, where a person who is not the   **A19.137** holder of a licence has been given a fixed penalty notice under section 54 of this Act in respect of an offence involving obligatory endorsement, his driving record may be endorsed in accordance with this section without any order of a court.

(2) A person's driving record may not be endorsed under this section if at the end of the suspended enforcement period—

(a) he has given notice, in the manner specified in the fixed penalty notice, requesting a hearing in respect of the offence to which the fixed penalty notice relates, and

(b) the fixed penalty has not been paid in accordance with this Part of this Act.

(3) If payment of the fixed penalty is made before the end of the suspended enforcement period and the person to whom the payment is made is the fixed penalty clerk, the fixed penalty clerk must send to the Secretary of State notice of the relevant particulars which are to be endorsed on the person's driving record.

(4) Where any sum determined by reference to the fixed penalty is registered under section 71 of this Act for enforcement against the person as a fine in a case where the fixed penalty is required to be paid to the fixed penalty clerk, the fixed penalty clerk must send to the Secretary of State notice of the relevant particulars which are to be endorsed on the person's driving record—

(a) if he is himself the person who registers the sum, on the registration of that sum, and

(b) in any other case, on being notified of the registration by the person who registers that sum.

(5) The Secretary of State must endorse the relevant particulars on the person's driving record if—

(a) he receives notice of them under subsection (3) or (4) above,

(b) the fixed penalty is paid to him before the end of the suspended enforcement period, or

(c) in a case where the fixed penalty is required to be paid to the Secretary of State, any sum determined by reference to the fixed penalty is registered under section 71 of this Act for enforcement against the person as a fine.

(6) References in this section to the relevant particulars are to—

(a) particulars of the offence, including the date when it was committed, and

(b) the number of penalty points to be attributed to the offence.]

A19.138   *[Section 57A is printed as inserted by the Road Safety Act 2006 s.9(5).*

With effect from a day to be appointed and in relation to endorsement (all drivers), s.57A (as inserted) will be amended as follows by the Road Safety Act 2006 s.10(9)–(11), s.59 and Sch.7(4):

1. *in s.57A(1), the words "who is not the holder of the licence" will be omitted;*

2. *in s.57A(3), the words "and return to that person any licence surrendered by him under section 54 of this Act" will be inserted at the end;*

3. *in s.57A(4), the words "and return to that person any licence surrendered by him under section 54 of this Act" will be inserted after the word "record".*

For the provisions relating to the commencement of s.10 of the 2006 Act, see ibid. s.61(8) below.]

Effect of endorsement [of counterpart] without hearing

A19.139   58.—(1) Where [the counterpart of] a person's licence is endorsed under section 57 of this Act he shall be treated for the purposes of sections 13(4), 28, 29 and 45 of this Act and of the Rehabilitation of Offenders Act 1974 as if—

    (a) he had been convicted of the offence,

    (b) the endorsement had been made in pursuance of an order made on his conviction by a court under section 44 of this Act, and

    (c) the particulars of the offence endorsed by virtue of section 57(5)(a) of this Act were particulars of his conviction of that offence.

(2) In relation to any endorsement of [the counterpart of] a person's licence under section 57 of this Act —

    (a) the reference in section 45(4) of this Act to the order for endorsement, and

    (b) the references in section 13(4) of this Act to any order made on a person's conviction,

are to be read as references to the endorsement itself.

[Section 58 is printed as amended by the Driving Licences (Community Driv-   **A19.140**
ing Licence) Regulations 1990 (SI 1990/144); the Road Safety Act 2006 s.9 and Sch.2, para.16.

With effect from a day to be appointed and in relation to endorsement (all drivers), s.58 will be omitted by the Road Safety Act 2006 s.10 and Sch.3, para.47, s.59 and Sch.7(4).

For the provisions relating to the commencement of ss.9 and 10 of and Schs 2 and 3 to the Road Safety Act 2006, see ibid. s.61(8).]

[Effect of endorsement of driving record without hearing

58A.—(1) Where a person's driving record is endorsed under section 57A of   **A19.141**
this Act he shall be treated for the purposes of sections 13(4), 28, 29 and 45A of this Act and of the Rehabilitation of Offenders Act 1974 as if—

    (a) he had been convicted of the offence,

    (b) the endorsement had been made in pursuance of an order made on his conviction by a court under section 44 of this Act, and

    (c) the particulars of the offence endorsed by virtue of section 57A(6)(a) of this Act were particulars of his conviction of that offence.

(2) In relation to any endorsement of a person's driving record under section 57A of this Act, the references in section 13(4) of this Act to any order made on a person's conviction are to be read as references to the endorsement itself.]

[Section 58A is printed as inserted by the Road Safety Act 2006 s.9 and Sch.2,   **A19.142**
para.17.

For the provisions relating to the commencement of s.9 of and Sch.2 to the Road Safety Act 2006, see ibid. s.61(8).]

Notification of court and date of trial in England and Wales

59. [...]   **A19.143**

[Repealed by the Statute Law (Repeals) Act 2004 s.1(1) and Sch.1, Pt 14.]

Court procedure in Scotland

60. [...]   **A19.144**

[Repealed by the Road Traffic Act 1991 s.83 and Sch.8.]

Fixed penalty notice mistakenly given [to licence holder]: exclusion of fixed penalty procedures

A19.145 　　**61.**—(1) This section applies where, on inspection of a licence [and its counterpart] [surrendered or delivered under section 54] of this Act, it appears to the fixed penalty clerk [or the Secretary of State] that the person whose licence it is would be liable to be disqualified under section 35 of this Act if he were convicted of the offence in respect of which the fixed penalty notice was given.

(2) The [counterpart of the] licence [must not be endorsed] under section 57 of this Act but [if it was sent to the fixed penalty clerk he] must instead send it to the chief officer of police.

(3) Nothing in this Part of this Act prevents proceedings being brought in respect of the offence in respect of which the fixed penalty notice was given where those proceedings are commenced before the end of the period of six months beginning with the date on which that notice was given.

(4) Where proceedings in respect of that offence are commenced before the end of that period, the case is from then on to be treated in all respects as if no fixed penalty notice had been given in respect of the offence.

(5) Accordingly, where proceedings in respect of that offence are so commenced, any action taken in pursuance of any provision of this Part of this Act by reference to that fixed penalty notice shall be void (including, but without prejudice to the generality of the preceding provision—

> (a) the registration under section 71 of this Act of any sum, determined by reference to the fixed penalty for that offence, for enforcement against the person whose licence it is as a fine, and
>
> (b) any proceedings for enforcing payment of any such sum within the meaning of sections 73 and 74 of this Act (defined in section 74(5)).

[(6) In determining for the purposes of subsection (1) above whether a person convicted of an offence would be liable to disqualification under section 35, it shall be assumed, in the case of an offence in relation to which a range of numbers is shown in the last column of Part I of Schedule 2 to this Act, that the number of penalty points to be attributed to the offence would be the lowest in the range.]

A19.146 　　*[Section 61 is printed as amended by the Driving Licences (Community Driving Licence) Regulations 1990 (SI 1990/144); the Road Traffic Act 1991 s.48 and Sch.4, para.104; the Road Safety Act 2006 s.5 and Sch.1, para.6, s.59 and Sch.7(2), s.9 and Sch.2, para.18.*

With effect from a day to be appointed and in relation to endorsement (all drivers), s.61 will be omitted by the Road Safety Act 2006 s.10 and Sch.3, para.48, s.59 and Sch.7(4).

For the provisions relating to the commencement of ss.9 and 10 of and Schs 2 and 3 to the Road Safety Act 2006, see ibid. s.61(8).]

[Fixed penalty notice mistakenly given to unlicensed person: exclusion of fixed penalty procedures

A19.147 　　**61A.**—(1) This section applies where, on accessing information held on the driving record of a person to whom a fixed penalty notice was given under section 54 of this Act, but who is not the holder of a licence, it appears to the fixed penalty clerk or the Secretary of State that the person would be liable to be disqualified under section 35 of this Act if he were convicted of the offence in respect of which the fixed penalty notice was given.

(2) The person's driving record must not be endorsed under section 57A of this Act.

(3) In a case where the fixed penalty is required to be paid to the fixed penalty clerk he must not send notice to the Secretary of State under section 57A of this Act but instead must notify the chief officer of police that the person to whom the fixed penalty notice was given would be liable to be disqualified under section 35 of this Act if he were convicted of the offence in respect of which the fixed penalty notice was given.

(4) Nothing in this Part of this Act prevents proceedings being brought in respect of the offence in respect of which the fixed penalty notice was given where those proceedings are commenced before the end of the period of six months beginning with the date on which that notice was given.

(5) Where proceedings in respect of that offence are commenced before the end of that period, the case is from then on to be treated in all respects as if no fixed penalty notice had been given in respect of the offence.

(6) Accordingly, where proceedings in respect of that offence are so commenced, any action taken in pursuance of this Part of this Act by reference to that fixed penalty notice shall be void (including, but without prejudice to the generality of the preceding provision—

    (a) the registration under section 71 of this Act of any sum, determined by reference to the fixed penalty for that offence, for enforcement against the person to whom the fixed penalty

notice was given, and

    (b) any proceedings for enforcing payment of any such sum within the meaning of sections 73 and 74 of this Act (defined in section 74(5)).

(7) In determining for the purposes of subsection (1) above whether a person convicted of an offence would be liable to disqualification under section 35, it shall be assumed, in the case of an offence in relation to which a range of numbers is shown in the last column of Part 1 of Schedule 2 to this Act, that the number of penalty points to be attributed to the offence would be the lowest in the range.]

[Section 61A is printed as inserted by the Road Safety Act 2006 s.9 and Sch.2, **A19.148**
para.19.

With effect from a day to be appointed and in relation to endorsement (all drivers), s.61A will be amended by the Road Safety Act 2006 s.10 and Sch.3, para.49, s.59 and Sch.7(4) as follows:

    1. *s.61A(1), the words "but who is not the holder of a licence," will be omitted;*

    2. *in s.61A(3), the words "and send the chief officer of police any licence sent to him under section 54(7) of this Act" will be inserted at the end;*

    3. *in the heading, the words "**to unlicensed person**" will be omitted.*

For the provisions relating to the commencement of ss.9 and 10 of and Schs 2 and 3 to the Road Safety Act 2006, see ibid. s.61(8).]

Notices fixed to vehicles

Fixing notices to vehicles

A19.149   **62.**—(1) Where on any occasion a constable [or a vehicle examiner] has reason to believe in the case of any stationary vehicle that a fixed penalty offence is being or has on that occasion been committed in respect of it, he may fix a fixed penalty notice in respect of the offence to the vehicle unless the offence appears to him to involve obligatory endorsement.

(2) A person is guilty of an offence if he removes or interferes with any notice fixed to a vehicle under this section, unless he does so by or under the authority of the driver or person in charge of the vehicle or the person liable for the fixed penalty offence in question.

A19.150   *[Section 62 is printed as amended by the Road Safety Act 2006 s.5 and Sch.1, para.7.]*

Service of notice to owner if penalty not paid

A19.151   **63.**—(1) This section applies where a fixed penalty notice relating to an offence has been fixed to a vehicle under section 62 of this Act.

(2) Subject to subsection (3) below, if at the end of the suspended enforcement period the fixed penalty has not been paid in accordance with this Part of this Act, a notice under this section may be served by or on behalf of the [relevant person] on any person who appears to him (or to any person authorised to act on his behalf for the purposes of this section) to be the owner of the vehicle.
Such a notice is referred to in this Part of this Act as a *"notice to owner"*.

[(2A) In this section *"the relevant person"* means—

    (a) if the fixed penalty notice was fixed by a constable, the chief officer of police, and

    (b) if it was fixed by a vehicle examiner, the Secretary of State.]

(3) Subsection (2) above does not apply where before the end of the suspended enforcement period—

    (a) any person has given notice requesting a hearing in respect of the offence in the manner specified in the fixed penalty notice, and

    (b) the notice so given contains a statement by that person to the effect that he was the driver of the vehicle at the time when the offence is alleged to have been committed.

That time is referred to in this Part of this Act as the *"time of the alleged offence"*.

(4) A notice to owner—

    (a) must give particulars of the alleged offence and of the fixed penalty concerned,

    (b) must state the period allowed for response to the notice, and

    (c) must indicate that, if the fixed penalty is not paid before the end of that period, the person on whom the notice is served is asked to provide before the end of that period to the [relevant person] a statutory statement of ownership (as defined in Part I of Schedule 4 to this Act).

(5) For the purposes of this Part of this Act, the period allowed for response to

a notice to owner is the period of twenty-one days from the date on which the notice is served, or such longer period (if any) as may be specified in the notice.

(6) A notice to owner relating to any offence must indicate that the person on whom it is served may, before the end of the period allowed for response to the notice, either—

(a) give notice requesting a hearing in respect of the offence in the manner indicated by the notice, or

(b) if—

  (i) he was not the driver of the vehicle at the time of the alleged offence, and

  (ii) a person purporting to be the driver wishes to give notice requesting a hearing in respect of the offence,

provide, together with a statutory statement of ownership provided as requested in that notice, a statutory statement of facts (as defined by Part II of Schedule 4 to this Act) having the effect referred to in paragraph 3(2) of that Schedule (that is, as a notice requesting a hearing in respect of the offence given by the driver).

(7) In any case where a person on whom a notice to owner relating to any offence has been served provides a statutory statement of facts in pursuance of subsection (6)(b) above—

(a) any notice requesting a hearing in respect of the offence that he purports to give on his own account shall be of no effect, and

(b) no sum may be registered for enforcement against him as a fine in respect of the offence unless, within the period of two months immediately following the period allowed for response to the notice to owner, no summons … in respect of the offence in question is served on the person identified in the statement as the driver.

[Section 63 is printed as amended by the Road Safety Act 2006 s.5 and Sch.1, **A19.152** *para.8.*

Words relating exclusively and expressly to Scotland have been omitted from s.63(7).

Forms FP1 to FP6, Forms EC1 to EC6 and Form H for use in connection with ss.63 and 66 are prescribed by Sch.1 to the Road Traffic (Owner Liability) Regulations 2000 (SI 2000/2546; not reproduced in this work); forms to the like effect may be used. Forms FP1 and FP4 have been amended by the Road Traffic (Owner Liability) (Amendment) (No.2) Regulations 2001 (SI 2001/1222; not reproduced in this work).]

Enforcement or proceedings against owner

64.—(1) This section applies where—   **A19.153**

(a) a fixed penalty notice relating to an offence has been fixed to a vehicle under section 62 of this Act,

(b) a notice to owner relating to the offence has been served on any person under section 63(2) of this Act before the end of the period of six months beginning with the day on which the fixed penalty notice was fixed to the vehicle, and

(c) the fixed penalty has not been paid in accordance with this Part of this

Act before the end of the period allowed for response to the notice to owner.

(2) Subject to subsection (4) below and to section 63(7)(b) of this Act, a sum equal to the fixed penalty plus one-half of the amount of that penalty may be registered under section 71 of this Act for enforcement against the person on whom the notice to owner was served as a fine.

(3) Subject to subsection (4) below and to section 65 of this Act, proceedings may be brought in respect of the offence against the person on whom the notice to owner was served.

(4) If the person on whom the notice to owner was served—

(a) was not the owner of the vehicle at the time of the alleged offence, and

(b) provides a statutory statement of ownership to that effect in response to the notice before the end of the period allowed for response to the notice,

he shall not be liable in respect of the offence by virtue of this section nor shall any sum determined by reference to the fixed penalty for the offence be so registered by virtue of this section for enforcement against him as a fine.

(5) Subject to subsection (6) below—

(a) for the purposes of the institution of proceedings by virtue of subsection (3) above against any person on whom a notice to owner has been served, and

(b) in any proceedings brought by virtue of that subsection against any such person,

it shall be conclusively presumed (notwithstanding that that person may not be an individual) that he was the driver of the vehicle at the time of the alleged offence and, accordingly, that acts or omissions of the driver of the vehicle at that time were his acts or omissions.

(6) That presumption does not apply in any proceedings brought against any person by virtue of subsection (3) above if, in those proceedings, it is proved that at the time of the alleged offence the vehicle was in the possession of some other person without the consent of the accused.

(7) Where—

(a) by virtue of subsection (3) above proceedings may be brought in respect of an offence against a person on whom a notice to owner was served, and

(b) section 74(1) of this Act does not apply,

section 127(1) of the Magistrates' Courts Act 1980 (information must be laid within six months of time offence committed) … shall have effect as if for the reference to six months there were substituted a reference to twelve months.

A19.154   *[Words relating exclusively and expressly to Scotland in s.64(7) have been omitted.]*

Restrictions on proceedings against owner and others

A19.155   **65.**—(1) In any case where a notice to owner relating to an offence may be served under section 63 of this Act, no proceedings shall be brought in respect of the offence against any person other than a person on whom such a notice has been served unless he is identified as the driver of the vehicle at the time of the alleged offence in a statutory statement of facts provided in pursuance of section 63(6)(b) of this Act by a person on whom such a notice has been served.

(2) Proceedings in respect of an offence to which a notice to owner relates shall not be brought against the person on whom the notice was served unless, before the end of the period allowed for response to the notice, he has given notice, in the manner indicated by the notice to owner, requesting a hearing in respect of the offence.

(3) Proceedings in respect of an offence to which a notice to owner relates may not be brought against any person identified as the driver of the vehicle in a statutory statement of facts provided in response to the notice if the fixed penalty is paid in accordance with this Part of this Act before the end of the period allowed for response to the notice.

(4) Once any sum determined by reference to the fixed penalty for an offence has been registered by virtue of section 64 of this Act under section 71 for enforcement as a fine against a person on whom a notice to owner relating to that offence has been served, no proceedings shall be brought against any other person in respect of that offence.

Hired vehicles

66.—(1) This section applies where—

    (a) a notice to owner has been served on a vehicle-hire firm,

    (b) at the time of the alleged offence the vehicle in respect of which the notice was served was let to another person by the vehicle-hire firm under a hiring agreement to which this section applies, and

    (c) within the period allowed for response to the notice the firm provides the [relevant person] with the documents mentioned in subsection (2) below.

(2) Those documents are a statement on an official form, signed by or on behalf of the firm, stating that at the time of the alleged offence the vehicle concerned was hired under a hiring agreement to which this section applies, together with—

    (a) a copy of that hiring agreement, and

    (b) a copy of a statement of liability signed by the hirer under that hiring agreement.

(3) In this section a *"statement of liability"* means a statement made by the hirer under a hiring agreement to which this section applies to the effect that the hirer acknowledges that he will be liable, as the owner of the vehicle, in respect of any fixed penalty offence which may be committed with respect to the vehicle during the currency of the hiring agreement and giving such information as may be prescribed.

(4) In any case where this section applies, sections 63, 64 and 65 of this Act shall have effect as if—

    (a) any reference to the owner of the vehicle were a reference to the hirer under the hiring agreement, and

    (b) any reference to a statutory statement of ownership were a reference to a statutory statement of hiring,

and accordingly references in this Part of this Act (with the exceptions mentioned below) to a notice to owner include references to a notice served under section 63 of this Act as it applies by virtue of this section.

This subsection does not apply to references to a notice to owner in this section or in section 81(2)(b) of or Part I of Schedule 4 to this Act.

(5) In any case where this section applies, a person authorised in that behalf by the [person] to whom the documents mentioned in subsection (2) above are provided may, at any reasonable time within six months after service of the notice to owner (and on the production of his authority), require the firm to produce the originals of the hiring agreement and statement of liability in question.

(6) If a vehicle-hire firm fails to produce the original of a document when required to do so under subsection (5) above, this section shall thereupon cease to apply (and section 64 of this Act shall apply accordingly in any such case after that time as it applies in a case where the person on whom the notice to owner was served has failed to provide a statutory statement of ownership in response to the notice within the period allowed).

(7) This section applies to a hiring agreement under the terms of which the vehicle concerned is let to the hirer for a fixed period of less than six months (whether or not that period is capable of extension by agreement between the parties or otherwise); and any reference in this section to the currency of the hiring agreement includes a reference to any period during which, with the consent of the vehicle-hire firm, the hirer continues in possession of the vehicle as hirer, after the expiry of the fixed period specified in the agreement, but otherwise on the terms and conditions so specified.

(8) In this section—

   "hiring agreement" refers only to an agreement which contains such particulars as may be prescribed and does not include a hire-purchase agreement within the meaning of the Consumer Credit Act 1974, and

   [*"relevant person"* means—

   (a) if the fixed penalty notice was fixed by a constable, the chief officer of police by or on whose behalf the notice to owner was served, and

   (b) if it was fixed by a vehicle examiner, the Secretary of State, and]

   "vehicle-hire firm" means any person engaged in hiring vehicles in the course of a business.

A19.157   *[Section 66 is printed as amended by the Road Safety Act 2006 s.5 and Sch.1, para.9.*

The particulars to be contained in hiring agreements for the purposes of s.66(8) are prescribed in Sch.2 to the Road Traffic (Owner Liability) Regulations 2000 (SI 2000/2546; not reproduced in this work). As to forms for use in connection with s.66 and s.63, see the note to s.63 above.]

False statements in response to notices to owner

A19.158   **67.** A person who, in response to a notice to owner, provides a statement which is false in a material particular and does so recklessly or knowing it to be false in that particular is guilty of an offence.

"Owner", "statutory statement" and "official form"

A19.159   **68.**—(1) For the purposes of this Part of this Act, the owner of a vehicle shall be taken to be the person by whom the vehicle is kept; and for the purposes of determining, in the course of any proceedings brought by virtue of section 64(3) of this Act, who was the owner of a vehicle at any time, it shall be presumed that the owner was the person who was the registered keeper of the vehicle at that time.

(2) Notwithstanding the presumption in subsection (1) above, it is open to the defence in any proceedings to prove that the person who was the registered keeper of a vehicle at a particular time was not the person by whom the vehicle was kept at that time and to the prosecution to prove that the vehicle was kept by some other person at that time.

(3) References in this Part of this Act to statutory statements of any description are references to the statutory statement of that description defined in Schedule 4 to this Act; and that Schedule shall also have effect for the purpose of requiring certain information to be provided in official forms for the statutory statements so defined to assist persons in completing those forms and generally in determining what action to take in response to a notice to owner.

(4) In this Part of this Act *"official form"*, in relation to a statutory statement mentioned in Schedule 4 to this Act or a statement under section 66(2) of this Act, means a document supplied by or on behalf of a chief officer of police [or the Secretary of State] for use in making that statement.

[Section 68 is printed as amended by the Road Safety Act 2006 s.5 and Sch.1, para.10.]   **A19.160**

The fixed penalty procedure

Payment of penalty

69.—(1) [Where a fixed penalty notice has been given or fixed by a constable   **A19.161** or authorised person under this Part of this Act, payment of the fixed penalty] must be made to such [designated officer for a magistrates' court] … as may be specified in the fixed penalty notice relating to that penalty.

[(1A) Where a fixed penalty notice has been given or fixed by a vehicle examiner, or given by the Secretary of State, under this Part of this Act, payment of the fixed penalty must be made to the Secretary of State.]

(2) Without prejudice to payment by any other method, payment of a fixed penalty under this Part of this Act may be made by properly addressing, prepaying and posting a letter containing the amount of the penalty (in cash or otherwise) and, unless the contrary is proved, shall be regarded as having been made at the time at which that letter would be delivered in the ordinary course of post.

(3) A letter is properly addressed for the purposes of subsection (2) above if it is addressed to the fixed penalty clerk[, or the Secretary of State,] at the address specified in the fixed penalty notice relating to the fixed penalty as the address at which the fixed penalty may be paid.

(4) References in this Part of this Act [(except in sections 75 to [77A])], in relation to any fixed penalty or fixed penalty notice, to the fixed penalty clerk are references to the [designated officer or] clerk specified in accordance with subsection (1) above in the fixed penalty notice relating to that penalty or (as the case may be) in that fixed penalty notice.

A19.162   *[Section 69 is printed as amended by the Road Traffic Act 1991 s.48 and Sch.4, para.105; the Access to Justice Act 1999 s.90(1) and Sch.13, paras 140 and 148; the Courts Act 2003 s.109(1) and Sch.8, para.315; the Road Safety Act 2006 s.5 and Sch.1, para.11, and s.9 and Sch.2, para.20.*

Words relating exclusively and expressly to Scotland in s.69(1) have been omitted.]

Registration certificates

A19.163   **70.**—(1) This section and section 71 of this Act apply where by virtue of section 55(3) or 64(2) of this Act a sum determined by reference to the fixed penalty for any offence may be registered under section 71 of this Act for enforcement against any person as a fine.

In this section and section 71 of this Act —

>(a) that sum is referred to as a *"sum payable in default"*, and
>
>(b) the person against whom that sum may be so registered is referred to as the *"defaulter"*.

(2) Subject to subsection (3) below, the [relevant person] may in respect of any sum payable in default issue a certificate (referred to in this section and section 71 as a *"registration certificate"*) stating that the sum is registrable under section 71 for enforcement against the defaulter as a fine.

[(2A) In subsection (2) above *"the relevant person"* means—

>(a) if the fixed penalty notice in question was given or fixed by a constable or given by an authorised person, the chief officer of police, and
>
>(b) if it was given or fixed by a vehicle examiner or given by the Secretary of State, the Secretary of State.]

(3) *[Applies to Scotland.]*

[(3A) *[Applies to Scotland.]*]

(4) Where [a person] issues a registration certificate under this section, he must—

>(a) if the defaulter appears to him to reside in England and Wales, cause it to be sent to the [designated officer for the local justice] area in which the defaulter appears to him to reside, [...]
>
>(b) *[applies to Scotland]*; [and
>
>(c) otherwise—
>
>>(i) if the offence to which the fixed penalty notice or conditional offer relates was committed in England or Wales, cause it to be sent to the designated officer for the local justice area in which the offence was committed, or
>>
>>(ii) *[applies to Scotland].*]

(5) A registration certificate issued under this section in respect of any sum payable in default must—

>(a) give particulars of the offence to which the fixed penalty notice relates,
>
>(b) indicate whether registration is authorised under section 55(3) or 64(2) of this Act, and
>
>(c) state the name and last known address of the defaulter and the amount of the sum payable in default.

[Section 70 is printed as amended by the Access to Justice Act 1999 s.90(1) **A19.164**
and Sch.13, paras 140 and 149; the Courts Act 2003 s.109(1) and Sch.8,
para.316; the Road Safety Act 2006 s.5 and Sch.1, para.12, s.9 and Sch.2,
para.21(1), s.59 and Sch.7(3).]

Registration of sums payable in default

71.—[(1) Where, in England and Wales, a [the designated officer for a local   **A19.165**
justice area] receives a registration certificate issued under section 70 of this Act
in respect of any sum payable in default—

    (a) if it appears to him that the defaulter resides in a [local justice area for
which he is the designated officer], he must register that sum for
enforcement as a fine in that area by entering it in the register of a
magistrates' court [acting in] that area, [or]

    (b) if it appears to him that the defaulter resides in any [other local justice]
area in England and Wales, he must send the certificate to the
[designated officer for] for that area, or

    (c) if it appears to him that the defaulter resides in Scotland, he must send
the certificate to the clerk of the court of summary jurisdiction for the
area in which the defaulter appears to him to reside;] [or

    (d) if it appears to him that the defaulter does not reside in England, Wales
or … —

        (i) in a case where the offence to which the fixed penalty notice or
conditional offer relates was committed in the local justice area
for which he is the designated officer, he must register that sum
for enforcement as a fine in that area by entering it in the register
of a magistrates' court acting in that area,

       (ii) in a case where it was committed in another local justice area in
England and Wales, he must send the certificate to the designated
officer for that area, and

     (iii) *[applies to Scotland].]*

[(2) Where, in Scotland, the clerk of a court receives a registration certificate
issued under section 70 of this Act in respect of any sum payable in default—

    (a) if it appears to him that the defaulter resides in the area of the court,
he must register that sum for enforcement as a fine by that court, [or]

    (b) if it appears to him that the defaulter resides in the area of any other
court of summary jurisdiction in Scotland, he must send the certificate
to the clerk of that court, or

    (c) if it appears to him that the defaulter resides in England and Wales, he
must send the certificate to the [designated officer for the local justice]
area in which the defaulter appears to him to reside;] [or

    (d) if it appears to him that the defaulter does not reside in England, Wales
or … —

        (i) in a case where the offence to which the fixed penalty notice or
conditional offer relates was committed in the area of the court,
he must register that sum for enforcement as a fine by that court,

       (ii) *[applies to Scotland]*, and

     (iii) in a case where it was committed in England or Wales, he must send the certificate to the designated officer for the local justice area in which the offence was committed.]

[(2A) Subsections (1) and (2) apply to [officers] and clerks who receive certificates pursuant to the provision they contain as they apply to the original recipients.]

(3) Where—

    (a) the fixed penalty notice in question was given to the defaulter under section 54 of this Act in respect of an offence committed in Scotland, and

    (b) the defaulter appears to the fixed penalty clerk to reside within the jurisdiction of the court of summary jurisdiction of which he is himself the clerk,

the fixed penalty clerk must register the sum payable in default for enforcement as a fine by that court.

(4), (5) [...]

(6) On registering any sum under this section for enforcement as a fine, the [designated officer for a local justice] area or, as the case may be, the clerk of a court of summary jurisdiction must give to the defaulter notice of registration—

    (a) specifying the amount of that sum, and

    (b) giving the information with respect to the offence and the authority for registration included in the registration certificate by virtue of section 70(5)(a) and (b) of this Act or (in a case within subsection (3) above) the corresponding information.

(7) On the registration of any sum in a magistrates' court or a court of summary jurisdiction by virtue of this section any enactment referring (in whatever terms) to a fine imposed or other sum adjudged to be paid on the conviction of such a court shall have effect in the case in question as if the sum so registered were a fine imposed by that court on the conviction of the defaulter on the date of the registration.

(8) Accordingly, in the application by virtue of this section of the provisions of the Magistrates' Courts Act 1980 relating to the satisfaction and enforcement of sums adjudged to be paid on the conviction of a magistrates' court, section 85 of that Act (power to remit a fine in whole or in part) is not excluded by subsection (2) of that section (references in that section to a fine not to include any other sum adjudged to be paid on a conviction) from applying to a sum registered in a magistrates' court by virtue of this section.

(9) For the purposes of this section, where the defaulter is a body corporate, the place where that body resides and the address of that body are either of the following—

    (a) the registered or principal office of that body, and

    (b) the address which, with respect to the vehicle concerned, is the address recorded in the record kept under [the Vehicle Excise and Registration Act 1994] as being that body's address.

A19.166   *[Section 71 is printed as amended by the Vehicle Excise and Registration Act 1994 s.63 and Sch.3, para.25(1); the Access to Justice Act 1999 ss.90(1) and 106, Schs 13 (paras 140 and 150) and 15 (Pt V(7)); the Courts Act 2003 s.109(1) and Sch.8, para.317; the Road Safety Act 2006 s.9 and Sch.2, para.22(1)–(3).*

Words omitted above apply exclusively to Scotland.

Where a person is liable for a sum due and registered for enforcement under s.71 of the Road Traffic Offenders Act 1988, that person comes within the definition of "existing defaulter", see the Courts Act 2003 Sch.5, para.3 (collection of fines).]

Notices on-the-spot [etc.]: when registration and endorsement invalid

72.—(1) This section applies where—

    (a) a person who has received notice of the registration, by virtue of section 55(3) of this Act, of a sum under section 71 of this Act for enforcement against him as a fine makes a statutory declaration to the effect mentioned in subsection (2) below, and

    (b) that declaration is, within twenty-one days of the date on which the person making it received notice of the registration, served on the [proper officer] of the relevant court.

(2) The statutory declaration must state—

    (a) that the person making the declaration was not the person to whom the relevant fixed penalty notice was given, or

    (b) that he gave notice requesting a hearing in respect of the alleged offence as permitted by the fixed penalty notice before the end of the suspended enforcement period.

(3) In any case within subsection (2)(a) above, the relevant fixed penalty notice, the registration and any proceedings taken before the declaration was served for enforcing payment of the sum registered shall be void.

(4) Where in any case within subsection (2)(a) above the person to whom the relevant fixed penalty notice was given surrendered [or delivered] a licence [and its counterpart] held by the person making the declaration, any endorsement of [that counterpart] made under section 57 of this Act in respect of the offence in respect of which that notice was given shall be void.

[(4A) Where in any case within subsection (2)(a) above the driving record of the person to whom the relevant fixed penalty notice was given was endorsed under section 57A of this Act in respect of the offence in respect of which the notice was given, the endorsement shall be void.]

(5) In any case within subsection (2)(b) above—

    (a) the registration, any proceedings taken before the declaration was served for enforcing payment of the sum registered, and any endorsement, in respect of the offence in respect of which the relevant fixed penalty notice was given, made under section 57 [or 57A] of this Act before the declaration was served, shall be void, and

    (b) the case shall be treated after the declaration is served as if the person making the declaration had given notice requesting a hearing in respect of the alleged offence as stated in the declaration.

(6) The [proper officer] of the relevant court must—

    (a) cancel an endorsement of [the counterpart of] a licence under section 57 of this Act that is void by virtue of this section on production of the licence [and its counterpart] to him for that purpose, and

    (b) send notice of the cancellation to the Secretary of State.

[(6A) The proper officer of the relevant court must send notice to the Secretary of State of any endorsement of a person's driving record that is void by virtue of this section and the Secretary of State must adjust the endorsements on that record accordingly.]

(7) References in this section to the relevant fixed penalty notice are to the fixed penalty notice relating to the fixed penalty concerned.

A19.168   *[Section 72 is printed as amended by the Driving Licences (Community Driving Licence) Regulations 1990 (SI 1990/144); the Access to Justice Act 1999 s.90(1) and Sch.13, paras 140 and 151; the Road Safety Act 2006 s.5 and Sch.1, para.13, s.9 and Sch.2, para.23.*

With effect from a day to be appointed and in relation to endorsement (all drivers), s.72 will be amended by the Road Safety Act 2006 s.10 and Sch.3, para.50, s.59 and Sch.7(4) as follows:

      1. *s.72(4) will be omitted;*

      2. *in s.72(5), "57 or" will be omitted;*

      3. *s.72(6) will be omitted.*

For the provisions relating to the commencement of ss.9 and 10 of and Schs 2 and 3 to the 2006 Act, see ibid. s.61(8) below.]

Notices fixed to vehicles: when registration invalid

A19.169   **73.**—(1) This section applies where—

    (a) a person who has received notice of the registration, by virtue of section 64(2) of this Act, of a sum under section 71 of this Act for enforcement against him as a fine makes a statutory declaration to the effect mentioned in subsection (2) below, and

    (b) that declaration is, within twenty-one days of the date on which the person making it received notice of the registration, served on the [proper officer] of the relevant court.

  (2) The statutory declaration must state either—

    (a) that the person making the declaration did not know of the fixed penalty concerned or of any fixed penalty notice or notice to owner relating to that penalty until he received notice of the registration, or

    (b) that he was not the owner of the vehicle at the time of the alleged offence of which particulars are given in the relevant notice to owner and that he has a reasonable excuse for failing to comply with that notice, or

    (c) that he gave notice requesting a hearing in respect of that offence as permitted by the relevant notice to owner before the end of the period allowed for response to that notice.

  (3) In any case within subsection (2)(a) or (b) above—

    (a) the relevant notice to owner,

    (b) the registration, and

    (c) any proceedings taken before the declaration was served for enforcing payment of the sum registered,

shall be void but without prejudice, in a case within subsection (2)(a) above, to the service of a further notice to owner under section 63 of this Act on the person making the declaration.

This subsection applies whether or not the relevant notice to owner was duly served in accordance with that section on the person making the declaration.

(4) In any case within subsection (2)(c) above—

(a) no proceedings shall be taken, after the statutory declaration is served until the end of the period of twenty-one days following the date of that declaration, for enforcing payment of the sum registered, and

(b) where before the end of that period a notice is served by or on behalf of [the relevant person] on the person making the declaration asking him to provide a new statutory statement of ownership to [the relevant person] before the end of the period of twenty-one days from the date on which the notice is served, no such proceedings shall be taken until the end of the period allowed for response to that notice.

[(4A) In subsection (4) above *"the relevant person"* means—

(a) if the fixed penalty notice concerned was fixed by a constable, the fixed penalty clerk, and

(b) if it was fixed by a vehicle examiner, the Secretary of State.]

(5) Where in any case within subsection (2)(c) above—

(a) no notice is served […] in accordance with subsection (4) above, or

(b) […] a notice is so served and the person making the declaration provides a new statutory statement of ownership in accordance with the notice,

then—

(i) the registration and any proceedings taken before the declaration was served for enforcing payment of the sum registered shall be void, and

(ii) the case shall be treated after the time mentioned in subsection (6) below as if the person making the declaration had given notice requesting a hearing in respect of the alleged offence as stated in the declaration.

(6) The time referred to in subsection (5) above is—

(a) in a case within paragraph (a) of that subsection, the end of the period of twenty-one days following the date of the statutory declaration,

(b) in a case within paragraph (b) of that subsection, the time when the statement is provided.

(7) In any case where notice is served […] in accordance with subsection (4) above, [the person by whom it is served] must cause the [proper officer] of the relevant court to be notified of that fact immediately on service of the notice.

(8) References in this section to the relevant notice to owner are to the notice to owner relating to the fixed penalty concerned.

[Section 73 is printed as amended by the Access to Justice Act 1999 s.90(1)   **A19.170**
and Sch.13, paras 140 and 151; the Road Safety Act 2006 s.5 and Sch.1, para.14, s.59 and Sch.7(2).].

Provisions supplementary to sections 72 and 73

74.—(1) In any case within section 72(2)(b) or 73(2) of this Act —   **A19.171**

(a) section 127(1) of the Magistrates' Courts Act 1980 (limitation of time), and

(b) *[applies to Scotland.]*

shall have effect as if for the reference to the time when the offence was committed or (as the case may be) the time when the contravention occurred there were substituted a reference to the date of the statutory declaration made for the purposes of section 72(1) or, as the case may be, 73(1).

(2) Where, on the application of a person who has received notice of the registration of a sum under section 71 of this Act for enforcement against him as a fine, it appears to the relevant court (which for this purpose may be composed of a single justice) that it was not reasonable to expect him to serve, within twenty-one days of the date on which he received the notice, a statutory declaration to the effect mentioned in section 72(2) or, as the case may be, 73(2) of this Act, the court may accept service of such a declaration by that person after that period has expired.

(3) A statutory declaration accepted under subsection (2) above shall be taken to have been served as required by section 72(1) or, as the case may be, section 73(1) of this Act.

(4) For the purposes of sections 72(1) and 73(1) of this Act, a statutory declaration shall be taken to be duly served on the [proper officer] of the relevant court if it is delivered to him, left at his office, or sent in a registered letter or by the recorded delivery service addressed to him at his office.

(5) In sections 72, 73 and this section —

(a) references to the relevant court are—

(i) in the case of a sum registered under section 71 of this Act for enforcement as a fine in a [local justice] area in England and Wales, references to any magistrates' court acting [in that area], and

(ii) *[applies to Scotland.]*

[(b) references to the *"proper officer"* of the relevant court are—

(i) in the case of a magistrates' court, references to the [designated officer] for the court, and

(ii) *[applies to Scotland]*, and]

(c) references to proceedings for enforcing payment of the sum registered are references to any process issued or other proceedings taken for or in connection with enforcing payment of that sum.

(6) For the purposes of sections 72, 73 and this section, a person shall be taken to receive notice of the registration of a sum under section 71 of this Act for enforcement against him as a fine when he receives notice either of the registration as such or of any proceedings for enforcing payment of the sum registered.

(7) Nothing in the provisions of sections 72 or 73 or this section is to be read as prejudicing any rights a person may have apart from those provisions by virtue of the invalidity of any action purportedly taken in pursuance of this Part of this Act which is not in fact authorised by this Part of this Act in the circumstances of the case; and, accordingly, references in those provisions to the registration of any sum or to any other action taken under or by virtue of any provision of this Part of this Act are not to be read as implying that the registration or action was validly made or taken in accordance with that provision.

A19.172   *[Section 74 is printed as amended by the Access to Justice Act 1999 s.90(1) and Sch.13, paras 140 and 152; the Courts Act 2003 s.109(1) and Sch.8, para.318.]*

[Conditional offer of fixed penalty]

A19.173

[The above heading was substituted by the Road Traffic Act 1991 s.34.]

[Issue of conditional offer

  75.—(1) Where in England and Wales—   **A19.174**
- (a) a constable has reason to believe that a fixed penalty offence has been committed, and
- (b) no fixed penalty notice in respect of the offence has been given under section 54 of this Act or fixed to a vehicle under section 62 of this Act,

a notice under this section may be sent to the alleged offender by or on behalf of the chief officer of police [or, if the constable is a member of the British Transport Police, by or on behalf of the chief constable of the British Transport Police].

  [(1A) Where in England and Wales—
- (a) a vehicle examiner has reason to believe that a fixed penalty offence has been committed, and
- (b) no fixed penalty notice in respect of the offence has been given under section 54 of this Act or fixed to a vehicle under section 62 of this Act,

a notice under this section may be sent to the alleged offender by the Secretary of State.]

  (2)–(4) *[Apply to Scotland.]*

  (5) A notice under this section is referred to in this section and sections 76[, 77 and 77A] as a *"conditional offer"*.

  (6) Where a [conditional offer is issued by a person under subsection (1), (2) or (3) above], he must notify the [designated officer] ... specified in it of its issue and its terms; and [he] is referred to in this section and sections 76[, 77 and 77A] as *"the fixed penalty clerk"*.

  (7) A conditional offer must—
- (a) give such particulars of the circumstances alleged to constitute the offence to which it relates as are necessary for giving reasonable information about the alleged offence,
- (b) state the amount of the fixed penalty for that offence, and
- (c) state that proceedings against the alleged offender cannot be commenced in respect of that offence until the end of the period of twenty-eight days following the date on which the conditional offer was issued or such longer period as may be specified in the conditional offer.

  (8) A conditional offer [sent to an alleged offender who is the holder of a licence] must indicate that if the following conditions are fulfilled, that is—
- (a) within the period of twenty-eight days following the date on which the offer was issued, or such longer period as may be specified in the offer, the alleged offender—

> (i) makes payment of the fixed penalty to [the appropriate person], and
>
> (ii) where the offence to which the offer relates is an offence involving obligatory endorsement, at the same time delivers his licence and its counterpart to [the appropriate person], and
>
> (b) where his licence and its counterpart are so delivered, that clerk is satisfied on inspecting them that, if the alleged offender were convicted of the offence, he would not be liable to be disqualified under section 35 of this Act,

any liability to conviction of the offence shall be discharged.

[(8A) A conditional offer sent to an alleged offender who is not the holder of a licence must indicate that if the following conditions are fulfilled, that is—

> (a) within the period of twenty-eight days following the date on which the offer was issued, or such longer period as may be specified in the offer, the alleged offender makes payment of the fixed penalty to the appropriate person, and
>
> (b) the appropriate person is satisfied, on accessing information held on the driving record of the alleged offender, that if he were convicted of the offence, he would not be liable to be disqualified under section 35 of this Act,

any liability to conviction of the offence shall be discharged.]

(9) For the purposes of the [conditions] set out in subsection[s] (8)(b) [and (8A)(b)] above, it shall be assumed, in the case of an offence in relation to which a range of numbers is shown in the last column of Part I of Schedule 2 to this Act, that the number of penalty points to be attributed to the offence would be the lowest in the range.

(10) The Secretary of State may by order provide for offences to become or (as the case may be) to cease to be offences in respect of which a conditional offer may be sent under subsection (2)(b) above, and may make such modifications of the provisions of this Part of this Act as appear to him to be necessary for the purpose.

(11) *[Applies to Scotland.]*

[(11A) In this section and sections 76 and 77 of this Act *"the appropriate person"* means—

> (a) where the conditional offer was issued under subsection (1), (2) or (3) above, the fixed penalty clerk, and
>
> (b) where the conditional offer was issued under subsection (1A) or (3B) above, the Secretary of State.]

(12) In relation to licences which came into force before 1st June 1990, the references in subsection (8) above to the counterpart of a licence shall be disregarded.]

A19.175 *[Section 75 is printed as substituted by the Road Traffic Act 1991 s.34 and is printed as amended by the Access to Justice Act 1999 s.90(1) and Sch.13, paras 140 and 153; the Police Reform Act 2002 s.76(1) and (3) (with respect to England and Wales only); the Courts Act 2003 s.109(1) and Sch.8, para.319; the Road Safety Act 2006 s.5 and Sch.1, para.15, s.9 and Sch.2, para.24.*

With effect from a day to be appointed and in relation to endorsement (all

drivers), s.75 will be amended by the Road Safety Act 2006 s.10 and Sch.3,
para.51, s.59 and Sch.7(4) as follows:

    1. *in s.75(5) and (6), the words "and 77A" will be substituted for ", 77*
       and 77A";

    2. *s.75(8) will be omitted;*

    3. *in s.75(8A), the words "who is not the holder of a licence" will be*
       omitted, and in para.(a), the following text will be substituted for the
       words after "offender":

         [(i) makes payment of the fixed penalty to the appropriate person, and

         (ii) where he is the holder of a licence and the offence to which the offer
             relates is an offence involving obligatory endorsement, at the same
             time delivers his licence to the appropriate person, and]

    4. *s.75(12) will be omitted.*

   For the provisions relating to the commencement of ss.9 and 10 of and Schs 2
and 3 to the 2006 Act, see ibid. s.61(8) below.

   Words in s.75(6) relating expressly and exclusively to Scotland have been
omitted.]

[Effect of offer and payment of penalty

   76.—(1) This section applies where a conditional offer has been [issued] to a   **A19.176**
person under section 75 of this Act.

   [(2) Where the alleged offender makes payment of the fixed penalty in accordance with the conditional offer, no proceedings shall be brought against him for
the offence to which the offer relates unless subsection (3) below applies.

   (3) This subsection applies where—

     (a) it appears to the appropriate person, on inspecting the licence and its
         counterpart [or (where the alleged offender is not the holder of a
         licence) accessing information held on his driving record], that the alleged offender would be liable to be disqualified under section 35 of
         this Act if he were convicted of the offence to which the conditional
         offer relates,

     (b) the appropriate person returns the payment to the alleged offender
         together with [(where he is the holder of a licence)] his licence and its
         counterpart, and

     (c) where the appropriate person is not the Secretary of State, the appropriate person gives notice that he has done so to the person
         required to be notified.

   (4) Where the requirements specified in the conditional offer in accordance
with sub-paragraphs (i) and (ii) of section 75(8)(a) [or (8A)(a)] of this Act have
not been fulfilled, no proceedings shall be brought against the alleged offender
for the offence to which the offer relates—

     (a) until the end of the period of twenty-eight days following the date on
         which the conditional offer was made, or such longer period as may
         be specified in the offer, and

     (b) where the appropriate person is not the Secretary of State, unless the
         appropriate person notifies the person required to be notified that
         proceedings may be brought by virtue of this subsection.

(5) In this section and section 77 of this Act *"the person required to be notified"* means—

(a) if the conditional offer was issued under subsection (1) of section 75 of this Act, the chief officer of police,

(b) if it was issued under subsection (2) of that section, the procurator fiscal, and

(c) if it was issued under subsection (3) of that section, the chief constable or (as the case may be) the chief constable of the British Transport Police Force.]

(6) In determining for the purposes of subsection [(3)(a)] above whether a person convicted of an offence would be liable to disqualification under section 35, it shall be assumed, in the case of an offence in relation to which a range of numbers is shown in the last column of Part I of Schedule 2 to this Act, that the number of penalty points to be attributed to the offence would be the lowest in the range.

(7) In any proceedings a certificate that by a date specified in the certificate payment of a fixed penalty was or was not received by [the appropriate person] shall, if the certificate purports to be signed by [the appropriate person], be evidence ... of the facts stated.

(8) In relation to licences which came into force before 1st June 1990, the references in subsection [(3)] above to the counterpart of a licence shall be disregarded.

(9) *[Applies to Scotland.]]*

A19.177   *[Section 76 is printed as substituted by the Road Traffic Act 1991 s.34 and as amended by the Police Reform Act 2002 s.76(1), (4) (with respect to England and Wales only); the Railways and Transport Safety Act 2003 s.109 and Sch.8; the Road Safety Act 2006 s.5 and Sch.1, para.16, s.9 and Sch.2, para.25.*

With effect from a day to be appointed, s.76 will be amended by the Road Safety Act 2006 s.10 and Sch.3, para.52, s.59 and Sch.7(4) in relation to endorsement (all drivers) as follows:

1. *in s.76(3)(a), the words "inspecting the licence and its counterpart or (where the alleged offender is not the holder of a licence)" will be omitted; and the words "the alleged offender's" will be substituted for "his";*

2. *in s.76(3)(b), the words "and its counterpart" will be omitted;*

3. *in s.76(4), "75(8A)(a)" will be substituted for "75(8)(a) or (8A)(a)"*

4. *s.76(8) will be omitted.*

For the provisions relating to the commencement of ss.9 and 10 of and Schs 2 and 3 to the 2006 Act, see ibid. s.61(8) below.

Words in s.76(7) relating expressly and exclusively to Scotland have been omitted.]

[Endorsement [of counterparts] where penalty paid

A19.178   77.—(1) Where—

(a) in pursuance of a conditional offer a person [who is the holder of a licence] (referred to in this section as the *"licence holder"*) makes payment of the fixed penalty to [the appropriate person] and delivers his licence and its counterpart to [the appropriate person], and

[(b) proceedings against the alleged offender for the offence to which the conditional offer relates are excluded by section 76 of this Act,]
the [appropriate person] must forthwith endorse the relevant particulars on the counterpart of the licence and return it to the licence holder together with the licence.

(2) *[Applies to Scotland.]*

(3) Subject to subsection (4) below, where a cheque tendered in payment is subsequently dishonoured—

(a) any endorsement made by [the appropriate person] under subsection (1) above remains effective, notwithstanding that the licence holder is still liable to prosecution in respect of the alleged offence to which the endorsement relates, and

(b) [unless the appropriate person is the Secretary of State, the appropriate person] must, upon the expiry of the period specified in the conditional offer or, if the period has expired, forthwith notify the person [required to be notified] that no payment has been made.

(4) When proceedings are brought against a licence holder [where subsection (3) above applies], the court—

(a) must order the removal of the fixed penalty endorsement from the counterpart of the licence, and

(b) may, on finding the licence holder guilty, make any competent order of endorsement or disqualification and pass any competent sentence.

(5) The reference in subsection (1) above to the relevant particulars is to—

(a) particulars of the offence, including the date when it was committed, and

(b) the number of penalty points to be attributed to the offence.

(6) [Where the appropriate person is the fixed penalty clerk, he] must send notice to the Secretary of State—

(a) of any endorsement under subsection (1) above and of the particulars endorsed,

(b) of any amendment under subsection (2) above, and

(c) of any order under subsection (4)(a) above.

(7) Where the counterpart of a person's licence is endorsed under this section he shall be treated for the purposes of sections 13(4), 28, 29 and 45 of this Act and of the Rehabilitation of Offenders Act 1974 as if—

(a) he had been convicted of the offence,

(b) the endorsement had been made in pursuance of an order made on his conviction by a court under section 44 of this Act, and

(c) the particulars of the offence endorsed by virtue of subsection (5)(a) above were particulars of his conviction of that offence.

(8) In relation to any endorsement of the counterpart of a person's licence under this section —

(a) the reference in section 45(4) of this Act to the order for endorsement, and

(b) the references in section 13(4) of this Act to any order made on a person's conviction, are to be read as references to the endorsement itself.

(9) In relation to licences which came into force before 1st June 1990, the references in this section to the counterpart of a licence shall be disregarded or, as the case may require, construed as references to the licence itself.]

[(10) Subsection (1) above is subject to section 2(4)(a) of and paragraph 7(4)(a) of Schedule 1 to the Road Traffic (New Drivers) Act 1995 [*q.v.*] and the fixed penalty clerk need not send a notice falling within subsection (6)(a) above in a case where he sends a person's licence and its counterpart to the Secretary of State under section 2(4)(b) of or paragraph 7(4)(b) of Schedule 1 to that Act.]

A19.179   *[Section 77 is printed as substituted by the Road Traffic Act 1991 s.34, and as subsequently amended by the Road Traffic (New Drivers) Act 1995 s.10(4) and Sch.2, paras 3 and 6; the Road Safety Act 2006 s.5 and Sch.1, para.17 and s.9 and Sch.2, para.26.*

With effect from a day to be appointed and in relation to endorsement (all drivers), s.77 will be omitted by the Road Safety Act 2006 s.10 and Sch.3, para.53, s.59 and Sch.7(4).

For the provisions relating to the commencement of ss.9 and 10 of and Schs 2 and 3 to the 2006 Act, see ibid. s.61(8) below.]

[Endorsement of driving records where penalty paid

A19.180   **77A.**—(1) Where—

(a) in pursuance of a conditional offer issued under subsection (1), (2) or (3) of section 75 of this Act a person who is not the holder of a licence (referred to in this section as the "alleged offender") makes payment of the fixed penalty to the fixed penalty clerk, and

(b) proceedings against the alleged offender for the offence to which the conditional offer relates are excluded by section 76 of this Act,

the fixed penalty clerk must forthwith send to the Secretary of State notice of the relevant particulars to be endorsed on the alleged offender's driving record.

(2) The Secretary of State must endorse the relevant particulars on a person's driving record—

(a) on receiving notice under subsection (1) above, or

(b) if, in pursuance of a conditional offer issued under subsection (1A) or (3B) of section 75 of this Act, a person who is not the holder of a licence (also referred to in this section as the "alleged offender") makes payment of the fixed penalty to him and proceedings against the alleged offender are excluded by section 76 of this Act.

(3) Where in Scotland the appropriate person is the fixed penalty clerk and it appears to him that there is an error in an endorsement made by virtue of this section on a person's driving record, he may send to the Secretary of State notice of the error.

(4) Subject to subsection (5) below, where a cheque tendered in payment is subsequently dishonoured—

(a) any endorsement made by the Secretary of State under subsection (2) above remains effective notwithstanding that the alleged offender is still liable to prosecution in respect of the alleged offence to which the endorsement relates, and

(b) unless the appropriate person is the Secretary of State, the appropriate person must upon expiry of the period specified in the conditional offer or, if the period has expired, forthwith notify the person required to be notified that no payment has been made.

(5) When proceedings are brought against an alleged offender where subsection (4) above applies, the court—

(a) must order the removal of the fixed penalty endorsement from the driving record of the alleged offender,

(b) may, on finding the alleged offender guilty, make any competent order of endorsement or disqualification and pass any competent sentence, and

(c) must send to the Secretary of State notice of any order made under paragraph (a) or (b) above.

(6) On receiving notice under subsection (3) above, the Secretary of State may correct the error in the endorsement on the driving record; and any endorsement corrected shall be treated for all purposes as if it had been correctly made on receipt of the fixed penalty.

(7) On receiving a notice under subsection (5)(c) above, the Secretary of State must make any necessary adjustments to the endorsements on the alleged offender's driving record.

(8) The references in subsection (1) and (2) above to the relevant particulars are to—

(a) particulars of the offence, including the date when it was committed, and

(b) the number of penalty points to be attributed to the offence.

(9) Where a person's driving record is endorsed under this section he shall be treated for the purposes of sections 13(4), 28, 29 and 45A of this Act and of the Rehabilitation of Offenders Act 1974 as if—

(a) he had been convicted of the offence,

(b) the endorsement had been made in pursuance of an order made on his conviction by a court under section 44 of this Act, and

(c) the particulars of the offence endorsed by virtue of subsection (8)(a) above were particulars of his conviction of that offence.

(10) In relation to any endorsement of a person's driving record under this section, the references in section 13(4) of this Act to any order made on a person's conviction are to be read as references to the endorsement itself.]

[Section 77A is printed as inserted by the Road Safety Act 2006 s.9 and Sch.2, **A19.181**
para.27.

With effect from a day to appointed and in relation to endorsement (all drivers), s.77A (as inserted) will be amended by the Road Safety Act 2006 s.10 and Sch.3, para.54, s.59 and Sch.7(4) as follows:

1. *in s.77A(1), the words "who is not the holder of a licence" will be omitted, the words "and (if he is the holder of a licence) delivers his licence to the fixed penalty clerk" will be inserted after the words "to the fixed penalty clerk", and the words "together with any licence delivered under paragraph (a) above" will be inserted at the end;*

2. *in s.77A(2), the words "and return any licence delivered to him under*

this section to the alleged offender" will be inserted after the word "record", the words "who is not the holder of a licence" will be omitted, and the words "and (if he is the holder of a licence) delivers his licence to him," will be inserted after the words "to him".

For the provisions relating to the commencement of ss.9 and 10 of and Schs 2 and 3 to the 2006 Act, see ibid. s.61(8) below.]

Proceedings in fixed penalty cases

General restriction on proceedings

A19.182   **78.**—(1) Proceedings shall not be brought against any person for the offence to which a fixed penalty notice relates until the end of the suspended enforcement period.

(2) Proceedings shall not be brought against any person for the offence to which a fixed penalty notice relates if the fixed penalty is paid in accordance with this Part of this Act before the end of the suspended enforcement period.

Statements by constables

A19.183   **79.**—(1) In any proceedings a certificate that a copy of a statement by a constable [or vehicle examiner] with respect to the alleged offence (referred to in this section as a *"constable's [relevant] witness statement"*) was included in or given with a fixed penalty notice or a notice under [54(4)] of this Act given to the accused on a date specified in the certificate shall, if the certificate purports to be signed by the [...] person who gave the accused the notice, be evidence of service of a copy of that statement by delivery to the accused on that date.

(2) In any proceedings a certificate that a copy of a [relevant] witness statement was included in or served with a notice to owner served on the accused in the manner and on a date specified in the certificate shall, if the certificate purports to be signed by any person employed by the police authority for the police area in which the offence to which the proceedings relate is alleged to have been committed [or on behalf of the Secretary of State], be evidence of service in the manner and on the date so specified both of a copy of that statement and of the notice to owner.

(3) Any address specified in any such certificate as is mentioned in subsection (2) above as being the address at which service of the notice to owner was effected shall be taken for the purposes of any proceedings in which the certificate is tendered in evidence to be the accused's proper address, unless the contrary is proved.

(4) Where a copy of a [relevant] witness statement is included in or served with a notice to owner served in any manner in which the notice is authorised to be served under this Part of this Act, the statement shall be treated as duly served for the purposes of section 9 of the Criminal Justice Act 1967 (proof by written statement) notwithstanding that the manner of service is not authorised by subsection (8) of that section.

(5) In relation to any proceedings in which service of a [relevant] witness statement is proved by certificate under this section —

(a) that service shall be taken for the purposes of subsection (2)(c) of that section (copy of statement to be tendered in evidence to be served before hearing on other parties to the proceedings by or on behalf of the party proposing to tender it) to have been effected by or on behalf of the prosecutor, and

(b) subsection (2)(d) of that section (time for objection) shall have effect with the substitution, for the reference to seven days from the service of the copy of the statement, of a reference to seven days from the relevant date.

(6) In subsection (5)(b) above *"relevant date"* means—

(a) where the accused gives notice requesting a hearing in respect of the offence in accordance with any provision of this Part of this Act, the date on which he gives that notice, and

(b) where a notice in respect of the offence was given to the accused under section 54(4) of this Act but no fixed penalty notice is given in respect of it, the last day for [delivery of the notice].

(7) This section does not extend to Scotland.

[Section 79 is printed as amended by the Road Safety Act 2006 s.58(4) and s.5 **A19.184**
and Sch.1, para.18.]

Certificates about payment

80. In any proceedings a certificate—   **A19.185**

(a) that payment of a fixed penalty was or was not received, by a date specified in the certificate, by the [person to whom it was required to be paid], or

(b) that a letter containing an amount sent by post in payment of a fixed penalty was marked as posted on a date so specified,

shall, if the certificate purports to be signed by the [person to whom it was required to be paid], be evidence … of the facts stated.

[Section 80 is printed as amended by the Road Safety Act 2006 s.5 and Sch.1, **A19.186**
para.19.

Words relating exclusively and expressly to Scotland in s.80 have been omitted.]

Documents signed by the accused

81.—(1) Where—   **A19.187**

(a) any person is charged with a fixed penalty offence, and

(b) the prosecutor produces to the court a document to which this subsection applies purporting to have been signed by the accused,

the document shall be presumed, unless the contrary is proved, to have been signed by the accused and shall be evidence … in the proceedings of any facts stated in it tending to show that the accused was the owner, the hirer or the driver of the vehicle concerned at a particular time.

(2) Subsection (1) above applies to any document purporting to be—

(a) a notice requesting a hearing in respect of the offence charged given in accordance with a fixed penalty notice relating to that offence, or

(b) a statutory statement of any description defined in Schedule 4 to this Act or a copy of a statement of liability within the meaning of section 66 of this Act provided in response to a notice to owner.

A19.188   *[Words relating exclusively and expressly to Scotland in s.81(1) have been omitted.]*

Miscellaneous

Accounting for fixed penalties: England and Wales

A19.189   **82.**—(1) In England and Wales, sums paid [to the fixed penalty clerk] by way of fixed penalty for an offence shall be treated for the purposes of [section 38 of the Courts Act 2003 (application of receipts of designated officers)] as if they were fines imposed on summary conviction for that offence.

    (2) [...]

    (2A) [...]

    (3) [...]

A19.190   *[Section 82 is printed as amended by the Police and Magistrates' Courts Act 1994 s.91(1) and Sch.8, para.32; the Justices of the Peace Act 1997 s.73(3) and Sch.5, para.25; the Access to Justice Act 1999 ss.83(3) and 90(1) and Schs 12 (para.3) and 13 (paras 140 and 154); the Courts Act 2003 s.109(1) and (3), Sch.8, para.320 and Sch.10; the Road Safety Act 2006 s.5 and Sch.1, para.20.]*

Powers of court [in cases of deception]

A19.191   **83.**—(1) This section applies where—

    (a) in endorsing [the counterpart of] any person's licence under section 57 of this Act, the fixed penalty clerk [or the Secretary of State] is deceived as to whether endorsement under that section is excluded by section 61(2) of this Act by virtue of the fact that the licence holder would be liable to be disqualified under section 35 of this Act if he were convicted of the offence, or

    (b) in endorsing [the counterpart of] any person's licence under section 77 of this [Act the appropriate person is deceived as to whether proceedings against the person are excluded by section 76 of this Act] by virtue of the fact that the licence holder would be liable to be disqualified under section 35 of this Act if he were convicted of the offence.

[(1A) This section also applies where—

    (a) particulars are endorsed on a person's driving record under section 57A of this Act because the fixed penalty clerk or the Secretary of State is deceived as to whether endorsement under that section is excluded by section 61A(2) of this Act by virtue of the fact that the person to whom the fixed penalty notice was given would be liable to be disqualified under section 35 of this Act if he were convicted of the offence, or

    (b) particulars are endorsed on a person's driving record under section 77A of this Act because the appropriate person or court is deceived as to whether proceedings against the person are excluded by section 76 of this Act by virtue of the fact that the person to whom the conditional offer is issued would be liable to be disqualified under section 35 of this Act if he were convicted of the offence.]

    (2) If—

(a) the deception constituted or was due to an offence committed by the [person to whom the fixed penalty notice was given or conditional offer was issued], and

(b) [he] is convicted of that offence,

the court by or before which he is convicted shall have the same powers and duties as it would have had if he had also been convicted by or before it of the offence of which particulars were endorsed under section 57 [or 57A] or, as the case may be, 77 [or 77A] of this Act.

[Section 83 is printed as amended by the Driving Licences (Community Driving Licence) Regulations 1990 (SI 1990/144); the Access to Justice Act 1999 s.90(1) and Sch.13, paras 140 and 155; the Courts Act 2003 s.109(1) and Sch.8, para.321; the Road Safety Act 2006 s.5 and Sch.1, para.21, s.9 and Sch.2, para.28.   **A19.192**

With effect from a day to be appointed and in relation to endorsement (all drivers), s.83 will be amended by the Road Safety Act 2006 s.10 and Sch.3, para.55, s.59 and Sch.7(4):

1. *s.83(1) will be omitted;*

2. *in s.83(1A), the word "also" will be omitted;*

3. *in s.83(2), "57 or" and "77 or" will be omitted.*

For the provisions relating to the commencement of ss.9 and 10 of and Schs 2 and 3 to the 2006 Act, see ibid. s.61(8) below.]

Regulations

84. *[Omitted.]*   **A19.193**

[Notices to Secretary of State

84A. Any notice sent to the Secretary of State under this Part must be sent in such manner and to such address and contain such particulars as the Secretary of State may determine.]   **A19.194**

[Section 84A is printed as inserted by the Road Safety Act 2006 s.9 and Sch.2, para.30.]   **A19.195**

Service of documents

85.—(1) Subject to any requirement of this Part of this Act with respect to the manner in which a person may be provided with any such document, he may be provided with the following documents by post (but without prejudice to any other method of providing him with them), that is to say—   **A19.196**

(a) any of the statutory statements mentioned in Schedule 4 to this Act, and

(b) any of the documents mentioned in section 66(2) of this Act.

(2) Where a notice requesting a hearing in respect of an offence is permitted by a fixed penalty notice or notice to owner relating to that offence to be given by post, section 7 of the Interpretation Act 1978 (service of documents by post) shall apply as if that notice were permitted to be so given by this Act.

(3) A notice to owner may be served on any person—

(a) by delivering it to him or leaving it at his proper address, or

(b) by sending it to him by post,

and where the person on whom such a notice is to be served is a body corporate it is duly served if it is served on the secretary or clerk of that body.

(4) For the purposes of this Part of this Act and of section 7 of the Interpretation Act 1978 as it applies for the purposes of subsection (3) above the proper address of any person in relation to the service on him of a notice to owner is—

(a) in the case of the secretary or clerk of a body corporate, that of the registered or principal office of that body or the registered address of the person who is or was the registered keeper of the vehicle concerned at the time of service, and

(b) in any other case, his last known address at the time of service.

(5) In subsection (4) above, *"registered address"*, in relation to the registered keeper of a vehicle, means the address recorded in the record kept under [the Vehicle Excise and Registration Act 1994] with respect to that vehicle as being that person's address.

A19.197   *[Section 85 is printed as amended by the Vehicle Excise and Registration Act 1994 s.63 and Sch.3, para.25(1).]*

Functions of traffic wardens

A19.198   **86.**—(1) An order under section 95(5) of the Road Traffic Regulation Act 1984 may not authorise the employment of a traffic warden to discharge any function under this Part of this Act in respect of an offence if the offence appears to the traffic warden to be an offence involving obligatory endorsement [unless that offence was committed whilst the vehicle concerned was stationary].

(2) In so far as an order under that section authorises the employment of traffic wardens for the purposes of this Part of this Act, references in this Part of this Act to a constable or, as the case may be, to a constable in uniform include a traffic warden.

A19.199   *[Section 86 is printed as amended by the Road Traffic Act 1991 s.48 and Sch.4, para.106.*

The Functions of Traffic Wardens Order 1970 (SI 1970/1958) (q.v.) has effect as if made under the Road Traffic Regulation Act 1984 s.95(5).]

Guidance on application of Part III

A19.200   **87.** *[Omitted.]*

Procedure for regulations and orders

A19.201   **88.** *[Omitted.]*

Interpretation

A19.202   **89.**—(1) In this Part of this Act —

"authorised person" has the meaning given by section 54(9) of this Act,

[*"British Transport Police"* means the force of constables appointed under the British Transport Commission Act 1949 (c.xxix);]

*   *   *

"chief officer of police" (except in the definition of *"authorised person"*)

means, in relation to any fixed penalty notice[, notice to owner or conditional offer], the chief officer of police for the police area in which the fixed penalty offence in question is alleged to have been committed,

*   *   *

"driver" except in section 62 of this Act means, in relation to an alleged fixed penalty offence, the person by whom, assuming the offence to have been committed, it was committed,

…

"proceedings", except in relation to proceedings for enforcing payment of a sum registered under section 71 of this Act, means criminal proceedings; [and

"vehicle examiner" means an examiner appointed under section 66A of the Road Traffic Act 1988.]

(2) In this Part of this Act —

    (a) references to a notice requesting a hearing in respect of an offence are references to a notice indicating that the person giving the notice wishes to contest liability for the offence or seeks a determination by a court with respect to the appropriate punishment for the offence,

    (b) references to an offence include an alleged offence, and

    (c) references to the person who is or was at any time the registered keeper of a vehicle are references to the person in whose name the vehicle is or was at that time registered under [the Vehicle Excise and Registration Act 1994].

[Section 89 is printed as amended by the Road Traffic Act 1991 s.48 and Sch.4, **A19.203** *para.107(1)–(3); the Vehicle Excise and Registration Act 1994 s.63 and Sch.3, para.25(1); the Access to Justice Act 1999 ss.105, 106 and Sch.15, Pt 5(1), (7); the Police Reform Act 2002 s.76(1), (6) (with respect to England and Wales only); the Road Safety Act 2006 s.5 and Sch.1, para.23.*

    Two definitions ("chief constable" and "court of summary jurisdiction") which are applicable exclusively to Scotland have been omitted from s.89(1).]

Index to Part III

90. The expressions listed in the left-hand column below are respectively **A19.204** defined or (as the case may be) fall to be construed in accordance with the provisions of this Part of this Act listed in the right-hand column in relation to those expressions.

Expression	Relevant provision
Authorised person	Section 54(9)
Conditional offer	[Section [75(5)]]
Fixed penalty	Section 53
Fixed penalty clerk	Section[s] 69(4) [and [75(6)]]
Fixed penalty notice	Section 52
Fixed penalty offence	Section 51

Expression	Relevant provision
Notice to owner	Sections 63(2) and 66(4)
Notice requesting a hearing in respect of an offence	Section 89(2)
Offence	Section 89(2)
Official form	Section 68(4)
Owner	Section 68(1)
Period allowed for response to a notice to owner	Section 63(5)
Proper address, in relation to the service of a notice to owner	Section 85(4)
Registered keeper	Section 89(2)
Statutory statement of facts	Part II of Schedule 4
Statutory statement of hiring	Part I of Schedule 4
Statutory statement of ownership	Part I of Schedule 4
Suspended enforcement period	Section 52(3)(a)
Time of the alleged offence	Section 63(3)

A19.205   *[Section 90 is printed as amended by the Road Traffic Act 1991 s.48 and Sch.4, para.108(a) and (b); the Road Safety Act 2006 s.58(5).*

     A "conditional offer" (which is defined in s.75(4)) is applicable only in Scotland.]

[PART 3A

FINANCIAL PENALTY DEPOSITS

Power to impose financial penalty deposit requirement

A19.206   **90A.**—(1) A constable or vehicle examiner may impose a financial penalty deposit requirement on a person on any occasion if the conditions in this section are satisfied.

(2) The constable or vehicle examiner must have reason to believe—

     (a) that the person is committing or has on that occasion committed an offence relating to a motor vehicle, and

     (b) that the person, the offence and the circumstances in which the offence is committed are of a description specified in an order made by the Secretary of State.

(3) The person must be—

     (a) given written notification that it appears likely that proceedings will be brought against him in respect of the offence, or

     (b) (if the offence is a fixed penalty offence) either given such notification or given a fixed penalty notice … in respect of the offence.

(4) The person must fail to provide a satisfactory address; and for this purpose "a satisfactory address" is an address in the United Kingdom at which the constable or vehicle examiner considers it likely that it would be possible to find the person whenever necessary to do so in connection with the proceedings, fixed penalty notice or conditional offer.

(5) The person who is to impose the financial penalty deposit requirement—

    (a) if a constable, must be in uniform, and

    (b) if a vehicle examiner, must produce his authority.

Financial penalty deposit requirement

90B.—(1) For the purposes of this Part of this Act a financial penalty   **A19.207**
deposit requirement is a requirement to make a payment of the appropriate amount to the
Secretary of State—

    (a) in a manner specified in an order made by him, and

    (b) either immediately or within the relevant period.

(2) In this Part of this Act "the appropriate amount", in relation to an offence
and a person, is an amount specified in relation to the offence in an order made by
the Secretary of State; and different amounts may be so specified—

    (a) by reference to whether the person is given notification that it appears
likely that proceedings will be brought against him or given a fixed
penalty notice …, and

    (b) otherwise by reference to the circumstances of the offence.

(3) In this Part of this Act *"the relevant period"* means—

    (a) if the person was given a fixed penalty notice and proceedings are not
brought in respect of the offence by virtue of this Act before the end
of the suspended enforcement period, the suspended enforcement period,

    (b) *[applies to Scotland]*, and

    (c) otherwise, the period ending with the person being charged with the
offence.

Making of payment in compliance with requirement

. **90C.**—(1) This section applies where a person on whom a financial penalty   **A19.208**
deposit requirement is imposed in respect of an offence makes a payment of the
appropriate amount in accordance with section 90B(1) of this Act (and any order
made under it).

(2) On payment by the person of the appropriate amount the person by whom
the payment is received must issue him with a written receipt for the payment
specifying the effect of the following provisions of this section.

(3) *[Applies to Scotland]*.

(4) In a case where—

    (a) a fixed penalty notice relating to the offence has been given to the
person or … has been handed to him,

    (b) the person does not give notice requesting a hearing in respect of the
offence before the end of the relevant period in the appropriate manner, and

    (c) proceedings are not brought in respect of the offence by virtue of this
Act, subsection (6) below applies.

(5) In subsection (4)(b) above *"the appropriate manner"* means—

    (a) if the person was given a fixed penalty notice, the manner specified in
the fixed penalty notice, and

(b) *[applies to Scotland]*.

(6) Where this subsection applies, the Secretary of State must—

    (a) apply so much of the payment as does not exceed the amount of the fixed penalty in or towards payment of the fixed penalty, and

    (b) take the appropriate steps to make any appropriate refund to the person.

(7) In any other case—

    (a) if the person is informed that he is not to be prosecuted for the offence, is acquitted of the offence or is convicted but not fined in respect of it, or the prosecution period comes to an end without a prosecution having been commenced against him in respect of it, subsection (9) below applies, and

    (b) if a fine is imposed on the person in respect of the offence (otherwise than as a result of a conviction obtained on a prosecution commenced after the end of the prosecution period), subsection (10) below applies.

(8) In this Part of this Act "*the prosecution period*" means the period of twelve months beginning with the imposition of the financial penalty deposit requirement or, if shorter, any period after which no prosecution may be commenced in respect of the offence.

(9) Where this subsection applies, the Secretary of State must take the appropriate steps to make the appropriate refund to the person.

(10) Where this subsection applies, the Secretary of State must—

    (a) apply so much of the payment as does not exceed the amount of the fine in or towards payment of the fine, and

    (b) take the appropriate steps to make any appropriate refund to the person.

(11) Where the Secretary of State is required by this section to take the appropriate steps to make an appropriate refund, he must take such steps to trace the person and to make the refund to him, by such means, as are specified in an order made by the Secretary of State.

(12) In this Part of this Act "*the appropriate refund*", in any case, is a refund of—

    (a) where subsection (6) above applies, so much of the payment as exceeds the amount of the fixed penalty,

    (b) where subsection (9) above applies, the amount of the payment, and

    (c) where subsection (10) above applies, so much of the amount of the payment as exceeds the amount of the fine,

together with interest calculated in accordance with provision made by order made by the Treasury.

Prohibition on driving on failure to make payment

A19.209   **90D.**—(1) This section applies where a person on whom a financial penalty deposit requirement is imposed does not make an immediate payment of the appropriate amount in accordance with section 90B(1) of this Act (and any order made under it).

(2) The constable or vehicle examiner by whom the requirement was imposed

may prohibit the driving on a road of any vehicle of which the person was in charge at the time of the offence by giving to the person notice in writing of the prohibition.

(3) The prohibition—

    (a) shall come into force as soon as the notice is given, and

    (b) shall continue in force until the happening of whichever of the events in subsection (4) below occurs first.

(4) Those events are—

    (a) the person making a payment of the appropriate amount in accordance with section 90B(1) of this Act (and any order made under it) at any time during the relevant period,

    (b) (where a fixed penalty notice was given, or …, to the person in respect of the offence) payment of the fixed penalty,

    (c) the person being convicted or acquitted of the offence,

    (d) the person being informed that he is not to be prosecuted for the offence, and

    (e) the coming to an end of the prosecution period.

(5) A constable or vehicle examiner may by direction in writing require the person to remove the vehicle to which the prohibition relates (and, if it is a motor vehicle drawing a trailer, also to remove the trailer) to such place and subject to such conditions as are specified in the direction; and the prohibition does not apply to the removal of the vehicle (or trailer) in accordance with the direction.

(6) A person who—

    (a) drives a vehicle in contravention of a prohibition under this section,

    (b) causes or permits a vehicle to be driven in contravention of such a prohibition, or

    (c) fails to comply within a reasonable time with a direction under subsection (5) above, is guilty of an offence.

(7) The Secretary of State may by order provide for exceptions from subsection (6) above.

(8) Schedule 4 to the Road Safety Act 2006 makes provision about the immobilisation of vehicles the driving of which has been prohibited under this section and about their removal and disposal.

[An offence under s.90D is a fixed penalty offence for the purposes of Pt 3 of **A19.210** *the Road Traffic Offenders Act 1988 (see the Fixed Penalty Offences Order 2009 (SI 2009/483) art.2). The amount for the fixed penalty offence is prescribed by the Fixed Penalty Order 2000 (SI 2000/2792), as amended by the Fixed Penalty (Amendment) Order 2009 (SI 2009/488).*

The Road Safety (Immobilisation, Removal and Disposal of Vehicles) Regulations 2009 (SI 2009/493) [q.v.] apply with respect to any case where the driving has been prohibited under this section.]

Orders about financial penalty deposits

90E. *[Omitted.]*   **A19.211**

Financial penalty deposits: interpretation

90F. In sections 90A to 90D of this Act—   **A19.212**

"the appropriate amount" has the meaning given by section 90B(2) of this Act,

"the appropriate refund" has the meaning given by section 90C(12) of this Act,

"conditional offer" means a notice under section 75(3)(a) [or (3B)(a)] of this Act,

"financial penalty deposit requirement" has the meaning given by section 90B(1) of this Act,

"fixed penalty notice" has the meaning given by section 52 of this Act,

"fixed penalty offence" is to be construed in accordance with section 51 of this Act,

"the prosecution period" has the meaning given by section 90C(8) of this Act,

"the relevant period" has the meaning given by section 90B(3) of this Act,

"suspended enforcement period" is to be construed in accordance with section 52(3)(a) of this Act, and

"vehicle examiner" means an examiner appointed under section 66A of the Road Traffic Act 1988.]

A19.213   *[Section 90F is printed as amended by the Local Transport Act 2008 s.128.*

Part 3A (ss.90A–90F) is printed as inserted by the Road Safety Act 2006 s.11. Words omitted in ss. 90A–90D relate exclusively to Scotland.

The following orders have been made under powers conferred by provisions of Pt 3A which specify certain matters in relation to the imposition of financial penalty deposits: the Road Safety (Financial Penalty Deposit) Order 2009 (SI 2009/491); the Road Safety (Financial Penalty Deposit) (Appropriate Amount) Order 2009 (SI 2009/492); the Road Safety (Financial Penalty Deposit) (Interest) Order 2009 (SI 2009/498); the Road Safety (Financial Penalty Deposit) (Amendment) Order 2010 (SI 2010/2721). These orders are not reproduced in this work.]

Part IV

Miscellaneous and General

Penalty for breach of regulations

A19.214   **91.** If a person acts in contravention of or fails to comply with—

(a) any regulations made by the Secretary of State under the Road Traffic Act 1988 other than regulations made under section 31, 45 or 132 [or under section 160 by virtue of Schedule 2A],

(b) any regulations made by the Road Traffic Regulation Act 1984, other than regulations made under section 28, Schedule 4, Part III of Schedule 9 or Schedule 12,

and the contravention of failure to comply is not made an offence under any other provision of the Traffic Acts, he shall for each offence be liable on summary conviction to a fine not exceeding level 3 on the standard scale.

[Application to Northern Ireland licence holders

91ZA.—(1) The references to a licence in the following provisions of this Act   **A19.216**
include references to a Northern Ireland licence—

    (a) section 7,

    (b) section 26(7) and (8) and (9)(b),

    (c) section 27,

    (d) section 29(1),

    (e) section 30,

    (f) section 31(1),

    (g) section 32,

    (h) section 42(5),

    (i) section 44(1) [and (3A)],

    (j) section 46(2),

    (k) section 47(2)[, (3) and (3A)],

    (l) section 48(1) and (2).

(2) Accordingly, the reference in section 27(3)(b) of this Act to the suspension of a licence is to be construed in relation to a Northern Ireland licence holder as a reference to his ceasing to be authorised by virtue of section 109(1) of the Road Traffic Act 1988 to drive in Great Britain a motor vehicle of any class.

(3) The references in sections 26(9)(a) and 27(3) of this Act to a new licence include references to a counterpart of a Northern Ireland licence.

(4) In relation to a Northern Ireland licence holder to whom a counterpart is issued under section 109A of the Road Traffic Act 1988, the references in Part 3 of this Act (except sections 75(12), 76(8) and 77(9)) to a licence include references to a Northern Ireland licence.

(5) Where a court orders the endorsement of the counterpart of any Northern Ireland licence held by a person, it must send notice of the endorsement to the Secretary of State.

(6) The notice must—

    (a) be sent in such manner and to such address, and

    (b) contain such particulars,

as the Secretary of State may determine.

(7) Where a court orders the holder of a Northern Ireland licence to be disqualified, it must send the Northern Ireland licence and its counterpart (if any), on their being produced to the court, to the Secretary of State.

(8) The licence and its counterpart must be sent to such address as the Secretary of State may determine.

(9) Where—

    (a) a notice is sent to the Secretary of State under subsection (5) above, and

    (b) the particulars contained in the notice include—

        (i) particulars of an offence in respect of which the holder of a Northern Ireland licence is disqualified by an order of a court, and

(ii) particulars of the disqualification,
the Secretary of State must send a notice containing the particulars mentioned in paragraph (b)(i) and (ii) to the licensing authority in Northern Ireland.]

A19.217   *[Section 91ZA was inserted by the Crime (International Co-operation) Act 2003 s.77(2); the Road Safety Act 2006 s.9 and Sch.2, para.31.*

With effect from a day to be appointed, in relation to endorsement (all drivers), s.91ZA (as amended above) will be further amended by the Road Safety Act 2006 s.10 and Sch.3, para.57, s.59 and Sch.7(4) as follows:

1. *in s.91ZA(1), in para.(b), the words "and (9)(b)" will be omitted, paras (d) to (f) and (h) to (j) will be omitted, in para.(k), ", (3) and (3A)" will be omitted, and para.(l) will be omitted;*
2. *s.91ZA(3)–(6) will be omitted;*
3. *in s.91ZA(7), the words "and its counterpart (if any)" will be omitted, and the word "its" will be substituted for the word "their";*
4. *in s.91ZA(8), the words "and its counterpart" will be omitted;*
5. *in s.91ZA(9)(a), the words "section 44A above of an order for the endorsement of a person's driving record" will be substituted for the words "subsection (5) above";*
6. *in s.91ZA(9)(b)(i), the words ", or a person normally resident in Northern Ireland who does not hold a licence" will be inserted after the word "licence".*

For the provisions relating to the commencement of ss.9 and 10 of and Schs 2 and 3 to the 2006 Act, see ibid. s.61(8) below.]

[Effect of endorsement on Northern Ireland licence holders

A19.218   **91ZB.** Section 91B applies in relation to Northern Ireland licences as it applies in relation to Community licences.]

A19.219   *[Section 91ZB was inserted by the Crime (International Co-operation) Act 2003 s.77(2).*

With effect from a day to be appointed in relation to endorsement (all drivers), s.91ZB will be omitted by the Road Safety Act 2006 s.10 and Sch.3, para.58, s.59 and Sch.7(4).]

[Application to Community licence holders

A19.220   **91A.**—(1) The references in sections 7, 26(7) and (8) and (9)(b), 27, 29(1), 30, 31(1), 32, 42(5), 44(1) [and (3A)], 46(2), 47(3) [and (3A)] and 48(1) and (2) of this Act to a licence includes references to a Community licence; and accordingly the reference in section 27(3)(b) of this Act to the suspension of a licence is to be construed in relation to a Community licence as a reference to the Community licence holder ceasing to be authorised by virtue of section 99(1)(a) of the Road Traffic Act 1988 to drive in Great Britain a motor vehicle of any class.

(2) The references in sections 26(9)(a) and 27(3) of this Act to a new licence include references to a counterpart of a Community licence.

(3) In relation to a Community licence holder to whom a counterpart is issued under section 99B of the Road Traffic Act 1988, the references in Part III of this Act (except sections 75(12), 76(8) and 77(9) of this Act) to a licence include references to a Community licence.

(4) Where a court orders the endorsement of the counterpart of any Community licence held by a person, it must send notice of the endorsement to the Secretary of State.

(5) Where a court orders the holder of a Community licence to be disqualified, it must send the Community licence and its counterpart (if any), on their being produced to the court, to the Secretary of State.

(6) A notice sent by a court to the Secretary of State in pursuance of subsection (4) above must be sent in such manner and to such address and contain such particulars as the Secretary of State may determine, and a Community licence and its counterpart (if any) so sent in pursuance of subsection (5) above must be sent to such address as the Secretary of State may determine.

(7) Where a Community licence held by a person who is ordered by the court to be disqualified is sent to the Secretary of State in pursuance of subsection (5) above, the Secretary of State—

    (a) must send to the licensing authority in the EEA State in respect of which the Community licence was issued the holder's name and address and particulars of the disqualification, and

    (b) must (subject to subsection (8) below) return the Community licence to the holder—

        (i) on the expiry of the period of disqualification, or

        (ii) if earlier, on being satisfied that the holder has left Great Britain and is not normally resident there.

(8) Where—

    (a) the Secretary of State would, apart from this subsection, be under a duty on the expiry of the period of disqualification to return a Community licence to a person in pursuance of subsection (7)(b)(i) above, but

    (b) at that time, the person would not be authorised by virtue of section 99A(1) of the Road Traffic Act 1988 to drive in Great Britain a motor vehicle of any class,

the Secretary of State must send the Community licence to the licensing authority in the EEA State in respect of which it was issued and explain to them his reasons for so doing.

(9) A Community licence to be returned to any person under subsection (7) above may be returned to him by delivering it to him or by leaving it at his proper address or by sending it to him by post; and for the purposes of this subsection and section 7 of the Interpretation Act 1978 in its application to this subsection the proper address of any person shall be his latest address as known to the person returning the Community licence.

(10) In this section *"period of disqualification"* means, in relation to a Community licence holder, the period for which he is ordered by the court to be disqualified (otherwise than under section 36 of this Act).]

[Section 91A was inserted by the Driving Licences (Community Driving   **A19.221**
Licence) Regulations 1996 (SI 1996/1974) reg.3 and Sch.2, para.4 (not reproduced in this work) and is printed as amended by the Road Safety Act 2006 s.9 and Sch.2, para.32.
With effect from a day to be appointed, in relation to endorsement (all driv-

ers), s.91A will be amended by the Road Safety Act 2006 s.10 and Sch.3, para.59, s.59 and Sch.7(4) as follows:

1. *in s.91A(1), the words "and 32" will be substituted for the words from "27" to "48(1) and (2)";*
2. *s.91A(2)–(4) will be omitted;*
3. *in s.91A(5), the words "and its counterpart (if any)" will be omitted and the word "its" will be substituted for the word "their";*
4. *s.91A(6) will be omitted;*
5. *the following text will be substituted for s.91A(7):*

[(7) Where—

(a) a notice is sent to the Secretary of State under section 44A above for the endorsement of a person's driving record with any particulars or penalty points, and

(b) the particulars contained in the notice include—

  (i) particulars of an offence in respect of which the holder of a Community licence, or a person normally resident in another EEA state who does not hold a licence, is disqualified by an order of a court, and

  (ii) particulars of the disqualification,

the Secretary of State must send a notice containing the particulars mentioned in paragraph (b)(i) and (ii) to the licensing authority in the EEA state in respect of which the Community licence was issued or, where the person disqualified is not the holder of a licence, the licensing authority in the EEA state where the person is normally resident.

(7A) Where a Community licence has been sent to the Secretary of State in pursuance of subsection (5) above, he must return the Community licence to the holder—

(a) on the expiry of the period of disqualification, or

(b) if earlier, on being satisfied that the holder has left Great Britain and is not normally resident there.]

6. *s.91A(8)–(10) will be omitted.*

For the provisions relating to the commencement of ss.9 and 10 of and Schs 2 and 3 to the 2006 Act, see ibid. s.61(8) below.

As to the European Economic Area (EEA), see the introductory note to Section C below.]

[Effect of endorsement on Community licence holders

A19.222   **91B.**—(1) An order that any particulars or penalty points are to be endorsed on the counterpart of any Community licence held by the person convicted shall operate as an order that—

(a) the counterpart of any Community licence which he may then hold, or

(b) the counterpart of any licence or Community licence which he may subsequently obtain,

is to be so endorsed until he becomes entitled under subsection (3) below to have a counterpart of his Community licence, or a licence and its counterpart, issued to him free from the particulars or penalty points.

(2) On the issue of a new counterpart of a Community licence or a new licence

to a person, any particulars or penalty points ordered to be endorsed on the counterpart of any Community licence held by him shall be entered on the new counterpart or the counterpart of the new licence (as the case may be) unless he has become entitled under subsection (3) below to have a new counterpart of his Community licence or a new licence issued to him free from those particulars or penalty points.

(3) A person the counterpart of whose Community licence has been ordered to be endorsed is entitled to have issued to him with effect from the end of the period for which the endorsement remains effective (as determined in accordance with section 45(5) of this Act) —

> (a) a new counterpart of any Community licence then held by him free from the endorsement if he makes an application to the Secretary of State for that purpose in such manner as the Secretary of State may determine, or
>
> (b) a new licence with a counterpart free from the endorsement if he applies for a new licence in pursuance of section 97(1) of the Road Traffic Act 1988, surrenders any subsisting licence and its counterpart, pays the fee prescribed by regulations under Part III of that Act and satisfies the other requirements of section 97(1).]

[Section 91B was inserted by the Driving Licences (Community Driving   **A19.223**
Licence) Regulations 1996 (SI 1996/1974) reg.3 and Sch.2, para.5 (not reproduced in this work).

With effect from a day to be appointed, s.91B will be omitted by the Road Safety Act 2006 s.10 and Sch.3, para.60, s.59 and Sch.7(4).]

Application to Crown

92. The following provisions of this Act apply to vehicles and persons in the   **A19.224**
public service of the Crown: sections 1, 2, 3, 15, 16 [, 20] and 49 and the provisions connected with the licensing of drivers.

[Section 92 is printed as amended by the Road Traffic Act 1991 s.48 and Sch.4,   **A19.225**
para.109.]

Application of sections 15 and 16 to persons subject to service discipline

93.—(1) Sections 15 and 16, in their application to persons subject to service   **A19.226**
discipline, apply outside as well as within Great Britain and have effect as if—

> (a) references to proceedings for an offence under an enactment included references to proceedings for the corresponding service offence,
>
> (b) references to the court included a reference to any naval, military, or air force authority before whom the proceedings take place,
>
> (c) references to a constable included references to a member of the provost staff, and
>
> (d) in section 15, subsection (4) were omitted.

(2) Expressions used in this section have the same meaning as in sections [3A] to 10 of the Road Traffic Act 1988 [*q.v.*]

[Section 93 is printed as amended by the Road Traffic Act 1991 s.48 and Sch.4,   **A19.227**
para.110.]

Proceedings in respect of offences in connection with Crown vehicles

94.—(1) Where an offence under the Traffic Acts is alleged to have been com-   **A19.228**

mitted in connection with a vehicle in the public service of the Crown, proceedings may be brought in respect of the offence against a person nominated for the purpose on behalf of the Crown.

(2) Subject to subsection (3) below, where any such offence is committed any person so nominated shall also be guilty of the offence as well as any person actually responsible for the offence (but without prejudice to proceedings against any person so responsible).

(3) Where any person is convicted of an offence by virtue of this section —

(a) no order is to be made on his conviction save an order imposing a fine,

(b) payment of any fine imposed on him in respect of that offence is not to be enforced against him, and

(c) apart from the imposition of any such fine, the conviction is to be disregarded for all purposes other than any appeal (whether by way of case stated or otherwise).

Destination of Scottish fines

A19.229   **95.** *[Omitted.]*

Meaning of "offence involving obligatory endorsement"

A19.230   **96.** For the purposes of this Act, an offence involves obligatory endorsement if it is an offence under a provision of the Traffic Acts specified in column 1 of Part I of Schedule 2 to this Act or an offence specified in column 1 of Part II of that Schedule and either—

(a) the word "obligatory" (without qualification) appears in column 6 (in the case of Part I) or column 3 (in the case of Part II) against the offence, or

(b) that word appears there qualified by conditions relating to the offence which are satisfied.

Meaning of "offence involving obligatory disqualification" and "offence involving discretionary disqualification"

A19.231   **97.**—(1) For the purposes of this Act, an offence involves obligatory disqualification if it is an offence under a provision of the Traffic Acts specified in column 1 of Part I of Schedule 2 to this Act or an offence specified in column 1 of Part II of that Schedule and either—

(a) the word "obligatory" (without qualification) appears in column 5 (in the case of Part I) or column 2 (in the case of Part II) against the offence, or

(b) that word appears there qualified by conditions or circumstances relating to the offence which are satisfied or obtain.

(2) For the purposes of this Act, an offence involves discretionary disqualification if it is an offence under a provision of the Traffic Acts specified in column 1 of Part I of Schedule 2 to this Act or an offence specified in column 1 of Part II of that Schedule and either—

(a) the word "discretionary" (without qualification) appears in column 5 (in the case of Part I) or column 2 (in the case of Part II) against the offence, or

(b) that word appears there qualified by conditions or circumstances relating to the offence which are satisfied or obtain.

[Meaning of "driving record"

97A.—(1) In this Act "*driving record*", in relation to a person, means a record   A19.232
in relation to the person maintained by the Secretary of State and designed to be endorsed with particulars relating to offences committed by the person under the Traffic Acts.

(2) The Secretary of State may make arrangements for the following persons to have access, by such means as the Secretary of State may determine, to information held on a person's driving record—

    (a) courts,

    (b) constables,

    (c) fixed penalty clerks,

    (d) the person in respect of whom the record is maintained and persons authorised by him, and

    (e) other persons prescribed in regulations made by the Secretary of State.

(3) The power to make regulations under subsection (2)(e) above shall be exercisable by statutory instrument.

(4) No regulations shall be made under subsection (2)(e) above unless a draft of the instrument containing them has been laid before, and approved by a resolution of, each House of Parliament.]

[Section 97A is printed as inserted by the Road Safety Act 2006 s.8.]   A19.233

General interpretation

98.—(1) In this Act —   A19.234

    "*disqualified*" means disqualified for holding or obtaining a licence and "*disqualification*" is to be construed accordingly,

    "*drive*" has the same meaning as in the Road Traffic Act 1988,

    "*licence*" means a licence to drive a motor vehicle granted under Part III of that Act …

    "*provisional licence*" means a licence granted by virtue of section 97(2) of that Act [*q.v.*],

    "*the provisions connected with the licensing of drivers*" means sections 7, 8, 22, 25 to 29, 31, 32, 34 to 48, [[91ZA to] 91B,] 96 and 97 of this Act,

    "*road*" —

        (a) in relation to England and Wales, means any highway and any other road to which the public has access, and includes bridges over which a road passes, and

        (b) *[applies to Scotland]*,

    "*the Road Traffic Acts*" means the Road Traffic Act 1988, the Road Traffic (Consequential Provisions) Act 1988 (so far as it reproduces the effect of provisions repealed by that Act) and this Act,

    "*the Traffic Acts*" means the Road Traffic Acts and the Road Traffic Regulation Act 1984 [and

"Community licence", "counterpart"[, "EEA State" and Northern Ireland licence] have the same meanings as in Part III of the Road Traffic Act 1988.]

(2) Sections 185 and 186 of the Road Traffic Act 1988 [q.v.] (meaning of "motor vehicle" and other expressions relating to vehicles) apply for the purposes of this Act as they apply for the purposes of that [Act].

(3) In the Schedules to this Act—

"RTRA" is used as an abbreviation for the Road Traffic Regulation Act 1984, and

"RTA" is used as an abbreviation for the Road Traffic Act 1988 [or, if followed by "1989", the Road Traffic (Driver Licensing and Information Systems) Act 1989].

(4) Subject to any express exception, references in this Act to any Part of this Act include a reference to any Schedule to this Act so far as relating to that Part.

A19.235   *[Section 98 is printed as amended by the Road Traffic (Driver Licensing and Information Systems) Act 1989 s.7 and Sch.3, para.26; the Road Traffic Act 1991 s.48 and Sch.4, para.111(2); the Driving Licences (Community Driving Licence) Regulations 1996 (SI 1996/1974) reg.3 and Sch.2, para.6 (not reproduced in this work); the Crime (International Co-operation) Act 2003 s.91 and Sch.5, para.35.*

With effect from a day to be appointed, the following text will be inserted at the appropriate place by the Road Safety Act 2006 s.18(4):

["special road" in England and Wales has the same meaning as in the Highways Act 1980 and in Scotland has the same meaning as in the Roads (Scotland) Act 1984,]

With effect from a day to be appointed, in relation to endorsement (all drivers), s.98(1) will be amended by the Road Safety Act 2006 s.10 and Sch.3, para.61, s.59 and Sch.7(4) as follows:

    1. *in the definition of "the provisions connected with the licensing of drivers", "91ZA, 91A" will be substituted for "91ZA to 91B";*

    2. *in the words following the definition of "the Traffic Acts", the word "counterpart" will be omitted.*

As to the European Economic Area (EEA), see the introductory note to Section C below.

As to the meaning of the term "drive" in the Road Traffic Act 1988, see ibid. s.192 above. As to the meaning of "licence" in Pt 3 of that Act, see ibid. s.108 above.]

Short title, commencement and extent

A19.236   **99.**—(1) This Act may be cited as the Road Traffic Offenders Act 1988.

(2) This Act, except so far as it may be brought into force under subsection (3) or (5) below, shall come into force at the end of the period of six months beginning with the day on which it is passed.

(3), (4) *[Apply to Scotland.]*

(5) [...]

(6) An order under subsection (3) or (5) above may contain such transitional provisions and savings (whether or not involving the modification of any provi-

sions contained in an Act or in subordinate legislation (within the meaning of the Interpretation Act 1978)) as appear to the Secretary of State necessary or expedient in connection with the provisions brought (wholly or partly) into force by the order, and different days may be appointed for different purposes.

(7) This Act, except as provided by section 93, does not extend to Northern Ireland.

[Section 99 is printed as amended by the Statute Law (Repeals) Act 2004 s.1(1)   **A19.237**
and Sch.1, Pt 14.]

Section 1, etc.   SCHEDULE 1

OFFENCES TO WHICH SECTIONS 1, 6, 11 AND 12(1) APPLY

1.—(1) Where section 1, 6, 11 or 12(1) of this Act is shown in column 3 of this Sched-   **A19.238**
ule against a provision of the Road Traffic Act 1988 specified in column 1, the section in question applies to an offence under that provision.

[1A. Section 1 also applies to—   **A19.239**

  (a) an offence under section 16 of the Road Traffic Regulation Act 1984 consisting in the contravention of a restriction on the speed of vehicles imposed under section 14 of that Act,

  (b) an offence under subsection (4) of section 17 of that Act consisting in the contravention of a restriction on the speed of vehicles imposed under that section, and

  (c) an offence under section 88(7) or 89(1) of that Act (speeding offences).]

(2) The general nature of the offence is indicated in column 2.

2. Section 6 also applies—   **A19.240**

  (a) to an offence under section 67 of this Act, …

  (b) *[applies to Scotland]* …

    […]

  [(d) to an offence under paragraph 3(5) of Schedule 1 to the Road Traffic (New Drivers) Act 1995.]

3. Section 11 also applies to—   **A19.241**

  (a) any offence to which section 112 of the Road Traffic Regulation Act 1984 [*q.v.*] (information as to identity of driver or rider) applies except an offence under section 61(5) of that Act,

  (b) any offence which is punishable under section 91 of this Act, …

    […]

  (c) any offence against any other enactment relating to the use of vehicles on roads.

4. Section 12(1) also applies to—   **A19.242**

  (a) any offence which is punishable under section 91 of this Act, …

    […]

  (b) any offence against any other enactment relating to the use of vehicles on roads.

(1) *Provision creating offence*	(2) *General nature of offence*	(3) *Applicable provisions of this Act*
RTA section 1	Causing death by [dangerous] driving.	Section 11 of this Act.

A19.243

(1) *Provision creating offence*	(2) *General nature of offence*	(3) *Applicable provisions of this Act*
RTA section 2	[Dangerous] driving.	Sections 1, 11 and 12(1) of this Act.
[RTA section 2B	Causing death by careless, or inconsiderate, driving.	Sections 11 and 12(1) of this Act.]
RTA section 3	Careless, and inconsiderate, driving.	Sections 1, 11 and 12(1) of this Act.
[RTA section 3ZB	Causing death by driving: unlicensed, disqualified or uninsured drivers.	Sections 11 and 12(1) of this Act.]
[RTA section 3A	Causing death by careless driving when under influence of drink or drugs.	Section 11 of this Act.]
RTA section 4	Driving or attempting to drive, or being in charge of a [mechanically propelled vehicle], when unfit to drive through drink or drugs.	Sections 11 and 12(1) of this Act.
RTA section 5	Driving or attempting to drive, or being in charge of a motor vehicle, with excess alcohol in breath, blood or urine.	Sections 11 and 12(1) of this Act.
RTA section 6	[Failing to co-operate with a preliminary test].	Sections 11 and 12(1) of this Act.
RTA section 7	Failing to provide specimen for analysis or laboratory test.	Sections 11 and 12(1) of this Act.
[RTA section 7A	Failing to allow specimen of blood to be subjected to laboratory test.	Sections 11 and 12(1).]
RTA section 12	Motor racing and speed trials.	Sections 11 and 12(1) of this Act.
RTA section 14	Driving or riding in a motor vehicle in contravention of regulations requiring wearing of seat belts.	Sections 11 and 12(1) of this Act.
RTA section 15	Driving motor vehicle with child not wearing seat belt [or with child in a rear-facing child restraint in front seat with an active air bag].	Sections 11 and 12(1) of this Act.
RTA section 19	Prohibition of parking of heavy commercial vehicles on verges and footways.	Sections 11 and 12(1) of this Act.
RTA section 22	Leaving vehicles in dangerous positions.	Sections 1, 11 and 12(1) of this Act.
RTA section 23	Carrying passenger on motor-cycle contrary to section 23.	Sections 11 and 12(1) of this Act.
RTA section 24	Carrying passenger on bicycle contrary to section 24.	Sections 11 and 12(1) of this Act.
RTA section 25	Tampering with motor vehicles.	Section 11 of this Act.
RTA section 26(1)	Holding or getting onto vehicle in order to be carried.	Section 11 of this Act.
RTA section 26(2)	Holding onto vehicle in order to be towed.	Sections 11 and 12(1) of this Act.
RTA section 28	[Dangerous] cycling.	Sections 1, 11 and 12(1) of this Act.

(1) Provision creating offence	(2) General nature of offence	(3) Applicable provisions of this Act
RTA section 29	Careless, and inconsiderate, cycling.	Sections 1, 11 and 12(1) of this Act.
RTA section 30	Cycling when unfit through drink or drugs.	Sections 11 and 12(1) of this Act.
RTA section 31	Unauthorised or irregular cycle racing, or trials of speed.	Sections 11 and 12(1) of this Act.
RTA section 33	Unauthorised motor vehicle trial on footpaths or bridleways.	Sections 11 and 12(1) of this Act.
RTA section 34	Driving motor vehicles elsewhere than on roads.	Sections 11 and 12(1) of this Act.
RTA section 35	Failing to comply with traffic directions.	Sections 1, 11 and 12(1) of this Act.
RTA section 36	Failing to comply with traffic signs.	Sections 1, 11 and 12(1) of this Act.
[RTA section 40A	Using vehicle in dangerous condition, etc.	Sections 11 and 12(1) of this Act.]
[RTA section 41A	Breach of requirement as to brakes, steering-gear or tyres.	Sections 11 and 12(1) of this Act.]
[RTA section 41B	Breach of requirement as to weight: goods and passenger vehicles.	Sections 11 and 12(1) of this Act.]
[RTA section 41D	Breach of requirements as to control of vehicle, mobile telephones etc.	Sections 11 and 12(1) of this Act.]
RTA section 42	[Breach of other construction and use requirements].	Sections 11 and 12(1) of this Act.
RTA section 47	Using, etc., vehicle without required test certificate being in force.	Sections 11 and 12(1) of this Act.
RTA section 53	Using, etc., goods vehicle without required plating certificate or goods vehicle test certificate being in force, or where Secretary of State is required by regulations under section 49 to be notified of an alteration to the vehicle or its equipment but has not been notified.	Sections 11 and 12(1) of this Act.
RTA section 63	Using, etc., vehicle without required certificate being in force showing that it, or a part fitted to it, complies with type approval requirements applicable to it, or using, etc., certain goods vehicles for drawing trailer when plating certificate does not specify maximum laden weight for vehicle and trailer, or using, etc., goods vehicle where Secretary of State has not been but is required to be notified under section 48 of alteration to it or its equipment.	Sections 11 and 12(1) of this Act.
RTA section 71	Driving, etc., ... vehicle in contravention of prohibition on driving it as being unfit for service or overloaded, or refusing, neglecting or otherwise failing to comply with a direction to remove a ... vehicle found overloaded.	Sections 11 and 12(1) of this Act.

(1) Provision creating offence	(2) General nature of offence	(3) Applicable provisions of this Act
RTA section 78	Failing to comply with requirement about weighing motor vehicle or obstructing authorised person.	Sections 11 and 12(1) of this Act.
RTA section 87(1)	Driving [otherwise than in accordance with] a licence.	Sections 11 and 12(1) of this Act.
RTA section 87(2)	Causing or permitting a person to drive [otherwise than in accordance with] a licence.	Section 11 of this Act.
[RTA section 92(10)	Driving after making false declaration as to physical fitness.	Sections 6, 11 and 12(1) of this Act.]
RTA [section 94(3)] [and that subsection as applied by RTA section 99D [or 109C]]	Failure to notify the Secretary of State of onset of, or deterioration in, relevant or prospective disability.	Section 6 of this Act.
[RTA section 94(3A) [and that subsection as applied by RTA section 99D(b) [or 109C(c)]]	Driving after such a failure.	Sections 6, 11 and 12(1) of this Act.]
[RTA section 94A [or 109B]	Driving after refusal of licence under section 92(3) [, revocation under section 93 or service of a notice under section 99C].	Sections 6, 11 and 12(1) of this Act.]
[RTA section 99(5)	Driving licence holder failing to surrender licence and counterpart.	Section 6 of this Act.]
[...]	[...]	[...]
RTA section 99B(11) [and that subsection as applied by RTA section 109A(5)]	Driving after failure to comply with a requirement under section 99B(6), (7) or (10) [or a requirement under section 99(B)(6) or (7) as applied by section 109A(5)].	Section 6 of this Act.]
RTA section 103(1)(a)	Obtaining driving licence while disqualified.	Section 6 of this Act.
RTA section 103(1)(b)	Driving while disqualified.	Sections 6, 11 and 12(1) of this Act.
[RTA section 114(1)	Failing to comply with conditions of LGV[, PCV licence or LGV Community licence].	Sections 11 and 12(1) of this Act.]
[RTA section 114(2)	Causing or permitting a person under 21 to drive LGV or PCV in contravention of conditions of that person's licence.	Section 11 of this Act.]
RTA section 143	Using motor vehicle, or causing or permitting it to be used, while uninsured or unsecured against third party risks.	Sections 6, 11 and 12(1) of this Act.

(1) Provision creating offence	(2) General nature of offence	(3) Applicable provisions of this Act
[RTA section 144A	Keeping vehicle which does not meet insurance requirements.	Sections 6, 11 and 12(1) of this Act.]
RTA section 163	Failing to stop vehicle when required […].	Sections 11 and 12(1) of this Act.
RTA section 164(6)	Failing to produce driving licence[, etc.] or to state date of birth.	Sections 11 and 12(1) of this Act.
RTA section 165(3)	Failing to give constable certain names and addresses or to produce certificate of insurance or certain test and other like certificates.	Sections 11 and 12(1) of this Act.
RTA section 165(6)	Supervisor of learner driver failing to give constable certain names and addresses.	Section 11 of this Act.
RTA section 168	Refusing to give, or giving false, name and address in case of reckless, careless or inconsiderate driving or cycling.	Sections 11 and 12(1) of this Act.
RTA section 170	Failure by driver to stop, report accident or give information or documents.	Sections 11 and 12(1) of this Act.
RTA section 171	Failure by owner of motor vehicle to give police information for verifying compliance with requirement of compulsory insurance or security.	Sections 11 and 12(1) of this Act.
RTA section 174(1) or [(5)]	Making false statements in connection with licences under this Act and with registration as an approved driving instructor; or making false statement or withholding material information in order to obtain the issue of insurance certificates, etc.	Section 6 of this Act.
RTA section 175	Issuing false documents.	Section 6 of this Act.

[Schedule 1 is printed as corrected by a correction slip dated November 1990 **A19.244**
and as amended by the Road Traffic (Driver Licensing and Information Systems) Act 1989 ss.7, 16, Sch.3, para.27(a)–(d), and Sch.6; the Driving Licences (Community Driving Licence) Regulations 1990 (SI 1990/144); the Road Traffic Act 1991 ss.22, 83, Sch.1, paras 1–17, and Sch.8; the Road Traffic (New Drivers) Act 1995 s.10(4) and Sch.2, paras 3 and 7; the Driving Licences (Community Driving Licence) Regulations 1996 (SI 1996/1974) reg.3 and Sch.2, para.7 (not reproduced in this work); the Driving Licences (Community Driving Licence) Regulations 1998 (SI 1998/1420) regs 2 and 16(1) and (2) (not reproduced in this work); the Police Reform Act 2002 s.56(4); the Railways and Transport Safety Act 2003 s.107 and Sch.7, para.7; the Crime (International Co-operation) Act 2003 s.91 and Sch.5, para.36; the Statute Law (Repeals) Act 2004 s.1(1) and Sch.1, Pt 14; the Traffic Management Act 2004 s.98 and Sch.12, Pt 2; the Motor Vehicles (Wearing of Seat Belts) (Amendment) Regulations 2006 (SI 2006/1892) reg.7; and the Road Safety Act 2006 ss.20(3), 21(2), 22(5), 26(3), 58(6) (s.58(6) only has effect in relation to offences committed after November 8, 2006).

Schedule 1 is also prospectively amended by the Transport Act 1982 s.24(3) (as itself amended by the Road Traffic (Consequential Provisions) Act 1988 s.4 and Sch.2, Pt 1, para.13(c)(iv)), which will add the words "falsely amending certificate of conformity" to column (2) of the entry relating to the Road Traffic Act 1988 s.175, with effect from a date to be announced; see the Transport Act 1982 s.76(2).

For the extension of offences to which s.6 applies, see the note to s.6 above.

A19.245   **Road Safety Act 2006 amendments.** *With effect from a day (or days) to be appointed, the following amendments will be made to Sch.1:*

1. *in para.3, the following new sub-paragraph will be inserted after para.(a) by the Road Safety Act 2006 s.15(3)(a):*

   [(aa) an offence under section 34D(12) of this Act,]

2. *in para.4, the following new sub-paragraph will be inserted before para.(a) by the Road Safety Act 2006 s.15(3)(b):*

   [(za) an offence under section 34D(12) of this Act,]

3. *after the entry relating to s.41B of the Road Traffic Act 1988, the following text will be inserted by the Road Safety Act 2006 s.18(5):*

[RTA section 41C	Breach of requirement as to speed assessment equipment detection device.	Sections 11 and 12(1) of this Act.]

4. *after the entry relating to s.94A of the Road Traffic Act 1988, the following text will be inserted by the Road Safety Act 2006 s.39(2):*

[RTA section 98A(7)	Driving licence holder failing to surrender licence and counterpart.	Section 6 of this Act.]

5. *in the entry relating to s.98A(7) of the Road Traffic Act 1988 (in relation to endorsement (all drivers)), the words "and counterpart" will be omitted by the Road Safety Act 2006 s.10 and Sch.3, para.62(2), s.59 and Sch.7(4);*

6. *in the entry relating to s.99(5) of the Road Traffic Act 1988 (in relation to endorsement (all drivers)), the words "and counterpart" will be omitted by the Road Safety Act 2006 s.10 and Sch.3, para.62(2), s.59 and Sch.7(4);*

7. *in the entry relating to s.164(6) of the Road Traffic Act 1988 (in relation to endorsement (all drivers)), the words "and counterpart etc." will be omitted by the Road Safety Act 2006 s.10 and Sch.3, para.62(3), s.59 and Sch.7(4).*

A19.246

SCHEDULE 2

PROSECUTION AND PUNISHMENT OF OFFENCES

PART I

OFFENCES UNDER THE TRAFFIC ACTS

Section 9, etc.

(1) Provision creating offence	(2) General nature of offence	(3) Mode of prosecution	(4) Punishment	(5) Disqualification	(6) Endorsement	(7) Penalty points
Offences under the Road Traffic Regulation Act 1984						
RTRA section 5	Contravention of traffic regulation order.	Summarily.	Level 3 on the standard scale.			
RTRA section 8	Contravention of order regulating traffic in Greater London.	Summarily.	Level 3 on the standard scale.			
RTRA section 11	Contravention of experimental traffic order.	Summarily.	Level 3 on the standard scale.			
RTRA section 13	Contravention of experimental traffic scheme in Greater London.	Summarily.	Level 3 on the standard scale.			
RTRA section 16(1)	Contravention of temporary prohibition or restriction.	Summarily.	Level 3 on the standard scale.	[Discretionary if committed in respect of a speed restriction.	Obligatory if committed in respect of a speed restriction.	3–6 or 3 (fixed penalty)]

(1) Provision creating offence	(2) General nature of offence	(3) Mode of prosecution	(4) Punishment	(5) Disqualification	(6) Endorsement	(7) Penalty points
[RTRA section 16C(1)	Contravention of prohibition or restriction relating to relevant event.	Summarily.	Level 3 on the standard scale.	—	—	—]
RTRA section 17(4)	Use of special road contrary to scheme or regulations.	Summarily.	Level 4 on the standard scale.	Discretionary if committed in respect of a motor vehicle otherwise than by unlawfully stopping or allowing the vehicle to remain at rest on a part of a special road on which vehicles are in certain circumstances permitted to remain at rest.	Obligatory if committed as mentioned in the entry in column 5.	[3–6 or 3 (fixed penalty) if committed in respect of a speed restriction, 3 in any other case].
RTRA section 18(3)	One-way traffic on trunk road.	Summarily.	Level 3 on the standard scale.			
RTRA section 20(5)	Contravention of prohibition or restriction for roads of certain classes.	Summarily.	Level 3 on the standard scale.			

(1) Provision creating offence	(2) General nature of offence	(3) Mode of prosecution	(4) Punishment	(5) Disqualification	(6) Endorsement	(7) Penalty points
RTRA section 25(5)	Contravention of pedestrian crossing regulations.	Summarily.	Level 3 on the standard scale.	Discretionary if committed in respect of a motor vehicle.	Obligatory if committed in respect of a motor vehicle.	3
RTRA section 28(3)	Not stopping at school crossing.	Summarily.	Level 3 on the standard scale.	Discretionary if committed in respect of a motor vehicle.	Obligatory if committed in respect of a motor vehicle.	3
RTRA section 29(3)	Contravention of order relating to street playground.	Summarily.	Level 3 on the standard scale.	Discretionary if committed in respect of a motor vehicle.	Obligatory if committed in respect of a motor vehicle.	2
...						

(1) Provision creating offence	(2) General nature of offence	(3) Mode of prosecution	(4) Punishment	(5) Disqualification	(6) Endorsement	(7) Penalty points
RTRA section [35A(1)]	Contravention of order as to use of parking place.	Summarily.	(a) Level 3 on the standard scale in the case of an offence committed by a person in a street parking place reserved for disabled persons' vehicles or in an off-street parking place reserved for such vehicles, where that person would not have been guilty of that offence if the motor vehicle in respect of which it was committed had been a disabled person's vehicle. (b) Level 2 on the standard scale in any other case.			

(1) Provision creating offence	(2) General nature of offence	(3) Mode of prosecution	(4) Punishment	(5) Disqualification	(6) Endorsement	(7) Penalty points
RTRA section [35A(2)]	[Misuse of apparatus for collecting charges or of parking device or connected apparatus].	Summarily.	Level 3 on the standard scale.			
RTRA section [35A(5)]	Plying for hire in parking place.	Summarily.	Level 2 on the standard scale.			
RTRA section 43(5)	Unauthorised disclosure of information in respect of licensed parking place.	Summarily.	Level 3 on the standard scale.			
RTRA section 43(10)	Failure to comply with term or conditions of licence to operate parking place.	Summarily.	Level 3 on the standard scale.			
	Operation of public off-street parking place without licence.	Summarily.	Level 5 on the standard scale.			

(1) Provision creating offence	(2) General nature of offence	(3) Mode of prosecution	(4) Punishment	(5) Disqualification	(6) Endorsement	(7) Penalty points
RTRA section 47(1)	Contraventions relating to designated parking places.	Summarily.	(a) Level 3 on the standard scale in the case of an offence committed by a person in a street parking place reserved for disabled persons' vehicles where that person would not have been guilty of that offence if the motor vehicle in respect of which it was committed had been a disabled person's vehicle. (b) Level 2 in any other case.			
RTRA section 47(3)	Tampering with parking meter.	Summarily.	Level 3 on the standard scale.			
RTRA section 52(1)	Misuse of parking device.	Summarily.	Level 2 on the standard scale.			
RTRA section 53(5)	Contravention of certain provisions of designation orders.	Summarily.	Level 3 on the standard scale.			

(1) Provision creating offence	(2) General nature of offence	(3) Mode of prosecution	(4) Punishment	(5) Disqualification	(6) Endorsement	(7) Penalty points
RTRA section 53(6)	Other contraventions of designation orders.	Summarily.	Level 2 on the standard scale.			
RTRA section 61(5)	Unauthorised use of loading area.	Summarily.	Level 3 on the standard scale.			
RTRA section 88(7)	Contravention of minimum speed limit.	Summarily.	Level 3 on the standard scale.			
RTRA section 89(1)	Exceeding speed limit.	Summarily.	Level 3 on the standard scale.	Discretionary.	Obligatory.	[3–6 or 3 (fixed penalty)].
RTRA section 104(5)	Interference with notice as to immobilisation device.	Summarily.	Level 2 on the standard scale.			
RTRA section 104(6)	Interference with immobilisation device.	Summarily.	Level 3 on the standard scale.			
RTRA section 105(5)	Misuse of disabled person's badge (immobilisation devices).	Summarily.	Level 3 on the standard scale.			
[RTRA section 105(6A)	Misuse of recognised badge (immobilisation devices).	Summarily.	Level 3 on the standard scale.			]

(1) Provision creating offence	(2) General nature of offence	(3) Mode of prosecution	(4) Punishment	(5) Disqualification	(6) Endorsement	(7) Penalty points
RTRA section 108(2) or that subsection as modified by section 109(2), (3))	Non-compliance with notice (excess charge).	Summarily.	Level 3 on the standard scale.			
RTRA section 108(3) (or that subsection as modified by section 109(2) and (3))	False response to notice (excess charge).	Summarily.	Level 5 on the standard scale.			
RTRA section 112(4)	Failure to give information as to identity of driver.	Summarily.	Level 3 on the standard scale.			
RTRA section 115(1)	Mishandling or faking parking documents.	(a) Summarily. (b) On indictment.	(a) The statutory maximum. (b) 2 years.			
RTRA section 115(2)	False statement for procuring authorisation.	Summarily.	Level 4 on the standard scale.			
RTRA section 116(1)	Non-delivery of suspect document or article.	Summarily.	Level 3 on the standard scale.			
RTRA section [117(1)]	Wrongful use of disabled person's badge.	Summarily.	Level 3 on the standard scale.			

(1) Provision creating offence	(2) General nature of offence	(3) Mode of prosecution	(4) Punishment	(5) Disqualification	(6) Endorsement	(7) Penalty points
[RTRA section 117(1A)	Wrongful use of recognised badge.	Summarily.	Level 3 on the standard scale.			]
RTA section 129(3)	Failure to give evidence at inquiry.	Summarily.	Level 3 on the standard scale.			
Offences under the Road Traffic Act 1988						
RTA section 1	Causing death by [dangerous] driving.	On indictment.	[14 years].	Obligatory.	Obligatory.	[3–11]
RTA section 2	[Dangerous] driving.	(a) Summarily.	(a) 6 months or the statutory maximum or both.	[Obligatory.]	Obligatory.	[3–11]
		(b) On indictment.	(b) 2 years or a fine or both.			
[RTA section 2B	Causing death by careless, or inconsiderate, driving.	(a) Summarily.	(a) 12 months (in England and Wales) or 6 months (in Scotland) or the statutory maximum or both.	Obligatory.	Obligatory.	3–11]
		(b) On indictment.	(b) 5 years or a fine or both.			
RTA section 3	Careless, and inconsiderate, driving.	Summarily.	[Level 5] on the standard scale.	Discretionary.	Obligatory.	3–9

(1) Provision creating offence	(2) General nature of offence	(3) Mode of prosecution	(4) Punishment	(5) Disqualification	(6) Endorsement	(7) Penalty points
[RTA section 3ZB	Causing death by driving: unlicensed, disqualified or uninsured drivers.	(a) Summarily.	(a) 12 months (in England and Wales) or 6 months (in Scotland) or the statutory maximum or both.	Obligatory.	Obligatory.	3–11]
		(b) On indictment.	(b) 2 years or a fine or both.			
[RTA section 3A	Causing death by careless driving when under influence of drink or drugs.	On indictment.	[14 years] or a fine or both.	Obligatory.	Obligatory.	3–11]
RTA section 4(1)	Driving or attempting to drive when unfit to drive through drink or drugs.	Summarily.	6 months or level 5 on the standard scale or both.	Obligatory.	Obligatory.	[3–11]
RTA section 4(2)	Being in charge of a [mechanically propelled vehicle] when unfit to drive through drink or drugs.	Summarily.	3 months or level 4 on the standard scale or both.	Discretionary.	Obligatory.	10

(1) Provision creating offence	(2) General nature of offence	(3) Mode of prosecution	(4) Punishment	(5) Disqualification	(6) Endorsement	(7) Penalty points
RTA section 5(1)(a)	Driving or attempting to drive with excess alcohol in breath, blood or urine.	Summarily.	6 months or level 5 on the standard scale or both.	Obligatory.	Obligatory.	[3–11]
RTA section 5(1)(b)	Being in charge of a motor vehicle with excess alcohol in breath, blood or urine.	Summarily.	3 months or level 4 on the standard scale or both.	Discretionary.	Obligatory.	10
RTA section 6	[Failing to co-operate with a preliminary test]	Summarily.	Level 3 on the standard scale.	Discretionary.	Obligatory.	4
RTA section 7	Failing to provide specimen for analysis or laboratory test.	Summarily.	(a) Where the specimen was required to ascertain ability to drive or proportion of alcohol at the time offender was driving or attempting to drive, 6 months or level 5 on the standard scale or both.	(a) Obligatory in case mentioned in column 4(a).	Obligatory.	(a) [3–11 in case mentioned in column 4(a).

(1) Provision creating offence	(2) General nature of offence	(3) Mode of prosecution	(4) Punishment	(5) Disqualification	(6) Endorsement	(7) Penalty points
[RTA section 7A	Failing to allow specimen to be subjected to laboratory test.	Summarily.	(a) Where the test would be for ascertaining ability to drive or proportion of alcohol at the time offender was driving or attempting to drive, 6 months or level 5 on the standard scale or both	(a) Obligatory in the case mentioned in column 4(a).	Obligatory.	3–11, in case mentioned in column 4(a).
			(b) In any other case, 3 months or level 4 on the standard scale or both.	(b) Discretionary in any other case.		(b) 10 in any other case.
RTA section 12	Motor racing and speed trials on public ways.	Summarily.	Level 4 on the standard scale.	(b) Discretionary in any other case. Obligatory.	Obligatory.	10, in any other case.] [3–11]

(1) Provision creating offence	(2) General nature of offence	(3) Mode of prosecution	(4) Punishment	(5) Disqualification	(6) Endorsement	(7) Penalty points
RTA section 13	Other unauthorised or irregular competitions or trials on public ways.	Summarily.	Level 3 on the standard scale.			
RTA section 14	Driving or riding in a motor vehicle in contravention of regulations requiring wearing of seat belts.	Summarily.	Level 2 on the standard scale.			
RTA section 15(2)	Driving motor vehicle with child in front not wearing seat belt [or with child in a rear-facing child restraint in front seat with an active air bag].	Summarily.	Level 2 on the standard scale.			
RTA section 15(4)	Driving motor vehicle with child in rear not wearing seat belt.	Summarily.	[Level 2] on the standard scale.			

(1) Provision creating offence	(2) General nature of offence	(3) Mode of prosecution	(4) Punishment	(5) Disqualification	(6) Endorsement	(7) Penalty points
[RTA section 15A(3) or (4)	Selling, etc. in certain circumstances equipment as conducive to the safety of children in motor vehicles.	Summarily.	Level 3 on the standard scale.	—	—	—
[RTA section 15B	Failure to notify bus passengers of the requirement to wear seat belts.	Summarily.	Level 4 on the standard scale.	—	—	—
RTA section 16	Driving or riding motor cycles in contravention of regulations requiring wearing of protective headgear.	Summarily.	Level 2 on the standard scale.			
RTA section 17	Selling, etc., helmet not of the prescribed type as helmet for affording protection for motor cyclists.	Summarily.	Level 3 on the standard scale.			
RTA section 18(3)	Contravention of regulations with respect to use of headworn appliances on motor cycles.	Summarily.	Level 2 on the standard scale.			

(1) Provision creating offence	(2) General nature of offence	(3) Mode of prosecution	(4) Punishment	(5) Disqualification	(6) Endorsement	(7) Penalty points
RTA section 18(4)	Selling, etc., appliance not of prescribed type as approved for use on motor cycles.	Summarily.	Level 3 on the standard scale.			
RTA section 19	Prohibition of parking of heavy commercial vehicles on verges, etc.	Summarily.	Level 3 on the standard scale.			
RTA section 21	Driving or parking on cycle track.	Summarily.	Level 3 on the standard scale.			
RTA section 22	Leaving vehicles in dangerous positions.	Summarily.	Level 3 on the standard scale.	Discretionary if committed in respect of a motor vehicle.	Obligatory if committed in respect of a motor vehicle.	3
[RTA section 22A	Causing danger to road-users.	(a) Summarily. (b) On indictment.	(a) 6 months or the statutory maximum or both. (b) 7 years or a fine or both.	—	—	—]
RTA section 23	Carrying passenger on motor cycle contrary to section 23.	Summarily.	Level 3 on the standard scale.	Discretionary.	Obligatory.	[3]
RTA section 24	Carrying passenger on bicycle contrary to section 24.	Summarily.	Level 1 on the standard scale.			

(1) Provision creating offence	(2) General nature of offence	(3) Mode of prosecution	(4) Punishment	(5) Disqualification	(6) Endorsement	(7) Penalty points
RTA section 25	Tampering with motor vehicles.	Summarily.	Level 3 on the standard scale.			
RTA section 26	Holding or getting on to vehicle, etc., in order to be towed or carried.	Summarily.	Level 1 on the standard scale.			
RTA section 27	Dogs on designated roads without being held on lead.	Summarily.	Level 1 on the standard scale.			
RTA section 28	[Dangerous] cycling.	Summarily.	[Level 4] on the standard scale.			
RTA section 29	Careless, and inconsiderate, cycling.	Summarily.	[Level 3] on the standard scale.			
RTA section 30	Cycling when unfit through drink or drugs.	Summarily.	Level 3 on the standard scale.			
RTA section 31	Unauthorised or irregular cycle racing or trials of speed on public ways.	Summarily.	Level 1 on the standard scale.			

(1) Provision creating offence	(2) General nature of offence	(3) Mode of prosecution	(4) Punishment	(5) Disqualification	(6) Endorsement	(7) Penalty points
RTA section 32	Contravening prohibition on persons under 14 driving electrically assisted pedal cycles.	Summarily.	Level 2 on the standard scale.			
RTA section 33	Unauthorised motor vehicle trial on footpaths or bridleways.	Summarily.	Level 3 on the standard scale.			
RTA section 34	Driving [mechanically propelled] vehicles elsewhere than on roads.	Summarily.	Level 3 on the standard scale.			
RTA section 35	Failing to comply with traffic directions.	Summarily.	Level 3 on the standard scale.	Discretionary, if committed in respect of a motor vehicle by failure to comply with a direction of a constable[, or traffic officer] or traffic warden.	Obligatory if committed as described in column 5.	3

(1) Provision creating offence	(2) General nature of offence	(3) Mode of prosecution	(4) Punishment	(5) Disqualification	(6) Endorsement	(7) Penalty points
RTA section 36	Failing to comply with traffic signs.	Summarily.	Level 3 on the standard scale.	Discretionary, if committed in respect of a motor vehicle by failure to comply with an indication given by a sign specified for the purposes of this paragraph in regulations under RTA section 36.	Obligatory if committed as described in column 5.	3
RTA section 37	Pedestrian failing to stop when directed [...].	Summarily.	Level 3 on the standard scale.			
[RTA section 40A	Using vehicle in dangerous condition, etc.	Summarily.	[(a) Level 5 on the standard scale if committed in respect of a goods vehicle or a vehicle adapted to carry more than eight passengers. (b) Level 4 on the standard scale in any other case.]	[(a) Obligatory if committed within three years of a previous conviction of the offender under section 40A. (b) Discretionary in any other case.]	Obligatory.	3]

(1) Provision creating offence	(2) General nature of offence	(3) Mode of prosecution	(4) Punishment	(5) Disqualification	(6) Endorsement	(7) Penalty points
[RTA section 41A	Breach of requirement as to brakes, steering gear or tyres.	Summarily.	(a) Level 5 on the standard scale if committed in respect of a goods vehicle or a vehicle adapted to carry more than eight passengers. (b) Level 4 on the standard scale in any other case.	Discretionary.	Obligatory.	3]
[RTA section 41B	Breach of requirement as to weight: goods and passenger vehicles.	Summarily.	Level 5 on the standard scale.	—	—	—]
[RTA section 41D	Breach of requirements as to control of vehicle, mobile telephones etc.	Summarily.	(a) Level 4 on the standard scale if committed in respect of a goods vehicle or a vehicle adapted to carry more than eight passengers. (b) Level 3 on the standard scale in any other case.	Discretionary.	Obligatory.	3]

(1) Provision creating offence	(2) General nature of offence	(3) Mode of prosecution	(4) Punishment	(5) Disqualification	(6) Endorsement	(7) Penalty points
[RTA section 42	Breach of other construction and use requirements.	Summarily.	(a) Level 4 on the standard scale if committed in respect of a goods vehicle or a vehicle adapted to carry more than eight passengers. (b) Level 3 on the standard scale in any other case.	—	—	—]
RTA section 47	Using, etc., vehicle without required test certificate being in force.	Summarily.	(a) Level 4 on the standard scale in the case of a vehicle adapted to carry more than eight passengers. (b) Level 3 on the standard scale in any other case.			

(1) Provision creating offence	(2) General nature of offence	(3) Mode of prosecution	(4) Punishment	(5) Disqualification	(6) Endorsement	(7) Penalty points
Regulations under RTA section 49 made by virtue of section 51(2)	Contravention of requirement of regulations (which is declared by regulations to be an offence) that driver of goods vehicle being tested be present throughout test or drive, etc., vehicle as and when directed.	Summarily.	Level 3 on the standard scale.			
RTA section 53(1)	Using, etc., goods vehicle without required plating certificate being in force.	Summarily.	Level 3 on the standard scale.			
RTA section 53(2)	Using, etc., goods vehicle without required goods vehicle test certificate being in force.	Summarily.	Level 4 on the standard scale.			

(1) Provision creating offence	(2) General nature of offence	(3) Mode of prosecution	(4) Punishment	(5) Disqualification	(6) Endorsement	(7) Penalty points
RTA section 53(3)	Using, etc. goods vehicle where Secretary of State is required by regulations under section 49 to be notified of an alteration to the vehicle or its equipment but has not been notified.	Summarily.	Level 3 on the standard scale.			
Regulations under RTA section 61 made by virtue of subsection (4)	Contravention of requirement of regulations (which is declared by regulations to be an offence) that driver of goods vehicle being tested after notifiable alteration be present throughout test and drive, etc., vehicle as and when directed.	Summarily.	Level 3 on the standard scale.			

(1) Provision creating offence	(2) General nature of offence	(3) Mode of prosecution	(4) Punishment	(5) Disqualification	(6) Endorsement	(7) Penalty points
RTA section 63(1)	Using, etc., goods vehicle without required certificate being in force showing that it complies with type approval requirements applicable to it.	Summarily.	Level 4 on the standard scale.			
RTA section 63(2)	Using, etc., certain goods vehicles for drawing trailer when plating certificate does not specify maximum laden weight for vehicle and trailer.	Summarily.	Level 3 on the standard scale.			
RTA section 63(3)	Using, etc., goods vehicle where Secretary of State is required to be notified under section 59 of alteration to it or its equipment but has not been notified.	Summarily.	Level 3 on the standard scale.			

(1) Provision creating offence	(2) General nature of offence	(3) Mode of prosecution	(4) Punishment	(5) Disqualification	(6) Endorsement	(7) Penalty points
RTA section 64	Using goods vehicles with unauthorised weights as well as authorised weights marked on it.	Summarily.	Level 3 on the standard scale.			
[RTA section 64A	Failure to hold EC certificate of conformity for unregistered light passenger vehicle [or motor cycle].	Summarily.	Level 3 on the standard scale.	—	—	—]
RTA section 65	Supplying vehicle or vehicle part without required certificate being in force showing that it complies with type approval requirements applicable to it.	Summarily.	Level 5 on the standard scale.			
[RTA section 65A	Light passenger vehicles [and motor cycles] not to be sold without EC certificate of conformity.	Summarily.	Level 5 on the standard scale.	—	—	—]

(1) Provision creating offence	(2) General nature of offence	(3) Mode of prosecution	(4) Punishment	(5) Disqualification	(6) Endorsement	(7) Penalty points
RTA section 67	Obstructing testing of vehicle by examiner on road or failing to comply with requirements of RTA section 67 or Schedule 2.	Summarily.	Level 3 on the standard scale.			
RTA section 68	Obstructing inspection, etc., of ... vehicle by examiner or failing to comply with requirement to take ... vehicle for inspection.	Summarily.	Level 3 on the standard scale.			
RTA section 71	Driving, etc., ... vehicle in contravention of prohibition on driving it as being unfit for service, or refusing, neglecting or otherwise failing to comply with direction to remove a ... vehicle found overloaded.	Summarily.	Level 5 on the standard scale.			

(1) Provision creating offence	(2) General nature of offence	(3) Mode of prosecution	(4) Punishment	(5) Disqualification	(6) Endorsement	(7) Penalty points
RTA section 74	Contravention of regulations requiring goods vehicle operator to inspect, and keep records of inspection of, goods vehicles.	Summarily.	Level 3 on the standard scale.			
RTA section 75	Selling, etc., unroadworthy vehicle or trailer or altering vehicle or trailer so as to make it unroadworthy.	Summarily.	Level 5 on the standard scale.			
RTA section 76(1)	Fitting of defective or unsuitable vehicle parts.	Summarily.	Level 5 on the standard scale.			
RTA section 76(3)	Supplying defective or unsuitable vehicle parts.	Summarily.	Level 4 on the standard scale.			
RTA section 76(8)	Obstructing examiner testing vehicles to ascertain whether defective or unsuitable part has been fitted, etc.	Summarily.	Level 3 on the standard scale.			

(1) Provision creating offence	(2) General nature of offence	(3) Mode of prosecution	(4) Punishment	(5) Disqualification	(6) Endorsement	(7) Penalty points
RTA section 77	Obstructing examiner testing condition of used vehicles at sale rooms, etc.	Summarily.	Level 3 on the standard scale.			
RTA section 78	Failing to comply with requirement about weighing motor vehicle or obstructing authorised person.	Summarily.	Level 5 on the standard scale.			
RTA section 81	Selling, etc., pedal cycle in contravention of regulations as to brakes, bells, etc.	Summarily.	Level 3 on the standard scale.			
RTA section 83	Selling, etc., wrongly made tail lamps or reflectors.	Summarily.	Level 5 on the standard scale.			
[RTA section 87(1)	Driving otherwise than in accordance with a licence.	Summarily.	Level 3 on the standard scale.	Discretionary in a case where the offender's driving would not have been in accordance with any licence that could have been granted to him.	Obligatory in the case mentioned in column 5.	3–6]

(1) Provision creating offence	(2) General nature of offence	(3) Mode of prosecution	(4) Punishment	(5) Disqualification	(6) Endorsement	(7) Penalty points
RTA section 87(2)	Causing or permitting a person to drive [otherwise than in accordance with] a licence.	Summarily.	Level 3 on the standard scale.			
[RTA section 92(7C)	Failure to deliver licence [and counterpart] revoked by virtue of section 92(7A) to Secretary of State.	Summarily.	Level 3 on the standard scale.	—	—	—]
[RTA section 92(10)	Driving after making false declaration as to physical fitness.	Summarily.	Level 4 on the standard scale.	Discretionary.	Obligatory.	3–6]
[RTA section 93(3)	Failure to deliver revoked licence [and counterpart] to Secretary of State.	Summarily.	Level 3 on the standard scale.	—	—	—]

(1) Provision creating offence	(2) General nature of offence	(3) Mode of prosecution	(4) Punishment	(5) Disqualification	(6) Endorsement	(7) Penalty points
RTA [section 94(3)]	Failure to notify Secretary of State of onset of, or deterioration in, relevant or prospective disability [and that subsection as applied by RTA section 99D [or 109C]].	Summarily.	Level 3 on the standard scale.			
[RTA section 94(3A)	Driving after such a failure [and that subsection as applied by RTA section 99D(b) [or 109C(c)]].	Summarily.	Level 3 on the standard scale.	Discretionary.	Obligatory.	3–6]
[RTA section 94A	Driving after refusal of licence under section 92(3) [, revocation under section 93 or service of a notice under section 99C [or 109B]].	Summarily.	6 months or level 5 on the standard scale or both.	Discretionary.	Obligatory.	3–6]

(1) Provision creating offence	(2) General nature of offence	(3) Mode of prosecution	(4) Punishment	(5) Disqualification	(6) Endorsement	(7) Penalty points
RTA section 96	Driving with uncorrected defective eyesight, or refusing to submit to test of eyesight.	Summarily.	Level 3 on the standard scale.	Discretionary.	Obligatory.	[3]
RTA section 99[(5)]	Driving licence holder failing [to surrender licence and counterpart].	Summarily.	Level 3 on the standard scale.	—	—	—
[RTA section 99B(11) [and that subsection as applied by RTA section 109A(5)]	Driving after failure to comply with a requirement under section 99B(6), (7) or (10) [or a requirement under section 99B(6) or (7) as applied by section 109A(5)].	Summarily.	Level 3 on the standard scale.			
[RTA section 99C(4)	Failure to deliver Community licence to Secretary of State when required by notice under section 99C.	Summarily.	Level 3 on the standard scale.	—	—	—
RTA section 103(1)(a)	Obtaining driving licence while disqualified.	Summarily.	Level 3 on the standard scale.			

(1) Provision creating offence	(2) General nature of offence	(3) Mode of prosecution	(4) Punishment	(5) Disqualification	(6) Endorsement	(7) Penalty points
RTA section 103(1)(b)	Driving while disqualified.	(a) Summarily, in England and Wales. (b) Summarily, in Scotland. (c) On indictment, in Scotland.	(a) 6 months or level 5 on the standard scale or both. (b) 6 months or the statutory maximum or both. (c) 12 months or a fine or both.	Discretionary.	Obligatory.	[6]
[...] [RTA section 109B(4)	[...] Failure to deliver Northern Ireland licence to Secretary of State when required by notice under section 109B	[...] Summarily	[...] Level 3 on the standard scale	—	—	—
[RTA section 114	Failing to comply with conditions of LGV[, PCV licence or LGV Community licence], or causing or permitting person under 21 to drive LGV or PCV in contravention of such conditions.	Summarily.	Level 3 on the standard scale.	—	—	—

(1) Provision creating offence	(2) General nature of offence	(3) Mode of prosecution	(4) Punishment	(5) Disqualification	(6) Endorsement	(7) Penalty points
[RTA section 115A(4)	Failure to deliver LGV or PCV Community licence when required by notice under section 115A.	Summarily.	Level 3 on the standard scale.	—	—	—
[RTA section 118	Failing to surrender revoked or suspended LGV or PCV licence [and counterpart].	Summarily.	Level 3 on the standard scale.	—	—	—
Regulations made by virtue of RTA [section 120(5)]	Contravention of provisions of regulations (which is declared by regulations to be an offence) about [LGV or PCV] drivers' licences [or LGV or PCV Community licence].	Summarily.	Level 3 on the standard scale.			
RTA section 123(4)	Giving of paid driving instruction by unregistered and unlicensed persons or their employers.	Summarily.	Level 4 on the standard scale.			

(1) Provision creating offence	(2) General nature of offence	(3) Mode of prosecution	(4) Punishment	(5) Disqualification	(6) Endorsement	(7) Penalty points
RTA section 123(6)	Giving paid instruction without there being exhibited on the motor car a certificate of registration or a licence under RTA Part V.	Summarily.	Level 3 on the standard scale.			
[RTA section 125A(4)	Failure, on application for registration as disabled driving instructor, to notify Registrar of onset of, or deterioration in, relevant or prospective disability.	Summarily.	Level 3 on the standard scale.	—	—	—]
[RTA section 133C(4)	Failure by registered or licensed disabled driving instructor to notify Registrar of onset of, or deterioration in, relevant or prospective disability.	Summarily.	Level 3 on the standard scale.	—	—	—]

(1) Provision creating offence	(2) General nature of offence	(3) Mode of prosecution	(4) Punishment	(5) Disqualification	(6) Endorsement	(7) Penalty points
[RTA section 133D	Giving of paid driving instruction by disabled persons or their employers without emergency control certificate or in unauthorised motor car.	Summarily.	Level 3 on the standard scale.	—	—	—]
RTA section 135	Unregistered instructor using title or displaying badge, etc., prescribed for registered instructor, or employer using such title, etc., in relation to his unregistered instructor or issuing misleading advertisement, etc.	Summarily.	Level 4 on the standard scale.			
RTA section 136	Failure of instructor to surrender to Registrar certificate or licence.	Summarily.	Level 3 on the standard scale.			

(1) Provision creating offence	(2) General nature of offence	(3) Mode of prosecution	(4) Punishment	(5) Disqualification	(6) Endorsement	(7) Penalty points
RTA section 137	Failing to produce certificate of registration or licence as driving instructor.	Summarily.	Level 3 on the standard scale.			
RTA section 143	Using motor vehicle while uninsured or unsecured against third-party risks.	Summarily.	[Level 5] on the standard scale.	Discretionary.	Obligatory.	6–8
[RTA section 144A	Keeping vehicle which does not meet insurance requirements.	Summarily.	Level 3 on the standard scale.			]
RTA section 147	Failing to surrender certificate of insurance or security to insurer on cancellation or to make statutory declaration of loss or destruction.	Summarily.	Level 3 on the standard scale.			
RTA section 154	Failing to give information, or wilfully making a false statement, as to insurance or security when claim made.	Summarily.	Level 4 on the standard scale.			

(1) Provision creating offence	(2) General nature of offence	(3) Mode of prosecution	(4) Punishment	(5) Disqualification	(6) Endorsement	(7) Penalty points
[Regulations under RTA section 160 made by virtue of paragraph 2(1) of Schedule 2A	Contravention of provision of regulations (which is declared by regulations to be an offence) prohibiting removal of or interference with immobilisation notice.	Summarily.	Level 2 on the standard scale.			
Regulations under RTA section 160 made by virtue of paragraph 2(2) of Schedule 2A	Contravention of provision of regulations (which is declared by regulations to be an offence) prohibiting removal or attempted removal of immobilisation device.	Summarily.	Level 3 on the standard scale.			
Regulations under RTA section 160 made by virtue of paragraph 2(3) of Schedule 2A	Contravention of provision of regulations (which is declared by regulations to be an offence) about display of disabled person's badge.	Summarily.	Level 3 on the standard scale.			

(1) Provision creating offence	(2) General nature of offence	(3) Mode of prosecution	(4) Punishment	(5) Disqualification	(6) Endorsement	(7) Penalty points
Regulations under RTA section 160 made by virtue of paragraph 2(4) of Schedule 2A	Contravention of provision of regulations (which is declared by regulations to be an offence) prohibiting making of false or misleading declaration to secure release of vehicle from immobilisation device.	(a) Summarily. (b) On indictment.	(a) The statutory maximum. (b) 2 years or a fine or both.			
Regulations under RTA section 160 made by virtue of paragraph 4 of Schedule 2A	Contravention of provision of regulations (which is declared by regulations to be an offence) prohibiting making of false or misleading declaration to secure possession of vehicle in person's custody.	(a) Summarily. (b) On indictment.	(a) The statutory maximum. (b) 2 years or a fine or both.			]

(1) Provision creating offence	(2) General nature of offence	(3) Mode of prosecution	(4) Punishment	(5) Disqualification	(6) Endorsement	(7) Penalty points
RTA section 163	Failing to stop [mechanically propelled] vehicle or cycle when required [...].	Summarily.	[(a) Level 5 on the standard scale if committed by a person driving a mechanically propelled vehicle. (b) Level 3 on the standard scale if committed by a person riding a cycle.]			
RTA section 164	Failing to produce driving licence[, etc.] or to state date of birth, or failing to provide the Secretary of State with evidence of date of birth, etc.	Summarily.	Level 3 on the standard scale.			
RTA section 165	Failing to give ... certain names and addresses or to produce certain documents.	Summarily.	Level 3 on the standard scale.			

(1) Provision creating offence	(2) General nature of offence	(3) Mode of prosecution	(4) Punishment	(5) Disqualification	(6) Endorsement	(7) Penalty points
RTA section 168	Refusing to give, or giving false, name and address in case of reckless, careless or inconsiderate driving or cycling.	Summarily.	Level 3 on the standard scale.			
RTA section 169	Pedestrian failing to give constable his name and address after failing to stop when directed by constable controlling traffic.	Summarily.	Level 1 on the standard scale.			
RTA section 170(4)	Failing to stop after accident and give particulars or report accident.	Summarily.	[Six months or level 5 on the standard scale or both].	Discretionary.	Obligatory.	[5–10]
RTA section 170(7)	Failure by driver, in case of accident involving injury to another, to produce evidence of insurance or security or to report accident.	Summarily.	Level 3 on the standard scale.			

(1) Provision creating offence	(2) General nature of offence	(3) Mode of prosecution	(4) Punishment	(5) Disqualification	(6) Endorsement	(7) Penalty points
RTA section 171	Failure by owner of motor vehicle to give police information for verifying compliance with requirement of compulsory insurance or security.	Summarily.	Level 4 on the standard scale.			
RTA section 172	Failure of person keeping vehicle and others to give police information as to identity of driver, etc., in the case of certain offences.	Summarily.	Level 3 on the standard scale.	[Discretionary, if committed otherwise than by virtue of subsection (5) or (11).	Obligatory, if committed otherwise than by virtue of subsection (5) or (11)	[6]
RTA section 173	Forgery, etc., of licences, [counterparts of licences,] test certificates, certificates of insurance and other documents and things.	(a) Summarily. (b) On indictment.	(a) The statutory maximum. (b) 2 years.			

(1) Provision creating offence	(2) General nature of offence	(3) Mode of prosecution	(4) Punishment	(5) Disqualification	(6) Endorsement	(7) Penalty points
RTA section 174	Making certain false statements, etc., and withholding certain material information.	[(a) Summarily (b) On indictment].	[(a) 6 months or the statutory maximum or both (b) 2 years or a fine or both].			
RTA section 175	Issuing false documents.	Summarily.	Level 4 on the standard scale.		—	...]
[[RTA section] [175(2)]	Falsely amending certificate of conformity.	Summarily.	[Level 4 on the standard scale.]			
RTA section 177	Impersonation of, or of person employed by, authorised examiner.	Summarily.	Level 3 on the standard scale.	—		
RTA section 178	Taking, etc., in Scotland a motor vehicle without authority or, knowing that it has been so taken, driving it or allowing oneself to be carried in it without authority.	(a) Summarily. (b) On indictment.	(a) 3 months or the statutory maximum or both. (b) 12 months or a fine or both.	Discretionary.	[—	—]

(1) Provision creating offence	(2) General nature of offence	(3) Mode of prosecution	(4) Punishment	(5) Disqualification	(6) Endorsement	(7) Penalty points
RTA section 180	Failing to attend, give evidence or produce documents to, inquiry held by Secretary of State, etc.	Summarily.	Level 3 on the standard scale.			
RTA section 181	Obstructing inspection of vehicles after accident.	Summarily.	Level 3 on the standard scale.			
RTA Schedule 1 paragraph 6	Applying warranty to [equipment, protective helmet, appliance or information in defending proceedings under RTA section 15A,] 17 or 18(4) where no warranty given, or applying false warranty.	Summarily.	Level 3 on the standard scale.			

(1) Provision creating offence	(2) General nature of offence	(3) Mode of prosecution	(4) Punishment	(5) Disqualification	(6) Endorsement	(7) Penalty points
			Offences under this Act			
Section 25 of this Act	Failing to give information as to date of birth or sex to court or to provide Secretary of State with evidence of date of birth, etc.	Summarily.	Level 3 on the standard scale.			
Section 26 of this Act	Failing to produce driving licence [and counterpart] to court making order for interim disqualification …	Summarily.	Level 3 on the standard scale.			

(1) Provision creating offence	(2) General nature of offence	(3) Mode of prosecution	(4) Punishment	(5) Disqualification	(6) Endorsement	(7) Penalty points
Section 27 of this Act	Failing to produce licence [and counterpart] to court for endorsement on conviction of offence involving obligatory endorsement or on committal for sentence, etc., for offence involving obligatory or discretionary disqualification when no interim disqualification ordered	Summarily.	Level 3 on the standard scale.			
...						
Section 62 of this Act	Removing fixed penalty notice fixed to vehicle.	Summarily.	Level 2 on the standard scale.			
Section 67 of this Act	False statement in response to notice to owner.	Summarily.	Level 5 on the standard scale.			
[...]						

[The entries in Pt 1 of Sch.2 are printed as amended by the Road Traffic **A19.247**
(Driver Licensing and Information Systems) Act 1989 ss.7, 16, Sch.3, paras.28
and 29, and Sch.6; the Parking Act 1989 s.4 and Schedule, para.11; the Driving
Licences (Community Driving Licence) Regulations 1990 (SI 1990/144); the Mo-
tor Vehicles (Safety Equipment for Children) Act 1991 s.3(2) and (3); the New
Roads and Street Works Act 1991 s.168(2) and Sch.9; the Road Traffic Act 1991
ss.26, 83, Sch.1, paras 1–31, and Sch.8; the Motor Vehicles (EC Type Approval)
Regulations 1992 (SI 1992/3107); the Road Traffic (Driving Instruction by Dis-
abled Persons) Act 1993 s.6 and Schedule, paras 1 and 11; the Criminal Justice
Act 1993 s.67(1); the Road Traffic Regulation (Special Events) Act 1994 s.1(2);
the Driving Licences (Community Driving Licence) Regulations 1996 (SI 1996/
1974) reg.3 and Sch.2, para.8 (not reproduced in this work); the Driving Licences
(Community Driving Licence) Regulations 1998 (SI 1998/1420) regs 2 and 16(1)
and (3) (not reproduced in this work); the Motor Cycles Etc. (EC Type Approval)
Regulations 1999 (SI 1999/2920); the Countryside and Rights of Way Act 2000
ss.67 and 103(2) and Sch.7, para.8; the Police Reform Act 2002 s.56(5); the
Railways and Transport Safety Act 2003 s.107 and Sch.7, para.8; the Crime
(International Co-operation) Act 2003 s.91 and Sch.5, para.37; the Criminal
Justice Act 2003 s.285 (s.285 will not affect the penalty for any offence commit-
ted before its commencement (February 27, 2004)) and s.286 (s.286 will not ap-
ply to any offences committed before its commencement (January 29, 2004)); the
Traffic Management Act 2004 s.6(5), s.98 and Sch.12, Pt 2; Statute Law (Repeals)
Act 2004 s.1(1) and Sch.1, Pt 14; the Disability Discrimination Act 2005 Sch.1,
Pt 2, para.45; the Motor Vehicles (Wearing of Seat Belts) (Amendment) Regula-
tions 2006 (SI 2006/1892) reg.8; the Road Safety Act 2006 ss.20(4), 21(3), 22(6)
and (7), 26(4), 27, 29.

The traffic signs specified for the purposes of column 5 of the entry relating to
s.36 of the Road Traffic Act 1988 are prescribed by reg.10(2) of the Traffic Signs
Regulations and General Directions 2002 (SI 2002/3113) below.

The entries in Pt 1 of Sch.2 are prospectively amended by the Transport Act
1982 s.24(3) (as itself amended by the Criminal Justice Act 1982 s.46(1) and
(3)(c), and the Road Traffic (Consequential Provisions) Act 1988 s.4 and Sch.2,
Pt 1, para.13(c)) (as to the entries relating to the Road Traffic Act 1988 s.175(1)
and (2)); when s.24(3) of the 1982 Act is brought into operation, the reference to
s.175 of the Road Traffic Act 1988 will read "s.175(1)" and the entry relating to
s.175(2) of that Act will become operative.

Further prospective amendments to Pt 1 of Sch.2 are as follows:

1. *in the entry for s.4(2) of the Road Traffic Act 1988, in column 4, the*
   words "51 weeks" will be substituted for the words "three months" by
   the Criminal Justice Act 2003 s.280(2) and Sch.26, para.38(2);
2. *in the entry for s.5(1)(b) of the Road Traffic Act 1988, in column 4, the*
   words "51 weeks" will be substituted for the words "three months" by
   the Criminal Justice Act 2003 s.280(2) and Sch.26, para.38(3);
3. *in the entry for s.7 of the Road Traffic Act 1988, in column 4, the words*
   "51 weeks" will be substituted for the words "three months" by the
   Criminal Justice Act 2003 s.280(2) and Sch.26, para.38(4);
4. *in the entry for s.7A of the Road Traffic Act 1988, in column 4, the*
   words "51 weeks" will be substituted for the words "three months" by
   the Criminal Justice Act 2003 s.280(2) and Sch.26, para.38(5).

A19.248   **Road Safety Act 2006 amendments**

Part I. *With effect from a day(or days) to be appointed, the following amendments will be made to Pt 1 of Sch.2:*

1. *in column (7), Penalty points, for the entry relating to s.17(4) of the Road Traffic Regulation Act 1984 the words "2–6 or appropriate penalty points (fixed penalty) if committed in respect of a speed limit, 3 in any other case" will be substituted by the Road Safety Act 2006 s.17(a);*

2. *in column (7), Penalty points, for the entry relating to s.89(1) of the Road Traffic Regulation Act 1984, the words "2–6 or appropriate penalty points (fixed penalty)" will be substituted by the Road Safety Act 2006 s.17(b);*

3. *after the entry relating to s.41B of the Road Traffic Act 1988, the following text will be inserted by the Road Safety Act 2006 s.18(6):*

[RTA section 41C.	Breach of requirement as to speed assessment equipment detection devices.	Summarily.	(a) Level 4 on the standard scale if committed on a special road.	Discretionary.	Obligatory.	3–6 or 3 (fixed penalty).
(b) Level 3 on the standard scale in any other case.						

4. *in the entry relating to s.92(7C) of the Road Traffic Act 1988 (in relation to endorsement (all drivers)), the words "and counterpart" will be omitted by the Road Safety Act 2006 s.10 and Sch.3, para.63(2)(a), s.59 and Sch.7(4);*

5. *in the entry relating to s.93(3) of the Road Traffic Act 1988 (in relation to endorsement (all drivers)), the words "and counterpart" will be omitted by the Road Safety Act 2006 s.10 and Sch.3, para.63(2)(b), s.59 and Sch.7(4);*

6. *after the entry relating to s.94A of the Road Traffic Act 1988, the following text will be inserted by the Road Safety Act 2006 s.39(3):*

[RTA section 98A(7).	Driving licence holder failing to surrender licence and counterpart.	Summarily.	Level 3 on the standard scale.			]

7. *in the entry relating to s.98A(7) of the Road Traffic Act 1988 (in relation to endorsement (all drivers)), the words "and counterpart" will be omitted by the Road Safety Act 2006 s.10 and Sch.3, para.63(2)(c), s.59 and Sch.7(4);*

8. *in the entry relating to s.99(5) of the Road Traffic Act 1988 (in relation to endorsement (all drivers)), the words "and counterpart" will be omitted by the Road Safety Act 2006 s.10 and Sch.3, para.63(2)(d), s.59 and Sch.7(4);*

9. *in the entry relating to s.118 of the Road Traffic Act 1988 (in relation to endorsement (all drivers)), the words "and counterpart" will be omitted by the Road Safety Act 2006 s.10 and Sch.3, para.63(2)(e), s.59 and Sch.7(4);*

10. *in the entry relating to s.123(4) of the Road Traffic Act 1988, in column (1), Provision creating offence, "123A(1) and (2)" will be substituted for "123(4)", and in column (2), General nature of offence, the words ", and carrying on of business in provision of driving instruction, by unregistered persons" will be substituted for the words "by unregistered and unlicensed persons or their employers" by the Road Safety Act 2006 s.42 and Sch.6, para.33(2);*

11. *in the entry relating to s.123(6) of the Road Traffic Act 1988, in column (1), Provision creating offence, "123A(4)" will be substituted for "123(6)"' and in column (2), General nature of offence, the words "and carrying on of business in provision of driving instruction, without prescribed requirements relating to displaying of evidence of registration under RTA Part 5 being complied with" will be substituted for the words "without there being exhibited on the motor car a certificate of registration or a licence under RTA Part 5" by the Road Safety Act 2006 s.42 and Sch.6, para.33(3);*

12. *in the entry relating to s.133C(4) of the Road Traffic Act 1988, in column (2), General nature of offence, the words "or licensed" will be omitted by the Road Safety Act 2006 s.42 and Sch.6, para.33(4), s.59 and Sch.7, Pt 14;*

13. *in the entry relating to s.133D of the Road Traffic Act 1988, in column (2), General nature of offence, the words "or their employers" will be omitted by the Road Safety Act 2006 s.42 and Sch.6, para.33(5), s.59 and Sch.7(14);*

14. *in the entry relating to s.135 of the Road Traffic Act 1988, for the words in column (2), General nature of offence, the words "Misuse of evidence of registration, etc." will be substituted by the Road Safety Act 2006 s.42 and Sch.6, para.33(6);*

15. *in the entry relating to s.136 of the Road Traffic Act 1988, in column (2), General nature of offence, the word "etc." will be substituted for the words "or licence" by the Road Safety Act 2006 s.42 and Sch.6, para.33(7);*

16. *in the entry relating to s.137 of the Road Traffic Act 1988, in column (2), General nature of offence, the word "etc." will be substituted for the words "or licence" by the Road Safety Act 2006 s.42 and Sch.6, para.33(7);*

17. *in the entry relating to s.164 of the Road Traffic Act 1988 (in relation to endorsement (all drivers)), the words "or counterpart etc." will be omitted by the Road Safety Act 2006 s.10 and Sch.3, para.63(3), s.59 and Sch.7(4);*

18.   *in the entry relating to s.173 of the Road Traffic Act 2006 (in relation to endorsement (all drivers)), the words "counterparts of Community licences," will be omitted by the Road Safety Act 2006 s.10 and Sch.3, para.63(4), s.59 and Sch.7(4);*

19.   *in the entry to s.26 of the Road Traffic Offenders Act 1988 (in relation to endorsement (all drivers)), the words "and counterpart" will be omitted by the Road Safety Act 2006 s.10 and Sch.3, para.63(2)(f), s.59 and Sch.7(4);*

20.   *in the entry to s.27 of the Road Traffic Offenders Act 1988 (in relation to endorsement (all drivers)), the words "and counterpart" will be omitted by the Road Safety Act 2006 s.10 and Sch.3, para.63(2)(g), Sch.7(4);*

21.   *after the entry relating to s.27 of the Road Traffic Offenders Act 1988, the following text will be inserted by the Road Safety Act 2006 s.15(4):*

[Section 34D(12) of this Act.	Interference etc. with alcohol ignition interlock.	Summarily.	Level 4 on the standard scale if the motor vehicle to which the alcohol ignition interlock is fitted is a goods vehicle or a vehicle adapted to carry more than eight passengers. Level 3 on the standard scale in any other case.			]

22.   *after the entry relating to s.67 of the Road Traffic Offenders Act 1988, the following text will be inserted by the Road Safety Act 2006 s.11(2):*

[Section 90D(6) of this Act.	Driving, etc., vehicle in contravention of prohibition for failure to pay financial penalty deposit, etc.	Summarily.	Level 5 on the standard scale.			]/

A19.249

Part II

Other Offences

(1) *Offence*	(2) *Disqualification*	(3) *Endorsement*	(4) *Penalty points*
Manslaughter or, in Scotland, culpable homicide by the driver of a motor vehicle.	Obligatory.	Obligatory.	[3–11]
[An offence under section 35 of the Offences against the Person Act 1861 (furious driving).	Discretionary.	Obligatory if committed in respect of a mechanically propelled vehicle.	3–9
[An offence under section 12A of the Theft Act 1968 (aggravated vehicle-taking).	Obligatory.	Obligatory.	[3–11]
Stealing or attempting to steal a motor vehicle.	Discretionary.	⌐	⌐
An offence or attempt to commit an offence in respect of a motor vehicle under section 12 of the Theft Act 1968 (taking conveyance without consent of owner, etc., or, knowing it has been so taken, driving it or allowing oneself to be carried in it).	Discretionary.	⌐	⌐
An offence under section 25 of the Theft Act 1968 (going equipped for stealing, etc.) committed with reference to the theft or taking of motor vehicles.	Discretionary.	⌐	⌐

A19.250   *[Part II of Sch.2 is printed as amended by the Road Traffic Act 1991 ss.26, 83, Sch.2, para.32(1)–(3), and Sch.8; the Aggravated Vehicle-Taking Act 1992 s.3(1); the Road Safety Act 2006 s.28.]*

SCHEDULE 3

FIXED PENALTY OFFENCES

A19.251

(1) Provision creating offence	(2) General nature of offence
[Offences under the Parks Regulation (Amendment) Act 1926]	
[section 2(1)	Breach of parks regulations but only where the offence is committed in relation to regulation 4(27) (driving or riding a trade vehicle), 4(28) (exceeding speed limit) or 4(30) (unauthorised waiting by a vehicle or leaving a vehicle unattended) of the Royal and other Parks and Gardens Regulations 1977 [*SI 1977/217; not reproduced in this work*].]
[Offences under the Highways Act 1835 and the Roads (Scotland) Act 1984]	
[Section 72 of the Highways Act 1835	Driving on the footway
	Cycling on the footway]
[Section 129(5) of the Roads (Scotland) Act 1984	Driving on the footway]
...	
[Offences under the Transport Act 1968 (c.73)	
[Section 96(11) of the Transport Act 1968	Contravention of any requirement of domestic drivers' hours code
Section 96(11A) of that Act	Contravention of any requirement of applicable Community rules as to periods of driving, etc.
Section 97(1) of that Act	Using vehicle in contravention of requirements relating to installation, use or repair of recording equipment in accordance with Community Recording Equipment Regulation
Section 98(4) of that Act	Contravention of regulations made under section 98 or any requirement as to books, records or documents of applicable Community rules
Section 99(4) of that Act	Failing to comply with requirements relating to inspection of records or obstructing an officer, but only insofar as the offence relates to:— (i) failing to comply with any requirement under section 99(1)(a); or (ii) obstructing an officer in exercise of powers under 99(2)(a) or 99(3).

(1) Provision creating offence	(2) General nature of offence
Section 99ZD(1) of that Act	Failing to comply with requirements relating to inspection of recording equipment or records (whether electronic or hard copy) made by or stored on recording equipment except where that offence is committed by:— (i) failing to sign a hard copy of downloaded data when required to do so under section 99ZC(1); or (ii) obstructing an officer in exercise of powers under section 99ZF.
Section 99C of that Act	Failure to comply with prohibition or direction in relation to driving vehicle.
Offence under the Road Traffic (Foreign Vehicles) Act 1972 (c.27)	
Section 3(1) of the Road Traffic (Foreign Vehicles) Act 1972.	Driving, etc., foreign goods vehicle or foreign public service vehicle in contravention of prohibition etc.]
Offence under the Greater London Council (General Powers) Act 1974	
Section 15 of the Greater London Council (General Powers) Act 1974.	Parking vehicles on footways, verges, etc.
Offence under the Highways Act 1980	
Section 137 of the Highways Act 1980.	Obstructing a highway, but only where the offence is committed in respect of a vehicle.
[*Offence under the Public Passenger Vehicles Act 1981 (c.14)*	
Section 12(5) of the Public Passenger Vehicles Act 1981	Using public service vehicle on road except under PSV operators' licence.]
Offences under the Road Traffic Regulation Act 1984	
RTRA section 5(1)	Using a vehicle in contravention of a traffic regulation order outside Greater London.
RTRA section 8(1)	Breach of traffic regulation order in Greater London.
RTRA section 11	Breach of experimental traffic order.
RTRA section 13	Breach of experimental traffic scheme regulations in Greater London.
RTRA section 16(1)	Using a vehicle in contravention of temporary prohibition or restriction of traffic in case of execution of works, etc.
RTRA section 17(4)	Wrongful use of special road.
RTRA section 18(3)	Using a vehicle in contravention of provision for one-way traffic on trunk road.
RTRA section 20(5)	Driving a vehicle in contravention of order prohibiting or restricting driving vehicles on certain classes of roads.

(1) *Provision creating offence*	(2) *General nature of offence*
RTRA section 25(5)	Breach of pedestrian crossing regulations, except an offence in respect of a moving motor vehicle [other than a contravention of regulations 23, 24, 25 and 26 of the Zebra, Pelican and Puffin Pedestrian Crossings Regulations and General Directions 1997 [*q.v.*]].
...	
RTRA section [35A(1)]	Breach of an order regulating the use, etc. of a parking place provided by a local authority, but only where the offence is committed in relation to a parking place provided on a road.
RTRA section 47(1)	Breach of a provision of a parking place designation order and other offences committed in relation to a parking place designated by such an order, except any offence of failing to pay an excess charge within the meaning of section 46.
RTRA section 53(5)	Using vehicle in contravention of any provision of a parking place designation order having effect by virtue of section 53(1)(a) (inclusion of certain traffic regulation provisions).
RTRA section 53(6)	Breach of a provision of a parking place designation order having effect by virtue of section 53(1)(b) (use of any part of a road for parking without charge).
RTRA section 88(7)	Driving a motor vehicle in contravention of an order imposing a minimum speed limit under section 88(1)(b).
RTRA section 89(1)	Speeding offences under RTRA and other Acts.
[*Offences under the Road Transport (International Passenger Services) Regulations 1984 (S.I. 1984/748)*	
Regulation 19(1) of the Road Transport (International Passenger Services) Regulations 1984	Using vehicle for Community regulated carriage of passengers by road otherwise than in accordance with authorisation or certificate, etc.
Regulation 19(2) of those Regulations	Using vehicle for ASOR regulated or Community regulated carriage of passengers by road without having correctly completed passenger waybill or without carrying top copy of waybill on vehicle throughout journey.]
Offences under the Road Traffic Act 1988	
RTA section 14	Breach of regulations requiring wearing of seat belts.
RTA section 15(2)	Breach of restriction on carrying children in the front of vehicles.
[RTA section 15(4)	Breach of restriction on carrying children in the rear of vehicles].

(1) *Provision creating offence*	(2) *General nature of offence*
RTA section 16	Breach of regulations relating to protective headgear for motor cycle drivers and passengers.
[RTA section 18(3)	Breach of regulations relating to head-worn appliances (eye protectors) for use on motor cycles]
RTA section 19	Parking a heavy commercial vehicle on verge or footway.
RTA section 22	Leaving vehicle in dangerous position.
RTA section 23	Unlawful carrying of passengers on motor cycles.
[RTA section 24	Carrying more than one person on a pedal cycle.]
RTA section 34	Driving [mechanically propelled] vehicles elsewhere than on a road.
RTA section 35	Failure to comply with traffic directions.
RTA section 36	Failure to comply with traffic signs.
[RTA section 40A	Using vehicle in dangerous condition, etc.]
[RTA section 41A	Breach of requirement as to brakes, steering-gear or tyres.]
[RTA section 41B	Breach of requirement as to weight: goods and passenger vehicles.]
RTA section 42	[Breach of other construction and use requirements.]
[RTA section 47	Using, etc, vehicle without required test certificate being in force]
[RTA section 71(1)	Driving, etc., vehicle in contravention of prohibition on driving it as being unfit for service or overloaded, or failing to comply with direction to remove a vehicle found overloaded.]
RTA section 87(1)	Driving vehicle [otherwise than in accordance with] requisite licence.
[RTA section 143	Using motor vehicle while uninsured or unsecured against third party risks]
…	
RTA section 163	Failure to stop vehicle on being so required […].
[RTA section 172	Failure of person keeping vehicle and others to give the police information as to identity of driver, etc, in the case of certain offences]
[Offence under this Act	
Section 90D(6)	Driving, etc., vehicle in contravention of prohibition on driving, or failing to comply with direction to remove vehicle on failure to make a financial penalty deposit payment.

(1) *Provision creating offence*	(2) *General nature of offence*
Offences under the Goods Vehicles (Community Authorisations) Regulations 1992 (S.I. 1992/3077)	
Regulation 3 of the Goods Vehicles (Community Authorisations) Regulations 1992	Using goods vehicle without Community authorisation.
Regulation 7 of those Regulations	Using vehicle under Community authorisation in contravention of conditions governing authorisation.]
[Offences under the Vehicle Excise and Registration Act 1994 (c.22)]	
[Section 33 of the Vehicle Excise and Registration Act 1994.	Using or keeping a vehicle on a public road without [vehicle licence, trade licence or nil licence] being exhibited in manner prescribed by regulations.]
[Section 34 of that Act	Using trade licence for unauthorised purposes or in unauthorised circumstances, etc.]
[RTA section 41D	Breach of requirement as to control of vehicle, mobile telephone etc.]
[Section 42 of that Act.	Driving or keeping a vehicle without required registration mark.]
[Section 43 of that Act.	Driving or keeping a vehicle with registration mark obscured, etc.]
[Section 43C of that Act	Using an incorrectly registered vehicle.]
[Section 59 of that Act	Failure to fix prescribed registration mark to a vehicle in accordance with regulations made under section 23(4)(a) of that Act]
[Offence under the Goods Vehicles (Licensing of Operators) Act 1995 (c. 23)	
Section 2(5) of the Goods Vehicles (Licensing of Operators) Act 1995	Using goods vehicle on road for carriage of goods except under operator's licence.
Offences under the Public Service Vehicles (Community Licences) Regulations 1999 (S.I.1999/1322)	
Regulation 3 of the Public Service Vehicles (Community Licences) Regulations 1999	Using public service vehicle on road without Community licence.
Regulation 7 of those Regulations	Using public service vehicle under Community licence in contravention of conditions governing use of licence.
Offences under the Road Transport (Passenger Vehicles Cabotage) Regulations 1999 (S.I. 1999/3413)	
Regulation 3 of the Road Transport (Passenger Vehicles Cabotage) Regulations 1999	Using vehicle on road for UK cabotage operations without Community licence.
Regulation 4 of those Regulations	Using vehicle on road for UK cabotage operations without control document.
Regulation 7(1) of those Regulations	Driver failing to produce Community licence on request when vehicle required to have licence on board.
Regulation 7(3) of those Regulations	Driver failing to produce control document on request when vehicle required to have control document on board.

(1)	(2)
Provision creating offence	*General nature of offence*
Offence under the Vehicle Drivers (Certificates of Professional Competence) Regulations 2007 (S.I. 2007/605)	
Regulation 11(7) of the Vehicle Drivers (Certificates of Professional Competence) Regulations 2007	Driver of relevant vehicle failing to produce on request evidence or document required to be carried under regulation 11(1), (3) or (5).]

[The entries in Sch.3 are printed as amended by the Crown Roads (Royal Parks) (Application of Road Traffic Enactments) Order 1987 (SI 1987/363; not reproduced in this work) as applied by the Road Traffic (Consequential Provisions) Act 1988 s.2(4); the Parking Act 1989 s.4 and Schedule; the Fixed Penalties Offences Order 1990 (SI 1990/335); the New Roads and Street Works Act 1991 s.168(2) and Sch.9; the Road Traffic Act 1991 ss.48, 83, Sch.4, para.112(1)–(4) and Sch.8; the Fixed Penalty Offences Order 1992 (SI 1992/345); the Vehicle Excise and Registration Act 1994 ss.63 and 65, Sch.3, para.25(2) and Sch.5; the Finance Act 1997 s.18 and Sch.3, paras 1 and 8(1); the Fixed Penalty Offences Order 1999 (SI 1999/1851); the Countryside and Rights of Way Act 2000 ss.67 and 103(2) and Sch.7, para.9; the Fixed Penalty Offences Order 2003 (SI 2003/1253); the Traffic Management Act 2004 s.98 and Sch.12, Pt 2; the Fixed Penalty Offences Order 2004 (SI 2004/2922); the Serious Organised Crime and Police Act 2005 s.150(2); the Road Safety Act 2006 s.26(5); the Fixed Penalty Offences Order 2009 (SI 2009/483) Sch.

A19.252

With effect from a day to be appointed, after the entry relating to s.41B of the Road Traffic Act 1988, the following text will be inserted by the Road Safety Act 2006 s.18(7):

[RTA section 41C	Breach of requirement as to speed assessment equipment detection devices.]

As to fixed penalty parking offences, see the Fixed Penalty Order 2000 (SI 2000/2792) and the Fixed Penalty Offences Order 2009 (SI 2009/483).]

Section 68   SCHEDULE 4

STATUTORY STATEMENTS

PART I

STATUTORY STATEMENT OF OWNERSHIP OR HIRING

1.—(1) For the purposes of Part III of this Act, a statutory statement of ownership is a statement on an official form signed by the person providing it and stating whether he was the owner of the vehicle at the time of the alleged offence and, if he was not the owner of the vehicle at that time, whether—

    (a) he was never the owner, or

    (b) he ceased to be the owner before, or became the owner after, that time,

and in a case within paragraph (b) above, stating, if the information is in his possession, the name and address of the person to whom, and the date on which, he disposed of the vehicle or (as the case may be) the name and address of the person from whom, and the date on which, he acquired it.

(2) An official form for a statutory statement of ownership shall—

A19.253

   (a) indicate that the person providing the statement in response to a notice to owner relating to an offence may give notice requesting a hearing in respect of the offence in the manner specified in the form, and

   (b) direct the attention of any person proposing to complete the form to the information provided in accordance with paragraph 3(3) below in any official form for a statutory statement of facts.

A19.254   **2.**—(1) For the purposes of Part III of this Act, a statutory statement of hiring is a statement on an official form, signed by the person providing it, being a person by whom a statement of liability was signed, and stating—

   (a) whether at the time of the alleged offence the vehicle was let to him under the hiring agreement to which the statement of liability refers, and

   (b) if it was not, the date on which he returned the vehicle to the possession of the vehicle-hire firm concerned.

   (2) An official form for a statutory statement of hiring shall—

   (a) indicate that the person providing the statement in pursuance of a notice relating to an offence served under section 63 of this Act by virtue of section 66 of this Act may give notice requesting a hearing in respect of the offence in the manner specified in the form, and

   (b) direct the attention of any person proposing to complete the form to the information provided in accordance with paragraph 3(3) below in any official form for a statutory statement of facts.

   (3) In sub-paragraph (1) above *"statement of liability"*, *"hiring agreement"* and *"vehicle-hire firm"* have the same meanings as in section 66 of this Act.

PART II

STATUTORY STATEMENT OF FACTS

A19.255   **3.**—(1) For the purposes of Part III of this Act, a statutory statement of facts is a statement on an official form, signed by the person providing it, which—

   (a) states that the person providing it was not the driver of the vehicle at the time of the alleged offence, and

   (b) states the name and address at the time when the statement is provided of the person who was the driver of the vehicle at the time of the alleged offence.

   (2) A statutory statement of facts has effect as a notice given by the driver requesting a hearing in respect of the offence if it is signed by the person identified in the statement as the driver of the vehicle at the time of the alleged offence.

   (3) An official form for a statutory statement of facts shall indicate—

   (a) that if a person identified in the statement as the driver of the vehicle at the time of the alleged offence signs the statement he will be regarded as having given notice requesting a hearing in respect of the offence,

   (b) that the person on whom the notice to owner relating to the offence is served may not give notice requesting a hearing in respect of the offence on his own account if he provides a statutory statement of facts signed by a person so identified, and

   (c) that if the fixed penalty is not paid before the end of the period stated in the notice to owner as the period for response to the notice, a sum determined by reference to that fixed penalty may be registered without any court hearing for enforcement as a fine against the person on whom the notice to owner is served, unless he has given notice requesting a hearing in respect of the offence,

but that, in a case within paragraph (c) above, the sum in question may not be so registered if the person on whom the notice to owner is served provides a statutory statement of facts as mentioned in paragraph (b) above until two months have elapsed from the end of the period so stated without service of a summons ...

A19.256   *[Words relating expressly and exclusively to Scotland have been omitted from para.3 of Sch.4.]*

Section 75

SCHEDULE 5

SCOTLAND; ADDITIONAL OFFENCES OPEN TO CONDITIONAL OFFER

[Omitted.]

A19.257

The London Regional Transport (No.2) Act 1989

(1989 c.xi)

A20.01   *An Act to empower London Underground Limited to construct works and to acquire lands; to confer powers on London Regional Transport; and for other purposes.*

[27th July 1989]

Whereas—

(1) By the London Regional Transport Act 1984 the London Transport Executive which were established by the Transport (London) Act 1969 were reconstituted on 29th June 1984 under the name of London Regional Transport (in this Act referred to as " the Corporation ")

A20.02   *[The Transport for London (Consequential Provisions) Order 2003 (SI 2003/1615), art.4 and Sch.2 apply this Act to Transport for London, or any subsidiary of Transport for London, as it applied to London Regional Transport or any subsidiary of London Regional Transport immediately before the coming into force of the Order (July 15, 2003).]*

*   *   *

PART V

PROVISIONS FOR CORPORATION

Application of [section 172 of the Road Traffic Act 1988] to British Transport Police Force

A20.03   **20.**—(1) In this section —

"*the British Transport Police Force*" means the force established by the Scheme set out in the Schedule to the British Transport Police Force Scheme 1963 (Approval) Order 1964 [*SI 1964/1456*] ;

"*level crossing*" has the same meaning as in section 1 of the Level Crossings Act 1983;

"*road*" has the same meaning as in [section 192 of the Road Traffic Act 1988]; and

"*subsidiary*" has the same meaning as in section 68 of the London Regional Transport Act 1984.

(2) In the application of [section 172 of the said Act of 1988] (which imposes a duty on the keeper of a vehicle to give information to a chief officer of police as to the identity of the driver, etc., in certain circumstances) to an offence alleged to be committed at a level crossing or on a road forming an access or approach to any garage, depot, railway or bus station, goods yard, workshop or other premises of the Corporation or any subsidiary of the Corporation, the expression "*chief of-*

ficer of police", where used in that section, shall include the chief constable of the British Transport Police Force.

   [Section 20 is printed as amended by the Interpretation Act 1978 s.17(2)(a).]   **A20.04**

The Radioactive Material (Road Transport) Act 1991

(1991 c.27)

A21.01 *An Act to make new provision with respect to the transport of radioactive material by road; to repeal section 5(2) of the Radioactive Substances Act 1948; and for connected purposes.*

[27th June 1991]

ARRANGEMENT OF SECTIONS

Section
1. Preliminary
2. Regulations
3. Prohibitions and directions
4. Enforcement notices
5. Powers of entry
6. Offences and penalties

*   *   *

Preliminary

A21.02   **1.**—(1) In this Act *"radioactive material"* means any material having a specific activity in excess of—

(a) 70 kilobecquerels per kilogram; or

(b) such lesser specific activity as may be specified in an order made by the Secretary of State;

and the power to make an order under this subsection shall be exercisable by statutory instrument which shall be subject to annulment in pursuance of a resolution of either House of Parliament.

(2) In this Act —

"examiner" means any examiner appointed under section 68(1) of the Road Traffic Act 1988;

"inspector" means any inspector appointed under subsection (3) below;

"packaging", in relation to radioactive material which has been consigned for transport, means an assembly of packaging components which encloses the material completely;

"packaging components" means components intended for use as part of the packaging of such material, and includes—

(a) receptacles, absorbent materials, spacing structures and radiation shielding; and

(b) devices for cooling, for absorbing mechanical shocks and for thermal insulation;

"radioactive package" means a package comprising radioactive material which has been consigned for transport and its packaging;

"transport" means transport by road.

(3) The Secretary of State may—

    (a) appoint as inspectors, to assist him in the execution of this Act and regulations made under it, such number of persons appearing to him to be qualified for the purpose as he may consider necessary; and

    (b) make to or in respect of any person so appointed such payments by way of remuneration, allowances or otherwise as he may with the approval of the Treasury determine.

[References to an examiner appointed under s.68(1) of the Road Traffic Act **A21.03** *1988 (see definition of "examiner" in s.1(2) above) are to be construed (as appropriate) as references to an examiner appointed under s.66A of the 1988 Act; see the Road Traffic Act 1991 s.9(2) below.*

0.1 kilobecquerels per kilogram have been specified as the specific activity for the purposes of s.1(1) above with effect from June 7, 2002 by the Radioactive Material (Road Transport) (Definition of Radioactive Material) Order 2002 (SI 2002/1092; not reproduced in this work). The 2002 Order therefore lowers the level of specific activity and widens the definition of "radioactive material" for the purposes of this Act.]

Regulations

    2.—(1)–(3) *[Power to make regulations.]*   **A21.04**

    (4) Any person who contravenes or fails to comply with any regulations under this section shall be guilty of an offence.

    (5) *[Power to make regulations exercisable by statutory instrument.]*

    (6) Subsection (2) of section 5 of the Radioactive Substances Act 1948 shall cease to have effect; and any regulations under that subsection which are in force at the commencement of this Act shall have effect as if made under this section.

[With effect from a day to be appointed, in s.2(4), the words "requirement **A21.05** *imposed by or by virtue of" will be inserted after the words "with any" by the Road Safety Act 2006 s.57(4).]*

Prohibitions and directions

    3.—(1) If it appears to an inspector or examiner, as respects any vehicle used   **A21.06** to transport radioactive packages—

    (a) that the vehicle, or any radioactive package which is being transported by it, fails to comply with any regulations under section 2 above;

    (b) that the vehicle, or any radioactive package which is or was being transported by it, has been involved in an accident;

    (c) that any radioactive package which was being transported by the vehicle, or any radioactive material which was contained in such a package, has been lost or stolen,

he may prohibit the driving of the vehicle.

    (2) If it appears to an inspector that any radioactive package or packaging component fails to comply with any regulations under section 2 above, he may prohibit the transport of that package or, as the case may require, the use of that component as part of the packaging of radioactive materials.

(3) A prohibition imposed under this section may apply either absolutely or for a specified purpose and either without any limitation of time or for a specified period.

(4) Where an inspector or examiner imposes a prohibition under subsection (1) above, he may also by a direction in writing require the person in charge of the vehicle to remove it (and, if it is a motor vehicle drawing a trailer, also to remove the trailer) to such place and subject to such conditions as are specified in the direction; and the prohibition shall not apply to the removal of the vehicle or trailer in accordance with the direction.

(5) Where an inspector or examiner imposes a prohibition under this section, he shall forthwith give notice of the prohibition to the person in charge of the vehicle, package or packaging component, specifying the failure to comply or, as the case may be, the accident or other incident in consequence of which the prohibition is imposed and—

> (a) stating whether the prohibition applies absolutely or for a specified purpose (and if the latter specifying the purpose); and
>
> (b) stating whether the prohibition applies without limitation of time or for a specified period;

and any direction under subsection (4) above may be given either in such a notice or in a separate notice given to the person in charge of the vehicle.

(6) A prohibition under this section shall come into force as soon as notice of it has been given in accordance with subsection (5) above and shall continue in force—

> (a) until it is removed under subsection (7) below; or
>
> (b) in the case of a prohibition imposed only for a specified period, until either it is removed or that period expires, whichever first occurs.

(7) A prohibition under subsection (1) above may be removed by any inspector or examiner, and a prohibition under subsection (2) above may be removed by any inspector, if he is satisfied—

> (a) in the case of a prohibition imposed in consequence of a failure to comply with any regulations under section 2 above, that appropriate action has been taken to remedy that failure;
>
> (b) in the case of a prohibition imposed in consequence of an accident or other incident, either that no failure so to comply was occasioned by that accident or incident or that appropriate action has been taken to remedy any such failure which was so occasioned;

and on doing so, the inspector or examiner shall forthwith give notice of the removal of the prohibition to the person in charge of the vehicle, package or packaging component.

(8) Any person who contravenes a prohibition under this section, or fails to comply with a direction under subsection (4) above, shall be guilty of an offence.

Enforcement notices

A21.07   4.—(1) If an inspector is of the opinion that any person is failing or is likely to fail to comply with any regulations under section 2 above which make provision for regulating the manufacture, or requiring the maintenance, of packaging components, he may serve a notice under this section on that person.

(2) A notice under this section shall—

    (a) state that the inspector is of the said opinion;

    (b) specify the matters constituting the failure to comply with the regulations in question or the matters making it likely that such a failure will occur, as the case may be;

    (c) specify the steps that must be taken in order to remedy those matters and the period within which those steps must be taken.

(3) Any person who fails to comply with a notice under this section shall be guilty of an offence.

Powers of entry

A21.08

5.—(1) An inspector or examiner shall, on producing, if so required, some duly authenticated document showing his authority, have a right at all reasonable hours—

    (a) to enter any vehicle used to transport radioactive packages for the purpose of ascertaining—

        (i) whether the vehicle, or any radioactive package which is being transported by it, fails to comply with any regulations under section 2 above;

        (ii) whether the vehicle, or any radioactive package which is or was being transported by it, has been involved in an accident; and

        (iii) whether any radioactive package which was being transported by the vehicle, or any radioactive material which was contained in such a package, has been lost or stolen; and

    (b) in the case of an inspector, to enter any premises for the purpose of ascertaining whether there is on the premises any vehicle used for transporting radioactive packages, or any radioactive package or packaging component which fails to comply with regulations under section 2 above.

(2) If a justice of the peace, on sworn information in writing ... is satisfied that there are reasonable grounds for entering any vehicle or premises for any such purpose as is mentioned in subsection (1) above and either—

    (a) that admission to the vehicle or premises has been refused, or a refusal is apprehended, and (in the case of premises) that notice of the intention to apply for the warrant has been given to the occupier; or

    (b) that an application for admission, or the giving of such a notice, would defeat the object of the entry, or that the case is one of urgency, or (in the case of premises) that they are unoccupied or the occupier temporarily absent,

he may by warrant signed by him authorise the inspector or examiner to enter and search the vehicle or premises, using reasonable force if need be.

(3) A warrant granted under this section shall continue in force until executed.

(4) An inspector or examiner who enters any vehicle or premises by virtue of this section, or of a warrant issued under it, may seize anything which he has reasonable grounds for believing is evidence in relation to an offence under section 2(4) above.

(5) Any person who intentionally obstructs any person exercising any power

conferred by this section, or by a warrant issued under it, shall be guilty of an offence.

(6) If any person who enters any vehicle or premises by virtue of this section, or of a warrant issued under it, discloses any information thereby obtained with respect to any manufacturing process or trade secret, he shall, unless the disclosure was made in the performance of his duty, be guilty of an offence.

(7) *[Application to Scotland.]*

A21.09   *[In s.5(2), words relating expressly and exclusively to Scotland have been omitted.]*

Offences and penalties

A21.10   **6.**—(1) Where an offence under this Act which has been committed by a body corporate is proved to have been committed with the consent or connivance of, or to be attributable to any neglect on the part of—

> (a) any director, manager, secretary or other similar officer of the body corporate; or
>
> (b) any person who was purporting to act in any such capacity,

he as well as the body corporate shall be deemed to be guilty of that offence and shall be liable to be proceeded against and punished accordingly.

(2) Any person guilty of an offence under section 5(5) above shall be liable on summary conviction to a fine not exceeding level 3 on the standard scale.

(3) Any person guilty of any other offence under this Act shall be liable—

> (a) on conviction on indictment, to a fine or to imprisonment for a term not exceeding two years or to both;
>
> (b) on summary conviction, to a fine not exceeding the statutory maximum or to imprisonment for a term not exceeding two months or to both.

(4) The court by or before which any person is convicted of an offence under section 2(4) or 3(8) above in respect of any radioactive material may order the material to be destroyed or disposed of and any expenses reasonably incurred in connection with the destruction or disposal to be defrayed by that person.

Expenses

A21.11   **7.** *[Omitted.]*

Corresponding provision for Northern Ireland

A21.12   **8.** *[Omitted.]*

Short title, repeals, commencement and extent

A21.13   **9.** *[Omitted.]*

SCHEDULE

REPEALS

A21.14   *[Omitted.]*

The Aggravated Vehicle-Taking Act 1992

(1992 c.11)

An Act to make provision with respect to persons who commit offences under section 12(1) of the Theft Act 1968 in relation to a mechanically propelled vehicle where additional circumstances are present relating to the driving of or damage to the vehicle. **A22.01**

[6th March 1992]

New offence of aggravated vehicle-taking

1.—(1) *[Inserts s.12A into the Theft Act 1968, q.v.]* **A22.02**

(2) The provisions of subsection (4) of section 12A of the Theft Act 1968 are without prejudice to the operation of—

> (a) [section 163 of the Criminal Justice Act 2003] (under which a Crown Court has a general power to fine an offender convicted on indictment); and

> (b) section 17 of, and Schedule 1 to, the Magistrates' Courts Act 1980 (under which, with certain exceptions not material to section 12A, offences under the Theft Act 1968 are triable either way).

(3) Nothing in section 12A of the Theft Act 1968 applies to—

> (a) an offence under section 12(1) of that Act which was committed before this section comes into force; or

> (b) any driving, injury or damage which occurred before this section comes into force.

[Section 1 is printed as amended by the Powers of Criminal Courts (Sentencing) Act 2000 s.165(1) and Sch.9, para.151; the Criminal Justice Act 2003 s.304 and Sch.32, para.65.] **A22.03**

Offence to be tried only summarily if value of damage is small

2.—(1) In Schedule 2 to the Magistrates' Courts Act 1980 (offences for which **A22.04**
the value involved is relevant to the mode of trial) after paragraph 2 there shall be inserted the following paragraph —

"3. Offences under section 12A of the Theft Act 1968 (aggravated vehicle-taking) where no allegation is made under subsection 1(b) other than of damage, whether to the vehicle or other property or both.	The total value of the damage alleged to have been caused.	(1) In the case of damage to any property other than the vehicle involved in the offence, as for the corresponding entry in paragraph 1 above, substituting a reference to the time of the accident concerned for any reference to the material time. (2) In the case of damage to the vehicle involved in the offence— (a) if immediately after the vehicle was recovered the damage was capable of repair— (i) what would probably then have been the market price for the repair of the damage, or (ii) what the vehicle would probably have cost to buy in the open market immediately before it was unlawfully taken, whichever is the less; or

		(b) if immediately after the vehicle was recovered the damage was beyond repair, what the vehicle would probably have cost to buy in the open market immediately before it was unlawfully taken."

(2) In the Magistrates' Courts Act 1980, at the end of section 22 (which introduces Schedule 2) there shall be added the following subsection—

"(12) Subsection (8) of section 12A of the Theft Act 1968 (which determines when a vehicle is recovered) shall apply for the purposes of paragraph 3 of Schedule 2 to this Act as it applies for the purposes of that section."

(3) In section 33 of the Magistrates' Courts Act 1980 (maximum penalties on summary conviction in pursuance of section 22)—

> (a) in subsection (1), at the beginning of paragraph (a) there shall be inserted the words "subject to subsection (3) below"; and
>
> (b) after subsection (2) there shall be inserted the following subsection—

"(3) Paragraph (a) of subsection (1) above does not apply to an offence under section 12A of the Theft Act 1968 (aggravated vehicle-taking)."

Obligatory disqualification

3. *[Amends the Road Traffic Offenders Act 1988.]*   **A22.05**

Short title, commencement and extent

4. *[Omitted.]*   **A22.06**

The Transport and Works Act 1992

(1992 c.42)

A23.01 *An Act to provide for the making of orders relating to, or to matters ancillary to, the construction or operation of railways, tramways, trolley vehicle systems, other guided transport systems and inland waterways ...; to make further provision in relation to railways, tramways, trolley vehicle systems and other guided transport systems; ... and for connected purposes.*

[16th March 1992]

PART I

ORDERS AUTHORISING WORKS, ETC.

*   *   *

PART II

SAFETY OF RAILWAYS, ETC.

A23.03 *[All the functions of a Minister of the Crown under Pt 2 of the Transport and Works Act 1992 exercisable in relation to Wales have been transferred to the National Assembly for Wales by the National Assembly for Wales (Transfer of Functions) Order 1999 (SI 1999/672; not reproduced in this work) art.2 and Sch.1.]*

Chapter I

Offences Involving Drink or Drugs
[Omitted.]   A23.04

Chapter II

Other Safety Provisions
[Omitted.]   A23.05

Chapter III

Supplementary

Duty to consult

57. *[Omitted.]*   A23.06

Prosecution

58. No proceedings shall be instituted in England and Wales in respect of an   A23.07
offence under this Part [, other than an offence under section 41 or 43 above]
except by or with the consent of the Secretary of State or the Director of Public
Prosecutions.

[Section 58 is printed as amended by the Railways Act 1993 s.117(5)(b). Sec-   A23.08
tion 117 applies to railways, tramways, trolley vehicle systems and any transport
system using any other mode of guided transport; ibid.s.117(6).

Neither s.41 nor s.43 of the Railways Act 1993 is concerned with matters relat-
ing to road traffic.]

Offences by bodies corporate

59.—(1) Where an offence under this Part committed by a body corporate is   A23.09
committed with the consent or connivance of, or is attributable to any neglect on
the part of, a director, manager, secretary or other similar officer of the body, or a
person purporting to act in such a capacity, he as well as the body corporate shall
be guilty of the offence.

(2) In subsection (1) above *"director"*, in relation to a body corporate whose
affairs are managed by its members, means a member of the body corporate.

(3) *[Applies to Scotland.]*

*   *   *

The Vehicle Excise and Registration Act 1994

(1994 c.22)

A24.01 *An Act to consolidate the enactments relating to vehicle excise duty and the registration of vehicles.*

[5th July 1994]

ARRANGEMENT OF SECTIONS
PART I
VEHICLE EXCISE DUTY AND LICENCES
Main provisions

PART II
REGISTRATION OF VEHICLES

* * *

SCHEDULES

* * *

* * *

[No excise duty is chargeable under the 1994 Act in respect of any vehicle in   **A24.02**
the service of a visiting force (as defined); see the Visiting Forces and Interna-
tional Headquarters (Application of Law) Order 1999 (SI 1999/1736; not
reproduced in this work) art.8(8).]

PART I

VEHICLE EXCISE DUTY AND LICENCES

Main provisions

Duty and licences

    1.—[(1) A duty of excise (*"vehicle excise duty"*) shall be charged in respect of   **A24.03**
every mechanically propelled vehicle that—

  (a) is registered under this Act (see section 21), or

  (b) is not so registered but is used, or kept, on a public road in the United
    Kingdom.]

    [(1A) Vehicle excise duty shall also be charged in respect of every thing
(whether or not it is a vehicle) that has been, but has ceased to be, a mechanically
propelled vehicle and—

  (a) is registered under this Act, or

  (b) is not so registered but is used, or kept, on a public road in the United
    Kingdom.]

    [(1B) In the following provisions of this Act *"vehicle"* means—

  (a) a mechanically propelled vehicle, or

  (b) any thing (whether or not it is a vehicle) that has been, but has ceased
    to be, a mechanically propelled vehicle.]

    [(1C) Vehicle excise duty charged in respect of a vehicle by subsection (1)(a)
or (1A)(a) shall be paid on a licence to be taken out—

    (a) by the person in whose name the vehicle is registered under this Act, or

    (b) if that person is not the person keeping the vehicle, by either of those persons.]

[(1D) Vehicle excise duty charged in respect of a vehicle by subsection (1)(b) or (1A)(b) shall be paid on a licence to be taken out by the person keeping the vehicle.]

(2) A licence taken out for a vehicle is in this Act referred to as a *"vehicle licence"*.

A24.04   *[Section 1 is printed as amended by the Finance Act 2002 s.19(1) and (2) and Sch.5, paras 1 and 2.]*

Annual rates of duty

A24.05   **2.**—(1) Vehicle excise duty in respect of a vehicle of any description is chargeable by reference to the annual rate currently applicable to it in accordance with the provisions of Schedule 1 which relate to vehicles of that description.

[(2) Subsection (1) applies subject to the following provisions of this section.]

[(3) Where vehicle excise duty is charged by section 1(1)(b) or (1A)(b) in respect of the keeping of a vehicle on a road (and not in respect of its use), duty in respect of such keeping is chargeable by reference to the general rate currently specified in paragraph 1(2) of Schedule 1.]

[(4) Subsections (5) and (6) apply where—

    (a) vehicle excise duty is charged by section 1(1)(a) or (1A)(a) in respect of a vehicle, and

    (b) were the vehicle not registered under this Act, duty would not be charged by section 1(1)(b) or (1A)(b) in respect of the use of the vehicle on a road.]

[(5) Where one or more use licences have previously been issued for the vehicle, the duty charged by section 1(1)(a) or (1A)(a) is chargeable by reference to the annual rate currently applicable to a vehicle of the same description as that of the vehicle on the occasion of the issue of that licence (or the last of those licences).]

[(6) In any other case, the duty charged by section 1(1)(a) or (1A)(a) is chargeable by reference to the general rate currently specified in paragraph 1(2) of Schedule 1.]

[(7) In subsection (5) *"use licence"* means—

    (a) a vehicle licence issued for the use of a vehicle, or

    (b) a vehicle licence that is issued by reason of a vehicle being registered under this Act but which would have been issued for the use of the vehicle if the vehicle had not been registered under this Act.]

A24.06   *[Section 2 is printed as amended by the Finance Act 1996 s.18(3) and (5); the Finance Act 2002 s.19(1) and (2) and Sch.5, paras 1 and 3.]*

Duration of licences

A24.07   **3.** *[Omitted.]*

Amount of duty

    4. *[Omitted.]*

Exempt vehicles

   5.—(1) No vehicle excise duty shall be charged in respect of a vehicle if it is   **A24.08**
an exempt vehicle.

   (2) Schedule 2 specifies descriptions of vehicles which are exempt vehicles.

Collection, etc., of duty

   6. *[Omitted.]*   **A24.09**

Vehicle licences

Issue of vehicle licences

   7.—(1) Every person applying for a vehicle licence shall—   **A24.10**

     (a) make [any] such declaration, and

     (b) furnish [any] such particulars [and any such documentary or other evidence],

(whether or not with respect to the vehicle for which the licence is to be taken
out) as may be [specified] by the Secretary of State.

   (2), (3) *[Content of declaration and particulars which may be prescribed.]*

   [(3A) A person applying for a licence shall not be required to make a declaration specified for the purposes of subsection (1)(a) if he agrees to comply with such conditions as may be specified in relation to him by the Secretary of State.]

   [(3B) The conditions which may be specified under subsection (3A) include—

     [(a)] a condition that particulars for the time being specified for the purposes of subsection (1)(b) are furnished by being transmitted to the Secretary of State by such electronic means as he may specify[; and]

     [(b) a condition requiring such payments as may be specified by the Secretary of State to be made to him in respect of—

        (i) steps taken by him for facilitating compliance by any person with any condition falling within paragraph (a); and

        (ii) in such circumstances as may be so specified, the processing of applications for vehicle licences where particulars are transmitted in accordance with that paragraph.]]

   [(4) A vehicle licence is issued for the vehicle specified in the application for the licence (and for no other).]

   (5) The Secretary of State is not required to issue a vehicle licence for which an application is made unless he is satisfied—

     (a) that the licence applied for is the appropriate licence for the vehicle specified in the application, and

     (b) in the case of an application for a licence for a vehicle purporting to be the first application for a licence for the vehicle, that a licence has not previously been issued for the vehicle.

   (6) *[Regulation-making power.]*

   (7) Where, following an application made in accordance with regulations under paragraph 13 of Schedule 1, a licence is issued for a goods vehicle at the rate of duty applicable to a weight specified in the application which is lower than its actual weight, that lower weight is to be shown on the licence.

[(8) In this section *"special vehicle"* has the same meaning as in paragraph 4 of Schedule 1.]

A24.11   *[Section 7 is printed as amended by the Finance Act 1995 s.19 and Sch.4, paras 1 and 30(1)(a) and (3); the Finance Act 1996 s.17(10), (14), and s.23 and Sch.2, paras 1 and 2(1)–(3); the Finance (No.2) Act 1997 s.14(1); the Vehicles (Crime) Act 2001 s.32(1)(a) and (b); the Finance Act 2002 s.19(1) and (2) and Sch.5, paras 1 and 4.*

With effect from a day to be appointed, the following amendments will be made to s.7 by the Road Safety Act 2006 s.47(1)–(3):

    1. *after s.7(1), the following new subsection will be inserted:*

[(1A) The particulars which may be so specified include any particulars which are required by regulations under section 22(1)(aa) to be recorded on the register in the case of the vehicle for which the licence is to be taken out; and the declarations and evidence which may be so specified include declarations and evidence relating to any such particulars.]

    2. *in s.7(5), the following new paragraph will be inserted after para.(a):*

[(za) that the requirements imposed by this section in the case of the vehicle specified in the application have been complied with,]*]*

Supplement payable on late renewal of a vehicle licence

A24.12   **7A.** *[Omitted.]*

Late-renewal supplements: further provisions

A24.13   **7B.** *[Omitted.]*

[Recovery of section 7A supplements: Scotland

A24.14   **7C.** *[Omitted.]*]

Vehicles removed into UK

A24.15   **8.** *[Omitted.]*

Temporary vehicle licences

A24.16   **9.**—(1) Where an application is made for a vehicle licence for a vehicle for any period, the Secretary of State may, if he thinks fit, instead of issuing immediately a vehicle licence for that period—

    (a) issue a vehicle licence (a *"temporary licence"*) for fourteen days, or such other period as may be prescribed by regulations made by the Secretary of State, having effect from such day as may be so prescribed, and

    (b) from time to time issue a further temporary licence for the vehicle.

(2) Nothing in this section affects the amount of any duty payable on a vehicle licence.

(3), (4) *[Payment of fee on application to an authorised body.]*

Transfer [...] of vehicle licences

A24.17   **10.**—(1) Any vehicle licence may be transferred in the manner prescribed by regulations made by the Secretary of State.

(2) [...]

(3) [...]

[Section 10 is printed as amended by the Finance Act 2008 s.144(2).]   **A24.18**

Trade licences

Issue of trade licences

11.—(1) Where—   **A24.19**

  (a) a motor trader or vehicle tester, or

  (b) a person who satisfies the Secretary of State that he intends to com-
      mence business as a motor trader or vehicle tester,

applies to the Secretary of State (in the manner [specified] by the Secretary of
State) to take out a licence under this section (a *"trade licence"*), the Secretary of
State may, subject to the conditions [prescribed by regulations made by the Secretary of State], issue such a licence to him on payment of vehicle excise duty at
the rate applicable to the licence.

[(1A) The power to prescribe conditions under subsection (1) includes, in particular, the power to prescribe conditions which are to be complied with after the
licence is issued.]

(2) In the case of a motor trader who is a manufacturer of vehicles, a trade
licence is a licence for—

  (a) all vehicles which are from time to time temporarily in his possession
      in the course of his business as a motor trader,

  (b) all vehicles kept and used by him solely for purposes of conducting
      research and development in the course of his business as such a
      manufacturer, and

  (c) all vehicles which are from time to time submitted to him by other
      manufacturers for testing on roads in the course of that business.

(3) In the case of any other motor trader, a trade licence is a licence for all
vehicles which are from time to time temporarily in his possession in the course
of his business as a motor trader.

(4) In the case of a vehicle tester, a trade licence is a licence for all vehicles
which are from time to time submitted to him for testing in the course of his business as a vehicle tester.

[Section 11 is printed as amended by the Finance Act 1995 s.19 and Sch.4,   **A24.20**
paras 1 and 30(2) and (3); the Finance Act 1996 s.23 and Sch.2, paras 1 and 3.]

Use of vehicles by holders of trade licences

12.—(1) The holder of a trade licence is not entitled by virtue of the licence—   **A24.21**

  (a) to use more than one vehicle at any one time,

  (b) to use a vehicle for any purpose other than a purpose prescribed by
      regulations made by the Secretary of State, or

  (c) except in such circumstances as may be so prescribed, to keep any ve-
      hicle on a road if it is not being used on the road.

(2) The Secretary of State shall by regulations prescribe—

  (a) the conditions subject to which trade licences are to be issued, and

(b) the purposes for which the holder of a trade licence may use a vehicle by virtue of the licence.

(3) The purposes which may be prescribed as those for which the holder of a trade licence may use a vehicle under the licence shall not include the conveyance of goods or burden of any description other than—

(a) a load which is carried solely for the purpose of testing or demonstrating the vehicle or any of its accessories or equipment and which is returned to the place of loading without having been removed from the vehicle except for that purpose or in the case of accident,

(b) in the case of a vehicle which is being delivered or collected, a load consisting of another vehicle used or to be used for travel from or to the place of delivery or collection,

(c) a load built in as part of the vehicle or permanently attached to it,

(d) a load consisting of parts, accessories or equipment designed to be fitted to the vehicle and of tools for fitting them to the vehicle, or

(e) a load consisting of a trailer other than a trailer which is for the time being a disabled vehicle.

(4) For the purposes of subsection (3), where a vehicle is so constructed that a trailer may by partial superimposition be attached to the vehicle in such a manner as to cause a substantial part of the weight of the trailer to be borne by the vehicle, the vehicle and the trailer are deemed to constitute a single vehicle.

(5) In subsection (3)(e) *"disabled vehicle"* includes a vehicle which has been abandoned or is scrap.

Trade licences: duration and amount of duty

A24.22   **13.** *[Omitted.]*

Trade licences: supplementary

A24.23   **14.**—(1) Nothing in sections 11 to 13 prevents a person entitled to take out a trade licence from holding two or more trade licences.

(2) The holder of a trade licence may at any time surrender the licence to the Secretary of State.

(3) *[Review of decision to refuse application for trade licence.]*

(4) *[Regulation-making power.]*

Additional duty, rebates, etc.

Vehicles becoming chargeable to duty at higher rate

A24.24   **15.**—(1) Where—

(a) a vehicle licence has been taken out for a vehicle at any rate of vehicle excise duty, and

(b) at any time while the licence is in force the vehicle is used so as to subject it to a higher rate,

duty at the higher rate becomes chargeable in respect of the licence for the vehicle.

(2) For the purposes of subsection (1) a vehicle is used so as to subject it to a

higher rate if it is used in an altered condition, in a manner or for a purpose which—

    (a) brings it within, or

    (b) if it was used solely in that condition, in that manner or for that purpose, would bring it within,

a description of vehicle to which a higher rate of duty is applicable.

[(2A) For the purpose of subsection (1) a vehicle is also used so as to subject it to a higher rate if—

    (a) the rate of vehicle excise duty paid on a vehicle licence taken out for the vehicle was the rate applicable to a vehicle of the same description with respect to which the reduced pollution requirements are satisfied, and

    (b) while the licence is in force, the vehicle is used at a time when those requirements are not satisfied with respect to it.]

(3) For the purposes of subsection (1) a vehicle in respect of which a lower rate of duty is chargeable by virtue of regulations under paragraph 13 of Schedule 1 is also used so as to subject it to a higher rate if it is used in contravention of a condition imposed under or by virtue of sub-paragraph (2) of that paragraph.

(4) [Subject to section 7(5),] where duty at a higher rate becomes chargeable under subsection (1) in respect of a vehicle licence, the licence may be exchanged for a new vehicle licence for the period—

    (a) beginning with the date on which the higher rate of duty becomes chargeable, and

    (b) ending with the period for which the original licence was issued.

(5) A new vehicle licence may be obtained under subsection (4) only on payment of the appropriate proportion of the difference between—

    (a) the amount of duty payable on the original licence, and

    (b) the amount of duty payable on a vehicle licence taken out for the period for which the original licence was issued but at the higher rate of duty.

(6) For the purposes of subsection (5) *"the appropriate proportion"* means the proportion which the number of months in the period—

    (a) beginning with the date on which the higher rate of duty becomes chargeable, and

    (b) ending with the period for which the original licence was issued,

        bears to the number of months in the whole of the period for which the original licence was issued (any incomplete month being treated as a whole month).

(7) If the higher rate has been changed since the issue of the original licence, the amount under subsection (5)(b) is calculated as if that rate had been in force at all material times at the level at which it is in force when it becomes chargeable.

[Section 15 is printed as amended by the Finance Act 1995 s.19 and Sch.4,   **A24.25** *paras 1, 16, 19 and 29; the Finance Act 1998 s.16 and Sch.1, paras 1, 13 and 17.]*

[Exception for tractive units from charge at higher rate

    15A.—(1) Where—   **A24.26**

(a) a vehicle licence has been taken out for a tractive unit, and

(b) the licence was taken out at a rate of vehicle excise duty applicable to a tractive unit which is to be used with semi-trailers with a minimum number of axles,

duty at a higher rate does not become chargeable under section 15 by reason only that while the licence is in force the tractive unit is used with a semi-trailer with fewer axles than that minimum number, if the condition in subsection (2) is satisfied.

(2) The condition is that the rate of duty at which the licence was taken out is equal to or exceeds the rate which would have been applicable if the revenue weight of the tractive unit had been a weight equal to the actual laden weight, at the time of the use, of the articulated vehicle consisting of the tractive unit and the semi-trailer.]

A24.27   *[Section 15A was inserted by the Finance Act 2003 s.16(1). Section 16 of the 2003 Act has effect in relation to the use of a tractive unit on or after April 9, 2003.]*

Exceptions from charge at higher rate in case of tractive units

A24.28   **16.** […]

[Revoked by the Finance Act 2003 s.16 and Sch.43, in relation to the use of a tractive unit on or after April 9, 2003.]

Other exceptions from charge at higher rate

A24.29   **17.**—(1) Where a vehicle licence has been taken out for a vehicle of any description, duty at a higher rate applicable to a vehicle of another description does not become chargeable under section 15 unless the vehicle as used while the licence is in force satisfies all the conditions which must be satisfied in order to bring the vehicle into the other description of vehicle for the purposes of vehicle excise duty.

(2) Where—

(a) duty has been paid in respect of a vehicle at a rate applicable under Part VIII of Schedule 1, and

(b) the vehicle is to a substantial extent being used for the conveyance of goods or burden belonging to a particular person (whether the person keeping the vehicle or not),

duty at a higher rate does not become chargeable under section 15 by reason only that the vehicle is used for the conveyance without charge in the course of their employment of employees of the person to whom the goods or burden belong.

(3)–(7) […]

(8) This section does not have effect where section 15 applies by reason of the use of a vehicle in contravention of a condition imposed under or by virtue of paragraph 13(2) of Schedule 1.

A24.30   *[Section 17 is printed as amended by the Finance Act 1995 s.19 and Sch.4, paras 1, 15 and 16 (see also ibid. s.162 and Sch.29, Pt 5(2)).]*

Vehicles for export becoming liable to VAT

A24.31   **18.**—(1) Where, by virtue of sub-paragraph (2) of paragraph 23 of Schedule 2, a vehicle which is an exempt vehicle under sub-paragraph (1) of that paragraph is deemed never to have been an exempt vehicle under that sub-paragraph, vehicle excise duty is payable—

(a) by the person by whom the vehicle was acquired from its manufacturer, in relation to the whole period since the registration of the vehicle, or

(b) by any other person who is for the time being the keeper of the vehicle, in relation to the period since the vehicle was first kept by him,

unless, or except to the extent that, the Secretary of State waives payment of the duty.

(2) Subsection (1) is without prejudice to section 30; but duty with respect to a vehicle is not payable by a person under that subsection in relation to any part of a period if an amount with respect to it has been ordered to be paid by him under that section in relation to the part of the period.

[Rebates]

19. *[Omitted.]*   A24.32

[Payment for licences by cheque

19A.—(1) The Secretary of State may, if he thinks fit, issue a vehicle licence   A24.33
or a trade licence on receipt of a cheque for the amount of the duty payable on it.

(2) In a case where—

(a) a vehicle licence or a trade licence is issued to a person on receipt of a cheque which is subsequently dishonoured, and

(b) the Secretary of State sends a notice by post to the person informing him that the licence is void as from the time when it was granted,

the licence shall be void as from the time when it was granted.

(3) In a case where—

(a) a vehicle licence or a trade licence is issued to a person on receipt of a cheque which is subsequently dishonoured,

(b) the Secretary of State sends a notice by post to the person requiring him to secure that the duty payable on the licence is paid within such reasonable period as is specified in the notice,

(c) the requirement in the notice is not complied with, and

(d) the Secretary of State sends a further notice by post to the person informing him that the licence is void as from the time when it was granted,

the licence shall be void as from the time when it was granted.

(4) Section 102 of the Customs and Excise Management Act 1979 (payment for excise licences by cheque) shall not apply in relation to a vehicle licence or a trade licence.]

[Section 19A was inserted by the Finance Act 1995 s.19 and Sch.4, paras 1   A24.34
and 32(1).]

[Issue of licences before payment of duty

19B.—(1) The Secretary of State may, if he thinks fit, issue a vehicle licence   A24.35

or a trade licence to a person who has agreed with the Secretary of State to pay the duty payable on the licence in a manner provided for in the agreement.

(2) In a case where—

    (a) a vehicle licence or a trade licence is issued to a person in accordance with subsection (1),

    (b) the duty payable on the licence is not received by the Secretary of State in accordance with the agreement, and

    (c) the Secretary of State sends a notice by post to the person informing him that the licence is void as from the time when it was granted,

the licence shall be void as from the time when it was granted.

(3) In a case where—

    (a) paragraphs (a) and (b) of subsection (2) apply,

    (b) the Secretary of State sends a notice by post to the person requiring him to secure that the duty payable on the licence is paid within such reasonable period as is specified in the notice,

    (c) the requirement in the notice is not complied with, and

    (d) the Secretary of State sends a further notice by post to the person informing him that the licence is void as from the time when it was granted,

the licence shall be void as from the time when it was granted.]

A24.36   *[Section 19B was inserted by the Finance Act 1997 s.19(1).]*

[Fee for payment of duty by credit card

A24.37   **19C.** *[Omitted.]*]

Combined road–rail transport of goods

A24.38   **20.**—(1) This section applies where—

    (a) goods are loaded on a relevant goods vehicle for transport between member States,

    (b) the vehicle is transported by rail between the nearest suitable rail loading station to the point of loading and the nearest suitable rail unloading station to the point of unloading, and

    (c) part of the rail transport of the vehicle takes place in the United Kingdom at a time when a vehicle licence for it is in force.

(2) Where this section applies, the holder of the licence is, on making a claim, entitled to receive from the Secretary of State (by way of rebate of the duty paid on the licence) an amount calculated by the method prescribed by regulations made by the Secretary of State.

[(3) In this section *"relevant goods vehicle"* means any vehicle the rate of duty applicable to which is provided for in Part VIII of Schedule 1 or which would be such a vehicle if Part VI of that Schedule did not apply to the vehicle.]

(4) *[Regulation-making power.]*

A24.39   *[Section 20 will come into force on a date to be appointed; see Sch.4, para.9 to this Act.*

Section 20 is printed as amended by the Finance Act 1995 s.19 and Sch.4, paras 1, 16, 21 and 29.]

PART II

REGISTRATION OF VEHICLES

Registration

Registration of vehicles

21. *[Omitted.]*   **A24.40**

Registration regulations

22. *[Omitted.]*

[Nil licences for vehicles for disabled persons: information

22ZA. *[Omitted.]]*   **A24.41**

Vehicle identity checks

22A. *[Regulation-making power.]*

Registration marks

Registration marks

23.—(1) Where the Secretary of State registers a vehicle under section 21(1)   **A24.42**
he shall assign to the vehicle a mark (a *"registration mark"*) indicating the
registered number of the vehicle.

(2) The Secretary of State may, in such circumstances as he may determine—

    (a) assign a registration mark to a vehicle to which another registration
    mark has previously been assigned,

    (b) assign to a vehicle (whether on its first registration or later) a registra-
    tion mark previously assigned to another vehicle,

    (c) (whether or not in connection with an assignment within paragraph
    (a) or (b)) withdraw any registration mark for the time being assigned
    to a vehicle, and

    (d) re-assign to a vehicle a registration mark previously assigned to it but
    subsequently withdrawn.

(3)–(5) *[Regulation-making power.]*

[For the construction of the term "for the time being" in s.23(2), see Sch.4,   **A24.43**
para.11, to this Act.

The Road Vehicles (Display of Registration Marks) Regulations 2001 (SI 2001/
561) below have been made (in part) under s.23.]

Assignment of registration marks by motor dealers

24.—(1) The Secretary of State may by regulations make such provision as he   **A24.44**
considers appropriate with respect to the allocation of registration marks for
vehicles to motor dealers who—

    (a) apply for such allocations, and

    (b) appear to the Secretary of State suitable to receive them, and with respect to the assigning of the marks to vehicles by motor dealers.

(2), (3) *[Regulation-making power.]*

(4)–(6) *[Review of refusal to allocate registration mark.]*

Charge on request for registration mark

A24.45   **25.** *[Omitted.]*

Retention of registration mark pending transfer

A24.46   **26.**—[(1) The Secretary of State may by regulations provide for—

(a) a person in whose name a vehicle is registered under this Act, or

(b) if that person so requests, another person,

to be granted a right of retention in respect of the registration mark for the time being assigned to the vehicle.

(1A) In subsection (1), the reference to a right of retention is to a right, exercisable on a single occasion falling within a period prescribed by regulations made by the Secretary of State, to have the registration mark assigned to some other vehicle which is registered under this Act in the name of—

(a) the person to whom the right is granted, or

(b) some other person nominated by him in accordance with regulations made by the Secretary of State.]

(2) Regulations under this section may, in particular, make provision—

(a) for the manner in which an application for the grant of [a right of retention] is to be made to the Secretary of State,

(b)–(m) *[Omitted.]*

(3) *[Exemptions from fees or charges under s.26(2)(f) or (m).]*

(4) *[Exemptions from fees under s.26(2)(f) or (l).]*

(5) *[Regulations providing for no charge in connection with assignments.]*

(6) *[Assignments of marks by Secretary of State.]*

A24.47   *[Section 26 is printed as amended by the Vehicle Registration Marks Act 2007 s.1(1) and (2).]*

Sale of rights to particular registration marks

A24.48   **27.**—(1) This section applies to registration marks which either—

(a) have never been assigned to a vehicle, or

(b) have been assigned to a vehicle but (as a result of having been subsequently withdrawn) are not for the time being so assigned,

and which are such as the Secretary of State may from time to time determine.

(2) The Secretary of State may by regulations make a scheme providing for registration marks to which this section applies to be assigned to vehicles registered under this Act in the names of, or of the nominees of, persons who have acquired rights under the scheme to have the marks so assigned.

(3) Regulations under this section may, in particular, make provision—

(a) for a person to acquire a right under the scheme to have a particular registration mark to which this section applies assigned to a vehicle registered under this Act in his name, or in the name of some other person nominated by him in accordance with the scheme, on payment of such sum as is payable in accordance with the scheme—

    (i) in respect of the acquisition of the right, and

    (ii) where no charge is to be made by virtue of paragraph in connection with an assignment pursuant to the right, in respect of such an assignment,

  (b) with respect to—

    (i) the manner in which agreements for the sale of such a right (a *"relevant right"*) may be effected,

    (ii) the terms which may be contained in, or incorporated into, such agreements, and

    (iii) rights and liabilities arising in connection with such agreements otherwise than under any such terms,

  (c)–(n) *[Omitted.]*

  (4), (5) *[Regulation-making powers.]*

  (6) *[Exemption from fees in certain cases.]*

  (7) *[Assignment of mark to be without prejudice to powers under s.23(2) .]*

[The Sale of Registration Marks Regulations 1995 (SI 1995/2880; not reproduced in this work) have been made in part under s.27.]   **A24.49**

[Registration plates]

[Registration plates

27A.—(1), (2) *[Regulation-making power.]*   **A24.50**

  (3) In this section *"registration plates"* means—

  (a) plates or other devices for displaying registration marks and for fixing them on vehicles or trailers in accordance with regulations under section 23(3), or

  (b) plates or other devices for displaying special registration marks and for fixing them on vehicles or trailers in accordance with regulations under section 22(2),

and includes plates or other devices which are also for containing or displaying information other than registration marks or (as the case may be) special registration marks (whether or not such information is to be contained or displayed by virtue of regulations under this section).

  (4) In this section—

    "special registration mark" means a mark indicating the registered number of a vehicle or trailer and assigned to the vehicle or trailer by virtue of regulations under section 22(2), and

    "trailer" has the same meaning as in Part 8 of Schedule 1.]

[Section 27A and the heading that precedes it will be inserted from a date to be appointed by the Vehicles (Crime) Act 2001 s.34.]   **A24.51**

Marking

Marking of engines and bodies

  28.—(1) The Secretary of State may by regulations make such provision as he   **A24.52**

thinks appropriate with respect to the marking of the engines and bodies of vehicles.

(2) *[Regulation-making power.]*

[Power of constables etc. to require production of documents

Power of constables etc. to require production of registration documents

A24.53   **28A.**—(1) A person using a vehicle in respect of which a registration document has been issued must produce the document for inspection on being so required by—

    (a) a constable, or

    (b) a person authorised by the Secretary of State for the purposes of this section (an "authorised person").

(2) An authorised person exercising the power conferred by subsection (1) must, if so requested, produce evidence of his authority to exercise the power.

(3) A person is guilty of an offence if he fails to comply with subsection (1).

(4) Subsection (3) does not apply if any of the following conditions is satisfied.

(5) The first condition is that—

    (a) the person produces the registration document, in person, at a police station specified by him at the time of the request, and

    (b) he does so within 7 days after the date on which the request was made or as soon as is reasonably practicable.

(6) The second condition is that—

    (a) the vehicle is subject to a lease or hire agreement,

    (b) the vehicle is not registered in the name of the lessee or hirer under that agreement and is not required to be so registered,

    (c) the person produces appropriate evidence of the agreement to the constable or authorised person at the time of the request or he produces such evidence in person, at a police station specified by him at the time of the request—

        (i) within 7 days after the date of the request, or

        (ii) as soon as is reasonably practicable, and

    (d) the person has reasonable grounds for believing, or it is reasonable for him to expect, that the person from whom the vehicle has been leased or hired is able to produce, or require the production of, the registration document.

(7) In subsection (6)(c) *"appropriate evidence"* means—

    (a) a copy of the agreement, or

    (b) such other documentary evidence of the agreement as is prescribed in regulations under this section.

(8) The third condition is that any exception prescribed in regulations under this section is met.

(9) Where a requirement is imposed under subsection (1) by an authorised person, a testing station provided under section 52(2) of the Road Traffic Act 1988 may be specified under subsection (5)(a) or (6)(c) instead of a police station.

(10) A person accused of an offence under this section is not entitled to the

benefit of an exception conferred by or under this section unless evidence is adduced that is sufficient to raise an issue with respect to that exception, but where evidence is so adduced it is for the prosecution to prove beyond reasonable doubt that the exception does not apply.

(11) A person guilty of an offence under this section is liable on summary conviction to a fine not exceeding level 2 on the standard scale.

(12) The Secretary of State may make regulations—

    (a) prescribing descriptions of evidence for the purposes of subsection (7);

    (b) prescribing, varying or revoking exceptions for the purposes of subsection (8).

(13) In this section *"registration document"* means a registration document issued in accordance with regulations under section 22(1)(e).]

[Section 28A and the heading above it are printed as inserted by the Serious Organised Crime and Police Act 2005 s.151.]   **A24.54**

PART III

OFFENCES

Offence of using or keeping unlicensed vehicle

Penalty for using or keeping unlicensed vehicle

29.—(1) If a person uses, or keeps, [a vehicle] which is unlicensed he is guilty   **A24.55**
of an offence.

(2) For the purposes of subsection (1) a vehicle is unlicensed if no vehicle licence or trade licence is in force for or in respect of the vehicle.

[(2A) Subsection (1) does not apply to a vehicle if—

    (a) it is an exempt vehicle in respect of which regulations under this Act require a nil licence to be in force and a nil licence is in force in respect of the vehicle, or

    (b) it is an exempt vehicle that is not one in respect of which regulations under this Act require a nil licence to be in force.

(2B) Subsection (1) does not apply to a vehicle if—

    (a) the vehicle is being neither used nor kept on a public road, and

    (b) the particulars and declaration required to be furnished and made by regulations under section 22(1D) have been furnished and made in accordance with the regulations and the terms of the declaration have at no time been breached.

(2C) Subsection (1) does not apply to a vehicle if the vehicle is kept by a motor trader or vehicle tester at business premises.

(2D) The Secretary of State may by regulations make provision amending this section for the purpose of providing further exceptions from subsection (1) (or varying or revoking any such further exceptions).

(2E) A person accused of an offence under subsection (1) is not entitled to the benefit of an exception from subsection (1) conferred by or under this section unless evidence is adduced that is sufficient to raise an issue with respect to that exception; but where evidence is so adduced it is for the prosecution to prove beyond reasonable doubt that the exception does not apply.]

(3) [Subject to subsection (3A)] a person guilty of an offence under subsection (1) is liable on summary conviction to an excise penalty of—

    (a) level 3 on the standard scale, or

    (b) five times the amount of the vehicle excise duty chargeable [in respect of using or keeping the vehicle on a public road],

whichever is the greater.

[(3A) In the case of a person who—

    (a) has provided the Secretary of State with a declaration or statement (in pursuance of regulations under section 22) that the vehicle will not during a period specified in the declaration or statement be used or kept on a public road, and

    (b) commits an offence under subsection (1) within a period prescribed by regulations,

subsection (3) applies as if the reference in paragraph (a) to level 3 were a reference to level 4.]

(4) Where a vehicle for which a vehicle licence is in force is transferred by the holder of the licence to another person, the licence is to be treated for the purposes of subsection (2) as no longer in force unless it is delivered to the other person with the vehicle.

(5) Where—

    (a) an application is made for a vehicle licence for any period, and

    (b) a temporary licence is issued pursuant to the application,

subsection (4) does not apply to the licence applied for if, on a transfer of the vehicle during the currency of the temporary licence, the temporary licence is delivered with the vehicle to the transferee.

(6) The amount of the vehicle excise duty chargeable in respect of a vehicle is to be taken for the purposes of subsection (3)(b) to be an amount equal to the annual rate of duty applicable to the vehicle at the date on which the offence was committed.

(7) Where in the case of a vehicle [not being used] on a public road that annual rate differs from the annual rate by reference to which the vehicle was at that date chargeable under [section 2(3) to (6)], the amount of the vehicle excise duty chargeable in respect of the vehicle is to be taken for those purposes to be an amount equal to the latter rate.

(8) In the case of a conviction for a continuing offence, the offence is to be taken for the purposes of subsections (6) and (7) to have been committed on the date or latest date to which the conviction relates.

A24.56   *[Section 29 is printed as amended by the Finance Act 1996 s.23 and Sch.2, paras 1 and 9(1), (2); the Finance Act 2002 s.19(1) and (2) and Sch.5, paras 1 and 7; the Finance Act 2008 s.145 and Sch.45, para.2.*

Proceedings under s.29(1) are specified by the Prosecution of Offences Act 1985 (Specified Proceedings) Order 1999 (SI 1999/904) below as being proceedings the conduct of which the Director of Public Prosecutions is not required to take over from the police under the Prosecution of Offences Act 1985 s.3(3)(a).

As to the admissibility of evidence in respect of offences under s.29(1), see the Road Traffic Offenders Act 1988 s.20.]

Additional liability for keeper of unlicensed vehicle

30.—(1) Where the person convicted of an offence under section 29 is the   **A24.57**
person by whom the vehicle in respect of which the offence was committed was
kept at the time at which it was committed, the court shall (in addition to any
penalty which it may impose under that section) order him to pay the amount
specified in subsection (2).

(2) The amount referred to in subsection (1) is an amount equal to one-twelfth
of the annual rate of vehicle excise duty [chargeable in respect of using or keeping the vehicle on a public road] for each month, or part of a month, in the relevant period (within the meaning of section 31).

(3) In relation to any month or part of a month in the relevant period, the reference in subsection (2) to the annual rate of vehicle excise duty appropriate to the
vehicle is a reference to the annual rate applicable to it at the beginning of that
month or part.

(4) A vehicle is to be taken for the purposes of this section to have belonged
throughout the relevant period to the description of vehicle to which it belonged
for the purposes of vehicle excise duty at—

    (a) the date on which the offence was committed, or

    (b) if the prosecution so elect, the date when a vehicle licence for it was
         last issued,

except so far as it is proved to have fallen within some other description for the
whole of any month or part of a month in that period.

(5) In the case of a conviction for a continuing offence, the offence is to be
taken for the purposes of this section to have been committed on the date or latest
date to which the conviction relates.

[Section 30 is printed as amended by the Finance Act 2008 s.145 and Sch.45,   **A24.58**
para.3.]

Relevant period for purposes of section 30

31.—(1) For the purposes of section 30 the relevant period is the period—   **A24.59**

    (a) ending with the date on which the offence was committed, and

    (b) beginning as provided by subsections (2) to (4).

(2) Subject to subsection (4), if the person convicted has before the date of the
offence notified the Secretary of State of his acquisition of the vehicle in accordance with regulations made by the Secretary of State, the relevant period begins
with—

    (a) the date on which the notification was received by the Secretary of
         State, or

    (b) the expiry of the vehicle licence last in force for the vehicle,

whichever is the later.

(3) Subject to subsection (4), in any other case the relevant period begins
with—

    (a) the expiry of the vehicle licence last in force for the vehicle before the
         date on which the offence was committed, or

    (b) if there has not at any time before that date been a vehicle licence in
         force for the vehicle, the date on which the vehicle was first kept by
         the person convicted.

(4) Where—

    (a) the person convicted has been ordered to pay an amount under section 30 on the occasion of a previous conviction for an offence in respect of the same vehicle, and

    (b) that offence was committed after the date specified in subsection (2) or (3) as the date with which the relevant period begins,

the relevant period instead begins with the month immediately following that in which the earlier offence was committed.

(5) Where the person convicted proves—

    (a) that throughout any month or part of a month in the relevant period the vehicle was not kept by him, or

    (b) that he has paid the duty due ... in respect of the vehicle for any such month or part of a month,

any amount which the person is ordered to pay under section 30 is to be calculated as if that month or part of a month were not in the relevant period.

(6) Where a person has previously been ordered under section 36 to pay an amount for a month or part of a month in the case of a vehicle, any amount which he is ordered to pay under section 30 in the case of the vehicle is to be calculated as if no part of that month were in the relevant period.

(7) In this section references to the expiry of a vehicle licence include a reference to—

    (a) its surrender [or ceasing to be in force under section 19(7)], and

    (b) its being treated as no longer in force for the purposes of subsection (2) of section 29 by subsection (4) of that section.

(8) In the case of a conviction for a continuing offence, the offence is to be taken for the purposes of this section to have been committed on the date or latest date to which the conviction relates.

A24.60   *[Section 31 is printed as amended by the Finance Act 1995, s.19 and Sch.4, paras 1 and 35(1) and (2) (see also ibid. s.162 and Sch.29, Pt 5(3)); the Finance Act 2008 s.144(5)(a).]*

[Offence of being registered keeper of unlicensed vehicle]

[Offence by registered keeper where vehicle unlicensed

A24.61   **31A.**—(1) If a vehicle registered under this Act is unlicensed, the person in whose name the vehicle is registered is guilty of an offence.

(2) For the purposes of this section a vehicle is unlicensed if no vehicle licence or trade licence is in force for or in respect of the vehicle.

(3) Subsection (1) does not apply to a vehicle if—

    (a) it is an exempt vehicle in respect of which regulations under this Act require a nil licence to be in force and a nil licence is in force in respect of the vehicle, or

    (b) it is an exempt vehicle that is not one in respect of which regulations under this Act require a nil licence to be in force.

(4) Where a vehicle for which a vehicle licence is in force is transferred by the holder of the licence to another person, the licence is to be treated for the purposes of subsection (2) as no longer in force unless it is delivered to the other person with the vehicle.

(5) Where—

  (a) an application is made for a vehicle licence for any period, and

  (b) a temporary licence is issued pursuant to the application,

subsection (4) does not apply to the licence applied for if, on a transfer of the vehicle during the currency of the temporary licence, the temporary licence is delivered with the vehicle to the transferee.]

[Section 31A (and the heading above) are printed as inserted by the Finance   **A24.62**
Act 2002 s.19(1) and (2) and Sch.5, paras 1 and 8.

  Article 3 of the Finance Act 2002, Section 19 (Appointed Days etc.) Order 2003 (SI 2003/3086) provides that s.31A shall not apply to a person in whose name a vehicle is registered upon the coming into force of the section, if before that date that person has sold, disposed of or permanently exported that vehicle or if it has been stolen and not recovered.]

[Exceptions to section 31A

31B.—(1) A person (*"the registered keeper"*) in whose name an unlicensed   **A24.63**
vehicle is registered at any particular time (*"the relevant time"*) does not commit an offence under section 31A at that time if any of the following conditions are satisfied.

(2) The first condition is that the registered keeper—

  (a) is not at the relevant time the person keeping the vehicle, and

  (b) if previously he was the person keeping the vehicle, he has by the relevant time complied with any requirements under section 22(1)(d) —

   (i) that are prescribed for the purposes of this condition, and

   (ii) that he is required to have complied with by the relevant or any earlier time.

(3) The second condition is that—

  (a) the registered keeper is at the relevant time the person keeping the vehicle,

  (b) at the relevant time the vehicle is neither kept nor used on a public road, and

  (c) the registered keeper has by the relevant time complied with any requirements under section 22(1D) —

   (i) that are prescribed for the purposes of this condition, and

   (ii) that he is required to have complied with by the relevant or any earlier time.

(4) The third condition is that—

  (a) the vehicle has been stolen before the relevant time,

  (b) the vehicle has not been recovered by the relevant time, and

  (c) any requirements under subsection (6) that, in connection with the theft, are required to have been complied with by the relevant or any earlier time have been complied with by the relevant time.

(5) The fourth condition is that the relevant time falls within a period (*"the grace days"*)—

  (a) beginning with the expiry of the last vehicle licence to be in force for the vehicle, and

    (b) of a prescribed length,

and a vehicle licence for the vehicle is taken out within the grace days for a period beginning with the grace days.

    (6) The Secretary of State may by regulations make provision for the purposes of subsection (4)(c) as to the persons to whom, the times at which and the manner in which the theft of a vehicle is to be notified.

    (7) The Secretary of State may by regulations make provision amending this section for the purpose of providing for further exceptions to section 31A(1) (or varying or revoking any such further exceptions).

    (8) A person accused of an offence under section 31A(1) is not entitled to the benefit of an exception conferred by or under this section unless evidence is adduced that is sufficient to raise an issue with respect to that exception, but where evidence is so adduced it is for the prosecution to prove beyond reasonable doubt that the exception does not apply.

    (9) In this section—

        (a) references to the expiry of a vehicle licence include a reference to—

            (i) its surrender [or ceasing to be in force under section 19(7)], and

            (ii) its being treated as no longer in force for the purposes of subsection (2) of section 31A by subsection (4) of that section;

        (b) *"prescribed"* means prescribed by regulations made by the Secretary of State.]

A24.64   *[Section 31B is printed as inserted by the Finance Act 2002 s.19(1) and (2) and Sch.5, paras 1 and 8 and as subsequently amended by the Finance Act 2008 s.144(5)(b).]*

[Penalties for offences under section 31A

A24.65   **31C.**—(1) A person guilty of an offence under section 31A(1) is liable on summary conviction to—

    (a) an excise penalty of—

        (i) level 3 on the standard scale, or

        (ii) five times the amount of vehicle excise duty chargeable in respect of the vehicle concerned,

        whichever is the greater; and

    (b) if subsection (3) applies to him, an excise penalty (in addition to any under paragraph (a)) of an amount that complies with subsection (2).

    (2) An amount complies with this subsection if it—

    (a) is not less than the greater of—

        (i) the maximum of the penalty to which the person is liable under subsection (1)(a), and

        (ii) the amount of the supplement (if any) that became payable by him by reason of non-renewal of the vehicle licence for the vehicle that last expired before the commission of the offence; and

    (b) is not more than the greatest of—

        (i) the maximum of the penalty to which the person is liable under subsection (1)(a),

        (ii) the amount mentioned in paragraph (a)(ii), and

(iii) ten times the amount of vehicle excise duty chargeable in respect of the vehicle.

(3) This subsection applies to the person if—

(a) he was, at the time proceedings for the offence were commenced, the person in whose name the vehicle concerned was registered under this Act, and

(b) that vehicle was unlicensed throughout the period beginning with the commission of the offence and ending with the commencement of those proceedings.

(4) The amount of vehicle excise duty chargeable in respect of a vehicle is to be taken for the purposes of subsections (1) and (2) to be an amount equal to the annual rate of duty applicable to the vehicle at the date on which the offence was committed.

(5) Where in the case of a vehicle kept (but not used) on a public road that annual rate differs from the annual rate by reference to which the vehicle was at that date chargeable under section 2(3) to (6), the amount of the vehicle excise duty chargeable in respect of the vehicle is to be taken for those purposes to be an amount equal to the latter rate.

(6) In the case of a conviction for a continuing offence, the offence is to be taken for the purposes of subsections (4) and (5) to have been committed on the date or latest date to which the conviction relates.

(7) In this section, references to the expiry of a vehicle licence include a reference to—

(a) its surrender [or ceasing to be in force under section 19(7)], and

(b) its being treated as no longer in force for the purposes of subsection (2) of section 31A by subsection (4) of that section.]

[Section 31C (and the heading below) are printed as inserted the Finance Act 2002 s.19(1) and (2) and Sch.5, paras 1 and 8 and as subsequently amended by the Finance Act 2008 s.144(5)(c).] **A24.66**

[Offences under sections 29 and 31A: supplementary]

Sections 29 to [31C]: supplementary

32.—(1) Where in the case of an offence under section 29 [or 31A] there is **A24.67** made against a person—

(a) an order under [section 12 of the Powers of Criminal Courts (Sentencing) Act 2000] discharging him absolutely or conditionally,

(b) *[applies in Scotland]*, or

(c) *[applies in Northern Ireland]*,

he is to be treated for the purposes of sections 29 to 31 [or (as the case may be) sections 31A to 31C] as having been convicted.

(2) Section 30 has effect subject to the provisions (applying with the necessary modifications) of any enactment relating to the imposition of fines by magistrates' courts and courts of summary jurisdiction, other than any conferring a discretion as to their amount.

(3) Where a sum is payable by virtue of an order under section 30 —

(a) in England and Wales, the sum is to be treated as a fine, and the order as a conviction, for the purposes of Part III of the Magistrates' Courts Act 1980 (including any enactment having effect as if contained in that Part) and of any other enactment relating to the recovery or application of sums ordered to be paid by magistrates' courts,

(b) *[applies in Scotland]*, and

(c) *[applies in Northern Ireland]*.

A24.68   *[Section 32 is printed as amended by the Powers of Criminal Courts (Sentencing) Act 2000 s.165(1) and Sch.9, para.158; the Finance Act 2002 s.19(1) and (2) and Sch.5, paras 1 and 9.]*

[Immobilisation, removal and disposal of vehicles

A24.69   **32A.** Schedule 2A (which relates to the immobilisation of vehicles as regards which it appears that an offence under section 29(1) is being committed and to their removal and disposal) shall have effect.]

A24.70   *[Section 32A was inserted by the Finance Act 1995 s.19 and Sch.4, paras 1 and 36(1).]*

Other offences relating to licences

Not exhibiting licence

A24.71   **33.**—(1) A person is guilty of an offence if—

(a) he uses, or keeps, on a public road a vehicle in respect of which vehicle excise duty is chargeable, and

(b) there is not fixed to and exhibited on the vehicle in the manner prescribed by regulations made by the Secretary of State a licence for, or in respect of, the vehicle which is for the time being in force.

[(1A) A person is guilty of an offence if—

(a) he uses, or keeps, on a public road an exempt vehicle,

(b) that vehicle is one in respect of which regulations under this Act require a nil licence to be in force, and

(c) there is not fixed to and exhibited on the vehicle in the manner prescribed by regulations made by the Secretary of State a nil licence for that vehicle which is for the time being in force.]

[(1B) A person is not guilty of an offence under subsection (1) or (1A) by using or keeping a vehicle on a public road during any of the 5 working days following the time when a licence or nil licence for the vehicle, or a relevant declaration applying to the vehicle, ceases to be in force, if an application for a licence or nil licence for or in respect of the vehicle to run from that time has been received before that time.

(1C) In subsection (1B) *"working day"* means any day other than—

(a) a Saturday or Sunday, or

(b) a day which is Christmas Eve, Christmas Day, Good Friday or a bank holiday under the Banking and Financial Dealings Act 1971 in any part of the United Kingdom.

(1D) For the purposes of subsection (1B)—

(a) there is a relevant declaration applying to a vehicle if the particulars and declaration required to be furnished and made by regulations under section 22(1D) have been furnished and made in relation to the vehicle in accordance with the regulations, and

(b) the relevant declaration ceases to be in force if, after the particulars and declaration have been furnished and made—

    (i) the vehicle is used or kept on a public road (otherwise than under a trade licence), or

    (ii) the period of 12 months beginning with the day on which the particulars and declaration were furnished and made expires.]

(2) A person guilty of an offence under subsection (1)[, or (1A)] is liable on summary conviction to a fine not exceeding level 1 on the standard scale.

[(3) Subsections (1) and (1A) —

(a) have effect subject to the provisions of regulations made by the Secretary of State, and

(b) are without prejudice to sections 29 [, 31A] and 43A.]

[(4) The Secretary of State may make regulations prohibiting a person from exhibiting on a vehicle [which is kept or used on a public road] anything—

(a) which is intended to be, or

(b) which could reasonably be,

mistaken for a licence which is for, or in respect of, the vehicle and which is for the time being in force.]

[(5) The reference to a licence in subsection (4) includes a reference to a nil licence.]

[Section 33 is printed as amended by the Finance Act 1996 s.23 and Sch.2, **A24.72** *paras 1 and 10; the Finance Act 1997 s.18 and Sch.3, paras 1, 4; the Finance Act 2002 s.19(1) and (2) and Sch.5, paras 1 and 10; the Finance Act 2008 s.147.*

For the application of the fixed penalty procedure to offences under s.33, see the Road Traffic Offenders Act 1988 Pt 3 and Sch.3 above.]

Trade licences: penalties

34.—(1) A person holding a trade licence or trade licences is guilty of an of- **A24.73** fence if he—

(a) uses at any one time on a public road a greater number of vehicles (not being vehicles for which vehicle licences are for the time being in force) than he is authorised to use by virtue of the trade licence or licences,

(b) uses a vehicle (not being a vehicle for which a vehicle licence is for the time being in force) on a public road for any purpose other than a purpose which has been prescribed under section 12(2)(b), or

(c) uses the trade licence, or any of the trade licences, for the purposes of keeping on a public road in any circumstances other than circumstances which have been prescribed under section 12(1)(c) a vehicle which is not being used on that road.

(2) A person guilty of an offence under subsection (1) is liable on summary conviction to an excise penalty of—

(a) level 3 on the standard scale, or

(b) five times the amount of the vehicle excise duty chargeable in respect of (in the case of an offence under subsection (1)(a)) the vehicles which he is not authorised to use or (in the case of an offence under subsection (1)(b) or (c)) the vehicle concerned,

whichever is the greater.

(3) The amount of the vehicle excise duty chargeable in respect of a vehicle is to be taken for the purposes of subsection (2) to be an amount equal to the annual rate of duty applicable to the vehicle at the date on which the offence was committed.

(4) Where in the case of a vehicle kept (but not used) on a public road that annual rate differs from the annual rate by reference to which the vehicle was at that date chargeable under [section 2(3) to (6)], the amount of the vehicle excise duty chargeable in respect of the vehicle is to be taken for those purposes to be an amount equal to the latter rate.

(5) In the case of a conviction for a continuing offence, the offence is to be taken for the purposes of subsections (3) and (4) to have been committed on the date or latest date to which the conviction relates.

A24.74   *[Section 34 is printed as amended by the Finance Act 2002 s.19(1) and (2) and Sch.5, paras 1 and 11.*

An offence under s.34 is a fixed penalty offence for the purposes of Pt 3 of the Road Traffic Offenders Act 1988 (see the Fixed Penalty Offences Order 2009 (SI 2009/483) art.2). The amount for the fixed penalty offence is prescribed by the Fixed Penalty Order 2000 (SI 2000/2792), as amended by the Fixed Penalty (Amendment) Order 2009 (SI 2009/488).]

Failure to return licence

A24.75   **35.**—(1) A person who knowingly fails to comply with section 10(3) is guilty of an offence.

(2) A person guilty of an offence under subsection (1) is liable on summary conviction to a fine not exceeding level 3 on the standard scale.

[Dishonoured cheques

A24.76   **35A.**—(1) In a case where—

    (a) a notice sent as mentioned in section 19A(2)(b) [or 19B(2)(c)] or a further notice sent as mentioned in section 19A(3)(d) [or 19B(3)(d)] [contains relevant information], and

    (b) the person fails to comply with the requirement [contained in the notice]

he shall be liable on summary conviction to a penalty of an amount found under subsection (2).

(2) The amount is whichever is the greater of—

    (a) level 3 on the standard scale;

    (b) an amount equal to five times the annual rate of duty that was payable on the grant of the licence or would have been so payable if it had been taken out for a period of twelve months.]

    [(3) For the purposes of subsection (1)(a), *a relevant requirement* is—

    (a) a requirement to deliver up the licence within such reasonable period as is specified in the notice; or

(b) a requirement to deliver up the licence within such reasonable period as is so specified and, on doing so, to pay the amount specified in subsection (4).]

[(4) The amount referred to in subsection (3)(b) is an amount equal to one-twelfth of the appropriate annual rate of vehicle excise duty for each month, or part of a month, in the relevant period.]

[(5) The reference in subsection (4) to the appropriate annual rate of vehicle excise duty is a reference [...]

    [(a) in the case of a vehicle licence, to the annual rate which at the beginning of the relevant period was applicable to a vehicle of the description specified in the application, or

    (b) in the case of a trade licence, to the basic goods vehicle rate (within the meaning of section 13) which was applicable at that time (or to the annual rate which at that time was applicable.]

[(6) For the purposes of subsection (4) the relevant period is the period—

    (a) beginning with the first day of the period for which the licence was applied for or, if later, the day on which the licence first was to have effect, and

    (b) ending with whichever is the earliest of the times specified in subsection (7).]

[(7) In a case where the requirement is a requirement to deliver up a vehicle licence, those times are—

    (a) the end of the month during which the licence was required to be delivered up,

    (b) the end of the month during which the licence was actually delivered up,

    (c) the date on which the licence was due to expire, and

    (d) the end of the month preceding that in which there first had effect a new vehicle licence for the vehicle in question;

and, in a case where the requirement is a requirement to deliver up a trade licence, those times are the times specified in paragraphs (a) to (c).]

[Section 35A was inserted by the Finance Act 1995 s.19 and Sch.4, paras 1   **A24.77**
and 32(2), and is printed as subsequently amended by the Finance Act 1997
s.19(2); the Finance Act 1998 s.19(1), (2) and (5); the Finance Act 1999 s.8(4)
and (5); the Finance Act 2005 s.7(6).]

Dishonoured cheques: additional liability

36.—(1) Where a person has been convicted of an offence under section [35A]   **A24.78**
in relation to a vehicle licence or a trade licence, the court shall (in addition to any penalty which it may impose under that section) order him to pay the amount specified in subsection (2).

(2) The amount referred to in subsection (1) is an amount equal to one-twelfth of the appropriate annual rate of vehicle excise duty for each month, or part of a month, in the relevant period.

(3) The reference in subsection (2) to the appropriate annual rate of vehicle excise duty is a reference [...]

    [(a) in the case of a vehicle licence, to the annual rate which at the beginning of the relevant period was applicable to a vehicle of the description specified in the application, or

(b) in the case of a trade licence, to the basic goods vehicle rate (within the meaning of section 13) which was applicable at that time (or to the annual rate which at that time was applicable.]

[(4) For the purposes of this section *the relevant period* is the period—

(a) beginning with the first day of the period for which the licence was applied for or, if later, the day on which the licence was first to have effect, and

(b) ending with whichever is the earliest of the times specified in subsection (4A).]

[(4A) In the case of a vehicle those times are—

(a) the end of the month in which the order is made,

(b) the date on which the licence was due to expire,

(c) the end of the month during which the licence was delivered up, and

(d) the end of the month preceding that in which there first had effect a new licence for the vehicle in question;

and, in the case of a trade licence, those times are the times specified in paragraphs (a) to (c).]

(5) Where a person has previously been ordered under section 30 to pay an amount for a month or part of a month in the case of a vehicle, any amount which he is ordered to pay under this section in the case of a vehicle licence for the vehicle is to be calculated as if no part of that month were in the relevant period.

[(6) Where—

(a) a person has been convicted of an offence under section 35A in relation to a vehicle licence or a trade licence, and

(b) a requirement to pay an amount with respect to that licence has been imposed on that person by virtue of section 35A(3)(b),

the order to pay an amount under this section shall have effect instead of that requirement and the amount to be paid under the order shall be reduced by any amount actually paid in pursuance of the requirement.]

A24.79   *[Section 36 is printed as amended by the Finance Act 1995 s.19 and Sch.4, paras 1, 6(2)(c), 16 and 32(3); the Finance Act 1996 s.18(4)(c) and (5); the Finance Act 1998 s.19(3)–(5); the Finance Act 1999 s.8(4) and (5); the Finance Act 2005 s.7(6).]*

Offence of not paying duty chargeable at higher rate

Penalty for not paying duty chargeable at higher rate

A24.80   37.—(1) Where—

(a) a vehicle licence has been taken out for a vehicle at any rate of vehicle excise duty,

(b) at any time while the licence is in force the vehicle is so used that duty at a higher rate becomes chargeable in respect of the licence for the vehicle under section 15, and

(c) duty at that higher rate was not paid before the vehicle was so used, the person so using the vehicle is guilty of an offence.

(2) A person guilty of an offence under subsection (1) is liable on summary conviction ... to an excise penalty of—

    (a) level 3 on the standard scale ..., or

    (b) five times the difference between the duty actually paid on the licence and the amount of the duty at the higher rate,

whichever is the greater.

[Section 37 is printed as amended by the Finance Act 1995 s.19 and Sch.4, **A24.81** *paras 1 and 37(1) (see also ibid. s.162 and Sch.29, Pt 5(3)).]*

Additional liability for keeper of vehicle chargeable at higher rate

38.—(1) Where the person convicted of an offence under section 37 is the **A24.82** person by whom the vehicle in respect of which the offence was committed was kept at the time at which it was committed, the court shall (in addition to any penalty which it may impose under that section) order him to pay the amount specified in subsection (2).

(2) The amount referred to in subsection (1) is an amount equal to one-twelfth of the difference between—

    (a) the rate of duty at which the licence in relation to which the offence was committed was taken out, and

    (b) the relevant higher rate of duty (within the meaning of section 39) in relation to the vehicle,

for each month, or part of a month, in the relevant period (within the meaning of section 40).

(3) A vehicle is to be taken for the purposes of subsection (2) to have belonged throughout the relevant period to the description of vehicle to which it belonged for the purposes of vehicle excise duty at the date on which the offence was committed, except so far as it is proved to have fallen within some other description for the whole of any month or part of a month in that period.

(4) Where a person is convicted of more than one offence under section 37 in respect of the same vehicle (whether or not in the same proceedings), the court shall (in calculating the amount payable under this section in respect of any of the offences) reduce the amount in relation to any period by any amount ordered to be paid under this section in relation to the period in respect of any other such offence.

Relevant higher rate of duty for purposes of section 38

39.—(1) For the purposes of section 38 the relevant higher rate of duty in rela- **A24.83** tion to a vehicle is the rate provided by this section.

(2) Where—

    (a) at the time of the offence the vehicle had a [revenue weight] which exceeded that which it had when the licence in relation to which the offence was committed was taken out, and

    (b) the licence was taken out at the rate applicable to the previous weight,

the relevant higher rate of duty is the rate which would have been applicable had the licence been taken out by reference to the higher weight.

(3) Where—

(a) the vehicle is a tractive unit,

(b) the licence in relation to which the offence was committed was taken out at a rate applicable to the use of the vehicle—

  (i) only with semi-trailers having not fewer than two axles, or

  (ii) only with semi-trailers having not fewer than three axles, and

(c) the offence consisted in using the vehicle with a semi-trailer with a smaller number of axles,

the relevant higher rate of duty is the rate which would have been applicable had the licence been taken out by reference to the use of the vehicle which constituted the offence.

(4) Where—

(a) the licence in relation to which the offence was committed was taken out at a rate applicable, by virtue of paragraph 13 of Schedule 1, to a weight lower than the [revenue weight] of the vehicle, and

(b) the offence consisted in using the vehicle in contravention of a condition imposed under or by virtue of sub-paragraph (2) of that paragraph,

the relevant higher rate of duty is the rate which would have been applicable had the licence been taken out by reference to the [revenue weight] of the vehicle.

(5) Where—

(a) the licence in relation to which the offence was committed was taken out at a rate lower than that applicable to it by reference to its [revenue weight], and

(b) none of subsections (2) to (4) apply,

the relevant higher rate of duty is the rate which would have been applicable had the licence been taken out by reference to the [revenue weight] of the vehicle.

(6) Where—

(a) the licence in relation to which the offence was committed was taken out at a rate lower than that at which duty was chargeable in respect of the condition, manner or purpose of use of the vehicle which constituted the offence, and

(b) none of subsections (2) to (5) apply,

the relevant higher rate of duty is the rate which would have been applicable had the licence been taken out by reference to the condition, manner or purpose of use of the vehicle which constituted the offence.

A24.84   *[Section 39 is printed as amended by the Finance Act 1995 s.19 and Sch.4, paras 1, 16, 22 and 29.]*

Relevant period for purposes of section 38

A24.85   40.—(1) For the purposes of section 38 the relevant period is the period—

(a) ending with the date on which the offence was committed, and

(b) beginning as provided by subsection (2) or (3).

(2) If the offence consists in the vehicle having a [revenue weight] which exceeds that which it had when the licence in relation to which the offence was committed was taken out, the relevant period begins with the date on which the vehicle [became a vehicle with a higher revenue weight].

(3) In any other case, the relevant period begins with the date on which the licence in relation to which the offence was committed first took effect.

(4) Where the person convicted proves—

    (a) that throughout any month or part of a month in the relevant period the vehicle was not kept by him, or

    (b) that he has paid the duty due (or an amount equal to the duty due) at the relevant higher rate in respect of the vehicle for any such month or part of a month,

any amount which the person is ordered to pay under section 38 is to be calculated as if that month or part of a month were not in the relevant period.

[Section 40 is printed as amended by the Finance Act 1995 s.19 and Sch.4,   **A24.86**
paras 1, 16, 23 and 29.]

Sections 37 to 40: supplementary

41.—(1) Where in the case of an offence under section 37 there is made against   **A24.87**
a person—

    (a) an order under [section 12 of the Powers of Criminal (Sentencing) Act 2000] discharging him absolutely or conditionally,

    (b) *[applies in Scotland]*, or

    (c) *[applies in Northern Ireland]*,

he is to be treated for the purposes of sections 38 to 40 as having been convicted.

(2) Section 38 has effect subject to the provisions (applying with the necessary modifications) of any enactment relating to the imposition of fines by magistrates' courts and courts of summary jurisdiction, other than any conferring a discretion as to their amount.

(3) Where a sum is payable by virtue of an order under section 38 —

    (a) in England and Wales, the sum is to be treated as a fine, and the order as a conviction, for the purposes of Part III of the Magistrates' Courts Act 1980 (including any enactment having effect as if contained in that Part) and of any other enactment relating to the recovery or application of sums ordered to be paid by magistrates' courts,

    (b) *[applies in Scotland]*, and

    (c) *[applies in Northern Ireland]*.

[Section 41 is printed as amended by the Powers of Criminal Courts (Sentenc-   **A24.88**
ing) Act 2000 s.165(1) and Sch.9, para.159.]

Offences relating to registration marks

Not fixing registration mark

42.—(1) If a registration mark is not fixed on a vehicle as required by virtue of   **A24.89**
section 23, the relevant person is guilty of an offence.

(2) A person guilty of an offence under subsection (1) is liable on summary conviction to a fine not exceeding level 3 on the standard scale.

(3) In subsection (1) *"the relevant person"* means the person driving the vehicle or, where it is not being driven, the person keeping it.

(4) It is a defence for a person charged with an offence under subsection (1) to prove that—

    (a) he had no reasonable opportunity to register the vehicle under this Act, and

(b) the vehicle was being driven for the purpose of being so registered.

(5) It is a defence for a person charged with an offence under subsection (1) in relation to a vehicle—

    (a) to which section 47 of the Road Traffic Act 1988 applies by virtue of subsection (2)(b) of that section, or

    (b) *[applies in Northern Ireland]*,

(vehicles manufactured before the prescribed period and used before registration) to prove that he had no reasonable opportunity to register the vehicle under this Act and that the vehicle was being driven in accordance with subsection (6).

(6) A vehicle is being driven in accordance with this subsection if—

    (a) it is being driven for the purposes of, or in connection with, its examination under section 45 of the Road Traffic Act 1988 in circumstances in which its use is exempted from subsection (1) of section 47 of that Act by regulations under subsection (6) of that section, or

    (b) *[applies in Northern Ireland]*,

A24.90   *[For the application of the fixed penalty procedure to offences under s.42, see the Road Traffic Offenders Act 1988 Pt 3 and Sch.3 above.]*

Obscured registration mark

A24.91   **43.**—(1) If a registration mark fixed on a vehicle as required by virtue of section 23 is in any way—

    (a) obscured, or

    (b) rendered, or allowed to become, not easily distinguishable,

the relevant person is guilty of an offence.

(2) A person guilty of an offence under subsection (1) is liable on summary conviction to a fine not exceeding level 3 on the standard scale.

(3) In subsection (1) *"the relevant person"* means the person driving the vehicle or, where it is not being driven, the person keeping it.

(4) It is a defence for a person charged with an offence under this section to prove that he took all steps which it was reasonably practicable to take to prevent the mark being obscured or rendered not easily distinguishable.

Other offences

[Failure to have nil licence for exempt vehicle

A24.92   **43A.**—(1) A person is guilty of an offence if—

    (a) he uses, or keeps, on a public road an exempt vehicle,

    (b) that vehicle is one in respect of which regulations under this Act require a nil licence to be in force, and

    (c) a nil licence is not for the time being in force in respect of the vehicle.

(2) A person guilty of an offence under subsection (1) is liable on summary conviction to a fine not exceeding level 2 on the standard scale.

(3) Subsection (1) has effect subject to the provisions of regulations made by the Secretary of State.

(4) The Secretary of State may, if he thinks fit, compound any proceedings for an offence under this section.]

[Section 43A was inserted by the Finance Act 1997 s.18 and Sch.3, paras 1 **A24.93**
and 5.]

[Vehicle identity checks: impersonation of authorised examiners

43B.—(1) A person is guilty of an offence if, with intent to deceive, he falsely   **A24.94**
represents himself to be a person entitled under regulations made by virtue of
section 22A(2) to carry out examinations of vehicles in accordance with regulations so made.

(2) A person guilty of an offence under subsection (1) is liable on summary
conviction to a fine not exceeding level 3 on the standard scale.]

[Section 43B was inserted by the Vehicles (Crime) Act 2001 s.43 and Sched- **A24.95**
ule, para.5.]

[Offence in respect of incorrectly registered vehicles

Offence of using an incorrectly registered vehicle

43C.—(1) A person is guilty of an offence if, on a public road or in a public   **A24.96**
place, he uses a vehicle to which subsection (2) applies and in respect of which—

   (a) the name and address of the keeper are not recorded in the register, or

   (b) any of the particulars recorded in the register are incorrect.

(2) This subsection applies to a vehicle if—

   (a) vehicle excise duty is chargeable in respect of it, or

   (b) it is an exempt vehicle in respect of which regulations under this Act
        require a nil licence to be in force.

(3) It is a defence for a person charged with an offence under subsection (1) to
show (as the case may be)—

   (a) that there was no reasonable opportunity, before the material time, to
        furnish the name and address of the keeper of the vehicle, or

   (b) that there was no reasonable opportunity, before the material time, to
        furnish particulars correcting the incorrect particulars.

(4) It is also a defence for a person charged with an offence under subsection
(1) to show—

   (a) that he had reasonable grounds for believing, or that it was reasonable
        for him to expect, that the name and address of the keeper or the other
        particulars of registration (as the case may be) were correctly recorded
        in the register, or

   (b) that any exception prescribed in regulations under this section is met.

(5) A person guilty of an offence under this section is liable on summary
conviction to a fine not exceeding level 3 on the standard scale.

(6) The Secretary of State may make regulations prescribing, varying or
revoking exceptions for the purposes of subsection (4)(b).

(7) In this section—

   "keeper", in relation to a vehicle, means the person by whom it is kept at
        the material time;

   *"the register"*means the register kept by the Secretary of State under Part
        2.]

[Section 43C and the heading which precedes it are printed as inserted by the Serious Organised Crime and Police Act 2005 s.150.]

Forgery and fraud

A24.98   **44.**—(1) A person is guilty of an offence if he forges, fraudulently alters, fraudulently uses, fraudulently lends or fraudulently allows to be used by another person anything to which subsection (2) applies.

(2) This subsection applies to—

    (a) a vehicle licence,

    (b) a trade licence,

    [(c) a nil licence,]

    (d) a registration mark,

    (e) a registration document, and

    (f) a trade plate (including a replacement trade plate).

(3) A person guilty of an offence under this section is liable—

    (a) on summary conviction, to a fine not exceeding the statutory maximum, and

    (b) on conviction on indictment, to imprisonment for a term not exceeding two years or to a fine or … to both.

A24.99   *[Section 44 is printed as amended by the Finance Act 1997 s.18 and Sch.3, paras 1, 6.*

The words omitted from s.44(3)(b) relate exclusively to Scotland.

For the application of the fixed penalty procedure to offences under s.44, see the Road Traffic Offenders Act 1988 Pt 3 and Sch.3 above.]

False or misleading declarations and information

A24.100   **45.**—(1) A person who in connection with—

    (a) an application for a vehicle licence or a trade licence,

    (b) a claim for a rebate under section 20, or

    (c) an application for an allocation of registration marks,

makes a declaration which to his knowledge is either false or in any material respect misleading is guilty of an offence.

(2) A person who makes a declaration which—

    (a) is required by regulations under this Act to be made in respect of a vehicle which is an exempt vehicle under paragraph 19 of Schedule 2, and

    (b) to his knowledge is either false or in any material respect misleading,

is guilty of an offence.

[(2A) A person who makes a declaration or statement which—

    (a) is required to be made in respect of a vehicle by regulations under section 22, and

    (b) to his knowledge is either false or in any material respect misleading,

is guilty of an offence.]

(3) A person who—

    (a) is required by [virtue of] this Act to furnish particulars relating to, or to the keeper of, a vehicle, and

(b) furnishes particulars which to his knowledge are either false or in any material respect misleading,

is guilty of an offence.

[(3A) A person who, in supplying information or producing documents for the purposes of any regulations made under section 61A [or 61B]—

(a) makes a statement which to his knowledge is false or in any material respect misleading or recklessly makes a statement which is false or in any material respect misleading, or

(b) produces or otherwise makes use of a document which to his knowledge is false or in any material respect misleading,

is guilty of an offence.]

[(3B) A person who—

(a) with intent to deceive, forges, alters or uses a certificate issued by virtue of section 61A [or 61B];

(b) knowing or believing that it will be used for deception lends such a certificate to another or allows another to alter or use it; or

(c) without reasonable excuse makes or has in his possession any document so closely resembling such a certificate as to be calculated to deceive,

is guilty of an offence.]

(4) A person guilty of an offence under this section is liable—

(a) on summary conviction, to a fine not exceeding the statutory maximum, and

(b) on conviction on indictment, to imprisonment for a term not exceeding two years or to a fine or … to both.

[Section 45 is printed as amended by the Finance Act 1995 s.19 and Sch.4, **A24.101**
paras 1, 16, 24 and 29; the Finance Act 1996 s.23 and Sch.2, paras 1 and 11; the Finance Act 1998 s.16 and Sch.1, paras 1, 15 and 17(2).

With effect from a day to be appointed, the following amendments will be made to s.45 by the Road Safety Act 2006 s.47(11)–(13):

1. *in s.45(1), the words ", or produces a document which to his knowledge is false or in any material respect misleading," will be inserted after the word "misleading";*

2. *in s.45(2A), the words "or produces a document" will be inserted after the word "statement"; and the words "made or produced" will be substituted for the words "made in respect of a vehicle".*

The words omitted from s.45(4)(b) relate exclusively to Scotland.

As to the reference in s.45(1)(b) to s.20, see Sch.4, para.9 below.

Section 45 has been expressly applied by the Finance Act 2000 s.20(10) (not reproduced in this work) to declarations made under s.20 of the 2000 Act in connection with applications for refunds of vehicle excise duty.]

Duty to give information

46.—(1) Where it is alleged that a vehicle has been used on a road in contraven-   **A24.102**
tion of section 29, 34[, 37 or 43A]—

(a) the person keeping the vehicle shall give such information as he may be required to give in accordance with subsection (7) as to the identity of the driver of the vehicle or any person who used the vehicle, and

(b) any other person shall give such information as it is in his power to give and which may lead to the identification of the driver of the vehicle or any person who used the vehicle if he is required to do so in accordance with subsection (7).

(2) Where it is alleged that a vehicle has been kept on a road in contravention of section 29 [or 43A]—

(a) the person keeping the vehicle shall give such information as he may be required to give in accordance with subsection (7) as to the identity of the person who kept the vehicle on the road, and

(b) any other person shall give such information as it is in his power to give and which may lead to the identification of the person who kept the vehicle on the road if he is required to do so in accordance with subsection (7).

(3) Where it is alleged that a vehicle has at any time been used on a road in contravention of section 29 [or 43A], the person who is alleged to have so used the vehicle shall give such information as it is in his power to give as to the identity of the person who was keeping the vehicle at that time if he is required to do so in accordance with subsection (7).

(4) A person who fails to comply with subsection (1), (2) or (3) is guilty of an offence.

(5) A person guilty of an offence under subsection (4) is liable on summary conviction to a fine not exceeding level 3 on the standard scale.

(6) If a person is charged with an offence under subsection (4) consisting of failing to comply with subsection (1)(a) or (2)(a), it is a defence for him to show to the satisfaction of the court that he did not know, and could not with reasonable diligence have ascertained, the identity of the person or persons concerned.

(7) A person is required to give information in accordance with this subsection if he is required to give the information by or on behalf of—

(a) a chief officer of police or, in Northern Ireland, the Chief Constable of the Royal Ulster Constabulary, or

(b) the Secretary of State.

A24.103   *[Section 46 is printed as amended by the Finance Act 1997 s.18 and Sch.3, paras 1, 7(1).*

With effect from November 4, 2001, the Royal Ulster Constabulary became known as the Police Service of Northern Ireland (incorporating the Royal Ulster Constabulary) (Police (Northern Ireland) Act 2000 s.1(1)). The reference in s.46(7)(a) above to the Chief Constable of the Royal Ulster Constabulary should be construed as a reference to the Chief Constable of the Police Service of Northern Ireland (2000 Act s.78(2)(a)).]

[Duty to give information: offences under regulations

A24.104   46A.—(1) Subsection (2) applies where it appears to the Secretary of State—

(a) that a person is a person by, through or to whom a vehicle has been sold or disposed of and that he has failed to comply with regulations made by virtue of section 22(1)(d) requiring him to furnish particulars prescribed by the regulations;

(b) that a person is a person by or through whom a vehicle has been sold or disposed of and that he has failed to comply with regulations made by virtue of section 22(1)(dd) requiring him to furnish a document prescribed by the regulations; or

(c) that a person is a person who is surrendering a vehicle licence, or who is not renewing a vehicle licence for a vehicle kept by him or who is keeping an unlicensed vehicle and that he has failed to comply with regulations made by virtue of section 22(1D) requiring him to furnish particulars or make a declaration prescribed by the regulations.

(2) The Secretary of State may serve a notice on the person in question requiring him to give the Secretary of State such information as it is in his power to give—

(a) as to the identity of any person who is keeping a specified vehicle or who has kept it at a specified time or during a specified period;

(b) as to the identity of any person by, through or to whom a specified vehicle has been sold or disposed of at a specified time or during a specified period; or

(c) which may lead to the identification of a person falling within paragraph (a) or (b).

(3) A person who fails to comply with a notice under subsection (2) is guilty of an offence.

(4) A person guilty of an offence under subsection (3) is liable on summary conviction to a fine not exceeding level 3 on the standard scale.

(5) In this section *"specified"* means specified in a notice under subsection (2).]

[Section 46A was inserted by the Finance Act 1996 s.23 and Sch.2, paras 1   **A24.105** *and 12.]*

Part IV

Legal Proceedings

Institution and conduct of proceedings

Proceedings in England and Wales or Northern Ireland

47.—(1) No proceedings for an offence under section 29, [31A,] 34[, 35A] or   **A24.106** 37 shall be instituted in England and Wales or Northern Ireland except by the Secretary of State or a constable; and no such proceedings shall be instituted there by a constable except with the approval of the Secretary of State.

(2) Proceedings for an offence under—

(a) section 29, [31A,] 34[, 35A] or 37, or

(b) regulations under this Act,

may be commenced in England or Wales or Northern Ireland by the Secretary of State or a constable at any time within six months from the date on which evidence sufficient in his opinion to justify the proceedings came to his knowledge.

(3) No proceedings for any offence may be commenced by virtue of subsection (2) more than three years after the commission of the offence.

(4) A certificate—

    (a) stating that the Secretary of State's approval is given for the institution by a constable of any proceedings specified in the certificate, and

    (b) signed by or on behalf of the Secretary of State,

is conclusive evidence of that approval.

(5) A certificate—

    (a) stating the date on which evidence such as is mentioned in subsection (2) came to the knowledge of the Secretary of State or a constable, and

    (b) signed by or on behalf of the Secretary of State or constable, is conclusive evidence of that date.

(6) A certificate—

    (a) including a statement such as is mentioned in paragraph (a) of subsection (4) or (5), and

    (b) purporting to be signed as mentioned in paragraph (b) of the subsection concerned,

is to be deemed to be so signed unless the contrary is proved.

(7) The following provisions of the Customs and Excise Management Act 1979 do not apply to proceedings in England and Wales or Northern Ireland for any offence under this Act—

    (a) section 145 (which would require such proceedings to be instituted by order of the Secretary of State and certain such proceedings to be commenced in the name of an officer of his), and

    (b) section 146A (which would impose time-limits for bringing such proceedings).

A24.107   *[Section 47 is printed as amended by the Finance Act 1996 s.23 and Sch.2, paras 1 and 14(1)(a); the Finance Act 2002 s.19(1) and (2) and Sch.5, paras 1 and 12.]*

Proceedings in Scotland

A24.108   **48.** *[Omitted.]*

Authorised persons

A24.109   **49.** A person authorised by the Secretary of State for the purposes of this section may on behalf of the Secretary of State conduct and appear in any proceedings by or against the Secretary of State under this Act—

    (a) in England and Wales, in a magistrates' court or before a district judge of a county court,

    (b) *[applies in Scotland]*, and

    (c) *[applies in Northern Ireland]*.

Time-limit for recovery of underpayments and overpayments

A24.110   **50.** No proceedings shall be brought—

    (a) by the Secretary of State for the recovery of any underpayment of duty on a vehicle licence, or

    (b) by any person for the recovery of any overpayment of duty on a vehicle licence taken out by him, after the end of the period of twelve months beginning with the end of the period in respect of which the licence was taken out.

Evidence

Admissions

51.—(1) This section applies where in any proceedings in England and Wales   **A24.111**
or Northern Ireland for an offence under section 29[, 34 or 43A]—

> (a) it is appropriately proved that there has been served on the accused by post a requirement under section 46(1) or (2) to give information as to the identity of—
>
> > (i) the driver of, or a person who used, a particular vehicle, or
> >
> > (ii) the person who kept a particular vehicle on a road,
> >
> > on the particular occasion on which the offence is alleged to have been committed, and
>
> (b) a statement in writing is produced to the court purporting to be signed by the accused that he was—
>
> > (i) the driver of, or a person who used, that vehicle, or
> >
> > (ii) the person who kept that vehicle on a road,
> >
> > on that occasion.

(2) Where this section applies, the court may accept the statement as evidence that the accused was—

> (a) the driver of, or a person who used, that vehicle, or
>
> (b) the person who kept that vehicle on a road,

on that occasion.

(3) In subsection (1) *"appropriately proved"* means proved to the satisfaction of the court—

> (a) on oath, or
>
> (b) in the manner prescribed—
>
> > (i) in England and Wales, by [Criminal Procedure Rules], or
> >
> > (ii) *[applies in Northern Ireland].*

[Section 51 is printed as amended by the Finance Act 1997 s.18 and Sch.3,   **A24.112**
paras 1, 7(2); the Courts Act 2003 s.109(1) and Sch.8, para.362(a).

The amendment to subs.(3)(b)(i) (see the Courts Act 2003 s.109(1) and Sch.8, para.362(a)) did not affect the general operation of the Vehicle Excise and Registration Act 1994 in so far as it relates to Criminal Procedure Rules during the period between the coming into force of the Courts Act 2003 (Commencement No.6 and Savings) Order 2004 (SI 2004/2066) (September 1, 2004) and the coming into force of the first Criminal Procedure Rules made under the Courts Act 2003 s.69 (April 4, 2005) (see the 2004 Order art.3).]

[Admissions: offences under regulations

51A.—(1) Subsection (2) applies in relation to any proceedings in England,   **A24.113**
Wales or Northern Ireland against a person for an offence on the grounds that—

> (a) a vehicle has been sold or disposed of by, through or to him and he has failed to furnish particulars prescribed by regulations made by virtue of section 22(1)(d);

(b) a vehicle has been sold or disposed of by or through him and he has failed to furnish a document prescribed by regulations made by virtue of section 22(1)(dd); or

(c) he has surrendered, or not renewed, a vehicle licence, or is keeping an unlicensed vehicle, and has failed to furnish any particulars or make a declaration prescribed by regulations made by virtue of section 22(1D).

(2) If—

(a) it is appropriately proved that there has been served on the accused by post a requirement under section 46A to give information as to the identity of the person keeping the vehicle at a particular time, and

(b) a statement in writing is produced to the court purporting to be signed by the accused that he was keeping the vehicle at that time,

the court may accept the statement as evidence that the accused was keeping the vehicle at that time.

(3) In subsection (2) *"appropriately proved"* has the same meaning as in section 51.]

A24.114   *[Section 51A was inserted by the Finance Act 1996 s.23 and Sch.2, paras 1 and 13.]*

Records

A24.115   52.—(1) A statement to which this section applies is admissible in any proceedings as evidence ... of any fact stated in it with respect to matters prescribed by regulations made by the Secretary of State to the same extent as oral evidence of that fact is admissible in the proceedings.

(2) This section applies to a statement contained in a document purporting to be—

(a) a part of the records maintained by the Secretary of State in connection with any functions exercisable by him under or by virtue of this Act,

(b) a copy of a document forming part of those records, or

(c) a note of any information contained in those records,

and to be authenticated by a person authorised to do so by the Secretary of State.

[(3) In this section as it has effect in England and Wales ...—

"document" means anything in which information of any description is recorded;

"copy", in relation to a document, means anything onto which information recorded in the document has been copied, by whatever means and whether directly or indirectly; and

"statement" means any representation of fact, however made.]

[(4) *[Applies to Scotland.]*]

[(5) [...]]

[(6) *[Applies to Scotland.]*]

A24.116   *[Section 52 is printed as amended by the Civil Evidence Act 1995 s.15(1) and Sch.1, para.19.*

Words in s.52(3) relating exclusively to Northern Ireland have been omitted.]

Burden of proof

53. Where in any proceedings for an offence under section 29, [31A,] 34, 37 or 45 any question arises as to—   **A24.117**

    (a) the number of vehicles used,

    (b) the character, weight or cylinder capacity of a vehicle,

    (c) the seating capacity of a vehicle, or

    (d) the purpose for which a vehicle has been used,

the burden of proof in respect of the matter lies on the accused.

[Section 53 is printed as amended by the Finance Act 2002 s.19(1) and (2) and   **A24.118** *Sch.5, paras 1 and 14.]*

Single witness sufficient in certain Scottish proceedings

54. *[Omitted.]*   **A24.119**

Guilty plea by absent accused

55.—(1) This section applies where, under section [12(5)] of the Magistrates'   **A24.120** Courts Act 1980 …, a person is convicted in his absence of [an offence under section 29 or 35A] and it is appropriately proved that a relevant notice was served on the accused with the summons.

    (2) In subsection (1) *"appropriately proved"* means—

      (a) in England and Wales, proved to the satisfaction of the court—

        (i) on oath, or

        (ii) in the manner prescribed by [Criminal Procedure Rules], and

      (b) *[applies in Northern Ireland].*

    (3) In this section *"relevant notice"*, in relation to an accused, means a notice stating that, in the event of his being convicted of the offence, it will be alleged that an order requiring him to pay an amount specified in the notice falls to be made by the court—

      (a) in a case within subsection (1)(a), under section 30, or

      (b) in a case within subsection (1)(b), under section 36.

    (4) Where this section applies, the court shall proceed under section 30, or section 36, as if the amount specified in the relevant notice were the amount calculated in accordance with that section.

    (5) The court shall not so proceed if it is stated in the notification purporting to be given by or on behalf of the accused under—

      (a) section [12(4)] of the Magistrates' Courts Act 1980, or

      (b) *[applies in Northern Ireland],*

that the amount specified in the relevant notice is inappropriate.

[Section 55 is printed as amended by the Finance Act 1996 s.23 and Sch.2,   **A24.121** *paras 1 and 14(2); the Magistrates' Courts (Procedure) Act 1998 s.4; the Courts Act 2003 s.109(1) and Sch.8, para.362(b).*

The amendment to subs.(2)(a)(ii) (see the Courts Act 2003 s.109(1) and Sch.8, para.362(b)) did not affect the general operation of the Vehicle Excise and Registration Act 1994 in so far as it relates to Criminal Procedure Rules during the period between the coming into force of the Courts Act 2003 (Commencement

No.6 and Savings) Order 2004 (SI 2004/2066) (September 1, 2004) and the coming into force of the first Criminal Procedure Rules made under the Courts Act 2003 s.69 (April 4, 2005) (see the 2004 Order art.3).]

Penalties, etc.

Application of penalties and fines

A24.122   **56.** *[Omitted.]*

PART V

SUPPLEMENTARY

Regulations and orders

Regulations

A24.123   **57.** *[Omitted.]*

Fees prescribed by regulations

58. *[Omitted.]*

Regulations: offences

A24.124   **59.**—(1) A person who contravenes or fails to comply with any regulations under this Act (other than any regulations under section 24, 26, 27 or 28) is guilty of an offence.

(2) A person guilty of an offence under subsection (1) is liable on summary conviction to a fine not exceeding—

    (a) in the case of regulations prescribed by regulations made by the Secretary of State as regulations to which this paragraph applies, level 3 on the standard scale, and

    (b) in any other case, level 2 on the standard scale.

(3) The prescribing of regulations as regulations to which subsection (2)(a) applies does not affect the punishment for a contravention of, or failure to comply with, the regulations before they were so prescribed.

(4) Regulations under section 24 or 28 may provide that a person who contravenes or fails to comply with any specified provision of the regulations is guilty of an offence.

(5) A person guilty of such an offence is liable on summary conviction to a fine not exceeding—

    (a) in the case of regulations under section 24, level 1 on the standard scale, and

    (b) in the case of regulations under section 28, level 3 on the standard scale.

[(6) The Secretary of State may, if he sees fit, compound any proceedings for an offence—

    (a) under subsection (1), or

    (b) under regulations under section 24 or 28.]

[Section 59 is printed as amended by the Finance Act 1996 s.23 and Sch.2, **A24.125**
paras 1 and 15.

*As to the person responsible for compliance with the Road Vehicles (Display
of Registration Marks) Regulations 2001 (SI 2001/561), see ibid. reg.19(1) below.*

*The Road Vehicles (Registration and Licensing) Regulations 2002 (SI 2002/
2742) were made in part under s.59(2)(a).*

*The Road Vehicles (Display of Registration Marks) Regulations 2001 (SI 2001/
561) are prescribed for the purposes of s.59(2)(a), see reg.11(1)–(3) below; as
are the Road Vehicles (Registration and Licensing) Regulations 2002 (SI 2002/
2742) reg.47 and Sch.8 below.]*

Exercise of power to make orders

60. *[Omitted.]*　　　　　　　　　　　　　　　　　　　　　　　**A24.126**

Interpretation

[Meaning of "revenue weight"

60A.—(1) Any reference in this Act to the revenue weight of a vehicle is a ref-　**A24.127**
erence—

    (a)　where it has a confirmed maximum weight, to that weight; and

    (b)　in any other case, to the weight determined in accordance with the
       following provisions of this section.

(2) For the purposes of this Act a vehicle which does not have a confirmed
maximum weight shall have a revenue weight which, subject to the following
provisions of this section, is equal to its design weight.

(3) Subject to subsection (4), the design weight of a vehicle is, for the purposes
of this section—

    (a)　in the case of a tractive unit, the weight which is required, by the
       design and any subsequent adaptations of that vehicle, not to be
       exceeded by an articulated vehicle which—

       (i)　consists of the vehicle and any semi-trailer capable of being
          drawn by it, and

       (ii)　is in normal use and travelling on a road laden;
       and

    (b)　in the case of any other vehicle, the weight which the vehicle itself is
       designed or adapted not to exceed when in normal use and travelling
       on a road laden.

(4) Where, at any time, a vehicle—

    (a)　does not have a confirmed maximum weight

    (b)　has previously had such a weight, and

    (c)　has not acquired a different design weight by reason of any adaptation
       made since the most recent occasion on which it had a confirmed
       maximum weight,

the vehicle's design weight at that time shall be equal to its confirmed maximum
weight on that occasion.

(5) An adaptation reducing the design weight of a vehicle shall be disregarded
for the purposes of this section unless it is a permanent adaptation.

(6) For the purposes of this Act where—

    (a) a vehicle which does not have a confirmed maximum weight is used on a public road in the United Kingdom, and

    (b) at the time when it is so used—

        (i) the weight of the vehicle, or

        (ii) in the case of a tractive unit used as part of an articulated vehicle consisting of the vehicle and a semi-trailer, the weight of the articulated vehicle,

        exceeds what, apart from this subsection, would be the vehicle's design weight,

it shall be conclusively presumed, as against the persons using the vehicle, that the vehicle has been temporarily adapted so as to have a design weight while being so used equal to the actual weight of the vehicle or articulated vehicle at that time.

(7) For the purposes of this Act limitations on the space available on a vehicle for carrying a load shall be disregarded in determining the weight which the vehicle is designed or adapted not to exceed when in normal use and travelling on a road laden.

(8) A vehicle which does not have a confirmed maximum weight shall not at any time be taken to have a revenue weight which is greater than the maximum laden weight at which that vehicle or, as the case may be, an articulated vehicle consisting of that vehicle and a semi-trailer may lawfully be used in Great Britain.

(9) A vehicle has a confirmed maximum weight at any time if at that time—

    (a) it has a plated gross weight or a plated train weight; and

    (b) that weight is the maximum laden weight at which that vehicle or, as the case may be, an articulated vehicle consisting of that vehicle and a semi-trailer may lawfully be used in Great Britain;

and the confirmed maximum weight of a vehicle with such a weight shall be taken to be the weight referred to in paragraph (a).

(10), (11) *[Apply to Northern Ireland.]]*

A24.128   *[Section 60A was inserted by the Finance Act 1995 s.19 and Sch.4, paras 1, 16, 26 and 29.*

    As to the modification of s.60A in its application to vehicles to which reference is made in the Goods Vehicles (Licensing of Operators) Act 1995 s.5(3), see the Goods Vehicles (Licensing of Operators) Regulations 1995 (SI 1995/2869) reg.36 below.]

Vehicle weights

A24.129   **61.**—(1) In this Act a reference to the plated gross weight of a goods vehicle or trailer is a reference—

    (a) in the case of a trailer which may lawfully be used in Great Britain without a Ministry plate (within the meaning of regulations under section 41 or 49 of the Road Traffic Act 1988), to the maximum laden weight at which the trailer may lawfully be used in Great Britain, and

    (b) otherwise, to the weight which is the maximum gross weight which may not be exceeded in Great Britain for the vehicle or trailer as indicated on the appropriate plate.

(2) In this Act a reference to the plated train weight of a vehicle is a reference to the weight which is the maximum gross weight which may not be exceeded in Great Britain for an articulated vehicle consisting of the vehicle and any semi-trailer which may be drawn by it as indicated on the appropriate plate.

(3) In subsections (1) and (2) *"appropriate plate"*, in relation to a vehicle or trailer, means—

(a) where a Ministry plate (within the meaning of regulations under section 41 or 49 of the Road Traffic Act 1988) has been issued, or has effect as if issued, for the vehicle or trailer following the issue or amendment of a plating certificate (within the meaning of Part II of that Act), that plate, [and]

(b) where paragraph (a) does not apply but such a certificate is in force for the vehicle or trailer, that certificate, ...

(c) [...].

[(3A) Where it appears to the Secretary of State that there is a description of document which—

(a) falls to be treated for some or all of the purposes of the Road Traffic Act 1988 as if it were a plating certificate, or

(b) is issued under the law of any state in the European Economic Area for purposes which are or include purposes corresponding to those for which such a certificate is issued,

he may by regulations provide for references in this section to a plating certificate to have effect as if they included references to a document of that description.]

(4), (5) [...]

(6) In this Act *"weight unladen"* —

(a) in England and Wales and Scotland, has the same meaning as it has for the purposes of the Road Traffic Act 1988 by virtue of section 190 of that Act, and

(b) *[applies in Northern Ireland]*.

(7) [...]

(8) In this section *"trailer"* has the same meaning as in Part VIII of Schedule 1.

[Section 61 is printed as amended by the Finance Act 1995 s.19 and Sch.4, paras 1, 16, 27 and 29 (see also ibid. s.162 and Sch.29, Pt 5(2)).] **A24.130**

Certificates, etc., as to vehicle weight

61A. *[Power to make regulations for the issue of certificates stating the design weight.]* **A24.131**

[Certificates as to reduced pollution

61B.—(1) *[Power to make regulations for applications, etc., for reduced pollution certificates for eligible vehicles.]* **A24.132**

[(2) For the purposes of this Act, the reduced pollution requirements are satisfied with respect to a vehicle at any time if, at that time, prescribed requirements relating to the vehicle's emissions are satisfied as a result of—

(a) the design, construction or equipment of the vehicle as manufactured; or

(b) adaptations of a prescribed description having been made to the vehicle after a prescribed date.]

[(2A) Different requirements may be prescribed under subsection (2) for vehicles first registered at different times.]

(3) *[Additional regulation-making powers.]*

(4) In this section *"eligible vehicle"* means—

(a) a bus, as defined in paragraph 3(2) of Schedule 1;

(b) a vehicle to which paragraph 6 of Schedule 1 applies;

(c) a haulage vehicle, as defined in paragraph 7(2) of Schedule 1, other than a showman's vehicle; or

(d) a goods vehicle, other then one falling within paragraph 9(2) or 11(2) of Schedule 1.

(5) In this section *"prescribed"* means prescribed by regulations made by the Secretary of State.]

A24.133   *[Section 61B was inserted by the Finance Act 1998 s.16 and Sch.1, paras 1, 2 and 17(2) and is printed as amended by the Finance Act 2006 s.14.]*

Other definitions

A24.134   62.—(1) In this Act, unless the context otherwise requires—

"axle", in relation to a vehicle, includes—

(a) two or more stub axles which are fitted on opposite sides of the longitudinal axis of the vehicle so as to form a pair in the case of two stub axles or pairs in the case of more than two stub axles,

(b) a single stub axle which is not one of a pair, and

(c) a retractable axle,

(*"stub axle"* meaning an axle on which only one wheel is mounted),

*   *   *

"business" includes the performance by a local or public authority of its functions,

"disabled person" means a person suffering from a physical or mental defect or disability,

"exempt vehicle" means a vehicle in respect of which vehicle excise duty is not chargeable,

[*"first vehicle licence"*, in relation to a vehicle, means (subject to subsections (1B) and (1C)) the vehicle licence for the vehicle on the issue of which the vehicle is first registered under this Act (so that, if the vehicle is first registered on the issue of a nil licence, there is no first vehicle licence in relation to it),]

*   *   *

"goods vehicle" means a vehicle constructed or adapted for use and used for the conveyance of goods or burden of any description, whether in the course of trade or not,

"motor dealer" means a person carrying on the business of selling or supplying vehicles,

"motor trader" means—

    (a) a manufacturer or repairer of, or dealer in, vehicles, or

    (b) any other description of person who carries on a business of such description as may be prescribed by regulations made by the Secretary of State,

and a person is treated as a dealer in vehicles if he carries on a business consisting wholly or mainly of collecting and delivering vehicles, and not including any other activities except activities as a manufacturer or repairer of, or dealer in, vehicles,

[*"nil licence"* means a document which is in the form of a vehicle licence and is issued by the Secretary of State in pursuance of regulations under this Act in respect of a vehicle which is an exempt vehicle,]

"public road" —

    (a) in England and Wales and Northern Ireland, means a road which is repairable at the public expense, and

    (b) *[applies in Scotland]*,

"registration mark" is to be construed in accordance with section 23(1),

"relevant right" is to be construed in accordance with section 27(3)(a) and (b),

"right of retention" is to be construed in accordance with section 26(1) and [(1A)],

"rigid goods vehicle" means a goods vehicle which is not a tractive unit,

*   *   *

"showman's goods vehicle" means a showman's vehicle which—

    (a) is a goods vehicle, and

    (b) is permanently fitted with a living van or some other special type of body or superstructure forming part of the equipment of the show of the person in whose name the vehicle is registered under this Act,

"showman's vehicle" means a vehicle—

    (a) registered under this Act in the name of a person following the business of a travelling showman, and

    (b) used solely by him for the purposes of his business and for no other purpose,

"temporary licence" is to be construed in accordance with section 9(1),

"tractive unit" means a goods vehicle to which a semi-trailer may be so attached that—

    (a) part of the semi-trailer is superimposed on part of the goods vehicle, and

    (b) when the semi-trailer is uniformly loaded, not less than twenty per cent. of the weight of its load is borne by the goods vehicle,

"trade licence" is to be construed in accordance with section 11,

[*"vehicle"* shall be construed in accordance with section 1(1B),]

"vehicle excise duty" is to be construed in accordance with section 1(1),

"*vehicle licence*" is to be construed in accordance with section 1(2), and

"*vehicle tester*" means a person, other than a motor trader, who regularly in the course of his business engages in the testing on roads of vehicles belonging to other persons.

[(1A) For the purposes of this Act, a vehicle is not an electrically propelled vehicle unless the electrical motive power is derived from—

(a) a source external to the vehicle, or

(b) an electrical storage battery which is not connected to any source of power when the vehicle is in motion.]

[(1B) Where a vehicle is first registered under this Act on the issue of a temporary licence, the "first vehicle licence" in relation to the vehicle is the first vehicle licence subsequently issued for it.

(1C) Where a vehicle—

(a) has been registered under the law of a country or territory outside the United Kingdom,

(b) is first registered under this Act more than 6 months after the time when it was first registered as mentioned in paragraph (a), and

(c) has travelled more than 6,000 kilometres under its own power before it is first registered under this Act,

there is no first vehicle licence in relation to the vehicle.]

(2) For the purposes of this Act and any other enactment relating to the keeping of vehicles on public roads, a person keeps a vehicle on a public road if he causes it to be on such a road for any period, however short, when it is not in use there.

A24.135   *[Section 62 is printed as amended by the Finance Act 1995 s.162 and Sch.29, Pt 5(2); the Finance Act 1996 s.15(3) and (4); the Finance Act 1997 s.18 and Sch.3, paras 1 and 7(3); the Finance Act 2002 s.19(1) and (2) and Sch.5, paras 1 and 17; the Vehicle Registration Marks Act 2007 s.1(3); the Finance Act 2009 s.14 and Sch.4, para.4 (the amendments made by Sch.4 to the Finance Act 2009 have effect in relation to licences taken out on or after April 1, 2010).*

The following definition (although repealed by the Finance Act 1995) is expressly incorporated into the Goods Vehicles (Plating and Testing) Regulations 1988 (SI 1988/1478) Sch.2, para.7 below:

"*road construction vehicle*" *means a vehicle—*

(a) *which is constructed or adapted for use for the conveyance of built-in road construction machinery, and*

(b) *which is not constructed or adapted for the conveyance of any other load except articles and material used for the purposes of such machinery.]*

Other supplementary provisions

Consequential amendments

A24.136   **63.** *[Omitted.]*

Transitionals, etc.

A24.137   **64.** Schedule 4 has effect for—

    (a) making transitional provisions in consequence of this Act and savings in connection with the repeals and revocations made by this Act,

    (b) re-enacting provisions repealed by this Act when not in force, and

    (c) making transitory modifications of this Act.

Repeals and revocations

65. *[Omitted.]*   **A24.138**

Commencement

66. *[Omitted.]*

Extent

67. This Act extends to Northern Ireland.   **A24.139**

Short title

68. *[Omitted.]*

SCHEDULES

Section 2   SCHEDULE 1

ANNUAL RATES OF DUTY

PART I

GENERAL

[**1.**—(1) The annual rate of vehicle excise duty applicable to a vehicle in respect of   **A24.140**
which no other annual rate is specified by this Schedule is [the general rate].

(2) [Except in the case of a vehicle with a cylinder capacity not exceeding [1,549 cubic centimetres], the] general rate is £—.

[(2A) In the case of a vehicle having an engine capacity not exceeding [1,549 cubic centimetres], the general rate is £—.]

[(2B) For the purposes of this Schedule the cylinder capacity of an engine shall be calculated in accordance with regulations made by the Secretary of State.]

(3)–(5) [...]

[Paragraph 1 of Sch.1 is printed as amended by the Finance Act 1999 s.8(2),   **A24.141**
(3) and (5); the Finance Act 2000 s.20(1); the Finance Act 2001 s.8(1); the Finance Act 2002 s.20(1). The references in para.1(2) and (2A) above to "1,549 cubic centimetres" apply to licences issued on or after July 1, 2001.

The amounts of duty (and amendments to those amounts) are not reproduced.]

PART IA

LIGHT PASSENGER VEHICLES: GRADUATED RATES OF DUTY

[Omitted.]   **A24.142**

PART IB

LIGHT GOODS VEHICLES

[Omitted.]   **A24.143**

PART II

MOTORCYCLES

A24.144   2.—(1) The annual rate of vehicle excise duty applicable to a motorcycle that does not exceed 450 kilograms in weight unladen is—

[(a) if the cylinder capacity of the engine does not exceed 150 cubic centimetres, £—;

(b) if the vehicle is a motorbicycle and the cylinder capacity of the engine exceeds 150 cubic centimetres but does not exceed 400 cubic centimetres, £—;

(c) if the vehicle is a motorbicycle and the cylinder capacity of the engine exceeds 150 cubic centimetres but does not exceed 600 cubic centimetres, £—;

(d) in any other case, £—.]

(2) Where a motorbicycle which was constructed before 1933 has an engine the cylinder capacity of which exceeds 150 cubic centimetres, it is to be treated for the purposes of sub-paragraph (1) as having an engine the cylinder capacity of which does not exceed 150 cubic centimetres.

(3) In this paragraph—

"*motorcycle*" means a motorbicycle or a motortricycle [but does not include an electrically propelled vehice],

"*motorbicycle*" includes a two-wheeled motor scooter, a bicycle with an attachment for propelling it by mechanical power and a motorbicycle to which a side-car is attached, and

"*motortricycle*" includes a three-wheeled motor scooter and a tricycle with an attachment for propelling it by mechanical power.

(4) [...]

A24.145   *[Paragraph 2 of Sch.1 is printed as amended by the Finance Act 1995 s.19 and Sch.4, paras 1, 7 and 16; the Finance Act 1996 ss.15(1) and (4) and 18(2) and (5) (see also ibid. s.205 and Sch.41, Pt 2(3)); the Finance Act 2001 s.13(2)(a) and (b) (in relation to licences issued on or after April 1, 2001 (ibid. s.13(4); see also ibid. s.110 and Sch.33, Pt 1(3)); the Finance Act 2002 ss.18(1), 20(2)(a), 141 and Sch.40, Pt 1(5). The text of para.2(1) above as substituted applies in relation to licences taken out after April 18, 2002 for a period beginning on or after May 1, 2002 (see s.18(3) of the Finance Act 2002).*

The amounts of duty are not reproduced.]

[PART III

BUSES]

A24.146   [3.—(1) The annual rate of vehicle excise duty applicable to a bus [with respect to which the reduced pollution requirements are not satisfied] is—

(a) if its seating capacity is nine to sixteen, the same as the basic goods vehicle rate;

(b) if its seating capacity is seventeen to thirty-five, 133 per cent of the basic goods vehicle rate;

(c) if its seating capacity is thirty-six to sixty, 200 per cent of the basic goods vehicle rate;

(d) if its seating capacity is over sixty, 300 per cent of the basic goods vehicle rate.

[(1A) The annual rate of vehicle excise duty applicable to a bus with respect to which the reduced pollution requirements are satisfied is [£—].]

(2) In this paragraph *"bus"* means a vehicle which—

(a) is a public service vehicle (within the meaning given by section 1 of the Public Passenger Vehicles Act 1981), and

(b) is not an excepted vehicle [or a special concessionary vehicle].

(3) For the purposes of this paragraph an *"excepted vehicle"* is—

(a) a vehicle which has a seating capacity under nine,

(b) a vehicle which is a community bus,

(c) a vehicle used under a permit granted under section 19 of the Transport Act 1985 (educational and other bodies) and used in circumstances where the requirements mentioned in subsection (2) of that section are met, or

(d) a vehicle used under a permit granted under section 10B of the Transport Act (Northern Ireland) 1967 (educational and other bodies) and used in circumstances where the requirements mentioned in subsection (2) of that section are met.

(4) In sub-paragraph (3)(b) *"community bus"* means a vehicle—

(a) used on public roads solely in accordance with a community bus permit (within the meaning given by section 22 of the Transport Act 1985), and

(b) not used for providing a service under an agreement providing for service subsidies (within the meaning given by section 63(10)(b) of that Act).

(5) For the purposes of this paragraph the seating capacity of a vehicle shall be determined in accordance with regulations made by the Secretary of State.

(6) In sub-paragraph (1) references to the *"basic goods vehicle rate"* are to the rate applicable, by virtue of sub-paragraph (1) of paragraph 9, to a rigid goods vehicle [which—

(a) is not a vehicle with respect to which the reduced pollution requirements are satisfied; and

(b) falls] within column (3) of the table in that sub-paragraph and has a revenue weight exceeding 3,500 kilograms and not exceeding 7,500 kilograms.

(7), (8) *[Rounding up or down of uneven amounts of duty.]*]

[Paragraph 3 of Sch.1 is printed as substituted by the Finance Act 1995 s.19 **A24.147** *and Sch.4, paras 1, 8 and 16, and is printed as subsequently amended by the Finance Act 1996 s.16(2) and (8); the Finance Act 1998 s.16 and Sch.1, paras 1, 3 and 17; the Finance Act 2006 s.14.*

The amounts of duty are not reproduced.]

[PART IV

SPECIAL VEHICLES]

[The heading to Pt 4 is printed as substituted by the Finance Act 1995 s.19 and **A24.148** *Sch.4, paras 1, 9(1) and (2) and 16.]*

4.—(1) The annual rate of vehicle excise duty applicable to a [special vehicle is the **A24.149** same as the basic goods vehicle rate].

(2) In sub-paragraph (1) [*"special vehicle"* means a vehicle which has a revenue weight exceeding 3,500 kilograms [which is not a special concessionary vehicle and which is]]

(a),

(b) [...],

[(bb) a vehicle falling within sub-paragraph (2A) or (2B),]

(c) a digging machine,

(d) a mobile crane,

[(dd) mobile pumping vehicle,]

(e) a works truck, or

[(ee) a road roller.]

(f) [...]

[(2A) A vehicle falls within this sub-paragraph if—

(a) it is designed or adapted for use for the conveyance of goods or burden of any description; but

(b) it is not so used or is not so used for hire or reward or for or in connection with a trade or business.]

[(2B) A vehicle falls within this sub-paragraph if—

  (a) it is designed or adapted for use with a semi-trailer attached; but

  (b) it is not so used or, if it is so used, the semi-trailer is not used for the conveyance of goods or burden of any description.]

(3) [...]

(4) In sub-paragraph (2)(c) *"digging machine"* means a vehicle which is designed, constructed and used for the purpose of trench digging, or any kind of excavating or shovelling work, and which—

  (a) is used on public roads only for that purpose or for the purpose of proceeding to and from the place where it is to be or has been used for that purpose, and

  (b) when so proceeding does not carry any load except such as is necessary for its propulsion or equipment.

(5) In sub-paragraph (2)(d) *"mobile crane"* means a vehicle which is designed and constructed as a mobile crane and which—

  (a) is used on public roads only as a crane in connection with work carried on on a site in the immediate vicinity or for the purpose of proceeding to and from a place where it is to be or has been used as a crane, and

  (b) when so proceeding does not carry any load except such as is necessary for its propulsion or equipment.

[(5A) In sub-paragraph (2)(dd) *"mobile pumping vehicle"* means a vehicle—

  (a) which is constructed or adapted for use and used for the conveyance of a pump and a jib satisfying the requirements specified in sub-paragraph (5B),

  (b) which is used on public roads only—

    (i) when the vehicle is stationary and the pump is being used to pump material from a point in the immediate vicinity to another such point, or

    (ii) for the purpose of proceeding to and from a place where the pump is to be or has been used, and

  (c) which, when so proceeding, does not carry—

    (i) the material that is to be or has been pumped, or

    (ii) any other load except such as is necessary for the propulsion or equipment of the vehicle or for the operation of the pump.]

[(5B) The requirements are that each of the pump and the jib is—

  (a) built in as part of the vehicle, and

  (b) designed so that material pumped by the pump is delivered to a desired height or depth through piping that—

    (i) is attached to the pump and the jib, and

    (ii) is raised or lowered to that height or depth by operation of the jib.]

(6) In sub-paragraph (2)(e) *"works truck"* means a goods vehicle which is—

  (a) designed for use in private premises, and

  (b) used on public roads only—

    (i) for carrying goods between private premises and a vehicle on a road in the immediate vicinity,

    (ii) in passing from one part of private premises to another or between private premises and other private premises in the immediate vicinity, or

    (iii) in connection with road works at or in the immediate vicinity of the site of the works.

[(7) In sub-paragraph (1) reference to the *"basic goods vehicle rate"* is to the rate applicable, by virtue of sub-paragraph (1) of paragraph (9), to a rigid goods vehicle [which—

  (a) is not a vehicle with respect to which the reduced pollution requirements are satisfied; and

  (b) falls] within column (3) of the table in that sub-paragraph and has a revenue weight exceeding 3,500 kilograms and not exceeding 7,500 kilograms.]

[Paragraph 4 of Sch.1 is printed as amended by the Finance Act 1995 s.19 and Sch.4, paras 1, 9(1) and (3), (6), and 16 (see also ibid. s.162 and Sch.29, Pt 5(2)); the Finance Act 1996 ss.16(3) and (8) and 17(1), (2), (3) and (11); the Finance Act 1998 s.16 and Sch.1, paras 1, 4 and 17; the Finance Act 2001 s.12(1)–(3) and (5) (in respect of licences issued after May 11, 2001). **A24.150**

The definition of "tractor" formerly contained in para.4(3) (repealed by the Finance Act 1995) is expressly saved for the purposes of the Goods Vehicles (Licensing of Operators) Regulations 1995 (SI 1995/2869) by ibid. Sch.3, para.1 below; the former para.4(3) is set out hereunder:

(3) In sub-paragraph (2)(a) *"tractor"* means—

    (a) an agricultural tractor, or

    (b) a tractor (other than an agricultural tractor) which is—

        (i) designed and constructed primarily for use otherwise than on roads, and

        (ii) incapable by reason of its construction of exceeding a speed of twenty-five miles per hour on the level under its own power.

The amount of duty is not reproduced.]

[PART IVA

SPECIAL CONCESSIONARY VEHICLES]

[Part 4A of Sch.1 (paras 4A–4H) was repealed by the Finance Act 2001 s.13(3), in relation to licences issued on or after April 1, 2001 (s.13(4); see also ibid. s.110 and Sch.33, Pt 1(3)).] **A24.151**

PART V

RECOVERY VEHICLES

5.—(1) The annual rate of vehicle excise duty applicable to a recovery vehicle [is— **A24.152**

    (a) if it has a revenue weight exceeding 3,500 kilograms and not exceeding 25,000 kilograms, the same as the basic goods vehicle rate;]

    (b) […]

    (c) if it has a revenue weight exceeding 25,000 kilograms, [250] per cent of the basic goods vehicle rate.]

(2) In sub-paragraph (1) *"recovery vehicle"* means a vehicle which is constructed or permanently adapted primarily for any one or more of the purposes of lifting, towing and transporting a disabled vehicle.

(3) A vehicle is not a recovery vehicle if at any time it is used for a purpose other than—

    (a) the recovery of a disabled vehicle,

    (b) the removal of a disabled vehicle from the place where it became disabled to premises at which it is to be repaired or scrapped,

    (c) the removal of a disabled vehicle from premises to which it was taken for repair to other premises at which it is to be repaired or scrapped,

    (d) carrying fuel and other liquids required for its propulsion and tools and other articles required for the operation of, or in connection with, apparatus designed to lift, tow or transport a disabled vehicle, and

    (e) any purpose prescribed for the purposes of this sub-paragraph by regulations made by the Secretary of State.

(4) At any time when a vehicle is being used for either of the purposes specified in paragraphs (a) and (b) of sub-paragraph (3), use for—

    (a) the carriage of a person who, immediately before the vehicle became disabled, was the driver of or a passenger in the vehicle,

(b) the carriage of any goods which, immediately before the vehicle became disabled, were being carried in the vehicle, or

(c) any purpose prescribed for the purposes of this sub-paragraph by regulations made by the Secretary of State,

shall be disregarded in determining whether the vehicle is a recovery vehicle.

(5) A vehicle is not a recovery vehicle if at any time the number of vehicles which it is used to recover exceeds a number specified for the purposes of this sub-paragraph by an order made by the Secretary of State.

[(5A) [...]]

[(6) In sub-paragraph (1) references to the *"basic goods vehicle rate"* are to the rate applicable, by virtue of sub-paragraph (1) of paragraph (9), to a rigid goods vehicle [which—

(a) is not a vehicle with respect to which the reduced pollution requirements are satisfied; and

(b) falls] within column (3) of the table in that sub-paragraph and has a revenue weight exceeding 3,500 kilograms and not exceeding 7,500 kilograms.]

[(7), (8) *[Rounding up or down of uneven amounts of duty.]*]

A24.153   *[Paragraph 5 of Sch.1 is printed as amended by the Finance Act 1995 s.19 and Sch.4, paras 1, 11 and 16; the Finance Act 1996 s.16(4) and (8); the Finance Act 1998 s.16 and Sch.1, paras 1, 5 and 17; the Finance Act 2001 s.11(1)–(4) (amendments to para.5(1), in respect of licences issued on or after December 1, 2001) and ibid. s.110 and Sch.33, Pt 1(3) (repeal of para.5(5A), in relation to licences issued on or after April 1, 2001).*

The amount of duty is not reproduced.

The Recovery Vehicles (Number of Vehicles Recovered) Order 1989 (SI 1989/ 1226; not reproduced in this work), which has effect as if made under para.5(5), prescribes two vehicles as the number prescribed for the purposes of para.5(5).]

Part VI

Vehicles used for Exceptional Loads

A24.154   **6.**—(1) This paragraph applies to a vehicle which is—

(a) a heavy motor car used for the carriage of exceptional loads, or

(b) a heavy locomotive, light locomotive or motor tractor used to draw trailers carrying exceptional loads,

[and which is not a special concessionary vehicle].

(2) The annual rate of vehicle excise duty applicable to a vehicle to which this paragraph applies in respect of use for the carriage of exceptional loads, or to draw trailers carrying exceptional loads, which is authorised by virtue of an order under—

(a) section 44 of the Road Traffic Act 1988, or

(b) *[applies in Northern Ireland]*,

is [the rate specified in sub-paragraph (2A)].

[(2A) The rate referred to in sub-paragraph (2) is—

(a) in the case of a vehicle with respect to which the reduced pollution requirements are not satisfied, £—; and

(b) in the case of a vehicle with respect to which those requirements are satisfied £—.]

(3) For the purposes of this paragraph an *exceptional load* is a load which—

(a) by reason of its dimensions cannot be carried by a heavy motor car or trailer, or a combination of a heavy motor car and trailer, which complies in all respects with requirements of regulations under section 41 of the Road Traffic Act 1988 ..., or

(b) by reason of its weight cannot be carried by a heavy motor car or trailer, or a combination of a heavy motor car and trailer, which has a total laden weight of not more than [41,000 kilograms] and which complies in all respects with such requirements.

[(3A) [...]]

(4) Expressions used in this paragraph and in the Road Traffic Act 1988 ... have the same meanings in this paragraph as in that Act ...

[Paragraph 6 of Sch.1 is printed as amended by the Finance Act 1995 s.19 and Sch.14, paras 1, 12 and 16; the Finance Act 1996 s.16(5) and (8); the Finance Act 1998 s.16 and Sch.1, paras 1, 6 and 17 (see also ibid. s.165 and Sch.27, Pt 1(3)); the Finance Act 1999 s.9 and Sch.1, paras 1 and 2. **A24.155**

The words omitted from para.6(3) and (4) relate exclusively to Northern Ireland.

The amounts of duty (and amendments of those amounts) are not reproduced.]

PART VII

HAULAGE VEHICLES

7.—(1) The annual rate of vehicle excise duty applicable to a haulage vehicle is—   **A24.156**

[(a) if it is a showman's vehicle, the same as the basic goods vehicle rate;

(b) in any other case, [the rate specified in sub-paragraph (3A)].]

(2) In sub-paragraph (1) *"haulage vehicle"* means a vehicle (other than a vehicle to which Part IV, ... V or VI applies) which is constructed and used on public roads solely for haulage and not for the purpose of carrying or having superimposed on it any load except such as is necessary for its propulsion or equipment.

[(3) In sub-paragraph (1) references to the *"basic goods vehicle rate"* is to the rate applicable, by virtue of sub-paragraph (1) of paragraph (9), to a rigid goods vehicle [which—

(a) is not a vehicle with respect to which the reduced pollution requirements are satisfied; and

(b) falls] within column (3) of the table in that sub-paragraph and has a revenue weight exceeding 3,500 kilograms and not exceeding 7,500 kilograms.]

[(3A) The rate referred to in sub-paragraph (1)(b) is—

(a) in the case of a vehicle with respect to which the reduced pollution requirements are not satisfied, £—; and

(b) in the case of a vehicle with respect to which those requirements are satisfied, [£—].]

[(4)–(6) [...]]

[Paragraph 7 of Sch.1 is printed as amended by the Finance Act 1995 s.19 and Sch.4, paras 1, 13 and 16; the Finance Act 1996 s.16(6) and (8); the Finance Act 1998 s.16 and Sch.1, paras 1, 7 and 17; the Finance Act 2001 s.110 and Sch.33, Pt 1(3) (repeal of the number "[IVA]," in para.7(2)(a), in relation to licences issued on or after April 1, 2001); the Finance Act 2006 s.14. **A24.157**

The amounts of duty are not reproduced.]

PART VIII

GOODS VEHICLES

Basic rate

8.—(1) *The annual rate of vehicle excise duty applicable to a goods vehicle to which this paragraph applies is £—.*   **A24.158**

(2) *This paragraph applies to a goods vehicle—*

(a) *which has a plated gross weight or plated train weight ... exceeding 3,500 kilograms but not exceeding 7,500 kilograms,*

(b) *which has a plated gross weight or plated train weight exceeding 7,500 kilograms but has such a weight only by virtue of section 61(3)(c) of this Act and is not a vehicle of a class prescribed by regulations made by the Secretary of State,*

(c) *which is a tower wagon with a plated gross weight ... exceeding 7,500 kilograms, or*

(d) *which does not have a plated gross weight or plated train weight ... but has a design weight exceeding 3,500 kilograms.*

(3) *In sub-paragraph (2)(c) "tower wagon" means a goods vehicle—*

(a) *into which there is built, as part of the vehicle, an expanding or extendible device designed for facilitating the erection, inspection, repair or maintenance of overhead structures or equipment, and*

(b) *which is not constructed or adapted for use, or used, for the conveyance of any load other than such a device or articles used in connection with it.*

(4) *This paragraph is subject to paragraph 12.*

A24.159   *[Paragraph 8 of Sch.1 has been repealed by the Finance Act 1995 s.19 and Sch.4, paras 1, 14(2) and 16 (see also ibid. s.162 and Sch.29, Pt 5(2)).*

The text of para.8 has been expressly saved for the purposes of the Goods Vehicles (Plating and Testing) Regulations 1988 (SI 1988/1478) Sch.2, para.6 below.

The words omitted from para.8(2)(a), (c) and (d) relate exclusively to Northern Ireland.

The amount of duty is not reproduced.]

Rigid goods vehicles

A24.160   9.—(1) [Subject to sub-paragraphs (2) and (3),] the annual rate of excise duty applicable to a rigid goods vehicle which [is not a vehicle with respect to which the reduced pollution requirements are satisfied and which] has a [revenue weight exceeding 3,500 kilograms] shall be determined in accordance with the following table by reference to—

(a) the [revenue weight] of the vehicle, and

(b) the number of axles on the vehicle.

TABLE OF RATES OF DUTY

[Omitted.]

[(2) The annual rate of vehicle excise duty applicable—

(a) to any rigid goods vehicle which is a showman's goods vehicle with a revenue weight exceeding 3,500 kilograms but not exceeding 44,000 kilograms, ...

(b) to any rigid goods vehicle which is an island goods vehicle with a revenue weight exceeding 3,500 kilograms, [and]

[(c) to any rigid goods vehicle which is used loaded only in connection with a person learning to drive the vehicle or taking a driving test,]

shall be the basic goods vehicle rate.]

[(3) The annual rate of vehicle excise duty applicable to a rigid goods vehicle [which—

(a) is not a vehicle with respect to which the reduced pollution requirements are satisfied,

(b) has a revenue weight exceeding 44,000 kilograms, and

(c) is not an island goods vehicle,

shall be £—.]]

[(4) In sub-paragraph (2) the reference to the *"basic goods vehicle rate"* is to the rate applicable, by virtue of sub-paragraph (1) of paragraph (9), to a rigid goods vehicle [which—

(a) is not a vehicle with respect to which the reduced pollution requirements are satisfied; and

(b) falls] within column (3) of the table in that sub-paragraph and has a revenue weight exceeding 3,500 kilograms and not exceeding 7,500 kilograms.]

[(5) [...]]

[Paragraph 9 of Sch.1 is printed as amended by the Finance Act 1995 s.19 and Sch.4, paras 1, 14 and 16; the Finance Act 1996 s.17(1), (4) and (11) (see also ibid. s.205 and Sch.41, Pt 2(2)); the Finance Act 1998 s.16 and Sch.1, paras 1 and 8 (and see also ibid. s.165 and Sch.27, Pt 1(3)).] **A24.161**

[9A.—(1) This paragraph applies to a rigid goods vehicle which— **A24.162**

  (a) is a vehicle with respect to which the reduced pollution requirements are satisfied;

  (b) is not a vehicle for which the annual rate of vehicle excise duty is determined under paragraph 9(2); and

  (c) has a revenue weight exceeding 3,500 kilograms.

(2) Subject to sub-paragraph (3), the annual rate of vehicle excise duty applicable to a rigid goods vehicle to which this paragraph applies shall be determined in accordance with the table set out in paragraph 9B by reference to—

  (a) the revenue weight of the vehicle, and

  (b) the number of axles on the vehicle.

(3) The annual rate of vehicle excise duty applicable to a rigid goods vehicle to which this paragraph applies which has a revenue weight exceeding 44,000 kilograms shall be £—.]

[Paragraph 9A of Sch.1 has been inserted by the Finance Act 1998 s.16 and Sch.1, paras 1, 9 and 17. **A24.163**

The amount of duty (and amendments to the amount) are not reproduced.]

9B. *[Rates of duty.]* **A24.164**

10.—(1) The annual rate of vehicle excise duty applicable, in accordance with [paragraphs 9 and 9A], to a rigid goods vehicle which has a [revenue weight] exceeding 12,000 kilograms[, which does not fall within paragraph 9(2)(b) or (c)] and which is used for drawing a trailer which— **A24.165**

  (a) has a [plated gross weight] exceeding 4,000 kilograms, and

  (b) when so drawn, is used for the conveyance of goods or burden,

shall be increased by the amount of the supplement (the *"trailer supplement"*) which is appropriate to the [plated gross weight] of the trailer being drawn.

(2) Where the plated gross weight ... of the trailer—

  (a) exceeds 4,000 kilograms, but

  (b) does not exceed 12,000 kilograms,

the amount of the trailer supplement is [£—].

(3) Where the plated gross weight ... of the trailer exceeds 12,000 kilograms, the amount of the trailer supplement is [£—].

[(3A), (3B) *[Revoked.]*]

(4) [...]

[Paragraph 10 of Sch.1 is printed as amended by the Finance Act 1995 s.19 and Sch.4, paras 1, 14(6)–(10) and 16 (see also ibid. s.162 and Sch.29, Pt 5(2)); the Finance Act 1996 s.17(1), (5) and (11); the Finance Act 1998 s.16 and Sch.1, paras 1, 10 and 17; the Finance Act 2001 s.110 and Sch.33, Pt 1(3) (amendment of percentage figure in para.10(3), in relation to licences issued on or after December 1, 2001; see the 2001 Act s.9(2)); the Finance Act 2005 s.7(12) and Sch.11. **A24.166**

The amounts of trailer supplement are not reproduced.]

Tractive units

11.—(1) [Subject to sub-paragraphs (2) and (3) [and paragraph 11C],] the annual rate of **A24.167**

vehicle excise duty applicable to a tractive unit which [is not a vehicle with respect to which the reduced pollution requirements are satisfied and which] has a [revenue weight exceeding 3,500 kilograms] shall be determined in accordance with the following table by reference to—

(a) the [revenue weight] of the tractive unit,

(b) the number of axles on the tractive unit, and

(c) the types of semi-trailers, distinguished according to the number of their axles, which are to be drawn by it.

TABLE OF RATES OF DUTY
[Omitted.]

[(2) The annual rate of vehicle excise duty applicable—

(a) to any tractive unit which is a showman's goods vehicle with a revenue weight exceeding 3,500 kilograms but not exceeding 44,000 kilograms, …

(b) to any tractive unit which is an island goods vehicle with a revenue weight exceeding 3,500 kilograms, [and]

[(c) to any tractive unit to which a semi-trailer is attached which is used loaded only in connection with a person learning to drive the vehicle or taking a driving test,]

shall be the basic goods vehicle rate.]

[(3) The annual rate of vehicle excise duty applicable to a tractive unit [which—

(a) is not a vehicle with respect to which the reduced pollution requirements are satisfied,

(b) has a revenue weight exceeding 44,000 kilograms, and

(c) is not an island goods vehicle,

shall be £—.]]

[(4) In sub-paragraph (2) references to the *"basic goods vehicle rate"* is to the rate applicable, by virtue of sub-paragraph (1) of paragraph (9), to a rigid goods vehicle [which—

(a) is not a vehicle with respect to which the reduced pollution requirements are satisfied; and

(b) falls] within column (3) of the table in that sub-paragraph and has a revenue weight exceeding 3,500 kilograms and not exceeding 7,500 kilograms.]

[(5) […]]

A24.168   *[Paragraph 11 of Sch.1 is printed as amended by the Finance Act 1995 s.19 and Sch.4, paras 1, 14(11) and (13) and 16; the Finance Act 1996 s.17(1), (6) and (11) (see also ibid. s.205 and Sch.41, Pt 2(2)); the Finance Act 1998 s.16 and Sch.1, paras 1, 11 and 17 (see also ibid. s.165 and Sch.27, Pt 1(3)); the Finance Act 2000 s.24 and Sch.5, paras 1 and 6(1)(a).*

The amount of duty (and amendments to the amount) are not reproduced.]

A24.169   [11A.—(1) This paragraph applies to a tractive unit which—

(a) is a vehicle with respect to which the reduced pollution requirements are satisfied;

(b) is not a vehicle for which the annual rate of vehicle excise duty is determined under paragraph 11(2); and

(c) has a revenue weight exceeding 3,500 kilograms.

(2) Subject to sub-paragraph (3) [and paragraph 11C] , the annual rate of vehicle excise duty applicable to a tractive unit to which this paragraph applies shall be determined, in accordance with the table set out in paragraph 11B, by reference to—

(a) the revenue weight of the tractive unit,

(b) the number of axles on the tractive unit, and

(c) the types of semi-trailers, distinguished according to the number of their axles, which are to be drawn by it.

(3) The annual rate of vehicle excise duty applicable to a tractive unit to which this paragraph applies which has a revenue weight exceeding 44,000 kilograms shall be £—.]

[Paragraph 11A of Sch.1 has been inserted by the Finance Act 1998 s.16 and Sch.1 paras 1, 12 and 17, and is printed as amended by the Finance Act 2000 s.24 and Sch.5, paras 1 and 6(1)(b).

The amount of duty is not reproduced.]   **A24.170**

11B. *[Rates of duty.]*   **A24.171**

11C. *[Rates of duty.]*

Farmers' goods vehicles and showmen's goods vehicles

12. […]   **A24.172**

[Repealed by the Finance Act 1995 s.19 and Sch.4, paras 1, 14(14) and 16.]

Vehicles with reduced plated weights

13.—(1) The Secretary of State may by regulations provide that, on an application relat-   **A24.173** ing to a goods vehicle which is made in accordance with the regulations, the vehicle is treated for the purposes of this Part as if [its revenue weight were such lower weight as may be specified] in the application.

(2) The regulations may provide that the treatment of the vehicle as being of a lower weight is subject to—

(a) conditions prescribed by the regulations, or

(b) such further conditions as the Secretary of State may think fit to impose in any particular case.

[Paragraph 13 of Sch.1 is printed as amended by the Finance Act 1995 s.19   **A24.174** *and Sch.4, paras 1, 14(15) and 16.]*

Vehicles for conveying machines

14. A vehicle which—   **A24.175**

(a) is constructed or adapted for use and used for the conveyance of a machine or device and no other load except articles used in connection with the machine or device,

(b),

(c) […],

is chargeable with vehicle excise duty at the rate which would be applicable to it if the machine or device were burden even if it is built in as part of the vehicle.

[Paragraph 14 of Sch.1 is printed as amended by the Finance Act 1995 s.19   **A24.176** *and Sch.4, paras 1, 14(16) and 16 (see also ibid. s.162 and Sch.29, Pt 5(2)).]*

Goods vehicles used partly for private purposes

15. […]   **A24.177**

[Repealed by the Finance Act 1996 s.17(1) and (15).]

Exceptions

16.—(1) This Part does not apply to—   **A24.178**

(a) a vehicle to which Part II, IV, … V or VII applies, …

(b) […]

(2) This Part applies to a goods vehicle which is a vehicle to which paragraph 6 applies only if it is used on a public road and the use is not such as is mentioned in sub-paragraph (2) of that paragraph.

[Paragraph 16 of Sch.1 is printed as amended by the Finance Act 1996 ss.16(7)   **A24.179**

and (8) and 17(1), (7) and (11) (see also ibid. s.205 and Sch.41, Pt 2(2)); the Finance Act 2001 s.110 and Sch.33, Pt 1(3) (repeal of the number "[IVA]," in para.16(1)(a), in relation to licences issued on or after April 1, 2001).]

Meaning of "trailer"

A24.180   17.—(1) In this Part *"trailer"* does not include—

    (a) an appliance constructed and used solely for the purpose of distributing on the road loose gritting material, [or]

    (b) a snow plough,

  (c)–(e) [...].

  (2) [...]

A24.181   *[Paragraph 17 of Sch.1 is printed as amended by the Finance Act 1995 s.19 and Sch.4, paras 1, 14(17) and (18) and 16 (see also ibid. s.162 and Sch.29, Pt 5(2)).]*

[Meaning of "island goods vehicle"]

A24.182   [18.—(1) In this Part *"island goods vehicle"* means any goods vehicle which—

    (a) is kept for use wholly or partly on the roads of one or more small islands; and

    (b) is not kept or used on any mainland road, except in a manner authorised by sub-paragraph (2) or (3).

  (2) The keeping or use of a goods vehicle on a mainland road is authorised by this sub-paragraph if—

    (a) the road is one used for travel between a landing place and premises where vehicles disembarked at that place are loaded or unloaded, or both;

    (b) the length of the journey, using that road, from that landing place to those premises is not more than five kilometres;

    (c) the vehicle in question is one which was disembarked at that landing place after a journey by sea which began on a small island; and

    (d) the loading or unloading of that vehicle is to take place, or has taken place, at those premises.

  (3) The keeping or use of a goods vehicle on a mainland road is authorised by this sub-paragraph if—

    (a) that vehicle has a revenue weight not exceeding 17,000 kilograms;

    (b) that vehicle is normally kept at a base or centre on a small island; and

    (c) the only journeys for which that vehicle is used are ones that begin or end at that base or centre.

  (4) References in this paragraph to a *small island* are references to any such island falling within sub-paragraph (5) as may be designated as a small island by an order made by the Secretary of State.

  (5) An island falls within this sub-paragraph if—

    (a) it has an area of 23,000 hectares or less; and

    (b) the absence of a bridge, causeway, tunnel, ford or other way makes it at all times impracticable for road vehicles to be driven under their own power from that island as far as the mainland.

  (6) The reference in sub-paragraph (5) to *driving a road vehicle as far as the mainland* is a reference to driving it as far as any public road in the United Kingdom which is not on an island with an area of 230,000 hectares or less and is not a road connecting two such islands.

  (7) In this paragraph —

    "island" includes anything that is an island only when the tide reaches a certain height;

"landing place" means any place at which vehicles are disembarked after sea journeys;

"mainland road" means any public road in the United Kingdom, other than one which is on a small island or which connects two such islands; and

"road vehicles" means vehicles which are designed or adapted primarily for being driven on roads and which do not have any special features for facilitating their being driven elsewhere;

and references in this paragraph to the loading or unloading of a vehicle include references to the loading or unloading of its trailer or semi-trailer.]

[Paragraph 18 of Sch.1 (and the italicised heading preceding para.18) were inserted by the Finance Act 1995 s.19 and Sch.4, paras 1, 14(19) and 16.   **A24.183**

The Vehicle Excise Duty (Designation of Small Islands) Order 1995 (SI 1995/ 1397) below has been made under para.18(4).]

[Other expressions]

[19.—(1) In this Part *"driving test"* means any test of competence to drive mentioned in section 89(1) of the Road Traffic Act 1988.   **A24.184**

(2) For the purposes of this Part a vehicle or a semi-trailer is used loaded if the vehicle or, as the case may be, the semi-trailer is used for the conveyance of goods or burden of any description.]

[Paragraph 19 of Sch.1 (and the italicised heading preceding para.19) were inserted by the Finance Act 1996 s.17(1), (8) and (11).]   **A24.185**

Section 5   SCHEDULE 2

EXEMPT VEHICLES

Electrically propelled vehicles

1. [...]   **A24.186**

[Repealed by the Finance Act 1995 s.19 and Sch.4, paras 1, 2(a) and 5.]

[Old vehicles]

[1A.—(1) Subject to sub-paragraph (2), a vehicle is an exempt vehicle at any time if it was constructed [before 1st January 1973].   **A24.187**

(2) A vehicle is not an exempt vehicle by virtue of sub-paragraph (1) if—

  (a) an annual rate is specified in respect of it by any provision of Part III, V, VI, VII or VIII of Schedule 1; or

  (b) it is a special vehicle, within the meaning of Part IV of Schedule 1, which—

    (i) falls within sub-paragraph (3) or (4); and

    (ii) is not a digging machine, mobile crane[, mobile pumping vehicle], works truck or road roller.

(3) A vehicle falls within this sub-paragraph if—

  (a) it is designed or adapted for use for the conveyance of goods or burden of any description;

  (b) it is put to a commercial use on a public road; and

  (c) that use is not a use for the conveyance of goods or burden of any description.

(4) A vehicle falls within this sub-paragraph if—

  (a) it is designed or adapted for use with a semi-trailer attached;

  (b) it is put to a commercial use on a public road; and

  (c) in a case where that use is a use with a semi-trailer attached, the semi-trailer is not used for the conveyance of goods or burden of any description.

(5) In sub-paragraph (2) *"digging machine"*, *"mobile crane"*[, *"mobile pumping vehicle"*] and *"works truck"* have the same meanings as in paragraph 4 of Schedule 1.

(6) In sub-paragraphs (3) and (4) *"commercial use"* means use for hire or reward or for or in connection with a trade or business.]

A24.188   *[Paragraph 1A of Sch.2 and the heading preceding it were inserted by the Finance Act 1996 s.18(1) and (5), and para.1A is printed as subsequently substituted by ibid. s.19(1) and (2); the Finance Act 1998 s.17; the Finance Act 2001 s.12(1), (4)(a) and (b).]*

Trams

A24.189   2. A vehicle used on tram lines is an exempt vehicle.

[Electrically assisted pedal cycles]

A24.190   [2A.—(1) An electrically assisted pedal cycle is an exempt vehicle.

(2) For the purposes of sub-paragraph (1) an electrically assisted pedal cycle is a vehicle of a class complying with such requirements as may be prescribed by regulations made by the Secretary of State for the purposes of this paragraph.]

A24.191   *[Paragraph 2A of Sch.2 and the heading preceding it were inserted by the Finance Act 1996 s.15(5).]*

Vehicles not for carriage

A24.192   3. A vehicle which is not constructed or adapted for use, or used, for the carriage of a driver or passenger is an exempt vehicle.

[Police vehicles]

A24.193   [3A. A vehicle is an exempt vehicle when it is being used for police purposes.]

[Paragraph 3A of Sch.2 and the heading preceding it were inserted by the Finance Act 1995 s.19 and Sch.4, paras 1, 3 and 5.]

Fire engines, etc.

A24.194   4.—(1) A fire engine is an exempt vehicle.

(2) In sub-paragraph (1) *"fire engine"* means a vehicle which—

    (a) is constructed or adapted for use for the purpose of fire fighting or salvage (or both), and

    [(b) is used solely for purposes in relation to which a fire and rescue authority under the Fire and Rescue Services Act 2004 has functions (whoever uses it for those purposes).]

A24.195   *[Paragraph 4 of Sch.2 is printed as amended by the Fire and Rescue Services Act 2004 s.53 and Sch.1, para.85(2).]*

A24.196   5. A vehicle which is kept by a [fire and rescue authority] is an exempt vehicle when it is being used or kept on a road for the purposes of the authority's [functions].

A24.197   *[Paragraph 5 of Sch.2 is printed as amended by the Fire and Rescue Services Act 2004 s.53 and Sch.1, para.85(3).]*

Ambulances and health service vehicles

A24.198   6.—(1) An ambulance is an exempt vehicle.

(2) In sub-paragraph (1) *"ambulance"* means a vehicle which—

    (a) is constructed or adapted for, and used for no purpose other than, the carriage of sick, injured or disabled people to or from welfare centres or places where medical or dental treatment is given, and

    (b) is readily identifiable as a vehicle used for the carriage of such people by being marked "Ambulance" on both sides.

7. A vehicle is an exempt vehicle when it is being used or kept on a road by—

A24.199

  (a) a health service body (as defined in section 60(7) of the National Health Service and Community Care Act 1990) or a health and social services body (as defined in Article 7(6) of the Health and Personal Social Services (Northern Ireland) Order 1991) [*SI 1991/194 (NI 1)*], or

  (b) a National Health Service trust established under [the National Health Service Act 2006, the National Health Service (Wales) Act 2006] or the National Health Service (Scotland) Act 1978 or a Health and Social Services Trust established under the Health and Personal Social Services (Northern Ireland) Order 1991, [or]

  [(ba) an NHS foundation trust, or]

  [(c) [...]]

  [(d) a Primary Care Trust established under [section 18 of the National Health Service Act 2006]

    ... [or

  [(f) the Care Quality Commission.]

[Paragraph 7 of Sch.2 is printed as amended by the Health Act 1999 (Supplementary and Consequential Provisions) Order 1999 (SI 1999/2795; not reproduced in this work) art.5; the Health Act 1999 (Supplementary, Consequential, etc., Provisions) Order 2000 (SI 2000/90; not reproduced in this work) art.3(1) and Sch.1, para.28); the Health and Social Care (Community Health and Standards) Act 2003 Sch.4, para.96; the Health and Social Care (Community Health and Standards) Act 2003 (Commission for Healthcare Audit and Inspection and Commission for Social Care Inspection) (Consequential Provisions) Order 2004 (SI 2004/2987) art.2(1)(g)(ii); the National Health Service (Consequential Provisions) Act 2006 s.2 and Sch.1, para.170; the Health and Social Care Act 2008 s.95 and Sch.5(3), para.62 and Sch.15(1).

A24.200

With effect from October 10, 2002 in relation to Wales only, the following sub-paragraph was inserted after sub-para.(d) by the National Health Service Reform and Health Care Professions Act 2002 ss.6(2), 42 and Sch.5, para.39 (see the National Health Service Reform and Health Care Professions Act 2002 (Commencement) (Wales) Order 2002 (SI 2002/2532)):

  [or

    (e) a Local Health Board established under [section 11 of the National Health Service (Wales) Act 2006]].

The words in square brackets in sub-para.(e) above were substituted by the National Health Service (Consequential Provisions) Act 2006 s.2 and Sch.1, para.170.]

8. A vehicle which is made available by the Secretary of State [or the Welsh Ministers]—

A24.201

  (a) to a person, body or local authority under [section 12 or 80 of the National Health Service Act 2006, or section 12 or 36 of the National Health Service (Wales) Act 2006], or

  (b) to a local authority, education authority or voluntary organisation in Scotland under section 15 or 16 of the National Health Service (Scotland) Act 1978,

and which is used in accordance with the terms on which it is so made available is an exempt vehicle.

[Paragraph 8 of Sch.2 is printed as amended by the National Health Service (Consequential Provisions) Act 2006 s.2 and Sch.1, para.171.]

A24.202

9.—(1) A veterinary ambulance is an exempt vehicle.

A24.203

(2) In sub-paragraph (1) *"veterinary ambulance"* means a vehicle which—

(a) is used for no purpose other than the carriage of sick or injured animals to or from places where veterinary treatment is given, and

(b) is readily identifiable as a vehicle used for the carriage of such animals by being marked "Veterinary Ambulance" on both sides.

Mine rescue vehicles, etc.

A24.204   **10.** A vehicle used solely—

(a) as a mine rescue vehicle, or

(b) for the purpose of conveying or drawing emergency winding-gear at a mine,

is an exempt vehicle.

Lifeboat vehicles

A24.205   **11.** A vehicle used or kept on a road for no purpose other than the haulage of a lifeboat and the conveyance of the necessary gear of the lifeboat which is being hauled is an exempt vehicle.

Road construction and maintenance vehicles

A24.206   **12–17.** [...]

[Repealed by the Finance Act 1995 s.19 and Sch.4, paras 1, 2(b)–(g) and 5.

The following definition contained in para.17(2) of Sch.2 (repealed by the Finance Act 1995) has been expressly saved for the purposes of the Goods Vehicles (Licensing of Operators) Regulations 1995 (SI 1995/2869) by ibid. reg.3(2) below and also for the Goods Vehicles (Plating and Testing) Regulations 1988 (SI 1988/1478) Sch.2 below:

"tower wagon" means a goods vehicle—

(a) into which there is built, as part of the vehicle, an expanding or extendible device designed for facilitating the erection, inspection, repair or maintenance of overhead structures or equipment, and

(b) which is not constructed or adapted for use, or used, for the conveyance of any load other than—

(i) such a device or articles used in connection with it, or

(ii) articles used in connection with the installation or maintenance (by means of such a device) of materials or apparatus for lighting streets, roads or public places. *]*

Vehicles for disabled people

A24.207   **18.** A vehicle (including a cycle with an attachment for propulsion by mechanical power) which—

(a) is adapted, and used or kept on a road, for an invalid, and

(b) does not exceed 508 kilograms in weight unladen,

is an exempt vehicle.

A24.208   **19.**—(1) A vehicle is an exempt vehicle when it is being used, or kept for use, by or for the purposes of a disabled person who satisfies sub-paragraph (2) if—

(a) the vehicle is registered under this Act in the name of the disabled person, and

(b) no other vehicle registered in his name under this Act is an exempt vehicle under this paragraph or paragraph 7 of Schedule 4.

(2) A disabled person satisfies this sub-paragraph if—

(a) he is in receipt of a disability living allowance by virtue of entitlement to the mobility component at the higher rate,

(b) he is in receipt of a mobility supplement, or ·

(c) he has obtained, or is eligible for, a grant under—

   [(i) paragraph 2 of Schedule 20 to the National Health Service Act 2006 or paragraph 2 of Schedule 15 to the National Health Service (Wales) Act 2006,]

   (ii) section 46(3) of the National Health Service (Scotland) Act 1978, or

   (iii) Article 30(3) of the Health and Personal Social Services (Northern Ireland) Order 1972 [*SI 1972/1265 (NI 14)*],

in relation to the vehicle.

[(2A) This paragraph shall have effect as if a person were in receipt of a disability living allowance by virtue of entitlement to the mobility component at the higher rate in any case where—

(a) he has ceased to be in receipt of it as a result of having ceased to satisfy a condition of receiving the allowance or of receiving the mobility component at that rate;

(b) that condition is either—

   (i) a condition relating to circumstances in which he is undergoing medical or other treatment as an in-patient in a hospital or similar institution; or

   (ii) a condition specified in regulations made by the Secretary of State;

   and

(c) he would continue to be entitled to receive the mobility component of the allowance at the higher rate but for his failure to satisfy that condition.]

(3) For the purposes of sub-paragraph (1) a vehicle is deemed to be registered under this Act in the name of a person in receipt of a disability living allowance by virtue of entitlement to the mobility component at the higher rate, or of a mobility supplement, if it is so registered in the name of—

(a) an appointee, or

(b) a person nominated for the purposes of this paragraph by the person or an appointee.

(4) In sub-paragraph (3) *"appointee"* means—

(a) a person appointed pursuant to regulations made under (or having effect as if made under) the Social Security Administration Act 1992 or the Social Security Administration (Northern Ireland) Act 1992 to exercise any of the rights and powers of a person in receipt of a disability living allowance, or

(b) a person to whom a mobility supplement is paid for application for the benefit of another person in receipt of the supplement.

(5) In this paragraph *"mobility supplement"* means a mobility supplement under—

(a) a scheme under the Personal Injuries (Emergency Provisions) Act 1939, or

(b) an Order in Council under section 12 of the Social Security (Miscellaneous Provisions) Act 1977,

   or a payment appearing to the Secretary of State to be of a similar kind and specified for the purposes of this paragraph by an order made by him.

[Paragraph 19 of Sch.2 is printed as amended by the Finance Act 1997 s.17, **A24.209**
the National Health Service (Consequential Provisions) Act 2006 s.2 and Sch.1,
para.172.

   The Motor Vehicles (Exemption from Vehicles Excise Duty) Order 1985 (SI
1985/722; not reproduced in this work) has effect as if made under para.19.]

20.—(1) A vehicle (other than an ambulance within the meaning of paragraph (6)) used **A24.210**
for the carriage of disabled people by a body for the time being recognised by the Secretary of State for the purposes of this paragraph is an exempt vehicle.

(2) The Secretary of State shall recognise a body for the purposes of this paragraph if, on an application made to him in such manner as he may specify, it appears to him that the body is concerned with the care of disabled people.

(3) The issue by the Secretary of State of a nil licence in respect of a vehicle under this paragraph is to be treated as recognition by him for the purposes of this paragraph of the body by reference to whose use of the vehicle the document is issued.

(4) [...]

(5) The Secretary of State may withdraw recognition of a body for the purposes of this paragraph if it appears to him that the body is no longer concerned with the care of disabled people.

A24.211   *[Paragraph 20 of Sch.2 is printed as amended by the Finance Act 1997 s.18 and Sch.3, paras 1, 7(4) and 9 (see also ibid. s.113 and Sch.18, Pt 3).]*

[Vehicles used between different parts of land]

A24.212   **[20A.** A vehicle is an exempt vehicle if—

    (a) it is used only for purposes relating to agriculture, horticulture or forestry,

    (b) it is used on public roads only in passing between different areas of land occupied by the same person, and

    (c) the distance it travels on public roads in passing between any two such areas does not exceed 1.5 kilometres.]

A24.213   *[Paragraph 20A of Sch.2 and the heading preceding it were inserted by the Finance Act 1995 s.19 and Sch.4, paras 1, 4 and 5.]*

[Tractors]

A24.214   **[20B.**—(1) A vehicle is an exempt vehicle if it is—

    (a) an agricultural tractor, or

    (b) an off-road tractor.

(2) In sub-paragraph (1) *"agricultural tractor"* means a tractor used on public roads solely for purposes relating to agriculture, horticulture, forestry or activities falling within sub-paragraph (3).

(3) The activities falling within this sub-paragraph are–

    (a) cutting verges bordering public roads;

    (b) cutting hedges or trees bordering public roads or bordering verges which border public roads.

(4) In sub-paragraph (1) *"off-road tractor"* means a tractor which is not an agricultural tractor (within the meaning given by sub-paragraph (2)) and which is—

    (a) designed and constructed primarily for use otherwise than on roads, and

    (b) incapable by reason of its construction of exceeding a speed of twenty-five miles per hour on the level under its own power.]

A24.215   *[Paragraph 20B of Sch.2 was inserted by the Finance Act 2001 s.13(1), in respect of licences issued on or after April 1, 2001 (see s.13(4)).*

As to the effect of licences issued before April 1, 2001, and as to refunds in respect of such licences, see the notes to para.20J.]

[Light agricultural vehicles]

A24.216   **[20C.**—(1) A vehicle is an exempt vehicle if it is a light agricultural vehicle.

(2) In sub-paragraph (1) *"light agricultural vehicle"* means a vehicle which—

    (a) has a revenue weight not exceeding 1,000 kilograms,

    (b) is designed and constructed so as to seat only the driver,

    (c) is designed and constructed primarily for use otherwise than on roads, and

    (d) is used solely for purposes relating to agriculture, horticulture or forestry.]

[Paragraph 20C of Sch.2 was inserted by the Finance Act 2001 s.13(1), in respect of licences issued on or after April 1, 2001 (see s.13(4)).   **A24.217**

As to the effect of licences issued before April 1, 2001, and as to refunds in respect of such licences, see the notes to para.20J.]

[Agricultural engines]

[20D. An agricultural engine is an exempt vehicle.]   **A24.218**

[Paragraph 20D of Sch.2 was inserted by the Finance Act 2001 s.13(1), in respect of licences issued on or after April 1, 2001 (see s.13(4)).

As to the effect of licences issued before April 1, 2001, and as to refunds in respect of such licences, see the notes to para.20J.]

[Mowing machines]

[20E. A mowing machine is an exempt vehicle.]   **A24.219**

[Paragraph 20E of Sch.2 was inserted by the Finance Act 2001 s.13(1), in respect of licences issued on or after April 1, 2001 (see s.13(4)).

As to the effect of licences issued before April 1, 2001, and as to refunds in respect of such licences, see the notes to para.20J.]

[Steam powered vehicles]

[20F. A steam powered vehicle is an exempt vehicle.]   **A24.220**

[Paragraph 20F of Sch.2 was inserted by the Finance Act 2001 s.13(1), in respect of licences issued on or after April 1, 2001 (see s.13(4)).

As to the effect of licences issued before April 1, 2001, and as to refunds in respect of such licences, see the notes to para.20J.]

[Electrically propelled vehicles]

[20G. An electrically propelled vehicle is an exempt vehicle.]   **A24.221**

[Paragraph 20G of Sch.2 was inserted by the Finance Act 2001 s.13(1), in respect of licences issued on or after April 1, 2001 (see s.13(4)).

As to the effect of licences issued before April 1, 2001, and as to refunds in respect of such licences, see the notes to para.20J.]

[Snow ploughs]

[20H. A vehicle is an exempt vehicle when it is—   **A24.222**

  (a) being used,

  (b) going to or from the place where it is to be or has been used, or

  (c) being kept for use,

for the purpose of clearing snow from public roads by means of a snow plough or similar device (whether or not forming part of the vehicle).]

[Paragraph 20H of Sch.2 was inserted by the Finance Act 2001 s.13(1), in respect of licences issued on or after April 1, 2001 (see s.13(4)).   **A24.223**

As to the effect of licences issued before April 1, 2001, and as to refunds in respect of such licences, see the notes to para.20J.]

[Gritters]

[20J. A vehicle is an exempt vehicle if it is constructed or adapted, and used, solely for   **A24.224**
the conveyance of machinery for spreading material on roads to deal with frost, ice or snow (with or without articles or material used for the purposes of the machinery).]

[Paragraph 20J of Sch.2 was inserted by the Finance Act 2001 s.13(1), in   **A24.225**

respect of licences issued on or after April 1, 2001 (see s.13(4)). There is no paragraph numbered "20I".

Licences issued before April 1, 2001 in respect of a vehicle of any of the descriptions in paras 20B–20J of this Schedule which were in force on that date (or which came into force on a later date) are deemed (from April 1, 2001, or the date on which they came into force, whichever is the later, until the end of the period for which they were issued) to be nil licences for the purposes of this Act; see the Finance Act 2001 s.13(5), (6) and (12), not reproduced in this work. As to refunds in respect of such licences, see ibid. s.13(7)–(9).]

Vehicles used for short journeys between different parts of person's land

A24.226   21. [...]

[Repealed by the Finance Act 1995 s.19 and Sch.4, paras 1, 2(b) and 5.]

Vehicle testing, etc.

A24.227   22.—(1) A vehicle is an exempt vehicle when it is being used solely for the purpose of—

> (a) submitting it (by previous arrangement for a specified time on a specified date) for a compulsory test[, a vehicle identity check][, a vehicle weight test or a reduced pollution test], or
>
> (b) bringing it away from [any such test [or check]].

[(1A) A vehicle is an exempt vehicle when it is being used solely for the purpose of—

> (a) taking it (by previous arrangement for a specified time on a specified date) for a relevant re-examination, or
>
> (b) bringing it away from such a re-examination.]

(2) A vehicle is an exempt vehicle when it is being used by an authorised person in the course of a compulsory test[, a vehicle weight test [or a vehicle identity check][, a reduced pollution test] or a relevant re-examination and is being so used] solely for the purpose of—

> (a) taking it to, or bringing it away from, a place where a part of the test[, check] [or re-examination] is to be, or has been, carried out, or
>
> (b) carrying out a part of the test[, check] [or re-examination].

[(2A) A vehicle is an exempt vehicle when it is being used by an authorised person solely for the purpose of warming up its engine in preparation for the carrying out of—

> (a) a compulsory test [or a reduced pollution test], or
>
> (b) a relevant re-examination that is to be carried out for the purposes of an appeal relating to a determination made on a compulsory test [or a reduced pollution test].]

(3) Where the relevant certificate is refused on a compulsory test[, or a reduced pollution test] of a vehicle [or as a result of a relevant re-examination,] the vehicle is an exempt vehicle when it is being used solely for the purpose of—

> (a) delivering it (by previous arrangement for a specified time on a specified date) at a place where relevant work is to be done on it, or
>
> (b) bringing it away from a place where relevant work has been done on it.

(4) In this paragraph *"compulsory test"* means, as respects England and Wales and Scotland—

> (a) in the case of a vehicle for which by virtue of section 66(3) of the Road Traffic Act 1988 a vehicle licence cannot be granted unless certain requirements are satisfied, an examination such as is specified in sub-paragraph (5), and
>
> (b) otherwise, an examination under section 45 of the Road Traffic Act 1988 with a view to obtaining a test certificate without which a vehicle licence cannot be granted for the vehicle.

(5) The examinations referred to in sub-paragraph (4)(a) are—

[(a) an examination under regulations under section 49(1)(b) or (c) of the Road Traffic Act 1988 (examination as to compliance with construction and use or safety requirements)],

(b) an examination for the purposes of sections 54 to 58 of that Act (examination as to a ... vehicle's compliance with type approval requirements), [and]

(c) [...]

(d) an examination under regulations under section 61(2)(a) of that Act (examinations in connection with alterations to ... vehicles subject to type approval requirements).

(6) *[Applies to Northern Ireland.]*

[(6ZA) In this paragraph *"a vehicle identity check"* means any examination of a vehicle for which provision is made by regulations made by virtue of section 22A(2) of this Act.]

[(6A) In this paragraph *"a vehicle weight test"* means any examination of a vehicle for which provision is made by regulations under—

(a) section 61A of this Act,

(b) section 49(1)(a) of the Road Traffic Act 1988 (tests for selecting plated weights and other plated particulars), or

(c) Article 65(1)(a) of the Road Traffic (Northern Ireland) Order 1995 [*SI 1995/2994 (NI 18)*].]

[(6AA) In this paragraph *"a reduced pollution test"* means any examination of a vehicle for which provision is made by regulations under sectio 61B of this Act.]

[(6B) In this paragraph *"a relevant re-examination"* means any examination or re-examination which is carried out in accordance with any provision or requirement made or imposed for the purposes of an appeal relating to a determination made on a compulsory test[, a vehicle identity check][, a vehicle weight test or a reduced pollution test].]

(7) In this paragraph *"authorised person"* means—

(a) in the case of an examination within sub-paragraph (4)(b), a person who is, or is acting on behalf of, an examiner or inspector entitled to carry out such an examination or a person acting under the personal direction of such a person,

(b) in the case of an examination within sub-paragraph (5), an examiner appointed under section 66A of the Road Traffic Act 1988, a person carrying out the examination under the direction of such an examiner or a person driving the vehicle in accordance with a requirement to do so under the regulations under which the examination is carried out, ...

(c) *[applies to Northern Ireland]* ...

[(ca) in the case of the examination of a vehicle for which provision is made by regulations made by virtue of section 22A(2) of this Act, the Secretary of State or a person authorised by him to carry out the examination;] [and]

[(d) in the case of a relevant re-examination—

(i) the person to whom the appeal in question is made, or

(ii) any person who, by virtue of an appointment made by that person, is authorised by or under any enactment to carry out that re-examination.]

(8) In this paragraph *"the relevant certificate"* means, as respects England and Wales and Scotland—

(a) a test certificate (as defined in section 45(2) of the Road Traffic Act 1988), [or]

(b) a goods vehicle test certificate (as defined in section 49 of that Act), or

(c) a type approval certificate or Minister's approval certificate (as defined in sections 54 to 58 of that Act), [or]

[(d) a certificate issued by virtue of section 61B of this Act.]

(9) *[Applies to Northern Ireland.]*

(10) In this paragraph *"relevant work"* means—

(a) where the relevant certificate which is refused is a test certificate …, work done or to be done to remedy for a further compulsory test the defects on the ground of which the relevant certificate was refused, and

(b) in any other case, work done or to be done to remedy the defects on the ground of which the relevant certificate was refused (including work to alter the vehicle in some aspect of design, construction, equipment or marking on account of which the relevant certificate was refused).

A24.228   *[Paragraph 22 of Sch.2 is printed as amended by the Finance Act 1996 ss.20 and 21(1), (5) and (6) (see also ibid. s.205 and Sch.41, Pt 2(4)); the Finance Act 1998 s.16 and Sch.1, paras 1 and 16; the Vehicles (Crime) Act 2001 s.43 and Schedule, para.6.*

Paragraph 22(7)(d) is expressed to take effect subject to s.21(3) of the Finance Act 1996, which substituted the text of para.22(7)(c) (not reproduced in this work). As to the effective date of the repeal of the words in para.22(10)(a) (which related to Northern Ireland), see the Finance Act 1996 s.21(6).]

Vehicles for export

A24.229   **23.**—(1) A vehicle is an exempt vehicle if—

(a) it has been supplied to the person keeping it by a taxable person within the meaning of section [3 of the Value Added Tax Act 1994], and

(b) the supply has been zero-rated under subsection [(8) of section 30] of that Act.

(2) If at any time the value added tax that would have been chargeable on the supply but for the zero-rating becomes payable under [subsection (10)] of that section (or would have become payable but for any authorisation or waiver under that subsection), the vehicle is deemed never to have been an exempt vehicle under sub-paragraph (1).

A24.230   *[Paragraph 23 of Sch.2 is printed as amended by the Value Added Tax Act 1994 s.100(1) and Sch.14, para.14.*

The term "taxable person" (in para.23(1)(a) above) is defined in the Value Added Tax Act 1994 s.3, as a person who is (or who is required to be) registered under the 1994 Act. Exempt supplies for value added tax purposes are listed in Sch.9 to the 1994 Act.]

Vehicles imported by members of foreign armed forces, etc.

A24.231   **24.** The Secretary of State may by regulations provide that, in such cases, subject to such conditions and for such period as may be prescribed by the regulations, a vehicle is an exempt vehicle if it has been imported by—

(a) a person for the time being appointed to serve with any body, contingent or detachment of the forces of any country prescribed by the regulations which is for the time being present in the United Kingdom on the invitation of Her Majesty's Government in the United Kingdom,

(b) a member of any country's military forces, except Her Majesty's United Kingdom forces, who is for the time being appointed to serve in the United Kingdom under the orders of any organisation so prescribed,

(c) a person for the time being recognised by the Secretary of State as a member of a civilian component of a force within sub-paragraph (a) or as a civilian member of an organisation within sub-paragraph (b), or

(d) any dependant of a description so prescribed of a person within sub-paragraph (a), (b) or (c).

A24.232   *[The Road Vehicles (Registration and Licensing) Regulations 2002 (SI 2002/ 2742) (q.v.) have effect as if made under para.24.]*

[Light passenger vehicles with low CO_2 emissions

A24.233   **25.**—[(1)] A vehicle is an exempt vehicle if—

(a) it is a vehicle to which Part 1A of Schedule 1 applies, and

(b) the applicable CO_2 emissions figure (as defined in paragraph 1A(3) and (4) of that Schedule) for the vehicle does not exceed 100 g/km.]

[(2) A vehicle is an exempt vehicle for the appropriate period if—

(a) it is a vehicle to which Part 1A of Schedule 1 applies, and

(b) the applicable CO_2 emissions figure (as defined in paragraph 1A(3) and (4) of that Schedule) exceeds 100g/ km but does not exceed 130g/km.

(3) *"The appropriate period"* is the period for which (if the vehicle were not an exempt vehicle by virtue of sub-paragraph (2)) the first vehicle licence for the vehicle would (if taken out) have effect.]

[Paragraph 25 of Sch.2 and the heading which precedes it were inserted by the Finance Act 2006 s.13(8). Paragraph 25 is printed as amended by the Finance Act 2009 s.14 and Sch.4, para.6 (the amendments made by Sch.4 to the Finance Act 2009 have effect in relation to licences taken out on or after April 1, 2010). **A24.234**

Nothing in s.13(8) of the Finance Act 2006 has the effect that a nil licence is required to be in force in respect of a vehicle while a vehicle licence is in force in respect of it.]

[SCHEDULE 2A

IMMOBILISATION, REMOVAL AND DISPOSAL OF VEHICLES

Immobilisation

1.—(1) The Secretary of State may make regulations under this Schedule with respect to any case where an authorised person has reason to believe that, on or after such date as may be prescribed, an offence under section 29(1) is being committed as regards a vehicle which is stationary [in any place other than a place to which this Schedule does not apply]. **A24.235**

[(1A) This Schedule does not apply to—

(a) any place which is within the curtilage of, or in the vicinity of, a dwelling-house, mobile home or houseboat and which is normally enjoyed with it, or

(b) any place which is within the curtilage of, or in the vicinity of, a building consisting entirely (apart from common parts) of two or more dwellings and which is normally enjoyed only by the occupiers of one or more of those dwellings.]

(2) The regulations may provide that the authorised person or a person acting under his direction may [enter the place and]—

(a) fix an immobilisation device to the vehicle while it remains in the place where it is stationary, or

(b) move it from that place to another place [...] and fix an immobilisation device to it in that other place.

(3) The regulations may provide that on any occasion when an immobilisation device is fixed to a vehicle in accordance with the regulations the person fixing the device shall also fix to the vehicle a notice—

(a) indicating that the device has been fixed to the vehicle and warning that no attempt should be made to drive it or otherwise put it in motion until it has been released from the device;

(b) specifying the steps to be taken to secure its release;

(c) giving such other information as may be prescribed.

(4) The regulations may provide that—

(a) a vehicle to which an immobilisation device has been fixed in accordance with the regulations may only be released from the device by or under the direction of an authorised person;

(b) subject to that, such a vehicle shall be released from the device if the first and second requirements specified below are met.

(5) The first requirement is that such charge in respect of the release as may be prescribed is paid in any manner specified in the immobilisation notice.

[(6) The second requirement is that—

(a) evidence that no offence under section 29(1) was being committed when the immobilisation device was fixed or the vehicle moved is produced in accordance with instructions specified in the immobilisation notice,

(b) such sum as may be prescribed is paid in any manner specified in the immobilisation notice, or

(c) any other prescribed conditions are fulfilled.

(6A) The conditions prescribed under sub-paragraph (6)(c) may include a condition that any of the following declarations is made—

(a) a declaration that an appropriate licence was in force for the vehicle at the time when the immobilisation device was fixed or the vehicle moved,

(b) (unless the vehicle was stationary on a public road) a declaration that a relevant declaration was in force for the vehicle at that time, or

(c) a declaration that at that time the vehicle was an exempt vehicle which was not one in respect of which regulations under this Act require a nil licence to be in force.]

(7) The regulations may provide that they shall not apply in relation to a vehicle if—

(a) a current disabled person's badge is displayed on the vehicle, or

(b) such other conditions as may be prescribed are fulfilled;

and *"disabled person's badge"* here means a badge issued, or having effect as if issued, under any regulations for the time being in force under section 21 of the Chronically Sick and Disabled Persons Act 1970 [*q.v.*] or any regulations for the time being in force under section 14 of the Chronically Sick and Disabled Persons (Northern Ireland) Act 1978 [*1978 c.53*].

(8) The regulations may provide that an immobilisation notice shall not be removed or interfered with except by or on the authority of a person falling within a prescribed description.

[(9) In sub-paragraph (6A)(a) *"appropriate licence"*, in relation to a vehicle, means—

(a) a vehicle licence,

(b) a trade licence which entitled the holder to keep the vehicle where it was stationary, or

(c) a nil licence.

(10) For the purposes of sub-paragraph (6A)(b)—

(a) *"relevant declaration"* means the declaration required to be made by regulations under section 22(1D), and

(b) a relevant declaration is in force for a vehicle if the vehicle is neither used nor kept on a public road (except under a trade licence) and the declaration has been made, and the particulars required to be furnished by regulations under section 22(1D) have been furnished, in relation to the vehicle in accordance within the regulations within the immediately preceding period of 12 months.]

A24.236   *[Schedule 2A was inserted by the Finance Act 1995 s.19 and Sch.4, para.36(2) and is printed as subsequently amended by the Finance Act 2008 s.145 and Sch.45, paras 4 and 5.]*

Offences connected with immobilisation

A24.237   **2.**—(1) The regulations may provide that a person contravening provision made under paragraph 1(8) is guilty of an offence and liable on summary conviction to a fine not exceeding level 2 on the standard scale.

(2) The regulations may provide that a person who, without being authorised to do so in accordance with provision made under paragraph 1, removes or attempts to remove an im-

mobilisation device fixed to a vehicle in accordance with the regulations is guilty of an offence and liable on summary conviction to a fine not exceeding level 3 on the standard scale.

(3) The regulations may provide that where they would apply in relation to a vehicle but for provision made under paragraph 1(7)(a) and the vehicle was not, at the time it was stationary, being used—

(a) in accordance with regulations under section 21 of the Chronically Sick and Disabled Persons Act 1970 or regulations under section 14 of the Chronically Sick and Disabled Persons (Northern Ireland) Act 1978, and

(b) in circumstances falling within section 117(1)(b) of the Road Traffic Regulation Act 1984 [*q.v.*] or Article 174A(2)(b) of the Road Traffic (Northern Ireland) Order 1981 [*SI 1981/154 (NI 1)*] (use where a disabled person's concession would be available),

the person in charge of the vehicle at that time is guilty of an offence and liable on summary conviction to a fine not exceeding level 3 on the standard scale.

(4) The regulations may provide that where—

[(a) a person makes a declaration described in paragraph 1(6A)(a), (b) or (c) with a view to securing the release of a vehicle from an immobilisation device purported to have been fixed in accordance with the regulations, and]

(b) [...]

(c) the declaration is to the person's knowledge either false or in any material respect misleading,

he is guilty of an offence.

(5) The regulations may provide that a person guilty of an offence by virtue of provision made under sub-paragraph (4) is liable—

(a) on summary conviction, to a fine not exceeding the statutory maximum, and

(b) on conviction on indictment, to imprisonment for a term not exceeding two years or to a fine or (except in Scotland) to both.

[*Paragraph 2 of Sch.2A was inserted by the Finance Act 1995 s.19 and Sch.4, para.36(2) and is printed as subsequently amended by the Finance Act 2008 s.145 and Sch.45, para.6.*]   **A24.238**

Removal and disposal of vehicles

3.—[(1) The regulations may make provision with respect to any case where—   **A24.239**

(a) an authorised person has reason to believe that an offence under section 29(1) —

(i) is being committed as regards a vehicle which is stationary [in any place other than a place to which this Schedule does not apply]; or

(ii) was being committed as regards a vehicle at a time when an immobilisation device which is fixed to the vehicle was fixed to it in accordance with the regulations;

and

(b) such conditions as may be prescribed are fulfilled.]

(2) The regulations may provide that [the authorised person, or a person acting under his direction], may [enter the place and] remove the vehicle and deliver it into the custody of a person—

(a) who is identified in accordance with prescribed rules, and

(b) who agrees to accept delivery in accordance with arrangements agreed between that person and the Secretary of State;

and the arrangements may include provision as to the payment of a sum to the person into whose custody the vehicle is delivered.

(3) The regulations may provide that the person into whose custody the vehicle is delivered may dispose of it, and in particular provision may be made as to—

    (a) the time at which the vehicle may be disposed of;

    (b) the manner in which it may be disposed of.

  (4) The regulations may make provision allowing a person to take possession of the vehicle if—

    (a) he claims it before it is disposed of, and

    (b) any prescribed conditions are fulfilled.

  (5) The regulations may provide for a sum of an amount arrived at under prescribed rules to be paid to a person if—

    (a) he claims after the vehicle's disposal to be or to have been its owner,

    (b) the claim is made within a prescribed time of the disposal, and

    (c) any other prescribed conditions are fulfilled.

  (6) The regulations may provide that—

    (a) the Secretary of State, or

    (b) a person into whose custody the vehicle is delivered under the regulations,

may recover from the vehicle's owner (whether or not a claim is made under provision made under sub-paragraph (4) or (5)) such charges as may be prescribed in respect of all or any of the following, namely, its release, removal, custody and disposal; and *"owner"* here means the person who was the owner [when the vehicle was removed].

  (7) The conditions prescribed under sub-paragraph (4) may include conditions as to—

    (a) satisfying the person with custody that the claimant is the vehicle's owner;

    (b) the payment of prescribed charges in respect of the vehicle's release, removal and custody;

    [(c) the production of evidence that no offence under section 29(1) was committed;

    (d) payment of a prescribed sum where such evidence is not produced;

    (e) the making of a declaration described in paragraph 1(6A)(a), (b) or (c).]

  (8) Without prejudice to anything in the preceding provisions of this paragraph, the regulations may include provision for purposes corresponding to those of sections 101 and 102 of the Road Traffic Regulation Act 1984 (disposal and charges) subject to such additions, omissions or other modifications as the Secretary of State thinks fit.

A24.240   *[Paragraph 3 of Sch.2A was inserted by the Finance Act 1995 s.19 and Sch.4, para.36(2) and is printed as subsequently amended by the Finance Act 1997 s.20; the Finance Act 2008 s.145 and Sch.45, para.8.]*

Offences as to securing possession of vehicles

A24.241   4.—(1) The regulations may provide that where—

    [(a) a person makes a declaration described in paragraph 1(6A)(a), (b) or (c) with a view to securing possession of a vehicle purported to have been delivered into the custody of a person in accordance with provision made under paragraph 3, and]

    (b) [...]

    (c) the declaration is to the person's knowledge either false or in any material respect misleading,

he is guilty of an offence.

  (2) The regulations may provide that a person guilty of such an offence is liable—

    (a) on summary conviction, to a fine not exceeding the statutory maximum, and

    (b) on conviction on indictment, to imprisonment for a term not exceeding two years or to a fine or (except in Scotland) to both.

A24.242   *[Paragraph 4 of Sch.2A was inserted by the Finance Act 1995 s.19 and Sch.4, para.36(2) and is printed as subsequently amended by the Finance Act 2008 s.145 and Sch.45, para.8.*

Payment of sum where licence not produced

A24.243   5.—(1) The regulations may make provision as regards a case where a person pays a prescribed sum in pursuance of provision made under—

(a) paragraph 1(6)(b), or

(b) paragraph 3(7)(d).

(2) The regulations may—

(a) provide for a voucher to be issued in respect of the sum;

(b) provide for setting the sum against the amount of any vehicle excise duty payable in respect of the vehicle concerned;

(c) provide for the refund of any sum;

(d) provide that where a voucher has been issued section 29(1) and any other prescribed provision of this Act shall not apply, as regards the vehicle concerned, in relation to events occurring in a prescribed period.

(3) The regulations may make provision—

(a) as to the information to be provided before a voucher is issued;

(b) as to the contents of vouchers;

(c) specifying conditions subject to which any provision under sub-paragraph (2)(b) to (d) is to have effect.

(4) The regulations may make provision as to any case where a voucher is issued on receipt of a cheque which is subsequently dishonoured, and in particular the regulations may—

(a) provide for a voucher to be void;

(b) provide that, where the sum concerned is set against the amount of any vehicle excise duty, the licence concerned shall be void;

(c) make provision under which a person is required to deliver up a void voucher or void licence.

[Paragraph 5 of Sch.2A; see the note to para.1 above.]   **A24.244**

Offences relating to vouchers

6.—(1) The regulations may provide that—   **A24.245**

(a) a person is guilty of an offence if within such reasonable period as is found in accordance with prescribed rules he fails to deliver up a voucher that is void by virtue of provision made under paragraph 5(4);

(b) a person guilty of such an offence shall be liable on summary conviction to a fine not exceeding level 3 on the standard scale.

(2) The regulations may provide that a person is guilty of an offence if within such reasonable period as is found in accordance with prescribed rules he fails to deliver up a licence that is void by virtue of provision made under paragraph 5(4), and that a person guilty of such an offence shall be liable on summary conviction to a penalty of whichever is the greater of—

(a) level 3 on the standard scale;

(b) an amount equal to five times the annual rate of duty that was payable on the grant of the licence or would have been so payable if it had been taken out for a period of twelve months.

(3) The regulations may provide that where a person is convicted of an offence under provision made by virtue of sub-paragraph (2) he must pay, in addition to any penalty, an amount found in accordance with prescribed rules.

(4) The regulations may provide that if—

(a) a voucher is void by virtue of provision made under paragraph 5(4),

(b) a person seeks to set the sum concerned against the amount of any vehicle excise duty, and

(c) he knows the voucher is void,

he is guilty of an offence and liable on summary conviction to a fine not exceeding level 5 on the standard scale.

(5) The regulations may provide that a person who in connection with—

   (a) obtaining a voucher for which provision is made under paragraph 5, or

   (b) obtaining a refund of any sum in respect of which such a voucher is issued,

makes a declaration which to his knowledge is either false or in any material respect misleading is guilty of an offence.

(6) The regulations may provide that a person is guilty of an offence if he forges, fraudulently alters, fraudulently uses, fraudulently lends or fraudulently allows to be used by another person a voucher for which provision is made under paragraph 5.

(7) The regulations may provide that a person guilty of an offence under provision made under sub-paragraph (5) or (6) is liable—

   (a) on summary conviction, to a fine not exceeding the statutory maximum, and

   (b) on conviction on indictment, to imprisonment for a term not exceeding two years or to a fine or (except in Scotland) to both.

A24.246   *[Paragraph 6 of Sch.2A; see the note to para.1 above.]*

Vouchers: general

A24.247   **7.** Without prejudice to anything in paragraphs 5(4) and 6 the regulations may include provision for purposes corresponding to those of sections 19A and 36 subject to such additions, omissions or other modifications as the Secretary of State thinks fit.

A24.248   *[Paragraph 7 of Sch.2A; see the note to para.1 above.]*

Disputes

A24.249   **8.** The regulations may make provision about the proceedings to be followed where a dispute occurs as a result of the regulations, and in particular provision may be made—

   (a) for an application to be made to a magistrates' court …;

   (b) for a court to order a sum to be paid by the Secretary of State.

A24.250   *[Paragraph 8 of Sch.2A; see the note to para.1 above.*

    The words omitted from para.8(a) relate exclusively to Northern Ireland.]

Authorised persons

A24.251   **9.** As regards anything falling to be done under the regulations (such as receiving payment of a charge or other sum or issuing a voucher) the regulations may provide that it may be done—

   (a) by an authorised person, or

   (b) by an authorised person or a person acting under his direction.

A24.252   *[Paragraph 9 of Sch.2A; see the note to para.1 above.]*

Application of provisions

A24.253   **10.**—(1) The regulations may provide that they shall only apply where the authorised person has reason to believe that the offence mentioned in paragraph 1(1) is being committed before such date as may be prescribed.

(2) The regulations may provide that they shall only apply where the vehicle mentioned in paragraph 1(1) is in a prescribed area.

(3) Different dates may be prescribed under paragraph 1(1) or sub-paragraph (1) above in relation to different areas prescribed under sub-paragraph (2) above.

A24.254   *[Paragraph 10 of Sch.2A; see the note to para.1 above.]*

Interpretation

A24.255   **11.**—(1) The regulations may make provision as to the meaning for the purposes of the regulations of *"owner"* as regards a vehicle.

(2) In particular, the regulations may provide that for the purposes of the regulations—

(a) the owner of a vehicle at a particular time shall be taken to be the person by whom it is then kept;

(b) the person by whom a vehicle is kept at a particular time shall be taken to be the person in whose name it is then registered by virtue of this Act.

[Paragraph 11 of Sch.2A; see the note to para.1 above.]   **A24.256**

12.—(1) The regulations may make provision as to the meaning in the regulations of   **A24.257**
"authorised person".

(2) In particular, the regulations may provide that—

(a) references to an authorised person are to a person authorised by the Secretary of State for the purposes of the regulations;

(b) an authorised person may be a local authority or an employee of a local authority or a member of a police force or some other person;

(c) different persons may be authorised for the purposes of different provisions of the regulations.

[Paragraph 12 of Sch.2A; see the note to para.1 above.]   **A24.258**

13. In this Schedule —   **A24.259**

(a) references to an immobilisation device are to a device or appliance which is an immobilisation device for the purposes of section 104 of the Road Traffic Regulation Act 1984 [*q.v.*] (immobilisation of vehicles illegally parked);

(b) references to an immobilisation notice are to a notice fixed to a vehicle in accordance with the regulations;

(c) *"prescribed"* means prescribed by regulations made under this Schedule.]

[Paragraph 13 of Sch.2A; see the note to para.1 above.   **A24.260**

The Vehicle Excise Duty (Immobilisation, Removal and Disposal of Vehicles) Regulations 1997 (SI 1997/2439) below have been made in part under Sch.2A.]

Section 63	SCHEDULE 3

CONSEQUENTIAL AMENDMENTS

*   *   *

Section 64	SCHEDULE 4	**A24.261**

TRANSITIONALS, ETC.

General transitionals and savings

1. The substitution of this Act for the provisions repealed or revoked by this Act does   **A24.263**
not affect the continuity of the law.

2.—(1) Anything done, or having effect as done (including the making of subordinate   **A24.264**
legislation and the issuing of licences), under or for the purposes of any provision repealed or revoked by this Act has effect as if done under or for the purposes of any corresponding provision of this Act.

(2) Sub-paragraph (1) does not apply to the Vehicle Licences (Duration and Rate of Duty) Order 1980 [*SI 1980/1183*].

3. Any reference (express or implied) in this Act or any other enactment, or in any   **A24.265**
instrument or document, to a provision of this Act is (so far as the context permits) to be read as (according to the context) being or including in relation to times, circumstances and purposes before the commencement of this Act a reference to the corresponding provision repealed or revoked by this Act.

4. Any reference (express or implied) in any enactment, or in any instrument or docu-   **A24.266**
ment, to a provision repealed or revoked by this Act is (so far as the context permits) to be

read as (according to the context) being or including in relation to times, circumstances and purposes after the commencement of this Act a reference to the corresponding provision of this Act.

A24.267   5. Paragraphs 1 to 4 have effect in place of section 17(2) of the Interpretation Act 1978 (but are without prejudice to any other provision of that Act).

Preservation of old transitionals and savings

A24.268   6.—(1) The repeal by this Act of an enactment previously repealed subject to savings (whether or not in the repealing enactment) does not affect the continued operation of those savings.

(2) The repeal by this Act of a saving made on the previous repeal of an enactment does not affect the operation of the saving in so far as it remains capable of having effect.

(3) Where the purpose of an enactment repealed by this Act was to secure that the substitution of the provisions of the Act containing that enactment for provisions repealed by that Act did not affect the continuity of the law, the enactment repealed by this Act continues to have effect in so far as it is capable of doing so.

Exemption for disabled passengers

A24.269   7.—(1) Where—

(a) a vehicle is suitable for use by persons having a particular disability that so incapacitates them in the use of their limbs that they have to be driven and cared for by a full-time constant attendant,

(b) the vehicle is registered under this Act in the name of a person who has such a disability and is a person to whom this paragraph applies,

(c) that person is sufficiently disabled to be eligible for an invalid tricycle under the National Health Service Act 1977, the National Health Service (Scotland) Act 1978 or the Health and Personal Social Services (Northern Ireland) Order 1972 [*SI 1972/1265 (NI 14)*] but too disabled to drive it, and

(d) no other vehicle registered in that person's name under this Act, or deemed to be so registered under sub-paragraph (3) of paragraph 19 of Schedule 2, is an exempt vehicle under that paragraph,

the vehicle is an exempt vehicle if used or kept for use by or for the purposes of that person.

(2) This paragraph applies to a person if—

(a) there remains valid a relevant certificate issued in respect of him before 13th October 1993 (the day on which the repeal of the provisions specified in section 12(1) of the Finance (No.2) Act 1992 came into force), or

(b) an application for a relevant certificate in respect of him had been received by the Secretary of State or the Department of Health and Social Services for Northern Ireland before that date and a relevant certificate issued pursuant to that application remains valid.

(3) In this paragraph a *"relevant certificate"* means—

(a) a certificate issued by the Secretary of State (or the Minister of Transport) containing a statement as described in Regulation 26(2)(b)(i) and (ii) of the Road Vehicles (Registration and Licensing) Regulations 1971 [*SI 1971/450*] (as in force on 29th December 1972) or a statement to similar effect, or

(b) a certificate issued by the Department of Health and Social Services for Northern Ireland (or the Ministry of Health and Social Services for Northern Ireland) containing a statement as described in Regulation 27(2)(b)(i) and (ii) of the Road Vehicles (Registration and Licensing) Regulations (Northern Ireland) 1973 [*SR & O (NI) 1973/490*] (as originally in force) or a statement to similar effect,

including (in either case) any renewal or continuation of such a certificate.

(4) For the purposes of sub-paragraph (2) a relevant certificate issued in respect of a person remains valid for as long as the matters stated in the certificate in relation to the person's disability remain unaltered.

(5) Where immediately before 13th October 1993 a person to whom this paragraph applies was under the age of five, the person ceases to be a person to whom this paragraph applies—

    (a) if a relevant licence document is in force on the day on which he attains the age of five in respect of a vehicle used or kept for use for his purposes, when that licence document expires, and

    (b) otherwise, on attaining the age of five.

(6) In sub-paragraph (5) *"relevant licence document"* means a document in the form of a licence issued under—

    (a) Regulation 26(3A)(b) of the Road Vehicles (Registration and Licensing) Regulations 1971,

    (b) Regulation 27(4)(b) of the Road Vehicles (Registration and Licensing) Regulations (Northern Ireland) 1973, or

    (c) paragraph 4 or 6 of the Schedule to the Finance (No.2) Act 1992 (Commencement No.6 and Transitional Provisions and Savings) Order 1993 [*SI 1993/2272 (q.v.)*],

        or any re-enactment (with or without modifications) of any of those provisions.

(7) Regulations under section 22(2) of this Act which require a person to furnish information relating to a vehicle which is an exempt vehicle under this paragraph may require him to furnish (in addition) such evidence of the facts giving rise to the exemption as is prescribed by the regulations.

(8) In spite of the repeal by this Act of section 12(2) of the Finance (No.2) Act 1992, paragraphs 4 to 8 of the Schedule to the Finance (No.2) Act 1992 (Commencement No.6 and Transitional Provisions and Savings) Order 1993 [*SI 1993/2272*] shall, until the coming into force of the first regulations made by virtue of sub-paragraph (7) (unless revoked and subject to any amendments), continue to have effect but subject to the modifications specified in sub-paragraph (9).

(9) The modifications referred to in sub-paragraph (8) are—

    (a) the substitution of a reference to this paragraph for any reference to paragraph 2 of that Schedule,

    (b) the addition of a reference to this Act after the first reference to the Vehicles (Excise) Act 1971 in paragraphs 4(4)(a) and 6(4)(a),

    (c) the substitution of a reference to this Act for each other reference to the Vehicles (Excise) Act 1971, and

    (d) the substitution of a reference to section 23 of this Act for any reference to section 19 of that Act and of a reference to subsection (3) of section 23 of this Act for any reference to subsection (2) of section 19 of that Act.

(10) Sections 44 and 45 of this Act have effect in relation to a vehicle which is an exempt vehicle under this paragraph as they have effect in relation to a vehicle which is an exempt vehicle under paragraph 19 of Schedule 2 to this Act.

(11) If and to the extent that, immediately before the coming into force of this Act, the Secretary of State had power to amend or revoke by order any provision of the Finance (No.2) Act 1992 (Commencement No.6 and Transitional Provisions and Savings) Order 1993, he has the same power in relation to so much of this paragraph as reproduces that provision.

[The reference in para.7(3)(a) to the "Minister of Transport" is presumed to **A24.270** *be of historical nature and is not directly affected by the Transfer of Functions (Transport, Local Government and the Regions) Order 2002 (SI 2002/2626).*

The Road Vehicles (Registration and Licensing) Regulations 1971 (SI 1971/ 450) and the Road Vehicles (Registration and Licensing) Regulations (Northern Ireland) 1973 (SR & O (NI) 1973/490) referred to in para.7(3)(a) and (b) and (6)(a) and (b) above have been revoked by the Road Vehicles (Registration and Licensing) Regulations 2002 (SI 2002/2742) reg.2 and Sch.1, Pts I and III.]

Trade licences

A24.271   **8.** *[Power to substitute by order different text for that of s.13.]*

Combined road-rail transport of goods

A24.272   **9.** Section 20 (and the references to it in sections 45(1)(b) and 57(5)) shall not come into force until such day as the Secretary of State may by order appoint.

Regulations about registration and licensing

A24.273   **10.** Regulation 12(1) of the Road Vehicles (Registration and Licensing) Regulations 1971 continues to have effect (until revoked) as if the amendments of section 23 of the Vehicles (Excise) Act 1971, as set out in paragraph 20 of Schedule 7 to that Act, which were made by paragraph 16(3) of Part III of Schedule 1 to the Finance Act 1987 had been in force when those Regulations were made.

A24.274   *[The Finance Act 1987 Sch.1, Pt 3, para.16, has been repealed by s.65 of and Sch.5, Pt 1, to this Act.*

Regulation 12(1) of the Road Vehicles (Registration and Licensing) Regulations 1971 (SI 1971/450) has been revoked by the Road Vehicles (Registration and Licensing) Regulations 2002 (SI 2002/2742) reg.2 and Sch.1, Pt 1.]

Assignment of registration marks

A24.275   **11.** The inclusion in this Act of subsection (2), and the words "for the time being" in subsection (3), of section 23 (which reproduce the amendments of the Vehicles (Excise) Act 1971 made by section 10(2) and (3) of the Finance Act 1989) shall not be construed as affecting the operation of—

   (a) the Vehicles (Excise) Act 1971 or the Vehicles (Excise) Act (Northern Ireland) 1972, or

   (b) any regulations made under either of those acts,

in relation to any time before 27th July 1989 (the day on which the Finance Act 1989 was passed).

Section 65   SCHEDULE 5

REPEALS AND REVOCATIONS

*   *   *

The Road Traffic (New Drivers) Act 1995

(1995 c.13)

An Act to make provision about newly qualified drivers who commit certain offences, including provision with respect to tests of competence to drive.

[28th June 1995]

ARRANGEMENT OF SECTIONS

*   *   *

Introductory

Probationary period for newly qualified drivers

1.—(1) For the purposes of this Act, a person's probationary period is, subject to section 7, the period of two years beginning with the day on which he becomes a qualified driver.

(2) For the purposes of this Act, a person becomes a qualified driver on the first occasion on which he passes—

    (a) any test of competence to drive mentioned in paragraph (a) or (c) of section 89(1) of the Road Traffic Act 1988 [*q.v.*];

(b) any test of competence to drive conducted under the law of—

[(i) another EEA State,

(ii) the Isle of Man,

(iii) any of the Channel Islands, or

(iv) Gibraltar.]

(3) In subsection (2) *"EEA State"* means a State which is a contracting party to the EEA Agreement but until the EEA Agreement comes into force in relation to Liechtenstein does not include the State of Liechtenstein.

(4) In subsection (3) *"EEA Agreement"* means the Agreement on the European Economic Area signed at Oporto on 2nd May 1992 as adjusted by the Protocol signed at Brussels on 17th March 1993.

A25.03 *[Section 1 is printed as amended by the Driving Licences (Community Driving Licence) Regulations 1996 (SI 1996/1974) reg.5 and Sch.4, para.5(1) and (2), read together with ibid. reg.1(2).*

As to the EEA Agreement, the protocol of March 17, 1993 and the date on which the EEA Agreement took effect in Liechtenstein, see the introductory note to Section C below.]

Surrender of licences

A25.04 **2.**—(1) Subsection (2) applies where—

(a) a person is the holder of a licence;

(b) he is convicted of an offence involving obligatory endorsement;

(c) the penalty points to be taken into account under section 29 of the Road Traffic Offenders Act 1988 [*q.v.*] on that occasion number six or more;

(d) the court makes an order falling within section 44(1)(b) of that Act in respect of the offence;

(e) the person's licence shows the date on which he became a qualified driver, or that date has been shown by other evidence in the proceedings; and

(f) it appears to the court, in the light of the order and the date so shown, that the offence was committed during the person's probationary period.

(2) Where this subsection applies, the court must send to the Secretary of State—

(a) a notice containing the particulars required to be endorsed on the counterpart of the person's licence in accordance with the order referred to in subsection (1)(d); and

(b) on their production to the court, the person's licence and its counterpart.

(3) Subsection (4) applies where—

(a) a person's licence and its counterpart have been sent to the fixed penalty clerk under section 54(7) of the Road Traffic Offenders Act 1988[, retained by a vehicle examiner under that section] or delivered to the [appropriate person in] response to a conditional offer issued under section 75 of that Act;

(b) the offence to which the fixed penalty notice or the conditional offer relates is one involving obligatory endorsement;

(c) the [appropriate person] endorses the number of penalty points to be attributed to the offence on the counterpart of the licence;

(d) the penalty points to be taken into account by the [appropriate person] in respect of the offence number six or more;

(e) the licence shows the date on which the person became a qualified driver; and

(f) it appears to the [appropriate person], in the light of the particulars of the offence endorsed on the counterpart of the licence and the date so shown, that the offence was committed during the person's probationary period.

(4) Where this subsection applies, the [...]

(a) [the appropriate person] may not return the licence and its counterpart under section 57(3) or (4) or 77(1) of the Road Traffic Offenders Act 1988; but

(b) [unless the appropriate person is the Secretary of State, he] must send them to the Secretary of State.

(5) For the purposes of subsection (3)(d) the penalty points to be taken into account [...] in respect of the offence are the penalty points which would have been taken into account under section 29 of the Road Traffic Offenders Act 1988 if—

(a) the person in question had been convicted of the offence; and

(b) the number of penalty points to be attributed to the offence on that occasion had been determined in accordance with section 28(3) of that Act.

[(6) In this section and section 3 *"licence"* includes a Northern Ireland licence.]

[(7) In this section and section 3—

"the appropriate person" , in relation to a conditional offer, means—

(a) if it was given by a constable or an authorised person, the fixed penalty clerk, and

(b) if it was given by a vehicle examiner or the Secretary of State, the Secretary of State, and

"the appropriate person" , in relation to a fixed penalty notice, means—

(a) where the conditional offer was issued under subsection (1), (2) or (3) of section 75 of the Road Traffic Offenders Act 1988, the fixed penalty clerk, and

(b) where it was issued under subsection (1A) or (3B) of that section, the Secretary of State.]

[Section 2 is printed as amended by the Crime (International Co-operation) **A25.05** *Act 2003 s.91 and Sch.5, para.46; the Road Safety Act 2006 s.5 and Sch.1, para.25 and Sch.7(2).*

With effect from a day (or days) to be appointed, the following amendments will be made to s.2:

1. *for s.2(2), in relation to endorsement (all drivers), the following text*

will be substituted by the Road Safety Act 2006 s.10 and Sch.3, para.67(2):

[(2) Where this subsection applies, the court must, together with the notice of the order referred to in subsection (1)(d) required to be sent to the Secretary of State under section 44A of the Road Traffic Offenders Act 1988, send the person's licence on its production to the court.]

2. *in s.2(3)(a), in relation to endorsement (all drivers), the word "has" will be substituted for the words "and its counterpart have" by the Road Safety Act 2006 s.10 and Sch.3, para.67(3)(a);*

3. *in s.2(3)(c), in relation to endorsement (all drivers) and as amended by the Road Safety Act 2006 s.5 and Sch.1, para.25(2)(b) above, the words "appropriate person endorses the number of" will be omitted by ibid. s.10 and Sch.3, para.67(3)(b)(i), s.59 and Sch.7(4); and the words "are to be endorsed on the person's driving record" will be substituted for the words "on the counterpart of the licence" by ibid. s.10 and Sch.3, para.67(3)(b)(ii);*

4. *in s.2(3)(f), in relation to endorsement (all drivers), the words "to be" will be inserted before the word "endorsed", and the words "person's driving record" will be substituted for the words "counterpart of the licence" by the Road Safety Act 2006 s.10 and Sch.3, para.67(3)(c);*

5. *in s.2(4)(a), in relation to endorsement (all drivers), the words "and its counterpart" will be omitted, and "57A(3) or (4) or 77A(2)" will be substituted for "57(3) or (4) or 77(1)" by the Road Safety Act 2006 s.10 and Sch.3, para.67(4)(a), s.59 and Sch.7(4);*

6. *in s.2(4)(b), in relation to endorsement (all drivers), the words "together with the notice he is required to send under section 57A or 77A of that Act of the particulars to be endorsed on the person's driving record" will be inserted at the end by the Road Safety Act 2006 s.10 and Sch.3, para.67(4)(b);*

For the provisions relating to the commencement of s.10 of and Sch.3 to the 2006 Act, see ibid. s.61(8) below.

The holder of a licence under s.2(1) above may liable to a penalty charge under the London Local Authorities and Transport for London Act 2003 ss.4 and 5.]

Revocation of licences

A25.06   3.—(1) Where the Secretary of State receives—

(a) a notice sent to him under section 2(2)(a) of particulars required to be endorsed on the counterpart of a person's licence, or

(b) a person's licence and its counterpart sent to him in accordance with section 2(2)(b) or [(4)(b)],

the Secretary of State must by notice served on that person revoke the licence.

[(1ZA) Where section 2(4)(a) applies but the appropriate person is the Secretary of State, the Secretary of State must by notice served on the person to whom the fixed penalty notice or conditional offer was given or issued, revoke that person's licence.]

[(1A) Where the Secretary of State serves on the holder of a Northern Ireland licence a notice under subsection (1) [or (1ZA)], the Secretary of State must send to the licensing authority in Northern Ireland—

    (a) particulars of the notice; and

    (b) the Northern Ireland licence.]

[(1B) Where the Secretary of State is sent by that licensing authority particulars of a notice served on the holder of a licence under a provision of Northern Ireland law corresponding to subsection (1) [or (1ZA)], he must by notice served on the holder revoke the licence.]

(2) A revocation under [this section] shall have effect from a date specified in the notice of revocation which may not be earlier than the date of service of that notice.

[(3) In this section references to the revocation of a person's Northern Ireland licence are references to its revocation as respects Great Britain; and, accordingly, the person ceases to be authorised by virtue of section 109(1) of the Road Traffic Act 1988 to drive in Great Britain a motor vehicle of any class.]

[Section 3 is printed as amended by the Crime (International Co-operation)   **A25.07** *Act 2003 s.91 and Sch.5, para.47; the Road Safety Act 2006 s.5 and Sch.1, para.26.*

With effect from a day to be appointed, in relation to endorsement (all drivers), s.3(1) will be substituted by the Road Safety Act 2006 s.10 and Sch.3, para.68 as follows:

    [(1) Where the Secretary of State receives—

        (a) a notice sent to him under section 44A, 57A or 77A of the Road Traffic Offenders Act 1988 of particulars required to be endorsed on a person's driving record, and

        (b) a person's licence sent to him in accordance with section 2(2) or (4)(b), the Secretary of State must by notice served on that person revoke the licence.]

For the provisions relating to the commencement of s.10 of and Sch.3 to the 2006 Act, see ibid. s.61(8) below.]

Retesting

4.—(1) Subject to subsection (5) and section 5, the Secretary of State may not   **A25.08** under Part III of the Road Traffic Act 1988 grant a person whose licence has been revoked under [section 3] a full licence to drive any class of vehicles in relation to which the revoked licence was issued as a full licence [or (as the case may be) full Northern Ireland licence] unless he satisfies the Secretary of State that within the relevant period he has passed a relevant driving test.

[(1A) Subject to subsection (5), the Secretary of State may not under that Part grant a person whose Northern Ireland licence has been revoked under a provision of Northern Ireland law corresponding to section 3(1) a full licence to drive any class of vehicles in relation to which the revoked licence was issued as a full Northern Ireland licence unless he satisfies the Secretary of State as mentioned in subsection (1).]

(2) In this section *"relevant driving test"* means, in relation to a person whose licence has been revoked, any test which—

    (a) falls within paragraph (a) or (b) of section 1(2); and

(b) is a test of competence to drive any vehicle included in any class of vehicles in relation to which the revoked licence was issued as a full licence [or (as the case may be) full Northern Ireland licence].

(3) If the Secretary of State grants a full licence to a person who is required to pass a relevant driving test in order to be granted that licence, the licence granted must (subject to section 92 and Part IV of the Road Traffic Act 1988) be one authorising that person to drive all the classes of vehicles in relation to which the revoked licence was issued as a full licence [or (as the case may be) full Northern Ireland licence].

(4) In subsection (1) *"the relevant period"* means the period beginning—
(a) after the date of the revocation of the licence; and
(b) not more than two years before the date on which the application for the full licence is made.

(5) [Subsections (1) and (1A) do] not apply to a person whose licence has been revoked under [section 3 or whose Northern Ireland licence has been revoked under a provision of Northern Ireland law corresponding to section 3(1)] if, before he passes a relevant driving test, an order is made in relation to him under section 36 of the Road Traffic Offenders Act 1988 (disqualification until test is passed).

A25.09   *[Section 4 is printed as amended by the Crime (International Co-operation) Act 2003 s.91 and Sch.5, para.48.]*

Restoration of licence without retesting in certain cases

A25.10   **5.**—(1) If the Secretary of State receives notice that a person whose licence has been revoked under [section 3] is appealing against a conviction or endorsement which was the basis or formed part of the basis for the revocation, he must grant that person free of charge a full licence for a period prescribed by regulations.

(2) Regulations under subsection (1) may in particular prescribe—
(a) a period expiring when the appeal is finally determined or abandoned; or
(b) a period expiring on the date on which the revoked licence would have expired if it had not been revoked.

(3) If the regulations prescribe a period other than that mentioned in subsection (2)(a), a licence granted under subsection (1) shall be treated as revoked if—
(a) following the appeal, the penalty points taken into account for the purposes of section 2 [or (as the case may be) the provision of Northern Ireland law corresponding to that section] are not reduced to a number smaller than six; or
(b) the appeal is abandoned.

(4) If, in the case of a person whose licence has been revoked under [section 3], the Secretary of State receives notice that a court—
(a) has quashed a conviction which was the basis or formed part of the basis for the revocation of the licence,
(b) has quashed an endorsement which was the basis or formed part of the basis for the revocation of the licence and has not on doing so ordered him to be disqualified, or
(c) has made an order which has the effect of reducing the penalty points

taken into account for the purposes of section 2 to a number smaller than six,

then, subject to subsection (5), the Secretary of State must grant that person free of charge a full licence for a period expiring on the date on which the revoked licence would have expired if it had not been revoked.

(5) Subsection (4) does not require the Secretary of State to grant a licence to a person who has been granted a previous licence which has not been surrendered unless that person provides the Secretary of State with an explanation for not surrendering the previous licence that the Secretary of State considers adequate.

(6) If, in accordance with subsection (1) or (4), the Secretary of State grants a full licence to a person whose licence has been revoked under [section 3], the licence granted must be one authorising that person to drive all the classes of vehicles in relation to which the revoked licence was issued as a full licence.

(7) Any licence granted in accordance with subsection (1) or (4) shall have effect for the purposes of the Road Traffic Acts as if it were a licence granted under Part III of the Road Traffic Act 1988.

(8) Regulations may make provision for requiring such courts as may be prescribed to give notice to the Secretary of State—

    (a) that a person whose licence has been or is due to be revoked under section 3(1) is appealing against a conviction or endorsement which is the basis or forms part of the basis for the revocation;

    (b) that such an appeal has been abandoned.

(9) Regulations under this section may—

    (a) include such incidental or supplementary provision as appears to the Secretary of State to be expedient;

    (b) make different provision for different cases.

(10) Any regulations made under this section shall be made by the Secretary of State by statutory instrument which shall be subject to annulment in pursuance of a resolution of either House of Parliament.

[(11) Nothing in this section applies in relation to a person whose Northern Ireland licence has been revoked under section 3(1).]

[Section 5 is printed as amended by the Crime (International Co-operation) **A25.11**
Act 2003 s.91 and Sch.5, para.49.

The New Drivers (Appeals Procedure) Regulations 1997 (SI 1997/1098) below have been made in part under this section.]

Miscellaneous and general

Newly qualified drivers holding test certificates

6. Schedule 1 (which makes provision about newly qualified drivers who hold   **A25.12**
test certificates) shall have effect.

Early termination of probationary period

7. For the purposes of this Act a person's probationary period comes to an end   **A25.13**
if—

    (a) an order is made in relation to him under section 36 of the Road Traffic Offenders Act 1988 (order that a person be disqualified until he passes the appropriate driving test);

(b) after his licence is revoked under [section 3], he is granted a full licence following the passing of a test which is a relevant driving test for the purposes of section 4; or

(c) after his test certificate is revoked under [paragraph 5] of Schedule 1, or his licence and test certificate are revoked under [paragraph 8] of that Schedule, he is granted a full licence following the passing of a test which is a relevant driving test for the purposes of paragraph 6 or 9 of that Schedule.

A25.14   *[Section 7 is printed as amended by the Crime (International Co-operation) Act 2003 s.91 and Sch.5, para.50.]*

The Crown

A25.15   **8.** This Act applies to persons in the public service of the Crown.

Interpretation, etc.

A25.16   **9.**—(1) Expressions used in this Act which are also used in Part III of the Road Traffic Act 1988 [*q.v.*] shall be construed in the same way as in that Act.

(2) Expressions used in this Act which are also used in the Road Traffic Offenders Act 1988 [*q.v.*] shall be construed in the same way as in that Act.

[(2A) In this Act—

"full Northern Ireland licence" means a Northern Ireland licence other than a Northern Ireland provisional licence,

"Northern Ireland provisional licence" means a Northern Ireland licence which corresponds to a provisional licence.]

(3) In this Act *"notice"* means notice in writing.

(4) Section 107 of the Road Traffic Act 1988 (service of notices) applies to a notice served under section 3 or paragraph 5 or 8 of Schedule 1 [as it applies to a notice served under Part III or IV of that Act].

(5) Any requirement under any provision of this Act that a licence and its counterpart, a test certificate or a notice must be sent to the Secretary of State is a requirement that the licence and its counterpart, the test certificate or the notice must be sent to the Secretary of State at such address as the Secretary of State may determine.

A25.17   *[Section 9 is printed as amended by the Driving Licences (Community Driving Licence) Regulations 1996 (SI 1996/1974) reg.5 and Sch.4, para.5(1) and (3), read together with ibid. reg.1(2); the Crime (International Co-operation) Act 2003 s.91 and Sch.5, para.51.*

With effect from a day to be appointed, the words "and its counterpart" will be omitted from s.9(5) by the Road Safety Act 2006 s.10 and Sch.3, para.69, s.59 and Sch.7(4) (for commencement provisions, see ibid. s.61(8) below).]

Short title, commencement, extent, etc.

A25.18   **10.**—(1) This Act may be cited as the Road Traffic (New Drivers) Act 1995.

(2) The provisions of this Act shall come into force on such day as the Secretary of State may by order made by statutory instrument appoint and different days may be so appointed for different provisions.

(3) Nothing in any provision of this Act applies to a person who becomes a qualified driver before the day on which the provision comes into force.

(4) The consequential amendments set out in Schedule 2 shall have effect.

(5) This Act does not extend to Northern Ireland.

[This Act was brought into force (in the main) on June 1, 1997 by the Road Traffic (New Drivers) Act 1995 (Commencement) Order 1997 (SI 1997/267; not reproduced in this work).] **A25.19**

SCHEDULES

Section 6   SCHEDULE 1

NEWLY QUALIFIED DRIVERS HOLDING TEST CERTIFICATES

PART I

GENERAL

Interpretation

1.—(1) In this Schedule *"test certificate"* means a certificate or other document which **A25.20** by virtue of regulations under section 89 of the Road Traffic Act 1988 is evidence that a person has not more than two years previously passed a test of competence to drive prescribed by virtue of such regulations.

(2) In this Schedule *"prescribed conditions"* means the prescribed conditions referred to in section 97(3) of the 1988 Act (subject to which provisional licences are granted).

[(2A) In this Schedule *"the appropriate person"* has the same meaning as in sections 2 and 3 of this Act.].

[(3) In this Schedule *"licence"* includes a Northern Ireland licence, *"full licence"* includes a full Northern Ireland licence and *"provisional licence"* includes a Northern Ireland provisional licence.]

[(4) In relation to the holder of a Northern Ireland licence, the following sub-paragraphs have effect for the purposes of this Schedule.]

[(5) References to a test certificate are references to a certificate or other document (in this Schedule referred to as a "Northern Ireland test certificate") which is evidence that he has not more than two years previously passed a Northern Ireland test of competence to drive corresponding to the test mentioned in sub-paragraph (1).]

[(6) References to prescribed conditions are references to conditions subject to which the Northern Ireland provisional licence was granted.]

[Paragraph 1 of Sch.1 is printed as amended by the Crime (International Co- **A25.21** *operation) Act 2003 s.91 and Sch.5, para.53; the Road Safety Act 2006 s.5 and Sch.1, para.27.].*

Application of Schedule

2.—(1) Part II of this Schedule applies to any person to whom Part III or IV of this **A25.22** Schedule applies.

(2) Part III of this Schedule applies to a person who holds—

    (a) a licence issued as a provisional licence; and

    (b) a test certificate.

(3) Part IV of this Schedule applies to a person who falls within sub-paragraph (4) or (5).

(4) A person falls within this sub-paragraph if—

    (a) he holds a licence issued as a full licence in relation to a class or certain classes of vehicles;

    (b) he is treated under section 98(2) of the Road Traffic Act 1988 as authorised by a provisional licence to drive another class or other classes of vehicles; and

(c) he holds a test certificate which relates to that other class of vehicles or any of those other classes of vehicles.

[(4A) In relation to the holder of a Northern Ireland licence, the reference in sub-paragraph (4)(b) to section 98(2) of the Road Traffic Act 1988 is a reference to the corresponding provision under the law of Northern Ireland.]

(5) A person falls within this sub-paragraph if he holds—

(a) a licence issued as a full licence in relation to a class or certain classes of vehicles and has a provisional licence in relation to another class or other classes of vehicles; and

(b) a test certificate which relates to that other class of vehicles or any of those other classes of vehicles.

A25.23   *[Paragraph 2 of Sch.1 is printed as amended by the Crime (International Co-operation) Act 2003 s.91 and Sch.5, para.54.]*

PART II

DUTY TO PROVIDE TEST CERTIFICATE

A25.24   **3.**—(1) Sub-paragraph (2) applies where—

(a) a person to whom this Part of this Schedule applies is prosecuted for an offence involving obligatory endorsement; and

(b) the time at which the offence for which he is prosecuted is alleged to have occurred is a time during his probationary period.

(2) Any obligations imposed on the person under section 7 of the Road Traffic Offenders Act 1988 as respects his licence and its counterpart shall also apply as respects his test certificate.

(3) If, in a case where sub-paragraph (2) applies—

(a) the person is convicted in the proceedings in question of an offence involving obligatory endorsement, and

(b) he has not previously caused his test certificate to be delivered or posted it to the [proper officer] of the court,

he must produce his test certificate to the court.

[(3A) In sub-paragraph (3) *"proper officer"* means—

(a) in relation to a magistrates' court in England and Wales, the [designated officer] for the court, and

(b) in relation to any other court, the clerk of the court.]

(4) In a case where—

(a) the licence of a person to whom this Part of this Schedule applies has (with its counterpart) been sent to the [appropriate person] under section 54(7) of the Road Traffic Offenders Act 1988 or delivered to the [appropriate person] in response to a conditional offer issued under section 75 of that Act,

(b) the offence to which the fixed penalty notice or the conditional offer relates is one involving obligatory endorsement and occurring during his probationary period, and

(c) the person proposes to pay the fixed penalty to the [appropriate person],

the person must ensure that when the fixed penalty is paid his test certificate is sent to the [appropriate person].

(5) A person who without reasonable excuse fails to comply with sub-paragraph (3) or (4) is guilty of an offence and shall be liable on summary conviction to a fine not exceeding level 3 on the standard scale.

A25.25   *[Paragraph 3 of Sch.1 is printed as amended by the Access to Justice Act 1999 s.90(1) and Sch.13, para.173; the Courts Act 2003 s.109(1) and Sch.8, para.365; the Road Safety Act 2006 s.5 and Sch.1, para.27.*

With effect from a day (or days) to be appointed, the following amendments will be made to para.3:

1. *in para.3(2), in relation to endorsement (all drivers), the words "and its counterpart" will be omitted by the Road Safety Act 2006 s.10 and Sch.3, para.70(2)(a), s.59 and Sch.7(4);*

2. *in para.3(4)(a), in relation to endorsement (all drivers), the words- "(with its counterpart)" will be omitted by the Road Safety Act 2006 s.10 and Sch.3, para.70(2)(a), s.59 and Sch.7(4).*

For the provisions relating to the commencement of s.10 and Sch.3 to the 2006 Act, see ibid. s.61(8) below.]

PART III

NEWLY QUALIFIED DRIVER WITH PROVISIONAL LICENCE AND TEST CERTIFICATE

Surrender of test certificate

4.—(1) Where the circumstances mentioned in section 2(1) exist with respect to a person to whom this Part of this Schedule applies, sub-paragraph (2) applies instead of section 2(2).   **A25.26**

(2) The court must send to the Secretary of State—

  (a) a notice containing the particulars required to be endorsed on the counterpart of the person's licence in accordance with the order referred to in section 2(1)(d); and

  (b) on its production to the court, the person's test certificate.

(3) Where—

  (a) the circumstances mentioned in section 2(3)(a) to (d) and (f) exist with respect to a person to whom this Part of this Schedule applies,

  (b) the [appropriate person] has received the person's test certificate in accordance with paragraph 3(4), and

  (c) the test certificate shows the date on which the person became a qualified driver,

[section 2(4) does not apply but if the appropriate person is the fixed penalty clerk subparagraph (4) applies instead].

(4) The fixed penalty clerk must send to the Secretary of State—

  (a) a notice containing the particulars endorsed on the counterpart of the person's licence; and

  (b) the person's test certificate.

[Paragraph 4 of Sch.1 is printed as amended by the Road Safety Act 2006 s.5 and Sch.1, para.27.   **A25.27**

With effect from a day (or days) to be appointed, the following amendments will be made to para.4:

1. *for para.4(2), in relation to endorsement (all drivers), the following text will be substituted by the Road Safety Act 2006 s.10 and Sch.3, para.70(3)(a):*

    [(2) The court must send to the Secretary of State, on its production to the court, the person's test certificate, together with the notice of the order referred to in section 2(1)(d).]

2. *in para.4(4), in relation to endorsement (all drivers), the words "the person's test certificate together with the notice he is required to send under section 57A or 77A of the particulars to be endorsed on the person's driving record" will be substituted for the words following "State" by the Road Safety Act 2006 s.10 and Sch.3, para.70(3)(b).*

For the provisions relating to the commencement of s.10 of and Sch.3 to the 2006 Act, see ibid. s.61(8) below.]

Revocation of test certificate

A25.28   **5.**—(1) Where the Secretary of State—

(a) has received a notice sent to him under paragraph 4 of particulars required to be endorsed or endorsed on the counterpart of a person's licence, and

(b) has received the person's test certificate sent to him under paragraph 4(2)(b) or (4)(b) or is satisfied that the person has been issued with a test certificate,

the Secretary of State must by notice served on that person revoke the test certificate.

[(1ZA) Where section 2(4) is disapplied by paragraph 4(3) and the appropriate person is the Secretary of State, the Secretary of State must by notice served on the person to whom the fixed penalty notice or conditional offer was given or issued revoke that person's test certificate.]

[(1A) Where the Secretary of State serves on the holder of a Northern Ireland licence a notice under sub-paragraph (1) [or (1ZA)], the Secretary of State must send to the licensing authority in Northern Ireland particulars of the notice together with the Northern Ireland test certificate.]

[(1B) Where the Secretary of State is sent by that licensing authority particulars of a notice served on the holder of a licence under a provision of Northern Ireland law corresponding to sub-paragraph (1) [or (1ZA)], he must by notice served on that person revoke his test certificate.]

(2) A revocation under [this paragraph] shall have effect from a date specified in the notice of revocation which may not be earlier than the date of service of that notice.

(3) The effect of the revocation of a person's test certificate is that any prescribed conditions to which his provisional licence ceased to be subject when he became a qualified driver shall again apply.

[(4) In this paragraph and paragraph 8 references to the revocation of a person's Northern Ireland test certificate are references to its revocation as respects Great Britain.]

[(5) The effect of the revocation of a person's Northern Ireland test certificate as respects Great Britain is that any prescribed conditions to which his Northern Ireland provisional licence ceased to be subject when he became a qualified driver shall again apply for the purposes of section 109(1) of the Road Traffic Act 1988.]

A25.29   *[Paragraph 5 of Sch.1 is printed as amended by the Crime (International Co-operation) Act 2003 s.91 and Sch.5, para.55; the Road Safety Act 2006 s.5 and Sch.1, para.27.*

With effect from a day (or days) to be appointed, the following amendments will be made to para.5: in para.5(1), in relation to endorsement (all drivers), the words "section 44A, 57A or 77A of the Road Traffic Offenders Act 1988" will be substituted for "paragraph 4"; the words "on a person's driving record" will be substituted for "or endorsed on the counterpart of a person's licence"; and "(4)" will be substituted for "(4)(b)" by the Road Safety Act 2006 s.10 and Sch.3, para.70(4).

For the provisions relating to the commencement of s.10 and Sch.3 to the 2006 Act, see ibid. s.61(8) below.]

Re-testing

A25.30   **6.**—(1) Subject to Part V of this Schedule, the Secretary of State may not under Part III of the Road Traffic Act 1988 grant a person whose test certificate has been revoked under [paragraph 5, or whose Northern Ireland test certificate has been revoked under a provision of Northern Ireland law corresponding to paragraph 5(1)] [or (1ZA)] a full licence to drive any class of vehicles that, immediately before his test certificate was revoked, he was permitted to drive without observing prescribed conditions, unless he satisfies the Secretary of State that within the relevant period he has passed a relevant driving test.

(2) In this paragraph *"relevant driving test"* means, in relation to a person whose test certificate has been revoked, any test which—

    (a) falls within paragraph (a) or (b) of section 1(2); and

    (b) is a test of competence to drive any vehicle included in any class of vehicles that, immediately before his test certificate was revoked, he was permitted to drive without observing prescribed conditions.

(3) If the Secretary of State grants a full licence to a person who is required to pass a relevant driving test in order to be granted that licence, the licence granted must (subject to section 92 and Part IV of the Road Traffic Act 1988) be one authorising that person to drive all the classes of vehicles that, immediately before his test certificate was revoked, he was permitted to drive without observing prescribed conditions.

(4) In sub-paragraph (1) *"the relevant period"* means the period beginning—

    (a) after the date of the revocation of the test certificate; and

    (b) not more than two years before the date on which the application for the full licence is made.

[Paragraph 6 of Sch.1 is printed as amended by the Crime (International Co-operation) Act 2003 s.91 and Sch.5, para.56; the Road Safety Act 2006 s.5 and Sch.1, para.27.]. **A25.31**

Part IV

Newly Qualified Driver with full and Provisional Entitlements and Test Certificate

Surrender of licence and test certificate

7.—(1) Where the circumstances mentioned in section 2(1) exist with respect to a person **A25.32** to whom this Part of this Schedule applies, sub-paragraph (2) applies instead of section 2(2).

(2) The court must send to the Secretary of State—

    (a) a notice containing the particulars required to be endorsed on the counterpart of the person's licence in accordance with the order referred to in section 2(1)(d);

    (b) on their production to the court, the person's licence and its counterpart; and

    (c) on its production to the court, the person's test certificate.

(3) Where—

    (a) the circumstances mentioned in section 2(3) exist with respect to a person to whom this Part of this Schedule applies, and

    (b) the [appropriate person] has received the person's test certificate in accordance with paragraph 3(4),

sub-paragraph (4) applies instead of section 2(4).

(4) The [appropriate person]—

    (a) may not return the person's licence and its counterpart under section 57(3) or (4) or 77(1) of the Road Traffic Offenders Act 1988; but

    (b) [unless the appropriate person is the Secretary of State,] must send them and the person's test certificate to the Secretary of State.

[Paragraph 7 of Sch.1 is printed as amended the Road Safety Act 2006 s.5 and **A25.33** *Sch.1, para.27.*

With effect from a day (or days) to be appointed, the following amendments will be made to para.7:

    1. for para.7(2), in relation to endorsement (all drivers), the following text will be substituted by the Road Safety Act 2006 s.10 and Sch.3, para.70(5)(a):

[(2) The court must, together with the notice of the order referred to in section 2(1)(d), send to the Secretary of State—

(a) on its production to the court, the person's licence, and

(b) on its production to the court, the person's test certificate.]

2. *in para.7(4)(a), in relation to endorsement (all drivers), the words "and its counterpart" will be omitted; and the words "57A(3) or (4) or 77A(2)" will be substituted for the words "57(3) or (4) or 77(1)" by the Road Safety Act 2006 s.10 and Sch.3, para.70(5)(b)(i), (ii), s.59 and Sch.7(4);*

3. *in para.7(4)(b), in relation to endorsement (all drivers), the word "it" will be substituted for the word "them" and the words "together with the notice he is required to send under section 57A or 77A of that Act of the particulars to be endorsed on the person's driving record" will be inserted at the end by the Road Safety Act 2006 s.10 and Sch.3, para.70(5)(b)(iii).*

For the provisions relating to the commencement of s.10 of and Sch.3 to the 2006 Act, see ibid. s.61(8) below.]

Revocation of licence and test certificate

A25.34   **8.**—(1) Where the Secretary of State—

(a) has received a notice sent to him under paragraph 7(2)(a) of particulars required to be endorsed on the counterpart of a person's licence or has received the licence and its counterpart under paragraph 7(2)(b) or (4)(b), and

(b) has received the person's test certificate sent to him under paragraph 7(2)(b) or (4)(b) or is satisfied that the person has been issued with a test certificate,

the Secretary of State must by notice served on that person revoke the licence and the test certificate.

[(1ZA) Where paragraph 7(4) applies and the appropriate person is the Secretary of State, the Secretary of State must by notice served on the person to whom the fixed penalty notice or conditional offer was given or issued revoke that person's licence and test certificate.]

[(1A) Where the Secretary of State serves on the holder of a Northern Ireland licence a notice under sub-paragraph (1) [or (1ZA)], the Secretary of State must send to the licensing authority in Northern Ireland particulars of the notice together with the Northern Ireland licence and the Northern Ireland test certificate.]

[(1B) Where the Secretary of State is sent by that licensing authority particulars of a notice served on the holder of a licence under a provision of Northern Ireland law corresponding to sub-paragraph (1) [or (1ZA)], he must by notice served on that person revoke his licence and test certificate.]

(2) A revocation under [this paragraph] shall have effect from a date specified in the notice of revocation which may not be earlier than the date of service of that notice.

[(3) In this paragraph references to the revocation of a person's Northern Ireland licence are references to its revocation as respects Great Britain; and, accordingly, the person clases to be authorised by virtue of section 109(1) of the Road Traffic Act 1988 to drive in Great Britain a motor vehicle of any class.]

A25.35   *[Paragraph 8 of Sch.1 is printed as amended by the Crime (International Co-operation) Act 2003 s.91 and Sch.5, para.57; the Road Safety Act 2006 s.5 and Sch.1, para.27.*

With effect from a day to be appointed, in para.8(1)(a), in relation to endorse-

ment (all drivers), the words "section 44A, 57A or 77A of the Road Traffic Of-fenders Act 1988" will be substituted for the words "paragraph 7(2)(a)"; the words "a person's driving record" will be substituted for the words "the counterpart of a person's licence"; the words "and its counterpart" will be omitted; and "7(2)(a)" will be substituted for "7(2)(b)" by the Road Safety Act 2006 s.10 and Sch.3, para.70(6), s.59 and Sch.7(4).

For the provisions relating to the commencement of s.10 of and Sch.3 to the 2006 Act, see ibid. s.61(8) below.]

Re-testing

9.—(1) Subject to Part V of this Schedule, the Secretary of State may not under Part III   **A25.36** of the Road Traffic Act 1988 grant a person whose licence and test certificate have been revoked under [paragraph 8, or whose Northern Ireland licence and Northern Ireland test certificate have been revoked under a provision of Northern Ireland law corresponding to paragraph 8(1) [or (1ZA)],] a full licence to drive any class of vehicles mentioned in subparagraph (4), unless he satisfies the Secretary of State that within the relevant period he has passed a relevant driving test.

(2) In this paragraph *"relevant driving test"* means any test which—

    (a) falls within paragraph (a) or (b) of section 1(2); and

    (b) is a test of competence to drive any vehicle included in any class of vehicles mentioned in sub-paragraph (4).

(3) If the Secretary of State grants a full licence to a person who is required to pass a relevant driving test in order to be granted that licence, the licence granted must (subject to section 92 and Part IV of the Road Traffic Act 1988) be one authorising that person to drive all the classes of vehicles mentioned in sub-paragraph (4).

(4) The classes of vehicles are—

    (a) any class of vehicles in relation to which the revoked licence was issued as a full licence; and

    (b) any class of vehicles—

        (i) that he was treated under section 98(2) of the Road Traffic Act 1988 [, or under a provision of Northern Ireland law corresponding to that section,] as authorised to drive under a provisional licence, or

        (ii) in relation to which the revoked licence was issued as a provisional licence, and that, immediately before the test certificate was revoked, he was permitted to drive without observing prescribed conditions.

(5) In sub-paragraph (1) *"the relevant period"* means the period beginning—

    (a) after the date of the revocation of the licence and the test certificate; and

    (b) not more than two years before the date on which the application for the full licence is made.

[Paragraph 9 of Sch.1 is printed as amended by the Crime (International Co-   **A25.37** *operation) Act 2003 s.91 and Sch.5, para.58; the Road Safety Act 2006 s.5 and Sch.1, para.27.]*

PART V

SUPPLEMENTARY

Effect of disqualification until test is passed on re-testing rule

10. Where—   **A25.38**

    (a) a person's test certificate has been revoked under [paragraph 5 (or a person's Northern Ireland test certificate has been revoked under a provision of Northern Ireland law corresponding to paragraph 5(1) [or (1ZA)])] or his licence and test certificate have been revoked under [paragraph 8 (or a person's Northern Ireland licence and Northern Ireland test certificate have been revoked under a provision of Northern Ireland law corresponding to paragraph 8(1) [or (1ZA)])], but

(b) before he passes a relevant driving test, an order is made in relation to him under section 36 of the Road Traffic Offenders Act 1988 (disqualification until test is passed),

paragraph 6(1) or, as the case may be, paragraph 9(1) shall not apply to him.

A25.39   *[Paragraph 10 of Sch.1 is printed as amended by the Crime (International Co-operation) Act 2003 s.91 and Sch.5, para.59; the Road Safety Act 2006 s.5 and Sch.1, para.27.]*

Regulations

A25.40   **11.**—(1) The Secretary of State may by regulations make provision for cases where, after the Secretary of State has revoked a person's test certificate under [paragraph 5], or a person's licence and test certificate under [paragraph 8], he receives notice—

(a) that the person is appealing against a conviction or endorsement which was the basis or formed part of the basis for the revocation;

(b) that a court has quashed a conviction which was the basis or formed part of the basis for the revocation;

(c) that a court has quashed an endorsement which was the basis or formed part of the basis for the revocation and has not on doing so ordered that person to be disqualified;

(d) that a court has made an order which has the effect of reducing the penalty points taken into account for the purposes of section 2 [or (as the case may be) the provision of Northern Ireland law corresponding to that section] to a number smaller than six.

(2) Regulations under sub-paragraph (1) may in particular make provision for—

(a) issuing licences for such period as may be prescribed;

(b) licences issued under the regulations to be treated as revoked in such circumstances as may be prescribed;

(c) re-issuing a test certificate which has been revoked under paragraph 5(1) or 8(1);

(d) suspending or terminating any prescribed conditions applied by virtue of paragraph 5(3);

(e) requiring such courts as may be prescribed to give notice to the Secretary of State of the matters mentioned in sub-paragraph (3).

(3) The matters referred to are—

(a) that a person whose certificate has been or is due to be revoked under paragraph 5(1) or whose licence and certificate have been or are due to be revoked under paragraph 8(1) is appealing against a conviction or endorsement which is the basis or forms part of the basis for the revocation;

(b) that such an appeal has been abandoned.

(4) Any regulations under this paragraph may—

(a) include such incidental or supplementary provision as appears to the Secretary of State to be expedient;

(b) make different provision for different cases.

(5) Any regulations under this paragraph shall be made by statutory instrument which shall be subject to annulment in pursuance of a resolution of either House of Parliament.

A25.41   *[Paragraph 11 of Sch.1 is printed as amended by the Crime (International Co-operation) Act 2003 s.91 and Sch.5, para.60.*

The New Drivers (Appeals Procedure) Regulations 1997 (SI 1997/1098) below have been made in part under this paragraph.]

SCHEDULE 2

CONSEQUENTIAL AMENDMENTS

[Amends the Road Traffic Act 1988 (q.v.) and the Road Traffic Offenders Act   **A25.42**
1988 (q.v.).]

The Goods Vehicles (Licensing of Operators) Act 1995

(1995 c.23)

A26.01 *An Act to consolidate Part V of the Transport Act 1968 and related provisions concerning the licensing of operators of certain goods vehicles.*

[19th July 1995]

ARRANGEMENT OF SECTIONS

Functions of traffic commissioners

Section

*   *   *

A26.02   *[This Act is modified in its application to foreign goods vehicles; see further the Goods Vehicles (Licensing of Operators) (Temporary Use in Great Britain) Regulations 1996 (SI 1996/2186) below.]*

Functions of traffic commissioners

Functions of traffic commissioners

A26.03   **1.** *[Omitted.]*

Operators' licences

Obligation to hold operator's licence

A26.04   **2.**—(1) Subject to subsection (2) and section 4, no person shall use a goods vehicle on a road for the carriage of goods—

(a) for hire or reward, or

(b) for or in connection with any trade or business carried on by him,

except under a licence issued under this Act; and in this Act such a licence is referred to as an *"operator's licence"*.

(2) Subsection (1) does not apply to—

(a) the use of a small goods vehicle within the meaning given in Schedule 1;

(b) the use of a goods vehicle for international carriage by a haulier established in a member State other than the United Kingdom and not established in the United Kingdom;

(c) the use of a goods vehicle for international carriage by a haulier established in Northern Ireland and not established in Great Britain; or

(d) the use of a vehicle of any class specified in regulations.

(3) In subsection (2)(b) and (c) *"established"*, *"haulier"* and *"international carriage"* have the same meaning as in Community Council Regulation (EEC) No.881/92 dated 26 March 1992 [*q.v.*] concerning access to the market in the carriage of goods by road within the Community to or from the territory of a member State or passing across the territory of one or more member States.

(4) It is hereby declared that, for the purposes of this Act, the performance by a local or public authority of their functions constitutes the carrying on of a business.

(5) A person who uses a vehicle in contravention of this section is guilty of an offence and liable on summary conviction to a fine not exceeding [level 5] on the standard scale.

[Section 2 is printed as amended by the Transport Act 2000 s.261(1) (with ef-   **A26.05**
fect from February 1, 2001; see the Transport Act 2000 (Commencement No.3)
Order 2001 (SI 2001/57; not reproduced in this work)) (the subsequent amend-
ment of SI 2001/57 by the Transport Act 2000 (Commencement No.3) (Amend-
ment) Order 2001 (SI 2001/115; not reproduced in this volume) does not affect
the amendment of s.2).

As to the vehicles specified under s.2(2)(d), see Sch.3, Pt I, to the Goods
Vehicles (Licensing of Operators) Regulations 1995 (SI 1995/2869) below.

An offence under s.2(5) is a fixed penalty offence for the purposes of Pt 3 of
the Road Traffic Offenders Act 1988 (see the Fixed Penalty Offences Order 2009
(SI 2009/483) art.2). The amount for the fixed penalty offence is prescribed by
the Fixed Penalty Order 2000 (SI 2000/2792), as amended by the Fixed Penalty
(Amendment) Order 2009 (SI 2009/488).]

[Detention of vehicle used without operator's licence

2A. Schedule 1A (which relates to the detention, removal and disposal of goods   **A26.06**
vehicles in respect of which it appears that section 2 is contravened) shall have
effect.]

[Section 2A was inserted by the Transport Act 2000 s.262(1) (with effect from   **A26.07**
February 1, 2001; see the Transport Act 2000 (Commencement No.3) Order
2001 (SI 2001/57; not reproduced in this work)) (the subsequent amendment of
SI 2001/57 by the Transport Act 2000 (Commencement No.3) (Amendment) Or-
der 2001 (SI 2001/115; not reproduced in this volume) does not affect the inser-
tion of s.2A).

Use of a vehicle on a road in contravention of s.2 may result in the detention of
the vehicle; see reg.2 of the Goods Vehicles (Enforcement Powers) Regulations
2001 (SI 2001/3981) below.]

"Standard" and "restricted" licences

3.—(1) An operator's licence may be either a standard licence or a restricted   **A26.08**
licence.

(2) A *standard licence* is an operator's licence under which a goods vehicle
may be used on a road for the carriage of goods—

    (a) for hire or reward, or

    (b) for or in connection with any trade or business carried on by the holder
        of the licence.

(3) A *restricted licence* is an operator's licence under which a goods vehicle
may be used on a road for the carriage of goods for or in connection with any
trade or business carried on by the holder of the licence, other than that of carrying goods for hire or reward.

(4) Notwithstanding subsections (2) and (3), a company may use a goods vehicle on a road for the carriage of goods for hire or reward under a restricted
licence instead of a standard licence if (but only if) the goods concerned are the
property of a company which is—

    (a) a subsidiary of the first company,

    (b) a holding company for the first company, or

    (c) a subsidiary of a company which is a holding company both for that
        subsidiary and for the first company.

(5) A standard licence may authorise a goods vehicle to be used for the carriage of goods—

    (a) on both national and international transport operations; or

    (b) on national transport operations only.

(6) Except as provided in subsection (4) and subject to section 4, a person who uses a goods vehicle under a restricted licence for carrying goods for hire or reward is guilty of an offence and liable on summary conviction to a fine not exceeding £500.

(7) A person who uses a goods vehicle for carrying goods for hire or reward on international transport operations under a standard licence which covers the carriage of goods on national transport operations only is guilty of an offence and liable on summary conviction to a fine not exceeding £500.

Temporary exemptions

A26.09   **4.**—(1) A traffic commissioner may, for the purpose of—

    (a) enabling an emergency to be dealt with, or

    (b) enabling some other special need to be met,

by notice in writing grant to any person falling within subsection (2) a temporary exemption from any requirement to hold a standard licence which would otherwise be imposed on him by sections 2 and 3 in respect of any vehicle specified in the notice or any vehicle of a class so specified.

(2) A person falls within this subsection if he is engaged exclusively in national transport operations which have only a minor impact on the transport market because of the nature of the goods carried or the short distances over which goods are carried.

(3) A temporary exemption granted under subsection (1) permits the person to whom it is granted to use the specified vehicle or (as the case may be) any vehicle of the specified class for the carriage of goods for hire or reward for the purposes of transport operations of his such as are referred to in subsection (2) (and, accordingly, sections 2(1) and 3(6) shall not to that extent apply to that person's use of goods vehicles).

(4) A temporary exemption has effect until consultations with the European Commission for the purposes of Article 2(2) of the 1974 Council Directive are completed.

Vehicles authorised to be used under a licence

Vehicles authorised to be used under operator's licence

A26.10   **5.**—(1) Subject to the following provisions of this section, the vehicles authorised to be used under an operator's licence are—

    (a) any motor vehicle in the lawful possession of the licence-holder (whether that motor vehicle is specified in the licence or not); and

    (b) any trailer in the lawful possession of the licence-holder.

(2) An operator's licence may provide—

    (a) that no motor vehicle, or no trailer, whose relevant weight exceeds a weight specified in the licence is authorised to be used under it;

    (b) that no trailers are authorised to be used under the licence; or

(c) that no motor vehicle that is not specified in the licence is authorised to be used under it.

(3) In subsection (2) *"relevant weight"*, in relation to a motor vehicle or trailer of any prescribed class, means a weight of the description specified in relation to motor vehicles or trailers of that class by regulations.

(4) An operator's licence shall not authorise the use of any vehicle unless the place which is for the time being its operating centre—

(a) is in the area of the traffic commissioner by whom the licence was issued; or

(b) is outside that area but has not been the operating centre of that vehicle for a period of more than three months.

(5) For the purposes of subsection (4)(b), two or more successive periods which are not separated from each other by an interval of at least three months shall be treated as a single period having a duration equal to the total duration of those periods.

(6) A motor vehicle which is not specified in an operator's licence is not authorised to be used under that licence by virtue of subsection (1) after the period of one month beginning with—

(a) the day on which the vehicle was first in the lawful possession of the licence-holder, or

(b) (if later) the day on which the licence came into force,

unless, during that period, the licence-holder has given to the traffic commissioner by whom the licence was issued a notice in such form and containing such information about the vehicle as the commissioner may require, and has paid to him [the prescribed fee (if any)].

(7) Where notice of a vehicle has been duly given and the prescribed fee [(if any)] has been duly paid under subsection (6), the traffic commissioner shall vary the licence by directing that the vehicle be specified in it.

(8) A motor vehicle specified in an operator's licence shall not, while it remains so specified, be capable of being effectively specified in any other operator's licence.

(9) Where it comes to the knowledge of the traffic commissioner by whom an operator's licence (*"the first licence"*) was issued that a vehicle specified in that licence—

(a) has ceased to be used under the licence (otherwise than because of a fluctuation in business or because it is undergoing repair or maintenance), or

(b) is specified in another operator's licence,

he may vary the first licence by directing that the vehicle be removed from it.

[Section 5 is printed as amended by the Local Transport Act 2008 s.125(1).   **A26.11**

[With effect from a date to be announced under the Transport Act 2000 s.275(1), the following text will be substituted by ibid. s.263 for s.5(6):

[(6) A motor vehicle which is not specified in an operator's licence is not authorised to be used under that licence by virtue of subsection (1) [on or after the relevant day] unless the licence-holder—

(a) has given to the traffic commissioner by whom the licence was issued a notice in such form and containing such information about the vehicle as the commissioner may require, and

(b) has paid to him [the prescribed fee, if any].]

[(6A) For the purposes of subsection (6) *"the relevant day"* is the latest of the following days—

(a) the day on which the vehicle was first in the lawful possession of the licence holder,

(b) the day on which the licence came into force,

(c) if a day not more than one month after the later of those days is prescribed for the purpose, the day so prescribed.]

Section 5(6), as substituted above by the Transport Act 2000 s.275(1) (when in force), is printed as amended by the Local Transport Act 2008 s.125(3).

Subsection (6A) was inserted by the Local Transport Act 2008 s.125(4).

Section 5 is modified in its application to old-style licences by para.5 of the Schedule to the Goods Vehicles (Licensing of Operators) Act 1995 (Commencement and Transitional Provisions) Order 1995 (SI 1995/2181; not reproduced in this work). As to firms, see the Goods Vehicles (Licensing of Operators) Regulations 1995 (SI 1995/2869) reg.29(2) below. As to the vehicles to which reference is made in s.5(3), see SI 1995/2869 reg.36 below.]

Maximum numbers of vehicles

A26.12   **6.**—(1) An operator's licence—

(a) shall specify a maximum number for motor vehicles, and

(b) may specify a maximum number for motor vehicles whose relevant weight exceeds a weight specified in the licence.

(2) An operator's licence that does not contain a provision such as is mentioned in section 5(2)(b) —

(a) shall specify a maximum number for trailers, and

(b) may specify a maximum number for trailers whose relevant weight exceeds a weight specified in the licence.

(3) The number of motor vehicles which at any one time are being used under an operator's licence while not specified in that licence may not exceed the maximum number specified in the licence under subsection (1)(a) less however many motor vehicles are specified in the licence.

(4) Where, under subsection (1)(b), an operator's licence specifies a maximum number for motor vehicles whose relevant weight exceeds a specified weight—

(a) the number of such motor vehicles which at any one time are being used under the licence while not specified in it may not exceed that maximum number less however many motor vehicles whose relevant weight exceeds the specified weight are specified in the licence, and

(b) the number of such motor vehicles that are specified in the licence and are being used under it at any one time may not exceed that maximum number.

(5) The number of trailers being used under an operator's licence at any one time may not exceed the maximum number specified in the licence under subsection (2)(a).

(6) Where, under subsection (2)(b), an operator's licence specifies a maximum number for trailers whose relevant weight exceeds a specified weight, the number of such trailers being used under the licence at any one time may not exceed that maximum number.

(7) The definition of *"relevant weight"* in section 5(3) applies for the purposes of this section as it applies for the purposes of section 5(2).

(8) If subsection (3), (4)(a) or (b), (5) or (6) is contravened, the licence-holder is guilty of an offence and liable on summary conviction to a fine not exceeding level 4 on the standard scale.

[Section 6 does not apply to old-style licences; see para.5(6) of the Schedule to the Goods Vehicles (Licensing of Operators) Act 1995 (Commencement and Transitional Provisions) Order 1995 (SI 1995/2181; not reproduced in this work).]   **A26.13**

Operating centres

Operating centres to be specified in operators' licences

7.—(1) A person may not use a place in the area of any traffic commissioner as   **A26.14** an operating centre for vehicles authorised to be used under any operator's licence issued to him by that commissioner unless that place is specified as an operating centre of his in that licence.

(2) Any person who contravenes subsection (1) is guilty of an offence and liable on summary conviction to a fine not exceeding level 4 on the standard scale.

(3) In this Act *"operating centre"*, in relation to any vehicle, means the base or centre at which the vehicle is normally kept, and references to an operating centre of the holder of an operator's licence are references to any place which is an operating centre for vehicles used under that licence.

Applications for licences

Applications for operators' licences

8.—(1) An application for an operator's licence shall be made to the traffic   **A26.15** commissioner for each area in which, if the licence is issued, the applicant will have an operating centre or operating centres.

(2) Accordingly, a person may hold separate operators' licences in respect of different areas; but he shall not at any time hold more than one such licence in respect of the same area.

(3) *[Statement by applicant for operator's licence.]*

(4) *[Provision of further information by applicant.]*

(5) *[Provision of particulars by applicant.]*

(6) *[Form of statement, information and particulars.]*

[As to firms, see the Goods Vehicles (Licensing of Operators) Regulations   **A26.16** *1995 (SI 1995/2869) reg.29(1) and (10) below.]*

Convictions, etc., subsequent to the making of an application

9.—(1) A person who has made an application for an operator's licence shall   **A26.17** forthwith notify the traffic commissioner to whom it was made if, in the interval between the making of the application and the date on which it is disposed of, there occurs a notifiable conviction within the meaning given in paragraph 4 of Schedule 2 [or there is issued a notifiable fixed penalty notice within the meaning given in paragraph 7 of that Schedule].

(2) A person who—

    (a) has made an application for a standard licence, and

    (b) has included in that application particulars of a transport manager,

shall forthwith notify the traffic commissioner to whom the application was made if, in the interval between the making of the application and the date on which it is disposed of, there occurs any event affecting any information about the transport manager given to the commissioner under section 8.

(3) A person is guilty of an offence if he—

    (a) knowingly fails to comply with subsection (1), or

    (b) knowingly fails to comply with subsection (2) in a case where the event which occurs as mentioned in that subsection is the conviction of the transport manager of an offence such as is mentioned in paragraph 5 of Schedule 2;

and a person who is guilty of an offence under paragraph (a) or (b) is liable on summary conviction to a fine not exceeding level 4 on the standard scale.

(4) For the purposes of this section an application shall be taken to be disposed of—

    (a) in a case where the traffic commissioner is required, by virtue of regulations under section 57(2)(a), to cause a statement containing his decision on the application to be issued, on the date on which that statement is issued, and

    (b) in any other case, on the date on which the applicant receives notice from the traffic commissioner of his decision on the application [or the issue to the transport manager of a fixed penalty notice or conditional offer under Part 3 of the Road Traffic Offenders Act 1988 in respect of such an offence].

A26.18   *[Section 9 is printed as amended by the Road Safety Act 2006 s.6(1)–(3).*

    As to firms, see the Goods Vehicles (Licensing of Operators) Regulations 1995 (SI 1995/2869) reg.29(10) below.]

Publication by traffic commissioner of notice of application for licence

A26.19   **10.** *[Omitted.]*

Publication in locality affected of notice of application for licence

A26.20   **11.** *[Omitted.]*

Objections to, and representations against, issue of operators' licences

A26.21   **12.** *[Omitted.]*

Determination of applications

Determination of applications for operators' licences

A26.22   **13.**—(1) Subject to sections 11 and 45(2), on an application for a standard licence a traffic commissioner shall consider—

    (a) whether the requirements of subsections (3) and (5) are satisfied, and

    (b) if he thinks fit, whether the requirements of subsection (6) are satisfied.

(2) Subject to sections 11 and 45(2), on an application for a restricted licence a traffic commissioner shall consider—

    (a) whether the requirements of subsections (4) and (5) are satisfied, and

    (b) if he thinks fit, whether the requirements of subsection (6) are satisfied.

(3) For the requirements of this subsection to be satisfied the traffic commissioner must be satisfied that the applicant fulfils the following requirements, namely—

    (a) that he is of good repute,

    (b) that he is of the appropriate financial standing, and

    (c) that he is professionally competent;

and the traffic commissioner shall determine whether or not that is the case in accordance with Schedule 3.

(4) For the requirements of this subsection to be satisfied the applicant must not be unfit to hold an operator's licence by reason of—

    (a) any activities or convictions of which particulars may be required to be given under section 8(4) by virtue of paragraph 1(e) or (f) of Schedule 2, or

    (b) any conviction required to be notified in accordance with section 9(1).

(5) For the requirements of this subsection to be satisfied it must be possible (taking into account the traffic commissioner's powers under section 15(3) to issue a licence in terms that differ from those applied for) to issue a licence on the application in relation to which paragraphs (a) to (e) will apply—

    (a) there are satisfactory arrangements for securing that—

        (i) Part VI of the Transport Act 1968 [*q.v.*] (drivers' hours), and

        (ii) the applicable Community rules, within the meaning of that Part, are complied with in the case of the vehicles used under the licence;

    (b) there are satisfactory arrangements for securing that the vehicles used under the licence are not overloaded;

    (c) there are satisfactory facilities and arrangements for maintaining the vehicles used under the licence in a fit and serviceable condition;

    (d) at least one place in the traffic commissioner's area is specified in the licence as an operating centre of the licence-holder, and each place so specified is available and suitable for use as such an operating centre (disregarding any respect in which it may be unsuitable on environmental grounds);

    (e) the capacity of the place so specified (if there is only one) or of both or all the places so specified taken together (if there are more than one) is sufficient to provide an operating centre for all the vehicles used under the licence.

(6) For the requirements of this subsection to be satisfied the provision of such facilities and arrangements as are mentioned in subsection (5)(c) must not be prejudiced by reason of the applicant's having insufficient financial resources for that purpose.

(7) In considering whether any of the requirements of subsections (3) to (6) are satisfied, the traffic commissioner shall have regard to any objection duly made under section 12(1)(a) in respect of the application.

(8) In considering whether the requirements of subsection (5) are satisfied, the traffic commissioner may take into account any undertakings given by the applicant (or procured by him to be given) for the purposes of the application, and may assume that those undertakings will be fulfilled.

(9) In considering whether subsection (5)(d) will apply in relation to a licence, the traffic commissioner may take into account any conditions that could be attached to the licence under section 21, and may assume that any conditions so attached will not be contravened.

(10) In considering whether subsection (5)(d) or (e) will apply in relation to a licence, the traffic commissioner may take into account (if that is the case) that any proposed operating centre of the applicant would be used—

    (a) as an operating centre of the holders of other operators' licences as well as of the applicant; or

    (b) by the applicant or by other persons for purposes other than keeping vehicles used under the licence.

(11) If the traffic commissioner determines that any of the requirements that he has taken into consideration in accordance with subsection (1) or (2) are not satisfied he shall refuse the application, but in any other case he shall, subject to sections 14 and 45(2), grant the application.

A26.23   *[As to firms, see the Goods Vehicles (Licensing of Operators) Regulations 1995 (SI 1995/2869) reg.29(3)–(5) below.]*

Determination where objections, etc., are made on environmental grounds

A26.24   **14.** *[Omitted.]*

Issue of operators' licences

A26.25   **15.** *[Omitted.]*

Duration of operators' licences

A26.26   **16.**—(1) The date on which an operator's licence is to come into force shall be specified in the licence.

(2) Subject to its revocation or other termination under any provision of this Act or any other statutory provision, an operator's licence (other than an interim licence issued under section 24) shall continue in force indefinitely.

(3) If the holder of an operator's licence requests the traffic commissioner by whom it was issued to terminate it at any time, the commissioner shall, subject to subsection (4), comply with the request.

(4) The traffic commissioner may refuse to comply with the request if he is considering giving a direction in respect of the licence under section 26 or 27.

(5) An operator's licence held by an individual terminates if he dies, if he becomes a patient within the meaning of Part VII of the Mental Health Act 1983, or ...

A26.27   *[The words omitted from s.16(5) relate expressly and exclusively to Scotland.*

As to the application of s.16(2) to licences with expiry dates before the appointed day, see para.2 of the Schedule to the Goods Vehicles (Licensing of Operators) Act 1995 (Commencement and Transitional Provisions) Order 1995 (SI 1995/2181; not reproduced in this work). As to prematurely terminated licences, see ibid. para.3. As to firms, see the Goods Vehicles (Licensing of Operators) Regulations 1995 (SI 1995/2869) reg.29(11) below.]

Variation of licences

Variation of operators' licences

17. *[Omitted.]* **A26.28**

Publication of notice of applications for variation in any locality affected

18. *[Omitted.]* **A26.29**

Objection to, and refusal of, applications to vary operators' licences on environmental grounds

19. *[Omitted.]* **A26.30**

Variation of licences: further provisions

20.—(1) Where the holder of a restricted licence makes an application under **A26.31** section 17 to the traffic commissioner by whom the licence was issued to vary it by directing that it be converted into a standard licence—

    (a) section 9(2) and (3)(b) and (without prejudice to the generality of section 17(5)) section 13(1) shall apply in relation to that application as they apply in relation to an application for a standard licence; and

    (b) if the application is granted, section 22(2) shall apply to the giving of the direction to vary the restricted licence as it applies to the issuing of a standard licence.

(2) *[Application to vary standard licence so as to add international transport operations.]*

Conditions attached to licences

Conditions for securing road safety

21.—(1) On issuing an operator's licence, or on varying such a licence under **A26.32** section 17, a traffic commissioner may attach to the licence such conditions as he thinks fit for preventing vehicles that are authorised to be used under it from causing danger to the public—

    (a) at any point where vehicles first join a public road on their way from an operating centre of the licence-holder (or last leave a public road on their way to such an operating centre); and

    (b) on any road (other than a public road) along which vehicles are driven between such a point and the operating centre.

(2) *[Variation or removal of conditions.]*

(3), (4) *[Representations as to conditions.]*

(5) In this section *"public road"* —

    (a) in relation to England and Wales, means a highway maintainable at the public expense for the purposes of the Highways Act 1980; and

    (b) *[applies to Scotland].*

(6) Any person who contravenes any condition attached under this section to a

licence of which he is the holder is guilty of an offence and liable on summary conviction to a fine not exceeding level 4 on the standard scale.

Conditions as to matters required to be notified to traffic commissioner

A26.33   22.—(1) On issuing an operator's licence, a traffic commissioner may attach to the licence such conditions as he thinks fit for requiring the holder to inform him—

(a) of any change of a kind specified in the conditions in the organisation, management or ownership of the trade or business in the course of which vehicles are used under the licence or, if the licence is at any time suspended under section 26 or 28, were used under the licence immediately before its suspension;

(b) where the licence-holder is a company, of any change, or of any change of a kind specified in the conditions, in the persons holding shares in the company; or

(c) of any other event of a kind specified in the conditions which affects the licence-holder and which is relevant to the exercise of any powers of the traffic commissioner in relation to the licence.

(2) On issuing a standard licence, a traffic commissioner shall attach to it the following conditions, namely—

(a) a condition requiring the licence-holder to inform the commissioner of any event which could affect the fulfilment by the licence-holder of any of the requirements of section 13(3), and to do so within 28 days of the event; and

(b) a condition requiring the licence-holder to inform the commissioner of any event which could affect the fulfilment by a relevant transport manager of the requirements mentioned in section 13(3)(a) or (c), and to do so within 28 days of the event coming to the licence-holder's knowledge.

(3) In subsection (2)(b) the reference to a *"relevant transport manager"* is a reference to any transport manager employed by the licence-holder who is relied on by the licence-holder to fulfil the requirements of section 13(3)(c).

(4) In a case where the licence-holder is a company, no condition attached under subsection (2) shall be taken to require the company to inform the traffic commissioner of any change in the identity of the persons holding shares in the company unless the change is such as to cause a change in the control of the company.

(5) For the purposes of subsection (4), a change in the control of a company occurs when the beneficial ownership of more than half its equity share capital (as defined in section 744 of the Companies Act 1985) passes from one person to another person or from one group of persons to a wholly or substantially different group of persons.

(6) Any person who contravenes any condition attached under this section to a licence of which he is the holder is guilty of an offence and liable on summary conviction to a fine not exceeding level 4 on the standard scale.

A26.34   *[As to holding companies and their subsidiaries, see the Goods Vehicles (Licensing of Operators) Regulations 1995 (SI 1995/2869) Sch.2, para.2(i) below.]*

Conditions as to use of operating centres

23.—(1) On issuing an operator's licence, or on varying such a licence on an application of which notice has been published under section 17(3), a traffic commissioner may attach to the licence such conditions as he thinks fit for preventing or minimising any adverse effects on environmental conditions arising from the use of a place in his area as an operating centre of the licence-holder. **A26.35**

(2) The conditions which may be attached to a licence under this section shall be of such description as may be prescribed; and; without prejudice to the generality of the preceding provision, the descriptions which may be prescribed include conditions regulating—

(a) the number, type and size of motor vehicles or trailers which may at any one time be at any operating centre of the licence-holder in the area of the traffic commissioner for any prescribed purpose;

(b) the parking arrangements to be provided at or in the vicinity of any such centre; and

(c) the hours at which operations of any prescribed description may be carried on at any such centre.

(3) *[Variation or removal of conditions.]*

(4), (5) *[Representations as to conditions.]*

(6) Any person who contravenes any condition attached under this section to a licence of which he is the holder is guilty of an offence and liable on summary conviction to a fine not exceeding level 4 on the standard scale.

Interim licences and interim variations

Interim operators' licences

24.—(1) On an application for an operator's licence (a *"full"* licence), a traffic commissioner may, if the applicant so requests, issue to him an interim licence. **A26.36**

(2) An *interim licence* is an operator's licence that (subject to its revocation or other termination under any provision of this Act or any other statutory provision) will continue in force until it terminates under subsection (4), (5) or (6).

(3) *[Terms in which interim licence issued.]*

(4)–(6) *[Termination of interim licence.]*

(7) *[Full licence taking effect on termination of interim licence.]*

(8) A request for the issuing of an interim licence—

(a) shall not be treated as an application for an operator's licence for the purposes of section 10, 11, 12, 13, 14, 15(1) to (4), 36 or 37 or Schedule 4, but

(b) shall be treated as such an application for the purposes of any other provision of this Act.

(9) *[Date on which an application is finally disposed of.]*

Interim variations

25. *[Omitted.]* **A26.37**

Revocation, suspension and curtailment of operators' licences

A26.38   26. *[Omitted.]*

Revocation of standard licences

A26.39   27. *[Omitted.]*

Disqualification

A26.40   28.—(1) Where, under section 26(1) or 27(1), a traffic commissioner directs that an operator's licence be revoked, the commissioner may order the person who was the holder of the licence to be disqualified (either indefinitely or for such period as the commissioner thinks fit) from holding or obtaining an operator's licence; and so long as the disqualification is in force—

> (a) any operator's licence held by him at the date of the making of the order (other than the licence revoked) shall be suspended, and

> (b) notwithstanding anything in section 13 or 24, no operator's licence may be issued to him.

(2) If a person applies for or obtains an operator's licence while he is disqualified under subsection (1) —

> (a) he is guilty of an offence and liable on summary conviction to a fine not exceeding level 4 on the standard scale, and

> (b) any operator's licence issued to him on the application, or (as the case may be) the operator's licence obtained by him, shall be void.

(3) An order under subsection (1) may be limited so as to apply only to the holding or obtaining of an operator's licence in respect of one or more specified traffic areas and, if the order is so limited—

> (a) paragraphs (a) and (b) of that subsection and subsection (2) shall apply only to any operator's licence to which the order applies, but

> (b) notwithstanding section 5(4)(b), no other operator's licence held by the person in question shall authorise the use by him of any vehicle at a time when its operating centre is in a traffic area in respect of which he is disqualified by virtue of the order.

(4) Where the traffic commissioner makes an order under subsection (1) in respect of any person, the commissioner may direct that if that person, at any time or during such period as the commissioner may specify—

> (a) is a director of, or holds a controlling interest in—

>> (i) a company which holds a licence of the kind to which the order in question applies, or

>> (ii) a company of which such a company is a subsidiary, or

> (b) operates any goods vehicles in partnership with a person who holds such a licence,

that licence of that company or, as the case may be, of that person, shall be liable to revocation, suspension or curtailment under section 26.

(5) The powers conferred by subsections (1) and (4) in relation to the person who was the holder of a licence shall be exercisable also—

(a) where that person was a company, in relation to any director of that company, and

(b) where that person operated vehicles under the licence in partnership with other persons, in relation to any of those other persons;

and any reference in this section or in section 26 or 29 to subsection (1) or (4) above includes a reference to that subsection as it applies by virtue of this subsection.

(6) *[Cancellation or variation of any order or direction.]*

(7) *[Effect of suspension of operator's licence.]*

(8) *[Criterion for holding controlling interest in company.]*

[As to firms, see the Goods Vehicles (Licensing of Operators) Regulations 1995 (SI 1995/2869) reg.29(8) and (9) below. As to holding companies and their subsidiaries, see SI 1995/2869 Sch.2, para.2(n)–(p) below.] **A26.41**

Revocation and disqualification, etc., supplementary provisions

29. *[Omitted.]*   **A26.42**

Review of operating centres

Periods of review for operating centres

30. *[Omitted.]*   **A26.43**

Power to remove operating centres on review

31. *[Omitted.]*

Power to attach conditions on review

32. *[Omitted.]*

Transfer of operating centres

Transfer of operating centres

33. *[Omitted.]*   **A26.44**

Environmental matters

Determinations as to environmental matters

34. *[Omitted.]*   **A26.45**

Inquiries

Power of traffic commissioners to hold inquiries

35. *[Omitted.]*   **A26.46**

Review of decisions and appeals

Review of decisions

36. *[Omitted.]*   **A26.47**

Rights of appeal in connection with operators' licences

37. *[Omitted.]*

Forgery, false statements, etc.

Forgery of documents, etc.

A26.48   **38.**—(1) A person is guilty of an offence if, with intent to deceive, he—

(a) forges, alters or uses a document or other thing to which this section applies;

(b) lends to, or allows to be used by, any other person a document or other thing to which this section applies; or

(c) makes or has in his possession any document or other thing so closely resembling a document or other thing to which this section applies as to be calculated to deceive.

(2) This section applies to the following documents and other things, namely—

(a) any operator's licence;

(b) any document, plate, mark or other thing by which, in pursuance of regulations, a vehicle is to be identified as being authorised to be used, or as being used, under an operator's licence;

(c) any document evidencing the authorisation of any person for the purposes of sections 40 and 41;

(d) any certificate of qualification under section 49; and

(e) any certificate or diploma such as is mentioned in paragraph 13(1) of Schedule 3.

(3) A person guilty of an offence under subsection (1) is liable—

(a) on summary conviction, to a fine not exceeding the statutory maximum;

(b) on conviction on indictment, to imprisonment for a term not exceeding two years or to a fine or to both.

(4) In the application of subsection (1) to England and Wales, *"forges"* means makes a false document or other thing in order that it may be used as genuine.

A26.49   *[With effect from a date to be announced, s.38(2)(c) will be amended by s.50 of and para.5(1) of Sch.5 to this Act.]*

False statements

A26.50   **39.**—(1) A person is guilty of an offence if he knowingly makes a false statement for the purpose of—

(a) obtaining the issue to himself or any other person of an operator's licence;

(b) obtaining the variation of any such licence;

(c) preventing the issue or variation of any such licence;

(d) procuring the imposition of a condition or limitation in relation to any such licence; or

(e) obtaining the issue to himself or any other person of a certificate of qualification under section 49 or a certificate or diploma such as is mentioned in paragraph 13(1) of Schedule 3.

(2) A person guilty of an offence under subsection (1) is liable on summary conviction to a fine not exceeding level 4 on the standard scale.

Enforcement, etc.

Inspection of maintenance facilities

40.—(1) An officer may, at any time which is reasonable having regard to the circumstances of the case, enter any premises of an applicant for an operator's licence or of the holder of such a licence and inspect any facilities on those premises for maintaining the vehicles used under the licence in a fit and service-able condition.   **A26.51**

(2) Any person who obstructs an officer in the exercise of his powers under subsection (1) is guilty of an offence and liable on summary conviction to a fine not exceeding level 3 on the standard scale.

Power to seize documents, etc.

41.—(1) If an officer has reason to believe that—   **A26.52**

    (a) a document or article carried on or by the driver of a vehicle, or

    (b) a document produced to him in pursuance of this Act,

is a document or article in relation to which an offence has been committed under section 38 or 39, he may seize that document or article.

(2) Where—

    (a) a document or article is seized under subsection (1),

    (b) no person has, within six months of the date on which the document or article was seized, been charged since that date with an offence in relation to it under section 38 or 39, and

    (c) the document or article is still detained,

then any of the persons mentioned in subsection (3) may make an application to a magistrates' court …

(3) The persons who may make an application under subsection (2) are—

    (a) an officer;

    (b) the driver or owner of the vehicle;

    (c) the person from whom the document was seized.

(4) On an application under subsection (2), the magistrates' court … shall—

    (a) make such order respecting the disposal of the document or article, and

    (b) award such costs …,

as the justice of the case may require.

(5) *[Applies to Scotland.]*

[With effect from a date to be announced, s.41(1) and (2)(b) will be amended by s.50 of and para.5(2) of Sch.5 to this Act.   **A26.53**

The words omitted from s.41(2) and (4) relate exclusively to Scotland.]

Meaning of "officer" and powers of police constables

42.—(1) In sections 40 and 41 *"officer"* means—   **A26.54**

(a) an examiner appointed under section 66A of the Road Traffic Act 1988, or

(b) any person authorised for the purposes of sections 40 and 41 by the traffic commissioner for any area.

(2) The powers conferred by sections 40 and 41 on an officer shall be exercisable also by a police constable.

A26.55 *[With effect from a date to be announced, s.42(1)(b) will be amended by s.50 of and para.5(1) of Sch.5 to this Act.]*

Evidence by certificate

A26.56 **43.**—(1) In any proceedings for an offence under this Act a certificate such as is mentioned in subsection (2) shall be evidence … of the facts stated in it.

(2) The certificate referred to in subsection (1) is a certificate signed by or on behalf of a traffic commissioner which states—

(a) that, on any date, a person was or was not the holder of an operator's licence issued by the commissioner;

(b) that, by virtue of a direction given by the commissioner under regulations made under section 48(2)(b) or (3), a person is to be treated as having been the holder of an operator's licence on any date;

(c) the date of the coming into force of any operator's licence issued by the commissioner;

(d) the date on which any operator's licence issued by the commissioner ceased to be in force;

(e) the terms and conditions of any operator's licence issued by the commissioner;

(f) that a person is by virtue of an order of the commissioner disqualified from holding or obtaining an operator's licence, either indefinitely or for a specified period;

(g) that a direction, having effect indefinitely or for a specified period, has been given by the commissioner under section 28(4) in relation to any person;

(h) that an operator's licence was on any date or during any specified period suspended by virtue of a direction given by the commissioner under section 26(1); or

(i) that, by virtue of a direction given by the commissioner under regulations made under section 48(2)(a), an operator's licence is to be treated as having been suspended on any date or during any specified period.

(3) Any such certificate which purports to be signed by or on behalf of a traffic commissioner shall be taken to be so signed unless the contrary is proved.

A26.57 *[The words omitted from s.43(1) relate exclusively to Scotland.]*

Miscellaneous

Assessors

A26.58 **44.** *[Omitted.]*

Fees

45. *[Omitted.]*

Holding companies and subsidiaries

46.—(1) The Secretary of State may by regulations make provision for the **A26.59** purpose of enabling any company or other body corporate which has one or more subsidiaries to hold an operator's licence under which the vehicles authorised to be used consist of or include vehicles belonging to or in the possession of any of its subsidiaries.

(2) Regulations under this section may—

    (a) modify or supplement any of the provisions of this Act, other than the excepted provisions, so far as appears to the Secretary of State to be necessary or expedient for or in connection with the purpose mentioned in subsection (1), and

    (b) may contain such other supplementary and incidental provisions as appear to the Secretary of State to be requisite.

(3) In this Act *"the excepted provisions"* means the following provisions (which are provisions that reproduce the effect of provisions of the Goods Vehicles (Operators' Licences, Qualifications and Fees) Regulations 1984 [*SI 1984/176 (revoked)*]), namely—

    (a) sections 3, 4, 9(2) and (3)(b), 13(3), 15(5) and (6), 20, 22(2) to (5), 27 and 49;

    (b) in section 58, in subsection (1), the definitions of *"international transport operations"*, *"national transport operations"*, *"road transport undertaking"* and *"transport manager"*, and subsection (4); and

    (c) Schedule 3.

Partnerships

47. Regulations may provide for this Act to apply in relation to partnerships **A26.60** with such modifications as may be specified in the regulations; but nothing in any such regulations may make modifications in any of the excepted provisions (within the meaning given in section 46(3)).

Operators' licences not to be transferable, etc.

48.—(1) Subject to any regulations under section 46, an operator's licence is **A26.61** neither transferable nor assignable.

(2) Regulations may make provision enabling a traffic commissioner, where the holder of an operator's licence issued by him has died or become a patient within the meaning of Part VII of the Mental Health Act 1983, to direct that the licence be treated—

    (a) as not having terminated at the time when the licence-holder died or became a patient but as having been suspended (that is, as having remained in force but subject to the limitation that no vehicles were authorised to be used under it) from that time until the time when the direction comes into force; and

    (b) as having effect from the time when the direction comes into force for a specified period and as being held during that period (for such purposes and to such extent as may be specified) not by the person to whom it was issued but by such other person carrying on that person's business, or part of that person's business, as may be specified.

(3) Regulations may make provision enabling a traffic commissioner in prescribed circumstances to direct that any operator's licence issued by him is to be treated (for such purposes, for such period and to such extent as may be specified) as held not by the person to whom it was issued but by such other person carrying on that person's business, or part of that person's business, as may be specified.

(4) Regulations may make provision enabling a traffic commissioner to direct, for the purpose of giving effect to or supplementing a direction given by him by virtue of subsection (2) or (3), that this Act is to apply with specified modifications in relation to the person who is to be treated under the direction as the holder of an operator's licence; but nothing in any such regulations shall permit the commissioner to modify the operation of any of the excepted provisions (within the meaning given in section 46(3)).

(5) *[Applies to Scotland.]*

(6) In this section *"specified"*, in relation to a direction, means specified—

    (a) in the regulations under which the direction was given; or

    (b) in the direction in accordance with those regulations.

Certificates of qualification

A26.62 **49.**—(1) On an application made to him by a person wishing to engage in a road transport undertaking in a member State other than the United Kingdom, the appropriate person shall issue to the applicant a certificate (a *"certificate of qualification"*) as to such matters relating to—

    (a) the applicant's repute,

    (b) his professional competence, or

    (c) (where relevant) his financial standing,

as the appropriate person is satisfied he may properly certify and as appear to him to be of assistance to the applicant in satisfying any requirements imposed by the law of the other member State as regards the repute, professional competence and financial standing of persons engaged in road transport undertakings in that member State.

(2) A certificate of qualification shall—

    (a) be in such form as the Secretary of State … may specify; and

    (b) have effect for the purposes of Article 3, 4 or (as the case may be) 5 of the 1977 Council Directive.

(3) *[Fee for certificate.]*

(4) *[Information relating to application.]*

(5) *[Meaning of "the appropriate person".]*

(6) *[Fees to be paid into Consolidated Fund.]*

A26.63 *[Section 49 is printed as amended by the Secretary of State for the Environment, Transport and the Regions Order 1997 (SI 1997/2971).]*

Large goods vehicles

Large goods vehicles

A26.64 **50.**—(1) Schedule 5 (which requires certain documents to be carried by the drivers of large goods vehicles and makes other provision in connection with such vehicles) shall have effect.

(2) This section and Schedule 5 shall come into force on such day as the Secretary of State may by order appoint; and different days may be appointed for different purposes and different provisions.

[No date has been appointed under s.50(2) for s.50 or Sch.5 to come into force; **A26.65**
these provisions were expressly excluded from the operation of the Goods
Vehicles (Licensing of Operators) Act 1995 (Commencement and Transitional
Provisions) Order 1995 (SI 1995/2181) by ibid. art.2.]

General provisions

Time for bringing proceedings

51. Section 6 of the Road Traffic Offenders Act 1988 (time for bringing sum-   **A26.66**
mary proceedings for certain offences) shall apply to an offence under section
9(3)(a) or (b), 38 or 39.

Destination of fines: Scotland

52. *[Omitted.]*   **A26.67**

Method of calculating weight of motor vehicles

53. For the purposes of this Act the weight unladen of a vehicle shall be taken   **A26.68**
to be the weight of the vehicle inclusive of the body and all parts (the heavier being taken where alternative bodies or parts are used) which are necessary to or
ordinarily used with the vehicle when working on a road, but exclusive of the
weight of water, fuel or accumulators used for the purpose of the supply of power
for the propulsion of the vehicle, and of loose tools and loose equipment.

Saving for law of nuisance

54. Nothing in this Act shall authorise a person to use on a road a vehicle so   **A26.69**
constructed or used as to cause a public or private nuisance ... or affect the liability, whether under statute or common law, of the driver or owner so using
such a vehicle.

[The words omitted from s.54 relate exclusively to Scotland.]   **A26.70**

Protection of public interests

55. It is hereby declared that nothing in this Act is to be treated as conferring   **A26.71**
on the holder of an operator's licence any right to the continuance of any benefits
arising from this Act or from any such licence or from any conditions attached to
any such licence.

Secretary of State's power to hold inquiries

56. *[Revoked.]*   **A26.72**

Regulations and orders

Regulations and orders

57.—(1) The Secretary of State may make regulations for any purpose for   **A26.73**
which regulations may be made under this Act, and for prescribing anything

which may be prescribed under this Act, and generally for carrying this Act into effect.

(2) In particular, but without prejudice to the generality of subsection (1), the Secretary of State may make regulations with respect to the following matters—

    (a) the procedure on applications for, and the determination of questions in connection with, the issuing and variation of operators' licences and the procedure under, and the determination of questions for the purposes of, sections 26 to 32 and 36;

    (b) the issue of operators' licences and the issue on payment of the prescribed fee of copies of such licences in the case of licences lost or defaced;

    (c) the forms which operators' licences are to take in order to show a distinction—

        (i) between a standard licence and a restricted licence; and

        (ii) between a licence covering both international and national transport operations and a licence covering national transport operations only;

    (d) the means by which vehicles may be identified, whether by plates, marks or otherwise, as being used or authorised to be used under an operator's licence;

    (e) the custody, production, return and cancellation of operators' licences and of documents, plates and any other means of identification prescribed under paragraph (d);

    (f) the payment of a prescribed fee in respect of any document, plate or other means of identification so prescribed that has been lost, defaced or broken;

    (g) the notification to a traffic commissioner of vehicles which have ceased to be used under an operator's licence;

    (h) the repayment (or partial repayment) in the prescribed circumstances of fees paid under this Act;

    (i) the circumstances in which goods are to be treated for the purposes of this Act as carried for hire or reward and the circumstances in which goods are to be treated for those purposes as carried by any person for or in connection with a trade or business carried on by him.

(3) The power under subsection (2)(a) shall include power to require a person applying for an operator's licence to state in his application—

    (a) whether his application is for a standard licence or a restricted licence, and

    (b) (if his application is for a standard licence) whether his application is for a licence to cover both international and national transport operations or for one to cover national transport operations only.

(4) The power under subsection (2)(d) shall include power to require that any means of identification prescribed for a vehicle shall be carried notwithstanding that for the time being the vehicle is not being used for a purpose for which an operator's licence is required.

(5) The power under subsection (2)(d) shall also include power to make provision with respect to the means by which—

(a) any vehicle may be identified as being used under a standard licence or, as the case may be, a restricted licence; and

(b) any vehicle which is being used under a standard licence may be identified as being used under a licence that permits it to be used—

(i) for both international and national transport operations, or

(ii) for national transport operations only.

(6) The Secretary of State may make regulations for providing that any provision of this Act shall, in relation to vehicles brought temporarily into Great Britain, have effect subject to such modifications as may be prescribed.

(7) Any regulations under this Act may make—

(a) different provision for different cases or classes of case and different circumstances, and

(b) transitional provision,

and regulations made by virtue of subsection (2)(d) may make different provision for different traffic areas.

(8) A definition or description of a class of vehicles for the purposes of any regulation under this Act may be framed by reference to any characteristic of the vehicles or to any other circumstances whatever.

(9) Any person who contravenes a provision of regulations under this section, a contravention of which is declared by the regulations to be an offence, is guilty of an offence and liable on summary conviction to a fine not exceeding level 1 on the standard scale.

(10)–(12) *[Regulations under s.30(3) subject to approval by each House of Parliament; other regulations subject to annulment; consultation with representative organisations.]*

(13) Any power to make orders or regulations conferred on the Secretary of State by any provision of this Act shall be exercisable by statutory instrument.

[The Goods Vehicles (Licensing of Operators) Regulations 1995 (SI 1995/ 2869) below, the Goods Vehicles (Licensing of Operators) (Fees) Regulations 1995 (SI 1995/3000; not reproduced in this work), and the Goods Vehicles (Licensing of Operators) (Temporary Use in Great Britain) Regulations 1996 (SI 1996/2186) below have been made (in part) under this section.]   **A26.74**

Interpretation

General interpretation

58.—(1) In this Act, unless the context otherwise requires—   **A26.75**

"*area*", in relation to a traffic commissioner, means the traffic area for which he is the traffic commissioner;

"*articulated combination*" means a combination made up of—

(a) a motor vehicle which is so constructed that a trailer may by partial superimposition be attached to the vehicle in such a manner as to cause a substantial part of the weight of the trailer to be borne by the vehicle, and

(b) a trailer attached to it as described in paragraph (a);

"*carriage of goods*" includes haulage of goods;

"*contravention*", in relation to any condition or provision, includes a failure to comply with the condition or provision, and *"contravenes"* shall be construed accordingly;

"the 1974 Council Directive" means Community Council Directive No.74/ 561/EEC dated 12 November 1974 [*O.J. No.L308, November 19, 1974, p.18*] on admission to the occupation of road haulage operator in national and international transport operations, as amended by Community Council Directive No.89/438/EEC dated 21 June 1989 [*O.J. No.L212, July 22, 1989, p.101*] ;

"the 1977 Council Directive" means Community Council Directive No.77/ 796/EEC dated 12 December 1977 [*O.J. No.L334, December 24, 1977, p.37*] concerning the mutual recognition of diplomas, certificates and other evidence of formal qualifications for goods haulage operators and road passenger transport operators, including measures to encourage such operators effectively to exercise their right of freedom of establishment, as amended by Community Council Directive No.89/438/EEC dated 21 June 1989;

"driver" —

    (a) where a separate person acts as steersman of a motor vehicle, includes that person as well as any other person engaged in the driving of the vehicle; and

    (b) in relation to a trailer, means the driver of the vehicle by which the trailer is drawn;

and *"drive"* shall be construed accordingly;

"functions" includes powers, duties and obligations;

"goods" includes goods or burden of any description;

"goods vehicle" means a motor vehicle constructed or adapted for use for the carriage of goods, or a trailer so constructed or adapted, but does not include a tramcar or trolley vehicle within the meaning of the Road Traffic Act 1988;

"holding company" and *"subsidiary"* have the meaning given by section 736 of the Companies Act 1985 [*not reproduced in this work*];

"international transport operations" and *"national transport operations"* have the same meaning as in the 1974 Council Directive;

"modification" includes addition, omission and alteration, and related expressions shall be construed accordingly;

"motor vehicle" and *"trailer"* have the same meaning as in section 253 of the Road Traffic Act 1960;

"operating centre" has the meaning given in section 7(3);

"operator's licence" has the meaning given in section 2(1);

"owner", in relation to any land in England and Wales, means a person, other than a mortgagee not in possession, who, whether in his own right or as trustee for any other person, is entitled to receive the rack rent of the land or, where the land is not let at a rack rent, would be so entitled if it were so let;

"plated weight", in relation to a vehicle, means a weight required to be marked on it by means of a plate in pursuance of regulations made by

virtue of section 41 of the Road Traffic Act 1988 or required to be so marked by section 57 or 58 of that Act;

"prescribed" means prescribed by regulations;

"regulations" means regulations made by the Secretary of State under this Act;

"restricted licence" has the meaning given in section 3(3);

"road" —

    (a) in relation to England and Wales, means any highway and any other road to which the public has access, and includes bridges over which a road passes; and

    (b) *[applies to Scotland]*;

"road transport undertaking" means an undertaking which involves the use of goods vehicles—

    (a) under an operator's licence, or

    (b) in accordance with the law of Northern Ireland or the law of any member State other than the United Kingdom;

"standard licence" has the meaning given in section 3(2);

"statutory provision" means a provision contained in an Act or in subordinate legislation within the meaning of the Interpretation Act 1978;

"traffic area" means a traffic area constituted for the purposes of the Public Passenger Vehicles Act 1981;

"transport manager", in relation to a business, means an individual who is in, or who is engaged to enter into, the employment of the holder of a standard licence and who, either alone or jointly with one or more other persons, has continuous and effective responsibility for the management of the transport operations of the business in so far as they relate to the carriage of goods;

"vehicle combination" means a combination of goods vehicles made up of one or more motor vehicles and one or more trailers all of which are linked together when travelling.

(2) For the purposes of this Act, the driver of a vehicle, if it belongs to him or is in his possession under an agreement for hire, hire-purchase or loan, and in any other case the person whose servant or agent the driver is, shall be deemed to be the person using the vehicle; and references to using a vehicle shall be construed accordingly.

(3) In this Act references to vehicles being authorised to be used under an operator's licence are to be read in accordance with section 5.

(4) For the purposes of this Act, a person who is an applicant for, or a holder of, a standard licence, or who is a transport manager, shall be regarded as being engaged in a road transport undertaking if—

    (a) in a case where that person is an individual, he is either—

      (i) the holder, or one of the joint holders, of an operator's licence, or

      (ii) in the employment of a person who carries on a road transport undertaking and that undertaking gives him responsibility for the operation of goods vehicles used under an operator's licence; or

    (b) in a case where that person is a company, either—

> (i) the company is the holder of an operator's licence, or
>
> (ii) the company is a subsidiary of the holder of an operator's licence and goods vehicles used under that licence belong to the company or are in its possession.

(5) Anything required or authorised by this Act to be done by or to a traffic commissioner by whom a licence was issued may be done by or to any person for the time being acting as traffic commissioner for the area for which the first-mentioned commissioner was acting at the time of the issuing of the licence.

A26.76 *[The term "motor vehicle" (to which reference is made in s.58(1)) is defined in the Road Traffic Act 1960 s.253(1), as "a mechnically propelled vehicle intended or adapted for use on roads"; and the same provision defines the term "trailer" as "a vehicle drawn by a motor vehicle".]*

Supplementary provisions

Transitional provisions, etc.

A26.77 **59.**—(1) The transitional provisions and transitory modifications of this Act contained in Schedule 6 shall have effect.

(2) Without prejudice to the generality of paragraphs 2 to 4 of that Schedule, an existing licence shall continue in force as if it had been issued under this Act, and in this Act or any other enactment, instrument or document, any reference to, or including a reference to, an operator's licence issued under this Act shall, so far as the nature of the reference permits, be construed as including a reference to an existing licence.

(3) In subsection (2) *"existing licence"* means any operator's licence within the meaning of Part V of the Transport Act 1968 which was in force immediately before the commencement of this Act.

A26.78 *[This Act was, in the main, brought into force on January 1, 1996; see the Goods Vehicles (Licensing of Operators) Act 1995 (Commencement and Transitional Provisions) Order 1995 (SI 1995/2181) art.2. By reference to the definitions of "appointed day" and "existing licence" in para.1 of the Schedule to that order, it is clear that January 1, 1996 should be treated for the purposes of s.59(3) as the commencement date of this Act.]*

Consequential amendments and repeals

A26.79 **60.** *[Omitted.]*

Commencement

A26.80 **61.**—(1) Subject to section 50(2) (which makes provision in relation to the commencement of section 50 and Schedule 5) this Act shall come into force on such day as the Secretary of State may by order appoint.

(2) An order under subsection (1) may contain such transitional provisions and savings as appear to the Secretary of State to be necessary or expedient in connection with the coming into force of any provision of this Act which reproduces the effect of any provision of the Deregulation and Contracting Out Act 1994 which was not brought into force before the appointed day.

(3) Where any provision of the Deregulation and Contracting Out Act 1994 was brought into force before the appointed day by an order containing

transitional provisions or savings in connection with the coming into force of that provision, an order under subsection (1) may contain corresponding transitional provisions or savings in connection with the coming into force of any provision of this Act which reproduces the effect of that provision of that Act.

(4) In subsections (2) and (3) *"the appointed day"* means the day appointed under subsection (1).

[The Goods Vehicles (Licensing of Operators) (Commencement and Transi-   **A26.81**
tional Provisions) Order 1995 (SI 1995/2181) was made under this section. It
brought this Act (other than s.50 and Sch.5) into force on January 1, 1996.]

Short title and extent

62.—(1) This Act may be cited as the Goods Vehicles (Licensing of Opera-   **A26.82**
tors) Act 1995.

(2) The amendments specified in Schedule 7 and the repeals and revocations specified in Schedule 8 have the same extent as the enactments and instruments to which they relate.

(3) Subject to subsection (2), this Act does not extend to Northern Ireland.

SCHEDULES

Section 2   SCHEDULE 1

MEANING OF "SMALL GOODS VEHICLE"

1. For the purposes of section 2 a *"small goods vehicle"* is a goods vehicle falling   **A26.83**
within any of paragraphs 2 to 4.

2. A goods vehicle falls within this paragraph if it does not form part of a vehicle   **A26.84**
combination and—

    (a) has a relevant plated weight not exceeding 3.5 tonnes, or

    (b) if it does not have a relevant plated weight, has an unladen weight not exceeding
        1525 kilograms.

3.—(1) A goods vehicle falls within this paragraph if it forms part of a vehicle combina-   **A26.85**
tion, other than an articulated combination, and the combination is such that—

    (a) in a case where all the vehicles comprised in it, or all of those vehicles except any
        small trailer, have relevant plated weights, the aggregate of the relevant plated
        weights of those vehicles, exclusive of any such trailer, does not exceed 3.5 tonnes,
        or

    (b) in any other case, the aggregate of the unladen weights of the vehicles comprised
        in the combination, exclusive of any small trailer, does not exceed 1525 kilograms.

(2) In this paragraph *"small trailer"* means a trailer having an unladen weight not exceeding 1020 kilograms.

4. A goods vehicle falls within this paragraph if it forms part of an articulated combina-   **A26.86**
tion which is such that—

    (a) in a case where the trailer comprised in the combination has a relevant plated
        weight, the aggregate of—

        (i) the unladen weight of the motor vehicle comprised in the combination,and

        (ii) the relevant plated weight of that trailer,

      does not exceed 3.5 tonnes, or

    (b) in any other case, the aggregate of the unladen weights of the motor vehicle and
        the trailer comprised in the combination does not exceed 1525 kilograms.

A26.87   **5.** In any provision of paragraphs 2 to 4 *"relevant plated weight"* means a plated weight of the description specified in relation to that provision by regulations.

[SCHEDULE 1A

A26.88   *[Most of the paragraphs of this Schedule merely provide for the making of regulations for the purposes indicated in the italicised heading preceding the various paragraphs. As to the regulations, see further the note at the end of this Schedule.]*

Interpretation

A26.89   **1.**—(1) In this Schedule —

"authorised person" means—

    (a) an examiner appointed by the Secretary of State under section 66A of the Road Traffic Act 1988 [*q.v.*], or

    (b) a person acting under the direction of such an examiner;

"contents", in relation to a goods vehicle, means any goods carried by that vehicle;

"immobilisation device" means any device or appliance which is an immobilisation device for the purposes of section 104 of the Road Traffic Regulation Act 1984 [*q.v.*] .

(2) Regulations may, for the purposes of regulations made by virtue of this Schedule, make provision as to the meaning of *"owner"* as regards a goods vehicle.

(3) Regulations made by virtue of sub-paragraph (2) may, in particular, provide that the owner of a motor vehicle at a particular time shall be taken to be—

    (a) any person in whose name it is then registered by virtue of the Vehicle Excise and Registration Act 1994, or

    (b) any person in whose operator's licence it is then specified.

Detention of property

A26.90   **2., 3.** *[Omitted.]*

Immobilisation and removal

4–7. *[Omitted.]*

Return or disposal of vehicle

8–12. *[Omitted.]*

Return or disposal of contents of vehicle

A26.91   **13.** *[Omitted.]*

Custody of property

14. *[Omitted.]*

Proceeds of sale

15. *[Omitted.]*

Disputes

A26.92   **16.** *[Omitted.]*

Obstruction of authorised persons

A26.93   **17.** Regulations may provide that a person who intentionally obstructs an authorised person in the exercise of his powers under regulations made by virtue of paragraph 2 or 6 is guilty of an offence and liable on summary conviction to a fine not exceeding level 3 on the standard scale.

Offences as to securing possession of property

18.—(1) Regulations may provide that where—   **A26.94**

(a) a person makes a declaration with a view to securing the return of a goods vehicle under the regulations made by virtue of paragraph 10,

(b) the declaration is that the vehicle was not being, or had not been, used in contravention of section 2, and

(c) the declaration is to the person's knowledge either false or in any material respect misleading,

he is guilty of an offence.

(2) Regulations may provide that a person guilty of such an offence is liable—

(a) on summary conviction, to a fine not exceeding the statutory maximum, and

(b) on conviction on indictment, to imprisonment for a term not exceeding two years or to a fine or to both.]

[Schedule 1A was inserted by the Transport Act 2000 s.262(2) (with effect **A26.95**
from February 1, 2001; see the Transport Act 2000 (Commencement No.3) Order 2001 (SI 2001/57; not reproduced in this work)) (the subsequent amendment of SI 2001/57 by the Transport Act 2000 (Commencement No.3) (Amendment) Order 2001 (SI 2001/115; not reproduced in this volume) does not affect the insertion of Sch.1A).

The Goods Vehicles (Enforcement Powers) Regulations 2001 (SI 2001/3603) below have been made under this Schedule.]

Sections 8, 9 and 26   SCHEDULE 2

INFORMATION ABOUT, AND CONVICTIONS OF, APPLICANTS FOR AND HOLDERS OF OPERATORS' LICENCES

Information to be given under section 8

1. The information referred to in section 8(4) is the following—   **A26.96**

(a) such particulars as the traffic commissioner may require with respect to the purposes for which the vehicles referred to in the statement under section 8(3) are proposed to be used;

(b) particulars of the arrangements for securing that—

(i) Part VI of the Transport Act 1968 (drivers' hours), and

(ii) the applicable Community rules, within the meaning of that Part,

will be complied with in the case of those vehicles;

(c) particulars of the arrangements for securing that those vehicles will not be overloaded;

(d) particulars of the facilities and arrangements for securing that those vehicles will be maintained in a fit and serviceable condition;

(e) particulars of any relevant activities carried on, at any time before the making of the application, by any relevant person;

(f) particulars of any notifiable convictions which have occurred during the five years preceding the making of the application;

[(fa) particulars of any notifiable fixed penalty notices which have been issued during those five years;]

(g) particulars of the financial resources which are or are likely to be available to the applicant;

(h) where the applicant is a company, the names of the directors and officers of—

(i) the company, and

(ii) any company of which that company is a subsidiary;

(i) where the vehicles referred to in the statement under section 8(3) are proposed to be operated by the applicant in partnership with other persons, the names of those other persons.

A26.97   *[Paragraph 1 of Sch.2 is printed as amended by the Road Safety Act 2006 s.6(6).]*

"Relevant person"

A26.98   **2.** In this Schedule *"relevant person"* means any of the following persons, namely—

(a) the applicant;

(b) any company of which the applicant is or has been a director;

(c) where the applicant is a company, any person who is a director of the company;

(d) where the applicant proposes to operate the vehicles referred to in the statement under section 8(3) in partnership with other persons, any of those other persons;

(e) any company of which any such person as is mentioned in sub-paragraph (c) or (d) is or has been a director; or

(f) where the applicant is a company, any company of which the applicant is a subsidiary.

"Relevant activities"

A26.99   **3.** In paragraph 1(e) *"relevant activities"* means any of the following—

(a) activities in carrying on any trade or business in the course of which vehicles of any description are operated;

(b) activities as a person employed for the purposes of any such trade or business; or

(c) activities as a director of a company carrying on any such trade or business.

"Notifiable convictions"

A26.100   **4.** The following are *"notifiable convictions"*, namely—

(a) any conviction of a relevant person of an offence such as is mentioned in paragraph 5, and

(b) any conviction of a servant or agent of a relevant person of an offence such as is mentioned in sub-paragraph (a), (b), (d), (f), (g), (i) or (j) of that paragraph.

Offences

A26.101   **5.** The offences are—

(a) an offence under section 53 of the Road Traffic Act 1988 (plating certificates and goods vehicle test certificates);

(b) an offence committed in relation to a goods vehicles consisting in the contravention of any provision (however expressed) contained in or having effect under any enactment (including any enactment passed after this Act) relating to—

(i) the maintenance of vehicles in a fit and serviceable condition;

(ii) limits of speed and weight laden and unladen, and the loading of goods vehicles; or

(iii) the licensing of drivers;

(c) an offence under—

(i) this Act;

(ii) Part V of the Transport Act 1968 or section 233 or 235 of the Road Traffic Act 1960 so far as applicable (by virtue of Schedule 10 to the 1968 Act) to licences or means of identification under that Part;

(iii) regulation 33(2) or (3) of the Goods Vehicles (Operators' Licences, Qualifications and Fees) Regulations 1984; or

    (iv) any regulation made under this Act or the Transport Act 1968 which is prescribed for the purposes of this paragraph;

  (d) an offence under, or of conspiracy to contravene, Part VI of the Transport Act 1968 (drivers' hours) committed in relation to a goods vehicle;

  (e) an offence under, or of conspiracy to contravene, section 13 of the Hydrocarbon Oil Duties Act 1979 (unlawful use of rebated fuel oil) committed in relation to a goods vehicle;

  (f) an offence under section 173 or 174 of the Road Traffic Act 1988 (forgery, false statements and withholding of information) committed in relation to an international road haulage permit within the meaning of that Act;

  (g) an offence under section 2 of the International Road Haulage Permits Act 1975 (removing, or causing or permitting the removal of, a goods vehicle or trailer from the United Kingdom in contravention of a prohibition imposed under that section);

  (h) an offence under section 74 of the Road Traffic Act 1988 (operator's duty to inspect, and keep records of inspection of, goods vehicles);

  (i) an offence under—

    (i) section 3 of the Control of Pollution Act 1974;

    (ii) section 2 of the Refuse Disposal (Amenity) Act 1978;

    (iii) section 1 of the Control of Pollution (Amendment) Act 1989; or

    (iv) section 33 of the Environmental Protection Act 1990;

[(ia) an offence under regulation 38(1)(a) or 38(1)(b) of the Environmental Permitting (England and Wales) Regulations 2007 committed in relation to a waste operation (within the meaning of those Regulations);]

  (j) an offence committed in relation to a goods vehicle consisting in the contravention of—

    (i) any provision (however expressed) prohibiting or restricting the waiting of vehicles which is contained in an order made under section 1, 6, 9 or 12 of the Road Traffic Regulation Act 1984, including any such order made by virtue of paragraph 3 of Schedule 9 to that Act (local authority powers to be exercisable also by Secretary of State); or

    (ii) any provision which is contained in a traffic regulation order, within the meaning of section 1 of that Act, by virtue of section 2(4) of that Act (lorry routes).

[Paragraph 5 of Sch.2 is printed as amended by the Environmental Permitting (England and Wales) Regulations 2007 (SI 2007/3538) reg.24.]   **A26.102**

Repealed enactments

6.—(1) In paragraph 5 any reference to an offence under a provision of the Road Traffic   **A26.103**
Act 1988 includes a reference to an offence under any corresponding provision of the Road Traffic Act 1972 repealed by the Road Traffic (Consequential Provisions) Act 1988.

  (2) In paragraph 5(j) —

  (a) the reference to a provision contained in an order made under section 1, 6, 9 or 12 of the Road Traffic Regulation Act 1984 includes a reference to a provision contained in an order made under any enactment repealed by the 1984 Act and re-enacted by any of those sections, including any such order made by virtue of section 84A(2) of the Road Traffic Regulation Act 1967; and

  (b) the reference to a provision contained in a traffic regulation order by virtue of section 2(4) of the 1984 Act includes a reference to a provision included in such an order by virtue of section 1(3AA) of the 1967 Act.

["Notifiable fixed penalty notices"

7. In paragraph 1(fa) *"notifiable fixed penalty notice"* means any fixed penalty notice or   **A26.104**
conditional offer under Part 3 of the Road Traffic Offenders Act 1988—

(a) issued to a relevant person in respect of an offence such as is mentioned in paragraph 5, or

(b) issued to a servant or agent of a relevant person in respect of an offence within paragraph 4(b).]

A26.105   *[Paragraph 7 of Sch.2 is printed as inserted by the Road Safety Act 2006 s.6(7).]*

<table>
<tr><td>**Sections 13 and 27**</td><td>SCHEDULE 3</td></tr>
</table>

QUALIFICATIONS FOR STANDARD LICENCE

Good repute

A26.106   **1.**—(1) In determining whether an individual is of good repute, a traffic commissioner may have regard to any matter but shall, in particular, have regard to—

(a) any relevant convictions of the individual or of his servants or agents; and

(b) any other information in his possession which appears to him to relate to the individual's fitness to hold a licence.

(2) In determining whether a company is of good repute, a traffic commissioner shall have regard to all the material evidence including, in particular—

(a) any relevant convictions of the company or of any of its officers, servants or agents; and

(b) any other information in his possession as to the previous conduct of—

(i) any of the company's officers, servants or agents, or

(ii) any of its directors, in whatever capacity,

if that conduct appears to him to relate to the company's fitness to hold a licence.

(3) For the purposes of this paragraph, the relevant convictions of any person are—

(a) any conviction of that person of an offence such as is mentioned in paragraph 5 of Schedule 2;

(b) any conviction of that person of an offence under the law of Northern Ireland or of the law of any country or territory outside the United Kingdom corresponding to an offence such as is mentioned in that paragraph;

(c) any conviction of that person of a serious offence within the meaning given in paragraph 3; and

(d) any conviction of that person of a road transport offence within the meaning given in paragraph 4.

A26.107   *[As to firms, see the Goods Vehicles (Licensing of Operators) Regulations 1995 (SI 1995/2869) reg.29(12)(a) below.]*

A26.108   [**2.** Without prejudice to the generality of a traffic commissioner's power under paragraph 1 to determine that a person is not of good repute, a commissioner shall determine that an individual is not of good repute if that individual has—

(a) more than one conviction of a serious offence; or

(b) been convicted of road transport offences.]

A26.109   *[Paragraph 2 of Sch.3 is printed as substituted by the Goods Vehicle Operators (Qualifications) Regulations 1999 (SI 1999/2430) reg.2(1) below.]*

A26.110   **3.**—(1) A person has a conviction of a *"serious offence"* if—

(a) he has been convicted of any offence under the law of any part of the United Kingdom or under the law of a country or territory outside the United Kingdom, and

(b) on such conviction there was imposed on him for that offence a punishment falling within sub-paragraph (2).

(2) The punishments are—

(a) a sentence of imprisonment for a term exceeding three months;

(b) a fine exceeding level 4 on the standard scale;

(c) a [community order] requiring him to perform work for more than 60 hours; and

(d) in the case of an offence committed under the law of a country or territory outside the United Kingdom, any punishment corresponding to those mentioned in paragraphs (a) to (c).

(3) In sub-paragraph (2) —

(a) the reference to a *sentence of imprisonment* includes a reference to any form of custodial sentence or order, other than one imposed under the enactments relating to mental health; and

[(b) *"community order"* means a community order under section 177 of the Criminal Justice Act 2003, a community punishment order made under section 46 of the Powers of Criminal Courts (Sentencing) Act 2000 or a community service order under the Community Service by Offenders (Scotland) Act 1978.]

[Paragraph 3 of Sch.3 is printed as amended by the Powers of Criminal Courts (Sentencing) Act 2000 s.165(1) and Sch.9, para.174; the Criminal Justice Act 2003 s.304 and Sch.32, para.68(3) and (4).   **A26.111**

With effect from a day to be appointed, para.3(2)(a) of Sch.3 will be amended by the Criminal Justice Act 2003 s.304 and Sch.32, para.68(2) so that the words "of 12 months or more or, before the commencement of section 181 of the Criminal Justice Act 2003, a term exceeding 3 months" are substituted for the words "exceeding three months".]

[4. *"Road transport offence"* means—   **A26.112**

(a) an offence under the law of any part of the United Kingdom relating to road transport including, in particular—

(i) an offence relating to drivers' hours of work or rest periods, the weights or dimensions of commercial vehicles, road or vehicle safety or the protection of the environment; and

(ii) any other offence concerning professional liability; or

(b) any corresponding offence under the law of a country or territory outside the United Kingdom.]

[Paragraph 4 of Sch.3 is printed as substituted by the Goods Vehicle Operators (Qualifications) Regulations 1999 (SI 1999/2430) reg.2(2) below.]   **A26.113**

5.—[(1) In paragraph 1(3)(a) the reference to an offence mentioned in paragraph 5 of Schedule 2 includes an offence under section 42 of the Armed Forces Act 2006 as respects which the corresponding offence under the law of England and Wales (within the meaning given by that section) is an offence mentioned in that paragraph.   **A26.114**

(1A) In paragraphs 3 and 4, reference to an offence under the law of any part of the United Kingdom include an offence under section 42 of that Act.

(1B) In paragraph 3(2)(c) the reference to a community order includes a service community order or overseas community order under that Act.]

[Paragraph 5 of Sch.3 is printed as substituted by the Armed Forces Act 2006 s.378 and Sch.16, para.13.]   **A26.115**

Appropriate financial standing

6. *[Omitted.]*   **A26.116**

Professional competence

7–12. *[Omitted.]*

A26.117   **13.**—(1) An individual shall be regarded as professionally competent if, and only if—

(a) he has demonstrated that he possesses the requisite skills by passing a written examination organised by an approved body and is the holder of a certificate to that effect issued by that body; or

(b) he is the holder of any other certificate of competence, diploma or other qualification recognised for the purposes of this sub-paragraph by the Secretary of State.

[(2) The written examination mentioned in sub-paragraph (1)(a) may be supplemented by an oral examination organised by the approved body in the form set out in Annex I to Council Directive No.96/26/EC.]

[(2A) The certificate mentioned in sub-paragraph (1)(a) must take the form of the certificate set out in Annex IA to that Directive.]

(3) In sub-paragraph (1) —

"*approved body*" means—

(a) a body approved by the Secretary of State for the purposes of that sub-paragraph;

(b) a body approved by the Department of the Environment for Northern Ireland for the purposes of section 46A(5)(c) of the Transport Act (Northern Ireland) 1967 [*1967 c.37 (NI)*]; or

(c) a body or authority designated for the purposes of Article 3.4 of [Council Directive No.96/26/EC] by a member State other than the United Kingdom; and

[*"the requisite skills"* means knowledge corresponding to the level of training, for either national or international transport operations as the case may be, provided for in Annex I to that Directive in the subjects there listed.]

A26.118   *[Paragraph 13 of Sch.3 is printed as amended by the Goods Vehicles Operators (Qualifications) Regulations 1999 (SI 1999/2430) reg.4 below (subject to transitional provisions set out in SI 1999/2430 reg.5(3)–(5)).*

The transitional provisions apply the text of para.13 before its amendment by SI 1999/2430 to (inter alia) certificates of professional competence issued before October 1, 1999. The unamended text read as follows:

A26.119   **13.**—(1) An individual shall be regarded as professionally competent if, and only if—

(a) he has demonstrated that he possesses the requisite skills by passing a written examination organised by an approved body and is the holder of a certificate to that effect issued by that body; or

(b) he is the holder of any other certificate of competence, diploma or other qualification recognised for the purposes of this sub-paragraph by the Secretary of State.

(2) The written examination mentioned in sub-paragraph (1)(a) may take the form of a multiple-choice examination.

(3) In sub-paragraph (1) —

"*approved body*" means—

(a) a body approved by the Secretary of State for the purposes of that sub-paragraph;

(b) a body approved by the Department of the Environment for Northern Ireland for the purposes of s.46A(5)(c) of the Transport Act (Northern Ireland) 1967 [*1967 c.37 (NI)*]; or

(c) a body or authority designated for the purposes of Article 3.4 of the 1974 Council Directive by a member State other than the United Kingdom; and

"*the requisite skills*" means skills in the subjects listed in Part A and, in the

case of a licence to cover international operations, Part B, of the Annex to the 1974 Council Directive. *]*

14. In relation to a certificate of professional competence which was issued before 4   **A26.120**
February 1991, or which was issued on or after that date to a person who before that date
passed the whole or any part of the examination leading to the issue of that certificate,
paragraph 13 has effect with the following modifications—

(a) for sub-paragraph (1)(a) there shall be substituted—

    (a) he is the holder of a certificate issued by an approved body to the effect that
he possesses the requisite skills; or;

(b) sub-paragraph (2) shall be omitted; and

(c) references in sub-paragraph (3) to the 1974 Council Directive shall be construed
as references to that Directive as it had effect immediately before it was amended
by Community Council Directive No.89/438/EEC dated 21 June 1989.

[As to the revocation of para.14 of Sch.3 in accordance with transitional pro-   **A26.121**
visions relating to certificates of professional competence issued before Febru-
ary 4, 1991 or issued on or after that date to a person who had previously passed
the examination leading to the issue of that certificate, see the Goods Vehicle
Operators (Qualifications) Regulations 1999 (SI 1999/2430) reg.5(4) and (5)
below.]

Transport manager to be notified of proceedings

15. *[Omitted.]*   **A26.122**

SCHEDULE 4

TRANSFER OF OPERATING CENTRES

[Omitted.]   **A26.123**

Section 50   <center>SCHEDULE 5</center>

LARGE GOODS VEHICLES

Meaning of "large goods vehicle"

1.—(1) For the purposes of this Schedule, a large goods vehicle is a goods vehicle, other   **A26.124**
than a hauling vehicle, falling within any of sub-paragraphs (2) to (4).

(2) A goods vehicle falls within this sub-paragraph if—

(a) it has a relevant plated weight exceeding 16260 kilograms, or

(b) in the case of a vehicle which does not have a relevant plated weight, it has an
unladen weight exceeding 5080 kilograms.

(3) A goods vehicle falls within this sub-paragraph if it forms part of a vehicle combination, other than an articulated combination, and the combination is such that—

(a) in a case where all the vehicles comprised in the combination, or all of those
vehicles except any small trailer, have relevant plated weights, the aggregate of
the relevant plated weights of the vehicles comprised in the combination, exclusive
of any such trailer, exceeds 16260 kilograms, or

(b) in any other case, the aggregate of the unladen weights of the vehicles comprised
in it, exclusive of any small trailer, exceeds 5080 kilograms;

and in this sub-paragraph *"small trailer"* means a trailer having an unladen weight not
exceeding 1020 kilograms.

(4) A goods vehicle falls within this sub-paragraph if it forms part of an articulated
combination which is such that—

(a) in a case where the trailer comprised in the combination has a relevant plated weight, the aggregate of—

(i) the unladen weight of the motor vehicle comprised in the combination, and

(ii) the relevant plated weight of that trailer,

exceeds 16260 kilograms, or

(b) in any other case, the aggregate of the unladen weights of the motor vehicle and the trailer comprised in the combination exceeds 5080 kilograms.

(5) In any provision of sub-paragraphs (2) to (4) *"relevant plated weight"* means a plated weight of the description specified in relation to that provision by regulations.

(6) In sub-paragraph (1) *"hauling vehicle"* means a motor tractor, a light locomotive, a heavy locomotive or the motor vehicle comprised in an articulated combination; and in this sub-paragraph *"motor tractor"*, *"light locomotive"* and *"heavy locomotive"* have the same meaning as in the Road Traffic Act 1960.

A26.125   *[The terms "motor tractor", "light locomotive" and "heavy locomotive" (to which reference is made in para.1(6)) are defined in the Road Traffic Act 1960 s.253(6), (7) and (8), respectively (as amended by the Road Traffic Acts 1960 and 1972, Road Traffic Regulation Act 1984 and Transport Act 1968 (Metrication) Regulations 1981 (SI 1981/1373)) in the following terms:*

(6) In this Act *"motor tractor"* means a mechanically propelled vehicle which is not constructed itself to carry a load, other than the following articles, that is to say, water, fuel, accumulators and other equipment used for the purpose of propulsion, loose tools and loose equipment, and the weight of which unladen does not exceed [7370 kilograms].

(7) In this Act *"light locomotive"* means a mechanically propelled vehicle which is not constructed itself to carry a load, other than any of the articles aforesaid, and the weight of which unladen does not exceed [11690 kilograms] but does exceed [7370 kilograms].

(8) In this Act *"heavy locomotive"* means a mechnically propelled vehicle which is not constructed itself to carry a load, other than any of the articles aforesaid, and the weight of which unladen exceeds [11690 kilograms]. *]*

Consignment notes

A26.126   2.—(1) Subject to sub-paragraph (2), no goods shall be carried on a large goods vehicle unless a document (a *"consignment note"*) in the prescribed form and containing the prescribed particulars has been completed and signed in the prescribed manner and is carried by the driver of the vehicle.

(2) Sub-paragraph (1) shall not apply—

(a) to the carriage of goods on any journey or on a vehicle of any class exempted from that sub-paragraph by regulations; or

(b) to any carriage of goods which is lawful without the authority of an operator's licence.

(3) Subject to the provisions of regulations, a traffic commissioner may dispense with the observance, as respects the carriage of goods under an operator's licence issued by him, of any requirement of sub-paragraph (1), where he is satisfied that it is not reasonably practicable for that requirement to be observed.

(4) Such a dispensation may be granted—

(a) generally;

(b) as respects a particular vehicle; or

(c) as respects the use of vehicles for a particular purpose.

(5) The consignment note relating to the goods carried on a vehicle on any journey shall, at the conclusion of that journey, be preserved for the prescribed period by the person who used the vehicle for carrying the goods on that journey.

(6) Any person who—

    (a) uses or drives a vehicle in contravention of sub-paragraph (1), or

    (b) fails to comply with sub-paragraph (5),

is guilty of an offence and liable on summary conviction to a fine not exceeding level 4 on the standard scale.

Powers of entry and inspection

3.—(1) An officer may require any person to produce and permit him to inspect and copy—　　**A26.127**

    (a) any document which is required by or under paragraph 2 to be carried by that person as driver of a vehicle; or

    (b) any document which that person is required by or under that paragraph to preserve;

and that document shall, if the officer so requires by notice in writing served on that person, be produced at the office of the traffic commissioner specified in the notice within such time (not being less than 10 days) from the service of the notice as may be so specified.

(2) An officer may at any time enter any large goods vehicle and inspect that vehicle and any goods carried on it.

(3) Where an officer has reason to believe—

    (a) that a large goods vehicle is being kept on any premises, or

    (b) that any such documents as are mentioned in sub-paragraph (1) are to be found on any premises,

he may, at any time which is reasonable having regard to the circumstances of the case, enter those premises and inspect any such vehicle, and inspect and copy any such document, which he finds there.

(4) For the purpose of exercising his powers under sub-paragraph (1)(a) or (2), an officer may detain the vehicle in question during such time as is required for the exercise of that power.

(5) The powers conferred by sub-paragraphs (1) to (4) are exercisable on production by the officer, if so required, of his authority.

(6) Any person who—

    (a) fails to comply with any requirement under sub-paragraph (1), or

    (b) obstructs any officer in the exercise of his powers under sub-paragraph (2), (3) or (4),

is guilty of an offence and liable on summary conviction to a fine not exceeding level 3 on the standard scale.

(7) In this paragraph *"officer"* has the meaning given in section 42(1) (as amended by paragraph 5 below).

(8) The powers conferred by this paragraph on an officer shall be exercisable also by a police constable who shall not, if wearing uniform, be required to produce any authority.

Falsification of consignment notes and records

4.—(1) Any person who—　　**A26.128**

    (a) makes, or causes to be made, any document required to be made under paragraph 2 which he knows to be false, or

    (b) with intent to deceive, alters or causes to be altered any document required to be made under that paragraph,

is guilty of an offence.

(2) A person guilty of an offence under sub-paragraph (1) is liable—

    (a) on summary conviction, to a fine not exceeding the statutory maximum;

    (b) on conviction on indictment, to imprisonment for a term not exceeding two years or to a fine or to both.

Amendment of sections 38, 41 and 42 of this Act

5.—(1) The following amendments shall take effect on the day appointed for the coming　　**A26.129**

into force of paragraph 3, namely, in sections 38(2)(c) and 42(1)(b), after the words "sections 40 and 41" there shall be inserted the words "and paragraph 3 of Schedule 5".

(2) The following amendments shall take effect on the day appointed for the coming into force of paragraph 4, namely, in section 41(1) and (2)(b), after the words "section 38 or 39" there shall be inserted the words "or paragraph 4(1) of Schedule 5".

Section 59   SCHEDULE 6

TRANSITIONAL PROVISIONS, TRANSITORY MODIFICATIONS AND SAVINGS

General transitional provisions

A26.130 1. The substitution of this Act for the provisions repealed and revoked by it shall not affect the continuity of the law.

A26.131 2. In so far as any thing done (including any subordinate legislation made or other instrument issued) under a provision repealed or revoked by this Act could have been done under the corresponding provision of this Act, it shall have effect as if done under that corresponding provision.

A26.132 3. Any reference (express or implied) in this Act or any other enactment, instrument or document to—

    (a) any provision of this Act, or

    (b) things done or falling to be done under or for the purposes of any provision of this Act,

shall, so far as the nature of the reference permits, be construed as including, in relation to the times, circumstances or purposes in relation to which the corresponding provision repealed or revoked by this Act had effect, a reference to that corresponding provision or (as the case may be) to things done or falling to be done under or for the purposes of that corresponding provision.

A26.133 4. Any reference (express or implied) in any enactment, instrument or document to—

    (a) a provision repealed or revoked by this Act, or

    (b) things done or falling to be done under or for the purposes of such a provision,

shall, so far as the nature of the reference permits, be construed as including, in relation to the times, circumstances or purposes in relation to which the corresponding provision of this Act has effect, a reference to that corresponding provision or (as the case may be) to things done or falling to be done under or for the purposes of that corresponding provision.

A26.134 5. Paragraphs 1 to 4 have effect, in relation to the substitution of this Act for the provisions repealed and revoked by it, in place of section 17(2) of the Interpretation Act 1978 (but without prejudice to any other provision of that Act).

Meaning of "local authority" in relation to Scotland or Wales

A26.135 6. *[Revoked.]*

Meaning of "holding company" and "subsidiary"

A26.136 7. For the purposes of this Act as it applies in relation to licences granted before 11 November 1990 (the date on which section 144(1) of the Companies Act 1989 came into force) the expressions *"holding company"* and *"subsidiary"* have the meaning given by section 736 of the Companies Act 1985 as originally enacted.

Section 60(1)   SCHEDULE 7

CONSEQUENTIAL AMENDMENTS

A26.137   *[Omitted.]*

Section 60(2)   SCHEDULE 8

REPEALS AND REVOCATIONS

A26.138   *[Omitted.]*

The Private Hire Vehicles (London) Act 1998

(1998 c.34)

An Act to provide for the licensing and regulation of private hire vehicles, and drivers and operators of such vehicles, within the metropolitan police district and the City of London; and for connected purposes.

A27.01

[28th July 1998]

ARRANGEMENT OF SECTIONS

Introductory

*   *   *

A27.02 *[A table of commencement dates of the provisions of the Private Hire Vehicles (London) Act 1998 is set out in the twenty-third edition of this work at § A27.63.]*

Introductory

Meaning of "private hire vehicle", "operator" and related expressions

A27.03 **1.**—(1) In this Act —

  (a) *"private hire vehicle"* means a vehicle constructed or adapted to seat fewer than nine passengers which is made available with a driver [...] for hire for the purpose of carrying passengers, other than a licensed taxi or a public service vehicle; and

  (b) *"operator"* means a person who makes provision for the invitation or acceptance of, or who accepts, private hire bookings.

  (2) Any reference in this Act to a vehicle being *"used as a private hire vehicle"* is a reference to a private hire vehicle which—

  (a) is in use in connection with a hiring for the purpose of carrying one or more passengers; or

  (b) is immediately available to an operator to carry out a private hire booking.

  (3) Any reference in this Act to the operator of a vehicle which is being used as a private hire vehicle is a reference to the operator who accepted the booking for the hiring or to whom the vehicle is immediately available, as the case may be.

  (4) In this Act *"private hire booking"* means a booking for the hire of a private hire vehicle for the purpose of carrying one or more passengers (including a booking to carry out as sub-contractor a private hire booking accepted by another operator).

(5) In this Act *"operating centre"* means premises at which private hire book-ings are accepted by an operator.

[Section 1 is printed as amended by the Road Safety Act 2006 s.54, s.59 and   **A27.04**
Sch.7(17).]

Regulation of private hire vehicle operators in London

Requirement for London operator's licence

2.—(1) No person shall in London make provision for the invitation or accep-   **A27.05**
tance of, or accept, private hire bookings unless he is the holder of a private hire
vehicle operator's licence for London (in this Act referred to as a *"London PHV
operator's licence"*).

(2) A person who makes provision for the invitation or acceptance of private
hire bookings, or who accepts such a booking, in contravention of this section is
guilty of an offence and liable on summary conviction to a fine not exceeding
level 4 on the standard scale.

[Under the Disability Discrimination Act 1995 s.37A (as inserted by the   **A27.06**
*Private Hire Vehicles (Carriage of Guide Dogs, etc.) Act 2002 s.1) it is an of-
fence for an operator or driver of a private hire vehicle licensed under this Act to
refuse to carry a disabled person accompanied by an assistance dog or make an
additional charge for carrying an assistance dog.]*

London operator's licences

3.—(1) Any person may apply to the [licensing authority] for a London PHV   **A27.07**
operator's licence.

(2) An application under this section shall state the address of any premises in
London which the applicant proposes to use as an operating centre.

(3) The [licensing authority] shall grant a London PHV operator's licence to
the applicant if [the authority] is satisfied that—

    (a) the applicant is a fit and proper person to hold a London PHV
operator's licence; and

    (b) any further requirements that may be prescribed (which may include
requirements relating to operating centres) are met.

(4) A London PHV operator's licence shall be granted subject to such conditions as may be prescribed and such other conditions as the [licensing authority]
may think fit.

(5) A London PHV operator's licence shall be granted for five years or such
shorter period as the [licensing authority] may consider appropriate in the circumstances of the case.

(6) A London PHV operator's licence shall—

    (a) specify the address of any premises in London which the holder of
the licence may use as an operating centre;

    (b) be in such form and contain such particulars as the [licensing author-
ity] may think fit.

(7) An applicant for a London PHV operator's licence may appeal to a magistrates' court against—

    (a) a decision not to grant such a licence;

(b) a decision not to specify an address proposed in the application as an operating centre; or

(c) any condition (other than a prescribed condition) to which the licence is subject.

A27.08   *[Section 3 is printed as amended by the Greater London Authority Act 1999 s.254 and Sch.21, paras 1–3.*

The Private Hire Vehicles (London) (Operators' Licences) Regulations 2000 (SI 2000/3146) below have been made (in part) under s.3.]

Obligations of London operators

A27.09   **4.**—(1) The holder of a London PHV operator's licence (in this Act referred to as a *"London PHV operator"*) shall not in London accept a private hire booking other than at an operating centre specified in his licence.

(2) A London PHV operator shall secure that any vehicle which is provided by him for carrying out a private hire booking accepted by him in London is—

(a) a vehicle for which a London PHV licence is in force driven by a person holding a London PHV driver's licence; or

(b) a London cab driven by a person holding a London cab driver's licence.

(3) A London PHV operator shall—

(a) display a copy of his licence at each operating centre specified in the licence;

(b) keep at each specified operating centre a record in the prescribed form of the private hire bookings accepted by him there;

(c) before the commencement of each journey booked at a specified operating centre, enter in the record kept under paragraph (b) the prescribed particulars of the booking;

(d) keep at each specified operating centre such records as may be prescribed of particulars of the private hire vehicles and drivers which are available to him for carrying out bookings accepted by him at that centre;

(e) at the request of a constable or authorised officer, produce for inspection any record required by this section to be kept.

(4) If a London PHV operator ceases to use an operating centre specified in his licence he shall preserve any record he was required by this section to keep there for such period as may be prescribed.

(5) A London PHV operator who contravenes any provision of this section is guilty of an offence and liable on summary conviction to a fine not exceeding level 3 on the standard scale.

(6) It is a defence in proceedings for an offence under this section for an operator to show that he exercised all due diligence to avoid committing such an offence.

A27.10   *[With effect from a day to be appointed, s.4(3)(d) will be substituted by the Transport for London Act 2008 s.25 as follows:*

[(d) keep at the specified operating centre or, where more than one operating centre is specified, at one of the operating centres such records as may be prescribed of particulars of the private hire vehicles and drivers which are available to him for carrying out bookings accepted by him at that or, as the case may be, each centre;

  (da) where more than one operating centre is specified—

    (i) give notice to the licensing authority, and

    (ii) display at each specified operating centre a notice,

      stating the address of the operating centre at which the records are kept under paragraph (d);]

The Private Hire Vehicles (London) (Operators' Licences) Regulations 2000 (SI 2000/3146) below have been made (in part) under s.4.]

Hirings accepted on behalf of another operator

5.—(1) A London PHV operator (*"the first operator"*) who has in London ac- **A27.11** cepted a private hire booking may not arrange for another operator to provide a vehicle to carry out that booking as a sub-contractor unless—

  (a) the other operator is a London PHV operator and the sub-contracted booking is accepted at an operating centre in London;

  (b) the other operator is licensed under section 55 of the Local Government (Miscellaneous Provisions) Act 1976 (in this Act referred to as *"the 1976 Act"*) by the council of a district and the sub-contracted booking is accepted in that district; or

  (c) the other operator accepts the sub-contracted booking in Scotland.

(2) A London PHV operator who contravenes subsection (1) is guilty of an offence and liable on summary conviction to a fine not exceeding level 3 on the standard scale.

(3) It is a defence in proceedings for an offence under this section for an operator to show that he exercised all due diligence to avoid committing such an offence.

(4) It is immaterial for the purposes of subsection (1) whether or not sub-contracting is permitted by the contract between the first operator and the person who made the booking.

(5) For the avoidance of doubt (and subject to any relevant contract terms), a contract of hire between a person who made a private hire booking at an operating centre in London and the London PHV operator who accepted the booking remains in force despite the making of arrangements by that operator for another contractor to provide a vehicle to carry out that booking as a sub-contractor.

Regulation of private hire vehicles in London

Requirements for private hire vehicle licence

6.—(1) A vehicle shall not be used as a private hire vehicle on a road in London **A27.12** unless a private hire vehicle licence is in force for that vehicle.

(2) The driver and operator of a vehicle used in contravention of this section are each guilty of an offence.

(3) The owner of a vehicle who permits it to be used in contravention of this section is guilty of an offence.

(4) It is a defence in proceedings for an offence under subsection (2) for the

driver or operator to show that he exercised all due diligence to prevent the vehicle being used in contravention of this section.

(5) A person guilty of an offence under this section is liable on summary conviction to a fine not exceeding level 4 on the standard scale.

(6) In this section *"private hire vehicle licence"* means—

    (a) except where paragraph (b) or (c) applies, a London PHV licence;

    (b) if the vehicle is in use for the purposes of a hiring the booking for which was accepted outside London in a controlled district, a licence under section 48 of the 1976 Act issued by the council for that district; and

    (c) if the vehicle is in use for the purposes of a hiring the booking for which was accepted in Scotland, a licence under section 10 of the Civic Government (Scotland) Act 1982 (in this Act referred to as *"the 1982 Act"*),

and for the purposes of paragraph (b) or (c) it is immaterial that the booking in question is a sub-contracted booking.

(7) This section does not apply to a vehicle used for the purposes of a hiring for a journey beginning outside London in an area of England and Wales which is not a controlled district.

London PHV licences

A27.13   7.—(1) The owner of any vehicle constructed or adapted to seat fewer than nine passengers may apply to the [licensing authority] for a private hire vehicle licence for London (in this Act referred to as a *"London PHV licence"*) for that vehicle.

(2) The [licensing authority] shall grant a London PHV licence for a vehicle if [the authority] is satisfied—

    (a) that the vehicle—

        (i) is suitable in type, size and design for use as a private hire vehicle;

        (ii) is safe, comfortable and in a suitable mechanical condition for that use; and

        (iii) is not of such design and appearance as would lead any person to believe that the vehicle is a London cab;

    (b) that there is in force in relation to the use of the vehicle a policy of insurance or such security as complies with the requirements of Part VI of the Road Traffic Act 1988; and

    (c) that any further requirements that may be prescribed are met.

(3) A London PHV licence may not be granted in respect of more than one vehicle.

(4) A London PHV licence shall be granted subject to such conditions as may be prescribed and such other conditions as the [licensing authority] may think fit.

(5) A London PHV licence shall be in such form and shall contain such particulars as the [licensing authority] may think fit.

(6) A London PHV licence shall be granted for one year or for such shorter period as the [licensing authority] may consider appropriate in the circumstances of the case.

(7) An applicant for a London PHV licence may appeal to a magistrates' court against a decision not to grant such a licence or against any condition (other than a prescribed condition) to which the licence is subject.

[Section 7 is printed as amended by the Greater London Authority Act 1999 **A27.14**
s.254 and Sch.21, paras 1, 2 and 4.]

Obligations of owners of licensed vehicles

8.—(1) This section applies to the owner of any vehicle to which a London   **A27.15**
PHV licence relates.

(2) The owner shall present the vehicle for inspection and testing by or on behalf of the [licensing authority] within such period and at such place as [the authority] may by notice reasonably require.
The vehicle shall not be required to be presented under this subsection on more than three separate occasion during any one period of 12 months.

(3) The owner shall (without prejudice to section 170 of the Road Traffic Act 1988) report any accident to the vehicle materially affecting—

   (a) the safety, performance or appearance of the vehicle, or

   (b) the comfort or convenience of persons carried in the vehicle,

to the [licensing authority] as soon as reasonably practical and in any case within 72 hours of the accident occurring.

(4) If the ownership of the vehicle changes, the person who was previously the owner shall within 14 days of the change give notice to the Secretary of State of that fact and the name and address of the new owner.

(5) A person who, without reasonable excuse, contravenes any provision of this section is guilty of an offence and liable on summary conviction to a fine not exceeding level 3 on the standard scale.

[Section 8 is printed as amended by the Greater London Authority Act 1999   **A27.16**
s.254 and Sch.21, paras 1, 2 and 5.]

Fitness of licensed vehicles

9.—(1) A constable or authorised officer has power at all reasonable times to   **A27.17**
inspect and test, for the purpose of ascertaining its fitness, any vehicles to which a London PHV licence relates.

(2) If a constable or authorised officer is not satisfied as to the fitness of such a vehicle he may by notice to the owner of the vehicle—

   (a) require the owner to make the vehicle available for further inspection and testing at such reasonable time and place as may be specified in the notice; and

   (b) if he thinks fit, suspend the London PHV licence relating to that vehicle until such time as a constable or authorised officer is satisfied as to the fitness of the vehicle.

(3) A notice under subsection (2)(b) shall state the grounds on which the licence is being suspended and the suspension shall take effect on the day on which it is served on the owner.

(4) A licence suspended under subsection (2)(b) shall remain suspended until such time as a constable or authorised officer by notice to the owner directs that the licence is again in force.

(5) If a licence remains suspended at the end of the period of two months beginning with the day on which a notice under subsection (2)(b) was served on the owner of the vehicle—

    (a) a constable or authorised officer may by notice to the owner direct that the licence is revoked; and

    (b) the revocation shall take effect at the end of the period of 21 days beginning with the day on which the owner is served with that notice.

(6) An owner may appeal against a notice under subsection (2)(b) or (5) to a magistrates' court.

Identification of licensed vehicles

A27.18   **10.**—(1) The [licensing authority] shall issue a disc or plate for each vehicle to which a London PHV licence relates which identifies that vehicle as a vehicle for which such a licence is in force.

(2) No vehicle to which a London PHV licence relates shall be used as a private hire vehicle on a road in London unless the disc or plate issued under this section is exhibited on the vehicle in such manner as may be prescribed.

(3) The [licensing authority] may by notice exempt a vehicle from the requirement under subsection (2) when it is being used to provide a service specified in the notice if [the authority] considers it inappropriate (having regard to that service) to require the disc or plate in question to be exhibited.

(4) The driver and operator of a vehicle used in contravention of subsection (2) are each guilty of an offence.

(5) The owner of a vehicle who permits it to be used in contravention of subsection (2) is guilty of an offence.

(6) It is a defence in proceedings for an offence under subsection (4) for the driver or operator to show that he exercised all due diligence to prevent the vehicle being used in contravention of subsection (2).

(7) A person guilty of an offence under this section is liable on summary conviction to a fine not exceeding level 3 on the standard scale.

A27.19   *[Section 10 is printed as amended by the Greater London Authority Act 1999 s.254 and Sch.21, paras 1, 2 and 6.]*

Prohibition of taximeters

A27.20   **11.**—(1) No vehicle to which a London PHV licence relates shall be equipped with a taximeter.

(2) If such a vehicle is equipped with a taximeter, the owner of that vehicle is guilty of an offence and liable on summary conviction to a fine not exceeding level 3 on the standard scale.

(3) In this section *"taximeter"* means a device for calculating the fare to be charged in respect of any journey by reference to the distance travelled or time elapsed since the start of the journey (or a combination of both).

Regulation of drivers of private hire vehicles in London

Requirement for private hire vehicle driver's licence

A27.21   **12.**—(1) No vehicle shall be used as a private hire vehicle on a road in London unless the driver holds a private hire vehicle driver's licence.

(2) The driver and operator of a vehicle used in contravention of this section are each guilty of an offence.

(3) The owner of a vehicle who permits it to be used in contravention of this section is guilty of an offence.

(4) It is a defence in proceedings against the operator of a vehicle for an offence under subsection (2) for the operator to show that he exercised all due diligence to prevent the vehicle being used in contravention of this section.

(5) A person guilty of an offence under this section is liable on summary conviction to a fine not exceeding level 4 on the standard scale.

(6) In this section *"private hire vehicle driver's licence"* means—

    (a) except where paragraph (b) or (c) applies, a London PHV driver's licence;

    (b) if the vehicle is in use for the purposes of a hiring the booking for which was accepted outside London in a controlled district in England and Wales, a licence under section 51 of the 1976 Act issued by the council for that district; and

    (c) if the vehicle is in use for a hiring the booking for which was accepted in Scotland, a licence under section 13 of the 1982 Act,

and for the purposes of paragraph (b) or (c) it is immaterial that the booking in question is a sub-contracted booking.

(7) This section does not apply to the use of a vehicle for the purposes of a hiring for a journey beginning outside London in an area of England and Wales which is not a controlled district.

London PHV driver's licences

13.—(1) Any person may apply to the [licensing authority] for private hire vehicle driver's licence for London (in this Act referred to as a *"London PHV driver's licence"*).   **A27.22**

(2) The [licensing authority] shall grant a London PHV driver's licence to an applicant if [the authority] is satisfied that—

    (a) the applicant has attained the age of 21, is (and has for at least three years been) authorised to drive a motor car and is a fit and proper person to hold a London PHV driver's licence; and

    (b) the requirement mentioned in subsection (3), and any further requirements prescribed by the [licensing authority], are met.

(3) The [licensing authority] shall require applicants to show to [the authority's] satisfaction (whether by taking a test or otherwise) that they possess a level—

    (a) of knowledge of London or parts of London; and

    (b) of general topographical skills,

which appears to [the authority] to be appropriate.

The [licensing authority] may impose different requirements in relation to different applicants.

(4) The [licensing authority] may send a copy of an application to the Commissioner of Police of the Metropolis or the Commissioner of Police for the City of London with a request for the Commissioner's observations; and the Commissioner shall respond to the request.

(5) A London PHV driver's licence—

    (a) may be granted subject to such conditions as the [licensing authority] may think fit;

    (b) shall be in such form and shall contain such particulars as the [licensing authority] may think fit; and

    (c) shall be granted for three years or for such shorter period as the [licensing authority] may consider appropriate in the circumstances of the particular case.

(6) An applicant may appeal to a magistrates' court against a decision not to grant a London PHV driver's licence or against any condition to which such a licence is subject.

(7) For the purposes of subsection (2), a person is authorised to drive a motor car if—

    (a) he holds a licence granted under Part III of the Road Traffic Act 1988 (other than a provisional licence) authorising him to drive a motor car; or

    (b) he is authorised by virtue of section 99A(1) or 109(1) of that Act (Community licences and Northern Ireland licences) to drive a motor car in Great Britain.

A27.23   *[Section 13 is printed as amended by the Greater London Authority Act 1999 s.254 and Sch.21, paras 1, 2 and 7.*

In relation to an application for a London PHV driver's licence who is an existing driver and the holder of a temporary permit or London PHV driver's licence, this section shall have effect subject to the following modifications:

    1. in subs.(2) for the words "the requirement mentioned in subsection (3), and any further" there shall be substituted "any";

    2. subs.(3) shall be omitted;

see the Private Hire Vehicles (London) (Transitional and Saving Provisions) Regulations 2003 (SI 2003/655) reg.7.]

Issue of driver's badges

A27.24   **14.**—(1) The [licensing authority] shall issue a badge to each person to whom [the authority] has granted a London PHV driver's licence.

(2) The [licensing authority] may prescribe the form of badges issued under this section.

(3) A person issued with such a badge shall, when he is the driver of a vehicle being used as a private hire vehicle, wear the badge in such position and manner as to be plainly and distinctly visible.

(4) The [licensing authority] may by notice exempt a person from the requirement under subsection (3), when he is the driver of a vehicle being used to provide a service specified in the notice if [the authority] considers it inappropriate (having regard to that service) to require the badge to be worn.

(5) Any person who without reasonable excuse contravenes subsection (3) is guilty of an offence and liable on summary conviction to a fine not exceeding level 3 in the standard scale.

A27.25   *[Section 14 is printed as amended by the Greater London Authority Act 1999 s.254 and Sch.21, paras 1, 2 and 8.*

With effect from a day to be appointed, the following amendments will be made to s.14 by the Transport for London Act 2008 s.23:

    1. in s.14(3), "(a)" will be inserted before the words "wear the badge in such position and manner as to be plainly and distinctly visible", and after those words the following text will be inserted:

        [and—

        (b) at the request of any person, produce the badge for inspection.]

    2. in s.14(4), the words "subsection (3)(a)" will be substituted for the words "subsection (3)".]

Licences: general provisions

Applications for licences

15.—(1) An application for the grant of a licence under this Act shall be made   **A27.26** in such form, and include such declarations and information, as the [licensing authority] may require.

(2) The [licensing authority] may require an applicant to furnish such further information as [the authority] may consider necessary for dealing with the application.

(3) The information which an applicant for a London PHV operator's licence may be required to furnish includes in particular information about—

    (a) any premises in London which he proposes to use as an operating centre;

    (b) any convictions recorded against him;

    (c) any business activities he has carried on before making the application;

    (d) if the applicant is or has been a director or secretary of a company, that company;

    (e) if the applicant is a company, information about the directors or secretary of that company;

    (f) if the applicant proposes to act as an operator in partnership with any other person, information about that person.

(4) An applicant for a London PHV driver's licence may be required by the [licensing authority]—

    (a) to produce a certificate signed by a registered medical practitioner to the effect that—

        (i) he is physically fit to be the driver of a private hire vehicle; and

        (ii) if any specific requirements of physical fitness have been prescribed for persons holding London PHV licences, that he meets those requirements; and

    (b) whether or not such a certificate has been produced, to submit to examination by a registered medical practitioner selected by the [licensing authority] as to his physical fitness to be the driver of such a vehicle.

(5) The provisions of this Act apply to the renewal of a licence as they apply to the grant of a licence.

A27.27   *[Section 15 is printed as amended by the Greater London Authority Act 1999 s.254 and Sch.21, paras 1, 2 and 8.]*

Power to suspend or revoke licences

A27.28   **16.**—(1) The [licensing authority] may suspend or revoke a licence under this Act for any reasonable cause including (without prejudice to the generality of this subsection) any ground mentioned below.

(2) A London PHV operator's licence may be suspended or revoked where—

    (a) the [licensing authority] is no longer satisfied that the licence holder is fit to hold such a licence; or

    (b) the licence holder has failed to comply with any condition of the licence or any other obligation imposed on him by or under this Act.

(3) A London PHV licence may be suspended or revoked where—

    (a) the [licensing authority] is no longer satisfied that the vehicle to which it relates is fit for use as a private hire vehicle; or

    (b) the owner has failed to comply with any condition of the licence or any other obligation imposed on him by or under this Act.

(4) A London PHV driver's licence may be suspended or revoked where—

    (a) the licence holder has, since the grant of the licence, been convicted of an offence involving dishonesty, indecency or violence;

    (b) the [licensing authority] is for any other reason no longer satisfied that the licence holder is fit to hold such a licence; or

    (c) the licence holder has failed to comply with any condition of the licence or any other obligation imposed on him by or under this Act.

A27.29   *[Section 16 is printed as amended by the Greater London Authority Act 1999 s.254 and Sch.21, paras 1 and 2.]*

Suspension and revocation under section 16: procedure

A27.30   **17.**—(1) Where the [licensing authority] has decided to suspend or revoke a licence under section 16 —

    (a) [the authority] shall give notice of the decision and the grounds for the decision to the licence holder or, in the case of a London PHV licence, the owner of the vehicle to the which the licence relates; and

    (b) the suspension or revocation takes effect at the end of the period of 21 days beginning with the day on which that notice is served on the licence holder or the owner.

(2) If the [licensing authority] is of the opinion that the interests of public safety require the suspension or revocation of a licence to have immediate effect, and [the authority] includes a statement of that opinion and the reasons for it in the notice of suspension or revocation, the suspension or revocation takes effect when the notice is served on the licence holder or vehicle owner (as the case may be).

(3) A licence suspended under this section shall remain suspended until such time as the [licensing authority] by notice directs that the licence is again in force.

(4) The holder of a London PHV operator's or driver's licence, or the owner

of a vehicle to which a PHV licence relates, may appeal to a magistrates' court against a decision under section 16 to suspend or revoke that licence.

[Section 17 is printed as amended by the Greater London Authority Act 1999   **A27.31** *s.254 and Sch.21, paras 1, 2 and 10.]*

Variation of operator's licence at the request of the operator

18.—(1) The [licensing authority] may, on the application of a London PHV   **A27.32** operator, vary his licence by adding a reference to a new operating centre or removing an existing reference to an operating centre.

(2) An application for the variation of a licence under this section shall be made in such form, and include such declarations and information, as the [licensing authority] may require.

(3) The [licensing authority] may require an applicant to furnish such further information as he may consider necessary for dealing with the application.

(4) The [licensing authority] shall not add a reference to a new operating centre unless [the authority] is satisfied that the premises in question meet any requirements prescribed under section 3(3)(b).

(5) An applicant for the variation of a London PHV operator's licence under this section may appeal to a magistrates' court against a decision not to add a new operating centre to the licence.

[Section 18 is printed as amended by the Greater London Authority Act 1999   **A27.33** *s.254 and Sch.21, paras 1, 2 and 11.]*

[Variation of operator's licence by the licensing authority]

19.—(1) The [licensing authority] may—   **A27.34**

     (a) suspend the operation of a London PHV operator's licence so far as relating to any operating centre specified in the licence; or

     (b) vary such a licence by removing a reference to an operating centre previously specified in the licence,

if [the authority] is no longer satisfied that the operating centre in question meets any requirements prescribed under section 3(3)(b) or for any other reasonable cause.

(2) Where the [licensing authority] has decided to suspend the operation of a licence as mentioned in subsection (1)(a) or vary a licence as mentioned in subsection (1)(b) —

     (a) [the authority] shall give notice of the decision and the grounds for it to the licence holder; and

     (b) the decision shall take effect at the end of the period of 21 days beginning with the day on which the licence holder is served with that notice.

(3) If the [licensing authority] is of the opinion that the interests of public safety require [the authority's] decision to have immediate effect, and [the authority] includes a statement of that opinion and the reasons for it in the notice, [the authority's] decision shall take effect when the notice is served on the licence holder.

(4) If a licence is suspended in relation to an operating centre, the premises in question shall not be regarded for the purposes of this Act as premises at which

the licence holder is authorised to accept private hire bookings, until such time as the [licensing authority] by notice states that the licence is no longer suspended in relation to those premises.

(5) The holder of a London PHV operator's licence may appeal to a magistrates' court against a decision under subsection (1).

A27.35 *[Section 19 is printed as amended by the Greater London Authority Act 1999 s.254 and Sch.21, paras 1, 2 and 12.]*

Fees for grant of licences, etc.

A27.36 **20.** *[Omitted.]*

Production of documents

A27.37 **21.**—(1) The holder of a London PHV operator's licence or a London PHV driver's licence shall at the request of a constable or authorised officer produce his licence for inspection.

(2) The owner of a vehicle to which a London PHV licence relates shall at the request of a constable or authorised officer produce for inspection—

    (a) the London PHV licence for that vehicle;

    (b) the certificate of the policy of insurance or security required in respect of the vehicle by Part VI of the Road Traffic Act 1988.

(3) A document required to be produced under this section shall be produced either forthwith or—

    (a) if the request is made by a constable, at any police station within London nominated by the licence holder or vehicle owner when the request is made, or

    (b) if the request is made by an unauthorised officer, at such place as the officer may reasonably require,

before the end of the period of 6 days beginning with the day on which the request is made.

(4) A person who without reasonable excuse contravenes this section is guilty of an offence and liable on summary conviction to a fine not exceeding level 3 on the standard scale.

Return of licences, etc.

A27.38 **22.**—(1) The holder of a London PHV operator's licence shall return the licence to the [licensing authority] after the expiry or revocation of that licence, within the period of 7 days after the day on which the licence expires or the revocation takes effect.

(2) The owner of a vehicle to which a London PHV licence relates shall return the licence and the plate or disc which was issued for the vehicle under section 10 to the [licensing authority] after the expiry or revocation of that licence within the period of 7 days after the day on which the licence expires or the revocation takes effect.

(3) The holder of a London PHV driver's licence shall return the licence and his driver's badge to the [licensing authority] after the expiry or revocation of that licence, within the period of 7 days after the day on which the licence expires or the revocation takes effect.

(4) On the suspension of a licence under this Act, the [licensing authority], a constable or an authorised officer may by notice direct the holder of the licence, or the owner of the vehicle, to return the licence to [the authority, constable or officer (as the case may be)] within the period of 7 days after the day on which the notice is served on that person.

A direction under this subsection may also direct—

    (a) the return by the vehicle owner of the disc or plate which was issued for the vehicle under section 10 (in the case of a London PHV licence); or

    (b) the return by the licence holder of the driver's badge (in the case of a London PHV driver's licence).

(5) A person who without reasonable excuse fails to comply with any requirement or direction under this section to return a licence, disc, plate or badge is guilty of an offence.

(6) A person guilty of an offence under this section is liable on summary conviction—

    (a) to a fine not exceeding level 3 on the standard scale; and

    (b) in the case of a continuing offence, to a fine not exceeding ten pounds for each day during which an offence continues after conviction.

(7) A constable or authorised officer is entitled to remove and retain the plate or disc from a vehicle to which an expired, suspended or revoked London PHV licence relates following—

    (a) a failure to comply with subsection (2) or a direction under subsection (4);

    (b) a suspension or revocation of the licence which has immediate effect by virtue of section 9(3) or 17(2).

[Section 22 is printed as amended by the Greater London Authority Act 1999 **A27.39** *s.254 and Sch.21, paras 1, 2 and 13.*

With effect from a day to be appointed, the following amendments will be made to s.22 by the Transport for London Act 2008 s.24:

    1. *in s.22(1), the words "Without prejudice to subsection (1A)," will be inserted at the beginning;*

    2. *after s.22(1), the following new subsection will be inserted:*

      [(1A) Where the suspension or revocation of a London PHV operator's licence has immediate effect by virtue of section 17(2), the holder of the licence shall, at the request of a constable or authorised officer, forthwith return the licence to the constable or officer.]

    3. *in s.22(2), the words "Without prejudice to subsection (2A)," will be inserted at the beginning, the words "every plate or disc" will be substituted for the words "plate or disc", and the words "or any regulations made under this Act" will be inserted after the words "section 10";*

    4. *after s.22(2), the following text will be inserted:*

      [(2A) Where the suspension or revocation of a London PHV licence has immediate effect by virtue of section 9(3) or 17(2), the owner of the vehicle to which the licence relates shall, at the request of a constable or authorised officer, forthwith return to the constable or officer the licence and every plate or disc which was issued for the vehicle under section 10 or any regulations made under this Act.]

5. in s.22(3), the words "Without prejudice to subsection (3A)," will be inserted at the beginning;

6. after s.22(3), the following text will be inserted:

[(3A) Where the suspension or revocation of a London PHV driver's licence has immediate effect by virtue of section 17(2), the holder of the licence shall, at the request of a constable or authorised officer, forthwith return his driver's badge to the constable or officer.]

7. in s.22(4), the words "Without prejudice to subsections (1A), (2A) and (3A)," will be inserted at the beginning, in para.(a) the words "every disc or plate" will be substituted for the words "the disc or plate", and the words "or any regulations made under this Act" will be inserted after "section 10";

8. in s.22(7), the words "every disc or plate" will be substituted for the words "the plate or disc".]

Register of licences

A27.40   23. *[Omitted.]*

[Delegation of functions by the licensing authority]

A27.41   24. *[Omitted.]*

Appeals

A27.42   25.—(1) This section applies to any appeal which lies under this Act to a magistrates' court against a decision of the [licensing authority], a constable or an authorised officer in relation to, or to an application for, a licence under this Act.

(2) If the [licensing authority] has exercised the power to delegate functions under section 24, such an appeal shall be heard by [a magistrates' court].

(3) Any such appeal shall be by way of complaint for an order and the Magistrates' Courts Act 1980 shall apply to the proceedings.

(4) The time within which a person may bring such an appeal is 21 days from the date on which notice of the decision appealed against is served on him.

(5) In the case of a decision where an appeal lies, the notice of the decision shall state the right of appeal to a magistrates' court and the time within which an appeal may be brought.

(6) An appeal against any decision of a magistrates' court in pursuance of an appeal to which this section applies shall lie to the Crown Court at the instance of any party to the proceedings in the magistrates' court.

(7) Where on appeal a court varies or reverses any decision of the [licensing authority], a constable or an authorised officer, the order of the court shall be given effect to by the [licensing authority] or, as the case may be, a constable or authorised officer.

A27.43   *[Section 25 is printed as amended by the Greater London Authority Act 1999, s.254 and Sch.21, paras 1 and 2; the Courts Act 2003 (Consequential Provisions) Order 2005 (SI 2005/886) art.2 and Sch., para.54.]*

Effect of appeal on decision appealed against

26.—(1) If any decision of the [licensing authority] against which a right of   **A27.44**
appeal is conferred by this Act —

    (a) involves the execution of any work or the taking of any action;

    (b) makes it unlawful for any person to carry on a business which he was
        lawfully carrying on at the time of the decision,

the decision shall not take effect until the time for appealing has expired or (where
an appeal is brought) until the appeal is disposed of or withdrawn.

(2) This section does not apply in relation to a decision to suspend, vary or
revoke a licence if the notice of suspension, variation or revocation directs that,
in the interests of public safety, the decision is to have immediate effect.

[Section 26 is printed as amended by the Greater London Authority Act 1999   **A27.45**
s.254 and Sch.21, paras 1 and 2.]

Obstruction of authorised officers, etc.

27.—(1) A person who wilfully obstructs a constable or authorised officer act-   **A27.46**
ing in pursuance of this Act is guilty of an offence and liable on summary conviction to a fine not exceeding level 3 on the standard scale.

(2) A person who, without reasonable excuse—

    (a) fails to comply with any requirement properly made to such person
        by a constable or authorised officer acting in pursuance of this Act; or

    (b) fails to give a constable or authorised officer acting in pursuance of
        this Act any other assistance or information which he may reasonably
        require of such person for the purpose of performing his functions
        under this Act,

is guilty of an offence and liable on summary conviction to a fine not exceeding
level 3 on the standard scale.

(3) A person who makes any statement which he knows to be false in giving
any information to an authorised officer or constable acting in pursuance of this
Act is guilty of an offence and liable on summary conviction to a fine not exceeding level 5 on the standard scale.

Penalty for false statements

28. A person who knowingly or recklessly makes a statement or furnishes in-   **A27.47**
formation which is false or misleading in any material particular for the purpose
of procuring the grant or renewal of a licence under this Act, or the variation of
an operator's licence under section 18, is guilty of an offence and liable on summary conviction to a fine not exceeding level 5 on the standard scale.

Saving for vehicle used for funerals and weddings

29. Nothing in this Act applies to any vehicle whose use as a private hire vehi-   **A27.48**
cle is limited to use in connection with funerals or weddings.

Further controls

Prohibition of certain signs, notices, etc.

30.—(1) The [licensing authority] may make regulations prohibiting the   **A27.49**

display in London on or from vehicles (other than licensed taxis and public service vehicles) of any sign, notice or other feature of a description specified in the regulations.

  (2) *[Consultation before making regulations.]*

  (3) Any person who—

    (a) drives a vehicle in respect of which a prohibition imposed by regulations under this section is contravened; or

    (b) causes or permits such a prohibition to be contravened in respect of any vehicle,

is guilty of an offence and liable on summary conviction to a fine not exceeding level 4 on the standard scale.

A27.50 *[Section 30 is printed as amended by the Greater London Authority Act 1999 s.254 and Sch.21, paras 1 and 2.]*

Prohibition of certain advertisements

A27.51 31.—(1) This section applies to any advertisement—

    (a) indicating that vehicles can be hired on application to a specified address in London;

    (b) indicating that vehicles can be hired by telephone on a telephone number being the number of premises in London; or

    (c) on or near any premises in London, indicating that vehicles can be hired at those premises.

  (2) No such advertisement shall include—

    (a) any of the following words, namely "taxi", "taxis", "cab" or "cabs", or

    (b) any word so closely resembling any of those words as to be likely to be mistaken for it,

(whether alone or as part of another word), unless the vehicles offered for hire are London cabs.

  (3) An advertisement which includes the word "minicab", "mini-cab" or "mini cab" (whether in the singular or plural) does not by reason only of that fact contravene this section.

  (4) Any person who issues, or causes to be issued, an advertisement which contravenes this section is guilty of an offence and liable on summary conviction to a fine not exceeding level 4 on the standard scale.

  (5) It is a defence for a person charged with an offence under this section to prove that—

    (a) he is a person whose business it is to publish or arrange for the publication of advertisements;

    (b) he received the advertisement in question for publication in the ordinary course of business; and

    (c) he did not know and had no reason to suspect that its publication would amount to an offence under this section.

  (6) In this section —

    "advertisement" includes every form of advertising (whatever the medium) and references to the issue of an advertisement shall be construed accordingly;

"telephone number" includes any number used for the purposes of communicating with another by electronic means; and *"telephone"* shall be construed accordingly.

Miscellaneous and supplementary

Regulations

32. *[Omitted.]*   **A27.52**

Offences due to fault of other person

33.—(1) Where an offence by any person under this Act is due to the act or **A27.53** default of another person, then (whether proceedings are taken against the first mentioned person or not) that other person is guilty of the offence and is liable to be proceeded against and punished accordingly.

(2) Where an offence under this Act committed by a body corporate is proved to have been committed with the consent or connivance of, or attributable to any neglect on the part of, any director, manager, secretary or other similar officer of the body corporate (or any person purporting to act in that capacity), he as well as the body corporate is guilty of the offence is liable to be proceeded against and punished accordingly.

Service of notices

34.—(1) Any notice authorised or required under this Act to be given to any **A27.54** person may be served by post.

(2) For the purposes of section 7 of the Interpretation Act 1978 any such notice is properly addressed to a London PHV operator if it is addressed to him at any operating centre of his in London.

(3) Any notice authorised or required under this Act to be given to the owner of a vehicle shall be deemed to have been effectively given if it is given to the person who is for the time being notified to the [licensing authority] for the purposes of this Act as the owner of the vehicle (or, if more than one person is currently notified as the owner, if it is given to any of them).

[Section 34 is printed as amended by the Greater London Authority Act 1999   **A27.55** *s.254 and Sch.21, paras 1 and 2.]*

References to the owner of a vehicle

35.—(1) For the purposes of this Act the owner of a vehicle shall be taken to **A27.56** be the person by whom it is kept.

(2) In determining, in the course of any proceedings for an offence under this Act, who was the owner of a vehicle at any time it shall be presumed that the owner was the person who was the registered keeper of the vehicle at that time.

(3) Notwithstanding that presumption—

    (a) it is open to the defence to show that the person who was the registered keeper of a vehicle at any particular time was not the person by whom the vehicle was kept at the time; and

    (b) it is open to the prosecution to prove that the vehicle was kept at that time by some person other than the registered keeper.

(4) In this section *"registered keeper"*, in relation to a vehicle, means the person in whose name the vehicle was registered under the Vehicle Excise and Registration Act 1994.

Interpretation

A27.57   **36.** In this Act, unless the context otherwise requires—

"authorised officer" means an officer authorised in writing by the [licensing authority] for the purposes of this Act;

[*"controlled district"* means any area for which Part II of the 1976 Act is in force by virtue of—

(a) a resolution passed by a district council under section 45 of that Act; or

(b) section 255(4) of the Greater London Authority Act 1999;]

"driver's badge" means the badge issued to the holder of a London PHV driver's licence;

"hackney carriage" means a vehicle licensed under section 37 of the Town Police Clauses Act 1847 or any similar enactment;

"licensed taxi" means a hackney carriage, a London cab or a taxi licensed under Part II of the 1982 Act;

[*"the licensing authority"* means Transport for London;]

"London" means the area consisting of the metropolitan police district and the City of London (including the Temples);

"London cab" means a vehicle licensed under section 6 of the Metropolitan Public Carriage Act 1869;

"London PHV driver's licence" means a licence under section 13;

"London PHV licence" means a licence under section 7;

"London PHV operator" has the meaning given in section 4(1);

"London PHV operator's licence" means a licence under section 2;

"notice" means notice in writing;

"operating centre" has the meaning given in section 1(5);

"operator" has the meaning given in section 1(1);

"prescribed" means prescribed in regulations under section 32(1);

"private hire vehicle" has the meaning given in section 1(1);

"public service vehicle" has the same meaning as in the Public Passenger Vehicles Act 1981;

"road" means any length of highway or of any other road to which the public has access (including bridges over which a road passes);

"the 1976 Act" means the Local Government (Miscellaneous Provisions) Act 1976;

"the 1982 Act" means the Civic Government (Scotland) Act 1982; and

"vehicle" means a mechanically propelled vehicle (other than a tramcar) intended or adapted for use on roads.

A27.58   *[Section 35 is printed as amended by the Greater London Authority Act 1999 s.254 and Sch.21, paras 1, 2 and 17; the Greater London Authority Act 1999*

(Commencement No.8 and Consequential Provisions) Order 2000 (SI 2000/3145; not reproduced in this work).]

Power to make transitional, etc., provisions

 37. *[Omitted.]*   **A27.59**

Financial provisions

 38. [...]   **A27.60**

Consequential amendments and repeals

 39.—(1) Schedule 1 (minor and consequential amendments) shall have effect. **A27.61**
(2) The enactments mentioned in Schedule 2 are repealed to the extent specified.

Short title, commencement and extent

 40. *[Omitted.]*   **A27.62**

SCHEDULES   **A27.63**

SCHEDULE 1
MINOR AND CONSEQUENTIAL AMENDMENTS
[Omitted.]

SCHEDULE 2
REPEALS
[Omitted.]

The Finance Act 2000

(2000 c.17)

A28.01 *An Act to grant certain duties, to alter other duties, and to amend the law relating to the National Debt and the Public Revenue, and to make further provisions in connection with Finance.*

[28th July 2000]

* * *

Enforcement provisions for graduated rates

A28.02 **23.** Schedule 4 to this Act has effect with respect to vehicle licences for vehicles in respect of which vehicle excise duty is chargeable at different rates.

* * *

Section 23 **SCHEDULE 4**

VEHICLE EXCISE DUTY: ENFORCEMENT PROVISIONS FOR GRADUATED RATES

Introduction

A28.03 **1.**—(1) This Schedule applies to vehicles in respect of which different rates of vehicle excise duty are, under the provisions listed below, chargeable in respect of vehicles by reference to characteristics of the vehicle.

(2) The provisions referred to in sub-paragraph (1) are—

Part I of Schedule 1 to the Vehicle Excise and Registration Act 1994 (the general rate),

Part IA of that Schedule (graduated rates for light passenger vehicles first registered on or after 1st March 2001), or

Part II of that Schedule (motorcycles).

Particulars to be furnished on application for licence

A28.04 **2.** *[Regulation-making power.]*

Power to require evidence in support of application

A28.05 **3.** *[Regulation-making power.]*

Powers exercisable where licence issued on basis of incorrect application

A28.06 **4.** The powers conferred by paragraphs 5 to 11 below are exercisable in a case where—

(a) a vehicle licence is issued to a person on the basis of an application stating that the vehicle—

(i) is a vehicle to which this Schedule applies, or

(ii) is a vehicle to which this Schedule applies in respect of which a particular amount of vehicle excise duty falls to be paid, and

(b) the vehicle is not such a vehicle or, as the case may be, is one in respect of which duty falls to be paid at a higher rate.

Power to declare licence void

A28.07 **5.** The Secretary of State may by notice sent by post to the person inform him that the licence is void as from the time when it was granted.

If he does so, the licence shall be void as from the time when it was granted.

Power to require payment of balance of duty

6.—(1) The Secretary of State may by notice sent by post to the person require him to secure that the additional duty payable is paid within such reasonable period as is specified in the notice.

(2) If that requirement is not complied with, the Secretary of State may by notice sent by post to the person inform him that the licence is void as from the time when it was granted. If he does so, the licence shall be void as from the time when it was granted.

A28.08

Power to require delivery up of licence

7. The Secretary of State may in a notice under paragraph 5 or 6(2) require the person to whom it is sent to deliver up the licence within such reasonable period as is specified in the notice.

A28.09

Power to require delivery up of licence and payment in respect of duty

8.—(1) The Secretary of State may in a notice under paragraph 5 or 6(2) require the person to whom it is sent—

(a) to deliver up the licence within such reasonable period as is specified in the notice, and

(b) on doing so to pay an amount equal to the monthly duty shortfall for each month, or part of a month, in the relevant period.

(2) The *"monthly duty shortfall"* means one-twelfth of the difference between—

(a) the duty that would have been payable for a licence for a period of twelve months if the vehicle had been correctly described in the application, and

(b) that duty payable in respect of such a licence on the basis of the description in the application made

For this purpose the amount of the duty payable shall be ascertained by reference to the rates in force at the beginning of the relevant period.

A28.10

Failure to deliver up licence

9.—(1) A person who—

(a) is required by notice under paragraph 7 or 8(1)(a) above to deliver up a licence, and

(b) fails to comply with the requirement contained in the notice, commits an offence.

(2) A person committing such an offence is liable on summary conviction to a penalty not exceeding whichever is the greater of—

(a) level 3 on the standard scale, and

(b) five times the annual duty shortfall.

(3) The *"annual duty shortfall"* means the difference between—

(a) the duty that would have been payable for a licence for a period of twelve months if the vehicle had been correctly described in the application, and

(b) that duty payable in respect of a licence for period of twelve months in respect of the vehicle as described in the application.

For this purpose the amount of the duty payable shall be ascertained by reference to the rates in force at the beginning of the relevant period.

A28.11

Failure to deliver up licence: additional liability

10.—(1) Where a person has been convicted of an offence under paragraph 9, the court shall (in addition to any penalty which it may impose under that paragraph) order him to pay an amount equal to the monthly duty shortfall for each month, or part of a month, in the relevant period (or so much of the relevant period as falls before the making of the order).

A28.12

(2) In sub-paragraph (1) the *"monthly duty shortfall"* has the meaning given by paragraph 8(2).

(3) Where—

(a) a person has been convicted of an offence under paragraph 9, and

(b) a requirement to pay an amount with respect to that licence has been imposed on that person by virtue of paragraph 8(1)(b),

the order to pay an amount under this paragraph has effect instead of that requirement and the amount to be paid under the order shall be reduced by any amount actually paid in pursuance of the requirement.

Meaning of the *"relevant period"*

A28.13   **11.** References in this Schedule to the *"relevant period"* are to the period—

(a) beginning with the first day of the period for which the licence was applied for or, if later, the day on which the licence first was to have effect, and

(b) ending with whichever is the earliest of the following times—

(i) the end of the month during which the licence was required to be delivered up;

(ii) the end of the month during which the licence was actually delivered up;

(iii) the date on which the licence was due to expire;

(iv) the end of the month preceding that in which there first had effect a new vehicle licence for the vehicle in question.

Construction and effect

A28.14   **12.**—(1) This Schedule and the Vehicle and Excise Registration Act 1994 shall be construed and have effect as if this Schedule were contained in that Act.

(2) References in any other enactment to that Act shall be construed and have effect accordingly as including references to this Schedule.

The Police Reform Act 2002

(2002 c.30)

An Act to make new provision about the supervision, administration, functions and conduct of police forces, police officers and other persons serving with, or carrying out functions in relation to, the police; to amend police powers and to provide for the exercise of police powers by persons who are not police officers; ... and for connected purposes.   **A29.01**

[24th July 2002]

PART 4

POLICE POWERS ETC.

CHAPTER 2

PROVISIONS MODIFYING AND SUPPLEMENTING POLICE POWERS

*　　*　　*

Seizure of motor vehicles

Vehicles used in manner causing alarm, distress or annoyance

59.—(1) Where a constable in uniform has reasonable grounds for believing   **A29.02**
that a motor vehicle is being used on any occasion in a manner which—

(a) contravenes section 3 or 34 of the Road Traffic Act 1988 (c.52) (careless and inconsiderate driving and prohibition of off-road driving) [*q.v.*], and

(b) is causing, or is likely to cause, alarm, distress or annoyance to members of the public,

he shall have the powers set out in subsection (3).

(2) A constable in uniform shall also have the powers set out in subsection (3) where he has reasonable grounds for believing that a motor vehicle has been used on any occasion in a manner falling within subsection (1).

(3) Those powers are—

(a) power, if the motor vehicle is moving, to order the person driving it to stop the vehicle;

(b) power to seize and remove the motor vehicle;

(c) power, for the purposes of exercising a power falling within paragraph (a) or (b), to enter any premises on which he has reasonable grounds for believing the motor vehicle to be;

(d) power to use reasonable force, if necessary, in the exercise of any power conferred by any of paragraphs (a) to (c).

(4) A constable shall not seize a motor vehicle in the exercise of the powers conferred on him by this section unless—

(a) he has warned the person appearing to him to be the person whose use falls within subsection (1) that he will seize it, if that use continues or is repeated; and

(b) it appears to him that the use has continued or been repeated after the the warning.

(5) Subsection (4) does not require a warning to be given by a constable on any occasion on which he would otherwise have the power to seize a motor vehicle under this section if—

(a) the circumstances make it impracticable for him to give the warning;

(b) the constable has already on that occasion given a warning under that subsection in respect of any use of that motor vehicle or of another motor vehicle by that person or any other person;

(c) the constable has reasonable grounds for believing that such a warning has been given on that occasion otherwise than by him; or

(d) the constable has reasonable grounds for believing that the person whose use of that motor vehicle on that occasion would justify the seizure is a person to whom a warning under that subsection has been given (whether or not by that constable or in respect the same vehicle or the same or a similar use) on a previous occasion in the previous twelve months.

(6) A person who fails to comply with an order under subsection (3)(a) is guilty of an offence and shall be liable, on summary conviction, to a fine not exceeding level 3 on the standard scale.

(7) Subsection (3)(c) does not authorise entry into a private dwelling house.

(8) The powers conferred on a constable by this section shall be exercisable only at a time when regulations under section 60 are in force.

(9) In this section—

"*driving*" has the same meaning as in the Road Traffic Act 1988 (c. 52);

"*motor vehicle*" means any mechanically propelled vehicle, whether or not it is intended or adapted for use on roads; and

"*private dwelling house*" does not include any garage or other structure occupied with the dwelling house, or any land appurtenant to the dwelling house.

A29.03   *[For the exercise of the powers set out in subs.(3) above by civilians designated as community support officers by a chief officer of police, see the Police Reform Act 2002 s.38 and Sch.4, Pt 1 para.9; not reproduced in this work.]*

Retention etc. of vehicles seized under section 59

A29.04   **60.**—(1) The Secretary of State may by regulations make provision as to—

(a) the removal and retention of motor vehicles seized under section 59; and

(b) the release or disposal of such motor vehicles.

(2) Regulations under subsection (1) may, in particular, make provision—

(a) for the giving of notice of the seizure of a motor vehicle under section 59 to a person who is the owner of that vehicle or who, in accordance with the regulations, appears to be its owner;

(b) for the procedure by which a person who claims to be the owner of a motor vehicle seized under section 59 may seek to have it released;

(c) for requiring the payment of fees, charges or costs in relation to the removal and retention of such a motor vehicle and to any application for its release;

(d) as to the circumstances in which a motor vehicle seized under section 59 may be disposed of;

(e) as to the destination—

  (i) of any fees or charges payable in accordance with the regulations; and

  (ii) of the proceeds (if any) arising from the disposal of a motor vehicle seized under section 59;

(f) for the delivery to a local authority, in circumstances prescribed by or determined in accordance with the regulations, of any motor vehicle seized under section 59.

(3) Regulations under subsection (1) must provide that a person who would otherwise be liable to pay any fee or charge under the regulations shall not be liable to pay it if—

(a) the use by reference to which the motor vehicle in question was seized was not a use by him; and

(b) he did not know of the use of the vehicle in the manner which led to its seizure, had not consented to its use in that manner and could not, by the taking of reasonable steps, have prevented its use in that manner.

(4) In this section—

"local authority" —

  (a) in relation to England, means the council of a county, metropolitan district or London borough, the Common Council of the City of London or Transport for London; and

  (b) in relation to Wales, means the council of a county or county borough;

"motor vehicle" has the same meaning as in section 59.

[The Police (Retention and Disposal of Motor Vehicles) Regulations 2002 (SI **A29.05**
2002/3049) below have been made (in part) under s.60.]

The Crime (International Co-operation) Act 2003

(2003 c.32)

A30.01 *An Act to make provision for furthering co-operation with other countries in respect of criminal proceedings and investigations; ... and for connected purposes.*

[30th October 2003]

ARRANGEMENT OF SECTIONS

* * *

*   *   *

*   *   *

[The Crime (International Co-operation) Act 2003 (Commencement No.4) Or-   **A30.02**
der 2008 (SI 2008/3009) brings into force, with effect from a day specified in
ibid. art.2(1)(a) and (b), Pt 3, Chap.1 of this Act as between the United Kingdom
and Ireland. Sections 54 and 55 come into force only in relation to an offender
who is normally resident in Ireland (SI 2008/3009 art.2(3)). Sections 56 to 70
come into force only in relation to an offence of which an offender has been
convicted in Ireland (SI 2008/3009 art.2(4)).

The Mutual Recognition of Driving Disqualifications (Great Britain and
Ireland) Regulations 2008 (SI 2008/3010; not reproduced in this work) have
been made under Pt 3 of this Act.]

PART 3

ROAD TRAFFIC

CHAPTER 1

CONVENTION ON DRIVING DISQUALIFICATIONS

Road traffic offences in UK

Application of section 55

54.—(1) Section 55 applies where—   **A30.03**

     (a) an individual ("the offender") who is normally resident in a member
         State other than the United Kingdom is convicted of an offence
         mentioned in Schedule 3,

     (b) no appeal is outstanding in relation to the offence, and

     (c) the driving disqualification condition is met in relation to the offence.

(2) The driving disqualification condition is met—

     (a) in relation to an offence mentioned in Part 1 of Schedule 3, if an order
         of disqualification is made in respect of the offence,

     (b) in relation to an offence mentioned in Part 2 of that Schedule, if an or-
         der of disqualification for a period not less than the minimum period
         is made in respect of the offence.

(3) The minimum period is—

     (a) a period of six months, or

     (b) where the State in which the offender normally resides is a prescribed
         State, a shorter period equal to the period prescribed in relation to the
         State.

(4) Section 55 does not apply in prescribed circumstances.

(5) For the purposes of this section no appeal is outstanding in relation to an offence if—

> (a) no appeal is brought against an offender's conviction of the offence, or any order made on his conviction, within the time allowed for making such appeals, or
>
> (b) such an appeal is brought and the proceedings on appeal are finally concluded.

A30.04   *[With effect from a day to be appointed, the following new subsection will be inserted in s.54 by the Coroners and Justice Act 2009 s.177 and Sch.21, Pt 9, para.93:*

> [(3A) When determining whether the period of disqualification is not less than the minimum period, any extension period imposed pursuant to any of the following is to be disregarded—
>
> (a) Article 8A of the Criminal Justice (Northern Ireland) Order 1980;
>
> (b) section 35A or 35C of the Road Traffic Offenders Act 1988;
>
> (c) section 248D of the Criminal Procedure (Scotland) Act 1995;
>
> (d) Article 40A of the Road Traffic Offenders (Northern Ireland) Order 1996;
>
> (e) section 147A of the Powers of Criminal Courts (Sentencing) Act 2000;
>
> (f) Article 91A of the Criminal Justice (Northern Ireland) Order 2008.]*]*

Duty to give notice to foreign authorities of driving disqualification of a non-UK resident

A30.05   **55.**—(1) Where this section applies, the appropriate Minister must give the central authority of the State in which the offender is normally resident a notice under this section.

(2) A notice under this section must—

> (a) give the name, address and date of birth of the offender,
>
> (b) give particulars of the offence,
>
> (c) state that no appeal is outstanding in relation to it,
>
> (d) give particulars of the disqualification,
>
> (e) state whether or not the offender took part in the proceedings in which the disqualification was imposed,
>
> (f) state that the offender has been informed that any decision made for the purposes of the convention on driving disqualifications will have no effect on the disqualification.

(3) A notice under this section may contain such other information as the appropriate Minister considers appropriate.

(4) A notice under this section must be accompanied by the original or a certified copy of the order of disqualification.

(5) Where the offender did not take part in the proceedings mentioned in subsection (2)(e), a notice under this section must also be accompanied by evidence that the offender was duly notified of those proceedings.

(6) Where the offender is the holder of a Community licence, a notice under this section must also be accompanied by the licence unless it has been returned to the driver—

    (a) under section 91A(7)(b)(ii) of the Road Traffic Offenders Act 1988 (c. 53), or

    (b) under Article 92A(7)(b)(ii) of the Road Traffic Offenders (Northern Ireland) Order 1996 (S.I. 1996/1320 (N.I.10)).

(7) Where the period of disqualification is reduced by virtue of section 34A of that Act or Article 36 of that Order, the appropriate Minister must give the central authority particulars of the reduction.

(8) Where the disqualification is removed by an order under section 42 of that Act or Article 47 of that Order, the appropriate Minister must give the central authority particulars of the removal.

(9) The appropriate Minister must provide—

    (a) the central authority, or

    (b) the competent authority of the State mentioned in subsection (1),

with any further information which it requires for the purposes of the convention on driving disqualifications.

Disqualification in respect of road traffic offences outside UK

Application of section 57

56.—(1) Section 57 applies where—   **A30.06**

    (a) an individual ("the offender") who is normally resident in the United Kingdom is convicted in another member State of an offence falling within subsection (5),

    (b) no appeal is outstanding in relation to the offence,

    (c) the driving disqualification condition is met in relation to the offence, and

    (d) the offender was duly notified of the proceedings ("the relevant proceedings") in which the disqualification was imposed and was entitled to take part in them.

(2) The driving disqualification condition is met—

    (a) in relation to an offence falling within subsection (5)(a), if, as a result of the offence, the offender is disqualified in the State in which the conviction is made,

    (b) in relation to an offence falling within subsection (5)(b), if, as a result of the offence, the offender is disqualified in that State for a period not less than the minimum period.

(3) For the purposes of this section an offender is disqualified in a State if he is disqualified in that State for holding or obtaining a licence to drive a motor vehicle granted under the law of that State (however the disqualification is described under that law).

(4) The minimum period is—

    (a) a period of six months, or

    (b) where the State in which the conviction is made is a prescribed State, a shorter period equal to the period prescribed in relation to that State.

(5) An offence falls within this subsection if it is constituted by—

    (a) conduct falling within any of paragraphs 1 to 5 of the Annex to the convention on driving disqualifications, or

    (b) other conduct which constitutes a road traffic offence for the purposes of that convention.

(6) Section 57 does not apply if the relevant proceedings were brought later than the time at which summary proceedings for any corresponding offence under the law of the part of the United Kingdom in which the offender is normally resident could have been brought.

(7) An offence is a corresponding offence if—

    (a) the conduct constituting the offence outside the United Kingdom took place in any part of the United Kingdom, and

    (b) that conduct is, or corresponds to, conduct which would constitute an offence under the law of that part.

(8) The appropriate Minister may make regulations treating offences under the law of a part of the United Kingdom as corresponding to offences under the law of a member State other than the United Kingdom.

(9) For the purposes of this section no appeal is outstanding in relation to an offence if—

    (a) no appeal is brought against an offender's conviction of the offence, or any decision made as a result of his conviction, within the time allowed for making such appeals, or

    (b) such an appeal is brought and the proceedings on appeal are finally concluded.

Recognition in United Kingdom of foreign driving disqualification

A30.07   57.—(1) Where this section applies, the appropriate Minister—

    (a) must give the offender a notice under this section if the unexpired period of the foreign disqualification is not less than one month, and

    (b) may give him a notice under this section if that period is less than one month.

(2) The unexpired period of the foreign disqualification is—

    (a) the period of the foreign disqualification, less

    (b) any period of that disqualification which is treated by regulations made by the appropriate Minister as having been served in the State in which the offender was convicted.

(3) The provision which may be made by regulations under subsection (2)(b) includes provision for treating any period during which a central authority or competent authority of a State has seized a licence without returning it as a period which has been served in that State.

(4) If the appropriate Minister gives the offender a notice under this section, the offender is disqualified in each part of the United Kingdom—

    (a) for the relevant period, and

    (b) if the foreign disqualification is also effective until a condition is satisfied, until the condition or a corresponding prescribed condition is satisfied.

(5) The relevant period is the period which—

    (a) begins at the end of the period of 21 days beginning with the day on which the notice is given, and

(b) is equal to the unexpired period of the foreign disqualification.

(6) But if the foreign disqualification is at any time removed otherwise than in prescribed circumstances, the offender ceases to be disqualified in each part of the United Kingdom from that time.

(7) The appropriate Minister may make regulations substituting a longer period for the period for the time being mentioned in subsection (5)(a).

(8) Where the foreign disqualification is for life—

    (a) the condition in subsection (1)(a) is to be treated as satisfied, and

    (b) the other references in this section and section 58 to the unexpired period of the foreign disqualification are to be read as references to a disqualification for life.

Notice under section 57

58.—(1) A notice under section 57 must—   **A30.08**

    (a) give particulars of the offence in respect of which the foreign disqualification was imposed and the period of that disqualification,

    (b) state that the offender is disqualified in each part of the United Kingdom for a period equal to the unexpired period of the foreign disqualification,

    (c) state the date from which, and period for which, he is disqualified,

    (d) give particulars of any relevant condition mentioned in section 57(4)(b),

    (e) give details of his right to appeal under section 59.

(2) A notice under section 57 must be in writing.

(3) A notice under section 57 may contain such other information as the appropriate Minister considers appropriate.

Appeals

Appeal against disqualification

59.—(1) A person who is disqualified by virtue of section 57 may, after giving   **A30.09** notice to the appropriate Minister of his intention to do so, appeal to the appropriate court against the disqualification.

(2) The appropriate court is—

    (a) in relation to England and Wales, a magistrates' court [...],

    (b) in relation to Scotland, the sheriff within whose jurisdiction the applicant resides,

    (c) in relation to Northern Ireland, a court of summary jurisdiction acting for the petty sessions district in which the applicant resides.

(3) The appeal must be made before the end of the period of 21 days beginning with the day on which the notice under section 57 is given to the applicant.

(4) But the appropriate Minister may make regulations substituting a longer period for the period for the time being mentioned in subsection (3).

(5) If the appropriate court is satisfied that section 57 does not apply to the applicant's case, it must allow the appeal.

(6) Otherwise it must dismiss the appeal.

(7) Where on an appeal against the disqualification the appeal is allowed, the court by which the appeal is allowed must send notice of that fact to the appropriate Minister.

(8) The notice must—

(a) be sent in such manner and to such address, and

(b) contain such particulars,

as the appropriate Minister may determine.

A30.10   *[Section 59 is printed as amended by the Courts Act 2003 (Consequential Provisions) Order 2005 (SI 2005/886) art.2 and Sch., para.97.]*

Power of appellate courts in England and Wales to suspend disqualification

A30.11   **60.**—(1) This section applies where a person is disqualified by virtue of section 57.

(2) Where the person appeals to a magistrates' court against the disqualification, the court may, if it thinks fit, suspend the disqualification.

(3) Where the person makes an application in respect of the decision of the court under section 111 of the Magistrates' Courts Act 1980 (c. 43) (statement of case), the High Court may, if it thinks fit, suspend the disqualification.

(4) Where the person has appealed, or applied for leave to appeal, to the [Supreme Court] under section 1 of the Administration of Justice Act 1960 (c. 65) from any decision of the High Court which is material to the disqualification, the High Court may, if it thinks fit, suspend the disqualification.

(5) Any power of a court under this section to suspend the disqualification is a power to do so on such terms as the court thinks fit.

(6) Where, by virtue of this section, a court suspends the disqualification, it must send notice of the suspension to the Secretary of State.

(7) The notice must—

(a) be sent in such manner and to such address, and

(b) contain such particulars,

as the Secretary of State may determine.

A30.12   *[Section 60 is printed as amended by the Constitutional Reform Act 2005 s.40 and Sch.9, para.79.]*

Power of appellate courts in Scotland to suspend disqualification

A30.13   **61.** *[Applies to Scotland.]*

Power of appellate courts in Northern Ireland to suspend disqualification

A30.14   **62.**—(1) This section applies where a person is disqualified by virtue of section 57.

(2) Where the person appeals to a court of summary jurisdiction against the disqualification, the court may, if it thinks fit, suspend the disqualification.

(3) Where the person makes an application in respect of the decision of the court under Article 146 of the Magistrates' Courts (Northern Ireland) Order 1981 (S.I. 1981/1675 (N.I. 26)) (statement of case), the Court of Appeal may, if it thinks fit, suspend the disqualification.

(4) Where the person has appealed, or applied for leave to appeal, to the

[Supreme Court] under section 41 of the Judicature (Northern Ireland) Act 1978 (c. 23) from any decision of the Court of Appeal which is material to the disqualification, the Court of Appeal may, if it thinks fit, suspend the disqualification.

(5) Any power of a court under this section to suspend the disqualification is a power to do so on such terms as the court thinks fit.

(6) Where, by virtue of this section, a court suspends the disqualification, it must send notice of the suspension to the Department.

(7) The notice must—

    (a) be sent in such manner and to such address, and

    (b) contain such particulars,

as the Department may determine.

[Section 62 is printed as amended by the Constitutional Reform Act 2005 s.40   **A30.15** *and Sch.9, para.79.]*

Production of licence

Production of licence: Great Britain

63.—(1) A person who—   **A30.16**

    (a) is given a notice under section 57 by the Secretary of State, and

    (b) is the holder of a licence,

must deliver his licence and its counterpart to the Secretary of State before the end of the period of 21 days beginning with the day on which the notice is given.

(2) The Secretary of State may make regulations substituting a longer period for the period for the time being mentioned in subsection (1).

(3) If—

    (a) a person delivers a current receipt for his licence and its counterpart to the Secretary of State within the period for the time being mentioned in subsection (1), and

    (b) on the return of his licence and its counterpart immediately delivers them to the Secretary of State,

the duty under subsection (1) is to be taken as satisfied.

    "Receipt" means a receipt issued under section 56 of the Road Traffic Offenders Act 1988 (c. 53).

(4) Subsection (1) does not apply if the competent authority of the relevant State—

    (a) has the licence and its counterpart, or

    (b) has delivered them to the Secretary of State.

(5) The relevant State is the State in which the offence in relation to which the notice was given was committed.

(6) If the holder of a licence does not deliver his licence and its counterpart to the Secretary of State as required by subsection (1), he is guilty of an offence.

(7) A person is not guilty of an offence under subsection (6) if he satisfies the court that he has applied for a new licence and has not received it.

In relation to the holder of a Northern Ireland licence or Community licence, a new licence includes the counterpart of such a licence.

(8) A person guilty of an offence under subsection (6) is liable on summary conviction to a fine not exceeding level 3 on the standard scale.

(9) *"Licence"* means a Great Britain licence, a Northern Ireland licence or a Community licence.

A30.17   *[With effect from a day to be appointed, in relation to endorsement (all drivers), s.63 will be amended by the Road Safety Act 2006 s.10 and Sch.3, para.75, s.59 and Sch.7(4) as follows:*

1. *the words "and its counterpart" will be omitted in each place;*
2. *in s.63(3)(b) and s.63(4)(b), the word "it" will be substituted for the word "them";*
3. *in s.63(7), the second sentence will be omitted.]*

Production of licence: Northern Ireland

A30.18   **64.**—(1) A person who—

(a) is given a notice under section 57 by the Department, and

(b) is the holder of a licence,

must deliver his licence and its counterpart to the Department before the end of the period of 21 days beginning with the day on which the notice is given.

(2) The Department may make regulations substituting a longer period for the period for the time being mentioned in subsection (1).

(3) If—

(a) a person delivers a current receipt for his licence and its counterpart to the Department within the period for the time being mentioned in subsection (1), and

(b) on the return of his licence and its counterpart immediately delivers them to the Department,

the duty under subsection (1) is to be taken as satisfied.

"Receipt" means a receipt issued under Article 62 of the Road Traffic Offenders (Northern Ireland) Order 1996 (S.I. 1996/1320 (N.I.10)).

(4) Subsection (1) does not apply if the competent authority of the relevant State—

(a) has the licence and its counterpart, or

(b) has delivered them to the Department.

(5) The relevant State is the State in which the offence in relation to which the notice was given was committed.

(6) If the holder of a licence does not deliver his licence and its counterpart to the Department as required by subsection (1), he is guilty of an offence.

(7) A person is not guilty of an offence under subsection (6) if he satisfies the court that he has applied for a new licence and has not received it.

In relation to the holder of a Great Britain licence or Community licence, a new licence includes the counterpart of such a licence.

(8) A person guilty of an offence under subsection (6) is liable on summary conviction to a fine not exceeding level 3 on the standard scale.

(9) *"Licence"* means a Northern Ireland licence, a Great Britain licence or a Community licence.

A30.19   *[With effect from a day to be appointed, in relation to endorsement (all driv-*

ers), s.64 will be amended by the Road Safety Act 2006 s.10 and Sch.3, para.76, s.59 and Sch.7(4) as follows:

    1. *the words "and its counterpart" will be omitted in each place;*

    2. *in s.64(3)(b) and s.64(4)(b), the word "it" will be substituted for the word "them";*

    3. *in s.64(7), the second sentence will be omitted.]*

Production of licence: Community licence holders

65.—(1) This section applies where—   **A30.20**

    (a) the holder of a Community licence is disqualified by virtue of section 57, and

    (b) the licence is sent to the Secretary of State or the Department under section 63 or 64.

(2) The Secretary of State or (as the case may be) the Department must send—

    (a) the holder's name and address, and

    (b) particulars of the disqualification,

to the licensing authority in the EEA State in respect of which the licence was issued.

(3) But subsection (2) does not apply if the EEA State is the same as the State in which the offence in relation to which the holder is disqualified was committed.

(4) The Secretary of State or (as the case may be) the Department must return the licence to the holder—

    (a) on the expiry of the relevant period of the disqualification (within the meaning of section 57), or

    (b) if earlier, on being satisfied that the holder has left Great Britain or (as the case may be) Northern Ireland and is no longer normally resident there.

(5) But subsection (4) does not apply at any time where—

    (a) the Secretary of State or the Department would otherwise be under a duty under paragraph (a) of that subsection to return the licence, and

    (b) the holder would not at that time be authorised by virtue of section 99A(1) of the Road Traffic Act 1988 (c. 52) or Article 15A(1) of the Road Traffic (Northern Ireland) Order 1981 (S.I. 1981/154 (N.I.1)) to drive in Great Britain or Northern Ireland a motor vehicle of any class.

(6) In that case the Secretary of State or (as the case may be) the Department must—

    (a) send the licence to the licensing authority in the EEA State in respect of which it was issued, and

    (b) explain to that authority the reasons for so doing.

(7) *"EEA State"* has the same meaning as in Part 3 of the Road Traffic Act 1988.

Disqualification

Effect of disqualification by virtue of section 57

66. Where the holder of a Great Britain licence or Northern Ireland licence is   **A30.21**

disqualified by virtue of section 57, the licence is to be treated as revoked with effect from the beginning of the period of disqualification.

Rule for determining end of period of disqualification

A30.22   **67.** In determining the expiration of the period for which a person is disqualified by virtue of section 57, any time during which—

    (a) the disqualification is suspended, or

    (b) he is not disqualified,

is to be disregarded.

Endorsement

Endorsement of licence: Great Britain

A30.23   **68.**—(1) This section applies where a person who is normally resident in Great Britain is disqualified by virtue of section 57.

(2) The Secretary of State must secure that particulars of the disqualification are endorsed on the counterpart of any Great Britain licence or of any Northern Ireland licence or Community licence which the person—

    (a) may then hold, or

    (b) may subsequently obtain,

until he becomes entitled under subsection (4) or (5) to have a Great Britain licence and its counterpart, or a counterpart of his Northern Ireland licence or Community licence, issued to him free from those particulars.

(3) On the issue to the person of—

    (a) a new Great Britain licence, or

    (b) a new counterpart of a Northern Ireland licence or Community licence,

those particulars must be entered on the counterpart of the new licence or the new counterpart unless he has become so entitled.

(4) The person is entitled to have issued to him with effect from the end of the period for which the endorsement remains effective a new Great Britain licence with a counterpart free from the endorsement if he—

    (a) applies for a new licence under section 97(1) of the Road Traffic Act 1988 (c. 52),

    (b) surrenders any subsisting licence and its counterpart,

    (c) pays the fee prescribed by regulations under Part 3 of that Act, and

    (d) satisfies the other requirements of section 97(1).

(5) The person is entitled to have issued to him with effect from the end of that period a new counterpart of any Northern Ireland licence or Community licence then held by him free from the endorsement if he makes an application to the Secretary of State for that purpose in such manner as the Secretary of State may determine.

(6) The endorsement remains effective until four years have elapsed since he was convicted of the offence in relation to which he is disqualified by virtue of section 57.

(7) Where the person ceases to be disqualified by virtue of section 57(6), the

Secretary of State must secure that the relevant particulars are endorsed on the counterpart of the Great Britain licence or of any Northern Ireland licence or Community licence previously held by him.

[With effect from a day to be appointed, in relation to endorsement (all drivers), s.68 will be amended by the Road Safety Act 2006 s.10 and Sch.3, para.77 as follows: **A30.24**

1. *s.68(2)–(5) will be substituted by the following text:*

[(2) The Secretary of State must secure that the particulars of the disqualification are endorsed on the person's driving record until the end of the period for which the endorsement remains effective.

(3) At the end of the period for which the endorsement remains effective the Secretary of State must remove the endorsement from the person's driving record.]

2. *s.68(7) will be substituted as follows:*

[(7) Where the person ceases to be disqualified by virtue of section 57(6), the Secretary of State must endorse the relevant particulars on his driving record.

In this section and section 69 "*driving record*" has the meaning given by section 97A of the Road Traffic Offenders Act 1988.]*]*

Endorsement of licence: Northern Ireland

69.—(1) This section applies where a person who is normally resident in Northern Ireland is disqualified by virtue of section 57. **A30.25**

(2) The Department must secure that particulars of the disqualification are endorsed on the counterpart of any Northern Ireland licence or the counterpart of any Great Britain licence or Community licence which the person—

(a) may then hold, or

(b) may subsequently obtain,

until he becomes entitled under subsection (4) or (5) to have a Northern Ireland licence and its counterpart, or a counterpart of his Great Britain licence or Community licence, issued to him free from those particulars.

(3) On the issue to the person of—

(a) a new Northern Ireland licence, or

(b) a new counterpart of a Great Britain licence or Community licence,

those particulars must be entered on the counterpart of the new licence or the new counterpart unless he has become so entitled.

(4) The person is entitled to have issued to him with effect from the end of the period for which the endorsement remains effective a new Northern Ireland licence with a counterpart free from the endorsement if he—

(a) applies for a new licence under Article 13(1) of the Road Traffic (Northern Ireland) Order 1981 (S.I. 1981/154 (N.I.1)),

(b) surrenders any subsisting licence and its counterpart,

(c) pays the fee prescribed by regulations under Part 2 of that Order, and

(d) satisfies the other requirements of Article 13(1).

(5) The person is entitled to have issued to him with effect from the end of that

period a new counterpart of any Great Britain licence or Community licence then held by him free from the endorsement if he makes an application to the Department for that purpose in such manner as it may determine.

(6) The endorsement remains effective until four years have elapsed since he was convicted of the offence in relation to which he is disqualified by virtue of section 57.

(7) Where the person ceases to be disqualified by virtue of section 57(6), the Department must secure that the relevant particulars are endorsed on the counterpart of the Northern Ireland licence or the counterpart of any Great Britain licence or Community licence previously held by him.

A30.26   *[With effect from a day to be appointed, in relation to endorsement (all drivers), s.69 will be amended by the Road Safety Act 2006 s.10 and Sch.3, para.78 as follows:*

   1. *s.69(2)–(5) will be substituted by the following text:*

   [(2) The Department must secure that the particulars of the disqualification are endorsed on the person's driving record until the end of the period for which the endorsement remains effective.

   (3) At the end of the period for which the endorsement remains effective the Department must secure that the endorsement is removed from the person's driving record.]

   2. *s.69(7) will be substituted as follows:*

   [(7) Where the person ceases to be disqualified by virtue of section 57(6), the Department must secure that the relevant particulars are endorsed on his driving record.]*]*

General

Duty of appropriate Minister to inform competent authority

A30.27   70.—(1) This section applies where a competent authority of any State gives the appropriate Minister a notice under the convention on driving disqualifications in respect of any person.

(2) If the appropriate Minister gives a notice under section 57 to that person, he must give the competent authority particulars of the disqualification which arises by virtue of that section.

(3) If the appropriate Minister does not give such a notice, he must give his reasons to the competent authority.

Notices

A30.28   71.—(1) A notice authorised or required under this Chapter to be given by the appropriate Minister to an individual, or a Community licence required to be returned to its holder by section 65, may be given or returned to him by—

   (a) delivering it to him,

   (b) leaving it at his proper address, or

   (c) sending it to him by post.

(2) For the purposes of—

   (a) subsection (1), and

(b) section 7 of the Interpretation Act 1978 (c. 30) in its application to
    that subsection,

the proper address of any individual is his latest address as known to the appropriate Minister.

Regulations: Great Britain

72. *[Omitted.]*   **A30.29**

Regulations: Northern Ireland

73. *[Omitted.]*   **A30.30**

Interpretation

74.—(1) In this Chapter—   **A30.31**

"appropriate Minister" means—

    (a) in relation to Great Britain, the Secretary of State,

    (b) in relation to Northern Ireland, the Department,

"central authority", in relation to a State, means an authority designated
by the State as a central authority for the purposes of the convention
on driving disqualifications,

"Community licence" —

    (a) in relation to Great Britain, has the same meaning as in Part 3
       of the Road Traffic Act 1988 (c. 52),

    (b) in relation to Northern Ireland, has the same meaning as in
       Part 2 of the Road Traffic (Northern Ireland) Order 1981 (S.I.
       1981/154 (N.I.1)),

"competent authority", in relation to a State, means an authority which is a
competent authority in relation to the State for the purposes of the
convention on driving disqualifications,

"the convention on driving disqualifications" means the Convention drawn
up on the basis of Article K.3 of the Treaty on European Union on
Driving Disqualifications signed on 17th June 1998,

"counterpart" —

    (a) in relation to Great Britain, has the same meaning as in Part 3
       of the Road Traffic Act 1988 (c. 52),

    (b) in relation to Northern Ireland, has the same meaning as in
       Part 2 of the Road Traffic (Northern Ireland) Order 1981 (S.I.
       1981/154 (N.I.1)),

"the Department" means the Department of the Environment,

"disqualified", except in section 56, means —

    (a) in relation to Great Britain, disqualified for holding or obtaining a Great Britain licence,

    (b) in relation to Northern Ireland, disqualified for holding or
       obtaining a Northern Ireland licence,

  and *"disqualification"* is to be interpreted accordingly,

"foreign disqualification" means the disqualification mentioned in section
56,

"*Great Britain licence*" means a licence to drive a motor vehicle granted under Part 3 of the Road Traffic Act 1988,

"*motor vehicle*"—

    (a) in relation to Great Britain, has the same meaning as in the Road Traffic Act 1988,

    (b) in relation to Northern Ireland, has the same meaning as in the Road Traffic (Northern Ireland) Order 1995 (S.I. 1995/2994 (N.I.18)),

"*Northern Ireland licence*" means a licence to drive a motor vehicle granted under Part 2 of the Road Traffic (Northern Ireland) Order 1981,

"*prescribed*" means prescribed by regulations made by the appropriate Minister.

(2) In this Chapter a disqualification, or foreign disqualification, for life is to be treated as being for a period of not less than six months.

A30.32   *[With effect from a day to be appointed, in relation to endorsement (all drivers), the definition of "counterpart" in s.74(1) will be omitted by the Road Safety Act 2006 s.10 and Sch.3, para.79, s.59 and Sch.7(4).]*

Application to Crown

A30.33   **75.** This Chapter applies to vehicles and persons in the public service of the Crown.

A30.34   *[The Crime (International Co-operation) Act 2003 (Commencement No.4) Order 2008 (SI 2008/3009) brings into force, with effect from a day specified in ibid. art.2(1)(a) and (b), Sch.3 to this Act as between the United Kingdom and Ireland.]*

Section 54   SCHEDULE 3

OFFENCES FOR THE PURPOSES OF SECTION 54

PART I

OFFENCES WHERE ORDER OF DISQUALIFICATION FOR A MINIMUM PERIOD UNNECESSARY

A30.35   **1.**—(1) Manslaughter or culpable homicide by the driver of a motor vehicle.

(2) "*Driver*"—

    (a) in relation to Great Britain, has the same meaning as in the Road Traffic Act 1988 (c. 52),

    (b) in relation to Northern Ireland, has the same meaning as in Article 2(2) of the Road Traffic (Northern Ireland) Order 1995 (S.I. 1995/2994 (N.I.18)).

A30.36   **2.** An offence under section 89(1) of the Road Traffic Regulation Act 1984 (c. 27) or Article 43(1) of the Road Traffic Regulation (Northern Ireland) Order 1997 (S.I. 1997/276 (N.I.2)) (exceeding speed limit).

A30.37   **3.** An offence under any of the following sections of the Road Traffic Act 1988 or Articles of the Road Traffic (Northern Ireland) Order 1995 —

    (a) section 1 or Article 9 (causing death by dangerous driving),

    (b) section 2 or Article 10 (dangerous driving),

[(ba) section 2B (causing death by careless, or inconsiderate, driving),]

    (c) section 3 or Article 12 (careless, and inconsiderate, driving),

[(ca) section 3ZB (causing death by driving: unlicensed, disqualified or uninsured drivers),]

   (d) section 3A or Article 14 (causing death by careless driving when under influence of drink or drugs),

   (e) section 4 or Article 15 (driving, or being in charge, when under influence of drink or drugs),

   (f) section 5 or Article 16 (driving, or being in charge, of a motor vehicle with alcohol concentration above prescribed limit),

   (g) section 6 or Article 17 (failing to provide a specimen of breath for a breath test),

   (h) section 7 or Article 18 (failing to provide specimen for analysis or laboratory test).

[Paragraph 3 of Sch.3 is printed as amended by the Road Safety Act 2006 s.20(6) and s.21(5).] **A30.38**

4. An offence under section 12 of the Road Traffic Act 1988 (motor racing and speed trials on public ways). **A30.39**

5. An offence under section 103(1)(b) of the Road Traffic Act 1988 or Article 167(1) of the Road Traffic (Northern Ireland) Order 1981 (S.I. 1981/154 (N.I.1)) (driving while disqualified). **A30.40**

6. An offence under section 170(4) of the Road Traffic Act 1988 or Article 175(2) of the Road Traffic (Northern Ireland) Order 1981 (failing to stop after accident and give particulars or report of accident). **A30.41**

Part II

OFFENCES WHERE ORDER OF DISQUALIFICATION FOR MINIMUM PERIOD NECESSARY

7. An offence which— **A30.42**

   (a) is mentioned in Part 1 of Schedule 2 to the Road Traffic Offenders Act 1988 (c. 53) or Part 1 of Schedule 1 to the Road Traffic Offenders (Northern Ireland) Order 1996 (S.I. 1996/1320 (N.I.10)), but

   (b) is not an offence mentioned in Part 1 of this Schedule.

The Criminal Justice Act 2003

(2003 c.44)

A31.01 *An Act to make provision about criminal justice (including the powers and duties of the police) and about dealing with offenders; ... and for connected purposes.*

[20th November 2003]

ARRANGEMENT OF SECTIONS

* * *

PART 12
SENTENCING
CHAPTER 1
GENERAL PROVISIONS ABOUT SENTENCING

* * *

Fines

* * *

CHAPTER 5
DANGEROUS OFFENDERS

* * *

CHAPTER 8

OTHER PROVISIONS ABOUT SENTENCING

* * *

Fine defaulters

* * *

301.   Fine defaulters: driving disqualification

* * *

SCHEDULES

* * *

* * *

PART 12

SENTENCING

CHAPTER 1

GENERAL PROVISIONS ABOUT SENTENCING

* * *   **A31.02**

Fines

Powers to order statement as to offender's financial circumstances

162.—(1) Where an individual has been convicted of an offence, the court may, before sentencing him, make a financial circumstances order with respect to him.

(2) Where a magistrates' court has been notified in accordance with section 12(4) of the Magistrates' Courts Act 1980 (c. 43) that an individual desires to plead guilty without appearing before the court, the court may make a financial circumstances order with respect to him.

(3) In this section *"a financial circumstances order"* means, in relation to any individual, an order requiring him to give to the court, within such period as may be specified in the order, such a statement of his financial circumstances as the court may require.

(4) An individual who without reasonable excuse fails to comply with a financial circumstances order is liable on summary conviction to a fine not exceeding level 3 on the standard scale.

(5) If an individual, in furnishing any statement in pursuance of a financial circumstances order—

(a) makes a statement which he knows to be false in a material particular,

(b) recklessly furnishes a statement which is false in a material particular, or

(c) knowingly fails to disclose any material fact,

he is liable on summary conviction to a fine not exceeding level 4 on the standard scale.

(6) Proceedings in respect of an offence under subsection (5) may, notwithstanding anything in section 127(1) of the Magistrates' Courts Act 1980 (c. 43) (limitation of time), be commenced at any time within two years from the date of the commission of the offence or within six months from its first discovery by the prosecutor, whichever period expires the earlier.

General power of Crown Court to fine offender convicted on indictment

A31.03　　　**163.** *[Omitted.]*

Fixing of fines

A31.04　　　**164.**—(1) Before fixing the amount of any fine to be imposed on an offender who is an individual, a court must inquire into his financial circumstances.

(2) The amount of any fine fixed by a court must be such as, in the opinion of the court, reflects the seriousness of the offence.

(3) In fixing the amount of any fine to be imposed on an offender (whether an individual or other person), a court must take into account the circumstances of the case including, among other things, the financial circumstances of the offender so far as they are known, or appear, to the court.

(4) Subsection (3) applies whether taking into account the financial circumstances of the offender has the effect of increasing or reducing the amount of the fine.

[(4A) In applying subsection (3), a court must not reduce the amount of a fine on account of any surcharge it orders the offender to pay under section 161A, except to the extent that he has insufficient means to pay both.]

(5) Where—

(a) an offender has been convicted in his absence in pursuance of section 11 or 12 of the Magistrates' Courts Act 1980 (c. 43) (non-appearance of accused), or

(b) an offender—

(i) has failed to furnish a statement of his financial circumstances in response to a request which is an official request for the purposes of section 20A of the Criminal Justice Act 1991 (c.53) (offence of making false statement as to financial circumstances),

(ii) has failed to comply with an order under section 162(1), or

(iii) has otherwise failed to co-operate with the court in its inquiry into his financial circumstances,

and the court considers that it has insufficient information to make a proper determination of the financial circumstances of the offender, it may make such determination as it thinks fit.

A31.05　　　*[Section 164 is printed as amended by the Domestic Violence, Crime and Victims Act 2004 s.14(2).]*

Remission of fines

165. *[Omitted.]*   **A31.06**

*   *   *

CHAPTER 5

DANGEROUS OFFENDERS

Meaning of "specified offence", etc.

224.—(1) An offence is a "specified offence" for the purposes of this Chapter if   **A31.07**
it is a specified violent offence or a specified sexual offence.

(2) An offence is a "serious offence" for the purposes of this Chapter if and
only if—

    (a) it is a specified offence, and

    (b) it is, apart from section 225, punishable in the case of a person aged
        18 or over by—

        (i) imprisonment for life, or

        (ii) imprisonment for a determinate period of ten years or more.

(3) In this Chapter—

    [...]

    "serious harm" means death or serious personal injury, whether physical
        or psychological;

    "specified violent offence" means an offence specified in Part 1 of Sched-
        ule 15;

    …

*[Section 224 is printed as amended by the Criminal Justice and Immigration
Act 2008 s.148 and Sch.26, para.69 and s.149 and Sch.28, Pt 2.*

*Words omitted after the definition of "specified violent offence" refer to sexual
offences.*

With effect from April 4, 2005, in relation to any time before the coming into   **A31.08**
*force of s.61 of the Criminal Justice and Court Services Act 2000 (abolition of
sentences in a young offender institution, custody for life, etc.), s.224 shall have
effect subject to the following modifications (see the Criminal Justice Act 2003
(Sentencing) (Transitory Provisions) Order 2005 (SI 2005/643) art.3(3)):*

    1. *in subs.(2)(b)(i), after the words "imprisonment for life" insert the
        words "or, in the case of a person aged at least 18 but under 21,
        custody for life";*

    2. *in subs.(2)(b)(ii), after the word "imprisonment" insert the words "or,
        in the case of a person aged at least 18 but under 21, detention in a
        young offender institution,".]*

Life sentence or imprisonment for public protection for serious offences

225.—(1) This section applies where—   **A31.09**

    (a) a person aged 18 or over is convicted of a serious offence committed
        after the commencement of this section, and

(b) the court is of the opinion that there is a significant risk to members of the public of serious harm occasioned by the commission by him of further specified offences.

(2) If—

(a) the offence is one in respect of which the offender would apart from this section be liable to imprisonment for life, and

(b) the court considers that the seriousness of the offence, or of the offence and one or more offences associated with it, is such as to justify the imposition of a sentence of imprisonment for life,

the court must impose a sentence of imprisonment for life.

[(3) In a case not falling within subsection (2), the court may impose a sentence of imprisonment for public protection if the condition in subsection (3A) or the condition in subsection (3B) is met.

(3A) The condition in this subsection is that, at the time the offence was committed, the offender had been convicted of an offence specified in Schedule 15A.

(3B) The condition in this subsection is that the notional minimum term is at least two years.

(3C) The notional minimum term is the part of the sentence that the court would specify under section 82A(2) of the Sentencing Act (determination of tariff) if it imposed a sentence of imprisonment for public protection but was required to disregard the matter mentioned in section 82A(3)(b) of that Act (crediting periods of remand).]

(4) A sentence of imprisonment for public protection is a sentence of imprisonment for an indeterminate period, subject to the provisions of Chapter 2 of Part 2 of the Crime (Sentences) Act 1997 (c. 43) as to the release of prisoners and duration of licences.

(5) An offence the sentence for which is imposed under this section is not to be regarded as an offence the sentence for which is fixed by law.

A31.10   *[Section 225 is printed as amended by the Criminal Justice and Immigration Act 2008 s.13. The coming into force of s.13 of the Criminal Justice and Immigration Act 2008 is of no effect in relation to any person sentenced under s.225 of the Criminal Justice Act 2003 before July 14, 2008 (see the Criminal Justice and Immigration Act 2008 (Commencement No.2 and Transitional and Saving Provisions) Order 2008 (SI 2008/1586) art.2(3) and Sch.2, para.2).*

For modifications to s.225 for the sentencing of offenders aged at least 18 but under 21, see the Criminal Justice and Immigration Act 2008 (Transitory Provisions) Order 2008 (SI 2008/1587).]

Detention for life or detention for public protection for serious offences committed by those under 18

A31.11   **226.**—(1) This section applies where—

(a) a person aged under 18 is convicted of a serious offence committed after the commencement of this section, and

(b) the court is of the opinion that there is a significant risk to members of the public of serious harm occasioned by the commission by him of further specified offences.

(2) If—

(a) the offence is one in respect of which the offender would apart from this section be liable to a sentence of detention for life under section 91 of the Sentencing Act, and

(b) the court considers that the seriousness of the offence, or of the offence and one or more offences associated with it, is such as to justify the imposition of a sentence of detention for life,

the court must impose a sentence of detention for life under that section.

[(3) In a case not falling within subsection (2), the court may impose a sentence of detention for public protection if the notional minimum term is at least two years.

(3A) The notional minimum term is the part of the sentence that the court would specify under section 82A(2) of the Sentencing Act (determination of tariff) if it imposed a sentence of detention for public protection but was required to disregard the matter mentioned in section 82A(3)(b) of that Act (crediting periods of remand).]

(4) A sentence of detention for public protection is a sentence of detention for an indeterminate period, subject to the provisions of Chapter 2 of Part 2 of the Crime (Sentences) Act 1997 (c. 43) as to the release of prisoners and duration of licences.

(5) An offence the sentence for which is imposed under this section is not to be regarded as an offence the sentence for which is fixed by law.

[Section 226 is printed as amended by the Criminal Justice and Immigration   **A31.12**
Act 2008 s.14.

The coming into force of s.14 of the Criminal Justice and Immigration Act 2008 is of no effect in relation to any person sentenced under s.226 of the Criminal Justice Act 2003 before July 14, 2008 (see the Criminal Justice and Immigration Act 2008 (Commencement No.2 and Transitional and Saving Provisions) Order 2008 (SI 2008/1586) art.2(3) and Sch.2, para.2).]

Extended sentence for certain violent or sexual offences: persons 18 or over

227. *[Omitted.]*   **A31.13**

Extended sentence for certain violent or sexual offences: persons under 18

228. *[Omitted.]*   **A31.14**

The assessment of dangerousness

229.—(1) This section applies where—   **A31.15**

(a) a person has been convicted of a specified offence, and

(b) it falls to a court to assess under any of sections 225 to 228 whether there is a significant risk to members of the public of serious harm occasioned by the commission by him of further such offences.

(2) [...], the court in making the assessment referred to in subsection (1)(b)—

(a) must take into account all such information as is available to it about the nature and circumstances of the offence,

[(aa) may take into account all such information as is available to it about the nature and circumstances of any other offences of which the offender has been convicted by a court anywhere in the world,]

  (b) may take into account any information which is before it about any pattern of behaviour of which [any of the offences mentioned in paragraph (a) or (aa)] forms part, and

  (c) may take into account any information about the offender which is before it.

 [(2A) The reference in subsection (2)(aa) to a conviction by a court includes a reference to—

  [(a) a conviction of an offence in any service disciplinary proceedings, and]

  (b) a conviction of a service offence within the meaning of the Armed Forces Act 2006 ("conviction" here including anything that under section 376(1) and (2) of that Act is to be treated as a conviction).]

 [(2B) For the purposes of subsection (2A)(a) *"service disciplinary proceedings"* means—

  (a) any proceedings under the Army Act 1955, the Air Force Act 1955 or the Naval Discipline Act 1957 (whether before a court-martial or any other court or person authorised under any of those Acts to award a punishment in respect of any offence), and

  (b) any proceedings before a Standing Civilian Court; and "conviction" includes the recording of a finding that a charge in respect of the offence has been proved.]

  (3) [...]

  (4) [...]

A31.16 *[Section 229 is printed as amended by the Criminal Justice and Immigration Act 2008 s.17 and s.149 and Sch.28, Pt 2; the Coroners and Justice Act 2009 s.177 and Sch.21, Pt 10, para.95.*

 Nothing in para.95 of Sch.21 to the 2009 Act has effect in relation to any person sentenced under s.225, 226, 227 or 228 of the Criminal Justice Act 2003 before the passing of the 2009 Act (Coroners and Justice Act 2009 s.177 and Sch.22, Pt 5, para.47).]

Imprisonment or detention for public protection: release on licence

A31.17 **230.** *[Omitted.]*

Appeals where previous convictions set aside

A31.18 **231.**—[(1) This section applies where—

  (a) a sentence has been imposed on any person under section 225(3) or 227(2),

  (b) the condition in section 225(3A) or (as the case may be) 227(2A) was met but the condition in section 225(3B) or (as the case may be) 227(2B) was not, and

  (c) any previous conviction of his without which the condition in section 225(3A) or (as the case may be) 227(2A) would not have been met has been subsequently set aside on appeal.]

 (2) Notwithstanding anything in section 18 of the Criminal Appeal Act 1968 (c.19), notice of appeal against the sentence may be given at any time within 28 days from the date on which the previous conviction was set aside.

[Section 231 is printed as amended by the Criminal Justice and Immigration Act 2008 s.18(1).] **A31.19**

Certificates of convictions for purposes of [sections 225 and 227]

232. Where— **A31.20**

(a) on any date after [the commencement of Schedule 15A] a person is convicted in England and Wales of [an offence specified in that Schedule], and

(b) the court by or before which he is so convicted states in open court that he has been convicted of such an offence on that date, and

(c) that court subsequently certifies that fact,

that certificate shall be evidence, for the purposes of [sections 225(3A) and 227(2A)], that he was convicted of such an offence on that date.

[Section 232 is printed as amended by the Criminal Justice and Immigration Act 2008 s.18(2).] **A31.21**

Offences under service law

233. *[Omitted.]* **A31.22**

Determination of day when offence committed

234. [...] **A31.23**

[Section 234 was omitted by the Criminal Justice and Immigration Act 2008 s.18(3) and s.149 and Sch.28, Pt 2.] **A31.24**

Detention under sections 226 and 228

235. A person sentenced to be detained under section 226 or 228 is liable to be detained in such place, and under such conditions, as may be determined by the Secretary of State or by such other person as may be authorised by him for the purpose. **A31.25**

Conversion of sentences of detention into sentences of imprisonment

236. *[Omitted.]* **A31.26**

*   *   *

CHAPTER 8

OTHER PROVISIONS ABOUT SENTENCING

*   *   * **A31.27**

Fine defaulters

*   *   *

Fine defaulters: driving disqualification

301.—(1) Subsection (2) applies in any case where a magistrates' court—

    (a) has power under Part 3 of the Magistrates' Courts Act 1980 (c. 43) to issue a warrant of commitment for default in paying a sum adjudged to be paid by a conviction (other than a sum ordered to be paid under section 6 of the Proceeds of Crime Act 2002 (c. 29)), or

    (b) would, but for section 89 of the Sentencing Act (restrictions on custodial sentences for persons under 18), have power to issue such a warrant for such default.

(2) The magistrates' court may, instead of issuing a warrant of commitment or, as the case may be, proceeding under section 81 of the Magistrates' Courts Act 1980 (enforcement of fines imposed on young offenders), order the person in default to be disqualified, for such period not exceeding twelve months as it thinks fit, for holding or obtaining a driving licence.

(3) Where an order has been made under subsection (2) for default in paying any sum—

    (a) on payment of the whole sum to any person authorised to receive it, the order shall cease to have effect, and

    (b) on payment of part of the sum to any such person, the total number of weeks or months to which the order relates is to be taken to be reduced by a proportion corresponding to that which the part paid bears to the whole sum.

(4) In calculating any reduction required by subsection (3)(b) any fraction of a week or month is to be disregarded.

(5) The Secretary of State may by order amend subsection (2) by substituting, for the period there specified, such other period as may be specified in the order.

(6) A court which makes an order under this section disqualifying a person for holding or obtaining a driving licence shall require him to produce—

    (a) any such licence held by him together with its counterpart; or

    (b) in the case where he holds a Community licence (within the meaning of Part 3 of the Road Traffic Act 1988 (c. 52)), his Community licence and its counterpart (if any).

(7) In this section—

    "driving licence" means a licence to drive a motor vehicle granted under Part 3 of the Road Traffic Act 1988;

    "counterpart" —

        (a) in relation to a driving licence, has the meaning given in relation to such a licence by section 108(1) of that Act; and

        (b) in relation to a Community licence, has the meaning given by section 99B of that Act.

A31.28   *[With effect from a day to be appointed, in relation to endorsement (all drivers), s.301 will be amended by the Road Safety Act 2006 s.10 and Sch.3, para.80, s.59 and Sch.7(4) as follows:*

    1. in s.301(6)(a), the words "together with its counterpart" will be omitted;

    2. in s.301(6)(b), the words "and its counterpart (if any)" will be omitted;

    3. in s.301(7), the definition of "counterpart" will be omitted.]

* * *

Section 224   SCHEDULE 15

SPECIFIED OFFENCES FOR PURPOSES OF CHAPTER 5 OF PART 12

PART 1

SPECIFIED VIOLENT OFFENCES

* * *

17. An offence under section 35 of that Act (injuring persons by furious driving).   **A31.29**

* * *

34. An offence under section 12A of that Act (aggravated vehicle-taking) involving an accident which caused the death of any person.   **A31.30**

* * *

48. An offence under section 1 of the Road Traffic Act 1988 (c. 52) (causing death by dangerous driving).   **A31.31**

49. An offence under section 3A of that Act (causing death by careless driving when under influence of drink or drugs).   **A31.32**

* * *

The Clean Neighbourhoods and Environment Act 2005

(2005 c.16)

A32.01 *An Act to amend section 6 of the Crime and Disorder Act 1998; to make provision for the gating of certain minor highways; to make provision in relation to vehicles parked on roads that are exposed for sale or being repaired; to make provision in relation to abandoned vehicles and the removal and disposal of vehicles; ... and for connected purposes.*

[7th April 2005]

PART 2

VEHICLES

Nuisance parking offences

Exposing vehicles for sale on a road

A32.02   **3.**—(1) A person is guilty of an offence if at any time—

(a) he leaves two or more motor vehicles parked within 500 metres of each other on a road or roads where they are exposed or advertised for sale, or

(b) he causes two or more motor vehicles to be so left.

(2) A person is not to be convicted of an offence under subsection (1) if he proves to the satisfaction of the court that he was not acting for the purposes of a business of selling motor vehicles.

(3) A person guilty of an offence under subsection (1) is liable on summary conviction to a fine not exceeding level 4 on the standard scale.

(4) In this section—

"motor vehicle" has the same meaning as in the Refuse Disposal (Amenity) Act 1978 (c.3);

"road" has the same meaning as in the Road Traffic Regulation Act 1984 (c.27).

Repairing vehicles on a road

A32.03   **4.**—(1) A person who carries out restricted works on a motor vehicle on a road is guilty of an offence, subject as follows.

(2) For the purposes of this section *"restricted works"* means—

(a) works for the repair, maintenance, servicing, improvement or dismantling of a motor vehicle or of any part of or accessory to a motor vehicle;

(b) works for the installation, replacement or renewal of any such part or accessory.

(3) A person is not to be convicted of an offence under this section in relation

to any works if he proves to the satisfaction of the court that the works were not carried out—

    (a) in the course of, or for the purposes of, a business of carrying out restricted works; or

    (b) for gain or reward.

(4) Subsection (3) does not apply where the carrying out of the works gave reasonable cause for annoyance to persons in the vicinity.

(5) A person is also not to be convicted of an offence under this section in relation to any works if he proves to the satisfaction of the court that the works carried out were works of repair which—

    (a) arose from an accident or breakdown in circumstances where repairs on the spot or elsewhere on the road were necessary; and

    (b) were carried out within 72 hours of the accident or breakdown or were within that period authorised to be carried out at a later time by the local authority for the area.

(6) A person guilty of an offence under this section is liable on summary conviction to a fine not exceeding level 4 on the standard scale.

(7) In this section—

    "motor vehicle" has the same meaning as in the Refuse Disposal (Amenity) Act 1978;

    "road" has the same meaning as in the Road Traffic Regulation Act 1984;

    "local authority" has the meaning given in section 9.

Liability of directors etc

5.—(1) Where an offence under section 3 or 4 committed by a body corporate is proved to have been committed with the consent or connivance of, or to have been attributable to any neglect on the part of—   **A32.04**

    (a) any director, manager, secretary or other similar officer of the body corporate, or

    (b) a person who was purporting to act in any such capacity,

he as well as the body corporate is guilty of the offence and liable to be proceeded against and punished accordingly.

(2) Where the affairs of a body corporate are managed by its members, subsection (1) applies in relation to the acts or defaults of a member in connection with his functions of management as if he were a director of the body.

Nuisance parking offences: fixed penalty notices

Power to give fixed penalty notices

6.—(1) Where on any occasion an authorised officer of a local authority has reason to believe that a person has committed an offence under section 3 or 4 in the area of that authority, the officer may give that person a notice offering him the opportunity of discharging any liability to conviction for that offence by payment of a fixed penalty to the local authority.   **A32.05**

(2) Where a person is given a notice under this section in respect of an offence—

(a) no proceedings may be instituted for that offence before the expiration of the period of fourteen days following the date of the notice; and

(b) he may not be convicted of that offence if he pays the fixed penalty before the expiration of that period.

(3) A notice under this section must give such particulars of the circumstances alleged to constitute the offence as are necessary for giving reasonable information of the offence.

(4) A notice under this section must also state—

(a) the period during which, by virtue of subsection (2), proceedings will not be taken for the offence;

(b) the amount of the fixed penalty; and

(c) the person to whom and the address at which the fixed penalty may be paid.

(5) Without prejudice to payment by any other method, payment of the fixed penalty may be made by pre-paying and posting a letter containing the amount of the penalty (in cash or otherwise) to the person mentioned in subsection (4)(c) at the address so mentioned.

(6) Where a letter is sent in accordance with subsection (5) payment is to be regarded as having been made at the time at which that letter would be delivered in the ordinary course of post.

(7) The form of a notice under this section is to be such as the appropriate person may by order prescribe.

(8) The fixed penalty payable to a local authority under this section is, subject to subsection (9), £100.

(9) The appropriate person may by order substitute a different amount for the amount for the time being specified in subsection (8).

(10) The local authority to which a fixed penalty is payable under this section may make provision for treating it as having been paid if a lesser amount is paid before the end of a period specified by the authority.

(11) The appropriate person may by regulations restrict the extent to which, and the circumstances in which, a local authority may make provision under subsection (10).

(12) In any proceedings a certificate which—

(a) purports to be signed on behalf of the chief finance officer of the local authority, and

(b) states that payment of a fixed penalty was or was not received by a date specified in the certificate,

is evidence of the facts stated.

(13) In this section *"chief finance officer"*, in relation to a local authority, means the person having responsibility for the financial affairs of the authority.

Power to require name and address

A32.06   7.—(1) If an authorised officer of a local authority proposes to give a person a notice under section 6, the officer may require the person to give him his name and address.

(2) A person commits an offence if—

    (a) he fails to give his name and address when required to do so under subsection (1), or

    (b) he gives a false or inaccurate name or address in response to a requirement under that subsection.

(3) A person guilty of an offence under subsection (2) is liable on summary conviction to a fine not exceeding level 3 on the standard scale.

8. *[Omitted.]*   **A32.07**

Fixed penalty notices: supplementary

9.—(1) For the purposes of this section, *"this group of sections"* means sec- **A32.08**
tions 6 to 8 and this section.

(2) In this group of sections—

    "local authority" means—

        (a) a district council in England;

        (b) a county council in England for an area for which there is no district council;

        (c) a London borough council;

        (d) the Common Council of the City of London;

        (e) the Council of the Isles of Scilly;

        (f) a county or county borough council in Wales;

    "appropriate person" means—

        (a) in relation to England, the Secretary of State;

        (b) in relation to Wales, the National Assembly for Wales;

    "authorised officer", in relation to a local authority, means an employee of the authority who is authorised in writing by the authority for the purposes of giving notices under section 6.

(3)–(5) *[Omitted.]*

The Road Safety Act 2006

(2006 c.49)

A33.01 *An Act to make provision about road traffic, registration plates, vehicle and driver information, hackney carriages and private hire vehicles, and trunk road picnic areas*

[8th November 2006]

* * *

Supplementary

Repeals and revocations

A33.02 **59.** *[Omitted.]*

Power to make amendments

A33.03 **60.** *[Omitted.]*

Commencement

A33.04 **61.**—(1) The preceding provisions of this Act come into force on such day as the Secretary of State may by order made by statutory instrument appoint (but subject to subsections (7) to (10)).

(2) Different days may be appointed for different purposes.

(3) Any provision of this Act which alters any penalty for an offence has effect only in relation to offences committed after the coming into force of the provision.

(4) Section 2B of the Road Traffic Act 1988 (c.52) (inserted by section 20) has effect only in relation to driving occurring after the coming into force of that section; and section 3ZB of that Act (inserted by section 21) has effect only in relation to driving occurring after the coming into force of that section.

(5) In relation to an offence under section 2B or 3ZB of the Road Traffic Act 1988 committed before the commencement of section 154(1) of the Criminal Justice Act 2003 (c.44), the references in column 4 of Part 1 of Schedule 2 to the Road Traffic Offenders Act 1988 (c.53) relating to offences under those sections have effect with the omission of the words "12 months (in England and Wales) or" and "(in Scotland)".

(6) The Secretary of State may by order made by statutory instrument make such transitional provisions and savings as he considers appropriate in connection with the coming into force of any provision of this Act.

(7) The following provisions come into force at the end of the period of two months beginning with the day on which this Act is passed—

(a) section 1, and

(b) section 49.

(8) The day on which sections 8 and 9 and Schedule 2 (and the repeals contained in Schedule 7 under the heading "Endorsement: unlicensed and foreign drivers") come into force must be—

(a) later than the day on which section 5 and Schedule 1 (and the repeals contained in Schedule 7 under the heading "Giving of fixed penalty notices by vehicle examiners") come into force, but

(b) earlier than the day on which section 10 and Schedule 3 (and the repeals contained in Schedule 7 under the heading "Endorsement: all drivers") come into force.

(9) Sections 51, 58 and 60, and the repeals contained in Schedule 7 under the heading "Spent enactments" (and section 59 so far as relating to them), come into force on the day on which this Act is passed; but—

(a) section 51(2) does not affect anything done or omitted to be done before that day, and

(b) section 58(6) has effect only in relation to offences committed on or after that day.

(10) Any power to make an order or regulations which is conferred by any provision of this Act may be exercised at any time after the passing of this Act.

Extent

62.—(1) Section 1 extends only to England and Wales.   **A33.05**

(2) Section 11(3) and Schedule 4, section 16 and section 51 extend only to England and Wales and Scotland.

(3) Section 49(2) extends only to Northern Ireland.

(4) Apart from the amendments made by sections 1 and 46, the amendments (and repeals and revocations) made by this Act have the same extent as the enactments and instruments amended (or repealed or revoked).

Short title

63. This Act may be cited as the Road Safety Act 2006.   **A33.06**

*   *   *

Section 11   SCHEDULE 4

PROHIBITION ON DRIVING: IMMOBILISATION, REMOVAL AND DISPOSAL OF VEHICLES

Cases to which regulations may apply

1. The Secretary of State may make regulations with respect to any case where, on or af-   **A33.07**
ter such date as may be prescribed, the driving of a vehicle has been prohibited under—

(a) section 99A(1) of the Transport Act 1968 (c.73) (powers to prohibit driving of vehicles in connection with contravention of provisions about drivers' hours),

(b) section 1 of the Road Traffic (Foreign Vehicles) Act 1972 (c.27) (powers to prohibit driving of foreign goods vehicles and foreign public service vehicles),

(c) section 69 or 70 of the Road Traffic Act 1988 (c.52) (powers to prohibit driving of unfit or overloaded vehicles), or

(d) section 90D of the Road Traffic Offenders Act 1988 (c.53) (power to prohibit driving of vehicle on failure to make payment in compliance with financial penalty deposit requirement).

Immobilisation

2.—(1) The regulations may provide that an authorised person or a person acting under   **A33.08**
his direction may—

   (a) fix an immobilisation device to the vehicle, and

   (b) move the vehicle, or direct it to be moved, for the purpose of enabling an immobilisation device to be fitted it.

(2) The regulations may provide that on any occasion when an immobilisation device is fixed to a vehicle in accordance with the regulations the person fixing the device must also fix to the vehicle a notice—

   (a) indicating that the device has been fixed to the vehicle and warning that no attempt should be made to drive it or otherwise put it in motion until it has been released from the device,

   (b) specifying the steps to be taken to secure its release, and

   (c) giving such other information as may be prescribed.

(3) The regulations may provide that a vehicle to which an immobilisation device has been fixed in accordance with the regulations—

   (a) may only be released from the device by or under the direction of an authorised person, but

   (b) subject to that, must be released from the device if the first and second requirements specified below are met.

(4) The first requirement is that such charge in respect of the release as may be prescribed is paid in any manner specified in the immobilisation notice.

(5) The second requirement is that, in accordance with instructions specified in the immobilisation notice, there is produced such evidence as may be prescribed establishing that the prohibition has been removed.

(6) The regulations may provide that they do not apply in relation to a vehicle if—

   (a) a current disabled person's badge is displayed on the vehicle, or

   (b) such other conditions as may be prescribed are fulfilled,

and *"disabled person's badge"* means a badge issued, or having effect as if issued, under any regulations for the time being in force under section 21 of the Chronically Sick and Disabled Persons Act 1970 (c.44).

(7) The regulations may provide that an immobilisation notice is not to be removed or interfered with except by or on the authority of a person falling within a prescribed description.

Offences connected with immobilisation etc.

A33.09   **3.**—(1) The regulations may provide that a person who fails to comply within a reasonable time with a direction under provision made under paragraph 2(1)(b) is guilty of an offence and liable on summary conviction to a fine not exceeding level 5 on the standard scale.

(2) The regulations may provide that a person contravening provision made under paragraph 2(7) is guilty of an offence and liable on summary conviction to a fine not exceeding level 2 on the standard scale.

(3) The regulations may provide that a person who, without being authorised to do so in accordance with provision made under paragraph 2, removes or attempts to remove an immobilisation device fixed to a vehicle in accordance with the regulations is guilty of an offence and liable on summary conviction to a fine not exceeding level 3 on the standard scale.

(4) The regulations may provide that where they would otherwise have applied in relation to a vehicle but for provision made under paragraph 2(6)(a) and the vehicle was not, at the time at which they would otherwise have applied, being used—

   (a) in accordance with regulations under section 21 of the Chronically Sick and Disabled Persons Act 1970 (c.44), and

   (b) in circumstances falling within section 117(1)(b) of the Road Traffic Regulation Act 1984 (c.27) (use where a disabled person's concession would be available), the person in charge of the vehicle at that time is guilty of an offence and liable on summary conviction to a fine not exceeding level 3 on the standard scale.

(5) The regulations may provide that where—

(a) a person makes a declaration with a view to securing the release of a vehicle from an immobilisation device purported to have been fixed in accordance with the regulations,

(b) the declaration is that the prohibition has been removed, and

(c) the declaration is to the person's knowledge either false or in any material respect misleading,

he is guilty of an offence.

(6) The regulations may provide that a person guilty of an offence for which provision is made under sub-paragraph (5) is liable—

(a) on summary conviction, to a fine not exceeding the statutory maximum, or

(b) on conviction on indictment, to imprisonment for a term not exceeding two years, or to a fine, or both.

Removal and disposal of vehicles

4.—(1) The regulations may provide that where such conditions as may be prescribed are fulfilled an authorised person, or a person acting under his direction, may remove the vehicle or direct it to be removed.   **A33.10**

(2) The regulations may provide that where such conditions as may be prescribed are fulfilled an authorised person, or a person acting under his direction, may deliver the vehicle, or direct it to be delivered, into the custody of a person—

(a) who is identified in accordance with prescribed rules, and

(b) who agrees to accept delivery in accordance with arrangements agreed between that person and the Secretary of State,

and the arrangements may include provision as to the payment of a sum to the person into whose custody the vehicle is delivered.

(3) The regulations may make provision for such persons as may be prescribed to be informed that a vehicle has been removed and delivered into a person's custody and may, in particular, include provision requiring—

(a) the publication by an authorised person of such notices as may be prescribed, and

(b) the giving of notice by an authorised person to such persons as may be prescribed.

(4) The regulations may provide that the person into whose custody the vehicle is delivered may dispose of it, and may in particular make provision as to—

(a) the time at which the vehicle may be disposed of, and

(b) the manner in which it may be disposed of.

(5) The regulations may make provision allowing a person to take possession of the vehicle if–

(a) he claims it before it is disposed of, and

(b) any prescribed conditions are fulfilled.

(6) The regulations may provide for a sum of an amount arrived at under prescribed rules to be paid to a person if—

(a) he claims after the vehicle's disposal to be or to have been its owner or to have been the person in charge of the vehicle when it was removed,

(b) the claim is made within a prescribed time of the disposal, and

(c) any other prescribed conditions are fulfilled.

(7) The regulations may provide that (whether or not a claim is made under provision made under sub-paragraph (5) or (6))—

(a) the Secretary of State, or

(b) a person into whose custody the vehicle is delivered under the regulations, may recover from the vehicle's owner or the person in charge of the vehicle such charges as may be prescribed in respect of all or any of its release, removal, custody and disposal.

(8) In sub-paragraph (7) *"person in charge"* and *"owner"*, in relation to a vehicle, means the person who was in charge of the vehicle or was the vehicle's owner when it was removed.

(9) The conditions prescribed under sub-paragraph (5) may include conditions as to—

    (a) satisfying the person with custody that the claimant is the vehicle's owner or was the person in charge of the vehicle when it was removed,

    (b) the payment of prescribed charges in respect of the vehicle's release, removal and custody, and

    (c) the production of such evidence as may be prescribed establishing that the prohibition has been removed.

(10) The regulations may in particular include provision for purposes corresponding to those of sections 101 and 102 of the Road Traffic Regulation Act 1984 (c.27) (disposal and charges) subject to such additions, omissions or other modifications as the Secretary of State thinks fit.

Offences as to securing possession of vehicles

A33.11 **5.**—(1) The regulations may provide that a person who fails to comply within a reasonable time with a direction under provision made under subparagraph (1) or (2) of paragraph 4 is guilty of an offence and liable on summary conviction to a fine not exceeding level 5 on the standard scale.

(2) The regulations may provide that where—

    (a) a person makes a declaration with a view to securing possession of a vehicle purported to have been delivered into the custody of a person in accordance with provision made under paragraph 4,

    (b) the declaration is that the prohibition has been removed, and

    (c) the declaration is to the person's knowledge either false or in any material respect misleading,

he is guilty of an offence.

(3) The regulations may provide that a person guilty of an offence for which provision is made under sub-paragraph (2) is liable—

    (a) on summary conviction, to a fine not exceeding the statutory maximum, or

    (b) on conviction on indictment, to imprisonment for a term not exceeding two years, or to a fine, or both.

Disputes

A33.12 **6.** The regulations may make provision about the proceedings to be followed where a dispute occurs as a result of the regulations, and may in particular make provision—

    (a) for an application to be made to a magistrates' court or (in Scotland) to the sheriff, or

    (b) or a court to order a sum to be paid by the Secretary of State.

Authorised persons

A33.13 **7.** As regards anything falling to be done under the regulations (such as receiving payment of a charge or other sum) the regulations may provide that it may be done—

    (a) by an authorised person, or

    (b) by an authorised person or a person acting under his direction.

Application of Road Traffic Offenders Act 1988 (c.53)

A33.14 **8.** The regulations may make provision for the application of any or all of sections 1, 6, 11 and 12(1) of the Road Traffic Offenders Act 1988 to an offence for which provision is made by the regulations.

Interpretation

9. References in this Schedule to a vehicle include references to any trailer drawn by the vehicle.   **A33.15**

10.—(1) This paragraph makes provision about the meaning of "authorised person" for the purposes of this Schedule.   **A33.16**

(2) Where the driving of the vehicle has been prohibited under section 99A(1) of the Transport Act 1968 (c.73), section 1(2) of the Road Traffic (Foreign Vehicles) Act 1972 (c.27) or section 69 of the Road Traffic Act 1988 (c.52), *"authorised person"* means—

(a) an examiner appointed by the Secretary of State under section 66A of the Road Traffic Act 1988, or

(b) a constable authorised by or on behalf of a chief officer of police to act for the purposes of the provision under which the driving of the vehicle has been prohibited.

(3) Where the driving of the vehicle has been prohibited under section 1(3) of the Road Traffic (Foreign Vehicles) Act 1972 (c.27), *"authorised person"* means a person authorised to exercise the powers of section 78 of the Road Traffic Act 1988 (c.52) with respect to the weighing of motor vehicles and trailers.

(4) Where the driving of the vehicle has been prohibited under section 70 of the Road Traffic Act 1988, *"authorised person"* means a person mentioned in sub-paragraph (2) or a person authorised with the consent of the Secretary of State to act for the purposes of subsection (1) of that section by—

(a) a highway authority other than the Secretary of State, or

(b) a local roads authority in Scotland.

(5) Where the driving of the vehicle has been prohibited under section 90D of the Road Traffic Offenders Act 1988 (c.53), *"authorised person"* means—

(a) an examiner appointed by the Secretary of State under section 66A of the Road Traffic Act 1988, or

(b) a constable.

11. In this Schedule—   **A33.17**

(a) references to an immobilisation device are to a device or appliance which is an immobilisation device for the purposes of section 104 of the Road Traffic Regulation Act 1984 (c.27) (immobilisation of vehicles illegally parked), and

(b) references to an immobilisation notice are to a notice fixed to a vehicle in accordance with the regulations.

12. In this Schedule *"prescribed"* means prescribed by the regulations.   **A33.18**

13.—(1) The regulations may make provision as to the meaning for the purposes of the regulations of "owner" as regards a vehicle.   **A33.19**

(2) In particular, the regulations may provide that for the purposes of the regulations the owner of a vehicle is taken to be the person in whose name it is then registered under the Vehicle Excise and Registration Act 1994 (c. 22).

Supplementary provisions about regulations

14. *[Omitted.]*   **A33.20**

*   *   *

Section B

Statutory Instruments

ALPHABETICAL LIST

Vehicle Drivers (Certificates of Professional Competence)
  Regulations 2007
  (SI 2005/1606)
  regs 1–5, 5A, 5B, 6, 6A, 7–8, 8A, 8B, 9–14   B64.01
Vehicle Excise Duty (Designation of Small Islands) Order 1995
  (SI 1995/1397)
  art.2, Schedule   B31.01
Vehicle Excise Duty (Immobilisation, Removal and Disposal of
  Vehicles) Regulations 1997
  (SI 1997/2439)
  regs 2–9, 11–13, 15–17   B38.01
Zebra, Pelican and Puffin Pedestrian Crossings Regulations and
  General Directions 1997
  (SI 1997/2400)
  regs 2–26, Schs 1–4, directions 2–10   B37.01

Scottish statutory instruments. References are not included in this work to
amendments to statutory instruments which have been effected by Scottish
statutory instruments.

The Drivers' Hours (Passenger Vehicles) (Exemptions) Regulations 1970

(SI 1970/145)

[The text of these regulations is printed as amended by: **B1.01**

    the Drivers' Hours (Passenger Vehicles) (Exemptions) (Amendment) Regulations 1970 (SI 1970/649) (May 12, 1970); and

    the Communications Act 2003 (Consequential Amendments) Order 2003 (SI 2003/2155) (September 17, 2003).

The amending instruments are referred to in the notes to the principal regulations only by their years and numbers. The dates referred to above are the dates on which the amending instruments came into force.]

Commencement and citation

1. *[Omitted.]* **B1.02**

Interpretation

2.—(1) In these Regulations, unless the context otherwise requires,— **B1.03**

    "the Act" means the Transport Act 1968,

    "emergency" means an event which—

        (a) causes or is likely to cause such—

            (i) danger to the life or health of one or more individuals, or

            (ii) a serious interruption in the maintenance of public services for the supply of water, gas, electricity or drainage or of [electronic communications] or postal services, or

            (iii) a serious interruption in the use of roads, or

            (iv) a serious interruption in private transport or in public transport (not being an interruption caused by a trade dispute (within the meaning of the Trade Disputes Act 1906) involving persons who carry passengers for hire or reward), or

        (b) is likely to cause such serious damage to property,

    as to necessitate the taking of immediate action to prevent the occurrence or continuance of such danger or interruption or the occurrence of such damage;

and any other expression which is also used in Part VI of the Act has the same meaning as in that Part of that Act.

(2) Any reference in these Regulations to an enactment or instrument shall be construed, unless the context otherwise requires, as a reference to that enactment or instrument as amended by any subsequent enactment or instrument.

(3) The [Interpretation Act 1978] shall apply for the interpretation of these Regulations as it applies for the interpretation of an Act of Parliament.

B1.04   *[Regulation 2 is printed as amended by SI 2003/2155.*

The Trade Disputes Act 1906 was repealed by the Industrial Relations Act 1971 s.169 and Sch.9; cf. now the Trade Union and Labour Relations (Consolidation) Act 1992 s.244(1).]

Exemptions from requirements as to drivers' hours

B1.05   3.—(1) Any driver of a passenger vehicle who spends time on duty to deal with an emergency is, in accordance with paragraphs (2) and (3) of this Regulation, hereby exempted from the requirements of subsections (1) to (6) of section 96 of the Act in respect of the time so spent.

(2) Any time so spent by such a driver for the purposes of—

    (a) subsection (1) of the said section 96 be deemed not to have been spent in driving vehicles to which Part VI of the Act applies, and

    (b) subsections (1) to (6) of the said section 96 (including the expression "working day" used therein)—

        (i) be deemed to have been spent by him off duty, and

        (ii) if it would apart from the emergency have been spent in taking an interval for rest or an interval for rest and refreshment be deemed to have been so spent by him.

(3) The requirements of subsection (6) of the said section 96 shall, in relation to such a driver, be deemed to be satisfied in respect of a working week in which he spends time on such duty if he is off duty for a period of twenty-four hours in accordance with that subsection less a period equal to the total time which he spends on such duty in that week.

B1.06   4. Any driver of a passenger vehicle who spends time on duty during a working day to meet a special need, that is to say work done solely in connection with the collection and delivery of blood for the purposes of transfusion, is hereby exempted from the requirements of section 96(3) in relation to that day, subject to the conditions that—

    (a) he is able to obtain rest and refreshment during that day for a period which is, or for periods which taken together are, not less than the time by which the working day exceeds ten hours,

    (b) that day does not exceed fourteen hours, and

    (c) he has not taken advantage of this exemption from the requirements of section 96(3) on more than one previous working day which forms part of the working week of which that day forms part.

B1.07   [5. Any driver of a passenger vehicle who spends time on duty during a working day to meet a special need, that is to say work done in connection with the carriage of persons suffering from physical or mental disability to or from any place at which social or recreational facilities for them are specially provided, is hereby exempted from the requirements of section 96(3) in relation to that day, subject to the conditions that—

    (a) he is able to obtain rest and refreshment during that day for a period which is, or for periods which taken together are, not less than the time by which the working day exceeds ten hours,

(b) that day does not exceed fourteen hours, and

(c) he has not taken advantage of this exemption from the requirements of section 96(3) on more than one previous working day which forms part of the working week of which that day forms part.]

[Regulation 5 was added by SI 1970/649.]   **B1.08**

The Drivers' Hours (Goods Vehicles) (Modifications) Order 1970

(SI 1970/257)

B2.01   *[The text of this order is printed as amended by:*

the Drivers' Hours (Passenger and Goods Vehicles) (Modifications) Order 1971 (SI 1971/818) (May 29, 1971); and

the Drivers' Hours (Goods Vehicles) (Modifications) Order 1986 (SI 1986/1459) (September 29, 1986).

The amending orders are referred to in the notes to the principal order by their years and numbers. The dates referred to above are the dates on which the orders came into force.]

Commencement and citation
B2.02   **1.** *[Omitted.]*

Interpretation

B2.03   **2.**—(1) In this Order, unless the context otherwise requires, *"the Act"* means the Transport Act 1968 and any other expression which is also used in Part VI of the Act has the same meaning as in that Part of the Act.

(2) Any reference in this Order to a numbered section is a reference to the section bearing that number in the Act except where otherwise expressly provided.

(3) Any reference in this Order to any enactment or instrument shall be construed, unless the context otherwise requires, as a reference to that enactment or instrument as amended by any subsequent enactment or instrument.

(4) The [Interpretation Act 1978] shall apply for the interpretation of this Order as it applies for the interpretation of an Act of Parliament.

B2.04   **3.** […]
[Revoked by SI 1986/1459.]

Exemptions for drivers engaged [in quarrying operations or] on building, construction and civil engineering work

B2.05   **4.** There shall be added to the exemption provided for by section 96(9) (which provides that for the purposes of subsections (1) and (7) of section 96 no account is to be taken of any time spent in driving a vehicle elsewhere than on a road if the vehicle is being so driven in the course of operations of agriculture or forestry) the following exemption, that is to say—

"For the purposes of subsections (1) and (7) of section 96 no account shall be taken of any time spent in driving a goods vehicle elsewhere than on a road if the vehicle is being so driven in the course of [operations of quarrying or of] carrying out any work in the construction, reconstruction, alteration, extension or maintenance of, or of a part of, a building, or of any other fixed works of construction or civil engineering (including works for the construction, improvement or maintenance of a road) and, for the purposes of this exemption, where the vehicle is being driven on, or on a part of, a road in the course of carrying out any work for the improvement or maintenance of, or of that part of, that road, it shall be treated as if it were being driven elsewhere than on a road."

[Article 4 is printed as amended by SI 1971/818.]   **B2.06**

The Functions of Traffic Wardens Order 1970

(SI 1970/1958)

*   *   *

B3.01   **2.** In this Order —

> *"[the Act of 1988]"* and *"[the Act of 1984]"* mean respectively [the Road Traffic Act 1988] and [the Road Traffic Regulation Act 1984] ;
>
> *"street parking place order"* means an order made under [the Act of 1984] relating to a street parking place;
>
> *"traffic order"* means an order made under [section 1, 6, 9, 12 or 37 of or Schedule 9 to the Act of 1984] .

B3.02   *[Article 2 is printed as amended by the Road Traffic Act 1972 s.205(2) and Sch.10, para.3; the Road Traffic Regulation Act 1984 s.144(1) and Sch.10, para.2.]*

B3.03   **3.**—(1) The functions set out in the Schedule to this Order are hereby prescribed as appropriate for discharge by traffic wardens.

(2) For the purposes of the discharge by traffic wardens of such functions, references to a constable or police constable in the following enactments shall include references to a traffic warden—

> (a) section 52 of the Metropolitan Police Act 1839 so far as it relates to the giving by the commissioner of directions to constables for preventing obstruction;
>
> (b) section 22 of the local Act of the second and third year of the reign of Queen Victoria, chapter 94, so far as it makes similar provision with respect to the City of London;
>
> (c) [sections 35 and 37 of the Act of 1988] (drivers and pedestrians to comply with traffic directions given by police constables);
>
> (d) [section 169 of the Act of 1988] (the power of constables to obtain the names and addresses of pedestrians failing to comply with traffic directions);
>
> (e) [section 11 of the Road Traffic Offenders Act 1988] (the giving of evidence of an admission by certificate).
>
> [(f) section 100(3) of the Road Traffic Regulation Act 1984 (the interim disposal of vehicles removed under section 99 of that Act);]
>
> [(g) sections 104 and 105 of the Road Traffic Regulation Act 1984 (the immobilisation of illegally parked vehicles);]
>
> [(h) section 67(3) of the Road Traffic Act 1988 (power to stop vehicles for testing);]
>
> [(i) section 163 of the Road Traffic Act 1988 (power to stop vehicles).]

(3) For the purposes of the discharge by traffic wardens of the functions set out in the Schedule to this Order, references in section [165(1) of the Act of 1988] to a police constable shall, in so far as it applies to the furnishing of names

and addresses, include references to a traffic warden if the traffic warden has reasonable cause to believe that there has been committed an offence—

(a) in respect of a vehicle by its being left or parked on a road during the hours of darkness (as defined by the [Act of 1988]) without the lights or reflectors required by law;

(b) in respect of a vehicle by its obstructing a road, or waiting, or being left or parked, or being loaded or unloaded, in a road;

(c) in contravention of [section 35 of the Act of 1988];

(d) in contravention of a provision of [the Vehicle Excise and Registration Act 1994];

(e) created by [section 47 of the Act of 1984] (offences relating to parking places on highways where charges made).

[(4) References in section 164(1), (2) and (6) of the Road Traffic Act of 1988 to a constable or police constable shall include references to a traffic warden only where—

(a) the traffic warden has reasonable cause to believe that there has been committed an offence by causing a vehicle, or any part of it, to stop in contravention of regulations made under section 25 of the Road Traffic Regulation Act 1984 or an offence in contravention of section 22 of the Road Traffic Act 1988 (leaving vehicles in dangerous positions); or

(b) the traffic warden is employed to perform functions in connection with the custody of vehicles removed from a road or land in the open air in pursuance of regulations made under section 99 of the Road Traffic Regulation Act 1984 or from a parking place in pursuance of a street parking place order, and he has reasonable cause to believe that there has been committed an offence in respect of a vehicle by its obstructing a road, or waiting, or being left or parked, or being loaded or unloaded, in a road.]

[Article 3 is printed as amended by the Vehicles (Excise) Act 1971 s.39(4) and **B3.04** *Sch.7, Pt II, para.11; the Road Traffic Act 1972 s.205(2) and Sch.10, para.3; the Road Traffic Regulation Act 1984 s.144(1) and Sch.10, para.2; the Functions of Traffic Wardens (Amendment) Order 1993 (SI 1993/1334); the Vehicle Excise and Registration Act 1994 s.64 and Sch.4, para.4; the Functions of Traffic Wardens (Amendment) Order 2002 (SI 2002/2975) art.2.*

The definition of "hours of darkness" (to which reference is made in art.3(3)(a) above) had been included in earlier legislation and was re-enacted in the Road Traffic Act 1972 s.82. The definition was repealed, however, by the Road Traffic Act 1974. The term is now defined in the Road Vehicles Lighting Regulations 1989 (SI 1989/1796) reg.3(2) (q.v.).]

Article 3   SCHEDULE

FUNCTIONS OF TRAFFIC WARDENS

1.—(1) Traffic wardens may be employed to enforce the law with respect to an of- **B3.05** fence—

(a) committed in respect of a vehicle by its being left or parked on a road during the hours of darkness (as defined by [the Act of 1988]) without the lights or reflectors required by law; or

(b) committed in respect of a vehicle by its obstructing a road, or waiting, or being left or parked, or being loaded or unloaded, in a road or other public place; or

(c) committed in contravention of a provision of [the Vehicle Excise and Registration Act 1994];

(d) created by [section 47 of the Act of 1984] (offences relating to parking places on highways where charges made).

[(e) committed by causing a vehicle, or any part of it, to stop in contravention of regulations made under section 25 of the Road Traffic Regulation Act 1984,]

[(2) For the purposes of the enforcement of the law with respect to such of the offences described in sub-paragraph (1) of this paragraph as are fixed penalty offences within the meaning of [section 51(1) of the Road Traffic Offenders Act 1988], ... traffic wardens may exercise the functions conferred on constables by [Part III of the Road Traffic Offenders Act 1988].]

B3.06   **2.**—(1) Traffic wardens may, under arrangements made with the Secretary of State or a local authority, be employed to act as parking attendants at street parking places provided or controlled by the Secretary of State or local authority.

(2) A traffic warden may exercise functions conferred on a traffic warden by a traffic order or a street parking place order.

B3.07   **3.** Without prejudice to the generality of paragraph 1 above, traffic wardens may be employed in connection with obtaining information under [section 172 of the Act of 1988] or [section 112 of the Act of 1984] (duty to give information as to identity of driver, etc., in certain cases).

B3.08   **4.** Traffic wardens may be employed to perform functions in connection with the custody of vehicles removed from a road or land in the open air in pursuance of regulations under [section 99 of the Act of 1984] or from a parking place in pursuance of a street parking place order.

B3.09   **5.** Where a police authority provides school crossing patrols under [section 26 of the Act of 1984], whether as the appropriate authority or by agreement with the appropriate authority, traffic wardens appointed by that police authority may be employed to act as school crossing patrols.

B3.10   [**5A.** Traffic wardens may be employed to stop vehicles for the purposes of a test under subsection (1) of section 67 of the Road Traffic Act 1988 (testing of conditions of vehicles on roads).]

B3.11   [**5B.** Traffic wardens may be employed to escort vehicles or trailers carrying loads of exceptional dimensions the use of which is authorised by an order made by the Secretary of State under section 44(1)(d) of the Road Traffic Act 1988.]

B3.12   **6.**—(1) Subject to the foregoing paragraphs, traffic wardens may be employed in the control and regulation of traffic (including foot passengers) or vehicles whether on a highway or not and to discharge any other functions normally undertaken by the police in connection with the control and regulation of traffic (including foot passengers) or vehicles.

(2) [...]

B3.13   *[The Schedule is printed as amended by the Vehicles (Excise) Act 1971 s.39(4) and Sch.7, Pt II, para.11; the Road Traffic Act 1972 s.205(2) and Sch.10, para.3; the Road Traffic Regulation Act 1984 s.144(1) and Sch.10, para.2; the Functions of Traffic Wardens (Amendment) Order 1986 (SI 1986/1328); the Functions of Traffic Wardens (Amendment) Order 1993 (SI 1993/1334); the Vehicle Excise and Registration Act 1994 s.64 and Sch.4, para.4; the Functions of Traffic Wardens (Amendment) Order 2002 (SI 2002/2975) art.3.*

As to the definition of "hours of darkness" (to which reference is made in para.1(1)(a) above), see the note to art.3 of this order.]

The Vehicle and Driving Licences Records (Evidence) Regulations 1970

(SI 1970/1997)

* * *

Matters prescribed for [section 13(5) of the Road Traffic Offenders Act 1988]

3. The following matters are prescribed for the purposes of [section 13(5) of the Road Traffic Offenders Act 1988] — **B4.01**

(1) in connection with the licensing of drivers under [Part III of the Road Traffic Act 1988] —

    (a) a document being, forming part of, or submitted in connection with, an application for a driving licence;

    (b) a driving licence;

    (c) a certificate of competence to drive;

    (d) the conviction of an offence specified in [Part I of Schedule 2 to the Road Traffic Offenders Act 1988 or the offence of manslaughter (or culpable homicide) specified in Part II of that Schedule] of any person or any order made by the Court as a result of any such conviction;

(2) [...]

(3) in connection with the examination of a goods vehicle under regulations under [section 49 of the Road Traffic Act 1988] —

    (a) an application for an examination of a vehicle under the said regulations;

    (b) a notifiable alteration made to a vehicle and required by the said regulations to be notified to the [Secretary of State for Transport];

    (c) a plating certificate, goods vehicle test certificate, notification of the refusal of a goods vehicle test certificate, Ministry plate, Ministry test date disc or certificate of temporary exemption.

[Regulation 3 is printed as amended by the Vehicles (Excise) Act 1971 Sch.7, **B4.02**
para.11; the Road Traffic Act 1972 Sch.10, para.3; the Minister of Transport Order 1979 (SI 1979/571); the Transfer of Functions (Transport) Order 1981 (SI 1981/238); the Vehicle Excise and Registration Act 1994 s.64 and Sch.4, para.4; the Secretary of State for the Environment, Transport and the Regions Order 1997 (SI 1997/2971); the Secretaries of State for Transport, Local Government and the Regions and for Environment, Food and Rural Affairs Order 2001 (SI 2001/2568); the Transfer of Functions (Transport, Local Government and the Regions) Order 2002 (SI 2002/2626); the Road Vehicles (Registration and Licensing) Regulations 2002 (SI 2002/2742) Sch.1 Pt II.

For the regulations under s. 49 of the Road Traffic Act 1988, see the Goods Vehicles (Plating and Testing) Regulations 1988 (SI 1988/1478) below.]

The Drivers' Hours (Passenger and Goods Vehicles) (Modifications) Order 1971

(SI 1971/818)

B5.01 *[The text of s.96 of the Transport Act 1968 as modified by this order is set out as an appendix to this order.]*

PART I

GENERAL

*   *   *

B5.02 2.—(1) In this Order, *"the Act"* means the Transport Act 1968 and any other expression which is also used in Part VI of the Act has the same meaning as in that Part.

(2) The [Interpretation Act 1978] shall apply for the interpretation of this Order as it applies for the interpretation of an Act of Parliament, and as if for the purposes of [sections 16(1) and 17(2)(a)] of that Act this Order were an Act of Parliament and the Order revoked by Article 3 below were an Act of Parliament thereby repealed.

B5.03 *[Article 2 is printed as amended by the Interpretation Act 1978 s.17(2)(a).]*

PART II

DRIVERS OF PASSENGER VEHICLES

B5.04 3. *[Revokes SI 1970/356.]*

B5.05 4.—(1) Where during any working day, or during each working day which falls wholly or partly within any working week, a driver spends all or the greater part of the time when he is driving vehicles to which Part VI of the Act applies in driving one or more passenger vehicles, then, as respects that driver and that working day or working week (as the case may be), the provisions of section 96 of the Act (permitted driving time and periods of duty of drivers of certain vehicles) and of section 103 thereof (interpretation of Part VI of the Act) mentioned in paragraphs (2) to (8) below shall have effect with the modifications or amendments respectively specified in those paragraphs.

(2) Section 96(2) (interval for rest between periods of duty) shall have effect as if for the words from "if on any working day" onwards there were substituted the following words:—

"if on any working day a driver has been driving a vehicle or vehicles to which this Part of this Act applies—

(a) for a period of five and a half hours and the end of that period does not mark the end of the working day; or

(b) for periods amounting in the aggregate to five and a half hours and there has not been between any of those periods an interval

2/888

of not less than half an hour in which the driver was able to obtain rest and refreshment and the end of the last of those periods does not mark the end of the working day,

there shall, as respects the period mentioned in paragraph (a) above, at the end of that period or, in the case of the periods mentioned in paragraph (b) above, at the end of the last of those periods, be such an interval as aforesaid; but the requirements of the foregoing provisions of this subsection need not be satisfied in relation to a driver who, within any continuous period of eight and a half hours in the working day, drives for periods amounting in the aggregate to not more than seven and three-quarter hours, being periods of driving between which there is a period of, or there are periods amounting in the aggregate to, not less than forty-five minutes driving which the driver has not been driving, if—

(i) the end of the last of those periods of driving marks the end of the working day, or

(ii) at the end of the last of those periods, there is such an interval as is mentioned in paragraph (b) above."

(3) Section 96(3) (the working day of a driver) shall have effect as if for paragraph (c) there were substituted the following paragraph: —

"(c) if during that day all or the greater part of the time when he is driving vehicles to which this Part of this Act applies is spent in driving one or more passenger vehicles, shall not exceed sixteen hours."

(4) Section 96(4) (interval for rest between working days) shall have effect as if for paragraphs (a) and (b) there were substituted the words "shall not be of less than ten hours except that on not more than three occasions in any working week the said interval may be of less than ten hours but not of less than eight and a half hours;".

(5) Section 96(5) and (8)(b) (maximum duty periods in a working week) shall not apply.

(6) Section 96(6) (off-duty periods in a working week) shall have effect as if for the words from "in the case of each working week of a driver" onwards there were substituted the following words:—

"in the case of every two successive working weeks of a driver, a period of not less than twenty-four hours for which he is off duty, being a period either falling wholly in those weeks or beginning in the second of those weeks and ending in the first of the next two successive weeks; but where the requirements of the foregoing provisions of this subsection have been satisfied in the case of any two successive working weeks by reference to a period ending in the first of the next two successive weeks, no part of that period (except any part after the expiration of the first twenty-four hours of it) shall be taken into account for the purpose of satisfying those requirements in the case of the said next two successive weeks."

(7) For section 96(7) there shall be substituted the following subsections:—

"(7) If in the case of the working week of any driver the following requirements are satisfied, that is to say, that—

(a) the driver does not drive any vehicle to which this Part of this Act applies for a period of, or for periods amounting in the aggregate to, more than four hours in more than two of the periods of twenty-four hours beginning at midnight which make up that working week (any such period of twenty-four hours in which the driver does drive for a period of, or for periods amounting in the aggregate to, more than four hours being in this subsection, and in subsection (7B) below, referred to as '*a full time day*'); and

    (b) the provisions of subsection (7B) of this section are complied with in relation to him as respects each full time day in that week,

then, subject to subsection (7A) of this section, the provisions of subsections (1) to (4) of this section shall not apply to that driver in that week, and where the said requirements are satisfied in the case of two successive working weeks of that driver the provisions of subsection (6) of this section shall not apply to him as respects those working weeks.

(7A) Where in the case of the working week of a driver the requirements mentioned in subsection (7) above are satisfied but there is a working day of the driver which falls partly in that working week and partly in a working week in the case of which the said requirements are not satisfied, then the provisions of subsections (1), (2) and (3) of this section shall nevertheless have effect in relation to the whole of that working day.

(7B) The following provisions shall apply as respects each full time day in a working week of a driver in the case of which the requirement mentioned in subsection (7)(a) above is satisfied, that is to say—

    (a) each period of duty of that driver shall fall wholly within the full time day;

    (b) there shall be an interval for rest of not less than ten hours immediately before his first period of duty and immediately after his last period of duty in the full time day or, if there is only one such period of duty therein, immediately before and after that period of duty;

    (c) the driver shall not in the full time day drive a vehicle or vehicles to which this Part of this Act applies for periods amounting in the aggregate to more than ten hours;

    (d) if in the full time day the driver has been driving a vehicle or vehicles to which this Part of this Act applies—

        (i) for a period of five and a half hours and the end of that period of driving does not mark the end of his period of duty, or of the last of his periods of duty, in that day, or

       (ii) for periods amounting in the aggregate to five and a half hours and there has not been between any of those periods of driving an interval of not less than half an hour in which the driver was able to obtain rest and refreshment and the end of the last of those periods of driving does not mark the end of his period of duty, or of the last of his periods of duty, in that day,

          there shall be such an interval as aforesaid at the end of the period of driving mentioned in sub-paragraph (i) above or of the last of the periods of driving mentioned in sub-paragraph (ii) above: provided however that the foregoing requirements of this paragraph need not be satisfied in relation to a driver who, within any continuous period of eight and a half hours falling wholly within the full time day, drives for periods amounting in the aggregate to not more than seven and three-quarter hours, being periods of driving between which there is a period of, or there are periods amounting in the aggregate to, not less than forty-five minutes during which the driver has not been driving, if the end of the last of those periods of driving marks the end of his period, or of the last of his periods, of duty in that day, or at the end of the last of those periods of driving there is such an interval as is mentioned in sub-paragraph (ii) above; and

(e) the period during which the driver is on duty in the full time day or, if there is more than one such period, the period between the beginning of his first period of duty in that day and the end of his last period of duty therein, shall not exceed 16 hours.

(8) The definition of *'working day'* in section 103 shall have effect for the purposes of subsections (1) to (4) and (6) to (8) of section 96 as if for the words from 'eleven hours' to the words 'nine and a half hours' there were substituted the words 'ten hours or (where permitted by virtue of section 96(4) of this Act) of not less than eight and a half hours'."

PART III

DRIVERS OF GOODS VEHICLES

5. *[Amends the Drivers' Hours (Goods Vehicles) (Modification) Order 1970* **B5.06**
(SI 1970/257) (q.v.).]

APPENDIX (TRANSPORT ACT 1968, S.96, AS APPLIED TO DRIVERS OF
PASSENGER VEHICLES)

Permitted driving time and periods of duty

96.—(1) Subject to the provisions of this section, a driver shall not on any working day   **B5.07**
drive a vehicle or vehicles to which this Part of this Act applies for periods amounting in
the aggregate to more than ten hours.

(2) Subject to the provisions of this section, if on any working day a driver has been
driving a vehicle or vehicles to which this Part of this Act applies—

(a) for a period of five and a half hours and the end of that period does not mark the
end of the working day; or

(b) for periods amounting in the aggregate to five and a half hours and there has not
been between any of those periods an interval of not less than half an hour in
which the driver was able to obtain rest and refreshment and the end of the last of
those periods does not mark the end of the working day,

there shall, as respects the period mentioned in paragraph (a) above, at the end of that period or, in the case of the periods mentioned in paragraph (b) above, at the end of the last
of those periods, be such an interval as aforesaid; but the requirements of the foregoing

provisions of this subsection need not be satisfied in relation to a driver who, within any continuous period of eight and a half hours in the working day, drives for periods amounting in the aggregate to not more than seven and three-quarter hours, being periods of driving between which there is a period of, or there are periods amounting in the aggregate to, not less than forty-five minutes during which the driver has not been driving, if—

 (i) the end of the last of those periods of driving marks the end of the working day, or

 (ii) at the end of the last of those periods there is such an interval as is mentioned in paragraph (b) above.

 (3) Subject to the provisions of this section, the working day of a driver—

 (a) except where paragraph (b) or (c) of this subsection applies, shall not exceed eleven hours;

 (b) if during that day he is off duty for a period which is, or periods which taken together are, not less than the time by which his working day exceeds eleven hours, shall not exceed twelve and a half hours;

 (c) if during that day all or the greater part of the time when he is driving vehicles to which this Part of this Act applies is spent in driving one or more passenger vehicles, shall not exceed sixteen hours.

 (4) Subject to the provisions of this section, there shall be, between any two successive working days of a driver, an interval for rest which shall not be of less than ten hours except that on not more than three occasions in any working week the said interval may be of less than ten hours but not of less than eight and a half hours, and for the purposes of this Part of this Act a period of time shall not be treated, in the case of an employee-driver, as not being an interval for rest by reason only that he may be called upon to report for duty if required.

 (5) *[Inapplicable.]*

 (6) Subject to the provisions of this section, there shall be, in the case of every two successive working weeks of a driver, a period of not less than twenty-four hours for which he is off duty, being a period either falling wholly in those weeks or beginning in the second of those weeks and ending in the first of the next two successive weeks; but where the requirements of the foregoing provisions of this subsection have been satisfied in the case of any two successive working weeks by reference to a period ending in the first of the next two successive weeks, no part of that period (except any part after the expiration of the first twenty-four hours of it) shall be taken into account for the purpose of satisfying those requirements in the case of the said next two successive weeks.

 (7) If in the case of the working week of any driver the following requirements are satisfied, that is to say, that—

 (a) the driver does not drive any vehicle to which this Part of this Act applies for a period of, or for periods amounting in the aggregate to, more than four hours in more than two of the periods of twenty-four hours beginning at midnight which make up that working week (any such period of twenty-four hours in which the driver does drive for a period of, or for periods amounting in the aggregate to, more than four hours being in this subsection, and in subsection (7B) below, referred to as "*a full time day*"); and

 (b) the provisions of subsection (7B) of this section are complied with in relation to him as respects each full time day in that week,

then, subject to subsection (7A) of this section, the provisions of subsections (1) to (4) of this section shall not apply to that driver in that week, and where the said requirements are satisfied in the case of two successive working weeks of that driver the provisions of subsection (6) of this section shall not apply to him as respects those working weeks.

 (7A) Where in the case of the working week of a driver the requirements mentioned in subsection (7) above are satisfied but there is a working day of the driver which falls partly in that working week and partly in a working week in the case of which the said requirements are not satisfied, then the provisions of subsections (1), (2) and (3) of this section shall nevertheless have effect in relation to the whole of that working day.

(7B) The following provisions shall apply as respects each full time day in a working week of a driver in the case of which the requirement mentioned in subsection (7)(a) above is satisfied, that is to say—

(a) each period of duty of that driver shall fall wholly within the full time day;

(b) there shall be an interval for rest of not less than ten hours immediately before his first period of duty and immediately after his last period of duty in the full time day or, if there is only one such period of duty therein, immediately before and after that period of duty;

(c) the driver shall not in the full time day drive a vehicle or vehicles to which this Part of this Act applies for periods amounting in the aggregate to more than ten hours;

(d) if in the full time day the driver has been driving a vehicle or vehicles to which this Part of this Act applies—

    (i) for a period of five and a half hours and the end of that period of driving does not mark the end of his period of duty, or of the last of his periods of duty, in that day, or

    (ii) for periods amounting in the aggregate to five and a half hours and there has not been between any of those periods of driving an interval of not less than half an hour in which the driver was able to obtain rest and refreshment and the end of the last of those periods of driving does not mark the end of his period of duty, or of the last of his periods of duty, in that day,

there shall be such an interval as aforesaid at the end of the period of driving mentioned in sub-paragraph (i) above or of the last of the periods of driving mentioned in sub-paragraph (ii) above: provided however that the foregoing requirements of this paragraph need not be satisfied in relation to a driver who, within any continuous period of eight and a half hours falling wholly within the full time day, drives for periods amounting in the aggregate to not more than seven and three-quarter hours, being periods of driving between which there is a period of, or there are periods amounting in the aggregate to, not less than forty-five minutes during which the driver has not been driving, if the end of the last of those periods of driving marks the end of his period, or of the last of his periods, of duty in that day, or at the end of the last of those periods of driving there is such an interval as is mentioned in sub-paragraph (ii) above; and

(e) the period during which the driver is on duty in the full time day or, if there is more than one such period, the period between the beginning of his first period of duty in that day and the end of his last period of duty therein, shall not exceed sixteen hours.

(8) If on any working day a driver does not drive any vehicle to which this Part of this Act applies—

(a) subsections (2) and (3) of this section shall not apply to that day, and

(b) *[inapplicable.]*

(9) For the purposes of subsections (1) and (7) of this section no account shall be taken of any time spent driving a vehicle elsewhere than on a road if the vehicle is being so driven in the course of operations of agriculture or forestry.

(10) For the purposes of enabling drivers to deal with cases of emergency or otherwise to meet a special need, the [Secretary of State for Transport] may by regulations—

(a) create exemptions from all or any of the requirements of subsections (1) to (6) of this section in such cases and subject to such conditions as may be specified in the regulations;

(b) empower the traffic commissioner for any area, subject to the provisions of the regulations—

    (i) to dispense with the observance of all or any of those requirements (either generally or in such circumstances or to such extent as the commissioner thinks fit) in any particular case for which provision is not made under paragraph (a) of this subsection;

    (ii) to grant a certificate (which, for the purposes of any proceedings under this Part of this Act, shall be conclusive evidence of the facts therein stated) that any particular case falls or fell within any exemption created under the said paragraph (a)

and regulations under this subsection may enable any dispensation under paragraph (b)(i) of this subsection to be granted retrospectively and provide for a document purporting to be a certificate granted by virtue of paragraph (b)(ii) of this subsection to be accepted in evidence without further proof.

(11) If any of the requirements of the domestic drivers' hours code is contravened in the case of any driver—

    (a) that driver; and

    (b) any other person (being that driver's employer or a person to whose orders that driver was subject) who caused or permitted the contravention,

shall be liable on summary conviction to a fine not exceeding level 4 on the standard scale; but a person shall not be liable to be convicted under this subsection if he proves to the court—

    (i) that the contravention was due to unavoidable delay in the completion of a journey arising out of circumstances which he could not reasonably have foreseen; or

    (ii) in the case of a person charged under paragraph (b) of this subsection, that the contravention was due to the fact that the driver had for any particular period or periods driven or been on duty otherwise than in the employment of that person or, as the case may be, otherwise than in the employment in which he is subject to the orders of that person, and that the person charged was not, and could not reasonably have become, aware of that fact.

(11A) Where, in the case of a driver of a motor vehicle, there is in Great Britain a contravention of any requirement of the applicable Community rules as to period of driving, or distance driven, or periods on or off duty, then the offender and any other person (being the offender's employer or a person to whose orders the offender was subject) who caused or permitted the contravention shall be liable on summary conviction to a fine not exceeding level 4 on the standard scale.

(11B) But a person shall not be liable to be convicted under subsection (11A) if—

    (a) he proves the matters specified in paragraph (i) of subsection (11); or

    (b) being charged as the offender's employer or a person to whose orders the offender was subject, he proves the matters specified in paragraph (ii) of that subsection.

(12) The [Secretary of State for Transport] may by order—

    (a) direct that subsection (1) of this section shall have effect with the substitution for the reference to ten hours of a reference to nine hours, either generally or with such exceptions as may be specified in the order;

    (b) direct that paragraph (a) of subsection (3) of this section shall have effect with the substitution for the reference to eleven hours of a reference to any shorter period, or remove, modify or add to the provisions of that subsection containing exceptions to the said paragraph (a);

    (c) remove, modify or add to any of the requirements of subsections (2), (4), (5) or (6) of this section or any of the exemptions provided for by subsections (7), (8) and (9) thereof;

and any order under this subsection may contain such transitional and supplementary provisions as the [Secretary of State for Transport] thinks necessary or expedient, including provisions amending any definition in section 103 of this Act which is relevant to any of the provisions affected by the order.

(13) In this Part of this Act *"the domestic drivers' hours code"* means the provisions of subsections (1) to (6) of this section as for the time being in force (and, in particular, as modified, added to or substituted by or under any instrument in force under section 95(1) of this Act or subsection (10) or (12) of this section) .

B5.08

[This version of the Transport Act 1968 s.96, is the text of s.96 as modified by the Drivers' Hours (Passenger and Goods Vehicles) (Modifications) Order 1971 (SI 1971/818) above.

This version of s.96 is printed as further amended by the Secretary of State for the Environment Order 1970 (SI 1970/1681); the European Communities Act 1972 s.4, and Sch.4, para.9(2); the Road Traffic (Drivers' Ages and Hours of Work) Act 1976 s.2(1); the Secretary of State for Transport Order 1976 (SI 1976/1775); the Transport Act 1978 s.10; the Minister of Transport Order 1979 (SI 1979/571); the Transfer of Functions (Transport) Order 1981 (SI 1981/238); the Criminal Justice Act 1982 ss.38 and 46(1); the Transport Act 1985 s.3 and Sch.2, Pt II, para.1(2); the Community Drivers' Hours and Recording Equipment Regulations 1986 (SI 1986/1457) reg.2; the Secretary of State for the Environment, Transport and the Regions Order 1997 (SI 1997/2971); the Secretaries of State for Transport, Local Government and the Regions and for Environment, Food and Rural Affairs Order 2001 (SI 2001/2568); the Transfer of Functions (Transport, Local Government and the Regions) Order 2002 (SI 2002/2626).]

The Motor Vehicles (Third Party Risks) Regulations 1972

(SI 1972/1217)

B6.01   *[The text of these regulations is printed as amended by:*

> *the Motor Vehicles (Third Party Risks) (Amendment) Regulations 1973 (SI 1973/1821) (January 1, 1974);*
>
> *the Motor Vehicles (Third Party Risks) (Amendment) Regulations 1974 (SI 1974/792) (May 27, 1974);*
>
> *the Motor Vehicles (Third Party Risks) (Amendment) (No.2) Regulations 1974 (SI 1974/2187) (January 31, 1975);*
>
> *the Motor Vehicles (Third Party Risks) (Amendment) Regulations 1981 (SI 1981/1567) (December 1, 1981);*
>
> *the Motor Vehicles (Third Party Risks) (Amendment) Regulations 1992 (SI 1992/1283) (July 1, 1992);*
>
> *the Motor Vehicles (Third Party Risks) (Amendment) Regulations 1997 (SI 1997/97) (February 21, 1997);*
>
> *the Motor Vehicles (Third Party Risks) (Amendment) Regulations 2001 (SI 2001/2266) (July 16, 2001); and*
>
> *the Motor Vehicles (Electronic Communication of Certificates of Insurance) Order 2010 (SI 2010/1117) (April 30, 2010).*

The amending instruments are referred to in the notes to the principal regulations only by their years and numbers. The dates referred to above are the dates on which the amending instruments came into force.

The principal regulations have also been amended by the Motor Vehicles (Third Party Risks) (Amendment) Regulations 1999 (SI 1999/2392), the Motor Vehicles (Third Party Risks) (Amendment) Regulations 2010 (SI 2010/1115), but these regulations do not affect the text of any provision which is printed in this work.]

Commencement and citation

B6.02   **1., 2.** *[Omitted.]*

Temporary use of existing forms

B6.03   **3.** *[Omitted.]*

Interpretation

B6.04   **4.**—(1) In these Regulations, unless the context otherwise requires, the following expressions have the meanings hereby respectively assigned to them:—

> *"the Act"* means [the Road Traffic Act 1988] ;
>
> [*"a certificate delivered by electronic means"* means a certificate delivered

as described in section 147(1A)(a) or (b) of the Road Traffic Act 1988;]

"*company*" means an authorised insurer within the meaning of [Part VI] of the Act or a body of persons by whom a security may be given in pursuance of the said [Part VI] ;

["*Motor Insurers' Bureau*" means the company referred to in section 145(5) of the Road Traffic Act 1988;]

"*motor vehicle*" has the meaning assigned to it by [sections 185, 186, 188 and 189] of the Act, but excludes any invalid carriage, tramcar or trolley vehicle to which [Part VI] of the Act does not apply;

"*policy*" means a policy of insurance in respect of third party risks arising out of the use of motor vehicles which complies with the requirements of [Part VI] of the Act and includes a covering note;

"*security*" means a security in respect of third party risks arising out of the use of motor vehicles which complies with the requirements of [Part VI] of the Act;

"*specified body*" means—

    (a) any of the local authorities referred to in [paragraph (a) of section 144(2)] of the Act; or

    (b) a Passenger Transport Executive established under an order made under section 9 of the Transport Act 1968, or a subsidiary of that Executive, being an Executive or subsidiary to whose vehicles [section 144(2)(a)] of the Act has been applied; or

    (c) *[lapsed.]*

(2) Any reference in these Regulations to a certificate in Form A, B, C, D, E or F shall be construed as a reference to a certificate in the form so headed and set out in Part 1 of the Schedule to these Regulations which has been duly made and completed subject to and in accordance with the provisions set out in Part 2 of the said Schedule.

(3) Any reference in these Regulations to any enactment shall be construed as a reference to that enactment as amended by any subsequent enactment.

(4) The Interpretation Act [1978] shall apply for the interpretation of these Regulations as it applies for the interpretation of an Act of Parliament, and as if for the purposes of [sections 16(1) and 17(2)(a)] of that Act these Regulations were an Act of Parliament and the Regulations revoked by Regulation 2 of these Regulations were Acts of Parliament thereby repealed.

[(5) Any reference in these Regulations to the issue of a certificate of insurance shall be construed, in the case of a certificate delivered by electronic means, as a reference—

    (a) in the case of a certificate transmitted as described in section 147(1A)(a) of the Road Traffic Act 1988, to its transmission in accordance with section 147(1B) of that Act;

    (b) in the case of a certificate made available as described in section 147(1A)(b) of that Act, to its being made available in accordance with section 147(1C) of that Act.]

[Regulation 4 is printed as amended by the Interpretation Act 1978 s.17(2)(a);   **B6.05**
SI 2001/2266; SI 2010/1117.]

Issue of certificates of insurance or security

B6.06   5.—(1) A company shall issue to every holder of a security or of a policy other than a covering note issued by the company:—

(a) in the case of a policy or security relating to one or more specified vehicles a certificate of insurance in Form A or a certificate of security in Form D in respect of each such vehicle;

(b) in the case of a policy or security relating to vehicles other than specified vehicles such number of certificates in Form B or Form D as may be necessary for the purpose of complying with the requirements of [section 165(1) and (2)] of the Act and of these Regulations as to the production of evidence that a motor vehicle is not being driven in contravention of [section 143] of the Act:

Provided that where a security is intended to cover the use of more than ten motor vehicles at one time the company by whom it was issued may issue one certificate only and the holder of the security may issue duplicate copies of such certificate duly authenticated by him.]

(2) Notwithstanding the foregoing provisions of this Regulation, where as respects third party risks a policy or security relating to a specified vehicle extends also to the driving by the holder of other motor vehicles, not being specified vehicles, the certificate may be in Form A or Form D, as the case may be, containing a statement in either case that the policy or security extends to such driving of other motor vehicles. Where such a certificate is issued by a company they may, and shall in accordance with a demand made to them by the holder, issue to him a further such certificate or a certificate in Form B.

(3) Every policy in the form of a covering note issued by a company shall [contain] a certificate of insurance in Form C.

B6.07   *[Regulation 5 is printed as amended by the Interpretation Act 1978 s.17(2)(a) (cf. reg.4(4) above); SI 1997/97; SI 2010/1117.]*

B6.08   6. Every certificate of insurance or certificate of security shall be issued not later than four days after the date on which the policy or security to which it relates is issued or renewed.

Production of evidence as alternatives to certificates

B6.09   7. The following evidence that a motor vehicle is not or was not being driven in contravention of [section 143] of the Act may be produced in pursuance of [section 165] of the Act as an alternative to the production of a certificate of insurance or a certificate of security:—

(1) a duplicate copy of a certificate of security issued in accordance with the proviso to sub-paragraph (b) of paragraph (1) of Regulation 5 of these Regulations;

(2) in the case of a motor vehicle of which the owner has for the time being deposited with the Accountant-General of the Supreme Court [the sum for the time being specified in section 144(1) of the Road Traffic Act 1988], a certificate in Form E signed by the owner of the motor vehicle or by some person authorised by him in that behalf that such sum is on deposit;

(3) in the case of a motor vehicle owned by a specified body, a police author-

ity or the Receiver for the metropolitan police district, a certificate in Form F signed by some person authorised in that behalf by such specified body, police authority or Receiver as the case may be that the said motor vehicle is owned by the said specified body, police authority or Receiver.

[(4) in the case of a vehicle normally based [in the territory other than the United Kingdom and Gibraltar of a member state of the Communities or of [Austria, Czechoslovakia, Finland, the German Democratic Republic, Hungary, Norway, Sweden or Switzerland]] a document issued by the insurer of the vehicle which indicates the name of the insurer, the number or other identifying particulars of the insurance policy issued in respect of the vehicle and the period of the insurance cover. In this paragraph the territory of the state in which a vehicle is normally based is

(a) the territory of the state in which the vehicle is registered, or

(b) in cases where no registration is required for the type of vehicle, but the vehicle bears an insurance plate or distinguishing sign analogous to a registration plate, the territory of the state in which the insurance plate or the sign is issued, or

(c) in cases where neither registration plate nor insurance plate nor distinguishing sign is required for the type of vehicle, the territory of the state in which the keeper of the vehicle is permanently resident.]

[Regulation 7 is printed as amended by SI 1973/1821; SI 1974/792; SI 1974/ 2187; the Interpretation Act 1978 s.17(2)(a) (cf. reg.4(4) above); SI 1992/1283.   **B6.10**

The German Democratic Republic has been incorporated into the Federal Republic of Germany and is (in effect) a member of the European Union. Austria, Finland and Sweden formally acceded to the European Union on January 1, 1995. The Czech Republic and the Slovak Republic (formerly Czechoslovakia) and Hungary acceded to the European Union on May 1, 2004. Romania and Bulgaria acceded to the European Union on January 1, 2007.]

8. Any certificate issued in accordance with paragraph (2) or (3) of the preceding Regulation shall be destroyed by the owner of the vehicle to which it relates before the motor vehicle is sold or otherwise disposed of.   **B6.11**

*   *   *

Return of certificates to issuing company

12.—(1) [Except in the case of a certificate of insurance delivered by electronic means, the following provisions shall apply] in relation to the transfer of a policy or security with the consent of the holder to any other person:—   **B6.12**

(a) the holder shall, before the policy or security is transferred, return any relative certificates issued for the purposes of these Regulations to the company by whom they were issued; and

(b) the policy or security shall not be transferred to any other person unless and until the certificates have been so returned or the company are satisfied that the certificates have been lost or destroyed.

(2) [Except in the case of a certificate of insurance delivered by electronic means, in any case where] with the consent of the person to whom it was issued a policy or security is suspended or ceases to be effective, otherwise than by effluxion of time, in circumstances in which the provisions of [section 147(4)] of the Act (relating to the surrender of certificates) do not apply, the holder of the policy

or security shall within seven days from the date when it is suspended or ceases to be effective return any relative certificates issued for the purposes of these Regulations to the company by whom they were issued and the company shall not issue a new policy or security to the said holder in respect of the motor vehicle or vehicles to which the said first mentioned policy or security related unless and until the certificates have been returned to the company or the company are satisfied that they have been lost or destroyed.

(3) Where a policy or security is cancelled by mutual consent or by virtue of any provision in the policy or security, any statutory declaration that a certificate has been lost or destroyed made in pursuance of [section 147(4)] (which requires any such declaration to be made within a period of seven days from the taking effect of the cancellation) shall be delivered forthwith after it has been made to the company by whom the policy was issued or the security given.

(4) The provisions of the last preceding paragraph shall be without prejudice to the provisions of [paragraph (c) of subsection (1) of section 152] of the Act as to the effect for the purposes of that subsection of the making of a statutory declaration within the periods therein stated.

B6.13   *[Regulation 12 is printed as amended by the Interpretation Act 1978 s.17(2)(a) (cf. reg.4(4) above); SI 2010/1117.]*

Issue of fresh certificates

B6.14   **13.** Where any company by whom a certificate of insurance [(other than a certificate of insurance delivered by electronic means)] or a certificate of security has been issued are satisfied that the certificate has become defaced or has been lost or destroyed they shall, if they are requested to do so by the person to whom the certificate was issued, issue to him a fresh certificate. In the case of a defaced certificate the company shall not issue a fresh certificate unless the defaced certificate is returned to the company.

B6.15   *[Regulation 13 is printed as amended by SI 2010/1117.]*

THE SCHEDULE

PART 1

FORMS OF CERTIFICATES

B6.16

FORM A

Certificate of Motor Insurance

Certificate No. ....   Policy No. ....(Optional)
  1. Registration mark of vehicle.
  2. Name of policy holder.
  3. Effective date of the commencement of insurance for the purposes of the relevant law.
  4. Date of expiry of insurance.

5. Persons or classes of persons entitled to drive.
6. Limitations as to use.

I/We hereby certify that the policy to which this certificate relates satisfies the requirements of the relevant law applicable in Great Britain.

....

Authorised Insurers

Note: For full details of the insurance cover
reference should be made to the policy.

Form B

Certificate of Motor Insurance

Certificate No. ....   Policy No. ....(Optional)
1. Description of vehicle.
2. Name of policy holder.
3. Effective date of the commencement of insurance for the purposes of the relevant law.
4. Date of expiry of insurance.
5. Persons or classes of persons entitled to drive.
6. Limitations as to use.

I/We hereby certify that the policy to which this certificate relates satisfies the requirements of the relevant law applicable in Great Britain.

....

Authorised Insurers

Note: For full details of the insurance cover
reference should be made to the policy.

Form C

Certificate of Motor Insurance

I/We hereby certify that this covering note satisfies the requirements of the relevant law applicable in Great Britain.

....

Authorised Insurers

Form D

Certificate No. ....   Policy No. ....(Optional)

1. Name of holder of security.
2. Effective date of the commencement of security for the purposes of the relevant law.
3. Date of expiry of security.
4. Conditions to which security is subject.

I/We hereby certify that the security to which this certificate relates satisfies the requirements of the relevant law applicable in Great Britain.

....

Persons giving security

Note: For full details of the cover
reference should be made to the security.

FORM E

Certificate of Deposit

I/We hereby certify that I am/we are the owner(s) of the vehicle of which the registration mark is..........................and that in pursuance of the relevant law applicable in Great Britain I/we have on deposit with the Accountant-General of the Supreme Court [the sum for the time being specified in section 144(1) of the Road Traffic Act 1988]

Signed ....
on behalf of ....

FORM F

Certificate of Ownership

We hereby certify that the vehicle of which the registration mark is
................................is owned by ....

Signed ....
on behalf of ....

B6.17   *[Part I of the Schedule is printed as amended by SI 1992/1283.]*

PART 2

PROVISIONS RELATING TO THE FORMS AND COMPLETION OF CERTIFICATES

B6.18   [1. Every certificate [(except a certificate delivered by electronic means)] shall be printed and completed in black [on a white background]. This provision shall not prevent the reproduction of a seal or monogram or similar device referred to in paragraph 2 of this Part of this Schedule, or the presence of a background pattern (of whatever form and whether coloured or not) on the face of the form which does not materially affect the legibility of the certificate.]

B6.19   [2. No certificate shall contain any advertising matter [...]:

Provided that the name and address of the company by whom the certificate is issued, or a reproduction of the seal of the company or any monogram or similar device of the company, or the name and address of an insurance broker, shall not be deemed to be advertising matter for the purposes of this paragraph if it is printed or stamped at the foot or on the back of such certificate, or if it forms, or forms part of, any such background pattern as is referred to in the foregoing paragraph.]

B6.20   3. [Except in the case of a certificate of insurance delivered by electronic means, the whole of each form] as set out in Part 1 of this Schedule shall in each case appear on the face of the form, the items being in the order so set out and the certification being set out at the end of the form.

B6.21   [3A. In the case of a certificate of insurance delivered by electronic means, the items in each form as set out in Part 1 of this Schedule shall in each case appear in the order so set out and the certification shall be set out at the end of the form.]

4. [Except in the case of a certificate of insurance delivered by electronic means, the particulars to be inserted] on the said forms shall so far as possible appear on the face of the form, but where in the case of any of the numbered headings in Forms A, B, or D, this cannot conveniently be done, any part of such particulars may be inserted on the back of the form, provided that their presence on the back is clearly indicated under the relevant heading. **B6.22**

5. The particulars to be inserted on any of the said forms shall not include particulars relating to any exceptions purporting to restrict the insurance under the relevant policy or the operation of the relevant security which are by [subsections (1) and (2) of section 148] of the Act rendered of no effect as respects the third party liabilities required by [sections 145 and 146] of the Act to be covered by a policy or security. **B6.23**

6.—(1) In any case where it is intended that a certificate of insurance, certificate of security or a covering note shall be effective not only in Great Britain, but also in any of the following territories, that is to say, Northern Ireland, the Isle of Man, the Island of Guernsey, the Island of Jersey or the Island of Alderney, Forms A, B, C and D may be modified by the addition thereto, where necessary, of a reference to the relevant legal provisions of such of those territories as may be appropriate. **B6.24**

(2) A certificate of insurance or a certificate of security may contain [...] a statement as to whether or not the policy or security to which it relates satisfies the requirements of the relevant law in any of the territories referred to in this paragraph.

7. Every certificate of insurance or certificate of security shall be duly authenticated by or on behalf of the company by whom it is issued. **B6.25**

8. A certificate in Form F issued by a subsidiary of a Passenger Transport Executive or by a wholly-owned subsidiary of the [London Regional Transport] shall indicate under the signature that the issuing body is such a subsidiary of an Executive, which shall there be specified. **B6.26**

[Part 2 of the Schedule is printed as amended by the Interpretation Act 1978 s.17(2)(a) (cf. reg.4(4) above); SI 1981/1567; the London Regional Transport Act 1984 s.71(4); SI 1992/1283; SI 2010/1117. **B6.27**

As to the dissolution of London Regional Transport and its replacement by Transport for London, see the Greater London Authority Act 1999 Pt IV, Chap.XVI (particularly ss.297 and 302). The London Regional Transport (Dissolution) Order 2003 (SI 2003/1913) art.2 provides for the dissolution of London Regional Transport on July 16, 2003. All London Regional Transport's remaining property, rights and liabilities were transferred to Transport for London on July 15, 2003.]

The Motor Vehicles (International Circulation) Order 1975

(SI 1975/1208)

B7.01   *[The text of this order is printed as amended by:*

the Motor Vehicles (International Circulation) (Amendment) Order 1985 (SI 1985/459) (March 21, 1985);

the Motor Vehicles (International Circulation) (Amendment) Order 1989 (SI 1989/993) (June 14, 1989 (arts 1–4), September 1, 1989 (art.5) and on a date to be announced under art.1 (art.6));

the Motor Vehicles (International Circulation) (Amendment) Order 1991 (SI 1991/771) (April 3, 1991);

the Motor Vehicles (International Circulation) (Amendment) (No.2) Order 1991 (SI 1991/1727) (July 25, 1991);

the Motor Vehicles (International Circulation) (Amendment) Order 1996 (SI 1996/1929) (August 6, 1996);

the Driving Licences (Community Driving Licence) Regulations 1996 (SI 1996/1974) (January 1, 1997);

the Motor Vehicles (International Circulation) (Amendment) Order 2004 (SI 2004/1992) (August 10, 2004); and

the Motor Vehicles (International Circulation) (Amendment) Order 2010 (SI 2010/771) (May 14, 2010; except for the purposes of art.4, December 4, 2011).

The amending instruments are referred to in the notes to the principal order only by their years and numbers. The dates referred to above are the dates on which the amendments took (or will take) effect. (SI 1996/1974 came into force for certain purposes, not concerning the text of the principal order set out below on an earlier date.)]

Documents for drivers and vehicles going abroad

B7.02   **1.**—(1) The Secretary of State may issue for use outside the United Kingdom a driving permit in each or either of the forms A and B in Schedule 1 to this Order to a person who has attained the age of eighteen years and satisfies the Secretary of State—

>   (a) that he is competent to drive motor vehicles of the classes for which the permit is to be issued, and

>   (b) that he is resident in the United Kingdom:

Provided that a permit in form A which is restricted to motor cycles or invalid carriages may be issued to a person who is under eighteen years of age.

(2) The Secretary of State may issue for use outside the United Kingdom a document in the form D in Schedule 1 to this Order for any motor vehicle registered under [the Vehicle Excise and Registration Act 1994].

(3), (4) [...]

(5) The Secretary of State may assign to a motor vehicle to which the Decision of 1957 of the Council of the Organisation for European Economic Co-operation applies, an identification mark in the form of such a trade plate as may be required to be carried on such a vehicle under the provisions of section 1 of the Regulation attached to that Decision.

In this paragraph, *"the Decision of 1957 of the Council of the Organisation for European Economic Co-operation"* means the decision of the Council of the Organisation for European Economic Co-operation concerning the International Circulation of Hired Private Road Motor Vehicles adopted by that Council at its 369th Meeting, in June 1957.

(6) [The Secretary of State may charge a fee of £— for the issue of any such document as is mentioned in paragraph (1) or (2) of this Article.]

(7) The Secretary of State may for the purpose of his functions under this Article carry out tests of the competency of applicants for driving permits and examination of vehicles.

(8) The Secretary of State may delegate any of his functions under this Article (including any power of charging fees and the carrying out of tests or examinations) to any body concerned with motor vehicles or to any Northern Ireland department.

[(9) Sections 173 and 174 of the Road Traffic Act 1988 (forgery of documents, etc., false statements and withholding material information) and Article 174 of the Road Traffic (Northern Ireland) Order 1981 [*SI 1981/154*] (false statements in connection with forgery of, and fraudulent use of, documents, etc.) shall apply to a Convention driving permit as they apply to licences under that Act or under that Order.]

[(10) Section 13 of the Road Traffic Offenders Act 1988 and Article 190 of the said Order of 1981 (admissibility of records as evidence) shall apply to records maintained by the Secretary of State in connection with his functions under this Article, or by a body or Northern Ireland department to which in accordance with paragraph (8) of this Article he has delegated the function in connection with which the records are maintained, as that section or that Article apply to records maintained in connection with functions under that Act or under that Order, and the powers conferred by section 13(5) of the said Act of 1988 and Article 190(4) of the said Order of 1981 to prescribe a description of matter which may be admitted as evidence under that section or under that Article shall have effect in relation to the application of that section and that Article by this Article.]

[Article 1 is printed as amended by SI 1989/993 art.4; the Vehicle Excise and Registration Act 1994 s.64 and Sch.4, para.4; SI 1996/1929; SI 2004/1992. **B7.03**
The amount of the fee referred to in art.1(6) is not reproduced.]

[Visitors' driving permits

2.—(1) Subject to the provisions of this Article, it shall be lawful for a person resident outside the United Kingdom who is temporarily in Great Britain and holds— **B7.04**

    (a) a Convention driving permit, or
    (b) a domestic driving permit issued in a country outside the United Kingdom, or

(c) [...]

during a period of twelve months from the date of his last entry into the United Kingdom to drive, for any person to cause or permit such a person to drive [...], in Great Britain a motor vehicle of any class [other than a medium-sized goods vehicle, a large goods vehicle, a privately-operated passenger vehicle or a passenger-carrying vehicle] which he is authorised by that permit or that licence to drive, notwithstanding that he is not the holder of a driving licence under Part III of the Road Traffic Act 1988.

[(2) Subject to the provisions of this Article, it shall be lawful for a person resident outside the United Kingdom who is temporarily in Great Britain and holds—

(a) a Convention driving permit, or

(b) a domestic driving permit issued in a country outside the United Kingdom,

during a period of twelve months from the date of his last entry into the United Kingdom to drive, or for any person to cause or permit such a person to drive, in Great Britain—

(i) in the case of any such person who is resident in an EEA State, the Isle of Man, Jersey or Guernsey, a medium-sized goods vehicle, a large goods vehicle, a privately-operated passenger vehicle or a passenger-carrying vehicle; and

(ii) in the case of any other such person, a medium-sized goods vehicle, a large goods vehicle, a privately-operated passenger vehicle or a passenger-carrying vehicle brought temporarily into Great Britain,

which he is authorised by that permit to drive, notwithstanding that he is not the holder of a medium-sized goods vehicle driver's licence, a large goods vehicle driver's licence, a privately-operated passenger vehicle driver's licence or a passenger-carrying vehicle driver's licence.]

(3) [...]

(4) Nothing in the preceding provisions of this Article shall authorise any person to drive, or any person to cause or permit any person to drive, a vehicle of any class at a time when he is disqualified by virtue of section 101 of the Road Traffic Act 1988 (persons under age) [q.v.], for holding or obtaining a driving licence authorising him to drive vehicles of that class, but in the case of any such person as is mentioned in [paragraphs (1) or (2)] of this Article, who is driving a vehicle which—

(a) in the case of a person not resident in [an EEA State], [the Isle of Man[, Jersey or Guernsey]] is brought temporarily into Great Britain, and

(b) is within the class specified in the first column of [paragraph (7)] of the Table in subsection (1) of that section, and

(c) is either a vehicle registered in a Convention country or a goods vehicle in respect of which that person holds a certificate of competence which satisfies the international requirements,

the second column of that paragraph, in its application for the purposes of this paragraph, shall have effect as if for "21" there were substituted "18".

In this paragraph the following expressions have the meanings respectively assigned to them—

"*the international requirements*" means—

(i) in relation to a person who is driving a goods vehicle on a journey to which Council Regulation (EEC) No.3820/85 of 20th December 1985 [*q.v.*], on the harmonisation of certain social legislation relating to road transport applies, the requirements of Article 5(1)(b) (minimum ages for goods vehicle drivers) of that Regulation;

(ii) in relation to a person who is driving a goods vehicle on a journey to which the European Agreement concerning the work of crews engaged in International Road Transport (AETR) signed at Geneva on 25th March 1971 [*q.v.*] applies, the requirements of Article 5(1)(b) (conditions to be fulfilled by drivers) of that Agreement;

"*Convention country*" means a country which is not [an EEA State] nor a party to the aforementioned European Agreement but is a party to the Convention on Road Traffic concluded at Geneva in the year 1949 [*Cmnd. 7991*], or the International Convention relative to Motor Traffic concluded at Paris in the year 1926 [*Cmnd. 3510*] .

(5) This Article shall not authorise a person to drive a motor vehicle of any class if, in consequence of a conviction or of the order of a court, he is disqualified for holding or obtaining a driving licence under Part III of the Road Traffic Act 1988 [*q.v.*].

[(6) The Secretary of State for Transport may by order made by statutory instrument withdraw one or both of the rights conferred by paragraphs (1)(b) and (2)(b) of this Article in respect of—

(a) all domestic driving permits;

(b) domestic driving permits of a description specified in the order; or

(c) domestic driving permits held by persons of a description specified in the order.]

(7) In this Article —

"*Convention driving permit*" means a driving permit in the form A in Schedule 1 to this Order issued under the authority of a country outside the United Kingdom; whether or not that country is a party to the Convention on Road Traffic concluded at Geneva in the year 1949 [to a person who has given proof of his competence to drive], or a driving permit in the form B in the said Schedule issued under the authority of a country outside the United Kingdom which is a party to the International Convention relative to Motor Traffic concluded at Paris in the year 1926 but not to the Convention of 1949 [to a person who has given proof of his competence to drive];

"*domestic driving permit*" in relation to a country outside the United Kingdom means a document issued under the law of that country [to a person who has given proof of his competence to drive] and authorising the holder to drive motor vehicles, or a specified class of motor vehicles, in that country, and includes a driving permit issued [to such a person] by the armed forces of any country outside the United

Kingdom for use in some other country outside the United Kingdom [but does not include a Community licence (within the meaning of Part III of the Road Traffic Act 1988)] ;

[...]

"dependants" in relation to such a member of the British Forces or the civilian component thereof, means any of the following persons, namely—

> (a) the wife or husband of that member; and
>
> (b) any other person wholly or mainly maintained by him or in his custody, charge or care; and

[*"EEA Agreement"* means the Agreement on the European Economic Area signed at Oporto on 2nd May 1992 as adjusted by the Protocol signed at Brussels on 17th March 1993;]

[*"EEA State"* means a State which is a Contracting Party to the EEA Agreement;]

[*"medium-sized goods vehicle"* has the same meaning as in Part III of the Road Traffic Act 1988;]

[*"medium-sized goods vehicle driver's licence"* means a licence under Part III of the Road Traffic Act 1988 in so far as it authorises a person to drive medium-sized goods vehicles of any class;]

[*"privately-operated passenger vehicle"* means a vehicle, not used for carrying passengers for hire or reward, which is constructed or adapted to carry more than eight but not more than 16 passengers;]

[*"privately-operated passenger vehicle driver's licence"* means a licence under Part III of the Road Traffic Act 1988 in so far as it authorises a person to drive privately-operated passenger vehicles of any class;]

"public service vehicle" has the same meaning as in the Public Passenger Vehicles Act 1981 [*q.v.*];

[and *"large goods vehicle"*, *"passenger-carrying vehicle"*, *"large goods vehicle driver's licence"* and *"passenger-carrying vehicle driver's licence"* have the same meaning as in Part IV of the Road Traffic Act 1988 [*q.v.*].]

(8) The provisions of this Article which authorise the holder of a permit or a licence to drive a vehicle during a specified period shall not be construed as authorising the driving of a vehicle at a time when the permit or the licence has ceased to be valid.]

B7.05   *[Article 2 is printed as substituted by SI 1989/993 art.4, and as subsequently amended by SI 1991/771; SI 1996/1929 and 1974; SI 2004/1992.*

As to the European Economic Area, see the introductory note to Section C below.]

B7.06   [3.—(1) It shall be lawful—

> (a) for a member of a visiting force of a country to which Part I of the Visiting Forces Act 1952, for the time being applies who holds a driving permit issued under the law of any part of the sending country or issued by the service authorities of the visiting force, or
>
> (b) for a member of a civilian component of such a visiting force who holds such a driving permit, or

(c) for a dependant of any such member of a visiting force or of a civilian component thereof who holds such a driving permit,

to drive, or for any person to cause or permit any such person to drive, in Great Britain, a motor vehicle of any class ... which he is authorised by that permit to drive, notwithstanding that he is not the holder of a driving licence under Part III of the Road Traffic Act 1988 [*q.v.*].

(2) This Article shall not authorise a person to drive a motor vehicle of any class if, in consequence of a conviction or of the order of a court, he is disqualified for holding or obtaining a driving licence under Part III of the Road Traffic Act 1988.

(3) Nothing in this Article shall authorise any person to drive, or any person to cause or permit any other person to drive, a vehicle of any class at a time when he is disqualified by virtue of section 101 of the Road Traffic Act 1988 (persons under age) [*q.v.*], for holding or obtaining a driving licence authorising him to drive vehicles of that class.

(4) The interpretative provisions of the Visiting Forces Act 1952 shall apply for the interpretation of this Article and *"dependant"*, in relation to a member of any such visiting force or a civilian component thereof, means any of the following persons namely—

(a) the wife or husband of that member; and

(b) any other person wholly or mainly maintained by him or in his custody, charge or care.]

[Article 3 is printed as substituted by SI 1989/993 art.4, and as subsequently   **B7.07**
amended by SI 1991/771; SI 1996/1929.

As to persons who are members of visiting forces, see Vol.1, § 2.31.]

4. Schedule 3 to this Order shall have effect as respects the driving permits   **B7.08**
referred to in Articles 2 and 3 of this Order.

Excise exemption and documents for vehicles brought temporarily into [United Kingdom]

5.—(1) The next following paragraph shall apply to a vehicle brought   **B7.09**
temporarily into [United Kingdom] by a person resident outside the United Kingdom if the person bringing that vehicle into [United Kingdom]—

(a) satisfies a registration authority that he is resident outside the United Kingdom and that the vehicle is only temporarily in [United Kingdom], and

(b) complies with any regulations made under paragraph (4) of this Article.

[(2) A vehicle to which this paragraph applies, and to which the temporary importation arrangements referred to in the Council Regulation on temporary importation from third countries do not apply and which would, but for this Order, be chargeable with excise duty under the Excise Act, shall be exempt from any duty of excise under that Act to the following extent,—

(a) in the case of a vehicle to which the Council Directive on the temporary importation of a private vehicle from another member State applies, the vehicle shall be exempt from excise duty if its importation is in accordance with the provisions of that Directive and it shall continue to be so exempt for as long as those provisions continue to be satisfied;

[(b) in a case of a vehicle being used for or in connection with—

(i) international carriage or a cabotage operation within the scope of the Regulation of the European Parliament and of the Council on common rules for access to the international market for coach and bus services or the Regulation of the European Parliament and of the Council on common rules for access to the international road haulage market, or

(ii) a type of carriage which is exempt from any Community authorisation and from any carriage authorisation under the Directive of the European Parliament and of the Council on the establishment of common rules for certain types of carriage of goods by road,

the vehicle shall be exempt from excise duty if and so long as the vehicle is being used in accordance with whichever of those instruments is applicable to the use of the vehicle.]

(3) A vehicle registered in the Isle of Man and brought temporarily into [United Kingdom] by a person resident outside the United Kingdom shall be exempt from any duty of excise under the Excise Act for a period not exceeding one year from the date of importation, if the person bringing that vehicle into [United Kingdom]—

(a) satisfies a registration authority that he is resident outside the United Kingdom and that the vehicle is only temporarily in [United Kingdom], and

(b) complies with any regulations made under paragraph (4) of this Article.

(4) The Secretary of State may be regulations provide—

(a) for the furnishing to a registration authority by a person who imports a vehicle to which either of the two last preceding paragraphs applies of such particulars as may be prescribed, and

[(b) for the recording by a registration authority of any particulars which the Secretary of State may by the regulations direct to be recorded, and for the manner of such recording, and for the making of any such particulars available for use by such persons as may be specified in the regulations on payment, in such cases as may be so specified, of such fee as may be prescribed, and]

(c) for the production to a registration authority of prescribed documents, and

(d) for the registration of vehicles which by virtue of this Article are exempt from excise duty and for the assignment of registration marks to, and for the issue of registration cards for, such vehicles.

(5) The following provisions of the Excise Act, that is to say:—

(a) [paragraphs (e), (f) and (h) of section 22(1) of] the Excise Act (which enable the Secretary of State to make regulations as respects registration books for vehicles in respect of which excise licences are issued), and

(b) [section 23(4) of the Excise Act] (which enables the Secretary of

State to make regulations as to the display on a vehicle of the registration mark assigned to it), and

(c) [section 44 of the Excise Act] (which relates to forgery of licences, registration marks or registration documents),

shall apply in relation to a registration card issued, or a registration mark assigned, in pursuance of this Article as they apply in relation to a registration book or registration document issued, or a registration mark assigned, under the Excise Act.

(6) If regulations under this Article provide for the assignment of a registration mark on production of some document relating to a vehicle which is exempt from excise duty by virtue of this Article, then [paragraphs (e) and (f) of section 22(1) of the Excise Act] shall apply in relation to that document so as to authorise the Secretary of State to make regulations under that section requiring the production of that document for inspection by persons of classes prescribed by regulations made under that section.

(7) [Paragraphs (e) and (f) of section 22(1), section 23(4) and section 44] of the Excise Act shall, in [United Kingdom], apply in like manner in relation to a registration card issued, or a registration mark assigned, in pursuance of provisions corresponding to paragraph (4) of this Article in Northern Ireland.

(8) In relation to a motor vehicle brought temporarily into [United Kingdom] by a person resident outside the United Kingdom, references in [section 23] of the Excise Act and in [sections 22(1) and 23(4)] thereof to registration marks shall, where appropriate, include references to nationality signs.

(9) In this Article —

[*"the Directive of the European Parliament and of the Council on the establishment of common rules for certain types of carriage of goods by road"* means Directive 2006/94 of the European Parliament and of the Council of 12th December 2006 on the establishment of common rules for certain types of carriage of goods by road;]

[*"the Council Directive on the temporary importation of a private vehicle from another member State"* means Council Directive (EEC) No.83/182 of 28th March 1983 on tax exemptions within the community for certain means of transport temporarily imported into one Member State from another [*O.J. No.L105, April 23, 1983, p.59*];]

[*"the Council Regulation on temporary importation from third countries"* means Council Regulation (EEC) No.1855/89 of 14th June 1989 on the temporary importation of means of transport [*O.J. No.L186, June 30, 1989, p.8*];]

[*"the Regulation of the European Parliament and of the Council on common rules for access to the international market for coach and bus services"* means Regulation (EC) No. 1073/2009 of 21 October 2009 of the European Parliament and of the Council on common rules for access to the international market for coach and bus services and amending Regulation (EC) No. 561/2006 [*q.v.*]; and

"the Regulation of the European Parliament and of the Council on common rules for access to the international road haulage market" means Regulation (EC) No.1072/2009 of 21 October 2009 of the European Parliament and of the Council on common rules for access to the international road haulage market [*q.v.*].]

> *"the Excise Act"* means [the Vehicle Excise and Registration Act 1994];
>
> *"the date of importation"*, in relation to a vehicle, means the date on which that vehicle was last brought into the United Kingdom;
>
> [*"registration authority"* means the Automobile Association, the Royal Automobile Club, the Royal Scottish Automobile Club, or the Secretary of State;]

and references to registration marks shall, where appropriate, include references to nationality signs.

> [(10) *[Applies to vehicles imported into Northern Ireland.]*]

B7.10   *[Article 5 is printed as amended by SI 1985/459; SI 1991/1727; SI 1996/1929; SI 2010/771.]*

B7.11   **5A.** [...]
[Revoked by SI 1996/1929.]

B7.12   **6.**—(1) An application under Part V of the Transport Act 1968 for an operator's licence for a motor vehicle or trailer brought temporarily into Great Britain by a person resident outside the United Kingdom shall be made to the licensing authority for the purpose of the said Part V for the area where the vehicle is landed.

(2) Regulations made or having effect as if made, under sections 68–82 (provisions as to lighting of vehicles) of the Road Traffic Act 1972, may, either wholly or partially, and subject to any conditions, vary or grant exemptions from, the requirements of those sections in the case of motor vehicles or trailers brought temporarily into Great Britain by persons resident outside the United Kingdom or in the case of any class of such vehicles.

B7.13   *[Sections 68–80 and 81(1) of the Road Traffic Act 1972 were repealed by the Road Traffic Act 1974 s.24(3) and Sch.7. Regulations relating to vehicle lighting are now principally made under s.41 of the Road Traffic Act 1988.]*

Interpretation, repeals, citation and commencement

B7.14   **7.**—(1) In this Order —

> *"the Secretary of State"* means [the Secretary of State for Transport];
>
> *"prescribed"* means prescribed by regulations made by the Secretary of State.

(2) The Interpretation Act [1978] shall apply for the interpretation of this Order (except as provided by the next following paragraph of this Article) as it applies for the interpretation of an Act of Parliament and as if for the purposes of [sections 16(1) and 17(2)(a)] of that Act this Order (except as aforesaid) was an Act of Parliament and the Orders revoked by Article 8(1) of this Order were Acts of Parliament thereby repealed.

(3) *[Applies to Northern Ireland.]*

(4) Any reference in this Order to any enactment shall be taken as a reference to that enactment as amended by or under any other enactment; and any reference to an enactment which has effect subject to modifications specified in an enactment shall, when those modifications cease to have effect, then be construed as a reference to the first mentioned enactment as having effect without those modifications.

B7.15   *[Article 7 is printed as amended by the Secretary of State for Transport Order*

1976 (SI 1976/1775); the Interpretation Act 1978 s.17(2)(a); the Minister of Transport Order 1979 (SI 1979/571); the Transfer of Functions (Transport) Order 1981 (SI 1981/238); the Secretary of State for the Environment, Transport and the Regions Order 1997 (SI 1997/2971); the Secretaries of State for Transport, Local Government and the Regions and for Environment, Food and Rural Affairs Order 2001 (SI 2001/2568); the Transfer of Functions (Transport, Local Government and the Regions) Order 2002 (SI 2002/2626).]

*   *   *

SCHEDULE 1

[Omitted.]   **B7.16**

SCHEDULE 2

[...]   **B7.17**

[Revoked by SI 1996/1929.]

Article 4   SCHEDULE 3

VISITORS' DRIVING PERMITS

1. In this Schedule *"driving permit"* means a driving permit which by virtue of this Or-   **B7.18**
der authorises a person to drive a motor vehicle without holding a driving licence under [Part III of the Road Traffic Act 1988] ; [*"Convention driving permit"* has the meaning assigned it by article 2(7) of this Order]; and *"driving licence"* means a driving licence under the said [Part III] .

2.—(1) A court by whom the holder of a driving permit is convicted shall—   **B7.19**
  (a) if in consequence of the conviction or of the order of the court he is disqualified for holding or obtaining a driving licence, or
  (b) if the court orders particulars of the conviction to be endorsed on any driving licence held by him,
send particulars of the conviction to the Secretary of State.

(2) A court shall in no circumstances enter any particulars in a driving permit.

3.—(1) The holder of a driving permit disqualified in consequence of a conviction or of   **B7.20**
the order of a court for holding or obtaining a driving licence shall, if so required by the court, produce his driving permit within five days, or such longer time as the court may determine, and the court shall forward it to the Secretary of State.

[(2) The Secretary of State on receiving a permit forwarded under the foregoing sub-paragraph, shall—
  (a) retain the permit until the disqualification ceases to have effect or until the holder leaves Great Britain, whichever is the earlier;
  (b) send the holder's name and address, together with the particulars of the disqualification, to the authority by whom the permit was issued; and
  (c) if the permit is a Convention driving permit, record the particulars of the disqualification on the permit.]

(3) A person failing to produce a driving permit in compliance with this paragraph shall be guilty of an offence which shall be treated for the purposes of [section 9 of the Road Traffic Offenders Act 1988] and of [Part I of Schedule 2 thereto as an offence against the provision specified in column 1 of that Part as section 27] and he shall be liable to be prosecuted and punished accordingly.

4.—(1) A court, on ordering the removal under [section 42(2) of the Road Traffic   **B7.21**

Offenders Act 1988] of a disqualification for holding or obtaining a driving licence, shall, if it appears that particulars of the disqualification have been forwarded to the Secretary of State under paragraph 2 of this Schedule, cause particulars of the order also to be forwarded to him ...

[(2) The Secretary of State, on receiving particulars of a court order removing such a disqualification, shall—

    (a) in the case of a permit on which particulars of a disqualification were recorded in accordance with paragraph 3(2)(c) of this Schedule, enter on the permit particulars of the order removing the disqualification;

    (b) send the particulars of the order to the authority by whom the permit was issued; and

    (c) return the permit to the holder.]

B7.22   **5.**—(1) In the following provisions of [the Road Traffic Act 1988], references to a driving licence shall include references to a driving permit.

(2) The said provisions are—

    (a) [subsections (1) and (6) of section 164 (which authorises a police constable to require the production of a driving licence and in certain cases statement of date of birth by a person who is, or in certain circumstances has been, driving a vehicle),

    (b) *[Lapsed.]*

    (c) subsections (1) and (2) of section [173] (which relate to the use of a driving licence by a person other than the holder and to forgery of such a licence).

B7.23   *[Schedule 3 is printed as amended by the Interpretation Act 1978 s.17(2)(a) (cf. art.7(2) above); SI 1989/993 art.2.]*

SCHEDULE 4

REVOCATIONS

B7.24   *[Omitted.]*

The 70 miles per hour, 60 miles per hour and 50 miles per hour (Temporary Speed Limit) Order 1977

(SI Not Published)

[This order was varied by the 70 miles per hour, 60 miles per hour and 50 **B8.01**
miles per hour (Temporary Speed Limit) (Variation) Order 1978 with effect from
August 23, 1978. This order, which would otherwise have expired on November
30, 1978, was continued in force indefinitely by the 70 miles per hour (Temporary
Speed Limit) (Continuation) Order 1978 (SI 1978/1548).]

* * *

2. Subject to Article 4 below, no person shall during the period of this Order **B8.02**
drive a motor vehicle—
- (a) at a speed exceeding 50 miles per hour on the lengths of dual carriageway road specified in Part I of Schedule 1 to this Order,
- (b) at a speed exceeding 60 miles per hour on the lengths of dual carriageway road specified in Schedule 2 to this Order, or
- (c) at a speed exceeding 70 miles per hour on any other length of dual
  carriageway road.

3. Subject to Article 4 below, no person shall during the period of this Order **B8.03**
drive a motor vehicle—
- (a) at a speed exceeding 50 miles per hour on the lengths of single carriageway road specified in Part II of Schedule 1 to this Order, or
- (b) at a speed exceeding 60 miles per hour on any length of single carriageway road.

4. Nothing in this Order shall prohibit a person from driving a motor vehicle **B8.04**
on a length of road at a speed exceeding that which would apply to that length
under Article 2 or 3 above in a case where a higher speed limit is, after the coming into operation of this Order, prescribed in relation to that length by means of
an Order under [section 84 of the Road Traffic Regulation Act 1984].

[Article 4 is printed as amended by the Road Traffic Regulation Act 1984 **B8.05**
s.144(1) and Sch.10, para.2.]

SCHEDULE 1

Part I

LENGTHS OF DUAL CARRIAGEWAY ROAD FOR WHICH A 50 MILES PER HOUR SPEED LIMIT IS
PRESCRIBED

Any dual carriageway sections of any of the lengths of road described in Part II of this **B8.06**
Schedule.

Part II

LENGTHS OF SINGLE CARRIAGEWAY ROAD FOR WHICH A 50 MILES PER HOUR SPEED LIMIT IS
PRESCRIBED

[In certain instances the lengths of road described below in this Part of this Schedule **B8.07**

include short sections of dual carriageway road. These sections are covered by Pt I of this Schedule.]

A Trunk Roads

*   *   *

B Other Roads

*   *   *

SCHEDULE 2

LENGTHS OF DUAL CARRIAGEWAY ROAD FOR WHICH A 60 MILES PER HOUR SPEED LIMIT IS PRESCRIBED

A Trunk Roads

*   *   *

B Other Roads

*   *   *

The Public Service Vehicles (Conditions of Fitness, Equipment, Use and Certification) Regulations 1981

(SI 1981/257)

[As to the disapplication of the provisions of these regulations in respect of **B9.01**
certain vehicles, see the Road Transport (International Passenger Services)
Regulations 1984 (SI 1984/748) reg.23 below.

None of the provisions of Pts II, III, IV or V of these regulations had effect in
relation to a vehicle which is carrying out a cabotage transport operation in
Great Britain in accordance with Council Regulation (EC) 12/98 (O.J. No.L4,
January 8, 1998, p.10); see the Road Transport (Passenger Vehicles Cabotage)
Regulations 1999 (SI 1999/3413) regs 1(2) and 10(6) below. With effect from
December 4, 2011, Regulation (EEC) 12/98 was repealed by European and
Council Regulation (EC) 1073/2009 of October 21, 2009 on common rules for
access to the international market for coach and bus services, and amending
Regulation (EC) 561/2006 (O.J. No.L300, November 14, 2009, p.88) art.30. Ref-
erences to the repealed Regulation shall be construed as references to Regula-
tion (EC) 1073/2009 and shall be read in accordance with the correlation table
set out in ibid. Annex III.

The text of these regulations is printed as amended by: **B9.02**
  the Public Service Vehicles (Conditions of Fitness, Equipment, Use
  and Certification) (Amendment) Regulations 1982 (SI 1982/20) (Feb-
  ruary 22, 1982);
  the Public Service Vehicles (Conditions of Fitness, Equipment, Use
  and Certification) (Amendment) (No.2) Regulations 1982 (SI 1982/
  1058) (September 2, 1982);
  the Public Service Vehicles (Conditions of Fitness, Equipment, Use
  and Certification) (Amendment) (No.3) Regulations 1982 (SI 1982/
  1482) (November 22, 1982);
  the Public Service Vehicles (Conditions of Fitness, Equipment, Use
  and Certification) (Amendment) (No.2) Regulations 1986 (SI 1986/
  1812) (November 26, 1986);
  the Public Service Vehicles (Conditions of Fitness, Equipment, Use
  and Certification) (Amendment) (No.2) Regulations 1989 (SI 1989/
  2359, with correction slip dated January 1990) (January 11, 1990);
  the Public Service Vehicles (Conditions of Fitness, Equipment, Use
  and Certification) (Amendment) Regulations 1995 (SI 1995/305)
  (March 14, 1995);
  the Public Service Vehicles (Conditions of Fitness, Equipment, Use
  and Certification) (Amendment) Regulations 2002 (SI 2002/335)
  (March 18, 2002);
  the Public Service Vehicles (Conditions of Fitness, Equipment, Use

and Certification) (Amendment) (No.3) Regulations 2005 (SI 2005/ 2986) (December 12, 2005); and

the Public Service Vehicles (Conditions of Fitness, Equipment, Use and Certification) (Amendment) Regulations 2009 (SI 2009/141) (March 3, 2009).

The amending regulations are referred to in the notes to the principal regulations only by their years and numbers. The dates referred to above are the dates on which the amending regulations came into force.

The principal regulations have also been amended by the Public Service Vehicles (Conditions of Fitness, Equipment, Use and Certification) (Amendment) Regulations 1984 (SI 1984/1763), the Public Service Vehicles (Conditions of Fitness, Equipment, Use and Certification) (Amendment) Regulations 1986 (SI 1986/370), the Public Service Vehicles (Conditions of Fitness, Equipment, Use and Certification) (Amendment) Regulations 1988 (SI 1988/340), the Public Service Vehicles (Conditions of Fitness, Equipment, Use and Certification) (Amendment) Regulations 1989 (SI 1989/322), the Public Service Vehicles (Conditions of Fitness, Equipment, Use and Certification) (Amendment) Regulations 1990 (SI 1990/450), the Public Service Vehicles (Conditions of Fitness, Equipment, Use and Certification) (Amendment) Regulations 1991 (SI 1991/456), the Public Service Vehicles (Conditions of Fitness, Equipment, Use and Certification) (Amendment) Regulations 1992 (SI 1992/565), the Public Service Vehicles (Conditions of Fitness, Equipment, Use and Certification) (Amendment) Regulations 1993 (SI 1991/3012), the Public Service Vehicles (Conditions of Fitness, Equipment, Use and Certification) (Amendment) Regulations 1997 (SI 1997/84), the Public Service Vehicles (Conditions of Fitness, Equipment, Use and Certification) (Amendment) Regulations 1998 (SI 1998/1670), and the Public Service Vehicles (Conditions of Fitness, Equipment, Use and Certification (Amendment) Regulations 2000 (SI 2000/1431), the Public Service Vehicles (Conditions of Fitness, Equipment, Use and Certification) (Amendment) Regulations 2001 (SI 2001/1649), the Public Service Vehicles (Conditions of Fitness, Equipment, Use and Certification) (Amendment) Regulations 2002 (SI 2002/489), the Public Service Vehicles (Conditions of Fitness, Equipment, Use and Certification) Regulations (SI 2003/ 1817), the Public Service Vehicles (Conditions of Fitness, Equipment, Use and Certification) (Amendment) Regulations 2004 (SI 2004/1880), the Public Service Vehicles (Conditions of Fitness, Equipment, Use and Certification) (Amendment) Regulations 2005 (SI 2005/1403), the Public Service Vehicles (Conditions of Fitness, Equipment, Use and Certification) (Amendment) (No.2) Regulations 2005 (SI 2005/2342), the Public Service Vehicles (Conditions of Fitness, Equipment, Use and Certification) (Amendment) (No.4) Regulations 2005 (SI 2005/3128), the Public Service Vehicles (Conditions of Fitness, Equipment, Use and Certification) (Amendment) Regulations 2007 (SI 2007/502) and the Public Service Vehicles (Conditions of Fitness, Equipment, Use and Certification) (Amendment) Regulations 2008 (SI 2008/1458), the Public Service Vehicles (Conditions of Fitness, Equipment, Use and Certification) (Amendment) (No.2) Regulations 2009 (SI 2009/877), but these do not affect the text of any provision printed in this work.]

ARRANGEMENT OF REGULATIONS

PART I
PRELIMINARY

Regulation

*   *   *

PART II
REGULATIONS RELATING TO THE CONDITIONS AS TO FITNESS OF PUBLIC SERVICE VEHICLES

Regulation

*   *   *

*   *   *

*   *   *

*   *   *

*   *   *

*   *   *

*   *   *

PART III
REGULATIONS RELATING TO THE EQUIPMENT OF PUBLIC SERVICE VEHICLES

Regulation

PART IV
REGULATIONS RELATING TO THE USE OF PUBLIC SERVICE VEHICLES

Regulation

* * *

SCHEDULES

Schedule

* * *

* * *

Commencement and citation

B9.04   **1.** *[Omitted.]*

Revocation

B9.05   **2.** *[Omitted.]*

Interpretation

B9.06   **3.**—(1) In these Regulations, unless the context otherwise requires, the following exceptions have the meanings hereby respectively assigned to them:—

"*the Act*" means the [Public Passenger Vehicles Act 1981] ;

["*the 1995 Act*" means the Disability Discrimination Act 1995 [*not reproduced in this work*];]

["*the 2000 Regulations*" means the Public Service Vehicles Accessibility Regulations 2000 [*SI 2000/1970, as amended ; not reproduced in this work*];]

"*articulated bus*" means a passenger vehicle so constructed that—

(a) it can be divided into two parts, both of which are vehicles and one of which is a motor vehicle, but cannot be so divided without the use of facilities normally available only at a workshop; and

(b) passengers carried by it when not so divided can at all times pass from either part to the other;

"*certificate of conformity*" means a certificate issued by the Minister in pursuance of [section 10(2)] of the Act;

"*certificate of initial fitness*" has the same meaning as in [section 6(1)] of the … Act …

"the Commissioners" means the traffic commissioners for any traffic area constituted for the purposes of [Part I] of the Act;

[*"crew seat"* means a seat fitted to a vehicle and intended for use by crew (other than the driver), including any arm rests and foot rest with which the vehicle is fitted in relation to the seat, and which complies with the requirements specified in Regulation 28A;]

"deck" means a floor or platform upon which seats are provided for the accommodation of passengers;

"double-decked vehicle" means a vehicle having two decks one of which is wholly or partly above the other and each deck of which is provided with a gangway serving seats on that deck only;

[*"ECE Regulation 36"* means Regulation No. 36 (uniform provisions concerning the construction of public service vehicles) which came into force on 1st March 1976 as an Annex to the UNECE Agreement;

"ECE Regulation 52" means Regulation No. 52 (uniform provisions concerning the approval of M2 and M3 small capacity vehicles with regard to their general construction) which came into force on 1st November 1982 as an Annex to the UNECE Agreement;

"ECE Regulation 52.01" means Regulation No. 52 as amended by the 01 series of amendments on 12th September 1995;

"ECE Regulation 107" means Regulation No. 107 (uniform provisions concerning the approval of M2 and M3 vehicles with regard to their general construction) which came into force on 18th June 1998 as an Annex to the UNECE Agreement;

"ECE Regulation 107.01" means Regulation No. 107 as amended by the 01 series of amendments on 12th August 2004;

"ECE Regulation 107.02" means Regulation No. 107 as amended by the 02 series of amendments on 10th November 2007;]

"emergency exit" means an exit which is provided for use only in case of emergency;

"entrance" means any aperture or space provided to enable passengers to board the vehicle;

"exit" means any aperture or space provided to enable passengers to leave the vehicle;

"gangway" means the space provided for obtaining access from any entrance to the passengers' seats or from any such seat to an exit other than an emergency exit but does not include a staircase or any space in front of a seat or row of seats which is required only for the use of passengers occupying that seat or that row of seats;

"half-decked vehicle" means any vehicle not being a single-decked vehicle or a double-decked vehicle;

[*"minibus"* means a motor vehicle which is constructed or adapted to carry more than 8 but not more than 16 seated passengers in addition to the driver;]

"permanent top" means any covering of a vehicle other than a hood made of canvas or other flexible material which is capable of being readily

folded back so that no portion of such hood or any fixed structure of
the roof remains vertically above any part of any seat of the vehicle,
or, in the case of a double-decked vehicle, of any seat on the upper
deck of the vehicle;

[*"priority seat"* means a seat which is designated as such in accordance
with paragraph 3 of Schedule 2 to the 2000 Regulations (priority
seats);]

"registered" in relation to a vehicle, means registered under the Roads Act
1920 or, as the case may be, the Vehicles (Excise) Act 1949, the
Vehicles (Excise) Act 1962 or the Vehicles (Excise) Act 1971 [or the
Vehicle Excise and Registration Act 1994] and references to a vehicle being registered are references to the date on which it was first so
registered;

[*"regulated public service vehicle"* means a public service vehicle to which
the 2000 Regulations apply;]

"safety glass", *"safety glazing"* and *"specified safety glass"* have the same
meanings as are respectively assigned to them in [Regulation 32(13)]
of the Road Vehicles (Construction and Use) Regulations 1986] [*SI
1986/1078, q.v.*];

"single-decked vehicle" means a vehicle on which no part of a deck or
gangway is placed vertically above another deck or gangway;

"type approval certificate" means a certificate issued by the Minister in
pursuance of [section 10(1)] of the Act;

[*"the UNECE Agreement"* means the Agreement of the United Nations
Economic Commission for Europe concluded at Geneva on 20th
March 1958 as amended concerning the adoption of uniform technical prescriptions for wheeled vehicles, equipment and parts which
can be fitted to and/or used on wheeled vehicles and the conditions
for the reciprocal recognition of approvals granted on the basis of
these prescriptions, to which the United Kingdom is a party by virtue
of an instrument of accession dated 14th January 1963 deposited
with the Secretary General of the United Nations on 15th January
1963;]

"vehicle" means a public service vehicle within [section 1(1)] of the ...
Act ...; and

"vehicle in the service of a visiting force or headquarters" has the same
meaning as in Article 8(6) of the Visiting Forces and International
Headquarters (Application of Law) Order 1965 [*SI 1965/1536*].

[*"wheelchair user"* has the same meaning as in paragraph 1 of Schedule 1
to the 2000 Regulations;]

(2) For the purpose of these Regulations, the date when a motor vehicle is first
used shall be taken to be such date as is the earlier of the undermentioned relevant dates applicable to that vehicle, that is to say—

(a) in the case of a vehicle registered under the Roads Act 1920, the
Vehicles (Excise) Act 1949, the Vehicles (Excise) Act 1962 or the
Vehicles (Excise) Act 1971 [or the Vehicle Excise and Registration
Act 1994] the relevant date is the date on which it was first so
registered; and

(b) in each of the following cases, that is to say—

    (i) in the case of a vehicle which is being or has been used under a trade licence within the meaning of section 16(1) of the Vehicles (Excise) Act 1971 (otherwise than for the purposes of demonstration or testing or of being delivered from premises of the manufacturer by whom it was made, or of a distributor of vehicles or dealer in vehicles to premises of a distributor of vehicles, dealer in vehicles or purchaser thereof, or to premises of a person obtaining possession thereof under a hiring agreement or hire purchase agreement);

    (ii) in the case of a vehicle belonging, or which has belonged, to the Crown which is or was used or appropriated for use for naval, military or air force purposes;

    (iii) in the case of a vehicle belonging, or which has belonged, to a visiting force or a headquarters within the meaning of Article 3 of the Visiting Forces and International Headquarters (Application of Law) Order 1965;

    (iv) in the case of a vehicle which has been used on roads outside Great Britain and which has been imported into Great Britain; and

    (v) in the case of a vehicle which has been used otherwise than on roads after being sold or supplied by retail and before being registered,

the relevant date is the date of manufacture of the vehicle.

In case (v) above *"sold or supplied by retail"* means sold or supplied otherwise than to a person acquiring the vehicle solely for the purpose of resale or re-supply for valuable consideration.

(3) Unless the context otherwise requires, any reference in these Regulations—

    (a) to a numbered Regulation or Schedule is a reference to the Regulation or Schedule bearing that number in these Regulations, and

    (b) to a numbered paragraph is to the paragraph bearing that number in the Regulation in which the reference occurs.

(4) The provisions of the Regulations in Part IV of these Regulations are in addition to, and not in derogation of, the provisions of any other Regulations made or having effect as if made under [section 41 of the Road Traffic Act 1988].

[Regulation 3 is printed as amended by the Interpretation Act 1978 ss.17(2)(a) and 23(1); SI 1982/1058; SI 1986/1812; the Vehicle Excise and Registration Act 1994 s.64 and Sch.4, para.4; SI 2002/335; SI 2009/141. **B9.07**

The Visiting Forces and International Headquarters (Application of Law) Order 1965 (to which reference is made in reg.3(1) and (2)(b)(iii)) has been revoked and replaced by the Visiting Forces and International Headquarters (Application of Law) Order 1999 (SI 1999/1736; not reproduced in this work). No textual amendment had been made to reg.3 in consequence of that revocation; but by the Interpretation Act 1978 ss.17(2)(a) and 23(1) references to the earlier order may be treated as references to SI 1999/1736.]

Exemptions—

B9.08   **4.**—(1) Part IV of these Regulations does not apply to any vehicle in the public service of the Crown or in the service of a visiting force or headquarters.

(2) Parts III and IV of these Regulations do not apply to a motor vehicle belonging to a local education authority and which is from time to time used by that authority to provide free school transport whether the vehicle is being used wholly or partly to provide such transport or to provide a local bus service.

[(2A) Notwithstanding regulation 5, regulations 6 to 33, 35 to 44 and 45A shall not apply to a minibus which either complies with, or is required to comply with, or is exempted from the requirements specified in regulations 41 to 43 of the Road Vehicles (Construction and Use) Regulations 1986 for a minibus first used within the meaning of those Regulations on or after 1st April 1988.]

(3) Regulation 43 does not apply to a motor vehicle not belonging to a local education authority at any time when that vehicle is being used by that authority to provide free school transport, and to carry as the only fare-paying passengers pupils other than those for whom free school transport is provided.

(4) In this Regulation: —

> (a) *"free school transport"* has the meaning given by section 46(3) of the Public Passenger Vehicles Act 1981 [*as amended, q.v.*] as regards England and Wales ...;
>
> (b) *"pupil"* has the meaning given by [section 3(1) of the Education Act 1996 as regards England and Wales ...; and
>
> (c) [*applies to Scotland.*]]

B9.09   *[Regulation 4 is printed as substituted by SI 1982/20 and as amended by SI 1986/1812; the Education Act 1996 s.582(3) and Sch.39, para.1(4).*

Words relating expressly and exclusively to Scotland have been omitted from subs.(4)(a) and (b).

The term "pupil" is defined in the Education Act 1996; s.3(1) of which provides that the term "pupil" means any person for whom education is being provided at a school, other than (a) a person who has attained the age of 19 for whom further education is being provided, or (b) a person for whom part-time education suitable to the requirements of persons of any age over compulsory school age is being provided.]

[Alternative prescribed conditions

B9.10   **4A.**—[(1)] The prescribed conditions as to the fitness of a vehicle contained in Part II may alternatively be met by a vehicle satisfying the requirements in such of the Annexes to Directive 2001/85/EC of the European Parliament and of the Council of 20 November 2001, relating to special provisions for vehicles used for the carriage of passengers comprising more than eight seats in addition to the drivers seat, and amending Directives 70/156/EEC and 97/27/EC, as apply to it.]

[(2) The prescribed conditions as to the fitness of a vehicle contained in regulations 6 to 33 in Part 2 may alternatively be met by a vehicle satisfying such requirements of ECE Regulation 107.01 or 107.02 as apply to it.]

(3) The prescribed conditions as to the fitness of a vehicle contained in regulations 13, 15 to 17, 20 to 28A and 31 in Part 2 may alternatively be met by a vehicle satisfying such requirements of ECE Regulation 52.01 as apply to it.]

[Regulation 4A is printed as inserted by SI 2005/2986 and as amended by SI   **B9.11**
2009/141.]

PART II

REGULATIONS RELATING TO THE CONDITIONS AS TO FITNESS OF PUBLIC
SERVICE VEHICLES

Conditions of fitness

5. *[Omitted.]*   **B9.12**

Stability

6.—(1) The stability of a vehicle shall be such that—   **B9.13**

(a) in the case of a double-decked vehicle, the point at which overturning occurs would not be passed if, when the vehicle is complete, fully equipped for service and loaded with weights placed in the correct relative positions to represent the driver, a full complement of passengers on the upper deck only and a conductor (if carried), the surface on which the vehicle stands were tilted to either side to an angle of 28 degrees from the horizontal; and

(b) in the case of a single-decked vehicle and of a half-decked vehicle, the point at which overturning occurs would not be passed if, when the vehicle is complete, fully equipped for service and loaded with weights placed in the correct relative positions to represent [a full complement of passengers [(including any passengers who are wheelchair users)], a driver, any crew for whom a crew seat is provided, and any conductor intended to be carried on the vehicle otherwise than in a crew seat], the surface on which the vehicle stands were tilted to either side to an angle of 35 degrees from the horizontal.

(2) For the purpose of ascertaining whether the requirements of paragraph (1) have been complied with, the height of any stop used to prevent a wheel of the vehicle from slipping sideways shall not be greater than two-thirds of the distance between the surface upon which the vehicle stands before it is tilted and that part of the rim of that wheel which is nearest to that surface when the vehicle is loaded in accordance with the said requirements.

[(3) For the purpose of this Regulation —

(a) 63.5 kilograms shall be deemed to represent the weight of one person other than a wheelchair user, and

(b) 180 kilograms shall be deemed to represent the weight of one wheelchair and wheelchair user.]

[Regulation 6 is printed as amended by SI 1982/1058; SI 2002/335.]   **B9.14**

7. [...]   **B9.15**
[Revoked by SI 1989/2359.]

8. *[Omitted.]*

9–12. [...]   **B9.16**

[Revoked by SI 1989/2359.]

13–15. *[Omitted.]*

Artificial lighting

B9.17   **16.** Subject to paragraph 4 of Schedule 2, adequate internal lighting shall be provided in every vehicle for the illumination—

(a) of each deck having a permanent top; and

(b) of any step or platform forming part of any entrance or exit other than an emergency exit;

and all lighting circuits shall be so arranged that an electrical failure of any lighting sub-circuit shall not be capable of extinguishing all the lights on any deck and at least one lamp shall be provided as near as practicable to the top of every staircase leading to an upper deck not having a permanent top.

Electrical equipment

B9.18   **17.** *[Omitted.]*

Body

18. *[Omitted.]*

Height of sides of body

B9.19   **19.** *[Omitted.]*

Steps, platforms and stairs

20. *[Omitted.]*

Number, position and size of entrances and exits

B9.20   **21.**—(1) For the purposes of this Regulation and Regulations 13, 22, 23, 24, 25 and 26 —

(a) *"primary emergency exit"* means an emergency exit being an exit provided in a single-decked vehicle or in the lower deck of a double-decked vehicle which, subject to paragraph 8 of Schedule 2 —

(i) is situated so that passengers can step directly from the passage referred to in Regulation 26(1)(g) to the outside of the vehicle,

(ii) has a clear height—

(a) in the case of a vehicle which has a seating capacity not exceeding 14 passengers, of not less than 1.21 metres, and

(b) in the case of any other vehicle, of not less than 1.37 metres,

(iii) has a width of not less than 530 millimetres;

(b) *"secondary emergency exit"* means an emergency exit of which the dimensions are not less than 910 millimetres by 530 millimetres and which does not satisfy all the requirements of a primary emergency exit and which is not in the roof of a vehicle;

(c) neither of the foregoing definitions shall apply in relation to an emergency exit as required by paragraphs (7) and (8) but the exit so required shall be of dimensions not less than 1.52 metres by 455 millimetres;

(d) references to the seating capacity of a vehicle shall, in the case of a double-decked vehicle, be treated as references to the seating capacity of its lower deck;

(e) references to the distance between the centres or between the nearest points of the openings of two exits in a vehicle are references to the distance between lines drawn at right-angles to the longitudinal axis of the vehicle and passing respectively through the centres or, as the case may be, the nearest points of the openings of the exits at gangway level; and

(f) the references to the distance between the centre of an exit placed at the front end of a vehicle and the foremost part of the vehicle is a reference to the distance between lines drawn at right-angles to the longitudinal axis of the vehicle and passing through the centre of that exit and the said foremost part and the reference to the distance between the centre of an exit placed at the rear end of a vehicle and the rearmost part of the vehicle is a reference to the distance between lines drawn as aforesaid and passing through the centre of that exit and the said rearmost part.

(2) In this Regulation —

(a) *"pre-October 1981 vehicle"* means a vehicle manufactured before 1st October 1981 or first used before 1st April 1982; and

(b) *"post-October 1981 vehicle"* means a vehicle manufactured on or after 1st October 1981 and first used on or after 1st April 1982.

(3) Subject to paragraph 8 of Schedule 2, the following provisions of this Regulation shall apply with respect to the number and position of entrances and exits which shall be provided in a vehicle but a vehicle shall not be treated as failing to comply with any of those provisions by reason only that a number of exits is provided in a vehicle in excess of the number specified in relation to it by any provision of this Regulation.

(4) Subject to paragraphs (5) and (11), a vehicle which has a seating capacity for not more than 45 passengers shall be provided with two exits so placed as not to be on the same side of the vehicle, and

(a) in the case of a pre-October 1981 vehicle, one of which may be a primary emergency exit but neither of which shall be a secondary emergency exit;

(b) in the case of a post-October 1981 vehicle, one of which shall be a primary emergency exit and the other of which shall have dimensions which are not less than those specified in paragraph (1)(a) above in relation to a primary emergency exit;

Provided that this paragraph shall not apply in the case of a vehicle which has a seating capacity—

(i) exceeding 23 passengers and which is provided with an exit by virtue of its having a platform of a type described in [Regulation 20(1)(a)] which communicates with a deck (being in the case of a double-decked vehicle, the lower deck) by means of a doorless opening and has a doorless opening on the nearside of the vehicle contiguous with another such opening at the rear of the vehicle, these openings serving together as a means of entrance to or exit from the vehicle, and

(ii) not exceeding 12 passengers and of which the fuel tank is not placed behind the rear wheels if one exit of which, in the case of a post-October 1981 vehicle, the dimensions are not less than 1.21 metres in height by 530 millimetres in width is provided and is placed at the rear of the vehicle.

(5) Where the exits provided in accordance with paragraph (4) are so placed that the distance between their centres is—

(a) in the case of a vehicle first used before 1st January 1974 which has a seating capacity exceeding 30 passengers, less than 3.05 metres;

(b) in the case of a vehicle first used on or after 1st January 1974 which has a seating capacity exceeding 23 passengers, less than 3.05 metres;

(c) in the case of a vehicle first used on or after 1st January 1974 which has a seating capacity exceeding 14 but not exceeding 23 passengers, less than 2.44 metres,

a primary or secondary emergency exit shall be provided and placed so that there is a distance between the nearest points of the openings of that exit and one of the two exits mentioned in paragraph (4) of—

(i) in the cases mentioned in sub-paragraphs (a) and (b) above, not less than 3.05 metres, and

(ii) in the case mentioned in sub-paragraph (c) above, not less than 2.44 metres.

(6) Subject to paragraph (11), a vehicle which has a seating capacity exceeding 45 passengers shall be provided with three exits in respect of which the following provisions shall apply:—

(a) in the case of a pre-October 1981 vehicle one of the exits, but not more than one, may be a secondary emergency exit, and in the case of a post-October 1981 vehicle one of the exits shall be a primary emergency exit and any other exit (not being a secondary emergency exit) shall have dimensions not less than those specified in paragraph (1)(a) above in relation to primary emergency exits;

(b) two of the exits (neither being a secondary emergency exit) shall be so placed as not to be on the same side of the vehicle;

(c) where two exits are placed on the same side of the vehicle, the distance between their centres shall not be less than 3.05 metres; and

(d) one of the exits (not being a secondary emergency exit) shall be placed at the front end of the vehicle so that the distance between its centre and the foremost part of the vehicle is not more than 3.05 metres and another of the exits (not being a secondary emergency exit) shall be placed at the rear end of the vehicle so that the distance between its centre and the rearmost part of the vehicle is not more than 3.05 metres:

Provided that—

    (i) in the case of a vehicle registered on or after 28th October 1964 and before 19th June 1968 the reference in sub-paragraph (c) above to 3.05 metres shall be replaced by a reference to 4.75 metres and sub-paragraph (d) shall not apply, and

    (ii) in the case of any other vehicle first used before 1st January 1974 sub-paragraph (d) above shall apply with the omission of the words "(not being a secondary emergency exit)" in both places where they occur.

(7) In the case of a half-decked vehicle an emergency exit shall be provided in the roof of the vehicle so placed that the transverse centre line of that exit lies within 610 millimetres of the mid-point between the front edges of the foremost and of the rearmost passenger seats in the vehicle.

(8) Where, in the case of a double-decked vehicle which has a permanent top, access to the upper deck is obtained by means of an enclosed staircase, an emergency exit shall be provided on that deck and placed otherwise than on the nearside of the vehicle.

(9) Every entrance provided in a vehicle shall be placed on the nearside of the vehicle, but one or more entrances may be provided on the offside of the vehicle if—

    (a) as respects any entrance so provided it is not also an exit provided in accordance with any of the foregoing provisions in this Regulation;

    (b) every such entrance is fitted with a door which can be controlled only by the driver while sitting in his seat; and

    (c) the device available to the driver for opening or closing that door is a separate and readily distinguishable device from that available to the driver for opening or closing any door fitted to the nearside of the vehicle:

        [and one or more entrances may be provided on the rear face of the vehicle if each of those entrances is provided with a lifting platform or ramp for the benefit of disabled passengers;]

        Provided that this paragraph shall not apply in the case of any such vehicle as is mentioned in the proviso to paragraph (4).

(10) A grab handle shall be fitted to every entrance and exit (other than an emergency exit) to assist passengers to board or alight from the vehicle.

(11) In the case of a vehicle—

    (a) being a post-October 1981 vehicle,

    (b) having a seating capacity for more than 16 passengers, and

    (c) being a single-decked vehicle or a half-decked vehicle,

there shall be at least one emergency exit which complies with the requirements specified in paragraph (12) and which is either—

    (i) in the front face of the vehicle, or

    (ii) in the rear face of the vehicle, or

    (iii) in the roof of the vehicle.

(12) The requirements referred to in paragraph (11) are, in respect of each exit therein referred to, as follows:—

    (a) the dimensions of the aperture shall be such that it has a total area of not less than 4,000 square centimetres and shall include a rectangular area the dimensions of which are not less than 70 centimetres by 50 centimetres;

(b) the exit shall be so constructed that it can be opened by means available to persons inside the vehicle, and it may be so constructed that it can be opened also by persons outside the vehicle; and

(c) the exit shall be—

(i) ejectable, or

(ii) constructed of specified safety glass which can be readily broken by the application of reasonable force so as to afford a clear aperture having the dimensions referred to in sub-paragraph (a) above, and provided in a position adjacent to the exit with a suitable means, readily available to persons inside the vehicle, for breaking the glass, or

(iii) except where the exit is an exit in the roof, hinged.

[(13) The width requirements of paragraphs (4)(b) and (6)(a) shall not apply to those parts of an exit which have a clear unobstructed width of not less than 800 millimetres for wheelchair access.]

B9.21 *[Regulation 21 is printed as amended by SI 1989/2359; SI 2002/335.]*

Width of entrances and exits

B9.22 22. *[Omitted.]*

Doors

B9.23 23.—(1) Subject to paragraph 9 of Schedule 2 and paragraph (4) the following conditions shall be complied with in the case of every vehicle:—

(a) means shall be provided for holding every entrance and exit door securely in the closed position and, where any such door is capable of remaining open when the vehicle is in motion or of being accidentally closed by the movement of the vehicle, means shall also be provided for holding that door securely in the open position;

(b) subject to paragraph (2) [and paragraph (5)], every entrance and exit door shall be provided with at least two devices (of which one may be a device provided for use in circumstances of normal operation only by a person authorised by the owner of the vehicle, and one, but not more than one, shall be provided on the outside of the vehicle) being in each case a device for operating the means for holding the door securely in the closed position, and every such device shall be so designed that a single movement of it will allow that door to be readily opened;

(c) the method of operation of any device mentioned in condition (b) above, the position of such a device where it is not placed on the door and the direction and points of application of any manual effort required to open any door, shall be clearly indicated; and there shall, in the case of a power-operated door, also be an indication that the said device may not be used by passengers except in an emergency;

(d) where any device mentioned in condition (b) above is not placed on the door, it shall be placed so as to be readily associated with that door and so that a person of normal height may conveniently operate the device without risk of being injured by movement of the door;

(e) in the case of every entrance and exit, any device mentioned in condition (b) above, other than such a device provided on the outside of an emergency exit on the upper deck of a double-decked vehicle or in the roof of a vehicle, shall be easily accessible to persons of normal height;

(f) the means and devices mentioned in conditions (a) and (b) above shall be so designed and fitted that they are unlikely to become dislodged or be operated accidentally but [(subject to paragraph (5))] there shall be in the vehicle no means of a mechanical nature the operation of which would prevent the devices mentioned in the said condition (b) (devices for allowing entrance and exit doors to be opened in an emergency) when deliberately used, from allowing the entrance or exit doors for which they are provided to be readily opened;

(g) every door shall operate so as not to obstruct clear access to any entrance or exit from inside or outside the vehicle;

(h) being a vehicle having a power-operated door which, when open or being operated, projects laterally beyond the body of the vehicle at its widest point by more than 80 millimetres, shall be so constructed or adapted that it cannot move from rest under its own power when the door is open, and the door shall not be capable of being operated while the vehicle is in motion, except by the operation of such a device as is mentioned in condition (b) above;

(i) the storage and transmission system of the power for operating any power-operated door shall be such that operation of the doors does not adversely affect the efficient operation of the braking system of the vehicle and the apparatus shall be so designed and constructed that in the event of the system becoming inoperative the door shall be capable of being operated manually from inside and outside the vehicle; and

(j) the design of power-operated doors and their associated equipment at entrances and exits shall be such that, when opening or closing, the doors are unlikely to injure any passengers, and the vertical edges of any power-operated door which, when open or being operated, projects laterally beyond the body of the vehicle at its widest point by not more than 80 millimetres and which is installed in a vehicle not constructed or adapted as mentioned in condition (h) above shall be fitted with soft rubber.

[(1A) Schedule 3A shall have effect for the purpose of supplementing paragraph (1) in relation to power-operated doors fitted to certain vehicles.]

(2) A vehicle shall not be deemed to fail to comply with condition (b) or (f) of paragraph (1) by reason only of the fact that, for the purposes of securing the vehicle when unattended, any entrance or exit door has been fitted with a supplementary lock with or without an actuating mechanism if the lock is so designed and constructed that a single movement of any device mentioned in condition (b)

above, being a device provided on the inside of the vehicle, will at all times allow that door to be readily opened.

(3) In determining for the purposes of conditions (h) and (j) of paragraph (1) whether, or the distance by which, a power-operated door, when open or being operated, projects laterally beyond the body of the vehicle at its widest point any moulding on the outside of the vehicle shall be disregarded.

(4) The references to exits in paragraph (1) do not include an emergency exit provided in accordance with the provisions of Regulation 21(11) unless such exit is a primary emergency exit or a secondary emergency exit.

[(5) In relation to securing the closed position of an entrance or exit door of a vehicle whilst that vehicle is in motion, any such door may be fitted with a device so designed that the motion of the vehicle will operate to prevent that door from being readily opened.]

B9.24   *[Regulation 23 is printed as amended by SI 1989/2359; SI 2002/335.]*

Marking, positioning and operation of emergency exits

B9.25   **24.**—(1) Subject to the provisions of paragraph 10 of Schedule 2, every emergency exit, other than an emergency exit with which a vehicle is required to be fitted under Regulation 21(11) shall comply with the following conditions—

(a) the emergency exit shall—

(i) be clearly marked as such inside and outside the vehicle;

(ii) be fitted with doors which open outwards or, in the case of a secondary emergency exit, be constructed of specified safety glass which can be readily broken by the application of reasonable force so as to afford a clear aperture of dimensions not less than those referred to in Regulation 21(1)(b);

(iii) except in the case of an emergency exit provided in the roof of a vehicle, be readily accessible to passengers;

(iv) in the case of a single-decked or half-decked vehicle or the lower deck of a double-decked vehicle, be so situated that passengers can step directly from the passage referred to in Regulation 26(1)(g) to the outside of the vehicle:

Provided that this requirement shall not apply in the case of an emergency exit provided in the roof of the vehicle or in the case of a secondary emergency exit;

(b) the means of operation of doors fitted to the emergency exit shall be clearly indicated;

(c) the doors of the emergency exit shall not be fitted with any system of power operation; and

(d) the means of operation of the doors of the emergency exit, other than those provided in the upper deck of a double-decked vehicle or in the roof of a vehicle, shall be readily accessible to persons of normal height standing at ground level outside the vehicle.

(2) Every emergency exit with which a vehicle is required to be fitted under Regulation 21(11) shall—

(a) be clearly marked as an emergency exit—

(i) on the inside of the vehicle, and

    (ii) in a case where the emergency exit can be opened from the outside, on the outside of the vehicle;

(b) be accessible to persons inside the vehicle when the vehicle is tilted to either side through an angle of 99 degrees, measured from the normal vertical plane of the vehicle;

(c) be clearly marked with its means of operation;

(d) if hinged, open outwards; and

(e) if ejectable, be fitted with a restraint which will prevent the part of the emergency exit which is ejected from becoming completely detached from the vehicle but which will not prevent egress from the vehicle by persons within it.

Access to exits

25. *[Omitted.]*   **B9.26**

Width of gangways

26.—(1) [Subject to [paragraphs (2), (3) and (4) and] to paragraph 11 of Sched-   **B9.27** ule 2], the following conditions shall be complied with in the case of every vehicle:—

(a) the width of every gangway shall be not less than—

    (i) 305 millimetres up to a height of 765 millimetres above the level of the deck of the vehicle,

    (ii) 355 millimetres at heights exceeding 765 millimetres but not exceeding 1.22 metres above the level of the deck of the vehicle, and

    (iii) 455 millimetres at heights exceeding 1.22 metres above the level of the deck of the vehicle;

(b) a vertical line projected upwards from the centre line of any gangway at deck level shall, to the height prescribed in Regulation 27 as the height of the gangway, be laterally not less than 150 millimetres from any part of the vehicle other than the roof above the gangway;

(c) being a vehicle which has a seating capacity exceeding 12 passengers, no part of any gangway which is within 910 millimetres of an entrance or exit (other than an emergency exit) to which it provides access shall be less than 530 millimetres in width; ...

(d) [...]

(e) where a part of a gangway which adjoins an entrance or exit is divided by a handrail, the width of that part of the gangway at any point on each side of the handrail shall not be less than 455 millimetres;

(f) where two seats (being either two seats each for one passenger only or two portions of a continuous seat, each of such portions being for one passenger only measured in accordance with condition (b) of Regulation 28(1)) are placed parallel to the longitudinal axis of a vehicle and face each other and the space between those seats is not required for the purpose of obtaining access from an entrance to any other seat or from any other seat to an exit (not being an emergency exit), that space shall not for the purposes of this Regulation and Regulation 27 be treated as forming part of the gangway;

(g) between every exit, not being either—

(i) an emergency exit provided in the roof of a vehicle, or

(ii) an exit provided in accordance with the provisions of Regulation 21(11) unless it be a primary or secondary emergency exit,

and a gangway there shall be a passage—

a. of dimensions not less than those prescribed for a gangway in condition (a) of paragraph (1);

b. so designed that a vertical line projected upwards from the centre line of the passage at floor level to a height of 760 millimetres from the level of the deck is laterally not less than 150 millimetres from any part of the vehicle (excluding any cowling or cover which projects not more than 230 millimetres from the bulkhead of the vehicle into the passage at floor level and not more than 230 millimetres above the deck level and the provision of which is required by the projection of part of the chassis or mechanism of the vehicle into the body);

c. which has a clear height at every point along the centre line of the passage of 1.52 metres from the deck level:Provided that—

(i) for the purposes of sub-paragraphs A and B of this paragraph a seat placed below or in front of an emergency exit, being such an exit provided on the upper deck of a double-decked vehicle or in the roof of a vehicle or which is a secondary emergency exit within the meaning of Regulation 21 shall be deemed to form part of such a passage, and

(ii) sub-paragraph C of this paragraph shall not apply in the case of a passage leading to an emergency exit, being such an exit provided on the upper deck of a double-decked vehicle or in the roof of a vehicle or which is a secondary emergency exit within the meaning of Regulation 21, nor shall it apply in the case of a passage in a single-decked vehicle having a permanent top if the vehicle has a seating capacity not exceeding 14 passengers.

(2) Subject to paragraph 11 of Schedule 2, where any space in front of a seat in a vehicle adapted to carry more than 12 passengers is required for the accommodation of seated passengers, the space within 225 millimetres of the seat shall not be taken into account in measuring the width of a gangway;

[...]

[(3) The provisions of paragraph (1)(c) and (g) do not apply as regards a crew seat occupied by crew.]

[(4) The provisions of paragraph (1)(a) shall not apply to a gangway of a vehicle if the width of that gangway is not less than—

(i) 450 millimetres up to a height of 1400 millimetres measured vertically from the floor of the vehicle, and

(ii) 550 millimetres at heights exceeding 1400 millimetres measured vertically from the floor of the vehicle.]

[Regulation 26 is printed as amended by SI 1982/1058; SI 2002/335.]   **B9.28**

Height of gangways

27. *[Omitted.]*   **B9.29**

Seats

28.—(1) Subject to [paragraph (5) of this regulation and to] paragraph 13 of   **B9.30**
Schedule 2, [the following conditions shall, as regards every passenger seat, be
complied with] in the case of every vehicle—

(a) the supports of all seats shall be securely fixed in position;

(b) a length of at least 400 millimetres measured horizontally along the front of each seat shall be allowed for the accommodation of a seated passenger:
Provided that in the case of a continuous seat fitted with arms for the purpose of separating the seating spaces, being arms so constructed that they can be folded back or otherwise put out of use, the seat shall be measured for the purposes of this paragraph as though it were not fitted with arms;

(c) every seat shall have a back rest so closed or otherwise constructed as to prevent, as far as practicable, the pockets of passengers from being picked;

(d) all passenger seats shall be so fitted—

(i) that the distance between any part of the back rest of any seat placed lengthwise and the corresponding part of the back rest of the seat facing it shall be, in the case of a vehicle which has a seating capacity not exceeding 12 passengers, not less than 1.37 metres, and in any other case, not less than 1.60 metres, and

(ii) that there is a clear space of at least 610 millimetres in front of the back rest of any seat measured from the centre of each complete length of the seat allowed for the accommodation of a seated passenger in accordance with condition (b) above and a clear space of 200 millimetres in front of any part of that seat:
Provided that in the case of a seat for more than three passengers—

(a) in the case of a vehicle being used as a stage carriage, and

(b) in the case of any vehicle to which this regulation applies and which is first used on or after 1st April 1982

where access to that seat can be obtained only from one end of the seat, the said clear spaces shall respectively be at least 685 millimetres and 300 millimetres;

(e) there shall be a clear space of at least 480 millimetres between any part of the front edge of any transverse seat and any part of any other seat which faces it:

Provided that any support provided for a table shall be disregarded if there is a clear space of at least 225 millimetres between that support and the front edge of the nearest seat and the support is not in such a position as to cause discomfort to passengers occupying the seats;

(f) [...]

(g) there shall, as respects every seat, be a clear space measured vertically from the centre of each complete length of the seat allowed for the accommodation of a seated passenger in accordance with condition (b) above which shall be, in the case of a vehicle which has a seating capacity not exceeding 12 passengers, not less than 910 millimetres, and, in any other case, not less than 965 millimetres;

(h) where any seat is so placed that a passenger seated upon it is liable to be thrown through any entrance to or exit from the vehicle or down a stairway in the vehicle, an effective screen or guard shall be placed so as to afford adequate protection against that occurrence to a passenger occupying that seat; and

(i) the shortest distances between the edge of the well of any step in the vehicle and a vertical plane passing through the front edge of any seat shall be not less than 225 millimetres:

Provided that this condition shall not apply in the case of the well of a step provided as a means of obtaining access only to any forward-facing front passenger seat placed alongside the driver in a vehicle which has a seating capacity not exceeding 12 passengers.

(2) In this Regulation and in paragraph 13 of Schedule 2 the expression "back rest" includes any part of the vehicle which is available for seated passengers to lean against.

[(3) Paragraph (1)(b) above shall not apply to a wheelchair carried in a vehicle.]

[(4) Where a table is fitted to the rear of a seat and is so constructed that it can be folded back or otherwise put out of use, distances shall be measured for the purposes of paragraph (1)(d) with the table folded or put out of use.]

[(5) In the case of a regulated public service vehicle, the provisions of this regulation shall apply with the following modifications—

(a) where in accordance with paragraph 3(1) of Schedule 2 to the 2000 Regulations, such a vehicle is fitted with priority seats that comply with the requirements set out in paragraph 3(2) of that Schedule, paragraph (1)(d)(ii) and paragraph (1)(g) shall not apply to such seats; and

(b) where seats fitted to such a vehicle comply with the requirements set out in paragraph 3(1) of Schedule 3 to the 2000 Regulations, paragraph (1)(d)(ii) shall not apply to such seats:

Provided that in the case of a seat for more than three passengers, or one or more priority seats in a seat for more than three passengers, and where access to that seat can be obtained only from one end of the seat, there shall be clear space of—

(i) at least 685 millimetres in front of the back rest of any of those seats (measured from the centre of each complete length of the seat allowed for the accommodation of a seated passenger in accordance with paragraph (1)(b)), and

(ii) 300 millimetres in front of any part of those seats.]

[Regulation 28 is printed as amended by SI 1982/1058; SI 1989/2359; SI 2002/ **B9.31**
335.

The expression "stage carriage" was formerly defined in the Public Passenger
Vehicles Act 1981 s.82(1), but the definition was revoked by the Transport Act
1985 s.139(3) and Sch.9; for the meaning of that expression, see now Sch.1,
para.16, to the 1985 Act above.]

[Crew seats

28A.—(1) Every crew seat shall be so constructed and located that when it is   **B9.32**
in use—

    (a) the person by whom it is occupied—

        (i) is adequately protected by means of arm rests from falling
sideways either to the left or the right,

        (ii) may conveniently place his feet either on a deck of the vehicle or
on a foot rest, and

        (iii) does not impede the driving of the vehicle either by obstructing
the driver's field of vision or otherwise; and

    (b) a space of at least 300 millimetres exists, along the whole width of the
seat, between the foremost edge of the seat and any other part of the
vehicle.

(2) Every crew seat shall be so constructed and located that when it is not in
use—

    (a) no part of it impedes the driving of the vehicle either by obstructing
the driver's field of vision or otherwise; and

    (b) every part of it which, when the seat is ready for or in use, protrudes
into a gangway so that the provisions of Regulation 26(1)(c) and (g)
are not complied with, is, as a result of automatic mechanism,
retracted so that those provisions are complied with.

(3) The words "FOR CREW USE ONLY" shall be marked either on or near and in
relation to every crew seat in letters not less than 10 millimetres tall and in a colour which contrasts with their background.

(4) The provisions of [paragraph (1)(a) to (e) of Regulation 28] apply as
respects a crew seat in the same manner as they apply as respects a seat to which
that Regulation applies.]

[Regulation 28A was inserted by SI 1982/1058 and is printed as amended by   **B9.33**
SI 2002/335.]

29–34. *[Omitted.]*   **B9.34**

PART III

REGULATIONS RELATING TO THE EQUIPMENT OF PUBLIC SERVICE VEHICLES

Fire extinguishing apparatus

35.—[(1) There shall be carried by every vehicle suitable and efficient appara-   **B9.35**
tus for extinguishing fire which is of one or more of the types specified in Schedule 4.]

(2) The apparatus referred to in paragraph (1) shall be—

    (a) readily available for use,

    (b) clearly marked with the appropriate British Standards Institution specification number, and

    (c) maintained in good and efficient working order.

[(3) Paragraph (1) shall not apply to a vehicle if it carries apparatus for extinguishing fire which would meet the requirements of that paragraph were there substituted—

    (a) for a reference in Schedule 4 to any British Standard, a reference to a corresponding standard;

    (b) for the reference in Schedule 4 to a test fire rating of 8A or the reference in that Schedule to a test fire rating of 21B, a reference to an equivalent level of performance specified in the corresponding standard; and

    (c) for the reference in paragraph (2)(b) to the appropriate British Standards Institution specification number, a reference to a marking indicating compliance with the corresponding standard.]

[(4) For the purposes of this regulation, *"corresponding standard"* in relation to a British Standard, means—

    (a) a standard or code of practice of a national standards body or equivalent body of any EEA State;

    (b) any international standard recognised for use as a standard by any EEA State; or

    (c) a technical specification or code of practice which, whether mandatory or not, is recognised for use as a standard by a public authority of any EEA State,

      where the standard code of practice, international standard or technical specification provides, in relation to fire extinguishers, a level of safety equivalent to that provided by the British Standard and contains a requirement as respects the markings of fire extinguishers equivalent to that provided by the British Standard.]

[(5) For the purposes of this regulation—

    "EEA State" means a state which is a contracting party to the EEA Agreement but, until the EEA Agreement comes into force as regards Liechtenstein, does not include the State of Liechtenstein; and

    "EEA Agreement" means the Agreement on the European Economic Area signed at Oporto on 2 May 1992 [*Cm. 2073*] as adjusted by the Protocol signed at Brussels on 17 March 1993 [*Cm. 2183*].]

B9.36   *[Regulation 35 is printed as amended by SI 1989/2359; SI 1995/305.*

As to the European Economic Area, see the introductory note to Section C below.]

First aid equipment

B9.37   **36.**—(1) There shall be carried by every vehicle being used as an express carriage or as a contract carriage a receptacle which contains the items specified in Schedule 5.

(2) The receptacle referred to in paragraph (1) shall be—

    (a) maintained in a good condition,

    (b) suitable for the purpose of keeping the items referred to in the said paragraph in good condition,

    (c) readily available for use, and

    (d) prominently marked as a first aid receptacle.

(3) The items referred to in paragraph (1) shall be maintained in good condition and shall be of a good and reliable quality and of a suitable design.

[Section 82(1) of the Public Passenger Vehicles Act 1981 formerly included **B9.38**
definitions of "contract carriage" and "express carriage". These definitions were repealed by the Transport Act 1985 s.139(3) and Sch.8. For the meanings of these expressions, see now Sch.1, para.16, to the 1985 Act above.]

PART IV

REGULATIONS RELATING TO THE USE OF PUBLIC SERVICE VEHICLES

Obstruction of entrances, exits and gangways

37. No person shall, while passengers are being carried by a vehicle, cause or **B9.39** permit any unnecessary obstruction to any entrance or exit or gangway of the vehicle.

Obstruction of driver

38. No person shall cause or permit any unnecessary obstruction of the driver **B9.40** of a vehicle.

Body maintenance

39. No person shall use a vehicle while it is carrying passengers or cause or **B9.41** permit it to be so used unless the inside and the outside of the body of the vehicle and all windows and fittings and all passengers' seats are maintained in clean and good condition.

Lamps

40.—(1) No person shall use a vehicle during the hours of darkness while it is **B9.42** carrying passengers or cause or permit it to be so used unless every lamp provided in compliance with Regulation 16 for the internal illumination of the vehicle is at all times during such use kept lighted to such extent as is necessary to provide adequate illumination of every access from any seat in the vehicle to every exit in the vehicle and of every such marking as is required by Regulation 24 to be provided in relation to every emergency exit in the vehicle:

Provided that it shall not be necessary to keep lighted any lamp provided on the upper deck of a double-decked vehicle if a barrier is secured across the bottom of all staircases leading to that deck so as effectively to prevent passengers using any such staircase.

(2) In this Regulation, *"hours of darkness"* means the time between half-an-hour after sunset and half-an-hour before sunrise.

Use of device for operating power-operated doors

B9.43   41.—(1) Except as provided by paragraph (2), no person shall use or cause or permit to be used any device for operating the doors of a vehicle having power-operated doors, being a device such as is mentioned in condition (b) of Regulation 23(1) or, as the case may be, in paragraph 9(b)(ii) of Schedule 2.

(2) Paragraph (1) shall not apply—

(a) in an emergency, as to the use of a device by any person;

(b) otherwise than in an emergency, as to the use of a device by a person in accordance with an authorisation by the operator of the vehicle, save that no such use shall occur if—

(i) the vehicle is in motion, and

(ii) the doors, when fully opened, project more than 80 millimetres from the side of the vehicle.

Filling of petrol tank

B9.44   42. While the engine of a vehicle is running no person shall cause or permit the filler cap fitted to the petrol tank of the vehicle to be removed or petrol to be put in its petrol tank.

Carriage of conductor

B9.45   43. No person shall use or cause or permit to be used as a stage carriage any vehicle which has a seating capacity exceeding 20 passengers unless a person authorised to act as conductor of the vehicle is carried thereby:

Provided that this Regulation shall not apply—

(i) in the case of a single-decked vehicle which has a seating capacity not exceeding 32 passengers and which is provided with only one emergency exit, if that exit and the entrance to the vehicle are both placed at the front of the vehicle and are readily visible to the driver from his seat and means are provided for the driver to be aware if any person outside the vehicle has been trapped by the closure of any door provided at that entrance, or

(ii) in the case of any other vehicle, if a certifying officer has stated in writing that the construction and design of the vehicle is such that a conductor is not required for the purpose of the safety of the passengers.

Carriage of inflammable or dangerous substances

B9.46   44.—(1) No person shall use or cause or permit to be used any vehicle by which any highly inflammable or otherwise dangerous substance is carried unless that substance is carried in containers so designed and constructed, or unless the substance is so packed, that, notwithstanding an accident to the vehicle, it is unlikely that damage to the vehicle or injury to passengers carried by the vehicle will be caused by reason of the presence on it of that substance.

(2) The requirements of this Regulation are in addition to and not in derogation of the requirements of regulations made under the Petroleum (Consolidation) Act 1928 or under any other Act.

Markings

45. No vehicle in respect of which, by virtue of [section 6(1)] of the … Act …, **B9.47**
a certificate of initial fitness, or a certificate under [section 10] of the … Act …,
or a certificate under [section 57 of the Road Traffic Act 1988] is required shall be
used on a road unless the vehicle is marked with clearly legible characters—

  (i) not less than 25 millimetres tall,
  (ii) in a conspicuous position on the nearside of the vehicle,
  (iii) in colours which contrast with their background, and
  (iv) indicating the name of the owner (as defined in [section 82(1)] of
      the … Act … in relation to a vehicle to which that definition ap-
      plies) of the vehicle and the owner's principal place of business.

[Regulation 45 is printed as amended by the Interpretation Act 1978 ss.17(2)(a) **B9.48**
and 23(1).]

[Use of seats

45A.—(1) No passenger shall be permitted to use a seat provided for a pas- **B9.49**
senger unless it complies with the requirements specified in Regulation 28.

(2) No crew shall be permitted to use a crew seat unless it complies with the
requirements specified in Regulation 28A.]

[Regulation 45A was inserted by SI 1982/1058.] **B9.50**

[Route and destination displays

45B.—(1) No person shall use or cause or permit to be used on a road any **B9.51**
regulated public service vehicle unless any route number or any destination fitted
in the positions provided for such displays with respect to the vehicle in accordance (as the case may be) with either paragraph 8 of Schedule 2 or paragraph 7
of Schedule 3 to the 2000 Regulations is displayed in characters which—

  (a) in the case of a route number, are not less than 200 millimetres in
      height on the front and rear of the vehicle and not less than 70 milli-
      metres in height on the side of the vehicle,
  (b) in the case of a destination, are not less than 125 millimetres in height
      on the front of the vehicle and not less than 70 millimetres in height
      on the side of the vehicle,
  (c) contrast with the display background, and
  (d) in the case of destination information, is not written in capital letters
      only.

(2) In this regulation—
  "character" means capital letters or numbers of a height (as specified in
      paragraph (1)(a) and (b) above) and lower case letters of a size rela-
      tive to the text of a capital letter for a given typeface;
  "destination" means a word or words to describe the route or final destina-
      tion; and
  "route number" means any combination of numbers or letters which desig-
      nate a route.]

[Regulation 45B was inserted by SI 2002/335.] **B9.52**

Part V

Regulations Relating to Certificates of Initial Fitness, Approval as a Type Vehicle and Conformity to an Approved Type Vehicle

B9.53   46–57. *[Omitted.]*

SCHEDULES

SCHEDULE 1

Regulations Revoked by Regulation 2

B9.54   *[Omitted.]*

SCHEDULE 2

Exceptions from the Conditions Prescribed in Part II as Applicable to Vehicles Registered before Certain Dates

*   *   *

B9.55   4. Regulation 16 (Artificial lighting) in so far as it consists of sub-paragraph (b), shall not apply in the case of a vehicle registered before 1st April 1959 and the requirements as to lighting circuits in that Regulation shall not apply in the case of a vehicle registered before 28th October 1964.

*   *   *

B9.56   8. Regulation 21 (Number, position and size of entrances and exits) shall not apply—

   (a) in so far as it consists of paragraphs (4) and (6) in the case of a vehicle registered before 1st April 1959 if it is provided with two exits so placed as not to be on the same side of the vehicle;

   (b) in so far as it consists of paragraph (6) in the case of a vehicle registered on or after 1st April 1959 and before 28th October 1964 which has a seating capacity exceeding 45 passengers if—

    (i) the vehicle is provided with two exits (of which neither is a secondary emergency exit) and those exits are not on the same side of the vehicle, and

    (ii) in a case where those exits are so placed that the distance between their centres is less than 3.05 metres, a secondary emergency exit is provided in such a position that there is a distance of not less than 3.05 metres between the nearest points of the openings of that exit and of whichever of the exits mentioned in sub-paragraph (i) above is the nearer to that exit. For the purpose of this paragraph the reference to the distance between the centres and between the nearest points of the openings of the two exits there mentioned shall be construed in accordance with Regulation 21(1)(e);

   (c) in so far as it consists of paragraph (9) —

    (i) in the case of a vehicle registered before 1st April 1959 (not being a single-decked vehicle having a permanent top) if it is provided with two exits so placed as not to be on the same sides of the vehicle; or

    (ii) in the case of a vehicle which—

        a. is provided with a platform such as is mentioned in proviso (i) to Regulation 21(4); or

        b. has a seating capacity not exceeding 14 passengers, if one means of exit and entrance is provided and is placed behind the rear wheels.

9. Regulation 23(1) (Doors) shall not apply—   **B9.57**

(a) in so far as it consists of sub-paragraph (j) in the case of a vehicle registered before 1st August 1968;

(b) save in so far as it consists of sub-paragraph (j) in the case of a vehicle registered before 19th June 1968 if—

    (i) every entrance door and every exit door can be readily opened from inside and outside the vehicle by one operation of the locking mechanism:Provided that a vehicle shall not be deemed to fail to comply with this sub-paragraph by reason only of the fact that, for the purpose of securing the vehicle when unattended, any entrance or exit door has been fitted with a supplementary lock with or without an actuating mechanism if the lock is so designed and constructed that the door can at all times be opened by a person inside the vehicle by one operation of the ordinary locking mechanism;

    (ii) except in the case of a vehicle registered before 1st April 1959, the device provided outside the vehicle for operating the locking mechanism of the door (not being a device provided in relation to an emergency exit on the upper deck of a double-decked vehicle or in the roof of a half-decked vehicle) is readily accessible to persons of normal height standing at ground level outside the vehicle;

    (iii) except in the case of a vehicle registered before 1st April 1959, means are provided for holding every entrance and exit door securely in the closed position;

    (iv) except in the case of a vehicle registered before 1st April 1959, all locks and fastenings fitted to entrance and exit doors are so designed and fitted that they are not likely to become dislodged or be operated accidentally, and, in the said excepted case, door handles or levers to door catches are so designed and fitted that they are not likely to become dislodged or be operated accidentally;

    (v) where any entrances are provided with doors which are designed to remain open when the vehicle is in motion, suitable fastenings are provided to hold such doors securely in the opened position;

    (vi) except in the case of a vehicle registered before 1st April 1959, every sliding door and every folding door fitted to an entrance or exit is provided with suitable fastenings to prevent it from being closed by any movement of the vehicle;

    (vii) all doors can open so as not to obstruct clear access to any entrance or exit from inside or outside the vehicle; and

    (viii) except in the case of a vehicle registered before 1st April 1959, the means by which a power-operated door may be opened are provided inside the vehicle on or adjacent to the door and their position is clearly indicated and there is also an indication that the said means may be used by passengers only in an emergency; and the storage and transmission system of the power for operating the door is such that operation of the doors does not adversely affect the efficient operation of the braking system of the vehicle and the apparatus is so designed and constructed that in the event of the system becoming inoperative the door can be operated manually from inside and outside the vehicle.

10. Regulation 24(1)(b)(iv) (Marking, positioning and operation of emergency exits)   **B9.58** shall not apply in the case of a vehicle registered before 1st April 1959, being a vehicle which is provided with a rear platform, if an emergency exit (of which the clear height at the centre line is not less than 1.52 metres and of which the width is not less than 455 millimetres) is provided from that platform to the rear of the vehicle and is enclosed by means of a door placed on the near-side of that platform.

B9.59   **11.** The provisions of Regulation 26 (Width of gangways) specified in column 1 of the Table below shall not apply in the case of a vehicle specified, in relation to those provisions, in column 2 of that Table.

Table

1	2
Paragraph (1)(e) [...]	A vehicle registered before 19th June 1968.
Paragraph (1)(a), (c) and (g) c.	A vehicle registered before 1st April 1959 if the width of every gangway is not less than 305 millimetres up to a height of 765 millimetres above the level of the deck and not less than 355 millimetres above that height.
Paragraph 1(c)	A vehicle registered after 1st April 1959 and before 19th June 1968 if no part of any gangway which is within 915 millimetres of an exit (other than an emergency exit) to which it leads is less than 530 millimetres in width.

B9.60   *[The Table to para.11 is printed as amended by SI 2002/335.]*

*   *   *

B9.61   **13.** Regulation 28 (Seats) shall not apply—

(a) in so far as it consists of paragraph (1)(d) in the case of a vehicle registered before 1st April 1959 if all the passengers' seats in the vehicle are so fitted—

(a) that no part of the back rest of any seat placed lengthwise is less than 1.37 metres from the corresponding part of the back rest of the seat facing it; and

(b) there is in relation to every transverse seat in the vehicle a clear space of at least 660 millimetres in front of the whole length of the top of the back rest of that seat measured from the centre of each complete length of the seat allowed for the accommodation of a seated passenger in accordance with condition (b) of the said paragraph (1) but disregarding any handles or grips which do not project more than 105 millimetres from the back rest;

(b) in so far as it consists of [paragraph (1)(g)] in the case of a vehicle registered before 1st April 1959 if no seat placed over the arch of a wheel of the vehicle is in such a position as to cause discomfort to passengers;

(c) in so far as it consists of paragraph (1)(h) in the case of a vehicle registered before 1st April 1959 if, as respects any transverse seat in the vehicle which is so placed that a passenger seated upon it is liable to be thrown through any entrance to or exit from the vehicle or down a stairway in the vehicle, an effective screen or guard is placed so as to afford adequate protection against that occurrence to a passenger occupying that seat.

B9.62   *[Paragraph 13 is printed as amended by SI 2002/335.]*

SCHEDULE 3

Conditions Prescribed in Regulations in Part II, or Provisions Thereof, Applicable to Certain Vehicles Bearing a Designated Approval Mark

B9.63   *[Omitted.]*

(see regulation 23(1A))   [SCHEDULE 3A

Application

B9.64   **1.** This Schedule applies to every vehicle registered on or after the 1st April 1980.

Conditions

2. Save as provided below, the following conditions shall be complied with in relation   **B9.65**
to every power-operated door which is—

- (a) fitted to a vehicle to which this Schedule applies, and
- (b) so situated in a vehicle that the whole of the door opening is more than 500 milli-
      metres behind the transverse vertical plane that touches the back of the driver's
      seat when the seat is in its rearmost position.

3.—(1) The first condition is that when the door is prevented from closing by the pres-   **B9.66**
ence of a fixed vertical surface that is 60 millimetres high placed at right angles to the
direction of movement of the closing edge—

- (a) the force exerted on the surface does not exceed 150 newtons and
- (b) the door re-opens automatically and remains open until a closing control is oper-
      ated manually.

(2) This condition shall not have to be met when a door is within 30 millimetres of its
fully closed position, but shall otherwise apply wherever the surface is placed within the
door opening (regardless of the stage of closure when the door first strikes the surface or of
the part of the closing edge that strikes the surface).

4.—(1) The second condition is that whenever the door is closed on to the fingers or the   **B9.67**
palm of the hand—

- (a) the door re-opens automatically and remains open until a closing control is oper-
      ated manually, or
- (b) the fingers or hand can be readily extracted from the door without injury.

(2) This condition shall not apply to a door fitted to a coach manufactured before the 1st
of October 1992 or registered before the 1st of April 1993.

(3) In this paragraph *"coach"* has the same meaning as in the Road Vehicles (Construction and Use) Regulations 1986 [*SI 1986/1078, as amended, q.v.*].

5. The third condition is that a visual device, clearly visible to the driver at all times, is   **B9.68**
activated whenever the door is not fully closed.

Transitional and savings

6.—(1) This Schedule shall not have effect until 1st April 1993 in relation to a vehicle   **B9.69**
manufactured before the 14th May 1990 or first used before the 1st of October 1990.

(2) Nothing in this Schedule shall be construed as derogating from the requirements of
regulation 23(1).]

[Schedule 3A was inserted by SI 1989/2359.]   **B9.70**

(see regulation 35)   [SCHEDULE 4

FIRE EXTINGUISHING APPARATUS

A fire extinguisher which complies in all respects with the specification for portable fire   **B9.71**
extinguishers issued by the British Standards Institution numbered BS 5423: 1977 or BS
5423: 1980 or BS 5423: 1987 and which—

- (a) has a minimum test [fire] rating of 8A or 21B, and
- (b) contains water or foam or contains and is marked to indicate that it contains, halon
      1211 or halon 1301.]

*[Schedule 4 is printed as substituted by SI 1989/2359 and as subsequently   **B9.72**
amended by SI 1995/305.]*

(see regulation 36)   SCHEDULE 5

FIRST AID EQUIPMENT

- (i) Ten antiseptic wipes, foil packed.   **B9.73**

   (ii) One conforming disposable bandage (not less than 7.5 centimetres wide).

  (iii) Two triangular bandages.

  (iv) One packet of 24 assorted adhesive dressings.

   (v) Three large sterile unmedicated ambulance dressings (not less than 15.0 centimetres $\times$ 20.0 centimetres).

  (vi) Two sterile eye pads, with attachments.

 (vii) Twelve assorted safety pins.

(viii) One pair of rustless blunt-ended scissors.

*   *   *

The Motorways Traffic (England and Wales) Regulations 1982

(SI 1982/1163)

[Nothing contained in these regulations precludes any person, acting in accordance with Pt IV (regs 15 and 16) of the Traffic Signs (Temporary Obstructions) Regulations 1997 (SI 1997/3053), from placing a flat traffic delineator, a keep right sign, a traffic cone, a traffic pyramid, a traffic triangle, or a warning lamp on a special road to which these regulations apply; nor, having so placed such item, from removing it; see SI 1997/3053 reg.17 below. **B10.01**

The text of these regulations is printed as amended by: **B10.02**

> *the Motorways Traffic (England and Wales) (Amendment) Regulations 1983 (SI 1983/374) (April 16, 1983);*

> *the Motorways Traffic (England and Wales) (Amendment) Regulations 1984 (SI 1984/1479) (October 17, 1984);*

> *the Motorways Traffic (England and Wales) (Amendment) Regulations 1992 (SI 1992/1364) (July 1, 1992);*

> *the Motorways Traffic (England and Wales) (Amendment) Regulations 1995 (SI 1995/158) (January 1, 1996);*

> *the Motorways Traffic (England and Wales) (Amendment) Regulations 1996 (SI 1996/3053) (January 1, 1997);*

> *the Fire and Rescue Services Act 2004 (Consequential Amendments) (England) Order 2004 (SI 2004/3168) (December 30, 2004);*

> *the Motorways Traffic (England and Wales) (Amendment) Regulations 2004 (SI 2004/3258) (January 1, 2005); and*

> *the Serious Organised Crime and Police Act 2005 (Consequential and Supplementary Amendments to Secondary Legislation) Order 2006 (SI 2006/594) (April 1, 2006).*

The amending instruments are referred to in the notes to the principal regulations only by their years and numbers. The dates referred to above are the dates on which the amending instruments came into force.]

ARRANGEMENT OF REGULATIONS

Regulation **B10.03**

Commencement and citation

B10.04   **1.** *[Omitted.]*

Revocation

B10.05   **2.** *[Omitted.]*

Interpretation

B10.06   **3.**—(1) In these Regulations, the following expressions have the meanings hereby respectively assigned to them:—

[(a) *"the 1984 Act"* means the Road Traffic Regulation Act 1984 [*q.v.*];]

(b) [*"carriageway"* means that part of a motorway which—

(i) is provided for the regular passage of vehicular motor traffic along the motorway; and

(ii) where a hard shoulder is provided, has the approximate position of its left-hand or near-side edge marked with a traffic sign of the type shown in diagram 1012.1 in [Schedule 6 to the Traffic Signs Regulations and General Directions 2002] [*SI 2002/ 3113*]];

(c) *"central reservation"* means that part of a motorway which separates the carriageway to be used by vehicles travelling in one direction from the carriageway to be used by vehicles travelling in the opposite direction;

(d) *"excluded traffic"* means traffic which is not traffic of Classes I or II;

(e) *"hard shoulder"* means a part of the motorway which is adjacent to and situated on the left hand or near side of the carriageway when facing in the direction in which vehicles may be driven in accordance with Regulation 6, and which is designed to take the weight of a vehicle;

(f) *"motorway"* means any road or part of a road to which these Regulations apply by virtue of Regulation 4;

[(ff) *"traffic officer"* means an individual designated as such by, or under an authority given by, the Secretary of State or the National Assembly for Wales in accordance with section 2 of the Traffic Management Act 2004;]

(g) *"verge"* means any part of a motorway which is not a carriageway, a hard shoulder, or a central reservation.

(2) A vehicle shall be treated for the purposes of any provision of these Regulations as being on any part of a motorway specified in that provision if any part of the vehicle (whether it is at rest or not) is on the part of the motorway so specified.

(3) Any provision of these Regulations containing any prohibition or restriction relating to the driving, moving or stopping of a vehicle, or to its remaining at rest, shall be construed as a provision that no person shall use a motorway by driving, moving or stopping the vehicle or by causing or permitting it to be driven or moved, or to stop or remain at rest, in contravention of that prohibition or restriction.

(4) In these Regulations references to numbered classes of traffic are references to the classes of traffic set out in Schedule 4 to the Highways Act 1980 [*q.v.*]

[Regulation 3 is printed as amended by the Road Traffic Regulation Act 1984 **B10.07** *s.144(1) and Sch.10, para.2; SI 1984/1479; SI 1992/1364; the Interpretation Act 1978 ss.17(2)(a) and 23(1); SI 2004/3258.]*

[**4.** Subject to section 17(5) of the 1984 Act, these Regulations apply to every **B10.08** special road or part of a special road which can be used only by traffic of Class I or II.]

[Regulation 4 is printed as substituted by SI 1992/1364.]   **B10.09**

Vehicles to be driven on the carriageway only

5. Subject to the following provisions of these Regulations, no vehicle shall be **B10.10** driven on any part of a motorway which is not a carriageway.

Direction of driving

6.—(1) Where there is a traffic sign indicating that there is no entry to a carriageway at a particular place, no vehicle shall be driven or moved onto that carriageway at that place.

(2) Where there is a traffic sign indicating that there is no left or right turn into a carriageway at a particular place, no vehicle shall be so driven or moved as to cause it to turn to the left or (as the case may be) to the right into that carriageway at that place.

(3) Every vehicle on a length of carriageway which is contiguous to a central reservation, shall be driven in such a direction that the central reservation is at all times on the right hand or off side of the vehicle.

(4) Where traffic signs are so placed that there is a length of carriageway (being a length which is not contiguous to a central reservation) which can be entered at one end only by vehicles driven in conformity with paragraph (1) of this Regulation, every vehicle on that length of carriageway shall be driven in such a direction only as to cause it to proceed away from that end of that length of carriageway towards the other end thereof.

(5) Without prejudice to the foregoing provisions of this Regulation, no vehicle which—

(a) is on a length of carriageway on which vehicles are required by any of the foregoing provisions of this Regulation to be driven in one direction only and is proceeding in or facing that direction, or

(b) is on any other length of carriageway and is proceeding in or facing one direction,

shall be driven or moved so as to cause it to turn and proceed in or face the opposite direction.

Restriction on stopping

B10.12   7.—(1) Subject to the following provisions of this Regulation, no vehicle shall stop or remain at rest on a carriageway.

(2) Whether it is necessary for a vehicle which is being driven on a carriageway to be stopped while it is on a motorway—

(a) by reason of a breakdown or mechanical defect or lack of fuel, oil or water, required for the vehicle; or

(b) by reason of any accident, illness or other emergency; or

(c) to permit any person carried in or on the vehicle to recover or move any object which has fallen onto a motorway; or

(d) to permit any person carried in or on the vehicle to give help which is required by any other person in any of the circumstances specified in the foregoing provisions of this paragraph,

the vehicle shall, as soon and in so far as is reasonably practicable, be driven or moved off the carriageway on to, and may stop and remain at rest on, any hard shoulder which is contiguous to that carriageway.

(3) (a) A vehicle which is at rest on a hard shoulder shall so far as is reasonably practicable be allowed to remain at rest on that hard shoulder in such a position only that no part of it or of the load carried thereby shall obstruct or be a cause of danger to vehicles using the carriageway.

(b) A vehicle shall not remain at rest on a hard shoulder for longer than is necessary in the circumstances or for the purposes specified in paragraph 2 of this Regulation.

(4) Nothing in the foregoing provisions of this Regulation shall preclude a vehicle from stopping or remaining at rest on a carriageway while it is prevented from proceeding along the carriageway by the presence of any other vehicle or any person or object.

Restriction on reversing

B10.13   8. No vehicle on a motorway shall be driven or moved backwards except in so far as it is necessary to back the vehicle to enable it to proceed forwards or to be connected to any other vehicle.

Restriction on the use of hard shoulders

B10.14   9. No vehicle shall be driven or stop or remain at rest on any hard shoulder except in accordance with paragraphs (2) and (3) of Regulation 7.

Vehicles not to use the central reservation or verge

10. No vehicle shall be driven or moved or stop or remain at rest on a central **B10.15**
reservation or verge.

Vehicles not to be driven by learner drivers

11.—[(1) Subject to paragraph (3), a person shall not drive on a motorway a **B10.16**
motor vehicle to which this regulation applies if he is authorised to drive that vehicle only by virtue of his being the holder of a provisional licence.

(2) This regulation applies to—

  (a) a motor vehicle in category A or B or sub-category C1+E (8.25
      tonnes), D1 (not for hire or reward), D1+E (not for hire or reward) or
      P, and

  (b) a motor vehicle in category B+E or sub-category C1 if the provisional
      licence authorising the driving of such a motor vehicle was in force at
      a time before 1st January 1997.

(3) Paragraph (1) shall not apply in relation to a vehicle if the holder of the
provisional licence has passed a test of competence prescribed under section 89
of the Road Traffic Act 1988 [*q.v.*] for the grant of a licence to drive that vehicle.

(4) In this regulation—

  (a) the expression *"in force"* and expressions relating to vehicle catego-
      ries shall be construed in accordance with regulations 3(2) and 4(2)
      respectively of the Motor Vehicles (Driving Licences) Regulations
      1996 [*SI 1996/2824*];

  (b) *"provisional licence"*, in relation to any vehicle, means a licence—

      (i) granted under section 97(2) of the Road Traffic Act 1988, or

      (ii) treated, by virtue of section 98 of that Act and regulations made
           thereunder, as authorising its holder to drive that vehicle as if
           he were authorised by a provisional licence to do so.]

[Regulation 11 is printed as substituted by SI 1996/3053. **B10.17**

*The Motor Vehicles (Driving Licences) Regulations 1996 (to which reference
is made in reg.11(4)(a)) have been revoked and replaced with effect from
November 12, 1999 by the Motor Vehicles (Driving Licences) Regulations 1999
(SI 1999/2864) below. Attention is drawn in particular to regs 3(2) and 4(2) of SI
1999/2864.]*

Restriction on use of right hand or off-side lane

12.—[(1) This Regulation applies to— **B10.18**

  [(a) a goods vehicle having a maximum laden weight exceeding 7.5
      tonnes,]

  [(aa) a goods vehicle—

      (i) having a maximum laden weight exceeding 3.5 tonnes but not
          exceeding 7.5 tonnes, and

      (ii) to which regulation 36B of the Road Vehicles (Construction and
           Use) Regulations 1986 [*SI 1986/1078, q.v.*] applies or would ap-
           ply but for paragraph (14)(a) or (b) of that regulation;]

[(b) a passenger vehicle which is constructed or adapted to carry more than eight seated passengers in addition to the driver the maximum laden weight of which exceeds 7.5 tonnes;]

[(bb) a passenger vehicle—

(i) which is constructed or adapted to carry more than eight seated passengers in addition to the driver the maximum laden weight of which does not exceed 7.5 tonnes, and

(ii) to which regulation 36A of the Road Vehicles (Construction and Use) Regulations 1986 (Speed limiters) applies or would apply but for paragraph (13)(a) or (b) of that regulation;]

(c) a motor vehicle drawing a trailer; and

[(d) a vehicle which is a motor tractor, a light locomotive or a heavy locomotive.]

(2) Subject to the provisions of paragraph (3) below, no vehicle to which this Regulation applies shall be driven or moved or stop or remain at rest on the right hand or off-side lane of a length of carriageway which has three or more traffic lanes at any place where all the lanes are open for use by traffic proceeding in the same direction.

(3) The prohibition contained in paragraph (2) above shall not apply to a vehicle whilst it is being driven on any right hand or off-side lane such as is mentioned in that paragraph in so far as it is necessary for the vehicle to be driven to enable it to pass another vehicle which is carrying or drawing a load of exceptional width.

[(4) Nothing in this regulation shall have effect so as to require a vehicle to change lane during a period when it would not be reasonably practicable for it to do so without involving danger of injury to any person or inconvenience to other traffic.]

[(5) In this Regulation *"goods vehicle"*, *"passenger vehicle"* and *"maximum laden weight"* have the same meanings as in Schedule 6 to the 1984 Act.]

B10.19   *[Regulation 12 is printed as substituted by SI 1983/374, and as subsequently amended by SI 1992/1364; SI 1995/158; SI 2004/3258.]*

Restrictions affecting persons on foot on a motorway

B10.20   13. [...]
[Revoked by SI 1992/1364.]

Restrictions affecting animals carried in vehicles

B10.21   14. The person in charge of any animal which is carried by a vehicle using a motorway shall, so far is practicable, secure that—

(a) the animal shall not be removed from or permitted to leave the vehicle while the vehicle is on a motorway, and

(b) if it escapes from, or it is necessary for it to be removed from, or permitted to leave, the vehicle—

(i) it shall not go or remain on any part of the motorway other than a hard shoulder, and

(ii) it shall whilst it is not on or in the vehicle be held on a lead or otherwise kept under proper control.

Use of motorway by excluded traffic

15.—(1) Excluded traffic is hereby authorised to use a motorway on the occasions or in the emergencies and to the extent specified in the following provisions of this paragraph, that is to say— **B10.22**

    (a) traffic of Classes III or IV may use a motorway for the maintenance, repair, cleaning or clearance of any part of a motorway or for the erection, laying, placing, maintenance, testing, alteration, repair or removal of any structure, works or apparatus in, on, under or over any part of a motorway;

    (b) pedestrians may use a motorway—

        (i) when it is necessary for them to do so as a result of an accident or emergency or of a vehicle being at rest on a motorway in any of the circumstances specified in paragraph (2) of Regulation 7, or

        (ii) in any of the circumstances specified in sub-paragraphs (b), (d), (e) or (f) of paragraph (1) of Regulation 16.

(2) The Secretary of State may authorise the use of a motorway by any excluded traffic on occasion or in emergency or for the purpose of enabling such traffic to cross a motorway or to secure access to premises abutting on or adjacent to a motorway.

(3) Where by reason of any emergency the use of any road (not being a motorway) by any excluded traffic is rendered impossible or unsuitable the Chief Officer of Police of the police area in which a motorway or any part of a motorway is situated, or any officer of or above the rank of superintendent authorised in that behalf by that Chief Officer, may—

    (a) authorise any excluded traffic to use that motorway or that part of a motorway as an alternative road for the period during which the use of the other road by such traffic continues to be impossible or unsuitable, and

    (b) relax any prohibition or restriction imposed by these Regulations in so far as he considers it necessary to do so in connection with the use of that motorway or that part of a motorway by excluded traffic in pursuance of any such authorisation as aforesaid.

Exceptions and relaxations

16.—(1) Nothing in the foregoing provisions of these Regulations shall preclude any person from using a motorway otherwise than in accordance with the provisions in any of the following circumstances, that is to say— **B10.23**

    (a) where he does so in accordance with any direction or permission given by a constable in uniform[, a traffic officer in uniform] or with the indication given by a traffic sign;

    (b) where, in accordance with any permission given by [a traffic officer in uniform or] a constable, he does so for the purpose of investigating any accident which has occurred on or near a motorway;

    (c) where it is necessary for him to do so to avoid or prevent an accident or to obtain or give help required as the result of an accident or emergency, and he does so in such manner as to cause as little danger or inconvenience as possible to other traffic on a motorway;

(d) where he does so in the exercise of his duty as a constable[, a traffic officer, when in uniform] [as a member of the Serious Organised Crime Agency for the purposes of that Agency] or as a member of [an ambulance service or as an employee of a fire and rescue authority employed for the purposes of that authority];

(e) where it is necessary for him to do so to carry out in an efficient manner—

(i) the maintenance, repair, cleaning, clearance, alteration or improvement of any part of a motorway, or

(ii) the removal of any vehicle from any part of a motorway, or

(iii) the erection, laying, placing, maintenance, testing, alteration, repair or removal of any structure, works or apparatus in, on, under or over any part of a motorway; or

(f) where it is necessary for him to do so in connection with any inspection, survey, investigation or census which is carried out in accordance with any general or special authority granted by the Secretary of State.

(2) Without prejudice to the foregoing provisions of these Regulations, the Secretary of State may relax any prohibition or restriction imposed by these Regulations.

B10.24   *[Regulation 16 is printed as amended by SI 2004/3168; SI 2004/3258 and SI 2006/594.]*

The Road Transport (International Passenger Services) Regulations 1984

(SI 1984/748)

[These regulations refer to the Agreement on the Carriage of Passengers by **B11.01**
Road by means of Occasional Coach and Bus Services (ASOR) (O.J. No.L230,
August 5, 1982, p.38). A new Agreement on the International Occasional Car-
riage of Passengers by Coach and Bus (the Interbus Agreement) entered into
force on January 1, 2003 (O.J. No.L321, November 26, 2002, p.13; q.v.). The
contracting parties, which had signed and ratified the Interbus Agreement by the
entry into force date, are as follows: the Czech Republic, the European Com-
munity, Hungary, Lithuania, Latvia, Romania and Slovenia. The Interbus Agree-
ment has also been ratified by Albania, Bosnia and Herzegovina, Bulgaria,
Croatia, Macedonia, Moldova, Montenegro, Poland and Turkey. The text of the
ASOR Agreement, so far as is material, is reproduced in the twenty-third edition
of this work.

The text of these regulations is printed as amended by: **B11.02**

> *the Road Transport (International Passenger Services) (Amendment)*
> *Regulations 1987 (SI 1987/1755) (November 1, 1987);*

> *the Road Transport (International Passenger Services) (Amendment)*
> *Regulations 1988 (SI 1988/1809) (November 18, 1988); and*

> *the Road Transport (International Passenger Services) Regulations*
> *2004 (SI 2004/1882) (August 30, 2004).*

The amending regulations are referred to in the notes to the principal regula-
tions by their years and numbers. The dates referred to above are the dates on
which the amending regulations came into force.

The principal regulations have been further amended by the Road Transport
(International Passenger Services) (Amendment) Regulations 1990 (SI 1990/
1103), the Road Transport (International Passenger Services) (Amendment)
Regulations 2003 (SI 2003/1118) and the Road Transport (International Pas-
senger Services) (Amendment) Regulations 2008 (SI 2008/1577), the Road
Transport (International Passenger Services) (Amendment) Regulations 2009 (SI
2009/879); but the amending regulations do not affect the text of any provision
which is printed in this work.]

ARRANGEMENT OF REGULATIONS
PART I
GENERAL
B11.03

Regulation

* * *

SCHEDULES

Schedules 1, 2

PART I

GENERAL

Citation, commencement and revocation

1. *[Omitted.]*   **B11.04**

Interpretation

2.—(1) In these Regulations —   **B11.05**

    (a) the references to the following provisions, that is to say—

Council Regulation No.117/66

Council Regulation No.516/72

Council Regulation No.517/72 and

Commission Regulation No.1016/68

are references, respectively, to the Community provisions more particularly described in Schedule 1 and references to *"the Council Regulations"* or *"the Commission Regulation"* shall be construed accordingly;

    (b) *"ASOR"* means the Agreement on the International Carriage of Passengers by Road by means of Occasional Coach and Bus Services (ASOR), approved on behalf of the Economic Community pursuant to Council Decision (EEC) of 20th July 1982 concluding the Agreement *[O.J. No.L230, August 5, 1982, p.38]*, entering into force for the Economic Community on 1st December 1983, as read with Council Regulation (EEC) No.56/83 on measures implementing the Agreement *[O.J. No.L10, January 13, 1983, p.1]*.

    (c) *"ASOR State"* means—

        (i) a state, not being a member State, which is a Contracting Party to ASOR and to which the provisions of Sections II and III of ASOR apply in accordance with Article 18 thereof; or

        (ii) the Economic Community;

    (d) *"ASOR regulated"* means, in relation to the carriage of passengers, the international carriage of passengers by road to which ASOR applies, namely in the circumstances specified in Article 1 thereof, that is to say, by means of occasional services (within the meaning of that Agreement) effected—

        (i) between the territories of two ASOR States, or starting and finishing in the territory of the same ASOR State; and

        (ii) should the need arise during such services, in transit through the territory of another ASOR State or through the territory of a state which is not an ASOR State; and

        (iii) using vehicles registered in the territory of an ASOR State which by virtue of their construction and their equipment, are suitable for carrying more than nine persons, including the driver, and are intended for that purpose and references to the carriage of passengers which is ASOR regulated include unladen journeys of the vehicles concerned with such carriage;

(e) *"Community regulated"* means, in relation to the carriage of passengers, the international carriage of passengers by road to which Council Regulation No.117/66 applies, namely in the circumstances mentioned in Article 4(1) thereof, that is to say—

    (i) where the place of departure is in the territory of a member State and the destination is in the territory of the same or another member State; and

    (ii) the vehicle is registered in a member State and in construction and equipment is suitable for carrying more than nine persons, including the driver, and is intended for that purpose,

and references to the carriage of passengers which is Community regulated include unladen journeys of the vehicles concerned with such carriage;

(f) *"ECMT State"* means a State which is a member of the European Conference of Ministers of Transport of the 17th November 1953 but not a member State or an ASOR State;

(g) *"the Secretary of State"* means [the Secretary of State for the Environment, Transport and the Regions];

(h) *"examiner"* has the same meaning as in section 7(1) of the Road Traffic (Foreign Vehicles) Act 1972;

(i) *"public service vehicle"* shall be construed in accordance with section 1 of the Act of 1981 [*q.v.*];

(j) *"the Act of 1981"* means the Public Passenger Vehicles Act 1981.

(2) Any reference in these Regulations to a numbered Regulation or Schedule is a reference to the Regulations or Schedule bearing that number in these Regulations.

B11.06   *[Regulation 2 is printed as amended by the Secretary of State for the Environment, Transport and the Regions Order 1997 (SI 1997/2971); the Secretaries of State for Transport, Local Government and the Regions and for Environment, Food and Rural Affairs Order 2001 (SI 2001/2568); the Transfer of Functions (Transport, Local Government and the Regions) Order 2002 (SI 2002/2626); SI 2004/1882.*

Council Regulations (EEC) 117/66, 516/72 and 517/72 (to which references are made in reg.2(1)) were repealed by Regulation (EEC) 684/92 art.21(1) Regulation (EEC) 684/92 was itself repealed by European and Council Regulation (EC) 1073/2009 of October 21, 2009 on common rules for access to the international market for coach and bus services, and amending Regulation (EC) 561/2006 (O.J. No.L300, November 14, 2009, p.88) (q.v.) with effect from December 4, 2011. References to Council Regulations (EEC) 117/66, 516/72 and 517/72 should be construed as references to Regulation (EC) 1073/2009. Commission Regulation (EEC) 1016/68 (to which reference is made in reg.2(1)) was repealed (subject to transitional provisions) by Regulation (EEC) 1839/92 arts 10, 11 (O.J. No.L187, July 7, 1992, p.5).]

Extent

B11.07   **3.** These Regulations do not extend to Northern Ireland.

PART II

MODIFICATIONS OF THE ACT OF 1981 IN RELATION TO VEHICLES REGISTERED IN THE UNITED KINGDOM WHEN USED FOR THE INTERNATIONAL CARRIAGE OF PASSENGERS

Community regulated regular, shuttle and works services by vehicles registered in the United Kingdom

4.—(1) This Regulation applies to a vehicle registered in the United Kingdom   **B11.08**
which is being used for Community regulated carriage of passengers in so far as the vehicle—

    (a) is used to provide any service for the carriage of passengers such as is mentioned in Article 1, 2 or 6 of Council Regulation No.117/66; and

    (b) is so used in accordance with such of the requirements of the Council Regulations as apply in relation to the service in question.

(2) The provisions of the Act of 1981 shall have effect as if—

    (a) *[lapsed.]*

    (b) in relation to a vehicle to which this Regulation applies registered in Northern Ireland, sections 6, 12, 18, 22 ... of the Act of 1981 were omitted.

[Regulation 4 is printed as it has effect after the repeal of s.30 of the Public   **B11.09**
Passenger Vehicles Act 1981.]

Non-Community regulated regular and shuttle services by public service vehicles registered in the United Kingdom

5.—(1) This Regulation applies to a public service vehicle registered in the   **B11.10**
United Kingdom which is being used for the international carriage of passengers by road which is not Community regulated but where the vehicle is being used to provide a service for the carriage of passengers of a description such as is mentioned in Article 1 or 2 of Council Regulation 117/66 (that is to say, a regular service, a special regular service or a shuttle service as defined in those Articles).

(2) The provisions of the Act of 1981 [and Parts I and II of the Transport Act 1985] shall have effect as if—

    (a) in relation to a vehicle to which this Regulation applies registered in Northern Ireland, sections 6, 12, 18 and 22 of the Act of 1981 were omitted; and

    (b) in relation to a vehicle to which this Regulation applies registered in Great Britain or in Northern Ireland, for [section 6 of the Transport Act 1985 there shall be substituted the following section and section 35 of that Act shall be omitted]:—

"**[6.]**—(1) No person shall cause or permit a public service vehicle to be used on a road for the international carriage of passengers unless there is in force in relation to the use of the vehicle, and is carried on the vehicle, an international passenger transport authorisation.

(2) A certifying officer or a public service vehicle examiner may at any time, on production if so required of his authority, require the operator or

the driver of any such vehicle as is referred to in subsection (1) above, to produce and to permit him to inspect and copy an international passenger transport authorisation relating to the use of the vehicle, and for that purpose may require the vehicle to be stopped and may detain the vehicle for such time as is requisite for the purpose of inspecting and copying the authorisation.

(3) A person who—

    (a) without reasonable excuse contravenes subsection (1) of this section, or

    (b) without reasonable excuse fails to comply with a requirement of a certifying officer or public service vehicle examiner, or wilfully obstructs such officer or examiner, in the exercise of his powers under subsection (2) of this section,

shall be guilty of an offence and shall be liable on summary conviction to a fine not exceeding level 3 on the standard scale (within the meaning of section 75 of the Criminal Justice Act 1982).

(4) In this section *'international passenger transport authorisation'* means a licence, permit, authorisation or other document issued by the Secretary of State in pursuance of an international agreement or arrangement to which the United Kingdom is for the time being a party. "

B11.11   *[Regulation 5 is printed as amended by SI 1987/1755.]*

Occasional services by vehicles registered in the United Kingdom (whether ASOR or Community regulated or not)

B11.12   **6.**—(1) This Regulation applies to a vehicle registered in the United Kingdom which is being used for the international carriage of passengers by road—

    (a) in so far as the vehicle is used to provide a service for the carriage of passengers which is Community regulated and is such as is mentioned—

        (i) in paragraph 1(a) of Article 3 of Council Regulation No.117/66 (that is to say, an occasional service described in that paragraph as a closed-door tour), or

        (ii) in paragraph 1(b) of the said Article 3 (that is to say, an occasional service described in that paragraph where the passengers are carried on the outward journey and the return journey is made unladen), or

        (iii) in paragraph 1(c) of the said Article 3 (that is to say, an occasional service, as mentioned in that paragraph, of any other description); or

    (b) in so far as the vehicle is used to provide a service for the carriage of passengers which is ASOR regulated; or

    (c) in so far as the vehicle is used as a public service vehicle for the carriage of passengers which is not ASOR regulated or Community regulated but is a service of a description such as is mentioned in any of the paragraphs of Article 3 of Council Regulation No.117/66.

(2) The provisions of the Act of 1981 [and Parts I and II of the Transport Act 1985] shall have effect as if—

(a) in relation to a vehicle to which this Regulation applies registered in Northern Ireland, sections 6, 12, 18 and 22 of the Act of 1981 were omitted; and

(b) in relation to a vehicle to which this Regulation applies registered in Great Britain or in Northern Ireland, for [section 6 of the Transport Act 1985 there shall be substituted the following section and section 35 of that Act shall be omitted]:—

"[6.]—(1) No person shall cause or permit a vehicle to be used on a road for the international carriage of passengers unless—

(a) in relation to the use of the vehicle, in the case of such carriage which is ASOR regulated, the requirements of Articles 7, 8 and 9 of, and the Annex to, ASOR (which provide for the completion by the person by whom, or on whose behalf, a vehicle is used to provide an occasional service of a passenger waybill in respect of the service in question and for the carrying of the top copy of such waybill on the vehicle at all times while it is used on that service) are complied with and, in the case of any other such carriage, the requirements of Articles 2, 3 and 4 of, and of Annex 2 to, Commission Regulation No.1016/68 (which provide as aforesaid) are complied with, or would be complied with if those provisions applied to the service; and

(b) the vehicle is used on the service in question in circumstances which accord in all respects with the particulars which have been specified in the said passenger waybill as applicable to that service.

(2) A certifying officer or a public service vehicle examiner may, at any time which is reasonable having regard to the circumstances of the case, enter any premises from which he has reason to believe that a vehicle is or is to be operated on a service for the international carriage of passengers and may, on production if so required of his authority, require the operator of the vehicle to produce and to permit him to inspect and copy a control document duly completed for the service, in the case of ASOR regulated carriage, in accordance with Articles 7, 8 and 9 of, and the Annex to, ASOR and, in the case of any other such carriage, in accordance with Articles 2, 3, and 4 of, and Annex 2 to, Commission Regulation No.1016/68.

(3) A certifying officer or a public service vehicle examiner may, on production if so required of his authority—

(a) require the driver of a vehicle used for the international carriage of passengers to produce and to permit him to inspect and copy and to mark with an official stamp, in the case of a vehicle used for ASOR regulated carriage, the document required by Article 8(2) of ASOR and, in the case of any other such carriage, the document required by Article 3(2) of Commission Regulation No.1016/68, to be kept on a vehicle to which that Article applies; and

(b) detain the vehicle for such time as is required for the purpose of inspecting, copying and marking the document.

(4) A person who—

    (a) without reasonable excuse contravenes subsection (1) above, or

    (b) without reasonable excuse fails to comply with a requirement of an officer or examiner, under subsection (2) or (3) above, or

    (c) wilfully obstructs an officer or examiner in the exercise of his powers under either of those subsections,

shall be guilty of an offence and shall be liable on summary conviction to a fine not exceeding level 3 on the standard scale (within the meaning of section 75 of the Criminal Justice Act 1982).

    (5) In this section —

'ASOR' means the Agreement on the International Carriage of Passengers by Road by means of Occasional Coach and Bus Services (ASOR) approved on behalf of the Economic Community pursuant to Council Decision (EEC) of 20th July 1982 concluding the Agreement entering into force for the Economic Community on 1st December 1983, as read with Council Regulation (EEC) No.56/83 on measures implementing the Agreement;

'ASOR State' means—

    (a) a state, not being a member State, which is a Contracting Party to ASOR and to which the provisions of Section II and III of ASOR apply in accordance with Article 18 thereof; or

    (b) the Economic Community;

'ASOR regulated' means, in relation to the carriage of passengers, the international carriage of passengers by road to which ASOR applies namely in the circumstances specified in Article 1 thereof, that is to say, by means of occasional services (within the meaning of that Agreement) effected—

    (a) between the territories of two ASOR States, or starting and finishing in the territory of the same ASOR State; and

    (b) should the need arise during such services, in transit through the territory of another ASOR State or through the territory of a state which is not an ASOR State; and

    (c) using vehicles registered in the territory of an ASOR State which, by virtue of their construction and their equipment, are suitable for carrying more than nine persons, including the driver, and are intended for that purpose,

and references to the carriage of passengers which is ASOR regulated include unladen journeys of the vehicles concerned with such carriage;

'Commission Regulation No.1016/68' means Regulation (EEC) No.1016/68 of the Commission of 9th July 1968 prescribing the model control documents referred to in Articles 6 and 9 of Council Regulation No.117/66/EEC as amended by and as read with Regulation (EEC) No.2485/82 of the Commission of 13th September 1982; and

'Council Regulation No.117/66' means Regulation No.117/66/EEC of the Council of 28th July 1966 on the introduction of common rules for the international carriage of passengers by coach and bus. "

[Regulation 6 is printed as amended by SI 1987/1755.]   **B11.13**

PART III

MODIFICATIONS OF THE ACT OF 1981 IN RELATION TO VEHICLES REGISTERED OUTSIDE THE UNITED KINGDOM

Small vehicles registered outside the United Kingdom visiting Great Britain temporarily

7.—(1) This Regulation applies to a public service vehicle registered outside   **B11.14**
the United Kingdom which—

    (a) in construction and equipment is suitable for carrying not more than nine persons, including the driver, and is intended for that purpose;

    (b) is brought into Great Britain for the purpose of carrying passengers who are travelling to Great Britain from a place outside the United Kingdom, or who are travelling from the United Kingdom to any such place; and

    (c) remains in Great Britain for a period not exceeding three months from the date of its entry therein.

(2) The provisions of the Act of 1981 shall, in relation to a vehicle to which this Regulation applies, have effect as if sections 6, 12, 18, 22 ... of the Act of 1981 were omitted.

[Regulation 7 is printed as it has effect after the repeal of s.30 of the Public   **B11.15**
Passenger Vehicles Act 1981.]

Community regulated regular, shuttle and works services by vehicles registered outside the United Kingdom

8.—(1) This Regulation applies to a vehicle registered outside the United   **B11.16**
Kingdom which is being used for Community regulated carriage of passengers in so far as the vehicle—

    (a) is being used to provide any service for the carriage of passengers such as is mentioned in Article 1, 2 or 6 of Council Regulation 117/66; and

    (b) is being so used in accordance with such of the requirements of the Council Regulations or, as the case may be, the Commission Regulation as apply to the service in question.

(2) The provisions of the Act of 1981 shall, in relation to a vehicle to which this Regulation applies, have effect as if sections 6, 12, 18, 22 ... of the Act of 1981 were omitted.

[Regulation 8 is printed as it has effect after the repeal of s.30 of the Public   **B11.17**
Passenger Vehicles Act 1981.]

Non-Community regulated regular and shuttle services by vehicles registered outside the United Kingdom

9.—(1) This Regulation applies to a public service vehicle registered outside   **B11.18** the United Kingdom which is being used for the international carriage of passengers which is not Community regulated in so far as the vehicle—

    (a) is being used to provide a service for the carriage of passengers of a description such as is mentioned in Article 1 or 2 of Council Regulation 117/66 (that is to say, a regular service, a special regular service or a shuttle service as defined in those Articles), and

    (b) is so used by or on behalf of a person who is authorised, under the law of the country in which the vehicle is registered, to use the vehicle for the carriage of passengers on the journey in question or such parts thereof as are situated within that country.

    (2) The provisions of the Act of 1981 shall in relation to a vehicle to which this Regulation applies, have effect as if sections 6, 18, 22 ... of the Act of 1981 were omitted, and as if for section 12 of the Act of 1981 there were substituted the section set out in Schedule 2.

B11.19   *[Regulation 9 is printed as it has effect after the repeal of s.30 of the Public Passenger Vehicles Act 1981.]*

ASOR or Community regulated occasional services by vehicles registered outside the United Kingdom

B11.20   **10.**—(1) This Regulation applies to a vehicle registered outside the United Kingdom which is being used for ASOR or Community regulated carriage of passengers—

    (a) in so far as the vehicle is used to provide a service for the carriage of passengers such as is mentioned—

        (i) in paragraph 1(a) of Article 2 of ASOR or paragraph 1(a) of Article 3 of Council Regulation No.117/66 (that is to say, an occasional service described in that paragraph as a closed-door tour), or

        (ii) in paragraph 1(b) of each of those Articles (that is to say an occasional service as described in that paragraph where passengers are carried on the outward journey and the return journey is made unladen), or

        (iii) in paragraph 1(c) of each of those Articles (that is to say, an occasional service as mentioned in that paragraph of any other description); and

    (b) in so far as, in relation to the use of the vehicle—

        (i) in the case of a vehicle being used for ASOR regulated carriage, the requirements of Articles 7, 8 and 9 of, and Annex to, ASOR (which provides for the completion, by the person by whom or on whose behalf a vehicle is used to provide such an occasional service as aforesaid, of a passenger waybill in respect of the service in question and for the carrying of the top copy of such waybill on the vehicle at all times while it is used on that service) and in the case of a vehicle being used for Community regulated carriage, the requirements of Articles 2, 3 and 4 of, and Annex 2 to, Commission Regulation No.1016/68 (which provides as aforesaid), have been complied with, and

(ii) the vehicle is used on the service in question in circumstances which accord in all respects with particulars which, in pursuance of the said requirements, have been specified in the said passenger waybill as applicable to that service.

(2) In relation to a vehicle to which this Regulation applies, the provisions of the Act of 1981 shall have effect as if sections 6, 18, 22 ... of the Act of 1981 were omitted and—

(a) in so far as the vehicle is used to provide a service for the carriage of passengers such as is mentioned—

(i) in Article 2(1)(a) or (b) of ASOR or Article 3(1)(a) or (b) of Council Regulation No.117/66, or

(ii) in a case where the service is ASOR regulated and all the conditions mentioned in Article 5(2) of ASOR are fulfilled, in Article 2(1)(c) of ASOR, or

(iii) in a case where the service is Community regulated and all the conditions mentioned in Article 5(2) of the said Council Regulation are fulfilled, in Article 2(1)(c) of that Regulation,

as if section 12 of the Act of 1981 were omitted; and

(b) in so far as the vehicle is used as a public service vehicle to provide a service for the carriage of passengers such as is mentioned in Article 2(1)(c) of ASOR or Article 2(1)(c) of the said Council Regulation and—

(i) in a case where the service is ASOR regulated any of the conditions mentioned in Article 5(2) of ASOR are not fulfilled, or

(ii) in a case where the service is Community regulated, any of the conditions mentioned in Article 5(2) of the said Council Regulation are not fulfilled,

as if for the said section 12 there were substituted the section set out in Schedule 2.

[Regulation 10 is printed as it has effect after the repeal of s.30 of the Public   **B11.21**
Passenger Vehicles Act 1981.]

Certain occasional services by vehicles registered in ECMT States

11.—(1) This Regulation applies to a public service vehicle—   **B11.22**

(a) which is registered in the territory of a State which is an ECMT State;

(b) which is brought into Great Britain for the purpose of carrying passengers who are making only a temporary stay therein or are in transit; and

(c) which remains in Great Britain for a period not exceeding three months from the date of its entry therein,

in so far as the vehicle—

(i) is used to provide a service for the carriage of passengers which is not ASOR or Community regulated but which is of a description such as is mentioned in Article 3(1)(a), (b) or (c) of Council Regulation No.117/66, where the journey made by the vehicle in providing that service starts from a place situated in the territory of an ECMT State and ends at a place situated in the territory of such a State or in Great Britain, and

(ii) is so used by or on behalf of a person who is authorised, under the law in force in the State, in the territory of which it is registered to use the vehicle for the carriage of passengers on the journey in question or such part thereof as lies within the territory of that State.

(2) In relation to a vehicle to which this Regulation applies, the provisions of the Act of 1981 shall have effect as if sections 6, 18, 22 ... of the Act of 1981 were omitted and as if—

(a) in so far as the vehicle is used to provide a service for the carriage of passengers such as is mentioned in paragraph 1(a) and 1(b) of Article 3 of Council Regulation No.117/66, for section 12 of the Act of 1981 there were substituted the following sections [*sic*]: —

"**12.** No person shall cause or permit a public service vehicle to be used on a road for the international carriage of passengers unless there is in force in relation to the use of the vehicle, and is carried on the vehicle, a document which is issued by the competent authority of the country in which the vehicle is registered in the form set out in Schedule 3 to the Road Transport (International Passenger Service) Regulations 1984 and which is duly completed.";
and

(b) in so far as the vehicle is used for the carriage of passengers such as is mentioned in paragraph 1(c) of the said Article 3, for section 12 of the Act of 1981 there were substituted the section set out in Schedule 2.

B11.23   *[Regulation 11 is printed as it has effect after the repeal of s.30 of the Public Passenger Vehicles Act 1981.]*

Certain occasional services by vehicles not registered in a member State, an ASOR State or an ECMT State

B11.24   12.—(1) This Regulation applies to a public service vehicle—

(a) which is registered in the territory of a State which is not a member State, an ASOR State or an ECMT State;

(b) which is brought into Great Britain for the purpose of carrying passengers who are making only a temporary stay therein or are in transit, being passengers who commenced their journey from the state in the territory of which the vehicle is registered or, as the case may be, from Northern Ireland; and

(c) which remains in Great Britain for a period not exceeding three months from the date of its entry therein,

in so far as the vehicle—

(i) is used to provide a service for the carriage of passengers which is not Community regulated but which is of a description such as is mentioned in Article 3(1)(a), (b) or (c) of Regulation No.117/66, and

(iii) is so used by or on behalf of a person who is authorised, under the law in force in the state in the territory of which it is registered to use the vehicle for the carriage of passengers on the journey in question or such part thereof as lies within the territory of that state.

(2) The provisions of the Act of 1981 shall, in relation to a vehicle to which this Regulation applies, have effect as if sections 6, 18, 22 … of the Act of 1981 were omitted and as if for section 12 of the Act of 1981 there were substituted

[(a) in the case of a public service vehicle registered in the Union of Soviet Socialist Republics used to provide a service of a description such as is mentioned in Article 3(1)(a) or (b) of Regulation No.117/66, the following section:—

"**12.** No person shall cause or permit a public service vehicle to be used on a road for the international carriage of passengers unless there is carried on the vehicle a list of the passengers carried by the vehicle;"

and

(b) in any other case, the section set out in Schedule 2.]

[Regulation 12 is printed as it has effect after the repeal of s.30 of the Public **B11.25**
Passenger Vehicles Act 1981; and as subsequently amended by SI 1988/1809.]

PART IV

APPLICATIONS FOR ISSUE OF AUTHORISATIONS AND OTHER DOCUMENTS AND
FEES IN RESPECT THEREOF

*   *   *

Applications for, and issue of, certificates and control documents for works and occasional services

15.—(1)–(3) *[Omitted.]*   **B11.26**

(4) The top copy of every passenger waybill (being the document which, as mentioned in Article 7 of ASOR or Article 2 of the Commission Regulation is the document applicable in respect of the provision of a service for the carriage of passengers such as is mentioned in Article 2 of ASOR or Article 3 of Council Regulation No.117/66), shall be retained, after the service in question has been provided, by the person by whom or on whose behalf it was provided and shall be sent to the Secretary of State so as to reach him not later than 31st March next following the end of the calendar year in which the service to which the waybill relates was provided.

(5) The duplicate of every such passenger waybill (being the duplicate which, by virtue of Article 7(1) of ASOR or Article 2(1) of Commission Regulation No.1016/68 is required to be contained in a control document such as is mentioned in those Articles) shall not be detached from that document at any time during its period of validity.

PART V

PENALTIES, ENFORCEMENT, SUPPLEMENTARY AND CONSEQUENTIAL

Production, inspection and copying of documents in relation to ASOR or Community regulated services

16.—(1) Paragraph (2) below shall have effect in relation to a vehicle where it   **B11.27**
appears to an examiner that the vehicle—

    (a) is being used for the provision of an ASOR regulated or Community regulated service; and

    (b) is being used, or has been brought into Great Britain for the purpose of being used, in such circumstances as, by virtue of any of the provisions specified in paragraph (3) below, to require a document of a description referred to in that provision to be kept or carried on the vehicle.

(2) An examiner may, on production if so required of his authority—

    (a) require the driver of a vehicle referred to in paragraph (1) above to produce the document and to permit him to inspect and copy it and (in the case of a document of a description referred to in any of the provisions specified in paragraph (3)(c) or (e) below) to mark it with an official stamp; and

    (b) may detain the vehicle for such time as is required for the purpose of inspecting, copying and marking the document.

(3) The provisions referred to in paragraph (1) above as being specified in this paragraph are—

    (a) Article 17 of Council Regulation No.517/72 (which provides, inter alia, that the authorisation required by that Regulation for the use of a vehicle to provide a service for the carriage of passengers such as is mentioned in Article 1 thereof shall be carried on the vehicle);

    (b) Article 17 and 18 of Council Regulation No.516/72 (which respectively provide, inter alia, that the authorisation required by that Regulation for the use of a vehicle to provide a service for the carriage of passengers such as is mentioned in Article 1 thereof shall be carried on the vehicle and that passengers using that service shall be provided with a ticket throughout the journey in question);

    (c) Article 8(2) of ASOR and Article 3(2) of Commission Regulation No.1016/68 (which provide that the top copy of the passenger waybill being the document which, by virtue of Article 7 of ASOR or Article 2 of Commission Regulation No.1016/68, has been detached from the control document such as is mentioned in those Articles, and is the document applicable in respect of the provision of a service for the carriage of passengers such as is mentioned in Article 2 of ASOR or Article 3 of Council Regulation No.117/66, shall be kept on the vehicle);

    (d) Article 11(3) of ASOR and Article 5a(3) of Commission Regulation No.1016/68 (which provide that the model document with stiff green covers referred to in Article 11 of ASOR must be carried on the vehicle); and

    (e) Regulation 17.

B11.28 *[The text of reg.16(3)(d) has been printed as it is believed that it was intended to read: the word "of" has been substituted editorially for the word "or" immediately before the first reference to "ASOR", and the reference to "Commission Regulation No.1016/68" has similarly been substituted for a reference to "Commission Regulation No.1018/68"in the original text.]*

Carriage on the vehicle of certificate issued under Article 6 of Council Regulation No.117/66

17.—(1) In relation to a vehicle being used to provide a Community regulated service for the carriage of passengers such as is mentioned in Article 6 of Council Regulation No.117/66 there shall be carried on the vehicle, at all times while it is being used, the certificate specified in Article 1 of Commission Regulation No.1016/68, being the certificate which, by virtue of the said Article 6, is required to be in force in respect of the provision of that service.   **B11.29**

(2) An examiner may, on production if so required of his authority—

   (a) require the driver of a vehicle referred to in paragraph (1) above to produce the document and to permit him to inspect and copy it and to mark it with an official stamp; and

   (b) may detain the vehicle for such time as is required for the purpose of inspecting, copying and marking the document.

Withdrawal of regular, special regular and shuttle service authorisations

18.—(1) If the Secretary of State is at any time satisfied that a holder of a regular, special regular or shuttle service authorisation issued by him—   **B11.30**

   (a) has failed to comply with the relevant Council Regulation, with the authorisation or any conditions specified therein; or

   (b) has failed to operate, or is no longer operating, a service under the authorisation,

he may, by notice in writing to the holder, withdraw the authorisation.

(2) Where the Secretary of State decides to withdraw an authorisation in exercise of his powers under Council Regulation No.516/72 or Council Regulation No.517/72 he may do so by notice in writing to the holder of the authorisation.

(3) The withdrawal of an authorisation in accordance with this Regulation shall take effect on the date specified in the notice which shall be not earlier than 28 days after the date of the notice.

(4) Where an authorisation is withdrawn in accordance with this Regulation it shall be of no effect and the holder shall forthwith surrender the authorisation to the Secretary of State.

(5) At any time that is reasonable having regard to the circumstances of the case, an examiner may, on production if so required of his authority, enter any premises of the holder of an authorisation which has been withdrawn in accordance with this Regulation and may require the holder to produce the authorisation and, on its being produced, may seize it and deliver it to the Secretary of State.

(6) Where it appears to an examiner that a document produced to him in pursuance of Regulation 16 is an authorisation which has been withdrawn in accordance with this Regulation he may seize it and deliver it to the Secretary of State.

(7) In paragraph 1 of this Regulation *"relevant Council Regulation"* means in the case of a regular or special regular service authorisation Council Regulation No.517/72 and in the case of a shuttle service authorisation Council Regulation No.516/72.

Penalty for contravention of ASOR, the Council Regulations or the Commission Regulation

B11.31   **19.**—(1) A person is guilty of an offence under this Regulation if without reasonable excuse, he uses a vehicle for Community regulated carriage of passengers by road or causes or permits such a vehicle to be used—

    (a) to provide a service for the carriage of passengers such as is mentioned in Article 1 of Council Regulation No.117/66 (that is to say, a regular service or a special regular service as defined in that Article), not being, in either such case, a service such as is mentioned in Article 6 of that Regulation, otherwise than under and in accordance with the terms of an authorisation issued under Article 2 of Council Regulation No.517/72; or

    (b) to provide a service for the carriage of passengers such as is mentioned in Article 2 of Council Regulation No.117/66 (that is to say, a shuttle service as defined in that Article), not being a service such as is mentioned in Article 6 of that Regulation, otherwise than under and in accordance with the terms of an authorisation issued under Article 2 of Council Regulation No.516/72; or

    (c) to provide a service for the carriage of passengers such as is mentioned in Article 6 of Council Regulation No.117/66 (that is to say, a service provided by an undertaking for its own workers in relation to which the conditions mentioned in paragraph 1(a) and (b) of that Article are fulfilled) without there being in force in relation to the service a certificate issued under Article 1 of Commission Regulation No.1016/68.

(2) A person shall be guilty of an offence under this Regulation if, without reasonable excuse, he uses a vehicle for ASOR regulated or Community regulated carriage by road, or causes or permits a vehicle to be so used, to provide a service for the carriage of passengers such as is mentioned in paragraph 1 of Article 2 of ASOR or Article 3 of Council Regulation No.117/66 when there is not duly and correctly completed for the vehicle a passenger waybill, or when the top copy of the passenger waybill is not kept on the vehicle throughout the journey to which it refers, as required, in the case of a vehicle being used for ASOR regulated carriage, by Articles 2 and 8 of ASOR and, in the case of a vehicle being used for Community regulated carriage, by Articles 2 and 3 of Council Regulation No.1016/68.

(3) A person guilty of an offence under this Regulation shall be liable on summary conviction to a fine not exceeding [level 3 on the standard scale].

B11.32   *[Regulation 19 is printed as amended by the Criminal Justice Act 1988 s.52.*

Offences under reg.19(1) and (2) are fixed penalty offences for the purposes of Pt 3 of the Road Traffic Offenders Act 1988 (see the Fixed Penalty Offences Order 2009 (SI 2009/483) art.2). The amounts for the fixed penalty offences are prescribed by the Fixed Penalty Order 2000 (SI 2000/2792), as amended by the Fixed Penalty (Amendment) Order 2009 (SI 2009/488).]

Penalty relating to documents required in respect of ASOR and Community regulated services

B11.33   **20.** A person who—

(a) without reasonable excuse contravenes, or fails to comply with a requirement imposed by or under Regulation 15(4) or (5), 16(2)(a), 17(1) or (2), or 18(4) or (5), or by or under any provision of ASOR, the Council Regulations or the Commission Regulation referred to in any of those provisions; or

(b) wilfully obstructs an examiner in the exercise of his powers under Regulation 16(2), 17(1) or (2), or 18(5) or (6), or under any provision of ASOR, the Council Regulations or Commission Regulation referred to in any of those provisions

shall be liable on summary conviction to a fine not exceeding [level 3 on the standard scale].

[Regulation 20 is printed as amended by the Criminal Justice Act 1988 s.52.]   **B11.34**

Forgery and false statements, etc.

21. In sections 65(1)(a) (forgery) and 66(a) (false statements) of the Act of   **B11.35** 1981 the references to a licence under any Part of that Act shall include references to an authorisation, certificate or other document required by ASOR, any of the Council Regulations or the Commission Regulation, or by these Regulations, or by the Act of 1981 as modified by these Regulations, to be in force in relation to a vehicle, or to be kept or carried on a vehicle, used for the international carriage of passengers.

22. *[Amended the Road Traffic (Foreign Vehicles) Act 1972.]*   **B11.36**

Disapplication of requirements as to fitness, equipment type approval and certification of public service vehicles

23. None of the provisions of Parts II, III, IV and V of the Public Service   **B11.37** Vehicles (Conditions of Fitness, Equipment, Use and Certification) Regulations 1981 [*SI 1981/257, as amended (q.v.)*] shall have effect in relation to a vehicle to which any provision of Part III of these Regulations applies or to a vehicle registered in Northern Ireland to which any provision of Part II of these Regulations applies.

(see regulation 2)   SCHEDULE 1

THE COUNCIL REGULATIONS AND THE COMMISSION REGULATION

"Council Regulation No.117/66" means Regulation No.117/66/EEC of the Council of 28th   **B11.38** July 1966 on the introduction of common rules for the international carriage of passengers by coach and bus [*O.J. No.L147, August 9, 1966, p.2688*];

"Council Regulation No.516/72" means Regulations (EEC) No.516/72 of the Council of 28th February 1972 on the introduction of common rules for shuttle services by coach and bus between Member States [*O.J. No.L67, March 20, 1972, p.13*];

"Council Regulation No.517/72" means Regulation (EEC) No.517/72 of the Council of 28th February 1972 on the introduction of common rules for regular and special regular services by coach and bus between Member States [*O.J. No.L67, March 20, 1972, p.19*] as amended by Regulation (EEC) No.1301/78 of the Council of 12th June 1978 [*O.J. No.L158, June 16, 1978, p.1*];

"Commission Regulation No.1016/68" means Regulation (EEC) No.1016/68 of the Commission of 9th July 1968 prescribing the model control documents referred to in Articles 6

and 9 of Council Regulation No.117/66 EEC [*O.J. No.L173, July 22, 1968, p.8*] as amended by and as read with Regulation (EEC) No.2485/82 of the Commission of 13th September 1982 [*O.J. No.L265, September 15, 1982, p.5*].

B11.39   *[Council Regulations (EEC) 117/66, 516/72 and 517/72 (to which references are made in Sch.1) were repealed by Regulation (EEC) 684/92 art.21(1). Regulation (EEC) 684/92 was itself repealed by European and Council Regulation (EC) 1073/2009 of October 21, 2009 on common rules for access to the international market for coach and bus services, and amending Regulation (EC) 561/2006 (O.J. No.L300, November 14, 2009, p.88) (q.v.) with effect from December 4, 2011. References to Council Regulations (EEC) 117/66, 516/72 and 517/72 should be construed as references to Regulation (EC) 1073/2009. Commission Regulation (EEC) 1016/68 (to which reference is made in Sch.1) was repealed (subject to transitional provisions) by Regulation (EEC) 1839/92 arts 10, 11 (O.J. No.L187, July 7, 1992, p.5).]*

(see regulations 9, 10 and 11)   SCHEDULE 2

B11.40

"**12.**—(1) No person shall cause or permit a public service vehicle to be used on a road for the international carriage of passengers unless there is in force and is carried on the vehicle, an international passenger transport authorisation.

(2) An authorisation under this section may authorise the use of the vehicle or vehicles to which it relates on a specified occasion or during a specified period.

(3) In this section —

'specified' means specified in the authorisation; and

'international passenger transport authorisation' means a licence, permit, authorisation or other document issued by the Secretary of State in pursuance of an international agreement or arrangement to which the United Kingdom is for the time being a party."

(see regulation 11(2))   SCHEDULE 3

WAYBILL

B11.41   *[Omitted.]*

The Traffic Signs (Welsh and English Language Provisions) Regulations and General Directions 1985

(SI 1985/713)

The Secretary of State for Wales, in exercise of the powers conferred by section 28(4) of the Road Traffic Regulation Act 1984 (hereinafter referred to as "the Act of 1984") and the Secretary of State for Wales, the Secretary of State for Transport and the Secretary of State for Scotland acting jointly in exercise of the powers conferred by sections 64(1) and 65(1) of the Act of 1984 and by the provision in column 5 of Part I of Schedule 4 to the Road Traffic Act 1972 which relates to section 22 of that Act as that provision is amended by paragraph 9 of Schedule 3 to the Secretary of State for Transport Order 1976 [SI 1976/1775; not reproduced in this work] and in exercise of the powers conferred by section 2(2) and (3) of the Welsh Language Act 1967 and now vested in them and all other enabling powers, and after consultation with representative organisations in accordance with section 134(2) of the Act of 1984 and section 199(2) of the Road Traffic Act 1972 hereby make these Regulations and give these Directions. **B12.01**

[Although the Road Traffic Act 1972 has been repealed, the references to that Act in the recital of enabling powers have been retained for historical reasons. For ss.22 and 199(2) of the 1972 Act, see now ss.36 and 195(2), respectively, of the Road Traffic Act 1988; for Sch.4, Pt I, column 5, to the 1972 Act, see now Sch.2, Pt I, column 5, to the Road Traffic Offenders Act 1988.] **B12.02**

PART I

TRAFFIC SIGNS REGULATIONS

*   *   *

Interpretation

2.—(1) In these Regulations the Main Regulations means the Traffic Signs Regulations and General Directions 1981 [*SI 1981/859*] as amended and a reference in Schedule 1 to these Regulations and Directions to *"Main Regulations"* or to *"Prif Reolau"* is similarly a reference to the Traffic Signs Regulations 1981 amended as aforesaid. **B12.03**

(2) References in these Regulations to a numbered Regulation or numbered Schedule shall be construed, unless the context otherwise requires, as a reference to the Regulation bearing that number in these Regulations or to the Schedule bearing that number in these Regulations and Directions.

(3) References in these Regulations to a sign shown in a diagram in Schedule 1 shall include references to a variant of the sign which is specified in Schedule 1 as being a permitted variant.

(4) References in Schedule 1 to a sign without the prefix "W" before a diagram number are references to the sign bearing the same diagram number in Parts I and

II of Schedule I to the Main Regulations and references in Schedule I to a sign with the prefix "W" before a diagram number are references to the sign bearing the same diagram number which is prescribed for use in Wales by regulation 4(1).

(5) Nothing in these Regulations shall have effect so as to authorise any person not otherwise authorised to do so to place on or near a road any object or device for warning traffic of a temporary obstruction.

B12.04   *[The Traffic Signs Regulations 1981 (SI 1981/859) were revoked and replaced by the Traffic Signs Regulations and General Directions 1994 (SI 1994/1519), except for the purposes of these Regulations; see SI 1994/1519 reg.2. The text of SI 1981/859, so far as material, is reproduced in the sixteenth edition of this work. The 1994 Regulations have now been revoked by the Traffic Signs Regulations 2002 (SI 2002/3113, Pt I) (q.v.); see SI 2002/3113 reg.2. The text of SI 1994/1519, so far as material, can be found in the twentieth edition of this work.]*

Authorisation by the Secretary of State

B12.05   **3.** Nothing in these Regulations shall be taken to limit the power of the Secretary of State under section 64 of the Act of 1984 to authorise the erection or retention of traffic signs of a character not prescribed by these Regulations.

Traffic Signs shown in Schedule 1

B12.06   **4.**—(1) A sign shown in a diagram in Schedule 1 with the prefix "W" followed by a diagram number may be used in Wales in place of a sign bearing the same diagram number without the prefix "W" in Parts I or II of Schedule 1 to the Main Regulations.

(2) In the signs shown in the diagrams in Schedule 1, other than the signs shown in diagrams W605.1 and W629.1 and other than the signs therein which specifically prescribe the manner in which the two texts are to be displayed, either the Welsh or English text shall be placed above the other text.

B12.07   *[Diagram W605.1 was the sign exhibited by a school crossing patrol (see now the School Crossing Patrol Sign (England and Wales) Regulations 2006 (SI 2006/2215), which prescribe, as respects England and Wales, the size, colour and type of sign). Diagram W629.1 is the sign prohibiting vehicles or combinations of vehicles exceeding the length indicated; see now the Traffic Signs Regulations 2002 (SI 2002/3113, Pt I).]*

Application of the Main Regulations

B12.08   **5.**—(1) Subject to the provisions of this Regulation, the provisions of the Main Regulations shall apply to a sign shown in a diagram in Schedule 1 with the prefix "W" followed by a diagram number as if it were a sign bearing the same diagram number without the prefix "W" in Schedule 1 to the Main Regulations. Provided that—

(a) except as provided in paragraph (2) of this Regulation, references in subparagraphs (c), (d) and (e) of Regulation 12(1) of the Main Regulations to the signs specified in those subparagraphs showing distances in miles or in yards shall be construed as references to such signs in Schedule 1 showing distances in both the Welsh and English texts;

(b) references in subparagraph (g) of Regulation 12(1) of the Main Regulations to signs showing a period of time, day of the week, days of the month or months of the year shall be construed as references to such signs in Schedule 1 indicating these matters in both the Welsh and English texts;

(c) where, in accordance with the provisions of Regulation 12(1) of the Main Regulations, the indication given by a sign shown in a diagram in Schedule 1 is varied, the variation shall be made to both the Welsh and English texts of the sign; and

(d) Regulation 28(1) of the Main Regulations shall not apply to the sign shown in diagram 562 of Schedule 1 to the Main Regulations when used as directed in proviso (a) to Direction 3 in Part II of this Instrument in combination with any of the signs shown in diagrams W552, W554 and W554.1 in Schedule 1.

(2) A reference in Regulation 12(1)(c) of the Main Regulations to the sign shown in diagram 565.4 of Schedule 1 to the Main Regulations expressing distances in miles shall be construed as a reference to the sign showing distances by means of the letter "m" in diagram W564.4 in Schedule 1 and a similar reference in Regulation 12(1)(e) of the Main Regulations to the signs shown in diagrams 557.2 and 557.3 expressing distances in miles or yards shall be construed as references to the signs showing distances by means of the letters "m" or "yds" in diagrams W557.2 and W557.3 in Schedule 1.

(3) The provisions of Regulation 14 of and Schedule 7 to the Main Regulations shall apply as if in that Part of Schedule 7 specified in Column 1 of the following Table there were inserted the characters shown in that Part of Schedule 2 to these Regulations specified in Column 2 of the said Table opposite the Part in Column 1 to which it relates.

TABLE

Column 1 Part of Schedule 7 to Main Regulations	Column 2 Part of Schedule 2 to these Regulations to be inserted
Part I	Part A
Part II	Part B
Part IV	Part C
Part V	Part D
Part VI	Part E
Part VIII	Part F

[Diagrams 557.2 and 557.3 are plates for use in connection with diagram 557.1 (road hump ahead); diagram 562 is a warning sign of other danger ahead; diagrams W552 (cattle grid), W554 (ford) and W554.1 (try your brakes) are plates for use in connection with diagram 562; and diagrams W557.2 and W557.3 are plates for use in connection with diagram 557.1. See now the Traffic Signs Regulations 2002 (SI 2002/3113, Pt I), q.v.]   **B12.09**

Application of other enactments

6. A reference in any enactment to a traffic sign shown in a numbered diagram   **B12.10**

in the Main Regulations shall be construed as including a reference to a sign bearing the same diagram number with the prefix "W" in Schedule 1.

SCHEDULE 1

B12.11   *[Warning and regulating signs; omitted.]*

SCHEDULE 2

B12.12   *[Proportion and form of letters, numerals and other characters; omitted.]*

PART II

GENERAL DIRECTIONS

*   *   *

Interpretation

B12.13   **2.**—(1) References in these Directions to " *Schedule 1* " shall be construed as references to Schedule 1 to these Regulations and Directions.

(2) In these Directions *"the Main Regulations"* means the Traffic Signs Regulations 1981 as amended; *"the Main Directions"* means the Traffic Signs General Directions 1981 [*SI 1981/859*] as amended and a reference in Schedule 1 to these Regulations and Directions to "Main Directions" or to "Prif Gyfarwyddiadau" is similarly a reference to the Traffic Signs General Directions 1981 as amended.

(3) References in these Directions to a sign in a diagram in Schedule 1 shall include references to a variant of the sign which is specified in Schedule 1 as being a permitted variant.

(4) Nothing in these Directions shall have effect so as to authorise any person not otherwise authorised to do so to place on or near a road any object or device for warning traffic of a temporary obstruction.

B12.14   *[The Traffic Signs General Directions 1981 (SI 1981/859) were revoked and replaced by the Traffic Signs General Directions 1994 (SI 1994/1519), except for the purposes of these Directions; see SI 1994/1519 direction 2. The text of SI 1981/859, so far as material, is reproduced in the sixteenth edition of this work. The Traffic Signs General Directions 1994 have now been revoked by the Traffic Signs General Directions 2002 (SI 2002/3113, Pt II) (q.v.); see SI 2002/3113 direction 2. The text of SI 1994/1519, so far as material, can be found in the twentieth edition of this work.]*

Application of the Main Directions

B12.15   **3.** The Main Directions shall apply to a sign shown in a diagram in Schedule 1 with the prefix "W" followed by a diagram number as if it were a sign bearing the equivalent diagram number without the prefix "W" in Schedule 1 to the Main Regulations and the reference in Direction 12 of the Main Directions to signs which are specified beneath the diagrams showing the plates referred to in Direction 12 shall be construed as references to such signs beneath the corresponding diagrams in Schedule 1.

Provided that: —

   (a) notwithstanding anything to the contrary contained in Direction 11(3) of the Main Directions the plates shown in diagrams W552, W554 and W554.1 in Schedule 1 shall be used only in combination with the sign shown in diagram 562 of Schedule 1 to the Main Regulations; and

   (b) the references in Direction 17(ii) of the Main Directions to the sign shown in diagram 565.2 in Schedule 1 to the Main Regulations bearing words in the English language shall be construed as a reference to such sign in Schedule 1 in both the Welsh and English texts.

[Diagram 565.2 was a warning sign (slow—wet tar; and a number of specified **B12.16** *variants). As to the other diagrams mentioned in direction 3, see the note to reg.5. See now the Traffic Signs General Directions 2002 (SI 2002/3113, Pt II), q.v.]*

The Removal and Disposal of Vehicles Regulations 1986

(SI 1986/183)

B13.01 *[The text of the principal regulations is printed as amended by:*

> *the Removal and Disposal of Vehicles (Amendment) Regulations 1993 (SI 1993/278) (June 1, 1993);*

> *the Removal and Disposal of Vehicles (Amendment) (No.2) Regulations 1993 (SI 1993/1475) (July 5, 1993);*

> *the Removal and Disposal of Vehicles (Amendment) (No.3) Regulations 1993 (SI 1993/1708) (July 12, 1993);*

> *the Removal and Disposal of Vehicles (Amendment) Regulations 1994 (SI 1994/1503) (July 4, 1994);*

> *the Local Government Reorganisation (Wales) (Consequential Amendments No.2) Order 1996 (SI 1996/1008) (April 29, 1996); and*

> *the Greater London Road Traffic (Various Provisions) Order 2001 (SI 2001/1353) (April 4, 2001);*

> *the Removal and Disposal of Vehicles (England) (Amendment) Regulations 2002 (SI 2002/746) (April 9, 2002);*

> *the Removal and Disposal of Vehicles (Amendment) (No.2) Regulations 2002 (SI 2002/2777) (December 2, 2002); and*

> *the Removal and Disposal of Vehicles (Amendment) (England) Regulations 2007 (SI 2007/3484) (March 31, 2008).*

The amending regulations are referred to in the notes to the principal regulations only by their years and numbers. The dates referred to above are the dates on which the amending regulations came into force.

The principal regulations have also been amended by the Removal and Disposal of Vehicles (Amendment) Regulations 1998 (SI 1998/2019), and the Removal and Disposal of Vehicles (Amendment) (Scotland) Regulations 1999 (SI 1999/490), but the amending regulations do not affect any provision printed in this work.]

ARRANGEMENT OF REGULATIONS

B13.02

PART I
GENERAL

Regulation

*   *   *

2.   Interpretation

PART II
REMOVAL OF VEHICLES

*   *   *

SCHEDULES

*   *   *

PART I

GENERAL

Commencement, citation and revocation

1. *[Omitted.]*   **B13.03**

Interpretation

2. In these Regulations, unless the contrary intention appears, the following   **B13.04**
expressions have the meanings hereby assigned to them respectively, that is to
say:—

   "the 1978 Act" means the Refuse Disposal (Amenity) Act 1978;

   "the 1984 Act" means the Road Traffic Regulation Act 1984;

   "motor vehicle" has the meaning assigned to it in section 11(1) of the 1978
      Act;

   "road", in England and Wales, means any highway and any other road to
      which the public has access …;

   "vehicle", in relation to any matter prescribed by these Regulations for the
      purposes of any provision in sections 3 and 4 of the 1978 Act, means
      a motor vehicle, and in relation to any matter prescribed by these
      Regulations for the purposes of any provision in sections 99 and 101
      of the 1984 Act has the meaning assigned to it in section 99(5) of that
      Act, and, in relation to any matter prescribed by these Regulations
      for the purposes of section 99 of the 1984 Act, any reference to a ve-

hicle which has been permitted to remain at rest or which has broken down includes a reference to a vehicle which has been permitted to remain at rest or which has broken down before the coming into force of these Regulations.

B13.05   *[Words relating expressly and exclusively to Scotland have been omitted from the definition of "road" above.]*

PART II

REMOVAL OF VEHICLES

Power of constable to require removal of vehicles from roads

B13.06   **3.**—(1) Except as provided by regulation 7 of these Regulations, this regulation applies to a vehicle which—

(a) has broken down, or been permitted to remain at rest, on a road in such a position or in such condition or in such circumstances as to cause obstruction to persons using the road or as to be likely to cause danger to such persons, or

(b) has been permitted to remain at rest or has broken down and remained at rest on a road in contravention of a prohibition or restriction contained in, or having effect under, any of the enactments mentioned in Schedule 1 to these Regulations.

(2) A constable may require the owner, driver or other person in control or in charge of any vehicle to which this regulation applies to move or cause to be moved the vehicle and any such requirement may include a requirement that the vehicle shall be moved from that road to a place which is not on that or any other road, or that the vehicle shall not be moved to any such road or to any such position on a road as may be specified.

(3) A person required to move or cause to be moved a vehicle under this regulation shall comply with such requirement as soon as practicable.

Power of constable to remove vehicles

B13.07   **4.** Except as provided by regulation 7 of these Regulations, where a vehicle—

(a) is a vehicle to which regulation 3 of these Regulations applies, or

(b) having broken down on a road or on any land in the open air, appears to a constable to have been abandoned without lawful authority, or

(c) has been permitted to remain at rest on a road or on any land in the open air in such a position or in such condition or in such circumstances as to appear to a constable to have been abandoned without lawful authority,

then, subject to the provisions of sections 99 and 100 of the 1984 Act, a constable may remove or arrange for the removal of the vehicle, and, in the case of a vehicle which is on a road, he may remove it or arrange for its removal from that road to a place which is not on that or any other road, or may move it or arrange for its removal to another position on that or another road.

[Power of traffic warden to remove vehicles

B13.08   **4A.**—(1) Except as provided by regulation 7 of these Regulations, a traffic warden[, a designated person to whom paragraph 10 of Schedule 4 to the Police Reform Act 2002 applies, or an accredited person to whom paragraph 7 of Schedule 5 to that Act applies] may, subject to sections 99 and 100 of the 1984 Act, remove or arrange for the removal of a vehicle to which regulation 3 of these Regulations applies to a place which is not on that or any other road, or may move it or arrange for its removal to another position on that or another road.

(2) This regulation applies only in respect of—

(a) a vehicle which is on a road in, and

(b) its removal in and to a place in,

England or Wales.]

[Regulation 4A was inserted by SI 1993/278 and is printed as amended with respect to England only by SI 2002/2777.]   **B13.09**

Power of traffic wardens to remove vehicles

4B. *[Applies to Scotland.]*

Power of local authority to remove certain vehicles

5.—(1) Except as provided by regulation 7 of these Regulations, where a vehicle (other than a motor vehicle which a local authority have a duty to remove under section 3 of the 1978 Act) —   **B13.10**

(a) having broken down on a road or on any land in the open air in the area of a local authority, appears to them to have been abandoned without lawful authority, or

(b) has been permitted to remain at rest on a road or on any land in the open air in the area of a local authority in such a position or in such condition or in such circumstances as to appear to them to have been abandoned without lawful authority,

the local authority may, subject to the provisions of sections 99 and 100 of the 1984 Act, remove or arrange for the removal of the vehicle to a place which is not on any road.

(2) In this regulation *"local authority"* means, in the case of a vehicle situate at a place—

(a) in England, the council of the district or of the London borough, or the Common Council of the City of London;

(b) *[applies to Scotland]*; or

(c) in Wales, the council of the [county or county borough],

within whose area is situate that place.

[Regulation 5 is printed as amended by SI 1996/1008.   **B13.11**

The provisions of these regulations in their application to land within airports at Bournemouth, Bristol, Coventry, Gloucester, Cheltenham, Liverpool, London Luton, Manchester and Southend have been modified by the Airports (Designation) (Removal and Disposal of Vehicles) Order 1990 (SI 1990/54), as amended by the Airports (Designation) (Removal and Disposal of Vehicles) (Amendment) Order 1993 (SI 1993/2117) and the Airports (Designation) (Removal and Disposal of Vehicles) (Amendment) (Order) 2000 (SI 2000/707) (not reproduced in this work) so as to confer on the airport operators the functions exercisable under s.3 by local authorities. In relation to such airports, the regulations apply as if (inter alia) regs 5 and 7 were omitted and as if reg.10 were amended.]

[Powers of parking attendants to remove vehicles

B13.12   **5A.**—(1) Except as provided by regulation 7 of these Regulations where, in the area of a particular local authority, a vehicle—

(a) has been permitted to remain at rest or has broken down and remained at rest on a road in Greater London in contravention of a prohibition or restriction contained in an order having effect under—

(i) section 6 of the 1984 Act so far as the order designates any parking place; or

(ii) section 9 of the 1984 Act so far as the order designates any parking place in an area in respect of which section 65 of the Road Traffic Act 1991 [*q.v.*] is in force;

(iii) section 46 of the 1984 Act so far as the order relates to a parking place in such an area;

(b) has been permitted to remain at rest or has broken down and remained at rest on a road outside Greater London in contravention of a prohibition or restriction contained in an order under section 46 of the 1984 Act in circumstances in which an offence would have been committed in respect of the vehicle but for paragraph 1(4)(b) of Schedule 3 to the Road Traffic Act 1991 (permitted parking areas); or

(c) has been permitted to remain at rest or has broken down and remained at rest on a road in contravention of a statutory prohibition or restriction in circumstances in which an offence would have been committed with respect to the vehicle but for section 76(3) of, or paragraph 1(4)(a) or 2(4) of Schedule 3 to, the Road Traffic Act 1991 (permitted parking areas or special parking areas),

a parking attendant acting on behalf of the local authority may, subject to the provisions of sections 99 and 100 of the 1984 Act, remove or arrange for the removal of the vehicle from the road to a place which is not on that or any other road, or may move it or arrange for its removal to another position on that or another road.

(2) Sub-paragraphs (ii) and (iii) of paragraph (1)(a) and paragraph (1)(b) above shall not apply in relation to a vehicle if—

(a) not more than 15 minutes have elapsed since the end of any period for which the appropriate charge was duly paid at the time of parking; or

(b) not more than 15 minutes have elapsed since the end of any unexpired time (in respect of another vehicle) which is available at the relevant parking meter at the time of parking.

(3) This regulation applies only in respect of—

(a) a vehicle which is on a road in, and

(b) its removal in and to a place in,

England or Wales.

[(4) In this regulation —

"local authority" —

(a) in relation to a vehicle which is on a road in Greater London, shall be construed in accordance with paragraphs (5) and (6) below; and,

(b) in relation to any other vehicle, has the same meaning as in section 100 of the 1984 Act;

"*London local authority*" means the council of a London borough or the Common Council of the City of London;

"*parking meter*" has the same meaning as in section 46(2)(a) of that Act.]

[(5) In relation to a vehicle which falls within paragraph (1)(a) above (vehicle parked in contravention of an order designating a parking place on a road in Greater London)—

(a) if the parking place is on a GLA road or GLA side road and the parking place was designated by Transport for London, "*local authority*" means Transport for London;

(b) in any other case, "*local authority*" means the London local authority in whose area the parking place is.]

[(6) In relation to a vehicle which has been permitted to remain at rest, or having broken down has been permitted to remain at rest, on a GLA road or GLA side road in contravention of a statutory prohibition or restriction in circumstances in which an offence would have been committed with respect to the vehicle but for section 76(3) of the Road Traffic Act 1991 (offence provisions not applying within a special parking area) "*local authority*" means Transport for London.]

[(7) For the purposes of this regulation the area of Transport for London shall be taken to be Greater London.]

[(8) This regulation shall not apply to a vehicle found in a civil enforcement area for parking contraventions (as defined by regulation 5C(4)) on or after 31st March 2008.]

[*Regulation 5A was inserted by SI 1993/1475 and is printed as subsequently substituted by SI 1993/1708, and as later amended by SI 2001/1353; SI 2007/3484.*]   **B13.13**

5B. [*Applies only to Scotland.*]   **B13.14**

[Power of civil enforcement officers to remove vehicles in a civil enforcement area for parking contraventions in England

5C.—(1) Paragraph (2) applies where—   **B13.15**

(a) a vehicle has been permitted to remain at rest on a road in a civil enforcement area for parking contraventions in England; and

(b) a civil enforcement officer has, in accordance with regulation 9 of the Civil Enforcement of Parking Contraventions (England) General Regulations 2007 [*SI 2007/3483; not reproduced in this work*], fixed a penalty charge notice to the vehicle or handed such a notice to the person appearing to him to be in charge of the vehicle.

(2) Where this paragraph applies, a civil enforcement officer or a person acting under his direction may subject to paragraph (3) remove the vehicle concerned—

     (a) to another position on the road where it is found;

     (b) to another road; or

     (c) to a place which is not on a road.

(3) The power conferred by paragraph (2) is not exercisable where the vehicle concerned is in a parking place and a penalty charge notice has been served as mentioned in paragraph (1)(b) in respect of a contravention consisting of, or arising out of, a failure—

     (a) to pay a parking charge with respect to the vehicle;

     (b) properly to display a ticket or parking device; or

     (c) to remove the vehicle from the parking place by the end of the period for which the appropriate charge was paid,

until the appropriate period has elapsed since the giving of that penalty charge notice in respect of the contravention.

(4) In this regulation—

"the appropriate period" means—

     (a) in the case of a vehicle as respects which there are 3 or more penalty charges outstanding, 15 minutes;

     (b) in any other case 30 minutes;

"civil enforcement area for parking contraventions" and *"civil enforcement officer"* have the same meanings as in the Traffic Management Act 2004 (see Schedule 8 and section 76 of that Act);

"outstanding" in relation to a penalty charge has the same meaning as in the Civil Enforcement of Parking Contraventions (England) General Regulations 2007 (see regulation 2(2), (3) and (4) of those Regulations);

"parking place" has the meaning given by section 79(7) of the Traffic Management Act 2004;

"penalty charge" has the same meaning as in the Civil Enforcement of Parking Contraventions (England) General Regulations 2007 (see regulation 2(1) of those Regulations); and

"penalty charge notice" has the same meaning as in the Civil Enforcement of Parking Contraventions (England) General Regulations 2007 (see regulation 8(1) of those Regulations).]

B13.16   *[Regulation 5C was inserted by SI 2007/3484.]*

Method of removing vehicles

B13.17   **6.** Any person removing or moving a vehicle under [regulation 4, 4A or 5 of these Regulations] may do so by towing or driving the vehicle or in such other manner as he may think necessary and may take such measures in relation to the vehicle as he may think necessary to enable him to remove or move it as aforesaid.

B13.18   *[Regulation 6 is printed as amended by SI 1993/278. (Regulation 6 has been further amended by SI 1999/490, but the amendment has not been noted as it applies only to Scotland.)]*

Exception for Severn Bridge

B13.19   **7.** [Regulations 3, 4, 4A and 5] of these Regulations shall not apply in relation to any vehicle while on the central section of the specified carriageways (as defined in section 1 of the Severn Bridge Tolls Act 1965) of a road which crosses the Rivers Severn and Wye.

[Regulation 7 is printed as amended by SI 1993/278. **B13.20**
See also the note to reg.5 above.]

Manner of giving notice to occupier of land before removing a vehicle therefrom

8. *[Omitted.]*   **B13.21**

Manner and period during which occupier of land may object

9. *[Omitted.]*   **B13.22**

Period before which notice must be affixed to a vehicle in certain cases before removing it for destruction

10. For the purposes of section 3(5) of the 1978 Act and section 99(4) of the **B13.23** 1984 Act, the period before the commencement of which a notice must be caused to be affixed to a vehicle by an authority who propose to remove it, before they remove it, being a vehicle which in the opinion of the authority is in such a condition that it ought to be destroyed, shall be [24 hours].

[Regulation 10 is printed as amended with respect to England only by SI 2002/ **B13.24** *746; the words "24 hours" were substituted for the words "seven days". See also the note to reg.5 above.]*

PART III

DISPOSAL OF ABANDONED VEHICLES

11–16. *[Omitted.]*   **B13.25**

Regulation 3   SCHEDULE 1

CERTAIN ENACTMENTS BY OR UNDER WHICH ARE IMPOSED PROHIBITIONS OR RESTRICTIONS ON THE WAITING OF VEHICLES ON ROADS

...   **B13.26**

Section 52 of the Metropolitan Police Act 1839 and section 22 of the local Act of the second and third year of the reign of Queen Victoria, chapter 94 (relating to the prevention of obstruction in streets in London).

Section 21 of the Town Police Clauses Act 1847 (relating to the prevention of obstructions in streets in England and Wales elsewhere than in London).

Section 2 of the Parks Regulation (Amendment) Act 1926 (authorising the making of regulations as to Royal Parks).

[Section 36 of the Road Traffic Act 1988] (which makes it an offence to fail to conform to the indications given by certain traffic signs).

Section 1 of the 1984 Act (which authorises the making of orders regulating traffic on roads outside Greater London) ...

Section 6 of the 1984 Act (authorising the making of orders regulating traffic on roads in Greater London).

Section 9 of the 1984 Act (authorising the making of experimental traffic orders).

Section 12 of the 1984 Act (relating to experimental traffic schemes in Greater London).

Section 14 of the 1984 Act (which provides for the restriction or prohibition of the use of roads in consequence of the execution of works).

[Section 16A of the Road Traffic Regulation Act 1984 (which provides for the restriction or prohibition of the use of roads in connection with the holding of certain special events).]

Section 17 of the 1984 Act (authorising the making of regulations with respect to the use of special roads).

Section 25 of the 1984 Act (authorising the making of regulations for crossings for foot passengers).

Sections 35 and 45 to 49 of the 1984 Act (relating to parking places for vehicles).

Section 57 of the 1984 Act (relating to the provision of parking places in England and Wales for bicycles and motor cycles).

Sections 66 and 67 of the 1984 Act (which empower the police to place traffic signs relating to local traffic regulations and temporary signs for dealing with traffic congestion and danger).

Any enactment in any local Act for the time being in force, and any byelaw having effect under any enactment for the time being in force, being an enactment or byelaw imposing or authorising the imposition of a prohibition or restriction similar to any prohibition or restriction which is or can be imposed by or under any of the above-mentioned enactments.

B13.27   *[Schedule 1 is printed as amended by the Interpretation Act 1978 ss.17(2)(a) and 23(1); SI 1994/1503.*

References to Scottish legislation have been omitted from Sch.1.]

SCHEDULE 2

FORM OF NOTICE TO OCCUPIER OF LAND BEFORE REMOVING ABANDONED VEHICLES

B13.28   *[Omitted.]*

The Removal and Disposal of Vehicles (Loading Areas) Regulations 1986

(SI 1986/184)

PART I

GENERAL

Citation, commencement and revocation

1. *[Omitted.]* B14.01

Interpretation

2. In these Regulations — B14.02

"*the 1984 Act*" means the Road Traffic Regulation Act 1984;

"*loading area*" has the same meaning as in section 61 of the 1984 Act [*q.v.*];

"*vehicle*" has the same meaning as in section 99 of the 1984 Act [*q.v.*].

PART II

REMOVAL OF VEHICLES

Power to require the removal of vehicles from loading areas

3.—(1) This regulation applies to a vehicle which is in any part of a loading area while the parking of it in that part is prohibited by virtue of section 61 of the 1984 Act. B14.03

(2) Subject to paragraph (3) below, an officer of the local authority, duly authorised in writing by that authority, may require the owner, driver or other person in control or in charge of any vehicle to which this regulation applies to move it or cause it to be removed, and any such requirement may include a requirement that the vehicle shall be moved from the part of the loading area where it is to some other part of that loading area, or to a place on a highway, or to some other place which is not on a highway (being a place where the vehicle can be lawfully parked).

(3) When making any requirement under paragraph (2) above an officer of the local authority, if requested so to do by the owner, driver or other person in control or in charge of the vehicle, shall produce evidence of his authorisation.

(4) In this regulation and in regulation 4 below "*the local authority*" means—

(a) in Greater London, the Council of the London borough or, as the case may be, the Common Council of the City,

(b) elsewhere in England, ... the council of the district in whose area is situated the part of the loading area where the vehicle in question is while parking is prohibited as mentioned in paragraph (1) above.

[(c) in Wales, the council of the county or county borough.]

B14.04   *[Regulation 3 is printed as amended by the Local Government Reorganisation (Wales) (Consequential Amendments No.2) Order 1996 (SI 1996/1008; not reproduced in this work).]*

Power to remove vehicles

B14.05   **4.**—(1) Where, in the case of a vehicle to which regulation 3 above applies—

(a) the owner, driver or other person in control or in charge of the vehicle refuses or fails to comply with a requirement, made under that regulation by a duly authorised officer of the local authority, to move it or cause it to be moved, or

(b) no person who is in control or in charge of the vehicle and who is capable of moving it or causing it to be moved is present on or in the vicinity of the vehicle,

an officer of the local authority (who need not be the officer who has made any requirement as respects the vehicle under regulation 3 above) may move or arrange for the removal of the vehicle to another part of the loading area, or may remove it or arrange for its removal from the loading area to some other place which is not on a highway.

(2) Any person removing or moving a vehicle under this regulation may do so by towing or driving the vehicle or in such other manner as he may think necessary, and may take such measures in relation to the vehicle as he may think necessary to enable him to remove or move it as aforesaid.

PART III

DISPOSAL OF ABANDONED VEHICLES

Disposal of abandoned vehicles

B14.06   **5.** *[Omitted.]*

The Road Vehicles (Construction and Use) Regulations 1986

(SI 1986/1078)

[The text of these regulations is printed as amended by: **B15.01**

> *the Road Vehicles (Construction and Use) (Amendment) Regulations 1986 (SI 1986/1597) (October 10, 1986);*
>
> *the Road Vehicles (Construction and Use) (Amendment) Regulations 1987 (SI 1987/676) (except as otherwise indicated, May 6, 1987);*
>
> *the Road Vehicles (Construction and Use) (Amendment) (No.2) Regulations 1987 (SI 1987/1133) (July 31, 1987);*
>
> *the Road Vehicles (Construction and Use) (Amendment) Regulations 1988 (SI 1988/271) (March 18, 1988);*
>
> *the Road Vehicles (Construction and Use) (Amendment) (No.4) Regulations 1988 (SI 1988/1178) (July 25, 1988);*
>
> *the Road Vehicles (Construction and Use) (Amendment) (No.5) Regulations 1988 (SI 1988/1287) (January 1, 1989);*
>
> *the Road Vehicles (Construction and Use) (Amendment) (No.6) Regulations 1988 (SI 1988/1524) (October 1, 1988);*
>
> *the Road Vehicles (Construction and Use) (Amendment) (No.7) Regulations 1988 (SI 1988/1871) (January 1, 1989);*
>
> *the Road Vehicles (Construction and Use) (Amendment) Regulations 1989 (SI 1989/1478) (September 7, 1989);*
>
> *the Road Vehicles (Construction and Use) (Amendment) (No.2) Regulations 1989 (SI 1989/1695) (October 30, 1989);*
>
> *the Road Vehicles (Construction and Use) (Amendment) (No.3) Regulations 1989 (SI 1989/1865) (November 8, 1989);*
>
> *the Road Vehicles (Construction and Use) (Amendment) (No.4) Regulations 1989 (SI 1989/2360) (January 11, 1990);*
>
> *the Road Vehicles (Construction and Use) (Amendment) Regulations 1990 (SI 1990/317) (March 19, 1990);*
>
> *the Road Vehicles (Construction and Use) (Amendment) (No.2) Regulations 1990 (SI 1990/1131) (June 26, 1990);*
>
> *the Road Vehicles (Construction and Use) (Amendment) (No.3) Regulations 1990 (SI 1990/1163) (June 29, 1990);*
>
> *the Road Vehicles (Construction and Use) (Amendment) (No.4) Regulations 1990 (SI 1990/1981) (November 2, 1990);*
>
> *the Road Vehicles (Construction and Use) (Amendment) (No.5) Regulations 1990 (SI 1990/2212) (December 10, 1990);*
>
> *the Road Vehicles (Construction and Use) (Amendment) (No.1) Regulations 1991 (SI 1991/1526) (November 1, 1991);*

the Road Vehicles (Construction and Use) (Amendment) (No.2) Regulations 1991 (SI 1991/1527) (August 1, 1991);

the Road Vehicles (Construction and Use) (Amendment) (No.3) Regulations 1991 (SI 1991/2003) (October 7, 1991);

the Road Vehicles (Construction and Use) (Amendment) (No.4) Regulations 1991 (SI 1991/2125) (October 17, 1991);

the Road Vehicles (Construction and Use) (Amendment) (No.5) Regulations 1991 (SI 1991/2710) (January 1, 1992);

the Road Vehicles (Construction and Use) (Amendment) Regulations 1992 (SI 1992/352) (April 1, 1992);

the Road Vehicles (Construction and Use) (Amendment) (No.2) Regulations 1992 (SI 1992/422) (for the purposes of reg.8, August 1, 1993; for all other purposes, August 1, 1992);

the Road Vehicles (Construction and Use) (Amendment) (No.3) Regulations 1992 (SI 1992/646) (April 1, 1992);

the Tramcars and Trolley Vehicles (Modification of Enactments) Regulations 1992 (SI 1992/1217), reg.13 (July 1, 1992);

the Road Vehicles (Construction and Use) (Amendment) (No.4) Regulations 1992 (SI 1992/2016) (January 1, 1993);

the Road Vehicles (Construction and Use) (Amendment) (No.5) Regulations 1992 (SI 1992/2137) (December 31, 1992);

the Road Vehicles (Construction and Use) (Amendment) (No.6) Regulations 1992 (SI 1992/2909) (December 31, 1992);

the Road Vehicles (Construction and Use) (Amendment) (No.7) Regulations 1992 (SI 1992/3088) (January 1, 1993);

the Road Vehicles (Construction and Use) (Amendment) (No.8) Regulations 1992 (SI 1992/3285) (February 1, 1993);

the Road Vehicles (Construction and Use) (Amendment) (No.1) Regulations 1993 (SI 1993/1946) (September 1, 1993);

the Road Vehicles (Construction and Use) (Amendment) (No.2) Regulations 1993 (SI 1993/2199) (October 1, 1993);

the Road Vehicles (Construction and Use) (Amendment) (No.3) Regulations 1993 (SI 1993/3048) (January 1, 1994);

the Road Vehicles (Construction and Use) (Amendment) Regulations 1994 (SI 1994/14) (July 1, 1994);

the Road Vehicles (Construction and Use) (Amendment) (No.2) Regulations 1994 (SI 1994/329) (March 24, 1994);

the Road Vehicles (Construction and Use) (Amendment) (No.3) Regulations 1994 (SI 1994/2192) (October 1, 1994);

the Road Vehicles (Construction and Use) (Amendment) (No.4) Regulations 1994 (SI 1994/3270) (February 1, 1995), with corrigendum dated May 1995;

the Road Vehicles (Construction and Use) (Amendment) Regulations 1995 (SI 1995/551) (April 1, 1995);

the Road Vehicles (Construction and Use) (Amendment) (No.2) Regulations 1995 (SI 1995/737) (March 31, 1995);

the Road Vehicles (Construction and Use) (Amendment) (No.3) Regulations 1995 (SI 1995/1201) (June 1, 1995);

the Road Vehicles (Construction and Use) (Amendment) (No.4) Regulations 1995 (SI 1995/1458) (July 1, 1995);

the Road Vehicles (Construction and Use) (Amendment) (No.5) Regulations 1995 (SI 1995/2210) (September 25, 1995 and January 1, 1996);

the Road Vehicles (Construction and Use) (Amendment) (No.6) Regulations 1995 (SI 1995/3051) (January 1, 1996);

the Road Vehicles (Construction and Use) (Amendment) Regulations 1996 (SI 1996/16) (February 1, 1996);

the Road Vehicles (Construction and Use) (Amendment) (No.2) Regulations 1996 (SI 1996/163) (March 6, 1996 and February 10, 1997);

the Gas Act 1995 (Consequential Modifications of Subordinate Legislation) Order 1996 (SI 1996/252) (March 1, 1996);

the Road Vehicles (Construction and Use) (Amendment) (No.3) Regulations 1996 (SI 1996/2064) (September 1, 1996 and September 1, 1997);

the Road Vehicles (Construction and Use) (Amendment) (No.4) Regulations 1996 (SI 1996/2085) (September 2, 1996);

the Road Vehicles (Construction and Use) (Amendment) (No.5) Regulations 1996 (SI 1996/2329) (October 1, 1996);

the Road Vehicles (Construction and Use) (Amendment) (No.6) Regulations 1996 (SI 1996/3017) (July 1, 1997);

the Road Vehicles (Construction and Use) (Amendment) (No.7) Regulations 1996 (SI 1996/3033) (January 1, 1997);

the Road Vehicles (Construction and Use) (Amendment) (No.8) Regulations 1996 (SI 1996/3133) (January 3, 1997);

the Road Vehicles (Construction and Use) (Amendment) Regulations 1997 (SI 1997/530) (October 1, 1997);

the Road Vehicles (Construction and Use) (Amendment) (No.2) Regulations 1997 (SI 1997/1096) (April 22, 1997);

the Road Vehicles (Construction and Use) (Amendment) (No.3) Regulations 1997 (SI 1997/1340) (July 1, 1997);

the Road Vehicles (Construction and Use) (Amendment) (No.4) Regulations 1997 (SI 1997/1458) (June 30, 1997);

the Road Vehicles (Construction and Use) (Amendment) (No.5) Regulations 1997 (SI 1997/1544) (August 1, 1997);

the Road Vehicles (Construction and Use) (Amendment) (No.6) Regulations 1997 (SI 1997/2935) (December 31, 1997);

the Road Vehicles (Construction and Use) (Amendment) Regulations 1998 (SI 1998/1) (February 2, 1998);

the Road Vehicles (Construction and Use) (Amendment) (No.2) Regulations 1998 (SI 1998/1000) (April 30, 1998);

the Road Vehicles (Construction and Use) (Amendment) (No.3) Regulations 1998 (SI 1998/1188) (June 1, 1998);

the Road Vehicles (Construction and Use) (Amendment) (No.4) Regulations 1998 (SI 1998/1281) (August 1, 1998);

the Road Vehicles (Construction and Use) (Amendment) (No.5) Regulations 1998 (SI 1998/1563) (August 1, 1998);

the Road Vehicles (Construction and Use) (Amendment) (No.6) Regulations 1998 (SI 1998/2429) (November 1, 1998);

the Road Vehicles (Construction and Use) (Amendment) (No.7) Regulations 1998 (SI 1998/3112) (January 1, 1999);

the Road Vehicles (Construction and Use) (Amendment) Regulations 1999 (SI 1999/1521) (August 1, 1999);

the Road Vehicles (Construction and Use) (Amendment No.2) Regulations 1999 (SI 1999/1959) (July 31, 1999);

the Road Vehicles (Construction and Use) (Amendment) Regulations 2000 (SI 2000/1434) (August 1 and October 1, 2000);

the Road Vehicles (Construction and Use) (Amendment) (No.2) Regulations 2000 (SI 2000/1971) (August 30, 2000);

the Road Vehicles (Construction and Use) (Amendment) (No.3) Regulations 2000 (SI 2000/3197) (January 1, 2001);

the Road Vehicles (Construction and Use) (Amendment) Regulations 2001 (SI 2001/306) (March 1, 2001);

the Road Vehicles (Construction and Use) (Amendment) (No.2) Regulations 2001 (SI 2001/1043) (October 1, 2001);

the Postal Services Act 2000 (Consequential Modifications No.1) Order 2001 (SI 2001/1149) (March 26, 2001);

the Road Vehicles (Construction and Use) (Amendment) (No.3) Regulations 2001 (SI 2001/1825) (August 1, 2001);

the Road Vehicles (Construction and Use) (Amendment) (No.4) Regulations 2001 (SI 2001/3208) (October 16, 2001 and May 1, 2002);

the Road Vehicles (Construction and Use) (Amendment) Regulations 2002 (SI 2002/227) (March 1, 2002);

the Road Vehicles (Construction and Use) (Amendment) (No.2) Regulations 2002 (SI 2002/1474) (July 1, 2002 and August 1, 2002);

the Road Vehicles (Construction and Use) (Amendment) (No.3) Regulations 2002 (SI 2002/2126) (September 4, 2002);

the Road Vehicles (Construction and Use) (Amendment) Regulations 2003 (SI 2003/182) (April 1, 2003);

the Road Vehicles (Construction and Use) (Amendment) (No.2) Regulations 2003 (SI 2003/1690) (August 1, 2003);

the Road Vehicles (Construction and Use) (Amendment) (No.3) Regulations 2003 (SI 2003/1946) (September 1, 2003);

the Communications Act 2003 (Consequential Amendments) Order 2003 (SI 2003/2155) (September 17, 2003);

the Road Vehicles (Construction and Use) (Amendment) (No.4) Regulations 2003 (SI 2003/2695) (December 1, 2003);

the Road Vehicles (Construction and Use) (Amendment) (No.5) Regulations 2003 (SI 2003/3145) (January 1, 2004);

the Road Vehicles (Construction and Use) (Amendment) Regulations 2004 (SI 2004/1706) (August 1, 2004);

the Road Vehicles (Construction and Use) (Amendment) (No.2) Regulations 2004 (SI 2004/2102) (January 1, 2005);

the Fire and Rescue Services Act 2004 (Consequential Amendments) (England) Order 2004 (SI 2004/3168) (December 30, 2004);

the Road Vehicles (Construction and Use) (Amendment) Regulations 2005 (SI 2005/1641) (August 1, 2005);

the Road Vehicles (Construction and Use) (Amendment) (No.2) Regulations (SI 2005/2560) (October 21, 2005);

the Fire and Rescue Services Act 2004 (Consequential Amendments) (Wales) Order 2005 (SI 2005/2929) (October 25, 2005);

the Road Vehicles (Construction and Use) (Amendment) (No.3) Regulations 2005 (SI 2005/2987) (December 12, 2005);

the Road Vehicles (Construction and Use) (Amendment) (No.4) Regulations 2005 (SI 2005/3165) (December 12, 2005);

the Road Vehicles (Construction and Use) (Amendment) (No.5) Regulations 2005 (SI 2005/3170 (December 12, 2005);

the Serious Organised Crime and Police Act 2005 (Consequential and Supplementary Amendments to Secondary Legislation) Order 2006 (SI 2006/594) (April 1, 2006);

the Road Vehicles (Construction and Use) (Amendment) Regulations 2006 (SI 2006/1756) (August 1, 2006);

the Road Vehicles (Construction and Use) and Motor Vehicles (Type Approval for Goods Vehicles) (Great Britain) (Amendment) Regulations 2006 (SI 2006/2565) (October 20, 2006 and November 9, 2006);

the Motor Vehicles (Type Approval for Goods Vehicles) (Great Britain) (Amendment) Regulations (SI 2007/361) (March 14, 2007);

the Road Vehicles (Construction and Use) (Amendment) Regulations 2007 (SI 2007/1817) (August 1, 2007);

the Road Vehicles (Construction and Use) (Amendment) (No.2) Regulations 2007 (SI 2007/2544) (October 1, 2007);

the Road Vehicles (Construction and Use) (Amendment) (No.3) Regulations 2007 (SI 2007/3132) (December 1, 2007);

the Consumer Protection from Unfair Trading Regulations 2008 (SI 2008/1277) (May 26, 2008);

the Road Vehicles (Construction and Use) (Amendment) Regulations 2008 (SI 2008/1702) (August 1, 2008);

the Road Vehicles (Construction and Use) (Amendment) Regulations 2009 (SI 2009/142) (March 3, 2009; March 31, 2009);

the Road Vehicles (Construction and Use) (Amendment) (No.2) Regulations 2009 (SI 2009/1806) (August 1, 2009);

the Road Vehicles (Construction and Use) (Amendment) (No.3) Regulations 2009 (SI 2009/2196) (September 7, 2009);

the Road Vehicles (Construction and Use) (Amendment) (No.4) Regulations 2009 (SI 2009/3221) (January 4, 2010);

the Road Vehicles (Construction and Use) (Amendment) Regulations 2010 (SI 2010/312) (March 23, 2010);

the Road Vehicles (Construction and Use) (Amendment) (No.2) Regulations 2010 (SI 2010/964) (April 20, 2010); and

the Road Vehicles (Construction and Use) (Amendment) Regulations 2011 (SI 2011/427) (March 11, 2011).

The amending instruments are referred to in the notes to the principal regulations only by their years and numbers. The dates referred to above are the dates on which the amending instruments came into force.

The Road Vehicles (Construction and Use) (Amendment) (No.2) Regulations 1988 (SI 1988/1102) were revoked on July 12, 1988 (before they were due to take effect) by the Road Vehicles (Construction and Use) (Amendment) (No.3) Regulations 1988 (SI 1988/1177); reg.3 of the latter regulations expressly stated that the principal regulations should have effect as if the Amendment No.2 regulations had never been made.

The Amendment No.2 regulations of 1988, have, in effect, been replaced by the Amendment No.4 regulations of 1988 (see above), and hence neither the Amendment No.2 regulations of 1988 nor the Amendment No.3 regulations of 1988 are referred to in the notes to the principal regulations.

The Road Vehicles (Construction and Use) (Amendment No.2) Regulations 1999 (SI 1999/1959) amended the Road Vehicles (Construction and Use) (Amendment) Regulations 1999 (SI 1999/1521) before the latter took effect.]

ARRANGEMENT OF REGULATIONS

PART III

PLATES, MARKINGS, TESTING AND INSPECTION

SCHEDULES

PART I

PRELIMINARY

Commencement and citation

1. *[Omitted.]* **B15.03**

Revocation

2. *[Omitted.]* **B15.04**

Interpretation

3.—(1) In these Regulations, unless the context otherwise requires— **B15.05**
  (a) any reference to a numbered regulation or a numbered Schedule is a reference to the regulation or Schedule bearing that number in these Regulations,
  (b) any reference to a numbered or lettered paragraph or sub-paragraph is a reference to the paragraph or sub-paragraph bearing that number or letter in the regulation or Schedule or (in the case of a sub-paragraph) paragraph in which the reference occurs, and
  (c) any reference to a Table, or to a numbered Table, is a reference to the Table, or to the Table bearing that number, in the regulation or Schedule in which that reference occurs.

(2) In these Regulations, unless the context otherwise requires, the expressions specified in column 1 of the Table have the meaning, or are to be interpreted in accordance with the provisions, specified for them in column 2 of the Table.

TABLE

(regulation 3(2))

1	2
Expression	*Meaning*
The 1971 Act	The Vehicles (Excise) Act 1971.
The [1988 Act]	The [Road Traffic Act 1988].
The 1981 Act	The Public Passenger Vehicles Act 1981.
The 1984 Act	The Road Traffic Regulation Act 1984.
[The 1988 Act	The Road Traffic Act 1988].
[The 1994 Act]	[The Vehicle Excise and Registration Act 1994].
The Approval Marks Regulations	The Motor Vehicles (Designation of Approval Marks) Regulations 1979 [SI 1979/1088, as amended].
[The EC Whole Vehicle Type Approval Regulations	The Motor Vehicles (EC Type Approval) Regulations 1998 [SI 1998/2051, as amended].]

1	2
Expression	*Meaning*
The Lighting Regulations	[The Road Vehicles Lighting Regulations 1989 [*SI 1989/1796, q.v.*]].
The Plating and Testing Regulations	The [Goods Vehicles (Plating and Testing) Regulations 1988] [*SI 1988/1478, q.v.*].
The Type Approval Regulations	The Motor Vehicles (Type Approval) Regulations 1980 [*SI 1980/1182, as amended*].
The Type Approval (Great Britain) Regulations	The Motor Vehicles (Type Approval) (Great Britain) Regulations 1984 [*SI 1984/981, as amended*].
The Type Approval for Goods Vehicles Regulations	The Motor Vehicles (Type Approval for Goods Vehicles) (Great Britain) Regulations 1982 [*SI 1982/1271, as amended*].
The Type Approval for Agricultural Vehicles Regulations	The Agricultural or Forestry Tractors and Tractor Components (Type Approval) Regulations 1988 [*SI 1988/1567, as amended*].
[*The Vehicle Approval Regulations*	The Road Vehicles (Approval) Regulations 2009 [*SI 2009/717*].
The Act of Accession	The Treaty concerning the Accession of the Kingdom of Denmark, Ireland, the Kingdom of Norway and the United Kingdom of Great Britain and Northern Ireland to the European Economic Community and the European Atomic Energy Community [*Cmnd. 5179-1*].
[*agricultural or forestry tractor*	an agricultural or forestry tractor within the meaning of Community Directive 82/890.]
agricultural motor vehicle	a motor vehicle which is constructed or adapted for use off roads for the purpose of agriculture, horticulture or forestry and which is primarily used for one or more of those purposes, not being a dual-purpose vehicle.
agricultural trailer	a trailer which is constructed or adapted for the purpose of agriculture, horticulture or forestry and which is only used for one or more of those purposes, not being an agricultural trailed appliance.

1	2
Expression	*Meaning*

agricultural trailed appliance	a trailer—
	(a) which is an implement constructed or adapted—
	  (i) for use off roads for the purpose of agriculture, horticulture or forestry and whichis only used for one or more of those purposes, and
	  (ii) so that, save in the case of an appliance manufactured before 1st December 1985, or a towed roller, its maximum gross weight is not more than twice its unladen weight; but
	(b) which is not—
	  (i) a vehicle which is used primarily as living accommodation by one or more persons, and which carries no goods or burden except those needed by such one or more persons for the purpose of their residence in the vehicle; or
	  (ii) an agricultural, horticultural or forestry implement rigidly but not permanently mounted on any vehicle whether or not any of the weight of the implement is supported by one or more of its own wheels; so however that such an implement is an agricultural trailed appliance if
	    — part of the weight of the implement is supported by one or more of its own wheels, and
	    — the longitudinal axis of the greater part of the implement is capable of articulating in the horizontal plane in relation to the longitudinal axis of the rear portion of the vehicle which is mounted.

agricultural trailed appliance conveyor	an agricultural trailer which— (a) has an unladen weight which does not exceed 510kg; (b) is clearly and indelibly marked with its unladen weight; (c) has a pneumatic tyre fitted to each one of its wheels; (d) is designed and constructed for the purpose of conveying one agricultural trailed appliance or one agricultural, horticultural or forestry implement.
[anti-lock braking system ("ABS")	a part of a service braking system which automatically controls the degree of slip, in the direction of rotation of the wheel or wheels, on one or more wheels of the vehicle during braking.]

1	*2*
Expression	*Meaning*
articulated bus	a bus so constructed that— (a) it can be divided into two parts, both of which are vehicles and one of which is a motor vehicle, but cannot be so divided without the use of facilities normally available only at a workshop; and (b) passengers carried by it can at all times pass from either part to the other.
articulated vehicle	a heavy motor car or motor car, not being an articulated bus, with a trailer so attached that part of the trailer is superimposed on the drawing vehicle and, when the trailer is uniformly loaded, not less than 20% of the weight of its load is borne by the drawing vehicle.
axle	any reference to the number of axles of a vehicle is to be interpreted in accordance with paragraph (8).
axle weight	in relation to each axle of a vehicle, the sum of the weights transmitted to the road surface by all the wheels of that axle, having regard to the provisions of paragraph (8).
braking efficiency	the maximum braking force capable of being developed by the brakes of a vehicle, expressed as a percentage of the weight of the vehicle including any persons or load carried in the vehicle.
braking system	is to be interpreted in accordance with paragraph (6).
bus	a motor vehicle which is constructed or adapted to carry more than eight seated passengers in addition to the driver.
[car transporter	a trailer which is constructed and normally used for the purpose of carrying at least two other wheeled vehicles.]
cc	cubic centimetre(s).
close-coupled	in relation to wheels on the same side of a trailer, fitted so that at all times while the trailer is in motion they remain parallel to the longitudinal axis of the trailer, and that the distance between the centres of their respective areas of contact with the road surface does not exceed 1m.
closely spaced	[...]
cm	centimetre(s).
cm²	square centimetre(s).
[coach	a large bus with a maximum gross weight of more than 7.5 tonnes and with a maximum speed exceeding 60mph.]

1	*2*
Expression	*Meaning*
Community Directive, followed by a number	the Directive adopted by the Council or the Commission of the European Communities [or the European Parliament and the Council of the European Union] of which identifying particulars are given in the item in column 3 of Table I in Schedule 2 in which that number appears in column 2; where such a Directive amends a previous Directive mentioned in column 3(d) of the Table [the reference to the amending Directive includes a reference to] that previous Directive as so amended. Any reference to a Directive which has been amended by the Act of Accession is a reference to the Directive as so amended.
the Community Recording Equipment Regulation	[Council Regulation (EEC) No.3821/85 on recording equipment in road transport [*O.J. No.L370, December 31, 1985, p.8., q.v.*] as read with the Community Drivers' Hours and Recording Equipment Regulations 2007 [SI 2007/1819].]
[*combined transport operation*	shall be construed in accordance with paragraph 9 of Schedule 11A.]
composite trailer	a combination of a converter dolly and a semi-trailer.
container	an article of equipment, not being a motor vehicle or trailer, having a volume of at least 8 cubic metres, constructed wholly or mostly of metal and intended for repeated use for the carriage of goods or burden.

converter dolly	[(a) a trailer which is—
	   (i) equipped with 2 or more wheels,
	   (ii) designed to be used in combination with a semi-trailer without any part of the weight of the semi-trailer being borne by the drawing vehicle, and
	   (iii) not itself a part either of the semi-trailer or the drawing vehicle when being so used; or
	(b) a trailer which is—
	   (i) equipped with 2 or more wheels;
	   (ii) designed to be used in combination with a semitrailer with part of the weight of the semi-trailer being borne by the drawing vehicle;
	   (iii) not itself a part either of the semi-trailer or the drawing vehicle when being so used; and
	   (iv) used solely for the purposes of agriculture, horticulture or forestry, or for any two or for all of those purposes.]

Council Regulation (EEC), followed by a number	the Regulation adopted by the Council of the European Communities.
deck	a floor or platform on which seats are provided for the accommodation of passengers.

1	2
Expression	*Meaning*
design weight	in relation to the gross weight, each axle weight or the train weight of a motor vehicle or trailer, the weight at or below which in the opinion of the Secretary of State or of a person authorised in that behalf by the Secretary of State the vehicle could safely be driven on roads.
double-decked vehicle	a vehicle having two decks one of which is wholly or partly above the other and each of which is provided with a gangway serving seats on that deck only.

dual-purpose vehicle	a vehicle constructed or adapted for the carriage both of passengers and of goods or burden of any description, being a vehicle of which the unladen weight does not exceed 2040kg, and which either—
	
	(i) is so constructed or adapted that the driving power of the engine is, or by the appropriate use of the controls of the vehicle can be, transmitted to all the wheels of the vehicle; or
	(ii) satisfies the following conditions as to construction, namely—
	  (a) the vehicle must be permanently fitted with a rigid roof, with or without a sliding panel;
	  (b) the area of the vehicle to the rear of the driver's seat must—
	    (i) be permanently fitted with at least one row of transverse seats (fixed or folding) for two or more passengers and those seats must be properly sprung or cushioned and provided with upholstered back-rests, attached either to the seats or to a side or the floor of the vehicle; and
	    (ii) be lit on each side and at the rear by a window or windows of glass or other transparent material having an area or aggregate area of not less that 1850 square centimetres on each side and not less than 770 square centimetres at the rear; and
	  (c) the distance between the rearmost part of the steering wheel and the back-rests of the row of transverse seats satisfying the requirements specified in head (i) of sub-paragraph (b) (or, if there is more than one such row of seats, the distance between the rearmost part of the steering wheel and the back-rests of the rearmost such row) must, when the seats are ready for use, be not less than one-third of the distance between the rearmost part of the steering wheel and the rearmost part of the floor of the vehicle.

1	*2*
Expression	*Meaning*
ECE Regulation, followed by a number	the Regulation, annexed to the Agreement concerning the adoption of uniform conditions of approval for Motor Vehicles Equipment and Parts and reciprocal recognition thereof concluded at Geneva on 20th March 1958 [*Cmnd. 2535*] as amended [*Cmnd. 3562*], to which the United Kingdom is party [*instrument of accession dated January 14, 1963 deposited with the Secretary-General of the United Nations on January 15, 1963*], of which identifying particulars are given in the item in column (3)(a), (b) and (c) of Table II in Schedule 2 in which that number appears in column (2); and where that number contains more than two digits, it refers to that Regulation with the amendments in force at the date specified in column (3)(d) in that item.
engine power in kilowatts (kW)	the maximum net power ascertained in accordance with Community Directive 80/1269.
engineering plant	(a) movable plant or equipment being a motor vehicle or trailer specially designed and constructed for the special purposes of engineering operations, and which cannot, owing to the requirements of those purposes, comply with all the requirements of these Regulations and which is not constructed primarily to carry a load other than a load being either excavated materials raised from the ground by apparatus on the motor vehicle or trailer or materials which the vehicle or trailer is specially designed to treat while carried thereon; or (b) a mobile crane which does not comply in all respects with the requirements of these Regulations.
[*engineering equipment*	engineering plant and any other plant or equipment designed and constructed for the purpose of engineering operations.]
exhaust system	a complete set of components through which the exhaust gases escape from the engine unit of a motor vehicle including those which are necessary to limit the noise caused by the escape of those gases.
first used	is to be interpreted in accordance with paragraph (3).

1	2
Expression	*Meaning*
[*Framework Directive*	Council Directive 70/156/EEC [*O.J. L42, February 23, 1970, p.1*] as amended by Council Directive 87/403/EEC [*O.J. L220, August 8, 1987, p.44*], Council Directive 92/53/EEC [*O.J. L225, August 10, 1992, p.1*], Commission Directive 93/81/EEC [*O.J. No.L264, October 23, 1993, p.49*] and Commission Directive 98/14/EC [*O.J. No.L91, March 25, 1998, p.1*].]
gangway	the space provided for obtaining access from any entrance to the passengers' seats or from any such seat to an exit other than an emergency exit, but excluding a staircase and any space in front of a seat which is required only for the use of passengers occupying that seat or a seat in the same row of seats.
gas	any fuel which is wholly gaseous at 17.5°C under a pressure of 1.013 bar absolute.
gas-fired appliance	a device carried on a motor vehicle or trailer when in use on a road, which consumes gas and which is neither— (a) a device owned or operated by or with the authority of the British Gas Corporation for the purpose of detecting gas, nor (b) an engine for the propulsion of a motor vehicle, nor (c) a lamp which consumes acetylene gas.
goods vehicle	a motor vehicle or trailer constructed or adapted for use for the carriage or haulage of goods or burden of any description.
gritting trailer	a trailer which is used on a road for the purpose of spreading grit or other matter so as to avoid or reduce the effect of ice or snow on the road.
gross weight	(a) in relation to a motor vehicle, the sum of the weights transmitted to the road surface by all the wheels of the vehicle, (b) in relation to a trailer, the sum of the weights transmitted to the road surface by all the wheels of the trailer and of any weight of the trailer imposed on the drawing vehicle.
heavy motor car	a mechanically propelled vehicle, not being a locomotive, a motor tractor, or a motor car, which is constructed itself to carry a load or passengers and the weight of which unladen exceeds 2540kg.
indivisible load	a load which cannot without undue expense or risk of damage be divided into two or more loads for the purpose of conveyance on a road.

1	2
Expression	*Meaning*
industrial tractor	a tractor, not being an agricultural motor vehicle, which— (a) has an unladen weight not exceeeding 7370kg, (b) is designed and used primarily for work off roads, or for work on roads in connection only with road construction or maintenance (including any such tractor when fitted with an implement or implements designed primarily for use in connection with such work, whether or not any such implement is of itself designed to carry a load), and (c) has a maximum speed not exceeding 20mph.
invalid carriage	a mechanically propelled vehicle the weight of which unladen does not exceed 254kg and which is specially designed and constructed, and not merely adapted, for the use of a person suffering from some physical defect or disability and is solely used by such a person.
[ISO	International Organisation for Standardisation.]
[ISO 7638 connector	An electrical connector that complies with standard ISO 7638: 1997-1 or ISO 7368: 1997-2 and is used to provide a dedicated power supply and a communication link between the tow vehicle and trailer.]
kerbside weight	the weight of a vehicle when it carries— (a) in the case of a motor vehicle, (i) no person; and (ii) a full supply of fuel in its tank, an adequate supply of other liquids incidental to its propulsion and no load other than the loose tools and equipment with which it is normally equipped; (b) in the case of a trailer, no person and is otherwise unladen.
kg	kilogram(s).
km/h	kilometre(s) per hour.
kW	kilowatt(s).
[large bus	a vehicle constructed or adapted to carry more than 16 seated passengers in addition to the driver.]
[light trailer	a trailer with a maximum gross weight which does not exceed 3500kg.]
living van	a vehicle used primarily as living accommodation by one or more persons, and which is not also used for the carriage of goods or burden which are not needed by such one or more persons for the purpose of their residence in the vehicle.

1	*2*
Expression	*Meaning*
locomotive	a mechanically propelled vehicle which is not constructed itself to carry a load other than the following articles, that is to say, water, fuel, accumulators and other equipment used for the purpose of propulsion, loose tools and loose equipment, and the weight of which unladen exceeds 7370kg.
longitudinal plane	a vertical plane parallel to the longitudinal axis of a vehicle.

[low loader	a semi-trailer which is constructed and normally used for the carriage of engineering equipment so constructed that the major part of the load platform does not extend over or between the wheels and the upper surface of which is below the height of the topmost point of the tyres of those wheels, measured on level ground and when—
	    (a) any adjustable suspension is at the normal travelling height,
	    (b) all pneumatic tyres are suitably inflated for use when the vehicle is fully laden, and
	    (c) the semi-trailer is unladen,
	(see also the definition of stepframe low loader).]

[low platform trailer	a trailer fitted with tyres with a rim diameter size code less than 20 and displaying a rectangular plate which—
	    (a) is at least 225mm wide and at least 175mm high; and
	    (b) bears two black letters "L" on a white ground each at least 125mm high and 90mm wide with a stroke width of 12mm.]

m	metre(s).
m²	square metre(s).
m³	cubic metre(s).

[maximum permitted axle weight	in relation to an axle—
	    (a) in the case of a vehicle which is equipped with a Ministry plate in accordance with regulation 70, the axle weight shown in column (2) of that plate (where the plate is in the form required by [Schedule 10 or 10B]) or in column (2) of that plate (where the plate is in the form required by [Schedule 10A or 10C]) in relation to that axle;
	    (b) in the case of a vehicle which is not equipped with a Ministry plate but which is equipped with a plate in accordance with regulation 66, the maximum axle weight shown for that axle on the plate in respect of item 9 of Part I of Schedule 8 in the case of a motor vehicle and item 7 of Part II of Schedule 8 in the case of a trailer; and

1	2
Expression	*Meaning*
[*maximum permitted axle weight— cont.*	(c) in any other case, the weight which the axle is designed or adapted not to exceed when the vehicle is travelling on the road.]
maximum gross weight	(a) in the case of a vehicle equipped with a Ministry plate in accordance with regulation 70, the design gross weight shown in column (3) of that plate [(where the plate is in the form required by [Schedule 10 or 10B]) or in column (4) of that plate (where the plate is in the form required by [Schedule 10A or 10C])] or, if no such weight is shown, the gross weight shown in column (2) of that plate;
	(b) in the case of a vehicle not equipped with a Ministry plate, but which is equipped with a plate in accordance with regulation 66, the maximum gross weight shown on the plate in respect of item 7 of Part 1 of Schedule 8 in the case of a motor vehicle and item 6 of Part II of Schedule 8 in the case of a trailer;
	(c) in any other case, the weight which the vehicle is designed or adapted not to exceed when the vehicle is travelling on a road.
[*maximum total design axle weight* (an expression used only in relation to trailers)	(a) in the case of a trailer equipped with a Ministry plate in accordance with regulation 70, the sum of the relevant axle weights;
	(b) in the case of a trailer which is not equipped with a Ministry plate, but which is equipped with a plate in accordance with regulation 66, the sum of the maximum axle weights shown on the plate in respect of item 4 of Part II of Schedule 8; or
	(c) in the case of any other trailer, the sum of the axle weights which the trailer is designed or adapted not to exceed when the vehicle is travelling on a road;
	and for the purposes of sub-paragraph (a) the relevant axle weight, in respect to an axle, is the design axle weight shown in column (3) of the Ministry plate (where the plate is in the form required by [Schedule 10 or 10B]) or in column (4) of that plate (where the plate is in the form required by [Schedule 10A or 10C]) in relation to that axle or if no such weight is shown, the axle weight shown in column (2) of that plate in relation to that axle.]
maximum speed	the speed which a vehicle is incapable, by reason of its construction, of exceeding on the level under its own power when fully laden.

1	2
Expression	Meaning
minibus	a motor vehicle which is constructed or adapted to carry more than 8 but not more than 16 seated passengers in addition to the driver.
Ministry plate	[is to be interpreted in accordance with regulation 70].
mm	millimetre(s).
motor ambulance	a motor vehicle which is specially designed and constructed (and not merely adapted) for carrying, as equipment permanently fixed to the vehicle, equipment used for medical, dental, or other health purposes and is used primarily for the carriage of persons suffering from illness, injury or disability.
motor car	a mechanically propelled vehicle, not being a motor tractor, a motor cycle or an invalid carriage, which is constructed itself to carry a load or passengers and the weight of which unladen— (a) if it is constructed solely for the carriage of passengers and their effects and is adapted to carry not more than seven passengers exclusive of the driver does not exceed 3050kg; (b) if it is constructed for use for the conveyance of goods or burden of any description, does not exceed 3050kg; (c) does not exceed 2540kg in a case falling within neither of the foregoing paragraphs.
[motor caravan	a motor vehicle which is constructed or adapted for the carriage of passengers and their effects and which contains, as permanently installed equipment, the facilities which are reasonably necessary for enabling the vehicle to provide mobile living accommodation for its users.]
motor cycle	a mechanically propelled vehicle, not being an invalid carriage, having less than four wheels and the weight of which unladen does not exceed 410kg.
motor tractor	a mechanically propelled vehicle which is not constructed itself to carry a load, other than the following articles, that is to say, water, fuel, accumulators and other equipment used for the purpose of propulsion, loose tools and loose equipment, and the weight of which unladen does not exceed 7370kg.
motor vehicle	a mechanically propelled vehicle intended or adapted for use on roads.
mph	mile(s) per hour.
N/mm^2	newton(s) per square millimetre.
[off-road vehicle	an off-road vehicle as defined in Annex I to Council Directive 70/156/EEC of 6th February 1970 as read with Council Directive 87/403/EEC of 25th June 1987.]

1	2
Expression	*Meaning*
overall height	the vertical distance between the ground and the point on the vehicle which is furthest from the ground, calculated when— (a) the tyres of the vehicle are suitably inflated for the use to which it is being put; (b) the vehicle is at its unladen weight; and (c) the surface of the ground under the vehicle is reasonably flat; but, in the case of a trolley bus, exclusive of the power collection equipment mounted on the roof of the vehicle.
overall length	in relation to a vehicle, the distance between transverse planes passing through the extreme forward and rearward projecting points of the vehicle inclusive of all parts of the vehicle, of any receptacle which is of a permanent character and accordingly strong enough for repeated use, and any fitting on, or attached to, the vehicle except— (i) for all purposes— (a) any driving mirror; (b) any expanding or extensible contrivance forming part of a turntable fire escape fixed to a vehicle; (c) any snow-plough fixed in front of a vehicle; (d) any receptacle specially designed to hold and keep secure a seal issued for the purposes of customs clearance; (e) any tailboard which is let down while the vehicle is stationary in order to facilitate its unloading; (f) any tailboard which is let down in order to facilitate the carriage of, but which is not essential for the support of, loads which are in themselves so long as to extend at least as far as the tailboard when upright; (g) any fitting attached to part of, or to a receptacle on, a vehicle which does not increase the carrying capacity of the part or receptacle but which enables it to be — transferred from a road vehicle to a railway vehicle or from a railway vehicle to a road vehicle; — secured to a railway vehicle by a locking device; and — carried on a railway vehicle by the use of stanchions;

1	2
Expression	*Meaning*
overall length—cont.	(h) any plate, whether rigid or movable, fitted to a trailer constructed for the purpose of carrying other vehicles and designed to bridge the gap between that trailer and a motor vehicle constructed for that purpose and to which the trailer is attached so that, while the trailer is attached to the motor vehicle, vehicles which are to be carried by the motor vehicle may be moved from the trailer to the motor vehicle before a journey begins, and vehicles which have been carried on the motor vehicle may be moved from it to the trailer after a journey ends; (i) any sheeting or other readily flexible means of covering or securing a load; (j) [...] (k) any empty receptacle which itself forms a load; (l) any receptacle which contains an indivisible load of exceptional length; (m) any receptacle manufactured before 30th October 1985, not being a maritime container (namely a container designed primarily for carriage on sea transport without an accompanying road vehicle); ... (n) any special appliance or apparatus as described in regulation 81(c) which does not itself increase the carrying capacity of the vehicle; [or] [(o) any rearward projecting buffer made of rubber or other resilient material.] (ii) for the purposes of [regulations 7, 13A, 13B and 13C] (a) any part of a trailer (not being in the case of an agricultural trailed appliance a drawbar or other thing with which it is equipped for the purpose of being towed) designed primarily for use as a means of attaching it to another vehicle and any fitting designed for use in connection with any such part; (b) the thickness of any front or rear wall on a semi-trailer and of any part forward of such front wall or rearward of such rear wall which does not increase the vehicle's load-carrying space.

1	*2*
Expression	*Meaning*
overall width	the distance between longitudinal planes passing through extreme lateral projecting points of the vehicle inclusive of all parts of the vehicle, of any receptacle which is of permanent character and accordingly strong enough for repeated use, and any fitting on, or attached to, the vehicle except—

(a) any driving mirror;

(b) any snow-plough fixed in front of the vehicle;

(c) so much of the distortion of any tyre as is caused by the weight of the vehicle;

(d) any receptacle specially designed to hold and keep secure a seal issued for the purpose of customs clearance;

(e) any lamp or reflector fitted to the vehicle in accordance with the Lighting Regulations;

(f) any sideboard which is let down while the vehicle is stationary in order to facilitate its loading or unloading;

(g) any fitting attached to part of, or to a receptacle on, a vehicle which does not increase the carrying capacity of the part or receptacle but which enables it to be
— transferred from a road vehicle to a railway vehicle or from a railway vehicle to a road vehicle;
— secured to a railway vehicle by a locking device; and
— carried on a railway vehicle by the use of stanchions;

(h) any sheeting or other readily flexible means of covering or securing a load;

(i) any receptacle with an external width, measured at right angles to the longitudinal axis of the vehicle, which does not exceed 2.5m;

(j) any empty receptacle which itself forms a load;

(k) any receptacle which contains an indivisible load of exceptional width;

(l) any receptacle manufactured before 30th October 1985, not being a maritime container (namely a container designed primarily for carriage on sea transport without an accompanying road vehicle); ...

(m) any special appliance or apparatus as described in regulation 81(c) which does not itself increase the carrying capacity of the vehicle [; or]

1	2
Expression	*Meaning*
overall width—cont.	[(n) any apparatus fitted to a bus which enables it to be guided wholly or mainly by means of wheels bearing outwards against fixed apparatus, provided that no part of the apparatus projects more than 75mm beyond the side of the bus when the wheels of the bus are parallel to its longitudinal axis;

and the reference in paragraph above to the side of a bus is a reference to the longitudinal plane passing through the extreme lateral projecting points of the vehicle inclusive of all parts of the vehicle, of any receptacle which is of permanent character and accordingly strong enough for repeated use, and any fitting on, or attached to, the vehicle except those items referred to in paragraphs (a) to (n).] |
| overhang | the distance measured horizontally and parallel to the longitudinal axis of a vehicle between two transverse planes passing through the following two points—
(a) the rearmost point of the vehicle exclusive of—
    (i) any expanding or extensible contrivance forming part of a turntable fire escape fixed to a vehicle;
    (ii) in the case of a motor car constructed solely for the carriage of passengers and their effects and adapted to carry not more than eight passengers exclusive of the driver, any luggage carrier fitted to the vehicle; and
(b)
    (i) in the case of a motor vehicle having not more than three axles of which only one is not a steering axle, the centre point of that axle;
    (ii) in the case of a motor vehicle having three axles of which the front axle is the only steering axle and of a motor vehicle having four axles of which the two foremost are the only steering axles, a point 110mm behind the centre of a straight line joining the centre points of the two rearmost axles; and
    (iii) in any other case a point situated on the longitudinal axis of the vehicle and such that a line drawn from it at right angles to that axis will pass through the centre of the minimum turning circle of the vehicle. |
| passenger vehicle | a vehicle constructed solely for the carriage of passengers and their effects. |
| pedestrian-controlled vehicle | a motor vehicle which is controlled by a pedestrian and not constructed or adapted for use or used for the carriage of a driver or passenger. |

1	2
Expression	Meaning
pneumatic tyre	a tyre which— (a) is provided with, or together with the wheel upon which it is mounted forms, a continuous closed chamber inflated to a pressure substantially exceeding atmospheric pressure when the tyre is in the condition in which it is normally used, but is not subjected to any load; (b) is capable of being inflated and deflated without removal from the wheel or vehicle; and (c) is such that, when it is deflated and is subjected to a normal load, the sides of the tyre collapse.
public works vehicle	[a mechanically propelled vehicle which is used on a road by or on behalf of— (a) the Central Scotland Water Development Board; (b) a ferry undertaking; (c) a highway or roads authority; (d) a local authority; (e) a market undertaking; (f) the National Rivers Authority; (g) an operator of [an electronic communications code network]; (h) a police authority; (i) [a universal provider (within the meaning of the Postal Services Act 2000) in connection with the provision of a universal postal service (within the meaning of that Act)]; (j) a public electricity supplier within the meaning of Part I of the Electricity Act 1989; (k) [a public gas transporter within the meaning of Part I of the Gas Act 1986]; (l) a statutory undertaker within the meaning of section 329(1) of the Highways Act 1980 [q.v.]; (m) an undertaking for the supply of district heating; (n) a water authority within the meaning of the Water (Scotland) Act 1980; or (o) a water or sewerage undertaking within the meaning of the Water Act 1989; for the purpose of works which such a body has a duty or power to carry out, and which is used only for the carriage of— (i) the crew, and (ii) goods which are needed for works in respect of which the vehicle is used.]
recut pneumatic tyre	a pneumatic tyre in which all or part of its original tread pattern has been cut deeper or burnt deeper or a different tread pattern has been cut deeper or burnt deeper than the original tread pattern.

1	*2*
Expression	*Meaning*
refuse vehicle	a vehicle designed for use and used solely in connection with street cleansing, the collection or disposal of refuse, or the collection or disposal of the contents of gullies or cesspools.
registered	registered under any of the following enactments— (a) the Roads Act 1920 (b) the Vehicles (Excise) Act 1949 (c) the Vehicles (Excise) Act 1962, or (d) the 1971 Act [or the 1994 Act] and, in relation to the date on which a vehicle was registered, the date on which it was first registered under any of those enactments.
relevant braking requirement	a requirement that the brakes of a motor vehicle (as assisted, where a trailer is being drawn, by the brakes on the trailer) comply— (i) in a case to which item 1 in Table 1 in regulation 18 applies, with the requirements specified in regulation 18(3) for vehicles falling in that item; (ii) in any other case, with the requirements specified in regulation 18(3) for vehicle classes (a) and (b) in item 2 of that Table (whatever the date of first use of the motor vehicle and the date of manufacture of any trailer drawn by it may be).
resilient tyre	a tyre, not being a pneumatic tyre, which is of soft or elastic material, having regard to paragraph (5).
[*restricted speed vehicle*	a vehicle displaying at its rear a "50" plate in accordance with the requirements of Schedule 13.]
[*retreaded tyre*	a tyre which has been reconditioned to extend its useful life by replacement of the tread rubber or by replacement of the tread rubber and renovation of the sidewall rubber.]
rigid vehicle	a motor vehicle which is not constructed or adapted to form part of an articulated vehicle or articulated bus.
[*rim diameter*	is to be interpreted in accordance with the British Standard BS AU 50: Part 2: Section 1: 1980 entitled "British Standard Automobile Series: Specification for Tyres and Wheels Part 2. Wheels and rims Section 1. Rim profiles and dimensions (including openings for valves)" which came into effect on 28th November 1980.]
[*rim diameter size code*	is to be interpreted in accordance with the British Standard referred to in the meaning given in this Table to "rim diameter".]

1	2
Expression	*Meaning*
secondary braking system	a braking system of a vehicle applied by a secondary means of operation independent of the service braking system or by one of the sections comprised in a split braking system.
service braking system	the braking system of a vehicle which is designed and constructed to have the highest braking efficiency of any of the braking systems with which the vehicle is equipped.
semi-trailer	a trailer which is constructed or adapted to form part of an articulated vehicle [including (without prejudice to the generality of that) a vehicle which is not itself a motor vehicle but which has some or all of its wheels driven by the drawing vehicle].
silencer	a contrivance suitable and sufficient for reducing as far as may be reasonable the noise caused by the escape of exhaust gases from the engine of a motor vehicle.
single-decked vehicle	a vehicle upon which no part of a deck or gangway is vertically above another deck or gangway.
split braking system	in relation to a motor vehicle, a braking system so designed and constructed that— (a) it comprises two independent sections of mechanism capable of developing braking force such that, excluding the means of operation, a failure of any part (other than a fixed member or a brake shoe anchor pin) of one of the said sections will not cause a decrease in the braking force capable of being developed by the other section; (b) the said two sections are operated by a means of operation which is common to both sections; (c) the braking efficiency of either of the said two sections can be readily checked.
[staircase	a staircase by means of which passengers on a double-decked vehicle may pass to and from the upper deck of the vehicle.]
[stepframe low loader	a semi-trailer (not being a low loader) which is constructed and normally used for the carriage of engineering equipment and is so constructed that the upper surface of the major part of the load platform is at a height of less than 1m above the ground when measured on level ground and when— (a) any adjustable suspensions are at the normal travelling height, (b) all pneumatic tyres are suitably inflated for use when the vehicle is fully laden, and (c) the semi-trailer is unladen.]

1	2
Expression	*Meaning*
stored energy	in relation to a braking system of a vehicle, energy (other than the muscular energy of the driver or the mechanical energy of a spring) stored in a reservoir for the purpose of applying the brakes under the control of the driver, either directly or as a supplement to his muscular energy.
straddle carrier	a motor vehicle constructed to straddle and lift its load for the purpose of transportation.
statutory power of removal	a power conferred by or under any enactment to remove or move a vehicle from any road or from any part of a road.
temporary use spare tyre	a pneumatic tyre which is designed for use on a motor vehicle only— (a) in the event of a failure of one of the tyres normally fitted to a wheel of the vehicle, and (b) at a speed lower than that for which such normally fitted tyres are designed.
three-wheeled motor cycle	a motor cycle having three wheels, not including a two-wheeled motor cycle with a sidecar attached.
towing implement	a device on wheels designed for the purpose of enabling a motor vehicle to draw another vehicle by the attachment of that device to that other vehicle in such a manner that part of that other vehicle is secured to and either rests on or is suspended from the device and some but not all of the wheels on which that other vehicle normally runs are raised off the ground.
track-laying	in relation to a vehicle, so designed and constructed that the weight thereof is transmitted to the road surface either by means of continuous tracks or by a combination of wheels and continuous tracks in such circumstances that the weight transmitted to the road surface by the tracks is not less than half the weight of the vehicle.
trailer	means a vehicle drawn by a motor vehicle and is to be interpreted in accordance with paragraphs (9) and (11).
train weight	in relation to a motor vehicle which may draw a trailer, the maximum laden weight for the motor vehicle together with any trailer which may be drawn by it.
transverse plane	a vertical plane at right angles to the longitudinal axis of a vehicle.
trolley bus	a bus adapted for use on roads without rails and moved by power transmitted thereto from some external source.

1	2
Expression	*Meaning*
unbraked trailer	any trailer other than one which, whether or not regulation 15 or 16 applies to it, is equipped with a braking system in accordance with one of those regulations.
unladen weight	the weight of a vehicle or trailer inclusive of the body and all parts (the heavier being taken where alternative bodies or parts are used) which are necessary to or ordinarily used with the vehicle or trailer when working on a road, but exclusive of the weight of water, fuel or accumulators used for the purpose of the supply of power for the propulsion of the vehicle or, as the case may be, of any vehicle by which the trailer is drawn, and of loose tools and loose equipment.
vehicle in the service of a visiting force or of a headquarters	a vehicle so described in Article 8(6) of the Visiting Forces and International Headquarters (Application of Law) Order 1965 [*SI 1965/1536*].
wheel	a wheel the tyre or rim of which when the vehicle is in motion on a road is in contact with the ground; two wheels are to be regarded as one wheel in the circumstances specified in paragraph (7).
wheeled	in relation to a vehicle, so constructed that the whole weight of the vehicle is transmitted to the road surface by means of wheels.
wide tyre	a pneumatic tyre of which the area of contact with the road surface is not less than 300mm in width when measured at right angles to the longitudinal axis of the vehicle.
works trailer	a trailer designed for use in private premises and used on a road only in delivering goods from or to such premises to or from a vehicle on a road in the immediate neighbourhood, or in passing from one part of any such premises to another or to other private premises in the immediate neighbourhood or in connection with road works while at or in the immediate neighbourhood of the site of such works.
works truck	a motor vehicle (other than a straddle carrier) designed for use in private premises and used on a road only in delivering goods from or to such premises to or from a vehicle on a road in the immediate neighbourhood, or in passing from one part of any such premises to another or to other private premises in the immediate neighbourhood or in connection with road works while at or in the immediate neighbourhood of the site of such works.

[(2A) Without prejudice to section 17 of the Interpretation Act 1978 and subject to the context, a reference in these Regulations to any enactment comprised in subordinate legislation (within the meaning of that Act) is a reference to that enactment as from time to time amended or re-enacted with or without modification.]

(3) For the purpose of these Regulations, the date on which a motor vehicle is first used is—

(a) in the case of a vehicle not falling within sub-paragraph (b) and which is registered, the date on which it was registered;

(b) in each of the following cases—

(i) a vehicle which is being or has been used under a trade licence as defined in [section 11 of the 1994 Act] (otherwise than for the purposes of demonstration or testing or of being delivered from premises of the manufacturer by whom it was made or of a distributor of vehicles, or dealer in vehicles, to premises of a distributor of vehicles, dealer in vehicles or purchaser thereof or to premises of a person obtaining possession thereof under a hiring agreement or hire purchase agreement);

(ii) a vehicle belonging, or which has belonged, to the Crown and which is or was used or appropriated for use for naval, military or air force purposes;

(iii) a vehicle belonging, or which has belonged, to a visiting force or a headquarters or defence organisation to which in each case the Visiting Forces and International Headquarters (Application of Law) Order 1965 applies;

(iv) a vehicle which has been used on roads outside Great Britain before being imported into Great Britain; and

(v) a vehicle which has been used otherwise than on roads after being sold or supplied by retail and before being registered;

the date of manufacture of the vehicle.

In sub-paragraph (b)(v) of this paragraph *"sold or supplied by retail"* means sold or supplied otherwise than to a person acquiring it solely for the purpose of resale or re-supply for a valuable consideration.

(4) The date of manufacture of a vehicle to which the Type Approval for Goods Vehicles Regulations apply shall be the date of manufacture described in regulation 2(4)(a) of those Regulations.

(5) Save where otherwise provided in these Regulations a tyre shall not be deemed to be of soft or elastic material unless the said material is either—

(a) continuous round the circumference of the wheel; or

(b) fitted in sections so that so far as reasonably practicable no space is left between the ends thereof,

and is of such thickness and design as to minimise, so far as reasonably possible, vibration when the vehicle is in motion and so constructed as to be free from any defect which might in any way cause damage to the surface of a road.

(6) For the purpose of these Regulations a brake drum and a brake disc shall be deemed to form part of the wheel and not of the braking system.

(7) For the purpose of these Regulations other than regulations 26 and 27 any two wheels of a motor vehicle or trailer shall be regarded as one wheel if the distance between the centres of the areas of contact between such wheels and the road surface is less than 460mm.

(8) For the purpose of these Regulations other than regulations 26 and 27 in counting the number of axles of, and in determining the sum of the weights transmitted to the road surface by any one axle of, a vehicle, all the wheels of which the centres of the areas of contact with the road surface can be included between any two transverse planes less than [0.5] m apart shall be treated as constituting one axle.

[(8A) For the purposes of these Regulations, a reference to axles being closely-spaced is a reference to—

> (a) two axles (not being part of a group of axles falling within sub-paragraph (b) or (c)) which are spaced at a distance apart of not more than 2.5m;
>
> (b) three axles (not being part of a group of axles falling within sub-paragraph (c)) the outermost of which are spaced at a distance apart of not more than 3.25m; or
>
> (c) four or more axles the outermost of which are spaced at a distance apart of not more than 4.6m;

the number of axles for the purposes of these paragraphs being determined in accordance with paragraph (8); and a reference to any particular number of closely-spaced axles shall be construed accordingly.]

(9) The provisions of these Regulations relating to trailers do not apply to any part of an articulated bus.

(10) For the purpose of [paragraph (8A) above,] of regulations 51, [76, 77 and 79] and [Schedules 11 and 11A] …, the distance between any two axles shall be obtained by measuring the shortest distance between the line joining the centres of the areas of contact with the road surface of the wheels of one axle and the line joining the centres of the areas of contact with the road surface of the wheels of the other axle.

(11) For the purpose of the following provisions only, a composite trailer shall be treated as one trailer (not being a semi-trailer or a converter dolly)—

> (a) regulations 7, 76 and 83;
>
> (b) paragraph (2) of, and items 3 and 10 in the Table in, regulation 75;
>
> (c) item 2 in the Table in regulation 78.

[Regulation 3 is printed as amended by the Interpretation Act 1978 ss.17(2)(a)　**B15.06**
and 23(1); SI 1987/676; SI 1987/1133; SI 1988/1287; SI 1989/1865; SI 1990/ 317; SI 1990/1131; SI 1990/1981; SI 1991/1526; SI 1991/2125; SI 1992/2016; SI 1993/2199; SI 1994/329; the Vehicle Excise and Registration Act 1994 s.64 and Sch.4, para.4; SI 1995/3051; SI 1996/252; SI 1996/2329; SI 1998/118; SI 1998/ 3112; SI 2001/1149; SI 2001/3208; SI 2003/182; SI 2003/2155; SI 2005/3165; SI 2006/2565; SI 2009/2196; SI 2010/2060.

The Visiting Forces and International Headquarters (Application of Law) Order 1965 (to which reference is made both in the table to reg.3(2) and in reg.3(3)(b)(iii)) has been revoked and replaced by the Visiting Forces and International Headquarters (Application of Law) Order 1999 (SI 1999/1736; not reproduced in this work). No textual amendment had been made to reg.3 in consequence of that revocation; but by the Interpretation Act 1978 ss.17(2)(a) and 23(1) references to the earlier order may be treated as references to SI 1999/ 1736.

The categories of motor vehicles formerly set out in Annex I of Directive 70/

156/EEC (O.J. No.L42, February 23, 1970, p.1) are now set out in Annex II of Directive 2007/46/EC (O.J. No.L263, October 9, 2007, p.1), which repealed Directive 70/156/EEC with effect from April 29, 2009. As to "off-road" vehicles, see para.4 of Annex II of Directive 2007/46/EEC.]

[Modification of Regulations in relation to vehicles for which a Minister's approval certificate has been issued under the Motor Vehicles (Approval) Regulations 1996

B15.07   **3A.** Schedule 2A shall have effect for the purpose of modifying these Regulations in relation to vehicles in respect of which a Minister's approval certificate has been issued by virtue of the Motor Vehicles (Approval) Regulations 1996 [*SI 1996/3013*].]

B15.08   *[Regulation 3A was inserted by SI 1996/3017.*

The Motor Vehicles (Approval) Regulations 1996 (to which reference is made in reg.3A) have been revoked and replaced by the Motor Vehicles (Approval) Regulations 2001 (SI 2001/25); see further the note to Sch.2A, para.2 below.]

Application and exemptions

B15.09   **4.**—(1) Save where the context otherwise requires, these Regulations apply to both wheeled vehicles and track-laying vehicles.

(2) Where a provision is applied by these Regulations to a motor vehicle first used on or after a specified date it does not apply to that vehicle if it was manufactured at least six months before that date.

(3) Where an exemption from, or relaxation of, a provision is applied by these Regulations to a motor vehicle first used before a specified date it shall also apply to a motor vehicle first used on or after that date if it was manufactured at least six months before that date.

(4) [Subject to paragraph (7),] the regulations specified in an item in column 3 of the Table do not apply in respect of a vehicle of a class specified in that item in column 2.

TABLE

regulation 4(4)

1	2	3
Item	Class of vehicle	Regulations which do not apply
1	A vehicle proceeding to a port for export.	The regulations in Part II in so far as they relate to construction and equipment, except regulations 16 (in so far as it concerns parking brakes), 20, 30, 34, 37, [and 53] . Regulations 66 to 69 and 71.

1	2	3
Item	Class of vehicle	Regulations which do not apply
2	A vehicle brought temporarily into Great Britain by a person resident abroad, provided that the vehicle complies in every respect with the requirements relating to motor vehicles or trailers contained in— (a) article 21 and paragraph (1) article 22 of the Convention on Road Traffic concluded at Geneva on 19th September 1949 [*Cmnd. 7997*] and [Part I,] Part II (so far as it relates to direction indicators and stop lights) and Part III of Annex 6 to that Convention; or (b) paragraphs I, III and VIII of article 3 of the International Convention relative to Motor Traffic concluded at Paris on 24th April 1926 [*Treaty Series No.11 (1930)*].	The regulations in Part II in so far as they relate to construction and equipment except regulations 7, 8, ..., 10, [10A,] 40, [and 53] [; and (a) additionally, in respect of any passenger vehicle with a maximum gross weight exceeding 10 tonnes registered in one or more member States, regulations 36A(2), 36A(7) and 36A(9); (b) additionally, in respect of any goods vehicle with a maximum gross weight exceeding 12 tonnes registered in one or more member States, regulations 36B(2), 36B(9) and 36B(11)]. Regulations 66 to 69 and 71.
3	A vehicle manufactured in Great Britain which complies with the requirements referred to in item 2 above and contained in the Convention of 1949, or, as the case may be, 1926 referred to in that item as if the vehicle had been brought temporarily into Great Britain, and either— (a) is exempt from car tax by virtue of [section 7(1), (2) and (3) of the Car Tax Act 1983], or (b) has been zero rated under [regulation 132 or 133 of the Value Added Tax Regulations 1995].	The regulations in Part II in so far as they relate to construction and equipment, except regulations 7, 8, ..., 10, [10A,] 40, [and 53] . Regulations 66 to 69 and 71.

1	2	3
Item	Class of vehicle	Regulations which do not apply
4	A vehicle in the service of a visiting force or of a headquarters.	The regulations in Part II in so far as they relate to construction and equipment, except regulations …, 16 (in so far as it concerns parking brakes), 21, 53, … and 61. Regulations 66 to 69, [71 and 75 to 79 and 93A] .
5	A vehicle which has been submitted for an examination under [section 45 or section 67A of the 1988 Act] while it is being used on a road in connection with the carrying out of that examination and is being so used by a person who is empowered under that section to carry out that examination, or by a person acting under the direction of a person so empowered.	The regulations in Part II … Regulations 75 to 79 and 100.
6	A motor car or a motor cycle in respect of which a certificate has been issued by the Officer in Charge of a National Collection of Road Transport, the Science Museum, London SW7, that it was designed before 1st January 1905 and constructed before 31st December 1905.	Regulation 16 (except in so far as it applies requirements 3 and 6 in Schedule 3), 21, 37(4), 63 and 99(4).
7	(a) A towing implement which is being drawn by a motor vehicle while it is not attached to any vehicle except the one drawing it if— (i) the towing implement is not being so drawn during the hours of darkness, and (ii) the vehicle by which it is being so drawn is not driven at a speed exceeding 20mph; or (b) a vehicle which is being drawn by a motor vehicle in the exercise of a statutory power of removal.	The regulations in Part II in so far as they relate to the construction and equipment of trailers, except regulation 20.
[8	Tramcars.	The regulations in Parts II, III and IV.]

1	2	3
Item	Class of vehicle	Regulations which do not apply
[9	A public works vehicle which has a maximum design weight of 7500kg and is specifically designed for use and used solely for the purpose of street cleansing.	Regulation 15(1E) and (5B) in respect of the requirements in Community Directive 98/12/EC and ECE Regulation 13/09 which require the fitting of ABS to goods vehicles over 3500kg in weight.]
[10	A vehicle being used by a Police Authority which has been authorised by a Chief Constable to perform accident reconstruction duties.	Regulation 15(1E) and (5B) in respect of the requirements in Community Directive 98/12/EC and ECE Regulation 13.09 which prohibit the use of an isolation switch for the operation of ABS.]
[11	A vehicle being used on a road by a vehicle examiner, who has been authorised in writing by the Secretary of State for the purpose of— (a) submitting the vehicle for an examination under section 45 of the Road Traffic Act 1988 in order to ascertain whether the examination is carried out in accordance with regulations made under that section; or (b) removing the vehicle following that examination.	The regulations in Part 2. Regulations 67, 75, to 79 and 100.]

(5) Any reference to a broken down vehicle shall include a reference to any towing implement which is being used for the drawing of any such vehicle.

(6) The Secretary of State is satisfied that it is requisite that the provisions of regulation 40(2) should apply, as from the date on which these Regulations come into operation, to track-laying vehicles registered before the expiration of one year from the making of these Regulations; and that, notwithstanding that those provisions will then apply to these vehicles, no undue hardship or inconvenience will be caused thereby.

[(7) The exemption provided by item 11 in the Table in paragraph (4) shall only apply to the extent that the vehicle examiner using the vehicle in question reasonably believes that any defects in that vehicle do not give rise to a danger of injury to any person while it is being used by that person for a purpose mentioned in that item.]

[(8) In item 11 in the Table in paragraph (4) and paragraph (7), *"vehicle examiner"* means an examiner appointed under section 66A of the Road Traffic Act 1988.]

B15.10   *[Regulation 4 is printed as corrected by a corrigendum dated October 1986 and as amended by the Interpretation Act 1978 ss.17(2)(a) and 23(1); SI 1988/ 271; SI 1992/1217; SI 1994/14; SI 1995/1201; SI 1996/3133; SI 1997/530; SI 2001/3208; SI 2003/1946; SI 2005/3165.*

Section 7(1)–(3) of the Car Tax Act 1983 (see item 3(a) in the table) together with the rest of the 1983 Act has now been repealed by the Statute Law (Repeals) Act 2004 s.1(1) and Sch.1, Pt 9, Group 5.]

Trade Descriptions Act 1968

B15.11   **5.** [...]

[Regulation 5 was revoked by the Consumer Protection from Unfair Trading Regulations 2008 (SI 2008/1277) Sch.2, para.78 and Sch.4(2).]

Compliance with Community Directives and ECE Regulations

B15.12   **6.**—(1) For the purpose of any regulation which requires or permits a vehicle to comply with the requirements of a Community Directive or an ECE Regulation, a vehicle shall be deemed so to have complied at the date of its first use only if—

(a) one of the certificates referred to in paragraph (2) has been issued in relation to it; or

(b) the marking referred to in paragraph (3) has been applied; ...

(c) it was, before it was used on a road, subject to a relevant type approval requirement as specified in paragraph (4) [or]

[(d) a sound-level measurement certificate issued by the Secretary of State under regulation 4 of the Motorcycles (Sound Level Measurement Certificates) Regulations 1980 [*SI 1980/765, as amended; not reproduced in this work*].

(2) The certificates mentioned in paragraph (1) are—

(a) a type approval certificate issued by the Secretary of State under regulation 5 of the Type Approval Regulations or of the Type Approval for Agricultural Vehicles Regulations;

(b) a certificate of conformity issued by the manufacturer of the vehicle under regulation 6 of either of those Regulations; or

(c) a certificate issued under a provision of the law of any member state of the European Economic Community which corresponds to the said regulations 5 or 6,

being in each case a certificate issued by reason of the vehicle's conforming to the requirements of the Community Directive in question.

(3) The marking mentioned in paragraph (1) is a marking designated as an approval mark by regulation 4 of the Approval Marks Regulations, being in each case a mark shown in column 2 of an item in Schedule 2 to those Regulations which refers, in column 5, to the ECE Regulation in question, applied as indicated in column 4 in that item.

(4) A relevant type approval requirement is a requirement of the Type Ap-

proval (Great Britain) Regulations or that Type Approval for Goods Vehicles Regulations which appears—

    (a) in column 4 of Table I in Schedule 2 in that item in which the Community Directive in question appears in column 3, or

    (b) in column 4 of Table II in Schedule 2 in the item in which the ECE Regulation in question appears in column 3.

[Regulation 6 is printed as amended by SI 1989/1865.]   **B15.13**

PART II

REGULATIONS GOVERNING THE CONSTRUCTION, EQUIPMENT AND MAINTENANCE OF VEHICLES

A Dimensions and Manoeuvrability

[Length

7.—(1) Subject to paragraphs (2) to (6), the overall length of a vehicle or   **B15.14** combination of vehicles of a class specified in an item in column 2 of the Table shall not exceed the maximum length specified in that item in column 3 of the Table, the overall length in the case of a combination of vehicles being calculated in accordance with regulation 81(g) and (h).

TABLE

(regulation 7(1))

1	2	3
Item	*Class of vehicle*	*Maximum length (metres)*
	Vehicle combinations	
[1	A motor vehicle (other than a motor vehicle such as is mentioned in item 1A) drawing one trailer which is not a semi-trailer.	18.75]
[1A	Subject to paragraph (3C), a motor vehicle manufactured before 1st June 1998 and drawing one trailer, where the combination does not meet the requirements of paragraph (5A) and the trailer is not a semi-trailer.	18]
2	An articulated bus.	[18.75]
[2A	A bus drawing a trailer	18.75]
3	An articulated vehicle, the semi-trailer of which does not meet the requirements of paragraph (6) and is not a low loader.	15.5
3A	An articulated vehicle, the semi-trailer of which meets the requirements of paragraph (6) and is not a low loader.	16.5

1	2	3
Item	Class of vehicle	Maximum length (metres)
3B	An articulated vehicle, the semi-trailer of which is a low loader.	18
	Motor vehicles	
4	A wheeled motor vehicle [other than a bus].	12
[4A	A bus with two axles	13.5]
[4B	A bus with more than two axles	13.5]
5	A track-laying motor vehicle.	9.2
	Trailers	
6	An agricultural trailed appliance manufactured on or after 1st December 1985.	15
7	A semi trailer manufactured on or after 1st May 1983 which does not meet the requirements of paragraph (6) and is not a low loader.	12.2
7A	A composite trailer drawn by— (a) a goods vehicle being a motor vehicle having a maximum gross weight exceeding 3500kg; or (b) an agricultural motor vehicle.	14.04
8	A trailer (not being a semi-trailer or composite trailer) with at least 4 wheels which is— (a) drawn by a goods vehicle being a motor vehicle having a maximum gross weight exceeding 3500kg; or (b) an agricultural trailer.	12
9	Any other trailer not being an agricultural trailed appliance or a semi-trailer.	7

(2) In the case of a motor vehicle drawing one trailer where—

(a) the motor vehicle is a showman's vehicle as defined in paragraph 7 of Schedule 3 to the 1971 Act; and

(b) the trailer is used primarily as living accommodation by one or more persons and is not also used for the carriage of goods or burden which are not needed for the purpose of such residence in the vehicle,

item 1 in the Table applies with the substitution of 22m for 18m and item 1A in the Table does not apply.

(3) Items 1, 1A, 3, 3A and 3B of the Table do not apply to—

(a) a vehicle combination which includes a trailer which is constructed and normally used for the conveyance of indivisible loads of exceptional length, or

(b) a vehicle combination consisting of a broken down vehicle (including an articulated vehicle) being drawn by a motor vehicle in consequence of a breakdown, or

(c) an articulated vehicle, the semi-trailer of which is a low loader manufactured before It April 1991.

(3A) Items 6, 7, 7A, 8 and 9 of the Table do not apply to—

(a) a trailer which is constructed and normally used for the conveyance of indivisible loads of exceptional length,

(b) a broken down vehicle (including an articulated vehicle) which is being drawn by a motor vehicle in consequence of a breakdown, or

(c) a trailer being a drying or mixing plant designed for the production of asphalt or of bituminous or tar macadam and used mainly for the construction, repair or maintenance of roads, or a road planing machine so used.

(3B) Furthermore item 7 does not apply to—

(a) a semi-trailer which is a car transporter,

(b) a semi-trailer which is normally used on international journeys any part of which takes place outside the United Kingdom.

[(3C) Item 1A and the words "(other than a motor vehicle such as is mentioned in item 1A)" in item 1 of the Table shall cease to have effect after 31st December 2006.]

(4) Where a motor vehicle is drawing—

(a) two trailers, then only one of those trailers may exceed an overall length of 7m;

(b) three trailers, then none of those trailers shall exceed an overall length of 7m.

(5) Where a motor vehicle is drawing—

(a) two or more trailers; or

(b) one trailer constructed and normally used for the conveyance of indivisible loads of exceptional length—

then—

(i) the overall length of that motor vehicle shall not exceed 9.2m; and

(ii) the overall length of the combination of vehicles, calculated in accordance with regulation 81(g) and (h), shall not exceed 25.9m, unless the conditions specified in paragraphs 1 and 2 of Schedule 12 have been complied with.

[(5XA) A motor vehicle drawing a trailer which is not a semi-trailer shall (unless it is a vehicle such as is mentioned in item 1A of the Table in paragraph (1)) comply with the requirements of paragraph (5A).

The words in parenthesis in this paragraph shall cease to have effect after 31st December 2006.]

(5A) The requirements of this paragraph, in relation to a combination of vehicles, are that at least one of the vehicles in the combination is not a goods vehicle or, if both vehicles in the combination are goods vehicles that—

(a) the maximum distance measured parallel to the longitudinal axis of the combination of vehicles from the foremost point of the loading area behind the driver's cab to the rear of the trailer, less the distance between the rear of the motor vehicle and the front of the trailer, does not exceed 15.65m; and

(b) the maximum distance measured parallel to the longitudinal axis of the combination of vehicles from the foremost point of the loading area behind the driver's cab to the rear of the trailer does not exceed [16.4m];

but sub-paragraph (a) shall not apply if both vehicles in the combination are car transporters.

(6) The requirements of this paragraph, in relation to a semi-trailer, are that—

(a) the longitudinal distance from the axis of the king-pin to the rear of the semi-trailer does not exceed—

(i) 12.5m in the case of a car transporter, or

(ii) 12m in any other case; and

(b) no point in the semi-trailer forward of the transverse plane passing through the axis of the king-pin is more than—

(i) 4.19m from the axis of the king-pin, in the case of a car trans-porter, or

(ii) 2.04m from the axis of the king-pin, in any other case.

(6A) For the purposes of paragraph (5A) —

(a) where the forward end of the loading area of a motor vehicle is bounded by a wall, the thickness of the wall shall be regarded as part of the loading area; and

(b) any part of a vehicle designed primarily for use as a means of attaching another vehicle to it and any fitting designed for use in connection with any such part shall be disregarded in determining the distance between the rear of a motor vehicle and the front of a trailer being drawn by it.

(7) For the purpose of paragraph (6) the longitudinal distance from the axis of the kingpin to the rear of a semi-trailer is the distance between a transverse plane passing through the axis of the king-pin and the rear of the semi-trailer.

(7A) Where a semi-trailer has more than one king-pin or is constructed so that it can be used with a king-pin in different positions, references in this regulation to a distance from the king-pin shall be construed

[(a) in relation to a vehicle which was manufactured after [1st January 1999], as a reference to the foremost king-pin or, as the case may be, the foremost king-pin position; and]

[(b) in relation to any other vehicle, as a reference to the rearmost king-pin or, as the case may be, the rearmost king-pin position.]

(7B) For the purposes of paragraphs (5A), (6) and (7) —

(a) a reference to the front of a vehicle is a reference to the transverse plane passing through the extreme forward projecting points of the vehicle; and

(b) a reference to the rear of a vehicle is a reference to the transverse plane passing through the extreme rearward projecting points of the vehicle,

inclusive (in each case) of all parts of the vehicle, of any receptacle which is of a permanent character and accordingly strong enough for repeated use, and any fitting on, or attached to, the vehicle but exclusive of—

(i) the things set out in sub-paragraph (i) of the definition of "overall length" in the Table in regulation 3(2), and

(ii) in the case of a semi-trailer, the things set out in sub-paragraph (ii)(a) of that definition.

(8) Where a broken down articulated vehicle is being towed by a motor vehicle in consequence of a breakdown—

(a) paragraph (5) shall have effect in relation to the combination of vehicles as if sub-paragraph (b) were omitted, and

(b) for the purposes of paragraph (4) and of paragraph (5) as so modified, the articulated vehicle shall be regarded as a single trailer.

(9) No person shall use or cause or permit to be used on a road, a trailer with an overall length exceeding 18.65m unless the requirements of paragraphs 1 and 2 of Schedule 12 are complied with.]

B15.15

[Regulation 7 is printed as amended by SI 1990/317; SI 1990/1163; SI 1991/2125; SI 1998/1188; SI 1998/3112; SI 2003/182.

Following the 1991 amendments, the amended text of reg.7 was reproduced in the Schedule to SI 1991/2125 and that version is reproduced above with subsequent amendments.]

Width

8.—(1) Save as provided in paragraph (2), overall width of a vehicle of a class specified in an item in column 2 of the Table shall not exceed the maximum width specified in column 3 in that item.

B15.16

TABLE

(regulation 8(1))

1	2	3
Item	Class of vehicle	Maximum width (metres)
1	A locomotive, other than an agricultural motor vehicle.	2.75
2	A refrigerated vehicle.	[2.60]
4	[A trailer drawn by a motor vehicle other than a motor cycle]	[2.55]
5	[...]	[...]
6	[...]	[...]
7	[...]	[...]
8	A trailer drawn by a motor cycle.	1.5

(2) Paragraph (1) does not apply to a broken down vehicle which is being drawn in consequence of the breakdown.

(3) No person shall use or cause or permit to be used on a road a wheeled agricultural motor vehicle drawing a wheeled vehicle trailer if, when the longitudinal axes of the vehicles are parallel but in different vertical planes, the overall width of the two vehicles, measured as if they were on one vehicle, exceeds [2.55] metres.

(4) In this regulation *"refrigerated vehicle"* means any vehicle which is

specially designed for the carriage of goods at a low temperature and of which the thickness of each of the side walls, inclusive of insulation, is at least 45mm.

B15.17   *[Regulation 8 is printed as amended by SI 1988/1871; SI 1995/3051; SI 2010/ 964.]*

Height

B15.18   **9.**—(1) The overall height of a bus shall not exceed 4.57m.

(2) [...]

[(2A) [...]]

(3) [...]

B15.19   *[Regulation 9 is printed as amended by SI 1994/329; SI 1995/1201.]*

Indication of overall travelling height

B15.20   **10.**—[(1) Subject to the provisions of this regulation, no person shall drive or cause or permit to be driven on a road a motor vehicle with an overall travelling height exceeding 3m unless a notice is displayed in the cab, in such a manner that it can easily be read by the driver, and the notice meets the requirements of paragraph (3).

(2) Subject to the provisions of this regulation, no person shall use or cause or permit to be used on a road a motor vehicle with an overall travelling height exceeding 3m if any letters or numbers are displayed in the cab, otherwise than in a notice which meets the requirements of paragraph (3) —

(a) where they could be read by the driver; and

(b) which could be understood as indicating a height associated with the vehicle or any trailer drawn by it.

(3) The requirements of this paragraph in respect of a notice are that—

(a) the notice gives an indication of vehicle height expressed in feet and inches, or in both feet and inches and in metres;

(b) the numbers giving the indication in feet and inches are at least 40mm tall;

(c) the height expressed in feet and inches and (where applicable) the height expressed in metres are—

(i) if the vehicle is a vehicle to which regulation 10A applies, not less than the predetermined height mentioned in regulation 10A(2)(a) or the overall travelling height (whichever is the greater), or

(ii) if the vehicle is not a vehicle to which regulation 10A applies, not less than the overall travelling height;

(d) if the vehicle is not a relevant vehicle, the height expressed in feet and inches does not exceed the overall travelling height by more than 150mm;

(e) if the vehicle is a relevant vehicle, the height expressed in feet and inches does not exceed the overall travelling height by more than 1m;

(f) if the height is expressed in both feet and inches and in metres, the height expressed in feet and inches and the height expressed in metres do not differ by more than 50mm; and

(g) no other letters or numbers which could be understood as being an indication of any height associated with the vehicle or any trailer drawn by it are displayed in the notice.

(4) Paragraph (1) shall not apply if, having regard to the lengths of road which the driver might drive along in the course of fulfilling the purpose of the journey taking into account any possibility of unforeseen diversions and the driver having difficulty in finding his way, it is highly unlikely that the driver would during the course of the journey encounter any bridge or other overhead structure which does not exceed by at least 1m—

(a) in the case of a vehicle to which regulation 10A applies, the maximum travelling height; or

(b) in any other case, the overall travelling height.

(5) Paragraph (1) shall not apply to a vehicle on a particular journey and at a particular time if—

(a) one or more documents are being carried in the vehicle which are within the easy reach of the driver and that or those documents describe a route or a choice of routes which the driver must take in order to fulfil the purpose of the journey without risk of the vehicle, its load or equipment or any trailer drawn by the vehicle, its load or equipment, colliding with any bridge or other overhead structure; and

(b) the vehicle is on such a route which is so described or is off that route by reason of a diversion that could not reasonably have been foreseen at the beginning of the journey.

(6) Paragraph (1) shall not apply to a vehicle on a particular journey if—

(a) one or more documents are being carried in the vehicle which are within the easy reach of the driver and that or those documents contain informations as to—

(i) the height of bridges and other overhead structures under which the vehicle and any trailer drawn by it could pass, and

(ii) the height of bridges and other overhead structures under which the vehicle and any trailer drawn by it could not pass,

without the vehicle, its load or equipment or any such trailer, its load or equipment, colliding with any bridge or other overhead structure; and

(b) the information is such that, having regard in particular to the matters referred to in paragraph (7), it would enable any driver to fulfil the purpose of the journey without there being any risk of the vehicle, its load or equipment or any trailer, its load or equipment, colliding with any bridge or other overhead structure while on the journey.

(7) The matters referred to in paragraph (6) are—

(a) the roads which the driver might drive along in the course of fulfilling the purpose of the journey taking into account any possibility of unforeseen diversions and of the driver having difficulty in finding his way;

(b) the height of bridges and other overhead structures that would be encountered were the vehicle to proceed along any of those roads; and

(c) the setting of any device of a description specified in regulation 10A(2).

(8) Paragraphs (1) and (2) shall not apply to motor vehicle if it has an overall travelling height of not more than 4m and—

(a) it is a vehicle registered or put into circulation in an EEA State and is being used in international traffic; or

(b) it is a motor vehicle drawing a trailer registered or put into circulation in an EEA State and that trailer is being used in international traffic.

(9) For the purposes of this regulation—

(a) *"EEA State"*, and *"high level equipment"* and *"maximum travelling height"* have the meanings given in regulation 10C;

(b) *"overall travelling height"* in relation to a motor vehicle means—

(i) if it is not drawing a trailer, the overall height for the time being of the vehicle, its equipment and load, or

(ii) if it is drawing one or more trailers, the overall height for the time being of the combination of vehicles, their equipment and loads.

(c) a motor vehicle is a *"relevant vehicle"* if at any particular time—

(i) the vehicle or any trailer drawn by it is fitted with high level equipment with a maximum, height of more than 3m; and

(ii) the overall travelling height is less than the maximum travelling height.

(10) In paragraph (8), *"international traffic"* and *"registered or put into circulation"* have the same meanings as in article 3 of Community Directive 85/3 [*O.J. No.L2, January 3, 1985, p.14*].]

B15.21   [*Regulation 10 was substituted (together with regs 10A, 10B and 10C) by SI 1997/530.*

As to the terms "international traffic" and "registered or put into circulation" (to which reference is made in reg.10(10)), see now art.3(1) and (2) of Directive 96/53/EC below, which has repealed and replaced Directive 85/3/EEC.]

[Warning devices where certain high level equipment is fitted to a vehicle

B15.22   10A.—(1) Subject to the provisions of this regulation and regulations 10B and 10C, no person shall drive or cause or permit to be driven on a road a vehicle to which this regulation applies unless the vehicle is fitted with a warning device and the requirements specified in paragraph (2) are satisfied in respect of the device, the vehicle and any relevant trailer drawn by the vehicle.

(2) The requirements are—

(a) that the device, the vehicle and any relevant trailer drawn by it shall be constructed, maintained and adjusted, and the connections between the vehicle and those trailers are such, that the device would give a visible warning to the driver if, whilst the vehicle was being driven, the height of the highest point of any high level equipment fitted to the vehicle or any of those trailers were to exceed a predetermined height; and

(b) the predetermined height referred to in sub-paragraph (a) shall not exceed the overall travelling height by more than 1m.

(3) No person shall be taken to have failed to comply with paragraph (1) on the ground that a motor vehicle or a relevant trailer was not fitted with a warning device and the requirements in paragraph (2) were not being satisfied as mentioned in paragraph (1) —

(a) before 1st October 1998—

(i) if the motor vehicle was first used before 1st April 1998; or

(ii) the relevant trailer was manufactured before that date; or

(b) before 1st April 1998 in relation to any other motor vehicle or relevant trailer.

(4) Paragraph (1) shall not apply in relation to a particular journey if, having regard to the lengths of road which the driver might drive along in the course of fulfilling the purpose of the journey and taking into account any possibility of unforeseen diversions and the driver having difficulty in finding his way, it is highly unlikely that the driver would during the course of the journey be confronted with any bridge or other overhead structure which does not exceed the maximum travelling height by at least 1m.]

[Regulation 10A was inserted by SI 1997/530.]

[Vehicles to which regulation 10A applies

10B.—(1) Subject to the provisions of this regulation, regulation 10A applies to—   **B15.23**

(a) a motor vehicle first used on or after 1st April 1993, if the vehicle or any relevant trailer drawn by it, is fitted with high level equipment with a maximum height of more than 3m; and

(b) a motor vehicle first used before 1st April 1993, if any relevant trailer drawn by it is fitted with such equipment.

(2) Regulation 10A does not apply to a motor vehicle if it has an overall travelling height of not more than 4m and—

(a) it is a vehicle registered or put into circulation in an EEA State and is being used in international traffic; or

(b) it is a motor vehicle drawing a trailer registered or put into circulation in an EEA State and that trailer is being used in international traffic, and

in this paragraph, *"international traffic"* and *"registered or put into circulation"* have the same meanings as in article 3 of Community Directive 85/3.

(3) Regulation 10A does not apply to—

(a) an agricultural motor vehicle;

(b) an industrial tractor;

(c) a works truck;

(d) a motor vehicle owned by the Secretary of State for Defence and used for naval, military or air force purposes or a motor vehicle so used while being driven by a person for the time being subject to orders of a member of the armed forces of the Crown;

(e) a motor vehicle drawing a trailer owned by the Secretary of State for Defence and used for naval, military or air force purposes or a motor vehicle drawing such a trailer while being driven by a person for the time being subject to orders of a member of the armed forces of the Crown;

    (f) a motor vehicle used by a fire brigade maintained under the Fire Services Act 1947 [or, in England [or Wales], a motor vehicle used by employees of a fire and rescue authority for the purposes of that authority under the Fire and Rescue Services Act 2004];

    (g) a motor vehicle that is constructed and normally used for the purpose of carrying at least two other vehicles;

    (h) a motor vehicle drawing a car transporter; or

    (i) a motor vehicle whose maximum travelling height does not exceed its overall travelling height.]

B15.24   *[Regulation 10B was inserted by SI 1997/530 and is printed as amended by SI 2004/3168 and SI 2005/2929.*

See note to reg.10 with regard to the repeal of art.3 of Community Directive 85/3/EEC.]

[Interpretation of regulations 10A and 10B

B15.25   **10C.**—(1) The following provisions of this regulation apply for the interpretation of this regulation and regulations 10A and 10B.

(2) Subject to paragraphs (4) and (5), a reference to high level equipment, in relation to a motor vehicle, is a reference to equipment which is so fitted to the vehicle that—

    (a) the equipment can be raised by means of a power operated device, and

    (b) the raising or lowering of the equipment is capable of altering the overall travelling height of the motor vehicle when the vehicle and every trailer drawn by it is unladen.

(3) Subject to paragraph (4) and (5), a reference to high level equipment, in relation to a trailer drawn by a motor vehicle, is a reference to equipment which is so fitted to the trailer that—

    (a) the equipment can be raised by means of a power operated device, and

    (b) the raising or lowering of the equipment is capable of altering the overall travelling height of the motor vehicle when the vehicle and every trailer drawn by it is unladen.

(4) A reference to high level equipment in relation to a tipper which is—

    (a) a motor vehicle first used before 1st April 1998, or

    (b) a trailer manufactured before that date,

shall be construed as not including the relevant part of the tipper.

(5) Where equipment fitted to a vehicle would otherwise be high level equipment, that equipment shall not be regarded as high level equipment if—

    (a) the equipment is so designed and constructed that—

        (i) it can be fixed in a stowed position by a locking device when travelling; and

        (ii) it is not possible for a person in the cab to interfere with the locking device; and

(b) the equipment is fixed in that position by the locking device.

(6) The following expressions shall bear the following meanings—

(a) *"EEA State"* means a state which is a contracting party to the EEA Agreement; and

(b) *"EEA Agreement"* means the Agreement on the European Economic Area signed at Oporto on 2 May 1992 as adjusted by the Protocol signed at Brussels on 17 March 1993;

(c) *"maximum height"*, in relation to any high level equipment fitted to a vehicle, means the height of the highest point of that equipment above the ground when it is raised as far as possible by means of that device and the vehicle is unladen;

(d) *"maximum travelling height"*, in relation to a motor vehicle to which regulation 10A applies, means—

(i) if the overall travelling height could be increased by raising any high level equipment fitted to the vehicle or to any relevant trailer drawn by [it] that is not for the time being at its maximum height, the greatest overall travelling height that could be achieved by raising such equipment (without making any other changes to the vehicle, its load or equipment or to any trailer drawn by it, its load or equipment); or

(ii) in any other case, the overall travelling height;

(e) *"overall travelling height"* has the meaning given by regulation 10(9)(b);

(f) *"relevant part"*, in relation to a tipper, shall be construed in accordance with sub-paragraph (g);

(g) *"tipper"* means a vehicle that is so constructed that it can be unloaded by part of the vehicle (in this regulation referred to as the *"relevant part"*) being tipped sideways or rearwards, and

a reference to equipment fitted to a vehicle includes part of the vehicle.

(7) *"Relevant trailer"* means a trailer manufactured on or after 1st April 1993 not being—

(a) an agricultural trailer;

(b) an agricultural trailed appliance;

(c) a works trailer;

(d) a trailer used by a fire brigade maintained under the Fire Services Act 1947 [or, in England [or Wales], a trailer used by employees of a fire and rescue authority for the purposes of that authority under the Fire and Rescue Services Act 2004];

(e) a broken down vehicle (including an articulated vehicle) being drawn by a motor vehicle in consequence of a breakdown.

[Regulation 10C was inserted by SI 1997/530 and is printed as subsequently amended by SI 1998/1188; SI 2004/3168 and SI 2005/2929. **B15.26**

As to the European Economic Area and the EEA agreement, see the introductory note to Section C below.]

Overhang

11.—(1) The overhang of a wheeled vehicle of a class specified in an item in **B15.27**

column 2 of the Table [*see table on next page*] shall not, subject to any exemption specified in that item in column 4, exceed the distance specified in that item in column 3.

TABLE 1

(regulation 11(1))

1 Item	*2* Class of vehicle	*3* Maximum overhang	*4* Exemptions
1	Motor tractor	1.83m.	(a) a track-laying vehicle (b) an agricultural motor vehicle
2	Heavy motor car and motor car	60% of the distance between the transverse plane which passes through the centre or centres of the foremost wheel or wheels and the transverse plane which passes through the foremost point from which the overhang is to be measured as provided in regulation 3(2).	(a) a bus (b) a refuse vehicle (c) a works truck (d) a track-laying vehicle (e) an agricultural motor vehicle (f) a motor car which is an ambulance (g) a vehicle designed to dispose of its load to the rear, if the overhang does not exceed 1.15m (h) a vehicle first used before 2nd January 1933

1 Item	2 Class of vehicle	3 Maximum overhang	4 Exemptions
			(i) a vehicle first used before 1st January 1966 if— (i) the distance between the centres of the rearmost and foremost axles does not exceed 2.29m, and (ii) the distance specified in column 3 is not exceeded by more than 767mm (j) heating plant on a vehicle designed and mainly used to heat the surface of a road or other similar surface in the process of construction, repair or maintenance shall be disregarded.

(2) In the case of an agricultural motor vehicle the distance measured horizontally and parallel to the longitudinal axis of the rear portion of the vehicle between the transverse planes passing through the rearmost point of the vehicle and through the centre of the rear or the rearmost axle should not exceed 3m.

[(3) A heavy motor car shall be taken to comply with the requirements of paragraph (1) if it meets the requirements of paragraph 7.6.2 of Annex I of Community Directive 97/27 [*O.J. No.L233, August 25, 1997, p.1*].]

[Regulation 11 is printed as amended by SI 1998/1188.]   **B15.28**

Minimum ground clearance

12.—(1) Save as provided in paragraph (2), a wheeled trailer which is—   **B15.29**

    (a) a goods vehicle; and

    (b) manufactured on or after 1st April 1984,

shall have a minimum ground clearance of not less than 160mm if the trailer has an axle interspace of more than 6m but less than 11.5m, and a minimum ground clearance of not less than 190mm if the trailer has an axle interspace of 11.5m or more.

(2) Paragraph (1) shall not apply in the case of a trailer—

    (a) which is fitted with a suspension system which, by the operation of a control, the trailer may be lowered or raised, while that system is being operated to enable the trailer to pass under a bridge or other obstruction over a road provided that at such time the system is operated so that no part of the trailer (excluding any wheel) touches the ground or is likely to do so; or

    (b) while it is being loaded or unloaded.

(3) In this regulation—

"axle interspace" means—

    (a) in the case of a semi-trailer, the distance between the point of support of the semi-trailer at its forward end and, if it has only one axle, the centre of that axle or, if it has more than one axle, the point halfway between the centres of the foremost and rearmost of those axles; and

    (b) in the case of any other trailer, the distance between the centre of its front axle or, if it has more than one axle at the front, the point halfway between the centres of the foremost and rearmost of those axles, and the centre of its rear axle or, if it has more than one axle at the rear, the point halfway between the centre of the foremost and rearmost of those axles; and

"ground clearance" means the shortest distance between the ground and the lowest part of that portion of the trailer (excluding any part of a suspension, steering or braking system attached to any axle, any wheel and any air skirt) which lies within the area formed by the overall width of the trailer and the middle 70% of the axle interspace, such distance being ascertained when the trailer—

    (a) is fitted with suitable tyres which are inflated to a pressure recommended by the manufacturer, and

    (b) is reasonably horizontal and standing on ground which is reasonably flat.

[Turning circle—buses]

B15.30   13.—(1) This regulation applies to a bus first used on or after 1st April 1982.

(2) Every vehicle to which this regulation applies shall be able to move on either lock so that[, both with and without all its wheels in contact with the ground,] no part of it projects outside the area contained between concentric circles with radii of [12.5m] and 5.3m.

[(2A) In relation to a vehicle manufactured before 1st June 1998 paragraph (2) shall have effect as if the words ", both with and without all its wheels in contact with the ground," were omitted.]

(3) When a vehicle to which this regulation applies moves forward from rest, on either lock, so that its outermost point describes a circle of [12.5m] radius, no part of the vehicle shall project beyond the longitudinal plane which, at the beginning of the manoeuvre, defines the overall width of the vehicle on the side opposite to the direction in which it is turning by more than—

(a) 0.8m if it is a rigid vehicle [of 12m or less in overall length]; or

(b) 1.2m if it is [a rigid bus of over 12m in overall length or] an articulated bus

(4) For the purpose of paragraph (3) the two rigid portions of an articulated bus shall be in line at the beginning of the manoeuvre.

B15.31   *[Regulation 13 is printed as amended by SI 1998/1188; SI 2003/182.]*

[Turning circle—articulated vehicles other than those incorporating a car transporter

B15.32   13A.—[(1) Every vehicle to which this regulation applies shall be able to move on either lock so that, both with and without all its wheels in contact with the surface of the road and disregarding the things set out in paragraphs (a) to (m) in the definition of "overall width" and in paragraphs (i)(a) to (o) in the definition of "overall length" in the Table in regulation 3, no part of it projects outside the area contained between concentric circles with radii of 12.5m and 5.3m.

(2) This regulation applies to all articulated vehicles except the following:

(a) an articulated vehicle, the semi-trailer of which—

(i) was manufactured before 1st April 1990 and has an overall length that does not exceed the overall length it had on that date,

(ii) is a car transporter,

(iii) is a low loader,

(iv) is a stepframe low loader, or

(v) is constructed and normally used for the conveyance of indivisible loads of exceptional length;

(b) an articulated vehicle having an overall length not exceeding 15.5m and of which the drawing vehicle was first used before 1st June 1998 or the trailer was first used before that date; or

(c) an articulated vehicle when an axle of the trailer is raised to aid traction.

(3) In relation to a vehicle manufactured before 1st June 1998 paragraph (1) shall have effect as if the words "both with and without all its wheels in contact with the surface of the road and" were omitted.]

(4) An articulated vehicle shall be taken to comply with paragraph (1) if the semi-trailer comprised in it is, by virtue of paragraph 7.6.1.2 of Annex I of Community Directive 97/27/EC [*O.J. No.L233, August 25, 1997, p.1*], deemed to comply with paragraph 7.6.1 of that Annex.]]

[Regulation 13A was inserted by SI 1990/317 and was later amended by SI 1990/1163; SI 1998/1188.   **B15.33**

The text of reg.13A as printed above was substituted by SI 2000/3197.]

[Turning circle—articulated vehicles incorporating a car transporter

13B.—(1) Subject to paragraphs (2) and (3) this regulation applies to an   **B15.34**
articulated vehicle having an overall length exceeding 15.5m, the semi-trailer of which is a car transporter.

(2) This regulation does not apply to an articulated vehicle, the semi-trailer of which satisfied the following conditions—

    (a) it was manufactured before the 1st April 1990, and

    (b) the distance from the front of the trailer to the rearmost axle is no greater than it was on that date.

(3) This regulation does not apply to an articulated vehicle the semi-trailer of which is—

    (a) a low loader, or

    (b) a stepframe low loader.

(4) Every articulated vehicle to which this regulation applies shall be able to move on either lock so that, [both with and without all its wheels in contact with the surface of the road and] disregarding the things set out in [paragraphs (a) to (m) in the definition of "overall width" and in paragraphs (i)(a) to (o) in the definition of "overall length"] in the Table in regulation 3(2), no part of—

    (a) the motor vehicle drawing the car transporter, or

    (b) the car transporter to the rear of the transverse plane passing through the king pin,

projects outside the area between the concentric circles with radii of 12.5m and 5.3m.]

[(5) In relation to a vehicle manufactured before 1st June 1998 paragraph (4) shall have effect as if the words "both with and without all its wheels in contact with the surface of the road" were omitted.]

[(6) An articulated vehicle shall be taken to comply with paragraph (4) if the semi-trailer comprised in it is, by virtue of paragraph 7.6.1.2 of Annex I of Community Directive 97/27/EC, deemed to comply with paragraph 7.6.1 of that Annex.]

[Regulation 13B was inserted by SI 1990/317 and is printed as subsequently   **B15.35**
amended by SI 1998/1188.]

[Turning circle—heavy motor car

13C.—(1) This regulation applies to a vehicle which—   **B15.36**

    (a) is a heavy motor car or a vehicle combination which consists of a heavy motor car drawing one trailer which is not a semi-trailer;

    (b) was manufactured or, in the case of a vehicle combination, the part consisting of a heavy motor car, was manufactured after 31st May 1998; and

(c) is not a vehicle falling within any of the descriptions specified in paragraph (2).

(2) The descriptions of vehicle referred to in paragraph (1)(c) are—

(a) a vehicle having 4 or more axles where the distance between the foremost and rearmost axles exceeds 6.4 metres;

(b) a vehicle or a vehicle combination to which regulation 13, 13A or 13B applies;

(c) a vehicle constructed and normally used for the carriage of indivisible loads of abnormal length.

(3) Every vehicle to which this regulation applies shall be able to move on either lock so that, both with and without all its wheels in contact with the surface of the road and disregarding the things set out in paragraphs (a) to (m) in the definition of "overall width" and in paragraphs (i)(a) to (o) in the definition of "overall length" in the Table in regulation 3(2), no part of it projects outside the area contained between concentric circles with radii of 12.5m and 5.3m.]

B15.37   *[Regulation 13C was inserted by SI 1998/1188.]*

Connecting section and direction-holding of articulated buses

B15.38   14.—(1) This regulation applies to every articulated bus first used on or after 1st April 1982.

(2) The connecting section of the two parts of every articulated bus to which this regulation applies shall be constructed so as to comply with the provisions relating to such a section specified in paragraph 5.9 in ECE Regulation 36 as regards vehicles within the scope of that Regulation.

(3) Every articulated bus to which this regulation applies shall be constructed so that when the vehicle is moving in a straight line the longitudinal median planes of its two parts coincide and form a continuous plane without any deflection.

B Brakes

Braking systems of certain vehicles first used on or after 1st April 1983

B15.39   15.—[(1) Save as provided in paragraphs (2), (3) and (4), the braking system of every wheeled vehicle of a class specified in an item in column 2 of the Table which, in the case of a motor vehicle, is first used on or after 1st April 1983 or which, in the case of a trailer, is manufactured on or after 1st October 1982 shall comply with the construction, fitting and performance requirements specified in Annexes I, II and VII to Community Directive 79/489, and if relevant, Annexes III, IV, V, VI and VIII to that Directive in relation to the category of vehicles specified in that item in column 3.

Provided that it shall be lawful for any vehicle of such a class which, in the case of a motor vehicle, was first used before 1st April 1983 or which, in the case of a trailer, was manufactured before 1st October 1982 to comply with the said requirements instead of complying with regulations 16 and 17.

(1A) Save as provided in paragraphs (2), (3), (3A) and (5), the braking system of every wheeled vehicle of a class specified in an item in column 2 of the Table which, in the case of a motor vehicle, is first used on or after the revelant date or which, in the case of a trailer, is manufactured on or after the relevant date shall comply with the construction, fitting and performance requirements specified in Annexes I, II and VII to Community Directive 85/647, and if relevant, Annexes III, IV, V, VI, VIII, X, XI and XII to that Directive in relation to the category of vehicles specified in that item in column 3.

Provided that it shall be lawful for any vehicle of such a class which, in the case of a motor vehicle, was first used before the relevant date or which, in the case of a trailer, was manufactured before the relevant date to comply with the said requirements instead of complying with paragraph (1) or with regulations 16 and 17.

(1B) In paragraph (1A), the relevant date in relation to a vehicle of a class specified in item 1 or 2 of the Table is 1st April 1990, in relation to a vehicle specified in item 4 of that Table is 1st April 1992, in relation to a vehicle in items 7, 8, 9 or 10 of that Table is 1st October 1988 and in relation to a vehicle of any other class is 1st April 1989.

(1C) Save as provided in paragraphs (2), (3), (3A) and (5A), the braking system of every wheeled vehicle of a class specified in an item in column 2 of the Table which, in the case of a motor vehicle, is first used on or after 1st April 1992 or which, in the case of a trailer, is manufactured on or after 1st October 1991 shall comply with the construction, fitting and performance requirements specified in Annexes I, II and VII to Community Directive 88/194, and if relevant, Annexes III, IV, V, VI, VIII, X, XI and XII to that Directive in relation to the category of vehicles specified in that item in column 3.

Provided that it shall be lawful for any vehicle of such a class which, in the case of a motor vehicle, was first used before 1st April 1992 or which, in the case of a trailer, was manufactured before 1st October 1991 to comply with the said requirements instead of complying with paragraph (1) or (1A) or with regulations 16 and 17.

(1D) Save as provided in paragraphs (2), (3), (3A) and (5A), the braking system of every wheeled vehicle of a class specified in an item in column 2 of the Table which, in the case of a motor vehicle, is first used on or after 1st April 1995 or which, in the case of a trailer, is manufactured on or after that date shall comply with the construction, fitting and performance requirements specified in Annexes I, II, and VII to Community Directive 91/422, and if relevant, Annexes III, IV, V, VI, VIII, X, XI and XII to that Directive in relation to the category of vehicles specified in that item in column 3.

Provided that it shall be lawful for any vehicle of such a class which, in the case of a motor vehicle, was first used before 1st April 1995 or which, in the case of a trailer, was manufactured before that date to comply with the said requirements instead of complying with paragraph (1), (1A) or (1C) or with regulations 16 and 17.

[(1E) Save as provided in paragraphs (2), (3), (3A), (5A) and (5B) the braking system of every wheeled vehicle of a class specified in an item in column 2 of the Table which, in the case of a motor vehicle, is first used on or after 1st May 2002 or which, in the case of a trailer, is manufactured on or after 1st May 2002 shall comply with the construction, fitting and performance requirements of Annexes I, II and VII to Community Directive 98/12/EC and if relevant, Annexes III, IV,

V, VI, VIII, X, XI, XII, XIII and XIV to that Directive in relation to the category of vehicles specified in that item in column 3.

Provided that it shall be lawful for any vehicle of such a class which, in the case of a motor vehicle, was first used before 1st May 2002 or which, in the case of a trailer, was manufactured before 1st [May] 2002 to comply with the said requirements instead of complying with paragraphs (1), (1A), (1C) or (1D) or with regulations 16 and 17.]

(2) The requirements specified in paragraphs (1), (1A), [(1C), (1D) and (1E)] do not apply to—

(a) an agricultural trailer or agricultural trailed appliance that is not, in either case, drawn at a speed exceeding 20mph;

(b) a locomotive;

(c) a motor tractor;

(d) an agricultural motor vehicle unless it is first used after 1st June 1986 and is driven at more than 20mph;

(e) a vehicle which has a maximum speed not exceeding 25 km/h;

(f) a works trailer;

(g) a works truck;

(h) a public works vehicle;

(i) a trailer designed and constructed, or adapted, to be drawn exclusively by a vehicle to which sub-paragraph (b), (c), (e), (g) or (h) of this paragraph applies;

(j) a trailer falling within regulation 16(3)(b), (bb), (bc), (d), (e), (f) or (g);

[(ja) a trailer which is manufactured before 1st January 1997 and has a maximum total design axle weight that does not exceed 750kg, or]

(k) a vehicle manufactured by Leyland Vehicles Limited and known as the Atlantean Bus, if first used before 1st October 1984.

(3) The requirements specified in paragraphs (1), (1A), [(1C), (1D) and (1E)] shall apply to the classes of vehicles specified in the Table so that—

(a) in item 3, the testing requirement specified in paragraph 1.5.1 and 1.5.2 of Annex II to Community Directives 79/489, 85/647, [88/194, 91/422 and 98/12] shall apply to every vehicle specified in that item other than—

(i) a double-decked vehicle first used before 1st October 1983, or

(ii) a vehicle of a type in respect of which a member state of the European Economic Community has issued a type approval certificate in accordance with Community Directive 79/489, 85/647, [88/194, 91/422 or 98/12];

(b) in items 2 and 3—

(i) the requirements specified in paragraph 1.1.4.2 of Annex II to Community Directive 79/489, 85/647, [88/194, 91/422 and 98/12] shall not apply in relation to any vehicle first used before 1st April 1996;

(ii) those requirements shall not apply in relation to any relevant bus first used on or after that date;

    (iii) sub-note (2) to paragraph 1.17.2 of Annex I to Community Directive 85/647, [88/194, 91/422 and 98/127] shall not apply in relation to any vehicle,

and for the purposes of this sub-paragraph *"relevant bus"* means a bus that is not a coach;

(c) in items 1, 2, 3, 4, 5 and 6, in the case of vehicles constructed or adapted for use by physically handicapped drivers, the requirement in paragraph 2.1.2.1 of Annex I to Community Directive 79/489 that the driver must be able to achieve the braking action mentioned in that paragraph from his driving seat without removing his hands from the steering control shall be modified so as to require that the driver is able to achieve that action while continuing to steer the vehicle; and

(d) in items 1, 4, 5, 6, 7, 8, 9 and 10, the requirement specified in paragraph 1.1.4.2 of Annex II to Community Directive 79/489 shall not apply to a vehicle first used (in the case of a motor vehicle) or manufactured (in the case of a trailer) before the relevant date as defined in paragraph (1B) if either—

    (i) following a test in respect of which the fee numbered 26024/26250 to 26257, prescribed in Schedule 1 to the Motor Vehicles (Type Approval and Approval Marks) (Fees) Regulations 1990, or the corresponding fee prescribed under any corresponding previous enactment is payable, a document is issued by the Secretary of State indicating that, at the date of manufacture of the vehicle, the type to which it belonged complied with the requirements specified in Annex 13 to ECE Regulation 13.03, 13.04, [13.05, 13.06, 13.07, 13.08 or 13.09]; or

    (ii) as a result of a notifiable alteration to the vehicle within the meaning of regulation 3 of the Plating and Testing Regulations, a fitment has been approved as complying with the requirements mentioned in sub-paragraph (i).

(3A) The requirements specified in paragraphs (1A), [(1C), (1D) and (1E)] shall apply to a road tanker subject to the exclusion of paragraph 4.3 of Annex X to Community Directive 85/647.

(3B) No motor vehicle to which [paragraph (1D) or (1E)] applies and which is first used on or after 1st April 1996 shall be fitted with an integrated retarder unless either—

(a) the motor vehicle is fitted with an anti-lock device which acts on the retarder and which complies with the requirements specified in Annex X to Community Directive 91/422 [or Community Directive 98/12]; or

(b) the retarder is fitted with a cut-out device which allows the combined control to apply the service braking system alone and which can be operated by the driver from the driving seat;

and expressions (other than the word *"vehicle"*) used in this paragraph which are also used in Annex I to Community Directive 85/647 shall, for the purposes of this paragraph, have the same meanings as in that Annex save that *"retarder"* shall not in any circumstances include a regenerative braking system.

(4) Instead of complying with paragraph (1) of this regulation, a vehicle to

which this regulation applies may comply with ECE Regulation 13.03, 13.04, [13.05, 13.06, 13.07, 13.08 or 13.09].

(5) Instead of complying with paragraph (1A) of this regulation, a vehicle to which this regulation applies may comply with ECE Regulation [13.05, 13.06, 13.07, 13.08 or 13.09].

(5A) Instead of complying with paragraph (1C) or (1D) of this regulation, a vehicle to which this regulation applies may comply—

    (a) in the case of a trailer manufactured before 1st April 1992, with ECE Regulation 13.05 or 13.06; or

    (b) in the case of any vehicle not falling within sub-paragraph (a), with ECE Regulation 13.06 [13.07, 13.08 or 13.09].

[(5B) Instead of complying with paragraph (1E) of this regulation, a vehicle to which this regulation applies may comply with ECE Regulation 13.09.]

(6) In paragraph (3A), the expression *"road tanker"* means any vehicle or trailer which carries liquid fuel in a tank forming part of the vehicle or trailer other than that containing the fuel which is used to propel the vehicle, and also includes any tank with a capacity exceeding 3m^3 carried on a vehicle.

(7) In this regulation, and in relation to the application to any vehicle of any provision of Community Directive 85/647, 88/194 or 91/422, the definitions of *"semi-trailer"*, *"full trailer"* and *"centre-axle trailer"* set out in that Directive shall apply and the meaning of *"semitrailer"* in column 2 of the Table in regulation 3(2) shall not apply.

[(8) For the purposes of the preceding provisions of this regulation the date on which a trailer was manufactured shall be taken to be the date on which its manufacture was completed except that, in the case of a trailer whose manufacture has been completed for more than eight years and which has been the subject of a notifiable alteration under regulation 30 of the Goods Vehicles (Plating and Testing) Regulations 1988, it shall be taken to be the date on which the notifiable alteration was completed.]

[(9) A trailer, whose manufacture has been completed for more than eight years and which has been the subject of a notifiable alteration under regulation 30 of the Goods Vehicles (Plating and Testing) Regulations 1988, shall comply with all requirements of Community Directives relating to braking systems which applied to the trailer at the date when the notifiable alteration was completed.]

Table

(regulation 15(1))

1	2	3
Item	Class of Vehicle	Vehicle category in the Community Directive
1	Passenger vehicles and dual-purpose vehicles which have 3 or more wheels except—	M1

1	2	3
Item	Class of Vehicle	Vehicle category in the Community Directive
	(a) dual-purpose vehicles constructed or adapted to carry not more than 2 passengers exclusive of the driver; (b) motor cycles with sidecar attached; (c) vehicles with three wheels, an unladen weight not exceeding 410kg, a maximum design speed not exceeding 50 km/h and an engine capacity not exceeding 50cc; (d) buses.	
2	Buses having a maximum gross weight which does not exceed 5000kg.	M2
3	Buses having a maximum gross weight which exceeds 5000kg.	M3
4	Dual-purpose vehicles not within item 1; and goods vehicles, having a maximum gross weight which does not exceed 3500kg, and not being motor cycles with a sidecar attached.	N1
	Goods vehicles with a maximum gross weight which—	
5	exceeds 3500kg but does not exceed 12,000kg;	N2
6	exceeds 12,000kg.	N3
	Trailers with a maximum total design axle weight which—	
7	does not exceed 750kg;	01
8	exceeds 750kg but does not exceed 3500kg;	02
9	exceeds 3500kg but does not exceed 10,000kg;	03
10	exceeds 10,000kg.	04]

[Regulation 15 is printed as amended by SI 1987/676; SI 1990/1981; SI 1992/ 352; SI 1995/551; SI 1995/737; SI 1996/3033; SI 2001/3208; SI 2002/1474. **B15.40**

The text reproduced above is based on a consolidated text (as subsequently amended) scheduled to SI 1995/551 which incorporated the amendments effected by that instrument, by earlier instruments and by SI 1995/737; it also incorporated a number of minor changes to spellings and punctuation.

SI 1996/3033 (which substituted reg.15(2)(j) and (ja) for reg.15(2)(j)) disapplied the exemption from compliance in respect of trailers manufactured on or after January 1, 1997. SI 1996/3033 expressly states (reg.2(2)) that so far as any requirement is imposed by it such requirement is imposed in exercise of powers conferred by s.41 of the Road Traffic Act 1988 to the exclusion of powers under s.2(2) of the European Communities Act 1972.

The Motor Vehicles (Type Approval and Approval Marks) (Fees) Regulations 1990 (SI 1990/461) to which reference is made in reg.15(3)(d) have been revoked; see now the Motor Vehicles (Type Approval and Approval Marks) (Fees) Regulations 1999 (SI 1999/2149) (as amended); no formal amendment has, however, been made to reg.15(3)(d) in consequence of the revocation of SI 1990/461.

The following definitions (which are referred to in reg.15(7)) are taken from Commission Directive 85/647/EEC:

"*Semi-trailer*" means a towed vehicle in which the axle(s) is (are) positioned behind the centre of gravity of the vehicle (when uniformly loaded) and which is equipped with a connecting device permitting horizontal and vertical forces to be transmitted to the drawing vehicle.

"*Full trailer*" means a towed vehicle having at least two axles, and equipped with a towing device which can move vertically (in relation to the trailer) and controls the direction of the front axle(s), but which transmits no significant static load to the drawing vehicle.

"*Centre-axle trailer*" means a towed vehicle equipped with a towing device which cannot move vertically (in relation to the trailer), and in which the axle(s) is (are) positioned close to the centre of gravity of the vehicle (when uniformly loaded) such that only a small static vertical load, not exceeding 10% of the maximum mass of the trailer or 1,000kg (whichever is the lesser) is transmitted to the drawing vehicle. The maximum mass to be taken into consideration when classifying a centre-axle trailer shall be the mass transmitted to the ground by the axle(s) of the centre-axle trailer when coupled to the drawing vehicle and laden with a maximum load. *]*

Braking systems of vehicles to which regulation 15 does not apply

B15.41   **16.**—(1) Save as provided in paragraphs (2) and (3), this regulation applies to every vehicle to which regulation 15 does not apply.

[(2) Paragraph (4) of this regulation does not apply to a vehicle which complies with regulation 15 by virtue of the proviso to regulation 15(1), (1A), (1C), (1D) or (1E), or which complies with Community Directive 79/489, 85/647, 88/194, 91/422 or 98/12 or ECE Regulation 13.03, 13.04, 13.05, 13.06, 13.07, 13.08 or 13.09.]

(3) This regulation does not apply to the following vehicles, except in the case of a vehicle referred to in (a) in so far as the regulation concerns parking brakes (requirements 16 to 18 in Schedule 3) —

(a) a locomotive first used before 2nd January 1983, propelled by steam, and with an engine which is capable of being reversed;

[(b) a trailer which is designed for use and used for street cleansing and does not carry any load other than its necessary gear and equipment;]

[(ba) a trailer which has a maximum total design axle weight that does not exceed 750kg;]

[(bb) a trailer which—

(i) is an agricultural trailer manufactured before 1st July 1947;

(ii) is being drawn by a motor tractor or an agricultural motor vehicle at a speed not exceeding 10mph;

(iii) has a laden weight not exceeding 4070kg; and

(iv) is the only trailer being drawn;]

[(bc) a trailer which is being drawn by a motor cycle in accordance with regulation 84;]

(c) an agricultural trailed appliance;

(d) an agricultural trailed appliance conveyor;

(e) a broken down vehicle;

(f) before 1st October 1986—

(i) a trailer with an unladen weight not exceeding 102kg which was manufactured before 1st October 1982; and

(ii) a gritting trailer; or

(g) on or after 1st October 1986, a gritting trailer with a maximum gross weight not exceeding 2000kg.

(4) Save as provided in paragraph (7), a vehicle of a class specified in an item in column 2 of the Table shall comply with the requirements shown in column 3 in that item, subject to any exemptions or modifications shown in column 4 in that item, references to numbers in column 3 being references to the requirements so numbered in Schedule 3.

Provided that wheeled agricultural motor vehicles not driven at more than 20mph are excluded from all items other than items 21 to 23.

TABLE

(regulation 16(4))

1	2	3	4
Item	Class of vehicle	Requirement in Schedule 3	Exemptions or modifications
1	*Motor cars* First used before 1st January 1915.	3, 6, 7, 13, 16	Requirements 13 and 16 do not apply to a motor car with less than 4 wheels.
2	First used on or after 1st January 1915 but before 1st April 1938.	1, 4, 6, 7, 9, 16	A works truck within items 1 to 11 is not subject to requirements 1, 2, 3 or 4 if it is equipped with one braking system with one means of operation.

1	2	3	4
Item	Class of vehicle	Requirement in Schedule 3	Exemptions or modifications
3	First used on or after 1st April 1938 and being either a track-laying vehicle or a vehicle first used before 1st January 1968.	1, 4, 6, 7, 8, 9, 16	
4	Wheeled vehicles first used on or after 1st January 1968.	1, 4, 6, 7, 8, 9, [15,] 18	
	Heavy motor cars		
5	First used before 15th August 1928.	1, 6, 16	
6	First used on or after 15th August 1928 but before 1st April 1938.	1, 4, 6, 7, 8, 16	
7	First used on or after 1st April 1938 and being either a track-laying vehicle or a vehicle first used before 1st January 1968.	1, 4, 6, 7, 8, 9, 16	
8	Wheeled vehicles first used on or after 1st January 1968.	1, 4, 6, 7, 8, 9, [15,] 18	
	Motor cycles		
9	First used before 1st January 1927.	3, and, in the case of three-wheeled vehicles, 16	
10	First used on or after 1st January 1927 but before 1st January 1968.	2, 7, and, in the case of three-wheeled vehicles, 16	
11	First used on or after 1st January 1968 and not being a motor cycle to which paragraph (5) applies.	2, 7, and, in the case of three-wheeled vehicles, 18	
	Locomotives		
12	Wheeled vehicles first used before 1st June 1955.	3, 6, 12, 16	
13	Wheeled vehicles first used on or after 1st June 1955 but before 1st January 1968.	3, 4, 6, 7, 8, 9, 18	

1	2	3	4
Item	Class of vehicle	Requirement in Schedule 3	Exemptions or modifications
14	Wheeled vehicles first used on or after 1st January 1968.	3, 4, 6, 7, 8, 9, 18	
15	Track-laying vehicles.	3, 6, 16	
	Motor tractors		
16	Wheeled vehicles first used before 14th January 1931 and track-laying vehicles first used before 1st April 1938.	3, 4, 6, 7, 16	Industrial tractors within items 16 to 19 are subject to requirement 5 instead of requirement 4.
17	Wheeled vehicles first used on or after 14th January 1931 but before 1st April 1938.	3, 4, 6, 7, 9, 16	
18	Wheeled vehicles first used on or after 1st April 1938 but before 1st January 1968.	3, 4, 7, 8, 9, 16	
19	Wheeled vehicles first used on or after 1st January 1968.	3, 4, 6, 7, 8, 9, 18	
20	Track-laying vehicles first used on or after 1st April 1938.	3, 4, 6, 7, 8, 16	
	Wheeled agricultural motor vehicles not driven at more than 20mph		
21	First used before 1st January 1968.	3, 4, 6, 7, 8, 16	
22	First used on or after 1st January 1968 but before 9th February 1980.	3, 4, 6, 7, 8, 18	
23	First used on or after 9th February 1980.	3, 5, 6, 7, 8, 18	
	Invalid carriages		
24	Whenever first used.	3, 13	
	Trailers		
25	Manufactured before 1st April 1938.	3, 10, 14, 17	

1	2	3	4
Item	Class of vehicle	Requirement in Schedule 3	Exemptions or modifications
26	Manufactured on or after 1st April 1938 and being either a track-laying vehicle, an agricultural trailer or a vehicle manufactured before 1st January 1968.	3, 8, 10, 14, 17	Agricultural trailers are not subject to requirement 8.
27	Wheeled vehicles manufactured on or after 1st January 1968, not being an agricultural trailer.	3, 4, 8, 11, 15, 18	Trailers equipped with brakes which come into operation on the overrun of the vehicle are not subject to requirement 15.

[(5) Subject to paragraphs (5B) and (6), the braking system of a motor cycle to which this regulation applies and which is—

(a) of a class specified in an item in column 2 of the Table below; and

(b) first used on or after 1st April 1987 and before 22nd May 1995;

shall comply with ECE Regulation 13.05, 78 or 78.01 [or Community Directive 93/143] in relation to the category of vehicles specified in that item in column 3.]

[(5A) Subject to paragraph (6), the braking system of a motor cycle to which this regulation applies and which is—

(a) of a class specified in an item in column 2 of the Table below; and

(b) first used on or after 22nd May 1995;

shall comply with ECE Regulation 78.01 [or Community Directive 93/143] in relation to the category of vehicles specified in that item in column 3.]

[TABLE

(Regulation 16(5) and (5A))

1 Item	2 Class of vehicle	3 [Vehicle category in ECE Regulations or Community Directive 93/14 (as the case may be)]
1	Vehicles (without a sidecar attached) with two wheels, an engine capacity not exceeding 50cc and a maximum design speed not exceeding 50 km/h.	L1
2	Vehicles with three wheels (including two-wheeled vehicles with a sidecar attached) and with an engine capacity not exceeding 50cc and a maximum design speed not exceeding 50 km/h.	L2
3	Vehicles with two wheels (without a sidecar attached) and with— (a) an engine capacity exceeding 50cc, or (b) a maximum design speed exceeding 50 km/h.	L3
4	Vehicles with two wheels, a sidecar attached and— (a) an engine capacity exceeding 50cc, or (b) a maximum design speed exceeding 50 km/h.	L4]
[5	Vehicles with three wheels (excluding two-wheeled vehicles with a sidecar attached) and with— (a) an engine capacity exceeding 50cc, or (b) a maximum design speed exceeding 50km/h.	L5]

[[(5B)] In relation to a motor cycle with two wheels manufactured by Piaggio Veicoli Europei Societa per Azione and known as the Cosa 125, the Cosa 125E, the Cosa L125, the Cosa LX125, the Cosa 200, the Cosa 200E, the Cosa L200 or the Cosa LX200, paragraph (5) shall have effect as if ECE Regulation 13.05 were modified by—

(a) the omission of paragraph 4.4 (approval marks), and

(b) in paragraph 5.3.1.1, (independent braking devices and controls), the omission of the word "independent" in the first place where it appears, but this paragraph shall not apply to a motor cycle first used on or after 1st July 1991.]

(6) Paragraph (5) does not apply to a works truck or to a vehicle constructed or assembled by a person not ordinarily engaged in the business of manufacturing vehicles of that description.

[(6A) Paragraph (5A) does not apply to—

(a) a vehicle with a maximum speed not exceeding 25 km/h; or

(b) a vehicle fitted for an invalid driver.]

(7) Instead of complying with the provisions of paragraph (4) of this Regulation an agricultural motor vehicle may comply with Community Directive 76/432 [or 96/63].

B15.42 *[Regulation 16 is printed as amended by SI 1987/676; SI 1990/1981; SI 1992/352; SI 1995/551; SI 1996/3033; SI 1998/2429; SI 2001/3208.]*

Vacuum or pressure brake warning devices

B15.43 **17.**—(1) Save as provided in paragraph (2), every motor vehicle which is equipped with a braking system which embodies a vacuum or pressure reservoir or reservoirs shall be equipped with a device so placed as to be readily visible to the driver of the vehicle and which is capable of indicating any impending failure of, or deficiency in, the vacuum or pressure system.

(2) The requirement specified in paragraph (1) does not apply in respect of—

[(a) a vehicle to which paragraph (1), (1A), (1C), (1D) or (1E) of regulation 15 applies, or which complies with the requirements of that regulation, of Community Directives 79/489, 85/647, 88/194, 91/422 or 98/12 or of ECE Regulation 13.03, 13.04, 13.05, 13.06, 13.07, 13.08 or 13.09;]

(b) an agricultural motor vehicle which complies with Community Directive 76/432 [or 96/63];

(c) a vehicle with an unladen weight not exceeding 3050kg propelled by an internal combustion engine, if the vacuum in the reservoir or reservoirs is derived directly from the inclusion system of the engine, and if, in the event of a failure of, or deficiency in, the vacuum system, the brakes of that braking system are sufficient under the most adverse conditions to bring the vehicle to rest within a reasonable distance; or

(d) a vehicle first used before 1st October 1937.

B15.44 *[Regulation 17 is printed as amended by SI 1987/676; SI 1990/1981; SI 1992/352; SI 1995/551; SI 1998/2429; SI 2001/3208.]*

[Couplings on trailer pneumatic braking systems

B15.45 **17A.**—(1) In this regulation—

[*"BS coupling"* means a coupling which—

(a) is of the type, shown in figure 1, 4 or 5 of the British Standard specification BS AU 138a: 1980 or figure 1, 2 or 3 of the British Standard specification BS AU 138b: 2000; and

(b) complies with the dimensions shown in figure 1, 4 or 5 of the British Standard specification BS AU 138a: 1980 or figure 1,

2 or 3 of the British Standard specification BS AU 138b: 2000;]

"the British Standard specification" means the British Standard specification for dimensions of "contact" type couplings for air pressure braking systems on trailers and semitrailers and their towing vehicles, and the arrangements of these couplings on articulated and drawbar combinations, published by the British Standards Institution under reference number BS AU 138a: 1980 [or BS AU 138b: 2000];

"coupling", *"emergency line"*, *"secondary line"* and *"service line"* have the same meanings as in the British Standard specification;

"EEA Agreement" means the Agreement on the European Economic Area signed at Oporto on the 2nd May 1992 as adjusted by the Protocol signed at Brussels on 17th March 1993; and

"EEA State" means a state which is a Contracting Party to the EEA Agreement.

(2) For the purposes of this regulation, a relevant coupling is a coupling that is physically capable of being connected to a BS coupling.

(3) Subject to paragraphs (6) and (7), no service line comprised in a pneumatic braking system fitted to a trailer shall be equipped with a relevant coupling unless that coupling—

[(a) is of the type shown in figure 2 of the British Standard specification BS AU 138a:1980 or figure 4 of the British Standard specification BS AU 138b: 2000;]

(b) complies with the dimensions shown in that figure; and

(c) complies with paragraph 3.4.3 of that specification (except so far as it requires it to be of a type shown in that figure).

(4) Subject to paragraphs (6), (7) and (8) no emergency line comprised in a pneumatic braking system fitted to a trailer shall be equipped with a relevant coupling unless that coupling—

[(a) is of the type shown in figure 3 of the British Standard specification BS AU 138a: 1980 or figure 5 of the British Standard specification BS AU 138b: 2000;] and

(b) complies with the dimensions shown in that figure.

(5) Subject to paragraphs (6), (7) and (8) no secondary line comprised in a pneumatic braking system fitted to a trailer shall be equipped with a relevant coupling unless that coupling—

[(a) is of the type shown in figure 6 of the British Standard specification BS AU 138a: 1980 or figure 6 of the British Standard specification BS AU 138b: 2000;] and

(b) complies with the dimensions shown in that figure.

(6) For the purposes of paragraphs (3), (4) and (5), a reference to the dimensions shown in a figure in the British Standard specification does not include any dimension marked "M22×1.5".

[(7) Paragraph (3) does not prevent a line being equipped with a relevant coupling which fulfils the requirements of—

(a) a standard or code of practice of a national standards body or equivalent body of any EEA State;

(b) any international standard recognised for use as a standard by any EEA State; or

(c) a technical specification or code of practice which, whether mandatory or not, is recognised for use as a standard by a public authority of any EEA State,

where the standard, code of practice, international standard or technical specification provides, in relation to couplings, a level of safety and compatibility with BS couplings of the type shown in figure 1 of the British Standard specification BS AU 13a: 1980 or figure 1 of the British Standard specification BS AU 138b: 2000 equivalent to that provided by those specifications as modified in accordance with paragraph (6).]

[(8) Paragraph (7) shall have effect—

(a) in relation to paragraph (4), as if for the words "paragraph (3)" there were substituted the words "paragraph (4)" and for the words "figure 1" in the first and second places in which they occur there were substituted the words "figure 4" and "figure 2" respectively; and

(b) in relation to paragraph (5), as if for the words "paragraph (3)" there were substituted the words "paragraph (5)" and for the words "figure 1" in the first and second places in which they occur there were substituted the words "figure 5" and "figure 3" respectively.]

B15.46   *[Regulation 17A was inserted by SI 1996/3033 and is printed as subsequently amended by SI 2001/3208.*

SI 1996/3033 expressly states (reg.2(2)) that so far as any requirement is imposed by it such requirement is imposed in exercise of powers conferred by s.41 of the Road Traffic Act 1988 to the exclusion of the powers under s.2(2) of the European Communities Act 1972.

As to the European Economic Area and the EEA agreement, see the introductory note to Section C below.]

Maintenance and efficiency of brakes

B15.47   **18.**—(1) Every part of every braking system and of the means of operation thereof fitted to a vehicle shall be maintained in good and efficient working order and be properly adjusted.

[(1A) Without prejudice to paragraph (3), where a vehicle is fitted with an anti-lock braking system ("the ABS"), then while the condition specified in paragraph (1B) is fulfilled, any fault in the ABS shall be disregarded for the purposes of paragraph (1).]

[(1B) The condition is fulfilled while the vehicle is completing a journey at the beginning of which the ABS was operating correctly or is being driven to a place where the ABS is to undergo repairs.]

[(1C) Where a goods vehicle of category N_2 or N_3 is being used to tow a trailer of category O_3 or O_4 and both vehicles are fitted with an ISO 7638 connector to provide a dedicated power supply to the ABS, then these connectors shall be used regardless of any alternative method available on the vehicles to provide such power.]

(2) Paragraph (3) applies to every wheeled motor vehicle except—

(a) an agricultural motor vehicle which is not driven at more than 20mph;

(b) a works truck; ...

(c) a pedestrian-controlled vehicle [; and]

[(d) an industrial tractor.]

(3) Every vehicle to which this paragraph applies and which is of a class specified in an item in column 2 of Table I shall, subject to any exemption shown for
that item in column 4, be so maintained that—

(a) its service braking system has a total braking efficiency not less than
that shown in column (3)(a) for that item; and

(b) if the vehicle is a heavy motor car, a motor car first used on or after
1st January 1915 or a motor cycle first used on or after 1st January
1927, its secondary braking system has a total braking efficiency not
less than that shown in column 3(b) for those items.

Provided that a reference in Table I to a trailer is a reference to a trailer required
by regulation 15 or 16 to be equipped with brakes.

TABLE I

(regulation 18(3))

1	2	3		4
Item	Class of vehicle	Efficiencies %		Exemptions
		(a)	(b)	
1	A vehicle to which regulation 15 applies or which complies in all respects other than its braking efficiency with the requirements of that regulation or with [Community Directives 79/489, 85/647, 88/194, 91/422 or 98/12 or with ECE Regulation 13.03, 13.04, 13.05, 13.06, 13.07, 13.08 or 13.09] —			A motor cycle.
	(a) when not drawing a trailer;	50	25	
	(b) when drawing a trailer	45	25	
2	A vehicle, not included in item 1 and not being a motor cycle, which is first used on or after 1st January 1968—			
	(a) when not drawing a trailer;	50	25	
	(b) when drawing a trailer manufactured on or after 1st January 1968;	50	25	

1	2	3		4
Item	Class of vehicle	Efficiencies %		Exemptions
		(a)	(b)	
	(c) when drawing a trailer manufactured before 1st January 1968	40	15	
3	Goods vehicles [and buses (in each case)] first used on or after 15th August 1928 but before 1st January 1968 having an unladen weight exceeding 1525kg being—			
	(a) rigid vehicles with 2 axles not constructed to form part of an articulated vehicle—			
	(i) when not drawing a trailer	45	20	
	(ii) when drawing a trailer	40	15	
	(b) other vehicles, including vehicles constructed to form part of an articulated vehicle, whether or not drawing a trailer	40	15	
4	Vehicles not included in items 1 to 3—			(a) a bus;
	(a) having at least one means of operation applying to at least 4 wheels;	50	25	(b) an articulated vehicle;
	(b) having 3 wheels and at least one means of operation applying to all 3 wheels and not being a motor cycle with sidecar attached			(c) a vehicle constructed or adapted to form part of an articulated vehicle;
	(i) when not drawing a trailer	40	25	(d) a heavy motor car which is a goods vehicle first used before 15th August 1928.
	(ii) in the case of a motor cycle when drawing a trailer	40	25	
	(c) other			

1	2	3		4
Item	Class of vehicle	Efficiencies %		Exemptions
		(a)	(b)	
	(i) when not drawing a trailer	30	25	
	(ii) in the case of a motor cycle when drawing a trailer.	30	25	

(4) A goods vehicle shall not be deemed to comply with the requirements of paragraph (3) unless it is capable of complying with those requirements both at the laden weight at which it is operating at any time and when its laden weight is equal to—

(a) if a plating certificate has been issued and is in force for the vehicle, the design gross weight shown in column (3) of that certificate or, if no such weight is so shown, the gross weight shown in column (2) of that certificate; and

(b) in any other case, the design gross weight of the vehicle.

Provided that in the case of a goods vehicle drawing a trailer, references in this paragraph to laden weight refer to the combined laden weight of the drawing vehicle and the trailer and references to gross weight and design gross weight are to be taken as references to train weight and design train weight respectively.

[(4A) A bus shall be deemed not to comply with the requirements of paragraph (3) unless it is capable of complying with those requirements both at its laden weight for the time being and at its relevant weight.]

[(4B) For the purposes of paragraph (4A), the relevant weight,—

(a) in relation to a bus first used on or after 1st April 1982, is its maximum gross weight; and

(b) in relation to a bus first used before that date, is the weight specified in paragraph (4C).]

[(4C) The weight referred to in paragraph (4B)(b) is—

$$X + 63.5 (Y + Z)kg$$

where—

X is the unladen weight of that bus in kilograms;

Y is the number of passengers that the bus is constructed or adapted to carry seated in addition to the driver; and

Z is—

(a) in the case of a PSV which is not an articulated bus and has a standing capacity exceeding 8 persons, the standing capacity minus 8;

(b) in the case of a PSV which is an articulated bus, the standing capacity; or

(c) in any other case, nil.]

(5) The brakes of every agricultural motor vehicle which is first used on or af-

ter 1st June 1986 and is not driven at more than 20mph, and of every agricultural trailer manufactured on or after 1st December 1985 shall be capable of achieving a braking efficiency of not less than 25% when the weight of the vehicle is equal to the total maximum axle weights which the vehicle is designed to have.

(6) Every vehicle or combination of vehicles specified in an item in column 2 of Table II shall be so maintained that its brakes are capable, without the assistance of stored energy, of holding it stationary on a gradient of at least the percentage specified in column 3 in that item.

(7) For the purpose of this regulation the date of manufacture of a trailer which is a composite trailer shall be deemed to be the same as the date of manufacture of the semitrailer which forms part of the composite trailer.

TABLE II

(regulation 18(6))

1	2	3
Item	Class of vehicle or combination	Percentage gradient
1	A vehicle specified in item 1 of Table I— (a) when not drawing a trailer (b) when drawing a trailer.	16 12
2	A vehicle to which requirement 18 in Schedule 3 applies by virtue of regulation 16.	16
3	A vehicle, not included in item 1, drawing a trailer manufactured on or after 1st January 1968 and required, by regulation 15 or 16, to be fitted with brakes.	16

(8) A vehicle which is subject to, and which complies with the requirements in, item 1 and Tables I and II shall not be treated as failing, by reason of its braking efficiency, to comply with regulation 15 or with [Community Directives 79/489, 85/647, 88/194, 91/422 or 98/12 or with ECE Regulation 13.03, 13.04, 13.05, 13.06, 13.07, 13.08 or 13.09].

[(9) In this regulation—

"*PSV*" means a public service vehicle within the meaning of section 1 of the Public Passenger Vehicles Act 1981 [*as amended by the Transport Act 1985, Sch.8*] ;

"*standing capacity*", in relation to a PSV, means the number of persons that can be carried standing without an offence being committed under section 26 of the Public Passenger Vehicles Act 1981.]

B15.48   *[Regulation 18 is printed as amended by SI 1987/676; SI 1990/1981; SI 1992/352; SI 1995/551; SI 2001/3208.]*

Application of brakes of trailers

B15.49   **19.** Where a trailer is drawn by a motor vehicle the driver (or in the case of a locomotive one of the persons employed in driving or tending the locomotive) shall be in a position readily to operate any brakes required by these Regulations to be fitted to the trailer as well as the brakes of the motor vehicle unless a person other than the driver [(or in the case of a locomotive a person other than one of the persons employed in driving or tending the locomotive)] is in a position and competent efficiently to apply the brakes of the trailer.

Provided that this regulation shall not apply to a trailer which—

    (a) in compliance with these Regulations, is fitted with brakes which automatically come into operation on the overrun of the trailer; or

    (b) ... is a broken down vehicle being drawn, whether or not in consequence of a breakdown, in such a manner that it cannot be steered by its own steering gear.

[Regulation 19 is printed as amended by SI 1990/1981.]   **B15.50**

C Wheels, Springs, Tyres and Tracks

General requirements as to wheels and tracks

20. Every motor cycle and invalid carriage shall be a wheeled vehicle, and   **B15.51** every other motor vehicle and every trailer shall be either a wheeled vehicle or a track-laying vehicle.

Diameter of wheels

21. [...]   **B15.52**
[Revoked by SI 1995/1201.]

Springs and resilient material

22.—(1) Save as provided in paragraphs (3) and (4), every motor vehicle and   **B15.53** every trailer be equipped with suitable and sufficient springs between each wheel and the frame of the vehicle.

(2) Save as provided in paragraphs (3) and (4), in the case of a track-laying vehicle—

    (a) resilient material shall be interposed between the rims of the weight-carrying rollers and the road surface so that the weight of the vehicle, other than that borne by any wheel, is supported by the resilient material, and

    (b) where the vehicle is a heavy motor car, motor car, or trailer it shall have suitable springs between the frame of the vehicle and the weight-carrying rollers.

(3) This regulation does not apply to—

    (a) a wheeled vehicle with an unladen weight not exceeding 4070kg and which is—

        (i) a motor tractor any unsprung wheel of which is fitted with a pneumatic tyre;

        (ii) a motor tractor used in connection with railway shunting and which is used on a road only when passing from one railway track to another in connection with such use;

        (iii) a vehicle specially designed, and mainly used, for work on rough ground or unmade roads and every wheel of which is fitted with a pneumatic tyre and which is not driven at more than 20mph;

          (iv) a vehicle constructed or adapted for, and being used for, road sweeping and every wheel of which is fitted with either a pneumatic tyre or a resilient tyre and which is not driven at more than 20mph;

    (b) an agricultural motor vehicle which is not driven at more than 20mph;

    (c) an agricultural trailer, or an agricultural trailed appliance;

    (d) a trailer used solely for the haulage of felled trees;

    (e) a motor cycle;

    (f) a mobile crane;

    (g) a pedestrian-controlled vehicle all the wheels of which are equipped with pneumatic tyres;

    (h) a road roller;

    (i) a broken down vehicle; or

    (j) a vehicle first used on or before 1st January 1932.

(4) Paragraphs (1) and (2)(b) do not apply to a works truck or a works trailer.

Wheel loads

B15.54   **23.**—(1) Subject to paragraph (2) this regulation applies to—

    (a) a semi-trailer with more than 2 wheels;

    (b) a track-laying vehicle with more than 2 wheels; and

    (c) any other vehicle with more than 4 wheels.

(2) This regulation does not apply to a road roller.

(3) Save as provided in paragraphs (4) and (5), every vehicle to which this regulation applies shall be fitted with a compensating arrangement which will ensure that under the most adverse conditions every wheel will remain in contact with the road and will not be subject to abnormal variations of load.

(4) Paragraph (3) does not apply in respect of a steerable wheel on which the load does not exceed—

    (a) if it is a wheeled vehicle, [4250kg]; and

    (b) if it is a track-laying vehicle, 2540kg.

(5) In the application of paragraph (3) to an agricultural motor vehicle, wheels which are in line transversely on one side of the longitudinal axis of the vehicle shall be regarded as one wheel.

B15.55   *[Regulation 23 is printed as amended by SI 1998/3112.]*

Tyres

B15.56   **24.**—(1) Save as provided in paragraph (2), every wheel of a vehicle of a class specified in an item in column 2 of the Table shall be fitted with a tyre of a type specified in that item in column 3 which complies with any conditions specified in that item in column 4.

(2) The requirements referred to in paragraph (1) do not apply to a road-roller and are subject, in the case of any item in the Table, to the exemptions specified in that item in column 5.

TABLE

(regulation 24(1))

1	2	3	4	5
Item	Class of vehicle	Type of tyre	Conditions	Exemptions
1	Locomotives not falling into item 6	Pneumatic or resilient		
2	Motor tractors not falling in item 6	Pneumatic or resilient	No re-cut pneumatic tyre shall be fitted to any wheel of a vehicle with an unladen weight of less than 2540kg unless the diameter of the rim of the wheel is at least 405mm	
3	Heavy motor cars not falling in item 6	Pneumatic		The following, if every wheel not fitted with a pneumatic tyre is fitted with a resilient tyre— (a) a vehicle mainly used for work on rough ground; (b) a tower wagon; (c) a vehicle fitted with a turntable fire escape; (d) a refuse vehicle; (e) a works truck; (f) a vehicle first used before 3rd January 1933.

1	2	3	4	5
Item	Class of vehicle	Type of tyre	Conditions	Exemptions
4	Motor cars not falling in item 6	Pneumatic	No re-cut tyre shall be fitted to any wheel of a vehicle unless it is— (a) an electrically propelled goods vehicle or, (b) a goods vehicle with an unladen weight of at least 2540 kg and the diameter of the rim of the wheel is at least 405mm	The following, if every wheel not fitted with a pneumatic tyre is fitted with a resilient tyre— (a) a vehicle mainly used for work on rough ground; (b) a refuse vehicle; (c) a works truck; (d) a vehicle with an unladen weight not exceeding— (i) 1270kg if electrically propelled; (ii) 1020kg in any other case; (e) a tower wagon; (f) a vehicle fitted with a turntable fire escape; (g) a vehicle first used before 3rd January 1933.
5	Motor cycles	Pneumatic	No re-cut tyre shall be fitted	The following, if every wheel not fitted with a pneumatic tyre is fitted with a resilient tyre— (a) a works truck; (b) a pedestrian-controlled vehicle

1	2	3	4	5
Item	Class of vehicle	Type of tyre	Conditions	Exemptions
6	Agricultural motor vehicles which are not driven at more than 20mph	Pneumatic or resilient	The same as for item 2	The requirement in column 3 does not apply to a vehicle of which— (a) every steering wheel is fitted with a smooth-soled tyre which is not less than 60mm wide where it touches the road; and (b) in the case of a wheeled vehicle, every driving wheel is fitted with a smooth-soled tyre which— (i) is not less than 150mm wide if the unladen weight of the vehicle exceeds 3050kg, or 76mm wide in any other case, and either (ii) is shod with diagonal cross-bars not less than 76mm wide or more than 20mm thick extending the full breadth of the tyre and so arranged that the space between adjacent bars is not more than 76mm; or (iii) is shod with diagonal cross-bars of resilient material not less than 60mm wide extending the full breadth of the tyre and so arranged that the space between adjacent bars is not more than 76mm.

1	2	3	4	5
Item	Class of vehicle	Type of tyre	Conditions	Exemptions
7	Trailers	Pneumatic	Except in the case of a trailer mentioned in paragraph (d) of column 5, no recut tyre shall be fitted to any wheel of a trailer drawn by a heavy motor car or a motor car if the trailer— (a) has an unladen weight not exceeding— (i) if it is a living van, 2040kg; or (ii) in any other case, 1020kg; or (b) is not constructed or adapted to carry any load, other than plant or other special appliance which is a permanent or essentially permanent fixture and has a gross weight not exceeding 2290kg	(a) an agricultural trailer manufactured before 1st December 1985; (b) an agricultural trailed appliance; (c) a trailer used to carry water for a road roller being used in connection with road works; (d) the following if every wheel which is not fitted with a pneumatic tyre is fitted with a resilient tyre— (i) a works trailer; (ii) a refuse vehicle; (iii) a trailer drawn by a heavy motor car every wheel of which is not required to be fitted with a pneumatic tyre; (iv) a broken down vehicle; or (v) a trailer drawn by a vehicle which is not a heavy motor car or a motor car.

(3) Save as provided in paragraph (4) a wheel of a vehicle may not be fitted with a temporary use spare tyre unless either—

  (a) the vehicle is a passenger vehicle (not being a bus) first used before 1st April 1987; or

  (b) the vehicle complies at the time of its first use with ECE Regulation 64 [or Community Directive 92/23].

(4) Paragraph (3) does not apply to a vehicle constructed or assembled by a person not ordinarily engaged in the trade or business of manufacturing vehicles of that description.

[Regulation 24 is printed as amended by SI 1992/3088.]   **B15.57**

Tyre loads and speed ratings

25.—[(1) Save as provided in [paragraphs (3), (4), (7A) and (7B)] any tyre fit-   **B15.58**
ted to the axle of a vehicle—

(a) which is a class of vehicle specified in an item in column 2 of Table I; and

(b) in relation to which the date of first use is as specified in that item in column 3 of that Table;

shall comply with the requirements specified in that item in column 4 of that Table.

[TABLE I

(regulation 25(1))

1 Item	2 Class of vehicle	3 Date of first use	4 Requirements
1	Vehicles which are of one or more of the following descriptions, namely— (a) goods vehicles, (b) trailers, (c) buses, (d) vehicles of a class mentioned in column 2 in Table III	Before 1st April 1991	The requirements of paragraphs (5) and (6)
2	Vehicles which are of one or more of the following descriptions— (a) goods vehicles, (b) trailers, (c) buses, (d) vehicles of a class mentioned in column 2 in Table III and do not fall within item 3 below	On or after 1st April 1991	The requirements of paragraphs (5), (6) and (7)
3	Vehicles of a class mentioned in paragraph (2)	On or after 1st April 1991	The requirements of paragraph (5)]

[(2) The classes of vehicle referred to in item 3 in column 2 of Table I are—

(a) engineering plant;

(b) track-laying vehicles;

(c) vehicles equipped with tyres of speed category Q:

(d) works trucks; and

(e) motor vehicles with a maximum speed not exceeding 30mph, not being vehicles of a class specified in—

(i) items 2 and 3 of Table II; or

(ii) paragraph (7A) or sub-paragraphs (a) to (d) of this paragraph;

or trailers while being drawn by such vehicles.]

(3) Paragraph (1) shall not apply to any tyre fitted to the axle of a vehicle if the vehicle is—

(a) broken down or proceeding to a place where it is to be broken up; and

(b) being drawn by a motor vehicle at a speed not exceeding 20mph.

(4) Where in relation to any vehicle first used on or after 1st April 1991 a tyre supplied by a manufacturer for the purposes of tests or trials of that tyre is fitted to an axle of that vehicle, [paragraph (7) shall not apply to that tyre while it is being used for those purposes.]

(5) The requirements of this paragraph are that the tyre, as respects strength, shall be designed and manufactured adequately to support the maximum permitted axle weight for the axle.

(6) The requirements of this paragraph are that the tyre shall be designed and [manufactured] adequately to support the maximum permitted axle weight for the axle when the vehicle is driven at the speed shown in column 3 in Table II in the item in which the vehicle is described in column 2 (the lowest relevant speed being applicable to a vehicle which is described in more than one item).

TABLE II

(regulation 25(6))

1	2	3	4	
Item	Class of vehicle	Speed (mph)	Variation to the [load-capacity index] expressed as a percentage	
			[Tyres marked in accordance with ECE Regulation 30, 30.01 or 30.02] [and relevant car tyres]	Tyres marked in accordance with ECE Regulation 54 [and relevant commercial vehicle tyres]
1	A vehicle of a class for which maximum speeds are prescribed by Schedule 6 to the 1984 Act [other than an agricultural motor vehicle]	The highest speed so prescribed	Single wheels: none Dual wheels: 95.5%	None
2	An electrically propelled vehicle used as a multi-stop local collection and delivery vehicle and having a maximum speed of not more than 25mph	[The maximum speed of the vehicle]	None	150%
3	An electrically propelled vehicle used as a multi-stop local collection and delivery vehicle and having a maximum speed of more than 25mph and not more than 40mph	[The maximum speed of the vehicle]	None	130%

1	*2*	*3*	*4*	
Item	Class of vehicle	Speed (mph)	Variation to the [load-capacity index] expressed as a percentage	
			[Tyres marked in accordance with ECE Regulation 30, 30.01 or 30.02] [and relevant car tyres]	Tyres marked in accordance with ECE Regulation 54 [and relevant commercial vehicle tyres]
4	An electrically propelled vehicle used only within a radius of 25 miles from the permanent base at which it is normally kept and having a maximum speed of more than 40mph and not more than 50mph	[The maximum speed of the vehicle]	None	115%
5	A local service bus	50	None	110%
6	A restricted speed vehicle	50	None	The relevant % variation specified in Annex 8 to ECE Regulation 54 [or Appendix 8 to Annex II to Community Directive 92/23]
7	A low platform trailer[, an agricultural motor vehicle, an agricultural trailer, an agricultural trailed appliance or an agricultural trailed appliance conveyor]	40	None	The relevant % variation specified in Annex 8 to ECE Regulation 54 [or Appendix 8 to Annex II to Community Directive 92/23]
8	A municipal vehicle	40	None	115%

1	2	3	4	
Item	Class of vehicle	Speed (mph)	Variation to the [load-capacity index] expressed as a percentage	
			[Tyres marked in accordance with ECE Regulation 30, 30.01 or 30.02] [and relevant car tyres]	Tyres marked in accordance with ECE Regulation 54 [and relevant commercial vehicle tyres]
9	A multi-stop local collection and delivery vehicle if not falling within the class of vehicle described in items 2 or 3 above	40	None	115%
10	A light trailer or any trailer equipped with tyres of speed category F or G	60	Single wheels: 110% Dual wheels: 105%	The relevant variation specified in Annex 8 to ECE Regulation 54 [or Appendix 8 to Annex II to Community Directive 92/23]
11	A trailer not falling in items 6–10	60	Single wheels: none Dual wheels: 95.5%	None
12	A [motor] vehicle not falling in items 1–11	70	Single wheels: none Dual wheels: 95.5%	None

(7) The requirement of this paragraph is that the tyre when first fitted to the vehicle [was marked with a designated approval mark or] complied with the

requirements of [ECE Regulation 30, 30.01, 30.02] or 54, but this requirement shall not apply to a retreaded tyre.

[(7A) The requirements of paragraphs (6) and (7) shall not apply to [any tyre fitted to the axle of] a vehicle of a class specified in an item in column 2 of Table III while [the vehicle] is being driven or drawn at a speed not exceeding that specified in that item in column 3 of that Table.

TABLE III

(regulation 25(7A))

1	2	3
Item	Class of vehicle	Speed (mph)
1	Agricultural motor vehicles	20
2	Agricultural trailers	20
3	Agricultural trailed appliances	20
4	Agricultural trailed appliance conveyors	20
5	Works trailers	18]

[(7B) Paragraph (7C) applies where a tyre fitted to the axle of a vehicle—

(a) bears a speed category symbol and load-capacity index, being marks that were moulded on to or into the tyre at the time that it was manufactured;

(b) is designed and manufactured so as to be capable of operating safely at the speed and load indicated by those marks; and

(c) is designed so as to be capable of being fitted to the axle of a vehicle of a class specified in item 1, 2, 3 or 4 in column 2 of Table III above.]

[(7C) In the circumstances mentioned in paragraph (7B), paragraph (7) shall not apply to the tyre if—

(a) the vehicle is being driven or drawn at a speed that does not exceed the speed indicated by the speed category symbol or 50mph (which-ever is the less), and

(b) the load on the tyre does not exceed the load indicated by the load-capacity index.]

(8) A vehicle of a class described in column 2 in Table II first used on or after 1st April 1991 shall not be used on a road—

(a) in the case where there is no entry in column 4 specifying a variation to the [load-capacity index] expressed as a percentage, if the load ap-plied to any tyre fitted to the axle of the vehicle exceeds that indicated by the [load-capacity index]; or

(b) in the case where there is such an entry in column 4, if the load ap-plied to any tyre fitted to the axle of the vehicle exceeds the variation to the [load-capacity index] expressed as a percentage.

(9) In this regulation—

"designated approval mark" means the marking designated as an approval mark by regulation 5 of the Approval Marks Regulations and shown at item 33 in Schedule 4 to those Regulations (that item being a mark-ing relating to Community Directive 92/23);]

"*dual wheels*" means two or more wheels which are to be regarded as one wheel by virtue of paragraph 7 of regulation 3 in the circumstances specified in that paragraph;

"*load-capacity index*" has the same meaning as in [paragraph 2.28 of Annex II to Community Directive 92/23 or] paragraph 2.29 of ECE Regulation 30.02 or [paragraph 2.27] of ECE Regulation 54;

"*local service bus*" means a bus being used in the provision of a local service as defined in section 2 of the Transport Act 1985 [*q.v.*];

"*municipal vehicle*" means a motor vehicle or trailer limited at all times to use by a local authority, or a person acting in pursuance of a contract with a local authority, for road cleansing, road watering or the collection and disposal of refuse, night soil or the contents of cesspools, or the purposes of the enactments relating to weights and measures or the sale of food and drugs;

"*multi-stop local collection and delivery vehicle*" means a motor vehicle or trailer used for multistop collection and delivery services to be used only within a radius of 25 miles from the permanent base at which it is normally kept;

"*single wheels*" means wheels which are not dual wheels; and

"*speed category*" has the same meaning as in [paragraph 2.29 of Annex II to Community Directive 92/23 or] [paragraph 2.28] of ECE Regulation 54.

[(9A) For the purposes of this regulation, a tyre is a "*relevant car tyre*" if—

    (a) it has been marked with a designated approval mark, and

    (b) the first two digits of the approval number comprised in the mark are "02".]

[(9B) For the purposes of this regulation, a tyre is a "*relevant commercial vehicle tyre*" if—

    (a) it has been marked with a designated approval mark, and

    (b) the first two digits of the approval number comprised in the mark are "00".]

[(10) In this regulation any reference to the first use shall, in relation to a trailer, be construed as a reference to the date which is 6 months after the date of manufacture of the trailer.]

[Regulation 25 was substituted by SI 1990/1981; and is printed as subsequently amended by SI 1991/2710; SI 1992/3088; SI 1995/551.   **B15.59**

Paragraphs 2.28 and 2.29 of Annex II to Directive 92/23/EEC (O.J. No.L129, May 14, 1992, p.95; to which reference is made in reg.25(9)) and related paragraphs read as follows:

2.28.   "*load-capacity index*" means one or two numbers which indicate the load the tyre can carry in single or in single and dual formation at the speed corresponding to the associated speed category and when operated in conformity with the requirements governing utilization specified by the manufacturer. The list of these indices and their corresponding masses is given in Annex II, Appendix 2;

2.28.1.   on passenger car tyres there must be one load index only;

2.28.2.   on commercial vehicle tyres there may be one or two load indices, the first one for single formation and the second one, when present, for dual (twin) formation in which case the two indices are divided by a slash (/);

2.28.3.   a type of tyre may have either one or two sets of load capacity indices depending on whether or not the provisions of section 6.2.5 are applied;

2.29.   *"speed category"*, expressed by the speed category symbol as shown in the table in 2.29.3;

2.29.1.   in the case of a passenger car tyre, the maximum speed which the tyre can sustain;

2.29.2.   in the case of a commercial vehicle tyre, the speed at which the tyre can carry the mass corresponding to the load capacity index;

2.29.3.   The speed categories are as shown in the table below:

Speed category symbol	Corresponding speed (km/h)
F	80
G	90
J	100
K	110
L	120
M	130
N	140
P	150
Q	160
R	170
S	180
T	190
U	200
H	210
V	240

2.29.4.   tyres suitable for maximum speeds higher than 240 km/h are identified by means of the letter code "Z" placed within the tyre size designation;

2.29.5   a type of tyre may have either one or two sets of speed category symbols depending on whether or not the provisions of section 6.2.5 are applied; *]*

[Tyre noise

B16.60   **25A.**—(1) Subject to paragraphs (2) and (3), any replacement tyre (not being a retreaded or part-worn tyre) must be marked with an S mark where it is to be fitted to an axle of—

(a) a passenger vehicle with 4 wheels or more,

(b) a goods vehicle,

(c) a dual-purpose vehicle, or

(d) a trailer constructed or adapted for use with a passenger vehicle, a goods vehicle or a dual-purpose vehicle.

(2) Paragraph (1) applies to—

    (a) Class C1d tyres on or after 1st October 2010; and

    (b) Class C1e tyres on or after 1st October 2011.

(3) Paragraph (1) does not apply to—

    (a) tyres whose speed rating is less than 80 km/h;

    (b) tyres whose nominal rim diameter does not exceed 254mm (code 10) or is 635mm (code 25) or more;

    (c) T-type temporary-use spare tyres; or

    (d) tyres designed only to be fitted to vehicles described in paragraph (1) that were registered for the first time before 1st October 1980.

(4) In this regulation—

    "Class C1d tyre" means a tyre designed for a passenger vehicle with a nominal section width greater than 185mm but less than or equal to 215mm;

    "Class C1e tyre" means a tyre designed for a passenger vehicle with a nominal section width greater than 215mm;

    "nominal rim diameter" has the same meaning as in section 2.18 of Annex II of Community Directive 92/23;

    "part-worn tyre" means a tyre that is not new when fitted;

    "replacement tyre" means—

        (a) a Class C1d tyre sold, or intended to be sold, on or after 1st October 2010;

        (b) a Class C1e tyre sold, or intended to be sold, on or after 1st October 2011; or

        (c) any other tyre sold, or intended to be sold, on or after the date these Regulations come into force,

    where that tyre replaces, or is intended to replace, a tyre fitted to the axle of any vehicle to which paragraph (1) applies.

    "rim" has the same meaning as in section 2.19 of Annex II of Community Directive 92/23;

    "S mark" means a designated approval mark of a description specified in item 30B of Schedule 2 or item 33 of Schedule 4 of the Approval Marks Regulations including the relevant suffix indicating conformity with the requirements on tyre noise emissions;

    "section width" has the same meaning as in section 2.12 of Annex II of Community Directive 92/23; and

    "T-type temporary-use spare tyre" has the same meaning as in section 2.3.6 of Annex II of Community Directive 92/23, and *"temporary-use spare tyre"* has the same meaning as in section 2.3.5 if Annex II of Community Directive 92/23.]

[Regulation 25A is printed as inserted by SI 2010/312.]   **B15.61**

Mixing of tyres

26.—(1) Save as provided in paragraph (5) pneumatic tyres of different types **B15.62** of structure shall not be fitted to the same axle of a wheeled vehicle.

(2) Save as provided in paragraphs (3) or (5), a wheeled motor vehicle having

only two axles each of which is equipped with one or two single wheels shall not be fitted with—

    (a) a diagonal-ply tyre or a bias-belted tyre on its rear axle if a radial-ply tyre is fitted on its front axle; or

    (b) a diagonal-ply tyre on its rear axle if a bias-belted tyre is fitted on the front axle.

(3) Paragraph (2) does not apply to a vehicle to an axle of which there are fitted wide tyres not specially constructed for use on engineering plant or to a vehicle which has a maximum speed not exceeding 30mph.

(4) Save as provided in paragraph (5) pneumatic tyres fitted to—

    (a) the steerable axles of a wheeled vehicle; [or]

    (b) the driven axles of a wheeled vehicle, not being steerable axles,

shall all be of the same type of structure.

(5) Paragraphs (1), (2), and (4) do not prohibit the fitting of a temporary use spare tyre to a wheel of a passenger vehicle (not being a bus) unless it is driven at a speed exceeding 50mph.

(6) In this regulation—

    "axle" includes—

      (i) two or more stub axles which are fitted on opposite sides of the longitudinal axis of the vehicle so as to form—

        (a) a pair in the case of two stub axles; and

        (b) pairs in the case of more than two stub axles; and

      (ii) a single stub axle which is not one of a pair;

    "a bias-belted tyre" means a pneumatic tyre, the structure of which is such that the ply cords extend to the bead so as to be laid at alternate angles of substantially less than 90 degrees to the peripheral line of the tread, and are constrained by a circumferential belt comprising two or more layers of substantially inextensible cord material laid at alternate angles smaller than those of the ply cord structure;

    "a diagonal-ply tyre" means a pneumatic tyre, the structure of which is such that the ply cords extend to the bead so as to be laid at alternate angles of substantially less than 90 degrees to the peripheral line of the tread, but not being a bias-belted tyre;

    "a driven axle" means an axle through which power is transmitted from the engine of a vehicle to the wheels on that axle;

    "a radial-ply tyre" means a pneumatic tyre, the structure of which is such that the ply cords extend to the bead so as to be laid at an angle of substantially 90 degrees to the peripheral line of the tread, the ply cord structure being stabilised by a substantially inextensible circumferential belt;

    "stub-axle" means an axle on which only one wheel is mounted; and

    "type of structure", in relation to a tyre, means a type of structure of a tyre of a kind defined in the foregoing provisions of this paragraph.

B15.63   *[Regulation 26 is printed as amended by SI 1990/1981.]*

Condition and maintenance of tyres

B15.64   27.—(1) Save as provided in paragraphs (2), (3) and (4), a wheeled motor vehicle or trailer a wheel of which is fitted with a pneumatic tyre shall not be used on a road, if—

    (a) the tyre is unsuitable having regard to the use to which the motor vehicle or trailer is being put or to the types of tyres fitted to its other wheels;

    (b) the tyre is not so inflated as to make it fit for the use to which the motor vehicle or trailer is being put;

    (c) the tyre has a cut in excess of 25mm or 10% of the section width of the tyre, whichever is the greater, measured in any direction on the outside of the tyre and deep enough to reach the ply or cord;

    (d) the tyre has any lump, bulge or tear caused by separation or partial failure of its structure;

    (e) the tyre has any of the ply or cord exposed;

    (f) the base of any groove which showed in the original tread pattern of the tyre is not clearly visible;

    (g) either—

        (i) the grooves of the tread pattern of the tyre do not have a depth of at least 1mm throughout a continuous band measuring at least three-quarters of the breadth of the tread and round the entire outer circumference of the tyre; or

        (ii) if the grooves of the original tread pattern of the tyre did not extend beyond three-quarters of the breadth of the tread, any groove which showed in the original tread pattern does not have a depth of at least 1mm; or

    (h) the tyre is not maintained in such condition as to be fit for the use to which the vehicle or trailer is being put or has a defect which might in any way cause damage to the surface of the road or damage to persons on or in the vehicle or to other persons using the road.

(2) Paragraph (1) does not prohibit the use on a road of a motor vehicle or trailer by reason only of the fact that a wheel of the vehicle or trailer is fitted with a tyre which is deflated or not fully inflated and which has any of the defects described in sub-paragraph (c), (d) or (e) of paragraph (1), if the tyre and the wheel to which it is fitted are so constructed as to make the tyre in that condition fit for the use to which the motor vehicle or trailer is being put and the outer sides of the wall of the tyre are so marked as to enable the tyre to be identified as having been constructed to comply with the requirements of this paragraph.

(3) Paragraph (1)(a) does not prohibit the use on a road of a passenger vehicle (not being a bus) by reason only of the fact that a wheel of the vehicle is fitted with a temporary use spare tyre, unless the vehicle is driven at a speed exceeding 50mph.

(4) (a) Nothing in paragraph (1)(a) to (g) applies to—

        (i) an agricultural motor vehicle that is not driven at more than 20mph;

        (ii) an agricultural trailer;

        (iii) an agricultural trailed appliance; or

        (iv) a broken down vehicle or a vehicle proceeding to a place where it is to be broken up, being drawn, in either case, by a motor vehicle at a speed not exceeding 20mph.

   (b) Nothing in paragraph (1)(f) and (g) applies to—
      (i) a three-wheeled motor cycle the unladen weight of which does
          not exceed 102kg and which has a maximum speed of 12mph; or
      (ii) a pedestrian-controlled works truck.
   (c) Nothing in paragraph (1)(g) applies to a motor cycle with an engine
       capacity which does not exceed 50cc.
   [(d) With effect from 1st January 1992, paragraph 1(f) and (g) shall not
       apply to the vehicles specified in sub-paragraph (e) of this paragraph
       but such vehicles shall comply with the requirements specified in sub-
       paragraph (f) of this paragraph.]
   [(e) The vehicles mentioned in sub-paragraph (d) are—
      (i) passenger vehicles other than motor cycles constructed or
          adapted to carry no more than 8 seated passengers in addition to
          the driver;
      (ii) goods vehicles with a maximum gross weight which [does] not
           exceed 3500kg; and
      (iii) light trailers not falling within sub-paragraph (ii);
      first used on or after 3rd January 1933.]
   [(f) The requirements referred to in sub-paragraph (d) are that the grooves
       of the tread pattern of every tyre fitted to the wheels of a vehicle
       mentioned in sub-paragraph (e) shall be of a depth of at least 1.6mm
       throughout a continuous band [comprising] the central three-quarters
       of the breadth of tread and round the entire outer circumference of the
       tyre.]

(5) A recut pneumatic tyre shall not be fitted to any wheel of a motor vehicle
or trailer if—
   (a) its ply or cord has been cut or exposed by the recutting process; or
   (b) it has been wholly or partially recut in a pattern other than the
       manufacturer's recut tread pattern.

(6) (a) In this regulation—
   "breadth of tread" means the breadth of that part of the tyre which can
       contact the road under normal conditions of use measured at 90
       degrees to the peripheral line of the tread;
   "original tread pattern" means in the case of—
              a re-treaded tyre, the tread pattern of the tyre immediately af-
              ter the tyre was re-treaded;
              a wholly recut tyre, the manufacturer's recut tread pattern;
              a partially recut tyre, on that part of the tyre which has been
              recut, the manufacturer's recut tread pattern, and on the other
              part, the tread pattern of the tyre when new; and
              any other tyre, the tread pattern of the tyre when the tyre was
              new;
   "tie-bar" means any part of a tyre moulded in the tread pattern of the tyre
       for the purpose of bracing two or more features of such tread pattern;
   "tread pattern" means the combination of plain surfaces and grooves
       extending across the breadth of the tread and round the entire outer
       circumference of the tyre but excludes any—

(i) tie-bars or tread wear indicators;

(ii) features which are designed to wear out substantially before the rest of the pattern under normal conditions of use; and

(iii) other minor features; and

"tread wear indicator" means any bar, not being a tie-bar, projecting from the base of a groove of the tread pattern of a tyre and moulded between two or more features of the tread pattern of a tyre for the purpose of indicating the extent of the wear of such tread pattern.

(b) The references in [this regulation] to grooves are references—

if a tyre has been recut, to the grooves of the manufacturer's recut tread pattern; and

if a tyre has not been recut, to the grooves which showed when the tyre was new.

[(c) A reference in this regulation to first use shall, in relation to a trailer, be construed as a reference to the date which is 6 months after the date of manufacture of the trailer.]

[Regulation 27 is printed as amended by SI 1990/1981; SI 1991/2710.]   **B15.65**

Tracks

28.—(1) Every part of every track of a track-laying vehicle which comes into   **B15.66**
contact with the road shall be flat and have a width of not less than 12.5mm.

(2) The area of the track which is in contact with the road shall not at any time be less than 225cm^2 in respect of every 1000kg of the total weight which is transferred to the roads by the tracks.

(3) The tracks of a vehicle shall not have any defect which might damage the road or cause danger to any person on or in the vehicle or using the road, and shall be properly adjusted and maintained in good and efficient working order.

D Steering

Maintenance of steering gear

29. All steering gear fitted to a motor vehicle shall at all times while the vehi-   **B15.67**
cle is used on a road be maintained in good and efficient working order and be properly adjusted.

E Vision

View to the front

30.—(1) Every motor vehicle shall be so designed and constructed that the   **B15.68**
driver thereof while controlling the vehicle can at all times have a full view of the road and traffic ahead of the motor vehicle.

(2) Instead of complying with the requirement of paragraph (1) a vehicle may comply with Community Directive 77/649, 81/643 [, 88/366, 90/630] or, in the case of an agricultural motor vehicle, 79/1073.

(3) All glass or other transparent material fitted to a motor vehicle shall be maintained in such condition that it does not obscure the vision of the driver while the vehicle is being driven on a road.

[Regulation 30 is printed as amended by SI 1991/2003.]

Glass

B15.70 **31.**—(1) This regulation applies to a motor vehicle which is—

 (a) a wheeled vehicle, not being a caravan, first used before 1st June 1978;

 (b) a caravan first used before 1st September 1978; or

 (c) a track-laying vehicle.

(2) The glass fitted to any window specified in an item in column 3 of the Table of a vehicle of a class specified in that item in column 2 shall be safety glass.

Table

(regulation 31(2))

1	2	3
Item	Class of vehicle	Windows
1	Wheeled vehicles first used on or after 1st January 1959, being passenger vehicles or dual-purpose vehicles.	Windscreens and all outside windows.
2	Wheeled vehicles first used on or after 1st January 1959, being goods vehicles (other than dual-purpose vehicles), locomotives or motor tractors.	Windscreens and all windows in front of and on either side of the driver's seat.
3	Wheeled vehicles not mentioned in item 1 or 2.	Windscreens and windows facing to the front on the outside, except glass fitted to the upper decks of a double-decked vehicle.
4	Track-laying vehicles.	Windscreens and windows facing to the front.

(3) For the purposes of this regulation any windscreen or window at the front of the vehicle the inner surface of which is at an angle exceeding 30 degrees to the longitudinal axis of the vehicle shall be deemed to face to the front.

[(4) In this regulation and in regulation 32 —

 "caravan" means a trailer which is constructed (and not merely adapted) for human habitation; and

 [*"designated approval mark"* means the marking designated as an approval mark by Regulation 5 of the Approval Marks Regulations and shown at item 31 or 32 in Schedule 4 to those Regulations (those items being markings relating to Community Directive 92/22) ; and]

 "safety glass" means glass so constructed or treated if fractured it does not fly into fragments likely to cause severe cuts.]

[(5) Paragraph (2) does not apply to glass which is legibly and permanently marked with a designated approval mark.]

B15.71 *[Regulation 31 is printed as amended by SI 1987/676; SI 1992/3088.]*

32.—(1) This regulation applies to—

    (a) a caravan first used on or after 1st September 1978, and

    (b) a wheeled motor vehicle and a wheeled trailer, not being a caravan, first used on or after 1st June 1978.

(2) Save as provided in paragraphs (3) to (9) the windows specified in column 2 of Table I in relation to a vehicle of a class specified in that column shall be constructed of the material specified in column 3 of the Table.

TABLE I

(regulation 32(2))

1	*2*	*3*
Item	*Window*	*Material*
1	Windscreens and other windows wholly or partly on either side of the driver's seat fitted to motor vehicles first used on or after 1st April 1985.	Specified safety glass (1980).
2	Windscreens and other windows wholly or partly on either side of the driver's seat fitted to a motor vehicle first used before 1st April 1985.	Specified safety glass, or specified safety glass (1980).
3	All other windows.	Specified safety glass, specified safety glass (1980), or safety glazing.

(3) The windscreens and all other windows of security vehicles or vehicles being used for police purposes shall not be subject to the requirements specified in paragraph (2), but shall be constructed of either safety glass or safety glazing.

(4) The windscreens of motor cycles not equipped with an enclosed compartment for the driver or for a passenger shall not be subject to the requirements specified in paragraph (2), but shall be constructed of safety glazing.

(5) Any windscreens or other windows which are wholly or partly in front of or on either side of the driver's seat, and which are temporarily fitted to motor vehicles to replace any windscreens or other windows which have broken, shall—

    (a) be constructed of safety glazing; and

    (b) be fitted only while the vehicles are being driven or towed either to premises where new windscreens or other windows are to be permanently fitted to replace the windscreens or other windows which have broken, or to complete the journey in the course of which the breakage occurred.

(6) Windows forming all or part of a screen or door in the interior of a bus first used on or after 1st April 1988, shall be constructed either of safety glazing or of specified safety glass (1980).

(7) Windows being—

    (a) windows (other than windscreens) of motor vehicles being engineering plant, industrial tractors, agricultural motor vehicles (other than agricultural motor vehicles first used on or after 1st June 1986 and driven at more than 20mph) which are wholly or partly in front of or on either side of the driver's seat;

(b) windows of the upper deck of a double-decked bus; or

(c) windows in the roof of a vehicle,

shall be constructed of either specified safety glass, specified safety glass (1980) or safety glazing.

(8) In the case of motor vehicles and trailers which have not at any time been fitted with permanent windows and which are being driven or towed to a place where permanent windows are to be fitted, any temporary windscreens and any other temporary windows shall be constructed of either specified safety glass, specified safety glass (1980) or safety glazing.

(9) No requirement in this regulation that a windscreen or other window shall be constructed of specified safety glass or of specified safety glass (1980) shall apply to a windscreen or other window which is—

(a) manufactured in France;

(b) marked with a marking consisting of the letters "TP GS" or "TP GSE"; and

(c) fitted to a vehicle first used before 1st October 1986.

(10) Save as provided in paragraph (11), the windscreens or other windows constructed in accordance with the foregoing provisions of this regulation of specified safety glass, specified safety glass (1980) or safety glazing and specified in column 3 of Table II in relation to a vehicle of a class specified in column 2 of that Table shall have a visual transmission for light of not less than the percentage specified in relation to those windows in column 4 when measured perpendicular to the surface in accordance with the procedure specified in a document specified in relation to those windows in column 5.

TABLE II

(regulation 32(10))

1	2	3	4	5
Item	Class of vehicle	Windows	Percentage	Documents specifying procedure
1	Motor vehicles first used before 1st April 1985	All windows	70	British Standard Specification No.857 or No.5282
2	Motor vehicles first used on or after 1st April 1985 and trailers	(a) Windscreens	75	The documents mentioned in sub-paragraph (i), (ii) or (iii) of the definition in paragraph (13) of "specified safety glass (1980)".
		(b) All other windows	70	

(11) Paragraph (10) does not apply to—

(a) any part of any windscreen which is outside the vision reference zone;

(b) windows through which the driver when in the driver's seat is unable at any time to see any part of the road on which the vehicle is waiting or proceeding;

  (c) windows in any motor ambulance which are not wholly or partly in front of or on either side of any part of the driver's seat; or

  (d) windows in any bus, goods vehicle, locomotive, or motor tractor other than windows which—

    (i) are wholly or partly in front of or on either side of any part of the driver's seat;

    (ii) face the rear of the vehicle; or

    (iii) form the whole or part of a door giving access to or from the exterior of the vehicle.

[(11A) Paragraphs (10) and (11) have effect in relation to any tint, film or other substance or material applied to a windscreen or window as they have effect in relation to the windscreen or window itself.]

(12) For the purposes of this regulation any window at the rear of the vehicle is deemed to face the rear of the vehicle if the inner surface of such window is at an angle exceeding 30 degrees to the longitudinal axis of the vehicle.

[(12A) Paragraphs (2), (6), (7) and (8) do not apply to a window which is legibly and permanently marked with a designated approval mark.]

[(12B) Paragraph (10) does not apply to a window if—

  (a) it is a window to which paragraph 12C applies and is legibly and permanently marked with a designated approval mark which does not comprise the Roman numeral "V" (other than as part of the combination "VI"); or

  (b) it is not a window to which paragraph 12C applies and is legibly and permanently marked with a designated approval mark.]

[(12C) This paragraph applies to a side or rear window if—

  (a) any part of it is on either side of or forward of the driver's seat; or

  (b) any part of it is within the driver's indirect field of view obtained by means of the mirror or mirrors which are required to be fitted by regulation 33 when such mirrors are properly adjusted;

and for the purposes of this paragraph a mirror shall not be regarded as being required to be fitted by regulation 33 if, were it to be removed, the vehicle would nevertheless meet the requirements of regulation 33.]

(13) In this regulation, unless the context otherwise requires—

  "British Standard Specification No.857" means the British Standard Specification for Safety Glass for Land Transport published on 30th June 1967 under the number BS 857 as amended by Amendment Slip No.1 published on 15th January 1973 under the number AMD 1088;

  "British Standard Specification No.5282" means the British Standard Specification for Road Vehicle Safety Glass published in December 1975 under the number BS 5282 as amended by Amendment Slip No.1 published on 31st March 1976 under the number AMD 1927, and as amended by Amendment Slip No.2 published on 31st January 1977 under the number AMD 2185;

  "British Standard Specification BS AU 178" means the British Standard

Specification for Road Vehicle Safety Glass published on 28th November 1980 under the number BS AU 178;

...

[*"designated approval mark"* means—

    (a) in relation to a windscreen, the marking designated as an approval mark by regulation 5 of the Approval Marks Regulations and shown at item 31 in Schedule 4 to those Regulations, and

    (b) in relation to a window other than a windscreen, the markings designated as approval marks by regulation 5 of those Regulations and shown at item 32 in Schedule 4 to those Regulations.]

"safety glazing" means material (other than glass) which is so constructed or treated that if fractured it does not fly into fragments likely to cause severe cuts;

"security vehicle" means a motor vehicle which is constructed (and not merely adapted) for the carriage of either—

    (i) persons who are likely to require protection from any criminal offence involving violence; or

    (ii) dangerous substances, bullion, money, jewellery, documents or other goods or burden which, by reason of their nature or value, are likely to require protection from any criminal offence;

"specified safety glass" means glass complying with the requirements of either—

    (i) British Standard Specification No.857 (including the requirements as to marking); or

    (ii) British Standard Specification No.5282 (including the requirements as to marking);

"specified safety glass (1980)" means glass complying with the requirements of either—

    (i) the British Standard Specification for Safety Glass for Land Transport published on 30th June 1967 under the number BS 857 as amended by Amendment Slip No.1 published on 15th January 1973 under the number AMD 1088, Amendment Slip No.2 published on 30th September 1980 under the number AMD 3402, and Amendment Slip 4 published on 15th February 1981 under the number AMD 3548 (including the requirements as to marking); or

    (ii) British Standard Specification BS AU 178 (including the requirements as to marking); or

    (iii) ECE Regulation 43 (including the requirements as to marking);

"vision reference zone" means either—

    (i) the primary vision area as defined in British Standard Specification No.857;

    (ii) Zone 1, as defined in British Standard Specification No.5282;

(iii) Zone B (as regards passenger vehicles other than buses) and Zone 1 (as regards all other vehicles) as defined in British Standard Specification BS AU 178 and in ECE Regulation 43; and

"windscreen" includes a windshield.

[Regulation 32 is printed as amended by SI 1987/676; SI 1992/3088; SI 2003/ 3145.   **B15.73**

As to the application of the provisions of reg.32 to vehicles in respect of which approval certificates have been issued under the "Approval Regulations", see Sch.2A, para.3, to these regulations.]

[Mirrors and other devices for indirect vision

33.—(1) Save as provided in [paragraphs (5) to (6H)], a motor vehicle (not be-   **B15.74** ing a road roller) which is of a class specified in an item in column 2 of the Table shall be fitted with such mirror or mirrors or other device for indirect vision, if any, as are specified in that item in column 3; and any mirror or other device for indirect vision which is fitted to such a vehicle shall, whether or not it is required to be fitted, comply with the requirements, if any, specified in that item in columns 4 and 5.

(2) Save as provided in paragraph (5), each exterior mirror with which a vehicle is required to be fitted in accordance with item 2 or 8 of the Table shall, if the vehicle has a technically permissible maximum weight (as mentioned in Annex 1 to Community Directive 71/127) exceeding 3500 kg, be a Class II mirror (as described in that Annex) and shall in any other case be a Class II or a Class III mirror (as described in that Annex).

(3) Save as provided in paragraph (5), in the case of a wheeled motor vehicle described in item 1, 2, 10 or 11 of the Table which is first used on or after 1st April 1969 the edges of any interior mirror shall be surrounded by some material such as will render it unlikely that severe cuts would be caused if the mirror or that material were struck by any occupant of the vehicle.

(4) Save as provided in paragraph (5), in the case of a motor vehicle falling within paragraph (a) in column 4 of items 1 and 7, or within item 8, of the Table—

(a) each mirror shall be fixed to the vehicle in such a way that it remains steady under normal driving conditions;

(b) each exterior mirror on a vehicle fitted with windows and a windscreen shall be visible to the driver, when in his driving position, through a side window or through the portion of the windscreen which is swept by the windscreen wiper;

(c) where the bottom edge of an exterior mirror is less than 2 m above the road surface when the vehicle is laden, that mirror shall not project more than 20 cm beyond the overall width of the vehicle or, in a case where the vehicle is drawing a trailer which has an overall width greater than that of the drawing vehicle, more than 20 cm beyond the overall width of the trailer;

(d) where the bottom edge of an exterior mirror, which complies with the requirements of Community Directive 2003/97 or 2005/27 or ECE Regulation 46.02, is less than 2 m above the road surface when the vehicle is laden, that mirror shall not project more than 25 cm beyond the overall width of the vehicle or, in the case where the vehicle is drawing a trailer which has an overall width greater than that of the drawing vehicle, more than 25 cm beyond the overall width of the trailer;

(e) each interior mirror shall be capable of being adjusted by the driver when in his driving position; and

(f) except in the case of a mirror which, if knocked out of its alignment, can be returned to its former position without needing to be adjusted, each exterior mirror on the driver's side of the vehicle shall be capable of being adjusted by the driver when in his driving position, but this requirement shall not prevent such a mirror from being locked into position from the outside of the vehicle.

(5) Instead of complying with paragraphs (1) to (4) a vehicle may comply—

(a) if it is a goods vehicle with a maximum gross weight exceeding 3500kg first used on or after 1st April 1985 and before 1st August 1989, with Community Directive 79/795, 85/205[, 86/562 or 88/321 or ECE Regulation 46.01];

(b) if it is a goods vehicle first used on or after 1st August 1989 and before 26th January 2007—

(i) in the case of a vehicle with a maximum gross weight exceeding 3500kg but not exceeding 12,000kg with Community Directive 79/795, 85/205[, 86/562 or 88/321 or ECE Regulation 46.01]; and

(ii) in the case of a vehicle with a maximum gross weight exceeding 12,000kg with Community Directive 85/205[, 86/562 or 88/321 or ECE Regulation 46.01];

(c) if it is an agricultural motor vehicle with Community Directive 71/127, 74/346, 79/795, 85/205[, 86/562 or 88/321 or ECE Regulation 46.01];

(d) if it is a two-wheeled motor cycle with or without a side-car with Community Directive 71/127, 79/795, 80/780, 85/205[, 86/562 or 88/321 or ECE Regulation 46.01]; and

(e) if it is any other vehicle with Community Directive 71/127, 79/795, 85/205[, 86/562 or 88/321 or ECE Regulation 46.01].]

(6) Instead of complying with the provisions of column 4 in items 3, 4, 7 or 8 of the Table a mirror may comply with the requirements as to construction and testing set out either in—

(a) Annex I to Community Directive 71/127, excluding paragraphs 2.3.4 and 2.6;

(b) Annex I to Community Directive 79/795, excluding paragraphs 2.3.3 and 2.6;

(c) Annex II to Community Directive 2003/97, excluding paragraph 3.4; or

(d) Annex II to Community Directive 2005/27, excluding paragraph 3.4.

[(6A) The requirements set out in paragraph (1) and the Table are modified as set out in paragraphs (6C) and (6D) in so far as those requirements relate to a relevant vehicle and to the fitting of class IV and class V mirrors on the passenger's side of that vehicle.

(6B) The alternative requirements set out in paragraph (5) do not apply in so far as those requirements relate to a relevant vehicle and to the fitting of class IV and class V mirrors on the passenger's side of the vehicle.

(6C) Subject to paragraph (6F), a relevant vehicle which would otherwise be required to meet the requirements set out in item 3 of the Table shall instead meet the requirements set out in item 4 which are applicable to a vehicle of the same maximum gross weight.

(6D) Subject to paragraph (6F), a relevant vehicle which would otherwise be required to meet the requirements set out in item 5 of the Table shall instead meet the requirements set out in item 6.

(6E) For the purposes of paragraphs (6C) and (6D)—

    (a) the words "and other devices for indirect vision" are omitted from item 4; and

    (b) the words "or other devices for indirect vision" are omitted from items 4 and 6.

(6F) A relevant vehicle does not have to comply with paragraph (6C) or (6D) (whichever is applicable to the vehicle) in the circumstances set out in paragraph (6G) or (6H).

(6G) The first set of circumstances is where the vehicle is equipped in the manner described in article 3(2) of Community Directive 2007/38.

(6H) The second set of circumstances is where the vehicle cannot, for want of available, economically viable, technical solutions—

    (a) comply with paragraph (6C) or (6D) (whichever is applicable to the vehicle); or

    (b) be equipped in the manner described in article 3(2) of Community Directive 2007/38,

but is equipped in the manner described in article 3(3) of Community Directive 2007/38.]

(7) In this regulation—

    (a) *"devices for indirect vision"* mean devices to observe the traffic area adjacent to the vehicle which cannot be observed by direct vision and may include conventional mirrors, camera-monitors or other devices able to present information about the indirect field of vision to the driver;

    (b) *"mirror"* means any device with a reflecting surface, excluding devices such as periscopes, intended to give a clear view to the rear, side or front of the vehicle;

    (c) *"interior mirror"* means a device defined in sub-paragraph (a), which can be fitted in the passenger compartment of a vehicle;

    (d) *"exterior mirror"* means a device defined in sub-paragraph (a), which can be fitted on the external surface of a vehicle;

    [(e) *"class IV"* and *"class V"*, in relation to mirrors, have the meanings given in point 1.1.1.14 of Annex I to Community Directive 2003/97; and

    (f) *"a relevant vehicle"* means a vehicle which—

(i) would be a goods vehicle of a class referred to in column 2 of item 4 or 6 of the Table if "1st January 2000" were substituted for "26th January 2007"; and

(ii) is not outside the scope of Community Directive 2007/38 by virtue of article 2(2)(b) or (c) of that Directive.]

(8) In the case of—

(a) an agricultural motor vehicle, or

(b) a vehicle described in items 2 or 8 in the Table,

when drawing a trailer the references to a vehicle in the definitions in paragraph (7) shall be construed as including references to that trailer.

[(9) Where a provision is applied by paragraph (6C) or (6D) to a vehicle which was first used on or after 1st January 2000, that provision applies to the vehicle whatever the date of manufacture of the vehicle, and regulation 4(2) is disapplied accordingly.]

TABLE

(regulation 33(1))

1	2	3	4	5
Item	*Class of vehicle*	*Mirrors or other devices for indirect vision to be fitted*	*Requirements to be complied with by any mirrors fitted*	*Requirements to be complied with by any other devices for indirect vision where fitted*
1.	A motor vehicle which is— (a) drawing a trailer, if a person is carried on the trailer so that he has an uninterrupted view to the rear and has an efficient means of communicating to the driver the effect of signals given by the drivers of other vehicles to the rear; (b) (i) a works truck; (ii) a track-laying agricultural motor vehicle; and (iii) a wheeled agricultural motor vehicle first used before 1st June 1978, if, in each case, the driver can easily obtain a view to the rear; (c) a pedestrian-controlled vehicle;	No requirement.	(a) If the vehicle is a wheeled vehicle first used on or after 1st June 1978, Item 2 of Annex I to Community Directive 71/127 or 79/795 or Annex II to Community Directive 86/562 or 88/321 or paragraphs 4 to 8 of ECE Regulation 46.01 and paragraph (4) of this regulation. (b) In other cases, none, except as specified in paragraph (3).	None

1	2	3	4	5
Item	Class of vehicle	Mirrors or other devices for indirect vision to be fitted	Requirements to be complied with by any mirrors fitted	Requirements to be complied with by any other devices for indirect vision where fitted

	(d) a chassis being driven from the place where it has been manufactured to the place where it is to receive a vehicle body; or
	
	(e) an agricultural motor vehicle which has an unladen weight exceeding 7370 kg and which—
	  (i) is a track-laying vehicle or
	  (ii) is a wheeled vehicle first used before 1st June 1978.			

1	2	3	4	5
Item	Class of vehicle	Mirrors or other devices for indirect vision to be fitted	Requirements to be complied with by any mirrors fitted	Requirements to be complied with by any other devices for indirect vision where fitted
2.	A motor vehicle not included in item 1, which is— (a) a wheeled locomotive or a wheeled motor tractor first used in either case on or after 1st June 1978; (b) an agricultural motor vehicle, not being a track-laying vehicle with an unladen weight not exceeding 7370 kg (which falls in item 11) or a wheeled agricultural motor vehicle first used after 1st June 1986 which is driven at more than 20 mph (which falls in item 8); or (c) a works truck.	At least one exterior mirror fitted on the offside.	None, except as specified in paragraphs (2) and (3).	None.

1	2	3	4	5
Item	*Class of vehicle*	*Mirrors or other devices for indirect vision to be fitted*	*Requirements to be complied with by any mirrors fitted*	*Requirements to be complied with by any other devices for indirect vision where fitted*
3.	A wheeled motor vehicle not included in items 1 or 4 first used on or after 1st April 1983 which is— (a) a bus; or (b) a goods vehicle with a maximum gross weight exceeding 3500 kg (not being an agricultural motor vehicle or one which is not driven at more than 20 mph) other than a vehicle described in item 5.	Mirrors complying with item 3 of Annex I to Community Directive 79/795 or with paragraph 2.1 of Annex III to Community Directive 86/562 or 88/321 or paragraph 16.2.1 of ECE Regulation 46.01 or, except in the case of a goods vehicle first used on or after 1st April 1985, mirrors as required in the entry in this column in item 8.	Item 2 of Annex I to Community Directive 71/127 or 79/795 or Annex II to Community Directive 86/562 or 88/321 or paragraphs 4 to 8 of ECE Regulation 46.01.	None.

1	2	3	4	5
Item	Class of vehicle	Mirrors or other devices for indirect vision to be fitted	Requirements to be complied with by any mirrors fitted	Requirements to be complied with by any other devices for indirect vision where fitted

4.	A wheeled motor vehicle not included in item 1 first used on or after 26th January 2007 which is—
	
	(a) a bus;
	(b) a goods vehicle with a maximum gross weight—
	  (i) exceeding 3500 kg but not exceeding 7500 kg; or
	  (ii) exceeding 7500 kg but not exceeding 12,000 kg;
	  (not being an agricultural motor vehicle or one which is not driven at more than 20 mph).
		(a) and (b)(ii) Mirrors and other devices for indirect vision complying with Annex III to Community Directive 2003/97 or 2005/27 or paragraph 15 of ECE Regulation 46.02.
		(b)(i) Mirrors or other devices for indirect vision complying with Community Directive 2005/27.
			Paragraph 6 of Annex I and Annex II to Community Directive 2003/97 or 2005/27 or paragraphs 4, 5 and 6.1 of ECE Regulation 46.02.	Part B of Annex II to Community Directive 2003/97 or paragraph 4, 5 and 6.2 of ECE Regulation 46.02.

5.	A goods vehicle not being an agricultural motor vehicle with a maximum gross weight exceeding 12,000 kg which is first used on or after 1st October 1988 and before 26th January 2007.	Mirrors complying with paragraph 2.1 of Annex III to Community Directive 86/562 or 88/321 or paragraph 16.2.1 of ECE Regulation 46.01.	Annex II to Community Directive 86/562 or 88/321 or paragraphs 4 to 8 of ECE Regulation 46.01.	None

1	2	3	4	5
Item	Class of vehicle	Mirrors or other devices for indirect vision to be fitted	Requirements to be complied with by any mirrors fitted	Requirements to be complied with by any other devices for indirect vision where fitted
6.	A goods vehicle not being an agricultural motor vehicle with a maximum gross weight exceeding 12,000 kg which is first used on or after 26th January 2007.	Mirrors or other devices for indirect vision complying with Annex III to Community Directive 2003/97 or 2005/27 or paragraph 15 of ECE Regulation 46.02.	Paragraph 6 of Annex I and Annex II to Community Directive 2003/97 or 2005/27 or paragraphs 4, 5 and 6.1 of ECE Regulation 46.02.	Part B of Annex II to Community Directive 2003/97 or paragraph 4, 5 and 6.2 of ECE Regulation 46.02.
7.	A two-wheeled motor cycle with or without a sidecar attached.	No requirement.	(a) If the vehicle is first used on or after 1st October 1978, Item 2 of Annex I to Community Directive 71/127, 79/795 or 80/780 or Annex II to Community Directive 86/562 or 88/321 or paragraphs 4 to 8 of ECE Regulation 46.01 and paragraph (4) of this regulation. (b) In other cases, none.	None.

1	2	3	4	5
Item	Class of vehicle	Mirrors or other devices for indirect vision to be fitted	Requirements to be complied with by any mirrors fitted	Requirements to be complied with by any other devices for indirect vision where fitted
8.	A wheeled motor vehicle not in items 1 to 7, which is first used on or after 1st June 1978 (or, in the case of a Ford Transit motor car, 10th July 1978) and before 26th January 2010.	(i) At least one exterior mirror fitted on the offside of the vehicle; and (ii) at least one interior mirror, unless a mirror so fitted would give the driver no view to the rear of the vehicle; and (iii) at least one exterior mirror fitted on the nearside of the vehicle unless an interior mirror gives the driver an adequate view to the rear.	Item 2 of Annex I to Community Directive 71/127 or 79/795 or Annex II to Community Directive 86/562 or 88/321 or paragraphs 4 to 8 of ECE Regulation 46.01 and paragraphs (2) and (4) of this regulation.	None.
9.	A wheeled motor vehicle not in items 1 to 7, which is first used on or after 26th January 2010.	Mirrors complying with Annex III to Community Directive 2003/97 or 2005/27 or paragraph 15 of ECE Regulation 46.02.	Paragraph 6 of Annex I and Annex II to Community Directive 2003/97 or 2005/27 or paragraphs 4, 5 and 6.1 of ECE Regulation 46.02.	If fitted to comply with Part B of Annex II to Community Directive 2003/97 or paragraphs 4, 5 and 6.2 of ECE Regulation 46.02.

1	2	3	4	5
Item	Class of vehicle	Mirrors or other devices for indirect vision to be fitted	Requirements to be complied with by any mirrors fitted	Requirements to be complied with by any other devices for indirect vision where fitted
10.	A wheeled motor vehicle, not in items 1 to 7, first used before 1st June 1978 (or in the case of a Ford Transit motor car, 10th July 1978) and a track-laying motor vehicle which is not an agricultural motor vehicle first used on or after 1st January 1958, which in either case is— (a) a bus; (b) a dual-purpose vehicle; or (c) a goods vehicle.	At least one exterior mirror fitted on the offside of the vehicle and either one interior mirror or one exterior mirror fitted on the near-side of the vehicle.	None, except as specified in paragraph (3).	None.
11.	A motor vehicle, whether wheeled or track-laying, not in items 1 to 10.	At least one interior or exterior mirror.	None, except as specified in paragraph (3).	None.]

B15.75   [*Regulation 33 is printed as inserted by SI 2005/3165; SI 2009/142.*

The explanatory note which accompanies SI 2009/142 stated that the instrument gives effect to ECE Regulations 52.01, 107.01 and 107.02 (construction requirements for minibuses and coaches) and also implements Directive 2007/38/EC (O.J. No.L184, July 14, 2007, p.25) in respect of provisions imposing requirements as to the fitting of mirrors. SI 2009/142 also removes time-expired provisions relating to the speed limiter requirements for passenger-carrying vehicles and goods vehicles.

As to the application of the provisions of reg.33 to vehicles in respect of which approval certificates have been issued under the "Approval Regulations", see Sch.2A, para.4, to these regulations.]

Windscreen wipers and washers

B15.76   **34.**—(1) Subject to paragraphs (4) and (5), every vehicle fitted with a windscreen shall, unless the driver can obtain an adequate view to the front of the vehicle without looking through the windscreen, be fitted with one or more efficient automatic windscreen wipers capable of clearing the windscreen so that the driver has an adequate view of the road in front of both sides of the vehicle and to the front of the vehicle.

(2) Save as provided in paragraphs (3), (4) and (5), every wheeled vehicle required by paragraph (1) to be fitted with a wiper or wipers shall also be fitted with a windscreen washer capable of cleaning, in conjunction with the windscreen wiper, the area of the windscreen swept by the wiper of mud or similar deposit.

(3) The requirement specified in paragraph (2) does not apply in respect of—

(a) an agricultural motor vehicle (other than a vehicle first used on or after 1st June 1986 which is driven at more than 20mph);

(b) a track-laying vehicle;

(c) a vehicle having a maximum speed not exceeding 20mph; or

(d) a vehicle being used to provide a local service, as defined in the Transport Act 1985.

(4) Instead of complying with paragraphs (1) and (2), a vehicle may comply with Community Directive 78/318.

(5) Instead of complying with paragraph (1) an agricultural motor vehicle may comply with Community Directive 79/1073.

(6) Every wiper and washer fitted in accordance with this regulation shall at all times while a vehicle is being used on a road be maintained in efficient working order and be properly adjusted.

F Instruments and Equipment

Speedometers

35.—(1) Save as provided in paragraphs (2) and (3), every motor vehicle shall **B15.77** be fitted with a speedometer which, if the vehicle is first used on or after 1st April 1984, shall be capable of indicating speed in both miles per hour and kilometers per hour, either simultaneously or, by the operation of a switch, separately.

(2) Paragraph (1) does not apply to—

(a) a vehicle having a maximum speed not exceeding 25mph;

(b) a vehicle which is at all times unlawful to drive at more than 25mph;

(c) an agricultural motor vehicle which is not driven at more than 20mph;

(d) a motor cycle first used before 1st April 1984 the engine of which has a cylinder capacity not exceeding 100cc;

(e) an invalid carriage first used before 1st April 1984;

(f) a works truck first used before 1st April 1984;

(g) a vehicle first used before 1st October 1937; or

(h) a vehicle equipped with recording equipment marked with a marking designated as an approval mark by regulation 5 of the Approval Marks Regulations and shown at item 3 in Schedule 4 to those Regulations (whether or not the vehicle is required to be equipped with that equipment) and which, as regards the visual indications given by that equipment of the speed of the vehicle, complies with the requirements relating to the said indications and installations specified in the Community Recording Equipment Regulation.

(3) Instead of complying with paragraph (1) a vehicle may comply with [Community Directive 97/39 [*O.J. No.L177, July 3, 1997, p.1*]] or with ECE Regulation 39.

B15.78   *[Regulation 35 is printed as amended by SI 1998/1188.*

As to the application of the provisions of reg.35 to vehicles in respect of which approval certificates have been issued under the "Approval Regulations", see Sch.2A, para.5, to these regulations.]

Maintenance of speedometers

B15.79   36.—(1) Every instrument for indicating speed fitted to a motor vehicle—

     (a) in compliance with the requirements of regulation 35(1) or (3); or

     (b) to which regulation 35(2)(h) relates and which is not, under the Community Recording Equipment Regulation, required to be equipped with the recording equipment mentioned in that paragraph,

shall be kept free from any obstruction which might prevent it being easily read and shall at all material times be maintained in good working order.

(2) In this regulation *"all material times"* means all times when the motor vehicle is in use on a road except when—

     (a) the vehicle is being used on a journey during which, as a result of a defect, the instrument ceased to be in good working order; or

     (b) as a result of a defect, the instrument has ceased to be in good working order and steps have been taken to have the vehicle equipped with all reasonable expedition, by means of repairs or replacement, with an instrument which is in good working order.

[Speed limiters

B15.80   36A.—[(1) Subject to paragraph (13), this regulation applies to every coach which—

     (a) was first used on or after 1st April 1974 and before 1st January 1988; and

     (b) has, or if a speed limiter were not fitted to it would have, a maximum speed exceeding [112.65 km/h];

and a reference to this regulation to a paragraph (1) vehicle is a reference to a vehicle to which this regulation applies by virtue of this paragraph.

(2) Subject to paragraph (13), this regulation also applies to every bus which—

     (a) is first used on or after 1st January 1988;

     (b) has a maximum gross weight exceeding 7.5 tonnes; and

     (c) has, or if a speed limiter were not fitted to it would have, a maximum speed exceeding [100 km/h];

and a reference in this regulation to a paragraph (2) vehicle is a reference to a vehicle to which this regulation applies by virtue of this paragraph.

[(2A) Subject to paragraph (13), this regulation also applies to every bus, not being a bus to which paragraph (2) applies, which—

     (a) is first used on or after 1st January 2005;

     (b) has a maximum gross weight exceeding 5 tonnes but not exceeding 10 tonnes; and

(c) has, or if a speed limiter were not fitted to it would have, a maximum speed exceeding 100 km/h;

and a reference in this regulation to a paragraph (2A) vehicle is a reference to a vehicle to which this regulation applies by virtue of this paragraph.]

[(2B) Subject to [paragraph 13], this regulation also applies to every bus which—

(a) is first used on or after 1st January 2005;

(b) has a maximum gross weight not exceeding 5 tonnes; and

(c) has, or if a speed limiter were not fitted to it would have, a maximum speed exceeding 100 km/h;

and a reference in this regulation to a paragraph (2B) vehicle is a reference to a vehicle to which this regulation applies by virtue of this paragraph.]

[(2C) Subject to [paragraph 13], this regulation also applies to every bus, not being a bus to which paragraph (2) applies, which—

(a) was first used on or after 1st October 2001 and before 1st January 2005;

[(b) complies with the limit values in respect of Euro III emission standards set out in Council Directive 88/77/EEC, as amended by amendments up to and including those effected by Commission Directive 2001/27/EC;]

(c) has a maximum gross weight not exceeding 10 tonnes; and

(d) has, or if a speed limiter were not fitted to it would have, a maximum speed exceeding 100 km/h;

and a reference in this regulation to a paragraph (2C) vehicle is a reference to a vehicle to which this regulation applies by virtue of this paragraph.]

[(2D) [...]]

[(2E) [...]]

(3) [...]

(4) Every vehicle to which this regulation applies shall be fitted with a speed limiter in respect of which such of the requirements of paragraphs (5) to (9) are met as apply to that speed limiter.

(5) Subject to paragraph (10), the requirements of this paragraph are that a speed limiter fitted to any vehicle must—

(a) be sealed by an authorised sealer in such a manner as to protect the limiter against any improper interference or adjustment and against any interruption of its power supply; and

(b) be maintained in good and efficient working order.

(6) The requirements of this paragraph are that a speed limiter fitted to a paragraph (1) vehicle must be calibrated to a set speed not exceeding [112.65 km/h].

[(7) Subject to paragraph (7A), the requirements of this paragraph are that a speed limiter fitted to a paragraph (2) vehicle, a paragraph (2A) vehicle, a paragraph (2B) vehicle or a paragraph (2C) vehicle, must be set so that the speed of the vehicle cannot exceed 100 km/h.]

[(7A) A speed limiter fitted to a paragraph (2) vehicle which—

(a) was first used before 1st January 2005 and has a maximum gross weight exceeding 10 tonnes; or

(b) was first used before 1st October 2001 and has a maximum gross weight exceeding 7.5 tonnes but not exceeding 10 tonnes;

may be set at a maximum speed of 100 km/h.]

(8) Subject to paragraphs (11) and (12), the requirements of this paragraph are that a speed limiter fitted at any time to any paragraph (1) vehicle or a speed limiter fitted before 1st October 1994 to a paragraph (2) vehicle first used before that date must comply with—

(a) Part 1 of the British Standard; or

(b) the Annexes to Community Directive 92/24 [as amended by Directive 2004/11/EC of the European Parliament and of the Council] [*O.J. No. L44, February 14, 2004, p.19*].

(9) The requirements of this paragraph are that a speed limiter (not being a speed limiter to which paragraph (8) applies) fitted to a paragraph (2) vehicle[, a paragraph (2A) vehicle, a paragraph (2B) vehicle and a paragraph (2C) vehicle] must comply with the Annexes to Community Directive 92/24 [as amended by Directive 2004/11/EC of the European Parliament and of the Council].

(9A) [...]

(10) Paragraph (5)(a) shall have effect in relation to—

(a) a speed limiter fitted before 1st August 1992 to a vehicle first used before that date; or

(b) a speed limiter sealed outside the United Kingdom,

as if the words "by an authorised sealer" were omitted.

(11) Paragraph (8) does not apply to a speed limiter fitted before 1st October 1988.

(12) Paragraph (8) does not apply to a speed limiter fitted to a vehicle if the speed limiter complies with an equivalent standard.

(13) This regulation does not apply to a vehicle—

(a) being taken to a place where a speed limiter is to be installed, calibrated, repaired or replaced; [...]

(b) completing a journey in the course of which the speed limiter has accidentally ceased to function;

[(c) which is owned by the Secretary of State for Defence and used for naval, military or air force purposes;

(d) which is used for naval, military or air force purposes while being driven by a person for the time being subject to the orders of a member of the armed forces of the Crown; [...]

(e) while it is being used for fire and rescue authority purposes or for or in connection with the exercise of any function of a relevant authority as defined in section 6 of the Fire (Scotland) Act 2005, for ambulance purposes or police purposes [; or

(f) which is operated by or on behalf of Her Majesty's Prison Service and used primarily for the purpose of moving Category A prisoners.]

(14) In this regulation—

"*authorised sealer*" has the meaning given in Schedule 3B;

["*Category A prisoners*" means that prison security category which is applied to prisoners whose escape would be highly dangerous to the public or the police or to the security of the state, no matter how unlikely that escape might be, and for whom the aim must be to make escape impossible.]

"equivalent standard" means—

    (a) a standard or code of practice of a national standards body or equivalent body of any member State;

    (b) any international standard recognised for use as a standard by any member State; or

    (c) a technical specification or code of practice which, whether mandatory or not, is recognised for use as a standard by a public authority of any member State,

where the standard, code of practice, international standard or technical specification provides, in relation to speed limiters, a level of speed control equivalent to that provided by Part 1 of the British Standard.

[*"Euro III emission standards"* means the emission limits given in rows A of the tables in section 6.2.1 of Annex 1 to Directive 1999/96/EC of the European Parliament and of the Council (amending Council Directive 88/77/EEC);]

[*"international transport operations"* means transport operations outside the United Kingdom;]

[*"national transport operations"* means transport operations within the United Kingdom;]

"Part 1 of the British Standard" means the British Standard for Maximum Road Speed Limiters for Motor Vehicles which was published by the British Standards Institution under the number BS AU 217: Part 1: 1987 and which came into effect on 29th May 1987; as amended by Amendment Slip No.1 under the number AMD 5969 which was published and came into effect on 30th June 1988;

"set speed", in relation to a calibrated speed limiter fitted to a vehicle, means the speed intended by the person who calibrated the speed limiter to be the mean speed of the vehicle when operating in a stabilised condition;

"speed limiter" means a device designed to limit the maximum speed of a motor vehicle by controlling the power output from the engine of the vehicle;

[*"transport operations"* means the transportation of passengers in vehicles designed for such a purpose and to which this regulation applies.]

...]

[*Regulation 36A was inserted by SI 1988/271 and was later amended by SI* **B15.81** *1988/1524; SI 1992/422 and substituted by SI 1993/1946. The text of reg.36A as printed above was substituted by SI 1993/3048 and is printed as subsequently amended by the Vehicle Excise and Registration Act 1994 s.64 and Sch.4, para.4; SI 1997/1340; SI 2003/1946; SI 2004/2102; SI 2005/3170; SI 2009/142.*

The explanatory note accompanying SI 1997/1340 stated that reg.36A implements Directive 92/6/EEC (O.J. No.L57, April 2, 1992, p.27) and Directive 92/ 24/EEC (O.J. No.L129, May 14, 1992, p.154).]

B15.82   [**36B.**—(1) Subject to [paragraph 14], this regulation applies to every motor vehicle [, not being a motor vehicle to which paragraph (1B) applies,] which—

    (a) is a goods vehicle;

    (b) has a maximum gross weight exceeding 7,500kg but not exceeding 12,000kg;

    (c) is first used on or after 1st August 1992 [and before 1st January 2005]; and

    (d) has, or if a speed limiter were not fitted to it would have, a relevant speed exceeding 60mph;

and a reference in this regulation to a paragraph (1) vehicle is a reference to a vehicle to which this regulation applies by virtue of this paragraph.

[(1A) Subject to [paragraph 14], this regulation also applies to every motor vehicle which—

    (a) is a goods vehicle;

    (b) has a maximum gross weight exceeding 3,500 kg but not exceeding 12,000 kg;

    (c) is first used on or after 1st January 2005; and

    (d) has, or if a speed limiter were not fitted to it would have, a relevant speed exceeding 90 km/h;

and a reference in this regulation to a paragraph (1A) vehicle is a reference to a vehicle to which this regulation applies by virtue of this paragraph.]

[(1B) Subject to [paragraph 14], this regulation also applies to every motor vehicle, [...] which—

    (a) is a goods vehicle;

    (b) has a maximum gross weight exceeding 3,500 kg but not exceeding 12,000 kg;

    (c) was first used on or after 1st October 2001 and before 1st January 2005;

    (d) complies with the limit values in respect of Euro III emission standards set out in Council Directive 88/77/EEC, as amended by amendments up to and including those effected by Commission Directive 2001/27/EC; and

    (e) has, or if a speed limiter were not fitted to it would have, a relevant speed exceeding 90km/h;

and a reference in this regulation to a paragraph (1B) vehicle is a reference to a vehicle to which this regulation applies by virtue of this paragraph.]

[(1C) [...]]

[(1D) [...]]

(2) Subject to [paragraph (14)], this regulation also applies to every vehicle which—

    (a) is a goods vehicle;

    (b) has a maximum gross weight exceeding 12,000kg;

    (c) is first used on or after 1st January 1988; and

    (d) has, or if a speed limiter were not fitted to it would have, a relevant speed exceeding [90 km/h];

and a reference in this regulation to a paragraph (2) vehicle is a reference to a vehicle to which this regulation applies by virtue of this paragraph.

(3)–(5) [...]

(6) Every vehicle to which this regulation applies shall be fitted with a speed limiter in respect of which such of the requirements of paragraphs (7) to (11) are met as apply to that speed limiter.

(7) Subject to paragraph (12), the requirements of this paragraph are that a speed limiter fitted to any vehicle must—

    (a) be sealed by an authorised sealer in such a manner as to protect the limiter against any improper interference or adjustment or against any interruption of its power supply; and

    (b) be maintained in good and efficient working order.

(8) The requirements of this paragraph are that a speed limiter fitted to a paragraph (1) vehicle [...] must be calibrated to a set speed not exceeding 60mph.

[(9) [...] [T]he requirements of this paragraph are that a speed limiter fitted to [a paragraph (1A) vehicle, a paragraph (1B) vehicle or] a paragraph (2) vehicle must be set [so that] the stabilised speed of the vehicle must not exceed 90 km/h.]

(10) Subject to paragraph (13), the requirements of this paragraph are that a speed limiter fitted at any time to a paragraph (1) vehicle, a speed limiter fitted before 1st October 1994 to a paragraph (2) vehicle first used before that date [...] must comply with—

    (a) Part 1 of the British Standard; or

    (b) the Annexes to Community Directive 92/24 [as amended by Directive 2004/11/EC of the European Parliament and of the Council].

(11) The requirements of this paragraph are that a speed limiter (not being a speed limiter to which paragraph (10) applies) fitted to [a paragraph (1A) vehicle, a paragraph (1B) vehicle and] a paragraph (2) vehicle must comply with the Annexes to Community Directive 92/24 [as amended by Directive 2004/11/EC of the European Parliament and of the Council].

(11A) [...]

(12) Paragraph (7)(a) shall have effect in relation to—

    (a) a speed limiter fitted before 1st August 1992 to a vehicle first used before that date; or

    (b) a speed limiter sealed outside the United Kingdom,

as if the words "by an authorised sealer" were omitted.

(12A) [...]

(13) Paragraph (10) does not apply to a speed limiter fitted to a vehicle if the speed limiter complies with an equivalent standard.

(14) This regulation does not apply to a vehicle—

    (a) which is being taken to a place where a speed limiter is to be installed, calibrated, repaired or replaced;

    (b) which is completing a journey in the course of which the speed limiter has accidentally ceased to function;

    (c) is owned by the Secretary of State for Defence and used for naval, military or air force purposes;

    (d) is used for naval, military or air force purposes while being driven by a person for the time being subject to the orders of a member of the armed forces of the Crown;

(e) while it is being used for fire brigade [or, in England, fire and rescue authority], ambulance or police purposes; [...]

[(f) at a time when it is being used on a public road during any calendar week if—

  (i) it is being used only in passing from land in the occupation of the person keeping the vehicle to other land in his occupation, and

  (ii) it has not been used on public roads for distances exceeding an aggregate of six miles in that calendar week[; or

(g) which is an emergency tactical response vehicle operated by or on behalf of Her Majesty's Prison Service and used primarily for the purpose of transporting people or equipment (or both) to restore order within Her Majesty's prisons or immigration detention centres.]

and for the purposes of this paragraph *"public road"* has the meaning given in section 62(1) of the Vehicle Excise and Registration Act 1994 [*q.v.*].]

(15) In this regulation—

"equivalent standard" "Part 1 of the British Standard", ... *"speed limiter"* and *"stabilised speed"* have the same meanings as in regulation 36A;

[*"Euro III emission standards"*, means the emission limits given in rows A of the tables in section 6.2.1 of Annex 1 to Directive 1999/96/EC of the European Parliament and of the Council (amending Council Directive 88/77/EEC);]

[*"international transport operations"* means transport operations outside the United Kingdom;]

[*"national transport operations"* means transport operations within the United Kingdom;]

"relevant speed" means a speed which a vehicle is incapable, by means of its construction, of exceeding on the level under its own power when unladen;

[*"set speed"*, in relation to a paragraph (1) vehicle, has the same meaning as in regulation 36A;

[...], *"set"*, in relation to a speed limiter fitted to [a paragraph (1A) vehicle, a paragraph (1B) vehicle and] a paragraph (2) vehicle, has the same meaning as in Community Directive 92/6 [*q.v.*] ; and references to the speed at which a speed limiter is set shall be construed accordingly;] and

[*"transport operations"* means the transportation of goods in vehicles designed for such a purpose and to which this regulation applies.]

(16) For the purposes of this regulation, a motor vehicle has a maximum gross trailer weight exceeding 5,000kg if—

(a) in the case of a vehicle equipped with a Ministry plate in accordance with regulation 70, the difference between its maximum gross weight and the relevant train weight exceeds 5,000kg;

(b) in the case of a vehicle not equipped with a Ministry plate, but which is equipped with a plate in accordance with regulation 66, the difference between its maximum gross weight and the weight shown on the plate in respect of item 8 of Part I of Schedule 8 exceeds 5,000kg; and

(c) in the case of any other vehicle, the vehicle is designed or adapted to

be capable of drawing a trailer with a laden weight exceeding 5,000kg
    when travelling on a road;
and in sub-paragraph (a) *"the relevant train weight"* is the train weight shown in
column (3) of the plate or, if no such weight is shown, the train weight shown in
column (2) of the plate (where the plate is in the form required by [Schedule 10
or 10B]) or in column (4) of the plate (where the plate is in the form required by
[Schedule 10A or 10C]).]

[Regulation 36B was inserted by SI 1991/1527 and was later amended by SI   **B15.83**
1992/422 and substituted by SI 1993/1946.

The text of reg.36B as printed above was substituted by SI 1993/3048 and is
printed as subsequently amended by SI 1994/329; SI 1995/1458; SI 1996/2064;
SI 2003/1946; SI 2004/2102; SI 2004/3168; SI 2005/2929; SI 2005/3170; SI
2009/142.]

[Speed limiters—authorised sealers

36C. Schedule 3B (authorised sealers) shall have effect.]   **B15.84**
[Regulation 36C was inserted by SI 1992/422.]   **B15.85**

Audible warning instruments

37.—(1)(a) Subject to sub-paragraph (b), every motor vehicle which has a   **B15.86**
maximum speed of more than 20mph shall be fitted with a horn, not being a
reversing alarm or a two-tone horn.

(b) Sub-paragraph (a) shall not apply to an agricultural motor vehicle,
    unless it is being driven at more than 20mph.

(2) Subject to paragraph (6), the sound emitted by any horn, other than a
reversing alarm[, a boarding aid alarm] or a two-tone horn, fitted to a wheeled vehicle first used on or after 1st August 1973 shall be continuous and uniform and
not strident.

(3) A reversing alarm [or a boarding aid alarm] fitted to a wheeled vehicle
shall not be strident.

(4) Subject to paragraphs (5), (6) and (7) no motor vehicle shall be fitted with
a bell, gong, siren or two-tone horn.

(5) The provisions of paragraph (4) shall not apply to motor vehicles—

(a) used for fire brigade [or, in England [or Wales], fire and rescue author-
    ity], ambulance or police purposes;

[(aa) as regards England and Wales, and so far as relating to the functions
    of the Serious Organised Crime Agency which are exercisable in or
    as regards Scotland and which relate to reserved matters (within the
    meaning of the Scotland Act 1998), used for Serious Organised Crime
    Agency purposes;]

(b) owned by a body formed primarily for the purposes of fire salvage
    and used for those or similar purposes;

(c) owned by the Forestry Commission or by local authorities and used
    from time to time for the purposes of fighting fires;

(d) owned by the Secretary of State for Defence and used for the purposes
    of the disposal of bombs or explosives;

(e) used for the purposes of the Blood Transfusion Service provided under the National Health Service Act 1977 or under the National Health Service (Scotland) Act 1947;

(f) used by her Majesty's Coastguard or the Coastguard Auxiliary Service to aid persons in danger or vessels in distress on or near the coast;

(g) owned by the National Coal Board and used for the purposes of rescue operations at mines;

(h) owned by the Secretary of State for Defence and used by the Royal Air Force Mountain Rescue Service for the purposes of rescue operations in connection with crashed aircraft or any other emergencies; [...]

(i) owned by the Royal National Lifeboat Institution and used for the purposes of launching lifeboats.

[(j) a vehicle under the lawful control of the Commissioners for Her Majesty's Revenue and Customs and used from time to time for the purposes of investigation of serious crime (which, save for the omission of the words "and, where the authorising officer is within subsection (5)(h), it relates to an assigned matter within the meaning of section 1(1) of the Customs and Excise Management Act 1979", has the meaning given by section 93(4) of the Police Act 1997); [...]

[(k) owned or operated by the Secretary of State for Defence and used for the purpose of any activity—

(i) which prevents or decreases the exposure of persons to radiation arising from a radiation accident or radiation emergency; or

(ii) in connection with an event which could lead to a radiation accident or radiation emergency[; or

(l) used for mountain rescue purposes.]

(6) The provisions of paragraphs (2) and (4) shall not apply so as to make it unlawful for a motor vehicle to be fitted with an instrument or apparatus (not being a two-tone horn) designed to emit a sound for the purpose of informing members of the public that goods are on the vehicle for sale.

(7) Subject to paragraph (8), the provisions of paragraph (4) shall not apply so as to make it unlawful for a vehicle to be fitted with a bell, gong or siren—

(a) if the purpose thereof is to prevent theft or attempted theft of the vehicle or its contents; or

(b) in the case of a bus, if the purpose thereof is to summon help for the driver, the conductor or an inspector.

(8) Every bell, gong or siren fitted to a vehicle by virtue of paragraph (7)(a), and every device fitted to a motor vehicle first used on or after 1st October 1982 so as to cause a horn to sound for the purpose mentioned in paragraph (7)(a), shall be fitted with a device designed to stop the bell, gong, siren or horn emitting noise for a continuous period of more than five minutes; and every such device shall at all times be maintained in good working order.

(9) Instead of complying with paragraphs (1), (2) and (4) to (8), a vehicle may comply with Community Directive 70/388 or ECE Regulation 28 or, if the vehicle is an agricultural motor vehicle, with Community Directive 74/151.

[(9A) In this regulation "radiation accident" and "radiation emergency" shall have the same meaning as in the Radiation (Emergency Preparedness and Public Information) Regulations 2001.]

(10) In this regulation and in regulation 99 —

(a) *"horn"* means an instrument, not being a bell, gong or siren, capable of giving audible and sufficient warning of the approach or position of the vehicle to which it is fitted;

(b) references to a bell, gong or siren include references to any instrument or apparatus capable of emitting a sound similar to that emitted by a bell, gong or siren;

(c) *"reversing alarm"* means a device fitted to a motor vehicle and designed to warn persons that the vehicle is reversing or is about to reverse; ...

(d) *"two-tone horn"* means an instrument which, when operated, automatically produces a sound which alternates at regular intervals between two fixed notes [; and]

[(e) *"boarding aid alarm"* means an alarm for a power operated lift or ramp fitted to a bus to enable wheelchair users to board and alight and designed to warn persons that the lift or ramp is in operation.]

[Regulation 37 is printed as amended by SI 2000/1971; SI 2004/3168; SI 2005/ 2560; SI 2005/2929; SI 2006/564; SI 2009/3221.]   **B15.87**

Motor cycle sidestands

38.—(1) No motor cycle first used on or after 1st April 1986 shall be fitted   **B15.88** with any sidestand which is capable of—

(a) disturbing the stability of direction of the motor cycle when it is in motion under its own power; or

(b) closing automatically if the angle of the inclination of the motor cycle is inadvertently altered when it is stationary.

(2) In this regulation *"sidestand"* means a device fitted to a motor cycle which, when fully extended or pivoted to its open position, supports the vehicle from one side only and so that both the wheels of the motor cycle are on the ground.

G Fuel

Fuel tanks

39.—[(1) This regulation applies to every fuel tank which is fitted to a wheeled   **B15.89** vehicle for the purpose of supplying fuel to the propulsion unit or to an ancillary engine or to any other equipment forming part of the vehicle.]

[(2) Subject to paragraphs (3)[, (3A)] and (4), every fuel tank to which this regulation applies—

(a) shall be constructed and maintained so that the leakage of any liquid from the tank is adequately prevented;

(b) shall be constructed and maintained so that the leakage of vapour from the tank is adequately prevented; and

(c) if it contains petroleum spirit (as defined in section 23 of the Petroleum (Consolidation) Act 1928) and is fitted to a vehicle first used on or after 1st July 1973, shall be—

(i) made only of metal; and

(ii) fixed in such a position and so maintained as to be reasonably secure from damage.]

[(3) Notwithstanding the requirement of paragraph (2)(b), the fuel tank may be fitted with a device which, by the intake of air or the emission of vapour, relieves changes of pressure in the tank.]

[(3A) Sub-paragraph (i) of paragraph 2(c) shall not have effect in relation to a two-wheeled motor cycle (with or without a side-car) first used on or after 1st February 1993.]

[(4)] Instead of complying with the requirements of paragraphs (2) and (3) as to construction, a vehicle may comply with the requirement of Community Directive 70/221 (in so far as they relate to fuel tanks) or ECE Regulation 34 or 34.01 or, if the vehicle is an agricultural motor vehicle, of Community Directive 74/151.

B15.90   *[Regulation 39 is printed as amended by SI 1990/2212; SI 1992/3285.*

As to the application of reg.39(2)(c)(i) to vehicles in respect of which approval certificates have been issued under the "Approval Regulations", see Sch.2A, para.6, to these regulations.]

B15.91   [**39A.**—(1) Every vehicle to which this regulation applies shall be designed and constructed for running on unleaded petrol.

(2) No person shall use or cause or permit to be used a vehicle to which this regulation applies on a road if it—

(a) has been deliberately altered or adjusted for running on leaded petrol, and

(b) as a direct result of such alteration or adjustment it is incapable of running on unleaded petrol.

(3) Subject to paragraph (4) this regulation applies to every motor vehicle which is—

(a) propelled by a spark ignition engine which is capable of running on petrol, and

(b) is first used on or after the 1st April 1991.

(4) Part I of Schedule 3A shall have effect for the purpose of excluding certain vehicles first used before specified dates from the application of this legislation.

(5) In this regulation *"petrol"*, *"leaded petrol"* and *"unleaded petrol"* have the same meaning as in Community Directive 85/210.

(6) A vehicle shall be regarded for the purposes of this regulation as incapable of running on unleaded petrol at any particular time if and only if in its state of adjustment at that time prolonged continuous running on such petrol would damage the engine.]

B15.92   *[Regulation 39A was inserted by SI 1988/1524.*

"Petrol" is defined by Directive 85/210/EEC (O.J. No.L96, April 3, 1985, p.25) art.1, as "any volatile mineral oil intended for the operation of internal combustion spark-ignited engines used for the propulsion of vehicles". "Unleaded petrol" is defined by art.1 as "any petrol the contamination of which by lead compounds calculated in terms of lead, does not exceed 0.013 g Pb/1".]

B15.93   [**39B.**—(1) Subject to paragraph (2), every fuel tank fitted to a vehicle to which regulation 39A applies shall be so constructed and fitted that it cannot readily be filled from a petrol pump delivery nozzle which has an external diameter of 23.6mm or greater without the aid of a device (such as a funnel) not fitted to the vehicle.

(2) Paragraph (1) does not apply to a vehicle in respect of which both of the following conditions are satisfied, that is to say—

    (a) that at the time of its first use the vehicle is so designed and constructed that prolonged continuous running on leaded petrol would not cause any device designed to control the emission of carbon monoxide, hydrocarbons or nitrogen oxides to malfunction, and

    (b) that it is conspicuously and legibly marked in a position immediately visible to a person filling the fuel tank with—

        (i) the word "UNLEADED", or

        (ii) the symbol shown in Part II of Schedule 3A.

(3) In this regulation *"fuel tank"*, in relation to a vehicle, means a fuel tank used in connection with the propulsion of the vehicle.]

[Regulation 39B was inserted by SI 1988/1524.]   **B15.94**

Gas propulsion systems and gas-fired appliances

40.—(1) A vehicle which is—   **B15.95**

    (a) a motor vehicle which first used gas as a fuel for its propulsion before 19th November 1982; or

    (b) a trailer manufactured before 19th November 1982 to which there is fitted a gas container,

shall be so constructed that it complies either with the provisions of Schedule 4 or with the provisions of Schedule 5.

(2) [Subject to paragraph (2A), a vehicle which is]—

    (a) a motor vehicle which first used gas as a fuel for its propulsion on or after 19th November 1982; or

    (b) a motor vehicle first used on or after 1st May 1984 or a trailer manufactured on or after 19th November 1982 which is in either case equipped with a gas container or a gas-fired appliance,

shall comply with the provisions of Schedule 5 [or with ECE Regulation 67 or 67.01].

[(2A) A vehicle which first used gas as a fuel for its propulsion on or after 13th November 1999 shall comply with the provisions of Schedule 5 or ECE Regulation 67.01.]

(3) The requirements of this regulation are in addition to, and not in derogation from, the requirements of any regulations made under powers conferred by the Petroleum (Consolidation) Act 1928, the Health and Safety at Work, etc., Act 1974, the Control of Pollution Act 1974 or any other Act or of any codes of practice issued under the Health and Safety at Work etc., Act 1974.

(4) In this regulation *"gas container"* has the meaning given in Schedule 4 where compliance with the provisions of that Schedule is concerned and otherwise has the meaning given in Schedule 5.

[Regulation 40 is printed as amended by SI 2003/1690.]   **B15.96**

Minibuses

B15.97   41. The requirements specified in Schedule 6 shall apply to every minibus first used on or after 1st April 1988 except a vehicle—

    (a) manufactured by Land Rover UK Limited and known as the Land Rover; or

    (b) constructed or adapted for the secure transport of prisoners.

[Alternative means of compliance

B15.98   41A.—[(1)] A minibus which is required by regulation 41 to meet the requirements specified in Schedule 6 need not meet them if it meets the requirements of such of the Annexes to Directive 2001/85/EC of the European Parliament and of the Council of 20 November 2001, relating to special provisions for vehicles used for the carriage of passengers comprising more than eight seats in addition to the driver's seat, and amending Directives 70/156/EEC and 97/27/EC, as apply to that minibus.]

[(2) A minibus which is required by regulation 41 to meet the requirements specified in Schedule 6 need not meet the requirements set out in items 2 to 4 and 7 to 12 of that Schedule if it meets such requirements of ECE Regulation 52.01 or 107.01 or 107.02 as apply to that minibus.]

B15.99   *[Regulation 41A was inserted by SI 2005/2987; SI 2009/142.]*

Fire extinguishing apparatus

B15.100   42.—(1) No person shall use, or cause or permit to be used, on a road a minibus first used on or after 1st April 1988 unless it carries suitable and efficient apparatus for extinguishing fire which is of a type specified in Part I of Schedule 7.

(2) The apparatus referred to in paragraph (1) above shall be—

    (a) readily available for use;

    (b) clearly marked with the appropriate British Standards Institution specification number; and

    (c) maintained in good and efficient working order.

(3) This regulation does not apply to a vehicle manufactured by Land Rover U.K. Limited and known as the Land Rover.

First-aid equipment

B15.101   43.—(1) No person shall use, or cause or permit to be used, on a road a minibus first used on or after 1st April 1988 unless it carries a receptacle which contains the items specified in Part II of Schedule 7.

(2) The receptacle referred to in paragraph (1) above shall be—

    (a) maintained in a good condition;

    (b) suitable for the purpose of keeping the items referred to in the said paragraph in good condition;

    (c) readily available for use; and

    (d) prominently marked as first aid receptacle.

(3) The items referred to in paragraph (1) above shall be maintained in good condition and shall be of a good and reliable quality and of a suitable design.

(4) This regulation does not apply to a vehicle manufactured by Land Rover UK Limited and known as the Land Rover.

Carriage of dangerous substances

44.—(1) Save as provided in paragraph (2), no person shall use or cause or permit to be used on a road a minibus by which any highly inflammable or otherwise dangerous substance is carried unless that substance is carried in containers so designed and constructed, and unless the substance is so packed, that, notwithstanding an accident to the vehicle, it is unlikely that damage to the vehicle or injury to passengers in the vehicle will be caused by the substance.   **B15.102**

(2) Paragraph (1) shall not apply in relation to the electrolyte of a battery installed in an electric wheelchair provided that the wheelchair is securely fixed to the vehicle.

(3) This regulation does not apply to a vehicle manufactured by Land Rover UK Limited and known as Land Rover.

I Power-to-Weight Ratio

Power-to-weight ratio

45. [...]   **B15.103**
[Revoked by SI 1995/1201.]

J Protective Systems

[Seat belt anchorage points

46.—(1) This regulation applies to a motor vehicle which is not an excepted vehicle and is—   **B15.104**
  (a) a bus first used on or after 1st April 1982;
  (b) a wheeled motor car first used on or after 1st January 1965;
  (c) a three-wheeled motor cycle which has an unladen weight exceeding 255kg and which was first used on or after 1st September 1970; or
  (d) a heavy motor car first used on or after 1st October 1988.

(2) Each of the following is an excepted vehicle—
  (a) a goods vehicle (other than a dual-purpose vehicle)—
    (i) first used before 1st April 1967;
    (ii) first used on or after 1st April 1980 and before 1st October 1988 and having a maximum gross weight exceeding 3500kg; or
    (iii) first used before 1st April 1980 or, if the vehicle is of a model manufactured before 1st October 1979, first used before 1st April 1982 and, in either case, having an unladen weight exceeding 1525kg;
  (b) an agricultural motor vehicle;
  (c) a motor tractor;

(d) a works truck;

(e) an electrically propelled goods vehicle first used before 1st October 1988;

(f) a pedestrian-controlled vehicle;

(g) a vehicle which has been used on roads outside Great Britain, whilst it is being driven from the place at which it arrived in Great Britain to a place of residence of the owner or driver of the vehicle, or from any such place to a place where, by previous arrangement, it will be provided with such anchorage points as are required by this regulation and with such seat belts as are required by regulation 47;

(h) a vehicle having a maximum speed not exceeding 16mph;

(i) a motor cycle equipped with a driver's seat of a type requiring the driver to sit astride it, and which is constructed or assembled by a person not ordinarily engaged in the trade or business of manufacturing vehicles of that description;

(j) a locomotive.

(3) A vehicle which falls within a description specified in column (2) of an item in the Table below shall be equipped with anchorage points for seat belts for the use of persons sitting in the seats specified in column (3) of that item and those anchorage points (*"mandatory anchorage points"*) shall comply with the requirements specified in column (4).

TABLE

(1) Item	(2) Description of vehicle	(3) Seats for which mandatory anchorage points are to be provided	(4) Technical and installation requirements
1.	Any vehicle first used before 1st April 1982	The driver's seat and specified passenger seat (if any)	Anchorage points must be designed to hold seat belts securely in position on the vehicle
2.	Minibus constructed or adapted to carry not more than 12 seated passengers in addition to the driver, motor ambulance or motor caravan which, in any such case, was first used on or after 1st April 1982 but before 1st October 1988	The driver's seat and specified passenger seat (if any)	The technical and installation (but not the testing) requirements of Community Directive 76/115, 81/575, 82/318, 90/629 or 96/38 or ECE Regulation 14, 14.01, 14.02. 14.03, 14.04 or 14.05 whether or not those instruments apply to the vehicle

(1) Item	(2) Description of vehicle	(3) Seats for which mandatory anchorage points are to be provided	(4) Technical and installation requirements
3.	Minibus (not being a vehicle falling within item 7 or 8) having a gross weight not exceeding 3500kg, motor ambulance or motor caravan which, in any such case, was first used on or after 1st October 1988	The driver's seat and each forward-facing front seat	The requirements specified in column (4) of item 2
4.	Goods vehicle first used on or after 1st October 1988 but before 1st October 2001 and having a maximum gross weight exceeding 3500kg	The driver's seat and each forward-facing front seat	2 or 3 anchorage points designed to hold seat belts securely in position
5.	Goods vehicle first used on or after 1st October 2001 and having a maximum gross weight exceeding 3500kg	All forward-facing front seats	The technical and installation requirements of Community Directive 96/38 or ECE Regulation 14.04 or 14.05
6.	Coach first used on or after 1st October 1988 but before 1st October 2001	All exposed forward-facing seats	The requirements specified in column (4) of item 2 or, if the anchorage points were fitted before 1st October 2001 and form part of a seat, a requirement that they do not, when a forward horizontal force is applied ot them, become detached from the seat before the seat becomes detached from the vehicle

(1) Item	(2) Description of vehicle	(3) Seats for which mandatory anchorage points are to be provided	(4) Technical and installation requirements
7.	Bus (other than an urban bus) having a gross vehicle weight exceeding 3500kg and first used on or after 1st October 2001	Anchorage points for every forward-facing and every rearward-facing seat	The requirements specified in column (4) of item 5
8.	Bus (other than an urban bus) having a gross vehicle weight not exceeding 3500kg and first used on or after 1st October 2001	Every forward-facing and every rearward-facing seat	The requirements specified in column (4) of item 5
9.	Passenger or dual-purpose vehicle (other than a bus) first used on or after 1st April 1982 and not falling within any of items 2 to 8	Every forward-facing seat constructed or adapted to accommodate no more than one adult	The requirements specified in column (4) of item 2
10.	Vehicle (other than a bus) first used on or after 1st April 1982 and not falling within any of items 2 to 9	Every forward-facing front seat and every non-protected seat	The requirements specified in column (4) of item 2

(4) Any anchorage fitted after 1st October 2001 to a bus not falling within item 7 or 8 of the Table in paragraph (3) must comply with the technical and installation (but not the testing) requirements of Community Directive 76/115, 81/575, 82/318, 90/629 or 96/38 or ECE Regulation 14, 14.01, 14.02, 14.03, 14.04 or 14.05 whether or not those instruments apply to the vehicle.

(5) Subject to paragraph (6), where a vehicle to which this regulation applies and which falls within a class specified in an item of the Table in paragraph (3) is fitted with non-mandatory anchorage points, those anchorage points shall comply with the requirements applicable to the mandatory anchorage points specified for that item.

(6) Paragraph (5) does not apply to non-mandatory anchorage points fitted to—

    (a) a minibus before 1st April 1986; or

    (b) any other vehicle before 1st October 1988.

(7) For the purposes of this regulation—

    (a) the expressions *"exposed forward-facing seat"*, *"forward-facing front seat"*, *"lap belt"*, *"seat belt"* and *"specified passenger's seat"* have the same meaning as in regulation 47(8);

(b) *"mandatory anchorage points"* has the meaning given in paragraph (3) and *"non-mandatory anchorage points"* means anchorage points which are not mandatory anchorage points;

(c) a seat is a *"non-protected seat"* if it is not a front seat and the screen zones within the protected area have a combined surface area of less than 800 cm^2 ;

(d) *"screen zone"* and *"protected area"* in relation to a seat shall be construed in accordance with paragraph 4.3.3 of Annex I to Community Directive 81/575; and

(e) *"urban bus"* means a bus designed for urban use with standing passengers and includes a vehicle which is—

   (i) a Class I vehicle as defined by paragraph 2.1.2.1.3.1.1 of Annex I of Community Directive 97/27/EC [*O.J. No.L233, August 25, 1997, p.1*];

   (ii) a Class II vehicle as defined by paragraph 2.1.2.1.3.1.2 of that Annex; or

   (iii) a Class A vehicle as defined by paragraph 2.1.2.1.3.2.1 of that Annex.

(8) A vehicle which is not required by this regulation to comply with the technical and installation requirements of Community Directive 76/115, 81/575, 82/318, 90/629 or 96/38 or ECE Regulation 14, 14.01, 14.02, 14.03, 14.04 or 14.05 shall nevertheless be taken to comply with the provisions of this regulation if it does comply with those requirements.]

[Regulation 46 is printed as substituted by SI 2001/1043. The explanatory   **B15.105**
notes which accompanied SI 2001/1043 stated that that instrument gives effect to Directive 96/36/EC (O.J. No.L178, June 17, 1996, p.15), Directive 96/38/EC (O.J. No.L187, July 26, 1996, p.95) and Directive 2000/3/EC (O.J. No.L53, February 25, 2000, p.1).

As to the application of the provisions of reg.46 to vehicles in respect of which approval certificates have been issued under the "Approval Regulations", see Sch.2A, para.7, to these regulations.]

[Seat belts

47.—(1) This regulation applies to every vehicle to which regulation 46   **B15.106**
applies.

(2) Save as provided in paragraph (4) a vehicle to which—

(a) this regulation applies which was first used before 1st April 1981 shall be provided with—

   (i) a body-restraining belt, designed for use by an adult, for the driver's seat; and

   (ii) a body-restraining belt for the specified passenger's seat (if any);

(b) this regulation applies which is first used on or after 1st April 1981 shall be provided with three-point belts for the driver's seat and for the specified passenger's seat (if any);

(c) [item 9 or 10 of the Table in regulation 46(3)] applies which is first used on or after 1st April 1987 shall be fitted with seat belts additional to those required by sub-paragraph (b) as follows—

  (i) for any forward-facing front seat alongside the driver's seat, not being a specified passenger's seat, a seat belt which is a three-point belt, or a lap belt installed in accordance with paragraph 3.1.2.1 of Annex 1 to Community Directive 77/541 or a disabled person's belt;

 (ii) in the case of a passenger or dual-purpose vehicle having not more than two forward-facing seats behind the driver's seat with either—

    (a) an inertia reel belt for at least one of those seats, or

    (b) a three-point belt, a lap belt, a disabled person's belt or a child restraint for each of those seats;

(iii) in the case of a passenger or dual-purpose vehicle having more than two forward-facing seats behind the driver's seat, with either—

    (a) an inertia reel belt for one of those seats being an outboard seat and a three-point belt, a lap belt, a disabled person's belt or a child restraint for at least one other of those seats;

    (b) a three-point belt for one of those seats and either a child restraint or a disabled person's belt for at least one other of those seats; or

    (c) a three-point belt, a lap belt, a disabled person's belt or a child restraint for each of those seats;

 (d) [item 3 of the Table in regulation 46(3)] applies shall be fitted with seat belts as follows—

  (i) for the driver's seat and the specified passenger's seat (if any) a three-point belt; and

 (ii) for any forward-facing front seat which is not a specified passenger's seat, a three-point belt or a lap belt installed in accordance with the provisions of sub-paragraph (c)(i);

 (e) [item 6 of the Table in regulation 46(3)] applies shall be equipped with seat belts which shall be three-point belts, lap belts or disabled person's belts;

[(f) item 5 of the Table in regulation 46(3) applies shall be fitted—

  (i) as respects the driver's seat with a three-point belt or a lap belt; and

 (ii) as respects every other forward-facing front seat with a three-point belt, a lap belt installed in accordance with paragraph 3.1.2.1 of Annex I to Community Directive 77/541 or a disabled person's belt;]

[(g) item 7 of the Table in regulation 46(3) applies shall be fitted, as respects every forward-facing seat, with—

  (i) an inertia reel belt;

 (ii) a retractable lap belt installed in compliance with paragraph 3.1.10 of Annex I to Community Directive 96/36 or 2000/3;

(iii) a disabled person's belt; or

(iv) a child restraint;]
[(h) item 7 of the Table in regulation 46(3) applies shall be fitted, as respects every rearward-facing seat, with—
    (i) an inertia reel belt;
    (ii) a retractable lap belt;
    (iii) a disabled person's belt; or
    (iv) a child restraint;]
[(i) item 8 of the Table in regulation 46(3), as respects every forward-facing seat, with—
    (i) an inertia reel belt;
    (ii) a disabled person's belt; or
    (iii) a child restraint;]
[(j) item 8 of the Table in regulation 46(3), as respects every rearward-facing seat, with—
    (i) an inertia reel belt;
    (ii) a retractable lap belt;
    (iii) a disabled person's belt; or
    (iv) a child restraint;]

Where a lap belt is fitted to a forward-facing front seat of a minibus, a motor ambulance or a motor caravan, or to an exposed forward-facing seat [(other than the driver's seat or any crew seat) of a coach either—

    (i) there shall be provided padding to a depth of not less than 50mm, on that part of the surface or edge of any bar, or the top or edge of any screen or partition, which would be likely to be struck by the head of a passenger wearing the lap belt in the event of an accident; or

    (ii) the technical and installation requirements of Annex 4 to ECE Regulation 21 shall be met, in respect of any such bar, screen or partition,

but nothing in sub-paragraph (i) above shall require padding to be provided on any surface more than 1m from the centre of the line of intersection of the seat cushion and the back rest or more than 150mm on either side of the longitudinal vertical plane which passes through the centre of that line, nor shall it require padding to be provided on any instrument panel of a minibus.]

(3) Every seat belt for an adult, other than a disabled person's belt, provided for a vehicle in accordance with [any of paragraphs (2)(b) to (j)] shall, except as provided in paragraph (6), comply with the installation requirements specified in paragraph 3.2.2 to 3.3.4 of Annex I to Community Directive 77/541 [, 82/319, 90/628, 96/36 or 2000/3] whether or not [those Directives apply] to the vehicle.

(4) The requirements specified in paragraph (2) do not apply—

(a) to a vehicle while it is being used under a trade licence within the meaning of [section 11 of the Vehicle Excise and Registration Act 1994 [q.v.]];

(b) to a vehicle, not being a vehicle to which the Type Approval (Great Britain) Regulations apply, while it is being driven from premises of the manufacturer by whom it was made, or of a distributor of vehicles or dealer in vehicles—

        (i) to premises of a distributor of or dealer in vehicles or of the purchaser of the vehicle, or

        (ii) to premises of a person obtaining possession of the vehicle under a hiring agreement or hire-purchase agreement;

    (c) in relation to any seat for which there is provided—

        (i) a seat belt which bears a mark including the specification number of the British Standard for Passive Belt Systems, namely BSAU 183: 1983 and including the registered certification trade mark of the British Standards Institution; ...

        (ii) a seat belt designed for use by an adult which is a harness belt comprising a lap belt and shoulder straps which bears a British Standard mark or a mark including the specification number for the British Standard for Seat Belt Assemblies for Motor Vehicles, namely BS 3254: 1960 or [BS 3254: Part 1: 1988] and including the registered certification trade mark of the British Standards Institution, or [the marking designated as an approval mark by regulations 4 of the Approval Marks Regulations and shown at item 16 or 16A in Schedule 2 to those Regulations];

        [(iii) a seat belt which satisfies the requirements of a standard corresponding to the British Standard referred to in sub-paragraph (i); or]

        [(iv) a seat belt designated for use by an adult which is a harness belt comprising a lap belt and shoulder straps and which satisfies the requirements of a standard corresponding to any of the British Standards referred to in sub-paragraph (ii).]

    (d) in relation to the driver's seat or the specified passenger's seat (if any) of a vehicle which has been specially designed and constructed, or specially adapted, for the use of a person suffering from some physical defect or disability, in a case where a disabled person's belt for an adult person is provided for use for that seat;

    (e) to a vehicle to which [item 4 of the Table in regulation 46(3)] applies.

    [(4A) Vehicles constructed or adapted for the secure transport of prisoners shall not be required to comply with the requirements of paragraph (2) in relation to seats for persons other than the driver and any front seat passenger provided that those seats shall have seat belt anchorage points provided for them in accordance with regulation 46.]

    (5) Every seat belt provided in pursuance of paragraph (2) shall be properly secured to the anchorage points provided for it in accordance with regulation 46; or, in the case of a child restraint, to anchorages specially provided for it or, in the case of a disabled person's belt [first fitted before 1st October 2001], secured to the vehicle or to the seat which is being occupied by the person wearing the belt.

    (6) Paragraph (3), in so far as it relates to the second paragraph of paragraph 3.3.2 of the Annex there mentioned (which concerns the locking or releasing of a seat belt by a single movement) does not apply in respect of a seat belt fitted for—

    (a) a seat which is treated as a specified passenger's seat by virtue of the provisions of sub-paragraph (ii) in the definition of "specified passenger's seat" in paragraph (8); or

(b) any forward-facing seat for a passenger alongside the driver's seat of a goods vehicle which has an unladen weight of more than 915kg and has more than one such seat, any such seats for passengers being joined together in a single structure; or

(c) any seat (other than the driver's seat) fitted to a coach.

(7) Every seat belt, other than a disabled person's belt or a seat belt of a kind mentioned in paragraph [4(c)] above, provided for any person in a vehicle to which this regulation applies shall be legibly and permanently marked—

(a) … with a British Standard mark or a designated approval mark[; or]

[(b) with an EC Component Type-Approval Mark complying with Annex III to Community Directive 2000/3].

Provided this paragraph shall not operate so as to invalidate the exception permitted in paragraph (6).

[(7A) Paragraph (7) does not apply to—

(a) a seat belt for an adult … that satisfies the requirements of a standard corresponding to either of the British Standards referred to in sub-paragraph (i)(a) of the definition of "British Standard mark" in paragraph (8); or

(b) a child restraint that satisfies the requirements of a standard corresponding to any of the British Standards referred to in sub-paragraph (i)(b) of that definition.]

[(7B) For the purposes of this regulation a reference to a standard corresponding to a specified British Standard is a reference to—

(a) a standard or code of practice of a national standards body or equivalent body of any EEA State;

(b) any international standard recognised for use as a standard by any EEA State; or

(c) a technical specification recognised for use as a standard by a public authority of any EEA State,

where the standard, code of practice, international standard or technical specification provides in relation to seat belts, a level of safety equivalent to that provided by the British Standard and contains a requirement as respects the marking of seat belts equivalent to that provided by the British Standard.]

[(7C) For the purposes of paragraph (7B) —

(a) "EEA State" means a State which is a contracting Party to the EEA Agreement but, until the EEA Agreement comes into force in relation to Liechtenstein, does not include the state of Liechtenstein; and

(b) "EEA Agreement" [Cm. 2073] means the Agreement on the European Economic Area signed at Oporto on 2nd May 1992 as adjusted by the Protocol signed at Brussels on 17th March 1993 [Cm. 2183].]

(8) In this regulation—

"body-restraining belt" means a seat belt designed to provide restraint for both the upper and lower parts of the trunk of the wearer in the event of an accident to the vehicle;

"British Standard mark" means a mark consisting of—

(i) the specification number of one of the following British Standards for Seat Belt Assemblies for Motor Vehicles, namely—

      (a) if it is a seat belt for an adult, BS 3254: 1960 [BS 3254: Part 1: 1988]; or

      (b) if it is a child restraint, BS 3254: 1960, or BS 3254:1960 as amended by Amendment No.16 published on 31st July 1986 under the number AMD 5210, [BS 3254: Part 2: 1988] [or BS 3254: Part 2: 1991], BS AU 185, BS AU 186 or 186a, BS AU 202[, BS AU 202a or BS AU 202b]; and, in either case,

    (ii) the registered certification trade mark of the British Standards Institution;

"child restraint" means a seat belt for the use of a young person which is designed either to be fitted directly to a suitable anchorage or to be used in conjunction with a seat belt for an adult and held in place by the restraining action of that belt; Provided that for the purposes of paragraph (2)(c)(ii)(B) and (2)(c)(iii) it means only such seat belts fitted directly to a suitable anchorage and excludes belts marked with the specification numbers BS AU 185 and BS AU 186 or 186a;

"crew seat" has the same meaning as in regulation 3(1) of the Public Service Vehicles (Conditions of Fitness, Equipment, Use and Certification) Regulations 1981 [*q.v.*];

"designated approval mark" means

      (a) if it is a seat belt other than a child restraint, the marking designated as an approval mark by regulation 4 of the Approval Marks Regulations and shown at [items 16 and 16A] of Schedule 2 to those Regulations or the marking designated as an approval mark by regulation 5 of those Regulations and shown at item 23[, 23A and 23B] in Schedule 4 to those Regulations and

      (b) if it is a child restraint, [any] of the markings designated as approval marks by regulation 4 of those Regulations and shown at [items 44, 44A[, 44B and 44C]] in Schedule 2 to those Regulations;

"disabled person's belt" means a seat belt which has been specially designed or adapted for use by an adult or young person suffering from some physical defect or disability and which is intended for use solely by such a person;

"exposed forward-facing seat" means—

    (i) a forward-facing front seat (including any crew seat) and the driver's seat; and

    (ii) any other forward-facing seat which is not immediately behind and on the same horizonal plane as a forward-facing high-backed seat;

"forward-facing seat" means a seat which is attached to a vehicle so that it faces towards the front of the vehicle in such a manner that a line passing through the centre of both the front and the back of the seat is at an angle of 30° or less to the longitudinal axis of the vehicle;

"forward-facing front seat" means—

(i) any forward-facing seat alongside the driver's seat; or

(ii) if the vehicle normally has no seat which is a forward-facing front seat under sub-paragraph (i) of this definition, each forward-facing seat for a passenger which is foremost in the vehicle;

"forward-facing high-backed seat" means a forward-facing seat which is also a high-backed seat;

"high-backed seat" means a seat the highest part of which is at least 1 metre above the deck of the vehicle;

"inertia reel belt" means a three-point belt of either of the types required for a front out-board seating position by paragraph 3.1.1 of Annex 1 to Community Directive 77/541;

"lap belt" means a seat belt which passes across the front of the wearer's pelvic region and which is designed for use by an adult;

[*"retractable lap belt"* means a lap belt with either an automatically locking retractor (as defined in paragraph 1.8.3 of Annex I to Community Directive 77/541) or an emergency locking retractor (as defined in paragraph 1.8.4 of Annex I to Community Directive 77/541);]

"seat" includes any part designed for the accommodation of one adult of a continuous seat designed for the accommodation of more than one adult;

"seat belt" means a belt intended to be worn by a person in a vehicle and designed to prevent or lessen injury to its wearer in the event of an accident to the vehicle and includes, in the case of a child restraint, any special chair to which the belt is attached;

"specified passenger's seat" means—

(i) in the case of a vehicle which has one forward-facing front seat alongside the driver's seat, that seat, and in the case of a vehicle which has more than one such seat, the one furthest from the driver's seat; or

(ii) if the vehicle normally has no seat which is the specified passenger's seat under sub-paragraph (i) of this definition the forward-facing front seat for a passenger which is the foremost in the vehicle and furthest from the driver's seat, unless there is a fixed partition separating that seat from the space in front of it alongside the driver's seat; and

"three-point belt" means a seat belt which—

(i) restrains the upper and lower parts of the torso;

(ii) includes a lap belt;

(iii) is anchored at not less than three points; and

(iv) is designed for use by an adult.]

[Regulation 47 was substantially amended by SI 1987/1133. The text of reg.47, **B15.107** *as so amended, was set out in the Schedule to SI 1987/1133 and the above text is the text so printed as subsequently amended by SI 1989/1478; SI 1991/2003; SI 1994/3270; SI 1996/163; SI 1998/2429; SI 2001/1043.*

As to the European Economic Area and the EEA agreement, see the introductory note to Section C below.

As to the application of the provisions of reg.47 (so far as it relates to seat belts for adults) to vehicles in respect of which approval certificates have been issued under the "Approval Regulations", see Sch.2A, para.8, to these regulations.]

Maintenance of seat belts and anchorage points

B15.108   **48.**—(1) This regulation applies to every seat belt with which a motor vehicle is required to be provided in accordance with regulation 47 and to the anchorages, fastenings, adjusting device and retracting mechanism (if any) of every such seat belt [and also to every anchorage with which a goods vehicle is required to be provided in accordance with [regulation 46(3) and item 4 in the Table in that regulation].

(2) For the purposes of this regulation the anchorages and anchorage points of a seat belt shall, in the case of a seat which incorporates integral seat belt anchorages, include the system by which the seat assembly itself is secured to the vehicle structure.

(3) The anchorage points provided for seat belts shall be used only as anchorages for the seat belts for which they are intended to be used or capable of being used.

(4) Save as provided in paragraph (5) below—

(a) all load-bearing members of the vehicle structure or panelling within 30cm of each anchorage point shall be maintained in a sound condition and free from serious corrosion, distortion or fracture;

(b) the adjusting device and (if fitted) the retracting mechanism of the seat belt shall be so maintained that the belt may be readily adjusted to the body of the wearer, either automatically or manually, according to the design of the device and (if fitted) the retracting mechanism;

(c) the seat belt and its anchorages, fastenings and adjusting device shall be maintained free from any obvious defect which would be likely to affect adversely the performance by the seat belt of the function of restraining the body of the wearer in the event of an accident to the vehicle;

(d) the buckle or other fastening of the seat belt shall—

(i) be so maintained that the belt can be readily fastened or unfastened;

(ii) be kept free from any temporary or permanent obstruction; and

(iii) except in the case of a disabled person's seat belt, be readily accessible to a person sitting in the seat for which the seat belt is provided;

(e) the webbing or other material which forms the seat belt shall be maintained free from cuts or other visible faults (as, for example, extensive fraying) which would be likely to affect adversely the performance of the belt when under stress;

(f) the ends of every seat belt, other than a disabled person's seat belt, shall be securely fastened to the anchorage points provided for them; and

(g) the ends of every disabled person's seat belt shall, when the seat belt is being used for the purpose for which it was designed and constructed, be securely fastened either to some part of the structure of the vehicle or to the seat which is being occupied by the person wearing the belt so that the body of the person wearing the belt would be restrained in the event of an accident to the vehicle.

(5) No requirement specified in paragraph (4) above applies if the vehicle is being used—

(a) on a journey after the start of which the requirement ceased to be complied with; or

(b) after the requirement ceased to be complied with and steps have been taken for such compliance to be restored with all reasonable expedition.

(6) Expressions which are used in this regulation and are defined in regulation 47 have the same meaning in this regulation as they have in regulation 47.

[Regulation 48 is printed as amended by SI 1987/1133; SI 2001/1043.]   **B15.109**

[Minibuses and coaches to be fitted with additional seat belts when used in certain circumstances

48A.—(1) No person shall use or cause or permit to be used on a road a coach   **B15.110**
or minibus wholly or mainly for the purpose of carrying a group of 3 or more children in the following circumstances unless the appropriate number of forward-facing passenger seats fitted to the vehicle meet the requirements of this regulation.

(2) The circumstances are that—

(a) the group of children are on an organised trip; and

(b) the journey is being made for the purposes of the trip.

(3) In paragraph (1), the reference to the appropriate number is a reference to the number of children being carried in the vehicle (excluding disabled children in wheel-chairs).

[(3A) For the purposes of this regulation a rearward-facing seat shall be treated as a forward-facing seat which meets the requirements of this regulation if the coach or minibus concerned was first used on or after 1st October 2001, and the rearward-facing seat complies with the requirements of regulations 46 and 47.]

(4) Without prejudice to the generality of paragraph (2)(a), a group of children shall, for the purposes of this regulation, be regarded as being on an organised trip if they are being carried to or from their school or from one part of their school premises to another.

(5) Without prejudice to the meaning of paragraph (2)(b), paragraph (1) shall not apply to a vehicle if it is being used in the provision of a bus service of a description specified in paragraph 2 of the Schedule to the Fuel Duty Grant (Eligible Bus Services) Regulations 1985 [*SI 1985/1886; not reproduced in this work*] or if it is otherwise being used wholly or mainly for the purpose of providing a transport service for the general public.

(6) For a forward-facing passenger seat to meet the requirements of this regulation a seat belt must be provided for it, and—

(a) if paragraph (3) of regulation 47 does not (in whole or part) apply to the seat belt and the seat belt was first fitted to the vehicle after 10th

February 1997, the seat belt must comply with that paragraph to the extent (if any) that it would have to so comply were—

  (i) that regulation to apply to all motor vehicles, and

  (ii) there substituted for the words "provided" to "or (e)", in that paragraph, the words "provided for any person in a vehicle to which this regulation applies";

(b) if paragraph (5) of regulation 47 does not apply to the seat belt and the seat belt is a seat belt for an adult (not being a disabled person's belt) that was first fitted to the vehicle after 10th February 1997, the seat belt must comply with the requirements specified in paragraph (7) below;

(c) if paragraph (5) of regulation 47 does not apply to the seat belt and the seat belt is a child restraint that was first fitted to the vehicle after 10th February 1997, the seat belt must be properly secured to anchorages provided for it;

(d) if paragraph (5) of regulation 47 does not apply to the seat belt and the seat belt is a disabled person's belt that was first fitted to the vehicle after 10th February 1997, the seat belt must be properly secured to the vehicle or to the seat;

(e) if regulation 47 does not apply to the vehicle and the seat belt was first fitted to the vehicle after 10th February 1997, the seat belt must comply with paragraph (7) of that regulation to the extent (if any) that it would have to so comply were that regulation to apply to all motor vehicles; and

(f) if regulation 48 does not apply to the seat belt and the seat belt was first fitted to the vehicle after 10th February 1997, the requirements of paragraph (4) of that regulation must be met in relation to the anchorages, fastenings, adjusting device and retracting mechanism (if any) of the seat belt to the extent (if any) that those requirements would have to be met were that paragraph to apply to all anchorages, fastenings, adjusting devices and retracting mechanisms of seat belts fitted to motor vehicles,

and paragraph (2) of regulation 48 shall apply for the purposes of sub-paragraph (f) above as it applies for the purposes of that regulation.

(7) The requirements referred to in paragraph (6)(b) are that the seat belt must be properly secured to the anchorage points provided for it and, in a case where any of those anchorage points is first fitted to the vehicle after 10th February 1997 the anchorage points to which it is secured must comply—

(a) if the vehicle is a coach, with the requirements specified in regulation 46(4)(b) or (4A)(b)(ii); or

(b) in any other case, with the requirements specified in regulation 46(4)(b).

(8) Until 10th February 1998, this regulation shall not apply to a coach first used before 1st October 1988.

(9) In this regulation—

  "school" has the meaning given by [section 4(1) of the Education Act 1996];

"forward-facing passenger seat" means a forward-facing seat which is not the driver's seat; and

"child restraint", *"disabled person's belt"*, *"forward-facing seat"*, *"seat"*, and *"seat belt"* have the meanings given in regulation 47.

(10) For the purpose of this regulation, a child is a person who is aged 3 years or more but is under the age of 16 years.]

[Regulation 48A was inserted by SI 1996/163 and is printed as subsequently amended by the Education Act 1996 s.582(3) and Sch.39, para.1(4); SI 2001/ 1043.   **B15.111**

SI 1996/163 is expressly stated (in relation to this provision) to have been made in exercise of powers under s.41 of the Road Traffic Act 1988 to the exclusion of powers under s.2(2) of the European Communities Act 1972.

Section 4(1) of the Education Act 1996 (as substituted by the Education Act 1997 s.51) defines a "school" (see reg.48A(9) above) as an educational institution which is outside the further education sector and the higher education sector and is an institution for providing—(a) primary education, (b) secondary education, or (c) both primary and secondary education, whether or not the institution also provides part-time education suitable to the requirements of junior pupils or further education. The words "part-time education suitable to the requirements of junior pupils or" have been repealed in relation to Wales only by the Education Act 2002 Sch.22, Pt 3.]

Rear under-run protection

49.—(1) Save as provided in paragraph (2), this regulation applies to a wheeled goods vehicle being either—   **B15.112**

   (a) a motor vehicle with a maximum gross weight which exceeds 3500kg and which was first used on or after 1st April 1984; or

   (b) a trailer manufactured on or after 1st May 1983 with an unladen weight which exceeds 1020kg.

(2) This regulation does not apply to—

   (a) a motor vehicle which has a maximum speed not exceeding 15mph;

   (b) a motor car or a heavy motor car constructed or adapted to form part of an articulated vehicle;

   (c) an agricultural trailer;

   (d) engineering plant;

   (e) a fire engine;

   (f) an agricultural motor vehicle;

   (g) a vehicle fitted at the rear with apparatus specially designed for spreading material on a road;

   (h) a vehicle so constructed that it can be unloaded by part of the vehicle being tipped rearwards;

   (i) a vehicle owned by the Secretary of State for Defence and used for naval, military or air force purposes;

   (j) a vehicle to which no bodywork has been fitted and which is being driven or towed—

      (i) for the purpose of a quality or safety check by its manufacturer or a dealer in, or distributor of, such vehicles; or

    (ii) to a place where, by previous arrangement, bodywork is to be fitted or work preparatory to the fitting of bodywork is to be carried out; or

    (iii) by previous arrangement to premises of a dealer in, or distributor of, such vehicles;

  (k) a vehicle which is being driven or towed to a place where by previous arrangement a device is to be fitted so that it complies with this regulation;

  (l) a vehicle specially designed and constructed, and not merely adapted, to carry other vehicles loaded onto it from the rear;

  (m) a trailer specially designed and constructed, and not merely adapted, to carry round timber, beams or girders, being items of exceptional length;

  (n) a vehicle fitted with a tail lift so constructed that the lift platform forms part of the floor of the vehicle and this part has a length of at least 1m measured parallel to the longitudinal axis of the vehicle;

  (o) a trailer having a base or centre in a country outside Great Britain from which it normally starts its journeys, provided that a period of not more than 12 months has elapsed since the vehicle was last brought into Great Britain;

  (p) a vehicle specially designed, and not merely adapted, for the carriage and mixing of liquid concrete;

  (q) a vehicle designed and used solely for the delivery of coal by means of a special conveyor which is carried on the vehicle and when in use is fitted to the rear of the vehicle so as to render its being equipped with a rear under-run protective device impracticable; or

  (r) an agricultural trailed appliance.

(3) Subject to the provisions of paragraphs (4), (5) and (6), every vehicle to which this regulation applies shall be equipped with a rear under-run protective device.

(4) A vehicle to which this regulation applies and which is fitted with a tail lift, bodywork or other part which renders its being equipped with a rear under-run protective device impracticable shall instead be equipped with one or more devices which do not protrude beyond the overall width of the vehicle (excluding any part of the device or the devices) and which comply with the following requirements—

  (a) where more than one device is fitted, not more than 50cm shall lie between one device and the device next to it;

  (b) not more than 30cm shall lie between the outermost end of a device nearest to the outermost part of the vehicle to which it is fitted and a longitudinal plane passing through the outer end of the rear axle of the vehicle on the same side of the vehicle or, in a case where the vehicle is fitted with more than one rear axle, through the outer end of the widest rear axle on the same side of the vehicle, and paragraph II.5.4.2 in the Annex to Community Directive 79/490 shall not have effect in a case where this requirement is met; and

  (c) the device or, where more than one device is fitted, all the devices together, shall have the characteristics specified in paragraphs II.5.4.5.1 to II.5.4.5.5.2 in the Annex to the said Directive save—

    (i) as provided in sub-paragraphs (a) and (b) above;

    (ii) that for the reference in paragraph II.5.4.5.1 in that Annex to 30cm there is substituted a reference to 35cm; and

    (iii) that the distance of 40cm specified in paragraph II.5.4.5 in that Annex may be measured exclusive of the said tail-lift, bodywork or other part.

(5) The provisions of paragraph (3) shall have effect so that in the case of—

    (a) a vehicle which is fitted with a demountable body, the characteristics specified in paragraph II.5.4.2 in the Annex to the said Directive have effect as if the reference to 10cm were a reference to 30cm and as if in paragraph II.5.4.5.1 the reference to 30cm were a reference to 35cm; and

    (b) a trailer with a single axle to two close-coupled axles, the height of 55cm referred to in paragraph II.5.4.5.1 in that Annex is measured when the coupling of the trailer to the vehicle by which it is drawn is at the height recommended by the manufacturer of the trailer.

(6) Instead of complying with paragraphs (3) to (5) a vehicle may comply with [Community Directive 97/19 [*O.J. No.L125, May 16, 1997, p.1*].

(7) In this regulation—

    "rear under-run protective device" means a device within the description given in paragraph II.5.4 in the Annex to Community Directive 79/490 [*see O.J. No.L128, May 26, 1979, p.22*].

[Regulation 49 is printed as amended by SI 1998/1188.]   **B15.113**

Maintenance of rear under-run protective device

50. Every device fitted to a vehicle in compliance with the requirements of regulation 49 shall at all times when the vehicle is on a road be maintained free from any obvious defect which would be likely to affect adversely the performance of the device in the function of giving resistance in the event of an impact from the rear.   **B15.114**

Sideguards

51.—(1) Save as provided in paragraph (2), this regulation applies to a wheeled goods vehicle being—   **B15.115**

    (a) a motor vehicle first used on or after 1st April 1984 with a maximum gross weight which exceeds 3500kg; or

    (b) a trailer manufactured on or after 1st May 1983 with an unladen weight which exceeds 1020kg; or

    (c) a semi-trailer manufactured before 1st May 1983 which has a relevant plate showing a gross weight exceeding 26,000kg and which forms part of an articulated vehicle with a relevant train weight exceeding 32,520kg.

(2) This regulation does not apply to—

    (a) a motor vehicle which has a maximum speed not exceeding 15mph;

(b) an agricultural trailer;

(c) engineering plant;

(d) a fire engine;

(e) an agricultural motor vehicle;

(f) a vehicle so constructed that it can be unloaded by part of the vehicle being tipped sideways or rearwards;

(g) a vehicle owned by the Secretary of State for Defence and used for naval, military or air force purposes;

(h) a vehicle to which no bodywork has been fitted and which is being driven or towed—

   (i) for the purpose of a quality or safety check by its manufacturer or a dealer in, or distributor of, such vehicles;

   (ii) to a place where, by previous arrangement, bodywork is to be fitted or work preparatory to the fitting of bodywork is to be carried out; or

   (iii) by previous arrangement to premises of a dealer in, or distributor of, such vehicles;

(i) a vehicle which is being driven or towed to a place where by previous arrangement a sideguard is to be fitted so that it complies with this regulation;

(j) a refuse vehicle;

(k) a trailer specially designed and constructed, and not merely adapted, to carry round timber, beams or girders, being items of exceptional length;

(l) a motor car or a heavy motor car constructed or adapted to form part of an articulated vehicle;

(m) a vehicle specially designed and constructed, and not merely adapted, to carry other vehicles loaded onto it from the front or the rear;

(n) a trailer with a load platform—

   (i) no part of any edge of which is more than 60mm inboard from the tangential plane; and

   (ii) the upper surface of which is not more than 750mm from the ground throughout that part of its length under which a sideguard would have to be fitted in accordance with paragraph (5)(d) to (g) if this exemption did not apply to it;

(o) a trailer having a base or centre in a country outside Great Britain from which it normally starts its journeys, provided that a period of not more than 12 months has elapsed since the vehicle was last brought into Great Britain; or

(p) an agricultural trailed appliance.

[(2A) This regulation also applies to a wheeled goods vehicle, whether of a description falling within paragraph (2) or not, which is a semi-trailer some or all of the wheels of which are driven by the drawing vehicle.]

(3) Every vehicle to which this regulation applies shall be securely fitted with a sideguard to give protection on any side of the vehicle where—

   (a) if it is a semi-trailer, the distance between the transverse planes passing through the centre of its foremost axle and through the centre of its king pin or, in the case of a vehicle having more than one king pin, the rearmost one, exceeds 4.5m; or

(b) if it is any other vehicle, the distance between the centres of any two consecutive axles exceeds 3m.

(4) Save as provided in paragraphs (6) and (7), a sideguard with which a vehicle is by this regulation required to be fitted shall comply with all the specifications listed in paragraph (5).

(5) Those specifications are—

(a) the outermost surface of every sideguard shall be smooth, essentially rigid and either flat or horizontally corrugated, save that—

   (i) any part of the surface may overlap another provided that the overlapping edges face rearwards or downwards;

   (ii) a gap not exceeding 25mm measured longitudinally may exist between any two adjacent parts of the surface provided that the foremost edge of the rearward part does not protrude outboard of the rearmost edge of the forward part; and

   (iii) domed heads of bolts or rivets may protrude beyond the surface to a distance not exceeding 10mm;

(b) no part of the lowest edge of a sideguard shall be more than 550mm above the ground when the vehicle to which it is fitted is on level ground and, in the case of a semi-trailer, when its load platform is horizontal;

(c) in a case specified in an item in column 2 of the Table the highest edge of a sideguard shall be as specified in that item in column 3;

(d) the distance between the rearmost edge of a sideguard and the transverse plane passing through the foremost part of the tyre fitted to the wheel of the vehicle nearest to it shall not exceed 300mm;

(e) the distance between the foremost edge of a sideguard fitted to a semi-trailer and a transverse plane passing through the centre of the vehicle's king pin or, if the vehicle has more than one king pin, the rearmost one, shall not exceed 3m;

(f) the foremost edge of a sideguard fitted to a semi-trailer with landing legs shall, as well as complying with sub-paragraph (e), not be more than 250mm to the rear of a transverse plane passing through the centre of the leg nearest to that edge;

(g) the distance between the foremost edge of a sideguard fitted to a vehicle other than a semi-trailer and a transverse plane passing through the rearmost part of the tyre fitted to the wheel of the vehicle nearest to it shall not exceed 300mm if the vehicle is a motor vehicle and 500mm if the vehicle is a trailer;

(h) the external edges of a sideguard shall be rounded at a radius of at least 2.5mm;

(i) no sideguard shall be more than 30mm inboard from the tangential plane;

(j) no sideguard shall project beyond the longitudinal plane from which, in the absence of a sideguard, the vehicle's overall width would fall to be measured;

(k) every sideguard shall cover an area extending to at least 100mm upwards from its lowest edge, 100mm downwards from its highest edge, and 100mm rearwards and inwards from its foremost edge, and no sideguard shall have a vertical gap measuring more than 300mm nor any vertical surface measuring less than 100mm; and

(l) except in the case of a vehicle described in paragraph (1)(c) every sideguard shall be capable of withstanding a force of 2 kilonewtons applied perpendicularly to any part of its surface by the centre of a ram the face of which is circular and not more than 220mm in diameter, and during such application—

    (i) no part of the sideguard shall be deflected by more than 150mm, and

    (ii) no part of the sideguard which is less than 250mm from its rearmost part shall be deflected by more than 30mm.

TABLE

(regulation 51(5))

1	2	3
Item	Case	Requirement about highest edge of sideguard
1	Where the floor of the vehicle to which the sideguard is fitted— (i) extends laterally outside the tangential plane; (ii) is not more than 1.85m from the ground; (iii) extends laterally over the whole of the length of the sideguard with which the vehicle is required by this regulation to be fitted; and (iv) is wholly covered at its edge by a side-rave the lower edge of which is not more than 150mm below the underside of the floor.	Note more than 350mm below the lower edge of the side-rave.
2	Where the floor of the vehicle to which the sideguard is fitted— (i) extends laterally outside the tangential plane; and (ii) does not comply with all of the provisions specified in sub-paragraphs (ii), (iii) and (iv) in item 1 above, and any part of the structure of the vehicle is cut within 1.85m of the ground by the tangential plane.	Not more than 350mm below the structure of the vehicle where it is cut by the tangential plane.

1	2	3
Item	Case	Requirement about highest edge of sideguard
3	Where— (i) no part of the structure of the vehicle is cut within 1.85m of the ground by the tangential plane; and (ii) the upper surface of the load carrying structure of the vehicle is less than 1.5m from the ground.	Not less than the height of the upper surface of the load carrying structure of the vehicle.
4	A vehicle specially designed, and not merely adapted, for the carriage and mixing of liquid concrete.	Not less than 1m from the ground.
5	Any other case.	Not less than 1.5m from the ground.

(6) The provisions of paragraph (4) apply—

(a) in the case of an extendible trailer when it is, by virtue of the extending mechanism, extended to a length greater than its minimum, so as not to require, in respect of any additional distance solely attributed to the extension, compliance with the specifications mentioned in paragraph (5)(d) to (g);

(b) in the case of a vehicle designed and constructed, and not merely adapted, to be fitted with a demountable body or to carry a container, when it is not fitted with a demountable body or carrying such a container as if it were fitted with such a body or carrying such a container; and

(c) only so far as it is practicable in the case of—

(i) a vehicle designed solely for the carriage of a fluid substance in a closed tank which is permanently fitted to the vehicle and provided with valves and hose or pipe connections for loading or unloading; and

(ii) a vehicle which requires additional stability during loading or unloading or while being used for operations for which it is designed or adapted and is fitted on one or both sides with an extendible device to provide such stability.

(7) In the case of a motor vehicle to which this regulation applies and which is of a type which was required to be approved by the Type Approval for Goods Vehicles Regulations before 1st October 1983—

(a) if the bodywork of the vehicle covers the whole of the area specified as regards a sideguard in paragraph (5)(b), (c), (d) and (g) above the other provisions of that paragraph do not apply to that vehicle; and

(b) if the bodywork of the vehicle covers only part of that area the part of that area which is not so covered shall be fitted with a sideguard which complies with the provisions of paragraph (5) above save that there shall not be a gap between—

    (i) the rearmost edge of the sideguard or the rearmost part of the bodywork (whichever is furthest to the rear) and the transverse plane mentioned in paragraph (5)(d) of more than 300mm;

    (ii) the foremost edge of the sideguard or the foremost part of the bodywork (whichever is furthest to the front) and the transverse plane mentioned in paragraph (5)(g) of more than 300mm; or

    (iii) any vertical or sloping edge of any part of the bodywork in question and the edge of the sideguard immediately forwards or rearwards thereof of more than 25mm measured horizontally.

(8) In this regulation—

"relevant plate" means a Ministry plate, where fitted, and in other cases a plate fitted in accordance with regulation 66;

"relevant train weight" means the train weight shown in column 2 of the Ministry plate, where fitted, and in other cases the maximum train weight shown at item 8 of the plate fitted in accordance with regulation 66; and

"tangential plane", in regulation to a sideguard, means the vertical plane tangential to the external face of the outermost part of the tyre (excluding any distortion caused by the weight of the vehicle) fitted to the outermost wheel at the rear and on the same side of the vehicle.

[(9) Instead of complying with the foregoing provisions of this regulation a vehicle may comply with Community Directive 89/297.]

B15.116   *[Regulation 51 is printed as amended by SI 1987/676; SI 1989/1695.]*

Maintenance of sideguards

B15.117   **52.** Every sideguard fitted to a vehicle in compliance with the requirements of regulation 51 shall at all times when the vehicle is on a road be maintained free from any obvious defect which would be likely to affect adversely its effectiveness.

Mascots

B15.118   **53.**—(1) Subject to paragraph (2), no mascot, emblem or other ornamental object shall be carried by a motor vehicle first used on or after 1st October 1937 in any position where it is likely to strike any person with whom the vehicle may collide unless the mascot is not liable to cause injury to such person by reason of any projection thereon.

(2) Instead of complying with the requirements of paragraph (1) a vehicle may comply with Community Directive 74/483 or 79/488 or ECE Regulation 26.01.

[Strength of superstructure

B15.119   **53A.**—(1) This regulation applies to every coach which is—

    (a) a single decked vehicle;

    (b) equipped with a compartment below the deck for the luggage of passengers; and

(c) first used on or after [1st April 1993].

(2) Every vehicle to which this regulation applies shall comply with the requirements of ECE Regulation 66.]

[Regulation 53A was inserted by SI 1987/1133 and is printed as subsequently amended by SI 1989/2360.] **B15.120**

[Additional exits from double-decked coaches

53B.—(1) This regulation applies to every coach which is— **B15.121**

    (a) a double-decked vehicle; and

    (b) first used on or after 1st April 1990.

(2) Subject to the following provisions of this regulation, every vehicle to which this regulation applies shall be equipped with two staircases, one of which shall be located in one half of the vehicle and the other in the other half of the vehicle.

(3) Instead of being equipped with two staircases in accordance with paragraph (2), a vehicle to which this regulation applies may be equipped in accordance with the following provisions of this regulation with a hammer or other similar device with which in case of emergency any side window of the vehicle may be broken.

(4) Where a vehicle is equipped with—

    (a) a staircase located in one half of the vehicle; and

    (b) an emergency exit complying with regulation 21(8) of the Public Service Vehicles (Conditions of Fitness, Equipment, Use and Certification) Regulations 1981 [*SI 1981/257 (q.v.)*] located in the same half of the upper deck of the vehicle;

the hammer or the similar device shall be located in the other half of that deck.

(5) Any hammer or other similar device with which a vehicle is equipped pursuant to this regulation shall be located in a conspicuous and readily accessible position in the upper deck of the vehicle.

(6) There shall be displayed, in a conspicuous position in close proximity to the hammer or other similar device, a notice which shall contain in clear and indelible lettering—

    (a) in letters not less than 25mm high, the heading *"in emergency"*; and

    (b) in letters not less than 10mm high, instructions that in case of emergency the hammer or device is to be used first to break any side window by striking the glass near the edge of the window and then to clear any remaining glass from the window aperture.

(7) For the purposes of this regulation a staircase, emergency exit, hammer or other similar device (as the case may be) shall be considered to be located in the other half of the vehicle if the shortest distance between any part of that staircase, exit, hammer or device (as the case may be) and any part of any other staircase, emergency exit, hammer or device is not less than one half of the overall length of the vehicle.]

[Regulation 53B was inserted by SI 1987/1133.] **B15.122**

[Alternative means of compliance

53C.—[(1)] A coach which is required by either regulation 53A or 53B, as the **B15.123**

case may be, to meet the requirements specified in that particular provision, need not meet them if it meets the requirements of such of the Annexes to Directive 2001/85/EC of the European Parliament and of the Council of 20 November 2001, relating to special provisions for vehicles used for the carriage of passengers comprising more than eight seats in addition to the driver's seat, and amending Directives 70/156/EEC and 97/27/EC, as apply to that coach.]

[(2) A coach which is required by either regulation 53A or 53B, as the case may be, to meet the requirements specified in that particular provision, need not meet them if it meets such requirements of ECE Regulation 107.01 or 107.02 as apply to that coach.]

B15.124   *[Regulation 53C was inserted by SI 2005/2987; SI 2009/142.]*

K Control of Emissions

[Silencers—general]

B15.125   54.—(1) Every vehicle propelled by an internal combustion engine shall be fitted with an exhaust system including a silencer and the exhaust gases from the engine shall not escape into the atmosphere without first passing through the silencer.

(2) Every exhaust system and silencer shall be maintained in good and efficient working order and [shall not after the date of manufacture be altered] so as to increase the noise made by the escape of exhaust gases.

(3) Instead of complying with paragraph (1) a vehicle may comply with Community Directive 77/212, 81/334, 84/372 [, 84/424 or 92/97 or ECE Regulation 51.02] or, in the case of a motor cycle other than a moped, 78/1015, 87/56 or 89/235.

(4) In this regulation *"moped"* has the meaning given to it in paragraph (5) [*sic*] of Schedule 9.

B15.126   *[Regulation 54 is printed as amended by SI 1994/14; SI 1996/2329.]*

[Noise limits—certain vehicles with 3 or more wheels—general]

B15.127   55.—(1) Save as provided in [paragraphs (1A) and (2)] and regulation 59, this regulation applies to every wheeled motor vehicle having at least three wheels and first used on or after 1st October 1983 which is—

(a) a vehicle, not falling within sub-paragraph (b) or (c), with or without bodywork;

(b) a vehicle not falling within sub-paragraph (c) which is—

(i) engineering plant;

(ii) a locomotive other than an agricultural motor vehicle;

(iii) a motor tractor other than an industrial tractor or an agricultural motor vehicle;

(iv) a public works vehicle;

(v) a works truck; or

(vi) a refuse vehicle; or

(c) a vehicle which—

(i) has a compression ignition engine;

    (ii) is so constructed or adapted that the driving power of the engine is, or by appropriate use of the controls can be, transmitted to all wheels of the vehicle; and

    (iii) falls within category I.1.1, I.1.2, or I.1.3 specified in Article 1 of Community Directive 77/212.

[(1A)　This regulation does not apply to a vehicle to which an item in the Table in regulation 55A applies.]

(2)　This regulation does not apply to—

    (a) a motor cycle with a sidecar attached;

    (b) an agricultural motor vehicle which is first used before 1st June 1986 or which is not driven at more than 20mph;

    (c) an industrial tractor;

    (d) a road roller;

    (e) a vehicle specially constructed, and not merely adapted, for the purposes of fighting fires or salvage from fires at or in the vicinity of airports, and having an engine power exceeding 220kW;

    (f) a vehicle which runs on rails; or

    (g) a vehicle manufactured by Leyland Vehicles Ltd. and known as the Atlantean Bus, if first used before 1st October 1984.

(3)　Save as provided in paragraphs (4) and (5), every vehicle to which this regulation applies shall be so constructed that it complies with the requirements set out in item 1, 2, 3 or 4 of the Table [*see table at § B15.126*]; a vehicle complies with those requirements if—

    (a) its sound level does not exceed the relevant limit specified in column 2(a), (b) or (c), as the case may be, in the relevant item when measured under the conditions specified in column 3 in that item and by the method specified in column 4 in that item using the apparatus prescribed in paragraph (6); and

    (b) in the case of a vehicle referred to in paragraph 1(a) (other than one having less than four wheels or a maximum speed not exceeding 25 km/h) or 1(c), the device designed to reduce the exhaust noise meets the requirements specified in column 5 in that item.

(4)　Save as provided in paragraph (5), paragraph (3) applies to every vehicle to which this regulation applies and which is first used on or after 1st April 1990, unless it is equipped with 5 or more forward gears and has a maximum power to maximum gross weight ratio not less than 75kW per 1000kg, and is of a type in respect of which a type approval certificate has been issued under the Type Approval (Great Britain) Regulations as if, for the reference to items 1, 2, 3 or 4 of the Table there were substituted a reference to item 4 of the Table.

(5)　Paragraph (4) does not apply to a vehicle in category 5.2.2.1.3 as defined in Annex I to Directive 84/424 and equipped with a compression ignition engine, a vehicle in category 5.2.2.1.4 as defined in that Annex, or a vehicle referred to in paragraph 1(b) unless it is first used on or after 1st April 1991.

(6)　The apparatus prescribed for the purposes of paragraph 3(a) and [regulation 56(2)(a) and Schedule 7A] is a sound level meter of the type described in Publication No.179 of the International Electrotechnical Commission, in either its first or second edition, a sound level meter complying with the specification for Type 0 or Type 1 in Publication No.651 (1979) "Sound Level Meters" of the International Electrotechnical Commission, or a sound level meter complying with the specifications of the British Standard Number BS 5969: 1981 which came into effect on 29th May 1981.

[(6A) A vehicle shall be deemed to satisfy the requirements of this regulation if it is so constructed that it complies with the requirements specified in column 4 of item 2 in the Table in regulation 55A as they apply to a vehicle first used on or after the date specified in column 3 of that item.]

(7) Instead of complying with the preceding provisions of this regulation a vehicle may comply at the time of its first use with Community Directive 77/212, 81/334, 84/372 [, 84/424, 92/97 or 96/20 or ECE Regulation 51.02].

B15.128   *[Regulation 55 is printed as amended by SI 1989/1865; SI 1994/14; SI 1996/2329.]*

B15.129

[TABLE
(regulation 55(3))

1		2 Limits of sound level		3	4	5
Item		(a) Vehicle referred to in paragraph (1)(a)	(b) Vehicle referred to in paragraph (1)(c)	(c) Vehicle referred to in paragraph (1)(c)	Conditions of measurement	Method of measurement	Requirements for exhaust device
1		Limits specified in paragraph I.1 of the Annex to Community Directive 77/212.	89dB(a)	82dB(a)	Conditions specified in paragraph I.3 of the Annex to Community Directive 77/212.	Method specified in paragraph I.4.1 of the Annex to Community Directive 77/212.	Requirements specified in heading II of the Annex to Community Directive 77/212 (except paragraphs II.2 and II.5).

1	2 Limits of sound level			3	4	5
Item	(a) Vehicle referred to in paragraph (1)(a)	(b) Vehicle referred to in paragraph (1)(c)	(c) Vehicle referred to in paragraph (1)(c)	Conditions of measurement	Method of measurement	Requirements for exhaust device
2	Limits specified in paragraph 5.2.2.1 of Annex I to Community Directive 81/334.	89dB(a)	82dB(a)	Conditions specified in paragraph 5.2.2.3 of Annex I to Community Directive 81/334.	Method specified in paragraph 5.2.2.4 of Annex I to Community Directive 81/334. Interpretation of results as specified in paragraph 5.2.2.5 of that Annex.	Requirements specified in section 3 and paragraphs 5.1 and 5.3.1 of Annex I to Community Directive 81/334.

1	2 Limits of sound level			3	4	5
Item	(a) Vehicle referred to in paragraph (1)(a)	(b) Vehicle referred to in paragraph (1)(c)	(c) Vehicle referred to in paragraph (1)(c)	Conditions of measurement	Method of measurement	Requirements for exhaust device
3	Limits specified in paragraph 5.2.2.1 of Annex I to Community Directive 84/372.	89dB(a)	82dB(a)	Conditions specified in paragraph 5.2.2.3 of Annex I to Community Directive 84/372.	Method specified in paragraph 5.2.2.4 of Annex I to Community Directive 84/372, except that vehicles with 5 or more forward gears and a with 5 or more forward gears and a maximum power to maximum gross weight ratio not less than 75kW per 1000 kg may be tested in 3rd gear only. Interpretation of results as specified in paragraph 5.2.2.5 of that Annex.	Requirements specified in section 3 and paragraphs 5.1 and 5.3.1 of Annex I to Community Directive 84/372.

1	2			3	4	5
	Limits of sound level					
Item	(a) Vehicle referred to in paragraph (1)(a)	(b) Vehicle referred to in paragraph (1)(c)	(c) Vehicle referred to in paragraph (1)(c)	Conditions of measurement	Method of measurement	Requirements for exhaust device
4	Limits specified in paragraph 5.2.2.1 of Annex I to Community Directive 84/424.	Vehicles with engine power— —less than 75kW —84dB(a) —not less than 75kW —86dB(a)	Limits specified in paragraph 5.2.2.1 of Annex I to Community Directive 84/424.	Conditions specified in paragraph 5.2.2.3 of Annex I to Community Directive 84/424.	Method specified in paragraph 5.2.2.4 of Annex I to Community Directive 84/424, except that vehicles with 5 or more forward gears and a maximum power to maximum gross weight ratio not less than 75kW per 1000 kg may be tested in 3rd gear only. Interpretation of results as specified in paragraph 5.2.2.5 of that Annex.	Requirements specified in section 3 and paragraphs 5.1 and 5.3.1 of Annex I to Community Directive 84/424.

[**Noise limits—certain vehicles first used on or after 1st October 1996—general**

55A.—(1) A motor vehicle to which an item in the Table below applies shall   **B15.130** be so constructed that it meets the requirements specified in column 4 of that item; and an item in that Table applies to a vehicle if it is of the description specified in column 2 of that item.

This paragraph has effect subject to the following provisions of this regulation, regulation 59 and Schedule 7XA.

THE TABLE

(1) Item	(2) Vehicles to which the item applies	(3) Earliest date of first use (see column 2)	(4) The requirements	(5) Modification of Community Directives in relation to special vehicles (see paragraph (4)(c))
1	1. All motor vehicles with less than 4 wheels and first used on or after the date specified in column 3 of this item. 2. All special vehicles first used on or after the date specified in column 3 of this item. 3. All motor vehicles first first used on or after the date specified in column 3 of this item with a maximum speed not exceeding 25 km/h.	1st October 1996	The requirement of— (a) regulation 55 as they would apply to the vehicle but for paragraph (1A) of that regulation; or (b) paragraphs 3 and 5.2 of Annex I to Community Directive 92/97 or 96/20.	For paragraph 5.2.2.1 of Annex I, substitute— "The sound level measured in accordance with 5.2.2.2 to 5.2.2.5 of this Annex shall not exceed—in the case of vehicles with engine power of less than 75kW, 84 dB(a)in the case of vehicles with engine power not less than 75 kW, 86 dB(a)."

(1) Item	(2) Vehicles to which the item applies	(3) Earliest date of first use (see column 2)	(4) The requirements	(5) Modification of Community Directives in relation to special vehicles (see paragraph (4)(c))
2	All motor vehicles first used on or after the date specified in column 3 of this item, not being a vehicle to which item 1 applies.	1st October 1996	The requirements of paragraphs 3 and 5 of Annex I to Community Directive 92/97 or 96/20.	

(2) (b) Paragraph (1) does not apply to—

    (a) a vehicle with fewer than 3 wheels; or

    (b) a vehicle of a description mentioned in regulation 55(2).

(3) In this regulation, *"special vehicle"* means a vehicle which is—

    (a) engineering plant;

    (b) a locomotive other than an agricultural motor vehicle;

    (c) a motor tractor other than an industrial tractor or an agricultural motor vehicle;

    (d) a public works vehicle; or

    (e) a works truck.

(4) For the purposes of this regulation—

    (a) subject to paragraphs (b), (c), (d) and (e), the Community Directives referred to in this regulation shall have effect in relation to a vehicle that is not a "vehicle" within the meaning of the Framework Directive but is of a class of a description specified in column 2 of an item in the Table in regulation 15 (whether or not regulation 15 applies to the vehicle) as it has effect in relation to a vehicle of the category specified in column 3 of that item;

    (b) subject to paragraphs (c), (d) and (e), a vehicle that does not fall within sub-paragraph (a) and is not a "vehicle" within the meaning of the Framework Directive shall be regarded as meeting the requirements of paragraph 5 of a Community Directive mentioned in the Table if it meets—

        (i) the requirements of that paragraph as it applies to a vehicle in category M_1 or N_1 within the meaning of the Community Directive, or

        (ii) the requirements of that paragraph as it applies to a vehicle that is not in either of those categories;

(c) subject to sub-paragraphs (d) and (e), in relation to a special vehicle the Community Directives mentioned in column 4 of an item in the Table shall have effect with the modifications (if any) specified in column 5 of the item;

(d) a requirement in paragraph 5.2.2.1 of Annex I to Community Directive 92/97 for a sound level not to exceed a specified limit in specified circumstances shall be read as a requirement for the sound level not to exceed that limit by more than the amount mentioned in paragraph 4.1 of Annex V to the Community Directive in those circumstances;

(e) a requirement in paragraph 5.2.2.1 of Annex I to Community Directive 96/20 for a sound level not to exceed a specified limit in specified circumstances shall be read as a requirement for the sound level not to exceed that limit by more than the amount mentioned in paragraph 4.1 of Annex III to the Directive in those circumstances.

(5) Instead of complying with paragraph (1) a vehicle may comply at the time of its first use—

(a) in the case of a vehicle to which item 1 of the Table applies, with Community Directive 77/212, 81/334, 84/424, 92/97 or 96/20 or ECE Regulation 51.02; or

(b) in the case of a vehicle to which item 2 of the Table applies, with Community Directive 92/97 or 96/20 or ECE Regulation 51.02.]

[Regulation 55A was inserted by SI 1996/2329.   **B15.131**

With effect from April 29, 2009, the Framework Directive (i.e. Directive 2007/46/EC (O.J. No.L263, October 9, 2007, p.1)) defines a motor vehicle in art.3 as:

any power-driven vehicle which is moved by its own means, having at least four wheels, being complete, completed or incomplete, with a maximum design speed exceeding 25 km/h;

The definition of "vehicle" includes any motor vehicle (as defined above) or its trailer. A trailer is defined as:

any non-self-propelled vehicle on wheels which is designed and constructed to be towed by a motor vehicle.]

Noise limits—agricultural motor vehicles and industrial tractors

56.—(1) Save as provided in regulation 59, this regulation applies to every   **B15.132**
wheeled vehicle first used on or after 1st April 1983 being an agricultural motor vehicle or an industrial tractor, other than—

(a) an agricultural motor vehicle which is first used on or after 1st June 1986 and which is driven at more than 20mph; or

(b) a road roller.

(2) Every vehicle to which this regulation applies should be so constructed—

(a) that its sound level does not exceed—

(i) if it is a vehicle with engine power of less than 65kW, 89 dB(a);

(ii) if it is a vehicle with engine power of 65kW or more, and first used before 1st October 1991, 92 dB(a); or

(iii) if it is a vehicle with engine power of 65kW or more, and first used on or after 1st October 1991, 89 dB(a), when measured under the conditions specified in paragraph I.3 of Annex VI of Community Directive 74/151 by the method specified in paragraph I.4.1 of that Annex using the apparatus prescribed in regulation 55(6); and

(b) that the device designed to reduce the exhaust noise meets the requirements specified in paragraph II.1 of the Annex and, if fibrous absorbent material is used, the requirements specified in paragraphs II.4.1 to II.4.3 of that Annex.

[Noise limits—construction requirements relating to motor cycles

B15.133   57.—(1) Subject to regulation 59, this regulation applies to every motor vehicle first used on or after 1st April 1983 which is—

(a) a moped; or

(b) a two-wheeled motor cycle, whether or not with sidecar attached, which is not a moped.

(2) A vehicle to which this regulation applies shall be so constructed that it meets,—

(a) if it is first used before 1st April 1991, the requirements of item 1 or 2 of the Table in Part I of Schedule 7A;

(b) if it is used on or after that date, the requirements of item 2 of that Table.

(3) Instead of complying with paragraph (2), a vehicle first used before 1st April 1991 may comply at the time of its first use with Community Directive 78/1015, 87/56 or 89/235.

(4) Instead of complying with paragraph (2), a vehicle first used on or after 1st April 1991 may comply at the time of its first use with Community Directive 87/56 or 89/235.

(5) In this regulation *"moped"* has the meaning given to it in paragraph 5 of Schedule 9.]

B15.134   *[Regulation 57 was originally amended by SI 1989/1865. The text of reg.57 printed above was substituted by SI 1994/14.]*

[Exhaust systems—motor cycles

B15.135   57A.—(1) Any original silencer forming part of the exhaust system of a vehicle to which regulation 57 applies, being a vehicle first used before 1st February 1996, shall—

(a) be so constructed that the vehicle meets the requirements specified in paragraph 3 (other than sub-paragraphs 3.2 and 3.3) of Annex I to Community Directive 78/1015 and be marked in accordance with sub-paragraph 3.3 of that Annex; or

(b) be so constructed that the vehicle meets the requirements specified in paragraph 3 (other than sub-paragraphs 3.2 and 3.3) of Annex I to Community Directive 89/235 and be marked in accordance with sub-paragraph 3.3 of that Annex.

(2) Any original silencer forming part of the exhaust system of a vehicle to which regulation 57 applies, being a vehicle first used on or after 1st February

1996, shall be so constructed that the vehicle meets the requirements specified in paragraph 3 (other than sub-paragraphs 3.2 and 3.3) of Annex I to Community Directive 89/235 and be marked in accordance with sub-paragraph 3.3 of that Annex.

(3) A vehicle fitted with an original silencer may,—

    (a) if the vehicle is first used before 1st February 1996, instead of complying with paragraph (1), comply at the time of first use with Community Directive 78/1015, 87/56 or 89/235; or

    (b) if the vehicle is first used on or after that date, instead of complying with paragraph (2), comply at the time of first use with Community Directive 89/235.

(4) Where any replacement silencer forms part of the exhaust system of a vehicle to which regulation 57 applies, being a vehicle first used on or after 1st January 1985, the first requirement or the second requirement as set out below must be met in respect of the silencer.

(5) In order for the first requirement to be met in respect of a silencer forming part of the exhaust system of a vehicle (in this paragraph referred to as *"the vehicle in question"*),—

    (a) if the vehicle in question is first used before 1st April 1991, the silencer must be so constructed that, were it to be fitted to an unused vehicle of the same model as the vehicle in question, the unused vehicle would meet—

        (i) the requirements of item 1 or 3 of the Table in Part I of Schedule 7A; and

        (ii) the requirements specified in paragraph 3 (other than sub-paragraphs 3.2 and 3.3) of Annex I to Community Directive 78/1015 or 89/235,

    and the silencer must be marked in accordance with sub-paragraph 3.3 of Annex I to Community Directive 78/1015 or 89/235;

    (b) if the vehicle in question is first used on or after the 1st April 1991 but before 1st February 1996, the silencer must be so constructed that, were it to be fitted to an unused vehicle of the same model as the vehicle in question, the unused vehicle would meet—

        (i) the requirements of item 3 of the Table in Part I of Schedule 7A; and

        (ii) the requirements specified in paragraph 3 (other than sub-paragraphs 3.2 and 3.3) of Annex I to Community Directive 78/1015 or 89/235,

    and the silencer must be marked in accordance with sub-paragraph 3.3 of Annex I to Community Directive 78/1015 or 89/235;

    (c) if the vehicle in question is first used on or after 1st February 1996, the silencer must be so constructed that, were it to be fitted to an unused vehicle of the same model as the vehicle in question, the unused vehicle would meet—

        (i) the requirements of item 3 of the Table in Part I of Schedule 7A; and

        (ii) the requirements specified in paragraph 3 (other than sub-paragraphs 3.2 and 3.3) of Annex I to Community Directive 89/235,

and the silencer must be marked in accordance with sub-paragraph 3.3 of Annex I to that Directive.

(6) In order for the second requirement to be met in respect of a silencer forming part of the exhaust system of a vehicle (in Part II of Schedule 7A referred to as *"the vehicle in question"*),—

(a) if the vehicle is first used before 1st April 1991, the silencer must meet the requirements of paragraph 2, 3 or 4 of Part II of Schedule 7A; or

(b) if the vehicle is first used on or after that date, the silencer must meet the requirements of paragraph 4 of Part II of Schedule 7A.

(7) Any requirements specified in paragraph (5) or in Part II of Schedule 7A relating to the silencer were it to be fitted to an unused vehicle of the same model as the vehicle in question (as defined in that paragraph or in paragraph (6) for the purposes of that Part, as the case may be) shall be deemed to be met if they are met by the silencer as fitted to the vehicle in question at the time that it is first fitted.

(8) For the purposes of this regulation, Community Directive 89/235 shall have effect as if—

(a) in Annex I, for sub-paragraph 3.4.1, there were substituted—

"3.4.1. After removal of the fibrous material, the vehicle must meet the relevant requirements"; and

for sub-paragraph 3.4.3 there were substituted—

"3.4.3. After the exhaust system has been put into a normal state for road use by one of the following conditioning methods, the vehicle must meet the relevant requirements:";

(b) references in Annex I as so modified to a vehicle meeting the relevant requirements were,—

(i) in relation to an original silencer, references to a vehicle meeting the requirements of item 2 of the Table in Part I of Schedule 7A; and

(ii) in relation to a replacement silencer, references to a vehicle meeting the requirements of item 3 of that Table;

(c) in Annex II there were omitted sub-paragraphs 3.1.2, 3.4 and 3.5 and in sub-paragraph 3.2—

(i) the words "and the name referred to in 3.1.2", and

(ii) the words after "legible".

[(8A) For the purposes of paragraphs (1)(b) and (2) in their application to vehicles with a design speed not exceeding 50 km/h, Community Directive 89/235/EEC shall have effect as if it were not only modified in accordance with paragraph (8) but were further modified by the omission of—

(a) sub-paragraph 3.1.3 of Annex II; and

(b) in sub-paragraph 3.2 of that Annex, the words "and 3.1.3".]

(9) In relation to a replacement silencer which is—

(a) fitted to a vehicle before 1st February 1997; and

    (b) clearly and indelibly marked with the name or trade mark of the manufacturer of the silencer and with that manufacturer's part number relating to it,

paragraphs (5) and (6) of this regulation and Parts II and III of Schedule 7A shall have effect as if they contained no reference to a silencer being marked.

(10) For the purposes of this regulation, a silencer forming part of the exhaust system of a vehicle shall not be regarded as being marked in accordance with sub-paragraph 3.3 of Annex I to Community Directive 78/1015 or 89/235, paragraph (9) of this regulation or any paragraph of Part II of Schedule 7A if the marking is so obscured by any part of the vehicle that it cannot easily be read.

(11) Until 1st February 1996, for the purposes of paragraph (6), a vehicle first used on or after 1st April 1991 shall be treated as a vehicle first used before 1st April 1991.

(12) Part III of Schedule 7A shall have effect for the purpose of exempting certain silencers from the provisions of paragraph (4).

(13) No person shall use a motor cycle on a road or cause or permit such a vehicle to be so used if any part of the exhaust system has been indelibly marked by the manufacturer of that part with the words "NOT FOR ROAD USE" or words to that effect.

(14) In this regulation—

    "original silencer", in relation to a vehicle, means a silencer which was fitted to the vehicle when it was manufactured;

    "replacement silencer", in relation to a vehicle, means a silencer fitted to the vehicle, not being an original silencer; and

    "trade mark" has the same meaning as in the Trade Marks Act 1938.]

[Regulation 57A was inserted by SI 1994/14 and is printed as subsequently **B15.136** *amended by SI 1996/16.*

    The Trade Marks Act 1938 (see reg.57A(14)) has been repealed by the Trade Marks Act 1994; the term "trade mark" is defined in s.1(1) of the 1994 Act.]

[Noise limits—maintenance requirements relating to motor cycles

57B.—(1) No person shall use or cause or permit to be used on a road a motor   **B15.137** cycle to which regulation 57 applies if the three conditions specified below are all fulfilled.

(2) The first condition is fulfilled if the vehicle does not meet the noise limit requirements.

(3) The second condition is fulfilled if—

    (a) any part of the vehicle is not in good and efficient working order, or

    (b) the vehicle has been altered.

(4) The third condition is fulfilled if the noise made by the vehicle would have been materially less (so far as applicable)—

    (a) were all parts of the vehicle in good and efficient working order, or

    (b) had the vehicle not been altered.

(5) For the purposes of this regulation, a vehicle meets the noise limit requirements if,—

    (a) in the case of a vehicle first used before 1st April 1991 and not fitted with a replacement silencer, it meets the requirements of item 1 or 2 of the Table in Part I of Schedule 7A;

(b) in the case of a vehicle first used before 1st April 1991 and fitted with a replacement silencer, it meets the requirements of item 1 or 3 of that Table;

(c) in the case of a vehicle first used on or after 1st April 1991 and not fitted with a replacement silencer, it meets the requirements of item 2 of that Table;

(d) in the case of a vehicle first used on or after 1st April 1991 and fitted with a replacement silencer, it meets the requirements of item 3 of that Table.

(6) In this regulation, *"replacement silencer"* has the same meaning as in regulation 57A.]

B15.138   *[Regulation 57B was inserted by SI 1994/14.]*

Noise limits—vehicles not subject to regulations 55 to 57, first used on or after 1st April 1970

B15.139   **58.** […]
[Revoked by SI 1995/1201.]

[Exceptions to regulations 55 to 57B]

B15.140   **59.** Regulations 55, [55A,] 56, [57, [57A and 57B]] do not apply to a motor vehicle which is—

(a) proceeding to a place where, by previous arrangement—

    (i) noise emitted by it is about to be measured for the purpose of ascertaining whether or not the vehicle complies with such of those provisions as apply to it; or

    (ii) the vehicle is about to be mechanically adjusted, modified or equipped for the purpose of securing that it so complies; or

(b) returning from such a place immediately after the noise has been so measured.

B15.141   *[Regulation 59 is printed as amended by SI 1989/1865; SI 1994/14; SI 1995/1201; SI 1996/2329.]*

Radio interference suppression

B15.142   **60.**—[(1) Subject to paragraphs (1B), (1D), (1E) and (2)—

(a) every vehicle to which this sub-paragraph applies shall be so constructed that it complies with the requirements of paragraph 6 of Annex I to Community Directive 72/245 or paragraph 6 (as read with paragraph 8) of Annex I to Community Directive 95/54 (whether or not those Community Directives apply to the vehicle); and

(b) every agricultural and forestry tractor which is propelled by a spark ignition engine and is first used on or after 1st April 1974 shall be so constructed that it meets the requirements of paragraph 6 of Community Directive 72/245, 75/322 or 95/54.]

[(1A) Paragraph (1)(a) applies to every wheeled vehicle which is propelled by a spark ignition engine and—

(a) is first used on or after 1st April 1974 and before 1st January 1996; or

(b) is first used on or after 1st January 1996 and is a "vehicle" within the meaning of the Framework Directive.]

[(1B) For the purposes of paragraph (1) —

(a) a requirement in paragraph 6.2.2 of Community Directive 72/245 or 75/322 for any description of radiation level not to exceed a specified limit when measured in specified circumstances shall be read as a requirement for that description of radiation level not to exceed that limit by more than the amount mentioned in paragraph 9.2 of those Community Directives when measured in those circumstances; and

(b) a requirement in paragraph 6.2.2 or 6.3.2 of Community Directive 95/54 for any description of radiation level not to exceed a specified limit when measured in specified circumstances shall be read as a requirement for that description of radiation level not to exceed that limit by more than the amount mentioned in paragraph 7.3.1 of the Community Directive when measured in those circumstances.]

[(1C) Subject to paragraph (1F), the requirements of Community Directive 72/245/EC as amended by Community Directive 95/54/EC shall be met by electrical/electronic sub-assemblies as components or separate technical units first used on or after 1 October 2002.]

[(1D) Instead of complying with paragraph (1)(a) a vehicle may comply at the time of first use with Community Directive 72/245 or 95/54 or [ECE Regulations 10, 10.01 or 10.02].]

[(1E) Instead of complying with paragraph (1)(b) a vehicle may comply at the time of first use with Community Directive 75/322.]

[(1F) The requirements of paragraph (1C) shall not apply to electrical/ electronic sub-assemblies of the following descriptions—

(a) replacement parts intended for use on vehicles manufactured in accordance with type approvals granted before 1 January 1996 in compliance with Community Directive 72/245/EEC or Community Directive 72/306/EEC including any subsequent extension that may have been granted to such type approvals;

(b) electrical/electronic sub-assemblies fitted to any vehicle under an authorisation having effect under Part III of the Police Act 1997 or Part II of the Regulation of Investigatory Powers Act 2000.]

(2) This regulation does not apply to a vehicle constructed or assembled by a person not ordinarily engaged in the trade or business of manufacturing vehicles of that description, but nothing in this paragraph affects the application to such vehicles of the Wireless Telegraphy (Control of Interference from Ignition Apparatus) Regulations 1973 [*SI 1973/1217; not reproduced in this work*].

[(3) In this regulation *"electrical/electronic sub-assembly"* has the same meaning as in Community Directive 95/54.]

[Regulation 60 is printed as amended by SI 1996/2329; SI 2002/2126.   **B15.143**

The term "electrical/electronic sub-assembly" (see reg.60(3)) is defined by Directive 95/54/EC Annex I, para.2.1.10 as follows:

> *"Electrical/electronic sub-assembly"* (ESA) means an electrical and/or electronic device or set(s) of devices intended to be part of a vehicle,

together with any associated electrical connections and wiring, which performs one or more specialized functions. An ESA may be approved at the request of a manufacturer as either a "component" or a "separate technical unit (STU)" (see Directive 70/156/EEC, Article 2).]

Emission of smoke, vapour, gases, oily substances, etc.

B15.144　　**61.**—(1) Subject to [paragraph (3B)], every vehicle shall be constructed [and maintained] so as not to emit any avoidable smoke or avoidable visible vapour.

(2) Every motor vehicle using solid fuel shall be fitted with—

(a) a tray or shield to prevent ashes and cinders from falling onto the road; and

(b) an efficient appliance to prevent any emission of sparks or grit.

[(2A) Paragraphs (3), (3A), (3C), (4A), (5)(b), (5)(c), (6), (7), (8), (9), (10) and (11) shall not apply to motor vehicles first used on or after 1st January 2001.]

(3) Subject to paragraph (3B)], and to the exemptions specified in an item in column 4 of [Table I] [*see § B15.143*], every wheeled vehicle of a class specified in that item in column 2 shall be constructed so as to comply with the requirements specified in that item in column 3.

[(3A) A motor vehicle to which an item in Table II [*see § B15.144*] applies shall be so constructed as to comply with the requirements relating to conformity of production models set out in the provisions specified in that item in column 4 of that Table.]

[(3B) Instead of complying with paragraph (1) a vehicle may comply with a relevant instrument.]

[(3C) Instead of complying with such provisions of items 1, 2 and 3 in Table I as apply to it, a vehicle may at the time of its first use comply with a relevant instrument.]

(4) [For the purposes of paragraphs (3B) and (3C), a reference to a vehicle complying with a relevant instrument is a reference to a vehicle complying]—

[(a) if it is propelled by a compression ignition engine—

(i) in the case of an agricultural vehicle first used before 1st January 2001, with Community Directive 77/537, or

(ii) in the case of any other vehicle, either—

(aa) Community Directive 72/306, as last amended by Community Directive 2005/21, or

(bb) ECE Regulation 24.01, 24.02 or 24.03;]

[(b) if it is propelled by a spark ignition engine, with an instrument mentioned in column (4)(a) of Table II.]

[(4A) In relation to a vehicle which—

(a) has an engine the cyclinder capacity of which is less than 700cc and has a rated power speed of more than 3,000 revolutions per minute;

(b) is first used before 1st October 1998,

Community Directive 91/542 shall have effect for the purposes of this regulation as if for the figure "0.15" in the Table in paragraph 6.2.1 and 8.3.1.1 there were substituted "0.25".

For the purposes of this paragraph, *"rated power speed"* has the same meaning as in Community Directive 96/1.]

(5) No person shall use, or cause or permit to be used, on a road any motor vehicle—

    (a) from which any smoke, visible vapour, grit, sparks, ashes, cinders or oily substance is emitted if that emission causes, or is likely to cause, damage to any property or injury or danger to any person who is, or who may reasonably be expected to be, on the road;

    (b) which is subject to the requirement in item 2 of [Table I] [*see § B15.146*] (whether or not it is deemed to comply with that requirement by virtue of paragraph (4)), if the fuel injection equipment, the engine speed governor or any other parts of the engine by which it is propelled have been altered or adjusted so as to increase the emission of smoke; or

    (c) which is subject to the requirement in item 1 of [Table I] [*see § B15.146*] if the device mentioned in column 2 in that item is used while the vehicle is in motion.

(6) No person shall use, or cause or permit to be used, on a road a motor vehicle to which item 3 of [Table I] applies unless it is so maintained that the means specified in column 3 of that item are in good working order.

[(7) Subject to paragraphs … (8), (9) and (10), no person shall use, or cause or permit to be used, on a road a motor vehicle to which an item in Table II [*see § B15.147*] applies if, in relation to the emission of the substances specified in column (6) of the item, the vehicle does not comply with the requirements relating to conformity of production models specified in column (4) unless the following conditions are satisfied in respect to it—

    (a) the failure to meet those requirements in relation to the emission of those substances does not result from an alteration to the propulsion unit or exhaust system of the vehicle,

    (b) [neither would those requirements] be met in relation to the emission of those substances nor would such emissions be materially reduced if maintenance work of a kind which would fall within the scope of a normal periodic service of the vehicle were to be carried out on the vehicle, and

    (c) the failure to meet those requirements in relation to such emissions does not result from any device designed to control the emission of carbon monoxide, hydrocarbons, oxides of nitrogen, or particulates fitted to the vehicle being other than in good and efficient working order.]

(7A)–(7H) [...]

[(8) Paragraph (7) shall not apply to a vehicle first used before 26th June 1990.]

[(9) Where—

    (a) a vehicle is fitted with a device of the kind referred to in sub-paragraph (c) of paragraph (7),

    (b) the vehicle does not comply with the requirements specified in that paragraph in respect to it, and

    (c) the conditions specified in sub-paragraphs (a) and (b) of that paragraph are satisfied in respect to the vehicle, nothing in paragraph (7) shall prevent the vehicle being driven to a place where the device is to be repaired or replaced.]

[(10) Where a vehicle is constructed or assembled by a person not ordinarily engaged in the business of manufacturing motor vehicles of that description [and is first used before [July 1st, 1998]], the date on which it is first used shall, for the purposes of paragraphs (3A), (7), (8) and (9), be regarded as being the 1st January immediately preceding the date of manufacture of the engine by which it is propelled.

However, the date on which a vehicle is first used shall not, by virtue of the foregoing provisions of this paragraph, be regarded in any circumstances as being later than the date on which it would otherwise have been regarded as being first used had those provisions been omitted.]

[(10A) Without prejudice to paragraphs (1) and (7) and subject to the following provisions of this regulation, no person shall use, or cause or permit to be used on a road, a vehicle first used on or after 1st August 1975 and propelled by a four-stroke spark ignition engine, if the vehicle is in such a condition and running on such fuel that—

    (a) when the engine is idling the carbon monoxide content of the exhaust emissions from the engine exceeds—

        (i) in the case of a vehicle first used before 1st August 1986, 4.5%; or

        (ii) in the case of a vehicle first used on or after 1st August 1986, 3.5%;

      of the total exhaust emissions from the engine by volume; and

    (b) when the engine is running without load at a rotational speed of 2,000 revolutions per minute, the hydrocarbon content of those emissions exceeds 0.12% of the total exhaust emissions from the engine by volume.]

[(10AA) Without prejudice to paragraphs (1) and (7) and subject to the following provisions of this regulation, no person shall use, or cause or permit to be used on a road, a vehicle to which this paragraph applies and which is propelled by a spark ignition engine, if the vehicle is in such a condition and running on such fuel that Part I of Schedule 7B applies to the vehicle.]

[(10AB) [Subject to paragraph (10B)], paragraph (10AA) applies to—

    (a) a passenger car which—

        (i) is first used on or after 1st August 1992 and before [1st August 1995], and

        (ii) is of a description mentioned in the Annex to the emissions publication;

    (b) a vehicle which—

        (i) is not a passenger car,

        (ii) is first used on or after 1st August 1994 … and

        (iii) is of a description mentioned in the Annex to the emissions publication; [...]

    (c) a passenger car which is first used on or after [1st August 1995]; … [or]

    [(ca) a vehicle which—

(i) is not a passenger car,

(ii) is first used on or after 1st July 2002, and

(iii) has a maximum gross weight not exceeding 3,500kg;]

and in this paragraph, *"emissions publication"* has the meaning given in Part I of Schedule 7B.]

[(10AC) [...]]

[(10AD) Paragraph (10A) does not apply to—

(a) a vehicle to which paragraph (10AA) applies; or

(b) a vehicle if, at the date that the engine was manufactured, that engine was incapable of meeting the requirements specified in that paragraph.]

[(10AE) Paragraph (10AA) does not apply to a vehicle if, at the date that the engine was manufactured, that engine was incapable of meeting the requirements specified in that paragraph.]

[(10B) [Paragraphs (10A) and (10AA) do not] apply to—

(a) [...]

(b) a vehicle being driven to a place where it is to undergo repairs;

(c) a vehicle which was constructed or assembled by a person not ordinarily engaged in the business of manufacturing motor vehicles of that description [and is first used before [1st July 1998]];

(d) an exempt vehicle within the meaning given by paragraph (12)(a) ...;

(e) a goods vehicle with a maximum gross weight exceeding 3,500kg;

(f) engineering plant, an industrial tractor, or a works truck; ...

(g) [...]

[(h) a vehicle first used before 1st August 1987 if the engine is a rotary piston engine; and for the purposes of this paragraph *"the engine"*, in relation to a vehicle, means the engine by which it is propelled.]

[(10BA) Without prejudice to paragraphs (1) and (7), no person shall use, or cause or permit to be used on a road, a vehicle propelled by a compression ignition engine, if the vehicle is in such a condition and running on such fuel that Part II of Schedule 7B applies to the vehicle.]

[(10BB) Paragraph (10BA) shall not apply to—

(a) a vehicle if, at the date that the engine was manufactured, that engine was incapable of meeting the requirements specified in that paragraph;

(b) a vehicle being driven to a place where it is to undergo repairs;

(c) an exempt vehicle within the meaning given by paragraph (12)(a);

(d) engineering plant, an industrial tractor or a works truck; and

(e) a vehicle in Class III, IV, V[, VI] or VII within the meaning of the Motor Vehicles (Tests) Regulations 1981 and first used before 1st August 1979.]

[(10BC) [...]]

[(10C) For the purposes of this regulation—

(a) any rotary piston engine shall be deemed to be a four-stroke engine; and

(b) *"rotary piston engine"* means an engine in which the torque is provided by means of one or more rotary pistons and not by any reciprocating piston.]

[(11) Subject to Schedule 7XA] in this regulation, a reference to a vehicle to which an item in Table II [*see § B15.147*] applies is a reference to a vehicle which—

(a) is of a class specified in that item in column (2) of that Table,

(b) is first used on or after the date specified in that item in column (3) of that Table, and

(c) is not exempted by the entry in that item in column (5) of that Table,] [and for the purposes of determining whether a vehicle is a vehicle to which [any item numbered 8 or more] in that Table applies, regulation 4(2) shall be disregarded.]

[(11A) In this regulation, *"passenger car"* means a motor vehicle which—

(a) is constructed or adapted for use for the carriage of passengers and is not a goods vehicle;

(b) has no more than five seats in addition to the driver's seat; and

(c) has a maximum gross weight not exceeding 2,500kg.]

[(12) In Table II [and paragraphs (10B) and (10BB)]—

(a) *"exempt vehicle"* means—

(i) a vehicle with less than 4 wheels,

(ii) a vehicle with a maximum gross weight of less than 400kg,

(iii) a vehicle with a maximum speed of less than 25 km/h, or

(iv) an agricultural motor vehicle;

(b) *"direct injection"* means a fuel injection system in which the injector communicates with an open combustion chamber or the main part of a divided combustion chamber;

(c) *"indirect injection"* means a fuel injection system in which the injector communicates with the subsidiary part of a divided combustion chamber;

(d) a reference in column (5) to a vehicle complying with an item is a reference to a vehicle that complies with the provisions specified in that item in column (4) whether the vehicle is or is not within the class of vehicles to which that item applies and any instrument mentioned in that item shall for the purposes of the reference have effect as if it applied to the vehicle in question (whether it would otherwise have done so or not).]

B15.145   *[Regulation 61 is printed as amended by SI 1988/1524; SI 1990/1131; SI 1991/ 1526; SI 1992/2016, 2137, 2909, 3285; SI 1993/2199; SI 1994/2192; SI 1995/ 2210; SI 1996/2085, 2329 and 3017; SI 1997/1458, 1544 and 2935; SI 1998/ 1000 and 1563; SI 2000/3197; SI 2003/3145; SI 2007/3132.*

As to the modification of the provisions of reg.61 in relation to vehicles in respect of which approval certificates containing the letter "A" have been issued under the "Approval Regulations", see Sch.2A, para.9, to these regulations.

As to the issue of fixed penalty notices for contraventions of reg.61, see the Road Traffic (Vehicle Emissions) (Fixed Penalty) (England) Regulations 2002 (SI 2002/1808); the Road Traffic (Vehicle Emissions) (Fixed Penalty) (Scotland) Regulations 2003 (SI 2003/212) and the Road Traffic (Vehicle Emissions) (Fixed Penalty) (Wales) Regulations 2003 (SI 2003/300) (W.42).]

[TABLE I]

(regulation 61(3))

1	2	3	4
Item	*Class of vehicle*	*Requirements*	*Exemptions*
1	Vehicles propelled by a compression ignition engine and equipped with a device designed to facilitate starting the engine by causing it to be supplied with excess fuel.	Provision shall be made to ensure the device cannot readily be operated by a person inside the vehicle.	(a) a works truck; (b) a vehicle on which the device is so designed and maintained that— (i) its use after the engine has started cannot cause the engine to be supplied with excess fuel, or (ii) it does not cause any increase in the smoke or visible vapour emitted from the vehicle.

1	2	3	4
Item	*Class of vehicle*	*Requirements*	*Exemptions*
2	Vehicles first used on or after 1st April 1973 and propelled by a compression ignition engine.	The engine of the vehicle shall be of a type for which there has been issued by a person authorised by the Secretary of State a type test certificate in accordance with the British Standard Specification for the Performance of Diesel Engines for Road Vehicles published on 19th May 1971 under number BS AU 141a: 1971. In the case of an agricultural motor vehicle (other than one which is first used after 1st June 1986 and is driven at more than 20mph), an industrial tractor, a works truck or engineering plant, for the purposes of that Specification as to the exhaust gas opacity, measurements shall be made with the engine running at 80% of its full load over the speed range from maximum speed down to the speed at which maximum torque occurs as declared by the manufacturer of the vehicle for those purposes.	(a) a vehicle manufactured before 1st April 1973 and propelled by an engine known as the Perkins 6.354 engine; (b) a vehicle propelled by an engine having not more than 2 cylinders and being an agricultural motor vehicle (other than one which is first used on or after 1st June 1986 and which is driven at more than 20 mph), an industrial tractor, a works truck or engineering plant.

1		2	3	4
Item		Class of vehicle	Requirements	Exemptions
3		Vehicles first used on or after 1st January 1972 and propelled by a spark ignition engine other than a 2-stroke engine.	The engine shall be equipped with means sufficient to ensure that, while the engine is running, any vapours or gases in the engine crank case, or in any other part of the engine to which vapours or gases may pass from that case, are prevented, so far as is reasonably practicable, from escaping into the atmosphere otherwise than through the combustion chamber of the engine.	(a) a two-wheeled motor cycle with or without a sidecar attached; (b) … [(c) a vehicle to which any item in Table II applies.]
4		…	…	…

[Table I is printed as amended by SI 1990/1131; SI 1993/2199.]

B15.147

TABLE II

(regulation 61(3A), (3C), (7), (11) and (12))

(1) Item	(2) Class of Vehicle	(3) Date of First Use	(4) Design, construction and equipment requirements		(5) Vehicles exempted from requirements	(6) Emitted substances
			(a) Instrument	(b) Place in instrument where requirements are stated		
1	Vehicles propelled by a spark ignition engine.	1st October 1982	Community Directive 78/665 or ECE Regulation 15.03	Annex I, paragraphs 3 and 5. Paragraphs 5, 8 and 11.	(a) A vehicle whose maximum gross weight exceeds 3,500kg; (b) A vehicle which complies with the requirements of item 2, 4, 5, 8, 11, 12 or 13; (c) A vehicle whose maximum speed is less than 50 km/h; (d) An exempt vehicle.	Carbon monoxide, hydrocarbons and oxides of nitrogen.

(1) Item	(2) Class of Vehicle	(3) Date of First Use	(4) Design, construction and equipment requirements		(5) Vehicles exempted from requirements	(6) Emitted substances
			(a) Instrument	(b) Place in instrument where requirements are stated		
2	All vehicles.	1st April 1991	Community Directive 83/351 or ECE Regulation 15.04	Annex I, paragraphs 5, 7 and 8. Paragraphs 5, 8 and 12.	(a) A vehicle propelled by a compression ignition engine and whose maximum gross weight exceeds 3,500kg; (b) A vehicle which complies with the requirements of item 4, 5, 8, 11, 12 or 13; (c) A vehicle within the meaning given by Article 1 of Community Directive 88/77 which complies with the requirements of item 6, 9, or 10; (d) An industrial tractor, works truck, or engineering plant;	Carbon monoxide, hydrocarbons and oxides of nitrogen.

(1) Item	(2) Class of Vehicle	(3) Date of First Use	(4) Design, construction and equipment requirements		(5) Vehicles exempted from requirements	(6) Emitted substances
			(a) Instrument	(b) Place in instrument where requirements are stated		
					(e) A vehicle whose maximum speed is less than 50 km/h (f) An exempt vehicle.	
3	Industrial tractors, works trucks and engineering plant propelled in each case by a compression ignition engine.	1st April 1993	ECE Regulation 49	Paragraphs 5 and 7.	A vehicle which complies with the requirements of item 6, 9, 10, 11, 12 or 13.	Carbon monoxide, hydrocarbons and oxides of nitrogen.

(1) Item	(2) Class of Vehicle	(3) Date of First Use	(4) Design, construction and equipment requirements		(5) Vehicles exempted from requirements	(6) Emitted substances
			(a) Instrument	(b) Place in instrument where requirements are stated		
4	Passenger vehicles which— (a) are constructed or adapted to carry not more than 5 passengers excluding the driver, and (b) have a maximum gross weight of not more than 2,500kg, not being off-road vehicles.	1st April 1991	Community Directive 88/76 or Community Directive 89/458 or EEC Regulation 83	Annex I, paragraphs 5, 7, and 8. Annex I, paragraphs 5, 7 and 8. Paragraphs 5, 8 and 13.	(a) A vehicle which complies with the requirements of item 2, 8, 11, 12 or 13; (b) A vehicle whose maximum speed is less than 50 km/h; (c) An exempt vehicle.	Carbon monoxide, hydrocarbons and oxides of nitrogen.

(1) Item	(2) Class of Vehicle	(3) Date of First Use	(4) Design, construction and equipment requirements		(5) Vehicles exempted from requirements	(6) Emitted substances
			(a) Instrument	(b) Place in instrument where requirements are stated		
5	Vehicles which are not of a description specified in this column in item 4 but which— (a) are propelled by a spark ignition engine and have a maximum gross weight of not more than 2,000kg, or	1st April 1992	Community Directive 88/76 or ECE Regulation 8.3	Annex I, paragraphs 5, 7 and 8. Paragraphs 5, 8 and 13.	(a) A vehicle within the meaning given by Article 1 of Community Directive 88/77 and which complies with the requirements of item 6, 9, 10, 11, 12 or 13; (b) An industrial tractor, works truck or engineering plant; (c) A vehicle whose maximum speed is less than 50 km/h;	Carbon monoxide, hydrocarbons and oxides of nitrogen.

(1) Item	(2) Class of Vehicle	(3) Date of First Use	(4) Design, construction and equipment requirements		(5) Vehicles exempted from requirements	(6) Emitted substances
			(a) Instrument	(b) Place in instrument where requirements are stated		
	(b) are propelled by a compression ignition engine and have a maximum gross weight of more than 3,500kg.	1st April 1991			(d) A vehicle which complies with the requirements of item 8; (e) An exempt vehicle.	
6	All vehicles propelled by compression ignition engines.	1st April 1991	Community Directive 88/77 or ECE Regulation 49.01	Annex I, paragraphs 6, 7 and 8. Paragraphs 5, 6 and 7.	(a) A vehicle whose maximum gross weight is less than 3,500kg and which complies with the requirements of item 2; (b) A vehicle which complies with the requirements of item 4, 5, 8, 9, 10, 11, 12 or 13; (c) A fire appliance which is first used before 1st October 1992;	Carbon monoxide, hydrocarbons and oxides of nitrogen.

(1) Item	(2) Class of Vehicle	(3) Date of First Use	(4) Design, construction and equipment requirements — (a) Instrument	(4) (b) Place in instrument where requirements are stated	(5) Vehicles exempted from requirements	(6) Emitted substances
					(d) An industrial tractor, works truck or engineering plant; (e) An exempt vehicle.	
7	Passenger vehicles which— (a) are constructed or adapted to carry not more than 5 passengers excluding the driver, (b) have a maximum gross weight of not more than 2,500kg, and	1st April 1991	Community Directive 88/436	Annex I, paragraphs 5, 7 and 8 as far as they relate to particulate emissions.	(a) A vehicle which complies with the requirements of item 8, 11, 12 or 13; (b) A vehicle whose maximum speed is less than 50 km/h; (c) An off-road vehicle; (d) An exempt vehicle.	Particulates.

(1) Item	(2) Class of Vehicle	(3) Date of First Use	(4) Design, construction and equipment requirements		(5) Vehicles exempted from requirements	(6) Emitted substances
			(a) Instrument	(b) Place in instrument where requirements are stated		
	(c) are propelled by a compression ignition engine of the indirect injection type.					
8	All vehicles.	31st December 1992	Community Directive 91/441 or ECE Regulation 83.01	Annex I, paragraphs 5, 7 and 8. Paragraphs 5, 8 and 13.	(a) A vehicle within the meaning given by Article 1 of Community Directive 88/77 and which— (i) complies with the requirements of item 6 and is first used before 1st October 1993, or (ii) complies with the requirements of item 9, 10, 11, 12 or 13;	Carbon monoxide, hydrocarbons, oxides of nitrogen and particulates.

(1) Item	(2) Class of Vehicle	(3) Date of First Use	(4) Design, construction and equipment requirements		(5) Vehicles exempted from requirements	(6) Emitted substances
			(a) Instrument	(b) Place in instrument where requirements are stated		
					(b) An industrial tractor, works truck or engineering plant; (c) A vehicle whose maximum speed is less than 50 km/h; (d) An exempt vehicle.	
9	All vehicles propelled by a compression ignition engine.	1st October 1993	Community Directive 91/542 or	Annex I, paragraphs 6, 7 and 8 (excluding line B in the Tables in sub-paragraphs 6.2.1 and 8.3.1.1).	(a) A vehicle which complies with the requirements of item 8, 10, 11, 12 or 13; (b) An industrial tractor, works truck or engineering plant;	Carbon monoxide, hydrocarbons, oxides of nitrogen and particulates.

(1) Item	(2) Class of Vehicle	(3) Date of First Use	(4) Design, construction and equipment requirements		(5) Vehicles exempted from requirements	(6) Emitted substances
			(a) Instrument	(b) Place in instrument where requirements are stated		
			ECE Regulation 49.02	Paragraphs 5, 6 and 7 (excluding line B in the Tables in sub-paragraphs 5.2.1 and 7.4.2.1).	(c) An exempt vehicle.	
10	All vehicles propelled by a compression ignition engine.	1st October 1996	Community Directive 91/542 or ECE Regulation 49.02	Annex I, paragraphs 6, 7 and 8 (excluding line A in the Tables in sub-paragraphs 6.2.1 and 8.3.1.1). Paragraphs 5, 6 and 7 (excluding line A in the Tables in sub-paragraphs 5.2.1 and 7.4.2.1).	(a) A vehicle which complies with the requirements of item 8, 11, 12 or 13; (b) An industrial tractor, works truck or engineering plant; (c) An exempt vehicle.	Carbon monoxide, hydrocarbons, oxides of nitrogen and particulates.

(1) Item	(2) Class of Vehicle	(3) Date of First Use	(4) Design, construction and equipment requirements		(5) Vehicles exempted from requirements	(6) Emitted substances
			(a) Instrument	(b) Place in instrument where requirements are stated		
11	All vehicles.	1st October 1994	Community Directive 93/59	Annex I, paragraphs 5, 7 and 8.	(a) A vehicle within the meaning given by Article 1 of Community Directive 88/77 and which complies with the requirements of items 9, 10, 12 or 13 [or ECE Regulation 83.02]; (b) An industrial tractor, works truck or engineering plant; (c) Vehicles whose maximum speed is less than 50 km/h; (d) An exempt vehicle.	Carbon monoxide, hydrocarbons, oxides of nitrogen and particulates.

(1) Item	(2) Class of Vehicle	(3) Date of First Use	(4) Design, construction and equipment requirements		(5) Vehicles exempted from requirements	(6) Emitted substances
			(a) Instrument	(b) Place in instrument where requirements are stated		
12	All vehicles.	1st January 1997	Community Directive 94/12	Annex I, paragraphs 5, 7 and 8.	(a) A vehicle within the meaning given by Article 1 of Community Directive 88/77 and which complies with the requirements of items 9, 10, 11 or 13 [or ECE Regulation 83.03]; (b) An industrial tractor, works truck or engineering plant; (c) Vehicles whose maximum speed is less than 50 km/h; (d) An exempt vehicle.	Carbon monoxide, hydrocarbons, oxides of nitrogen and particulates.

(1) Item	(2) Class of Vehicle	(3) Date of First Use	(4) Design, construction and equipment requirements		(5) Vehicles exempted from requirements	(6) Emitted substances
			(a) Instrument	(b) Place in instrument where requirements are stated		
13	All vehicles.	1st October 1997	Community Directive 96/69	Annex I, paragraphs 5, 7 and 8.	(a) A vehicle within the meaning given by Article 1 of Community Directive 88/77 and which complies with the requirements of items 9, 10, or 12 [or ECE Regulation 83.04]; (b) A vehicle as defined in column 2 of item 14; (c) An industrial tractor, works truck or engineering plant; (d) Vehicles whose maximum speed is less than 50 km/h; (e) An exempt vehicle.	Carbon monoxide, hydrocarbons, oxides of nitrogen and particulates.

(1) Item	(2) Class of Vehicle	(3) Date of First Use	(4) Design, construction and equipment requirements		(5) Vehicles exempted from requirements	(6) Emitted substances
			(a) Instrument	(b) Place in instrument where requirements are stated		
14	Vehicles falling within (a) Class II or III, as specified in the Annex to Community Directive 96/69, of category N_1, or (b) Category M and specified in footnote (^{2}) of that Annex. Note: references to categories M and N_1 are to those categories as specified in Annex II of the Framework Directive.	1st October 1998	Community Directive 96/69	Annex 1, paragraphs 5, 7 and 8.		Carbon monoxide, hydrocarbons, oxides of nitrogen and particulates.

[Table II was inserted by SI 1990/1131 and is printed as substituted by SI 1997/1544; and subsequently amended by SI 2000/3197.

SI 2000/3197 purported to add the words "or ECE Regulation 83.04" to the entry in column (4)(a) in item 14 above, but there is no such entry.]

[Emission of smoke, vapour, gases, oily substances, etc.—further requirements for certain motor vehicles first used on or after 1st January 2001

B15.148   **61A.**—(1) This regulation shall apply to motor vehicles first used on or after 1st January 2001.

(2) Subject to paragraphs (5) to (7) and Schedule 7XA, a motor vehicle in any category shall comply with such design, construction and equipment requirements and such limit values as may be specified for a motor vehicle of that category and weight by any Community Directive specified in item 1 or 2 of the Table and from such date as is specified by that Community Directive.

(3) Subject to paragraphs (4) to (7) and Schedule 7XA, no person shall use, or cause or permit to be used, on a road a motor vehicle if the motor vehicle does not comply with such limit values as may apply to it by virtue of any Community Directive specified in item 1 or 2 of the Table, and from such date as is specified by that Community Directive, unless the following conditions are satisfied with respect to it—

(a) the failure to meet the limit values does not result from an alteration to the propulsion unit or exhaust system of the motor vehicle;

(b) neither would those limit values be met nor the emissions of gaseous and particulate pollutants and smoke and evaporative emissions be materially reduced if maintenance work of any kind which would fall within the scope of a normal periodic service of the vehicle were carried out on the motor vehicle; and

(c) the failure to meet those limit values does not result from any device designed to control the emission of gaseous and particulate pollutants and smoke and evaporative emissions which is fitted to the motor vehicle being other than in good and efficient working order.

(4) [Where]—

(a) a motor vehicle is fitted with a device of the kind referred to in sub-paragraph (c) of [this paragraph];

(b) the motor vehicle does not comply with the limit values applying to it which are referred to in that paragraph; and

(c) the conditions specified in sub-paragraphs (a) and (b) of paragraph (3) are satisfied in respect of the motor vehicle

nothing in this paragraph shall prevent the motor vehicle being driven to a place where the device is to be repaired or replaced.

(5) Subject to paragraph (6), if the Secretary of State has exempted any motor vehicle produced in a small series from one or more of the provisions of the Community Directive specified in item 1 of the Table in accordance with the procedure in Article 8(2)(a) of the Framework Directive then paragraphs (2) to (4) shall not apply to that motor vehicle insofar as it has been so exempted.

(6) If any motor vehicle has been exempted from one or more of the provi-

sions of a Community Directive specified in item 1 of the Table in accordance with paragraph (5), then in the Table as it applies to that motor vehicle there shall be deemed to be substituted, for the reference to Community Directive 96/69/EC or ECE Regulation 83.04, Community Directive 98/69/EC and 1999/102/EC —

    (a) in the case of passenger cars as defined in regulations 61(11A), a reference to Community Directive 94/12/EC or ECE Regulation 83.03; and

    (b) in the case of other motor vehicles of category M, a reference to Community Directive 93/59/EEC or ECE Regulation 83.02

and in any such case paragraphs (2) to (4) shall apply to the motor vehicle as if they referred to the substituted Community Directives or ECE Regulations.

[(7) If a vehicle has, in accordance with Schedule 7XA, been exempted from the need to comply with any provision of a Community Directive specified in item 1 or 2 in the Table ("the exempted provision"), it shall, in substitution for the exempted provision, comply with the equivalent provision (if any) that would have applied by virtue of this regulation in relation to such a vehicle immediately before the coming into force of the requirement to comply with the exempted provision; and in relation to that equivalent provision paragraphs 2 to 4 shall apply as if they referred to the Community Directive under which that equivalent provision arose.]

(8) In this regulation—

    (a) *"category"* means a category for the purpose of Annex II of the Framework Directive;

    [(b) *"date as is specified"* means, in relation to any vehicle and—

        (i) in relation to limit values set by a Community Directive specified in item 1 or 2 in the Table, the date specified by that Community Directive as that from which Member States are required to prohibit the registration or the entry into service of that vehicle if it does not comply with those limit values; or

        (ii) in relation to emission control and monitoring systems and devices, the date specified by a Community Directive specified in item 1 or 2 in the Table as that from which Member States are required to ensure that such equipment is fitted to that vehicle,

    provided that, where a Community Directive specified in item 2 in the Table re-enacts a requirement imposed by a Community Directive that had been specified in that item immediately before 9th November 2006, the date as is specified shall be the date that had been specified by that previous Directive;]

    (c) *"limit values"* means the permitted amounts of gaseous and particulate pollutants and smoke and evaporative emissions;

    (d) *"small series"* means the motor vehicles within a family of types as defined in Annex XII of the Framework Directive which are registered or enter into service in a period of twelve months beginning on 1st January in any year where the total number of motor vehicles does not exceed the small series limits specified in that Annex.

[(9) Regulation 4(2) does not apply to any requirement imposed on a vehicle by or under this Regulation.]

Table
(Regulation 61A)

Item	Community Directive of ECE Regulation	Amending Community Directive or ECE Regulation
1.	70/220/EEC	96/69/EC or ECE Regulation 83.04 98/69/EC 1999/102/EC [2001/1/EC]
[2.	2005/55/EC or EEC Regulation 49.02	2005/78/EC or 2006/51/EC]

B15.149   *[Regulation 61A was inserted by SI 2000/3197; and is printed as amended by SI 2001/306; SI 2001/1825; SI 2001/3208; SI 2002/1474; SI 2006/2565.*

As to the issue of fixed penalty notices in England for contravention of reg.61A, see the Road Traffic (Vehicle Emissions) (Fixed Penalty) (England) Regulations 2002 (SI 2002/1808); the Road Traffic (Vehicle Emissions) (Fixed Penalty) (Scotland) Regulations 2003 (SI 2003/212) and the Road Traffic (Vehicle Emissions) (Fixed Penalty) (Wales) Regulations 2003 (SI 2003/300) (W.42).]

[Retrofitting and refilling of certain air conditioning systems

B15.150   **61B.**—(1) Subject to paragraphs (7), (8), (9) and (10) and Schedule 7XA, this regulation applies to vehicles set out in Article 2 of Directive 2006/40, regardless of their date of manufacture.

(2) Regulation 4(2) does not apply in relation to a vehicle to which this regulation applies.

(3) A vehicle type approved on or after 1st January 2011 may not be retrofitted with an air conditioning system designed to contain high-GWP fluorinated greenhouse gases.

(4) On or after 1st January 2017, a vehicle may not be retrofitted with an air conditioning system designed to contain high-GWP fluorinated greenhouse gases.

(5) A vehicle type approved on or after 1st January 2011 may not be fitted with an air conditioning system containing high-GWP fluorinated greenhouse gases.

(6) On or after 1st January 2017, a vehicle may not be fitted with an air conditioning system containing high-GWP fluorinated greenhouse gases.

(7) Paragraph (5) does not apply to a vehicle where—

    (a) it was type approved on or after 1st January 2011, and

    (b) on the date it was type approved, it was not prevented from being fitted with an air conditioning system containing high-GWP fluorinated greenhouse gases by any pre-requisite for type approval imposed by—

        (i) the 1988 Act or any regulations made under it, except for this regulation;

        (ii) the Road Traffic (Northern Ireland) Order 1981 or any regulations made under it; or

        (iii) the Vehicle Approval Regulations.

(8) Paragraph (6) does not apply to a vehicle where—

    (a) it was registered on or after 1st January 2017, and

    (b) on the date it was registered, it was not prevented from being fitted with an air conditioning system containing high-GWP fluorinated greenhouse gases by any pre-requisite for registration imposed by—

        (i) the 1988 Act or any regulations made under it, except for this regulation;

        (ii) the Road Traffic (Northern Ireland) Order 1981 or any regulations made under it; or

        (iii) the Vehicle Approval Regulations.

(9) Paragraph (6) does not apply to a vehicle where—

    (a) it was used for the first time on a road in Great Britain on or after 1st January 2017 (this date not being determined, for the purposes of this sub-paragraph, in accordance with regulation 3(3)), and

    (b) on the date it was first used, it was not prevented from being fitted with an air conditioning system containing high-GWP fluorinated greenhouse gases by any pre-requisite for use imposed by—

        (i) the 1988 Act or any regulations made under it, except for this regulation;

        (ii) the Road Traffic (Northern Ireland) Order 1981 or any regulations made under it; or

        (iii) the Vehicle Approval Regulations.

(10) Paragraph (6) does not apply to a vehicle which before 1st January 2017 was fitted with an air conditioning system containing high-GWP fluorinated greenhouse gases.

(11) For the purposes of this regulation, a vehicle was type approved if—

    (a) there has been issued in relation to it—

        (i) an EC type approval certificate under regulation 4(5) of the EC Whole Vehicle Type Approval Regulations;

        (ii) an EC type approval certificate under a provision of the law of any EEA State which corresponds to regulation 4(5) of the EC Whole Vehicle Type Approval Regulations;

        (iii) an EC type approval certificate under regulation 13(3) of the Vehicle Approval Regulations;

        (iv) an EC type approval certificate under a provision of the law of any EEA State which corresponds to regulation 13(3) of the Vehicle Approval Regulations;

        (v) a type approval certificate under section 55 of the 1988 Act; or

        (vi) a Minister's Approval certificate under section 58(1) of the 1988 Act; or

        (vii) a certificate under section 58(4) of the 1988 Act by reason of the vehicle conforming with another vehicle in respect of which a Minister's Approval Certificate was issued under section 58(1) of that Act.

(12) In this regulation—

    "air conditioning system" means any system whose main purpose is to

decrease the air temperature and humidity of the passenger compartment of a vehicle;

"*high-GWP fluorinated greenhouse gases*" means fluorinated greenhouse gases having a global warming potential higher than 150, "*fluorinated greenhouse gases*" has the same meaning as in Article 3(5) of Community Directive 2006/40, and "*global warming potential*" has the same meaning as in Article 3(8) (including the footnote) of Community Directive 2006/40, read in conjunction with the second sentence of Article 3(9) (including the footnote) of the same Directive;

"*retrofitted*" means fitted to a vehicle after it has been first used.]

B15.151   *[Regulation is printed as inserted by SI 2009/2196.*

The Vehicle Approval Regulations referred to above are the Road Vehicles (Approval) Regulations 2009 (SI 2009/717), not reproduced in this work. The 2009 Regulations implement Directive 2007/46/EC of the European Parliament and of the Council establishing a framework for the approval of motor vehicles and trailers and of systems, components and separate technical units intended for such vehicles, known as the "Framework Directive" (O.J. No.L263, 9.10.2007, p.1).]

[End-of-series exemption

B15.152   61C.—(1) The emissions requirements in European Community Regulation 715/2007 shall have effect for category N1 class I end-of-series vehicles from the first anniversary of the relevant date.

(2) The emissions requirements in European Community Regulation 595/2009 shall have effect for category N2 and N3 end-of-series vehicles from the first anniversary of the relevant date.

(3) For the purpose of this regulation, "*relevant date*" means—

   (a) for category N1 class I vehicles, 1st January 2011, and

   (b) for category N2 and N3 vehicles, 31st December 2013.

(4) For the purpose of paragraphs (1) and (2), a vehicle is an end-of-series vehicle if—

   (a) at least three months before the relevant date, a certificate of conformity or a sub-MAC was in force for the vehicle, and the MAC or TAC (as the case may be) had been issued by virtue of an emissions requirement that—

      (i) then applied to the vehicle, but

      (ii) ignoring this regulation, would have ceased to apply on the relevant date; and

   (b) it is in the territory of an EEA state on the relevant date.

(5) In this regulation—

"*category N1 class I*" means a motor vehicle with at least 4 wheels designed or constructed for the carriage of goods and having a reference mass not exceeding 1,305 kilograms;

"*category N2 and N3*" have the meaning given in Annex II to Community Directive 2007/46;

"MAC" means a Minister's approval certificate issued under section 58(1) of the 1988 Act;

"reference mass" has the meaning given in Article 3(3) of European Community Regulation 715/2007;

"reference mass" has the meaning given in Article 3(3) of European Community Regulation 715/2007;

"TAC" means a type approval certificate.]

[Regulation 61C is printed as inserted by SI 2011/427.]   **B15.153**

Closets, etc.

62.—(1) No wheeled vehicle first used after 15th January 1931 shall be   **B15.154** equipped with any closet or urinal which can discharge directly on to a road.

(2) Every tank into which a closet or urinal with which a vehicle is equipped empties, and every closet or urinal which does not empty into a tank, shall contain chemicals which are non-inflammable and non-irritant and provide an efficient germicide.

Wings

63.—(1) Save as provided in paragraph (4), this regulation applies to—   **B15.155**
   (a) invalid carriages;
   (b) heavy motor cars, motor cars and motor cycles, not being agricultural motor vehicles or pedestrian-controlled vehicles;
   (c) agricultural motor vehicles driven at more than 20mph; and
   (d) trailers.

(2) Subject to paragraphs (3) and (5), every vehicle to which this regulation applies shall be equipped with wings or other similar fittings to catch, so far as practicable, mud or water thrown up by the rotation of its wheels or tracks.

(3) The requirements specified in paragraph (2) apply, in the case of a trailer with more than two wheels, only in respect of the rearmost two wheels.

(4) Those requirements do not apply in respect of—
   (a) a works truck;
   (b) a living van;
   (c) a water cart;
   (d) an agricultural trailer drawn by a motor vehicle which is not driven at a speed in excess of 20mph;
   (e) an agricultural trailed appliance;
   (f) an agricultural trailed appliance conveyor;
   (g) a broken down vehicle;
   (h) a heavy motor car, motor car or trailer in an unfinished condition which is proceeding to a workshop for completion;
   (i) a trailer used for or in connection with the carriage of round timber and the rear wheels of any heavy motor car or motor car drawing a semi-trailer so used; or
   (j) a trailer drawn by a motor vehicle the maximum speed of which is restricted to 20mph or less under Schedule 6 to the 1984 Act.

(5) Instead of complying with paragraph (2) a vehicle may comply with Community Directive 78/549.

Spray suppression devices

B15.156   64.—(1) Save as provided in paragraph (2), this regulation applies to every wheeled goods vehicle which is—

    (a) a motor vehicle first used on or after 1st April 1986 having a maximum gross weight exceeding 12,000kg;

    (b) a trailer manufactured on or after 1st May 1985 having a maximum gross weight exceeding 3500kg; or

    (c) a trailer, whenever manufactured, having a maximum gross weight exceeding 16,000kg and 2 or more axles.

(2) This regulation does not apply to—

    (a) a motor vehicle so constructed that the driving power of its engine is, or can by use of its controls be, transmitted to all the wheels on at least one front axle and on at least one rear axle;

    (b) a motor vehicle of which no part which lies within the specified area is less than 400mm vertically above the ground when the vehicle is standing on reasonably flat ground;

    (c) a works truck;

    (d) a works trailer;

    (e) a broken down vehicle;

    (f) a motor vehicle which has a maximum speed not exceeding 30mph;

    (g) a vehicle of a kind specified in sub-paragraphs (b), (c), (d), (e), (f), (g), (h), (j), (o) or (p) or regulation 51(2);

    (h) a vehicle specially designed, and not merely adapted, for the carriage and mixing of liquid concrete; or

    (i) a vehicle which is being driven or towed to a place where by previous arrangement a device is to be fitted so that it complies with the requirements specified in paragraph (3).

[(2A) This regulation shall not apply to a vehicle fitted with a spray-suppression system in accordance with the requirements of Annex III of Community Directive 91/226 if the spray-suppression devices with which the vehicle is equipped are legibly and permanently marked with a designated approval mark.]

(3) A vehicle to which this regulation applies and which is of a class specified in an item in column 2 of the Table shall not be used on a road on or after the date specified in column 3 in that item, unless it is fitted in relation to the wheels on each of its axles, with such containment devices as satisfy the technical requirements and other provisions about containment devices specified in the British Standard Specification, provided that in the case of a containment device fitted before 1st January 1985 the said requirements shall be deemed to be complied with if that containment device substantially conforms to those requirements.

TABLE

(regulation 64(3))

1	2	3
Item	Class of vehicle	Date
1	A trailer manufactured before 1st January 1975	1st October 1987
2	A trailer manufactured on or after 1st January 1975 but before 1st May 1985	1st October 1986
3	A trailer manufactured on or after 1st May 1985	1st May 1985
4	A motor vehicle	1st April 1986

(4) In this regulation—

["*the British Standard Specification*" means—

    (a) in relation to a containment device fitted before 1st May 1987, Part 1a of the amended Specification and Part 2 of the original Specification; and

    (b) in relation to a containment device fitted on or after 1st May 1987, Part 1a and Part 2a of the amended Specification;]

["*designated approval mark*" means the marking designated as an approval mark by regulation 5 of the Approval Marks Regulations [*i.e. as amended by SI 1992/634*] and shown at item 30 in Schedule 4 to those Regulations;]

["*the original Specification*" means the British Standard Specification for Spray Reducing Devices for Heavy Goods Vehicles published under the reference BS AU 200: Part 1: 1984 and BS AU 200: Part 2: 1984;]

["*the amended Specification*" means the original Specification as amended and published under the reference BS AU 200: Part 1a: 1986 and BS AU 200: Part 2a: 1986;]

["*containment device*" means any device so described in the original Specification or the amended Specification;]

"*the specified area*" means the area formed by the overall length of the vehicle and the middle 80% of the shortest distance between the inner edges of any two wheels on opposite sides of the vehicle (such distance being ascertained when the vehicle is fitted with suitable tyres inflated to a pressure recommended by the manufacturer, but excluding any bulging of the tyres near the ground).

(5) Nothing in this regulation derogates from any requirement in regulation 63.

[Regulation 64 is printed as amended by SI 1986/1597; SI 1992/646.]   **B15.157**

Maintenance of spray suppression devices

65. Every part of every containment device with which a vehicle is required to   **B15.158**
be fitted by the provisions of regulation 64 shall at all times when the vehicle is
on a road be maintained free from any obvious defect which would be likely to
affect adversely the effectiveness of the device.

PART III

PLATES, MARKINGS, TESTING AND INSPECTION

Plates for goods vehicles and buses

B15.159   66.—(1) This regulation applies to—

(a) a wheeled heavy motor car or motor car first used on or after 1st January 1968 not being—

(i) a dual-purpose vehicle;

(ii) an agricultural motor vehicle;

(iii) a works truck;

(iv) a pedestrian-controlled vehicle; …

(v) save as provided in sub-paragraph (b) below, a passenger vehicle; [or]

[(vi) a vehicle which is exempt from section 63(1) of the Road Traffic Act 1988 by virtue of regulation 14(6) of the Motor Vehicles (Approval) Regulations 1996.]

(b) a bus (whether or not it is an articulated bus) first used on or after 1st April 1982;

(c) a wheeled locomotive or motor tractor first used on or after 1st April 1973 not being—

(i) an agricultural motor vehicle;

(ii) an industrial tractor;

(iii) a works truck;

(iv) engineering plant; or

(v) a pedestrian-controlled vehicle;

(d) a wheeled trailer manufactured on or after 1st January 1968 which exceeds 1020kg in weight unladen not being—

(i) a trailer not constructed or adapted to carry any load, other than plant or special appliances or apparatus which is a permanent or essentially permanent fixture, and not exceeding 2290kg in total weight;

(ii) a living van not exceeding 2040kg in weight unladen and fitted with pneumatic tyres;

(iii) a works trailer;

(iv) a trailer mentioned in regulation 16(3)(b) to (g); or

(v) a trailer which was manufactured and used outside Great Britain before it was first used in Great Britain; and

(e) a converter dolly manufactured on or after 1st January 1979.

(2) Every vehicle to which this regulation applies shall be equipped with a plate securely attached to the vehicle in a conspicuous and readily accessible position which either—

(a) contains the particulars required, in the case of a motor vehicle by Part I of Schedule 8 or, in the case of a trailer, by Part II of that Schedule and complies with the provisions of Part III of that Schedule; or

(b) complies with the requirements specified in the Annex to Community Directive 78/507 or, in the case of a vehicle first used before 1st October 1982, in the Annex to Community Directive 76/114, such requirements being in any case modified as provided in paragraph (3).

(3) Instead of the particulars required by items 2.1.4 to 2.1.7 of that Annex, the plate required by paragraph (2)(b) shall show, for a vehicle of a class specified in column 2 of the Table against an item of that Annex so specified in column 1, the following particulars—

(a) the maximum permitted weight for that class, if any, shown in column 3 of the Table;

(b) where the maximum weight shown in column 4 of the Table exceeds the maximum permitted weight, the maximum weight in a column on the plate to the right of the maximum permitted weight; and

(c) if no weight is shown in column 3 of the Table, the maximum weight shown in column 4 of the Table, in the right hand column of the plate.

TABLE

(regulation 66(3))

1	2	3	4
Item in Annex to Directive	Class of vehicle	Maximum permitted weight	Maximum weight
2.1.4 (Laden weight of vehicle)	(i) Motor vehicles	The maximum gross weight in Great Britain referred to in item 10 in Part I of Schedule 8.	The maximum gross weight referred to in item 7 in Part I of Schedule 8.
	(ii) Trailers, other than semi-trailers	The maximum gross weight in Great Britain referred to in item 8 in Part II of Schedule 8.	The maximum gross weight referred to in item 6 in Part II of Schedule 8.
	(iii) Semi-trailers		The maximum gross weight referred to in item 6 in Part II of Schedule 8.
2.1.5 (Train weight of motor vehicle)	Motor vehicles constructed to draw a trailer	The lower of— (a) the maximum train weight referred to in item 8 in Part I of Schedule 8; and	The maximum train weight referred to in item 8 in Part I of Schedule 8.

1	2	3	4
Item in Annex to Directive	Class of vehicle	Maximum permitted weight	Maximum weight
		(b) the maximum laden weight specified, in the case of vehicles constructed to form part of an articulated vehicle, in regulation 77, and, in other cases, in regulation 76.	
2.1.6 (Axle weight of vehicle)	(i) Motor vehicles	The maximum weight in Great Britain for each axle referred to in item 9 in Part I of Schedule 8.	The maximum weight for each axle referred to in item 6 in Part I of Schedule 8.
	(ii) Trailers	The maximum weight in Great Britain for each axle referred to in item 7 in Part II of Schedule 8.	The maximum weight for each axle referred to in item 4 in Part II of Schedule 8.
2.1.7 (Load imposed by semi-trailer)	Semi-trailers		The maximum load imposed on the drawing vehicle referred to in item 5 in Part II of Schedule 8.

(4) Part III of Schedule 8 applies for determining the relevant weights to be shown on a plate in accordance with this regulation.

[(5) Where, in accordance with the provisions of this regulation and of Schedule 8, a motor vehicle first used, or a trailer manufactured, after 31st December 1998, is required to be equipped with a plate showing the maximum gross weight in Great Britain or the maximum weight in Great Britain for each axle of the vehicle, the plate may instead show particulars of the maximum authorised weight for the vehicle of, as the case may be, the maximum authorised weight for each axle of the vehicle.]

[(6) In paragraph (5) the references to the *maximum authorised weight* for a vehicle and *maximum authorised* [*weight*] for each axle of a vehicle mean those weights determined in accordance with the Motor [*sic*] Vehicles (Authorised Weight) Regulations 1998 [*SI 1998/3111 below*].]

[(7) The plate for a vehicle which falls within paragraph (1)(a) and which is a motor vehicle first used after 31st December 1998 need not include the particulars referred to in paragraph 9 or 10 of Part I of Schedule 8.]

B15.160   *[Regulation 66 is printed as amended by SI 1996/3017; SI 1998/3112.*

The Motor Vehicles (Approval) Regulations 1996 (to which reference is made in reg.66(1)(a)(vi)) have been revoked and replaced by the Motor Vehicles (Approval) Regulations 2001 (SI 2001/25); see further the note to Sch.2A, para.2 below.

The word "weight" (in the second place where it occurs in reg.66(6)) has been added editorially.]

Vehicle identification numbers

67.—(1) This regulation applies to a wheeled vehicle which is first used on or after 1st April 1980 and to which the Type Approval (Great Britain) Regulations apply.   **B15.161**

(2) A vehicle to which this regulation applies shall be equipped with a plate which is in a conspicuous and readily accessible position, is affixed to a vehicle part which is not normally subject to replacement and shows clearly and indelibly—

> (a) the vehicle identification number in accordance with the requirements specified—
>> (i) in the case of a vehicle first used before 1st April 1987, in paragraphs 3.1.1. and 3.1.2 of the Annex to Community Directive 76/114/EEC; or
>> (ii) in any case, in sections 3 and 4 of the Annex to Community Directive 78/507/EEC;
> (b) the name of the manufacturer; and
> (c) the approval reference number of either—
>> (i) the type approval certificate which relates to the vehicle model or the model variant of the vehicle model, as the case may be, issued in accordance with the provisions of regulation 9(1) of, and Part I of Schedule 3 to, the Type Approval (Great Britain) Regulations; or
>> (ii) the Minister's approval certificate which relates to the vehicle, issued in accordance with the provisions of regulation 9(2) of, and Part 1A of Schedule 4 to, the said Regulations.

Provided that the information required under sub-paragraph (c) above may be shown clearly and indelibly on an additional plate which is fitted in a conspicuous and readily accessible position and which is affixed to a vehicle part which is not normally subject to replacement.

(3) The vehicle identification number of every vehicle to which this regulation applies shall be marked on the chassis, frame or other similar structure, on the offside of the vehicle, in a clearly visible and accessible position, and by a method such as hammering or stamping, in such a way that it cannot be obliterated or deteriorate.

[As to the application of the provisions of reg.67 to vehicles in respect of which approval certificates have been issued under the "Approval Regulations", see Sch.2A, para.10, to these regulations.]   **B15.162**

Plates—agricultural trailed appliances

68.—(1) Save as provided in paragraph (3) below, every wheeled agricultural   **B15.163**

trailed appliance manufactured on or after 1st December 1985 shall be equipped with a plate affixed to the vehicle in a conspicuous and readily accessible position and which is clearly and indelibly marked with the particulars specified in paragraph (2) below.

(2) Those particulars are—

   (a) the name of the manufacturer of the appliance;

   (b) the year in which the appliance was manufactured;

   (c) the maximum gross weight;

   (d) the unladen weight; and

   (e) the maximum load which would be imposed by the appliance on the drawing vehicle.

(3) In the case of a towed roller consisting of several separate rollers used in combination, a single plate shall satisfy the requirements specified in paragraph (2) above.

Plates—motor cycles

B15.164   **69.**—(1) This regulation applies to every motor cycle first used on or after 1st August 1977 which is not—

   (a) propelled by an internal combustion engine with a cylinder capacity exceeding 150cc if the vehicle was first used before 1st January 1982 or 125cc if it was first used on or after 1st January 1982;

   (b) a mowing machine; or

   (c) a pedestrian-controlled vehicle.

(2) Every vehicle to which this regulation applies shall be equipped with a plate which is securely affixed to the vehicle in a conspicuous and readily accessible position and which complies with the requirements of Schedule 9.

Ministry plates

B15.165   **70.**—(1) Every goods vehicle to which the Plating and Testing Regulations apply and in respect of which a plating certificate has been issued shall, from the date specified in paragraph (2), be equipped with a Ministry plate securely affixed, so as to be legible at all times, in a conspicuous and readily accessible position, and in the cab of the vehicle if it has one.

(2) That date is in the case of—

   (a) a vehicle to which the Type Approval for Goods Vehicles Regulations apply, the date of the fourteenth day after the plate was issued; or

   (b) any other vehicle, the date by which it is required, by the said Regulations, to be submitted for examination for plating.

[(3) In these Regulations *"Ministry plate"* means a plate which—

   (a) is issued by the Secretary of State following the issue or amendment of a plating certificate; and

   (b) subject to paragraph (4), contains the particulars required by Schedule 10, 10A, 10B or 10C.]

[(4) Instead of particulars of the gross weight, train weight and axle weights of the vehicle to which it relates, a Ministry plate may contain particulars of the maximum authorised weight for the vehicle, maximum authorised weight for a combination of which the vehicle forms part and maximum authorised axle weights for the vehicle, determined in accordance with the Road Vehicles (Authorised Weight) Regulations 1998 [*SI 1998/3111 below*] and the form of the plate shall be amended accordingly.]

[Regulation 70 is printed as amended by SI 1998/3112.]   **B15.166**

[Speed limiters—plates

70A.—[(1) This regulation applies to every vehicle to which regulation 36A or   **B15.167**
36B applies and which is fitted with a speed limiter.

(2) Every vehicle to which this regulation applies shall be equipped with a plate which meets the requirements specified in paragraph (3).

(3) [...] [T]he requirements are that the plate is in a conspicuous position in the driving compartment of the vehicle and is clearly and indelibly marked with the speed at which the speed limiter has been set.]

[Regulation 70A was inserted by SI 1988/271 and was later amended by SI   **B15.168**
1988/1524; SI 1992/422; and substituted by SI 1993/1946.

The text of reg.70A as printed above was substituted by SI 1993/3048 and is printed as subsequently amended by SI 1996/2064; SI 2004/2102.]

[Plate relating to dimensions

70B.—(1) This regulation applies to a vehicle which is not a goods vehicle fit-   **B15.169**
ted in accordance with regulation 70 with a Ministry plate containing the particulars required by Schedule 10A or 10C and which is either—

    (a) a bus or a heavy motor car and which is manufactured after 31st May 1998; or

    (b) a trailer used in combination with a vehicle falling within paragraph (a) and manufactured after 31st May 1998.

(2) A vehicle to which this regulation applies shall not be used unless—

    (a) the vehicle is equipped with a plate securely attached to the vehicle in a conspicuous and readily accessible position and containing the particulars as to the dimensions of the vehicle specified in Annex III of Community Directive 96/53/EC [*q.v.*]; or

    (b) those particulars are included in the particulars shown on the plate with which the vehicle is equipped in accordance with regulation 66.]

[Regulation 70B was inserted by SI 1998/1188.]   **B15.170**

Marking of weights on certain vehicles

71.—(1) This regulation applies to a vehicle (other than an agricultural motor   **B15.171**
vehicle which is either a track-laying vehicle not exceeding 3050kg in unladen weight or a wheeled vehicle) which is—

    (a) a locomotive;

    (b) a motor tractor;

    (c) [a bus] which is registered under [the 1994 Act] (or any enactment repealed thereby) ...; or

(d) an unbraked wheeled trailer, other than one mentioned in [regulation 16(3)(b), (bb), (c), (d), (e), (f), or (g)].

(2) There shall be plainly marked in a conspicuous place on the outside of a vehicle to which this regulation applies, on its near side—

(a) if it is a vehicle falling in paragraph (1)(a), (b) or (c), its unladen weight; and

(b) if it is a vehicle falling in paragraph (1)(d), its maximum gross weight.

B15.172   *[Regulation 71 is printed as amended by SI 1990/1981; SI 1994/329; the Vehicle Excise and Registration Act 1994 s.64 and Sch.4, para.4; SI 1996/3033.]*

[Marking of date of manufacture of trailers

B15.173   71A.—(1) This regulation applies to a trailer that—

(a) is not a motor vehicle;

(b) is manufactured on or after 1st January 1997; and

(c) has a maximum total design axle weight not exceeding 750kg.

(2) The year of manufacture of every trailer to which this regulation applies shall be marked on the chassis, frame or other similar structure on the nearside of the vehicle, in a clearly visible and accessible position, and by a method such as hammering or stamping, in such a way that it cannot be obliterated or deteriorate.]

B15.174   *[Regulation 71A was inserted by SI 1996/3033.*

SI 1996/3033 expressly states (reg.2(2)) that so far as any requirement is imposed by it such requirement is imposed in exercise of powers conferred by s.41 of the Road Traffic Act 1988 to the exclusion of the powers under s.2(2) of the European Communities Act 1972.]

Additional markings

B15.175   72.—(1) This regulation applies to every goods vehicle to which the Plating and Testing Regulations apply and for which a plating certificate has been issued.

(2) Without prejudice to the provisions of regulation 70, any weight which by virtue of regulation 80 may not be exceeded in the case of a goods vehicle to which this regulation applies may be marked on either side, or on both sides, of the vehicle.

(3) Where at any time by virtue of any provision contained in regulation 75 a goods vehicle to which this regulation applies may not be used in excess of a weight which is less than the gross weight which may not be exceeded by that vehicle by virtue of regulation 80, the first mentioned weight may be marked on either side, or on both sides, of the vehicle.

(4) Where at any time by virtue of any provision contained in regulation 76 and 77 a goods vehicle to which this regulation applies is drawing, or being drawn by, another vehicle and those vehicles may not be used together in excess of a laden weight applicable to those vehicles by virtue of any such provision, that weight may be marked on either side, or on both sides, of that goods vehicle.

Test date discs

B15.176   73.—(1) Every Ministry test date disc which is issued, following the issue of a goods vehicle test certificate, in respect of a trailer to which the Plating and Testing Regulations apply and for which a plating certificate has been issued shall be carried on the trailer in a legible condition and in a conspicuous and readily accessible position in which it is clearly visible by daylight from the near side of the road, from the date of its issue until but not beyond the date of expiry of that test certificate or the date of issue of a further test certificate for that trailer, whichever date is the earlier.

(2) In this regulation *"Ministry test date disc"* means a plate issued by the Secretary of State for a goods vehicle, being a trailer, following the issue of a goods vehicle test certificate for that trailer under the Plating and Testing Regulations and containing the following particulars—

(a) the identification mark allotted to that trailer and shown in that certificate;

(b) the date until which that certificate is valid; and

(c) the number of the vehicle testing station shown in that certificate.

Testing and inspection

74.—(1) Subject to the conditions specified in paragraph (2), the following persons are hereby empowered to test and inspect the brakes, silencers, steering gear and tyres of any vehicle, on any premises where that vehicle is located— **B15.177**

(a) a police constable in uniform;

(b) a person appointed by the Commissioner of Police of the Metropolis to inspect public carriages for the purposes of the Metropolitan Public Carriage Act 1869;

(c) a person appointed by the police authority for a police area to act for the purposes of [section 67 of the 1988 Act];

(d) a goods vehicle examiner as defined in [section 68 of the 1988 Act];

(e) a certifying officer as defined in section 7(1) of the 1981 Act; and

(f) a public service vehicle examiner appointed as mentioned in section 7(2) of the 1981 Act.

(2) Those conditions are—

(a) any person empowered as there mentioned shall produce his authorisation if required to do so;

(b) no such person shall enter any premises unless the consent of the owner of those premises has first been obtained;

(c) no such person shall test or inspect any vehicle on any premises unless—

(i) the owner of the vehicle consents thereto;

(ii) notice has been given to that owner personally or left at his address not less than 48 hours before the time of the proposed test or inspection, or has been sent to him at least 72 hours before that time by the recorded delivery service to his address last known to the person giving the notice; or

(iii) the test or inspection is made within 48 hours of an accident to which [section 170 of the 1988 Act] applies and in which the vehicle was involved.

(3) For the purposes of this regulation, the owner of the vehicle shall be deemed to be in the case of a vehicle—

(a) which is for the time being registered under [the 1994 Act], and is not being used under a trade licence under that Act the person appearing as the owner of the vehicle in the register kept by the Secretary of State under that Act;

(b) used under a trade licence, the holder of the licence; or

(c) exempt from excise duty by virtue of the Motor Vehicles (International Circulation) Order 1975 [*SI 1975/1208 (q.v.)*], the person resident outside the United Kingdom who has brought the vehicle into Great Britain;

and in cases (a) and (b) the address of the owner as shown on the said register or, as the case may be, on the licence may be treated as his address.

B15.178   *[Regulation 74 is printed as amended by the Interpretation Act 1978 ss.17(2)(a) and 23(1); the Vehicle Excise and Registration Act 1994 s.64 and Sch.4, para.4.]*

PART IV

CONDITIONS RELATING TO USE

A Laden Weight

Maximum permitted laden weight of a vehicle

B15.179   75.—(1) Save as provided in paragraph (2), the laden weight of the vehicle of a class specified in an item in column 2 of the Table shall not exceed the maximum permitted laden weight specified in that item in column 3.

(2) The maximum permitted laden weight of a vehicle first used before 1st June 1973 which falls in item 1 or 2 shall not be less than would be the case if the vehicle fell in item 9.

TABLE

(regulation 75(1))

1	2	3
Item	Class of vehicle	Maximum permitted laden weight (kg)
1	A wheeled heavy motor car or motor car which is not described in items [1A, 2], 4 or 5 and which complies with the relevant braking requirement [(see regulation 78(3) to (6) in relation to buses)]	[The weight determined in accordance with Part I of Schedule 11]
[1A	A wheeled heavy motor car or motor car which is not described in item 2, 4 or 5, which complies with the relevant braking requirement and in which—	The weight determined in accordance with Part IA of Schedule 11]

1	2	3
Item	Class of vehicle	Maximum permitted laden weight (kg)
	(a) every driving axle not being a steering axle is fitted with twin tyres; and (b) either every driving axle is fitted with road friendly suspension or no axle has an axle weight exceeding 9,500 kg	
2	A wheeled heavy motor car or motor car (not being an agricultural motor vehicle) which forms part of an articulated vehicle and which complies with the relevant braking requirement	The weight specified in column (5) in Part II of Schedule 11 in the item which is appropriate having regard to columns (2), (3) and (4) in that Part
3	A wheeled trailer, including a composite trailer, but not including a semi-trailer, which is drawn by a motor tractor, heavy motor car or motor car which complies with the relevant braking requirement, other than a trailer described in items 6, 7, 8 or 11	As for item 1
[4	An articulated bus (see regulation 78(3) to (5))	27,000]
5	A wheeled agricultural motor vehicle	As for item 1, but subject to a maximum of 24,390
6	A balanced agricultural trailer, as defined in paragraph (4), which is not described in items 8, 11 or 16	As for item 1, but subject to a maximum of 18,290
7	An unbalanced agricultural trailer, as defined in paragraph (4), which is not described in items 8, 11 or 16	18,290 inclusive of the weight imposed by the trailer on the drawing vehicle

1	2	3
Item	Class of vehicle	Maximum permitted laden weight (kg)
8	A wheeled trailer manufactured on or after 27th February 1977 and fitted with brakes which automatically come into operation on the over-run of the trailer (whether or not it is fitted with any other brake), except an agricultural trailer which is being drawn by an agricultural motor vehicle, which complies with the requirements specified in items 3, 14 and 17 of Schedule 3 and of which the brakes can be applied either by the driver of the drawing vehicle or by some other person on that vehicle or on the trailer	3,500
9	A wheeled heavy motor car or motor car not described in items 1, 2, 4 or 5—	
	(a) with not more than 4 wheels	14,230
	(b) with more than 4 but not more than 6 wheels	20,330
	(c) with more than 6 wheels	24,390
10	A wheeled trailer not described in items 3, 6, 7, 8 or 11 having less than 6 wheels, and not forming part of an articulated vehicle; and an agricultural trailed appliance	14,230
11	A trailer manufactured before 27th February 1977 and having no brakes other than—	
	(i) a parking brake and	
	(ii) brakes which come into operation on the over-run of the trailer	3,560
12	A wheeled locomotive, not described in item 5, which is equipped with suitable and sufficient springs between each wheel and the vehicle's frame and with a pneumatic tyre or a tyre of soft or elastic material fitted to each wheel—	
	(a) if having less than 6 wheels	22,360

1	2	3
Item	Class of vehicle	Maximum permitted laden weight (kg)
	(b) if having 6 wheels	26,420
	(c) if having more than 6 wheels	30,490
13	A track-laying locomotive with resilient material interposed between the rims of the weight-carrying rollers and the road so that the weight of the vehicle (other than that borne by any wheels and the portion of the track in contact with the road) is supported by the resilient material	22,360
14	A locomotive not described in items 5, 12 or 13	20,830
15	A track-laying heavy motor car or motor car	22,360
16	A track-laying trailer	13,210

(3) The maximum total weight of all trailers, whether laden or unladen, drawn at any one time by a locomotive shall not exceed [44,000kg].

[(3A) Nothing in item 1 or 1A of the Table shall prevent a vehicle being used on a road if—

(a) a plating certificate in respect of the vehicle was in force immediately before the 1st January 1993; and

(b) the laden weight of the vehicle does not exceed the weight shown in that certificate as being the weight not to be exceeded in Great Britain.]

(4) [In this Part of these Regulations and in Schedule 11—]

[*"air spring"* means a spring operated by means of air or other compressible fluid under pressure;]

[*"air suspension"* means a suspension system in which at least 75 per cent of the spring effect is caused by an air spring;]

"balanced agricultural trailer" means an agricultural trailer the whole of the weight of which is borne by its own wheels; and

"unbalanced agricultural trailer" means an agricultural trailer of which some, but not more than 35 per cent, of the weight is borne by the drawing vehicle and the rest of the weight is borne by its own wheels.

[(5) For the purposes of this Part of these Regulations and Schedule 11, an axle shall be regarded as fitted with a road friendly suspension if its suspension is—

(a) an air suspension, or

(b) a suspension, not being an air suspension, which is regarded as being equivalent to an air suspension for the purposes of Community Directive 92/7.]

[(6) For the purposes of this Part of these Regulations and Schedule 11, an axle shall be regarded as fitted with twin tyres if it would be regarded as fitted with twin tyres for the purposes of Community Directive 92/7.]

B15.180   *[Regulation 75 is printed as amended by SI 1992/2016; SI 1998/3112.]*

Maximum permitted laden weight of a vehicle and trailer, other than an articulated vehicle

B15.181   **76.**—(1) The total laden weight of a motor vehicle and the trailer or trailers (other than semi-trailers) drawn by it shall not, in a case specified in an item in column 2 of the Table, exceed the maximum permitted train weight specified in that item in column 3.

[(1A) This regulation is subject to Schedule 11A (exemptions relating to combined transport operations).]

[(2) In this regulation, the expressions *"road friendly suspension"*, *"twin tyres"* and *"unbalanced agricultural trailer"* shall be construed in accordance with regulation 75(4), (5) and (6).]

TABLE
(regulation 76(1))

1	2	3
Item	*Vehicle combination*	*Maximum permitted laden weight (kg)*
[1	A wheeled trailer which is drawn by a wheeled motor tractor, heavy motor car (not being in any case an agricultural motor vehicle), where— (a) the combination has a total of 4 axles and is being used for international transport; and (b) the drawing vehicle is a vehicle which was first used on or after 1st April 1973 and complies with the relevant braking requirement	35,000]
[1A	A wheeled trailer which is drawn by a wheeled motor tractor, heavy motor car or motor car (not being in any case an agricultural motor vehicle), where the combination has a total of 4 axles and the following conditions are satisfied in relation to the drawing vehicle, namely—	

1	*2*	*3*
Item	*Vehicle combination*	*Maximum permitted laden weight (kg)*
	(a) it was first used on or after 1st April 1973; (b) it complies with the relevant braking requirement; (c) every driving axle not being a steering axle is fitted with twin tyres; and (d) every driving axle is fitted with road friendly suspension	35,000]
[1AA	A wheeled trailer which is drawn by a wheeled motor tractor, heavy motor car or motor car (not being in any case an agricultural motor vehicle), where the combination has a total of 5 or more axles and the following conditions are satisfied in relation to the drawing vehicle, namely— (a) it was first used on or after 1st April 1973; (b) it complies with the relevant braking requirement; (c) every driving axle not being a steering axle is fitted with twin tyres; and (d) either every driving axle is fitted with road friendly suspension or no axle has an axle weight exceeding 8,500kg	38,000]
[1B	A wheeled trailer, not being part of a combination described in items 1, 1A or 1AA which is drawn by a wheeled motor tractor heavy motor car or motor car (not being in any case an agricultural motor vehicle), where— (a) the trailer is fitted with power-assisted brakes which can be operated by the driver of the drawing vehicle and are not rendered ineffective by the non-rotation of its engine; and	

1	2	3
Item	Vehicle combination	Maximum permitted laden weight (kg)
	(b) the drawing vehicle is equipped with a warning device so placed as to be readily visible to the driver of the vehicle and which is capable of indicating any impending failure of, or deficiency in, the vacuum or pressure system	32,520]
1C	A wheeled trailer which is of a description specified in item 8 in the Table of regulation 75 drawn by a wheeled motor tractor, heavy motor car or motor car (not being in any case an agricultural motor vehicle), the drawing vehicle being a vehicle which— (a) was first used on or after 1st April 1973; and (b) complies with the relevant braking requirement	29,500
2	A wheeled agricultural motor vehicle drawing a wheeled unbalanced agricultural trailer, if the distance between the rearmost axle of the trailer and the rearmost axle of the drawing vehicle does not exceed 2.9m	20,000
3	A wheeled trailer or trailers drawn by a wheeled motor tractor, heavy motor car, motor car or agricultural motor vehicle, not being a combination of vehicles mentioned in items 1 [, 1A, [1AA,] 1B, 1C] or 2	24,390

1	2	3
Item	Vehicle combination	Maximum permitted laden weight (kg)
4	A track-laying trailer drawn by a motor tractor, heavy motor car or motor car, whether wheeled or track-laying and a wheeled trailer, drawn by a track-laying vehicle being a motor tractor, heavy motor car or motor car	22,360

[Regulation 76 is printed as amended by SI 1992/2016; SI 1994/329.]   **B15.182**

Maximum permitted laden weight of an articulated vehicle

77.—(1) Except as provided in paragraph (2), the laden weight of an articulated   **B15.183**
vehicle of a class specified in an item in column 2 of the Table shall not exceed
the weight specified in column 3 in that item.

TABLE
(regulation 77(1))

1	2	3
Item	Class of vehicle	Maximum permitted laden weight (kg)
1	An articulated vehicle which complies with the relevant braking requirement	Whichever is the lower of— (a) the weight specified in column (3) of Part III of Schedule 11 in the item in which the spacing between the rearmost axles of the motor vehicle and the semi-trailer is specified in column (2), …; and (b) if the vehicle is of a description specified in an item in column (2) of Part IV of Schedule 11, the weight specified in column (3) of that item
2	An articulated vehicle which does not comply with the relevant braking requirement if the trailer has— (a) less than 4 wheels (b) 4 wheels or more	20,330 24,390

(2) This regulation does not apply to an agricultural motor vehicle, an agricultural trailer or an agricultural trailed appliance.

[(2A) This regulation is subject to Schedule 11A (exemptions relating to combined transport operations).]

[(3) In Part IV of Schedule 11, *"road friendly suspension"* and *"twin tyres"* shall be construed in accordance with regulation 75(5) and (6).]

B15.184   *[Regulation 77 is printed as amended by SI 1992/2016; SI 1994/329.]*

Maximum permitted wheel and axle weights

B15.185   **78.**—(1) The weight transmitted to the road by one or more wheels of a vehicle as mentioned in an item in column 2 of the Table shall not exceed the maximum permitted weight specified in that item in column 3.

(2) The Parts of the Table have the following application—

  (a) Part I applies to wheeled heavy motor cars, motor cars and trailers which comply with the relevant braking requirement and to wheeled agricultural motor vehicles, agricultural trailers and agricultural trailed appliances; items 1(b) and 2 also apply to buses;

  (b) Part II applies to wheeled heavy motor cars, motor cars and trailers which do not fall in Part I;

  (c) Part III applies to wheeled locomotives; and

  (d) Part IV applies to track-laying vehicles.

Table
(regulation 78(1)) (Part I)
(wheeled heavy motor cars, motor cars and trailers which comply with the relevant braking requirement and wheeled agricultural motor vehicles, agricultural trailers and agricultural trailed appliances; and, in respect of items 1(b) and 2, buses)

1	2	3
Item	Wheel criteria	Maximum permitted weight (kg)
1	Two wheels in line transversely each of which is fitted with a wide tyre or with two pneumatic tyres having the centres of their areas of contact with the road not less than 300mm apart, measured at right angles to the longitudinal axis of the vehicle—	
	(a) if the wheels are on the sole driving axle of a motor vehicle [not being a bus],	10,500
	(b) if the vehicle is a bus which has 2 axles and of which the weight transmitted to the road surface by its wheels is calculated in accordance with regulation 78(5),	10,500
	(c) in any other case	10,170

1	2	3
Item	Wheel criteria	Maximum permitted weight (kg)
2	Two wheels in line transversely otherwise than as mentioned in item 1	9,200
3	More than two wheels in line transversely— (a) in the case of a vehicle manufactured before 1st May 1983 [where] the wheels are on one axle of a group of ... closely spaced axles ..., (b) in the case of a vehicle manufactured on or after 1st May 1983, (c) in any other case	 10,170 10,170 11,180
4	One wheel not transversely in line with any other wheel— (a) if the wheel is fitted as described in item 1, (b) in any other case	 5,090 4,600

(Part II)

(wheeled heavy motor cars, motor cars and trailers not falling in Part I)

1	2	3
Item	Wheel criteria	Maximum permitted weight (kg)
5	More than two wheels transmitting weight to a strip of the road surface on which the vehicle rests contained between two parallel lines at right angles to the longitudinal axis of the vehicle— (a) less than 1.02m apart, (b) 1.02m or more apart but less than 1.22m apart, (c) 1.22m or more apart but less than 2.13m apart	 11,180 16,260 18,300
6	Two wheels in line transversely	9,200
7	One wheel, where no other wheel is in the same line transversely	4,600

(Part III)
(wheeled locomotives)

1	2	3
Item	Wheel criteria	Maximum permitted weight (kg)
8	Two wheels in line transversely (except in the case of a road roller, or a vehicle with not more than four wheels first used before 1st June 1955)	11,180
9	Any two wheels in the case of a wheeled locomotive having not more than four wheels first used before 1st June 1955 (not being a road roller or an agricultural motor vehicle which is not driven at more than 20mph)	Three quarters of the total weight of the locomotive

(Part IV)
(track-laying vehicles)

1	2	3
Item	Wheel criteria	Maximum permitted weight (kg)
10	The weight of a heavy motor car, motor car or trailer transmitted to any strip of the road surface on which the vehicle rests contained between two parallel lines 0.6m apart at right angles to the longitudinal axis of the vehicle	10,170
11	Two wheels in line— (a) heavy motor cars or motor cars with 2 wheels,	8,130
	(b) heavy motor cars or motor cars with more than 2 wheels	7,630
12	One wheel, where no other wheel is in the same line transversely, on a heavy motor car or a motor car	4,070

(3) In the case of an articulated bus, or, subject to paragraph (4), of a bus first used before 1st April 1988, the laden weight, for the purposes of ... regulation 75, and the weight transmitted to the road surface by wheels of the vehicle, for the purposes of items 1 and 2 of the Table in this regulation, shall be calculated with reference to the vehicle when it is complete and fully equipped for service with—

    (a) a full supply of water, oil and fuel; and

    (b) weights of 63.5kg for each person (including crew)—

    (i) for whom a seat is provided in the position in which he may be seated; and

    (ii) who may by or under any enactment be carried standing, the total of such weights being reasonably distributed in the space in which such persons may be carried, save that in the case of a bus (not being an articulated bus) only the number of such persons exceeding 8 shall be taken into account.

(4) The weights for the purposes referred to in paragraph (3) may, in the case of a bus to which that paragraph applies, be calculated in accordance with paragraph (5) instead of paragraph (3).

(5) In the case of a bus first used on or after 1st April 1988, the weights for the purposes referred to in paragraph (3) shall be calculated with reference to the vehicle when it is complete and fully equipped for service with—

  (a) a full supply of water, oil and fuel;

  (b) a weight of 65kg for each person (including crew)—

    (i) for whom a seat is provided, in the position in which he may be seated; and

    (ii) who may by or under any enactment be carried standing, the total of such weights being reasonably distributed in the space in which such persons may be so carried, save that in the case of a bus (not being an articulated bus) only the number of such persons exceeding 4 shall be taken into account;

  (c) all luggage space within the vehicle but not with the passenger compartment loaded at the rate of 100kg per m³ or 10kg per person mentioned in sub-paragraph (b) above, whichever is the less; and

  (d) any area of the roof of the vehicle constructed or adapted for the storage of luggage loaded with a uniformly distributed load at the rate of 75kg per m² .

[(6) Regulation 75 shall not apply to a two axle bus if—

  (a) its laden weight as calculated in accordance with paragraph (5) does not exceed 17,000kg; and

  (b) the distance between the two axles is at least 3.0m.]

[Regulation 78 is printed as amended by SI 1987/676; SI 1992/2016.]   **B15.186**

Maximum permitted weights for certain closely spaced axles, etc.

79.—(1) This regulation applies to—   **B15.187**

  (a) a wheeled motor vehicle which complies with the relevant braking requirement;

  (b) a wheeled trailer which is drawn by such a motor vehicle; and

  (c) an agricultural motor vehicle, an agricultural trailer and an agricultural trailed appliance.

[(2) Save as provided in paragraph (5), where a vehicle to which this regulation applies is of a description specified in an item in column 2 of Part V of Schedule 11 and has two closely-spaced axles, the total weight transmitted to the road surface by all the wheels of those axles shall not exceed the maximum permitted weight specified in column 3 of that item.]

[(3) Save as provided in paragraph (5), where a vehicle to which this regulation applies is of a description specified in an item in column 2 of Part VI of

Schedule 11 and has three closely-spaced axles, the total weight transmitted to the road surface by all the wheels of those axles shall not exceed the weight specified in column 3.]

[(4) Save as provided by paragraph (5), where a vehicle is fitted with four or more closely-spaced axles, the weight transmitted to the road surface by all the wheels of those axles shall not exceed 24,000kg.]

(5) Nothing in paragraphs (2), (3) or (4) of this regulation shall apply so as to prevent a vehicle first used before 1st June 1973 from being used on a road at a weight as respects those axles at which it could be used if it fell within item 5 in the Table in regulation 78 [and nothing in those paragraphs shall prevent a vehicle being used on a road if—

(a) a plating certificate in respect of the vehicle was in force immediately before the 1st January 1993; and

(b) no axle has an axle weight exceeding the weight shown in that certificate as being the weight not to be exceeded in Great Britain for that axle.]

[(6) In Parts V and VI of Schedule 11, *"air suspension"*, *"road friendly suspension"* and *"twin tyres"* shall be construed in accordance with regulation 75(4), (5) and (6).]

[(7) Paragraph (6) applies to a semi-trailer if—

(a) it has a total of three axles;

(b) the outermost axles are spaced at a distance apart of at least 0.7m but not more than 3.25m, such distances being obtained as provided in regulation 3(10);

(c) each axle is fitted with suspension devices in which air springs are used to support a substantial part of the weight borne on that axle; and

(d) the devices are so interconnected and maintained that under any relevant condition of load the weight transmitted to the road surface by all the wheels of any one axle does not exceed the total weight transmitted to the road surface by all the wheels of any other axle by more than 500kg.]

[(8) For the purposes of paragraphs (6) and (7), in relation to a semi-trailer any two adjoining axles of which are spaced at such a distance apart as is specified in an item in column 2 of Part VI of Schedule 11—

(a) *"air spring"* means a spring operated by means of air or other compressible fluid under pressure;

(b) *"relevant condition of load"* means a condition of load which causes the weight transmitted to the road surface by all the wheels of any one axle to exceed the weight shown in column 3 of that item;

(c) *"relevant weight"* means the weight shown in column 4 of that item.]

B15.188   *[Regulation 79 is printed as amended by SI 1988/1287; SI 1992/2016.]*

[Saving for the Road Vehicles (Authorised Weight) Regulations 1998

B15.189   79A. Nothing in regulations 75 to 79 shall be taken to prohibit the use of a vehicle in circumstances where the maximum authorised weight for the vehicle, for any vehicle combination of which the vehicle forms part and for any axle of the vehicle, as determined in accordance with the Road Vehicles (Authorised Weight) Regulations 1998 [*SI 1998/3111 below*], is not exceeded.]

[*Regulation 79A was inserted by SI 1998/3112.*]

Over-riding weight restrictions

80.—(1) Subject to [paragraphs (2), (2A), (2B), (2C) and (4)], no person shall   **B15.190**
use, or cause or permit to be used, on a road a vehicle—

    (a) fitted with a plate in accordance with regulation 66, but for which no plating certificate has been issued, if any of the weights shown on the plate is exceeded;

    (b) for which a plating certificate has been issued, if any of the weights shown in column (2) of the plating certificate is exceeded; or

    (c) required by regulation 68 to be fitted with a plate, if the maximum gross weight referred to in paragraph (2)(c) of that regulation is exceeded.

(2) Where any two or more axles are fitted with a compensating arrangement in accordance with regulation 23 the sum of the weights shown for them in the plating certificate shall not be exceeded. In a case where a plating certificate has not been issued the sum of the weights referred to shall be that shown for the said axles in the plate fitted in accordance with regulation 66.

[(2A) Paragraph (1) shall not apply to a vehicle for which a plating certificate has been issued in the form set out in Schedule 10A or 10C where—

    (a) the vehicle is being used for international transport; and

    (b) none of the weights shown in column (3) of the plating certificate is exceeded.]

[(2B) Where both a train weight and a maximum train weight are shown in column (2) of a plating certificate issued for a motor vehicle, paragraph (1)(b) in so far as it relates to train weights shall not apply to the motor vehicle if—

    (a) the motor vehicle is a wheeled heavy motor car drawing a wheeled trailer and the requirements set out in Part II of Schedule 11A are for the time being fulfilled; or

    (b) the motor vehicle is comprised in an articulated vehicle and the requirements set out in Part III of Schedule 11A are for the time being fulfilled,

and the train weight of the motor vehicle does not exceed the maximum train weight shown in column (2) of the certificate.]

(3) Nothing in regulations 75 to 79 [or in the Road Vehicles (Authorised Weight) Regulations 1998 [*SI 1998/3111 below*]] shall permit any such weight as is mentioned in the preceding provisions of this regulation to be exceeded and nothing in this regulation shall permit any weight prescribed by regulations 75 to 79 [or in the Road Vehicles (Authorised Weight) Regulations 1998] in relation to the vehicle in question to be exceeded.

[(4) Paragraph (1) shall not apply where a vehicle is used on a road before 1st January 2000 if—

    (a) the vehicle is fitted with a plate in accordance with regulation 66(1)(b) and the maximum gross weight and the maximum weight for any axle of the vehicle are not exceeded; or

(b) there is in force a plating certificate for the vehicle that was issued before 1st January 1999 and the design weight of the vehicle is not exceeded; and

(c) in either case the maximum authorised weight for the vehicle, maximum authorised weight for a combination of which the vehicle forms part and maximum authorised weight for any axle of the vehicle, determined in accordance with the Road Vehicles (Authorised Weight) Regulations 1998, are not exceeded.]

B15.191   *[Regulation 80 is printed as amended by SI 1994/329; SI 1997/1096; SI 1998/ 3112.*

The reference to para.(2C) in reg.80(1) seems to have been made in error. There is no provision designated as reg.80(2C); a reference to para.(2C) was inserted by SI 1994/329 and deleted by SI 1997/1096; but a further amendment to reg.80(1) (effected by SI 1998/3112) seems to have been made on the basis that the reference to para.(2C) was extant, and renewed it.

Other than as stated, compliance with the Road Vehicles (Authorised Weight) Regulations 1998 (SI 1998/3111 below) provides no defence to a contravention of this regulation; see SI 1998/3111 reg.5(1) below. But as to the application of reg.80 after January 1, 2002 to vehicles fitted with one or more retractable (or loadable) axles, see SI 1998/3111 reg.5(2).]

B Dimensions of Laden Vehicles

Restrictions on use of vehicles carrying wide or long loads or having fixed appliances or apparatus

B15.192   **81.** For the purpose of this regulation, regulation 82 and Schedule 12—

(a) *"lateral projection"*, in relation to a load carried by a vehicle, means that part of the load which extends beyond a side of the vehicle;

(b) the width of any lateral projection shall be measured between longitudinal planes passing through the extreme projecting point of the vehicle on that side on which the projection lies and the part of the projection furthest from that point;

(c) references to a special appliance or apparatus, in relation to a vehicle, are references to any crane or other special appliance or apparatus fitted to the vehicle which is a permanent or essentially permanent fixture;

(d) *"forward projection"* and *"rearward projection"*—

(i) in relation to a load carried in such a manner that its weight [is borne by] only one vehicle, mean respectively that part of the load which extends beyond the foremost point of the vehicle and that part which extends beyond the rearmost point of the vehicle;

(ii) in relation to a load carried in such a manner that part of its weight [is borne by] more than one vehicle, mean respectively that part of the load which extends beyond the foremost point of the foremost vehicle by which the load is carried except where the context otherwise requires and that part of the load which extends beyond the rearmost point of the rearmost vehicle by which the load is carried; and

    (iii) in relation to any special appliance or apparatus, mean respectively that part of the appliance or apparatus which, if it were deemed to be a load carried by the vehicle, would be a part of a load extending beyond the foremost point of the vehicle and that part which would be a part of a load extending beyond the rearmost point of the vehicle,

and references in regulation 82 and Schedule 12 to a forward projection or to a rearward projection in relation to a vehicle shall be construed accordingly;

(e) the length of any forward projection or of any rearward projection shall be measured between transverse planes passing—

    (i) in the case of a forward projection, through the foremost point of the vehicle and that part of the projection furthest from that point; and

    (ii) in the case of a rearward projection, through the rearmost point of the vehicle and that part of the projection furthest from that point.

In this and the foregoing sub-paragraph *"vehicle"* does not include any special appliance or apparatus or any part thereof which is a forward projection or a rearward projection;

(f) references to the distance between vehicles, in relation to vehicles carrying a load, are references to the distance between the nearest points of any two adjacent vehicles by which the load is carried, measured when the longitudinal axis of each vehicle lies in the same vertical plane.

For the purposes of this sub-paragraph, in determining the nearest point of two vehicles any part of either vehicle designed primarily for use as a means of attaching the one vehicle to the other and any fitting designed for use in connection with any such part shall be disregarded;

(g) references to a combination of vehicles, in relation to a motor vehicle which is drawing one or more trailers, are references to the motor vehicle and the trailer or trailers drawn thereby, including any other motor vehicle which is used for the purpose of assisting in the propulsion of the trailer or the trailers on the road;

(h) the overall length of a combination of vehicles shall be taken as the distance between the foremost point of the drawing vehicle comprised in the combination and the rearmost point of the rearmost vehicle comprised therein, measured when the longitudinal axis of each vehicle comprised in the combination lies in the same vertical plane;

(i) the extreme projecting point of a vehicle is the point from which the overall width of the vehicle is calculated in accordance with the definition of overall width contained in regulation 3(2);

(j) without prejudice to sub-paragraph (e) the foremost or, as the case may be, the rearmost point of a vehicle is the foremost or rearmost point from which the overall length of the vehicle is calculated in accordance with the definition of overall length contained in regulation 3(2); and

(k) an agricultural, horticultural or forestry implement rigidly but not permanently mounted on an agricultural motor vehicle, agricultural trailer or agricultural trailed appliance, whether or not part of its weight is supported by one or more of its own wheels, shall not be treated as a load, or special appliance, on that vehicle.

B15.193   *[Regulation 81 is printed as amended by SI 1991/2125.]*

B15.194   82.—(1) No load shall be carried on a vehicle so that the overall width of the vehicle together with the width of any lateral projections or projection of its load exceeds 4.3m.

(2) Subject to the following provisions of this regulation, no load shall be carried on a vehicle so that—

  (a) the load has a lateral projection or projections on either side exceeding 305mm; or

  (b) the overall width of the vehicle and of any lateral projection or projections of its load exceeds 2.9m.

Provided that this paragraph does not apply to the carriage of—

    (i) loose agricultural produce not baled or crated; or

    (ii) an indivisible load if—

      (A) it is not reasonably practicable to comply with this paragraph and the conditions specified in [paragraphs 1 and 5] of Schedule 12 are complied with; and plied with; and

      (B) where the overall width of the vehicle together with the width of any lateral projection or projections of its loads exceeds 3.5m, the conditions specified in paragraph 2 of Schedule 12 are complied with.

(3) Where a load is carried so that its weight rests on a vehicle or vehicles, the length specified in paragraph (5) shall not exceed 27.4m.

[(4) A load shall not be carried so that its weight is borne by a vehicle or vehicles if either—

  (a) the length specified in paragraph (5) exceeds 18.65m; or

  (b) the load is borne by a trailer or trailers and the length specified in paragraph (6) exceeds 25.9m,

unless the conditions specified in paragraphs 1 and 2 of Part I of Schedule 12 are complied with.]

(5) The length referred to in paragraphs (3) and (4)(a) is—

  (a) where the [weight of the load is borne by] a single vehicle, the overall length of the vehicle together with the length of any forward and rearward projection of the load;

  (b) where the [weight of the load is borne by] a motor vehicle and one trailer, whether or not forming an articulated vehicle, the overall length of the trailer together with the length of any projection of the load in front of the foremost point of the trailer and of any rearward projection of the load; and

  (c) in any other case, the overall length of all the vehicles [which bear the weight of the load], together with the length of any distance between them and of any forward or rearward projection of the load.

(6) The length referred to in paragraph (4)(b) is the overall length of the combination of vehicles, together with the length of any forward or rearward projection of the load.

(7) Subject to the following provisions of this regulation no person shall use, or cause or permit to be used, on a road a vehicle, not being a straddle carrier, carrying a load or fitted with a special appliance or apparatus if the load, appliance or apparatus has a forward projection of a length specified in an item in column 2 of the Table, or rearward projection of a length specified in an item in column 3, unless the conditions specified in that item in column 4 are complied with.

TABLE

(regulation 82(7))

1	2	3	4	
Item	Length of forward projection	Length of rearward projection	Conditions to be complied with	
			(a) if the load consists of a racing boat propelled solely by oars	(b) in any other case
1	Exceeding 1m but not exceeding 2m	—	Para 4 of Schedule 12	—
2	Exceeding 2m but not exceeding 3.05m	—	Para 4 of Schedule 12	Paras 2 and 3 of Schedule 12
3	Exceeding 3.05m	—	Paras 1 and 4 of Schedule 12	Paras 1, 2 and 3 of Schedule 12
4	—	Exceeding 1m but not exceeding 2m	Para 4 of Schedule 12	Para 4 of Schedule 12
5	—	Exceeding 2m but not exceeding 3.05m	Para 4 of Schedule 12	Para 3 of Schedule 12
6	—	Exceeding 3.05m	Paras 1 and 4 of Schedule 12	Paras 1, 2 and 3 of Schedule 12

(8) Subject to the following provisions of this regulation, no person shall use, or cause or permit to be used, on a road a straddle carrier carrying a load if—

(a) the load has a rearward projection exceeding 1m unless the conditions specified in paragraph 4 of Schedule 12 are met;

(b) the load has a forward projection exceeding 2m or a rearward projection exceeding 3m; or

(c) the overall length of the vehicle together with the length of any forward projection and of any rearward projection of its load exceeds 12.2m;

Provided that—

   (i) sub-paragraph (a) does not apply to a vehicle being used in passing from one of private premises to another part thereof or to other private premises in the immediate neighbourhood;

   (ii) sub-paragraphs (b) and (c) do not apply to a vehicle being used as in proviso (i) above if—

      (A) the vehicle is not being driven at a speed exceeding 12mph; and

      (B) where the overall length of the vehicle together with the length of any forward projection and of any rearward projection of its load exceeds 12.2m, the conditions specified in paragraphs 1 and 2 of Schedule 12 are complied with.

(9) Where another vehicle is attached to that end of a vehicle from which a projection extends, then for the purposes of any requirement in this regulation to comply with paragraph 3 or 4 of Schedule 12, that projection shall be treated as a forward or rearward projection only if, and to the extent that it extends beyond the foremost point or, as the case may be, the rearmost point, of that other vehicle, measured when the longitudinal axis of each vehicle lies in the same vertical plane.

(10) In the case of a vehicle being used—

   (a) for fire brigade [or, in England [or Wales], fire and rescue authority], ambulance or police purposes or for defence purposes (including civil defence purposes); or

   (b) in connection with the removal of any obstruction to traffic,

if compliance with any provision of this regulation would hinder or be likely to hinder the use of the vehicle for the purpose for which it is being used, that provision does not apply to that vehicle while it is being so used.

(11) No person shall use, or cause or permit to be used, on a road an agricultural, horticultural or forestry implement rigidly, but not permanently, mounted on a wheeled agricultural motor vehicle, agricultural trailer, or agricultural trailed appliance, whether or not part of its weight is supported by one or more of its own wheels if—

   (a) the overall width of the vehicle together with the lateral projection of the implement exceeds [2.55]m; or

   (b) the implement projects more than 1m forwards or rearwards of the vehicle,

so however, that this restriction shall not apply in a case where—

      (i) part of the weight of the implement is supported by one or more of its own wheels; and

      (ii) the longitudinal axis of the greater part of the implement is capable of articulating in the horizontal plane in relation to the longitudinal axis of the rear portion of the vehicle.

B15.195   *[Regulation 82 is printed as amended by SI 1991/2125; SI 1995/3051; SI 2004/ 3168; SI 2005/2929.]*

C Trailers and Sidecars

Number of trailers

83.—(1) No person shall use, or cause or permit to be used, on a road a wheeled **B15.196** vehicle of a class specified in an item in column 2 of the Table drawing a trailer, subject to any exceptions which may be specified in that item in column 3.

TABLE

(regulation 83(1))

1	2	3
Item	Class of vehicles	Exceptions
1	A straddle carrier	—
2	An invalid carriage	—
3	An articulated bus	—
4	A bus not being an articulated bus or a mini-bus	(a) 1 broken down bus where no person other than the driver is carried in either vehicle or [(b) 1 trailer]
5	A locomotive	3 trailers
6	A motor tractor	[1 trailer] 2 trailers if neither is laden
7	A heavy motor car or a motor car not described in items 1, 3 or 4	2 trailers if one of them is a towing implement and part of the other is secured to and either rests on or is suspended from that implement 1 trailer in any other case
8	An agricultural motor vehicle	(a) in respect of trailers other than agricultural trailers and agricultural trailed appliances, such trailers as are permitted under items 5, 6 or 7 above, as the case may be; or (b) in respect of agricultural trailers and agricultural trailed appliances— (i) 2 unladen agricultural trailers, or (ii) 1 agricultural trailer and 1 agricultural trailed appliance, or (iii) 2 agricultural trailed appliances

(2) For the purposes of items 5, 6 and 7 of the Table—

(a) an unladen articulated vehicle, when being drawn by another motor vehicle because it has broken down, shall be treated as a single trailer; and

(b) a towed roller used for the purposes of agriculture, horticulture or forestry and consisting of several separate rollers shall be treated as one agricultural trailed appliance.

(3) No track-laying motor vehicle which exceeds 8m in overall length shall draw a trailer other than a broken down vehicle which is being drawn in consequence of the breakdown.

[(4) For the purpose of this regulation, the word *"trailer"* does not include a vehicle which is drawn by a steam powered vehicle and which is used solely for carrying water for the purpose of the drawing vehicle.]

B15.197   *[Regulation 83 is printed as amended by SI 1987/676; SI 1989/2360.]*

Trailers drawn by motor cycles

B15.198   **84.**—(1) Save as provided in paragraph (2), no person shall use, or cause or permit to be used, on a road a motor cycle—

> (a) drawing behind it more than one trailer;
>
> (b) drawing behind it any trailer carrying a passenger;
>
> (c) drawing behind it a trailer with an unladen weight exceeding 254kg;
>
> (d) with not more than 2 wheels, without a sidecar, and with an engine capacity which does not exceed 125cc, drawing behind it any trailer; or
>
> (e) with not more than 2 wheels, without a sidecar and with an engine capacity exceeding 125cc, drawing behind it any trailer unless—
>
>> (i) the trailer has an overall width not exceeding 1m;
>>
>> (ii) the distance between the rear axle of the motor cycle and the rearmost part of the trailer does not exceed 2.5m;
>>
>> (iii) the motor cycle is clearly and indelibly marked in a conspicuous and readily accessible position with its kerbside weight;
>>
>> (iv) the trailer is clearly and indelibly marked in a conspicuous and readily accessible position with its unladen weight; and
>>
>> (v) the laden weight of the trailer does not exceed 150kg or two-thirds of the kerbside weight of the motor cycle, whichever is the less.

(2) The provisions of paragraph (1)(b), (d) and (e) do not apply if the trailer is a broken down motor cycle and one passenger is riding it.

Trailers drawn by agricultural motor vehicles

B15.199   **85.**—(1) No person shall use, or cause or permit to be used, on a road a wheeled agricultural motor vehicle drawing one or more wheeled trailers if the weight of the drawing vehicle is less than a quarter of the weight of the trailer or trailers, unless the brakes fitted to each trailer in compliance with regulation 15 or 16 are operated directly by the service braking systems fitted to the motor vehicle.

(2) No person shall use, or cause or permit to be used, on a road any motor vehicle drawing an agricultural trailer of which—

> (a) more than 35 per cent of the weight is borne by the drawing vehicle; or
>
> (b) the gross weight exceeds 14,230kg, unless it is fitted with brakes as mentioned in paragraph (1).

(3) No person shall use, or cause or permit to be used, on a road an agricul-

tural trailer manufactured on or after 1st December 1985 which is drawn by a motor vehicle first used on or after 1st June 1986 unless the brakes fitted to the trailer—

(a) in accordance with regulation 15 can be applied progressively by the driver of the drawing vehicle, from his normal driving position and while keeping proper control of that vehicle, using a means of operation mounted on the drawing vehicle; or

(b) automatically come into operation on the over-run of the trailer.

Distance between motor vehicles and trailers

86.—(1) Where a trailer is attached to the vehicle immediately in front of it solely by means of a rope or chain, the distance between the trailer and that vehicle shall not in any case exceed 4.5m; and shall not exceed 1.5m unless the rope or chain is made clearly visible to any other person using the road within a reasonable distance from either side.   **B15.200**

(2) For the purpose of determining the said distance any part of either vehicle designed primarily for use as a means of attaching the one vehicle to the other and any fitting designed for use in connection with any such part shall be disregarded.

[Use of secondary coupling on trailers

86A.—(1) No person shall use or cause or permit to be used on a road a motor vehicle drawing one trailer if the trailer—   **B15.201**

(a) is a trailer to which regulation 15 applies; and

(b) is not fitted with a device which is designed to stop the trailer automatically in the event of the separation of the main coupling while the trailer is in motion,

unless the requirements of paragraph (2) are met in relation to the motor vehicle and trailer.

(2) The requirements of this paragraph, in relation to a motor vehicle drawing a trailer, are that a secondary coupling is attached to the motor vehicle and trailer in such a way that, in the event of the separation of the main coupling while the trailer is in motion,—

(a) the drawbar of the trailer would be prevented from touching the ground; and

(b) there would be some residual steering of the trailer.

(3) No person shall use or cause or permit to be used on a road a motor vehicle drawing one trailer if—

(a) the trailer is a trailer to which regulation 15 applies;

(b) the trailer is fitted with a device which is designed to stop the trailer automatically in the event of the separation of the main coupling while the trailer is in motion;

(c) the operation of the device in those circumstances depends upon a secondary coupling linking the device to the motor vehicle; and

(d) the trailer is not also fitted with a device which is designed to stop the trailer automatically in those circumstances in the absence of such a secondary coupling, unless the requirements of paragraph (4) are met in relation to the motor vehicle and trailer.

(4) The requirements of this paragraph, in relation to a motor vehicle drawing a trailer, are that the secondary coupling is attached to the motor vehicle and trailer in such a way that, in the event of the separation of the main coupling while the trailer is in motion, the device of the kind referred to in paragraph (3)(b) and (c) fitted to the trailer would stop the trailer.

(5) This regulation is without prejudice to any other provision in these Regulations.]

B15.202   *[Regulation 86A was inserted by SI 1995/1201.]*

Use of mechanical coupling devices

B15.203   **86B.**—(1) This regulation applies to every light passenger vehicle first used on or after 1st August 1998 in respect of which an EC certificate of conformity has effect.

(2) No person shall use or cause or permit to be used on a road any vehicle to which this regulation applies unless any mechanical coupling device which is attached to it complies with the relevant technical and installation requirements of Annexes I, V, VI and VII of Community Directive 94/20 [*O.J. No.L195, July 29, 1994, p.1*] and is marked in accordance with sub-paragraphs 3.3.4 to 3.3.5 of Annex I to that Directive.

(3) For the purposes of this regulation, in a case where a vehicle is drawing a trailer a mechanical coupling device shall not be regarded as being attached to that vehicle if it forms part of the trailer.

(4) In this regulation *"mechanical coupling device"* shall be construed in accordance with paragraph 2.1 of Annex I to Community Directive 94/20.]

B15.204   *[Regulation 86B was inserted by SI 1998/1281.]*

Unbraked trailers

B15.205   **87.**—(1) Save as provided in paragraph (2), no person shall use, or cause or permit to be used, on a road an unbraked wheeled trailer if—

    (a) its laden weight exceeds its maximum gross weight; or

    (b) it is drawn by a vehicle of which the kerbside weight is less than twice the sum of the unladen weight of the trailer and the weight of any load which the trailer is carrying.

(2) This regulation does not apply to—

    (a) an agricultural trailer; or

    (b) a trailer mentioned in [paragraph (b), (bb), (bc), (c), (d), (e), (f) or (g) of regulation 16(3)].

B15.206   *[Regulation 87 is printed as amended by SI 1987/676; SI 1996/3033.]*

Use of bridging plates between motor vehicle and trailer

B15.207   **88.** […]
[Revoked by SI 1998/2429.]

Leaving trailers at rest

B15.208   **89.** No person in charge of a motor vehicle, or trailer drawn thereby, shall cause or permit such trailer to stand on a road when detached from the drawing vehicle unless one at least of the wheels of the trailer is (or, in the case of a track-laying trailer, its tracks are) prevented from revolving by the setting of [a parking brake] or the use of a chain, chock or other efficient device.

[Regulation 89 is printed as amended by SI 1996/3033.]   **B15.209**

Passengers in trailers

90.—(1) Save as provided in paragraph (2), no person shall use, or cause or permit to be used, on a road any trailer for the carriage of passengers for hire or reward.   **B15.210**

(2) The provisions of paragraph (1) do not apply in respect of a wheeled trailer which is, or is carrying, a broken down motor vehicle if—

    (a) the trailer is drawn at a speed not exceeding 30mph; and

    (b) where the trailer is, or is carrying, a broken down bus, it is attached to the drawing vehicle by a rigid draw bar.

(3) Save as provided in paragraph (4), no person shall use, or cause or permit to be used, on a road a wheeled trailer in which any person is carried and which is a living van having either—

    (a) less than 4 wheels; or

    (b) 4 wheels consisting of two close-coupled wheels on each side.

(4) The provisions of paragraph (3) do not apply in respect of a trailer which is being tested by—

    (a) its manufacturer;

    (b) a person by whom it has been, or is being, repaired; or

    (c) a distributor of, or dealer in, trailers.

Attendance on trailers and certain other vehicles

91. [...]   **B15.211**

[Revoked by the Road Traffic (Consequential Provisions) Act 1988.]

Attachment of sidecars

92. Every sidecar fitted to a motor cycle shall be so attached that the wheel thereof is not wholly outside the space between transverse planes passing through the extreme projecting points at the front and at the rear of the motor cycle.   **B15.212**

Use of sidecars

93. No person shall use or cause or permit to be used on a road any two-wheeled motor cycle registered on or after 1st August 1981, not being a motor cycle brought temporarily into Great Britain by a person resident abroad, if there is a sidecar attached to the right (or off) side of the motor cycle.   **B15.213**

[CA Use of Motor Vehicles for the Carriage or Haulage of Dangerous Goods]

[Additional braking requirements for motor vehicles carrying or hauling dangerous goods

93A.—(1) Subject to paragraph (5), no person shall use or cause or permit to   **B15.214**

be used a motor vehicle for the carriage or haulage of dangerous goods on a road if it is a vehicle within the meaning of the Framework Directive and—

> (a) its maximum gross weight exceeds 16,000kg; or
>
> (b) it is drawing a trailer which has a maximum total design axle weight exceeding 10,000kg,

unless the vehicle meets the requirements of paragraph (2).

(2) Subject to paragraph (6), in order for a motor vehicle to meet the requirements of this paragraph —

> (a) it must not be drawing more than one trailer;
>
> (b) without prejudice to regulation 15, it must be fitted with an anti-lock braking system that meets the requirements of paragraph (1) of marginal 220 521 of Appendix B.2 to Annex B to the ADR;
>
> (c) it must be fitted with an endurance braking system (which may consist of one device or a combination of several devices) that meets the requirements of sub-paragraphs (a) to (d) of paragraph (2) of marginal 220 522 of Appendix B.2 to Annex B to the ADR;
>
> (d) if it is not drawing a trailer, it must meet the requirements of the 4th, 5th, 6th and 7th sub-paragraphs of paragraph (2) of marginal 10 221 of Annex B to the ADR;
>
> (e) without prejudice to regulation 15, if it is drawing a trailer with a maximum total design axle weight exceeding 10,000kg—
>
>> (i) the trailer must be fitted with an anti-lock braking system that meets the requirements of paragraph (2) of marginal 220 521 of Appendix B.2 to Annex B to the ADR, and
>>
>> (ii) the electrical connections between the motor vehicle and the trailer must meet the requirements of paragraph (3) of marginal 220 521 of Appendix B.2 to Annex B to the ADR;
>
> (f) if it is drawing a trailer, the combination of vehicles must meet the requirements of the 4th, 5th, 6th and 7th sub-paragraphs of paragraph (2) of marginal 10 221 of Annex B to the ADR;
>
> (g) if it is drawing a trailer fitted with an endurance braking system, the trailer must meet the requirements of paragraph (3) of marginal 220 522 of Appendix B.2 to Annex B to the ADR; and
>
> (h) if it is drawing a trailer, the requirements of either paragraph (3) or (4) must be met.

(3) The requirements of this paragraph are that the motor vehicle meets the requirements of paragraph (2)(e) of marginal 220 522 of Appendix B.2 to Annex B to the ADR.

(4) The requirements of this paragraph are that the motor vehicle—

> (a) does not contravene the restriction mentioned in sub-paragraph (f) of paragraph (2) of marginal 220 522 of Appendix B.2 to Annex B to the ADR; and
>
> (b) meets the requirements of the second sentence of that sub-paragraph in relation to the trailer.

(5) Paragraph (1) does not apply to a motor vehicle manufactured before 1st January 1997.

(6) Sub-paragraph (e) of paragraph (2) does not apply to a trailer manufactured before 1st January 1997.

(7) For the purposes of this regulation, Annex B to the ADR (including the Appendices to that Annex) shall have effect as if—

  (a) references to ECE Regulation 13 (however expressed) were references to ECE Regulation 13.06 or 13.07;

  (b) references to Directive 71/320/EEC [*O.J. No.L202, September 6, 1971, p.37*] were references to Community Directive 91/422 [*O.J. No.L233, September 22, 1991, p.21*];

  (c) references to the corresponding EEC Directive, an relation to Annex 5 to ECE Regulation 13, were references to paragraph 1.5 of Annex II to Community Directive 91/422.

(8) Subject to paragraph (9), a reference in this regulation to dangerous goods is a reference to a load comprising explosives of such type and in such quantity that it could not be carried by road in a single transport unit of Type I and II without there being a contravention of the restrictions set out in marginal 11 401 of Annex B to the ADR as read with marginal 11 402 of that Annex.

(9) For the purposes of paragraph (8)—

  (a) marginal 11 402 of Annex B to the ADR shall have effect with the omission of the words "in conformity with the prohibitions of mixed loading contained in 11 403"; and

  (b) *"transport unit of Type I or II"* means a transport unit of Type I or a transport unit of Type II as defined in marginal 11 204 of that Annex.

(10) In this regulation, *"ADR"* means the 1995 edition of the " European Agreement concerning the International Carriage of Dangerous Goods by Road (ADR)" produced by the Department of Transport and published by Her Majesty's Stationery Office (ISBN 0-11-551265-9).]

[Regulation 93A was inserted by SI 1996/3133.   **B15.215**

The 1995 edition of the ADR (see reg.93A(10)) has been superseded. See now the consolidated text (applicable from January 1, 2011) published by the United Nations (ISBN 9789211391404) and available from the TSO.]

D Use of Gas Propulsion Systems and Gas-fired Appliances

Use of gas propulsion systems

94.—(1) No person shall use, or cause or permit to be used, on a road a vehicle   **B15.216** with a gas propulsion system unless the whole of such system is in a safe condition.

(2) No person shall use, or cause or permit to be used, in any gas supply system for the propulsion of a vehicle when the vehicle is on a road any fuel except liquefied petroleum gas.

(3) No person shall use, or cause or permit to be used, on a road a vehicle which is propelled by gas unless the gas container in which such fuel is stored is on the motor vehicle, and not on any trailer, and in the case of an articulated vehicle on the portion of the vehicle to which the engine is fitted.

(4) In this regulation and in regulation 95 *"liquefied petroleum gas"* means—

  (a) butane gas in any phase which meets the requirements contained in the specification of commercial butane and propane issued by the British Standards Institution under the number BS4250: 1975 published on 29th August 1975; or

(b) propane gas in any phase which meets the requirements contained in the said specification; or

(c) any mixture of such butane gas and such propane gas.

Use of gas-fired appliances—general

B15.217   **95.**—(1) No person shall use, or cause or permit to be used, in or on a vehicle on a road any gas-fired appliance unless the whole of such appliance and the gas system attached thereto is in an efficient and safe condition.

(2) No person shall use, or cause or permit to be used, in any gas-fired appliance in or on a vehicle on a road any fuel except liquefied petroleum gas as defined in regulation 94(4).

(3) No person shall use, or cause or permit to be used, in or on a vehicle on a road any gas-fired appliance unless the vehicle is so ventilated that—

(a) an ample supply of air is available for the operation of the appliance;

(b) the use of the appliance does not adversely affect the health or comfort of any person using the vehicle; and

(c) any unburnt gas is safely disposed of to the outside of the vehicle.

(4) No person shall use, or cause or permit to be used, on a road a vehicle in or on which there is—

(a) one gas-fired appliance unless the gas supply for such appliance is shut off at the point where it leaves the container or containers at all times when the appliance is not in use;

(b) more than one gas-fired appliance each of which has the same supply of gas unless the gas supply for such appliances is shut off at the point where it leaves the container or containers at all times when none of such appliances is in use; or

(c) more than one gas-fired appliance each of which does not have the same supply of gas unless each gas supply for such appliances is shut off at the point where it leaves the container or containers at all times when none of such appliances which it supplies is in use.

Use of gas-fired appliances when a vehicle is in motion

B15.218   **96.**—(1) Subject to paragraph (2), this regulation applies to every motor vehicle and trailer.

(2) Paragraphs (3) and (4) do not apply to a vehicle constructed or adapted for the conveyance of goods under controlled temperatures.

(3) No person shall use, or cause or permit to be used, in any vehicle to which this paragraph applies, while the vehicle is in motion on a road, any gas-fired appliance except—

(a) a gas-fired appliance which is fitted to engineering plant while the plant is being used for the purposes of the engineering operations for which it was designed;

(b) a gas-fired appliance which is permanently attached to a bus, provided that any appliance for heating or cooling the interior of the bus for the comfort of the driver and any passengers does not expose a naked flame on the outside of the appliance; or

(c) in any other vehicle, a refrigerating appliance or an appliance which does not expose a naked flame on the outside of the appliance and which is permanently attached to the vehicle and designed for the purpose of heating any part of the interior of the vehicle for the comfort of the driver and any passengers.

(4) No person shall use, or cause or permit to be used, in any vehicle to which this paragraph applies, while the vehicle is in motion on a road, any gas-fired appliance to which—

(a) sub-paragraph (3)(a) refers, unless the appliance complies with the requirements specified in paragraphs 12 and 13 of Schedule 5 and the gas system to which it is attached complies with the requirements specified in paragraphs 2 to 9 and 15 of Schedule 5; or

(b) sub-paragraph (3)(b) refers, unless the appliance complies with the requirements specified in paragraphs 12, 13 and 14 of Schedule 5 and the gas system to which it is attached complies with the requirements specified in paragraphs 2 to 9, 11 and 15 of Schedule 5; or

(c) sub-paragraph (3)(c) refers, unless the appliance complies—

(i) if it is fitted to a motor vehicle, with the requirements specified in paragraphs 12, 13 and 14 of Schedule 5; and

(ii) in any other case, with the requirements specified in paragraphs 12 and 13 of Schedule 5;

and the gas system to which the appliance is attached complies with the requirements specified in paragraphs 2 to 9 and 15 of Schedule 5.

(5) No person shall use, or cause or permit to be used, in a vehicle to which this regulation applies which is in motion on a road any gas-fired appliance unless it is fitted with a valve which stops the supply of gas to the appliance if the appliance fails to perform its function and causes gas to be emitted.

E Control of Noise

Avoidance of excessive noise

97. No motor vehicle shall be used on a road in such manner as to cause any excessive noise which could have been avoided by the exercise of reasonable care on the part of the driver.   **B15.219**

Stopping of engine when stationary

98.—(1) Save as provided in paragraph (2), the driver of a vehicle shall, when the vehicle is stationary, stop the action of any machinery attached to or forming part of the vehicle so far as may be necessary for the prevention of noise [or of exhaust emissions].   **B15.220**

(2) The provisions of paragraph (1) do not apply—

(a) when the vehicle is stationary owing to the necessities of traffic;

(b) so as to prevent the examination or working of the machinery where the examination is necessitated by any failure or derangement of the machinery or where the machinery is required to be worked for a purpose other than driving the vehicle; or

(c) in respect of a vehicle propelled by gas produced in plant carried on the vehicle, to such plant.

B15.221   *[Regulation 98 is printed as amended by SI 1998/1.*

As to the issue of fixed penalty notices in England for contravention of reg.98, see the Road Traffic (Vehicle Emissions) (Fixed Penalty) (England) Regulations 2002 (SI 2002/1808); the Road Traffic (Vehicle Emissions) (Fixed Penalty) (Scotland) Regulations 2003 (SI 2003/212) and the Road Traffic (Vehicle Emissions) (Fixed Penalty) (Wales) Regulations 2003 (SI 2003/300) (W.42).]

Use of audible warning instruments

B15.222   **99.**—(1) Subject to the following paragraphs, no person shall sound, or cause or permit to be sounded, any horn, gong, bell or siren fitted to or carried on a vehicle which is—

(a) stationary on a road, at any time, other than at times of danger due to another moving vehicle on or near the road; or

(b) in motion on a restricted road, between 23.30 hours and 07.00 hours in the following morning.

(2) The provisions of paragraph (1)(a) do not apply in respect of the sounding of a reversing alarm when the vehicle to which it is fitted is about to move backwards and its engine is running [or in respect of the sounding of a boarding aid alarm.]

(3) No person shall sound, or cause or permit to be sounded, on a road any reversing alarm [or any boarding aid alarm] fitted to a vehicle—

(a) unless the vehicle is a goods vehicle which has a maximum gross weight not less than 2000kg, a bus, engineering plant, [a refuse vehicle,] or a works truck; or

(b) if the sound of the alarm is likely to be confused with a sound emitted in the operation of a pedestrian crossing established, or having effect as if established, under Part III of the 1984 Act.

(4) Subject to the provisions of the following paragraphs, no person shall sound, or cause or permit to be sounded a gong, bell, siren or two-tone horn, fitted to or otherwise carried on a vehicle (whether it is stationary or not).

(5) Nothing in paragraph (1) or (4) shall prevent the sounding of—

(a) an instrument or apparatus fitted to, or otherwise carried on, a vehicle at a time when the vehicle is being used for one of the purposes specified in regulation 37(5) and it is necessary or desirable to do so either to indicate to other road users the urgency of the purposes for which the vehicle is being used, or to warn other road users of the presence of the vehicle on the road; or

(b) a horn (not being a two-tone horn), bell, gong or siren—

(i) to raise alarm as to the theft or attempted theft of the vehicle or its contents, or

(ii) in the case of a bus, to summon help for the driver, the conductor or an inspector.

(6) Subject to the provisions of section 62 of the Control of Pollution Act 1974 and notwithstanding the provisions of paragraphs (1) and (4) above, a person may, between 12.00 hours and 19.00 hours, sound or cause or permit to be sounded an instrument or apparatus, other than a two-tone horn, fitted to or otherwise carried on a vehicle, being an instrument or apparatus designed to emit a sound for the purpose of informing members of the public that the vehicle is conveying goods for sale, if when the apparatus or instrument is sounded, it is sounded only for that purpose.

(7) For the purposes of this regulation the expressions which are referred to in regulation 37(10) have the meanings there given to them and the expression *"restricted road"* in paragraph (1) means a road which is a restricted road for the purpose of section 81 of the 1984 Act [*q.v.*].

[Regulation 99 is printed as amended by SI 1987/676; SI 2000/1971.   **B15.223**

The Control of Pollution Act 1974 s.62, regulates the use of loudspeakers in streets.]

F Avoidance of Danger

Maintenance and use of vehicle so as not to be a danger, etc.

100.—(1) A motor vehicle, every trailer drawn thereby and all parts and acces-   **B15.224**
sories of such vehicle and trailer shall at all times be in such condition, and the number of passengers carried by such vehicle or trailer, the manner in which any passengers are carried in or on such vehicle or trailer, and the weight, distribution, packing and adjustment of the load of such vehicle or trailer shall at all times be such, that no danger is caused or is likely to be caused to any person in or on the vehicle or trailer or on a road.

Provided that the provisions of this regulation with regard to the number of passengers carried shall not apply to a vehicle to which the Public Service Vehicles (Carrying Capacity) Regulations 1984 [*SI 1984/1406; not reproduced in this work*] apply.

(2) The load carried by a motor vehicle or trailer shall at all times be so secured, if necessary by physical restraint other than its own weight, and be in such a position, that neither danger nor nuisance is likely to be caused to any person or property by reason of the load or any part thereof falling or being blown from the vehicle or by reason of any other movement of the load or any part thereof in relation to the vehicle.

(3) No motor vehicle or trailer shall be used for any purpose for which it is so unsuitable as to cause or be likely to cause danger or nuisance to any person in or on the vehicle or trailer or on a road.

[Speed of low platform trailers and restricted speed vehicles

100A.—(1) No person shall use, or cause or permit to be used, on a road a ve-   **B15.225**
hicle displaying the rectangular plate described in the definition of "low platform trailer" in the Table in regulation 3(2) or anything resembling such a plate at a speed exceeding 40mph.

(2) No person shall use, or cause or permit to be used on a road a vehicle displaying the rectangular plate described in Schedule 13 (Plate for restricted speed vehicle) or anything resembling such a plate at a speed exceeding 50mph.]

B15.226   *[Regulation 100A was inserted by SI 1990/1981.]*

Parking in darkness

B15.227   **101.**—(1) Save as provided in paragraph (2) no person shall, except with the permission of a police officer in a uniform, cause or permit any motor vehicle to stand on a road at any time between ... sunset and ... sunrise unless the near side of the vehicle is as close as may be to the edge of the carriageway.

(2) The provisions of paragraph (1) do not apply in respect of any motor vehicle—

(a) being used for fire brigade [or, in England [or Wales], fire and rescue authority], ambulance or police purposes or for defence purposes (including civil defence purposes) if compliance with those provisions would hinder or be likely to hinder the use of the vehicle for the purpose for which it is being used on that occasion;

(b) being used in connection with—

(i) any building operation or demolition;

(ii) the repair of any other vehicle;

(iii) the removal of any obstruction to traffic;

(iv) the maintenance, repair or reconstruction of any road; or

(v) the laying, erection, alteration or repair in or near to any road of any sewer, main pipe or apparatus for the supply of gas, water or electricity, of any [electronic communications apparatus] as defined in Schedule 2 to the Telecommunication Act 1984 or of the apparatus of any electric transport undertaking;

if, in any such case, compliance with those provisions would hinder or be likely to hinder the use of the vehicle for the purpose for which it is being used on that occasion;

(c) on any road in which vehicles are allowed to proceed in one direction only;

(d) standing on a part of a road set aside for the parking of vehicles or as a stand for hackney carriages or as a stand for buses or as a place at which such vehicles may stop for a longer time than is necessary for the taking up and setting down of passengers where compliance with those provisions would conflict with the provisions of any order, regulations or byelaws governing the use of such part of a road for that purpose; or

(e) waiting to set down or pick up passengers in accordance with regulations made or directions given by a chief officer of police in regard to such setting down or picking up.

B15.228   *[Regulation 101 is printed as amended by SI 1991/2125; SI 2003/2155; SI 2004/3168; SI 2005/2929.]*

Passengers on motor cycles

B15.229   **102.** If any person in addition to the driver is carried astride a two-wheeled motor cycle on a road (whether a sidecar is attached to it or not) suitable supports or rests for the feet shall be available on the motor cycle for that person.

Obstruction

103. No person in charge of a motor vehicle or trailer shall cause or permit the   **B15.230**
vehicle to stand on a road so as to cause any unnecessary obstruction of the road.

[Offences under reg.103 have been designated as fixed penalty parking of-   **B15.231**
fences by the Schedule to the Fixed Penalty Order 2000 (SI 2000/2792) (not
reproduced in this work).]

Driver's control

104. No person shall drive or cause or permit any other person to drive, a mo-   **B15.232**
tor vehicle on a road if he is in such a position that he cannot have proper control
of the vehicle or have a full view of the road and traffic ahead.

Opening of doors

105. No person shall open, or cause or permit to be opened, any door of a vehi-   **B15.233**
cle on a road so as to injure or endanger any person.

Reversing

106. No person shall drive, or cause or permit to be driven, a motor vehicle   **B15.234**
backwards on a road further than may be requisite for the safety or reasonable
convenience of the occupants of the vehicle or other traffic, unless it is a road
roller or is engaged in the construction, maintenance or repair of the road.

Leaving motor vehicle unattended

107.—(1) Save as provided in paragraph (2), no person shall leave or cause or   **B15.235**
permit to be left, on a road a motor vehicle which is not attended by a person
licensed to drive it unless the engine is stopped and any parking brake with which
the vehicle is required to be equipped is effectively set.

(2) The requirement specified in paragraph (1) as to the stopping of the engine
shall not apply in respect of a vehicle—

    (a) being used for ambulance, fire brigade [or, in England [or Wales], fire
        and rescue authority] or police purposes; or

    (b) in such a position and condition as not to be likely to endanger any
        person or property and engaged in an operation which requires its
        engine to be used to—

        (i) drive machinery forming part of, or mounted on, the vehicle and
            used for purposes other than driving the vehicle; or

        (ii) maintain the electrical power of the batteries of the vehicle at a
            level required for driving that machinery or apparatus.

(3) In this regulation *"parking brake"* means a brake fitted to a vehicle in accordance with requirement 16 or 18 in Schedule 3.

[Regulation 107 is printed as amended by SI 2004/3168; SI 2005/2929.]   **B15.236**

Securing of suspended implements

108. Where a vehicle is fitted with any apparatus or appliance designed for lift-   **B15.237**
ing and part of the apparatus or appliance consists of a suspended implement, the

implement shall at all times while the vehicle is in motion on a road and when the
implement is not attached to any load supported by the appliance or apparatus be
so secured either to the appliance or apparatus or to some part of the vehicle that
no danger is caused or is likely to be caused to any person on the vehicle or on
the road.

Television sets

B15.238   109.—(1) No person shall drive, or cause or permit to be driven, a motor vehicle on a road, if the driver is in such a position as to be able to see, whether
directly or by reflection, a television receiving apparatus or other cinematographic
apparatus used to display anything other than information—

    (a) about the state of the vehicle or its equipment;

    (b) about the location of the vehicle and the road on which it is located;

    (c) to assist the driver to see the road adjacent to the vehicle; or

    (d) to assist the driver to reach his destination.

(2) In this regulation *"television receiving apparatus"* means any cathode ray
tube carried on a vehicle and on which there can be displayed an image derived
from a television broadcast, a recording or a camera or computer.

Mobile telephones

B15.239   [110.—(1) No person shall drive a motor vehicle on a road if he is using—

    (a) a hand-held mobile telephone; or

    (b) a hand-held device of a kind specified in paragraph (4).

(2) No person shall cause or permit any other person to drive a motor vehicle
on a road while that other person is using—

    (a) a hand-held mobile telephone; or

    (b) a hand-held device of a kind specified in paragraph (4).

(3) No person shall supervise a holder of a provisional licence if the person
supervising is using—

    (a) a hand-held mobile telephone; or

    (b) a hand-held device of a kind specified in paragraph (4),

at a time when the provisional licence holder is driving a motor vehicle on a road.

(4) A device referred to in paragraphs (1)(b), (2)(b) and (3)(b) is a device,
other than a two-way radio, which performs an interactive communication function by transmitting and receiving data.

(5) A person does not contravene a provision of this regulation if, at the time
of the alleged contravention—

    (a) he is using the telephone or other device to call the police, fire,
        ambulance or other emergency service on 112 or 999;

    (b) he is acting in response to a genuine emergency; and

    (c) it is unsafe or impracticable for him to cease driving in order to make
        the call (or, in the case of an alleged contravention of paragraph (3)(b),
        for the provisional licence holder to cease driving while the call was
        being made).

(6) For the purposes of this regulation—

(a) a mobile telephone or other device is to be treated as hand-held if it is, or must be, held at some point during the course of making or receiving a call or performing any other interactive communication function;

(b) a person supervises the holder of a provisional licence if he does so pursuant to a condition imposed on that licence holder prescribed under section 97(3)(a) of the Road Traffic Act 1988 (grant of provisional licence);

(c) *"interactive communication function"* includes the following:

    (i) sending or receiving oral or written messages;

    (ii) sending or receiving facsimile documents;

    (iii) sending or receiving still or moving images; and

    (iv) providing access to the internet;

(d) *"two-way radio"* means any wireless telegraphy apparatus which is designed or adapted—

    (i) for the purpose of transmitting and receiving spoken messages; and

    (ii) to operate on any frequency other than 880 MHz to 915 MHz, 925 MHz to 960 MHz, 1710 MHz to 1785 MHz, 1805 MHz to 1880 MHz, 1900 MHz to 1980 MHz or 2110 MHz to 2170 MHz; and

(e) *"wireless telegraphy"* has the same meaning as in section 19(1) of the Wireless Telegraphy Act 1949.]

[Regulation 110 was inserted by SI 2003/2695.]   **B15.240**

SCHEDULE 1

REGULATIONS REVOKED BY REGULATION 2

[Omitted.]   **B15.241**

B15.242

(see regulation 3)

SCHEDULE 2

Community Directives and ECE Regulations

Table I

Community Directives

1	2	3			4		
Item	Reference No	Community Directives			Item No. in Schedule 1 to —		
		(a) Date	(b) Official Journal Reference	(c) Subject matter	(d) Previous Directives included	(a) The Type Approval (Great Britain) Regulations	(b) The Type Approval for Goods Vehicles Regulations
1	70/157	6.2.70	L42, 23.2.70, p.16	The permissible sound level and the exhaust system of motor vehicles			
2	70/220	20.3.70	L76, 6.4.70, p.1	Measures to be taken against air pollution by gases from spark ignition engines of motor vehicles			
3	70/221	20.3.70	L76, 6.4.70, p.23	Liquid fuel tanks and rear protective devices for motor vehicles and their trailers			
4	70/388	27.7.70	L176, 10.8.70, p.12	Audible warning devices for motor vehicles			
5	71/127	1.3.71	L68, 22.3.71, p.1	The rear-view mirrors of motor vehicles		10	

1	2	3 Community Directives				4 Item No. in Schedule 1 to —	
Item	Reference No	(a) Date	(b) Official Journal Reference	(c) Subject matter	(d) Previous Directives included	(a) The Type Approval (Great Britain) Regulations	(b) The Type Approval for Goods Vehicles Regulations
6	71/320	[26.7.71]	L202, 6.9.71, p.37	The braking devices of certain categories of motor vehicles and their trailers			
7	72/245	20.6.72	L152, 6.7.72, p.15	The suppression of radio interference produced by spark ignition engines fitted to motor vehicles		2A	5A
8	72/306	2.8.72	L190, 20.8.72, p.1	The emission of pollutants from diesel engines for use in vehicles		5	3
9	73/350	7.11.73	L321, 22.11.73, p.33	The permissible sound level and the exhaust system of motor vehicles	70/157		4A
10	74/132	11.2.74	L74, 19.3.74, p.7	The braking devices of certain categories of motor vehicles and their trailers	71/320		
11	74/151	4.3.74	L84, 28.3.74, p.25	Parts and characteristics of agricultural motor vehicles (see Note 1)			

1	2	3				4	
		Community Directives				Item No. in Schedule 1 to—	
Item	Reference No	(a) Date	(b) Official Journal Reference	(c) Subject matter	(d) Previous Directives included	(a) The Type Approval (Great Britain) Regulations	(b) The Type Approval for Goods Vehicles Regulations
12	74/290	28.5.74	L159, 15.6.74, p.61	Measures to be taken against air pollution by gases from spark ignition engines for motor vehicles	70/220		
13	74/346	25.6.74	L191, 15.7.74, p.1	Rear-view mirrors for agricultural motor vehicles (see Note 1);			
14	74/347	25.6.74	L191, 15.7.74, p.1	Field of vision and windscreen wipers for agricultural motor vehicles (see Note 1)			
15	74/483	17.9.74	L266, 2.10.74, p.4	External projections of motor vehicles		19	
16	75/322	20.5.75	L147, 9.6.75, p.28	Suppression of radio interference from spark ignition engines of agricultural motor vehicles (see Note 1)			
17	75/443	26.6.75	L196, 26.7.75, p.1	Reverse and speedometer equipment of motor vehicles		20	

1	2	3				4	
		Community Directives				Item No. in Schedule 1 to —	
Item	Reference No	(a) Date	(b) Official Journal Reference	(c) Subject matter	(d) Previous Directives included	(a) The Type Approval (Great Britain) Regulations	(b) The Type Approval for Goods Vehicles Regulations
18	75/524	25.7.75	L236, 8.9.75, p.3	The braking devices of certain categories of motor vehicles and their trailers	71/320 as amended by 74/132	13A	
19	76/114	18.12.75	L24, 30.1.76, p.1	Statutory plates and inscriptions for motor vehicles and trailers			
20	76/115	18.12.75	L24, 30.1.76, p.6	Anchorages for motor vehicle seat belts		12A	
21	76/432	6.4.76	L122, 8.5.76, p.1	Braking devices of agricultural vehicles (see Note 1)			
22	77/102	30.11.76	L32, 3.2.77, p.32	Measures to be taken against air pollution by gases from spark ignition engines of motor vehicles	70/220 as amended by 74/290		
23	77/212	8.3.77	L66, 12.3.77, p.33	The permissible sound level and the exhaust system of motor vehicles	70/157 as amended by 73/350	14B	4B, 4C, 4D
24	77/537	28.6.77	L220, 29.8.77, p.38	Emission of pollution from diesel engines for agricultural motor vehicles (see Note 1)			

1	2	3			4	
		Community Directives			Item No. in Schedule 1 to —	
Item	Reference No	(a) Date	(b) Official Journal Reference	(c) Subject matter	(d) Previous Directives included	(a) The Type Approval (Great Britain) Regulations	(b) The Type Approval for Goods Vehicles Regulations
25	77/541	28.6.77	L220, 29.8.77, p.95	Seat belts and restraint systems for motor vehicles		12A	
26	77/649	27.9.77	L267, 19.10.77, p.1	Field of vision of motor vehicle drivers			
27	78/318	21.12.77	L81, 28.3.78, p.49	Wiper and washer systems of motor vehicles		22	
28	78/507	19.5.78	L155, 13.6.78, p.31	Statutory plates and inscriptions for motor vehicles and trailers	76/114		
29	78/549	12.6.78	L168, 26.6.78, p.45	Wheel guards of motor vehicles			
30	78/665	14.7.78	L223, 14.8.78, p.48	Measures to be taken against air pollution by gases from spark ignition engines of motor vehicles	70/220 amended by 74/290 and 77/102	4B, 4C	2
31	78/1015	23.11.78	L349, 13.12.78, p.21	The permissible sound level and exhaust system of motor cycles			
32	79/488	18.4.79	L128, 26.5.79, p.1	External projections of motor vehicles	74/483	19A	

1	2	3					4	
		Community Directives					Item No. in Schedule 1 to —	
Item	Reference No	(a) Date	(b) Official Journal Reference	(c) Subject matter	(d) Previous Directives included		(a) The Type Approval (Great Britain) Regulations	(b) The Type Approval for Goods Vehicles Regulations
33	79/489	18.4.79	L128, 26.5.79, p.12	The braking devices of certain categories of motor vehicles and their trailers	71/320 as amended by 74/132 and 75/524		13B	6, 6C
34	79/490	18.4.79	L128, 26.5.79, p.22	Liquid fuel tanks and rear under-run protection	70/221			
35	79/795	20.7.79	L239, 22.9.79, p.1	The rear-view mirrors of motor vehicles	71/127		10A	
36	79/1073	22.11.79	L331, 27.12.79, p.20	Field of vision and windscreen wipers for agricultural motor vehicles	74/347			
37	80/780	22.7.80	L229, 30.8.80, p.49	Rear-view mirrors for motor cycles				
38	80/1269	16.12.80	L375, 31.12.80, p.46	The engine power of motor vehicles				
39	81/334	13.4.81	L131, 18.5.81, p.6	The permissible sound level and exhaust system of motor vehicles	70/157 as amended by 73/350 and 77/212		14C	4B, 4C, 4D

| 1 | 2 | 3 | | | | 4 | |
| Item | Reference No | Community Directives | | | | Item No. in Schedule 1 to — | |
		(a) Date	(b) Official Journal Reference	(c) Subject matter	(d) Previous Directives included	(a) The Type Approval (Great Britain) Regulations	(b) The Type Approval for Goods Vehicles Regulations
40	81/575	29.7.81	L209, 29.7.81, p.30	Anchorages for motor vehicle seat belts	76/115	12A	
41	81/576	29.7.81	L209, 29.7.81, p.32	Seat belts and restraint systems for motor vehicles	77/541	12A	
42	81/643	29.7.81	L231, 15.8.81, p.41	Field of vision of motor vehicle drivers	77/649	12A	
43	82/318	2.4.82	L139, 19.5.82, p.9	Anchorages for motor vehicle seat belts	76/115 as amended by 81/575	12A	
44	82/319	2.4.82	L139, 19.5.82, p.17	Seat belts and restraint systems for motor vehicles	77/541 as amended by 81/576	12A	
45	82/890	17.12.82	L378, 31.12.82, p.45	Agricultural motor vehicles			
46	83/351	16.6.83	L197, 20.7.82, p.1	Air pollution by gases from positive ignition engines of motor vehicles	70/220 as amended by 74/290, 77/102 and 78/665	4C	

| 1 | 2 | 3 | | | | | 4 | |
| Item | Reference No | Community Directives | | | | | Item No. in Schedule 1 to — | |
		(a) Date	(b) Official Journal Reference	(c) Subject matter	(d) Previous Directives included		(a) The Type Approval (Great Britain) Regulations	(b) The Type Approval for Goods Vehicles Regulations
47	84/372	3.7.84	L196, 26.7.84, p.47	The permissible sound level and exhaust system of motor vehicles	70/157 as amended by 73/350, 77/212 and 81/334			
48	84/424	3.9.84	L238, 6.9.84, p.31	The permissible sound level and exhaust system of motor vehicles	70/157 as amended by 73/350, 77/212, 81/334 and 84/372			
[48A	85/3	19.12.84	L2, 3.1.85, p.14	The weights, dimensions and other technical characteristics of certain road vehicles				
49	85/205	18.2.85	L90, 29.3.85, p.1	Mirrors	71/127 as amended by 79/795		10B	
[49A	85/210	20.3.85	L96, 3.4.85, p.25	The lead content of petrol]				]

1	2	3				4	
Item	Reference No	Community Directives				Item No. in Schedule 1 to —	
		(a) Date	(b) Official Journal Reference	(c) Subject matter	(d) Previous Directives included	(a) The Type Approval (Great Britain) Regulations	(b) The Type Approval for Goods Vehicles Regulations
[50	85/647	23.12.85	L380, 31.12.85, p.1	The braking devices of certain motor vehicles and their trailers	71/320 as amended by 74/132, 75/524 and 79/489]		
[50A	86/360	24.7.86	L217, 5.8.86, p.19	The weights, dimensions and other technical characteristics of certain road vehicles	85/3		]
[51	86/562	6.11.86	L327, 27.11.86, p.49	Mirrors	71/127 as amended by 79/795 and 85/205]		
[51A	87/56	18.12.86	L24, 27.1.87, p.42	The permissible sound level and exhaust system of motor cycles	78/1015		
[52	88/76	3.12.87	L36, 9.2.88, p.1	Measures to be taken against air pollution by gases from the engines of motor vehicles	70/220 as amended by 74/290 77/102, 78/665, and 83/351	4D	] 2B]

| 1 | 2 | 3 | | | | 4 | |
| Item | Reference No | Community Directives | | | | Item No. in Schedule 1 to — | |
		(a) Date	(b) Official Journal Reference	(c) Subject matter	(d) Previous Directives included	(a) The Type Approval (Great Britain) Regulations	(b) The Type Approval for Goods Vehicles Regulations
[53	89/297	13.4.89	L124, 5.5.89, p.1	Lateral protection (side guards) of certain motor vehicles and their trailers			]
[54	88/77	3.12.87	L36, 9.2.88, p.33	Measures to be taken against the emission of gaseous pollutants from diesel engines for use in vehicles		4E	2D]
[54A	88/194	24.3.88	L92, 9.4.88, p.47	The braking devices of certain categories of motor vehicles and their trailers	71/320 as amended by 74/132, 75/524, 79/489 and 85/647		]
[55	88/195	24.3.88	L92, 9.4.88, p.50	Engine power of motor vehicles	80/1269		]
[55A	88/218	11.4.88	L98, 15.4.88, p.48	The weights, dimensions and other technical characteristics of certain road vehicles	85/3 as amended by 86/360		]

| 1 | 2 | 3 Community Directives | | | | 4 Item No. in Schedule 1 to — | |
Item	Reference No	(a) Date	(b) Official Journal Reference	(c) Subject matter	(d) Previous Directives included	(a) The Type Approval (Great Britain) Regulations	(b) The Type Approval for Goods Vehicles Regulations
[55B	88/321	16.5.88	L147, 14.6.88, p.77	Mirrors	71/127 as amended by 79/795, 85/205 and 86/562	10C	]
[55C	88/366	17.5.88	L181, 12.7.88, p.40	Field of vision of motor vehicle drivers	77/649 as amended by 81/643		]
[56	88/436	16.6.88	L124, 6.8.88, p.1	Measures to be taken against air pollution by gases from engines of motor vehicles (restriction of particulate pollution emissions from diesel engines)	70/220 as amended by 74/290, 77/102, 78/665, 83/351 and 88/76	4D	2C]
[56A	89/235	13.3.89	L98, 11.4.89. p.1	The permissible sound level and exhaust systems of motor cycles	78/1015 amended by 87/56	—	—]

| 1 | 2 | 3 | | | | 4 | |
| Item | Reference No | Community Directives | | | | Item No. in Schedule 1 to — | |
		(a) Date	(b) Official Journal Reference	(c) Subject matter	(d) Previous Directives included	(a) The Type Approval (Great Britain) Regulations	(b) The Type Approval for Goods Vehicles Regulations
[[56 AA]	89/338	27.4.89	L142, 25.5.89, p.3	The weights, dimensions and other technical characteristics of certain road vehicles	85/3 as amended by 86/360 and 88/218		]
[57	89/458	18.7.89	L226, 3.8.89, p.1	Measures to be taken against air pollution by emissions from motor vehicles	70/220 as amended by 74/290, 77/102, 78/665, 83/351, 88/76 and 88/436		]
[57A	89/460	18.7.89	L226, 3.8.89, p.5	The weights, dimensions and other technical characteristics of certain road vehicles	85/3 as amended by 86/360, 88/218 and 89/338		]

1	2	3				4	
Item	Reference No	Community Directives				Item No. in Schedule 1 to —	
		(a) Date	(b) Official Journal Reference	(c) Subject matter	(d) Previous Directives included	(a) The Type Approval (Great Britain) Regulations	(b) The Type Approval for Goods Vehicles Regulations
[57B	89/461	18.7.89	L226, 3.8.89, p.7	The weights, dimensions and other technical characteristics of certain road vehicles	85/3 as amended by 86/360, 88/218, 89/338 and 89/460		]
[57C	89/491	17.7.89	L238, 15.08.89, p.43	Motor vehicles	72/306		]
[58	90/628	30.10.90	L341, 6.12.90, p.1	Safety belts and restraint systems of motor vehicles	77/541 as amended by 81/576 and 82/319	12A	]
[59	[90/629]	30.10.90	L341, 6.12.90, p.14	Anchorages for motor vehicle safety belts	76/115 as amended by 81/575 and 82/318	12A	]
[60	90/630	30.10.90	L341, 6.12.90, p.20	Field of vision of motor vehicle drivers	77/649 as amended by 81/643 and 88/366		]

1	2	3 Community Directives				4 Item No. in Schedule 1 to —	
Item	Reference No	(a) Date	(b) Official Journal Reference	(c) Subject matter	(d) Previous Directives included	(a) The Type Approval (Great Britain) Regulations	(b) The Type Approval for Goods Vehicles Regulations
[60A	91/60	4.2.91	L37, 9.2.91, p.37	The weights, dimensions and other technical characteristics of certain vehicles	85/3 as amended by 86/360, 88/218, 89/338, 89/460 and 89/641		
[61	91/226	27.3.91	L103, 23.4.91, p.5	Spray-suppression systems of certain categories of motor vehicles and their trailers			]
[61A	91/422	15.7.91	L233, 22.8.91, p.21	The braking devices of certain categories of motor vehicles and their trailers	71/320 as amended by 74/132, 75/524, 79/489, 85/647 and 88/194		]

| 1 | 2 | 3 Community Directives | | | | 4 Item No. in Schedule 1 to — | |
Item	Reference No	(a) Date	(b) Official Journal Reference	(c) Subject matter	(d) Previous Directives included	(a) The Type Approval (Great Britain) Regulations	(b) The Type Approval for Goods Vehicles Regulations
[62	92/7	10.2.91	L57, 2.3.92, p.29	The weights, dimensions and other technical characteristics of certain road vehicles	85/3 as amended by 86/360, 88/218, 89/338, 89/460 and 89/641		
[63	91/441	26.6.91	L242, 30.8.91, p.1	Measures to be taken against air pollution by emissions from motor vehicles	70/220 as amended by 74/290 77/102, 78/665, 83/351, 88/76, 88/436 and 89/458	4G	] 2F]
[64	91/542	1.10.91	L295, 25.10.91, p.1	Measures to be taken against the emission of gaseous pollutants from diesel engines for use in vehicles	88/77	4H	2G]

| 1 | 2 | 3 Community Directives | | | | 4 Item No. in Schedule 1 to — | |
Item	Reference No	(a) Date	(b) Official Journal Reference	(c) Subject matter	(d) Previous Directives included	(a) The Type Approval (Great Britain) Regulations	(b) The Type Approval for Goods Vehicles Regulations
[64A	92/6	10.2.92	L57, 2.4.92, p.27	The installation and use of speed limitation devices			]
[65	92/22	31.3.92	L129, 14.5.92, p.11	Safety glazing and glazing materials on motor vehicles and their trailers			]
[66	92/23	31.3.92	L129, 14.5.92, p.95	Tyres of motor vehicles and their trailers and their fittings			]
[67	92/24	31.3.92	L 129, 14.5.92, p.154	Speed limitation devices or similar speed limitation on-board certain categories of motor vehicles			]
[67A	93/14	5.4.93	L121, 15.5.93, p.1	The braking of two or three-wheel motor vehicles	—	—	]

1	2	3				4	
		Community Directives				*Item No. in Schedule 1 to —*	
Item	Reference No	(a) Date	(b) Official Journal Reference	(c) Subject matter	(d) Previous Directives included	(a) The Type Approval (Great Britain) Regulations	(b) The Type Approval for Goods Vehicles Regulations
[68	93/59	28.6.93	—	Measures to be taken against air pollution by emissions from motor vehicles	70/220 as amended by 74/290, 77/102, 78/665, 83/351, 88/76, 88/436, 89/458 and 91/441	4K	2I]
[69	94/12	23.3.94	L100, 19.4.94, p.42	Measures to be taken against air pollution by emissions from motor vehicles	70/220 as amended by 74/290, 77/102, 78/665,	4L	2J]
[69A	94/20	30.5.94	L195, 29.7.94, p.1	Mechanical coupling devices of motor vehicles and their trailers	83/351, 88/76, 88/436, 89/458, 91/441 and 93/59		]

1	2	3					4	
Item	Reference No	Community Directives					Item No. in Schedule 1 to —	
		(a) Date	(b) Official Journal Reference	(c) Subject matter	(d) Previous Directives included		(a) The Type Approval (Great Britain) Regulations	(b) The Type Approval for Goods Vehicles Regulations
[70	92/97	10.11.92	L371, 19.12.92, p.1	Permissible sound level and the exhaust system of motor vehicles	70/157 as amended by 73/350, 77/212, 81/334, 84/372 and 84/424		14G	4F
[71	95/54	31.10.95	L266, 8.11.95, p.1	The suppression of radio interference of motor vehicles	72/245		2B	5B]
[72	96/1	22.1.96	L40, 17.2.96, p.1	Measures to be taken against the emission of gaseous pollutants from diesel engines for use in vehicles	88/77 as amended by 91/542		4N	2L]
[73	96/20	27.3.96	L92, 13.4.96, p.23	Permissible sound level and the exhaust system of motor vehicles	70/157 as amended by 73/350, 77/212, 81/334, 84/372 84/424 and 92/97		14I	4G]

| 1 | 2 | 3 | | | | 4 | |
| Item | Reference No | Community Directives | | | | Item No. in Schedule 1 to — | |
		(a) Date	(b) Official Journal Reference	(c) Subject matter	(d) Previous Directives included	(a) The Type Approval (Great Britain) Regulations	(b) The Type Approval for Goods Vehicles Regulations
[73A	96/36	17.6.96	L178, 17.6.96, p.15	Safety belts and restraint systems of motor vehicles	77/541 as amended by 81/576, 82/319 and 90/628		]
[73B	96/38	17.6.96	L187, 26.7.96, p.95	Anchorage for motor vehicle safety belts	76/115 as amended by 81/575, 82/318 and 90/629		]
[74	96/53	25.7.96	L234, 17.9.96, p.59	Maximum dimensions in national and international traffic and maximum weights in international traffic			]
[74A	96/63	30.9.96	L253, 5.10.96, p.13	Braking devices of wheeled agricultural or forestry tractors	76/432		]

| 1 | 2 | 3 Community Directives | | | | 4 Item No. in Schedule 1 to — | |
Item	Reference No	(a) Date	(b) Official Journal Reference	(c) Subject matter	(d) Previous Directives included	(a) The Type Approval (Great Britain) Regulations	(b) The Type Approval for Goods Vehicles Regulations
[74B	96/69	08.10.96	L282, 1.11.96, p.64	Measures to be taken against air pollution by emissions from motor vehicles	70/220 as amended by 74/290, 77/102, 78/665, 83/351, 88/76, 88/436, 89/491, 91/441, 93/59, 94/12, and 96/44		]
[74C	96/69	20.12.96	L46, 17.2.97, p.1	Roadworthiness tests for motor vehicles and their trailers			]
[75	97/19	18.4.97	L125, 16.5.97, p.1	Liquid fuel tanks and rear under-run protection of motor vehicles and their trailers	70/221 as amended by 79/490 and 81/333		]
[75A	97/20	18.4.97	L125, 16.5.97, p.21	The measures to be taken against the emission of pollutants from diesel engines for use in vehicles	72/306 as amended by 89/491		]

1	2	3				4	
Item	Reference No	Community Directives				Item No. in Schedule 1 to —	
		(a) Date	(b) Official Journal Reference	(c) Subject matter	(d) Previous Directives included	(a) The Type Approval (Great Britain) Regulations	(b) The Type Approval for Goods Vehicles Regulations
[76	97/27	22.7.97	L233, 25.8.97, p.1	Masses and dimensions of certain categories of vehicle and their trailers			]
[77	97/39	27.4.97	L177, 5.7.97, p.15	Reverse and speedometer equipment of motor vehicles	75/443		]
[77A	98/12	27.1.98	L81, 18.3.98, p.1	The braking devices of certain vehicles and their trailers	71/320 as amended by 74/132, 75/524, 79/489, 85/647, 88/184, 91/422 and 98/12		]

1	2	3 Community Directives				4 Item No. in Schedule 1 to —	
Item	Reference No	(a) Date	(b) Official Journal Reference	(c) Subject matter	(d) Previous Directives included	(a) The Type Approval (Great Britain) Regulations	(b) The Type Approval for Goods Vehicles Regulations
[78	98/69	13.10.98	L350, 28.12.98, p.1	Measures to be taken against air pollution by emissions from motor vehicles	70/220 as amended by 74/290, 77/102, 78/665, 83/351, 88/76, 88/436, 89/491, 91/441, 93/59, 94/12, 96/44 and 96/69		]
[79	1999/96	13.12.99	L44, 16.2.2000, p.1	Measures to be taken against the emission of gaseous and particulate pollutants from compression ignition engines for use in vehicles and the emission of gaseous pollutants from positive ignition engines fuelled with natural gas or liquefied petroleum gas for use in vehicles	88/77 as amended by 91/542 and 96/1		]

1	2	3 Community Directives				4 Item No. in Schedule 1 to —	
Item	Reference No	(a) Date	(b) Official Journal Reference	(c) Subject matter	(d) Previous Directives included	(a) The Type Approval (Great Britain) Regulations	(b) The Type Approval for Goods Vehicles Regulations
[80	1999/102	15.12.99	L334, 28.12.99, p.43	Measures to be taken against air pollution by emissions from motor vehicles	70/220 as amended by 74/290, 77/102, 78/665, 83/351, 88/76, 88/436, 89/491, 91/441, 93/59, 94/12, 96/44, 96/69 and 98/69		]

| 1 | 2 | 3 | | | | 4 | |
| Item | Reference No | Community Directives | | | | Item No. in Schedule 1 to — | |
		(a) Date	(b) Official Journal Reference	(c) Subject matter	(d) Previous Directives included	(a) The Type Approval (Great Britain) Regulations	(b) The Type Approval for Goods Vehicles Regulations
[81	2001/1	22.01.2001	L35, 06.2.2001, p.34	Measures to be taken against air pollution by emissions from motor vehicles	70/220 as amended by 74/290, 77/102, 78/665, 83/351, 88/76, 88/436, 89/491, 91/441, 93/59, 94/12, 96/44, 96/69, 98/69, and 1999/02		]

| 1 | 2 | 3 | | | | 4 | |
| Item | Reference No | Community Directives | | | | Item No. in Schedule 1 to — | |
		(a) Date	(b) Official Journal Reference	(c) Subject matter	(d) Previous Directives included	(a) The Type Approval (Great Britain) Regulations	(b) The Type Approval for Goods Vehicles Regulations
[82	2001/27	10.4.01	L107, 18.4.2001, p.10	Measures to be taken against the emission of gaseous and particulate pollutants from compression-ignition engines for use in vehicles, and the emission of gaseous pollutants from positive-ignition engines fuelled with natural gas or liquefied petroleum gas for use in vehicles	88/77 as amended by 91/542 and 1999/96		]
[82A	2001/43	4.8.2001	L211, 4.8.2001, p.25	Tyres for motor vehicles and their trailers and to their fitting	92/23		]
[83	2000/30	6.6.2000	L203, 10.8.2000, p.1	Technical roadside inspection of the roadworthiness of commercial vehicles circulating in the Community			]
[84	2002/85	5.11.2002	L57, 4.12.2002, p.327	Installation and use of speed limitation devices for certain categories of motor vehicles in the Community	92/6		]

1	2	3				4	
		Community Directives				Item No. in Schedule 1 to —	
Item	Reference No	(a) Date	(b) Official Journal Reference	(c) Subject matter	(d) Previous Directives included	(a) The Type Approval (Great Britain) Regulations	(b) The Type Approval for Goods Vehicles Regulations
[85	2003/26	3.4.2003	L90, 8.4.2003, p.37	Speed limiters and exhaust emissions of commercial vehicles	2000/30		]
[86	2003/27	3.4.2003	L90, 8.4.2003, p.41	Testing of exhaust emissions from motor vehicles	96/96		]
[87	2003/97	10.11.2003	L25, 29.1.2004, p.1	Devices for indirect vision	71/127 as amended by 79/795, 85/205, 86/562 and 88/321		]
[88	2004/11	11.2.2004	L44, 14.2.2004, p.19	Speed limitation devices or similar speed limitation on-board systems of certain categories of motor vehicles	92/24	9A	]

1	2	3				4	
		Community Directives				Item No. in Schedule 1 to —	
Item	Reference No	(a) Date	(b) Official Journal Reference	(c) Subject matter	(d) Previous Directives included	(a) The Type Approval (Great Britain) Regulations	(b) The Type Approval for Goods Vehicles Regulations
[88A	2005/21	7.3.2005	L61, 08.3.2005, p.25	The measures to be taken against the emission of pollutants from diesel engines for use in vehicles	72/306, as amended by 89/491, 97/20		]
[89	2005/27	30.3.2005	L81, 30.3.2005, p.44	Devices for indirect vision	71/127 as replaced by 2003/97		]
[90	2005/55	28.9.05	L275, 20.10.2005, p.1	The measures to be taken against the emission of gaseous and particulate pollutants from compression-ignition engines for use in vehicles, and the emission of gaseous pollutants from positive-ignition engines fuelled with natural gas or liquefied petroleum gas for use in vehicles			]

1	2	3				4	
		Community Directives				*Item No. in Schedule 1 to —*	
Item	Reference No	(a) Date	(b) Official Journal Reference	(c) Subject matter	(d) Previous Directives included	(a) The Type Approval (Great Britain) Regulations	(b) The Type Approval for Goods Vehicles Regulations
[91	2005/78	14.11.05	L31, 29.11.2005, p.1	The measures to be taken against the emission of gaseous and particulate pollutants from compression-ignition engines for use in vehicles, and the emission of gaseous pollutants from positive-ignition engines fuelled with natural gas or liquefied petroleum gas for use in vehicles	2005/55		]
[91A	2006/40	17.5.2006	L161, 14.6.2006, p.2	Emissions from air conditioning systems in motor vehicles.			]
[92	2006/51	6.6.06	L152, 7.6.2006, p.11	The measures to be taken against the emission of gaseous and particulate pollutants from compression-ignition engines for use in vehicles, and the emission of gaseous pollutants from positive-ignition engines fuelled with natural gas or liquefied petroleum gas for use in vehicles	2005/55, 2005/78		]

1	2	3				4	
		Community Directives				Item No. in Schedule 1 to —	
Item	Reference No	(a) Date	(b) Official Journal Reference	(c) Subject matter	(d) Previous Directives included	(a) The Type Approval (Great Britain) Regulations	(b) The Type Approval for Goods Vehicles Regulations
[93	2005/21	7.3.05	L61, 08.03.2005, p.251	The 72/306, as amended by 89/491, 97/20] measures to be taken against the emission of pollutants from diesel engines for use in vehicles	72/306, as amended by 89/491, 97/20		]
[94	2007/46	5.9.2007	L263, 09.10.2007, p.1	Framework Directive for the approval of motor vehicles and their trailers, and of systems, components and separate technical units intended for such vehicles.			]

NOTE 1. This item is to be interpreted as including reference to the amendments made by Community Directive 82/890 (item 45).

[Table I in Sch.2 is printed as amended by SI 1987/676; SI 1988/1178 and   **B15.243**
1524; SI 1989/1695 and 1865; SI 1990/1131, 1981; SI 1991/2003; SI 1992/646,
2016, 2137 and 3088; SI 1993/1946 and 2199; SI 1994/14; SI 1995/551 and
2210; SI 1996/2064, 2329 and 3033; SI 1998/1188, 1281 and 2429; SI 2000/
3197; SI 2001/1825 and 3298; SI 2002/1474; SI 2005/3165; SI 2006/2565; SI
2007/3132; SI 2009/142; SI 2009/2196; SI 2010/312.]

B15.244

Table II
ECE Regulations

| 1 | 2 | 3 | | | | 4 | |
| Item | Reference No. | ECE Regulations | | | | Item No. in Schedule 1 to — | |
		(a) Number	(b) Date	(c) Subject matter	(d) Date of amendment	(a) The Type Approval (Great Britain) Regulations	(b) The Type Approval for Goods Vehicles Regulations
1	10	10	17.12.68	Radio interference suppression	—	2A	5A
2	10.01	10	17.12.68	Radio interference suppression	19.3.78	2A	5A
[2A	10.02	—	8.12.97	Radio interference suppression	—	—	—
[2B	10.02	Amend. 1	9.7.99	Radio interference suppression	—	—	—
[2C	10.02	Corr. 1	11.2.00	Radio interference suppression	—	—	—
3	13.03	13	29.5.69	Brakes	4.1.79	13C, 13D	6A, 6B, 6D
4	13.04	13	29.5.69	Brakes	11.8.81	13C, 13D	6A, 6B, 6D
[4A]	13.05	13	29.5.69	Brakes	26.11.84	—	—
[4B	13.06	13	29.5.69	Brakes	22.11.90	—	—
[4C	13.07	13	29.5.69	Brakes	18.9.94	—	—
[4D	13.08	13	29.5.69	Brakes	26.3.95	—	—
[4E	13.09	13	29.5.69	Brakes	28.8.96	—	—

1	2	3					4	
		ECE Regulations					Item No. in Schedule 1 to —	
Item	Reference No.	(a) Number	(b) Date	(c) Subject matter	(d) Date of amendment		(a) The Type Approval (Great Britain) Regulations	(b) The Type Approval for Goods Vehicles Regulations
[5A	14	14	30.1.70	Anchorages for seat belts	—		—	—
6	14.01	14	30.1.70	Anchorages for seat belts	28.4.76		12A	—
[6A	14.02	14	30.1.70	Anchorages for seat belts	22.11.84		12A	—
[6B	14.03	14	30.1.70	Anchorages for seat belts	29.1.92		—	—
[6C	14.04	14	30.1.70	Anchorages for seat belts	18.1.98		—	—
[6D	14.05	14	30.1.70	Anchorages for seat belts	4.2.99		—	—
[6C	14.03	—	30.1.70	Anchorages for seat belts	29.1.92		12A	—
7	15.03	15	11.3.70	Emission of gaseous pollutants	6.3.78		4B	2A
8	15.04	15	11.3.70	Emission of gaseous pollutants	20.10.81		4C	2A
9	16.03	16	14.8.70	Seat belts and restraint systems	9.12.79		12A	—
10	24.01	24	23.8.71	Emission of pollutants by a diesel engine	11.9.73		5A	3A
11	24.02	24	23.8.71	Emission of pollutants by a diesel engine	11.2.80		5A	3A
12	24.03	24	23.8.71	Emission of pollutants by a diesel engine	20.4.86		—	—

| 1 | 2 | 3 | | | | 4 | |
| Item | Reference No. | ECE Regulations | | | | Item No. in Schedule 1 to — | |
		(a) Number	(b) Date	(c) Subject matter	(d) Date of amendment	(a) The Type Approval (Great Britain) Regulations	(b) The Type Approval for Goods Vehicles Regulations
13	26.01	26	28.4.72	External projections	11.9.73	19A	—
[13A	30	30	1.4.75	Pneumatic tyres for motor vehicles and their trailers	—	17, 17A	⌉
[13B	30	30.01	1.4.75	Pneumatic tyres for motor vehicles and their trailers	25.9.77	17, 17A	⌉
[[13C]	30.02	30	1.4.75	Pneumatic tyres for motor vehicles and their trailers	5.10.87	17, 17A	⌉
14	34	34	25.7.75	Prevention of fire risks	—	—	—
15	34.01	34	25.7.75	Prevention of fire risks	18.1.79	—	—
16	36	36	21.11.75	Construction of public service vehicles	—	—	—
17	39	39	11.7.78	Speedometers	—	20B	—
18	43	43	15.9.80	Safety glass and glazing materials	—	15B	—
19	43.01	43	15.9.80	Safety glass and glazing materials	12.11.82	15B	—
20	44	44	1.2.81	Child restraints	—	—	—
21	44.01	44	1.2.81	Child restraints	1.2.84	—	—
[21A	46.01	46	21.10.84	Mirrors	30.5.88	—	⌉

1	2	3				4	
		ECE Regulations				Item No. in Schedule 1 to —	
Item	Reference No.	(a) Number	(b) Date	(c) Subject matter	(d) Date of amendment	(a) The Type Approval (Great Britain) Regulations	(b) The Type Approval for Goods Vehicles Regulations
[21A(1)]	46.02	46	21.10.84	Mirrors	23.06.05	—	—
[21AA]	49.01	49	14.5.90	Emissions of gaseous pollutants	30.12.92	—	—
[21AB]	49.02	49	15.4.82	Emissions of gaseous pollutants	—	—	—
[[21B]	49	49	15.4.82	Emissions of gaseous pollutants	—	—	—
[21BA]	51.02	51	18.4.95	Noise emissions from motor vehicles having at least 4 wheels	—	14E	4D(4) or 4E
[21BB]	52.01	52	1.11.82	Construction of small buses and coaches (M2 and M3)	12.9.95	—	—
[[21C]	54	54	1.3.83	Pneumatic tyres for commercial vehicles and their trailers	—	17A	—
22	64	64	1.8.85	Vehicles with temporary-use spare wheels/tyres	—	—	—
[22A]	67	67	27.04.90	Vehicles using liquefied petroleum gas	—	—	—
[22B]	67.01	67	13.11.99	Vehicles using liquefied petroleum gas	—	—	—
[23]	78	78	15.10.88	Brakes	—	—	—
[24]	78.01	78	15.10.88	Brakes	22.11.90	—	—

1	2	3				4	
		ECE Regulations				Item No. in Schedule 1 to —	
Item	Reference No.	(a) Number	(b) Date	(c) Subject matter	(d) Date of amendment	(a) The Type Approval (Great Britain) Regulations	(b) The Type Approval for Goods Vehicles Regulations
[25	83	83	5.11.89	Emissions of gaseous pollutants	—	4F	2H]
[26	83.01	83	5.11.89	Emissions of gaseous pollutants	30.12.92	4K	2F]
[27	107.01	107	18.6.98	Construction of small buses and coaches (M2 and M3)	12.8.04	—	—]
[28	107.02	107	18.6.98	Construction of small buses and coaches (M2 and M3)	10.11.07	—	—]
[29	117.01	117	6.4.2005	Tyres—Rolling sound emissions and adhesion to wet surfaces	2.2.2007	—	—]

[Table II in Sch.2 in printed as amended by SI 1989/1478; SI 1990/1131 and   **B15.245**
1981; SI 1991/2710; SI 1992/352, 2016, 2137 and 3088; SI 1993/2199; SI 1994/
3270; SI 1996/2329 and 3133; SI 2001/1043 and 3208; SI 2002/2126; SI 2003/
1690; SI 2005/3165; SI 2009/142; SI 2010/312.

Item 21AA in table II was positioned after what is now item 21B before that
item (formerly 21A) was re-numbered by SI 1992/3088.]

Regulation 3A   SCHEDULE 2A

VEHICLES FOR WHICH A MINISTER'S APPROVAL CERTIFICATE HAS BEEN ISSUED UNDER THE MOTOR
VEHICLES (APPROVAL) REGULATIONS 1996

PART I

INTERPRETATION

General interpretation
  1.—(1) In this Schedule —   **B15.246**
    "the Approval Regulations" means the Motor Vehicles (Approval) Regulations 1996;
    "approval certificate" means a Minister's approval certificate in the form prescribed
        by the Approval Regulations;
    "approval date", in relation to a vehicle in respect of which an approval certificate
        has been issued, is the date that the certificate was issued;
    "goods vehicle approval certificate" means an approval certificate which appears to
        have been issued on the basis that the vehicle to which Part III of the Approval
        Regulations applies;
    [*"individual approval certificate"* means a certificate issued under regulation 27(10)
        of the Vehicle Approval Regulations;]
    "passenger vehicle approval certificate" means an approval certificate which appears
        to have been issued on the basis that the vehicle is a vehicle to which Part II of
        the Approval Regulations applies.

[Schedule 2A (paras 1–9 and 10) was inserted by SI 1996/3017. Paragraph 1   **B15.247**
is printed as subsequently amended by SI 2009/2196.

As to the "Approval Regulations", see the note to para.2 of this Schedule
below. The reference to the "Vehicle Approval Regulations" in the definition of
"individual approval certificate" is to the Road Vehicles (Approval) Regulations
2009 (SI 2009/717).]

Interpretation of references to a vehicle complying with the approval requirements
and to a vehicle exempt from the approval requirements
  2.—(1) Subject to paragraph 3, references in this Schedule to a vehicle complying with   **B15.248**
or being exempt from the approval requirements shall be construed in accordance with the
following provisions of this paragraph.

  (2) Subject to sub-paragraphs (4) and (5), a vehicle in respect of which a goods vehicle
approval certificate has been issued shall be regarded as complying with or exempt from
the approval requirements in relation to a specified subject matter if and only if it for the
time being satisfies at least one of the conditions in regulation 6(5) of the Approval Regulations in relation to that subject matter.

  (3) Subject to sub-paragraphs (4) and (5), a vehicle in respect of which a passenger vehicle approval certificate has been issued shall be regarded as complying with or exempt
from the approval requirements in relation to a specified subject matter if and only if it for
the time being satisfies at least one of the conditions in regulation 4(5) of the Approval
Regulations in relation to that subject matter.

(4) A vehicle in respect of which an approval certificate has been issued shall be regarded as neither complying with nor being exempt from the approval requirements in relation to any subject matter if—

    (a) the certificate is a goods vehicle approval certificate and the vehicle is not for the time being a vehicle to which Part III of the Approval Regulations applies; or

    (b) the certificate is a passenger vehicle approval certificate and the vehicle is not for the time being a vehicle to which Part II of the Approval Regulations applies.

(5) For the purposes of this paragraph, the Approval Regulations shall have effect with the omission of regulations 4(8) and 6(7).

B15.249   *[Schedule 2A (paras 1–9 and 10) was inserted by SI 1996/3017.*

The "Approval Regulations" (i.e. the Motor Vehicles (Approval) Regulations 1996, to which reference is made in para.2 of Sch.2A) have been revoked and replaced by the Motor Vehicles (Approval) Regulations 2001 (SI 2001/25) (not reproduced in this work). The Interpretation Act 1978 ss.17(2)(a) and 23, which enables references to the 1996 Regulations to be construed as references to the 2001 Regulations is only applicable in the absence of a contrary intention (see 1978 Act s.17(2)(a)); the fact that the scheme of the 2001 Regulations differs from that of the 1996 Regulations (e.g. there are no Parts in the 2001 Regulations corresponding to Pt II ("Passenger Vehicles") and Pt III ("Goods Vehicles") of the 1996 Regulations) suggests that a "contrary intention" should be inferred.]

PART II

MODIFICATION OF THE REGULATIONS

Part exemption from regulation 32 (glazing)

B15.250   3. Regulation 32(2), (7) and (10) shall not apply to a vehicle in respect of which a passenger vehicle approval certificate has been issued, if it complies with or is exempt from the approval requirements relating to glazing.

B15.251   *[Schedule 2A (paras 1–9 and 10) was inserted by SI 1996/3017.*

References in these paragraphs to approval certificates are to approval certificates issued under the "Approval Regulations". As to the "Approval Regulations", see the note to para.2 of this Schedule.]

Exemption from regulation 33 (mirrors)

B15.252   4. Regulation 33 shall not apply to a vehicle in respect of which a passenger vehicle approval certificate has been issued, if it complies with or is exempt from the approval requirements relating to rear view mirrors.

B15.253   *[Schedule 2A (paras 1–9 and 10) was inserted by SI 1996/3017.*

References in these paragraphs to approval certificates are to approval certificates issued under the "Approval Regulations". As to the "Approval Regulations", see the note to para.2 of this Schedule.]

Exemption from regulation 35 (speedometers)

B15.254   5. Regulation 35 shall not apply to a vehicle in respect of which a passenger approval certificate has been issued, if it complies with or is exempt from the approval requirements relating to speedometers.

B15.255   *[Schedule 2A (paras 1–9 and 10) was inserted by SI 1996/3017.*

References in these paragraphs to approval certificates are to approval certificates issued under the "Approval Regulations". As to the "Approval Regulations", see the note to para.2 of this Schedule.]

Exemption from regulation 39(2)(c)(i) (fuel tanks to be made of metal)

6. Regulation 39(2)(c)(i) shall not apply to a vehicle in respect of which either a pas-   **B15.256**
senger vehicle approval certificate or a goods vehicle approval certificate has been issued,
if it complies with the approval requirements relating to general vehicle construction.

[Schedule 2A (paras 1–9 and 10) was inserted by SI 1996/3017.   **B15.257**

*References in these paragraphs to approval certificates are to approval certif-
icates issued under the "Approval Regulations". As to the "Approval Regulations", see the note to para.2 of this Schedule.]*

Exemption from regulation 46 (seat belt anchorages)

7. Regulation 46 shall not apply to a vehicle in respect of which a passenger vehicle ap-   **B15.258**
proval certificate has been issued, if it complies with or is exempt from the approval
requirements relating to anchorage points.

[Schedule 2A (paras 1–9 and 10) was inserted by SI 1996/3017.   **B15.259**

*References in these paragraphs to approval certificates are to approval certif-
icates issued under the "Approval Regulations". As to the "Approval Regulations", see the note to para.2 of this Schedule.]*

Part exemption from regulation 47 (seat belts)

8. Regulation 47, so far as it relates to seat belts for adults, shall not apply to a vehicle in   **B15.260**
respect of which a passenger vehicle approval certificate has been issued, if it complies
with or is exempt from the approval requirements relating to seat belts (including the
requirements relating to the installation of seat belts).

[Schedule 2A (paras 1–9 and 10) was inserted by SI 1996/3017.   **B15.261**

*References in these paragraphs to approval certificates are to approval certif-
icates issued under the "Approval Regulations". As to the "Approval Regulations", see the note to para.2 of this Schedule.]*

Modifications to regulation 61 (emissions)

9.—(1) Regulation 61 shall have effect with the following modifications in relation to a   **B15.262**
vehicle in respect of which there has been issued an approval certificate containing the letter "A" pursuant to regulation 12(2)(c) of the Approval Regulations.

(2) For the purposes of paragraphs (3A), (7), (8) and (9), the date of first use of the vehicle shall be regarded as being 1st January immediately preceding the date of manufacture
of the engine by which it is propelled.

However, the date on which the vehicle is first used shall not, by virtue of this paragraph,
be regarded in any circumstances as being later than the date on which it would otherwise
have been regarded as being first used had this paragraph been omitted.

(3) Paragraphs 10(A) and 10(AA) shall not apply to the vehicle if it complies with or is
exempt from the approval requirements relating to exhaust emissions.

[Schedule 2A (paras 1–9 and 10) was inserted by SI 1996/3017.   **B15.263**

*References in these paragraphs to approval certificates are to approval certif-
icates issued under the "Approval Regulations". As to the "Approval Regulations", see the note to para.2 of this Schedule.]*

[**9A.** Paragraphs (10A), (10AA) and (10BA) of regulation 61 shall not apply to a vehicle   **B15.264**
in respect of which either a passenger vehicle approval certificate or a goods vehicle approval certificate has been issued, if it complies with, or is exempt from, the approval
requirements relating to exhaust or smoke emissions.]

[Paragraph 9A was inserted into Schedule 2A by SI 2000/3197.   **B15.265**

*References in para.9A to approval certificates are to approval certificates is-
sued under the "Approval Regulations". As to the "Approval Regulations", see
the note to para.2 of this Schedule.]*

[Modifications to regulation 61A (emissions)

B15.266   **9B.**—(1) Regulation 61A shall not apply to a vehicle in respect of which either a passenger vehicle approval certificate or a goods vehicle approval certificate has been issued, if it complies with or is exempt from the approval requirements relating to exhaust or smoke emissions.

(2) Regulation 61A shall have effect with the following modifications in relation to a vehicle in respect of which there has been issued an approval certificate containing the letter "A" pursuant to regulation 12(2)(c) of the Approval Regulations.

(3) For the purposes of paragraphs (2) and (3) of regulation 61A, the date as is specified (as defined in regulation 61A) shall be regarded as being the 1st January immediately preceeding the date of manufacture of the engine by which the vehicle is propelled; provided that the date as is specified shall not in any circumstances be regarded as being later than the date on which the motor vehicle would otherwise have been regarded as being first used.]

B15.267   *[Paragraph 9B was inserted into Sch.2A by SI 2000/3197.*

References in para.9B to approval certificates are to approval certificates issued under the "Approval Regulations". As to the "Approval Regulations", see the note to para.2 of this Schedule.

Vehicles in respect of which approval certificates have been issued under reg.12(2)(c) of the Approval Regulations which were in force when reg.9B was enacted (i.e. the Motor Vehicles (Approval) Regulations 1996 (SI 1996/3013)), are, by reference to ibid. Sch.1, para.3, vehicles constructed for the personal use of the constructor, etc. As to the revocation of SI 1996/3013, see the note to para.2 of this Schedule.]

[Modification to regulation 61B (retrofitting and refilling of certain air conditioning systems)

B15.268   **9C.** Paragraphs (5) and (6) of regulation 61B shall not apply to a vehicle in relation to which a passenger vehicle approval certificate, a goods vehicle approval certificate or an individual approval certificate has been issued if it complies with the approval requirements for air conditioning systems designed to contain high-GWP fluorinated greenhouse gases.]

B15.269   *[Paragraph 9C was inserted into Sch.2A by SI 2009/2196.]*

Modification to regulation 67 (vehicle identification numbers)

B15.270   **10.** Regulation 67 shall not apply to a vehicle in respect of which an approval certificate has been issued if—

(a) the vehicle is equipped with a plate which is in a conspicuous and readily accessible position, is affixed to a vehicle part which is not normally subject to replacement and shows clearly and indelibly the identification number shown on the certificate and the name of the manufacturer; and

(b) that number is marked on the chassis, frame or other similar structure, on the offside of the vehicle, in a clearly visible and accessible position, and by a method such as hammering or stamping, in such a way that it cannot be obliterated or deteriorate.

B15.271   *[Schedule 2A (paras 1–9 and 10) was inserted by SI 1996/3017.*

References in these paragraphs to approval certificates are to approval certificates issued under the "Approval Regulations". As to the "Approval Regulations", see the note to para.2 of this Schedule.]

(see regulation 16)   SCHEDULE 3

Bʀᴀᴋɪɴɢ Rᴇǫᴜɪʀᴇᴍᴇɴᴛs

1. The braking requirements referred to in regulation 16(4) are set out in the Table and **B15.272**
are to be interpreted in accordance with paragraphs 2 to 5 of this Schedule.

Tᴀʙʟᴇ

(Schedule 3)

Number	Requirement
1	The vehicle shall be equipped with— (a) one efficient braking system having two means of operation; (b) one efficient split braking system having one means of operation; or (c) two efficient braking systems each having a separate means of operation, and in the case of a vehicle first used on or after 1st January 1968, no account shall be taken of a multi-pull means of operation unless, at first application, it operates a hydraulic, electric or pneumatic device which causes the application of brakes with total braking efficiency not less than 25%.
2	The vehicle shall be equipped with— (a) one efficient braking system having two means of operation; or (b) two efficient braking systems each having a separate means of operation.
3	The vehicle shall be equipped with an efficient braking system.
4	The braking system shall be so designed that in the event of failure of any part (other than a fixed member or a brake shoe anchor pin) through or by means of which the force necessary to apply the brakes is transmitted, there shall still be available for application by the driver brakes sufficient under the most adverse conditions to bring the vehicle to rest within a reasonable distance. The brakes so available shall be applied to— (a) in the case of a track-laying vehicle, one track on each side of the vehicle; (b) in the case of a wheeled motor vehicle, one wheel if the vehicle has 3 wheels and otherwise to at least half the wheels; and (c) in the case of a wheeled trailer, at least one wheel if it has only 2 wheels and otherwise at least 2 wheels. This requirement applies to the braking systems of both a trailer and the vehicle by which it is being drawn except that if the drawing vehicle complies with regulation 15 [Community Directive [79/489, 85/647, 88/194, 91/422 or 98/12 or ECE Regulation 13.03, 13.04, 13.05, 13.06, 13.07, 13.08 or 13.09]], the requirement applies only to the braking system of the drawing vehicle. It does not apply to vehicles having split braking systems (which are subject to regulation 18(3)(b)) or to road rollers. (The expressions *"part"* and *"half the wheels"* are to be interpreted in accordance with paragraphs (3) and (4) respectively.)
5	The braking system shall be so designed and constructed that, in the event of the failure of any part thereof, there shall still be available for application by the driver a brake sufficient under the most adverse conditions to bring the vehicle to rest within a reasonable distance.

Number	Requirement
6	The braking system of a vehicle, when drawing a trailer which complies with regulation 15 [Community Directive [79/489, 85/647, 88/194, 91/422 or 98/12 or ECE Regulation 13.03, 13.04, 13.05, 13.06, 13.07, 13.08 or 13.09]] , shall be so constructed that, in the event of a failure of any part (other than a fixed member or brake shoe anchor pin) of the service braking system of the drawing vehicle (excluding the means of operation of a split braking system) the driver can still apply brakes to at least one wheel of the trailer, if it has only 2 wheels, and otherwise to at least 2 wheels, by using the secondary braking system of the drawing vehicle. (The expression *"part"* is to be interpreted in accordance with paragraph 3.)
7	The application of any means of operation of a braking system shall not affect or operate the pedal or hand lever of any other means of operation.
8	The braking system shall not be rendered ineffective by the non-rotation of the engine of the vehicle or, in the case of a trailer, the engine of the drawing vehicle (steam-propelled vehicles, other than locomotives and buses, are excluded from this requirement).
9	At least one means of operation shall be capable of causing brakes to be applied directly, and not through the transmission gear, to at least half the wheels of the vehicle. This requirement does not apply to a works truck with an unladen weight not exceeding 7370kg, or to an industrial tractor; and it does not apply to a vehicle with more than 4 wheels if— (a) the drive is transmitted to all wheels other than the steering wheels without the interposition of a differential driving gear or similar mechanism between the axles carrying the driving wheels; and (b) the brakes applied by one means of operation apply directly to 2 driving wheels on opposite sides of the vehicle; and (c) the brakes applied by another means of operation act directly on all the other driving wheels. (The expression *"half the wheels"* is to be interpreted in accordance with paragraph (4).)
10	The brakes of a trailer shall come into operation automatically on its overrun or, in the case of a track-laying trailer drawn by a vehicle having steerable wheels at the front or a wheeled trailer, the driver of, or some other person on, the drawing vehicle or on the trailer shall be able to apply the brakes on the trailer.
11	The brakes of a trailer shall come into operation automatically on its overrun or the driver of the drawing vehicle shall be able to apply brakes to all the wheels of the trailer, using the means of operation which applies the service brakes of the drawing vehicle.
12	The brakes of the vehicle shall apply to all wheels other than the steering wheels.
13	The brakes of the vehicle shall apply to at least 2 wheels.
14	The brakes of the vehicle shall apply in the case of a wheeled vehicle to at least 2 wheels if the vehicle has no more than 4 wheels and to at least half the wheels if the vehicle has more than 4 wheels; and in the case of a track-laying vehicle to all the tracks.
15	The brakes shall apply to all the wheels.

Number	Requirement
16	The parking brake shall be so designed and constructed that— (a) in the case of a wheeled heavy motor car or motor car, its means of operation is independent of the means of operation of any split braking system with which the vehicle is fitted; (b) in the case of a motor vehicle other than a motor cycle or an invalid carriage, either— (i) it is capable of being applied by direct mechanical action without the intervention of any hydraulic, electric or pneumatic device; or (ii) the vehicle complies with requirement 15; and (c) it can at all times when the vehicle is not being driven or is left unattended be set so as— (i) in the case of a track-laying vehicle, to lock the tracks; and (ii) in the case of a wheeled vehicle, to prevent the rotation of at least one wheel in the case of a three wheeled vehicle and at least two wheels in the case of a vehicle with more than three wheels.
17	The parking brake shall be capable of being set so as effectively to prevent two at least of the wheels from revolving when the trailer is not being drawn.
18	The parking brake shall be so designed and constructed that— (a) in the case of a motor vehicle, its means of operation (whether multi-pull or not) is independent of the means of operation of any braking system required by regulation 18 to have a total braking efficiency of not less than 50%; and (b) in the case of a trailer, its brakes can be applied and released by a person standing on the ground by a means of operation fitted to the trailer; and (c) in either case, its braking force, when the vehicle is not being driven or is left unattended (and in the case of a trailer, whether the braking force is applied by the driver using the service brakes of the drawing vehicle or by a person standing on the ground in the manner indicated in sub-paragraph (b)) can at all times be maintained in operation by direct mechanical action without the intervention of any hydraulic, electric or pneumatic device and, when so maintained, can hold the vehicle stationary on a gradient of at least 16% without the assistance of stored energy.

[Paragraph 1 of Sch.3 is printed as amended by SI 1987/676; SI 1990/1981; SI 1992/352; SI 1995/551; SI 2001/3208.] **B15.273**

2. For the purposes of requirement 3 in the Table, in the case of a motor car or heavy **B15.274** motor car propelled by steam and not used as a bus, the engine shall be deemed to be an efficient braking system with one means of operation if the engine is capable of being reversed and, in the case of a vehicle first used on or after 1st January 1927, is incapable of being disconnected from any of the driving wheels of the vehicle except by the sustained effort of the driver.

3. For the purpose of requirements 4 and 6 in the Table, in the case of a wheeled motor **B15.275** car and of a vehicle first used on or after 1st October 1938 which is a locomotive, a motor tractor, a heavy motor car or a track-laying motor car, every moving shaft which is connected to or supports any part of a braking system shall be deemed to be part of the system.

4. For the purpose of [requirements 4, 9 and 14] in the Table, in determining whether **B15.276** brakes apply to at least half the wheels of a vehicle, not more than one front wheel shall be treated as a wheel to which brakes apply unless the vehicle is—

(a) a locomotive or motor tractor with more than 4 wheels;

(b) a heavy motor car or motor car first used before 1st October 1938;

  (c) a motor car with an unladen weight not exceeding 1020kg;

  (d) a motor car which is a passenger vehicle but is not a bus;

  (e) a works truck;

  (f) a heavy motor car or motor car with more than 3 wheels which is equipped in re-
      spect of all its wheels with brakes which are operated by one means of operation;
      or

  (g) a track-laying vehicle.

[Paragraph 4 of Sch.3 is printed as amended by SI 1987/676.]

B15.277   **5.** In this Schedule a *"multi-pull means of operation"* means a device forming part of a braking system which causes the muscular energy of the driver to apply the brakes of that system progressively as a result of successive applications of that device by the driver.

(see regulations 39A and 39B)   [SCHEDULE 3A

EXCLUSION OF CERTAIN VEHICLES FROM THE APPLICATION OF REGULATION 39A

PART I

B15.278   **1.**—(1) In this Part —

  "EEC type approval certificate" means a certificate issued by a member state of the European Economic Community in accordance with Community Directive 70/220 as originally made or with any amendments which have from time to time been made before 5th September 1988;

  "engine capacity" means in the case of a reciprocating engine, the nominal swept volume and, in the case of a rotary engine, double the nominal swept volume;

                    *   *   *

  "relevant authority" means—

      (a) in relation to an EEC type approval certificate issued by the United Kingdom, the Secretary of State, and

      (b) in relation to an EEC type approval certificate issued by any other member state of the European Economic Community, the authority having power under the law of that state to issue that certificate.

  (2) The reference in this Schedule to a M1 category vehicle is reference to a vehicle described as M1 in Council Directive 70/156/EEC of 6th February 1970 as amended at 5th September 1988.

  [2] A vehicle of a description specified in column 2 of the Table below is excluded from the application of regulation 39A if it is first used before the date specified in column 3 and the conditions specified in paragraph 3 are satisfied in respect to it on that date.

  [3] The conditions referred to in paragraph 2 are—

      (a) that the vehicle is a model in relation to which there is in force an EEC type approval certificate issued before 1st October 1989;

      (b) that the manufacturer of the vehicle has supplied to the relevant authority which issued the EEC type approval certificate, a certificate stating that adapting vehicles of that model to the fuel requirements specified in the Annexes to Community Directive 88/76 would entail a change in material specification of the inlet or exhaust valve seats or a reduction in the compression ratio or an increase in the engine capacity to compensate for loss of power; and

      (c) that the relevant authority has accepted the certificate referred to in sub-paragraph (b).

TABLE

Item (1)	Description of vehicle (2)	Date before which vehicle must be first used (3)
1.	Vehicles with an engine capacity of less than 1400cc.	1.4.92
2.	Vehicles with an engine capacity of not less than 1400cc and not more than 2000cc.	1.4.94
3.	M1 category vehicles with an engine capacity of more than 2000cc and which— (a) are constructed or adapted to carry not more than 5 passengers excluding the driver, or (b) have a maximum gross weight of not more than 2500kg not being in either case, an off-road vehicle.	1.4.93

PART II

SYMBOL INDICATING THAT VEHICLE CAN RUN ON UNLEADED PETROL

[Omitted.]   **B15.279**

[Schedule 3A was inserted by SI 1988/1524 and is printed as subsequently amended by SI 1990/1131.]

(see regulation 36C)   [SCHEDULE 3B

AUTHORISED SEALERS

PART I

GENERAL

1. The Secretary of State may authorise—   **B15.280**

    (a) an individual proposing to seal speed limiters other than on behalf of another person;

    (b) a firm; or

    (c) a corporation;

to seal speed limiters for the purposes of regulation 36A or 36B and a person or body so authorised is referred to in this Schedule as an *"authorised sealer"*.

2. An authorised sealer shall comply with the conditions set out in Part II of this Schedule and with such other conditions as may from time to time be imposed by the Secretary of State.   **B15.281**

3. *[Entitlement to charge for sealing a speed limiter.]*

4. *[Withdrawal of authorisation granted under para.1.]*

5. *[Events terminating an authorisation granted under para.1.]*

PART II

THE CONDITIONS

[6. An authorised sealer shall not—   **B15.282**

(a) seal a speed limiter fitted to a vehicle to which regulation 36A applies unless he is satisfied that the speed limiter fulfils the requirements of—

    (i) paragraph (5)(b);

    (ii) paragraph (6), (7) or (7A); and

    (iii) paragraph (8) or (9),

of that regulation, or

(b) seal a speed limiter fitted to a vehicle to which regulation 36B applies unless he is satisfied that the speed limiter fulfils the requirements of—

    (i) paragraph (7)(b);

    (ii) paragraph (8) or (9); and

    (iii) paragraph (10) or (11),

of that regulation.]

B15.283   7. When sealing a speed limiter fitted to a vehicle to which regulation 36A applies, an authorised sealer shall do so in such a manner that the speed limiter fulfils the requirements of [paragraph (5)(a)] of that regulation.

B15.284   8. When sealing a speed limiter fitted to a vehicle to which regulation 36B applies, an authorised sealer shall do so in such a manner that the speed limiter fulfils the requirements of [paragraph (7)(a)] of that regulation.

B15.285   9. When an authorised sealer has sealed a speed limiter fitted to a vehicle to which section 36A applies he shall supply the owner with a plate which fulfils the requirements of regulation 70A.

B15.286   10. When an authorised sealer has sealed a speed limiter fitted to a vehicle to which section 36B applies he shall supply the owner with a plate which fulfils the requirements of [regulation 70A].]

B15.287   *[Schedule 3B was inserted by SI 1992/422 and is printed as subsequently amended by SI 2003/1946; SI 2007/3132.]*

(see regulation 40)   SCHEDULE 4

Gas Containers

Part I

Definitions relating to gas containers

B15.288   1. In this Schedule, unless the context otherwise requires, the following expressions have the meanings hereby assigned to them respectively, that is to say—

    "gas container" means a container fitted to a motor vehicle or a trailer and intended for the storage of gaseous fuel for the purpose of the propulsion of the vehicle or the drawing vehicle as the case may be;

    "gas cylinder" means a container fitted to a motor vehicle or a trailer and intended for the storage of compressed gas for the purpose of the propulsion of the vehicle or the drawing vehicle as the case may be;

    "compressed gas" means gaseous fuel under a pressure exceeding 1.0325 bar above atmospheric pressure;

    "pipeline" means all pipes connecting a gas container or containers—

        (a) to the engine or the mixing device for the supply of a mixture of gas and air to the engine; and

        (b) to the filling point on the vehicle;

    "pressure pipeline" means any part of a pipeline intended for the conveyance of compressed gas; and

    "reducing valve" means an apparatus which automatically reduces the pressure of the gas passing through it.

Gas containers

  2. Every gas container shall—   **B15.289**
    (a) be securely attached to the vehicle in such manner as not to be liable to displacement or damage due to vibration or other cause; and
    (b) be so placed or insulated as not to be adversely affected by the heat from the exhaust system.

Pipelines

  3.—(1) Every pipeline shall be supported in such manner as to be protected from excessive vibration and strain.   **B15.290**
  (2) No part of a pipeline shall be in such a position that it may be subjected to undue heat from the exhaust system.
  (3) Every pressure pipeline shall be made of steel solid drawn.
  (4) The maximum unsupported length of a pressure pipeline shall not exceed 920mm.

Unions

  4.—(1) Every union shall be so constructed and fitted that it will—   **B15.291**
    (a) not be liable to work loose or develop leakage when in use; and
    (b) be readily accessible for inspection and adjustment.
  (2) No union on a pressure pipeline or on a gas cylinder shall contain a joint other than a metal to metal joint.

Reducing valves

  5. Every reducing valve shall be—   **B15.292**
    (a) so fitted as to be readily accessible; and
    (b) so constructed that there can be no escape of gas when the engine is not running.

Valves and cocks

  6.—(1) Every valve or cock intended to be subjected to a pressure exceeding 6.8948 bar shall be of forged steel or of brass or bronze complying with the specification contained in Part II of this Schedule.   **B15.293**
  (2) A valve or cock shall be fitted to the pipeline to enable the supply of gas from the container or containers to the mixing device to be shut off.
  (3)
    (a) In the case of a pressure pipeline the valve or cock shall be placed between the reducing valve and the container and shall be readily visible and accessible from the outside of the vehicle and a notice indicating its position and method of operation shall be affixed in a conspicuous position on the outside of the vehicle carrying the gas container or containers.
    (b) In other cases, if the valve or cock is not so visible and accessible as aforesaid, a notice indicating its position shall be affixed in a conspicuous position on the outside of the vehicle carrying the container or containers.

Pressure gauges

  7. Every pressure gauge connected to a pressure pipeline shall be so constructed as not to be liable to deterioration under the action of the particular gases employed and shall be so constructed and fitted that—   **B15.294**
    (a) in the event of failure of such pressure gauge no gas can escape into any part of the vehicle;
    (b) it is not possible owing to leakage of gas into the casing of the pressure gauge for pressure to increase therein to such extent as to be liable to cause a breakage of the glass thereof; and
    (c) in the event of failure of such pressure gauge the supply of gas thereto may be readily cut off.

Charging connections

B15.295   8.—(1) Every connection for charging a gas container shall be outside the vehicle and in the case of a public service vehicle no such connection shall be within 610mm of any entrance or exit.

(2) An efficient shut-off valve shall be fitted as near as practicable to the filling point. Provided that in cases where compressed gas is not used a cock or an efficient non-return valve may be fitted in lieu thereof.

(3) Where compressed gas is used an additional emergency shut-off valve shall be fitted adjacent to the valve referred to in sub-paragraph (2) of this paragraph.

(4) A cap shall be fitted to the gas filling point on the vehicle and where compressed gas is used this cap shall be made of steel with a metal to metal joint.

Trailers

B15.296   9.—(1) Where a trailer is used for the carriage of a gas cylinder, a reducing valve shall be fitted on the trailer.

(2) No pipe used for conveying gas from a trailer to the engine of a vehicle shall contain compressed gas.

Construction, etc., of system

B15.297   10. Every part of a gas container propulsion system shall be—

(a) so placed or protected as not to be exposed to accidental damage and shall be soundly and properly constructed of suitable and well-finished materials capable of withstanding the loads and stresses likely to be met with in operation and shall be maintained in an efficient, safe and clean condition; and

(b) so designed and constructed that leakage of gas is not likely to occur under normal working conditions, whether or not the engine is running.

PART II

SPECIFICATION FOR BRASS OR BRONZE VALVES

Manufacture of valves

B15.298   1. The stamping or pressing from which each valve is manufactured shall be made from bars produced by (a) extrusion, (b) rolling, (c) forging, (d) extrusion and drawing, or (e) rolling and drawing.

Heat treatment

B15.299   2. Each stamping or pressing shall be heat treated so as to produce an equiaxed microstructure in the material.

Freedom from defects

B15.300   3. All stampings or pressings and the bars from which they are made shall be free from cracks, laminations, hard spots, segregated materials and variations in composition.

Tensile test

B15.301   4. Tensile tests shall be made on samples of stampings or pressings taken at random from any consignment. The result of the tensile test shall conform to the following conditions—

Yield Stress.—Not less than 231.6 N/mm^2 .

Ultimate Tensile Stress.—Not less than 463.3 N/mm^2 .

Elongation on 50mm gauge length.—Not less than 25%.

Note. —When the gauge length is less than 50mm the required elongation shall be proportionately reduced.

The fractured test piece shall be free from piping and other defects (see paragraph 3 of this Part of this Schedule).

(see regulations 40 and 96)   SCHEDULE 5

GAS SYSTEMS

Definitions

1. In this Schedule —   **B15.302**

"*check valve*" means a device which permits the flow of gas in one direction and prevents the flow of gas in the opposite direction;

"*design pressure*" means the pressure which a part of a gas system has been designed and constructed safely to withstand;

"*double-check valve*" means a device which consists of two check valves in series and which permits the flow of gas in one direction and prevents the flow of gas in the opposite direction;

["*electrically operated valve*" means a device which is electrically operated and opens when the ignition is switched on and closes when the ignition is switched off or the power is otherwise cut off;]

"*excess flow valve*" means a device which automatically and instantaneously reduces to a minimum the flow of gas through the valve when the flow rate exceeds a set value;

"*fixed gas container*" means a gas container which is attached to a vehicle permanently and in such a manner that the container can be filled without being moved;

"*gas container*" means any container, not being a container for the carriage of gas as goods, which is fitted to or carried on a motor vehicle or trailer and is intended for the storage of gas for either—

(a) the propulsion of the motor vehicle, or

(b) the operation of a gas-fired appliance;

"*high pressure*" means a pressure exceeding 1.0325 bar absolute;

"*high pressure pipeline*" means a pipeline intended to contain gas at high pressure;

"*pipeline*" means any pipe or passage connecting any two parts of a gas propulsion system of a vehicle or of a gas-fired appliance supply system on a vehicle or any two points on the same part of any such system;

"*portable gas container*" means a gas container which may be attached to a vehicle but which can readily be removed;

"*pressure relief valve*" means a device which opens automatically when the pressure in the part of the gas system to which it is fitted exceeds a set value, reaches its maximum flow capacity when the set value is exceeded by 10% and closes automatically when the pressure falls below a set value; and

"*reducing valve*" means a device which automatically reduces the pressure of the gas passing through it, and includes regulator devices.

[Paragraph 1 of Sch.5 is printed as amended by SI 2003/1690.]   **B15.303**

Gas containers

2.—(1) Every gas container shall—   **B15.304**

(a) be capable of withstanding the pressure of the gas which may be stored in the container at the highest temperature which the gas is likely to reach,

(b) if fitted inside the vehicle be so arranged as to prevent so far as is practicable the possibility of gas entering the engine, passenger or living compartments due to leaks or venting from the container or valves connections and gauges immediately adjacent to it, and the space containing those components shall be so ventilated and drained as to prevent the accumulation of gas,

(c) be securely attached to the vehicle in such a manner as not to be liable to displacement or damage due to vibration or other cause, and

(d) be so placed and so insulated or shielded as not to suffer any adverse effect from the heat of the exhaust system of any engine or any other source of heat.

(2) Every portable gas container shall be either—
- (a) hermetically sealed, or
- (b) fitted with a valve or cock to enable the flow of gas from the container to be stopped.

(3) Every fixed gas container shall—
- (a) be fitted with—
  - (i) at least one pressure relief valve, and
  - (ii) at least one manually operated valve which may be extended by an internal dip tube inside the gas container so as to indicate when the container has been filled to the level corresponding to the filling ratio specified in the British Standards Institution Specification for Filling Ratios and Developed Pressure for Liquefiable and Permanent Gases (as defined, respectively, in paragraphs 3.2 and 3.5 of the said Specification) published in May 1976 under the number BS 5355, and
- (b) be conspicuously and permanently marked with its design pressure.

(4) If any fixed gas container is required to be fitted in a particular attitude or location, or if any device referred to in sub-paragraph (3) above requires the container to be fitted in such a manner, then it shall be conspicuously and permanently marked to indicate that requirement.

(5) If the operation of any pressure relief valve or other device referred to in sub-paragraph (3) above may cause gas to be released from the gas container an outlet shall be provided to lead such gas to the outside of the vehicle so as not to suffer any adverse effect from the heat of the exhaust system of any engine or any other source of heat, and that outlet from the pressure relief valve shall not be fitted with any other valve or cock.

Filling systems for fixed gas containers

B15.305   3.—(1) Every connection for filling a fixed gas container shall be on the outside of the vehicle.

(2) There shall be fitted to every fixed gas container either—
- (a) a manually operated shut-off valve and an excess flow valve, or
- (b) a manually operated shut-off valve and a single check valve, or
- (c) a double-check valve,

and all parts of these valves in contact with gas shall be made entirely of suitable metal except that they may contain non-metal washers and seals provided that such washers and seals are supported and constrained by metal components.

(3) In every case where a pipe is attached to a gas container for the purpose of filling the gas container there shall be fitted to the end of the pipe furthest from the gas container a check valve or a double-check valve.

(4) There shall be fitted over every gas filling point on a vehicle a cap which shall—
- (a) prevent any leakage of gas from the gas filling point,
- (b) be secured to the vehicle by a chain or some other suitable means,
- (c) be made of suitable material; and
- (d) be fastened to the gas filling point by either a screw thread or other suitable means.

Pipelines

B15.306   4.—(1) Every pipeline shall be fixed in such a manner and position that—
- (a) it will not be adversely affected by the heat of the exhaust system of any engine or any other source of heat,
- (b) it is protected from vibration and strain in excess of that which it can reasonably be expected to withstand, and
- (c) in the case of a high pressure pipeline it is so far as is practicable accessible for inspection.

(2) Save as provided in sub-paragraph (4) below, every high pressure pipeline shall be—

(a) a rigid line of steel, copper or copper alloy of high pressure hydraulic grade, suit-able for service on road vehicles and designed for a minimum service pressure rat-ing of not less than 75 bar absolute, and

(b) effectively protected against, or shielded from, or treated so as to be resistant to, external corrosion throughout its length unless it is made from material which is corrosion resistant under the conditions which it is likely to encounter in service.

(3) No unsupported length of any high pressure pipeline shall exceed 600mm.

[(4) Flexible hose may be used in a high pressure pipeline either if—

(a)

    (i) it is reinforced either by stainless steel wire braid or by textile braid,

    (ii) its length does not exceed 500mm, and

    (iii) save in the case of a pipeline attached to a gas container for the purpose of filling that container the flexibility which it provides is necessary for the construction or operation of the gas system of which it forms a part, or

(b) its length exceeds 500mm and it complies with Annex 8 of ECE Regulation 67.01 and is approved and marked in accordance with that Regulation.]

[(4A) In the case of a motor vehicle which first used gas as a fuel for its propulsion on or after 1st January 2004 a flexible hose of any length used in a high pressure pipe line shall comply with the requirements of Annex 8 of ECE Regulation 67.01 shall be approved and marked in accordance with that Regulation and shall be no longer than is reasonably necessary.]

[Paragraph 4 of Sch.5 is printed as amended by SI 2003/1690.]   **B15.307**

Unions and joints

5.—(1) Every union and joint on a pipeline or gas container shall be so constructed and   **B15.308**
fitted that it will—

(a) not be liable to work loose or leak when in use, and

(b) be readily accessible for inspection and maintenance.

(2) Every union on a high pressure pipeline or on a gas container shall be made of suit-able metal but such a union may contain non-metal washers and seals provided that such washers and seals are supported and constrained by metal components.

Reducing valves

6. Every reducing valve shall be made of suitable materials and be so fitted as to be   **B15.309**
readily accessible for inspection and maintenance.

Pressure relief valves

7.—(1) Every pressure relief valve which is fitted to any part of a gas system (including   **B15.310**
a gas container) shall—

(a) be made entirely of suitable metal and so constructed and fitted as to ensure that the cooling effect of the gas during discharge shall not prevent its effective opera-tion,

(b) be capable, under the most extreme temperatures likely to be met (including exposure to fire), of a discharge rate which prevents the pressure of the contents of the gas system from exceeding its design pressure,

(c) have a maximum discharge pressure not greater than the design pressure of the gas container,

(d) be so designed and constructed as to prevent unauthorised interference with the relief pressure setting during service, and

(e) have outlets which are—

    (i) so sited that so far as is reasonably practicable in the event of an accident the valve and its outlets are protected from damage and the free discharge from such outlets is not impaired, and

    (ii) so designed and constructed as to prevent the collection of moisture and other foreign matter which could adversely affect their performance.

(2) The pressure at which a pressure relief valve is designed to start lifting shall be clearly and permanently marked on every such valve.

(3) Every pressure relief valve which is fitted to a gas container shall communicate with the vapour space in the gas container and not with any liquefied gas.

Valves and cocks

B15.311

8.—(1) A valve or cock shall be fitted to every supply pipeline as near as practicable to every fixed gas container and such valve or cock shall by manual operation enable the supply of gas from the gas container to the gas system to be stopped, and save as provided in sub-paragraph (2) below, shall—

    (a) if fitted on the outside of the vehicle, be readily visible and accessible from the outside of the vehicle, or

    (b) if fitted inside the vehicle be readily accessible for operation and be so arranged as to prevent so far as is practicable the possibility of gas entering the engine, passenger or living compartments due to leaks, and the space containing the valve or cock shall be so ventilated and drained as to prevent the accumulation of gas in that space.

[(2) Where a fixed gas container supplies no gas system other than a gas propulsion system—

    (a) an electrically operated valve may be fitted in place of the valve or cock referred to in sub-paragraph (1) above; and

    (b) either—

        (i) it shall be fitted as near as practicable to the gas container; or

        (ii) if fitted in addition to the valve or cock referred to in sub-paragraph (1) above it shall either be incorporated into that valve or cock or be fitted immediately downstream from it; and

    (c) it shall if fitted inside the vehicle be so arranged as to prevent as far as is practicable the possibility of gas entering the engine, passenger or living compartments due to leaks, and the space containing the valve shall be so ventilated and drained as to prevent the accumulation of gas in that space.]

(3) A notice clearly indicating the position, purpose and method of operating every valve or cock referred to in sub-paragraphs (1) and (2) above shall be fixed—

    (a) in all cases, in a conspicuous position on the outside of the vehicle, and

    (b) if every case where the valve or cock is located inside the vehicle in a conspicuous position adjacent to the gas container.

(4) In the case of a high pressure pipeline for the conveyance of gas from the gas container an excess flow valve shall be fitted as near as practicable to the gas container and such valve shall operate in the event of a fracture of the pipeline or other similar failure.

(5) All parts of every valve or cock referred to in this paragraph which are in contact with gas shall be made of suitable metal, save that they may contain non-metal washers and seals provided that such washers and seals are supported and constrained by metal components.

B15.312

[Paragraph 8 of Sch.5 is printed as amended by SI 2003/1690.]

Gauges

B15.313

9. Every gauge connected to a gas container or to a pipeline shall be so constructed as to be unlikely to deteriorate under the action of the gas used or to be used and shall be so constructed and fitted that—

(a) no gas can escape into any part of the vehicle as a result of any failure of the gauge, and

(b) in the event of any failure of the gauge the supply of gas to the gauge can be readily stopped.

Provided that the requirement specified in sub-paragraph (b) above shall not apply in respect of a gauge as an integral part of a gas container.

Propulsion systems

10.—(1) Every gas propulsion system shall be so designed and constructed that—   **B15.314**

(a) the supply of gas to the engine is automatically stopped by the operation of a valve when the engine is not running at all or is not running on the supply of gas, and,

(b) where a reducing valve is relied on to comply with sub-paragraph (a) above, the supply of gas to the engine is automatically stopped by the operation of an additional valve when the engine is switched off.

(2) Where the engine of a vehicle is constructed or adapted to run on one or more fuels as alternatives to gas, the safety and efficiency of the engine and any fuel system shall not be impaired by the presence of any other fuel system.

Special requirements for buses

11. In the case of a bus there shall be fitted as near as practicable to the gas container a   **B15.315** valve which shall stop the flow of gas into the gas supply pipeline in the event of—

(a) the angle of tilt of the vehicle exceeding that referred to in regulation 6 of the Public Services Vehicles (Conditions of Fitness, Equipment, Use and Certification) Regulations 1981 [*SI 1981/257, q.v.*], and

(b) the deceleration of the vehicle exceeding 5 g.

Gas-fired appliances

12. Every part of a gas-fired appliance shall be—   **B15.316**

(a) so designed and constructed that leakage of gas is unlikely to occur, and

(b) constructed of materials which are compatible both with each other and with the gas used.

13. Every gas-fired appliance shall be—   **B15.317**

(a) so located as to be easily inspected and maintained,

(b) so located and either insulated or shielded that its use shall not cause or be likely to cause danger due to the presence of any flammable material,

(c) so constructed and located as not to impose undue stress on any pipe or fitting, and

(d) so fastened or located as not to work loose or move in relation to the vehicle.

14. With the exception of catalytic heating appliances, every appliance of the kind   **B15.318** described in regulation 96(3)(b) or (c) which is fitted to a motor vehicle shall be fitted with a flue which shall be—

(a) connected to an outlet which is on the outside of the vehicle,

(b) constructed and located so as to prevent any expelled matter from entering the vehicle, and

(c) located so that it will not cause any adverse effect to, or suffer any adverse effect from, the exhaust outlet of any engine or any other source of heat.

General requirements

15. Every part of a gas propulsion system or a gas-fired appliance system, excluding the   **B15.319** appliance itself, shall be—

(a) so far as is practicable so located or protected as not to be exposed to accidental damage,

(b) soundly and properly constructed of materials which are compatible with one another and with the gas used or to be used and which are capable of withstanding the loads and stresses likely to be met in operation, and

(c) so designed and constructed that leakage of gas is unlikely to occur.

(see regulation 41)   SCHEDULE 6

Construction of Minibuses

B15.320   The requirements referred to in regulation 41 are as follows—

Exhaust pipes

1. The outlet of every exhaust pipe fitted to a minibus shall be either at the rear or on the off side of the vehicle.

Doors—number and position

B15.321   **2.**—(1) Every minibus shall be fitted with at least—

(a) one service door on the near side of the vehicle; and

(b) one emergency door either at the rear or on the off side of the vehicle so, however, that any emergency door fitted on the off side of the vehicle shall be in addition to the driver's door and there shall be no requirement for an emergency door on a minibus if it has a service door at the rear in addition to the service door on the near side.

(2) No minibus shall be fitted with any door on its off side other than a driver's door and an emergency door.

Emergency doors

B15.322   **3.** Every emergency door fitted to a minibus, whether or not required pursuant to these Regulations, shall—

(a) be clearly marked, in letters not less than 25mm high, on both the inside and the outside, "EMERGENCY DOOR" or "FOR EMERGENCY USE ONLY", and the means of its operation shall be clearly indicated on or near the door;

(b) if hinged, open outwards;

(c) be capable of being operated manually; and

(d) when fully opened, give an aperture in the body of the vehicle not less than 1210mm high nor less than 530mm wide.

Power-operated doors

B15.323   **4.**—(1) Every power-operated door fitted to a minibus shall—

(a) incorporate transparent panels so as to enable a person immediately inside the door to see any person immediately outside the door;

(b) be capable of being operated by a mechanism controlled by the driver of the vehicle when in the driving seat;

(c) be capable, in the event of an emergency or a failure of the supply of power for the operation of the door, of being opened from both inside and outside the vehicle by controls which—

(i) over-ride all other controls;

(ii) are placed on, or adjacent to, the door, and

(iii) are accompanied by markings which clearly indicate their position and method of operation and state that they may not be used by passengers except in an emergency;

(d) have a soft edge so that a trapped finger is unlikely to be injured; and

(e) be controlled by a mechanism by virtue of which if the door, when closing, meets a resistance exceeding 150 Newtons, either

—the door will cease to close and begin to open, or

—the closing force will cease and the door will become capable of being opened manually.

(2) No minibus shall be equipped with a system for the storage or transmission of energy in respect of the opening or closing of any door which, either in normal operation or if the system fails, is capable of adversely affecting the operation of the vehicle's braking system.

Locks, handles and hinges of doors

5. No minibus shall be fitted with—

B15.324

(a) a door which can be locked from the outside unless, when so locked, it is capable of being opened from inside the vehicle when stationary;

(b) a handle or other device for opening any door, other than the driver's door, from inside the vehicle unless the handle or other device is designed so as to prevent, so far as is reasonably practicable, the accidental opening of the door, and is fitted with a guard or transparent cover or so designed that it must be raised to open the door;

(c) a door which is not capable of being opened, when not locked, from inside and outside the vehicle by a single movement of the handle or other device for opening the door;

(d) a door in respect of which there is not a device capable of holding the door closed so as to prevent any passenger falling through the doorway;

(e) a side door which opens outwards and is hinged at the edge nearest the rear of the vehicle except in the case of a door having more than one rigid panel;

(f) a door, other than a power-operated door, in respect of which there is not either—

(i) a slam lock of the two-stage type; or

(ii) a device by means of which the driver, when occupying the driver's seat, is informed if the door is not securely closed, such device being operated by movement of the handle or other device for opening the door or, in the case of a handle or other device with a spring-return mechanism, by movement of the door as well as of the handle or other device.

Provided that the provisions of sub-paragraphs (a), (c), (d) and (f) of this paragraph shall not apply in respect of a near side rear door forming part of a pair of doors fitted at the rear of a vehicle if that door is capable of being held securely closed by the other door of that pair.

View of doors

6.—(1) Save as provided in sub-paragraph (2), every minibus shall be fitted with mirrors or other means so that the driver, when occupying the driver's seat, can see clearly the area immediately inside and outside every service door of the vehicle.

B15.325

(2) The provisions of sub-paragraph (1) shall be deemed to be satisfied in respect of a rear service door if a person 1.3 metres tall standing 1 metre behind the vehicle is visible to the driver when occupying the driver's seat.

Access to doors

7.—(1) Save as provided in sub-paragraph (2), there shall be unobstructed access from every passenger seat in a minibus to at least two doors one of which must be on the near-side of the vehicle and one of which must be either at the rear or on the offside of the vehicle.

B15.326

(2) Access to one only of the doors referred to in sub-paragraph (1) may be obstructed by either or both of—

(a) a seat which when tilted or folded does not obstruct access to that door, and

(b) a lifting platform or ramp which—

(i) does not obstruct the handle or other device on the inside for opening the door with which the platform or ramp is associated, and

       (ii) when the door is open, can be pushed or pulled out of the way from the inside so as to leave the doorway clear for use in an emergency.

Grab handles and hand rails

B15.327   **8.** Every minibus shall be fitted as respects every side service door with a grab handle or a hand rail to assist passengers to get on or off the vehicle.

Seats

B15.328   **9.**—(1) No seat shall be fitted to any door of a minibus.

(2) Every seat and every wheelchair anchorage fitted to a minibus shall be fixed to the vehicle.

(3) No seat, other than a wheelchair, fitted to a minibus shall be less than 400mm wide, and in ascertaining the width of a seat no account shall be taken of any arm-rests, whether or not they are folded back or otherwise put out of use.

(4) No minibus shall be fitted with an anchorage for a wheelchair in such a manner that a wheelchair secured to the anchorage would face either side of the vehicle.

(5) No minibus shall be fitted with a seat—

    (a) facing either side of the vehicle and immediately forward of a rear door unless the seat is fitted with an arm-rest or similar device to guard against a passenger on that seat falling through the doorway; or

    (b) so placed that a passenger on it would, without protection, be liable to be thrown through any doorway which is provided with a power-operated door or down any steps, unless the vehicle is fitted with a screen or guard which affords adequate protection against that occurrence.

Electrical equipment and wiring

B15.329   **10.**—(1) Save as provided in sub-paragraph (2) no minibus shall be fitted with any—

    (a) electrical circuit which is liable to carry a current exceeding that for which it was designed;

    (b) cable for the conduct of electricity unless it is suitably insulated and protected from damage;

    (c) electrical circuit, other than a charging circuit, which includes any equipment other than—

        (i) a starter motor,

        (ii) a glow plug,

        (iii) an ignition circuit, and

        (iv) a device to stop the vehicle's engine,

    unless it includes a fuse or circuit breaker so, however, that one fuse or circuit breaker may serve more than one circuit; or

    (d) electrical circuit with a voltage exceeding 100 volts unless there is connected in each pole of the main supply of electricity which is not connected to earth a manually operated switch which is—

        (i) capable of disconnecting the circuit, or, if there is more than one, every circuit, from the main supply,

        (ii) not capable of disconnecting any circuit supplying any lamp with which the vehicle is required to be fitted, and

        (iii) located inside the vehicle in a position readily accessible to the driver.

(2) The provisions of sub-paragraph (1) do not apply in respect of a high tension ignition circuit or a circuit within a unit of equipment.

Fuel tanks

B15.330   **11.** No minibus shall be fitted with a fuel tank or any apparatus for the supply of fuel which is in the compartments or other spaces provided for the accommodation of the driver or passengers.

Lighting of steps

12. Every minibus shall be provided with lamps to illuminate every step at a passenger **B15.331**
exit or in a gangway.

General construction and maintenance

13. Every minibus, including all bodywork and fittings, shall be soundly and properly **B15.332**
constructed of suitable materials and maintained in good and serviceable condition, and
shall be of such design as to be capable of withstanding the loads and stresses likely to be
met in the normal operation of the vehicle.

Definitions

14. In this Schedule — **B15.333**

"*driver's door*" means a door fitted to a minibus for use by the driver;

"*emergency door*" means a door fitted to a minibus for use by passengers in an
emergency; and

"*service door*" means a door fitted to a minibus for use by passengers in normal
circumstances.

SCHEDULE 7

FIRE-EXTINGUISHING APPARATUS AND FIRST-AID EQUIPMENT FOR MINIBUSES

(SEE REGULATION 42)

[PART I

FIRE EXTINGUISHING APPARATUS

A fire extinguisher which complies in all respects with the specification for portable fire **B15.334**
extinguishers issued by the British Standards Institution numbered BS 5423: 1977 or BS
5423: 1980 or BS 5423: 1987 and which—

(a) has a minimum test fire rating of 8A or 21B, and

(b) contains water or foam or contains, and is marked to indicate that it contains halon
1211 or halon 1301.]

[Part I of Sch.7 was substituted by SI 1989/2360.] **B15.335**

(SEE REGULATION 43)

PART II

FIRST AID EQUIPMENT

(i) Ten antiseptic wipes, foil packed; **B15.336**

(ii) One conforming disposable bandage (not less than 7.5cm wide);

(iii) Two triangular bandages;

(iv) One packet of 24 assorted adhesive dressings;

(v) Three large sterile unmedicated ambulance dressings (not less than
15.0cm $\times$ 20.0cm);

(vi) Two sterile eye pads, with attachments;

(vii) Twelve assorted safety pins; and

(viii) One pair of rustless blunt-ended scissors.

**(Regulations 55A(1) and
61(11))**

[SCHEDULE 7XA

End of Series Exemptions

B15.337

Part I

Modification of [Regulations 55A, 61 and 61A] in Relation to End of Series Vehicles

[The heading to Pt I is printed as amended by SI 2000/3197.]

Modification of [regulations 55A, 61 and 61A]

B15.338   **1.**—(1) An item numbered 2 or higher in the Table in regulation 55A shall not apply to—

(a) a type approval end of series vehicle;

(b) a non-type approval end of series vehicle; or

(c) a late entry into service vehicle,

if it is first used before the first anniversary of the date specified in column 3 of the item.

(2) An item numbered 8, 9 or 11 in Table II of regulation 61 shall not apply to a type approval end of series vehicle if it is first used before the first anniversary of the date specified in column 3 of the item.

(3) An item numbered 9 or 11 in Table II of regulation 61 shall not apply to a non-type approval end of series vehicle if it is first used before the first anniversary of the date specified in column 3 of the item.

(4) An item numbered 10 or higher (other than 11) in Table II of regulation 61 shall not apply to—

(a) a type approval end of series vehicle;

(b) a non-type approval end of series vehicle; or

(c) a late entry into service vehicle,

if it is first used before the first anniversary of the date specified in column 3 of the item.

[(4A) No provision of any Community Directive specified in an item numbered 1 or 2 in the Table in regulation 61A shall be deemed to be a design, construction or equipment requirement applying to, or to impose limit values in relation to, a vehicle by virtue of paragraphs (2) and (3) of regulation 61A, if the vehicle is——

(a) a type approval end of series vehicle,

(b) a non-type-approval end of series vehicle, or

(c) a late entry into service vehicle,

in relation to such a provision, and the vehicle is first used before the first anniversary of the date as is specified (as defined in regulation 61A) by the relevant Community Directive in item 1 or 2 in the Table in regulation 61A.]

[(4B) Paragraphs (5) and (6) of regulation 61B shall not apply to a type approval end of series vehicle, if it has been first used before 1st January 2018 and is lawfully equipped with an air conditioning system designed to contain high-GWP fluorinated greenhouse gases.]

(5) Parts II, III and IV of this Schedule shall have effect for the purpose of interpreting the expressions *"type approval end of series vehicle"*, *"non-type approval end of series vehicle"* and *"late entry into service vehicle"* respectively for the purposes of this paragraph.

B15.339   *[Schedule 7XA (paras 1–13) was inserted by SI 1996/2329. Paragraph 1 is printed as subsequently amended by SI 2000/3197; SI 2006/2565; SI 2009/2196.]*

Part II

Meaning of "Type Approval End of Series Vehicle" in Part I

Meaning of "type approval end of series vehicle" for the purposes of paragraph 1

B15.340   **2.**—(1) For the purposes of paragraph 1[, and subject to regulation 3 of the Motor Vehicles (Type Approval for Goods Vehicles) (Great Britain) (Amendment) Regulations 2007], a vehicle is a type approval end of series vehicle, in relation to item 8, 9 or 11 in

Table II in regulation 61, if it meets the requirements of sub-paragraph (3) in relation to the item.

(2) For the purposes of paragraph 1, a vehicle is a type approval end of series vehicle, in relation to an item numbered 2 or higher in the Table in regulation 55A or an item numbered 10 or higher (other than item 11) in Table II in regulation 61 [or any provision of any Community Directive specified in item 1 or 2 in the Table in regulation 61A] [or paragraph (5) or (6) of regulation 61B] if—

(a) by virtue of [either item 2J of Schedule 1 or] Schedule 1C to the Type Approval for Goods Vehicles Regulations, [or]

(b) by virtue of Schedule 1C to the Type Approval (Great Britain) Regulations, [...]

(c) [...]

[which] [, other than item 2J of Schedule 1,] Schedules in certain circumstances defer the date on which certain requirements relating to exhaust emissions, [air conditioning systems] noise and silencers cease to apply) the type approval requirements that applied to the vehicle on the date specified in column 3 of the item [or, in relation to any provision of any Community Directive specified in item 1 or 2 in the Table in regulation 61A, on the date as is specified (as defined in regulation 61A) by the relevant Community Directive] [or, in relation to paragraph (5) or (6) of regulation 61B, 1st January 2017,] are the same as the type approval requirements that applied to the vehicle immediately before the date so specified in that column of that item [or in relation to any provision of any Community Directive specified in item 1 or 2 in the Table in regulation 61A, the date as is specified by the relevant Community Directive [or, in relation to paragraph (5) or (6) of regulation 61B, immediately before 1st January 2017]]].

[(2A) For the purposes of paragraph 1, a vehicle is a type-approval end of series vehicle in relation to an item in the Table in regulation 55A, or in Table II in regulation 61, or any provision in any Community Directive specified in item 1 or 2 in the Table in regulation 61A [or paragraph (5) or (6) of regulation 61B], if it has been exempted from that item or provision under—

(a) the laws of a relevant State (as defined by paragraph 5(1)(c)) other than the United Kingdom, or

(b) the laws applicable in Northern Ireland,

pursuant to Article 8(2)(b) of the Framework Directive[, or Article 27 of Community Directive 2007/46].]

[(2B) For the purposes of paragraph 1, a vehicle is a type approval end of series vehicle in relation to—

(a) an item numbered 2 or higher in the Table in regulation 55A,

(b) an item numbered 10 or higher (other than item 11) in Table II in regulation 61,

if a direction given under regulation 12 or 13 of the EC Whole Vehicle Type Approval Regulations or regulation 31 or 32 of the Vehicle Approval Regulations is in force in relation to the vehicle.]

(3) A vehicle meets the requirements of this sub-paragraph, in relation to the item, if—

(a) it was manufactured during the relevant period;

(b) one of the following conditions is satisfied—

(i) a certificate of conformity was issued in respect of the vehicle before the date specified in column 3 of the item by virtue of a TAC issued before the date specified in column 4 of the Table in paragraph 6 in relation to the item, or

(ii) a sub-MAC was issued in respect of the vehicle before the date specified in column 3 of the item by virtue of a MAC issued before the date specified in column 4 of that Table;

(c) it was in the territory of a relevant state at some time before the date specified in column 3 of the item; and

    (d) the number of relevant vehicles which were—

        (i) manufactured before that vehicle was manufactured, and

        (ii) still in existence on the date specified in column 3 of that item, was less than the specified number of 50 (whichever is the greater).

    (4) For the purposes of sub-paragraph (3) —

      (a) *"MAC"* means a Minister's approval certificate issued under section 58(1) of the Road Traffic Act 1988;

      (b) *"sub-MAC"* means a Minister's approval certificate issued under section 58(4) of the Road Traffic Act 1988; and

      (c) *"TAC"* means a type approval certificate.

B15.341   *[Schedule 7XA (paras 1–13) was inserted by SI 1996/2329. Paragraph 2 is printed as subsequently amended by SI 2000/3197; SI 2006/2565; SI 2007/361; SI 2007/2544; SI 2009/2196.]*

Meaning of "relevant vehicle" for the purposes of this Part

B15.342   **3.**—(1) For the purposes of paragraph 2(3)(d), in relation to a particular vehicle to which Type Approval for Goods Vehicles Regulations apply (in this paragraph referred to as *"the vehicle in question"*) and a particular item, a *"relevant vehicle"* is a vehicle (other than the vehicle in question) which—

    (a) is a vehicle to which those Regulations apply;

    (b) meets the requirements specified in paragraphs (a) to (c) of paragraph 2(3);

    (c) was manufactured by the manufacturer of the vehicle in question; and

    (d) had not been registered under the Vehicles (Excise) Act 1971 or the Vehicle Excise and Registration Act 1994 before the date specified in column 3 of the item.

    (2) For the purposes of paragraph 2(3)(d) in relation to a particular vehicle to which the Type Approval (Great Britain) Regulations apply (in this paragraph referred to as *"the vehicle in question"*) and a particular item, a *"relevant vehicle"* is a vehicle (other than the vehicle in question) which—

    (a) is a vehicle to which these Regulations apply;

    (b) meets the requirements specified in paragraphs (a) to (c) of paragraph 2(3);

    (c) was manufactured by the manufacturer of the vehicle in question; and

    (d) had not been registered under the Vehicle Excise and Registration Act 1994 before the date specified in column 3 of the item.

B15.343   *[Schedule 7XA (paras 1–13) was inserted by SI 1996/2329.]*

Meaning of "specified number" for the purposes of this Part

B15.344   **4.**—(1) For the purposes of paragraph 2(3)(d), in relation to a particular vehicle to which the Type Approval (Great Britain) Regulations apply (in this paragraph referred to as *"the vehicle in question"*) and a particular item, *"the specified number"* is 10% of the total number of vehicles to which those Regulations apply that were both—

    (a) manufactured by the manufacturer of the vehicle in question; and

    (b) registered under the Vehicles Excise Act 1971 or the Vehicle Excise and Registration Act 1994 during the one-year period ending immediately before the date specified in column 3 of the item.

    (2) For the purposes of paragraph 2(3)(d), in relation to a particular vehicle to which the Type Approval for Goods Vehicles Regulations apply (in this paragraph referred to as *"the vehicle in question"*) and a particular item, *"the specified number"* is 10% of the total number of vehicles to which those Regulations apply that were both—

    (a) manufactured by the manufacturer of the vehicle in question, and

    (b) registered under the Vehicles Excise Act 1971 or the Vehicle Excise and Registration Act 1994 during the one-year period ending immediately before the date specified in column 3 of the item.

[Schedule 7XA (paras 1–13) was inserted by SI 1996/2329.]   **B15.345**

Circumstances in which a vehicle is to be regarded as having been in the territory of a relevant state for the purposes of this Part

5.—(1) For the purposes of paragraph 2(3)(c) —   **B15.346**

(a) at any material time before the 5th November 1993, *"relevant state"* means a member State;

(b) in relation to any time on or after 5th November 1993 but before 1st May 1995, *"relevant state"* means an EEA State other than Liechtenstein; and

(c) in relation to any time on or after 1st May 1995, *"relevant state"* means any EEA State.

(2) For the purposes of this paragraph —

"EEA agreement" means the Agreement on the European Economic Area signed at Oporto on the 2nd May 1992 as adjusted by the protocol signed at Brussels on the 17th March 1993; and

"EEA State" means a State which is a contracting party to the EEA agreement.

[Schedule 7XA (paras 1–13) was inserted by SI 1996/2329.   **B15.347**

As to the European Economic Area and the EEA agreement (see para.5(2) above), see the introductory note to Section C below.]

Meaning of "relevant period" for the purposes of this Part

6. For the purposes of this Part, *"the relevant period"* in relation to an item numbered 8, 9 or 11 in Table II in regulation 61 is the period—   **B15.348**

(a) beginning on the date specified in column 2 of the Table below against that item; and

(b) ending immediately before the date specified in column 3 of the Table below against that item.

THE TABLE

1	2	3	4	5
Item in Table II in regulation 61	*Date on which the relevant period begins*	*Date immediately before which the relevant period ends*	*Date before which type approval, etc. needs to be granted*	*Date in column 3 of Table II in regulation 61*
8	1st August 1990	1st September 1992	1st July 1992	31st December 1992
9	1st April 1991	1st October 1993	1st October 1993	1st October 1993
11	1st August 1992	1st August 1994	1st October 1993	1st October 1994

[Schedule 7XA (paras 1–13) was inserted by SI 1996/2329.]   **B15.349**

PART III

MEANING OF "NON-TYPE APPROVAL END OF SERIES VEHICLE" IN PART I

Meaning of "non-type approval end of series vehicle" in paragraph 1

7.—[(1) For the purposes of paragraph 1, a vehicle is a non-type approval end of series vehicle in relation to an item or provision if it meets the requirements of sub-paragraph (2) in relation to the item or provision.]   **B15.350**

[(2) A vehicle meets the requirements of this sub-paragraph in relation to an item or provision if—]

(a) it is a vehicle to which neither the Type Approval (Great Britain) Regulations nor the Type Approval for Goods Vehicles Regulations [nor the EC Whole Vehicle Type Approval Regulations] [nor the Vehicle Approval Regulations] apply;

(b) it was manufactured during the relevant period;

(c) no EC certificate of conformity has been issued in respect of the vehicle;

(d) it was in the territory of a relevant state at some time before the end of the relevant period; and

(e) the number of relevant vehicles which were both—

    (i) manufactured before that vehicle was manufactured, and

    (ii) still in existence on the date specified in column 3 in the item [or in relation to any provision of any Community Directive specified in item 1 or 2 in the Table in regulation 61A, on the date as is specified (as defined in regulation 61A) by the relevant Community Directive, is less than the specified number, or 100, whichever is the greater.]

B15.351   *[Schedule 7XA (paras 1–13) was inserted by SI 1996/2329. Paragraph 7 is printed as subsequently amended by SI 2000/3197 and SI 2006/2565; SI 2009/2196.]*

Meaning of "relevant vehicle" for the purposes of this Part

B15.352   **8.** For the purposes of paragraph 7(2)(e), in relation to a particular vehicle (in this paragraph referred to as *"the vehicle in question"*) and a particular item [or provision], a *"relevant vehicle"* is a vehicle (other than the vehicle in question) which—

(a) meets the requirements specified in paragraphs (a) to (d) of paragraph 7(2);

[(b) is a "vehicle" within the meaning of Community Directive 70/220 (as amended by Community Directive 83/351) or Community Directive 2005/55 (as amended by Community Directives 2005/78 and 2006/51);]

(c) was manufactured by the manufacturer of the vehicle in question;

(d) had not been registered under the Vehicles (Excise) Act 1971 or the Vehicle Excise and Registration Act 1994 during the relevant period.

B15.353   *[Schedule 7XA (paras 1–13) was inserted by SI 1996/2329. Paragraph 8 is printed as subsequently amended by SI 2006/2565.*

The term "vehicle" is defined in art.1 of Directive 2005/55/EC, as amended by Directive 2008/74/EC (O.J. No.L192, July 19, 2008, pp.51–59), as—

any motor vehicle as defined in Article 2 of Directive 70/156/EEC with a reference mass exceeding 2610 kg;

The categories of motor vehicles are set out in Annex II to Directive 2007/46/EC (O.J. No.L263, October 9, 2007, p.1), which repealed Directive 70/156/EEC (O.J. No.L42, February 23, 1970, p.1) with effect from April 29, 2009.]

Meaning of "specified number" for the purposes of this Part

B15.354   **9.**—(1) For the purposes of paragraph 7(2)(e), in relation to a particular vehicle (in this paragraph referred to as *"the vehicle in question"*) and a particular item [or provision], *"the specified number"* is [30%] of the total number of vehicles that—

(a) are vehicles to which neither the Type Approval (Great Britain) Regulations nor the Type Approval for Goods Vehicles Regulations [nor the EC Whole Vehicle Type Approval Regulations] apply; and

(b) meet the requirements of sub-paragraph (2).

(2) A vehicle meets the requirements of this paragraph if it—

[(a) is a "vehicle"within the meaning of Community Directive 70/220 (as amended by Community Directive 83/351) or Community Directive 2005/55 (as amended by Community Directives 2005/78 and 2006/51);]

(b) was manufactured by the manufacturer of the vehicle in question; and

(c) was registered under the Vehicles (Excise) Act 1971 or the Vehicle Excise and Registration Act 1994 during the one-year period ending immediately before the date specified in column 3 of that item [or, in relation to [any provision of any Community Directive specified in] item 1 or 2 of the Table in regulation 61A, before the date as is specified (as defined in regulation 61A) by the relevant Community Directive].

[Schedule 7XA (paras 1–13) was inserted by SI 1996/2329. Paragraph 9 is **B15.355**
printed as subsequently amended by SI 2000/3197 and SI 2006/2565.

As to the meaning of "vehicle" (see para.9(2)(a) above), see the note to para.8 above.]

Circumstances in which a vehicle is to be regarded as having been in the territory of a relevant state for the purposes of this Part

10. Paragraph 5 in Part II of this Schedule shall have effect for the purposes of paragraph **B15.356** 7(2)(d) as it has effect for the purposes of paragraph 2(3)(c).

[Schedule 7XA (paras 1–13) was inserted by SI 1996/2329.]   **B15.357**

Meaning of "relevant period" for the purposes of this Part

11. For the purposes of paragraphs [*sic*] 7(2)(d), *"the relevant period"*—   **B15.358**

(a) in relation to an item numbered 9 or 11 in Table II in regulation 61 is the period—

   (i) beginning on the date specified in column 2 of the Table below against the item, and

   (ii) ending immediately before the date specified in column 3 of the Table below against the item; and

(b) in relation to any item in the Table in regulation 55A or any item numbered 10 or higher (other than 11) in the said Table II is the two-year period ending immediately before the date specified in column 3 of that item [; and]

[(c) in relation to an item [any provision of any Community Directive specified in] numbered 1 or 2 in the Table in regulation 61A is the two year period ending immediately before the date as is specified (as defined in regulation 61A) by the relevant Community Directive in the Table].

Tʜᴇ Tᴀʙʟᴇ

1	*2*	*3*	*4*
Item in Table II in regulation 61	*Date on which relevant period begins*	*Date immediately before which the relevant period ends*	*Date in column 3 of Table II in regulation 61*
9	1st April 1991	1st October 1993	1st October 1993
11	1st August 1992	1st August 1994	1st October 1994

[Schedule 7XA (paras 1–13) was inserted by SI 1996/2329. Paragraph 11 is **B15.359**
printed as subsequently amended by SI 2000/3197 and SI 2006/2565.]

Pᴀʀᴛ IV

Mᴇᴀɴɪɴɢ ᴏꜰ "Lᴀᴛᴇ Eɴᴛʀʏ ɪɴᴛᴏ Sᴇʀᴠɪᴄᴇ Vᴇʜɪᴄʟᴇ" ɪɴ Pᴀʀᴛ I

Meaning of "late entry into service vehicle" in paragraph 1

12. For the purposes of paragraph 1, a vehicle is a late entry into service vehicle, in rela- **B15.360** tion to an item [or provision], if—

(a) no EC certificate of conformity has been issued in respect of the vehicle;

(b) it was in the territory of a relevant state at some time before the date specified in column 3 of the item [or, in relation to [any provision of any Community Directive specified in] item 1 or 2 of the Table in regulation 61A, before the date as is specified (as defined in regulation 61A) by the relevant Community Directive];

(c) it was manufactured at least two years before that date.

B15.361   *[Schedule 7XA (paras 1–13) was inserted by SI 1996/2329. Paragraph 12 is printed as subsequently amended by SI 2000/3197 and SI 2006/2565.]*

Circumstances in which a vehicle is to be regarded as having been in the territory of a relevant state for the purposes of this Part

B15.362   13. Paragraph 5 in Part II of this Schedule shall have effect for the purposes of paragraph 12(b) as it has effect for the purposes of paragraph 2(3)(c).]

B15.363   *[Schedule 7XA (paras 1–13) was inserted by SI 1996/2329.]*

Regulations 57, 57A and 57B   [SCHEDULE 7A

MOTOR CYCLE NOISE AND MOTOR CYCLE SILENCERS

PART I

B15.364   **1.**—(1) For the purposes of these Regulations a vehicle meets the requirements of an item in the Table below if its sound level does not exceed by more than 1 dB(a) the relevant limit specified in column 2 in that item when measured under the conditions specified in column 3 in that item by the method specified in column 4 in that item using the apparatus prescribed in regulation 55(6).

(2) In this Part of this Schedule, *"moped"* has the same meaning as in regulation 57.

TABLE

1	2		3	4
	Limits of sound level			
Item	*Mopeds*	*Vehicles other than mopeds*	*Conditions of measurement*	*Methods of measurement*
1	73 dB(a)	Limit determined in accordance with paragraph 2.1.1 of Annex I to Community Directive 78/1015 by reference to the cubic capacity of the vehicle	Conditions specified in paragraph 2.1.3 of Annex I to Community Directive 78/1015	Methods specified in paragraph 2.1.4 of Annex I to Community Directive 78/1015
2	73 dB(a)	First stage limit determined in accordance with paragraph 2.1.1 of Annex I to Community Directive 87/56 by reference to the cubic capacity of the vehicle	Conditions specified in paragraph 2.1.3 of Annex I to Community Directive 87/56	Methods specified in paragraph 2.1.4 of Annex I to Community Directive 87/56

1	2		3	4
	Limits of sound level			
Item	Mopeds	Vehicles other than mopeds	Conditions of measurement	Methods of measurement
3	74 dB(a)	The limit specified in item 2 plus 1 dB(a)	As in item 2	As in item 2

PART II

2. The requirements of this paragraph are that the silencer—   **B15.365**

  (a) is so constructed that—

      (i) it meets the requirements of paragraphs 3 and 4 of British Standard BS AU 193:1983;

      (ii) were it to be fitted to an unused vehicle of the same model as the vehicle in question, the unused vehicle would meet the requirements of paragraph 5.2 of that Standard; and

  (b) is clearly and indelibly marked "BS AU 193/T2".

3. The requirements of this paragraph are that the silencer—   **B15.366**

  (a) is so constructed that—

      (i) it meets the requirements of paragraphs 3 and 4 of British Standard BS AU 193a: 1990;

      (ii) were it to be fitted to an unused vehicle of the same model as the vehicle in question, the unused vehicle would meet the requirements of paragraph 5.2 of that Standard; and

  (b) is clearly and indelibly marked "BS AU 193a: 1990/T2".

4. The requirements of this paragraph are that the silencer—   **B15.367**

  (a) is so constructed that—

      (i) it meets the requirements of paragraphs 3 and 4 of British Standard BS AU 193a: 1990;

      (ii) were it to be fitted to an unused vehicle of the same model as the vehicle in question, the unused vehicle would meet the requirements of paragraph 5.3 of that Standard; and

  (b) is clearly and indelibly marked "BS AU 193a: 1990/T3".

5. In this Part of this Schedule —   **B15.368**

  (a) *"British Standard BS AU 193: 1983"* means the British Standard Specification for replacement motor cycle and moped exhaust systems published by the British Standards Institution under reference number BS AU 193: 1983;

  (b) *"British Standard BS AU 193a: 1990"* means the British Standard Specification for replacement motor cycle and moped exhaust systems published by the British Standards Institution under reference number BS AU 193a: 1990.

PART III

6. Paragraph (4) of regulation 57A shall not apply to a replacement silencer if the second   **B15.369** requirement referred to in that regulation would be met were there substituted in Part II of this Schedule, —

  (a) for the references to provisions in either of the British Standard Specifications, references to equivalent provisions in a corresponding standard; and

  (b) for the references to a mark, references to a mark made pursuant to that corresponding standard indicating that the silencer complies with those equivalent provisions.

B15.370   7. In this Part of this Schedule, *"corresponding standard"*, in relation to a British Standard Specification, means—

(a) a standard or code of practice of a national standards body or equivalent body of any member State;

(b) any international standard recognised for use as a standard by any member State; or

(c) a technical specification or code of practice which, whether mandatory or not, is recognised for use as a standard by a public authority of any member State,

> where the standard, code of practice, international standard or technical specification provides, in relation to motor cycles, a level of noise limitation and safety equivalent to that provided by the British Standard Specification and contains a requirement as respects the marking of silencers equivalent to that provided by that instrument.

B15.371   8. A reference in this part of this Schedule to a British Standard Specification is a reference to British Standard BS AU 193: 1983 or British Standard BS AU 193a: 1990; and *"either of the British Standard Specifications"* shall be construed accordingly.

B15.372   9. In this Part of this Schedule, *"British Standard BS AU 193: 1983"* and *"British Standard BS AU 193a: 1990"* have the same meanings as in Part II of this Schedule.]

B15.373   *[Schedule 7A was inserted by SI 1994/14.]*

**Regulation 61(10AA), (10AB)   [SCHEDULE 7B
and 10(BA)**

EMISSIONS FROM CERTAIN MOTOR VEHICLES

PART I

VEHICLES PROPELLED BY SPARK IGNITION ENGINES

B15.374   1. This Part of this Schedule applies to a vehicle if, when the engine is running without load at a normal idling speed, the carbon monoxide content of the exhaust emissions from the engine exceeds the relevant percentage of the total exhaust emissions from the engine by volume.

B15.375   *[Schedule 7B (paras 1–9) was inserted by SI 1995/2210.]*

B15.376   2. This Part of this Schedule also applies to a vehicle if, when the engine is running without load at a fast idling speed,—

(a) the carbon monoxide content of the exhaust emissions from the engine exceeds [the relevant percentage] of the total exhaust emissions from the engine by volume;

(b) the hydrocarbon content of those emissions exceeds 0.02% of the total exhaust emissions from the engine by volume; or

(c) the lambda value is not within the relevant limits.

B15.377   *[Schedule 7B (paras 1–9) was inserted by SI 1995/2210 and is printed as subsequently amended by SI 2002/227.]*

B15.378   3. For the purposes of [paragraph 1 of] this Part of this Schedule the relevant percentage, in respect of a vehicle, is—

(a) if the vehicle is of a description specified in the Annex to the emissions publication, the percentage shown against that description of vehicle in column 2(a) of that Annex; [...]

[(b) if the vehicle is not of such a description and is first used before 1st July 2002, 0.5%; or]

[(c) if the vehicle is not of such a description and is first used on or after 1st July 2002, 0.3%.]

B15.379   *[Schedule 7B (paras 1–9) was inserted by SI 1995/2210 and is printed as* *subsequently amended by SI 2002/227. Paragraph 3 is further amended by SI 2003/3145.]*

[3A. For the purposes of paragraph 2(a) of this Part of this Schedule the relevant percentage, in respect of a vehicle, is, when the engine is running without load at a fast idling speed—   **B15.380**

  (a) if the vehicle is of a description specified in the Annex to the emissions publication, the percentage shown against that description of vehicle in column 3(a) of that Annex; […]

  [(b) if the vehicle is not of such a description and is first used before 1st July 2002, 0.3%; or]

  [(c) if the vehicle is not of such a description and is first used on or after 1st July 2002, 0.2%.]

[Schedule 7B (para.3A) was inserted by SI 2002/227. Paragraph 3A is printed as subsequently amended by SI 2003/3145.]   **B15.381**

4. For the purposes of this Part of this Schedule, in the case of a vehicle of a description specified in the Annex to the emissions publication, the engine shall be regarded as running at a normal idling speed if and only if the engine is running at a rotational speed between the minimum and maximum limits shown against that description of vehicle in columns 2(b) and (c) respectively of that Annex.   **B15.382**

[Schedule 7B (paras 1–9) was inserted by SI 1995/2210.]   **B15.383**

5. For the purposes of this Part of this Schedule an engine shall be regarded as running at a fast idling speed if—   **B15.384**

  (a) the vehicle is of a description specified in the Annex to the emissions publication and the engine is running at a rotational speed between the minimum and maximum limits shown against that description of vehicle in columns 3(e) and (f) respectively of that Annex; or

  (b) the vehicle is not of such a description and the engine is running at a rotational speed between 2,500 and 3,000 revolutions per minute.

[Schedule 7B (paras 1–9) was inserted by SI 1995/2210.]   **B15.385**

6. For the purposes of this Part of this Schedule, the lambda value, in respect of a vehicle, shall be regarded as being within relevant limits, if and only if—   **B15.386**

  (a) the vehicle is of a description specified in the Annex to the emissions publication and the lambda value is between the minimum and maximum limits shown against that description of vehicle in columns 3(c) and (d) respectively of that Annex; or

  (b) the vehicle is not of such a description and the lambda value is between 0.97 and 1.03.

[Schedule 7B (paras 1–9) was inserted by SI 1995/2210.]   **B15.387**

7. In this Part of this Schedule —   **B15.388**

  (a) a reference to the lambda value, in relation to a vehicle at any particular time, is a reference to the ratio by mass of air to petrol vapour in the mixture entering the combustion chambers divided by 14.7; and

  [(b) *"the emissions publication"* is the publication entitled "In Service Exhaust Emission Standards for Road Vehicles—Sixteenth Edition" (ISBN 978-0-9549352-6-9) published by the Department for Transport.]

[Schedule 7B (paras 1–9) was inserted by SI 1995/2210. Paragraph 7 is printed as subsequently amended by SI 1996/2085; SI 1997/1544; SI 1998/1563, SI 1999/1521 and 1959; SI 2000/1434; SI 2001/1825; SI 2002/1474; the Transfer of Functions (Transport, Local Government and the Regions) Order 2002 (SI 2002/2626); SI 2003/1690; SI 2004/1706; SI 2005/1641; SI 2006/1756; SI 2007/ 1817; SI 2008/1702; SI 2010/2060.]   **B15.389**

PART II

VEHICLES PROPELLED BY COMPRESSION IGNITION ENGINES

B15.390   [8.—(1) This Part of this Schedule applies to a vehicle if, when subjected to a relevant test, the coefficient of absorption of the exhaust emissions from the engine of the vehicle immediately after leaving the exhaust system exceeds—

    (a) if the vehicle is first used before 1st July 2008 and the engine of that vehicle is turbo-charged, 3.0 per metre;

    (b) if the vehicle is first used before 1st July 2008 and the engine of that vehicle is not turbo-charged, 2.5 per metre; or

    (c) if the vehicle is first used on or after 1st July 2008, 1.5 per metre.

(2) In paragraph (1) *"a relevant test"* means a test conducted in accordance with—

    (a) point 8.2.2 of Annex II of Council Directive 96/96/EC [*O.J. No.L46, February 17, 1997, p.1*] as replaced by Article 1 of Commission Directive 2003/27/EC [*O.J. No.L90, April 8, 2003, p.41*]; or

    (b) point 2.2 of Annex II of Directive 2000/30/EC [*O.J. No.L203, August 10, 2000, p.1*] of the European Parliament and the Council as replaced by Article 1 of Commission Directive 2003/26/EC [*O.J. No.L90, April 8, 2003, p.37*].]

B15.391   *[Schedule 7B (paras 1–9) was inserted by SI 1995/2210. Paragraph 8 is printed as substituted by SI 2003/3145.]*

B15.392   **9.** In this Part of this Schedule —

    (a) *"coefficient of absorption"* shall be construed in accordance with paragraph 3.5 of Annex VII to Community Directive 72/306.

    (b) [...]

B15.393   *[Schedule 7B (paras 1–9) was inserted by SI 1995/2210. Paragraph 9 is printed as subsequently amended by SI 2000/1434.*

Paragraph 3.5 of (what is now) Annex VI to Directive 72/306/EEC (to which reference is made at para.9(a) above) provides:

3.5 **Measuring scales**

3.5.1. The light-absorption coefficient k shall be calculated by the formula $\Phi = \Phi_o\, e^{-kL}$, where L is the effective length of the light path through the gas to be measured, Φ_o the incident flux and Φ the emergent flux. When the effective length L of a type of opacimeter cannot be assessed directly from its geometry, the effective length L shall be determined

    — either by the method described in item 4 of this Annex; or

    — through correlation with another type of opacimeter for which the effective length is known.

3.5.2. The relationship between the 0–100 linear scale and the light absorption coefficient k is given by the formula

$$k = -\frac{1}{L}\log_e\left(1 - \frac{N}{100}\right)$$

where N is a reading on the linear scale and k the corresponding value of the absorption coefficient.

3.5.3. The indicating dial of the opacimeter shall enable an absorption coefficient of $1.7\,\mathrm{m}^{-1}$ to be read with an accuracy of $0.025\,\mathrm{m}^{-1}$]

(see regulation 66)   SCHEDULE 8

PLATES FOR CERTAIN VEHICLES

PART I

Particulars to be shown on plate for motor vehicles (including motor vehicles forming part   **B15.394**
of articulated vehicles)

1. Manufacturer's name.
2. Vehicle type.
3. Engine type and power (a).
4. Chassis or serial number.
5. Number of axles.
6. Maximum axle weight for each axle (b).
7. Maximum gross weight (c).
8. Maximum train weight (d).
9. Maximum weight in Great Britain for each axle (b), (e).
10. Maximum gross weight in Great Britain (c), (e).

   (a) The power need not be shown in the case of a motor vehicle manufactured before 1st October 1972 (hereinafter in this Schedule referred to as *"an excepted vehicle"*) and shall not be shown in the case of any motor vehicle which is propelled otherwise than by a compression ignition engine.

   (b) This weight as respects each axle is the sum of the weights to be transmitted to the road surface by all the wheels of that axle.

   (c) This weight is the sum of the weights to be transmitted to the road surface by all the wheels of the motor vehicle (including any load imposed by a trailer, whether forming part of an articulated vehicle or not, on the motor vehicle).

   (d) This weight is the sum of the weights to be transmitted to the road surface by all the wheels of the motor vehicle and of any trailer drawn, but this item need not be completed where the motor vehicle is not constructed to draw a trailer.

(b), (c),

   (d) References to the weights to be transmitted to the road surface by all or any of the wheels of the vehicle or any trailer drawn are references to the weights so to be transmitted both of the vehicle or trailer and of any load or persons carried by it.

   (e) This item need not be completed in the case of an excepted vehicle or in the case of a vehicle which is a locomotive or motor tractor.

PART II

Particulars to be shown on plate for trailers (including trailers forming part of articulated   **B15.395**
vehicles)

1. Manufacturer's name.
2. Chassis or serial number.
3. Number of axles.
4. Maximum weight for each axle (a).
5. Maximum load imposed on drawing vehicle (b).
6. Maximum gross weight (c).
7. Maximum weight in Great Britain for each axle (a), (e).
8. Maximum gross weight in Great Britain (c), (f).

9. Year of manufacture (d).

(a) This weight as respects each axle is the sum of the weights to be transmitted to the road surface by all the wheels of that axle.

(b) Only for trailers forming part of articulated vehicles or where some of the weight of the trailer or its load is to be imposed on the drawing vehicle. This item need not be completed in the case of a converter dolly [manufactured before 1st February 1992].

(c) This weight is the sum of the weights to be transmitted to the road surface by all the wheels of the trailer, including any weight of the trailer to be imposed on the drawing vehicle.

(a), (b), (c) References to the weights to be transmitted to the road surface by all or any of the wheels of the trailer are references to the weight so to be transmitted both of the trailer and of any load or persons carried by it and references to the weights to be imposed on the drawing vehicle are references to the weights so to be imposed both of the trailer and of any load or persons carried by it except where only the load of the trailer is imposed on the drawing vehicle.

(d) This item need not be completed in the case of a trailer manufactured before 1st April 1970.

(e) This item need not be completed in the case of a trailer manufactured before 1st October 1972.

(f) This item need not be completed in the case of a trailer manufactured before 1st October 1972 or which forms part of an articulated vehicle.

B15.396   *[Part II of Sch.8 is printed as amended by SI 1991/1526.]*

Part III

B15.397   1. The power of an engine, which is to be shown only in the case of a compression ignition engine on the plate in respect of item 3 in Part I of this Schedule, shall be the amount in kilowatts equivalent to the installed power output shown in a type test certificate issued—

(a) by a person authorised by the Secretary of State for the type of engine to which the engine conforms; and

(b) in accordance with either—

(i) the provisions relating to the installed brake power output specified in the British Standard Specification for the Performance of Diesel Engines for Road Vehicles published on 19th May 1971 under the number BS AU 141a: 1971;

(ii) the provisions relating to the net power specified in Community Directive 80/1269 but after allowance has been made for the power absorbed by such equipment, at its minimum power setting, driven by the engine of the vehicle as is fitted for the operation of the vehicle (other than its propulsion) such power being measured at the speed corresponding to the engine speed at which maximum engine power is developed; or

(iii) the provisions of Annex 10 of ECE Regulations 24.02 as further amended with effect from 15th February 1984 [or Annex 10 of ECE Regulation 24.03 or Community Directive 88/195] relating to the method of measuring internal combustion engine net power, but after allowance has been made for the power absorbed by any disconnectable or progressive cooling fan, at its maximum setting, and by any other such equipment, at its minimum power setting, driven by the engine of the vehicle as is fitted for the operation of the vehicle (other than its propulsion), such power being measured at the speed corresponding to the engine speed at which maximum engine power is developed.

[Paragraph 1 of Pt III of Sch.8 is printed as amended by SI 1990/1131.]   **B15.398**

2.—(1) [Subject to paragraph 3A,] the weights to be shown on the plate in relation to   **B15.399**
items 6, 7 and 8 in Part I and in relation to items 4, 5 and 6 in Part II shall be the weight
limits at or below which the vehicle is considered fit for use, having regard to its design,
construction and equipment and the stresses to which it is likely to be subject in use, by
the Secretary of State if the vehicle is one to which the Type Approval for Goods Vehicles
Regulations [or the Motor Vehicles (Approval) Regulations 2001] [*SI 2001/25*] apply, and
by the manufacturer if the vehicle is one to which those Regulations do not apply.

Provided that, where alterations are made to a vehicle which may render the vehicle fit for
use at weights which exceed those referred to above in this paragraph and shown on the
plate—

(a) there may be shown on the plate, in place of any of those weights, such new
weights as the manufacturer of the vehicle or any person carrying on business as a
manufacturer of motor vehicles or trailers (or a person duly authorised on behalf
of that manufacturer or any such person) or a person authorised by the Secretary
of State considers to represent the weight limits at or below which the vehicle will
then be fit for use, having regard to its design, construction and equipment and to
those alterations and to the stresses to which it is likely to be subject in use; and

(b) the name of the person who has determined the new weights shall be shown on the
plate as having made that determination and, where he is a person authorised by
the Secretary of State, his appointment shall be so shown.

(2) In relation to a vehicle manufactured on or after 1st October 1972, in the foregoing
paragraph —

(a) the references to equipment shall not be treated as including a reference to the type
of tyres with which the vehicle is equipped; and

(b) for the words "weight limits at or below" in both places where they occur there
shall be substituted the words "maximum weights at".

[Paragraph 2 of Pt III of Sch.8 is printed as amended by SI 2001/306.]   **B15.400**

3. [Subject to paragraph 3A,] the weights to be shown on the plate in respect of—   **B15.401**

(a) item 9 in Part I of this Schedule shall be the weights shown at item 6 in that Part
and in respect of item 7 in Part II of this Schedule shall be the weights shown at
item 4 in that Part, in each case reduced so far as necessary to indicate the
maximum weight applicable to each axle of the vehicle, if the vehicle is not to be
used in contravention of regulations 23, 75, 78 or 79, and if the tyres with which
the vehicle is equipped are not, as respects strength, to be inadequate to support
the weights to be so shown at item 9 and item 7;

(b) item 10 in the said Part I shall be the weight shown at item 7 in that Part and in respect of item 8 in the said Part II shall be the weight shown at item 6 in that Part,
in each case reduced so far as necessary to indicate the maximum permissible
weight applicable if the vehicle is not to be used in contravention of regulation 75
if the tyres with which the vehicle is equipped are not, as respects strength, to be
inadequate to support the weights to be so shown at item 10 and item 8.

[Paragraph 3 of Pt III of Sch.8 is printed as amended by SI 2001/306.]   **B15.402**

[**3A.** In the case of a vehicle—   **B15.403**

(a) which complies with the requirements specified in regulation 4(2) of the Motor
Vehicles (Approval) Regulations 2001;

(b) in respect of which a Minister's approval certificate has been issued under section
58 of the 1988 Act for the purposes of the type approval requirements prescribed
by those Regulations; and

(c) in respect of which a Minister's approval certificate has not subsequently been issued under that section for the purposes of the type approval requirements
prescribed by the Type Approval for Goods Vehicles Regulations,

the weight shown on the plate in relation to items 7 and 10 in Part I of this Schedule shall be 3,500 kg.]

B15.404   *[Paragraph 3A of Pt III of Sch.8 was inserted by SI 2001/306.]*

B15.405   **4.**—(1) Subject to sub-paragraph (2) of this paragraph weights on plates first affixed to a vehicle on or after 1st October 1972 shall be shown in kilograms and weights on plates first so affixed before that date shall be shown in tons and decimals thereof.

(2) Where a new weight is first shown on a plate by virtue of the proviso to paragraph 2(1) the weight shall be shown as if it was on a plate first affixed to a vehicle on the date it was first shown.

B15.406   **5.** All letters and figures shown on the plate shall be not less than 6mm in height.

B15.407   **6.** In this Schedule references to the manufacturer of a motor vehicle or trailer are in relation to—

(a) a vehicle constructed with a chassis which has not previously formed part of another vehicle, references to the person by whom that chassis was made;

(b) any other vehicle, references to the person by whom that vehicle was constructed.

(see regulation 69)   SCHEDULE 9

PLATES FOR MOTOR CYCLES

B15.408   **1.** The plate required by regulation 69 shall be firmly attached to a part of the motor cycle which is not normally subject to replacement during the life of the motor cycle.

B15.409   **2.** The plate shall be in the form shown in the diagram in this paragraph, shall have dimensions not less than those shown in that diagram and shall show the information provided for in that diagram and detailed in the Notes below.

Diagram of Plate

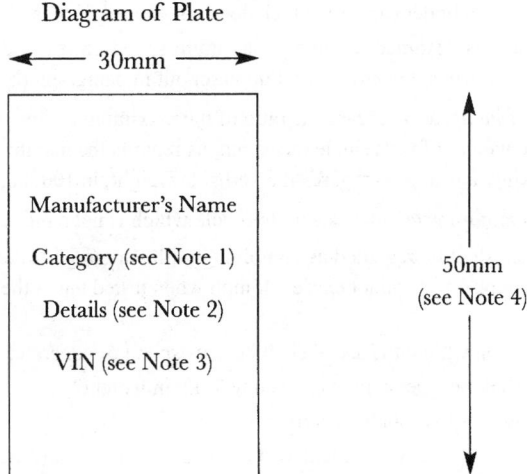

Notes:

    1. The categories are "standard motor cycle" and "moped".

    2. The details are—

      (a) for standard motor cycles—

         (i) the engine capacity,

         (ii) the maximum engine power, and

         (iii) the power to weight ratio,

       provided that the details under (ii) and (iii) need not be shown for a vehicle first used before 1st January 1982;

      (b) for mopeds—

         (i) the engine capacity,

         (ii) the kerbside weight, and

         (iii) the maximum speed.

    3. The vehicle identification number (VIN) shall be marked in the form used by the manufacturer to identify any one individual vehicle.

    4. In the case of a plate fitted to a vehicle first used before 1st January 1982 or to a moped this dimension shall be 40mm.

3. The information on the plate shall be shown in characters not less than 4mm in height **B15.410** and in the positions on the plate indicated in the diagram above.

4. No information, other than that provided for in the diagram above, shall be marked **B15.411** within the rectangle which is shown in that diagram.

5. In this Schedule and, in respect of the definition of "moped", in regulations 54 and **B15.412** 57—

      "maximum engine power" means the maximum net power the motor cycle engine will develop, in kilowatts, when measured in accordance with the test conditions specified in the International Standard number ISO 4106 developed by the technical committee of the International Organisation for Standardisation, and approved by member bodies, including the United Kingdom, and published under the reference ISO 1978 4106-09-01;

      "moped" means a motor cycle which—

         (a) has a kerbside weight not exceeding 250kg, and

(b) if propelled by an internal combustion engine, has an engine with a cylinder capacity which does not exceed 50cc, and

(c) is designed to have a maximum speed not exceeding 30mph when driven under the conditions set out in paragraph 6;

"power to weight ratio" means the ratio of the maximum engine power to the kerbside weight of the vehicle measured, as regards the maximum engine power, in kilowatts and, as regards the kerbside weight, in 1000kg;

"standard motor cycle" means a motor cycle which is not a moped.

B15.413   6. A motor cycle shall be regarded as complying with paragraph (c) of the definition of "moped" in paragraph 5 if it cannot exceed 35mph when tested under the following conditions—

(a) the surface on which it is tested shall be dry asphalt or concrete;

(b) the rider shall be a person not exceeding 75kg in weight;

(c) no passenger or load shall be carried;

(d) the test route shall be so located that acceleration to, and deceleration from, maximum speed can take place elsewhere than on the test route itself;

(e) the test route shall not have a gradient exceeding 5%;

(f) when being driven along the test route, the motor cycle shall be driven in such manner and in such gear as to achieve the maximum speed of which it is capable; and

(g) if the motor cycle is fitted with a device which can, without the use of specialist tools or equipment, be readily modified or removed so as to increase its maximum speed, the test shall be carried out with the device in the modified condition or, as the case may be, without the device.

(see regulation 70)   SCHEDULE 10

MINISTRY PLATE

PLATE	DEPARTMENT OF TRANSPORT [Road Traffic Act 1988, Sections 41 and 54] Examination of Goods Vehicles			Serial No. DTp REF. No.
REGISTRATION/IDENTIFICATION MARK	YEAR OF ORIGINAL REGISTRATION	YEAR OF MANUFACTURE	FUNCTION	MAKE AND MODEL
CHASSIS/SERIAL No.		UNLADEN WEIGHT		

(1) DESCRIPTION OF WEIGHTS APPLICABLE TO VEHICLE	(2) WEIGHTS NOT TO BE EXCEEDED IN GREAT BRITAIN KILOGRAMS	(3) DESIGN WEIGHTS (if higher than shown in col (2)) KILOGRAMS	
AXLE WEIGHT (Axles numbered from front to rear) — AXLE 1			
AXLE 2			
AXLE 3			
AXLE 4			
GROSS WEIGHT (see warning opposite)			
TRAIN WEIGHT (see warning opposite)			DATE OF ISSUE

WARNING
1. A reduced gross weight may apply in certain cases to a vehicle towing or being towed by another.
2. A reduced train weight may apply depending on the type of trailer drawn.
3. All weights shown are subject to fitting of correct tyres.

NOTES: 1. A Ministry plate may contain the words "MINISTRY OF TRANSPORT" or "DEPARTMENT OF TRANSPORT" instead of the words "DEPARTMENT OF TRANSPORT", and may contain the words "Road Safety Act 1967, Sections 8 and 9" or the words "Road Traffic Act 1972, Sections 40 and 45" [or the words "Road Traffic Act 1988, Sections 41 and 49"]. (In a case where the Type Approval for Goods Vehicles Regulations do not apply.) It may also contain additional columns in Columns (2) and (3) showing the weights in tons.

2. Entries in respect of train weight are required in the case of—(a) a motor vehicle constructed or adapted to draw a trailer and is first used on or after 1st April 1983.

3. A Ministry plate shows the unladen weight and function of the vehicle in a case where the Type Approval for Goods Vehicles Regulations apply.

4. A Ministry plate may have separate spaces for the "make" and "model" of the vehicle.

5. A Ministry plate may have no "Reference Number" or may refer to the "Department of the Environment Reference No".

B15.415

MINISTRY PLATE

DEPARTMENT OF TRANSPORT
[Road Traffic Act 1988, Sections 41, 49 and 54]
Examination of Goods Vehicles

SERIAL NUMBER		
UNLADEN WEIGHT	DTp REF No	

PLATE VTG 6A

REGISTRATION/IDENTIFICATION MARK	YEAR OF ORIGINAL REG	
MANUFACTURER/MODEL	YEAR OF MANUFACTURE	FUNCTION
TYPE APPROVAL/VARIANT No		
VEHICLE IDENTIFICATION No		

(1) DESCRIPTION OF WEIGHTS APPLICABLE TO VEHICLE	(2) WEIGHT NOT TO BE EXCEEDED IN Gt. BRITAIN	(3) EEC MAXIMUM PERMITTED WEIGHTS (See Note 4)	(4) DESIGN WEIGHTS (if higher than shown in column 2)
GROSS WEIGHT (See warning below)			
TRAIN WEIGHT (See warning below)			
MAXIMUM TRAIN WEIGHT (See Note 3)			
AXLE WEIGHTS (Axles numbered from front to rear) Axle 1			
Axle 2			
Axle 3			
Axle 4			
MAXIMUM KINGPIN LOAD (Semi-trailers only)			

5. VEHICLE DIMENSIONS

	MAXIMUM	MINIMUM
LENGTH (L)		
WIDTH (W)		
a. (See Note 1) COUPLING CENTRE TO VEHICLE FOREMOST PART	MAXIMUM	MINIMUM
b. (See Note 2) COUPLING CENTRE TO VEHICLE REARMOST PART		

DATE OF ISSUE

N.B. ALL WEIGHTS IN KILOGRAMS/ALL DIMENSIONS IN MILLIMETRES.

WARNING

a. A reduced gross weight may apply in certain cases to a vehicle towing or being towed by another.
b. A reduced train weight may apply depending on the type of trailer drawn.
c. All weights shown are subject to the fitting of correct tyres.

NOTES

1. This dimension only applies to drawing vehicles of trailers and semi-trailers.
2. This dimension only applies to trailers and semi-trailers.
3. This weight only applies to a 3 axle tractor with a 2 or 3 axle semi-trailer carrying a 40 foot ISO container as a combined transport operation.
4. Where there is no weight shown in the EEC maximum permitted weights column this is because there is no EEC standard relating to that weight.

NOTES

1. Entries in respect of train weight are required in the case of—(a) a motor vehicle constructed or adapted to form an articulated vehicle; and (b) a rigid vehicle which is constructed or adapted to draw a trailer and is first used on or after 1st April 1983.
2. A Ministry plate shows the unladen weight and function of the vehicle in a case where the Type Approval for Goods Vehicles Regulations apply.
3. A Ministry plate may have no "Reference Number".]

[Schedule 10A was inserted by SI 1987/676 and is printed as amended by the **B15.416**
Interpretation Act 1978 ss.17(2)(a) and 23(1).]

(see regulation 3(2))   [SCHEDULE 10B

B15.417

Department of Transport *ROAD TRAFFIC ACT 1988 SECTIONS 41, 49, 57 & 59* *EXAMINATION OF GOODS VEHICLES*		Serial No.	**V**	
Plate VTG 6T Rev. 92		DTp Ref. No.		

Reg./Ident. Mark		Vehicle Identification No.		Type Approval No./Variant	
Manufacturer/ Model					Speed Limiter Exempt
Function *(See note 3 below)*		Year of Original Registration			Year of Manufacture

(1) Description of Weights applicable to vehicle	(2) Weights not to be exceeded in GL Britain		(3) Design Weights *(If higher than shown in column 2)*	
Gross Weight *(See notes 1 & 4 below)*				
Train Weight *(See note 2 below)*				
Max. Train Weight *(See note 5 below)*				Date of Issue
Axle Weights *(Axles numbered from front to rear) (See note 1 overleaf)* Axle 1				
Axle 2				DEPARTMENT OF
Axle 3				TRANSPORT GREAT BRITAIN
Axle 4				

NOTES 1. A reduced gross weight and/or axle weight may apply in certain cases to a vehicle towing or being towed by another. 2. The MAXIMUM permissible train weight can vary depending on the type of suspension and trailer drawn. 3. If the last letter in the function box is "R" road friendly suspension is fitted. 4. All weights shown are subject to the fitting of correct tyres. 5. This weight applies to combined transport operations.	Tyre use conditions applicable to vehicle N. B. All weights in Kilograms

Note: A weight is not required in the box for Maximum Train Weight unless the vehicle is capable of being lawfully used on a road in Great Britain, having regard to Schedule 11A, at a greater train weight than the train weight at which it could lawfully be used ignoring that Schedule.]

B15.418   *[Schedule 10B was inserted by SI 1994/329.]*

(see regulation 3(2))   [SCHEDULE 10C

Department of Transport ROAD TRAFFIC ACT 1988 SECTIONS 41, 49, 57 & 59 EXAMINATION OF GOODS VEHICLES This is issued as proof of compliance with the Weights and Dimensions Directive 86/3/EEC **Plate** VTG 6A					Serial No. **B** DTp Ref. No.			
Reg./Ident. Mark		Vehicle Identification No.				Type Approval No./Variant		
Manufacturer/ Model						Speed Limiter Exempt		
Function (See note 3 below)		Year of Original Registration				Year of Manufacture		
(1) Description of Weights applicable to vehicle	(2) Weights not to be exceeded in Gt. Britain	(3) EEC Maximum permitted weights (See note 8 below)	(4) Design Weights (If higher than shown in column 2)	Length			Width	
Gross Weight (See notes 1 & 4 below)				a Coupling centre to vehicle foremost part (See note 6 below)			Max	Min
Train Weight (See note 2 below)				b Coupling centre to vehicle rearmost part (See note 7 below)			Max	Min
Max. Train Weight (See note 5 below)				Date of Issue				
Axle Weights (Axles numbered from front to rear) (See note 1 overleaf)	Axle 1			👑 DEPARTMENT OF TRANSPORT GREAT BRITAIN				
	Axle 2							
	Axle 3							
	Axle 4			Tyre use conditions applicable to vehicle				
Maximum Kingpin Load (Semi-Trailers only)				NOTES (cont'd) 6. This dimension only applies to drawing vehicles of trailers and semi-trailers.				

NOTES
1. A reduced gross weight and/or axle weight may apply in certain cases to a vehicle towing or being towed by another.
2. The MAXIMUM permissible train weight can vary depending on the type of suspension and trailer drawn.
3. If the last letter in the function box is "R" road friendly suspension is fitted.
4. All weights shown are subject to the fitting of correct tyres.
5. This weight applies to combined transport operations.

7. This dimension only applies to trailers and semi-trailers.
8. Where there is no weight shown in the EEC maximum permitted weights column this is because there is no EEC standard relating to that weight.

N. B. All weights in Kilograms

Note: A weight is not required in the box for Maximum Train Weight unless the vehicle is capable of being lawfully used on a road in Great Britain, having regard to Schedule 11A, at a greater train weight than the train weight at which it could lawfully be used ignoring that Schedule.]

[Schedule 10C was inserted by SI 1994/329.]

(see regulations 75, 77 and 79)   SCHEDULE 11

MAXIMUM PERMITTED WEIGHTS, ETC.

(SEE REGULATION 75)

[PART I

MAXIMUM PERMITTED LADEN WEIGHTS OF (1) TRAILERS AND (2) HEAVY MOTOR CARS AND MOTOR CARS NOT FITTED WITH ROAD FRIENDLY SUSPENSION; IN EACH CASE NOT FORMING PART OF AN ARTICULATED VEHICLE

1. The maximum permitted laden weight of a two or three axle vehicle to which this Part applies of a description specified in column 2 of Table I below shall, for the purposes of regulation 75, be the weight specified in column 3 of that item.

B15.422   2. In the case of a vehicle to which this Part applies and which is not of a description specified in an item in column 2 of Table I below, the maximum permitted laden weight shall, for the purposes of regulation 75, be the weight specified in column 4 of Table II below in the item which is appropriate having regard to columns 2 and 3 of that Table.

TABLE I

MAXIMUM PERMITTED LADEN WEIGHTS OF CERTAIN TWO AND THREE AXLE VEHICLES

(1) Item	(2) Description of Vehicle	(3) Maximum permitted laden weight (kg)
1	A two axle trailer in which— (a) the two axles are closely spaced, and (b) the distance between the foremost axle of the trailer and the rearmost axle of the drawing vehicle is at least 4.2m	18,000
2	A three axle trailer in which— (a) the three axles are closely spaced, and (b) the distance between the foremost axle of the trailer and the rearmost axle of the drawing vehicle is at least 4.2m	24,000
3	A two axle motor vehicle which is a goods vehicle in which the distance between the foremost and rearmost axles is at least 3.0m	17,000
4	A two axle trailer in which the distance between the foremost axle and the rearmost axle is at least 3.0m	18,000

TABLE II

MAXIMUM PERMITTED LADEN WEIGHTS OF VEHICLES NOT FALLING WITHIN TABLE I

(1) Item	(2) No. of axles	(3) Distance between foremost and rearmost axles (metres)	(4) Maximum permitted laden weight (kg)
1	2	Less than 2.65	14,230
2	2	At least 2.65	16,260
3	3 or more	Less than 3.0	16,260
4	3 or more	At least 3.0 but less than 3.2	18,290
5	3 or more	At least 3.2 but less than 3.9	20,330
6	3 or more	At least 3.9 but less than 4.9	22,360
7	3	At least 4.9	25,000
8	4 or more	At least 4.9 but less than 5.6	25,000
9	4 or more	At least 5.6 but less than 5.9	26,420
10	4 or more	At least 5.9 but less than 6.3	28,450
11	4 or more	At least 6.3	30,000]

B15.423   *[Part I of Sch.11 is printed as substituted by SI 1992/2016.]*

[PART IA

MAXIMUM PERMITTED GROSS WEIGHTS FOR HEAVY CARS AND MOTOR CARS IF THE DRIVING AXLES
ARE FITTED WITH ROAD FRIENDLY SUSPENSION, ETC., AND IN EACH CASE NOT FORMING PART OF
AN ARTICULATED VEHICLE

1. Subject to paragraph 2, the maximum permitted gross weight of a vehicle to which **B15.424**
this Part applies shall, for the purposes of regulation 75, be the weight shown in column 4
of the Table below in the item which is appropriate, having regard to columns 2 and 3 in
that Table.

2. In the case of a vehicle to which this Part applies being a two axle goods vehicle **B15.425**
which has a distance between its axles of at least 3.0m, the maximum permitted laden
weight for the purposes of regulation 75 shall be 17,000kg.

TABLE
MAXIMUM PERMITTED LADEN WEIGHT

(1) Item	(2) No. of axles	(3) Distance between foremost and rearmost axles (metres)	(4) Maximum permitted laden weight (kg)
1	2	Less than 2.65	14,230
2	2	At least 2.65	16,260
3	3 or more	Less than 3.0	16,260
4	3 or more	At least 3.0 but less than 3.2	18,290
5	3 or more	At least 3.2 but less than 3.9	20,330
6	3 or more	At least 3.9 but less than 4.9	22,360
7	3 or more	At least 4.9 but less than 5.2	25,000
8	3	At least 5.2	26,000
9	4 or more	At least 5.2 but less than 6.4	The distance in metres between the foremost and rearmost axles multiplied by 5,000, rounded up to the next 10kg
10	4 or more	At least 6.4	32,000]

[Part IA of Sch.11 was inserted by SI 1992/2016.]   **B15.426**

(see regulation 75)

Part II

MAXIMUM PERMITTED LADEN WEIGHTS FOR HEAVY MOTOR CARS AND MOTOR CARS FORMING PART OF ARTICULATED VEHICLES

B15.427

1	2	3	4	5
Item	No. of axles	Distance between foremost and rearmost axles (metres)	Weight not exceeded by any axle not being the foremost or rearmost (kg)	Maximum permitted laden weight (kg)
1	2	At least 2.0	—	14,230
2	2	At least 2.4	—	16,260
3	2	At least 2.7	—	17,000
4	3 or more	At least 3.0	8,390	20,330
5	3 or more	At least 3.8	8,640	22,360
6	3 or more	At least 4.0	10,500	22,500
7	3 or more	At least 4.3	9,150	24,390
8	3 or more	At least 4.9	10,500	24,390

B15.428   *[Part II of Sch.11 is printed as amended by SI 1987/676.]*

(see regulation 77)

Part III

MAXIMUM PERMITTED LADEN WEIGHT OF ARTICULATED VEHICLES

B15.429

1	2		3
Item	Relevant axle spacing (metres)		Maximum weight (kg)
	(a) Where motor vehicle has 2 axles	(b) Where motor vehicle has more than 2 axles	
1	At least 2.0	At least 2.0	20,330
2	At least 2.2	At least 2.2	22,360
3	At least 2.6	At least 2.6	23,370
4	At least 2.9	At least 2.9	24,390
5	At least 3.2	At least 3.2	25,410
6	At least 3.5	At least 3.5	26,420
7	At least 3.8	At least 3.8	27,440
8	At least 4.1	At least 4.1	28,450
9	At least 4.4	At least 4.4	29,470
10	At least 4.7	At least 4.7	30,490
11	At least 5.0	At least 5.0	31,500
12	At least 5.3	At least 5.3	32,520
13	At least 5.5	At least 5.4	33,000

1	2		3
Item	Relevant axle spacing (metres)		Maximum weight (kg)
	(a) Where motor vehicle has 2 axles	(b) Where motor vehicle has more than 2 axles	
14	At least 5.8	At least 5.6	34,000
15	At least 6.2	At least 5.8	35,000
16	At least 6.5	At least 6.0	36,000
17	At least 6.7	At least 6.2	37,000
18	At least 6.9	At least 6.3	38,000

[Part III of Sch.11 is printed as amended by SI 1994/329.]   **B15.430**

(SEE REGULATION 77)

[PART IV

MAXIMUM PERMITTED LADEN WEIGHT OF ARTICULATED VEHICLES

B15.431

(1) Item	(2) Type of articulated vehicle	(3) Maximum permitted weight (kg)
1	Motor vehicle first used on or after 1st April 1973 and semi-trailer having a total of 5 or more axles	38,000
2	Motor vehicle with 2 axles first used on or after 1st April 1973 and semi-trailer with 2 axles while being used for international transport	35,000
3	Motor vehicle with 2 axles first used on or after 1st April 1973 in which— (a) every driving axle not being a steering axle is fitted with twin tyres; and (b) every driving axle is fitted with road friendly suspension; and a semi-trailer with 2 axles	35,000
4	[Motor vehicle and semi-trailer having a total of 4 or more axles and not described in item 1, 2 or 3]	32,520
5	Motor vehicle with 2 axles first used on or after 1st April 1973 in which— (a) every driving axle not being a steering axle is fitted with twin tyres; and (b) every driving axle is fitted with road friendly suspension; and a semi-trailer with 1 axle	26,000
6	Motor vehicle with 2 axles and a semi-trailer with 1 axle being a combination not described in item 5	25,000]

[Part IV of Sch.11 is printed as substituted by SI 1992/2016 and as subsequently amended by SI 1994/329.]   **B15.432**

[Part V

Vehicles with Two Closely-Spaced Axles

B15.433

(1) Item	(2) Description of vehicle	(3) Maximum permitted weight of the two closely-spaced axles (kg)
1	A motor vehicle or trailer in which (in either case) the distance between the two closely-spaced axles is less than 1.3 metres	16,000
2	A vehicle being— (a) a motor vehicle in which the distance between the two closely-spaced axles is at least 1.3m, or (b) a trailer in which that distance is at least 1.3m and less than 1.5m, not being a vehicle described in item 3 or 4	18,000
3	A motor vehicle in which the distance between the two closely-spaced axles is at least 1.3m and— (a) every driving axle not being a steering axle is fitted with twin tyres; and (b) either every driving axle is fitted with road friendly suspension or neither of the two closely-spaced axles has an axle weight exceeding 9,500kg	19,000
4	A trailer in which— (a) the two closely-spaced axles are driven from the motor vehicle drawing the trailer and are fitted with twin tyres; and (b) either those axles are fitted with road friendly suspension or neither of them has an axle weight exceeding 9,500kg	19,000
5	A trailer in which the distance between the two closely-spaced axles is at least 1.5m and less than 1.8m	19,320
6	A trailer in which the distance between the two closely-spaced axles is at least 1.8m	20,000]

B15.434   *[Part V of Sch.11 is printed as substituted by SI 1992/2016.]*

(REGULATION 79(3))

[PART VI

VEHICLES WITH THREE CLOSELY-SPACED AXLES

B15.435

(1) Item	(2) Description of vehicle	(3) Maximum permitted weight of the three closely-spaced axles (kg)
1	A vehicle in which the smallest distance between any two of the three closely-spaced axles is less than 1.3m	21,000
2	A vehicle in which the smallest distance between any two of the three closely-spaced axles is at least 1.3m and at least one of those axles does not have air suspension	22,500
3	A vehicle in which the smallest distance between any two of the three closely-spaced axles is at least 1.3m and all three axles are fitted with air suspension	24,000]

[Part VI of Sch.11 is printed as substituted by SI 1992/2016.]   **B15.436**

PART VII

[...]   **B15.437**

[Revoked by SI 1992/2016.]

(see regulations 76(1A),   [SCHEDULE 11A
77(2A) and [80(2B)])

EXEMPTIONS RELATING TO COMBINED TRANSPORT OPERATIONS

[Schedule 11A was inserted by SI 1994/329 and the heading to the Schedule is   **B15.438**
printed as amended by SI 1997/1096.]

PART I

GENERAL

1. Regulation 76 does not apply to a wheeled heavy motor car drawing one wheeled   **B15.439**
trailer if the requirements set out in Part II of this Schedule are for the time being fulfilled.

[Schedule 11A (paras 1, 2, 3–8, and 9) was inserted by SI 1994/329.]

2. Regulation 77 does not apply to an articulated vehicle if the requirements set out in   **B15.440**
Part III of this Schedule are for the time being fulfilled.

[Schedule 11A (paras 1, 2, 3–8, and 9) was inserted by SI 1994/329.]

[2A. Regulation 75, 76, 77 and 78 do not apply to an articulated vehicle if the require-   **B15.441**
ments set out in Part IIIA of this Schedule are for the time being fulfilled.]

[Paragraph 2A of Sch.11A was inserted by SI 1998/3112.]

PART II

DRAWBAR COMBINATIONS

3.—(1) The drawing vehicle and trailer must each be carrying a relevant receptacle as   **B15.442**
part of a combined transport operation, each such receptacle being on a journey—

    (a) to a railhead from which the relevant receptacle is, as part of the operation, to be transported in a relevant manner by railway pursuant to a relevant contract made before the journey began; or

   (b) from a railhead to which the relevant receptacle has, as part of the operation, been transported in a relevant manner by railway.

(2) There must be carried in the cab of the drawing vehicle a document or documents—

   (a) if the vehicle is on a journey to a railhead, specifying the railhead, the date the relevant contract was made and the parties thereto;

   (b) if the vehicle is on a journey from a railhead, specifying the railhead and the date and time at which the receptacles were collected from that railhead.

B15.443   *[Schedule 11A (paras 1, 2, 3–8, and 9) was inserted by SI 1994/329.]*

B15.444   4. The following conditions must be satisfied in relation to the drawing vehicle, namely—

   (a) it complies with the relevant braking requirement;

   (b) every driving axle not being a steering axle is fitted with twin tyres; and

   (c) either every driving axle is fitted with road friendly suspension or no axle has an axle weight exceeding 8,500kg.

B15.445   *[Schedule 11A (paras 1, 2, 3–8, and 9) was inserted by SI 1994/329.]*

B15.446   5.—(1) The motor vehicle and trailer must have a total of at least 6 axles.

(2) The total laden weight of the motor vehicle and trailer must not exceed 44,000kg.

B15.447   *[Schedule 11A (paras 1, 2, 3–8, and 9) was inserted by SI 1994/329.]*

PART III

ARTICULATED VEHICLES

B15.448   6.—(1) The motor vehicle comprised in the articulated vehicle must be being used for the conveyance of a loading unit as part of a combined transport operation, the loading unit being on a journey—

   (a) to a railhead from which the loading unit is, as part of the operation, to be transported in a relevant manner by railway pursuant to a relevant contract made before the journey began; or

   (b) from a railhead to which the loading unit has, as part of the operation, been transported in a relevant manner by railway.

(2) If the loading unit is a bi-modal vehicle, the semi-trailer comprised in the articulated vehicle must be the bi-modal vehicle in its semi-trailer mode.

(3) If the loading unit is a relevant receptacle, the relevant receptacle must be being carried on the semi-trailer comprised in the articulated vehicle.

(4) There must be carried in the cab of the motor vehicle a document or documents—

   (a) if the vehicle is on a journey to a railhead, specifying the railhead, the date the contract was made and the parties thereto;

   (b) if the vehicle is on a journey from a railhead, specifying the railhead and the date and time at which the loading unit was collected from that railhead.

B15.449   7. The following conditions must be satisfied in relation to the motor vehicle, namely—

   (a) it complies with the relevant braking requirements;

   (b) it has at least three axles;

   (c) every driving axle not being a steering axle is fitted with twin tyres; and

   (d) either every driving axle is fitted with road friendly suspension or no axle has an axle weight exceeding 8,500kg.

B15.450   *[Schedule 11A (paras 1, 2, 3–8, and 9) was inserted by SI 1994/329.]*

B15.451   [8.—(1) The articulated vehicle must have a total of at least 6 axles.

(2) The laden weight of the articulated vehicle must not exceed the weight determined in accordance with sub-paragraph (3).

(3) The weight for the purposes of sub-paragraph (2) is the number of kilograms equal to the product of the distance measured in metres between the king-pin and the centre of the rearmost axle of the semi-trailer by 5500 and rounded up to the nearest 10kg, if that number is less than 44000kg.]

[Schedule 11A (paras 1, 2, 3–8, and 9) was inserted by SI 1994/329. Paragraph 8 is printed as substituted by SI 1998/3112.]   **B15.452**

[Pᴀʀᴛ IIIA

Aʀᴛɪᴄᴜʟᴀᴛᴇᴅ Vᴇʜɪᴄʟᴇs (Aʟᴛᴇʀɴᴀᴛɪᴠᴇ RᴇQᴜɪʀᴇᴍᴇɴᴛs)]

[8A.—(1) The requirements of paragraph 6 are fulfilled.   **B15.453**

(2) The vehicle is one which falls within the first indent of paragraph 1 of Article 3 of Community Directive 96/53 [*q.v.*] (vehicles used in international traffic or put into circulation in any other Member State) and complies with the limit values specified in paragraph 2.2.2 of Annex I and the other relevant requirements of that Directive.]

[Paragraph 8A of Sch.11A, and the Pt IIIA heading immediately preceding it, was inserted by SI 1998/3112.]   **B15.454**

Pᴀʀᴛ IV

Iɴᴛᴇʀᴘʀᴇᴛᴀᴛɪᴏɴ

9.—(1) In this Schedule —   **B15.455**

"*bi-modal vehicle*" means a semi-trailer which can be adapted for use as a railway vehicle;

"*journey*", except in sub-paragraph (3), means a journey by road;

"*loading unit*" means a bi-modal vehicle[, road-rail semi-trailer] or a relevant receptacle;

"*railhead*" means a facility for the transhipment of—

    (a) bi-modal vehicles from the ground onto the track of a railway, or

    (b) relevant receptacles from road vehicles onto railway vehicles situated on the track of a railway, [or]

    [(c) road-rail semi-trailers from the ground onto railway vehicles on the track of a railway,]

  or vice versa;

"*relevant contract*" means a contract for the transport of a loading unit by railway;

"*relevant receptacle*" means a receptacle (not being a vehicle) having a length of at least 6.1m designed and constructed for repeated use for the carriage of goods on, and for transfer between, road vehicles and railway vehicles;

["*road-rail semi-trailer*" means a semi-trailer constructed or adapted so as to be capable of being both used as a semi-trailer on roads and carried on a railway vehicle;]

"*road friendly suspension*" and "*twin tyres*" have the meanings given by regulation 75; and

"*network*", "*network licence*", "*railway vehicle*", "*track*" and "*train*" have the meanings given by section 83 of the Railways Act 1993.

(2) The definition of "*railway*" in section 67(1) of the Transport and Works Act 1992 shall have effect for the purposes of this Schedule as it has effect for the purposes of that Act, and cognate expressions shall be construed accordingly.

(3) In these Regulations, a reference to a combined transport operation is a reference to the transport of a loading unit on a journey where—

    (a) part of the journey is by railway on a network operated by the British Railways Board or under a network licence;

(b) part of the journey is by road; and

(c) no goods are added to or removed from the loading unit between the time when the journey begins and the time when it ends.

(4) Subject to sub-paragraph (5), for the purposes of this Schedule —

(a) a bi-modal vehicle shall be regarded as being transported by railway in a relevant manner if and only if the vehicle in its railway vehicle mode is travelling by railway as part of a train; ...

(b) a relevant receptacle shall be regarded as being transported by railway in a relevant manner if and only if it is being carried on a railway vehicle which forms part of a train [; and]

[(c) a road-rail semi-trailer shall be regarded as being transported by railway in a relevant manner if and only if it is being carried on a railway vehicle which forms part of a train.]

(5) A relevant receptacle shall be regarded, for the purposes of this Schedule, as not being transported by railway in a relevant manner at any time when—

(a) the relevant receptacle is in or on a motor vehicle or trailer; and

(b) the motor vehicle or trailer is being carried on a railway vehicle.]

[(6) A road-rail semi-trailer shall be regarded, for the purposes of this Schedule, as not being transported by railway in a relevant manner at any time when it is being carried on a railway vehicle as part of an articulated vehicle.]

B15.456   *[Schedule 11A (paras 1, 2, 3–8, and 9) was inserted by SI 1994/329. Paragraph 9 is printed as amended by SI 1997/1096.*

The Railways Act 1993 s.83(1), defines "network", "network licence", "railway vehicle", "track" and "train" in the following terms:

"network" means—

(a) any railway line, or combination of two or more railway lines, and

(b) any installations associated with any of the track comprised in that line or those lines,

together constituting a system of track and other installations which is used for and in connection with the support, guidance and operation of trains;

"network licence" means a licence authorising a person—

(a) to be the operator of a network;

(b) to be the operator of a train being used on a network for any purpose comprised in the operation of that network; and

(c) to be the operator of a train being used on a network for a purpose preparatory or incidental to, or consequential on, using a train as mentioned in paragraph (b) above;

"railway vehicle" includes anything which, whether or not it is constructed or adapted to carry any person or load, is constructed or adapted to run on flanged wheels over or along track;

"track" means any land or other property comprising the permanent way of any railway, taken together with the ballast, sleepers and metals laid thereon, whether or not the land or other property is also used for other purposes; and any reference to track includes a reference to—

(a) any level crossings, bridges, viaducts, tunnels, culverts, retaining walls, or other structures used or to be used for the support of, or otherwise in connection with, track; and

(b) any walls, fences or other structures bounding the railway or bounding any adjacent or adjoining property;

"train" means—

        (a) two or more items of rolling stock coupled together, at least one of which is a locomotive; or

        (b) a locomotive not coupled to any other rolling stock;

The Transport and Works Act 1992 s.67(1), defines "railway" in the following terms:

        "railway" means a system of transport employing parallel rails which—

        (a) provide support and guidance for vehicles carried on flanged wheels, and

        (b) form a track which either is of a gauge of at least 350 millimetres or crosses a carriageway (whether or not on the same level),

but does not include a tramway; *]*

(see regulations 81 and 82)   SCHEDULE 12

Cᴏɴᴅɪᴛɪᴏɴs ᴛᴏ ʙᴇ Cᴏᴍᴘʟɪᴇᴅ ᴡɪᴛʜ ɪɴ Rᴇʟᴀᴛɪᴏɴ ᴛᴏ ᴛʜᴇ Usᴇ ᴏꜰ Vᴇʜɪᴄʟᴇs Cᴀʀʀʏɪɴɢ Wɪᴅᴇ ᴏʀ Lᴏɴɢ Lᴏᴀᴅs ᴏʀ Vᴇʜɪᴄʟᴇs Cᴀʀʀʏɪɴɢ Lᴏᴀᴅs ᴏʀ ʜᴀᴠɪɴɢ Fɪxᴇᴅ Aᴘᴘʟɪᴀɴᴄᴇs ᴏʀ Aᴘᴘᴀʀᴀᴛᴜs ᴡʜɪᴄʜ Pʀᴏᴊᴇᴄᴛ

Pᴀʀᴛ I

Advance notice to police

1. (a) Before using on a road a vehicle or vehicles to which this paragraph applies, the owner shall give notice of the intended use to the Chief Officer of Police for any area in which he proposes to use the vehicle or vehicles. The notice shall be given so that it is received by the date after which there are at least two working days before the date on which the use of the vehicle or vehicles is to begin, and shall include the following details— **B15.457**

    (i) time, date and route of the proposed journey, and

    [(ia) in a case to which regulation 7(9) applies, the overall length of the trailer,]

    (ii) in a case to which regulation 82(2) applies, the overall length and width of the vehicle by which the load is carried and the width of the lateral projection or projections of its load,

    (iii) in a case to which regulation 82(4)(a) applies, the overall length and width of each vehicle by which the load is carried, the length of any forward or rearward projection and, where the load rests on more than one vehicle, the distance between the vehicles,

    (iv) in a case to which regulation 82(4)(b) applies, the overall length of the combination of vehicles and the length of any forward or rearward projection of the load, and

    (v) in a case to which regulation 82(7) and (8) applies, the overall length of the vehicle and the length of any forward or rearward projection of the load or special appliance or apparatus.

The Chief Officer of Police for any police area may, at his discretion, accept a shorter period of notice or fewer details.

(b) The vehicle or vehicles shall be used only in accordance with the details at (a) subject to any variation in the time, date or route which may be directed by—

    (i) any such Chief Officer of Police to the owner of the vehicle or vehicles, or

    (ii) a police constable to the driver in the interests of road safety or in order to avoid undue traffic congestion by halting the vehicle or vehicles in a place on or adjacent to the road on which the vehicle or vehicles are travelling.

(c) In this paragraph —

 (i) *"Chief Officer of Police"* has, in relation to England and Wales, the same meaning as in the Police Act 1964 …,

 (ii) *"working day"* means a day which is not a Sunday, a bank holiday, Christmas Day or Good Friday, and

 (iii) *"bank holiday"* means a day which is a bank holiday by or under the Banking and Financial Dealings Act 1971, either generally or in the locality in which the road is situated.

B15.458 *[Paragraph 1 of Pt I of Sch.12 is printed as amended by SI 1991/2125.*

Words relating expressly and exclusively to Scotland have been omitted from para.1(c) above.

The term "chief officer of police" was defined in the Police Act 1964 s.62, as substituted by the Police and Magistrates' Courts Act 1994 s.44 and Sch.5, para.15; s.62 has, however, been repealed by the Police Act 1996 s.104(2) and Sch.9, Pt II. Reference should now be made (by virtue of s.103(2) of and Sch.8, para.1(4), to the 1996 Act) to s.1 of that Act (as amended) for the meaning of "police area" and to s.101(1) for the meaning of "chief officer of police".

The following are stated by the Banking and Financial Dealings Act 1971 Sch.1, para.1, to be bank holidays in England and Wales:

Easter Monday.
The last Monday in May.
The last Monday in August.
26th December, if it be not a Sunday.
27th December in a year in which 25th or 26th December is a Sunday.

Days may be substituted for or added to the above list by royal proclamation. In recent years January 1 (or 2), and the first Monday in May have been so added.]

Attendants

B15.459 **2.** At least one person in addition to the person or persons employed in driving a motor vehicle to which this paragraph applies shall be employed—

(a) in attending to that vehicle and its load and any other vehicle or vehicles drawn by that vehicle and the load or loads carried on the vehicle or vehicles so drawn, and

(b) to give warning to the driver of the said motor vehicle and to any person of any danger likely to be caused to any such person by reason of the presence of the said vehicle or vehicles on the road.

Provided that, where three or more vehicles as respects which the conditions in this paragraph are applicable are travelling together in convoy, it shall be a sufficient compliance with this paragraph if only the foremost and rearmost vehicles in the convoy are attended in the manner prescribed in this paragraph.

For the purpose of this paragraph when a motor vehicle is drawing a trailer or trailers—

 (i) any person employed in pursuance of section 34 of the 1972 Act in attending that vehicle or any such trailer shall be treated as being an attendant required by this paragraph so long as he is also employed to discharge the duties mentioned in this paragraph; and

 (ii) when another motor vehicle is used for the purpose of assisting in their propulsion on the road, the person or persons employed in driving that other motor vehicle shall not be treated as a person or persons employed in attending to the first-mentioned vehicle or any vehicle or vehicles drawn thereby.

[Section 34 of the Road Traffic Act 1972 (to which reference is made in para.2   **B15.460**
of Sch.12 above) was repealed by the Road Traffic (Consequential Provisions)
Act 1988 but not re-enacted. It seems therefore that para.2(i) above has lapsed.]

Marking of longer projections

3.(a) Every forward and rearward projection to which this paragraph applies shall be fit-   **B15.461**
ted with—

    (i) an end marker, except in the case of a rearward projection which is fitted
      with a rear marking in accordance with the Lighting Regulations, and

    (ii) where required by sub-paragraphs (c) and (d) of this paragraph, two or
      more side markers;

which shall be of the size, shape and colour described in Part II of this Schedule;

(b) the end marker shall be so fitted that—

    (i) it is as near as is practicable in a transverse plane,

    (ii) it is not more than 0.5m from the extreme end of the projection,

    (iii) the vertical distance between the lowest point of the marker and the road
      surface is not more than 2.5m,

    (iv) it, and any means by which it is fitted to the projection, impedes the view of
      the driver as little as possible, and

    (v) it is clearly visible within a reasonable distance to a person using the road at
      the end of the vehicle from which the projection extends;

(c) where the forward projection exceeds 2m or the rearward projection exceeds 3m,
one side marker shall be fitted on the right hand side and one on the left hand side
of the projection so that—

    (i) each marker is as near as is practicable in a longitudinal plane,

    (ii) no part extends beyond the end of the projection,

    (iii) the vertical distance between the lowest part of each marker and the surface
      of the road is not more than 2.5m,

    (iv) the horizontal distance between each marker and the end marker or as the
      case may be, the rear marking carried in accordance with the Lighting
      Regulations does not exceed 1m, and

    (v) each marker is clearly visible within a reasonable distance to a person using
      the road on that side of the projection;

(d) where—

    (i) a forward projection exceeds 4.5m, or

    (ii) a rearward projection exceeds 5m,

extra side markers shall be fitted on either side of the projection so that the horizontal distance between the extreme projecting point of the vehicle from which
the projection extends and the nearest point on any side marker from that point,
and between the nearest points of any adjacent side markers on the same side does
not exceed—

2.5m in the case of a forward projection, or

3.5m in the case of a rearward projection.

For the purposes of this sub-paragraph the expression *"the vehicle"* shall not
include any special appliance or apparatus or any part thereof which is a forward
projection or a rearward projection within the meaning of regulation 81;

(e) the extra side markers required by this sub-paragraph shall also meet the requirements of (i), (iii) and (v) of sub-paragraph (c);

(f) every marker fitted in accordance with this paragraph shall be kept clean and unobscured and [between sunset and sunrise] be illuminated by a lamp which renders
it readily visible from a reasonable distance and which is so shielded that its light,
except as reflected from the marker, is not visible to other persons using the road.

B15.462   *[Paragraph 3 of Pt I of Sch.12 is printed as amended by SI 1991/2125.]*

Marking of shorter projections

B15.463   **4.** A projection to which this paragraph applies shall be rendered clearly visible to other persons using the road within a reasonable distance, in the case of a forward projection, from the front thereof or, in the case of a rearward projection, from the rear thereof and, in either case, from either side thereof.

[Marking of wide loads

B15.464   **5.**(a) Subject to sub-paragraph (d), every load carried on a vehicle in circumstances where this paragraph applies shall be fitted on each side and in the prescribed manner, with—

> (i) a prescribed marker in such a position that it is visible from the front of the vehicle, and
>
> (ii) a prescribed marker in such a position that it is visible from the rear of the vehicle.

> (b) For the purposes of sub-paragraph (a) —
>
> > (i) a marker on a side of the load is fitted in the prescribed manner if at least part of it is within 50mm of a longitudinal plane passing through the point on that side of the load which is furthest from the axis of the vehicle; and
> >
> > (ii) a prescribed marker is a marker of the size, shape and colour described in Part II of this Schedule.

> (c) Every marker fitted pursuant to this paragraph shall be kept clean and between sunset and sunrise be illuminated by a lamp which renders it readily visible from a reasonable distance and which is so shielded that its light, except as reflected from the marker, is not visible to other persons using the road.

> (d) If the load does not extend beyond the longitudinal plane passing through the extreme projecting point on one side of the vehicle, it shall not be necessary for a marker to be fitted to the load on that side.]

B15.465   *[Paragraph 5 of Pt I of Sch.12 was inserted by SI 1991/2125.]*

[(SEE PARAGRAPHS 3(A) AND 5(B) OF THIS SCHEDULE)]

PART II

PROJECTION MARKERS

B15.466

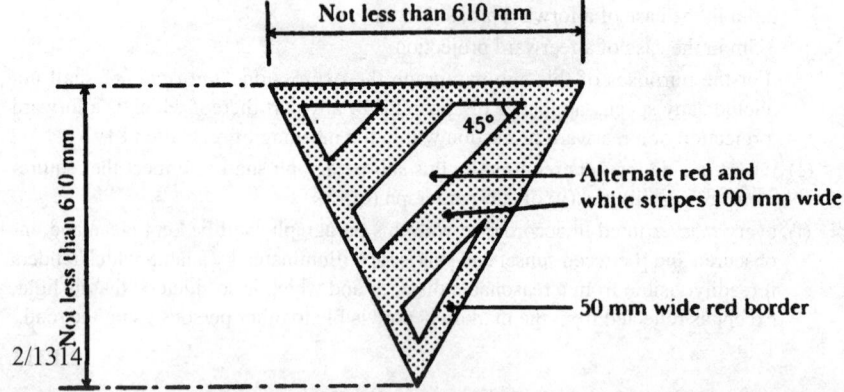

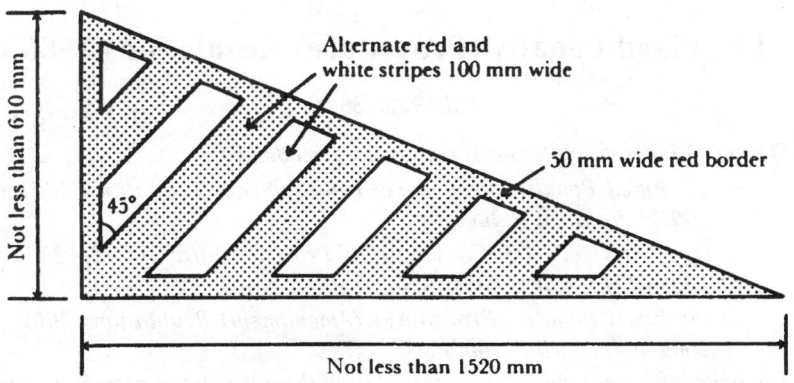

Alternate red and
white stripes 100 mm wide

50 mm wide red border

Not less than 610 mm

45°

Not less than 1520 mm

[Part II of Sch.12 is printed as amended by SI 1991/2125.]   **B15.467**

(see regulation 3(2))   [SCHEDULE 13

Pʟᴀᴛᴇ ꜰᴏʀ Rᴇꜱᴛʀɪᴄᴛᴇᴅ Sᴩᴇᴇᴅ Vᴇʜɪᴄʟᴇ

1.—[(1)] A vehicle displays a plate in accordance with the requirements of this Sched-   **B15.468**
ule if a plate in respect of which the following conditions are satisfied is displayed on the
vehicle in a prominent position.

(2) The conditions are—

    (a) the plate must be in the form shown in the diagram below;

    (b) the plate must be at least 150mm wide and at least 120mm high;

    (c) the figures "5" and "0" must be at least 100mm high and 50mm wide with a stroke
        width of at least 12mm, the figures being black on a white background; and

    (d) the border must be black and between 3mm and 5mm wide.

[Schedule 13 was inserted by SI 1990/1981.   **B15.469**

*The reference "(1)" at the beginning of the text of para.1 of this Schedule has
been added editorially. There are no numbered paragraphs after para.1.]*

The Fixed Penalty (Procedure) Regulations 1986

(SI 1986/1330)

B16.01   *[The text of these regulations is printed as amended by:*

the Fixed Penalty (Procedure) (Amendment) Regulations 2001 (SI 2001/926) (April 1, 2001);

the Courts Act 2003 (Consequential Provisions) (No.2) Order 2005 (SI 2005/617) (April 1, 2005); and

the Fixed Penalty (Procedure) (Amendment) Regulations 2009 (SI 2009/494) (April 1, 2009).

The amending instruments are referred to in the notes to the principal instruments only by their years and numbers. The dates referred to above are the dates on which the amending regulations came into force.]

B16.02   **1.**—(1) *[Omitted.]*

(2) In these Regulations any reference to a section is a reference to a section of [the Road Traffic Offenders Act 1988].

(3) These Regulations do not extend to Scotland.

[(4) These Regulations shall not apply if the fixed penalty notice is given or affixed by a vehicle examiner in accordance with the Road Traffic Offenders Act 1988.]

B16.03   *[Regulation 1 is printed as amended by the Interpretation Act 1978; SI 2009/494..]*

B16.04   **2.**—(1) Subject to paragraph (2) below, in the documents described in column 1 of the Schedule to these Regulations and referred to in the provisions of the Act specified in column 2 of the Schedule there shall be provided the information or, as the case may be, further information prescribed in column 3 of the Schedule.

(2) The information prescribed in the Schedule in relation to a fixed penalty notice need not be provided if the offender's driving licence [(if the offender holds a driving licence) or driving record (if the offender does not hold a driving licence)] would not be subject to endorsement on conviction of the offence in respect of which the notice was given.

B16.05   *[Regulation 2 is printed as amended by SI 2009/494.]*

B16.06   **3.**—(1) A copy of any fixed penalty notice given or affixed under [section 54 or section 62] shall be forwarded by or on behalf of the constable or traffic warden giving or affixing the notice to the fixed penalty clerk unless the fixed penalty clerk has notified the chief officer of police that he does not wish to receive a copy of any such notice.

(2) Where a fixed penalty notice has been given to a person under [section 54] and that person has surrendered his driving licence [(if held)] in accordance with that section the driving licence shall be forwarded by or on behalf of the constable to the fixed penalty clerk.

B16.07   *[Regulation 3 is printed as amended by the Interpretation Act 1978; SI 2009/494.]*

4.—(1) Where a constable has issued a fixed penalty notice to a person under **B16.08**
[section 54(5)], he shall send a notice indicating that fact to the chief officer of
police together with that person's driving licence [(if that person is a holder of a
licence which has been surrendered or delivered)].

(2) Subject to paragraph (3) below, on receipt of the documents referred to in
paragraph (1) above the chief officer of police shall send the driving licence and a
copy of the notice issued under [section 54(4)] to the fixed penalty clerk and
notify him that a fixed penalty notice has been issued under [section 54(5)].

(3) The chief officer of police shall not send a copy of the notice issued under
[section 54(4)] to the fixed penalty clerk under paragraph (2) above if the fixed
penalty clerk has notified the chief officer of police that he does not wish to
receive a copy of any such notice.

[Regulation 4 is printed as amended by the Interpretation Act 1978 ss.17(2)(a) **B16.09**
and 23(1); SI 2009/494.]

5.—(1) On receipt of the remittance in respect of a fixed penalty the fixed **B16.10**
penalty clerk shall notify the chief officer of police that the remittance has been
received.

(2) If payment of the fixed penalty is made by a person otherwise than as
required by the fixed penalty notice the fixed penalty clerk shall return the remittance to that person.

(3) Where a remittance in respect of a fixed penalty is sent by a person to a
[the designated officer for a magistrates' court] who is not the fixed penalty clerk
specified in the fixed penalty notice, the [designated officer] shall return the remittance to that person.

[Regulation 5 is printed as amended by SI 2001/926; SI 2005/617.] **B16.11**

6. Where— **B16.12**
    (a) the suspended enforcement period has expired; and
    (b) the fixed penalty has not been paid; and
    (c) either the person to whom the fixed penalty notice was given has
        requested a hearing under [section 55(2)] or [63(3)] or no registration
        certificate has been issued under [section 70(2)],

the chief officer of police shall notify the fixed penalty clerk accordingly and
the fixed penalty clerk shall, where an endorsable offence is involved, return the
driving licence to the person to whom the fixed penalty notice was given[, if that
person holds a driving licence].

[Regulation 6 is printed as amended by the Interpretation Act 1978 ss.17(2)(a) **B16.13**
and 23(1); SI 2009/494.]

7. Where— **B16.14**
    (a) the suspended enforcement period has expired; and
    (b) the fixed penalty has not been paid; and
    (c) a registration certificate has been issued under [section 70(2)],

the chief officer of police shall notify the fixed penalty clerk accordingly.

[Regulation 7 is printed as amended by the Interpretation Act 1978 ss.17(2)(a) **B16.15**
and 23(1).]

B16.16   **8.** Where in a case involving an endorsable offence any sum determined by reference to the fixed penalty is registered under [section 71] for enforcement against the licence holder as a fine the [designated officer for] the court where the sum is registered shall notify the fixed penalty clerk [...] that the sum has been registered.

B16.17   *[Regulation 8 is printed as amended by the Interpretation Act 1978 ss.17(2)(a) and 23(1); SI 2001/926; SI 2005/617; SI 2009/494.]*

B16.18   **9.** Where a fixed penalty notice is issued under [section 54(2)] or [(5)] the fixed penalty clerk shall not accept payment of the fixed penalty after the expiry of the suspended enforcement period.

B16.19   *[Regulation 9 is printed as amended by the Interpretation Act 1978 ss.17(2)(a) and 23(1).]*

B16.20   **10.** Where a fixed penalty is paid within the suspended enforcement period the fixed penalty clerk shall send a receipt for the payment, if requested, to the payer.

B16.21   **11.** For the purposes of [section 56(3)(a) (which provides that a licence receipt issued by a constable is to cease to have effect on the expiration of the period of one month beginning with the date of issue) there shall be prescribed a longer period of two months beginning with the same date.

B16.22   *[Regulation 11 is printed as amended by the Interpretation Act 1978 ss.17(2)(a) and 23(1).]*

Regulation 2   SCHEDULE

INFORMATION OR FURTHER INFORMATION TO BE PROVIDED IN CERTAIN DOCUMENTS MENTIONED IN [PART III OF THE ROAD TRAFFIC OFFENDERS ACT 1988]

B16.23

Document	Provision of Act	Information or further information to be provided
1. Fixed penalty notice	[Section 52(1)]	(i) The name of the police force of which the constable giving the notice is a member.
		(ii) The serial number of the fixed penalty notice.
		(iii) Whether the notice relates to an endorsable offence.
		(iv) The name, date of birth and address of the person to whom the notice is given.
		(v) The date, time and place of the alleged offence.
		(vi) The details of the vehicle including the registration number.
		(vii) The documents, if any, to be produced at a police station and the period within which they must be produced.
		(viii) An explanation of the action to be taken by the driver where (a) he has not or (b) he has surrendered the licence[, if he holds such a licence].
		(ix) The fact that the person to whom the notice is given may opt for trial.
		(x) The method of paying the fixed penalty.

Document	Provision of Act	Information or further information to be provided
		(xi) The name, rank and number of the constable issuing the fixed penalty notice.
		(xii) Guidance to the driver as to the legal consequences of a fixed penalty notice.
2. Receipt for driving licence	[Section 56(1)]	(i) Whether the driving licence [if the offender holds a driving licence] is full or provisional.
		(ii) The driver number as shown on the licence.
		(iii) The groups of vehicles which the driver is entitled to drive.
		(iv) The expiry date of the licence.
		(v) The duration of the validity of the licence receipt.
		(vi) The method of obtaining a new receipt on the expiry of an old receipt.
		(vii) The name, rank and number of the constable issuing the fixed penalty notice.
3. Receipt for driving licence	[Section 56(2)]	(i) The date of issue of receipt.
		(ii) The code of the magistrates' court issuing receipt.
		(iii) The name, address and date of birth of driver.
		(iv) Whether the driving licence [if the offender holds a driving licence] is full or provisional.
		(v) The driver number as shown on the licence.
		(vi) The groups of vehicles which the driver is entitled to drive.
		(vii) The expiry date of the licence.
		(viii) The duration of the validity of the licence receipt.
4. Registration certificate	[Section 70]	(i) The serial number and date, time and place of issue of the notice to owner, notice to hirer or fixed penalty notice (as case may be).
		(ii) The vehicle registration number.
		(iii) The driver number.
		(iv) The amount of the appropriate fixed penalty.
		(v) The sum to be registered in default of payment of the fixed penalty.
5. Notice requesting new statutory statement	[Section 73(4)]	(i) The particulars of the statutory declaration.
		(ii) The details of the alleged fixed penalty offence.
		(iii) A request to furnish a statutory statement of ownership.

Document	Provision of Act	Information or further information to be provided
		(iv) The period allowed for a response to the notice. (v) The consequences of providing, or, as the case may be, not providing the statutory statement of ownership.
6. Statement of liability	[Section 66(2)]	(i) The name, date of birth and address of hirer. (ii) The duration of the hiring agreement.

B16.24   *[The Schedule is printed as amended by the Interpretation Act 1978 ss.17(2)(a) and 23(1); SI 2009/494.]*

The Drivers' Hours (Harmonisation with Community Rules) Regulations 1986

(SI 1986/1458)

Citation, commencement, interpretation and revocation

1.—(1) *[Omitted.]*   **B17.01**

(2) In these Regulations *"the 1968 Act"* means the Transport Act 1968.

(3) *[Revocation.]*

Domestic drivers' hours code, etc.

2.—(1) Subject to the provisions of this Regulation, the domestic drivers'   **B17.02** hours code shall not apply in relation to any Community driving or work of a driver of a vehicle to which Part VI of the 1968 Act applies.

(2) Paragraphs (3) and (4) below apply where during any working day a driver of a vehicle to which Part VI of the 1968 Act applies spends time both on Community driving or work and on domestic driving or work.

(3) Any time spent on Community driving or work shall be regarded for the purpose of—

    (a) applying the limits in the domestic drivers' hours code on periods of driving or length of working day; or

    (b) calculating periods of driving for the purposes of section 96(7) of the 1968 Act,

as time spent on domestic driving, or as the case may be, domestic work.

(4) Without prejudice to paragraph (3) above, any time spent on Community driving or work shall not be regarded for the purposes of any of the provisions of the domestic drivers' hours code as constituting or forming part of an interval for rest or an interval for rest and refreshment.

(5) In this Regulation *"the domestic drivers' hours code"* has the meaning given by section 96(13) of the 1968 Act [*q.v.*].

(6) In this Regulation —

    (a) any reference to Community driving or work is a reference to driving or, as the case may be, work to which the applicable Community Rules apply; and

    (b) any reference to domestic driving or work is a reference to driving or, as the case may be, work to which Part VI of the 1968 Act applies and those Rules do not apply.

Meaning of "working week"

3. *[Amends s.103(1) and (5) of the 1968 Act, q.v.]*   **B17.03**

The Drivers' Hours (Goods Vehicles) (Modifications) Order 1986

(SI 1986/1459)

B18.01   *[The text of s.96 of the Transport Act 1968 as modified by this order is set out as an appendix to this order.]*

Citation, commencement, interpretation and revocation

B18.02   **1.**—(1) *[Omitted.]*

(2) In this Order *"the 1968 Act"* means the Transport Act 1968.

(3) *[Revokes SI 1970/257 art.3, and SI 1971/818 art.5(a).]*

Goods vehicles generally

B18.03   **2.** Where during any working day a driver spends all or the greater part of the time when he is driving vehicles to which Part VI of the 1968 Act applies in driving goods vehicles, that Part of that Act shall have effect, as respects that driver and that working day, as if—

(a) subsections (2), (3)(b), (4) to (6) and (8)(b) of section 96 were omitted;

(b) for the words "subsections (1), (2) and (3)" in subsection (7) of that section there were substituted the words "subsections (1) and (3)(a)";

(c) for the words "subsections (2) and (3)" in subsection (8)(a) of that section there were substituted the words "subsection (3)(a)"; and

(d) for the definition of *"working day"* in section 103(1) there were substituted the following definition—

" *'working day'*, in relation to any driver, means—

(a) any working period (that is to say, any period during which he is on duty) which does not fall to be aggregated with the whole or part of any other such period or periods by virtue of paragraph (b) of this definition; and

(b) where a working period is followed by one or more other such periods beginning within the 24 hours next after the beginning of that working period, the aggregate of that working period and so much of the other such period or periods as fall within those 24 hours;".

Light goods vehicles

B18.04   **3.**—(1) Where during any working week a driver spends all of the time when he is driving vehicles to which Part VI of the 1968 Act applies in driving light goods vehicles and, in so far as he drives such a vehicle during that week otherwise than for social, domestic or pleasure purposes, he does so—

(a) solely in connection with the carrying on by him or by his employer of the profession of medical practitioner, nurse, midwife, dentist or veterinary surgeon;

    (b) wholly or mainly in connection with the carrying out of any service of inspection, cleaning, maintenance, repair, installation or fitting;

    (c) solely while he is acting as a commercial traveller and is carrying in the vehicle (apart from the effects of any person carried in it) no goods other than goods carried for the purpose of soliciting orders;

    (d) solely while he is acting in the course of his employment by the Automobile Association, the Royal Automobile Club or Royal Scottish Automobile Club; or

    (e) solely in connection with the carrying on by him or by his employer of the business of cinematography or of radio or television broadcasting,

that Part of that Act shall have effect, as respects that driver and any working day falling wholly within that working week, not only with the modifications made by article 2 above but also as if subsections (3)(a) and (8)(a) of section 96 were omitted.

  (2) In this article *"light goods vehicle"* means a vehicle which—

    (a) is a goods vehicle which has a permissible maximum weight within the meaning of [section 108 of the Road Traffic Act 1988] not exceeding 3.5 tonnes; or

    (b) is a dual purpose vehicle within the meaning of [Regulation 3(2) of the Road Vehicles (Construction and Use) Regulations 1986] [*SI 1986/1078, q.v.*],

and (in either case) is a vehicle to which Part VI of the 1968 Act applies.

  [Article 3 is printed as amended by the Interpretation Act 1978 ss.17(2)(a) and 23.]   **B18.05**

APPENDIX (TRANSPORT ACT 1986, S.96, AS APPLIED TO DRIVERS OF GOODS VEHICLES)

Permitted driving time and periods of duty

  96.—(1) Subject to the provisions of this section, a driver shall not on any working day **B18.06** drive a vehicle or vehicles to which this Part of this Act applies amounting in the aggregate to more than ten hours.

  (2) *[Inapplicable.]*

  (3) Subject to the provisions of this section, the working day of a driver—

    (a) except where paragraph (b) or (c) of this subsection applies, shall not exceed eleven hours;

    (b) *[inapplicable.]*

  (4)–(6) *[Inapplicable.]*

  (7) If in the case of the working week of any driver the following requirement is satisfied, that is to say, that, in each of the periods of twenty-four hours beginning at midnight which make up that week, the driver does not drive a vehicle to which this Part of this Act applies for a period of, or periods amounting in the aggregate to, more than four hours, the foregoing provisions of this section shall not apply to him in that week, except that the provisions of subsections (1) and (3)(a) shall nevertheless have effect in relation to the whole of any working day falling partly in that week and partly in a working week in the case of which that requirement is not satisfied.

  (8) If on any working day a driver does not drive any vehicle to which this Part of this Act applies—

(a) subsection (3)(a) of this section shall not apply to that day, and

(b) *[inapplicable.]*

(9) For the purposes of subsections (1) and (7) of this section no account shall be taken of any time spent driving a vehicle elsewhere than on a road if the vehicle is being so driven in the course of operations of agriculture or forestry.

(10) For the purpose of enabling drivers to deal with cases of emergency or otherwise to meet a special need, the [Secretary of State for Transport] may by regulations—

(a) create examinations from all or any of the requirements of subsections (1) to (6) of this section in such cases and subject to such conditions as may be specified in the regulations;

(b) empower the traffic commissioner for any area, subject to the provisions of the regulations—

(i) to dispense with the observance of all or any of those requirements (either generally or in such circumstances or to such extent as the commissioner thinks fit) in any particular case for which provision is not made under paragraph (a) of this subsection;

(ii) to grant a certificate (which, for the purposes of any proceedings under this Part of this Act, shall be conclusive evidence of the facts therein stated) that any particular case falls or fell within any exemption created under the said paragraph (a)

and regulations under this subsection may enable any dispensation under paragraph (b)(i) of this subsection to be granted retrospectively and provide for a document purporting to be a certificate granted by virtue of paragraph (b)(ii) of this subsection to be accepted in evidence without further proof.

(11) If any of the requirements of the domestic drivers' hours code is contravened in the case of any driver—

(a) that driver; and

(b) any other person (being that driver's employer or a person to whose orders that driver was subject) who caused or permitted the contravention,

shall be liable on summary conviction to a fine not exceeding level 4 on the standard scale; but a person shall not be liable to be convicted under this subsection if he proves to the court—

(i) that the contravention was due to unavoidable delay in the completion of a journey arising out of circumstances which he could not reasonably have foreseen; or

(ii) in the case of a person charged under paragraph (b) of this subsection, that the contravention was due to the fact that the driver had for any particular period or periods driven or been on duty otherwise than in the employment of that person or, as the case may be, otherwise than in the employment in which he is subject to the orders of that person, and that the person charged was not, and could not reasonably have become, aware of that fact.

(11A) Where, in the case of a driver of a motor vehicle, there is in Great Britain a contravention of any requirement of the applicable Community rules as to period of driving, or distance driven, or periods on or off duty, then the offender and any other person (being the offender's employer or a person to whose orders the offender was subject) who caused or permitted the contravention shall be liable on summary conviction to a fine not exceeding level 4 on the standard scale.

(11B) But a person shall not be liable to be convicted under subsection (11A) if—

(a) he proves the matters specified in paragraph (i) of subsection (11); or

(b) being charged as the offender's employer or a person to whose orders the offender was subject, he proves the matters specified in paragraph (ii) of that subsection.

(12) The [Secretary of State for Transport] may by order—

(a) direct that subsection (1) of this section shall have effect with the substitution for the reference to ten hours of a reference to nine hours, either generally or with such exceptions as may be specified in the order;

(b) direct that paragraph (a) of subsection (3) of this section shall have effect with the substitution for the reference to eleven hours of a reference to any shorter period, or remove, modify or add to the provisions of that subsection containing exceptions to the said paragraph (a);

(c) remove, modify or add to any of the requirements of subsections (2), (4), (5) or (6) of this section or any of the exemptions provided for by subsections (7), (8) and (9) thereof;

and any order under this subsection may contain such transitional and supplementary provisions as the [Secretary of State for Transport] thinks necessary or expedient, including provisions amending any definition in section 103 of this Act which is relevant to any of the provisions affected by the order.

(13) In this Part of this Act *"the domestic drivers' hours code"* means the provisions of subsections (1) to (6) of this section as for the time being in force (and, in particular, as modified, added to or substituted by or under any instrument in force under section 95(1) of this Act or subsection (10) or (12) of this section) .

[This version of the Transport Act 1968, s.96, is the text of s.96 as modified by **B18.07**
the Drivers' Hours (Goods Vehicles) (Modifications) Order 1986 (SI 1986/1459) art.2 (goods vehicles generally); in relation to light goods vehicles, subss.(3)(a) and (8)(a) are also inapplicable (see SI 1986/1459 art.3).

This version of s.96 is printed as further amended by the Secretary of State for the Environment Order 1970 (SI 1970/1681); the European Communities Act 1972 s.4, and Sch.4, para.9(2); the Road Traffic (Drivers' Ages and Hours of Work) Act 1976 s.2(1); the Secretary of State for Transport Order 1976 (SI 1976/1775); the Transport Act 1978 s.10; the Minister of Transport Order 1979 (SI 1979/571); the Transfer of Functions (Transport) Order 1981 (SI 1981/238); the Criminal Justice Act 1982 ss.38 and 46(1); the Transport Act 1985 s.3 and Sch.2, Pt II, para.1(2); the Community Drivers' Hours and Recording Equipment Regulations 1986 (SI 1986/1457) reg.2; the Secretary of State for the Environment, Transport and the Regions Order 1997 (SI 1997/2971); the Secretaries of State for Transport, Local Government and the Regions and for Environment, Food and Rural Affairs Order 2001 (SI 2001/2568); the Transfer of Functions (Transport, Local Government and the Regions) Order 2002 (SI 2002/2626).]

The Drivers' Hours (Goods Vehicles) (Exemptions) Regulations 1986

(SI 1986/1492)

Citation, commencement and revocation

B19.01   **1.** *[Omitted.]*

Exemptions from requirements as to drivers' hours

B19.02   **2.**—(1) A driver who during any working day spends all or the greater part of the time when he is driving vehicles to which Part VI of the Transport Act 1968 applies in driving goods vehicles and who spends time on duty during that working day to deal with any of the cases of emergency specified in paragraph (2) below is exempted from the requirements of section 96(1) and (3)(a) of that Act in respect of that working day subject to the condition that he does not spend time on such duty (otherwise than to deal with the emergency) for a period of or periods amounting in the aggregate to more than 11 hours.

(2) The cases of emergency referred to in paragraph (1) above are—

    (a) events which cause or are likely to cause such—

        (i) danger to life or health of one or more individuals or animals, or

        (ii) a serious interruption in the maintenance of public services for the supply of water, gas, electricity or drainage or of [electronic communications] or postal services, or

        (iii) a serious interruption in the use of roads, railways, ports or airports,

    as to necessitate the taking of immediate action to prevent the occurrence or continuance of such danger or interruption and

    (b) events which are likely to cause such serious damage to property as to necessitate the taking of immediate action to prevent the occurrence of such damage.

B19.03   *[Regulation 2 is printed as amended by the Communications Act 2003 (Consequential Amendments) Order 2003 (SI 2003/2155).]*

The Drivers' Hours (Goods Vehicles) (Keeping of Records) Regulations 1987

(SI 1987/1421)

ARRANGEMENT OF REGULATIONS

Commencement and citation

1. *[Omitted.]*   **B20.02**

Revocation

2. *[Omitted.]*   **B20.03**

Interpretation

3. In these Regulations, unless the context otherwise requires—   **B20.04**

   "the Act" means the Transport Act 1968;

   "driver's record book" means a book which complies with regulation 5, and any reference in relation to a driver's record book to a front sheet, instructions to drivers for completion of sheets, and weekly record sheets is a reference to those components of a driver's record book referred to in regulation 5;

   "operator's licence" has the same meaning as in section 60(1) of the Act; and

"passenger vehicles" and *"goods vehicles"* have the same meaning as in section 95(2) of the Act.

Application of Regulations

B20.05   4. Subject to the provisions of regulations 12 and 13 these Regulations apply to drivers of goods vehicles and to employers of employee-drivers of such vehicles but they do not so apply in relation to a journey made or work done by a driver in a case where the journey or, as the case may be, the work is a journey or work to which the applicable Community rules apply.

Form of driver's record book

B20.06   5. A driver's record book shall contain—
    (a) a front sheet;
    (b) instructions to drivers for completion of sheets;
    (c) notes for guidance on use of the book; and
    (d) weekly record sheets divided up into boxes for entry of information relating to each day of the week and a duplicate of each weekly record sheet together with one sheet of carbon paper or other means whereby an entry on a weekly record sheet may be simultaneously reproduced on the duplicate of that sheet

each of which shall conform to the model in the Schedule to these Regulations and shall have the standard A6 format (105 × 148mm) or a larger format.

Issue of driver's record books

B20.07   6.—(1) Where an employee-driver is required by these Regulations to enter information in a driver's record book the employer shall issue to him and from time to time as may be necessary while the employee-driver remains in the employment of that employer supply him with a new driver's record book.

(2) If on the date of the coming into operation of these Regulations or at any time thereafter an employee-driver has more than one employer in relation to whom he is an employee-driver of a vehicle, the employer who is to issue a new driver's record book to him shall be the employer for whom the employee-driver first acts in the course of his employment on or after the said date or time.

(3) Where during the currency of a driver's record book an employee-driver ceases to be employed by an employer who has issued that book to him he shall return that book, (including all unused weekly record sheets), to that employer and, if he is at that time employed by some other person or persons in relation to whom he is an employee-driver of a vehicle, that other person, or if there is more than one such other person, that one of them for whom he first acts in the course of his employment after ceasing to be so employed as aforesaid, shall issue a new driver's record book to him in accordance with the provisions of paragraph (1) above.

Entries in driver's record books

B20.08   7.—(1) An employer of an employee-driver or an owner-driver shall enter or secure that there is entered on the front sheet the information specified in items 4 and 6 of that sheet.

(2) The entries referred to in paragraph (1) shall be made—

    (a) in the case of an employer, before the driver's record book is issued to the driver pursuant to regulation 6, and

    (b) in the case of an owner-driver before the book is used.

(3) (a) For the purpose of entering the information specified in item 4, the address shall, in the case of an owner-driver, be the address of the driver's place of business.

    (b) For the purpose of entering the information specified in item 6 the Operator's Licence No. shall be the serial number of the operator's licence granted under Part V of the Act by virtue of which each goods vehicle used by the driver during the currency of the record book is an authorised vehicle for the purposes of the said Part V.

(4) A driver shall enter, and where he is an employee-driver, his employer shall cause him to enter, in accordance with the instructions to drivers for the completion of sheets—

    (a) on the front sheet the information specified in relation to the front sheet in those instructions; and

    (b) in the appropriate boxes in the weekly record sheet the information specified in relation to weekly record sheets in those instructions.

(5) A driver when making an entry in a weekly record sheet (including signing such a sheet) shall ensure, by the use of the carbon paper or otherwise, that the entry is simultaneously reproduced on the duplicate of that sheet.

Manner of keeping driver's record books—supplementary

8.—(1) Where a weekly record sheet has been completed by an employee-driver he shall deliver the driver's record book (including the duplicate of the weekly record sheet which has been completed) to the employer who issued or should have issued the record book to him within a period of seven days from the date when the weekly record sheet was completed or earlier if so required by the employer.   **B20.09**

(2) An employer to whom a driver's record book has been delivered pursuant to paragraph 1 above shall—

    (a) examine the weekly record sheeet which has been completed and sign it and its duplicate;

    (b) detach the duplicate sheet; and

    (c) return the book to the driver before he is next on duty.

(3) When all the weekly record sheets in a driver's record book have been used, the driver shall retain the book for a period of fourteen days from the date on which the book was last returned to him pursuant to paragraph (2)(c) above and shall then return the book to the employer as soon as is reasonably practicable.

(4) When a weekly record sheet has been completed by an owner-driver he shall, within a period of seven days from the date of its being completed, detach the duplicate sheet and deliver it to the address which is required to be entered in item 4 on the front sheet.

(5) An employee-driver or an owner-driver shall not be treated as having failed to comply with any of the requirements of paragraphs (1) and (4) above with respect to the period within which the duplicate of a weekly record sheet shall be delivered if he can show that it was not reasonably practicable to comply with that requirement and that the duplicate of the weekly record sheet was delivered as soon as it was reasonably practicable to do so.

(6) A driver who is in possession of a driver's record book in which he has made any entry pursuant to regulation 7 shall not, until all the weekly record sheets in that book have been completed, make any entry in any other record book.

(7) An employee-driver shall not make any entry in a driver's record book pursuant to regulation 7 if the book was not supplied to him by his employer unless a driver's record book so supplied was not available to him.

(8) No person shall erase or obliterate any entry once made in a driver's record book, and if a correction is required it shall be made by striking the original entry through in such a way that it may still be read and by writing the appropriate correction near to the entry so struck through, and any person making such a correction shall initial it.

Production of driver's record book by employee-drivers

B20.10   9.—(1) Where an employee-driver has or has had during any period more than one employer in relation to whom he is an employee-driver each employer, who is not the employer who is required by these Regulations to issue a driver's record book to that employee-driver, shall require that driver to produce his current driver's record book and shall enter on the front sheet the information contained in item 5.

(2) An employee-driver shall produce his current driver's record book for inspection by the employer who issued it to him, or by any other person in relation to whom he is at any time during the period of the currency of that book an employee-driver, whenever required to do so by that employer or that other person.

Driver's record books to be carried by drivers

B20.11   10. A driver shall have his current driver's record book (including all unused record sheets) in his possession at all times when he is on duty.

Preservation of driver's record books

B20.12   11.—(1) An owner-driver shall preserve his driver's record book intact when it has been completed or he has ceased to use it, and the employer of an employee-driver to whom any driver's record book relating to that employee-driver has been returned shall preserve that book intact, for the period specified in paragraph (3) below.

(2) An employer of an employee-driver or an owner-driver who has detached duplicates of weekly sheets pursuant to regulation 8(2)(b) or as the case may be regulation 8(4) shall preserve those sheets for the period specified in paragraph (3) below.

(3) The period for which driver's record books and duplicates of weekly rec-

ord sheets must be preserved as required by this regulation shall be one year reckoned, in the case of an owner-driver, from the day on which that book was completed or ceased to be used by him, or in the case of an employee-driver, from the day on which that book was returned to his employer pursuant to regulation 8(3).

Exemptions

12.—(1) Where a driver does not during any working day drive any goods vehicle other than a vehicle the use of which is exempted from any requirement to have an operator's licence or, in the case of a vehicle in the public service of the Crown, would be so exempted by virtue of section 60(2) of the Act, were it not such a vehicle, that driver and, if he is an employee-driver, his employer, shall be exempted for that period from the specified requirements.   **B20.13**

(2) (a) Where in any working day a driver does not drive a goods vehicle for more than four hours and does not drive any such vehicle outside a radius of 50 kilometres from the operating centre of the vehicle, then he and, if he is an employee-driver, his employer shall be exempted for that period from the specified requirements.

(b) For the purposes of computing the period of four hours mentioned in sub-paragraph (a) above no account shall be taken of any time spent in driving a vehicle elsewhere than on a road if the vehicle is being so driven in the course of operations of agriculture, forestry or quarrying or in the course of carrying out work in the construction, reconstruction, alteration or extension or maintenance of, or of a part of, a building, or of any other fixed works of construction of [*sic*] civil engineering (including works for the construction, improvement or maintenance of a road) and, for the purposes of this sub-paragraph, where the vehicle is being driven on, or on a part of, a road in the course of carrying out of any work for the improvement or maintenance of, or that part of, that road, it shall be treated as being driven elsewhere than on a road.

(3) Where during any working day a driver does not spend all or the greater part of the time when he is driving vehicles to which Part VI of the Act applies in driving goods vehicles, then he and, if he is an employee-driver, his employer shall be exempted for that working day from the specified requirements.

(4) Where a vehicle is used in such circumstances that by virtue of regulation 5 of the Community Drivers' Hours and Recording Equipment (Exemptions and Supplementary Provisions) Regulations 1986 [*SI 1986/1456, q.v.*] Council Regulation (EEC) No.3821/85 of 20th December 1985 on recording equipment in road transport [*q.v.*] applies to the vehicle, the driver of the vehicle and, if he is an employee-driver, his employer shall be exempted from the specified requirements in relation to the use of the vehicle in those circumstances.

(5) (a) In this regulation *"the specified requirements"* means the provisions of regulations 7 and 10.

(b) In paragraph (2)(a) above *"operating centre"* has the same meaning as in section 92 of the Act [*as amended*] [*q.v.*].

Drivers of goods vehicles and passenger vehicles

13.—(1) Subject to the provisions of regulation 12(3), regulations 7 and 10   **B20.14**

apply to a driver who in any working week drives goods and passenger vehicles as they apply to a driver who only drives a goods vehicle and the information to be entered in the driver's record book pursuant to regulation 7 shall be information in relation to his employment in connection with both goods and passenger vehicles.

(2) If a driver of both goods vehicles and passenger vehicles has a different employer in relation to his employment in connection with goods vehicles from his employer in relation to his employment in connection with passenger vehicles his employer for the purpose of regulation 6 shall be his employer in relation to his employment in connection with goods vehicles notwithstanding the provisions of regulation 6(2).

SCHEDULE

MODEL FOR DRIVER'S RECORD BOOK

B20.15   (a) *Front sheet*

RECORD BOOK FOR DRIVERS IN ROAD TRANSPORT

1. Date book first used . . . .

2. Date book last used . . . .

3. Surname, first name(s), and address of holder of book . . . .

. . . .

. . . .

4. Name, address, telephone number and stamp (if any) of employer/undertaking . . . . . .

. . . .

. . . .

5. Name, address, telephone number and stamp (if any) of any other employer(s) . . . . . .

. . . .

. . . .

6. Operator's Licence No. (Nos) . . . .

B20.16   (b) *Instructions to drivers for completion of sheets*

INSTRUCTIONS TO DRIVERS FOR COMPLETION OF SHEETS

FRONT SHEET

1. Enter your surname, first name(s) and address (item 3). Owner-drivers need not make any entry in item 3 unless their personal address is different from the address of their place of business.

2. Enter the date on which you first use the book (item 1).

3. Immediately after you have completed all the weekly sheets enter in item 2 the date on which you last made an entry in a weekly sheet. If you cease to be employed by the employer who issued you with a record book enter the last date on which you were employed in item 2.

WEEKLY RECORD SHEET

4. Use a new sheet each week. A week runs from midnight on Sunday/Monday to midnight the next Sunday/Monday.

5. Complete boxes 1 and 2 at the beginning of each week in which you work as a driver.

6. Each day on which you do not work as a driver complete boxes 3–9 in accordance with the instructions below.

7. Enter in box 3 for the day in question the registration number of any vehicle used during that day.

8. Complete boxes 4 and 5 at the beginning of each day on which you do work as a driver.

9. Complete boxes 6, 7, 8 and 9 at the end of the day's work.

(c) *Notes for guidance on the use of book*   **B20.17**

NOTES FOR GUIDANCE ON THE USE OF RECORD BOOKS

FOR EMPLOYERS

1. After completing items 4 and 6 on the front sheet, issue a record book to the drivers employed by you.

2. Give the holder the necessary instructions for correct use of the book.

3. When the record book is handed in to you by the drivers employed by you within seven days of the end of each week of driving, examine and sign the weekly record sheet (including the duplicate sheet) for the week to which it relates. Tear out and keep the duplicate sheets, leaving the top sheets in the book and return the book to the driver before he is next on duty.

4. When the used books have been handed back to you by the drivers employed by you preserve them together with the duplicate sheets for not less than one year.

FOR EMPLOYEE-DRIVERS

5. Ensure that items 1 and 3 on the front sheet are completed before you use the book.

6. This record book is personal. Carry it with you when on duty and produce it to any authorised inspecting officer on request. Hand it over to your employer when you leave the undertaking.

7. Produce this record book to your employer within 7 days of the end of each week of driving, so that he can check and countersign your entries. Keep the top sheets in the book.

8. When the book is completed, complete item 2 on the front sheet and keep the book for 2 weeks so that it can be produced at any time to an authorised inspecting officer and then hand it to your employer.

FOR OWNER-DRIVERS

9. Ensure that items 1, 3 (if applicable), 4 and 6 on the front sheet are completed before you use the record book. Enter your business address in item 4.

10. This record book is personal. Carry it with you when on duty and produce it to any authorised inspecting officer on request.

11. Tear out and keep the duplicate of each weekly record sheet at the end of the week to which it relates.

12. When the book is completed, complete item 2 on the front sheet. Preserve the used books and the duplicate sheets for not less than a year.

GENERAL

13. All entries must be made in ink or with a ball-point pen.

14. If you have to correct an entry, strike the incorrect entry through, write the correct entry near it and initial the correction.

(These notes are for guidance only and reference should be made to Part VI of the Transport Act 1968 and the Drivers' Hours (Keeping of Records) Regulations 1987 for particulars of the statutory provisions.)

[The weekly sheet is set out on the next page.]

(d) *Weekly record sheets*

WEEKLY SHEET

1. DRIVER'S NAME

2. PERIOD COVERED BY SHEET

WEEK COMMENCING (DATE) ....

TO WEEK ENDING (DATE) ....

DAY ON WHICH DUTY COMMENCED	REGISTRATION NO. OF VEHICLE(S) 3	PLACE WHERE VEHICLE(S) BASED 4	TIME OF GOING ON DUTY 5	TIME OF GOING OFF DUTY 6	TIME SPENT DRIVING 7	TIME SPENT ON DUTY 8	SIGNATURE OF DRIVER 9
MONDAY							
TUESDAY							
WEDNESDAY							
THURSDAY							
FRIDAY							
SATURDAY							
SUNDAY							

10. CERTIFICATION BY EMPLOYER

I HAVE EXAMINED THE ENTRIES IN THIS SHEET

SIGNATURE ....

POSITION HELD ....

The Goods Vehicles (Plating and Testing) Regulations 1988

(SI 1988/1478)

B21.01   *[The text of these regulations is printed as amended by:*

the Goods Vehicles (Plating and Testing) (Amendment) Regulations 1990 (SI 1990/448) (April 2, 1990);

the Goods Vehicles (Plating and Testing) (Amendment) (No.1) Regulations 1991 (SI 1991/252) (March 18, 1991);

the Goods Vehicles (Plating and Testing) (Amendment) Regulations 1993 (SI 1993/2048) (October 1, 1993);

the Goods Vehicles (Plating and Testing) (Amendment) (No.2) Regulations 1993 (SI 1993/3013) (January 2, 1994);

the Goods Vehicles (Plating and Testing) (Amendment) Regulations 1994 (SI 1994/328) (March 24, 1994);

the Goods Vehicles (Plating and Testing) (Amendment) Regulations 1995 (SI 1995/1456) (July 1, 1995);

the Goods Vehicles (Plating and Testing) (Amendment) Regulations 1997 (SI 1997/82) (March 3, 1997);

the Goods Vehicles (Plating and Testing) (Amendment) (No.2) Regulations 1997 (SI 1997/263) (March 5, 1997);

the Goods Vehicles (Plating and Testing) (Amendment) Regulations 2000 (SI 2000/1433) (June 26, 2000);

the Goods Vehicles (Plating and Testing) (Amendment) Regulations 2001 (SI 2001/307) (March 1, 2001);

the Good Vehicles (Plating and Testing) (Amendment) Regulations 2002 (SI 2002/487) (April 1, 2002);

the Goods Vehicles (Plating and Testing) (Amendment) Regulations 2003 (SI 2003/1816) (August 11, 2003);

the Goods Vehicles (Plating and Testing) (Amendment) Regulations 2005 (SI 2005/2343) (September 30, 2005);

the Goods Vehicles (Plating and Testing) (Amendment) Regulations 2008 (SI 2008/1460) (July 13, 2008); and

the Goods Vehicles (Plating and Testing) (Amendment) Regulations 2010 (SI 2010/448) (April 1, 2010).

The amending regulations are referred to in the notes to the principal regulations only by their years and numbers. The dates referred to above are the dates on which the amending regulations came into force.

The principal regulations have also been amended by the Goods Vehicles (Plating and Testing) (Amendment) Regulations 1989 (SI 1989/320), the Goods Vehicles (Plating and Testing) (Amendment) (No.2) Regulations 1989 (SI 1989/1693), the Goods Vehicles (Plating and Testing) (Amendment) (No.2) Regulations 1991 (SI 1991/454), the Goods Vehicles (Plating and Testing) (Amendment)

Regulations 1992 (SI 1992/564), the Goods Vehicles (Plating and Testing) (Amendment) (No.2) Regulations 1992 (SI 1992/2447), the Goods Vehicles (Plating and Testing) (Amendment) Regulations 1998 (SI 1998/1671), the Goods Vehicles (Plating and Testing) (Amendment) (No.2) Regulations 1998 (SI 1998/ 3113), the Goods Vehicles (Plating and Testing) (Amendment) Regulations 2001 (SI 2001/1650), the Goods Vehicles (Plating and Testing) (Amendment) Regulations 2004 (SI 2004/1873), the Goods Vehicles (Plating and Testing) (Amendment) Regulations 2007 (SI 2007/503), the Goods Vehicles (Plating and Testing) (Amendment) Regulations 2009 (SI 2009/799) and the Road Vehicles Lighting and Goods Vehicles (Plating and Testing) (Amendment) Regulations 2009 (SI 2009/3220), but these do not affect the text of any provision which is printed in this publication.]

PART I

GENERAL

Commencement and citation

1. *[Omitted.]*   **B21.02**

Revocation

2. *[Omitted.]*   **B21.03**

Interpretation

3.—(1) In these Regulations, except where the context otherwise requires, the **B21.04** following expressions have the meanings hereby respectively assigned to them:—

[*"the 1994 Act"* means the Vehicle Excise and Registration Act 1994;]

[*"the 1988 Act"* means the Road Traffic Act 1988] [*q.v.*];

"the Construction and Use Regulations" means the Road Vehicles (Construction and Use) Regulations 1986 [*SI 1986/1078, as amended (q.v.)*];

"the National Type Approval for Goods Vehicles Regulations" means the Motor Vehicles (Type Approval for Goods Vehicles) (Great Britain) Regulations 1982 [*SI 1982/1271, as amended*];

"agricultural motor vehicle", *"agricultural trailer"*, *"agricultural trailed appliance"*, *"agricultural trailed appliance conveyor"*, *"articulated vehicle"*, *"converter dolly"*, *"dual-purpose vehicle"*, *"engineering plant"*, [*exhaust system,*] *"Ministry plate"*, *"registered"*, *"semi-trailer"*, *"straddle carrier"*, *"track-laying"*, *"works trailer"*, and *"works truck"* have the same meanings respectively as in the Construction and Use Regulations;

"appeal officer" means the person appointed by the Secretary of State for the purposes of appeals to the Secretary of State;

[*"appropriate day"*, means—

(a) in relation to a vehicle which is a motor vehicle, the last day of the calendar month in which falls the first anniversary of the date on which it was registered; and

(b) in relation to a vehicle which is a trailer, the last day of the calendar month in which falls the first anniversary of the date on which it was first sold or supplied by retail;]

*   *   *

"auxiliary station" means a vehicle testing station which is regularly not open for the carrying out of re-tests on certain normal working days;

"break-down vehicle" means a motor vehicle—

(a) on which is permanently mounted apparatus designed for raising one disabled vehicle partly from the ground and for drawing that vehicle when so raised; and

(b) which is not equipped to carry any load other than articles required for the operation of, or in connection with, that apparatus or for repairing disabled vehicles;

[*"design gross weight"* means—

(a) in the case of a vehicle equipped with a Ministry plate, the weight shown thereon as the design weight or, if no weight is so shown thereon, the weight shown thereon as the weight not to be exceeded in Great Britain;

(b) in the case of a vehicle which is not equipped with a Ministry plate, but which is equipped with a plate in accordance with regulation 66 of the Construction and Use Regulations, the maximum gross weight shown on the plate in respect of item 7 of Part I of Schedule 8 to those Regulations; and

(c) in any other case, the weight which the vehicle is designed or adapted not to exceed when in normal use and travelling on a road laden;]

"examination" means any operation being—

(a) a first examination;

(b) a re-test;

(c) a periodical test;

(d) a re-examination under regulation 33; or

[(e) an examination or re-examination for the purposes of an appeal against a determination made under these Regulations;]

[*"first examination"* means an examination or, as the case may be, examinations for which a vehicle is submitted under regulation 9;]

"Goods Vehicle Centre" means the Goods Vehicle Centre at [such office of the Vehicle and Operator Services Agency as the Secretary of State might direct];

"living van" means a vehicle whether mechanically propelled or not which is used as living accommodation by one or more persons, and which is also used for the carriage of goods or burden which are not needed by such one or more persons for the purpose of their residence in the vehicle;

"Ministry test date disc" means a plate issued by the Secretary of State for a goods vehicle being a trailer, following the issue of a goods vehicle test certificate for that trailer under these Regulations and containing—

(a) the identification mark allotted to that trailer and shown in that certificate;

(b) the date until which that certificate is valid; and

(c) the number of the vehicle testing station shown in the said certificate;

"notifiable alteration", in relation to a vehicle, means—

(a) an alteration made in the structure or fixed equipment of the vehicle which varies the carrying capacity or towing capacity of the vehicle;

(b) an alteration, affecting any part of a braking system or the steering system with which the vehicle is equipped or of the means of operation of either of those systems; or

(c) any other alteration made in the structure or fixed equipment of the vehicle which renders or is likely to render the vehicle unsafe to travel on roads at any weight equal to any plated weight shown in the plating certificate for that vehicle;

[*"out of hours"* means at any time either—

(a) on any day which is a Saturday, Sunday, Good Friday, Christmas Day or a Bank holiday (as defined in the Banking and Financial Dealings Act 1971); or

[(b) on any other day, other than between 6.00 am and 8.00 pm;]]

"periodical test", in relation to a vehicle, means a goods vehicle test carried out under Part IV of these Regulations on a vehicle in respect of which a goods vehicle test certificate has been issued on a first examination of it or as a result of a re-test following that examination or as a result of an appeal under any provision in these Regulations;

"plated particulars" means those particulars which are required to be shown in a Ministry plate under Schedule [10B] to the Construction and Use Regulations;

"plated weights" means such of the plated particulars related to gross weight, axle weight for each axle and train weight as are required to be shown in column (2) on the Ministry plate;

"play bus" means a motor vehicle which was originally constructed to carry more than 12 passengers but which has been adapted primarily for the carriage of play things for children (including articles required in connection with the use of those things);

[*"the prescribed construction and use requirements"*, in relation to a vehicle, mean those of the requirements specified in Part I of Schedule 3 which apply to the vehicle and the requirements of Part II of that Schedule;]

"re-test", in relation to a vehicle, means an examination which is

(a) an examination for plating and a goods vehicle test carried out on a vehicle under Part III of these Regulations subsequent to a first examination of that vehicle as a result of which a notice of refusal was issued; or

(b) a goods vehicle test carried out on a vehicle under Part IV of these Regulations subsequent to a periodical test of that vehicle as a result of which a notice of refusal was issued;

"*Secretary of State*" means the [Secretary of State for Transport];

"*sender*" means a person who informs the Secretary of State of a notifiable alteration under regulation 30;

"*sold or supplied by retail*", in relation to a trailer, means sold or supplied otherwise than to a person acquiring solely for the purpose of resale or of resupply for a valuable consideration;

* * *

["*vehicle testing station*" means a station provided by the Secretary of State under section 52(2) of the 1988 Act or such other place as he may consider appropriate for the purposes of carrying out an examination.]

(2) Any reference in these Regulations to—

(a) an examination for plating includes, in relation to a vehicle to which regulation 18 applies, an examination provided for in that regulation; and

(b) a vehicle of a make, model and type shall, in relation to a trailer, include a reference to a vehicle of a make and bearing a serial number.

(3) For the purpose of these Regulations, in counting the number of axles of a vehicle, where the centres of the areas of contact between all the wheels and the road surface can be included between any two vertical planes at right angles to the longitudinal axis of the vehicle less than [0.5] metres apart, those wheels shall be treated as constituting one axle.

(4) For the purpose of these Regulations, in determining when a trailer is first sold or supplied by retail the date of such first sale or supply by retail shall in the case of a trailer which is constructed with a chassis be taken to be the date on which that chassis (with or without a body mounted on it) is first sold or supplied by retail and in the case of any other trailer be taken to be the date the trailer is first sold or supplied by retail.

[(4A) Without prejudice to section 17 of the Interpretation Act 1978 and subject to the context, a reference in these Regulations to any enactment comprised in subordinate legislation (within the meaning of that Act) is a reference to that enactment as from time to time amended or as from time to time re-enacted with or without modification.]

(5) Unless the context otherwise requires, any reference in these Regulations to—

(a) a numbered regulation or Schedule is a reference to the regulation or Schedule bearing that number in these Regulations;

(b) a numbered paragraph is a reference to the paragraph bearing that number in the regulation or Schedule in which the reference appears;

(c) a vehicle is a reference to a vehicle to which these Regulations apply.

B21.05 *[Regulation 3 is printed as amended by SI 1990/448; SI 1991/252; SI 1993/ 2048 and 3013; SI 1994/328; the Vehicle Excise and Registration Act 1994, s.64 and Sch.4, para.4; SI 1997/82 and 263; the Secretary of State for the Environ- ment, Transport and the Regions Order 1997 (SI 1997/2971); SI 2000/1433; the Secretaries of State for Transport, Local Government and the Regions and for Environment, Food and Rural Affairs Order 2001 (SI 2001/2568); the Transfer* *of Functions (Transport, Local Government and the Regions) Order 2002 (SI 2002/2626); SI 2008/1460; SI 2010/448.*

The Goods Vehicle Department was a department of the Vehicle Inspectorate, now known as the Vehicle and Operator Services Agency (VOSA). For information on the range of services provided and VOSA locations, go to www.vosa.gov.uk [accessed March 2, 2011].

As to the Banking and Financial Dealings Act 1971, see the note to the Road Vehicles (Construction and Use) Regulations 1986 (SI 1986/1078) Sch.12, para.1 above.]

Application

4.—(1) Subject to paragraph (2), these Regulations apply to goods vehicles be-   **B21.06**
ing—

    (a) heavy motor cars and motor cars constructed or adapted for the purpose of forming part of an articulated vehicle;

    (b) other heavy motor cars;

    [(c) other motor cars, the design gross weight of which exceeds 3500 kilograms;]

    (d) semi-trailers;

    (e) converter dollies of any unladen weight manufactured on or after 1st January 1979; or

    (f) trailers, not being converter dollies or semi-trailers, the unladen weight of which exceeds 1020 kilograms.

(2) Nothing in these Regulations applies to goods vehicles of any of the classes of vehicle specified in Schedule 2.

[Regulation 4 is printed as amended by SI 1991/252.]   **B21.07**

Prescribed requirements for tests

5. *[Omitted.]*   **B21.08**

Supervision of tests

6. *[Omitted.]*   **B21.09**

Authority to drive and duties of driver

7.—(1) The person who drove the vehicle to an examination shall, except so   **B21.10**
far as he is permitted to be absent by the person who is carrying out the examination, be present throughout the whole of the examination, and shall drive the vehicle and operate its controls when and in such a manner as he may be directed by the person who is carrying out the examination to do so.

(2) The person who is carrying out an examination is authorised to drive the vehicle on a road or elsewhere.

(3) A contravention of this regulation is hereby declared to be an offence.

*   *   *

Part V

Regulations Governing Notifiable Alterations, Amendments of Plating Certificates and Re-Examination in Connection therewith

Secretary of State to be informed of notifiable alterations

B21.11   **30.** In the event of a notifiable alteration being made to a vehicle in respect of which a plating certificate has been issued, and before the vehicle to which the alteration has been made is used on roads, particulars of that alteration on a form approved by the Secretary of State shall be sent to him at the Goods Vehicle Centre, and any such form may contain a request by the sender for an amendment to be made as respects a plated weight shown on the plating certificate for the vehicle.

B21.12   *[As to the consequences of failure to notify the Secretary of State, see the Road Traffic Act 1988 s.53(3) above.*

With regard to the reference to the Goods Vehicle Centre, see the note to reg.3 above.]

Part VI

Miscellaneous Matters

*   *   *

General provisions as to fees

B21.13   **39.**—(1) In this Regulation *"exceptional circumstances"* means an accident, a fire, an epidemic, severe weather, a failure in the supply of essential services or other unexpected happening (excluding a breakdown or mechanical defect in a vehicle or non-delivery of spare parts therefor).

(2), (3) *[Omitted.]*

B21.14   *[The definition of "exceptional circumstances" in reg.39(1) is applied by reg.46.]*

*   *   *

Part VIII

Exemptions

[Exemptions from section 53(1) and (2) of the 1988 Act]

B21.15   **44.**—(1) The provisions of [section 53(1) and (2) of the 1988 Act] do not apply to the use of a vehicle for any of the following purposes—

(a) the purpose of submitting it by previous arrangement for, or of bringing it away from, or being used in the course of or in connection with any examination;

(b) where a goods vehicle test certificate is refused on an examination—

    (i) the purpose of delivering it by previous arrangement at, or bring-
ing it away from, a place where work is to be or has been done
on it to remedy the defects on the grounds of which the certificate was refused; or

    (ii) the purpose of delivering it, by towing it, to a place where it is to
be broken up;

(c) when unladen, the purpose of being driven or drawn by a vehicle
driven under a trade licence issued under [section 11 of the 1994 Act];

(d) the purpose of being driven or drawn where it has been imported into
Great Britain after arrival in Great Britain on the journey from the
place where it has arrived in Great Britain to a place where it is to be
kept by the person importing the vehicle or by any other person on
whose behalf the vehicle has been imported, and in this sub-paragraph
the reference to a vehicle being imported into Great Britain is a reference, in the case of a vehicle which has been so imported more than
once, to the first such importation, and in determining for the purposes
of this sub-paragraph when a vehicle was first so imported any such
importation as is referred to in paragraph 24 of Schedule 2 shall be
disregarded;

(e) any purpose for which it is authorised to be used on roads by an order
under [section 44 of the 1988 Act];

(f) any purpose connected with its seizure or detention [by a constable];

(g) any purpose connected with its removal, detention, seizure, condem-
nation or forfeiture under any provision in the Customs and Excise
Management Act 1979; and

(h) the purpose of removing it under section 3 of the Refuse Disposal
(Amenity) Act 1978, or under section 99 of the Road Traffic Regulation Act 1984 or of removing it from a parking place in pursuance of
an order under section 35(1) of the Road Traffic Regulation Act 1984,
an order relating to a parking place designated under section 45
thereof, or a provision of a designation order having effect by virtue
of section 53(3) thereof.

(2) The provisions of [section 53(1) and (2) of the 1988 Act] shall not apply to
the use of a vehicle in so far as such use occurs in any place (excluding the Isle of
Wight, the islands of Lewis, Mainland (Orkney), Mainland (Shetland) and Skye)
being an island or to any area mainly surrounded by water, being an island or
area from which motor vehicles not constructed for special purposes can at no
time be conveniently driven to a road in any other part of Great Britain by reason
of the absence of any bridge, tunnel, ford or other way suitable for the passage of
such motor vehicles.

[Regulation 44 is printed as amended by SI 1990/448; the Vehicle Excise and **B21.16**
Registration Act 1994 s.64 and Sch.4, para.4.]

[Exemption from section 63(2) of the 1988 Act]

45. Motor vehicles other than those manufactured on or after 1st October 1982 **B21.17**
and first used on or after 1st April 1983, not constructed or adapted to form part
of an articulated vehicle, are hereby exempted from the provisions of [section
63(2) of the 1988 Act].

B21.18   *[Regulation 45 is printed as amended by SI 1990/448.]*

Certificates of temporary exemption

B21.19   46.—(1) [The Secretary of State] may issue in respect of a vehicle a certificate of temporary exemption, by virtue of which that vehicle shall not, during the period specified in paragraph (2)(d), be subject to the provisions of [section 53(1) or (2) of the 1988 Act], where—

(a) he is satisfied that by reason of exceptional circumstances, as defined in regulation 39(1) affecting either a vehicle testing station or the vehicle, an examination cannot be completed by a date fixed under these Regulations for carrying out the examination; and

(b) the use of the vehicle on or after that date would be unlawful by virtue of the said provisions.

(2) Every certificate of temporary exemption shall be on a form approved by the Secretary of State and shall be signed by a person duly authorised on his behalf and shall contain—

(a) in the case of a certificate issued for a motor vehicle, the registration mark (if any) exhibited on the vehicle or, if no such mark is so exhibited, the chassis or serial number marked on the vehicle or, if no such number is so marked, the identification mark which shall have been allotted to the vehicle by the Secretary of State in the notice of appointment relating to the first examination of the vehicle;

(b) in the case of a certificate issued for a trailer, the identification mark which shall have been allotted to the trailer by the Secretary of State in the notice of appointment (if any) relating to the first examination of the trailer or shall have otherwise been allotted to the trailer by the Secretary of State under these Regulations;

(c) the date on which the certificate is issued; and

(d) the period during which the vehicle is exempted from the provisions of [section 53(1) or (2) of the 1988 Act] so, however, that no such period shall exceed three months in duration.

B21.20   *[Regulation 46 is printed as amended by SI 1990/448; SI 1997/82.]*

*   *   *

Regulation 4   SCHEDULE 2

CLASSES OF VEHICLE TO WHICH THESE REGULATIONS DO NOT APPLY

B21.21   1. Dual-purpose vehicles not constructed or adapted to form part of an articulated vehicle.

B21.22   2. Mobile cranes as defined in [paragraph 4(5) of Schedule 1 to the 1994 Act].

B21.23   3. Break-down vehicles.

B21.24   4. Engineering plant and plant, not being engineering plant, which is movable plant or equipment being a motor vehicle or trailer (not constructed primarily to carry a load) especially designed and constructed for the special purposes of engineering operations.

B21.25   5. Trailers being drying or mixing plant designed for the production of asphalt or of bituminous or tar macadam.

B21.26   [6. Tower wagons as defined in—

(a) paragraph 8 of Schedule 1 to the Vehicle Excise and Registration Act 1994 as originally enacted; or

(b) paragraph 17 of Schedule 2 to that Act as originally enacted.]

7. Road construction vehicles as defined in [section 61 of the Vehicle Excise and Registration Act 1994 as originally enacted [*q.v.*]] and road rollers. **B21.27**

8. Vehicles designed [and used solely] for fire fighting or fire salvage purposes. **B21.28**

9. Works trucks, straddle carriers used solely as works trucks, and works trailers. **B21.29**

10. Electrically-propelled motor vehicles. **B21.30**

11. Vehicles used solely for one or both of the following purposes— **B21.31**

(a) clearing frost, ice or snow from roads by means of a snow plough or similar contrivance, whether forming part of the vehicle or not, and

(b) spreading material on roads to deal with frost, ice or snow.

12. Motor vehicles used for no other purpose than the haulage of lifeboats and the conveyance of the necessary gear of the lifeboats which are being hauled. **B21.32**

[**13.** Living vans the design gross weight of which does not exceed 3500 kilograms.] **B21.33**

14. Vehicles constructed or adapted for, and used primarily for the purpose of, carrying equipment permanently fixed to the vehicle which equipment is used for medical, dental, veterinary, health, educational, display, clerical or experimental laboratory purposes such use— **B21.34**

(a) not directly involving the sale, hire or loan of goods from the vehicle; and

(b) not directly or indirectly involving drain cleaning or sewage or refuse collection.

15. Trailers which have no other brakes than a parking brake and brakes which automatically come into operation on the over-run of the trailer. **B21.35**

[**16.** A motor vehicle at a time when it is being used on a public road during any calendar week if— **B21.36**

(a) it is being used only in passing from land in the occupation of the person keeping the vehicle to other land in his occupation, and

(b) it has not been used on public roads for distances exceeding an aggregate of six miles in that calendar week,

and to a trailer drawn by a motor vehicle that is being used on a public road in such circumstances.

For the purposes of this paragraph *"public road"* has the meaning given in section 62(1) of the Vehicle Excise and Registration Act 1994.]

17. Agricultural motor vehicles and agricultural trailed appliances. **B21.37**

18. Agricultural trailers and agricultural trailed appliance conveyors drawn on roads only by an agricultural motor vehicle. **B21.38**

[**18A.** Converter dollies used solely for the purposes of agriculture, horticulture and forestry, or for any one or two of those purposes.] **B21.39**

19. Public service vehicles (as defined in section 1 of the Public Passenger Vehicles Act 1981 [*q.v.*]). **B21.40**

20. Licensed taxis (as defined in section 13(3) of the Transport Act 1985 [*q.v.*]). **B21.41**

21. Vehicles used solely for the purposes of funerals. **B21.42**

22. Goods vehicles to which any of the prescribed construction and use requirements do not apply by virtue of either of the following items in the Table in regulation 4(4) of the Construction and Use Regulations [*q.v.*] namely— **B21.43**

(a) item 1 (which relates to vehicles proceeding to a port for export);

(b) item 4 (which relates to vehicles in the service of a visiting force or of a headquarters).

23. Vehicles equipped with a new or improved equipment or types of equipment and used, solely by a manufacturer of vehicles or their equipment or by an importer of vehicles, for or in connection with the test or trial of any such equipment. **B21.44**

B21.45 **24.** Motor vehicles brought into Great Britain and displaying a registration mark mentioned in regulation 5 of the Motor Vehicles (International Circulation) Regulations 1971 [*SI 1971/937*], a period of twelve months not having elapsed since the vehicle in question was last brought into Great Britain.

B21.46 **25.** Motor vehicles [in respect of which a test certificate issued in accordance with Article 34 of the Road Traffic (Northern Ireland) Order 1981 [*SI 1981/154 (NI I), as amended; not reproduced in this work*] is in force or which are] for the time being licensed under the Vehicles (Excise) Act (Northern Ireland) 1972.

B21.47 **26.** Vehicles having a base or centre in any of the following islands, namely, Arran, Bute, Great Cumbrae, Islay, Mull, Tiree or North Uist from which the use of the vehicle on a journey is normally commenced.

B21.48 **27.** Trailers brought into Great Britain and having a base or centre in a country outside Great Britain from which the use of the vehicle on a journey is normally commenced, a period of twelve months not having elapsed since the vehicle in question was last brought into Great Britain.

B21.49 **28.** Track-laying vehicles.

B21.50 **29.** Steam propelled vehicles.

B21.51 **30.** Motor vehicles first used before 1st January 1960, used unladen and not drawing a laden trailer, and trailers manufactured before 1st January 1960 and used unladen.

For the purposes of this paragraph any determination as to when a motor vehicle is first used shall be made as provided in regulation 3(3) of the Construction and Use Regulations [*q.v.*].

B21.52 **31.** Motor vehicles constructed, and not merely adapted, for the purpose of street cleansing, or the collection or disposal of refuse or the collection or disposal of the contents of gullies and which are either—

    (a) three-wheeled vehicles, or

    (b) vehicles which—

        (i) are incapable by reason of their construction of exceeding a speed of 20 miles per hour on the level under their own power, or

        (ii) have an inside track width [of not more than 1100mm].

B21.53 **32.** Vehicles designed and used for the purpose of servicing or controlling or loading or unloading aircraft while so used—

    (a) on an aerodrome as defined in section 105(1) of the Civil Aviation Act 1982;

    (b) on roads outside such an aerodrome if, except when proceeding directly from one part of such an aerodrome to another part thereof, the vehicles are unladen and are not drawing a laden trailer.

B21.54 **33.** Vehicles designed for use, and used on an aerodrome mentioned in paragraph 32, solely for the purpose of road cleansing, the collection or disposal of refuse or the collection or disposal of the contents of gullies or cesspools.

B21.55 **34.** Vehicles provided for police purposes and maintained in workshops approved by the Secretary of State as suitable for such maintenance, being vehicles provided in England and Wales by a police authority or the Receiver for the metropolitan police district, or, in Scotland, by a police authority or a joint police committee.

B21.56 **35.** Heavy motor cars or motor cars constructed or adapted for the purpose of forming part of an articulated vehicle and which are used for drawing only a trailer falling within a class of vehicle specified in paragraph 13, 14 or 15 of this Schedule or a trailer being used for or in connection with any purpose for which it is authorised to be used on roads by an order under [section 44(1) of the 1988 Act] being an order authorising that trailer or any class or description of trailers comprising that trailer to be used on roads.

B21.57 **36.** Play buses.

B21.58 [**37.** A vehicle—

(a) which complies with the requirements specified in regulation 4(2) of the Motor Vehicles (Approval) Regulations 2001 [*SI 2001/25*];

(b) in respect of which a Minister's approval certificate has been issued under section 58 of the 1988 Act for the purposes of the type approval requirements prescribed by those Regulations; and

(c) in respect of which a Minister's approval certificate has not subsequently been issued under that section for the purposes of the type approval requirements prescribed by the National Type Approval for Goods Vehicles Regulations [*as defined in reg.3 above*].]

[Schedule 2 is printed as amended by SI 1990/448; SI 1991/252; SI 1995/ 1456; SI 2001/307; SI 2002/487; SI 2003/1816; SI 2005/2343. **B21.59**

The reference in para.7 above to s.61 of the Vehicle Excise and Registration Act 1994 would appear to be intended to be a reference to s.62(1) of that Act.]

The Use of Invalid Carriages on Highways Regulations 1988

(SI 1988/2268)

Citation and commencement

B22.01   **1.** *[Omitted.]*

Revocation and saving

B22.02   **2.**—(1) Subject to paragraph (2), the Use of Invalid Carriages on Highways Regulations 1970 [*SI 1970/1391*] (*"the 1970 Regulations"*) are hereby revoked.

(2) Nothing in these Regulations shall apply to invalid carriages manufactured before 30th January 1989, and the 1970 Regulations shall continue to apply to such invalid carriages as if these Regulations had not been made.

Interpretation

B22.03   **3.** In these Regulations —

the *"1970 Act"* means the Chronically Sick and Disabled Persons Act 1970;

the *"1986 Regulations"* means the Road Vehicles (Construction and Use) Regulations 1986 [*SI 1986/1078 (q.v.)*] ;

a *"Class 1 invalid carriage"* means an invalid carriage which is not mechanically propelled;

a *"Class 2 invalid carriage"* means a mechanically propelled invalid carriage which is so constructed or adapted as to be incapable of exceeding a speed of 4 miles per hour on the level under its own power;

a *"Class 3 invalid carriage"* means a mechanically propelled invalid carriage which is so constructed or adapted as to be capable of exceeding a speed of 4 miles per hour but incapable of exceeding a speed of 8 miles per hour on the level under its own power;

"horn" has the meaning given by regulation 37(10)(a) of the 1986 Regulations;

"reversing alarm" has the meaning given by regulation 37(10)(c) of the 1986 Regulations;

"road" has the meaning given by section 142(1) of the Road Traffic Regulation Act 1984 [*q.v.*];

"two-tone horn" has the meaning given by regulation 37(10)(d) of the 1986 Regulations.

Prescribed conditions for purposes of section 20(1) of the 1970 Act

B22.04   **4.** The conditions in accordance with which an invalid carriage must be used, in order that the modifications of the statutory provisions mentioned in subsection (1) of section 20 of the 1970 Act [*q.v.*] shall have effect in the case of the invalid carriage (being modifications of certain statutory provisions which relate to the use of vehicles on footways and roads) shall be—

    (a) in the case of Class 1, Class 2 and Class 3 invalid carriages that the invalid carriage must be used—

        (i) by a person falling within a class of persons for whose use it was constructed or adapted, being a person suffering from some physical defect or physical disability;

        (ii) by some other person for the purposes only of taking the invalid carriage to or bringing it away from any place where work of maintenance or repair is to be or has been carried out to the invalid carriage;

        (iii) by a manufacturer for the purposes only of testing or demonstrating the invalid carriage;

        (iv) by a person offering to sell the invalid carriage for the purpose only of demonstrating it; or

        (v) by a person giving practical training in the use of the invalid carriage for that purpose only;

    (b) in the case of Class 1, Class 2 and Class 3 invalid carriages, that any horn fitted to it must not be sounded in the circumstances set out in regulation 5;

    (c) in the case of Class 3 invalid carriages only—

        (i) that the invalid carriage must not be used by a person who is aged under 14 years;

        (ii) that, when being used on a footway, the invalid carriage must not be driven at a speed greater than 4 miles per hour;

        (iii) that the invalid carriage must not be used on a footway unless the device fitted in accordance with regulation 10(1)(a) is operating; and

        (iv) that the invalid carriage must not be used at any time unless the speed indicator fitted to it in accordance with regulation 10(1)(b) is operating.

5. The circumstances referred to in regulation 4(b) are that the invalid carriage is either—   **B22.05**

    (a) stationary on a road, at any time, other than at times of danger due to another moving vehicle on or near the road; or

    (b) in motion on a road which is a restricted road for the purposes of section 81 of the Road Traffic Regulation Act 1984 between 23.30 hours and 07.00 hours in the following morning.

Prescribed requirements for purposes of section 20(1) of the 1970 Act

6. The requirements with which an invalid carriage must comply in order that the modifications of the statutory provisions mentioned in subsection (1) of section 20 of the 1970 Act [*q.v.*] shall have effect in the case of the invalid carriage (being modifications of certain statutory provisions which related to the use of vehicles on footways and roads) shall be—   **B22.06**

    (a) that it shall be a Class 1, Class 2 or Class 3 invalid carriage; and

(b) the requirements specified in regulations 7 to 14.

Unladen weight

B22.07   7.—(1) The unladen weight of a Class 1 or Class 2 invalid carriage shall not exceed 113.4 kilograms.

(2) The unladen weight of a Class 3 invalid carriage shall not exceed 150 kilograms.

(3) In this regulation *"unladen weight"* means the weight of the invalid carriage inclusive of the weight of water, fuel or accumulators used for the purpose of the supply of power for its propulsion and of loose tools, but exclusive of the weight of any other load or of a person carried by the invalid carriage.

Means of stopping

B22.08   8.—(1) A Class 2 or Class 3 invalid carriage shall be so constructed and maintained that it meets the requirements set out in paragraphs (2) to (4).

(2) The invalid carriage shall be capable of being brought to rest in all conditions of use with reasonable directional stability and within a reasonable distance.

(3) When the invalid carriage is not being propelled or is left unattended it shall be capable of being held stationary indefinitely in all conditions of use on a gradient of at least 1 in 5.

(4) The requirements of paragraphs (2) and (3) shall not be regarded as met unless the necessary braking effect can be achieved by the appropriate use—

    (a) of the invalid carriage's propulsion unit transmission gear or of both the propulsion unit and transmission gear;

    (b) of a separate system fitted to the vehicle (which may be a system which operates upon the propulsion unit or transmission gear); or

    (c) of a combination of the means of achieving a braking effect referred to in sub-paragraphs (a) and (b);

and in the case of paragraph (3) without depending upon any hydraulic or pneumatic device or on the flow of electrical current.

Lighting

B22.09   9. A Class 2 or Class 3 invalid carriage when on the carriageway of any road shall comply with the requirements specified in [the Road Vehicles Lighting Regulations 1989 [*SI 1989/1796 (q.v.)*]] as if it was a motor vehicle within the meaning of [the Road Traffic Act 1988] and as if any reference to an invalid carriage in those Regulations included an invalid carriage within the meaning of the 1970 Act.

B22.10   *[Regulation 9 is printed as amended by the Interpretation Act 1978 ss.17(2)(a) and 23(1).]*

Speed device and speed indicator

B22.11   10.—(1) A Class 3 invalid carriage shall be fitted with—

    (a) a device which is capable of limiting the maximum speed of the invalid carriage to 4 miles per hour on the level under its own power and which can be put into operation by the user; and

(b) a speed indicator.

(2) A speed indicator fitted in accordance with this regulation shall be kept free from any obstruction which might prevent it being easily seen by the user of the invalid carriage and shall be maintained in efficient working order.

(3) In this regulation, *"speed indicator"* means a device fitted to an invalid carriage for the purpose of indicating to the user of the invalid carriage whether the device referred to in paragraph (1)(a) is in operation.

Width

11. The overall width of a Class 3 invalid carriage shall not exceed 0.85 metres.   **B22.12**

Audible warning instrument

12.—(1) A Class 3 invalid carriage shall be fitted with a horn, not being a   **B22.13** reversing alarm or a two-tone horn.

(2) The sound emitted by any horn fitted to an invalid carriage shall be continuous and uniform and not strident.

Vision

13.—(1) A Class 2 or Class 3 invalid carriage shall be so constructed that the   **B22.14** user of the invalid carriage can at all times have a full view of the road and traffic ahead when controlling the invalid carriage.

(2) Any windscreen or window fitted to a Class 2 or Class 3 invalid carriage shall be made of safety glass or safety glazing and shall be maintained in such condition that it does not obscure the vision of the user of the invalid carriage while the invalid carriage is being driven.

(3) In this regulation—

"*safety glass*" means glass so manufactured or treated that if fractured it does not fly into fragments likely to cause severe cuts; and

"*safety glazing*" means material other than glass so manufactured or treated that if fractured it does not fly into fragments likely to cause severe cuts.

Rear view mirrors

14.—(1) A Class 3invalid carriage shall be fitted either internally or externally   **B22.15** with a rear view mirror.

(2) Any rear view mirror fitted to an invalid carriage shall be so constructed or treated that if fractured it does not fly into fragments likely to cause severe cuts.

(3) In this regulation *"rear view mirror"* means a mirror to assist the user of the invalid carriage to become aware of traffic to the rear of the invalid carriage.

The Road Vehicles Lighting Regulations 1989

(SI 1989/1796)

B23.01 *[The explanatory note accompanying the 1989 Regulations draws attention specifically to the drafting of certain of the provisions in the regulations relating to contraventions. These, unlike the corresponding provisions in the earlier regulations, are drafted so that contraventions are offences under s.42(1)(b) of the Road Traffic Act 1988 (q.v.), rather than under s.42(1)(a).*

The explanatory notes also included the following explanation of European approval marks:

7. The following explanation of European approval marks is added for convenience—

EXPLANATION OF EUROPEAN APPROVAL MARKS EXAMPLES OF MARKINGS

HCR

021507

UN: ECE Dipped and
Main-Beam Halogen Headlamp

III

011471

E.C. Class III Triangular Shaped
Rectro Reflector

Notes—

1. An E within a circle indicates a device which has been approved to a UN: ECE Regulation. (United Nations: Economic Commission for Europe, based in Geneva.)

2. An e within a rectangle indicates a device which has been approved to an EEC Directive. (European Economic Community, based in Brussels.)

3. The number within the circle or rectangle beside the E or e is the distinguishing number of the country that issued the approval. 11 stands for the United Kingdom.

4. An arrow below the circle or rectangle means, in the case of a headlamp, that it dips to the left. A double-headed arrow means that the headlamp bulb holder can be adjusted so as to dip either to the left or to the right.

5. In the case of a motor vehicle registered for use in the United Kingdom which is fitted with European-approved headlamps, an arrow (single or double headed) is required to be present below the approval mark on the lenses of the headlamps.

6. An arrow below the circle or rectangle means, in the case of any other type of lamp, that the lamp is "handed" and must be fitted to the side of the vehicle to which the arrow points except in the case of a direction indicator of category 3, 4 or 5, in which case the lamp is fitted on the side of the vehicle and the arrow points towards the front of the vehicle.

7. The symbols above the circle or rectangle identify the function, category or class of device as follows—

A	Front position lamp (or end-outline marker lamp)
C	Dipped-beam headlamp
R	Main-beam headlamp
S	Sealed-beam headlamp
H	Halogen headlamp
B	Front fog lamp (white or yellow)
1	Category 1 front direction indicator
	(suitable for fitting at least 40mm from a headlamp or front fog lamp)
1a	Category 1a front direction indicator
	(suitable for fitting at least 20mm from a headlamp or front fog lamp)
1b	Category 1b front direction indicator
	(suitable for fitting less than 20mm from a headlamp or front fog lamp)
2a	Category 2a rear direction indicator
	(with single level of intensity)
2b	Category 2b rear director indicator
	(with dual level of intensity)
3	Category 3 front-side direction indicator
4	Category 4 front-side direction indicator
5	Category 5 side-repeater direction indicator
11	Category 11 front
12	Category 12 rear direction indicators for motor cycles only
13	Category 13 side repeater
SM	Side marker lamp
R	Rear position lamp
B or F	Rear fog lamp (red)
S1	Stop lamp with single level of intensity
S2	Stop lamp with two levels of intensity
AR	Reversing lamp
I	Class I retro reflector
IA	Class IA retro reflector
III	Class III retro reflector
	(triangular—for trailers only)
IIIA	Class IIIA retro reflector
	(triangular—for trailers only)
No symbol	No A, R, S1 or S2 is required on a position lamp or a stop lamp approved for use only on motor cycles
	Common combinations of symbols—
R–S1	Rear position lamp which is also a stop lamp
HCR	Halogen headlamp emitting both main and dipped-beam
	Other combinations of symbols are possible.

The text of these regulations has been amended by: **B23.02** *the Tramcars and Trolley Vehicles (Modification of Enactments) Regulations 1992 (SI 1992/1217), reg.14 (July 1, 1992);*

the Road Vehicles Lighting (Amendment) Regulations 1994 (SI 1994/2280) (October 1, 1994 and April 1, 1995);

the Road Vehicles Lighting (Amendment) Regulations 1996 (SI 1996/3016) (July 1, 1997);

the Road Vehicles Lighting (Amendment) Regulations 2001 (SI 2001/560) (March 21, 2001);

the Fire and Rescue Services Act 2004 (Consequential Amendments) (England) Order 2004 (SI 2004/3168) (December 30, 2004);

the Road Vehicles Lighting (Amendment) Regulations 2005 (SI 2005/2559) (October 21, 2005);

the Fire and Rescue Services Act 2004 (Consequential Amendments) (Wales) Order 2005 (SI 2005/2929) (October 25, 2005); and

the Road Vehicles Lighting (Amendment) (No.2) Regulations 2005 (SI 2005/3169) (December 12, 2005).

the Serious Organised Crime and Police Act 2005 (Consequential and Supplementary Amendments to Secondary Legislation) Order 2006 (SI 2006/594) (April 1, 2006);

the Medical Act 1983 (Amendment) and Miscellaneous Amendments Order 2006 (SI 2006/1914) (October 19, 2007);

the Consumer Protection from Unfair Trading Regulations 2008 (SI 2008/1277) (May 26, 2008); and

the Road Vehicles Lighting and Goods Vehicles (Plating and Testing) (Amendment) Regulations (SI 2009/3220) (January 4, 2010).

The amending instruments are referred to in the notes to the principal regulations only by their years and numbers. The dates referred to above are the dates on which the amending instruments came into force.]

ARRANGEMENT OF REGULATIONS

B23.03

PART I

PRELIMINARY

Regulation

*　　*　　*

10.   Rear position lamps
11.   Rear fog lamps
12.   Stop lamps
13.   End-outline marker lamps
14.   Reversing lamps
15.   Rear registration plate lamps
16.   Warning beacons
17.   Side retro reflectors
18.   Rear retro reflectors
19.   Rear markings
20.   Pedal retro reflectors
21.   Front retro reflectors
22.   Diagram showing where unlit parking is not permitted near a junction
23.   Example of marking showing the vertical downwards inclination of the dipped-beam headlamps

PART I

PRELIMINARY

Commencement, citation and revocations

B23.04   **1.** *[Omitted.]*

Statement under section 43(3) of the Road Traffic Act 1988

B23.05   **2.** *[Omitted.]*

Interpretation

B23.06   **3.**—(1) Unless the context otherwise requires, any reference in these Regulations —

     (a) to a numbered regulation or Schedule is a reference to the regulation or Schedule bearing that number in these Regulations,

     (b) to a numbered paragraph is to the paragraph bearing that number in the regulation or Schedule in which the reference occurs, and

     (c) to a numbered or lettered sub-paragraph is to the sub-paragraph bearing that number in the paragraph in which the reference occurs.

(2) In these Regulations, unless the context otherwise requires, any expressions for which there is an entry in column 1 of the Table has the meaning given against it in column 2 or is to be construed in accordance with directions given against it in that column.

TABLE

1 *Expression*	2 *Meaning*
"The Act"	The Road Traffic Act 1988 [*q.v.*].

1 *Expression*	2 *Meaning*
"The Construction and Use Regulations"	The Road Vehicles (Construction and Use) Regulations 1986 [*SI 1986/1078 (q.v.)*].
"The Designation of Approval Marks Regulations"	The Motor Vehicles (Designation of Approval Marks) Regulations 1979 [*SI 1979/1088, as amended; not reproduced in this work*].
["Abnormal load escort vehicle"	A vehicle which is clearly identifiable to other road users as a vehicle used for the purposes of escorting abnormal loads by having on its front suitable markings and on its sides and rear retro-reflective markings.]
"Agricultural vehicle"	A vehicle constructed or adapted for agriculture, grass cutting, forestry, land levelling, dredging or similar operations and primarily used for one or more of these purposes, and includes any trailer drawn by an agricultural vehicle.
"Angles of visibility"	A requirement for a lamp or reflector fitted to a vehicle to have specified horizontal and vertical angles of visibility is a requirement that at least 50 per cent of the apparent surface must be visible from any point within those angles when every door, tailgate, boot lid, engine cover, cab or other movable part of the vehicle is in the closed position.
"Apparent surface"	For any given direction of observation, is the orthogonal projection of a light-emitting surface in a plane perpendicular to the direction of observation and touching that surface.
"Articulated bus"	Has the same meaning as in the Construction and Use Regulations.
"Articulated vehicle"	Has the same meaning as in the Construction and Use Regulations.
"Breakdown vehicle"	A vehicle used to attend an accident or breakdown or to draw a broken down vehicle.
"Bus"	Has the same meaning as in the Construction and Use Regulations.
"Caravan"	A trailer which is constructed (and not merely adapted) for human habitation.
"cc"	Cubic centimetre or centimetres (as the case may be).
"Circuit-closed tell-tale"	A light showing that a device has been switched on.
"cm"	Centimetre or centimetres (as the case may be).
"cm²"	Square centimetre or centimetres (as the case may be).

1 Expression	2 Meaning
"Combat vehicle"	A vehicle of a type described at item 1, 2 or 3 in column 1 of Schedule 1 to the Motor Vehicles (Authorisation of Special Types) General Order 1979 [*SI 1979/1198*].
[*"Community Directive 76/756/EEC, as last amended by Directive 89/278/EEC"*]	Council Directive 76/756/EEC of 27.7.76 (O.J. L262, 27.9.76, p.1) as amended by Commission Directive 80/233/EEC of 21.11.79 (O.J. L51, 25.2.80, p.8), Commission Directive 82/244/EEC of 17.3.82 (O.J. L109, 22.4.82, p.31), Council Directive 83/276/EEC of 26.5.83 (O.J. L151, 9.6.83, p.47), Commission Directive 84/8/EEC of 14.12.83 (O.J. L9, 12.1.84, p.24) and Commission Directive 89/278/EEC of 23.3.89 (O.J. L109, 20.4.89, p.38).
[*"Community Directive 76/756/EEC, as last amended by Directive 91/663/EEC"*]	Council Directive 76/756/EEC as last amended by Directive 89/278/EEC and further amended by Commission Directive 91/663/EEC (O.J. L366, 31.12.91, p.17).]
[*"Conspicuity marking"*]	A device intended to increase the conspicuity of a vehicle, when viewed from the side or rear, by the reflection of light emanating from a light source not connected to the vehicle, the observer being situated near the source.]
"Daytime hours"	The time between half an hour before sunrise and half an hour after sunset.
"Dim-dip device"	A device which is capable of causing a dipped-beam headlamp to operate at reduced intensity.
"Dipped beam"	A beam of light emitted by a lamp which illuminates the road ahead of the vehicle without causing undue dazzle or discomfort to oncoming drivers or other road users.
"Direction indicator"	A lamp on a vehicle used to indicate to other road users that the driver intends to change direction to the right or to the left.
"Dual-purpose vehicle"	Has the same meaning as in the Construction and Use Regulations.

1	2
Expression	Meaning
"Emergency vehicle"	A [vehicle] of any of the following descriptions—
	(a) a vehicle used for fire brigade [or, in England [or Wales], fire and rescue authority], ambulance or police purposes;
	[(aa) as regards England and Wales, and so far as relating to the functions of the Serious Organised Crime Agency which are exercisable in or as regards Scotland and which relate to reserved matters (within the meaning of the Scotland Act 1998), a vehicle used for Serious Organised Crime Agency purposes;]
	(b) an ambulance, being a vehicle (other than an invalid carriage) which is constructed or adapted for the purposes of conveying sick, injured or disabled persons and which is used for such purposes;
	(c) a vehicle owned by a body formed primarily for the purposes of fire salvage and used for those or similar purposes;
	(d) a vehicle owned by the Forestry Commission or by a local authority and used from time to time for the purposes of fighting fires;
	(e) [a vehicle owned or operated by the Secretary of State for Defence and used]—
	(i) for the purposes of the disposal of bombs or explosives,
	[(ii) for the purposes of any activity—
	(aa) which prevents or decreases the exposure of persons to radiation arising from a radiation accident or radiation emergency, or
	(bb) in connection with an event which could lead to a radiation accident or radiation emergency;] [or]
	(iii) by the Royal Air Force Mountain Rescue Service for the purposes of rescue operations or any other emergencies, [...]
	(iv) [...]

1 *Expression*	2 *Meaning*
	(f) a vehicle primarily used for the purposes of the Blood Transfusion Service provided under the National Health Service Act 1977 or under the National Health Service (Scotland) Act 1978; (g) a vehicle used by Her Majesty's Coastguard or Coastguard Auxiliary Service for the purposes of giving aid to persons in danger or vessels in distress on or near the coast; (h) a vehicle owned by the British Coal Corporation and used for the purposes of rescue operations at mines; (i) a vehicle owned by the Royal National Lifeboat Institution and used for the purposes of launching lifeboats; [...] (j) a vehicle primarily used for the purposes of conveying any human tissue for transplanting or similar purposes; [...] (k) a vehicle under the lawful control of the Commissioners for Her Majesty's Revenue and Customs and used from time to time for the purposes of the investigation of serious crime (which, save for the omission of the words "and, where the authorising officer is within subsection (5)(h), it relates to an assigned matter within the meaning of section 1(1) of the Customs and Excise Management Act 1979", has the meaning given in section 93(4) of the Police Act 1997)[; and (l) a vehicle used for mountain rescue purposes.]
"End-outline marker lamp"	A lamp fitted near the outer edge of a vehicle in addition to the front and rear position lamps to indicate the presence of a wide vehicle.
"Engineering plant"	Has the same meaning as in the Construction and Use Regulations.

1 *Expression*	2 *Meaning*
"Extreme outer edge"	In relation to a side of a vehicle, the vertical plane parallel with the longitudinal axis of the vehicle, and coinciding with its lateral outer edge, disregarding the projection of— (a) so much of the distortion of any tyre as is caused by the weight of the vehicle, (b) any connections for tyre pressure gauges, (c) any anti-skid devices which may be mounted on the wheels, (d) rear-view mirrors, (e) lamps and reflectors, (f) customs seals affixed to the vehicle, and devices for securing and protecting such seals, and (g) special equipment.
"Front fog lamp"	A lamp used to improve the illumination of the road in front of a motor vehicle in conditions of seriously reduced visibility.
"Front position lamp"	A lamp used to indicate the presence and width of a vehicle when viewed from the front.
"First used"	References to the date of first use of a vehicle shall be construed in accordance with regulation 3(3) of the Construction and Use Regulations.
"Hazard warning signal device"	A device which is capable of causing all the direction indicators with which a vehicle, or a combination of vehicles, is fitted to operate simultaneously.
"Headlamp"	A lamp used to illuminate the road in front of a vehicle and which is not a front fog lamp.
"Headlamp levelling device"	Either— (a) an automatic headlamp levelling device by means of which the downward inclination of any dipped-beam headlamp is automatically maintained regardless of the load on the vehicle, or (b) a manual headlamp levelling device by means of which the downward inclination of any dipped-beam headlamp may be adjusted by a manual control operable from the driving seat of the vehicle.
"Home forces"	The naval, military or air forces of Her Majesty raised in the United Kingdom.
"Home forces' vehicle"	A vehicle owned by, or in the service of, the home forces and used for naval, military or air force purposes.

1 Expression	2 Meaning
"Horse-drawn"	In relation to a vehicle, means that the vehicle is drawn by a horse or other animal.
"Hours of darkness"	The time between half an hour after sunset and half an hour before sunrise.
"Illuminated area"	The expression, in relation to a headlamp, front fog lamp and reversing lamp, in each case fitted with a reflector, means the orthogonal projection of the full aperture of the reflector on a plane (touching the surface of the lamp) at right angles to the longitudinal axis of the vehicle to which the lamp is fitted. If the light-emitting surface extends over only part of the full aperture of the reflector, then the projection of only that part shall be taken into account. In the case of a dipped-beam headlamp, the illuminated area is limited by the apparent trace of the cut-off on the lens.
	The expression, in relation to any other lamp, means the part of the orthogonal projection of the light-emitting surface on a plane (touching the surface of the lamp) at right angles to the longitudinal axis of the vehicle to which it is fitted, the boundary of which is such that if the straight edge of an opaque screen touches it at any point 98 per cent of the total intensity of the light is shown in the direction parallel to the longitudinal axis of the vehicle. Accordingly, for the purposes of determining the lower, upper and lateral edges of the lamp, only a screen placed with its straight edge horizontally or vertically needs to be considered.
"Industrial tractor"	Has the same meaning as in the Construction and Use Regulations.
"Installation and performance requirements"	In relation to any lamp, reflector, rear marking or device, the requirements specified in the Schedules to these Regulations relating to that lamp, reflector, rear marking or device.
"Invalid carriage"	A mechanically propelled vehicle constructed or adapted for the carriage of one person, being a person suffering from some physical defect or disability.
"Kerbside weight"	Has the same meaning as in the Construction and Use Regulations.
"kg"	Kilogram or kilograms (as the case may be).
[*"km/h"*	Kilometre per hour or kilometres per hour (as the case may be).]

1 Expression	2 Meaning
"Light-emitting surface"	In relation to a lamp, that part of the exterior surface of the lens through which light is emitted when the lamp is lit, and in relation to a retro reflector that part of the exterior surface of the retro reflector from which light can be reflected.
"m"	Metre or metres (as the case may be).
"Main beam"	A beam of light emitted by a headlamp which illuminates the road over a long distance ahead of the vehicle.
["Mandatory ECE conspicuity requirements"	The requirements specified in— (a) paragraph 5.15. of ECE Regulation 48 in respect of a conspicuity marking; and (b) paragraph 6.21. of ECE Regulation 48 as relating to vehicles for which the fitting of conspicuity markings is mandatory.]
"Matched pair"	In relation to lamps, a pair of lamps in respect of which— (a) both lamps emit light of substantially the same colour and intensity, and (b) both lamps are of the same size and of such a shape that they are symmetrical to one another.
"Maximum distance from the side of the vehicle"	The expression means— (a) in relation to a lamp fitted to a vehicle, the shortest distance from the boundary of the illuminated area to an extreme outer edge of the vehicle, and (b) in relation to a retro reflector fitted to a vehicle, the shortest distance from the boundary of the reflecting area to an extreme outer edge of the vehicle.
"Maximum gross weight"	Has the same meaning as in the Construction and Use Regulations.
"Maximum height above the ground"	The height above which no part of the illuminated area in the case of a lamp, or the reflecting area in the case of a retro reflector, extends when the vehicle is at its kerbside weight and when each tyre with which the vehicle is fitted is inflated to the pressure recommended by the manufacturer of the vehicle.
"Maximum speed"	Has the same meaning as in the Construction and Use Regulations.

1 Expression	2 Meaning
"Minimum height above the ground"	The height below which no part of the illuminated area in the case of a lamp, or the reflecting area in the case of a retro reflector, extends when the vehicle is at its kerbside weight and when each tyre with which the vehicle is fitted is inflated to the pressure recommended by the manufacturer of the vehicle.
"mm"	Millimetre or millimetres (as the case may be).
"Motor bicycle combination"	A combination of a solo motor bicycle and a sidecar.
"Motor tractor"	Has the same meaning as in the Construction and Use Regulations.
"Motorway"	Has the same meaning as in Schedule 6 of the Road Traffic Regulation Act 1984 [*q.v.*].
"Movable platform"	A platform which is attached to, and may be moved by means of, an extendible boom.
"mph"	Mile per hour or miles per hour (as the case may be).
"Obligatory"	In relation to a lamp, reflector, rear marking or device, means a lamp, reflector, rear marking or device with which a vehicle, its load or equipment is required by these Regulations to be fitted.
"Operational tell-tale"	A warning device readily visible or audible to the driver and showing whether a device that has been switched on is operating correctly or not.
"Optional"	In relation to a lamp, reflector, rear marking or device, means a lamp, reflector, rear marking or device with which a vehicle, its load or equipment is not required by these Regulations to be fitted. [But, when used in the expression *"Optional ECE conspicuity requirements"*, shall be construed in accordance with the definition of that expression.]
[*"Optional ECE conspicuity requirements"*	The requirements specified in— (a) paragraph 5.15. of ECE Regulation 48 in respect of a conspicuity marking; and (b) paragraph 6.21. of ECE Regulation 48 as relating to vehicles for which the fitting of conspicuity markings is optional.]
"Overall length"	Has the same meaning as in the Construction and Use Regulations.
"Overall width"	Has the same meaning as in the Construction and Use Regulations.

1 Expression	2 Meaning
"Pair"	In relation to lamps, reflectors or rear markings means a pair of lamps, reflectors or rear markings, including a matched pair, one on each side of the vehicle, in respect of which the following conditions are met— (a) each lamp, reflector or rear marking is at the same height above the ground, and (b) each lamp, reflector or rear marking is at the same distance from the extreme outer edge of the vehicle. In the case of an asymmetric vehicle, those conditions shall be deemed to be met if they are as near as practicable to being met.
"Passenger vehicle"	Has the same meaning as in the Construction and Use Regulations.
"Pedal cycle"	A vehicle which is not constructed or adapted to be propelled by mechanical power and which is equipped with pedals, including an electrically assisted pedal cycle prescribed for the purposes of section 189 of the Act and section 140 of the Road Traffic Regulation Act 1984.
"Pedal retro reflector"	A retro reflector attached to or incorporated in the pedals of a pedal cycle or motor bicycle.
"Pedestrian-controlled vehicle"	Has the same meaning as in the Construction and Use Regulations.
[*"Prescribed sign"*	A sign which is of a type shown in Schedule 21A and complies with the requirements of that Schedule.]
[*"Radiation accident"* and *"radiation emergency"*	Have the same meaning as in the Radiation (Emergency Preparedness and Public Information) Regulations 2001 [*SI 2001/2975; not reproduced in this work.*]]
"Rear fog lamp"	A lamp used to render a vehicle more readily visible from the rear in conditions of seriously reduced visibility.
"Rear position lamp"	A lamp used to indicate the presence and width of a vehicle when viewed from the rear.
"Rear retro reflector"	A retro reflector used to indicate the presence and width of a vehicle when viewed from the rear.
"Rear registration plate lamp"	A lamp used to illuminate the rear registration plate.

1 Expression	2 Meaning

"Reflecting area"	In relation to a retro reflector fitted to a vehicle, the area of the orthogonal projection on a vertical plane (touching the surface of the reflector)—
	    (a) at right angles to the longitudinal axis of the vehicle of that part of the reflector designed to reflect light in the case of a front or a rear retro reflector, and
	    (b) parallel to the longitudinal axis of the vehicle of that part of the reflector designed to reflect light in the case of a side retro reflector.

"Reversing lamp"	A lamp used to illuminate the road to the rear of a vehicle for the purpose of reversing and to warn other road users that the vehicle is reversing or about to reverse.
"Road clearance vehicle"	A mechanically propelled vehicle used for dealing with frost, ice or snow on roads.
"Running lamp"	A lamp (not being a front position lamp, an end-outline marker lamp, headlamp or front fog lamp) used to make the presence of a moving motor vehicle readily visible from the front.
"Separation distance"	In relation to two lamps or two retro reflectors the expression means, except where otherwise specified, the shortest distance between the orthogonal projections in a plane perpendicular to the longitudinal axis of the vehicle of the illuminated areas of the two lamps or the reflecting areas of the two reflectors.
"Service braking system"	Has the same meaning as in the Construction and Use Regulations.
"Side marker lamp"	A lamp fitted to the side of a vehicle or its load and used to render the vehicle more visible to other road users.
"Side retro reflector"	A reflector fitted to the side of a vehicle or its load and used to render the vehicle more visible from the side.
"Solo motor bicycle"	A motor bicycle without a sidecar.
"Special equipment"	A movable platform fitted to a vehicle, the apparatus for moving the platform and any jacks fitted to the vehicle for stabilising it while the movable platform is in use.
"Special warning lamp"	A lamp, fitted to the front or rear of a vehicle, capable of emitting a blue flashing light and not any other kind of light.

1 Expression	2 Meaning
"Stop lamp"	A lamp used to indicate to road users that the brakes of a vehicle or combination of vehicles are being applied.
["Traffic officer"	Has the same meaning as in section 15 of the Traffic Management Act 2004.]
"Traffic sign"	Has the same meaning given by section 64(1) of [the Road Traffic Regulation Act 1984] .
"Trailer"	A vehicle constructed or adapted to be drawn by another vehicle.
"Unrestricted dual-carriageway road"	A dual-carriageway within the meaning given by paragraph 2 of Schedule 6 to the Road Traffic Regulation Act 1984 on which a motor vehicle may lawfully be driven at a speed exceeding 50mph.
"Unladen weight"	Has the same meaning as in the Construction and Use Regulations.
"Vehicle in the service of a visiting force or of a headquarters"	Has the same meaning as in the Construction and Use Regulations.
"Visiting vehicle"	Has the meaning given by regulation 3(1) of the [Motor Vehicles (International Circulation) Regulations 1985 [SI 1985/610; not reproduced in this work]].
"Warning beacon"	A lamp that is capable of emitting a flashing or rotating beam of light throughout 360° in the horizontal plane.
"Wheel"	Has the same meaning as in the Construction and Use Regulations (see also paragraph (7)).
"Wheeled"	Has the same meaning as in the Construction and Use Regulations.
"Work lamp"	A lamp used to illuminate a working area or the scene of an accident, breakdown or roadworks in the vicinity of the vehicle to which it is fitted.
"Works trailer"	Has the same meaning as in the Construction and Use Regulations.
"Works truck"	Has the same meaning as in the Construction and Use Regulations.

(3) Material designed primarily to reflect light is, when reflecting light, to be treated for the purposes of these Regulations as showing a light, and material capable of reflecting an image is not, when reflecting the image of a light, to be so treated.

(4) In these Regulations a reference to one lamp, except in the case of a dipped-beam headlamp, a main-beam headlamp and a front fog lamp, includes any combination of two or more lamps, whether identical or not, having the same function and emitting light of the same colour, if it comprises devices the aggre-

gate illuminated area of which occupies 60 per cent or more of the area of the smallest rectangle circumscribing those illuminated areas.

(5) In these Regulations a reference to two lamps includes—

(a) a single illuminated area which—

(i) is placed symmetrically in relation to the longitudinal axis of the vehicle,

(ii) extends on both sides to within 400mm of the extreme outer edge of the vehicle,

(iii) is not less than 800mm long, and

(iv) is illuminated by not less than two sources of light, and

(b) any number of illuminated areas which—

(i) are juxtaposed,

(ii) if on the same transverse plane have illuminated areas which occupy not less than 60 per cent of the area of the smallest rectangle circumscribing their illuminated areas,

(iii) are placed symmetrically in relation to the median longitudinal plane of the vehicle,

(iv) extend on both sides to within 400mm of the extreme outer edge of the vehicle,

(v) do not have a total length of less than 800mm, and

(vi) are illuminated by not less than two sources of light.

(6) Where a part fitted to a vehicle is required by these Regulations to be marked with a British Standard mark, the requirements shall not be regarded as met unless, in addition to being marked as required, the part complied with the relevant British Standard at the time when the part was first fitted to the vehicle.

(7) A reference in these Regulations to the number of wheels of a vehicle shall be construed in accordance with regulation 3 of the Construction and Use Regulations.

(8) A reference in a Schedule to there being no requirement in relation to a lamp, reflector, rear marking or device is without prejudice to any other provision in these Regulations affecting same.

[(9) In these Regulations, a reference to "ECE Regulation" followed by a number is a reference to the regulation of the same number annexed to the Agreement concerning the adoption of uniform conditions of approval for Motor Vehicle Equipment and Parts and reciprocal recognition thereof concluded at Geneva on 2nd March 1958 as revised and retitled the Agreement Concerning the Adoption of Uniform Technical Prescriptions for Wheeled Vehicles, Equipment and Parts which can be fitted and/or be used on Wheeled Vehicles and the Conditions for reciprocal recognition of approvals granted on the basis of these Prescriptions by an agreement at Geneva on 5th October 1995.

(10) In these Regulations, a reference to ECE Regulation 48 is to that Regulation as amended by the 03 series of amendments (as in force on 12th June 2007) with the following modifications—

(a) footnote 6 is omitted;

(b) paragraph 6.21.4.1.3. is deemed to read "In the case of a motor vehicle first used before 10th October 2011 or a trailer manufactured before 10th October 2011, where it is impossible to achieve the value referred to in paragraph 6.21.4.1.2. above, the cumulative length may be reduced to 60 per cent.";

(c) paragraph 6.21.4.2.3. is deemed to read "In the case of a motor vehicle first used before 10th October 2011 or a trailer manufactured before 10th October 2011, where it is impossible to achieve the value referred to in paragraph 6.21.4.2.2. above, the cumulative length may be reduced to 60 per cent.";

(d) footnote 10 is omitted;

(e) in paragraph 6.21.7.3. the reference to a "mandatory stop lamp" is deemed to be a reference to an obligatory stop lamp;

(f) in paragraph 6.21.7.4. the words "at the discretion of the manufacturer" are omitted; and

(g) paragraph 6.21 is deemed to contain the following paragraph inserted after paragraph 6.21.7.5.—

"**6.21.7.6.** No conspicuity marking may be fitted unless it bears the international approval mark referred to in paragraph 5.4. of ECE Regulation 104 (as in force on 11th July 2008)."]

[Regulation 3 is printed as amended by SI 1994/2280; SI 2004/3168; SI 2005/2559; SI 2005/2929; SI 2006/594; SI 2009/3220.   **B23.07**

In reg.3(2), table, the Motor Vehicles (Authorisation of Special Types) General Order 1979 (SI 1979/1198) referred to in the definition of "Combat vehicle" has been revoked and replaced by the Road Vehicles (Authorisation of Special Types) (General) Order 2003 (SI 2003/1998, q.v.).

In reg.3(2), table, reference is made in the definition of "visiting vehicle" to the Motor Vehicles (International Circulation) Regulations 1985 (SI 1985/610). By reg.3 of the 1985 Regulations, the term is defined as "a vehicle brought temporarily into Great Britain by a person resident outside the United Kingdom". See further reg.5(b) of these regulations.]

[Equivalent standards

3A.—(1) Nothing in these Regulations shall render unlawful any act or omission which would have been lawful were—   **B23.08**

(a) there to be substituted for any reference to a British Standard in these Regulations a reference to a corresponding standard, and

(b) regulation 3(6) to apply in relation to that corresponding standard and the markings relating to that corresponding standard as it applies to a British Standard.

(2) For the purposes of this regulations, *"corresponding standard"*, in relation to a relevant British Standard Specification, means—

(a) a standard or code of practice of a national standards body or equivalent body of any State within the European Economic Area;

(b) any international standard recognised for use as a standard by any State within the European Economic Area;

(c) a technical specification or code of practice which, whether mandatory or not, is recognised for use as a standard by a public authority of any State within the European Economic Area, where the standard, code of practice, international standard or technical specification provides, in relation to lamps, retro reflectors and rear markings, a level of safety equivalent to that provided by that British Standard Specification and contains a requirement as respects the marking of such parts equivalent to that provided by that instrument.]

B23.09   *[Regulation 3A was inserted by SI 1994/2280.*

As to the European Economic Area, see the introductory note to Section C below.]

Exemptions—General

B23.10   **4.**—(1) Where a provision is applied by these Regulations to a motor vehicle first used on or after a specified date it does not apply to any vehicle manufactured at least six months before that date.

(2) Where an exemption from, or a relaxation of, a provision is applied by these Regulations to a motor vehicle first used before a specified date it shall also apply to a motor vehicle first used on or after that date if it was manufactured at least six months before that date.

(3) Nothing in these Regulations shall require any lamp or reflector to be fitted between sunrise and sunset to—

     (a) a vehicle not fitted with any front or rear position lamp,

     (b) an incomplete vehicle proceeding to a works for completion,

     (c) a pedal cycle,

     (d) a pedestrian-controlled vehicle,

     (e) a horse-drawn vehicle,

     (f) a vehicle drawn or propelled by hand, or

     (g) a combat vehicle.

(4) Without prejudice to regulation 16, for the purposes of these Regulations a lamp shall not be treated as being a lamp if it is—

     (a) so painted over or masked that it is not capable of being immediately used or readily put to use; or

     (b) an electric lamp which is not provided with any system of wiring by means of which that lamp is, or can readily be, connected with a source of electricity.

[Exemptions—Vehicle examiners

B23.11   **4A.**—(1) Parts 2 and 3 of these Regulations do not apply where a vehicle is being used on a road by a vehicle examiner and it is so used in order—

     (a) to submit the vehicle for an examination under section 45 of the Road Traffic Act 1988 for the purpose of ascertaining whether the examination is carried out in accordance with Regulations made under that section; or

     (b) to remove the vehicle following that examination.

(2) This regulation shall only apply to a vehicle examiner who—

     (a) has been authorised in writing by the Secretary of State to use a vehicle for the purposes described in paragraph (1)(a) and (b); and

(b) when using the vehicle for such a purpose, reasonably believes that any defects in that vehicle do not give rise to a danger of injury to any person while being so used.

(3) In this regulation *"vehicle examiner"* means an examiner appointed under section 66A of the Road Traffic Act 1988.]

[Regulation 4A was inserted by SI 2005/3169.]   **B23.12**

Exemptions—Temporarily imported vehicles and vehicles proceeding to a port for export

5. Part II of these Regulations does not apply to—   **B23.13**

(a) any vehicle having a base or centre in a country outside Great Britain from which it normally starts its journeys, provided that a period of not more than 12 months has elapsed since the vehicle was last brought into Great Britain;

(b) a visiting vehicle;

(c) any combination of two or more vehicles, one of which is drawing the other or others, if the combination includes any vehicle of the type mentioned in sub-paragraph (a) or (b); or

(d) a vehicle proceeding to a port for export,

if in each case the vehicle or combination of vehicles complies in every respect with the requirements about lighting equipment and reflectors relating thereto contained in the Convention on Road Traffic concluded at Geneva on 19th September 1949 [*Cmnd. 7997*] or the International Convention relating to Motor Traffic concluded at Paris on 24th April 1926 [*T.S. No.11 (1930)*].

Exemptions—Vehicles towing or being towed

6.—(1) No motor vehicle first used before 1st April 1986 and no pedal cycle or   **B23.14** trailer manufactured before 1st October 1985 is required by regulation 18 to be fitted with any rear position lamp, stop lamp, rear direction indicator, rear fog lamp or rear reflector whilst a trailer fitted with any such lamp or reflector is attached to its rear.

(2) No trailer manufactured before 1st October 1985 is required by regulation 18 to be fitted with any front position lamp whilst being drawn by a passenger vehicle.

(3) No trailer is required by regulation 18 to be fitted with any stop lamp whilst being drawn by a vehicle which is not required by regulation 18 to be fitted with any such lamp.

(4) Paragraph (3) shall apply respectively to rear fog lamps and direction indicators as it applies to stop lamps.

(5) No trailer manufactured before 1st October 1990 is required by regulation 18 to be fitted with any stop lamp or direction indicator whilst being drawn by a motor vehicle fitted with one or two stop lamps and two or more direction indicators if the dimensions of the trailer are such that when the longitudinal axes of the drawing vehicle and the trailer lie in the same vertical plane such stop lamps and at least one direction indicator on each side of the vehicle are visible to an observer in that vertical plane from a point 6m behind the rear of the trailer whether it is loaded or not.

(6) No rear marking is required to be fitted to any vehicle by regulation 18 if another vehicle in a combination of which it forms part would obscure any such marking.

(7) Where a broken-down vehicle is being drawn by another vehicle—

    (a) regulations 18 and 23 shall not apply to the broken-down vehicle between sunrise and sunset, and

    (b) between sunset and sunrise those regulations shall apply to the broken-down vehicle only in respect of rear position lamps and reflectors.

(8) The references in paragraphs (3) and (4) to a vehicle which is required to be fitted with a lamp shall be construed as if paragraph (1) did not have effect.

Exemptions—Military vehicles

B23.15　　7.—(1) Regulation 18 does not apply to a home forces' vehicle or to a vehicle in the service of a visiting force or of a headquarters whilst being used—

    (a) in connection with training which is certified in writing for the purposes of this regulation by a person duly authorised in that behalf to be training on a special occasion and of which not less than 48 hours' notice has been given by that person to the chief officer of police of every police area in which the place selected for the training is wholly or partly situate; or

    (b) on manoeuvres within such limits and during such period as may from time to time be specified by Order in Council under the Manoeuvres Act 1958.

(2) Where not less than 6 nor more than 12 vehicles being home forces' vehicles or vehicles of a visiting force or of a headquarters are proceeding together in a convoy on tactical or driving exercises which are authorised in writing by a person duly authorised in that behalf, and of which not less than 48 hours' notice in writing has been given by that person to the chief officer of police of every police area through which it is intended that the convoy shall pass and the interval between any two vehicles in such convoy does not exceed 20m—

    (a) front position lamps shall be required only on the vehicle leading the convoy; and

    (b) rear position lamps shall be required only on the rearmost vehicle provided that every other vehicle in the convoy carries a bright light under the vehicle illuminating either a part of the vehicle or anything attached to the vehicle or the road surface beneath the vehicle, in such a manner that the presence of the vehicle can be detected from the rear.

(3) No lamp is required to be fitted to any home forces' vehicle or any vehicle in the service of a visiting force or of a headquarters if the vehicle is constructed or adapted for combat and is such that compliance with these provisions is impracticable and it is fitted with two red rear position lamps and two red rear retro reflectors when on a road between sunset and sunrise. Such lamps and reflectors need not meet any of the requirements specified in Schedules 10 and 18.

(4) Part II of these Regulations does not apply to a vehicle in the service of a visiting force or of a headquarters if the vehicle complies in every respect with

the requirements as to lighting equipment and reflectors relating thereto contained in a Convention referred to in regulation 5.

Exemptions—Invalid carriages

8. An invalid carriage having a maximum speed not exceeding 4mph is required by these Regulations to be fitted with lamps and reflectors only when it is used on the carriageway of a road between sunset and sunrise otherwise than for the sole purpose of crossing it.   **B23.16**

Exemptions—Vehicles drawn or propelled by hand

9. A vehicle drawn or propelled by hand which has an overall width, including any load, not exceeding 800mm is required by these Regulations to be fitted with lamps and reflectors only when it is used on the carriageway of a road between sunset and sunrise other than—   **B23.17**

(a) close to the near side or left-hand edge of the carriageway, or

(b) to cross the carriageway.

[Exemptions—Tramcars

9A. Parts II to IV of these Regulations do not apply to tramcars.]   **B23.18**

[Regulation 9A was inserted by SI 1992/1217.]   **B23.19**

[Modifications in relation to vehicles approved under the Motor Vehicles (Approval) Regulations 1996

9B.—(1) In this regulation—   **B23.20**

"*the Approval Regulations*" means the Motor Vehicles (Approval) Regulations 1996 [*SI 1996/3013*];

"*coefficient of luminous intensity*" has the same meaning as in [ECE Regulation 3 as amended by the 01 series of amendments (as in force on 20th March 1982)];

[...]

"*passenger vehicle approval certificate*" means a Minister's approval certificate in the form prescribed by the Approval Regulations which appears to have been issued on the basis that the vehicle is a vehicle to which Part II of those Regulations applies;

"*relevant vehicle*" means a vehicle—

(a) in respect of which a passenger vehicle approval certificate containing the letter "P" has been issued pursuant to regulation 12(2)(b) of the Approval Regulations; or

(b) which is a "transitional provision vehicle" as defined by Schedule 6 to the Approval Regulations in respect of which a passenger vehicle approval certificate containing the letter "A" has been issued pursuant to regulation 12(2)(c) of the Approval Regulations;

"*standard mark*" means a mark which when applied to a lamp, reflector or device indicates compliance with the requirements of a particular instrument; and a reference to the instrument to which a standard mark relates shall be construed accordingly.

(2) The requirements of the Schedules to these Regulations, so far as they require any lamp, reflector or device to bear a particular standard mark (or one of two or more standard marks), shall not apply to a lamp, reflector or device if it is fitted to a relevant vehicle and—

     (a) in the case of a lamp or device, it meets the requirements as to intensity; and

     (b) in the case of a reflector, it meets the requirements as to coefficient of luminous intensity,

of the instrument to which the standard mark (or as the case may be one of those standard marks) relates.

(3) The requirements of these Regulations so far as they require headlamps (including a filament lamp fitted to a headlamp) fitted to a vehicle to bear a particular standard mark (or one of two or more standard marks) shall not apply to the headlamps fitted to a relevant vehicle if they emit sufficient light to illuminate the road in front of the vehicle on both main beam and dipped beam.

(4) Table 1 of Schedule 1 shall apply to a vehicle in respect of which a passenger vehicle approval certificate has been issued as if the entry that relates to dim-dip devices and running lamps were omitted.

(5) Paragraph (5) (markings) of Part I of Schedule 7 shall apply to a vehicle in respect of which a passenger approval certificate has been issued as if the vehicle were of a description falling within sub-paragraph (b) of that paragraph.]

B23.21   *[Regulation 9B was inserted by SI 1996/3016; SI 2009/3220.*

The Motor Vehicles (Approval) Regulations 1996 (to which reference is made in reg.9B(1)) have been revoked and replaced by the Motor Vehicles (Approval) Regulations 2001 (SI 2001/25). The Interpretation Act 1978 ss.17(2)(a) and 23, which enables references to the 1996 Regulations to be construed as references to the 2001 Regulations is only applicable in the absence of a contrary intention (see 1978 Act s.17(2)(a)); the fact that the scheme of the 2001 Regulations differs from that of the 1996 Regulations (e.g. there is no Part in the 2001 Regulations corresponding to Pt II ("Passenger Vehicles") of the 1996 Regulations) suggests that a "contrary intention" should be inferred.]

Provision as respects Trade Descriptions Act 1968

B23.22   **10.** [...]

     [Regulation 10 is revoked by SI 2008/1277 Sch.2, para.82 and Sch.4(2).]

PART II

REGULATIONS GOVERNING THE FITTING OF LAMPS, REFLECTORS, REAR MARKINGS AND DEVICES

Colour of light shown by lamps and reflectors

B23.23   **11.**—(1) No vehicle shall be fitted with a lamp [or retro reflective material] which is capable of showing a red light to the front, except—

     (a) a red and white chequered domed lamp, or a red and white segmented mast-mounted warning beacon, fitted to a fire service control vehicle and intended for use at the scene of an emergency;

(b) a side marker lamp or a side retro reflector;

(c) retro reflective material or a retro reflector designed primarily to reflect light to one or both sides of the vehicle and attached to or incorporated in any wheel or tyre of—

[(i) a pedal cycle;

(ii) a trailer drawn by, or a sidecar attached to, a pedal cycle;

(iii) a solo motor bicycle or motor bicycle combination; or

(iv) an invalid carriage; or]

(d) a traffic sign.

(2) No vehicle shall be fitted with a lamp [or retro reflective material] which is capable of showing any light to the rear, other than a red light, except—

(a) amber light from a direction indicator or side marker lamp;

(b) white light from a reversing lamp;

(c) white light from a work lamp;

(d) light to illuminate the interior of a vehicle;

(e) light from an illuminated rear registration plate;

(f) light for the purposes of illuminating a taxi meter;

(g) in the case of a bus, light for the purposes of illuminating a route indicator;

(h) blue light and white light from a chequered domed lamp fitted to a police control vehicle and intended for use at the scene of an emergency;

(i) white light from a red and white chequered domed lamp, or a red and white segmented mast-mounted warning beacon, fitted to a fire service control vehicle and intended for use at the scene of an emergency;

(j) green light and white light from a chequered domed lamp fitted to an ambulance control vehicle and intended for use at the scene of an emergency;

(k) blue light from a warning beacon or rear special warning lamp fitted to an emergency vehicle, or from any device fitted to a vehicle used for police purposes;

(l) amber light from a warning beacon fitted to—

(i) a road clearance vehicle;

(ii) a vehicle constructed or adapted for the purpose of collecting refuse;

(iii) a breakdown vehicle;

(iv) a vehicle having a maximum speed not exceeding 25mph or any trailer drawn by such a vehicle;

(v) a vehicle having an overall width (including any load) exceeding 2.9m;

(vi) a vehicle used for the purposes of testing, maintaining, improving, cleansing or watering roads or for any purpose incidental to any such use;

(vii) a vehicle used for the purpose of inspecting, cleansing, maintaining, adjusting, renewing or installing any apparatus which is in, on, under or over a road, or for any purpose incidental to any such use;

(viii) a vehicle used for or in connection with any purpose for which it is authorised to be used on roads by an order under section 44 of the Act;

[(ix) a vehicle used for escort purposes;]

(x) a vehicle used by the Commissioners of Customs and Excise for the purpose of testing fuels;

(xi) a vehicle used for the purpose of surveying;

(xii) a vehicle used for the removal or immobilisation of vehicles in exercise of a statutory power or duty;

(m) green light from a warning beacon fitted to a vehicle used by a medical practitioner registered by the General Medical Council (whether with [full or provisional] registration);

(n) yellow light from a warning beacon fitted to a vehicle for use at airports;

(o) light of any colour from a traffic sign which is attached to a vehicle;

[(oa) amber light from a lamp attached to or incorporated in a pedal of a pedal cycle;]

[(ob) white light or amber light from a lamp which is designed to emit light primarily to one or both sides of the vehicle, and is attached to or incorporated in any wheel or tyre of—

(i) a pedal cycle or;

(ii) a trailer drawn by, or a sidecar attached to, a pedal cycle;]

(p) reflected light from amber pedal retro reflectors;

(q) reflected light of any colour from retro reflective material or a retro reflector designed primarily to reflect light to one or both sides of the vehicle and attached to or incorporated in any wheel or tyre of—

[(i) a pedal cycle;

(ii) a trailer drawn by, or a sidecar attached to, a pedal cycle;

(iii) a solo motor bicycle or motor bicycle combination; or

(iv) an invalid carriage;]

(r) reflected light from amber retro reflective material on a road clearance vehicle;

(s) reflected light from yellow retro reflective registration plates;

[(sa) reflected blue, yellow and white light from a retro reflective plate displaying a distinguishing sign in accordance with Council Regulation (EC) No.2411/98 [*Council Regulation of November 3, 1998 on the recognition in intra-Community traffic of the distinguishing sign of the Member State in which motor vehicles and their trailers are registered; O.J. No.L299, November 10, 1998, p.1*]];

(t) reflected light from yellow retro reflective material incorporated in a [prescribed rear marking fitted in the appropriate manner to]—

(i) a motor vehicle having a maximum gross weight exceeding 7500kg;

(ii) a motor vehicle first used before 1st August 1982 having an unladen weight exceeding 3000kg;

(iii) a trailer having a maximum gross weight exceeding 3500kg;

(iv) a trailer manufactured before 1st August 1982 having an unladen weight exceeding 1000kg;

(v) a trailer which forms part of a combination of vehicles one of which is of a type mentioned in a previous item of this sub-paragraph;

(vi) a load carried by any vehicle; ...

(u) reflected light from orange retro reflective material incorporated in a sign fitted to the rear of a vehicle carrying a dangerous substance within the meaning of the Dangerous Substances (Conveyance by Road in Road Tankers and Tank Containers) Regulations 1981 [*SI 1981/1059*] or the Road Traffic (Carriage of Dangerous Substances in Packages, etc.) Regulations 1986 [*SI 1986/1951*].

[(v) reflected light from yellow retro reflective material incorporated in a prescribed sign and fitted to the rear of a bus;] [...] [;

[(w) reflected light from yellow retro reflective material incorporated in a sign fitted to the rear of a bus in accordance with paragraph (4).]

(x) reflected light from a yellow conspicuity marking where the fitting of that marking complies with the mandatory or optional ECE conspicuity requirements; or

(y) reflected light from yellow or orange retro reflective material fitted to the rear of a vehicle used for—

(i) police,

(ii) relevant authority (as defined by section 6 of the Fire (Scotland) Act 2005) or, in England and Wales, fire and rescue authority,

(iii) ambulance,

(iv) Vehicle and Operator Services Agency, or

(v) traffic officer,

purposes.]

[(3) For the purposes of paragraph (2)(t), a rear marking fitted to a vehicle is a prescribed rear marking fitted in the appropriate manner if the rear marking—

(a) is a rear marking of a description specified in the entry applicable to that vehicle in the right hand column of paragraph 1 of Part I of Schedule 19, and

(b) complies with paragraphs 2 to 7 of that Part of that Schedule.]

[(4) For the purposes of paragraph (2)(w), a sign (*"the secondary sign"*) is fitted to the rear of a bus in accordance with this paragraph if—

(a) a prescribed sign is also fitted to the rear of a bus;

(b) the total area of the retro reflective material incorporated in the secondary sign is no greater than the area of the prescribed sign; and

(c) the secondary sign satisfies the requirements specified—

(i) in the case of a bus which is owned or hired by a local education authority or any person managing an education establishment attended by children under the age of 16 years, in paragraphs (5) or (6); or

(ii) in any other case, in paragraph (6).]

[(5) The requirements referred to in paragraph (4)(c)(i) are that the secondary sign contains no words or other markings apart from words or markings identifying the local education authority or the educational establishment (as the case may be).]

[(6) The requirements referred to in paragraph (4)(c)(ii) are that the secondary sign contains no words or other markings apart from words or other markings which—

    (a) indicate that children are on board the bus when it is in motion or likely to be on board the bus or in its vicinity when it is stationary, and

    (b) are calculated to reduce the risk of road accidents involving such children.]

B23.24   *[Regulation 11 is printed as amended by SI 1994/2280; SI 2001/560; SI 2005/2559; SI 2006/1914; SI 2009/3220*

    SI 1981/1059 (to which reference is made in reg.11(2)(u)) was revoked by the Road Traffic (Carriage of Dangerous Substances in Road Tankers and Tank Containers) Regulations 1992 (SI 1992/743) and SI 1986/1951 (to which reference is also made) was revoked by the Road Traffic (Carriage of Dangerous Substances in Packages, etc.) Regulations 1992 (SI 1992/743); see now the Carriage of Dangerous Goods and Use of Transportable Pressure Equipment Regulations 2009 (SI 2009/1348), not reproduced in this work).]

Movement of lamps and reflectors

B23.25   **12.**—(1) Save as provided in paragraph (2), no person shall use, or cause or permit to be used, on a road any vehicle to which, or to any load or equipment of which, there is fitted a lamp, reflector or marking which is capable of being moved by swivelling, deflecting or otherwise while the vehicle is in motion.

(2) Paragraph (1) does not apply in respect of—

    (a) a headlamp which can be dipped only by the movement of the headlamp or its reflector;

    (b) a headlamp which is capable of adjustment so as to compensate for the effect of the load carried by the vehicle;

    (c) a lamp or reflector which can be deflected to the side by the movement of, although not necessarily through the same angle as, the front wheel or wheels of the vehicle when turned for the purpose of steering the vehicle;

    (d) a headlamp or front fog lamp which can be wholly or partially retracted or concealed;

    (e) a direction indicator fitted to a motor vehicle first used before 1st April 1986;

    (f) a work lamp;

    (g) a warning beacon;

    (h) an amber pedal retro reflector; [...]

    (i) retro reflective material or a retro reflector of any colour which is fitted so as to reflect light primarily to one or both sides of the vehicle and is attached to or incorporated in any wheel or tyre of—

[(i) a pedal cycle;

(ii) a trailer drawn by, or a sidecar attached to, a pedal cycle;

(iii) a solo motor bicycle or motor bicycle combination, or

(iv) an invalid carriage.]

[(j) a lamp which is designed to emit light primarily to one or both sides of the vehicle, and is attached to or incorporated in any wheel or tyre of—

(i) a pedal cycle;

(ii) a trailer drawn by, or a sidecar attached to, a pedal cycle; or

[(k) a lamp attached to or incorporated in a pedal of a pedal cycle.]

[Regulation 12 is printed as amended by SI 2005/2559.]   **B23.26**

Lamps to show a steady light

13.—(1) Save as provided in paragraph (2), no vehicle shall be fitted with a   **B23.27**
lamp which automatically emits a flashing light.

(2) Paragraph (1) does not apply in respect of—

(a) a direction indicator;

(b) a headlamp fitted to an emergency vehicle;

(c) a warning beacon or special warning lamp;

(d) a lamp or illuminated sign fitted to a vehicle used for police purposes;

(e) a green warning lamp used as an anti-lock brake indicator; [...]

(f) lamps forming part of a traffic sign;

[(g) a front position lamp capable of emitting a flashing light (whether or not it is also capable of emitting a steady light) which is fitted to—

(i) a pedal cycle; or

(ii) a trailer drawn by, or a sidecar attached to, a pedal cycle;

and which, if it is a lamp which is required to be fitted pursuant to regulation 18, is capable, when emitting a flashing light, of emitting light to the front of the pedal cycle, trailer or sidecar (as the case may be) of an intensity of not less than 4 candelas; or

(h) a rear position lamp capable of emitting a flashing light (whether or not it is also capable of emitting a steady light) which is fitted to—

(i) a pedal cycle; or

(ii) a trailer drawn by, or a sidecar attached to, a pedal cycle;

and which, if it is a lamp which is required to be fitted pursuant to regulation 18, is capable, when emitting a flashing light, of emitting light to the rear of the pedal cycle, trailer or sidecar (as the case may be) of an intensity of not less than 4 candelas.]

[Regulation 13 is printed as amended by SI 2005/2559.]   **B23.28**

Filament lamps

14.—(1) Where a motor vehicle first used on or after 1st April 1986 or any   **B23.29**
trailer manufactured on or after 1st October 1985 is equipped with any lamp of a type that is required by any Schedule to these Regulations to be marked with an approval mark, no filament lamp other than a filament lamp referred to in the Designation of Approval Marks Regulations in—

(a) regulation 4 and Schedule 2, items 2 or 2A, 8, 20, 37 or 37A; or

(b) regulation 5 and Schedule 4, item 18,

shall be fitted to any such lamp.

(2) [...]

B23.30   *[Regulation 14 is printed as amended by SI 1994/2280.]*

General requirements for electrical connections

B23.31   **15.**—(1) Every motor vehicle first used on or after 1st April 1991 shall be so constructed that every position lamp, side marker lamp, end-outline marker lamp and rear registration plate lamp with which the vehicle is fitted is capable of being switched on and off by the operation of one switch and, save as provided in paragraph (2), not otherwise.

(2) Sub-paragraph (a) of paragraph (1) shall not prevent one or more position lamps from being capable of being switched on and off independently of any other lamp referred to in that sub-paragraph.

Restrictions on fitting blue warning beacons, special warning lamps and similar devices

B23.32   **16.** No vehicle, other than an emergency vehicle, shall be fitted with—

(a) a blue warning beacon or special warning lamp, or

(b) a device which resembles a blue warning beacon or a special warning lamp, whether the same is in working order or not.

Obligatory warning beacons

B23.33   **17.**—(1) Subject to paragraph (2), no person shall use, or cause or permit to be used, on an unrestricted dual-carriageway road any motor vehicle with four or more wheels having a maximum speed not exceeding 25mph unless it or any trailer drawn by it is fitted with at least one warning beacon which—

(a) complies with Schedule 16, and

(b) is showing an amber light.

(2) Paragraph (1) shall not apply in relation to—

(a) any motor vehicle first used before 1st January 1947; and

(b) any motor vehicle, or any trailer being drawn by it, to which paragraph (1) would otherwise apply, when that vehicle or trailer is on any carriageway of an unrestricted dual-carriageway road for the purpose only of crossing that carriageway in the quickest manner practicable in the circumstances.

[Signs on buses carrying children

B23.34   **17A.**—(1) Subject to paragraph (2), no person shall use or cause or permit to be used on a road a bus when it is carrying a child to or from his school unless—

(a) a prescribed sign is fitted to the front of the bus and is plainly visible to road users ahead of the bus, and

(b) a prescribed sign is fitted to the rear of the bus and is plainly visible to road users behind the bus.

(2) Paragraph (1) does not apply where a bus is on a bus service of a description specified in paragraph 2 of the Schedule to the Fuel Duty Grant (Eligible Bus Services) Regulations 1985 [*SI 1985/1886; not reproduced in this work*].

(3) For the purposes of this regulation—

    (a) a reference to a bus carrying a child to or from his school is a reference to a bus carrying a child—

        (i) to, or to a place within the vicinity of, his school on a day during term time before he has attended the school on that day; or

        (ii) from, or from a place within the vicinity of, his school on a day during term time after he has finished attending the school on that day;

    (b) *"school"* has the meaning given by [section 4(1) of the Education Act 1996]; and

    (c) a reference to a child is a reference to a child under the age of 16 years.]

[Regulation 17A was inserted by SI 1994/2280, and is printed as subsequently   **B23.35** *amended by the Education Act 1996 s.582(3) and Sch.39, para.1(4).*

For the definition of "school" in s.4(1) of the Education Act 1996, see the notes to the Road Vehicles (Construction and Use) Regulations 1986 (SI 1986/ 1078) reg.48A above.]

Obligatory lamps, reflectors, rear markings and devices

18.—(1) Save as provided in the foregoing provisions of these Regulations[, in   **B23.36** regulation 20A(a)] and in [paragraphs (2), (2A) and (2B)], every vehicle of a class specified in a Table in Schedule 1 shall be fitted with lamps, reflectors, rear markings and devices which—

    (a) are of a type specified in column 1 of that Table, and

    (b) comply with the relevant installation, alignment and performance requirements set out in the Schedule or Part of a Schedule shown against that type in column 2 of that Table.

(2) The requirements specified in paragraph (1) do not apply in respect of a lamp, reflector, rear marking or device of a type specified in column 1 of a Table in the case of a vehicle shown against it in column 3 of that Table.

[(2A) The requirements specified in paragraph 5(c) and (ca) of Schedule 2 shall not apply in the case of a front position lamp capable of emitting a flashing light which is fitted to—

    (i) a pedal cycle; or

    (ii) a trailer drawn by, or a sidecar attached to, a pedal cycle,

unless the lamp is also capable of emitting a steady light.]

[(2B) The requirements specified in paragraph 5(d) and (e) of Schedule 10 shall not apply in the case of a rear position lamp capable of emitting a flashing light which is fitted to—

    (i) a pedal cycle; or

    (ii) a trailer drawn by, or a sidecar attached to, a pedal cycle,

unless the lamp is also capable of emitting a steady light.]

(3) The requirements specified in paragraph (1) apply without prejudice to any additional requirements specified in regulations 20[, 20A] and 21.

(4) The Schedules referred to in the Tables in Schedule 1 are Schedules 2 to 21.

B23.37   *[Regulation 18 as amended by SI 2005/2559; SI 2009/3220.]*

Restrictions on the obscuration of certain obligatory lamps and reflectors

B23.38   **19.** Every vehicle shall be so constructed that at least part of the apparent surface of any—

        (a) front and rear position lamp,

        (b) front and rear direction indicator, and

        (c) rear retro reflector,

which is required by these Regulations to be fitted to a vehicle is visible when the vehicle is viewed from any point directly in front of or behind the lamp or reflector, as appropriate, when every door, tailgate, boot lid, engine cover, cab or other movable part of the vehicle is in a fixed open position.

Optional lamps, reflectors, rear markings and devices

B23.39   **20.** [Subject to regulation 20A(a), every optional lamp], reflector, rear marking or device fitted to a vehicle, being of a type specified in an item in column 2 of the Table below, shall comply with the provisions shown in column 3 of that Table.

TABLE

(1) Item No	(2) Type of lamp, reflector, rear marking or device	(3) Provisions with which compliance is required	
1	Front position lamp	Schedule 2, Part II	
2	Dim-dip device and running lamp	Schedule 3, Part II	
3	Dipped-beam headlamp	Schedule 4, Part II	
4	Main-beam headlamp	Schedule 5, Part II	
5	Front fog lamp	Schedule 6	
7	Direction indicator	Schedule 7, Part II	and Parts I of Schedules 2 to 5, 7, 9 to 13 and 17 to 21 to the extent specified in Parts II of those Schedules.
8	Hazard warning signal device	Schedule 8	
9	Side marker lamp	Schedule 9, Part II	
10	Rear position lamp	Schedule 10, Part II	
11	Rear fog lamp	Schedule 11, Part II	
12	Stop lamp	Schedule 12, Part II	
13	End-outline marker lamp	Schedule 13, Part II	
14	Reversing lamp	Schedule 14	
15	Warning beacon	Schedule 16	

(1) Item No	(2) Type of lamp, reflector, rear marking or device	(3) Provisions with which compliance is required	
16	Side retro reflector	Schedule 17, Part II	
17	Rear retro reflector	Schedule 18, Part II	
18	Rear marking	Schedule 19, Part II	
19	Pedal retro reflector	Schedule 20, Part II	
20	Front retro reflector	Schedule 21, Part II	

[Regulation 20 is printed as amended by SI 2009/3220.]   **B23.40**

[Application of the ECE conspicuity requirements

20A.—(1) Subject to paragraphs (2), (4) and (5), a goods vehicle which is—   **B23.41**

(a) a motor vehicle first used on or after 10th July 2011, or

(b) a trailer manufactured on or after 10th July 2011,

shall be fitted with conspicuity markings which comply with the mandatory ECE conspicuity requirements.

(2) Paragraph (1) does not apply in respect of a goods vehicle which is—

(a) a motor vehicle with a maximum gross weight not exceeding 7500 kg;

(b) a trailer with a maximum gross weight not exceeding 3500 kg;

(c) an incomplete vehicle proceeding to a works for completion or to a place where it is to be stored or displayed for sale; or

(d) a motor car or heavy motor car intended to form part of an articulated vehicle.

(3) A goods vehicle to which paragraph (1) applies is referred to in this regulation as a "relevant goods vehicle".

(4) If the overall length of a relevant goods vehicle does not exceed 6 m, conspicuity markings that comply with the mandatory ECE conspicuity requirements need not be fitted to the side of that vehicle.

(5) If the overall width of a relevant goods vehicle does not exceed 2.1 m, conspicuity markings that comply with the mandatory ECE conspicuity requirements need not be fitted to the rear of that vehicle.

(6) To the extent that, pursuant to paragraph (4) or (5), a relevant goods vehicle is not required to be fitted with conspicuity markings to the side or rear that comply with the mandatory ECE conspicuity requirements, conspicuity markings which comply with the optional ECE conspicuity requirements may be fitted to the side or rear (as the case may be).

(7) Subject to paragraph (8), a vehicle which is not a relevant goods vehicle may be fitted with conspicuity markings which comply with the optional ECE conspicuity requirements.

(8) Paragraph (7) does not apply in respect of—

(a) a passenger vehicle (other than a bus); or

(b) a trailer with a maximum gross weight not exceeding 750 kg.

(9) A requirement imposed under regulation 18 or 20 is to be disregarded to the extent it is incompatible with paragraph (1), (6) or (7).

(10) In this regulation *"motor car"* and *"heavy motor car"* have the same meaning as in the Construction and Use Regulations.]

B24.42   *[Regulation 20A is printed as inserted by SI 2009/3220.]*

Projecting trailers and vehicles carrying overhanging or projecting loads or equipment

B23.43   **21.**—(1) No person shall use, or cause or permit to be used, on a road in the circumstances mentioned in paragraph (2) —

(a) any trailer which forms part of a combination of vehicles which projects laterally beyond any preceding vehicle in the combination; or

(b) any vehicle [or] combination of vehicles which carries a load or equipment

in either case under the conditions specified in an item in column 2 of the Table below, unless the vehicle or combination of vehicles complies with the requirements specified in that item in column 3 of that Table.

TABLE

(1) *Item No*	(2) *Conditions*	(3) *Requirements*
1	A trailer which is not fitted with front position lamps and which projects laterally on any side so that the distance from the outermost part of the projection to the outermost part of the illuminated area of the obligatory front position lamp on that side fitted to any preceding vehicle in the combination exceeds 400mm.	A lamp showing white light to the front shall be fitted to the trailer so that the outermost part of the illuminated area is not more than 400mm from the outermost projection of the trailer. The installation and performance requirements relating to front position lamps do not apply to any such lamp.
2	A trailer which is not fitted with front position lamps and which carries a load or equipment which projects laterally on any side of the trailer so that the distance from the outermost projection of the load or equipment to the outermost part of the illuminated area of the obligatory front position lamp on that side fitted to any preceding vehicle in the combination exceeds 400mm.	A lamp showing white light to the front shall be fitted to the trailer or the load or equipment so that the outermost part of the illuminated area is not more than 400mm from the outermost projection of the load or equipment. The installation and performance requirements relating to front position lamps do not apply to any such lamp.

(1) Item No	(2) Conditions	(3) Requirements
3	A vehicle which carries a load or equipment which projects laterally on any side of the vehicle so that the distance from the outermost part of the load or equipment to the outermost part of the illuminated area of the obligatory front or rear position lamp on that side exceeds 400mm.	Either— (a) the obligatory front or rear position lamp shall be transferred from the vehicle to the load or equipment to which must also be attached a white front or a red rear reflecting device; or (b) an additional front or rear position lamp and a white front or a red rear reflecting device shall be fitted to the vehicle, load or equipment. All the installation, performance and maintenance requirements relating to front or rear position lamps shall in either case be complied with except that for the purpose of determining the lateral position of such lamps and reflecting devices any reference to the vehicle shall be taken to include the load or equipment except special equipment on a vehicle fitted with a movable platform or the jib of any crane.
4	A vehicle which carries a load or equipment which projects beyond the rear of the vehicle or, in the case of a combination of vehicles, beyond the rear of the rearmost vehicle in the combination, more than— (a) 2m in the case of an agricultural vehicle or a vehicle carrying a fire escape; or (b) 1m in the case of any other vehicle.	An additional rear lamp capable of showing red light to the rear and a red reflecting device, both of which are visible from a reasonable distance, shall be fitted to the vehicle or the load in such a position that the distance between the lamp and the reflecting device, and the rearmost projection of the load or equipment does not exceed 2m in the case mentioned in sub-paragraph (a) in column 2 of this item or 1m in any other case. The installation and performance requirements relating to rear position [lamps and rear retro reflectors do not apply to any such additional lamp and reflecting device].

(1) Item No	(2) Conditions	(3) Requirements
5	A vehicle which carries a load or equipment which projects beyond the front of the vehicle more than— (a) 2m in the case of an agricultural vehicle or a vehicle carrying a fire fire escape; or (b) 1m in the case of any other vehicle.	An additional front lamp capable of showing white light to the front and a white reflecting device, both visible from a reasonable distance shall be fitted to the vehicle or the load in such a position that the distance between the lamp and the the reflecting device, and the foremost projection of the load or equipment, does not exceed 2m in the case mentioned in sub-paragraph (a) in column 2 of this item or 1m in any other case. The installation and performance requirements relating to front position lamps and front retro reflectors do not apply to any such additional lamp and reflecting device.
6	A vehicle which carries a load or equipment which obscures any obligatory lamp, reflector or rear marking.	Either— (a) the obligatory lamp, reflector or rear marking shall be transferred to a position on the vehicle, load or equipment where it is not obscured; or (b) an additional lamp, reflector or rear marking shall be fitted to the vehicle, load or equipment. All the installation, performance and maintenance requirements relating to obligatory lamps, reflectors or rear markings shall in either case be complied with.

(2) The circumstances referred to in paragraph (1) are—

    (a) as regards item 6 in the Table, in so far as it relates to obligatory stop lamps and direction indicators, all circumstances; and

    (b) as regards items 1 to 5 in the Table and item 6 in the Table, except in so far as it relates to obligatory stop lamps and direction indicators, the time between sunset and sunrise or, except in so far as it relates to obligatory reflectors, when visibility is seriously reduced between sunrise and sunset.

B23.44   *[Regulation 21 is printed as amended by SI 1994/2280.]*

Additional side marker lamps

22.—(1) Save as provided in paragraph (2), no person shall use, or cause or   **B23.45**
permit to be used, on a road between sunset and sunrise, or in seriously reduced
visibility between sunrise and sunset, any vehicle or combination of vehicles of a
type specified in an item in column 2 of the Table below unless each side of the
vehicle or combination of vehicles is fitted with the side marker lamps specified
in that item in column 3 and those lamps are kept lit.

TABLE

(1) Item No	(2) Vehicle or combination of vehicles	(3) Side marker lamps
1	Any vehicle or combination of vehicles the overall length of which (including any load) exceeds 18.3m.	There shall be fitted— (a) one lamp no part of the light-emitting surface of which is more than 9.15m from the foremost part of the vehicle or vehicles (in either case inclusive of any load); (b) one lamp no part of the light-emitting surface of which is more than 3.05m from the rearmost part of the vehicle or vehicles (in either case inclusive of any load); and (c) such other lamps as are required to ensure that not more than 3.05m separates any part of the light-emitting surface of one lamp and any part of the light-emitting surface of the next lamp.

(1) Item No	(2) Vehicle or combination of vehicles	(3) Side marker lamps
2	A combination of vehicles the overall length of which (including any load) exceeds 12.2m but does not exceed 18.3m and carrying a load supported by any two of the vehicles but not including a load carried by an articulated vehicle.	There shall be fitted— (a) one lamp no part of the light-emitting surface of which is forward of, or more than 1530mm rearward of, the rearmost part of the drawing vehicle; and (b) if the supported load extends more than 9.15m rearward of the rearmost part of the drawing vehicle, one lamp no part of the light-emitting surface of which is forward of, or more than 1530mm rearward of, the centre of the length of the load.

(2) The requirements specified in paragraph (1) do not apply to—

    (a) a combination of vehicles where any vehicle being drawn in that combination has broken down; or

    (b) a vehicle (not being a combination of vehicles) having an appliance or apparatus or carrying a load of a kind specified in the Table to regulation 82(7) or in regulation 82(8) of the Construction and Use Regulations [q.v.], if the conditions specified in paragraphs 3 and 4 (which provide for the special marking of projections from vehicles) of Schedule 12 to those Regulations are complied with in relation to the special appliance or apparatus or load as if the said conditions had been expressed in the said regulation 82 to apply in the case of every special appliance or apparatus or load of a kind specified in that regulation.

(3) Every side marker lamp fitted in accordance with this regulation shall comply with Part I of Schedule 9.

Part III

Regulations Governing the Maintenance and Use of Lamps, Reflectors, Rear Markings and Devices

Maintenance of lamps, reflectors, rear markings and devices

B23.46   23.—(1) No person shall use, or cause or permit to be used, on a road a vehicle unless every lamp, reflector, rear marking and device to which this paragraph applies is in good working order and, in the case of a lamp, clean.

    (2) Save as provided in paragraph (3), paragraph (1) applies to—

        (a) every—

            (i) front position lamp,

  (ii) rear position lamp,

  (iii) headlamp,

  (iv) rear registration plate lamp,

  (v) side marker lamp,

  (vi) end-outline marker lamp,

  (vii) rear fog lamp,

  (viii) retro reflector, and

  (ix) rear marking of a type specified in Part I of … Schedule 19,

with which the vehicle is required by these Regulations to be fitted; and

 (b) every—

  (i) stop lamp,

  (ii) direction indicator,

  (iii) running lamp,

  (iv) dim-dip device,

  (v) headlamp levelling device, and

  (vi) hazard warning signal device,

with which it is fitted.

 (3) Paragraph (2) does not apply to—

 (a) a rear fog lamp on a vehicle which is part of a combination of vehicles any part of which is not required by these Regulations to be fitted with a rear fog lamp;

 (b) a rear fog lamp on a motor vehicle drawing a trailer;

 (c) a defective lamp, reflector, dim-dip device or headlamp levelling device on a vehicle in use on a road between sunrise and sunset, if any such lamp, reflector or device became defective during the journey which is in progress or if arrangements have been made to remedy the defect with all reasonable expedition; or

 (d) a lamp, reflector, dim-dip device, headlamp levelling device or rear marking on a combat vehicle in use on a road between sunrise and sunset.

[Regulation 23 is printed as amended by SI 1994/2280.] **B23.47**

Requirements about the use of front and rear position lamps, rear registration plate lamps, side marker lamps and end-outline marker lamps

24.—(1) Save as provided in paragraphs (5) and (9), no person shall— **B23.48**

 (a) use, or cause or permit to be used, on a road any vehicle which is in motion—

  (i) between sunset and sunrise, or

  (ii) in seriously reduced visibility between sunrise and sunset; or

 (b) allow to remain at rest, or cause or permit to be allowed to remain at rest, on a road any vehicle between sunset and sunrise

unless every front position lamp, rear position lamp, rear registration plate lamp, side marker lamp and end-outline marker lamp with which the vehicle is required by these Regulations to be fitted is kept lit and unobscured.

(2) Save as provided in paragraphs (5) and (9), where a solo motor bicycle is not fitted with a front position lamp, no person shall use it, or cause or permit it to be used, on a road (other than when it is parked) between sunset and sunrise or in seriously reduced visibility between sunrise and sunset, unless a headlamp is kept lit and unobscured.

(3) Save as provided in paragraphs (5) and (9), no person shall allow to remain parked, or cause or permit to be allowed to remain parked between sunset and sunrise—

    (a) a motor bicycle combination which is required to be fitted only with a front position lamp on the sidecar; or

    (b) a trailer to the front of which no other vehicle is attached and which is not required to be fitted with front position lamps,

unless a pair of front position lamps is fitted and kept lit and unobscured.

(4) Save as provided in paragraphs (5) and (9), no person shall allow to remain parked, or cause or permit to be allowed to remain parked between sunset and sunrise a solo motor bicycle which is not required to be fitted with a front position lamp, unless a front position lamp is fitted and kept lit and unobscured.

(5) Paragraphs (1), (2), (3) and (4) shall not apply in respect of a vehicle of a class specified in paragraph (7) which is parked on a road on which a speed limit of 30mph or less is in force and the vehicle is parked—

    (a) in a parking place for which provision is made under section 6, or which is authorised under section 32 or designated under section 45 of the Road Traffic Regulation Act 1984, or which is set apart as a parking place under some other enactment or instrument and the vehicle is parked in a manner which does not contravene the provision of any enactment or instrument relating to the parking place; or

    (b) in a lay-by—

        (i) the limits of which are indicated by a traffic sign consisting of the road marking shown in diagram 1010 in [Schedule 6 of the Traffic Signs Regulations and General Directions 2002] [*SI 2002/ 3113, q.v.*]; or

        (ii) the surface of which is of a colour or texture which is different from that of the part of the carriageway of the road used primarily by through traffic; or

        (iii) the limits of which are indicated by a continuous strip of surface of a different colour or texture from that of the surface of the remainder of the carriageway of the road; or

    (c) elsewhere than in such a parking place or lay-by if—

        (i) the vehicle is parked in one of the circumstances described in paragraph (8); and

        (ii) no part of the vehicle is less than 10m from the junction of any part of the carriageway of any road with the carriageway of the road on which it is parked whether that junction is on the same side of the road as that on which the vehicle is parked or not.

(6) Sub-paragraph (5)(c)(ii) shall be construed in accordance with the diagram in Schedule 22.

(7) The classes of vehicle referred to in paragraph (5) are—

(a) a motor vehicle being a goods vehicle [the gross vehicle weight of which does not exceed 2500 kg];

(b) a passenger vehicle other than a bus;

(c) an invalid carriage; and

(d) a motor cycle or a pedal cycle in either case with or without a sidecar;

not being—

    (i) a vehicle to which a trailer is attached;

    (ii) a vehicle which is required to be fitted with lamps by regulation 21; or

    (iii) a vehicle carrying a load, if the load is required to be fitted with lamps by regulation 21.

(8) The circumstances referred to in paragraph (5)(c) are that—

(a) the vehicle is parked on a road on which the driving of vehicles otherwise than in one direction is prohibited at all times and its left or near side is as close as may be and parallel to the left-hand edge of the carriageway or its right or off side is as close as may be and parallel to the right-hand edge of the carriageway; or

(b) the vehicle is parked on a road on which such a prohibition does not exist and its left or near side is as close as may be and parallel to the edge of the carriageway.

(9) Paragraphs (1), (2), (3) and (4) do not apply in respect of—

(a) a solo motor bicycle or a pedal cycle being pushed along the left-hand edge of a carriageway;

(b) a pedal cycle waiting to proceed provided it is kept to the left-hand or near side edge of a carriageway; or

(c) a vehicle which is parked in an area on part of a highway on which roadworks are being carried out and which is bounded by amber lamps and other traffic signs so as to prevent the presence of the vehicle, its load or equipment being a danger to persons using the road.

[Regulation 24 is printed as amended by the Interpretation Act 1978 ss.17(2)(a) and 23(1); SI 2009/3220.]   **B23.49**

Requirements about the use of headlamps and front fog lamps

25.—(1) Save as provided in paragraph (2), no person shall use, or cause or **B23.50** permit to be used, on a road a vehicle which is fitted with obligatory dipped-beam headlamps unless every such lamp is kept lit—

(a) during the hours of darkness, except on a road which is a restricted road for the purposes of section 81 of the Road Traffic Regulation Act 1984 [*q.v.*] by virtue of a system of street lighting when it is lit; and

(b) in seriously reduced visibility.

(2) The provisions of paragraph (1) do not apply—

(a) in the case of a motor vehicle fitted with one obligatory dipped-beam headlamp or a solo motor bicycle or motor bicycle combination fitted with a pair of obligatory dipped-beam headlamps, if a main-beam headlamp or a front fog lamp is kept lit;

(b) in the case of a motor vehicle, other than a solo motor bicycle or motor bicycle combination, fitted with a pair of obligatory dipped-beam headlamps, if—

  (i) a pair of main-beam headlamps is kept lit; or

  (ii) in seriously reduced visibility, a pair of front fog lamps which is so fitted that the outermost part of the illuminated area of each lamp in the pair is not more than 400mm from the outer edge of the vehicle is kept lit;

 (c) to a vehicle being drawn by another vehicle;

 (d) to a vehicle while being used to propel a snow plough; or

 (e) to a vehicle which is parked.

(3) For the purposes of this regulation a headlamp shall not be regarded as lit if its intensity is reduced by a dim-dip device.

Requirements about the use of warning beacons

B23.51 **26.** No person shall use, or cause or permit to be used, on an unrestricted dual-carriageway road a vehicle which is required to be fitted with at least one warning beacon by regulation 17 unless every such beacon is kept lit.

Restrictions on the use of lamps other than those to which regulation 24 refers

B23.52 **27.** No person shall use, or cause or permit to be used, on a road any vehicle on which any lamp, hazard warning signal device or warning beacon of a type specified in an item in column 2 of the Table below is used in a manner specified in that item in column 3.

TABLE

(1) Item No	(2) Type of lamp, hazard warning signal device or warning beacon	(3) Manner of use prohibited
1	Headlamp	(a) Used so as to cause undue dazzle or discomfort to other persons using the road. (b) Used so as to be lit when a vehicle is parked.
2	Front fog lamp	(a) Used so as to cause undue dazzle or discomfort to other persons using the road. (b) Used so as to be lit at any time other than in conditions of seriously reduced visibility. (c) Used so as to be lit when a vehicle is parked.

(1) Item No	(2) Type of lamp, hazard warning signal device or warning beacon	(3) Manner of use prohibited
3	Rear fog lamp	(a) Used so as to cause undue dazzle or discomfort to the driver of a following vehicle. (b) Used so as to be lit at any time other than in conditions of seriously reduced visibility. (c) Save in the case of an emergency vehicle, used so as to be lit when a vehicle is parked.
4	Reversing lamp	Used so as to be lit except for the purpose of reversing the vehicle.
5	Hazard warning signal device	Used other than— (i) to warn persons using the road of a temporary obstruction when the vehicle is at rest; or (ii) on a motorway or unrestricted dual-carriageway, to warn following drivers of a need to slow down due to a temporary obstruction ahead; or (iii) in the case of a bus, to summon assistance for the driver or any person acting as a conductor or inspector on the vehicle. [or] [(iv) in the case of a bus to which prescribed signs are fitted as described in sub-paragraphs (a) and (b) of regulation 17A(1), when the vehicle is stationary and children under the age of 16 years are entering or leaving, or are about to enter or leave, or have just left the vehicle.]
6	Warning beacon emitting blue light and special warning lamp	Used so as to be lit except— (i) at the scene of an emergency; or

(1) Item No	(2) Type of lamp, hazard warning signal device or warning beacon	(3) Manner of use prohibited
		(ii) when it is necessary or desirable either to indicate to persons using the road the urgency of the purpose for which the vehicle is being used, or to warn persons of the presence of the vehicle or a hazard on the road.
7	Warning beacon emitting amber light	Used so as to be lit except— (i) at the scene of an emergency; (ii) when it is necessary or desirable to warn persons of the presence of the vehicle; [...] (iii) in the case of a breakdown vehicle, while it is being used in connection with, and in the immediate vicinity of, an accident or breakdown, or while it is being used to draw a broken-down vehicle. [(iv) in the case of an abnormal load escort vehicle, while it is being used in connection with the escort of another vehicle which has— (aa) an overall width (including any load) exceeding 2.9 metres; (bb) an overall length (including any load) exceeding 18.65 metres, or (cc) been authorised by the Secretary of State under section 44 of the Act; and [(v) in the case of a vehicle, used for escort purposes other than an abnormal load escort vehicle, while it is being used in connection with the escort of any vehicle and travelling at a speed not exceeding 25 mph.]

(1) *Item No*	(2) *Type of lamp, hazard warning signal device or warning beacon*	(3) *Manner of use prohibited*
8	Warning beacon emitting green light	Used so as to be lit except whilst occupied by a medical practitioner registered by the General Medical Council (whether with [full or provisional] registration) and used for the purposes of an emergency.
9	Warning beacon emitting yellow light	Used so as to be lit on a road.
10	Work lamp	(a) Used so as to cause undue dazzle or discomfort to the driver of any vehicle. (b) Used so as to be lit except for the purpose of illuminating a working area, accident, breakdown or works in the vicinity of the vehicle.
11	Any other lamp	Used so as to cause undue dazzle or discomfort to other persons using the road.

[Regulation 27 is printed as amended by SI 1994/2280; SI 2005/2559; SI 2006/ **B23.53**
1914.]

PART IV

TESTING AND INSPECTION OF LIGHTING EQUIPMENT AND REFLECTORS

Testing and inspection of lighting equipment and reflectors

28. The provisions of regulation 74 of the Construction and Use Regulations   **B23.54**
[*q.v.*] apply in respect of lighting equipment and reflectors with which a vehicle is
required by these Regulations to be fitted in the same way as they apply in respect
of brakes, silencers, steering gear and tyres.

SCHEDULE 1

OBLIGATORY LAMPS, REFLECTORS, REAR MARKINGS AND DEVICES

TABLE I   **B23.55**

Motor vehicle having three or more wheels not being a vehicle to which any other Table
in this Schedule applies

(1) *Type of lamp, reflector, rear marking or device*	(2) *Schedule in which relevant installation and performance requirements are specified*	(3) *Exceptions*
Front position lamp	Schedule 2: Part I	None.
Dim-dip device or running lamp	Schedule 3: Part I	A vehicle having a maximum speed not exceeding 40mph; A vehicle first used before 1st April 1987; A home forces' vehicle; A vehicle in respect of which the following conditions are satisfied— (a) there is fitted to the vehicle all the lighting and light-signalling devices listed in items 1.5.7 to 1.5.20 of Annex I of [Community Directive 76/756/EEC as last amended by Directive 89/278/EEC or Community Directive 76/756/EEC as last amended by Directive 91/663/EEC] which are required to be fitted under that Annex; and (b) all those devices are so installed that they comply with the requirements set out in items 3 and 4 of that Annex including, in particular, item 4.2.6 (Alignment of dipped-beam headlamps).
Dipped-beam headlamp	Schedule 4: Part I	A vehicle having a maximum speed not exceeding 15mph; A vehicle first used before 1st April 1986 being an agricultural vehicle or a works truck; A vehicle first used before 1st January 1931.
Main-beam headlamp	Schedule 5: Part I	A vehicle having a maximum speed not exceeding 25mph; A vehicle first used before 1st April 1986 being an agricultural vehicle or a works truck; A vehicle first used before 1st January 1931.
Direction indicator	Schedule 7: Part I	An invalid carriage having a maximum speed not exceeding 4mph and any other vehicle having a maximum speed not exceeding 15mph; An agricultural vehicle having an unladen weight not exceeding 255kg;

(1) Type of lamp, reflector, rear marking or device	(2) Schedule in which relevant installation and performance requirements are specified	(3) Exceptions
Hazard warning signal device	Schedule 8: Part I	A vehicle first used before 1st April 1986 being an agricultural vehicle, an industrial tractor or a works truck; A vehicle first used before 1st January 1936. A vehicle not required to be fitted with direction indicators; A vehicle first used before 1st April 1986.
Side marker lamp	Schedule 9: Part I	A vehicle having a maximum speed not exceeding 25mph; A passenger vehicle; An incomplete vehicle proceeding to a works for completion or to a place where it is to be stored or displayed for sale; A vehicle the overall length of which does not exceed 6m; A vehicle first used before 1st April 1991; [A vehicle first used before 1st April 1996 in respect of which the following conditions are satisfied]— (a) there is fitted to the vehicle all the lighting and light-signalling devices listed in items 1.5.7 to 1.5.20 of Annex I of [Community Directive 76/756/EEC as last amended by Directive 89/278/EEC or Community Directive 76/756/EEC as last amended by Directive 91/663/EEC] which are required to be fitted under that Annex; and (b) all those devices are so installed that they comply with the requirements set out in items 3 and 4 of that Annex including, in particular, item 4.2.6 (Alignment of dipped-beam headlamps).
Rear position lamp	Schedule 10: Part I	None.
Rear fog lamp	Schedule 11: Part I	A vehicle having a maximum speed not exceeding 25mph; A vehicle first used before 1st April 1986 being an agricultural vehicle or a works truck; A vehicle first used before 1st April 1980;

(1) *Type of lamp, reflector, rear marking or device*	(2) *Schedule in which relevant installation and performance requirements are specified*	(3) *Exceptions*
Stop lamp	Schedule 12: Part I	A vehicle having an overall width which does not exceed 1300mm. A vehicle having a maximum speed not exceeding 25mph; A vehicle first used before 1st April 1986 being an agricultural vehicle or a works truck; A vehicle first used before 1st January 1936.
End-outline marker lamp	Schedule 13: Part I	A vehicle having a maximum speed not exceeding 25mph; A motor vehicle having an overall width not exceeding 2100mm; An incomplete vehicle proceeding to a works for completion or to a place where it is to be stored or displayed for sale; A motor vehicle first used before 1st April 1991.
Rear registration plate lamp	Schedule 15	A vehicle not required to be fitted with a rear registration plate; A works truck.
Side retro reflector	Schedule 17: Part I	A vehicle having a maximum speed not exceeding 25mph; A goods vehicle— (a) first used on or after 1st April 1986, the overall length of which does not exceed 6m; or (b) first used before 1st April 1986, the overall length of which does not exceed 8m; A passenger vehicle; An incomplete vehicle proceeding to a works for completion or to a place where it is to be stored or displayed for sale; A vehicle primarily constructed for moving excavated material and being used by virtue of an Order under section 44 of the Act; A mobile crane or engineering plant.
Rear retro reflector	Schedule 18: Part I	None.
Rear marking	Schedule 19: Part I	A vehicle having a maximum speed not exceeding 25mph; A vehicle first used before 1st August 1982, the unladen weight of which does not exceed 3050kg;

(1) Type of lamp, reflector, rear marking or device	(2) Schedule in which relevant installation and performance requirements are specified	(3) Exceptions
		A vehicle the maximum gross weight of which does not exceed 7500kg;
		A passenger vehicle not being an articulated bus;
		A tractive unit for an articulated vehicle;
		An incomplete vehicle proceeding to a works for completion or to a place where it is to be stored or displayed for sale;
		A vehicle first used before 1st April 1986 being an agricultural vehicle, a works truck or engineering plant;
		A vehicle first used before 1st January 1940;
		A home forces' vehicle;
		A vehicle constructed or adapted for— (a) fire fighting or fire salvage; (b) servicing or controlling aircraft; (c) heating and dispensing tar or other material for the construction or maintenance of roads; or (d) transporting two or more vehicles or vehicle bodies or two or more boats[;]
		[A vehicle fitted with conspicuity markings to the rear where the fitting of those markings complies with the mandatory or optional ECE conspicuity requirements.]

Tᴀʙʟᴇ II

Solo motor bicycle and motor bicycle combination   **B23.56**

(1) Type of lamp or reflector	(2) Schedule in which relevant installation and performance requirements are specified	(3) Exceptions
Front position lamp	Schedule 2: Part I	A solo motor bicycle fitted with a headlamp.
Dipped-beam headlamp	Schedule 4: Part I	A vehicle first used before 1st January 1931.
Main-beam headlamp	Schedule 5: Part I	A vehicle having a maximum speed not exceeding 25mph;

(1) Type of lamp or reflector	(2) Schedule in which relevant installation and performance requirements are specified	(3) Exceptions
Direction indicator	Schedule 7: Part I	A vehicle first used before 1st January 1972 and having an engine with a capacity of less than 50cc; A vehicle first used before 1st January 1931. A vehicle having a maximum speed not exceeding 25mph; A vehicle first used before 1st April 1986; A vehicle which is constructed or adapted primarily for use off roads (whether by reason of its tyres, suspension, ground clearance or otherwise) and which can carry only one person or which, in the case of a motor bicycle combination, can carry only the rider and one passenger in the sidecar.
Rear position lamp	Schedule 10: Part I	None.
Stop lamp	Schedule 12: Part I	A vehicle having a maximum speed not exceeding 25mph; A vehicle first used before 1st April 1986 and having an engine with a capacity of less than 50cc; A vehicle first used before 1st January 1936.
Rear registration plate lamp	Schedule 15	A vehicle not required to be fitted with a rear registration plate.
Rear retro reflector	Schedule 18: Part I	None.

Table III

Pedal cycle

(1) Type of lamp or reflector	(2) Schedule in which relevant installation and performance requirements are specified	(3) Exceptions
Front position lamp	Schedule 2: Part I	None.
Rear position lamp	Schedule 10: Part I	None.

(1) Type of lamp or reflector	(2) Schedule in which relevant installation and performance requirements are specified	(3) Exceptions
Rear retro reflector	Schedule 18: Part I	None.
Pedal retro reflector	Schedule 20: Part I	A pedal cycle manufactured before 1st October 1985.

Tᴀʙʟᴇ IV

Pedestrian-controlled vehicle, horse-drawn vehicle and track-laying vehicle   **B23.58**

(1) Type of lamp or reflector	(2) Schedule in which relevant installation and performance requirements are specified	(3) Exceptions
Front position lamp	Schedule 2: Part I	None.
Rear position lamp	Schedule 10: Part I	None.
Rear retro reflector	Schedule 18: Part I	None.

Tᴀʙʟᴇ V

Vehicle drawn or propelled by hand   **B23.59**

(1) Type of lamp or reflector	(2) Schedule in which relevant installation and performance requirements are specified	(3) Exceptions
Front position lamp	Schedule 2: Part I	None.
Rear position lamp	Schedule 10: Part I	A vehicle fitted with a rear retro reflector.
Rear retro reflector	Schedule 18: Part I	A vehicle fitted with a rear position lamp.

TABLE VI

B23.60   Trailer drawn by a motor vehicle

(1) Type of lamp, reflector or rear marking	(2) Schedule in which relevant installation and performance requirements are specified	(3) Exceptions
Front position lamp	Schedule 2: Part I	A trailer with an overall width not exceeding 1600mm; A trailer manufactured before 1st October 1985 the overall length of which, excluding any drawbar and any fitting for its attachment, does not exceed 2300mm; A trailer constructed or adapted for the carriage and launching of a boat.
Direction indicator	Schedule 7: Part I	A trailer manufactured before 1st September 1965; An agricultural vehicle or a works trailer in either case manufactured before 1st October 1990.
Side marker lamp	Schedule 9: Part I	A trailer the overall length of which, excluding any drawbar and any fitting for its attachment, does not exceed— (a) 6m, (b) 9.15m in the case of a trailer manufactured before 1st October 1990; An incomplete trailer proceeding to a works for completion or to a place where it is to be stored or displayed for sale; An agricultural vehicle or a works trailer; A caravan; A trailer constructed or adapted for the carriage and launching of a boat;

(1) Type of lamp, reflector or rear marking	(2) Schedule in which relevant installation and performance requirements are specified	(3) Exceptions
		[A trailer manufactured before 1st October 1995 in respect of which the following conditions are satisfied]— (a) there is fitted to the trailer all the lighting and light-signalling devices listed in items 1.5.7 to 1.5.20 of Annex I of [Community Directive 76/756/EEC as last amended by Directive 89/278/EEC or Community Directive 76/756/EEC as last amended by Directive 91/663/EEC] which are required to be fitted under that Annex; and (b) all those devices are so installed and maintained that they comply with the requirements set out in items 3 and 4 of that Annex.
Rear position lamp	Schedule 10: Part I	None.
Rear fog lamp	Schedule 11: Part I	A trailer manufactured before 1st April 1980; A trailer the overall width of which does not exceed 1300mm; An agricultural vehicle or a works trailer.
Stop lamp	Schedule 12: Part I	An agricultural vehicle or a works trailer.
End-outline marker lamp	Schedule 13: Part I	A trailer having an overall width not exceeding 2100mm; An incomplete trailer proceeding to a works for completion or to a place where it is to be stored or displayed for sale; An agricultural vehicle or a works trailer; A trailer manufactured before 1st October 1990.
Rear registration plate lamp	Schedule 15	A trailer not required to be fitted with a rear registration plate.
Side retro reflector	Schedule 17: Part I	A trailer the overall length of which, excluding any drawbar, does not exceed 5m; An incomplete trailer proceeding to a works for completion or to a place where it is to be stored or displayed for sale; Engineering plant;

(1) Type of lamp, reflector or rear marking	(2) Schedule in which relevant installation and performance requirements are specified	(3) Exceptions
		A trailer primarily constructed for moving excavated material and which is being used by virtue of an Order under section 44 of the Act.
Front retro reflector	Schedule 21: Part I	A trailer manufactured before 1st October 1990;
		An agricultural vehicle or a works trailer.
Rear retro reflector	Schedule 18: Part I	None.
Rear marking	Schedule 19: Part I	A trailer manufactured before 1st August 1982 the unladen weight of which does not exceed 1020kg;
		A trailer the maximum gross weight of which does not exceed 3500kg;
		An incomplete trailer proceeding to a works for completion or to a place where it is to be stored or displayed for sale;
		An agricultural vehicle, a works trailer or engineering plant;
		A trailer drawn by a bus;
		A home forces' vehicle;
		A trailer constructed or adapted for— (a) fire fighting or fire salvage; (b) servicing or controlling aircraft; (c) heating and dispensing tar or other material for the construction or maintenance of roads; (d) carrying asphalt or macadam, in each case being mixing or drying plant; or (e) transporting two or more vehicles or vehicle bodies or two or more boats[;]
		[A trailer fitted with conspicuity markings to the rear where the fitting of those markings complies with the mandatory or optional ECE conspicuity requirements.]

TABLE VII

Trailer drawn by a pedal cycle   **B23.61**

(1) *Type of lamp, reflector or rear marking*	(2) *Schedule in which relevant installation and performance requirements are specified*	(3) *Exceptions*
Rear position lamp	Schedule 10: Part I	None.
Rear retro reflector	Schedule 18: Part I	None.

[Tables I and VI in Sch.1 are printed as amended by SI 1994/2280; SI 2009/ 3220.]   **B23.62**

(Regulations 18 and 20)   SCHEDULE 2

PART I

REQUIREMENTS RELATING TO OBLIGATORY FRONT POSITION LAMPS AND TO OPTIONAL FRONT POSITION LAMPS TO THE EXTENT SPECIFIED IN PART II

B23.63

1. Number—
    (a) Any vehicle not covered by sub-paragraph (b), (c), (d), (e) or (f):   Two
    (b) A pedal cycle with less than four wheels and without a sidecar: One
    (c) A solo motor bicycle: One
    (d) A motor bicycle combination with a headlamp on the motor bicycle: One, on the sidecar
    (e) An invalid carriage: One
    (f) A vehicle drawn or propelled by hand: One

2. Position—
    (a) Longitudinal: No requirement
    (b) Lateral—
        (i) Where two front position lamps are required to be fitted—
        (A) Maximum distance from the side of the vehicle—
            (1) A motor vehicle first used on or after 1st April 1986:   400mm
            (2) A trailer manufactured on or after 1st October 1985:   150mm
            (3) Any other vehicle manufactured on or after 1st October 1985:   400mm
            (4) A motor vehicle first used before 1st April 1986 and any other vehicle manufactured before 1st October 1985:   510mm

		(B)	Minimum separation distance between front position lamps:	No requirement
	(ii)		Where one front position lamp is required to be fitted—	
		(A)	A sidecar forming part of a motor bicycle combination:	On the centre-line of the sidecar or on the side of the sidecar furthest from the motor bicycle
		(B)	Any other vehicle:	On the centre-line or offside of the vehicle
(c)	Vertical—			
	(i)		Maximum height above the ground—	1500mm or, if the structure of the vehicle makes this impracticable, 2100mm
		(A)	Any vehicle not covered by sub-paragraph (b), (c) or (d):	
		(B)	A motor vehicle first used before 1st April 1986 and a trailer manufactured before 1st October 1985:	2300mm
		(C)	A motor vehicle, first used on or after 1st April 1986, having a maximum speed not exceeding 25mph:	2100mm
		(D)	A [bus] and a road clearance vehicle	No requirement
	(ii)		Minimum height above the ground	No requirement

3.   Angles of visibility—

(a)	A motor vehicle (not being a motor bicycle combination or an agricultural vehicle) first used on or after 1st April 1986 and a trailer manufactured on or after 1st October 1985—			
	(i)		Horizontal—	
		(A)	Where one lamp is required to be fitted:	80° to the left and to the right
		(B)	Where two lamps are required to be fitted:	80° outwards and 45° inwards (5° inwards in the case of a trailer)
	(ii)		Vertical—	
		(A)	Any case not covered by sub-paragraph (B):	15° above and below the horizontal
		(B)	Where the highest part of the illuminated area of the lamp is less than 750 mm above the ground:	15° above and 5° below the horizontal
(b)	Any other vehicle:			Visible to the front

4.   Alignment: To the front

5.   Markings [(see also regulation 3(6))] —

(a)	A motor vehicle (other than a solo motor bicycle or a motor bicycle combination) first used on or after 1st January 1972 and a trailer manufactured on or after 1st October 1985:	An approval mark
(b)	A solo motor bicycle and a motor bicycle combination in either case first used on or after 1st April 1986:	An approval mark
(c)	Any other vehicle manufactured or first used on or after 1st October 1990 [and before the 1st October 1995]:	An approval mark or a British Standard mark
[(ca)	Any other vehicle manufactured on or after 1st October 1995:	An approval mark or the British Standard mark which is specified in [sub-paragraph (b), (c) or (d)] of the definition of "British Standard mark" below.]
(d)	Any other vehicle:	No requirement

6. Size of illuminated area: No requirement

7. Colour: White or, if incorporated in a headlamp which is capable of emitting only a yellow light, yellow

8. Wattage: No requirement

9. Intensity—

    (a) A front position lamp bearing any of the markings mentioned in paragraph 5: No requirement

    (b) Any other front position lamp: Visible from a reasonable distance

10. Electrical connections: No individual requirement

11. Tell-tale: No requirement

12. Other requirements—

(a) Except in the case of a vehicle covered by sub-paragraph (b), where two front position lamps are required to be fitted they shall form a pair.

(b) In the case of a trailer manufactured before 1st October 1985 and a motor bicycle combination, where two front position lamps are required to be fitted they shall be fitted on each side of the longitudinal axis of the vehicle.

[(c) in the case of a front position lamp capable of emitting a flashing light which is fitted to—

    (i) a pedal cycle; or

    (ii) a trailer drawn by, or a sidecar attached to, a pedal cycle;

the light shown by the lamp when flashing shall be displayed not less than 60 nor more than 240 equal times per minute and the intervals between each display of light shall be constant.]

13. Definitions—

In this Schedule —

    "approval mark" means—

        (a) in relation to a solo motor bicycle or a motor bicycle combination, a marking designated as an approval mark by regulation 4 of the Designation of Approval Marks Regulations and shown at item 50A of Schedule 2 to those Regulations, and

(b) in relation to any other ... vehicle ..., either—

   (i) a marking designated as an approval mark by regulation 5 of the Designation of Approval Marks Regulations and shown at item 5 of Schedule 4 to those Regulations, or

   (ii) a marking designated as an approval mark by regulation 4 of the Designation of Approval Marks Regulations and shown at item 7 of Schedule 2 to those Regulations;

[*"British Standard mark"* means—

(a) the mark indicated in the specification for photometric and physical requirements for lighting equipment published by the British Standards Institution under the references BS 6102: Part 3: 1986 namely "6102/3"; or

(b) the mark indicated in the specification for photometric and physical requirements for lighting equipment published by the British Standards Institution under the references BS 6102: Part 3: 1986 as amended by AMD 5821 published on the 29th April 1988, namely "6102/3"] [or

(c) the mark indicated in the specification for photometric and physical requirements for lighting equipment published by the British Standards Institution under the reference BS 6102: Part 3: 1986 as amended by AMD 8438 published on the 15th April 1995, namely "6102/3"; or

(d) the mark indicated in the specification for photometric and physical requirements for lighting equipment published by the British Standards under the reference BS 6102: Part 3: 1986 as amended by AMD 14621 published on the 1st September 2003, namely "6102/3".]

B23.64   *[Part I of Sch.2 is printed as amended by SI 1994/2280; SI 2005/2559.]*

PART II

REQUIREMENTS RELATING TO OPTIONAL FRONT POSITION LAMPS

B23.65   1. In the case of a solo motor bicycle first used on or after 1st April 1991 which is not fitted with any obligatory front position lamp, not more than two may be fitted which must comply with the requirement specified in paragraph 7 of Part I. Where two are fitted these shall be situated as close together as possible.

B23.66   2. In the case of a solo motor bicycle first used on or after 1st April 1991 which is fitted with one obligatory front position lamp, not more than one additional lamp may be fitted which must comply with the requirement specified in paragraph 7 of Part I and shall be situated as close as possible to the obligatory front position lamp.

B23.67   [3. In the case of any other vehicle any number of front position lamps may be fitted and the only requirements prescribed by these Regulations in respect of any which are fitted are those in paragraph 7 and 12(c) of Part I.]

B23.68   *[Part II of Sch.2 is printed as amended by SI 2005/2559.]*

(Regulations 18 and 20)   SCHEDULE 3

PART I

REQUIREMENTS RELATING TO OBLIGATORY DIM-DIP DEVICES AND RUNNING LAMPS

B23.69   1. A dim-dip device fitted to satisfy regulation 18 shall cause light to be emitted from the dipped-beam filament of each obligatory dipped-beam headlamp, each such light having, so far as is practicable, an intensity of between 10 and 20 per cent of the intensity of the normal dipped beam.

B23.70   2. Running lamps fitted to satisfy regulation 18 shall be in the form of a matched pair of front lamps, each of which—

(a) is fitted in a position in which an obligatory front position lamp may lawfully be fitted, and

(b) is capable of emitting white light to the front having an intensity of not less than 200 candelas, measured from directly in front of the centre of the lamp in a direction parallel to the longitudinal axis of the vehicle, and of not more than 800 candelas in any direction.

[3. The electrical connections to the obligatory dim-dip device shall be such that the light output specified in paragraph 1 above is automatically emitted whenever the following four conditions are satisfied, namely—   **B23.71**

(a) the engine is running, or the key or devices which control the starting or stopping of the engine are in the normal position for when the vehicle is being driven

(b) the obligatory main beam and dipped beam headlamps are switched off;

(c) any front fog lamp fitted to the vehicle is switched off; and

(d) the obligatory front position lamps are switched on.]

[4. The electrical connections to the obligatory running lamps shall be such that the light output specified in paragraph 2 above is automatically emitted, whenever the conditions set out in sub-paragraphs (a), (b) and (c) of paragraph 3 are satisfied.]   **B23.72**

[Part I of Sch.3 is printed as amended by SI 1994/2280.]   **B23.73**

PART II

REQUIREMENTS RELATING TO OPTIONAL DIM-DIP DEVICES AND RUNNING LAMPS

There is no requirement relating to an optional dim-dip device or an optional running lamp.   **B23.74**

(Regulations 18 and 20)   SCHEDULE 4

PART I

REQUIREMENTS RELATING TO OBLIGATORY DIPPED-BEAM HEADLAMPS AND TO OPTIONAL DIPPED-BEAM HEADLAMPS TO THE EXTENT SPECIFIED IN PART II

     B23.75

1.   Number—

(a)	Any vehicle not covered by sub-paragraph (b), (c), (d) or (e):	Two
(b)	A solo motor bicycle and a motor bicycle combination:	One
(c)	A motor vehicle with three wheels, other than a motor bicycle combination, first used before 1st January 1972:	One
(d)	A motor vehicle with three wheels, other than a motor bicycle combination, first used on or after 1st January 1972 and which has an unladen weight of not more than 400kg and an overall width of not more than 1300mm:	One
(e)	A bus first used before 1st October 1969:	One

2.   Position—

(a)	Longitudinal:	No requirement
(b)	Lateral—	
	(i) Where two dipped-beam headlamps are required to be fitted—	
	(A) Maximum distance from the side of the vehicle—	

	(1)	Any vehicle not covered by sub-paragraph (2) or (3):	400mm
	(2)	A vehicle first used before 1st January 1972:	No requirement
	(3)	An agricultural vehicle, engineering plant and an industrial tractor:	No requirement
(B)		Minimum separation distance between a pair of dipped-beam headlamps:	No requirement
(ii)		Where one dipped-beam headlamp is required to be fitted—	
	(A)	Any vehicle not covered by sub-paragraph (B):	(i) On the centre-line of the motor vehicle (disregarding any sidecar forming part of a motor bicycle combination), or (ii) At any distance from the side of the motor vehicle (disregarding any sidecar forming part of a motor bicycle combination) provided that a duplicate lamp is fitted on the other side so that together they form a matched pair. In such a case, both lamps shall be regarded as obligatory lamps.
	(B)	A bus first used before 1st October 1969:	No requirement
(c)		Vertical—	
(i)		Maximum height above the ground—	
	(A)	Any vehicle not covered by sub-paragraph (b):	1200mm
	(B)	A vehicle first used before 1st January 1952, an agricultural vehicle, a road clearance vehicle, an aerodrome fire tender, an aerodrome runway sweeper, an industrial tractor, engineering plant and a home forces' vehicle:	No requirement
(ii)		Minimum height above the ground—	
	(A)	Any vehicle not covered by sub-paragraph (b):	500mm
	(B)	A vehicle first used before 1st January 1956:	No requirement

3.   Angles of visibility: No requirement

4.   Alignment—

When a vehicle is at its kerbside weight and has a weight of 75kg on the driver's seat, and any manual headlamp levelling device control is set to the stop position, the alignment of every dipped-beam headlamp shall, as near as practicable, be as follows:

(a)   In the case of a vehicle having a maximum speed exceeding 25mph—

    (i)   If the dipped-beam headlamp bears an approval mark its aim shall be set so that the horizontal part of the cut-off of the beam pattern is inclined downwards as indicated by the vehicle manufacturer in a marking on the vehicle, as mentioned in sub-paragraph 12(b) or, where no such marking is provided—

        (A)   1.3 per cent if the height of the centre of the headlamp is not more than 850mm above the ground, or

        (B)   2 per cent if the height of the centre of the headlamp is more than 850mm above the ground;

    (ii)   If the dipped-beam headlamp does not bear an approval mark and the headlamp can also be used as a main-beam headlamp its aim shall be set so that the centre of the main-beam pattern is horizontal or inclined slightly below the horizontal;

    (iii)   If the dipped-beam headlamp does not bear an approval mark and the headlamp cannot also be used as a main-beam headlamp its aim shall be set so as not to cause undue dazzle or discomfort to other persons using the road;

(b)   In the case of a vehicle having a maximum speed not exceeding 25mph—

    (i)   If the dipped-beam headlamp bears an approval mark or not and the headlamp can also be used as a main-beam headlamp its aim shall be set so that the centre of the main-beam pattern is horizontal or inclined slightly below the horizontal;

    (ii)   If the dipped-beam headlamp bears an approval mark or not and the headlamp cannot also be used as a main-beam headlamp its aim shall be set so as not to cause undue dazzle or discomfort to other persons using the road.

5.   Markings—

(a)   Any vehicle not covered by sub-paragraph (b), (c) or (d):   An approval mark or a British Standard mark

(b)   A motor vehicle first used before 1st April 1986:   No requirement

(c)   A three-wheeled motor vehicle, not being a motor bicycle combination, first used on or after 1st April 1986 and having a maximum speed not exceeding 50mph: No requirement

(d)   A solo motor bicycle and a motor bicycle combination: No requirement

6.   Size of illuminated area: No requirement

7.   Colour: White or yellow

8.   Wattage—

(a)   A motor vehicle with four or more wheels first used on or after 1st April 1986:   No requirement

(b)   A three-wheeled motor vehicle, not being a motor bicycle combination, first used on or after 1st April 1986—

(i) having a maximum speed not exceeding 50mph:	15 watts minimum
(ii) having a maximum speed exceeding 50mph:	No requirement
(c) A motor vehicle with four or more wheels first used before 1st April 1986:	30 watts minimum
(d) A three-wheeled motor vehicle, not being a motor bicycle combination, first used before 1st April 1986:	24 watts minimum
(e) A solo motor bicycle and a motor bicycle combination—	
(i) having an engine not exceeding 250cc and a maximum speed not exceeding 25mph:	10 watts minimum
(ii) having an engine not exceeding 250cc and a maximum speed exceeding 25mph:	15 watts minimum
(iii) having an engine exceeding 250cc:	24 watts minimum

9.   Intensity: No requirement

10.   Electrical connections—

Where a matched pair of dipped-beam headlamps is fitted they shall be capable of being switched on and off simultaneously and not otherwise.

11.   Tell-tale: No requirement

12. Other requirements—

(a) Every dipped-beam headlamp shall be so constructed that the direction of the beam of light emitted therefrom can be adjusted whilst the vehicle is stationary.

(b) Every vehicle which—

    (i) is fitted with dipped-beam headlamps bearing an approval mark,

    (ii) has a maximum speed exceeding 25mph, and

    (iii) is first used on or after 1st April 1991

shall be marked with a clearly legible and indelible marking, as illustrated in Schedule 23, close to either the headlamps or the manufacturer's plate showing the setting recommended by the manufacturer for the downward inclination of the horizontal part of the cut-off of the beam pattern of the dipped-beam headlamps when the vehicle is at its kerbside weight and has a weight of 75kg on the driver's seat. That setting shall be a single figure—

    (A) between 1 and 1.5 per cent if the height of the centre of the headlamp is not more than 850mm above the ground, and

    (B) between 1 and 2 per cent if the height of the centre of the headlamp is more than 850mm above the ground.

(c) Every dipped-beam headlamp fitted to a vehicle first used on or after 1st April 1986 in accordance with this part of this Schedule shall be designed for a vehicle which is intended to be driven on the left-hand side of the road.

(d) Where two dipped-beam headlamps are required to be fitted they shall form a matched pair.

13. Definitions—

In this Schedule —

"approval mark" means either—

    (a) a marking designated as an approval mark by regulation 5 of the Designation of Approval Marks Regulations and shown at item 12 or 13 or 14 or 16 or, in the case of a vehicle having a maximum speed not exceeding 25mph, 27 or 28 of Schedule 4 to those Regulations, or

    (b) a marking designated as an approval mark by regulation 4 of the Designation of Approval Marks Regulations and shown at item 1A or 1B or 1C or 1E or 5A or 5B or 5C or 5E or 8C or 8D or 8E or 8F or 8G or 8H or 8K or 8L or 20C or 20D or 20E or 20F or 20G or 20H or 20K or 20L or 31A or 31C or, in the case of a vehicle having a maximum speed not exceeding 25mph, 1H or 1I or 5H or 5I or Schedule 2 to those Regulations; and

"British Standard mark" means the specification for sealed beam headlamps published by the British Standards Institution under the reference BS AU 40: Part 4A: 1966 as amended by Amendment AMD 2188 published in December 1976, namely "B.S. AU40".

PART II

REQUIREMENTS RELATING TO OPTIONAL DIPPED-BEAM HEADLAMPS

1. In the case of a vehicle with three or more wheels having a maximum speed exceeding 25mph first used on or after 1st April 1991, two and not more than two may be fitted and the only requirements prescribed by these Regulations in respect of any which are fitted are—   **B23.76**

(a) those specified in paragraphs 2(c), 4, 7, 10 and 12 (a) of Part I,

(b) that they are designed for a vehicle which is intended to be driven on the right-hand side of the road,

(c) that they form a matched pair, and

(d) that their electrical connections are such that not more than one pair of dipped-beam headlamps is capable of being illuminated at a time.

2. In the case of any other vehicle, any number may be fitted and the only requirements prescribed by these Regulations in respect of any which are fitted are those specified in paragraphs 2(c), 4, 7 and 12(a) of Part I.   **B23.77**

(Regulations 18 and 20)   SCHEDULE 5

PART I

REQUIREMENTS RELATING TO OBLIGATORY MAIN-BEAM HEADLAMPS AND TO OPTIONAL MAIN-BEAM HEADLAMPS TO THE EXTENT SPECIFIED IN PART II

B23.78

1. Number—

   (a) Any vehicle not covered by sub-paragraph (b), (c) or (d):   Two

   (b) A solo motor bicycle and motor bicycle combination: One

   (c) A motor vehicle with three wheels, other than a motor bicycle combination, first used before 1st January 1972:   One

   (d) A motor vehicle with three wheels, other than a motor bicycle combination, first used on or after 1st January 1972 and which has an unladen weight of not more than 400kg and an overall width of not more than 1300mm: One

2. Position—

   (a) Longitudinal: No requirement

   (b) Lateral—

     (i) Where two dipped-beam headlamps are required to be fitted—

	(A)	Maximum distance from the side of the vehicle:	The outer edges of the illuminated areas must in no case be closer to the side of the vehicle than the outer edges of the illuminated areas of the obligatory dipped-beam headlamps.
	(B)	Maximum separation distance between a pair of main-beam headlamps:	No requirement
(ii)		Where one main-beam headlamp is required to be fitted:	(i) On the centre-line of the motor vehicle (disregarding any sidecar forming part of a motor bicycle combination), or
			(ii) At any distance from the side of the vehicle (disregarding any sidecar, forming part of a motor bicycle combination) provided that a duplicate lamp is fitted on the other side so that together they form a matched pair. In such a case, both lamps shall be treated as obligatory lamps.
	(c)	Vertical:	No requirement
3.		Angles of visibility:	No requirement
4.		Alignment:	To the front
5.		Markings—	
	(a)	Any vehicle not covered by sub-paragraph (b), (c), or (d):	An approval mark or a British Standard mark
	(b)	A motor vehicle first used before 1st April 1986:	No requirement
	(c)	A three-wheeled motor vehicle, not being a motor bicycle combination, first used on or after 1st April 1986 and having a maximum speed not exceeding 50mph:	No requirement
	(d)	A solo motor bicycle and a motor bicycle combination:	No requirement
6.		Size of illuminated area:	No requirement
7.		Colour:	White or yellow
8.		Wattage—	

(a)　A motor vehicle, other than a solo motor　　　No requirement
bicycle or motor bicycle combination, first
used on or after 1st April 1986:

(b)　A motor vehicle, other than a solo motor　　　30 watts minimum
bicycle or a motor bicycle combination, first
used before 1st April 1986:

(c)　A solo motor bicycle and a motor bicycle
combination—

(i)　having an engine not exceeding 250cc:　　15 watts minimum

(ii)　having an engine exceeding 250cc:　　30 watts minimum

9.　Intensity:　　　No requirement

10.　Electrical connections—

(a)　Every main-beam headlamp shall be so constructed that the light
emitted therefrom—

(i)　can be deflected at the will of the driver to become a dipped
beam, or

(ii)　can be extinguished by the operation of a device which at the
same time either—

(ᴀ)　causes the lamp to emit a dipped
beam, or

(ʙ)　causes another lamp to emit a dipped beam.

(b)　Where a matched pair of main-beam headlamps is fitted they shall be
capable of being switched on and off simultaneously and not
otherwise.

11.　Tell-tale—

(a)　Any vehicle not covered by sub-paragraph (b):　　A circuit-closed
tell-tale shall be
fitted

(b)　A motor vehicle first used before 1st April　　No requirement
1986:

12. Other requirements—

(a) Every main-beam headlamp shall be so constructed that the direction of the beam
of light emitted therefrom can be adjusted whilst the vehicle is stationary.

(b) Except in the case of a bus first used before 1st October 1969, where two main-
beam headlamps are required to be fitted they shall form a matched pair.

13. Definitions—

In this Schedule —

"approval mark" means—

(a) a marking designated as an approval mark by regulation 5 of the Designation of Approval Marks Regulations and shown at item 12 or 13 or 17 of
Schedule 4 to those Regulations; or

(b) a marking designated as an approval mark by regulation 4 of the Designation of Approval Marks Regulations and shown at item 1A or 1B or 1F or
5A or 5B or 5F or 8C or 8D or 8E or 8F or 8M or 8N or 20C or 20D or 20E
or 20F or 20M or 20N or 31A or 31D of Schedule 2 to those Regulations;
and

"British Standard mark" means the specification for sealed beam headlamps
published by the British Standards Institution under the reference BS AU 40:
Part 4a: 1966 as amended by Amendment AMD 2188 published in December
1976, namely "B.S. AU40".

PART II

REQUIREMENTS RELATING TO OPTIONAL MAIN-BEAM HEADLAMPS

B23.79   Any number may be fitted and the only requirements prescribed by these Regulations in respect of any which are fitted are those specified in paragraphs 7, 10 and 12(a) of Part I and, in the case of a motor vehicle first used on or after 1st April 1991, paragraph 5 of Part I.

(Regulation 20)   SCHEDULE 6

REQUIREMENTS RELATING TO OPTIONAL FOG LAMPS

B23.80   **1.**   Number—

(a)	Any vehicle not covered by sub-paragraph (b):	No requirement
(b)	A motor vehicle, other than a motor bicycle or motor bicycle combination, first used on or after 1st April 1991:	Not more than two

2.   Position—

(a)	Longitudinal:	No requirement
(b)	Lateral—	
(i)	Where a pair of front fog lamps is used in conditions of seriously reduced visibility in place of the obligatory dipped beam headlamps—	
	Maximum distance from side of vehicle:	400mm
(ii)	in all other cases:	No requirement
(c)	Vertical—	
(i)	Maximum height above the ground—	
(A)	Any vehicle not covered by sub-paragraph (B):	1200mm
(B)	An agricultural vehicle, a road clearance vehicle, an aerodrome fire tender, an aerodrome runway sweeper, an industrial tractor, engineering plant and a home forces' vehicle:	No requirement
(ii)	Minimum height above the ground:	No requirement

3.   Angles of visibility: No requirement

4.   Alignment: To the front and so aimed that the upper edge of the beam is, as near as practicable, 3 per cent below the horizontal when the vehicle is at its kerbside weight and has a weight of 75kg on the driver's seat

5.   Markings—

(a)	A vehicle first used on or after 1st April 1986:	An approval mark
(b)	A vehicle first used before 1st April 1986:	No requirement

6.   Size of illuminated area: No requirement

7.	Colour:	White or yellow
8.	Wattage:	No requirement
9.	Intensity:	No requirement
10.	Electrical connections:	No individual requirement
11.	Tell-tale:	No requirement

12. Other requirements—

Every front fog lamp shall be so constructed that the direction of the beam of light emitted therefrom can be adjusted whilst the vehicle is stationary.

13. Definitions—

In this Schedule *"approval mark"* means either—

    (a)   a marking designated as an approval mark by regulation 5 of the Designation of Approval Marks Regulations and shown at item 19 of Schedule 4 to those Regulations; or

    (b)   a marking designated as an approval mark by regulation 4 of the Designation of Approval Marks Regulations and shown at item 19 or 19A of Schedule 2 to those Regulations.

(Regulations 18 and 20)　　　　　SCHEDULE 7

Pᴀʀᴛ I

RᴇQᴜɪʀᴇᴍᴇɴᴛs Rᴇʟᴀᴛɪɴɢ ᴛᴏ Oʙʟɪɢᴀᴛᴏʀʏ Dɪʀᴇᴄᴛɪᴏɴ Iɴᴅɪᴄᴀᴛᴏʀs ᴀɴᴅ ᴛᴏ Oᴘᴛɪᴏɴᴀʟ Dɪʀᴇᴄᴛɪᴏɴ
Iɴᴅɪᴄᴀᴛᴏʀs ᴛᴏ ᴛʜᴇ Exᴛᴇɴᴛ Sᴘᴇᴄɪғɪᴇᴅ ɪɴ Pᴀʀᴛ II

B23.81

1.　Number (on each side of a vehicle)—

    (a)   A motor vehicle with three or more wheels, not being a motor bicycle combination, first used on or after 1st April 1986:　　One front indicator (Category 1, 1a or 1b), one rear indicator (Category 2, 2a or 2b) and one side repeater indicator [(Category 5 or 6 above)] or, in the case of a motor vehicle having a maximum speed not exceeding 25mph, one front indicator (Category 1, 1a or 1b) and one rear indicator (Category 2, 2a or 2b).

    (b)   A trailer manufactured on or after 1st October 1985 drawn by a motor vehicle:　　One rear indicator (Category 2, 2a or 2b) or, in the case of a trailer towed by a solo motor bicycle or a motor bicycle combination, one rear indicator (Category 12).

(c)	A solo motor bicycle and a motor bicycle combination, in each case first used on or after 1st April 1986:	One front indicator (Category 1, 1a, 1b or 11) and one rear indicator (Category 2, 2a, 2b or 12).
(d)	A motor vehicle first used on or after [1st April 1936] and before 1st April 1986, a trailer manufactured on or after [1st April 1936] and before 1st October 1985, a pedal cycle with or without a sidecar or a trailer, a horse-drawn vehicle and a vehicle drawn or propelled by hand:	Any arrangement of indicators so as to satisfy the requirements for angles of visibility in paragraph 3.
(e)	A motor vehicle first used before 1st April 1936 and any trailer manufactured before that date:	Any arrangement of indicators so as to make the intention of the driver clear to other road users.

2. Position—

(a) Longitudinal—

(i) A side repeater indicator which is required to be fitted in accordance with paragraph 1(a): — Within 2600mm of the front of the vehicle

(ii) Any other indicator: — No requirement

(b) Lateral—

(i) Maximum distance from the side of the vehicle—

(A) Any vehicle not covered by sub-paragraph (b): — 400mm

(B) A motor vehicle first used before 1st April 1986, a trailer manufactured before 1st October 1985, a solo motor bicycle, a pedal cycle, a horse-drawn vehicle and a vehicle drawn or propelled by hand: — No requirement

(ii) Minimum separation distance between indicators on opposite sides of a vehicle—

(A) A motor vehicle (other than a solo motor bicycle or a motor bicycle combination or an invalid carriage having a maximum speed not exceeding 8mph) first used on or after 1st April 1986, a trailer manufactured on or after 1st October 1985, a horse-drawn vehicle, a pedestrian-controlled vehicle and a vehicle drawn or propelled by hand: — 500mm or, if the overall width of the vehicle is less than 1400mm, 400mm

(B) A solo motor bicycle having an engine exceeding 50cc and first used on or after 1st April 1986—

(1) Front indicators: — 300mm

(2) Rear indicators: — 240mm

(C) A solo motor bicycle having an engine not exceeding 50cc and first used on or after 1st April 1986 and a pedal cycle—

    (1) Front indicators: 240mm

    (2) Rear indicators: 180mm

(D) A motor bicycle combination first used on or after 1st April 1986:   400mm

(E) An invalid carriage having a maximum speed not exceeding 8mph—

    (1) Front indicators: 240mm

    (2) Rear indicators: 300mm

(F) A motor vehicle first used before 1st April 1986 and a trailer manufactured before 1st October 1985:   No requirement

(iii) Minimum separation distance between a front indicator and any dipped-beam headlamp or front fog lamp—

(A) Fitted to a motor vehicle, other than a solo motor bicycle or a motor bicycle combination, first used on or after [1st April 1995]:   (a) in the case of a Category 1 indicator, 40mm;

(b) in the case of a Category 1a indicator, 20mm;

(c) in the case of a Category 1b indicator, no requirement

(B) Fitted to a solo motor bicycle or a motor bicycle combination in either case first used on or after 1st April 1986:   100mm

(C) Fitted to any other vehicle: No requirement

(c) Vertical—

  (i) Maximum height above the ground—

(A) Any vehicle not covered by sub-paragraph (b) or (c):   1500mm or, if the structure of the vehicle makes this impracticable, 2300mm

(B) A motor vehicle first used before 1st April 1986 and a trailer manufactured before 1st October 1985:   No requirement

(C) A motor vehicle having a maximum speed not exceeding 25mph: No requirement

  (ii) Minimum height above the ground: 350mm

3. Angles of visibility—

(a) A motor vehicle first used on or after 1st April 1986 and a trailer manufactured on or after 1st October 1985—

(i) Horizontal (see diagrams in Part III of this Schedule) —

(A)	A front or rear indicator fitted to a motor vehicle, other than a solo motor bicycle or a motor bicycle combination, having a maximum speed exceeding 25mph and every rear indicator fitted to a trailer:	80° outwards and 45° inwards
(B)	A front or rear indicator fitted to a solo motor bicycle or a motor bicycle combination:	80° outwards and 20° inwards
(C)	A front or rear indicator fitted to a motor vehicle, other than a solo motor bicycle or a motor bicycle combination, having a maximum speed not exceeding 25mph:	80° outwards and 3° inwards
(D)	A side repeater indicator fitted to a motor vehicle or a trailer:	Between rearward angles of 5° outboard and 60° outboard or, in the case of a motor vehicle having a maximum speed not exceeding 25mph where it is impracticable to comply with the 5° angle, this may be replaced by 10°.

(ii) Vertical—

(A)	Except as provided by sub-paragraph [(B), (C) or (D)]:	15° above and below the horizontal
(B)	Where the highest part of the illuminated area of the lamp is less than 1900mm above the ground and the vehicle is a motor vehicle having a maximum speed not exceeding 25mph:	15° above and 10° below the horizontal
(C)	Where the highest part of the illuminated area of the lamp is less than 750mm above the ground:	15° above and 5° below the horizontal
[(D)	But where the indicator is a category 6 indicator:	30° above and 5° below the horizontal]

(b) A motor vehicle first used before 1st April 1986, a trailer manufactured before 1st October 1985, a pedal cycle, a horse-drawn vehicle and a vehicle drawn or propelled by hand: Such that at least one (but not necessarily the same) indicator on each side is plainly visible to the rear in the case of a trailer and both to the front and rear in the case of any other vehicle.

4. Alignment—

(a)   A front indicator: To the front

(b)   A rear indicator: To the rear

(c)   A side repeater indicator (Category 5 [or 6]):   As shown in the
                                                                 first sketch in Part
                                                                 III of this Schedule

5.   Markings—

(a)   A motor vehicle, other than a solo motor   An approval mark
        bicycle or a motor bicycle combination, first   and, above such
        used on or after 1st April 1986 and a trailer,   mark, the following
        other than a trailer drawn by a solo motor   numbers—
        bicycle or a motor bicycle combination,
        manufactured on or after 1st October 1985:   (a) in the case of a
                                                         front indicator, "1",
                                                         "1a", or "1b",

                                                         (b) in the case of a
                                                         rear indicator, "2",
                                                         "2a" or "2b";

                                                         (c) in the case of a
                                                         side repeater
                                                         indicator, "5" [or
                                                         "6"].

(b)   A solo motor bicycle and a motor bicycle   An approval mark
        combination in either case first used on or after and, above such
        1st April 1986, a trailer, manufactured on or   mark, the following
        after 1st October 1985, drawn by such a solo   numbers—
        motor bicycle or a motor bicycle combination, a
        pedal cycle, a horse-drawn vehicle and a   (a) in the case of a
        vehicle drawn or propelled by hand: front indicator, "1",
                                                         "1a", "1b" or "11";

                                                         (b) in the case of a
                                                         rear indicator, "2",
                                                         "2a", "2b" or "12";

                                                         (c) in the case of a
                                                         side repeater
                                                         indicator, "5".

(c)   A motor vehicle first used before 1st April 1986   No requirement
        and a trailer manufactured before 1st October
        1985:

6.   Size of illuminated area: No requirement

7.   Colour—

(a)   Any vehicle not covered by sub-paragraph (b):   Amber

(b)   An indicator fitted to a motor vehicle first used
        before 1st September 1965 and any trailer
        drawn thereby—

        (i)   if it shows only the front: White or amber

        (ii) if it shows only the rear: Red or amber

        (iii) if it shows both to the front and to the   Amber
              rear.

8.   Wattage—

(a)   Any front or rear indicator which emits a   15 to 36 watts
        flashing light and does not bear an approval
        mark:

(b)   Any other indicator: No requirement

9.   Intensity—

(a)   An indicator bearing an approval mark: No requirement

(b) An indicator not bearing an approval mark: Such that the light is plainly visible from a reasonable distance

10. Electrical conditions—

(a) All indicators on one side of a vehicle together with all indicators on that side of any trailer drawn by the vehicle, while so drawn, shall be operated by one switch.

(b) All indicators on one side of a vehicle or combination of vehicles showing a flashing light shall flash in phase, except that in the case of a solo motor bicycle, a motor bicycle combination and a pedal cycle, the front and rear direction indicators on one side of the vehicle may flash alternately.

11. Tell-tale—

(a) One or more indicators on each side of a vehicle to which indicators are fitted shall be so designed and fitted that the driver when in his seat can readily be aware when it is in operation; or

(b) The vehicle shall be equipped with an operational tell-tale for front and rear indicators (including any rear indicator on the rearmost of any trailers drawn by the vehicle).

12. Other requirements—

(a) Every indicator (other than a semaphore arm, that is an indicator in the form of an illuminated sign which when in operation temporarily alters the outline of the vehicle to the extent of at least 150mm measured horizontally and is visible from both the front and rear of the vehicle) shall when in operation show a light which flashes constantly at the rate of not less than 60 nor more than 120 flashes per minute. However, in the event of a failure, other than a short-circuit of an indicator, any other indicator on the same side of the vehicle or combination of vehicles may continue to flash, but the rate may be less than 60 or more than 120 flashes per minute. Every indicator shall when in operation perform efficiently regardless of the speed of the vehicle.

(b) Where two front or rear direction indicators are fitted to a motor vehicle first used on or after 1st April 1986, and two rear direction indicators are fitted to a trailer manufactured on or after 1st October 1985, in each case they shall be fitted so as to form a pair.

(c) [...]

13. Definitions—

In this Schedule *"approval mark"* means either—

(a) a marking designated as an approval mark by regulation 5 of the Designation of Approval Marks Regulations and shown at item 9 of Schedule 4 to those Regulations; or

(b) a marking designated as an approval mark by regulation 4 of the Designation of Approval Marks Regulations and shown at item 6 or, in the case of a solo motor bicycle or a motor bicycle combination, a pedal cycle, a horse-drawn vehicle or a vehicle drawn or propelled by hand, at item 50 of Schedule 2 to those Regulations.

B23.82   *[Part I of Sch.7 is printed as amended by SI 1994/2280; SI 2009/3220.]*

Part II

Requirements Relating to Optional Direction Indicators

B23.83   **1.** No vehicle shall be fitted with a total of more than one front indicator nor more than two rear indicators, on each side.

B23.84   **2.** Any number of side indicators may be fitted to the side (excluding the front and rear) of a vehicle.

3. The only other requirements prescribed by these Regulations in respect of any which are fitted are those specified in paragraphs 5, 7, 8, 9, 10, 11, 12(a) and 12(b) of Part I.　　**B23.85**

B23.86

PART III

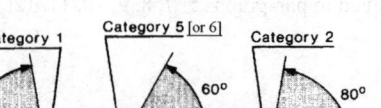

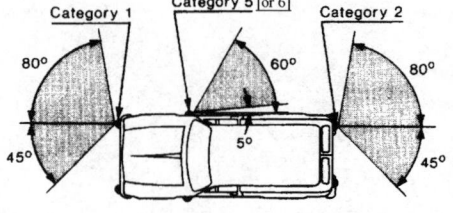

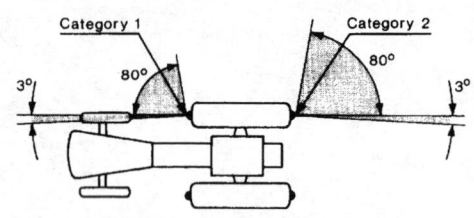

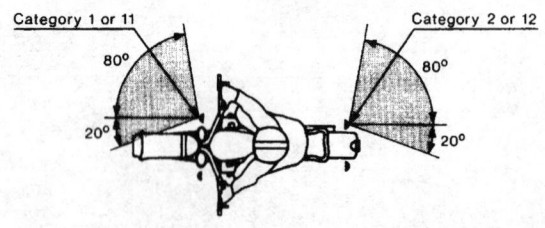

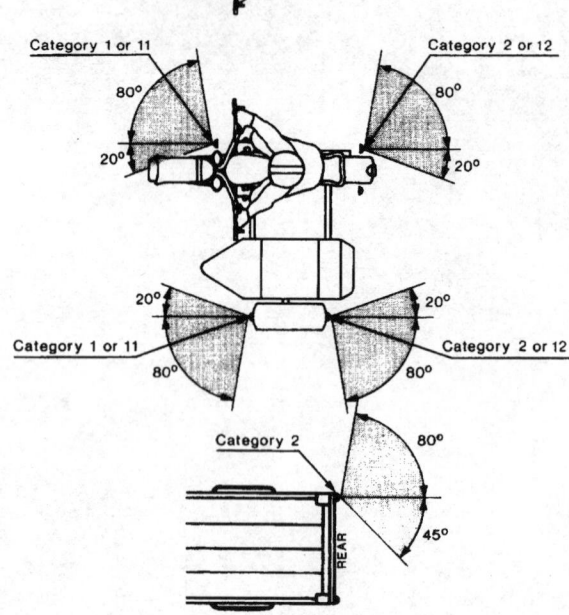

B23.87 *[Part III of Sch.7 is printed as amended by SI 2009/3220.]*

(Regulations 18 and 20)   SCHEDULE 8

REQUIREMENTS RELATING TO OBLIGATORY AND OPTIONAL HAZARD WARNING SIGNAL DEVICES

Every hazard warning signal device shall—   **B23.88**

(a) be operated by one switch;

(b) cause all the direction indicators with which a vehicle or a combination of vehicles is equipped to flash in phase;

(c) be provided with a circuit-closed tell-tale in the form of a flashing light which may operate in conjunction with any direction indicator tell-tale; and

(d) be able to function even if the device which controls the starting and stopping of the engine is in a position which makes it impossible to start the engine.

(Regulations 18, 20 and 22)   SCHEDULE 9

PART I

REQUIREMENTS RELATING TO OBLIGATORY SIDE MARKER LAMPS AND TO OPTIONAL SIDE MARKER LAMPS TO THE EXTENT SPECIFIED IN PART II

B23.89

1.   Number—

   (a)   A vehicle not covered by sub-paragraph (b) which is—

(i)	a motor vehicle first used on or after 1st April 1991 or a trailer manufactured on or after 1st October 1990:	On each side: two and as many more as are sufficient to satisfy the requirements of paragraph 2(a)
(ii)	a trailer manufactured before 1st October 1990:	One on each side

   (b)   Long vehicles and vehicle combinations to which regulation 22 applies: The numbers required by regulation 22

2.   Position—

   (a)   Longitudinal—

      (i)   A vehicle of a type mentioned in sub-paragraph 1(a)(i) —

(A)	Maximum distance from the front of the vehicle, including any drawbar, in respect of the foremost side marker lamp on each side:	4m
(B)	Maximum distance from the rear of the vehicle in respect of the rearmost side marker lamp on each side:	1m
(C)	Maximum separation distance between the light-emitting surfaces of adjacent side marker lamps on the same side of the vehicle:	3m or, if this is not practicable, 4m

(ii)	A vehicle of a type mentioned in sub-paragraph 1(a)(ii):	Such that no part of the light-emitting surface is forward of, or more than 1530mm to the rear of, the centre point of the overall length of the trailer
(b)	Lateral:	
(c)	Vertical—	No requirement
	(i) Maximum height above the ground:	2300mm
	(ii) Minimum height above the ground:	No requirement
3.	Angles of visibility—	
(a)	Horizontal:	45° to the left and to the right when viewed in a direction at right angles to the longitudinal axis of the vehicle
(b)	Vertical:	No requirement
4.	Alignment: To the side	
5.	Markings: No requirement	
6.	Size of illuminated area:	No requirement
7.	Colour:	Amber or, if within 1m of the rear of the vehicle it may be red or, if the vehicle is a trailer manufactured before 1st October 1990, it may be white when viewed from the front and red when viewed from the rear
8.	Wattage:	No requirement
9.	Intensity:	Visible from a reasonable distance
10.	Electrical connections:	No individual requirement
11.	Tell-tale:	No requirement

PART II

REQUIREMENTS RELATING TO OPTIONAL SIDE MARKER LAMPS

B23.90   Any number may be fitted and the only requirement prescribed by these Regulations in respect of any which are fitted is that specified in paragraph 7 of Part I.

(Regulations 18 and 20)   SCHEDULE 10

PART I

REQUIREMENTS RELATING TO OBLIGATORY REAR POSITION LAMPS AND TO OPTIONAL REAR POSITION LAMPS TO THE EXTENT SPECIFIED IN PART II

B23.91

1.   Number—

(a)	Any vehicle not covered by sub-paragraph (b), (c), (d), (e), (f), (g) or (h):	Two
(b)	A bus first used before 1st April 1955:	One
(c)	A solo motor bicycle:	One
(d)	A pedal cycle with less than four wheels and without a sidecar:	One
(e)	A trailer drawn by a pedal cycle and a trailer, the overall width of which does not exceed 800mm, drawn by a solo motor bicycle or by a motor bicycle combination:	One
(f)	An invalid carriage having a maximum speed not exceeding 4mph:	One
(g)	A vehicle drawn or propelled by hand:	One
(h)	A motor vehicle having three or more wheels and a maximum speed not exceeding 25mph and a trailer drawn by any such vehicle if, in either case, the structure of the vehicle makes it impracticable to meet all of the relevant requirements of paragraphs 2 and 3 below with two lamps:	Four

2.   Position—

(a)	Longitudinal:			At or near the rear
(b)	Lateral—			
	(i)	Where two lamps are required to be fitted—		
		(A)	Maximum distance from the side of the vehicle—	
			(1) Any vehicle not covered by sub-paragraph (2):	400mm
			(2) A motor vehicle first used before 1st April 1986 and any other vehicle manufactured before 1st October 1985:	800mm
		(B)	Minimum separation distance between a pair of rear position lamps—	
			(1) Any vehicle not covered by sub-paragraph (2):	500mm. If the overall width of the vehicle is less than 1400mm, 400mm or if less than 800mm, 300mm

	(2)		A motor vehicle first used before 1st April 1986 and any other vehicle manufactured before 1st October 1985:	No requirement
(ii)			Where one lamp is required to be fitted:	On the centre-line or off side of the vehicle
(iii)			Where four lamps are required to be fitted—	
	(A)		Maximum distance from the side of the vehicle—	
		(1)	One pair of lamps:	Such that they satisfy the relevant requirements in sub-paragraph 2(b)(i) (A)
		(2)	The other pair of lamps:	No requirement
	(B)		Minimum separation distance between rear position lamps—	
		(1)	One pair of lamps:	Such that they satisfy the relevant requirements in sub-paragraph 2(b)(i) (B)
		(2)	The other pair of lamps:	No requirement
(c)			Vertical—	
(i)			Maximum height above the ground where one or two rear position lamps are required to be fitted—	
	(A)		Any vehicle not covered by sub-paragraph (B) or (C):	1500mm or, if the structure of the vehicle makes this impracticable, 2100mm
	(B)		A bus first used before 1st April 1986:	No requirement
	(C)		A motor vehicle first used before 1st April 1986 not being a bus, a trailer manufactured before 1st October 1985, an agricultural vehicle, a horse-drawn vehicle, an industrial tractor and engineering plant:	2100mm
(ii)			Maximum height above the ground where four rear position lamps are required to be fitted—	
	(A)		One pair of lamps:	Such that they satisfy the relevant requirements in paragraph 2(c)(i)
	(B)		The other pair of lamps:	No requirement
(iii)			Minimum height above the ground—	
	(A)		A vehicle not covered by sub-paragraph (B):	350mm

	(B)	A motor vehicle first used before 1st April 1986 and any other vehicle manufactured before 1st October 1985:		No requirement

3.   Angles of visibility—

   (a)   A motor vehicle, other than a motor bicycle combination, first used on or after 1st April 1986 and a trailer manufactured on or after 1st October 1985—

	(i)	Horizontal—		
		(A)	Where two lamps are required to be fitted:	45° inwards and 80° outwards
		(B)	Where one lamp is required to be fitted:	80° to the left and to the right
		(C)	Where four lamps are required to be fitted—	
			(1) The outer pair of lamps:	0° inwards and 80° outwards
			(2) The inner pair of lamps:	45° inwards and 80° outwards
	(ii)	Vertical—		
		(A)	Where one or two rear position lamps are required to be fitted—	
			(1) Any vehicle not covered by sub-paragraph (2) or (3):	15° above and below the horizontal
			(2) Where the highest part of the illuminated area of the lamp is less than 1500mm above the ground:	15° above and 10° below the horizontal
			(3) Where the highest part of the illuminated area of the lamp is less than 750mm above the ground:	15° above and 5° below the horizontal
		(B)	Where four rear position lamps are required to be fitted—	
			(1) One pair of lamps:	Such that they satisfy the relevant requirements in paragraph 3(a)(ii) (A)
			(2) The other pair of lamps:	Visible to the rear
	(b)	A motor vehicle, other than a motor bicycle combination, first used before 1st April 1986 and any other vehicle manufactured before 1st October 1985:		Visible to the rear
	(c)	A vehicle drawn or propelled by hand, a pedal cycle, a horse-drawn vehicle and a motor bicycle combination:		Visible to the rear

4.   Alignment: To the rear

5.   Markings [(see also regulation 3(6))] —

	(a)	A motor vehicle or a trailer not covered by sub-[paragraph (b), (c), (d) or (e)]:	An approval mark

(b)	A motor vehicle first used before 1st January 1974 and a trailer, other than a trailer drawn by a pedal cycle, manufactured before that date:	No requirement
(c)	A solo motor bicycle and a motor bicycle combination, in each case first used before 1st April 1986, and a trailer manufactured before 1st October 1985 and drawn by a solo motor bicycle or a motor bicycle combination:	No requirement
(d)	A pedal cycle, a trailer drawn by a pedal cycle, an invalid carriage having a maximum speed not exceeding 4mph, a horse-drawn vehicle and a vehicle drawn or propelled by hand [in each case manufactured before 1st October 1995]:	An approval mark or a British Standard mark
[(e)	A pedal cycle, a trailer drawn by a pedal cycle, an invalid carriage having a maximum speed not exceeding 4mph, a horse-drawn vehicle and a vehicle drawn or propelled by hand in each case manufactured on or after 1st October 1995.	An approval mark or the British Standard mark which is specified in [sub-paragraph (c), (d) or (e)] of the definition of "British Standard mark".]

6.	Size of illuminated area:	No requirement
7.	Colour:	Red
8.	Wattage:	No requirement
9.	Intensity—	
	(a) A rear position lamp bearing any of the markings mentioned in paragraph 4:	No requirement
	(b) Any other rear position lamp:	Visible from a reasonable distance
10.	Electrical connections:	No individual requirement
11.	Tell-tale:	No requirement

12. Other requirements—

(a) Except in the case of a motor vehicle first used before 1st April 1986, any other vehicle manufactured before 1st October 1985 and a motor bicycle combination, where two rear position lamps are required to be fitted they shall form a matched pair and where four rear position lamps are required to be fitted they shall form two matched pairs.

[(b) In the case of a rear position lamp capable of emitting a flashing light which is fitted to—

    (i) a pedal cycle; or

    (ii) a trailer drawn by, or a sidecar attached to, a pedal cycle

the light shown by the lamp when flashing shall be displayed not less than 60 nor more than 240 equal times per minute and the intervals between each display of light shall be constant.]

13. Definitions—

In this Schedule —

    "approval mark" means—

        (a) in relation to a solo motor bicycle, a motor bicycle combination and a trailer drawn by a solo motor bicycle or a motor bicycle combination, a marking designated as an approval mark by regulation 4 of the Designation of Approval Marks Regulations and shown at item 50A of Schedule 2 to those Regulations, and

  (b) in relation to any other motor vehicle or any other trailer, either—

     (i) a marking designated as an approval mark by regulation 5 of the Designation of Approval Marks Regulations and shown at item 6 or, if combined with a stop lamp, at item 8 of Schedule 4 to those Regulations, or

     (ii) a marking designated as an approval mark by regulation 4 of the Designation of Approval Marks Regulations and shown at item 7A or, if combined with a stop lamp, at item 7C of Schedule 2 to those Regulations; and

"British Standard mark" means—

  (a) the mark indicated in the specification for cycle rear lamps and published by the British Standards Institution under the reference 3648: 1963 as amended by Amendment PD 6137 published in May 1967 and by AMD 4753 published in July 1985, or

  (b) the mark indicated in the specification for photometric and physical requirements for lighting equipment published by the British Standards Institution under the reference BS 6102: Part 3: 1986, namely "BS 6102/3", [or]

  [(c) the mark indicated in the specification for photometric and physical requirements for lighting equipment published by the British Standards Institution under the reference BS 6102: Part 3: 1986 as amended by AMD 5821 published on the 29th April 1988, namely "6102/3",] [or

  (d) the mark indicated in the specification for photometric and physical requirements for lighting equipment published by the British Standards Institution under the reference BS 6102: Part 3: 1986 as amended by AMD,

  (e) the mark indicated in the specification for photometric and physical for lighting equipment published by the British Standards Institution under the references BS 6102: part 3: 1986 as amended by AMD 14621 published on the 1st September 2003, namely 6102/3.]

[Part I of Sch.10 is printed as amended by SI 1994/2280; SI 2005/2559.]   **B23.92**

Part II

Requirements Relating to Optional Rear Position Lamps

Any number may be fitted and [the only requirement prescribed by these Regulations in respect of any which are fitted are those specified in paragraphs 7 and 12(b) of Part I].   **B23.93**

[Part II of Sch.10 is printed as amended by SI 2005/2559.]   **B23.94**

(Regulations 18 and 20)   SCHEDULE 11

Part I

Requirements Relating to Obligatory Rear Fog Lamps and to Optional Rear Fog Lamps to the Extent Specified in Part II

B23.95

1.	Number:	One
2.	Position—	
	(a) Longitudinal:	At or near the rear of the vehicle
	(b) Lateral—	

	(i)	Where one rear fog lamp is fitted:	On the centre-line or off side of the vehicle (disregarding any sidecar forming part of a motor bicycle combination)
	(ii)	Where two lamps are fitted:	No requirement
(c)	Vertical—		
	(i)	Maximum height above the ground—	
	(A)	Any vehicle not covered by sub-paragraph (B):	1000mm
	(B)	An agricultural vehicle, engineering plant and a motor tractor:	2100mm
	(ii)	Minimum height above the ground:	250mm
(d)	Minimum separation distance between a rear fog lamp and a stop lamp—		
	(i)	In the case of a rear fog lamp which does not share a common lamp body with a stop lamp:	A distance of 100mm between the light-emitting surfaces of the lamps when viewed in a direction parallel to the longitudinal axis of the vehicle
	(ii)	In the case of a rear fog lamp which shares a common lamp body with a stop lamp:	100mm
3.	Angles of visibility—		
(a)	Horizontal:		25° inwards and outwards. However, where two rear fog lamps are fitted it shall suffice if throughout the sector so defined at least one lamp (but not necessarily the same lamp) is visible
(b)	Vertical:		5° above and below the horizontal
4.	Alignment:		To the rear
5.	Markings:		An approval mark
6.	Size of illuminated area:		No requirement
7.	Colour:		Red
8.	Wattage:		No requirement
9.	Intensity:		No requirement

10.	Electrical connections:	No rear fog lamp shall be fitted to any vehicle so that it can be illuminated by the application of any braking system on the vehicle
11.	Tell-tale:	A circuit-closed tell-tale shall be fitted

12. Other requirements—

Where two rear fog lamps are fitted to a motor vehicle first used on or after 1st April 1986 or to a trailer manufactured on or after 1st October 1985 they shall form a matched pair.

13. Definitions—

In this Schedule *"approval mark"* means either—

    (a) a marking designated as an approval mark by regulation 5 of the Designation of Approval Marks Regulations and shown at item 20 of Schedule 4 to those Regulations; or

    (b) a marking designated as an approval mark by regulation 4 of the Designation of Approval Marks Regulations and shown at item 38 of Schedule 2 to those Regulations.

PART II

REQUIREMENTS RELATING TO OPTIONAL REAR FOG LAMPS

1. In the case of a motor vehicle first used before 1st April 1980 and any other vehicle manufactured before 1st October 1979, any number may be fitted and the only requirements prescribed by these Regulations in respect of any which are fitted are those specified in paragraphs 2(d), 7 and 10 of Part I.   **B23.96**

2. In the case of a motor vehicle first used on or after 1st April 1980 and any other vehicle manufactured on or after 1st October 1979, not more than two may be fitted and the requirements prescribed by these Regulations in respect of any which are fitted are all those specified in this Schedule.   **B23.97**

(Regulations 18 and 20)   SCHEDULE 12

PART I

REQUIREMENTS RELATING TO OBLIGATORY STOP LAMPS AND TO OPTIONAL STOP LAMPS TO THE EXTENT SPECIFIED IN PART II

B23.98

1.	Number—		
	(a)	Any vehicle not covered by sub-paragraph (b) or (c):	Two
	(b)	A solo motor bicycle, a motor bicycle combination, an invalid carriage and a trailer drawn by a solo motor bicycle or a motor bicycle combination:	One
	(c)	Any other motor vehicle first used before 1st January 1971 and any other trailer manufactured before that date:	One
2.	Position—		
	(a)	Longitudinal:	No requirement

(b)   Lateral—

   (i)   Maximum distance from the side of the vehicle—

      (A)   Where two stop lamps are fitted: One each side of the longitudinal axis of the vehicle

      (B)   Where only one stop lamp is fitted: On the centre-line or off side of the vehicle (disregarding any sidecar forming part of a motor bicycle combination)

   (ii)   Minimum separation distance between two obligatory stop lamps: 400mm

(c)   Vertical—

   (i)   Maximum height above ground—

      (A)   Any vehicle not covered by sub-paragraph (B):   1500mm or, if the structure of the vehicle makes this impracticable, 2100mm

      (B)   A motor vehicle first used before 1st January 1971, a trailer manufactured before that date and a motor vehicle having a maximum speed not exceeding 25mph: No requirement

   (ii)   Minimum height above the ground—

      (A)   Any vehicle not covered by sub-paragraph (B):   350mm

      (B)   A motor vehicle first used before 1st January 1971 and a trailer manufactured before that date: No requirement

3.   Angles of visibility—

  (a)   A motor vehicle first used on or after 1st January 1971 and a trailer manufactured on or after that date—

   (i)   Horizontal: 45° to the left and to the right

   (ii)   Vertical—

      (A)   Except in a case specified in sub-paragraph (B) or (C):   15° above and below the horizontal

      (B)   Where the highest part of the illuminated area of the lamp is less than 1500 mm above the ground: 15° above and 10° below the horizontal

      (C)   Where the highest part of the illuminated area of the lamp is less than 750 mm above the ground: 15° above and 5° below the horizontal

  (b)   A motor vehicle first used before 1st January 1971 and a trailer manufactured before that date: Visible to the rear

4.   Alignment: To the rear

5.   Markings—

    (a)   Any vehicle not covered by sub-paragraph (b)   An approval mark
         or (c):

    (b)   A motor vehicle first used before 1st February   No requirement
         1974 and a trailer manufactured before that
         date:

    (c)   A solo motor bicycle and a motor bicycle   No requirement
         combination, in each case first used before 1st
         April 1986, and a trailer manufactured before
         1st October 1985 drawn by a solo motor
         bicycle or a motor bicycle combination:

6.   Size of illuminated area: No requirement

7.   Colour: Red

8.   Wattage—

    (a)   A stop lamp fitted to a motor vehicle first used   No requirement
         before 1st January 1971 or a trailer
         manufactured before that date and a stop lamp
         bearing an approval mark:

    (b)   Any other stop lamp: 15 to 36 watts

9.   Intensity: No requirement

10.   Electrical connections—

    (a)   Every stop lamp fitted to—

        (i)   a solo motor bicycle or a motor bicycle combination first used
            on or after 1st April 1986 shall be operated by the application
            of every service brake control provided for the use of the rider;

        (ii)   any other motor vehicle, shall be operated by the application of
            the service braking system.

    (b)   Every stop lamp fitted to a trailer drawn by a motor vehicle shall be
         operated by the application of the service braking system of that motor
         vehicle.

11.   Tell-tale: No requirement

12. Other requirements—

Where two stop lamps are required to be fitted, they shall form a pair.

13. Definitions—

In this Schedule *"approval mark"* means—

    (a)   in relation to a solo motor bicycle, a motor bicycle combination or a trailer
       drawn by a solo motor bicycle or a motor bicycle combination, a marking
       designated as an approval mark by regulation 4 of the Designation of Ap-
       proval Marks Regulations and shown at item 50A of Schedule 2 to those
       Regulations; and

    (b)   in relation to any other vehicle, either—

    (i)   a marking designated as an approval mark by regulation 5 of the Designation
      of Approval Marks Regulations and shown at item 7 or, if combined with a
      rear position lamp, at item 8 of Schedule 4 to those Regulations; or

    (ii)   a marking designated as an approval mark by regulation 4 of the Designation
      of Approval Marks Regulations and shown at item 7B or, if combined with a
      rear position lamp, at item 7C of Schedule 2 to those Regulations.

PART II

REQUIREMENTS RELATING TO OPTIONAL STOP LAMPS

Any number may be fitted, and the requirements prescribed by these Regulations in re-   **B23.99**
spect of any which are fitted are all those specified in Part I except—

(a) those specified in paragraphs 1, 2 and 3; and

(b) in the case of a stop lamp fitted to a pedal cycle, those specified in paragraphs 5 and 8; and

(c) in the case of a stop lamp fitted to a motor vehicle not being a motor bicycle, first used on or after 1st April 1991 either centrally or in such a manner as to project light through the rear window the intensity of the light emitted to the rear of the vehicle shall be not less than 20 candelas and not more than 60 candelas when measured from directly behind the centre of the lamp in a direction parallel to the longitudinal axis of the vehicle.

(Regulations 18 and 20)   SCHEDULE 13

PART I

REQUIREMENTS RELATING TO OBLIGATORY END-OUTLINE MARKER LAMPS AND TO OPTIONAL END-OUTLINE MARKER LAMPS TO THE EXTENT SPECIFIED IN PART II

B23.100

1.	Number:		Two visible from the front and two visible from the rear
2.	Position—		
	(a)	Longitudinal:	No requirement
	(b)	Lateral—	
		(i) Maximum distance from the side of the vehicle:	400mm
		(ii) Minimum separation distance between a pair of end-outline marker lamps:	No requirement
	(c)	Vertical—	
		(i) At the front of a motor vehicle	The horizontal plane tangential to the upper edge of the illuminated area of the lamp shall not be lower than the horizontal plane tangential to the upper edge of the transparent zone of the windscreen
		(ii) At the front of a trailer and at the rear of any vehicle:	At the maximum height compatible with: (a) the requirements relating to the lateral position and to being a pair, and (b) the use for which the vehicle is constructed
3.	Angles of visibility—		
	(a)	Horizontal:	0° inwards and 80° outwards
	(b)	Vertical:	5° above and 20° below the horizontal

4.	Alignment:	Such that white light is shown towards the front and red light is shown towards the rear
5.	Markings:	An approval mark
6.	Size of illuminated area:	No requirement
7.	Colour:	White towards the front and red towards the rear
8.	Wattage:	No requirement
9.	Intensity:	No requirement
10.	Electrical connections:	No individual requirement
11.	Tell-tale:	No requirement

12. Other requirements—

The two lamps which emit white light towards the front, and the two lamps which emit red light towards the rear, shall in each case form a matched pair. The white front lamp and red rear lamp on one side of a vehicle may be combined into a single lamp with a single light source.

13. Definitions—

In this Schedule, *"approval mark"* means the approval mark for a front or rear position lamp, as the case may be.

PART II

REQUIREMENTS RELATING TO OPTIONAL END OUTLINE MARKER LAMPS

Any number may be fitted, and the only requirement prescribed by these Regulations in respect of any which are fitted is that specified in paragraph 7 of Part I.   **B23.101**

(Regulation 20)   SCHEDULE 14

REQUIREMENTS RELATING TO OPTIONAL REVERSING LAMPS

1.	Number:	[Not more than two but if the vehicle has an overall length which exceeds 6 m and is—
		(a) a bus; or
		(b) a vehicle which is not a passenger vehicle,
		four may be fitted.]
2.	Position:	No requirement
3.	Angles of visibility:	No requirement

B23.102

4. Alignment:

[To the rear but if, in accordance with paragraph 1, four are fitted the configuration shall be—
 (a) four to the rear; or
 (b) two to the rear and one on each side.]

5. Markings—

    (a) A motor vehicle first used on or after 1st April 1986 and a trailer manufactured on or after 1st October 1985:   An approval mark

    (b) A motor vehicle first used before 1st April 1986 and a trailer manufactured before 1st October 1985:   No requirement

6. Size of illuminated area: No requirement

7. Colour: White

8. Wattage—

    (a) A reversing lamp bearing an approval mark: No requirement

    (b) A reversing lamp not bearing an approval mark: The total wattage of any one reversing lamp shall not exceed 24 watts

9. Intensity: No requirement

10.	Electrical connections:	[No requirement except that if, in accordance with paragraph 4, reversing lamps have been fitted to the side, the following requirements shall apply in relation to those lamps—

        (a) it shall not be possible for the reversing lamps to be illuminated unless the front and rear position lamps of the vehicle are illuminated at the same time; and

        (b) the reversing lamps shall be switched on and off by the manual operation of one switch which shall have no other function; but

        (c) the reversing lamps shall switch off automatically if the vehicle is moving forward at a speed of 10km/h or more.]

11.	Tell-tale—	
	(a)	A motor vehicle first used on or after 1st July 1954, provided that the electrical connections [are such that any] reversing lamp or lamps [fitted to the rear] cannot be illuminated other than automatically by the selection of the reverse gear of the vehicle:	No requirement
	(b)	Any other motor vehicle first used on or after 1st July 1954:	A circuit-closed tell-tale shall be fitted
	(c)	A motor vehicle first used before 1st July 1954:	No requirement
	(d)	Any vehicle which is not a motor vehicle:	No requirement

12. Definitions—

In this Schedule *"approval mark"* means either—

    (a) a marking designated as an approval mark by regulation 5 of the Designation of Approval Marks Regulations and shown at item 21 of Schedule 4 to those Regulations; or

    (b) a marking designated as an approval mark by regulation 4 of the Designation of Approval Marks Regulations and shown at item 23 or 23A of Schedule 2 to those Regulations.

B23.103   *[Schedule 14 is printed as amended by SI 2009/3220.]*

(Regulation 18)   SCHEDULE 15

Requirements Relating to Obligatory Rear Registration Plate Lamps

B23.104

1.	Number:	
2.	Position:	Such that the lamp or lamps are capable of adequately illuminating the rear registration plate
3.	Angles of visibility:	
4.	Alignment:	
5.	Markings—	
(a)	A motor vehicle first used on or after 1st April 1986 and a trailer manufactured on or after 1st October 1985:	An approval mark
(b)	A motor vehicle first used before 1st April 1986 and a trailer manufactured before 1st October 1985:	No requirement
6.	Size of illuminated area:	No requirement
7.	Colour:	White
8.	Wattage:	No requirement
9.	Intensity:	No requirement
10.	Electrical connections:	No individual requirement
11.	Tell-tale:	No requirement

12. Definitions—

In this Schedule *"approval mark"* means—

(a) in relation to a solo motor bicycle, a motor bicycle combination and a trailer drawn by a solo motor bicycle or a motor bicycle combination, a marking designated as an approval mark by regulation 4 of the Designation of Approval Marks Regulations and shown at item 50A of Schedule 2 to those Regulations; and

(b) in relation to any other motor vehicle and any other trailer, either—

(i) a marking designated as an approval mark by regulation 5 of the Designation of Approval Marks Regulations and shown at item 10 of Schedule 4 to those Regulations; or

(ii) a marking designated as an approval mark by regulation 4 of the Designation of Approval Marks Regulations and shown at item 4 of Schedule 2 to those Regulations.

(Regulations 17 and 20)   SCHEDULE 16

Requirement Relating to Obligatory and Optional Warning Beacons

B23.105

1.	Number:	Sufficient to satisfy the requirements of paragraph 3
2.	Position—	

Every warning beacon shall be so mounted on the vehicle that the centre of the lamp is at a height not less than 1200mm above the ground.

3. Angles of visibility—

The light shown from at least one beacon (but not necessarily the same beacon) shall be visible from any point at a reasonable distance from the vehicle or any trailer being drawn by it.

4.	Markings:	No requirement
5.	Size of illuminated area:	No requirement
6.	Colour:	Blue, amber, green or yellow in accordance with Regulation 11
7.	Wattage:	No requirement
8.	Intensity:	No requirement
9.	Electrical connections:	No requirement
10.	Tell-tale:	No requirement

11. Other requirements—

The light shown by any one warning beacon shall be displayed not less than 60 nor more than 240 equal times per minute and the intervals between each display of light shall be constant.

(Regulations 18 and 20)   SCHEDULE 17

PART I

REQUIREMENTS RELATING TO OBLIGATORY SIDE RETRO REFLECTORS AND OPTIONAL SIDE RETRO REFLECTORS TO THE EXTENT SPECIFIED IN PART II

B23.106

1. Number—

(a)	A motor vehicle first used on or after 1st April 1986 and a trailer manufactured on or after 1st October 1985:	On each side: two and as many more as are sufficient to satisfy the requirements of paragraph 2(a)
(b)	A motor vehicle first used before 1st April 1986 and a trailer manufactured before 1st October 1985:	On each side: Two

2. Position—

   (a) Longitudinal—

(i)	A motor vehicle first used on or after 1st April 1986 and a trailer manufactured on or after 1st October 1985—		
	(A)	Maximum distance from the front of the vehicle, including any drawbar, in respect of the foremost reflector on each side:	4m
	(B)	Maximum distance from the rear of the vehicle in respect of the rearmost reflector on each side:	1m
	(C)	Maximum separation distance between the reflecting areas of adjacent reflectors on the same side of the vehicle:	3m or, if this is not practicable, 4m
(ii)	A motor vehicle first used before 1st April 1986 and a trailer manufactured before 1st October 1985—		

	(A)	Maximum distance from the rear of the vehicle in respect of the rearmost reflector on each side:	1m
	(B)	The other reflector on each side of the vehicle:	Towards the centre of the vehicle
(b)	Lateral:		No requirement
(c)	Vertical—		
	(i)	Maximum height above the ground:	1500mm
	(ii)	Minimum height above the ground:	350mm

3. Angles of visibility—

(a) A motor vehicle first used on or after 1st April 1986 and a trailer manufactured on or after 1st October 1985—

    (i) Horizontal: 45° to the left and to the right when viewed in a direction at right angles to the longitudinal axis of the vehicle

    (ii) Vertical—

        (A) Except in a case specified in sub-paragraph (b):   15° above and below the horizontal

        (B) Where the highest part of the reflecting area is less than 750mm above the ground: 15° above and 5° below the horizontal

(b) A motor vehicle first used before 1st April 1986 and a trailer manufactured before 1st October 1985:   Plainly visible to the side

4. Alignment: To the side

5. Markings: An approval mark

6. Size of reflecting area: No requirement

7. Colour—

(a) Any vehicle not covered by sub-paragraph (b):   Amber or if within 1m of the rear of the vehicle it may be red

(b) A solo motor bicycle, a motor bicycle combination, a pedal cycle with or without a sidecar or an invalid carriage: No requirement

8. Other requirements: No side retro reflector shall be triangular

9. Definitions—

  (a) In this Schedule *"approval mark"* means either—

    (i) a marking designated as an approval mark by regulation 4 of the Designation of Approval Marks Regulations and shown at item 3 or 3B of Schedule 2 to those Regulations and which includes the marking I or IA; or

    (ii) a marking designated as an approval mark by regulation 5 of the Designation of Approval Marks Regulations and shown at item 4 of Schedule 4 to those Regulations and which includes the marking I; and

  (b) In this Schedule references to *"maximum distance from the front of the vehicle"* and *"maximum distance from the rear of the vehicle"* are references to the maximum distance from that end of the vehicle (as determined by reference to the overall length of the vehicle exclusive of any special equipment) beyond which no part of the reflecting area of the side retro reflector extends.

[Part II

Requirements Relating to Optional Side Retro Reflectors

Any number may be fitted and the only requirements in respect of any which are fitted are those specified in paragraphs 7 and 8 of Part I. But, in respect of a vehicle to which paragraph 7(a) applies which is used for the purposes listed in column (1) of the Table, the permitted colours are those listed in column (2).   **B23.107**

Table

Police	amber, yellow, blue, white or if within 1 m of the rear of the vehicle it may be red
Relevant authority (as defined by section 6 of the Fire (Scotland) Act 2005) or, in England and Wales, fire and rescue authority	amber, yellow, red
Ambulance	amber, yellow, green, white or if within 1 m of the rear of the vehicle it may be red
Vehicle and Operator Services Agency	amber, yellow, silver, white or if within 1 m of the rear of the vehicle it may be red
Traffic officer	amber, yellow, white or if within 1 m of the rear of the vehicle it may be red.]

[Part II of Sch.17 is printed as substituted by SI 2009/3220.]   **B23.108**

(Regulations 18 and 20)   SCHEDULE 18

Part I

Requirements Relating to Obligatory Rear Retro Reflectors and Optional Rear Retro Reflectors to the Extent Specified in Part II

B23.109

1. Number—

   (a) Any vehicle not covered by sub-paragraph (b) or (c):   Two

   (b) A solo motor bicycle, a pedal cycle with less than four wheels and with or without a sidecar, a trailer drawn by a pedal cycle, a trailer the overall width of which does not exceed 800mm drawn by a solo motor bicycle or a motor bicycle combination, an invalid carriage having a maximum speed not exceeding 4mph and a vehicle drawn or propelled by hand: One

   (c) A motor vehicle having three or more wheels and a maximum speed not exceeding 25mph and a trailer drawn by any such vehicle if, in either case, the structure of the vehicle makes it impracticable to meet all of the requirements of paragraphs 2 and 3 below with two reflectors: Four

2. Position—

(a)   Longitudinal: At or near the rear

(b)   Lateral—

     (i)   Where two rear reflectors are required to be fitted—

         (A)   Maximum distance from the side of the vehicle—

	(1)	Any vehicle not covered by sub-paragraph (2), (3) or (4):	400mm
	(2)	A bus first used before 1st October 1954 and a horse-drawn vehicle manufactured before 1st October 1985:	No requirement
	(3)	A vehicle constructed or adapted for the carriage of round timber:	765mm
	(4)	Any other motor vehicle first used before 1st April 1986 and any other vehicle manufactured before 1st October 1985:	610mm

         (B)   Minimum separation distance between a pair of rear reflectors—

	(1)	Any vehicle not covered by sub-paragraph (2):	600mm. If the overall width of the vehicle is less than 1300mm, 400mm or if less than 800mm, 300mm
	(2)	A motor vehicle first used before 1st April 1986 and any other vehicle manufactured before 1st October 1985:	No requirement

     (ii)   Where one rear reflector is required to be fitted: On the centre-line or off side of the vehicle

     (iii)   Where four rear reflectors are required to be fitted—

         (A)   Maximum distance from the side of the vehicle—

	(1)	One pair of reflectors:	Such that they satisfy the relevant requirements in sub-paragraph 2(b)(i) (A)
	(2)	The other pair of reflectors:	No requirement

         (B)   Minimum separation distance between rear reflectors—

	(1)	One pair of reflectors:	Such that they satisfy the relevant requirements in sub-paragraph 2(b)(i) (B)
	(2)	The other pair of reflectors:	No requirement

(c)   Vertical—

    (i)   Maximum height above the ground where one or two rear reflectors are required to be fitted—

(A) Any vehicle not covered by sub-paragraph (b):	900mm or, if the structure of the vehicle makes this impracticable, [1500mm]
(B) A motor vehicle first used before 1st April 1986 and any other vehicle manufactured before 1st October 1985:	1525mm

    (ii) Maximum height above the ground where four rear reflectors are required to be fitted—

(A) One pair of reflectors:	Such that they satisfy the relevant requirements in paragraph 2(c)(i)
(B) The other pair of reflectors:	2100mm

    (iii) Minimum height above the ground—

(A) Any vehicle not covered by sub-paragraph (b):	[250mm]
(B) A motor vehicle first used before 1st April 1986 and any other vehicle manufactured before 1st October 1985:	No requirement

3.   Angles of visibility—

(a)   A motor vehicle (not being a motor bicycle combination) first used on or after 1st April 1986 and a trailer manufactured on or after 1st October 1985—

    (i)   Where one or two rear reflectors are required to be fitted—

       (A)   Horizontal—

(1) Where two rear reflectors are required to be fitted:	30° inwards and outwards
(2) Where one rear reflector is required to be fitted:	30° to the left and to the right

       (B)   Vertical—

(1) Except in a case specified in sub-paragraph (2):	[10°] above and below the horizontal
(2) Where the highest part of the reflecting area is less than 750 mm above the ground:	15° above and 5° below the horizontal

    (ii) Where four rear reflectors are required to be fitted—

(A) One pair of reflectors:	Such that they satisfy the relevant requirements in paragraph 3(a)(i)

	(B) The other pair of reflectors:	Plainly visible to the rear
(b)	A motor vehicle (not being a motor bicycle combination) first used before 1st April 1986 and a trailer manufactured before 1st October 1985:	Plainly visible to the rear
(c)	A motor bicycle combination, a pedal cycle, a sidecar attached to a pedal cycle, a horse-drawn vehicle and a vehicle drawn or propelled by hand:	Plainly visible to the rear
4.	Alignment:	To the rear
5.	Markings—	
(a)	A motor vehicle first used—	
	(i) On or after 1st April 1991:	An approval mark incorporating "I" or "IA"
	(ii) On or after 1st July 1970 and before 1st April 1991:	(A) An approval mark incorporating "I" or "IA", or (B) A British Standard mark which is specified in sub-paragraph (i) of the definition of "British Standard mark" below followed by "LI" or "LIA"; or (C) In the case of a vehicle manufactured in Italy, an Italian approved marking
	(iii) Before 1st July 1970:	No requirement
(b)	A trailer (other than a broken-down motor vehicle) manufactured—	
	(i) On or after 1st October 1989:	An approval mark incorporating "III" or "IIIA"
	(ii) On or after 1st July 1970 and before 1st October 1989:	(A) An approval mark incorporating "III" or "IIIA"; or (B) A British Standard mark which is specified in sub-paragraph (i) of the definition of "British Standard mark" below followed by "LIII" or "LIIIA", or (C) In the case of a trailer manufactured in Italy, an Italian approved marking

(iii) Before 1st July 1970:	No requirement

(c) A pedal cycle, an invalid carriage having a maximum speed not exceeding 4mph, a horse-drawn vehicle and a vehicle drawn or propelled by hand, in each case manufactured—

(i) On or after 1st October 1989:	(A) An approval mark incorporating "I" or "IA"; or
	(B) A British Standard mark which is specified in sub-paragraph (ii) of the definition of "British Standard mark" below
(ii) On or after 1st July 1970 and before 1st October 1989:	(A) Any of the markings mentioned in sub-paragraph (c)(i) above; or
	(B) A British Standard mark which is specified in sub-paragraph (i) of the definition of "British Standard mark" below followed by "LI" or "LIA"
(iii) Before 1st July 1970:	No requirement
6. Size of reflecting area:	No requirement
7. Colour:	Red

8. Other requirements—

(a) Except in the case of a motor vehicle first used before 1st April 1986, any other vehicle manufactured before 1st October 1985 and a motor bicycle combination, where two rear reflectors are required to be fitted they shall form a pair. Where four rear reflectors are required to be fitted they shall form two pairs.

(b) No vehicle, other than a trailer or a broken-down motor vehicle being towed, may be fitted with triangular-shaped rear reflectors.

(c) [...]

9. Definitions—

In this Schedule —

(a) *"approval mark"* means either—

(i) a marking designated as an approval mark by regulation 4 of the Designation of Approval Marks Regulations and shown at item 3 or 3A or 3B of Schedule 2 to those Regulations; or

(ii) a marking designated as an approval mark by regulation 5 of the Designation of Approval Marks Regulations and shown at item 4 of Schedule 4 to those Regulations;

(b) *"British Standard mark"* means either—

(i) the mark indicated in the specification for retro reflectors for vehicles, including cycles, published by the British Standards Institution under the reference B.S. AU40: Part 2: 1965, namely "AU 40"; or

(ii) the mark indicated in the specification for photometric and physical requirements of reflective devices published by the British Standards Institution under the reference BS6102: Part 2: 1982, namely "BS 6102/2"; and

(c) *"Italian approved marking"* means—

a mark approved by the Italian Ministry of Transport, namely, one including two separate groups of symbols consisting of "IGM" or "DGM" and "C.1." or "C.2.".

B23.110   *[Part I of Sch.18 is printed as amended by SI 1994/2280; SI 2009/3220.]*

[Part II

Requirements Relating to Optional Rear Retro Reflectors

B23.111   Any number may be fitted and the only requirements in respect of any which are fitted are those specified in paragraphs 7 and 8(b) of Part I. But the colour of rear retro reflectors fitted to a vehicle used for—

(a) police,

(b) relevant authority (as defined by section 6 of the Fire (Scotland) Act 2005) or, in England and Wales, fire and rescue authority,

(c) ambulance,

(d) Vehicle and Operator Services Agency, or

(e) traffic officer,

purposes may be red, yellow or orange (or any combination).]

B23.112   *[Part II of Sch.18 is printed as substituted by SI 2009/3220.]*

(Regulations 18 and 20)   SCHEDULE 19

Part I

Requirements Relating to Obligatory Rear Markings and Optional Rear Markings to the Extent Specified in Part II

B23.113   General Requirements

1.   Description

(a)   A motor vehicle first used on or after 1 April 1996, the overall length of which—

(i) does not exceed 13m:	A rear marking of a type shown in diagram 1, 2, 3 or 4 of this Schedule
(ii) exceeds 13m:	A rear marking of a type shown in diagram 5, 6, 7 or 8 in Part IV of this Schedule

(b)   A motor vehicle first used before 1 April 1996, the overall length of which—

(i)	does not exceed 13m:	A rear marking of a type shown in diagram 1, 2 or 3 in Part III of this Schedule or a rear marking of a type shown in diagram 1, 2, 3 or 4 of Part IV of this Schedule
(ii)	exceeds 13m:	A rear marking of a type shown in diagram 4 or 5 in Part III of this Schedule or a rear marking of a type shown in diagram 5, 6, 7 or 8 in Part IV of this Schedule

(c) A trailer manufactured on or after 1 October 1995 if it forms part of a combination of vehicles the overall length of which—

(i)	does not exceed 11m:	A rear marking of a type shown in diagram 1, 2, 3 or 4 in Part IV of this Schedule
(ii)	exceeds 11m but does not exceed 13m:	A rear marking of a type shown in Part IV of this Schedule
(iii)	exceeds 13m:	A rear marking of a type shown in diagram 5, 6, 7 or 8 in Part IV of this Schedule

(d) A trailer manufactured before 1 October 1995 if it forms part of a combination of vehicles the overall length of which—

(i)	does not exceed 11m:	A rear marking of a type shown in diagram 1, 2 or 3 in Part III of this Schedule or a rear marking of a type shown in diagram 1, 2, 3 or 4 in Part IV of this Schedule
(ii)	exceeds 11m but does not exceed 13m:	A rear marking of a type shown in Part III or Part IV of this Schedule

(iii)	exceeds 13m:	A rear marking of a type shown in diagram 4 or 5 in Part III of this Schedule or a rear marking of a type shown in diagram 5, 6, 7 or 8 in Part IV of this Schedule

2.   Position—

(a)	Longitudinal:	At or near the rear of the vehicle
(b)	Lateral—	
	(i) A rear marking of a type shown in diagram 2, 3 or 5 in Part III of this Schedule and a rear marking of a type shown in diagram 2, 3, 4, 6, 7 or 8 in Part IV of this Schedule:	Each part shall be fitted as near as practicable to the outermost edge of the vehicle on the side thereof on which it is fitted so that no part of the marking projects beyond the outermost part of the vehicle on either side
	(ii) A rear marking of a type shown in diagram 1 or 4 in Part III of this Schedule and a rear marking of a type shown in diagram 1 or 5 in Part IV of this Schedule:	The marking shall be fitted so that the vertical centre-line of the marking lies on the vertical plane through the longitudinal axis of the vehicle and no part of the marking projects beyond the outermost part of the vehicle on either side
(c)	Vertical:	The lower edge of every rear marking shall be at a height of not more than 1700mm nor less than 400mm above the ground whether the vehicle is laden or unladen

3.   Visibility: Plainly visible to the rear

| 4. | Alignment: | The lower edge of every rear marking shall be fitted horizontally. Every part of a rear marking shall lie within 20° of a transverse vertical plane at right angles to the longitudinal axis of the vehicle and shall face to the rear |

5.	Markings—	
	(a) A motor vehicle or trailer not covered by sub-paragraph (b) [or (c)]:	In respect of any rear marking of a type shown in Part III of this Schedule a British Standard mark or in respect of any rear marking of a type shown in Part IV of this Schedule an approval mark
	(b) [Unless covered by sub-paragraph (c), a motor vehicle] first used on or after 1 April 1996 and a trailer manufactured on or after 1 October 1995:	An approval mark
	[(c) A motor vehicle first used on or after 10th July 2011 and a trailer manufactured on or after 10th July 2011:	A 70.01 mark]

| 6. | Colour: | Red fluorescent material in the stippled areas shown in any of the diagrams in Part III or IV of this Schedule and yellow retro reflective material in any of the areas so shown, being areas not stippled and not constituting a letter. All letters shall be coloured black |

7. Other requirements—

A rear marking of a type shown in a diagram in Part III of this Schedule shall comply with the requirements of that Part.

The two parts of every rear marking of a type shown in diagrams 2, 3 or 5 in Part III and diagrams 2, 3, 6 and 7 in Part IV of this Schedule shall form a pair and the four parts of every rear marking of a type shown in diagrams 4 and 8 in Part IV of this Schedule shall form two pairs.

8. Definitions—

In this Schedule —

   (a) *"approval mark"* means a marking designated as an approval mark by regulation 3 of the Designation of Approval Marks Regulations and shown at item 70 of Schedule 2 to those Regulations; [...]

   (b) *"British Standard mark"* means the specification for rear markings for vehicles published by the British Standards Institution under the reference BS AU 152: 1970, namely "BS AU 152"[; and

(c) *"70.01 mark"* means the international approval mark referred to in paragraph 5.4.1 of ECE Regulation 70 as amended by the 01 series of amendments (as in force on 15th October 2008).]

B23.114   *[Part II of Sch.19 is printed as amended by SI 2009/3220.]*

PART II

REQUIREMENTS RELATING TO OPTIONAL REAR MARKINGS

B23.115   Subject to regulation 11(2), any number of rear markings shown in Parts III and IV may be fitted to the rear of a vehicle.

Part III

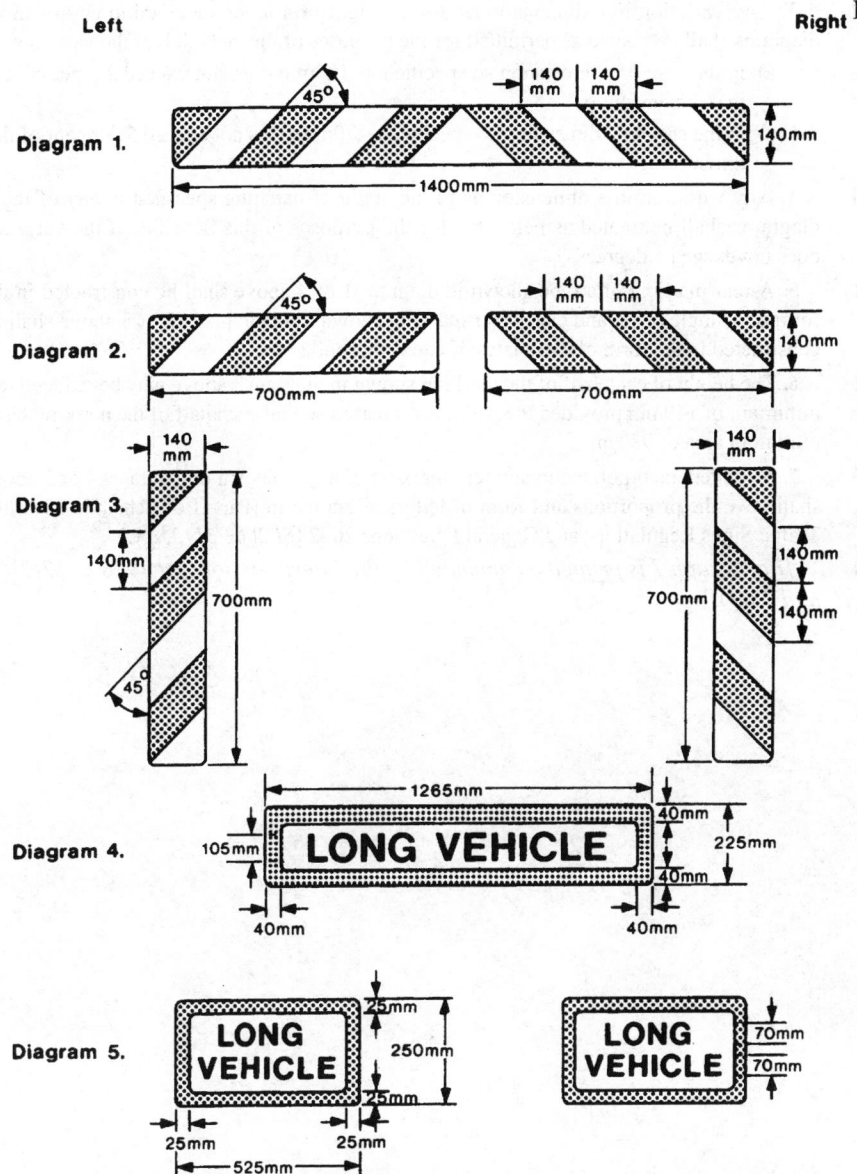

Left   **Right** B23.116

Diagram 1.

Diagram 2.

Diagram 3.

Diagram 4.

LONG VEHICLE

Diagram 5.

LONG VEHICLE

LONG VEHICLE

ADDITIONAL PROVISIONS RELATING TO THE ABOVE DIAGRAMS

1. A rear marking of a type shown in one of the above diagrams shall have the dimensions shown in relation to that diagram.   **B23.117**

2. Any variation in a dimension (other than as to the height of a letter) specified in any of the diagrams shall be treated as permitted for the purposes of this Schedule if the variation—   **B23.118**

    (a) in the case of a dimension so specified as 250mm or as over 250mm does not exceed 2.5 per cent of that dimension;

    (b) in the case of a dimension so specified as 40mm or as over 40mm but as under 250mm does not exceed 5 per cent of that dimension; or

    (c) in the case of a dimension so specified as under 40mm does not exceed 10 per cent of that dimension.

B23.119   **3.** Any variation in a dimension as to the height of a letter specified in any of those diagrams shall be treated as permitted for the purposes of this Schedule if the variation—

    (a) in the case of a dimension so specified as 105mm does not exceed 2.5 per cent of that dimension; or

    (b) in the case of a dimension so specified as 70mm does not exceed 5 per cent of that dimension.

B23.120   **4.** Any variation in a dimension as to the angle of hatching specified in any of those diagrams shall be treated as permitted for the purposes of this Schedule if the variation does not exceed 5 degrees.

B23.121   **5.** A rear marking of a type shown in diagram 1 or 4 above shall be constructed in the form of a single plate, and every rear marking shown in diagrams 2, 3 or 5 above shall be constructed in the form of two plates of equal size and shape.

B23.122   **6.** The height of each half of the marking shown in diagram 3 above may be reduced to a minimum of 140mm provided the width is increased so that each half of the marking has a minimum area of 980cm^2 .

B23.123   **7.** All letters incorporated in any rear marking of a type shown in diagrams 4 or 5 above shall have the proportions and form of letters as shown in [Part II of Schedule 13 to the Traffic Signs Regulations and General Directions 2002 [*SI 2002/3113, q.v.*].

B23.124   *[Paragraph 7 is printed as amended by the Interpretation Act 1978 ss.17(2)(a) and 23(1).]*

PART IV

REAR MARKINGS PRESCRIBED FOR MOTOR VEHICLES WHENEVER FIRST USED AND TRAILERS WHEN-
EVER MANUFACTURED

B23.125

Left   Right

Diagram 1.

Diagram 2.

Diagram 3.

Diagram 4.

Left   **Right**

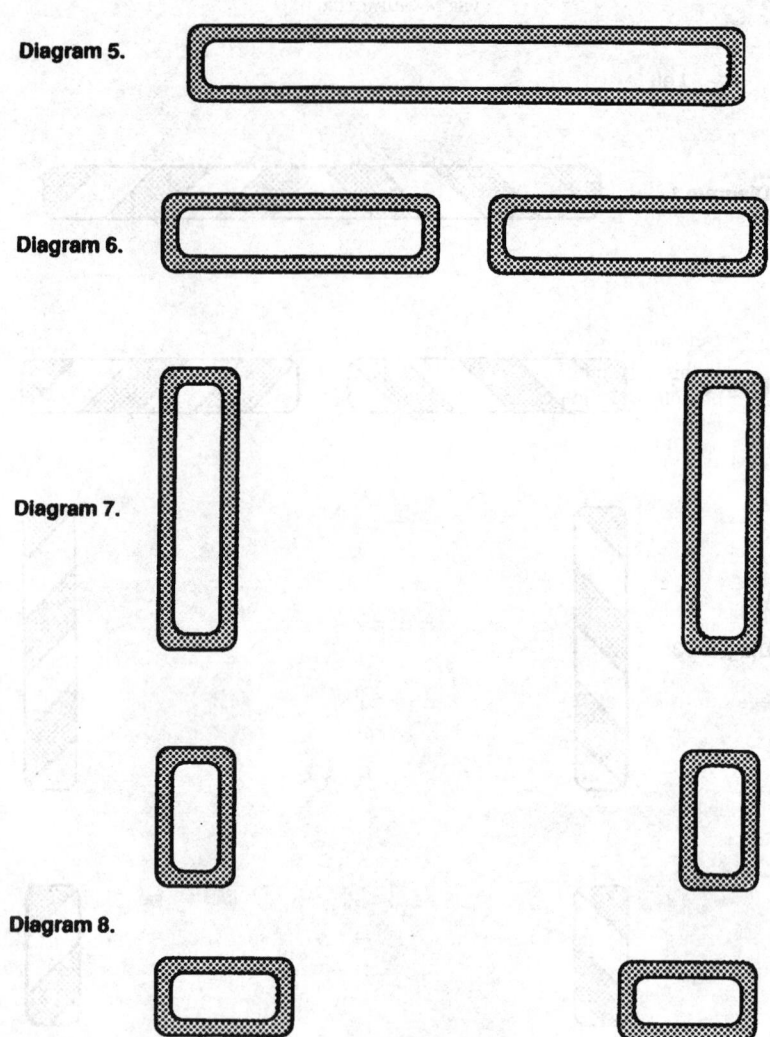

Diagram 5.

Diagram 6.

Diagram 7.

Diagram 8.

,,

B23.126   *[Schedule 19 is printed as substituted by SI 1994/2280.]*

(Regulations 18 and 20)   SCHEDULE 20

PART I

REQUIREMENTS RELATING TO OBLIGATORY PEDAL RETRO REFLECTORS AND OPTIONAL PEDAL
RETRO REFLECTORS TO THE EXTENT SPECIFIED IN PART II

B23.127   **1.**   Number: Two reflectors on each
                                                                      pedal

               2.   Position—
                          (a)   Longitudinal: On the leading edge
                                                                      and the trailing edge
                                                                      of each pedal

(b)	Lateral:	No requirement
(c)	Vertical:	No requirement
3.	Angles of visibility:	Such that the reflector on the leading edge of each pedal is plainly visible to the front and the reflector on the trailing edge of each pedal is plainly visible to the rear
4.	Markings:	A British Standard mark
5.	Size of reflecting area:	No requirement
6.	Colour:	Amber
7.	Definitions—	

In this Schedule *"British Standard mark"* means the specification for photometric and physical requirements of reflective devices published by the British Standards Institution under the reference BS 6102: Part 2: 1982, namely "BS 6102/2".

PART II

REQUIREMENTS RELATING TO OPTIONAL PEDAL RETRO REFLECTORS

Any number may be fitted and the only requirement prescribed by these Regulations in respect of any which are fitted is that specified in paragraph 6 of Part I.

B23.128

(Regulations 18 and 20)   SCHEDULE 21

PART I

REQUIREMENTS RELATING TO OBLIGATORY FRONT RETRO REFLECTORS AND TO OPTIONAL FRONT RETRO REFLECTORS TO THE EXTENT SPECIFIED IN PART II

B23.129

1.	Number:		Two
2.	Position—		
	(a)	Longitudinal:	No requirement
	(b)	Lateral—	
		(i) Maximum distance from the side of the trailer:	150mm
		(ii) Minimum separation distance between a pair of front reflectors:	600mm or, if the overall width of the trailer is less than 1400mm, 400mm
	(c)	Vertical—	
		(i) Maximum height above the ground:	900mm or, if the structure of the trailer makes this impracticable, 1500mm
		(ii) Minimum height above the ground:	[250mm]
3.	Angles of visibility—		
	(a)	Horizontal:	30° outwards and 5° inwards
	(b)	Vertical—	

| (i) | Any case not covered by sub-paragraph (ii): | [10°] above and below the horizontal |
| (ii) | Where the highest point of the reflecting area is less than 750mm above the ground: | 15° above and 5° below the horizontal |

4.	Alignment:	To the front
5.	Markings:	An approval mark
6.	Size of reflecting area:	No requirement
7.	Colour:	White

8. Other requirements—

    (a) Where two front reflectors are required to be fitted they shall form a pair.

    (b) Triangular shaped retro reflectors shall not be fitted to the front of any trailer.

9. Definitions—

In this Schedule —

    "approval mark" means either—

        (a) a marking designated as an approval mark by regulation 4 of the Designation of Approval Marks Regulations and shown at item 3 or 3A or 3B of Schedule 2 to those Regulations; or

        (b) a marking designated as an approval mark by regulation 5 of the Designation of Approval Marks Regulations and shown at item 4 of Schedule 4 to those Regulations.

B23.130   *[Part I of Sch.21 is printed as amended by SI 2009/3220.]*

PART II

REQUIREMENTS RELATING TO OPTIONAL FRONT RETRO REFLECTORS

B23.131   Any number may be fitted and the only requirements prescribed by these Regulations in respect of any which are fitted are those specified in paragraph 8(b) of Part I and that the colour shall not be red.

Colour

Shaded areas—yellow retro reflective material

Border and silhouette—black

Dimensions

A	Front—not less than 250mm.	B	Front—not more than 20mm.
A	Rear—not less than 400mm.	B	Rear—not more than 30mm.]

[Schedule 21A was inserted by SI 1994/2280.]   **B23.133**

(Regulation 24(3))   SCHEDULE 22

DIAGRAM SHOWING WHERE UNLIT PARKING IS NOT PERMITTED NEAR A JUNCTION

B23.134

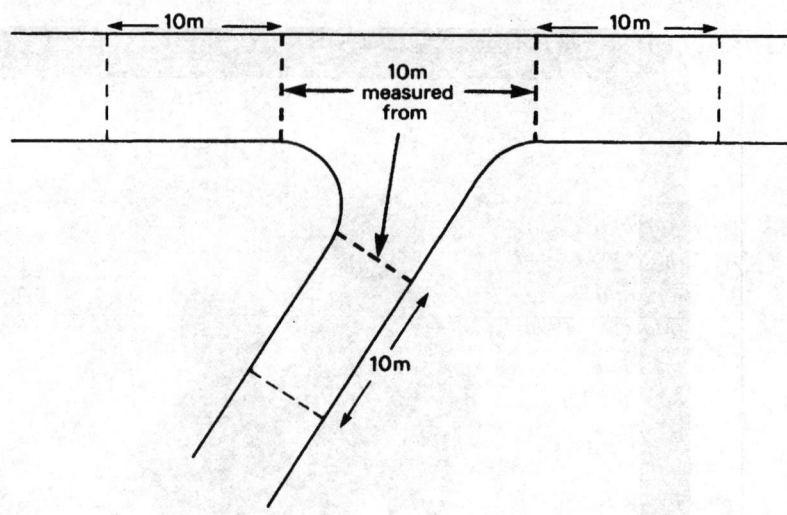

(Schedule 4, Part I,   SCHEDULE 23
paragraphs 4 and 12)

EXAMPLE OF MARKING SHOWING THE VERTICAL DOWNWARDS INCLINATION OF THE DIPPED-BEAM
HEADLAMPS WHEN THE VEHICLE IS AT ITS KERBSIDE WEIGHT AND HAS A WEIGHT OF 75KG ON THE
DRIVER'S SEAT

B23.135

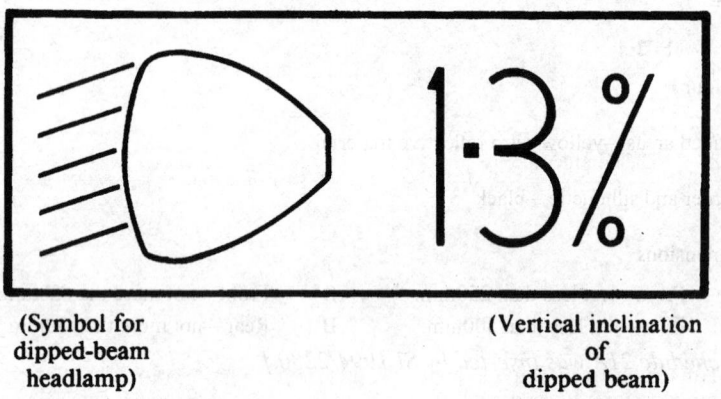

(Symbol for   (Vertical inclination
dipped-beam   of
headlamp)   dipped beam)

The Public Service Vehicles (Conduct of Drivers, Inspectors, Conductors and Passengers) Regulations 1990

(SI 1990/1020)

[The text of these regulations is printed as amended by:

the Public Service Vehicles (Conduct of Drivers, Inspectors, Conductors and Passengers) (Amendment) Regulations 1995 (SI 1995/186) (March 1, 1995); and

the Public Service Vehicles (Conduct of Drivers, Inspectors, Conductors and Passengers) (Amendment) Regulations 2002 (SI 2002/1724) (October 1, 2002).

The amending regulations are referred to in the notes to the principal regulations only by their years and numbers. The dates referred to above are the dates on which the amending regulations came into force.]

B24.01

ARRANGEMENT OF REGULATIONS

B24.02

17.   Extent of driver's and conductor's duty

Part I

Citation and commencement

B24.03   **1.** *[Omitted.]*

Revocation

B24.04   **2.** *[Omitted.]*

Part II

Interpretation

B24.05   **3.**—(1) In this Part of the Regulations unless the context otherwise requires—

"*the 1981 Act*" means the Public Passenger Vehicles Act 1981;

"*the 1985 Act*" means the Transport Act 1985;

["*the 1995 Act*" means the Disability Discrimination Act 1995 [*not reproduced in this work*];]

["*the 1984 Regulations*" means the Public Service Vehicles (Carrying Capacity) Regulations 1984 [*SI 1984/1406; not reproduced in this work*];]

["*the 2000 Regulations*" means the Public Service Vehicles Accessibility Regulations 2000 [*SI 2000/1970, as amended; not reproduced in this work*];]

["*assistance dog*" means a dog which—

    (a) is trained by a specified charity to assist a disabled person with a physical impairment for the purpose of section 1 of the 1995 Act which—

        (i) consists of epilepsy; or

        (ii) otherwise affects his mobility, manual dexterity, physical coordination or ability to lift, carry or otherwise move everyday objects; and

    (b) at the time it is providing assistance to a disabled person, is wearing a jacket inscribed with the name of one of the following charities, that is to say—

        (i) "Dogs for the Disabled" registered with the Charity Commission under registration number 700454;

        (ii) "Support Dogs" registered with the Charity Commission under registration number 1017237; or

        (iii) "Canine Partners for Independence" registered with the Charity Commission under registration number 803680;]

["*boarding lift*" means a lift fitted to a regulated public service vehicle for the purpose of allowing wheelchair users to board and alight from the vehicle;]

["*boarding ramp*" means a ramp fitted to a regulated public service vehicle for the purpose of allowing wheelchair users to board and alight from the vehicle;]

[*"disabled person"* has the same meaning as in section 1 of the 1995 Act;]

[*"guide dog"* has the same meaning as in section 37(11) of the 1995 Act;]

[*"hearing dog"* has the same meaning as in section 37(11) of the 1995 Act;]

"licence" means a licence to drive a vehicle granted under section 22 of the 1981 Act [*q.v.*];

[*"local service"* has the same meaning as in section 2 of the 1985 Act [*q.v.*];]

[*"maximum seating capacity"* has the same meaning as in regulation 4 of the 1984 Regulations;]

[*"maximum standing capacity"* has the same meaning as in regulation 6 of the 1984 Regulations;

"portable ramp" means a ramp which is carried on a regulated public service vehicle for the purpose of allowing wheelchair users to board or alight from the vehicle;]

[*"regulated public service vehicle"* means a public service vehicle to which the 2000 Regulations apply;]

[*"scheduled service"* means a service, using one or more public service vehicles, for the carriage of passengers at separate fares—

    (a) along specified routes,

    (b) at specified times, and

    (c) with passengers being taken up and set down at predetermined stopping points,

but does not include a tour service (being a service where a public service vehicle is used for or in conjunction with the carriage of passengers to a particular location, or particular locations, and back to their point of departure);]

"ticket" means a document which, in accordance with the terms and conditions under which it has been issued, constitutes a valid authority to travel on a vehicle;

"vehicle" means any vehicle used as a public service vehicle as defined in the 1981 Act but excluding any vehicle used under a permit granted by virtue of section 19 of the 1985 Act [*q.v.*];

[*"wheelchair restraint system"* means a system which is designed to keep a wheelchair restrained within the wheelchair space;]

[*"wheelchair space"* means a space for a wheelchair with which a regulated public service vehicle is fitted in accordance with paragraph 2 of Schedule 1 to the 2000 Regulations;]

[*"wheelchair user"* means a disabled person using a wheelchair; and]

[*"wheelchair user restraint"* means a system which is designed to keep a wheelchair user restrained in the wheelchair.]

(2) For the purposes of this Part of the Regulations, a sum payable by a passenger on the vehicle shall not be regarded as a fare unless—

    (a) it is computed in accordance with a fare table available on the vehicle; and

(b) the fare table contains sufficient information to enable the passenger to ascertain the fare for his journey or the manner in which it is computed.

(3) In this Part of the Regulations, in relation to a vehicle—

"*conductor*" means a person, not being the driver, who is authorised by the operator to act as a conductor on the vehicle, but does not include an inspector; and

"*driver*" means a person who is the holder of a licence and who is for the time being responsible for driving the vehicle.

(4) In this Part of the Regulations, any reference to a numbered regulation is a reference to the regulation bearing that number in this Part of the Regulations.

(5) In this Part of the Regulations, any reference to a numbered or lettered paragraph or sub-paragraph is a reference to the paragraph or sub-paragraph bearing that number or letter in the regulation or (in the case of a sub-paragraph) paragraph in which the reference appears.

B24.06   *[Regulation 3 is printed as amended by SI 2002/1724.]*

The conduct of drivers, inspectors and conductors

B24.07   **4.**—(1) A driver shall not, when a vehicle is in motion, hold a microphone or any attachment thereto unless it is necessary for him, either in an emergency or on grounds of safety, to speak into the microphone.

(2) Subject to paragraph (3), a driver shall not, when a vehicle is in motion, speak to any person either directly or by means of a microphone.

(3) Nothing in paragraph (2) shall prevent—

(a) the driver of a vehicle from—

(i) speaking in circumstances when he is obliged to do so by reason of an emergency or on grounds of safety; or

(ii) speaking to a relevant person in relation to the operation of the vehicle provided that he can do so without being distracted from his driving of the vehicle; and

(b) the driver of a vehicle which is being used to provide a relevant service from making short statements from time to time limited to indicating the location of the vehicle or operational matters provided that he can do so without being distracted from his driving of the vehicle.

(4) In this regulation—

(a) "*relevant person*" is a person fulfilling one of the following descriptions—

(i) an employee of the operator;

(ii) when the operator is a firm, a partner of the firm;

(iii) if the operator is an individual, that individual; or

(iv) if the operator is a company, a director; and

(b) "*relevant service*" is a service for the carriage of passengers for hire or reward at separate fares which is neither—

(i) an excursion or tour within the meaning of section 137(1) of the 1985 Act [*q.v.*]; nor

    (ii) a service the primary purpose of which is sightseeing, not falling within sub-paragraph (i).

5. *[Omitted.]* **B24.08**

The conduct of passengers

6.—(1) No passenger on a vehicle shall— **B24.09**

  (a) where the vehicle has a door which passengers are by a notice informed is for a particular purpose, use that door for any other purpose, unless otherwise directed or authorised by a driver, inspector or conductor;

  (b) put at risk or unreasonably impede or cause discomfort to any person travelling on or entering or leaving the vehicle, or a driver, inspector, conductor or employee of the operator when doing his work on the vehicle;

  (c) throw or trail any article from the vehicle;

  (d) smoke or carry lighted tobacco or light a match or a cigarette lighter in or on any part of the vehicle where passengers are by a notice informed that smoking is prohibited, unless the vehicle has been hired as a whole and both the operator and the hirer have given their permission to the contrary;

  (e) except with the permission of the operator, distribute any paper or other article for the purpose of giving or seeking information about or comment upon any matter;

  (f) except with the permission of the operator, sell or offer for sale any article;

  [(g) speak to the driver whilst the vehicle is in motion except—

     (i) in an emergency;

    (ii) for reasons of safety; or

   (iii) to give directions as to the stopping of the vehicle;]

  (h) without reasonable cause distract the driver's attention, obstruct his vision or give any signal which might reasonably be interpreted by the driver as a signal—

     (i) to stop the vehicle in an emergency; or

    (ii) to start the vehicle;

  (j) travel on any part of the vehicle which is not provided for the carriage of passengers;

  (k) remain on the vehicle, when directed to leave by the driver, inspector or conductor on the following grounds—

     (i) that his remaining would result in the number of passengers exceeding the maximum seating capacity or the maximum standing capacity marked on the vehicle in accordance with the Public Service Vehicles (Carrying Capacity) Regulations 1984 [*SI 1984/ 1406; not reproduced in this work*];

    (ii) that he has been causing a nuisance, or

   (iii) that his condition is such as would be likely to cause offence to a reasonable passenger or that the condition of his clothing is such that his remaining would be reasonably expected to soil the fittings of the vehicle or the clothing of other passengers;

(l) play or operate any musical instrument or sound reproducing equipment to the annoyance of any person on the vehicle or in a manner which is likely to cause annoyance to any person on the vehicle; or

(m) intentionally interfere with any equipment with which the vehicle is fitted.

[(1A) Paragraph (1)(k)(ii) and (iii) shall not apply to a direction given by a driver, inspector or conductor solely on the grounds that a person is a disabled person.]

(2) Subject to paragraph (3), a passenger on a vehicle who has with him any article or substance mentioned in paragraph (4) or any animal—

(a) if directed by the driver, inspector or conductor to put it in a particular place on the vehicle, shall put it where directed; and

(b) if requested to move it from the vehicle by the driver, inspector or conductor, shall remove it.

[(3) Paragraph (2)(b) does not require the removal of an animal where the passenger is a disabled person and the animal is an assistance dog, a guide dog or a hearing dog.]

[(3A) Without prejudice to regulation 5(7), a disabled person shall comply with any direction given by a driver, inspector or conductor to remove his assistance dog, guide dog or hearing dog from the gangway.]

(4) The article or substance referred to in paragraph (2) is—

(a) any bulky or cumbersome article;

(b) any article or substance which causes or is likely to cause annoyance to any person on the vehicle; or

(c) any article or substance which would be reasonably expected to constitute—

(i) a risk of injury to any person on the vehicle; or

(ii) a risk of damage to the property of any person on the vehicle or to the vehicle.

(5) [...]

B24.10 *[Regulation 6 is printed as amended by SI 1995/186; SI 2002/1724.*

Regulation 5(7) (to which reference is made in reg.6(3A)) was inserted by SI 2002/1724 and requires a driver, inspector or a conductor to allow a disabled person and an assistance dog, a guide dog or a hearing dog to board and travel in the vehicle.]

B24.11   7.—(1) No passenger on a vehicle being used for the carriage of passengers at separate fares shall use any ticket which has—

(a) been altered or defaced;

(b) been issued for use by another person on terms that it is not transferable; or

(c) expired.

(2) Save as provided in paragraph (3), every passenger on a vehicle being used for the carriage of passengers at separate fares shall—

(a) declare, if so requested by the driver, inspector or conductor, the journey which he intends to take, is taking or has taken in the vehicle;

(b) where the vehicle is being operated by the driver without a conductor—

    (i) save as provided in (ii) below, immediately on boarding the vehicle, pay the fare for the journey he intends to take to the driver or, where appropriate, by inserting in any fare-collection equipment provided on the vehicle the money or token required to pay that fare; or

    (ii) if otherwise directed by the driver, an inspector or a notice displayed on the vehicle, shall pay the fare for his journey in accordance with the direction;

(c) where the vehicle is being operated by the driver with a conductor, pay the fare for the journey which he intends to take, is taking, or has taken in the vehicle to the conductor immediately on being requested to do so by the conductor or an inspector;

(d) accept and retain for the rest of his journey any ticket which is provided on payment of a fare in accordance with sub-paragraph (b) or (c);

(e) produce during his journey any ticket which has been issued to him either under sub-paragraph (d) or before he started his journey for inspection by the driver, inspector or conductor on being requested to do so by the driver, inspector or conductor; and

(f) as soon as he has completed the journey for which he has a ticket, either—

    (i) leave the vehicle; or

    (ii) pay the fare for any further journey which he intends to take on the vehicle.

(3) Paragraph (2)(b) and (c) do not apply to a passenger who has with him a ticket which was issued to him before his journey in respect of that journey, provided he complies with all such directions in relation to the ticket as may be—

(a) printed on the ticket;

(b) displayed on the vehicle; or

(c) given by the driver, inspector or conductor.

(4) Any passenger who—

(a) fails to comply with paragraph (2)(b) or (c); or

(b) does not have with him a ticket which was issued to him before his journey in respect of that journey;

shall pay the fare for his journey to the driver, inspector or conductor on request and in any case before he leaves the vehicle unless otherwise agreed by the driver, inspector or conductor.

(5) Any passenger on a vehicle being used for the carriage of passengers at separate fares who has with him a ticket which he is not entitled to retain for any reason including—

(a) the alteration or defacement of the ticket;

(b) the fact that the ticket, having been issued for use by another person, was not transferable to him;

(c) the expiry of the ticket; or

(d) a mistake in consequence of which the ticket was issued;

shall surrender the ticket to a driver, inspector or conductor on being required to do so.

B24.12   **8.**—(1) Any passenger on a vehicle who is reasonably suspected by the driver, inspector or conductor of the vehicle of contravening any provision of these Regulations shall give his name and address to the driver, inspector or conductor on demand.

(2) Any passenger on a vehicle who contravenes any provision of these Regulations may be removed from the vehicle by the driver, inspector or conductor of the vehicle or on the request of the driver, inspector or conductor by a police constable.

B24.13   **9.** *[Applies to Scotland.]*

Part III

Amendment of Regulations

B24.14   **10.** *[Omitted.]*

Part IV

The Conduct of Drivers and Conductors of Regulated Public Service Vehicles with Respect to Wheelchair Users and Other Disabled Persons

[Interpretation of Part IV

B24.15   **11.** In this Part—

"*Schedule 1*" means Schedule 1 (wheelchair accessibility requirements) to the 2000 Regulations;

"*Schedule 2*" means Schedule 2 (general accessibility requirements for single-deck and double-deck buses) to the 2000 Regulations;

"*Schedule 3*" means Schedule 3 (general accessibility requirements for single-deck and double-deck coaches) to the 2000 Regulations;

a "*Schedule 1 vehicle*" means a regulated public service vehicle which is required to comply with the provisions of Schedule 1; and

a "*Schedule 2 or 3 vehicle*" means a regulated public service vehicle which is required to comply (as the case may be) with the provisions of either Schedule 2 or Schedule 3.]

B24.16   *[Part IV (regs 11–17) was inserted by SI 2002/1724.]*

[Duties towards wheelchair users of Schedule 1 vehicles

B24.17   **12.**—(1) This regulation applies (subject to regulation 15(1) (duties requiring the proper functioning of equipment)) in relation to a driver and a conductor of a Schedule 1 vehicle.

(2) If there is an unoccupied wheelchair space on the vehicle, a driver and a conductor shall allow a wheelchair user to board if—

(a) the wheelchair is of a type or size that can be correctly and safely located in that wheelchair space, and

(b) in so doing, neither the maximum seating nor standing capacity of the vehicle would be exceeded.

(3) For the purpose of paragraph (2), a wheelchair space is occupied if—

(a) there is a wheelchair user in that space; or

(b) passengers or their effects are in that space and they or their effects cannot readily and reasonably vacate it by moving to another part of the vehicle.

(4) A driver and a conductor shall ensure—

(a) where the carriage of a portable ramp is required by Schedule 1, that a portable ramp is carried on the vehicle where the vehicle is operating on a local service or on a scheduled service;

(b) that any boarding lift, boarding ramp or portable ramp is in its normal position for vehicle travel and is securely stowed before the vehicle is driven;

(c) where the vehicle is operating on a local or a scheduled service and it is fitted with a boarding lift or a boarding ramp which, in order to comply with Schedule 1, requires a means of control for it to be capable of being operated manually in the event of a power failure, that such a separate means of control is carried on the vehicle;

(d) that wheelchair users can gain access into and can get out of a wheelchair space;

(e) before the vehicle is driven, that any wheelchair user is correctly and safely positioned in a wheelchair space and that any retractable rail (being a rail fitted in accordance with the requirements of paragraph 4(3)(b) of Schedule 1) or any similar device is in a position to restrict the lateral movement of the wheelchair; and

(f) where a wheelchair user using a wheelchair space faces the front of the vehicle, that the wheelchair restraint system is attached in accordance with the relevant instructions pursuant to paragraph 8(3) of Schedule 1.

(5) If the vehicle has a seat in a wheelchair space which is capable of being quickly dismantled or removed, a driver and a conductor shall ensure that any such seat—

(a) when it is not in use and is stowed on the vehicle, is safely stowed; and

(b) whenever it is in position for use within the wheelchair space, is secured.]

[See note reg.11 above.]

[Duties concerning kneeling systems etc towards disabled persons using Schedule 2 or 3 vehicles

13.—(1) This regulation (subject to regulations 15 (effects of faulty or malfunctioning equipment) and 17 (extent of driver's and conductor's duty)) applies in relation to a driver and to a conductor of a Schedule 2 and 3 vehicle where that vehicle is equipped with— **B24.18**

    (a) a kneeling system, or

    (b) a folding or retractable step.

(2) A driver and a conductor shall operate the kneeling system or the folding or retractable step—

    (a) whenever they consider that a disabled person will need the system to be operated or the step to be deployed, or

    (b) if requested to do so,

for the purpose of enabling that person to board or to alight from the vehicle, and in such a manner that the distance between the vehicle and the ground or the vehicle and the kerb is the minimum that is reasonably practicable.

(3) *"Kneeling system"* means any system which enables the bodywork of the vehicle to be lowered relative to its normal height of travel and a *"folding or retractable step"* means a step which can either fold or retract and which meets the requirements applicable to external steps pursuant to paragraph 4 of Schedule 2 or Schedule 3 (as the case may be).

(4) A driver and a conductor shall ensure that disabled persons who are not wheelchair users may, when boarding or alighting from the vehicle, use an entrance or an exit which is provided in compliance with (as the case may be) the provisions of either Schedule 2 or Schedule 3.]

[See note reg.11 above.]

[General duties towards wheelchair users and other disabled persons

B24.19   **14.**—(1) Where a wheelchair user wishes to board or to alight from a Schedule 1 vehicle, a driver and a conductor shall first safely deploy (subject to regulation 15(1) (duties requiring the proper functioning of equipment)) any boarding lift, boarding ramp or portable ramp in its correct operating position.

(2) Where a wheelchair user wishes to board or to alight from a Schedule 1 vehicle and requests assistance to do so, a driver and a conductor shall provide assistance to him.

(3) Where a disabled person who is not a wheelchair user wishes to board or to alight from a Schedule 2 or 3 vehicle and requests assistance to do so, a driver and a conductor shall provide assistance to him.

(4) Where a wheelchair user wishes to occupy a wheelchair space in a Schedule 1 vehicle which is fitted with a wheelchair user restraint, a driver and a conductor shall—

    (a) offer to provide such assistance as may be required so as to enable the wheelchair user to wear that restraint, and

    (b) in providing that assistance, apply (subject to regulation 15(1) (duties requiring the proper functioning of equipment)) the wheelchair user restraint only in accordance with the user instructions which are displayed pursuant to paragraph 8(3) of Schedule 1.]

[See note reg.11 above.]

[Effects of faulty or malfunctioning equipment

B24.20   **15.**—(1) Where the fulfilment of a duty owed by a driver or a conductor under—

(a) regulation 12 (duties towards wheelchair users of Schedule 1 vehicles),

(b) regulation 13 (duties concerning kneeling systems etc towards disabled persons using Schedule 2 or 3 vehicles) or

(c) regulation 14 (general duties towards wheelchair users and other disabled persons),

requires the use or operation of any equipment, kneeling system or folding or retractable step and there is a fault in, or a failure in the operation of, that equipment, system or step, the person owing the duty shall not permit a wheelchair user, or other disabled person or any other passenger to board or alight from the vehicle or (if already on board) to travel on the vehicle unless he is satisfied that such persons can do so in safety.

(2) A driver or a conductor shall not be considered to have failed to ensure fulfilment of the duty under either regulation 13(2) (duties concerning kneeling systems etc) or regulation 16 (display of route numbers etc) if, and to the extent that, the performance of that duty involves the proper functioning of equipment on the vehicle but there is a fault in, or a failure in the operation of, that equipment which prevents it being used.

(3) In this regulation—

"*equipment*" means any equipment fitted to a regulated public service vehicle in order to comply with Schedule 1, Schedule 2 or Schedule 3 and which a driver and a conductor must operate for the safe fulfilment of the relevant duty; and

"*kneeling system or folding or retractable step*" has the same meaning as in regulation 13(3).]

[See note reg.11 above.]

[Route numbers, etc.

16.—(1) Subject to regulation 15(2) (equipment failure preventing use), a **B24.21** driver and a conductor of a regulated public service vehicle shall ensure that—

(a) a route number (if any) and a destination is displayed in the positions provided for such displays with respect to the vehicle in accordance (as the case may be) with either paragraph 8 of Schedule 2 or paragraph 7 of Schedule 3;

(b) a route number and a destination displayed in accordance with sub-paragraph (a) which is required to be provided with a means of illumination shall have characters that are kept illuminated between sunset and sunrise; and

(c) the vehicle shall at all times display the correct route number and destination.

(2) Sub-paragraphs (a) and (b) of paragraph (1) shall not apply to an emergency replacement vehicle or to a temporary service vehicle until 21 days has elapsed from the day when the vehicle is first used as an emergency replacement vehicle or as a temporary service vehicle, provided that—

(a) the route number (if any) and a destination shall be displayed either on the front or on the nearside of the vehicle as close as practical to the foremost passenger entrance; and

(b) the requirement of sub-paragraph (c) of paragraph (1) is complied with.

(3) In this regulation, *"destination"* and *"route number"* have the same meanings as in paragraph 7(6) of Schedule 3 to the 2000 Regulations and—

"emergency replacement vehicle" means a public service vehicle which has been brought into service on the route in question to provide emergency cover; and

"temporary service vehicle" means a public service vehicle which is in service on a temporary route or service.]

[See note reg.11 above.]

[Extent of driver's and conductor's duty

B24.22   17.—(1) Where, in any of the preceding provisions of this Part, a duty is expressed to be owed by the driver and the conductor of a vehicle, but a function to be performed to fulfil that duty is, according to arrangements made by the operator of the vehicle, the responsibility of one only of them, then that one only, and not the other, owes that duty in relation to that function.

(2) The duties which a driver or a conductor owes under regulation 13 (duties concerning kneeling systems etc) and 14 (general duties towards wheelchair users and other disabled persons) are duties—

(a) to take such care as in all the circumstances of the case is reasonable to see that the wheelchair user or other disabled person will be reasonably safe in boarding or in alighting from the vehicle, and

(b) shall not oblige the person owing the duty to take any steps if, on reasonable grounds, he considers that—

(i) there will be a risk to his health, safety or security or to that of the wheelchair user or other disabled person or to that of any other passenger or member of the public; or

(ii) there will be a risk to the safety and security of the vehicle.

(3) The duties which a driver or a conductor owes under regulations 13 (duties concerning kneeling systems etc) and 14 (general duties towards wheelchair users and other disabled persons) are duties to operate the kneeling system or the folding or retractable step, or to deploy the boarding lift, boarding ramp or portable ramp to the extent that it is practicable having regard to the construction of the vehicle and the condition of the road.]

[See note reg.11 above.]

SCHEDULE

(Regulations revoked by reg.2)

[Omitted.]

B24.23

The Tramcars and Trolley Vehicles (Modification of Enactments) Regulations 1992

(SI 1992/1217)

PART I

PRELIMINARY

Citation and commencement

1. *[Omitted.]* **B25.01**

Interpretation

2.—(1) In these Regulations — **B25.02**

"*the 1984 Act*" means the Road Traffic Regulation Act 1984 [*q.v.*];

"*the 1988 Act*" means the Road Traffic Act 1988 [*q.v.*];

"*duobus*" means a trolley vehicle which—

    (a) is adapted to operate under power provided from a source on board when it is not operating from power transmitted to it from some external source;

    (b) has a maximum speed when it is operating solely under power provided from a source on board which is at least—

        (i) 75% of its maximum speed when it is operating solely under power transmitted to it from an external source, or

        (ii) 30 miles per hour, whichever is the less; and

    (c) is designed to have a range of at least 10 miles when operating solely under power provided from a source on board;

"*maximum speed*", in relation to a trolley vehicle and a source of power, means the speed which the trolley vehicle is incapable, by reason of its construction, of exceeding on the level under that source of power when unladen.

(2) A reference in these Regulations to an order or regulations made under an enactment shall be read as including a reference to an order or regulations having effect as if made under that enactment.

PART II

MODIFICATIONS TO THE 1984 ACT

Modifications relating to tramcars

3.—(1) Subject to Part IV of these Regulations, the following sections of the 1984 Act — **B25.03**

    (a) section 1 (traffic regulation orders),

    (b) section 6 (orders similar to traffic orders in London),

    (c) section 9 (experimental orders), and

    (d) section 18 (one-way traffic on trunk roads),

shall have effect in relation to tramcars so that such vehicles are exempt from any order under any of those sections.

B25.04   **4.**—(1) Save as provided below, section 14 (temporary prohibition or restriction of traffic on roads) shall have effect in relation to tramcars so that such vehicles are exempt from any order or notice under that section.

    (2) Nothing in paragraph (1) above shall affect the operation of any provision in an order or notice under that section restricting the speed of vehicles.

Modifications relating to trolley vehicles

B25.05   **5.**—(1) Subject to Part IV of these Regulations and save as provided below, the following sections of the 1984 Act —

    (a) section 1 (traffic regulation orders),

    (b) section 6 (orders similar to traffic orders in London),

    (c) section 9 (experimental orders), and

    (d) section 18 (one-way traffic on trunk roads),

shall have effect in relation to trolley vehicles so that such vehicles are exempt from any order under any of those sections.

    (2) Nothing in paragraph (1) above shall affect the operation of any provision in an order under section 1 of the 1984 Act prohibiting or restricting the waiting of vehicles or the loading or unloading of vehicles.

    (3) Nothing in paragraph (1) above shall affect the operation of an order under section 6 of the 1984 Act in so far as it is made in respect of the matters referred to in paragraph 15 of Schedule 1 to that Act.

    (4) Nothing in paragraph (1) above shall affect the operation of any provision in an order under section 9 of the 1984 Act prohibiting or restricting the waiting of vehicles or the loading or unloading of vehicles.

    (5) Nothing in paragraph (1) above shall affect the operation of an order under section 9 of the 1984 Act as respects traffic on roads in Greater London in so far as it is made in respect of the matters referred to in paragraph 15 of Schedule 1 to that Act or imposes a speed limit.

B25.06   **6.**—(1) Save as provided below, section 14 (temporary prohibition or restriction of traffic on roads) shall have effect in relation to trolley vehicles so that such vehicles are exempt from any order or notice under that section.

    (2) Nothing in paragraph (1) above shall affect the operation of any provision in an order or notice under that section —

    (a) prohibiting or restricting the waiting of vehicles or the loading and unloading of vehicles;

    (b) restricting the speed of vehicles;

    (c) prohibiting or restricting overtaking; or

    (d) prohibiting or restricting the use of a road or part of the width of a road by vehicular traffic or by any class of vehicular traffic.

Part III

Modifications to the 1988 Act

Modifications relating to tramcars

7. The following provisions of the 1988 Act shall not apply to tramcars—   **B25.07**
    section 40A (using vehicle in dangerous condition, etc.);
    section 68 (inspection of public passenger vehicles and goods vehicles);
    sections 69 to 73 (prohibition of unfit vehicles);
    section 75 (vehicles not to be sold in unroadworthy condition or as altered
      so as to be unroadworthy);
    section 76 (fitting and supply of defective or unsuitable vehicle parts);
    section 77 (testing condition of used vehicles at sale rooms, etc.);
    sections 78 and 79 (weighing of motor vehicles);
    section 83 (offences to do with reflectors and tail lamps);
    section 190 (method of calculating weight of motor vehicles and trailers);
      and
    section 191 (interpretation of statutory references to carriages).

8. *[Amends s.87 of the Road Traffic Act 1988 (q.v.) as it applies to tramcars.]* **B25.08**

Modifications relating to trolley vehicles

9. Subject to Part IV of these Regulations, the following provisions of the 1988 **B25.09**
Act shall not apply to trolley vehicles—
    section 40A (using a vehicle in a dangerous condition);
    section 77 (testing condition of used vehicle in sale rooms, etc.); and
    sections 78 and 79 (weighing of motor vehicles).

10. Subject to Part IV of these Regulations, section 68 of the 1988 Act (inspec- **B25.10**
tion of public passenger vehicles and goods vehicles) shall apply to trolley
vehicles as if subsection (4) were omitted.

Part IV

Duobuses

11. Nothing in Parts II or III of these Regulations affects the operation of the **B25.11**
1984 Act or the 1988 Act in relation to duobuses.

Part V

Amendments to Subordinate Legislation

12–14. *[Omitted.]*   **B25.12**

Part VI

Transitional

15. An order made under—   **B25.13**
    (a) section 1, 14, 18 or 84 of the 1984 Act; or

    (b) as respects any road outside Greater London under section 9 of that Act, before the coming into force of these Regulations shall not apply to tramcars or trolley vehicles (other than duobuses).

B25.14   *[The regulations came into force on July 1, 1992; reg.1.]*

B25.15   **16.** An order made under—

    (a) section 1, 14, 18 or 84 of the 1984 Act; or

    (b) as respects any road outside Greater London under section 9 of that Act,

before the coming into force of these Regulations shall have effect thereafter, in relation to duobuses, as if the provisions of section 141 of that Act (as originally enacted) and the corresponding provisions of earlier enactments had never been passed.

B25.16   *[See the note to reg.15 above.]*

B25.17   **17.** Any regulations made under section 41 of the 1988 Act before the coming into force of these Regulations shall have effect thereafter in relation to trolley vehicles as if section 193 of and Schedule 4 to that Act (as originally enacted) and the corresponding provisions of earlier enactments had never been passed.

B25.18   *[See the note to reg.15 above.]*

The Road Vehicles (Prohibition) Regulations 1992

(SI 1992/1285)

[These regulations have been amended by the Road Vehicles (Prohibition) (Amendment) Regulations 1997 (SI 1997/83), but these regulations do not affect any of the provisions reproduced in this work.].   **B26.01**

Preliminary

1. *[Citation and commencement.]*   **B26.02**

Interpretation

2.—(1) In these Regulations —   **B26.03**

"the 1981 Regulations" means the Motor Vehicles (Tests) Regulations 1981 [*SI 1981/1694*] as from time to time amended;

"the 1988 Regulations" means the Goods Vehicles (Plating and Testing) Regulations 1988 [*SI 1988/1478 (q.v.)*] as from time to time amended;

"the 1988 Act" means the Road Traffic Act 1988 [*q.v.*];

"authorised constable" means a constable authorised to act for the purpose of section 72 of the 1988 Act by or on behalf of a chief officer of police;

"vehicle examiner" has the meaning given by section 66A of the 1988 Act;

"prohibition" means a prohibition under section 69 of the 1988 Act; and

"relevant test certificate", in relation to a prohibition, means a test certificate issued in respect of the vehicle after the prohibition had been imposed.

(2) A reference to an inspection by a vehicle examiner shall be read as including a reference to an inspection under the direction of a vehicle examiner.

Exemptions from section 71(1) of the 1988 Act

3.—(1) The driving of a vehicle on a road—   **B26.04**

(a) solely for the purpose of submitting it by previous arrangement for a specified time on a specified date for an inspection by a vehicle examiner or authorised constable with a view to the removal of the prohibition;

(b) solely for the purpose of submitting it by previous arrangement for a specified time on a specified date for an inspection by a vehicle examiner with a view to the removal of the prohibition and the issue of either a test certificate or a goods vehicle test certificate;

(c) in the course of an inspection with a view to the removal of a prohibition; or

(d) within 3 miles from where it is being, or has been, repaired solely for the purpose of its test or trial with a view to the removal of a prohibition, is exempted from section 71(1)(a) and (b) of the 1988 Act.

(2) Where a prohibition has been imposed with a direction under section 69A(3) of the 1988 Act, the driving of the vehicle on a road solely for the purpose of submitting it by previous arrangement at a specified time for an examination under section 45(3) of the 1988 Act with a view to obtaining a test certificate or bringing it away from such an examination is exempted from section 71(1)(a) and (b) of that Act.

(3) Where—

    (a) a prohibition has been imposed with a direction under section 69A(3) of the 1988 Act, and

    (b) a relevant test certificate has been issued,

the driving of the vehicle on a road to a police station with a view to the prohibition being removed under regulation 4(3) of these Regulations is exempted from section 71(1)(a) and (b) of that Act.

Removal of prohibitions imposed with a direction under section 69A(3) of the 1988 Act

B26.05   **4.**—(1) This regulation applies where a prohibition has been imposed with a direction under section 69A(3) of the 1988 Act.

(2) Where a vehicle examiner has issued a relevant test certificate, the prohibition may be removed by—

    (a) the vehicle examiner who issued the certificate, or

    (b) a person who has been authorised for the purpose by or on behalf of the Secretary of State and to whom the certificate has been produced.

(3) The prohibition may also be removed by a person who has been authorised for the purpose by or on behalf of a chief officer of police and to whom a relevant test certificate has been produced at a police station.

Removal of prohibitions imposed with a direction under section 69A(4)

B26.06   **5.**—(1) This regulation applies where a prohibition has been imposed under section 69A(4) of the 1988 Act.

(2) The requirements relating to the inspection of the vehicle which have to be complied with before the prohibition can be removed are that the vehicle must have been inspected by a vehicle examiner or an authorised constable.

Appeals to the Secretary of State relating to prohibitions

B26.07   **6.** *[Omitted.]*

Fees relating to inspection of goods vehicles

B26.08   **7.** *[Omitted.]*

Fees relating to the inspection of vehicles other than goods vehicles

B26.09   **8.** *[Omitted.]*

Revocations

B26.10   **9.** *[Omitted.]*

The Goods Vehicles (Community Authorisations) Regulations 1992

(SI 1992/3077)

[The Goods Vehicles (Community Authorisations) Regulations 1992 were made under the European Communities Act 1972, s.2(2), and are expressly stated (in the explanatory note) to give effect to Council Regulation (EEC) 881/92 below.]

B27.01

ARRANGEMENT OF REGULATIONS

Regulation

B27.02

Commencement and citation

1. *[Omitted.]*

B27.03

Purpose and interpretation

2.—(1) These Regulations implement the Council Regulation.

B27.04

(2) In these Regulations —

"*actual holder*", in relation to a person established as a haulier in Great Britain, has the meaning which it bears in regulation 32A(1) of the 1984 Regulations;

"*Community authorisation*" means a Community authorisation issued under the Council Regulation;

"*competent authority*" has the meaning given by regulation 4 of these Regulations;

"*the Council Regulation*" means Council Regulation (EEC) No.881/92 of

26th March 1992 [*q.v.*] on access to the market in the carriage of goods by road within the Community to or from the territory of a member State or passing across the territory of one or more member States;

"*the First Council Directive*" means the First Council Directive of 23 July 1962 on the establishment of common rules for certain types of carriage of goods by road [*O.J. No.L70, August 6, 1962, p.2005/62, as amended; not reproduced in this work*];

"*operating centre*" has the meaning which it bears in section 92(1) of the Transport Act 1968 [*q.v.*];

"*operator's licence*" means an operator's licence within the meaning of section 60(1) of the Transport Act 1968 or section 14 of the Transport Act (Northern Ireland) 1967;

"*standard operator's licence*" means an operator's licence which is a standard licence within the meaning of regulation 3(2) of the 1984 Regulations;

"*the 1984 Regulations*" means the Goods Vehicles (Operators' Licences, Qualifications and Fees) Regulations 1984 [*SI 1984/176, as amended*]; and

"*traffic area*" means a traffic area constituted for the purposes of the Public Passenger Vehicles Act 1981 [*as amended by the Traffic Areas (Reorganisation) (No.2) Order 1983 (SI 1983/1714; not reproduced in this work) and the Traffic Areas (Reorganisation) Order 1991 (SI 1991/288; not reproduced in this work)*],

and, subject thereto, expressions used which are also used in the Council Regulation have the meaning which they bear in that Regulation.

B27.05   *[The Goods Vehicles (Operators' Licences, Qualifications and Fees) Regulations 1984 (SI 1984/176) have been revoked by the Goods Vehicles (Licensing of Operators) Regulations 1995 (SI 1995/2869) below.*

With effect from December 4, 2011, Regulation (EEC) 881/92 was repealed by European Parliament and Council Regulation (EC) 1072/2009 on common rules for access to the international haulage market (O.J. No.L300, November 14, 2009, p.72).]

Use of goods vehicle without Community authorisation

B27.06   3. A person who uses a vehicle in the United Kingdom in contravention of Article 3.1 of the Council Regulation shall be guilty of an offence and liable on summary conviction to a fine not exceeding level 4 on the standard scale.

B27.07   *[An offence under reg.3 is a fixed penalty offence for the purposes of Pt 3 of the Road Traffic Offenders Act 1988 (see the Fixed Penalty Offences Order 2009 (SI 2009/483) art.2). The amount for the fixed penalty offence is prescribed by the Fixed Penalty Order 2000 (SI 2000/2792), as amended by the Fixed Penalty (Amendment) Order 2009 (SI 2009/488).]*

Competent authorities

B27.08   4. The competent authority for the purposes of the Council Regulation and of these Regulations shall be—

   (a) in relation to a haulier with an operating centre in a traffic area in Great Britain, the traffic commissioner for that area, and

   (b) in relation to a haulier established in Northern Ireland, the Department of the Environment for Northern Ireland.

Entitlement to the issue of Community authorisation

5. *[Omitted.]*   **B27.09**

Rights of appeal

6. *[Omitted.]*

Effect of failure to comply with conditions governing use of Community authorisation

7. A person who uses a vehicle in the United Kingdom under a Community authorisation and, without reasonable excuse, fails to comply with any of the conditions governing the use of that authorisation under the Council Regulation shall be guilty of an offence and liable on summary conviction to a fine not exceeding level 4 on the standard scale.   **B27.10**

[An offence under reg.7 is a fixed penalty offence for the purposes of Pt 3 of the Road Traffic Offenders Act 1988 (see the Fixed Penalty Offences Order 2009 (SI 2009/483) art.2). The amount for the fixed penalty offence is prescribed by the Fixed Penalty Order 2000 (SI 2000/2792), as amended by the Fixed Penalty (Amendment) Order 2009 (SI 2009/488).]   **B27.11**

Authorised inspecting officers

8. Authorised inspecting officers for the purposes of the Council Regulation shall be police constables and—   **B27.12**

   (a) in Great Britain, examiners appointed under section 56(1) of the Road Traffic Act 1972 or section 66A(1) of the Road Traffic Act 1988 [*q.v.*], and

   (b) *[applies to Northern Ireland]*.

Return of documents

9.—(1) The holder of a Community authorisation which is withdrawn by the competent authority in accordance with Article 8.2 of the Council Regulation shall within 7 days of such withdrawal return to the competent authority which issued it the original authorisation and all certified true copies of it.   **B27.13**

(2) The holder of a Community authorisation shall return to the competent authority which issued it such certified true copies of the authorisation as the authority may require pursuant to any reduction in the number of vehicles at the disposal of the holder or any decision of the authority under Article 8.3 of the Council Regulation to suspend certified true copies of that authorisation.

(3) A person who, without reasonable excuse, fails to comply with any provision of paragraphs (1) or (2) above shall be guilty of an offence and liable on summary conviction to a fine not exceeding level 4 on the standard scale.

Supply of information

B27.14   10.—(1) The holder of a Community authorisation shall furnish such information as the competent authority which issued it may reasonably require from time to time to enable the authority to decide whether the holder is entitled to retain that authorisation.

(2) A person who, without reasonable excuse, fails to supply any information required under paragraph (1) above shall be guilty of an offence and liable on summary conviction to a fine not exceeding level 4 on the standard scale.

Death, bankruptcy, etc., of holder of Community authorisation

B27.15   11. Where a person is treated as the holder of an operator's licence by virtue of a direction under Regulation 32A of the 1984 Regulations or by virtue of regulations made under section 33(2) of the Transport Act (Northern Ireland) 1967, such person shall also be treated as the holder of any Community authorisation held by the actual holder of that operator's licence, for the same period as is specified in that direction or under such regulations.

B27.16   *[The 1984 Regulations have been revoked; see the note to reg.2 above.*

As to the continuance of an operator's licence by the direction of a traffic commissioner following the death, bankruptcy, etc., of the holder, see the Goods Vehicles (Licensing of Operators) Regulations 1995 (SI 1995/2869) reg.31 below.]

Bodies corporate

B27.17   12.—(1) Where an offence under these Regulations has been committed by a body corporate and it is proved to have been committed with the consent or connivance of, or to be attributable to any neglect on the part of, any director, manager, secretary or other similar officer of the body corporate or any person who was purporting to act in any such capacity, he as well as the body corporate shall be guilty of the offence and shall be liable to be proceeded against and punished accordingly.

(2) Where the affairs of a body corporate are managed by its members, paragraph (1) above shall apply in relation to the acts and defaults of a member in connection with his functions of management as if he were a director of the body corporate.

(3) Where an offence under these Regulations has been committed by a Scottish partnership and it is proved to have been committed with the consent or connivance of, or to be attributable to any neglect on the part of, a partner, he as well as the partnership shall be guilty of the offence and shall be liable to be proceeded against and punished accordingly.

B27.18   13. [...]

[Revoked by the Goods Vehicles (International Road Haulage Permits) (Revocation) Regulations 1995 (SI 1995/1290).]

B27.19   14. [...]

[Revoked by the Goods Vehicles (Licensing of Operators) Act 1995, s.60(2) and Sch.8, Pt II.]

15. […]   **B27.20**

[Revoked by the Goods Vehicles (Licensing of Operators) (Temporary Use in Great Britain) Regulations 1996 (SI 1996/2186).]

The Motor Vehicles (Wearing of Seat Belts by Children in Front Seats) Regulations 1993

(SI 1993/31)

B28.01 *[The Motor Vehicles (Wearing of Seat Belts by Children in Front Seats) Regulations 1993 are expressly stated (in the explanatory note) to implement partially Council Directive 91/671/EEC (O.J. No.L373, December 31, 1991, p.26). The explanatory note adds that the Directive applies only to vehicles of less than 3.5 tonnes which have four or more wheels and a design speed of more than 25 km/h; and it continues to the effect that the Directive does not apply to passenger vehicles with more than eight passenger seats if they are designed to carry standing passengers. (Article 1(1) of the Directive as amended by Directive 2003/20/EC (O.J. No.L115, May 9, 2003, p.63) with effect from May 9, 2003 now provides: "This Directive shall apply to all motor vehicles in categories M1, M2, M3, N1, N2 and N3 as defined in Annex II to Directive (EEC) 70/156 [O.J. No.L42, February 23, 1970, p.1; as substituted by Directive 2001/116/EC], intended for use on the road, having at least four wheels and a maximum design speed exceeding 25 km/h." The categories of motor vehicles are now set out in Annex II of Directive 2007/46/EC (O.J. No.L263, October 9, 2007, p.1), which repealed Directive 70/156/EEC with effect from April 29, 2009. References to re-pealed Directive 70/156/EEC are to be construed as references to the 2007 Directive.)*

The text of these regulations is printed as amended by:

> *the Motor Vehicles (Wearing of Seat Belts by Children in Front Seats) (Amendment) Regulations 2006 (SI 2006/2213) (September 18, 2006).*

The amending regulations are referred to in the notes to the principal regulations only by their year and number. The date referred to above is the date on which the amending regulations came into force.]

ARRANGEMENT OF REGULATIONS

B28.02 Regulation

Citation, commencement and revocations

1. *[Omitted.]*   **B28.03**

General interpretation

2.—(1) In these Regulations —   **B28.04**
"*the Act*" means the Road Traffic Act 1988;
"*Construction and Use Regulations*" means the Road Vehicles (Construction and Use) Regulations 1986 [*SI 1986/1078, as amended (q.v.)*];
"*front seat*", in relation to a vehicle, means a seat which is wholly or
partially in the front of the vehicle and "*rear seat*", in relation to a
vehicle, means any seat which is not a front seat (see also regulation
4);
"*maximum laden weight*" has the meaning given by Part IV of Schedule 6
to the Road Traffic Regulation Act 1984 [*q.v.*];
"*medical certificate*" has the meaning given by Schedule 1 to these Regulations;
["*operator*", in relation to a bus means—
(a) the owner of the bus, or
(b) if the bus is in the possession of any other person under an
agreement for hire, hire-purchase, conditional sale, loan or
otherwise, that person;]
"*restraint system*" means a system combining a seat fixed to the structure
of the vehicle by appropriate means and a seat belt for which at least
one anchorage point is located on the seat structure;
"*seat belt*", except in this Regulation, includes a child restraint and references to wearing a seat belt shall be construed accordingly;
"*disabled person's belt*", "*lap belt*", "*seat*", and "*three point belt*" have
the meanings given by regulation 47(8) of the Construction and Use
Regulations [*q.v.*].

(2) Without prejudice to section 17 of the Interpretation Act 1978, a reference
to a provision of the Construction and Use Regulations is a reference to that provision as from time to time amended or as from time to time re-enacted with or
without modification.

(3) In these Regulations —
"*child*" means a person under the age of 14 years;
"*large child*" means a child who is not a small child; and
"*small child*" means a child who is—
(a) aged under 12 years; and
(b) under [135] centimetres in height.

(4) In these Regulations, "*adult belt*" means a seat belt in respect of which
one or more of the following requirements is satisfied, namely that—
(a) it is a three-point belt which has been marked in accordance with regulation 47(7) of the Construction and Use Regulations;
(b) it is a lap belt which has been so marked;
(c) it is a seat belt that falls within regulation 47(4)(c)(i) or (ii) of those
Regulations;

(d) it is a seat belt fitted [in a vehicle] and comprised in a restraint system—

    (i) of a type which has been approved by an authority of another member State for use by all persons who are either aged 13 years or more or of 150 centimetres or more in height, and

    (ii) in respect of which, by virtue of such approval, the requirements of the law of another member State corresponding to these Regulations would be met were it to be worn by persons who are either aged 13 years or more or of 150 centimetres or more in height when travelling [in that vehicle in that State].

(5) In these Regulations, *"child restraint"* means a seat belt or other device in respect of which the following requirements are satisfied, namely that—

    (a) it is a seat belt or any other description of restraining device for the use of a child which is—

        (i) designed either to be fitted directly to a suitable anchorage or to be used in conjunction with an adult belt and held in place by the restraining action of the belt, and

        (ii) marked in accordance with regulation 47(7) of the Construction and Use Regulations; or

    (b) it is a seat belt consisting of or comprised in a restraint system fitted [in a vehicle], being a restraint system—

        (i) of a type which has been approved by an authority of another member State for use by a child, and

        (ii) in respect of which, by virtue of such approval, the requirements of the law of that State corresponding to these Regulations would be met were it to be worn by a child when travelling [in that vehicle in that State].

(6) Subject to paragraph (7), for the purposes of these Regulations, a seat shall be regarded as provided with an adult belt if an adult belt is fixed in such a position that it can be worn by an occupier of that seat.

(7) A seat shall not be regarded as provided with an adult belt if the belt—

    (a) has an inertia reel mechanism which is locked as a result of the vehicle being, or having been, on a steep incline, or

    (b) does not comply with the requirements of regulation 48 of the Construction and Use Regulations.

(8) For the purposes of these Regulations, a seat shall be regarded as provided with a child restraint if a child restraint is—

    (a) fixed in such a position that it can be worn by an occupier of that seat, or

    (b) elsewhere in or on the vehicle but—

        (i) could readily be fixed in such a position without the aid of tools, and

        (ii) is not being worn by a child for whom it is appropriate and who is occupying another seat.

[(9) For the purposes of these Regulations, a seat belt is appropriate—

    (a) in relation to a small child, if it is a child restraint of a description prescribed for a child of his height and weight by regulation 5;

    (b) in relation to a large child, if it is a child restraint of a description prescribed for a child of his height and weight by regulation 5 or an adult belt; or

    (c) in relation to a person aged 14 years or more, if it is an adult belt.]

[(9A) For the purposes of these Regulations, references to a bus being used to provide a service in a "built-up area" shall be construed in the same way as in section 15B(6) of the Act.]

(10) Unless the context otherwise requires, in these Regulations —

    (a) any reference to a numbered regulation is a reference to the regulation bearing that number in these Regulations; and

    (b) a numbered paragraph is a reference to the paragraph bearing that number in the regulation or Schedule in which the reference appears.

[Regulation 2 is printed as amended by SI 2006/2213.]   **B28.05**

Interpretation of references to relevant vehicles

3. [...]   **B28.06**

[Regulation 3 was omitted by SI 2006/2213.]   **B28.07**

Interpretation of reference to the front of a vehicle

4.—(1) This regulation has effect for the purpose of defining in relation to a ve-   **B28.08**
hicle what part of the vehicle is to be regarded as the front of the vehicle for the purposes of section 15(1) of the Act and these Regulations.

(2) Subject to paragraph (3), every part of the vehicle forward of the transverse vertical plane passing through the rearmost part of the driver's seat shall be regarded as the front of the vehicle; and accordingly no part of the vehicle to the rear of that plane shall be regarded as being in the front of the vehicle.

(3) Where a vehicle has a deck which is above the level of the driver's head when he is in the normal driving position, no part of the vehicle above that level shall be regarded as being in the front of the vehicle.

Description of seat belts to be worn by children

5.—(1) For a child of any particular height and weight travelling in a particular   **B28.09**
vehicle, the description of seat belt prescribed for the purpose of section 15(1) of the Act to be worn by him is—

    (a) if he is a small child [...], a child restraint of a description specified in sub-paragraph (a) or (b) of paragraph (2);

    (b) [...];

    (c) if he is a large child, a child restraint of a description specified in sub-paragraph (a) of paragraph (2) or an adult belt.

(2) The descriptions of seat belt referred to in paragraph (1) are—

    (a) a child restraint with the marking required under regulation 47(7) of the Construction and Use Regulations if the marketing indicates that it is suitable for his weight and either indicates that it is suitable for his height or contains no indication as respects height;

    (b) a child restraint which would meet the requirements of the law of another member State corresponding to these Regulations were it to be worn by that child when travelling in that vehicle in that State.

B28.10   *[Regulation 5 is printed as amended by SI 2006/2213.]*

Vehicles to which section 15(1) of the Act does not apply

B28.11   **6.** Two-wheeled motor cycles with or without sidecars are exempt from the prohibition in section 15(1) of the Act.

Exemptions

B28.12   **7.**—[(1) The prohibition in section 15(1) of the Act shall not apply in relation to—

(a) a small child aged 3 years or more who is riding in a bus and is wearing an adult belt if an appropriate seat belt is not available for him in the front or rear of the vehicle;

(b) a child for whom there is a medical certificate; or

(c) a disabled child who is wearing a disabled person's belt.]

[(2) The prohibition in section 15(1) of the Act shall not apply in relation to a child riding in a bus—

(a) which is being used to provide a local service (within the meaning of the Transport Act 1985) in a built-up area, or

(b) which is constructed or adapted for the carriage of standing passengers and on which the operator permits standing.]

(3) The prohibition in section 15(1) of the Act shall not apply in relation to a large child if no appropriate seat belt is available for him in the front of the vehicle.

(4) For the purpose of this regulation, a reference to a seat belt being available shall be construed in accordance with Schedule 2.

B28.13   *[Regulation 7 is printed as amended by SI 2006/2213.]*

Regulation 2(1)   SCHEDULE 1

MEANING OF "MEDICAL CERTIFICATE"

PART I

B28.14   **1.** Subject to paragraph 2, in these Regulations, *"medical certificate"*, in relation to a person driving or riding in a vehicle, means—

(a) a valid certificate signed by a medical practitioner to the effect that it is inadvisable on medical grounds for him to wear a seat belt, or

(b) a valid certificate to such effect issued by the authority having power to issue such a certificate under the law of another member State corresponding to these Regulations.

B28.15   **2.** A certificate shall not be regarded as a medical certificate in relation to a person driving or riding in a vehicle for the purposes of these Regulations unless—

(a) it specifies its period of validity and bears the symbol shown in Part II of this Schedule; or

(b) the person is aged under 14 years [...].

B28.16   **3.** Paragraph 2 does not apply in relation to a certificate issued before 1st January 1995.

B28.17   *[Part I of Sch.1 is printed as amended by SI 2006/2213.]*

(SEE PARAGRAPH 2(A) IN PART I OF THIS SCHEDULE)

PART II

B28.18

Regulation 7(4)   SCHEDULE 2

INTERPRETATION OF REFERENCE TO AVAILABILITY OF SEAT BELTS

1. For the purposes of these Regulations, in relation to a child riding in a vehicle,—   **B28.19**

    (a) if any front seat in the vehicle (other than the driver's seat) is provided with an [appropriate seat belt], that belt shall be regarded as being available for him in the front of the vehicle unless the requirements of paragraph 2 are satisfied in relation to [that child], that seat and that belt; and

    (b) if any rear seat in the vehicle is provided with an [appropriate seat belt], that belt shall be regarded as being available for him in the rear of the vehicle unless the requirements of paragraph 2 are satisfied in relation to [that child], the seat and that belt.

2. The requirements of this paragraph are satisfied in relation to a particular child (*"the*   **B28.20**
child in question") and a particular seat (*"the relevant seat"*) provided with a particular seat belt (*"the relevant belt"*) if—

    (a) another person is wearing the relevant belt;

    (b) another child is occupying the relevant seat and wearing a child restraint which is an appropriate child restraint for that child;

    (c) another person, being a person holding a medical certificate, is occupying the relevant seat;

    (d) a disabled person (not being the child in question) is occupying the relevant seat and wearing a disabled person's belt;

    (e) by reason of his disability, it would not be practicable for the child in question to wear the relevant belt;

    (f) [...]

    (g) the child in question is prevented from occupying the relevant seat by the presence of a child restraint which could not readily be removed without the aid of tools; or

    (h) the relevant seat is specially designed so that—

        (i) its configuration can be adjusted in order to increase the space in the vehicle available for goods or personal effects, and

        (ii) when it is so adjusted the seat cannot be used as such,

    and the configuration is adjusted in the manner described in sub-paragraph (i) above and it would not be reasonably practicable for the goods and personal effects being carried in the vehicle to be so carried were the configuration not so adjusted.

3. Paragraphs 2(b) and (d) shall not apply unless the presence of the other person renders   **B28.21**
it impracticable for the child in question to wear the relevant belt.

4. [...]   **B28.22**

5. Paragraph 2(g) shall not apply if the child restraint is appropriate for the child in   **B28.23**
question.

B28.24   *[Schedule 2 is printed as amended by SI 2006/2213.]*

The Motor Vehicles (Wearing of Seat Belts) Regulations 1993

(SI 1993/176)

[The Motor Vehicles (Wearing of Seat Belts) Regulations 1993 are expressly **B29.01**
stated (in the explanatory note) to implement partially Council Directive 91/671/
EEC (O.J. No.L373, December 31, 1991, p.26). As to the vehicles to which the
Directive applies, see the editorial note to the Motor Vehicles (Wearing of Seat
Belts by Children in Front Seats) Regulations 1993 (SI 1993/31) above.
The text of these regulations is printed as amended by:

> *the Fire and Rescue Services Act 2004 (Consequential Amendments)*
> *(England) Order 2004 (SI 2004/3168) (December 30, 2004);*

> *the Motor Vehicles (Wearing of Seat Belts) (Amendment) Regulations*
> *2005 (SI 2005/27) (March 1, 2005);*

> *the Fire and Rescue Services Act 2004 (Consequential Amendments)*
> *(Wales) Order 2005 (SI 2005/2929) (October 25, 2005);*

> *the Serious Organised Crime and Police Act 2005 (Consequential and*
> *Supplementary Amendments to Secondary Legislation) Order 2006 (SI*
> *2006/594) (April 1, 2006); and*

> *the Motor Vehicles (Wearing of Seat Belts) (Amendment) Regulations*
> *2006 (SI 2006/1892) (September 18, 2006).*

The amending instruments are referred to in the notes to the principal regula-
tions by their years and numbers. The dates referred to above are the dates on
which the amending instruments came into force.]

ARRANGEMENT OF REGULATIONS

PART I   **B29.02**
INTRODUCTION

PART II
ADULTS IN THE FRONT OR REAR OF A VEHICLE

*   *   *

PART I

INTRODUCTION

Citation, commencement and revocations

B29.03   **1.** *[Omitted.]*

General interpretation

B29.04   **2.**—(1) In these Regulations —

"*the Act*" means the Road Traffic Act 1988;

"*the Construction and Use Regulations*" means the Road Vehicles (Construction and Use) Regulations 1986 [*SI 1986/1078, as amended (q.v.)*];

[*"large bus"* means a motor vehicle which—

(a) is constructed or adapted for use for the carriage of passengers,

(b) has more than eight seats in addition to the driver's seat,

(c) has four or more wheels,

(d) has a maximum design speed exceeding 25 kilometres per hour, and

(e) has a maximum laden weight exceeding 3.5 tonnes;]

"*licensed hire car*" has the meaning given by section 13(3) of the Transport Act 1985 [*q.v.*];

"*licensed taxi*" has the meaning given by section 13(3) of the Transport Act 1985;

[*"light goods vehicle"* means a motor vehicle which—

(a) has four or more wheels,

(b) has a maximum design speed exceeding 25 kilometres per hour, and

(c) has a maximum laden weight not exceeding 3.5 tonnes;]

"*maximum laden weight*" has the meaning given by Part IV of Schedule 6 to the Road Traffic Regulation Act 1984 [*q.v.*];

"medical certificate" has the meaning given in Schedule 1 to these Regulations;

[*"operator"* , in relation to a small or large bus, means—

    (a) the owner of the bus, or

    (b) if the bus is in the possession of any other person under an agreement for hire, hire-purchase, conditional sale, loan or otherwise, that person;]

"passenger car" has the same meaning as in section 15 of the Act;

"private hire vehicle" means a motor vehicle which has no more than 8 seats in addition to the driver's seat, other than a licensed taxi or a public service vehicle (within the meaning of the Public Passenger Vehicles Act 1981 [*q.v.*]), which is provided for hire with the services of a driver for the purpose of carrying passengers and which displays a sign pursuant to either section 21 of the Vehicles (Excise) Act 1971 or section 48(2) of the Local Government (Miscellaneous Provisions) Act 1976 or any similar enactment;

"rear seat" in relation to a vehicle means a seat not being the driver's seat, a seat alongside the driver's seat or a specified passenger seat;

"restraint system" means a system combining a seat fixed to the structure of the vehicle by appropriate means and a seat belt for which at least one anchorage point is located on the seat structure;

"seat belt" except in this regulation, includes a child restraint and references to wearing a seat belt shall be construed accordingly;

[*"small bus"* means a motor vehicle which—

    (a) is constructed or adapted for use for the carriage of passengers,

    (b) has more than eight seats in addition to the driver's seat,

    (c) has four or more wheels,

    (d) has a maximum design speed exceeding 25 kilometres per hour, and

    (e) has a maximum laden weight not exceeding 3.5 tonnes;]

"trade licence" has the meaning given by [section 11(1) of the Vehicle Excise and Registration Act 1994] [*q.v.*];

"disabled person's belt", *"lap belt"*, *"seat"*, *"specified passenger seat"* and *"three point belt"* have the meanings given by regulation 47(8) of the Construction and Use Regulations.

(2) Without prejudice to section 17 of the Interpretation Act 1978, a reference to a provision in any subordinate legislation (within the meaning of that Act) is a reference to that provision as from time to time amended or as from time to time re-enacted with or without modification.

(3) In these Regulations —

"child" means a person under the age of 14 years;

"large child" means a child who is not a small child; and

"small child" means a child who is—

    (a) aged under 12 years, and

    (b) under [135] centimetres in height.

(4) In these Regulations, *"adult belt"* means a seat belt in respect of which one or more of the following requirements is satisfied, namely that—

(a) it is a three-point belt which has been marked in accordance with regulation 47(7) of the Construction and Use Regulations,

(b) it is a lap belt which has been so marked,

(c) it is a seat belt that falls within regulation 47(4)(c)(i) or (ii) of those Regulations;

(d) it is a seat belt fitted [in a vehicle] and comprised in a restraint system—

(i) of a type which has been approved by an authority of another member State for use by all persons who are either aged 13 years or more or of 150 centimetres or more in height, and

(ii) in respect of which, by virtue of such approval, the requirements of the law of another member State corresponds to these Regulations would be met were it to be worn by persons who are either aged 13 years or more or of 150 centimetres or more in height when travelling [in that vehicle in that State].

(5) In these Regulations, *"child restraint"* means a seat belt or other device in respect of which the following requirements are satisfied, namely that—

(a) it is a seat belt or any other description of restraining device for the use of a child which is—

(i) designed either to be fitted directly to a suitable anchorage or to be used in conjunction with an adult seat belt and held in place by the restraining action of that belt, and

(ii) marked in accordance with regulation 47(7) of the Construction of Use Regulations; or

(b) it is a seat belt consisting of or comprised in a restraint system fitted [in a vehicle], being a restraint system—

(i) of a type which has been approved by an authority of another member State for use by a child, and

(ii) in respect of which, by virtue of such approval, the requirements of the law of that State corresponding to these Regulations would be met were it to be worn by a child when travelling [in that vehicle in that State].

(6) Subject to paragraph (7), for the purposes of these Regulations, a seat shall be regarded as provided with an adult seat belt if it is fixed in such a position that it can be worn by an occupier of that seat.

(7) A seat shall not be regarded as provided with an adult belt if the seat belt—

(a) has an inertia reel mechanism which is locked as a result of the vehicle being, or having been, on a steep incline, or

(b) does not comply with the requirements of regulation 48 of the Construction and Use Regulations.

[(8) For the purposes of these Regulations, a seat belt is appropriate—

(a) in relation to a small child, if it is a child restraint of a description prescribed for a child of his height and weight by regulation 8;

(b) in relation to a large child, if it is a child restraint of a description prescribed for a child of his height and weight by regulation 8 or an adult belt; or

(c) in relation to a person aged 14 years or more, if it is an adult belt.]

(9) For the purposes of these Regulations, any reference to a seat belt being available shall be construed in accordance with Schedule 2 to these Regulations.

[(9A) For the purposes of these Regulations, references to a bus being used to provide a service in a "built-up area" shall be construed in the same way as in section 15B(6) of the Act.]

(10) Unless the context otherwise requires, in these Regulations —

    (a) any reference to a numbered regulation is a reference to the regulation bearing that number in these Regulations; and

    (b) a numbered paragraph is a reference to the paragraph bearing that number in the regulation or Schedule in which the reference appears.

[Regulation 2 is printed as amended by the Vehicle Excise and Registration **B29.05**
Act 1994 s.64 and Sch.4, para.4 and SI 2006/1892.

Section 21 of the Vehicles (Excise) Act 1971 was repealed by the Finance Act 1994 s.258 and Sch.26.]

Interpretation of reference to relevant vehicles

3. [...]   **B29.06**
[Regulation 3 was omitted by SI 2006/1892.]   **B29.07**

PART II

ADULTS IN THE FRONT OR REAR OF A VEHICLE

General

4. This Part of these Regulations shall have effect for the purpose of section 14   **B29.08**
of the Act.

Requirement for adults to wear adult belts

5.—[(1) Subject to the following provisions of these Regulations, every   **B29.09**
person—

    (a) driving a motor vehicle (other than a two-wheeled motor cycle with or without a sidecar); or

    (b) riding in a front seat or rear seat of a motor vehicle (other than a two-wheeled motor cycle with or without a sidecar),

shall wear an adult belt.]

(2) Paragraph (1) does not apply to a person under the age of 14 years.
[Regulation 5 is printed as amended by SI 2006/1892.]   **B29.10**

Exemptions

6.—(1) The requirements of regulation 5 do not apply to—   **B29.11**

    (a) a person holding a medical certificate;

    [(b) the driver of or a passenger in a motor vehicle constructed or adapted for carrying goods, while on a journey which does not exceed 50 metres and which is undertaken for the purpose of delivering or collecting any thing;]

    (c) a person driving a vehicle while performing a manoeuvre which includes reversing;

    (d) a qualified driver (within the meaning given by [regulation 17 of the Motor Vehicles (Driving Licences) Regulations 1999]) who is supervising the holder of a provisional licence (within the meaning of Part III of the Act) while that holder is performing a manoeuvre which includes reversing;

    (e) a person by whom, as provided in the [Motor Vehicles (Driving Licences) Regulations 1999], a test of competence to drive is being conducted and his wearing a seat belt would endanger himself or any other person;

    (f) a person driving or riding in a vehicle while it is being used for fire brigade [or, in England [or Wales], fire and rescue authority] or police purposes or for carrying a person in lawful custody (a person who is being so carried being included in this exemption);

  [(fa) as regards England and Wales, and so far as relating to the functions of the Serious Organised Crime Agency which are exercisable in or as regards Scotland and which relate to reserved matters (within the meaning of the Scotland Act 1998), a person driving or riding in a vehicle while it is being used for Serious Organised Crime Agency purposes;]

    (g) the driver of—

        (i) a licensed taxi while it is being used for seeking hire, or answering a call for hire, or carrying a passenger for hire, or

        (ii) a private hire vehicle while it is being used to carry a passenger for hire;

    (h) a person riding in a vehicle, being used under a trade licence, for the purpose of investigating or remedying a mechanical fault in the vehicle;

    (j) a disabled person who is wearing a disabled person's belt; or

    (k) a person riding in a vehicle while it is taking part in a procession organised by or on behalf of the Crown.

(2) Without prejudice to paragraph (1)(k), the requirements of regulation 5 do not apply to a person riding in a vehicle which is taking part in a procession held to mark or commemorate an event if either—

    (a) the procession is one commonly or customarily held in the police area or areas in which it is being held, or

    (b) notice in respect of the procession was given in accordance with section 11 of the Public Order Act 1986.

(3) The requirements of regulation 5 do not apply to—

    (a) a person driving a vehicle if the driver's seat is not provided with an adult belt;

    (b) a person riding in the front of a vehicle if no adult belt is available for him in the front of the vehicle;

    (c) a person riding in the rear of a vehicle if no adult belt is available for him in the rear of the vehicle.

[(4) The requirements of regulation 5(1)(b) do not apply to a person riding in a small or large bus—

(a) which is being used to provide a local service (within the meaning of the Transport Act 1985) in a built-up area, or

(b) which is constructed or adapted for the carriage of standing passengers and on which the operator permits standing.]

[Regulation 6 is printed as amended by SI 2004/3168; SI 2005/27; SI 2005/2929; SI 2006/594; SI 2006/1892.]   **B29.12**

PART III

CHILDREN IN THE REAR OF A VEHICLE

General

7. This Part of these Regulations has effect for the purposes of section 15(3)   **B29.13**
and (3A) of the Act.

Description of seat belts to be worn by children

8.—(1) For a child of any particular height and weight travelling in a particular   **B29.14**
vehicle, the description of seat belt prescribed for the purpose of section 15(3) of
the Act to be worn by him is—

(a) if he is a small child [...], a child restraint of a description specified in sub-paragraph (a) or (b) of paragraph (2);

(b) [...];

(c) if he is a large child, a child restraint of a description specified in sub-paragraph (a) of paragraph (2) or an adult belt.

(2) The descriptions of seat belt referred to in paragraph (1) are—

(a) a child restraint with the marking required under regulation 47(7) of the Construction and Use Regulations if the marking indicates that it is suitable for his weight and either indicates that it is suitable for his height or contains no indication as respects height;

(b) a child restraint which would meet the requirements of the law of another member State corresponding to these Regulations were it to be worn by that child when travelling in that vehicle in that State.

[Regulation 8 is printed as amended by SI 2006/1892.]   **B29.15**

Vehicles to which section 15(3) and (3A) of the Act do not apply

9. The following classes of vehicles are exempt from the prohibition in section   **B29.16**
15(3) and (3A) of the Act, that is to say—

[(a) large buses;]

(b) licensed taxis and licensed hire cars in which (in each case) the rear seats are separated from the driver by a fixed partition.

[Regulation 9 is printed as amended by SI 2006/1892.]   **B29.17**

Exemptions

10.—[(1) The prohibitions in section 15(3) and (3A) of the Act do not apply in   **B29.18**
relation to—

(a) a child for whom there is a medical certificate;

(b) a small child aged under 3 years who is riding in a licensed taxi or licensed hire car, if no appropriate seat belt is available for him in the front or rear of the vehicle;

(c) a small child aged 3 years or more who is riding in a licensed taxi, a licensed hire car or a small bus and wearing an adult belt if an appropriate seat belt is not available for him in the front or rear of the vehicle;

(d) a small child aged 3 years or more who is wearing an adult belt and riding in a passenger car or light goods vehicle where the use of child restraints by the child occupants of two seats in the rear of the vehicle prevents the use of an appropriate seat belt for that child and no appropriate seat belt is available for him in the front of the vehicle;

(e) a small child who is riding in a vehicle being used for the purposes of the police, security or emergency services to enable the proper performance of their duty;

(f) a small child aged 3 years or more who is wearing an adult belt and who, because of an unexpected necessity, is travelling a short distance in a passenger car or light goods vehicle in which no appropriate seat belt is available for him; or

(g) a disabled child who is wearing a disabled person's belt or whose disability makes it impracticable to wear a seat belt where a disabled person's belt is unavailable to him.]

[(2) The prohibition in section 15(3) of the Act does not apply in relation to a child aged under 3 years riding in a rear seat of a small bus.]

[(3) The prohibition in section 15(3) of the Act does not apply to a small child aged 3 years or more riding in a rear seat of a small bus if neither an appropriate seat belt nor an adult belt is available for him in the front or rear of the vehicle.]

[(3A) For the purposes of paragraph (3) of this regulation, a reference to an appropriate seat belt in paragraphs 2 and 3 of Schedule 2 shall be read as including reference to an adult belt.]

(4) The prohibition in section 15(3) of the Act does not apply in relation to a large child in any vehicle if no appropriate seat belt is available for him in the rear of the vehicle.

[(4A) The prohibition in section 15(3) of the Act does not apply to a child riding in a small bus—

(a) which is being used to provide a local service (within the meaning of the Transport Act 1985) in a built-up area, or

(b) which is constructed or adapted for the carriage of standing passengers and on which the operator permits standing.]

(5) The prohibition in section 15(3A) of the Act does not apply in relation to a child if no appropriate seat belt is available for him in the front of the vehicle.

B29.19   *[Regulation 10 is printed as amended by SI 2006/1892.]*

Regulation 2(1)   SCHEDULE 1

MEANING OF "MEDICAL CERTIFICATE"

PART I

1. Subject to paragraph 2, in these Regulations, *"medical certificate"*, in relation to a person driving or riding in a vehicle, means—   **B29.20**

    (a) a valid certificate signed by a medical practitioner to the effect that it is inadvisable on medical grounds for him to wear a seat belt, or

    (b) a valid certificate to such effect issued by the authority having power to issue such a certificate under the law of another member State corresponding to these Regulations.

2. A certificate shall not be regarded as a medical certificate in relation to a person driving or riding in a vehicle for the purposes of these Regulations unless—   **B29.21**

    (a) it specifies its period of validity and bears the symbol shown in Part II of this Schedule; [...]

    (b) [...]

3. Paragraph 2 does not apply in relation to a certificate issued before 1st January 1995.   **B29.22**

[Part I of Sch.1 is printed as amended by SI 2006/1892.]   **B29.23**

(SEE PARAGRAPH 2(A) IN PART I OF THIS SCHEDULE)

PART II

    B29.24

Regulation 2(9)   SCHEDULE 2

INTERPRETATION OF REFERENCES TO AVAILABILITY OF SEAT BELTS

1. For the purpose of these Regulations, in relation to a person aged 14 years or more riding in a vehicle—   **B29.25**

    (a) if any front seat in a vehicle (other than the driver's seat) is provided with an adult belt, that belt shall be regarded as being available for him in the front of the vehicle unless the requirements of paragraph 3 are satisfied in relation to that person, that seat and that belt; and

    (b) if any rear seat in the vehicle is provided with an adult belt, that belt shall be regarded as being available for him in the rear of the vehicle unless the requirements of paragraph 3 are satisfied in relation to that person, that seat and that belt.

2. For the purpose of these Regulations, in relation to a child riding in a vehicle—   **B29.26**

    (a) if any front seat in the vehicle (other than the driver's seat) is provided with an appropriate seat belt, that belt shall be regarded as an appropriate seat belt available for him in the front of the vehicle unless the requirements of paragraph 3 are satisfied in relation to that child, that seat and that belt; and

    (b) if any rear seat in a vehicle is provided with an appropriate seat belt, that belt shall be regarded as an appropriate seat belt available for him in the rear of the vehicle unless the requirements of paragraph 3 are satisfied in relation to that child, that seat and that belt.

B29.27   **3.** The requirements of this paragraph are satisfied in relation to a particular person (*"the person in question"*) and a particular seat (*"the relevant seat"*) provided with a particular seat belt (*"the relevant belt"*) if—

    (a) another person is wearing the relevant belt;

    (b) a child is occupying the relevant seat and wearing a child restraint which is an appropriate child restraint for that child;

    (c) another person, being a person holding a medical certificate, is occupying the relevant seat;

    (d) a disabled person (not being the person in question) is occupying the relevant seat and wearing a disabled person's belt;

    (e) by reason of his disability, it would not be practicable for the person in question to wear the relevant belt;

    (f) [...]

    (g) the person in question is prevented from occupying the relevant seat by the presence of a child restraint which could not readily be removed without the aid of tools; or

    (h) the relevant seat is specially designed so that—

        (i) its configuration can be adjusted in order to increase the space in the vehicle available for goods or personal effects, and

        (ii) when it is so adjusted the seat cannot be used as such, and the configuration is adjusted in the manner described in sub-paragraph (i) and it would not be reasonably practicable for the goods and personal effects being carried in the vehicle to be so carried were the configuration not so adjusted.

B29.28   **4.** Paragraph 3 shall have effect in relation to regulation 10(5) as if sub-paragraphs (a) to (d) of that paragraph were omitted.

B29.29   **5.** Paragraph (3b) and (d) shall not apply unless the presence of the other person renders it impracticable for the person in question to wear the relevant belt.

B29.30   **6.** [...]

B29.31   **7.** Paragraph 3(g) shall not apply if—

    (a) the person in question is a child; and

    (b) the child restraint is appropriate for him.

B29.32   **8.** A child restraint shall be regarded as provided for a seat for the purposes of this Schedule if—

    (a) it is fixed in such a position that it can be worn by an occupier of that seat, or

    (b) it is elsewhere in or on the vehicle but—

        (i) it could readily be fixed in such a position without the aid of tools, and

        (ii) it is not being worn by a child for whom it is appropriate and who is occupying another seat.

B29.33   *[Schedule 2 is printed as amended by SI 2006/1892.]*

Regulation 1(2)   SCHEDULE 3

REVOCATIONS

B29.34   *[Omitted.]*

The Finance (No.2) Act 1992 (Commencement No.6 and Transitional Provisions and Savings) Order 1993

(SI 1993/2272)

[As to the saving of paras 4–8 of the Schedule to this order following the repeal **B30.01**
of s.12(2) of the Finance (No.2) Act 1992, see the Vehicle Excise and Registra-
tion Act 1994 Sch.4, para.7(8) and (9) above.]

1., 2. *[Omitted.]* **B30.02**

Transitional provisions and savings

3. The transitional provisions and savings set out in the Schedule to this Order **B30.03**
shall have effect.

Article 3   SCHEDULE

TRANSITIONAL PROVISIONS AND SAVINGS

1.—(1) In this Schedule — **B30.04**

"*appropriate authority*" means the Secretary of State for Social Security, the Secretary of State for Scotland or the Department of Health and Social Services for
Northern Ireland;

"*licence*" means a licence under the Act for a mechanically propelled vehicle;

"*qualified disabled person*" has the meaning given in paragraph 2(2) below;

"*relevant certificate*" has the meaning given in paragraph 2(3) below;

"*the Act*" means the Vehicles (Excise) Act 1971;

"*the appointed day*" means 13th October 1993;

"*the 1971 Regulations*" means the Road Vehicles (Registration and Licensing)
Regulations 1971 [*SI 1971/450, as amended*] ; and

"*the 1973 Regulations*" means the Road Vehicles (Registration and Licensing)
Regulations (Northern Ireland) 1973 [*SR & O (NI) 1973/490*] .

(2) In this Schedule any reference to the Secretary of State for Social Security shall
include a reference to his statutory predecessor.

(3) In this Schedule any reference to the Department of Health and Social Services for
Northern Ireland shall include a reference to its statutory predecessor.

(4) Without prejudice to section 17 of the Interpretation Act 1978, a reference in this
Schedule to a provision of either the 1971 Regulations or the 1973 Regulations is, unless
otherwise stated, a reference to that provision as from time to time amended or as from
time to time re-enacted with or without modification.

[The Vehicles (Excise) Act 1971 has been repealed and replaced by the Vehi- **B30.05**
cle Excise and Registration Act 1994.

The Road Vehicles (Registration and Licensing) Regulations 1971 (SI 1971/
450) and the Road Vehicles (Registration and Licensing) Regulations (Northern
Ireland) 1973 (SR & O (NI) 1973/490) have been repealed and replaced, with
amendments, by the Road Vehicles (Registration and Licensing) Regulations
2002 (SI 2002/2742).]

2., 3. *[Lapsed.]* **B30.06**

[The provisions of paras 2 and 3 of the Schedule have been re-enacted in the **B30.07**
Vehicle Excise and Registration Act 1994 Sch.4, para.7(1)–(5) above.]

B30.08   **4.**—(1) This paragraph applies only to Great Britain.

(2) The owner of a mechanically propelled vehicle which is exempt from duty by virtue of [paragraph 7 of Schedule 4 to the Vehicle Excise and Registration Act 1994] shall annually—

(a) make the prescribed declaration and furnish the prescribed particulars as if, subject to sub-paragraph (3) below, he desired to take out a licence for the vehicle; and

(b) include with the prescribed declaration and particulars, the relevant certificate issued in respect of him.

(3) Such declaration, particulars and certificate shall be forwarded to the Secretary of State.

(4) Upon receipt of such declaration, particulars and certificate, the Secretary of State shall—

(a) if the vehicle has not previously been registered under the Act [or the 1994 Act], register the vehicle, assign to the vehicle a registration mark and issue to the owner a registration book with the appropriate particulars of the vehicle in respect of which it is issued entered therein, and any registration mark so assigned shall be deemed to be assigned under [section 23 of the 1994 Act] for the purposes of [subsection (3) of section 23 of the 1994 Act] and the 1971 Regulations; and

(b) issue to the owner of the vehicle a document in respect thereof in the form of a licence valid for a period of twelve months running from the beginning of the month in which the document first has effect with the word "NIL" marked in the space provided for indicating the amount of duty payable.

(5) If at any time duty becomes chargeable under the Act in respect of a mechanically propelled vehicle to which this paragraph applies the owner of the vehicle shall forthwith return to the Secretary of State any document issued by him for exhibition on the vehicle which indicates that no duty was payable in respect of it.

(6) The provisions of regulation 7 (which relates to the alteration of licences and similar offences) and regulation 16 (which relates to the exhibition of licences) of the 1971 Regulations shall apply in relation to a vehicle to which this paragraph applies as if each reference therein to a licence issued under [the 1994 Act] included a reference to any such document issued in respect of the vehicle as is mentioned in sub-paragraph (5) above.

(7) In this paragraph, the expressions *"prescribed"* and *"owner"* have the meanings given in Part I of the 1971 Regulations.

B30.09   *[Paragraph 4 of the Schedule is printed as amended by the Vehicle Excise and Registration Act 1994 s.64 and Sch.4, para.7(9).]*

B30.10   **5.** The provisions of Parts II and III of the 1971 Regulations as to registration and matters incidental thereto shall extend to the vehicles to which paragraph 4 above applies subject to the modifications specified in that paragraph.

[See the note to art.1 above.]

B30.11   **6., 7.** *[Apply to Northern Ireland.]*

B30.12   **8.**—(1) Paragraphs 4 to 7 above shall have effect as if they were contained in regulations made under the Act.

(2) Without prejudice to the generality of sub-paragraph (1), any vehicle registered under either paragraph 4(4)(a) or paragraph 6(4)(a) shall be deemed to be registered under [the 1994 Act].

B30.13   *[Paragraph 8 of the Schedule is printed as amended by the Vehicle Excise and Registration Act 1994 s.64 and Sch.4, para.7(9).]*

The Vehicle Excise Duty (Designation of Small Islands) Order 1995

(SI 1995/1397)

[The text of this order has been amended by: **B31.01**
    the Vehicle Excise Duty (Designation of Small Islands) (Amendment)
    Order 2002 (SI 2002/1072) (June 1, 2002).
*The amending order is referred to in the notes to the principal order only by its
year and number. The date referred to above is the date on which the amending
order came into force.]*

1. *[Omitted.]*   **B31.02**

2. The islands listed in the Schedule to this Order are hereby designated as   **B31.03**
small islands for the purposes of paragraph 18 (meaning of island goods vehicle)
of Schedule 1 to the Vehicle Excise and Registration Act 1994.

THE SCHEDULE

DESIGNATED SMALL ISLANDS

Inner Hebrides	Egilsay	Berneray	**B31.04**
Canna	Fara	Eriskay	
Coll	Faray	[Harris and	
Colonsay	Flotta	Lewis]	
Eigg	Graemsay	North Uist	
Gigha	Hoy	Scalpay	
Iona	[Mainland]	South Uist	
Islay	North	Vatersay	
Jura	Ronaldsay		
Kerrera	Papa Stronsay	*Scilly Isles*	
Lismore	Papa Westray	Bryher	
Luing	Pentland	St Agnes	
Muck	Skerries	St Martin's	
Mull	Rousay	St Mary's	
Pabay	Sanday	Tresco	
Raasay	[Shapinsay]		
Rum	South Walls	*Shetland*	
Scarba	Stroma	*Islands*	
Shuna	Stronsay	Bressay	
Tiree	Westray	Fair Isle	
Ulva	Wyre	Fetlar	
		Foula	
Orkney Islands	*Outer*	[Mainland]	
Copinsay	*Hebrides*	Out Skerries	
Eday	Barra	Papa Stour	
	Benbecula	Unst	

Uyea	Bute	Lundy
Whalsay	Caldey Island	Isle of May
Yell	Isle of Ewe	Rathlin
	Flat Holm	St Kilda
Other Islands	Great	Sanda
Arran	Cumbrae	Scalpay
Bardsey Island	Inch Marnock	Skokholm
Brownsea	Little	
Island	Cumbrae	

B31.05   *[The Schedule is printed as amended by SI 2002/1072.]*

The Goods Vehicles (Licensing of Operators) Regulations 1995

(SI 1995/2869)

[These regulations are modified in relation to their application to foreign **B32.01**
goods vehicles by the Goods Vehicles (Licensing of Operators) (Temporary Use
in Great Britain) Regulations 1996 (SI 1996/2186) below.

The text of these regulations is printed as amended by:

the Fire and Rescue Services Act 2004 (Consequential Amendments)
(England) Order 2004 (SI 2004/3168) (December 30, 2004);

the Fire and Rescue Services Act 2004 (Consequential Amendments)
(Wales) Order 2005 (SI 2005/2929) (October 25, 2005);

the Serious Organised Crime and Police Act 2005 (Consequential and
Supplementary Amendments to Secondary Legislation) Order 2006 (SI
2006/594) (April 1, 2006); and

the Goods Vehicles (Licensing of Operators) (Amendment) Regula-
tions 2010 (SI 2010/455) (April 1, 2010; except for the purposes of
reg.2(4) and (5), May 14, 2010; December 4, 2011 respectively).

The amending instruments are referred to in the notes to the principal regula-
tions only by their years and numbers. The dates referred to above are the dates
on which the amending order came into force.]

ARRANGEMENT OF REGULATIONS

PART I   **B32.02**

GENERAL

Regulation

*   *   *

SCHEDULES

Schedule

*   *   *

*   *   *

PART I

GENERAL

Commencement and citation

B32.03   **1.** *[Omitted.]*

Revocation

B32.04   **2.** *[Omitted.]*

Interpretation

B32.05   **3.**—(1) In these Regulations, unless the context otherwise requires, any reference to—

(a) a numbered section is a reference to the section bearing that number in the Goods Vehicles (Licensing of Operators) Act 1995 [*q.v.*];

(b) a numbered regulation or Schedule is a reference to the regulation or, as the case may be, the Schedule bearing that number in these Regulations; and

(c) a numbered paragraph is a reference to the paragraph bearing that number in the regulation in which the reference appears.

(2) In these Regulations, unless the context otherwise requires—

"the 1995 Act" means the Goods Vehicles (Licensing of Operators) Act 1995;

"application for a licence" means an application for an operator's licence for which publication is required by section 10(1);

"application for the variation of a licence" means an application for the variation of an operator's licence for which publication is required by section 17(3) and *"application"* when used otherwise than as part of those expressions means—

(a) an application for a licence, or

(b) an application for the variation of a licence;

"Applications and Decisions" means a statement issued by a traffic commissioner under regulation 21;

"company" shall be construed as provided in section 735 of the Companies Act 1985;

"disc" means a disc issued in accordance with regulation 23(1) and (2) or 27(2);

"dual purpose vehicle" has the meaning given in column 2 of the Table in regulation 3(2) of the Road Vehicles (Construction and Use) Regulations 1986 [*SI 1986/1078, as amended (q.v.)*];

"farm" includes a market garden;

"firm" has the same meaning as in section 4 of the Partnership Act 1890 [*not reproduced in this work*];

"goods vehicle" has the same meaning as in section 58(1) but excludes a small goods vehicle as described in Schedule 1 to the 1995 Act;

"keeper", in relation to a goods vehicle, is the person in whose name the vehicle is registered under the Vehicle Excise and Registration Act 1994 [*q.v.*];

[*"interim licence"* means a licence issued under section 24;

"interim direction" means a direction given by a traffic commissioner pursuant to section 25;]

"licence" means an operator's licence (whether standard or restricted) as defined in section 2(1) and, where the context so requires, includes the documentation which evidences the grant of an application;

"licence-holder", and *"holder"* in relation to a licence, mean the person to whom the licence was issued;

"motor vehicle" means a mechanically propelled vehicle intended or adapted for use on roads;

"maintenance" in relation to a goods vehicle includes inspection, repair and fuelling;

"officer" has the meaning given in section 42;

"recovery vehicle" has the same meaning as in Part V of Schedule 1 to the Vehicle Excise and Registration Act 1994;

"relevant conviction" means any conviction mentioned in paragraph 5 of Schedule 2 to the 1995 Act or any conviction of contravening any provision of the law of Northern Ireland or of a country or territory outside the United Kingdom corresponding to any such conviction, not being in either case a spent conviction within the meaning of section 1(1) of the Rehabilitation of Offenders Act 1974 [*not reproduced in this work*];

"showman's goods vehicle" has the same meaning as in section 62 of the Vehicle Excise and Registration Act 1994;

"tower wagon" has the same meaning as in paragraph 17(2) of Schedule 2 to the Vehicle Excise and Registration Act 1994 (as originally enacted);

"trade licence" is a licence granted under section 11 of the Vehicle Excise and Registration Act 1994;

"visiting force", *"headquarters"* and *"vehicle in the service of a visiting force or a headquarters"* have the same meanings as in the Visiting Forces and International Headquarters (Application of Law) Order 1965 [*SI 1965/1536.*]

B32.06 *[Regulation 3 is printed as amended by SI 2010/455.*

The Visiting Forces and International Headquarters (Application of Law) Order 1965 (to which reference is made in reg.3(2)) has been revoked and replaced by the Visiting Forces and International Headquarters (Application of Law) Order 1999 (SI 1999/1736; not reproduced in this work). No textual amendment has been made to reg.3 in consequence of that revocation; but by the Interpretation Act 1978 ss.17(2)(a) and 23(1) references to the earlier order may be treated as references to SI 1999/1736.]

PART II

APPLICATIONS

B32.07 **4–9.** *[Omitted.]*

PART III

OBJECTIONS AND REPRESENTATIONS

B32.08 **10–13.** *[Omitted.]*

PART IV

OPERATING CENTRES

B32.09 **14–19.** *[Omitted.]*

PART V

INQUIRIES

B32.10 **20.** *[Omitted.]*

PART VI

APPLICATIONS AND DECISIONS

B32.11 **21–22.** *[Omitted.]*

PART VII

OTHER MATTERS

Identification of motor vehicles

B32.12 **23.**—(1) The traffic commissioner shall, when any motor vehicle to be used under a licence is specified in the licence, issue to the licence-holder a disc in respect of the vehicle.

(2) The disc shall clearly indicate (by colour or other means)—

  (a) whether a vehicle is being used under a standard licence or under a restricted licence;

  (b) in the case of a vehicle being used under a standard licence, whether the vehicle covers both international and national transport operations or [national transport operations;]

  [(c) where applicable, that the vehicle is being used under an interim licence, or pursuant to an interim direction, and in such a case, the date the interim licence was issued or the interim direction was given; and

  (d) subject to paragraph (5)(b), the date on which the disc expires under paragraph (5)(a).]

(3) The licence-holder shall, during such time as any motor vehicle is specified in the licence and whether or not for the time being the vehicle is being used for the purpose for which a licence is required, cause a disc appropriate to the vehicle to be fixed to, and exhibited in a legible condition on, that vehicle in a waterproof container—

  (a) in the case of a vehicle fitted with a front windscreen, on the near side and near the lower edge of the windscreen with the obverse side facing forwards;

  (b) in the case of a vehicle not fitted with a front windscreen, in a conspicuous position on the front or near side of the vehicle.

(4) At no time shall any person except the traffic commissioner, or a person authorised to do so on his behalf, write on or make any other alteration to a disc.

  [(5) (a) Subject to paragraph (b) and without prejudice to regulation 28, a disc will expire at the end of the last day of the month in which the continuation fee for a licence falls due.

  (b) Neither paragraph (a) nor paragraph (2)(d) apply where a disc is issued under an interim licence or pursuant to an interim direction.

(6) For the purposes of paragraph (5)(a)—

  (a) *"continuation fee"* means the fee numbered (iii) as specified in the Schedule to the Goods Vehicles (Licensing of Operators) (Fees) Regulations 1995 [*not reproduced in this work*]; and

  (b) the month in which such a fee falls due is determined in accordance with that Schedule.]

[*Regulation 23 is printed as amended by SI 2010/455.*   **B32.13**

The amendments to reg.23 by SI 2010/455 do not apply to the modified version of reg.23, which applies to certain foreign goods vehicles and which is set out in Sch.6 to the Goods Vehicles (Licensing of Operators) (Temporary Use in Great Britain) Regulations 1996 (SI 1996/2186), q.v.

A contravention of reg.23(3) or reg.23(4) is an offence under s.57(9) of the 1995 Act; see reg.32 below.]

Temporary addition of a motor vehicle

24. *[Omitted.]*   **B32.14**

Notification of change of address

25. If during the currency of a licence the address for correspondence as noti-   **B32.15**

fied in the licence-holder's application or as subsequently notified under this regulation ceases to be an effective address for correspondence the licence-holder shall within 28 days from the date of such event notify the traffic commissioner by whom the licence was granted of an effective address for correspondence.

B32.16   *[A contravention of reg.25 is an offence under s.57(9) of the 1995 Act; see reg.32 below.]*

Production of licence for examination

B32.17   26.—(1) The licence-holder shall produce the licence for inspection by an officer or a police constable on being required by such a person to do so, and the licence-holder may do so at any operating centre covered by the licence or at his head or principal place of business within the traffic area in which any such operating centre lies or, if the requirement is made by a police constable, at a police station chosen by the licence-holder.

(2) The licence-holder shall comply with any requirement mentioned in paragraph (1) within 14 days of the day on which the requirement is made.

B32.18   *[A contravention of reg.26 is an offence under s.57(9) of the 1995 Act; see reg.32 below.*

As to holding companies and their subsidiaries, see Sch.2, para.3(b), to these regulations below.]

Issue of copies of licences and discs

B32.19   27.—(1) If a licence or disc has been lost, destroyed or defaced, the person to whom it was issued shall forthwith notify in writing the traffic commissioner by whom the licence or disc was issued.

(2) If—

    (a) the traffic commissioner is satisfied that a licence or disc has been lost, destroyed or defaced; and

    (b) in the case of a licence or disc which has been defaced, it is surrendered to the traffic commissioner,

the traffic commissioner shall issue a copy (so marked) which shall have effect as the original licence or disc.

(3) Where a licence or disc has been lost and after a copy has been issued the lost licence or disc is found by or comes into the possession of the licence-holder he shall forthwith return the original licence or disc to the traffic commissioner.

B32.20   *[A contravention of reg.27(1) or reg.27(3) is an offence under s.57(9) of the 1995 Act; see reg.32 below.]*

Return of licences and discs

B32.21   28.—(1) If the licence-holder ceases to use under the licence any motor vehicle specified in the licence he shall within 21 days beginning with the date of ceasing to use the vehicle or vehicles notify the traffic commissioner by whom the licence was issued and return to that traffic commissioner the licence for variation and the disc relating to the vehicle.

(2) If a licence is varied under section 17, 31, 32 or 36 its holder shall, when required by the traffic commissioner so to do, return to the traffic commissioner—

(a) the licence; and

(b) if the number of motor vehicles specified in the licence has been reduced, the disc relating to any vehicle no longer specified in the licence.

(3) If a licence is revoked, surrendered, suspended, curtailed or terminated for any other reason, or if a traffic commissioner has given a direction in respect of a licence under section 26(2), the licence-holder shall on or before the date specified in a notice to that effect, send or deliver to the office of the traffic area of the traffic commissioner by whom the licence was issued—

(a) the licence; and

(b) the disc relating to any motor vehicle which the traffic commissioner may specify,

for cancellation, retention during the time of suspension, or alteration as the case may be.

(4) The notice referred to in paragraph (3) shall be delivered personally to the licence-holder or sent to him by recorded delivery service at the address shown in his application or last notified in accordance with regulation 25.

(5) In the event of the traffic commissioner deciding to make a variation under paragraph 9 of the Schedule to the Goods Vehicles (Licensing of Operators) Act 1995 (Commencement and Transitional Provisions) Order 1995 [*SI 1995/2181*] the licence-holder shall return the licence to the traffic commissioner for him to amend the licence so that it conforms to the variation before returning it to the holder.

[A contravention of reg.28(1), reg.28(2), reg.28(3) or reg.28(5) is an offence **B32.22** *under s.57(9) of the 1995 Act; see reg.32 below and the note thereto.]*

Partnerships

29.—(1) The provision in section 8(2) that a person shall not at the same time **B32.23** hold more than one operator's licence in respect of the same area shall apply so that a firm shall be treated as a person separate from any partner of that firm or an individual in any other partnership.

(2) For the purposes of authorising goods vehicles to be used under section 5(1) when the licence-holder is a firm, any vehicle in the lawful possession of any partner of a firm shall be regarded as in the lawful possession of the firm.

(3) The provisions of section 13(3) shall apply in any case where an applicant for a standard licence is a firm so that the traffic commissioner is required to satisfy himself that—

(a) every one of the partners of that firm is of good repute;

(b) the firm satisfies the requirement of appropriate financial standing; and

(c) either—

(i) if one of the firm's partners manage the road transport business carried on by the firm, he, or if more than one each of whom, is professionally competent, or

(ii) the firm employs a transport manager or transport managers who, or if more than one each of whom, is of good repute and professionally competent.

(4) The provisions of section 13(4) shall apply in any case where an applicant for a restricted licence is a firm so that the traffic commissioner is required to satisfy himself that every one of the partners of that firm is not unfit to hold an operator's licence by reason of any activities or convictions covered by section 34(a) or (b).

(5) The provisions of section 13(6) shall apply in any case where an applicant is a firm and in such case the financial resources referred to in that subsection shall be those of the firm.

(6) *[Application of s.26 to firms.]*

(7) *[Application of s.27(1) to firms.]*

(8) The provisions of section 28 shall apply to the revocation of an operator's licence held by a firm and in such a case the powers conferred by subsections (1) and (4) shall be exercisable in respect of each and every partner of that firm.

(9) Except in a case falling within paragraph (9) [*sic*] any requirement, obligation or prohibition (however expressed) placed on a person making an application or on the licence-holder by, or in pursuance of, a provision in the 1995 Act or these Regulations, shall apply where the licence-holder is a firm and the duty to meet the requirement or obligation or to comply with the prohibition shall apply to the partners of that firm severally as well as jointly.

(10) Where an application is made by, or the licence-holder is a firm a requirement or obligation placed on the applicant or licence-holder by virtue of sections 8(4), 9(1) or 17(2) of the 1995 Act to inform the traffic commissioner of a notifiable conviction within the meaning given in paragraph 4 of Schedule 2 to the 1995 Act shall apply in relation to the notifiable conviction of each partner of that firm, and the duty to meet the requirement shall apply to the person convicted.

(11) The provisions in section 16(5) as to the events on which an operator's licence held by an individual terminates apply in a case where such a licence is held by a firm, if—

    (a) the partnership is dissolved; or

    (b) one or more of the persons dies or becomes a patient within the meaning of Part VII of the Mental Health Act 1983, or …

(12) In Schedule 3 to the 1995 Act —

    (a) the provisions in paragraph 1 as regards determining whether an individual is of good repute apply, in a case of a firm in respect of each of the partners of that firm as they apply to an individual;

    (b) *[applies to para.6 (not reproduced in this work)]*;

    (c) *[applies to para.8(2) (not reproduced in this work)]*; and

    (d) *[applies to paras 10 and 11 (not reproduced in this work)]*.

B32.24   *[The reference in reg.29(9) to "paragraph (9)" is a drafting or typographical error and a reference to "paragraph (10)" might have been intended.*

    The words omitted from reg.29(11)(b) refer expressly and exclusively to Scotland.]

Holding companies and subsidiaries

B32.25   **30.**—(1) A holding company may apply to the traffic commissioner for any traffic area—

(a) if it does not already hold a licence in respect of that area, for the issue of a licence; or

(b) if it already holds a licence in respect of that area, for a variation of its licence by a direction under section 17(1)(a),

which would have the effect, if the application were granted, of including in the licence to be issued to, or already held by, the holding company, goods vehicles in the lawful possession of a subsidiary of that company specified in the application.

(2) An application by a holding company under paragraph (1) shall, unless

(a) the subsidiary is not the licence-holder; or

(b) the licence or variation applied for by the holding company will not take effect until any licence held by the subsidiary has been surrendered or has otherwise terminated,

be accompanied by an application by the subsidiary for the variation of the licence held by the subsidiary by a direction under section 17(1)(b) for the removal therefrom of all or some of the goods vehicles authorised to be used thereunder, being the vehicles to which the application of the holding company relates.

(3) Where a holding company, on an application under paragraph (1), signifies to the traffic commissioner its desire that the provisions of this regulation should have effect as respects a subsidiary of that company, then, in relation to the application and to any licence granted to the holding company, or held by the holding company and varied, on that application, and to the use of any goods vehicles authorised to be used under any such licence, the 1995 Act and these Regulations shall have effect subject to the modifications specified in Schedule 2.

(4) The provisions of this regulation shall cease to have effect as respects a holding company and its subsidiary—

(a) if the holding company gives notice to the traffic commissioner who issued or varied its licence that it desires that this regulation should, as from any date, cease to apply to the holding company and that subsidiary, as from that date; or

(b) as from the date on which that subsidiary ceases to be a subsidiary of that holding company.

(5) *[Publication of notice of application under reg.30(4)(a).]*

(6) Where the provisions of this regulation cease to have effect as respects a holding company and its subsidiary by virtue of paragraph (4)(b) the company which was the holding company shall within 21 days of the event which caused the subsidiary to cease to be a subsidiary of that company—

(a) notify the traffic commissioner by whom the licence was issued, and

(b) supply all material details of the event, and

(c) return to the traffic commissioner the licence and the discs relating to the motor vehicles authorised to be used thereunder,

and in so far as the holding company fails to satisfy those requirements the company which was the subsidiary company shall, on being so directed by the traffic commissioner, within 7 days of that direction supply the details, or return the licence and the discs, as the case may require.

(7) In a case where the applicant for, or the holder of, a standard licence is a holding company and the goods vehicles used, or to be used, under the licence

belong to, or are in the possession of, a subsidiary of that holding company, the provisions of these Regulations apply as if—

    (a) the road transport undertaking and any operating centre of the subsidiary were the road transport undertaking and an operating centre of the holding company;

    (b) for purposes of, or relating to, the reputation and financial standing of the holding company, the activities, relevant convictions and financial resources of the subsidiary were activities, convictions and resources of the holding company; and

    (c) in relation to a transport manager, his employment by the subsidiary were employment by the holding company.

B32.26   *[A contravention of reg.30(6) is an offence under s.57(9) of the 1995 Act; see reg.32 below.]*

Continuance of licence on death, bankruptcy, etc.

B32.27   **31.**—(1) In this regulation, *"actual holder"* in relation to a licence means the person to whom the licence was issued.

(2) This regulation applies in the event—

    (a) of the death of the actual holder of a licence;

    (b) of the actual holder of a licence becoming a patient under Part VII of the Mental Health Act 1983, or …;

    (c) of the bankruptcy of the actual holder of a licence;

    (d) in the case of a company, of the actual holder of a licence going into liquidation or an administration order being made in relation to the actual holder; or

    (e) of the appointment of a receiver or manager of the trade or business of the actual holder of a licence.

(3) After the happening of either of the events mentioned in paragraphs (2)(a) or (b) the traffic commissioner may direct that the licence shall not be treated as terminated when the actual holder died or became a patient but suspended until the date when a direction under paragraph (4) comes into force.

(4) After the happening of any of the events mentioned in paragraph (2) the traffic commissioner may direct that a person carrying on the trade or business of the actual holder of the licence is to be treated for the purposes of the 1995 Act as if he were the holder thereof for such purpose and to such extent as is specified in the direction for a period not exceeding—

    (a) if it appears to the traffic commissioner that there are special circumstances, 18 months;

    (b) in any other case, 12 months,

from the date of the coming into force of that direction.

(5) The powers under paragraph (4) shall be exercisable in relation to a standard licence whether or not the person carrying on the trade or business of the actual holder of the licence satisfies the requirement of professional competence.

(6) Where a person is treated as if he were the licence-holder by virtue of a direction under this regulation—

    (a) any goods vehicle which had been in the lawful possession of the actual holder of the licence shall for the purposes of the 1995 Act be treated as if it was in the lawful possession of that person; and

(b) if the licence is a standard licence, nothing in section 27 shall oblige the traffic commissioner to revoke the licence by reason only of that person not satisfying the requirement of professional competence.

[The words omitted from reg.31(2)(b) relate expressly and exclusively to Scotland.]   **B32.28**

Offences

32. Any contravention of, or failure to comply with, a provision in regulations   **B32.29**
23(3), 23(4), 25, 26, 27(1), 27(3), 28(1), 28(2), 28(3), 28(4) *[sic]* or 30(6), is hereby declared to be an offence and for the purposes of section 57(9) any provision mentioned above shall be regarded as made under the 1995 Act.

*[The reference in reg.32 to reg."28(4)" would appear to be a drafting or   **B32.30**
typographical error; it is probable that a reference to reg.28(5) was intended.]*

Classes of vehicle for which a licence is not required

33.—(1) The classes of vehicle specified under section 2(2)(d) as those to   **B32.31**
which section 2(1) does not apply are the classes mentioned in Part I of Schedule 3.

(2) The relevant plated weight of a goods vehicle, for the purposes of Schedule 1 to the 1995 Act (meaning of *"small goods vehicle"*) is the gross weight not to be exceeded in Great Britain of the vehicle as shown on a Ministry plate as defined in column 2 of the Table in regulation 3(2) of the Road Vehicles (Construction and Use) Regulations 1986 or, if no such plate has been issued in respect of that vehicle, the maximum gross weight of the vehicle as shown on a plate affixed to the vehicle by virtue of regulation 66 of those Regulations.

Period for service of notice of review on ground of procedural irregularity

34. *[Omitted.]*   **B32.32**

Manner of service of notice of review on ground of procedural irregularity

35. *[Omitted.]*   **B32.33**

Meaning of "relevant weight"

36.—(1) A motor vehicle or trailer of any prescribed class referred to in sec-   **B32.34**
tion 5(3) means any vehicle described in section 2(1) as needing an operator's licence, and the relevant weight of such a vehicle is its revenue weight.

(2) For purposes of this regulation *"revenue weight"* shall have the meaning given in section 60A of the Vehicle Excise and Registration Act 1994 *[q.v.]*.

(3) In its application to this regulation, section 60A of that Act shall have effect as if—

(a) subsection (6) of that section were omitted; and

(b) no provision had been made under section 61A(2) of that Act.

SCHEDULE 1

NOTICE OF APPLICATION FOR A LICENCE OR A VARIATION OF A LICENCE

[Omitted.]   **B32.35**

MODIFICATIONS IN RELATION TO HOLDING COMPANIES AND SUBSIDIARIES

B32.36   1. The 1995 Act and these Regulations have effect as if any reference (except in this Schedule) to a provision which is modified by this Schedule were a reference to that provision as so modified.

B32.37   2. The 1995 Act has effect as if—

(a) goods vehicles in the lawful possession of the subsidiary were in the lawful possession of the holding company;

(b) where a goods vehicle is used in circumstances in which, but for the provisions of regulation 30, the subsidiary would be deemed to be the user, the holding company were the user;

(c) a trade or business carried on by the subsidiary were carried on by the holding company;

(d) the subsidiary were an applicant for the grant or variation of the licence;

(e) any operating centre of the subsidiary were an operating centre of the holding company;

(f) any person who is a director of the subsidiary were a director of the holding company;

(g) any person who is an employee of the subsidiary were an employee of the holding company;

(h) *[modification of s.10(1) (not reproduced in this work)]*;

(i) in section 22(1) the reference in paragraph (b) to persons holding shares in the company included a reference to persons holding shares in the subsidiary, and the reference in paragraph (c) to the licence-holder included a reference to the subsidiary;

(j) *[modification of s.17(3) (not reproduced in this work)]*;

(k)–

(m) *[modification of s.26(1) and s.26(5) (not reproduced in this work)]*;

(n) in section 28(1) the reference to the licence-holder included a reference to the subsidiary;

(o) in section 28(4)(a) after sub-paragraph (ii) there were inserted the following sub-paragraph —

"(iii) a company which is a subsidiary of such a company; or";

(p) in section 28(5) there were substituted for paragraph (a) "where that person is a company or other body corporate which is the licence-holder in respect of a subsidiary of that company or other body corporate in pursuance of Regulations made under section 46 of this Act, in relation to any director of that company or other body corporate or of that subsidiary.".

B32.38   3. These Regulations shall have effect as if—

(a) *[modifies reg.8 (not reproduced in this work)]*;

(b) in regulation 26 the reference to the licence-holder included a reference to the subsidiary.

CLASSES OF VEHICLES FOR WHICH A LICENCE IS NOT REQUIRED

PART I

B32.39   1. Any tractor as defined in paragraph 4(3) of Part IV of Schedule 1 to the Vehicle Excise and Registration Act 1994 (as originally enacted) while being used for one or more of the purposes specified in Part II of this Schedule.

B32.40   2. A dual-purpose vehicle and any trailer drawn by it.

3. A vehicle used on a road only in passing from private premises to other private premises in the immediate neighbourhood belonging (except in the case of a vehicle so used only in connection with excavation or demolition) to the same person, provided that the distance travelled on a road by any such vehicle does not exceed in the aggregate 9.654 kilometres, (6 miles), in any one week.   **B32.41**

4. A motor vehicle constructed or adapted primarily for the carriage of passengers and their effects, and any trailer drawn by it, while being so used.   **B32.42**

5. A vehicle which is being used for funerals.   **B32.43**

6. A vehicle which is being used for police, fire brigade [or, in England [or Wales], fire and rescue authority] or ambulance [or Serious Organised Crime Agency] purposes.   **B32.44**

7. A vehicle which is being used for fire-fighting or rescue operations at mines.   **B32.45**

8. A vehicle on which no permanent body has been constructed, which is being used only for carrying burden which either is carried solely for the purpose of test or trial, or consists of articles and equipment which will form part of the completed vehicle when the body is constructed.   **B32.46**

9. A vehicle which is being used under a trade licence.   **B32.47**

10. A vehicle in the service of a visiting force or of a headquarters.   **B32.48**

11. A vehicle used by or under the control of Her Majesty's United Kingdom forces.   **B32.49**

12. A trailer not constructed primarily for the carriage of goods but which is being used incidentally for that purpose in connection with the construction, maintenance or repair of roads.   **B32.50**

13. A road roller and any trailer drawn by it.   **B32.51**

14. A vehicle while being used under the direction of HM Coastguard or of the Royal National Lifeboat Institution for the carriage of life-boats, life-saving appliances or crew.   **B32.52**

15. A vehicle fitted with a machine, appliance, apparatus or other contrivance which is a permanent or essentially permanent fixture, provided that the only goods carried on the vehicle are—   **B32.53**

    (a) required for use in connection with the machine, appliance, apparatus or contrivance or the running of the vehicle;

    (b) to be mixed by the machine, appliance, apparatus or contrivance with other goods not carried on the vehicle on a road in order to thrash, grade, clean or chemically treat grain;

    (c) to be mixed by the machine, appliance, apparatus or contrivance with other goods not carried on the vehicle in order to make fodder for animals; or

    (d) mud or other matter swept up from the surface of a road by the use of the machine, appliance, apparatus or other contrivance.

16. A vehicle while being used by a local authority for the purposes of the enactments relating to weights and measures or the sale of food and drugs.   **B32.54**

17. A vehicle while being used by a local authority in the discharge of any function conferred on or exercisable by that authority under Regulations made under the Civil Defence Act 1948.   **B32.55**

18. A steam-propelled vehicle.   **B32.56**

19. A tower wagon or trailer drawn thereby, provided that the only goods carried on the trailer are goods required for use in connection with the work on which the tower wagon is ordinarily used as such.   **B32.57**

20. A vehicle while being used for the carriage of goods within an aerodrome within the meaning of section 105(1) of the Civil Aviation Act 1982.   **B32.58**

21. An electrically propelled vehicle.   **B32.59**

22. A showman's goods vehicle and any trailer drawn thereby.   **B32.60**

[**23.** A vehicle which is being used to carry out a cabotage operation consisting of   **B32.61** national carriage for hire or reward on a temporary basis in the United Kingdom in accordance with the provisions of Regulation (EC) No.1072/2009 of the European Parliament and of the Council of 21 October 2009 on common rules for access to the international road haulage market.]

B32.62   **24.** A goods vehicle first used before 1 January 1977 which has an unladen weight not exceeding 1525 kilograms and for which the maximum gross weight, as shown on a plate affixed to the vehicle by virtue of regulation 66 of the Motor Vehicles (Construction and Use) Regulations 1986 or any provision which that regulation replaced, exceeds 3500 kilograms but does not exceed 3556.21 kilograms (3^1/$_2$ tons).

B32.63   **25.** A vehicle while being used by a highway authority for the purposes of section 196 of the Road Traffic Act 1988.

B32.64   **26.** A vehicle being held ready for use in an emergency by an undertaking for the supply of water, electricity, gas or telephone services.

B32.65   **27.** A recovery vehicle.

B32.66   **28.** A vehicle which is being used for snow clearing, or for the distribution of grit, salt or other materials on frosted, icebound or snow-covered roads or for going to or from the place where it is to be used for the said purposes or for any other purpose directly connected with those purposes.

B32.67   **29.** A vehicle proceeding to or from a station provided by the Secretary of State under section 45 of the Road Traffic Act 1988 for the purposes of an examination of that vehicle under that section provided that—

    (a) the only load being carried is a load required for the purposes of the examination; and

    (b) it is being carried at the request of the Secretary of State.

B32.68   *[Part I of Sch.3 is printed as amended by SI 2004/3168; SI 2005/2929; SI 2006/594; SI 2010/455.]*

Part II

Purposes Referred to in Paragraph 1 of Part I of this Schedule

B32.69   **1.** Hauling—

    (a) threshing appliances;

    (b) farming implements;

    (c) a living van for the accommodation of persons employed to drive the tractor; or

    (d) supplies of water or fuel required for the tractor.

B32.70   **2.** Hauling articles for a farm required by the keeper, being either the occupier of the farm or a contractor employed to do agricultural work on the farm by the occupier of the farm.

B32.71   **3.** Hauling articles for a forestry estate required by the keeper where the keeper is the occupier of that estate or employed to do forestry work on the estate by the occupier or a contractor employed to do forestry work on the estate by the occupier.

B32.72   **4.** Hauling within 24.135 kilometres, (15 miles), of a farm or a forestry estate occupied by the keeper, agricultural or woodland produce of that farm or estate.

B32.73   **5.** Hauling within 24.135 kilometres, (15 miles), of a farm or a forestry estate occupied by the keeper, material to be spread on roads to deal with frost, ice or snow.

B32.74   **6.** Hauling a snow plough or a similar contrivance for the purpose of clearing snow; and

B32.75   **7.** Hauling—

    (a) soil for landscaping or similar works; or

    (b) a mowing machine,

where the keeper is a local authority.

SCHEDULE 4

Inquiries

[Omitted.] **B32.76**

SCHEDULE 5

List of Regulations Revoked

[Omitted.] **B32.77**

The Public Service Vehicles (Operators' Licences) Regulations 1995

(SI 1995/2908)

B33.01 *[The text of these regulations has been amended by:*

the Postal Services Act 2000 (Consequential Modifications No.1) Order 2001 (SI 2001/1149) (March 26, 2001);

the Public Service Vehicles (Operators' Licences) (Amendment) Regulations 2009 (SI 2009/786) (April 20, 2009); and

the Public Service Vehicles (Operators' Licences) (Amendment) Regulations 2010 (SI 2010/452) (April 1, 2010).

The amending instruments are referred to in the principal regulations only by their years and numbers. The dates referred to above are the dates on which the amending instruments came into force.]

ARRANGEMENT OF REGULATIONS

Regulation

Citation and commencement

B33.02   **1.** *[Omitted.]*

Revocation

  2. *[Omitted.]*   **B33.03**

Interpretation

  3.—(1) In these Regulations, unless the context otherwise requires—   **B33.04**
       "the 1981 Act" means the Public Passenger Vehicles Act 1981 [*q.v.*];
       "the 1985 Act" means the Transport Act 1985;
       "designated sporting event" has the same meaning as in the Sporting
          Events (Control of Alcohol) Act 1985;
       "disc" means an operator's disc issued under section 18 [*q.v.*];
       "fax" means the making of a facsimile copy of a document by the trans-
          mission of electronic signals;
       "holder" in relation to a licence means the person to whom that licence
          was granted;
       "licence" means a PSV operator's licence and *"special licence"* has the
          same meaning as in section 12(2) of the 1985 Act [*q.v.*];
       "local authority" has the meaning given by section 14A(4);
      [*"notice of election"* means a notice for the purposes of regulation 11(4) of
          these Regulations served prior to 20th April 2009;]
       "Notices and Proceedings" has the same meaning as in regulation 3 of the
          Public Service Vehicles (Traffic Commissioners: Publications and
          Inquiries) Regulations 1986 [*SI 1986/1629; not reproduced in this
          work*];
       "traffic regulation conditions" has the meaning given by section 7(1) of
          the 1985 Act; and
       "vehicle examiner" means an examiner appointed under section 66A of the
          Road Traffic Act 1988 [*q.v.*].
   (2) Unless the context otherwise requires, any reference in these Regulations
to:
     (a) a numbered section is a reference to the section bearing that number
         in the 1981 Act;
     (b) a numbered regulation is a reference to the regulation bearing that
         number in these Regulations;
     (c) a numbered paragraph is a reference to the paragraph bearing that
         number in the regulation in which the reference appears.
  [Regulation 3 is printed as amended by SI 2009/786.]   **B33.05**

Inspection of applications

  4. *[Omitted.]*   **B33.06**

Objections to applications for licences

  5. *[Omitted.]*   **B33.07**

Determination of applications

  6. *[Omitted.]*   **B33.08**

Description of conditions attached to licences

B33.09   7. *[Omitted.]*

Requirements of notice and consideration of representations

B33.10   **8., 9.** *[Omitted.]*

Forms of and particulars to be contained on discs

B33.11   **10.**—(1) There shall be specified on every disc the date on which it [...] expires.

(2) The disc shall clearly indicate (by colour or other means)—

(a) whether a vehicle is being used under a standard licence or under a restricted licence; and

(b) in the case of a vehicle being used under a standard licence, whether the licence covers both international and national transport operations or national transport operations only.

B33.12   *[Regulation 10 is printed as amended by SI 2010/452.]*

[The expiry of discs

B33.13   **11.**—(1) Without prejudice to regulations 14 and 15, a disc shall expire at the end of the 5 year period specified in paragraph (2).

(2) The 5 year period referred to in paragraph (1) is the latest of—

(a) the period of 5 years beginning with the first day of the month in which the relevant licence comes into force and ending immediately before the fifth anniversary of that day; and

(b) each subsequent consecutive period of 5 years.]

B33.14   *[Regulation 11 was amended by SI 2009/786 and is printed as substituted by SI 2010/452.]*

Manner in which discs are to be fixed and exhibited

B33.15   **12.** The prescribed manner in which a disc is to be fixed and exhibited for the purposes of section 18 is by so fixing it to the vehicle that it—

(a) is adjacent to the licence issued under the Vehicle Excise and Registration Act 1994 [*q.v.*];

(b) does not interfere unduly with the driver's view; and

(c) can easily be read in daylight from the outside of the vehicle.

Issue of a duplicate licence or disc and prohibition on unauthorised alteration of a disc

B33.16   **13.**—(1) If a licence or disc has been lost or destroyed, the holder shall forthwith notify the traffic commissioner who granted the licence or disc so that he may provide a duplicate, marked as such.

(2) If a licence or disc has been notified as lost or destroyed in accordance with paragraph (1) and is subsequently recovered by the holder, then the holder shall use the duplicate licence or disc and return the original to the traffic commissioner.

(3) At no time shall any person except the traffic commissioner, or a person authorised to do so on his behalf, write on or otherwise alter a disc, but in the event that a disc becomes illegible by ordinary wear and tear the holder shall forthwith return the illegible disc so that the traffic commissioner may provide a duplicate, marked as such.

Compulsory return of licences and discs

14.—(1) In the event of the suspension, surrender or other termination—   **B33.17**

    (a) at any time of a continuous licence; or

    (b) prior to the date of expiry specified in a term licence,

the holder shall return that licence to the traffic commissioner by whom it was granted for retention during the time of the suspension, or for cancellation, as the case may be, and shall at the same time return to that commissioner any discs which have been issued in relation to the licence.

(2) On the removal of a suspension referred to in paragraph (1) the commissioner shall return the licence together with any discs which were issued in relation to the licence.

(3) In the event of the traffic commissioner deciding—

    (a) to attach an additional condition or any traffic regulation conditions to a licence;

    (b) to alter or remove a condition or any traffic regulation conditions attached to a licence; or

    (c) to vary or remove any undertaking in a licence,

the holder shall return that licence to the traffic commissioner for him to make the appropriate addition, alteration, variation or removal before returning it to the holder.

(4) In the event of the traffic commissioner deciding to vary one or more conditions attached to a licence under section 16(1), so reducing the maximum number of vehicles which may be used under the licence below the number of discs which have been issued to the holder, the holder shall return to that commissioner such number of discs as will leave the holder with only the same number of discs as is equal to the reduced maximum number of vehicles.

(5) In the event of a disc ceasing to have effect prior to the date of expiry, the holder shall return the disc to the traffic commissioner who issued it.

(6) For the purposes of this regulation, a requirement to return a licence or disc to a traffic commissioner is a requirement for it to be—

    (a) delivered to the office of his traffic area; or

    (b) sent to the traffic commissioner at the office of his traffic area by recorded delivery service,

within the period of 14 days beginning with the date on which the holder receives the notice from the traffic commissioner requiring it to be returned.

(7) For the purposes of this regulation, if a licence or disc is sent by recorded delivery service in accordance with paragraph (6), it shall be regarded as having been returned at the date that it is delivered at the appropriate office in the traffic area.

(8) In this regulation—

"*term licence*" means a licence which by virtue of the Deregulation and Contracting Out (Commencement) (No.4) Order 1995 [*SI 1995/2835*], has an expiry date; and

"*continuous licence*" means a licence that is not a term licence.

Voluntary return of discs

B33.18   **15.** *[Omitted.]*

Production of licences and discs for examination

B33.19   **16.**—(1) Unless its loss or destruction has been previously notified to the traffic commissioner in accordance with regulation 13(1) or (2), a licence or a disc shall be produced by the holder for examination if he is so required by any police constable, vehicle examiner or by any person authorised by the traffic commissioner for any traffic area to examine the licence or disc, and any such requirement shall be complied with in not more than 14 days.

(2) Any such requirement as is mentioned in paragraph (1) may be complied with by the holder producing the licence or disc within the traffic area of the traffic commissioner by whom the licence was granted at the operating centre or principal place of business of the holder.

Notification of decisions

B33.20   **17.** *[Omitted.]*

Review of decisions

B33.21   **18.** *[Omitted.]*

Notices generally

B33.22   **19.** *[Omitted.]*

Notification of change of address

B33.23   **20.** If during the currency of a licence the address for correspondence as notified in the licence holder's application or as subsequently notified under this regulation ceases to be an effective address for correspondence the holder shall within 28 days from the date of such event notify the traffic commissioner by whom the licence was granted of an effective address for correspondence.

Relevant convictions

B33.24   **21.** The convictions specified in the Schedule hereto are hereby prescribed as relevant convictions for the purposes of the 1981 Act.

Operators under hiring arrangements

B33.25   **22.** The person who is to be regarded as the operator of a vehicle which is made available by one holder of a licence to another under a hiring arrangement is the holder from whom the vehicle is hired in a case where—

(a) the holder to whom the vehicle is hired is not, under the hiring arrangement, entitled to keep the vehicle in his possession for a total period of more than 14 days;

(b) not less than 14 days have elapsed between the finish of any previous period (of whatever duration) in which the hirer to whom the vehicle is hired was entitled to the use of the vehicle under a hiring arrangement with the holder from whom the vehicle is hired and the start of the period mentioned in sub-paragraph (a) above;

(c) at all times when the vehicle is being used for carrying passengers for hire or reward during the period mentioned in sub-paragraph (a) above there is affixed to the vehicle a disc which has been issued to the holder from whom the vehicle is hired;

(d) the vehicle, if made available to the holder of a restricted licence, is not adapted to carry more than sixteen passengers; and

(e) the vehicle is not a licensed taxi made available to or by the holder of a special licence.

Termination of licences held by companies

23. In a case where a licence is held by a company the events relating to the holder on the occurrence of which the licence is to terminate are as follows— **B33.26**

    (a) the making of a winding-up order; and

    (b) the passing of a resolution for voluntary winding-up.

Computation of time

24. Any day which is a bank holiday under the Banking and Financial Dealings Act 1971 shall be excluded from the computation of any period of a specified number of days prescribed in these Regulations. **B33.27**

[As to bank holidays under the Banking and Financial Dealings Act 1971, see the note to the Road Vehicles (Construction and Use) Regulations 1986 (SI 1986/ 1078) Sch.12, para.1 above.] **B33.28**

[Universal Service Providers]

25. Section 16(1A) (limit on number of vehicles to be used under a restricted licence) shall not apply in respect of a licence held at any time by [a universal service provider (within the meaning of the Postal Services Act 2000) for any purposes in connection with the provision of a universal postal service (within the meaning of that Act)]. **B33.29**

[Regulation 25 is printed as amended by SI 2001/1149.] **B33.30**

Savings

26. Notwithstanding the revocation of the Public Service Vehicles (Operators' Licences) Regulations 1986 by these Regulations, regulation 12(3) of those Regulations (which require a licence to be returned if its period of validity is curtailed) shall continue to have effect in relation to a licence if its period of validity is curtailed before 1st January 1996. **B33.31**

Regulation 21   SCHEDULE

RELEVANT CONVICTIONS PRESCRIBED BY REGULATION 21

1. A conviction of any of the offences specified in paragraph 2 below— **B33.32**

(a) of the holder of a licence, or the applicant for a licence;

(b) where the holder of a licence, or the applicant for a licence, is a partnership, of a partner in that partnership;

(c) of any transport manager whom the holder of a licence employs or proposes to employ, and of any transport manager whom an applicant for a licence employs or proposes to employ; and

(d) of any person appointed or otherwise engaged as an officer, employee or agent of the holder of, or of an applicant for, a licence in relation to any business which such holder or applicant carries on, or proposes to carry on.

B33.33 **2.** The offences referred to in paragraph 1 above are offences in relation to a public service vehicle or the operation thereof—

(a) under or by virtue of the 1981 Act;

(b) under sections 5(1), 8(1), 11, 13, 16(1), 17(4) and 18(3) of the Road Traffic Regulation Act 1984;

(c) under section 1(2) of the Sporting Events (Control of Alcohol, etc.) Act 1985;

(d) under or by virtue of Parts I and II and section 101 of the 1985 Act;

(e) under or by virtue of Parts I, II, III, IV and VI and sections 164(6) and (9), 165(3) and (6), 168, 170(7), 171(2), 172(3) and (4), 173(1), 174(1) and (2) and (5) in Part VII of the Road Traffic Act 1988;

(f) under section 91 of the Road Traffic Offenders Act 1988;

(g) relating to—

　(i) the speed at which vehicles may be driven,

　(ii) drivers' hours or the keeping of drivers' records under or by virtue of Part VI of the Transport Act 1968,

　(iii) new bus grants under section 32 of, and Schedule 8 to, the Transport Act 1968, grants towards bus fuel duty under section 92 of the Finance Act 1965,

　(iv) a duty of excise imposed by or under the Vehicles (Excise) Act 1971 or the Vehicle Excise and Registration Act 1994, and

(h) *[applies to Scotland;]*

or other offences under the law in force in any part of Great Britain which are serious offences as defined in paragraph 1(4) of Schedule 3 [*q.v.*] or road transport offences as defined in paragraph 1(5) of that Schedule.

B33.34 *[The Sporting Events (Control of Alcohol, etc.) Act 1985 s.1(2) (to which reference is made in para.2(c)) prohibits specified persons from knowingly causing or permitting alcohol to be carried on a vehicle to which s.1 applies, e.g. a public service vehicle used to carry passengers to or from a designated sporting event.]*

The Private Crossings (Signs and Barriers) Regulations 1996

(SI 1996/1786)

ARRANGEMENT OF REGULATIONS

PART I
PRELIMINARY

*   *   *

PART I

PRELIMINARY

Citation and commencement

B34.02   **1.** *[Omitted.]*

Interpretation

B34.03   **2.**—(1) In these Regulations, where the context so admits, the following expressions have the meanings hereby respectively assigned to them—

> *"crossing"* means a level crossing;
>
> *"crossing operator"* means an operator of a railway or tramway that is crossed in any place by a relevant road or a private path;
>
> *"relevant road"* means a private road that crosses, or a private road and a private path that cross, a railway or tramway;
>
> *"retroreflecting material"* means material which reflects a ray of light back towards the source of that light;
>
> *"sign"* includes a road marking and a light signal;
>
> *"the 1992 Act"* means the Transport and Works Act 1992 [*q.v.*];
>
> *"the 1994 Regulations"* means the Traffic Signs Regulations and General Directions 1994 [*SI 1994/1519*].

(2) Except where otherwise provided, any reference in these Regulations to a numbered regulation or Schedule shall be construed as a reference to the regulation or Schedule bearing that number in these Regulations and any reference in these Regulations to a numbered diagram shall be construed as a reference to the diagram bearing that number in Schedule 1 to these Regulations.

B34.04   *[The 1994 Regulations referred to in reg.2(1) above have been revoked by the Traffic Signs Regulations and General Directions 2002 (SI 2002/3113) (q.v.). The 1994 Regulations may be found in the twentieth edition of this work.]*

PART II

GENERAL PROVISIONS

Signs to be of the size, colour and type shown in diagrams

B34.05   **3.** Subject to the provisions of these Regulations, for the purposes of section 52 of the 1992 Act, a crossing operator may cause or permit the placement on or near the relevant road or private path of a sign of a size, colour and type described and shown—

> (a) in a diagram in Schedule 1; or
>
> (b) in a diagram in Schedule 3 to the 1994 Regulations; or
>
> (c) in one of the diagrams numbered 601.1, 602, 953.1 and 953.2, 963.3, 966, 971, 1001, 1002.1, 1003, 1003.2, 1004, 1004.1, 1005, 1005.1, 1008, 1008.1, 1010, 1012.1, 1013.1, 1014, 1022, 1023, 1026, 1045, 3000.3, 3000.4, 3000.5, 3000.6, 3013, 3013.1, 3013.2, 3013.3,

3013.4, 3013.5 and 3014 in Schedules 2, 5, 6 and 8 to the 1994 Regulations.

[The 1994 Regulations have been revoked by the Traffic Signs Regulations   **B34.06**
and General Directions 2002 (SI 2002/3113) (q.v.). References to the 1994
Regulations should be construed in the light of the 2002 Regulations. The 1994
Regulations may be found in the twentieth edition of this work.]

PART III

SIGNS SHOWN IN SCHEDULE 1

Colours of backs of signs

4. The back of any sign shown in a diagram in Schedule 1 and any post or   **B34.07**
other structure specially provided for mounting the sign shall be coloured black
or grey.

Dimensions

5.—(1) Any variation in a dimension specified in Schedule 1 shall be treated as   **B34.08**
permitted by these Regulations if the variation is not more than 5% more or less
than the dimension specified.

(2) In the diagrams in Schedule 1 the dimensions given are expressed in
millimetres.

Permitted variants

6.—(1) Where the circumstances so require the indication given by a sign   **B34.09**
shown in a diagram in Schedule 1 may be varied in the respect (if any) shown
below the diagram relating to that sign.

(2) Where a sign in a diagram in Schedule 1 contains an indication as to the
penalty relating to a failure to obey the requirements on that sign, the indication
of the penalty may be varied when necessary to accord with changes in the legislation governing the nature and level of penalty.

Illumination of signs

7.—(1) Subject to paragraphs (2) and (3) of this regulation all parts other than   **B34.10**
the back of every sign shown in a diagram in Schedule 1 shall be illuminated by
means of retroreflecting material.

(2) No retroreflecting material shall be applied to—

    (a) any part of a sign coloured black; or

    (b) the red and green lights in the signs shown in diagrams 107 and 108
        and prescribed in regulation 8.

(3) Retroreflecting material need not be applied to a sign at a crossing which is
not used by motor vehicles.

Miniature stop lights

8.—(1) The signs shown in diagrams 107 and 108 shall contain red and green   **B34.11**
lamps which are internally illuminated by a steady light in such a manner that—

(a) when one light is illuminated the other is not illuminated;

(b) the green lamp is and remains illuminated for so long as no railway or tramway vehicle is approaching the vicinity of the crossing from either direction; and

(c) the red lamp is and remains illuminated for so long as the green lamp is not illuminated.

(2) The lenses of the lamps shall be—

(a) circular and not less than 60 millimetres in diameter; or

(b) rectangular with each side measuring not less than 60 millimetres;

and the distance between the edges of the lenses of the green lamp and the red lamp shall be not less than 40 millimetres.

(3) The information, warnings, requirements and prohibitions conveyed by the lamps described in paragraphs (1) and (2) shall be as follows—

(a) the red lamp when illuminated shall convey the warning that a railway or tramway vehicle is approaching the vicinity of the crossing and the prohibition that persons must not proceed across the crossing;

(b) the green lamp when illuminated shall convey the information that no railway or tramway vehicle is approaching the vicinity of the crossing and persons may proceed across the crossing;

(c) if neither the red nor green lamp is illuminated persons should either telephone the crossing operator or proceed across the crossing with caution after having ascertained that no railway or tramway vehicle is approaching the vicinity of the crossing in accordance with the instructions shown on the sign.

PART IV

SIGNS SHOWN IN THE 1994 REGULATIONS

Proportions and significance, etc., of signs

B34.12   9. The provisions made by the 1994 Regulations in relation to the proportions, illumination and significance of, and requirements conveyed by, a sign shall have effect where the sign is placed under the authority of these Regulations, as if the relevant road or private path on or near to which it is placed were a road within the meaning of the Road Traffic Regulation Act 1984 [*q.v.*].

B34.13   *[The 1994 Regulations referred to above have been revoked by the Traffic Signs Regulations and General Directions 2002 (SI 2002/3113) (q.v.). The 1994 Regulations may be found in the twentieth edition of this work.]*

PART V

BARRIERS

Barriers to be of the character described in Schedule 2 or Schedule 3

B34.14   10. For the purposes of section 52 of the 1992 Act, where a railway or tramway is crossed in any place by a relevant road, the operator of that railway or tramway may cause or permit a barrier to be placed on or near the relevant road near the crossing if it is, in the case of a gate, of the character described in Schedule 2, or, in the case of any other form of barrier, of the character described in Schedule 3.

PART VI

SIGNS RELATING TO TELEPHONES

Placement of signs relating to telephones

11. The authority which these Regulations give for the placement of signs re-   **B34.15**
lating to telephones at a crossing shall only apply where telephones are, or are to be, provided on both sides of the crossing and connected direct to the crossing operator.

Regulation 3   SCHEDULE 1

CROSSING SIGNS

[The diagrams representing the actual traffic signs are not reproduced in this   **B34.16**
*work, but the signs in Schedule 1 are described below by means of (in the main)
the legends accompanying the signs. The dimensions of the components of the
various signs are specified in marks accompanying the diagrams (not reproduced) and variations of wording (where permissible) are referred to in notes accompanying the diagrams (not reproduced).*

101   warning signs for non-vehicular crossing ("Stop Look Listen
        Beware of trains") (black lettering on white background with red
        border) (permitted variant: "tram" for "trains")

102   instructions for use at vehicular crossing without telephone (top
        panel: "Stop Look Listen Notify crossing operator before crossing
        with a vehicle which is unusually long, wide, low, heavy or slow
        moving"; lower panel includes advice on crossing and maximum
        penalty for offence) (top panel, white lettering on red background;
        lower panel, black lettering on white background) (permitted
        variant: telephone number of crossing operator may be added)

103   instructions for use at vehicular crossing with telephone (top panel:
        "Stop Always telephone before crossing with vehicles or animals
        to find out if there is time to cross. Tell the crossing operator if the
        vehicle is large or slow moving"; lower panel includes advice on
        crossing and maximum penalty for offence) (top panel, white
        lettering on red background; lower panel, black lettering on white
        background)

104   operating instructions for barrier ("Hold down to lower Maximum
        penalty for not closing barriers £1000 Pump to raise both barriers
        In the event of failure phone crossing operator") (black lettering
        and border on white background)

105   indication of penalty for failure to shut gate at vehicular crossing
        (black lettering and border on white background)

106   target for crossing gate (circle on red background)

107   sign for use with miniature stop lights at crossing with telephone ("Red [circular lamp on black square] STOP Green [circular lamp on black square] Clear IF NO LIGHT—PHONE CROSSING OPERATOR") (black lettering and border on white background) (permitted variant: lenses of lamps may be rectangular instead of circular)

108   sign for use with miniature stop lights at crossing without telephone ("Red [circular lamp on black square] STOP Green [circular lamp on black square] Clear IF NO LIGHT—PROCEED WITH CAUTION") (black lettering and border on white background) (permitted variant: lenses of lamps may be rectangular instead of circular)

109   instructions for use at crossing with miniature stop lights and user-operated gates (black lettering and border on white background)

110   instructions for use at crossing with miniature stop lights and user-operated barriers (black lettering and border on white background)

111   reminder to close gates at crossing with user-operated gates (black lettering and border on white background)

112   reminder to lower barriers at crossing with user-operated barriers (black lettering and border on white background)

113   special sign for use at vehicular crossing where railway or tramway is equipped with overhead electric wire and road approaches are on a gradient (black lettering, symbols and border with white background) (permitted variant: telephone number of operator may be added)

114   instructions to non-vehicular traffic at crossing with miniature stop lights (black lettering and border on white background)

115   instructions to shut and fasten gate at crossing with gates (black lettering and border on white background)

116   danger sign for use at crossing where railway or tramway is equipped with overhead electric wires (word "DANGER" and flash symbol in red; other lettering in black; white background with no border)

117   danger sign for use at crossing where track has electric live rail or rails (word "DANGER"and flash symbol in red; other lettering in black; white background with no border)

118   supplementary sign for use with diagram 103 or diagram 107 where crossing used for animal traffic (black lettering on white background with red border)

119   instructions to horse riders to dismount at crossing where railway or tramway is equipped with overhead electric wires]

Regulation 10   SCHEDULE 2

GATES

B34.17   *[Omitted.]*

Regulation 10   SCHEDULE 3

BARRIERS OTHER THAN GATES

B34.18   *[Omitted.]*

The Goods Vehicles (Licensing of Operators) (Temporary Use in Great Britain) Regulations 1996

(SI 1996/2186)

[The text of these regulations has been amended by: **B35.01**

the Postal Services Act 2000 (Consequential Modifications No.1) Order 2001 (SI 2001/1149) (March 26, 2001);

the Goods Vehicles (Licensing of Operators) (Temporary Use in Great Britain) (Amendment) Regulations 2004 (SI 2004/462) (March 19, 2004); and

the Goods Vehicles (Licensing of Operators) (Temporary Use in Great Britain) (Amendment) Regulations 2010 (SI 2010/804) (April 19, 2010; except for the purposes of reg.2(1), (2) and (3), May 14, 2010; and reg.2(4) and (5), December 4, 2011).

The amending instruments are referred to in the principal regulations only by their years and numbers. The dates referred to above are the dates on which the amending instruments came into force.]

ARRANGEMENT OF REGULATIONS

Regulation

SCHEDULES

Schedule

*   *   *

Citation and commencement

B35.02   **1.** *[Omitted.]*

Revocation

B35.03   **2.** *[Omitted.]*

Interpretation

B35.04   **3.**—(1) In these Regulations —

"*the Act*" means the Goods Vehicles (Licensing of Operators) Act 1995 [*q.v.*];

[...]

"*foreign goods vehicle*" means a goods vehicle—

(a) which is operated by a person who is not established in the United Kingdom and has been brought temporarily into Great Britain;

(b) which is not being used for international carriage by a haulier who is established in a Member State other than the United Kingdom;

(c) which is engaged in carrying goods by road on a journey some part of which has taken place, or will take place, outside the United Kingdom; and

(d) which, [(except in the case of use in a cabotage operation permitted under Regulation (EC) No.1072/2009)], is not used at any time during the said journey for the carriage of goods loaded at one place in the United Kingdom and delivered at another place in the United Kingdom;

[*"international carriage"* has the meaning which it bears in Article 2 of Regulation (EC) No.1072/2009;]

"loading" includes attaching to a drawing vehicle a trailer which has been loaded with goods before it is so attached, and *"loaded"* shall be construed accordingly;

"Northern Ireland goods vehicle" means a goods vehicle of which the operating centre is in Northern Ireland and—

(a) which has been brought temporarily into Great Britain;

(b) which is not being used for international carriage by a haulier who is established in Northern Ireland and is not established in Great Britain;

(c) which is engaged in carrying goods by road on a journey some part of which has taken place, or will take place, outside Great Britain; and

(d) which—

(i) in the case of a motor vehicle, is registered in Northern Ireland or Great Britain; or

(ii) in the case of a trailer, is drawn in Great Britain only by a motor vehicle which is a Northern Ireland goods vehicle; [...]

[*" Regulation (EC) No.1072/2009"* means Regulation (EC) No.1072/2009 of the European Parliament and of the Council of 21st October 2009 on common rules for access to the international road haulage market; and]

"relief vehicle" means a vehicle used for transporting goods which is sent to replace a vehicle which has broken down, and which continues the haul under cover of the licence, permit, or other document issued for the vehicle which has broken down.

(2) For the purposes of these Regulations —

(a) the permissible laden weight and the permissible pay load of a vehicle shall be determined by reference to the law of the country where the vehicle is registered or, in the case of a trailer which is not registered, by reference to the law of the country where the drawing vehicle is registered; and

(b) a combination of a motor vehicle drawing a trailer shall be treated, for the purpose of determining the permissible laden weight or the permissible pay load, as the case may be, as a single vehicle.

(3) In these Regulations, unless the context otherwise requires, a reference to a numbered regulation or Schedule is a reference to the regulation or Schedule bearing that number in these Regulations.

B35.05   *[Regulation 3 is printed as amended by SI 2010/804.]*

Exemptions for foreign vehicles used for certain purposes

B35.06   **4.** Notwithstanding anything in [regulations 8 to 30E], section 2(1) of the Act (Users of certain goods vehicles to hold operators' licences) shall not apply to the use in Great Britain of a foreign goods vehicle for the carriage of any goods specified in paragraph 1, 2, 4, 5, 6, 7 or 8 of Schedule 2.

B35.07   *[Regulation 4 is printed as amended by SI 2004/462.]*

Exemptions for Northern Ireland or foreign goods vehicles used for the carriage of goods between Member States of the European Community

B35.08   **5.** Notwithstanding anything in [regulations 8 to 30E], section 2(1) of the Act shall not apply to the use in Great Britain of a Northern Ireland or foreign goods vehicle for the carriage of goods between Member States of the European Community—

(a) where the vehicle is—

(i) loaded or unloaded at a place not more than 25 kilometres from the coast of Great Britain and unloaded or loaded (as the case may be) at a place not more than 25 kilometres from the coast of another Member State, and the distance between the place where the goods are loaded on to the vehicle and the place where they are off-loaded from the vehicle, when measured in a straight line (but disregarding so much of that distance as lies over the sea in a case where the vehicle is carried on sea transport specially constructed and equipped for the carriage of commercial vehicles and operated as a regular service) does not exceed 100 kilometres; or

(ii) a motor vehicle, or trailer drawn by a foreign goods vehicle, having a permissible laden weight not exceeding 6 metric tons or a permissible pay load not exceeding 3.5 metric tons; or

(iii) a relief vehicle; or

(b) where the goods so carried are those specified in paragraphs 9, 16, 17, 18, 20, 21, 26 or 28 of Schedule 2; or

(c) where the vehicle is being used on a journey for combined transport as defined in Article 1 of Council Directive (EEC) No.92/106 on the establishment of common rules for certain types of combined transport of goods between Member States [*O.J. No.L368, December 17, 1992, p.38*], and there is carried on the vehicle, or, in the case of a trailer, on the vehicle drawing it, a document which satisfies the requirements of Article 3 of that Directive, or a document issued by the competent authority of the Member State where the vehicle, or, in the case of a trailer, the vehicle drawing it, is registered certifying that the vehicle is being used on such a journey; or

(d) where the goods are being carried for or in connection with any trade or business carried on by the undertaking carrying them and each of the following conditions are fulfilled:—

(i) the goods are the property of the undertaking carrying them or have been sold, bought, let out on hire or hired, produced, extracted, processed or repaired by that undertaking;

(ii) the purpose of the journey is to carry the goods to or from the undertaking carrying them or to move them either inside that undertaking, or outside for that undertaking's own requirements;

(iii) the vehicle used for such carriage is being driven by an employee of the undertaking;

(iv) except in the case of a replacement vehicle during a short breakdown of the vehicle normally used, the vehicle used for carrying the goods is owned by the undertaking carrying them or has been bought by it on deferred terms or hired in accordance with the conditions on the use of vehicles hired without drivers for the carriage of goods by road contained in Council Directive (EEC) No.84/647 [*O.J. No.L335, December 22, 1984, p.72*].

[Regulation 5 is printed as amended by SI 2004/462.   **B35.09**

The term "combined transport" is defined for the purposes of Directive 92/106/EEC, by ibid. art.1, as—

the transport of goods between Member States where the lorry, trailer, semi-trailer, with or without tractor unit, swap body or container of 20 feet or more uses the road on the initial or final leg of the journey and, on the other leg, rail or inland waterway or maritime services where this section exceeds 100 km as the crow flies and make the initial or final road transport leg of the journey;

— between the point where the goods are loaded and the nearest suitable rail loading station for the initial leg, and between the nearest suitable rail unloading station and the point where the goods are unloaded for the final leg, or;

— within a radius not exceeding 150 km as the crow flies from the inland waterway port or seaport of loading or unloading. *]*

Exemption for Northern Ireland or foreign goods vehicles with international licences

6. Notwithstanding anything in [regulations 8 to 30E], section 2(1) of the Act   **B35.10** shall not apply to the use in Great Britain of a Northern Ireland or foreign goods vehicle for the carriage of goods for hire or reward if the vehicle is being used by virtue of a licence issued pursuant to the scheme adopted by Resolution of the Council of Ministers of Transport on 14th June 1973 [*CM(73)5 Final, ECMT 20th Annual Report and Resolutions of the Council of Ministers (1973), pp.64, 65, ISBN 92–821*] and the licence is carried on the vehicle or, if the vehicle is a trailer, on the motor vehicle by which it is drawn.

[Regulation 6 is printed as amended by SI 2004/462.]   **B35.11**

Exemption for foreign goods vehicles [being used to carry out Community cabotage authorisations] and for Northern Ireland goods vehicles carrying goods in Great Britain or between Northern Ireland and Great Britain

B35.12   **7.**—[(1) Notwithstanding anything in regulations 8 to 30E, section 2(1) of the Act shall not apply in the case of a foreign goods vehicle being used to carry out a cabotage operation consisting of national carriage for hire or reward on a temporary basis in Great Britain in accordance with the provisions of [Regulation (EC) No.1072/2009].]

(2) Section 2(1) of the Act shall not apply to the use in Great Britain of a Northern Ireland goods vehicle for the carriage of goods between places of loading or unloading in Great Britain or between one such place in Northern Ireland and another such place in Great Britain.

B35.13   *[Regulation 7 is printed as amended by SI 2004/462; SI 2010/804.]*

Exemption for Albanian goods vehicles

B35.14   **8.**—(1) In this regulation *"Albanian goods vehicle"* means a foreign goods vehicle which is owned or operated by a person who is authorised under the law of the Republic of Albania to engage in the international carriage of goods by road for hire or reward or on his own account and which, in the case of a motor vehicle, is registered in the Republic of Albania.

(2) Section 2(1) of the Act shall not apply to the use in Great Britain of an Albanian goods vehicle for the carriage of any goods.

Exemptions and modifications for Austrian goods vehicles

B35.15   **9.**—(1) In this regulation *"Austrian goods vehicle"* means a foreign goods vehicle—

    (a) which, in the case of a motor vehicle, is owned by or operated by or on behalf of a person—

        (i) who is authorised under Austrian law to use that vehicle for the carriage of goods in the Republic of Austria; or

        (ii) who, if Austrian law permits him so to use that vehicle without being so authorised, uses that vehicle primarily or substantially for that purpose in that country; and

    (b) which, in the case of a trailer, is drawn in Great Britain only by a motor vehicle which is an Austrian goods vehicle.

(2) Section 2(1) of the Act shall not apply to the use in Great Britain of an Austrian goods vehicle for the carriage of any goods specified in paragraph 1, 2, 4, 5, 6, 7, 8, 9, 10, 15, 17, 18, 19, 20, 21, 24, 26 or 27 of Schedule 2.

(3) Section 2(1) of the Act shall not apply to the use in Great Britain of an Austrian goods vehicle which is a vehicle specified in Schedule 3.

(4) In relation to an Austrian goods vehicle used for the carriage of any goods, for or in connection with any trade or business carried on by the user of the vehicle, in a case to which neither of the preceding exemptions applies, section 2(1) of the Act shall have effect as set out in Schedule 4.

(5) In relation to an Austrian goods vehicle used for the carriage of goods in a

case to which neither of the preceding exemptions nor the preceding modification apply, section 2(1) of the Act shall have effect as set out in Schedule 5.

Exemption for Bulgarian goods vehicles

10.—(1) In this regulation *"Bulgarian goods vehicle"* means a foreign goods vehicle—   **B35.16**

    (a) which, in the case of a motor vehicle, is registered in the Republic of Bulgaria; and

    (b) which, in the case of a trailer, is drawn in Great Britain only by a motor vehicle which is a Bulgarian goods vehicle.

(2) Section 2(1) of the Act shall not apply to the use in Great Britain of a Bulgarian goods vehicle for the carriage of any goods.

Exemption for Channel Islands goods vehicles

11.—(1) In this regulation *"Channel Islands goods vehicle"* means a foreign goods vehicle—   **B35.17**

    (a) which, in the case of a motor vehicle, is registered in the Channel Islands; and

    (b) which, in the case of a trailer, is drawn in Great Britain only by a motor vehicle which is a Channel Islands goods vehicle.

(2) Section 2(1) of the Act shall not apply to the use in Great Britain of a Channel Islands goods vehicle for the carriage of any goods.

Exemptions and modifications for Cypriot goods vehicles

12.—(1) In this regulation *"Cypriot goods vehicle"* means a foreign goods vehicle which is owned by, or operated by or on behalf of, a person who is authorised under the law of the Republic of Cyprus to use the vehicle in that country for the international carriage of goods, and which, in the case of a motor vehicle, is registered in the Republic of Cyprus.   **B35.18**

(2) Section 2(1) of the Act shall not apply to the use in Great Britain of a Cypriot goods vehicle for the carriage of any goods specified in paragraph 1, 2, 3, 5, 9, 10, 16, 22, 23 or 24 of Schedule 2.

(3) Section 2(1) of the Act shall not apply to the use in Great Britain of a Cypriot goods vehicle specified in Schedule 3.

(4) Section 2(1) of the Act shall not apply to the use in Great Britain of a Cypriot goods vehicle which is a vehicle used for the recovery of a damaged vehicle.

(5) In relation to a Cypriot goods vehicle used for the carriage of goods, for or in connection with any trade or business carried on by the user of the vehicle, in a case to which none of the preceding exemptions apply, section 2(1) of the Act shall have effect as if for the words from "(a) hire or reward" to the end of that subsection there were substituted the words "for or in connection with any trade or business carried on by him unless there is carried on the vehicle or, if that vehicle is a trailer, on the motor vehicle by which it is drawn a document containing the following particulars:—

    (a) the place at which and the date on which the document was made out;

    (b) the name and address of the carrier and a description of the nature of his business;

(c) if the goods carried, or to be carried, or any of them, are to be collected from or delivered to, any person other than the carrier, the name and address of that person and a description of the nature of his business;

(d) the place or places at which the vehicle is to be loaded or unloaded;

(e) the nature and gross weight, or other indication of quantity, of the goods;

(f) the carrying capacity of the vehicle by weight;

(g) the index mark and registration number of the vehicle, or if the vehicle does not carry an index mark or any registration number, the chassis number of the vehicle;

(h) the place of entry of the vehicle into, or of exit from, the United Kingdom;

(i) the signature of the carrier or his authorised agent.".

(6) In relation to a Cypriot goods vehicle used for the carriage of goods in a case to which none of the preceding exemptions nor the preceding modification apply, section 2(1) of the Act shall have effect as set out in Schedule 5.

[Exemption for Czech goods vehicles

B35.19   13.—(1) In this regulation—

"*Czech goods vehicle*" means a goods vehicle which—

(a) is owned or operated by a person who is authorised under the law of the Czech Republic to engage in the international carriage of goods by road for hire or reward or on his own account;

(b) in the case of a motor vehicle, is registered in the Czech Republic;

(c) has been temporarily brought into Great Britain; and

(d) is engaged in carrying goods by road on a journey some part of which has taken place, or will take place, outside the United Kingdom.

"*relevant date*" means the date on which the Agreement between the Government of the United Kingdom of Great Britain and Northern Ireland and the Government of the Czech Republic on international road transport signed on 27th of May 1998 [*Cm. 6246, June 2004*] comes into force.

(2) Where a Czech goods vehicle is not used at any time during the journey upon which it is engaged for the carriage of goods loaded at one place in the United Kingdom and delivered at another place in the United Kingdom—

(a) regulations 4, 5, 6 and 7 shall apply to the Czech goods vehicle as they apply to a foreign goods vehicle; and

(b) section 2(1) of the Act shall not apply to the use in Great Britain of the Czech goods vehicle for the carriage of any goods.

(3) On and after the relevant date, where a Czech goods vehicle is used at any time for the carriage of goods loaded at one place in the United Kingdom and delivered at another place in the United Kingdom section 2(1) of the Act shall have effect as set out in Schedule 5.]

[Regulation 13 is printed as substituted by SI 2004/462.   **B35.20**
The Agreement with the Czech Republic came into force on April 30, 2004.]

Exemption for Faroese goods vehicles

14.—(1) In this regulation *"Faroese goods vehicle"* means a foreign goods ve-   **B35.21**
hicle—

    (a) which, in the case of a motor vehicle, is registered in the Faroe Islands;
       and

    (b) which, in the case of a trailer, is drawn in Great Britain only by a motor
       vehicle which is a Faroese goods vehicle.

(2) Section 2(1) of the Act shall not apply to the use in Great Britain of a
Faroese goods vehicle for the carriage of any goods.

Exemptions and modifications for Estonian goods vehicles

15.—(1) In this regulation—   **B35.22**

    "Estonian goods vehicle" means a foreign goods vehicle—

        (a) which, in the case of a motor vehicle, is registered in the Re-
           public of Estonia; and

        (b) which, in the case of a trailer, is owned by or operated by or
           on behalf of a person who under Estonian law is authorised to
           use that vehicle for the carriage of goods in the Republic of
           Estonia.

    "relevant date" means the date on which the Agreement between the
        Government of the United Kingdom of Great Britain and Northern
        Ireland and the Republic of Estonia on international road transport
        signed on 16th August 1995 [*Cm. 3105*] comes into force.

(2) On and after the relevant date, section 2(1) of the Act shall not apply to the
use in Great Britain of an Estonian goods vehicle for the carriage of any goods
specified in paragraphs 4, 5, 9, 18, 20, 21, 22, 23 or 24 of Schedule 2 and in such
a case these provisions shall have effect as if the words "or broken-down" were
added after "damaged" in paragraph 5.

(3) Section 2(1) of the Act shall not apply to the use in Great Britain of an
Estonian goods vehicle specified in paragraph 1 of Schedule 3.

(4) In relation to an Estonian goods vehicle being used for the carriage of
goods in a case to which the preceding exemptions do not apply, section 2(1) of
the Act shall have effect as set out in Schedule 5.

Exemption for Hungarian goods vehicles

16.—(1) In this regulation *"Hungarian goods vehicle"* means a foreign goods   **B35.23**
vehicle—

    (a) which, in the case of a motor vehicle, is registered in the Republic of
       Hungary; and

    (b) which, in the case of a trailer, is drawn in Great Britain only by a motor
       vehicle which is a Hungarian goods vehicle.

(2) Section 2(1) of the Act shall not apply to the use in Great Britain of a Hungarian goods vehicle for the carriage of any goods.

Exemption for Jordanian goods vehicles

B35.24   **17.**—(1) In this regulation *"Jordanian goods vehicle"* means a foreign goods vehicle which is owned or operated by a person who is authorised under the law of the Hashemite Kingdom of Jordan to engage in the international carriage of goods by road for hire or reward or on his own account and which, in the case of a motor vehicle, is registered in the Hashemite Kingdom of Jordan.

(2) Section 2(1) of the Act shall not apply to the use in Great Britain of a Jordanian goods vehicle for the carriage of any goods.

Exemption for Latvian goods vehicles

B35.25   **18.**—(1) In this regulation—

> *"Latvian goods vehicle"* means a foreign goods vehicle which is owned or operated by a person who is authorised under the law of the Republic of Latvia to engage in the international carriage of goods by road for hire or reward or on his own account and which, in the case of a motor vehicle, is registered in the Republic of Latvia; and

> *"relevant date"* means the date on which the Agreement between the Government of the United Kingdom of Great Britain and Northern Ireland and the Government of the Republic of Latvia on international road transport signed on 6th December 1993 [*Cm. 2526*] comes into force.

(2) On and after the relevant date, section 2(1) of the Act shall not apply to the use in Great Britain of a Latvian goods vehicle for the carriage of any goods.

Exemption for Lithuanian goods vehicles

B35.26   **19.**—(1) In this regulation—

> *"Lithuanian goods vehicle"* means a foreign goods vehicle which is owned or operated by a person who is authorised under the law of the Republic of Lithuania to engage in the international carriage of goods by road for hire or reward or on his own account and which, in the case of a motor vehicle, is registered in the Republic of Lithuania; and

> *"relevant date"* means the date on which the Agreement between the Government of the United Kingdom of Great Britain and Northern Ireland and the Government of the Republic of Lithuania on international road transport signed on 2nd November 1994 [*Cm. 2999*] comes into force.

(2) On and after the relevant date, section 2(1) of the Act shall not apply to the use in Great Britain of a Lithuanian goods vehicle for the carriage of any goods.

Exemption for Manx goods vehicles

B35.27   **20.**—(1) In this regulation *"Manx goods vehicle"* means a foreign goods vehicle—

> (a) which, in the case of a motor vehicle, is registered in the Isle of Man; and

> (b) which, in the case of a trailer, is drawn in Great Britain only by a motor vehicle which is a Manx goods vehicle.

(2) Section 2(1) of the Act shall not apply to the use in Great Britain of a Manx goods vehicle for the carriage of any goods.

Exemption and modification for Moroccan goods vehicles

21.—(1) In this regulation—   **B35.28**

"Moroccan goods vehicle" means a foreign goods vehicle which is owned or operated by a person who is authorised under the law of the Kingdom of Morocco to engage in the international carriage of goods by road for hire or reward or on his own account and which, in the case of a motor vehicle, is registered in the Kingdom of Morocco; and

"relevant date" means the date on which the Agreement between the Government of the United Kingdom of Great Britain and Northern Ireland and the Government of the Kingdom of Morocco on international road transport signed on 15th April 1994 [*Cm. 2703, replaced by Cm. 3480*] comes into force.

(2) On and after the relevant date, section 2(1) of the Act shall not apply to the use in Great Britain of a Moroccan goods vehicle for the carriage of any goods specified in paragraph 2, 9, or 31 of Schedule 2.

(3) In relation to a Moroccan goods vehicle used for the carriage of goods in a case to which the preceding exemption applies, section 2(1) of the Act shall have effect as set out in Schedule 5.

[The agreement with Morocco entered into force on April 12, 2000 and is   **B35.29** *supplemented by an administrative memorandum (see ibid.).]*

Exemption and modification for Northern Ireland goods vehicles

22.—(1) Section 2(1) of the Act shall not apply to the use of a Northern Ireland   **B35.30** goods vehicle for the carriage of goods for hire or reward where there is in force in relation to the use of that vehicle in Northern Ireland or, in the case of a trailer, the vehicle by which it is drawn, a licence under section 17 of the Transport Act (Northern Ireland) 1967 [*c.37 (NI)*].

(2) In relation to a Northern Ireland goods vehicle used for the carriage of goods otherwise than for hire or reward, section 2(1) of the Act shall have effect as set out in Schedule 4.

Exemption for Polish goods vehicles

23.—(1) In this regulation *"Polish goods vehicle"* means a foreign goods ve-   **B35.31** hicle—

(a) which, in the case of a motor vehicle, is registered in the Republic of Poland; and

(b) which, in the case of a trailer, is drawn in Great Britain only by a motor vehicle which is a Polish goods vehicle.

(2) Section 2(1) of the Act shall not apply to the use in Great Britain of a Polish goods vehicle for the carriage of any goods.

Exemption for Romanian goods vehicles

24.—(1) In this regulation *"Romanian goods vehicle"* means a foreign goods   **B35.32** vehicle—

(a) which, in the case of a motor vehicle, is registered in Romania; and

(b) which, in the case of a trailer, is drawn in Great Britain only by a motor vehicle which is a Romanian goods vehicle.

(2) Section 2(1) of the Act shall not apply to the use in Great Britain of a Romanian goods vehicle for the carriage of any goods.

[Exemption for Slovak goods vehicles

B35.33   **25.**—(1) In this regulation—

"Slovak goods vehicle" means a foreign goods vehicle which is owned or operated by a person who is authorised under the law of the Slovak Republic to engage in the international carriage of goods by road for hire or reward or on his own account and which, in the case of a motor vehicle, is registered in the Slovak Republic; and

"relevant date" means the date on which the Agreement between the Government of the United Kingdom of Great Britain and Northern Ireland and the Government of the Slovak Republic on international road transport signed on 11th of January 2001 [*Cm. 6248, June 2004*] comes into force.

(2) On and after the relevant date, section 2(1) of the Act shall not apply to the use in Great Britain of a Slovak goods vehicle for the carriage of any goods.]

B35.34   *[Regulation 25 is printed as substituted by SI 2004/462.*

The Agreement with the Slovak Republic entered into force on April 1, 2004.]

Exemptions and modification for the Republics of the former Soviet Union goods vehicles

B35.35   **26.**—(1) In this regulation *"Republic of the former Soviet Union goods vehicle"* means a foreign goods vehicle which is not provided for elsewhere in these Regulations —

(a) which is owned by, or operated on behalf of, a person who is authorised under the law of a Republic of the former Union of Soviet Socialist Republics to use the vehicle in that country for the international carriage of goods; and

(b) which, in the case of a motor vehicle, is registered in a Republic of the former Union of Soviet Socialist Republics; and

(c) which, in the case of a trailer, is drawn in Great Britain only by a motor vehicle which is a Republic of the former Soviet Union goods vehicle.

(2) Subject to paragraphs (6) and (7) below, section 2(1) of the Act shall not apply to the use of a Republic of the former Soviet Union goods vehicle for the carriage of any goods specified in paragraph 4, 5 or 8 of Schedule 2.

(3) Subject to paragraphs (6) and (7) below, section 2(1) of the Act shall not apply to the use of a Republic of the former Soviet Union goods vehicle for the carriage of any goods specified in paragraph 21, 22 or 23 of Schedule 2 if the goods are to be, or are being, returned to the country of origin of the vehicle or are to be, or are being, taken to another country.

(4) Subject to paragraphs (6) and (7) below, section 2(1) of the Act shall not apply to the use of a Republic of the former Soviet Union goods vehicle which is a vehicle specified in paragraph 2 or 3 of Schedule 3.

(5) Subject to paragraphs (6) and (7) below, in relation to a Republic of the former Soviet Union goods vehicle being used for the carriage of goods in a case to which none of the preceding exemptions apply, section 2(1) shall have effect as set out in Schedule 5.

(6) The foregoing exemptions and modification shall not apply unless there is carried on the vehicle or, if the vehicle is a trailer, on the motor vehicle by which it is drawn—

(a) in the case of the carriage of goods under a contract to which the Convention on the Contract for the International Carriage of Goods by Road (as given the force of law in the United Kingdom by section 1 of the Carriage of Goods by Road Act 1965 [*not reproduced in this work*]) applies, a consignment note made out in accordance with that Convention and containing the particulars specified therein, or

(b) in the case of the carriage of goods otherwise than under such a contract, a document or documents containing the following particulars:

(i) the date of the document and the place at which it is made out;

(ii) the name and address of the sender of the goods, if any;

(iii) the name and address of the carrier;

(iv) the date and place of taking over of the goods, if any, and the place designated for delivery, if any;

(v) the name and address of the consignee, if any;

(vi) the description in common use of the nature of the goods and the method of packing, and, in the case of dangerous goods, their generally recognised description;

(vii) the number of packages and their special marks and numbers;

(viii) the gross weight of the goods and their quantity otherwise expressed;

(ix) charges relating to the carriage (carriage charges, supplementary charges, Customs duties and other charges incurred during the journey); and

(x) the requisite instructions for Customs and other formalities.

(7) The foregoing exemptions and modification shall not apply to the use of a Republic of the former Soviet Union goods vehicle for the carriage of goods between a place in Great Britain and a place in a country other than Great Britain or a Republic of the former Soviet Union, or vice versa, unless there is carried on the vehicle, or if the vehicle is a trailer, on the motor vehicle by which it is drawn, a permit for the use of the vehicle for that purpose issued with the authority of the Secretary of State.

Exemption for Swiss goods vehicles

27.—(1) In this regulation *"Swiss goods vehicle"* means a foreign goods vehi-   **B35.36**
cle—

(a) which, in the case of a motor vehicle, is registered in the Swiss Confederation; and

(b) which, in the case of a trailer, is drawn in Great Britain only by a motor vehicle which is a Swiss goods vehicle.

(2) Section 2(1) of the Act shall not apply to the use in Great Britain of a Swiss goods vehicle for the carriage of any goods.

Exemptions and modification for Tunisian goods vehicles

B35.37   **28.**—(1) In this regulation *"Tunisian goods vehicle"* means a foreign goods vehicle which—

(a) in the case of a motor vehicle, is registered in the Republic of Tunisia; and

(b) in the case of a trailer, is operated by a person who is authorised under Tunisian law to use that vehicle for the international carriage of goods for hire or reward or on his own account.

(2) Section 2(1) of the Act shall not apply to the use in Great Britain of a Tunisian goods vehicle for the carriage of any goods specified in paragraph 1, 2, 3, 4, 5, 6, 7, 8, 9, 10, 13, 18, 19, 21, 24 or 30 of Schedule 2.

(3) Section 2(1) of the Act shall not apply to the use in Great Britain of a Tunisian goods vehicle which is a vehicle specified in Schedule 3.

(4) In relation to a Tunisian goods vehicle being used for the carriage of goods in a case to which none of the preceding exemptions apply, section 2(1) of the Act shall have effect as set out in Schedule 5.

[Exemption for Turkish goods vehicles

B35.38   **29.**—(1) In this regulation *"Turkish goods vehicle"* means a foreign goods vehicle—

(a) which, in the case of a motor vehicle, is registered in the Republic of Turkey; and

(b) which, in the case of a trailer, is owned by or operated by or on behalf of a person who is authorised under Turkish law to use that vehicle for the carriage of goods in the Turkish Republic.

(2) Section 2(1) of the Act shall not apply to the use in Great Britain of a Turkish goods vehicle for the carriage of any goods.]

B35.39   *[Regulation 29 is printed as substituted by SI 2010/804.]*

Exemptions and modification for Ukrainian goods vehicles

B35.40   **30.**—(1) In this regulation—

"Ukrainian goods vehicle" means a foreign goods vehicle—

(a) which, in the case of a motor vehicle, is registered in the Ukraine; and

(b) which, in the case of a trailer, is owned by or operated by or on behalf of a person who under Ukrainian law is authorised to use that vehicle for the carriage of goods in the Ukraine.

"relevant date" means the date on which the Agreement between the Government of the United Kingdom of Great Britain and Northern Ireland and the Government of the Ukraine on international road transport signed on 13th December 1995 [*Cm. 3158*] comes into force.

(2) On and after the relevant date, section 2(1) of the Act shall not apply to the

use in Great Britain of a Ukrainian goods vehicle for the carriage of any goods specified in paragraphs 4, 5, 9, 18 and 20 to 24 of Schedule 2 and in such a case these provisions shall have effect as if the words "or broken-down" were added after "damaged" in paragraph 5.

(3) Section 2(1) of the Act shall not apply to the use in Great Britain of a Ukrainian goods vehicle—

(a) specified in paragraph 1 of Schedule 3, or

(b) where the goods are being carried for or in connection with any trade or business carried on by the undertaking carrying them and each of the following conditions are fulfilled—

(i) the goods are the property of the undertaking carrying them or have been sold, bought, let out on hire or hired, produced, extracted, processed or repaired by that undertaking;

(ii) the purpose of the journey is to carry the goods to or from the undertaking carrying them or to move them either inside that undertaking or outside for that undertaking's own requirements;

(iii) the vehicle used for such carriage is being driven by an employee of the undertaking;

(iv) except in the case of a replacement vehicle during a short breakdown of the vehicle normally used, the vehicle used for carrying the goods is owned by the undertaking carrying them or has been bought by it on deferred terms or hired in accordance with the conditions on the use of vehicles hired without drivers for the carriage of goods by road contained in Council Directive (EEC) No.84/647;

(v) the carriage in Great Britain is part of a journey between Great Britain and the Ukraine.

(4) In relation to a Ukrainian goods vehicle being used for the carriage of goods in a case to which the preceding exemptions do not apply, section 2(1) of the Act shall have effect as set out in Schedule 5.

[The agreement with the Ukraine entered into force on June 10, 2000 and has been reissued as Cm. 4879.]   **B35.41**

[Exemption for Macedonian goods vehicles

30A.—(1) In this regulation—   **B35.42**

"Macedonian goods vehicle" means a foreign goods vehicle which is owned or operated by a person who is authorised under the law of Macedonia to engage in the international carriage of goods by road for hire or reward or on his own account and which, in the case of a motor vehicle, is registered in Macedonia; and

"relevant date" means the date on which the Agreement between the Government of the United Kingdom of Great Britain and Northern Ireland and the Macedonian Government on international road transport signed on 18th of June 1996 comes into force.

(2) On and after the relevant date, section 2(1) of the Act shall not apply to the use in Great Britain of a Macedonian goods vehicle for the carriage of any goods.]

[Regulation 30A is printed as inserted by SI 2004/462.]   **B35.43**

[Exemption for Moldovan goods vehicles

B35.44   **30B.**—(1) In this regulation—

"*Moldovan goods vehicle*" means a foreign goods vehicle which is owned or operated by a person who is authorised under the law of the Republic of Moldova to engage in the international carriage of goods by road for hire or reward or on his own account and which, in the case of a motor vehicle, is registered in the Republic of Moldova; and

"*relevant date*" means the date on which the Agreement between the Government of the United Kingdom of Great Britain and Northern Ireland and the Government of the Republic of Moldova on international road transport signed on 15th of October 1996 comes into force.

(2) On and after the relevant date, section 2(1) of the Act shall not apply to the use in Great Britain of a Moldovan goods vehicle for the carriage of any goods.]

B35.45   *[Regulation 30B is printed as inserted by SI 2004/462.]*

[Exemption for Georgian goods vehicles

B35.46   **30C.**—(1) In this regulation—

"*Georgian goods vehicle*" means a foreign goods vehicle which is owned or operated by a person who is authorised under the law of the Republic of Georgia to engage in the international carriage of goods by road for hire or reward or on his own account and which, in the case of a motor vehicle, is registered in the Republic of Georgia; and

"*relevant date*" means the date on which the Agreement between the Government of the United Kingdom of Great Britain and Northern Ireland and the Government of the Republic of Georgia on international road transport signed on 13th of November 1997 comes into force.

(2) On and after the relevant date, section 2(1) of the Act shall not apply to the use in Great Britain of a Georgian goods vehicle for the carriage of any goods—

(a) specified in paragraphs 4, 5, 9, 21, 29, 30, 31 and 32 of Schedule 2; or

(b) on the owner's or operator's own account between the territories of Great Britain and the Republic of Georgia.

(3) In relation to a Georgian goods vehicle used for the carriage of goods in a case to which paragraph (2) does not apply, section 2(1) of the Act shall have effect as set out in Schedule 5.]

B35.47   *[Regulation 30C is printed as inserted by SI 2004/462.]*

[Exemption for Croatian goods vehicles

B35.48   **30D.**—(1) In this regulation—

"*Croatian goods vehicle*" means a foreign goods vehicle which is owned or operated by a person who is authorised under the law of the Republic of Croatia to engage in the international carriage of goods by road for hire or reward or on his own account and which, in the case of a motor vehicle, is registered in the Republic of Croatia; and "*relevant date*" means the date on which the Agreement between the Government of the United Kingdom of Great Britain and Northern Ireland and the Government of the Republic of Croatia on international road transport signed on 22nd of February 1999 comes into force.

(2) On and after the relevant date, section 2(1) of the Act shall not apply to the use in Great Britain of a Croatian goods vehicle for the carriage of any goods.]

[Regulation 30D is printed as inserted by SI 2004/462.]   **B35.49**

[Exemption for Slovenian goods vehicles

30E.—(1) In this regulation—   **B35.50**

"*Slovenian goods vehicle*" means a foreign goods vehicle which is owned or operated by a person who is authorised under the law of the Republic of Slovenia to engage in the international carriage of goods by road for hire or reward or on his own account and which, in the case of a motor vehicle, is registered in the Republic of Slovenia; and

"*relevant date*" means the date on which the Agreement between the Government of the United Kingdom of Great Britain and Northern Ireland and the Government of the Republic of Slovenia on international road transport signed on 30th of May 2000 comes into force.

(2) On and after the relevant date, section 2(1) of the Act shall not apply to the use in Great Britain of a Slovenian goods vehicle for the carriage of any goods.]

[Regulation 30E is printed as inserted by SI 2004/462.]   **B35.51**

Simplified procedure for the grant, etc., of operators' licences

31.—(1) The Act shall have effect subject to the modifications set out in Part I   **B35.52**
of Schedule 6 in relation to any foreign goods vehicles [to which [regulations 4 to 30E] do not apply].

(2) The Goods Vehicles (Licensing of Operators) Regulations 1995 [*SI 1995/2869 (q.v.)*] shall have effect subject to the amendments set out in Part II of the said Schedule in relation to foreign goods vehicles [to which Regulations 4 to 30E do not apply].

(3) The Goods Vehicles (Licensing of Operators) Act 1995 (Commencement and Transitional Provisions) Order 1995 [*SI 1995/2181*] and the Goods Vehicles (Licensing of Operators) (Fees) Regulations 1995 [*SI 1995/3000; not reproduced in this work*] shall not have effect in relation to any foreign goods vehicles.

[Regulation 31 is printed as amended by SI 2004/462.]   **B35.53**

Regulation 2	SCHEDULE 1

REVOCATIONS

[Omitted.]   **B35.54**

Regulations 4, 5, 9(2), 12(2),   SCHEDULE
215(2) and (3), 21(2), 26(2),
26(3), 28(2), 29(2) and 30(2)

EXEMPTION FROM SECTION 2(1) OF THE ACT FOR CERTAIN GOODS CARRIED BY CERTAIN GOODS VEHICLES

1. Luggage being carried to or from an airport.   **B35.55**

2. Goods being carried to or from an airport in a case where an air service has been diverted.

3. Luggage being carried in trailers drawn by passenger vehicles.

4. Postal packets (as defined by [section 125(1) of the Postal Services Act 2000 [*not reproduced in this work*]]).

B35.56   *[Paragraph 4 is printed as amended by SI 2001/1149.]*

B35.57   **5.** Damaged vehicles.

6. Animal corpses (other than those intended for human consumption) for the purpose of disposal.

7. Bees or fish stock.

8. The body of a deceased person.

9. Goods for medical or surgical care in emergency relief and in particular for relief in natural disasters.

B35.58   **10.** Goods carried in connection with household removals by undertakings using specialised personnel and equipment for that purpose.

11. Household effects.

12. Live animals, other than animals intended for slaughter.

13. Spare parts for ocean-going ships.

14. Spare parts and provisions for ships.

B35.59   **15.** Spare parts and provisions for ocean-going ships where such ships have been rerouted.

16. Spare parts and provisions for ocean-going ships and aircraft.

17. Goods which by reason of their value are carried in vehicles constructed or adapted for the carriage of goods requiring special security precautions and which are accompanied by guards.

18. Works of art.

19. Antiques.

B35.60   **20.** Goods carried exclusively for publicity or educational purposes.

21. Properties, equipment or animals being carried to or from theatrical, musical, cinematographic or circus performances or sporting events, exhibitions or fairs, or to or from the making of radio or television broadcasts or films.

22. Goods, properties or animals being carried to or from theatrical, musical, film or circus programmes, or sporting events.

23. Goods or properties intended for the making of radio or television broadcasts or films.

24. Goods carried for fairs and exhibitions.

B35.61   **25.** Goods carried for international fairs and exhibitions.

26. Refuse.

27. Garbage.

28. Sewage.

29. Perishable foodstuffs in a state of refrigeration.

B35.62   **30.** Broken down vehicles.

[**31.** Objects and works of art for exhibitions.]

[**32.** Samples of objects and materials exclusively for publicity or information purposes.]

B35.63   *[Schedule 2 is printed as amended by SI 2004/462.]*

Regulations 9(3), 12(3), 15(3),   SCHEDULE 3
26(4), 28(3) and 30(3)

Exemptions from Section 2(1) of the Act for Certain Foreign Goods Vehicles

B35.64   **1.** A vehicle having a permissible laden weight not exceeding 6 metric tons or a permissible pay load not exceeding 3.5 metric tons.

2. A goods vehicle used for the carriage of an abnormal indivisible load or other wide load provided that the requirements of the Motor Vehicles (Authorisation of Special Types) General Order 1979 [*SI 1979/1198*] are complied with.

3. A relief vehicle.

[The Motor Vehicles (Authorisation of Special Types) General Order 1979 (SI 1979/1198) referred to in para.2 above has been revoked and replaced by the Road Vehicles (Authorisation of Special Types) (General) Order 2003 (SI 2003/1998, q.v.).]   **B35.65**

Regulations 9(4) and 22(2)   SCHEDULE 4

MODIFICATION TO SECTION 2(1) OF THE ACT IN RELATION TO CERTAIN FOREIGN GOODS VEHICLES AND NORTHERN IRELAND VEHICLES

"**2.**—(1) Subject to subsection (2) of this section and to the other provisions of this Part of this Act, no person shall use a goods vehicle on a road for the carriage of goods for or in connection with any trade or business carried on by him unless there is carried on the vehicle, or, if that vehicle is a trailer, on the motor vehicle by which it is drawn, a document containing particulars of the user of the goods vehicle, his trade or business, the goods being carried, their loading and unloading points, the vehicle, and the route."   **B35.66**

Regulations 9(5), 12(6), 15(4),   SCHEDULE
521(3), 26(5), 28(5),
29(3) and 30(4)

MODIFICATION TO SECTION 2(1) OF THE ACT IN RELATION TO CERTAIN FOREIGN GOODS VEHICLES

"**2.**—(1) Subject to subsection (2) of this section and to the other provisions of this Part of this Act, no person shall use a goods vehicle on a road for the carriage of goods—   **B35.67**

    (a) for hire or reward, or

    (b) for or in connection with any trade or business carried on by him,

except under a permit carried on the vehicle or, if the vehicle is a trailer, on the motor vehicle by which it is drawn, issued with the authority of the Secretary of State, and authorising the vehicle to be used for the carriage of goods on the journey on which the goods are being carried."

Regulation 31   SCHEDULE 6

PART I

MODIFICATIONS TO THE GOODS VEHICLES (LICENSING OF OPERATORS) ACT 1995 IN RELATION TO FOREIGN GOODS VEHICLES

The Act shall have effect—   **B35.68**

    (a) as if for section 5(1) there were substituted the following—

    "(1) The vehicles authorised to be used under an operator's licence are—

        (a) any motor vehicle in the lawful possession of the licence-holder that is specified in the licence;

        (b) any trailer in the lawful possession of the licence-holder, and for the purposes of this section different types of trailers may be distinguished in a licence and a maximum number may be specified in the licence for trailers of each type.";

    (b) as if sections 5(4) to (7), 6(1)(a), (3) and (4), and 7 were omitted;

    (c) as if for section 8(1), there were substituted the following—

    "(1) A person applying for an operator's licence with a view to enabling goods vehicles brought temporarily into Great Britain to be used shall apply to such traffic commissioner as the Secretary of State may from time to time direct and shall not at any time hold more than one such licence";

(d) as if sections 8(2), (3)(b) and (5) were omitted;

(e) as if for section 8(4), there were substituted the following—

"(4) A person applying for an operator's licence shall also give to the traffic commissioner details of—

> (a) the notifiable convictions within the meaning given in paragraph 4 of Schedule 2, and
>
> (b) a prohibition under section 69 or 70 of the Road Traffic Act 1988 of the driving of a vehicle of which he was the owner when the prohibition was imposed.";

(f) as if in section 9(1), there was inserted at the end of the subsection ", or a prohibition under section 69 or 70 of the Road Traffic Act 1988 of the driving of a vehicle which he owned", and section 9(2) was omitted;

(g) as if sections 10, 11, 12, 13(2) to (11), 14 and 15 were omitted;

(h) as if for section 13(1) there were substituted the following—

"(1) On an application for an operator's licence the traffic commissioner shall consider whether the applicant satisfies the requirement that he is a fit and proper person to hold an operator's licence having regard in particular to his previous known conduct in respect of the use and operation of motor vehicles in the United Kingdom.";

(i) as if in section 16(1) there were substituted the following—

"(1) The operator's licence shall specify in the licence—

> (a) the date on which it is to come into force, and
>
> (b) the date when it will terminate, which date shall not be less than three months after the coming into force of the licence.";

(j) as if section 16(2) and (4) and the words "subject to subsection (4)" in section 16(3) were omitted;

(k) as if in section 17(1) there were substituted the following—

"(1) On the application of the holder of an operator's licence, the traffic commissioner by whom the licence was issued may vary the licence by directing that any vehicle may cease to be specified in the licence and at the same time direct that another [similar] vehicle shall be specified in the licence as a substitute.";

(l) as if sections 17(3) to (5), and 18 to 21 were omitted;

as if in section 22(1) there were substituted the following—

"(1) On issuing an operator's licence, a traffic commissioner may attach to the licence such conditions as he thinks fit for requiring the holder to inform him of any event of a kind specified in the conditions which affect the licence-holder and which is relevant to the exercise of any powers of the traffic commissioner in relation to the licence.";

as if section 22(2) to (6), and 23 to 25 were omitted;

(o) as if in section 26(1) there were substituted the following—

"(1) Subject to the provisions of section 29, the traffic commissioner by whom an operator's licence was issued may direct that it be revoked, suspended or curtailed on the grounds—

> (a) that during the five years ending with the date on which the direction is given there has been either a conviction of the licence-holder of a notifiable conviction within the meaning of paragraph 4 of Schedule 2, or a prohibition under section 69 or 70 of the Road Traffic Act 1988 of the driving of a vehicle of which the licence-holder was the owner when the prohibition was imposed, or
>
> (b) that since the licence was issued or varied he has learned that a statement of fact was false or statement of expectation has not been fulfilled.";

(p) as if sections 26(2) to (10) and (11)(c) and (d), and 27 were omitted;

(q) as if in section 28(1) there were substituted the following—

"(1) Where, under section 26(1) a traffic commissioner directs that an operator's licence be revoked, the commissioner may order the person who was the holder of the licence to be disqualified (either indefinitely or for such period as the commissioner thinks fit) from holding or obtaining an operator's licence in Great Britain.";

(r) as if section 28(3) were omitted;

(s) as if sections 30 to 34 and sections 40, 44 and 49 were omitted.

[In para.(k) of Pt I of Sch.6, the square brackets used in the substituted text of **B35.69**
s.17(1) are part of the official text and do not represent editorial emendations.]

Part II

MODIFICATIONS TO THE GOODS VEHICLES (LICENSING OF OPERATORS) REGULATIONS 1995 IN RELATION TO FOREIGN GOODS VEHICLES

The Goods Vehicles (Licensing of Operators) Regulations 1995 [*SI 1995/2869 (q.v.)*] **B35.70**
shall have effect:—

(a) as if regulations 4(c), 7, 9(1) and (3), 10 to 19, 21(1)(a)(i) and (iii), 21(1)(d), 22(1)(b) and (c), 22(2)(b), 22(3), 28(2) and (5), 29(1), (3) to (5), (7), and (12), 31 and 36 were omitted;

(b) as if in regulation 8(1) for the words "grant of that application would lead to a contravention of section 8(2)" there were substituted "applicant already holds an operator's licence in Great Britain";

(c) as if in regulation 21(1)(b) the words "or section 27" were omitted;

(d) as if in regulation 23(2) there were substituted the following—

"The disc shall clearly indicate (by colour or other means) that the vehicle is a foreign goods vehicle.";

(e) as if in regulation 26(1), for the words "and the licence-holder may do so" to the end there were substituted "at a place specified by the person requiring its production";

(f) as if in regulation 33(2) for the words "on a plate affixed to the vehicle by virtue of regulation 66 of those Regulations" there were substituted "in accordance with the legal requirements of the State of establishment of the operator of the foreign goods vehicle".

The New Drivers (Appeals Procedure) Regulations 1997

(SI 1997/1098)

Citation, commencement and interpretation

B36.01   **1.**—(1) *[Omitted.]*

(2) In these Regulations —

"*the Act*" means the Road Traffic (New Drivers) Act 1995;

"*appellate court*" means—

(a) in England and Wales, the Crown Court, the High Court or the Court of Appeal, as the case may be;

(b) *[applies to Scotland.]*

"*relevant appeal*" means an appeal against—

(a) a conviction, or

(b) an order of a court in England and Wales for the endorsement of a licence or ...;

which is, or forms part of, the basis for the revocation of the licence or a test certificate.

B36.02   *[The words omitted from the definition of "relevant appeal" relate exclusively to Scotland.]*

Licences granted pending appeal

B36.03   **2.**—(1) There is prescribed for the purposes of section 5(1) of the Act (duration of licences granted without retesting pending appeal) a period expiring on the date on which the revoked licence would have expired if it had not been revoked.

(2) Where the Secretary of State has—

(a) revoked a person's test certificate under paragraph 5(1) of Schedule 1 to the Act or, as the case may be, revoked a person's licence and test certificate under paragraph 8(1) of that Schedule, and

(b) received notice that the person is making a relevant appeal, he must, if that person surrenders to him any previous licence granted to him or provides an explanation for not surrendering it that the Secretary of State considers adequate, grant to that person a full licence in accordance with paragraph (3) below.

(3) A licence granted under paragraph (2) above shall—

(a) have effect for the purposes of the Road Traffic Acts as if it were a licence granted under Part III of the Road Traffic Act 1988,

(b) subject to section 92 and Part IV of that Act, authorise the driving of all classes of vehicle which, immediately before his test certificate was revoked, the person was permitted to drive without observing the prescribed conditions, and

   (c) subject to paragraph (4) below be for a period expiring on the date on which a licence granted under Part III of that Act would have expired.

(4) A licence granted under paragraph (2) shall be treated as revoked if—

   (a) following the appeal, the penalty points taken into account for the purposes of section 2(1) of the Act are not reduced to a number smaller than six, or

   (b) the appeal is abandoned.

Notices of appeal

3.—(1) Subject to paragraphs (2) and (3) below, notice of a relevant appeal shall be given to the Secretary of State—   **B36.04**

   (a) in England and Wales, by the magistrates' court or Crown Court in which the case is heard;

   (b) *[applies to Scotland.]*

(2) Notice of a relevant appeal from a magistrates' court or Crown Court by case stated shall be given to the Secretary of State by the High Court.

(3) Notice of a further appeal from a decision of an appellate court shall be given to the Secretary of State by the appellate court from which the appeal is made.

(4) A notice pursuant to this regulation shall be given—

   (a) in the case of an appeal by case stated, as soon as reasonably practicable after the day on which the case is lodged in the High Court;

   (b) in the case of any other appeal—

     (i) where leave to appeal or for abridgement of time is necessary, as soon as reasonably practicable after the court has granted such leave or abridgement, or

     (ii) in any other case, as soon as reasonably practicable after notice of appeal is duly given by the appellant.

Notice of abandonment of appeal

4. Notice of the abandonment of any relevant appeal shall be given to the Secretary of State—   **B36.05**

   (a) in England and Wales, by the appellate court to which the appeal is made, or

   (b) *[applies to Scotland]*,

as soon as reasonably practicable after the day on which notice of the abandonment of the appeal is duly given.

The Zebra, Pelican and Puffin Pedestrian Crossings Regulations and General Directions 1997

(SI 1997/2400)

B37.01 *[All the functions of a Minister of the Crown under the Zebra, Pelican and Puffin Pedestrian Crossings and General Directions 1997 which are exercisable in relation to Scotland have been transferred to the Scottish Ministers by the Scotland Act 1998 (Transfer of Functions to the Scottish Ministers etc.) Order 1999 (SI 1999/1750; not reproduced in this work) art.2 and Sch.1.*

B37.02 *The regulations and directions have been amended by:*

> *the Pelican and Puffin Pedestrian Crossings General (Amendment) Directions 1998 (SI 1998/901) (April 1, 1998);*
>
> *the Communications Act 2003 (Consequential Amendments) Order 2003 (SI 2003/2155) (September 17, 2003);*
>
> *the Fire and Rescue Services Act 2004 (Consequential Amendments) (England) Order 2004 (SI 2004/3168) (December 30, 2004);*
>
> *the Fire and Rescue Services Act 2004 (Consequential Amendments) (Wales) Order 2005 (SI 2005/2929) (October 25, 2005); and*
>
> *the Serious Organised Crime and Police Act 2005 (Consequential and Supplementary Amendments to Secondary Legislation) Order 2006 (SI 2006/594) (April 1, 2006).*

The amending instruments are referred to in the notes to the regulations and directions only by their years and numbers. The dates referred to above are the dates on which the amending instruments came into force.]

B37.03

6. Pedestrian demand units at Puffin crossings
7. Additional traffic signs
8. Colouring of containers and posts
9. Approval of equipment
10. Special directions by the Secretary of State

*   *   *

PART I

THE ZEBRA, PELICAN AND PUFFIN PEDESTRIAN CROSSINGS REGULATIONS 1997

SECTION I

Preliminary

Citation and commencement

B37.04   **1.** *[Omitted.]*

Revocation

B37.05   **2.**—(1) The "Zebra" Pedestrian Crossings Regulations 1971 [*SI 1971/1524*], the "Zebra" Pedestrian Crossings (Amendment) Regulations 1990 [*SI 1990/1828*] and, so far as they consist of or comprise regulations, the "Pelican" Pedestrian Crossings Regulations and General Directions 1987 [*SI 1987/16*] are hereby revoked.

(2) Any crossing which, immediately before the coming into force of these Regulations, was constituted a Pelican or a Zebra crossing in accordance with the regulations revoked by paragraph (1) which were applicable to it (*"the applicable regulations"*) shall, notwithstanding the revocation of the applicable regulations, be treated as constituted in accordance with these Regulations for so long as the traffic signs situated at or near it and the manner in which its presence and limits are indicated comply with the applicable regulations.

(3) Paragraph (2) shall cease to have effect on 15th December 2002.

B37.06   *[The text of the "Zebra" Pedestrian Crossings Regulations 1971 (SI 1971/ 1524) and that of the "Pelican" Pedestrian Crossings Regulations and General Directions 1987 (SI 1987/16) may be found in the eighteenth edition of this work.]*

Interpretation

B37.07   **3.**—(1) In these Regulations unless the context otherwise requires—

"*the 1984 Act*" means the Road Traffic Regulation Act 1984;

"*the 1994 Regulations*" means the Traffic Signs Regulations 1994 [*Pt I of SI 1994/1519*];

"*carriageway*" means—

(a) in relation to a crossing on a highway in England or Wales ..., a way constituting or comprised in the highway or road being a way over which the public has a right of way for the passage of vehicles; and

(b) in relation to a crossing on any other road in England or Wales to which the public has access, that part of the road to which vehicles have access,

but does not include in either case any central reservation (whether within the limits of the crossing or not);

"central reservation" means—

(a) in relation to a road comprising a single carriageway, any provision (including a refuge for pedestrians) which separates one part of the carriageway from another part;

(b) in relation to a road which comprises two or more carriageways any land or permanent work which separates those carriageways from one another;

"controlled area" means a Pelican controlled area, a Puffin controlled area or a Zebra controlled area;

"crossing" means a crossing for pedestrians established—

(a) in the case of a trunk road, by the Secretary of State pursuant to section 24 of the 1984 Act; and

(b) in the case of any other road, by a local traffic authority pursuant to section 23 of that Act;

"driver" in relation to a vehicle which is a motor cycle or pedal cycle means the person riding the vehicle who is in control of it;

"give-way line" means a road marking placed adjacent to a Zebra crossing in accordance with regulation 6(1) and Schedule 1;

"indicator for pedestrians" means the traffic sign of that description prescribed for the purposes of a Pelican crossing by regulation 5(2)(a) and paragraphs 2(c) and 5 of Part I and Part II of Schedule 2;

"layout or character" in relation to a road means the layout or character of the road itself and does not include the layout or character of any land or premises adjacent to the road;

"mm" means millimetres;

"one-way street" means a road on which the driving of vehicles otherwise than in one particular direction is prohibited;

"pedestrian demand unit" means the traffic sign of that description prescribed for the purposes of a Puffin crossing by regulation 5(3)(a) and paragraphs 1(b) and 3 of Part I and Part II of Schedule 3;

"pedestrian light signals" means the traffic sign of that description prescribed for the purposes of a Pelican crossing by regulation 5(2)(a) and paragraphs 2(b) and 4 of Part I of Schedule 2;

"Pelican controlled area" means an area of carriageway in the vicinity of a Pelican crossing the limits of which are indicated in accordance with regulation 6(2) and Schedule 4;

"Pelican crossing" means a crossing—

(a) at which there are traffic signs of the size, colour and type prescribed by regulation 5(2)(a) and Schedule 2;

(b) the limits of which are indicated in accordance with regulation 5(2)(b) and Schedule 4;

"primary signal" means vehicular light signals so placed as to face

vehicular traffic approaching a Pelican or a Puffin crossing and placed beyond the stop line and in front of the line of studs nearest the stop line indicating the limits of the crossing in accordance with regulation 6(3) and Schedule 4;

"Puffin controlled area" means an area of the carriageway in the vicinity of a Puffin crossing the limits of which are indicated in accordance with regulation 6(2) and Schedule 4;

"Puffin crossing" means a crossing—

    (a) at which there are traffic signs of the size, colour and type prescribed by regulation 5(3)(a) and Schedule 3;

    (b) the limits of which are indicated in accordance with regulation 5(3)(b) and Schedule 4;

"refuge for pedestrians" means a part of a road to which vehicles do not have access and on which pedestrians may wait after crossing one part of the carriageway and before crossing the other;

"retroreflecting material" means material which reflects a ray of light back towards the source of that light;

"road marking" means a traffic sign consisting of a line or mark or legend on a road and includes a stud;

"secondary signal" means vehicular light signals so placed as to face vehicular traffic approaching a Pelican or Puffin crossing but sited beyond the furthest limit of the crossing as viewed from the direction of travel of the traffic;

"stop line" means, in relation to a vehicle approaching a Pelican or Puffin crossing, the transverse continuous white line (indicated in accordance with regulation 6(3) and Schedule 4 and parallel to the limits of the crossing) which is on the same side of the crossing as the vehicle;

"stud" means a mark or device on the carrriageway, whether or not projecting above the surface of the carriageway;

"system of staggered crossings" means two or more Pelican crossings or two or more Puffin crossings provided on a road on which there is a central reservation and where—

    (a) there is one crossing on each side of the central reservation; and

    (b) taken together the two crossings do not lie along a straight line;

"two-way street" means a road which is not a one-way street;

"vehicular light signals" means, in relation to a Pelican or Puffin crossing, the traffic sign of that description prescribed (in the case of a Pelican crossing) by regulation 5(2)(a) and paragraphs 2(a) and 3 of Part I of Schedule 2 or (in the case of a Puffin crossing) by regulation 5(3)(a) and paragraphs 1(a) and 2 of Part I of Schedule 3;

"Zebra controlled area" means an area of carriageway in the vicinity of a Zebra crossing the limits of which are indicated in accordance with regulation 6(1) and Part II of Schedule 1; and

"Zebra crossing" means a crossing—

(a) at which there are traffic signs of the size, colour and type prescribed by regulation 5(1)(a) and Part I of Schedule 1; and

(b) the limits of which are indicated in accordance with regulation 5(1)(b) and Part II of Schedule 1.

(2) In these Regulations, unless it is expressly provided otherwise or the context otherwise requires—

(a) a reference to a numbered regulation or Schedule is a reference to the regulation or, as the case may be, the Schedule so numbered in these Regulations;

(b) a reference in a regulation or Schedule to a numbered paragraph is a reference to the paragraph so numbered in the regulation or, as the case may be, in the Schedule in which the reference occurs; and

(c) a reference to a sub-paragraph followed by a number or letter is a reference to the sub-paragraph bearing that number or letter in the paragraph in which the reference occurs.

[The 1994 Regulations referred to in reg.3(1) above have been revoked by the **B37.08** *Traffic Signs Regulations 2002 (SI 2002/3113 Pt I) (q.v.). The 1994 Regulations may be found in the twentieth edition of this work.*

The words omitted from the definition of "carriageway" relate exclusively to Scotland.]

Application of Regulations

4. These Regulations apply to a crossing which is a Zebra, Pelican or Puffin   **B37.09** crossing.

SECTION II

Form of crossings

Traffic signs and road markings for indicating crossings

5.—(1) A Zebra crossing shall be indicated by—   **B37.10**

(a) the placing at or near the crossing of traffic signs of the size, colour and type specified in Part I of Schedule 1;

(b) the placing on the carriageway to indicate the limits of the crossing of road markings of the size, colour and type specified in Part II of Schedule 1.

(2) A Pelican crossing shall be indicated by—

(a) the placing at or near the crossing of traffic signs of the size, colour and type specified in Schedule 2;

(b) the placing on the carriageway to indicate the limits of the crossing of road markings of the size, colour and type specified in Schedule 4.

(3) A Puffin crossing shall be indicated by—

(a) the placing at or near the crossing of traffic signs of the size, colour and type specified in Schedule 3;

(b) the placing on the carriageway to indicate the limits of the crossing of road markings of the size, colour and type specified in Schedule 4.

Give-way and stop lines and controlled areas

B37.11   6.—(1) On each side of a Zebra crossing, there shall be laid out a Zebra controlled area (including a give-way line) indicated by road markings of the size, colour and type, and generally in the manner, specified in Part II of Schedule 1.

(2) On each side of a Pelican or Puffin crossing, there shall be laid out a Pelican controlled area or a Puffin controlled area indicated by road markings of the size, colour and type, and generally in the manner, specified in Schedule 4.

(3) A stop line or stop lines of the size, colour and type specified in Schedule 4 shall be placed next to a Pelican or Puffin crossing in the manner specified in that Schedule.

Dimensions

B37.12   7.—(1) Dimensions indicated on any diagram shown in the Schedules to these Regulations are expressed in millimetres.

(2) A dimension (other than one specified as a maximum or minimum dimension) specified in a diagram in Schedule 2 or 3 may be varied if, in the case of a dimension of the length specified in column (2) of an item in the table below, the variation does not exceed the extent specified in column (3) of the item.

TABLE

(1) Item	(2) Length of dimension	(3) Extent of variation
(1)	less than 10mm	1mm
(2)	10mm or more but less than 50mm	10% of the dimension
(3)	50mm or more but less than 300mm	7.5% of the dimension
(4)	300mm or more	5% of the dimension

(3) A dimension (other than one specified as a maximum or minimum dimension) specified in any diagram in Schedule 1 or in Schedule 4 may be varied if, in the case of a dimension of the length specified in column (2) of an item in the table below, the variation does not exceed the extent specified in column (3) of the item.

TABLE

(1) Item	(2) Length of dimension	(3) Extent of variation
(1)	300mm or more	(i) 20% of the dimension where the varied dimension is greater than the specified dimension; or (ii) 10% of the dimension where the varied dimension is less than the specified dimension

(1) Item	(2) Length of dimension	(3) Extent of variation
(2)	less than 300mm	(i) 30% of the dimension where the varied dimension is greater than the specified dimension; or
		(ii) 10% of the dimension where the varied dimension is less than the specified dimension.

(4) Where maximum and minimum dimensions are specified for any element of a traffic sign or road marking, the dimension chosen for that element must not be less than the minimum and must not exceed the maximum.

(5) Where any diagram in a Schedule to these Regulations specifies a dimension for an element of a traffic sign or road marking together with a dimension for that element in brackets, the dimensions so specified shall be alternatives.

(6) A dimension specified in the 1994 Regulations in relation to a traffic sign prescribed by those Regulations and referred to in these Regulations may be varied to the extent permitted by the 1994 Regulations.

[The 1994 Regulations referred to in reg.7(6) above have been revoked by the **B37.13** *Traffic Signs Regulations 2002 (SI 2002/3113 Pt I) (q.v.). The 1994 Regulations may be found in the twentieth edition of this work.]*

Additional equipment

8. A traffic authority may provide at, or fix to any traffic sign or post placed for   **B37.14** the purposes of, a crossing in accordance with these Regulations any object, device, apparatus or equipment—

(a) in connection with the proper operation of the crossing; or

(b) which they consider appropriate for giving information or assistance to disabled persons wishing to use the crossing.

Additional traffic signs

9. In addition to the traffic signs prescribed in regulation 5 a traffic sign shown   **B37.15** in diagram 610, 611, 612, 613 or 616 in Schedule 2 or diagram 810 in Schedule 4, or a road marking shown in diagram 1029 or the white triangular markings included in the road marking shown in diagram 1061 of Schedule 6, to the 1994 Regulations may, if the traffic authority think fit, be placed at or near a crossing.

[The 1994 Regulations referred to above have been revoked by the Traffic **B37.16** *Signs Regulations 2002 (SI 2002/3113 Pt I) (q.v.). References to the 1994 Regulations should be construed in the light of the 2002 Regulations. The 1994 Regulations may be found in the twentieth edition of this work.]*

Non-compliance with requirements of this Section

10.—(1) Where, as respects a crossing or controlled area, the requirements of   **B37.17** this Section of these Regulations as to the placing of traffic signs and road markings to indicate the crossing or controlled area have not been complied with in every respect, the crossing or, as the case may be, the controlled area shall nevertheless be treated as complying with these Regulations if the non-compliance—

(a) is not such as materially to affect the general appearance of the crossing or the controlled area;

(b) does not, in the case of a Pelican or Puffin crossing, affect the proper operation of the vehicular and pedestrian signals at the crossing; and

(c) does not relate to the size of the controlled area.

(2) Nothing in any other provision of these Regulations shall be taken to restrict the generality of paragraph (1).

SECTION III

Significance of traffic signs at crossings

Scope of Section III

B37.18   11. The provisions of this Section of these Regulations (except regulation 16) are made under section 64(1) of the Road Traffic Regulation Act 1984 for the purpose of prescribing the warnings, information, requirements, restrictions and prohibitions which are to be conveyed to traffic by traffic signs and road markings of the size, colour and type prescribed by Section II.

Significance of vehicular light signals at Pelican crossings

B37.19   12.—(1) The significance of the vehicular light signals prescribed by regulation 5(2)(a) and paragraph 3 of Schedule 2 for the purpose of indicating a Pelican crossing shall be as follows—

(a) the green signal shall indicate that vehicular traffic may proceed beyond the stop line and across the crossing;

(b) the green arrow signal shall indicate that vehicular traffic may proceed beyond the stop line and through the crossing only for the purpose of proceeding in the direction indicated by the arrow;

(c) except as provided by sub-paragraph (e) [and sub-paragraph (ea)] the steady amber signal shall convey the same prohibition as the red signal except that, as respects a vehicle which is so close to the stop line that it cannot safely be stopped without proceeding beyond the stop line, it shall convey the same indication as the green signal or, if the amber signal was immediately preceded by a green arrow signal, as that green arrow signal;

(d) except as provided in sub-paragraph (e) [and sub-paragraph (ea)], the red signal shall convey the prohibition that vehicular traffic shall not proceed beyond the stop line;

(e) when a vehicle is being used for fire brigade [or, in England, fire and rescue authority], ambulance, national blood service or police purposes and the observance of the prohibition conveyed by the steady amber or the red signal in accordance with sub-paragraph (c) or (d) would be likely to hinder the use of that vehicle for the purpose for which it is being used, then those sub-paragraphs shall not apply to the vehicle, and the steady amber and the red signal shall each convey the information that the vehicle may proceed beyond the stop line if the driver—

   (i) accords precedence to any pedestrian who is on that part of the carriageway which lies within the limits of the crossing or on a central reservation which lies between two crossings which do not form part of a system of staggered crossings; and

   (ii) does not proceed in a manner or at a time likely to endanger any person or any vehicle approaching or waiting at the crossing, or to the driver of any such vehicle to change its speed or course in order to avoid an accident; [...]

[(ea) as regards England and Wales, and so far as relating to the functions of the Serious Organised Crime Agency which are exercisable in or as regards Scotland and which relate to reserved matters (within the meaning of the Scotland Act 1998), when a vehicle is being used for Serious Organised Crime Agency purposes and the observance of the prohibition conveyed by the steady amber or the red signal in accordance with sub-paragraph (c) or (d) would be likely to hinder the use of that vehicle for those purposes, then those sub-paragraphs shall not apply to the vehicle, and the steady amber and the red signal shall each convey the information that the vehicle may proceed beyond the stop line if the driver—

   (i) accords precedence to any pedestrian who is on that part of the carriageway which lies within the limits of the crossing or on a central reservation which lies between two crossings which do not form part of a system of staggered crossings; and

   (ii) does not proceed in a manner or at a time likely to endanger any person or any vehicle approaching or waiting at the crossing, or to cause the driver of any such vehicle to change its speed or course in order to avoid an accident; and]

 (f) the flashing amber signal shall convey the information that traffic may proceed across the crossing but that every pedestrian who is on the carriageway or a central reservation within the limits of the crossing (but not if he is on a central reservation which lies between two crossings forming part of a system of staggered crossings) before any part of a vehicle has entered those limits, has the right of precedence within those limits over that vehicle, and the requirement that the driver of a vehicle shall accord such precedence to any such pedestrian.

(2) Vehicular traffic proceeding beyond a stop line in accordance with paragraph (1) shall proceed with due regard to the safety of other road users and subject to any direction given by a constable in uniform or a traffic warden or to any other applicable prohibition or restriction.

(3) In this regulation, references to the *"stop line"* in relation to a Pelican crossing where the stop line is not visible are to be treated as references to the post or other structure on which the primary signal is mounted.

[Regulation 12 is printed as amended by SI 2004/3168; SI 2005/2929; SI 2006/594.]   **B37.20**

Significance of vehicular light signals at Puffin crossings

13.—(1) The significance of the vehicular light signals at a Puffin crossing   **B37.21**

prescribed by regulation 5(3)(a) and paragraph 2 of Schedule 3 shall be as follows—

(a) the green signal shall indicate that vehicular traffic may proceed beyond the stop line and across the crossing;

(b) the green arrow signal shall indicate that vehicular traffic may proceed beyond the stop line and through the crossing only for the purpose of proceeding in the direction indicated by the arrow;

(c) except as provided by sub-paragraph (f) [and sub-paragraph (g)], the amber signal shall, when shown alone, convey the same prohibition as the red signal, except that, as respects any vehicle which is so close to the stop line that it cannot safely be stopped without proceeding beyond the stop line, it shall convey the same indication as the green signal or, if the amber signal was immediately preceded by a green arrow signal, as that green arrow signal;

(d) except as provided in sub-paragraph (f) [and sub-paragraph (g)], the red signal shall convey the prohibition that vehicular traffic shall not proceed beyond the stop line;

(e) except as provided by sub-paragraph (f) [and sub-paragraph (g)], the red-with-amber signal shall denote an impending change to green in the indication given by the signals but shall convey the same prohibition as the red signal;

(f) when a vehicle is being used for fire brigade [or, in England [or Wales], fire and rescue authority], ambulance, national blood service or police purposes and the observance of the prohibition conveyed by the amber, red or red-with-amber signal in accordance with sub-paragraph (c), (d) or (e) would be likely to hinder the use of that vehicle for the purpose for which it is being used, then those sub-paragraphs shall not apply to the vehicle, and the red signal, red-with-amber and amber signals shall each convey the information that the vehicle may proceed beyond the stop line if the driver—

(i) accords precedence to any pedestrian who is on that part of the carriageway which lies within the limits of the crossing or on a central reservation which lies between two crossings which do not form part of a system of staggered crossings; and

(ii) does not proceed in a manner or at a time likely to endanger any person or any vehicle approaching or waiting at the crossing, or to cause the driver of any such vehicle to change its speed or course in order to avoid an accident;

[(g) as regards England and Wales, and so far as relating to the functions of the Serious Organised Crime Agency which are exercisable in or as regards Scotland and which relate to reserved matters (within the meaning of the Scotland Act 1998), when a vehicle is being used for Serious Organised Crime Agency purposes and the observance of the prohibition conveyed by the amber, red or red-with-amber signal in accordance with sub-paragraph (c), (d) or (e) would be likely to hinder the use of that vehicle for those purposes, then those sub-paragraphs shall not apply to the vehicle, and the red signal, red-with-amber and amber signals shall each convey the information that the vehicle may proceed beyond the stop line if the driver——

     (i) accords precedence to any pedestrian who is on that part of the carriageway which lies within the limits of the crossing or on a central reservation which lies between two crossings which do not form part of a system of staggered crossings; and

     (ii) does not proceed in a manner or at a time likely to endanger any person or any vehicle approaching or waiting at the crossing, or to cause the driver of any such vehicle to change its speed or course in order to avoid an accident.]

(2) Vehicular traffic proceeding beyond a stop line in accordance with paragraph (1) shall proceed with due regard to the safety of other road users and subject to any direction given by a constable in uniform or a traffic warden or to any other applicable prohibition or restriction.

(3) In this regulation, references to the *"stop line"* in relation to a Puffin crossing where the stop line is not visible are to be treated as references to the post or other structure on which the primary signal is mounted.

[Regulation 13 is printed as amended by SI 2004/3168; SI 2005/2929; SI 2006/594.]   **B37.22**

Significance of give-way lines at Zebra crossings

14. A give-way line included in the markings placed pursuant to regulation 5(1)(b) and Part II of Schedule 1 shall convey to vehicular traffic proceeding towards a Zebra crossing the position at or before which a vehicle should be stopped for the purpose of complying with regulation 25 (precedence of pedestrians over vehicles at Zebra crossings).   **B37.23**

Significance of pedestrian light signals and figures on pedestrian demand units

15.—(1) The significance of the red and steady green pedestrian light signals whilst they are illuminated at a Pelican crossing and of the red and green figures on a pedestrian demand unit whilst they are illuminated at a Puffin crossing shall be as follows—   **B37.24**

    (a) the red pedestrian light signal and the red figure shall both convey to a pedestrian the warning that, in the interests of safety, he should not cross the carriageway; and

    (b) the steady green pedestrian light signal and the steady green figure shall both indicate to a pedestrian that he may cross the carriageway and that drivers may not cause vehicles to enter the crossing.

(2) The flashing green pedestrian light signal at a Pelican crossing shall convey—

    (a) to a pedestrian who is already on the crossing when the flashing green signal is first shown the information that he may continue to use the crossing and that, if he is on the carriageway or a central reservation within the limits of that crossing (but not if he is on a central reservation which lies between two crossings which form part of a system of staggered crossings) before any part of a vehicle has entered those limits, he has precedence over that vehicle within those limits; and

    (b) to a pedestrian who is not already on the crossing when the flashing green light is first shown the warning that he should not, in the interests of safety, start to cross the carriageway.

(3) Any audible signal emitted by any device for emitting audible signals provided in conjunction with the steady green pedestrian light signal or the green figure, and any tactile signal given by any device for making tactile signals similarly provided, shall convey to a pedestrian the same indication as the steady green pedestrian light signal or as the green figure as the case may be.

Significance of additional traffic signs

B37.25   **16.** A traffic sign placed in accordance with regulation 9 shall convey the information, prohibition or requirement specified in relation to it by the 1994 Regulations.

B37.26   *[The 1994 Regulations referred to above have been revoked by the Traffic Signs Regulations 2002 (SI 2002/3113 Pt I) (q.v.). The 1994 Regulations may be found in the twentieth edition of this work.]*

SECTION IV

Movement of traffic at crossings

Scope of Section IV

B37.27   **17.** This Section of these Regulations is made under section 25 of the 1984 Act with respect to the movement of traffic at and in the vicinity of crossings.

Prohibition against the stopping of vehicles on crossings

B37.28   **18.** The driver of a vehicle shall not cause the vehicle or any part of it to stop within the limits of a crossing unless he is prevented from proceeding by circumstances beyond his control or it is necessary for him to stop to avoid injury or damage to persons or property.

Pedestrians not to delay on crossings

B37.29   **19.** No pedestrian shall remain on the carriageway within the limits of a crossing longer than is necessary for that pedestrian to pass over the crossing with reasonable despatch.

Prohibition against the stopping of vehicles in controlled areas

B37.30   **20.**—(1) For the purposes of this regulation and regulations 21 and 22 the word *"vehicle"* shall not include a pedal bicycle not having a sidecar attached to it, whether or not additional means of propulsion by mechanical power are attached to the bicycle.

(2) Except as provided in regulations 21 and 22 the driver of a vehicle shall not cause it or any part of it to stop in a controlled area.

Exceptions to regulation 20

B37.31   **21.** Regulation 20 does not prohibit the driver of a vehicle from stopping it in a controlled area—

(a) if the driver has stopped it for the purpose of complying with regulation 25 or 26;

(b) if the driver is prevented from proceeding by circumstances beyond his control or it is necessary for him to stop to avoid injury or damage to persons or property; [...]

(c) when the vehicle is being used for police, fire brigade [or, in England [or Wales], fire and rescue authority] or ambulance purposes; [or

(d) as regards England and Wales, and so far as relating to the functions of the Serious Organised Crime Agency which are exercisable in or as regards Scotland and which relate to reserved matters (within the meaning of the Scotland Act 1998), when the vehicle is being used for Serious Organised Crime Agency purposes.]

[Regulation 21 is printed as amended by SI 2004/3168; SI 2005/2929; SI 2006/ 594.]   **B37.32**

Further exceptions to regulation 20

22.—(1) Regulation 20 does not prohibit the driver of a vehicle from stopping   **B37.33** it in a controlled area—

(a) for so long as may be necessary to enable the vehicle to be used for the purposes of—

   (i) any building operation, demolition or excavation;

  (ii) the removal of any obstruction to traffic;

 (iii) the maintenance, improvement or reconstruction of a road; or

 (iv) the laying, erection, alteration, repair or cleaning in or near the crossing of any sewer or of any main, pipe or apparatus for the supply of gas, water or electricity, or of any [electronic communications apparatus] kept installed for the purposes of [an electronic communications code network] or of any other [electronic communications apparatus] lawfully kept installed in any position,

but only if the vehicle cannot be used for one of those purposes without stopping in the controlled area; or

(b) if the vehicle is a public service vehicle being used—

   (i) in the provision of a local service; or

  (ii) to carry passengers for hire or reward at separate fares,

and the vehicle, having proceeded past the crossing to which the controlled area relates, is waiting in that area in order to take up or set down passengers; or

(c) if he stops the vehicle for the purposes of making a left or right turn.

(2) In paragraph (1) *"local service"* has the meaning given in section 2 of the Transport Act 1985 [*q.v.*] but does not include an excursion or tour as defined by section 137(1) of that Act.

[Regulation 22 is printed as amended by SI 2003/2155. For the meaning of   **B37.34** *"electronic communications apparatus" and "an electronic communications code network", see SI 2003/2155 art.2(1) and the Communications Act 2003 Pt 2, Ch.1.]*

Prohibition against vehicles proceeding across Pelican or Puffin crossings

B37.35   23. When vehicular light signals at a Pelican or Puffin crossing are displaying the red light signal the driver of a vehicle shall not cause it to contravene the prohibition given by that signal by virtue of regulation 12 or 13.

Prohibition against vehicles overtaking at crossings

B37.36   24.—(1) Whilst any motor vehicle (in this regulation called *"the approaching vehicle"*) or any part of it is within the limits of a controlled area and is proceeding towards the crossing, the driver of the vehicle shall not cause it or any part of it—

    (a) to pass ahead of the foremost part of any other motor vehicle proceeding in the same direction; or

    (b) to pass ahead of the foremost part of a vehicle which is stationary for the purpose of complying with regulation 23, 25 or 26.

  (2) In paragraph (1) —

    (a) the reference to a motor vehicle in sub-paragraph (a) is, in a case where more than one motor vehicle is proceeding in the same direction as the approaching vehicle in a controlled area, a reference to the motor vehicle nearest to the crossing; and

    (b) the reference to a stationary vehicle is, in a case where more than one vehicle is stationary in a controlled area for the purpose of complying with regulation 23, 25 or 26, a reference to the stationary vehicle nearest the crossing.

B37.37   *[For the application of the fixed penalty procedure to overtaking a moving or stationary vehicle on a zebra, pelican or puffin crossing contrary to reg.24, see the Road Traffic Offenders Act 1988 Pt III and Sch.3 above.]*

Precedence of pedestrians over vehicles at Zebra crossings

B37.38   25.—(1) Every pedestrian, if he is on the carriageway within the limits of a Zebra crossing, which is not for the time being controlled by a constable in uniform or traffic warden, before any part of a vehicle has entered those limits, shall have precedence within those limits over that vehicle and the driver of the vehicle shall accord such precedence to any such pedestrian.

  (2) Where there is a refuge for pedestrians or central reservation on a Zebra crossing, the parts of the crossing situated on each side of the refuge for pedestrians or central reservation shall, for the purposes of this regulation, be treated as separate crossings.

Precedence of pedestrians over vehicles at Pelican crossings

B37.39   26. When the vehicular light signals at a Pelican crossing are showing the flashing amber signal, every pedestrian, if he is on the carriageway or a central reservation within the limits of the crossing (but not if he is on a central reservation which forms part of a system of staggered crossings) before any part of a vehicle has entered those limits, shall have precedence within those limits over that vehicle and the driver of the vehicle shall accord such precedence to any such pedestrian.

Regulations 5(1) and 6(1)   SCHEDULE 1

TRAFFIC SIGNS AND ROAD MARKINGS TO INDICATE ZEBRA CROSSINGS AND ZEBRA CONTROLLED AREAS

PART I

TRAFFIC SIGNS

1.—(1) Subject to the following provisions of this Part of this Schedule the traffic signs which are to be placed at or near a Zebra crossing for the purpose of indicating it shall consist of globes each of which is—   **B37.40**

  (a) coloured yellow or fluorescent yellow;

  (b) not less than 275 nor more than 335mm in diameter;

  (c) illuminated by a flashing light or, where the Secretary of State so authorises in writing in relation to a particular crossing a constant steady light; and

  (d) mounted on a post or bracket so that the lowest part of a globe is not less than 2.1 metres nor more than 3.1 metres above the surface of the ground immediately beneath it.

(2) One globe shall be placed at each end of the crossing and, if there is a refuge for pedestrians or central reservation on the crossing, one or more globes may, if the traffic authority thinks fit, be placed on the refuge or central reservation.

2. Where a globe is mounted on or attached to a post, whether or not specially provided for the purpose—   **B37.41**

  (a) the post shall be coloured in alternate black and white bands, the lowest band being coloured black;

  (b) the bands shall be not less than 275mm nor more than 335mm wide except that the lowest band may be up to 1 metre wide; and

  (c) the post may be internally illuminated.

3. A globe or the post on which it is mounted may be fitted with all or any of the following—   **B37.42**

  (a) a backing board or other device designed to improve the conspicuousness of the globe;

  (b) a shield or other device designed to prevent or reduce light shining into adjacent premises;

  (c) a light to illuminate the crossing.

4. A crossing shall not be taken to have ceased to be indicated in accordance with this Part of this Schedule by reason only of—   **B37.43**

  (a) the imperfection, disfigurement or discolouration of any globe or post, or

  (b) the failure of illumination of any of the globes.

5. Nothing in this Part of this Schedule shall be taken to restrict regulation 8 or 9.   **B37.44**

PART II

ROAD MARKINGS

Road markings

6. Subject to the following provisions of this Part of this Schedule —   **B37.45**

  (a) within the limits of a Zebra crossing the carriageway shall be marked with a series of alternate black and white stripes;

  (b) the Zebra controlled areas shall be marked with give-way lines, a line of studs and zig-zag lines,

of the size and type, and generally in the manner, shown in the diagram at the end of this Part of this Schedule.

Number of studs and stripes

B37.46   7. The number of studs and stripes may be varied.

Limits of the crossing

B37.47   8.—(1) If it provides a reasonable contrast with the white stripes, the colour of the surface of the carriageway may be used to indicate the stripes shown coloured black in the diagram.

(2) The white stripes may be illuminated by retroreflecting material.

(3) Subject to paragraph (4) each black and each white stripe shall be of the same size and not less than 500mm nor more than 715mm wide as measured across the carriageway.

(4) The first stripe at each end may be up to 1300mm wide and, if the traffic authority consider it appropriate in relation to a particular crossing having regard to the layout of the carriageway or other special circumstances, the other stripes may be not less than 380mm nor more than 840mm wide as measured across the carriageway.

Studs

B37.48   9.—(1) The studs may be omitted altogether.

(2) If studs are provided—

    (a) they shall be coloured white, silver or light grey;

    (b) they shall be either—

        (i) circular in shape with a diameter of not less than 95mm nor more than 110mm; or

        (ii) square in shape with each side not less than 95mm nor more than 110mm long;

    (c) they may be illuminated by retroreflecting material;

    (d) if they consist of a device fixed to the carriageway, they shall—

        (i) not be fitted with reflecting lenses;

        (ii) be so fixed that they do not project more than 20mm above the adjacent surface of the carriageway at their highest points nor more than 6mm at their edges;

    (e) the distance from the centre of any stud to the centre of the next stud in the same line shall not be less than 250mm nor more than 715mm and the distance between the edge of the carriageway at each end of a line of studs and the centre of the nearest stud shall be not more than 1.3 metres; and

    (f) the two lines of studs need not be at right angles to the edge of the carriageway, but shall form straight lines and, so far as is reasonably practicable, shall be parallel to each other.

Zig-zag lines

B37.49   10.—(1) The pattern of the central zig-zag lines may be reversed or, on a road having a carriageway not more than 6 metres wide, those lines may be omitted altogether so long as they are replaced by the road marking shown in diagram 1004 in Schedule 6 to the 1994 Regulations.

(2) Subject to sub-paragraph (4) the number of marks in a zig-zag line shall not be less than 8 nor more than 18 and a zig-zag line need not contain the same number of marks as any other zig-zag line.

(3) Each mark in a zig-zag line shall be coloured white and may be illuminated by retroreflecting material.

(4) Where the traffic authority is satisfied that, by reason of the layout or character of any roads in the vicinity of a Zebra crossing, it would be impracticable to lay out a Zebra controlled area in accordance with this Schedule —

    (a) the number of marks in any zig-zag line in that area may be reduced to not less than 2; and

(b) the length of any of the marks may be varied to not less than 1 metre.

Give-way line

11.—(1) The give-way line shall be coloured white and may be illuminated by retrore-   **B37.50**
flecting material.

(2) The angle of the give-way line in relation to, and its distance from, the edge of the crossing may be varied, if the traffic authority is satisfied that the variation is necessary having regard to the angle of the crossing in relation to the edge of the carriageway.

(3) The maximum distance of 3 metres between the give-way line and the limits of the crossing shown in the diagram in this Part of this Schedule may, if the traffic authority think fit having regard to the layout or character of the road in the vicinity of the crossing, be increased to not more than 10 metres.

Discolouration or partial displacement of markings

12. A Zebra crossing or a Zebra controlled area shall not be deemed to have ceased to be   **B37.51**
indicated in accordance with this Schedule by reason only of the discolouration or partial displacement of any of the road markings prescribed by this Schedule, so long as the general appearance of the pattern of the lines is not impaired.

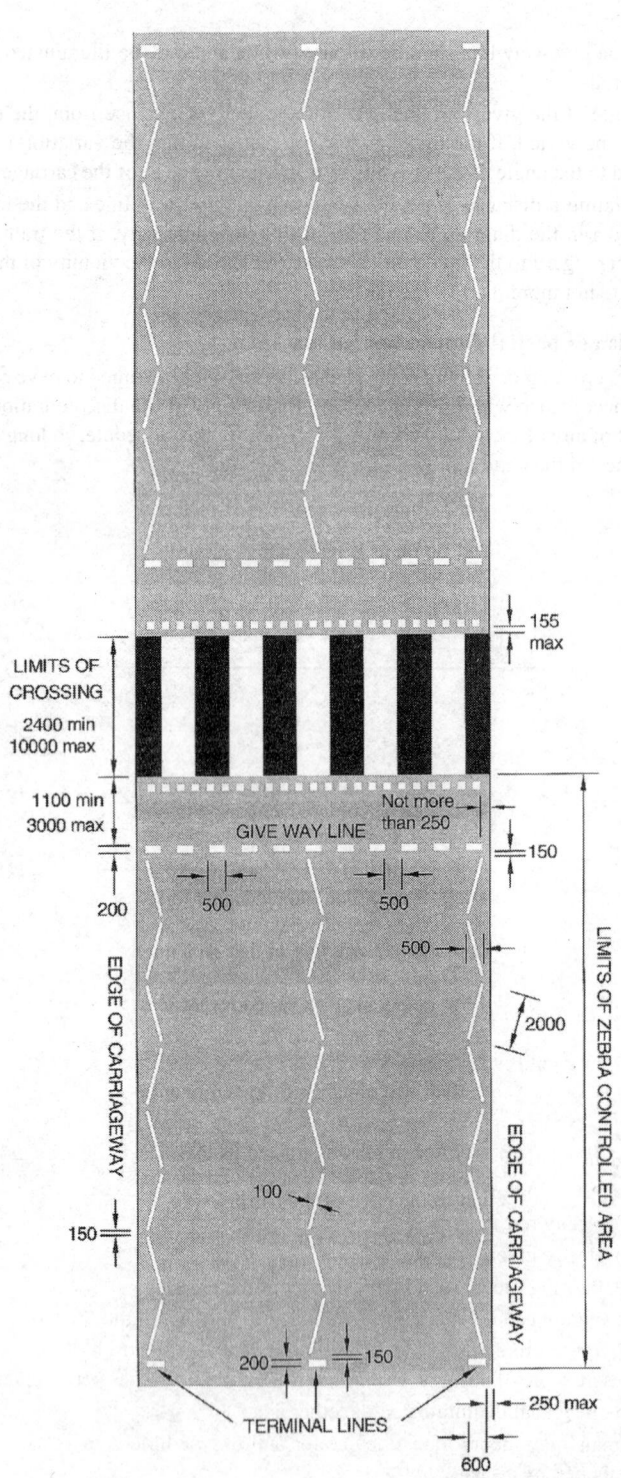

Regulation 5(2)(a)   SCHEDULE 2

Traffic Signs to Indicate Pelican Crossings

Part I

Traffic Signs to be Placed at or Near Pelican Crossings

Interpretation

1. In this Schedule *"push button"* has the meaning given by paragraph 5(c).   **B37.52**

Traffic signs

2. The traffic signs which are to be placed at or near a Pelican crossing shall consist of a   **B37.53**
combination of—

(a) vehicular light signals;

(b) pedestrian light signals; and

(c) indicators for pedestrians,

of the size, colour and type specified in the following provisions of this Part of this
Schedule, together with any additional traffic signs placed in accordance with regulation 9.

Vehicular light signals

3.—(1) The vehicular light signals shall be of the size, colour and type of the signals   **B37.54**
shown in diagram 3000 in Schedule 8 to the 1994 Regulations, except that a green arrow
may be substituted for the green aspect in the manner shown in diagram 3003 in that
Schedule or in accordance with any variant permitted by those Regulations in respect of
that diagram.

(2) The lamp showing an amber light shall be capable of showing a light which is either
steady or which flashes at a rate of not less than 70 nor more than 90 flashes per minute.

(3) The vehicular light signals shall be illuminated in the following sequence—

(a) steady green,

(b) steady amber,

(c) steady red,

(d) flashing amber.

[The 1994 Regulations referred to above have been revoked by the Traffic   **B37.55**
Signs Regulations 2002 (SI 2002/3113 Pt I) (q.v.). References to the 1994 Regula-
tions should be construed in the light of the 2002 Regulations. The 1994 Regula-
tions may be found in the twentieth edition of this work.]

Pedestrian light signals

4.—(1) The pedestrian light signals shall be of the size, colour and type of the signals   **B37.56**
shown in diagram 4002 in Schedule 9 to the 1994 Regulations.

(2) The signals shall be so designed that—

(a) they operate in the following sequence—

(i) steady red,

(ii) steady green,

(iii) flashing green;

(b) the red figure can be internally illuminated by a steady light;

(c) the green figure can be internally illuminated by a steady light or a light which
flashes at a rate of not less than 70 nor more than 90 flashes per minute; and

(d) when one signal is illuminated the other is not.

(3) The signals may incorporate a device for emitting audible signals whilst the green
figure is illuminated by a steady light.

[The 1994 Regulations referred to above have been revoked by the Traffic   **B37.57**

Signs Regulations 2002 (SI 2002/3113 Pt I) (q.v.). References to the 1994 Regulations should be construed in the light of the 2002 Regulations. The 1994 Regulations may be found in the twentieth edition of this work.]

Indicators for pedestrians

B37.58   5. The indicators for pedestrians—

(a) shall be of the size, colour and type shown in the diagram in Part II of this Schedule;

(b) shall be so constructed that the word "WAIT" as shown on the diagram can be illuminated;

(c) shall incorporate a push button or other switching device (referred to in this Schedule as a *"push button"*) which can be used by pedestrians with the effect described in paragraphs 6 and 7;

(d) shall be so constructed that the instruction for pedestrians shown in the diagram can be internally illuminated; and

(e) may be so constructed that a device giving audible or tactile signals is provided for use when the green figure shown in the diagram is illuminated by a steady light.

Co-ordination of light signals and indicators for pedestrians

B37.59   6.—(1) The vehicular light signals, pedestrian light signals and the indicators for pedestrians shall be so constructed that—

(a) before the signals and indicators are operated by the pressing of a push button (or by remote control in accordance with paragraph 7) —

(i) the vehicular light signals show a green or red light,

(ii) the pedestrian light signals show a red light,

(iii) the word "WAIT" on the indicators for pedestrians is not illuminated,

(iv) any device for giving tactile signals is inactive; and

(v) any device for giving audible signals is silent;

(b) when a push button is pressed or the signals and indicators are operated by remote control—

(i) the signals and indicators show lights in the sequences specified in descending order in—

(a) column (1) in the case of vehicular light signals;

(b) in column (2) in the case of pedestrian light signals; and

(c) in column (3) in the case of indicators for pedestrians, of either Part III or Part IV of this Schedule;

(ii) when the pedestrian light signals are showing a steady green light, the word "WAIT" in the indicators for pedestrians is not illuminated;

(iii) when the pedestrian light signals are showing a flashing green light, the word "WAIT" in the indicators for pedestrians is illuminated immediately and the signals and indicators are caused to show lights in the sequence specified in paragraph (i) above at the end of the next vehicle period; and

(iv) when the pedestrian light signals are showing a red light, the word "WAIT" in the indicators for pedestrians is illuminated immediately and the vehicular light signals and indicators for pedestrians are caused to show lights in the sequence specified in paragraph (i);

(c) the periods during which lights are shown by the signals and indicators, begin and end in relation to each other as shown in either Part III or Part IV of this Schedule as if each horizontal line in those Parts represented one moment of time, subsequent moments occurring in descending order, but the distances between the horizontal lines do not represent the lengths of the periods during which lights shown by the signals and indicator are, or are not, lit.

(2) Where a device for emitting audible signals is provided pursuant to paragraph 4(3) or (5)(e), it shall be so constructed that the device operates only when the pedestrian light signals are showing a steady green light and at the same time the vehicular light signals are showing a red light.

(3) Where a device for giving tactile signals is provided pursuant to paragraph 5(e), it shall be so constructed that, when it is operating, a regular movement perceptible to touch by pedestrians is made only when the pedestrian light signals are showing a steady green light and at the same time the vehicular light signals are showing a red light.

(4) In this paragraph *"vehicle period"* means such period as may be fixed from time to time in relation to a Pelican crossing, being a period which begins when the vehicular light signals cease to show a flashing amber light and during which those signals show a green light.

Operation by remote control

7. The vehicular light signals, pedestrian light signals, indicators for pedestrians and any device for giving tactile signals or emitting audible signals, when they are placed at or near a Pelican crossing may also be so constructed that they can be operated by remote control.   **B37.60**

PART II

INDICATOR FOR PEDESTRIANS

[Diagram omitted.]   **B37.61**

PART III

SEQUENCE OF OPERATION OF VEHICULAR AND PEDESTRIAN LIGHT SIGNALS AND INDICATOR FOR
PEDESTRIANS (BUT NOT THE AUDIBLE OR TACTILE SIGNALS)

B37.62

Sequence of vehicular traffic light signals (1)	Sequence of pedestrian signals	
	Pedestrian light signals (2)	*Indicator for pedestrians* (3)
Green light	Red light	The word "WAIT" is illuminated
Amber light		
Red light		
	Green light	The word "WAIT" is not illuminated
Flashing amber light	Flashing green light	The word "WAIT" is illuminated
	Red light	
Green light		

Part IV

Alternative Sequence of Operation of Vehicular and Pedestrian Light Signals and
Indicator for Pedestrians (But not the Audible or Tactile Signals)

B37.63

Sequence of vehicular traffic light signals	Sequence of pedestrian signals	
	Pedestrian light signals	Indicator for pedestrians
(1)	(2)	(3)
Green light	Red light	The word "WAIT" is illuminated
Amber light		
Red light		
	Green light	The word "WAIT" is not illuminated
Flashing amber light	Flashing green light	The word "WAIT" is illuminated
	Red light	
Green light		

Regulation 5(3)(a)   SCHEDULE 3

Traffic Signs to Indicate Puffin Crossings

Part I

Traffic Signs to Indicate Puffin Crossings

Traffic signs at or near a Puffin crossing

B37.64   1. The traffic signs which are to be placed at or near a Puffin crossing by virtue of regulation 5(3)(a) shall consist of a combination of—

(a) vehicular light signals: and

(b) pedestrian demand units,

of the size, colour and type specified in the following provisions of this Schedule, together with any additional traffic signs placed in accordance with regulation 9.

Vehicular light signals

B37.65   2.—(1) The vehicular light signals shall be of the size, colour and type shown in diagram 3000 in Schedule 8 to the 1994 Regulations, except that a green arrow may be substituted for the green aspect in the manner shown in diagram 3003 in that Schedule or in accordance with any variant permitted by those Regulations in respect of that diagram.

(2) The vehicular lights shall be illuminated in the following sequence—

(a) red,

(b) red and amber together,

(c) green,

(d) amber.

B37.66   *[The 1994 Regulations referred to above have been revoked by the Traffic Signs Regulations 2002 (SI 2002/3113 Pt I) (q.v.). References to the 1994 Regulations should be construed in the light of the 2002 Regulations. The 1994 Regulations may be found in the twentieth edition of this work.]*

Pedestrian demand unit

3.—(1) A pedestrian demand unit shall be placed at each end of a crossing.   **B37.67**

(2) Each such unit shall consist of a device the principal features of which are a signal display of the size, colour and type shown in the diagram in Part II of this Schedule and which—

(a) complies with the requirements of sub-paragraph (3); and

(b) includes a push button or other switching device which in some way indicates to pedestrians that it has been operated.

(3) The requirements referred to in sub-paragraph (2)(a) are—

(a) the signal display must comprise a red figure and a green figure, both of which can be internally illuminated;

(b) while one figure is illuminated the other figure must not be capable of being illuminated; and

(c) the green figure must be capable of being illuminated only whilst there is conveyed to vehicular traffic, by means of the red vehicular light signal prescribed by paragraph 2, a prohibition against entering the limits of the Puffin crossing at or near which the unit is displayed and at no other time.

(4) The pedestrian demand unit may incorporate a device for emitting tactile or audible signals whilst the green figure is illuminated.

(5) Units consisting of only the red and green figures or the push button and legend comprised in a pedestrian demand unit may be provided at a crossing in addition to pedestrian demand units.

PART II

Pedestrian Demand Unit

[Diagram omitted.]   **B37.68**

Regulation 5(2)(b)   SCHEDULE 4
and (3)(b) and 6(2) and (3)

PART I

Road Markings to Indicate Pelican and Puffin Crossings, Pelican and Puffin Controlled Areas and Stop Lines

Interpretation of Schedule

1. In this Schedule except where otherwise stated,—   **B37.69**

(a) a reference to a *"crossing"* is to a Pelican crossing or a Puffin crossing;

(b) a reference to a *"controlled area"* is to a Pelican controlled area or a Puffin controlled area;

(c) a reference to a numbered diagram is a reference to the diagram in Part II of this Schedule so numbered.

Indication of limits of crossings and of controlled areas and stop lines

2.—(1) Subject to the provisions of this Schedule, the limits of a crossing on a two-way   **B37.70** street and of its controlled areas and stop lines shall be indicated by road markings consisting of lines and studs on the carriageway of the size and type shown—

(a) in diagram 1 where there is no central reservation;

(b) in diagram 2 where there is a central reservation, but the crossing does not form part of a system of staggered crossings; and

(c) in diagram 3 where the crossing forms part of a system of staggered crossings.

(2) Subject to the provisions of this Schedule, the limits of a crossing on a one-way street and of its controlled areas and stop lines shall be indicated by road markings consisting of lines and studs placed on the carriageway of the size and type shown—

(a) in diagram 4 where there is no central reservation;

(b) in diagram 5 where there is a central reservation but the crossing does not form part of a system of staggered crossings; and

(c) in diagram 6 where the crossing forms part of a system of staggered crossings.

(3) The two lines of studs indicating the limits of a crossing need not be at right angles to the edge of the carriageway, but shall form straight lines and shall, as near as is reasonably practicable, be parallel to each other.

Controlled areas and stop lines on a two-way street

B37.71   3.—(1) Where a crossing is on a two-way street the road markings to indicate each controlled area and stop line shall consist of—

(a) a stop line parallel to the nearer row of studs indicating the limits of the crossing and extending, in the manner indicated in the appropriate diagram, across the part of the carriageway used by vehicles approaching the crossing from the side on which the stop line is placed; and

(b) two or more longitudinal zig-zag lines or, in the case of a road having more than one carriageway, two or more such lines on each carriageway, each zig-zag line containing not less than 8 nor more than 18 marks and extending away from the crossing.

(2) Subject to paragraph (3), where a central reservation is provided, the road marking shown in diagram 1040 in Schedule 6 to the 1994 Regulations may be placed between the zig-zag lines on the approaches to the central reservation.

(3) Where a central reservation is provided connecting crossings which form part of a system of staggered crossings, the road marking shown in diagram 1040.2 in Schedule 6 to the 1994 Regulations shall be placed in the manner indicated in diagram 3.

(4) The distance between the studs and the terminal marks on the exit sides shall be not less than 1700mm nor more than 3000mm.

B37.72   *[The 1994 Regulations referred to above have been revoked by the Traffic Signs Regulations 2002 (SI 2002/3113 Pt I) (q.v.). References to the 1994 Regulations should be construed in the light of the 2002 Regulations. The 1994 Regulations may be found in the twentieth edition of this work.]*

Controlled areas and stop line on a one-way street

B37.73   4.—(1) Where a crossing is on a one-way street the road markings to indicate a controlled area and stop line shall consist of—

(a) a stop line parallel to the nearer row of studs indicating the limits of the crossing and extending—

    (i) in the case of a crossing of the type shown in diagram 4 or 5, from one edge of the carriageway to the other; and

    (ii) in the case of a crossing of the type shown in diagram 6, from the edge of the carriageway to the central reservation; and

(b) two or more zig-zag lines, each containing not less than 8 nor more than 18 marks and extending away from the crossing.

(2) Subject to paragraph (3), where a central reservation is provided, the road marking shown in diagram 1041 in Schedule 6 to the 1994 Regulations may be placed between the zig-zag lines on the approaches to the central reservation.

(3) Where a central reservation is provided connecting crossings which form part of a system of staggered crossings, the road marking mentioned in paragraph (2) shall be placed in the manner indicated in diagram 6.

B37.74   *[The 1994 Regulations referred to in para.4(2) above have been revoked by the Traffic Signs Regulations 2002 (SI 2002/3113 Pt I) (q.v.). References to the 1994 Regulations should be construed in the light of the 2002 Regulations. The 1994 Regulations may be found in the twentieth edition of this work.]*

Variations in relation to a controlled area or stop line

5.—(1) Where the traffic authority is satisfied that, by reason of the layout or character **B37.75** of the roads in the vicinity of a crossing, it is impracticable to indicate a controlled area in accordance with the requirements of the preceding provisions of this Schedule, the following variations shall be permitted—

(a) the number of marks in each zig-zag line may be reduced to not less than 2;

(b) the marks comprised in a zig-zag line may be varied to a length of not less than 1 metre, in which case—

(i) each mark in each zig-zag line must be of the same or substantially the same length as the other marks in the same line;

(ii) and the number of marks in each line must be not more than 8 nor less than 2.

(2) The angle of a stop line in relation to the nearer line of studs indicating the limits of a crossing may be varied, if the traffic authority is satisfied that the variation is necessary having regard to the angle of the crossing in relation to the edge of the carriageway.

(3) The maximum distance of 3 metres between a stop line and the nearer line of studs indicating the limits of the crossing shown in the diagrams in this Schedule may be increased to such greater distance, not exceeding 10 metres, as the traffic authority may decide.

(4) Each zig-zag line in a controlled area need not contain the same number of marks as the others and the pattern of the central lines may be reversed or, if the carriageway is not more than 6 metres wide, may be omitted altogether if replaced by the road marking shown in diagram 1004 in Schedule 6 to the 1994 Regulations.

[The 1994 Regulations referred to above have been revoked by the Traffic **B37.76** *Signs Regulations 2002 (SI 2002/3113 Pt I) (q.v.). References to the 1994 Regulations should be construed in the light of the 2002 Regulations. The 1994 Regulations may be found in the twentieth edition of this work.]*

Colour and illumination of road markings

6. Subject to paragraph 7, the road markings shown in the diagrams in this Schedule **B37.77** shall be coloured white and may be illuminated by retroreflecting material.

Form and colour of studs

7.—(1) The studs shown in the diagrams in this Schedule shall be— **B37.78**

(a) coloured white, silver or light grey and shall not be fitted with reflective lenses; and

(b) either circular in shape with a diameter of not less than 95mm nor more than 110mm or square in shape with the length of each side being not less than 95mm nor more than 110mm.

(2) Any stud which is fixed or embedded in the carriageway shall not project more than 20mm above the carriageway at its highest point nor more than 6mm at its edges.

Supplementary

8. The requirements of this Schedule shall be regarded as having been complied with in **B37.79** the case of any crossing or controlled area, if most of the road markings comply with those requirements, even though some of the studs or lines do not so comply by reason of discolouration, temporary removal or a displacement or for some other reason, so long as the general appearance of the road markings as a whole is not thereby materially impaired.

Part II

B37.80

Diagram 1

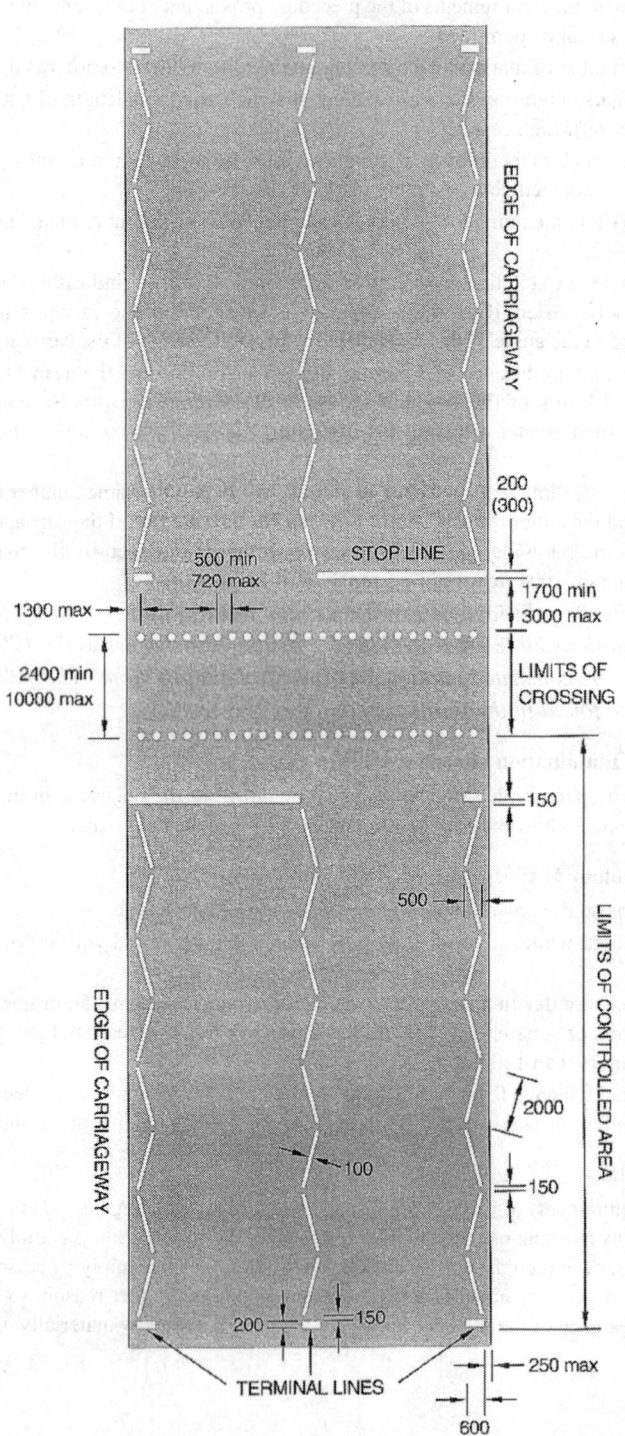

Dɪᴀɢʀᴀᴍ 2

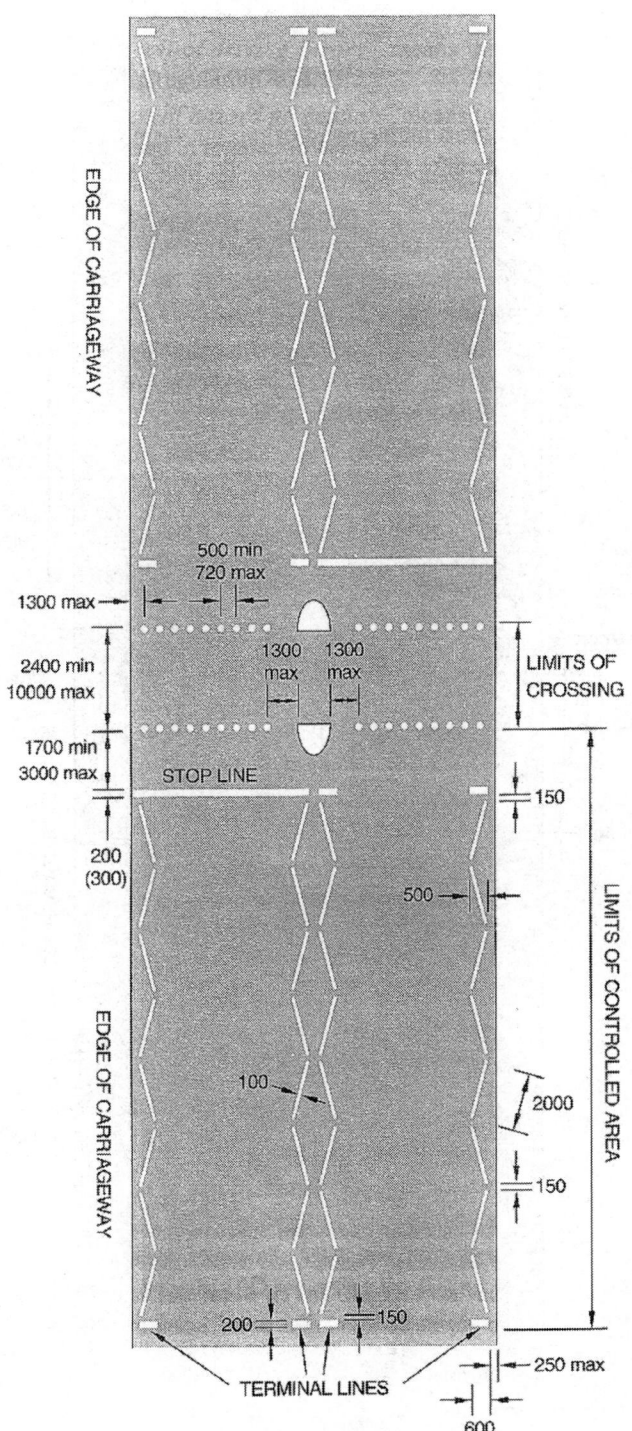

DIAGRAM 3

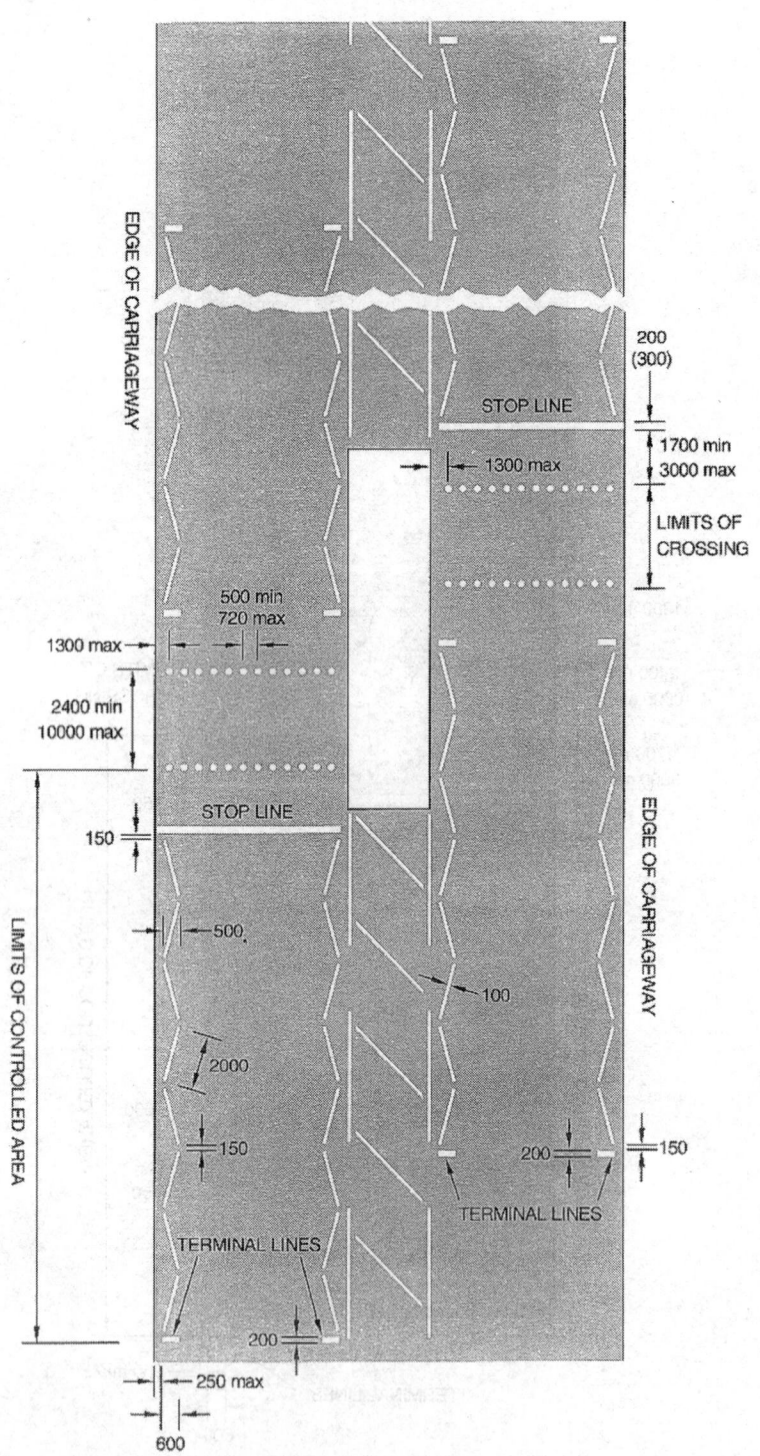

DIAGRAM 4

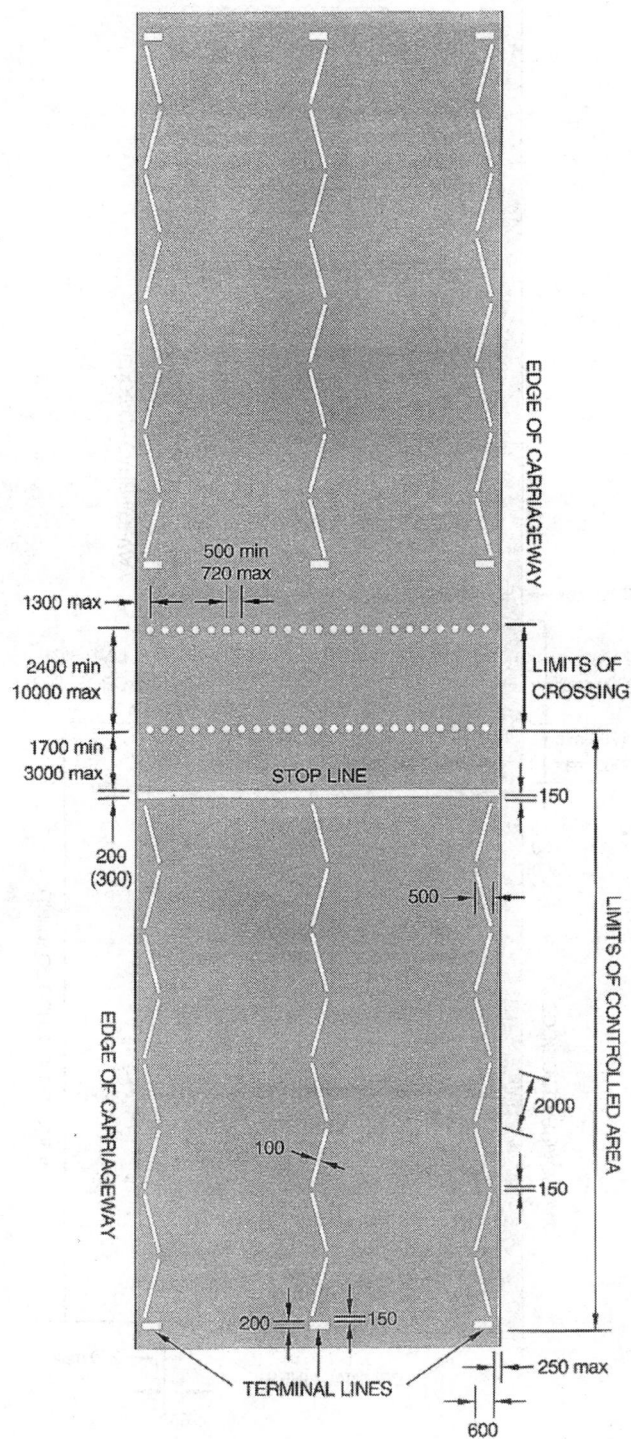

Diagram 5

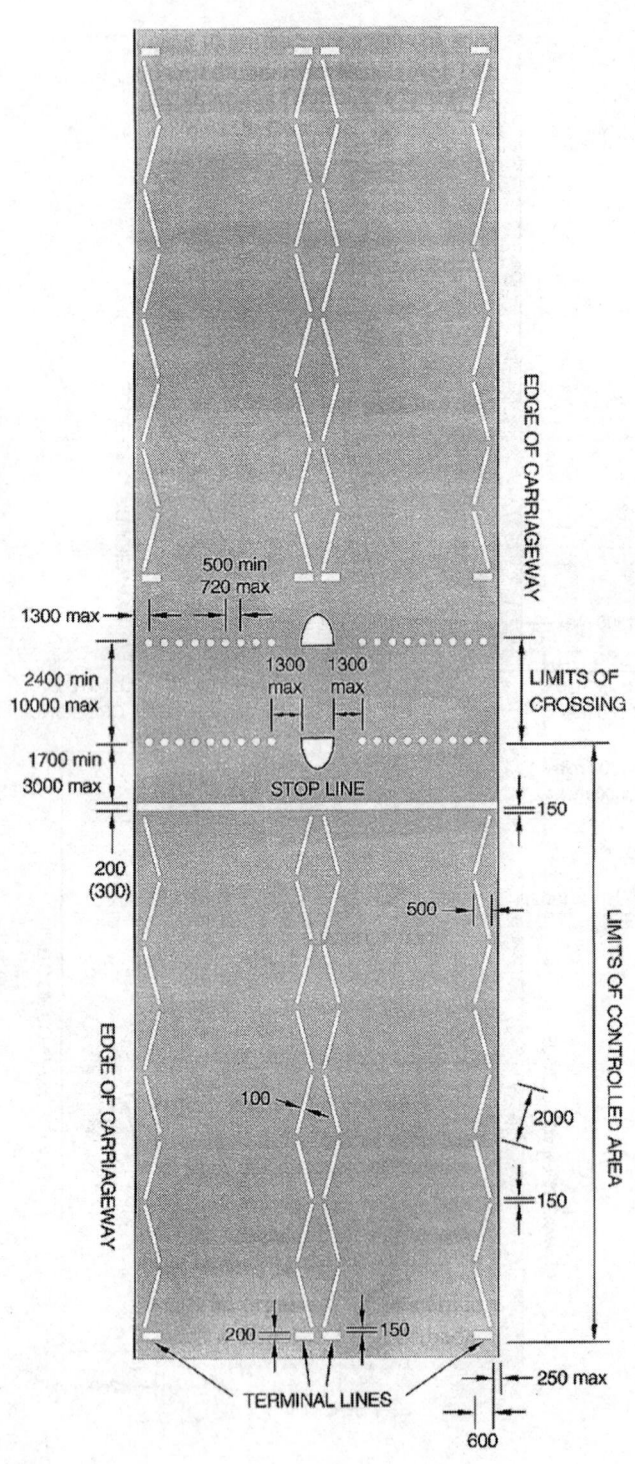

Dɪᴀɢʀᴀᴍ 6

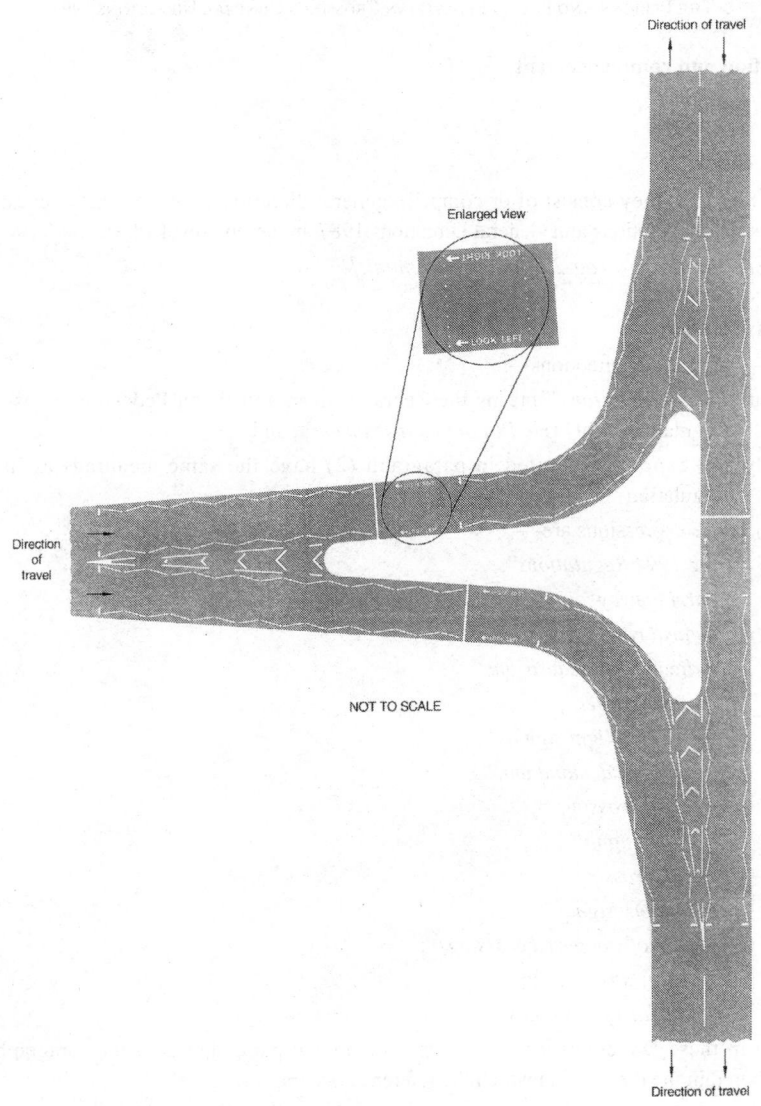

Part II

The Pelican and Puffin Pedestrian Crossings General Directions 1997

Citation and commencement

B37.81   **1.** *[Omitted.]*

Revocation

B37.82   **2.** So far as they consist of or comprise general directions, the "Pelican" Pedestrian Crossings Regulations and General Directions 1987 are hereby revoked.

[See the note to reg.2 of this instrument.]

Interpretation

B37.83   **3.**—(1) In these Directions—

    (a) *"the Regulations"* means the Zebra, Pelican and Puffin Pedestrian Crossings Regulations 1997 [*i.e. Pt I of this Instrument*] , and

    (b) the expressions listed in paragraph (2) have the same meanings as in the Regulations.

    (2) Those expressions are—

        "the 1994 Regulations";

        "carriageway";

        "central reservation";

        "indicator for pedestrians";

        "one-way street";

        "pedestrian light signals";

        "pedestrian demand unit";

        "Pelican crossing";

        "primary signal";

        "Puffin crossing";

        "secondary signal";

        "system of staggered crossings";

        "two-way street"; and

        "vehicular light signals".

    (3) In these Directions a reference to a numbered paragraph is to the paragraph so numbered in the direction in which the reference occurs.

B37.84   *[The 1994 Regulations referred to in direction 3(2) above have been revoked by the Traffic Signs Regulations 2002 (SI 2002/3113 Pt I) (q.v.). The 1994 Regulations may be found in the twentieth edition of this work.]*

Vehicular light signals at Pelican and Puffin crossings

B37.85   **4.**—(1) In this direction references to the left or right hand side of a crossing are to the left or right hand side as viewed from the direction of travel of vehicular traffic approaching the crossing.

    (2) Subject to paragraph (4) the vehicular light signals to be provided facing each direction of approaching traffic at a Pelican or Puffin crossing which is on a two-way street and is of a type specified in column (1) of the table below shall be as specified in relation to that type of crossing in column (2).

TABLE

(1) Type of crossing on a two-way street	(2) Vehicular light signals facing each direction of traffic
Crossing not forming part of a system of staggered crossings and not having a refuge for pedestrians or central reservation within the limits of the crossing	One primary signal on the left hand side of the crossing and one secondary signal on the right hand side of the crossing
Crossing not forming part of a system of staggered crossings and having a refuge for pedestrians or central reservation within the limits of the crossing	One primary signal on the left hand side of the crossing and one secondary signal on the right hand side or on the refuge for pedestrians or central reservation
Crossing forming part of a system of staggered crossings	One primary signal on the left hand side of the crossing and one other signal, which may be either a primary signal or a secondary signal, on the right hand side of the crossing

(3) Subject to paragraph (4) the vehicular light signals to be provided facing the direction of approaching traffic at a Pelican or Puffin crossing which is on a one-way street and is of a type specified in column (1) of the table below shall be as specified in relation to that type of crossing in column (2).

TABLE

(1) Type of crossing on a one-way street	(2) Vehicular light signals to be provided
Crossing not forming part of a system of staggered crossings and not having a refuge for pedestrians or central reservation within the limits of the crossing	One primary signal on the left hand side of the crossing and one other signal, which may be either a primary or a secondary signal, on the right hand side of the crossing
Crossing not forming part of a system of staggered crossings and having a refuge for pedestrians or central reservation within the limits of the crossing	One primary signal on each side of the crossing and one other signal which may be either a primary signal (in which case it must be on the refuge for pedestrians or the central reservation) or a secondary signal
Crossing forming part of a system of staggered crossings	One primary signal on the left hand side of the crossing and a signal, which may be either a primary or a secondary signal, on the right hand side of the crossing

(4) In addition to the signals required to be placed by paragraph (2) or (3) the traffic authority may place such other primary or secondary signals at a Pelican or Puffin crossing as it thinks fit.

Pedestrian light signals and indicators for pedestrians at Pelican crossings

5.—(1) At least one pedestrian light signal and at least one indicator for pedestrians shall be placed at each end of a Pelican crossing.   **B37.86**

(2) Each pedestrian light signal shall be so placed as to be clearly visible to any person on the other side of the carriageway who wishes to use the crossing.

(3) Where there is a central reservation in a Pelican crossing, at least one indicator for pedestrians shall be placed on the central reservation.

(4) Each indicator for pedestrians shall be so placed that the push button on it may be reached by any person wishing to press it.

Pedestrian demand units at Puffin crossings

B37.87   **6.**—(1) At least one pedestrian demand unit shall be placed at each end of a Puffin crossing.

(2) Each pedestrian demand unit shall be so placed that the push button on it may be reached by any person wishing to press it.

Additional traffic signs

B37.88   **7.** A traffic sign of the size, colour and type shown in diagram 610 or 611 in Schedule 2 to the 1994 Regulations may only be placed on a refuge for pedestrians or a central reservation within the limits of a Pelican or Puffin crossing or on a central reservation which lies between two Pelican or Puffin crossings which form part of a system of staggered crossings.

B37.89   *[The 1994 Regulations referred to above have been revoked by the Traffic Signs Regulations 2002 (SI 2002/3113) (q.v.). References to the 1994 Regulations should be construed in the light of the 2002 Regulations. The 1994 Regulations may be found in the twentieth edition of this work.]*

Colouring of containers and posts

B37.90   **8.**—(1) The containers of vehicular light signals at a Pelican or Puffin crossing—

    (a) shall be coloured black; and

    (b) may be mounted on a backing board,

and, if so mounted the backing board shall be coloured black and may have a white border not less than 45mm nor more than 55mm wide which may be made of reflective material.

(2) The containers of pedestrian light signals at a Pelican crossing shall be coloured black.

(3) Where, at a Pelican or Puffin crossing, vehicular light signals, pedestrian light signals, an indicator for pedestrians or a pedestrian demand unit is mounted on a post specially provided for the purpose, the part of the post extending above ground level shall be of a single colour, which may be grey, [black,] brown, dark green or dark blue but may have marked on it one yellow or white band not less than 140mm nor more than 160mm deep, the lower edge of the band being not less than 1.5 metres nor more than 1.7 metres above the level of the immediately adjacent ground.

(4) Any box attached to a post or other structure on which vehicular light signals, pedestrian light signals, an indicator for pedestrians or a pedestrian demand unit are mounted and housing apparatus designed to control, or to monitor, the operation of the signals or unit shall be coloured grey, black, brown, dark green or dark blue.

B37.91   *[Direction 8 is printed as amended by SI 1998/901.]*

Approval of equipment

B37.92   **9.**—(1) In this direction *"equipment"* means all equipment (including the content of all instructions stored in, or executable by it) capable of giving visible, audible or tactile signals used in connection with vehicular light signals, pedestrian light signals, indicators for pedestrians or pedestrian demand units to secure that those signals, indicators or units comply with the relevant provisions of the Regulations.

(2) All equipment placed on a road for the purposes of a Pelican or Puffin crossing shall be of a type approved in writing by the Secretary of State.

(3) If, after equipment has been placed in accordance with an approval under paragraph (2), the signals, indicator or unit used in connection with it is altered, the signal, indicator or unit shall not be further used unless that alteration is approved in writing by the Secretary of State.

(4) When any equipment which has been placed at a Pelican or Puffin crossing is of a type approved under paragraph (2), the equipment shall, subject to paragraph (3), be regarded as continuing to be approved until notice is given in writing by the Secretary of State—

(a) to the traffic authority; and

(b) either—

    (i) to the supplier of the equipment; or

    (ii) where an alteration has been approved in accordance with paragraph (3), to the person who carried out the alteration,

of a date which the equipment is no longer to be so regarded.

(5) Where notice is given under paragraph (4) that equipment is no longer to be regarded as being approved, the equipment and, unless the Secretary of State approves any alternative equipment for the same purpose, any signal, indicator or unit in connection with it shall be removed from the road on or before the date given in the notice.

Special directions by the Secretary of State

10. Nothing in these Directions shall be taken to limit the power of the Secretary of State by any special direction to dispense with, add to or modify any of the requirements of these Directions in their application to any particular case. **B37.93**

APPENDIX

Exercise of Powers

[Omitted.] **B37.94**

The Vehicle Excise Duty (Immobilisation, Removal and Disposal of Vehicles) Regulations 1997

(SI 1997/2439)

B38.01 *[The text of the regulations is printed as amended by:*

> *the Vehicle Excise Duty (Immobilisation, Removal and Disposal of Vehicles) (Amendment) Regulations 1997 (SI 1997/3063) (February 2, 1998);*
>
> *the Vehicle Excise Duty (Immobilisation, Removal and Disposal of Vehicles (Amendment) Regulations 1998 (SI 1998/1217) (June 15, 1998);*
>
> *the Postal Services Act 2000 (Consequential Modifications No.1) Order 2001 (SI 2001/1149) (March 26, 2001); and*
>
> *the Vehicle Excise Duty (Immobilisation, Removal and Disposal of Vehicles) (Amendment) Regulations 2008 (SI 2008/2266) (October 1, 2008).*

The amending instruments are referred to in the notes to the principal regulations only by their years and numbers. The dates referred to above are the dates on which the amending instruments came into force.

The principal regulations have also been amended by the Vehicle Excise Duty (Immobilisation, Removal and Disposal of Vehicles) (Amendment) Regulations 1999 (SI 1999/35); the Vehicle Excise Duty (Immobilisation, Removal and Disposal of Vehicles) (Amendment) Regulations 2001 (SI 2001/936); the Vehicle Excise Duty (Immobilisation, Removal and Disposal of Vehicles) (Amendment) Regulations 2002 (SI 2002/745), but these do not affect the text of any provision printed in this work.]

ARRANGEMENT OF REGULATIONS

B38.02

PART I
PRELIMINARY

Regulation

PART II
IMMOBILISATION OF VEHICLES

Regulation

PART I

PRELIMINARY

Citation, commencement and revocation

1. *[Omitted.]***B38.03**

Interpretation

2.—(1) In these Regulations—**B38.04**

"*the 1994 Act*" means the Vehicle Excise and Registration Act 1994;

"*authorised person*" has the meaning given by regulation 3;

"*custodian*" in relation to a vehicle has the meaning given by regulation 9(3);

"*disabled person's badge*" has the meaning given by paragraph 1(7) of Schedule 2A to the 1994 Act;

"*G.B. records*" means the records kept under the 1994 Act by the Driver and Vehicle Licensing Agency on behalf of the Secretary of State and "*G.B. registration mark*" means a registration mark assigned to a vehicle registered in those records;

[*"local authority"* means—

    (a) in relation to England, a county council, a district council, a London borough council or the Common Council of the City of London;

(b) in relation to Wales, a county council or county borough council;

(c) *[applies to Northern Ireland]*;]

[(d) *[applies to Scotland]*];

"*N.I. records*" means the records kept under the 1994 Act by Driver and Vehicle Licensing Northern Ireland on behalf of the Secretary of State and "*N.I. registration mark*" means a registration mark assigned to a vehicle registered in those records;

[*"public service vehicle"* —

(a) in relation to [Great Britain] has the meaning given by section 1 of the Public Passenger Vehicles Act [*q.v.*]; and

(b) *[applies to Northern Ireland]*;]

"*release*" in relation to a vehicle means release from an immobilisation device;

[*"relevant place"* means a place to which Schedule 2A to the 1994 Act applies;]

"*surety payment*" means a sum payable by virtue of regulation 6(3)(b) or regulation 12(2)(c)(ii) where a vehicle licence is not produced; and

"*voucher*" means a voucher issued under regulation 15(2).

(2) References to the prescribed charge for any matter are to the charge specified in relation to that matter in Schedule 1 to these Regulations.

(3) References to the "*owner*" of a vehicle at a particular time are to the person by whom it was then kept and the person in whose name the vehicle is registered at a particular time shall be taken, unless the contrary is shown, to be the person by whom the vehicle was kept at that time.

(4) Except where it is expressly provided otherwise, references in these Regulations to a numbered regulation are to the regulation in these Regulations so numbered and references to a numbered paragraph are to the paragraph so numbered in the regulation in which the reference occurs.

B38.05 *[Regulation 2 is printed as amended by SI 1997/3063; SI 1998/1217; SI 2008/ 2266.]*

Authorised persons

B38.06 3.—(1) In these Regulations a reference to an authorised person is to a person authorised by the Secretary of State for the purposes of these Regulations.

(2) An authorised person may be a local authority, an employee of a local authority, a member of a police force or any other person.

(3) Different persons may be authorised for different purposes, but a person who is an authorised person for the purposes of regulation 17 shall not act as an authorised person for any other purpose.

Disapplication of the Regulations

B38.07 4.—(1) These Regulations shall not apply in relation to a vehicle [...] in any of the circumstances specified in paragraph (2).

(2) The circumstances are that—

(a) a current disabled person's badge is displayed on the vehicle;

(b) [...];

(c) a badge issued pursuant to the British Medical Association car badge scheme is displayed on the vehicle;

(d) the vehicle appears to an authorised person to have been abandoned;

(e) the vehicle is a public service vehicle being used for the carriage of passengers;

(f) the vehicle is being used for the purpose of the removal of any obstruction to traffic, the maintenance, improvement or reconstruction of a public road, or the laying, erection, alteration, repair or cleaning in or near a road of any traffic sign or sewer or of any main, pipe or apparatus for the supply of gas, water or electricity, or of any telegraph or telephone wires, cables, posts or supports;

(g) the vehicle is being used by [a universal service provider (within the meaning of the Postal Services Act 2000) in relation to the provision of a universal postal service (within the meaning of that Act)] and each side of the vehicle is clearly marked with [the name of the universal service provider concerned]; or

(h) the vehicle is stationary at a time when, having been immobilised or removed under these Regulations, less than 24 hours have elapsed since it was released or, as the case may be, removed.

(3) [...]

[Regulation 4 is printed as amended by SI 1997/3063; SI 2001/1149; SI 2008/2266.] **B38.08**

PART II

IMMOBILISATION OF VEHICLES

Power to immobilise vehicles

5.—(1) This regulation applies where an authorised person has reason to believe that an offence under section 29(1) of the 1994 Act is being committed as regards a vehicle which is stationary [in a relevant place] ... **B38.09**

(2) Where this regulation applies, without prejudice to the institution of proceedings for any offence under the 1994 Act, the authorised person or a person acting under his direction may—

(a) fix an immobilisation device to the vehicle while it remains [in that place], or

(b) move it from that place to another [relevant place] and fix an immobilisation device to it in that other place.

(3) Where an immobilisation device is fixed to a vehicle in accordance with this regulation, the person fixing the device shall also fix to the vehicle an immobilisation notice which—

(a) indicates that the device has been fixed to the vehicle and warns that no attempt should be made to drive it or otherwise put it in motion until it has been released from the device;

(b) states the reason why the device has been fixed;

(c) specifies the steps to be taken to secure its release including the charges payable under these Regulations and the person to whom and the means by which those charges may be paid.

B38.10   *[Regulation 5 is printed as amended by SI 1997/3063; SI 1998/1217; SI 2008/ 2266.]*

Release of immobilised vehicles

B38.11   **6.**—(1) A vehicle to which an immobilisation device has been fixed in accordance with regulation 5 —

(a) may be released only by or under the direction of an authorised person; and

(b) subject to sub-paragraph (a) above, shall be released—

(i) [...];

(ii) where an authorised person is satisfied that the vehicle was immobilised in any of the circumstances specified in regulation 4(2) [...]; or

(iii) if the first and second requirements specified in paragraphs (2) and (3) are met.

(2) The first requirement is that the prescribed charge for the release of the vehicle from the immobilisation device is paid in any manner specified in the immobilisation notice.

[(3) The second requirement is that—

(a) evidence that no offence under section 29(1) of the 1994 Act was being committed when the immobilisation device was fixed or the vehicle moved is produced in accordance with instructions specified in the immobilisation notice;

(b) the prescribed charge for a surety payment is paid in any manner specified in the immobilisation notice;

(c) a vehicle licence for the vehicle, which is in force, is produced; or

(d) a declaration is made that—

(i) an appropriate licence was in force for the vehicle at the time when the immobilisation device was fixed or the vehicle moved;

(ii) save in the case of a vehicle stationary on a public road, a relevant declaration was in force for the vehicle at that time; or

(iii) at that time the vehicle was an exempt vehicle which was not one in respect of which regulations under the 1994 Act require a nil licence to be in force.]

B38.12   *[Regulation 6 is printed as amended by SI 2008/2266.]*

Removal of or interference with immobilisation notice or device

B38.13   **7.**—(1) An immobilisation notice shall not be removed or interfered with except by or under the authority of an authorised person.

(2) A person contravening paragraph (1) shall be guilty of an offence and liable on summary conviction to a fine not exceeding level 2 on the standard scale.

(3) Any person who, without being authorised to do so in accordance with regulation 6, removes or attempts to remove an immobilisation device fixed to a

vehicle in accordance with these Regulations is guilty of an offence and shall be liable on summary conviction to a fine not exceeding level 3 on the standard scale.

Other offences connected with immobilisation

8.—(1) Where these Regulations would apply in relation to a vehicle but for　**B38.14**
the provisions of regulation 4(1) and (2)(a) and the vehicle was not, at the time it was stationary, being used—

(a) in accordance with regulations under section 21 of the Chronically Sick and Disabled Persons Act 1970 [*q.v.*] or with regulations under section 14 of the Chronically Sick and Disabled Persons (Northern Ireland) Act 1978, and

(b) in circumstances falling within section 117(1)(b) of the Road Traffic Regulation Act 1984 [*q.v.*] or Article 174A(2)(b) of the Road Traffic (Northern Ireland) Order 1981 [*SI 1981/154*] (use where a disabled person's concession would be available),

the person in charge of the vehicle at that time is guilty of an offence and liable on summary conviction to a fine not exceeding level 3 on the standard scale.

(2) Where—

[(a) a person makes a declaration of a type referred to in regulation 6(3)(d) with a view to securing the release of a vehicle from an immobilisation device purported to have been fixed in accordance with the regulations; and]

(b) [...]

(c) the declaration is to the person's knowledge either false or in any material respect misleading,

that person is guilty of an offence.

(3) A person guilty of an offence by virtue of paragraph (2) is liable—

(a) on summary conviction, to a fine not exceeding the statutory maximum, and

(b) on conviction on indictment, to imprisonment for a term not exceeding two years or to a fine or to both.

[Regulation 8 is printed as amended by SI 2008/2266.]　　　**B38.15**

PART III

REMOVAL AND DISPOSAL OF VEHICLES

Removal of vehicles

9.—(1) This regulation applies where an authorised person has reason to　**B38.16**
believe that an offence under section 29(1) of the 1994 Act —

(a) is being committed as regards a vehicle which is stationary [in a relevant place] ...; or

(b) was being committed as regards a vehicle at a time when an immobilisation device which is fixed to the vehicle was fixed to it in accordance with these Regulations and the conditions prescribed in paragraph (2) are fulfilled.

(2) The conditions are—

    (a) 24 hours have elapsed since the device was fixed to the vehicle, and

    (b) the vehicle has not been released in accordance with these Regulations.

(3) In a case where this regulation applies, the authorised person or a person acting under his direction, may [enter the relevant place and] remove the vehicle and deliver it to a person authorised by the Secretary of State to keep vehicles so removed in his custody (in these Regulations called a *"custodian"*).

B38.17   *[Regulation 9 is printed as amended by SI 1997/3063; SI 1998/1217; SI 2008/2266.]*

Disposal of removed vehicles

B38.18   **10.** *[Omitted.]*

Recovery of prescribed charges

B38.19   **11.**—(1) Where a vehicle has been removed and delivered into the custody of a custodian in accordance with regulation 9(3), the Secretary of State or the custodian may (whether or not any claim is made under regulation 12 or 14) recover from the person who was the owner of the vehicle when the vehicle was removed the prescribed charges for—

    (a) its removal and storage; and

    (b) if the vehicle has been disposed of, its disposal.

(2) Where, by virtue of paragraph (1)(a), any sum is recoverable in respect of a vehicle by a custodian, he shall be entitled to retain custody of it until that sum is paid.

Taking possession of a vehicle

B38.20   **12.**—(1) A person (*"the claimant"*) may take possession of a vehicle which has been removed and delivered to a custodian and has not been disposed of under regulation 10, if the conditions specified in paragraph (2) are satisfied.

(2) The conditions are—

    (a) the claimant satisfies the custodian that he is the owner of the vehicle or that he is authorised by the owner to take possession of the vehicle;

    (b) except where the claimant produces [evidence that no offence under section 29(1) of the 1994 Act was committed] or the custodian is satisfied that these Regulations did not apply to the vehicle at the time it was immobilised or removed, the claimant pays to the custodian—

        (i) the prescribed charge in respect of the removal of the vehicle; and

        (ii) the prescribed charge for the storage of the vehicle during the period whilst it was in the custody of the custodian; and

    [(c) the claimant—

        (i) produces to the custodian evidence that no offence under section 29(1) was committed;

        (ii) produces to the custodian a vehicle licence for the vehicle which is then in force; or

(iii) pays to the custodian the prescribed charge for the surety payment.]

(3) On giving the claimant possession of a vehicle pursuant to this regulation, the custodian shall give the claimant a statement of the right of the owner or person in charge of the vehicle at the time it was immobilised or, where it was not immobilised, it was removed to appeal pursuant to regulation 17(2), of the steps to be taken in order to appeal and of the address to which representations to an authorised person made as mentioned in that regulation should be sent.

[Regulation 12 is printed as amended by SI 2008/2266.] **B38.21**

Offences as to securing possession of vehicles

13.—(1) Where— **B38.22**

   (a) a person makes a declaration with a view to securing possession of a vehicle purported to have been delivered into the custody of a custodian in accordance with regulation 9(3);

   (b) the declaration is that the vehicle is or was an exempt vehicle, and

   (c) the declaration is to the person's knowledge either false or in any material respect misleading,

that person is guilty of an offence.

(2) A person guilty of an offence under paragraph (1) is liable—

   (a) on summary conviction, to a fine not exceeding the statutory maximum, and

   (b) on conviction on indictment, to imprisonment for a term not exceeding two years or to a fine or to both.

Claim by owner of a vehicle after its disposal

14. *[Omitted.]* **B38.23**

PART IV

PAYMENT OF SUM WHERE LICENCE IS NOT PRODUCED

Issue of vouchers

15.—(1) This regulation applies where a surety payment has been made in respect of a vehicle under either— **B38.24**

   (a) regulation 6(3)(b); or

   (b) regulation 12(2)(c)(ii).

(2) Where this regulation applies a voucher shall be issued in respect of the surety payment to the person making the payment by an authorised person, in a case falling within paragraph (1)(a), or by the custodian, in a case falling within paragraph (1)(b).

(3) Where a voucher is so issued section 29(1) of the 1994 Act shall not apply as regards the vehicle concerned if it is used or kept on a public road without a vehicle licence being in force for it at any time during the period of 24 hours beginning with the time when the voucher was issued.

(4) Neither an authorised person nor a custodian shall issue a voucher unless

they have been furnished with information as to the identity of the owner of the vehicle.

(5) A voucher shall contain the following information—

  (a) the registration mark of the vehicle concerned;

  (b) the date and time of day when the vehicle was released from the immobilisation device; or, as the case may be, possession of it was taken;

  (c) the name and address of the owner or assumed owner;

  (d) the amount paid and the means by which it was paid;

  (e) the name and address of the person procuring the release of the vehicle or, as the case may be, taking possession of it;

  (f) particulars as to how a refund may be obtained in accordance with paragraph (6).

(6) The owner of a vehicle as respects which a voucher has been issued under this regulation shall be entitled to a refund of the amount of the surety payment represented by the voucher if—

  (a) within the period of 15 days beginning with the date on which the voucher was issued, the voucher is surrendered to a person authorised to issue vouchers or a custodian; and

  (b) a valid vehicle licence for the vehicle whose registration mark is given in the voucher is produced at the same time.

(7) Where a voucher is issued on receipt of a cheque which is subsequently dishonoured—

  (a) the voucher shall be void;

  (b) the person to whom the voucher is issued shall be required to deliver it up; and

  (c) no refund shall be payable under paragraph (6).

Offences relating to vouchers

B38.25   16.—(1) Where a person who, in connection with—

  (a) obtaining a voucher under regulation 15, or

  (b) obtaining a refund of any sum in respect of which a voucher was issued,

makes a declaration which to his knowledge is either false or in any material respect misleading, he is guilty of an offence.

(2) A person is guilty of an offence if he forges, fraudulently alters, fraudulently uses or fraudulently lends a voucher or fraudulently allows a voucher to be used by another person.

(3) A person guilty of an offence under paragraph (1) or (2) is liable—

  (a) on summary conviction, to a fine not exceeding the statutory maximum, and

  (b) on conviction on indictment, to imprisonment for a term not exceeding two years or to a fine or to both.

PART V

DISPUTES

Disputes

17.—(1) This regulation applies to a dispute which has arisen because—   **B38.26**

    (a) a person (*"the claimant"*), in order to secure the release or to obtain possession of a vehicle, has paid a charge in accordance with regulation 6 or 12 and alleges that the charge (*"the disputed charge"*) should be refunded to him on the ground that, at the time the vehicle was immobilised or, where it was not immobilised, it was removed,—

        (i) a vehicle licence was in force for the vehicle; or

        (ii) any of the circumstances specified in regulation 4(2) applied to the vehicle; and

    (b) the person to whom the disputed charge was paid refuses to refund the charge.

(2) The claimant under a dispute to which this regulation applies may appeal against the refusal of a refund by sending, to the authorised person whose name is given for this purpose in the statement under regulation 12(3) at the address so given, written representations stating the grounds on which a refund is claimed.

(3) The authorised person to whom the appeal is made may disregard any representations which are received by him after the end of the period of 28 days beginning with the date on which the vehicle was released or, as the case may be, on which possession was taken of it.

(4) The authorised person shall consider any representations duly made and any evidence provided in support of them and notify the claimant whether or not he accepts that either of the grounds mentioned in paragraph (1)(a) have been established and—

    (a) if the authorised person notifies the claimant that one of those grounds has been established, the Secretary of State shall refund the disputed charge;

    (b) if the authorised person rejects the appeal he shall so inform the claimant and at the same time notify him of his right to make a further appeal under paragraph (5).

[(5) A claimant who has made an appeal to an authorised person under paragraph (2) may make a further appeal to the appropriate court in accordance with paragraph (6) —

    (a) if his appeal under paragraph (2) has been rejected under paragraph (4) and the further appeal is made within 28 days of his being served with notification to that effect under paragraph (4)(b); or

    (b) if the authorised person has not notified him of the outcome of his appeal in accordance with paragraph (4) and 56 days have elapsed since he appealed,

and, if the court finds that either of the gounds mentioned in paragraph (1)(a) have been established, it shall order the Secretary of State to refund the disputed charge.]

[(6) A further appeal in accordance with paragraph (5) lies—

      (a) in relation to a vehicle that was stationary [in a relevant place] in England or Wales, to a magistrates' court by way of complaint;

      (b) *[applies to Scotland]*;

      (c) *[applies to Northern Ireland].*]

B38.27 *[Regulation 17 is printed as amended by SI 1998/1217; SI 2008/2266.]*

SCHEDULE 1

THE PRESCRIBED CHARGES

B38.28 *[Omitted.]*

SCHEDULE 2

STEPS TO BE TAKEN TO ASCERTAIN OWNERSHIP OF A REMOVED VEHICLE

B38.29 *[Omitted.]*

The Traffic Signs (Temporary Obstructions) Regulations 1997

(SI 1997/3053)

ARRANGEMENT OF REGULATIONS

PART I

PRELIMINARY

Regulation

*   *   *

PART II

SIGNIFICANCE OF TRAFFIC SIGNS

Regulation

PART III

SIZE, COLOUR AND TYPE OF TRAFFIC SIGNS

Regulation

PART IV

PLACING OF TRAFFIC SIGNS

Regulation

PART V

SAVINGS

Regulation

SCHEDULES TO REGULATIONS

Schedule

2.   The traffic pyramid
3.   The traffic triangle

PART I

PRELIMINARY

B39.02   **1., 2.** *[Omitted.]*

Interpretation

B39.03   **3.**—(1) In these Regulations —

"*the 1994 Regulations*" means the Traffic Signs Regulations 1994 [*Pt I of SI 1994/1519*] ;

"*EEA State*" means a State which is a contracting Party to the Agreement on the European Economic Area signed at Oporto on 2nd May 1992 [*Cm. 2073*] as adjusted by the protocol signed at Brussels on 17th March 1993 [*Cm. 2183*] ;

"*flat traffic delineator*" means a traffic sign which is of the size, colour and type prescribed by regulation 9;

"*keep right sign*" means a traffic sign which is of the size, colour and type prescribed by regulation 8;

"*reflectorised*" means illuminated with retroreflecting material, that is to say material which reflects a ray of light back towards the source of that light;

"*road vehicle sign*" means a traffic sign which is of the size, colour and type prescribed by regulation 10;

"*traffic cone*" means a traffic sign which is of the size, colour and type prescribed by regulation 11;

"*traffic pyramid*" means a traffic sign which is of the size, colour and type prescribed by regulation 12;

"*traffic triangle*" means a traffic sign which is of the size, colour and type prescribed by regulation 13; and

"*warning lamp*" means a traffic sign which is of the size, colour and type prescribed by regulation 14.

(2) Unless otherwise specified, a reference in these Regulations to a numbered regulation or to a numbered Schedule is a reference to the regulation of or, as the case may be, the Schedule to these Regulations so numbered.

(3) The dimensions given in the diagrams in the Schedules to these Regulations are all in millimetres.

B39.04   *[The 1994 Regulations referred to in reg.3(1) above have been revoked by the Traffic Signs Regulations 2002 (SI 2002/3113 Pt I) (q.v.). The 1994 Regulations may be found in the twentieth edition of this work.*

As to the European Economic Area agreement, see the introductory note to Section C below.]

PART II

SIGNIFICANCE OF TRAFFIC SIGNS

Keep right sign

4.—(1) In addition to the requirement conveyed by the sign shown in diagram **B39.05**
610 of the 1994 Regulations in accordance with those Regulations, a keep right
sign shall convey to vehicular traffic a warning of a temporary obstruction.

(2) Section 36 of the Road Traffic Act 1998 [*q.v.*] shall apply to the keep right
sign.

Flat traffic delineator and traffic cone

5. In addition to indicating the edge of a route for vehicular traffic through or **B39.06**
past a temporary obstruction, in accordance with the 1994 Regulations, a traffic
cone and a flat traffic delineator shall each convey to such traffic on a road a
warning of an obstruction in the road.

[The 1994 Regulations have been revoked by the Traffic Signs Regulations **B39.07**
2002 (SI 2002/3113, Pt I) (q.v.). The 1994 Regulations may be found in the
twentieth edition of this work.]

Road vehicle sign

6. A road vehicle sign shall convey to vehicular traffic using a road a warning **B39.08**
of a temporary obstruction in the road caused by a stationary vehicle.

Traffic pyramid, traffic triangle and warning lamp

7. A traffic pyramid, a traffic triangle and a warning lamp shall each convey to **B39.09**
vehicular traffic using a road a warning of a temporary obstruction in the road,
other than an obstruction caused by the carrying out of works.

PART III

SIZE, COLOUR AND TYPE OF TRAFFIC SIGNS

Keep right sign

8. A keep right sign shall consist of a device which is— **B39.10**

    (a) of the colour and type of the traffic sign shown in diagram 610 of
        Schedule 2 to the 1994 Regulations varied so that the arrow points
        downwards to the right;

    (b) of the size shown in that diagram except that its minimum diameter
        shall be 900 millimetres instead of 270 millimetres; and

    (c) illuminated in accordance with the provisions of paragraph (2) in col-
        umn (3) of item 1 of Schedule 17 to the 1994 Regulations.

[The 1994 Regulations have been revoked by the Traffic Signs Regulations **B39.11**
2002 (SI 2002/3113) (q.v.). References to the 1994 Regulations should be
construed in the light of the 2002 Regulations. The 1994 Regulations may be
found in the twentieth edition of this work.]

Flat traffic delineator

B39.12   9. A flat traffic delineator shall consist of a device which is of the type specified in, and complies with the provisions of, regulation 44(3) of the 1994 Regulations and is of the colour and type of the traffic sign shown in the two parts of diagram 7102 in Schedule 12 to those Regulations, except that—

(a) its minimum height may be 450 millimetres instead of 750 millimetres; and

(b) it shall not have the optional white strip on its base referred to in regulation 44(3)(a) and shown in the second part of diagram 7102.

B39.13   *[The 1994 Regulations have been revoked by the Traffic Signs Regulations 2002 (SI 2002/3113 Pt I) (q.v.). References to the 1994 Regulations should be construed in the light of the 2002 Regulations. The 1994 Regulations may be found in the twentieth edition of this work.]*

Road vehicle sign

B39.14   10. A road vehicle sign shall consist of a device which is of the size, colour and type specified in the diagram in Schedule 1.

Traffic cone

B39.15   11. A traffic cone shall consist of a device which—

(a) complies with the requirements of regulation 44(1) of the 1994 Regulations; and

(b) is of the size, colour and type of the traffic sign shown in diagram 7101 in Schedule 12 to the 1994 Regulations.

B39.16   *[The 1994 Regulations have been revoked by the Traffic Signs Regulations 2002 (SI 2002/3113 Pt I) (q.v.). References to the 1994 Regulations should be construed in the light of the 2002 Regulations. The 1994 Regulations may be found in the twentieth edition of this work.]*

Traffic pyramid

B39.17   12. A traffic pyramid shall consist of a device which is—

(a) pyramidically shaped with at least 3 visible faces, each of which is of the size and colour specified in one of the diagrams in Schedule 2;

(b) made of rubber or flexible plastic material; and

(c) so constructed that it can stand upright firmly on the surface of a road.

Traffic triangle

B39.18   13. A traffic triangle shall consist of a device which is—

(a) of the size, colour and type specified in either of the diagrams in Schedule 3; and

(b) legibly and permanently marked—

(i) in the case of a triangle of the size, colour and type specified in the first diagram in Schedule 3, with the specification number of the British Standard for an Advance Warning Triangle to indicate a temporary obstruction, namely BS:AU47: 1965 as amended by amendment No.1 of 6th May 1966, or the specification number of an equivalent standard which has been approved by a recognised standardising body in an EEA State; or

(ii) in the case of a triangle of the size, colour and type specified in the second diagram in Schedule 3, with the marking designated as an approval mark by regulation 4 of the Motor Vehicles (Designation of Approval Marks) Regulations 1979 [*SI 1979/ 1088; not reproduced in this work*] and shown in item 27 of Schedule 2 to those Regulations.

Warning lamp

14. A warning lamp shall consist of a device which—   **B39.19**

(a) shows an intermittent amber light having a flashing rate of not less than 55 nor more than 150 flashes per minute; and

(b) is illuminated by either—

(i) a single source of light; or

(ii) two or more sources of light mounted adjacent to each other and flashing in such a manner that all the sources of light are illuminated and extinguished simultaneously.

PART IV

PLACING OF TRAFFIC SIGNS

Authorisation to place traffic signs

15.—(1) Subject to paragraph (4) of this regulation, a person who is in charge   **B39.20** of or accompanies an emergency or a breakdown vehicle which is temporarily obstructing a road is hereby authorised to place a keep right sign for the purpose of warning vehicular traffic of the obstruction created by the vehicle and to indicate the way past the vehicle.

(2) Subject to paragraph (4) of this regulation, any person not otherwise authorised to do so is hereby authorised to place a road vehicle sign on a vehicle or a flat traffic delineator, traffic cone, traffic pyramid, traffic triangle or warning lamp on any road for the purpose of warning traffic of a temporary obstruction in the road, other than one caused by the carrying out of works.

(3) In paragraph (1) above, the expressions *"emergency vehicle"* and *"breakdown vehicle"* have the meanings given in regulation 3(2) of the Road Vehicles Lighting Regulations 1989 [*SI 1989/1796, q.v.*].

(4) The authorisations given by paragraphs (1) and (2) of this regulation are subject to the conditions specified in regulation 16.

Conditions of authorisation

16.—(1) In this regulation —   **B39.21**

(a) *"placed"* in relation to a traffic sign means placed in pursuance of an authorisation given by regulation 15;

(b) references to *"the obstruction"* are to the temporary obstruction in relation to which a traffic sign is placed; and

(c) references to *"the road"* are to the road on which the obstruction is
situated.

(2) A traffic sign which has been placed shall be removed as soon as the
obstruction has been removed.

(3) A flat traffic delineator, keep right sign, traffic cone, traffic pyramid or traffic triangle shall be placed in an upright position.

(4) A flat traffic delineator, keep right sign, traffic cone or traffic pyramid shall
be placed so as to guide traffic past the obstruction.

(5) A traffic sign referred to in column (2) of an item in the table below may
be placed only if the conditions specified in column (3) of the item are complied
with.

TABLE

(1) Item	(2) Traffic sign	(3) Conditions
1.	Flat traffic delineator	1. At least three other flat traffic delineators must also be placed in relation to the obstruction. 2. Each flat traffic delineator must be so placed as to face traffic approaching the obstruction from the side of the obstruction on which it is placed.
2.	Road vehicle sign	1. It must be placed to face traffic approaching the stationary vehicle from the front, rear or side of the vehicle on which it is placed. 2. It must be securely fixed to the stationary vehicle. 3. It must not obscure any registration plate, lamps or reflectors of the stationary vehicle.
3.	Traffic cone	At least three other traffic cones must also be placed in relation to the obstruction.
4.	Traffic pyramid	At least three other traffic pyramids must also be placed in relation to the obstruction.
5.	Traffic triangle	1. A traffic triangle must be placed at least 45 metres away from the obstruction. 2. A traffic triangle must be so placed as to face traffic approaching the obstruction from the side of the obstruction on which it is placed.

(1) Item	(2) Traffic sign	(3) Conditions
6.	Warning lamp	1. A warning lamp may be used only in conjunction with another traffic sign lawfully placed in accordance with these Regulations being— (a) a flat traffic delineator; (b) a keep right sign; (c) a road vehicle sign; (d) a traffic cone; (e) a traffic pyramid; or (f) a traffic triangle and shall be so placed as not to obscure that other traffic sign from the view of approaching traffic. 2. Not more than one warning lamp shall be placed in conjunction with each such other traffic sign.

PART V

SAVINGS

Saving for the 1994 Regulations

17. Nothing in these Regulations shall affect regulation 41 (temporary traffic signs) of the 1994 Regulations.   **B39.22**

[The 1994 Regulations have been revoked by the Traffic Signs Regulations 2002 (SI 2002/3113 Pt I) (q.v.). References to the 1994 Regulations should be construed in the light of the 2002 Regulations. The 1994 Regulations may be found in the twentieth edition of this work.]   **B39.23**

The Motorways Traffic (England and Wales) Regulations 1982 and the Motorways Traffic (Scotland) Regulations 1995

18. Nothing in the Motorways Traffic (England and Wales) Regulations 1982   **B39.24**
[*SI 1982/1163, as amended, q.v.*] or the Motorways Traffic (Scotland) Regulations 1995 [*SI 1995/2507, as amended; not reproduced in this work*] shall preclude any person, acting in accordance with an authorisation conferred by Part IV of these Regulations, from placing a flat traffic delineator, keep right sign, traffic cone, traffic pyramid, traffic triangle or warning lamp on, or having placed it there removing it from, a special road to which either of those Regulations apply.

The Road Vehicle Sign

B39.25

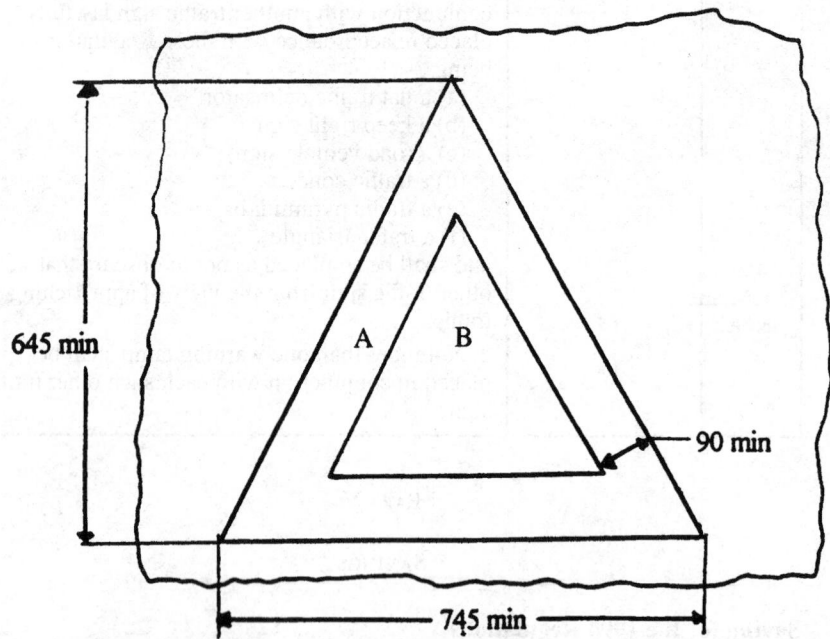

645 min

90 min

745 min

B39.26   1. A road vehicle sign shall be a flexible sheet on which appears a triangle.

B39.27   2. The triangle shall be equilateral. The area marked A in the diagram shall be coloured red, and shall be reflectorised to Class 1 of British Standard BS 873 Part 6 or an equivalent standard which has been approved by a recognised standardising body in an EEA State.

B39.28   3. The area marked B in the diagram may be coloured white, in which case it shall be reflectorised to Class 1 of British Standard BS 873 Part 6 or an equivalent standard which has been approved by a recognised standardising body in an EEA State. If the area marked B is not coloured white it shall be of the same colour as the background specified in note 4 below.

B39.29   4. The background shall be coloured yellow which shall be fluorescent and may also be reflectorised.

B39.30   5. The total area of the sheet, including the red triangle, shall be not less than 0.8 square metres.

The Traffic Pyramid—First Diagram   B39.31

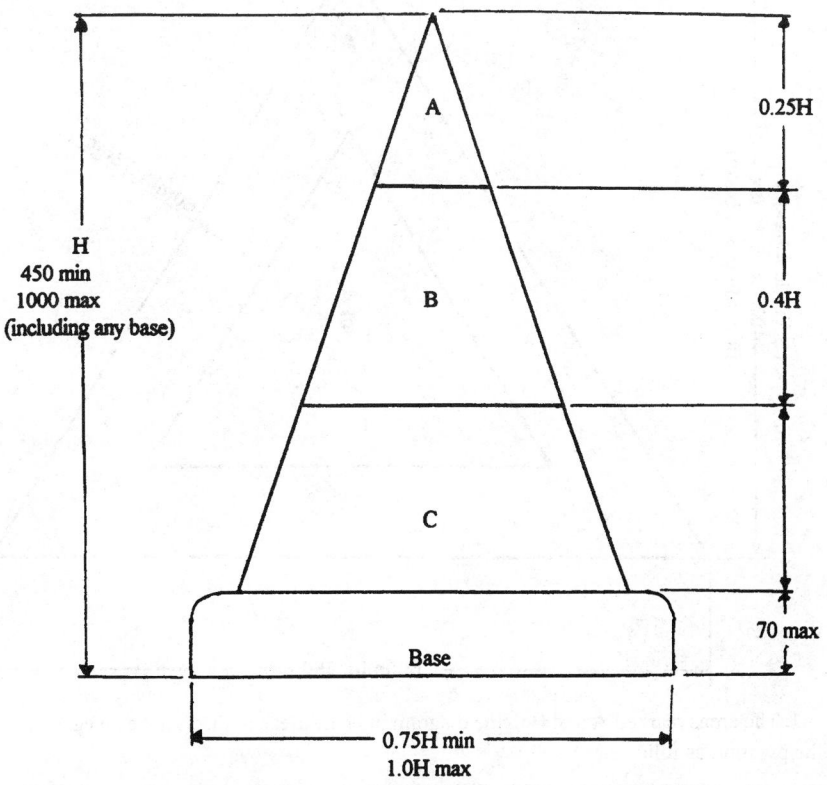

1. The areas marked A B and C in the diagram indicate areas of the surface on each face   **B39.32**
of the pyramid as follows:

    A —Surface coloured red which may be reflectorised.

    B —White surface which must be reflectorised.

    C —Surface coloured red which may be reflectorised. Up to 50% of this surface
       may be obscured by constructional components.

2. The pyramid shall not be directly illuminated either internally or externally.   **B39.33**

3. The base may be of any colour or it may be omitted.   **B39.34**

B39.35   The Traffic Pyramid—Second Diagram

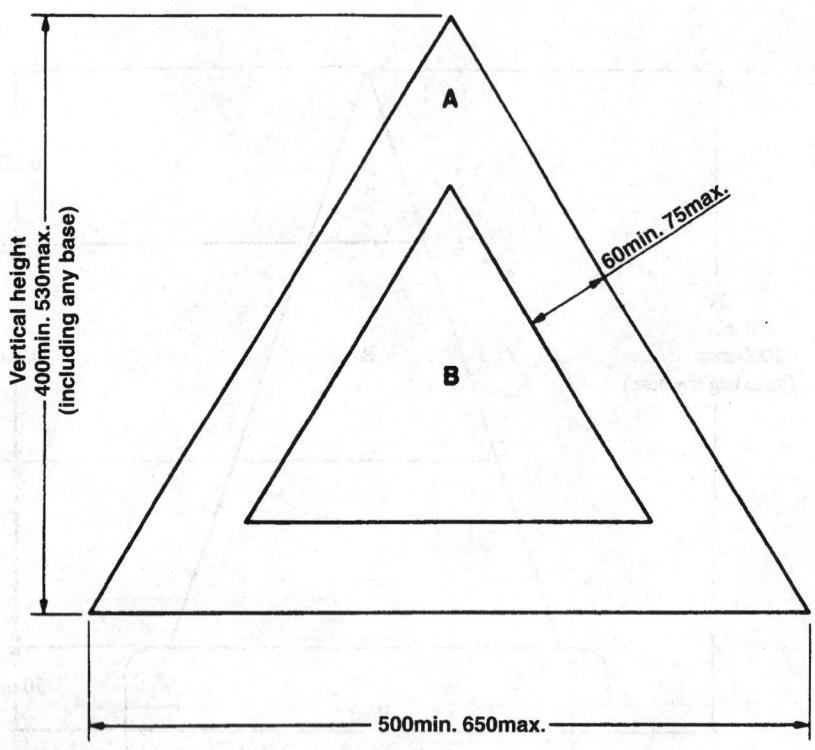

B39.36   **1.** The areas marked A and B in the diagram indicate areas of the surface on each face of the pyramid as follows:

       A —Surface coloured red which may be reflectorised.

       B —White surface which must be reflectorised.

B39.37   **2.** Each outer edge of the triangular face shall be the same length.

B39.38   **3.** The pyamid shall not be directly illuminated either internally or externally.

Regulation 13   SCHEDULE 3

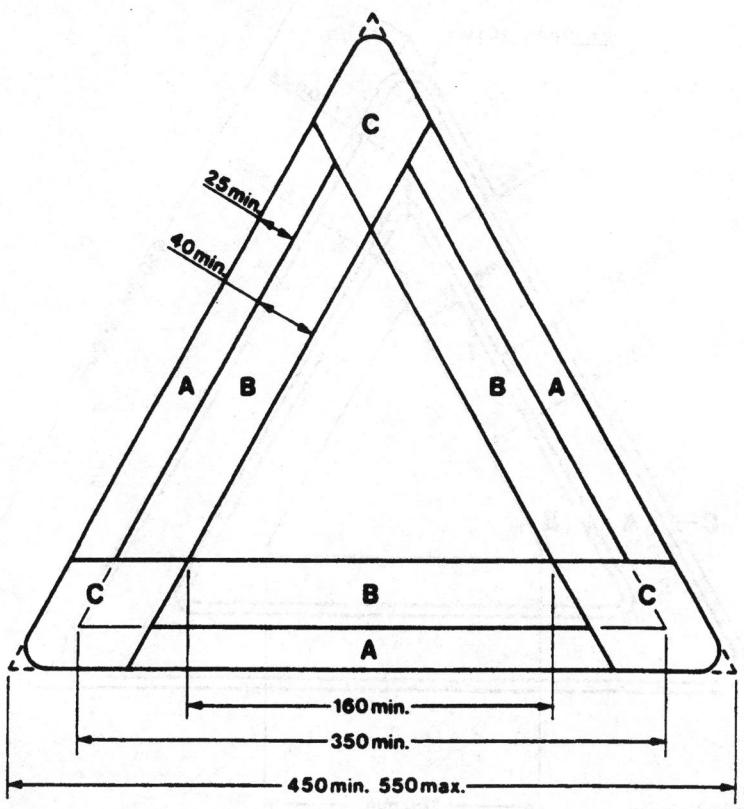

1. The areas marked A B and C in the diagram indicate areas of the surface on the face   **B39.40**
of the triangle as follows:

    A —Red reflectorised surface. Not more than a total of 15 square centimetres may
      be obscured by constructional components.

    B —Red fluorescent surface.

    C —May have either red reflectorised surface or a combination of both red reflec-
      torised and red fluorescent surface. Not more than 10 square centimetres in each
      corner may be obscured by constructional components.

2. The corners shall be radiused.   **B39.41**

3. All sides shall be the same length.   **B39.42**

4. The reflectorised areas of the surface may be internally illuminated provided that such   **B39.43**
illumination is steady, presents a uniform appearance throughout that area and does not
impair the retroreflecting properties of that area of the surface. The triangle shall not be
directly illuminated externally.

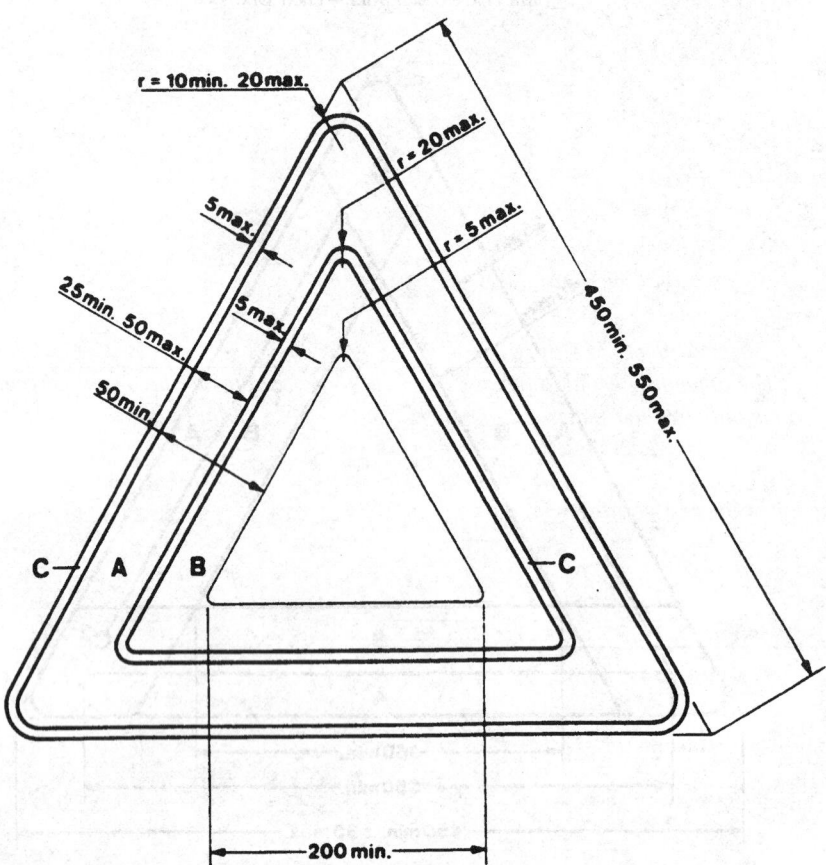

B39.45   1. The areas marked A B and C in the diagram indicate areas of the surface on the face of the triangle as follows:

    A —Red reflectorised surface.

    B —Red fluorescent surface (having an area of not less than 315 square centimetres).

    C —Red edging which may be omitted.

B39.46   2. The corners shall be radiused.

B39.47   3. All sides shall be the same length.

B39.48   4. The reflectorised areas of the surface may be internally illuminated provided that such illumination is steady, presents a uniform appearance throughout that area and does not impair the retroreflecting properties of that area of the surface. The triangle shall not be directly illuminated externally.

The Motor Cycles (Protective Helmets) Regulations 1998

(SI 1998/1807)

[The text of these regulations is printed as amended by:

    the Motor Cycles (Protective Helmets) (Amendment) Regulations 2000 (SI 2000/1488) (June 30, 2000); and

    the Consumer Protection from Unfair Trading Regulations 2008 (SI 2008/1277) (May 26, 2008).

The amending regulations are referred to in the notes to the principal regulations only by their years and numbers. The dates referred to above are the dates on which the amending regulations came into force.]

                                            B40.01

Citation and commencement

1. *[Omitted.]*   **B40.02**

Revocation

2. *[Omitted.]*   **B40.03**

Interpretation

3. In these Regulations —   **B40.04**

    (a) *"EEA State"* means a state which is a contracting party to the Agreement on the European Economic Area signed at Oporto on 2nd May 1992 as adjusted by the Protocol signed at Brussels on 17th March 1993 [*Cm. 2073 and Cm. 2183*] ;

    [(aa) *"ECE Regulation 22"* means Regulation No.22 set out in Addendum 21 to the UN ECE Agreement;

    [(aaa) *"ECE Regulation 22.05"* means ECE Regulation 22 as amended by the 05 series of amendments and all previous amendments in force on 30th June 2000;]

    [(aaaa) *"the UN ECE Agreement"* means the Agreement of the United Nations Economic Commission for Europe concluded at Geneva on 20th March 1958 as amended [*Cmnd. 2535 and Cmnd. 3562*] concerning the adoption of uniform technical prescriptions for wheeled vehicles, equipment and parts which can be fitted to and/or used on wheeled vehicles and the condition for the reciprocal recognition of approvals granted on the basis of these prescriptions, to which the United Kingdom is a part by virtue of an instrument of accession dated 14th January 1963 deposited with the Secretary General of the United Nations on 15th January 1963;]

    (b) a reference to a numbered regulation is a reference to the regulation so numbered in these Regulations; and

(c) a reference to a numbered paragraph is a reference to the paragraph so numbered in the regulation in which the reference occurs.

B40.05   *[Regulation 3 is printed as amended by SI 2000/1488.*

As to the European Economic Area, see further the introductory note to Section C below.]

Protective headgear

B40.06   **4.**—(1) Save as provided in paragraph (2), every person driving or riding (otherwise than in a side-car) on a motor bicycle when on a road shall wear protective headgear.

(2) Nothing in paragraph (1) shall apply to any person driving or riding on a motor bicycle if—

(a) it is a mowing machine; or

(b) it is for the time being propelled by a person on foot.

(3) In this regulation —

"motor bicycle" means a two-wheeled motor cycle, whether or not having a side-car attached, and for the purposes of this definition where the distance measured between the centre of the area of contact with the road surface of any two wheels of a motor cycle is less than 460 millimetres, those wheels shall be counted as one wheel;

"protective headgear" means a helmet which—

(a) either—

(i) bears a marking applied by its manufacturer indicating compliance with the specifications contained in one of the British Standards (whether or not as modified by any amendment) mentioned in Schedule 2 to these Regulations; or

(ii) is of a type manufactured for use by persons on motor cycles which by virtue of its shape, material and construction could reasonably be expected to afford to the wearer a degree of protection from accidental injury similar to or greater than that provided by a helmet of a type prescribed by regulation 5.

(b) if worn with a chin cup attached to or held in position by a strap, is provided with an additional strap (to be fastened under the wearer's jaw) for securing the helmet to the head; and

(c) is securely fastened to the head by means of straps provided for that purpose; and

"strap" includes any fastening device.

Prescribed types of recommended helmet

B40.07   **5.**—(1) The types of helmet hereby prescribed as types of helmet recommended as affording protection to persons on or in motorcycles from injury in the event of an accident are helmets which as regards their shape, construction and other qualities conform—

(a) with British Standard 6658: 1985 as amended by Amendment Slip number 1 published on 28th February 1986 and are marked with the number of that standard, …

(b) with any other standard accepted by an EEA State which offers in use equivalent levels of safety, suitability and fitness for purpose and are marked with a mark to indicate that standard,

[and in each case] are marked with an approved certification mark of an approved body (whether or not they are required to be so marked by the standard in point)[, or]

[(c) with ECE Regulation 22.05 including the approval, marking and conformity of production requirements of that Regulation].

(2) For the purposes of this regulation—

(a) an approved certification mark is—

(i) the certification mark of the British Standards Institution; or

(ii) a certification mark which indicates that a conformity assessment equivalent to that of the British Standards Institution has been undertaken, and

(b) an approved body is—

(i) the British Standards Institution; or

(ii) any body approved by an EEA State to undertake conformity assessments equivalent to those undertaken by the British Standards Institution.

[Regulation 5 is printed as amended by SI 2000/1488.]   **B40.08**

Saving for [...] the Consumer Protection Act 1987

6. Nothing in regulation 5(1) shall be taken to authorise any person to apply   **B40.09**
any number or mark referred to therein in contravention of [...] the Consumer
Protection Act 1987.

[Regulation 6 is printed as amended by SI 2008/1277 Sch.2, para.89 and   **B40.10**
Sch.4(2).]

Regulation 2   SCHEDULE 1

REVOCATIONS

[Omitted.]   **B40.11**

SCHEDULE 2

BRITISH STANDARDS

1. British Standard 2001: 1956 as amended by the following Amendment Slips—   **B40.12**

Number	Date of Publication
1	11th January 1957
2	23rd November 1959
3	27th February 1962
4	11th June 1964
5	13th March 1968

Number	Date of Publication
6	18th February 1972

B40.13   2. British Standard 1869: 1960 as amended by the following Amendment Slips—

Number	Date of Publication
1	29th May 1963
4	3rd December 1965
5	13th March 1968
6	10th August 1971
7	3rd January 1972
8	15th May 1973
9	1st February 1974
10	2nd September 1974
11	1st March 1975

B40.14   3. British Standard 2495: 1960 as amended by the following Amendment Slips—

Number	Date of Publication
1	29th May 1963
2	22nd February 1965
3	7th December 1965
4	22nd July 1966
5	10 August 1971
6	3rd January 1972
7	1st February 1974
8	1st March 1975

B40.15   4. British Standard 2001: 1972 as amended by the following Amendment Slips—

Number	Date of Publication
1	12th December 1972
2	26th January 1973
3	1st February 1974
4	2nd September 1974
5	1st March 1975

B40.16   5. British Standard 5361: 1976

B40.17   6. British Standard 2495: 1977

B40.18   7. British Standard 5361: 1976 as amended by the following Amendment Slips—

Number	Date of Publication
1	30th September 1977
2	31st August 1978
3	31st August 1979
4	29th February 1980

B40.19   8. British Standard 2495: 1977 as amended by the following Amendment Slips—

Number	Date of Publication
1	30th September 1977
2	31st August 1978
3	31st August 1979
4	29th February 1980

9. British Standard 5361: 1976 as amended by the following Amendment Slips—   **B40.20**

Number	Date of Publication
1	30th September 1977
2	31st August 1978
3	31st August 1979
4	29th February 1980
5	27th February 1981

10. British Standard 2495: 1977 as amended by the following Amendment Slips—   **B40.21**

Number	Date of Publication
1	30th September 1977
2	31st August 1978
3	31st August 1979
4	29th February 1980
5	27th February 1981

11. British Standard 6658: 1985 as amended by the following Amendment Slips—   **B40.22**

Number	Date of Publication
1	28th February 1986

The Road Vehicles (Authorised Weight) Regulations 1998

(SI 1998/3111)

B41.01

[The text of these regulations is printed as amended by:

the Road Vehicles (Authorised Weight) (Amendment) Regulations 2000 (SI 2000/3224) (January 1, 2001; February 1, 2001; and January 1, 2002); and

the Road Vehicles (Authorised Weight) (Amendment) Regulations 2001 (SI 2001/1125) (April 17, 2001).

The amending regulations are referred to in the notes to the principal regulations only by their years and numbers. The dates referred to above are the dates on which the amending regulations came into force (the dates on which the amendments effected by SI 2000/3224 took effect are noted against the amended provisions, as appropriate).

SI 2001/1125 also amended SI 2000/3224; as to this amendment, see the notes to reg.2 of the principal regulations below.

The Arrangement of regulations set out below has been added editorially and does not form part of the text of the regulations.]

ARRANGEMENT OF REGULATIONS

B41.02   Regulation

Citation and commencement

B41.03   **1.** *[Omitted.]*

Interpretation

B41.04   **2.**—(1) In these Regulations

"*the 1986 Regulations*" means the Road Vehicles (Construction and Use) Regulations 1986 [*SI 1986/1078, as amended (q.v.)*];

2/1620

"articulated bus or coach" means a single vehicle which is a bus or coach consisting of 2 or more rigid sections which—

    (a) articulate relative to one another;

    (b) are intercommunicating so that passengers can move freely between them; and

    (c) are permanently connected so that they can only be separated by an operation using facilities normally found only in a workshop;

"articulated vehicle" means a tractor unit to which a semi-trailer is attached;

"axle weight" means the sum of the weights transmitted to the road surface by all the wheels of an axle, and for the purpose of calculating axle weight the 2 axles comprised in a tandem axle and all the axles comprised in a triaxle shall be treated as one axle;

"axle-lift device" means a device permanently fitted to the vehicle for the purpose of reducing or increasing the load on the axles, according to the loading conditions of the vehicle either—

    (a) by means of raising the wheels clear off the ground or by lowering them to the ground, or

    (b) without raising the wheels off the ground,

in order to reduce wear on the tyres when the vehicle is not fully laden and, or alternatively, to make it easier for the vehicle to move off on slippery ground by increasing the load on the driving axle;

"centre-axle trailer" means a trailer having only a single axle or group of axles which is positioned at or close to the centre of gravity so that, when the trailer is uniformly loaded, the static vertical load transmitted to the towing vehicle does not exceed 10 per cent of the maximum authorised weight for the axle or group of axles or 1000kg, whichever is the less;

[*"complies with"* shall, in relation to the requirements of a Community Directive, be construed in accordance with regulation 6 of the 1986 Regulations [*SI 1986/1078, as amended*];]

[*"diesel engine"* shall be construed in accordance with para.2.2 of Directive 88/77/EEC as amended by Directive 91/542/EEC, Annex 1;]

[*"Directive 88/77/EEC"* means Council Directive 88/77 of 3 December 1987 on the approximation of the laws of the member states relating to the measures to be taken against the emission of gaseous and particulate pollutants from diesel engines for use in vehicles;]

[*"Directive 91/542/EEC"* means Council Directive 91/542 of 1 October 1991 amending Directive 88/77/EEC;]

[*"first used"* shall be construed in accordance with regulation 3(3) of the 1986 Regulations;]

[*"gas"* has the meaning given in regulation 3(2) of the 1986 Regulations;]

"kg" means kilograms;

"low pollution engine" means an engine which—

    (a) is fuelled solely by gas; or

    (b) is fuelled predominantly by gas and has a minimum gas tank capacity of 400 litres; or

(c) being a diesel engine, complies with at least the requirements for the emission of gaseous and particulate pollutants specified in paragraphs 6.2.1 of Annex I to Directive 88/77/EEC [*O.J. No.L36, February 9, 1988, p.33*] as amended by Directive 91/542/EEC [*O.J. No.L295, October 25, 1991, p.1*] , the maximum masses of which as shown on line B in the table to that paragraph are—

Mass of carbon monoxide (CO)g/kWh	Mass of hydrocarbons (HC)g/kWh	Mass of nitrogen oxides (NOx)g/kWh	Mass of particulates (PT)g/kWh
4.0	1.1	7.0	0.15

"loadable axle" means an axle the load on which can be varied without the axle being raised by the use of an axle-lift device;

"m" means metres;

"maximum authorised weight" in relation to a vehicle, vehicle combination or axle means the maximum authorised weight for the vehicle, vehicle combination or axle determined in accordance with these Regulations;

"retractable axle" means an axle which is raised or lowered by an axle-lift device, either by raising the wheels of the vehicle clear off the ground or by lowering them to the ground.

"rigid motor vehicle" means a motor vehicle which is not a tractor unit or an articulated bus;

"road friendly suspension" means a suspension system whereby at least 75 per cent of the spring effect is produced by air or other compressible fluid under pressure or suspension recognised as being equivalent within the Community as defined in Annex II of Council Directive 96/53/EC [*O.J. No.L235, September 17, 1996, p.59*];

"semi-trailer" means a trailer which is constructed or adapted to be drawn by a tractor unit and includes a vehicle which is not itself a motor vehicle but has some or all of its wheels driven by the drawing vehicle;

"steering axle" means an axle that can be positively steered by the action of the driver;

"tandem axle" means a group of 2 axles not more than 2.5m apart so linked together that the load applied to one axle is applied to the other; references to *"driving tandem axle"* include a tandem axle where either or both the axles comprising the tandem axle are driven and references to a *"non-driving tandem axle"* are to a tandem axle where neither of the axles comprising it is driven;

"tractor unit" means a motor vehicle by which a trailer partially superimposed on it may be drawn so that, when the trailer is fully loaded, not less than 20 per cent of its load is borne by the drawing vehicle;

[*"trailer"* and *"semi-trailer"* have the meanings given in regulation 3(2) of the 1986 Regulations; and]

"triaxle" means—

(a) a group of 3 axles in which no axle is more than 3.25m apart from any other axle; or

(b) a group of more than 3 axles in which no axle is more than 4.6m from any other axle,

and in either case so linked together that the load applied to one axle is transferred to both or all the others; and

"*vehicle combination*" means an articulated vehicle or a rigid motor vehicle drawing a trailer[;]

[*"wheel"* has the meaning given in regulation 3(2) of the 1986 Regulations.]

(2) For the purposes of these Regulations the distance between any 2 axles of a vehicle or vehicle combination shall be taken to be the shortest distance between the line joining the centres of the areas of contact with the road surface of the wheels of one axle and the line joining the centres of the areas of contact with the road surface of the wheels of the other axle.

(3) In these Regulations, except where otherwise specified,—

(a) a reference to a numbered regulation is a reference to the regulation in these Regulations so numbered;

(b) a reference to a numbered paragraph is a reference to the paragraph so numbered in the regulation or the Schedule in which the reference occurs;

(c) a reference to a numbered sub-paragraph is a reference to the sub-paragraph so numbered in the paragraph in which the reference occurs; and

(d) a reference to a numbered Schedule is a reference to the Schedule to these Regulations so numbered.

[Regulation 2 is printed as amended by SI 2000/3224 (on January 1, 2001) **B41.05** *and SI 2001/1125.*

The amendment effected by SI 2000/3224 was set out in reg.3(1) of that instrument, ibid. reg.3(2), provided as follows:

The expressions listed below shall be construed in accordance with the provisions indicated—

first used	regulation 3(3) of the 1986 Regulations [*SI 1986/1078*]
complies with	regulation 6 of the 1986 Regulations
diesel engine	paragraph 2.2 Directive 88/77/EEC
	as amended by Directive 91/542/EEC, Annex 1
gas	regulation 3(2) of the 1986 Regulations
trailer	regulation 3(2) of the 1986 Regulations
wheel	regulation 3(2) of the 1986 Regulations

The effect of ibid. reg.3(2) (which also took effect on January 1, 2001) is not clear; in particular, it is not clear whether the expressions referred to were intended to be introduced as textual amendments into reg.2 of the principal regulations. However, SI 2000/3224 reg.3(2) was prospectively revoked by SI 2001/1125 with effect from April 17, 2001. Nevertheless, if SI 2000/3224 reg.3(2) is properly to be regarded as textually amending reg.2 of the principal regulations it would seem that the textual amendment would survive the revocation of SI 2000/3224 reg.3(2) (see the Interpretation Act 1978 ss.16(1)(b) and 23(1)). SI 2001/1125 inserted the definitions of "complies with", "diesel engine", "Direc-

tive 88/77/EEC", "Directive 91/542/EEC", "first used", "gas", "trailer" and "semi-trailer" and "wheel"(at the appropriate places) into reg.2 of the principal regulations (and such definitions seem to be intended to supersede the substance of SI 2000/3224 reg.3(2)) with effect from April 17, 2001.]

Application of Regulations

B41.06   **3.** These Regulations apply to all wheeled motor vehicles and trailers which fall within category M_2, M_3, N_2, N_3, O_3 or O_4 of the vehicle categories defined in Annex II of Directive 70/156/EEC as substituted by Directive 92/53/EC [*q.v.*] except where vehicle combinations which for the time being fulfil the requirements of Part II, III or IIIA of Schedule 11A to the 1986 Regulations (exemptions relating to combined transport operations).

B41.07   *[The categories of motor vehicles formerly set out in Annex II of Directive 70/156/EEC are now set out in Annex II of Directive 2007/46/EC (O.J. No.L263, October 9, 2007, p.1), which repealed Directive 70/156/EEC with effect from April 29, 2009.]*

Maximum authorised weights

B41.08   **4.**—(1) Subject to paragraph (2) and regulation 5, no vehicle to which these Regulations apply and which is of a description specified in a Schedule to these Regulations shall be used on a road if—

     (a) the weight of the vehicle exceeds the maximum authorised weight for the vehicle determined in accordance with Schedule 1;

     (b) where the vehicle is used as part of a vehicle combination, the weight of the combination exceeds the maximum authorised weight for the combination determined in accordance with Schedule 2; or

     (c) the axle weight of any axle of the vehicle exceeds the maximum authorised axle weight for that axle determined in accordance with Schedule 3 [or if any of the other requirements of that Schedule are not complied with.]

     (2) A vehicle to which any of the provisions of regulations 75 to 79 of the 1986 Regulations apply, so long as it is so used that those provisions are complied with, shall be taken to comply with these Regulations [except, in the case of a vehicle fitted with one or more retractable loadable axles, for the provisions of paragraphs 3 or 4 of Schedule 3.]

B41.09   *[Regulation 4 is printed as amended by SI 2000/3224 (with effect from January 1, 2002).]*

[Compliance with] regulation 80 of the 1986 Regulations (over-riding weight restrictions)

B41.10   **5.**—(1) [Subject to paragraph (2),] [n]othing in these Regulations shall prejudice or affect regulation 80 of the 1986 Regulations and a person using or permitting a vehicle to be used contrary to the provisions of that regulation commits an offence even if the weights authorised by these Regulations are not exceeded.

     [(2) Regulation 80 of the 1986 Regulations [*SI 1986/1078, as amended*] shall not be contravened when a vehicle to which paragraph 3 of Schedule 3 applies is operated in accordance with sub-paragraph (3) of that paragraph.]

[Regulation 5 is printed as amended by SI 2000/3224 (with effect from Janu- **B41.11**
ary 1, 2002).]

Regulation 4(1)(a)   SCHEDULE 1

MAXIMUM AUTHORISED WEIGHTS FOR VEHICLES

Weight not to be exceeded in any circumstances

1.—(1) Subject to paragraph 2, the maximum authorised weight for a vehicle of a de- **B41.12**
scription specified in column (2) of an item in Table 1 below and having the number of
axles specified in column (3) shall be the weight specified in column (4) of the item.

TABLE 1

(1) Item	(2) Description of vehicle	(3) Number of axles	(4) Maximum authorised weight (kg)
1.	Rigid motor vehicle	2	18000
2.	Tractor unit	2	18000
3.	Trailer which is not a semi-trailer or a centre-axle trailer	2	18000
4.	Trailer which is not a semi-trailer or centre-axle trailer	3 or more	2400
5.	Rigid motor vehicle which satisfies at least one of the conditions specified in sub-paragraph (2)	3	26000
6.	Rigid motor vehicle not falling within item 5	3	2500
7.	Tractor unit which satisfies at least one of the conditions specified in sub-paragraph (2)	3 or more	26000
8.	Tractor unit not falling within item 7	3 or more	25000
9.	Articulated bus	Any number	28000
10.	Rigid motor vehicle which satisfies at least one of the conditions specified in sub-paragraph (2)	4 or more	32000
11.	Rigid motor vehicle not falling within item 10	4 or more	30000

(2) The conditions referred to in items 5, 7 and 10 of Table 1 are that—

(a) the driving axle if it is not a steering axle is fitted with twin tyres and road friendly
suspension; or

(b) each driving axle is fitted with twin tyres and the maximum weight for each axle
does not exceed 9500kg.

Weight by reference to axle spacing

2. For a vehicle of a description specified in column (2) of an item in Table 2 below and **B41.13**
having the number of axles specified in column (3) of that item, the authorised weight in
kilograms shall be the number equal to the product of the distance measured in metres between the foremost and rearmost axles of the vehicle multiplied by the factor specified in
column (4) and rounded up to the nearest 10kg, if that number is less than the maximum
authorised weight determined in accordance with paragraph 1.

TABLE 2

(1) Item	(2) Description of vehicle	(3) Number of axles	(4) Factor to determine maximum authorised weight
1.	Rigid motor vehicle	2	6000
2.	Tractor unit	2	6000
3.	Trailer which is not a semi-trailer or centre-axle trailer	2	6000
4.	Rigid motor vehicle	3	5500
5.	Tractor unit	3 or more	6000
6.	Trailer which is not a semi-trailer or centre-axle trailer	3 or more	5000
7.	Rigid motor vehicle	4 or more	5000
8.	Articulated bus	Any number	5000

Regulation 4(1)(b)   SCHEDULE 2

MAXIMUM AUTHORISED WEIGHTS FOR VEHICLE COMBINATIONS

Weight not to be exceeded in any circumstances

B41.14   **1.**—(1) Subject to paragraph 2, the maximum authorised weight for a vehicle combination of a description of vehicle specified in column (2) of an item in Table 3 below and having the number of axles specified in column (3) shall be the weight specified in column (4) of the item.

TABLE 3

(1) Item	(2) Description of combination	(3) Number of axles	(4) Maximum authorised weight (kg)
1.	Articulated vehicle	3	26000
2.	Rigid motor vehicle towing a trailer satisfying the condition specified in sub-paragraph (2)	3	26000
3.	Rigid motor vehicle not falling within item 2 drawing a trailer	3	22000
4.	Articulated vehicle satisfying the conditions specified in sub-paragraph (3)	4	38000
5.	Articulated vehicle not falling within item 4	4	36000
6.	Rigid motor vehicle towing a trailer satisfying the condition specified in sub-paragraph (2)	4	36000
7.	Rigid motor vehicle not falling within item 6 drawing a trailer	4	30000
8.	Articulated vehicle	5 or more	40000

(1) Item	(2) Description of combination	(3) Number of axles	(4) Maximum authorised weight (kg)
9.	Rigid motor vehicle towing a trailer satisfying the condition specified in sub-paragraph (2)	5 or more	40000
10.	Rigid motor vehicle not falling within item 9 drawing a trailer	5 or more	34000
11.	Articulated vehicle satisfying the conditions specified in sub-paragraph (4)	6 or more	41000
12.	Rigid motor vehicle towing a trailer satisfying each of the conditions specified in sub-paragraphs (2) and (4)	6 or more	41000
[13.	Articulated vehicles satisfying each of the conditions specified in sub-paragraphs (4) and (5)	6 or more	44000]
[14.	Rigid motor vehicles towing a trailer satisfying each of the conditions specified in sub-paragraphs (2), (4) and (5)	6 or more	44000]

(2) The condition referred to in items 2, 6, 9[, 12 and 14] of Table 3 is that the distance between the rear axle of the motor vehicle and the front axle of the trailer is not less than 3m.

(3) The conditions referred to in item 4 of Table 3 are that—

(a) the combination consists of a 2-axle tractor unit and a 2-axle semi-trailer;

(b) the weight of the tractor unit comprised in the combination does not exceed 18000kg;

(c) the sum of the axle weights of the semi-trailer does not exceed 20000kg; and

(d) the driving axle is fitted with twin tyres and road friendly suspension.

(4) The conditions referred to in items 11[, 12, 13 and 14] of Table 3 are that—

(a) the axle weight of each driving axle does not exceed 10500kg; and

(b) either—

(i) each driving axle is fitted with twin tyres and road friendly suspension; or

(ii) each driving axle which is not a steering axle is fitted with twin tyres and the axle weight of each such axle does not exceed 8500kg;

(c) each axle of the trailer is fitted with road friendly suspension; and

(d) each vehicle comprised in the combination has at least 3 axles.

[(5) The condition referred to in items 13 and 14 of Table 3 is that the vehicle is fitted with a low pollution engine.]

[Paragraph 1 of Sch.2 is printed as amended (on February 1, 2001) by SI **B41.15** *2000/3224 and (on April 17, 2001) by SI 2001/1125.*

(It has been assumed that the addition of sub-para.(5) to para.1 was intended by SI 2000/3224, although the text of ibid. reg.6(b) is ambiguous. The matter was clarified, however, by SI 2001/1125 which revoked the original amendment and inserted a like-worded provision as sub-para.(5) of para.1; but the latter instrument only took effect on April 17, 2001.)]

Weight by reference to axle spacing

B41.16   2. For a vehicle combination of a description specified in column (2) in Table 4 below and having the number of axles specified in column (3), the maximum authorised weight in kilograms shall be the product of the distance measured in metres between the king-pin and the centre of the rearmost axle of the semi-trailer multiplied by the factor specified in column (4) and rounded up to the nearest 10kg, if that weight is less than the authorised weight determined in accordance with paragraph 1.

TABLE 4

(1) *Item*	(2) *Description of vehicle combination*	(3) *Number of axles*	(4) *Factor to determine maximum authorised weight*
1.	Articulated vehicle	3 or more	5500

Regulation 4(1)(c)   SCHEDULE 3

Maximum Authorised Axle Weights

Weight not to be exceeded in any circumstances

B41.17   1.—(1) Subject to [paragraphs 2 to 4] , the maximum authorised weight for an axle of a description specified in column (2) of an item in Table 5 below shall be the weight specified in column (3) of the item.

TABLE 5

(1) *Item*	(2) *Description of axle*	(3) *Maximum authorised weight (kg)*
1.	Single driving axle	11500
2.	Single non-driving axle	10000
3.	Driving tandem axle which meets either of the conditions specified in sub-paragraph (2)	19000
4.	Driving tandem axle not falling within item 3	18000
5.	Non-driving tandem axle	20000
6.	Triaxle	24000

(2) The conditions referred to in item 3 of Table 5 are that—
   (a) the driving axle is fitted with twin tyres and road friendly suspension; or
   (b) each driving axle is fitted with twin tyres and no axle has an axle weight exceeding 9500kg.

B41.18   *[Paragraph 1 is printed as amended, with effect from January 1, 2002, by SI 2000/3224.]*

Weight by reference to axle spacing

B41.19   2. For an axle of a description specified in column (2) of an item in Table 6 below, if the dimension specified in column (3) is of the length specified in column (4), the maximum authorised weight shall be the weight specified in column (5) of the item, if that weight is less than the maximum authorised weight determined in accordance with paragraph 1.

Table 6

(1) Item	(2) Description of axle	(3) Specified dimension	(4) Length m	(5) Maximum authorised weight (kg)
1.	Driving tandem axle	Distance between the 2 axles comprised in the tandem axle	Less than 1	11500
2.	Driving tandem axle	Distance between the 2 axles comprised in the tandem axle	Not less than 1 but less than 1.3	16000
3.	Non-driving tandem axle	Distance between the 2 axles comprised in the tandem axle	Less than 1	11000
4.	Non-driving tandem axle	Distance between the 2 axles comprised in the tandem axle	Not less than 1 but less than 1.3	16000
5.	Non-driving tandem axle	Distance between the 2 axles comprised in the tandem axle	Not less than 1.3 but less than 1.8	18000
6.	Triaxle	Distance between any one axle comprised in the triaxle and the nearer of the other 2 axles	1.3 or less	21000

[Requirements relating to retractable and loadable axles

3.—(1) This paragraph applies to a vehicle which—   **B41.20**

(a) is fitted with one or more retractable axles or with one or more loadable axles; and

(b) is first used on or after 1 January 2002.

(2) Subject to sub-paragraph (3), under all driving conditions other than those described in sub-paragraph (3), the maximum authorised weight on any axle shall be the weight specified in column (3) of Table 5 or in column (5) of Table 6 (as may be appropriate) and the retractable axle or the loadable axle shall lower to the ground automatically if—

(a) the front axle on the vehicle is laden to that maximum authorised weight, or

(b) in the case of a vehicle having a group of axles, the nearest axle or axles is or are laden to that maximum authorised weight;

and in paragraph (a) above *"axle"* is a reference to an axle described in column (2) of items 1 or 2 of Table 5 in Sch.3 and in paragraph (b) above *"group of axles"* is a reference to an axle described in column (2) of items 3 to 6 of that Table.

(3) The driving conditions referred to in sub-paragraph (2) exist where a vehicle is on a slippery surface and, accordingly in order to help vehicles or vehicle combinations to move off on slippery ground, and to increase the traction of their tyres on slippery surfaces, the axle-lift device may also actuate the retractable axle or the loadable axle of the vehicle or semi-trailer to increase the weight on the driving axle of the vehicle, subject as follows:—

(a) the weight corresponding to the load on each axle of the vehicle may exceed the relevant maximum authorised weight by up to 30 per cent, so long as it does not exceed the value stated by the manufacturer for this special purpose;

(b) the weight corresponding to the remaining load on the front axle shall remain above zero;

(c) the retractable axle or the loadable axle shall be actuated only by a special control device; and

(d) after the vehicle has moved off and reached a speed of 30 kms per hour, the axle shall automatically lower again to the ground or be reloaded.]

B41.21 *[Paragraph 3 was inserted by SI 2000/3224, with effect from January 1, 2002.]*

B41.22 [4. Every retractable axle or loadable axle fitted to a vehicle to which these Regulations apply, and any system for its operation, shall be designed and installed in such a manner as to protect it against improper use or tampering.]]

B41.23 *[Paragraph 4 was inserted by SI 2000/3224, with effect from January 1, 2002.]*

The Motor Cycles (Eye Protectors) Regulations 1999

(SI 1999/535)

[The text of these regulations is printed as amended by:

the Motor Cycles (Eye Protectors) (Amendment) Regulations 2000 (SI 2000/1489) (June 30, 2000).

The amending regulations are referred to in the notes to the principal regulations only by their year and number. The date referred to above is the date on which the amending regulations came into force.]

B42.01

Citation and commencement

1. *[Omitted.]*

B42.02

Interpretation

2. In these Regulations —

B42.03

[(aa) *"ECE Regulation 22"* means Regulation No.22 set out in Addendum 21 to the UN ECE Agreement;]

[(aaa) *"ECE Regulation 22.05"* means ECE Regulation 22 as amended by the 05 series of amendments and all previous amendments in force on 30th June 2000;]

[(aaaa) *"the UN ECE Agreement"* means the Agreement of the United Nations Economic Commission for Europe concluded at Geneva on 20th March 1958 at amended [*Cmnd. 2535 and Cmnd. 3562*] concerning the adoption of uniform technical prescriptions for wheeled vehicles, equipment and parts which can be fitted to and/or used on wheeled vehicles and the conditions for the reciprocal recognition of approvals granted on the basis of these prescriptions, to which the United Kingdom is a party by virtue of an instrument of accession dated 14th January 1963 deposited with the Secretary General of the United Nations on 15th January 1963;]

(a) *"EEA State"* means a State which is a contracting party to the Agreement on the European Economic Area signed at Oporto on 2nd May 1992 as adjusted by the Protocol signed at Brussels on 17th March 1993 [*Cm. 2073 and Cm. 2183*] ;

(b) *"eye protector"* means an appliance designed or adapted for use with any headgear or by being attached to or placed upon the head by a person driving or riding on a motor bicycle and intended for the protection of the eyes;

(c) *"motor bicycle"* means a two-wheeled motor cycle, whether or not having a side-car attached, and for the purposes of this definition, where the distance measured between the centre of the area of contact with the road surface of any two wheels of a motor cycle is less than 460 millimetres, those wheels shall be counted as one wheel.

B42.04   *[Regulation 2 is printed as amended by SI 2000/1489.*
As to the EEA states, see the introductory note to Section C below.]

Revocation

B42.05   **3.** *[Omitted.]*

Prescribed types of authorised eye protector

B42.06   **4.**—(1) Subject to paragraph (3), the types of eye protector hereby prescribed as authorised for use by persons driving or riding (otherwise than in a side-car) on a motor bicycle are—

    (a) those which conform—

        (i) to the requirements relating to Grade X in British Standard BS 4110: 1979 and are marked with that Grade and the number of that standard,

        (ii) to the requirements relating to Grades XA, YA or ZA in British Standards BS 4110:1979 as amended by Amendment No.1 (AMD 3368), Amendment No.2 (AMD 4060) and Amendment No.3 (AMD 4630) and are marked with the number of that standard and the Grade to which they conform, or

        (iii) to any other standard accepted by an EEA State, which offers in use levels of safety, suitability and fitness for purpose equivalent to those offered by the standards referred to in paragraph (i) or (ii) above, and are marked with a mark to indicate that standard,

    and in each case are marked with an approved certification mark of an approved body (whether or not they are required to be so marked by the standard in point);

    [(aa) those which conform with ECE Regulation 22.05 including the approval, marking and conformity of production requirements of that Regulation;]

    (b) those which comply with the requirements of Council Directive 89/686/EEC [*O.J. No.L399, December 30, 1989, p.18*] of the 21st December 1989 on the approximation of the laws of the Member States relating to personal protective equipment as amended by Council Directives 93/68/EEC [*O.J. No.L220, August 30, 1993, p.1*] of 22nd July 1993, 93/95/EEC [*O.J. No.L276, November 9, 1993, p.11*] of 29th October 1993 and 96/58/EEC [*O.J. No.L236, September 18, 1996, p.44*] of 3rd September 1996; or

    (c) those which were first used before 1st April 1989 and fulfil all of the following requirements—

        (i) they are fitted with lenses that are designed to correct a defect in sight,

        (ii) they transmit 50 per cent or more of the light, and

        (iii) they do not fly into fragments if fractured.

    (2) For the purposes of this regulation:

    (a) an approved certification mark is—

        (i) the certification mark of the British Standards Institution; or

(ii) a certification mark which indicates that a conformity assessment equivalent to that of the British Standards Institution has been undertaken, and

(b) an approved body is—

(i) the British Standards Institution; or

(ii) any body approved by an EEA State to undertake conformity assessments equivalent to those undertaken by the British Standards Institution.

(3) The types of eye protector prescribed by paragraph (1) are not prescribed as authorised for use by persons to whom paragraph (4) applies.

(4) This paragraph applies to any person driving or riding on a motor bicycle if—

(a) it is a mowing machine;

(b) it is for the time being propelled by a person on foot;

(c) it is a vehicle brought temporarily into Great Britain by a person resident outside the United Kingdom which has not remained in the United Kingdom for a period of more than one year from the date it was last brought into the United Kingdom; or

(d) that person is in the armed forces of the Crown, is on duty and is wearing an eye protector supplied to him as part of his service equipment.

[Regulation 4 is printed as amended by SI 2000/1489.]   **B42.07**

Regulation 3   SCHEDULE

[Revocations.]   **B42.08**

The Prosecution of Offences Act 1985 (Specified Proceedings) Order 1999

(SI 1999/904)

B43.01   **1., 2.** *[Omitted.]*

B43.02   **3.**—(1) Subject to paragraphs (2) and (3) below, proceedings for the offences mentioned in the Schedule to this Order are hereby specified for the purposes of section 3 of the Prosecution of Offences Act 1985 (which, amongst other things, places a duty on the Director of Public Prosecutions to take over the conduct of all criminal proceedings, other than specified proceedings, instituted on behalf of a police force).

(2) Where a summons has been issued in respect of an offence mentioned in the Schedule to this Order, proceedings for that offence cease to be specified when the summons is served on the accused unless the documents described in section 12(3)(b) of the Magistrates' Courts Act 1980 (pleading guilty by post etc.) are served upon the accused with the summons.

(3) Proceedings for an offence cease to be specified if at any time a magistrates' court begins to receive evidence in those proceedings; and for the purpose of this paragraph nothing read out before the court under section 12(7) of the Magistrates' Courts Act 1980 shall be regarded as evidence.

Article 3   SCHEDULE

OFFENCES PROCEEDINGS FOR WHICH ARE SPECIFIED BY ARTICLE 3(1)

B43.03   **1.** Fixed penalty offences within the meaning of section 51(1) of the Road Traffic Offenders Act 1988.

B43.04   **2.** The offences under section 29(1) of the Vehicle Excise and Registration Act 1994.

B43.05   **3.** The offences under sections 17(2), 18(3), 24(3), 26(1) and (2), 29, 31(1), 42(b), 47(1), 87(2), 143, 164(6) and (9), 165(3) and (6), 168 and 172(3) of the Road Traffic Act 1988.

B43.06   **4.** All offences under the Road Traffic Regulation Act 1984 other than those under sections 35A(2), 43(5) and (12), 47(3), 52(1), 108(3), 115(1) and (2), 116(1) and 129(3) or those mentioned in paragraph 1 above.

B43.07   **5.** The offences arising by contravention of Regulations 3(9)(a) (involving a pedal cycle) and 3(9)(b) and 4(27), (28) and (30) of the Royal and Other Open Spaces Regulations 1997 [*SI 1997/1639; not reproduced in this work*].

The Public Service Vehicles (Community Licences) Regulations 1999

(SI 1999/1322)

B44.01

ARRANGEMENT OF REGULATIONS

*   *   *

Citation, commencement and extent

1.—(1) *[Omitted.]*   **B44.03**

(2) These Regulations shall not extend to Northern Ireland.

Purpose and interpretation

2.—(1) These Regulations implement Article 3A of the Council Regulation.   **B44.04**

(2) In these Regulations —

"*the 1981 Act*" means the Public Passenger Vehicles Act 1981 [*q.v.*];

"*the Council Regulation*" means Council Regulation (EEC) No.684/92 of 16 March 1992 on common rules for the international carriage of passengers by coach and bus, as amended by Council Regulation (EC) No.11/98 of 11 December 1997;

"*international operations*", "*national operations*", "*operating centre*", "*PSV operator's licence*", "*restricted licence*", "*standard licence*" and "*traffic commissioner*" have the meaning given to them by section 82(1) of the 1981 Act [*q.v.*];

"*operator*" has the meaning given by section 81 of the 1981 Act;

"*public service vehicle*" has the meaning given by section 1 of the 1981 Act [*q.v.*];

"*traffic area*" means a traffic area constituted for the purposes of the 1981 Act;

"*Transport Tribunal*" means the Transport Tribunal constituted as provided in Schedule 4 to the Transport Act 1985;

and subject thereto, expressions used which are also used in the Council Regulation have the meaning which they bear in that Regulation.

B44.05   *[With effect from December 4, 2011, Regulation (EEC) 684/92 will be repealed by European and Council Regulation (EC) 1073/2009 of October 21, 2009 on common rules for access to the international market for coach and bus services, and amending Regulation (EC) 561/2006 (O.J. No.L300, November 14, 2009, p.88).]*

Use of public service vehicles without Community licence

B44.06   **3.** A person who uses a vehicle in Great Britain in contravention of Article 3 A (1) of the Council Regulation shall be guilty of an offence and liable on summary conviction to a fine not exceeding level 4 on the standard scale.

B44.07   *[An offence under reg.3 is a fixed penalty offence for the purposes of Pt 3 of the Road Traffic Offenders Act 1988 (see the Fixed Penalty Offences Order 2009 (SI 2009/483) art.2). The amount for the fixed penalty offence is prescribed by the Fixed Penalty Order 2000 (SI 2000/2792), as amended by the Fixed Penalty (Amendment) Order 2009 (SI 2009/488).]*

Competent authorities

B44.08   **4.** The competent authority for the purposes of Article 3 A of the Council Regulation and of these Regulations shall be, in relation to the operator of a public service vehicle who has an operating centre in a traffic area in Great Britain, the traffic commissioner for that area.

Entitlement to the issue of a Community licence

B44.09   **5.** A person shall be entitled to be issued by the competent authority with a Community licence under Article 3A(2) of the Council Regulation if he holds a standard licence which authorises use on both national and international operations, or a restricted licence.

Rights of appeal

B44.10   **6.** A person who—

(a) is aggrieved by the refusal of the competent authority to issue a Community licence to him, or

(b) being the holder of a Community licence, is aggrieved by the decision of the competent authority who issued it to withdraw it,

may appeal to the Transport Tribunal.

Effect of failure to comply with conditions governing use of Community licences

B44.11   **7.** A person who uses a public service vehicle in Great Britain under a Community licence and, without reasonable excuse, fails to comply with any of the conditions governing the use of that licence under the Council Regulation, shall be guilty of an offence and liable on summary conviction to a fine not exceeding level 4 on the standard scale.

[An offence under reg.7 is a fixed penalty offence for the purposes of Pt 3 of   **B44.12**
the Road Traffic Offenders Act 1988 (see the Fixed Penalty Offences Order 2009 (SI 2009/483) art.2). The amount for the fixed penalty offence is prescribed by the Fixed Penalty Order 2000 (SI 2000/2792), as amended by the Fixed Penalty (Amendment) Order 2009 (SI 2009/488).]

Authorised inspecting officers

8. Authorised inspecting officers for the purposes of the Council Regulation   **B44.13** shall be examiners appointed under section 66A(1) of the Road Traffic Act 1988 [*q.v.*] and police constables.

Return of documents

9.—(1) Where a Community licence is withdrawn by the competent authority   **B44.14** in accordance with condition 5 of the model Community licence set out in the Annex to the Council Regulation, the holder of that licence shall within 7 days of such withdrawal return to the competent authority which issued it the original licence and all certified true copies of it.

(2) The holder of a Community licence shall return to the competent authority which issued it such certified true copies of the licence as the authority may require pursuant to—

    (a) any decision of the authority to reduce the maximum number of vehicles (being vehicles having their operating centre in the area of that authority) which the holder is authorised, under section 16(1) of the 1981 Act, to use under the PSV operator's licence held by him, or

    (b) any decision of the authority under the condition 5 referred to in paragraph (1) to suspend or withdraw certified true copies of the Community licence.

(3) A person who, without reasonable excuse, fails to comply with any provision of paragraph (1) or (2) shall be guilty of an offence and liable on summary conviction to a fine not exceeding level 4 on the standard scale.

Supply of information

10.—(1) The holder of a Community licence shall furnish such information as   **B44.15** the competent authority which issued it may reasonably require from time to time to enable the authority to decide whether the holder is entitled to retain that licence.

(2) A person who, without reasonable excuse, fails to supply any information required under paragraph (1) shall be guilty of an offence and liable on summary conviction to a fine not exceeding level 4 on the standard scale.

Death, bankruptcy, etc., of holder of Community licence

11. Where a person is authorised to carry on the business of the holder of a   **B44.16** PSV operator's licence by virtue of an authorisation under section 57(4)(b) of the

1981 Act, such person shall be treated as the holder of any Community licence held by the holder of the PSV operator's licence, for the same period as is specified in that authorisation.

Bodies corporate

B44.17   **12.**—(1) Where an offence under these Regulations has been committed by a body corporate and it is proved to have been committed with the consent or connivance of, or to be attributable to any neglect on the part of, any director, manager, secretary or other similar officer of the body corporate or any person who was purporting to act in any such capacity, he as well as the body corporate shall be guilty of the offence and shall be liable to be proceeded against and punished accordingly.

(2) Where the affairs of a body corporate are managed by its members, paragraph (1) shall apply in relation to the acts and defaults of a member in connection with his functions of management as if he were a director of the body corporate.

(3) Where an offence under these Regulations has been committed by a Scottish partnership and it is proved to have been committed with the consent or connivance of, or to be attributable to any neglect on the part of, a partner, he as well as the partnership shall be guilty of the offence and shall be liable to be proceeded against and punished accordingly.

Modification of the Road Traffic (Foreign Vehicles) Act 1972

B44.18   **13.** *[Amends the 1972 Act, q.v.]*

The Goods Vehicle Operators (Qualifications) Regulations 1999

(SI 1999/2430)

*   *   *

Transitional provisions and savings

5.—(1), (2) *[Transitional provisions relating to matters of financial standing.]*   **B45.01**

(3) The amendments made by Regulation 4 above shall not apply in relation to a certificate of professional competence—

(a) which was issued before 1st October 1999; or

(b) which was issued on or after that date to a person who before that date passed the whole or any part of the examination leading to the issue of that certificate.

(4) In relation to a certificate of professional competence which was issued before 4th February 1991, or which was issued on or after that date to a person who before that date passed the whole or any part of the examination leading to the issue of that certificate, Schedule 3 to the Act shall have effect as if for paragraph 13 there was substituted the following paragraph —

"**13.**—(1) An individual shall be regarded as professionally competent if, and only if—

(a) he is the holder of a certificate issued by an approved body to the effect that he possesses the requisite skills; or

(b) he is the holder of any other certificate of competence, diploma or other qualification recognised for the purposes of this sub-paragraph by the Secretary of State.

(2) In sub-paragraph (1) —

'*approved body*' means—

(a) a body approved by the Secretary of State for the purposes of that sub-paragraph;

(b) a body approved by the Department of the Environment for Northern Ireland for the purposes of section 46A(5)(c) of the Transport Act (Northern Ireland) 1967; or

(c) a body or authority designated by a member state other than the United Kingdom for the purposes of Article 3.4 of Council Directive No.74/561/EEC as it had effect immediately before it was amended by Council Directive No.89/438/EEC; and

'*the requisite skills*' means skills in the subjects listed in Part A and, in the case of a licence to cover international operations, Part B, of the Annex to Council Directive No.74/561/EEC as it had effect immediately before it was amended by Council Directive No.89/438/EEC."

(5) Paragraph 14 of Schedule 3 to the Act [*Goods Vehicles (Licensing of Operators) Act 1995*] (which is superseded by paragraph (4) above) shall be omitted.

The Motor Vehicles (Driving Licences) Regulations 1999

(SI 1999/2864)

[The text of these regulations is printed as amended by: **B46.01**

the Motor Vehicles (Driving Licences) (Amendment) Regulations 2000 (SI 2000/2766) (November 1, 2000);

the Motor Vehicles (Driving Licences) (Amendment) (No.2) Regulations 2000 (SI 2000/3157) (January 1, 2001);

the Motor Vehicles (Driving Licences) (Amendment) Regulations 2001 (SI 2001/53) (February 1, 2001);

the Motor Vehicles (Driving Licences) (Amendment) (No.2) Regulations 2001 (SI 2001/236) (February 1, 2001);

the Motor Vehicles (Driving Licences) (Amendment) (No.3) Regulations 2001 (SI 2001/937) (April 5, 2001);

the Motor Vehicles (Driving Licences) (Amendment) Regulations 2002 (SI 2002/2641) (November 14, 2002);

the Motor Vehicles (Driving Licences) (Amendment) Regulations 2003 (SI 2003/166) (February 21, 2003);

the Motor Vehicles (Driving Licences) (Amendment) (No.2) Regulations 2003 (SI 2003/222) (March 1, 2003);

the Motor Vehicles (Driving Licences) (Amendment) (No.3) Regulations 2003 (SI 2003/636) (April 1, 2003 and July 1, 2003);

the Motor Vehicles (Driving Licences) (Amendment) Regulations 2004 (SI 2004/265) (March 1, 2004);

the Health and Social Care (Community Health and Standards) Act 2003 (Supplementary and Consequential Provision) (NHS Foundation Trusts) Order 2004 (SI 2004/696) (April 1, 2004);

the Motor Vehicles (Driving Licences) (Amendment) (No.2) Regulations 2004 (SI 2004/1519) (July 26, 2004);

the Motor Vehicles (Driving Licences) (Amendment) (No.2) Regulations 2005 (SI 2005/2717) (November 1, 2005);

the Motor Vehicles (Driving Licences) (Amendment) Regulations 2006 (SI 2006/524) (April 1, 2006; July 1, 2007 (for the purposes of reg.9(3));

the Vehicle Drivers (Certificates of Professional Competence) Regulations 2007 (SI 2007/605) (September 10, 2008 and 10 September, 2009 (in accordance with reg.1(2)(b)));

the Motor Vehicles (Driving Licences) (Amendment) Regulations 2007 (SI 2007/698) (April 2, 2007);

the Motor Vehicles (Driving Licences) (Amendment) (No.4) Regulations 2008 (SI 2008/1435) (July 7, 2008);

the Motor Vehicles (Driving Licences) (Amendment) Regulations 2009 (SI 2009/788) (March 30, 2009; April 6, 2009 (for the purposes of reg.28)); and

the Motor Vehicles (Driving Licences) (Amendment) Regulations 2010 (SI 2010/1203) (May 1, 2010; October 4, 2010 (for the purposes of reg.24)).

The amending instruments are referred to in the notes to the principal regulations only by their years and numbers. The dates referred to above are the dates on which the amending instruments came into force.

The Motor Vehicles (Driving Licences) (Amendment) (No.2) Regulations 2001 (SI 2001/236) amended the Motor Vehicles (Driving Licences) (Amendment) Regulations 2001 (SI 2001/53) on the day on which the earlier regulations came into force.

These regulations have been further amended by the Motor Vehicles (Driving Licences) (Amendment) (No.4) Regulations 2001 (SI 2001/2779), the Motor Vehicles (Driving Licences) (Amendment) (No.5) Regulations 2001 (SI 2001/3486), the Motor Vehicles (Driving Licences) (Amendment) (No.4) Regulations 2003 (SI 2003/2003), the Motor Vehicles (Driving Licences) (Amendment) (No.5) Regulations 2003 (SI 2003/3313), the Motor Vehicles (Driving Licences) (Amendment) (No.3) Regulations 2004 (SI 2004/3028) the Fire and Rescue Services Act 2004 (Consequential Amendments) (England) Order 2004 (SI 2004/3168), the Motor Vehicles (Driving Licences) (Amendment) Regulations 2005 (SI 2005/1975), the Motor Vehicles (Driving Licences) (Amendment) Regulations 2008 (SI 2008/508), the Motor Vehicles (Driving Licences) (Amendment) (No.5) Regulations 2008 (SI 2008/2508), the Motor Vehicles (Driving Licences) (Amendment) (No.2) Regulations 2009 (SI 2009/2362), the Vehicles Regulations (Amendment) Order 2010 (SI 2010/1111), but the amending regulations do not affect the text of any provision of the principal regulations which is printed in this work.]

ARRANGEMENT OF REGULATIONS

B46.02

PART I

Preliminary

Regulation

*   *   *

PART II

Licences

Categories of entitlement

Regulation

SCHEDULES

* * *

* * *

* * *

PART I

PRELIMINARY

Citation and commencement

1. *[Omitted.]* **B46.03**

Revocation and saving

2.—(1) The regulations specified in Schedule 1 [*not reproduced*] are hereby **B46.04** revoked.

(2) Subject to otherwise herein provided, and without prejudice to the operation of sections 16 and 17 of the Interpretation Act 1978, the revocation of those regulations shall not affect the validity of any application or appointment made, notice or approval given, licence, certificate or other document granted or issued or other thing done thereunder and any reference in such application, appointment, notice, approval, licence, certificate or other document or thing to a provision of any regulation hereby revoked, whether specifically or by means of a general description, shall, unless the context otherwise requires, be construed as a reference to the corresponding provision of these Regulations.

Interpretation

3.—(1) In these Regulations, unless the context otherwise requires, the follow- **B46.05** ing expressions have the following meanings—

   "1981 Act" means the Public Passenger Vehicles Act 1981 [*q.v.*];

   "1985 Act" means the Transport Act 1985 [*q.v.*];

   [*"abridged standard test of driving theory"* means the test described in regulation 40B(1A);]

"ambulance" means a motor vehicle which—

    (a) is constructed or adapted for, and used for no other purpose than, the carriage of sick, injured or disabled people to or from welfare centres or places where medical or dental treatment is given, and

    (b) is readily identifiable as such a vehicle by being marked "Ambulance" on both sides;

"appropriate driving test" and *"extended driving test"* have the same meanings respectively as in section 36 of the Offenders Act [*q.v.*];

[*"certified direct access instructor"* has the meaning given by regulation 64(2);]

"Construction and Use Regulators" means the Road Vehicles (Construction and Use) Regulations 1986 [*SI 1986/1078, q.v.*];

"controlled by a pedestrian" in relation to a vehicle means that the vehicle either—

    (a) is constructed or adapted for use under such control; or

    (b) is constructed or adapted for use either under such control or under the control of a person carried on it but is not for the time being in use under, or proceeding under, the control of a person carried on it;

[*"disability assessment test"* means a test of competence to drive for which a person is required, by notice under section 94(5)(c) of the Traffic Act, to submit himself; and *"disability assessment licence"* means a provisional licence granted to enable him to drive a motor vehicle for the purposes of preparing for, and taking, such a test];

"dual purpose vehicle" means a motor vehicle which is constructed or adapted both to carry or haul goods and to carry more than eight persons in addition to the driver;

"exempted goods vehicle" and *"exempted military vehicle"* have the meanings respectively given in regulation 51;

"extended driving test" means a test of a kind prescribed by regulation 41;

"full", in relation to a licence of any nature, means a licence granted otherwise than as a provisional licence;

"Group 1 licence" and *"Group 2 licence"* have the meanings respectively given in regulation 70;

"incomplete large vehicle" means—

    (a) an incomplete motor vehicle, typically consisting of a chassis and a complete or incomplete cab, which is capable of becoming, on the completion of its construction, a medium-sized or large goods vehicle or a passenger-carrying vehicle, or

    (b) a vehicle which would be an articulated goods vehicle but for the absence of a fifth-wheel coupling,

and which is not drawing a trailer;

"large motor bicycle" means—

    (a) in the case of a motor bicycle without a side-car, a bicycle the engine of which has a maximum net power output exceeding 25 kilowatts or which has a power to weight ratio exceeding 0.16 kilowatts per kilogram, or

(b) in the case of a motor bicycle and side-car combination, a combination having a power to weight ratio exceeding 0.16 kilowatts per kilogram;

[*"large vehicle test of driving theory"* means the test of driving theory described in regulation 40B(2);

"large vehicle test of hazard perception" means the test of hazard perception described in regulation 40B(4);

"large vehicle theory test pass certificate" means a certificate in the form specified in regulation 47B(1);]

"LGV trainee driver's licence" has the meaning given in regulation 54;

[*"manoeuvres test"* means a test consisting of the activities and manoeuvres specified in Schedule 8A and includes such a test conducted as part of an extended driving test;]

"maximum authorised mass" —

(a) in relation to a goods vehicle, has the same meaning as "permissible maximum weight" in section 108(1) of the Traffic Act [*q.v.*];

(b) in relation to an incomplete large vehicle, means its working weight, and

(c) in relation to any other motor vehicle or trailer, has the same meaning as "maximum gross weight" in regulation 3(2) of the Construction and Use Regulations [*q.v.*];

"maximum speed" means the speed which the vehicle is incapable, by reason of its construction, of exceeding on the level under its own power when fully laden;

"maximum net power output" has the same meaning as in section 97 of the Traffic Act [*q.v.*];

"mobile project vehicle" means a vehicle which has a maximum authorised mass exceeding 3.5 tonnes, is constructed or adapted to carry not more than eight persons in addition to the driver and carries principally goods or burden consisting of—

(a) play or educational equipment and articles required in connection with the use of such equipment, or

(b) articles required for the purposes of display or of an exhibition,

and the primary purpose of which is use as a recreational, educational or instructional facility when stationary;

[*"module 1 pass certificate"* means a certificate relating to the passing of a manoeuvres test in the form set out in Part 1 of Schedule 10D;

"module 1 statement of failure" means a statement in the form set out in Part 2 of Schedule 10D regarding the failing of a manoeuvres test;]

"Northern Ireland test" means a test of competence to drive conducted under the law of Northern Ireland;

"Offenders Act" means the Road Traffic Offenders Act 1988 [*q.v.*];

"passenger-carrying vehicle recovery vehicle" means a vehicle (other than an articulated goods vehicle combination as defined in section 108(1) of the Traffic Act) which—

(a) has an unladen weight not exceeding 10.2 tonnes,

(b) is being operated by the holder of a PSV operator's licence, and

(c) is being used for the purpose of—

  (i) proceeding to, or returning from, a place where assistance is to be, or has been, given to a damaged or disabled passenger-carrying vehicle; or

  (ii) giving assistance to or moving a disabled passenger-carrying vehicle or moving a damaged vehicle;

"penalty points" means penalty points attributed to an offence under section 28 of the Offenders Act [q.v.];

"power to weight ratio", in relation to a motor bicycle, means the ratio of the maximum net power output of the engine of the vehicle to its weight (including the weight of any side-car) with—

(a) a full supply of fuel in the tank,

(b) an adequate supply of other liquids needed for its propulsion, and

(c) no load other than its normal equipment, including loose tools;

"practical test" means a practical test of driving skills and behaviour or, where a test is by virtue of these Regulations required to be conducted in two [or three] parts, [the part of it consisting of that test; and the term—

(a) includes such a test conducted as part of an extended driving test; and

(b) excludes the manoeuvres test;]

"propelled by electrical power", in relation to a motor vehicle, means deriving motive power solely from an electrical storage battery carried on the vehicle and having no connection to any other source of power when the vehicle is in motion;

"PSV operator's licence" has the meaning given by section 82(1) of the 1981 Act [q.v.];

"standard access period" has the meaning given by regulation 22;

"standard motor bicycle" means a motor bicycle which is not a large motor bicycle;

["standard test of driving theory" means the test described in regulation 40B(1);

"standard test of hazard perception" means the test described in regulation 40B(3);

"standard theory test pass certificate" means a certificate in the form specified in regulation 47(2)(a);]

"test" means any test of competence to drive conducted pursuant to section 89 of the Traffic Act including an extended driving test;

["test pass certificate"] means a certificate in the form specified in regulation 48(1)(a);

[...]

"Traffic Act" means the Road Traffic Act 1988 [q.v.];

"*traffic commissioner*" means, in relation to an applicant for or the holder of a licence, the traffic commissioner in whose area the applicant or holder resides;

"*unitary test*" means a test which, by virtue of these Regulations, is to consist of a single test of both practical driving skills and behaviour and knowledge of the Highway Code and other matters and includes such a test conducted as an extended driving test;

"*unladen weight*" has the same meaning as in regulation 3(2) of the Construction and Use Regulations [*q.v.*] and, in the case of a road roller, includes the weight of any object for the time being attached to the vehicle, being an object specially designed to be so attached for the purpose of temporarily increasing the vehicle's weight;

"*vehicle with automatic transmission*" means a class of vehicle in which either—

  (a) the driver is not provided with any means whereby he may vary the gear ratio between the engine and the road wheels independently of the accelerator and the brakes, or

  (b) he is provided with such means but they do not include a clutch pedal or lever which he may operate manually,

(and accordingly a vehicle with manual transmission is any other class of vehicle);

"*working weight*" means the weight of a vehicle in working condition on a road but exclusive of the weight of any liquid coolant and fuel used for its propulsion.

(2) In these Regulations, unless the context otherwise requires—

  (a) a reference to a licence being in force is a reference to it being in force in accordance with section 99 of the Traffic Act, save that for the purpose of these Regulations a licence shall remain in force notwithstanding that it is—

    (i) surrendered to the Secretary of State or is revoked otherwise than by notice under section 93(1) or (2) of the Traffic Act (revocation because of disability or prospective diability), or

    (ii) treated as revoked by virtue of sections 37(1) of the Offenders Act, and

  (b) a reference to the expiry of a licence is a reference to the time at which it ceases to be so in force (and "*expired*" shall be construed accordingly).

(3) Except where otherwise expressly provided, any reference in these Regulations to a numbered regulation or Schedule is a reference to the regulation or Schedule bearing that number in these Regulations, and any reference to a numbered paragraph (otherwise than as part of a reference to a numbered regulation) is a reference to the paragraph bearing that number in the regulation or Schedule in which the reference occurs.

(4) Where a statement or certificate (but not a distinguishing mark specified in regulation 16) is required under these Regulations to be in a form prescribed herein, the reference is to a certificate or statement in that form (or as nearly in that form as circumstances permit), adapted to the circumstances of the case and duly completed and signed where required.

(5) For the purposes of section 97(3)(d) of the Traffic Act and these Regulations the date of first use of a motor bicycle means—

(a) except in a case to which paragraph (b) applies, the date on which it was first registered under the Roads Act 1920, the Vehicles (Excise) Act 1949, the Vehicles (Excise) Act 1962 or the Vehicles (Excise) Act 1971;

(b) in the case of a motor bicycle which was used in any of the following circumstances before the date on which it was first registered, namely:—

(i) where the bicycle was used under a trade licence as defined in section 16 of the Vehicles (Excise) Act 1971, otherwise than for the purposes of demonstration or testing or of being delivered from premises of the manufacturer by whom it was made, or of a distributor of vehicles or dealer in vehicles to premises of a distributor of vehicles, dealer in vehicles or purchaser thereof, or to premises of a person obtaining possession thereof under a hiring agreement or hire purchase agreement,

(ii) where the bicycle belonged to the Crown and is or was used or appropriated for use for naval, military or air force purposes,

(iii) where the bicycle belonged to a visiting force or a headquarters or defence organisation to which the Visiting Forces and International Headquarters (Application of Law) Order 1965 [*SI 1965/ 1536*] applied,

(iv) where the bicycle had been used on roads outside Great Britain and was imported into Great Britain, or

(v) where the bicycle had been used otherwise than on roads after being sold or supplied by retail and before being registered,

the date of manufacture of the bicycle.

(6) In paragraph (5)(b)(v) *"sold or supplied by retail"* means sold or supplied otherwise than to a person acquiring solely for the purpose of re-sale or re-supply for a valuable consideration.

B46.06 *[Regulation 3 is printed as amended by SI 2000/3157; SI 2001/53; SI 2002/ 2641; SI 2008/1435; SI 2009/788; SI 2010/1203.*

The Visiting Forces and International Headquarters (Application of Law) Order 1965 (to which reference is made in reg.3(5)(b)(iii)) has been revoked and replaced by the Visiting Forces and International Headquarters (Application of Law) Order 1999 (SI 1999/1736; not reproduced in this work). No textual amendment has been made to reg.3 in consequence of that revocation; but by the Interpretation Act 1978 ss.17(2)(a) and 23(1) references to the earlier order may be treated as references to SI 1999/1736.]

[Meaning of "theory test"

B46.07 3A.—(1) In these Regulations, *"theory test"* means—

(a) where a test is to be conducted, by virtue of regulation 40(2), in two parts, the part, described in regulation 40(2)(a), which consists of the standard test of driving theory and the standard test of hazard perception; [...]

[(aa) where a test is to be conducted, by virtue of regulation 40(1A), in three parts, the part, described in regulation 40(1A)(a), which consists of the standard test of driving theory and the standard test of hazard perception; […]]

[(ab) the part of a test which consists of the abridged standard test of driving theory and the standard test of hazard perception where the test is to be conducted in—

    (i) three parts by virtue of regulation 40(2B); or

    (ii) two parts by virtue of regulation 40(2C); and]

(b) in any other case, each of the large vehicle test of driving theory and the large vehicle test of hazard perception.

(2) Any reference in these Regulations to a "*theory test*" includes such a test conducted as part of an extended driving test.]

[Regulation 3A is printed as inserted by SI 2008/1435 and as amended by SI 2009/788; SI 2010/1203.]   **B46.08**

PART II

LICENCES

Categories of entitlement

Classification of vehicles

4.—(1) Subject to regulations 5 and 78, the Secretary of State shall grant   **B46.09**
licences authorising the driving of motor vehicles in accordance with the categories and sub-categories specified in column (1) and defined in column (2) of Schedule 2 and those categories and sub-categories are designated as groups for the purposes of section 89(1)(b) of the Traffic Act.

(2) In these Regulations, expressions relating to vehicle categories have the following meanings—

(a) any reference to a category or sub-category identified by letter, number or word or by any combination of letters, numbers and words is a reference to the category or sub-category defined in column (2) of Schedule 2 opposite that letter or combination in column (1) of the Schedule,

(b) "*sub-category*" means, in relation to category A, B, C, C+E, D or D+E, a class of vehicles comprising part of the category and identified as a sub-category thereof in column (2) of Schedule 2, and

(c) unless the context otherwise requires, a reference to a category includes a reference to sub-categories of that category.

Classes for which licences may be granted

5.—(1) A licence authorising the driving of motor vehicles of a class included   **B46.10**
in a category or sub-category shown in Part 1 of Schedule 2 may be granted to a person who is entitled thereto by virtue of—

(a) holding or having held a full licence, a full Northern Ireland licence, full British external licence, full British Forces licence, exchangeable licence or Community licence authorising the driving of vehicles of that class, or

(b) having passed a test for a licence authorising the driving of motor vehicles of that class or a Northern Ireland or Gibraltar test corresponding to such a test.

(2) A licence authorising the driving of motor vehicles of a class included in any category or sub-category shown in Part 2 of Schedule 2 may not be granted to a person unless, at a time before 1st January 1997—

(a) in the case of a person applying for a full licence—

(i) he held a full licence authorising the driving of motor vehicles of that class or a class which by virtue of these Regulations corrresponds to a class included in that category or sub-category, or

(ii) he passed a test which at the time it was passed authorised the driving of motor vehicles of such a class or a Northern Ireland test corresponding to such a test;

(b) in the case of a person applying for a provisional licence, he held a provisional licence authorising the driving of vehicles of that class or a class which by virtue of these Regulations corresponds to a class included in that category or sub-category.

(3) A licence authorising the driving of motor vehicles included in sub-category B1 (invalid carriages), which are specified in Part 3 of Schedule 2, may not be granted to a person unless, at a time before 12th November 1999—

(a) in the case of a person applying for a full licence, he held a full licence authorising the driving of motor vehicles included in sub-category B1 (invalid carriages) or a class of motor vehicles which by virtue of these Regulations corresponds to vehicles included in that sub-category, or

(b) in the case of a person applying for a provisional licence, he held a provisional licence authorising the driving of motor vehicles included in sub-category B1 (invalid carriages) or a class of motor vehicles which by virtue of these Regulations corresponds to vehicles included in that sub-category.

Competence to drive classes of vehicle: general

B46.11   **6.**—(1) Where a person holds, or has held, a relevant full licence authorising him to drive vehicles included in any category or, as the case may be, sub-category he is deemed competent to drive—

(a) vehicles of all classes included in that category or sub-category unless by that licence he is or was authorised to drive—

(i) only motor vehicles of a specified class within that category or sub-category, in which case he shall be deemed competent to drive only vehicles of that class, or

(ii) only motor vehicles adapted on account of a disability, in which case he shall be deemed competent to drive only such classes of vehicle included in that category or sub-category as are so adapted (and for the purposes of this paragraph, a motor bicycle with a side-car may be treated in an appropriate case as a motor vehicle adapted on account of a disability), and

(b) all classes of vehicle included in any other category or sub-category which is specified in column (3) of Schedule 2 as an additional category or sub-category in relation to that category or sub-category unless by that licence he is or was authorised to drive—

    (i) only motor vehicles having automatic transmission, in which case he shall, subject to paragraph (2), be deemed competent to drive only such classes of motor vehicle included in the additional category or sub-category as have automatic transmission, or

    (ii) only motor vehicles adapted on account of a disability, in which case he shall be deemed competent to drive only such classes of vehicle included in the additional category or sub-category as are so adapted.

(2) Where the additional category is F, K or P, paragraph (1)(b)(i) shall not apply.

(3) In this regulation and regulations 7 and 8, *"relevant full licence"* means a full licence granted under Part III of the Traffic Act, a full Northern Ireland licence or a Community licence.

Competence to drive classes of vehicle: special cases

7.—(1) A person who has held, for a period of at least two years, a relevant full licence authorising the driving of vehicles included in category C, other than vehicles included in sub-category C1, may also drive a motor vehicle of a class included in category D which is— **B46.12**

(a) damaged or defective and being driven to a place of repair or being road tested following repair, and

(b) is not used for the carriage of any person who is not connected with its repair or road testing,

unless by that licence he is authorised to drive only vehicles having automatic transmission, in which case he shall be deemed competent to drive only such of the vehicles mentioned in sub-paragraphs (a) and (b) as have automatic transmission.

(2) A person who holds a relevant full licence authorising the driving of vehicles included in category D, other than vehicles included in sub-category D1 or D1 (not for hire or reward), may drive a passenger-carrying vehicle recovery vehicle unless by that licence he is authorised to drive only vehicles having automatic transmission, in which case he shall be deemed competent to drive only passenger-carrying vehicle recovery vehicles having automatic transmission.

(3) A person may drive an incomplete large vehicle—

(a) having a working weight exceeding 3.5 tonnes but not exceeding 7.5 tonnes if he holds a relevant full licence authorising the driving of vehicles in sub-category C1, or

(b) having a working weight exceeding 7.5 tonnes if he holds a relevant full licence authorising the driving of vehicles in category C, other than vehicles in sub-category C1,

unless by that licence he is authorised to drive only motor vehicles having automatic transmission, in which case he shall be deemed competent to drive only incomplete large vehicles of the appropriate weight specified in paragraph (a) or (b) which have automatic transmission.

(4) A person who holds a relevant full licence authorising the driving of vehicles included in category B, other than vehicles in sub-categories B1 and B1 (invalid carriages), may drive—

    (a) an exempted goods vehicle other than—

        (i) a passenger-carrying vehicle recovery vehicle, or

        (ii) a mobile project vehicle,

    (b) an exempted military vehicle, and

    (c) a passenger-carrying vehicle in respect of which the conditions specified in regulation 50(2) or (3) are satisfied,

unless by that licence he is authorised to drive only motor vehicles having automatic transmission, in which case he shall be deemed competent to drive only such of the vehicles mentioned in sub-paragraphs (a), (b) and (c) as have automatic transmission.

(5) A person who—

    (a) holds a relevant full licence authorising the driving of vehicles of a class included in category B, other than vehicles in sub-categories B1 or B1 (invalid carriages),

    (b) has held that licence for an aggregate period of not less than 2 years, and

    (c) is aged 21 or over,

may drive a mobile project vehicle on behalf of a non-commercial body—

        (i) to or from the place where the equipment it carries is to be, or has been, used, or the display or exhibition is to be, or has been, mounted, or

        (ii) to or from the place where a mechanical defect in the vehicle is to be, or has been, remedied, or

        (iii) in such circumstances that by virtue of paragraph 22 of Schedule 2 to the Vehicle Excise and Registration Act 1994 [q.v.] the vehicle is not chargeable with duty in respect of its use on public roads,

unless by that licence he is authorised to drive only vehicles having automatic transmission, in which case he shall be deemed competent to drive only mobile project vehicles having automatic transmission.

(6) A person who—

    (a) holds a relevant full licence authorising the driving of vehicles of a class included in category B, other than vehicles in sub-categories B1 or B1 (invalid carriages),

    (b) has held that licence for an aggregate period of not less than 2 years,

    (c) is aged 21 or over,

    (d) if he is aged 70 or over, is not suffering from a relevant disability in respect of which the Secretary of State would be bound to refuse to grant him a Group 2 licence, and

    (e) receives no consideration for so doing, other than out-of-pocket expenses, may drive, on behalf of a non-commercial body for social purposes but not for hire or reward, a vehicle of a class included in sub-category D1 which has no trailer attached and has a maximum authorised mass—

> (i) not exceeding 3.5 tonnes, excluding any part of that weight which is attributable to specialised equipment intended for the carriage of disabled passengers, and
>
> (ii) not exceeding 4.25 tonnes otherwise,

unless such a person is by that licence authorised to drive only vehicles having automatic transmission, in which case he shall be deemed competent to drive only such vehicles in sub-category D1 as conform to the above specification and have automatic transmission.

(7) A person who holds a relevant full licence authorising the driving of vehicles of a class included in category B, other than vehicles in sub-categories B1 or B1 (invalid carriages), may drive a vehicle of a class included in category B+E where—

> (a) the trailer consists of a vehicle which is damaged or defective and is likely to represent a road safety hazard or obstruction to other road users,
>
> (b) the vehicle is driven only so far as is reasonably necessary in the circumstances to remove the hazard or obstruction, and
>
> (c) he receives no consideration for driving the vehicle,

unless by that licence he is authorised to drive only motor vehicles having automatic transmission, in which case he shall be deemed competent to drive, in the circumstances mentioned above, only vehicles included in category B+E having automatic transmission.

Competence to drive classes of vehicle: dual purpose vehicles

8.—(1) Subject to paragraph (2), a person who is a member of the armed forces **B46.13** of the Crown may drive a dual purpose vehicle when it is being used to carry passengers for naval, military or air force purposes—

> (a) where the vehicle has a maximum authorised mass not exceeding 3.5 tonnes, if he holds a relevant full licence authorising the driving of vehicles included in category B other than vehicles in sub-categories B1 or B1 (invalid carriages),
>
> (b) where the vehicle has a maximum authorised mass exceeding 3.5 tonnes but not exceeding 7.5 tonnes, if he holds a relevant full licence authorising the driving of vehicles included in sub-category C1,
>
> (c) in any other case, if he holds a relevant full licence authorising the driving of vehicles included in category C other than vehicles in sub-category C1.

(2) Where the person is authorised by his licence to drive only motor vehicles included in the relevant category or sub-category having automatic transmission, he may drive only dual purpose vehicles having automatic transmission.

Minimum ages for holding or obtaining licences

Minimum ages for holding or obtaining licences

9.—(1) Subsection (1) of section 101 of the Traffic Act shall have effect as if **B46.14**

for the classes of vehicle and the ages specified in the Table in that subsection there were substituted classes of vehicle and ages in accordance with the following provisions of this regulation.

(2) In item 3 (motor bicycles), the age of 21 is substituted for the age of 17 in a case where the motor bicycle is a large motor bicycle except in the following cases, namely—

(a) a case where a person has passed a test on or after 1st January 1997 for a licence authorising the driving of a motor vehicle of a class included in category A, other than sub-category A1, and the standard access period has elapsed,

(b) a case where the large motor bicycle—

(i) is owned or operated by the Secretary of State for Defence, or

(ii) is being driven by a person for the time being subject to the orders of a member of the armed forces of the Crown

and is being used for naval, military or air force purposes, and

(c) a case where a person holds a licence authorising the driving of a large motor bicycle by virtue of having passed a test before 1st January 1997.

(3) In item 4 (agricultural and forestry tractors), in the case of an agricultural or forestry tractor which—

(a) is so constructed that the whole of its weight is transmitted to the road surface by means of wheels,

(b) has an overall width not exceeding 2.45 metres, and

(c) is driven either—

(i) without a trailer attached to it, or

(ii) with a trailer which has an overall width not exceeding 2.45 metres and is either a two-wheeled or close-coupled four-wheeled trailer,

the age of 16 is substituted for the age of 17 in the case of a person who has passed a test prescribed in respect of category F, or is proceeding to, taking or returning from, such a test.

(4) In item 5 (small vehicles), the age of 16 is substituted for the age of 17 in the case of a small vehicle driven without a trailer attached where the driver of the vehicle is a person in respect of whom an award of the higher rate component of the disability living allowance made in pursuance of section 73 of the Social Security Contributions and Benefits Act 1992 (whether before or after his 16th birthday) is still in force.

(5) [...]

(6) In item 7 (other vehicles, including large goods and passenger-carrying vehicles), the age of 18 is substituted for the age of 21 in the case of a person driving a vehicle of a class included in sub-category D1 which is an ambulance and which is owned or operated by—

(a) a health service body (as defined in section 60(7) of the National Health Service and Community Care Act 1990), or

(b) a National Health Service Trust established under Part I of that Act or under the National Health Service (Scotland) Act 1978 [, or

[(bb) an NHS foundation trust within the meaning of section 1(1) of the

Health and Social Care (Community Health and Standards) Act 2003, or]

(c) a Primary Care Trust established under section 16A of the National Health Service Act 1977].

[(7) In item 7, the age of 18 is substituted for the age of 21 in relation to a motor vehicle of a class included in category C or C+E where the person driving the vehicle—

(a) has an initial qualification authorising him to drive motor vehicles of that class,

(b) is using the vehicle as described in regulation 3(2)(e) of the Vehicle Drivers (Certificates of Professional Competence) Regulations 2007,

(c) is authorised by such document as is referred to in regulation 4(5)(d) of those Regulations to drive motor vehicles of that class, or

(d) by reason of being a person in relation to whom regulation 4(7) of those Regulations applies, is not required to have an initial qualification as described in sub-paragraph (a).]

(8) [...]

[(9) In item 7, the age of 18 is substituted for the age of 21 in relation to a motor vehicle of a class included in category D or D+E, other than sub-category D1 or D1+E, where the person driving the vehicle—

(a) has an initial qualification authorising him to drive motor vehicles of that class and is either—

(i) engaged in the carriage of passengers on a regular service over a route which does not exceed 50 kilometres, or

(ii) not engaged in the carriage of passengers,

(b) is using the vehicle as described in regulation 3(2)(e) of the Vehicle Drivers (Certificates of Professional Competence) Regulations 2007,

(c) is authorised by such document as is referred to in regulation 4(5)(d) of those Regulations to drive motor vehicles of that class, or

(d) by reason of being a person in relation to whom regulation 4(7) of those Regulations applies, is not required to have an initial qualification relating to motor vehicles of that class.

(9A) In item 7, the age of 18 is substituted for the age of 21 in relation to a motor vehicle of a class included in sub-category D1 or D1+E where the person driving the vehicle—

(a) has an initial qualification authorising him to drive motor vehicles of that class,

(b) is using the vehicle as described in regulation 3(2)(e) of the Vehicle Drivers (Certificates of Professional Competence) Regulations 2007,

(c) is authorised by such document as is referred to in regulation 4(5)(d) of those Regulations to drive motor vehicles of that class, or

(d) by reason of being a person to whom regulation 4(7) of those Regulations applies, is not required to have an initial qualification relating to motor vehicles of that class.

(9B) In item 7, the age of 20 is substituted for the age of 21 in relation to a motor vehicle of a class include in category D or D+E, other than sub-category D1 or D1+E, where the person driving the vehicle—

    (a) has an initial qualification authorising him to drive motor vehicles of that class, and

    (b) is engaged in the carriage of passengers otherwise than on such a service as is described in paragraph (9)(a)(i).]

(10) In items 6 and 7, the age of 17 is substituted for the ages of 18 and 21 respectively in the case of—

    (a) motor vehicles owned or operated by the Secretary of State for Defence, or

    (b) motor vehicles driven by persons for the time being subject to the orders of a member of the armed forces of the Crown,

when they are being used for naval, military or air force purposes.

(11) In item 7, in the case of an incomplete large vehicle—

    (a) which has a working weight not exceeding 3.5 tonnes, the age of 17 is substituted for the age of 21;

    (b) which has a working weight exceeding 3.5 tonnes but not exceeding 7.5 tonnes, the age of 18 is substituted for the age of 21.

(12) In item 7, the age of 17 is substituted for the age of 21 in the case of a road roller which—

    (a) is propelled otherwise than by steam,

    (b) has no wheel fitted with pneumatic, soft or elastic tyres,

    (c) has an unladen weight not exceeding 11.69 tonnes, and

    (d) is not constructed or adapted for the conveyance of a load other than the following things, namely water, fuel or accumulators used for the purpose of the supply of power to or propulsion of the vehicle, loose tools and objects specially designed to be attached to the vehicle for the purpose of temporarily increasing its weight.

(13) In this regulation—

    (a) for the purposes of paragraph (3) —

        (i) any implement fitted to a tractor shall be deemed to form part of the tractor notwithstanding that it is not a permanent or essentially permanent fixture,

        (ii) *"closed-coupled"*, in relation to wheels on the same side of a trailer, means fitted so that at all times while the trailer is in motion the wheels remain parallel to the longitudinal axis of the trailer and that the distance between the centres of their respective areas of contact with the road surface does not exceed 840 millimetres, and

        (iii) *"overall width"*, in relation to a vehicle, means the width of the vehicle measured between vertical planes parallel to the longitudinal axis of the vehicle and passing through the extreme projecting points thereof exclusive of any driving mirror and so much of the distortion of any tyre as is caused by the weight of the vehicle;

    (b), (c) *[Omitted.]*

    [(d) in paragraphs (7), (9), (9A) and (9B), *"initial qualification"* means such initial qualification as is provided for in Article 3(1)(a) of

Council Directive 2003/59/EC [*O.J. No.L226, September 10, 2003, p.4*] of the European Parliament and of the Council on the initial qualification and periodic training of drivers of certain road vehicles for the carriage of goods or passengers;

   (e) in paragraphs (9) and (9B), expressions which are also used in that Directive have the same meanings as in that Directive.]

[Regulation 9 is printed as amended by SI 2003/166; SI 2004/696; SI 2007/605.]   **B46.15**

Applications for licences

10–12. *[Omitted.]*   **B46.16**

13. [...]   **B46.17**
[Revoked by SI 2001/53.]

14. *[Omitted.]*   **B46.18**

Provisional licences

Duration of provisional licences authorising the driving of motor bicycles

15.—(1) Subject to paragraph (2), there is prescribed for the purposes of section 99(2) of the Traffic Act —   **B46.19**

   (a) a motor bicycle of any class, and

   [(b) the same period as is provided by section 99(1) of the Traffic Act in relation to a licence to which section 99(1) applies.]

(2) There are prescribed for the purposes of section 99(2)(b)(ii) of that Act the circumstances that—

   (a) the previous licence was surrendered or revoked, otherwise than under subsection (3) or (4) of section 99 of the Traffic Act, or treated as being revoked under section 37(1) of the Offenders Act,

   (b) if it has not been so surrendered or revoked, a period of at least one month, commencing on the date of surrender or revocation, would have elapsed before the previous licence would have expired, and

   (c) the licence when granted would come into force within the period of one year beginning on the date of surrender or revocation of the previous licence.

[Regulation 15 is printed as amended by SI 2001/53.]   **B46.20**

Conditions attached to provisional licences

16.—(1) A provisional licence of any class is granted subject to the conditions prescribed in relation to a licence of that class in the following paragraphs.   **B46.21**

(2) Subject to the following paragraphs, the holder of a provisional licence shall not drive a vehicle of a class which he is authorised to drive by virtue of that licence—

   (a) otherwise than under the supervision of a qualified driver who is present with him in or on the vehicle,

   (b) unless a distinguishing mark in the form set out in Part 1 of Schedule

4 is displayed on the vehicle in such manner as to be clearly visible to other persons using the road from within a reasonable distance from the front and and from the back of the vehicle, or

(c) while it is being used to draw a trailer.

(3) The condition specified in paragraph (2)(a) shall not apply when the holder of the provisional licence—

(a) is driving a motor vehicle of a class included in sub-category B1 or B1 (invalid carriages) or in category F, G, H or K which is constructed to carry only one person and not adapted to carry more than one person;

[(aa) is driving a motor vehicle of a class included in sub-category B1 which is adapted to carry only one person and has at any time between 1st August 2002 and 1st March 2003, had the use of an NHS invalid carriage that was issued to him by reason of his having a relevant disability;]

(b) is riding a moped or a motor bicycle with or without a side-car; or

(c) is driving a motor vehicle, other than a vehicle of a class included in category C, C+E, D or D+E, on a road in an exempted island.

(4) The condition specified in paragraph (2)(b) shall not apply—

(a) when the holder of the provisional licence is driving a motor vehicle on a road in Wales, and

(b) a distinguishing mark in the form set out in Part 2 of Schedule 4 is displayed on the motor vehicle in the manner described in paragraph (2)(b).

(5) The condition specified in paragraph (2)(c) shall not apply to the holder of a provisional licence authorising the driving of a vehicle of a class included in category B+E, C+E, D+E or F, in relation to motor vehicles of that class.

(6) The holder of a provisional licence authorising the driving of—

(a) a moped, or

(b) a motor bicycle with or without a side-car,

shall not drive such a vehicle while carrying on it another person.

(7) The holder of a provisional licence authorising the driving of a motor bicycle other than a learner motor bicycle shall not drive such a vehicle otherwise than under the supervision of a certified direct access instructor ... who is—

(a) present with him on the road while riding another motor bicycle,

(b) able to communicate with him by means of a radio which is not hand-held while in operation,

(c) supervising only that person or only that person and another person who holds such a provisional licence, and

(d) carrying a valid certificate issued in respect of him by the Secretary of State under regulation 65(4),

while he and the instructor are wearing apparel which is fluorescent or (during hours of darkness) is either fluorescent or luminous.

[(7A) The holder of a provisional licence authorising the driving of a moped or a learner motor bicycle shall not drive such a vehicle on a road when undergoing relevant training, unless the instructor giving the training is at all times—

(a) present with him on the road while riding another moped or learner motor bicycle or any motor bicycle, and

(b) supervising only him or him and not more than 3 other persons each of whom holds such a provisional licence.]

[(7B) In paragraph (7A) —

(a) *"relevant training"* means training (otherwise than as part of an approved training course for motor cyclists) in how to drive a moped or learner motor cycle given by a professional instructor; and

(b) *"professional instructor"* means an instructor paid money or money's worth for giving such training.]

(8) The holder of a passenger-carrying vehicle driver's provisional licence shall not drive a vehicle which he is authorised to drive by that licence while carrying any passenger in the vehicle other than—

(a) the person specified in paragraph (2)(a), or

(b) a person who holds a passenger-carrying vehicle driver's licence and either is giving or receiving instruction in the driving of passenger-carrying vehicles, or has given or received or is to give or receive, such instruction.

(9) The conditions specified in paragraphs (2)(a), (7) and (8) shall not apply when the holder of the provisional licence is undergoing a test.

(10) The conditions specified in paragraphs (2), (6), (7) and (8) shall not apply in relation to the driving of motor vehicles of a class in respect of which the provisional licence holder has been furnished with a valid test pass certificate stating that he has passed a test for the grant of a licence authorising him to drive vehicles of that class.

(11) The condition specified in paragraph (7)(b) shall not apply in the case of a provisional licence holder who is unable, by reason of impaired hearing, to receive directions from the supervising instructor by radio where the licence holder and the instructor are employing a satisfactory means of communication which they have agreed before the start of the journey.

[(11A) The holder of a disability assessment licence shall not drive a vehicle of a class which he is authorised to drive by virtue of the licence otherwise than during a period which—

(a) commences with the beginning of such period prior to the taking of the disability assessment test required by a relevant notice as is specified in writing by the Secretary of State when serving that notice; and

(b) ends with the completion of the test;

and, for these purposes, a *"relevant notice"* is a notice under section 94(5)(c) of the Traffic Act requiring the person to submit to a disability assessment test.]

(12) In the case of an LGV trainee driver's licence issued as a provisional licence, this regulation shall apply as modified by regulation 54.

(13) In this regulation—

(a) *"exempted island"* means any island outside the mainland of Great Britain from which motor vehicles, unless constructed or adapted specially for that purpose, cannot at any time be conveniently driven to a road in any other part of Great Britain by reason of the absence of any bridge, tunnel, ford or other way suitable for the passage of such motor vehicles but excluding any of the following islands, namely, the Isle of Wight, St. Mary's (Isles of Scilly), the islands of Arran, Barra, Bute, Great Cumbrae, Islay, the island which comprises Lewis and Harris, Mainland Orkney, Mainland Shetland, Mull, the island which comprises North Uist, Benbecula and South Uist and Tiree;

  (b) *"provisional licence"*, in relation to a class of vehicles, includes a full licence which is treated, by virtue of section 98 of the Traffic Act, as authorising its holder to drive vehicles of that class as if he held a provisional licence therefor;

  (c) *"qualified driver"* shall be interpreted in accordance with regulation 17.

  [(aa) *"NHS invalid carriage"* means a motor vehicle included in sub-category B1 (invalid carriages) that is owned by the Department for Health.]

B46.22   *[Regulation 16 is printed as amended by SI 2000/3157; SI 2001/53; SI 2003/222.]*

Meaning of "qualified driver"

B46.23   17.—(1) Subject to [paragraphs (2) and (2A)], a person is a qualified driver for the purposes of regulation 16 if he—

  (a) is 21 years of age or over,

  (b) holds a relevant licence,

  (c) has the relevant driving experience, and

  (d) in the case of a disabled driver, he is supervising a provisional licence holder who is driving a vehicle of a class included in [categories B, C, D, C+E, or D+E] and would in an emergency be able to take control of the steering and braking functions of the vehicle in which he is a passenger.

(2) In the case of a person who is a member of the armed forces of the Crown acting in the course of his duties for naval, military or air force purposes sub-paragraphs (a) and (c) of paragraph (1) shall not apply.

[(2A) For the purposes of supervising the holder of a provisional licence driving a vehicle of a class included in sub-category C1, C1+E, D1 or D1+E ("the learner vehicle") which the holder is authorised to drive by that licence, a person is not a qualified driver unless that person has, in addition to meeting the requirements specified in paragraph (1), passed a test in which the vehicle used in the practical test fell within the same sub-category as that of the learner vehicle.]

(3) For the purposes of this regulation—

  (a) *"disabled driver"* means a person who holds a relevant licence which is limited by virtue of a declaration made with his application for the licence or a notice served under section 92(5)(b) of the Traffic Act to vehicles of a particular class;

  (b) *"full licence"* includes a full Northern Ireland licence and a Community licence;

  [(c) *"relevant licence"* means, subject to sub-paragraph (d), a full licence authorising—

      (i) the driving of vehicles of the same class as the vehicle being driven by the provisional licence holder, and

(ii) where sub-paragraph (f) applies—

    (aa) where that class of vehicle is included within any sub-category specified in column 1 of the table at the end of this regulation, the driving of vehicles in the sub-category specified in column 2 which is opposite that sub-category, or

    (bb) where sub-paragraph (aa) does not apply, the driving of vehicles in the category specified in column 2 of that table which is opposite the category specified in column 1 that includes the class of vehicle being driven by the provisional licence holder;]

[(d) in the case of a disabled driver who holds a licence authorising the driving of vehicles in category B, a relevant licence must authorise the driving of vehicles other than vehicles in sub-category B1 or B1 (invalid carriages);]

[(e) [subject to sub-paragraph (ea)] a person has relevant driving experience if—

(i) where sub-paragraph (c)(i) only applies, he has held the relevant licence for a period of 3 years, or

(ii) where sub-paragraph (c)(ii) applies, he has held the relevant licence authorising the driving of vehicles—

    (aa) of the same class as the vehicle being driven by the provisional licence holder for a minimum period of 1 year, and

    (bb) in the category or sub-category specified in column 2 described in sub-paragraph (c)(ii) for a minimum period of 3 years;]

[(ea) a period before 1st May 2010 during which a person ("the supervising driver") has held a licence authorising the driving of vehicles included in sub-category C1, C1+E, D1, or D1+E may only be taken into account in assessing whether the supervising driver has the relevant driving experience to supervise the holder of a provisional licence driving such a vehicle, if the supervising driver has passed a test before 1st May 2010 in which the vehicle used for the practical test fell within one of those sub-categories;]

[(f) this sub-paragraph applies if—

(i) a person holds a full licence authorising the driving of vehicles of the same class as the vehicle being driven by the provisional licence holder;

(ii) that class is included in a category or sub-category specified in column 1 of the table at the end of this regulation, and

(iii) that person has held that licence for less than a minimum period of 3 years;]

[(g) for the purposes of sub-paragraphs (e) and (f), the minimum period of time for holding a full licence may be met either by holding that licence continuously for that period or for periods amounting in aggregate to not less than that period.]

[Table

Column (1)	Column (2)
Categories and sub-categories which include the vehicle being driven by the provisional licence holder	Categories and sub-categories authorised by the relevant licence
C	D
C1	D1
C+E	D+E
C1+E	D1+E
D	C
D1	C1
D+E	C+E
D1+E	C1+E]

B46.24   *[Regulation 17 is printed as amended by SI 2005/2717; SI 2006/524; SI 2010/ 203.]*

Conditions attached to provisional licences: holders of driving permits other than licences granted under Part III of the Traffic Act

B46.25   **18.** A holder of a provisional licence authorising the driving of vehicles of any class who also holds a permit by virtue of which he is at any time—

(a) treated, by virtue of regulation 80, as the holder, for the purposes of section 87 of the Traffic Act, of a licence authorising the driving of vehicles of that class, or

(b) entitled, pursuant to article 2(1) of the Motor Vehicles (International Circulation) Order 1975 [*SI 1975/1208, q.v.*], to drive motor vehicles of that class,

need not comply with regulation 16 at that time.

Full licences not carrying provisional entitlement

B46.26   **19.**—(1) The application of sections 98(2) and 99A(5) of the Traffic Act is limited or excluded in accordance with the following paragraphs.

(2) Subject to paragraphs (3), (4), (5), (6), (11) and (12), the holder of a full licence which authorises the driving of motor vehicles of a class included in a category or sub-category specified in column (1) of the table at the end of this regulation may drive motor vehicles—

(a) of other classes included in that category or sub-category, and

(b) of a class included in each category or sub-category specified, in relation to that category or sub-category, in column (2) of the table,

as if he were authorised by a provisional licence to do so.

(3) Section 98(2) shall not apply to a full licence if it authorises the driving only of motor vehicles adapted on account of a disability, whether pursuant to an application in that behalf made by the holder of the licence or pursuant to a notice served under section 92(5)(b) of the Traffic Act.

(4) In the case of a full licence which authorises the driving of a class of standard motor bicycles, other than bicycles included in sub-category A1, section 98(2) shall not apply so as to authorise the driving of a large motor bicycle by a person under the age of 21 before the expiration of the standard access period.

(5) In the case of a full licence which authorises the driving of motor bicycles of a class included in sub-category A1 section 98(2) shall not apply so as to authorise the driving of a large motor bicycle by a person under the age of 21.

(6) In the case of a full licence which authorises the driving of a class of vehicles included in category C or C+E, paragraph (2) applies subject to the provisions of regulation 54.

(7) Subject to paragraphs (8), (9), (10), (11) and (12), the holder of a Community licence to whom section 99A(5) of the Traffic Act applies and who is authorised to drive in Great Britain motor vehicles of a class included in a category or sub-category specified in column (1) of the Table at the end of this regulation may drive motor vehicles—

(a) of other classes included in that category or sub-category, and

(b) of a class included in each category or sub-category specified, in relation to that category or sub-category, in column (2) of the Table,

as if he were authorised by a provisional licence to do so.

(8) Section 99A(5) shall not apply to a Community licence if it authorises the driving only of motor vehicles adapted on account of a disability.

(9) In the case of a Community licence which authorises the driving of a class of standard motor bicycle other than bicycles included in sub-category A1, section 99A(5) shall not apply so as to authorise the driving of a large motor bicycle by a person under the age of 21 before the expiration of the period of two years commencing on the date when that person passed a test for a licence authorising the driving of that class of standard motor bicycle (and in calculating the expiration of that period, any period during which that person has been disqualified for holding or obtaining a licence shall be disregarded).

(10) In the case of a Community licence which authorises the driving only of motor bicycles of a class included in sub-category A1 section 98(2) shall not apply so as to authorise the driving of a large motor bicycle by a person under the age of 21.

(11) Except to the extent provided in paragraph (12), section 98(2) shall not apply to a full licence, and section 99A(5) shall not apply to a Community licence, in so far as it authorises its holder to drive motor vehicles of any class included in category B+E, C+E, D+E, or K or in sub-category B1 (invalid carriages), C1 or D1 (not for hire or reward).

(12) A person—

(a) who holds a full licence authorising the driving only of those classes of vehicle included in a category or sub-category specified in paragraph (11) which have automatic transmission (and are not otherwise adapted on account of a disability), or

(b) who holds a Community licence, to whom section 99A(5) of the Traffic Act applies and who is authorised to drive in Great Britain only those classes of vehicle included in a category or sub-category specified in paragraph (11) which have automatic transmission (and are not otherwise adapted on account of a disability), may drive motor vehicles of all other classes included in that category or sub-category which have manual transmission as if he were authorised by a provisional licence to do so.

TABLE

(1) *Full licence held*	(2) *Provisional entitlement included*
A1	A, B, F and K
A	B and F
B1	A, B and F
B	A, B+E, G and H
C	C1+E, C+E
D1	D1+E
D	D1+E, D+E
F	B and P
G	H
H	G
P	A, B, F and K

Miscellaneous

Signatures on licences

B46.27 **20.** In order that a licence may show the usual form of signature of its holder—

(a) where the Secretary of State so requires, a person applying for a licence shall provide the Secretary of State with a specimen of his signature which can be electronically recorded and reproduced on the licence;

(b) where no such requirement is made, a person to whom a licence is granted shall forthwith sign it in ink in the space provided.

Lost or defaced licences

B46.28 **21.** *[Omitted.]*

PART III

TESTS OF COMPETENCE TO DRIVE

Preliminary

Interpretation of Part III

B46.29 **22.** In this Part of these Regulations —

"*applicant in person*" means a person making an application for an appointment for a test or a part of a test with a view to taking the test or that part thereof himself;

[*"appointed person"* means—

    (a) in the case of a safe road use test, a person appointed by the Secretary of State to conduct such a test under paragraph (1)(a) of regulation 22A; and

    (b) in the case of a theory test, a person appointed by the Secretary of State to conduct such a test under paragraph (1)(a)(ii) or (2)(a) of regulation 23;]

["*the CPC subjects*" means the list of subjects set out in section 1 of Annex I to Directive 2003/59/EC of the European Parliament and of the Council of 15 July 2003 on the initial qualification and periodic training of drivers of certain road vehicles for the carriage of goods or passengers, amending Council Regulation (EEC) No.3820/85 and Council Directive 91/439/EEC and repealing Council Directive 76/914/EEC in so far as these subjects are not already covered by the matters specified in regulation 40C(5) in respect of a vehicle of the relevant class;]

"*DSA examiner*" means a person appointed by the Secretary of State to conduct [manoeuvres test, practical tests] or unitary tests under paragraph (1)(a) or (2)(a) of regulation 24;

["*educational qualification*" means—

    (a) a qualification awarded by the Scottish Qualifications Authority pursuant to section 2(1) of the Education (Scotland) Act 1996;

    (b) a qualification accredited by the Scottish Qualifications Authority pursuant to section 3(1) of the Education (Scotland) Act 1996;

    (c) a qualification accredited by the Qualifications and Curriculum Authority under section 24(2)(g) or 30(1)(e) of the Education Act 1997;

    (d) a qualification accredited by the Welsh Ministers under section 30(1)(e) of the Education Act 1997;

    (e) a qualification which has been awarded or authenticated by an awarding body recognised for either of those purposes by the Office of Qualifications and Examinations Regulation ("Ofqual") under section 132 of the Apprenticeships, Skills, Children and Learning Act 2009 and, where that qualification is subject to the accreditation requirement under section 138 of that Act, which has been accredited by Ofqual under section 139 of that Act; or

    (f) a qualification which has been awarded or authenticated by a person recognised for either of those purposes by the Welsh Ministers under section 30(1)(e) of the Education Act 1997 (as substituted by the 2009 Act) and, where they have determined, under section 30(1)(f) of that Act (as so substituted) that that qualification shall be subject to a requirement of accreditation, which has been accredited by them under section 30(1)(h) of that Act (as so substituted);

"*excepted matters*" means the matters falling within Schedule 7, Part 2, section B paragraph 2, section C paragraph 3, section D paragraph 2, section E and section F paragraphs 1 and 3;]

"*large vehicle instructor*" means a person operating an establishment for providing instruction in the driving of vehicles included in category B+E, C, C+E, D or D+E, including an establishment which provides tuition to prepare persons for the theory test;

"*motor bicycle instructor*" means a person operating an establishment for providing instruction in the driving of vehicles included in categories A or P, including an establishment which provides tuition to prepare persons for the theory test;

["*motor car instructor*" means a person operating an establishment for providing instruction in the driving of vehicles included in category B, including an establishment which provides tuition to prepare persons for the theory test;]

["*qualification award certificate*" means a certificate which certifies that the person to whom it has been issued has been awarded the Safe Road User Award;

"*relevant awarding authority*" means a body which awards or authenticates relevant qualifications;

"*relevant qualification*" means an educational qualification in respect of which a safe road use test must be passed before the qualification can be awarded;

"*relevant qualification certificate*" means a certificate issued by a relevant awarding authority which certifies that the person to whom it has been issued has been awarded a relevant qualification;

"*safe road use test*" means an examination the content of which is set out in regulation 40B(ZA1) [*not reproduced*];

"*Safe Road User Award*" means the qualification of that name which is awarded by the Scottish Qualifications Authority before 1st May 2010;]

"*standard access period*" means the period of two years commencing on the date when a person passes a test for a licence authorising the driving of standard motor bicycles of any class, other than a class included in the sub-category A1, but disregarding—

(a) any period during which the person is disqualified under section 34 or 35 of the Offenders Act [*q.v.*],

(b) in a case where the person has been disqualified under section 36 of the Offenders Act [*q.v.*], the period beginning on the date of the court order under subsection (1) of that section and ending on the date when the disqualification is deemed by virtue of that section to have expired in relation to standard motor bicycles of that class,

(c) in a case where the Secretary of State has revoked the person's licence or test pass certificate under section 3(2) of, or Schedule 1 to, the Road Traffic (New Drivers) Act 1995 [*q.v.*], the period beginning on the date of the notice of revocation under that Act and ending on the date when the person passes the relevant driving test within the meaning of that Act, and

(d) any period during which the licence has ceased to be in force;

"*working day*" means [(other than in regulation 35)] a day other than a [...]

Sunday, bank holiday, Christmas Day or Good Friday (and *"bank holiday"* means a day to be observed as such under section 1 of and Schedule 1 to [the Banking and Financial Dealings Act 1971]).

[Regulation 22 is printed as amended by SI 2005/2717; SI 2006/524; SI 2008/ 1435; SI 2009/788; SI 2010/1203. **B46.30**

For the Banking and Financial Dealings Act 1971 Sch.1, see the note to the Road Vehicles (Construction and Use) Regulations 1986 (SI 1986/1078) Sch.12, para.1 above.]

Appointment of persons to conduct tests

22A, 22B, 23–25. *[Omitted.]* **B46.31**

Applications for tests

26–36. *[Omitted.]* **B46.32**

Requirements at tests

37–39. *[Omitted.]* **B46.33**

Nature and conduct of tests

40–42. *[Omitted.]* **B46.34**

Entitlements upon passing test

Entitlement upon passing a test other than an appropriate driving test

43.—(1) Where a person passes a test other than an appropriate driving test **B46.35** prescribed in respect of any category for a licence which (by virtue of regulation 37) authorises the driving of motor vehicles included in that category or in a sub-category thereof, or has passed a Northern Ireland test of competence corresponding to that test, the Secretary of State shall grant to him a licence in accordance with [the following provisions of this regulation].

(2) Subject to [regulations 44 and 44A], the licence shall authorise the driving of all classes of motor vehicle included in that category or sub-category unless—

    (a) the test[, practical test (other than in relation to a vehicle of a class included in category A or P) or two-part practical test, as the case may be,] is passed on a motor vehicle with automatic transmission, in which case it shall authorise the driving only of such classes of vehicle included in that category or sub-category as have automatic transmission;

    (b) the test[, practical test (other than in relation to a vehicle of a class included in category A or P) or two-part practical test, as the case may be,] is passed on a motor vehicle which is adapted on account of a disability of the person taking the test, in which case it shall authorise the driving only of such classes of vehicle included in that category or sub-category as are so adapted (and for the purposes of this paragraph, a motor bicycle with a side-car may be treated in an appropriate case as a motor vehicle adapted on account of a disability).

(3) [Subject to paragraphs (5) and (6), the licence shall] in addition authorise the driving of all classes of motor vehicle included in a category or sub-category which is specified in column (3) of Schedule 2 as an additional category or sub-category in relation to a category or sub-category specified in column (1) of that Schedule unless—

(a) the test[, practical test (other than in relation to a vehicle of a class included in category A or P) or two-part practical test, as the case may be,] is passed on a motor vehicle with automatic transmission, in which case it shall (subject to paragraph (4)) authorise the driving only of such classes of vehicle included in the additional category or sub-category as have automatic transmission;

(b) the test[, practical test (other than in relation to a vehicle of a class included in category A or P) or two-part practical test, as the case may be,] is passed on a motor vehicle which is adapted on account of a disability of the person taking the test in which case it shall authorise the driving only of such classes of vehicle included in the additional category or sub-category as are so adapted.

(4) Where the additional category is F, K or P, paragraph (3)(a) shall not apply.

[(5) Where a person has passed a test (or Northern Ireland test of competence corresponding to such a test) for a licence authorising the driving of vehicles included in category B, the effect of paragraph (3) in relation to the driving of vehicles in category P shall be as follows—

(a) the licence granted by the Secretary of State shall authorise the driving of vehicles within class P if and only if—

(i) the test was passed before 1st February 2001;

(ii) the person concerned held at the date on which he passed the test the prescribed certificate of successful completion by him of an approved training course for motor cyclists and that certificate was at that time valid in accordance with regulation 68(2); or

(iii) the person concerned holds the prescribed certificate of successful completion by him of an approved training course for motor cyclists and that certificate was furnished to him after the date on which he passed the test, and

(b) where a certificate referred to in sub-paragraph (a)(ii) or (iii) shows that the person concerned has successfully completed an approved training course for riders of three-wheeled mopeds, the only vehicles in category P authorised by the licence to be driven shall be three-wheeled mopeds.

[(6) In relation to the first item of Schedule 2 (category A), the effect of paragraph (3) shall be that a licence authorising the driving of vehicles in category A shall in addition authorise the driving of vehicles in category B1, if and only if, the test, or as the case may be the practical test, is passed before 1st February 2001.]

[(7) In this regulation " two-part practical test" means—

(a) in relation to a vehicle of a class included in category A or P, the manoeuvres test and the practical test in respect of a vehicle of a class included in category A or P, as appropriate;

(b) in relation to a vehicle of a class included in sub-category A1, the manoeuvres test and the practical test in respect of a vehicle of a class included in sub-category A1.]

[Regulation 43 is printed as amended by SI 2001/53; SI 2001/236; SI 2009/788.]   **B46.36**

Entitlement upon passing a test other than an appropriate driving test: category A

44.—(1) This regulation applies where a person has passed a test (or a Northern   **B46.37**
Ireland test of competence corresponding to such a test) for a licence authorising the driving of motor bicycles of any class other than a class included in sub-category A1.

(2) Where this regulation applies the Secretary of State shall grant to the person who passed the test—

(a) in a case where he has passed the [manoeuvres test and practical test] (or the Northern Ireland test of competence corresponding to the practical test) on a motor bicycle without a side-car, the engine of which has a maximum net power output of not less than 35 kilowatts, a licence authorising him to drive all classes of motor vehicle included in category A;

(b) subject to paragraph (3), in a case where the practical test (or the Northern Ireland test of competence corresponding to the practical test) was passed on any other motor bicycle without a side-car, a licence authorising him to drive standard motor bicycles;

(c) in a case where he has passed the practical test (or the Northern Ireland test of competence corresponding to the practical test) on a motor bicycle and side-car combination and the engine of the bicycle has a maximum net power output of not less than 35 kilowatts, a licence authorising him to drive all classes of motor bicycle and side-car combinations included in category A;

(d) subject to paragraph (4), in a case where the practical test (or the Northern Ireland test of competence corresponding to the practical test) was passed on a motor bicycle and a side-car combination the power to weight ratio of which does not exceed 0.16 kw/kg but which does not fall within paragraph (c), a licence authorising him to drive standard motor bicycles and side-car combinations.

(3) A licence granted to a person by virtue of paragraph (2)(b) shall authorise him to drive all classes of motor vehicle included in category A upon the expiration of the standard access period.

(4) A licence granted to a person by virtue of paragraph (2)(d) shall authorise him to drive all classes of motor bicycle and side-car combinations included in category A upon the expiration of the standard access period.

[Regulation 44 is printed as amended by SI 2009/788.]   **B46.38**

[Entitlement upon passing a test other than an appropriate driving test: category P

44A.—(1) This regulation applies where a person has passed a test (or Northern   **B46.39**

Ireland test of competence corresponding to such a test) for a licence authorising the driving of vehicles included in category P.

(2) Where this regulation applies the Secretary of State shall grant to the person who passed the test—

    (a) in a case where the test was passed on a three-wheeled moped, a licence authorising the driving of all vehicles having three wheels included in category P;

    (b) in any other case, a licence authorising the driving of all vehicles included in category P.]

B46.40   *[Regulation 44A was inserted by SI 2001/53.]*

Upgrading of entitlements by virtue of passing second test

B46.41   **45.**—(1) A person who has passed tests for a licence authorising the driving of motor vehicles included in—

    (a) category D or sub-category D1 as specified in column (1) of Table A in Schedule 9, and

    (b) category C+E or sub-category C1+E as respectively specified at the top of columns (2) and (3) of Table A,

is deemed, subject to the following paragraphs of this regulation, competent to drive (in addition to the classes of motor vehicle in respect of which the tests were passed) vehicles included in the category or sub-category shown in column (2) or (3) of Table A in relation to the relevant test pass in column (1).

(2) Where, in a case to which paragraph (1) applies, each practical test is passed on a vehicle having automatic transmission the person pasing the tests is deemed competent to drive only such classes of vehicle in the upgrade category as have automatic transmission.

(3) A person who has passed a test for a licence authorising the driving of—

    (a) motor vehicles included in a category or sub-category specified in column (A) of Table B in Schedule 9 which have automatic transmission, and

    (b) motor vehicles included in a category or sub-category specified at the head of one of the columns in that table numbered (1) to (8) which have manual transmission,

is, subject to the following paragraphs of this regulation, deemed competent to drive in addition to the classes of vehicle in respect of which the tests were passed all vehicles included in the category or sub-category shown in the relevant numbered column of Table B in relation to the relevant test pass mentioned in column (A).

(4) Where a person has passed tests for a licence authorising the driving of—

    (a) motor vehicles in category D not more than 5.5 metres in length having automatic transmission, and

    (b) motor vehicles in category C, other than vehicles in sub-category C1, having manual transmission,

he is deemed competent to drive vehicles in category D not more than 5.5 metres in length which have manual transmission.

(5) In the case of a person who holds a licence which, by virtue of regulation

76 (notwithstanding that he may not have passed a test authorising the driving of such vehicles), authorises the driving of a class of vehicles in category D when used under a section 19 permit or (if not so used) are driven otherwise than for hire or reward, Tables A and B shall be read as if—

    (a) for "D" there were substituted "vehicles in category D, driven otherwise than for hire or reward", and

    (b) for "D+E" there were substituted "vehicles in category D+E driven otherwise than for hire or reward".

(6) In the case of a person who has passed a test for a licence authorising the driving only of those classes of vehicle in category C+E which are drawbar trailer combinations, paragraphs (1), (2) and (3) and Tables A and B in Schedule 9 shall apply as if he had passed a test for a licence authorising only the driving of the corresponding classes of vehicle in category C.

(7) Where, in Table B, the upgrade category is qualified by the expression "(a)", the person is deemed competent to drive only such classes of vehicle therein as have automatic transmission.

(8) Where a person has passed a test prescribed in respect of category B+E which authorises the driving only of classes of vehicle having automatic transmission and a test prescribed in respect of any class of vehicle in category C or D which authorises the driving of vehicles with manual transmission, he is deemed competent to drive vehicles in category B+E with manual transmission.

(9) Where a person, who is the holder of a licence which authorises the driving of motor vehicles included in categories B and B+E and sub-categories C1, C1+E (8.25 tonnes), D1 (not for hire or reward) and D1+E (not for hire or reward) which have automatic transmission, passes a test prescribed in respect of category B, B+E, C or D which authorises the driving of vehicles with manual transmission, he is deemed competent to drive vehicles in category B+E and in sub-categories C1, C1+E (8.25 tonnes), D1 (not for hire or reward) and D1+E (not for hire or reward) which have manual transmission.

(10) Where a person has passed tests for a licence authorising the driving of—

    (a) motor vehicles included in category B, other than vehicles included in sub-categories B1 and B1 (invalid carriages), having automatic transmission, and

    (b) motor vehicles included in category B+E, C or D having manual transmission,

he is deemed competent to drive vehicles in category B which have manual transmission.

(11) In this regulation—

    (a) *"upgrade category"* means the additional category or sub-category which the person passing the tests (or holding the licence and passing the test) is deemed competent to drive by virtue of the relevant provision of this regulation, and

    (b) a reference to a test or a practical test includes, as the case may be, a reference to a Northern Ireland test of competence or a Northern Ireland practical test corresponding thereto.

Entitlement upon passing an appropriate driving test

    46.—(1) Where a person—

B46.42

(a) is disqualified by order of a court under section 36 of the Offenders Act until he passes the appropriate driving test, and

(b) passes the appropriate driving test for a licence authorising the driving of a class of motor vehicles included in any category or sub-category,

the disqualification shall, subject to paragraph (8), be deemed to have expired in relation to that class and such other classes of motor vehicle as are specified in paragraphs (2), (3), (4), (5) and (6).

(2) Subject to paragraph (4), the disqualification shall be deemed to have expired in relation to all classes of vehicle included in the category or sub-category referred to in paragraph (1)(b) unless—

(a) the test [practical test (other than in relation to a vehicle of a class included in category A or P) or two-part practical test, as the case may be,] is passed on a motor vehicle with automatic transmission, in which case the disqualification shall be deemed to have expired only in relation to such classes of vehicle included in that category or sub-category as have automatic transmission;

(b) the test [practical test (other than in relation to a vehicle of a class included in category A or P) or two-part practical test, as the case may be,] is passed on a motor vehicle which is adapted on account of a disability of the person taking the test, in which case the disqualification shall be deemed to have expired only in relation to such classes of motor vehicle included in that category or sub-category as are so adapted (and for the purposes of this paragraph, a motor bicycle with a side-car may be treated in an appropriate case as a motor vehicle adapted on account of a disability).

(3) The disqualification shall be deemed to have expired in relation to all classes of vehicle included in any other category which is specified in column (3) of Schedule 2 as being an additional category or sub-category in relation to that category or sub-category unless—

(a) subject to paragraph (5), the test [practical test (other than in relation to a vehicle of a class included in category A or P) or two-part practical test, as the case may be,] is passed on a vehicle with automatic transmission, in which case the disqualification shall be deemed to have expired only in relation to such classes of motor vehicle included in the additional category or sub-category as have automatic transmission;

(b) the test [practical test (other than in relation to a vehicle of a class included in category A or P) or two-part practical test, as the case may be,] is passed on a vehicle which is adapted on account of a disability of the person taking the test, in which case the disqualification shall be deemed to have expired only in relation to such classes of motor vehicle included in the additional category or sub-category as are so adapted.

(4) Where, at the date on which a person is disqualified—

(a) he holds a licence which was granted pursuant to regulation 44(2)(b) or (d), and

(b) the standard access period has not expired,

the disqualification shall not, by virtue of paragraph (2) or (7), be deemed to have expired—

> (i) in a case to which regulation 44(2)(b) applies, in relation to large motor bicycles, or
>
> (ii) in a case to which regulation 44(2)(d) applies, in relation to large motor bicycle and side-car combinations,

until the standard access period has expired.

(5) Paragraph (3)(a) shall not apply where the additional category is F, G, H, K, L or P.

(6) Where a person who is disqualified passes the [two-part practical test] on a vehicle of a class included in category A, other than sub-category A1, the disqualification shall be deemed to have expired additionally in relation to all classes of vehicle included in—

> (a) categories B, B+E, C, C+E, D and D+E, unless that test is passed on a vehicle with automatic transmission, in which case the disqualification shall be deemed to have expired only in relation to such classes of motor vehicle included in those categories as have automatic transmission;
>
> (b) categories F, G, H and L.

(7) Where the person who is disqualified passes the practical test on a vehicle of a class included in category B, other than a vehicle included in sub-category B1, the disqualification shall be deemed to have expired additionally in relation to all classes of vehicle included in—

> (a) categories A, B+E, C, C+E, D and D+E, unless that test is passed on a vehicle with automatic transmission, in which case the disqualification shall be deemed to have expired only in relation to such classes of motor vehicle included in those categories as have automatic transmission;
>
> (b) categories G, H and L.

(8) Where a person is, pursuant to regulation 56, disqualified by the Secretary of State until he passes a driving test prescribed in respect of a class of large goods or passenger-carrying vehicle, the disqualification shall not be deemed to have expired in relation to any class of large goods or passenger-carrying vehicle until he passes that test.

[(9) In this regulation *"two-part practical test"* means—

> (a) in relation to a vehicle of a class included in category A or P, the manoeuvres test and the practical test in respect of a vehicle of a class included in category A or P, as appropriate;
>
> (b) in relation to a vehicle of a class included in sub-category A1, the manoeuvres test and the practical test in respect of a vehicle of a class included in sub-category A1.]

[Regulation 46 is printed as amended by SI 2009/788.] **B46.43**

Test results

[Results of safe road use test and validity of certificates

46A.—(1) The person conducting a safe road use test shall arrange for the test **B46.44**

to be marked on the day it was undertaken and shall upon completion of the marking of the test furnish the person who undertook it with notification of the result of that test.

(2) A qualification award certificate or a relevant qualification certificate shall be valid for the purposes of regulation 38(3)(a)(iia) for a period commencing on the date of the certificate and ending—

    (a) three years later,

    (b) on the date on which the person to whom the certificate is issued is disqualified by order of a court under section 34 or 35 of the Offenders Act,

    (c) on the date on which that person is disqualified by order of a court under section 36 of the Offenders Act until that person passes an appropriate driving test, or

    (d) on the date on which that person's driving licence is revoked under section 3 of the New Drivers Act 1995, whichever is the earliest.]

B46.45   *[Regulation 46A is printed as inserted by SI 2010/1203.]*

Evidence of result of theory test[: vehicles other than category C or D]

B46.46   **47.**—[(1) The person conducting a theory test described in regulation [40(2)(a), (2B)(b) or (2C)(a)] shall arrange for the test to be marked on the day of the test.]

(2) A person conducting the theory test shall, upon completion of the marking of the test, furnish—

    (a) a person who passes the test with a [standard theory test pass certificate] in the form set out in Part 1 of Schedule 10;

    (b) a person who fails to pass the test with a failure statement in the form set out in Part 2 of Schedule 10.

(3)–(8) *[Omitted.]*

B46.47   *[Regulation 47 is printed as amended by SI 2008/1435; SI 2010/1203.]*

[Evidence of result of theory test: category C and D

B46.48   **47(A) [sic]**—(1) The person conducting—

    (a) a large vehicle test of driving theory; or

    (b) a large vehicle test of hazard perception,

shall arrange for the test to be marked on the day of the test.

(2) The person conducting a large vehicle test of driving theory shall, upon completion of the marking of the test, furnish—

    (a) a person who passes the test with a statement of performance in the form set out in Part 1 of Schedule 10A;

    (b) a person who fails to pass the test with a statement of performance in the form set out in Part 2 of Schedule 10A.

(3) The person conducting a large vehicle test of hazard perception shall, upon completion of the test, furnish—

    (a) a person who passes the test with a statement of performance in the form set out in Part 1 of Schedule 10B;

    (b) a person who fails to pass the test with a statement of performance in the form set out in Part 2 of Schedule 10B.

(4) Where a person who has conducted a large vehicle test of driving theory or a large vehicle test of hazard perception is satisfied that a statement of performance has been furnished in error to a person who took the test, he shall, upon receipt of that document from that person, and subject to paragraph (5), furnish that person with a correct statement.

(5) Where the person who took the test alleges that a statement of performance has been furnished under paragraph (2)(b) or (3)(b) in error he may return the statement not later than 14 days after it is furnished to him to the person who conducted the test with a request in writing that the test be remarked.

(6) The person who conducted the test shall comply with a request under paragraph (5) for the purpose of ascertaining whether an error has been made but otherwise shall not be obliged to remark any test.

(7) A statement of performance is not valid for the purposes of regulation 47B(1)—

  (a) if the person to whom it is furnished is at that time ineligible, by virtue of an enactment contained in the Traffic Act or these Regulations, to take the test to which the statement relates; or

  (b) if the statement is furnished in error or with an error in the particulars required to be specified in it.]

[Regulation 47A is printed as inserted by SI 2008/1435.]   **B46.49**

[Large vehicle theory test pass certificates

47B.—(1) Where a person has obtained statements of performance under   **B46.50**
regulation 47A(2)(a) and (3)(a) he shall be entitled to be furnished with a large vehicle theory test pass certificate in the form set out in Schedule 10C.

(2) The large vehicle theory test pass certificate shall be furnished as soon as practicable to a person entitled to it under paragraph (1) by the person who conducted the test to which the later of the two statements relates.

(3) A large vehicle theory test pass certificate furnished in error, or with an error in the particulars required to be specified in it, may not be presented in support of an application for a licence as evidence that the person has passed the tests mentioned in such a certificate.

(4) A large vehicle theory test pass certificate shall be valid for the purposes of regulation 38(4) [or 40A(2)(b)(i)] for a period commencing on the earlier of the dates on which a person passes the large vehicle test of driving theory or the large vehicle hazard perception test and ending—

  (a) two years later, or

  (b) on the date on which that person is disqualified by order of a court under section 36 of the Offenders Act until he passes the appropriate driving test,

whichever is the earlier.

(5) A large vehicle theory test pass certificate is not valid for the purposes of regulation 38(4) if—

  (a) it is furnished in error or with an error in the particulars required to be specified in it; or

  (b) the person to whom it is furnished is at that time ineligible, by virtue of an enactment contained in the Traffic Act or these Regulations, to take any test to which the certificate relates.

(6) Where a person who has furnished a large vehicle theory test pass certificate is satisfied that it has been furnished with an error in the particulars specified in it, he shall upon receipt of that document from the person to whom it was furnished, furnish that person with a correct certificate.

(7) A large vehicle theory test pass certificate shall cease to be valid if the person to whom it is furnished is disqualified by order of a court under section 36 of the Offenders Act until he passes the appropriate driving test.

(8) A person authorised to conduct theory tests by virtue of paragraphs (b), (c), (da), (db), (e) or (f) of regulation 23(1) or regulation 23(2)(b) shall issue large vehicle theory test pass certificates using forms supplied by the Secretary of State.]

B46.51   *[Regulation 47B is printed as inserted by SI 2008/1435; SI 2009/788.]*

Evidence of the result of [manoeuvres] practical or unitary test

B46.52   **48.**—[(ZA1) A person conducting a manoeuvres test shall upon completion of the test furnish—

(a) a person who passes the test with a module 1 pass certificate which, save where the person is exempt from the requirement to pass a theory test by virtue of regulation 42, shall record the date of the standard theory test as recorded in the standard theory test pass certificate which was produced in accordance with regulation 38(4) when that person submitted to the manoeuvres test;

(b) a person who fails to pass the test with a module 1 failure statement.]

(1) A person conducting a practical or unitary test shall upon completion of the test furnish—

(a) a person who passes the test with a test pass certificate in the form set out in Part 1 of Schedule 11;

(b) a person who fails to pass the test with a statement in the form set out in Part 2 of Schedule 11.

[(1A) A module 1 pass certificate is invalid if—

(a) the person to whom it is issued is at that time ineligible, by virtue of an enactment contained in the Traffic Act or these Regulations, to take the manoeuvres test to which the certificate relates; or

(b) at the time when it was issued, the standard theory test pass certificate produced to the person conducting the test in accordance with regulation 38(4) is invalid by virtue of regulation 47(7).

(1B) A module 1 pass certificate is not valid for the purpose of regulation 38(8A)(a) if—

(a) it is furnished in error or with an error in the particulars required to be specified in it; or

(b) it is invalid by virtue of paragraph (1A).]

(2), (3) *[Omitted.]*

B46.53   *[Regulation 48 is printed as amended by SI 2009/788.]*

PART IV

GOODS AND PASSENGER-CARRYING VEHICLES

General

Part III of the Traffic Act: prescribed classes of goods and passenger-carrying vehicle

49.—(1) All classes of motor vehicle included in categories C, C+E, D and D+E, except vehicles of classes included in sub-categories C1, C1+E (8.25 tonnes) D1 (not for hire or reward) and D1+E (not for hire or reward), are prescribed for the purposes of section 89A(3) of the Traffic Act. **B46.54**

(2) Subject to paragraph (3), all classes of motor vehicle included in categories C, C+E, D and D+E, except vehicles of classes included in sub-categories C1+E (8.25 tonnes), D1 (not for hire or reward) and D1+E (not for hire or reward), are prescribed for the purposes of section 99(1) and (1A) of the Traffic Act.

(3) In the case of a licence in force at a time before 1st January 1997, paragraph (2) above shall apply as if "C1," was inserted after "sub-categories".

(4) All classes of motor vehicle included in categories C, C+E, D and D+E, except vehicles of classes included in sub-categories C1+E (8.25 tonnes), D1 (not for hire or reward) and D1+E (not for hire or reward), are prescribed for the purposes of section 99A(3) and (4) of the Traffic Act.

Part IV of the Traffic Act: prescribed classes of large goods and passenger-carrying vehicle

50.—(1) Part IV of the Traffic Act and regulations 54 to 57 shall not apply to a large goods vehicle— **B46.55**

  (a) of a class included in category F, G or H or sub-category C1+E (8.25 tonnes), or

  (b) which is an exempted goods vehicle or an exempted military vehicle.

(2) Part IV of the Traffic Act and regulations 54 to 57 shall not apply to a passenger-carrying vehicle manufactured more than 30 years before the date when it is driven and not used for hire or reward or for the carriage of more than eight passengers;

(3) Part IV of the Traffic Act and regulations 54 to 57 shall not apply to a passenger-carrying vehicle when it is being driven by a constable for the purpose of removing or avoiding obstruction to other road users or other members of the public, for the purpose of protecting life or property (including the passenger-carrying vehicle and its passengers) or for other similar purposes.

(4) All classes of large goods and passenger-carrying vehicle to which Part IV of the Traffic Act applies are prescribed for the purposes of section 117(7) and 117A(6) of the Traffic Act.

Exempted goods vehicles and military vehicles

51.—(1) For the purposes of this Part of these Regulations, an exempted goods vehicle is a vehicle falling within any of the following classes— **B46.56**

(a) a goods vehicle propelled by steam;

(b) any road construction vehicle used or kept on the road soley for the conveyance of built-in road construction machinery (with or without articles or materials used for the purpose of that machinery);

(c) any engineering plant other than a mobile crane;

(d) a works truck;

(e) an industrial tractor;

(f) an agricultural motor vehicle which is not an agricultural or forestry tractor;

(g) a digging machine;

(h) a goods vehicle which, in so far as it is used on [public roads]—

    (i) is used only in passing from land in the occupation of a person keeping the vehicle to other land in the occupation of that person, and

    (ii) is not used on [public roads] for distances exceeding an aggregate of 9.7 kilometres in any calendar week;

(j) a goods vehicle, other than an agricultural motor vehicle, which—

    (i) is used only for purposes relating to agriculture, horticulture or forestry,

    (ii) is used on [public roads] only in passing between different areas of land occupied by the same person, and

    (iii) in passing between any two such areas does not travel a distance exceeding 1.5 kilometres on [public roads];

(k) a goods vehicle used for no other purpose than the haulage of lifeboats and the conveyance of the necessary gear of the lifeboats which are being hauled;

(l) a goods vehicle manufactured before 1st January 1960, used unladen and not drawing a laden trailer;

(m) an articulated goods vehicle the unladen weight of which does not exceed 3.05 tonnes;

(n) a goods vehicle in the service of a visiting force or headquarters as defined in the Visiting Forces and International Headquarters (Application of Law) Order 1965;

(o) a goods vehicle driven by a constable for the purpose of removing or avoiding obstruction to other road users or other members of the public, for the purpose of protecting life or property (including the vehicle and its load) or for other similar purposes;

(p) a goods vehicle fitted with apparatus designed for raising a disabled vehicle partly from the ground and for drawing a disabled vehicle when so raised (whether by partial superimposition or otherwise) being a vehicle which—

    (i) is used solely for dealing with disabled vehicles;

    (ii) is not used for the conveyance of any goods other than a disabled vehicle when so raised and water, fuel, accumulators and articles required for the operation of, or in connection with, such apparatus or otherwise for dealing with disabled vehicles; and

    (iii) has an unladen weight not exceeding 3.05 tonnes;

(q) a passenger-carrying vehicle recovery vehicle; and

(r) a mobile project vehicle.

(2) For the purposes of this Part of these Regulations, an exempted military vehicle is a large goods or passenger-carrying vehicle falling within any of the following classes—

    (a) a vehicle designed for fire fighting or fire salvage purposes which is the property of, or for the time being under the control of, the Secretary of State for Defence, when being driven by a member of the armed forces of the Crown;

    (b) a vehicle being driven by a member of the armed forces of the Crown in the course of urgent work of national importance in accordance with an order of the Defence Council in pursuance of the Defence (Armed Forces) Regulations 1939 which were continued permanently in force, in the form set out in Part C of Schedule 2 to the Emergency Laws (Repeal) Act, 1959, by section 2 of the Emergency Powers Act 1964; or

    (c) an armoured vehicle other than a track-laying vehicle which is the property of, or for the time being under the control of, the Secretary of State for Defence.

(3) In this Regulation —

    "digging machine" has the same meaning as in paragraph 4(4) of Schedule 1 to the Vehicle Excise and Registration Act 1994 [*q.v.*];

    "agricultural motor vehicle", *"engineering plant"*, *"industrial tractor"* and *"works truck"* have the same meaning as in regulation 3(2) of the Construction and Use Regulations [*q.v.*];

    "public road" has the same meaning as in section 62(1) of the Vehicle Excise and Registration Act 1994 [*q.v.*];

    "road construction machinery" means a machine or device suitable for use for the construction and repair of roads and used for no purpose other than the construction and repair of roads; and

    "road construction vehicle" means a vehicle which—

        (a) is constructed or adapted for use for the conveyance of road construction machinery which is built in as part of, or permanently attached to, that vehicle, and

        (b) is not constructed or adapted for the conveyance of any other load except articles and materials used for the purposes of such machinery.

[Regulation 51 is printed as amended by SI 2003/166.   **B46.57**

The Visiting Forces and International Headquarters (Application of Law) Order 1965 (to which reference is made in reg.51(1)(n)) has been revoked and replaced by the Visiting Forces and International Headquarters (Application of Law) Order 1999 (SI 1999/1736; not reproduced in this work). No textual amendment has been made to reg.3 in consequence of that revocation; but by the Interpretation Act 1978 ss.17(2)(a) and 23(1) references to the earlier order may be treated as references to SI 1999/1736.]

Correspondences

52.—(1) For the purposes of section 89A(5) of the Traffic Act, a heavy goods vehicle or public service vehicle of a class specified in column (1) of the table at the end of this regulation corresponds to a class of large goods vehicle or passenger-carrying vehicle, as the case may be, specified in column (2) of that table in relation to the class of vehicle in column (1).

(2) For the purposes of paragraph (1), where a heavy goods vehicle driver's licence held before 1st April 1991 was restricted to vehicles having a permissible maximum weight not exceeding 10 tonnes by virtue of—

    (a) paragraph 3(3) and (5) of Schedule 2 to the Road Traffic (Drivers' Ages and Hours of Work) Act 1976; or

    (b) paragraph (1) or (2) of regulation 31 of the Heavy Goods Vehicles (Drivers' Licences) Regulations 1977 [*SI 1977/1309*];

before those enactments ceased to have effect, such restriction shall be disregarded.

TABLE

(1) *Class of heavy goods or public service vehicle*	(2) *Corresponding class of large goods or passenger-carrying vehicle*
Heavy goods vehicles	*Large goods vehicles*
1	Categories C and C+E
1A	Categories C and C+E (limited, in each case, to vehicles with automatic transmission)
2	Category C and vehicles in category C+E which are drawbar trailer combinations
2A	Category C and vehicles in category C+E which are drawbar trailer combinations (limited, in each case, to vehicles with automatic transmission)
3	Category C and vehicles in category C+E which are drawbar trailer combinations
3A	Category C and vehicles in category C+ E which are drawbar trailer combinations (limited, in each case, to vehicles with automatic transmission)
Public service vehicles	*Passenger-carrying vehicles*
1	Categories D and D+E
1A	Categories D and D+E (limited, in each case, to vehicles with automatic transmission)
2	Categories D and D+E
2A	Categories D and D+E (limited, in each case, to vehicles with automatic transmission)
3	Category D
3A	Category D (limited to vehicles with automatic transmission)

(1) *Class of heavy goods or public service vehicle*	(2) *Corresponding class of large goods or passenger-carrying vehicle*
4	Sub-category D1 and vehicles in category D not more than 5.5 metres in length
4A	Sub-category D1 and vehicles in category D not more than 5.5 metres in length (limited, in each case, to vehicles with automatic transmission)

Part IV of the Traffic Act: dual purpose vehicles

53.—(1) Except in the case of a vehicle mentioned in paragraph (2), Part IV of the Traffic Act and regulations 54 to 57 shall apply to dual purpose vehicles to the extent that they apply to passenger-carrying vehicles.   **B46.59**

(2) Part IV of the Traffic Act and regulations 54 to 57 shall apply to any dual purpose vehicle which is—

(a) driven by a member of the armed forces of the Crown, and

(b) used to carry passengers for naval, military or air force purposes,

to the extent that they apply to large goods vehicles.

Persons under the age of 21

[Large goods vehicles drivers' licences granted to persons under the age of 21

54.—(1) A large goods vehicle driver's licence granted to a person under the   **B46.60**
age of 21 is subject to the conditions prescribed in relation thereto, for the purposes of section 114(1) of the Traffic Act [*i.e.* the Road Traffic Act 1988], in the following paragraphs.

(2) An LGV trainee driver's licence is subject to the condition that its driver shall not drive a large goods vehicle of any class which the licence authorises him to drive unless—

(a) he is a registered employee of a registered employer, and

(b) the vehicle is a large goods vehicle of a class to which his training agreement applies and is owned or operated by that registered employer or by a registered LGV driver training establishment.

(3) A large goods vehicle driver's licence held by a member of the armed forces of the Crown is subject to the condition that he shall not drive a large goods vehicle of any class unless it is owned or operated by the Secretary of State for Defence and is being used for naval, military or air force purposes.

(4) A large goods vehicle which—

(a) authorises the driving of a class of vehicles included in category C, and

(b) is a full licence,

is subject to the condition that its holder shall not drive large goods vehicles of a class included in category C+E, other than vehicles included in sub-category C1+E the maximum authorised mass of which does not exceed 7.5 tonnes, as if he were authorised to do so by a provisional licence before the expiration of a period of six months commencing on the date on which he passed the test for that licence.

(5) In this regulation—

"*LGV trainee driver's licence*" means a large goods vehicle driver's licence which—

(a) authorises its holder to drive vehicles of a class included in category C or C+E,

(b) is held by a person, other than a member of the armed forces of the Crown, and

(c) is in force for a period during the whole or part of which that person is under the age of 21;

"*registered*", in relation to an employee, employer or training establishment, means registered for the time being by the [Skills for Logistics Council] in accordance with the Training Scheme;

"*training agreement*", in relation to an individual who is undergoing, or is to undergo, driver training under the Training Scheme, means the agreement between that individual and a registered employer;

"*the Training Committee*" means the Young LGV Driver Committee which is referred to in the Training Scheme;

[*"the Training Scheme"* means the Young Large Goods Vehicle (LGV) Driver Training Scheme which was established by Skills for Logistics and approved by the Secretary of State for the purpose of regulations under section 101(2) of the Traffic Act on 24 February 2004 for training young drivers of large goods vehicles.]

B46.61   *[Regulation 54 is printed as substituted by SI 2003/636, and as amended by SI 2004/1519.]*

Drivers' conduct

Large goods vehicle drivers' licences and LGV Community licences: obligatory revocation or withdrawal and disqualification

B46.62   55.—(1) The prescribed circumstances for the purposes of section 115(1)(a) of the Traffic Act are that, in the case of the holder of a large goods vehicle driver's licence who is under the age of 21, he has been convicted (or is, by virtue of section 58 of the Offenders Act, to be treated as if he had been convicted) of an offence as a result of which the number of penalty points to be taken into account under section 29 of the Offenders Act [*q.v.*] exceeds three.

(2) The prescribed circumstances for the purposes of section 115A(1)(a) of the Traffic Act are that, in the case of the holder of an LGV Community licence who is under the age of 21, he has been convicted (or is, by virtue of section 58 of the Offenders Act, to be treated as if he had been convicted) of an offence as a result of which the number of penalty points to be taken into account under section 29 of the Offenders Act exceeds three.

(3) Where—

(a) a large goods vehicle drivers' licence is revoked under section 115(1)(a) of the Traffic Act, or

(b) the Secretary of State serves a notice on a person in pursuance of section 115A(1)(a) of that Act,

the cases in which the person whose licence has been revoked or, as the case may be, on whom the notice has been served must be disqualified indefinitely or for a fixed period shall be determined by the Secretary of State.

(4) Where the Secretary of State makes a determination under paragraph (3) that a person is to be disqualified for a fixed period he shall be disqualified until he reaches 21 years of age or for such longer period as the Secretary of State shall determine.

Holders of licences who are disqualified by order of a court

56.—(1) This regulation applies where a person's large goods vehicle or **B46.63** passenger-carrying vehicle driver's licence is treated is revoked by virtue of section 37(1) of the Offenders Act (effect of disqualification by court order) and where it applies subsections (1) and (2) of section 117 of the Traffic Act are modified in accordance with paragraphs (2) to (6).

(2) Where the licence which is treated as revoked is a large goods vehicle driver's licence held by a person under the age of 21—

(a) the Secretary of State must order that person to be disqualified either indefinitely or for a fixed period, and

(b) where the Secretary of State determines that he shall be disqualified for a fixed period, he must be disqualified until he reaches the age of 21 or for such longer period as the Secretary of State determines.

(3) Where the licence which is treated as revoked is a large goods vehicle driver's licence held by any other person or is a passenger-carrying vehicle driver's licence—

(a) the Secretary of State may order that person to be disqualified either indefinitely or for such fixed period as he thinks fit, or

(b) except where the licence is a provisional licence, if it appears to the Secretary of State that, owing to that person's conduct, it is expedient to require him to comply with the prescribed conditions applicable to provisional licences until he passes a test, the Secretary of State may order him to be disqualified for holding or obtaining a full licence until he passes a test.

(4) Where the Secretary of State orders him to be disqualified until he passes a test, that test shall be a test prescribed by these Regulations for a licence authorising the driving of any class of vehicle in category C (other than sub-category C1), C+E, D or D+E which, prior to his disqualification by order of the court, he was authorised to drive by the revoked licence.

(5) Any question as to whether a person—

(a) shall be disqualified indefinitely or for a fixed period or until he passes a test, or

(b) if he is to be disqualified for a fixed period, what that period should be, or

(c) if he is to be disqualified until he passes a test, which test he should be required to pass,

may be referred by the Secretary of State to the traffic commissioner.

(6) Where the Secretary of State determines that a person shall be disqualified for a fixed period, that period shall commence on the expiration of the period of disqualification ordered by the court.

(7) Where this regulation applies, subsections (3) to (6) of section 116 of the Traffic Act shall apply, but as if—

(a) subsection (4)(a) were omitted,

(b) for the words "in any other case, revoke the licence or suspend it" in subsection (4)(b) there were substituted "suspend the licence", and

(c) the references to sections 115(1) and 116(1) of that Act were references to this regulation.

Removal of disqualification

B46.64   **57.**—(1) Subject to paragraphs (2) and (3), the Secretary of State may remove a disqualification for a period of more than two years imposed under section 117(2)(a) of the Traffic Act, after consultation with the traffic commissioner in a case which was referred to him, if an application for the removal of the disqualification is made after the expiration of whichever is relevant of the following periods commencing on the date of the disqualification—

(a) two years, if the disqualification is for less than four years;

(b) one half of the period of the disqualification, if it is for less than ten years, but not less than four years;

(c) five years in any other case.

(2) An application may not be made if the applicant has during the relevant period been convicted (or treated as convicted) of an offence by virtue of which he has incurred—

(a) penalty points, or

(b) an endorsement of a Northern Ireland driving licence held by him, or of its counterpart, with particulars of a conviction pursuant to provisions for the time being in force in Northern Ireland that correspond to sections 44 and 45 of the Offenders Act.

(3) Where an application under paragraph (1) for the removal of a disqualification is refused, a further such application shall not be entertained if made within three months after the date of refusal.

Part V

Approved Training Courses for Riders of Motor Bicycles and Mopeds

Approved training courses

Provision of approved training courses

B46.65   **58.**—(1) For the purposes of section 97(3)(e) of the Traffic Act an approved training course is a course for riders of motor bicycles or mopeds both complying with and conducted in accordance with this Part of these Regulations and approved by the Secretary of State.

(2)–(5) *[Omitted.]*

Nature and conduct of training courses

B46.66   **59.** *[Omitted.]*

Instructors

Certified instructors

　60. *[Omitted.]*　　　　　**B46.67**

Persons authorised as assistant instructors

　61. *[Omitted.]*　　　　　**B46.68**

Withdrawal of approval to provide training courses or to act as instructor

　62. *[Omitted.]*　　　　　**B46.69**

Cessation of conduct of training

　63. *[Omitted.]*　　　　　**B46.70**

Approved training courses conducted on large motor bicycles

　64.—(1) An approved training course for a person holding a provisional licence　**B46.71**
authorising the driving of large motor bicycles and undertaken by him on a motor
bicycle other than a learner motor bicycle must be conducted by a certified direct
access instructor.

　(2) *"Certified direct access instructor"* means a person authorised (or deemed
to have been authorised) in accordance with regulation 65.

Certified direct access instructors

　65.—(1) An approved training body may, subject to the following provisions　**B46.72**
of this regulation, authorise instructors to conduct on his behalf the instruction of
persons who hold provisional licences authorising the riding of large motor
bicycles in the riding of motor bicycles other than learner motor bicycles.

　(2) A person may not be authorised under paragraph (1) unless he—

　　(a) holds a full licence to drive motor bicycles,

　　(b) either—

　　　(i) was authorised on 30th January 1998 to conduct instruction by
　　　　an approved training body in accordance with [the Motor
　　　　Vehicles (Driving Licences) Regulations 1996 [*SI 1996/2824*]]
　　　　and has held that licence for a period of, or periods amounting in
　　　　aggregate to, not less than 2 years, or

　　　(ii) if he was not so authorised, is at least 21 years of age and has
　　　　held that licence for a period of, or periods amounting in aggre-
　　　　gate to, not less than 3 years.

　　(c) is a certified instructor, and

　　(d) has successfully completed the Secretary of State's assessment course
　　　for certified direct access instructors.

　(3)–(9) *[Omitted.]*

[Regulation 65 is printed as amended by SI 2000/2766.]　　　　　**B46.73**

Miscellaneous

Eligibility to undertake approved training course

B46.74   **66.** *[Omitted.]*

Ratio of trainees to instructors

B46.75   **67.** *[Omitted.]*

Evidence of successful completion of course

B46.76   **68.**—(1) The certified instructor or the certified direct access instructor who conducted element (E) of the prescribed training course shall furnish a person who successfully completes an approved training course with a certificate in the form set out in Part 3 of Schedule 13 and signed by that instructor.

(2)–(4) *[Omitted.]*

Exemptions from Part V

B46.77   **69.**—(1) Subject to paragraph (2), section 98(3)(c) of the Traffic Act shall not apply to a person who is a provisional entitlement holder by virtue of having passed a test for the time being prescribed in respect of category P on or after 1st December 1990 and such a person shall be exempt from the requirement imposed by section 89(2A) of that Act.

(2) Paragraph (1) shall cease to apply to a person if he is disqualified by order of a court under section 36 of the Offenders Act.

[(2A) Subject to paragraph (2C), section 89(2A) of the Traffic Act shall not apply to a person who is for the time being a holder of a full licence for a class of vehicle included in category A in respect of a test of competence to drive a vehicle of any other class included in that category.]

[(2B) Subject to paragraph (2C), a person who is for the time being the holder of a full licence for a class of vehicle included in category A shall be exempt from the restriction imposed by section 97(3)(e) on his driving a vehicle of another class included in that category.]

[(2C) The exemptions conferred by paragraphs (2A) and (2B) shall not apply in relation to the holder of a full licence authorising him only to drive a vehicle included in category A having automatic transmission in respect of—

    (a) a test of competence to drive a vehicle having manual transmission; or

    (b) his driving a vehicle having manual transmission.]

(3) A provisional licence or provisional entitlement holder who is resident on an exempted island shall be exempt from the requirement imposed by section 89(2A) of the Traffic Act in respect of a test of competence to drive a motor bicycle of any class taken, or to be taken, on an island, whether or not that island is an exempted island.

(4) A provisional licence holder who is resident on an exempted island shall be exempt from the restriction imposed by section 97(3)(e) of the Traffic Act if he satisfies either of the conditions set out in paragraph (6).

(5) Section 98(3)(c) of the Traffic Act shall not apply to a provisional entitlement holder who is resident on an exempted island if he satisfies either of the conditions set in paragraph (6).

(6) The conditions referred to in paragraphs (4) and (5) are that he is—

    (a) driving on an exempted island, whether or not he is also resident on that island; or

    (b) driving on an island which is not an exempted island for the purpose of—

        (i) undertaking, or travelling to or from, an approved training course,

        (ii) undergoing, or travelling to or from a place where he is to take or where he has taken, a test of competence prescribed in respect of category A or P.

(7) In this regulation—

"exempted island" means any island in Great Britain other than—

    (a) the Isle of Wight, the island which comprises Lewis and Harris, the island which comprises North Uist, Benbecula and South Uist, Mainland Orkney and Mainland Shetland, and

    (b) any other island from which motor vehicles vehicles not constructed or adapted for special purposes can at some time be conveniently driven to a road in any other part of Great Britain because of the presence of a bridge, tunnel, ford or other way suitable for the passage of such motor vehicles;

"provisional licence holder" means a person who holds a provisional licence which, subject to section 97(3) of the Traffic Act, authorises the driving of motor bicycles of any class; and

"provisional entitlement holder" means a person who holds a full licence which is treated, by virtue of section 98 of the Traffic Act and regulation 19, as authorising him to drive motor bicycles of any class as if he held a provisional licence therefor.

[Regulation 69 is printed as amended by SI 2001/53.]   **B46.78**

PART VI

DISABILITIES

Licence groups

70.—(1) In this Part of these Regulations —   **B46.79**

"Group 1 licence" means a licence in so far as it authorises its holder to drive classes of motor vehicle included in—

    (a) categories A, B, B+E, F, G, H, K, L and P,

    (b) the former category N,

"Group 2 licence" means, subject to paragraphs (2) and (3), a licence in so far as it authorises its holder to drive classes of motor vehicle included in any other category, and

"licence" includes, unless the context otherwise requires, a Northern Ireland licence and a Community licence.

(2) In so far as a licence authorises its holder to drive vehicles of a class included in sub-categories C1, C1+E (8.25 tonnes), D1 (not for hire or reward) and D1+E (not for hire or reward) it is a Group 1 licence while it remains in force if—

  (a) it was in force at a time before 1st January 1997, or

  (b) it is granted upon the expiry of a licence which was in force at a time before 1st January 1997 and comes into force not later than 31st December 1997.

(3) Subject to paragraph (6)(d) of regulation 7, a licence shall be a Group 1 licence in so far as it authorises, by virtue of paragraphs (4), (5) and (6) of that regulation, the driving of a class of motor vehicles which is not included in a category or sub-category specified in relation to a Group 1 licence in paragraph (1) or (2) above.

Disabilities prescribed in respect of Group 1 and 2 licences

B46.80   **71.**—(1) The following disabilities are prescribed for the purposes of section 92(2) of the Traffic Act as relevant disabilities in relation to an applicant for, or a person who holds, a Group 1 or Group 2 licence—

  (a) epilepsy;

  (b) severe mental disorder;

  (c) liability to sudden attacks of disabling giddiness or fainting which are caused by any disorder or defect of the heart as a result of which the applicant for the licence or, as the case may be, the holder of the licence has a device implanted in his body, being a device which, by operating on the heart so as to regulate its action, is designed to correct the disorder or defect;

  (d) liability to sudden attacks of disabling giddiness or fainting, other than attacks falling within paragraph (1)(c); and

  (e) persistent misuse of drugs or alcohol, whether or not such misuse amounts to dependency.

(2) The disability prescribed in paragraph (1)(c) is prescribed for the purpose of section 92(4)(b) of the Traffic Act in relation to an applicant for a Group 1 or Group 2 licence if the applicant suffering from that disability satisfies the Secretary of State that—

  (a) the driving of a vehicle by him in pursuance of the licence is not likely to be a source of danger to the public; and

  (b) he has made adequate arrangements to receive regular medical supervision by a cardiologist (being a supervision to be continued throughout the period of the licence) and is conforming to those arrangements.

(3) The following disabilities are prescribed for the purposes of paragraphs (a) and (c) of section 92(4) of the Traffic Act namely, any disability consisting solely of any one or more of—

  (a) the absence of one or more limbs,

  (b) the deformity of one or more limbs, or

  (c) the lost of use of one or more limbs, which is not progressive in nature.

(4) In this regulation—

    (a) in paragraph (1)(b), the expression *"severe mental disorder"* includes mental illness, arrested or incomplete development of the mind, psychopathic disorder and severe impairment of intelligence or social functioning;

    (b) in paragraph (2)(b), the expression *"cardiologist"* means a registered medical practitioner who specialises in disorders or defects of the heart and who, in that connection, holds a hospital appointment;

    (c) in paragraph (3), references to a limb include references to a part of a limb, and the reference to loss of use, in relation to a limb, includes a reference to a deficiency of limb movement or power.

Disabilities prescribed in respect of Group 1 licences

72.—[(1) There is prescribed for the purposes of section 92(2) of the Traffic **B46.81** Act as a relevant disability in relation to an applicant for, or a holder of, a Group 1 licence, the inability to read in good daylight, with the aid of corrective lenses if worn, a registration mark which is affixed to a motor vehicle and contains characters of the prescribed size.

(1A) In paragraph (1) the *"prescribed size"* means —

    (a) characters 79 millimetres high and 57 millimetres wide in a case where they are viewed from a distance of—

        (i) 12.3 metres, by an applicant for, or the holder of, a licence authorising the driving of a vehicle of a class included in category K, and

        (ii) 20.5 metres, in any other case; or

    (b) characters 79 millimetres high and 50 millimetres wide in a case where they are viewed from a distance of—

        (i) 12 metres, by an applicant for, or the holder of, a licence authorising the driving of a vehicle of a class included in category K, and

        (ii) 20 metres, in any other case.]

(2) Epilepsy is prescribed for the purposes of section 92(4)(b) of the Traffic Act in relation to an applicant for a Group 1 licence who either—

    (a) has been free from any epileptic attack during the period of one year immediately preceding the date when the licence is granted; or

    (b) (if not so free from attack) has had an epileptic attack whilst asleep more than three years before the date when the licence is granted and has had attacks only whilst asleep between the date of that attack and the date when the licence is granted,

[where the conditions set out in paragraph (2A) are satisfied.]

[(2A) The conditions are that—

    (a) so far as is practicable, he complies with the directions regarding his treatment for epilepsy, including directions as to regular medical check-ups made as part of that treatment, which may from time to time be given to him by the registered medical practitioner supervising the treatment,

    (b) if required to do so by the Secretary of State, he has provided a declaration signed by him that he will observe the condition in sub-paragraph (a), and

(c) the Secretary of State is satisfied that the driving of a vehicle by him in accordance with the licence is not likely to be a source of danger to the public.]

(3) The disability described in paragraph (1) is prescribed for the purposes of section 94(5)(b) of the Traffic Act in relation to an applicant for, or a person who holds, a Group 1 licence.

B46.82   *[Regulation 72 is printed as amended by SI 2003/166.]*

Disabilities prescribed in respect of Group 2 licences

B46.83   **73.**—[(1) There is prescribed for the purposes of section 92(2) of the Traffic Act as a relevant disability in relation to an applicant for, or the holder of, a Group 2 licence the disability described in regulation 72(1).]

(2) There is also prescribed for the purposes of section 92(2) of the Traffic Act as a relevant disability in relation to a person other than an excepted licence holder who is an applicant for or who holds a Group 2 licence, such abnormality of sight in one or both eyes that he cannot meet the relevant standard of visual acuity.

(3) The relevant standard of visual acuity for the purposes of paragraph (2) means—

    (a) in the case of a person who—
        (i) was the holder of a valid Group 2 licence or obsolete vocational licence upon each relevant date specified in column (1) of Table 1 at the end of this regulation, and
        (ii) if he is an applicant for a Group 2 licence, satisfies the Secretary of State that he has had adequate recent driving experience and has not during the period of 10 years immediately before the date of the application been involved in any road accident in which his defective eyesight was a contributory factor,
        the standard prescribed in relation to him in column (2) of Table 1;
    (b) in the case of a person who—
        (i) does not fall within sub-paragraph (a), and
        (ii) was or is the holder of a valid Group 2 licence upon the relevant date specified in column (1) of Table 2 at the end of this regulation,
        the standard prescribed in relation to him in column (2) of Table 2;
    [(c) in the case of any other person, a standard of visual acuity (with the aid of corrective lenses if necessary) of at least 6/9 in the better eye and at least 6/12 in the worse eye and, if corrective lenses are necessary, an uncorrected acuity of at least 3/60 in both eyes.]

(4) There is prescribed for the purposes of section 92(2) of the traffic Act in relation to a person—

    (a) to whom paragraph (3)(c) applies, and
    (b) who is able to meet the relevant standard of visual acuity prescribed in that sub-paragraph only with the aid of corrective lenses,
poor toleration of the correction made by the lenses.

(5) There is prescribed for the purposes of section 92(2) as a relevant disabil-

ity in relation to a person who is an applicant for or who holds a Group 2 licence, sight in only one eye unless—

(a) he held an obsolete vocational licence on 1st April 1991, the traffic commissioner who granted the last such licence knew of the disability before 1st January 1991, and—

(i) in a case of a person who also held such a licence on 1st Janaury 1983, the visual acuity in his sighted eye is no worse than 6/12, or

(ii) in any other case, the visual acuity in his sighted eye is no worse than 6/9, and

if he is an applicant for a Group 2 licence, he satisfies the Secretary of State that he has had adequate recent driving experience and has not during the period of 10 years immediately before the date of the application been involved in any road accident in which his defective eyesight was a contributory factor; or

(b) the person is an excepted licence holder.

(6) Diabetes requiring insulin treatment is prescribed for the purposes of section 92(2) in relation to an applicant for or a person who holds a Group 2 licence unless the person suffering from the disability held an obsolete vocational licence on 1st April 1991 and the traffic commissioner who granted the last obsolete vocational licence knew of the disability before 1st January 1991.

(7) Liability to seizures arising from a cause other than epilepsy is prescribed for the purposes of section 92(2) in relation to an applicant for or a person who holds a Group 2 licence.

(8) Epilepsy is prescribed for the purposes of section 92(4)(b) of the Traffic Act in the case of an applicant for a Group 2 licence suffering from epilepsy who satisfies the Secretary of State that—

(a) during the period of 10 years immediately preceding the date when the licence is granted—

(i) he has been free from any epileptic attack, and

(ii) he has not required any medication to treat epilepsy, and

(b) that the driving of a vehicle by him in accordance with the licence is not likely to be a source of danger to the public.

[(9) Diabetes requiring insulin treatment is prescribed for the purposes of section 92(4)(b) in the case of a person who—

(a) is an applicant for a licence authorising the driving of vehicles in sub-category C1, C1+E or C1+E (8.25 tonnes), and

(c) satisfies the Secretary of State that he has for at least 4 weeks been undergoing treatment with insulin,

provided that he satisfies the conditions mentioned in paragraph (10).]

(10) The conditions referred to in paragraph (9) are that—

(a) [...]

(b) he has not, during the period of 12 months ending on the date of the application, required the assistance of another person to treat an episode of hypoglycaemia suffered whilst he was driving,

(c) he makes an arrangement to undergo at intervals of not more than 12 months an examination by a hospital consultant specialising in the treatment of diabetes and so far as is reasonably practicable conforms to that arrangement,

(d) his application is supported by a report from such a consultant sufficient to satisfy the Secretary of State that he has a history of responsible diabetic control with a minimal risk of incapacity due to hypoglycaemia …

[(dd) he provides a declaration signed by him that he will—

(i) so far as reasonably practicable comply with such directions regarding his treatment for diabetes as may for the time being be given to him by the doctor supervising that treatment;

(ii) immediately report to the Secretary of State in writing any significant change in his condition; and

(iii) provide such evidence as the Secretary of State may request that he continues to carry out the monitoring referred to in sub-paragraph (e) below,]

(e) he regularly monitors his condition and, in particular, undertakes blood glucose monitoring at least twice daily and at times relevant to—

(i) if he has held a licence authorising the driving of vehicles in sub-category C1, C1+E or C1+E (8.25 tonnes) for at least 12 months since starting his insulin treatment, the driving of such vehicles, and

(ii) in any other case, the driving of motor vehicles generally,]

(f) the Secretary of State is satisfied that the driving of such a vehicle in pursuance of the licence is not likely to be a source of danger to the public.

(11) In this regulation—

(a) references to measurements of visual acuity are references to visual acuity measured on the Snellen Scale;

(b) *"excepted licence holder"* means a person who—

(i) was the holder of a licence authorising the driving of vehicles included in sub-categories C1 and C1+E (8.25 tonnes) which was in force at a time before 1st January 1997, and

(ii) is an applicant for, or the holder of, a Group 2 licence solely by reason that the licence applied for or held authorises (or would, if granted, authorise) the driving of vehicles included in those sub-categories.

(c) *"obsolete vocational licence"* means a licence to drive heavy goods vehicles granted under Part IV of the Traffic Act as originally enacted or a licence to drive public service vehicles granted under section 22 of the 1981 Act which was in force a time before 1 April 1991.

TABLE 1

(1) *Person holding Group 2 licence or obsolete vocational licence on:*	(2) *Standard of visual acuity applicable:*
1. 1 January 1983 and 1 April 1991	Acuity (with the aid of corrective lenses if necessary) of at least 6/12 in the better eye or at least 6/36 in the worse eye or uncorrected acuity of at least 3/60 in at least one eye.
2. 1 March 1992, but not on 1 January 1983	Acuity (with the aid of corrective lenses if necessary) of at least 6/9 in the better eye or at least 6/12 in the worse eye, or uncorrected acuity of at least 3/60 in at least one eye.

TABLE 2

(1) *Person holding Group 2 licence on:*	(2) *Standard of visual acuity applicable:*
1. 31 December 1996, but not on 1 March 1992.	Acuity (with the aid of corrective lenses if necessary) of at least 6/9 in the better eye and at least 6/12 in the worse eye and, if corrected lenses are needed to meet that standard, uncorrected acuity of at least 3/60 in at least one eye.
[...]	[...]

[Regulation 73 is printed as amended by SI 2001/937; SI 2003/166; SI 2007/698.]   **B46.84**

Disabilities requiring medical investigation: high risk offenders

74.—(1) Subject to paragraph (2), the circumstances prescribed for the purposes of subsection (5) of section 94 of the Traffic Act, under subsection (4) of that section, are that the person who is an applicant for, or holder of, a licence—   **B46.85**

(a) has been disqualified by an order of a court by reason that the proportion of alcohol in his body equalled or exceeded—
  (i) 87.5 microgrammes per 100 millilitres of breath, or
  (ii) 200 milligrammes per 100 millilitres of blood, or
  (iii) 267.5 milligrammes per 100 millilitres of urine;
(b) has been disqualified by order of a court by reason that he has failed, without reasonable excuse, to provide a specimen when required to do so pursuant to section 7 of the Traffic Act; or
(c) has been disqualified by order of a court on two or more occasions within any period of 10 years by reason that—
  (i) the proportion of alcohol in his breath, blood or urine exceeded the limit prescribed by virtue of section 5 of the Traffic Act, or
  (ii) he was unfit to drive through drink contrary to section 4 of that Act.

(2) For the purposes of paragraph (1)(a) and (b) a court order shall not be taken into account unless it was made on or after 1st June 1990 and paragraph (1)(c) shall not apply to a person unless the last such order was made on or after 1st June 1990.

Examination by an officer of the Secretary of State

B46.86 75.—(1) There are prescribed for the purposes of section 94(5)(b)(ii) (examination of a licence applicant or holder by an officer of the Secretary of State) the following disabilities—

    (a) impairment of visual acuity or of the central or peripheral visual field;

    (b) a disability consisting of any one or more of the following—

        (i) the absence of one or more limbs,

        (ii) the deformity of one or more limbs,

        (iii) the loss of use of one or more limbs whether or not progressive in nature, and

        (iv) impairment of co-ordination of movement of the limbs or of co-ordination between a limb and the eye;

    (c) impairment of cognitive functions or behaviour;

(2) In paragraph (1)(b), a reference to a limb includes a reference to part of a limb, and the reference to loss of use in relation to a limb includes a reference to impairments of limb movement, power or sensation.

PART VII

SUPPLEMENTARY

Transitional provisions

Effect of change in classification of vehicles for licensing purposes

B46.87 76.—(1) In a licence (whether full or provisional) granted before 1st January 1997, a reference to motor vehicles in an old category shall be construed as a reference to motor vehicles in the new category corrresponding thereto and a reference to motor vehicles of a class included in an old category shall be construed as a reference to vehicles of the corresponding class included in the new category.

(2) Where a licence granted before 1st January 1997 authorises only the driving of a class of motor vehicles included in an old category having automatic transmission, it shall authorise the driving of the corresponding class of vehicles in the new category having automatic transmission.

(3) For the purposes of paragraphs (1) and (2), a reference in a licence to motor vehicles in an old category (or a class included in that category) includes a reference in a licence granted before 1st June 1990 to a group or class of motor vehicles which is, by virtue of any enactment, to be construed as a reference to vehicles in the old category (or a class included in that category).

(4) In this regulation—

    "old category" and *"class included in an old category"* mean respectively a category and a class of vehicles specified in column (1) of the table at the end of this regulation,

"*new category*" and "*class included in a new category*", in relation to an old category, mean respectively the category (or, as the case may be, the sub-category) and the class of vehicles specified in column (2) of the table as corresponding to the relevant old category or class included therein, and

"*section 19 permit*" means a permit granted under section 19 of the 1985 Act.

TABLE

(1) *Old category or class*	(2) *Corresponding new category or class*
A	A
B1	B1
B1, limited to invalid carriages	B1 (invalid carriages)
B	B
B plus E	B+E
C1	C1
C1 plus E	C1+E (8.25 tonnes)
C	C
C plus E	C+E
C plus E, limited to drawbar trailer combinations only	Vehicles in category C+E which are drawbar trailer combinations
D1	D1 (not for hire or reward)
D1 plus E	D1+E (not for hire or reward)
D, limited to 16 seats	D1
D, limited to vehicles not more than 5.5 metres in length	D1 and vehicles in category D not more than 5.5 metres in length
D, limited to vehicles not driven for hire or reward	Vehicles in category D which are either driven while being used in accordance with a section 19 permit or, if not being so used, driven otherwise than for hire or reward
D	D
D plus E	D+E
F	F
G	G
H	H
K	K
L	L
P	P

Saving in respect of entitlement to Group M

77.—(1) Where a person was authorised by virtue of regulations revoked by these Regulations (whether or not he is also the holder of a licence granted before 1st October 1982) to drive, or to apply for the grant of a licence authorising the driving of, vehicles of a class included in the former group M (trolley vehicles

B46.88

used for the carriage of passengers with more than 16 seats in addition to the driver's seat), he shall continue to be so authorised and any licence granted to such a person shall be construed as authorising the driving of vehicles of that class.

(2) A person who is authorised to drive vehicles of a class included in the former group M shall, to the extent that he is so authorised, be deemed to be the holder of a Group 1 licence.

Saving in respect of entitlement to former category N

B46.89   78.—(1) Where on 31st December 1996 a person was, by virtue of regulations then in force, the holder of, or entitled to apply for the grant of, a licence authorising the driving of vehicles included in—

     (a) the former category N (vehicles exempt from vehicle excise duty under section 7(1) of the Vehicles (Excise) Act 1971) alone, or

     (b) category F or A and the former category N,

the Secretary of State may, notwithstanding anything otherwise contained in these Regulations, grant to such a person a licence authorising the driving of vehicles in the former category N (with or without vehicles in either or both of the other categories as the case may be) and a person holding such a licence shall be authorised to drive such vehicles.

(2) Where on 31st December 1996 a person was the holder of, or entitled to apply for the grant of, a licence authorising the driving of vehicles included in category B and the former category N, he shall continue to be authorised to drive vehicles in that former category and any licence granted to such a person authorising the driving of vehicles included in category B shall be construed as authorising also the driving of vehicles in that former category.

Saving in respect of entitlement to drive mobile project vehicles

B46.90   79. In relation to a person who was at a time before 1st January 1997 the holder of a licence authorising the driving of vehicles of a class included in category B (except a licence authorising only the driving of vehicles included in sub-category B1 or B1 (invalid carriages)), regulation 7(5) shall apply as if paragraphs (b) and (c) and the words "on behalf of a noncommercial body" were omitted.

Miscellaneous

Persons who become resident in Great Britain

B46.91   80.—(1) A person who becomes resident in Great Britain who is—

     (a) the holder of a relevant permit, and

     (b) not disqualified for holding or obtaining a licence in Great Britain

shall, during the period of one year after he becomes so resident, be treated for the purposes of section 87 of the Traffic Act as the holder of a licence authorising him to drive all classes of small vehicle, motor bicycle or moped which he is authorised to drive by that permit.

(2) A person who becomes resident in Great Britain who is—

     (a) the holder of a British external licence granted in the [Isle of Man,

Jersey or Guernsey] authorising the driving of [large and medium-sized goods vehicles] of any class, and

(b) not disqualified for holding or obtaining a licence in Great Britain

shall, during the period of one year after he becomes so resident, be treated for the purposes of section 87 of the Traffic Act as the holder of a licence authorising him to drive large goods vehicles of all classes which he is authorised to drive by that licence.

(3) A person who becomes resident in Great Britain who is—

(a) the holder of a British external licence granted in the [Isle of Man, Jersey or Guernsey] authorising the driving of passenger-carrying vehicles of any class, and

(b) not disqualified for holding or obtaining a licence in Great Britain

shall, during the period of one year after he becomes so resident, be treated for the purposes of section 87 of the Traffic Act as the holder of a licence authorising him to drive passenger-carrying vehicles of all classes which he is authorised to drive by that licence.

(4) The enactments mentioned in paragraph (5) shall apply in relation to—

(a) holders of relevant permits and holders of British external licences of the classes mentioned in paragraphs (2) and (3), or

(b) (as the case may be) those licences and permits,

with the modifications contained in paragraph (5).

(5) The modifications referred to in paragraph (4) are that—

(a) section 7 of the Offenders Act shall apply as if—

(i) the references to a licence were references to a relevant permit or a British external licence, and

(ii) the words after paragraph (c) thereof were omitted;

(b) section 27(1) and (3) of the Offenders Act shall apply as if—

(i) the references to a licence were references to a relevant permit or a British external licence,

(ii) the references to the counterpart of a licence were omitted, and

(iii) in subsection (3) the words ", unless he satisfies the Court that he has applied for a new licence and has not received it" were omitted;

(c) section 42(5) of the Offenders Act shall apply as if for the words "endorsed on the counterpart of the licence" onwards there were substituted the words "notified to the Secretary of State";

(d) section 47 of the Offenders Act shall apply as if for subsection (2) there were substituted—

"(2) Where a court orders the holder of a relevant permit or a British external licence to be disqualified it must send the permit or the licence, on its being produced to the court, to the Secretary of State who shall keep it until the disqualification has expired or been removed or the person entitled to it leaves Great Britain and in any case has made a demand in writing for its return to him.

'Relevant permit' has the meaning given by regulation 80 of the Motor Vehicles (Driving Licences) Regulations 1999.";

(e) section 164(1), (6) and (8) of the Traffic Act shall apply as if the references therein to a licence were references to a relevant permit or a British external licence and the references to a counterpart of a licence were omitted; and

(f) section 173 of the Traffic Act (e) shall apply as if after paragraph (aa) there were added—

"(ab) a relevant permit (within the meaning of regulation 80 of the Motor Vehicles (Driving Licences) Regulations 1999,

(ac) a British external licence,".

(6) In this regulation *"relevant permit"* means—

(i) a "domestic driving permit",

(ii) a "Convention driving permit", or

(iii) a "British Forces (BFG) driving licence",

within the meaning of article 2(7) of the Motor Vehicles (International Circulation) Order 1975 which is—

(a) for the time being valid for the purposes for which it was issued, and

(b) is not a domestic driving permit or a British Forces (BFG) driving licence in respect of which any order made, or having effect as if made, by the Secretary of State is for the time being in force under article 2(6) of that Order.

B46.92   *[Regulation 80 is printed as amended by SI 2003/166.]*

Service personnel

B46.93   **81.** The traffic commissioner for the South Eastern and Metropolitan Traffic Areas is hereby prescribed for the purposes of section 183(6) of the Traffic Act (discharge of Part IV functions in relation to HM Forces).

Northern Ireland licences

B46.94   **82.**—(1) The traffic commissioner for the North Western Traffic Area is hereby prescribed for the purposes of section 122(2) of the Traffic Act.

(2) For the purposes of section 122(4) of the Traffic Act, the magistrates' court or sheriff to whom an appeal shall lie by the holder of a Northern Ireland licence, being a person who is not resident in Great Britain and who is aggrieved by the suspension or revocation of the licence or by the ordering of disqualification for holding or obtaining a licence, shall be—

(a) such a magistrates' court or sheriff as he may nominate at the time he makes the appeal; or

(b) in the absence of a nomination of a particular court under sub-paragraph (a), the magistrates' court in whose area the office of the traffic commissioner for the North Western Traffic Area is situated.

Statement of date of birth

B46.95   **83.**—(1) The circumstances in which a person specified in section 164(2) of the Traffic Act shall, on being required by a police constable, state his date of birth are—

(a) where that person fails to produce forthwith for examination his licence on being required to do so by a police constable under that section; or

(b) where, on being so required, that person produces a licence—

(i) which the police constable in question has reason to suspect was not granted to that person, was granted to that person in error or contains an alteration in the particulars entered on the licence (other than as described in paragraph (ii)) made with intent to deceive; or

(ii) in which the driver number has been altered, removed or defaced;

(c) where that person is a person specified in subsection (1)(d) of that section and the police constable has reason to suspect that he is under 21 years of age.

(2) In paragraph (1), *"driver number"* means the number described as the driver number in the licence.

Regulation 2   SCHEDULE 1

[Regulations revoked]   **B46.96**

Regulations 4 to 6 and 43   SCHEDULE 2

CATEGORIES AND SUB-CATEGORIES OF VEHICLE FOR LICENSING PURPOSES

PART 1

B46.97

(1) *Category or*	(2) *Classes of vehicle included sub-category*	(3) *Additional categories and sub-categories*
A	Motor bicycles.	B1, K and P
A1	A sub-category of category A comprising learner motor bicycles.	P
B	Motor vehicles, other than vehicles included in category A, F, K or P, having a maximum authorised mass not exceeding 3.5 tonnes and not more than eight seats in addition to the driver's seat, including: (i) a combination of any such vehicle and a trailer where the trailer has a maximum authorised mass not exceeding 750 kilograms, and (ii) a combination of any such vehicle and a trailer where the maximum authorised mass of the combination does not exceed 3.5 tonnes and the maximum authorised mass of the trailer does not exceed the unladen weight of the tractor vehicle.	F, K and P
B1	A sub-category of category B comprising motor vehicles having three or four wheels and an unladen weight not exceeding 550 kilograms.	K and P

(1) Category or	(2) Classes of vehicle included sub-category	(3) Additional categories and sub-categories
B+E	Combinations of a motor vehicle and trailer where the tractor vehicle is in category B but the combination does not fall within that category.	None
C	Motor vehicles having a maximum authorised mass exceeding 3.5 tonnes, other than vehicles falling within category D, F, G or H, including any such vehicle drawing a trailer having a maximum authorised mass not exceeding 750 kilograms.	None
C1	A sub-category of category C comprising motor vehicles having a maximum authorised mass exceeding 3.5 tonnes but not exceeding 7.5 tonnes, including any such vehicle drawing a trailer having a maximum authorised mass not exceeding 750 kilograms.	None
D	Motor vehicles constructed or adapted for the carriage of passengers having more than eight seats in addition to the driver's seat, including any such vehicle drawing a trailer having a maximum authorised mass not exceeding 750 kilograms.	None
D1	A sub-category of category D comprising motor vehicles having more than eight but not more than 16 seats in addition to the driver's seat and including any such vehicle drawing a trailer with a maximum authorised mass not exceeding 750 kilograms.	None
C+E	Combinations of a motor vehicle and trailer where the tractor vehicle is in category C but the combination does not fall within that category.	B+E
C1+E	A sub-category of category C+E comprising combinations of a motor vehicle and trailer where: (a) the tractor vehicle is in sub-category C1, (b) the maximum authorised mass of the trailer exceeds 750 kilograms but not the unladen weight of the tractor vehicle, and (c) the maximum authorised mass of the combination does not exceed 12 tonnes.	B+E
D+E	Combinations of a motor vehicle and trailer where the tractor vehicle is in category D but the combination does not fall within that category	B+E

(1) Category or	(2) Classes of vehicle included sub-category	(3) Additional categories and sub-categories
D1+E	A sub-category of category D+E comprising combination of a motor vehicle and trailer where: (a) the tractor vehicle is in sub-category D1, (b) the maximum authorised mass of the trailer exceeds 750 kilograms but not the unladen weight of the tractor vehicle, (c) the maximum authorised mass of the combination does not exceed 12 tonnes, and (d) the trailer is not used for the carriage of passengers.	B+E
F	Agricultural or forestry tractors, including any such vehicle drawing a trailer but excluding any motor vehicle included in category H.	K
G	Road rollers.	None
H	Track-laying vehicles steered by their tracks.	None
K	Mowing machines which do not fall within category A and vehicles controlled by a pedestrian.	None
P	Mopeds.	None

PART 2

B46.98

(1) Sub-category	(2) Classes of vehicle included	(3) Additional categories and sub-categories
C1+E (8.25 tonnes)	[A sub-category of category C+E comprising combinations of a motor vehicle and trailer in sub-category C1+E where: (a) the maximum authorised mass of the trailer exceeds 750 kilograms and may exceed the unladen weight of the tractor vehicle, and (b) the maximum authorised mass of the combination does not exceed 8.25 tonnes.]	None
D1 (not for hire or reward)	A sub-category of category D comprising motor vehicles in sub-category D1 driven otherwise than for hire or reward.	None
D1+E (not for hire or reward)	[A sub-category of category D+E comprising motor vehicles in sub-category D1+E where: (a) the motor vehicles are driven otherwise than for hire or reward, and (b) the maximum authorised mass of the trailer exceeds 750 kilograms and may exceed the unladen weight of the tractor vehicle.]	None

(1) Sub-category	(2) *Classes of vehicle included*	(3) *Additional categories and sub-categories*
L	Motor vehicles propelled by electrical power.	None

B46.99   *[Part 2 of Sch.2 is printed as amended by SI 2005/2717.]*

PART 3

B46.100

(1) Sub-category	(2) *Classes of vehicle included*	(3) *Additional categories and sub-sub-categories*
B1 (invalid carriages)	A sub-category of category B comprising motor vehicles which are invalid carriages.	None

B46.101   *[The categories of driving licences issued by EC Member States have been harmonised by Directive 91/439/EEC of July 29, 1991 (O.J. No.L237, August 24, 1991, p.1), as amended. The Directive requires the mutual recognition of driving licences issued in the various Member States, including those issued before the implementation of the Directive. Tables of equivalences between the categories of driving licences issued before the implementation of the Directive and the harmonised categories of driving licences have been published as an Annex to Decision 2000/275/EC (O.J. No.L91, April 12, 2000, pp.1–50). When an existing driving licence is exchanged for a Community model driving licence, the entitlement to drive under the latter will be determined by reference to the published equivalences.*

Directive 91/439/EEC will be wholly repealed with effect from January 19, 2013 by Directive 2006/126/EC on driving licences (recast) (O.J. No.L403, December 30, 2006, p.18). References to the repealed Directive should be construed as references to the 2006 Directive.]

    Regulation 14   SCHEDULE 3

LICENCE FEES

PART 1

B46.102   *[Omitted.]*

[PART 2

INTERPRETATION

B46.103   In Part 1 of this Schedule—

       "first licence" means a licence (other than a licence granted in exchange for a full Northern Ireland licence or to a person who has held a full Northern Ireland licence which was granted on or after 1st January 1976 or in exchange for a Community licence which is required to be delivered to the Secretary of State) granted to a person—

          (a) who has not held a licence before, or

          (b) whose last licence was a full licence which expired before 31st December 1978, or

          (c) whose last licence was a provisional licence which was granted before 1st October 1982.]

Regulation 16   SCHEDULE 4

DISTINGUISHING MARKS TO BE DISPLAYED ON A MOTOR VEHICLE BEING DRIVEN UNDER A PROVISIONAL LICENCE

PART 1

Diagram of distinguishing mark to be displayed on a motor vehicle in England, Wales   **B46.105**
or Scotland.

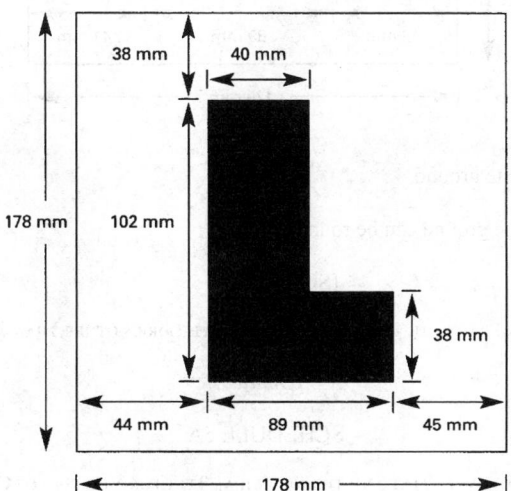

Red letter on white ground.

The corners of the ground can be rounded off.

PART 2

Diagram of optional distinguishing mark to be displayed on a motor vehicle in Wales if   **B46.106**
a mark in the form set out in Part 1 is not displayed.

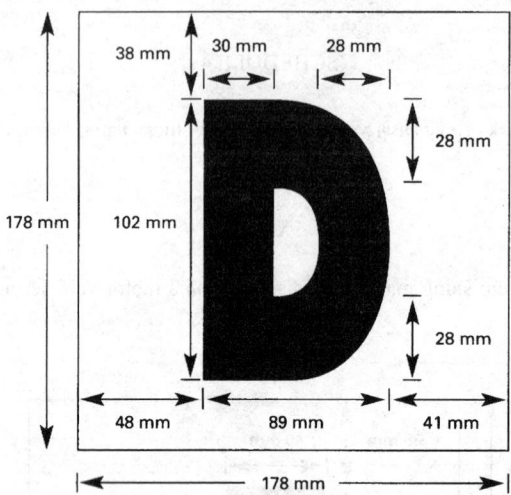

Red letter on white ground

The corners of the ground can be rounded off.

Regulation 35   [SCHEDULE 5

FEES FOR PRACTICAL TESTS: VEHICLES OR CATEGORIES OTHER THAN A OR P

B46.107   *[Omitted.]*

Regulation 35   SCHEDULE 5A

FEES FOR THE MANOEUVRES TEST AND THE PRACTICAL TEST FOR VEHICLES OF CATEGORY A OR P

B46.108   *[Omitted.]*]

Regulation 38   SCHEDULE 6

EVIDENCE OF IDENTITY OF TEST CANDIDATES

B46.109   *[Revoked.]*

Regulation 40   SCHEDULE 7

SPECIFIED MATTERS FOR THEORY TEST

B46.110   *[Omitted.]*

Regulation 40   SCHEDULE 8

SPECIFIED REQUIREMENTS FOR PRACTICAL OR UNITARY TEST

B46.111   *[Omitted.]*

Regulations 3 and 40C(7)   [SCHEDULE 8A

SPECIFIED REQUIREMENTS FOR MANOEUVRES TEST

B46.112   *[Omitted.]*]

Regulation 45   SCHEDULE 9

Upgraded Entitlements on Passing Second Test

TABLE A   **B46.113**

(1) *Test prescribed in respect of:*—	*Prescribed test also passed for:*— (2) *Category C+E*	(3) *Sub-category C1+E*
D D1	D+E D1+E	D1+E D1+E

TABLE B

(A) Automatic test pass: —	*Manual test pass in category (or sub-category):*—							
	(1) *C1*	(2) *C*	(3) *C1+E*	(4) *C+E*	(5) *D1*	(6) *D*	(7) *D1+E*	(8) *D+E*
C1	—	—	C1	C1 & C1+E	C1	C1	C1	C1
C	—	—	—	C	C1	C	C1	C
C1+E	—	C1+E	—	—	D1+E (a)	C1+E	C1+E	C1+E
C+E	—	—	—	—	D1+E (a)	D+E (a)	—	C+E
D1	D1	D1	D1 & D1+E	D1 & D1+E	—	—	—	D1&D1+E
D	—	D	—	D1 & D+E	—	—	—	D
D1+E	—	D1+E	D1+E	D1+E	—	D1+E	—	—
D+E	—	—	—	D+E	—	—	—	—

B46.114

Regulation 47   SCHEDULE 10

Forms of Certificate and Statement of Theory Test Result

[Omitted.]   **B46.115**

Regulation 47A(2)   [SCHEDULE 10A

Large Vehicle Test of Driving Theory

[Omitted.]]   **B46.116**

Regulation 47A(3)   [SCHEDULE 10B

Large Vehicle Test of Hazard Perception

[Omitted.]]   **B46.117**

Regulation 47B(1)   [SCHEDULE 10C

Large Vehicle Theory Test Pass Certificate

[Omitted.]]   **B46.118**

Regulation 3   [SCHEDULE 10D

Forms of Certificate and Statement

[Omitted.]]   **B46.119**

Regulation 48   SCHEDULE 11

FORMS OF CERTIFICATE AND STATEMENT OF PRACTICAL OR UNITARY TEST RESULT

B46.120   *[Omitted.]*

Regulation 59   SCHEDULE 12

ELEMENTS OF AN APPROVED TRAINING COURSE

B46.121   *[Omitted.]*

Regulations 60, 65 and 68   SCHEDULE 13

APPROVED MOTOR BICYCLE TRAINING COURSES: FORMS OF CERTIFICATE

B46.122   *[Omitted.]*

The Road Transport (Passenger Vehicles Cabotage) Regulations 1999

(SI 1999/3413)

[The Arrangement of regulations set out below has been added editorially and **B47.01**
does not form part of the text of the regulations.

The text of these regulations is printed as amended by: **B47.02**
the Road Transport (Passenger Vehicles Cabotage) (Amendment)
Regulations 2000 (SI 2000/3114) (December 28, 2000).

The amending regulations are referred to in the notes to the principal regula-
tions only by their year and number. The date referred to above is the date on
which the amending regulations came into force.

Council Regulation (EC) No.12/98 ("the Council Regulation") referred to
below in these regulations was, with effect from December 4, 2011, repealed by
European and Council Regulation (EC) 1073/2009 of October 21, 2009 on com-
mon rules for access to the international market for coach and bus services, and
amending Regulation (EC) 561/2006 (O.J. No.L300, November 14, 2009, p.88)
art.30. References to the repealed Regulation shall be construed as references to
Regulation (EC) 1073/2009 and shall be read in accordance with the correlation
table set out in ibid. Annex III.]

ARRANGEMENT OF REGULATIONS

Commencement, citation and interpretation

1.—(1) *[Omitted.]* **B47.04**

(2) In these Regulations —

"*the Council Regulation*" means Council Regulation (EC) No.12/98 of 11 December 1997 laying down the conditions under which non-resident carriers may operate national road passenger transport services within a member State;

"*the 1981 Act*" means the Public Passenger Vehicles Act 1981 [*q.v.*];

"*Community carrier*" means a road passenger transport carrier established in a member state of the European Community other than the United Kingdom;

"*road*" has the meaning given in section 192(1) of the Road Traffic Act 1988 [*q.v.*];

"*traffic commissioner*" has the meaning given in section 4 of the 1981 Act;

"*UK cabotage operations*" means cabotage transport operations in Great Britain or between Great Britain and Northern Ireland.

Extent

B47.05   2. These Regulations apply in Great Britain.

Cabotage without a Community licence

B47.06   3.—(1) A person commits an offence if he uses a vehicle on a road, or causes or permits a vehicle to be so used, for the purpose of UK cabotage operations which are carried out by a Community carrier without a valid Community licence.

(2) A person who is guilty of an offence under paragraph (1) above shall be liable on summary conviction to a fine not exceeding level 4 on the standard scale.

B47.07   *[An offence under reg.3 is a fixed penalty offence for the purposes of Pt 3 of the Road Traffic Offenders Act 1988 (see the Fixed Penalty Offences Order 2009 (SI 2009/483) art.2). The amount for the fixed penalty offence is prescribed by the Fixed Penalty Order 2000 (SI 2000/2792), as amended by the Fixed Penalty (Amendment) Order 2009 (SI 2009/488).]*

Use of a vehicle in Great Britain without a control document

B47.08   4.—(1) A person commits an offence if he uses a vehicle on a road, or causes or permits a vehicle to be so used, for the purposes of UK cabotage operations which—

(a) take the form of occasional services in Great Britain or between Great Britain and Northern Ireland, and

(b) are carried out in contravention of Article 6(1) of the Council Regulation.

(2) A person who is guilty of an offence under paragraph (1) above shall be liable on summary conviction to a fine not exceeding level 4 on the standard scale.

B47.09   *[An offence under reg.4 is a fixed penalty offence for the purposes of Pt 3 of the Road Traffic Offenders Act 1988 (see the Fixed Penalty Offences Order 2009 (SI 2009/483) art.2). The amount for the fixed penalty offence is prescribed by the Fixed Penalty Order 2000 (SI 2000/2792), as amended by the Fixed Penalty (Amendment) Order 2009 (SI 2009/488).]*

Competent authorities in Great Britain

B47.10   5.—(1) For the purposes of Article 11(4) of the Council Regulation the competent authority of the member State of establishment shall be the traffic commissioner for the area in which the carrier has his operating centre (*"the appropriate traffic commissioner"*).

[(2) For the purposes of Articles 7, 9 and 11(2) and (3) of the Council Regulation the competent authority shall be the Secretary of State.]

[Regulation 5 is printed as amended by SI 2000/3114.]   **B47.11**

Appeals

6.—(1) A carrier who is aggrieved by an administrative penalty imposed on   **B47.12**
him by the Secretary of State under Article 11(2) of the Council Regulation may request the Secretary of State to review that decision.

(2) A carrier who is aggrieved by an administrative penalty imposed on him by the appropriate traffic commissioner under Article 11(4) of the Council Regulation may appeal to the Transport Tribunal.

Production of documents

7.—(1) The driver of a vehicle which is required, under Article 5 of the Council   **B47.13**
Regulation, to have on board a Community licence commits an offence if he fails, without reasonable cause, to produce the licence when requested to do so by an authorised inspecting officer.

(2) References in paragraph (1) above to a Community licence include references to a certified true copy of a licence.

(3) The driver of a vehicle which is required, under Article 6(1) of the Council Regulation, to have on board a control document commits an offence if he fails, without reasonable cause, to produce the control document when requested to do so by an authorised inspecting officer.

(4) A person who is guilty of an offence under paragraph (1) or (3) above is liable on summary conviction to a fine not exceeding level 3 on the standard scale.

[Offences under reg.7(1) and (3) are fixed penalty offences for the purposes of   **B47.14**
Pt 3 of the Road Traffic Offenders Act 1988 (see the Fixed Penalty Offences Order 2009 (SI 2009/483) art.2). The amounts for the fixed penalty offences are prescribed by the Fixed Penalty Order 2000 (SI 2000/2792), as amended by the Fixed Penalty (Amendment) Order 2009 (SI 2009/488).]

Authorised inspecting officers

8. Authorised inspecting officers for the purposes of the Council Regulation   **B47.15**
shall in Great Britain be constables in uniform, and examiners appointed under section 66A of the Road Traffic Act 1988.

Bodies corporate

9.—(1) Where an offence under these Regulations has been committed by a   **B47.16**
body corporate and it is proved to have been committed with the consent or connivance of, or to be attributable to any neglect on the part of, any director, manager, secretary or other similar officer of the body corporate or any person who was purporting to act in any such capacity, he as well as the body corporate shall be guilty of the offence and shall be liable to be proceeded against and punished accordingly.

(2) Where the affairs of a body corporate are managed by its members, paragraph (1) above shall apply in relation to the acts and defaults of a member in

connection with his functions of management as if he were a director of the body corporate.

(3) Where an offence under these Regulations has been committed by a Scottish partnership and is proved to have been committed with the consent or connivance of, or to be attributable to any neglect on the part of a partner, he as well as the partnership shall be guilty of the offence and shall be liable to be proceeded against and punished accordingly.

Modification of certain enactments and of the Public Service Vehicles (Conditions of Fitness, Equipment, Use and Certification) Regulations 1981

B47.17   **10.**—(1)–(5) *[Amend, inter alia, the Road Traffic (Foreign Vehicles) Act 1972, q.v., and the Public Passenger Vehicles Act 1981, q.v.]*

(6) None of the provisions of Parts II, III, IV and V of the Public Service Vehicles (Conditions of Fitness, Equipment, Use and Certification) Regulations 1981 [*SI 1981/257, as amended, q.v.*] shall have effect in relation to a vehicle which is carrying out a cabotage transport operation in Great Britain in accordance with the Council Regulation.

The Disabled Persons (Badges for Motor Vehicles) (England) Regulations 2000

(SI 2000/682)

[These regulations provide for a Community-model parking card for disabled persons in conformity with Council Recommendation 98/37/EC of June 4, 1998 (O.J. No.L167, June 12, 1998, p.25).   **B48.01**

Corresponding Welsh regulations are the Disabled Persons (Badges for Motor Vehicles) (Wales) Regulations 2000 (SI 2000/1786). These regulations are not reproduced below, but may be found in the twenty-first edition of this work.

The text of the regulations is printed as amended by: **B48.02**

> *the Disabled Persons (Badges for Motor Vehicles) (England) (Amendment) Regulations 2000 (SI 2000/1507) July 1, 2000); and*

> *the Disabled Persons (Badges for Motor Vehicles) (England) (Amendment) Regulations 2007 (SI 2007/2531) (October 15, 2007).*

The amending regulations are referred to in notes to the principal regulations only by their years and numbers. The dates referred to above are the dates on which the amending regulations came into force.]

ARRANGEMENT OF REGULATIONS

*   *   *

PART I

PRELIMINARY

Citation, commencement and extent

B48.04   **1.**—(1) *[Omitted.]*

(2) These Regulations extend to England.

Interpretation

B48.05   **2.**—(1) In these Regulations —

"the 1970 Act" means the Chronically Sick and Disabled Persons Act 1970 [*q.v.*] ;

"the 1982 Regulations" has the meaning given by regulation 3(1);

"the 1984 Act" means the Road Traffic Regulation Act 1984 [*q.v.*];

"disabled person" means a person more than 2 years old and falling within at least one of the prescribed descriptions in regulation 4;

"disabled person's badge" means, [subject to paragraph (1A), a badge in the form prescribed by regulation 11 issued by a local authority for display on a motor vehicle driven by a disabled person, or used for the carriage of a disabled person, and includes a replacement badge issued in accordance with regulation 7;

"disabled person's concession" has the meaning given by section 117(3) of the 1984 Act;

"holder", in relation to a disabled person's badge, means the individual or [organisation] to whom a disabled person's badge was issued;

[...]

"individual's badge" means a disabled person's badge issued to an individual disabled person;

[...]

"issuing authority", in relation to a disabled person's badge, means the local authority which issued the badge; [...]

[*"local authority"* means a county council, district council, the Council of the Isles of Scilly, a London borough council or the Common Council of the City of London;

"organisation" means an organisation concerned with the care of disabled persons to which a disabled person's badge may be issued in accordance with section 21(4) of the 1970 Act; and

"organisational badge" means a disabled person's badge issued to an organisation.]

[(1A) For the purposes of regulations 12 to 16, the definition of *"disabled person's badge"* in paragraph (1) shall include a badge issued under regulations having effect in Scotland or Wales under section 21 of the Chronically Sick and Disabled Persons Act 1970.]

(2) In these Regulations a reference to an order made under any provision of the 1984 Act is to an order made, or having effect as if made, under that provision including an order varying or revoking an order made or having effect as if made under that Act.

(3) In these Regulations *"relevant conviction"* means—

   (a) any conviction of—
      (i) the holder of a disabled person's badge; or
      (ii) any other person using such a badge with the holder's consent, for an offence specified in paragraph (4); or
   (b) any conviction of a person other than the holder of a disabled person's badge of an offence under section 117(1) of the 1984 Act where the badge was displayed on the vehicle with the consent of the holder at any time during which the offence was being committed.

(4) The offences mentioned in paragraph (3)(a) are—

   (a) any offence under section 5, 8, 11 or 16(1) of the 1984 Act so far as it relates to any contravention of or failure to comply with any provision of an order made under section 1, 6, 9 or 14 of that Act —
      (i) prohibiting or restricting the waiting of vehicles on any road; or
      (ii) relating to any of the matters mentioned in paragraph 7 or 8 of Schedule 1 to that Act; or
   (b) any offence under section 35A(1) and (2), 47(1), 53(5), 53(6) or 117(1) of that Act.

(5) Any notice given under these Regulations shall be in writing.

[Regulation 2 is printed as amended by SI 2000/1507; SI 2007/2531.] **B48.06**

[Transitional provisions]

3. [...] **B48.07**

[Revoked; see now the Disabled Persons (Badges for Motor Vehicles) (Wales) Regulations (SI 2000/1786) reg.3(2) and (3).]

PART II

ISSUE, DURATION AND REVOCATION OF BADGES

Descriptions of disabled persons

4.—[(1) The prescribed descriptions of disabled person to whom a disabled **B48.08** person's badge may be issued are—

   (a) a person who is more than 2 years old and falls within one or more of the descriptions specified in paragraph (2);
   (b) a person who is not more than 2 years old and falls within either or both of the descriptions specified in paragraph (3).]

(2) The descriptions [referred to in paragraph (1)(a)] are a person who—

   (a) receives the higher rate of the mobility component of the disability living allowance in accordance with section 73 of the Social Security and Benefits Act [1992];

    (b) [...] is in receipt of a grant pursuant to [paragraph 10(3) of Schedule 1 to the National Health Service Act 2006] or section 46 of the National Health Service (Scotland) Act 1978;

    (c) is registered as blind under section 29(4)(g) of the National Assistance Act 1948 or, in Scotland, is a blind person within the meaning of section 64(1) of that Act;

    (d) receives a mobility supplement under article 26A of the Naval, Military and Air Forces etc. (Disablement and Death) Service Pensions Order 1983 [*SI 1983/883, as amended*] including such a supplement by virtue of any scheme or order under article 25A of the Personal Injuries (Civilians) Scheme 1983 [*SI 1983/686; as amended*];

    [(e) drives a vehicle regularly, has a severe disability in both arms and is unable to operate, or has considerable difficulty in operating, all or some types of parking meter;]

    (f) has a permanent and substantial disability which causes inability to walk or very considerable difficulty in walking.

  [(3) The descriptions referred to in paragraph (1)(b) are—

    (a) a child who, on account of a condition, must always be accompanied by bulky medical equipment which cannot be carried around with the child without great difficulty;

    (b) a child who, on account of a condition, must always be kept near a motor vehicle so that, if necessary, treatment for that condition can be given in the vehicle or the child can be taken quickly in the vehicle to a place where such treatment can be given.

  (4) In this regulation—

    (a) *"bulky medical equipment"* includes in particular any of the following—

      (i) ventilators;

      (ii) suction machines;

      (iii) feed pumps;

      (iv) parenteral equipment;

      (v) syringe drivers;

      (vi) oxygen administration equipment;

      (vii) continual oxygen saturation monitoring equipment; and

      (viii) casts and associated medical equipment for the correction of hip dysplasia; and

    (b) *"parking meter"* has the same meaning as in the Road Traffic Regulation Act 1984 (see sections 46(2)(a) and 142(1)).]

B48.09   *[Regulation 4 is printed as amended by SI 2000/1507; SI 2007/2531.]*

[Organisational badges

B48.10   **5.** An organisational badge may be issued to an organisation for a motor vehicle which is to be used to carry disabled persons falling within one or more of the descriptions specified in regulation 4(2) or (3).

B48.11   *[Regulation 5 is printed as substituted by SI 2007/2531.]*

Fee for issue and period of issue of a badge

    6. *[Omitted.]*   **B48.12**

Replacement badges

    7. *[Omitted.]*   **B48.13**

Grounds for refusal to issue a badge

    8. *[Omitted.]*   **B48.14**

Return of badge to issuing authority

    9. *[Omitted.]*   **B48.15**

Appeals

    10. *[Omitted.]*   **B48.16**

PART III

FORM AND DISPLAY OF BADGES

Form of badge

    11. A disabled person's badge is in the prescribed form if—   **B48.17**
        (a) the front and reverse of the badge are in the form shown in—
            (i) Part I of the Schedule to these Regulations in the case of an individual's badge; or
            (ii) Part II of the Schedule in the case of an [organisational] badge, and
        (b) the badge complies with the specifications in Part III of the Schedule.
[Regulation 11 is printed as amended by SI 2007/2531.   **B48.18**
The text of the Schedule is not reproduced.]

Manner in which a badge is to be displayed

    12. For the purposes of section 21(4A) of the 1970 Act a disabled person's   **B48.19**
badge is displayed on a vehicle in the prescribed manner if—
        (a) the badge is exhibited on the dashboard or fascia of the vehicle, or
        (b) where the vehicle is not fitted with a dashboard or fascia, the badge is exhibited in a conspicuous position on the vehicle,

so that the front of the badge is clearly legible from the outside of the vehicle.

Display of an individual's badge when a vehicle is being driven

    13.—(1) This regulation prescribes for the purposes of section 21(4A) of the   **B48.20**
1970 Act the circumstances in which an individual's badge may be displayed
while a vehicle is being driven.

    (2) An individual's badge may be displayed on a vehicle while the holder is
either driving or being carried in it.

(3) An individual's badge may also be displayed on a vehicle if—

    (a) the vehicle is being used for the collection of the holder and no other purpose;

    (b) a disabled person's concession (other than a concession relating to parking) would be available to a vehicle lawfully displaying a disabled person's badge; and

    (c) it would not be practicable for the vehicle to be lawfully driven to, or to stop at, the place at which the holder is to be collected if the concession did not apply to the vehicle.

(4) An individual's badge may be displayed on a vehicle if—

    (a) the vehicle, after being driven by or carrying the holder, is leaving the place where he got out;

    (b) a disabled person's concession (other than a concession relating to parking) is available to a vehicle lawfully displaying a disabled person's badge; and

    (c) it would not have been practicable for the vehicle to have left that place if the concession did not apply to the vehicle.

Display of an individual's badge when a vehicle is parked

B48.21   **14.**—(1) This regulation prescribes for the purposes of section 21(4A) of the 1970 Act the circumstances in which an individual's badge may be displayed while a vehicle is parked.

(2) An individual's badge may be displayed on a vehicle while it is parked if it—

    (a) has been driven by the holder, or has been used to carry the holder, to the place where it is parked; or

    (b) is to be driven by the holder, or is to be used to carry the holder, from that place.

Display of an [organisational] badge when a vehicle is being driven

B48.22   **15.**—(1) This regulation prescribes for the purposes of section 21(4A) of the 1970 Act the circumstances in which an [organisational] badge may be displayed while a vehicle is being driven.

(2) An [organisational] badge may be displayed on a vehicle while it is being driven by or on behalf of the holder and is carrying a disabled person.

(3) An [organisational] badge may also be displayed on a vehicle while it is being driven by or on behalf of the holder and—

    (a) the vehicle is being used for the collection of a disabled person and for no other purpose;

    (b) a disabled person's concession (other than a concession relating to parking) is available to a vehicle lawfully displaying a disabled person's badge; and

    (c) it would not have been practicable for the vehicle to be lawfully driven to or to stop at the place at which the disabled person is to be collected if that concession did not apply to the vehicle.

(4) An [organisational] badge may also be displayed on a vehicle while it is being driven by or on behalf of the holder and—

(a) the vehicle, after carrying a disabled person, is leaving the place where he got off;

(b) a disabled person's concession (other than a concession relating to parking) is available to a vehicle lawfully displaying a disabled person's badge; and

(c) it would not have been practicable for the vehicle to have left that place if the concession had not applied to the vehicle.

[Regulation 15 is printed as amended by SI 2007/2531.]   **B48.23**

Display of an [organisational] badge when a vehicle is parked

16.—(1) This regulation prescribes for the purposes of section 21(4A) of the 1970 Act the circumstances in which an [organisational] badge may be displayed while a vehicle is parked.   **B48.24**

(2) An [organisational] badge may be displayed on a vehicle while it is parked if it has been, or is to be, used by or on behalf of the holder for carrying a disabled person to or from the place where it is parked.

[Regulation 16 is printed as amended by SI 2007/2531.]   **B48.25**

(Regulation 11)   THE SCHEDULE

PART I

[INDIVIDUAL'S BADGE]

[Omitted.]   **B48.26**

PART II

[ORGANISATIONAL BADGE]

[Omitted.]   **B48.27**

PART III

SPECIFICATIONS FOR BADGE

[Omitted.]   **B48.28**

The Private Hire Vehicles (London) (Operators' Licences) Regulations 2000

(SI 2000/3146)

ARRANGEMENT OF REGULATIONS

B49.01

PART I
GENERAL

Regulation

PART III
LICENCES

Regulation

PART IV
RECORDS

Regulation

PART V
OTHER MATTERS

Regulation

PART I

GENERAL

Citation and commencement

B49.02　**1.** *[Omitted.]*

2/1720

Interpretation

2. In these Regulations, unless the context otherwise requires—   **B49.03**

"the 1998 Act" means the Private Hire Vehicles (London) Act 1998 [*q.v.*];

"application" means an application for the grant or variation of a licence;

"business name" means a name which if used by a person for the purpose of carrying on business would make him subject to the Business Names Act 1985;

"CB apparatus" means wireless telegraphy apparatus known as *"Citizens' Band"* which is designed or adapted, or has facilities permitting its adaptation, for the purpose of transmitting spoken messages on the frequency band 26.1 MHz to 28 MHz;

"certificate of insurance" and *"certificate of security"* shall be construed in accordance with section 147 of the Road Traffic Act 1988 [*q.v.*];

"Community licence" and *"Northern Ireland licence"* have the same meanings as in section 108(1) of the Road Traffic Act 1988 [*q.v.*];

"driving licence" means a licence to drive a motor car granted under Part III of the Road Traffic Act 1988 [*q.v.*] (other than a provisional licence), or a licence authorising the driving of a motor car by virtue of section 99A(1) or 109(1) of that Act (Community licences and Northern Ireland licences);

"firm" has the same meaning as in section 4 of the Partnership Act 1890;

"licence" means a London PHV operator's licence;

"licensing authority" means the person appointed under section 24(1) of the 1998 Act for the purpose of exercising the functions of the Secretary of State under that Act or, where no such appointment has been made, the Secretary of State;

"MOT test certificate" means, in relation to a vehicle to which section 47 of the Road Traffic Act 1998 [*q.v.*] applies, a test certificate issued in respect of the vehicle as mentioned in subsection (1) of that section;

"national insurance number" has the same meaning as in [regulation 1(2) of the Social Security (Contributions) Regulations 2001] [*SI 2001/ 1004*];

"officer", in relation to a body corporate, shall be construed in accordance with section 744 of the Companies Act 1985;

"operator" means a London PHV operator and in relation to a licence means the operator to whom the licence was granted;

"registered keeper" means, in relation to a vehicle, the person in whose name the vehicle is registered under the Vehicle Excise and Registration Act 1994 [*q.v.*];

"registration mark" means, in relation to a vehicle, the mark assigned to the vehicle in accordance with section 23 of the Vehicle Excise and Registration Act 1994 [*q.v.*];

"variation" means a variation of a licence at the operator's request under section 18 of the 1998 Act [*q.v.*]; and

"wireless telegraphy apparatus" shall be construed in accordance with section 19(1) of the Wireless Telegraphy Act 1949.

B49.04   *[Regulation 2 is printed as amended by the Interpretation Act 1978 ss.17(2)(a) and 23(1).]*

Part II

Applications

Manner of making applications

B49.05   3. *[Omitted.]*

Fees

B49.06   4. *[Omitted.]*

Determination of applications

B49.07   5. *[Omitted.]*

Part III

Licences

Grant and variation

B49.08   6. *[Omitted.]*

Fees

B49.09   7. *[Omitted.]*

Refund of fees

B49.10   8. *[Omitted.]*

Conditions

B49.11   **9.**—(1) Every licence shall be granted subject to the conditions set out in the following provisions of this regulation.

(2) In respect of any operating centre specified in the licence which is accessible to members of the public, the operator shall maintain in force a policy of insurance against public liability risks which provides a minimum indemnity of £5,000,000 in respect of any one event.

(3) The operator shall, if required to do so by a person making a private hire booking—

      (a) agree the fare for the journey booked, or

      (b) provide an estimate of that fare.

(4) If, during the currency of the licence—

      (a) any conviction is recorded—

            (i) where the operator is an individual, against him,

            (ii) where the operator is a firm, against any partner of that firm, or

> (iii) where the operator is another type of body or group of persons, against that body or group or any officer of that body or group;

(b) any information provided in the application for the grant of the licence, or for any variation thereof, changes; or

(c) any driver ceases to be available to the operator for carrying out bookings, by virtue of that driver's unsatisfactory conduct in connection with the driving of a private hire vehicle,

the operator shall, within 14 days of the date of such event, give the licensing authority notice containing details of the conviction or change, as the case may be, or, in the case falling within sub-paragraph (c), the name of the driver and the circumstances of the case.

(5) No CB apparatus shall be used in connection with a private hire booking at any operating centre specified in the licence or in any private hire vehicle available for carrying out bookings accepted at any such operating centre.

(6) The operator shall preserve records in accordance with regulation 16(1)(a) and (b).

(7) The operator shall establish and maintain a procedure for dealing with—

(a) complaints, and

(b) lost property,

arising in connection with any private hire booking accepted by him and shall keep and preserve records in accordance with regulations 14, 15 and 16(1)(c).

(8) Where an operator provides a London cab for the purpose of carrying out a private hire booking, any fare payable in respect of the booking shall be calculated as if the vehicle was a private hire vehicle unless the fare shown on the taximeter is less.

(9) In the case of a licence granted following an election made under regulation 7(2) or (5), the operator must, during the currency of the licence, continue to meet the requirement that no more than two private hire vehicles are available to him for carrying out bookings accepted by him at all the operating centres specified in his licence.

PART IV

RECORDS

Form of record of private hire bookings

10. The record which an operator is required to keep by virtue of section 4(3)(b)   **B49.12** of the 1998 Act at each operating centre specified in his licence of the private hire bookings accepted by him there shall be kept—

(a) in writing, or

(b) in such other form that the information contained in it can easily be reduced to writing.

Particulars of private hire bookings

11. Before the commencement of each journey booked at an operating centre   **B49.13** specified in his licence an operator shall enter the following particulars of the booking in the record referred to in regulation 10 —

(a) the date on which the booking is made and, if different, the date of the proposed journey,

(b) the name of the person for whom the booking is made or other identification of him, or, if more than one person, the name or other identification of one of them;

(c) the agreed time and place of collection, or, if more than one, the agreed time and place of the first;

(d) the main destination specified at the time of the booking;

(e) any fare or estimated fare quoted;

(f) the name of the driver carrying out the booking or other identification of him;

(g) if applicable, the name of the other operator to whom the booking has been subcontracted, and

(h) the registered number of the vehicle to be used or such other means of identifying it as may be adopted.

Particulars of private hire vehicles

B49.14   12.—(1) For the purposes of section 4(3)(d) of the 1998 Act, an operator shall keep at each operating centre specified in his licence a record, containing the particulars set out in paragraph (2), of each private hire vehicle which is available to him for carrying out bookings accepted by him at that centre.

(2) In relation to each vehicle the particulars referred to in paragraph (1) are—

(a) the make, model and colour;

(b) the registration mark;

(c) the name and address of the registered keeper;

(d) in the case of a vehicle to which section 47 of the Road Traffic Act 1988 applies, a copy of the current MOT test certificate;

(e) a copy of the current certificate of insurance or certificate of security;

(f) the date on which the vehicle became available to the operator; and

(g) the date on which the vehicle ceased to be so available.

Particulars of drivers

B49.15   13.—(1) For the purposes of section 4(3)(d) of the 1998 Act, an operator shall keep at each operating centre specified in his licence a record, containing the particulars set out in paragraph (2); of each driver who is available to him for carrying out bookings accepted by him at that centre.

(2) In relation to each driver the particulars referred to in paragraph (1) are—

(a) his surname, forenames, address and date of birth;

(b) his national insurance number;

(c) a photocopy of his driving licence;

(d) a photograph of him;

(e) the date on which he became available to the operator, and

(f) the date on which he ceased to be so available.

Record of complaints

B49.16   14.—(1) An operator shall keep at each operating centre specified in his licence a record containing—

(a) the particulars set out in paragraph (2) of any complaint made in respect of a private hire booking accepted by him at that centre; and

(b) the particulars set out in paragraph (2)(d), (e), and (f) of any other complaint made in respect of his undertakings as an operator at that centre.

(2) In relation to each complaint the particulars referred to in paragraph (1) are—

(a) the date of the related booking;

(b) the name of the driver who carried out the booking;

(c) the registration mark of the vehicle used;

(d) the name of the complainant and any address, telephone number or other contact details provided by him;

(e) the nature of the complaint, and

(f) details of any investigation carried out and subsequent action taken as a result.

Record of lost property

15.—(1) An operator shall keep at each operating centre specified in his licence   **B49.17** a record, containing the particulars set out in paragraph (2), of any lost property found—

(a) at that centre, or

(b) in any private hire vehicle used to carry out a booking accepted by him there.

(2) In relation to each item of lost property the particulars referred to in paragraph (1) are—

(a) the date on which it was found;

(b) the place where it was found and if it was found in a vehicle, the registration mark of that vehicle;

(c) a description of the item;

(d) evidence to show that, where practical, an attempt was made to return the item to the owner and whether or not this was successful, and

(e) in the case of any unclaimed item which has been disposed of, how it was disposed of.

(3) An operator shall keep at each operating centre specified in his licence a record, containing the particulars set out in paragraph (4), of any property reported to him at that centre as having been lost.

(4) In relation to each item of property reported as having been lost the particulars referred to in paragraph (3) are—

(a) the date of the report;

(b) the date on which it is alleged to have been lost;

(c) the place where it is alleged to have been lost;

(d) a description of the item, and

(e) evidence to show that, where practical, an attempt was made to find the item.

Preservation of records

B49.18   **16.**—(1) Subject to paragraph (3), an operator shall preserve the particulars of—

> (a) each private hire booking recorded in accordance with regulation 11 for six months from the date on which the booking was accepted;
>
> (b) each private hire vehicle and driver recorded in accordance with regulations 12 and 13 for twelve months from the date on which the vehicle or, as the case may be, the driver ceased to be available for carrying out bookings;
>
> (c) each complaint and item of lost property recorded in accordance with regulations 14 and 15 for six months from the date on which they were entered in the respective record.

(2) Where an operator tape-records a private hire booking he shall preserve the taperecording of that conversation for a period of six months.

(3) For the purpose of section 4(4) of the 1998 Act, if an operator ceases to use an operating centre specified in his licence, he shall, in relation to that operating centre, preserve—

> (a) the record referred to in regulation 10 for six months; and
>
> (b) the records kept in accordance with regulations 12 and 13 for twelve months, from the date of the last entry.

PART V

OTHER MATTERS

Register of licences

B49.19   **17.** *[Omitted.]*

Issue of replacement licences

B49.20   **18.** *[Omitted.]*

Continuance of licence on death, bankruptcy, etc.

B49.21   **19.**—(1) This regulation applies in relation to a licence granted in the sole name of an individual in the event of—

> (a) the death of that individual;
>
> (b) the bankruptcy of that individual; or
>
> (c) that individual becoming a patient under Part VII of the Mental Health Act 1983.

(2) After the happening of the event mentioned in paragraph (1)(a) the licensing authority may direct that the licence shall not be treated as terminated when the individual died but suspended until the date when a direction under paragraph (3) comes into force.

(3) After the happening of any of the events mentioned in paragraph (1) the licensing authority may direct that a person carrying on the business of the operator is to be treated for the purposes of the 1998 Act as if he were the operator for

such purpose and to such extent as is specified in the direction for a period not exceeding—

    (a) six months from the date of the coming into force of that direction; or

    (b) if less, the remainder of the period of the licence.

Transitional provisions

20.—(1) Subject to paragraph (2), where an application is received by the licensing authority before 22nd August 2001 but no determination under regulation 5 has been made in relation to that application before 22nd October 2001, the licensing authority shall—   **B49.22**

    (a) issue the applicant with a temporary permit, in the terms applied for, to make provision for the invitation or acceptance of, or accept, private hire bookings, or

    (b) make a temporary variation of the applicant's licence in the terms applied for, which shall have effect from the latter date as if it were a licence granted or, as the case may be, variation made under the 1998 Act.

(2) Any temporary permit issued or variation made under paragraph (1) shall, unless the permit or, as the case may be, the licence to which the variation applies, has already been suspended or revoked under the 1998 Act, cease to have effect for the purposes of that Act —

    (a) on the grant or variation of a licence pursuant to the outstanding application; or

    (b) where no such licence is granted or varied, on the expiry of the period of 28 days commencing on the date specified in paragraph (3).

(3) The date referred to in paragraph (2)(b) is—

    (a) the date of service of the notice given in accordance with regulation 5 of a decision in relation to the outstanding application; or

    (b) where an appeal is brought against that decision, the date of disposal or withdrawal of that appeal.

The Road Vehicles (Display of Registration Marks) Regulations 2001

(SI 2001/561)

B50.01   *[These regulations give effect in national law to Regulation (EC) 2411/98, the text of which is reproduced below.*

The text of these regulations is printed as amended by:

> *the Road Vehicles (Display of Registration Marks) (Amendment) Regulations 2001 (SI 2001/1079) (September 1, 2001);*

> *the Road Vehicles (Display of Registration Marks) (Amendment) Regulations 2002 (SI 2002/2687) (November 22, 2002); and*

> *the Road Vehicles (Display of Registration Marks) (Amendment) Regulations 2009 (SI 2009/811) (April 27, 2009).*

The amending regulations are referred to in the notes to the principal regulations only by their years and numbers. The dates referred to above are the dates on which the amending regulations came into force.]

PART I

PRELIMINARY

Citation, commencement and revocation

1.—(1) These Regulations may be cited as the Road Vehicles (Display of   **B50.03** Registration Marks) Regulations 2001 and shall come into force—

(a) for the purposes of this paragraph and regulation 17, on 21st March 2001, and

(b) for all other purposes, on 1st September 2001.

(2) The regulations specified in Schedule 1 are hereby revoked.

Interpretation: general

2.—(1) In these Regulations the following expressions shall have the follow-   **B50.04** ing meanings—

"the Act" means the Vehicle Excise and Registration Act 1994 [*q.v.*];

"agricultural machine" means a vehicle which is—

    (a) an agricultural tractor, as defined in paragraph 4B(2) of Schedule 1 to the Act [*q.v.*], or

    (b) an off-road tractor, as defined in paragraph 4B(4) of that Schedule, or

    (c) a light agricultural vehicle, as defined in paragraph 4C(2) of that Schedule, or

    (d) an agricultural engine, or

    (e) a mowing machine;

  [...]

"EEA State" means a state which is a contracting party to the Agreement on the European Economic Area signed at Oporto on 2nd May 1992 as adjusted by the Protocol signed at Brussels on 17th March 1993;

"motor cycle" means a vehicle having two wheels and includes a vehicle of that description in combination with a sidecar;

"motor tricycle" means a vehicle having three wheels symmetrically arranged;

"quadricycle" means a vehicle having four wheels, a maximum net engine power not exceeding 15 kilowatts and an unladen mass (excluding the mass of batteries in the case of an electrically-powered vehicle) not exceeding—

(a) 550 kilograms in the case of a goods vehicle, and

(b) 400 kilograms in any other case;

"registration plate" means a plate or other device displaying the registration mark of the vehicle[, but does not include such part of a plate or device as is intended for the display of material specified in regulation 16(3) and (4);];

"prescribed font" means the style shown in Schedule 4 for a character of the height specified in that Schedule;

"relevant date" means—

(a) in Great Britain, 1st October 1938, and

(b) in Northern Ireland, 1st January 1948;

"works truck" means a vehicle which is—

(a) designed for use in private premises, and

(b) used on public roads only—

    (i) for carrying goods between private premises and a vehicle on a road in the immediate vicinity, or

    (ii) in passing from one part of private premises to another or between private premises and other private premises in the immediate vicinity, or

    (iii) in connection with road works at or in the immediate vicinity of the site of the works.

(2) Unless the context otherwise requires, a reference in these Regulations to—

(a) a registration plate fixed or to be fixed to a vehicle, or

(b) a registration mark displayed or to be displayed on a plate,

is to be construed, where the vehicle is towing a trailer, so as to include a reference to the registration plate which is required under these Regulations to be fixed to the trailer or a reference to the mark displayed on the plate fixed to that trailer.

B50.05   *[Regulation 2 is printed as amended by SI 2009/811.*

As to the EEA states, see further the introductory note to Section C below.]

Exempt vehicles

B50.06   3. Nothing in these Regulations applies to—

(a) an invalid vehicle, that is a vehicle the unladen weight of which does not exceed 254 kilograms and which is specially designed and constructed, and not merely adapted, for the use of a person suffering from a physical disability and solely used by that person; or

(b) a pedestrian-controlled vehicle, that is a vehicle the unladen weight of which does not exceed 450 kilograms which is neither constructed nor adapted for the carriage of a driver or passenger.

PART II

REGISTRATION PLATES

Interpretation of Part II

4. In this Part the following expressions shall have the following meanings—   **B50.07**

"diagonal length", in relation to a relevant area, means the length of a line drawn diagonally across the square enclosing the area (so that the extent of the relevant area is thereby delimited);

"relevant area", in relation to a registration plate, means the area contained in a square described on the ground—

     (a) in front of the vehicle in the case of a plate fixed on the front of the vehicle, and

     (b) behind the vehicle in the case of a plate fixed on the rear of the vehicle,

where one corner of the square is immediately below the middle of the plate and the diagonal of the square from that corner is parallel to the longitudinal axis of the vehicle;

"relevant type-approval directive" means—

     (a) in the case of a motor cycle, motor tricycle or quadricycle—

         (i) Council Directive 93/94/EEC [*O.J. No.L311, December 14, 1993, p.8*] (as amended by Commission Directive 99/26/EC [*O.J. No.L118, May 6, 1999, p.32*] as regards the space to be provided for fixing of the rear registration plate, and

         (ii) Council Directive 93/92/EEC [*O.J. No.L311, December 14, 1993, p.1*] as regards the rear registration plate lamp;

     (b) in the case of any other vehicle or a trailer—

         (i) Council Directive 70/222/EEC [*O.J. No.L75, April 6, 1970, p.25*] as regards the space to be provided for fixing of the rear registration plate, and

         (ii) Council Directive 76/760/EEC [*O.J. No.L262, September 27, 1976, p.85*] (as amended by Commission Directive 97/31/EC [*O.J. No.L171, June 30, 1997, p.49*] as regards the rear registration plate lamp.

Fixing of rear registration plates: vehicles registered on or after the relevant date

5.—(1) This regulation applies to vehicles, other than works trucks, road rollers and agricultural machines, first registered on or after the relevant date.   **B50.08**

(2) A registration plate must be fixed on the rear of—

     (a) the vehicle, or

     (b) where the vehicle is towing a trailer, the trailer, or

     (c) where the vehicle is towing more than one trailer, the rearmost trailer.

(3) Where a vehicle (or, in a case where the plate is required to be fixed on a

trailer, that trailer) has been constructed so as to satisfy the requirements of the relevant type-approval directive, whether or not it is required by law to satisfy them, the plate may be fixed in the space provided in accordance with those requirements but if it is not so fixed it must be fixed in the manner required by paragraph (5).

(4) Except as provided in paragraph (3) the plate must be fixed in the manner required by paragraph (5).

(5) This paragraph requires the plate to be fixed—

    (a) vertically or, where that is not reasonably practicable, in a position as close to the vertical as is reasonably practicable, and

    (b) in such a position that in normal daylight the characters of the registration mark are easily distinguishable from every part of a relevant area having the diagonal length specified in paragraph (6).

(6) The diagonal length of the relevant area is—

    (a) in the case of a mark having characters the width of which is at least 57 millimetres, 22 metres,

    (b) in the case of a mark having characters the width of which is 50 millimetres, 21.5 metres,

    (c) in the case of a mark having characters the width of which is 44 millimetres, 18 metres.

Fixing of front registration plates: vehicles registered on or after the relevant date

B50.09   **6.**—(1) This regulation applies to vehicles, other than works trucks, road rollers and agricultural machines, first registered on or after the relevant date.

(2) Except as provided in paragraph (5), a registration plate must be fixed on the front of the vehicle in the manner required by paragraph (3).

(3) This paragraph requires the plate to be fixed—

    (a) vertically or, where that is not reasonably practicable, in a position as close to the vertical as is reasonably practicable,

    (b) in such a position that in normal daylight the characters of the registration mark are easily distinguishable from every part of a relevant area having the diagonal length specified in paragraph (4).

(4) The diagonal length of the relevant area is—

    (a) in the case of a mark having characters the width of which is at least 57 millimetres, 22 metres,

    (b) in the case of a mark having characters the width of which is 50 millimetres, 21.5 metres,

    (c) in the case of a mark having characters the width of which is 44 millimetres, 18 metres.

(5) In the case of a motor cycle or a motor tricycle which does not have a body of a type which is characteristic of the body of a four-wheeled vehicle—

    (a) a registration plate must not be fixed on the front of a vehicle if it was first registered on or after 1st September 2001,

    (b) a plate need not be fixed on the front of the vehicle if it was first registered before 1st September 2001.

Fixing of registration plates: vehicles registered before the relevant date

7.—(1) This regulation applies to vehicles, other than works trucks, road rollers and agricultural machines, first registered before the relevant date. **B50.10**

(2) Except as provided in paragraph (4), a registration plate must be fixed in the manner required by paragraph (3) on—

    (a) the front of the vehicle, and

    (b) the rear of—

        (i) the vehicle or,

        (ii) where the vehicle is towing a trailer, the trailer or,

        (iii) where the vehicle is towing more than one trailer, the rearmost trailer.

(3) This paragraph requires each plate to be fixed—

    (a) in a vertical position or, where that is not possible, in a position as close to the vertical as is reasonably practicable, and

    (b) in such a position that in normal daylight the characters of the registration mark are easily distinguishable, in the case of a plate fixed on the front of the vehicle, from in front of the vehicle and, in the case of a plate fixed on the rear of the vehicle or trailer, from behind the vehicle or trailer.

(4) In the case of a motor cycle and a motor tricycle which does not have a body of a type which is characteristic of the body of a four-wheeled vehicle, a registration plate need not be fixed on the front of the vehicle.

Fixing of registration plates: works trucks, road rollers and agricultural machines

8.—(1) This regulation applies to works trucks, road rollers and agricultural machines. **B50.11**

(2) A registration plate must be fixed on the vehicle in a vertical position or, where that is not possible, in a position as close to the vertical as is reasonably practicable—

    (a) on both sides of the vehicles, so that the characters of the mark are easily distinguishable from both sides of the vehicle, or

    (b) on the rear of the vehicle, so that the characters of the mark are easily distinguishable from behind the vehicle, or

    (c) where the vehicle is towing a trailer or trailers and the plate is not fixed on the sides of the vehicle, on the trailer or the rearmost trailer (as the case may be) so that the characters of the mark are easily distinguishable from behind the trailer.

(3) Where the towing vehicle is an agricultural machine, a plate fixed on the trailer may, instead of displaying the registration mark of the towing vehicle, display the mark of any other agricultural machine kept by the keeper of the towing vehicle.

Lighting of rear registration plates

9.—(1) This regulation applies to vehicles other than— **B50.12**

    (a) works trucks,

    (b) road rollers,

    (c) agricultural machines, and

    (d) vehicles first registered before the relevant date.

(2) Where the vehicle is being used on a road between sunset and sunrise the registration plate fixed on the rear of—

    (a) the vehicle, or

    (b) where the vehicle is towing a trailer, the trailer or,

    (c) where the vehicle is towing more than one trailer, the rearmost trailer,
        must be lit in accordance with this regulation.

(3) Where a vehicle (or, in a case where the plate is required to be fixed on a trailer, that trailer) has been constructed so as to satisfy the requirements of the relevant type-approval directive, whether or not it is required by law to satisfy them, that plate may be lit by a lamp which complies with those requirements but if it is not so lit it must be lit in the manner required by paragraph (5).

(4) Except as provided in paragraph (3) that plate must be lit in the manner required by paragraph (5).

(5) This paragraph requires the plate to be lit so that it is easily distinguishable from every part of a relevant area having a diagonal length

    (a) in the case of a plate displaying a mark having characters with a width of 44 millimetres, of 15 metres, and

    (b) in any other case, of 18 metres.

Specifications for registration plates

B50.13   **10.**—(1) A registration mark must be displayed on a registration plate conforming to the requirements prescribed by this regulation.

(2) In the case of a vehicle first registered on or after 1st September 2001 the registration plate must conform to the requirements set out in Part 1 of Schedule 2.

(3) Subject to paragraph (4), in the case of a vehicle first registered on or after 1st January 1973 but before 1st September 2001 the registration plate must conform either to the requirements set out in Part 2 of Schedule 2 or to the requirements set out in Part 1 of that Schedule.

(4) Where on or after 1st September 2001 a new registration plate is fixed to a vehicle to which paragraph (3) applies to replace a plate previously fixed thereto, the plate must conform to the requirements set out in Part 1 of Schedule 2.

(5) In the case of a vehicle first registered before 1st January 1973, the registration plate must conform either to one of the requirements set out in Part 3 of Schedule 2 or to the requirements set out in Part 2 of that Schedule or to the requirements set out in Part 1 of that Schedule.

(6) The corners of a registration plate may be rounded off provided that the requirements of regulation 14(9) (margins around registration marks) are not thereby infringed.

Further requirements for registration plates

B50.14   **11.**—(1) No reflex-reflecting material may be applied to any part of a registration plate and the plate must not be treated in such a way that the characters of the registration mark become, or are caused to act as, retroreflective characters.

[(1A) The surface of a registration plate must not compromise or incorporate any design, pattern or texture, or be treated in any way which gives to any part of the plate the appearance of a design, pattern or texture.]

(2) A registration plate must not be treated in any other way which renders the characters of the registration mark less easily distinguishable to the eye or which would prevent or impair the making of a true photographic image of the plate through the medium of camera and film or any other device.

(3) A registration plate must not be fixed to a vehicle—

    (a) by means of a screw, bolt or other fixing device of any type or colour,

    (b) by the placing of a screw, bolt or other fixing device in any position, or

    (c) in any other manner,

which has the effect of changing the appearance or legibility of any of the characters of the registration mark, which renders the characters of the registration mark less easily distinguishable to the eye or which prevents or impairs the making of a true photographic image of the plate through the medium of camera and film or any other device.

(4) Section 59(2)(a) of the Act (regulations the contravention of which attracts a level 3 fine) applies to paragraphs (1), (2) and (3) of this regulation.

[Regulation 11 is printed as amended by SI 2002/2687.] **B50.15**

PART III

REGISTRATION MARKS

Interpretation of Part III

12.—(1) In this Part and in Schedule 3, the following expressions shall have **B50.16** the following meanings—

    (a) *"diagram"* means a diagram shown in Part 2 of Schedule 3 and a reference to a numbered diagram is a reference to the diagram identified by that number in that part of that Schedule,

    (b) *"Table A"* means the table in Part 1 of Schedule 3,

    (c) *"Table B"* means the table in Part 3 of Schedule 3,

    (d) a reference to *"relevant character height"* [, except in relation to a vehicle to which regulation 14A applies] is a reference to the height of the characters in the registration mark shown at the head of column (2), (3) or (4) of Table B as the case may be.

(2) Any provision as to measurement contained in this Part or in Schedule 3 shall be taken to be complied with—

    (a) in the case of a provision prescribing character height, if the height of the character is not more than 1 millimetre more or less than the measurement prescribed herein, and

    (b) in the case of a provision prescribing any other dimension, if the dimension of the character or the space in question is not more than 0.5 millimetres more or less than the measurement prescribed herein.

(3) For the purpose of any provision contained in this Part or in Schedule 3 as to the spacing between characters or between groups of characters or as to the width of a margin the measurement shall be made—

    (a) in the case of a horizontal spacing requirement, between vertical lines passing through the extreme edges of each character or group of characters or between a vertical line passing through the extreme edge of a character and the lateral edge of the plate (as the case may be), and

    (b) in the case of a vertical spacing requirement, between horizontal lines passing through the extreme edges of each group of characters or between a horizontal line passing through the extreme edge of a group of characters and the top or bottom edge of the plate (as the case may be).

B50.17   *[Regulation 12 is printed as amended by SI 2002/2687.]*

Layout of marks

B50.18   **13.**—(1) Subject to paragraphs (2) and (3), a registration mark of a description specified in column (1) of Table A must be laid out on the registration plate in conformity with one of the diagrams specified in relation to that description in column (2) of Table A.

(2) A mark displayed on a motor cycle may not be laid out in conformity with diagram 1a, 2a, 3a, 4a, 5a, 6a, 7a, 8a or 9a.

(3) A mark may not be laid out in conformity with diagram 2c, 3c, 4b or 7b if it is displayed on—

    (a) a registration plate fixed to a vehicle first registered on or after 1st September 2001, or

    (b) a new registration plate fixed to a vehicle on or after 1st September 2001 to replace a plate previously fixed thereto (except where the vehicle was first registered before 1st January 1973).

Size and spacing of characters

B50.19   **14.**—(1) Except in the cases mentioned in paragraphs (2) and (3) [and regulation 14A], each character in a registration mark must be 79 millimetres high.

(2) In the case of a registration mark displayed on a vehicle first registered before 1st September 2001, a character in a registration mark may be 89 millimetres high unless—

    (a) the vehicle was first registered on or after 1st January 1973 and the mark is displayed on a new registration plate fixed to the vehicle to replace a plate previously fixed thereto, or

    (b) the vehicle is a motor cycle, motor tricycle, quadricycle, agricultural machine, works truck or road roller.

(3) In the case of a registration mark fixed on a motor cycle, motor tricycle, quadricycle, agricultural machine, works truck or road roller, each character of the mark may be 64 millimetres high.

(4) [Subject to regulation 14A, the] width of each character of a mark other than the letter "I" and the figure "1" must be—

(a) in the case of a mark displayed—

    (i) on a registration plate fixed to a vehicle first registered on or after 1st September 2001, or

    (ii) on a new registration plate fixed to a vehicle on or after 1st September 2001 to replace a plate previously fixed thereto (except where the vehicle was first registered before 1st January 1973),

    that shown in line 1 of Table B in relation to the relevant character height,

(b) in any other case, that shown in line 2 of Table B in relation to the relevant character height.

(5) [Subject to regulation 14A, the] width of every part of the stroke forming a character in a mark must be that shown in line 3 of Table B in relation to the relevant character height.

(6) Except in a case to which paragraph (11) [or regulation 14A] applies, the spacing between any two characters within a group must be that shown in line 4 of Table B in relation to the relevant character height.

(7) [Subject to regulation 14A, the] horizontal spacing between groups of characters in a mark must be that shown in line 5 of Table B in relation to the relevant character height.

(8) [Subject to regulation 14A, the] vertical spacing between groups of characters must be shown in line 6 of Table B in relation to the relevant character height.

(9) [Subject to regulation 14A, the] width of a margin between the mark and the top, bottom and lateral edges of the registration plate must be not less than that shown in line 7 of Table B in relation to the relevant character height.

(10) Paragraph (11) applies where—

(a) one or both of the characters is "I" or "1",

(b) those characters are either 79 millimetres or 89 millimetres high,

(c) the mark is displayed on a vehicle first registered before 1st September 2001,

(d) the registration plate displaying the mark was fixed to the vehicle before 1st September 2001 or, if that is not the case, the vehicle was first registered before 1st January 1973 and,

(e) the plate is made of cast or pressed metal with raised characters.

(11) Where this paragraph applies the spacing between—

[(a)] two characters one of which is "I" or "1" must be within the limits shown in line 8 of Table 8 in relation to the relevant character height, and

[(b)] two characters both of which are "I" or "1" must be within the limits shown in line 9 of Table B in relation to the relevant character height,

but where one or more characters in a group is "I" or "1" all the characters within that group must be evenly spaced.

[Regulation 14 is printed as amended by SI 2001/1079; SI 2002/2687.]   **B50.20**

[Size and spacing of characters: special cases

14A.—(1) This regulation applies in relation to any vehicle imported into the United Kingdom which—   **B50.21**

    (a) does not have European Community Whole Vehicle Type Approval; and

    (b) is so constructed that the area available for the fixing of the registration plate precludes the display on the plate of a registration mark in conformity with the requirements of regulation 14.

  (2) In relation to a vehicle to which this regulation applies—

    (a) each character in the registration mark must be 64 millimetres high;

    (b) the width of each character of the mark, other than the letter "I" and the figure "1", must be 44 millimetres;

    (c) the width of every part of the stroke forming a character in a mark must be 10 millimetres;

    (d) the spacing between any two characters within a group must be 10 millimetres;

    (e) the vertical spacing between groups of characters must be 5 millimetres;

    (f) the width of a margin between the mark and the top and lateral sides of the registration plate must be not less than 5 millimetres;

    (g) the space between the bottom of the mark and the bottom of the registration plate must be not less than 13 millimetres; but, within that space, the space between the bottom of the mark and the top of the name and postcode of the person by whom the plate was supplied must be not less than 5 millimetres.]

B50.22   *[Regulation 14A was inserted by SI 2002/2687.]*

Style of characters

B50.23   15.—(1) In the case of a registration mark displayed—

    (a) on a registration plate fixed to a vehicle first registered on or after 1st September 2001, or

    (b) on a new registration plate fixed to a vehicle on or after 1st September 2001 to replace a plate previously fixed thereto (except where the vehicle was first registered before 1st January 1973),

each of the characters of the mark must be in the prescribed font.

  (2) Except in a case to which paragraph (1) applies, each of the characters of the registration mark must either be in the prescribed font or in a style which is substantially similar to the prescribed font so that the character is easily distinguishable and in particular, but without prejudice to the generality of those requirements, characters must not be formed in any way described in paragraph (4) or in a manner which is similar to any of those ways.

  (3) For the purposes of paragraph (2), a character shall not be treated as being in a style which is not substantially similar to the prescribed font merely by virtue of the fact that it has, or does not have, serifs.

  (4) The ways of forming characters referred to in paragraph (2) are their formation—

    (a) in italic script,

    (b) using a font, other than italic script, in which the characters are not vertical,

(c) using a font in which the curvature or alignment of the lines of the stroke is substantially different from the prescribed font,

(d) using multiple strokes,

(e) using a broken stroke,

(f) in such a way as to make a character or more than one character appear like a different character or characters.

PART IV

MISCELLANEOUS

International distinguishing signs and other material

[16.—(1) No material other than a registration mark and material complying **B50.24** with the requirements of any of the relevant standards mentioned in Schedule 2 may be displayed on a registration plate.

(2) Subject to the following paragraphs of this regulation, a registration plate may not be combined with any other plate or a device of any kind.

(3) The letters "GB" may be displayed on a plate or other device in accordance with the Annex to Council Regulation (EC) No.2411/98 on the recognition in intra-Community traffic of the distinguishing sign of the Member State in which motor vehicles and their trailers are registered.

(4) Subject to paragraphs (5) to (8), there may be displayed on a plate or other device an arrangement of letters corresponding with one of the sub-paragraphs of paragraph (9) and an emblem corresponding with one of the sub-paragraphs of paragraph (10).

(5) The arrangement of letters and emblem referred to in paragraph (4)—

(a) must be displayed to the left of the registration plate;

(b) must not encroach into the margin,

and for this purpose the expression "margin" is to have the same meaning as in regulations 14(9) and 14A(2)(f).

(6) The emblem referred to in paragraph (4) must be positioned above the arrangement of letters referred to in that paragraph.

(7) Neither the arrangement of letters referred to in paragraph (4), nor the emblem referred to in that paragraph, must be more than fifty millimetres wide.

(8) Paragraph (4) does not apply—

(a) if the letters "GB" are displayed in accordance with paragraph (3); or

(b) if the relevant vehicle is recorded in the part of the register relating to Northern Ireland.

(9) The arrangements of letters referred to in paragraph (4) are—

(a) "United Kingdom" or "UNITED KINGDOM";

(b) "UK";

(c) "Great Britain" or "GREAT BRITAIN";

(d) "GB";

(e) "England" or "ENGLAND";

(f) "Eng" or "ENG";

(g) "Scotland" or "SCOTLAND";

(h) "Sco" or "SCO";

(i) "Wales" or "WALES";

(j) "Cymru" or "CYMRU";

(k) "Cym" or "CYM".

(10) The emblems referred to in paragraph (4) are—

(a) an image of the Union flag;

(b) an image of the Cross of Saint George, as depicted on the flag of England;

(c) an image of the Cross of Saint Andrew (the Saltire), as depicted on the flag of Scotland;

(d) an image of the Red Dragon of Wales, as depicted on the flag of Wales.]

B50.25   *[Regulation 16 is printed as amended by SI 2001/1079; and is printed as substituted by SI 2009/811.]*

Optional early use of new-specification plates and prescribed font

B50.26   17.—(1) This regulation applies in a case where, on or after 21st March and before 1st September 2001 a registration mark on a vehicle—

(a) is displayed on a registration plate which conforms to the specification set out in Part 1 of Schedule 2 and is otherwise fixed on the vehicle and lit in accordance with the requirements of Part II of these Regulations,

(b) conforms to the requirements of regulations 13 and 14 as to layout and spacing of characters in so far as they apply to vehicles first registered on or after 1st September 2001, and

(c) is comprised of characters each of which is in the prescribed font.

(2) Where this regulation applies—

(a) regulations 17 to 22 of the Road Vehicles (Registration and Licensing) Regulations 1971 [*SI 1971/450, as amended*] or, as the case may be,

(b) regulations 18 to 23 of the Road Vehicles (Registration and Licensing) Regulations (Northern Ireland) 1973 [*SR & O (NI) 1973/490, as amended*],

(which provide for the format and means of display of registration plates and marks) shall cease to apply in respect of that vehicle and any trailer being towed by it and the provisions of these Regulations shall apply instead.

B50.27   *[The Road Vehicles (Registration and Licensing) Regulations 1971 (SI 1971/450) and the Road Vehicles (Registration and Licensing) Regulations (Northern Ireland) 1973 (SR & O (NI) 1973/490) have been repealed and replaced, with amendments, by the Road Vehicles (Registration and Licensing) Regulations 2002 (SI 2002/2742), q.v.]*

Saving for vehicles constructed before 1st January 1973

B50.28   18. For the purposes of these Regulations a vehicle which was first registered on or after 1st January 1973 shall be treated as if it was first registered before that date if—

    (a) it is an exempt vehicle for the purposes of paragraph 1A(1) of Schedule 2 to the Act, or

    (b) not being such a vehicle, it was constructed before 1st January 1973.

Offences under section 59 of the Act

19.—(1) For the purposes of section 59(1) of the Act (regulations: offences), the person responsible for complying with these Regulations is the person driving the vehicle or, where it is not being driven, the person keeping it   **B50.29**

(2) Paragraph (1) does not apply to a regulation the breach of which would constitute an offence under section 42(1) of the Act (not fixing a registration mark as required by virtue of section 23).

SCHEDULE 1

REGULATIONS REVOKED

Title of Regulations	Number	Extent of revocation
The Road Vehicles (Registration and Licensing) Regulations 1971	1971/450	Regulations 17 to 22 and Schedules 2 and 3.
The Road Vehicles (Registration and Licensing) (Amendment) Regulations 1972	1972/1865	Regulation 6.
The Road Vehicles (Registration and Licensing) Regulations (Northern Ireland) 1973	S.R. & O (N.I.) 1973 No.490	Regulations 18 to 23 and Schedule 2 and 3.
The Road Vehicles (Registration and Licensing) (Amendment) Regulations 1975	1975/1089	The whole instrument.
The Road Vehicles (Registration and Licensing) (Amendment) (No.2) Regulations (Northern Ireland) 1976	1976/2180	Regulations 2(6), (8) and (9).
The Road Vehicles (Registration and Licensing) (Amendment) Regulations 1984	1984/814	The whole instrument.

B50.30

[The Road Vehicles (Registration and Licensing) Regulations 1971 (SI 1971/450), the Road Vehicles (Registration and Licensing) (Amendment) Regulations 1972 (SI 1972/1865), the Road Vehicles (Registration and Licensing) Regulations (Northern Ireland) 1973 (SR & O (NI) 1973/490), and the Road Vehicles (Registration and Licensing) (Amendment) (No.2) Regulations (Northern Ireland) 1976 (SI 1976/2180) have been wholly revoked by the Road Vehicles (Registration and Licensing) Regulations 2002 (SI 2002/2742), q.v.]   **B50.31**

SCHEDULE 2

Requirements for Registration Plates

Part I

Vehicles Registered and New Registration Plates Fitted on or After 1st September 2001 (Mandatory Specification)

B50.32   1. The plate must be made of retroreflecting material which, as regards its construction, colour and other qualities, complies with the requirements of—

    (a) the British Standard specification for retroreflecting number plates published on 15 January 1998 under number BS AU 145d [*ISBN 0 580 28985 0*], or

    (b) any other relevant standard or specification recognised for use in an EEA State and which, when in use, offers a performance equivalent to that offered by a plate complying with the British Standard specification,

and which, in either case, is marked with the number (or such other information as is necessary to permit identification) of that standard or specification.

B50.33   2. Where the registration mark is displayed on the front of the vehicle, it must have black characters on a white background.

B50.34   3. Where the registration mark is displayed on the back of the vehicle, it must have black characters on a yellow background.

Part 2

Vehicles Registered on or after 1st January 1973 and before 1st September 2001 (Optional Specification)

B50.35   1. The plate must be made of reflex-reflecting material which, as regards its construction, colour and other qualities, complies with the requirements of—

    (a) the British Standard Specification for reflex-reflecting number plates, published on 11 September 1972 under the number BS AU 145a [*ISBN 0 580 07327 0*], or

    (b) any other relevant standard or specification recognised for use in an EEA State and which, when in use, offers a performance equivalent to that offered by a plate complying with the British Standard specification,

and which, in either case, is marked with the number (or such other information as is necessary to permit identification) of that standard or specification.

B50.36   2. Where the registration mark is displayed on the front of the vehicle, it must have black characters on a white background.

B50.37   3. Where the registration mark is displayed on the back of the vehicle, it must have black characters on a yellow background.

Part 3

Vehicles Registered before 1st January 1973 (Optional Specifications)

A. Requirements where the vehicle carries a registration plate which is constructed so that the mark may be illuminated from behind by virtue of the translucency of its characters

B50.38   1. The registration mark must be formed of white translucent characters on a black background on the surface of that plate.

B50.39   2. When the registration mark is illuminated during the hours of darkness, the characters on that plate must appear white against a black background.

B. Requirements where the vehicle carries a registration plate which is not so constructed

B50.40   Either of the following is permitted—

1. A plate made of reflex-reflecting material complying with the requirements of the British Standard Specification for reflex-reflecting number plates published on 31 October 1967 under the number BS AU 145 [*revised in 1972 to BS AU 145a*] and which displays black characters on a white background where it is fixed on the front of the vehicle and black characters on a yellow background where it fixed on the rear of the vehicle.

2. A plate displaying white, silver or light grey letters and numbers on a black surface having every character indelibly inscribed on the surface or so attached to the surface that it cannot readily be detached from it, which may either—   **B50.41**

(a) be made of cast or pressed metal with raised characters, or

(b) consist of a plate to which separate characters are attached, or

(c) consist of a plastic plate having either reverse engraved characters or characters of a foil type, or

(d) consist of an unbroken rectangular area on the surface of the vehicle which is either flat or, if there is no flat area where the mark is required to be displayed, an area which is almost flat.

Regulations 12, 13 and 14   SCHEDULE 3

LAYOUT OF REGISTRATION MARKS

PART 1

TABLE A   **B50.42**

PERMITTED LAYOUTS FOR REGISTRATION MARKS

(1) *Description of mark*	(2) *Permitted layouts*
1. A group consisting of two letters and two numbers followed by a group of 3 letters (for example DE51 ABC).	Diagrams 1a and 1b.
2. A group consisting of a single letter and not more than 3 numbers followed by a group of 3 letters (for example A123 ABC).	Diagrams 2a, 2b and 2c.
3. A group of 3 letters followed by a group consisting of not more than 3 numbers and a single letter (for example ABC 123A).	Diagrams 3a, 3b and 3c.
4. A group of 4 numbers followed by a single letter or a group of 2 letters (for example 1234 AB, 1234 A).	Diagrams 4a and 4b.
5. A group of not more than 3 numbers followed by a group of not more than 3 letters (for example 123 ABC, 123 AB, 12 A).	Diagrams 5a and 5b.
6. A group of not more than 3 letters followed by a group of not more than 3 numbers (for example ABC 123, AB 123, A 12).	Diagrams 6a and 6b.
7. A single letter or group of 2 letters followed by a group of 4 numbers (for example AB 1234, A 1234).	Diagrams 7a and 7b.
8. A group of 3 letters followed by a group of 4 numbers (for example ABZ 1234, being a form of mark issued only in Northern Ireland).	Diagrams 8a and 8b.
9. A group of 4 numbers followed by a group of 3 letters (for example 1234 ABZ, being a form of mark issued only in Northern Ireland).	Diagrams 9a and 9b.

PART 2

DIAGRAMS SHOWING PERMITTED LAYOUTS

[The diagrams are not reproduced. Reference can be made to the twenty-second edition of this work or to www.opsi.gov.uk [accessed March 2, 2009].]   **B50.43**

PART 3

B50.44

TABLE B

STROKE AND CHARACTER WIDTH, SPACING AND MARGINS

(1) *Relevant dimension*		*Relevant character height:*		
		(2) 89 mm.	(3) 79 mm.	(4) 64 mm.
1.	Character width (all new registration plates from 1.9.01 except replacement of "classic" plates)	—	50 mm.	44 mm.
2.	Character width (other registration plates)	64 mm.	57 mm.	44 mm.
3.	Stroke width	16 mm.	14 mm.	10 mm.
4.	Space between two characters within group: general rule	13 mm.	11 mm.	10 mm.
5.	Horizontal space between groups	38 mm.	33 mm.	30 mm.
6.	Vertical space between groups	19 mm.	19 mm.	13 mm.
7.	Minimum margin	13 mm.	11 mm.	11 mm.
8.	Pressed/embossed plates fixed before 1.9.01 and "classic" plates: space permitted between "I" or "1" and another character	13 to 37 mm.	11 to 33 mm.	—
9.	Pressed/embossed plates fixed before 1.9.01 and "classic" plates: space permitted between characters if both "I" or "1"	13 to 60 mm.	11 to 54 mm.	—

SCHEDULE 4

PRESCRIBED FONT

PART 1

FONT DESCRIBED FOR CHARACTERS 79 MILLIMETRES IN HEIGHT

B50.45   *[The prescribed font is not reproduced. Reference can be made to the twenty-second edition of this work or to* www.legislation.gov.uk/uksi *[accessed March 2, 2011].]*

PART 2

FONT DESCRIBED FOR CHARACTERS 64 MILLIMETRES IN HEIGHT

B50.46   *[The prescribed font is not reproduced. Reference can be made to the twenty-second edition of this work or to* www.legislation.gov.uk/uksi *[accessed March 2, 2011].]*

The Road Traffic Offenders (Additional Offences and Prescribed Devices) Order 2001

(SI 2001/1814)

1. *[Omitted.]* **B51.01**

2. In this Order, *"the 1988 Act"* means the Road Traffic Offenders Act 1988. **B51.02**

3. *[Amends the Road Traffic Offenders Act 1988, s.20(2), q.v.]* **B51.03**

4.—(1) The following device is prescribed for the purposes of section 20 of the **B51.04**
1988 Act: a device designed or adapted to register—

    (a) an image of a vehicle and its registration mark; and

    (b) the time at which the image is registered.

and to record that information if, according to data stored by or otherwise accessible by the device, that vehicle is unlicensed

(2) In this article, expressions which also occur in section 29 of the Vehicle Excise and Registration Act 1994 shall be construed in accordance with section 29 of that Act.

The Motor Vehicles (Access to Driver Licensing Records) Regulations 2001

(SI 2001/3343)

B52.01 *[The text of these regulations is printed as amended by:*

the Vehicle Drivers (Certificates of Professional Competence) (Amendment) (No.2) Regulations 2008 (SI 2008/1965) (September 1, 2008).

The amending regulations are referred to in the notes to the principal regulations by their year and number. The date referred to is the date on which the amending regulations came into force.]

Citation and commencement

B52.02 1. *[Omitted.]*

Purposes for which access may be given

B52.03 2. The purposes for which constables may be given access to information made available to the [National Policing Improvement Agency] under section 71(1) of the Criminal Justice and Court Services Act 2000 are—

    (a) the prevention, investigation or prosecution of a contravention of any provision of the following enactments—

        (i) the Road Traffic Act 1988;

        (ii) the Road Traffic Offenders Act 1988;

        (iii) the Road Traffic (Northern Ireland) Order 1981;

        (iv) the Road Traffic (Northern Ireland) Order 1995; [...]

        (v) the Road Traffic Offenders (Northern Ireland) Order 1996 [; and

        [(vi) the Vehicle Drivers (Certificates of Professional Competence) Regulations 2007;]

    (b) ascertaining whether a person has had an order made in relation to him under—

        (i) section 40B(1) or (5) (disqualification from driving: further provision) of the Child Support Act 1991;

        (ii) *[applies to Scotland]*; or

        (iii) section 39(1) (offenders) or 40(2) (fine defaulters) of the Crime (Sentences) Act 1997.

B52.04 *[Regulation 2 is printed as amended by SI 2008/1965.*

Section 39(1) of the Crime (Sentences) Act has been repealed; see now s.146(1) of the Powers of Criminal Courts (Sentencing) Act 2000, as amended.]

Further disclosure

B52.05 3.—(1) Paragraph (2) below specifies the circumstances in which information to which constables have been given access, in accordance with section 71(1) of the Criminal Justice and Court Services Act 2000 and regulation 2 above, may be further disclosed by them.

(2) The circumstances are that the information is passed to an employee of a police authority for any purpose ancillary to, or connected with, the use of the information by constables.

The Goods Vehicles (Enforcement Powers) Regulations 2001

(SI 2001/3981)

B53.01 *[The text of these regulations is printed as amended by:*

the Goods Vehicles (Enforcement Powers) (Amendment) Regulations 2009 (SI 2009/1965) (October 1, 2009).

The amending regulations are referred to in the notes to the principal regulations only by their year and number. The date referred to is the date on which the amending regulations came into force.

The Arrangement of regulations set out below has been added editorially and does not form part of the regulations.]

ARRANGEMENT OF REGULATIONS

Citation and commencement

B53.02 **1.** These Regulations may be cited as the Goods Vehicles (Enforcement Powers) Regulations 2001 and shall come into force on 4th January 2002.

Interpretation

2. In these Regulations—   **B53.03**

"*the 1995 Act*" means the Goods Vehicles (Licensing of Operators) Act
1995;

"*hiring agreement*" has the same meaning as in section 66 of the Road
Traffic Offenders Act 1988;

"*immobilisation notice*" has the meaning given in regulation 5(3);

"*licence*" means an operator's licence (whether standard or restricted) as
defined in section 2(1) of the 1995 Act;

"*owner*" means , in relation to a vehicle or trailer which has been detained
in accordance with regulation 3—

   (a) in the case of a vehicle which at the time of its detention was
not hired from a vehicle-hire firm under a hiring agreement
but was registered under the Vehicle Excise and Registration
Act 1994, the person who can show to the satisfaction of an
authorised person that he was at the time of its detention the
lawful owner (whether or not he was the person in whose
name it was so registered);

   (b) in the case of a vehicle or trailer which at the time of its detention was hired from a vehicle-hire firm under a hiring agreement, the vehicle-hire firm; or

   (c) in the case of any other vehicle or trailer, the person who can
show to the satisfaction of an authorised person that he was at
the time of its detention the lawful owner.

"*release*" in relation to a vehicle means release from an immobilisation device;

"*vehicle*" has the same meaning as "*goods vehicle*" in section 58(1) of the
1995 Act but excludes a small goods vehicle as described in Schedule 1 to that Act; and

"*vehicle-hire firm*" has the same meaning as in section 66 of the Road
Traffic Offenders Act 1988.

[These regulations were made under Sch.1A to the Goods Vehicles (Licensing   **B53.04**
of Operators) Act 1995. The terms "authorised person", "contents" and "immo-
bilisation device" are defined in para.1(1) of that Schedule.]

Detention of property

3.—(1) Where an authorised person has reason to believe that a vehicle is be-   **B53.05**
ing, or has been, used on a road in contravention of section 2 of the 1995 Act, he
may detain the vehicle and its contents.

(2) Paragraph (1) shall not authorise a person other than a constable in uniform
to stop a vehicle on any road.

Release of detained vehicles

4.—(1) In the circumstances described in paragraph (2), a vehicle detained by   **B53.06**
virtue of regulation 3 shall be returned to the owner, without the need for an application under regulation 10.

(2) The circumstances are that the authorised person is satisfied that one or more of the grounds specified in paragraph (3) is or are made out.

(3) The grounds are—

    (a) that, at the time the vehicle was detained, the person using the vehicle held a valid licence (whether or not authorising the use of the vehicle);

    (b) that, at the time the vehicle was detained, the vehicle was not being, and had not been, used in contravention of section 2 of the 1995 Act;

    (c) that, although at the time the vehicle was detained it was being, or had been, used in contravention of section 2 of the 1995 Act, the owner did not know that it was being, or had been, so used;

    (d) that, although knowing at the time the vehicle was detained that it was being, or had been, used in contravention of section 2 of the 1995 Act, the owner—

        (i) had taken steps with a view to preventing that use; and

        (ii) has taken steps with a view to preventing any further such use.]

B53.07   *[Regulation 4 is printed as substituted by SI 2009/1965.]*

Power to immobilise vehicles

B53.08   **5.**—(1) This regulation applies where a vehicle has been detained in accordance with regulation 3.

(2) Where this regulation applies, without prejudice to the institution of proceedings for any offence under the 1995 Act, the authorised person may—

    (a) fix an immobilisation device to the vehicle in the place where it has been detained; or

    (b) move the vehicle, or require it to be moved, to a more convenient place and fix an immobilisation device to the vehicle in that other place.

(3) Where an immobilisation device is fixed to a vehicle in accordance with this regulation, the person fixing the device shall also fix to the vehicle a notice (an *"immobilisation notice"*) which indicates that—

    (a) the device has been fixed to the vehicle;

    (b) the vehicle may only be released from the device by or under the direction of an authorised person [(and provides details as to where an authorised person may be contacted)];

    [(ba) an application may be made for the release of the vehicle (and provides information about the procedure under which such an application may be made);]

    (c) the notice shall not be removed or interfered with except by or on the authority of an authorised person; and

    (d) no attempt should be made to drive the vehicle or otherwise put it in motion.

B53.09   *[Regulation 5 is printed as amended by SI 2009/1965.]*

Removal of, or interference with, an immobilisation notice or device

B53.10   **6.**—(1) An immobilisation notice shall not be removed or interfered with except by or on the authority of an authorised person.

[(1A) A vehicle to which an immobilisation device has been fixed in accordance with regulation 5(2) may be released from the device only by or under the direction of an authorised person.]

(2) A person contravening paragraph (1) shall be guilty of an offence and liable on summary conviction to a fine not exceeding level 2 on the standard scale.

[(3) A person who removes or attempts to remove, otherwise than in accordance with paragraph (1A), an immobilisation device fixed to a vehicle in accordance with regulation 5(2), is guilty of an offence.

(4) A person guilty of an offence under paragaph (3) is liable on summary conviction to a fine not exceeding level 3 on the standard scale.]

[Regulation 6 is printed as amended by SI 2009/1965.]   **B53.11**

Release of immobilised vehicles

7. [...]   **B53.12**
[Revoked by SI 2009/1965.]   **B53.13**

Removal and delivery of property detained

8.—(1) An authorised person may direct in writing that any property detained **B53.14** in accordance with regulation 3 be removed and delivered into the custody of a person specified in the direction.

(2) A vehicle may be driven, towed or removed by such means as are reasonable in the circumstances and any necessary steps may be taken in relation to the vehicle in order to facilitate its removal.

(3) The contents of a vehicle may be removed separately in cases where—

    (a) it is reasonable to do so to facilitate removal of the vehicle;

    (b) there is good reason for storing them at a different place from the vehicle; or

    (c) their condition requires them to be disposed of without delay.

(4) A person may be specified in a direction only if—

    (a) he is a person appointed by an authorised person; and

    (b) he has made arrangements with the Secretary of State and agreed to accept delivery of the property in accordance with those arrangements; and

    (c) he has agreed with the Secretary of State to take such steps as are necessary for the safe custody of such property.

(5) The arrangements made by virtue of paragraph (4) may include the payment of a sum to a person into whose custody any property is delivered.

(6) Where an authorised person has given a direction by virtue of paragraph (1) in respect of a vehicle, he may allow the driver of the vehicle to deliver its contents to their destination or some other suitable place before delivering the vehicle into the custody of the person specified in the direction.

(7) Subject to the powers of a person specified in a direction by virtue of paragraph (1) to sell or destroy any property, it shall be the duty of that person while any property is in his custody to take such steps as are necessary for the safe custody of that property.

Notification of detention of a vehicle and its contents

B53.15
9.—(1) Where a vehicle has been detained in accordance with regulation 3, an authorised person shall—

   (a) publish a notice in the *London Gazette* if the vehicle was detained in England or Wales or in the *Edinburgh Gazette* if the vehicle was detained in Scotland—

      (i) giving a brief description of the property detained and the vehicle's registration mark (if any);

      (ii) indicating the time and place at which, and the powers under which, it was detained by the authorised person;

     [(iia) describing the procedure under which, and the period within which, an application may be made to the traffic commissioner for the return of any property so detained;]

      (iii) stating [...] that, if no-one establishes within the period specified in the notice that he is entitled to the return of the vehicle, the authorised person intends to dispose of it after the expiry of that period in accordance with regulation 15;

      (iv) stating that any contents which are not disposed of in accordance with regulation 17(1) may be claimed at the place and at the times specified in the notice and that, if no-one establishes within the period specified in the notice that he is entitled to the return of the contents, the authorised person intends to dispose of them after the expiry of that period in accordance with regulation 17(2); and

   (b) not less than 21 days before the expiry of the period given in the notice serve a copy of the notice on—

      (i) the owner of the vehicle;

      (ii) the traffic commissioner in whose area the vehicle was detained;

      (iii) the chief officer of the police force in whose area the property was detained;

      (iv) the Association of British Insurers; and

      (v) the British Vehicle Rental and Leasing Association[, where the vehicle was hired from a vehicle-hire firm under a hiring agreement].

(2) The period specified in a notice under paragraph (1)(a), [(iia),](iii) and (iv) shall be [a minimum of] 21 days, beginning with the date on which the notice is published under regulation 9(1)(a) or, if later, a copy of the notice is served under regulation 9(1)(b).

B53.16
[Regulation 9 is printed as amended by SI 2009/1965.]

Applications to a traffic commissioner

B53.17
10.—(1) The owner of a vehicle detained in accordance with regulation 3 may, within the period specified in regulation 9(2), apply to the traffic commissioner for the area in which the vehicle was detained for the return of the vehicle.

(2) An application under paragraph (1) shall be given in writing and shall be accompanied by—

(a) a statement of one or more of the grounds specified in [regulation 4(3)] on which the application is declared to be based; and

(b) a statement indicating whether the applicant wishes the traffic commissioner to hold a hearing.

(3) An application under paragraph (1) shall be served before the expiry of the period specified in regulation 9(2).

(4) [...]

[(5) The period referred to in paragraphs (1) and (3) is subject to regulation 23.]

[Regulation 10 is printed as amended by SI 2009/1965.]

B53.18

Hearings

11. *[Omitted.]*

B53.19

Notification of determinations

12. *[Omitted.]*

B53.20

Appeals from a determination of a traffic commissioner to the Transport Tribunal

13. *[Omitted.]*

B53.21

Return of a vehicle detained

14. If—

B53.22

(a) an application is made to a traffic commissioner in accordance with regulation 10; or

(b) an appeal is made to the Transport Tribunal in accordance with regulation 13,

and the traffic commissioner or the Transport Tribunal, as the case may be, determines that one or more of the grounds specified in [regulation 4(3)] is made out, the traffic commissioner or the Transport Tribunal shall order an authorised person to return the vehicle to the owner.

[Regulation 14 is printed as amended by SI 2009/1965.]

B53.23

Disposal of vehicles

15.—(1) If—

B53.24

(a) no application for the return of a vehicle is made in accordance with regulation 10; or

(b) such an application is made but the traffic commissioner, or the Transport Tribunal in the event of an appeal under regulation 13, determines that none of the grounds specified in [regulation 4(3)] is made out,

the authorised person may sell or destroy the vehicle as he thinks fit.

(2) After disposing of a vehicle under paragraph (1), the authorised person shall serve notice of the disposal on the following persons—

    (a) the owner of the vehicle;

    (b) the traffic commissioner in whose area the vehicle was detained;

    (c) the chief officer of the police force in whose area it was detained;

  [(ca) the Driver and Vehicle Licensing Agency;]

    (d) the Association of British Insurers; and

    (e) the British Vehicle Rental and Leasing Association[, where the vehicle was hired from a vehicle-hire firm under a hiring agreement].

B53.25   *[Regulation 15 is printed as amended by SI 2009/1965.]*

Return of contents

B53.26   **16.**—(1) The person specified in a direction by virtue of regulation 8 may retain custody of the contents of a vehicle until they are disposed of in accordance with regulation 17, or returned to a person who establishes that he is entitled to them in accordance with the provisions of this regulation.

(2) Unless the contents of a vehicle have already been disposed of in accordance with regulation 17, an authorised person shall return any contents detained under regulation 3 to a person who has given notice in writing of his claim to an authorised person within the period specified in the notice given under regulation 9(1)(a)(iv) and who—

    (a) produces satisfactory evidence of his entitlement to them and of his identity and address; or

    (b) where he seeks to recover the contents as the agent of another person, produces satisfactory evidence of his status as agent and of his principal's identity, address and entitlement to the contents.

(3) Where the person claiming to be entitled to a vehicle establishes his entitlement, he shall be treated for the purposes of this regulation as also entitled to its contents unless and to the extent that another person has claimed them.

(4) Where there is more than one claim to the contents, an authorised person shall determine which person is entitled to them on the basis of the evidence provided to him.

Disposal of contents

B53.27   **17.**—(1) Where the condition of the contents of a vehicle requires them to be disposed of without delay they may be disposed of without the authorised person complying with the requirements of regulation 9.

(2) Where the contents of a vehicle are not disposed of in accordance with paragraph (1) and either—

    (a) one or more persons has given notice of a claim in respect of them in accordance with regulation 16(2) but no person establishes his entitlement to them in accordance with regulation 16; or

    (b) no notice of a claim has been given in respect of them in accordance with regulation 16(2),

the authorised person may sell or destroy those contents as he thinks fit.

Application of proceeds of sale

B53.28   **18.**—[(1) Subject to paragraph (1A), the proceeds of sale of any property sold under regulation 15 or 17 shall—

(a) be applied towards meeting expenses incurred by any authorised person exercising functions by virtue of these Regulations in relation to the property in question; and

(b) in so far as they are not so applied, be applied in meeting any claim to the proceeds of sale which is made and established in accordance with paragraph (2).

(1A) Where the proceeds of sale of any property sold under regulation 15 or 17 exceed the expenses referred to in paragraph (1)(a) and—

(a) no person has established entitlement to the proceeds of sale of the property; or

(b) a person has established entitlement to the proceeds of sale of the property, but excess proceeds remain once the claim has been satisfied,

the excess proceeds may be applied towards meeting expenses incurred by any authorised person exercising functions in relation to any other property detained by virtue of regulation 3.

(2) For the purposes of paragraph (1), a claim to the proceeds of sale of any property is established if—

(a) the claim is made not later than one year after the date on which the property was sold; and

(b) the authorised person is satisfied that—

(i) if the property consists of a vehicle, the person making the claim was the owner of the vehicle immediately before it was sold by virtue of regulation 15; or

(ii) if the property consists of contents, the person making the claim would, had the person made an appropriate application at the prescribed time, have been entitled to the return of the property by virtue of regulation 16.]

(3) Where the conditions specified in [paragraph (2)] are fulfilled, there shall be payable to him by the authorised person a sum calculated in accordance with paragraph (5).

(4) [...]

(5) The sum payable under paragraph (2) shall be calculated by deducting from the proceeds of sale the expenses incurred by the authorised person in exercising his functions under these Regulations, including the detention, removal, storage and disposal of the property.

[Regulation 18 is printed as amended by SI 2009/1965.]   **B53.29**

Disputes

19. *[Omitted.]*   **B53.30**

Offences as to obstruction of an authorised person

20. Where a person intentionally obstructs an authorised person in the exercise   **B53.31** of his powers under regulation 3 or 8, he is guilty of an offence and shall be liable on summary conviction to a fine not exceeding level 3 on the standard scale.

Offences as to securing possession of property

21.—(1) Where a person makes a declaration with a view to securing the return   **B53.32**

of a vehicle and the declaration is that the vehicle was not being, or had not been, used in contravention of section 2 of the 1995 Act, and the declaration is to the person's knowledge either false or in any material respect misleading, he is guilty of an offence.

(2) A person guilty of an offence under paragraph (1) shall be liable—

(a) on summary conviction, to a fine not exceeding the statutory maximum, and

(b) on conviction on indictment, to imprisonment for a term not exceeding two years or to a fine or to both.

Giving of notice

B53.33   **22.** *[Omitted.]*

[Extension of time

B53.34   **23.**—(1) Where a traffic commissioner considers it to be necessary in order for a particular case to be dealt with fairly and justly, the traffic commissioner may extend any of the periods described in paragraph (3).

(2) A period described in paragraph (3) may only be extended for such period as the traffic commissioner considers appropriate in the circumstances of the case.

(3) The periods are those referred to in—

(a) regulation 10;

(b) regulation 11(1); and

(c) regulation 12.]

B53.35   *[Regulation 23 is printed as inserted by SI 2009/1965.]*

The Driving Licences (Disqualification until Test Passed) (Prescribed Offence) Order 2001

(SI 2001/4051)

Citation and commencement

1. *[Omitted.]*   B54.01

Offences to which section 36(1) of the Road Traffic Offenders Act 1988 applies

2. An offence under section 3A of the Road Traffic Act 1988 (causing death by   **B54.02**
careless driving when under the influence of drink or drugs) which is committed
on or after 31st January 2002, and any person committing such an offence, are
prescribed for the purposes of section 36(1) of the Road Traffic Offenders Act
1988.

The Road Vehicles (Registration and Licensing) Regulations 2002

(SI 2002/2742)

B55.01 *[The text of these regulations is printed as amended by:*

the Road Vehicles (Registration and Licensing) (Amendment) Regulations 2003 (SI 2003/2154) (October 1, 2003);

the End-of-Life Vehicles Regulations 2003 (SI 2003/2635) (in Great Britain, on November 3, 2003 in respect of Pts I–VI; in England and Wales, November 3, 2003 in respect of Pt VII; in Northern Ireland, on November 3, 2003 in respect of Pts I–IV, on December 31, 2003 in respect of Pts V and VI);

the Road Vehicles (Registration and Licensing) (Amendment) (No.3) Regulations 2003 (SI 2003/2981) (November 30, 2003);

the Road Vehicles (Registration and Licensing) (Amendment) (No.4) Regulations 2003 (SI 2003/3073 (December 19, 2003, January 31, 2004, June 1, 2004 and July 1, 2004);

the Road Vehicles (Registration and Licensing) (Amendment) Regulations 2004 (SI 2004/238) (March 1, 2004);

the Road Vehicles (Registration and Licensing) (Amendment No.2) Regulations 2004 (SI 2004/1773) (August 16, 2004);

the Road Vehicles (Registration and Licensing) (Amendment) (No.5) Regulations 2004 (SI 2004/3298) (January 15, 2004); and

the Road Vehicles (Registration and Licensing) (Amendment) (No.2) Regulations 2005 (SI 2005/2713) (October 31, 2005).

The amending regulations are referred to in the notes to the principal regulations by their years and numbers. The dates referred to above are the dates on which the amending regulations came into force.

These regulations have been further amended by the Road Vehicles (Registration and Licensing) (Amendment) (No.2) Regulations 2003 (SI 2003/2335), the Road Vehicles (Registration and Licensing) (Amendment) (No.5) Regulations 2003 (SI 2003/3110), the Road Vehicles (Registration and Licensing) (Amendment) (No.3) Regulations 2004 (SI 2004/1872), the Road Vehicles (Registration and Licensing) (Amendment) (No.4) Regulations 2004 (SI 2004/2099), the Road Vehicles (Registration and Licensing) (Amendment) Regulations 2005 (SI 2005/2344), the Road Vehicles (Registration and Licensing) (Amendment) Regulations 2006 (SI 2006/2320) and the Road Vehicles (Registration and Licensing) (Amendment) Regulations 2007 (SI 2007/498), the Road Vehicles (Registration and Licensing) (Amendment) (No.2) Regulations 2007 (SI 2007/1018), the Road Vehicles (Registration and Licensing) (Amendment) (No.3) Regulations 2007 (SI 2007/2553), the Road Vehicles (Registration and Licensing) (Amendment) Regulations 2008 (SI 2008/642), the Road Vehicles (Registration and Licensing) (Amendment) (No.2) Regulations 2008 (SI 2008/1444), the Road Vehicles (Registration and Licensing) (Amendment) (No.3) Regulations 2008 (SI 2008/

2849), the Road Vehicles (Registration and Licensing) (Amendment) Regulations 2009 (SI 2009/880), the Road Vehicles (Registration and Licensing) (Amendment) (No.2) Regulations 2009 (SI 2009/3103), the Road Vehicles (Registration and Licensing) (Amendment) Regulations 2010 (SI 2010/451), the Road Vehicles (Registration and Licensing) (Amendment) (No.2) Regulations 2010 (SI 2010/1092), but the amending regulations do not affect any provision of the principal regulations which is printed in this work.]

ARRANGEMENT OF REGULATIONS

PART I
PRELIMINARY

PART II
LICENCES

PART III
REGISTRATION AND REGISTRATION DOCUMENTS

PART IV
NOTIFICATION AND CHANGES

PART V

DISCLOSURE OF INFORMATION

*   *   *

PART VI

CROWN VEHICLES AND EXEMPT VEHICLES

Regulation

PART VII

TRADE LICENCES

Regulation

*   *   *

PART VIII

MISCELLANEOUS

Regulation

SCHEDULES

* * *

PART I

PRELIMINARY

Citation and commencement

1.—(1) *[Omitted.]*   **B55.02**

(2) These regulations except regulations 15(3) and 20(4) and (5) and Schedule 3 shall come into force on 30th November 2002.

(3) Regulations 15(3) and 20(4) and (5) and Schedule 3 shall come into force on 7th April 2003.

Revocation

2. *[Omitted.]*   **B55.03**

Interpretation

3.—(1) In these regulations—   **B55.04**

"the 1988 Act" means the Road Traffic Act 1988;

"the 1994 Act" means the Vehicle Excise and Registration Act 1994 and a reference to the *"predecessor legislation"* of the 1994 Act is a reference to any of the following Acts—

    (a) the Roads Act 1920;

    (b) the Vehicles (Excise) Act 1949;

    (c) the Vehicles (Excise) Act (Northern Ireland) 1954;

    (d) the Vehicles (Excise) Act 1962;

    (e) the Vehicles (Excise) Act 1971;

    (f) the Vehicles (Excise) Act (Northern Ireland) 1972;

"bicycle" means a mechanically propelled bicycle (including a motor scooter, a bicycle with an attachment for propelling it by mechanical power and a mechanically propelled bicycle used for drawing a trailer or sidecar) not exceeding 450 kgs in weight unladen;

[*"the Directive"* means Council Directive 1999/37/EC of 29 April 1999 on the registration documents for vehicles [*O.J. No.L138, June 1, 1999, p.57*] as amended by Commission Directive 2003/127/EC of 23 December 2003 [*O.J. No.L10, January 16, 2004, p.29*];]

"*GB records*" means the part of the register which is maintained on behalf of the Secretary of State by the Driver and Vehicle Licensing Agency;

"*insurer*" means an authorised insurer as defined by section 145 of the 1988 Act;

"*invalid vehicle*" means a vehicle (including a cycle with an attachment for propelling it by mechanical power) which does not exceed 508 kgs in weight unladen and is adapted and used or kept on a public road for an invalid;

"*keeper*" in relation to a vehicle means the person by whom that vehicle is kept;

"*kgs*" means kilograms;

"*local authority*" has, in relation to each part of the United Kingdom, the meaning given in the following table—

England	County council, district council, London borough council, Council of the Isles of Scilly, Common Council of the City of London
Northern Ireland	District Council as defined in the Local Government Act (Northern Ireland) 1972
Scotland	Council constituted under section 2 of the Local Government etc. (Scotland) Act 1994
Wales	County council, county borough council

"*mm*" means millimetres;

"*NI records*" means the part of the register which is maintained on behalf of the Secretary of State by Driver and Vehicle Licensing Northern Ireland;

"*reduced pollution certificate*" means a certificate issued with respect to a vehicle by virtue of Schedule 2;

"*register*" means the record kept by or on behalf of the Secretary of State of the vehicles registered by him, in Great Britain or in Northern Ireland, under section 21 of the 1994 Act;

"*registered keeper*" in relation to a vehicle means the person for the time being shown in the register as the keeper of that vehicle;

"*trade plates*" means plates issued in accordance with regulation 40 or 41;

"*tricycle*" means a mechanically propelled tricycle (including a motor scooter and a tricycle with an attachment for propelling it by mechanical power) not exceeding 450 kgs in weight unladen and not being a pedestrian controlled vehicle as defined by regulation 4(3)(b); and

"*valeting*" means the thorough cleaning of a vehicle before its registration by the Secretary of State under section 21 of the 1994 Act or in order to prepare it for sale and includes removing wax and grease from the exterior, engine and interior, and "*valeted*" shall be construed accordingly.

[(1A) For the purposes of these Regulations "the registration document fee exemption" applies in relation to the issue of a new registration document for a vehicle if the following conditions are satisfied—

   (a) the vehicle has sustained damage to its bodywork;

   (b) the insurer of the vehicle has notified the Secretary of State that the vehicle was capable of being repaired but that the cost to the insurer of having it repaired would exceed the value of the vehicle in the condition in which it was immediately before it sustained the damage; and

   (c) the last registration document to be issued for the vehicle was destroyed by the insurer in accordance with regulation 20(5).]

(2) In regulations 21 to 25 *"vehicle trader"* has the meaning given by regulation 20(6) and in Schedule 4 *"relevant vehicle trader"* has the meaning given by paragraph 1(4) of that Schedule.

(3) Any application, notification, notice, information, particulars, appeal, declaration or other document or thing given or made in pursuance of these Regulations shall, except where it is expressly provided otherwise, be in writing.

[Regulation 3 is printed as amended by SI 2004/1773 and SI 2004/3298.   **B55.05**

The text of Sch.2 to these regulations referred to above is not reproduced in this work.]

Electrically assisted pedal cycles and pedestrian controlled vehicles

4.—(1) The requirements specified in regulation 4 of the Electrically Assisted   **B55.06** Pedal Cycles Regulations 1983 [*SI 1983/1168; not reproduced in this work*] are hereby prescribed as requirements for the purposes of paragraph 2A of Schedule 2 to the 1994 Act (electrically assisted pedal cycles exempt vehicles if of a class complying with prescribed requirements).

(2) Nothing in the following provisions of these Regulations applies to a vehicle which is an electrically assisted pedal cycle or pedestrian controlled vehicle.

(3) In this regulation—

   (a) *"electrically assisted pedal cycle"* means a vehicle which, by virtue of paragraph (1), is an electrically assisted pedal cycle for the purposes of paragraph 2A of Schedule 2 to the 1994 Act; and

   (b) *"pedestrian controlled vehicle"* means a vehicle with three or more wheels which does not exceed 450 kgs in weight unladen and which is neither constructed nor adapted for use nor used for the carriage of a driver or passenger.

PART II

LICENCES

Application for a vehicle licence on the basis that the reduced pollution requirements are satisfied

5.—(1) Where an application is made for a vehicle licence on the basis that the   **B55.07** rate of vehicle excise duty applicable is a rate specified in one of the provisions of Schedule 1 to the 1994 Act specified in paragraph (2), the Secretary of State may require the applicant to furnish a reduced pollution certificate before he determines the rate at which vehicle excise duty is payable on the licence.

(2) The provisions of Schedule 1 to the 1994 Act referred to in paragraph (1) are—

    (a) paragraph 3(1A) (buses);

    (b) paragraph 6(2A)(b) (vehicles used to carry exceptional loads);

    (c) paragraph 7(3A)(b) (haulage vehicles);

    (d) paragraph 9A (rigid goods vehicles); and

    (e) paragraph 11A (tractive units).

(3) Schedule 2 shall have effect with respect to reduced pollution certificates and the reduced pollution requirements.

Exhibition of vehicle and nil licences

B55.08   **6.**—(1) When a vehicle licence or nil licence has been delivered to the Secretary of State with an application for a replacement licence, no licence need be fixed to and exhibited on the vehicle to which the licence relates until the replacement licence is obtained.

(2) Except where paragraph (1) applies, the manner in which any vehicle licence or nil licence in force for a vehicle is to be fixed to and exhibited on the vehicle in accordance with the provisions of section 33(1) or (1A) of the 1994 Act, when it is used or kept on a public road, is that specified in the following provisions of this regulation.

(3) Each such licence shall be fixed to the vehicle in a holder sufficient to protect the licence from the weather to which it would otherwise be exposed.

(4) The licence shall be exhibited on the vehicle—

    (a) in the case of an invalid vehicle, tricycle or bicycle, other than in a case specified in sub-paragraph (b) or (c) of this paragraph, on the near side of the vehicle;

    (b) in the case of a bicycle drawing a side-car or to which a side-car is attached, on the near side of the handlebars of the bicycle or on the near side of the side-car;

    (c) in the case of any vehicle fitted with a glass windscreen in front of the driver extending across the vehicle to its near side, on or adjacent to the near side of the windscreen;

    (d) in the case of any other vehicle—

        (i) if the vehicle is fitted with a driver's cab containing a near side window, on that window; or

        (ii) on the near side of the vehicle in front of the driver's seat and not less than 760 mm and not more than 1.8 metres above the surface of the road.

(5) In each case referred to in paragraph (4), the licence shall be so exhibited that all the particulars on the licence are clearly visible in daylight from the near side of the road.

Prohibition against exhibiting anything resembling a vehicle, trade or nil licence

B55.09   **7.** No person shall exhibit on a vehicle which is kept or used on a public road anything—

    (a) which is intended to be, or

    (b) which could reasonably be,

mistaken for a vehicle licence, a nil licence or a trade licence which is for the time being in force for, or in respect of, the vehicle.

Issue of duplicate vehicle, trade and nil licences

8. *[Omitted.]*   B55.10

Surrender of vehicle and trade licences

9. *[Omitted.]*   B55.11

[Supplement payable on late renewal of vehicle licence

9A. *[Omitted.]*]   B55.12

PART III

REGISTRATION AND REGISTRATION DOCUMENTS

Registration and issue of registration document

10.—(1) A vehicle shall not be registered under section 21 of the 1994 Act un-   B55.13
less a fee of £— has been paid to the Secretary of State.

(2) Paragraph (1) does not apply to a vehicle which is an exempt vehicle by virtue of paragraph 18 or 19 of Schedule 2 to the 1994 Act.

(3) The Secretary of State may register a vehicle in either the GB records or the NI records as he considers appropriate and may, if he thinks fit, remove the particulars of a vehicle included in one of those parts of the register and include them in the other.

(4) On registering a vehicle the Secretary of State shall issue a registration document to the keeper of the vehicle.

(5) Subject to paragraph (6) and regulation 11, the Secretary of State shall issue the registration document forthwith, except where the vehicle is registered in consequence of an application for a vehicle licence by a person applying as mentioned in section 7(3A) of the 1994 Act, in which case the registration document shall be issued when that person asks for it to be issued.

(6) Before issuing a registration document to the keeper of a vehicle, the Secretary of State may require him to produce the vehicle for inspection or to produce other evidence that the vehicle accords with the particulars furnished when a vehicle or nil licence was applied for in respect of it.

(7) The Secretary of State may refuse to issue a registration document or replacement registration document for a vehicle if he is not satisfied that the vehicle accords with those particulars.

[The amount of the fee (and amendments to it) are not reproduced.]

[Registration document

10A.—(1) [Subject to paragraph (1A),] this regulation applies to vehicles fall-   B55.14
ing within the definition of "vehicle" in Article 2 of Council Directive 70/156/
EEC on the approximation of the laws of the Member States relating to the type

approval of motor vehicles and their trailers [*O.J. No.42, February 23, 1970, p.1*] and in Article 2 of Council Directive 92/61/EEC relating to the type-approval of two or three-wheeled motor vehicles [*O.J. No.L225, August 10, 1992, p.72*].

[(1A) Paragraph (3A) applies to any vehicle registered under the 1994 Act or its predecessor legislation.]

(2) The Secretary of State shall not issue a new registration document on or after 31st January 2004 unless it complies with Annex I of [the Directive] as regards—

(a) dimensions;

(b) composition; and

(c) information contained within it;

except that in relation to a new registration document, the information contained may be limited to that available to the Secretary of State.

(3) Any registration document which does not comply with [the Directive] shall cease to have effect on the earlier of—

(a) the date on which the Secretary of State issues a new registration document under these Regulations; or

(b) 1st July 2005.

[(3A) Notwithstanding any other provision of these Regulations, the Secretary of State may, without charge and on surrender by the registered keeper of a registration document issued before 31st January 2004, issue to the registered keeper a registration document which is in a form provided for by the Directive in respect of the same vehicle if it appears proper and reasonable to him to do so.]

(4) In registering for the first time on or after 1st June 2004 a vehicle, which has been registered in another member State or Gibraltar, the Secretary of State shall recognise as a registration document a document which has been issued in respect of that vehicle by that other member State or Gibraltar if it complies with Annex I or Annexes I and II of [the Directive].

(5) Where the Secretary of State registers a vehicle in accordance with paragraph (4) he shall—

(a) retain the former registration document for not less than 6 months; and

(b) within 2 months of registration in the United Kingdom, notify the authorities in the member State or in Gibraltar where the vehicle was previously registered of his act of registration.]

B55.15 *[Regulation 10A was inserted by SI 2003/3073 and is printed as amended by SI 2004/3298.*

Directive 70/156/EEC and Directive 92/61/EEC have both been repealed, see now Directive 2007/46/EC (O.J. No.L263, October 9, 2007, p.1) and Directive 2002/24/EC (O.J. No.L124, May 9, 2002, p.1) respectively.]

Production of vehicle for inspection before assignment of registration mark

B55.16   **11.** Where at the request of the keeper of a vehicle a particular registration mark is to be assigned to it, having previously been assigned to another vehicle, that other vehicle shall be made available for inspection by the Secretary of State at a place designated by him, and the keeper of the first mentioned vehicle shall, before the registration mark is so assigned, pay to the Secretary of State a charge of £— for the assignment.

[The amount of the charge (and amendments to it) are not reproduced.]   **B55.17**

Production of registration document for inspection

12. The keeper of a vehicle in respect of which a registration document has   **B55.18**
been issued shall produce the document for inspection if he is required to do so at
any reasonable time by a constable or by a person acting on behalf of the Secretary of State.

Issue of replacement registration document

13.—(1) Where a registration document has been, or may have been, lost,   **B55.19**
stolen, destroyed or damaged, or it contains any particulars that have become illegible, the registered keeper shall apply to the Secretary of State for the issue of
a replacement document.

(2) In a case where the registration document has been damaged or contains
any particulars which have become illegible, an application under paragraph (1)
shall be accompanied by the document and, in any other case, the Secretary of
State may, if he thinks fit, accept an application made orally by telephone.

[(2A) Where the registration document has been, or may have been, lost,
stolen or destroyed, notification under paragraph (1) shall[, unless the registration
document fee exemption applies,] be accompanied by an application for the issue
of a new registration document and a fee of £—.]

(3) If the Secretary of State—

    (a) receives an application made in accordance with this regulation; and

    (b) he is satisfied that a registration document has been, or may have
        been, lost, stolen, destroyed or damaged, or that it contains any
        particulars that have become illegible,

he shall, subject to regulation 15, issue a replacement registration document to
the registered keeper.

(4) If a replacement registration document has been issued on the ground that
the original has been, or may have been, lost, stolen or destroyed, and the original
is subsequently found or recovered, the keeper of the vehicle—

    (a) if the original is in his possession, shall forthwith return it to the Sec-
        retary of State, or

    (b) if it is not in his possession but he becomes aware that it is found or
        recovered, shall take all reasonable steps to obtain possession of it
        and return it to the Secretary of State.

[Regulation 13 is printed as amended by SI 2004/238 and SI 2004/1773.   **B55.20**
The amount of the fee is not reproduced.]

Correction of registration document

14.—(1) Where the keeper of a vehicle believes that the particulars in the   **B55.21**
registration document issued in respect of that vehicle are, or have become, inaccurate, he shall forthwith notify the Secretary of State of the inaccuracy.

(2) Notification under paragraph (1) shall be accompanied by the registration
document, unless it has been, or may have been, lost stolen or destroyed.

[(2A) Where the registration document has been, or may have been, lost, stolen or destroyed, notification under paragraph (1) shall be accompanied by an application for the issue of a new registration document and[, except where the registration document fee exemption applies, by] a fee of £—.]

(3) Where the Secretary of State believes that the particulars in the registration document issued in respect of a vehicle are inaccurate—

    (a) if the document has not been sent to him [...], he may require the registered keeper of the vehicle to send it to him;

    (b) whether or not he has received the document, he may correct the particulars in the register; and

    [(c) after correcting the particulars in the register, he shall, provided that paragraphs (2) or (2A) have been complied with, and subject to regulation 15, issue a new registration document containing the correct particulars to the registered keeper.]

B55.22   *[Regulation 14 is printed as amended by SI 2004/238 and SI 2004/1773.*
The amount of the fee is not reproduced.]

Issue of new registration document

B55.23   **15.**—(1) Before issuing a new registration document in respect of a vehicle under any provision of these Regulations, the Secretary of State may require the keeper of the vehicle to satisfy him by the production of the vehicle or other sufficient evidence that the vehicle—

    (a) accords with the particulars furnished when a vehicle or nil licence was last applied for in respect of it; or

    (b) is the registered vehicle.

[(1A) Before issuing a new registration document the Secretary of State may take actions to satisfy himself that the identity and address of the person seeking to be the registered keeper accords with the information given to him.]

(2) The Secretary of State may refuse to issue a new registration document in respect of a vehicle if he is not satisfied as mentioned in [paragraphs (1) and (1A)].

(3) The provisions of Schedule 3 shall have effect in relation to the issue of a new registration document in respect of a vehicle (in this regulation and in Schedule 3 called *"the relevant vehicle"*) where—

    (a) the relevant vehicle falls within category M1 of Annex II to Council Directive 70/156/EEC [*O.J. No.L42, February 23, 1970, p.1; as substituted by Directive 2001/116/EC (O.J. No.L18, January 21, 2002, pp.1–115)*], and

    (b) either an insurer has informed the Secretary of State that it has decided to pay the value of the relevant vehicle to the owner in preference to paying for the cost of repairing it or the registration document has been surrendered to the Secretary of State under regulation 20(5).

(4) For the purposes of paragraph (3) and Schedule 3 the return of a registration document for a vehicle registered in the NI records in accordance with regulation 18(2)(b) shall be taken to be the issue of a new registration document.

B55.24   *[Regulation 15 is printed as amended by SI 2003/3073.*
Category M1 of vehicle referred to in para.3(a) above is now set out in Annex

II of Directive 2007/46/EC (O.J. No.L263, October 9, 2007, p.1), which repealed Directive 70/156/EEC (O.J. No.L42, February 23, 1970, p.1) with effect from April 29, 2009.]

PART IV

NOTIFICATION AND CHANGES

Notification of an alteration to a vehicle

16.—(1) Where any alteration is made to a vehicle so as to make any of the   **B55.25**
particulars set out in the registration document incorrect, the registered keeper
shall deliver to the Secretary of State—

    (a) notification of the alteration;

    (b) except where the registration document [has been, or may have been,]
        lost, stolen or destroyed, the registration document.

[(1A) Where the registration document has been, or may have been, lost,
stolen or destroyed, notification under paragraph (1) shall be accompanied by an
application for the issue of a new registration document and[, except where the
registration document fee exemption applies, by] a fee of £—.]

(2) If the alteration makes any of the particulars shown on the vehicle licence
or nil licence incorrect, the registered keeper shall also deliver to the Secretary of
State the appropriate licence, unless it is lost, stolen or destroyed.

(3) The Secretary of State may require the registered keeper to furnish such
evidence as he may reasonably require to show that the alteration has taken place.

(4) On receiving notification under this regulation the Secretary of State shall,
subject to regulation 15, if he is satisfied that the vehicle has been altered in the
way notified to him,—

    (a) record the alteration in the register;

    (b) [issue] to the registered keeper a new registration document showing
        the correct particulars; and

    (c) in a case falling within paragraph (2), send to the registered keeper a
        new vehicle [licence]or nil licence showing the correct particulars.

[Regulation 16 is printed as amended by SI 2004/238 and SI 2004/1773.   **B55.26**
The amount of the fee is not reproduced.

Contravention of reg.16(1) is a summary offence for which the offender is liable to a fine on level 3 of the standard scale under the Vehicle Excise and Registration Act 1994 s.59(2)(a).]

Notification of destruction or permanent export of a vehicle

17. Where a vehicle is […] sent permanently out of—   **B55.27**

    (a) Great Britain; or

    (b) Northern Ireland,

the registered keeper shall immediately notify the Secretary of State of the fact
[…].

[Regulation 17 is printed as amended by SI 2003/2635 and SI 2004/3298.   **B55.28**

Contravention of reg.17 is a summary offence for which the offender is liable to a fine on level 3 of the standard scale under the Vehicle Excise and Registration Act 1994 s.59(2)(a).]

[Vehicles to which the End-of-Life Vehicles Directive applies

B55.29   **17A.**—(1) This regulation applies to a vehicle to which Directive 2000/53 of the European Parliament and of the Council [*O.J. No.L269, 21.10.2000, p.34*] on end-of-life vehicles applies and which is—

> (a) registered in the GB or NI records; or
> (b) designed or adapted for use on a road and would be registered but for the fact that it falls within the exemption in regulation 29(2).

(2) Where a vehicle to which this regulation applies is transferred to an authorised treatment facility—

> (a) if that facility is in the United Kingdom, the owner or operator thereof shall notify the Secretary of State of the issue of a certificate of destruction pursuant to regulation 27 of the End-of-Life Vehicles Regulations and at the same time shall surrender the registration document to him, except where the registration document has been lost, stolen or destroyed; and
> (b) if that facility is in an EEA State other than the United Kingdom, the registered keeper of the vehicle shall notify the Secretary of State of the issue in that other EEA State of a certificate of destruction and at the same time the registered keeper shall surrender the registration document to him except where the registration document has been lost, stolen or destroyed.

(3) Where the Secretary of State has been notified of the issue of a certificate of destruction he shall not as respects the vehicle to which it relates—

> (a) record in the GB records or, in the case of a vehicle registered in Northern Ireland, in the NI records any further change of keeper;
> (b) accept the required declaration in paragraph 1(1) of Schedule 4.

(4) In this regulation *"authorised treatment facility", "certificate of destruction"* and *"EEA State"* have the meanings that those expressions have in the End-of-Life Vehicles Regulations 2003 [*SI 2003/2635, not reproduced in this work*].]

B55.30   *[Regulation 17A was inserted by SI 2003/2635.]*

Notification of a change of the keeper's name or address

B55.31   **18.**—(1) If the registered keeper of a vehicle changes his name or his address, he shall forthwith notify the new name or address to the Secretary of State and, except where the registration document has been[, or may have been,] lost, stolen or destroyed, shall deliver the registration document to him.

[(1A) Where the registration document has been, or may have been, lost, stolen or destroyed, notification under paragraph (1) shall be accompanied by an application for the issue of a new registration document and[, except where the registration document fee exemption applies, by] a fee of £—.]

(2) On receiving notification in accordance with [this regulation] the Secretary of State shall, subject to regulation 15, —

(a) record the alteration in the register, and

[(b) send to the registered keeper a new registration document showing the new name or address.]

[Regulation 18 is printed as amended by SI 2004/238 and SI 2003/3073.   **B55.32**
The amount of the fee is not reproduced.

Contravention of reg.18(1) is a summary offence for which the offender is liable to a fine on level 3 of the standard scale under the Vehicle Excise and Registration Act 1994 s.59(2)(a).]

Notification of a change of the name or address of the holder of a trade licence

19.—(1) If the holder of a trade licence changes the name of his business or his   **B55.33**
business address, he shall notify the Secretary of State of this fact and of the new name or address forthwith and shall at the same time deliver up the licence to the Secretary of State.

(2) On receiving notification in accordance with paragraph (1) the Secretary of State shall—

(a) record the alteration in the register of trade licences; and

(b) send to the holder a new trade licence showing the correct particulars.

[Contravention of reg.19(1) is a summary offence for which the offender is li-   **B55.34**
able to a fine on level 3 of the standard scale under the Vehicle Excise and Registration Act 1994 s.59(2)(a).]

Change of keeper: general provisions

20.—(1) Regulations 21 to 25 have effect subject to the provisions of this   **B55.35**
regulation.

(2) On a change in the keeper of a vehicle, any current vehicle licence for the vehicle may be delivered to the new keeper.

(3) So far as they provide for the issue of a new registration document, regulations 21 to 25 have effect subject to the provisions of regulation 15.

(4) Paragraph (5) shall apply and regulations 21 to 25 shall not apply where—

(a) a vehicle has sustained damage to its bodywork such that the cost of commercial repair would exceed the value of the vehicle when repaired; and

(b) either the keeper of the vehicle does not have the benefit of a policy of insurance or cover note which covers the damage or the keeper is an insurer.

(5) On a change of keeper to which this paragraph applies the keeper shall forthwith surrender the registration document to the Secretary of State or, if an insurer, destroy it.

(6) In regulations 21 to 25 *"vehicle trader"* means any person who—

(a) is the holder of a trade licence;

(b) carries on business as a dealer in motor vehicles;

(c) carries on business as an auctioneer of motor vehicles;

(d) carries on business as a dismantler of motor vehicles; or

(e) in relation to a particular vehicle, is—

(i) a finance company which has acquired that vehicle under an order for repossession; or

(ii) an insurer which has acquired that vehicle in satisfaction of a total loss claim.

Change of keeper: registration document issued in Great Britain before 24th March 1997

B55.36   **21.** [...]

B55.37   *[Regulation 21 was revoked on July 1, 2005 (see SI 2003/3073 regs 1 and 8).]*

Change of keeper: registration document issued in Great Britain on or after 24th March 1997 and the new keeper not a vehicle trader

B55.38   **22.**—(1) This regulation applies where—

(a) there is a change in the keeper of a vehicle;

(b) a vehicle registration document has been issued in respect of the vehicle [...]; and

(c) the new keeper is not a vehicle trader.

(2) The registered keeper of the vehicle—

(a) if the registration document issued in respect of the vehicle is in his possession, shall deliver to the new keeper that part of the document marked as the part which is to be given to the new keeper; and

(b) shall forthwith deliver [to the Secretary of State on the remainder of the registration document, or otherwise in writing, the following information]—

(i) the name and address of the new keeper;

(ii) the date on which the vehicle was sold or transferred to the new keeper;

(iii) a declaration signed by the registered keeper that the details given in accordance with paragraph (i) are correct to the best of his knowledge and that the details given in accordance with paragraph (ii) are correct; and

(iv) a declaration signed by the new keeper that the details given in accordance with paragraphs (i) and (ii) are correct.

[(3) Where all parts of the registration document have been, or may have been, lost, stolen or destroyed, the new keeper shall submit an application to the Secretary of State for the issue of a new registration document [and, except where the registration document fee exemption applies, that application shall be] accompanied by a fee of £—.

(4) Where the new keeper can produce to the Secretary of State that part of the document marked as the part which is to be given to the new keeper, the new keeper may submit an application to the Secretary of State for the issue of a new registration document accompanied by that part.

(5) On receiving notification of a change in keeper in accordance with paragraphs (2), (3) or (4), the Secretary of State shall, subject to regulation 15 —

(a) record the change in the register, and

(b) issue to the new registered keeper a new registration document.]

Change of keeper: obligations of registered keeper where vehicle registration document issued in Great Britain on or after 24th March 1997 and the new keeper a vehicle trader

23.—(1) Subject to regulation 24, this regulation applies where—   **B55.40**

    (a) there is a change in the keeper of a vehicle;

    (b) the person disposing of the vehicle is the registered keeper;

    (c) a vehicle registration document has been issued in respect of the vehicle; and

    (d) the new keeper is a vehicle trader.

(2) The registered keeper shall forthwith notify the Secretary of State, on that part of the registration document which relates to the transfer to a vehicle trader, or otherwise in writing, of the following—

    (a) the name and address of the vehicle trader;

    (b) the date on which the vehicle was transferred to the vehicle trader;

    (c) a declaration signed by the registered keeper that he transferred the vehicle to the vehicle trader on the date specified in accordance with sub-paragraph (b); and

    (d) a declaration signed by the vehicle trader that the vehicle was transferred to him on the date specified in accordance with sub-paragraph (b).

(3) If the registration document issued in respect of the vehicle is in his possession, the registered keeper shall deliver to the vehicle trader those parts of it not required to be sent to the Secretary of State under paragraph (2).

Change of keeper: obligations of vehicle traders where registration document issued in Great Britain on or after 24 March 1997

24.—(1) This regulation applies where a vehicle trader becomes the keeper of   **B55.42** a vehicle in respect of which a vehicle registration document has been issued [...].

(2) Where this regulation applies the vehicle trader shall, on or before the appropriate date and on that part of the registration document which relates to a change of keeper […], notify the Secretary of State as to—

    (a) the transfer of the vehicle to him; and

    (b) the date on which he became the keeper of the vehicle.

[(2A) Where the registration document has been, or may have been, lost, stolen or destroyed, notification in accordance with paragraph (2) shall be effected by an application to the Secretary of State for the issue of a new registration document [and, except where the registration document fee exemption applies, that application shall be] accompanied by a fee of £—.]

(3) For the purposes of paragraph (2) the appropriate date is whichever is the earliest of—

    (a) the day on which the vehicle trader first uses, or permits the use of, the vehicle on a public road otherwise than under a trade licence;

    (b) the day on which he first keeps the vehicle on such a road;

    (c) the day immediately following the expiration of the period of three months (*"the three months period of grace"*) beginning with the day after the date on which the vehicle was last kept by a person who was not a vehicle trader.

(4) Where this regulation applies and the vehicle trader transfers the vehicle to another vehicle trader before the expiration of the three months period of grace, he shall give to the new keeper any part of the registration document in his possession.

(5) Where the vehicle trader transfers the vehicle to another person in a case not falling within paragraph (4), he shall—

    (a) forthwith deliver to the Secretary of State, on that part of the registration document which relates to the change of keeper or otherwise in writing, the following—

       (i) the name and address of the new keeper;

       (ii) the date on which the vehicle was transferred to the new keeper;

       (iii) a declaration signed by the [vehicle trader] that the details given in accordance with paragraph (i) are correct to the best of his knowledge and that the details given in accordance with paragraph (ii) are correct; and

       (iv) a declaration signed by the new keeper that the details given in accordance with paragraphs (i) and (ii) are correct; and

    (b) if the registration document issued in respect of the vehicle is in his possession, deliver to the new keeper those parts of it not required to be sent to the Secretary of State under sub-paragraph (a).

[(6) Where all parts of the registration document have been, or may have been, lost, stolen or destroyed, the new keeper shall submit an application to the Secretary of State for the issue of a new registration document [and, except where the registration document fee exemption applies, that application shall be] accompanied by a fee of £—.]

[(7) Where the new keeper can produce to the Secretary of State that part of the document marked as the part which is to be given to the new keeper, the new keeper may submit an application to the Secretary of State for the issue of a new registration document accompanied by that part.]

[(8) On receiving notification of a change in keeper in accordance with paragraphs (2), (2A), (5), (6) or (7), the Secretary of State shall, subject to regulation 15—

    (a) record the change in the register, and

    (b) issue to the new registered keeper a new registration document.]

B55.43   *[Regulation 24 is printed as amended by SI 2003/3073, SI 2004/238, SI 2004/ 1773 and SI 2004/2154.*

The amounts of the fees are not reproduced.

Contravention of reg.24 is a summary offence for which the offender is liable to a fine on level 3 of the standard scale under the Vehicle Excise and Registration Act 1994 s.59(2)(a).]

Change of keeper: registration document issued in Northern Ireland

25. [...]   **B55.44**

[Regulation 25 was revoked on July 1, 2005 (see SI 2003/3073 regs 1 and 8).]   **B55.45**

Statutory off-road notification

26. Schedule 4 shall have effect for the purpose of prescribing, the particulars   **B55.46**
to be furnished and the declarations to be made, and the times at which and the
circumstances and manner in which they are to be made, by a person who—

(a) surrenders a vehicle licence;

(b) does not renew a vehicle licence on its expiration; or

(c) keeps an unlicensed vehicle.

[Contravention of reg.26 is a summary offence for which the offender is liable to a fine on level 3 of the standard scale under the Vehicle Excise and Registration Act 1994 s.59(2)(a).]

[Exceptions to section 31A

26A.—(1) The requirements prescribed for the purposes of the first condition   **B55.47**
in section 31B of the 1994 Act are whichever are applicable in the circumstances
of the requirements specified in—

(a) regulation 20(5) (surrender or destruction of registration document for damaged vehicle), in so far as it requires surrender of the registration document,

(b) [...],

(c) regulation 22(2)(b) (delivery of remainder of registration document to the Secretary of State),

(d) regulation 23(2) (notifying the Secretary of State when the transfer is to a vehicle trader),

(e) regulation 24(5) (vehicle trader notifying the Secretary of State of a transfer), and

(f) regulation 25(1)(a) (delivery of registration document and notification to the Secretary of State where the registration document was issued in Northern Ireland).

(2) The requirement prescribed for the purposes of the second condition in section 31B is the making of the required declaration and the furnishing of the prescribed particulars to the Secretary of State in accordance with Schedule 4.

(3) The requirement prescribed under subsection (6) of section 31B for the purposes of subsection (4)(c) (the third condition) is that before the expiry of 14 days beginning with the date on which the theft came to the knowledge of the registered keeper notification of the theft was given to—

(a) a member of a police force maintained for any police area in England and Wales or Scotland,

     (b) a member of the Police Service of Northern Ireland, or

     (c) a person employed to assist such a police force or that Police Service.

(4) The prescribed length of the period for the purpose of the fourth condition shall be 14 days.]

B55.48   *[Regulation 26A was inserted by SI 2003/3073.*

    Paragraph (1)(b) of reg.26A was revoked on July 1, 2005 by SI 2003/3073 reg.8. Regulation 25 referred to in para.(1)(f) of this regulation was also revoked on July 1, 2005 by SI 2003/3073 reg.8.]

PART V

DISCLOSURE OF INFORMATION

B55.49   *[Omitted.]*

PART VI

CROWN VEHICLES AND EXEMPT VEHICLES

Application of Regulations to Crown vehicles

B55.50   **29.**—(1) Except as provided by this Part of these Regulations, nothing in these Regulations applies to a vehicle kept by the Crown.

(2) Nothing in these Regulations or this Part of these Regulations applies to a vehicle kept by the Crown which is used or appropriated for use for naval, military or air force purposes.

Registration of Crown vehicles

B55.51   **30.**—(1) A Government Department which uses or keeps or, intends to use or keep, a vehicle on a public road shall—

     (a) make to the Secretary of State such declaration and furnish him with such particulars as would be required by section 7 of the 1994 Act if the Department desired to take out a vehicle licence for the vehicle; and

     (b) make to the Secretary of State a declaration that the vehicle is only to be used for the purposes of the Crown.

(2) Upon receipt of the declaration and particulars the Secretary of State shall—

     (a) register the vehicle in the name of the Government Department;

     (b) if there is no registration mark for the time being assigned to the vehicle, assign a registration mark to it; and

     (c) issue a registration document for the vehicle.

(3) Any registration mark assigned under paragraph (2) shall be deemed to be assigned under section 23 of the 1994 Act for the purposes of subsection (2) of that section and of these Regulations.

(4) No vehicle licence or nil licence shall be issued by the Secretary of State in respect of the vehicle so registered.

[(5) Where a Government department is the registered keeper of a vehicle—

(a) regulations 13, 14, 15, 16 and 18 shall apply;

(b) regulations 20, 21, 22, 23, 24 and 25 shall apply on a change in the keeper of a vehicle; and

(c) regulations 20, 21, 22 and 25 shall apply on a change in the keeper of a vehicle from one Government department to another.]

[Regulation 30 is printed as amended by SI 2004/238.]   **B55.52**

Certificates of Crown exemption

31.—(1) Subject to regulation 29(2), for the purposes of identification, a cer-   **B55.53**
tificate of Crown exemption shall be displayed on every vehicle belonging to the
Crown which is used or kept on a public road.

(2) A certificate of Crown exemption is a certificate—

(a) marked with the registration mark of the vehicle to which it relates;

(b) stating that the vehicle is exempt from vehicle excise duty as a Crown vehicle;

(c) signed by a duly authorised officer of the Government Department by which the vehicle is kept.

(3) Regulation 7 (exhibition of vehicle and nil licences) of these Regulations
shall apply as if references to a vehicle licence included a reference to a certificate of Crown exemption.

Application of Regulations to exempt vehicles

32. Subject to the provisions of these Regulations, these Regulations shall ap-   **B55.54**
ply to exempt vehicles so far as they are capable of being applied to such vehicles.

Nil licences

33.—(1) In this regulation *"nil licensable vehicle"* means a vehicle which is   **B55.55**
an exempt vehicle [otherwise than] by virtue of paragraph 2, 2A, 3, 22 or 23 of
Schedule 2 to the 1994 Act.

(2) A nil licence is required to be in force in respect of a nil licensable vehicle
which is used or kept on a public road.

(3) A nil licence shall—

(a) be granted for a period of 12 months beginning with the first day of the month in which the application for the licence is received by the Secretary of State; and

(b) be in the same form as a vehicle licence with the word "NIL" marked in the space provided for indicating the amount of vehicle excise duty payable.

(4) The keeper of a nil licensable vehicle may apply to the Secretary of State
for a nil licence by making to him such a declaration and furnishing him with
such particulars and such documentary or other evidence as might be specified
under section 7 of the 1994 Act if the keeper desired to take out a vehicle licence
for the vehicle.

(5) The Secretary of State may accept a declaration given, and particulars
furnished, orally by telephone.

(6) In the case of a vehicle which is an exempt vehicle by virtue of—

(a) paragraph 19 of Schedule 2 to the 1994 Act, or

(b) paragraph 7 of Schedule 4 to that Act,

the Secretary of State shall require the keeper to furnish him with a certificate that paragraph 19 of Schedule 2 or, as the case may be, paragraph 7 of Schedule 4 applies, unless the Secretary of State satisfies himself by other means that one of those paragraphs applies.

(7) The certificate shall be obtained by the keeper of the vehicle from the Secretary of State for Work and Pensions, the Secretary of State for Defence or the Department for Social Development for Northern Ireland, whichever is appropriate.

(8) Paragraphs (4) to (7) do not apply where the person applying for a nil licence agrees to comply with such conditions as may be specified in relation to him by the Secretary of State.

[(8A Section 22ZA of the 1994 Act shall apply to information of the following descriptions—

(a) the name of any person to whom—

(i) disability living allowance or mobility supplement is payable; or

(ii) disability living allowance has ceased to be payable and who would be entitled to receive the mobility component at the higher rate but for his failure to satisfy a condition referred to in paragraph 19(2A)(b) of Schedule 2 to the 1994 Act;

(b) that person's date of birth and National Insurance number; and

(c) if applicable, the date on which the allowance or supplement, as appropriate, will cease to be payable.]

[(8B) For the purposes of paragraph (8A)—

"disability living allowance" means a disability living allowance for the purposes of section 71 of the Social Security Contributions and Benefits Act 1992 (disability living allowance);

"mobility component" means the mobility component of a disability living allowance and *"higher rate"* means the higher rate of the mobility component for the time being prescribed under section 73 of that Act (the mobility component); and

"mobility supplement" has the meaning which that expression bears in paragraph 19 of Schedule 2 to the 1994 Act.].

(9) If, following an application made in accordance with this regulation, the Secretary of State is satisfied that a vehicle is a nil licensable vehicle, he shall issue a nil licence to the keeper of the vehicle.

(10) If at any time vehicle excise duty becomes chargeable under the 1994 Act in respect of a vehicle which immediately before that time was a nil licensable vehicle, the keeper of the vehicle shall forthwith return to the Secretary of State—

(a) any nil licence issued in respect of the vehicle; and

(b) any certificate obtained by him for the purposes of paragraph (6) in relation to the vehicle.

[Regulation 33 is printed as amended by SI 2003/2154 and SI 2005/2713.]

Exemptions from vehicle excise duty: vehicles imported by members of foreign armed forces and others

34. Schedule 5, which provides for the exemption from vehicle excise duty of vehicles imported into Great Britain by members of foreign armed forces and other persons, shall have effect.

B55.57

PART VII

TRADE LICENCES

Definition of "motor trader": descriptions of businesses

35. The following descriptions of business are hereby prescribed for the purposes of sub-paragraph (b) of the definition of *"motor trader"* in section 62(1) of the 1994 Act—

B55.58

    (a) the business of modifying vehicles, whether by the fitting of accessories or otherwise;

    (b) the business of valeting vehicles.

Period for review of decision refusing an application for a trade licence

36. *[Omitted.]*

B55.59

Conditions subject to which trade licences are to be issued

37. The conditions subject to which trade licences are to be issued, and with which every holder of a trade licence shall comply, shall be those specified in Part I of Schedule 6.

B55.60

Purposes for which the holder of a trade licence may use a vehicle by virtue of the licence

38. Part II of Schedule 6 shall have effect for prescribing the purposes for which a vehicle may be used by virtue of a trade licence.

B55.61

Assignment of general registration marks

39. On issuing a trade licence the Secretary of State shall assign to the holder of the licence a general registration mark in respect of that licence.

B55.62

Issue of trade plates

40.—(1) Subject to paragraphs (3) and (4), the Secretary of State shall issue to every holder of a trade licence, as respects each licence held by him, a set of trade plates appropriate to the class of vehicles for which the licence is to be used.

B55.63

(2) Each trade plate shall show the general registration mark assigned to the holder of the licence in respect of the licence, and one of the trade plates shall include a means whereby the licence may be fixed to it.

(3) Where the holder of a trade licence satisfies the Secretary of State that the vehicles which he will use by virtue of the licence include vehicles which would

otherwise be liable to vehicle excise duty under paragraph 2 of Schedule 1 to the 1994 Act (motorcycles) and other vehicles, the Secretary of State shall issue to the holder an additional trade plate in respect of the vehicles otherwise liable to vehicle excise duty under that paragraph.

(4) Where the licence is to be used only in respect of vehicles to which paragraph 2 of Schedule 1 to the 1994 Act applies (motorcycles), the Secretary of State shall issue only one trade plate to the holder of the licence and that plate shall include a means whereby the licence may be fixed to it.

(5) Each trade plate shall remain the property of the Secretary of State and shall be returned forthwith to the Secretary of State by the person to whom it was issued if that person ceases to be—

> (a) the holder of the trade licence in respect of which the trade plate was issued; or
>
> (b) a motor trader or a vehicle tester.

B55.64   *[Contravention of reg.40(5) is a summary offence for which the offender is liable to a fine on level 3 of the standard scale under the Vehicle Excise and Registration Act 1994 s.59(2)(a).]*

Issue of replacement trade plates

B55.65   **41.**—(1) If any trade plate issued by the Secretary of State to the holder of a trade licence is lost, stolen, destroyed or materially damaged, the holder of the licence shall apply to the Secretary of State for the issue to him of a replacement set of trade plates.

(2) On receipt of an application under paragraph (1) the Secretary of State shall so issue a replacement set if—

> (a) he has received all those trade plates in the set which are still in the possession of the holder of the licence;
>
> (b) except where paragraph (3) applies, the fee prescribed by paragraph (4) has been paid; and
>
> (c) he is satisfied that any plate has been lost, stolen, destroyed or materially damaged.

(3) If only that part of a trade plate which consists of a means whereby the trade licence may be fixed to it is lost, stolen, destroyed or materially damaged, the holder of the licence shall apply to the Secretary of State for the issue to him of a replacement means of fixing the licence and, upon payment of the fee prescribed by paragraph (4)(c), the Secretary of State shall issue such a replacement.

(4) *[Prescribes the fees payable.]*

(5) No fee shall be payable under paragraph (4)(a) or (b) on account of the replacement of a trade plate, if the Secretary of State is satisfied that the plate has become illegible or the colour of the plate has been altered (whether by fading or by other means) otherwise than by reason of any act or omission of the licence holder.

(6) If a replacement set of trade plates has been issued on the ground that any of the original trade plates has been lost, stolen or destroyed, and the original plate is subsequently found or recovered, the holder of the licence—

> (a) if the original plate is in his possession, shall forthwith return it to the Secretary of State, or

(b) if it is not in his possession but he becomes aware that it is found or recovered, shall take all reasonable steps to obtain possession of it and return it to the Secretary of State.

Display of general registration mark of holder of a trade licence and exhibition of licence

42.—(1) Where a vehicle is in use under a trade licence the general registration mark assigned to the holder of a trade licence shall be displayed on the vehicle in the manner specified in paragraph (2).   **B55.66**

(2) The trade plates issued by the Secretary of State shall be fixed to and displayed on the vehicle in such a manner that, if the general registration mark assigned to the holder were a registration mark assigned to the vehicle, the provisions of regulations 5 and 6 of the Road Vehicles (Display of Registration Marks) Regulations 2001 [*SI 2001/561, q.v.*] (the "2001 Regulations") would be complied with, notwithstanding the vehicle may not have been first registered on or after the relevant date, as defined in regulation 2(1) of the 2001 Regulations, or it is a works truck (as defined by paragraph 4(6) of Schedule 1 to the 1994 Act) or an agricultural machine (as defined by regulation 2(1) of the 2001 Regulations) or a road roller.

(3) The prescribed manner of exhibiting a trade licence on a vehicle for the purposes of section 33(1)(b) of the 1994 Act is that specified in paragraph (4).

(4) The trade licence shall be—

(a) exhibited on the front of the vehicle so as to be clearly visible at all times in daylight; and

(b) fixed by means of the trade plate issued to the licence holder which contains a means for fixing the licence to it.

[Contravention of reg.42 is a summary offence for which the offender is liable to a fine on level 3 of the standard scale under the Vehicle Excise and Registration Act 1994 s.59(2)(a).]   **B55.67**

PART VIII

MISCELLANEOUS

Cylinder capacity

43.—(1) For the purposes of Schedule 1 to the 1994 Act (annual rates of vehicle excise duty) the cylinder capacity of an internal combustion engine shall be taken to be—   **B55.68**

(a) in the case of a single-cylinder engine, the cylinder capacity attributable to the cylinder of the engine; and

(b) in the case of an engine having two or more cylinders, the sum of the cylinder capacities attributable to the separate cylinders.

(2) The cylinder capacity attributable to any cylinder of an internal combustion engine shall be deemed to be equal to—

(a) in the case of a cylinder having a single piston, the product expressed in cubic centimetres of the square of the internal diameter of the cylinder measured in centimetres, and the distance through which the piston associated with the cylinder moves during one half of a revolution of the engine measured in centimetres multiplied by 0.7854; and

(b) in the case of a cylinder having more than one piston, the sum of the products expressed in cubic centimetres of the square of the internal diameter of each part of the cylinder in which a piston moves measured in centimetres, and the distance through which the piston associated with that part of the cylinder moves during one half of a revolution of the engine measured in centimetres multiplied by 0.7854.

(3) In measuring cylinders for the purpose of calculating cylinder capacity, and in calculating cylinder capacity, fractions of centimetres are to be taken into account.

Seating capacity of buses

B55.69   44.—(1) For the purpose of Part III of Schedule 1 to the 1994 Act (annual rates of vehicle excise duty applicable to buses), the seating capacity of a bus shall be taken to be the number of persons that may be seated in the bus at any one time, as determined in accordance with the principles specified in paragraph (2).

(2) Those principles are—

(a) where separate seats for each person are provided one person shall be counted for each separate seat provided;

(b) where the vehicle is fitted with continuous seats one person shall be counted for each complete length of 410 mm measured in a straight line lengthwise on the front of each seat;

(c) where any continuous seat is fitted with arms in order to separate the seating spaces and the arms can be folded back or otherwise put out of use, the arms shall be ignored in measuring the seat;

(d) no account shall be taken of—

(i) the driver's seat; or

(ii) any seats alongside the driver's seat, whether separate from or continuous with it, if the Secretary of State is satisfied that the use of those seats by members of the public will not be permitted during the currency of the licence applied for.

(3) In paragraph (2) *"driver's seat"* means—

(a) any separate seat occupied by the driver; or

(b) where no such seat is provided and the driver occupies a portion of a continuous seat, so much of that seat as extends from the right edge of the seat if the vehicle is steered from the right-hand side, or from the left edge of the seat if the vehicle is steered from the left-hand side, to a point 460 mm left or right, as the case may be, of the point on the seat directly behind the centre of the steering column.

Recovery vehicles: prescribed purposes

B55.70   45.—(1) The purposes specified in Part I of Schedule 7 are hereby prescribed for the purposes of paragraph 5(3)(e) of Schedule 1 to the 1994 Act (purposes for which a recovery vehicle may be used).

(2) The purposes specified in Part II of Schedule 7 are hereby prescribed for

the purposes of paragraph 5(4) of Schedule 1 to the 1994 Act (purposes to be disregarded in determining whether a vehicle is a recovery vehicle).

Admissibility of evidence from records

46.—(1) The matters specified in paragraph (2) are hereby prescribed for the purposes of section 52(1) of the 1994 Act (matters with respect to which statements in documents are admissible in evidence).   **B55.71**

(2) The matters are anything relating to—

    (a) an application for—

        (i) a vehicle licence;

        (ii) a trade licence;

        (iii) a repayment of vehicle excise duty under section 19 of the 1994 Act (surrender of licences); or

        (iv) the recovery of overpaid vehicle excise duty;

    (b) a vehicle licence, trade licence, nil licence, registration document or registration mark;

    (c) a trade plate;

    (d) the recovery of underpaid vehicle excise duty;

    (e) the conviction of any person for an offence under the 1994 Act or its predecessor legislation;

    (f) the exemption of a vehicle from vehicle excise duty;

    (g) the liability of the person by whom a vehicle is kept to pay any sum in accordance with section 30 of the 1994 Act;

    (h) the immobilisation, removal or disposal of a vehicle pursuant to regulations made under Schedule 2A to the 1994 Act.

Regulations prescribed under section 59(2) of the 1994 Act

47. *[Omitted.]*   **B55.72**

Regulation 2   SCHEDULE 1

REGULATIONS REVOKED

[Omitted.]   **B55.73**

Regulation 5   SCHEDULE 2

REDUCED POLLUTION CERTIFICATES AND THE REDUCED POLLUTION REQUIREMENTS

[Omitted.]   **B55.74**

Regulation 15(3)   SCHEDULE 3

ISSUE OF NEW REGISTRATION DOCUMENT

Duty of the Secretary of State

1. Where this Schedule has effect, before issuing a new registration document for the relevant vehicle, the Secretary of State—   **B55.75**

    (a) shall require the keeper of the relevant vehicle to produce the vehicle for examination by a person authorised by the Secretary of State at a time and place fixed by the Secretary of State and notified to the keeper; and

(b) may require the keeper to provide such other evidence as he may specify,

for the purpose of ascertaining whether the relevant vehicle is the registered vehicle concerned.

Examination of vehicle

B55.76   **2.** A person authorised by the Secretary of State to conduct an examination under paragraph 1(a) may refuse to conduct the examination if—

(a) the Secretary of State has not received an application form completed and signed by or on behalf of the keeper and containing such information as the Secretary of State may specify;

(b) the vehicle is not presented at the time and place appointed for the examination;

(c) the prescribed fee has not been paid;

(d) the person presenting the vehicle is not willing, to the extent necessary for the purpose of properly carrying out the examination,—

    (i) to give the person authorised to conduct the examination access to the engine and the fuel and exhaust systems,

    (ii) to operate the controls of the vehicle, or

    (iii) generally to co-operate with that person;

(e) the vehicle is obviously unroadworthy;

(f) the vehicle is in so dangerous or dirty a condition that the examination cannot be carried out safely and properly;

(g) the vehicle has insufficient fuel or oil in it for the examination to be carried out; or

(h) the vehicle's engine has failed electrically or mechanically.

Determination of the Secretary of State

B55.77   **3.**—(1) The Secretary of State, having considered the report of the person who conducted any examination under paragraph 1(a) and the evidence (if any) provided under paragraph 1(b), shall give notice of his decision as to whether or not he is satisfied that the vehicle is the relevant vehicle.

(2) The Secretary of State's notification of a decision that he is not so satisfied shall state—

(a) the reasons for his decision;

(b) that the keeper of the vehicle may appeal against the decision on the ground that the reasons given are insufficient or that there has been an error in the conduct of the examination or the consideration of evidence;

(c) the name and address of the person to whom an appeal against the decision may be made; and

(d) that notice of the appeal stating the grounds on which it is made must be received by that person before the last day of the period of 28 days beginning with the day on which notification of the decision is sent or such later date as the Secretary of State may determine.

Appeals

B55.78   **4.**—(1) Where an appeal is received in accordance with paragraph 3(2)(d), the Secretary of State shall authorise a person (*"the appeal officer"*) to determine the appeal on his behalf.

(2) The appeal officer shall be an individual who has not previously examined the relevant vehicle or been involved in any other way in the taking of the decision appealed against.

(3) The appeal officer shall require the appellant to produce the relevant vehicle for re-examination by him at a specified time and place and may also require him—

(a) to produce the evidence provided under paragraph 1(b) for re-consideration; or

(b) to provide such other evidence as the appeal officer may specify.

(4) Paragraph 2 applies to a re-examination of the relevant vehicle on appeal.

(5) The appeal officer, having examined the relevant vehicle and considered the evidence (if any) provided to him, shall notify the appellant of his decision as to whether or not he is satisfied that the relevant vehicle is the registered vehicle.

Certificates

5. Where the Secretary of State is satisfied, whether on appeal or otherwise, that the relevant vehicle is the registered vehicle he shall issue a certificate to that effect and may at any time issue a replacement certificate to correct an error in a certificate.   **B55.79**

Giving of notices and certificates

6. A notice or certificate under this Schedule may be given or issued by—   **B55.80**

(a) handing it over to the person producing the relevant vehicle for examination or re-examination; or

(b) by sending it by pre-paid ordinary post addressed to the person who signed the application referred to in paragraph 2(a), and

shall be taken to have been given or issued at the time it was handed over or, as the case may be, put in the post.

The prescribed fee

7. *[Omitted.]*   **B55.81**

Refund of the prescribed fee

8. *[Omitted.]*   **B55.82**

| **Regulation 26** | SCHEDULE 4 |

STATUTORY OFF-ROAD NOTIFICATION

PART I

GENERAL

Interpretation of Schedule

1.—(1) In this Schedule—   **B55.83**

"authorised insurer" has the meaning given in section 145(5) of the 1988 Act;

"personal credit agreement" has the meaning given in section 8(1) of the Consumer Credit Act 1974;

"relevant vehicle" means a vehicle which is either a relevant GB vehicle or a relevant NI vehicle;

"the required declaration" means a declaration made to the Secretary of State by a person surrendering a vehicle licence or the keeper of a relevant vehicle to the effect that (except for use under a trade licence) he does not for the time being intend to use or keep the vehicle on a public road and will not use or keep the vehicle on a public road without first taking out a vehicle licence (or if appropriate a nil licence) for the vehicle;

"the required particulars" in relation to a relevant vehicle are particulars of—

(a) the registration mark of the vehicle;

(b) the make and model of the vehicle; and

(c) the address of the premises at which the vehicle is kept; and

"unlicensed vehicle" means a relevant vehicle for which no vehicle licence is for the time being in force and *"unlicensed"* shall be construed accordingly.

(2) In this Schedule, subject to sub-paragraph (3),—

(a) a *"relevant GB vehicle"* means a vehicle which is registered in the GB records and kept in Great Britain, but does not include a vehicle in relation to which each of the following conditions is satisfied—

  (i) neither a vehicle licence nor a nil licence was in force for the vehicle on 31st January 1998;

  (ii) such a licence has not been taken out for the vehicle for a period starting after that date; and

  (iii) the vehicle has not been used or kept on a public road on or after that date; and

(b) a *"relevant NI vehicle"* means a vehicle which is registered in the NI records and kept in Northern Ireland, but does not include a vehicle in relation to which each of the following conditions is satisfied—

  (i) neither a vehicle licence nor a nil licence was in force for the vehicle on 30th November 2002;

  (ii) such a licence has not been taken out for the vehicle for a period starting after that date; and

  (iii) the vehicle has not been used or kept on a public road on or after that date.

(3) A vehicle which is an exempt vehicle falling within a description specified in paragraph 2, 2A, 3, 23 or 24 of Schedule 2 to the 1994 Act is neither a relevant GB nor a relevant NI vehicle.

(4) For the purposes of this Schedule a person is a *"relevant vehicle trader"* in relation to a vehicle if he falls within a description mentioned in column (2) of an item in the Table below and the vehicle falls within a description mentioned in column (3) of that item.

TABLE

(1) Item	(2) Descriptions of person	(3) Descriptions of vehicle
1.	The holder of a trade licence	A vehicle temporarily in his possession in the course of the business by virtue of which he is a person eligible to hold such a licence
2.	An auctioneer of vehicles	A vehicle temporarily in his possession in the course of his business as such an auctioneer
3.	A motor dealer	A vehicle temporarily in his possession in the course of his business as a motor dealer
4.	A person who carries on business as a dismantler of vehicles	A vehicle temporarily in his possession in the course of that business
5.	An authorised insurer	A vehicle temporarily in his possession in consequence of settling a claim under a policy of insurance which related to the vehicle
6.	The holder of a licence under Part II of the Consumer Credit Act 1974 [*sic*] [*not reproduced in this work*]	A vehicle temporarily in his possession under an order for the repossession of the vehicle made in pursuance of a personal credit agreement relating to the vehicle

B55.84   *[The reference to Pt II of the Consumer Credit Act 1974 in item 6 of the table would appear in error. The reference should be to Pt III.]*

The term "personal credit agreement" is defined in the Consumer Credit Act 1974 s.8(1), as "an agreement between an individual ('the debtor') and any other person ('the creditor') by which the creditor provides the debtor with credit of any amount".

Contravention of Sch.4, paras 1–10 is a summary offence for which the offender is liable to a fine on level 3 of the standard scale under the Vehicle Excise and Registration Act 1994 s.59(2)(a).]

Manner in which declaration is to be made and particulars furnished

2.—(1) For the purposes of this Schedule the required declaration may be made and the required particulars furnished in such way as the Secretary of State may accept including—   **B55.85**

    (a) in writing on a form specified by the Secretary of State;

    (b) orally by telephone to a person authorised by the Secretary of State; or

    (c) by electronic means in a form specified by the Secretary of State.

(2) A person furnishing the required particulars need not provide particulars of the address at which the vehicle is kept unless required to do so—

    (a) in a case falling within sub-paragraph (1)(a) or (c), by the form on which those particulars are furnished; or

    (b) in a case falling within sub-paragraph (1)(b), by the person to whom they are furnished.

PART II

VEHICLES REGISTERED IN THE GB RECORDS AND KEPT IN GREAT BRITAIN

Surrender of a vehicle licence—relevant GB vehicle

3.—(1) When the holder of a vehicle licence for a relevant GB vehicle surrenders it under section 10(2) of the 1994 Act, he shall deliver to the Secretary of State the required declaration and the required particulars in relation to that vehicle.   **B55.86**

(2) Paragraph (1) does not apply where a relevant GB vehicle is no longer kept by the holder of the licence or the holder is a relevant vehicle trader in relation to that vehicle.

Expiry of vehicle licence or nil licence—relevant GB vehicle

4. Where a vehicle licence or nil licence ceases to be in force for a relevant GB vehicle by reason of the expiration of the period for which the licence was granted and a vehicle licence or nil licence for the vehicle is not taken out so as to run from the expiration of that period, the keeper of the vehicle shall deliver to the Secretary of State the required declaration and the required particulars in relation to the vehicle—   **B55.87**

    (a) if he is a relevant vehicle trader, not later than the end of the period of three months starting with the day following the expired period; or

    (b) in any other case, not later than that day.

Person keeping an unlicensed vehicle—relevant GB vehicle

5.—(1) Subject to sub-paragraph (2) this paragraph applies to a person who is the keeper of a relevant GB vehicle which is unlicensed and as respects which there has elapsed a period of 12 months (*"the unlicensed period"*) —   **B55.88**

    (a) throughout which the vehicle has been kept in Great Britain unlicensed; and

    (b) within which neither the required declaration nor the required particulars have been delivered to the Secretary of State in relation to the vehicle.

(2) For the purposes of sub-paragraph (1)(a), where a vehicle licence has been surrendered under section 10(2) of the 1994 Act, the vehicle to which it relates shall be taken to be unlicensed from the first day of the month in which the licence was surrendered.

(3) A person to whom this paragraph applies shall, unless a vehicle licence or a nil licence has been taken out so as to run from the end of the unlicensed period, deliver the required declaration and the required particulars to the Secretary of State in relation to the relevant GB vehicle not later than the day following the end of that period.

Change of keeper of unlicensed vehicle—relevant GB vehicle

B55.89   6. On a change in the keeper of a relevant GB vehicle which is unlicensed, unless a vehicle licence or nil licence is taken out for the vehicle, the new keeper shall deliver to the Secretary of State the required declaration and the required particulars in relation to the vehicle—

    (a) if he is a relevant vehicle trader, not later than the end of the period of three months beginning with the day following the day on which the change of keeper occurs; or

    (b) in any other case, not later than the day following the day on which the change of keeper occurs.

Part III

Vehicles Registered in the NI Records and kept in Northern Ireland

Surrender of a vehicle licence—relevant NI vehicle

B55.90   7.—(1) When after 30th November 2002 the holder of a vehicle licence for a relevant NI vehicle surrenders it under section 10(2) of the 1994 Act, he shall deliver to the Secretary of State the required declaration and the required particulars in relation to that vehicle.

(2) Paragraph (1) does not apply where a relevant NI vehicle is no longer kept by the holder of the licence or the holder is a relevant trader in relation to that vehicle.

Expiry of vehicle licence or nil licence—relevant NI vehicle

B55.91   8. Where, on or after 30th November 2002, a vehicle licence or nil licence ceases to be in force for a relevant NI vehicle by reason of the expiration of the period for which the licence was granted and a vehicle licence or nil licence for the vehicle is not taken out so as to run from the expiration of that period, the keeper of the vehicle shall deliver to the Secretary of State the required declaration and the required particulars in relation to the vehicle—

    (a) if he is a relevant vehicle trader, not later than the end of the period of three months starting with the day following the expired period; or

    (b) in any other case, not later than that day.

Person keeping an unlicensed vehicle—relevant NI vehicle

B55.92   9.—(1) Subject to sub-paragraph (2), this paragraph applies to a person who, at any time after 30th November 2003, is the keeper of a relevant NI vehicle which is unlicensed and as respects which there has elapsed a period of 12 months (*"the unlicensed period"*) —

    (a) throughout which the vehicle has been kept in Northern Ireland unlicensed; and

    (b) within which neither the required declaration nor the required particulars have been delivered to the Secretary of State in relation to the vehicle.

(2) For the purposes of sub-paragraph (1)(a), where a vehicle licence has been surrendered under section 10(2) of the 1994 Act, the vehicle to which it relates shall be taken to be unlicensed from the first day of the month on which the licence was surrendered.

(3) A person to whom this paragraph applies shall, unless a vehicle licence or a nil licence has been taken out so as to run from the end of the unlicensed period, deliver the required declaration and the required particulars to the Secretary of State in relation to the NI relevant vehicle not later than the day following the end of that period.

Change of keeper of unlicensed vehicle—relevant NI vehicle

B55.93   10. On a change occurring after 30th November 2002 in the keeper of a relevant NI vehicle which is unlicensed, unless a vehicle licence or nil licence is taken out for the vehicle, the new keeper shall deliver to the Secretary of State the required declaration and the required particulars in relation to the vehicle—

(a) if he is a relevant vehicle trader, not later than the end of the period of three months beginning with the day following the day on which the change of keeper occurs; or

(b) in any other case, not later than the day following the day on which the change of keeper occurs.

Regulation 34   SCHEDULE 5

EXEMPT VEHICLES: VEHICLES IMPORTED BY MEMBERS OF FOREIGN ARMED FORCES AND OTHERS

Scope of exemption

1.—(1) A vehicle is an exempt vehicle for the period specified in paragraph 2 if it was **B55.94** imported into Great Britain by or on behalf of—

(a) a member of a visiting force;

(b) a member of a headquarters or organisation; or

(c) a dependant of a person falling within paragraph (a) or (b),

and there is produced to the Secretary of State evidence that the person importing the vehicle has not been required to pay any tax or duty chargeable in respect of its importation.

(2) In sub-paragraph (1)—

(a) *"dependant"* means a member of the household of a person falling within sub-paragraph (1)(a) or (b) who is his spouse or any other person wholly or mainly maintained by him or in his custody, charge or care;

(b) *"member of a visiting force"* means a person for the time being appointed to serve with, or a member of the civilian component of, any body, contingent or detachment of the forces of any country specified in paragraph 3, which is for the time being present in the United Kingdom on the invitation of her Majesty's Government;

(c) *"member of a headquarters or organisation"* means a member of the military forces of any country, except the United Kingdom, who is for the time being appointed to serve in the United Kingdom under the orders of any headquarters or organisation specified in paragraph 4 and includes a person for the time being recognised by the Secretary of State as a civilian member of such a headquarters or organisation.

Period of exemption

2.—(1) The period during which a vehicle is an exempt vehicle by virtue of this Schedule shall be the period of 12 months beginning with the day on which a nil licence is issued in respect of that vehicle.   **B55.95**

(2) The exemption shall however cease to apply if, at any time during the period prescribed by sub-paragraph (1), the importer of the vehicle becomes liable to pay any duty or tax chargeable in respect of its importation.

[List of countries

3. The countries referred to in paragraph 1(2)(b) are—   **B55.96**

Albania	Austria
Antigua and Barbuda	Azerbaijan
Armenia	The Bahamas
Australia	Bangladesh

Barbados	Namibia
Belarus	Nauru
Belgium	The Netherlands
Belize	New Zealand
Botswana	Nigeria
Brunei	Norway
Bulgaria	Pakistan
Canada	Papua New Guinea
The Republic of	Poland
Cyprus	Portugal
The Czech Republic	Romania
Denmark	Russia
Dominica	Saint Christopher
Estonia	and Nevis
Fiji	Saint Lucia
Finland	Saint Vincent and
France	the Grenadines
The Gambia	Samoa
Georgia	Seychelles
Germany	Sierra Leone
Ghana	Singapore
Greece	Slovakia
Grenada	Slovenia
Guyana	Solomon Islands
Hungary	South Africa
India	Spain
Italy	Sri Lanka
Jamaica	Swaziland
Kazakhstan	Sweden
Kenya	Switzerland
Kiribati	Tanzania
Kyrgyzstan	Tonga
Latvia	Trinidad and Tobago
Lesotho	Turkey
Lithuania	Turkmenistan
Luxembourg	Tuvalu
The Former	Uganda
Yugoslav Republic	Ukraine
of Macedonia	United States of
Malawi	America
Malaysia	Uzbekistan
Maldives	Vanuatu
Malta	Zambia
Mauritius	Zimbabwe]
Moldova	

B55.97   *[Paragraph 3 of Sch.5 is printed as substituted by SI 2003/2154.]*

[**List of headquarters and organisations**

4. The headquarters and organisations referred to in paragraph 1(2)(c) are—   **B55.98**

    The Headquarters of the Supreme Allied Commander Atlantic (SACLANT)

    The Supreme Headquarters Allied Powers Europe (SHAPE)

    Headquarters Allied Forces North Western Europe (AFNORTHWEST)

    Headquarters Allied Air Forces North Western Europe (AIRNORTHWEST)

    Headquarters Allied Naval Forces North Western Europe (NAVNORTHWEST)

    Headquarters Maritime Air Forces North West (MARAIRNORTHWEST)

    Headquarters Submarine Forces North West (SUBNORTHWEST)

    Headquarters Allied Forces Eastern Atlantic Area (EASTLANT)

    Headquarters Maritime Air Forces Eastern Atlantic Area (MARAIREASTLANT)

    Headquarters Submarine Forces Eastern Atlantic Area (SUBEASTLANT)

    Headquarters United Kingdom—Netherlands Amphibious Force (UKNLAF)

    Headquarters United Kingdom—Netherlands Landing Force (UKNLLF)

    The NATO Airborne Early Warning Force Headquarters and the NATO E-3A
      Component]

    [Paragraph 4 of Sch.5 is printed as substituted by SI 2003/2154.]   **B55.99**

Regulations 37 and 38   SCHEDULE 6

TRADE LICENCES

PART I

CONDITIONS SUBJECT TO WHICH TRADE LICENCES ARE TO BE ISSUED

1. If the holder of a trade licence changes his name, the name of his business or his busi-   **B55.100**
ness address he shall forthwith—

    (a) notify the change and the new name or address to the Secretary of State; and

    (b) send the licence to the Secretary of State for any necessary amendment.

2. The holder of the licence shall not, and shall not permit any person to, alter, deface,   **B55.101**
mutilate or add anything to a trade plate.

3. The holder of the licence shall not, and shall not permit any person to, exhibit on any   **B55.102**
vehicle any trade licence or trade plate—

    (a) which has been altered, defaced multilated or added to;

    (b) upon which the figures or particulars have become illegible; or

    (c) the colour of which has altered whether by fading or otherwise.

4. The holder of the licence shall not, and shall not permit any person to, exhibit on any   **B55.103**
vehicle anything which could be mistaken for a trade plate.

5. The holder of the licence shall not permit any person to display the trade licence or   **B55.104**
any trade plates on a vehicle except a vehicle which that person is using for the purposes
of the holder under the licence.

6. The holder of the licence shall not, and shall not permit any person, to display the   **B55.105**
trade licence or any trade plates on any vehicle unless—

    (a) that vehicle is within the classes of vehicle specified in section 11(2) of the 1994
      Act (if the holder is a motor trader who is a manufacturer of vehicles), 11(3) (if the
      holder is any other motor trader) or 11(4) (if the holder is a vehicle tester); and

    (b) the vehicle is being used for one or more of the prescribed purposes for which the
      holder may use the vehicle in accordance with regulation 36 and this Schedule.

7. The holder of the licence shall not display any trade plate on a vehicle used under the   **B55.106**
licence unless that trade plate shows the general registration mark assigned to the holder in
respect of that licence.

Part II

General

Interpretation

B55.107   8. Where a vehicle is so constructed that a semi-trailer may by partial superimposition be attached to it in such a manner as to cause a substantial part of the weight of the semi-trailer to be borne by the vehicle, the vehicle and the semi-trailer shall be taken, for the purposes of this Part of this Schedule to constitute a single vehicle.

B55.108   9. The purposes prescribed by this Part of this Schedule as purposes for which the holder of a trade licence may use a vehicle on a public road by virtue of that licence—

(a) do not include the carrying of any person on the vehicle or any trailer drawn by it except a person carried in connection with such purposes; and

(b) are without prejudice to the provisions of subsections (4) to (6) of section 11 of the 1994 Act which specify the classes of vehicle which a trade licence is for, in the relation respectively to a motor trader who is a manufacturer of vehicles, any other motor trader and a vehicle tester.

Motor traders

Purposes for which a motor trader may use a vehicle by virtue of a trade licence

B55.109   10. The purposes for which the holder of a trade licence who is a motor trader may use a vehicle (other than a vehicle to which paragraph 14 applies) on a public road by virtue of that licence are purposes which meet each of the following requirements—

(a) they are business purposes;

(b) they are paragraph 12 purposes; and

(c) they are purposes that do not include the conveyance of goods or burden of any description except specified loads.

Business purposes

B55.110   11. A vehicle is used for *"business purposes"* if it is used for purposes connected with the motor trader's business—

(a) as a manufacturer or repairer of or dealer in vehicles,

(b) as a manufacturer or repairer of or dealer in trailers carried on in conjunction with his business as a motor trader,

(c) of modifying vehicles (whether by the fitting of accessories or otherwise); or

(d) of valeting vehicles.

Paragraph 12 purposes

B55.111   12. A vehicle is used for *" paragraph 12 purposes"* if it is used for any of the following purposes—

(a) for its test or trial or the test or trial of its accessories or equipment, in either case in the ordinary course of construction, modification or repair or after completion;

(b) for proceeding to or from a public weighbridge for ascertaining its weight or to or from any place for its registration or inspection by a person acting on behalf of the Secretary of State;

(c) for its test or trial for the benefit of a prospective purchaser, for proceeding at the instance of a prospective purchaser to any place for the purpose of such test or trial, or for returning after such test or trial;

(d) for its test or trial for the benefit of a person interested in promoting publicity in regard to it, for proceeding at the instance of such a person to any place for the purpose of such test or trial, or for returning after such test or trial;

(e) for delivering it to the place where the purchaser intends to keep it;

(f) for demonstrating its operation or the operation of its accessories or equipment when it is being handed over to the purchaser;

(g) for delivering it from one part of the licence holder's premises to another part of his premises, or for delivering it from his premises to premises of, or between parts of premises of, another manufacturer or repairer of or dealer in vehicles or removing it from the premises of another manufacturer or repairer of or dealer in vehicles direct to his own premises;

(h) for proceeding to or returning from a workshop in which a body or a special type of equipment or accessory is to be or has been fitted to it or in which it is to be or has been painted, valeted or repaired;

(i) for proceeding from the premises of a manufacturer or repairer of or dealer in vehicles to a place from which it is to be transported by train, ship or aircraft or for proceeding to the premises of such a manufacturer, repairer or dealer from a place to which it has been so transported;

(j) for proceeding to or returning from any garage, auction room or other place at which vehicles are usually stored or usually or periodically offered for sale and at which it is to be or has been stored or is to be or has been offered for sale as the case may be;

(k) for proceeding to or returning from a place where it is to be or has been inspected or tested; or

(l) for proceeding to a place where it is to be broken up or otherwise dismantled.

Specified loads

13.—(1) A specified load is one of the following kinds of load—   **B55.112**

(a) a test load;

(b) in the case of a vehicle which is being delivered or collected and is being used for a purpose falling within paragraph 12(f) to (k), a load which consists of another vehicle used or to be used for travel from or to the place of delivery or collection;

(c) a load which is built in as part of the vehicle or permanently attached to it;

(d) in the case of a vehicle which is being used for a purpose falling within paragraph 12(h), (i) or (j), a load which consists of a trailer or of parts, accessories or equipment designed to be fitted to the vehicle and of tools for fitting them.

(2) In paragraph (1) a *"test load"* means a load which—

(a) is carried by a vehicle being used for a purpose falling within paragraph 12(b), (d), (e) or (g);

(b) is carried solely for the purpose of testing or demonstrating the vehicle or any of its accessories or equipment; and

(c) is returned to the place of loading without its having been removed from the vehicle except—

(i) for the purpose of testing or demonstrating the vehicle or any of its accessories or equipment,

(ii) in the case of accident, or

(iii) where the load consists of water, fertiliser or refuse.

Manufacturers keeping vehicles for research and development

Vehicle kept by a motor trader for research and development in the course of his business as a manufacturer

14.—(1) This paragraph applies to a vehicle—   **B55.113**

(a) kept by a motor trader, being the holder of a trade licence who is a manufacturer of vehicles; and

(b) kept solely for the purposes of conducting research and development in the course of his business as such a manufacturer.

(2) The purposes for which such a person may, by virtue of the trade licence, use a vehicle to which this paragraph applies on a public road are the purposes of conducting research and development in the course of his business as a manufacturer of vehicles.

(3) Those purposes shall not be taken to include the conveyance of goods or burden of any description except—

(a) a load which is carried solely for the purpose of testing the vehicle or any of its accessories or equipment and which is returned to the place of loading without having been removed from the vehicle except for such purpose or in the case of accident; or

(b) any load built in as part of the vehicle or permanently attached to it.

Vehicle testers

Purposes for which a vehicle tester may use a vehicle by virtue of a trade licence

B55.114   **15.**—(1) Subject to sub-paragraph (2) the purposes for which the holder of a trade licence who is a vehicle tester may use a vehicle on a public road by virtue of that licence are the purposes of testing it or any trailer drawn by it or any of the accessories or equipment on the vehicle or trailer in the course of the business of the holder of the trade licence as a vehicle tester.

(2) The purposes prescribed by sub-paragraph (1) do not include the conveyance of goods or any other burden of any description on the vehicle except—

(a) a load which is carried solely for the purpose of testing or demonstrating the vehicle or any of its accessories or equipment and is returned to the place of loading without having been removed from the vehicle except for that purpose or in the case of accident, or

(b) a load which is built in as part of the vehicle or permanently attached to it.

Regulation 45   SCHEDULE 7

RECOVERY VEHICLES: PRESCRIBED PURPOSES

PART I

PURPOSES PRESCRIBED FOR THE PURPOSES OF PARAGRAPH 5(3)(E) OF SCHEDULE 1 TO THE 1994 ACT

B55.115   **1.** Carrying any person who, immediately before the vehicle became disabled was the driver of, or a passenger in that vehicle, together with his personal effects, from the premises at which the vehicle is to be repaired or scrapped to his original intended destination.

B55.116   **2.**—(1) At the request of a constable or a local authority empowered by or under statute to remove a vehicle from a road, removing such a vehicle to a place nominated by the constable or local authority.

(2) In sub-paragraph (1) *"road"* has the meaning given—

(a) in relation to England, Scotland or Wales by section 192 of the 1988 Act; and

(b) in relation to Northern Ireland by Article 2 of the Road Traffic (Northern Ireland) Order 1995.

B55.117   **3.** Proceeding to a place at which the vehicle will be available for use for a purpose specified in paragraph 5(3)(a) or (b) of Schedule 1 to the 1994 Act and remaining temporarily at such a place so as to be available for such use.

B55.118   **4.** Proceeding from—

(a) a place where the vehicle has remained temporarily so as to be available for such use;

(b) a place where the vehicle has recovered a disabled vehicle; or

(c) such premises as are mentioned in paragraph 5(3)(b) or (c) of Schedule 1 to the 1994 Act.

Part II

Purposes Prescribed for the Purposes of Paragraph 5(4)(c) of Schedule 1 to the 1994 Act

5. Repairing a disabled vehicle at the place where it became disabled or to which it has been moved in the interests of safety after becoming disabled.   **B55.119**

6. Drawing or carrying a single trailer if another vehicle had become disabled whilst drawing or carrying it.   **B55.120**

Regulation 47   SCHEDULE 8

Regulations to which Section 59(2)(a) of the 1994 Act Applies

[Omitted.]   **B55.121**

The Police (Retention and Disposal of Motor Vehicles) Regulations 2002

(SI 2002/3049)

B56.01 *[The text of these regulations is printed as amended by:*

> *the Police (Retention and Disposal of Motor Vehicles) (Amendment) Regulations (SI 2005/2702) (November 1, 2005); and*

> *the Police (Retention and Disposal of Motor Vehicles) (Amendment) Regulations 2008 (SI 2008/2096) (October 1, 2008).*

The amending regulations are referred to in the notes to the principal regulations only by their years and numbers. The dates referred to above are the dates on which the amending regulations came into force.

The Arrangement of regulations set out below has been added editorially and does not form part of the text of the regulations.]

ARRANGEMENT OF REGULATIONS

Regulation

Citation and commencement

B56.02   **1.** *[Omitted.]*

Interpretation

B56.03   **2.** In these Regulations—

> *"the 2002 Act"* means the Police Reform Act 2002 [*c.30*];

> *"the authority"* means a constable or such other person authorised by the chief officer under regulation 3(1);

> *"GB registration mark"* means a registration mark issued in relation to a vehicle under the Vehicle Excise and Registration Act 1994 [*q.v.*];

> [*"laden"* means that the vehicle is carrying a load;]

> [*"load"* means anything other than—

>> (a) the body and all parts of the vehicle which are necessary to or ordinarily used with the vehicle when working on a road;

>> (b) any water, fuel or accumulators used for the purpose of the supply of power for the propulsion of the vehicle;

(c) the driver, any passengers and their personal effects;

(d) a crane, works truck as defined in regulation 3(2) of the Road Vehicles (Construction and Use) Regulations 1986, or other special appliance or apparatus which is a permanent or essentially permanent fixture of the vehicle; and

(e) any containers or other equipment intended or adapted for the purpose of holding or carrying a load by the vehicle;]

[*"MAM"* means maximum authorised mass as defined in regulation 3(1) of the Motor Vehicles (Driving Licences) Regulations 1999;]

[*"off road"* means that no part of the vehicle is in contact with the road;]

[*"on road"* means that any part of the vehicle is in contact with the road;]

"owner" includes—

(a) the person by whom, according to the records maintained by the Secretary of State in connection with any functions exercisable by him by virtue of the Vehicle Excise and Registration Act 1994, the vehicle is kept and used;

(b) in relation to a vehicle which is the subject of a hiring agreement or a hire-purchase agreement, the person entitled to possession of the vehicle under the agreement;

"relevant motor vehicle" means a motor vehicle which has been seized and removed under section 59(3)(b) of the 2002 Act [*q.v.*];

[*"road"* means any length of highway or of any other road to which the public has access, and includes bridges over which a road passes;]

"seizure notice" means a notice complying with regulation 4;

"specified information", in relation to a vehicle, means such of the following information as can be or could have been ascertained from an inspection of the vehicle, or has been ascertained from any other source, that is to say—

(a) in the case of a vehicle which carries a GB registration mark, or a mark indicating registration in a place outside Great Britain, particulars of that mark; and

(b) the make of the vehicle.

[*"substantially damaged"* means such damage to a vehicle that in the reasonable opinion of a constable it cannot be driven safely on the road;]

[*"two wheeled vehicle"* means a mechanically propelled vehicle constructed or adapted to have two wheels or less and the MAM of which does not exceed 3.5 tonnes;]

[*"unladen"* means that the vehicle is not carrying a load;]

[*"working days"* shall be taken to exclude Saturdays, Sundays, Christmas Day, Good Friday and any day which, under the Banking and Financial Dealings Act 1971 is a bank holiday in England and Wales.]

[Regulation 2 is printed as amended by SI 2005/2702; SI 2008/2096.]   **B56.04**

Retention and safe keeping of motor vehicles

3.—(1) A relevant motor vehicle shall be passed into and remain in the custody   **B56.05**

of a constable or other person authorised under this regulation by the chief officer of the police force for the area in which the vehicle was seized (*"the authority"*) until—

    (a) the authority permit it to be removed from their custody by a person appearing to them to be the owner of the vehicle; or

    (b) it has been disposed of under these Regulations.

(2) While the vehicle is in the custody of the authority, they shall be under a duty to take such steps as are reasonably necessary for its safe keeping.

Giving of seizure notice

B56.06   **4.**—(1) The authority shall, as soon as they are able after a relevant motor vehicle has been taken into their custody, take such steps as are [reasonably] practicable to give a seizure notice to the person who is or appears to be the owner of that vehicle, except where the vehicle has been released from their custody in accordance with these Regulations.

(2) A seizure notice required to be given under these Regulations shall comply with, and be given in accordance with, the following provisions of this regulation.

(3) A seizure notice shall, in respect of the vehicle to which it relates, contain the specified information and shall state—

    (a) the place where the vehicle was seized;

    (b) the place where it is now being kept;

    (c) that the person to whom the notice is directed is required to claim the vehicle from the authority on or before the date specified in the notice, being a date not less than [7 working days] from the day when the notice is given to him;

    (d) that unless the vehicle is claimed on or before that date the authority intend to dispose of it;

    (e) that, subject to regulation 5(3), charges are payable under these Regulations by the owner of the vehicle in respect of the removal and retention of the vehicle, and that the vehicle may be retained until such charges are paid.

(4) The seizure notice shall be given—

    (a) by delivering it to the person to whom it is directed;

    (b) by leaving it at his usual or last known address;

    (c) by sending it in by the registered post service, addressed to him at his usual or last known address; or

    (d) if the person is a body corporate, by delivering it to the secretary or clerk of the body at its registered or principal office, or sending it by the registered post service, addressed to the secretary or clerk of the body at that office.

B56.07   *[Regulation 4 is printed as amended by SI 2005/2702.]*

Release of vehicles

B56.08   **5.**—(1) Subject to the provisions of these Regulations, if, before a relevant motor vehicle is disposed of by an authority, a person satisfies the authority that he is the owner of that vehicle and pays to the authority such a charge in respect of its removal and retention as is provided for in regulation 6, the authority shall permit him to remove the vehicle from their custody.

(2) In determining whether it is satisfied that a person who claims to be the owner of a relevant motor vehicle is in fact the owner, an authority may consider such documentary evidence as that person may supply to them.

(3) A person who would otherwise be liable to pay a charge under paragraph (1) shall not be liable to pay if—

(a) the use by reference to which the vehicle was seized under section 59 of the 2002 Act was not a use by him; and

(b) he did not know of the use of the vehicle in the manner which led to its seizure, had not consented to its use in that manner and could not, by the taking of reasonable steps, have prevented its use in that manner.

Charges in relation to the removal and retention of a motor vehicle

6. *[Omitted.]*   **B56.09**

[Disposal of motor vehicles

7.—(1) Subject to paragraph (2), the authority may, in such manner as they   **B56.10**
think fit, dispose of the vehicle at any time if—

(a) the person appearing to be the owner of the vehicle to whom a seizure notice is given under regulation 4(1) fails to comply with any requirement in that seizure notice; or

(b) the authority were not able, having taken such steps as were reasonably practicable, to give a seizure notice to the person appearing to be the owner of the vehicle.

(2) The authorised person may not dispose of the vehicle under this regulation—

(a) during the period of 14 days starting with the date on which the vehicle was seized;

(b) if the period in sub-paragraph (a) has expired, until after the date specified in the seizure notice in accordance with regulation 4(3)(c); or

(c) if not otherwise covered by sub-paragraph (a) or (b), during the period of 7 working days starting with the date on which the vehicle is claimed under regulation 5.]

[Regulation 7 is printed as substituted by SI 2005/2702.]   **B56.11**

Payment of proceeds of sale to owner of vehicle

8.—(1) Where the authority dispose of a motor vehicle in pursuance of these   **B56.12**
Regulations by means of sale, they shall pay the net proceeds of sale to any person who, before the end of the period of one year beginning with the date on which the vehicle is sold, satisfies the authority that at the time of the sale he was the owner of the vehicle.

(2) If it appears to the authority that more than one person is the owner of a particular vehicle, such one of them as the authority think fit shall be treated as its owner for the purposes of paragraph (1).

(3) In this regulation, *"the net proceeds of sale"* means any sum by which the proceeds of sale exceed the aggregate of such sums as may be payable under these Regulations in respect of the removal and retention of the vehicle.

The Traffic Signs Regulations and General Directions 2002

(SI 2002/3113)

[The Department of Transport published DfT Circular 02/2003, The Traffic **B57.01**
Signs Regulations and General Directions (TSRGD) 2002 on January 31, 2003.
The Circular should be read in conjunction with these regulations and is obtainable from the TSO (ISBN 0117536470).

The text of these regulations and general directions has been amended by:

> *the Traffic Signs (Amendment) General Directions 2003 (SI 2003/393) (March 1, 2003);*

> *the Communications Act 2003 (Consequential Amendments) Order 2003 (SI 2003/2155) (September 17, 2003);*

> *the Traffic Signs (Amendment) General Directions 2004 (SI 2004/1275) (May 27, 2004);*

> *the Fire and Rescue Services Act 2004 (Consequential Amendments) (England) Order 2004 (SI 2004/3168) (December 30, 2004);*

> *the Traffic Signs (Amendment) Regulations and General Directions 2005 (SI 2005/1670) (July 27, 2005);*

> *the Fire and Rescue Services Act 2004 (Consequential Amendments) (Wales) Order 2005 (SI 2005/2929) (October 25, 2005);*

> *the Serious Organised Crime and Police Act 2005 (Consequential and Supplementary Amendments to Secondary Legislation) Order 2006 (SI 2006/594) (April 1, 2006);*

> *the Traffic Signs (Amendment) Regulations 2006 (SI 2006/2083) (August 21, 2006); and*

> *the Traffic Signs (Amendment) Regulations and General Directions 2008 (SI 2008/2177) (September 15, 2008).*

The amending instruments are referred to in the notes to the principal general regulations and directions only by their years and numbers. The dates referred to above are the dates on which the amending instruments came into force.]

ARRANGEMENT OF ARTICLES

PART I
B57.02

THE TRAFFIC SIGNS REGULATIONS 2002
SECTION 1
Preliminary

SECTION 6

Miscellaneous traffic signs

SCHEDULES TO THE REGULATIONS

Schedule

*   *   *

PART II

THE TRAFFIC SIGNS GENERAL DIRECTIONS 2002

Direction

PART I

THE TRAFFIC SIGNS REGULATIONS 2002

SECTION 1

Preliminary

Citation and commencement

B57.03   **1.** This Part of this Instrument—

    (a) may be cited—

        (i) as the Traffic Signs Regulations 2002, and

        (ii) together with Part II below, as the Traffic Signs Regulations and General Directions 2002; and

(b) shall come into force on 31st January 2003.

Revocations

2. The Traffic Signs Regulations 1994 [*SI 1994/1519, Pt I*] and the Traffic   **B57.04**
Signs (Amendment) Regulations 1995 [*SI 1995/3107, Pt I*] are hereby revoked.

Savings

3.—(1) Subject to paragraph (2), any traffic sign which immediately before the   **B57.05**
coming into force of these Regulations was placed on or near a road shall be
treated as prescribed by these Regulations, notwithstanding any provisions of
these Regulations to the contrary, provided that—

    (a) it is a sign prescribed, or to be treated as if prescribed, by the 1981
        Regulations or by the 1994 Regulations; and

    (b) it continues to comply with those Regulations,

as if those Regulations had not been revoked.

  (2) Paragraph (1) shall cease to have effect—

    (a) on 1st January 2005 in relation to the signs shown in each of the fol-
        lowing diagrams—

        (i) in the Traffic Signs Regulations 1957 [*SR & O 1957/13, as
            amended*] , diagrams 403 to 405, 412A to 418, 422 to 433, 435 to
            459, 468 to 472, and 474 to 495;

        (ii) in the Traffic Signs Regulations 1964 [*SI 1964/1857, as
            amended*], diagrams 742, 746, 837 and 838;

        (iii) in the 1981 Regulations [*SI 1981/859*], diagrams 626.1, 627,
            628.1, 641, 642.1, 649.2, 653, 734.7, 739.3, 742.1, 742.2, 742.3,
            742.4, 742.5, 742.6, 747, 748, 749, 750, 751, 752, 752.1, 753,
            753.1, 758, 759, 837.1, 838.1 and 905;

        (iv) in the 1994 Regulations, diagrams 618.1 (when varied to include
            the legend "buses and coaches"), 784, 818.1 (when varied to
            show a distance greater than 2 miles), 820 (when varied to
            include the legend "buses and coaches"), 954.1 and 1028.2 (when
            varied to "COACHES"); and

        (v) in the 1994 Regulations, diagrams 958, 959 and 960, in each
            case when varied to include the legend "& coaches";

    (b) on 1st January 2007 in relation to the signs shown in diagrams 622.1A
        (when varied to show "17T"), 626.2 (when displaying "17T" or
        "25T"), 1025 and 1025.2 in the 1994 Regulations;

    (c) on 1st January 2010 in relation to—

        (i) the signals prescribed by regulation 31(3) of the 1981 Regula-
            tions;

        (ii) the sign shown in diagram 661 in the 1994 Regulations; and

        (iii) the signs shown in diagrams 618.1, 618.2, 618.3, 618.3A and
            620 in the 1994 Regulations when varied to include the orange
            badge symbol shown in diagram 661 in those Regulations;

    (d) on 1st January 2015 in relation to—

        (i) the signs shown in diagrams 728.1, 728.2, 729, 729.1, 729.2,

729.3, 730, 730.1, 732, 732.1, 732.2, 733, 733.1, 734.1, 734.2, 734.3, 734.4, 734.5, 734.6, 734.8, 734.9, 734.10, 736, 736.1, 737.1, 760 and 761 in the 1981 Regulations; and

(ii) the signs shown in diagrams 2308, 2309, 2310, 2311, 2313, 2314, 2315, 2315.1 and 2919 of the 1994 Regulations.

(3) Subject to paragraph (4), portable light signals which do not comply with regulation 35 shall be treated as prescribed by these Regulations if and so long as—

(a) those signals are of the size, colour and type prescribed by regulation 32 of the 1994 Regulations; and

(b) those signals and any apparatus (including the content of all instructions stored in, or executable by them) used in connection with them are the subject of an approval given and for the time being in force under direction 49 of the Traffic Signs General Directions 1994 [*SI 1994/1519, Pt II*] .

(4) Paragraph (3) shall cease to have effect on 1st January 2015.

(5) Notwithstanding regulation 2, the 1994 Regulations shall be treated, in relation to a paragraph (6) sign, as remaining in force during the extension period.

(6) In paragraph (5)—

(a) *"the extension period"* means the period of 12 weeks beginning with the day on which these Regulations come into force; and

(b) *"a paragraph (6) sign"* is a sign which is of the size, colour and type shown in diagram 547.5, 547.6, 626.2, 629, 639.1A, 642.2, 643, 644, 661, 661.2, 661.3, 780, 780.1, 780.2, 784, 785, 832.10, 864, 872, 2010, 2206, 2207, 2308, 2309, 2919, 2920, 3001, 3001.1, 4002, 7002, 7003, 7007 or 7010 of the 1994 Regulations.

Interpretation—general

B57.06   4. In these Regulations unless the context otherwise requires—

"the 1984 Act" means the Road Traffic Regulation Act 1984 [*q.v.*];

"the 1988 Act" means the Road Traffic Act 1988 [*q.v.*];

"the 1981 Regulations" means the Traffic Signs Regulations 1981;

"the 1994 Regulations" means the Traffic Signs Regulations 1994;

"articulated vehicle" means a motor vehicle with a trailer so attached to it as to be partially superimposed upon it;

"automatic half-barrier level crossing" means a level crossing where barriers are installed to descend automatically across part of the road when a railway vehicle or tramcar approaches and the operation of the barriers is monitored remotely from the crossing;

"automatic barrier crossing (L)" means a level crossing where barriers are installed to descend automatically across part of the road when a railway vehicle or tramcar approaches and the driver of the railway vehicle or tramcar is required to monitor the operation of the barriers when the railway vehicle or tramcar is at or near the crossing;

"automatic open crossing (L)" means a level crossing without automatic barriers where light signals are so installed as to be operated

automatically by a railway vehicle or tramcar approaching the crossing and the driver of the railway vehicle or tramcar is required to monitor the operation of the light signals when the railway vehicle or tramcar is at or near the crossing;

"automatic open crossing (R)" means a level crossing without automatic barriers where light signals are so installed as to be operated automatically by a railway vehicle or tramcar approaching the crossing and the operation of the light signals is monitored remotely from the crossing;

"automatic level crossing" means an automatic half-barrier level crossing, an automatic barrier crossing (L), an automatic open crossing (L) or an automatic open crossing (R);

"bus lane" has the meaning given in regulation 23;

"central reservation" means —

    (a) any land between the carriageways of a road comprising two carriageways; or

    (b) any permanent work (other than a traffic island) in the carriageway of a road,

which separates the carriageway or, as the case may be, the part of the carriageway which is to be used by traffic moving in one direction from the carriageway or part of the carriageway which is to be used (whether at all times or at particular times only) by traffic moving in the other direction;

"contra-flow" means a part of a carriageway of a road where—

    (a) traffic is authorised to proceed in the opposite direction to the usual direction of traffic on that part; or

    (b) a specified class of traffic is authorised to proceed in the opposite direction to other traffic on that carriageway;

"controlled parking zone" means either—

    (a) an area—

        (i) in which, except where parking places have been provided, every road has been marked with one or more of the road markings shown in diagrams 1017, 1018.1, 1019 and 1020.1; and

        (ii) into which each entrance for vehicular traffic has been indicated by the sign shown in diagram 663 or 663.1; or

    (b) an area—

        (i) in which at least one of the signs shown in diagram 640.2A has been placed on each side of every road; and

        (ii) into which each entrance for vehicular traffic has been indicated by the sign shown in diagram 665;

"cycle lane" means a part of the carriageway of a road which—

    (a) starts with the marking shown in diagram 1009; and

    (b) is separated from the rest of the carriageway—

        (i) if it may not be used by vehicles other than pedal cycles, by the marking shown in diagram 1049; or

(ii) if it may be used by vehicles other than pedal cycles, by the marking shown in diagram 1004 or 1004.1;

"cycle track", in relation to England and Wales, has the same meaning as in the Highways Act 1980 [*q.v.*] and, in relation to Scotland …;

"dual carriageway road" means a road which comprises a central reservation and *"all-purpose dual carriageway road"* means a dual carriageway road which is not a motorway;

"EEA Agreement" means the Agreement on the European Economic Area signed at Oporto on 2nd May 1992 as adjusted by the Protocol signed at Brussels on 17th March 1993 [*O.J. No.L1, January 3, 1994, p.3; Cmnd. 2073 and Cmnd. 2183*] ;

"EEA Standard" means —

(a) a standard or code of practice of a national standards body or equivalent body of any EEA State;

(b) any international standard recognised for use as a standard or code of practice by any EEA State; or

(c) a technical specification recognised for use as a standard by a public authority of any EEA State,

and a reference to a *"corresponding EEA Standard"*, in relation to a British or European Standard, is a reference to an EEA Standard which requires a level of performance equivalent to that required by the British or European Standard;

"EEA State" means a State which is a contracting Party to the EEA Agreement;

"enactment" includes any Act or subordinate legislation as defined in section 21(1) of the Interpretation Act 1978;

"equestrian crossing" means a place on the carriageway of a road—

(a) where provision is made for equestrian traffic to cross the carriageway; and

(b) whose presence is indicated by a combination of—

(i) traffic light signals to control vehicular traffic of the kind prescribed by regulation 33;

(ii) the signals shown in diagrams 4003.2 and 4003.3, or the signal shown in diagram 4003.4; and

(iii) the road marking shown in diagram 1055.1 or 1055.2;

"ES compliant" in relation to signal heads shall be construed in accordance with regulation 33(5);

"excursion or tour" has the meaning given in section 137(1) of the Transport Act 1985 [*q.v.*];

"goods vehicle" means a motor vehicle or trailer constructed or adapted for use for the carriage or haulage of goods or burden of any description;

[*"hard shoulder"*, in relation to a motorway in England or Wales, has the meaning given by regulation 3(1)(e) of the Motorways (England and Wales) Regulations … and *"actively managed hard shoulder"* means a hard shoulder along which, by virtue of regulations under section

17(2) and (3) of the Road Traffic Regulation Act 1984, vehicular traffic may be driven at times for the time being indicated by traffic signs in accordance with those regulations;]

"hours of darkness" means the time between half an hour after sunset and half an hour before sunrise;

"junction" means a road junction;

"level crossing" means a place where a road is crossed by a railway or a tramway on a reserved track on the same level;

"local bus" means a public service vehicle used for the provision of a local service not being an excursion or tour;

"local service" has the meaning given in section 2 of the Transport Act 1985 [*q.v.*];

"major road" means the road at a junction into which there emerges vehicular traffic from a minor road;

"manually operated" means a change from one sign to another or one signal aspect to another set in process by an operator;

"maximum gross weight" means —

    (a) in the case of a motor vehicle not drawing a trailer or in the case of a trailer, its maximum laden weight;

    (b) in the case of an articulated vehicle, its maximum laden weight (if it has one) and otherwise the aggregate maximum laden weight of all the individual vehicles forming part of that articulated vehicle; and

    (c) in the case of a motor vehicle (other than an articulated vehicle) drawing one or more trailers, the aggregate maximum laden weight of the motor vehicle and the trailer or trailers drawn by it;

"maximum laden weight" in relation to a vehicle (including a vehicle which is a trailer) means —

    (a) in the case of a vehicle as respects which a gross weight not to be exceeded in Great Britain is specified in construction and use requirements (as defined by [section 41(7)] of the 1988 Act), the weight so specified;

    (b) in the case of a vehicle as respects which no such weight is so specified, the weight which the vehicle is designed or adapted not to exceed when in normal use and travelling on a road laden;

"minor road" means a road on which, at its junction with another road, there is placed the sign shown in diagram 601.1 or 602 or the road marking shown in diagram 1003;

"mobile road works" means works on a road carried out by or from a vehicle or vehicles which move slowly along the road or which stop briefly from time to time along that road [*q.v.*];

"motorway" means a special road which—

    (a) in England or Wales (save as otherwise provided by or under regulations made under, or having effect as if made under, section 17 of the 1984 Act) can be used by traffic only of Class

I or II as specified in Schedule 4 to the Highways Act 1980
[*q.v.*]; or

(b) [*applies to Scotland*]

[*"Motorways (England and Wales) Regulations"* means the Motorways
Traffic (England and Wales) Regulations 1982 and ...;]

"mph" means miles per hour;

"non-primary route" means a route, not being a primary route or a motorway or part of a primary route or of a motorway;

"passenger vehicle" means a vehicle constructed or adapted for the carriage of passengers and their effects;

"pedal cycle" means a unicycle, bicycle, tricycle, or cycle having four or
more wheels, not being in any case mechanically propelled unless it
is an electrically assisted pedal cycle of such class as is to be treated
as not being a motor vehicle for the purposes of the 1984 Act;

"pedestrian zone" means an area—

(a) which has been laid out to improve amenity for pedestrians;
and

(b) to which the entry of vehicles is prohibited or restricted;

"plate" means a sign which by virtue of general directions given in exercise
of the power conferred by section 65 of the 1984 Act may be placed
only in combination or in conjunction with another sign and which is
supplementary to that other sign;

"police vehicle" means a vehicle being used for police purposes or operating under the instructions of a chief officer of police;

"primary route" means a route, not being a route comprising any part of a
motorway, in respect of which the Secretary of State—

(a) in the case of a trunk road is of the opinion, and

(b) in any other case after consultation with the traffic authority
for the road comprised in the route is of the opinion,

that it provides the most satisfactory route for through traffic between
places of traffic importance;

"primary signals" has the meaning given by regulation 43(5)(a);

"principal road" means a road for the time being classified as a principal
road—

(a) by virtue of section 12 of the Highways Act 1980 (whether as
falling within subsection (1) or classified under subsection
(3)), or

(b) [*applies to Scotland*];

"public service vehicle" has the meaning given in section 1 of the Public
Passenger Vehicles Act 1981 [*q.v.*];

"reflectorised" means illuminated by the use of retroreflecting material;

"retroreflecting material" means material which reflects a ray of light
back towards the source of that light;

"road maintenance vehicle" means a vehicle which—

(a) in England and Wales is specially designed or adapted for use
on a road by or on behalf of a highway authority for the

purposes of the Highways Act 1980 for the purposes of road maintenance; or

(b) [*applies to Scotland*];

"*road marking*" means a traffic sign consisting of a line or mark or legend on a road;

"*road works*" means works for the improvement, alteration or maintenance of a road and includes, in relation to England and Wales, street works as defined by section 48(3) of the New Roads and Street Works Act 1991 ...;

"*route*" includes any road comprised in a route;

"*school crossing place*" means a place in a road where children cross or seek to cross that road on their way to or from school or on their way from one part of a school to another;

"*secondary signals*" has the meaning given by regulation 43;

"*sign*" means a traffic sign;

"*signal-controlled crossing facility*" means —

(a) an equestrian crossing;

(b) a signal-controlled pedestrian facility; or

(c) a Toucan crossing;

"*signal-controlled pedestrian facility*" means a place on the carriageway of a road—

(a) which is not a "crossing" as defined by section 25(6) of the 1984 Act [*q.v.*];

(b) where provision is made for pedestrians to cross the carriageway; and

(c) whose presence is indicated by a combination of—

(i) traffic light signals to control vehicular traffic of the kind prescribed by regulation 33;

(ii) the signals shown in diagrams 4002.1 and 4003, or the signal shown in diagram 4003.1; and

(iii) the road marking shown in diagram 1055.1 or 1055.2;

"*single carriageway road*" means a road which is not a dual carriageway road;

"*solo motor cycle*" means a motor cycle without a side car and having two wheels;

"*stop line*" in relation to light signals for the control of vehicular traffic has the meaning given in regulation 43;

"*stud*" means a prefabricated device fixed or embedded as a mark in the carriageway of a road;

"*taxi*" means —

(a) in England and Wales, a vehicle licensed under—

(i) section 37 of the Town Police Clauses Act 1847 [*as amended by the Transport Act 1985 ss.16(a), 139(3) and Sch.8*]; or

(ii) section 6 of the Metropolitan Public Carriage Act

1869 [*as amended by the Statute Law (Repeals) Act 1976, and the Transport Act 1981 ss.35(1) and 40(1) and Sch.12, Pt III*]; or under any similar enactment; and

(b) [*applies to Scotland*];

"*taxi rank*" means an area of carriageway reserved for use by taxis waiting to pick up passengers;

"*telecommunications apparatus*" has the meaning given by paragraph 1(1) of Schedule 2 to the Telecommunications Act 1984;

"*temporary statutory provision*" means —

(a) a provision having effect under section 9 (experimental traffic orders) or section 14 (temporary restriction of traffic on roads) of the 1984 Act or under a provision referred to in section 66 (traffic signs for giving effect to local traffic regulations) of that Act;

(b) a prohibition, restriction or requirement indicated by a traffic sign placed pursuant to section 67 (emergencies and temporary obstructions) of the 1984 Act; or

(c) [*applies to Scotland*];

"*terminal sign*" means a sign placed in accordance with direction 8 or 9 of the Traffic Signs General Directions 2002 [*Pt II of this instrument below*];

"*Toucan crossing*" means a place on the carriageway of a road—

(a) where provision is made for both pedestrians and pedal cyclists to cross the carriageway; and

(b) whose presence is indicated by a combination of—

(i) traffic light signals to control vehicular traffic of the kind prescribed by regulation 33;

(ii) the signals shown in diagrams 4003.5 and 4003.6, or the signal shown in diagram 4003.7; and

(iii) the road marking shown in diagram 1055.1 or 1055.2;

"*tourist destination*" means a permanently established attraction or facility which—

(a) attracts or is used by visitors to an area;

(b) is open to the public without prior booking during its normal opening hours;

(c) [*applies to Scotland*]; and

(d) if located in Wales, is recognised by the Wales Tourist Board;

"*Tourist Information Centre*" means a staffed information service centre recognised and supported by the English or Wales Tourist Board …;

"*Tourist Information Point*" means a display of tourist information approved by a regional, area or local tourist board;

"*traffic calming features*" means —

(a) road humps constructed pursuant to section 90A of the Highways Act 1980 ("*the 1980 Act*") … and in accordance with the Highways (Road Humps) Regulations 1999 [*SI 1999/ 1025; not reproduced in this work*] …; or

(b) traffic calming works constructed in accordance with section 90G of the 1980 Act ... and in accordance with the Highways (Traffic Calming) Regulations 1999 [*SI 1999/1026; not reproduced in this work*] ...;

"traffic lane" means , in relation to a road, a part of the carriageway having, as a boundary which separates it from another such part, a road marking of the type shown in diagram 1004, 1004.1, 1005, 1005.1, 1008, 1008.1, 1010, 1013.1, 1013.3, 1013.4, 1040, 1040.2, 1041, 1041.1, 1042, 1042.1 or 1049;

"tramcar" has the meaning given in section 141A(4) of the 1984 Act [*q.v.*];

"trolley vehicle" has the meaning given in section 141A(4) of the 1984 Act;

"trunk road" as respects England and Wales has the meaning given in section 329(1) of the Highways Act 1980 ...;

"unladen vehicle" has the meaning given in Schedule 18;

"variable message sign" has the meaning given in regulation 58(1);

"with-flow lane" means a traffic lane reserved for a specified class of traffic proceeding in the same direction as general traffic in an adjoining traffic lane;

"Zebra crossing" has the meaning given by regulation 3(1) of the Zebra, Pelican and Puffin Pedestrian Crossings Regulations 1997 [*SI 1997/ 2400; q.v.*]; and

"zig-zag line" means a road marking of the size, colour and type shown in diagram 1001.3 which has been placed along a length of carriageway adjacent to a signal-controlled crossing facility.

[Regulation 4 is printed as amended by SI 2005/1670.   **B57.07**

As to the EEA Agreement and EEA states, see further the introductory note to Section C below.

In the definition of "maximum laden weight", the reference to s.41(7) of the 1988 Act has been inserted editorially in place of a reference to s.41(8).

The definition of "telecommunications apparatus" in the Telecommunications Act 1984 Sch.2, para.1(1) has now been repealed by the Communications Act 2003 Sch.19, para.1 (see now "electronic communications apparatus"; see further reg.26, as amended, below and the note to it).

Words omitted in reg.4 apply to Scotland.]

Interpretation of speed limit

5.—(1) In these Regulations *"speed limit"* means a maximum or minimum   **B57.08** limit of speed on the driving of vehicles on a road—

(a) imposed by an order under section 14 of the 1984 Act (temporary prohibition or restriction of traffic on roads);

(b) imposed by an order under section 16A of the 1984 Act (special events);

(c) imposed by regulations under section 17 of the 1984 Act (traffic regulation on special roads);

(d) arising by virtue of the road being restricted for the purposes of section 81 of the 1984 Act (general speed limit for restricted roads);

(e) imposed by an order under section 84 of the 1984 Act (speed limits on roads other than restricted roads);

(f) imposed by an order under section 88 of the 1984 Act (temporary speed limits); or

(g) imposed by or under a local Act,

and *"maximum speed limit"* and *"minimum speed limit"* shall be construed accordingly.

(2) In these Regulations *"national speed limit"* means any prohibition imposed on a road by the 70 miles per hour, 60 miles per hour and 50 miles per hour (Temporary Speed Limit) Order 1977 [*q.v.*] or by regulation 3 of the Motorways (Speed Limits) Regulations 1974 [*SI 1974/502; not reproduced in this work*].

Interpretation of references

B57.09   **6.** In these Regulations, unless it is expressly provided otherwise or the context otherwise requires—

(a) a reference to a numbered regulation is a reference to the regulation so numbered in these Regulations;

(b) a reference to a numbered paragraph is a reference to the paragraph so numbered in the regulation or Schedule in which the reference occurs;

(c) a reference to a sub-paragraph followed by a number or letter is a reference to the sub-paragraph bearing that number or letter in the paragraph in which the reference occurs;

(d) a reference to a numbered diagram is a reference to the diagram so numbered in a Schedule to these Regulations;

(e) a reference to a sign, signal, signals or road marking prescribed by a regulation or shown in a diagram in a Schedule to these Regulations means a sign, signal, signals or road marking of the size, colour and type—

(i) prescribed by that regulation and shown in any diagram to which that regulation refers; or as the case may be

(ii) shown in that diagram and prescribed by these Regulations,

and in either case includes a reference to that sign, signal, signals or road marking as varied in accordance with these Regulations;

(f) a reference to the information, warning, requirement, restriction, prohibition or speed limit conveyed by a sign, signal, signals or road marking prescribed by a regulation or shown in a diagram includes a reference to that information, warning, requirement, restriction, prohibition or speed limit, however expressed, as varied to accord with any variation of the sign, signal, signals or road marking made in accordance with these Regulations; and

(g) in any provision which includes a table, references to a table or to a numbered table are to the table or as the case may be to the table so numbered in that provision.

Interpretation of Schedules 1 to 12

B57.10   **7.**—(1) In any untitled table under or beside any diagram (in this paragraph referred to as *"the diagram"*) in Schedules 1 to 12—

(a) in item 1 any regulations which are specified are regulations in these Regulations in which a specific reference is made to the diagram, to a regulation or Schedule which refers to the diagram or to a symbol which appears in the diagram or a variant of the diagram;

(b) in item 2 any directions which are specified are directions in the Traffic Signs General Directions 2002 containing a reference to the particular diagram or to a regulation or Schedule which refers to the diagram;

(c) in item 3 any diagrams which are specified are diagrams in the Schedules to these Regulations which show signs which may or must be placed in conjunction or in combination with the sign shown in the diagram;

(d) in item 4 any item which is specified is an item in Schedule 16 which specifies permitted variants to the diagram; and

(e) in item 5 any item which is specified is an item in Schedule 17 which specifies the illumination requirements for the sign shown in the diagram.

(2) The table entitled "Table of combinations" under or beside any diagram in Part III of Schedule 12 indicates the manner in which the sign shown in that diagram may be varied in accordance with paragraphs (7) to (9) of regulation 17.

(3) Dimensions indicated on any diagram shown in Schedules 1 to 12 are expressed in millimetres unless otherwise specified.

SECTION 2

General Provisions

Authorisations

8. Nothing in these Regulations shall be taken to limit the powers of the Secretary of State, the Scottish Ministers and the National Assembly for Wales under section 64(1) and (2) of the 1984 Act to authorise the erection or retention of traffic signs of a character not prescribed by these Regulations.   **B57.11**

[As to the transfer of all of the functions of a Minister of the Crown under   **B57.12**
these regulations to the Scottish Ministers and to the National Assembly for Wales, see the Scotland Act 1998 (Transfer of Functions to the Scottish Ministers etc.) Order 1999 (SI 1999/1750; not reproduced in this work) and the National Assembly for Wales (Transfer of Functions) Order 1999 (SI 1999/672); not reproduced in this work.]

Temporary obstructions

9. Nothing in these Regulations shall have effect so as to authorise any persons   **B57.13**
not otherwise authorised to do so to place on or near a road any object or device for warning traffic of a temporary obstruction.

Application of section 36 of the Road Traffic Act 1988 to signs and disqualification for offences

10.—(1) Section 36 of the 1988 Act shall apply to each of the following   **B57.14**
signs—

    (a) the signs shown in diagrams 601.1, 602, 606, 609, 610, 611.1, 615, 616, 626.2A, 629.2, 629.2A, 784.1, 953, 953.1, 7023, 7029 (except when varied to omit the legend "NO OVERTAKING"), 7031 and 7403;

    (b) the road marking shown in diagram 1001.3;

    (c) the road marking shown in diagram 1003;

    (d) the road markings shown in diagrams 1013.1, 1013.3 and 1013.4 insofar as those markings convey the requirements specified in regulation 26;

    (e) the road markings shown in diagrams 1025.1, 1025.3 and 1025.4 insofar as those markings convey the prohibition specified by regulation 29(1) and Part I of Schedule 19;

    (f) the road markings shown in diagrams 1042, 1042.1, 1043, 1044 and 1045;

    (g) the red light signal when displayed by the light signals prescribed by regulation 33 or by regulation 35;

    (h) the light signals prescribed by regulation 33 as varied in accordance with regulation 34 when they are displaying one or more of the green arrow signals shown in diagrams 3001.2 or 3001.3 insofar as they convey any of the restrictions specified in regulation 36(1)(f) or (g);

    (i) the light signal shown in diagram 3013.1;

    (j) the intermittent red light signals when displayed by the sign shown in diagram 3014; and

    (k) the light signals prescribed by regulation 37 and shown in diagrams 6031.1 and 6032.1 when indicating one of the prohibitions prescribed by regulation 38.

(2) The following signs are hereby specified for the purposes of column 5 of the entry in Schedule 2 to the Road Traffic Offenders Act 1988 [*q.v.*] relating to offences under section 36 of the 1988 Act—

    (a) the signs shown in diagrams 601.1, 616, 629.2, 629.2A and 784.1;

    (b) the road marking shown in diagram 1001.3;

    (c) the road markings shown in diagram 1013.1, 1013.3 or 1013.4 insofar as those markings convey the requirements specified in regulation 26;

    (d) the red light signal when displayed by the light signals prescribed by regulation 33 or by regulation 35;

    (e) the light signals prescribed by regulation 33 as varied in accordance with regulation 34 when they are displaying one or more of the green arrow signals shown in diagrams 3001.2 or 3001.3 insofar as they convey any of the restrictions specified in regulation 36(1)(f) or (g);

    (f) the intermittent red light signals when displayed by the sign shown in diagram 3014; and

    (g) the light signals prescribed by regulation 37 and shown in diagrams 6031.1 and 6032.1 when indicating one of the prohibitions prescribed by regulation 38.

Signs, markings and signals to be of the size, colour and type shown in the diagrams

B57.15   **11.**—(1) Subject to the provisions of these Regulations, a sign for conveying information or a warning, requirement, restriction, prohibition or speed limit of the description specified under a diagram in Schedules 1 to 7, Part II of Schedule 10 and Schedule 12 to traffic on roads shall be of the size, colour and type shown in the diagram.

(2) The signs shown in diagrams 515.1, 515.1A, 515.2, 1012.2, 1012.3, 1049.1 and 7102 shall be of the size, colour and type shown in the two parts of those diagrams.

(3) In Schedule 6, a road marking shown in a diagram as a horizontal line indicates a marking to be laid on the carriageway of a road transversely, and a marking shown as a vertical line indicates a marking to be laid on the carriageway of a road longitudinally, to the flow of traffic, except so far as the nature of the diagram or the caption to the diagram indicates that it may or should be laid in another direction.

(4) The road markings shown in diagrams 1055.1 and 1055.2 shall be white, silver or light grey in colour.

Variations of dimensions

12.—(1) Where any diagram in Schedules 1 to 12 specifies a dimension for an element of a sign together with a dimension for that element in brackets, the dimensions so specified shall, subject to paragraph (2), be alternatives. **B57.16**

(2) Subject to paragraphs (3) and (4), where alternative dimensions are specified for more than one element of a sign, the dimensions chosen for each element must correspond with one another so that the shape and proportions of the sign are, so far as reasonably practicable, as shown in the diagram.

(3) Paragraph (2) does not apply to the road marking shown in diagram 1009 and the respective lengths of the lines comprised in that sign and of the gaps between them may be either—

    (a) 600 and 300 millimetres, in which case the width of the lines may be 100, 150 or 200 millimetres; or

    (b) 300 and 150 millimetres, in which case the width of the lines shall be 100 millimetres.

(4) Paragraph (2) does not apply to the road markings shown in diagrams 1001.2, 1013.3, 1013.4, 1040, 1040.2, 1040.4, 1041 and 1041.1.

(5) Where any diagram in Schedules 1 to 12 specifies a maximum and a minimum dimension for an element of a sign, the dimension chosen for that element shall, subject to the footnote to Table 1, be not more than the maximum and not less than the minimum.

(6) Where the maximum and minimum dimensions are specified for more than one element of a sign, the dimensions chosen for each element must (except in the case of diagrams 1003.4, 1028.2, 1028.3, 1028.4, 1032, 1033, 1043, 1044, 1045, 1050, 1055.1, 1055.2, 1066, 5001.1, 5001.2, 5003, 5003.1, 5005 and 5005.1) correspond with one another so that the shape and proportions of the sign are as shown in the diagram.

(7) Where a sign shown in diagram 606, 607, 609, 610, 611, 611.1, 612, 613, 614, 616, 642 or 645 is placed temporarily on a road by a constable or a person acting under the instructions (whether general or specific) of the chief officer of police for the purposes of indicating a temporary statutory provision, any dimen-

sion in the diagram for the diameter of a roundel, or for the sign may be reduced so long as any dimension shown in the diagram for the diameter of a roundel or for the measurement horizontally of the sign is at least 200 millimetres, and the height of any lettering is at least 20 millimetres.

(8) Where a sign shown in a diagram in Schedules 1 to 5 or Schedules 7 to 12 is varied in accordance with regulation 17, the shape, proportions and size of the sign shall be adjusted to the extent necessary to accommodate the variation.

(9) Any sign shown in a diagram in Part III of Schedule 12 shall be of such dimensions as, having regard to the character of the road and the speed of traffic generally using it, are necessary to accommodate the route symbols or arrows appropriate to the number of traffic lanes and the nature of the road works in relation to which the sign is placed.

(10) Any dimension (not being an angle or specified as a maximum or minimum) specified in these Regulations shall be treated as permitted by these Regulations if it is varied in accordance with the following Tables, subject, in the case of Tables 1, 2 and 3 to the Notes to those Tables.

TABLE 1

DIAGRAMS IN SCHEDULES 1 TO 5, 7, 10 AND 12—HEIGHT OF LETTERS OR
NUMBERS

(1) Item	*(2)* Dimensions shown in diagrams	*(3)* Permitted variations
1.	100 millimetres or more	Up to 5% of the dimension
2.	Less than 100 millimetres	Up to 7.5% of the dimension

NOTE: Where the height of letters or numbers is expressed as a range within maximum and minimum dimensions the permitted variations indicated in this Table shall apply to those dimensions shown as the maximum and minimum.

TABLE 2

DIAGRAMS IN SCHEDULE 6—ALL DIMENSIONS

(1) Item	*(2)* Dimensions shown in diagrams	*(3)* Permitted variations	
1.	3 metres or more	(i)	Up to 15% of the dimension where the varied dimension is greater than the specified dimension; or
		(ii)	Up to 10% of the dimension where the varied dimension is less than the specified dimension

(1) Item	*(2)* Dimensions shown in diagrams	*(3)* Permitted variations	
2.	300 millimetres or more, but less than 3 metres	(i)	Up to 20% of the dimension where the varied dimension is greater than the specified dimension; or
		(ii)	Up to 10% of the dimension where the varied dimension is less than the specified dimension
3.	50 millimetres or more but less than 300 millimetres	(i)	Up to 30% of the dimension where the varied dimension is greater than the specified dimension; or
		(ii)	Up to 10% of the dimension where the varied dimension is less than the specified dimension

NOTE: Where a dimension denoting the length or width of a road marking is varied in accordance with this Table, and there is a space between two parts of the marking, the dimensions of that space may be varied as required to accommodate the variation of the length or width of the marking, provided that the character of the marking is maintained.

TABLE 3

DIAGRAMS IN SCHEDULES 8 AND 9

(1) Item	*(2)* Dimensions shown in diagrams	*(3)* Permitted variations	
1.	200 millimetres	(i)	up to 10% of the dimension where the varied dimension is greater than the specified dimension
		(ii)	up to 2.5% of the dimension where the varied dimension is less than the specified dimension

NOTE: Where the dimensions of a signal which displays an arrow or symbol are varied in accordance with this table, the dimensions chosen for the arrow or symbol must be such as to maintain the shape and proportions shown in the diagram in which the signal is shown.

TABLE 4

ALL DIMENSIONS OTHER THAN THOSE IN TABLES 1, 2 AND 3

(1) Item	(2) Dimensions shown in diagrams	(3) Permitted variations
1.	300 millimetres or more	Up to 5% of the dimension
2.	50 millimetres or more, but less than 300 millimetres	Up to 7.5% of the dimension
3.	Less than 50 millimetres	Up to 10% of the dimension

(11) Any variation of any angle specified in any diagram in Schedule 1, 6 or 8, except diagrams 1043 and 1044, shall be treated as permitted by these Regulations if the variation does not exceed 5 degrees.

(12) Where—

(a) overall dimensions are given for a sign shown in any diagram in the Schedules to these Regulations; and

(b) the legend on that sign is varied in accordance with regulation 17 and with item 4 of the table appearing under or beside that diagram,

the overall dimensions or the number of lines filled by the legend, or both, may be varied so far as necessary to give effect to the variation of the legend.

Proportions and form of letters, numerals, symbols and other characters

B57.17
13.—(1) Subject to paragraphs (2), (5), (6) and (9) all letters, numerals and other characters incorporated in the signs or parts of the signs shown in the diagrams in Schedules 1 to 5 and 7, Part II of Schedule 10 and Schedule 12 which have a red, blue, brown, black or green background shall have the proportions and form shown in Part I of Schedule 13.

(2) Paragraph (1) does not apply to the letters, numerals and other characters incorporated in—

(a) the bottom panel of diagram 674;

(b) diagrams 970, 971, 973.2, 973.3, 2401 and 2403.1;

(c) the parts of diagrams 2505, 2505.1, 2506, 2507, 2508, 2509.1, 2510, 2511, 2512 and 2513 which indicate the availability of parking places in accordance with regulation 19(4)(c);

(d) diagrams 2607, 2610, 2610.1 and 2610.2;

(e) the top panels of diagrams 2919.1 and 2920.1;

(f) the petrol price display in diagram 2919.1;

(g) the reference to the traffic authority in diagrams 7003.1, 7006, 7006.1 and 7007.1;

(h) the top and bottom panels of diagram 7008; and

(i) [applies to Scotland].

(3) Subject to paragraphs (4), (5), (6), (8) and (9) all letters, numerals and other characters incorporated in the signs or the parts of signs shown in the diagrams in Schedules 1 to 5, 7, 10 and 12 which have a white, yellow or orange background shall have the proportions and form shown in Part II of Schedule 13.

(4) Paragraph (3) does not apply to the letters, numerals and other characters incorporated in—

    (a) the bottom panel of diagram 674;

    (b) diagrams 970, 971, 973.2, 973.3, 2401 and 2403.1;

    (c) diagrams 2607, 2610, 2610.1 and 2610.2;

    (d) the top panels of diagrams 2919.1 and 2920.1;

    (e) the references to the traffic authority in diagrams 7003.1, 7006, 7006.1 and 7007.1; and

    (f) the top and bottom panels of diagram 7008.

(5) Letters and numerals used for the purpose of indicating a route number on any sign shown in a diagram in Part X of Schedule 7 (other than those incorporated in diagrams 2913, 2913.2, 2913.3, 2913.4, 2914, 2915, 2927.1, 2929 and 2929.1) shall have the proportions and form shown in Part III of Schedule 13, except—

    (a) where a route number is indicated in brackets on a sign shown in diagram 2904, 2904.1, 2906, 2908, 2908.1, 2909, 2913.1 or 2914.1; or

    (b) where a route number is shown on a green or white panel indicating a route that is not a motorway on a sign shown in diagram 2913.1 or 2914.1,

in either of which cases those letters and numerals shall have the proportions and form shown in either Part I or Part III of Schedule 13 as appropriate.

(6) Letters and numerals used for the purpose of indicating a route number on any sign shown in a diagram in Part III of Schedule 12 when used on a motorway shall have the proportions and form shown in Part IV of Schedule 13.

(7) Subject to and within the limits of any dimension specified as a maximum or minimum in—

    (a) the bottom panel of diagram 674;

    (b) diagrams 970, 971, 973.2, 973.3, 2401 and 2403.1;

    (c) the parts of diagrams 2505, 2505.1, 2506, 2507, 2508, 2509.1, 2510, 2511, 2512 and 2513 which indicate the availability of spaces in accordance with regulation 19(4)(c);

    (d) diagrams 2607, 2610, 2610.1 and 2610.2;

    (e) the top panels of diagrams 2919.1 and 2920.1;

    (f) the petrol price display in diagram 2919.1;

    (g) the references to the traffic authority in diagrams 7003.1, 7006, 7006.1 and 7007.1;

    (h) the top and bottom panels of diagram 7008; and

    (i) [applies to Scotland],

any letters or numerals or other characters incorporated in those diagrams may have proportions and form other than the proportions and form shown in Schedule 13.

(8) Letters and numerals used on a sign in diagram 2714 or 2715 shall have the proportions and form shown in Part I of Schedule 13 where those letters and numerals are white and the proportions and form shown in Part II of Schedule 13 where they are black.

(9) All letters, numerals, symbols and other characters incorporated in variable message signs shall have the general proportions and form shown in Part V of Schedule 13 where the construction or method of operation of the sign does not permit the use of letters, numerals and other characters of the proportions and form shown in Part I, II, III or IV of Schedule 13 or of symbols shown in diagrams in Schedules 1 to 5, 10 or 12.

(10) All letters, numerals and other characters incorporated in the road markings shown in the diagrams in Schedule 6 shall have the proportions and form shown in Part VI of Schedule 13.

(11) Symbols incorporated in signs for the purpose of indicating diversion routes to be followed in an emergency shall have the proportions and form shown in Part VII of Schedule 13.

(12) Symbols incorporated in signs for the purpose of indicating types of tourist destination shall have the proportions and form shown in Schedule 14.

Signs attached to vehicles

B57.18   14.—(1) Any sign attached to a vehicle of the description specified in column (2) of an item in the Table and in the position on that vehicle specified in column (3) of the item, when the vehicle is on a road which is subject to a maximum speed limit specified in column (4) of that item, shall be of the size, colour and type shown in a diagram specified in column (5).

TABLE

(1) Item	(2) Description of vehicle	(3) Position on vehicle	(4) Maximum speed limit	(5) Diagrams
1.	Road maintenance vehicle	On the front	30 mph or under	610, 7001, 7001.1
2.	Road maintenance vehicle	On the rear	30 mph or under	610, 7001, 7001.1, 7402, 7403, 7404
3.	Road maintenance vehicle	On the rear	More than 30 mph	7402, 7403, 7404
4.	Road maintenance vehicle immediately ahead of a vehicle displaying the sign shown in diagram 7403	On the rear	More than 30 mph	610, 7402, 7403, 7404
5.	Police vehicle	On the front or the rear	70 mph or under	829.1, 829.2, 829.3, 829.4

(2) The operating requirements for the lamps that form part of the signs shown in diagrams 7402 and 7403 are that—

(a) the lamps shall be illuminated only when the signs are being used in accordance with the Table; and

(b) each lamp shall show an intermittent amber light at a rate of flashing of not less than 60 nor more than 90 flashes per minute, and in such a manner that the lights of one horizontal pair are always shown when the lights of the other horizontal pair are not shown.

(3) A sign attached to the rear of a vehicle used to escort traffic through road works, and indicating that the vehicle should not be overtaken, shall be of the size, colour and type shown in diagram 7029.

SECTION 3

Warning, Regulatory and Informatory Traffic Signs

Sign shown in diagram 610 and its significance

15.—(1) Except as provided in paragraphs (2)[, (2A)] and (3), the requirement **B57.19** conveyed by the sign shown in diagram 610 shall be that vehicular traffic passing the sign must keep to the left of the sign where the arrow is pointed downwards to the left, or to the right of the sign where the arrow is pointed downwards to the right.

(2) On an occasion where a vehicle is being used for fire brigade [or, in England [or Wales], fire and rescue authority], ambulance, bomb or explosive disposal, national blood service or police purposes and the observance of the requirement specified in paragraph (1) would be likely to hinder the use of that vehicle for one of those purposes then, instead of that requirement, the requirement conveyed by the sign in question shall be that the vehicle shall not proceed beyond that sign in such a manner or at such a time as to be likely to endanger any person.

[(2A) As regards England and Wales, and so far as relating to the functions of the Serious Organised Crime Agency which are exercisable in or as regards Scotland and which relate to reserved matters (within the meaning of the Scotland Act 1998), on an occasion where a vehicle is being used for Serious Organised Crime Agency purposes and the observance of the requirement specified in paragraph (1) would be likely to hinder the use of that vehicle for those purposes then, instead of that requirement, the requirement conveyed by the sign in question shall be that the vehicle shall not proceed beyond that sign in such a manner or at such a time as to be likely to endanger any person.]

(3) The requirement specified in paragraph (1) does not apply to a tramcar or trolley vehicle.

[Regulation 15 is printed as amended by SI 2004/3168; SI 2005/2929; SI 2006/ **B57.20** *594.]*

Signs shown in diagrams 601.1, 602, 611.1, 778, 778.1 and 784.1 and their significance

16.—(1) The requirements conveyed to vehicular traffic on roads by the sign **B57.21** shown in a diagram the number of which is specified in column (2) of an item in the Table are those specified in column (3) of that item.

TABLE

(1) Item	(2) Diagram	(3) Requirements	
1.	601.1	(a)	Every vehicle shall stop before crossing the transverse line shown in diagram 1002.1 or, if that line is not clearly visible, before entering the major road in respect of which the sign shown in diagram 601.1 has been provided; and
		(b)	no vehicle shall cross the transverse line shown in diagram 1002.1 or, if that line is not clearly visible, enter the major road in respect of which the sign shown in diagram 601.1 has been provided, so as to be likely to endanger the driver of or any passenger in any other vehicle or to cause that driver to change the speed or course of his vehicle in order to avoid an accident.
2.	601.1 when used at a level crossing	(a)	Every vehicle shall stop before crossing the transverse line shown in diagram 1002.1 or, if that line is not clearly visible, before entering the level crossing; and
		(b)	no vehicle shall cross the transverse line shown in diagram 1002.1 or, if that line is not clearly visible, enter the level crossing, so as to be likely to endanger the driver of or any passenger in any railway vehicle or tramcar or to cause that driver to change the speed of his vehicle in order to avoid an accident.
3.	602	No vehicle shall cross the transverse line shown in diagram 1003 nearer to the major road at the side of which that line is placed, or if that line is not clearly visible, enter that major road, so as to be likely to endanger the driver of or any passenger in any other vehicle or to cause that driver to change the speed or course of his vehicle in order to avoid an accident.	
4.	602 when placed in combination with 778 or 778.1	No vehicle shall cross the transverse line shown in diagram 1003 nearer to the level crossing at the side of which that line is placed, or if that line is not clearly visible, enter that level crossing, so as to be likely to endanger the driver of or any passenger in any railway vehicle or tramcar or to cause that driver to change the speed of his vehicle in order to avoid an accident.	

(1) Item	(2) Diagram	(3) Requirements
5.	611.1	(a) A vehicle entering the junction must give priority to vehicles coming from the right at the transverse road marking shown in diagram 1003.3 associated with the sign or, if the marking is not for the time being visible, at the junction; and (b) a vehicle proceeding through the junction must keep to the left of the white circle at the centre of the marking shown in diagram 1003.4, unless the size of the vehicle or the layout of the junction makes it impracticable to do so; and (c) no vehicle shall proceed past the marking shown in diagram 1003.4 in a manner or at a time likely— (i) to endanger any person, or (ii) to cause the driver of another vehicle to change its speed or course in order to avoid an accident.
6.	784.1	No abnormal transport unit shall proceed onto or over a level crossing unless— (a) the driver of the unit has used a telephone provided at or near the crossing for the purpose of obtaining from a person, authorised in that behalf by the railway or tramway authority, permission for the unit to proceed; (b) that permission has been obtained before the unit proceeds; and (c) the unit proceeds in accordance with any terms attached to that permission. Sub-paragraphs (b) and (c) above shall not apply if— (i) the driver uses the telephone at the crossing and receives an indication for not less than two minutes that the telephone at the other end of the telephone line is being called, but no duly authorised person answers it, or he receives no indication at all due to a fault or malfunction of the telephone; and

(1) Item	(2) Diagram	(3) Requirements	
		(ii)	the driver then drives the unit on to the crossing with the reasonable expectation of crossing it within times specified in a railway or tramway notice at the telephone as being times between which the railway vehicles or tramcars do not normally travel over that crossing.

(2) In this regulation—

"*abnormal transport unit*" means —

(a) a motor vehicle or a vehicle combination—

(i) the overall length of which, inclusive of the load (if any) on the vehicle or the combination, exceeds 61 feet 6 inches (18.75 metres); or

(ii) the overall width of which, inclusive of the load (if any) on the vehicle or the combination, exceeds 9 feet 6 inches (2.9 metres); or

(iii) the maximum gross weight of which exceeds 44 tonnes; or

(b) a motor vehicle, or a vehicle combination, which in either case is incapable of proceeding, or is unlikely to proceed, over an automatic level crossing at a speed exceeding 5 mph;

"*driver*" in relation to an abnormal transport unit, means where that unit is a single motor vehicle the driver of that vehicle and, where that unit is a vehicle combination, the driver of the only or the foremost motor vehicle forming part of that combination; and

"*vehicle combination*" means a combination of vehicles made up of one or more motor vehicles and one or more trailers all of which are linked together when travelling.

Permitted variants of upright signs

B57.22   17.—(1) This regulation applies to a sign shown in a diagram in a Schedule other than Schedule 6 and such a sign is in this regulation called an *"upright sign"*.

(2) The form of an upright sign shall, if the circumstances in which it is placed so require, or may, if appropriate in those circumstances, be varied—

(a) in the manner (if any) allowed or required in item 4 of the untitled table below or beside the diagram; or

(b) in the manner allowed or required in column (3) of an item in Schedule 16, if the diagram is one whose number is given in column (2) of that item.

(3) A symbol in the form of a prescribed sign to which direction 7 of the Traffic Signs General Directions 2002 applies shall not be incorporated in a sign in accordance with item 31 of Schedule 16, except in circumstances where it could be placed as a sign in accordance with that direction.

(4) A symbol incorporated as mentioned in paragraph (3) shall or may be varied in the same manner as the sign which the symbol represents or from which it is derived.

(5) In each of the signs shown in diagrams 780A, 780.1A and 780.2A the safe height shown on the sign shall be varied where necessary so that it is between 1 foot 3 inches and 2 feet (380 to 600 millimetres) less than the height of the lowest part of the overhead wire, of which the sign gives warning, over the highest part of the surface of the carriageway beneath that wire.

(6) Where a sign shown in a diagram in Schedule 7 indicates a road or a route, and that road or route is temporarily closed, there may be affixed to the sign or to that part of the sign where that road or route is indicated, in order to cancel temporarily the indication, a board coloured red and displaying in white lettering the words "Road temporarily closed" or "Route temporarily closed".

(7) In this paragraph and paragraphs (8) and (9)—

    (a) *"combination sign"* means a sign shown in diagram 7201, 7210, 7211.1, 7212, 7213, 7214, 7215, 7216, 7217, 7218, 7220, 7221, 7230, 7231, 7232, 7233, 7234, 7235, 7236, 7237, 7238, 7239 or 7240;

    (b) *"panel"* means a sign shown in diagram 7260, 7261, 7262, 7263, 7264, 7270, 7271, 7272, 7274 or 7275 when used as part of a combination sign and references to a panel whose number is shown in a table of combinations are to a sign shown in a diagram having a number so shown;

    (c) *"permitted combination"* means one of the combinations specified in paragraph (9);

    (d) *"the table"* in relation to a combination sign means the table of combinations appearing below or beside the diagram in which that sign is shown;

    (e) *"top panel"* means a panel shown at the top of a combination sign and *"bottom panel"* means a panel shown at the bottom of such a sign.

(8) If and only if the top and bottom panels of the sign as varied together constitute a permitted combination, a combination sign may be varied in the following ways—

    (a) by substituting for the top panel or, where a top panel is not shown, by adding as a top panel, a panel whose number is shown in item (1) of the table;

    (b) by substituting for the bottom panel or, where a bottom panel is not shown, by adding as a bottom panel, a panel whose number is shown in item (2) of the table;

    (c) if the word "none" appears in item (1) of the table, by omitting the top panel;

    (d) if the word "none" appears in item (2) of the table, by omitting the bottom panel.

(9) Each of the following is a permitted combination—

    (a) a top panel whose number appears in item (1) of a column in the table and a bottom panel whose number appears in item (2) of the same column;

(b) a top panel whose number appears in item (1) of a column in the table and, if the word "none" appears in item (2) of the same column, no bottom panel;

(c) a bottom panel whose number appears in item (2) of a column in the table and, if the word "none" appears in item (1) of the same column, no top panel;

(d) if the word "none" appears in both items of the same column of the table, no top panel and no bottom panel.

(10) Where an upright sign indicates a weight in tonnes using the symbol "T", that symbol may be varied to "t".

(11) Where the form of an upright sign is varied in accordance with these Regulations, the information, warning, requirement, restriction, prohibition or speed limit conveyed to traffic by the sign is varied to accord with the form of the sign as varied.

Illumination of signs

B57.23   **18.**—(1) Subject to paragraph (2), every sign shown in a diagram whose number is indicated in column (2) of an item in Schedule 17 shall be illuminated in the manner and at the times specified in column (3) of that item.

(2) Where a sign shown in a diagram whose number is indicated in column (2) of an item in Schedule 17 is placed for the purpose of conveying to vehicular traffic a warning, information, prohibition, restriction or requirement which applies only at certain times, the sign need only be illuminated, and in the case of the sign shown in diagram 776 shall only be illuminated, in accordance with that Schedule at those times.

(3) Where a sign shown in a diagram whose number is indicated in column (2) of an item in Schedule 17 is illuminated by a means of external lighting, then that means of lighting—

(a) shall be fitted to the sign or the structure on which the sign is mounted or which is otherwise specially provided; or

(b) if the sign is mounted on a bridge, tunnel or similar structure over a road or is provided temporarily at road works, the means of lighting may be mounted in any other manner such as to illuminate the face of the sign effectively.

Illumination of signs—further provisions

B57.24   **19.**—(1) Nothing in this regulation shall apply to the signs shown in diagrams 560, 561, 776 and 781.

(2) Subject to the provisions of regulation 18 and paragraph (1), any sign shown in a diagram in Schedules 1 to 5 and 7, Part II of Schedule 10 and Schedule 12 —

(a) when placed in consequence of the execution of road works must, and

(b) in other situations may,

be reflectorised in accordance with the following provisions of this regulation.

(3) Subject to paragraph (4), where retroreflecting material is used on any part of a sign shown in a diagram, all other parts of that sign shall also be reflectorised.

(4) No retroreflecting material shall be applied to—

    (a) any part of a sign coloured black;

    (b) that part of the sign shown in diagram 7031 which is coloured fluorescent yellow, unless the retroreflecting material is applied to that part in horizontal strips with a gap between each strip, or unless the retroreflecting material is itself also fluorescent;

    (c) those parts of the signs shown in diagrams 2505, 2505.1, 2506, 2507, 2508, 2509.1, 2510, 2511, 2512, and 2513 which give information about the availability of parking places when that information is conveyed by means of a legend which is internally illuminated or formed of light-emitting characters,

and in this paragraph the word *"part"*, in relation to a sign, means any part of that sign which is uniformly coloured and bounded by parts of a different colour.

Illumination of plates

20.—(1) Where a plate is placed in combination with a sign shown in a diagram in Schedules 1 to 5 or 12, and that sign is illuminated in accordance with regulation 18, the plate shall, subject to paragraph (2), be illuminated by the same means as the sign.   **B57.25**

(2) Paragraph (1) shall not apply where the means of lighting provided for the illumination of the sign adequately illuminates the plate.

Illumination of signs shown in diagrams 560 and 561

21.—(1) The signs shown in diagrams 560 and 561 shall not be illuminated by the fitting of a means of internal or external lighting.   **B57.26**

(2) A sign shown in a diagram whose number appears in column (2) of an item in the Table and having the dimension specified in column (3) of that item shall be illuminated by either of the methods prescribed by paragraph (3) which are shown in column (4) of the item, and by no other method.

TABLE

(1) Item	(2) Diagram	(3) Dimension	(4) Method of illumination
1.	560	150 millimetres diameter	Paragraph 3(a) or (b)
2.	560	75 millimetres or more but less than 150 millimetres diameter	Paragraph 3(c) or (d)
3.	561	180 square centimetres area	Paragraph 3(b) or (e)
4.	561	not less than 45 square centimetres but not more than 180 square centimetres area	Paragraph 3(d) or (e)

(3) The prescribed methods of illumination are—

    (a) the use of 14 circular reflectors of the corner cube type, each reflector having a diameter of 22 millimetres;

    (b) the use of retroreflecting material extending over the whole surface of the sign;

    (c) the use of a single circular reflector of the corner cube type extending over the whole surface of the sign;

    (d) the use of reflectors consisting of bi-convex lenses extending over the whole surface of the sign; and

    (e) the use of a single rectangular reflector of the corner cube type extending over the whole surface of the sign.

Buses

B57.27   **22.**—(1) In the signs shown in—

    (a) the permitted variants of diagrams 618.1, 618.2, 618.3, 618.3A, 620 and 820;

    (b) diagrams 877, 953.3. 954, 954.2, 954.3, 954.5, 954.6, 954.7, 970, 973.2, 973.3, 974, 975, 1025.1, 1025.3 and 1025.4;

    (c) the permitted variants of diagram 1028.3; and

    (d) diagrams 1048, 1048.1, 1048.2, 1048.3 and 1048.4,

the expressions *"bus"* and *"buses"* have the meanings given in paragraph (2).

    (2) *"Buses"* in the signs referred to in paragraph (1) means—

    (a) motor vehicles constructed or adapted to carry more than 8 passengers (exclusive of the driver); and

    (b) local buses not so constructed or adapted;

and *"bus"* shall be construed accordingly.

Bus lanes

B57.28   **23.**—(1) In the signs shown in the permitted variants of diagrams 877 and 878 in which the expression *"bus lane"* appears and in diagrams 962, 962.2, 963, 963.2, 964, 1048 and 1048.1, *"bus lane"* has the meaning given in paragraph (2).

    (2) *"Bus lane"* in the signs referred to in paragraph (1) means a traffic lane reserved for—

    (a) motor vehicles constructed or adapted to carry more than 8 passengers (exclusive of the driver);

    (b) local buses not so constructed or adapted; and

    (c) pedal cycles and taxis where indicated on the sign shown in diagram 958 or 959 and pedal cycles where indicated on the sign shown in diagram 960, 962.2, 963.2 or 1048.1.

Bus symbols

B57.29   **24.**—(1) A bus symbol when incorporated into any sign refers to—

    (a) motor vehicles constructed or adapted to carry more than 8 passengers (exclusive of the driver); or

    (b) local buses not so constructed or adapted.

    (2) In the signs shown in diagrams 958 and 959 and in the permitted variants of diagrams 953, 953.1 and 960, the word *"local"* on a bus symbol indicates that the road or the traffic lane on or near which the sign has been placed shall be used only by local buses.

(3) In this regulation *"bus symbol"* means a symbol depicting a bus in the form shown in diagram 952, 953 or 962.2.

SECTION 4

Road Markings

Road marking shown in diagram 1003: give way

25.—(1) The requirements conveyed to vehicular traffic on roads by the road marking consisting of the transverse lines shown in diagram 1003 shall be as follows.

(2) Except as provided by paragraphs (3) to (6), the requirement conveyed by the transverse lines shown in diagram 1003, whether or not they are placed in conjunction with the sign shown in diagram 602 or 1023, shall be that no vehicle shall proceed past such one of those lines as is nearer the major road into that road in a manner or at a time likely to endanger the driver of or any passenger in a vehicle on the major road or to cause the driver of such a vehicle to change its speed or course in order to avoid an accident.

(3) Wherever the transverse lines are placed in conjunction with the sign shown in diagram 602, and that sign is at the same time placed in combination with the sign shown in diagram 778 or 778.1 at a level crossing, then the requirement shall be that no vehicle shall proceed past such one of those lines as is nearer the level crossing in a manner or at a time likely to endanger the driver of or any passenger in a railway vehicle or tramcar, or to cause that driver to change the speed of his vehicle in order to avoid an accident.

(4) Wherever the transverse lines are placed in advance of a point in the road where the width of the carriageway narrows significantly, then the requirement shall be that no vehicle shall proceed past such one of those lines as is nearer to the point of narrowing in a manner or at a time likely to endanger the driver of or any passenger in a vehicle that is proceeding in the opposite direction to the first-mentioned vehicle, or to cause the driver of such a vehicle to change its speed or course in order to avoid an accident.

(5) Where the transverse lines are placed in conjunction with the sign shown in diagram 611.1 at a junction marked with the road marking shown in diagram 1003.4, then the requirement shall be that no vehicle shall proceed past such one of those lines as is nearer to the road marking shown in diagram 1003.4 in a manner or at a time likely to endanger the driver of or any passenger in a vehicle circulating past that road marking from the right of the first-mentioned vehicle or to cause the driver of the second-mentioned vehicle to change its speed or course in order to avoid an accident.

(6) Where the transverse lines are placed in advance of a length of the carriageway of the road where a cycle track crosses the road along a route parallel to the transverse lines, then the requirement shall be that no vehicle shall proceed past such one of those lines as is nearer the cycle track, in a manner or at a time likely to endanger any cyclist proceeding along the cycle track or to cause such a cyclist to change speed or course in order to avoid an accident.

Road markings shown in diagrams 1013.1, 1013.3 and 1013.4: double white lines

26.—(1) A road marking for conveying the requirements specified in paragraph

(2) and the warning specified in paragraph (7) shall be of the size, colour and type shown in diagram 1013.1, 1013.3 or 1013.4.

(2) The requirements conveyed by a road marking mentioned in paragraph (1) shall be that—

    (a) subject to paragraphs (3) and (5), no vehicle shall stop on any length of road along which the marking has been placed at any point between the ends of the marking; and

    (b) subject to paragraph (6), every vehicle proceeding on any length of road along which the marking has been so placed that, as viewed in the direction of travel of the vehicle, a continuous line is on the left of a broken line or of another continuous line, shall be so driven as to keep the first-mentioned continuous line on the right hand or off side of the vehicle.

(3) Nothing in paragraph (2)(a) shall apply so as to prevent a vehicle stopping on any length of road so long as may be necessary for any of the purposes specified in paragraph (4) if the vehicle cannot be used for such a purpose without stopping on the length of road.

(4) The purposes are—

    (a) to enable a person to board or alight from the vehicle,

    (b) to enable goods to be loaded on to or to be unloaded from the vehicle,

    (c) to enable the vehicle to be used in connection with—

        (i) any operation involving building, demolition or excavation;

        (ii) the removal of any obstruction to traffic;

        (iii) the maintenance, improvement or reconstruction of the length of road; or

        (iv) the laying, erection, alteration, repair or cleaning in or near the length of road of any sewer or of any main, pipe or apparatus for the supply of gas, water or electricity, or of any [electronic communications apparatus] kept installed for the purposes of [electronic communications code system [*sic*]] or of any other [electronic communications apparatus] lawfully kept installed in any position.

(5) Nothing in paragraph (2)(a) shall apply—

    (a) so as to prevent a vehicle stopping in a lay-by;

    (b) to a vehicle for the time being used for fire brigade [or, in England [or Wales], fire and rescue authority], ambulance or police purposes;

    [(ba) as regards England and Wales, and so far as relating to the functions of the Serious Organised Crime Agency which are exercisable in or as regards Scotland and which relate to reserved matters (within the meaning of the Scotland Act 1998), to a vehicle for the time being used for Serious Organised Crime Agency purposes;]

    (c) to a pedal bicycle not having a sidecar attached thereto, whether additional means of propulsion by mechanical power are attached to the bicycle or not;

    (d) to a vehicle stopping in any case where the person in control of the vehicle is required by law to stop, or is obliged to do so in order to avoid an accident, or is prevented from proceeding by circumstances outside his control;

(e) to anything done with the permission or at the direction of a constable in uniform or in accordance with the direction of a traffic warden; or

(f) to a vehicle on a road with more than one traffic lane in each direction.

(6) Nothing in paragraph (2)(b) shall be taken to prohibit a vehicle from being driven across, or so as to straddle, the continuous line referred to in that paragraph, if it is safe to do so and if necessary to do so—

(a) to enable the vehicle to enter, from the side of the road on which it is proceeding, land or premises adjacent to the length of road on which the line is placed, or another road joining that road;

(b) in order to pass a stationary vehicle;

(c) owing to circumstances outside the control of the driver;

(d) in order to avoid an accident;

(e) in order to pass a road maintenance vehicle which is in use, is moving at a speed not exceeding 10 mph, and is displaying to the rear the sign shown in diagram 610 or 7403;

(f) in order to pass a pedal cycle moving at a speed not exceeding 10 mph;

(g) in order to pass a horse that is being ridden or led at a speed not exceeding 10 mph; or

(h) for the purposes of complying with any direction of a constable in uniform or a traffic warden.

(7) The warning conveyed by a road marking mentioned in paragraph (1) shall be that no vehicle while travelling next to a broken line placed on the left of a continuous line, as viewed in the direction of travel of the vehicle, should cross or straddle the first-mentioned line unless it is seen by the driver of the vehicle to be safe to do so.

[Regulation 26 is printed as amended by SI 2003/2155; SI 2004/3168; SI 2005/2929; SI 2006/594.   **B57.32**

For the meaning of "electronic communications apparatus" and "electronic communications code system", see SI 2003/2155 art.2(1) and the Communications Act 2003 Pt 2, Ch.1.]

Road marking shown in diagram 1001.3: zig-zag lines—no stopping

27.—(1) In this regulation and regulation 28—   **B57.33**

"*controlled area*" means a length of carriageway—

(a) which is adjacent to a signal-controlled crossing facility and has a zig-zag line marked along each of its edges (with or without zig-zag lines also marked down its centre); and

(b) in or near which no other signs or markings have been placed except ones comprised in the combination of signs and markings indicating the presence of the facility or shown in diagram 610, 611, 612, 613, 616, 810, 1029 or 1062;

"*local service*" does not include an excursion or tour as defined by section 137(1) of the Transport Act 1985 [*q.v.*]; and

"*vehicle*" does not include a pedal bicycle not having a sidecar attached to it, whether or not additional means of propulsion by mechanical power are attached to the bicycle.

(2) Subject to paragraphs (3) and (4) and without prejudice to regulation 28, a zig-zag line shall convey the requirement that the driver of a vehicle shall not cause any part of it to stop in the controlled area in which it is marked.

(3) Paragraph (2) does not prohibit the driver of a vehicle from stopping it in a controlled area—

(a) if the driver has stopped it for the purpose of complying with an indication given by a light signal for the control of vehicular traffic or the direction of a constable in uniform or a traffic warden;

(b) if the driver is prevented from proceeding by circumstances beyond his control or it is necessary for him to stop to avoid injury or damage to persons or property; or

(c) when the vehicle is being used for police, fire brigade [or, in England [or Wales], fire and rescue authority] or ambulance purposes; [or

(d) as regards England and Wales, and so far as relating to the functions of the Serious Organised Crime Agency which are exercisable in or as regards Scotland and which relate to reserved matters (within the meaning of the Scotland Act 1998), when the vehicle is being used for Serious Organised Crime Agency purposes;]

(4) Paragraph (2) does not prohibit the driver of a vehicle from stopping it in a controlled area—

(a) for so long as may be necessary to enable the vehicle to be used for the purposes of—

(i) any operation involving building, demolition or excavation;

(ii) the removal of any obstruction to traffic;

(iii) the maintenance, improvement or reconstruction of a road; or

(iv) the laying, erection, alteration, repair or cleaning in or near the controlled area of any sewer or of any main, pipe or apparatus for the supply of gas, water or electricity, or of any [electronic communications apparatus] kept installed for the purposes of [electronic communications code system [*sic*]] or of any other [electronic communications apparatus] lawfully kept installed in any position;

(b) in the provision of a local service, and the vehicle, having proceeded past the light signals to which the controlled area relates, is waiting in that area in order to take up or set down passengers; or

(c) if he stops the vehicle for the purpose of making a left or right turn.

B57.34   *[Regulation 27 is printed as amended by SI 2003/2155; SI 2004/3168; SI 2005/ 2929; SI 2006/594.*

For the meaning of "electronic communications apparatus" and "electronic communications code system", see the note to reg.26 above.]

Road marking shown in diagram 1001.3: zig-zag lines—no overtaking

B57.35   **28.**—(1) Without prejudice to regulation 27, a zig-zag line shall convey the requirement that, whilst any motor vehicle (in this regulation called "the approaching vehicle") or any part of it is within the limits of a controlled area and is proceeding towards the signal-controlled crossing facility to which the controlled area relates, the driver of the vehicle shall not cause it or any part of it—

(a) to pass ahead of the foremost part of any other motor vehicle proceeding in the same direction; or

(b) to pass ahead of the foremost part of a vehicle which is stationary for the purpose of complying with the indication given by a traffic light signal for controlling vehicular traffic.

(2) In paragraph (1)—

(a) the reference to a motor vehicle in sub-paragraph (a) is, in a case where more than one motor vehicle is proceeding in the same direction as the approaching vehicle in a controlled area, a reference to the motor vehicle nearest to the signal-controlled crossing facility to which the controlled area relates; and

(b) the reference to a stationary vehicle is, in a case where more than one vehicle is stationary in a controlled area for the purpose of complying with the indication given by a traffic light signal for controlling vehicular traffic, a reference to the stationary vehicle nearest the signal-controlled crossing facility to which the controlled area relates.

Road markings shown in diagrams 1025.1, 1025.3, 1025.4, 1043 and 1044: bus stop and bus stand clearways and box junctions

29.—(1) The road markings shown in diagrams 1025.1, 1025.3 and 1025.4   **B57.36** shall convey the prohibition specified in Part I of Schedule 19.

(2) The road markings shown in diagrams 1043 and 1044 shall convey the prohibition specified in Part II of Schedule 19.

Permitted variants of road markings

30.—(1) Where the circumstances in which a road marking shown in a diagram   **B57.37** in Schedule 6 is to be placed so require or where appropriate in those circumstances, the form of the marking shall or may be varied as follows—

(a) in the manner (if any) allowed or required in item 4 of the untitled table below or beside the diagram; or

(b) in the manner allowed or required in column (3) of an item in Schedule 16, if the diagram is one whose number is given in column (2) of that item.

(2) In the road marking shown in diagram 1035, route numbers, place names and the direction in which any arrow-head points shall be varied to accord with the circumstances but the words "turn left", "ahead" or "turn right" shall not be included in the marking.

(3) Where the form of a road marking is varied in accordance with this regulation, the information, warning, requirement, restriction, prohibition or speed limit conveyed by the marking is varied to accord with the form of marking as varied.

Illumination of road markings

31.—(1) Subject to paragraph (2) a road marking shown in diagram 1001   **B57.38** (except when used in conjunction with the road marking shown in diagram 1001.3), 1001.1, 1001.2, 1002.1, 1003, 1003.1, 1003.3, 1003.4, 1004, 1004.1, 1005, 1005.1, 1008, 1008.1, 1009, 1010, 1012.1, 1012.2, 1012.3, 1013.1, 1013.3,

1013.4, 1014, 1022, 1023, 1024, 1024.1, 1036.1, 1036.2, 1037.1, 1039, 1040, 1040.2, 1040.3, 1040.4, 1040.5, 1041, 1041.1, 1042, 1042.1, 1046, 1049, 1062, 1064 or 1065 shall be reflectorised.

(2) Paragraph (1) shall not apply to a road marking shown in diagram 1003, 1023 or 1049 when varied for use on a cycle track.

(3) Subject to paragraph (4), studs incorporating reflectors or retroreflecting material and so spaced as to form a single line of studs not less than 3 nor more than 4.5 metres apart shall be fitted—

    (a) between the two lines constituting the marking shown in diagram 1013.1, except where that marking is so placed that the continuous lines shown in version B of diagram 1013.1 are more than 175 millimetres apart and are separated by an area of crosshatching so shown;

    (b) between the two continuous parallel lines forming part of the marking shown in diagrams 1013.3 and 1013.4.

(4) Where the marking shown in diagram 1013.1 is placed as mentioned in the exception to paragraph (3)(a), the studs mentioned in paragraph (3) shall be fitted either in opposite pairs within the width of each of the two lines or in a single line between those lines.

(5) Subject to the foregoing provisions of this regulation, and to paragraph (6), any road marking may be reflectorised, and studs incorporating reflectors or retroreflecting material may be used with a road marking shown in diagram 1004, 1004.1, 1005, 1005.1, 1008, 1008.1, 1010, 1012.1, 1012.2, 1012.3, 1025.3, 1025.4, 1035, 1040, 1040.2, 1040.3, 1040.4, 1040.5, 1041, 1041.1, 1042 or 1042.1 in such a manner that any such stud shall not be fitted to any part of the marking coloured white or yellow but shall be applied to the surface of the carriageway in the gaps between parts of a broken line, or alongside a solid line, forming part of the marking.

(6) In the case of a road marking shown in diagram 1012.1, 1012.2, 1012.3, 1042 or 1042.1 the studs shall, if fitted, be applied to the surface of the carriageway at the side of and adjacent to the line shown in the diagram.

(7) Reflectors or retroreflecting material incorporated in studs shall be white except that in the case of studs used with a road marking shown in diagram 1010, 1012.1, 1012.2, 1012.3, 1025.3, 1025.4, 1040.3, 1040.4, 1040.5, 1041, 1041.1, 1042 or 1042.1 the reflectors or retroreflecting material shall reflect—

    [(a) red light—

        (i) when placed in conjunction with the marking shown in diagram 1041, 1041.1, 1042 or 1042.1 to indicate the off side (as viewed in the direction of travel) edge of the carriageway of any road;

        (ii) when placed in conjunction with a road marking to indicate the near side (as viewed in the direction of travel) edge of the carriageway of any road, shoulder; or

        (iii) when placed in conjunction with the marking shown in diagram 1012.1 to indicate the boundary between the carriageway of a motorway and an actively managed hard shoulder;]

    (b) amber light to indicate the off side edge of a carriageway which—

        (i) is contiguous to a central reservation or to traffic cones or cylinders at road works or to the road marking shown in diagram 1040.3; or

(ii) carries traffic in one direction only; and

(c) green light when placed in conjunction with a road marking shown in diagram 1010, 1025.3 or 1025.4 where the edge of any part of the carriageway available for through traffic at a junction, a lay-by or a parking place is so indicated to drivers of approaching vehicles.

(8) The colour of the parts of the stud other than the reflectors or retroreflecting material shall either be the same as the reflectors or retroreflecting material, or be white, or be a natural metallic finish or other neutral colour, or shall be fluorescent green/yellow in the case of studs placed temporarily at road works.

[Regulation 31 is printed as amended by SI 2005/1670.] **B57.39**

Height of road markings and size of studs

32.—(1) The size and shape of a stud incorporating reflectors or retroreflecting **B57.40** material shall be such that the part which is visible above the surface of the road can be contained within—

(a) an overall length in the direction of travel of traffic of not less than 35 millimetres and not exceeding 250 millimetres; and

(b) an overall width of not less than 84 millimetres and not exceeding 190 millimetres.

(2) No road marking or stud shall project above the surface of the adjacent carriageway more than 6 millimetres at any point except—

(a) a depressible stud, which shall not project above that surface more than 25 millimetres at its highest point, whether depressed or not;

(b) a non-depressible stud, which shall not project above that surface more than 20 millimetres at its highest point;

(c) the central circular part of the road marking shown in diagram 1003.4, which shall not project above that surface more than 125 millimetres at its highest point or 6 millimetres at its perimeter;

(d) the road marking shown in diagram 1012.2, the raised ribs on which shall project above the surface of the remainder of the marking by not more than 11 millimetres; or

(e) the road marking shown in diagram 1012.3, the raised ribs on which shall project above the surface of the remainder of the marking by not more than 8 millimetres; and

(f) the road marking shown in diagram 1049.1, the height of which above the surface of the adjacent carriageway shall be within the range of dimensions indicated on the second part of that diagram illustrating the cross-section of the marking.

(3) In this regulation, the expression *"depressible stud"* means a stud so fitted that the height by which it, or part of it, projects above the surface of the adjacent carriageway is apt to be reduced when pressure is applied to the stud from above; and *"non-depressible stud"* and *"depressed"* shall be construed accordingly.

SECTION 5

Light Signals and Warning Lights

Light signals for the control of vehicular traffic—standard form

33.—(1) Subject to regulation 34, light signals for the control of vehicular traf- **B57.41**

fic (other than tramcars) at junctions, at places where the headroom or the width of the road is permanently restricted, or at signal-controlled crossing facilities—

    (a) shall be of the size, colour and type shown in diagram 3000, 3000.7, 3000.8, 3000.9 or 3000.10;

    (b) shall be illuminated in the sequence prescribed by paragraph (3); and

    (c) shall have ES compliant signal heads.

(2) Light signals for the control of vehicular traffic consisting exclusively of pedal cycles—

    (a) shall be of the size, colour and type shown in diagram 3000.2;

    (b) shall be illuminated in the sequence prescribed by paragraph (3); and

    (c) shall have ES compliant signal heads.

(3) The sequence of illumination of the lights shown by the signals prescribed by paragraphs (1) and (2) shall be as follows—

    (a) red,

    (b) red and amber together,

    (c) green,

    (d) amber.

(4) Where the light signals are varied as prescribed by regulation 34, one or more green arrows shown in diagram 3001.2 or 3001.3 may be illuminated whilst any of the lights referred to in paragraph (3) are illuminated.

(5) For the purposes of these Regulations a signal head is *"ES compliant"* if, in relation to each aspect of its performance specified in column (2) of an item in the Table, it complies with the requirement or test specification of European Standard EN12368: 2000 specified in column (3) of the item or to an equivalent requirement or test specification specified in a corresponding EEA standard.

TABLE

(1) Item	(2) Aspect of performance	(3) Requirement or test specification and class
1.	Protection rating	Class IV: IP 55
2.	Operating temperature range	Class A
3.	Luminous intensity	Performance level 3, class 2
4.	Distribution of luminous intensity	Type M
5.	Maximum signal phantom	Class 5
6.	Signal lights incorporating symbols	Class S1
7.	Background screen	Class C1
8.	Impact resistance	Class IR2

Green arrow light signals for the control of vehicular traffic

B57.42   **34.**—(1) A lens or lenses of the size and colour shown in diagram 3001.2 or 3001.3 which, when illuminated, shows a green arrow—

    (a) may be substituted for the lens showing the green light in the light signals referred to in regulation 33(1) using any of the methods shown in diagram 3000.8 or 3000.10; or

(b) may be affixed to the light signals referred to in regulation 33(1) or to those signals as altered in accordance with sub-paragraph (a) using any of the methods shown in diagrams 3000.7, 3000.8, 3000.9 and 3000.10.

(2) The direction of the arrow shown in indication B in diagram 3001.2 or 3001.3 may be varied so that the head of the arrow points to any position lying between indication A and indication C.

(3) The direction of the arrow shown in indication D in diagram 3001.2 or 3001.3 may be varied so that the head of the arrow points to any position lying between indication C and indication E.

Portable light signals for the control of vehicular traffic

35. Portable light signals for the control of vehicular traffic other than tramcars shall be—   **B57.43**

(a) of the size, colour and type shown in diagram 3000.1;

(b) illuminated in the sequence prescribed by regulation 33(3); and

(c) so constructed that, if European Standard EN12368: 2000 applied to portable signals, they would be ES compliant.

Significance of light signals prescribed by regulations 33 to 35

36.—(1) The significance of the light signals prescribed by regulations 33, 34 and 35 shall be as follows—   **B57.44**

(a) subject to sub-paragraph (b) [and sub-paragraph (ba)] and, where the red signal is shown at the same time as the green arrow signal, to sub-paragraphs (f) and (g), the red signal shall convey the prohibition that vehicular traffic shall not proceed beyond the stop line;

(b) when a vehicle is being used for fire brigade [or, in England [or Wales], fire and rescue authority], ambulance, bomb or explosive disposal, national blood service or police purposes and the observance of the prohibition conveyed by the red signal in accordance with sub-paragraph (a) would be likely to hinder the use of that vehicle for the purpose for which it is being used, then sub-paragraph (a) shall not apply to the vehicle, and the red signal shall convey the prohibition that that vehicle shall not proceed beyond the stop line in a manner or at a time likely to endanger any person or to cause the driver of any vehicle proceeding in accordance with the indications of light signals operating in association with the signals displaying the red signal to change its speed or course in order to avoid an accident;

[(ba) as regards England and Wales, and so far as relating to the functions of the Serious Organised Crime Agency which are exercisable in or as regards Scotland and which relate to reserved matters (within the meaning of the Scotland Act 1998), when a vehicle is being used for Serious Organised Crime Agency purposes and the observance of the prohibition conveyed by the red signal in accordance with sub-paragraph (a) would be likely to hinder the use of that vehicle for those purposes, then sub-paragraph (a) shall not apply to the vehicle, and the red signal shall convey the prohibition that that vehicle shall not proceed beyond the stop line in a manner or at a time likely to endanger any person or to cause the driver of any vehicle proceeding in accordance with the indications of light signals operating in association with the signals displaying the red signal to change its speed or course in order to avoid an accident;]

(c) the red-with-amber signal shall, subject in a case where it is displayed at the same time as the green arrow signal to sub-paragraph (f), denote an impending change to green or a green arrow in the indication given by the signals but shall convey the same prohibition as the red signal;

(d) the green signal shall indicate that vehicular traffic may proceed beyond the stop line and proceed straight on or to the left or to the right;

(e) the amber signal shall, when shown alone, convey the same prohibition as the red signal, except that, as respects any vehicle which is so close to the stop line that it cannot safely be stopped without proceeding beyond the stop line, it shall convey the same indication as the green signal or green arrow signal which was shown immediately before it;

(f) save as provided in sub-paragraphs (g) and (h), the green arrow signal shall indicate that vehicular traffic may, notwithstanding any other indication given by the signals, proceed beyond the stop line only in the direction indicated by the arrow for the purpose of proceeding in that direction through the junction controlled by those signals;

(g) where more than one green arrow is affixed to light signals in accordance with regulation 34(1)(b), vehicular traffic, notwithstanding any other indication given by the signals, may proceed beyond the stop line only in the direction indicated by any one of the green arrows for the purpose of proceeding in that direction through the junction controlled by those signals; and

(h) where the green arrow signal is displayed at the same time as the green signal, vehicular traffic may proceed in the direction indicated by the green arrow in accordance with sub-paragraph (g) or in any other direction in accordance with sub-paragraph (d).

(2) Vehicular traffic proceeding beyond a stop line in accordance with paragraph (1) shall proceed with due regard to the safety of other road users and subject to any direction given by a constable in uniform or a traffic warden or to any other applicable prohibition or restriction.

(3) In this regulation the expressions *"vehicle"* and *"vehicular traffic"* do not include tramcars.

B57.45   *[Regulation 36 is printed as amended by SI 2004/3168; SI 2005/2929; SI 2006/594.]*

Light signals for the control of vehicular traffic on motorways and all-purpose dual carriageway roads

B57.46   37.—(1) Subject to paragraph (4), light signals for the control of vehicular traffic entering or proceeding along a motorway, shall be—

    (a) of the size, colour and type shown in diagram 6031.1 or 6032.1; and

    (b) operated in accordance with the requirements specified in paragraph (2).

(2) The requirements are that—

    (a) each lamp shall show an intermittent red light at a rate of flashing of not less than 60 nor more than 90 flashes per minute, and in such a manner that the lights of one vertical pair are always shown when the lights of the other vertical pair are not shown; and

    (b) the red cross or the white symbol shown in diagram 6031.1 or 6032.1 shall be illuminated by a steady light when the red lights are flashing.

(3) Light signals for the control of vehicular traffic entering or proceeding along an all-purpose dual carriageway road may also be the size, colour and type prescribed by paragraph (1) and operated in accordance with the requirements specified in paragraph (2).

(4) Light signals for the control of vehicular traffic—

    (a) entering a motorway by means of a slip road; or

    (b) entering a motorway which is a roundabout may, instead of complying with paragraphs (1) and (2), be of the size, colour and type prescribed by regulation 33 or 34.

Significance of light signals prescribed by regulation 37(1)

[38.—(1) The significance of the light signals prescribed by regulation 37(1) shall be as follows.   **B57.47**

(2) The signals shown in diagram 6032.1 shall convey the prohibition that vehicular traffic (other than vehicles being used in the circumstances described in regulation 36(1)(b)) on the carriageway beside which the signals are mounted shall not proceed beyond the signals.

(3) When displayed over the carriageway of a road, the signals shown in diagram 6031.1 shall convey the prohibition that vehicular traffic (other than vehicles being used in the circumstances described in regulation 36(1)(b)) proceeding in the traffic lane immediately below the signals shall not proceed beyond them in that lane.

(4) When displayed over an actively managed hard shoulder, the signals shown in diagram 6031.1 shall convey the prohibition that vehicular traffic (other than vehicles being used in the circumstances described in regulation 36(1)(b)) shall not enter the hard shoulder beyond the signals for any purpose.]

[Regulation 38 is printed as substituted by SI 2005/1670.]   **B57.48**

Light signals to control traffic at level crossings etc

39.—(1) Light signals for the control of traffic at level crossings, swinging or   **B57.49**
lifting bridges, tunnels, airfields or in the vicinity of premises used regularly by fire, police or ambulance service vehicles shall—

    (a) be of the size, colour and type shown in diagram 3014;

    (b) be illuminated in the sequence prescribed by paragraph (2); and

    (c) have ES compliant signal heads.

(2) The sequence for the illumination of the light signals prescribed by paragraph (1) shall be as follows—

(a) a single steady amber light,

(b) two intermittent red lights, each of which will be shown at a rate of flashing of not less than 60 nor more than 90 flashes per minute, and in a such a manner that one light is always shown when the other light is not shown.

Significance of light signals prescribed by regulation 39

B57.50   **40.** The significance of the light signals prescribed by regulation 39 shall be as follows—

(a) the amber signal shall convey the prohibition that traffic shall not proceed beyond the stop line or the road marking shown in diagram 1003.2, except that a vehicle which is so close to the stop line that it cannot safely be stopped without proceeding beyond the stop line may proceed across the level crossing; and

(b) the intermittent red signals shall convey the prohibition that traffic shall not proceed beyond the stop line or the road marking shown in diagram 1003.2.

Light signals for the control of tramcars

B57.51   **41.**—(1) Light signals for the control of tramcars shall—

(a) be of the size, colour and type shown in diagram 3013; and

(b) display the aspects shown in diagrams 3013.1, 3013.2, 3013.3, 3013.4 and 3013.5 in the sequence prescribed by paragraph (2).

(2) The sequence for the illumination of the light signals prescribed by paragraph (1) shall be as follows—

(a) the horizontal line shown in diagram 3013.1,

(b) the vertical line shown in diagram 3013.2 or either of the diagonal lines shown in diagram 3013.3 or 3013.4,

(c) the central circle shown in diagram 3013.5.

(3) When the light signals prescribed by paragraph (1) ("tram signals") are affixed to the light signals mentioned in regulation 33 ("standard signals") in accordance with any of the options shown in diagrams 3000.7, 3000.8, 3000.9 and 3000.10 their aspect may be such that they convey to the driver of a tramcar a different significance from that conveyed at the same time in accordance with regulation 36 to the drivers of other vehicular traffic by the aspect of the standard signals to which the tram signals are affixed.

Significance of light signals prescribed by regulation 41

B57.52   **42.** The significance of the light signals prescribed by regulation 41 shall be as follows—

(a) the aspect shown in diagram 3013.1 shall convey the prohibition that a tramcar shall not proceed beyond the stop line;

(b) the aspect shown in diagram 3013.2 shall indicate that a tramcar may proceed beyond the stop line and proceed straight ahead;

(c) the aspect shown in diagram 3013.3 shall indicate that a tramcar may proceed beyond the stop line and proceed to the left;

(d) the aspect shown in diagram 3013.4 shall indicate that a tramcar may proceed beyond the stop line and proceed to the right; and

(e) the aspect shown in diagram 3013.5 shall convey the prohibition that a tramcar shall not proceed beyond the stop line except that, as respects a tramcar which is so close to the stop line that it cannot safely be stopped without proceeding beyond the stop line, it shall convey the same indication as the aspect which was shown immediately before it.

Meaning of stop line and references to light signals

43.—(1) Subject to paragraphs (2) and (3), *"stop line"* in relation to light signals for the control of vehicular traffic means—   **B57.53**

(a) in relation to any vehicle except a tramcar the road marking shown in diagram 1001 placed in conjunction with the light signals;

(b) in relation to a tramcar, the road marking shown in diagram 1001.1 placed in conjunction with those light signals, or when that marking has not been so placed, the marking shown in diagram 1001 so placed.

(2) Where the road marking shown in diagram 1001.2 has been placed in conjunction with light signals, *"stop line"* in relation to those light signals means—

(a) the first stop line, in the case of a vehicle (other than a pedal cycle proceeding in the cycle lane) which has not proceeded beyond that line; or

(b) the second stop line, in the case of a vehicle which has proceeded beyond the first stop line or of a pedal cycle proceeding in the cycle lane.

(3) Where no stop line has been provided in conjunction with light signals or the stop line is not visible, references in relation to those signals to the *"stop line"* are—

(a) in a case where the sign shown in diagram 7011, 7011.1 or 7027 is placed in conjunction with the light signals, to be treated as references to that sign; and

(b) in any other case, to be treated as references to the post or other structure on which the primary signals are mounted.

(4) A reference in this regulation or in regulations 33 to 42 to light signals, to the signals or to a signal of a particular colour is, where secondary signals as well as primary signals have been placed, a reference to the light signals displayed by both the primary and secondary signals or, as the case may be, by the primary signals operating without the secondary signals or by the secondary signals operating without the primary signals.

(5) In this regulation—

(a) *"primary signals"* means light signals erected on or near the carriageway of a road and—

(i) where a stop line is placed in conjunction with the signals, sited beyond that line and near one end or both ends of the line; or

(ii) where there is no stop line, sited at either edge or both edges of the carriageway or part of the carriageway which is in use by traffic approaching and controlled by the signals;

(b) *"secondary signals"* means light signals erected on or near the carriageway facing traffic approaching from the direction of the primary signals but sited beyond those signals as viewed from the direction of travel of such traffic; and

(c) in paragraph (2)—

   (i) *"the first stop line"* means the transverse white line or lines appearing below the pedal cycle symbol in the road markings shown in either version of diagram 1001.2;

   (ii) *"the second stop line"* means the transverse white line appearing above the pedal cycle symbol in the road markings shown in either version of that diagram; and

   (iii) *"the cycle lane"* means the lane so marked in either version of that diagram.

Light signals for lane control of vehicular traffic

B57.54   44.—(1) A light signal placed above the carriageway and facing the direction of oncoming vehicular traffic used for the control of that traffic proceeding along the traffic lane over which those signals have been placed shall be of the size, colour and type of any diagram shown in Part I of Schedule 10.

(2) The height of the centre of each light signal from the surface of the carriageway in the immediate vicinity shall be not less than 5.5 metres nor more than 9 metres.

(3) The signals prescribed by this regulation shall be so designed that—

(a) the red cross shown in diagram 5003 or 5003.1 (*"the red cross"*) can be internally illuminated in such a manner as to show a steady red light;

(b) the green arrow shown in diagram 5001.1 or 5001.2 (*"the downward green arrow"*) can be internally illuminated in such a manner as to show a steady green light;

(c) the white arrow shown in diagram 5005 or 5005.1 (*"the diagonal white arrow"*) can be internally illuminated in such a manner as to show a steady white light; and

(d) whenever one of the signals referred to in sub-paragraphs (a) to (c) is illuminated neither of the other signals referred to in those sub-paragraphs shall be illuminated when placed over the same traffic lane.

(4) The significance of the light signals prescribed by this regulation shall be as follows—

(a) the red cross [except when placed above an actively managed hard shoulder] shall convey to vehicular traffic proceeding in the traffic lane above which it is displayed the prohibition that such traffic shall not proceed beyond the red cross in the traffic lane until that prohibition is cancelled by a display over that traffic lane of the downward green arrow or diagonal white arrow or by a display over that traffic lane or beside the carriageway of the traffic sign shown in diagram 5015;

[(aa) when placed over an actively managed hard shoulder the red cross shall convey to vehicular traffic that the restrictions on the use of the hard shoulder imposed by regulation 9 of the Motorways (England and Wales) Regulations or regulation 8 of the Motorways (Scotland) Regulations for the time being apply to the hard shoulder, until those restrictions are—

    (i) cancelled by the display over the actively managed hard shoulder of the sign shown in diagram 670 by means of a variable message sign; or

    (ii) superseded by the display over the actively managed hard shoulder of the sign shown in diagram 6031.1;]

(b) the downward green arrow shall convey to vehicular traffic proceeding in the traffic lane above which it is displayed the information that such traffic may proceed or continue to do so in the lane beneath the arrow; and

(c) the diagonal white arrow shall convey to vehicular traffic proceeding in the traffic lane above which it is displayed the warning that such traffic should move into the adjacent traffic lane in the direction indicated by the arrow as soon as traffic conditions permit.

[Regulation 44 is printed as substituted by SI 2005/1670.]   **B57.55**

Warning signal for motorways and all-purpose dual carriageway roads

45.—(1) A traffic sign for conveying the warning specified in paragraph (2) to   **B57.56** vehicular traffic on a motorway or an all-purpose dual carriageway road shall be a light signal of the size, colour and type shown in diagram 6023.

(2) The warning conveyed by the light signal shall be that—

(a) there is a hazard ahead on the motorway or all-purpose dual carriageway road; and

(b) drivers should drive at a speed which does not exceed 30 mph until they are certain that the hazard has been passed or removed.

(3) When the light signal prescribed by this regulation is operated, each lamp shall show an intermittent amber light at a rate of flashing of not less than 60 nor more than 90 flashes per minute and in such a manner that one light is always shown when the other light is not shown.

Matrix signs for motorways and all-purpose dual carriageway roads

46.—(1) In this regulation *"matrix sign"* means a sign shown in a diagram in   **B57.57** Part I of Schedule 11 for conveying to traffic on a motorway or an all-purpose dual carriageway road information or a warning, requirement, restriction, prohibition or speed limit—

(a) relating to or arising out of temporary hazardous conditions on or near the motorway or dual carriageway road; and

(b) specified in the caption to a diagram contained in Part I of that Schedule.

(2) A matrix sign shall be a light signal and shall be of the size, colour and type prescribed by this regulation and shown in a diagram in Part I of Schedule 11.

(3) Where a matrix sign is placed beside the carriageway of a road the warn-

ing, requirement, restriction, prohibition or speed limit conveyed by the sign shall apply to all vehicular traffic facing that sign and proceeding along the carriageway beside which the sign is placed.

(4) For the purposes of this regulation a sign which is mounted on a post situated beside the carriageway but is projected over it or part of it shall be treated as a sign placed beside the carriageway of that road.

(5) Where a matrix sign mounted on a gantry or other structure is so placed that a traffic lane of the carriageway [or an actively managed hard shoulder] passes directly beneath it, the warning, requirement, restriction, prohibition or speed limit conveyed by the sign shall apply only to vehicular traffic facing that sign and proceeding along the traffic lane [or actively managed hard shoulder] passing directly beneath it.

(6) A legend or symbol shown on a matrix sign shall be displayed by means of white or off-white light and except in the case of the signs shown in diagrams 6006.2, 6008.1, 6009.3 and 6012 shall be accompanied by the four lamps prescribed by paragraph (7).

(7) The four lamps mentioned in paragraph (6)—

   (a) shall be of the size, colour and type shown in diagram 6022 when placed beside the carriageway or in diagram 6021 when mounted on a gantry or other structure over the carriageway; and

   (b) when a matrix sign other than those shown in diagrams 6006.2, 6008.1, 6009.3 and 6012 is displayed, each lamp shall show an intermittent amber light at a rate of flashing of not less than 60 nor more than 90 flashes per minute and in such a manner that one horizontal pair of lights is always shown when the other horizontal pair of lights is not shown.

(8) The signs shown in diagrams 6006.2, 6008.1 and 6009.3 shall be accompanied by the four red lamps prescribed by regulation 37.

B57.58   *[Regulation 46 is printed as amended by SI 2005/1670.]*

Light signals at signal-controlled pedestrian facilities

B57.59   **47.**—(1) In this regulation *"the crossing"*, in relation to a sign, means the signal-controlled pedestrian facility in relation to which the sign is placed.

(2) A sign for conveying to pedestrian traffic the warning and information specified in paragraph (4) shall—

   (a) be of the size, colour and type shown in diagram 4002.1; or

   (b) consist of either a single unit of the size, colour and type shown in diagram 4003.1 or of two units, one comprising the upper and the other the lower part of that unit placed close together,

and shall comply with the requirements of paragraph (3).

(3) The requirements are that the sign is so designed and constructed that—

   (a) the red figure in the sign ("the red signal") can be internally illuminated by a steady light;

   (b) the green figure in the sign ("the green signal") can be internally illuminated by a steady light;

   (c) when one signal is illuminated the other is not;

(d) the green signal is illuminated only when there is at the same time conveyed to vehicular traffic a prohibition against entering the crossing and the prohibition is indicated by—

    (i) the light signals prescribed by regulation 33 (whether or not varied in accordance with regulation 34) or 41; or

    (ii) those light signals and the sign shown in diagram 606, 612, 613 or 616;

(e) in the case of the sign shown in diagram 4003.1, a push button or other switching device is included which, whilst the red signal is illuminated, in some way indicates to pedestrians whether it has been activated; and

(f) in the case of the sign shown in diagram 4002.1, the signal heads are ES compliant.

(4) The red signal, whilst it is illuminated, shall indicate the period during which, in the interests of safety, pedestrians should not use the crossing and the green signal, whilst it is illuminated, shall indicate the period during which pedestrians may use the crossing.

(5) Where the sign shown in diagram 4003.1 is provided at a crossing, any additional device which—

(a) is of the size, colour and type of only the part of that sign which shows the red and green signals or of only the part which includes the push button and the legend above it;

(b) complies with the requirements of paragraph (3) so far as they are relevant to it; and

(c) is provided to supplement the indications given by the sign shown in diagram 4003.1,

shall give the same indication as the relevant part of the sign shown in that diagram.

(6) A push button device giving instructions to pedestrians on how to cause the green signal in the sign shown in diagram 4002.1 to become illuminated and explaining the significance of the red and green signals shall be of the size, colour and type shown in diagram 4003.

(7) The sign shown in diagram 4003 shall, whilst the word "WAIT" is illuminated, convey the same indication as the red signal.

(8) Any audible or tactile signal emitted by a device provided in conjunction with the green signal for the benefit of disabled persons shall convey to pedestrians the same indication as the green signal.

Light signals at equestrian crossings

48.—(1) In this regulation *"the crossing"* in relation to a sign means the equestrian crossing in relation to which the sign is placed.   **B57.60**

(2) A sign for conveying to equestrian traffic the warning and information specified in paragraph (4) shall—

(a) be of the size, colour and type shown in diagram 4003.2; or

(b) consist of either a single unit of the size, colour and type shown in diagram 4003.4 or of two units, one comprising the upper and the other the lower part of that unit placed close together, and shall comply with the requirements of paragraph (3).

    (3) The requirements are that the sign is so designed and constructed that—

    (a) the red symbol in the sign (*"the red signal"*) can be internally illuminated by a steady light;

    (b) the green symbol in the sign (*"the green signal"*) can be internally illuminated by a steady light;

    (c) when one signal is illuminated the other is not;

    (d) the green signal is illuminated only when there is at the same time conveyed to vehicular traffic a prohibition against entering the crossing and the prohibition is indicated by—

        (i) the light signals prescribed by regulation 33 (whether or not varied in accordance with regulation 34) or 41; or

        (ii) those light signals and the sign shown in diagram 606, 612, 613 or 616;

    (e) in the case of the sign shown in diagram 4003.4, a push button or other switching device is included which, whilst the red signal is illuminated, in some way indicates to equestrians whether it has been activated; and

    (f) in the case of the sign shown in diagram 4003.2, the signal heads are ES compliant.

    (4) The red signal, whilst it is illuminated, shall indicate the period during which, in the interests of safety, equestrian traffic should not use the crossing and the green signal, whilst it is illuminated, shall indicate the time during which such traffic may use the crossing.

    (5) Where the sign shown in diagram 4003.4 is provided at a crossing, any additional device which—

    (a) is of the size, colour and type of only the part of that sign which shows the red and green signals or of only the part which includes the push button and the legend above it;

    (b) complies with the requirements of paragraph (3) so far as they are relevant to it; and

    (c) is provided to supplement the indications given by the sign shown in diagram 4003.4,

shall give the same indication as the relevant part of the sign shown in that diagram.

    (6) A push button device giving instructions to equestrians on how to cause the green signal in the sign shown in diagram 4003.2 to become illuminated and explaining the significance of the red and green signals shall be of the size, colour and type shown in diagram 4003.3.

    (7) The sign shown in diagram 4003.3 shall, whilst the word "WAIT" is illuminated, convey the same indication as the red signal.

Light signals at Toucan crossings

B57.61   **49.**—(1) In this regulation *"the crossing"* in relation to a sign means the Toucan crossing in relation to which the sign is placed.

    (2) A sign for conveying to pedestrians and pedal cyclists the warning and information specified in paragraph (4) shall—

(a) be of the size, colour and type shown in diagram 4003.5; or

(b) consist of either a single unit of the size, colour and type shown in diagram 4003.7 or of two units, one comprising the upper and the other the lower part of that unit placed close together,

and shall comply with the requirements of paragraph (3).

(3) The requirements are that the sign is so designed and constructed that—

(a) the red figures in the signs shown in diagrams 4003.5 and 4003.7 and the red cycle symbol in diagram 4003.7 ("the red signal") can be internally illuminated by a steady light;

(b) the green figure and the green cycle symbol ("the green signal") can be internally illuminated by a steady light;

(c) when one signal is illuminated the other is not;

(d) the green signal is illuminated only when there is at the same time conveyed to vehicular traffic, other than pedal cyclists wishing to use the crossing, a prohibition against entering the crossing and the prohibition is indicated by—

(i) the light signals prescribed by regulation 33 (whether or not varied in accordance with regulation 34) or 41; or

(ii) those light signals and the sign shown in diagram 606, 612, 613 or 616;

(e) in the case of the sign shown in diagram 4003.7, a push button or other switching device is included which, whilst the red signal is illuminated, in some way indicates to pedestrians and pedal cyclists whether it has been activated; and

(f) in the case of the sign shown in diagram 4003.5, the signal heads are ES compliant.

(4) The red signal, whilst it is illuminated, shall indicate the period during which, in the interests of safety, pedestrians and pedal cyclists should not use the crossing and the green signal, whilst it is illuminated, shall indicate the period during which pedestrians and pedal cyclists may use the crossing.

(5) Where the sign shown in diagram 4003.7 is provided at a crossing, any additional device which—

(a) is of the size, colour and type of only the part of that sign which shows the red and green signals or of only the part which includes the push button and the legend above it;

(b) complies with the requirements of paragraph (3) so far as they are relevant to it; and

(c) is provided to supplement the indications given by the sign shown in diagram 4003.7,

shall give the same indication as the relevant part of the sign shown in that diagram.

(6) A push button device giving instructions to pedestrians and pedal cyclists on how to cause the green signal in the sign shown in diagram 4003.5 to become illuminated shall be of the size, colour and type shown in diagram 4003.6.

(7) The sign shown in diagram 4003.6 shall, whilst the word "WAIT" is illuminated, convey the same indication as the red signal.

(8) Any audible or tactile signal emitted by a device provided in conjunction

with the green signal for the benefit of disabled pedestrians shall convey to pedestrians the same indication as the green signal.

Warning lights at school crossing places

B57.62 **50.** A sign for conveying a warning to vehicular traffic that a school crossing place lies ahead and is being patrolled by a school crossing patrol or is otherwise in use by such children—

> (a) shall be a light signal of the size, colour and type shown in diagram 4004, each lamp of which when operated shall show an intermittent amber light at a rate of flashing of not less than 60 nor more than 90 flashes per minute and in such a manner that one light is always shown when the other light is not shown; and
>
> (b) may be erected on or near part of the road in advance of a crossing place in relation to oncoming traffic.

Cattle crossing signs and warning lights

B57.63 **51.**—(1) A sign of the size, colour and type shown in diagram 4005 may be erected on or near a road in advance of a place in that road where cattle under the supervision of a herdsman on their way from one part of a farm to another cross the road (*"a cattle crossing"*) to convey to oncoming traffic the warning specified in paragraph (2).

(2) The warning conveyed by the sign shall be that—

> (a) a cattle crossing lies ahead and may be in use; and
>
> (b) traffic should be prepared to stop.

(3) When the sign is operated, each lamp shall show an intermittent amber light at a rate of flashing of not less than 60 nor more than 90 flashes per minute and in such a manner that one light is always shown when the other light is not shown.

Light signals for pedestrian traffic at level crossings

B57.64 **52.**—(1) Light signals conveying to pedestrians at level crossings the prohibition specified in paragraph (2) shall be of the size, colour and type shown in diagram 4006 and so designed that—

> (a) the red figure shown in diagram 4006 is internally illuminated by an intermittent red light which is shown at a rate of flashing of not less than 60 nor more than 90 flashes per minute;
>
> (b) the red figure is illuminated only when the intermittent red lights prescribed by regulation 39(2)(b) are illuminated; and
>
> (c) the signal heads are ES compliant.

(2) The red figure when illuminated in the manner prescribed by paragraph (1) shall convey the prohibition that pedestrians shall not proceed beyond the transverse road marking shown in diagram 1003.2 on the footway or diagram 1001 on the carriageway.

SECTION 6

Miscellaneous Traffic Signs

Temporary signs

53.—(1) In this regulation *"temporary sign"* means a sign placed on or near a   **B57.65**
road for the purpose of conveying to traffic—
- (a) information about convenient routes to be followed on the occasion of—
  - (i) a sporting event;
  - (ii) an exhibition; or
  - (iii) any other public gathering, which is in each case likely to attract a large volume of traffic;
- (b) information about diversions or alternative traffic routes;
- (c) information about the availability of new routes or destinations;
- (d) information about changes in route numbers;
- (e) warnings about, or information on how to avoid, any temporary hazards caused by—
  - (i) works being executed on or near a road;
  - (ii) adverse weather conditions or other natural causes;
  - (iii) the failure of street lighting or malfunction of or damage to any other apparatus, equipment or facility used in connection with the road or anything situated on or near or under it; or
  - (iv) damage to the road itself; or
- (f) requests by the police for information in connection with road traffic accidents.

(2) A temporary sign—
- (a) which conveys to traffic any information, warning, requirement, restriction or prohibition of a description which can be conveyed by a sign shown in a diagram in Schedules 1 to 12 (whether on its own or in conjunction or in combination with another such sign) shall be of the size, colour and type shown in that diagram;
- (b) which does not fall within paragraph (a) ("a non-prescribed temporary sign") shall be of such size, colour and type as is specified in paragraphs (3) to (6).

(3) The shape of a non-prescribed temporary sign shall be—
- (a) rectangular but with the corners rounded; or
- (b) as in sub-paragraph (a) with a rounded point at one end.

(4) A non-prescribed temporary sign shall be of a size appropriate to the circumstances in which it is placed and may incorporate—
- (a) wording;
- (b) numerals;
- (c) arrows or chevrons;
- (d) any appropriate symbol taken from any diagram in any Schedule; and
- (e) the arms, badge or other device of a traffic authority, police authority or an organisation representative of road users.

(5) Every letter and numeral incorporated in a non-prescribed temporary sign

other than any letter incorporated in the sign in accordance with paragraph (4)(e) shall be not less than 40 nor more than 350 millimetres in height, and every arrow so incorporated shall be not less than 250 nor more than 1000 millimetres in length.

(6) Every letter, numeral, arrow, chevron or symbol, other than a sign shown in a diagram in Schedules 1 to 5 when used as a symbol, incorporated in a non-prescribed temporary sign shall be—

  (a) black on a background of white or of yellow;

  (b) white on a blue background;

  (c) blue on a white background;

  (d) if the sign conveys information or warnings of the kind mentioned in paragraph (1)(e), white on a red background, except where it is placed on a motorway when it shall be black on a yellow background; or

  (e) if the sign is a variable message sign, white, off-white or yellow on a black background or black on a yellow background, except when the sign is not in use when it shall display a plain black or grey face.

Flashing beacons

B57.66   **54.**—(1) A beacon—

  (a) showing an intermittent amber light and placed in combination with a temporary sign within the meaning of regulation 53 or the sign shown in diagram 562, 610, 7001, 7001.3, 7004, 7005, 7009, 7010.1, 7012, 7013, 7019, 7020, 7021, 7022, 7105, 7201, 7202 or 7207 and in compliance with the requirements in paragraph (2); or

  (b) showing an intermittent blue light and placed by a constable or a person acting under instructions (whether general or specific) of the chief officer of police in combination with a sign shown in diagram 606, 609, 610, 616, 633, 829.1, 829.2, 829.3, 829.4, 7101.1, 7102 or 7105, and in compliance with (c) and (d) of the requirements in paragraph (2),

shall convey the warning that drivers of vehicles should take special care.

(2) The requirements mentioned in paragraph (1) are—

  (a) the peak intensity of light emitted by the lens or lenses of each such beacon shall be—

    (i) if the period between individual flashes does not exceed $1/4$ of a second, not less than 100 candela on the principal axis of the relevant lens;

    (ii) if the period between individual flashes exceeds $1/4$ of a second, not less than 2000 candela on the principal axis; or

    (iii) if the period between the cessation of a double flash and the start of the succeeding double flash exceeds $1/4$ of a second, not less than 1000 candela on the principal axis;

  (b) each lens shall be of such a shape and size that the perimeter of its area projected horizontally onto a vertical plane shall be capable of lying wholly inside a square having sides of 200 millimetres in length and wholly outside a square having sides of 100 millimetres in length;

(c) the height of the centre of the lenses from the surface of the carriageway in the immediate vicinity shall be not less than 800 (or in the case of a beacon of the kind mentioned in paragraph (1)(b) 450) nor more than 1500 millimetres; and

(d) the rate of flashing shall be not less than 55 nor more than 150 individual or double flashes per minute.

Road danger lamps

55.—(1) A lamp showing a steady or intermittent amber light which—   **B57.67**
    (a) conforms to—
        (i) British Standard Specification BS3143: Part 1: 1985 amended by Amendment No.1 dated February 1985;
        (ii) BS3143: Part 2: 1990 amended by Amendment No.1 dated November 1993 and Amendment No.2 dated December 1998; or
        (iii) a corresponding EEA Standard; and
    (b) is illuminated separately and by a single source of light,
shall indicate to traffic the limits of a temporary obstruction of the road and in this regulation is called a *"road danger lamp"*.

(2) The height of the centre of each lens of a road danger lamp from the surface of the road in the immediate vicinity of the lamp shall not exceed 1500 millimetres where the speed limit on the road is 40 mph or less, or 1200 millimetres where the speed limit on the road is more than 40 mph.

(3) The rate of flashing of a road danger lamp which shows an intermittent light shall be—
    (a) if the lamp is placed not less than 50 metres from a street lamp lit by electricity on a road subject to a speed limit of 40 mph or less, either—
        (i) not less than 900 flashes per minute; or
        (ii) not less than 55 nor more than 150 flashes per minute;
    (b) in any other case not less than 900 flashes per minute.

Cones, delineators and cylinders

56.—(1) In this regulation—   **B57.68**
    "cone" means the sign shown in diagram 7101.1;
    "delineator" means the sign shown in diagram 7102;
    "cylinder" means the sign shown in diagram 7103.

(2) A cone shall consist of a conically shaped device made of rubber or flexible plastic material in respect of which—
    (a) the base is of any single colour; and
    (b) the base is a polygon having not more than eight sides, which would be contained wholly within a circle with a diameter of three quarters of the height of the cone.

(3) The part of a cone coloured white shall, subject to paragraph (5), be illuminated with white retroreflecting material and the part coloured red may be illuminated with red retroreflecting material.

(4) Information about the ownership of a cone may be moulded—

   (a) into the base in characters not more than 80 mm high in the same colour as the base;

   (b) into the conical body in characters not more than 40 mm high in the same colour as that body; or

   (c) as mentioned in both sub-paragraphs (a) and (b).

(5) Information about the manufacture of a cone, required to comply with British Standard Specification BS873: Part 8: 1985 or a corresponding EEA Standard and occupying an area not exceeding 30 square centimetres, may be indicated on the part coloured white in characters not exceeding 5 millimetres in height, leaving at least 90% of the remaining area of white colour illuminated with white retroreflecting material.

(6) A rotating device may be mounted on top of a cone and—

   (a) that device shall—

      (i) be red and not reflectorised; and

      (ii) display one or more signs shown in either diagram 560 or diagram 561; and

   (b) those signs shall be coloured amber, intermittently whilst rotating and constantly whilst static.

(7) A delineator shall consist of a flat device—

   (a) of which the side intended to be exposed to traffic is coloured as shown in diagram 7102 and the reverse side is either so coloured or coloured only grey or only red;

   (b) which is made of rubber or flexible plastic material; and

   (c) of which the base is of any single colour, except that a reflectorised white line 100 millimetres wide at an angle of not more than 60 degrees to the road surface may be marked on one side of the base at right angles to the face of the delineator.

(8) The white part of a delineator shall, subject to paragraph (10), be illuminated with white retroreflecting material and the red part (except on the reverse side when that side is coloured only red) may be illuminated with red retroreflecting material.

(9) Information about the ownership of a delineator may be moulded into the base in characters not more than 80 mm high and in the same colour as the base.

(10) Information about the manufacture of a delineator, required in order to comply with British Standard Specification BS 873: Part 8: 1985 or a corresponding EEA Standard and occupying an area not exceeding 30 square centimetres, may be indicated on the part coloured white in characters not exceeding 5 millimetres in height, leaving at least 90% of the remaining area of white colour illuminated with white retroreflecting material.

(11) A cylinder shall consist of a cylindrically shaped device made of rubber or flexible plastic material.

(12) The white part of a cylinder shall, subject to paragraph (14), be illuminated with white retroreflecting material and the part coloured red may be illuminated with red retroreflecting material.

(13) Information about the ownership of a cylinder may be moulded into the lower of the two red parts in red characters not more than 40 mm high.

(14) Information about the manufacture of a cylinder, required in order to comply with British Standard Specification BS873: Part 8: 1985 or a corresponding EEA Standard and occupying an area not exceeding 30 square centimetres, may be indicated on the part coloured white in characters not exceeding 5 millimetres in height, leaving at least 90% of the remaining area of white colour illuminated with white retroreflecting material.

Refuge indicator lamps

57. A lamp in the form of an illuminated spherical globe for conveying the   **B57.69** warning that drivers of vehicles are approaching a street refuge may be placed subject to the following conditions—

    (a) the globe shall be white;

    (b) the globe shall have a diameter of not less than 275 nor more than 335 millimetres; and

    (c) the height of the centre of the globe above the surface of the carriageway in the immediate vicinity shall be not less than 3800 millimetres nor more than 5000 millimetres.

Variable message signs

58.—(1) In these Regulations a *"variable message sign"* means a device   **B57.70** capable of displaying, at different times, two or more aspects falling within the following descriptions—

    (a) a sign shown in a diagram in Schedule 1, 2, 3, 4, 5, 7, 11 or 12;

    (b) a legend of a type shown in Schedule 15 in accordance with the provisions of that Schedule;

    (c) a non-prescribed temporary sign as defined by regulation 53(2)(b);

    (d) a blank grey or a blank black face.

(2) A variable message sign shall be of a size appropriate to display the messages referred to in sub-paragraphs (a) and (b) of paragraph (1), having regard to the normal speed of traffic on the road on or near which the sign is situated.

(3) If the construction or method of operation of a variable message sign prevents a sign from being displayed in the colours shown for it in the appropriate diagram in Schedule 1, 2, 3, 4, 5, 7 or 12, a black legend or symbol on a white or yellow background may be displayed as a white, off-white or yellow legend or symbol on a dark background, provided that any red triangle or red circle forming part of the sign is included.

(4) A legend or symbol [displayed] as mentioned in paragraph (3) may be in the form of a white, off-white or yellow outline of the legend or symbol.

(5) The size of any symbol or legend, including any red triangle or circle, displayed on a variable message sign, which is displayed by means of light-emitting characters or symbols, may be varied so that the size of the symbol or legend appears to road users to be the same as it appears to them to be when it is not displayed in this manner.

(6) When a variable message sign displays—

    (a) the sign shown in diagram 670;

    (b) any sign shown in a diagram in Part I of Schedule 11 except diagrams 6006.2, 6008.1, 6009.3 and 6012; or

(c) a legend of the type shown in Schedule 15,

it may also display four lamps, which are of the size, colour and type specified in regulation 46(7) and have a rate of flashing of not less than 60 nor more than 150 flashes per minute, and the distance between the lamps shall accord with the overall size of the variable message sign.

[(6A) Where a variable message sign displays the sign shown in diagram 670 by means of light emitting characters and symbols, the diameter of the sign may be varied to 1,300 millimetres.]

(7) Where a variable message sign displays by means of light-emitting characters or symbols—

(a) the sign shown in diagram 504.1, 505.1, 506.1, 507.1, 510, 512, 512.1, 512.2 or 513; or

(b) the sign shown in diagram 670 (when showing the numerals "20", "30", "40" or "50") in such a way that the sign is only visible when associated equipment detects the presence of a vehicle exceeding the speed limit indicated by the sign,

the variable message sign may display, beneath the sign displayed on it, the legend "SLOW DOWN" in characters having a height not less than one quarter of the height of the displayed sign.

(8) The display of a blank black or grey face on a variable message sign accompanied by four flashing lamps of the kind mentioned in paragraph (6) shall indicate to drivers that they should take special care.

(9) A variable message sign which displays alternately the signs shown in diagrams 7023 and 7024 shall be manually operated.

B57.71   *[Regulation 58 is printed as amended by SI 2005/1670.]*

Regulation 11(1)   SCHEDULE 1

WARNING SIGNS

B57.72   *[The diagrams representing the actual traffic signs are not reproduced in this work, but the signs in Sch.1 are described below by means of (in the main) the legends accompanying the signs. The dimensions of the components of the various signs are specified in marks accompanying the diagrams (not reproduced) and variations of wording (where permissible) are referred to in notes accompanying the diagrams (not reproduced), often by means of a cross-reference to Sch.16. The accompanying notes also cross refer to Sch.17 for information regarding the illumination requirements for the signs. The diagrams are reproduced in numerical sequence but there are gaps in the numbering.*

501	junction ahead controlled by a diagram 601.1 ("STOP") or diagram 602 ("GIVE WAY") sign (inverted red triangle)
502	distance to a junction ahead controlled by a diagram 601.1 ("STOP 100yds") sign
503	distance to a junction ahead controlled by a diagram 602 sign ("GIVE WAY 50yds")
504.1	crossroads ahead (black symbol within red triangle)
505.1	T-junction ahead (black symbol within red triangle)
506.1	side road ahead (black symbol within red triangle)
507.1	staggered junction ahead (black symbol within red triangle)

508.1	traffic merges from the left (black symbol within red triangle)
509.1	traffic merges ahead on to main carriageway (black symbol within red triangle)
510	roundabout ahead (black symbol within red triangle)
511	reduction in speed necessary for a change of road layout ahead ("REDUCE SPEED NOW" in white letters on red background edged in white)
512	bend ahead (black symbol within red triangle)
512.1	junction on bend ahead (black symbol within red triangle)
512.2	alternative to diagram 512.1
513	double bend or a series of bends ahead, first to the left (black symbol within red triangle)
513.1	adverse camber on a bend or roundabout ("Adverse camber" in black letters on white background)
513.2	advisory speed limit at a bend or other hazard ("Max speed 30" in black letters on white background)
515	sharp deviation of route (white chevrons on black background)
515.1	alternative to diagram 515
515.1A	sharp deviation of route at roundabout (white chevrons on black background)
515.2	sharp deviation of route at roundabout (black chevrons set between white paving blocks)
516	road narrows on both sides ahead (black symbol within red triangle)
517	road narrows on right ahead (black symbol within red triangle)
518	convergence of traffic to a single file in each direction ("Single file traffic" in black letters on white background)
519	road only wide enough for one line of vehicles ("Single track road" in black letters on white background)
520	dual carriageway ends ahead (black symbol within red triangle)
521	two-way traffic (black symbol within red triangle)
522	two-way traffic on route crossing ahead (black symbol within red triangle)
523.1	steep hill downwards ahead (black symbol within red triangle)
524.1	steep hill upwards ahead (black symbol within red triangle)
525	drivers should engage low gear for steep hill ("Low gear now" in black letters on white background)
526	drivers should keep in low gear for steep hill or tight bend ("Keep in low gear" in black letters on white background)
527	drivers should keep in low gear for distance indicated ("Low gear for 1 miles" in black letters on white background)
528	hump bridge ahead (black symbol within red triangle)
528.1	end of bridge parapet, abutment wall, tunnel mouth or other obstruction adjacent to the carriageway (vertical rectangles with diagonal yellow and black stripes)
529	opening or swing bridge ahead (black symbol within red triangle)
529.1	tunnel ahead (black symbol within red triangle)
530	maximum headroom available at hazard (alternatives in feet+inches and in metres) (black symbol within red triangle)
530.1	reduced headroom over part of road due to overhanging building ahead ("Overhanging building" in black letters on white background)

530.2	reduced headroom at hazard (alternative types) (horizontal rectangles with diagonal yellow and black stripes, one version culminating in inverted black triangle in middle)
531.1	maximum headroom available at arch bridge ahead (alternatives in feet+inches and in metres) (black symbol within red triangle)
531.2	high vehicles to use the middle of road at arch bridge ahead ("ARCH BRIDGE High vehicles use middle of road" in black letters on white background)
532.2	maximum headroom available in the centre of a road at an arch bridge (are with alternative black and yellow stripes surmounted by sign or signs as in diagram 531.1)
532.3	maximum headroom available at the side of and in the centre of a road at an arch bridge (sign or signs as in diagram 531.1 at side of bridge and sign or signs as in diagram 531.1 in centre of bridge)
543	traffic signs ahead (coloured lights symbol within red triangle)
543.1	traffic signals ahead which only operate at certain times ("Part time signals" in black letters on white background)
544	zebra crossing ahead (black symbol within red triangle)
544.1	pedestrians in road ahead (black symbol within red triangle)
544.2	frail or disabled pedestrians likely to cross road ahead (black symbol within red triangle)
545	children going to or from school of playground ahead (black symbol within red triangle)
546	school ahead ("School" in black letters on white background)
547.1	school crossing patrol ahead ("Patrol" in black letters on white background)
547.2	children's playground ahead ("Playground" in black letters on white background)
547.3	no footway for distance indicated ("No footway for 400 yards" in black letters on white background)
547.4	disabled pedestrians likely to cross road ahead ("Disabled people" in black letters on white background)
547.7	disabled children likely to cross road ahead ("Disabled children" in black letters on white background)
547.8	zebra crossing or signal-controlled crossing on road hump ahead ("Humped crossing" in black letters on white background)
548	cattle likely to be in road ahead (black symbol within red triangle)
548.1	supervised cattle crossing ahead ("When lights show 200yds" in black letters on white background)
549	sheep likely to be in road ahead (black symbol within red triangle)
550	wild horses or ponies likely to be in road ahead (black symbol within red triangle)
550.1	accompanied horses or ponies likely to be in or crossing road ahead (black symbol within red triangle)
550.2	horse drawn vehicles likely to be in road ahead (black symbol within red triangle)
551	wild animals likely to be in road ahead (black symbol within red triangle)
551.1	migratory toad crossing ahead (black symbol within red triangle)
551.2	wild fowl likely to be in road ahead (black symbol within red triangle)
552	cattle grid ahead ("Cattle grid" in black letters within red triangle)
553	by-pass of cattle grid ("Horse drawn vehicles and animals" and directional arrow in black letters on white background)

553.1	agricultural vehicles likely to be in road ahead (black symbol within red triangle)
553.2	agricultural vehicles likely to be in road ahead ("Farm traffic" in black letters on white background)
554	worded warning sign ("Ford" in black letters within red triangle)
554.1	risk of brake failure after crossing a ford or before descending a steep gradient ("Try your brakes" in black letters within red triangle)
554.2	risk of ice or packed snow ahead (black symbol within red triangle)
554.3	ice ahead ("Ice" in black letters on white background)
555	quayside or river bank ahead (black symbol within red triangle)
555.1	water course alongside road ahead (black symbol within red triangle)
556	uneven road ahead (black symbol within red triangle)
556.1	soft verges ahead (black symbol within red triangle)
566.2	soft verges for distance indicated ("Soft verges for 2 miles" in black letters on white background)
557	slippery road ahead (black symbol within red triangle)
557.1	road hump or series of road humps ahead (black symbol within red triangle)
557.2	road humps ahead for the distance indicated ("Humps for $^1/_2$ mile" in black letters on white background)
557.3	road humps ahead in the direction and for the distance indicated ("Humps for 300 yards" and directional arrow in black letters on white background)
557.4	road hump in the direction and at distance indicated ("Hump 20 yards" and directional arrow in black letters on white background)
558	low flying aircraft or sudden aircraft noise likely ahead (black symbol within red triangle)
558.1	low flying helicopters or sudden helicopter noise likely ahead (black symbol within red triangle)
558.2	gliders likely ahead ("Gliders" in black letters on white background)
559	risk of falling or fallen rocks likely (black symbol within red triangle)
560	edge of carriageway or obstruction near that edge (solid red circle)
561	alternative shape for the sign shown in diagram 560 (solid red rectangle (upright))
562	other danger ahead (black symbol within red triangle)
563	nature of other danger ahead ("Accident" in black letters on white background)
563.1	warning of light signals as shown in diagram 3014 ahead ("FIRE STATION STOP when lights show" in black letters on white background together with two red and one yellow lights on black background)
570	distance over which hazard or prohibition extends ("For 2 miles" in black letters on white background)
572	distance ahead to hazard ("400yds" in black letters on white background)
573	distance and direction to hazard ("250yds" and directional arrow in black letters on white background)
574	area infected by animal disease ahead ("ANIMAL DISEASE RABIES INFECTED AREA AHEAD" in white letters on red background)
575	large vehicles likely to be in middle of road because of narrowness of carriageway ("Oncoming vehicles in middle of road" in black letters on white background)
581	side winds likely ahead (black symbol within red triangle)

582   slow moving military vehicles likely to be crossing or in road ahead (black symbol within red triangle)

583   slow moving vehicles likely on incline ahead (black symbol within red triangle)

583.1   distance over which slow moving vehicles likely to be encountered ahead ("Slow lorries for 2 miles" in black letters on white background)

584   traffic queues likely on road ahead (black symbol within red triangle)

584.1   traffic queues likely on road ahead ("Queues likely" in black letters on white background)]

Regulation 11(1)   SCHEDULE 2

REGULATORY SIGNS (OTHER THAN THOSE EXCLUSIVELY FOR RAILWAY AND TRAMWAY LEVEL CROSSINGS, BUS AND PEDAL CYCLE FACILITIES, AND ROAD WORKS)

B57.73   *[The diagrams representing the actual traffic signs are not reproduced in this work, but the signs in Sch.2 are described below by means of (in the main) the legends accompanying the signs. The dimensions of the components of the various signs are specified in marks accompanying the diagrams (not reproduced) and variations of wording (where permissible) are referred to in notes accompanying the diagrams (not reproduced), often by means of a cross-reference to Sch.16. The accompanying notes also cross refer to Sch.17 for information regarding the illumination requirements for the signs. The diagrams are reproduced in numerical sequence but there are gaps in the numbering.*

601.1   vehicular traffic must comply with the requirements prescribed in reg.16 ("STOP" in white letters on a red hexagonal background edged with white)

602   vehicular traffic must comply with the requirements prescribed in reg.16 ("GIVE WAY" in black letters within an inverted red triangle)

606   vehicular traffic must proceed in the direction indicated by the arrow (horizontal arrow in white on blue background within circle edged in white)

607   one-way traffic ("One way" in black letters on white background)

608   dual carriageway ("Dual carriageway" in black letters on white background)

609   vehicular traffic must turn ahead in direction indicated by arrow (arrow in white on blue background within circle edged in white)

610   vehicular traffic must comply with requirements of reg.15 (angled arrow in white on blue background within circle edged in white)

611   vehicular traffic may reach the same destination by proceeding either side of sign (two white arrows within blue circle)

611.1   vehicular traffic entering junction must comply with the requirements prescribed in reg.16

612   no right turn for vehicular traffic (black arrow on white background pointing to right crossed through in red without red circle)

613   no left turn for vehicular traffic (black arrow on white background pointing to left crossed through in red within red circle)

614   no U-turns for vehicular traffic (black symbol on white background crossed through in red within red circle)

615   priority must be given to vehicles from the opposite direction (small red arrow and larger black arrow pointing in opposite directions on white background within red circle)

615.1	same as diagram 615 ("Give way to oncoming vehicles" in black letters on white background)
616	no entry for vehicular traffic (horizontal white bar on red background within circle edged in white)
617	all vehicles prohibited except non-mechanically propelled vehicles pushed by pedestrians (red circle with white centre)
618	all vehicles prohibited from "play street" during times indicated except for access ("Play Street [*time*] to sunset except for access" in black letters on white background)
618.1	all vehicles prohibited during the times indicated, except for access/specified vehicles ("No vehicles [*time*] except for ..." in black letters on white background)
618.2	entry to pedestrian zone restricted except for loading/specified vehicles (alternative types) ("PEDESTRIAN ZONE [red circle with white centre (with or without symbol)] except for [symbol] [times to be specified]")
618.3	entry to and waiting in pedestrian zone restricted, except for loading/specified vehicles (alternative types) ("PEDESTRIAN ZONE [red circle (with or without symbol)] except for ... [diagram 636] At any time")
618.3A	entry to and waiting in pedestrian zone restricted, except for loading/access/specified vehicles ("PEDESTRIAN ZONE [red circle with white centre] except for ... [symbol may be included] [diagram 636] At any time")
618.4	end of restrictions associated with pedestrian zone ([symbol] "Pedestrian Zone ENDS" in black letters on white background)
619	motor vehicles prohibited (black symbols (motorcyle and motor car) within red circle)
619.1	motor vehicles except solo motorcycles prohibited (black symbol (motor car) within red circle)
619.2	solo motorcycles prohibited (black symbol (motorcycle) within red circle)
620	vehicles requiring access to premises or land adjacent to the road exempt from prohibition conveyed by associated sign ("Except for access" in black letters on white background)
620.1	goods vehicles requiring to enter road for loading or unloading of goods exempt from prohibition conveyed by associated sign ("Except for loading by" [symbol] in black letters on white background)
622.1A	goods vehicles exceeding the maximum gross weight indicated on the goods vehicle symbol prohibited (black symbol [goods vehicle indicating weight] on white background within red circle)
622.2	end of prohibition of goods vehicles exceeding maximum gross weight indicated by diagram 622.1A (grey symbol on white background crossed through within grey circle)
622.4	articulated vehicles prohibited ("No articulated vehicles" in black letters on white background within red circle)
622.5	horse drawn vehicles prohibited (black symbol on white background within red circle)
622.6	ridden or accompanied horses prohibited (black symbol on white background within red circle)
622.7	towed caravans prohibited (black symbol within red triangle)
622.8	vehicles carrying explosives prohibited (black symbol within red triangle)
622.9	same as diagram 622.8 ("No explosives" in black letters on white background)

625.1	pedestrians prohibited (black symbol on white background within red circle)
626.2A	vehicles exceeding maximum gross weight indicated prohibited from crossing bridge or other structure ("WEAK BRIDGE" in black letters on white background above indication of "m g w" in black letters on white background within red circle on grey background)
627.1	exemption for unladen vehicles from prohibition conveyed by diagram 626.2A ("Except for empty vehicles" in black letters on white background set below diagram 626.2A)
629	vehicles exceeding width indicated prohibited (permitted width in black characters on white background preceded and followed by black arrow-heads pointing inwards within red circle)
629A	as diagram 629, with width indicated in both metric and imperial units
629.1	vehicles or combinations of vehicles exceeding length indicated prohibited (black symbol above permitted length and two arrows pointing outwards on white background within red circle)
629.2	vehicles exceeding height indicated prohibited (permitted height in black characters on white background above and below black arrowheads pointing inwards within red circle)
629.2A	as diagram 629.2, but height indicated in metric and imperial units.
632	no overtaking (black and red symbols (cars) on white background within red circle)
633	vehicular traffic must not proceed beyond the sign where displayed temporarily by uniformed police officer or traffic warden ("STOP [symbol] POLICE")
636	temporary prohibition of waiting except for loading and unloading (blue circle crossed with diagonal bar in red within red circle, on yellow background)
636.1	temporary prohibition of loading and unloading ("No loading" in black letters on yellow background)
636.2	temporary prohibition on stopping during the periods indicated ("No stopping" in black letters on yellow background [*times*])
637.1	continuous prohibition on waiting except for loading and unloading on verge or footway (rectangular panel displaying diagram 636 and "At any time on verge or footway" in black letters on yellow background)
637.2	prohibition on waiting (and loading and unloading) in pedestrian zone (alternative types) ("Pedestrian Zone" [diagram 636] "At any time" in black letters on yellow background (to which may be added "No loading" [*days*] and [*times*] in black letters on white background)
637.3	continuous prohibition on waiting except for loading and unloading for at least 4 consecutive months (rectangular panel displaying diagram 636 and "At any time [*dates*]" in black letters on yellow background)
638	continuous prohibition on loading and unloading ("No loading at any time" in black letters on white background)
638.1	loading and unloading prohibited during the periods and in the direction indicated ("No loading [*days*] [*times*]" together with directional arrow in black letters on white background)
639	waiting prohibited except for loading and unloading during the period and in the direction indicated (diagram 636 [*times*] together with directional arrow in black characters on yellow background)

639.1B   waiting prohibited during the periods indicated on the upper panel and restrictions on waiting during the period indicated on the lower panel (rectangular panel with diagram 636, [*dates*] and [*times*] in black letters on yellow background in upper panel; letter "P" in white on blue patch in lower panel with "[*Dates*] [*times*] *xx* hours No return within *xx* hours" in black letters on white background)

640   waiting prohibited during period and in direction indicated on upper panel and loading and unloading prohibited during periods and in the direction indicated on lower panel (rectangular panel with [*dates*] and [*times*] in black letters on yellow background and diagram 636 in upper portion; with "No loading [*days*] [*times*]" and directional arrow in black letters on white background in lower portion)

640.1   waiting, loading and unloading prohibited at parking place where parking temporarily suspended (indication on parking meter cover) (diagram 636 and "No loading" in black letters on yellow background)

640.2A   waiting by goods vehicles over maximum gross weight shown prohibited during the periods and in the direction indicated (yellow rectangular panel with black symbol displaying permitted weight, diagram 636, [*days*] and [*times*], in black letters and directional arrow)

640.3   entrance to designated off-highway loading area in which waiting restrictions apply ("Loading area diagram 636 Except by permitted vehicles [*days*] [*times*]" in black letters on yellow background)

640.4   waiting prohibited in designated off-highway loading area during period indicated except by permitted vehicles (diagram 636 "Except by permitted vehicles [*days*] [*times*]" in black letters on yellow background)

640.5   end of designated off-highway loading area in which waiting restrictions apply (rectangular panel, in left-hand portion diagram 636 displayed in grey and white crossed through; in right-hand portion "End of loading area" in black letters on yellow background)

642   no stopping on main carriageway (blue circle surrounded in red and crossed through diagonally in red)

642.2A   no stopping on the road marking shown in diagram 1027.1 (school entrance) during period indicated (diagram 642 "No stopping [*days*] [*times*] on entrance markings" in black letters on yellow background)

642.3   no stopping in lay-by except in emergency (diagram 642 "No stopping except in emergency")

645   end of restriction or prohibition conveyed by associated sign or, when used with diagram 7001 (road works or temporary obstruction of carriageway ahead), end of all restrictions or prohibitions associated with road works ("End" in black letters on white background)

646   no stopping during periods indicated except for so long as may be necessary for the purpose of picking up or setting down passengers (rectangular panel; in upper portion, diagram 636 "URBAN CLEARWAY" [*days*] ' in black letters on yellow background; in left-hand side of lower portion, "am [*times*]" in black letters on white background; in right-hand side of lower portion "pm [*times*]" in white letters on black background)

647   end of restriction on stopping (rectangular panel; in upper portion diagram 636 "URBAN CLEARWAY" in black letters on yellow background; in lower portion, "End" in black letters on white background)

650.1   prohibition on stopping by vehicles other than taxis during period indicated (diagram 642 "No stopping [*times*] except taxis" in black letters on yellow background)

650.2	prohibition on waiting by vehicles other than taxis during period indicated (diagram 636 "No waiting [*times*] except taxis" in black letters on yellow background)
650.3	continuous prohibition on waiting by vehicles with an exemption for taxis during the period indicated (diagram 642 "At any time except taxis" [*times*] in black letters on yellow background)
651	use of verge maintained in mown or ornamental condition by specified traffic prohibited ("No motor vehicles, cycles, animals, pedestrians on mown verge" in black letters on white background below three red circles enclosing black symbols on white backgrounds)
652	one-way traffic (directional arrow in white on blue background)
660	parking place reserved for permit holders ("P" in white on blue patch and "Permit holders only" in black letters on white background)
660.3	parking place reserved for holders of residents' permits ("P" in white on blue patch, "Resident permit holders only" in black letters on white background, and "A", "B" and "C" in white on black patches)
660.4	part of carriageway reserved for loading and unloading (white symbol on blue patch and "Loading only" in black letters on white background)
660.5	parking place reserved for voucher parking during period indicated ("P" in white and white coat of arms on blue patches, [*days*], [*times*], and "Voucher parking only *x* hour limit" in black letters on white background)
660.6	parking place for permit holders with limited waiting permitted by others at specified times (alternative types) ("P" in white on blue background, [*times*] specified permit holders, and "or 20 mins No return within 40 minutes" in black letters on white background)
660.7	Parking place for permit holders with paid limited waiting permitted by others at specified times (alternative types) ("P" in white on blue background, [*days*], directional arrow, [*times*] specified permit holders, and "or Pay at machine", directional arrow, "Display ticket Max stay 2 hours" in black letters on white background)
661A	parking place reserved for disabled badge holders ("P" in white on blue patch, disabled symbol in white on blue patch, and "Disabled badge holders only" in black letters on white background)
661.1	restrictions on length of waiting time and return period ("P" in white on blue patch; actual restrictions indicated in black letters on white background)
661.2A	"pay and display" ticket-regulated parking place ("P" in white on blue patch, "Pay at machine", one directional arrow and "Display ticket" in black letters on white background)
661.3A	location of "pay and display" ticket machine ("P" in white on blue patch, "Pay here at machine" and "Display ticket" in black letters on white background)
661.4	drivers must obtain and display parking tickets (alternative types) ("P" in white on blue patch and "Have you paid and displayed?" in black letters on white background)
662	period during which waiting is limited and display of disc is required at parking place in a disc zone ("Disc Zone", "P" in white on blue patch, [*days*], [*times*], and "*xx* mins No return within *x* hours" in black letters on white background)
663	entrance to controlled parking zone ("Controlled ZONE", diagram 636, [*days*], and [*times*] in black letters on white background)

663.1   entrance to voucher parking zone (coat of arms in white on blue patch, "Voucher parking ZONE" diagram 636 [*days*], [*times*] and "*x* hour limit" in black letters on white background)

664   end of controlled or voucher parking zone (diagram 636 reproduced in grey on white and crossed through above wording "Zone ENDS" in black letters on white background)

665   entrance to controlled parking zone applying to goods vehicles over maximum gross weight shown (diagram 636, black lorry symbol displaying permitted weight, "ZONE" and [*days*] and [*times*] in black letters on white background)

666   end of controlled parking zone applying to goods vehicles over a maximum weight shown (diagram 636 reproduced in grey on white and crossed through above goods vehicle symbol, and wording "Zone ENDS" in black letters on white background)

667   vehicles may be parked partially on verge or footway (blue panel, white "P" with white tilted symbol of car)

667.1   vehicles may be parked partially on verge or footway during period indicated (blue panel, white "P", white tilted car symbol, [*times*] in white)

667.2   end of area where vehicles may be parked partially on verge or footway (as diagram 667 with red diagonal stripe)

668   vehicles may be parked wholly on verge or footway (blue panel, white "P" with white symbol of car)

668.1   vehicles may be parked wholly on verge or footway during period indicated (blue panel, white "P", white car symbol, [*times*] in white)

668.2   end of area where vehicles may be parked wholly on verge or footway (as diagram 668 with red diagonal stripe)

[670   maximum speed limit in miles per hour (black numerals on white background within red circle)]

671   national speed limits apply (black diagonal bar across white circle)

672   minimum speed limit in miles per hour (white numerals within blue circle edged in white)

673   end of minimum speed limit (diagram 672 crossed through in red)

674   entrance to 20mph speed limit zone ("20" displayed within diagram 670 above "ZONE" [town name may be added])

675   end of 20mph speed limit zone ("30" displayed within diagram 670 above "20" in grey within grey circle and crossed through, and "Zone ENDS" in black on white background)

[Schedule 2 was amended by SI 2005/1670 (substitution of Diagram 670).]]   **B57.74**

Regulation 11(1)   SCHEDULE 3

SIGNS FOR RAILWAY AND TRAMWAY LEVEL CROSSINGS

[The diagrams representing the actual traffic signs are not reproduced in this   **B57.75**
work, but the signs in Sch.3 are described below by means of (in the main) the
legends accompanying the signs. The dimensions of the components of the vari-
ous signs are specified in marks accompanying the diagrams (not reproduced)
and variations of wording (where permissible) are referred to in notes ac-
companying the diagrams (not reproduced), often by means of a cross-reference
to Sch.16. The accompanying notes also cross refer to Sch.17 for information
regarding the illumination requirements for the signs. The diagrams are
reproduced in numerical sequence but there are gaps in the numbering.

770	level crossing with gate or barrier ahead (black symbol (gate) within red triangle)
771	railway level crossing without gate or barrier ahead (black symbol (engine) within red triangle)
772	tramcars crossing ahead (black symbol (tram) within red triangle)
773	light signals in diagram 3014 ahead (two red and one yellow lights on black background above "STOP when lights show" in black letters on white background)
774	location of railway or tramcar level crossing without gate or barrier (two white bars edged in red with arrow heads at their ends set diagonally to each other)
775	vehicular traffic must not stop within area of railway or tramway level crossing ("KEEP CROSSING CLEAR" in black letters on white background with black surround)
776	another train or tramcar may be about to pass over crossing ("ANOTHER TRAIN COMING" within circle in black letters on red background)
777	level crossing ahead is crossed by more than one railway or tramway track, and more than one train or tramcar may pass over it in quick succssion ("ANOTHER TRAIN COMING if lights continue to show" in black letters on white background with black surround)
778	open railway level crossing without light signals (black symbol on white background with black surround)
778.1	open tramway level crossing without light signals (black symbol on white background with black surround)
779	electrified overhead cable ahead (black symbol within red triangle)
780A	safe height beneath electrified overhead cable ahead
780.1A	safe height beneath electrified overhead cable in direction and at distance indicated
780.2A	safe height beneath electrified overhead cable ahead provided with a load gauge shown in diagram 781
781	load gauge giving audible warning to drivers where vehicle exceeds safe height under electrified overhead cables
782	risk of grounding at railway or tramway level crossing or hump backed bridge (black symbol (large vehicle) within red triangle)
783	drivers of long low vehicles must phone and get permission before using a railway or tramway level crossing ("DRIVERS OF LONG LOW VEHICLES phone before crossing" in white letters on blue background edged in white)
784	drivers of large or slow vehicles must stop and telephone before using an automatic railway or tramway level crossing ("DRIVERS OF LARGE or SLOW VEHICLES must phone and get permission to cross" in white letters on blue background edged in white; details of "LARGE" and "SLOW" in black letters on white lower panel)
785.1	name of level crossing and details of telephone number for contacting railway or tramway operator
786	place where large or slow, or long low vehicles should wait near a railway or tramway level crossing while the driver obtains permission to cross or confirms he has crossed
787	site of emergency telephone or telephone at or near railway or tramway level crossing
788	direction to emergency telephone, etc.
789	countdown markers to railway or tramway level crossing
789.1, 2	as diagram 789

790   new method of controlling traffic at railway or tramway level crossing
             ahead *]*

Regulation 11(1)   SCHEDULE 4

MISCELLANEOUS INFORMATORY SIGNS

[The diagrams representing the actual traffic signs are not reproduced in this   **B57.76**
work, but the signs in Sch. 4 are described below by means of (in the main) the
legends accompanying the signs. The dimensions of the components of the vari-
ous signs are specified in marks accompanying the diagrams (not reproduced)
and variations of wording (where permissible) are referred to in notes ac-
companying the diagrams (not reproduced), often by means of a cross-reference
to Sch.16. The accompanying notes also cross refer to Sch.17 for information
regarding the illumination requirements for the signs. The diagrams are
reproduced in numerical sequence but there are gaps in the numbering.

801	parking place ("P" in white on blue background edged in white)
804.1	parking place for goods vehicles (black symbol (lorry) on white background with black surround)
804.2	parking place for motor cars (black symbol (car) on white background with black surround)
804.3	parking place for motorised caravans or caravans drawn by motor vehicles (black symbol (car end and caravan) on white background with black surround)
804.4	parking place for solo motor cycles (black symbol on white background)
810	one-way traffic in direction indicated (sign for pedestrians)
811	traffic has priority over traffic from the opposite direction (large white arrow and smaller red arrow in opposite directions on blue background edged in white)
811.1	explanatory plate for diagram 811 ("Priority over oncoming vehicles" in black letters on white background with black surround)
814.1–4	signs for pedestrians relating to subway/overbridge
816	no through road for vehicular traffic (letter "T" on which horizontal is red edged in white and is broader than the vertical which is coloured white, all on a blue background edged in white)
816.1	alternative to diagram 816 with street nameplate to one side of sign
817	no through road for vehicular traffic in direction indicated from junction ahead (main road shown as white on blue background with side road from junction terminating with red bar (edged with white) at right angle to side road, all edged in white)
817.2	escape lane ahead for vehicles unable to stop on steep hill
818	section of dual carriageway begins directly ahead
818.1	distance to a section of dual carriageway ahead
818.1A	distance over which a short length of dual carriageway road beginning directly ahead extends
818.2	nature of and distance to a prohibition, restriction or requirement ahead (legend may vary to accord with the prohibition, restriction or requirement)
818.3	same as diagram 818.2
818.4	nature and location of a prohibition, restriction or requirement with indication of alternative route

820	road unsuitable for type of vehicle indicated
820.1	absence of hard shoulder for the distance shown
821	road ahead only wide enough for one line of vehicles, but has passing places at intervals
822	passing place on narrow road
823–825	distance in hundreds of yards to a roundabout or next point at which traffic may leave a route
826	depth of water at a ford
826.1	alternative to diagram 826 using metric and imperial units
827.1	hospital ahead without accident and emergency facilities
827.2	hospital ahead with accident and emergency facilities
827.3	hospital ahead with facilities for treating minor injuries
829.1	potential danger temporarily ahead and consequent need to proceed with caution ("POLICE SLOW" in white letters on blue background edged in white)
829.2	accident ahead and consequent need to proceed with caution ("POLICE ACCIDENT" in white letters on blue background edged in white)
829.3	traffic should use hard shoulder in emergency ("POLICE USE HARD SHOULDER" in white letters on blue background edged in white)
829.4	end of temporary permission for traffic to use hard shoulder ("POLICE REJOIN MAIN CARRIAGEWAY" in white letters on blue background edged in white)
829.5	area where police carry out checks on the speed of vehicles ("POLICE speed check area" in white letters on blue background edged in white)
829.6	waiting place at a lay-by or observation platform for police vehicles only ("Police patrol vehicles only" in white letters on blue background edged in white)
830	vehicles will be required to stop at traffic survey ahead ("STOP AT CENSUS POINT"in white letters on blue background edged in white)
830.1	vehicles may be directed to stop at traffic survey ahead ("CENSUS STOP if directed" in white letters on blue background edged in white)
830.2	goods vehicles may be directed to stop ahead by constable in uniform for purposes of sections 67, 68 or 78 of Road Traffic Act 1988 ("GOODS VEHICLES STOP if directed" in white letters on blue background edged in white)
830.3	vehicles should stay in lane for purposes of traffic survey, or a weight or vehicle check ahead ("STAY IN LANE" in white letters on blue background edged in white)
831	vehicles should reduce speed on approaching traffic survey ahead ("SLOW CENSUS POINT" in white letters on blue background edged in white)
831.2	vehicle excise licence check point ahead ("VEHICLE EXCISE LICENCE CHECK" in white letters on blue background edged in white)
832	location of traffic survey ("CENSUS POINT" in white letters on blue background edged in white)
832.1A	vehicle check point ahead ("Vehicle Inspectorate CHECK POINT AHEAD" in white letters on blue background)
832.2A	vehicle condition check point ahead ("Vehicle Inspectorate VEHICLE CONDITION INSPECTION" in white letters on blue background)
832.3	goods vehicles may be directed to leave motorway at junction ahead (rectangular panel displaying black symbol and "Leave m'way if directed" in black letters on yellow background)

832.4	goods vehicles may be directed to enter a check point ahead (square panel displaying black symbol and "Enter Check Point if directed" in black letters on yellow background)
832.5	goods vehicles should keep to left lane on approach to check point ahead (square panel displaying black symbol and "Keep to left lane" in black letters on yellow background)
832.6	goods vehicles should get into left lane and other vehicles should use right-hand lane of a two-lane carriageway on approach to goods vehicle check point ahead ([top panel] "GET IN LANE"; [second panel divided vertically into two by broken line] black symbol above arrow pointing upwards on left and "Other Vehicles" above arrow pointing upwards on right; [bottom panel] "Goods vehicle Check Point [*distance*]" in black letters on yellow background)
832.7	goods vehicles should get into left lane of a three-lane carriageway on approach to goods vehicle check point ahead ([top panel] "GET IN LANE"; [second panel divided vertically into three by broken lines] "Any Vehicle" above arrow pointing upwards on left and black symbol crossed through in red above arrow pointing upwards in each of other two panels; [bottom panel] "Goods vehicle Check Point [*distance*]" in black letters on yellow background)
832.8	goods vehicles should leave main carriageway of road on approach to goods vehicle check point (rectangular panel displaying arrow pointing diagonally and "All goods vehicles" in black letters on yellow background)
832.9	direction to a vehicle check point (rectangular panel with arrowhead displaying arrowhead and "Check Point" in black letters on yellow background)
832.10A	end of vehicle check point area (rectangular panel with "Check Point restrictions END" in black letters on yellow background)
833	entrance to a car park, private access road or property ("IN")
834	exit from a car park, private access road or property ("OUT")
835	exit from a car park, private access road or property to public road not allowed ("NO EXIT" in white letters on blue background edged in white)
836	entry to a car park, private access road or property from public road not allowed ("NO ENTRY" in white letters on blue background edged in white)
857	information for pedestrians about tourist attractions, etc.
857.1	information relating to taxi rank for number of taxis specified
864.1	Vehicle testing station approved by Vehicle Inspectorate
865	motor cycle test centre
868	additional traffic lane joining from left ahead
868.1	additional traffic lanes joining from right ahead
872.1	number of traffic lanes ahead on a dual carriageway road or on a one-way street reduces from three to two; traffic in the right-hand lane must move into the lane on the immidiate left
873	additional traffic lane joining from left ahead; traffic on main carriageway has priority over joining traffic from right-hand lane of slip road
874	additional traffic lanes joining from right ahead; traffic in right-hand lane joins main carriageway; traffic on main carriageway has priority over joining traffic
875	additional traffic lanes joining from right ahead; traffic in right-hand lane of slip road has priority over traffic in left-hand lane

876	distance to change in number of lanes indicated by diagrams 868 to 875
877	appropriate traffic lanes for different manoeuvres at a junction ahead (alternative types)
878	area in which cameras are used to enforce traffic light signal regulations (alternative types) (black symbol of camera, "Traffic signal cameras" in black letters on white background edged in black)
879	reminder to drivers within an area in which cameras are used to enforce traffic regulations (black symbol of camera in white background edged in black)
880	speed camera ahead and reminder of 30mph speed limit (black symbol of camera in white patch and "30" in red circle, both on blue background edged in white)]
[880.1	speed camera ahead on an unlit road and reminder that a national speed limit applies]
881	start of a home zone (alternative types)
882	end of designated home zone
883	start of area with traffic calming features of the type defined in reg.4 ("Traffic calmed area" in white letters on blue background edged in white)
884	start of a quiet lane in England designated under section 268 of the Transport Act 2000 (Alternative types)
885	end of designated quiet lane in England

B57.77   *[Schedule 4 was amended by SI 2006/2083 (addition of Diagrams 884 and 885 to indicate quiet lanes in England in accordance with the Quiet Lanes and Home Zones (England) Regulations 2006 (SI 2006/2082)) and by SI 2008/2177 (addition of Diagram 880.1).]]*

Regulation 11(1)   SCHEDULE 5

SIGNS FOR BUS, TRAM AND PEDAL CYCLE FACILITIES

B57.78   *[The diagrams representing the actual traffic signs are not reproduced in this work, but the signs in Sch.5 are described below by means of (in the main) the legends accompanying the signs. The dimensions of the components of the various signs are specified in marks accompanying the diagrams (not reproduced) and variations of wording (where permissible) are referred to in notes accompanying the diagrams (not reproduced), often by means of a cross-reference to Sch.16. The accompanying notes also cross refer to Sch.17 for information regarding the illumination requirements for the signs. The diagrams are reproduced in numerical sequence but there are gaps in the numbering.*

950	cycle route ahead (black symbol within red triangle)
950.1	training or testing of child cyclists ahead
951	riding of pedal cycles prohibited (black symbol within red circle)
952	buses prohibited (black symbol within red circle)
953	route for use by buses and pedal cycles only (white symbols on blue background within circle edged in white)
953.1	route for use by tramcars only (white symbol on blue background within circle edged in white)
953.2	explanatory plate for diagrams 953, 953.1 ("Only")

953.3	entrance to bus station, depot or garage ("BUSES ONLY" in white letters on blue background edged in white)
954	buses excluded from restriction or prohibition conveyed by associated sign ("Except buses")
954.2	same as diagram 954 applying to local buses ("Except local buses")
954.3	same as diagram 954 applying to buses and pedal cycles ("Except buses and cycles")
954.4	same as diagram 954 applying to pedal cycles ("Except cycles")
954.5	same as diagram 954 where the signs are mounted in combination with light signals prescribed by reg.33
954.6	same as diagram 954 applying to buses and pedal cycles where the signs are mounted in combination with light signals prescribed in reg.33
954.7	same as diagram 954 applying to buses, taxis and pedal cycles where the signs are mounted in combination with light signals prescribed in reg.33
955	route for use by pedal cycles only (white symbol on blue background within circle edged in white)
956	route for use by pedal cycles and pedestrians only (white symbols on blue background within circle edged in white)
957	route comprising two ways, separated, by marking in diagram 1049 or 1049.1 or by physical means, for use by pedal cycles only and by pedestrians only (white symbols separated by vertical white line on blue background within circle edged in white)
958	with-flow bus lane which pedal cycles and taxis may also use ahead
958.1	with-flow cycle lane ahead
959	with-flow bus lane which pedal cycles may also use (note: any vehicle may enter the bus lane to stop, load or unload where this is not prohibited)
959.1	with-flow cycle lane
960	contra-flow bus lane (note: any vehicle may enter the bus lane to stop, load or unload where this is not prohibited)
960.1	contra-flow cycle lane
961	times of operation of bus lane or cycle lane
962	bus lane on road junction ahead
962.1	cycle lane on road at junction ahead or cycle track crossing road
962.2	contra-flow bus lane which pedal cycles may also use on road at junction ahead
963	bus lane with traffic proceeding from right (sign for pedestrians)
963.1	cycle lane with traffic proceeding from right (sign for pedestrians)
963.2	contra-flow bus lane which pedal cycles may also use with traffic proceeding from right (sign for pedestrians)
963.3	tramway with traffic proceeding in both directions (sign for pedestrians)
964	end of bus lane
965	end of cycle lane, track or route
966	pedal cyclists to dismount at end of, or at break in, cycle lane, track or route
967	route recommended for pedal cycles on the main carriageway of a road
968, 968.1	parking place for pedal cycles
969	parking place for buses

970	stopping place for buses
971	stopping place for tramcars
972	stopping place for buses carrying tourists to allow passengers to take photographs
973.2	stopping place for buses operated by or on behalf of or under agreement with Transport for London
973.3	"request" stopping place for London buses
974	stopping by vehicles other than buses prohibited during periods indicated (rectangular panel displaying 642 and "No stopping [*times*] except buses" on yellow background)
975	place where buses may stand and stopping of other vehicles is prohibited during period indicated (square panel displaying diagram 642 and "BUS STAND No stopping [*times*] except buses" in black letters on yellow background)
976	maximum speed limit for tramcars in kilometres per hour *]*

Regulation 11(1) and (3)   SCHEDULE 6

Road Markings

B57.79   *[The diagrams representing the actual traffic signs are not reproduced in this work, but the signs in Sch.6 are described below by means of (in the main) the legends accompanying the signs. The dimensions of the components of the various signs are specified in marks accompanying the diagrams (not reproduced) and variations of wording (where permissible) are referred to in notes accompanying the diagrams (not reproduced), often by means of a cross-reference to Sch.16. The accompanying notes also cross refer to Sch.17 for information regarding the illumination requirements for the signs. The diagrams are reproduced in numerical sequence but there are gaps in the numbering.*

N.B. all diagrams included in Schedule 6 are marked on the surface of the roadway, usually in white.

1001	vehicular traffic must not proceed beyond the line when required to stop by light signals or by a constable in uniform or a traffic warden (solid white line)
1001.1	tramcars must not proceed beyond the line required to stop by light signals (solid white line)
1001.2	alternatives to the stop line shown in diagram 1001 showing separate stop lines at a junction for pedal cycles proceeding in the cycle lane (diagram 1957 (white symbol of cycle) between solid white lines)
1001.3	zig-zag lines to indicate the requirements of regs 27 and 28 at a Toucan or equestrian crossing facility controlled by signals (shown in combination with diagrams 1001 and 1055.1)
1002.1	vehicular traffic must not proceed beyond the line when required to stop by the sign shown in diagram 601.1 (solid white line)
1003	vehicular traffic must give way in accordance with regulation 25 (broken double white lines)
1003.1	vehicular traffic approaching roundabout should give way at or immediately beyond the line to vehicles circulating on carriageway of round about (broken single white line)

1003.2	pedestrians approaching level crossing should wait behind the line when barriers are closed or when the red figure shown in diagram 4006 or the light signals shown in diagram 3014 are showing or, if these are neither barriers nor light signals, until it is safe to proceed (broken single white line)
1003.3	vehicular traffic approaching roundabout with small central island or approaching junction marked by sign at diagram 611.1 should give way at or immediately beyond line to traffic circulating on carriageway of roundabout (broken white line)
1003.4	direction of traffic flow at junction marked by sign at diagram 611.1 and conveying requirements prescribed by reg.16 (alternative types) (three arrows circling small white circle on roadway)
1004	vehicular traffic on roads with speed limit of 40mph or less should not cross or straddle line unless safe to do so; when line used in conjunction with diagram 967, motor vehicles should not enter cycle lane unless lane is clear of pedal cycles (broken white line)
1004.1	as diagram 1004 on roads with speed limit of more than 40mph (broken white line (increased lengths of lines and intervals))
1005	division of carriageway into lanes where vehicles normally proceed in same direction on roads with speed limit of 40mph or less (except where diagram 1004 is used) (broken white line (long intervals between short lines))
1005.1	as diagram 1005 on roads with speed limit of more than 40mph (except when diagram 1004.1 is used) (broken white line (increased lengths of lines and intervals))
1008	division between opposing flows of traffic on carriageway with speed limit of 40mph or less (except when diagram 1004 is used) (broken white line))
1008.1	division between opposing flows of traffic on carriageway with speed limit of more than 40mph (except when diagram 1004.1 is used) (broken white line))
1009	edge of carriageway at road injunction, exit from private drive on to public road, or (laid diagonally) start of cycle lane (broken white line)
[1010	edge of carriageway at road junction or at a lay-by, or exit from private drive on to public road; (laid diagonally) start of traffic lane, the boundary of which is indicated by diagram 1049; most suitable path for high vehicles through arch bridge (used in conjunction with diagram 1014 or 1024.1); (laid alongside tram rails) edge of carriageway used by tramcars; or division between main carriageway and traffic lane leaving main carriageway at a junction ahead (broken white line)]
[1012.1	edge of carriageway available for through traffic other than at road junction, exit from a private drive on to public road or a lay-by; or the back edge of a hard shoulder; or the edge of a footway where it passes over a railway or tramway level crossing (unbroken white line)]
[1012.2	alternative to diagram 1012.1 incorporating audible and tactile warning (in form of raised rib) for use on motorways]
[1012.3	as diagram 1012.2, but for use on all-purpose roads with hard strips]
1013.1	alternative methods of showing warning prescribed in reg.26 (double white lines)
1013.3, 1013.4	as diagram 1013.1; adjacent part of carriageway which vehicular traffic should not enter unless it is seen by driver to be safe to do so

1014	direction in which vehicular traffic should pass (used in conjunction with diagram 1013.1, 1013.3, 1040, 1040.3, 1040.4 or 1049 ahead); obstruction on carriageway ahead; (used with diagram 1010) most suitable path for high vehicles through arch bridge (arrow); reduction in the number of traffic lanes ahead; path to be taken to avoid a route available for tramcars only
1017	waiting of vehicles on side of a length of road prohibited for less than that specified in caption (a) to diagram 1018.1 (single yellow line)
1018.1	(a) waiting of vehicles on side of a length of road prohibited at any time during period of at least four consecutive months; (b) stopping of vehicles in a lay-by prohibited except in emergency (double yellow lines)
1019	loading or unloading of vehicles on side of a length of road prohibited for a time less than that specified in caption to diagram 1020.1 (short yellow line at right angle to edge of carriageway)
1020.1	loading or unloading of vehicles on side of a length of road prohibited at any time during period of at least four consecutive months (two short yellow lines at right angle to edge of carriageway)
1022	approach to road junction or level crossing at or near which is placed the sign in diagram 601.1 and the road marking in diagram 1002.1 ("STOP")
1023	approach to road junction, level crossing or road narrowing at or near marking in diagram 1003 or 1003.3 (inverted triangle)
1024	vehicular traffic should proceed with caution because of potential danger ahead ("SLOW")
1024.1	path to be taken by high vehicles under a low bridge or to avoid an overhanging structure ("HIGH VEHS")
1025	stopping place for buses on part of carriageway also used by through traffic ("BUS STOP" in yellow inside yellow box with broken lines)
1025.1	bus stop at which vehicular traffic must comply with the requirements of reg.29(1) and Pt I of Sch.19 ("BUS STOP" in yellow inside box with broken lines and single yellow line at edge of carriageway)
1025.3	same as diagram 1025.1 but where the bus stop is located in part of a lay-by, the other part of which may be used by other vehicles
1025.4	same as diagram 1025.1 but where the bus stop occupies the whole of a lay-by
1026	part of carriageway to be kept clear of stationary vehicles ("KEEP CLEAR" preceded and followed by line at right angle to edge of carriageway)
1026.1	part of carriageway outside entrance to off-street premises or a private drive, or where kerb is dropped to provide convenient crossing place for pedestrians, to be kept clear of waiting vehicles (single line with short "bar" at each end)
1027.1	part of carriageway outside school entrance where vehicles should not stop ("SCHOOL—KEEP—CLEAR" in yellow preceded and followed by wavy lines in yellow)
1028.2	alternative types of taxi rank either at edge or in centre of carriageway ("TAXIS" in yellow; area boxed off with broken yellow lines)
1028.3	alternative types of parking bays reserved for disabled badge holders either at edge or in centre of carriageway ("DISABLED"; area boxed off with broken lines)
1028.4	alternative types of parking bays reserved for doctor permit holders either at edge or in centre of carriageway ("DOCTOR"; area boxed off with broken lines)
1029	direction in which pedestrians should look for approaching traffic

1032	parking bay marked with individual parking spaces (longitudinal marking)
1033	echelon parking spaces subject to such conditions (if any) as may be in force
1035	appropriate traffic lanes for different destinations
1036.1	vehicular traffic must turn left (alternative types)
1036.2	vehicular traffic must only proceed ahead (alternative types)
1037.1	vehicular traffic must turn right (alternative types)
1038	appropriate traffic lanes for different manoeuvres (longitudinal marking)
1038.1	appropriate direction to be taken by traffic turning within a junction (alternative types)
1039	place where traffic streams divide or bifurcate (longitudinal marking)
1040	part of carriageway which vehicular traffic should not enter unless it is seen by driver to be safe to do so (two broken lines converging on a point with diagonals between them)
1040.2	length of road along which drivers should not overtake by passing through marking unless it is seen by driver to be safe to do so (two parallel lines with diagonals between them)
1040.3	reduction in number of lanes on motorway/all-purpose dual carriageway
1040.4	part of carriageway adjacent to edge which vehicular traffic should not enter unless seen by driver to be safe to do so (broken line at angle from edge of carriageway with diagonals between it and edge of carriageway)
1040.5	end of hard shoulder
1041	part of carriageway where vehicular traffic passes in same direction on both sides of marking, and should not enter the area covered by the marking unless it is seen by driver to be safe to do so (two broken lines converging on a point with thick chevrons between them)
1041.1	length of road along which vehicular traffic travels in the same direction on both sides of the marking, and should not enter the area covered by the marking unless it is seen by the driver to be safe to do so (two broken lines with chevrons between them)
1042	part of verge or a hard shoulder on a motorway or all-purpose dual carriageway road between main motorway carriageway or all-purpose dual carriageway road and carriageway of slip road, or at bifurcation or convergence of motorways or all-purpose carriageway roads, or part of a carriageway between two lanes at a roundabout which vehicular traffic must not enter except in an emergency (two solid lines converging on a point with thick chevrons between them)
1042.1	division of traffic lanes on a length of carriageway, or between the main carriageway and slip road, of a motorway or all-purpose dual carriageway road, or part of a carriageway between two lanes at a roundabout which vehicular traffic must not enter except in an emergency (two solid lines with thick chevrons between them)
1043, 1044	Marking conveying the requirements prescribed by reg.29(2) and Pt II of Sch.19 (rhombus with several diagonals in each direction in yellow)
1045	area of carriageway at a level crossing which vehicles must not enter in a manner which then causes any part of the vehicle to remain at rest within the marked area due to the presence of stationary vehicles (yellow rectangle covering both carriageways with patterned cross hatching)
1046	no entry for vehiclar traffic (alternative type) ("NO ENTRY")

1048	with-flow lane reserved for buses and other vehicles as indicated in diagram 959 or a contra-flow lane reserved for buses ("BUS LANE")
1048.1	contra-flow reserved for buses and pedal cycles ("BUS AND [cycle symbol] LANE")
1048.2	road or part of a road with access permitted only for buses and tramcars ("TRAM & BUSES ONLY")
1048.3	road or part of a road with access permitted only for buses (alternative types) ("BUS ONLY")
1048.4	road or part of a road with access permitted only for buses and pedal cycles "(BUS AND [cycle symbol] ONLY")
1049	boundary of bus or cycle lane; where varied to 150mm wide and used in conjunction with diagram 957, the division of route into part reserved for pedal cycles and part for pedestrians (unbroken white line)
1049.1	division of route into part reserved for pedal cycles and part for pedestrians (raised white marking)
1050	direction of possible traffic movements at end of bus lane
1055.1	pedestrian crossing at which traffic subject to control by a constable in uniform or by a traffic warden, or the most suitable crossing for pedestrians near traffic signals or pedestrian crossing signals, or a Toucan crossing or equestrian only crossing (square marks)
1055.2	same as diagram 1055.1(c), (d) or (e) with an additional crossing point for pedestrians
1057	cycle lane, track or route
1058	end of cycle lane, track or route
1058.1	pedal cycles should proceed with caution because of potential danger ahead ("SLOW")
1059	directions in which pedal cycles should travel on cycle lane, track or route
1062	road hump
1063	limits of measured length of road for assessing speed of vehicular traffic (alternative types)
1064	chevron marking for use in conjunction with the sign shown in diagram 2933 (drivers should keep a distance of two chevron markings from the vehicle in front)
1065	maximum speed limit (alternative sizes)
1066	edge of the part of the road used by tramcars (yellow circles)

B57.80   *[Schedule 6 was amended by SI 2005/1670 (substitution of Diagrams 1010, 1012.1, 1012.2 and 1012.3).]]*

Regulation 11(1)   SCHEDULE 7

B57.81   *[The diagrams representing the traffic signs in Sch.7 being essentially for information are not listed.*

PART I

PRIMARY ROUTE DIRECTIONAL SIGNS

B57.82   Diagrams 2001 to 2035 *[not reproduced]*

PART II

NON-PRIMARY ROUTE DIRECTIONAL SIGNS

B57.83   Diagrams 2101 to 2141 *[not reproduced]*

Part III

Tᴏᴜʀɪꜱᴛ Dᴇꜱᴛɪɴᴀᴛɪᴏɴ Sɪɢɴꜱ

Diagrams 2201 to 2218 [*not reproduced*]   **B57.84**

Part IV

[Sɪɢɴꜱ ꜰᴏʀ Sᴇʀᴠɪᴄᴇꜱ ᴀɴᴅ Tᴏᴜʀɪꜱᴛ Fᴀᴄɪʟɪᴛɪᴇꜱ]

Diagrams 2301 to 2330 [*not reproduced*]   **B57.85**

Part V

Bᴏᴜɴᴅᴀʀʏ Sɪɢɴꜱ

Diagrams 2401 to 2403.1 [*not reproduced*]   **B57.86**

Part VI

Dɪʀᴇᴄᴛɪᴏɴᴀʟ Sɪɢɴꜱ ᴛᴏ Pᴀʀᴋɪɴɢ Pʟᴀᴄᴇꜱ

Diagrams 2501 to 2513 [*not reproduced*]   **B57.87**

Part VII

Dɪʀᴇᴄᴛɪᴏɴᴀʟ Sɪɢɴꜱ ꜰᴏʀ Cʏᴄʟɪꜱᴛꜱ ᴀɴᴅ Pᴇᴅᴇꜱᴛʀɪᴀɴꜱ

Diagrams 2601.1 to 2610.2 [*not reproduced*]   **B57.88**

Part VIII

Tᴇᴍᴘᴏʀᴀʀʏ ᴀɴᴅ Eᴍᴇʀɢᴇɴᴄʏ Dɪʀᴇᴄᴛɪᴏɴᴀʟ Sɪɢɴꜱ

Diagrams 2701 to 2717 [*not reproduced*]   **B57.89**

Part IX

Oᴛʜᴇʀ Nᴏɴ-Mᴏᴛᴏʀᴡᴀʏ Dɪʀᴇᴄᴛɪᴏɴᴀʟ Sɪɢɴꜱ

Diagrams 2801 to 2806.1 [*not reproduced*]   **B57.90**

Part X

Mᴏᴛᴏʀᴡᴀʏ Sɪɢɴꜱ

Diagrams 2901 to 2934 [*not reproduced*] *]*   **B57.91**

Regulations 33, 34, 35, 39, 41   SCHEDULE 8

Lɪɢʜᴛ Sɪɢɴᴀʟꜱ ꜰᴏʀ ᴛʜᴇ Cᴏɴᴛʀᴏʟ ᴏꜰ Vᴇʜɪᴄᴜʟᴀʀ Tʀᴀꜰꜰɪᴄ

[The diagrams representing the actual traffic signs are not reproduced in this   **B57.92**
work, but the signs in Sch.8 are described below by means of (in the main) the
legends accompanying the signs. The dimensions of the components of the vari-
ous signs are specified in marks accompanying the diagrams (not reproduced)
and variations of wording (where permissible) are referred to in notes ac-
companying the diagrams (not reproduced), often by means of a cross-reference
to Sch.16. The accompanying notes also cross refer to Sch.17 for information
regarding the illumination requirements for the signs. The diagrams are

reproduced in numerical sequence but there are gaps in the numbering.

3000	lights signals for the control of vehicular traffic at road junctions, at signal-controlled crossing facilities, or at places where the headroom or width of road is permanently reduced (red, yellow and green traffic signals)
3000.1	portable light signals (red, yellow and green traffic signals)
3000.2	light signals solely for pedal cycles (red, yellow and green traffic signals, the latter two displaying only a symbol of a cycle)
3000.7	as diagram 3000, but with additional signals as shown in diagram 3001.2, 3001.3 or 3013
3000.8	as diagram 3000, but without the green aspect and with additional signals as shown in diagram 3001.2, 3001.3 or 3013
3000.9	as diagram 3000 with additional signals as shown in diagram 3001.2, 3001.3 or 3013
3000.10	as diagram 3000, but without the green aspect and with additional signals as shown in diagram 3001.2, 3001.3 or 3013
3001.2	green arrow for inclusion within light signals (reg.34) (alternative indications)
3001.3	same as diagram 3001.2
3013	light signal for control of tramcars
3013.1	as diagram 3013, conveying prohibition prescribed by reg.42(a)
3013.2	as diagram 3013, conveying prohibition prescribed by reg.42(b)
3013.3	as diagram 3013, conveying prohibition prescribed by reg.42(c)
3013.4	as diagram 3013, conveying prohibition prescribed by reg.42(d)
3013.5	as diagram 3013, conveying prohibition prescribed by reg.42(e)
3014	light signals for control of traffic at level crossings, swing or lifting bridges, tunnels, airfields or in vicinity of premises used regularly by fire, police or ambulance service vehicles (two red and one orange light signals on black background mounted on red and white chequered surround) *]*

Regulations 47–52   SCHEDULE 9

LIGHT SIGNALS FOR PEDESTRIANS AND ANIMAL CROSSINGS

B57.93   *[The diagrams representing the actual traffic signs are not reproduced in this work, but the signs in Sch.9 are described below by means of (in the main) the legends accompanying the signs. The dimensions of the components of the various signs are specified in marks accompanying the diagrams (not reproduced) and variations of wording (where permissible) are referred to in notes accompanying the diagrams (not reproduced), often by means of a cross-reference to Sch.16. The accompanying notes also cross refer to Sch.17 for information regarding the illumination requirements for the signs.*

4002.1	light signals for pedestrians (red symbol of person standing, green symbol of person walking within black circles)
4003	instructions to pedestrians above push button control for calling up pedestrian phases at light signals
4003.1	near side light signals and instructions for pedestrians at a pedestrian facility controlled by light signals (red symbol of person standing, green symbol of person walking, "Push button Wait for signal"in white letters, all on black background)

4003.2	light signals for equestrian traffic (red and green symbols of horse and rider, both within black circles)
4003.3	instructions to horse riders above the push button control for calling up equestrian traffic phases at light signals
4003.4	near side light signals and instructions for horse riders at an equestrian traffic crossing facility controlled by light signals
4003.5	light signals for pedestrians and cycles at a Toucan crossing (red symbol of person standing, green symbol of person walking, green cycle symbol within black circles)
4003.6	instructions to pedestrians and cyclists above the push button control for calling up pedestrian and cycle phases at a Toucan crossing
4003.7	near side light signals and instructions for pedestrians and cyclists at a Toucan crossing
4004	children likely to be crossing road on their way to or from school ahead (alternative types) (two amber light signals on black background)
4005	cattle crossing ahead
4006	light signal at level crossings for pedestrians]

Regulation 44   SCHEDULE 10

[The diagrams representing the traffic signs in Sch.10 being in the main for in-   **B57.94**
formation are not listed.

PART I

LANE CONTROL SIGNALS

Diagrams 5001.1 to 5005.1 *[not reproduced]*   **B57.95**

PART II

LANE CONTROL SIGNS

Diagrams 5010 to 5015 *[not reproduced]*   **B57.96**

[Part II of Sch.10 was amended by SI 2005/1670 (substitution of Diagrams   **B57.97**
5003 and 5003.1).]]

Regulation 46   SCHEDULE 11

PART I

MATRIX SIGNS (FOR MOTORWAYS AND ALL-PURPOSE DUAL CARRIAGEWAY ROADS)

[The diagrams representing the actual traffic signs are not reproduced in this   **B57.98**
*work, but the signs in Sch.11 are described below by means of (in the main) the
legends accompanying the signs. The dimensions of the components of the various signs are specified in marks accompanying the diagrams (not reproduced)
and variations of wording (where permissible) are referred to in notes accompanying the diagrams (not reproduced), often by means of a cross-reference
to Sch.16. The accompanying notes also cross refer to Sch.17 for information
regarding the illumination requirements for the signs. The diagrams are
reproduced in numerical sequence but there are gaps in the numbering.*

| 6001 | temporary maximum speed advised |

[6002	vehicular traffic must move to next lane on the right]
6003	vehicular traffic must leave at next junction
6006	closure of one lane of a three-lane carriageway ahead
6006.1	closure of two lanes of a three-lane carriageway ahead
6006.2	closure of all lanes of a three-lane carriageway ahead
6008	closure of right-hand lane of a two-lane carriageway ahead
6008.1	closure of both lanes of a two-lane carriageway ahead
6009	closure of one lane or a four-lane carriageway ahead
6009.1	closure of two lanes of a four-lane carriageway ahead
6009.2	closure of three lanes of a four-lane carriageway ahead
6009.3	closure of all lanes of a four-lane carriageway ahead
6011	risk of fog ahead
6011.1	risk of ice ahead
6012	end of temporary restrictions indicated by previous signs
6021	gantry-mounted signal with flashing amber lamps displaying signs at diagram 6001, 6002, 6003, 6011 or 6011.1
6022	post-mounted signal with flashing amber lamps displaying signs at diagram 6001, 6003, 6006, 6006.1, 6008, 6009, 6009.1, 6009.2, 6011 or 6011.1

B57.99   *[Part I of Sch.11 was amended by SI 2005/1670 (substitution of Diagram 6002).]]*

REGULATIONS 37 AND 45

PART II

LIGHT SIGNALS (FOR MOTORWAYS AND DUAL CARRIAGEWAYS)

B57.100

6023	light signal conveying the warning under reg.45
[6031.1	light signals (motorways and dual carriageways) for conveying requirements of reg.38(b)]
[6032.1	light signals for conveying requirements of reg.38(a).]

B57.101   *[Part II of Sch.11 was amended by SI 2005/1670 (substitution of Diagrams 6031.1 and 6032.1).]]*

Regulation 11(1)   SCHEDULE 12

B57.102   *[The diagrams representing the traffic signs in Sch.12 being mainly for information, only selected signs are listed below. The dimensions of the components of the various signs are specified in marks accompanying the diagrams (not reproduced) and variations of wording (where permissible) are referred to in notes accompanying the diagrams (not reproduced), often by means of a cross-reference to Sch.16. The accompanying notes also cross refer to Sch.7 for information regarding the illumination requirements for the signs. The diagrams are reproduced in numerical sequence but there are gaps in the numbering.*

PART I

MISCELLANEOUS WARNING, INFORMATORY AND REGULATORY SIGNS FOR ROAD WORKS ETC.

B57.103

*   *   *

7011   point beyond which vehicular traffic must not proceed when required
              to stop by reg.36 in accordance with indication given by portable light
              signals in diagram 3000.1 and when road marking diagram 1001 is not
              placed on carriageway (rectangular panel with "WHEN RED LIGHT
              SHOWS WAIT HERE" in white letters on red background edged in white)

                          *   *   *

7023   vehicular traffic must not proceed into length of road where one-way
              working is temporarily necessary (manually operated sign) (octagonal
              panel with "STOP" in white letters on red background edged in white)

7024   vehicular traffic may proceed into length of road where one-way
              working is temporarily necessary (manually operated sign) (octagonal
              panel with "GO" in white letters on green background edged in white)

                          REGULATION 11(1)

                              PART II

                ROAD WORKS DELINEATORS AND BARRIERS

                                                                      B57.104
7101.1   edge of route for vehicular traffic through or past temporary
              obstruction (traffic cone)

7102   edge of route for vehicular traffic through or past temporary
              obstruction on motorway or dual carriageway road (flat traffic
              delineator)

7103   line of division of traffic flows on one carriageway, or edge of route
              for vehicular traffic through or past temporary obstruction, or
              boundary between two carriageways of a dual carriageway which may
              not be crossed except for fire brigade, ambulance or police purposes
              (traffic cylinder)

                          *   *   *

7105   position of barrier to mark length of road closed to traffic or to guide
              traffic past obstruction (barrier in alternate red and white stripes)

                          REGULATION 11(1)

                              PART III

        SIGNS FOR LANE CLOSURES AND CONTRA-FLOW WORKING AT ROAD WORKS

                Diagrams 7201 to 7294 [*not reproduced*]   **B57.105**

                          REGULATION 11(1)

                              PART IV

              SIGNS FOR ROAD WORKS ENTRANCES AND EXITS

                Diagrams 7301 to 7307 [*not reproduced*]   **B57.106**

Regulation 11(1)

Part V

Signs Mounted on Road Works Vehicles

B57.107

| 7402 | lanes closed to traffic ahead by vehicles carrying out mobile road works (alternative types) |
| 7403 | other traffic to keep to right of vehicles carrying out mobile road works (alternative types) *]* |

*   *   *

Regulation 13(1), 13(5), 13(8)   SCHEDULE 13

Part I

Proportions and form of Letters, Numerals and Other Characters (for Use on a Sign or Parts of a Sign with a Red, Blue, Brown, Black or Green Background and on the Signs Shown in Diagrams 2714 and 2715 where the Characters in those Diagrams are not Varied to Black)

B57.108   *[not reproduced]*

Regulation 13(3), 13(8)

Part II

Proportions and form of Letters, Numerals and Other Characters (for Use on a Sign or Parts of a Sign with a White, Yellow or Orange Background Other than the Signs Shown in Diagrams 2714 and 2715 Except where the Characters in those Diagrams are not Varied to Black)

B57.109   *[not reproduced]*

Regulation 13(5)

Part III

Proportions and form of Letters, Numerals and Other Characters (for Route Numbers on Permanent Motorway Signs with Blue Backgrounds)

B57.110   *[not reproduced]*

Regulation 13(6)

Part IV

Proportions and form of Letters, Numerals and Other Characters (for Route Numbers on Temporary Motorway Signs with Yellow Backgrounds)

B57.111   *[not reproduced]*

Regulation 13(9)

Part V

Proportions and form of Letters, Numerals and Other Characters for Use on Variable Message Signs (where the Characters Shown in Parts I, II, III and IV cannot be used because of The Method of Construction or Operation of the Sign)

B57.112   *[not reproduced]*

Rᴇɢᴜʟᴀᴛɪᴏɴ 13(10)

Pᴀʀᴛ VI

Pʀᴏᴘᴏʀᴛɪᴏɴs ᴀɴᴅ ғᴏʀᴍ ᴏғ Lᴇᴛᴛᴇʀs, Nᴜᴍᴇʀᴀʟs ᴀɴᴅ Oᴛʜᴇʀ Cʜᴀʀᴀᴄᴛᴇʀs ғᴏʀ Usᴇ ɪɴ ᴛʜᴇ Rᴏᴀᴅ
Mᴀʀᴋɪɴɢs Sʜᴏᴡɴ ɪɴ Sᴄʜᴇᴅᴜʟᴇ 6

(a) with a height of 1.6 metres [*not reproduced*]   **B57.113**

(b) with a height of 2.8 metres [*not reproduced*]

(c) for use in the road markings shown in diagrams 1027.1, 1028.2, 1028.3, 1028.4,
1029, 1032 and 1033 [*not reproduced*]

Rᴇɢᴜʟᴀᴛɪᴏɴ 13(11)

Pᴀʀᴛ VII

Pʀᴏᴘᴏʀᴛɪᴏɴs ᴀɴᴅ ғᴏʀᴍ ᴏғ Lᴇᴛᴛᴇʀs, Nᴜᴍᴇʀᴀʟs ᴀɴᴅ Oᴛʜᴇʀ Cʜᴀʀᴀᴄᴛᴇʀs (Sʏᴍʙᴏʟs ғᴏʀ Usᴇ ᴏɴ
Dɪʀᴇᴄᴛɪᴏɴᴀʟ Sɪɢɴs ᴛᴏ Iɴᴅɪᴄᴀᴛᴇ Dɪᴠᴇʀsɪᴏɴ Rᴏᴜᴛᴇs)

[*not reproduced*]   **B57.114**

SCHEDULE 14

Rᴇɢᴜʟᴀᴛɪᴏɴ 13(12)

Pᴀʀᴛ I

Pʀᴏᴘᴏʀᴛɪᴏɴs ᴀɴᴅ ғᴏʀᴍ ᴏғ Sʏᴍʙᴏʟs Iɴᴅɪᴄᴀᴛɪɴɢ Tʏᴘᴇs ᴏғ Tᴏᴜʀɪsᴛ Dᴇsᴛɪɴᴀᴛɪᴏɴ ɪɴ Eɴɢʟᴀɴᴅ,
Sᴄᴏᴛʟᴀɴᴅ ᴀɴᴅ Wᴀʟᴇs

Diagrams T1 to T12 [*not reproduced*]   **B57.115**

Rᴇɢᴜʟᴀᴛɪᴏɴ 13(12)

Pᴀʀᴛ II

Pʀᴏᴘᴏʀᴛɪᴏɴs ᴀɴᴅ ғᴏʀᴍ ᴏғ Sʏᴍʙᴏʟs Iɴᴅɪᴄᴀᴛɪɴɢ Tʏᴘᴇs ᴏғ Tᴏᴜʀɪsᴛ Dᴇsᴛɪɴᴀᴛɪᴏɴ ɪɴ Eɴɢʟᴀɴᴅ
ᴀɴᴅ Wᴀʟᴇs

Diagrams T101 to T164 [*not reproduced*]   **B57.116**

Rᴇɢᴜʟᴀᴛɪᴏɴ 13(12)

Pᴀʀᴛ III

Pʀᴏᴘᴏʀᴛɪᴏɴs ᴀɴᴅ ғᴏʀᴍ ᴏғ Sʏᴍʙᴏʟs Iɴᴅɪᴄᴀᴛɪɴɢ Tʏᴘᴇs ᴏғ Tᴏᴜʀɪsᴛ Dᴇsᴛɪɴᴀᴛɪᴏɴ ɪɴ Eɴɢʟᴀɴᴅ
Oɴʟʏ

Diagrams T201 to T205 [*not reproduced*]   **B57.117**

Rᴇɢᴜʟᴀᴛɪᴏɴ 13(12)

Pᴀʀᴛ IV

Pʀᴏᴘᴏʀᴛɪᴏɴs ᴀɴᴅ ғᴏʀᴍ ᴏғ Sʏᴍʙᴏʟs Iɴᴅɪᴄᴀᴛɪɴɢ Tʏᴘᴇs ᴏғ Tᴏᴜʀɪsᴛ Dᴇsᴛɪɴᴀᴛɪᴏɴ ɪɴ Sᴄᴏᴛʟᴀɴᴅ
Oɴʟʏ

Diagrams T301.1 to T303 [*not reproduced*]   **B57.118**

Rᴇɢᴜʟᴀᴛɪᴏɴ 13(12)

Pᴀʀᴛ V

Pʀᴏᴘᴏʀᴛɪᴏɴs ᴀɴᴅ ғᴏʀᴍ ᴏғ Sʏᴍʙᴏʟs Iɴᴅɪᴄᴀᴛɪɴɢ Tʏᴘᴇs ᴏғ Tᴏᴜʀɪsᴛ Dᴇsᴛɪɴᴀᴛɪᴏɴ ɪɴ Wᴀʟᴇs Oɴʟʏ

Diagrams T401 to T403 [*not reproduced*]   **B57.119**

Regulation 46   SCHEDULE 15

LEGENDS FOR USE ON VARIABLE MESSAGE SIGNS

PART I

PRELIMINARY

B57.120   Paragraph 1 [*not reproduced*]

PART II

SIGNS AUTOMATICALLY ACTIVATED BY VEHICULAR TRAFFIC

Paragraph 2 [*not reproduced*]

PART III

LEGENDS GIVING WARNINGS OF ADVERSE WEATHER OR OTHER TEMPORARY HAZARDS OR INCIDENTS

B57.121   Paragraph 3 [*not reproduced*]

PART IV

LEGENDS INDICATING LOCATION OF TEMPORARY HAZARD OR INCIDENT

B57.122   Paragraph 4 [*not reproduced*]

PART V

ADDITIONAL INFORMATION

B57.123   Paragraph 5 [*not reproduced*]

PART VI

OTHER LEGENDS

Paragraph 6 [*not reproduced*]

Regulation 17   SCHEDULE 16

PERMITTED VARIANTS

B57.124   Items 1 to 46 [*not reproduced*]

SCHEDULE 17

Regulation 18   **B57.125**

(1) Item	(2) Diagram numbers	(3) Method of illumination
1.	501, 504.1*, 505.1*, 506.1*, 507.1*, 508.1*, 509.1*, 510*, 512*, 512.1*, 512.2*, 513*, 516*, 517*, 520, 521*, 522*, 523.1*, 524.1*, 528*, 529*, 529.1*, 530, 531.1, 532.2 (in respect of the triangle symbols), 532.3 (in respect of the triangle symbols), 543, 544, 544.1, 544.2, 545*, 555, 557.1*, 601.1, 602, 606 (other than when used as described in item 6 or item 7), 609, 610 (other than when used as described in item 7), 611 (other than when used as described in item 7), 611.1, 612 (other than when used as described in item 6), 613 (other than when used as described in item 6), 614 (other than when used as described in item 6), 615, 616 (other than when used as described in item 7), 617 (other than when used with 618), 618.2, 618.3, 618.3A, 618.4, 619, 619.1, 619.2, 622.1A, 622.2, 622.4, 622.7, 622.8, 626.2A, 627.1, 629, 629A, 629.1, 629.2, 629.2A, 632, 642 (when used as a terminal sign), 652, 770, 771, 772, 779, 782, 784.1, 790, 950*, 952, 953, 953.1, 2901, 2902, 2902.1, 2908, 2908.1, 2909, 2913.4, 2930, 2931, 5010, 5011, 7001, 7001.3, 7004, 7005, 7006, 7009, 7010.1, 7011, 7011.1, 7012, 7013, 7027, 7201, 7201.1, 7202, 7203, 7203.1, 7204, 7205, 7206, 7207, 7208, 7210, 7211.1, 7212, 7213, 7214, 7215, 7216, 7217, 7218, 7220, 7221, 7230, 7231, 7232, 7233, 7234, 7235, 7236, 7237, 7238, 7239, 7240, 7241, 7242, 7250, 7251, 7252, 7253, 7254, 7255, 7256, 7260, 7261, 7262, 7263, 7264, 7270, 7271, 7272, 7274, 7275, 7290, 7291, 7292, 7293, 7294	(1) Subject to paragraphs (2) and (3) the signs shall be reflectorised in accordance with the provisions of regulation 19. (2) Subject to paragraph (3), where the sign is erected on a road within 50 metres of any lamp lit by electricity which forms part of a system of street-lighting for that road furnished by means of at least three such lamps placed not more than 183 metres (in Scotland 185 metres) apart, it shall be illuminated by a means of internal or external lighting either for so long as that system is illuminated, or throughout the hours of darkness and may also be reflectorised. (3) A sign to which this paragraph applies shall be illuminated as mentioned in paragraph (1) or (2). (4) Paragraph (3) applies to a sign erected as mentioned in paragraph (2) which falls within any of the following descriptions— (a) a sign placed temporarily— (i) for the purposes of a temporary statutory provision (other than in connection with road works); (ii) by reason of an emergency; or (iii) by reason of the execution of works, or of any obstruction, on a road subject to a speed limit (other than a temporary speed limit) of 40 mph or less; (b) a sign marked with an asterisk in column (2) when placed on a single carriageway road which is not a principal or trunk road and is subject to a speed limit of 30mph or less; (c) the sign shown in diagram 652 when placed on a road more than 50 metres from a junction with another road from which traffic can approach it; (d) the sign shown in diagram 7004 or 7005, in either case when varied to omit the sign shown in diagram 7001 and the distance plate.

(1) Item	(2) Diagram numbers	(3) Method of illumination
2.	2711	The sign shall be internally illuminated.
3.	955, 956, 957, other than when used as described in item 7	(1) Where the sign is a terminal sign and is erected on a road within 50 metres of any lamp lit by electricity which forms part of a system of street-lighting for that road furnished by means of at least three such lamps placed not more than 183 metres (in Scotland 185 metres) apart, that sign shall be illuminated by a means of internal or external lighting either for so long as that system is illuminated, or throughout the hours of darkness. (2) Where the sign is erected in such a manner that it is not required to be illuminated throughout the hours of darkness by a means of internal or external lighting, it shall be reflectorised in accordance with regulation 19.
4.	515, 515.1, 515.1A, 528.1, 548, 549, 550, 550.1, 550.2, 551, 551.1, 551.2, 552, 553.1, 554, 554.1, 554.2, 555.1, 556, 556.1, 557, 558, 558.1, 559, 562, 574, 581, 582, 583, 584, 633, 642 (when used other than as a terminal sign), 642.2A, 642.3, 646, 647, 650.1, 663, 663.1, 664, 665, 666, 774, 775, 777, 783, 785.1, 786, 787, 788, 789, 789.1, 789.2, 801, 811, 816, 817, 818, 818.1, 818.1A, 818.2, 818.3, 818.4, 820, 820.1, 821, 822, 823, 824, 825, 827.1, 827.2, 827.3, 829.1, 829.2, 829.3, 829.4, 829.5, 829.6, 830, 830.1, 830.2, 830.3, 831, 831.2, 832, 832.1A, 832.2A, 832.3, 832.4, 832.5, 832.6, 832.7, 832.8, 832.9, 832.10A, 868, 868.1, 872.1, 873, 874, 875, 876, 877, 878, 879, 880, [880.1], 881, 882, 883, [884, 885,] 951 (other than when used as described in item 7), 958, 958.1, 959, 959.1, 960, 960.1, 961, 962, 962.1, 962.2, 964, 969,	The sign may be illuminated by a means of internal or external lighting but, if not so illuminated throughout the hours of darkness, it shall be reflectorised in accordance with regulation 19.

(1) Item	*(2)* Diagram numbers	*(3)* Method of illumination
	974, 975, 2001, 2002, 2003, 2004, 2005, 2005.1, 2006, 2007, 2008, 2009, 2010.1, 2010.2, 2011, 2012, 2013, 2014, 2015, 2016, 2017, 2018, 2019, 2020, 2021, 2021.1, 2022, 2023, 2024, 2025, 2026, 2027, 2027.1, 2028, 2029, 2030, 2030.1, 2031, 2032, 2033, 2034, 2035, 2101, 2101.1, 2101.2, 2102, 2102.1, 2103, 2104, 2105.1, 2106.1, 2107, 2108, 2109, 2110, 2111, 2111.1, 2112, 2113, 2113.1, 2114, 2114.1, 2115, 2115.1, 2116, 2117, 2118, 2119, 2120, 2121, 2122, 2123, 2124, 2124.1, 2125, 2126, 2126.1, 2127, 2128, 2129, 2130, 2131, 2132, 2133, 2134, 2135, 2136, 2137, 2137.1, 2138, 2139, 2140, 2301, 2302, 2303, 2304, 2307, 2308.1, 2309.1, 2310.1, 2311.1, 2311.2, 2313.1, 2313.2, 2313.3, 2313.4, 2313.5, 2313.6, 2314.1, 2314.2, 2324, 2325, 2326, 2327, 2328, 2329, 2330, 2501, 2502, 2503, 2504, 2505, 2505.1, 2506, 2507, 2508, 2509.1, 2510, 2511, 2512, 2513, 2702, 2703, 2704, 2705, 2706, 2707, 2708, 2709, 2710, 2713.1, 2716, 2803, 2804, 2805, 2806, 2806.1, 2903, 2904, 2904.1, 2905, 2906, 2910, 2910.1, 2911, 2912, 2913, 2913.1, 2913.2, 2913.3, 2914, 2914.1, 2915, 2917, 2918, 2918.1, 2919.1, 2920.1, 2921, 2921.1, 2922, 2924, 2925, 2926, 2927, 2927.1, 2928, 2929, 2929.1, 2932, 2933, 2934, 4005 (in respect of the warning sign), 5012, 5013, 5014, 5015, 7002A, 7002B, 7002.1, 7003.1, 7006.1, 7014, 7015, 7019, 7020, 7025, 7026, 7028, 7029, 7032, 7104, 7105, 7301, 7302, 7303, 7304, 7305, 7306, 7307, 7402, 7403	
5.	7023, 7024, 7031	The sign shall be illuminated by a means of internal or external lighting throughout the hours of darkness.
6.	606, 612, 613, 614, 954.5, 954.6, 954.7	Where the sign is fixed to light signals prescribed by regulation 33, it shall be illuminated by a means of internal lighting at all times except when the light signals to which it is fixed are being maintained or repaired.

(1) Item	(2) Diagram numbers	(3) Method of illumination
7.	606, 610, 611, 616, 951, 955, 956, 957	Where the sign is mounted in a bollard fitted with a means of lighting it internally, the sign shall be illuminated throughout the hours of darkness by that means of internal lighting.
8.	502, 503, 511, 513.1, 513.2, 518, 519, 525, 526, 527, 530.1, 531.2, 543.1, 546, 547.1, 547.2, 547.3, 547.4, 547.7, 547.8, 548.1, 553, 553.2, 554.3, 556.2, 557.2, 557.3, 557.4, 558.2, 563, 563.1, 570, 572, 573, 575, 583.1, 584.1, 607, 608, 615.1, 618, 618.1, 620, 620.1, 622.9, 645, 773, 778, 778.1, 780A, 780.1A, 780.2A, 804.1, 804.2, 804.3, 804.4, 811.1, 817.2, 950.1, 953.2, 954, 954.2, 954.3, 954.4, 2602.3, 7001.1, 7001.2, 7021, 7022, 7030, 7209	See regulation 20.
9.	530.2, 532.2 and 532.3 in respect of parts of the signs other than the triangle symbols, 617 (when used with 618), 622.5, 622.6, 625.1, 636, 636.1, 636.2, 637.1, 637.2, 637.3, 638, 638.1, 639, 639.1B, 640, 640.1, 640.2A, 640.3, 640.4, 640.5, 650.2, 650.3, 651, 660, 660.3, 660.4, 660.5, 660.6, 660.7, 661A, 661.1, 661.2A, 661.3A, 661.4, 662, 667, 667.1, 667.2, 668, 668.1, 668.2, 810, 814.1, 814.2, 814.3, 814.4, 816.1, 826, 826.1, 833, 834, 835, 836, 857, 857.1, 864.1, 865, 953.3, 963, 963.1, 963.2, 963.3, 965, 966, 967, 968, 968.1, 970, 971, 972, 973.2, 973.3, 976, 2141, 2201, 2202, 2203, 2204, 2205, 2208, 2209, 2210, 2211, 2212, 2213, 2214, 2215, 2216, 2217, 2218, 2305, 2306, 2322, 2323, 2401, 2402.1, 2403.1, 2601.1, 2601.2, 2602.1, 2602.2, 2603, 2604, 2605, 2606, 2607, 2608, 2609, 2610, 2610.1, 2610.2, 2701, 2701.1, 2712, 2713, 2717, 2801, 2802, 7007.1, 7008, 7016, 7017, 7018, 7018.1, 7404	The sign or plate may be left unlit, or be illuminated either by means of internal or external lighting or by the use of retroreflecting material.

(1) Item	(2) Diagram numbers	(3) Method of illumination
10.	670, 671, 672, 673	(1) Where the sign is a terminal sign and is erected on a trunk or principal road within 50 metres of a street lamp lit by electricity, it shall throughout the hours of darkness— (a) be continuously illuminated by means of internal or external lighting and may also be reflectorised; or (b) while the street lamp is lit, be continuously illuminated by means of external lighting and shall also be reflectorised.
		(2) If any sign is required to be illuminated in the manner and at the times described in paragraph (1) above— (a) every sign shown in the same diagram as the first-mentioned sign which is erected at or near the same point on the road or the same junction for the same purpose as the first-mentioned sign shall be continuously illuminated throughout the same period by the same means of lighting as the first-mentioned sign; and (b) if any of the signs is reflectorised, every other such sign shall be similarly illuminated.
11.	670, 671, 672, 673, 674, 675	If the sign is not required by item 10 to be illuminated by lighting throughout the hours of darkness or throughout such hours while a street lamp is lit, it may be illuminated by a means of internal or external lighting; but if not so illuminated, it shall be reflectorised in accordance with regulation 19. Paragraph (2) of item 10 shall apply as if the sign were a sign required by paragraph (1) of item 10 to be illuminated by lighting throughout the hours of darkness or throughout those hours while a street lamp is lit.

(1) Item	(2) Diagram numbers	(3) Method of illumination
12.	1001, 1001.1, 1001.2, 1001.3, 1002.1, 1003, 1003.1, 1003.2, 1003.3, 1003.4, 1004, 1004.1, 1005, 1005.1, 1008, 1008.1, 1009, 1010, 1012.1, 1012.2, 1012.3, 1013.1, 1013.3, 1013.4, 1014, 1017, 1018.1, 1019, 1020.1, 1022, 1023, 1024, 1024.1, 1025.1, 1025.3, 1025.4, 1026, 1026.1, 1027.1, 1028.2, 1028.3, 1028.4, 1029, 1032, 1033, 1035, 1036.1, 1036.2, 1037.1, 1038, 1038.1, 1039, 1040, 1040.2, 1040.3, 1040.4, 1040.5, 1041, 1041.1, 1042, 1042.1, 1043, 1044, 1045, 1046, 1048, 1048.1, 1048.2, 1048.3, 1048.4, 1049, 1049.1, 1050, 1055.1, 1055.2, 1057, 1058, 1058.1, 1059, 1062, 1063, 1064, 1065, 1066	See regulation 31.
13.	560, 561	See regulation 21.
14.	776	When activated, the sign shall be illuminated by an intermittent red light flashing at a rate of not less than 54 nor more than 90 flashes per minute.
15.	515.2, 2714, 2715, 3014 (in respect of the backing board), 7031	(1) The parts of the sign coloured other than black or orange shall be reflectorised in accordance with regulation 19. (2) The parts coloured orange of the signs in diagrams 2714 and 2715 may be so illuminated and may be fluorescent. (3) The part of the sign in diagram 7031 coloured yellow shall be fluorescent, except as provided in regulation 19(4). The part of the sign in diagram 7031 coloured red may be fluorescent.
16.	7101.1, 7102, 7103	See regulation 56.

B57.126   [*Schedule 17 is printed as amended by SI 2006/2083; SI 2008/2177.*]

Regulation 4   SCHEDULE 18

Interpretation of "Unladen Vehicle"

B57.127   **1.** In these Regulations *"unladen vehicle"* means , subject to paragraph 3 —

     (a)   a motor vehicle not drawing a trailer or otherwise forming part of a combination of vehicles; or

     (b)   a combination of vehicles comprising one motor vehicle drawing one or more trailers,

       in relation to which the conditions specified in paragraph 2 below are satisfied.

B57.128   **2.** The conditions are—

(a) that the motor vehicle is a motor car, a heavy motor car, or a motor tractor;

(b) that no goods or burden are being carried in the motor vehicle or combination of vehicles; and

(c) that not more than 2 persons (excluding the driver) are being carried in the motor vehicle or combination of vehicles.

3. For the purposes of this Schedule, the following are to be deemed not to constitute goods or burden—   **B57.129**

(a) in the case of a motor vehicle constructed or adapted for use and used for the conveyance of a machine or device which is built in as part of the vehicle, that machine or device and any articles used in connection with it;

(b) water, fuel or accumulators used for the purpose of the supply of power for the propulsion of a vehicle or, as the case may be, of any vehicle by which a trailer is drawn, and loose tools and loose equipment.

Regulation 29   SCHEDULE 19

Bᴜs Sᴛᴏᴘ ᴀɴᴅ Bᴜs Sᴛᴀɴᴅ Cʟᴇᴀʀᴡᴀʏs ᴀɴᴅ Bᴏx Jᴜɴᴄᴛɪᴏɴs

Pᴀʀᴛ I

Sɪɢɴɪꜰɪᴄᴀɴᴄᴇ ᴏꜰ Bᴜs Sᴛᴏᴘ ᴀɴᴅ Bᴜs Sᴛᴀɴᴅ Cʟᴇᴀʀᴡᴀʏ Mᴀʀᴋɪɴɢs

Interpretation of Part I of Schedule

1. For the purposes of this Part of this Schedule—   **B57.130**

(a) *"clearway"* means an area of carriageway bounded by the continuous and broken straight yellow lines comprised in the road marking in diagram 1025.1, 1025.3 or 1025.4 and *"bus stop clearway"* means a clearway on which the words "BUS STOP" are marked; and

(b) a vehicle shall be taken to have stopped within a clearway if—

    (i) any point in the clearway is below the vehicle or its load (if any); and

    (ii) the vehicle is stationary.

Prohibition conveyed by road markings

2. The road markings in diagrams 1025.1, 1025.3 and 1025.4 shall each convey the prohibition that, subject to the exceptions specified in paragraphs 3 and 4, no person driving a vehicle shall cause it to stop within the clearway—   **B57.131**

(a) at any time, if the sign shown in diagram 974 or 975 placed in conjunction with the markings is varied so as to omit the reference to times of day; or

(b) in any other case, during the period specified on that sign.

Exceptions in favour of buses

3. Nothing in paragraph 2 applies to the driver of a bus being used in the provision of a local service who causes the bus to stop within the clearway for so long as may be necessary—   **B57.132**

(a) to maintain the published timetable for the service (provided, in the case of a bus stop clearway, the bus is not stopped within the clearway for a period exceeding two minutes);

(b) to enable passengers to board or alight from the bus; or

(c) to enable the crew of the bus to be changed.

Other exceptions

B57.133 **4.**—(1) Nothing in paragraph 2 applies in relation to—

(a) a vehicle being used for fire brigade [or, in England [or Wales], fire and rescue authority], ambulance or police purposes;

[(aa) as regards England and Wales, and so far as relating to the functions of the Serious Organised Crime Agency which are exercisable in or as regards Scotland and which relate to reserved matters (within the meaning of the Scotland Act 1998), a vehicle being used for Serious Organised Crime Agency purposes;]

(b) anything done with the permission or at the direction of—

(i) a constable in uniform;

(ii) a traffic warden; or

(iii) where the clearway is in a special parking area designated under Part II of the Road Traffic Act 1991 or Schedule 3 to that Act, a parking attendant appointed under section 63A of the 1984 Act;

(c) a vehicle which is prevented from proceeding by circumstances beyond the driver's control or which has to be stopped in order to avoid injury or damage to persons or property;

(d) a taxi which is stationary only for so long as may be reasonably necessary for a passenger to board or alight and to load or unload any luggage of the passenger;

(e) a marked vehicle which, whilst used by a universal service provider in the course of the provision of a universal postal service, is stationary only for so long as may be reasonably necessary for postal packets to be collected;

(f) a vehicle driven by a person whilst being trained to drive a bus operating local services who, as part of his training, stops the vehicle within a clearway for no longer than necessary to simulate the stopping of a bus at a bus stop for the purpose of picking up and setting down passengers;

(g) a vehicle which is stationary in order that it may be used for one or more of the purposes specified in paragraph 5 and which cannot be used for such a purpose without stopping in the clearway.

(2) In sub-paragraph (1)(e) the expressions *"universal service provider"*, *"provision of a universal postal service"* and *"postal packet"* shall bear the same meanings as in the Postal Services Act 2000.

B57.134 *[Paragraph 4 of Sch.19 is printed as amended by SI 2004/3168; SI 2005/2929; SI 2006/594.]*

Permitted purposes

B57.135 **5.** The purposes referred to in paragraph 4(g) are—

(a) any operation involving building, demolition or excavation;

(b) the removal of any obstruction to traffic;

(c) the maintenance, improvement or reconstruction of a road;

(d) constructing, improving, maintaining or cleaning any street furniture including bus stop infrastructure; or

(e) the laying, erection, alteration, repair or cleaning of any sewer or of any main, pipe or apparatus for the supply of gas, water or electricity, or of any [electronic communications apparatus] kept installed for the purposes of [electronic communications code system [*sic*]] or of any other [electronic communications apparatus] lawfully kept installed in any position.

B57.136 *[Paragraph 5 of Sch.19 is printed as amended by SI 2003/2155.*

For the meaning of "electronic communications apparatus" and "electronic communications code system", see the note to reg.26 above.]

Pᴀʀᴛ II

Sɪɢɴɪғɪᴄᴀɴᴄᴇ ᴏғ Bᴏx Jᴜɴᴄᴛɪᴏɴ Mᴀʀᴋɪɴɢs

Interpretation of Part II of Schedule

6. In this Part of this Schedule—   **B57.137**

(a) *"box junction"* means the area of carriageway marked with yellow cross-hatching at a junction between two or more roads on which there has been placed the road marking shown in diagram 1043 or 1044; and

(b) a reference (however expressed) to a vehicle which is stationary or stops within a box junction includes a vehicle which is stationary whilst part of it is within the box junction.

Prohibition conveyed by markings in diagram 1043 or 1044

7.—(1) Except when placed in the circumstances described in paragraph 8, the road   **B57.138**
markings shown in diagrams 1043 and 1044 shall each convey the prohibition that no person shall cause a vehicle to enter the box junction so that the vehicle has to stop within the box junction due to the presence of stationary vehicles.

(2) The prohibition in sub-paragraph (1) does not apply to any person—

(a) who causes a vehicle to enter the box junction (other than a box junction at a roundabout) for the purpose of turning right; and

(b) stops it within the box junction for so long as it is prevented from completing the right turn by oncoming vehicles or other vehicles which are stationary whilst waiting to complete a right turn.

Prohibition conveyed when markings are placed in conjunction with signs in diagrams 615 and 811

8. When the road marking shown in diagram 1043 or 1044 is placed in conjunction with   **B57.139**
the signs shown in diagrams 615 and 811 on an area of carriageway which is less than 4.5 metres wide at its narrowest point, the road marking shall convey the prohibition that no person shall cause a vehicle to enter the box junction so that the vehicle has to stop within the box junction due to the presence of oncoming vehicles or other stationary vehicles beyond the box junction.

Pᴀʀᴛ II

Tʜᴇ Tʀᴀғғɪᴄ Sɪɢɴs Gᴇɴᴇʀᴀʟ Dɪʀᴇᴄᴛɪᴏɴs 2002

Citation and commencement

1. This Part of this Instrument—   **B57.140**

(a) may be cited—

(i) as the Traffic Signs General Directions 2002, and

(ii) together with Part I above, as the Traffic Signs Regulations and General Directions 2002; and

(b) shall come into force on 31st January 2003.

Revocations

2. The Traffic Signs General Directions 1994 [*SI 1994/1519, Pt II*] , the Traffic   **B57.141**
Signs General (Amendment) Directions 1995 [*SI 1995/2769*] , the Traffic Signs General (Amendment) (No.2) Directions 1995 [*SI 1995/3107, Pt II*] and the Traffic Signs General (Amendment) Directions 1999 [*SI 1999/1723*] are hereby revoked.

Interpretation—general

B57.142   **3.**—(1) In these Directions—

(a) *"one-way road"* has the meaning given in paragraph 1 of the Schedule;

(b) *"the Regulations"* means the Traffic Signs Regulations 2002 [*q.v.*] ; and

(c) the expressions listed in paragraph (2) have the same meaning as in the Regulations.

(2) Those expressions are—

"the 1984 Act";

"central reservation";

"contra-flow";

"controlled parking zone";

"cycle lane";

"cycle track";

"dual carriageway road";

"EEA Standard";

"equestrian crossing";

["hard shoulder"];

["actively managed hard shoulder"];

"junction";

"level crossing";

"maximum gross weight";

"motorway";

"mph";

"non-primary route";

"pedal cycle";

"pedestrian zone";

"plate";

"primary route";

"primary signals";

"principal road";

"reflectorised";

"retroreflecting material";

"road marking";

"route";

"school crossing place";

"secondary signals";

"sign";

"signal-controlled crossing facility";

"signal-controlled pedestrian facility";

"speed limit" and "national speed limit";

"stud";

"temporary statutory provision";

"traffic lane";

"Toucan crossing";

"variable message sign";

"Zebra crossing"; and

"zig-zag line".

[*Direction 3 is printed as amended by SI 2005/1670.*]   **B57.143**

Interpretation of references

4. In these Directions, unless it is expressly provided otherwise or the context   **B57.144**
otherwise requires—

    (a) a reference to a numbered direction is a reference to the direction so numbered in these Directions;

    (b) a reference to a numbered paragraph is a reference to the paragraph so numbered in the direction in which the reference occurs;

    (c) a reference to a sub-paragraph followed by a number or letter is a reference to the sub-paragraph bearing that number or letter in the direction in which the reference occurs;

    (d) a reference to a numbered diagram is a reference to the diagram so numbered in a Schedule to the Regulations;

    (e) a reference to a sign shown in a diagram in a Schedule to the Regulations includes a reference to that sign as varied in accordance with the Regulations;

    (f) a reference to a numbered regulation or Schedule is a reference to the regulation of, or to the Schedule to, the Regulations so numbered; and

    (g) in any direction which includes a table, references to a table are to the table, or in the case of a numbered table to the table so numbered, in that direction.

Saving

5. Any sign, which immediately before the coming into force of these Direc-   **B57.145**
tions was—

    (a) placed on or near any road in conformity with the Traffic Signs General Directions 1994; or

    (b) was by virtue of those Directions to be treated as placed in conformity with those Directions,

shall, so long as it would have continued to conform or be treated as conforming with those Directions if they had not been revoked, be treated as if placed in conformity with these Directions, notwithstanding any provision of these Directions to the contrary.

Sign to be placed only at sites approved by the Secretary of State

6. The sign shown in diagram 601.1 shall not be placed for the first time at any   **B57.146**
site except with the approval of the Secretary of State, the Scottish Ministers or
the National Assembly for Wales.

Signs to be placed only to indicate the effect of a statutory prohibition

7.—(1) Except as provided by paragraph (3), the signs to which this paragraph   **B57.147**

applies may be placed on or near a road only to indicate the effect of an Act, order, regulation, byelaw or notice (*"the effect of a statutory provision"*) which prohibits or restricts the use of the road by traffic.

(2) Paragraph (1) applies to—

(a) the signs shown in diagrams 606, 607, 609, 612, 613, 614, 616, 617, 618, 618.1, 618.2, 618.3, 618.3A, 618.4, 619, 619.1, 619.2, 620, 620.1, 622.1A, 622.2, 622.4, 622.5, 622.6, 622.7, 622.8, 622.9, 625.1, 626.2A, 627.1, 629, 629A, 629.1, 629.2, 629.2A, 632, 636, 636.1, 636.2, 637.1, 637.2, 637.3, 638, 638.1, 639, 639.1B, 640, 640.2A, 640.3, 640.4, 640.5, 642, 642.2A, 642.3, 646, 647, 650.1, 650.2, 650.3, 651, 652, 660, 660.3, 660.4, 660.5, 660.6, 660.7, 661A, 661.1, 661.2A, 661.3A, 661.4, 662, 663, 663.1, 664, 665, 666, 667, 667.1, 667.2, 668, 668.1, 668.2, 670, 671, 672, 673, 674, 675, 804.1, 804.2, 804.3, 804.4, 810, 818.2, 818.3, 818.4, 951, 952, 953, 953.1, 953.2, 954, 954.2, 954.3, 954.4, 954.5, 954.6, 954.7, 955, 956, 957, 958, 958.1, 959, 959.1, 960, 960.1, 961, 962, 962.2, 963, 963.2, 963.3, 964, 969, 1017, 1018.1, 1019, 1020.1, 1028.2, 1028.3 (except when used in conjunction with the sign shown in diagram 786), 1028.4, 1032, 1033, 1036.1, 1036.2, 1037.1, 1046, 1048, 1048.1, 1048.2, 1048.3, 1048.4, 1049, 1049.1, 1050, 1065, 2003, 2007, 2009, 2010.1, 2010.2, 2107, 2108, 2123, 2124, 5001.1, 5001.2, 5003, 5003.1, 5005, 5005.1, 7201, 7201.1, 7203.1, 7204, 7207, 7210, 7211.1, 7212, 7213, 7214, 7215, 7216, 7217, 7218, 7220, 7230, 7231, 7232, 7233, 7234, 7235, 7260, 7261, 7282, 7283, 7283.1, 7284, 7284.1 and 7290; and

(b) any sign which, by virtue of regulation 17 and item 31 of Schedule 16, incorporates as a symbol a sign shown in a diagram specified in sub-paragraph (a).

(3) A sign shown in a diagram specified in an item in column (2) of the Table may be placed at a site or in circumstances specified in column (3) of that item notwithstanding that it does not at that site or in those circumstances indicate the effect of a statutory provision.

TABLE

(1) Item	(2) Diagram	(3) Site or circumstances
1.	606	On the central island of a roundabout or in combination with a plate of the type shown in diagram 608
2.	609	On a road approaching its junction with a dual carriageway road whether or not in combination with a plate of the type shown in diagram 608
3.	616, 1046	At a site which has been approved by the Secretary of State

(1) Item	(2) Diagram	(3) Site or circumstances
4.	629.2, 629.2A	On— (a) a road which passes under or through a bridge, tunnel or other structure which limits the height of vehicles using that road; or (b) any such bridge, tunnel or other structure
5.	2003, 2007, 2009, 2107, 2108 or a sign to which paragraph (1) applies by virtue of paragraph (2)(b)	When— (a) including a symbol representing diagram 629.2 or 629.2A in the circumstances specified in item 4; or (b) not including a symbol representing a sign to which paragraph (1) applies
6.	818.2, 818.3, 818.4	When placed in the circumstances specified in item 4 above to indicate that the prohibition indicated by the sign shown in diagram 629.2 or 629.2A is ahead

(4) The sign shown in diagram 626.2A may be placed only to indicate the effect of a statutory provision which restricts the use of a road carried by a bridge or other structure—

(a) in the case of vehicles required to be marked with their maximum gross weight, to any vehicle with a maximum gross weight not exceeding that indicated on the sign; or

(b) in the case of vehicles not required to be marked with their maximum gross weight but required to be marked with their unladen weight, to any vehicle with an unladen weight not exceeding the maximum gross weight indicated on the sign.

The placing of certain signs to indicate the beginning of a restriction, requirement, prohibition or speed limit

8.—(1) This direction applies to the signs shown in diagrams 616, 617, 618, **B57.148** 618.1, 618.2, 618.3, 618.3A, 619, 619.1, 619.2, 620, 620.1, 622.1A, 622.4, 622.5, 622.6, 622.7, 622.8, 622.9, 625.1, 626.2A, 627.1, 629, 629A, 629.1, 629.2, 629.2A, 632, 642, 646, 663, 663.1, 665, 667, 667.1, 668, 668.1, 670, 672, 674[, 675], 951, 952, 953, 953.1, 955, 956 and 957.

(2) In accordance with the following provisions of this direction and the provisions of direction 9, appropriate signs to which this direction applies shall be placed to indicate the point at which a restriction, requirement, prohibition or speed limit applying to traffic on a road (in this direction and in direction 9 called *"the relevant road"*) begins.

(3) Subject to paragraphs (4), (5) and (6) and to direction 9, a sign to which this direction applies shall be placed on the relevant road at or as near as practicable to the point referred to in paragraph (2)—

(a) where the relevant road has only one carriageway, on each side of that carriageway; or

(b) where the relevant road has more than one carriageway, on each side of each carriageway in relation to which the restriction, requirement, prohibition or speed limit begins.

(4) Where the relevant road has one carriageway, then signs to which this direction applies need only be placed on one side of the relevant road to indicate the point at which a restriction, requirement, prohibition (but not a speed limit) begins in the following cases—

(a) where the restriction, requirement or prohibition applies only to traffic on one side of the relevant road; or

(b) at a junction where—

(i) traffic proceeding on another road on which it is permitted to proceed only in one direction turns into the relevant road; or

(ii) the carriageway of the relevant road is less than 5 metres wide and the sign is so placed that its centre is within 2 metres of the edge of the carriageway.

(5) Where a length of road which passes under or through a bridge, tunnel or other structure is subject to a prohibition on vehicles exceeding a particular height, the sign shown in diagram 629.2 or 629.2A may be placed on the bridge, tunnel or other structure to indicate the prohibition in addition to or instead of the signs required to be placed by paragraph (3).

(6) Paragraphs (3) and (4) shall not apply to the signs shown in diagrams 667, 667.1, 668 and 668.1 which shall be placed on the side of the carriageway on which parking on a verge or footway is permitted and as near as is practicable to the point at which the length of the verge or footway concerned begins.

B57.149   *[Direction 8 is printed as amended by SI 2008/2177.]*

Beginning of a speed limit—further provisions

B57.150   9.—(1) Direction 8(3) does not apply where a speed limit in force on the relevant road begins—

(a) at a point where the relevant road begins, being a point where it has no junction with another road; or

(b) at a point where the relevant road has a junction with another road and the same speed limit is in force on both roads.

(2) This paragraph applies where the relevant road has a junction (*"the junction"*) with the side of another road (*"the other road"*) and a maximum speed limit is in force on the other road which is different from the speed limit in force on the relevant road.

(3) Where paragraph (2) applies, it is sufficient compliance with direction 8(2), for the purpose of indicating the beginning of the speed limit on the relevant road to traffic entering it from the other road, if the sign shown in diagram 670, 674 or 675 is placed not further than 20 metres from the junction, on the left hand or near side of the carriageway of the relevant road as viewed in the direction of travel of such traffic or, where the relevant road is a dual carriageway road, on the left hand or near side of the carriageway by which traffic may pass into the relevant road from the other road.

(4) Where paragraph (2) applies, for the purpose of indicating the speed limit in force on the other road to traffic entering that road from the relevant road, the sign shown in diagram 670, 674 or 675 shall (subject to paragraph (5)) be placed not further than 20 metres from the junction and so as to be visible to such traffic, on each side of the carriageway by which traffic may pass from the relevant road into the other road.

(5) Paragraph (4) does not apply if—

    (a) the maximum speed limit in force on the other road is greater than that in force on the relevant road; and

    (b) signs indicating the maximum speed limit have been placed on the other road in accordance with direction 11 on each side of, and not more than 100 metres from, the junction.

The placing of certain signs to indicate the end of a restriction, requirement, prohibition or speed limit

10.—(1) When the sign shown in diagram 618.4, 622.2, 645, 647, 664, 666, 667.2, 668.2, 673, 675 or 964 is placed to indicate the point at which traffic on a road ceases to be subject to a restriction, requirement, prohibition or speed limit, the sign shall be placed on the road as near as practicable to that point.   **B57.151**

(2) Subject to paragraph (3), where a length of road ceases to be subject to a speed limit and becomes subject to a national speed limit, the sign shown in diagram 671 shall be placed at or as near as practicable to the point where the speed limit ends and the national speed limit begins[, except where the sign shown in diagram 675 with the permitted variation shown in item 4 of the table below that diagram is placed at that point].

(3) Where a temporary restriction of speed has been imposed under section 14 of the 1984 Act along a length of road by reason of works which are being or are proposed to be executed on or near that road, there shall be placed at or as near as practicable to the point where the temporary restriction of speed ends—

    (a) the sign shown in diagram 7006 or in diagram 7001 (placed in combination with the plate shown in diagram 645); and

    (b) in a case where, but for the temporary speed limit, a change in speed limit would at some point have occurred along the length of road, the sign shown in diagram 670 (varied as appropriate) or 671.

(4) When the sign shown in diagram 671, 673 or 675 is placed to indicate the point at which traffic on a road ceases to be subject to a speed limit—

    (a) where the road has only one carriageway, one such sign shall be placed on each side of the carriageway of the road; or

    (b) where the road has more than one carriageway, one such sign shall be placed on each side of each carriageway on which the speed limit ends.

(5) Where a road (*"the relevant road"*) has a junction with the side of another road (*"the other road"*) and—

    (a) a maximum speed limit is in force on the other road; and

    (b) a national speed limit is in force on the relevant road,

then, for the purpose of indicating the national speed limit to traffic entering the relevant road from the other road, the sign shown in diagram 671 or 675 shall be placed on the relevant road in accordance with paragraph (6).

(6) The sign shall be placed not more than 20 metres from the junction with the other road on the left hand or near side of the relevant road as viewed in the direction of travel of a vehicle entering the relevant road from the other road or, if the relevant road is a dual carriageway road, on the left hand or near side of the carriageway by which a vehicle may pass into the relevant road from the other road.

(7) Where the relevant road has a junction with the side of the other road and—

(a) a national speed limit is in force on the other road; and

(b) a maximum speed limit is in force on the relevant road,

then, for the purpose of indicating the national speed limit to traffic entering the other road from the relevant road, traffic signs shown in diagram 671 or 675 shall be placed in accordance with paragraph (8) on the relevant road not further than 20 metres from the junction.

(8) If the relevant road has one carriageway, one such sign shall be placed on each side of that carriageway and, if the relevant road is a dual carriageway road, one such sign shall be placed on each side of the carriageway by which traffic may pass from the relevant road into the other road.

B57.152   *[Direction 10 is printed as amended by SI 2008/2177.]*

Repeater signs

B57.153   11.—(1) Paragraph (2) applies to the signs shown in diagrams 614, 632, 636, 636.1, 636.2, 637.1, 637.2, 637.3, 638, 638.1 when the arrow is omitted, 639 when the arrow is omitted, 639.1B, 640 when the arrow is omitted, 642, 646, 650.1, 650.2, 650.3, 660, 660.3, 660.4, 660.5, 660.6, 661A, 661.1, 662, 670 (except when displayed on a variable message sign in the manner mentioned in regulation 58(7)(b)), 672, 956, 957, 959, 959.1, 960, 960.1 and 961.

(2) Subject to [paragraphs (3), (4) and (7)], signs to which this paragraph applies shall be placed at regular intervals along a road which is subject to a restriction, requirement, prohibition or speed limit which can be indicated by the signs.

(3) Signs shown in diagram 670 when varied to "20" need not be placed in accordance with paragraph (2) on a road within an area into which each entrance for vehicular traffic has been indicated by the sign shown in diagram 674.

(4) The sign shown in diagram 670 (except when displayed on a variable message sign in the manner mentioned in regulation 58(7)(b)) shall not be placed along—

(a) a road on which there is provided a system of carriageway lighting furnished by lamps lit by electricity placed not more than 183 metres apart in England and Wales or not more than 185 metres apart in Scotland and which is subject to a speed limit of 30 mph; or

(b) a motorway on which a national speed limit is in force.

(5) The sign shown in diagram 671 shall be placed at regular intervals along the length of a road (other than a motorway) on which—

(a) there is a system of street or carriageway lighting furnished by lamps lit by electricity placed not more than 183 metres apart in England and Wales or not more than 185 metres apart in Scotland; and

(b) a national speed limit is in force.

[(6) Paragraph (7) applies if—

(a) direction 11(2) (in the case of the sign shown in diagram 670) or direction 11(5) (in the case of the sign shown in diagram 671) requires the sign shown in that diagram to be placed along a road at regular intervals; and

(b) an enforcement camera is from time to time in use along that road.

(7) Where this paragraph applies, an additional sign shown in diagram 670 or 671 respectively may be placed along the road at each approach to an enforcement camera, even if such an additional sign affects the regular intervals at which signs are placed along that road.]

[Direction 11 is printed as amended by SI 2008/2177.]   **B57.154**

Signs to be placed only on specified types of road

12.—(1) The signs shown in diagrams 2001, 2002, 2003, 2004, 2005, 2005.1,   **B57.155**
2006, 2007, 2008, 2009, 2010.1, 2010.2, 2011, 2012, 2013, 2014, 2015, 2016, 2017, 2018, 2019, 2020, 2021, 2021.1, 2022, 2023, 2024, 2025, 2030, 2030.1, 2032, 2033, 2034, 2035 and 2717 may be placed only on or near a primary route.

(2) The signs shown in diagrams 2026, 2027, 2027.1, 2028 and 2029 may be placed only on a primary route, or on a non-primary route at a junction with a primary route.

13.—(1) The signs shown in diagrams 2101, 2101.1, 2101.2, 2102, 2102.1,   **B57.156**
2103, 2104, 2105.1, 2106.1, 2107, 2108, 2109, 2110, 2111, 2111.1, 2112, 2113, 2113.1, 2114, 2114.1, 2115, 2115.1, 2116, 2117, 2118, 2119, 2120, 2121, 2122, 2123, 2124, 2124.1, 2128, 2129, 2130, 2131, 2133, 2135, 2137.1, 2138 and 2139 may be placed only on or near a non-primary route.

(2) The signs shown in diagrams 2125, 2126, 2126.1, 2127, 2132, 2134, 2136, 2137, 2140, 2322 and 2323 may be placed only on or near a non-primary route, or on a primary route at a junction with a non-primary route.

(3) The signs shown in diagrams 1012.3, 2031, 2201, 2202, 2203, 2204, 2205, 2208, 2209, 2210, 2211, 2212, 2213, 2214, 2215, 2216, 2217, 2218, 2301, 2302, 2303, 2304, 2305, 2306, 2307, 2308.1, 2309.1, 2310.1, 2311.1, 2311.2, 2313.1, 2313.2, 2313.3, 2313.4, 2313.5, 2313.6, 2314.1, 2314.2, 2324, 2325, 2326, 2327, 2328, 2329, 2330, 2401, 2402.1, 2403.1, 2501, 2502, 2504, 2505, 2505.1, 2506, 2507, 2508, 2509.1, 2510, 2511, 2512, 2513, 2601.1, 2601.2, 2602.1, 2602.2, 2602.3, 2603, 2604, 2605, 2606, 2607, 2608, 2609, 2610, 2610.1, 2610.2, 2701, 2701.1, 2702, 2703, 2704, 2705, 2706, 2707, 2708, 2709, 2710, 2712, 2713.1, 2801, 2802, 2803, 2804, 2805, 2806, 2806.1, 7031, 7242 and 7285 may not be placed on a motorway.

(4) The sign shown in diagram 2141 may only be placed on or near a minor route at a junction with another minor route and, for this purpose, *"minor route"* means any road except a road to which the Secretary of State, the Scottish Ministers or the National Assembly for Wales has assigned a number prefixed by the letter A, B or M.

14.—(1) The signs shown in diagrams 832.3, 1012.2, 1064, 2901, 2903, 2904,   **B57.157**
2904.1, 2905, 2906, 2908, 2908.1, 2909, 2910, 2910.1, 2911, 2912, 2913, 2913.1, 2913.2, 2913.3, 2913.4, 2914, 2914.1, 2915, 2917, 2918, 2918.1, 2919.1, 2920.1, 2921, 2921.1, 2922, 2924, 2925, 2926, 2927, 2927.1, 2928, 2929, 2929.1, 2930, 2931, 2932, 2933, 2934, 7241 and 7286 may be placed only on or near a motorway.

(2) The signs shown in diagrams 2902 and 2902.1 may be placed only on a motorway or on another road at a junction with a motorway.

15.—(1) The signs shown in diagrams 823, 824, 825, 868, 868.1, 872.1, 873,   **B57.158**
874, 875, 876 and 2713 may be placed only on or near—

(a) a motorway when the colour of the background of the sign is blue;

(b) a primary route when the colour of the background of the sign is green; or

(c) a non-primary route when the colour of the background of the sign is white.

(2) The sign shown in diagram 872.1 may only be placed on a dual carriageway road or a one-way road.

(3) The sign shown in diagram 877 may be placed only on or near—

(a) a motorway exit slip road when the colour of the background of the sign is blue;

(b) a primary route when the colour of the background of the sign is green; or

(c) a non-primary route when the colour of the background of the sign is white.

Speed limits of 20 mph

B57.159   16.—(1) The sign shown in diagram 674 may only be placed on a road if no point on any road (not being a cul-de-sac less than 80 metres long), to which the speed limit indicated by the sign applies, is situated more than 50 metres from a traffic calming feature.

(2) In paragraph (1) *"traffic calming feature"* means —

(a) a road hump constructed pursuant to section 90A of the Highways Act 1980 (*"the 1980 Act"*) … and in accordance with the Highways (Road Humps) Regulations 1999 [*SI 1999/1025; not reproduced in this work*] …;

(b) traffic calming works constructed in accordance with section 90G of the 1980 Act … and in accordance with the Highways (Traffic Calming) Regulations 1999 [*SI 1999/1026; not reproduced in this work*] …;

(c) a refuge for pedestrians which was constructed pursuant to section 68 of the 1980 Act … after 15th June 1999 and is so constructed as to encourage a reduction in the speed of traffic using the carriageway;

(d) a variation of the relative widths of the carriageway or of any footway pursuant to section 75 of the 1980 Act … which—

(i) was carried out after 15th June 1999 for the purpose of encouraging a reduction in the speed of traffic using the carriageway; and

(ii) had the effect of reducing the width of the carriageway; or

(e) a horizontal bend in the carriageway through which all vehicular traffic has to change direction by no less than 70 degrees within a distance of 32 metres as measured at the inner kerb radius.

(3) For the purposes of paragraph (1) the distance of 50 metres shall be measured along roads to which the speed limit indicated by the sign shown in diagram 674 applies.

B57.160   *[The words omitted from direction 16(2) relate exclusively to Scotland.]*

Signs to be placed only in conjunction with specified road markings (except signs for prohibitions and restrictions on waiting etc)

B57.161   17.—(1) Save as provided in paragraph (2), a sign shown in a diagram whose number appears and is placed in the circumstances (if any) or is in the form (if any) specified in column (2) of an item in the Table may be placed on a road only—

(a) in conjunction with the road marking shown in the diagram whose number appears and is in the form (if any) specified in column (3) of that item; or

(b) where the numbers of two or more road markings so appear, in conjunction with both or all of those markings.

TABLE

(1) Item	(2) Sign diagram number	(3) Road marking diagram number
1.	508.1, 509.1	1010
2.	557.1	1062
3.	601.1	1002.1 and 1022
4.	602	1003 and 1023
5.	611.1 if placed in conjunction with diagram 602	1003, 1003.4 and 1023
6.	611.1	1003.3 and 1003.4
7.	957	1057
8.	958	1010
9.	958.1	1009
10.	959	1048 and 1049
11.	959.1	1049 varied to a width of 150 millimetres and 1057
12.	960	1048 and 1049
13.	960 varied to include pedal cycle symbol	1048.1 and 1049
14.	960.1	1049 varied to a width of 150 millimetres and 1057
15.	2933	1064
16.	2934	1064

(2) The provisions of paragraph (1) requiring the placing of the sign shown in diagram 601.1, 602 or 611.1 in conjunction with a road marking shall not apply during the execution of works on a road near the sign—

(a) if those works necessitate the temporary removal of the marking; or

(b) if the sign is placed only temporarily in connection with the execution of works on a road.

Road markings to be placed only in conjunction with other road markings or specified signs (except road markings for prohibitions and restrictions on waiting etc)

18.—(1) A road marking shown in a diagram whose number appears and is placed in the circumstances (if any) specified in column (2) of an item in Table 1 may be placed on a road only in conjunction with a road marking or sign shown in a diagram whose number appears and is in the form, or is placed in the manner or circumstances (if any), specified in column (3) of that item. **B57.162**

Table 1

(1) Item	(2) Road marking diagram number	(3) Road marking or sign diagram number
1.	1001, except when placed at a site where traffic is from time to time controlled by a constable in uniform or traffic warden	3000, 3000.1, 3000.2, 3000.7, 3000.8, 3000.9, 3000.10 or 3014
2.	1001.1	3013
3.	1001.2	3000, 3000.7, 3000.8, 3000.9 or 3000.10 placed adjacent to the stop line appearing above the pedal cycle symbol in diagram 1001.2
4.	1001.3	1001 together with— (a) 1055.1 or 1055.2; and (b) 4002.1, 4003.1, 4003.2, 4003.4, 4003.5 or 4003.7
5.	1003.4	611.1
6.	1023	1003 or 1003.3
7.	1045	1013.1 (version A)
8.	1048.2 without any variation	953.1 varied to include the bus symbol shown in diagram 953 or the local bus symbol in diagram 958
9.	1048.2 varied to omit "& BUS"	953.1 as not varied
10.	1048.4	953
11.	1057	955, 956, 957, 959.1, 960.1, 965, 967, 1001.2 when used in conjunction with 1004 or 1004.1, 2601.2 or 2602.2
12.	1058	1057
13.	1059	1057
14.	1062 except when placed in a zone indicated by the sign shown in diagram 674	557.1, 543 and 547.8, or 544 and 547.8
15.	1062 except when placed at a signal-controlled crossing facility or at a "crossing" as defined by section 25(6) of the 1984 Act, or to indicate a road hump which extends across the carriageway for less than 5 metres	1004
16.	1062 when placed to indicate a road hump with tapered ends which does not extend across the whole width of the carriageway but ends within 300 millimetres of the kerb-line	1012.1, 1017 or 1018.1

(1) Item	(2) Road marking diagram number	(3) Road marking or sign diagram number
17.	1064	2933 and 2934
18.	1065	670, when placed to indicate the point at which a speed limit begins or as a repeater sign in accordance with direction 11(2)[, 674 or 880]

(2) The road marking shown in diagram 1001.2 may be placed only at a junction where traffic is regulated by light signals of the kind prescribed by regulation 33(1).

(3) A road marking shown in a diagram whose number appears in column (2) of an item in Table 2 may be placed on a road only in conjunction with the combination of road markings or signs specified in column (3) of that item.

TABLE 2

(1) Item	(2) Road marking diagram number	(3) Diagram numbers of road markings or signs in combination
1.	1002.1	601.1 and 1022
2.	1003 when used at a level crossing	602 and 1023
3.	1003.3 except when placed at a roundabout with a small central island	611.1 and 1003.4
4.	1022	601.1 and 1002.1
5.	1024.1	1010 and 1014
6.	1048	1049 and either 959 or 960
7.	1048.1	1049 and 960 varied to include the pedal cycle symbol
8.	1049 except when varied to a width of 150 millimetres	(a) 1048 and either 959 or 960; or (b) 1048.1 and 960 varied to include the pedal cycle symbol
9.	1049 when varied to a width of 150 millimetres	(a) 957 and 1057; (b) 959.1 and 1057; or (c) 960.1 and 1057
10.	1049.1	957 and 1057
11.	1050	964 and 1049

(4) The road marking shown in diagram 1048.3 may be placed on a road if and only if it is placed in conjunction with either—

    (a) a combination of the sign shown in diagram 616 and the sign shown in diagram 954 or 954.2; or

    (b) the sign shown in diagram 953 varied to show only the bus symbol.

(5) A road marking shown in diagram 1003 or 1023 when varied in size to

conform with any of the smaller dimensions prescribed for it may be placed on a road only in conjunction with the marking shown in diagram 1057 and with one or more of the signs shown in diagrams 955, 956 and 957, or where a contra-flow cycle lane ends at a junction with another road.

(6) The road marking shown in diagram 1009 when varied in size to conform with the smallest dimensions prescribed for it may be placed on a road only to mark the junction of a cycle track and another road and in conjunction with the road markings shown in diagrams 1003 and 1023 and having the smaller dimensions prescribed for them.

(7) The road marking shown in diagram 1064 may be placed on the carriageway of a road if and only if—

(a) it is placed as one of a series of such markings placed 40 metres apart;

(b) the carriageway on which a marking is placed has more than one traffic lane and such a series is placed in each lane;

(c) each series includes the same number of markings; and

(d) a straight line drawn across the carriageway at right angles to the direction of travel and passing through a marking would pass through a marking on each of the other traffic lanes of the carriageway.

B57.163   *[Direction 18, Table 1 is printed as amended by SI 2008/2177.]*

The placing of the signs shown in diagrams 615 and 811

B57.164   **19.** The signs shown in diagrams 615 and 811 may be placed on a road only in conjunction with one another.

Signs to be placed only in combination with specified plates or other signs

B57.165   **20.**—(1) A sign shown in a diagram whose number appears and is placed in the circumstances (if any) specified in column (2) of an item in the Table may be placed on a road only in combination with a plate shown in the diagram whose number appears in column (3) of that item.

TABLE

(1) Item	(2) Sign diagram number	(3) Plate diagram number
1.	501 when placed in advance of the sign shown in diagram 601.1	502
2.	501 when placed in advance of the sign shown in diagram 602	503
3.	553.1	553.2
4.	554.2	554.3
5.	556.1	556.2
6.	557.1	557.2, 557.3 or 557.4

(1) Item	(2) Sign diagram number	(3) Plate diagram number
7.	562	563, 563.1 or 7022
8.	583	583.1
9.	584	584.1
10.	601.1 when placed at a level crossing	783
11.	615	615.1 or 645
12.	617	618 or 618.1
13.	622.8	622.9
14.	779	780A, 780.1A or 780.2A
15.	811	645 or 811.1
16.	953	953.2
17.	953.1	953.2

(2) The sign shown in diagram 545 may be placed on a road only if it is used either—

(a) in combination with the plate shown in diagram 546, 547.1, 547.2, 547.3 or 547.7; or

(b) in combination with the plate shown in diagram 546, 547.1 or 547.7 and with the light signals shown in diagram 4004.

(3) The sign shown in diagram 515 (when placed on the central island of a roundabout), 515.1A or 515.2 may be placed on a road only in combination with the sign shown in diagram 606.

Plates to be placed only in combination with specified signs

21.—(1) A plate shown in a diagram whose number appears and is in the form (if any) specified in an item in column (2) of the Table may be placed on a road only in combination with a sign shown in a diagram whose number appears and is placed in the circumstances (if any) specified in column (3) of that item. **B57.166**

TABLE

(1) Item	(2) Plate diagram number	(3) Sign diagram number
1.	502	501
2.	503	501
3.	511	504.1, 505.1, 506.1, 507.1, 510, 512, 512.1, 512.2, 513, 516, 517, 520, 523.1, 524.1, 528 or 556
4.	511 when varied to "HEAVY PLANT CROSSING"	504.1, 505.1, 506.1, 507.1, 512.1 or 512.2
5.	513.1	510, 512, 512.1, 512.2 or 513
6.	513.2	512, 512.1, 512.2, 513 or 7009

(1) Item	(2) Plate diagram number	(3) Sign diagram number
7.	518	516, 517 or 520
8.	519	516 or 517
9.	525	523.1 or 524.1
10.	526	512, 512.1, 512.2, 513, 523.1, 524.1 or 554.1
11.	527	523.1 or 524.1
12.	530.1	530
13.	530.2	530, 629.2 or 629.2A
14.	531.2	531.1
15.	543.1	543, 3000, 3000.7, 3000.8, 3000.9 or 3000.10
16.	546	545
17.	547.1	545
18.	547.2	545
19.	547.3	544.1 or 545
20.	547.4	544.2
21.	547.7	545
22.	547.8	543 or 544
23.	548.1	548 when placed in advance of the sign shown in diagram 4005
24.	553	552
25.	553.2	553.1
26.	554.3	554.2, 622.1A, 622.4, 629, 629A, 629.1 or 632
27.	556.2	556.1
28.	557.2	557.1
29.	557.3	557.1
30.	557.4	557.1
31.	558.2	558
32.	563	562
33.	563 when varied to "Road liable to flooding"	554 or 562
34.	563.1	562
35.	570	513, 521, 523.1, 524.1, 548, 549, 550, 550.1, 550.2, 551, 551.1, 551.2, 554 (when varied to "Gates"), 555.1, 556, 557, 558, 558.1, 559, 581, 582, 614, 632, 642, 7001 or 7009
36.	572	504.1, 505.1, 506.1, 507.1, 508.1, 509.1, 510, 516, 517, 520, 521, 522, 523.1, 524.1, 528, 529, 529.1, 530, 531.1, 543, 544, 544.1, 544.2, 550.1, 552, 554, 555, 770, 771, 772, 782, 950, 7001 or 7009
37.	573	523.1, 524.1, 528, 529, 529.1, 530, 531.1, 543, 544, 544.1, 544.2, 550.1, 552, 554, 555, 770, 771, 772, 782, 950, 7001 or 7009

(1) Item	(2) Plate diagram number	(3) Sign diagram number
38.	575	512, 512.1, 512.2, 513, 516, 517, 528 or 529.1
39.	583.1	583
40.	584.1	584
41.	607	606 or 609
42.	608	501, 601.1, 602, 606, 609 or 610
43.	615.1	615
44.	618	617
45.	618.1	617
46.	620	619, 619.1, 619.2, 622.1A, 622.5, 622.6, 622.7, 622.8, 629, 629A, 629.1 or 952
47.	620.1	619 or 619.1
48.	622.9	622.8
49.	627.1	626.2A
50.	645	614, 615, 632, 642, 811 or 7001
51.	773	529, 529.1, 558, 770, 771 or 772
52.	778	602
53.	778.1	602
54.	780A	779
55.	780.1A	779
56.	780.2A	779
57.	804.1	801
58.	804.2	801
59.	804.3	801
60.	804.4	801
61.	811.1	811
62.	817.2	523.1 and either 525 or 526, or 554.1 and 526
63.	876	868, 868.1, 872.1, 873, 874 or 875
64.	950.1	950
65.	953.2	953 or 953.1
66.	954	606, 609, 612, 613, 616, 629, 629A or 629.1
67.	954.2	606, 609, 612, 613, 616, 629, 629A, 629.1 or 952
68.	954.3	606, 609, 612 or 613
69.	954.4	606, 609, 612, 613 or 816
70.	954.5	606, 612, 613
71.	954.6	606, 612, 613
72.	954.7	606, 612, 613
73.	961	958, 958.1, 959 or 959.1
74.	2602.3	955, 956 or 957
75.	7001.1	7001
76.	7001.2	7001

(1) Item	(2) Plate diagram number	(3) Sign diagram number
77.	7021	7001
78.	7022	562
79.	7030	543
80.	7208	7202, 7206 or 7207
81.	7209	7203, 7203.1, 7204 or 7205
82.	7256	7250, 7251, 7252, 7253, 7254 or 7255

(2) A plate shown in diagram 954.3 or 954.4 or the sign shown in diagram 954.6 or 954.7 shall not be placed in combination with the sign shown in diagram 616.

Placing of road markings and signs to indicate prohibitions and restrictions on waiting, loading and unloading and parking

B57.167   **22.**—(1) Subject to paragraphs (2) and (3)—

   (a) the road marking shown in diagram 1018.1 may be placed on a side of a road only for the purpose of indicating a statutory prohibition or restriction on the waiting of vehicles which applies on that side of the road at all times of day on every day of the year or on every day in a period of at least four consecutive months; and

   (b) the road marking shown in diagram 1017 may be placed on a side of a road only for the purpose of indicating a statutory prohibition or restriction on the waiting of vehicles which is not a restriction of the kind mentioned in sub-paragraph (a).

(2) In this direction, references to a statutory prohibition or restriction on the waiting of a vehicle do not include references to any such prohibition or restriction imposed—

   (a) on waiting for the purpose of loading or unloading goods from a vehicle or picking up or setting down passengers from a vehicle;

   (b) and expressly to limit the duration of waiting of vehicles within a particular period; or

   (c) on the waiting of goods vehicles (as defined by section 192(1) of the Road Traffic Act 1988) but of no other class of vehicle.

(3) The road marking shown in diagram 1017 or 1018.1 shall not be placed on a road on which is placed—

   (a) the marking shown in diagram 1025.1, 1025.3, 1025.4 or 1028.2 (in conjunction with the sign shown in diagram 650.1); or

   (b) the marking shown in diagram 1027.1 in conjunction with the sign shown in diagram 642.2A, unless there are times at which the restrictions to be indicated by the marking shown in diagram 1017 or 1018.1 apply and those indicated by that sign do not.

B57.168   **23.**—(1) The road marking shown in diagram 1020.1 may be placed on a side of the carriageway of a road only for the purpose of indicating a statutory prohibition or restriction on the waiting of vehicles for the purpose of their being loaded or unloaded which applies on that side of the road at all times of the day on every day of the year or on every day in a period of at least four consecutive months.

(2) The road marking shown in diagram 1019 may be placed on a side of the carriageway of a road only for the purpose of indicating a statutory prohibition or restriction on the waiting of vehicles for the purpose of their being loaded or unloaded (but not for indicating a statutory prohibition or restriction which expressly limits the duration of waiting by vehicles within a particular period for that purpose) which is not a restriction of the kind mentioned in paragraph (1).

24.—(1) Except where it is placed to indicate the effect of a temporary statutory provision and subject to paragraph (2), a sign shown in a diagram specified in column (2) of an item in the Table shall not be placed except—   **B57.169**

(a) on or near the side of a road; and

(b) in conjunction with, and on the same side of the road as, a road marking which is shown in a diagram and is in the form (if any) indicated in column (3) of that item.

TABLE

(1) Item	(2) Sign diagram number	(3) Road marking diagram number
1.	637.3	1018.1
2.	638	1020.1
3.	638.1	1019
4.	639	1017
5.	639.1B	1017 and 1028.3, 1028.4, 1032 or 1033
6.	639.1B when the sign shown in diagram 638.1 is added as a middle panel	1017 and 1019, and 1028.3, 1028.4, 1032 or 1033
7.	640	(a) 1017 or 1018.1; and (b) 1019 or (when the lower panel of the sign shown in diagram 640 is varied to "No loading at any time") 1020.1
8.	640 when the upper panel is varied to the sign shown in diagram 650.3	(a) 1028.2; (b) 1017 or 1018.1; and (c) 1019 or (when the lower panel of the sign shown in diagram 640 is varied to "No loading at any time") 1020.1
9.	642.2A	1027.1
10.	642.3	1018.1
11.	650.1	1028.2 when varied to include a continuous yellow line 200 or 300mm wide in the manner shown in diagram 1025.1
12.	650.2	1028.2
13.	650.3	1028.2, and 1017 or 1018.1

(1) Item	*(2)* Sign diagram number	*(3)* Road marking diagram number
14.	660	(a) 1028.3 (when varied to indicate "LARGE OR SLOW VEHICLES ONLY"); (b) 1028.4, 1032 or 1033 in each case when indicating "DOCTOR" or when no legend appears; or (c) 1028.4 when varied to indicate "PERMIT HOLDERS ONLY"
15.	660.3	(a) 1028.4, 1032 or 1033, in each case when indicating "DOCTOR" or when no legend appears; or (b) 1028.4 when varied to indicate "PERMIT HOLDERS ONLY"
16.	660.4	(a) 1028.3 or 1032 in each case when varied to indicate "LOADING ONLY"; or (b) 1033 when no legend appears
17.	660.5	1028.4, 1032 or 1033, in each case when no legend appears
18.	660.6	1028.4, 1032 or 1033 in each case when no legend appears
19.	660.7	1028.4, 1032 or 1033, in each case when no legend appears
20.	661A	1028.3, 1032 or 1033 in each case when varied to indicate "DISABLED" or when no legend appears
21.	661.1	1028.3 (when varied to "BUSES"), 1028.4 (when varied to "SOLO MOTORCYCLES ONLY", "SOLO M/CYCLES ONLY" or "SOLO M/CS ONLY" or when no legend appears), 1032 (when no legend appears) or 1033 (when no legend appears)
22.	661.2A	1028.4, 1032 or 1033, in each case when no legend appears
23.	661.3A	1028.4, 1032 or 1033, in each case when no legend appears
24.	662	1028.4, 1032 or 1033, in each case when no legend appears
25.	974	1025.1, 1025.3 or 1025.4, in each case when indicating "BUS STOP"
26.	975	1025.1, 1025.3 or 1025.4, in each case when varied to "BUS STAND"

(2) Paragraph (1) shall not apply to the signs shown in diagrams 637.3, 639 and 640 when placed to indicate restrictions applying to the same road as restrictions indicated by the sign shown in diagram 650.1, 974 or 975.

(3) Subject to paragraph (4) the sign shown in diagram 637.2 may be placed only on a road within a pedestrian zone where the sign shown in diagram 618.3 or 618.3A is placed at each entrance into the zone for vehicular traffic.

(4) The sign shown in diagram 637.2 shall not be used on a road within the pedestrian zone to which the sign relates except in conjunction with—

   (a) the road marking shown in diagram 1017 or 1018.1 unless—

      (i) the road does not comprise a carriageway and footway which are separately defined;

      (ii) the entry of vehicular traffic into the pedestrian zone is restricted at the same times as those at which the waiting of vehicles is prohibited as indicated on the upper panel of the sign in diagram 637.2; and

      (iii) the prohibition on the waiting of vehicles applies uniformly throughout every road in the zone, and

   (b) where there is a prohibition on the loading and unloading of vehicles, the road marking shown in diagram 1019 or 1020.1 unless—

      (i) the road does not comprise a carriageway and footway which are separately defined;

      (ii) the entry of vehicular traffic into the pedestrian zone is restricted at the same times as those at which the loading and unloading of vehicles is prohibited as indicated on the lower panel of the sign in diagram 637.2; and

      (iii) the prohibition on the loading and unloading of vehicles applies uniformly throughout every road in the zone.

25.—(1) Subject to paragraph (2) a road marking shown in a diagram whose   **B57.170** number appears and is in the form (if any) specified in an item in column (2) of the Table may be placed on a road only in conjunction with, and on the same side of the road as, a sign shown in a diagram whose number appears and in the form specified (if any) in column (3) of that item.

TABLE

(1) Item	(2) Road marking diagram number	(3) Sign diagram number
1.	1017	637.2, 639, 639.1B, 640 or 650.3
2.	1019	637.2, 638.1, 639.1B (when the sign shown in diagram 638.1 is added as a middle panel) or 640
3.	1020.1	637.2, 638 or 640 (when the lower panel is varied to "No loading at any time")
4.	1025.1	974 or 975
5.	1025.3	974 or 975
6.	1025.4	974 or 975
7.	1028.2	640 (when the upper panel is varied to the sign shown in diagram 650.3), 650.1, 650.2 or 650.3
8.	1028.3 when indicating "DISABLED"	661A or 639.1B (when the lower panel is varied to the sign shown in diagram 661A)

(1) Item	(2) Road marking diagram number	(3) Sign diagram number
9.	1028.3 when varied to "BUSES"	661.1 (when varied to include the bus symbol), 639.1B (when the lower panel is so varied) or 969
10.	1028.3 when varied to "LARGE OR SLOW VEHICLES ONLY"	660 (varied to "Large or slow vehicles only") or 639.1B (when the lower panel is so varied)
11.	1028.3 when no legend appears	661A, 639.1B (when the lower panel is varied to show the sign shown in diagram 661A), 786 or 801 in combination with 804.1
12.	1028.3 when varied to "LOADING ONLY"	660.4 or 639.1B (when the lower panel is varied to the sign shown in diagram 660.4)
13.	1028.4 when indicating "DOCTOR"	660 varied to "Doctor permit holders only" or 639.1B (when the lower panel is so varied)
14.	1028.4 when varied to "PERMIT HOLDERS ONLY"	(a) 639.1B when the lower panel is varied to the sign shown in diagram 660 (except the variants "Card holders only" and "Large or slow vehicles only") or 660.3; (b) 660 (except when varied to "Card holders only" or "Large or slow vehicles only"); or (c) 660.3
15.	1028.4 when no legend appears	639.1B, 660, 660.3, 660.5, 660.6, 660.7, 661.1, 661.2A, 661.3A, 662, 667, 667.1, 668, 668.1, or 801
16.	1032 when indicating "DOCTOR"	660 varied to "Doctor permit holders only" or 639.1B (when the lower panel is so varied)
17.	1032 when indicating "DISABLED"	661A or 639.1B (when the lower panel is varied to the sign shown in diagram 661A)
18.	1032 when indicating "LOADING ONLY"	660.4 or 639.1B (when the lower panel is varied to the sign shown in diagram 660.4)
19.	1033 when indicating "DISABLED"	661A or 639.1B (when the lower panel is varied to the sign shown in diagram 661A)
20.	1033 when indicating "DOCTOR"	660 varied to "Doctor permit holders only" or 639.1B (when the lower panel is so varied)

(2) Paragraph (1) shall not apply to a road marking placed on a road within a controlled parking zone, if signs shown in diagram 663 or 663.1 have been placed at the entrances for vehicular traffic into the zone, except where the road marking is placed to indicate restrictions different from the restrictions indicated on those signs.

26. The sign shown in diagram 663, 663.1, 664, 665 or 666 may be placed only   **B57.171**
at the boundary of a controlled parking zone.

Signs to be placed only at specified sites or for specified purposes

27. The sign shown in diagram 545, when placed in combination with—   **B57.172**
     (a) the plate shown in diagram 547.1; or
     (b) the plate shown in diagram 546, 547.1 or 547.7 together with the light
         signal shown in diagram 4004,

may be placed only at or near a school crossing place.

28. The sign shown in diagram 551.1 may be placed on or near a road only—   **B57.173**
     (a) at a site which is approved as a migratory toad crossing by or on behalf
         of the Secretary of State; and
     (b) during February, March, April and May in each year.

29. The sign shown in diagram 574 may be placed only in or near an infected   **B57.174**
place or area for the purposes of the Animal Health Act 1981 and shall be
removed as soon as it ceases to be in or near such a place or area.

30. The sign shown in diagram 601.1 may be placed on or near a road at a   **B57.175**
junction with another road only if a sign has not been placed on the other road so
as to control traffic passing through the junction on that other road.

31. The sign shown in diagram 833, 834, 835 or 836 may be placed only to   **B57.176**
regulate the movement of vehicular traffic into and out of premises with more
than one access to a road.

32.—[(1) A sign shown in diagram 878, 879, 880 or 880.1 may be placed only   **B57.177**
in an area or along a route where enforcement cameras are from time to time in
use.

(2) The sign shown in diagram 880 may be placed only on or near a road on
which—
     (a) there is provided a system of carriageway lighting furnished by means
         of lamps placed not more than 183 metres apart in England and Wales
         or 185 metres apart in Scotland; and
     (b) which is subject to a speed limit of 30 mph.

(3) The sign shown in diagram 880.1 may be placed only on or near a road on
which—
     (a) there is not a system of carriageway lighting furnished by means of
         lamps placed not more than 183 metres apart in England and Wales
         or 185 metres apart in Scotland; and
     (b) a national speed limit is in force.

(4) No more than two signs of the type shown in diagram 880 or 880.1 may be
placed on any approach to an enforcement camera.]

[Direction 32 is printed as substituted by SI 2008/2177.]   **B57.178**

33. The sign shown in diagram 957 may be placed on a road only when the   **B57.179**
road has been divided into a part reserved for the use of pedal cycles only and a

part reserved for use by pedestrians only by either or both of the following means—

> (a) the road marking shown in diagram 1049 (when that marking is varied to be 150 millimetres wide) or 1049.1;
>
> (b) the presence on the road of works such as distinctive colouring of the surface of each part, a kerb or other device.

B57.180   **34.**—(1) The marking shown in diagram 1003 may be placed on or near a road only in the following cases—

> (a) at a junction with another road on which no marking has been placed to control traffic passing through the junction on that other road;
>
> (b) at a roundabout in conjunction with the sign shown in diagram 602 and the road marking shown in diagram 1023;
>
> (c) at a level crossing in the circumstances described in regulation 25(3);
>
> (d) in the circumstances described in regulation 25(4), when such a marking has not been placed to control vehicles travelling in the opposite direction.

(2) The marking shown in diagram 1003 may only be placed on the carriageway of a road in circumstances such that regulation 25(6) (transverse lines placed in advance of a cycle track crossing a road) applies, if the length of the road which is crossed by a cycle track consists of a road hump extending across the full width of the carriageway and constructed pursuant to—

> (a) section 90A of the Highways Act 1980 and in accordance with the Highways (Road Humps) Regulations 1999; or
>
> (b) [*applies to Scotland*].

B57.181   **35.** The road marking shown in diagram 1043 or 1044 shall not be placed to indicate an area of carriageway on a roundabout unless the entry of traffic into the roundabout is at all times controlled by traffic light signals.

Restrictions on the placing of temporary signs

B57.182   **36.** The signs shown in Schedule 12, other than in diagrams 7014, 7019, 7020, 7032 and 7103, may be placed only in connection with the execution of works on or near a road or a temporary obstruction thereon, and any such sign so placed and any other sign shown in a diagram in Schedules 1 to 11 so placed shall not be retained on or near the road after the completion of the works or the removal of the obstruction, as the case may be, unless—

> (a) it is a sign of the type shown in diagram 7009, in which case that sign may be retained on or near a road after the completion of the works for so long as the traffic authority for the road thinks fit; or
>
> (b) it is a sign of the type shown in diagram 7012 bearing the words "NO GIVE WAY MARKINGS" or "NO STOP MARKINGS", in which case that sign shall be removed as soon as the road markings have been replaced and in any event not later than 28 days after the completion of the works.

B57.183   **37.**—(1) The sign shown in diagram 790 or 7014—

> (a) may be placed only in connection with works involving—

(i) an alteration in the layout of the carriageway of a road or level crossing; or

(ii) the placing, removal or alteration of traffic signs on or near a road or at a level crossing; and

(b) may be retained not later than the end of the period of 3 months beginning with completion of those works.

(2) The sign shown in diagram 7032—

(a) may be placed only to indicate the point at which a recently imposed speed limit of 30 mph begins on a road—

(i) on which there is a system of street or carriageway lighting furnished by lamps lit by electricity placed not more than 183 metres apart in England and Wales or not more than 185 metres apart in Scotland; and

(ii) which had previously been subject to a higher speed limit;

(b) shall be placed as near as practicable to that point;

(c) shall not be placed unless that point could not otherwise be indicated in accordance with these Directions;

(d) may be placed only during the period of 6 months beginning with the day on which the 30 mph speed limit comes into force; and

(e) shall not be retained after the end of that period.

38.—(1) No sign of the kind referred to in regulation 53 may be retained at any place for more than 6 months (or in the case of a sign of the kind referred to in regulation 53(1)(d) for more than 2 years) or such longer period as the Secretary of State may approve after the placing of the sign there or in any event after the sign has ceased to be needed at that place.   **B57.184**

(2) The sign shown in diagram 2701 or 2701.1 may be retained on or near a road for not more than six months after completion of the housing development to which it refers.

39.—(1) The sign shown in diagram 7023 or 7024 may be placed on or near a road only where—   **B57.185**

(a) one-way working is necessary along a length of road because part of the width of the carriageway has been temporarily closed to traffic; and

(b) either—

(i) there is no junction with another road along that length; or

(ii) the traffic authority has given express written approval to the placing of the sign in relation to a length of road having a junction with another road.

(2) The sign shown in diagram 543 may be placed in combination with the plate shown in diagram 7030 only on or near a road on which convoy working is in operation and indicated by one or more of the signs shown in diagrams 7025, 7026, 7027, 7028 and 7029.

(3) The sign shown in diagram—

(a) 554 when varied to "Flood" or "No smoking";

(b) 554.2 when placed in conjunction with the plate shown in diagram 554.3; or

(c) 562 when placed in combination with the plate shown in diagram 563 when indicating "Accident" or when varied to "Census", "Dust cloud", "Fallen tree", "Frost damage", "Overhead cable repairs", "Runners in road", "Smoke" or "Walkers in road",

may be retained only for so long as the hazard indicated by the sign continues to exist or is expected to recur in the near future.

(4) The sign shown in diagram 633, 636.2 (except when varied to show the name of a traffic authority), 829.1, 829.2, 829.3, 829.4, 829.5 or 1063 may be placed on or near a road only by a constable in uniform or a person acting under the instructions or authority of the chief officer of police.

(5) The sign shown in diagram 829.5 may only be placed on or near a road in an area where police speed checks are from time to time carried out.

(6) The sign shown in diagram 830, 830.1, 830.3, 831 or 832 may be placed on or near a road in connection with a traffic census, if and only if the taking of that census on that road has been approved—

(a) by the traffic authority for the road;

(b) by the chief officer of police of the police area in which the road is situated; and

(c) by or on behalf of the Secretary of State.

(7) The sign shown in diagram 950 may be placed in combination with the plate shown in diagram 950.1—

(a) when the plate is varied to "Cycle event", only while a cycle rally or similar event is in progress;

(b) in any other case except when the plate is varied to "Cycles crossing", only while the training or testing of child cyclists is in progress.

Placing of signs varied to show metric units

B57.186   **40.**—(1) Where the indication given by the sign shown in diagram 629.1 is varied in accordance with regulation 17 and item 2 of Schedule 16, that sign may be placed only in combination with another sign of the same type whose indication has not been so varied.

(2) Paragraph (1) shall also apply when the sign shown in diagram 629.1 is incorporated as a symbol into another sign.

Mounting and backing of signs

B57.187   **41.**—(1) Subject to paragraphs (2) and (3), where a sign (other than a sign referred to in paragraph (4), (5) or in direction 43 or 44) in a diagram in Schedules 1 to 5 and 7, Part II of Schedule 10 or Schedule 12, or a sign of the type prescribed by regulation 53, is mounted on a post or other support specially provided for the purpose ("the post"), that part of the post which extends above ground level shall be of any single colour or in its natural colour.

(2) Where the post is not likely to be readily visible to pedestrians or cyclists, a yellow or white band not less than 140 nor more than 160 millimetres deep may be provided on the post, the lower edge of the band being not less than 1500 nor more than 1700 millimetres above ground level.

(3) Where the support provided for a portable sign comprises several

components, instead of complying with paragraphs (1) and (2), the components need not all be of the same colour provided that each is of a single colour or in its natural colour.

(4) Where a beacon or lamp of a kind prescribed by regulation 54 or 55 is mounted on a structure specially provided for the purpose, the structure shall be coloured grey, red, white or yellow, or in alternate bands of red and white or of black and white.

(5) The post provided for the mounting of the sign shown in diagram 7031 shall be coloured in alternate black and yellow bands each 300 millimetres deep with a black band uppermost below the bottom of the sign face, and the yellow bands may be reflectorised.

(6) The sign shown in diagram 7104 or 7105 may be mounted on an object of the size, colour and type of the sign shown in diagram 7101.1.

(7) An identification code for maintenance purposes may be indicated, in characters not exceeding 25 millimetres in height, on the post on which a sign is mounted.

42.—(1) The back of any sign shown in a diagram in Schedules 1 to 5, 7, Part **B57.188** II of Schedule 10 or in Schedule 12, or prescribed by regulation 53, other than the sign shown in diagram 651, 970, 971, 972, 973.2, 973.3, 2610, 2610.1, 2610.2, 7101.1, 7102, 7103, 7104 or 7105 shall be coloured—

    (a) black if the sign is mounted on the same post as that on which light signals prescribed by regulation 33(1) (or those signals as varied in accordance with regulation 34) or light signals prescribed by regulation 33(2) and regulation 35 are mounted; or

    (b) grey, black or in a non-reflective metallic finish in any other case, except that—

        (i) information about sites for placing and the ownership of the sign and an identification code for maintenance purposes may be indicated on the back of the sign in characters not exceeding 25 millimetres in height, where they are shown in a contrasting colour, or in characters not exceeding 50 millimetres in height, where they are embossed in the same colour; and

        (ii) information about the manufacture of the sign required in order to comply with British Standard Specification BS 873 or a corresponding EEA Standard, occupying an area not exceeding 30 square centimetres, may be indicated on the back of the sign in characters not exceeding 5 millimetres in height.

(2) Paragraph (1) shall apply to the back of any backing board or other fitting provided for the assembly of such a sign as is referred to in paragraph (1) (including any container enclosing apparatus for the illumination of such a sign).

(3) The back of the sign shown in diagram 7104 or 7105 shall be coloured grey, red, white, black or yellow, except that—

    (a) information about sites for placing and the ownership of the sign may be indicated on the back of the sign in characters not exceeding 50 millimetres in height, where they are shown in a contrasting colour, or in characters not exceeding 80 millimetres in height, where they are embossed in the same colour; and

(b) information about the manufacture of the sign required in order to comply with British Standard Specification BS 873 or a corresponding EEA Standard, occupying an area not exceeding 30 square centimetres, may be indicated on the back of the sign in characters not exceeding 5 millimetres in height.

(4) The back of the sign shown in diagram 651, 970, 971, 972, 973.2, 973.3, 2610, 2610.1 or 2610.2 may be of any colour.

(5) The front of any backing board for a sign mounted otherwise than as described in paragraph (1)(a) shall be coloured either grey or yellow [and, if coloured yellow, may be—

(a) reflectorised;

(b) fluorescent; or

(c) both reflectorised and fluorescent.]

[(6) Except as provided in paragraph (7), a yellow backing board for a sign shall be rectangular in shape.]

[(7) A backing board for a combination of the sign shown in diagram 2402.1 with the sign shown in diagram 670 may be of any shape including rectangular.]

(8) The sign shown in diagram 2403.1 shall not be mounted on a backing board with any other sign.

(9) In this direction *"backing board"* in relation to a sign includes any background (except a wall to which the sign is affixed) against which the sign is displayed.

B57.189   *[Direction 42 is printed as amended by SI 2004/1275.]*

Mounting of the sign shown in diagram 781

B57.190   **43.** The sign shown in diagram 781 shall be mounted on two posts and so much of each post as extends above ground level shall be coloured black and white in alternate horizontal bands, each band being not less than 250 nor more than 335 millimetres deep.

Mounting of the signs shown in diagrams 560 and 561

B57.191   **44.**—(1) The sign shown in diagram 560 or 561 shall be so placed that the top of the sign is not less than 550 nor more than 1000 millimetres above the surface of the adjacent carriageway.

(2) Where the sign shown in diagram 560 or 561 is mounted on a post specially provided for the purpose that part of the post which extends above ground level may be—

(a) of any single colour; or

(b) coloured black and white in alternate horizontal bands, each band being not less than 225 nor more than 350 millimetres deep.

(3) The signs shown in diagrams 560 and 561 shall be so erected as to display—

(a) the colour red on the left hand edge of the carriageway as viewed by the drivers of approaching vehicles; and

(b) the colour white on the right hand edge of the carriageway when so viewed, unless the edge is the edge of the carriageway of a dual carriageway road or a one-way road when the colour amber shall be displayed.

Mounting of refuge indicator lamps

45.—(1) This paragraph applies where the lamp prescribed by regulation 57 is   **B57.192**
mounted on a post specially provided for the purpose.

(2) Subject to paragraph (4), if the post is placed at a zebra crossing and yellow globes are attached to the post, the part of the post between ground level and the point where the yellow globes are mounted or attached shall be coloured black and white in alternate horizontal bands and—

(a) the lowest band shall be coloured black and not less than 275 millimetres nor more than 1 metre deep; and

(b) each other band shall be not less than 275 nor more than 335 millimetres deep, and

the remaining part of the post shall be coloured in accordance with paragraph (3).

(3) Subject to paragraph (4), if the post is placed elsewhere or at a zebra crossing, but without yellow globes attached to it, the post shall be coloured grey or black but with two white bands (each band being not less than 275 nor more than 335 millimetres deep) so arranged that—

(a) not less than 275 nor more than 335 millimetres extend between the nearest edges of the two bands; and

(b) the upper edge of the uppermost band is not less than 275 nor more than 335 millimetres below the lowest part of the lamp,

and the white bands may be internally illuminated.

(4) Where the post consists of aluminium, concrete or galvanised metal it may remain in its natural colour.

(5) In this direction *"yellow globes"* means globes in relation to which Part I of Schedule 1 to the Zebra, Pelican and Puffin Pedestrian Crossings Regulations 1997 [*SI 1997/2400; q.v.*] is complied with.

Mounting and backing of light signals, matrix signs and warning lights

46.—(1) The light signals prescribed by regulation 33, 34, 35, 37, 39, 41, 44,   **B57.193**
45, 47, 48, 49 or 52, the matrix signals prescribed by regulation 46 and the warning lights prescribed by regulations 50 and 51 may be placed on or near a road only if they are so placed that they face the stream of traffic to which they are intended to convey the warnings, information, requirements, restrictions or prohibitions prescribed by the Regulations.

(2) A container enclosing the lamps of a type of light signals, matrix sign or warning light mentioned in paragraph (1) shall be coloured black except that—

(a) if a container encloses lamps of the light signals prescribed by regulation 37, 44 or 45, the matrix sign prescribed by regulation 46 or the warning lights prescribed by regulation 50 or 51, it may be coloured grey instead of black;

(b) the back of a container enclosing the signals shown in diagrams 4003, 4003.1, 4003.3, 4003.4, 4003.6 or 4003.7 may be coloured yellow; and

(c) the container may have a white border not less than 45 nor more than 55 millimetres wide.

(3) Any of the kinds of light signals mentioned in paragraph (1) other than the signals prescribed by regulation 39(1) may be mounted on a backing board, which shall be coloured black and may have a white border not less than 45 nor more than 55 millimetres wide.

(4) In the case of the light signals prescribed by regulation 39(1) the back of the backing board shown in diagram 3014 may be coloured black or grey.

(5) In the case of the matrix signs prescribed by regulation 46, an identification number may be shown on the front of the backing board below the signal or on the post on which the signal is mounted and, in the case of other light signals, an identification number and name, and a telephone number for use in an emergency, may be shown on the post on which the signals are mounted.

(6) Without prejudice to paragraph (8) and subject to the exceptions in paragraph (7), where light signals prescribed by any of the regulations specified in paragraph (1) or shown in a diagram in Part I of Schedule 10 or in Schedule 11 are mounted on a post specially provided for the purpose, that part of the post which extends above ground level shall be either—

(a) coloured grey, black, brown, dark green or dark blue; or

(b) in a non-reflective metallic finish.

(7) Paragraph (6) is subject to the following exceptions—

(a) the post may be marked with a yellow or white band not less than 140 nor more than 160 millimetres deep, the lower edge of the band being not less than 1500 nor more than 1700 millimetres above ground level; and

(b) where the light signals prescribed by regulation 33(1) or (2) are installed temporarily, the containers in which the posts are placed may be coloured with alternate red and white horizontal stripes.

(8) The portable light signals prescribed by regulation 35, instead of being mounted on a post coloured in accordance with paragraph (6), may be mounted on a post coloured yellow (but having no yellow or white band as specified in paragraph (7)) or on a tripod or other support coloured yellow.

Placing of road marking shown in diagram 1001 or 1001.2 in conjunction with light signals

B57.194   **47.**—(1) The light signals prescribed by regulation 33(1) may be placed only in conjunction with the road marking shown in diagram 1001 or, subject to direction 18(2), 1001.2.

(2) The light signals prescribed by regulation 33(2) or 39(1) may be placed only in conjunction with the road marking shown in diagram 1001.

(3) This direction shall not apply to light signals while works which necessitate the temporary removal of a road marking are being executed on a road near the light signals.

Placing of road marking shown in diagram 1014 in conjunction with the road marking shown in diagram 1013.1 or 1013.3

B57.195   **48.**—(1) At least one road marking of the type shown in diagram 1014 shall be placed in conjunction with a road marking of the type shown in diagram 1013.1 or 1013.3 on the length of carriageway which extends backwards from the commencement of any continuous line marked on the carriageway as a part of the road marking shown in diagram 1013.1 or 1013.3, such commencement being viewed in the direction of travel of a vehicle driven so as to have and keep that continuous line on its right hand or off side in accordance with regulation 26(2)(b).

(2) Paragraph (1) shall not apply where the commencement so viewed of a continuous line on the carriageway of a road falls immediately after—

    (a) the point where a central reservation ends; or

    (b) a roundabout from which traffic enters the carriageway.

(3) For the purposes of paragraph (1), where a continuous line marked on the carriageway of a road as part of the road marking shown in diagram 1013.1 or 1013.3 is interrupted at a junction or by a refuge and recommences immediately after the interruption, the line shall be treated as if it continued through the interruption.

(4) If more than one road marking of the type shown in diagram 1014 is placed on a length of carriageway, then the road markings shall be so spaced apart that one follows in line behind the other.

Placing of road marking shown in diagram 1001.3 (zig-zag lines)

49.—(1) In this direction *"relevant crossing facility"* means a signal-controlled   **B57.196** crossing facility—

    (a) at which there is placed the signal shown in diagram 4003.2, 4003.4, 4003.5 or 4003.7; and

    (b) which is not situated at a junction at which the priority between motor vehicles is regulated by traffic light signals.

(2) Subject to paragraphs (4) to (6), zig-zag lines shall be placed on the approaches to each side of a relevant crossing facility so as to form controlled areas as defined by regulation 27(1).

(3) Zig-zag lines shall not be placed on a road except in accordance with—

    (a) paragraph (2); or

    (b) regulations made, or having effect as if made, under section 25 of the 1984 Act (pedestrian crossings regulations).

(4) So long as the condition in paragraph (5) is complied with, paragraph (2) shall not apply where, in accordance with an authorisation given under section 64(1) or (2) of the 1984 Act, a relevant crossing facility has been provided on a road before 1st April 2003 but without the placing of zig-zag lines on the approaches as mentioned in paragraph (2).

(5) The condition is that the signs and markings indicating the facility are maintained in accordance with the authorisation under which they were placed and any special directions under section 65 of the 1984 Act that were given in conjunction with the authorisation.

(6) Paragraphs (4) and (5) shall cease to have effect on 1st January 2007.

Placing of signs and light signals shown in Schedule 11

50. The light signals prescribed by regulation 37(1) and 45 and the signs and   **B57.197**

light signals shown in any diagram in Schedule 11 may be displayed only on or near—

    (a) a motorway; or

    (b) an all-purpose dual carriageway road.

B57.198 **51.**—(1) The light signals prescribed by regulation 37(1) shall not be displayed over or in relation to a traffic lane in conjunction with the sign shown in diagram 6001, 6002, 6003, 6006, 6006.1, 6008, 6009, 6009.1, 6009.2, 6011, 6011.1 or 6012.

(2) Paragraph (1) shall not apply to the signs shown in diagrams 6006.2, 6008.1 and 6009.3 when the light signals prescribed by regulation 37(1) are placed at the side of a carriageway so as to convey prohibitions or requirements applying to all traffic proceeding along the carriageway in a particular direction.

B57.199 **52.** The sign shown in diagram 6002, 6021 or 6031.1 may be displayed only over a traffic lane and the sign shown in diagram 6006, 6006.1, 6006.2, 6008, 6008.1, 6009, 6009.1, 6009.2, 6009.3, 6022 or 6032.1 may be displayed only at the side of the carriageway to which the indications given by the sign relate, or projecting over part of that carriageway, so as to convey warnings, prohibitions or requirements applying to all traffic proceeding along the carriageway in a particular direction.

Placing of portable light signals prescribed by regulation 35

B57.200 **53.**—(1) A traffic authority may, pursuant to section 65(1) of the 1984 Act, cause or permit the placing of the portable light signals prescribed by regulation 35 if and only if—

    (a) permission is given in writing, or in a case of urgency, given orally and confirmed in writing as soon as reasonably practicable thereafter; and

    (b) either—

        (i) the written permission of the authority includes express approval to the placing of the signals at a particular site; or

        (ii) the authority is satisfied that the circumstances of the particular case fall within one of the sets of circumstances specified in paragraph (2).

(2) The sets of circumstances referred to in paragraph (1)(b)(ii) are—

    (a) where the signals are to be operated and maintained by, and are under the regular supervision of, a constable in uniform during the progress of a temporary scheme of traffic control;

    (b) where the signals are placed on a length of road along which—

        (i) there is no junction carrying vehicular traffic to or from it; and

        (ii) the width of the carriageway is temporarily restricted so as to carry only one line of traffic;

    (c) where the signals are placed at a level crossing when work in relation to that crossing is being carried out;

    (d) where the signals are placed on a road which is—

        (i) adjacent to the temporary site of road, building or engineering works; and

(ii) is used for the movement of vehicles, materials, plant or equipment within the site of the works.

(3) Nothing in this direction is to be taken to limit or affect the powers of a constable or the chief officer of police under section 67(1) of the 1984 Act (placing of temporary traffic signs on roads in extraordinary circumstances).

Placing of signals and other signs at crossings

54. The Schedule to these Directions shall have effect with regard to the placing of—   **B57.201**

   (a) vehicular light signals;

   (b) pedestrian light signals; and

   (c) other signs,

at signal-controlled crossing facilities where vehicular traffic is stopped only for the purpose of enabling pedestrians, cyclists or equestrians to cross the carriageway and not for the purpose of regulating the priority of vehicular traffic at a junction.

Placing of various light signals

55.—(1) The light signals shown in diagram 4004 may be placed only in   **B57.202**
combination with the sign shown in diagram 545 together with the plate shown in diagram 546, 547.1 or 547.7.

(2) The light signals shown in diagram 4005 may be placed on or near a road only when the sign shown in diagram 548 in conjunction with the plate shown in diagram 548.1 is placed in advance of those signals.

(3) The light signals shown in diagram 4006 may be placed only in conjunction with the light signals shown in diagram 3014.

(4) The sign shown in diagram 4003 may be placed only in conjunction with the light signals shown in diagram 4002.1.

(5) The sign shown in diagram 4003.3 may be placed only in conjunction with the light signals shown in diagram 4003.2.

(6) The sign shown in diagram 4003.6 may be placed only in conjunction with the light signals shown in diagram 4003.5.

(7) The light signals shown in diagram 4002.1 or 4003.1 may be placed only in conjunction with the light signals prescribed by regulation 33(1) or (2).

(8) The light signals shown in diagram 4003.2 or 4003.4 may be placed only in conjunction with the light signals prescribed by regulation 33(1).

(9) The light signals shown in diagram 4003.5 or 4003.7 may be placed only in conjunction with the light signals prescribed by regulation 33(1).

(10) The light signal shown in diagram 776 may be placed only at or near a level crossing and the legend shall be displayed to road traffic in black letters on a red background which is internally illuminated by means of electricity only when a railway vehicle or tramcar has just passed over the level crossing and another is approaching.

(11) The light signals of the kinds prescribed by regulation 33(1), 34 or 39 may be placed on or near a road to face traffic proceeding in a particular direction if and only if—

(a) at least two identical sets of signals are placed so as to face traffic proceeding in that direction; and

(b) at least one of those sets of signals is a set of primary signals.

[Signs used in conjunction with actively managed hard shoulders

B57.203   **55A.**—(1) The sign shown in diagram 5003 or 5003.1 may be displayed above an actively managed hard shoulder to convey the prohibition specified in regulation 44(4)(aa) only whilst variable message signs displaying the sign shown in diagram 670 or 671 are displayed above so much (if any) of the adjacent carriageway as is open to traffic.

(2) The sign shown in diagram 6002 may be displayed over an actively managed hard shoulder only whilst variable message signs displaying the sign shown in diagram 670 are displayed above so much of the adjacent carriageway as is open to traffic.

(3) The sign shown in diagram 6031.1 may be displayed over an actively managed hard shoulder to convey the prohibition specified in regulation 38(4) only whilst variable message signs displaying the sign shown in diagram 670 are displayed above so much (if any) of the adjacent carriageway as is open to traffic.]

B57.204   [*Direction 55A is printed as inserted by SI 2005/1670.*]

Approval of types of sign and signals by the Secretary of State

B57.205   **56.**—(1) The signs to which this direction applies may be placed on or near a road only if at the time that they are first placed they meet the requirements specified in paragraph (3).

(2) This direction applies to—

(a) the signals prescribed by regulations 33, 34, 35, 37, 39, 41, 44, 45, 47, 48, 49 and 52;

(b) the matrix signs prescribed by regulation 46;

(c) the warning lights prescribed by regulations 50 and 51;

(d) the audible and tactile signals prescribed by regulations 47 and 49;

(e) the signs shown in diagrams 618.3A, 776 and 2509.1;

(f) the signs shown in diagrams 2505, 2505.1, 2506, 2507, 2508, 2510, 2511, 2512 and 2513, if varied to include a variable element;

(g) any light signals or signs shown in a diagram in Schedule 11;

(h) variable message signs and any other signs not continuously in use over a period of 24 hours and which are capable of being brought into and taken out of use by the operation of any electrical or other apparatus.

(3) The requirements referred to in paragraph (1) are—

(a) in all cases, that any equipment (including the content of all instructions stored in, or executable by it) used in connection with the signal or sign is of a type approved in writing by the Secretary of State or the Scottish Ministers; and

(b) in the case of the signals prescribed by regulation 39 or regulation 52, that any such equipment is of a type so approved as appropriate having regard to the number and disposition and the site of those signals.

(4) Paragraph (3)(b) does not apply to signals displayed to indicate the effect of orders made, or having effect as if made, under section 1 of the Level Crossings Act 1983.

(5) If, after a signal or sign has been placed in accordance with an approval under paragraph (3), the signal, sign or any equipment used in connection with the signal or sign is altered, the signal or sign shall not be further used unless that alteration is approved in writing by or on behalf of the Secretary of State.

(6) When any signal or sign has been placed in accordance with an approval under paragraph (3), the signal, the sign or any equipment used in connection with the signal or sign, including any alterations approved in accordance with paragraph (5), shall be regarded as continuing to be approved until notice is given in writing by the Secretary of State—

    (a) to the traffic authority; and

    (b) either—

        (i) to the supplier of the sign, signal or equipment; or

        (ii) where an alteration has been approved in accordance with paragraph (3), to the person who carried out the alteration,

of a date after which the signal, sign or equipment is no longer to be so regarded.

(7) Where notice is given under paragraph (6) that a signal, sign or any equipment used in connection with the signal or sign is no longer to be regarded as being approved that signal, sign or equipment shall be removed from the road on or before the date given in the notice.

Studs

57.—(1) A stud incorporating reflectors or retroreflecting material, but no **B57.206** steady or intermittent light source, may be placed on a road if and only if—

    (a) it is a stud of a type which meets the requirements of paragraph (5); or

    (b) it is of a type approved by the Secretary of State in accordance with direction 58.

(2) A stud incorporating both reflectors or retroreflecting material and a steady or intermittent light source, may be placed on a road if and only if—

    (a) so far as it incorporates reflectors or retroreflecting material it is of a type that meets the requirements of paragraph (5) and, so far as it incorporates a steady or intermittent light source, it is of a type approved by the Secretary of State in accordance with direction 58; or

    (b) it is of a type approved by the Secretary of State in accordance with direction 58.

(3) A stud incorporating a steady or intermittent light source and no reflectors or retroreflecting material may be placed on a road if and only if it is of a type approved by the Secretary of State in accordance with direction 58.

(4) In paragraph (5) *"the European Standards"* means European Standards EN 1463–1: 1997 and 1463–2: 2000 for retroreflecting road studs.

(5) A type of stud meets the requirements of this paragraph if and only if, being a type of stud which falls within a description specified in column (2) of an item in the table, it meets the performance requirement or test specification of the

European Standards specified in column (3) of the item as it applies to studs within the class specified in that column.

TABLE

(1) Item	(2) Description of stud	(3) Requirement or test specification and class
1.	Non depressible road stud	Dimensions: height—class H1 or H2
2.	Depressible road stud	Dimensions: height—class H1, H2 or H3
3.	Permanent road stud	Dimensions: maximum horizontal dimension exposed to traffic: HD1
4.	Temporary road stud	Dimensions: minimum horizontal dimension exposed to traffic: HDT1
5.	Permanent road stud	Night-time visibility: photometric requirements—class PRP1
6.	Temporary road stud	Night-time visibility: photometric requirements—class PRT1
7.	Temporary road stud	Daytime visibility: colour of body of stud —class DCR1 fluorescent green-yellow —class DV1
8.	Any stud	Colorimetric requirements—class NCR1 for white, amber, red or green retroreflectors only
9.	Any stud	Primary assessment—class S1
10.	Any stud	Night-time visibility assessment—class R1, R2 or R3

NOTE: Expressions used in the table bear the same meanings as in the European Standards.

Approval of types of stud by the Secretary of State

B57.207   **58.**—(1) Subject to paragraph (2) the Secretary of State may approve in writing a type of stud for the purposes of direction 57(1)(b), (2) or (3).

(2) To the extent that a type of stud incorporates reflectors or retroreflecting material, the Secretary of State may approve it under paragraph (1) only for the purpose of testing it in order to determine whether it meets the requirements of direction 57(5).

(3) When any stud has been placed in accordance with an approval under paragraph (1), the stud shall cease to be regarded as being of an approved type—

(a) in a case where approval has been granted for a specified period only, on whichever is the earlier of—

(i) the date on which that period expires; or

(ii) the date specified in a notice in writing given by the Secretary of State to the supplier and to the traffic authority as the date after which the stud is no longer to be so regarded;

(b) in a case where approval has been granted without any express time limit, on the date specified in a notice in writing given by the Secretary of State to the supplier and to the traffic authority as the date after which the stud is no longer to be so regarded.

(4) All studs ceasing to be of an approved type shall be removed on or before the appropriate date in accordance with paragraph (2).

[(5) A stud which—

(a) is of a type which was approved by the Secretary of State under direction 50 of the Traffic Signs General Directions 1994; and

(b) is placed temporarily on a road in connection with road works,

shall be treated as having been approved under paragraph (1), even though it was not approved for the purpose mentioned in paragraph (2), and paragraphs (3) and (4) shall apply to it accordingly.

(6) Paragraph (5) shall cease to have effect on 31st January 2005.]

[Direction 58 is printed as amended by SI 2003/393.]   **B57.208**

Special directions

59. Nothing in these Directions shall be taken to limit the power of the Secre-   **B57.209**
tary of State, the Scottish Ministers and the National Assembly of Wales by special direction to dispense with, add to or modify any of the requirements of these Directions in their application to any particular case.

[As to the powers of the Scottish Ministers and the National Assembly for   **B57.210**
Wales, see the Scotland Act 1998 (Transfer of Functions to the Scottish Ministers etc.) Order 1999 (SI 1999/1750) and the National Assembly for Wales (Transfer of Functions) Order 1999 (SI 1999/672).]

Direction 54   SCHEDULE

PLACING OF SIGNALS AND OTHER SIGNS AT SIGNAL-CONTROLLED CROSSING FACILITIES

Interpretation

1. In this Schedule—   **B57.211**

"approaching vehicular traffic" in relation to a crossing means vehicular traffic approaching the crossing along the carriageway across which the crossing is placed;

"crossing" means a signal-controlled crossing facility;

"far side signals" means light signals of the size, colour and type shown in diagram 4002.1, 4003.2 and 4003.5;

"indicator" means a sign of the size, colour and type shown in diagram 4003, 4003.3 and 4003.6;

"near side signals" means a sign of the size, colour and type shown in diagram 4003.1, 4003.4 and 4003.7;

"one-way road" means a road on which the driving of vehicles otherwise than in one particular direction is prohibited;

"system of staggered crossings" means two crossings provided on a road on which there is a central reservation and where—

(a) there is one crossing on each side of the central reservation; and

(b) taken together the two crossings do not lie in a straight line;

"two-way street" means a road which is not a one-way road; and

references to the left or right hand side of a crossing are to the left or right hand side as viewed by approaching vehicular traffic.

Vehicular light signals on a two-way street

B57.212   **2.** Subject to paragraph 4, on a two-way street, the number and disposition of light signals of the kind prescribed by regulation 33 which are placed at a crossing to control approaching vehicular traffic shall, in the case of a crossing of the type specified in column (2) of an item in the table, be as specified in column (3) of that item.

TABLE

(1) Item	(2) Type of crossing on a two-way street	(3) Light signals to control approaching vehicular traffic
1.	Crossing not forming part of a system of staggered crossings and not having a refuge or central reservation within the limits of the crossing	One primary signal on the left hand side of the crossing and one secondary signal on the right hand side of the crossing
2.	Crossing not forming part of a system of staggered crossings and having a refuge or central reservation within the limits of the crossing	One primary signal on the left hand side of the crossing and one secondary signal on the right hand side of the crossing or on the refuge or central reservation
3.	Crossing forming part of a system of staggered crossings	One primary signal on the left hand side of the crossing and one other signal, which may be either a primary or a secondary signal, on the right hand side of the crossing

Vehicular light signals on a one-way road

B57.213   **3.** Subject to paragraph 4, on a one-way road, the number and disposition of light signals of the kind prescribed by regulation 33 to be placed at a crossing to control approaching vehicular traffic shall, in the case of a crossing of the type specified in column (2) of an item in the table, be as specified in column (3) of that item.

TABLE

(1) Item	(2) Type of crossing on a one-way road	(3) Light signals to control approaching vehicular traffic
1.	Crossing not forming part of a system of staggered crossings and not having a refuge or central reservation within the limits of the crossing	One primary signal on the left hand side of the crossing and a signal, which may be either a primary or a secondary signal, on the right hand side of the crossing
2.	Crossing not forming part of a system of staggered crossings and having a refuge or central reservation within the limits of the crossing	One primary signal on each side of the crossing and a signal, which may be either a primary signal (in which case it must be on the refuge or the central reservation) or a secondary signal
3.	Crossing forming part of a system of staggered crossings	One primary signal on the left hand side of the crossing and a signal, which may be either a primary signal or a secondary signal, on the right hand side of the crossing

Additional vehicular light signals

4. In addition to the signals required to be placed at a crossing by paragraph 2 or 3, the traffic authority may place such other primary or secondary signals as it thinks fit.

B57.214

Far side light signals at crossings

5.—(1) Except where near side signals have been placed at a crossing in accordance with paragraph 6, at least one set of far side signals and one indicator shall be placed at each end of a crossing.

B57.215

(2) Each set of far side signals shall be so placed as to be clearly visible to any person on the opposite side of the crossing who wishes to use the crossing.

(3) Where a crossing has a refuge or central reservation within its limits, at least one indicator shall be placed on the refuge or central reservation.

(4) Each indicator shall be so placed that the push button on it may be reached by any person wishing to press it.

(5) Where far side signals and indicators have been placed at a crossing in accordance with this paragraph—

    (a) there may be placed as many devices of the kind prescribed by regulation 49(8) as the traffic authority think fit; and

    (b) no near side signals shall be placed at that crossing.

Near side signals at crossings

6.—(1) Except where far side signals have been placed at a crossing in accor-

B57.216

dance with paragraph 5, at least one set of near side signals shall be placed at each end of a crossing.

(2) Where a crossing has a refuge or central reservation within its limits, at least one set of near side signals shall be placed on the refuge or central reservation.

(3) Each set of near side signals shall be so placed—

    (a) as to be clearly visible to any person who wishes to use the crossing; and

    (b) that the push button on it may be reached by any person wishing to press it.

(4) In addition to the near side signals required by this paragraph to be placed at a crossing—

    (a) there may be placed as many devices of the kind prescribed by regulation 49(5) or (8) as the traffic authority think fit; and

    (b) no far side signals or indicators shall be placed at that crossing.

The Private Hire Vehicles (London) (Transitional and Saving Provisions) Regulations 2003

(SI 2003/655)

[The text of these regulations has been amended by: **B58.01**

> *the Private Hire Vehicles (London) (Transitional and Savings Provisions) (Amendment) Regulations 2003 (SI 2003/3028) (December 18, 2003); and*
>
> *the Private Hire Vehicles (London) (Transitional and Savings Provisions) (Amendment) Regulations 2006 (SI 2006/584) (April 4, 2006).*

The amending regulations are referred to in the notes to the principal regulations by their years and numbers. The dates referred to above are the dates on which the amending regulations came into force.]

Citation and commencement

1. *[Omitted.]*   **B58.02**

Interpretation

2. In these Regulations—   **B58.03**

> *"the 1998 Act"* means the Private Hire Vehicles (London) Act 1998;
>
> *"application deadline"* in relation to an existing driver means the date specified under regulation 4(1) as the application deadline for that driver;
>
> *"existing driver"* means an individual who is registered with Transport for London as an existing driver in accordance with article 3(1);
>
> *"the first appointed day"* means 1st April 2003;
>
> *"the second appointed day"* means 1st June 2003; and
>
> *"temporary permit"* means a temporary permit issued under regulation 5(1).

Registration of existing drivers

3.—(1) Subject to the provisions of this regulation, an individual who has   **B58.04** been the driver of a vehicle used as a private hire vehicle on roads in London under a booking which was—

> (a) made through a London PHV operator ("the relevant operator"); and
>
> (b) accepted at an operating centre specified in the relevant operator's London PHV operator's licence,

may apply to be registered with Transport for London as an existing driver by delivering to Transport for London the form provided by it for the purpose completed to show such particulars as Transport for London may reasonably require.

(2) The form shall be signed by the applicant and countersigned by the relevant operator.

(3) The form shall be treated as validly delivered to Transport for London if, and only if, it is received by Transport for London on the second appointed day or at any time before that day, whether before or after the making of these Regulations.

Application deadlines

B58.05   **4.**—(1) Transport for London shall by notice given to each existing driver specify an application deadline by which that driver is invited to submit an application for a London PHV driver's licence.

(2) Transport for London shall not be required to consider any application for a London PHV driver's licence from an existing driver until after the application deadline.

Issue of temporary permits

B58.06   **5.**—[(1) Transport for London may issue a temporary permit to—

(a) any existing driver; or

(b) an applicant for a London PHV driver's licence who, at any time before [1st January 2007], has submitted an application which—

(i) meets all requirements of Transport for London made pursuant to section 15(1), (2) and (4) of the 1998 Act; and

(ii) for which any prescribed fee (or instalment) due in accordance with regulations made by Transport for London under section 20 has been paid.]

(2) Subject to regulation 6 and, except for the purposes of section 14(1) (driver's badges) of the 1998 Act, a temporary permit shall have effect as if it were London PHV driver's licence and may in particular be suspended or revoked under section 16 of that Act accordingly.

B58.07   *[Regulation 5 is printed as amended by SI 2003/3028 and SI 2006/584.]*

Duration of temporary permits

B58.08   **6.**—(1) A temporary permit shall cease to have effect on whichever of the following dates falls first—

(a) if a London PHV driver's licence is granted to the holder of the temporary permit, the date on which the licence was granted;

(b) if an application for a London PHV driver's licence by the holder of the temporary permit is refused, the date on which the time for appealing against the refusal of the application expires or (where an appeal is brought) the date on which the appeal is disposed of or withdrawn;

[(bb) in the case of a temporary permit issued pursuant to regulation 5(1)(b), on the last day of the period of 3 months beginning with the day on which the temporary permit is issued or such later date (if any) as Transport for London may from time to time notify to the holder;]

(c) if the temporary permit is revoked, the date on which the revocation takes effect in accordance with section 17(1) or (2) of the 1998 Act; or

    (d) if the temporary permit ceases to have effect in accordance with paragraph (3), the date specified or agreed as mentioned in paragraph (2).

(2) If an application for a London PHV driver's licence is not received from the holder of a temporary permit by the application deadline, Transport for London may give notice to the holder that, if an application is not received by Transport for London from him by the date specified in the notice or such later date as Transport for London may agree, the temporary permit is to cease to have effect.

(3) If no such application is received by the date so specified or agreed, the temporary permit shall thereupon cease to have effect.

[Regulation 6 is printed as amended by SI 2003/3028.]   **B58.09**

7., 8. *[Omitted.]*   **B58.10**

The Road Vehicles (Authorisation of Special Types) (General) Order 2003

(SI 2003/1998)

ARRANGEMENT OF THE ORDER

PART 1

GENERAL

PART 2

SPECIAL VEHICLES FOR HAULAGE, LIFTING, ENGINEERING AND VEHICLE RECOVERY

PART 3

SPECIAL VEHICLES FOR AGRICULTURE

*   *   *

8.   Marking of projections

*   *   *

10.   Local excavation vehicles
11.   Vehicles for tests, trials or non-UK use etc
12.   Vehicles propelled by compressed natural gas systems

Part 1

General

Preliminary

Citation and commencement

B59.02   **1.**—(1) *[Omitted.]*

(2) Except as stated in paragraph (3), this Order comes into force on 25th August 2003.

(3) Paragraphs 15 to 18 of Schedule 2 come into force on 1st December 2004.

Revocation

B59.03   **2.** *[Omitted.]*

Interpretation

Interpretation: general

B59.04   **3.**—(1) In this Order—

"abnormal indivisible load" has the meaning given in paragraph 2 of Schedule 1 to this Order;

"abnormal indivisible load vehicle" has the meaning given in paragraph 3 of Schedule 1 to this Order;

"agricultural motor vehicle", *"agricultural trailer"* and *"agricultural trailed appliance"* have the meaning given in article 19(3);

"AILV" has the meaning given in Schedule 1;

"articulated vehicle" has the same meaning as in the Construction and Use Regulations;

"authorisation requirements" has the meaning given in article 9(2);

"axle" has the meaning given in article 7(1);

"axle weight" has the meaning given in article 7(1);

"the Authorised Weight Regulations" means the Road Vehicles (Authorised Weight) Regulations 1998 *[SI 1998/3111, q.v.]*;

"chief officer of police" —

(a) in relation to England and Wales, has the same meaning as in the Police Act 1996; and

(b) in relation to Scotland, has the same meaning as in the Police (Scotland) Act 1967;

"the Construction and Use Regulations" means the Road Vehicles (Construction and Use) Regulations 1986 [*SI 1986/1078; q.v.*];

"engineering plant" has the meaning given in paragraph 2 of Schedule 3 to this Order;

"foremost point", in relation to a vehicle, has the meaning given in article 4(3);

"forward projection", in relation to a load carried on a vehicle, has the meaning given in article 6(1);

"gross weight" —

    (a) in relation to a motor vehicle, means the sum of the weights transmitted to the road surface by all the wheels of the vehicle; and

    (b) in relation to a trailer, means the sum of—

        (i) the weights transmitted to the road surface by all the wheels of the trailer; and

        (ii) any weight of the trailer imposed on the towing vehicle;

"group of axles" has the meaning given in article 7(1);

"lateral projection", in relation to a load carried on a vehicle, has the meaning given in article 5(1);

"the Lighting Regulations" means the Road Vehicles Lighting Regulations 1989 [*SI 1989/1796, q.v.*];

"local excavation vehicle" has the meaning given in paragraph 1 of Schedule 10 to this Order;

"mobile crane" has the meaning given in paragraph 2 of Schedule 2 to this Order;

"motor vehicle of category N3" means a motor vehicle of category N3 (motor vehicles over 12,000 kilograms maximum weight), as defined in Annex II of Council Directive 70/156/EEC on the approximation of the laws of the Member States relating to the type-approval of motor vehicles and their trailers [*O.J. No.L42, February 2, 1970, p.1; see now Annex II of Directive 2007/46/EC (O.J. No.L263, October 9, 2007, p.1)*];

"motorway" means a special road which—

    (a) in England or Wales (except as otherwise provided by or under regulations made under, or having effect as if made under, section 17 of the Road Traffic Regulation Act 1984) can be used by traffic only of Class I or II as specified in Schedule 4 to Highways Act 1980: or

    (b) in Scotland can be used by traffic only of Class I or Class II as specified in Schedule 3 to the Roads (Scotland) Act 1984;

"overall length", in relation to a vehicle, has the meaning given in article 4(2);

"overall width", in relation to a vehicle, has the meaning given in article 4(1);

"Part 2 vehicle" has the meaning given in article 10(2);

"Part 2 vehicle-combination" has the meaning given in article 10(3);

"pneumatic tyre" has the same meaning as in the Construction and Use Regulations;

"rearmost point", in relation to a vehicle, has the meaning given in article 4(4);

"rearward projection", in relation to a load carried on a vehicle, has the meaning given in article 6(2);

"recognised category of special vehicles" has the meaning given in article 8(2);

"road recovery vehicle" has the meaning given in paragraph 1 of Schedule 4 to this Order;

"special type agricultural vehicle" has the meaning given in article 19(2);

"track-laying", in relation to a vehicle, has the same meaning as in the Construction and Use Regulations;

"trailer of category O4" means a trailer of category O4 (trailers over 10,000 kilograms maximum weight), as defined in Annex II of Council Directive 70/156/EEC on the approximation of the laws of the Member States relating to the type-approval of motor vehicles and their trailers;

"vehicle-combination" means a motor vehicle towing one or more trailers, any trailer or trailers towed by it and any other motor vehicle used for the purpose of assisting the propulsion of the trailer or trailers on the road;

"warning beacon" has the same meaning as in the Lighting Regulations;

"wheel" is to be construed in accordance with article 7(2) and (3);

"wheeled", in relation to a vehicle, means a vehicle so constructed that the whole weight of the vehicle is transmitted to the road surface by means of wheels;

"wheel-track combination vehicle" has the meaning given in paragraph 1 of Schedule 3; and

"wheel weight" has the meaning given in article 7(1).

(2) In this Order, any reference to a motor vehicle towing a trailer in an offset manner is a reference to the vehicle towing the trailer so that the longitudinal axis of the trailer and the longitudinal axis of the towing vehicle are parallel but lie in different vertical planes.

(3) For the purposes of any provision of this Order requiring a person to do something within a specified number of days, no account is to be taken of any day which is a Saturday, a Sunday or a public holiday in any part of Great Britain.

Interpretation: vehicles and their measurement

B59.05   **4.**—(1) In this Order *"overall width"*, in relation to any vehicle, has the same meaning as in the Construction and Use Regulations.

(2) In this Order *"overall length"*—

(a) in relation to a single vehicle, has the same meaning as in the Construction and Use Regulations;

(b) in relation to a vehicle-combination, means the distance between the foremost point of the towing vehicle and the rearmost point of the rearmost vehicle, measured when the longitudinal axis of each vehicle in the combination lies in the same vertical plane.

(3) In this Order *"foremost point"*, in relation to any vehicle, means the foremost point from which its overall length is calculated when applying the definition of overall length contained in regulation 3(2) of the Construction and Use Regulations.

(4) In this Order *"rearmost point"*, in relation to any vehicle, means the rearmost point from which its overall length is calculated when applying the definition of overall length contained in regulation 3(2) of the Construction and Use Regulations.

(5) In this Order—

(a) any reference to the distance between vehicles bearing the weight of a load is a reference to the distance between the nearest points of any two adjacent vehicles by which each load is carried, measured when the longitudinal axis of each vehicle lies in the same vertical plane; and

(b) in determining the nearest point of two vehicles, any part of either vehicle designed primarily for use as a means of attaching the one vehicle to the other (and any fitting designed for use in connection with any such part) is to be disregarded.

Interpretation: lateral projections of loads and their measurement

5.—(1) In this Order *"lateral projection"*, in relation to a load carried on a vehicle, means that part of the load which extends beyond a side of the vehicle.   **B59.06**

(2) For the purposes of this Order, the width of any lateral projection is to be measured between longitudinal planes passing through the extreme projecting point of the vehicle on that side of the vehicle on which the projection lies and that part of the projection furthest from that point.

(3) The reference in paragraph (2) to the extreme projecting point of a vehicle is to the point of the vehicle from which its overall width is calculated when applying the definition of overall width contained in regulation 3(2) of the Construction and Use Regulations.

Interpretation: forward or rearward projections of loads and their measurement

6.—(1) In this Order *"forward projection"*, in relation to a load carried on a vehicle, means—   **B59.07**

(a) where the weight of the load is carried on a single vehicle, that part of the load that extends beyond the foremost point of the vehicle;

(b) where the weight of the load is carried on more than one vehicle, that part of the load that extends beyond the foremost point of the foremost vehicle on which the load is carried.

(2) In this Order *"rearward projection"*, in relation to a load carried on a vehicle, means—

(a) where the weight of the load is carried on a single vehicle, that part of the load that extends beyond the rearmost point of the vehicle;

(b) where the weight of the load is carried on more than one vehicle, that part of the load that extends beyond the rearmost point of the rearmost vehicle on which the load is carried.

(3) For the purposes of paragraphs (1) and (2), where a crane or other special appliance or apparatus is fitted to a vehicle so as to constitute a permanent (or essentially permanent) feature of it—

> (a) any part of that crane, appliance or apparatus that extends forwards beyond the foremost point of the vehicle (or, as the case may be, beyond the foremost point of the foremost vehicle by which its weight is carried) is to be treated as a forward projection; and

> (b) any part of that crane, appliance or apparatus that extends rearwards beyond the rearmost point of the vehicle (or, as the case may be, beyond the rearmost point of the rearmost vehicle by which its weight is carried) is to be treated as a rearward projection.

(4) In determining the foremost or rearmost point of a vehicle, any part of a crane or other special appliance or apparatus is to be disregarded.

(5) For the purposes of this Order, the length of any forward projection or rearward projection is to be measured between transverse planes passing—

> (a) in the case of a forward projection, through the foremost point of the vehicle and that part of the projection furthest from that point;

> (b) in the case of a rearward projection, through the rearmost point of the vehicle and that part of the projection furthest from that point.

Interpretation: axles, wheels, axle weights and wheel weights

B59.08   7.—(1) In this Order—

> "axle" means any number of wheels in a transverse line;

> "axle weight" means the sum of the weights transmitted to the road surface by all the wheels of any one axle;

> "group of axles" means a group of two or more axles that are so linked together that the load applied to one axle is applied to the other; and

> "wheel weight" means the weight transmitted to the road surface by any one wheel of an axle.

(2) For the purposes of this Order, any reference to a wheel of a vehicle is a reference to a wheel, the tyre or rim of which is, when the vehicle is in motion on a road, in contact with the ground.

(3) For the purposes of this Order, any two wheels of a vehicle are to be treated as one wheel if their centres of contact with the road are less than 460 millimetres apart.

(4) For the purposes of this Order, any wheels, or lines of wheels, whose centres can be contained between two transverse lines less than 0.5 metre apart are to be treated as one axle.

(5) For the purposes of this Order, the distance between any two axles of a vehicle or vehicle-combination is to be taken as the shortest distance between the line joining the centres of the areas of contact with the road surface of the wheels of one axle and the line joining the centres of the areas of contact with the road surface of the wheels of the other axle.

Authorisation of certain vehicles for use on roads

Application of this Order

8.—(1) This Order applies only to motor vehicles or trailers— **B59.09**

    (a) that do not comply in all respects with the standard construction and use requirements; and

    (b) that fall within a recognised category of special vehicles.

(2) In this Order *"recognised category of special vehicles"* means a description of vehicles that is stated by a provision of this Order to be a recognised category of special vehicles.

(3) In paragraph (1), *"standard construction and use requirements"*, in relation to a motor vehicle or trailer, means the requirements of such of the regulations made under section 41 of the Road Traffic Act 1988 [*q.v.*] as would, apart from this Order, apply to that motor vehicle or trailer.

Authorisation of particular vehicles falling within recognised category of special vehicles

9.—(1) A vehicle that falls within a recognised category of special vehicles is **B59.10** authorised to be used on roads by virtue of this Order if (but only if) it complies with the authorisation requirements applicable to vehicles in that category.

(2) In this Order *"authorisation requirements"*, in relation to a recognised category of special vehicles—

    (a) means all the requirements specified in this Order as being applicable to vehicles in that category; and

    (b) includes such of the requirements of regulations made under section 41 of the Road Traffic Act 1988 as are specified in this Order as being applicable to vehicles in that category (subject to any modifications or exceptions so specified).

(3) Where any provision of this Order specifies any of the regulations mentioned in paragraph (2)(b) as being applicable to any recognised category of special vehicles, that provision is not to be construed as applying any requirement of those regulations to a vehicle in that category if that requirement may reasonably be regarded, in all the circumstances, as not relevant to the vehicle in question (for example, if the requirement relates to trailers and the vehicle in question is not a trailer).

PART 2

SPECIAL VEHICLES FOR HAULAGE, LIFTING, ENGINEERING AND VEHICLE RECOVERY

Part 2 vehicles and Part 2 vehicle-combinations: recognised categories and defined terms

10.—(1) The following are recognised categories of special vehicles— **B59.11**

    (a) abnormal indivisible load vehicles;

    (b) mobile cranes;

    (c) engineering plant;

(d) road recovery vehicles.

(2) A vehicle that falls within any recognised category of special vehicles mentioned in paragraph (1) is referred to in this Order as a Part 2 vehicle.

(3) In this Order, a *"Part 2 vehicle-combination"* means—

(a) in the case of a road recovery vehicle, a vehicle-combination which consists of one motor vehicle of category N3 together with one trailer of category O4; or

(b) in any other case, a vehicle-combination which consists of, or includes, one motor vehicle (whether or not it is a Part 2 vehicle) together with one trailer that is a Part 2 vehicle.

(4) The categories of vehicles specified in sub-paragraph (a), (b), (c) or (d) of paragraph (1) are defined in Schedules 1 to 4 respectively.

Part 2 vehicles and Part 2 vehicle-combinations: authorisation requirements

B59.12   11.—(1) The authorisation requirements applicable to Part 2 vehicles or Part 2 vehicle-combinations are—

(a) as respects any vehicle or vehicle-combination falling within Schedule 1, 2, 3 or 4, the requirements specified in the Schedule in question; and

(b) as respects all such vehicles or vehicle-combinations, the requirements specified in articles 12 to 18.

(2) But the requirements specified in articles 12 to 17 do not apply to a mobile crane or road recovery vehicle in any case where—

(a) a civil emergency or road traffic accident has occurred;

(b) as a result, there is a danger to the public;

(c) the owner or user of the crane or vehicle has received a request made by the police for the vehicle to be used for the purposes of immediate clearance of an area affected by the emergency or accident;

(d) the crane or vehicle is used on roads within 24 hours of receipt of the request; and

(e) it is not reasonably practicable to comply with the requirements of those articles.

(3) Nothing in this article prevents a motor vehicle which falls within the definition of a mobile crane in paragraph 2 of Schedule 2, but which does not comply in all respects with the authorisation requirements for mobile cranes specified in that Schedule, from complying instead with the authorisation requirements for engineering plant specified in Schedule 3 provided that the motor vehicle in question also falls within the definition of engineering plant in paragraph 2 of that Schedule.

(4) For the purposes of this Order, a motor vehicle that complies with the authorisation requirements for engineering plant in the manner described in paragraph (3) is to be treated as engineering plant.

Length and width of vehicle and projections of load

Length: police notification and attendants

B59.13   12.—(1) Where either of the length limits set out in paragraph (2) or (3) is exceeded in relation to a Part 2 vehicle or Part 2 vehicle-combination, the user of the vehicle or vehicle-combination must—

    (a) before the start of any journey, notify in accordance with Schedule 5 the chief officer of police for each area in which the vehicle or vehicle-combination is to be used;

    (b) ensure that the vehicle or vehicle-combination is used in accordance with the requirements of that Schedule; and

    (c) ensure that the vehicle or vehicle-combination is accompanied during the journey by one or more attendants employed in accordance with Schedule 6.

(2) The first length limit is exceeded where the overall length of any single rigid unit together with the length of any forward or rearward projection of any load carried on the unit exceeds 18.75 metres.

(3) The second length limit is exceeded where the overall length of a Part 2 vehicle-combination exceeds 25.9 metres.

(4) The reference to a single rigid unit is a reference to—

    (a) a single vehicle, whether or not included in a Part 2 vehicle-combination; or

    (b) any two or more vehicles comprising or included in a Part 2 vehicle-combination which together bear the weight of one or more loads in such a way that, at all times when the vehicles are moving, the longitudinal axis of each vehicle lies in the same vertical plane.

Forward and rearward projections: police notification

13.—(1) This article applies where a Part 2 vehicle or Part 2 vehicle-combination is to carry a load and the length of any forward or rearward projection of the load exceeds 3.05 metres.   **B59.14**

(2) The user of the Part 2 vehicle or Part 2 vehicle-combination must, unless he has already notified the police under article 12(1)(a) —

    (a) before the start of any journey, notify in accordance with Schedule 5 the chief officer of police for each area in which the vehicle or vehicle-combination is to be used; and

    (b) ensure that the vehicle or vehicle-combination is used in accordance with the requirements of that Schedule.

Forward and rearward projections: attendants

14.—(1) If paragraph (2) or (3) applies, the user of a Part 2 vehicle or Part 2 vehicle-combination must ensure that the vehicle or vehicle-combination is accompanied during the journey by one or more attendants employed in accordance with Schedule 6.   **B59.15**

(2) This paragraph applies where a Part 2 vehicle or Part 2 vehicle-combination is carrying a load and the length of any forward projection of the load exceeds 2 metres.

(3) This paragraph applies where a Part 2 vehicle or Part 2 vehicle-combination is carrying a load and the length of any rearward projection of the load exceeds 3.05 metres.

Width and lateral projections: police notification, Secretary of State notification and attendants

B59.16   15.—(1) This article applies to a Part 2 vehicle or vehicle in a Part 2 vehicle-combination in respect of which one or more of the following width limits are exceeded—

(a) the first width limit is exceeded where the overall width of the vehicle together with the width of any lateral projection or projections of any load carried on it is 3 metres or less but the length of any lateral projection of a load carried on it exceeds 305 millimetres;

(b) the second width limit is exceeded where the overall width of the vehicle together with the width of any lateral projection or projections of any load carried on it exceeds 3 metres;

(c) the third width limit is exceeded where the overall width of the vehicle together with the width of any lateral projection or projections of any load carried on it exceeds 3.5 metres;

(d) the fourth width limit is exceeded where the overall width of the vehicle together with the width of any lateral projection or projections of any load carried on it exceeds 5 metres.

(2) Paragraphs (3), (4) and (5) apply cumulatively.

(3) Where the first or second width limit is exceeded, the user of the vehicle must—

(a) before the start of any journey, notify in accordance with Schedule 5 the chief officer of police for each area in which the vehicle or vehicle-combination is to be used; and

(b) ensure that the vehicle is used in accordance with the requirements of that Schedule.

(4) Where the third width limit is exceeded, the user of the vehicle must ensure that the vehicle is accompanied during the journey by one or more attendants employed in accordance with Schedule 6.

(5) Where the fourth width limit is exceeded, the user of the vehicle must—

(a) before the start of any journey, obtain in accordance with Schedule 7 the written consent of the Secretary of State; and

(b) ensure that the vehicle is used in accordance with the requirements of that Schedule.

Visibility and marking of forward, rearward and lateral projections of loads etc

B59.17   16. Schedule 8 (which makes provision as to the visibility and marking of projections exceeding a certain length or width) applies in relation to loads carried on a Part 2 vehicle or Part 2 vehicle-combination.

Weight of vehicle and load

Weight: police notification and road and bridge authority notification and indemnity

B59.18   17.—(1) In a case falling within paragraph (2), the user of a Part 2 vehicle or Part 2 vehicle-combination must before the start of any journey—

(a) notify in accordance with Part 1 of Schedule 9 the authority (within the meaning of that Schedule) for each road or bridge on which the vehicle or vehicle-combination is to be used; and

(b) give to each authority an indemnity in the form specified in Part 2 of that Schedule.

(2) A case falls within this paragraph where—

(a) the total weight of the Part 2 vehicle or Part 2 vehicle-combination (whether it is unladen or wholly or partly laden) exceeds 44,000 kilograms; or

(b) the vehicle or vehicle-combination does not comply in all respects with—

(i) the requirements of Schedule 3 to the Authorised Weight Regulations (axle weights); or

(ii) if that Schedule does not apply to it, the equivalent provisions of the Construction and Use Regulations.

(3) In a case falling within paragraph (4), the user of the Part 2 vehicle or Part 2 vehicle-combination must—

(a) before the start of any journey, notify in accordance with Schedule 5 the chief officer of police for each area in which the vehicle or vehicle-combination is to be used; and

(b) ensure that the vehicle is used in accordance with the requirements of that Schedule.

(4) A case falls within this paragraph if the total weight of the Part 2 vehicle or Part 2 vehicle-combination (whether it is unladen or wholly or partly laden) exceeds 80,000 kilograms.

(5) Paragraphs (1) and (3) apply cumulatively.

Use on bridges

18.—(1) The driver of a Part 2 vehicle or Part 2 vehicle-combination must not **B59.19** cause or permit any part of his vehicle (or any part of any vehicle in the vehicle-combination he is driving) to enter on a bridge if he knows that the whole or part of another such vehicle or vehicle-combination is already on the bridge or if he could reasonably be expected to ascertain that fact.

(2) Except in circumstances beyond his control, the driver of a Part 2 vehicle or Part 2 vehicle-combination must not cause or permit the Part 2 vehicle, or any vehicle in the vehicle-combination, to remain stationary on any bridge.

(3) If a Part 2 vehicle or Part 2 vehicle-combination that falls within article 17(2) or (4) is caused to stop on a bridge for any reason, the driver of the vehicle or vehicle-combination must ensure—

(a) that the vehicle or vehicle-combination is moved clear of the bridge as soon as practicable; and

(b) that no concentrated load is applied to the surface on that part of the road carried by the bridge.

(4) But where the action described in paragraph (3)(a) or (b) is not practicable and it becomes necessary to apply any concentrated load to the road surface by means of jacks, rollers or other similar means, the driver or other person in charge of the vehicle or vehicle-combination must—

(a) before the load is applied to the road surface, seek advice from the authority (within the meaning of Schedule 9) responsible for the maintenance of the bridge about the use of spreader plates to reduce the possibility of damage caused by the application of the load; and

(b) ensure that no concentrated load is applied without using spreader plates in accordance with any advice received.

(5) References to the driver of a Part 2 vehicle-combination are references to the driver of the foremost motor vehicle in the vehicle-combination.

PART 3

SPECIAL VEHICLES FOR AGRICULTURE

Agricultural vehicles: recognised categories and defined terms

B59.20   19.—(1) The following are recognised categories of special vehicles—

(a) agricultural motor vehicles;

(b) agricultural trailers;

(c) agricultural trailed appliances.

(2) A vehicle that falls within any recognised category of special vehicles mentioned in paragraph (1) is referred to in this Order as a special type agricultural vehicle.

(3) In this Order—

"agricultural motor vehicle" means a motor vehicle (not being a dual purpose vehicle) which—

(a) is constructed or adapted for use off-road for the purpose of agriculture, horticulture or forestry; and

(b) is primarily used for one or more of those purposes;

"agricultural trailer" has the same meaning as in the Construction and Use Regulations; and

"agricultural trailed appliance" has the same meaning as in the Construction and Use Regulations.

(4) In the definition of "agricultural motor vehicle" in paragraph (3), "dual purpose vehicle" has the same meaning as in the Construction and Use Regulations.

Agricultural vehicles: authorisation requirements

B59.21   20. The authorisation requirements applicable to special type agricultural vehicles are—

(a) the requirements specified in articles 21 to 27;

(b) the Construction and Use Regulations, apart from—

(i) regulation 8 (width);

(ii) paragraph (1) of regulation 75, in so far as that paragraph relates to item 13 or 15 of the Table referred to in it (maximum permitted laden weight of track-laying motor vehicles); and

(iii) regulation 82 (restrictions on vehicles carrying wide or long loads or having fixed appliance or apparatus);

(c) the Authorised Weight Regulations; and

(d) the Lighting Regulations.

General requirements as to construction and use

21.—(1) A special type agricultural vehicle that is a track-laying motor vehicle **B59.22**
may be used on roads only if the tracks operate on rubber or an alternative composite material that does not damage the road surface.

(2) The overall width of a special type agricultural vehicle together with the width of any lateral projection or projections of any load carried on it must not exceed 4.3 metres.

(3) For the purposes of paragraph (2) —

(a) the overall width of a special type agricultural vehicle that is a motor vehicle towing an agricultural trailer or agricultural trailed appliance in an offset manner, is to be taken as the overall width of the motor vehicle and trailer (or trailed appliance) measured as if they were one vehicle; and

(b) where any agricultural implement is rigidly (but not permanently) mounted on a special type agricultural vehicle, any part of the implement that extends beyond a side of the vehicle is to be treated as a lateral projection, regardless of whether any part of the weight of the implement is transmitted to the surface of the road otherwise than by the wheels or tracks of the vehicle.

(4) The gross weight of a special type agricultural motor vehicle that is a track-laying vehicle, together with the weight of any load carried on it, must not exceed 30,000 kilograms.

(5) All spikes, cutting blades or other protruding sharp appliances that are fitted to or mounted on a special type agricultural vehicle must be removed or effectively guarded so that no danger is caused (or likely to be caused) to any person.

(6) A special type agricultural vehicle must not at any time travel at speeds exceeding—

(a) 20 miles per hour in any case where the overall width of the vehicle is more than 2.55 metres but less than 3.5 metres;

(b) 12 miles per hour in any case where the overall width is 3.5 metres or more.

Restrictions on towing of trailers

22.—(1) This article applies in any of the following cases to a special type ag- **B59.23**
ricultural vehicle that is a motor vehicle:

CASE 1

Where the special type agricultural vehicle has an overall width exceeding 3 metres.

CASE 2

Where a special type agricultural vehicle is towing an agricultural trailer, or agricultural trailed appliance, in an offset manner and the overall width of the two vehicles (measured as if they were one) exceeds 3 metres.

CASE 3

Where a special type agricultural vehicle is towing an agricultural trailer, or agricultural trailed appliance, otherwise than in an offset manner and the overall width of either (or both) of the vehicles exceeds 3 metres.

(2) The special type agricultural vehicle must not either tow any trailer (where the vehicle falls within Case 1) or tow any other trailer (where the vehicle falls within Case 2 or 3), apart from a trailer that is of a description permitted by paragraph (3).

(3) The trailers permitted by this paragraph are—

    (a) a two wheeled trailer used solely for the carriage of equipment for use on the towing vehicle;

    (b) an agricultural trailed appliance; or

    (c) an unladen trailer specially designed for use with the towing vehicle when it is harvesting.

Forward and rearward projections: police notification, Secretary of State notification and attendants

B59.24   **23.**—(1) Paragraphs (2), (3) and (4) apply cumulatively.

(2) Where a special type agricultural vehicle is to carry a load and the length of any forward or rearward projection of the load exceeds 4 metres, the user of the vehicle must—

    (a) before the start of any journey, notify in accordance with Schedule 5 the chief officer of police for each area in which the special type agricultural vehicle is to be used; and

    (b) ensure that the vehicle is used in accordance with the requirements of that Schedule.

(3) Where a special type agricultural vehicle is carrying a load and the length of any forward or rearward projection of the load exceeds 6 metres, the user of the vehicle must ensure that the vehicle is accompanied during any journey by one or more attendants employed in accordance with Schedule 6.

(4) Where the length of any rearward projection of a load exceeds 12 metres, the user of the vehicle must—

    (a) before the start of any journey, obtain in accordance with Schedule 7 the written consent of the Secretary of State; and

    (b) ensure that the vehicle is used in accordance with the requirements of that Schedule.

(5) Where any agricultural implement is rigidly (but not permanently) mounted on a special type agricultural vehicle—

    (a) any part of the implement that extends forwards beyond the foremost point of the vehicle is to be treated as a forward projection; and

    (b) any part of the implement that extends rearwards beyond the rearmost point of the vehicle is to be treated as a rearward projection;

regardless of whether any part of the weight of the implement is transmitted to the surface of the road otherwise than by the wheels or tracks of the vehicle.

(6) In determining for the purposes of paragraph (5) the foremost or rearmost point of a special type agricultural vehicle, any part of the agricultural implement is to be disregarded.

Width: police notification and attendants

24.—(1) *"Width"*, in relation to a special type agricultural vehicle, means **B59.25**
whichever is the greater of—

    (a) the overall width of the vehicle; and

    (b) the overall width of the vehicle together with the width of any lateral
projection or projections of a load carried on it.

(2) Paragraphs (4) and (5) apply cumulatively.

(3) Paragraph (4) applies where the width of a special type agricultural vehicle exceeds 3 metres and—

    (a) there is a speed limit of 40 miles per hour or less on any road on which
the vehicle is to be used; or

    (b) the length of the journey to be made by the vehicle exceeds 5 miles.

(4) The user of the vehicle must—

    (a) before the start of any journey, notify in accordance with Schedule 5
the chief officer of police for each area in which the special type agricultural vehicle is to be used; and

    (b) ensure that the vehicle is used in accordance with the requirements of
that Schedule.

(5) Where the width of the vehicle exceeds 3.5 metres, the user of the vehicle
must ensure that the vehicle is accompanied during any journey by one or more
attendants employed in accordance with Schedule 6.

Visibility and marking of forward, rearward and lateral projections

25. Schedule 8 (which makes provision as to the visibility and marking of **B59.26**
projections exceeding a certain length or width) applies in relation to loads carried on a special type agricultural vehicle.

**Track-laying agricultural motor vehicles: road and bridge authority
notification and indemnity**

26.—(1) This article applies to a special type agricultural vehicle that is a **B59.27**
track-laying motor vehicle that does not comply with paragraph (1) of regulation
75 of the Construction and Use Regulations, in so far as that paragraph relates to
item 13 or 15 of the Table referred to in it (maximum permitted laden weight of
track-laying motor vehicles).

(2) Before the start of any journey, the user of the vehicle must—

    (a) notify in accordance with Part 1 of Schedule 9 the authority (within
the meaning of that Schedule) for each road or bridge on which vehicle is to be used; and

    (b) give to each authority an indemnity in the form specified in Part 2 of
that Schedule.

Track-laying agricultural motor vehicles: use on bridges

27.—(1) This article applies to a special type agricultural vehicle to which **B59.28**
article 26 applies.

(2) If the special type agricultural vehicle is caused to stop on a bridge for any
reason, the driver of the vehicle must ensure—

    (a) that the vehicle is moved clear of the bridge as soon as practicable; and

    (b) that no concentrated load is applied to the surface on that part of the road carried by the bridge.

(3) But where the action described in paragraph (2)(a) or (b) is not practicable and it becomes necessary to apply any concentrated load to the road surface by means of jacks, rollers or other similar means, the driver or other person in charge of the vehicle must—

    (a) before the load is applied to the road surface, seek advice from the authority (within the meaning of Schedule 9) responsible for the maintenance of the bridge about the use of spreader plates to reduce the possibility of damage caused by the application of the load; and

    (b) ensure that no concentrated load is applied without using spreader plates in accordance with any advice received.

Part 4

Other Special Vehicles Requiring Notifications or Attendants

Vehicles carrying loads of exceptional width

Motor vehicles or trailers carrying loads of exceptional width: recognised category

B59.29   **28.**—(1) Motor vehicles or trailers that are used for, or in connection with, the carriage of a load exceptional width are a recognised category of special vehicles.

(2) A vehicle carries a load of exceptional width where the overall width of the vehicle carrying a load, together with the width of any lateral projection or projections of the load, exceeds 4.3 metres.

Motor vehicles or trailers carrying loads of exceptional width: authorisation requirements

B59.30   **29.** The authorisation requirements applicable to vehicles falling within the recognised category of special vehicles mentioned in article 28(1) are—

    (a) the requirements specified in articles 30 and 31;

    (b) the Construction and Use Regulations, apart from regulation 82(1) and (2);

    (c) the Authorised Weight Regulations; and

    (d) the Lighting Regulations.

Motor vehicles or trailers carrying loads of exceptional width: restrictions on width and speed

B59.31   **30.**—(1) The overall width of a vehicle falling within the recognised category of special vehicles mentioned in article 28(1), together with the width of any lateral projection or projections of the load carried on it, must not exceed 6.1 metres.

(2) The vehicle must not travel at speeds exceeding—

    (a) 40 miles per hour on a motorway;

(b) 35 miles per hour on a dual carriageway;

(c) 30 miles per hour on any other road.

(3) Nothing in this article is to be taken to authorise travel at any speed in excess of any speed restriction imposed by or under any other enactment.

Motor vehicles or trailers carrying loads of exceptional width: requirements as to width

31.—(1) *"Width"*, in relation to a vehicle falling within the recognised category of special vehicles mentioned in article 28(1), means the overall width of the vehicle together with the width of any lateral projection or projections of the load carried on it.   **B59.32**

(2) Paragraphs (3) and (4) apply cumulatively.

(3) The user of any vehicle falling within the recognised category of special vehicles mentioned in article 28(1) must—

(a) before the start of any journey, notify in accordance with Schedule 5 the chief officer of police for each area in which the vehicle is to be used;

(b) ensure that the vehicle is used in accordance with the requirements of that Schedule; and

(c) ensure that the vehicle is accompanied during the journey by one or more attendants employed in accordance with Schedule 6.

(4) Where the width of the vehicle exceeds 5 metres, the user of the vehicle must—

(a) before the start of any journey obtain the written consent of the Secretary of State in accordance with Schedule 7; and

(b) ensure that the vehicle is used in accordance with the requirements of that Schedule.

Local excavation vehicles

Local excavation vehicles: recognised category

32.—(1) Local excavation vehicles are a recognised category of special vehicles.   **B59.33**

(2) Local excavation vehicles are defined in paragraph 1 of Schedule 10.

Local excavation vehicles: authorisation requirements

33. The authorisation requirements applicable to local excavation vehicles are—   **B59.34**

(a) the requirements specified in articles 34 and 35; and

(b) the requirements specified in Schedule 10.

Local excavation vehicles: requirements as to width

34.—(1) *"Width"*, in relation to a local excavation vehicle, means whichever is the greater of—   **B59.35**

(a) the overall width of the vehicle; and

(b) the overall width of the vehicle together with the width of any lateral projection or projections of a load carried on it.

(2) Paragraphs (3) to (5) apply cumulatively.

(3) Where the width of a local excavation vehicle exceeds 3 metres, the user of the vehicle must—

    (a) before the start of any journey, notify in accordance with Schedule 5 the chief officer of police for each area in which the vehicle is to be used; and

    (b) ensure that the vehicle is used in accordance with the requirements of that Schedule.

(4) Where the width of the vehicle exceeds 3.5 metres, the user of the vehicle must ensure that the vehicle is accompanied during the journey by one or more attendants employed in accordance with Schedule 6.

(5) Where the width of the vehicle exceeds 5 metres, the user of the vehicle must—

    (a) before the start of any journey obtain the written consent of the Secretary of State in accordance with Schedule 7; and

    (b) ensure that the vehicle is used in accordance with the requirements of that Schedule.

Local excavation vehicles: requirements as to weight

B59.36   **35.**—(1) This article applies to a local excavation vehicle—

    (a) which does not comply with the requirements of the Authorised Weight Regulations; or

    (b) if those Regulations do not apply to it, which does not comply with the requirements of regulations 75 to 79 of the Construction and Use Regulations.

(2) Before the start of any journey, the user of the vehicle must—

    (a) notify in accordance with Part 1 of Schedule 9 the authority (within the meaning of that Schedule) for each road or bridge on which vehicle is to be used; and

    (b) give to each authority an indemnity in the form specified in Part 2 of that Schedule.

Vehicles for tests, trials or non-UK use etc

Vehicles for tests, trials or non-UK use etc: recognised category

B59.37   **36.**—(1) The following are recognised categories of special vehicles—

    (a) any motor vehicle or trailer which is constructed for use outside the United Kingdom;

    (b) any type of motor vehicle or trailer which is constructed for use outside the United Kingdom;

    (c) any new or improved type of motor vehicle or trailer which is constructed for tests or trials;

    (d) any motor vehicle or trailer which is equipped with new or improved equipment;

    (e) any motor vehicle or trailer which is equipped with new or improved types of equipment.

(2) Paragraph (1) does not include—

    (a) any motor vehicle or trailer which is not a wheeled vehicle; or

    (b) any motor vehicle or trailer which is, or forms part of, a recognised category of special vehicles specified in sub-paragraph (a), (b), (c) or (d) of article 10(1).

Vehicles for tests, trials or non-UK use etc: authorisation requirements

37. The authorisation requirements applicable to vehicles falling within any of **B59.38** the recognised categories of special vehicles mentioned in article 36(1) are—

    (a) the requirements specified in articles 38 to 40; and

    (b) the requirements specified in Schedule 11.

Vehicles for tests, trials or non-UK use etc: requirements as to length

38.—(1) This article applies to—   **B59.39**

    (a) a vehicle falling within any of the recognised categories of special vehicles mentioned in article 36(1), where the overall length of the vehicle exceeds the overall length permitted for that description of vehicle under regulation 7 of the Construction and Use Regulations; and

    (b) a vehicle-combination, being a combination that includes one or more motor vehicles or trailers that fall within any of those recognised categories of special vehicles, where the overall length of the vehicle-combination exceeds the overall length for that combination permitted under regulation 7 of the Construction and Use Regulations.

(2) The user of the vehicle or vehicle-combination must—

    (a) before the start of any journey, notify in accordance with Schedule 5 the chief officer of police for each area in which the vehicle or vehicle-combination is to be used; and

    (b) ensure that the vehicle or vehicle-combination is used in accordance with the requirements of that Schedule.

Vehicles for tests, trials or non-UK use etc: requirements as to width

39.—(1) *"Width"*, in relation to a vehicle falling within any of the recognised **B59.40** categories of special vehicles mentioned in article 36(1), means whichever is the greater of—

    (a) the overall width of the vehicle; and

    (b) the overall width of the vehicle together with the width of any lateral projection or projections of a load carried on it.

(2) Where the width of a vehicle falling within any of the recognised categories of special vehicles mentioned in article 36(1) exceeds 3 metres, the user of the vehicle must—

    (a) before the start of any journey, notify in accordance with Schedule 5 the chief officer of police for each area in which the vehicle is to be used; and

    (b) ensure that the vehicle is used in accordance with the requirements of that Schedule.

Vehicles for tests, trials or non-UK use etc: requirements as to weight

B59.41   **40.**—(1) This article applies to a vehicle which is, or a vehicle-combination which includes, a vehicle falling within any of the recognised categories of special vehicles mentioned in article 36(1) and which—

(a) does not comply with the requirements of the Authorised Weight Regulations; or

(b) if those Regulations do not apply to it, does not comply with the requirements of regulations 75 to 79 of the Construction and Use Regulations.

(2) Before the start of any journey, the user of the vehicle or vehicle-combination must—

(a) notify in accordance with Part 1 of Schedule 9 the authority (within the meaning of that Schedule) for each road or bridge on which vehicle or vehicle-combination is to be used; and

(b) give to each authority an indemnity in the form specified in Part 2 of that Schedule.

Track-laying vehicles

Track-laying vehicles: recognised category

B59.42   **41.**—(1) Track-laying motor vehicles or trailers are a recognised category of special vehicles.

(2) Paragraph (1) does not include any track-laying vehicle that falls within any other recognised category of special vehicles.

Track-laying vehicles: authorisation requirements

B59.43   **42.** The authorisation requirements applicable to vehicles falling within the recognised category of special vehicles mentioned in article 41(1) are—

(a) the requirements specified in articles 43 and 44;

(b) regulation 100 of the Construction and Use Regulations (maintenance and use so as not to be a danger);

(c) the Authorised Weight Regulations; and

(d) the Lighting Regulations.

Track-laying vehicles: restrictions on use

B59.44   **43.**—(1) A vehicle falling within the recognised category of special vehicles mentioned in article 41 (1) may only be used for—

(a) demonstration;

(b) proceeding to the nearest suitable railway station for conveyance to a port for shipment; or

(c) where no suitable railway facilities are available, proceeding to a port for shipment.

(2) The vehicle must not be used for hire or reward.

(3) The vehicle must not be used in such a way as to cause a danger of injury to any person by reason of—

(a) the condition of the vehicle, its accessories or equipment;

(b) the purpose for which it is used;

(c) the number of passengers carried by it;

(d) the manner in which such passengers are carried;

(e) the weight, position or distribution of any load carried on the vehicle; or

(f) the manner in which any such load is secured.

Track-laying vehicles: consent of road authorities

44.—(1) Before the start of any journey, the user of a vehicle falling within the recognised category of special vehicles mentioned in article 41(1) must obtain from the road authority for each road on which the vehicle is to be used that authority's written consent to the vehicle being used on roads for which it is responsible. **B59.45**

(2) *"Road authority"*, in relation to any road, means the highway authority for that road.

Straddle carriers

Straddle carriers: recognised category

45. Straddle carriers are a recognised category of special vehicles. **B59.46**

Straddle carriers: authorisation requirements

46. The authorisation requirements for straddle carriers are— **B59.47**

(a) the requirements specified in article 47;

(b) the Construction and Use Regulations apart from—

    (i) regulation 7 (length);

    (ii) regulation 8 (width);

    (iii) regulation 11 (overhang);

    (iv) regulation 16(4) (braking systems);

    (v) regulation 18(1A) to (9) (braking; maintenance and efficiency);

    (vi) regulation 22 (springs and resilient material);

    (vii) regulation 66 (plates);

(c) the Authorised Weight Regulations; and

(d) the Lighting Regulations.

Straddle carriers: restrictions on use, speed and width

47.—(1) A straddle carrier may only be used— **B59.48**

(a) for demonstration;

(b) for delivery on sale;

(c) for proceeding to, or returning from, a manufacturer or repairer for construction, repair or overhaul; or

(d) if paragraph (2) applies to it, for proceeding between different parts of the same private premises or between private premises in the immediate neighbourhood.

(2) This paragraph applies to a straddle carrier—

   (a) that does not comply with regulation 11 of the Construction and Use Regulations (overhang); but

   (b) that does comply with regulations 8 (width) and 22 (springs and resilient material) of those Regulations.

(3) Nothing in this Order is to be taken to authorise use on roads beyond a radius of three miles drawn around the outermost perimeter of any work site on private premises.

(4) A straddle carrier must not carry any load.

(5) But a straddle carrier—

   (a) may carry its own necessary gear and equipment; and

   (b) may be laden in the course of any journey permitted under paragraph (1)(d).

(6) A straddle carrier must not travel at speeds exceeding 12 miles per hour.

(7) The overall width of a straddle carrier must not exceed 3 metres.

Straddle carriers: requirements as to length

B59.49   **48.**—(1) This article applies to a straddle carrier where its overall length, together with any forward or rearward projection of a load to be carried on it exceeds 9.2 metres.

(2) The user of the straddle carrier must—

   (a) before the start of any journey, notify in accordance with Schedule 5 the chief officer of police for each area in which the vehicle or vehicle-combination is to be used; and

   (b) ensure that the vehicle is used in accordance with the requirements of that Schedule.

PART 5

MISCELLANEOUS SPECIAL VEHICLES

Vehicles with moveable platforms

B59.50   **49.**—(1) Vehicles fitted with a moveable platform are a recognised category of special vehicles.

(2) The authorisation requirements applicable to vehicles falling within the recognised category of special vehicles mentioned in paragraph (1) are—

   (a) the requirements specified in paragraphs (3) to (5);

   (b) the Construction and Use Regulations, apart from—

      (i) regulations 7, 8 and 11 (length, width and overhang);

      (ii) regulation 20 (wheels and tracks);

      (iii) regulation 23 (wheel loads);

      (iv) regulation 82 (restrictions on wide/long loads or fixed appliances);

   (c) the Authorised Weight Regulations; and

   (d) the Lighting Regulations.

(3) The special equipment of the vehicle must be retracted at all times except when the vehicle is at a place where it is being used to facilitate overhead working.

(4) At all times when the special equipment of the vehicle is retracted, the provisions of the Construction and Use Regulations mentioned in paragraph (2)(b)(i) must be complied with (except that a vehicle that is a locomotive is permitted not to comply with regulation 11 (overhang)).

(5) Any jacks forming part of the vehicle's special equipment which project from the sides of the vehicle must be made clearly visible to any person who may be using the road within a reasonable distance of the vehicle.

(6) In this article—

> *"moveable platform"* means a platform that is attached to, and may be moved by means of, an extensible boom; and

> *"special equipment"*, in relation to a vehicle falling within the recognised category of special vehicles mentioned in paragraph (1), means a moveable platform, the apparatus for moving the platform and any jacks fitted to the vehicle for stabilising it whilst the vehicle is in use.

Pedestrian-controlled road maintenance vehicles

50.—(1) Pedestrian-controlled road maintenance vehicles that are not constructed or used to carry a driver or passenger are a recognised category of special vehicles. **B59.51**

(2) The authorisation requirements applicable to vehicles falling within the recognised category of special vehicles mentioned in paragraph (1) are—

> (a) the requirements specified in paragraphs (3) and (4);
> (b) the Construction and Use Regulations, apart from—
>> (i) regulation 16 (braking systems);
>> (ii) regulation 18(1A) to (9) (maintenance and efficiency of brakes);
>> (iii) regulation 23 (wheel loads);
>> (iv) regulation 61 (emission of smoke);
> (c) the Authorised Weight Regulations; and
> (d) the Lighting Regulations.

(3) The weight of the vehicle (whether laden or unladen) must not exceed 410 kilograms.

(4) The vehicle must be equipped with—

> (a) an efficient braking system capable of bringing the vehicle to a standstill and of being set so as to hold the vehicle stationary; or
> (b) if the vehicle does not have a braking system, sufficient other means capable of achieving the same results.

(5) *"Road maintenance vehicle"* means a motor vehicle that is specially constructed or adapted for the purposes of carrying out one or more of the following operations—

> (a) gritting roads;
> (b) laying road markings;
> (c) clearing frost, snow or ice from roads; or
> (d) any other work of maintaining roads.

Motor vehicles used for cutting grass or trimming hedges

B59.52   51.—(1) Motor cutters are a recognised category of special vehicles.

(2) The authorisation requirements applicable to motor cutters are—

(a) the requirements specified in paragraphs (3) to (5);

(b) the Construction and Use Regulations, apart from—

(i) regulation 8 (width);

(ii) regulation 82(11) (restrictions on wide/long loads or fixed appliances);

(c) the Authorised Weight Regulations; and

(d) the Lighting Regulations.

(3) The overall width of the motor cutter, together with any equipment mounted on it, must not exceed 2.55 metres.

(4) All cutting or trimming blades that form part of the machinery fitted to, or mounted on, the motor cutter must be effectively guarded so that no danger is caused (or is likely to be caused) to any person.

(5) But paragraphs (3) and (4) do not apply at any time when the motor cutter is cutting grass or trimming hedges.

(6) *"Motor cutters"* means motor vehicles that are specially constructed to—

(a) be used as grass cutters and hedge trimmers; and

(b) be controlled by a person other than a pedestrian.

Trailers used for cutting grass or trimming hedges

B59.53   52.—(1) Cutter trailers are a recognised category of special vehicles.

(2) The authorisation requirements applicable to vehicles falling within the recognised category of special vehicles mentioned in paragraph (1) are—

(a) the requirements specified in paragraphs (3) to (7);

(b) the following provisions of the Construction and Use Regulations—

(i) regulation 27 (condition and maintenance of tyres);

(ii) regulation 100 (maintenance and use so as not to be a danger);

(c) the Authorised Weight Regulations; and

(d) the Lighting Regulations.

(3) The overall width of—

(a) the motor vehicle towing the cutter trailer;

(b) the cutter trailer; or

(c) where a cutter trailer is being towed by a motor vehicle in an offset manner, the two vehicles measured as if they were one vehicle;

must not at any time exceed 2.6 metres.

(4) All cutting or trimming blades that form part of the machinery fitted to, or mounted on, the cutter trailer must be effectively guarded so that no danger is caused (or is likely to be caused) to any person.

(5) But—

(a) the restrictions on width applicable to vehicles falling within paragraph (3)(b) or (3)(c); and

(b) paragraph (4);

do not apply at any time when the cutter trailer is cutting grass or trimming hedges.

(6) The unladen weight of a cutter trailer must not exceed—

(a) 1020 kilograms in any case where it is towed by a locomotive, motor tractor or heavy motor car;

(b) 815 kilograms in any other case.

(7) A cutter trailer must not travel at speeds exceeding 20 miles per hour.

(8) *"Cutter trailer"* means a trailer that is specially constructed or adapted for use as a grass cutter and hedge trimmer.

Operational military vehicles

53.—(1) Operational military vehicles are a recognised category of special **B59.54** vehicles in any case where compliance with any regulations made under section 41 of the Road Traffic Act 1988 by any such vehicle would directly compromise the vehicle's operational capability.

(2) The authorisation requirements applicable to operational military vehicles are—

(a) the requirements specified in paragraphs (3) to (5); and

(b) the provisions of—

(i) the Construction and Use Regulations;

(ii) the Authorised Weight Regulations; and

(iii) the Lighting Regulations;

apart from the provisions specified, in respect of the vehicle in question, in the certificate required by paragraph (3).

(3) An operational military vehicle must be certified by the Secretary of State as being a vehicle, or type of vehicle, which for operational reasons cannot comply in all respects with such of the regulations mentioned in paragraph (1) as are specified in the certificate.

(4) An operational military vehicle must be the property of, or under the control of—

(a) the Secretary of State;

(b) a procurement contractor; or

(c) a procurement sub-contractor.

(5) In a case falling within paragraph (4)(b) or (c), the procurement contractor or procurement sub-contractor must, before any particular vehicle or type of vehicle is first used on roads, obtain from the Secretary of State written permission for such use.

(6) *"Operational military vehicles"* means any motor vehicle or trailer that is intended for—

(a) operational use for military action or the carrying out of a strategic, tactical, service or administrative military mission, the process of carrying on combat, including movement, supply, attack, defence and manoeuvres needed to gain the objectives of any battle or campaign or use for military support to the civil community;

(b) training in connection with such operational use;

(c) the carrying or recovery of vehicles or equipment in connection with such operational use or training.

(7) *"Procurement contractor"*, in relation to an operational military vehicle, means a person who, under a contract with the Secretary of State, is engaged in the design, manufacture or delivery of the vehicle with a view to its supply to the Secretary of State or to his direction.

(8) *"Procurement sub-contractor"*, in relation to an operational military vehicle, means a person—

(a) who has (directly or indirectly) entered into any kind of arrangement with a person who is a procurement contractor in relation to the vehicle; and

(b) who is, as a result, responsible for the performance of any of the procurement contractor's obligations under the contract mentioned in paragraph (7).

Track-laying vehicles belonging to Royal National Lifeboat Institution

B59.55   **54.**—(1) RNLI track-laying vehicles are a recognised category of special vehicles.

(2) The authorisation requirements applicable to RNLI track-laying vehicles are—

(a) the requirement specified in paragraph (3); and

(b) regulation 100 of the Construction and Use Regulations (maintenance and use so as not to be a danger).

(3) The vehicle may only be used on roads either—

(a) for the purpose of towing lifeboats; or

(b) in connection with the launching of lifeboats.

(4) *"RNLI track-laying vehicle"* means any track-laying motor vehicle or track-laying trailer that is the property of the Royal National Lifeboat Institution.

Highway testing vehicles

B59.56   **55.**—(1) Highway testing vehicles are a recognised category of special vehicles.

(2) The authorisation requirement applicable to highway testing vehicles is regulation 100 (maintenance and use so as not to be a danger) of the Construction and Use Regulations.

(3) *"Highway testing vehicle"* means any motor vehicle or trailer that is used in, or in connection with, the conduct of experiments or trials of roads or bridges as permitted under section 283 of the Highways Act 1980.

Vehicles propelled by natural gas

B59.57   **56.**—(1) Vehicles propelled by compressed natural gas are a recognised category of special vehicles.

(2) The authorisation requirements applicable to vehicles falling within the recognised category of special vehicles mentioned in paragraph (1) are the requirements specified in Schedule 12.

Article 10(4) and 11(1)(a)   SCHEDULE 1

Abnormal Indivisible Load Vehicles

Part 1

Defined Terms

General

1. In this Schedule—   **B59.58**

   "AILV" means an abnormal indivisible load vehicle within the meaning of paragraph 3;

   "AILV-combination" means a combination of two or more vehicles which includes an AILV;

   "Council Directive 71/320/EEC" means the Council Directive approximating the laws of the Member States relating to the braking devices of certain categories of motor vehicles and their trailers [*O.J. No.L202, September 6, 1971, p.37*]; and

   "semi-trailer" has the same meaning as in the Construction and Use Regulations.

Meaning of abnormal indivisible load

2. In this Order *"abnormal indivisible load"* means a load that cannot without undue   **B59.59**
expense or risk of damage be divided into two or more loads for the purpose of being carried on a road and that—

   (a) on account of its length, width or height, cannot be carried on a motor vehicle of category N3 or a trailer of category O4 (or by a combination of such vehicles) that complies in all respects with Part 2 of the Construction and Use Regulations; or

   (b) on account of its weight, cannot be carried on a motor vehicle of category N3 or a trailer of category O4 (or by a combination of such vehicles) that complies in all respects with—

      (i) the Authorised Weight Regulations (or, if those Regulations do not apply, the equivalent provisions in Part 4 of the Construction and Use Regulations); and

      (ii) Part 2 of the Construction and Use Regulations.

Meaning of abnormal indivisible load vehicle (AILV)

3. In this Order *"abnormal indivisible load vehicle"* means a vehicle of any of the fol-   **B59.60**
lowing descriptions—

   (a) a motor vehicle of category N3 specially designed and constructed for the carriage of abnormal indivisible loads;

   (b) a trailer of category O4 specially designed and constructed for the carriage of abnormal indivisible loads;

   (c) a locomotive specially designed and constructed to tow trailers falling within subparagraph (b); or

   (d) a motor vehicle of category N3 which is not constructed itself to carry a load but which is specially designed and constructed to tow trailers falling within subparagraph (b).

Category 1, 2 or 3 AILVs or AILV-combinations

4.—(1) For the purposes of this Schedule, an AILV or AILV-combination falls within   **B59.61**
Category 1 if—

   (a) it does not exceed the restrictions on vehicle or axle weight specified in paragraphs 28 and 29; and

   (b) it complies with any other requirements imposed by those paragraphs;

and references to a Category 1 AILV or AILV-combination are to be construed accordingly.

(2) For the purposes of this Schedule, an AILV or AILV-combination falls within Category 2 if—

(a) it does not fall within Category 1;

(b) it does not exceed the restrictions on vehicle, axle or wheel weight specified in paragraphs 30 and 31; and

(c) it complies with any other requirements imposed by those paragraphs;

and references to a Category 2 AILV or AILV-combination are to be construed accordingly.

(3) For the purposes of this Schedule, an AILV or AILV-combination falls within Category 3 if—

(a) it does not fall within Category 1 or 2;

(b) it does not exceed the restrictions on vehicle, axle or wheel weight specified in paragraphs 32 and 33; and

(c) it complies with any other requirements imposed by those paragraphs;

and references to a Category 3 AILV or AILV-combination are to be construed accordingly.

Part 2

Construction

Wheeled vehicles

B59.62   **5.** An AILV must be a wheeled vehicle.

Tyres

B59.63   **6.** Every wheel of an AILV must be fitted with a pneumatic tyre.

Braking requirements

B59.64   **7.** Paragraphs 8 to 12 apply to any AILV or AILV-combination which—

(a) falls within Category 2 or 3; and

(b) was manufactured on or after 1st October 1989.

B59.65   **8.**—(1) An AILV or AILV-combination must have a braking system that complies with the construction, fitting and performance requirements specified in sub-paragraph (2).

(2) The construction, fitting and performance requirements are those applicable to motor vehicles of category N3 and trailers of category O4 (according to the configuration of the AILV or AILV-combination) which are set out—

(a) in Annexes I, II and VII to Council Directive 71/320/EEC; and

(b) if appropriate, in Annexes III, IV, V, VI and X to that Directive.

(3) In their application to an AILV or AILV-combination, the requirements specified in sub-paragraph (2) are subject to the modifications in paragraphs 9 to 12.

B59.66   **9.**—(1) The following modifications apply for the purposes of each Type O test conducted in accordance with Annex II to Council Directive 71/320/EEC.

(2) References to a laden vehicle are to be taken to be references to a vehicle laden with the maximum technically permissible mass specified by the manufacturer for the vehicle speed specified for the test.

(3) For a trailer that is designed and constructed for use as part of an AILV-combination falling within Category 3—

(a) where X (stated in the Directive as being a percentage of the force corresponding to the maximum mass carried by the wheels of the stationary vehicle) is specified in paragraph 2.2.1.2.1 of Annex II as having the values of 45 or 50, X is to be taken to have the value of 30; and

(b) where the test speed is specified in that paragraph as 60km/h, the test speed is to be taken to be 48km/h.

(4) In relation to a towing vehicle of category N3 that is designed and constructed for use as part of an AILV-combination falling within Category 3—

(a) if the performance of a service braking device is determined by measuring the stopping distance in relation to the initial speed, the stopping distance in paragraph 2.1.1.1.1 of Annex II is to be taken to be—

$$0.15v + \frac{v^2}{77.5}$$

(b) if the performance of the service braking device is determined by measuring the reaction time and the mean deceleration, the mean braking deceleration at normal engine speed in paragraph 2.1.1.1.1 of Annex II is to be taken to be at least 3 m/s^2 ;

(c) if the performance of a secondary braking device is determined by measuring the stopping distance in relation to the initial speed, the stopping distance in paragraph 2.1.2.1 of Annex II is to be taken to be—

$$0.15v + \frac{v^2}{37.5}$$

(d) if the performance of the secondary braking device is determined by measuring the reaction time and the mean deceleration, the mean braking deceleration in paragraph 2.1.2.1 of Annex II is to be taken to be at least 1.45 m/s^2 .

10.—(1) The requirements of paragraphs 2.2.1.22 and 2.2.2.13 of Annex I to Council **B59.67** Directive 71/320/EEC do not apply.

(2) The requirements of paragraphs 1.1.4.2 and 1.4 of Annex II to Council Directive 71/320/EEC do not apply.

(3) In Annex I to Council Directive 71/320/EEC —

(a) in paragraph 2.2.1.23 the words "not mentioned in item 2.2.1.22 above" do not apply; and

(b) in paragraph 2.2.2.14 the words "not mentioned in item 2.2.2.13 above" do not apply.

11. For the purposes of Type I tests conducted, in accordance with paragraph 1.3 of An- **B59.68** nex II to Council Directive 71/320/EEC, on a vehicle that is designed and constructed for use as part of an AILV-combination falling within Category 3, the reference to a laden vehicle is to be taken to be a reference to a vehicle laden with the heaviest weight possible without the sum of the weights transmitted to the road surface by all the wheels of any one axle exceeding 12,500 kilograms.

12. The requirements of paragraph 2.1.3.2 of Annex II to Council Directive 71/320/EEC **B59.69** do not apply if wheel chocks are provided with the AILV or AILV-combination and the wheel chocks are—

(a) suitable and sufficient;

(b) readily accessible; and

(c) capable, when used in conjunction with any parking brakes fitted to the vehicle, of holding the vehicle stationary when loaded to its maximum mass on a gradient of 12%.

PART 3

PLATES AND SIGNS

Plates

B59.70   13.—(1) An AILV falling within Category 2 or 3 must be equipped with a plate that is—

(a) securely fixed to the vehicle in a conspicuous and readily accessible position;

(b) marked clearly with the words "SPECIAL TYPES USE"; and

(c) indelibly marked with letters and figures, not less than 4 millimetres high, containing the information specified in sub-paragraph (2).

(2) For each of the speeds listed in paragraph (a) to (e), the plate must indicate each of the relevant maximum weights at which, in the opinion of the manufacturer of the vehicle, the AILV may be used when travelling on roads at or below the speed in question—

(a) 20 miles per hour;

(b) 25 miles per hour;

(c) 30 miles per hour;

(d) 35 miles per hour;

(e) 40 miles per hour.

(3) The relevant maximum weights are—

(a) in the case of an AILV that is a motor vehicle—

(i) the maximum axle weight for each axle (within the meaning of the note to item 6 of Part 1 of Schedule 8 to the Construction and Use Regulations);

(ii) the maximum gross weight (within the meaning of the note to item 7 of that Part of that Schedule); and

(iii) the maximum train weight (within the meaning of the note to item 8 of that Part of that Schedule);

(b) in the case of an AILV that is a trailer—

(i) the maximum weight for each axle (within the meaning of the note to item 4 of Part 2 of Schedule 8 to the Construction and Use Regulations);

(ii) the maximum load to be imposed on the towing vehicle (within the meaning of the note to item 5 of that Part of that Schedule); and

(iii) the maximum gross weight (within the meaning of the note to item 6 of that Part of that Schedule).

(4) This paragraph does not apply to any vehicle that was manufactured before 29th July 1983.

B59.71   *[The date of July 29, 1983 referred to in sub-para.(4) above is the date when the Road Vehicles (Marking of Special Weights) Regulations 1983 (SI 1983/910) (not reproduced in this work) came into force.]*

B59.72   14. Where an AILV-combination consists of two or more modules, each module may be fitted with a separate plate if the information required from the plate in relation to the AILV as a whole can be readily determined from the individual plates.

Signs

B59.73   15.—(1) Each AILV or AILV-combination must be fitted with—

(a) a sign that indicates which of Categories 1, 2 or 3 the AILV or AILV-combination falls into; or

(b) a sign that is approved in connection with vehicles carrying loads of exceptional dimensions by the appropriate authority in another EEA State or in any other country which is a member of the United Nations Economic Commission for Europe.

(2) A sign falling within sub-paragraph (1)(a) must—

(a) be mounted in a clearly visible position on the front of the vehicle (or, in the case of an AILV-combination, on the front of the foremost motor vehicle);

(b) face forwards;

(c) be as near to the vertical plane as possible;

(d) be kept clean and unobscured at all times; and

(e) except as stated in sub-paragraph (3), consist of white letters on a black background in the following format (specifying Category 1, 2 or 3, as appropriate to the vehicle in question)—

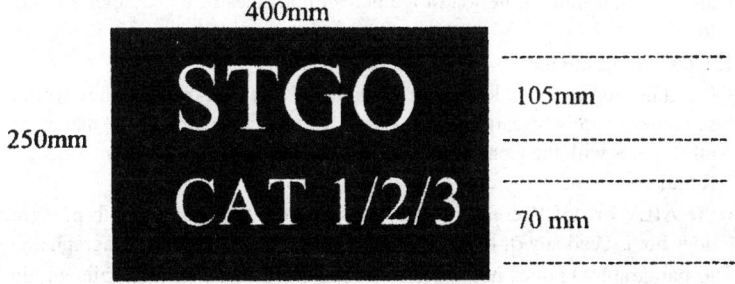

400mm

250mm

STGO

CAT 1/2/3

105mm

70 mm

(3) The dimensions of the sign specified for the purposes of sub-paragraph (2)(e) may vary up or down by a margin of 5 per cent.

Part 4

Conditions Relating to Use

General restrictions

16. An AILV must not be used on roads for, or in connection with, the carriage of any load that may safely be carried on a vehicle (or vehicle-combination) that complies in all respects with the Construction and Use Regulations and the Authorised Weight Regulations.   **B59.74**

17.—(1) Except as stated in paragraph 19, an AILV that falls within paragraph 3(a) or (b) may be used on roads only for, or in connection with—   **B59.75**

(a) the carriage of an abnormal indivisible load; or

(b) the carriage of a load of exceptional width.

(2) Where the overall width of such an AILV exceeds 3 metres, it must not be used for, or in connection with, the carriage of any load except one that can only safely be carried on an AILV with an overall width exceeding 3 metres.

(3) The reference to the carriage of a load of exceptional width is to be construed in accordance with article 28(2).

18.—(1) Except as stated in paragraph 19, an AILV that falls within paragraph 3(c) or (d) may be used on roads only for, or in connection with, the towing of another AILV which is a trailer.   **B59.76**

(2) Where the overall width of such a towing vehicle exceeds 3 metres, it must not be used unless—

(a) the trailer it is towing has an overall width exceeding 3 metres; and

(b) the load can only safely be carried on such a trailer.

19. At any time when an AILV-combination consisting of two or more modules—   **B59.77**

(a) is being used on roads in connection with the carriage of an abnormal indivisible load; but

(b) is not at that time carrying such a load;

the modules may be disassembled into two or more parts so that one part may carry any other.

Restrictions on carriage of multiple loads

B59.78   **20.**—(1) An AILV or AILV-combination may carry only one abnormal indivisible load at any one time.

(2) But that is subject to paragraphs 21 to 23.

B59.79   **21.**—(1) If the conditions specified in sub-paragraph (2) are satisfied, an AILV or AILV-combination which falls within Category 1 may carry—

    (a) two or more abnormal indivisible loads which are of the same character; or

    (b) an abnormal indivisible load together with articles of a character similar to the load.

(2) The conditions are that—

    (a) the abnormal indivisible load or loads to be carried cannot, if they were carried separately, safely be carried on a vehicle (or vehicle-combination) that complies in all respects with the Construction and Use Regulations and the Authorised Weight Regulations; and

    (b) the AILV or AILV-combination carrying items specified in sub-paragraph (1) does not exceed any of the restrictions on weight specified in paragraph 28 or 29.

(3) Sub-paragraph (1) does not apply to an AILV-combination that falls within Category 1 only by virtue of paragraph 28(3).

B59.80   **22.**—(1) If the conditions specified in sub-paragraph (2) are satisfied, an AILV or AILV-combination which falls within Category 1 or 2 may carry two or more abnormal indivisible loads if each load is of the same character, loaded at the same place and carried to the same destination.

(2) The conditions are that—

    (a) each of the abnormal indivisible loads to be carried cannot, if they were carried separately, safely be carried on a vehicle (or vehicle-combination) that complies in all respects with the Construction and Use Regulations and the Authorised Weight Regulations;

    (b) the overall width of any vehicle used does not exceed the width of vehicle necessary to carry the widest single load;

    (c) the overall length of the AILV or the AILV-combination does not exceed the length necessary to carry the longest single load;

    (d) the AILV or AILV-combination carrying the loads specified in sub-paragraph (1) does not exceed—

        (i) for a Category 1 AILV or AILV-combination, any of the restrictions on weight specified in paragraph 28 or 29;

        (ii) for a Category 2 AILV or AILV-combination, any of the restrictions on weight specified in paragraph 30 or 31; and

    (e) the loads carried by virtue of this paragraph are not in addition to any items permitted to be carried by paragraph 21.

B59.81   **23.** An AILV, or AILV-combination, that falls within Category 1 or 2 may carry an abnormal indivisible load consisting of engineering plant, together with constituent parts detached from the plant, if—

    (a) the engineering plant and its detached parts are loaded at the same place and carried to the same destination; and

    (b) the detached parts do not constitute any lateral, forward or rearward projection of the load that exceeds any projection that there would be without those parts.

Maximum width

B59.82   **24.**—(1) An AILV or AILV-combination must not exceed the maximum overall width.

(2) The maximum overall width is exceeded in any case where the overall width of the AILV (or of any AILV in the combination), together with the width of any lateral projection or projections of any load carried on it, exceeds 6.1 metres.

Maximum length

25.—(1) The maximum length of an AILV or AILV-combination used to carry an abnormal indivisible load must not exceed 30 metres.   **B59.83**

(2) The maximum length of an AILV or AILV-combination falling within any of sub-paragraphs (3) to (6) is to be determined in accordance with the sub-paragraph in question.

(3) Where the weight of the load rests wholly on an AILV that is a motor vehicle of category N3, the maximum length of the AILV is the overall length of the motor vehicle together with the length of any forward or rearward projection of the load.

(4) In the case of an AILV-combination that is configured so that the weight of the load rests wholly on a trailer of category O4, the maximum length of the AILV-combination is the overall length of the trailer together with the length of any forward or rearward projection of the load.

(5) In the case of an AILV-combination consisting only of a motor vehicle and a trailer, and which is configured so that the weight of the load rests on both vehicles (whether or not they form an articulated vehicle), the maximum length is the overall length of the trailer together with—

(a) the length of any projection of the load in front of the foremost part of the trailer; and

(b) the length of any rearward projection of the load.

(6) In the case of an AILV-combination (other than one falling within sub-paragraph (4) or (5)) which is configured so that that the weight of the load rests on at least two vehicles, the maximum length is the overall length of all the vehicles that bear the weight of the load together with—

(a) the length of any distance between them; and

(b) the length of any forward or rearward projection of the load.

Restrictions relating to weight: all AILVs and AILV-combinations

26. No AILV or AILV-combination may exceed the restrictions as to weight that apply to a Category 3 AILV or AILV-combination.   **B59.84**

27.—(1) An AILV falling within Category 1 must not exceed any of the maximum weights specified on any plate required to be fitted to it by regulation 66 of the Construction and Use Regulations.   **B59.85**

(2) An AILV falling within Category 2 or 3 must not exceed any of the maximum weights (for the speed at which it is travelling) specified on the plate required to be fitted to it by paragraph 13.

(3) Sub-paragraph (2) does not apply to any trailer first used before 29th July 1983.

Restrictions relating to weight: Category 1 AILVs and AILV-combinations

28.—(1) The total weight of any Category 1 AILV carrying a load must not exceed the maximum authorised weight for a vehicle of that description determined in accordance with Schedule 1 to the Authorised Weight Regulations.   **B59.86**

(2) The total weight of such of the vehicles comprised in a Category 1 AILV-combination as are carrying a load must not exceed 46,000 kilograms.

(3) But the weight restrictions imposed by sub-paragraphs (1) and (2) may be exceeded by a Category 1 AILV-combination if—

(a) the combination has at least 6 axles;

(b) the total weight of the vehicle or vehicles carrying the load does not exceed 50,000 kilograms; and

(c) the combination complies in all other respects with the Authorised Weight Regulations, as those Regulations apply to a vehicle or vehicle-combination of 44,000 kilograms.

(4) Where a Category 1 AILV or AILV-combination is one to which the Authorised Weight Regulations do not apply, references to provisions of those Regulations are to be taken as references to the equivalent provisions of the Construction and Use Regulations.

B59.87   **29.**—(1) The total weight of—

(a) any Category 1 AILV carrying a load; or

(b) such of the vehicles comprised in a Category 1 AILV-combination as are carrying a load;

must be transmitted to the road through 5 or more axles.

(2) In relation to any Category 1 AILV or AILV-combination (including one falling within paragraph 28(3)), the axle weight for an axle of any description must not exceed the maximum authorised weight for an axle of that description determined in accordance with Schedule 3 to the Authorised Weight Regulations.

(3) Where a Category 1 AILV or AILV-combination is one to which the Authorised Weight Regulations do not apply, the reference to Schedule 3 of those Regulations is to be taken as a reference to the equivalent provisions of the Construction and Use Regulations.

Restrictions relating to weight: Category 2 AILVs and AILV-combinations

B59.88   **30.**—(1) The total weight of—

(a) any Category 2 AILV carrying a load; or

(b) such of the vehicles comprised in a Category 2 AILV-combination as are carrying a load;

must not exceed 80,000 kilograms.

(2) Where the weight calculated in accordance with sub-paragraph (3), in relation to any Category 2 AILV or AILV-combination, is less than 80,000 kilograms, the total weight of the vehicle or vehicles described in sub-paragraph (1)(a) or (b) must not exceed that lesser weight.

(3) The weight calculated in accordance with this sub-paragraph is the number (expressed in kilograms) equal to the product of the following equation and then rounded up to the nearest 10 kilograms—

$$D \times 7,500$$

(4) In sub-paragraph (3), D is the distance (measured in metres) between—

(a) in the case of an AILV, the foremost axle and the rearmost axle of the AILV carrying the load;

(b) in the case of an AILV-combination that is an articulated vehicle, the kingpin and the rearmost axle on the semi-trailer; or

(c) in the case of any other description of AILV-combination, the foremost axle and the rearmost axle of the group comprising all those vehicles in the combination that are carrying a load.

B59.89   **31.**—(1) The total weight of—

(a) any Category 2 AILV carrying a load; or

(b) such of the vehicles comprised in a Category 2 AILV-combination as are carrying a load;

must be transmitted to the road through 6 or more axles.

(2) In sub-paragraphs (3) to (5) *"load-bearing vehicle"* means a vehicle mentioned in sub-paragraph (1)(a) or (b).

(3) The distance between any two adjacent axles of a load-bearing vehicle must not be less than 1 metre.

(4) Where the distance between two adjacent axles of a load-bearing vehicle is the

distance specified in column 1 of Table 1, the axle weight must not exceed the weight specified in column 2 and the wheel weight must not exceed the weight specified in column 3.

TABLE 1
CATEGORY 2: AXLES AND WHEELS

Distance between adjacent axles (Column 1)	Axle weight (Column 2)	Wheel weight (Column 3)
Less than 1.35 metres	12,000 kilograms	6,000 kilograms
1.35 metres or more	12,500 kilograms	6,250 kilograms

(5) But where—
   (a) a load-bearing vehicle has axles in two or more groups of axles;
   (b) the distance between the adjacent axles in each group is less than 2 metres; and
   (c) the distance between the adjacent axles in different groups is more than 2 metres;
the sum of the weights transmitted to the road surface by all the wheels in any group must not exceed 50,000 kilograms.

Restrictions relating to weight: Category 3 AILVs and AILV-combinations

32.—(1) The total weight of—   **B59.90**
   (a) any Category 3 AILV carrying a load; or
   (b) such of the vehicles comprised in a Category 3 AILV-combination as are carrying a load;
must not exceed 150,000 kilograms.

(2) Where the weight calculated in accordance with sub-paragraph (3), in relation to any Category 3 AILV or AILV-combination, is less than 150,000 kilograms, the total weight of the vehicle or vehicles described in sub-paragraph (1)(a) or (b) must not exceed that lesser weight.

(3) The weight calculated in accordance with this sub-paragraph is the number (expressed in kilograms) equal to the product of the following equation and then rounded up to the nearest 10 kilograms—

$$D \times 12{,}500$$

(4) In sub-paragraph (3), D is the distance (measured in metres) between—
   (a) in the case of an AILV, the foremost axle and the rearmost axle of the AILV carrying the load;
   (b) in the case of an AILV-combination that is an articulated vehicle, the kingpin and the rearmost axle on the semi-trailer; or
   (c) in the case of any other description of AILV-combination, the foremost axle and the rearmost axle of the group comprising all those vehicles in the combination that are carrying a load.

33.—(1) The total weight of—   **B59.91**
   (a) any Category 3 AILV carrying a load; or
   (b) such of the vehicles comprised in a Category 3 AILV-combination as are carrying a load;
must be transmitted to the road through 6 or more axles.

(2) In sub-paragraphs (3) to (5) *"load-bearing vehicle"* means a vehicle mentioned in sub-paragraph (1)(a) or (b).

(3) The distance between any two adjacent axles of a load-bearing vehicle must not be less than 1 metre.

(4) Where the distance between two adjacent axles of a load-bearing vehicle is the

distance specified in column 1 of Table 2, the axle weight must not exceed the weight specified in column 2 and the wheel weight must not exceed the weight specified in column 3.

TABLE 2
CATEGORY 3: AXLES AND WHEELS

Distance between adjacent axles (Column 1)	Axle weight (Column 2)	Wheel weight (Column 3)
Less than 1.35 metres	15,000 kilograms	7,500 kilograms
1.35 metres or more	16,500 kilograms	8,250 kilograms

(5) But where—

    (a) a load-bearing vehicle has axles in two or more groups of axles;

    (b) the distance between the adjacent axles in each group is less than 1.5 metres; and

    (c) the distance between the adjacent axles in different groups is more than 1.5 metres;

the sum of the weights transmitted to the road surface by all the wheels in any group must not exceed the overall maximum weight.

(6) The overall maximum weight is—

    (a) 90,000 kilograms if the distance specified in sub-paragraph (5)(b) is less than 1.35 metres; and

    (b) 100,000 kilograms in any other case.

Speed restrictions

B59.92   **34.**—(1) An AILV falling within Category 2 or 3 must not exceed any speed specified on the plate required by paragraph 13.

(2) An AILV, or AILV-combination, falling within Category 1, 2 or 3 must not travel on a motorway, dual carriageway or other description of road at speeds exceeding the speed specified in Table 3 for that Category in respect of the description of road in question.

TABLE 3
SPEED RESTRICTIONS FOR CATEGORY 1, 2 OR 3 AILVs OR AILV-COMBINATIONS

AILV or AILV-combination	Motorway	Dual carriageway	Other roads
Category 1	60 mph	50 mph	40 mph
Category 2 or 3	40 mph	35 mph	30 mph

(3) Nothing in this Schedule is to be taken to authorise travel at any speed in excess of any speed restriction imposed by or under any other enactment.

PART 5

APPLICATION OF REGULATIONS MADE UNDER SECTION 41 OF THE ROAD TRAFFIC ACT 1988

Category 1 AILVs and AILV-combinations

B59.93   **35.** Any AILV or AILV-combination falling within Category 1 must, unless it falls within paragraph 37, comply with—

    (a) the Construction and Use Regulations, apart from the provisions of those Regulations specified in Table 4;

    (b) the Authorised Weight Regulations; and

    (c) the Lighting Regulations.

Tᴀʙʟᴇ 4

Cᴀᴛᴇɢᴏʀʏ 1: Cᴏɴsᴛʀᴜᴄᴛɪᴏɴ ᴀɴᴅ Usᴇ Rᴇɢᴜʟᴀᴛɪᴏɴs ᴛʜᴀᴛ Dᴏ Nᴏᴛ Aᴘᴘʟʏ

Non-applicable Regulations	Subject
7	Length
8	Width
80	Over-riding weight regulations
82	Restrictions on use of vehicles carrying wide or long loads

Category 2 or 3 AILVs and AILV-combinations

36. Any AILV or AILV-combination falling within Category 2 or 3 must, unless it falls   **B59.94**
within paragraph 37, comply with—

(a) the Construction and Use Regulations, apart from the provisions of those Regulations specified in Table 5; and

(b) the Lighting Regulations.

Tᴀʙʟᴇ 5

Cᴀᴛᴇɢᴏʀʏ 2 ᴏʀ 3: Cᴏɴsᴛʀᴜᴄᴛɪᴏɴ ᴀɴᴅ Usᴇ Rᴇɢᴜʟᴀᴛɪᴏɴs ᴛʜᴀᴛ Dᴏ Nᴏᴛ Aᴘᴘʟʏ

Non-applicable Regulations	Subject
7	Length
8	Width
15, 16	Braking systems
18(1A) to (9)	Maintenance and efficiency of brakes
25	Tyre loads and speed ratings
64	Spray suppression devices
65	Maintenance of spray suppression devices
75(1), in so far as it relates to items 1–4, 6–11, 15 and 16 of the Table	Maximum permitted laden weight of vehicle
76 to 80	Other maximum permitted weight limits of vehicle and trailer, other than articulated vehicle
82	Restrictions on use of vehicles carrying wide or long loads
83(1)	Number of trailers

[The remaining items in the Table referred to in reg.75(1) continue to apply, in   **B59.95**
the terms there stated, to any AILV (or vehicle included in an AILV combination)
which is a wheeled agricultural motor vehicle (see Item 5), a wheeled locomotive
(see Item 12), a track laying locomotive (see Item 13) or a locomotive not
described in Items 5, 12 or 13 (see Item 14).]

AILVs manufactured before 1st October 1989

37. Instead of paragraphs 35 and 36, article 18(2)(p) of the Motor Vehicles (Authorisa-   **B59.96**
tion of Special Types) General Order 1979 [*SI 1979/1198*] continues to apply to any AILV
manufactured before 1st October 1989, to the same extent as it applied before the coming
into force of this Schedule.

SCHEDULE 2

MOBILE CRANES

PART 1

DEFINED TERMS

General

B59.97   1. In this Schedule—

"*Goods Vehicles Type Approval Regulations*" means the requirements applicable to goods vehicles which are prescribed by regulations made under section 54(1) of the Road Traffic Act 1988; and

"*manufacturer*" —

(a) in relation to a mobile crane constructed with a chassis that has not previously formed part of another vehicle, means the person by whom that chassis was made; and

(b) in relation to any other mobile crane, means the person by whom that mobile crane was constructed or adapted.

Meaning of mobile crane

B59.98   2.—(1) In this Order "*mobile crane*" means a motor vehicle which satisfies the five conditions specified in sub-paragraphs (2) to (6).

(2) The first condition is that the motor vehicle is specially designed and constructed, or is specially adapted, for the special purposes of lifting operations that cannot safely be carried out by a motor vehicle or trailer that complies in all respects with—

(a) the Construction and Use Regulations;

(b) the Authorised Weight Regulations; and

(c) the Goods Vehicles Type Approval Regulations.

(3) The second condition is that the gross weight of the crane exceeds 12,000 kilograms.

(4) The third condition is that the motor vehicle has crane apparatus permanently mounted as part of the vehicle chassis design.

(5) The fourth condition is that the motor vehicle is operated by a driver or other person riding on it.

(6) The fifth condition is that the motor vehicle meets the requirements for registered use as a mobile crane under Part 4 of Schedule 1 to the Vehicle and Excise Registration Act 1994.

(7) Any other motor vehicle which satisfies these conditions, but which does not comply in all respects with the authorisation requirements for mobile cranes specified in this Schedule, may nevertheless fall within the recognised category of special vehicles consisting of engineering plant if it satisfies the conditions specified in paragraph 2 of Schedule 3 and complies with the authorisation requirements applicable to engineering plant.

Category A, B or C mobile cranes

B59.99   3.—(1) For the purposes of this Schedule, a mobile crane falls within Category A if—

(a) it does not exceed the restrictions on plated vehicle or axle weight specified in paragraph 30; and

(b) it complies with any other requirements imposed by that paragraph;

and references to a Category mobile cranes are to be construed accordingly.

(2) For the purposes of this Schedule, a mobile crane falls within Category B if—

(a) it does not fall within Category A;

(b) it does not exceed the restrictions on plated vehicle or axle weight specified in paragraph 31; and

(c) it complies with any other requirements imposed by that paragraph;
and references to a Category B mobile crane are to be construed accordingly.

(3) For the purposes of this Schedule, a mobile crane falls within Category C if—

(a) it does not fall within Category A or B;

(b) it does not exceed the restrictions on plated vehicle or axle weight specified in paragraph 32; and

(c) it complies with any other requirements imposed by that paragraph;
and references to a Category C mobile crane are to be construed accordingly.

PART 2

CONSTRUCTION

Wheeled vehicles

4. A mobile crane must be a wheeled vehicle.   **B59.100**

Tyres

5. Every wheel of a mobile crane must be fitted with a pneumatic tyre.   **B59.101**

Suspension

6. A mobile crane must have suspension on all axles.   **B59.102**

Braking requirements

7. A mobile crane must be fitted with—   **B59.103**

(a) an efficient brake capable of braking the mobile crane at the maximum weight permitted under paragraphs 28 to 32 for a mobile crane of the Category in question when travelling at the maximum speeds for that Category permitted by this Schedule; and

(b) an efficient parking brake capable of holding the mobile crane stationary when necessary.

8.—(1) A mobile crane is to be treated as being fitted with a brake that complies with   **B59.104**
paragraph 7 if it is fitted with a braking system that meets the construction, fitting and performance requirements for motor vehicles of category N3 set out—

(a) in Annexes I, II and VII to Council Directive 71/320/EEC; and

(b) if appropriate, in Annexes III, IV, V, VI and X to that Directive.

(2) But, in their application to a mobile crane which has a maximum axle weight exceeding 12,500 kilograms, those requirements are subject to the modifications in paragraphs 9 to 12.

9.—(1) The following modifications apply for the purposes of each Type O test   **B59.105**
conducted in accordance with Annex II to Council Directive 71/320/EEC.

(2) References to a laden vehicle are to be taken to be references to a vehicle laden with the maximum technically permissible mass specified by the manufacturer for the vehicle speed specified for the test.

(3) If the performance of a service braking device is determined by measuring the stopping distance in relation to the initial speed, the stopping distance in paragraph 2.1.1.1.1 of Annex II is to be taken to be—

$$0.15v + \frac{v^2}{77.5}$$

(4) If the performance of the service braking device is determined by measuring the re-

action time and the mean deceleration, the mean braking deceleration at normal engine speed in paragraph 2.1.1.1.1 of Annex II is to be taken to be at least 3 m/s² .

(5) If the performance of a secondary braking device is determined by measuring the stopping distance in relation to the initial speed, the stopping distance in paragraph 2.1.2.1 of Annex II is to be taken to be—

$$0.15v + \frac{v^2}{37.5}$$

(6) If the performance of the secondary braking device is determined by measuring the reaction time and the mean deceleration, the mean braking deceleration in paragraph 2.1.2.1 of Annex II is to be taken to be at least 1.45 m/s² .

B59.106   10.—(1) The requirements of paragraphs 2.2.1.22 and 2.2.2.13 of Annex I to Council Directive 71/320/EEC do not apply.

(2) The requirements of paragraphs 1.1.4.2 and 1.4 of Annex II to Council Directive 71/320/EEC do not apply.

(3) In Annex I to Council Directive 71/320/EEC —

(a) in paragraph 2.2.1.23 the words "not mentioned in item 2.2.1.22 above" do not apply; and

(b) in paragraph 2.2.2.14 the words "not mentioned in item 2.2.2.13 above" do not apply.

B59.107   11. For the purposes of Type I tests conducted, in accordance with paragraph 1.3 of Annex II to Council Directive 71/320/EEC, on a mobile crane falling within paragraph 9(3) of this Schedule, the reference to a laden vehicle is to be taken to be a reference to a vehicle laden with the heaviest weight possible without the sum of the weights transmitted to the road surface by all the wheels of any one axle exceeding 12,500 kilograms.

B59.108   12. The requirements of paragraph 2.1.3.2 of Annex II to Council Directive 71/320/EEC do not apply if wheel chocks are provided with the mobile crane and the wheel chocks are—

(a) suitable and sufficient;

(b) readily accessible; and

(c) capable, when used in conjunction with any parking brakes fitted to the vehicle, of holding the vehicle stationary when loaded to its maximum mass on a gradient of 12 per cent.

Design speed

B59.109   13.—(1) A mobile crane that is specially adapted for the special purposes of lifting operations (as mentioned in paragraph 2(2)) must, when that adaptation is carried out, also be adapted as necessary so that it may operate on roads at speeds of 25 miles per hour or more.

(2) Any other mobile crane must be designed and constructed to operate on roads at speeds of 25 miles per hour or more.

Warning beacon

B59.110   14. A warning beacon emitting an amber light must be fitted to a mobile crane.

PART 3

PLATES

B59.111   15.—(1) A mobile crane must be equipped with a plate that is—

(a) securely fixed to the mobile crane in a conspicuous and readily accessible position; and

(b) indelibly marked with letters and figures, not less than 6 millimetres high, containing the information relating to the mobile crane which is specified in sub-paragraph (2).

(2) The information is—

(a) the maximum axle weight for each axle, determined in accordance with sub-paragraph (3); and

(b) the maximum gross weight, determined in accordance with that sub-paragraph.

(3) A maximum weight is determined in accordance with this sub-paragraph if—

(a) in the case of a vehicle which is specially adapted to be a mobile crane and to which the Goods Vehicles Type Approval Regulations applied immediately before such adaptation, it is the maximum weight at or below which the vehicle is considered fit for use by the Secretary of State; and

(b) in any other case, it is the maximum weight at or below which the mobile crane is considered fit for use by the manufacturer of the mobile crane.

(4) In determining a maximum weight for the purposes of sub-paragraph (3), the person making the determination must have regard to—

(a) the design, construction and equipment of the mobile crane; and

(b) the stresses to which it is likely to be subject when in use.

16.—(1) Where, in accordance with regulation 66 (plates for goods vehicles and buses) or 71 (marking of weights on certain vehicles) of the Construction and Use Regulations, a mobile crane is already fitted with a plate ("the original plate"), paragraph 15 does not require the crane— **B59.112**

(a) to be fitted with an additional plate; or

(b) to have additional information stamped on the original plate;

if the condition set out in sub-paragraph (2) is satisfied.

(2) The condition is that, at all times when the mobile crane is used on roads the gross weight of the crane does not exceed either the maximum gross weight stated on the original plate or, if no gross weight is so stated, the maximum unladen weight stated on the original plate.

17.—(1) In this paragraph *"qualified person"* means— **B59.113**

(a) the manufacturer of the vehicle (or a person duly authorised on his behalf);

(b) a person carrying on business as a manufacturer of motor vehicles or trailers (or a person duly authorised on his behalf); or

(c) a person authorised under this sub-paragraph by the Secretary of State.

(2) No person may make any alteration to a mobile crane with a view to making it fit for use at any weight exceeding the weights stated on a plate fitted to it as mentioned in paragraph 15 or 16 unless he is a qualified person.

(3) Where such an alteration is made—

(a) the existing plate must be updated to show, for each description of maximum weight referred to in paragraph 15(2)(a) or (b), the new maximum at or below which the qualified person considers that the mobile crane will then be fit for use; or

(b) an additional plate must be added showing such new maximum weights.

(4) The following details must also be shown on the plate that shows the new weights—

(a) the name of the qualified person;

(b) an indication that he is the person responsible for determining the new weights; and

(c) where he is a qualified person authorised by the Secretary of State under sub-paragraph (1)(c), an indication of that fact.

(5) In determining a maximum weight for the purposes of sub-paragraph (3), the qualified person must have regard to—

(a) the design, construction and equipment of the mobile crane;

(b) the alterations made to it; and

(c) the stresses to which it is likely to be subject when in use.

B59.114   **18.** Any additional plate that is specially fitted to a vehicle in order to comply with paragraph 15 or 17(3)(b) must be marked clearly with the words "SPECIAL TYPES USE".

PART 4

CONDITIONS RELATING TO USE

General restrictions

B59.115   **19.** A mobile crane may only be used on roads for—

(a) testing;

(b) demonstration;

(c) delivery on sale;

(d) proceeding to, or returning from, a manufacturer or repairer;

(e) proceeding to, or returning from, the site of lifting operations; or

(f) carrying out such operations.

B59.116   **20.** A mobile crane that has an overall width exceeding 3 metres may only be used on roads for, or in connection with, lifting operations that are of the character that the mobile crane is specially designed and constructed, or adapted, to carry out.

B59.117   **21.**—(1) When a mobile crane is used on roads, the beacon fitted to it under paragraph 14 must be kept lit—

(a) when the crane is stationary at the site of the operations at which it is to be used; or

(b) when the crane is unable, on account of the weather conditions or otherwise, to maintain speeds appropriate to the road.

(2) But, in the circumstances described in sub-paragraph (1)(a), the beacon may be switched off if—

(a) there is no reasonable prospect of the presence of the mobile crane causing a hazard to persons using the road (so that it is not necessary or desirable to warn persons of its presence); or

(b) it is likely that the use of the beacon could confuse or mislead other road users.

Restriction on carriage of loads etc

B59.118   **22.**—(1) Any mobile crane that is used on roads must not—

(a) carry any load; or

(b) transport any goods or burden.

(2) But that is subject to paragraphs 23 and 24.

B59.119   **23.** A mobile crane may carry its own necessary gear and equipment.

B59.120   **24.** A mobile crane may lift or transport goods or burden in the course of carrying out lifting operations.

Restriction on towing trailers

B59.121   **25.** A mobile crane must not tow any trailer.

Maximum width

B59.122   **26.** The overall width of a mobile crane, together with the width of any lateral projection or projections of any load carried on it in accordance with this Schedule, must not exceed 6.1 metres.

Maximum length

B59.123   **27.** The overall length of a mobile crane, together with any forward or rearward projections of any load carried on it in accordance with this Schedule, must not exceed 30 metres.

Restrictions relating to weight: all mobile cranes

28. No mobile crane may exceed any of the restrictions as to weight that apply to a Category C mobile crane.

B59.124

29. No mobile crane may exceed—

B59.125

    (a) any of the maximum weights, as determined by paragraphs 30 to 32, which are specified on the plate or plates fitted to it in accordance with paragraphs 15 to 18; or,

    (b) in the case of a Category C mobile crane, such lesser maximum weight as may result from the calculation set out in paragraph 32(3).

Restrictions relating to weight: Category A mobile cranes

30.—(1) For a Category A mobile crane, the maximum axle weight that may be specified on the plate fitted to it in accordance with paragraphs 15 to 18 is—

B59.126

    (a) 11,500 kilograms for a single driving axle; and

    (b) 10,000 kilograms for a single non-driving axle.

(2) No Category A mobile crane may have more than four axles.

(3) For a Category A mobile crane with the number of axles specified in column 1 of an entry in Table 6—

    (a) the distance between the two outermost axles of the crane must be at least the length specified in column 2 of the same entry; and

    (b) the maximum gross weight of the crane that may be specified on the plate fitted to the crane in accordance with paragraphs 15 to 18 is the weight specified in column 3 of the same entry.

TABLE 6
CATEGORY A: AXLES AND GROSS WEIGHT

Number of axles	Minimum distance between outermost axles	Maximum gross weight of crane
(Column 1)	*(Column 2)*	*(Column 3)*
2	3 metres	20,000 kilograms
3	5 metres	30,000 kilograms
4	6 metres	36,000 kilograms

Restrictions relating to weight: Category B mobile cranes

31.—(1) For a Category B mobile crane, the maximum axle weight that may be specified on the plate fitted to it in accordance with paragraphs 15 to 18 is 12,500 kilograms.

B59.127

(2) The maximum gross weight of a Category B mobile crane that may be specified on the plate fitted to it in accordance with paragraphs 15 to 18 is the number (expressed in kilograms) equal to the product of the following equation and then rounded up to the nearest 10 kilograms—

$$N \times 12{,}500$$

(3) In sub-paragraph (2), N is the number of axles on the crane.

Restrictions relating to weight: Category C mobile cranes

32.—(1) For a Category C mobile crane, the maximum axle weight that may be specified on the plate fitted to it in accordance with paragraphs 15 to 18 is 16,500 kilograms.

B59.128

(2) The maximum gross weight of a Category C mobile crane that may be specified on the plate fitted to it in accordance with paragraphs 15 to 18 is 150,000 kilograms.

(3) But where, in respect of any particular Category C mobile crane, the weight

calculated in accordance with sub-paragraph (4) is less than 150,000 kilograms, the gross weight of that crane must not exceed that lesser weight.

(4) The weight calculated in accordance with this sub-paragraph is the number (expressed in kilograms) equal to the product of the following equation and then rounded up to the nearest 10 kilograms—

$$N \times 16,500$$

(5) In sub-paragraph (4), N is the number of axles on the crane.

Speed restrictions

B59.129   33.—(1) A mobile crane falling within Category A, B or C must not travel on a motorway, dual carriageway or other description of road at speeds exceeding the speed specified in Table 7 for that Category in respect of the description of road in question.

TABLE 7

SPEED RESTRICTIONS FOR CATEGORY A, B OR C MOBILE CRANES

Category of mobile crane	Motorway	Dual carriageway	Other roads
Category A	60 mph	50 mph	40 mph
Category B	50 mph	45 mph	40 mph
Category C	40 mph	35 mph	30 mph

(2) Nothing in this Schedule is to be taken to authorise travel at—

(a) any speed in excess of any speed restriction imposed by or under any other enactment; or

(b) in the case of a mobile crane referred to in paragraph 2(7) which falls within the recognised category of special vehicles consisting of engineering plant, any speed in excess of those specified in paragraph 20 of Schedule 3.

PART 5

APPLICATION OF REGULATIONS MADE UNDER SECTION 41 OF THE ROAD TRAFFIC ACT 1988

Category A mobile cranes

B59.130   34.—(1) A Category A mobile crane must comply with—

(a) the Construction and Use Regulations, apart from the provisions of those Regulations specified in Table 8; and

(b) the Lighting Regulations.

TABLE 8

CATEGORY A: CONSTRUCTION AND USE REGULATIONS THAT DO NOT APPLY

Non-applicable Regulations	Subject
8	Width
80	Over-riding weight regulations

Category B or C mobile cranes

B59.131   35.—(1) A Category B or C mobile crane must comply with—

(a) the Construction and Use Regulations, apart from the provisions of those Regulations specified in Table 9; and

(b) the Lighting Regulations.

(2) But regulations 49, 51, 64 and 65 are disapplied in relation to a Category B or C

mobile crane only to the extent that it is not possible for the crane to comply with those regulations on account of the need to perform the lifting operations that it is specially designed and constructed (or specially adapted) to carry out.

TABLE 9

CATEGORIES B OR C: CONSTRUCTION AND USE REGULATIONS THAT DO NOT APPLY

Non-applicable Regulations	Subject
7	Length
8	Width
15, 16	Braking systems
18(1A) to (9)	Maintenance and efficiency of brakes
25	Tyre loads and speed ratings
49	Rear under-run protection
51	Sideguards
64	Spray suppression devices
65	Maintenance of spray suppression devices
75 to 80	Other maximum permitted weight limits of vehicle and trailer, other than articulated vehicle
82	Restrictions on use of vehicles carrying wide or long loads

Article 10(4) and 11(1)(a)   SCHEDULE 3

ENGINEERING PLANT

PART 1

DEFINED TERMS

General

1. In this Schedule—   **B59.132**

   "Goods Vehicles Type Approval Regulations" means the requirements applicable to goods vehicles which are prescribed by regulations made under section 54(1) of the Road Traffic Act 1988;

   "slow" has the meaning given in paragraph 20(2); and

   "wheel-track combination vehicle" means a track-laying vehicle designed and constructed so that the weight of the vehicle is transmitted to the road surface by a combination of wheels and continuous tracks.

Meaning of engineering plant

2.—(1) In this Order *"engineering plant"* means any moveable plant or equipment   **B59.133** which is a motor vehicle or trailer and which—

   (a) in the case of a motor vehicle that falls within the definition of a mobile crane in paragraph 2 of Schedule 2, satisfies the conditions specified in sub-paragraphs (2) to (5) of this paragraph;

   (b) in any other case, satisfies the conditions specified in sub-paragraphs (2) to (4) of this paragraph.

(2) The first condition is that the motor vehicle or trailer is specially designed and constructed for the special purposes of engineering operations that cannot safely be carried out by a motor vehicle or trailer that complies in all respects with—

   (a) the Construction and Use Regulations; and

   (b) the Goods Vehicles Type Approval Regulations.

(3) The second condition is that the motor vehicle or trailer is not constructed to carry any load apart from a load of a description specified in paragraph 13(2).

(4) The third condition is that the motor vehicle or trailer is operated by a driver or other person riding on it.

(5) The fourth condition is that the motor vehicle does not comply in all respects with the authorisation requirements for mobile cranes specified in Schedule 2.

Part 2

Construction

Wheeled or track-laying vehicles

B59.134   3. Engineering plant must be a wheeled vehicle, a track-laying vehicle or a wheel-track combination vehicle.

Provisions applying to wheeled vehicles

B59.135   4.—(1) Any wheel of engineering plant which is not fitted with a pneumatic tyre of soft or elastic material must be fitted with a smooth tyre and have the edges rounded to a radius of not less than 12 millimetres and not more than 25 millimetres.

(2) But, in the case of plant which is a gritting machine designed for use (and used) for gritting frosted and icebound roads, any tyre of the gritting machine may be fitted with diagonal cross bars which—

(a) are of equal width (which must not be less than 25 millimetres);

(b) extend the full breadth of the tyre; and

(c) are arranged so that the distance between the adjacent cross bars is not greater than the width of the crossbars.

(3) A tyre is not to be taken to be of soft or elastic material unless the material—

(a) is continuous around the circumference of the wheel, or fitted in sections so that, as far as is reasonably practicable, no space is left between the ends of each section;

(b) is of a thickness and design that, as far as is reasonably practicable, minimises vibration when the vehicle is in motion; and

(c) is free from any defect which might in any way cause damage to the surface of a road.

B59.136   5. Engineering plant which has wheels and may (in accordance with paragraph 21) travel on roads at speeds exceeding those specified for slow plant in paragraph 20, must be fitted with tyres marked with a load and speed rating that is greater than the maximum load and speed that the plant can achieve when used on roads under its own power.

Braking requirements

B59.137   6. Engineering plant that is designed and constructed to operate on roads at speeds exceeding 12 miles per hour must be fitted with a braking system that complies with regulation 16 of the Construction and Use Regulations.

B59.138   7.—(1) Any other engineering plant must be fitted with—

(a) an efficient brake capable of braking the vehicle at the maximum weight permitted under paragraphs 17 to 19 when travelling at the maximum speed permitted by this Schedule; and

(b) an efficient parking brake capable of holding the vehicle stationary when necessary.

(2) In the case of engineering plant that is a motor vehicle propelled by steam—

(a) the requirements of sub-paragraph (1)(a) are to be treated as met if the vehicle has an engine capable of being reversed; and

(b) the requirements of sub-paragraph (1)(b) are to be treated as met if the engine can be set to hold the vehicle stationary.

(3) Where engineering plant cannot be fitted with a parking brake on account of the nature of the engineering operations that it is specially designed and constructed to carry out, the requirements of sub-paragraph (1)(b) are to be treated as met if suitable scotches (or similar devices capable of holding the vehicle stationary when necessary) are fitted.

PART 3

CONDITIONS RELATING TO USE

General restrictions

8. Engineering plant must not be used on roads for, or in connection with, engineering operations of any description if those operations may safely be carried out by a vehicle that complies in all respects with the Construction and Use Regulations and the Goods Vehicles Type Approval Regulations.   **B59.139**

9. Engineering plant may only be used on roads for—   **B59.140**
  (a) testing;
  (b) demonstration;
  (c) delivery on sale;
  (d) proceeding to, or returning from, a manufacturer or repairer for repair or mainte-
      nance;
  (e) proceeding to, or returning from, the site of engineering operations; or
  (f) carrying out such operations.

10. Engineering plant which has an overall width exceeding 3 metres may only be used   **B59.141**
on roads for, or in connection with, engineering operations that are of the character that the plant is specially designed and constructed to carry out.

Restrictions on carriage of loads etc

11.—(1) Engineering plant which is used on roads must not—   **B59.142**
  (a) carry any load; or
  (b) lift or transport goods or burden.

(2) But that is subject to paragraphs 12 and 13.

12. Engineering plant may carry its own necessary gear and equipment.   **B59.143**

13.—(1) This paragraph applies at any time when engineering plant is engaged on the   **B59.144**
construction, maintenance or repair of roads.

(2) Engineering plant may carry—
  (a) materials that have been excavated and raised from the ground by apparatus on the
      plant; or
  (b) materials that the plant is specially designed to treat while carried on the plant.

Restrictions on towing of trailers

14.—(1) Except as stated in sub-paragraph (2), engineering plant must not tow a trailer.   **B59.145**

(2) Engineering plant falling within sub-paragraph (3) may tow—
  (a) a trailer which is itself engineering plant; or
  (b) a living van or office hut used in connection with the construction, maintenance or
      repair of roads.

(3) Engineering plant falls within this sub-paragraph if it is a motor vehicle with an overall length that does not exceed 8 metres.

Maximum width

15. The overall width of engineering plant, together with the width of any lateral projec-   **B59.146**
tion or projections of any load carried on it in accordance with this Schedule, must not exceed 6.1 metres.

Maximum length

B59.147   16. The overall length of engineering plant (or of any vehicle-combination permitted by this Schedule), together with any forward or rearward projections of any load carried on it in accordance with this Schedule, must not exceed 30 metres.

Restrictions relating to weight: gross weight

B59.148   17.—(1) The gross weight of engineering plant, together with the weight of any load carried on it in accordance with this Schedule, must not exceed 150,000 kilograms.

(2) The weight of the plant is to be calculated—

(a) in the case of plant which is a motor vehicle, by taking the sum of the weights transmitted to the road surface by all the wheels and tracks of the vehicle;

(b) in the case of plant which is a trailer, by taking the sum of the weights transmitted to the road surface by all the wheels and tracks of the trailer and of any weight of the trailer imposed on the towing vehicle.

Restrictions relating to weight: weight transmitted to road surface

B59.149   18.—(1) This paragraph applies to determine the maximum weight that may be transmitted to the road surface by the wheels of any engineering plant that is a wheeled vehicle or a wheel-track combination vehicle.

(2) The wheel weight of the plant must not exceed 11,250 kilograms.

(3) The weight transmitted to any strip of road surface on which the wheels of the plant are resting must not exceed the following limits (measuring the strip of road surface referred to in those limits as the distance contained between any two parallel lines drawn on the road surface at right angles to the longitudinal axis of the plant)—

(a) if the strip of road surface measures a distance of 0.5 metre or less, the weight must not exceed 45,000 kilograms;

(b) if the strip of road surface measures a distance that lies between 0.5 metre and any greater distance up to, and including, 2 metres, the weight must not exceed the sum of—

(i) 45,000 kilograms; and

(ii) an additional weight allowance which is to be calculated by reference to the difference between 0.5 metre and the overall measurement of the strip of road surface, with additional weight being allowed in respect of that difference at a rate of 30,000 kilograms per metre;

(c) if the strip of road surface measures a distance of more than 2 metres, the weight must not exceed the sum of—

(i) the weight determined in accordance with paragraph (b), as calculated in respect of the first 2 metres of the measurement of the strip of road surface; and

(ii) a further additional weight allowance which is to be calculated by reference to the difference between 2 metres and the overall measurement of the strip of road surface, with further additional weight being allowed in respect of that difference at a rate of 10,000 kilograms per metre.

(4) But where the plant has one or more wheels that are not fitted with a pneumatic tyre, the total weight transmitted to the road surface by—

(a) any such wheel (if no other wheel is in the same line transversely); or

(b) all such wheels as are in line transversely;

must be such that the average weight per 25 millimetres width of tyre in contact with the road surface does not exceed 750 kilograms.

B59.150   19.—(1) This paragraph applies to determine the maximum weight that may be transmitted to the road surface by the tracks of any engineering plant that is a track-laying vehicle or a wheel-track combination vehicle.

(2) The weight transmitted to any strip of road surface on which each track of the plant is resting must not exceed the following (measuring the strip of road surface referred to in those limits as the distance contained between any two parallel lines drawn on the road surface at right angles to the longitudinal axis of the plant)—

(a) if the strip of road surface measures a distance of 0.5 metre or less, the weight must not exceed 11,500 kilograms;

(b) if the strip of road surface measures a distance that lies between 0.5 metre and any greater distance up to, and including, 2 metres, the weight must not exceed the sum of—

  (i) 11,500 kilograms; and

  (ii) an additional weight allowance which is to be calculated by reference to the difference between 0.5 metre and the overall measurement of the strip of road surface, with additional weight being allowed in respect of that difference at a rate of 7,500 kilograms per metre;

(c) if the strip of road surface measures a distance of more than 2 metres, the weight must not exceed the sum of—

  (i) the weight determined in accordance with paragraph (b), as calculated in respect of the first 2 metres of the measurement of the strip of road surface; and

  (ii) a further additional weight allowance, which is to be calculated by reference to the difference between 2 metres and the overall measurement of the strip of road surface, with further additional weight being allowed in respect of that difference at a rate of 2,500 kilograms per metre.

Speed restrictions

20.—(1) Unless paragraph 21 applies, engineering plant must not travel on roads at speeds exceeding—   **B59.151**

(a) 30 miles per hour on a motorway; or

(b) 12 miles per hour on any other road.

(2) Engineering plant falling within sub-paragraph (1) is referred to in this Schedule as slow plant.

21.—(1) This paragraph—   **B59.152**

(a) applies to any engineering plant that satisfies the speed condition specified in sub-paragraph (2), and to any vehicle-combination that includes engineering plant and that satisfies that condition; but

(b) does not apply to engineering plant mentioned in paragraph 2(1)(a).

(2) The speed condition is that the plant or vehicle-combination would be able to comply with such requirements of Schedule 1 to this Order as are specified in sub-paragraph (3), if those requirements applied to it as they apply to an AILV (or AILV-combination) falling within Category 1, 2 or 3.

(3) The requirements of Schedule 1 referred to in sub-paragraph (2) are—

(a) the requirements as to brakes, plates and signs in paragraphs 7 to 15;

(b) the requirements as to weight in paragraphs 26 to 33; and

(c) such of the requirements of the Construction and Use Regulations, the Authorised Weight Regulations and the Lighting Regulations as are specified in paragraph 35 or 36.

(4) For the purposes of the remaining provisions of this Schedule, any engineering plant, or vehicle-combination that includes engineering plant, which complies with the requirements applicable to an AILV (or AILV-combination) falling within Category 1, 2, or 3 (as the case may be) is itself to be treated as falling within the Category in question.

22.—(1) Engineering plant, or a vehicle-combination that includes engineering plant, which falls within Category 1, 2 or 3 must not travel on a motorway, dual carriageway or   **B59.153**

other description of road at speeds exceeding the speed specified in Table 10 for that Category in respect of the description of road in question.

TABLE 10

Speed Restrictions for Engineering Plant Treated as Falling within Category 1, 2 or 3

Vehicle or vehicle-combination	Motorway	Dual carriageway	Other roads
Category 1	60 mph	50 mph	40 mph
Category 2 or 3	40 mph	35 mph	30 mph

(2) But where the plant or vehicle-combination does not have suspension on all axles, the plant or vehicle-combination must not travel at speeds exceeding 20 miles per hour.

B59.154   **23.** Nothing in this Schedule is to be taken to authorise travel at any speed in excess of any speed restriction imposed by or under any other enactment.

PART 4

Application of Regulations made under Section 41 of the Road Traffic Act 1988

Engineering plant treated as falling within Category 1, 2 or 3

B59.155   **24.** Engineering plant, or a vehicle-combination that includes engineering plant, which falls within Category 1, 2 or 3 must comply with—

(a) the Construction and Use Regulations;

(b) the Authorised Weight Regulations; and

(c) the Lighting Regulations;

to the same extent as an AILV (or AILV-combination) falling within the same Category must, by virtue of paragraph 35 or 36 of Schedule 1, comply with those Regulations.

Slow plant

B59.156   **25.**—(1) Slow plant must comply with—

(a) the Construction and Use Regulations, apart from the provisions of those Regulations specified in Table 11 and, in the case of slow plant to which any of paragraphs 26 to 29 apply, apart from such additional provisions of those Regulations as are specified in the paragraph in question; and

(b) the Lighting Regulations.

(2) But regulation 16 of the Construction and Use Regulations (braking systems) does apply to slow plant that is a wheeled motor vehicle.

TABLE 11

Slow Plant: Construction and Use Regulations that Do Not Apply to Any Slow Plant

Non-applicable Regulations	Subject
7	Length
8	Width
10A to 14	Other provisions as to dimensions and manoeuvrability
15, 16	Braking systems
17	Vacuum or pressure brake warning devices
18(1A) to (9)	Maintenance and efficiency of brakes
19	Application of brakes of trailers

Non-applicable Regulations	Subject
20 to 22, 24 to 26	Wheels, springs, tyres and tracks
35 to 36C	Instruments and equipment
39A, 39B	Fuel
49 to 53B	Protective systems
62 to 65	Control of emissions
66 to 74	Plates, markings, testings and inspection
75	Maximum permitted laden weight of vehicle
76 to 80	Other maximum permitted weight limits of vehicle and trailer, other than articulated vehicle
82	Restrictions on use of vehicles carrying wide or long loads

26.—(1) This paragraph applies to any slow plant that is a wheeled motor vehicle.   **B59.157**

(2) Regulation 23 (wheel loads) of the Construction and Use Regulations does not apply to any wheeled motor vehicle that is designed and used solely for the purpose of laying materials for the repair or construction of road surfaces if the weight transmitted to the road surface by any two wheels in line transversely does not exceed 11,180 kilograms.

(3) Regulation 27(1)(f) (tyre tread) of the Construction and Use Regulations does not apply to any wheeled motor vehicle that—

(a) is designed for use in work of construction and repair of road surfaces;

(b) has wheels fitted with pneumatic tyres with smooth treads for such use; and

(c) is incapable by reason of its construction of exceeding a speed of 20 miles per hour on the level under its own power.

27.—(1) This paragraph applies to any slow plant that is a wheeled trailer.   **B59.158**

(2) Regulation 27(1)(b) and (f) (tyre inflation level and tyre tread) of the Construction and Use Regulations does not apply to a wheeled trailer that—

(a) is designed for use in work of construction and repair of road surfaces; and

(b) has wheels fitted with pneumatic tyres with smooth treads for such use.

28.—(1) This paragraph applies to any slow plant that is a track-laying motor vehicle.   **B59.159**

(2) Regulation 28 (tracks) of the Construction and Use Regulations does not apply to a road roller.

(3) The following provisions of the Construction and Use Regulations do not apply to a vehicle which was registered (within the meaning of the Construction and Use Regulations) on or before 31st December 1951—

(a) regulation 31 (glass); and

(b) regulation 34 (windscreen wipers and washers).

29.—(1) This paragraph applies to any slow plant that is a track-laying trailer (including   **B59.160** a road roller).

(2) Regulation 28 (tracks) of the Construction and Use Regulations does not apply.

Article 10(4) and 11(1)(a)   SCHEDULE 4

ROAD RECOVERY VEHICLES

PART 1

DEFINED TERMS

1.—(1) In this Order *"road recovery vehicle"* means a vehicle that is—   **B59.161**

(a) a locomotive;

(b) a motor vehicle of category N3; or

(c) a vehicle-combination comprising a motor vehicle of category N3 and a trailer of category O4;

and that satisfies the three conditions in sub-paragraphs (2) to (4).

(2) The first condition is that the vehicle is specially designed and constructed for the purpose of recovering disabled road vehicles or is permanently adapted for that purpose.

(3) The second condition is that the vehicle is fitted with a crane, winch or other lifting system specially designed to be used for the purpose of recovering another vehicle.

(4) The third condition is that the vehicle meets the requirements for registered use as a recovery vehicle under Part 5 of Schedule 1 to the Vehicle Excise and Registration Act 1994.

Part 2

Construction

B59.162   **2.**—(1) A road recovery vehicle must be a wheeled vehicle.

(2) Every wheel must be fitted with a pneumatic tyre.

B59.163   **3.** A warning beacon emitting an amber light must be fitted to a road recovery vehicle.

Part 3

Plates

B59.164   **4.** A road recovery vehicle must be equipped with a plate that specifies the maximum weight that may be lifted by any crane, winch or other lifting system with which the vehicle is fitted.

Part 4

Conditions Relating to Use

Restriction on carriage of loads and towing of vehicles

B59.165   **5.**—(1) A road recovery vehicle must not carry or tow any load or transport any goods or burden.

(2) But that is subject to paragraphs 6 and 7.

B59.166   **6.** A road recovery vehicle may carry its own necessary gear and equipment.

B59.167   **7.**—(1) Except as stated in sub-paragraph (2), a road recovery vehicle may carry or tow a disabled vehicle or vehicle-combination when conveying it to a destination in accordance with the instructions of the owner or driver of the vehicle or when conveying it to an appropriate destination for repair.

(2) Where a recovery of a disabled vehicle or vehicle-combination is effected by using a drawbar or lift-and-tow method, the road recovery vehicle must not carry or tow the disabled vehicle or vehicle-combination any further than is reasonably necessary in order to clear any road obstructed by it and to facilitate the use of roads by other persons.

B59.168   **8.**—(1) At any time when a disabled vehicle or vehicle-combination is being towed by a road recovery vehicle, the braking system of the disabled vehicle or vehicle-combination must not be operated by any device other than an approved brake connection point that is fitted to both the road recovery vehicle and the disabled vehicle or vehicle-combination.

(2) In sub-paragraph (1), *"approved brake connection point"*, in relation to a road recovery vehicle, means a device which is—

(a) approved by the manufacturer of the vehicle;

(b) fitted to the vehicle in the course of its construction or adaptation; and

(c) specially designed for use in the course of recovering disabled vehicles or vehicle-combinations in order to provide a means by which the braking system of the disabled vehicle or vehicle-combination can be safely and effectively controlled from the road recovery vehicle.

B59.169   **9.** A road recovery vehicle must not tow a disabled vehicle or vehicle-combination if the weight of the road recovery vehicle, together with the weight of the vehicle or vehicles being towed, would exceed the maximum train weight shown on the plate required to be fitted to the road recovery vehicle by regulation 66 of the Construction and Use Regulations (plates for goods vehicles and buses).

Beacons

10.—(1) When a road recovery vehicle is used on roads, the beacon fitted to it under paragraph 3 must be kept lit— **B59.170**

(a) when the road recovery vehicle is stationary at the scene of the breakdown; or

(b) when the road recovery vehicle is unable, on account of any vehicle or vehicles it is towing, the weather conditions or otherwise, to maintain speeds appropriate to the road.

(2) But, in the circumstances described in sub-paragraph (1)(a), the beacon may be switched off if—

(a) there is no reasonable prospect of the presence of the road recovery vehicle causing a hazard to persons using the road (so that it is not necessary or desirable to warn persons of its presence); or

(b) it is likely that the use of the beacon could confuse or mislead other road users.

Maximum width

11.—(1) The overall width of a road recovery vehicle must not exceed the limits imposed by regulation 8 of the Construction and Use Regulations (restrictions as to width). **B59.171**

(2) But sub-paragraph (1) does not apply to a road recovery vehicle that satisfies the width conditions.

(3) The width conditions are that—

(a) the road recovery vehicle is a trailer;

(b) the trailer is used only for, or in connection with, the recovery of vehicles of a description that can only safely be recovered by a road recovery vehicle with an overall width exceeding the limits imposed by regulation 8 of the Construction and Use Regulations; and

(c) the overall width of the trailer does not exceed 3 metres.

Maximum length

12.—(1) The overall length of a road recovery vehicle must not exceed 18.75 metres. **B59.172**

(2) But sub-paragraph (1) does not apply to restrict the combined length of a road recovery vehicle together with any disabled vehicle or vehicle-combination carried or towed by it in the course of a recovery.

Maximum vehicle weight

13. The gross weight of a road recovery vehicle must not exceed— **B59.173**

(a) 36,000 kilograms in the case of a locomotive, the weight of which is transmitted to the road surface through 3 axles;

(b) 50,000 kilograms in the case of a locomotive, the weight of which is transmitted to the road surface through 4 or more axles;

(c) 80,000 kilograms in the case of a vehicle-combination comprising a motor vehicle of category N3 and a trailer of category O4, where the weight of the combination is transmitted to the road surface through 6 or more axles;

(d) in any other case, the maximum authorised weight (within the meaning of the Authorised Weight Regulations) for the description of vehicle in question.

Maximum axle and wheel weights

14.—(1) The distance between any two adjacent axles of a road recovery vehicle must not be less than 1.3 metres. **B59.174**

(2) The axle weight of a road recovery vehicle must not exceed 12,500 kilograms.

(3) The wheel weight of a road recovery vehicle must not exceed 6,250 kilograms.

(4) Where a road recovery vehicle has axles in two or more groups—

  (a) the distance between the adjacent axles in any group must not be less than 1.3 metres; and

  (b) the sum of the weights transmitted to the road surface by all the wheels in any group must not exceed 25,000 kilograms.

(5) But sub-paragraph (4)(b) does not apply to a road recovery vehicle falling within paragraph 13(c).

B59.175   **15.**—(1) If a road recovery vehicle has only one front steer axle, that axle must carry at least 40 per cent of the maximum axle weight shown on the plate required by regulation 66 of the Construction and Use Regulations (plates for goods vehicles and buses).

(2) If the vehicle has two or more front steer axles, all those axles taken together must carry at least 40 per cent of such weight.

Speed restrictions

B59.176   **16.**—(1) A road recovery vehicle must not, at any time when it is carrying or towing a disabled vehicle or vehicle-combination, travel at speeds exceeding—

  (a) 40 miles per hour on a motorway;

  (b) 30 miles per hour on a dual carriageway; or

  (c) 30 miles per hour on any other road.

(2) Nothing in this Schedule is to be taken to authorise travel at any speed in excess of any speed restriction imposed by or under any other enactment.

PART 5

APPLICATION OF REGULATIONS MADE UNDER SECTION 41 OF THE ROAD TRAFFIC ACT 1988

B59.177   **17.** A road recovery vehicle must comply with—

  (a) the Construction and Use Regulations, apart from the provisions of those Regulations specified in Table 12;

  (b) the Authorised Weight Regulations, but only to the extent specified in paragraph 13 of this Schedule; and

  (c) the Lighting Regulations.

TABLE 12

ROAD RECOVERY VEHICLES: CONSTRUCTION AND USE REGULATIONS THAT DO NOT APPLY

Non-applicable Regulations	Subjects
36A, 36B, 36C	Speed limiters
51	Sideguards
70, 70B	Plates
70A	Speed limiters
72	Additional markings
73	Test date disc
75	Maximum permitted laden weight of vehicle
76	Maximum permitted laden weight of vehicle and trailer, other than articulated vehicle
77	Maximum permitted laden weight of articulated vehicle
78	Maximum permitted wheel and axle weights

Non-applicable Regulations	Subjects
79	Maximum permitted weights for certain closely-spaced axles etc
79A	Savings for Authorised Weight Regulations
82	Restrictions on use of vehicles carrying wide or long loads
83(1)	Numbers of trailers

Article 12(1), 13(2), 17(3), 23(2), 24(4), 31(3), 34(3), 38(2), 39(2), and 48(2)   SCHEDULE 5

NOTICES TO POLICE

[Omitted.]   **B59.178**

Article 12(1), 14(1), 15(4), 23(3), 24(5), 31(3) and 34(4)   SCHEDULE 6

ATTENDANTS

[Omitted.]   **B59.179**

Article 15(5), 23(4) and 34(5)   SCHEDULE 7

NOTICES TO SECRETARY OF STATE

[Omitted.]   **B59.180**

Article 16 and 25   SCHEDULE 8

MARKING OF PROJECTIONS

PART 1

DEFINED TERMS

1. In this Schedule—   **B59.181**

"*end marker*" means a marker fitted to the end of any forward or rearward projection of a load which either—

    (a) has the dimensions and surface appearance specified in the first diagram in Part 5 of this Schedule; or

    (b) is a marker which, for the purpose of securing that any forward or rearward projection of a load or loads carried on a vehicle is made clearly visible to other persons using the roads, is designed to be fitted to the end of the projection and is approved for that purpose by the appropriate authority in—

        (i) another EEA State; or

        (ii) any other country which is a member of the United Nations Economic Commission for Europe;

"*relevant vehicle*" means—

    (a) a Part 2 vehicle;

    (b) a Part 2 vehicle-combination; or

    (c) a special type agricultural vehicle; and

"*side marker*" means a marker fitted to the side of any forward, rearward or lateral projection of a load which either—

    (a) has the dimensions and surface appearance specified in the second diagram in Part 5 of this Schedule; or

(b) is a marker which, for the purpose of securing that any forward, rearward or lateral projection of a load or loads carried on a vehicle is made clearly visible to other persons using the roads, is designed to be fitted to the side of the projection and is approved for that purpose by a recognised authority in—

    (i) another EEA State; or

    (ii) any other country which is a member of the United Nations Economic Commission for Europe.

Part 2

Forward and Rearward Projections

B59.182   2. Paragraphs 3 to 6 apply cumulatively.

General visibility of forward or rearward projections

B59.183   3. Where the length of a forward or rearward projection of a load carried on a relevant vehicle exceeds 1 metre—

(a) the projection must be made clearly visible, within a reasonable distance, to a person using the road at the end of the vehicle from which the projection extends; and

(b) it must be made clearly visible from the side of the vehicle.

Markers for the end of a forward or rearward projection

B59.184   4.—(1) Where the length of a forward or rearward projection of a load carried on a relevant vehicle exceeds 2 metres, an end marker must be fitted to the end of the projection.

(2) Sub-paragraph (1) does not apply if a rear marking has been fitted to the projection in accordance with regulation 21 of the Lighting Regulations.

(3) An end marker under sub-paragraph (1) must be fitted so that—

(a) it is as near as is practicable in a transverse plane;

(b) it is not more than 0.5 metre from the extreme end of the projection;

(c) the vertical distance between the lowest part of the end marker and the surface of the road is not more than 2.5 metres;

(d) the end marker, and any means by which it is fitted to the projection, impedes the view of the driver of the vehicle as little as possible; and

(e) the end marker is clearly visible, within a reasonable distance, to a person using the road at the end of the vehicle from which the projection extends.

Markers for the side of a forward or rearward projection

B59.185   5.—(1) Where the length of a forward or rearward projection of a load carried on a relevant vehicle exceeds 3 metres, one side marker must be fitted to the right hand side of the projection and one side marker must be fitted to its left hand side.

(2) The side markers under sub-paragraph (1) must be fitted so that—

(a) each side marker is, as near as is practicable, in a longitudinal plane;

(b) no part of a side marker extends beyond the end of the projection;

(c) the vertical distance between the lowest part of each side marker and the surface of the road is not more than 2.5 metres;

(d) the horizontal distance between each side marker and the end-marker (or, as the case may be, the rear marking fitted to the projection in accordance with the Lighting Regulations) does not exceed 1 metre; and

(e) each side marker is clearly visible, within a reasonable distance, to a person using the road on that side of the projection.

B59.186   6.—(1) This paragraph applies where any relevant vehicle is carrying a load and—

(a) the length of any forward projection of the load exceeds 4.5 metres; or

(b) the length of any rearward projection of the load exceeds 5 metres.

(2) Additional side markers must be fitted to the right hand side and the left hand side of a forward or rearward projection so that the horizontal distance between the extreme projecting points of the relevant vehicle and the nearest points of any adjacent side markers does not exceed—

(a) 2.5 metres in the case of a forward projection;

(b) 3.5 metres in the case of a rearward projection.

(3) The additional side markers also must be fitted to the projection so that—

(a) each additional side marker is, as near as is practicable, in a longitudinal plane;

(b) the vertical distance between the lowest part of each additional side marker and the surface of the road is not more than 2.5 metres; and

(c) each additional side marker is clearly visible, within a reasonable distance, to a person using the road on that side of the projection.

(4) In determining the extreme projecting points of a relevant vehicle for the purposes of sub-paragraph (2), any part of a crane or other special appliance or apparatus, which is treated as a forward projection or a rearward projection by virtue of article 6(3), is to be disregarded.

Part 3

Lateral Projections

Markers for a lateral projection

7.—(1) This paragraph applies where—   **B59.187**

(a) any relevant vehicle is carrying a load; and

(b) the load has a lateral projection or projections on either side exceeding 305 millimetres in length.

(2) Side markers must be fitted to the lateral projection so that, in respect of each side of the vehicle from which the projection extends, one marker is visible from the front of the vehicle and one marker is visible from the rear of the vehicle.

(3) Each side marker must be fitted so that at least part of it is within 50 millimetres of a longitudinal plane passing through the point on that side of the projection which is furthest from the axis of the vehicle.

8.—(1) If the user of the vehicle shows that it is not reasonably practicable to fit side   **B59.188** markers in accordance with paragraph 7, the load must be marked with tape so that the point at which the width of the load is at its greatest is clearly visible from the front, rear and side of the vehicle.

(2) The tape must be—

(a) red, yellow or white (or any combination); and

(b) made of day-glow, fluorescent or retro-reflective material which is of a standard approved by—

(i) the British Standards Institution; or

(ii) an equivalent body in another EEA State or in any other country which is a member of the United Nations Economic Commission for Europe.

(3) Nothing in this paragraph affects any requirement imposed by the Lighting Regulations, including, in particular, the requirements of regulation 11(1) (which states that no retro-reflective material is to be fitted to a vehicle which is capable of showing red light to the front of the vehicle) and regulation 11(2) (which states that no retro-reflective material is to be fitted to a vehicle which is capable of showing any light other than red to the rear).

Part 4

General Visibility of Markers

9. Any end marker or side marker which is required by any provision of this Schedule to   **B59.189** be fitted to a projection of a load must be kept clean and unobscured.

B59.190   **10.** Between sunset and sunrise, and at all times when visibility is seriously reduced, any end marker or side marker must be kept illuminated by a lamp which—

 (a) makes the marker readily visible from a reasonable distance; and

 (b) is shielded so that its light (except as reflected from the marker) is not visible to other persons using the road.

PART 5

APPEARANCE OF MARKERS

B59.191   DIAGRAM OF END MARKER SURFACE

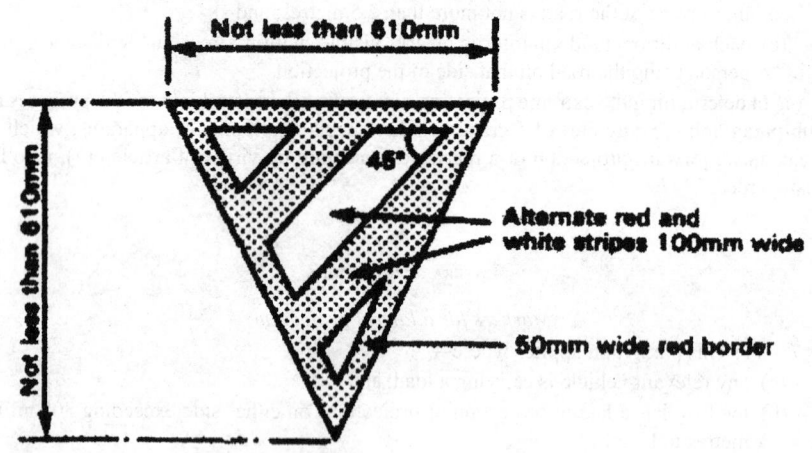

DIAGRAM OF SIDE MARKER SURFACE

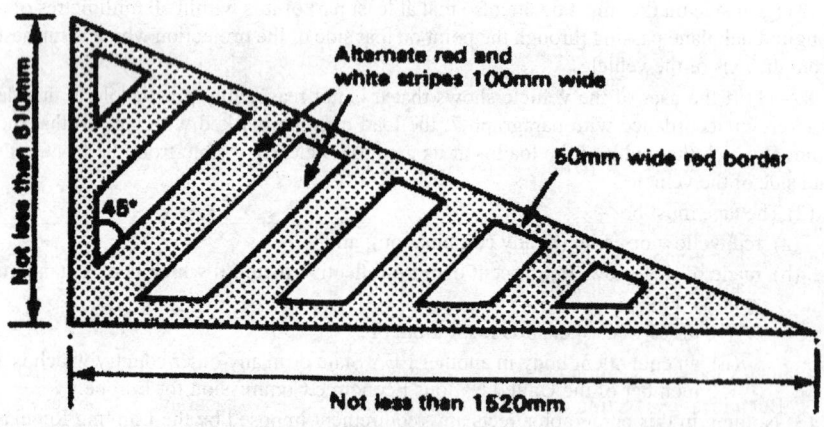

Article 17(1), 35(2) and 40(2)   SCHEDULE 9

ROAD AND BRIDGE AUTHORITIES

PART 1

NOTICES

B59.192   *[Omitted.]*

PART 2

INDEMNITIES

[Omitted.]   **B59.193**

Article 32(2) and 33(b)   SCHEDULE 10

LOCAL EXCAVATION VEHICLES

PART 1

MEANING OF LOCAL EXCAVATION VEHICLE

1.—(1) In this Schedule *"local excavation vehicle"* means any moveable plant or equip-   **B59.194**
ment which is a heavy motor car, trailer or articulated vehicle and which satisfies the four
conditions specified in sub-paragraphs (2) to (5).

(2) The first condition is that the vehicle is intended for use on a work site on private
premises.

(3) The second condition is that the vehicle is specially designed and constructed for the
primary purpose of moving excavated material.

(4) The third condition is that the vehicle is fitted with a tipping body, moving platform
or other similar device for discharging its load.

(5) The fourth condition is that the vehicle does not fall within the definition of engineering plant set out in paragraph 2 of Schedule 3.

PART 2

CONSTRUCTION

Wheels

2. Every wheel of a local excavation vehicle must be fitted with a pneumatic tyre.   **B59.195**

PART 3

CONDITIONS RELATING TO USE

General restrictions

3.—(1) A local excavation vehicle may only be used on roads—   **B59.196**
   (a) to proceed between different parts of the same private premises; or
   (b) to proceed between the private premises and a port.

(2) But nothing in this Order is to be taken to authorise use on roads of the local excavation vehicle beyond a radius of three miles drawn around the outermost perimeter of the
port or of any work site on the private premises on which the vehicle is used.

Restrictions on carriage of loads etc

4.—(1) A local excavation vehicle must not carry any load or transport goods or burden.   **B59.197**

(2) But a local excavation vehicle may carry its own necessary gear and equipment.

Restrictions on towing of trailers

5.—(1) A local excavation vehicle that is a heavy motor car must not tow any trailer.   **B59.198**

(2) But sub-paragraph (1) does not apply to a heavy motor car forming part of an
articulated vehicle.

6.—(1) This paragraph applies to a motor vehicle towing a trailer where—   **B59.199**
   (a) the motor vehicle or trailer is a local excavation vehicle; or
   (b) the motor vehicle and trailer together comprise an articulated vehicle that is a local
     excavation vehicle.

(2) A motor vehicle to which this paragraph applies must not tow any other trailer.

Maximum width

B59.200   7. The overall width of a local excavation vehicle must not exceed 6.1 metres.

Maximum length

B59.201   8. The overall length of a local excavation vehicle must not exceed—

(a) in the case of a heavy motor car, the maximum permitted by regulation 7 of the Construction and Use Regulations;

(b) in the case of a local excavation vehicle that is a trailer, 8.54 metres;

(c) in the case of a local excavation vehicle that is an articulated vehicle, 13.4 metres.

Restrictions relating to weight: gross weight

B59.202   9.—(1) The gross weight of a local excavation vehicle—

(a) must not exceed 50,800 kilograms for a vehicle that is—

    (i) a heavy motor car not forming part of an articulated vehicle; or

    (ii) an articulated vehicle; and

(b) in the case of a vehicle that is trailer, must not exceed the maximum authorised weight (within the meaning of Schedule 1 to the Authorised Weight Regulations) for a trailer of the same description.

(2) Where the trailer is one to which the Authorised Weight Regulations do not apply, the reference to Schedule 1 of those Regulations is to be taken as a reference to the equivalent provisions of regulations 75 to 79 of the Construction and Use Regulations.

Restrictions relating to weight: axle weight

B59.203   10.—(1) The axle weight for a local excavation vehicle—

(a) must not exceed 22,860 kilograms for a vehicle that is—

    (i) a heavy motor car not forming part of an articulated vehicle; or

    (ii) an articulated vehicle; and

(b) in the case of a vehicle that is trailer, must not exceed the maximum authorised axle weight (within the meaning of Schedule 3 to the Authorised Weight Regulations) for a trailer of the same description.

(2) Where the trailer is one to which the Authorised Weight Regulations do not apply, the reference to Schedule 3 of those Regulations is to be taken as a reference to the equivalent provisions of regulations 75 to 79 of the Construction and Use Regulations.

Speed restrictions

B59.204   11.—(1) A local excavation vehicle must not travel at speeds exceeding—

(a) 40 miles per hour on a motorway;

(b) 12 miles per hour on any other road.

(2) But nothing in this Order is to be taken to authorise travel at any speed in excess of any other speed restriction imposed by or under any other enactment.

Part 4

Application of Regulations made under Section 41 of the Road Traffic Act 1988

B59.205   12.—(1) A local excavation vehicle must comply with—

(a) the Construction and Use Regulations, apart from (according to the description of the vehicle in question) such provisions of those Regulations as are specified in paragraph 13;

(b) the Authorised Weight Regulations, if it is not excluded from complying with those Regulations by sub-paragraph (2) of this paragraph; and

(c) the Lighting Regulations.

(2) A local excavation vehicle is excluded from complying with the Authorised Weight Regulations if it is—

(a) a heavy motor car not forming part of an articulated vehicle; or

(b) an articulated vehicle.

13.—(1) In the case of a local excavation vehicle that is a heavy motor car not forming part of an articulated vehicle, the provisions of the Construction and Use Regulations specified in Table 13 do not apply.

B59.206

TABLE 13

Non-applicable Regulations	Subject
8	Width
16(4), Item 8 of Table	Braking system of certain vehicles
18(1A) to (9)	Maintenance and efficiency of brakes
22	Springs and resilient material
63	Wings
66	Plates for goods vehicles
75 to 80	Maximum permitted weights

TABLE 14

TRAILER NOT FORMING PART OF AN ARTICULATED VEHICLE: CONSTRUCTION AND USE REGULATIONS THAT DO NOT APPLY

Non-applicable Regulations	Subject
8	Width
18(1A) to (9)	Maintenance and efficiency of brakes
22	Springs and resilient material
63	Wings
66	Plates for goods vehicles

TABLE 15

ARTICULATED VEHICLE: CONSTRUCTION AND USE REGULATIONS THAT DO NOT APPLY

Non-applicable Regulations	Subject
7	Length
8	Width
16(4), Item 8 of Table	Braking system of certain vehicles
18(1A) to (9)	Maintenance and efficiency of brakes
22	Springs and resilient material
63	Wings
66	Plates for goods vehicles
75 to 80	Maximum permitted weights

Article 37(b)   SCHEDULE 11

VEHICLES FOR TESTS, TRIALS OR NON-UK USE ETC.

PART 1

INTERPRETATION

B59.207 **1.** In this Schedule *"relevant vehicle"* means any motor vehicle or trailer which falls within a recognised category of special vehicles specified in article 36(1)(a) to (e).

PART 2

CONDITIONS RELATING TO USE

General restrictions

B59.208 **2.** A relevant vehicle may only be used on roads for—

(a) testing;

(b) demonstration;

(c) delivery on sale;

(d) proceeding to, or returning from, a manufacturer or repairer for construction, repair or overhaul.

B59.209 **3.** Paragraph 2 does not apply in relation to a relevant vehicle where—

(a) a person ("A") has been approved by the Secretary of State for the purposes of this Schedule;

(b) the vehicle is registered under the Vehicle and Excise Registration Act 1994 and the registration is in A's name only; and

(c) the vehicle is being used either—

(i) by A for the sole purpose of making an evaluation of it; or

(ii) by another person ("B") in the circumstances described in sub-paragraph (2) and for the purpose of assisting A to make such an evaluation.

(2) The circumstances described in this sub-paragraph are—

(a) that A has lent the vehicle to B on terms that include a requirement for B to supply A with information or opinions derived from his use of it, and for B to return the vehicle to A on demand; and

(b) that the vehicle is being used by B in accordance with those terms.

B59.210 **4.** A relevant vehicle must not be used in such a way as to cause a danger of injury to any person by reason of—

(a) the condition of the vehicle, its accessories or equipment;

(b) the purpose for which it is used;

(c) the number of passengers carried by it;

(d) the manner in which such passengers are carried;

(e) the weight, position or distribution of any load carried on the vehicle; or

(f) the manner in which any such load is secured.

Restriction of carriage of loads etc

B59.211 **5.**—(1) A relevant vehicle that is used on roads must not carry any load or transport goods or burden.

(2) But that is subject to paragraphs 6 and 7.

B59.212 **6.** A relevant vehicle may carry—

(a) its own necessary gear and equipment; and

(b) any apparatus or ballast necessary for the purpose of carrying out a test or trial of the vehicle.

7.—(1) A relevant vehicle may carry a load if it complies with such of the requirements of the Authorised Weight Regulations as apply to a vehicle of that description.   **B59.213**

(2) Where the vehicle is one to which the Authorised Weight Regulations do not apply, the reference to requirements of those Regulations is to be taken as a reference to the applicable requirements of regulations 75 to 79 of the Construction and Use Regulations.

PART 3

CONDITIONS RELATING TO USE

8.—(1) A relevant vehicle must comply with—   **B59.214**

  (a) the provisions of the Construction and Use Regulations specified in Table 16, but subject to the modifications of those provisions which are specified in paragraph 9;

  (b) the Authorised Weight Regulations; and

  (c) the provisions of the Lighting Regulations specified in Table 17, but subject to the modifications of those provisions which are specified in paragraph 10.

9. In their application to a relevant vehicle, the Construction and Use Regulations specified in Table 16 are to be read subject to the following modifications—   **B59.215**

  (a) regulation 16 applies to all relevant vehicles (and not only those to which regulation 15 of those Regulations does not apply) except that, in the circumstances envisaged in the provisos to paragraphs (1), (1A), (1C) and (1D) of regulation 15, a relevant vehicle may comply instead with the requirements specified in each of those paragraphs respectively;

  (b) regulation 82(8)(c)(ii)(B) of the Construction and Use Regulations does not require any advance notice to be given to police in accordance with paragraph 1 of Schedule 12 to those Regulations.

10.—(1) In their application to a relevant vehicle, regulations 18 and 22 of the Lighting Regulations are to be read as if—   **B59.216**

  (a) the requirements relating to the markings of lamps, retro-reflectors and rear markings were omitted;

  (b) the requirements relating to angles of visibility were omitted; and

  (c) the requirements relating to the positioning of any lamp, retro-reflector or rear marking permitted any specified maximum measurement to be increased by 5 per cent and any specified minimum measurement to be decreased by 5 per cent.

(2) In its application to a relevant vehicle, regulation 18 of the Lighting Regulations is also to be read as if the requirements relating to the fitting of a dim-dip device or running lamp in Table 1 of Schedule 1 were omitted.

TABLE 16

VEHICLES FOR TESTS, TRIALS OR NON-UK USE ETC: CONSTRUCTION AND USE REGULATIONS THAT DO APPLY

Applicable Regulations	Subject
10	Indication of overall travelling height
16	Braking systems
18(1)	Maintenance and efficiency of brakes
20	General requirement as to wheels and tracks
26	Mixing of tyres
27	Condition and maintenance of tyres
29	Maintenance of steering gear
30	View to the front
34	Windscreen wipers and washers

Applicable Regulations	Subject
37	Audible warning instruments
53	Mascots
54	Silencers—general
61	Emissions
62	Closets
81,82	Restrictions on use of vehicles carrying wide or long loads
83	Number of trailers
84	Trailers drawn by motor cycles
86	Distance between motor vehicles and trailers
89	Leaving trailers at rest
90	Passengers in trailers
92	Attachment of sidecars
97	Avoidance of excessive noise
98	Stopping of engine when stationary
99	Use of audible warning instruments
100	Maintenance and use of vehicles so as not to cause danger
101	Parking in darkness
102	Passengers on motor-cycles
103	Obstruction
104	Driver's control
105	Opening of doors
106	Reversing
107	Leaving motor vehicle unattended
108	Securing of suspended implements
109	Television sets

TABLE 17

VEHICLES FOR TESTS, TRIALS OR NON-UK USE ETC: LIGHTING REGULATIONS THAT DO APPLY

Applicable Lighting Regulations	Subject
11	Colour of lights shown by lamps and reflectors
13	Lamps to show steady light
16	Restrictions on fitting blue warning beacons etc
17	Obligatory warning beacons
18	Obligatory lamps, reflectors, rear marking and devices
19	Restrictions on the obstruction of certain lamps etc
21	Projecting trailers, overhanging/projecting loads etc
22	Additional side marker lamps

Article 56   SCHEDULE 12

VEHICLES PROPELLED BY COMPRESSED NATURAL GAS SYSTEMS

Defined terms

B59.217   **1.** In this Schedule—

"an accredited testing laboratory" means a testing laboratory which has been accredited by the United Kingdom Accreditation Service or by an equivalent body in another EEA State under European Standard EN 45001: 1989 for general criteria for the operation of testing laboratories (British Standard BS 7501: 1989);

"articulating connector" means a connector bridging the space between two separate and rigid vehicle structures;

"bar" means bar gauge;

"BS 5430: Part I: 1990" means—

(a) Part I of the British Standard for the periodic inspection, testing and maintenance of transportable gas containers (excluding dissolved acetylene gas containers), published by the British Standards Institution under the reference BS 5430: Part I: 1990; or

(b) any equivalent standard published by a recognised testing body in another EEA State;

and, in a case falling within paragraph (b), a reference in this Schedule to any particular provision of the British Standard is to be taken as a reference to the equivalent provision of any such EEA equivalent standard;

"compressed natural gas" means natural gas stored at a pressure above 30 bar;

"design pressure" means the pressure that a part of a gas propulsion system has been designed to withstand;

"gas container" means a container for gas falling within paragraph 2(1);

"g" means gravity;

"high pressure" means a pressure exceeding 7 bar;

"large bus" means a vehicle constructed or adapted to carry more than 16 seated passengers in addition to the driver;

"low pressure" means a pressure not exceeding 75 millibars;

"medium pressure" means a pressure not exceeding 7 bar but exceeding 75 millibars;

  "millibars" means millibars gauge;

"mm" means millimetres;

"mm²" means square millimetres;

"N" means newtons;

"°C" means degrees Celsius;

"pipeline" means any pipe or passage connecting any two parts of a gas propulsion system;

"pressure relief device" means a device to protect a gas container against overpressure; and

"regulator" means a device that automatically reduces and controls the pressure of the gas flowing through it.

Gas containers

2.—(1) This paragraph applies to any container for gas which is fitted to a motor vehicle or a trailer and which is intended for the storage of natural gas for the purpose of the propulsion of the vehicle or of the towing vehicle, as the case may be. **B59.218**

(2) Before its first use on a vehicle, every gas container must be pressure tested by an accredited testing laboratory at a pressure of 1.5 times the working pressure of the gas container.

(3) The pressure test must be carried out in accordance with the procedure set out in paragraph 4.7 of BS 5430: Part I: 1990 or, where an equivalent procedure has been specified by the manufacturer, in accordance with that procedure.

3.—(1) The owner of any vehicle (or, if it is in the possession of a different person, that person) must ensure that any gas container used on that vehicle is subject to a periodic test by an accredited testing laboratory every three years, or with such greater frequency as the manufacturer specifies. **B59.219**

(2) The periodic test must include—

    (a) the pressure test specified in paragraph 2, and

    (b) an internal and external visual inspection carried out in accordance with paragraph 4.4.2 and 4.4.3 of BS 5430: Part I: 1990 or, where an equivalent procedure has been specified by the manufacturer, in accordance with that procedure.

(3) Nothing in sub-paragraph (1) affects the obligation imposed by regulation 100 of the Construction and Use Regulations.

B59.220   **4.**—(1) A gas container must—

    (a) be suitable to be fitted to the vehicle to which it is fitted and be constructed from suitable materials;

    (b) be capable of containing natural gas operating at a working pressure of 200 bar settled at 15°C with a maximum filling pressure of 260 bar;

    (c) be free from any visible damage or defect and not have been the subject of any alteration or repair subsequent to its manufacture;

    (d) be fitted with a manually operable isolation valve and a pressure relief device (but may in addition be fitted with an electrically operable isolation valve);

    (e) be used for no more than 30 years from the date of manufacture; and

    (f) be marked as follows in characters which, unless otherwise stated, are not less than 6mm high-

        (i) "CNG ONLY" in letters at least 25mm high;

        (ii) the date of manufacture;

        (iii) "DO NOT USE AFTER. . . . ." in characters at least 25mm high, and specifying the month and year of expiry;

        (iv) the design pressure at a temperature of 15°C;

        (v) the month and year of the original pressure test carried out in accordance with paragraph 2, together with the identity of the testing station;

        (vi) the month and year of any subsequent periodic pressure test carried out in accordance with paragraph 3, together with the identity of the testing station; and

        (vii) the design life of the gas container if less than 30 years.

(2) Where a gas container contains a mark from a previous pressure test carried out in accordance with paragraph 2 or 3, any additional test mark required by sub-paragraph (1)(f) must be placed adjacent to the previous test mark.

(3) Any gas container crumple zone must be so mounted that—

    (a) the effectiveness of any vehicle crumple zone is not impaired;

    (b) it is securely attached to the vehicle by suitable mountings that will protect the gas container from displacement or damage due to vibration or other cause;

    (c) the gas container and its mountings do not weaken the vehicle's structure or affect the vehicle's stability;

    (d) it is placed in such a position that the risk of impact damage to the gas container and its isolation valve is, as far as is practicable, reduced and it is placed or shielded so that the effects of any impact are, as far as is practicable, reduced;

    (e) it is placed in such a position or so shielded that the risk of damage from flying debris is minimised;

    (f) it is placed in such a position or so insulated or shielded that the effects of any source of heat are minimised;

    (g) it is suitably protected from external corrosion and abrasion; and

    (h) except as stated in sub-paragraph (4), any leaking or vented gas will be directed safely to the atmosphere preventing, as far as is practicable, the possibility of its entering the engine, passenger, driver or living compartments.

(4) Where a gas container is to be located in the driver, passenger or living compartment

or in the vehicle boot, or in any space which is not so ventilated as to prevent the accumulation of gas, the valves, connections and pipework must be enclosed in order to contain any gas leakage, either by—

(a) placing the gas container and its fittings within a durable enclosure which is sealed so that it is gas tight to the compartment, vehicle boot or space, as the case may be, and which is provided with permanent direct ventilation to the outside of the vehicle; or

(b) enclosing the neck and fittings of the gas container within a durable envelope which is gas tight to the compartment, vehicle boot or space, as the case may be, and which is provided with permanent direct ventilation to the outside of the vehicle.

(5) Any enclosure or envelope required for the purposes of sub-paragraph (4) must not contain any source of ignition.

(6) Any ventilation opening required under sub-paragraph (4) must—

(a) have a free area of not less than 600mm^2 ; and

(b) be terminated away from any openings into any vehicle compartment away from any source of ignition and in a position where it is not liable to blockage.

(7) Any pressure relief device contained within any enclosure must have a separate, dedicated vent line which may pass within the enclosure vent.

(8) In relation to every gas container, there must be provided (either on the gas container itself or in documents which are readily available) information concerning—

(a) any particular installation requirements;

(b) details of any pressure relief devices fitted or required to be fitted to the gas container;

(c) recommended inspection intervals (which must not be more than 3 years); and

(d) any recommended inspection procedure.

Gas container isolation

5.—(1) Any gas container must be capable of being isolated from its supply pipework   **B59.221**
by means of an isolation valve connected directly to each gas container but not between the gas container and its pressure relief device.

(2) Any isolation valve must be capable of shutting off all the gas flow from the gas container, except through the pressure relief device.

(3) Any isolation valve must be marked clearly and permanently with the direction of operation.

(4) Any isolation valve must be so protected as to ensure that its operation is unaffected by the collection of moisture and other foreign matter.

(5) Any gas container valve assembly must be so placed as, so far as is practicable, to be protected from damage.

(6) In this paragraph *"isolation valve"* means a manually operable isolation valve.

Pressure relief devices

6.—(1) Every gas container must be provided with a suitable pressure relief device that   **B59.222**
complies with sub-paragraphs (3) to (7).

(2) Where a pressure regulator is fitted to a gas container, any pressure relief device attached to it must comply with sub-paragraphs (3) to (7).

(3) Any pressure relief device must be such that—

(a) there is an adequate discharge rate to ensure the safety of the system;

(b) any cooling effect of the gas during discharge will not affect the discharge rate;

(c) its relieving characteristics will not be impaired on exposure to fire;

(d) operation of the device will not inhibit the discharge rate from the device;

(e) its outlet size is not less than the size of inlet or outlet pipework of the gas container;

(f) it cannot be installed in the reverse flow direction;

(g) it is so protected as to ensure that its operation is unaffected by the collection of moisture and other foreign matter;

(h) if the device is adjustable, unauthorised interference with its settings is prevented; and

(i) it is marked clearly with the set pressure or temperature and with the flow direction.

(4) Any pressure relief device must be placed so that—

(a) as far as is practicable, the device and its outlets are protected from damage and blockage in the event of an accident;

(b) its discharge rate is not inhibited if an associated gas container is located within an enclosure; and

(c) it is away from any source of heat which could impair the designed operation of the device.

(5) The discharge from a pressure relief device must terminate outside the vehicle and be directed or deflected away from any opening into the engine, driver, passenger or living compartment, vehicle boot, or any space which is not so ventilated as to prevent the accumulation of gas.

(6) The discharge from a pressure relief device must not terminate near any source of heat or other potential source of ignition.

(7) A pressure release device on any gas container or regulator located within the driver, passenger or living compartment, vehicle boot, or in any space which is not so ventilated as to prevent the accumulation of gas must have its discharge vented separately and directly to the outside of the vehicle.

Pipelines

B59.223   7.—(1) Every pipeline must be fixed in such a manner and position that—

(a) it will not be adversely affected by the heat of the exhaust system of any engine or by any other source of heat;

(b) it is protected from vibration and strain in excess of that which it can reasonably be expected to withstand;

(c) it is so placed or shielded as to minimise the risk from flying debris; and

(d) in the case of a medium or high pressure pipeline it is, so far as is practicable, accessible for inspection.

(2) Except as stated in sub-paragraph (4), every medium or high pressure pipeline must be—

(a) a rigid line of seamless steel of high pressure hydraulic grade, suitable for service on road vehicles and designed for the full range of operating temperatures, pressures and loading which may occur; and

(b) effectively protected against, or shielded from, or treated so as to be resistant to, external corrosion throughout its length unless it is made from material which is corrosion resistant under the conditions which it is likely to encounter in service.

(3) No unsupported length of any medium or high pressure pipeline may exceed 600mm.

(4) Flexible hose may be used in a medium or high pressure pipeline if—

(a) it is reinforced either by stainless steel wire braid or by textile braid; and

(b) except in the case of a pipeline attached to a gas container for the purpose of filling that gas container, the flexibility which it provides is necessary for the construction or operation of the gas propulsion system of which it forms a part.

Unions and joints

B59.224   8.—(1) Every union and joint on a pipeline or gas container must be constructed and fitted so that it will—

(a) not be liable to work loose or leak when in use; and

(b) be readily accessible for inspection and maintenance.

(2) Every union on a medium or high pressure pipeline or on a gas container must be made of suitable metal; but such a union may contain non-metal washers and seals provided that such washers and seals are supported and constrained by metal components.

Filling connectors

9.—(1) Any filling connector for the refuelling of the vehicle must be of a type which is used exclusively for natural gas filling and which is compatible with the filling nozzle without the use of an adapter fitting.   **B59.225**

(2) Gas must be prevented from flowing back from the gas container to the filling connector.

(3) Any filling connector must be covered with a dust cap, which is secured permanently to the vehicle.

(4) Where a filling connector is placed on the outside of the vehicle, it must be protected against unauthorised interference.

(5) The filling connector must be located outside the driver or passenger compartment in a suitably protected, well-ventilated and readily accessible position, away from any openings in the driver, passenger or living compartment.

Valves, safety devices and control equipment

10.—(1) Every gas propulsion system must be so designed and constructed that—   **B59.226**
  (a) the supply of gas to the engine is stopped by an automatic valve when—
      (i) the engine is not running at all;
      (ii) the engine is not running on the supply of gas; or
      (iii) the engine ignition is off;
  (b) where the valve mentioned in paragraph (a) is not integral with the regulator, it must be positioned upstream of the regulator so as to be able to isolate the gas container and filling point; and
  (c) in the event of a rapid deceleration of the vehicle in an accident or similar occurrence, the supply of gas to the engine is automatically stopped at a point as close as is possible to the gas container and may only be restored manually.

(2) Where the engine or vehicle is constructed or adapted to run on one or more fuels as an alternative to gas or in addition to gas, the safety of the engine or the gas fuel system must not be impaired by the presence of any other fuel system.

(3) Except as stated in sub-paragraph (4), every gas container must (in addition to the isolation valve required under paragraph 5 and the pressure relief device required under paragraph 6) be fitted with an automatically operated valve to prevent gas escaping from the gas container in the event of a fracture or failure of the pipeline or of any component in the gas supply system.

(4) In the case of a group of gas containers interconnected in such a manner that the pipework is protected in the event of an accident, the group of gas containers may be fitted with a single automatically operated valve or device to prevent gas escaping from the group of gas containers in the event of a fracture or failure of the pipeline or of any component in the gas supply system.

(5) Any electrically operated valve must be constructed so as to open when electrical power is applied and close when electrical power is removed.

(6) Where the vehicle is equipped to operate at any one time on one only of two or more alternative fuels, a fuel selection system that complies with sub-paragraph (7) must be installed.

(7) A fuel selection system complies with this sub-paragraph if—
  (a) it has a control switch that is readily accessible to the driver at all times and is clearly marked for the selection of each fuel;

(b) it has a change-over system, operated by the control switch mentioned in paragraph (a), which prevents the use at the same time of more than one of the alternative fuels, apart from where fuel remains in the common system during a change-over between alternatives; and

(c) it does not impair the safety of the engine or the fuel system.

(8) All the parts of every valve or cock which are in contact with gas must be made of suitable metal; but they may contain non-metal washers and seals if those washers and seals are supported and constrained by metal components.

Regulators

B59.227   11.—(1) Any regulator fitted must be designed so that—

(a) it has a pre-set pressure and flow rating suitable for the part of the system to which it is attached;

(b) it incorporates a means of protecting the system downstream of the regulator from the upstream pressure in the event of failure of or leakage from the regulator;

(c) it is marked clearly and permanently with the fuel type, pressure and flow direction; and

(d) if the engine cooling system is utilised within the regulator, passage of gas into the engine cooling system is prevented.

(2) Any pressure relief device on a regulator must comply with the requirements of paragraph 6(3) to (7).

(3) Any regulator must be so installed that—

(a) it is in an accessible position for inspection and maintenance;

(b) it is in a position where it is protected from heat sources;

(c) it is in a position where, as far as is practicable, any ventilation holes are prevented from being blocked; and

(d) it is securely attached to a secure mounting.

(4) Where a regulator is to be located in the driver, passenger or living compartment, or in the vehicle boot or in any other space which is not so ventilated as to prevent the accumulation of gas, it must be enclosed in order to contain any gas leakage, either by—

(a) placing the gas container and its fittings within a durable enclosure which is—

(i) sealed so that it is gas tight to the compartment, vehicle boot or space, as the case may be; and

(ii) provided with permanent direct ventilation to the outside of the vehicle; or

(b) enclosing the neck and fittings of the gas container within a durable envelope which is—

(i) gas tight to the compartment, vehicle boot or space, as the case may be; and

(ii) provided with direct permanent ventilation to the outside of the vehicle.

(5) A regulator may not be attached directly to the engine or to any part ancillary to the engine.

Special requirements for buses

B59.228   12. In the case of a large bus there must be fitted as near as practicable to the gas container a valve that stops the flow of gas into the gas supply pipeline in the event of—

(a) the angle of tilt of the vehicle exceeding that mentioned in regulation 6 of the Public Service Vehicles (Conditions of Fitness, Equipment, Use and Certification) Regulations 1981 [*SI 1982/1058*]; or

(b) the deceleration of the vehicle exceeding 5g.

Connections for articulated vehicles

B59.229   13.—(1) Where a trailer is used for the carriage of any part of the gas supply system—

(a) an articulating connector complying with sub-paragraphs (2) to (8) must be fitted between the part of the system on the vehicle and the part of the system on the trailer, and

(b) the articulating connector must not be subjected to more than medium pressure.

(2) Any articulating connector must—

(a) be of a type suitable for natural gas systems;

(b) be designed to accept a compatible nozzle without the use of adapter fittings; and

(c) not be interchangeable with connections for other services.

(3) The gas supply pipework at the terminal on each section of the articulated unit must be capable of withstanding a force of at least 200N in any direction before deformation or failure occurs.

(4) Any articulating connector must be designed so that separation can be achieved in a fail-safe manner, minimising the volume of gas released during the separation process and while the joint remains disconnected.

(5) Disconnection devices must be designed to prevent unauthorised interference.

(6) Dust caps must be fitted to exposed connections to keep out dirt and such dust caps must be attached to the system.

(7) The articulating connector must be properly supported and protected at all times.

(8) The articulating connector must incorporate a breakaway coupling which is designed to separate when a breakaway force of 200N (or greater) is applied in any direction and which has an automatic isolation system to minimise the release of gas in the event of the separation of the breakaway coupling.

Marking and labelling of the vehicle

14.—(1) Every vehicle which is equipped to be fuelled by natural gas must be fitted **B59.230** with a metal identification plate, located in a readily visible and accessible position, which is marked clearly and permanently to identify—

(a) that the vehicle has been constructed or adapted to run on natural gas; and

(b) the maximum system filling pressure.

This information is in addition to the information required by paragraph 4(1)(f) with respect to the gas container.

(2) The filling point for natural gas must be identified adjacent to the point by the words "NATURAL GAS" or other suitable wording.

General requirements

15. Every part of the gas system must—   **B59.231**

(a) so far as is practicable, be so located and protected as not to be exposed to accidental damage;

(b) be soundly and properly constructed of materials which are compatible with one another and with the gas used or likely to be used and which are capable of withstanding the loads or stresses likely to be met in operation; and

(c) be so designed and constructed that the number of joints is kept to a minimum, and that leakage of gas is unlikely to occur.

The Private Hire Vehicles (London) (Transitional Provisions) Regulations 2004

(SI 2004/242)

B60.01 *[The text of these regulations has been amended by:*

> *the Private Hire Vehicles (London) (Transitional Provisions) (Amendment) Regulations 2007 (SI 2007/3453) (December 31, 2007).*

The amending regulations are referred to in the notes to the principal regulations only by their year and number. The date referred to above is the date on which the amending regulations came into force.]

Citation and commencement

B60.02 **1.** These Regulations may be cited as the Private Hire Vehicles (London) (Transitional Provisions) Regulations 2004 and shall come into force on 8th March 2004.

Interpretation

B60.03 **2.** In these Regulations —

> *"the 1998 Act"* means the Private Hire Vehicles (London) Act 1998;
>
> *"existing private hire vehicle"* means a vehicle which is for the time being registered by Transport for London as an existing private hire vehicle in accordance with article 3;
>
> *"temporary permit"* means a temporary permit issued under regulation 5; and
>
> *"test certificate"* has the meaning given by section 45(2)(b) of the Road Traffic Act 1988.

Registration of existing private hire vehicles

B60.04 **3.**—(1) Subject to the provisions of this regulation, the holder of a London PHV Operator's licence may apply to Transport for London for a vehicle to be registered as an existing private hire vehicle.

(2) An application under paragraph (1) shall include a declaration by the applicant that—

> (a) the vehicle is constructed or adapted to seat fewer than nine passengers;
>
> (b) if the vehicle is one to which section 47 of the Road Traffic Act 1988 (obligatory test certificates) applies, a test certificate has been issued for it within the period of twelve months ending with the date on which the application is sent to Transport for London;
>
> (c) there is in force in relation to the use of the vehicle a policy of insurance or such security in respect of third party risks as complies with the requirements of Part VI (third-party insurance) of the Road Traffic Act 1988;

(d) the person in whose name the vehicle is registered under the Vehicle Excise and Registration Act 1994 raises no objection to the disclosure by the Secretary of State to Transport for London of any particulars the vehicle contained in the register of mechanically propelled vehicles maintained by the Secretary of State under that Act; and

(e) the vehicle has been used as a private hire vehicle on roads in London under a booking which was made through the applicant at an operating centre specified in the applicant's London PHV operator's licence.

(3) An application shall be made by sending by prepaid post or otherwise delivering to Transport for London at the Public Carriage Office, 15 Penton Street, London N1 9PU the form provided by it for the purpose—

(a) completed to include the declaration required by paragraph (2) and such other particulars as Transport for London may reasonably require; and

(b) signed by the applicant.

(4) The form shall be treated as validly delivered to Transport for London if, and only if, it is received by Transport for London before 8th June 2004, whether before or after the making of these Regulations.

(5) Transport for London shall register a vehicle as an existing private hire vehicle if it is satisfied that the form submitted by the applicant meets the requirements of paragraphs (2) and (3) and has been validly delivered.

(6) Transport for London shall, for the purposes of this regulation, maintain a register of existing private hire vehicles containing the following particulars with respect to each vehicle—

(a) the registration mark;

(b) the make, model and colour; and

(c) the name and address of the owner.

(7) Transport for London shall remove particulars of an existing private hire vehicle from the register if any temporary permit issued with respect to it ceases to have effect in accordance with regulation 6.

(8) Section 23(2) of the 1998 Act applies to the register maintained under this regulation as it applies to the register maintained under section 23(1).

Deemed applications for London PHV licences

4.—(1) The owner of an existing private hire vehicle shall be treated for the purposes of the 1998 Act as if he had made an application for a London PHV licence, unless and until he notifies Transport for London that he does not wish to proceed with the application, in which case any temporary permit issued in respect of the vehicle shall be treated as having been surrendered.   **B60.05**

(2) Transport for London shall, at such time as it thinks fit having regard to the need to spread the grant of licences for existing private hire vehicles, notify each owner of an existing private hire vehicle who, by virtue of paragraph (1), is treated as having applied for a London PHV licence of the time and place at which the owner is asked to produce the vehicle for an inspection to determine whether it meets the requirements of section 7(2) of the 1998 Act.

(3) Transport for London shall not be required to consider any other application for a London PHV licence for an existing private hire vehicle until after the time notified with respect to that vehicle in accordance with paragraph (2).

Issue of temporary permits

B60.06   **5.**—(1) Transport for London may issue to the owner a temporary permit with respect to any existing private hire vehicle.

(2) Subject to regulation 6 a temporary permit shall have effect for the purposes of the 1998 Act (other than those of section 10) as if it were a London PHV licence and may in particular be suspended or revoked under section 16 accordingly.

Duration of temporary permits

B60.07   **6.**—(1) A temporary permit shall cease to have effect with respect to an existing private hire vehicle on whichever of the following dates falls first—

>   (a) if a London PHV licence is granted in respect of the vehicle, the date on which the licence is granted;
>   (b) if an application for a London PHV licence for the vehicle is refused, the date specified in paragraph (2);
>   (c) if the temporary permit is revoked, the date on which the revocation takes effect in accordance with section 17(1) or (2) of the 1998 Act;
>   (d) if the temporary permit ceases to have effect in accordance with [paragraph (3)], the date specified or agreed as mentioned in paragraph (3);
>   (e) [...];
>   (f) if the temporary permit is surrendered by the holder, the date of the surrender.

(2) The date referred to in paragraph (1)(b) is the date on which the time for appealing against the refusal of the application expires or (where an appeal is brought) the date on which the appeal is disposed of or withdrawn.

(3) A temporary permit shall cease to have effect if a vehicle is not produced for inspection—

>   (a) at the time and place notified under regulation 4(2); or
>   (b) at an alternative time and place agreed between the owner and Transport for London being a time falling within the period of two months beginning with the time notified under regulation 4(2).

(4) For the purposes of paragraph (3) a vehicle shall not be taken to have been produced for inspection unless the fee prescribed by Transport for London for the application under section 20(1)(a) of the [1988] Act has been paid before the time fixed for the inspection.

B60.08   *[Regulation 6 is printed as amended by SI 2007/3453.]*

The Road Transport (Working Time) Regulations 2005

(SI 2005/639)

[The text of these regulations has been amended by:

> *the Road Transport (Working Time) (Amendment) Regulations 2007 (SI 2007/853) (April 11, 2007).*

The amending regulations are referred to in the notes to the principal regulations only by their year and number. The date referred to above is the date on which the amending regulations came into force.]

B61.01

Citation, commencement and extent

1.—(1) These Regulations may be cited as the Road Transport (Working Time) Regulations 2005 and shall come into force on 4th April 2005.

B61.02

(2) These Regulations extend to Great Britain only.

Interpretation

2. In these Regulations —

B61.03

"*AETR*" means the European agreement concerning the work of crews of vehicles engaged in international road transport [*q.v.*] of 1st July 1970;

"*collective agreement*" means a collective agreement within the meaning of section 178 of the Trade Union and Labour Relations (Consolidation) Act 1992, the trade union parties to which are independent trade unions within the meaning of section 5 of that Act;

["*the Community Drivers' Hours Regulation*" means Regulation (EC) No 561/2006 of the European Parliament and of the Council of 15 March 2006 on the harmonisation of certain social legislation relating to road transport (and amending and repealing certain Council Regulations);]

"*employer*" in relation to a worker, means the person by whom the worker is (or, where the employment has ceased, was) employed;

"*employment*" in relation to a worker, means employment under his contract, and "employed" shall be construed accordingly;

"*goods*" includes goods or burden of any description;

"*goods vehicle*" means a motor vehicle constructed or adapted for use for the carriage of goods, or a trailer so constructed or adapted;

"*inspector*" means a person appointed under paragraph 1 of Schedule 2;

"*mobile worker*" means any worker forming part of the travelling staff, including trainees and apprentices, who is in the service of an undertaking which operates transport services for passengers or goods by road for hire or reward or on its own account;

"night time" means in respect of goods vehicles the period between midnight and 4 a.m. and in respect of passenger vehicles the period between 1 a.m. and 5 a.m.;

"motor vehicle" means a mechanically propelled vehicle intended or adapted for use on roads;

"night work" means any work performed during night time;

"passenger vehicle" means a motor vehicle which is constructed or adapted to carry more than eight seated passengers in addition to the driver;

"period of availability" means a period during which the mobile worker is not required to remain at his workstation, but is required to be available to answer any calls to start or resume driving or to carry out other work, including periods during which the mobile worker is accompanying a vehicle being transported by a ferry or by a train as well as periods of waiting at frontiers and those due to traffic prohibitions;

"reference period" means the period for calculation of the average maximum weekly working time;

"relevant requirements" means regulations 4(8), 7(5), 8(2), 9(4), 10, 11 and 12;

"self-employed driver" means anyone whose main occupation is to transport passengers or goods by road for hire or reward within the meaning of Community legislation under cover of a Community licence or any other professional authorisation to carry out such transport, who is entitled to work for himself and who is not tied to an employer by an employment contract or by any other type of working hierarchical relationship, who is free to organise the relevant working activities, whose income depends directly on the profits made and who has the freedom, individually or through a cooperation between self-employed drivers, to have commercial relations with several customers;

"vehicle" means a goods vehicle or a passenger vehicle;

"week" means a period of seven days beginning at midnight between Sunday and Monday;

"worker" means an individual who has entered into or works under (or, where employment has ceased, worked under)—

    (a) a contract of employment; or

    (b) any other contract, whether express or implied and (if it is express) whether oral or in writing, whereby the individual undertakes to do or perform personally any work or services for another party to the contract;

and any reference to a worker's contract shall be construed accordingly;

"workforce agreement" means an agreement between an employer and mobile workers employed by him or their representatives in respect of which the conditions set out in Schedule 1 to these Regulations are satisfied;

"working time" means the time from the beginning to the end of work dur-

ing which the mobile worker is at his workstation, at the disposal of his employer and exercising his functions or activities, being

  (a) time devoted to all road transport activities, including, in particular—

    (i) driving;

    (ii) loading and unloading;

    (iii) assisting passengers boarding and disembarking from the vehicle;

    (iv) cleaning and technical maintenance;

    (v) all other work intended to ensure the safety of the vehicle, its cargo and passengers or to fulfil the legal or regulatory obligations directly linked to the specific transport operation under way, including monitoring of loading and unloading and dealing with administrative formalities with police, customs, immigration officers and others; or

  (b) time during which the mobile worker cannot dispose freely of his time and is required to be at his workstation, ready to take up normal work, with certain tasks associated with being on duty, in particular during periods awaiting loading or unloading where their foreseeable duration is not known in advance, that is to say either before departure or just before the actual start of the period in question, or under collective agreements or workforce agreements;

"workstation" means

  (a) the location of the main place of business of the undertaking for which the person performing mobile transport activities carries out duties, together with its various subsidiary places of business, regardless of whether they are located in the same place as its head office or its main place of business;

  (b) the vehicle which the person performing mobile road transport activities uses when he carries out duties; or

  (c) any other place in which activities connected with transport are carried out.

[Regulation 2 is printed as amended by SI 2007/853.]   **B61.04**

Application

3.—(1) These Regulations apply to mobile workers who are employed by, or who do work for, undertakings established in a Member State of the European Union, and to whom paragraph (2) or paragraph (3) applies.   **B61.05**

[(2) This paragraph applies to mobile workers who, in the course of that employment or work, drive or travel in or on vehicles—

  (a) which are vehicles within the meaning of Article 1 of the Community Drivers' Hours Regulation,

  (b) which are not vehicles described in Article 3 of that Regulation, and

  (c) which are not vehicles exempted from the provisions of that Regulation under regulation 2 of the Community Drivers' Hours and

Recording Equipment (Exemptions and Supplementary Provisions) Regulations 1986.]

(3) This paragraph applies to mobile workers, to whom paragraph (2) does not apply, who in the course of that employment or work drive, or travel in, vehicles

(a) which fall within the meaning of a *"vehicle"* in Article 1 of the AETR;

(b) which are not referred to in Article 2(2)(b) of the AETR; and

(c) which are performing international transport.

(4) These Regulations do not apply to—

(a) self-employed drivers, or

(b) any worker who does work which is included in the calculation of working time—

(i) where the reference period is shorter than 26 weeks, on fewer than 11 days in a reference period applicable to that worker, or

(ii) in any other case on fewer than 16 days in a reference period applicable to that worker.

B61.06   *[Regulation 3 is printed as amended by SI 2007/853.*

With effect from July 2, 2007, the Community Drivers' Hours and Recording Equipment (Exemptions and Supplementary Provisions) Regulations 1986 referred to in reg.3(2) above as substituted by SI 2007/853 have been revoked by the Community Drivers' Hours and Recording Equipment Regulations 2007 (SI 2007/1819), q.v.]

Working time

B61.07   **4.**—(1) Subject to paragraph (2) below, the working time, including overtime, of a mobile worker shall not exceed 60 hours in a week.

(2) In any reference period which is applicable to his case, a mobile worker's working time shall not exceed an average of 48 hours for each week.

(3) The reference periods which apply in the case of a mobile worker shall be—

(a) where a collective agreement or a workforce agreement provides for the application of this regulation in relation to successive periods of 17 weeks, each such period,

(b) in a case where—

(i) there is no such provision, and

(ii) the employer gives written notice to the mobile worker in writing that he intends to apply this subparagraph,

any period of 17 weeks in the course of the worker's employment, or

(c) in any other case, the period ending at midnight between Sunday 31st July 2005 and Monday 1st August 2005 and thereafter, in each year, the successive periods beginning at midnight at the beginning of the Monday which falls on, or is the first Monday after, a date in column 1 below and ending at midnight at the beginning of the Monday which falls on, or is the first Monday after, the date on the same line in column 2 below.

Column 1 (beginning)	Column 2 (end)
1st December	1st April
1st April	1st August
1st August	1st December

(4) The reference period may be extended in relation to particular mobile workers or groups of mobile workers for objective or technical reasons or reasons concerning the organisation of work, by a collective agreement or a workforce agreement, by the substitution for 17 weeks of a period not exceeding 26 weeks in the application of paragraphs (2) and (3)(a) above.

(5) A mobile worker's average weekly working time during a reference period shall be determined according to the formula—

$$(A+B) \div C$$

where—

A is the aggregate number of hours comprised in the mobile worker's working time during the course of the reference period;

B is the number of excluded hours during the reference period; and

C is the number of weeks in the reference period.

(6) In paragraph (5), *"excluded hours"* means hours comprised in—

    (a) any period of annual leave taken by the mobile worker in exercise of entitlement under regulation 13 of the Working Time Regulations 1998 [*SI 1998/1833; not reproduced in this work*];

    (b) any period of sick leave taken by the mobile worker;

    (c) any period of maternity, paternity, adoption or parental leave taken by the mobile worker;

(7) For the purposes of paragraph (5), the number of hours in a whole day shall be eight and the number of hours in a whole week shall be forty-eight.

(8) An employer shall take all reasonable steps, in keeping with the need to protect the health and safety of the mobile worker, to ensure that the limits specified above are complied with in the case of each mobile worker employed by him.

5. The times of breaks, rests and periods of availability shall not be included in the calculation of working time.   **B61.08**

Periods of availability

6.—(1) A period shall not be treated as a period of availability unless the   **B61.09** mobile worker knows before the start of the relevant period about that period of availability and its reasonably foreseeable duration.

(2) The time spent by a mobile worker, who is working as part of a team, travelling in, but not driving, a moving vehicle as part of that team shall be a period of availability for that mobile worker.

(3) Subject to paragraph (4) a period of availability shall not include a period of rest or a break.

(4) A period of availability may include a break taken by a mobile worker during waiting time or time which is not devoted to driving by the mobile worker and is spent in a moving vehicle, a ferry or a train.

Breaks

B61.10   7.—(1) No mobile worker shall work for more than six hours without a break.

(2) Where a mobile worker's working time exceeds six hours but does not exceed nine hours, the worker shall be entitled to a break lasting at least 30 minutes and interrupting that time.

(3) Where a mobile worker's working time exceeds nine hours, the worker shall be entitled to a break lasting at least 45 minutes and interrupting that period.

(4) Each break may be made up of separate periods of not less than 15 minutes each.

(5) An employer shall take all reasonable steps, in keeping with the need to protect the health and safety of the mobile worker, to ensure that the limits specified above are complied with in the case of each mobile worker employed by him.

Rest periods

B61.11   8.—(1) In the application of these Regulations, the provisions of the Community Drivers' Hours Regulation relating to daily and weekly rest shall apply to all mobile workers to whom they do not apply under that Regulation as they apply to other mobile workers under that Regulation.

(2) An employer shall take all reasonable steps, in keeping with the need to protect the health and safety of the mobile worker, to ensure that those provisions are complied with in the case of each mobile worker employed by him, to whom they are applied by paragraph (1).

Night work

B61.12   9.—(1) The working time of a mobile worker, who performs night work in any period of 24 hours, shall not exceed 10 hours during that period.

(2) The period of 10 hours may be extended in relation to particular mobile workers or groups of mobile workers for objective or technical reasons or reasons concerning the organisation of work, by a collective agreement or a workforce agreement.

(3) Compensation for night work shall not be given to a mobile worker in any manner which is liable to endanger road safety.

(4) An employer shall take all reasonable steps in keeping with the need to protect the health and safety of mobile workers to ensure that the limit specified in paragraph (1), or extended in accordance with paragraph (2), is complied with in the case of each mobile worker employed by him.

Information and records

B61.13   10. An employer of mobile workers shall notify each worker of the provisions of these Regulations and the provisions of any collective or workforce agreement which is capable of application to that worker

B61.14   11. An employer of a mobile worker shall

      (a) request from each mobile worker details of any time worked by that worker for another employer;

(b) include time worked for another employer in the calculation of the mobile worker's working time;

(c) keep records which are adequate to show whether the requirements of these Regulations are being complied with in the case of each mobile worker employed by him to whom they apply;

(d) retain such records for at least two years after the end of the period covered by those records;

(e) provide, at the request of a mobile worker, a copy of the record of hours worked by that worker;

(f) provide to an enforcement officer copies of such records relating to mobile workers as the officer may require;

(g) provide to a mobile worker or enforcement officer copies of such documentary evidence in the employer's possession as may be requested by the worker or officer in relation to records provided to him in accordance with paragraph (e) or (f) above.

12. A mobile worker shall, at the request of his employer under regulation 11(a), notify his employer in writing of time worked by the worker for another employer for inclusion in the calculation of the mobile worker's working time.   **B61.15**

13.—(1) The Secretary of State shall arrange for the publication, in such form and manner as he considers appropriate, of information and advice concerning the operation of these Regulations.   **B61.16**

(2) The information and advice shall be such as appear to him best calculated to enable employers and workers affected by these Regulations to understand their respective rights and obligations.

Agency workers not otherwise mobile workers

14.—(1) This regulation applies in any case where an individual ("the agency worker")—   **B61.17**

(a) is supplied by a person ("the agent") to do the work of a mobile worker for another ("the principal") under a contract or other arrangements made between the agent and the principal; but

(b) is not, as respects that work, a worker, because of the absence of a worker's contract between the individual and the agent or the principal; and

(c) is not a party to a contract under which he undertakes to do the work for another party to the contract whose status is, by virtue of the contract, that of a client or customer or any profession or business undertaking carried on by the individual.

(2) In a case where this regulation applies, the other provisions of these Regulations shall have effect as if there were a contract for the doing of the work by the agency worker made between the agency worker and—

(a) whichever of the agent and the principal is responsible for paying the agency worker in respect of the work; or

(b) if neither the agent nor the principal is so responsible, whichever of them pays the agency worker in respect of the work,

(c) and as if that person were the agency worker's employer.

[Individual carrying on trade or business

B61.18   **15.**—(1) This regulation applies to an individual who—

(a) for the purpose of a trade or business carried on by him, drives a vehicle described in paragraph (2) or (3) of regulation 3, and

(b) is neither—

(i) a self-employed driver, nor

(ii) an agency worker within the meaning of regulation 14.

(2) Where this regulation applies, these Regulations shall have effect as if—

(a) the individual were both a mobile worker and the employer of that mobile worker, and

(b) regulations 10, 11(a) and (e) and 12 were omitted.]

B61.19   *[Regulation 15 is printed as substituted by SI 2007/853.]*

Enforcement

B61.20   **16.**—(1) It shall be the duty of the Secretary of State to enforce the requirements of these Regulations.

(2) Schedule 2 shall apply in relation to the enforcement of the relevant requirements.

B61.21   **17.**—(1) Any person who fails to comply with any of the relevant requirements shall be guilty of an offence.

(2) The provisions of paragraph (3) shall apply where an inspector is exercising or has exercised any power conferred by Schedule 2.

(3) It is an offence for a person—

(a) to contravene any requirement imposed by an inspector under paragraph 2 of Schedule 2;

(b) to prevent or attempt to prevent any other person from appearing before an inspector or from answering any question to which an inspector may by virtue of paragraph 2(2)(e) of Schedule 2 require an answer;

(c) to contravene any requirement or prohibition imposed by an improvement notice or a prohibition notice referred to in paragraphs 3 and 4 of Schedule 2 (including any such notice as is modified on appeal);

(d) intentionally to obstruct an inspector in the exercise or performance of his powers;

(e) to use or disclose any information in contravention of paragraph 7 of Schedule 2;

(f) to make a statement which he knows to be false or recklessly to make a statement which is false where the statement is made in purported compliance with a requirement to furnish any information imposed by or under these Regulations.

(4) Any person guilty of an offence under paragraph (1) shall be liable—

(a) on summary conviction, to a fine not exceeding the statutory maximum;

(b) on conviction on indictment, to a fine.

(5) A person guilty of an offence under paragraph (3)(b) or (d) shall be liable on summary conviction to a fine not exceeding level 5 on the standard scale.

(6) A person guilty of an offence under paragraph (3)(c) shall be liable—

    (a) on summary conviction, to imprisonment for a term not exceeding three months, or a fine not exceeding the statutory maximum;

    (b) on conviction on indictment, to imprisonment for a term not exceeding two years, or a fine or both.

(7) A person guilty of an offence under paragraph (3)(a),(e) or (f) shall be liable—

    (a) on summary conviction, to a fine not exceeding the statutory maximum;

    (b) on conviction on indictment—

        (i) if the offence is under paragraph (3)(e), to imprisonment for a term not exceeding two years or a fine or both,

        (ii) if the offence is under paragraph (3)(a) or (f), to a fine.

(8) The provisions set out in regulations 18 to 22 shall apply in relation to the offences provided for in paragraphs (1) and (3).

Offences due to fault of other person

18. Where the commission by any person of an offence is due to the act or default of some other person, that other person shall be guilty of the offence, and a person may be charged with the conviction of the offence by virtue of this regulation whether or not proceedings are taken against the first-mentioned person.   **B61.22**

Offences by bodies corporate

19.—(1) Where an offence committed by a body corporate is proved to have been committed with the consent or connivance of, or to have been attributable to any neglect on the part of, any director, manager, secretary or other similar officer of the body corporate or a person who was purporting to act in any such capacity, he as well as the body corporate shall be guilty of that offence and shall be liable to be proceeded against and punished accordingly.   **B61.23**

(2) Where the affairs of a body corporate are managed by its members, the preceding paragraph shall apply in relation to the acts and defaults of a member in connection with his functions of management as if he were a director of the body corporate.

Restriction on institution of proceedings in England and Wales

20. Proceedings for an offence shall not be instituted in England or Wales except by an inspector or by, or with the consent of, the Director of Public Prosecutions.   **B61.24**

Prosecution by inspectors

21.—(1) If authorised in that behalf by the Secretary of State an inspector may prosecute proceedings for an offence before a magistrates court even though the inspector is not of counsel or a solicitor.   **B61.25**

(2) This regulation shall not apply in Scotland.

Power of court to order cause of offence to be remedied

B61.26   **22.**—(1) This regulation applies where a person is convicted of an offence in respect of any matter which appears to the court to be a matter which it is in his power to remedy.

(2) In addition to or instead of imposing any punishment, the court may order the person in question to take such steps as may be specified in the order for remedying the said matters within such time as may be fixed by the order.

(3) The time fixed by an order under paragraph (2) may be extended or further extended by order of the court on an application made before the end of that time as originally fixed or as extended under this paragraph, as the case may be.

(4) Where a person is ordered under paragraph (2) to remedy any matters, that person shall not be liable under these Regulations in respect of that matter in so far as it continues during the time fixed by the order or any further time allowed under paragraph (3).

Regulation 2	SCHEDULE 1

WORKFORCE AGREEMENTS

B61.27   *[Omitted.]*

Regulation 16(2)	SCHEDULE 2

ENFORCEMENT

Appointment of inspectors

B61.28   **1.**—(1) The Secretary of State may appoint as inspectors (under whatever title he may from time to time determine) such persons having suitable qualifications as he thinks necessary for carrying into effect these Regulations, and may terminate any appointment made under this paragraph.

(2) Every appointment of a person as an inspector under this paragraph shall be made by an instrument in writing specifying which of the powers conferred on inspectors by these Regulations are to be exercisable by the person appointed; and an inspector shall in right of his appointment under this paragraph be entitled to exercise only such of those powers as are so specified.

(3) So much of an inspector's instrument of appointment as specifies the powers which he is entitled to exercise may be varied by the Secretary of State.

(4) An inspector shall, if so required when exercising or seeking to exercise any power conferred on him by these Regulations, produce his instrument of appointment or a duly authenticated copy thereof.

Powers of inspectors

B61.29   **2.**—(1) Subject to the provisions of paragraph 1 and this paragraph, an inspector may for the purpose of carrying into effect these Regulations exercise the powers set out in sub-paragraph (2).

(2) The powers of an inspector are the following, namely—

    (a) at any reasonable time (or in a situation which in his opinion may be dangerous, at any time) to enter any premises which he has reason to believe it is necessary for him to enter for the purposes mentioned in sub-paragraph (1);

    (b) to take with him a constable if he has reasonable cause to apprehend any serious obstruction in the execution of his duty;

(c) without prejudice to paragraph (b), on entering any premises by virtue of paragraph (a) to take with him—

    (i) any other person duly authorised by the Secretary of State; and

    (ii) any equipment or material required for any purpose for which the power of entry is being exercised;

(d) to make such examination and investigation as may in any circumstances be necessary for the purpose mentioned in sub-paragraph (1);

(e) to require any person whom he has reasonable cause to believe to be able to give any information relevant to any examination or investigation under paragraph (d) to answer (in the absence of persons other than a person nominated by him to be present and any persons whom the inspector may allow to be present) such questions as the inspector thinks fit to ask and to sign a declaration of the truth of his answers;

(f) to require the production of, inspect, and take copies of, or of any entry in—

    (i) any records which by virtue of these Regulations are required to be kept, and

    (ii) any other books, records or documents which it is necessary for him to see for the purposes of any examination or investigation under paragraph (d);

(g) to require any person to afford him such facilities and assistance with respect to any matters or things within that person's control or in relation to which that person has responsibilities as are necessary to enable the inspector to exercise any of the powers conferred on him by this sub-paragraph;

(h) any other power which is necessary for the purpose mentioned in sub-paragraph (1).

(3) No answer given by a person in pursuance of a requirement imposed under sub-paragraph (2)(e) shall be admissible in evidence against that person or the husband or wife of that person in any proceedings.

(4) Nothing in this paragraph shall be taken to compel the production by any person of a document of which he would on grounds of legal professional privilege be entitled to withhold production on an order for discovery in an action in the High Court or, as the case may be, an order for the production of documents in an action in the Court of Session.

Improvement notices

3. If an inspector is of the opinion that a person—   **B61.30**

    (a) is contravening one or more of these Regulations; or

    (b) has contravened one or more of these Regulations in circumstances that make it likely that the contravention will continue or be repeated,

he may serve on him a notice (in this Schedule referred to as "an improvement notice") stating that he is of that opinion, specifying the provision or provisions as to which he is of that opinion, giving particulars of the reasons why he is of that opinion, and requiring that person to remedy the contravention or, as the case may be, the matter occasioning it within such period (ending not earlier than the period within which an appeal against the notice can be brought under paragraph (6)) as may be specified in the notice.

Prohibition notices

4.—(1) This paragraph applies to any activities which are being, or are likely to be, carried on by or under the control of any person, being activities to or in relation to which any of these Regulations apply or will, if the activities are so carried on, apply.   **B61.31**

(2) If as regards any activities to which this paragraph applies an inspector is of the opinion that, as carried on by or under the control of the person in question, the activities involve or, as the case may be, will involve a risk of serious personal injury, the inspector may serve on that person a notice (in this Schedule referred to as "a prohibition notice").

(3) A prohibition notice shall—

    (a) state that the inspector is of the said opinion;

    (b) specify the matters which in his opinion give or, as the case may be, will give rise to the said risk;

    (c) where in his opinion any of those matters involves or, as the case may be, will involve a contravention of any of these Regulations, state that he is of that opinion, specify the regulation or regulations as to which he is of that opinion, and give particulars of the reasons why he is of that opinion; and

    (d) direct that the activities to which the notice relates shall not be carried on by or under the control of the person on whom the notice is served unless the matters specified in the notice in pursuance of paragraph (b) and any associated contraventions of provisions so specified in pursuance of paragraph (c) have been remedied.

(4) A direction contained in a prohibition notice in pursuance of sub-paragraph (3)(d) shall take effect—

    (a) at the end of the period specified in the notice; or

    (b) if the notice so declares, immediately.

Provisions supplementary to paragraphs 3 and 4

B61.32   5.—(1) In this paragraph *"a notice"* means an improvement notice or a prohibition notice.

(2) A notice may (but need not) include directions as to the measures to be taken to remedy any contravention or matter to which the notice relates; and any such directions—

    (a) may be framed to any extent by reference to any approved code of practice; and

    (b) may be framed so as to afford the person on whom the notice is served a choice between different ways of remedying the contravention or matter.

(3) Where an improvement notice or prohibition notice which is not to take immediate effect has been served—

    (a) the notice may be withdrawn by an inspector at any time before the end of the period specified therein in pursuance of paragraph 3 or paragraph 4(4) as the case may be; and

    (b) the period so specified may be extended or further extended by an inspector at any time when an appeal against the notice is not pending.

Appeal against improvement or prohibition notice

B61.33   6.—(1) In this paragraph *"a notice"* means an improvement or prohibition notice.

(2) A person on whom a notice is served may within 21 days from the date of its service appeal to an employment tribunal; and on such an appeal the tribunal may either cancel or affirm the notice and, if it affirms it, may do so either in its original form or with such modifications as the tribunal may in the circumstances think fit.

(3) Where an appeal under this paragraph is brought against a notice within the period allowed under the preceding sub-paragraph, then—

    (a) in the case of an improvement notice, the bringing of the appeal shall have the effect of suspending the operation of the notice until the appeal is finally disposed of or, if the appeal is withdrawn, until the withdrawal of the appeal;

    (b) in the case of a prohibition notice, the bringing of the appeal shall have the like effect if, but only if, on the application of the appellant the tribunal so directs (and then only from the giving of the direction).

(4) One or more assessors may be appointed for the purposes of any proceedings brought before an employment tribunal under this paragraph.

Restrictions on disclosure of information

B61.34   7.—(1) In this paragraph —

      "relevant information" means information obtained by an inspector in pursuance of a requirement imposed under paragraph 2;

"relevant statutory provisions" means the provisions of Part 6 of the Transport Act 1968 and of any orders or regulations made under powers contained in that Part; and

"the recipient", in relation to any relevant information, means the person by whom that information was so obtained or to whom that information was so furnished, as the case may be.

(2) Subject to the following sub-paragraph, no relevant information shall be disclosed without the consent of the person by whom it was furnished.

(3) The preceding sub-paragraph shall not apply to—

    (a) disclosure of information to a government department;

    (b) without prejudice to paragraph (a), disclosure by the recipient of information to any person for the purpose of any function conferred on the recipient by or under any of the relevant statutory provisions or under these Regulations;

    (c) without prejudice to paragraph (a), disclosure by the recipient of information to—

        (i) an officer of a local authority who is authorised by that authority to receive it: or

        (ii) a constable authorised by a chief officer of police to receive it; or

    (d) disclosure by the recipient of information in a form calculated to prevent it from being identified as relating to a particular person or case.

(4) A person to whom information is disclosed in pursuance of sub-paragraph (3) shall not use the information for a purpose other than—

    (a) in a case falling within sub-paragraph (3)(a), a purpose of a government department or local authority in connection with these Regulations or with the relevant statutory provisions, or any enactment whatsoever relating to working time;

    (b) in the case of information given to a constable, the purposes of the police in connection with these Regulations, the relevant statutory provisions or any enactment relating to working time.

(5) A person shall not disclose any information obtained by him as a result of the exercise of any power conferred by paragraph 2 (including in particular any information with respect to any trade secret obtained by him in any premises entered by him by virtue of any such power) except—

    (a) for the purposes of his functions; or

    (b) for the purposes of any legal proceedings; or

    (c) with the relevant consent.

In this sub-paragraph *"the relevant consent"* means, in the case of information furnished in pursuance of a requirement imposed under paragraph 2, the consent of the person who furnished it, and, in any other case, the consent of a person having responsibilities in relation to the premises where the information was obtained.

(6) Notwithstanding anything in sub-paragraph (5) an inspector shall, in circumstances in which it is necessary to do so for the purpose of assisting in keeping persons (or the representatives of persons) adequately informed about matters affecting their health, safety and welfare or working time, give to such persons or their representatives the following descriptions of information, that is to say—

    (a) factual information obtained by him as mentioned in that sub-paragraph which relates to their working environment; and

    (b) information with respect to any action which he has taken or proposes to take in or in connection with the performance of his functions in relation to their working environment;

and, where an inspector does as aforesaid, he shall give the like information to the employer of the first-mentioned persons.

(7) Notwithstanding anything in sub-paragraph (5), a person who has obtained such information as is referred to in that sub-paragraph may furnish to a person who appears to

him to be likely to be a party to any civil proceedings arising out of any accident, occurrence, situation or other matter, a written statement of the relevant facts observed by him in the course of exercising any of the powers referred to in that sub-paragraph.

The Road Traffic Act 1988 (Retention and Disposal of Seized Motor Vehicles) Regulations 2005

(SI 2005/1606)

[The text of these regulations has been amended by: **B62.01**
     *the Road Traffic Act 1988 (Retention and Disposal of Seized Motor
     Vehicles) (Amendment) Regulations 2008 (SI 2008/2097) (October 1,
     2008).*
The amending regulations are referred to in the notes to the principal regulations only by their year and number. The date referred to is the date on which the amending regulations came into force.]

Citation and commencement

1. These Regulations may be cited as the Road Traffic Act 1988 (Retention and   **B62.02**
Disposal of Seized Motor Vehicles) Regulations 2005 and shall come into force
on 6th July 2005.

Interpretation

2. In these Regulations—   **B62.03**

     "the 1988 Act" means the Road Traffic Act 1988;

     "the 1994 Act" means the Vehicle Excise and Registration Act 1994;

     "authorised person" means a constable or such other person authorised by
         the chief officer under regulation 3(1);

     "certificate of insurance" is to be construed in accordance with sections
         147(1) and 161(2) of the 1988 Act;

     "GB registration mark" means a registration mark issued in relation to a
         vehicle under the 1994 Act;

     [*"laden"* means that the vehicle is carrying a load;]

     [*"load"* means anything other than—

         (a) the body and all parts of the vehicle which are necessary to or
             ordinarily used with the vehicle when working on a road;

         (b) any water, fuel or accumulators used for the purpose of the
             supply of power for the propulsion of the vehicle;

         (c) the driver, any passengers and their personal effects;

         (d) a crane, works truck as defined in regulation 3(2) of the Road
             Vehicles (Construction and Use) Regulations 1986, or other
             special appliance or apparatus which is a permanent or es-
             sentially permanent fixture of the vehicle; and

         (e) any containers or other equipment intended or adapted for the
             purpose of holding or carrying a load by the vehicle;]

     [*"MAM"* means maximum authorised mass as defined in regulation 3(1) of
         the Motor Vehicles (Driving Licences) Regulations 1999;]

["*off road*" means that no part of the vehicle is in contact with the road;]

["*on road*" means that any part of the vehicle is in contact with the road;]

"*owner*" includes—

    (a) the person by whom, according to the records maintained by the Secretary of State in connection with any functions exercisable by him by virtue of the 1994 Act, the vehicle is kept and used;

    (b) in relation to a vehicle which is the subject of a hiring agreement or a hire-purchase agreement, the person entitled to possession of the vehicle under the agreement;

"*the register*" means the register maintained by the Secretary of State under Part 2 of the 1994 Act;

"*registered keeper*", in relation to a motor vehicle, means the person in whose name the vehicle is registered under the 1994 Act;

"*relevant motor vehicle*" means a motor vehicle which has been seized and removed under section 165A of the 1988 Act;

["*road*" means any length of highway or of any other road to which the public has access, and includes bridges over which a road passes;]

"*seizure notice*" means a notice complying with regulation 4;

["*substantially damaged*" means such damage to a vehicle that in the reasonable opinion of a constable it cannot be driven safely on the road;]

["*two wheeled vehicle*" means a mechanically propelled vehicle constructed or adapted to have two wheels or less and the MAM of which does not exceed 3.5 tonnes;]

["*unladen*" means that the vehicle is not carrying a load;]

"*valid licence*" means a licence to drive a motor vehicle granted under Part 3 of the 1988 Act, a Community licence, an exchangeable licence or a Northern Ireland driving licence, and for this purpose the terms "Community licence" and "exchangeable licence" have the same meaning as given in section 108(1) of the 1988 Act;

"*working days*" shall be taken to exclude Saturdays, Sundays, Christmas Day, Good Friday and, in relation to a vehicle retained in England and Wales, any day which, under the Banking and Financial Dealings Act 1971, is a bank holiday in England and Wales and, in relation to a vehicle retained in Scotland, any day which, under that Act, is a bank holiday in Scotland.

B62.04   *[Regulation 2 is printed as amended by SI 2008/297.]*

Retention and safe keeping of motor vehicles

B62.05   3.—(1) A relevant motor vehicle shall be passed into and remain in the custody of a constable or other person authorised under this regulation by the chief officer of the police force for the area in which the vehicle was seized ("the authorised person") until—

    (a) the authorised person permits it to be removed from his custody by a person appearing to him to be the registered keeper or owner of the vehicle; or

(b) it has been disposed of under these Regulations.

(2) While the vehicle is in the custody of the authorised person, the authorised person shall be under a duty to take such steps as are reasonably necessary for its safe keeping.

Giving of seizure notice

4.—(1) A constable, on seizing a vehicle under section 165A of the 1988 Act, **B62.06** shall give a seizure notice in accordance with this regulation to the driver of the vehicle being seized unless the circumstances make it impracticable for him to do so.

(2) The authorised person shall, as soon as he is able after a relevant motor vehicle has been taken into his custody, take such steps as are reasonably practicable to give a seizure notice in accordance with this regulation to the person who is the registered keeper and to the owner, where that appears to be someone different, of that vehicle, except where—

>   (a) the authorised person is satisfied that a seizure notice has already been given to the registered keeper and to the owner, where that appears to be someone different, of the vehicle under paragraph (1); or

>   (b) the vehicle has been released from his custody in accordance with these Regulations.

(3) A seizure notice shall, in respect of the vehicle to which it relates, contain such of the following information as can be or could have been ascertained from an inspection of the vehicle, or has been ascertained from any other source, that is to say—

>   (a) in the case of a vehicle which carries a GB registration mark, or a mark indicating registration in a place outside Great Britain, particulars of that mark; and

>   (b) the make of the vehicle.

(4) A seizure notice shall, in respect of the vehicle to which it relates, state—

>   (a) the place where the vehicle was seized;

>   (b) the place where it is now being kept;

>   (c) that the registered keeper or owner of the vehicle is required to claim the vehicle from the authorised person on or before the date specified in the notice, being a date not less than 7 working days from the day when the notice is given to the registered keeper or owner as the case may be;

>   (d) that unless the vehicle is claimed on or before that date the authorised person intends to dispose of it;

>   (e) that, subject to regulation 5(5), charges are payable under these Regulations by the registered keeper, owner or driver of the vehicle in respect of the seizure and retention of the vehicle, and that the vehicle may be retained until such charges are paid; and

>   (f) that the registered keeper or owner of the vehicle must either—

>>   (i) produce at a specified police station a valid certificate of insurance covering his use of that vehicle and a valid licence authorising him to drive that vehicle; or

    (ii) nominate for this purpose a third person who produces at a specified police station a valid certificate of insurance covering that person's use of that vehicle and a valid licence authorising that person to drive that vehicle,

and that the vehicle may be retained until this requirement is satisfied.

(5) The seizure notice shall be given—

    (a) by delivering it to the person to whom it is directed;

    (b) in respect of the registered keeper—

        (i) by leaving it at the address which is entered on the register as being the address of the registered keeper; or

        (ii) by sending it by the registered post service, addressed to the registered keeper, to the address which is entered on the register as being the address of the registered keeper;

    (c) in respect of the owner—

        (i) by leaving it at his usual or last known address; or

        (ii) by sending it by the registered post service, addressed to the owner at his usual or last known address; or

    (d) if the person is a body corporate, by delivering it to the secretary or clerk of the body at its registered or principal office, or sending it by the registered post service, addressed to the secretary or clerk of the body at that office.

Release of vehicles

B62.07   **5.**—(1) Subject to the provisions of these Regulations, if, before a relevant motor vehicle is disposed of by an authorised person, a person—

    (a) satisfies the authorised person that he is the registered keeper or the owner of that vehicle;

    (b) pays to the authorised person such a charge in respect of its seizure and retention as is provided for in regulation 6; and

    (c) produces at a police station specified in the seizure notice a valid certificate of insurance covering his use of that vehicle and a valid licence authorising him to drive the vehicle,

the authorised person shall permit him to remove the vehicle from his custody.

(2) Where a person satisfies paragraph (1)(a) and (b) but cannot satisfy paragraph (1)(c), and nominates for this purpose a third person who produces a valid certificate of insurance covering that person's use of that vehicle and a valid driving licence authorising that person to drive that vehicle, the authorised person shall permit that person to remove the vehicle from his custody.

(3) In determining whether he is satisfied that a person who claims to be the owner of a relevant motor vehicle is in fact the owner, an authorised person may consider such documentary evidence as that person may supply them.

(4) In determining whether he is satisfied that a person who claims to be the registered keeper of a relevant motor vehicle is in fact the relevant keeper, an authorised person shall refer to the register.

(5) A person who would otherwise be liable to pay a charge under paragraph (1) shall not be liable to pay if—

(a) he was not driving the vehicle at the time it was seized under section 165A of the 1988 Act; and

(b) he did not know that the vehicle was being driven at that time, had not consented to its being driven and could not, by the taking of reasonable steps, have prevented it from being driven.

6. *[Omitted.]*   **B62.08**

Disposal of motor vehicles

7.—(1) Subject to paragraph (2), the authorised person may, in such manner as he thinks fit, dispose of the vehicle at any time if—   **B62.09**

(a) where the registered keeper and owner of the vehicle appear to be the same person—

    (i) that person fails to comply with any requirement in a seizure notice given to him under regulation 4(2); or

    (ii) the authorised person was not able, having taken such steps as were reasonably practicable, to give a seizure notice to that person;

(b) where the registered keeper and owner appear to be different—

    (i) where a seizure notice was given to both of those persons under regulation 4(2), neither the registered keeper nor the owner of the vehicle comply with all requirements in that seizure notice;

    (ii) where the authorised person was only able, having taken such steps as were reasonably practicable, to give a seizure notice to one of those persons under regulation 4(2), that person failed to comply with any requirement in that seizure notice; or

    (iii) the authorised person was not able, having taken such steps as were reasonably practicable, to give a seizure notice to either the registered keeper or the owner.

(2) The authorised person may not dispose of the vehicle under this regulation—

(a) during the period of 14 days starting with the date on which the vehicle was seized;

(b) if the period in sub-paragraph (a) has expired, until after the date specified in the seizure notice in accordance with regulation 4(4)(c); or

(c) if not otherwise covered by sub-paragraph (a) or (b), during the period of 7 working days starting with the date on which the vehicle is claimed under regulation 5.

Payment of proceeds of sale to owner of vehicle

8.—(1) Where the authorised person disposes of a motor vehicle in pursuance of these Regulations by means of sale, he shall pay the net proceeds of sale to any person who, before the end of the period of one year beginning with the date on which the vehicle is sold, satisfies the authorised person that at the time of the sale he was the owner of the vehicle.   **B62.10**

(2) If it appears to the authorised person that more than one person is the

owner of a particular vehicle, such one of them as the authorised person thinks fit shall be treated as its owner for the purposes of paragraph (1).

(3) In this regulation, *"the net proceeds of sale"* means any sum by which the proceeds of sale exceed the aggregate of such sums as may be payable under these Regulations in respect of the seizure and retention of the vehicle.

The Passenger and Goods Vehicles (Recording Equipment) (Tachograph Card) Regulations 2006

(SI 2006/1937)

[The text of these regulations has been amended by: **B63.01**

> *the Passenger and Goods Vehicles (Community Recording Equipment Regulation) Regulations 2006 (SI 2006/3276) (January 3, 2007); and*

> *the Passenger and Goods Vehicles (Community Recording Equipment Regulation) Regulations 2010 (SI 2010/892) (April 23, 2010).*

The amending regulations are referred to in the notes to the principal regulations by their years and numbers only. The dates referred to above are the dates when the amending regulations came into force.]

1. These Regulations may be cited as the Passenger and Goods Vehicles (Re-   **B63.02**
cording Equipment) (Tachograph Card) Regulations 2006 and shall come into
force on 21st August 2006.

2.—(1) In these Regulations—   **B63.03**

> [*"the Community Recording Equipment Regulation"* means Council Regulation (EEC) No.3821/85 [*q.v.*] on recording equipment in road transport as read with the Community Drivers' Hours and Recording Equipment Regulations 2007.]

> *"company card"*, *"control card"*, *"driver card"* and *"workshop card"* have the meanings given by Annex IB to the Community Recording Equipment Regulation;

> *"PIN"* means personal identification number for use in connection with a workshop card;

> *"relevant vehicle"* means a vehicle in which there is recording equipment

>> (i) which has been installed in accordance with the Community Recording Equipment Regulation; and

>> (ii) complies with Annexes IB and II to that regulation; and

> *"tachograph card"* means a company card, control card, driver card or workshop card.

[Regulation 2 is printed as amended by SI 2006/3276; SI 2010/892.]   **B63.04**

Driver cards

3.—(1) A person commits an offence—   **B63.05**

> (a) if, subject to paragraph (3), he uses, attempts to use or is in possession of, more than one driver card on which he is identified as the holder;

> (b) if he uses or attempts to use a driver card on which he is not identified as the holder;

> (c) if, with intent to deceive, he makes a false statement, or forges or alters a document, for the purpose of obtaining a driver card;

> (d) if he uses, or is in possession of, a driver card issued in consequence

of an application which included, with intent to deceive, a false statement or forged or altered document; or

    (e) if he uses, or is in possession of, a driver card which has been forged or altered.

(2) A person commits an offence if he causes or permits—

    (a) any use or possession of a driver card; or

    (b) the making of any false statement or forgery or alteration of a document

specified in paragraph (1).

(3) It shall not be an offence—

    (a) to hold a card which will become time-expired within one month and the card which has been issued by the Secretary of State in renewal of the former card; or

    (b) to hold a card, which has become time-expired, in combination with another card.

(4) A person guilty of an offence under paragraph (1)(a) or (b) is liable on summary conviction to a fine not exceeding level 5 on the standard scale.

(5) A person guilty of an offence under paragraph (1)(c) is liable—

    (a) on summary conviction, to imprisonment for a term not exceeding 3 months or to a fine not exceeding the statutory maximum, or to both; or

    (b) on conviction on indictment, to imprisonment for a term not exceeding two years, or to a fine, or to both.

(6) A person guilty of an offence under paragraph (1)(d) or (e) or paragraph (2) is liable—

    (a) on summary conviction, to a fine not exceeding the statutory maximum; or

    (b) on conviction on indictment, to imprisonment for a term not exceeding two years or to a fine, or to both.

Workshop cards

B63.06   **4.**—(1) A person commits an offence—

    (a) if, subject to paragraph (3) he uses, attempts to use or is in possession of more than one workshop card, on which he is identified as the holder, or more than one PIN, in respect of the same place of work;

    (b) if he uses or attempts to use a workshop card, or PIN, of which he is not the identified holder;

    (c) if he uses or attempts to use a workshop card, or PIN, in circumstances unconnected with the place of work for which that card, or PIN, was issued;

    (d) if, with intent to deceive, he makes a false statement, or forges or alters a document, for the purpose of obtaining a workshop card or PIN;

    (e) if he uses, or is in possession of, a workshop card, or PIN, issued in consequence of an application which included, with intent to deceive, a false statement or forged or altered document;

    (f) if he uses, or is in possession of, a workshop card, which has been forged or altered; or

    (g) if he divulges to another person, or permits another person to use, the PIN used in connection with a workshop card of which he is identified as the holder.

(2) A person commits an offence if he causes or permits—

    (a) any use, alteration or possession of a workshop card or PIN, or

    (b) the making of any false statement or forgery or alteration of a document,

specified in paragraph (1).

(3) It shall not be an offence —

    (a) to hold a workshop card which will become time-expired within one month and the workshop card which has been issued by the Secretary of State in renewal of the former workshop card; or

    (b) to hold a workshop card, which has become time-expired, in combination with another workshop card.

(4) A person guilty of an offence under paragraph (1)(a), (b), (c) or (g) is liable on summary conviction to a fine not exceeding level 5 on the standard scale.

(5) A person guilty of an offence under paragraph (1)(d) is liable—

    (a) on summary conviction, to imprisonment for a term not exceeding 3 months or to a fine not exceeding the statutory maximum, or to both; or

    (b) on conviction on indictment, to imprisonment for a term not exceeding two years, or to a fine, or to both.

(6) A person guilty of an offence under paragraph (1)(e) or (f) or paragraph (2) is liable—

    (a) on summary conviction, to a fine not exceeding the statutory maximum; or

    (b) on conviction on indictment, to imprisonment for a term not exceeding two years or to a fine, or both.

Lost, stolen, damaged or malfunctioning cards

5.—(1) If a tachograph card is lost or stolen, the person to whom that card was issued shall notify the Secretary of State in writing and shall provide such information or documents concerning the loss or theft as the Secretary of State may require.   **B63.07**

(2) If a tachograph card is found at any time after the Secretary of State has been notified in accordance with paragraph (1) of the loss or theft of it, the person to whom that card was issued, if it is in his possession, shall return it to the Secretary of State, or if it is not in his possession, but he becomes aware that it is found, shall take all reasonable steps to take possession of it and if successful shall return it as soon as may be to the Secretary of State

(3) If a tachograph card is damaged or malfunctions, the person to whom that card was issued shall return it to the Secretary of State and shall provide such information or documents concerning the damage or malfunction as the Secretary of State may require.

(4) A person who fails to comply with the requirements of paragraph (1), (2) or (3) commits an offence.

(5) A person guilty of an offence under paragraph (4) is liable on summary conviction to a fine not exceeding level 5 on the standard scale.

Card particulars

B63.08   **6.**—(1) Where the details of the holder of a tachograph card specified on the card cease to be correct, the holder—

   (a) must forthwith notify the Secretary of State of the details which require correction, and

   (b) must surrender the card when required to do so, to such address as may be specified, by the Secretary of State.

(2) Where it appears to the Secretary of State that a tachograph card issued by him to any person was issued in error or with an error or omission in the particulars specified in the card, he may serve notice in writing on that person requiring him to surrender that card and it shall be the duty of that person to comply with the requirement.

(3) Subject to paragraph (4), on surrender of a card by a person in accordance with paragraph (1) or (2) the Secretary of State shall, if so requested by that person, issue a replacement card to him.

(4) The Secretary of State may require the person surrendering the card to provide such information and documents as the Secretary of State may require to enable him to correct the details, error or omission before issuing a new card under paragraph (3).

(5) A person who fails to comply with the requirements of paragraph (1) or (2) commits an offence.

(6) A person guilty of an offence under paragraph (5) is liable on summary conviction to a fine not exceeding level 5 on the standard scale.

Unauthorised cards

B63.09   **7.**—(1) A person in possession of a tachograph card described in paragraph (3) shall surrender that card to the Secretary of State, by such means and to such address as may be specified by the Secretary of State.

(2) A constable or a vehicle examiner appointed under section 66A of the Road Traffic Act 1988 may remove and retain a tachograph card described in paragraph (3) which has not been surrendered to the Secretary of State.

(3) A tachograph card to which paragraphs (1) and (2) refer is a card—

   (a) on which the person using the card is not identified as the holder;

   (b) which has been falsified; or

   (c) which has been issued in consequence of an application which included a false statement or forged or altered document.

(4) A person who does not surrender a card in accordance with paragraph (1) commits an offence.

(5) A person guilty of an offence under paragraph (3) is liable on summary conviction to a fine not exceeding level 5 on the standard scale.

The Vehicle Drivers (Certificates of Professional Competence) Regulations 2007

(SI 2007/605)

[The text of these regulations has been amended by:

B64.01

> *the Vehicle Drivers (Certificates of Professional Competence) (Amendment) (No.2) Regulations 2008 (SI 2008/1965) (September 1, 2008);*
>
> *the Vehicle Drivers (Certificates of Professional Competence) (Amendment) Regulations 2010 (SI 2010/865) (April 21, 2010); and*
>
> *the Vehicles Regulations (Amendment) Order 2010 (SI 2010/1111) (April 27, 2010).*

The amending instruments are referred to in the notes to the principal regulations only by their years and numbers. The dates referred to are the dates on which the amending instruments came into force.

These regulations have been further amended by the Vehicle Drivers (Certificates of Professional Competence) (Amendment) Regulations 2008 (SI 2008/ 506), but the amending regulations do not affect any provision of the principal regulations which is printed in the main work.]

Citation, commencement and extent

1.—(1) These Regulations may be cited as the Vehicle Drivers (Certificates of   **B64.02**
Professional Competence) Regulations 2007.

(2) These Regulations shall come into force as follows—

(a) all regulations other than regulation 15 shall come into force on 27th March 2007;

(b) *[commencement of reg.15, amendment of the Driving Licences Regulations]*.

(3) These Regulations extend to Northern Ireland except regulation 15.

Interpretation

2.—(1) In these Regulations—   **B64.03**

> *"the Directive"* means Directive 2003/59/EC of the European Parliament and of the Council of 15th July 2003 on the initial qualification and periodic training of drivers of certain road vehicles for the carriage of goods or passengers, amending Council Regulation (EEC) No. 3820/85 and Council Directive 91/439EEC and repealing Council Directive 76/914/EEC;
>
> *"the Driving Licences Directive"* means Council Directive 91/439/EEC of 29th July 1991 on driving licences;
>
> *"the 1988 Act"* means the Road Traffic Act 1988;
>
> *"the 1981 Order"* means the Road Traffic (Northern Ireland) Order 1981;
>
> *"the Driving Licences Regulations"* means the Motor Vehicles (Driving Licences) Regulations 1999;

"armed forces" means the naval, military or air forces of the Crown and includes the reserve forces;

[*"bank holiday"* means a day to be observed as such under section 1 of, and Schedule 1 to, the Banking and Financial Dealings Act 1971;

"candidate" means a person submitting, or seeking to submit, to an initial CPC test;]

"Community code" has the meaning given by Article 10(2) of the Directive;

"Community licence"

    (a) in relation to Great Britain, has the same meaning as in section 108(1) of the 1988 Act, and

    (b) in relation to Northern Ireland, has the same meaning as in Article 2(2) of the 1981 Order;

"competent authority" means—

    (a) in relation to Great Britain, the Secretary of State, and

    (b) in relation to Northern Ireland, the Department of the Environment;

"CPC" has the meaning given by the seventh recital to the Directive;

"driving licence" means, except in regulation 4(8)(b) and (c)—

    (a) in relation to Great Britain, a full licence within the meaning of section 108(1) of the 1988 Act, and

    (b) in relation to Northern Ireland, a full licence within the meaning of Article 2(2) of the 1981 Order;

"driver qualification card" has the meaning given by Article 10(1) of the Directive;

"driving test" means—

    (a) in relation to Great Britain, a test of competence prescribed under section 89(3) of the 1988 Act, and

    (b) in relation to Northern Ireland, a test of competence prescribed under Article 5(3) of the 1981 Order;

"fire and rescue authority"—

    (a) in relation to Great Britain, has the same meaning as in section 1 of the Fire and Rescue Services Act 2004, and

    (b) in relation to Northern Ireland, has the same meaning as "fire authority" in Article 3 of the Fire Services (Northern Ireland) Order 1984;

"initial CPC" means a CPC within the meaning of Article 6 of the Directive (CPC certifying the initial qualification);

"initial CPC test" means the tests for initial qualification referred to in Article 3(1)(a)(ii) of the Directive;

[*"NVT certificate"* means an authorisation issued by the competent authority under regulation 4(5)(d) or 8B(3);]

"periodic CPC" means a CPC within the meaning of Article 8 of the Directive (CPC certifying periodic training);

"periodic training" means the training referred to in Article 3(1)(b) of the Directive;

"periodic training course" means a course of at least seven hours of periodic training within the meaning of Section 4 of Annex I to the Directive;

"relevant vehicle" means a vehicle for which is required a driving licence of category C, C+E, D or D+E as defined in Article 3(1) of the Driving Licences Directive, or a driving licence recognised as equivalent;

"reserve forces" has the same meaning as in section 1 of the Reserve Forces Act 1996;

"road" means any road open to the public;

"test pass certificate" in relation to Great Britain, has the same meaning as in regulation 3(1) of the Driving Licences Regulations [and in relation to Northern Ireland, means the certificate referred to in regulation 37(1) of the Motor Vehicles (Driving Licences) Regulations (Northern Ireland) 1996];

"third country" means a country which is not a member State;

[*"trainer"* means a person who provides training or instruction in relation to the initial CPC test;]

"vehicle examiner" means an examiner appointed under section 66A of the 1988 Act or under Article 74 of the Road Traffic (Northern Ireland) Order 1995;

"work permit" has the same meaning as in section 33 of the Immigration Act 1971.

[*"working day"* means—

    (a) in relation to Great Britain, save for the purposes of regulation 5(5B), (6ZA)(c), (6ZAD) and (6ZAE), a day other than a Saturday, Sunday, bank holiday, Christmas Day or Good Friday;

    (b) in relation to Northern Ireland, a day other than a Saturday, Sunday, bank holiday, Christmas Day or Easter Tuesday.]

(2) In these Regulations—

    (a) a reference to a member State includes a reference to an EEA State;

    (b) [save for the purposes of regulation 5A(2A),] a reference to a category of relevant vehicle includes references to its sub-categories as defined in Article 3(2) of the Driving Licences Directive.

[Regulation 2 is printed as amended by SI 2008/1965; SI 2010/865.]　　**B64.04**

Persons to whom these Regulations apply

3.—(1) These Regulations apply to any person who drives a relevant vehicle, **B64.05** other than a vehicle to which paragraph (2) applies, on a road and is—

    (a) a national of a member State; or

    (b) a national of a third country employed or used by an undertaking established in a member State.

(2) This paragraph applies to a vehicle—

    (a) which it is an offence for that person to drive on any road at a speed greater than 45 kilometres per hour in Great Britain under section 89 of the Road Traffic Regulation Act 1984 or in Northern Ireland under the Motor Vehicles (Speed Limits) Regulations (Northern Ireland) 1989;

(b) which is being used by, or is under the control of any of the following—

  (i) the armed forces;

  (ii) a police force;

  (iii) a local authority in the discharge of any function conferred on or exercisable by that authority under an order made under section 5 of the Civil Contingencies Act 2004 or regulations made under section 20 of that Act, or

  (iv) a fire and rescue authority;

(c) which is undergoing road tests for technical development, repair or maintenance purposes, or that is a new or rebuilt vehicle which has not yet been put into service;

(d) which is being used in a state of emergency or is assigned to a rescue mission;

(e) which is being used in the course of a driving lesson or driving test for the purpose of enabling that person to obtain a driving licence or a CPC;

(f) which is being used for the non-commercial carriage of passengers or goods for personal use;

(g) which is carrying material or equipment to be used by that person in the course of his work, provided that driving that vehicle is not his principal activity.

Persons who must take initial CPC test

B64.06   4.—(1) Except where paragraph (5) or (9) applies and subject to paragraph (7), a person to whom these Regulations apply is not permitted to drive a relevant vehicle on a road on or after the date specified in paragraph (3) unless he has successfully completed the appropriate initial CPC test.

(2) For the purposes of this regulation—

(a) the appropriate initial CPC test is the test relating to vehicles of the category into which that particular relevant vehicle falls;

(b) where Article 5(5) of the Directive applies, the appropriate initial CPC test must comply with the last paragraph of Section 2.2 of Annex I to the Directive.

(3) The specified date is 10th September 2008 in respect of vehicles in licence category D or D+E and 10th September 2009 in respect of vehicles in licence category C or C+E.

(4) A person may take the initial CPC test whether or not he has been granted a driving licence for a relevant vehicle.

(5) This paragraph applies where—

(a) a person is undergoing a vocational training course leading to a professional qualification relevant to the carriage by road of passengers or goods (or both) and which is approved by the competent authority as a course to which this paragraph applies;

(b) that course lasts at least six months;

(c) that person has produced to the competent authority's satisfaction such evidence as that authority may reasonably require that he is undergoing such a course;

(d) the competent authority has issued that person with a document authorising him to drive that relevant vehicle for a specified period of up to 12 months while undertaking such a course; and

(e) that person is driving within the United Kingdom.

[(5A) A person who wishes the competent authority to issue an NVT certificate to him under paragraph (5)(d) must make a written application to the competent authority and pay to it a fee of £—.]

[(5B) The competent authority may waive in whole or in part the fee payable under paragraph (5A).]

(6) The competent authority may authorise a person under paragraph (5)(d) in respect of only one specified period.

(7) A person is not required to take an initial CPC test relating to vehicles of the category into which that particular relevant vehicle falls if he holds a document described in paragraph (8)—

(a) on 10th September 2008, if that vehicle falls into category D or D+E;

(b) on 10th September 2009, if that vehicle falls into category C or C+E.

(8) That document may be—

(a) a current driving licence;

(b) a current driving licence issued by a member State other than the United Kingdom;

(c) a current driving licence recognised as equivalent to a document described in sub-paragraph (a) or (b); or

(d) a current test pass certificate entitling its holder to a driving licence authorising the driving of any relevant vehicle.

(9) This paragraph applies where a person holds a CPC certifying an initial qualification within the meaning of Article 6(1)(a) of the Directive (CPC awarded on the basis of course attendance and a test).

(10) A person who has passed the initial CPC test in respect of a vehicle which falls within—

(a) category C or C+E, or

(b) category D or D+E,

need not take another initial CPC test to drive any relevant vehicle that falls within the other category referred to in the same sub-paragraph.

[Regulation 4 is printed as amended by SI 2008/1965.   **B64.07**
The amount of the fee in reg.4(5A) is not reproduced.]

Initial CPC test

5.—(1) The initial CPC test may be organised by the competent authority or by   **B64.08**
a person approved by it.

(2) The competent authority may grant approval under paragraph (1) subject to such conditions as it thinks fit and provided it is satisfied that the person will—

    (a) make proper arrangements for the conduct of tests,

    (b) keep proper records of such tests and their results, and

    (c) notify the competent authority of those results as required by that authority.

[(2A) The competent authority may vary any conditions imposed under paragraph (2) by notice in writing to the person to whom the approval was given.]

(3) The competent authority may withdraw approval given by it under paragraph (1) by notice in writing to that person from a date specified in the notice.

(4) A person to whom these Regulations apply may take the initial CPC test under this regulation if that person—

    (a) is a national of a member State and normally resident in the United Kingdom, or

    (b) is a national of a third country, and—

        (i) employed or used by an undertaking established in the United Kingdom, or

        (ii) has been issued with a work permit in the United Kingdom.

(5) The competent authority or person who organises the initial CPC test may make arrangements that all or part of that test is taken at the same time as all or part of a driving test.

[(5A) A person must pass the theoretical test referred to in the table at the end of this regulation [*not reproduced*] before [applying to take] the practical test referred to there and must pass the practical test not more than 24 months after passing the theoretical test.]

[(5B) Where a person has failed to pass the theoretical test or the practical test (both as referred to in the table at the end of this regulation [*not reproduced*]), no application may be made by, or in respect of, that person for a test of the same part to be conducted on a day which falls before the expiry of a period of three clear working days commencing with the day after that on which that part of the test was failed.]

[(6) Subject to paragraph (6ZA), where an initial CPC test is organised by a competent authority, the candidate shall pay to the competent authority the fee specified in the table at the end of this regulation [*not reproduced*] for the part of the test for which an application for an appointment is made.]

[(6ZA) A trainer may, in respect of a candidate who has received, or will receive, from that trainer, training or instruction in Great Britain in relation to the initial CPC test, apply for an appointment in Great Britain for any part of a test referred to in the table at the end of this regulation if the trainer—

    (a) pays to the Secretary of State the fee specified in the table for that part of the test;

    (b) provides such details relating to the trainer's business in Great Britain, the appointment sought or the vehicle on which the test is to be taken as the Secretary of State may reasonably require; and

    (c) undertakes to provide the relevant details relating to the candidate no later than 1600 hours on the day before the last clear working day before the day for which the appointment is made.

(6ZAB) An application under paragraph (6ZA) may be refused where the appointment specified in that application is unavailable or where, in the opinion of the Secretary of State, it is reasonably necessary to do so in the general interests of candidates in Great Britain.

(6ZAC) Where an appointment ("the booked appointment") for part of a test has been made by or on behalf of a candidate in respect of a particular category of relevant vehicle, no application for a further appointment shall be made for that candidate in relation to that part of the test in respect of that category of relevant vehicle unless—

    (a) the booked appointment has been cancelled;

    (b) the part of the test due to take place on the day of the booked appointment does not otherwise take place; or

    (c) subject to paragraph (5B), the candidate fails to pass the test.

(6ZAD) A fee paid pursuant to paragraph (6) may be repaid if notice to cancel the appointment for the part of the test is given to the competent authority not less than three clear working days before the date of the appointment for that part of the test.

(6ZAE) A fee paid pursuant to paragraph (6ZA) may be repaid if notice to cancel the appointment for the part of the test is given to the Secretary of State not less than three clear working days before the date of the appointment for that part of the test.]

[(6A) A person approved under paragraph (1) shall pay to the competent authority in respect of each test which [that person is to conduct] a fee of £— for a practical test and £— for a theoretical test.]

[(6ZB) A fee paid pursuant to paragraph (6A) in respect of the practical test may be repaid if the person approved under paragraph (1) gives notice to the competent authority that the appointment for the conduct of that part of the test has been cancelled and the notice was given to the competent authority at any time before the time of the appointment.]

[(6B) The competent authority may waive in whole or in part the fee payable under paragraph (6) or (6A).]

(7) [The sums referred to in paragraphs (6) and (6A)] shall be payable in addition to any fee that is payable in respect of a driving test all or part of which is taken at the same time as the initial CPC test.

[(8) For the purposes of this regulation, a test commences during normal hours if the time for which the test appointment is made is at or after 0830 hours but not after 1630 hours on a working day.

[(9) In paragraphs (5B), (6ZA)(c), (6ZAD) and (6ZAE), *"working day"* means, in Great Britain, a day other than a Sunday, bank holiday, Christmas Day or Good Friday.]

[(10) In paragraph (6ZA) *"relevant details"*, in relation to a candidate, means the name and such further details relating to—

    (a) that candidate,

    (b) the licence that candidate holds,

    (c) the nature of the test, and

    (d) the vehicle on which the test is to be taken,

as the Secretary of State may reasonably request upon the making of the appointment for the test.]

Table [*Omitted.*]

B64.09   [*Regulation 5 is printed as amended by SI 2008/1965; SI 2010/865. The amounts of fees in reg.5(6A) are not reproduced.*]

[Further requirements at tests: initial CPC test

B64.10   **5A.**—(1) A person submitting himself for either the theoretical test or the practical test shall before the test commences—

(a) produce to the person conducting the test an appropriate licence authorising him to drive a motor vehicle of a class included in the category in respect of which the test is to be taken and, where that licence has a counterpart, the counterpart of that licence; and

(b) except where he has produced an appropriate licence containing his photograph, satisfy the person conducting the test as to his identity in accordance with paragraph (3).

(2) A person submitting himself for either the theoretical test or the practical test who produces a licence which fails to satisfy the person conducting the test, after an examination or otherwise, that it is an appropriate licence as required under paragraph (1) must surrender the licence forthwith to the person conducting the test.

[(2A) For the purposes of the conduct of the practical test referred to in the table in regulation 5 the candidate shall provide a relevant vehicle which falls within a category or sub-category shown in column (1) of the table in regulation 37 of the Driving Licences Regulations and which—

(a) has a power, mass, size or other specification equivalent to or greater than that shown in column (2) of the table in that regulation 37 in respect of the category or sub-category within which the vehicle falls;

(b) is reasonably representative of the category or sub-category to which it belongs and is otherwise suitable for the purposes of the test;

(c) complies with each requirement specified in column (1) of the following table where the vehicle is one which falls within the category or sub-category specified in relation to that requirement in column (2) of the table.

Table

(1) Requirement	(2) Category or sub-category of vehicle
The vehicle shall not be carrying goods or burden other than fixed items which are characteristic of the category or sub-category to which it belongs.	C1, C1+E, C, C+E, D1, D1+E, D, D+E
The vehicle shall be fitted with linkage and braking mechanisms which are designed for use when the trailer is fully laden.	C1+E, C+E, D1+E, D+ E

(1) Requirement	(2) Category or sub-category of vehicle
The vehicle shall be fitted with an anti-lock braking system and a tachograph.	C1, C1+E, C, C+E, D1, D1+E, D, D+E
The vehicle shall have eight or more forward ratios.	C, C+E]

(3) For the purposes of this regulation, a person conducting a test may be satisfied as to a person's identity from a valid passport [or a valid identity card issued under the Identity Cards Act 2006].

(4) In this regulation, "*appropriate licence*" means a licence authorising the person submitting himself for the test to drive a motor vehicle of a class included in the category in respect of which the test is to be taken which—

    (a) is either—

        (i) a driving licence;

        (ii) a provisional licence within the meaning of section 108(1) of the 1988 Act or article 19D(1) of the 1981 Order; or

        (iii) a Community licence;

    (b) is valid at the date of the test; and

    (c) bears the signature of the person who has submitted himself for the test.]

[Regulation 5A is printed as inserted by SI 2008/1965; SI 2010/865; SI 2010/ 1111.]   **B64.11**

[Examiner's right to refuse to conduct test

  5B.—(1) The examiner must refuse to conduct—   **B64.12**

    (a) the practical test where—

        (i) the vehicle submitted for that purpose does not fall within the category in respect of which the theoretical test referred to in regulation 5(5A) was passed; or

        (ii) the candidate fails to comply with regulation 5A(2A);

    (b) the theoretical test or the practical test where the candidate—

        (i) fails to comply with regulation 5A(1); or

        (ii) appears to the examiner to be someone other than the person whose details were provided pursuant to an undertaking under regulation 5(6ZA)(c).

(2) The examiner may refuse to conduct the theoretical test or the practical test where a trainer has failed to comply with an undertaking given under regulation 5(6ZA)(c).

(3) Any fee paid pursuant to regulation 5(6) or (6ZA)(a) may be repaid where—

    (a) the examiner refused to conduct the test under paragraph (1)(b)(i) because the candidate did not satisfy the examiner as to the candidate's identity in accordance with regulation 5A(3) and the candidate subsequently satisfies the competent authority as to the candidate's identity;

>   (b) the examiner refused to conduct the test under paragraph (1)(b)(ii)
>   and the candidate subsequently appears to the examiner to be the
>   person whose details were provided pursuant to an undertaking under
>   regulation 5(6ZA)(c).

(4) In this regulation—

"*examiner*" means the person approved under regulation 5(1), the person conducting the test on behalf of the person so approved or the person conducting the test on behalf of the competent authority;

"*practical test*" means the test of that name referred to in the table in regulation 5; and

"*theoretical test*" means the test of that name referred to in the table in regulation 5.]

B64.13 *[Regulation 5B is printed as inserted by SI 2010/865.]*

Persons providing periodic training courses

B64.14 **6.**—(1) *[Omitted.]*

(2) Such application must be accompanied by the documents specified in Section 5.1 of Annex I to the Directive and such other documents as the competent authority may reasonably require.

(3) The competent authority may approve in writing—

>   (a) that person to provide periodic training courses subject to the conditions specified in Section 5.2 of Annex I to the Directive, including the last two paragraphs of that Section;

>   (b) each periodic training course which that person wishes to provide.

(4) The competent authority's approval shall be valid for—

>   (a) five years under paragraph (3)(a), and

>   (b) one year under paragraph (3)(b).

[(5) Where it appears to the competent authority that—

>   (a) any conditions of an approval given under paragraph (3)(a) are not being complied with; or

>   (b) an approval under paragraph (3)(a) or (b) or (9) was given in error,

the competent authority may send notice to the person to whom the approval was given that it is minded to withdraw or suspend its approval.]

(6) Upon receiving a notice under paragraph (5), that person may make representations to the competent authority within 28 days.

(7) The competent authority shall take those representations into account and send notice to the person informing him whether or not its approval is withdrawn or suspended.

(8) A person approved under paragraph (3)(a) who wishes to provide a training course which has not been approved by the competent authority may at any time request that authority's approval for that course and shall pay to that authority a fee of £—.

(9) If the competent authority gives approval in response to a request under paragraph (8), that approval shall be valid for one year.

[(10) A person to whom these Regulations apply may take a periodic training course approved under this regulation if that person is—

(a) a national of a member State and normally resident in the United Kingdom;

(b) a national of a member State and works in the United Kingdom, or

(c) a national of a third country and authorised to work in the United Kingdom.]

[(11) The provisions of regulation 5A(1), (3) and (4) (further requirements at tests: initial CPC test) shall apply in respect of a periodic training course and for that purpose a reference in those provisions to a test shall be read as a reference to a periodic training course.]

[Regulation 6 is printed as amended by SI 2008/1965.   **B64.15**
The amount of fee is not reproduced.]

[Appeals

6A.—(1) A person who is aggrieved by a decision of the competent author-   **B64.16**
ity—

(a) not to approve a person to provide periodic training courses under regulation 6(3)(a) (persons providing periodic training courses);

(b) not to approve a periodic training course which a person wishes to provide under regulation 6(3)(b);

(c) to withdraw an approval under regulation 6(7);

(d) to suspend an approval under regulation 6(7); or

(e) not to approve a training course under regulation 6(9),

may by notice in writing appeal to the Transport Tribunal within the period of 28 days beginning with the day on which the notice of the decision was given.

(2) On the appeal the Transport Tribunal may make such order for the grant or refusal of approval for the person or course or for the withdrawal, suspension or continuation of an approval (as the case may be) as they think fit.

(3) An order on an appeal under paragraph (1)(a) or (c) may direct that an application by the appellant for an approval to provide periodic training courses under regulation 6(3)(a) shall not be entertained before the expiration of such period, not exceeding four years, beginning with the day on which the order is made, as may be specified in the order.

(4) If the Tribunal considers that any evidence adduced on an appeal has not been adduced to the competent authority before it gave the decision to which the appeal relates, the Tribunal may (instead of making the order under paragraph (2)) remit the matter to the competent authority for it to reconsider the decision.]

[Regulation 6A is printed as inserted by SI 2008/1965.]   **B64.17**

Record of periodic training by competent authority

7.—(1) A person approved by the competent authority under regulation 6(3)(a)   **B64.18**
shall—

(a) notify that authority each time a person to whom he has provided training has completed a periodic training course; and

(b) pay to the authority upon each notification [a fee equal to the sum of £— multiplied by the duration of the course in hours and for this purpose part of an hour shall be treated as an hour].

(2) The competent authority may waive in whole or in part the fee payable under paragraph (1).

(3) The competent authority shall maintain a record of the periodic training notified to it under paragraph (1).

B64.19   *[Regulation 7 is printed as amended by SI 2008/1965.*
The amount of fee is not reproduced.]

Driver Qualification Card

B64.20   **8.**—[(1) The competent authority shall issue a driver qualification card to a person to whom this regulation applies if—

    (a) it is satisfied that that person has passed the initial CPC test in accordance with regulation 5(1); or

    (b)(i) it is satisfied that that person has completed 35 hours of periodic training entitling him to a periodic CPC; and

      (ii) the completion of that training has been notified to a competent authority under regulation 7(1).]

(2) [...]

(3) [...]

(4) In respect of persons [to whom a driver qualification card is issued under paragraph (1), that card] shall be the CPC for the purposes of Article 6(1)(b) (CPC awarded on the basis of tests) or Article 8(1) (CPC certifying periodic training) of the Directive, as the case may be.

(5) [...]

(6) [...]

(7) [...]

[(8) This regulation applies to a person who—

    (a)(i) is a national of a member State and normally resident in the United Kingdom;

      (ii) is a national of a member State and works in the United Kingdom; or

      (iii) is a national of a third country and authorised to work in the United Kingdom; and

    (b) holds a driving licence in the form of a photocard.]

B64.21   *[Regulation 8 is printed as amended by SI 2008/1965.]*

B64.22   **[8A.**—(1) A person (other than a person to whom regulation 8 applies) may apply to the competent authority for a driver qualification card if he has passed the initial CPC test in accordance with regulation 5(1).

(2) A person who falls within regulation 6(10) may apply to the competent authority for a driver qualification card if he has completed 35 hours of periodic training entitling him to a periodic CPC and either—

    (a) he does not hold a driving licence in the form of a photocard; or

    (b) some or all of the periodic training which he has completed was undertaken outside the United Kingdom.

(3) The person shall send to the competent authority—

    (a) the fee specified in paragraph (6);

(b) if the competent authority so requests, a photograph of that person in such form as it may require; and

(c) in the case of an application made under paragraph (2), such documents or information as the competent authority may require in respect of periodic training undertaken by that person outside the United Kingdom.

(4) Upon receipt of the items specified in paragraph (3), the competent authority shall issue that person with a driver qualification card if it is satisfied that the person has (as the case may be)—

(a) passed the initial CPC test; or

(b) completed the periodic training entitling him to a periodic CPC.

(5) In respect of persons who make an application under this regulation, the driver qualification card issued under paragraph (4) shall be the CPC for the purposes of Article 6(1)(b) (CPC awarded on the basis of tests) or Article 8(1) (CPC certifying periodic training) of the Directive, as the case may be.

(6) The fee shall be £—.

(7) The competent authority may waive the fee specified in paragraph (6) in whole or in part if it thinks fit.

(8) For the purposes of paragraph (4)(b) the competent authority shall take account of periodic training undertaken outside the United Kingdom.]

[Regulation 8A is printed as inserted by SI 2008/1965.   **B64.23**
The amount of fee is not reproduced.]

[Damaged, lost or stolen documents

8B.—(1) If a driver qualification card or an NVT certificate is damaged, lost or   **B64.24** stolen, the person to whom that document was issued shall as soon as practicable notify the competent authority in writing and shall provide such information or documents concerning the damage, loss or theft as the competent authority may require.

(2) If a driver qualification card or an NVT certificate is found at any time after the competent authority has been notified in accordance with paragraph (1) of the loss or theft of it, the person to whom that document was issued shall, if it is in his possession, return it to the competent authority, or if it is not in his possession, but he becomes aware that it is found, he shall take all reasonable steps to take possession of it and, if successful, shall return it to the competent authority as soon as practicable.

(3) If a driver qualification card or an NVT certificate has been damaged, lost or stolen, the competent authority must upon payment to it of a fee of £— issue a replacement document to the person to whom that document was originally issued.

(4) The competent authority may waive the fee specified in paragraph (3) in whole or in part if it thinks fit.

(5) A person who does not comply with the requirements of paragraph (1) or (2) is guilty of an offence.

(6) A person guilty of an offence under this regulation is liable on summary conviction to a fine not exceeding level 3 on the standard scale.]

[Regulation 8B is printed as inserted by SI 2008/1965.   **B64.25**

The amount of fee is not reproduced.]

Time limits for obtaining a CPC

B64.26   9.—(1) Subject to paragraphs (2), (3), (4) and (5) of this regulation, a person to whom these Regulations apply is not permitted to drive a relevant vehicle on a road unless no more than five years have elapsed since he obtained a CPC relating to motor vehicles of the category into which that particular relevant vehicle falls.

(2) A person to whom regulation 4(7) applies is not required to hold an initial CPC relating to motor vehicles of the category into which that particular relevant vehicle falls, or

(a) a periodic CPC before 10th September 2013 where that regulation applies to him by virtue of sub-paragraph (a);

(b) a periodic CPC before 10th September 2014 where that regulation applies to him by virtue of sub-paragraph (b).

(3) A person is not required to hold a CPC where regulation 4(5) applies to him.

(4) Paragraph (1) does not apply to a person who holds an initial CPC granted to him by a member State other than the United Kingdom in accordance with the last paragraph of Article 8(2) of the Directive and the validity of that CPC has not expired.

(5) A person who holds a periodic CPC as described in paragraph (1) is not required to complete any further periodic training before the expiry of that CPC in respect of any category of relevant vehicle to which that CPC does not relate.

(6) [...]

B64.27   *[Regulation 9 is printed as amended by SI 2008/1965.]*

Offence of driving without a CPC

B64.28   10.—(1) A person who does not comply with regulation 4(1) or 9(1) is guilty of an offence.

(2) A person who causes or permits another person to drive a relevant vehicle on a road in breach of regulation 4(1) or 9(1) is guilty of an offence.

(3) A person guilty of an offence under this regulation shall be liable upon summary conviction to a fine not exceeding level 3 on the standard scale.

Requirement to carry and produce evidence of CPC or of training exemption in vehicle

B64.29   11.—(1) Subject to paragraph (4), a person who is required to hold a CPC by virtue of regulation 9(1) and who does not carry with him in the [relevant vehicle] which he is driving evidence of that CPC as specified in paragraph (2) is guilty of an offence.

(2) That evidence may be any of the following documents—

(a) a driver qualification card;

(b) a Community licence with the Community code;

(c) a driver's certificate granted to him by a member State other than the United Kingdom as referred to in Article 10(3)(a) of the Directive; or

(d) any other document issued to the driver by a member State other than the United Kingdom certifying an initial CPC or a periodic CPC.

(3) A person to whom regulation 4(9) or 9(4) applies who does not carry with him in the vehicle he is driving evidence as specified in paragraph (2) of the initial CPC he holds is guilty of an offence.

(4) Paragraph (1) does not apply to a person—

(a) who has been issued with a driver qualification card by the competent authority under regulation 8(1) or 8A(4) but has not yet received it; or

(b) whose driver qualification card has been damaged, lost or stolen, who has notified the competent authority under regulation 8B(1) and who has paid the fee specified in regulation 8B(3) but who has not yet received a replacement card.]

[(5) Subject to paragraph (5A), a person to whom regulation 4(5) applies who does not carry an NVT certificate with him in the relevant vehicle which he is driving is guilty of an offence.]

[(5A) Paragraph (5) does not apply to a person—

(a) who has been issued with an NVT certificate by the competent authority but has not yet received it; or

(b) whose NVT certificate has been damaged, lost or stolen, who has notified the competent authority under regulation 8B(1) and who has paid the fee specified in regulation 8B(3) but who has not yet received a replacement certificate.]

[(5B) In paragraphs (4)(b) and (5A)(b), the reference to the fee specified in regulation 8B(3) is a reference to the fee insofar as it has not been waived under regulation 8B(5).

(6) A police constable or vehicle examiner may at any time require a person to whom paragraph (1), (3) or (5) applies to produce to him the evidence or document, as the case may be, referred to in that paragraph.

(7) If a person fails to produce that evidence or document, as the case may be, when required to do so under paragraph (6) he shall be guilty of an offence.

(8) A person guilty of an offence under this regulation shall be liable upon summary conviction to a fine not exceeding level 3 on the standard scale.

[Regulation 11 is printed as amended by SI 2008/1965.　　　　　　**B64.30**

An offence under reg.11(7) is a fixed penalty offence for the purposes of Pt 3 of the Road Traffic Offenders Act 1988 (see the Fixed Penalty Offences Order 2009 (SI 2009/483) art.2). The amount for the fixed penalty offence is prescribed by the Fixed Penalty Order 2000 (SI 2000/2792), as amended by the Fixed Penalty (Amendment) Order 2009 (SI 2009/488).]

Document errors

12.—[(1) Where it appears to the competent authority that—　　　　　　**B64.31**

(a) an NVT certificate, or

(b) a driver qualification card issued by it under regulation 8(1), 8A(4) or 8B(3),

was granted in error, or with an error or omission in the particulars specified in it, it may serve a notice in writing on that person revoking it and requiring him to surrender it to the authority forthwith.]

(2) It shall be the duty of that person to comply with that requirement.

(3) Where the name of the holder of the driver qualification card as specified on that card ceases to be correct, its holder must as soon as reasonably practicable surrender the driver qualification card to the competent authority.

(4) On surrender of a driver qualification card under paragraph (2), the competent authority may issue a new driver qualification card to that person free of charge subject to paragraph (6).

(5) On surrender of a driver qualification card under paragraph (3) and payment to it of a fee of £—, the competent authority shall issue a new driver qualification card to that person.

(6) Where it appears to the competent authority that the driver qualification card surrendered to it under paragraph (2) was granted in consequence of an error, omission or other act attributable to the fault of the holder of that card, it may issue a new card upon payment of a fee of £—.

(7) The competent authority may require a person to provide evidence of his name, sex and place and date of birth before issuing him with a new driver qualification card under paragraph (4), (5) or (6).

(8) A person who fails to comply with the duty in paragraph (2) or (3) without reasonable excuse is guilty of an offence.

(9) A person guilty of an offence under this regulation shall be liable upon summary conviction to a fine not exceeding level 3 on the standard scale.

B64.32 *[Regulation 12 is printed as amended by SI 2008/1965.*
The amounts of fees are not reproduced.]

Forgery and false statements

B64.33 13.—(1) A person is guilty of an offence if, with intent to deceive he—

(a) forges, alters or uses any document referred to in regulation 11(2) [or an NVT certificate];

(b) lends to, or allows to be used by, any other person such a document; or

(c) makes or has in his possession any document so closely resembling such a document as to be calculated to deceive.

(2) In the application of paragraph (1) to England and Wales and Northern Ireland, *"forges"* means makes a false document in order that it may be used as genuine.

(3) A person who knowingly makes a false statement for the purpose of obtaining [the issue of a driver qualification card under regulation 8(1), 8A(4) or 8B(3) or the issue of an NVT certificate] is guilty of an offence.

(4) A person guilty of an offence under paragraph (1) or (3) shall be liable—

(a) on summary conviction, to imprisonment for a term not exceeding three months or a fine not exceeding the statutory maximum, or both, or

(b) on conviction on indictment, to imprisonment for a term not exceeding two years or a fine, or both.

(5) Subject to paragraph (6), summary proceedings for an offence to which this regulation relates may be brought within a period of six months from the date

on which evidence sufficient in the opinion of the prosecutor to warrant the proceedings came to his knowledge.

(6) No such proceedings shall be brought by virtue of this regulation more than three years after the commission of the offence.

(7) For the purposes of this regulation, a certificate signed by or on behalf of the prosecutor and stating the date on which evidence sufficient in his opinion to warrant the proceedings came to his knowledge shall be conclusive evidence of that fact.

(8) A certificate stating that matter and purporting to be so signed shall be deemed to be so signed unless the contrary is proved.

(9) *[Provision in relation to proceedings in Scotland.]*

[Regulation 13 is printed as amended by SI 2008/1965.]   **B64.34**

Power to seize document in respect of which offences may have been committed

14.—(1) If a constable or a vehicle examiner has reasonable cause to believe   **B64.35**
that a document carried in a motor vehicle or by the driver of the vehicle is a document in relation to which an offence has been committed under regulation 13, he may seize it.

(2) When a document is seized under paragraph (1) and paragraph (3) applies, either the driver or owner of the vehicle shall be summoned before a magistrates' court ... to account for his possession of the document.

(3) This paragraph applies where the document is detained and neither the driver nor owner of the vehicle has previously been charged with an offence in relation to the document under regulation 13.

(4) The court ... must make such order respecting the disposal of the document and award such costs as the justice of the case may require.

(5) For the purposes of paragraphs (2) and (3), *"owner"*, in relation to a vehicle which is the subject of a hiring or hire-purchase agreement, means the person in possession of the vehicle under that agreement.

[Words relating exclusively to Scotland have been omitted.]   **B64.36**

Amendment of the Driving Licences Regulations

15. *[Omitted.]*   **B64.37**

The Community Drivers' Hours and Recording Equipment Regulations 2007

(SI 2007/1819)

Citation, commencement, interpretation and revocation

B65.01   **1.**—(1) These Regulations may be cited as the Community Drivers' Hours and Recording Equipment Regulations 2007 and shall come into force on the seventh day after the day on which they are made.

(2) In these Regulations—

"*the Community Drivers' Hours Regulation*" means Regulation (EC) No 561/2006 of the European Parliament and of the Council as amended from time to time;

"*the Community Recording Equipment Regulation*" means Council Regulation (EEC) No 3821/85 as amended from time to time; and

"*the 1968 Act*" means the Transport Act 1968.

(3) Any expression used in these Regulations which is used in the Community Drivers' Hours Regulation has the same meaning as in that Regulation.

(4) The following provisions are revoked—

(a) the Community Drivers' Hours and Recording Equipment (Exemptions and Supplementary Provisions) Regulations 1986;

(b) the Community Drivers' Hours and Recording Equipment (Exemptions and Supplementary Provisions) (Amendment) Regulations 1986;

(c) the Community Drivers' Hours and Recording Equipment (Exemptions and Supplementary Provisions) (Amendment) Regulations 1987;

(d) the Community Drivers' Hours and Recording Equipment (Exemptions and Supplementary Provisions) (Amendment) Regulations 1988;

(e) the Community Drivers' Hours and Recording Equipment (Amendment) Regulations 1998; and

(f) paragraph 7 of the Schedule to the Railways Act 1993 (Consequential Modifications) Order 1994.

Exemption from the Community Drivers' Hours Regulation

B65.02   **2.**—(1) Pursuant to Article 13(1) of the Community Drivers' Hours Regulation, exemption is granted from Articles 6, 7, 8 and 9 of that Regulation in respect of—

(a) any vehicle falling within a description specified in Part 1 of the Schedule to these Regulations, and

(b) any vehicle—

    (i) which has a maximum permissible mass not exceeding 7.5 tonnes,

    (ii) which is being used to deliver items as part of a universal service by a universal service provider as defined in Article 2(13) of Directive 97/67/EC of the European Parliament and of the Council on common rules for the development of the internal market of Community postal services,

    (iii) which is being used within a 50 kilometre radius from the base of the universal service provider, and

    (iv) the driving of which does not constitute the driver's main activity.

(2) Pursuant to Article 14(1) of the Community Drivers' Hours Regulation, exemption is granted from Articles 6, 7, 8 and 9 of that Regulation in respect of any vehicle falling within a description specified in Part 2 of the Schedule to these Regulations.

Supplementary provisions relating to the Community Drivers' Hours Regulation

3. For the purpose of Article 3(i) of the Community Drivers' Hours Regulation **B65.03** a vehicle has a historic status if it is a vehicle which is by virtue of its construction and equipment suitable for carrying passengers or goods and which was manufactured more than 25 years before the date on which it is being driven.

Exemption from the Community Recording Equipment Regulation

4.—(1) Pursuant to Article 3(2) of the Community Recording Equipment **B65.04** Regulation, exemption is granted from the provisions of that Regulation in respect of any vehicle falling within a description specified in Part 1 of the Schedule to these Regulations.

(2) Pursuant to Article 3(3) of the Community Recording Equipment Regulation, exemption is granted from the provisions of that Regulation in respect of:

    (a) any vehicle falling within a description specified in Part 2 of the Schedule to these Regulations; and

    (b) any vehicle being used for collecting sea coal.

Amendment of Part 6 of the Transport Act 1968

5. *[Omitted.]*   **B65.05**

6. *[Omitted.]*

7. *[Omitted.]*

8. *[Omitted.]*

Regulations 2 and 4   THE SCHEDULE

EXEMPTED VEHICLES

PART 1

VEHICLES EXEMPTED BY REGULATIONS 2(1) AND 4(1)

1.—(1) Any vehicle which is owned or hired without a driver by a public authority to **B65.06**

undertake carriage by road otherwise than in competition with private transport undertakings.

(2) A vehicle does not fall within the description specified in this paragraph unless the vehicle—

> (a) is being used for the provision of ambulance services—
>
>> (i) by a relevant NHS body, or
>>
>> (ii) in pursuance of arrangements made by or at the request of a relevant NHS body, or made with the Secretary of State or with the Welsh or Scottish Ministers;
>
> (b) is being used for the transport of organs, blood, equipment, medical supplies or personnel—
>
>> (i) by a relevant NHS body, or
>>
>> (ii) in pursuance of arrangements of the kind mentioned in paragraph (a)(ii);
>
> (c) is being used by a local authority to provide, in the exercise of social services functions—
>
>> (i) services for old persons; or
>>
>> (ii) services for persons to whom section 29 of the National Assistance Act 1948 (welfare arrangements for physically and mentally handicapped persons) applies;
>
> (d) is being used by Her Majesty's Coastguard, a general lighthouse authority or a local lighthouse authority;
>
> (e) is being used for the purpose of maintaining railways by the British Railways Board, any holder of a network licence (within the meaning of Part 1 of the Railways Act 1993) which is a company wholly owned by the Crown (within the meaning of that Act), Transport for London, any wholly owned subsidiary of Transport for London, a Passenger Transport Executive or a local authority;
>
> (f) is being used by the British Waterways Board for the purpose of maintaining navigable waterways.

(3) In this paragraph—

> "general lighthouse authority" and "local lighthouse authority" have the same meaning as in Part 8 of the Merchant Shipping Act 1995;
>
> "local authority" means —
>
>> (a) in relation to England and Wales, a county or district council, a London borough council or the Common Council of the City of London; and
>>
>> (b) in relation to Scotland, a regional, islands or district council;
>
> "relevant NHS body" means —
>
>> (a) in England, a Strategic Health Authority, a Primary Care Trust, a National Health Service Trust, a Special Health Authority, and an NHS foundation trust;
>>
>> (b) in Wales, a Local Health Board, a National Health Service Trust, and a Special Health Authority; and
>>
>> (c) [applies to Scotland];
>
> "social services functions" —
>
>> (a) in relation to England and Wales, has the meaning given by section 1A of the Local Authority Social Services Act 1970; and
>>
>> (b) [applies to Scotland];
>
> "wholly owned subsidiary" in relation to Transport for London, has the meaning given by section 736(2) of the Companies Act 1985.

B65.07   **2.**—(1) Any vehicle which is being used or hired without a driver by an agricultural, horticultural, forestry, farming or fishery undertaking for carrying goods as part of its own entrepreneurial activity within a 100 kilometre radius from where the undertaking is based.

(2) A vehicle which is being used by a fishery undertaking does not fall within the description specified in this paragraph unless the vehicle is being used—

(a) to carry live fish; or

(b) to carry a catch of fish from the place of landing to a place where it is to be processed.

3. Any tractor which is used for agricultural or forestry work within a 100 kilometre radius of the base of the undertaking which owns, hires or leases the tractor. **B65.08**

4.—(1) Any vehicle which has a maximum permissible mass not exceeding 7.5 tonnes and is being used for carrying materials, equipment or machinery for the driver's use in the course of the driver's work. **B65.09**

(2) A vehicle does not fall within the description specified in this paragraph if—

(i) the vehicle is being used outside a 50 kilometre radius from the base of the undertaking; or

(ii) driving the vehicle constitutes the driver's main activity.

5. Any vehicle which operates exclusively on an island which does not exceed 2300 square kilometres in area and is not linked to the rest of Great Britain by a bridge, ford or tunnel open for use by motor vehicles. **B65.10**

6. Any vehicle which is used by an undertaking for the carriage of goods within a 50 kilometre radius from where the undertaking is based, is propelled by means of natural or liquefied gas or electricity and has a maximum permissible mass, including the mass of any trailer or semi-trailer drawn by it, not exceeding 7.5 tonnes. **B65.11**

7.—(1) Any vehicle which is being used for driving instruction and examination with a view to obtaining a driving licence or certificate of professional competence. **B65.12**

(2) A vehicle does not fall within the description specified in this paragraph if the vehicle or any trailer or semi-trailer drawn by it is being used for the commercial carriage of goods or passengers.

8. Any vehicle which is being used in connection with— **B65.13**

(a) sewerage, flood protection, water, gas or electricity maintenance services;

(b) road maintenance or control;

(c) door-to-door household refuse collection or disposal;

(d) telegraph or telephone services;

(e) radio or television broadcasting; or

(f) the detection of radio or television transmitters or receivers.

9. Any vehicle with not more than 17 seats, including the driver's seat, used exclusively for the non-commercial carriage of passengers. **B65.14**

10. Any specialised vehicle which is being used for transporting circus or funfair equipment. **B65.15**

11. Any mobile project vehicle the primary purpose of which is use as an educational facility when stationary and which is specially fitted for that purpose. **B65.16**

12. Any vehicle which is being used for the collection of milk from farms or for the return to farms of milk containers or milk products intended for animal feed. **B65.17**

13. Any vehicle which is being used to carry animal waste or carcasses which are not intended for human consumption. **B65.18**

14.—(1) Any vehicle which is used exclusively on roads inside hub facilities. **B65.19**

(2) For the purposes of this paragraph, examples of *"hub facilities"* include ports, interports and railway terminals.

15. Any vehicle which is being used to carry live animals from a farm to a market, or from a market to a slaughterhouse, where the distance between the farm and the market, or between the market and the slaughterhouse, does not exceed 50 kilometres. **B65.20**

PART 2

VEHICLES EXEMPTED BY REGULATIONS 2(2) AND 4(2)

B65.21   **16.** Any vehicle which is being used by the Royal National Lifeboat Institution for the purpose of hauling lifeboats.

B65.22   **17.** Any vehicle which was manufactured before 1st January 1947.

B65.23   **18.** Any vehicle which is propelled by steam.

The Removal and Disposal of Vehicles (Traffic Officers) (England) Regulations 2008

(SI 2008/2367)

PART 1

GENERAL

Citation, commencement and extent

1.—(1) These Regulations may be cited as the Removal and Disposal of **B66.01** Vehicles (Traffic Officers) (England) Regulations 2008 and shall come into force on 1st October 2008.

(2) These Regulations apply as respects England only.

Interpretation

2.—(1) In these Regulations— **B66.02**

"relevant road" means a road in England for which the Secretary of State is the traffic authority, other than:

(a) the eastbound carriageway of the M48 motorway from the boundary with Wales to a point 400 metres east of the outer edge of the eastern abutment of the Aust Viaduct;

(b) the westbound carriageway of that motorway from a point 500 metres east of the outer edge of the eastern abutment of the Aust Viaduct to that boundary;

(c) the eastbound carriageweay of the M4 motorway from the boundary with Wales to a point 60 metres east of the Binn Wall and 140 metres north of the Severn Tunnel Air Shaft; and

(d) the westbound carriageway of that motorway from a point 60 metres east of the Binn Wall and 140 metres north of the Severn Tunnel Air Shaft to that boundary; and

"traffic officer" means an individual designated as such by the Secretary of State, or by a person authorised by the Secretary of State, in accordance with section 2 of the Traffic Management Act 2004.

(2) In these Regulations a reference to—

(a) a numbered section is, unless expressly provided otherwise, a reference to the section so numbered in the Road Traffic Regulation Act 1984; and

(b) a vehicle which has been permitted to remain at rest, or which has broken down, includes a reference to a vehicle which has been permitted to remain at rest or which has broken down before their coming into force.

PART 2

REMOVAL OF VEHICLES

Power of traffic officer to require removal of vehicles from relevant roads

B66.03   3.—(1) This regulation applies to a vehicle which—

    (a) has broken down, or been permitted to remain at rest, on a relevant road in such a position or in such condition or in such circumstances as to cause obstruction to other persons using the road or as to be likely to cause danger to such persons; or

    (b) has been permitted to remain at rest, or has broken down and remained at rest, on a relevant road in contravention of a prohibition or restriction contained in, or having effect under, any enactment mentioned in Schedule 1.

(2) In relation to a vehicle to which this regulation applies, a traffic officer in uniform may require the owner, driver or other person in control or in charge of the vehicle and who is present, to remove it or have it removed.

(3) The exercise of this power may include a requirement that the vehicle—

    (a) be moved to another position on any road or to any other place; or

    (b) shall not be moved to any such part of, or position on, a road as is specified.

(4) A person required to remove a vehicle, or to have it removed, under this regulation shall comply as soon as practicable.

Power of traffic officer to remove vehicles from relevant roads

B66.04   4.—(1) This regulation applies to a vehicle which—

    (a) is a vehicle to which regulation 3 applies;

    (b) having broken down on a relevant road appears to a traffic officer in uniform to have been abandoned without lawful authority; or

    (c) has been permitted to remain at rest on a relevant road in such a position or in such condition or in such circumstances as to appear to a traffic officer in uniform to have been abandoned without lawful authority.

(2) In relation to a vehicle to which this regulation applies, a traffic officer in uniform may, subject to section 100, remove it or arrange for its removal.

(3) In exercising this power he may move it, or arrange for it to be moved, to another position on any road or to any other place.

Power of traffic officer to require removal of vehicles from roads other than relevant roads

B66.05   5.—(1) This regulation applies to a vehicle which—

    (a) has broken down, or been permitted to remain at rest, on a road which is not a relevant road in such a position or in such condition or in such circumstances as to cause obstruction to other persons using the road or as to be likely to cause danger to such persons; or

(b) has been permitted to remain at rest or has broken down and remained at rest on a road which is not a relevant road in contravention of a prohibition or restriction contained in, or having effect under, any enactment mentioned in Schedule 1.

(2) In relation to a vehicle to which this regulation applies, a traffic officer in uniform may, subject to regulation 7, require the owner, driver or other person in control or in charge of the vehicle and who is present, to remove it or have it removed.

(3) The exercise of this power may include a requirement that the vehicle—

(a) be moved to another position on any road or to any other place; or

(b) shall not be moved to any such part of, or position on, a road as is specified.

(4) A person required to remove a vehicle, or to have it removed, under this regulation shall comply as soon as practicable.

Power of traffic officer to remove vehicles from roads other than relevant roads

6.—(1) This regulation applies to a vehicle which—   **B66.06**

(a) is a vehicle to which regulation 5 applies;

(b) having broken down on a road which is not a relevant road, appears to a traffic officer in uniform to have been abandoned without lawful authority; or

(c) has been permitted to remain at rest on a road which is not a relevant road in such a position or in such condition or in such circumstances as to appear to a traffic officer in uniform to have been abandoned without lawful authority.

(2) In relation to a vehicle to which this regulation applies, a traffic officer in uniform may, subject to regulation 7 and section 100, remove it or arrange for its removal.

(3) In exercising this power he may move it, or arrange for it to be moved, to another position on any road or to any other place.

Restriction on the exercise of powers in regulations 5 and 6

7.—(1) The exercise of the powers contained in regulations 5(2) and 6(2) are   **B66.07** subject to the following restrictions.

(2) Those powers may only be exercised for one or more of the following purposes—

(a) avoiding danger to persons or other traffic using a relevant road or preventing risks of any such danger arising; and

(b) preventing an obstruction to anything on or near to a relevant road, or for a purpose incidental to either of those purposes.

(3) Subject to that, those powers may be exercised if the traffic officer is acting—

(a) at the direction of the chief officer of police for the area in which the road, from which the vehicle is to be removed, is situated; or

(b) with the consent of the traffic authority for that road.

Removing abandoned vehicles from land adjoining a relevant road

B66.08   **8.** Where a vehicle has been permitted to remain at rest on any land in the open air, which is adjacent to a relevant road, in such a position or in such condition or in such circumstances as to appear to a traffic officer in uniform to have been abandoned without lawful authority, a traffic officer in uniform may, subject to sections 99 and 100, remove it or arrange for its removal.

Manner of giving notice to occupier of land before removing a vehicle

B66.09   **9.**—(1) Any notice given by a traffic officer for the purposes of section 99(3) shall be in, or to the like effect as, the form in Schedule 2.

(2) Subject to paragraphs (3) and (4), the notice shall be—

    (a) addressed to the person who appears to be the occupier of the land—

        (i) by name; or

        (ii) by the title "The Occupier", followed by a description of the land; and

    (b) given by—

        (i) delivering it to that person;

        (ii) leaving it at his usual or last known place of residence; or

        (iii) sending it by prepaid registered or recorded delivery post, addressed to him at either of those places.

(3) Where it is not possible to identify—

    (a) the person who appears to be the occupier of the land; or

    (b) that person's usual or last known place of residence;

the notice may be affixed to an object on the land.

(4) If the person who appears to be the occupier is a body corporate, the notice shall be given by delivering it, or sending it by prepaid registered or recorded delivery post, to its registered or principal office.

(5) Any envelope containing the notice shall be clearly and legibly marked with the words "IMPORTANT — This communication affects your property".

Manner and period during which occupier of land may object

B66.10   **10.**—(1) For the purpose of section 99(3), where a notice is given in accordance with regulation 9, the occupier of the land may object, in the manner set out in paragraph (2), to the removal of the vehicle.

(2) The objection shall be—

    (a) in writing;

    (b) addressed to the person specified in the notice; and

    (c) delivered, or sent by post, to the address set out in that notice.

(3) The period within which the occupier may object shall be 15 days beginning with the day on which the notice is given.

Method of removing vehicles

B66.11   **11.**—(1) A person who removes or moves a vehicle under regulation 3, 4, 5, 6 or 8 may do so by towing or driving the vehicle or in such other manner as he may think necessary and may take such measures in relation to the vehicle as he may think necessary to enable him to remove or move it.

(2) Subject to paragraph (3), where, under regulation 3 or 5, a traffic officer requires a person to remove a vehicle and he determines that the manner of removal proposed to be used by that person may cause danger to other persons using the road, the traffic officer may require the vehicle to be moved in such other manner as he considers safe.

(3) Where a safe manner of removal cannot be agreed between the traffic officer and a person required to remove a vehicle, the traffic officer may remove, or arrange for the removal of the vehicle.

PART 3

DISPOSAL OF ABANDONED VEHICLES

12–18. *[Omitted.]*   **B66.12**

Regulations 3 and 5   SCHEDULE 1

CERTAIN ENACTMENTS BY OR UNDER WHICH ARE IMPOSED PROHIBITIONS OR RESTRICTIONS ON THE WAITING OF VEHICLES ON ROADS

1. Section 36 of the Road Traffic Act 1988 (drivers to comply with traffic signs).   **B66.13**

2. The following sections of the Road Traffic Regulation Act 1984:   **B66.14**

(1) Section 1 (traffic regulation orders outside Greater London).

(2) Section 6 (orders similar to traffic regulation orders).

(3) Section 9 (experimental traffic orders).

(4) Section 14 (temporary prohibition or restriction on roads).

(5) Section 16A (prohibition or restriction on roads in connection with certain events).

(6) Section 17 (traffic regulation on special roads).

(7) Section 25 (pedestrian crossing regulations).

(8) Section 66 (traffic signs for giving effect to local traffic regulations).

(9) Section 67 (emergencies and temporary obstructions).

3. Any enactment contained in any local Act for the time being in force and any byelaw   **B66.15**
having effect under any enactment for the time being in force, being an enactment or byelaw imposing or authorising the imposition of a prohibition or restriction similar to any prohibition or restriction which is or can be imposed by or under any of the enactments referred to in paragraphs 1 and 2.

Regulation 9   SCHEDULE 2

FORM OF NOTICE

[Omitted.]   **B66.16**

The Road Safety (Immobilisation, Removal and Disposal of Vehicles) Regulations 2009

(SI 2009/ 493)

CONTENTS

B67.01

PART 1

PRELIMINARY

Citation and commencement

1. These Regulations may be cited as the Road Safety (Immobilisation, Removal and Disposal of Vehicles) Regulations 2009 and shall come into force on 31st March 2009.

B67.02

Interpretation

2. In these Regulations—

B67.03

"*identified person*" has the meaning given in regulation 10(2);

"*immobilisation notice*" means a notice given in accordance with regulation 4(2);

"*owner*" means, in relation to a vehicle—

    (a) the person in whose name the vehicle is then registered under the Vehicle Excise and Registration Act 1994; or

    (b) if the vehicle is not so registered, the person appearing to the authorised person to own that vehicle;

"*recognised badge*" has the meaning given by section 21A(1) of the Chronically Sick and Disabled Persons Act 1970 ; and

"*release fee*" has the meaning given by regulation 4(7).

Application

3.—(1) These Regulations apply with respect to any case where the driving of a vehicle has been prohibited under—

B67.04

    (a) section 99A(1) of the Transport Act 1968 (powers to prohibit driving of vehicles in connection with contravention of provisions about drivers' hours);

    (b) section 1 of the Road Traffic (Foreign Vehicles) Act 1972 (powers to prohibit driving of foreign goods vehicles and foreign public service vehicles);

    (c) section 69 or 70 of the Road Traffic Act 1988 (powers to prohibit driving of unfit or overloaded vehicles); or

    (d) section 90D of the Road Traffic Offenders Act 1988 (power to prohibit driving of vehicle on failure to make payment in compliance with financial penalty deposit requirement).

(2) These Regulations do not apply in relation to a vehicle if a current disabled person's badge or current recognised badge is displayed on that vehicle.

PART 2

IMMOBILISATION OF VEHICLES

Power to immobilise vehicles

4.—(1) An authorised person or a person acting under the direction of the

B67.05

authorised person may, in relation to any vehicle in a case where these Regulations apply—

> (a) fix an immobilisation device to the vehicle; and
> (b) move the vehicle, or direct the driver or the person appearing to be in charge of the vehicle to move the vehicle, for the purpose of enabling an immobilisation device to be fitted to it.

(2) On any occasion when an immobilisation device is fixed to a vehicle in accordance with these Regulations, the person fixing the device must also fix to the vehicle a notice (*"an immobilisation notice"*)—

> (a) indicating that the device has been fixed to the vehicle and warning that no attempt should be made to drive it or otherwise put it in motion until it has been released from the device;
> (b) specifying the steps to be taken to secure its release, including—
>> (i) how payment of any release fee should be made; and
>> (ii) the evidence to be produced to show that the prohibition under which the driving of the vehicle was prohibited has been removed; and
> (c) giving any other relevant information, including the consequences of not securing release of the vehicle.

(3) A vehicle to which an immobilisation device has been fixed in accordance with these Regulations—

> (a) may only be released from the device by or under the direction of an authorised person; but
> (b) subject to sub-paragraph (a), must be released from the device if the first and second requirements specified below are met.

(4) The first requirement is that a charge of £80 in respect of the release is paid in any manner specified in the immobilisation notice.

(5) The second requirement is that, in accordance with instructions specified in the immobilisation notice, there is produced—

> (a) in the case of a prohibition issued under section 99A(1) of the Transport Act 1968 (powers to prohibit driving of vehicles in connection with contravention of provisions about drivers' hours), the notice referred to in section 99B(3) of that Act (notice to driver of the vehicle that the prohibition has been removed), or evidence that that prohibition has expired;
> (b) in the case of a prohibition issued under section 1 of the Road Traffic (Foreign Vehicles) Act 1972 (powers to prohibit driving of foreign goods vehicles and foreign public service vehicles), the notice referred to in section 2(3) of that Act (notice to driver of the vehicle that the prohibition has been removed), or evidence that that prohibition has expired;
> (c) In the case of a prohibition issued under sections 69 or 70 of the Road Traffic Act 1988 (powers to prohibit driving of unfit or overloaded vehicles), the notice referred to in section 72(7) of that Act (notice to owner that the prohibition has been removed); and
> (d) in the case of a prohibition issued under section 90D of the Road Traffic Offenders Act 1988 (power to prohibit driving of vehicle on

failure to make payment in compliance with financial penalty deposit requirement), evidence that one of the events referred to in section 90D(4) of that Act has occurred.

(6) An immobilisation notice may not be removed or interfered with except by an authorised person or a person acting on the authority of an authorised person.

(7) In this regulation, the *"release fee"* means the charge referred to in paragraph (4).

Offence of failing to move vehicle

5. A person who fails to comply within a reasonable time with a direction under regulation 4(1)(b) is guilty of an offence and liable on summary conviction to a fine not exceeding level 5 on the standard scale. **B67.06**

Offence of removing or interfering with immobilisation notice

6. A person, other than an authorised person or a person acting on the authority of an authorised person, who removes or interferes with an immobilisation notice is guilty of an offence and liable on summary conviction to a fine not exceeding level 2 on the standard scale. **B67.07**

Offence of removing or interfering with immobilisation device, etc.

7. A person, other than an authorised person or a person acting under the direction of an authorised person, who removes or attempts to remove an immobilisation device fixed to a vehicle in accordance with these Regulations is guilty of an offence and liable on summary conviction to a fine not exceeding level 3 on the standard scale. **B67.08**

False or misleading statements, etc.

8.—(1) Where— **B67.09**

    (a) a person makes a declaration with a view to securing the release of a vehicle from an immobilisation device purported to have been fixed in accordance with these Regulations;

    (b) the declaration is that the prohibition has been removed; and

    (c) the declaration is to the person's knowledge either false or in any material respect misleading,

that person is guilty of an offence.

(2) A person guilty of an offence under paragraph (1) is liable—

    (a) on summary conviction, to a fine not exceeding the statutory maximum; or

    (b) on conviction on indictment, to imprisonment for a term not exceeding two years, or to a fine, or both.

PART 3

REMOVAL AND DISPOSAL OF VEHICLES

Power to remove vehicles

9.—(1) Where any of the conditions specified in paragraph (2) are met, an au- **B67.10**

thorised person, or a person acting under the direction of an authorised person, may remove the vehicle or direct the driver or the person appearing to be in charge of the vehicle to remove the vehicle.

(2) The conditions are that the authorised person considers that the vehicle should be removed—

 (a) for the safety of traffic, the vehicle, its occupants or its load;

 (b) because there is insufficient space for the vehicle to remain at the location at which the vehicle was inspected; or

 (c) because it appears to the authorised person that the vehicle has been abandoned.

Delivery of vehicles

B67.11   **10.**—(1) An authorised person, or a person acting under the direction of an authorised person, may deliver a vehicle removed under regulation 9, or direct it to be delivered, into the custody of an identified person if—

 (a) the identified person agrees to accept delivery; and

 (b) a receipt is provided by the identified person to the authorised person, or the person acting under the direction of an authorised person, to confirm that the identified person has taken safe custody of the vehicle.

(2) An "*identified person*" is a person who–

 (a) is capable of accepting delivery of the vehicle; and

 (b) has agreed arrangements with the Secretary of State for accepting custody of vehicles, including arrangements regarding security and access.

(3) The arrangements made by virtue of sub-paragraph (2)(b) may include provision as to the payment of a sum to the identified person.

Notice of removal of vehicle

B67.12   **11.**—(1) Subject to paragraph (3), where a vehicle has been removed and delivered into the custody of an identified person under regulation 10, the authorised person must provide a notice to the person referred to in paragraph (2) specifying—

 (a) the statutory power under which the vehicle has been removed;

 (b) the particulars of the place to which the vehicle has been removed;

 (c) the identity of the person to whom the vehicle has been delivered;

 (d) the steps to be taken to reclaim the vehicle, including—

  (i) how payment of any release fee should be made; and

  (ii) the evidence to be produced to show that the prohibition under which the driving of the vehicle was prohibited has been removed or has expired;

 (e) the steps to be taken, in accordance with regulation 18, in the event of a dispute; and

 (f) any other relevant information, including the consequences of not reclaiming the vehicle.

(2) The notice shall be provided by the authorised person to the person who was the driver of the vehicle when the driving of the vehicle was prohibited.

(3) If it is not reasonably practicable to give the notice to the person referred to in paragraph (2), then the authorised person shall take reasonable steps to locate the owner of the vehicle and to give the notice to the owner in writing by post.

Taking possession of a vehicle

12. A person ("*the claimant*") may take possession of the vehicle if the claimant—   **B67.13**

- (a) claims it before it is disposed of;
- (b) claims it not more than three months from the date on which the vehicle was removed or the direction to remove it was given;
- (c) produces evidence to the satisfaction of the authorised person that the claimant—
  - (i) is either the owner of the vehicle; or
  - (ii) was the person in charge of the vehicle at the time it was removed or was directed to be removed;
- (d) pays the charges specified in the Schedule for the release, removal and custody of the vehicle, as applicable; and
- (e) produces such evidence as is required by regulation 4(5).

Compensation

13.—(1) An amount calculated in accordance with paragraph (2) may be paid to a person if—   **B67.14**

- (a) he claims after the vehicle's disposal to be or to have been its owner or to have been the person in charge of the vehicle when it was removed; and
- (b) the claim is made within three months of the date on which the vehicle was removed or the direction to remove the vehicle was given.

(2) The amount payable under paragraph (1) shall be calculated by deducting from any proceeds of sale the charges specified in the Schedule in respect of the release, removal, custody and disposal of the vehicle, as applicable.

Power to dispose, etc., of vehicles

14. The person into whose custody the vehicle is delivered pursuant to regulation 10 may dispose, sell or destroy the vehicle as that person sees fit if the vehicle has not been claimed in accordance with regulation 12 within three months from the date on which the vehicle was removed or the direction to remove the vehicle was given.   **B67.15**

Recovery of prescribed charges

15. Whether or not a claim is made under regulation 12 or 13—   **B67.16**

- (a) the Secretary of State; or
- (b) a person into whose custody the vehicle is delivered in accordance with regulation 10

may recover from the vehicle's owner or the person in charge of the vehicle the charges specified in the Schedule in respect of the release, removal, custody and disposal of the vehicle, as applicable.

Offences of failing to remove or deliver vehicles

B67.17 **16.** A person who fails to comply within a reasonable time with a direction under regulation 9(1) or 10(1) is guilty of an offence and liable on summary conviction to a fine not exceeding level 5 on the standard scale.

False or misleading statements, etc.

B67.18 **17.**—(1) Where—

    (a) a person makes a declaration with a view to securing possession of a vehicle purported to have been delivered into the custody of an identified person;

    (b) the declaration is that the prohibition has been removed; and

    (c) the declaration is to the person's knowledge either false or in any material respect misleading,

that person is guilty of an offence.

    (2) A person guilty of an offence under paragraph (1) is liable—

    (a) on summary conviction, to a fine not exceeding the statutory maximum; or

    (b) on conviction on indictment, to imprisonment for a term not exceeding two years, or to a fine, or both.

PART 4

GENERAL

Disputes

B67.19 **18.**—(1) A person may apply to the appropriate court on the grounds that the authorised person, or person acting under his direction, did not comply with any of the requirements of any of regulations 4(1), 9, 10(1), 11, 12, or 13 ("the specified requirements").

    (2) If the appropriate court finds that an authorised person, or person acting under his direction, did not comply with any of the specified requirements, it may order the Secretary of State to pay a sum to the person applying to the court to reflect any financial loss directly attributable to that failure to comply.

    (3) In this regulation, "*appropriate court*" means—

    (a) in England and Wales, a magistrates' court; or

    (b) *[applies to Scotland]*.

Application of Road Traffic Offenders Act 1988

B67.20 **19.** The following provisions of the Road Traffic Offenders Act 1988 shall apply to the offences created by these Regulations—

    (a) section 1 (requirement of warning etc. of prosecutions for certain offences);

(b) section 6 (timewithin which summary proceedings for certain offences must be commenced);

(c) section 11 (evidence by certificate as to driver, user or owner); and

(d) section 12(1) (proof, in summary proceedings, of identity of driver of vehicle).

*   *   *

The Fixed Penalty (Procedure) (Vehicle Examiners) Regulations 2009

(SI 2009/495)

Citation, commencement and extent

B68.01   **1.**—(1) These Regulations may be cited as the Fixed Penalty (Procedure) (Vehicle Examiners) Regulations 2009 and shall come into force on 1st April 2009.

(2) These Regulations do not extend to Scotland.

Interpretation

B68.02   **2.** In these Regulations, *"the Act"* means the Road Traffic Offenders Act 1988.

Application

B68.03   **3.** These Regulations apply in cases where a fixed penalty notice is given by a vehicle examiner in accordance with section 54 (notices on-the-spot etc) of the Act.

Documents or information to be provided

B68.04   **4.** The documents described in column 1 of the Schedule to these Regulations (as referred to in the provisions of the Act specified in column 2 of the Schedule) shall contain the information, or, as the case may be, further information prescribed in column 3 of the Schedule.

Remittance

B68.05   **5.** If payment of the fixed penalty is made by a person otherwise than as required by the fixed penalty notice, the Secretary of State shall return the remittance to that person.

Return of driving licence (if so held)

B68.06   **6.** Where—

(a) the person to whom the fixed penalty notice was given holds a driving licence;

(b) the suspended enforcement period has expired;

(c) the fixed penalty has not been paid; and

(d) either that person has requested a hearing under section 55(2) or no registration certificate has been issued under section 70(2) of the Act;

the Secretary of State shall, in the case of an endorseable offence, return the driving licence to that person.

Notification of registration of sum

B68.07   **7.** Where, in a case involving an endorseable offence, any sum is registered under section 71 of the Act for enforcement against that person as a fine, the designated officer for the court where the sum is registered shall notify the Secretary of State that the sum has been registered.

Receipt for payment

8. Where a fixed penalty is paid within the suspended enforcement period the Secretary of State shall send a receipt for the payment, if requested, to the payer.   **B68.08**

Licence receipts

9. For the purposes of section 56(3)(a) of the Act, there is prescribed a period of two months beginning with the same date of issue.   **B68.09**

Regulation 4   SCHEDULE

INFORMATION OR FURTHER INFORMATION TO BE PROVIDED IN CERTAIN DOCUMENTS MENTIONED IN PART 3 OF THE ACT

B68.10

Document	Provision of the Act	Information or further information to be provided
1. Fixed Penalty Notice	Section 52	(i) the name of the vehicle examiner giving the notice
		(ii) the serial number of the fixed penalty notice
		(iii) whether the notice relates to an endorseable offence
		(iv) the name, date of birth and address of the person to whom the notice is given
		(v) the date, time and place of the alleged offence
		(vi) the details of the vehicle including the registration number
		(vii) the documents, if any, to be provided to the Secretary of State and the period within which they must be provided and the address to which they must be sent
		(viii) an explanation of the action to be taken by the driver where (a) the driver has not or (b) the driver has, surrendered the licence, if the driver holds such a licence
		(ix) the fact that the person to whom the notice is given may opt for trial
		(x) the method of paying the fixed penalty
		(xi) guidance to the driver as to the legal consequences of a fixed penalty notice

Document	Provision of the Act	Information or further information to be provided
2. Receipt for driving licence (if the offender holds a driving licence)	Section 56	(i) whether the driving licence is full or provisional (ii) the driver number as shown on the licence (iii) the groups of vehicles which the driver is entitled to drive (iv) the expiry date of the licence (v) the duration of the validity of the licence receipt (vi) the method of obtaining a new receipt on expiry of an old receipt (vii) the name of the vehicle examiner issuing the fixed penalty notice
3. Registration certificate	Section 70	(i) the serial number and date, time and place of issue of the fixed penalty notice (ii) the vehicle registration number (iii) the driver number (either as shown on the licence or as allocated by the Secretary of State) (iv) the amount of the appropriate fixed penalty (v) the sum to be registered in default of payment of the fixed penalty

The Public Service Vehicles (Enforcement Powers) Regulations 2009

(SI 2009/1964)

CONTENTS

Citation and commencement

1. These Regulations may be cited as the Public Service Vehicles (Enforce-   **B69.02** ment Powers) Regulations 2009 and come into force on 1st October 2009.

Interpretation

2.—(1) In these Regulations—   **B69.03**

    "the Act" means the Public Passenger Vehicles Act 1981;

    "hiring agreement" and *" vehicle-hire firm"* have the same meaning as in section 66 of the Road Traffic Offenders Act 1988;

    "licence" means a PSV operator's licence;

    "owner", as regards a vehicle which has been detained by virtue of regulation 3, means —

    (a) in the case of a vehicle which, at the time of its detention, was hired from a vehicle-hire firm under a hiring agreement, the vehicle-hire firm; or

    (b) in the case of a vehicle to which paragraph (a) does not apply, the person who can show to the satisfaction of the authorised person that, at the time the vehicle was detained, the person lawfully owned the vehicle (whether or not that person was the person in whose name the vehicle was registered under the Vehicle Excise and Registration Act 1994); and

"vehicle" means a public service vehicle adapted to carry more than 8 passengers.

(2) In these Regulations, any reference to a person being entitled to the return of contents or personal effects is a reference to a person who satisfies the requirements prescribed in regulation 7(2).

Detention of vehicles and contents

B69.04   **3.**—(1) Where an authorised person has reason to believe that a vehicle is being, or has been, used on a road in contravention of section 12(1) of the Act, that person may detain the vehicle and its contents.

(2) Paragraph (1) does not authorise a person other than a constable in uniform to stop a vehicle on any road.

Passengers

B69.05   **4.**—(1) This regulation applies where a vehicle is detained by virtue of regulation 3 and, at the time of its detention, passengers are travelling on the vehicle.

(2) Where this regulation applies the authorised person must make provision for the passengers, with their personal effects, to be transported in safety—

    (a) to their destination; or

    (b) to a suitable place from which to continue their journey.

(3) In making provision under paragraph (2), the authorised person must have particular regard to the needs of passengers who appear to the authorised person to be—

    (a) under the age of 18 years; or

    (b) elderly or disabled persons.

Immobilisation of vehicle

B69.06   **5.**—(1) Where a vehicle has been detained by virtue of regulation 3 the authorised person may—

    (a) fix an immobilisation device to the vehicle in the place where the vehicle has been detained; or

    (b) move the vehicle, or require it to be moved, to a more convenient place and fix an immobilisation device to the vehicle in that other place.

(2) A vehicle to which an immobilisation device has been fixed in accordance with paragraph (1) may be released from the device only by or on the direction of an authorised person.

(3) Where an immobilisation device has been fixed to a vehicle in accordance with this regulation, the authorised person fixing the device must also fix to the vehicle an immobilisation notice—

    (a) indicating that an immobilisation device has been fixed to the vehicle;

    (b) indicating that the vehicle may be released from the device only by or under the direction of an authorised person;

    (c) providing details as to where the authorised person may be contacted, and information about the procedure under which an application may be made for the release of the vehicle from the device;

    (d) warning that the notice must not be removed or interfered with except by or on the authority of an authorised person; and

    (e) warning that no attempt must be made to drive the vehicle or otherwise put it in motion.

(4) An immobilisation notice fixed to a vehicle in accordance with paragraph (3) must not be removed or interfered with except by or on the authority of an authorised person.

Offences relating to immobilisation

6.—(1) A person who removes or attempts to remove, otherwise than in accordance with regulation 5(2), an immobilisation device fixed to a vehicle in accordance with regulation 5(1) is guilty of an offence. **B69.07**

(2) A person guilty of an offence under paragraph (1) is liable on summary conviction to a fine not exceeding level 3 on the standard scale.

(3) A person who removes or interferes with, otherwise than in accordance with regulation 5(4), an immobilisation notice fixed to a vehicle in accordance with regulation 5(3) is guilty of an offence.

(4) A person guilty of an offence under paragraph (3) is liable on summary conviction to a fine not exceeding level 2 on the standard scale.

Contents and personal effects

7.—(1) Where a vehicle is detained by virtue of regulation 3, the authorised person must take such steps as are reasonably practicable to return the contents and any personal effects remaining on the vehicle to the person who is entitled to their return. **B69.08**

(2) For the purposes of these Regulations a person is entitled to the return of contents or personal effects if—

    (a) the person has provided satisfactory evidence of entitlement to the authorised person; or

    (b) the person has, where the person seeks to recover contents or personal effects as the agent of another person, provided satisfactory evidence to the authorised person of the person's status as agent and of the principal's entitlement to the contents or personal effects.

(3) Where, by virtue of these Regulations, more than one person seeks to provide evidence of entitlement to any contents or personal effects, the authorised person must determine which of those persons is entitled to the contents or personal effects on the basis of the evidence provided by them.

Removal and delivery of property into custody of nominated custodian

B69.09   **8.**—(1) An authorised person may direct that—

    (a) a vehicle detained by virtue of regulation 3, or

    (b) any contents so detained, or any personal effects remaining on a vehicle so detained, which it has not been possible to return to the person entitled to their return,

be removed and delivered into the custody of a person specified in the direction ("*the nominated custodian*" [*defined in the Public Passenger Vehicles Act 1981 Sch.2A, para.1(1) and para.6(1), not reproduced in the main work*]).

(2) A direction under paragraph (1) must be given in writing.

(3) An authorised person may, in giving a direction under paragraph (1) in relation to a vehicle—

    (a) allow the vehicle to be driven, towed or removed by such means as the authorised person considers reasonable in the circumstances; and

    (b) provide for any other necessary steps to be taken in relation to the vehicle in order to facilitate its removal.

(4) An authorised person may, in giving a direction under paragraph (1), provide for any contents or personal effects to be removed separately from the vehicle if the authorised person considers that—

    (a) it is reasonable to do so to facilitate removal of the vehicle;

    (b) there is good reason for storing the contents or personal effects at a different place from the vehicle; or

    (c) the condition of the contents or personal effects requires them to be disposed of without delay.

(5) The authorised person may also, in giving a direction under paragraph (1), allow the driver of the vehicle to—

    (a) transport any passengers travelling on the vehicle at the time that it was detained,

    (b) deliver any contents of the vehicle, or

    (c) deliver any personal effects remaining on the vehicle,

to their destination, or to some other suitable place, before delivering the vehicle into the custody of the nominated custodian, provided the authorised person is satisfied that the passengers, contents or personal effects can be transported on the vehicle in safety.

(6) The nominated custodian must be a person who has agreed with the Secretary of State to accept delivery of any vehicle, contents and personal effects.

(7) The agreement made under paragraph (6) may include provision for the payment of a sum of money to the nominated custodian by the authorised person.

Informing persons that their property has been detained etc

B69.10   **9.**—(1) Subject to regulation 18(1), this regulation applies in relation to—

    (a) a vehicle detained by virtue of regulation 3; or

    (b) any contents so detained, or any personal effects remaining on a vehicle so detained, which it has not been possible to return to the person entitled to their return.

(2) Where this regulation applies an authorised person must—

    (a) publish a notice in at least one newspaper circulating in such areas as the authorised person considers appropriate in the circumstances of the case, and

    (b) publish a notice—

        (i) if the property was detained, or remained on a vehicle that was detained, in England or Wales, in the *London Gazette*, or

        (ii) if the property was detained, or remained on a vehicle that was detained, in Scotland, in the *Edinburgh Gazette*,

    containing the information described in paragraph (4).

(3) A copy of the notice published in accordance with paragraph (2) must be served by the authorised person on—

    (a) the owner of the vehicle;

    (b) the traffic commissioner for the traffic area in which the vehicle was detained;

    (c) the chief officer or, in Scotland, chief constable of the police force in whose area the vehicle was detained;

    (d) the Association of British Insurers; and

    (e) the British Vehicle Rental and Leasing Association, where the vehicle was hired from a vehicle-hire firm under a hiring agreement.

(4) The information is—

    (a) a brief description of the vehicle and contents detained, or personal effects remaining on a vehicle so detained, including the registration mark (if any) of any vehicle;

    (b) the time and place at which, and the powers under which, the vehicle was detained;

    (c) the procedure under which, and the date by which—

        (i) an application may be made to the traffic commissioner for the area in which the vehicle was detained for the return of any vehicle so detained; or

        (ii) a person may claim any contents or personal effects which have not been disposed of in accordance with regulation 18(1);

    (d) a statement that if, by the date specified by virtue of sub-paragraph (c), no person has made an application to the traffic commissioner in accordance with regulation 11, the authorised person intends to allow the vehicle to be disposed of in accordance with regulation 16; and

    (e) a statement that if, by the date specified by virtue of sub-paragraph (c), no person has sought to establish that they are entitled to the return of contents or personal effects, the authorised person intends to allow the contents or personal effects to be disposed of in accordance with regulation 18(2).

(5) The date specified by virtue of paragraph (4)(c) must be no less than 21 days after the date by which all the obligations prescribed in paragraph (2) have been fulfilled.

Return of vehicle

10.—(1) In the circumstances described in paragraph (2), a vehicle detained by **B69.11** virtue of regulation 3 must be returned to the owner, without the need for an application under regulation 11.

(2) The circumstances are that the authorised person is satisfied that one or more of the grounds specified in paragraph (3) is or are made out.

(3) The grounds are—

(a) that, at the time the vehicle was detained, the person using the vehicle held a valid licence (whether or not authorising the use of the vehicle);

(b) that, at the time the vehicle was detained, the vehicle was not being, and had not been, used in contravention of section 12(1) of the Act;

(c) that, although at the time the vehicle was detained it was being, or had been, used in contravention of section 12(1) of the Act, the owner did not know that it was being, or had been, so used;

(d) that, although knowing at the time the vehicle was detained that it was being, or had been, used in contravention of section 12(1) of the Act, the owner—

(i) had taken steps with a view to preventing that use; and

(ii) has taken steps with a view to preventing any further such use.

Application to traffic commissioner for return of vehicle

B69.12   **11.**—(1) The owner of a vehicle detained in accordance with regulation 3 may, no later than the date specified by virtue of regulation 9(4)(c), apply to the traffic commissioner for the area in which the vehicle was detained for the return of the vehicle.

(2) An application under paragraph (1) must—

(a) be made on one or more of the grounds specified in regulation 10(3);

(b) specify on which of those grounds the application is made;

(c) be made in writing; and

(d) include a statement of evidence to support the application.

(3) Where the applicant wishes the traffic commissioner to hold a hearing, the application under paragraph (1) must include a written statement to that effect.

(4) The period referred to in paragraph (1) is subject to regulation 25.

Hearings by traffic commissioner

B69.13   **12.** *[Omitted.]*

Notification of determinations

B69.14   **13.** *[Omitted.]*

Consequences of the traffic commissioner's determination

B69.15   **14.** *[Omitted.]*

Appeal to Upper Tribunal from traffic commissioner

B69.16   **15.** *[Omitted.]*

Sale or destruction of vehicle

16.—(1) Subject to paragraphs (2) and (3), and provided a notice containing **B69.17**
the information described in regulation 9(4) has been published and served in accordance with regulation 9(2) and (3), if—

(a) no application is made to the traffic commissioner under regulation 11
for the return of the vehicle, or

(b) such an application is made but the traffic commissioner, or the Upper
Tribunal where there is an appeal under regulation 15, determines
that none of the grounds specified in regulation 10(3) is made out,

the vehicle may be sold or destroyed by the nominated custodian.

(2) The nominated custodian must not sell or destroy the vehicle without the
permission of the authorised person.

(3) The nominated custodian must not sell or destroy the vehicle—

(a) until any period specified in the Tribunal Procedure (Upper Tribunal)
Rules 2008 for a notice of appeal to be provided to the Upper Tribunal
has expired with no such notice of appeal having been provided; or

(b) until, where a notice of appeal has been provided to the Upper
Tribunal, the appeal has been finally disposed of.

(4) After the sale or destruction of a vehicle by virtue of paragraph (1) the
nominated custodian must serve notice of the disposal on—

(a) the owner of the vehicle;

(b) the traffic commissioner for the traffic area in which the vehicle was
detained;

(c) the chief officer or, in Scotland, chief constable of the police force in
whose area the vehicle was detained;

(d) the Driver and Vehicle Licensing Agency;

(e) the Association of British Insurers; and

(f) the British Vehicle Rental and Leasing Association, where the vehicle was hired from a vehicle-hire firm under a hiring agreement.

(5) For the purposes of paragraph (3)(b), an appeal is "finally disposed of" on
the latest of the following dates—

(a) the date on which the appeal is finally determined,

(b) the date on which the time for any further appeal expires without any
such appeal having been made, or

(c) the date on which the appeal is abandoned or withdrawn,

and in this paragraph *"appeal"* includes a reference to any further appeal or
appeals.

Return or disposal of contents and personal effects

17.—(1) The nominated custodian must retain custody of any contents or **B69.18**
personal effects delivered into the custody of the nominated custodian by virtue
of regulation 8 until—

(a) the contents or personal effects are returned, in accordance with this
regulation, to the person who is entitled to their return; or

(b) the contents or personal effects are sold or destroyed by the nominated
custodian in accordance with regulation 18.

(2) A person seeking the return of any contents or personal effects described in paragraph (1) must give written notice to the nominated custodian no later than the date specified by virtue of regulation 9(4)(c).

(3) Except where the contents or personal effects have been disposed of in accordance with regulation 18(1), the nominated custodian must return any contents or personal effects to a person who has, by virtue of the notice given in accordance with paragraph (2), established that the person is entitled to the return of the contents or personal effects.

Disposal of contents and personal effects

B69.19   **18.**—(1) Where the authorised person is of the opinion that the condition of contents detained by virtue of regulation 3, or personal effects that remained on a vehicle so detained, (and which it has not been possible to return to the person entitled to their return), is such that they must be disposed of without delay, those contents or personal effects may be disposed of by the authorised person or the nominated custodian without the authorised person first complying with the requirements prescribed in regulation 9.

(2) Subject to paragraph (3), where such contents or personal effects are not disposed of in accordance with paragraph (1) and—

    (a) one or more persons has given written notice in accordance with regulation 17(2), but no person has established that they are entitled to the return of the property, or

    (b) no written notice has been given in accordance with regulation 17(2),

the nominated custodian may sell or destroy the contents or personal effects.

(3) The nominated custodian may not sell or destroy contents or personal effects in accordance with paragraph (2) unless—

    (a) the nominated custodian has the permission of the authorised person;

    (b) the authorised person has complied with the requirements prescribed in regulation 9; and

    (c) the date specified by virtue of regulation 9(4)(c) has passed.

Custody of property

B69.20   **19.**—(1) Subject to paragraph (2), it is the duty of the nominated custodian, at any time while property consisting of—

    (a) vehicles or contents detained by virtue of regulation 3, or

    (b) personal effects remaining on a vehicle so detained,

is in the custody of the nominated custodian, to take such steps as are necessary for the safe custody of the property.

(2) Paragraph (1) is subject to the powers of the nominated custodian to dispose of property by virtue of these Regulations.

Proceeds of sale

B69.21   **20.**—(1) Subject to paragraph (2), the proceeds of sale of any property sold under regulation 16 or 18 must—

    (a) be applied towards meeting expenses incurred by any authorised person exercising functions by virtue of these Regulations in relation to the property in question; and

(b) in so far as they are not so applied, be applied in meeting any claim to the proceeds of sale which is made and established in accordance with paragraph (3).

(2) Where the proceeds of sale of any property sold under regulation 16 or 18 exceed the expenses referred to in paragraph (1)(a) and—

(a) no person has established entitlement to the proceeds of sale of the property, or

(b) a person has established entitlement to the proceeds of sale of the property, but excess proceeds remain once the claim has been satisfied,

the excess proceeds may be applied towards meeting expenses incurred by any authorised person exercising functions in relation to any other property detained by virtue of regulation 3, or any personal effects remaining on a vehicle so detained.

(3) For the purposes of paragraph (1), a claim to the proceeds of sale of any property is established if—

(a) the claim is made not later than one year after the date on which the property was sold; and

(b) the authorised person is satisfied that—

(i) if the property consists of a vehicle, the person making the claim was the owner of the vehicle immediately before it was sold by virtue of regulation 16; or

(ii) if the property consists of contents or personal effects, the person making the claim would, had the person made an appropriate application at the prescribed time, have been entitled to the return of the property by virtue of regulation 17.

(4) Where the conditions specified in paragraph (3) are satisfied, the authorised person must pay the person a sum calculated in accordance with paragraph (5).

(5) Any sum payable under paragraph (4) is to be calculated by deducting from the proceeds of sale the expenses incurred by the authorised person in exercising functions under these Regulations in relation to the property, including for the detention, removal, storage and sale of the property.

Disputes

21. *[Omitted.]*   **B69.22**

Obstruction of an authorised person

22.—(1) A person who intentionally obstructs an authorised person in the   **B69.23**
exercise of the powers arising by virtue of these Regulations is guilty of an offence.

(2) A person guilty of an offence under paragraph (1) is liable on summary conviction to a fine not exceeding level 3 on the standard scale.

Offences as to securing possession of property

B69.24   23.—(1) Where a person makes a declaration with a view to securing the return of a vehicle under regulation 14 and the declaration—

   (a) is that the vehicle was not being, or had not been, used in contravention of section 12(1) of the Act, and

   (b) is to the person's knowledge either false or in any material respect misleading,

that person is guilty of an offence.

   (2) A person guilty of an offence under paragraph (1) is liable—

   (a) on summary conviction, to a fine not exceeding the statutory maximum; and

   (b) on conviction on indictment, to imprisonment for a term not exceeding two years or to a fine or to both.

Service of notice or application

B69.25   24. *[Omitted.]*

Extension of time

B69.26   25. *[Omitted.]*

The Motor Vehicles (Insurance Requirements) Regulations 2011

(SI 2011/20)

Citation, commencement and interpretation

1.—(1) These Regulations may be cited as the Motor Vehicles (Insurance **B70.01**
Requirements) Regulations 2011 and shall come into force on 4th February 2011.

(2) In these Regulations—

"*the 1988 Act*" means the Road Traffic Act 1988;

"*the 2002 Regulations*" means the Road Vehicles (Registration and Licensing) Regulations 2002 [*q.v.*]; and

"*certificate of destruction*" has the same meaning as that expression has in
the End-of-Life Vehicles Regulations 2003 [*SI 2003/2635, not
reproduced in this work*].

Exceptions to the offence under section 144A

2. For the purposes of section 144B(4)(b) of the 1988 Act (the third condi- **B70.02**
tion)—

    (a) where the vehicle has been sold or transferred by the registered keeper
(other than for the purpose of being destroyed or sent permanently
out of Great Britain) the registered keeper of the vehicle must, by the
relevant time and in relation to that vehicle, have furnished the information and documents and made the declarations in accordance with
regulation 22(2)(b), 23(2) or 24(5) (as the case may be) of the 2002
Regulations;

    (b) where the vehicle has been sold or transferred by the registered keeper
for the purpose of its destruction, the registered keeper must, by the
relevant time and in relation to that vehicle, have—

        (i) furnished the information and documents, and made the declara-
tions in accordance with regulation 23(2) or 24(5) (as the case
may be) of the 2002 Regulations; or

        (ii) been given a certificate of destruction; and

    (c) where the vehicle has been sent permanently out of Great Britain, the
registered keeper of the vehicle must, by the relevant time and in relation to that vehicle, have notified the Secretary of State in accordance
with regulation 17 of the 2002 Regulations.

3. For the purposes of section 144B(5)(c) of the 1988 Act (the fourth condi- **B70.03**
tion), the registered keeper of the vehicle must, by the relevant time and in relation to that vehicle, have delivered the required particulars, and made the required
declaration, in accordance with paragraph 5(3) of Schedule 4 to the 2002
Regulations.

4. For the purposes of section 144B(6)(c) of the 1988 Act (the fifth condition), **B70.04**

the registered keeper of the vehicle must, by the relevant time and in relation to that vehicle, have given notification in accordance with regulation 26A(3) of the 2002 Regulations.

Further exception to the offence under section 144A

B70.05   **5.** *[Omitted, amending, s.144B of the Road Traffic Act 1988.]*

Lesser amount of fixed penalty

B70.06   **6.**—(1) A fixed penalty payable under section 144C of the 1988 Act shall be treated as having been paid if the amount of £50 is paid before the end of the period of 21 days following the date of the notice given under that section.

(2) A fixed penalty notice under section 144C of the 1988 Act shall state that the fixed penalty payable under that section shall be treated as having been paid if the amount of £50 is paid before the end of the period of 21 days following the date of that notice.

Disclosure of information

B70.07   **7.** MIIC shall make available to the Secretary of State, for the purpose of the Secretary of State's functions in connection with the enforcement of an offence under Part 6 of the 1988 Act, the information referred to in regulation 4(a), (b) and (c) of the Motor Vehicles (Compulsory Insurance) (Information Centre and Compensation Body) Regulations 2003 [*SI 2003/37, not reproduced in this work*] or so much of that information as is required by the Secretary of State for that purpose.

Section C

European Union Legislation

Regulation (EC) 1073/2009
   on common rules for access to the international market for
      coach and bus services
   arts 1–28, 30, 31, Annexes I–III   C13.01

C0.01   *[Following the renumbering of the provisions of the EC Treaty and the EU
Treaty by art.12 of and the Annex to the Treaty of Amsterdam (O.J. No.C340,
November 10, 1997, pp.78 and 86–91) references in the notes in this volume to
articles in the EC Treaty as so renumbered are (in accordance with the practice
of the European Court of Justice) in the form "art.71 EC", whereas any reference to an article as numbered before the Treaty of Amsterdam took effect is in
the form "art.75 of the EC Treaty" or "EC Treaty art.75". No editorial change
in the style of citation has been incorporated into the texts of legislation. The
Treaty of Amsterdam entered into force in accordance with ibid. art.14(2), on
May 1, 1999 (see the information at O.J. No.C120, May 1, 1999, p.24).*

*For consolidated versions of the EU Treaty and EC Treaty following the entry
into force of the Treaty of Nice on February 1, 2003, see O.J. No.C325, December
24, 2002, pp.1–184. For consolidated versions of the EU Treaty and the Treaty
on the Functioning of the European Union, following the amendments introduced
by the Treaty of Lisbon, signed on December 13, 2007, see O.J. No.C115, May 9,
2008, p.1. The Treaty of Lisbon entered into force on December 1, 2009 in accordance with art.6, see* http://europa.eu/lisbon＿treaty/index＿en.htm *[accessed
March 1, 2011].*

European Economic Area

*The Agreement on the European Economic Area was signed at Oporto on May
2, 1992 and entered into force on January 1, 1994. The agreement was originally
signed by the EFTA countries (Austria, Finland, Iceland, Liechtenstein, Norway,
Sweden and Switzerland) and the EC Member States at that date (Belgium,
Denmark, France, Germany, Greece, Ireland, Italy, Luxembourg, the Netherlands, Portugal, Spain and the United Kingdom) (O.J. No.L1, January 3, 1994,
p.3). However, the agreement was not ratified by Switzerland and in consequence
a protocol adjusting the original agreement was signed by the remaining states
(op. cit., p.572). Following Switzerland's withdrawal from the original agreement, the position of Liechtenstein was for a time uncertain. Subsequently (on
January 1, 1995), Austria, Finland and Sweden became members of the European
Union. For practical purposes, the European Economic Area in effect became
the territory of the European Union (within which area Community law applies)
plus Iceland, Norway and (from May 1, 1995; see Decision 1/95 of the EEA
Council, O.J. No.L86, April 20, 1995, p.58) Liechtenstein. An EEA Enlargement
Agreement was signed on November 11, 2003 to parallel the enlargement of the
EU by the accession of the states of Cyprus, the Czech Republic, Estonia, Latvia,
Lithuania, Hungary, Malta, Poland, Slovenia and the Slovak Republic (see Cm.
6171, April 2004). Following the accession of the Republic of Bulgaria and
Romania to the European Union on January 1, 2007 an EEA Enlargement Agree-
ment was signed on July 25, 2007 (see* http://efta.int/eea/enlargement-of-the-
eea.aspx *[accessed March 1, 2011]).*

The agreement expressly adapts a number of provisions of Community law but does so expressly "for the purposes of the agreement". The agreement has itself been amended on a number of occasions since it came into operation. In view of the limited application of adaptations effected by the agreement, they are not expressly incorporated into this work.]

Regulation (EEC) 3821/85 of December 20, 1985 on recording equipment in road transport

C1.01 *THE COUNCIL OF THE EUROPEAN COMMUNITIES,*

Having regard to the Treaty establishing the European Economic Community, and in particular [Article 71] thereof,

Having regard to the proposal from the Commission [O.J. No.C100, April 12, 1984, p.3, O.J. No.C223, September 3, 1985, p.5],

Having regard to the opinion of the European Parliament [O.J. No.C122, May 20, 1985, p.168],

Having regard to the opinion of the Economic and Social Committee [O.J. No.C104, April 25, 1985, p.4, O.J. No.C303, November 25, 1985, p.29],

Whereas Regulation (EEC) No.1463/70 [O.J. No.L164, July 27, 1970, p.1] as last amended by Regulation (EEC) No.2828/77 [O.J. No.L334, December 24, 1977, p.11] introduced recording equipment in road transport;

Whereas, taking into account the amendments set out hereinafter, in order to clarify matters, all the relevant provisions should be brought together in a single text, and in consequence thereof, Regulation (EEC) No.1463/70 of the Council should be repealed; whereas, however, the exemptions set out in Article 3(1) for certain passenger services should be maintained in force for a certain time;

Whereas the use of recording equipment that may indicate the periods of time referred to in Regulation (EEC) No.3820/85 on the harmonisation of certain social legislation relating to road transport [q.v.] is intended to ensure effective checking on that social legislation;

Whereas the obligation to use such recording equipment can be imposed only for vehicles registered in Member States; whereas furthermore certain of such vehicles may, without giving rise to difficulty, be excluded from the scope of this Regulation;

Whereas the Member States should be entitled with the Commission's authorisation, to grant certain vehicles exemptions from the provisions of the Regulation in exceptional circumstances; whereas, in urgent cases, it should be possible to grant these exemptions for a limited time without prior authorisation from the Commission;

Whereas, in order to ensure effective checking, the equipment must be reliable in operation, easy to use and designed in such a way as to minimise any possibility of fraudulent use; whereas to this end recording equipment should in particular be capable of providing, on separate sheets for each driver and in a sufficiently precise and easily readable form, recorded details of the various periods of time;

Whereas automatic recording of other details of a vehicle's journey, such as speed and distance covered, will contribute significantly to road safety and will encourage sensible driving of the vehicle; whereas, consequently, it appears appropriate to provide for the equipment also to record those details;

Whereas it is necessary to set Community construction and installation standards for recording equipment and to provide for an EEC approval procedure, in order to avoid throughout the territory of the Member States any impediment to the registration of vehicles fitted with such recording equipment, to their entry into service or use, or to such equipment being used;

Whereas, in the event of differences of opinion between Member States concerning cases of EEC type approval, the Commission should be empowered to take a decision on a dispute within six months if the States concerned have been unable to reach a settlement;

Whereas it would be helpful in implementing this Regulation and preventing abuses to issue drivers who so request with a copy of their record sheets;

Whereas, in order to achieve the aims hereinbefore mentioned of keeping a check on work and rest periods, it is necessary that employers and drivers be responsible for seeing that the equipment functions correctly and that they perform with due care the operations described;

Whereas the provisions governing the number of records sheets that a driver must keep with him must be amended following the replacement of the flexible week by a fixed week;

Whereas technical progress necessitates rapid adaptation of the technical specifications set out in the Annexes to this Regulation; whereas, in order to facilitate the implementation of the measures necessary for this purpose, provision should be made for a procedure establishing close co-operation between the Member States and the Commission within an Advisory Committee;

Whereas Member States should exchange the available information on breaches established;

Whereas, in order to ensure that recording equipment functions reliably and correctly, it is advisable to lay down uniform requirements for the periodic checks and inspections to which the equipment is to be subject after installation,

[The preamble is printed as amended by the Treaty of Amsterdam art.12(1) and (3).]

HAS ADOPTED THIS REGULATION:

[As to the Agreement on the European Economic Area generally, see the **C1.02** *introductory note to Section C above.*

For the purposes of that agreement, Regulation (EEC) 3821/85 has been adapted by ibid. Annex XIII, Chap.II, para.21, as amended.

The text of this Regulation is printed as amended by:
    Commission Regulation (EEC) 3314/90 (O.J. No.L318, November 17, 1990, p.20) (November 20, 1990);
    Council Regulation (EEC) 3572/90, Art.3 (O.J. No.L353, December 17, 1990, p.12) (December 17, 1990);

Commission Regulation (EEC) 3688/92 (O.J. No.L374, December 22, 1992, p.12) (December 25, 1992);

Act of Accession of Austria, Finland and Sweden to the European Union (O.J. No.C241, August 29, 1994, p.21), as amended by Council Decision 95/1/EC (O.J. No.L1, January 1, 1995, p.1) ;

Commission Regulation (EC) 2479/95 (O.J. No.L256, October 26, 1995, p.8) (January 1, 1996);

Commission Regulation (EC) 1056/97 (O.J. No.L154, June 12, 1997, p.21) (January 1, 1996);

Council Regulation (EC) 2135/98 (O.J. No.L274, October 9, 1998, p.1) (October 10, 1998);

Commission Regulation (EC) 1360/2002 (O.J. No.L207, August 5, 2002, pp.1–252) (August 25, 2002);

Act of Accession of the Czech Republic, the Republic of Estonia, the Republic of Cyprus, the Republic of Latvia, the Republic of Lithuania, the Republic of Hungary, the Republic of Malta, the Republic of Poland, the Republic of Slovenia and the Slovak Republic (O.J. No.L236, September 23, 2003, p.33);

European Parliament and Council Regulation (EC) 1882/2003 (O.J. No.L284/24, October 31, 2003) (November 20, 2003);

Commission Regulation (EC) 432/2004(O.J. No.L71/3, March 10, 2004) (March 13, 2004);

European Parliament and Council Regulation (EC) 561/2006 (O.J. No.L102, April 11, 2006, p.1) (May 1, 2006 in relation to Arts 10(5), 26(3) and (4), and 27; April 11, 2007);

Council Regulation (EC) 1791/2006 (O.J. No.L363, December 12, 2006, p.1) (January 1, 2007);

Commission Regulation (EC) 68/2009 (O.J. No.L21, January 24, 2009, p.3) (February 17, 2009);

European Parliament and Council Regulation (EC) 219/2009 (O.J. No.L87/143, March 31, 2009, p.109) (April 20, 2009); and

Commission Regulation (EU) 1266/2009 (O.J. No.L339/2009, December 22, 2009, p.3) (January 11, 2010).

The amending Regulations are referred to in the notes to the principal Regulation only by their reference numbers. The dates referred to above in relation to Regulations are the dates on which the amending Regulations came into force.

CHAPTER I

PRINCIPLES AND SCOPE
ARTICLE 1

C1.03   Recording equipment within the meaning of this Regulation shall, as regards construction, installation, use and testing, comply with the requirements of this Regulation [and of Annexes I or IB and II thereto], which shall form an integral part of this Regulation.

C1.04   *[Article 1 is printed as amended by Regulation (EC) 2135/98.]*

[ARTICLE 2

For the purpose of this Regulation the definitions set out in Article 4 of Regula-   **C1.05**
tion (EC) No.561/2006 of the European Parliament and of the Council of 15
March 2006 on the harmonisation of certain social legislation relating to road
transport and amending Council Regulations (EEC) No.3821/85 and (EC)
No.2135/98 [*O.J. No.L102, April 11, 2006, p.1*] shall apply.]

[Article 2 is printed as substituted by Regulation (EC) 561/2006.]   **C1.06**

ARTICLE 3

[1. Recording equipment shall be installed and used in vehicles registered in a   **C1.07**
   Member State which are used for the carriage of passengers or goods by
   road, except the vehicles referred to in Article 3 of Regulation (EC) No.561/
   2006. Vehicles referred to in Article 16(1) of Regulation (EC) No.561/2006
   and vehicles, which were exempt from the scope of application of Regulation (EEC) No.3820/85, but which are no longer exempt under Regulation
   (EC) No.561/2006 shall have until 31 December 2007 to comply with this
   requirement.]

[2. Member States may exempt vehicles mentioned in Articles 13(1) and (3) of
   Regulation (EC) No.561/2006 from application of this Regulation.]

[3. Member States may, after authorisation by the Commission, exempt from
   application of this Regulation vehicles used for the transport operations
   referred to in Article 14 of Regulation (EC) No.561/2006.]

4. In the case of national transport operations, Member States may require the
   installation and use of recording equipment in accordance with this Regulation in any of the vehicles for which its installation and use are not required
   by paragraph 1.

[Article 3 is printed as amended by Regulation (EC) 561/2006.   **C1.08**

*For exemptions under national legislation in accordance with art.3(2), see the
Community Drivers' Hours and Recording Equipment Regulations 2007 (SI
2007/1819) reg.4 and Sch. above.]*

CHAPTER II

TYPE APPROVAL

ARTICLE 4

[For the purposes of this Chapter, the words *"recording equipment"* shall   **C1.09**
mean "recording equipment or its components".]

Applications for EEC approval of a type of recording equipment or of a model
record sheet [or memory card] shall be submitted, accompanied by the appropriate specifications, by the manufacturer or his agent to a Member State. No application in respect of any one type of recording equipment or of any one model
record sheet [or memory card] may be submitted to more than one Member State.

[Article 4 is printed as amended by Regulation (EC) 2135/98.]   **C1.10**

ARTICLE 5

[A Member State shall grant EC component type-approval to any type of re-   **C1.11**
cording equipment, to any model record sheet or memory card which conforms
to the requirements laid down in Annex I or IB to this Regulation, provided the

Member State is in a position to check that production models conform to the approved type.]

[The system's security must comply with the technical requirements laid down in Annex IB. The Commission shall ensure that the said Annex stipulates that recording equipment may not be granted EC component type approval until the whole system (the recording equipment itself, driver card and electrical gearbox connections) has demonstrated its capacity to resist attempts to tamper with or alter the data on driving times. Those measures, designed to amend non-essential elements of this Regulation, shall be adopted in accordance with the regulatory procedure with scrutiny referred to in Article 18(2). The tests necessary to establish this shall be carried out by experts familiar with up-to-date tampering techniques.]

Any modifications or additions to an approved model must receive additional EEC type approval from the Member State which granted the original EEC type approval.

C1.12   *[Article 5 is printed as amended by Regulation (EC) 2135/98; Regulation (EC) 219/2009.]*

ARTICLE 6

C1.13   Member States shall issue to the applicant an EEC approval mark, which shall conform to the model shown in Annex II, for each type of recording equipment or model record sheet [or memory card] which they approve pursuant to Article 5.

C1.14   *[Article 6 is printed as amended by Regulation (EC) 2135/98.]*

ARTICLE 7

C1.15   The competent authorities of the Member State to which the application for type approval has been submitted shall, in respect of each type of recording equipment or model record sheet [or memory card] which they approve or refuse to approve, either send within one month to the authorities of the other Member States a copy of the approval certificate accompanied by copies of the relevant specifications, or, if such is the case, notify those authorities that approval has been refused; in cases of refusal they shall communicate the reasons for their decision.

C1.16   *[Article 7 is printed as amended by Regulation (EC) 2135/98.]*

ARTICLE 8

C1.17   1. If a Member State which has granted EEC type approval as provided for in Article 5 finds that certain recording equipment or record sheets [or memory card] bearing the EEC type approval mark which it has issued do not conform to the prototype which it has approved, it shall take the necessary measures to ensure that production models conform to the approved prototype. The measures taken may, if necessary, extend to withdrawal of EEC type approval.

2. A Member State which has granted EEC type approval shall withdraw such approval if the recording equipment or record sheet [or memory card] which has been approved is not in conformity with this Regulation to its Annexes or displays in use any general defect which makes it unsuitable for the purpose for which it is intended.

3. If a Member State which has granted EEC type approval is notified by an-

other Member State of one of the cases referred to in paragraphs 1 and 2, it shall also, after consulting the latter Member State, take the steps laid down in those paragraphs, subject to paragraph 5.

4. A Member State which ascertains that one of the cases referred to in paragraph 2 has arisen may forbid until further notice the placing on the market and putting into service of the recording equipment or record sheets [or memory card]. The same applies in the cases mentioned in paragraph 1 with respect to recording equipment or record sheets [or memory card] which have been exempted from EEC initial verification, if the manufacturer, after due warning, does not bring the equipment into line with the approved model or with the requirements of this Regulation.

    In any event, the competent authorities of the Member States shall notify one another and the Commission, within one month, of any withdrawal of EEC type approval or of any other measures taken pursuant to paragraphs 1, 2 and 3 shall specify the reasons for such action.

5. If a Member State which has granted an EEC type approval disputes the existence of any of the cases specified in paragraphs 1 or 2 notified to it, the Member States concerned shall endeavour to settle the dispute and the Commission shall be kept informed.

    If talks between the Member States have not resulted in agreement within four months of the date of the notification referred to in paragraph 3 above, the Commission, after consulting experts from all Member States and having considered all the relevant factors, e.g. economic and technical factors, shall within six months adopt a decision which shall be communicated to the Member States concerned and at the same time to the other Member States. The Commission shall lay down in each instance the time limit for implementation of its decision.

[Article 8 is printed as amended by Regulation (EC) 2135/98.]   **C1.18**

ARTICLE 9

1. An applicant for EEC type approval of a model record sheet shall state on   **C1.19**
   his application the type or types of recording equipment on which the sheet in question is designed to be used and shall provide suitable equipment of such type or types for the purpose of testing the sheet.

2. The competent authorities of each Member State shall indicate on the approval certificate for the model record sheet the type or types of recording equipment on which that model sheet may be used.

ARTICLE 10

No Member State may refuse to register any vehicle fitted with recording   **C1.20**
equipment, or prohibit the entry into service or use of such vehicle for any reason connected with the fact that the vehicle is fitted with such equipment, if the equipment bears the EEC approval mark referred to in Article 6 and the installation plaque referred to in Article 12.

ARTICLE 11

All decisions pursuant to this Regulation refusing or withdrawing approval of   **C1.21**
a type of recording equipment or model record sheet [or memory card] shall specify in detail the reasons on which they are based. A decision shall be communicated to the party concerned, who shall at the same time be informed of the

remedies available to him under the laws of the Member States and of the time-limits for the exercise of such remedies.

C1.22   *[Article 11 is printed as amended by Regulation (EC) 2135/98.]*

CHAPTER III

INSTALLATION AND INSPECTION

ARTICLE 12

C1.23   1. Recording equipment may be installed or repaired only by fitters or workshops approved by the competent authorities of Member States for that purpose after the latter, should they so desire, have heard the views of the manufacturers concerned.

[The period of administrative validity of approved workshop and fitter cards shall not exceed one year.]

[If a card issued to an approved workshop or fitter is to be extended, is damaged, malfunctions, is lost or stolen, the authority shall supply a replacement card within five working days of receiving a detailed request to that effect.]

[Where a new card is issued to replace an old one, the new card shall bear the same "workshop" information number, but the index shall be increased by one. The authority issuing the card shall maintain a register of lost, stolen or defective cards.]

[Member States shall take any measure necessary to prevent the cards distributed to approved fitters and workshops being falsified.]

[2. The approved fitter or workshop shall place a special mark on the seals which it affixes and, in addition, shall enter for recording equipment in conformity with Annex IB, the electronic security data for carrying out, in particular, the authentification checks. The competent authorities of each Member State shall maintain a register of the marks and electronic security data used and of approved workshop and fitter cards issued.]

[3. The component authorities of the Member States shall forward to the Commission the lists of approved fitters and workshops and the cards issued to them and shall forward to it copies of the marks and of the necessary information relating to the electronic security data used.]

4. For the purpose of certifying that installation of recording equipment took place in accordance with the requirements of this Regulation an installation plaque affixed as provided in [Annexes I and IB] shall be used.

[5. Any seal may be removed by the fitters or workshops approved by competent authorities under paragraph 1 of this Article, or in the circumstances described in Annex I, Chapter V, paragraph 4 [or in Annex IB, section VI(c)] to this Regulation.]

C1.24   *[Article 12 is printed as amended by Regulation (EEC) 3688/92; Regulation (EC) 2135/98.]*

CHAPTER IV

USE OF EQUIPMENT

[ARTICLE 13

C1.25   The employer and drivers shall ensure the correct functioning and proper use of, on the one hand, the recording equipment and, on the other, the driver card where a driver is required to drive a vehicle fitted with recording equipment in conformity with Annex IB.]

[Article 13 is printed as substituted by Regulation (EC) 2135/98.]   **C1.26**

ARTICLE 14

[1. The employer shall issue a sufficient number of record sheets to drivers of   **C1.27**
vehicles fitted with recording equipment in conformity with Annex I, bearing in mind the fact that these sheets are personal in character, the length of the period of service and the possible obligation to replace sheets which are damaged, or have been taken by an authorised inspecting officer. The employer shall issue to drivers only sheets of an approved model suitable for use in equipment installed in the vehicle.]

[Where the vehicle is fitted with recording equipment in conformity with Annex IB, the employer and the driver shall ensure that, taking into account the length of the period of service, the printing on request referred to in Annex IB can be carried out correctly in the event of an inspection.]

[2. The undertaking shall keep record sheets and printouts, whenever printouts have been made to comply with Article 15(1), in chronological order and in a legible form for at least a year after their use and shall give copies to the drivers concerned who request them. The undertaking shall also give copies of downloaded data from the driver cards to the drivers concerned who request them and the printed papers of these copies. The record sheets, printouts and downloaded data shall be produced or handed over at the request of any authorised inspecting officer.]

[3. The driver card as defined in Annex IB shall be issued, at the request of the driver, by the competent authority of the Member State where the driver has his normal residence.]

[A Member State may require any driver subject to the provisions of Regulation (EEC) No.3820/85 and normally resident on its territory to hold a driver card.]

[(a) For the purposes of this Regulation *"normal residence"* means the place where a person usually lives, that is for at least 185 days in each calendar year, because of personal and occupational ties, or, in the case of a person with no occupational ties, because of personal ties which show close links between that person and the place where he is living.

However, the normal residence of a person whose occupational ties are in a different place from his personal ties and who consequently lives in turn in different places situated in two or more Member States shall be regarded as being the place of his personal ties, provided that such person returns there regularly. This last condition need not be met where the person is living in a Member State in order to carry out a fixed-term assignment.]

[(b) Drivers shall give proof of their place of normal residence by any appropriate means, such as their identity card or any other valid document.]

[(c) Where the competent authorities of the Member State issuing the driver card have doubts as to the validity of a statement as to normal residence made in accordance with point (b), or for the purposes of certain specific controls, they may request any additional information or evidence.]

[(d) The competent authorities of the issuing Member State shall, as far as this can be done, ensure that the applicant does not already hold a valid driver card.]

[4.(a) The competent authority of the Member State shall personalise the driver card in accordance with the provisions of Annex IB.

For administrative purposes, the driver card may not be valid for more than five years.

The driver may hold one valid driver card only. The driver authorised to use only his own personalised driver card. The driver shall not use a driver card which is defective or which has expired.

When a new driver card is issued replacing the old, the new card shall bear the same driver card issue number but the index shall be increased by one. The issuing authority shall keep records of issued, stolen, lost or defective driver cards for a period at least equivalent to their period of administrative validity.

If the driver card is damaged, malfunctions or is lost or stolen, the authority shall supply a replacement card within five working days of receiving a detailed request to that effect.

In the event of a request for the renewal of a card whose expiry date is approaching, the authority shall supply a new card before the expiry date provided that the request was sent to it within the time limits laid down in the second sub-paragraph of Article 15(1).]

[(b) Driver cards shall be issued only to applicants who are subject to the provisions of Regulation (EEC) No.3820/85.]

[(c) The driver card shall be personal. It may not, during its official period of validity, be withdrawn or suspended for whatever reason unless the competent authority of a Member State finds that the card has been falsified, or the driver is using a card of which he is not the holder, or that the card card held has been obtained on the basis of false declarations and/or forged documents. If such suspension or withdrawal measures are taken by a Member State other than the Member State of issue, the former shall return the card to the authorities of the Member State which issued it and shall indicate the reasons for returning it.]

[(d) Driver cards issued by Member States shall be mutually recognised.

Where the holder of a valid driver card issued by a Member State has established his normal place of residence in another Member State, he may ask for his card to be exchanged for an equivalent driver card; it shall be the responsibility of the Member State which carries out the exchange to verify if necessary whether the card produced is actually still valid.

Member States carrying out an exchange shall return the old card to the authorities of the Member State of issue and indicate the reasons for so doing.]

[(e) Where a Member State replaces or exchanges a driver card, the replacement or exchange, and any subsequent replacement or renewal, shall be registered in that Member State.]

[(f) Member States shall take all the necessary measures to prevent any possibility of driver cards being falsified.]

[5. Member States shall ensure that data needed to monitor compliance with Regulation (EEC) No.3820/85 and Council Directive 92/6/EEC of 10 February 1992 on the installation and use of speed limitation devices for certain categories of motor vehicles in the Community [*q.v.*] which are recorded and stored by recording equipment in conformity with Annex IB to this Regulation can be made available for at least 365 days after the date of their recording and that they can be made available under conditions that guarantee the security and accuracy of the data.]

[Member States shall take any measures necessary to ensure that the resale or decommissioning of recording equipment cannot detract, in particular, from the satisfactory application of this paragraph.]

[Article 14 is printed as amended by Regulation (EC) 2135/98 and Regulation (EC) 561/2006.]   **C1.28**

ARTICLE 15

1. Drivers shall not use dirty or damaged record sheets [or driver card]. The sheets shall be adequately protected on this account.   **C1.29**

[Where a driver wishes to renew his driver card, he shall apply to the competent authorities of the Member State in which he has his normal residence not later than 15 working days before the expiry date of the card.]

In case of damage to a sheet bearing recordings, drivers shall attach the damaged sheet to the spare sheet used to replace it.

[If the driver card is damaged, malfunctions or is lost or stolen, the driver shall apply within seven calendar days for its replacement to the competent authorities of the Member State in which he has his normal residence.]

[Where a driver card is damaged, malfunctions, or is not in the possession of the driver, the driver shall:

(a) at the start of his journey, print out the details of the vehicle the driver is driving, and shall enter onto that printout:

(i) details that enable the driver to be identified (name, driver card or driver's licence number), including his signature;

(ii) the periods referred to in paragraph 3, second indent (b), (c) and (d);

(b) at the end of his journey, print out the information relating to periods of time recorded by the recording equipment, record any periods of other work, availability and rest undertaken since the printout that was made at the start of the journey, where not recorded by the tachograph, and mark on that document details that enable the driver to be identified (name, driver card or driver's licence number), including the driver's signature.]

2. Drivers shall use the records sheets [or driver card] every day on which they are driving, starting from the moment they take over the vehicle. The record sheet [or driver card] shall not be withdrawn before the end of the daily working period unless its withdrawal is otherwise authorised. No record sheet [or driver card] be used to cover a period longer than that for which it is intended.

[When as a result of being away from the vehicle, a driver is unable to use the equipment fitted to the vehicle, the periods of time referred to in paragraph 3, second indent (b), (c) and (d) shall:

    (a) if the vehicle is fitted with recording equipment in conformity with Annex I, be entered on the record sheet, either manually, by automatic recording or other means, legibly and without dirtying the sheet; or

    (b) if the vehicle is fitted with recording equipment in conformity with Annex IB, be entered onto the driver card using the manual entry facility provided in the recording equipment.

Where there is more than one driver on board the vehicle fitted with recording equipment in conformity with Annex IB, each driver shall ensure that his driver card is inserted into the correct slot in the tachograph.]

Drivers shall amend the record sheets as necessary should there be more than one driver on board the vehicle, so that the information referred to in Chapter II(1) to (3) of Annex I is recorded on the record sheet of the driver who is actually driving.

3. Drivers shall:

    — ensure that the time recorded on the sheet agrees with the official time in the country of registration of the vehicle,

    — operate the switch mechanisms enabling the following periods of time to be recorded separately and distinctly:

    (a) under the sign

 :

    : driving time;

    (b) *"other work"* means any activity other than driving, as defined in Article 3(a) of Directive 2002/15/EC of the European Parliament and of the Council of 11 March 2002 on the organisation of the working time of persons performing mobile road transport activities [*O.J. No.L80, March 23, 2002, p.35*], and also any work for the same or another employer within or outside of the transport sector, and must be recorded under this sign

    (c) *"availability"* defined in Article 3(b) of Directive 2002/15/EC must be recorded under this sign

    (d) under the sign

    : breaks in work and daily rest periods.

4. [...]

5. Each crew member shall enter the following information on his record sheet:

(a) on beginning to use the sheet—his surname and first name;

(b) the date and place where use of the sheet begins and the date and place where such use ends;

(c) the registration number of each vehicle to which he is assigned, both at the start of the first journey recorded on the sheet and then, in the event of a change of vehicle, during the use of the sheet;

(d) the odometer reading:

— at the start of the first journey recorded on the sheet;

— at the end of the last journey recorded on the sheet;

— in the event of a change of vehicle during a working day (reading on the vehicle to which he was assigned and reading on the vehicle to which he is to be assigned);

(e) the time of any change of vehicle.

[5A. The driver shall enter in the recording equipment in conformity with Annex IB the symbols of the countries in which he begins and ends his daily work period. However, a Member State may require drivers of vehicles engaged in transport operations inside its territory to add more detailed geographic specifications to the country symbol provided that the Member State has notified them to the Commission before 1 April 1998 and that they do not number more than 20.]

[The above data entries shall be activated by the driver, and may be entirely manual or automatic if the recording equipment is linked to a satellite tracking system.]

6. The [recording equipment defined in Annex I] shall be so designed that it is possible for an authorised inspecting officer, if necessary after opening the equipment, to read the recordings relating to the nine hours preceding the time of the check without permanently deforming, damaging or soiling the sheet.

The equipment shall, furthermore, be so designed that it is possible, without opening the case, to verify that recordings are being made.

[7.(a) Where the driver drives a vehicle fitted with recording equipment in conformity with Annex I, the driver must be able to produce, whenever an inspecting officer so requests:

(i) the record sheets for the current week and those used by the driver in the previous 15 days;

(ii) the driver card if he holds one, and

(iii) any manual record and printout made during the current week and the previous 15 days as required under this Regulation and Regulation (EC) No.561/2006.

However, after 1 January 2008, the time periods referred to under (i) and (iii) shall cover the current day and the previous 28 days.

(b) Where the driver drives a vehicle fitted with recording equipment in conformity with Annex IB, the driver must be able to produce, whenever an inspecting officer so requests:

(i) the driver card of which he is holder;

(ii) any manual record and printout made during the current week and the previous 15 days as required under this Regulation and Regulation (EC) No.561/2006, and

(iii) the record sheets corresponding to the same period as the one referred to in the previous subparagraph during which he drove a vehicle fitted with recording equipment in conformity with Annex I.

However, after 1 January 2008, the time periods referred to under (ii) shall cover the current day and the previous 28 days.

(c) An authorised inspecting officer may check compliance with Regulation (EC) No.561/2006 by analysis of the record sheets, of the displayed or printed data which have been recorded by the recording equipment or by the driver card or, failing this, by analysis of any other supporting document that justifies non-compliance with a provision, such as those laid down in Article 16(2) and (3).]

[8. It shall be forbidden to falsify, suppress or destroy data recorded on the record sheet, stored in the recording equipment or on the driver card, or printouts from the recording equipment as defined in Annex IB. The same applies to any manipulation of the recording equipment, record sheet or driver card which may result in data and/or printed information being falsified, suppressed or destroyed. No device which could be used to this effect shall be present on the vehicle.]

C1.30   *[Article 15 is printed as amended by Regulation (EC) 2135/98 and Regulation (EC) 561/2006.]*

ARTICLE 16

C1.31   1. In the event of breakdown or faulty operation of the equipment, the employer shall have it repaired by an approved fitter or workshop, as soon as circumstances permit.

If the vehicle is unable to return to the premises within a period of one week calculated from the date of the breakdown or of the discovery of defective operation, the repair shall be carried out en route.

Measures taken by Member States pursuant to Article 19 may give the competent authorities power to prohibit the use of the vehicle in cases where breakdown or faulty operation has not been put right as provided in the foregoing subparagraphs.

[2. While the recording equipment is unserviceable or malfunctioning, drivers shall mark on the record sheet or sheets, or on a temporary sheet to be attached to the record sheet or to the driver card, on which he shall enter data enabling him to be identified (driver's card number and/or name and/or driving licence number), including his signature, all information for the various periods of time which are no longer recorded or printed out correctly by the recording equipment.]

[If a driver card is damaged, malfunctions or is lost or stolen, the driver shall, at the end of his journey, print out the information relating to the periods of time recorded by the recording equipment and mark on that document the details that enable him to be identified (the driver card number and/or name and/or driving licence number), including his signature.]

[3. If a driver card is damaged or if it malfunctions, the driver shall return it to the competent authority of the Member State in which he has his normal residence. Theft of the driver card shall be the subject of a formal declaration to the competent authorities of the State where the theft occurred.]

[Loss of the driver card must be reported in a formal declaration to the competent authorities of the State that issued it and to the competent authorities of the Member State of normal residence where they are different.]

[The driver may continue to drive without a driver card for a maximum period of 15 calendar days or for a longer period if this is necessary for the vehicle to return to its premises, provided he can prove the impossibility of producing or using the card during this period.]

[Where the authorities of the Member State in which the driver has his normal residence are different from those which issued his card and where the latter are requested to renew, replace or exchange the driver card, they shall inform the authorities which issued the old card of the precise reasons for its renewal, replacement or exchange.]

[Article 16 is printed as amended by Regulation (EC) 2135/98.]   **C1.32**

CHAPTER V

FINAL PROVISIONS

[ARTICLE 17

[1. The amendments required to adjust the annexes to technical progress,   **C1.33** designed to amend non-essential elements of this Regulation, shall be adopted in accordance with the regulatory procedure with scrutiny referred to in Article 18(2).]

2. The technical specifications relating to the following sections of Annex IB shall be adopted as soon as possible and if possible before 1 July 1998 by the same procedure:

(a) Chapter II
— (d) 17:
displaying and printing of faults in the recording equipment,
— (d) 18:
displaying and printing of faults in the driver card,
— (d) 21:
displaying and printing of summary reports;

(b) Chapter III
— (a) 6.3:
standards for the protection of vehicle electronics against electrical interference and magnetic fields,
— (a) 6.5:
protection (security) of the total system,
— (c) 1:
warning signals indicating the internal malfunctioning of the recording equipment
— (c) 5:
format of the warnings,

     — (f):

     maximum tolerances;

   (c) Chapter IV, A:

     — 4:

     standards,

     — 5:

     security, including data protection,

     — 6:

     temperature range,

     — 8:

     electrical characteristics,

     — 9:

     logical structure of the driver card,

     — 10:

     functions and commands,

     — 11:

     elementary files;

     and Chapter IV, B;

   (d) Chapter V:

     printer and standard print-outs.]

C1.34   *[Article 17 is printed as substituted by Regulation (EC) 2135/98; Regulation (EC) 219/2009.]*

[ARTICLE 18

C1.35   1. The Commission shall be assisted by a Committee.

   2. Where reference is made to this paragraph, Article 5a(1) to (4) and Article 7 of Decision 1999/468/EC shall apply, having regard to the provisions of Article 8 thereof.]

C1.36   *[Article 18 is printed as substituted by Regulation (EC) 219/2009.]*

ARTICLE 19

C1.37   1. Member States shall, in good time and after consulting the Commission, adopt such laws, regulations or administrative provisions as may be necessary for the implementation of this Regulation.

     Such measures shall cover, inter alia, the reorganisation of, procedure for, and means of carrying out, checks on compliance and the penalties to be imposed in case of breach.

   2. Member States shall assist each other in applying this Regulation and in checking compliance therewith.

   3. Within the framework of this mutual assistance the competent authorities of the Member States shall regularly send one another all available information concerning:

     — breaches of this Regulation committed by non-residents and any penalties imposed for such breaches,

     — penalties imposed by a Member State on its residents for such breaches committed in other Member States.

ARTICLE 20

C1.38   *[Repeal of Regulation (EEC) 1463/70.]*

[ARTICLE 20A

[Lapsed.]]

ARTICLE 21

[Commencement.]

This Regulation shall be binding in its entirety and directly applicable in all Member States.

ANNEX I

Requirements for Construction, Testing, Installation and Inspection

I   **Definitions**

In this Annex: **C1.39**

(a) Recording equipment means:

equipment intended for installation in road vehicles to show and record automatically or semi-automatically details of the movement of those vehicles and of certain working periods of their drivers;

(b) Record sheet means:

a sheet designed to accept and retain recorded data, to be placed in the recording equipment and on which the marking devices of the latter inscribe a continuous record of the information to be recorded;

(c) The constant of the recording equipment means:

the numerical characteristics giving the value of the input signal required to show and record a distance travelled of one kilometre; this constant must be expressed either in revolutions per kilometre ($k = \ldots$ rev/km), or in impulses per kilometre ($k = \ldots$ imp/km);

(d) Characteristic coefficient of the vehicle means:

the numerical characteristic giving the value of the output signal emitted by the part of the vehicle linking it with the recording equipment (gearbox output shaft or axle) while the vehicle travels a distance of one measured kilometre under normal test conditions (see Chapter VI, point 4 of this Annex). The characteristic coefficient is expressed either in revolutions per kilometre ($w = \ldots$ rev/km) or in impulses per kilometre ($w = \ldots$ imp/km);

(e) Effective circumference of wheel tyres means:

the average of the distances travelled by the several wheels moving the vehicle (driving wheels) in the course of one complete rotation. The measurement of these distances must be made under normal test conditions (see Chapter VI, point 4 of this Annex) and is expressed in the form: $1 = \ldots$ mm.

II   **General Characteristics and Functions of Recording Equipment**

The equipment must be able to record the following: **C1.40**

1. distance travelled by the vehicle;
2. speed of the vehicle;
3. driving time;
4. other periods of work or of availability;
5. breaks from work and daily rest periods;
6. opening of the case containing the record sheet;
[7. for electronic recording equipment which is equipment operating by signals

transmitted electrically from the distance and speed sensor, any interruption exceeding 100 milliseconds in the power supply of the recording equipment (except lighting), in the power supply of the distance and speed sensor and any interruption in the signal lead to the distance and speed sensor.]

For vehicles used by two drivers the equipment must be capable of recording simultaneously but distinctly and on two separate sheets details of the periods listed under 3, 4 and 5.

C1.41   *[Chapter II to Annex I is printed as amended by Regulation (EEC) 3314/90 which inserted item 7 into Chap.II.]*

III   Construction Requirements for Recording Equipment

(a)   General points

1. *Recording equipment shall include the following:*

C1.42   1.1. Visual instruments showing:
— distance travelled (distance recorder),
— speed (speedometer),
— time (clock).

        1.2. Recording instruments comprising:
— a recorder of the distance travelled,
— a speed recorder,
— one or more time recorders satisfying the requirements laid down in Chapter III (c) 4.

        [1.3. A means of marking showing on the record sheet individually:
— each opening of the case containing that sheet,
— for electronic recording equipment, as defined in point 7 of Chapter II, any interruption exceeding 100 milliseconds in the power supply of the recording equipment (except lighting), not later than at switching-on the power supply again,
— for electronic recording equipment, as defined in point 7 of Chapter II, any interruption exceeding 100 milliseconds in the power supply of the distance and speed sensor and any interruption in the signal lead to the distance and speed sensor.]

C1.43   2. Any inclusion in the equipment of devices additional to those listed above must not interfere with the proper operation of the mandatory devices or with the reading of them.

The equipment must be submitted for approval complete with any such additional devices.

3. *Materials*

C1.44   3.1. All the constituent parts of the recording equipment must be made of materials with sufficient stability and mechanical strength and stable electrical and magnetic characteristics.

        3.2. Any modification in a constituent part of the equipment or in the nature of the materials used for its manufacture must, before being applied in manufacture, be submitted for approval to the authority which granted type-approval for the equipment.

4. *Measurement of distance travelled*

C1.45   The distances travelled may be measured and recorded either:
— so as to include both forward and reverse movement; or
— so as to include only forward movement.

Any recording of reversing movements must on no account affect the clarity and accuracy of the other recordings.

5. *Measurement of speed*

    5.1. The range of speed measurement shall be as stated in the type approval certificate. **C1.46**

    5.2. The natural frequency and the damping of the measuring device must be such that the instruments showing and recording the speed can, within the range of measurement, follow acceleration changes of up to 2m/section 2, within the limits of accepted tolerances.

6. *Measurement of time (clock)*

    6.1. The control of the mechanism for resetting the clock must be located inside a case containing the record sheet; each opening of that case must be automatically recorded on the record sheet. **C1.47**

    6.2. If the forward movement mechanism of the record sheet is controlled by the clock, the period during which the latter will run correctly after being fully wound must be greater by at least 10% than the recording period corresponding to the maximum sheet-load of the equipment.

7. *Lighting and protection*

    7.1. The visual instruments of the equipment must be provided with adequate non-dazzling lighting. **C1.48**

    7.2. For normal conditions of use, all the internal parts of the equipment must be protected against damp and dust. In addition they must be made proof against tampering by means of casings capable of being sealed.

(b) Visual instruments

1. *Distance travelled indicator (distance recorder)*

    1.1. The value of the smallest grading on the instrument showing distance travelled must be 0.1 kilometres. Figures showing hectometres must be clearly distinguishable from those showing whole kilometres. **C1.49**

    1.2. The figures on the distance recorder must be clearly legible and must have an apparent height of at least 4mm.

    1.3. The distance recorder must be capable of reading up to at least 99,999.9 kilometres.

2. *Speed indicators (speedometer)*

    2.1. Within the range of measurement, the speed scale must be uniformly graduated by 1, 2, 5 or 10 kilometres per hour. The value of a speed graduation (space between two successive marks) must not exceed 10% of the maximum speed shown on the scale. **C1.50**

    2.2. The range indicated beyond that measured need not be marked by figures.

    2.3. The length of each space on the scale representing a speed difference of 10 kilometres per hour must not be less than 10 millimetres.

    2.4. On an indicator with a needle, the distance between the needle and the instrument face must not exceed three millimetres.

3. *Time indicator (clock)*

The time indicator must be visible from outside the equipment and give a clear, plain and unambiguous reading. **C1.51**

(c) Recording instruments

1. *General points*

C1.52

1.1. All equipment, whatever the form of the record sheet (strip or disc) must be provided with a mark enabling the record sheet to be inserted correctly, in such a way as to ensure that the time shown by the clock and the time-marking on the sheet correspond.

1.2. The mechanism moving the record sheet must be such as to ensure that the latter moves without play and can be freely inserted and removed.

1.3. For record sheets in disc form, the forward movement device must be controlled by the clock mechanism. In this case, the rotating movement of the sheet must be continuous and uniform, with a minimum speed of seven millimetres per hour measured at the inner border of the ring marking the edge of the speed recording area.

In equipment of the strip type, where the forward movement device of the sheets is controlled by the clock mechanism the speed of rectilinear forward movement must be at least 10 millimetres per hour.

1.4. Recording of the distance travelled, of the speed of the vehicle and of any opening of the case containing the record sheet or sheets must be automatic.

2. *Recording distance travelled*

C1.53

2.1. Every kilometre of distance travelled must be represented on the record by a variation of at least one millimetre on the corresponding coordinate.

2.2. Even at speeds reaching the upper limit of the range of measurement, the record of distances must still be clearly legible.

3. *Recording speed*

C1.54

3.1. Whatever the form of the record sheet, the speed recording stylus must normally move in a straight line and at right angles to the direction of travel of the record sheet.

However, the movement of the stylus may be curvilinear, provided the following conditions are satisfied:

— the trace drawn by the stylus must be perpendicular to the average circumference (in the case of sheets in disc form) or to the axis (in the case of sheets in strip form) of the area reserved for speed recording,

— the ratio between the radius of curvature of the trace drawn by the stylus and the width of the area reserved for speed recording must be not less than 2.4 to 1 whatever the form of the record sheet,

— the markings on the time-scale must cross the recording area in a curve of the same radius as the trace drawn by the stylus. The spaces between the markings on the time-scale must represent a period not exceeding one hour.

3.2. Each variation in speed of 10 kilometres per hour must be represented on the record by a variation of at least 1.5 millimetres on the corresponding coordinate.

4. *Recording time*

C1.55

4.1. Recording equipment must be so constructed that the period of driving time is always recorded automatically and that it is possible, through the operation where necessary of a switch device to record separately the other periods of time as indicated in Article 15(3), second indent (b), (c) and (d) of the Regulation.

4.2. It must be possible, from the characteristics of the traces, their relative positions and if necessary the signs laid down in Article 15 of the Regulation to distinguish clearly between the various periods of time.

The various periods of time should be differentiated from one another on the record by differences in the thickness of the relevant traces, or by any other system of at least equal effectiveness from the point of view of legibility and ease of interpretation of the record.

4.3. In the case of vehicles with a crew consisting of more than one driver, the recordings provided for in point 4.1 must be made on two separate sheets, each sheet being allocated to one driver. In this case, the forward movement of the separate sheets must be effected either by a single mechanism or by separate synchronised mechanisms.

(d) Closing device

1. The case containing the record sheet or sheets and the control of the mechanism for resetting the clock must be provided with a lock. **C1.56**

2. Each opening of the case containing the record sheet or sheets and the control of the mechanism for resetting the clock must be automatically recorded on the sheet or sheets.

(e) Markings

1. The following markings must appear on the instrument face of the equipment: **C1.57**
  — close to the figure shown by the distance recorder, the unit of measurement of distance, indicated by the abbreviation "km",
  — near the speed scale, the marking "km/h",
  — the measurement range of the speedometer in the form "Vmin … km/h, Vmax … km/h". This marking is not necessary if it is shown on the descriptive plaque of the equipment.

However, these requirements shall not apply to recording equipment approved before 10 August 1970.

2. The descriptive plaque must be built into the equipment and must show the following markings, which must be visible on the equipment when installed:
  — name and address of the manufacturer of the equipment,
  — manufacturer's number and year of construction,
  — approval mark for the equipment type,
  — the constant of the equipment in the form "k=… rev/km" or "k=… imp/km",
  — optionally, the range of speed measurement, in the form indicated in point 1,
  — should the sensitivity of the instrument to the angle of inclination be capable of affecting the readings given by the equipment beyond the permitted tolerances, the permissible angle expressed as:

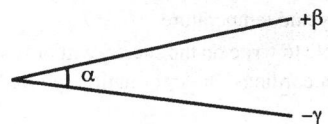

where a is the angle measured from the horizontal position of the front face (fitted the right way up) of the equipment for which the instrument is calibrated, while b and c represent respectively the maximum permissible upward and downward deviations from the angle of calibration a.

(f) Maximum tolerances (visual and recording instruments)

1. On the test bench before installation: **C1.58**
  (a) distance travelled:
  1% more or less than the real distance, where that distance is at least one kilometre;

(b) speed:

3 km/h more or less than the real speed;

(c) time:

± two minutes per day with a maximum of 10 minutes per seven days in cases where the running period of the clock after rewinding is not less than that period.

C1.59 2. On installation:

(a) distance travelled:

2% more or less than the real distance, where that distance is at least one kilometre;

(b) speed;

4 km/h more or less than the real speed;

(c) time:

± two minutes per day, or

± 10 minutes per seven days.

C1.60 3. In use:

(a) distance travelled:

4% more or less than the real distance, where that distance is at least one kilometre;

(b) speed:

6 km/h more or less than the real speed;

(c) time:

± two minutes per day, or

± 10 minutes per seven days.

C1.61 4. The maximum tolerances set out in points 1, 2 and 3 are valid for temperatures between 0° and 40°C, temperatures being taken in close proximity to the equipment.

C1.62 5. Measurement of the maximum tolerances set out in points 2 and 3 shall take place under the conditions laid down in Chapter VI.

[Chapter III to Annex I is printed as amended by Regulation (EEC) 3314/90.]

IV   Record Sheets

(a) General points

C1.63 1. The record sheets must be such that they do not impede the normal functioning of the instrument and that the records which they contain are indelible and easily legible and identifiable.

The record sheets must retain their dimensions and any records made on them under normal conditions of humidity and temperature.

In addition it must be possible to write on the sheets, without damaging them and without affecting the legibility of the recordings, the information referred to in Article 15(5) of the Regulation.

Under normal conditions of storage, the recordings must remain clearly legible for at least one year.

C1.64 2. The minimum recording capacity of the sheets, whatever their form, must be 24 hours.

If several discs are linked together to increase the continuous recording capacity which can be achieved without intervention by staff, the links between the various discs must be made in such a way that there are no breaks in or overlapping of recordings at the point of transfer from one disc to another.

(b) Recording areas and their graduation

C1.65 1. The record sheets shall include the following recording areas:

— an area exclusively reserved for data relating to speed,

— an area exclusively reserved for data relating to distance travelled,

— one or more areas for data relating to driving time, to other periods of work and availability to breaks from work and to rest periods for drivers.

2. The area for recording speed must be scaled off in divisions of 20 kilometres per hour or less. The speed corresponding to each marking on the scale must be shown in figures against that marking. The symbol "km/h" must be shown at least once within the area. The last marking on the scale must coincide with the upper limit of the range of measurement.

3. The area for recording distance travelled must be set out in such a way that the number of kilometres travelled may be read without difficulty.

4. The area or areas reserved for recording the periods referred to in point 1 must be so marked that it is possible to distinguish clearly between the various periods of time.

(c) Information to be printed on the record sheets

Each sheet must bear, in printed form, the following information: **C1.66**

— name and address or trade name of the manufacturer,

— approval mark for the model of the sheet,

— approval mark for the type or types of equipment in which the sheet may be used,

— upper limit of the speed measurement range, printed in kilometres per hour.

By way of minimal additional requirements, each sheet must bear, in printed form a time-scale graduated in such a way that the time may be read directly at intervals of fifteen minutes while each five minute interval may be determined without difficulty.

(d) Free space for handwritten insertions

A free space must be provided on the sheets such that drivers may as a minimum write   **C1.67**
in the following details:

— surname and first name of the driver,

— date and place where use of the sheet begins and date and place where such use ends,

— the registration number or numbers of the vehicle or vehicles to which the driver is assigned during the use of the sheet,

— odometer readings from the vehicle or vehicles to which the driver is assigned during the use of the sheet,

— the time at which any change of vehicle takes place.

V   Installation of Recording Equipment

1. Recording equipment must be positioned in the vehicle in such a way that the driver   **C1.68**
has a clear view from his seat of speedometer, distance recorder and clock while at the same time all parts of those instruments, including driving parts, are protected against damage.

2. It must be possible to adapt the constant of the recording equipment to the characteristic coefficient of the vehicle by means of a suitable device, to be known as an adaptor.

Vehicles with two or more rear axle ratios must be fitted with a switch device whereby these various ratios may be automatically brought into line with the ratio for which the equipment has been adapted to the vehicle.

3. After the equipment has been checked on installation, an installation plaque shall be   **C1.69**
affixed to the vehicle beside the equipment or in the equipment itself and in such a way as to be clearly visible. After every inspection by an approved fitter or workshop requiring a change in the setting of the installation itself, a new plaque must be affixed in place of the previous one.

The plaque must show at least the following details:
  — name, address or trade name of the approved fitter or workshop,
  — characteristic coefficient of the vehicle, in the form "w = … rev/km" or "w = … imp/km",
  — effective circumference of the wheel tyres in the form "1 = … mm",
  — the dates on which the characteristic coefficient of the vehicle was determined and the effective measured circumference of the wheel tyres.

4. *Sealing*

C1.70   The following parts must be sealed:
  (a) the installation plaque, unless it is attached in such a way that it cannot be removed without the markings thereon being destroyed;
  (b) the two ends of the link between the recording equipment proper and the vehicle;
  (c) the adaptor itself and the point of its insertion into the circuit;
  (d) the switch mechanism for vehicles with two or more axle ratios;
  (e) the links joining the adaptor and the switch mechanism to the rest of the equipment;
  (f) the casings required under Chapter III (a) 7.2.
  [(g) any cover giving access to the means of adapting the constant of the recording equipment to the characteristic coefficient of the vehicle.]

In particular cases, further seals may be required on approval of the equipment type and a note of the positioning of these seals must be made on the approval certificate.

[The seals mentioned in (b), (c) and (e) are authorised to be removed:
  — in case of emergency,
  — to install, to adjust or to repair a speed limitation device or any other device contributing to road safety,

provided that the recording equipment continues to function reliably and correctly and is resealed by an approved fitter or workshop immediately after fitting the speed limitation device or any other device contributing to road safety or within seven days in other cases]; for each occasion that these seals are broken a written statement giving the reasons for such action must be prepared and made available to the competent authority.

[5. The cables connecting the recording equipment to the transmitter must be protected by a continuous plastic-coated rust-protected steel sheath with crimped ends except where an equivalent protection against manipulation is guaranteed by other means (for example by electronic monitoring such as signal encryption) capable of detecting the presence of any device, which is unnecessary for the correct operation of the recording equipment and whose purpose is to prevent the accurate operation of the recording equipment by short circuiting or interruption or by modification of the electronic data from the speed and distance sensor. A joint, comprised of sealed connections, is deemed to be continuous within the meaning of this Regulation.

The aforementioned electronic monitoring may be replaced by an electronic control which ensures that the recording equipment is able to record any movement of the vehicle, independent from the signal of the speed and distance sensor.]

[For the purpose of the application of the present point, M 1 and N 1 vehicles are those defined in Part A of Annex II to Council Directive 70/156/EEC. For those vehicles that are equipped with tachographs in compliance with the Regulation and are not designed to install an armoured cable between the distance and speed sensors and the recording equipment, then an adaptor shall be fitted as close as possible to the distance and speed sensors.]

[The armoured cable shall be fitted from the adaptor to the recording equipment.]

C1.71   *[Chapter V to Annex I is printed as amended by Regulation (EEC) 3688/92; Regulation (EC) 2479/95; Regulation (EC) 1056/97.]*

VI   Checks and Inspections

The Member States shall nominate the bodies which shall carry out the checks and **C1.72**
inspections.

1. *Certification of new or repaired instruments*

Every individual device, whether new or repaired, shall be certified in respect of its correct operation and the accuracy of its readiness and recordings, within the limits laid down in Chapter III (f) 1, by means of sealing in accordance with Chapter V (4)(f).

For this purpose the Member States may stipulate an initial verification, consisting of a check on and confirmation of the conformity of a new or repaired device with the type-approved model and/or with the requirements of the Regulation and its Annexes, or may delegate the power to certify to the manufacturers or to their authorised agents.

2. *Installation*

When being fitted to a vehicle, the equipment and the whole installation must comply **C1.73**
with the provisions relating to maximum tolerances laid down in Chapter III (f) 2.

The inspection tests shall be carried out by the approved fitter or workshop on his or its responsibility.

3. *Periodic inspections*

(a) Periodic inspections of the equipment fitted to vehicles shall take place at least **C1.74**
every two years and may be carried out in conjunction with roadworthiness tests of vehicles.

These inspections shall include the following checks:

— that the equipment is working correctly,
— that the equipment carries the type approval mark,
— that the installation plaque is affixed,
— that the seals on the equipment and on the other parts of the installation are intact,
— the actual circumference of the tyres.

(b) An inspection to ensure compliance with the provision of Chapter III (f) 3 on the maximum tolerances in use shall be carried out at least once every six years, although each Member State may stipulate a shorter interval or such inspection in respect of vehicles registered in its territory. Such inspections must include replacement of the installation plaque.

4. *Measurement of errors*

The measurement of errors on installation and during use shall be carried out under the **C1.75**
following conditions, which are to be regarded as constituting standard test conditions:

— vehicle unladen, in normal running, order
— tyre pressures in accordance with the manufacturer's instructions,
— tyre wear within the limits allowed by law,
— movement of the vehicle: the vehicle must proceed, driven by its own engine, in a straight line and on a level surface, at a speed of 50 ± 5 km/h; provided that it is of comparable accuracy, the test may also be carried out on an appropriate test bench.

[ANNEX IB

Requirements for Construction, Testing, Installation, and Inspection

I   Definitions

In this Annex: **C1.76**

(a) "activation" means:

phase where the recording equipment becomes fully operational and implements all functions, including security functions;

Activating a recording equipment requires the use of a workshop card and the entry of its PIN code;

(b) "authentication" means:

a function intended to establish and verify a claimed identity;

(c) "authenticity" means:

the property that an information is coming from a party whose identity can be verified;

(d) "built-in-test (BIT)" means:

tests run at request, triggered by the operator or by an external equipment;

(e) "calendar day" means:

a day ranging from 00.00 hours to 24.00 hours. All calendar days relate to UTC time (universal time coordinated);

[(f) "calibration" means:

updating or confirming vehicle parameters to be held in the data memory. Vehicle parameters include vehicle identification (VIN, VRN and registering Member State) and vehicle characteristics (w, k, l, tyre size, speed limiting device setting (if applicable), current UTC time, current odometer value);

Any update or confirmation of UTC time only, shall be considered as a time adjustment and not as a calibration, provided it does not contradict Requirement 256 [*Annex IB, Chap.VI, para.4*].

Calibrating a recording equipment requires the use of a workshop card;]

(g) "card number" means:

C1.77   a 16 alpha-numerical characters number that uniquely identifies a tachograph card within a Member State. The card number includes a consecutive index (if applicable), a replacement index and a renewal index;

a card is therefore uniquely identified by the code of the issuing Member State and the card number;

(h) "card consecutive index" means:

the 14th alpha-numerical character of a card number that is used to differentiate the different cards issued to a company or a body entitled to be issued several tachograph cards. The company or the body is uniquely identified by the 13 first characters of the card number;

(i) "card renewal index" means:

the 16th alpha-numerical character of a card number which is incremented each time a tachograph card is renewed;

(j) "card replacement index" means:

the 15th alpha-numerical character of a card number which is incremented each time a tachograph card is replaced;

(k) "characteristic coefficient of the vehicle" means:

the numerical characteristic giving the value of the output signal emitted by the part of the vehicle linking it with the recording equipment (gearbox output shaft or axle) while the vehicle travels a distance of one kilometre under standard test conditions (see Chapter VI(5)). The characteristic coefficient is expressed in impulses per kilometre (w =... imp/km);

[(l) "company card" means:

A tachograph card issued by the authorities of a Member State to the owner or holder of **C1.78** vehicles fitted with recording equipment;

The company card identifies the company and allows for displaying, downloading and printing of the data stored in the recording equipment which has been locked by this company or which has not been locked by any company.]

(m) "constant of the recording equipment" means:

the numerical characteristic giving the value of the input signal required to show and record a distance travelled of one kilometre; this constant shall be expressed in impulses per kilometre (k =... imp/km);

(n) "continuous driving time" is computed within the recording equipment as

[*this way of computing the continuous driving time and the cumulative break time serves into the recording equipment for computing the continuous driving time warning; It does not prejudge the legal interpretation to be made of these times.*] [*Alternative ways of computing the continuous driving time and the cumulative break time may be used to replace these definitions if they have been made obsolete by updates in other relevant legislation.*]:

the continuous driving time is computed as the current accumulated driving times of a particular driver, since the end of his last AVAILABILITY or BREAK/REST or UNKNOWN [*UNKNOWN periods correspond to periods where the driver's card was not inserted in a recording equipment and for which no manual entry of driver activities was made*] period of 45 minutes or more (this period may have been split in several periods of 15 minutes or more). The computations involved take into account, as needed, past activities stored on the driver card. When the driver has not inserted his card, the computations involved are based on the data memory recordings related to the current period where no card was inserted and related to the relevant slot;

(o) "control card" means:

a tachograph card issued by the authorities of a Member State to a national competent control authority;

the control card identifies the control body and possibly the control officer and allows for getting access to the data stored in the data memory or in the driver cards for reading, printing and/or downloading;

(p) "cumulative break time" is computed within the recording equipment as

[*see note at heading (n) above*]:   **C1.79**

the cumulative break from driving time is computed as the current accumulated AVAILABILITY or BREAK/REST or UNKNOWN times of 15 minutes or more of a particular driver, since the end of his last AVAILABILITY or BREAK/REST or UNKNOWN period of 45 minutes or more (this period may have been split in several periods of 15 minutes or more).

The computations involved take into account, as needed, past activities stored on the driver card. Unknown periods of negative duration (start of unknown period end of unknown period) due to time overlaps between two different recording equipments, are not taken into account for the computation.

When the driver has not inserted his card, the computations involved are based on the data memory recordings related to the current period where no card was inserted and related to the relevant slot;

(q) "data memory" means:

an electronic data storage device built into the recording equipment;

(r) "digital signature" means:

data appended to, or a cryptographic transformation of, a block of data that allows the recipient of the block of data to prove the authenticity and integrity of the block of data;

[(rr) "adaptor" means:

a part of the recording equipment, providing a signal permanently representative of vehicle speed and/or distance travelled, and which is:

— installed and used only in M1 and N1 type vehicles (as defined in Annex II to Council Directive 70/156/EEC) put into service for the first time between 1 May 2006 and 31 December 2013,

— installed where it is not mechanically possible to install any other type of existing motion sensor which is otherwise compliant with the provisions of this Annex and its Appendixes 1 to 11,

— installed between the vehicle unit and where the speed/distance impulses are generated by integrated sensors or alternative interfaces.

Seen from a vehicle unit, the adaptor behaviour is the same as if a motion sensor, compliant the provisions of this Annex and its Appendixes 1 to 11, was connected to the vehicle unit.

Use of such an adaptor in those vehicles described above shall allow for the installation and correct use of a vehicle unit compliant with all the requirements of this Annex.

For those vehicles, the recording equipment includes cables, an adaptor, and a vehicle unit.]

[(s) "downloading" means:

Copying, together with the digital signature, of a part, or of a complete set of data files stored in the data memory of the vehicle or in the memory of the tachograph card, for which these data are necessary to establish compliance with the provisions set out in Regulation (EC) No.561/2006.

Manufacturers of digital tachograph vehicle units and manufacturers of equipment designed and intended to download data files shall take all reasonable steps to ensure that the downloading of such data can be performed with the minimum delay to transport undertakings or drivers.

Downloading may not alter or delete stored data. The downloading of the detailed speed file may not be necessary to establish compliance with Regulation (EC) No.561/2006, but may be used for other purposes, such as accident investigation.]

(t) "driver card" means:

a tachograph card issued by the authorities of a Member State to a particular driver;
the driver card identifies the driver and allows for storage of driver activity data;

(u) "effective circumference of the wheel tyres" means:

C1.80   the average of the distances travelled by each of the wheels moving the vehicle (driving wheels) in the course of one complete rotation. The measurement of these distances shall be made under standard test conditions (Chapter VI(5)) and is expressed in the form "l =... mm". Vehicle manufacturers may replace the measurement of these distances by a theoretical calculation which takes into account the distribution of the weight on the axles, vehicle unladen in normal running order [*Directive 97/27/EC, July 22, 1997, amending Directive 70/156/EEC (O.J. No.L233, August 25, 1997, p.1)*]. The methods for such theoretical calculation will be approved by a competent Member State authority;

(v) "event" means:

abnormal operation detected by the recording equipment which may come from a fraud attempt;

(w) "fault" means:

abnormal operation detected by the recording equipment which may come from an equipment malfunction or failure;

(x) "installation" means:

mounting of the recording equipment in a vehicle;

(y) "motion sensor" means:

part of the recording equipment, providing a signal representative of vehicle speed and/or distance travelled;

(z) "non valid card" means:

a card detected as faulty, or which initial authentication failed, or which start of validity date is not yet reached, or which expiry date has passed;

(aa) "out of scope" means:

when the use of the recording equipment is not required, according to the provisions of Council Regulation (EEC) No.3820/85;   **C1.81**

(bb) "over speeding" means:

exceeding the authorised speed of the vehicle, defined as any period of more than 60 seconds during which the vehicle's measured speed exceeds the limit for setting the speed limitation device laid down in Council Directive 92/6/EEC of 10 February 1992 on the installation and use of speed limitation devices for certain categories of motor vehicles in the Community [*O.J. No.L57, March 2, 1992, p.27*];

(cc) "periodic inspection" means:

set of operations performed to control that the recording equipment works properly and that its settings correspond to the vehicle parameters;

(dd) "printer" means:

component of the recording equipment which provides printouts of stored data;

(ee) "recording equipment" means:

the total equipment intended for installation in road vehicles to show, record and store automatically or semi-automatically details of the movement of such vehicles and of certain work periods of their drivers;

(ff) "renewal" means:

issue of a new tachograph card when an existing card reaches its expiry date, or is malfunctioning and has been returned to the issuing authority. Renewal always implies the certainty that two valid cards do not co-exist;

(gg) "repair" means:

any repair of a motion sensor or of a vehicle unit that requires disconnection of its   **C1.82** power supply, or disconnection from other recording equipment components, or opening of it;

(hh) "replacement" means:

issue of a tachograph card in replacement of an existing card, which has been declared lost, stolen or malfunctioning and has not been returned to the issuing authority. Replacement always implies a risk that two valid cards may co-exist;

(ii) "security certification" means:

process to certify, by an ITSEC [*Council Recommendation 95/144/EC, April 7, 1995 (O.J. No.L93, April 26, 1995, p.27)*] certification body, that the recording equipment (or component) or the tachograph card under investigation fulfils the security requirements defined in Appendix 10 Generic security targets [*not reproduced in this work*];

(jj) "self test" means:

tests run cyclically and automatically by the recording equipment to detect faults;

(kk) "tachograph card" means:

smart card intended for use with the recording equipment. Tachograph cards allow for identification by the recording equipment of the identity (or identity group) of the cardholder and allow for data transfer and storage. A tachograph card may be of the following types:

— driver card,
— control card,
— workshop card,
— company card;

(ll) "type approval" means:

C1.83   process to certify, by a Member State, that the recording equipment (or component) or the tachograph card under investigation fulfils the requirements of this regulation;

(mm) "tyre size" means:

the designation of the dimensions of the tyres (external driving wheels) in accordance with Directive 92/23/EEC of 31 March 1992 [*O.J. No.L129, May 15, 1992, p.95*];

(nn) "vehicle identification" means:

numbers identifying the vehicle: vehicle registration number (VRN) with indication of the registering Member State and vehicle identification number (VIN) [*Directive 76/114/ EEC, December 18, 1975 (O.J. No.L24, January 30, 1976, p.1)*];

(oo) "vehicle unit (VU)" means:

the recording equipment excluding the motion sensor and the cables connecting the motion sensor. The vehicle unit may either be a single unit or be several units distributed in the vehicle, as long as it complies with the security requirements of this regulation;

(pp) for computing sake in the recording equipment "week" means:

the period between 00.00 hours UTC on Monday and 24.00 UTC on Sunday;

(qq) "workshop card" means:

a tachograph card issued by the authorities of a Member State to a recording equipment manufacturer, a fitter, a vehicle manufacturer or workshop, approved by that Member State.

The workshop card identifies the cardholder and allows for testing, calibration and/or downloading of the recording equipment;

[Chapter 1 to Annex IB is printed as amended by Regulation (EC) 68/2009;   **C1.84**
Regulation (EU) 1266/2009.]

II   General Characteristics and Functions of the Recording Equipment

Any vehicle fitted with the recording equipment complying with the provisions of this   **C1.85**
Annex, must include a speed display and an odometer. These functions may be included
within the recording equipment.

1. General characteristics

The purpose of the recording equipment is to record, store, display, print, and output   **C1.86**
data related to driver activities.

The recording equipment includes cables, a motion sensor, and a vehicle unit.

[The interface between motion sensors and vehicle units shall be compliant with ISO
16844-3:2004, Cor 1:2006.]

The vehicle unit includes a processing unit, a data memory, a real time clock, two smart
card interface devices (driver and co-driver), a printer, a display, a visual warning, a
calibration/downloading connector, and facilities for entry of user's inputs.

The recording equipment may be connected to other devices through additional
connectors.

Any inclusion in or connection to the recording equipment of any function, device, or
devices, approved or otherwise, shall not interfere with, or be capable of interfering with,
the proper and secure operation of the recording equipment and the provisions of the
Regulation.

Recording equipment users identify themselves to the equipment via tachograph cards.

The recording equipment provides selective access rights to data and functions according to user's type and/or identity.

The recording equipment records and stores data in its data memory and in tachograph
cards.

This is done in accordance with Directive 95/46/EC of 24 October 1995 on the protection of individuals with regard to the processing of personal data and on the free movement of such data [*O.J. No.L281, November 23, 1995, p.31*].

2. Functions

The recording equipment shall ensure the following functions: **C1.87**

— monitoring cards insertions and withdrawals,
— speed and distance measurement,
— time measurement,
— monitoring driver activities,
— monitoring driving status,
— drivers manual entries:
  — entry of places where daily work periods begin and/or end,
  — manual entry of driver activities,
  — entry of specific conditions,
— company locks management,
— monitoring control activities,
— detection of events and/or faults,
— built-in and self tests,

— reading from data memory,
— recording and storing in data memory,
— reading from tachograph cards,
— recording and storing in tachograph cards,
— displaying,
— printing,
— warning,
— data downloading to external media,
— output data to additional external devices,
— calibration,
— time adjustment.

3. Modes of operation

C1.88　　The recording equipment shall possess four modes of operation:
— operational mode,
— control mode,
— calibration mode,
— company mode.

The recording equipment shall switch to the following mode of operation according to the valid tachograph cards inserted into the card interface devices:

Mode of operation		Driver slot				
		No card	Driver card	Control card	Workshop card	Company card
Co-driver slot	No card	Operational	Operational	Control	Calibration	Company
	Driver card	Operational	Operational	Control	Calibration	Company
	Control card	Control	Control	Control (*)	Operational	Operational
	Workshop card	Calibration	Calibration	Operational	Calibration (*)	Operational
	Company card	Company	Company	Operational	Operational	Company (*)

(*) In these situations the recording equipment shall use only the tachograph card inserted in the driver slot.

The recording equipment shall ignore non-valid cards inserted, except displaying, printing or downloading data held on an expired card which shall be possible.

All functions listed in II.2. shall work in any mode of operation with the following exceptions:
— the calibration function is accessible in the calibration mode only,
— the time adjustment function is limited when not in the calibration mode,
— [...]
— the company locks management function is accessible in the company mode only,
— the monitoring of control activities function is operational in the control mode only,
[— The downloading function is not accessible in the operational mode (except as provided for in Requirement 150 [*Annex IB, Chap.III, para.18, second subparagraph*]), and except downloading a driver card when no other card is inserted into the VU.]

The recording equipment can output any data to display, printer or external interfaces with the following exceptions:

— in the operational mode, any personal identification (surname and first name(s)) not corresponding to a tachograph card inserted shall be blanked and any card number not corresponding to a tachograph card inserted shall be partially blanked (every odd character—from left to right—shall be blanked),

[— in the company mode, driver related data (requirements 081, 084 and 087 [*Annex IB, Chap.III, paras 12.2, 12.4, 12.5*]) can be output only for periods where no lock exists or no other company holds a lock (as identified by the first 13 digits of the company card number).]

— when no card is inserted in the recording equipment, driver related data can be output only for the current and eight previous calendar days.

4. Security

The system security aims at protecting the data memory in such a way as to prevent unauthorised access to and manipulation of the data and detecting any such attempts, protecting the integrity and authenticity of data exchanged between the motion sensor and the vehicle unit, protecting the integrity and authenticity of data exchanged between the recording equipment and the tachograph cards, and verifying the integrity and authenticity of data downloaded. **C1.89**

In order to achieve the system security, the recording equipment shall meet the security requirements specified in the motion sensor and vehicle unit generic security targets (Appendix 10 [*not reproduced in this work*]).

[Chapter II to Annex IB is printed as amended by Regulation (EU) 1266/2009.] **C1.90**

III   Construction and Functional Requirements for Recording Equipment

1.   Monitoring cards insertion and withdrawal

The recording equipment shall monitor the card interface devices to detect card insertions and withdrawals. **C1.91**

Upon card insertion the recording equipment shall detect whether the card inserted is a valid tachograph card and in such a case identify the card type. The recording equipment shall be so designed that the tachograph cards are locked in position on their proper insertion into the card interface devices.

The release of tachograph cards may function only when the vehicle is stopped and after the relevant data have been stored on the cards. The release of the card shall require positive action by the user.

2.   Speed and distance measurement

This function shall continuously measure and be able to provide the odometer value corresponding to the total distance travelled by the vehicle. **C1.92**

This function shall continuously measure and be able to provide the speed of the vehicle.

The speed measurement function shall also provide the information whether the vehicle is moving or stopped. The vehicle shall be considered as moving as soon as the function detects more than 1 imp/sec for at least five seconds from the motion sensor, otherwise the vehicle shall be considered as stopped.

Devices displaying speed (speedometer) and total distance travelled (odometer) installed in any vehicle fitted with a recording equipment complying with the provisions of this Regulation, shall comply with the requirements relating to maximum tolerances laid down in this Annex (Chapters III(2)(1) and III(2)(2)).

[To detect manipulation of motion data, information from the motion sensor shall be corroborated by vehicle motion information derived from one or more source(s) independent from the motion sensor.]

2.1. *Measurement of distance travelled*

C1.93   The distance travelled may be measured either:

— so as to cumulate both forward and reverse movements, or

— so as to include only forward movement.

The recording equipment shall measure distance from 0 to 9 999 999,9 km.

Distance measured shall be within the following tolerances (distances of at least 1 000 m):

— ± 1% before installation,

— ± 2% on installation and periodic inspection,

— ± 4% in use.

Distance measured shall have a resolution better than or equal to 0,1 km.

2.2. *Measurement of speed*

C1.94   The recording equipment shall measure speed from 0 to 220 km/h.

To ensure a maximum tolerance on speed displayed of ± 6 km/h in use, and taking into account:

— a ± 2 km/h tolerance for input variations (tyre variations, …),

— a ± 1 km/h tolerance in measurements made during installation or periodic inspections,

the recording equipment shall, for speeds between 20 and 180 km/h, and for characteristic coefficients of the vehicle between 4000 and 25000 imp/km, measure the speed with a tolerance of ± 1 km/h (at constant speed).

Note: The resolution of data storage brings an additional tolerance of ± 0,5 km/h to speed stored by the recording equipment.

The speed shall be measured correctly within the normal tolerances within 2 seconds of the end of a speed change when the speed has changed at a rate up to 2 m/s2.

Speed measurement shall have a resolution better than or equal to 1 km/h.

3. Time measurement

C1.95   The time measurement function shall measure permanently and digitally provide UTC date and time.

[UTC date and time shall be used for dating data inside the recording equipment (recordings, data exchange) and for all printouts specified in Appendix 4 'Printouts' [*not reproduced in this work*].]

[In order to visualise the local time, it shall be possible to change the offset of the time displayed, in half hour steps. No other offsets than negative or positive multiples of half hours shall be allowed.]

Time drift shall be within ± 2 seconds per day in type approval conditions. Time measured shall have a resolution better than or equal to 1 second.

Time measurement shall not be affected by an external power supply cut-off of less than 12 months in type approval conditions.

4. Monitoring driver activities

C1.96   This function shall permanently and separately monitor the activities of one driver and one co-driver.

Driver activity shall be DRIVING, WORK, AVAILABILITY, or BREAK/REST.

It shall be possible for the driver and/or the co-driver to manually select WORK, AVAILABILITY, or BREAK/REST.

When the vehicle is moving, DRIVING shall be selected automatically for the driver and AVAILABILITY shall be selected automatically for the co-driver.

When the vehicle stops, WORK shall be selected automatically for the driver.

The first change of activity arising within 120 seconds of the automatic change to WORK due to the vehicle stop shall be assumed to have happened at the time of vehicle stop (therefore possibly cancelling the change to WORK).

This function shall output activity changes to the recording functions at a resolution of one minute.

[...]

[The first change of activity to REST or AVAILABILITY arising within 120 seconds of the automatic change to WORK due to the vehicle stop shall be assumed to have happened at the time of vehicle stop (therefore possibly cancelling the change to WORK).]

[Given a calendar minute, if DRIVING is registered as the activity of both the immediately preceding and immediately succeeding minute, the whole minute shall be regarded as DRIVING.]

[Given a calendar minute that is not regarded as DRIVING according to the previous requirement 041, the whole minute shall be regarded to be of the same type of activity as the longest continuous activity within the minute (or the latest of equally long activities).]

This function shall also permanently monitor the continuous driving time and the cumulative break time of the driver.

5. Monitoring driving status

This function shall permanently and automatically monitor the driving status.   **C1.97**

The driving status CREW shall be selected when two valid driver cards are inserted in the equipment, the driving status SINGLE shall be selected in any other case.

6. Drivers manual entries

6.1 *Entry of places where daily work periods begin and/or end*

This function shall allow for the entry of places where the daily work periods begin   **C1.98**
and/or end for a driver and/or a co-driver.

Places are defined as the country and, in addition where applicable, the region. At the time of a driver (or workshop) card withdrawal, the recording equipment shall prompt the (co-)driver to enter a "place where the daily work period ends".

The recording equipment shall allow this request to be disregarded.

[It shall be possible to input places where daily work periods begin and/or end through commands in the menus. If more than one such input is done within one calendar minute, only the last begin place input and the last end place input done within that time shall be kept recorded.]

6.2 *Manual entry of driver activities*

[Upon driver (or workshop) card insertion, and only at this time, the recording equip-   **C1.99**
ment shall allow manual entries of activities. It shall be possible to make manual entries, if required, at the first insertion of a previously unused driver (or workshop) card.

Manual entries of activities shall be performed using local time and date values of the time zone (UTC offset) currently set for the vehicle unit.

At driver or workshop card insertion the cardholder shall be reminded of:

— The date and time of his last card withdrawal.

— Optionally: the local time offset currently set for the vehicle unit.

It shall be possible to input activities with the following restrictions:

— Activity type shall be WORK, AVAILABILITY or BREAK/REST.

— Start and end times for each activity shall be within the period of the last card withdrawal—current insertion only.

Activities shall not be allowed to overlap mutually in time.

The procedure for manual entries of activities shall include as many consecutive steps as necessary to set a type, a start time and an end time for each activity. For any part of the time period between last card withdrawal and current card insertion, the cardholder shall have the option not to declare any activity.

During the manual entries associated with card insertion and if applicable, the card holder shall have the opportunity to input:

— a place where a previous daily work period ended, associated to the relevant time (if not already entered at the last card withdrawal),

— a place where the current daily work period begins, associated to the relevant time.

If a location is entered, it shall be recorded in the relevant tachograph card. Manual entries shall be interrupted if:

— the card is withdrawn or,

— the vehicle is moving and the card is in the driver slot.

Additional interruptions are allowed, e.g. a timeout after a certain period of user inactivity. If manual entries are interrupted, the recording equipment shall validate any complete place and activity entries (having either unambiguous place and time, or activity type, begin time and end time) already made.

If a second driver or workshop card is inserted while manual entries of activities are in progress for a previously inserted card, the manual entries for this previous card shall be allowed to be completed before manual entries start for the second card.

The cardholder shall have the option to insert manual entries according to the following minimum procedure:

Enter activities manually, in chronological order, for the period last card withdrawal—current insertion.

Begin time of the first activity shall be set to card withdrawal time. For each subsequent entry, the start time shall be preset to immediately follow the end time of the previous entry. Activity type and end time shall be selected for each activity.

The procedure shall end when the end time of a manually entered activity equals the card insertion time. The recording equipment may then optionally allow the card holder to modify any activity manually entered, until validation by selection of a specific command. Thereafter, any such modification shall be forbidden.]

6.3 *Entry of specific conditions*

C1.100   [The recording equipment shall allow the driver to enter, in real time, the following two specific conditions:

         "OUT OF SCOPE" (begin, end)

         "FERRY/TRAIN CROSSING"

A "FERRY/TRAIN CROSSING" may not occur if an "OUT OF SCOPE" condition is opened.

An opened "OUT OF SCOPE" condition shall be automatically closed, by the recording equipment, if a driver card is inserted or withdrawn.

An opened "OUT OF SCOPE" condition shall inhibit the following events and warnings:

— Driving without an appropriate card,

— Warnings associated with continuous driving time.]

7. Company locks management

C1.101   This function shall allow the management of the locks placed by a company to restrict data access in company mode to itself.

Company locks consist in a start date/time (lock-in) and an end date/time (lock-out) associated with the identification of the company as denoted by the company card number (at lock-in).

Locks may be turned "in" or "out" in real time only.

Locking-out shall only be possible for the company whose lock is "in" (as identified by the first 13 digits of the company card number), or,

locking-out shall be automatic if another company locks in.

In the case where a company locks in and where the previous lock was for the same company, then it will be assumed that the previous lock has not been turned "out" and is still "in".

8. Monitoring control activities

This function shall monitor DISPLAYING, PRINTING, VU and card DOWNLOAD-   **C1.102**
ING activities carried while in control mode.

This function shall also monitor OVER SPEEDING CONTROL activities while in control mode. An over speeding control is deemed to have happened when, in control mode, the "over speeding" printout has been sent to the printer or to the display, or when "events and faults" data have been downloaded from the VU data memory.

9. Detection of events and/or faults

This function shall detect the following events and/or faults: **C1.103**

9.1. *Insertion of a "non-valid card" event*

This event shall be triggered at the insertion of any non-valid card and/or when an inserted valid card expires.

9.2. *"Card conflict" event*

This event shall be triggered when any of the valid cards combination noted X in the following table arise:

Card conflict		Driver slot				
		No card	Driver card	Control card	Workshop card	Company card
Co-driver slot	No card					
	Driver card				X	
	Control card			X	X	X
	Workshop card		X	X	X	X
	Company card			X	X	X

9.3. *"Time overlap" event*

This event shall be triggered when the date/time of last withdrawal of a driver card, as   **C1.104**
read from the card, is later than the current date/time of the recording equipment in which the card is inserted.

9.4. *"Driving without an appropriate card" event*

This event shall be triggered for any tachograph cards combination noted X in the fol-   **C1.105**
lowing table, when driver activity changes to DRIVING, or when there is a change of the mode of operation while driver activity is DRIVING:

Driving without an appropriate card		Driver slot				
		No (or non-valid) card	Driver card	Control card	Workshop card	Company card
Co-driver slot	No (or non-valid) card	X		X		X
	Driver card	X		X	X	X
	Control card	X	X	X	X	X
	Workshop card	X	X	X		X
	Company card	X	X	X	X	X

9.5. *"Card insertion while driving" event*

C1.106   This event shall be triggered when a tachograph card is inserted in any slot, while driver activity is DRIVING.

9.6. *"Last card session not correctly closed" event*

C1.107   This event shall be triggered when at card insertion the recording equipment detects that, despite the provisions laid down in paragraph III(1), the previous card session has not been correctly closed (the card has been withdrawn before all relevant data have been stored on the card). This event shall be triggered by driver and workshop cards only.

9.7. *"Over speeding" event*

C1.108   [This event shall be triggered for each over-speeding. This requirement shall apply only to vehicles falling within category M2, M3, N2 or N3, as defined in Annex II of Directive 2007/46/EC, establishing a framework for the approval of motor vehicles and their trailer.]

9.8. *"Power supply interruption" event*

C1.109   This event shall be triggered, while not in calibration mode, in case of any interruption exceeding 200 milliseconds of the power supply of the motion sensor and/or of the vehicle unit. The interruption threshold shall be defined by the manufacturer. The drop in power supply due to the starting of the engine of the vehicle shall not trigger this event.

9.9. *"Motion data error" event*

C1.110   This event shall be triggered in case of interruption of the normal data flow between the motion sensor and the vehicle unit and/or in case of data integrity or data authentication error during data exchange between the motion sensor and the vehicle unit.

9.9 bis. *"Vehicle Motion Conflict" event*

C1.111   This event shall also be triggered when a zero speed measurement is contradicted by motion information from at least one independent source for more than one uninterrupted minute.

In cases where the vehicle unit can receive or elaborate speed values from external independent source of motion information, this event may also be triggered if such speed values significantly contradict those elaborated from the motion sensor speed signal for more than one minute.]

9.10. *"Security breach attempt" event*

C1.112   This event shall be triggered for any other event affecting the security of the motion sensor and/or of the vehicle unit as specified within the generic security targets of these components, while not in calibration mode.

9.11. *"Card" fault*

This fault shall be triggered when a tachograph card failure occurs during operation.   **C1.113**

9.12. *"Recording equipment" fault*

This fault shall be triggered for any of these failures, while not in calibration mode: **C1.114**
— VU internal fault,
— printer fault,
— display fault,
— downloading fault,
— sensor fault.

10. Built-in and self tests

The recording equipment shall self-detect faults through self tests and built-in-tests, according to the following table: **C1.115**

Sub-assembly to test	Self test	Built-in-test
Software		Integrity
Data memory	Access	Access, data integrity
Card interface devices	Access	Access
Keyboard		Manual check
Printer	(up to manufacturer)	Printout
Display		Visual check
Downloading (performed only during downloading)	Proper operation	
Sensor	Proper operation	Proper operation

11. Reading from data memory

The recording equipment shall be able to read any data stored in its data memory.   **C1.116**

12. Recording and storing in the data memory

For the purpose of this paragraph,   **C1.117**
— "365 days" is defined as 365 calendar days of average drivers activity in a vehicle. The average activity per day in a vehicle is defined as at least six drivers or co-drivers, six card insertion withdrawal cycles, and 256 activity changes. "365 days" therefore include at least 2 190 (co-)drivers, 2 190 card insertion withdrawal cycles, and 93 440 activity changes,
— times are recorded with a resolution of one minute, unless otherwise specified,
— odometer values are recorded with a resolution of one kilometre,
— speeds are recorded with a resolution of 1 km/h.

Data stored into the data memory shall not be affected by an external power supply cut-off of less than twelve months in type approval conditions.

The recording equipment shall be able to record and store implicitly or explicitly in its data memory the following:

12.1. *Equipment identification data*

12.1.1. VEHICLE UNIT IDENTIFICATION DATA   **C1.118**

The recording equipment shall be able to store in its data memory the following vehicle unit identification data:

— name of the manufacturer,

— address of the manufacturer,

— part number,

— serial number,

— software version number,

— software version installation date,

— year of equipment manufacture,

— approval number.

Vehicle unit identification data are recorded and stored once and for all by the vehicle unit manufacturer, except the software-related data and the approval number which may be changed in case of software upgrade.

12.1.2. MOTION SENSOR IDENTIFICATION DATA

The motion sensor shall be able to store in its memory the following identification data:

— name of the manufacturer,

— part number,

— serial number,

— approval number,

— embedded security component identifier (e.g. internal chip/processor part number),

— operating system identifier (e.g. software version number).

Motion sensor identification data are recorded and stored once and for all in the motion sensor, by the motion sensor manufacturer.

The vehicle unit shall be able to record and store in its data memory the following currently paired motion sensor identification data:

— serial number,

— approval number,

— first pairing date.

12.2. *Security elements*

C1.119   The recording equipment shall be able to store the following security elements:

— European public key,

— Member State certificate,

— equipment certificate,

— equipment private key.

Recording equipment security elements are inserted in the equipment by the vehicle unit manufacturer.

12.3. *Driver card insertion and withdrawal data*

C1.120   For each insertion and withdrawal cycle of a driver or workshop card in the equipment, the recording equipment shall record and store in its data memory:

— the card holder's surname and first name(s) as stored in the card,

— the card's number, issuing Member State and expiry date as stored in the card,

— the insertion date and time,

— the vehicle odometer value at card insertion,

— the slot in which the card is inserted,

— the withdrawal date and time,

— the vehicle odometer value at card withdrawal,

— the following information about the previous vehicle used by the driver, as stored in the card:

    — VRN and registering Member State,

    — card withdrawal date and time,

— a flag indicating whether, at card insertion, the card holder has manually entered activities or not.

The data memory shall be able to hold these data for at least 365 days.

When storage capacity is exhausted, new data shall replace oldest data.

12.4. *Driver activity data*

The recording equipment shall record and store in its data memory whenever there is a change of activity for the driver and/or the co-driver, and/or whenever there is a change of driving status, and/or whenever there is an insertion or withdrawal of a driver or workshop card: **C1.121**

    — the driving status (CREW, SINGLE),

    — the slot (DRIVER, CO-DRIVER),

    — the card status in the relevant slot (INSERTED, NOT INSERTED) (see Note),

    — the activity (DRIVING, AVAILABILITY, WORK, BREAK/REST),

    — the date and time of the change.

Note: INSERTED means that a valid driver or workshop card is inserted in the slot. NOT INSERTED means the opposite, i.e. no valid driver or workshop card is inserted in the slot (e.g. a company card is inserted or no card is inserted).

Note: Activity data manually entered by a driver are not recorded in the data memory.

The data memory shall be able to hold driver activity data for at least 365 days.

When storage capacity is exhausted, new data shall replace oldest data.

12.5. *Places where daily work periods start and/or end*

The recording equipment shall record and store in its data memory whenever a (co-) driver enters the place where a daily work period begins and/or ends: **C1.122**

    — if applicable, the (co-)driver card number and card issuing Member State,

    — the date and time of the entry (or the date/time related to the entry when the entry is made during the manual entry procedure),

    — the type of entry (begin or end, condition of entry),

    — the country and region entered,

    — the vehicle odometer value.

The data memory shall be able to hold daily work periods start and/or end data for at least 365 days (with the assumption that one driver enters two records per day).

When storage capacity is exhausted, new data shall replace oldest data.

12.6. *Odometer data*

The recording equipment shall record in its data memory the vehicle odometer value and the corresponding date at midnight every calendar day. **C1.123**

The data memory shall be able to store midnight odometer values for at least 365 calendar days.

When storage capacity is exhausted, new data shall replace oldest data.

12.7. *Detailed speed data*

The recording equipment shall record and store in its data memory the instantaneous speed of the vehicle and the corresponding date and time at every second of at least the last 24 hours that the vehicle has been moving. **C1.124**

12.8. *Events data*

For the purpose of this subparagraph, time shall be recorded with a resolution of one second. **C1.125**

The recording equipment shall record and store in its data memory the following data for each event detected according to the following storage rules:

Event	Storage rules	Data to be recorded per event
Card conflict	— the 10 most recent events.	— date and time of beginning of event, — date and time of end of event, — cards' type, number and issuing Member State of the two cards creating the conflict.
Driving without an appropriate card	— the longest event for each of the 10 last days of occurrence, — the five longest events over the last 365 days.	— date and time of beginning of event, — date and time of end of event, — cards' type, number and issuing Member State of any card inserted at beginning and/or end of the event, — number of similar events that day.
Card insertion while driving	— the last event for each of the 10 last days of occurrence.	— date and time of the event, — card's type, number and issuing Member State, — number of similar events that day.
Last card session not correctly closed	— the 10 most recent events.	— date and time of card insertion, — card's type, number and issuing Member State, — last session data as read from the card, — date and time of card insertion, — VRN and Member State of registration.
Over speeding (^{1})	— the most serious event for each of the last 10 days of occurrence (i.e. the one with the highest average speed), — the five most serious events over the last 365 days, — the first event having occurred after the last calibration.	— date and time of beginning of event, — date and time of end of event, — maximum speed measured during the event, — arithmetic average speed measured during the event, — card's type, number and issuing Member State (if applicable), — number of similar events that day.
Power supply interruption (^{2})	— the longest event for each of the 10 last days of occurrence, — the five longest events over the last 365 days.	— date and time of beginning of event, — date and time of end of event, — cards' type, number and issuing Member State of any card inserted at beginning and/or end of the event, — number of similar events that day.

Event	Storage rules	Data to be recorded per event
Motion data error	— the longest event for each of the 10 last days of occurrence, — the five longest events over the last 365 days.	— date and time of beginning of event, — date and time of end of event, — cards' type, number and issuing Member State of any card inserted at beginning and/or end of the event, — number of similar events that day.
[Vehicle Motion Conflict	— the longest event for each of the 10 last days of occurrence, — the 5 longest events over the last 365 days.	— date and time of beginning of event, — date and time of end of event, — cards' type, number and issuing Member State of any card inserted at beginning and/or end of the event, — number of similar events that day]
Security breach attempt	— the 10 most recent events per type of event.	— date and time of beginning of event, — date and time of end of event (if relevant), — cards' type, number and issuing Member State of any card inserted at beginning and/or end of the event, — type of event.

(^{1})   The recording equipment shall also record and store in its memory:
— the date and time of the last OVER SPEEDING CONTROL,
— the date and time of the first over speeding following this OVER SPEEDING CONTROL,
— the number of over speeding events since the last OVER SPEEDING CONTROL.
(^{2})   These data may be recorded at power supply reconnection only, times may be known with an accuracy to the minute.

12.9. *Faults data*

For the purpose of this subparagraph, time shall be recorded with a resolution of one **C1.126** second.

The recording equipment shall attempt to record and store in its data memory the following data for each fault detected according to the following storage rules:

Fault	Storage rules	Data to be recorded per fault
Card fault	— the 10 most recent driver card faults.	— date and time of beginning of fault, — date and time of end of fault, — card's type, number and issuing Member State.
Recording equipment faults	— the 10 most recent faults for each type of fault, — the first fault after the last calibration.	— date and time of beginning of fault, — date and time of end of fault, — type of fault, — cards' type, number and issuing Member State of any card inserted at beginning and/or end of the fault.

12.10. *Calibration data*

C1.127   The recording equipment shall record and store in its data memory data relevant to:
— known calibration parameters at the moment of activation,
— its very first calibration following its activation,
— its first calibration in the current vehicle (as identified by its VIN),
— the five most recent calibrations (if several calibrations happen within one calendar day, only the last one of the day shall be stored).

The following data shall be recorded for each of these calibrations:
— purpose of calibration (activation, first installation, installation, periodic inspection),
— workshop name and address,
— workshop card number, card issuing Member State and card expiry date,
— vehicle identification,
— parameters updated or confirmed: w, k, l, tyre size, speed limiting device setting, odometer (old and new values), date and time (old and new values).

The motion sensor shall record and store in its memory the following motion sensor installation data:
— first pairing with a VU (date, time, VU approval number, VU serial number),
— last pairing with a VU (date, time, VU approval number, VU serial number).

12.11. *Time adjustment data*

C1.128   The recording equipment shall record and store in its data memory data relevant to:
— the most recent time adjustment,
— the five largest time adjustments, since last calibration,
performed in calibration mode outside the frame of a regular calibration (definition (f)).
The following data shall be recorded for each of these time adjustments:
— date and time, old value,
— date and time, new value,
— workshop name and address,
— workshop card number, card issuing Member State and card expiry date.

12.12. *Control activity data*

C1.129   The recording equipment shall record and store in its data memory the following data relevant to the 20 most recent control activities:
— date and time of the control,
— control card number and card issuing Member State,
— type of the control (displaying and/or printing and/or VU downloading and/or card downloading).

In case of downloading, the dates of the oldest and of the most recent days downloaded shall also be recorded.

12.13. *Company locks data*

C1.130   [The recording equipment shall record and store in its data memory the following data relevant to the 255 most recent company locks.
— lock-in date and time,
— lock-out date and time,
— Company Card number and card issuing Member States,
— Company name and address.

Data previously locked by a lock removed from memory due to the limit above, shall be treated as not locked.]

12.14. *Download activity data*

The recording equipment shall record and store in its data memory the following data **C1.131** relevant to the last data memory downloading to external media while in company or in calibration mode:

— date and time of downloading,
— company or workshop card number and card issuing Member State,
— company or workshop name.

12.15. *Specific conditions data*

The recording equipment shall record in its data memory the following data relevant to **C1.132** specific conditions:

— date and time of the entry,
— type of specific condition.

The data memory shall be able to hold specific conditions data for at least 365 days (with the assumption that on average, one condition is opened and closed per day). When storage capacity is exhausted, new data shall replace oldest data.

13. Reading from tachograph cards

The recording equipment shall be able to read from tachograph cards, where applicable, **C1.133** the necessary data:

— to identify the card type, the card holder, the previously used vehicle, the date and time of the last card withdrawal and the activity selected at that time,
— to check that last card session was correctly closed,
— to compute the driver's continuous driving time, cumulative break time and cumulated driving times for the previous and the current week,
— to print requested printouts related to data recorded on a driver card,
— to download a driver card to external media.

In case of a reading error, the recording equipment shall try again, three times maximum, the same read command, and then if still unsuccessful, declare the card faulty and non-valid.

14. Recording and storing on tachograph cards

The recording equipment shall set the "card session data" in the driver or workshop card **C1.134** right after the card insertion.

The recording equipment shall update data stored on valid driver, workshop and/or control cards with all necessary data relevant to the period while the card is inserted and relevant to the card holder. Data stored on these cards are specified in Chapter IV.

The recording equipment shall update driver activity and location data (as specified in Chapter IV, paragraphs 5.2.5 and 5.2.6), stored on valid driver and/or workshop cards, with activity and location data manually entered by the cardholder.

[The "Vehicle Motion Conflict" event shall not be stored on the driver and workshop cards.]

Tachograph cards data update shall be such that, when needed and taking into account card actual storage capacity, most recent data replace oldest data.

In the case of a writing error, the recording equipment shall try again, three times maximum, the same write command, and then if still unsuccessful, declare the card faulty and non valid.

Before releasing a driver card, and after all relevant data have been stored on the card, the recording equipment shall reset the card session data.

15. Displaying

The display shall include at least 20 characters.   **C1.135**

The minimum character size shall be 5 mm high and 3,5 mm wide.

[The display shall support the characters specified in Appendix 1 Chapter 4 'Character sets' [*not reproduced in this work*]. The display may use simplified glyphs (e.g. accented characters may be displayed without accent, or lower case letters may be shown as upper case letters).]

The display shall be provided with adequate non-dazzling lighting.

Indications shall be visible from outside the recording equipment.

The recording equipment shall be able to display:

— default data,

— data related to warnings,

— data related to menu access,

— other data requested by a user.

Additional information may be displayed by the recording equipment, provided that it is clearly distinguishable from information required above.

The display of the recording equipment shall use the pictograms or pictogram combinations listed in Appendix 3 [*not reproduced in this work*]. Additional pictograms or pictogram combinations may also be provided by the display, if clearly distinguishable from the aforementioned pictogram or pictogram combinations.

The display shall always be ON when the vehicle is moving.

The recording equipment may include a manual or automatic feature to turn the display OFF when the vehicle is not moving.

Displaying format is specified in Appendix 5 [*not reproduced in this work*].

15.1. *Default display*

C1.136   [When no other information needs to be displayed, the recording equipment shall display, by default, the following:

— the local time (as a result of UTC time + offset as set by the driver),

— the mode of operation,

— the current activity of the driver and the current activity of the co-driver.

Information related to the driver:

— if his current activity is DRIVING, his current continuous driving time and his current cumulative break time,

— if his current activity is not DRIVING, the current duration of this activity (since it was selected) and his current cumulative break time.]

Display of data related to each driver shall be clear, plain and unambiguous. In the case where the information related to the driver and the co-driver cannot be displayed at the same time, the recording equipment shall display by default the information related to the driver and shall allow the user to display the information related to the co-driver.

In the case where the display width does not allow to display by default the mode of operation, the recording equipment shall briefly display the new mode of operation when it changes.

The recording equipment shall briefly display the card holder name at card insertion.

When an "OUT OF SCOPE" condition is opened, then the default display must show using the relevant pictogram that the condition is opened (It is acceptable that the driver's current activity may not be shown at the same time).

15.2. *Warning display*

C1.137   The recording equipment shall display warning information using primarily the pictograms of Appendix 3 [*not reproduced in this work*], completed where needed by an additional numerically coded information. A literal description of the warning may also be added in the driver's preferred language.

15.3. *Menu access*

The recording equipment shall provide necessary commands through an appropriate **C1.138**
menu structure.

15.4. *Other displays*

[It shall be possible to display selectively on request: **C1.139**
— the UTC date and time, and local time offset,
— the content of any of the six printouts under the same formats as the printouts
themselves,
— the continuous driving time and cumulative break time of the driver,
— the continuous driving time and cumulative break time of the co-driver,
— the cumulated driving time of the driver for the previous and the current week,
— the cumulated driving time of the co-driver for the previous and the current
week.

Optional:
— the current duration of co-driver activity (since it was selected),,
— the cumulated driving time of the driver for the current week,
— the cumulated driving time of the driver for the current daily work period,
— the cumulated driving time of the co-driver for the current daily work period.]

Printout content display shall be sequential, line by line. If the display width is less than
24 characters the user shall be provided with the complete information through an appropriate mean (several lines, scrolling, …). Printout lines devoted to hand-written information may be omitted for display.

16. Printing

The recording equipment shall be able to print information from its data memory and/or **C1.140**
from tachograph cards in accordance with the six following printouts:
— driver activities from card daily printout,
— driver activities from Vehicle Unit daily printout,
— events and faults from card printout,
— events and faults from Vehicle Unit printout,
— technical data printout,
— over speeding printout.

The detailed format and content of these printouts are specified in Appendix 4 [*not
reproduced in this work*].

Additional data may be provided at the end of the printouts.

Additional printouts may also be provided by the recording equipment, if clearly distinguishable from the six aforementioned printouts.

The "driver activities from card daily printout" and "events and faults from card
printout" shall be available only when a driver card or a workshop card is inserted in the
recording equipment. The recording equipment shall update data stored on the relevant
card before starting printing.

In order to produce the "driver activities from card daily printout" or the "events and
faults from card printout", the recording equipment shall:
— either automatically select the driver card or the workshop card if one only of
these cards is inserted,
— or provide a command to select the source card or select the card in the driver
slot if two of these cards are inserted in the recording equipment.

The printer shall be able to print 24 characters per line.

The minimum character size shall be 2,1 mm high and 1,5 mm wide.

[The printer shall support the characters specified in Appendix 1 Chapter 4 "Character sets" [*not reproduced in this work*].]

Printers shall be so designed as to produce these printouts with a degree of definition likely to avoid any ambiguity when they are read.

Printouts shall retain their dimensions and recordings under normal conditions of humidity (10 to 90%) and temperature.

[The printout paper used by the recording equipment shall bear the relevant type approval mark and an indication of the type(s) of recording equipment with which it may be used.]

[Printouts shall remain clearly legible and identifiable under normal conditions of storage, in terms of light intensity, humidity and temperature, for at least two years.

The printout paper shall conform at least to the test specifications defined on the website of the laboratory appointed to carry out interoperability testing, as set out in Requirement 278 [*Annex IB, Chap.VIII, para.4, "Interoperability certificate"*].

Any amendment or updating of the specifications described in the above paragraph shall only be made after the appointed laboratory has consulted the type approved digital tachograph vehicle unit manufacturer in conjunction with the type approval authorities.]

It shall also be possible to add handwritten notes, such as the driver's signature, to these documents.

The recording equipment shall manage "paper out" events while printing by, once paper has been re-loaded, restarting printing from printout beginning or by continuing printing and providing an unambiguous reference to previously printed part.

17. Warnings

C1.141   The recording equipment shall warn the driver when detecting any event and/or fault.

Warning of a power supply interruption event may be delayed until the power supply is reconnected.

[The recording equipment shall warn the driver 15 minutes before and at the time of exceeding the maximum allowed continuous driving time'.]

Warnings shall be visual. Audible warnings may also be provided in addition to visual warnings.

Visual warnings shall be clearly recognisable by the user, shall be situated in the driver's field of vision and shall be clearly legible both by day and by night.

Visual warnings may be built into the recording equipment and/or remote from the recording equipment.

[In the latter case it shall bear a "T" symbol.]

Warnings shall have a duration of at least 30 seconds, unless acknowledged by the user by hitting any key of the recording equipment. This first acknowledgement shall not erase warning cause display referred to in next paragraph.

Warning cause shall be displayed on the recording equipment and remain visible until acknowledged by the user using a specific key or command of the recording equipment.

Additional warnings may be provided, as long as they do not confuse drivers in relation to previously defined ones.

18. Data downloading to external media

C1.142   The recording equipment shall be able to download on request data from its data memory or from a driver card to external storage media via the calibration/downloading connector. The recording equipment shall update data stored on the relevant card before starting downloading.

In addition and as an optional feature, the recording equipment may, in any mode of operation, download data through another connector to a company authenticated through this channel. In such a case, company mode data access rights shall apply to this download.

Downloading shall not alter or delete any stored data.

The calibration/downloading connector electrical interface is specified in Appendix 6 [*not reproduced in this work*].

Downloading protocols are specified in Appendix 7 [*not reproduced in this work*].

19. Output data to additional external devices

When the recording equipment does not include speed and/or odometer display func-   **C1.143**
tions, the recording equipment shall provide output signal(s) to allow for displaying the speed of the vehicle (speedometer) and/or the total distance travelled by the vehicle (odometer).

The vehicle unit shall also be able to output the following data using an appropriate dedicated serial link independent from an optional CAN bus connection (ISO 11898 Road vehicles—Interchange of digital information—Controller Area Network (CAN) for high speed communication), to allow their processing by other electronic units installed in the vehicle:

— current UTC date and time,

— speed of the vehicle,

— total distance travelled by the vehicle (odometer),

— currently selected driver and co-driver activity,

— information if any tachograph card is currently inserted in the driver slot and in the co-driver slot and (if applicable) information about the corresponding cards identification (card number and issuing Member State).

Other data may also be output in addition to this minimum list.

When the ignition of the vehicle is ON, these data shall be permanently broadcast. When the ignition of the vehicle is OFF, at least any change of driver or co-driver activity and/or any insertion or withdrawal of a tachograph card shall generate a corresponding data output. In the event that data output has been withheld whilst the ignition of the vehicle is OFF, that data shall be made available once the ignition of the vehicle is ON again.

20. Calibration

The calibration function shall allow: **C1.144**

— to automatically pair the motion sensor with the VU,

— to digitally adapt the constant of the recording equipment (k) to the characteristic coefficient of the vehicle (w) (vehicles with two or more axle ratios shall be fitted with a switch device whereby these various ratios will automatically be brought into line with the ratio for which the equipment has been adapted to the vehicle),

— to adjust (without limitation) the current time,

— to adjust the current odometer value,

— to update motion sensor identification data stored in the data memory,

— to update or confirm other parameters known to the recording equipment: vehicle identification, w, l, tyre size and speed limiting device setting if applicable.

Pairing the motion sensor to the VU shall consist, at least, in:

— updating motion sensor installation data held by the motion sensor (as needed),

— copying from the motion sensor to the VU data memory necessary motion sensor identification data.

The calibration function shall be able to input necessary data through the calibration/ downloading connector in accordance with the calibration protocol defined in Appendix 8 [*not reproduced in this work*]. The calibration function may also input necessary data through other connectors.

21. Time adjustment

C1.145 The time adjustment function shall allow for adjusting the current time in amounts of one minute maximum at intervals of not less than seven days.

The time adjustment function shall allow for adjusting the current time without limitation, in calibration mode.

22. Performance characteristics

C1.146 The Vehicle Unit shall be fully operational in the temperature range -20 °C to 70 °C, and the motion sensor in the temperature range -40 °C to 135 °C. Data memory content shall be preserved at temperatures down to -40 °C.

The recording equipment shall be fully operational in the humidity range 10% to 90%.

The recording equipment shall be protected against over-voltage, inversion of its power supply polarity, and short circuits.

[Motion sensors shall either:

 — react to a magnetic field which disturbs vehicle motion detection. In such circumstances, the vehicle unit will record and store a sensor fault (Requirement 070 [*Annex IB, Chap.III, para.9.12, "'Recording equipment' fault"*]), or

 — have a sensing element that is protected from, or immune to, magnetic fields.]

The recording equipment shall conform to Commission Directive 95/54/EC of 31 October 1995 [*O.J. No.L266, November 8, 1995, p.1*] adapting to technical progress Council Directive 72/245/EEC [*O.J. No.L152, July 6, 1972, p.15*], related to electromagnetic compatibility, and shall be protected against electrostatic discharges and transients.

23. Materials

C1.147 All the constituent parts of the recording equipment shall be made of materials of sufficient stability and mechanical strength and with stable electrical and magnetic characteristics.

For normal conditions of use, all the internal parts of the equipment shall be protected against damp and dust.

The Vehicle Unit shall meet the protection grade IP 40 and the motion sensor shall meet the protection grade IP 64, as per standard IEC 529.

The recording equipment shall conform to applicable technical specifications related to ergonomic design.

The recording equipment shall be protected against accidental damage.

24. Markings

C1.148 If the recording equipment displays the vehicle odometer value and speed, the following details shall appear on its display:

 — near the figure indicating the distance, the unit of measurement of distance, indicated by the abbreviation "km",

 — near the figure showing the speed, the entry "km/h".

The recording equipment may also be switched to display the speed in miles per hour, in which case the unit of measurement of speed shall be shown by the abbreviation "mph".

A descriptive plaque shall be affixed to each separate component of the recording equipment and shall show the following details:

 — name and address of the manufacturer of the equipment,

 — manufacturer's part number and year of manufacture of the equipment,

 — equipment serial number,

 — approval mark for the equipment type.

When physical space is not sufficient to show all abovementioned details, the descriptive plaque shall show at least: the manufacturer's name or logo, and the equipment's part number.

[Chapter III to Annex IB is printed as amended by Regulation (EU) 1266/ **C1.149**
2009.]

IV   Construction and Functional Requirements for Tachograph Cards

1. Visible data

The front page will contain: **C1.150**

the words "Driver card" or "Control card" or "Workshop card" or "Company card"
printed in large type in the official language or languages of the Member State issuing the
card, according to the type of the card;

[the same words in the other official languages of the Community, printed to form the
background of the card:

	КАРТА НА ВОДАЧА	КОНТРОЛНА КАРТА	КАРТА ЗА МОНТА И НАСТРОЙКИ	КАРТА НА ПРЕВОЗВАЧА]
[BG				
ES	TARJETA DEL CONDUCTOR	TARJETA DE CONTROL	TARJETA DEL CENTRO DE ENSAYO	TARJETA DE LA EMPRESA
CS	KARTA ŘIDIČE	KONTROLNÍ KARTA	KARTA DÍLNY	KARTA PODNIKU
DA	FØRERKORT	KONTROLKORT	VÆRKSTEDSKORT	VIRKSOMHEDSKORT
DE	FAHRERKARTE	KONTROLLKARTE	WERKSTATTKARTE	UNTERNEHMENSKARTE
ET	AUTOJUHI KAART	KONTROLLIJA KAART	TÖÖKOJA KAART	TÖÖANDJA KAART
EL	[ΚΑΡΤΑ ΟΔΗΓΟΥ]	ΚΑΡΤΑ ΕΛΕΓΧΟΥ	ΚΑΡΤΑ ΚΕΝΤΡΟΥ ΔΟΚΙΜΝ	ΚΑΡΤΑ ΕΠΙΧΕΙΡΗΣΗΣ
EN	DRIVER CARD	CONTROL CARD	WORKSHOP CARD	COMPANY CARD
FR	CARTE DE CONDUCTEUR	CARTE DE CONTROLEUR	CARTE D'ATELIER	CARTE D'ENTREPRISE
GA	CÁRTA TIOMÁNAÍ	CÁRTA STIÚRTHA	CÁRTA CEARDLAINNE	CÁRTA COMHLACHTA
IT	CARTA DEL CONDUCENTE	CARTA DI CONTROLLO	CARTA DELL'OFFICINA	CARTA DELL' AZIENDA
LV	VADĪTĀJA KARTE	KONTROLKARTE	DARBNĪCAS KARTE	UZŅĒMUMA KARTE
LT	VAIRUOTOJO KORTELE	KONTROLES KORTELE	DIRBTUVES KORTELE	JMONES KORTELE
HU	GÉPJÁRMŰVEZETŐI KÁRTYA	ELLENŐRI KÁRTYA	MŰHELYKÁRTYA	ÜZEMBENTARTÓI KÁRTYA
MT	KARTA TAS-SEWWIEQ	KARTA TAL-KONTROLL	KARTA TAL-ISTAZZJON TAT-TESTIJIET	KARTA TAL-KUMPANNIJA
NL	BESTUURDERS KAART	CONTROLEKAART	WERKPLAATSKAART	BEDRIJFSKAART
PL	KARTA KIEROWCY	KARTA KONTROLNA	KARTA WARSZTATOWA	KARTA PRZEDSIEBIORSTWA
PT	CARTÃO DE CONDUTOR	CARTÃO DE CONTROLO	CARTÃO DO CENTRO DE ENSAIO	CARTÃO DE EMPRESA
[RO	CARTELA CONDUCĂ-TORULUI AUTO	CARTELA DE CONTROL	CARTELA AGENTULUI ECONOMIC AUTORIZAT	CARTELA OPERATORULUI DE TRANSPORT]
SK	KARTA VODICA	KONTROLNÁ KARTA	DIELENSKÁ KARTA	PODNIKOVÁ KARTA
SL	VOZNIKOVA KARTICA	KONTROLNA KARTICA	KARTICA PREIZKUŠEVALIŠČA	KARTICA PODJETJA
FI	KULJETTAJAKORTTI	VALVONTAKORTTI	KORJAAMOKORTTI	YRITYSKORTTI
SV	FÖRARKORT	KONTROLLKORT	VERKSTADSKORT	FÖRETAGSKORT]

the name of the Member State issuing the card (optional);

[the distinguishing sign of the Member State issuing the card, printed in negative in a blue rectangle and encircled by 12 yellow stars. The distinguishing signs shall be as follows:

B: Belgium	LV: Latvia
BG: Bulgaria	H: Hungary
CZ: The Czech Republic	M: Malta
DK: Denmark	NL: The Netherlands
D: Germany	A: Austria
EST: Estonia	PL: Poland
GR: Greece	P: Portugal
E: Spain	RO: Romania
F: France	SLO: Slovenia
IRL: Ireland	SK: Slovakia
I: Italy	FIN: Finland
CY: Cyprus	S: Sweden
LT: Lithuania	UK: United Kingdom]
L: Luxembourg	

information specific to the card issued, numbered as follows:

	Driver Card	Control Card	Company or workshop card
1.	Surname of the driver	Control body name	Company or workshop card
2.	First name(s) of the driver	Surname of the controller (if applicable)	Surname of card holder (if applicable)
3.	Birth date of the driver	First name(s) of the controller (if applicable)	First name(s) of the card holder (if applicable)
4.(a)	Card start of validity date		
(b)	Card expiry date (if any)		
(c)	The name of the issuing authority (may be printed on page 2)		
(d)	A different number from the one under heading 5, for administrative purposes (optional)		
5.(a)	Driving licence number (at the date of issue of the driver card)		
(b)	Card number		
6.	Photograph of the driver	Photograph of the controller (optional)	—
7.	Signature of the driver	Signature of the holder (optional)	
8.	Normal place of residence, or postal address of the holder (optional)	Postal address of the control body	Postal address of company or workshop

dates shall be written using a "dd/mm/yyyy" or "dd.mm.yyyy" format (day, month, year);

the reverse page will contain:

an explanation of the numbered items which appear on the front page of the card;

with the specific written agreement of the holder, information which is not related to the administration of the card may also be added, such addition will not alter in any way the use of the model as a tachograph card.

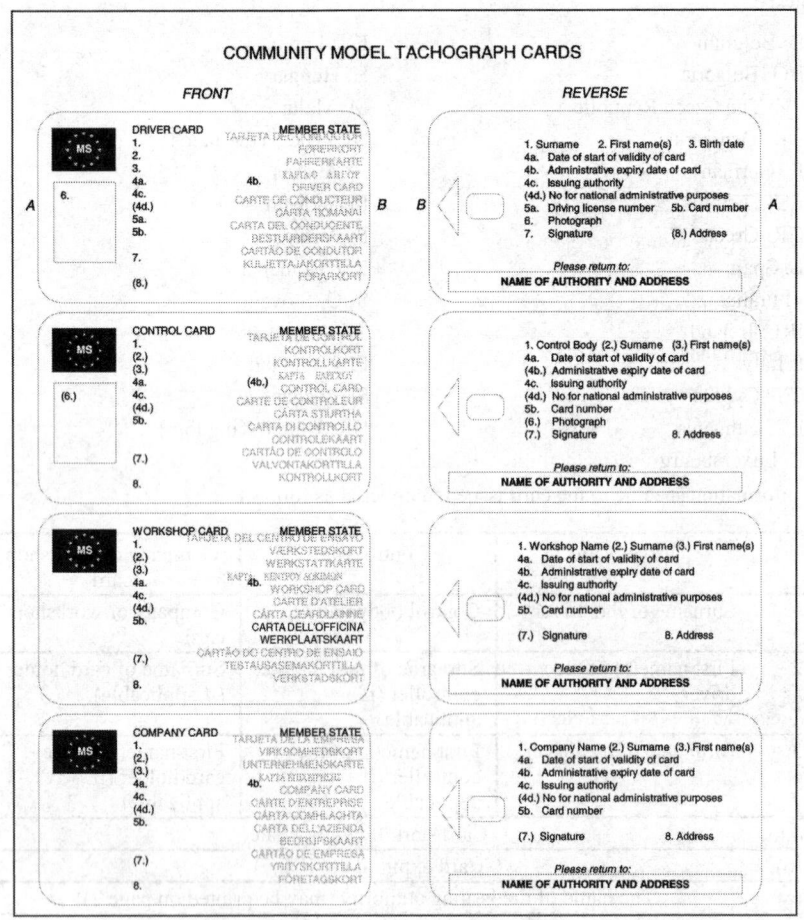

Tachograph cards shall be printed with the following background predominant colours:

— driver card: white,
— control card: blue,
— workshop card: red,
— company card: yellow.

Tachograph cards shall bear at least the following features for protection of the card body against counterfeiting and tampering:

— a security design background with fine guilloche patterns and rainbow printing,
— in the area of the photograph, the security design background and the photograph shall overlap,
— at least one two-coloured microprint line.

After consulting the Commission, Member States may add colours or markings, such as national symbols and security features, without prejudice to the other provisions of this Annex.

C1.151   *[Paragraph 1 of Chap.IV to Annex 1B is printed as amended by the Act of Accession of the Czech Republic, the Republic of Estonia, the Republic of Cyprus, the Republic of Latvia, the Republic of Lithuania, the Republic of Hungary, the*

Republic of Malta, the Republic of Poland, the Republic of Slovenia and the Slovak Republic to the European Union, Annex II, with effect from May 12, 2004; Regulation (EC) 432/2004; Regulation (EC) 1791/2006.]

2. Security

The system security aims at protecting integrity and authenticity of data exchanged be-   **C1.152**
tween the cards and the recording equipment, protecting the integrity and authenticity of data downloaded from the cards, allowing certain write operations onto the cards to recording equipment only, ruling out any possibility of falsification of data stored in the cards, preventing tampering and detecting any attempt of that kind.

In order to achieve the system security, the tachograph cards shall meet the security requirements defined in the tachograph cards generic security target (Appendix 10 [*not reproduced in this work*]).

Tachograph cards shall be readable by other equipment such as personal computers.

3. Standards

The tachograph cards shall comply with the following standards: **C1.153**

— ISO/IEC 7810 Identification cards—Physical characteristics,
— ISO/IEC 7816 Identification cards—Integrated circuits with contacts:
   — Part 1: Physical characteristics,
   — Part 2: Dimensions and location of the contacts,
   — Part 3: Electronic signals and transmission protocols,
   — Part 4: Inter-industry commands for interchange,
   — Part 8: Security related inter-industry commands,
— ISO/IEC 10373 Identification cards—Test methods.

4. Environmental and electrical specifications

The tachograph cards shall be capable of operating correctly in all the climatic condi-   **C1.154**
tions normally encountered in Community territory and at least in the temperature range -25 °C to +70 °C with occasional peaks of up to +85 °C, "occasional" meaning not more than 4 hours each time and not over 100 times during the lifetime of the card.

The tachograph cards shall be capable of operating correctly in the humidity range 10% to 90%.

The tachograph cards shall be capable of operating correctly for a five-year period if used within the environmental and electrical specifications.

During operation, the tachograph cards shall conform to Commission Directive 95/ 54/EC of 31 October 1995 [*O.J. No.L266, November 8, 1995, p.1*], related to electromagnetic compatibility, and shall be protected against electrostatic discharges.

5. Data storage

For the purpose of this paragraph,   **C1.155**

— times are recorded with a resolution of one minute, unless otherwise specified,
— odometer values are recorded with a resolution of one kilometre,
— speeds are recorded with a resolution of 1 km/h.

The tachograph cards functions, commands and logical structures, fulfilling data storage requirements are specified in Appendix 2 [*not reproduced in this work*].

This paragraph specifies minimum storage capacity for the various application data files. The tachograph cards shall be able to indicate to the recording equipment the actual storage capacity of these data files.

Any additional data that may be stored on tachograph cards, related to other applications eventually borne by the card, shall be stored in accordance with Directive 95/46/EC of 24

October 1995 on the protection of individuals with regard to the processing of personal data and on the free movement of such data [*O.J. No.L281, November 23, 1995, p.31*].

5.1. *Card identification and security data*

C1.156 5.1.1. Application identification

The tachograph cards shall be able to store the following application identification data:

— tachograph application identification,

— type of tachograph card identification.

5.1.2. Chip identification

The tachograph cards shall be able to store the following integrated circuit (IC) identification data:

— IC serial number,

— IC manufacturing references.

5.1.3. IC card identification

The tachograph cards shall be able to store the following smart card identification data:

— card serial number (including manufacturing references),

— card type approval number,

— card personaliser identification (ID),

— embedder ID,

— IC identifier.

5.1.4. Security elements

The tachograph cards shall be able to store the following security elements data:

— European public key,

— Member State certificate,

— card certificate,

— card private key.

5.2. *Driver card*

C1.157 5.2.1. Card identification

The driver card shall be able to store the following card identification data:

— card number,

— issuing Member State, issuing authority name, issue date,

— card beginning of validity date, card expiry date.

5.2.2. Card holder identification

The driver card shall be able to store the following card holder identification data:

— surname of the holder,

— first name(s) of the holder,

— date of birth,

— preferred language.

5.2.3. Driving licence information

The driver card shall be able to store the following driving licence data:

— issuing Member State, issuing authority name,

— driving licence number (at the date of the issue of the card).

5.2.4. Vehicles used data

The driver card shall be able to store, for each calendar day where the card has been used, and for each period of use of a given vehicle that day (a period of use includes all consecutive insertion/withdrawal cycle of the card in the vehicle, as seen from the card point of view), the following data:

— date and time of first use of the vehicle (i.e. first card insertion for this period of use of the vehicle, or 00.00 if the period of use is on-going at that time),
— vehicle odometer value at that time,
— date and time of last use of the vehicle, (i.e. last card withdrawal for this period of use of the vehicle, or 23.59 if the period of use is on-going at that time),
— vehicle odometer value at that time,
— VRN and registering Member State of the vehicle.

The driver card shall be able to store at least 84 such records.

5.2.5. DRIVER ACTIVITY DATA   **C1.158**

The driver card shall be able to store, for each calendar day where the card has been used or for which the driver has entered activities manually, the following data:

— the date,
— a daily presence counter (increased by one for each of these calendar days),
— the total distance travelled by the driver during this day,
— a driver status at 00.00,
— whenever the driver has changed of activity, and/or has changed of driving status, and/or has inserted or withdrawn his card:
    — the driving status (CREW, SINGLE),
    — the slot (DRIVER, CO-DRIVER),
    — the card status (INSERTED, NOT INSERTED),
    — the activity (DRIVING, AVAILABILITY, WORK, BREAK/REST),
    — the time of the change.

The driver card memory shall be able to hold driver activity data for at least 28 days (the average activity of a driver is defined as 93 activity changes per day).

The data listed under requirements 197 and 199 shall be stored in a way allowing the retrieval of activities in the order of their occurrence, even in case of a time overlap situation.

5.2.6. PLACES WHERE DAILY WORK PERIODS START AND/OR END

The driver card shall be able to store the following data related to places where daily work periods begin and/or end, entered by the driver:

— the date and time of the entry (or the date/time related to the entry if the entry is made during the manual entry procedure),
— the type of entry (begin or end, condition of entry),
— the country and region entered,
— the vehicle odometer value.

The driver card memory shall be able to hold at least 42 pairs of such records.

5.2.7. EVENTS DATA   **C1.159**

For the purpose of this subparagraph, time shall be stored with a resolution of one second.

The driver card shall be able to store data related to the following events detected by the recording equipment while the card was inserted:

— time overlap (where this card is the cause of the event),
— card insertion while driving (where this card is the subject of the event),
— last card session not correctly closed (where this card is the subject of the event),

— power supply interruption,

— motion data error,

— security breach attempts.

The driver card shall be able to store the following data for these events:

— event code,

— date and time of beginning of the event (or of card insertion if the event was on-going at that time),

— date and time of end of the event (or of card withdrawal if the event was on-going at that time),

— VRN and registering Member State of vehicle in which the event happened.

Note: For the "time overlap" event:

— date and time of beginning of the event shall correspond to the date and time of the card withdrawal from the previous vehicle,

— date and time of end of the event shall correspond to the date and time of card insertion in current vehicle,

— vehicle data shall correspond to the current vehicle raising the event.

Note: For the "last card session not correctly closed" event:

— date and time of beginning of event shall correspond to the card insertion date and time of the session not correctly closed,

— date and time of end of event shall correspond to the card insertion date and time of the session during which the event was detected (current session),

— vehicle data shall correspond to the vehicle in which the session was not correctly closed.

The driver card shall be able to store data for the six most recent events of each type (i.e. 36 events).

C1.160 5.2.8. FAULTS DATA

For the purpose of this subparagraph, time shall be recorded with a resolution of one second.

The driver card shall be able to store data related to the following faults detected by the recording equipment while the card was inserted:

— card fault (where this card is the subject of the event),

— recording equipment fault.

The driver card shall be able to store the following data for these faults:

— fault code,

— date and time of beginning of the fault (or of card insertion if the fault was on-going at that time),

— date and time of end of the fault (or of card withdrawal if the fault was on-going at that time),

— VRN and registering Member State of vehicle in which the fault happened.

The driver card shall be able to store data for the twelve most recent faults of each type (i.e. 24 faults).

5.2.9. CONTROL ACTIVITY DATA

The driver card shall be able to store the following data related to control activities:

— date and time of the control,

— control card number and card issuing Member State,

— type of the control (displaying and/or printing and/or VU downloading and/or card downloading (see note)),

— period downloaded, in case of downloading,

— VRN and registering Member State of the vehicle in which the control happened.

Note: security requirements imply that card downloading will only be recorded if performed through a recording equipment.

The driver card shall be able to hold one such record.

5.2.10. CARD SESSION DATA   **C1.161**

The driver card shall be able to store data related to the vehicle which opened its current session:

— date and time the session was opened (i.e. card insertion) with a resolution of one second,

— VRN and registering Member State.

5.2.11. SPECIFIC CONDITIONS DATA

The driver card shall be able to store the following data related to specific conditions entered while the card was inserted (whatever the slot):

— date and time of the entry,

— type of specific condition.

The driver card shall be able to hold 56 such records.

5.3. *Workshop card*

5.3.1. SECURITY ELEMENTS   **C1.162**

The workshop card shall be able to store a personal identification number (PIN code).

The workshop card shall be able to store the cryptographic keys needed for pairing motion sensors to vehicle units.

5.3.2. CARD IDENTIFICATION

The workshop card shall be able to store the following card identification data:

— card number,

— issuing Member State, issuing authority name, issue date,

— card beginning of validity date, card expiry date.

5.3.3. CARD HOLDER IDENTIFICATION

The workshop card shall be able to store the following card holder identification data:

— workshop name,

— workshop address,

— surname of the holder,

— first name(s) of the holder,

— preferred language.

5.3.4. VEHICLES USED DATA

The workshop card shall be able to store vehicles used data records in the same manner as a driver card.

The workshop card shall be able to store at least 4 such records.

5.3.5. DRIVER ACTIVITY DATA

The workshop card shall be able to store driver activity data in the same manner as a driver card.

The workshop card shall be able to hold driver activity data for at least one day of average driver activity.

5.3.6. DAILY WORK PERIODS START AND/OR END DATA   **C1.163**

The workshop card shall be able to store daily works period start and/or end data records in the same manner as a driver card.

The workshop card shall be able to hold at least three pairs of such records.

5.3.7. EVENTS AND FAULTS DATA

The workshop card shall be able to store events and faults data records in the same manner as a driver card.

The workshop card shall be able to store data for the three most recent events of each type (i.e. 18 events) and the six most recent faults of each type (i.e. 12 faults).

5.3.8. CONTROL ACTIVITY DATA

The workshop card shall be able to store a control activity data record in the same manner as a driver card.

5.3.9. CALIBRATION AND TIME ADJUSTMENT DATA

The workshop card shall be able to hold records of calibrations and/or time adjustments performed while the card is inserted in a recording equipment.

Each calibration record shall be able to hold the following data:

— [purpose of calibration (activation, first installation, installation, periodic inspection)],
— vehicle identification,
— parameters updated or confirmed (w, k, l, tyre size, speed limiting device setting, odometer (new and old values), date and time (new and old values),
— recording equipment identification (VU part number, VU serial number, motion sensor serial number).

The workshop card shall be able to store at least 88 such records.

The workshop card shall hold a counter indicating the total number of calibrations performed with the card.

The workshop card shall hold a counter indicating the number of calibrations performed since its last download.

5.3.10. SPECIFIC CONDITIONS DATA

The workshop card shall be able to store data relevant to specific conditions in the same manner as the driver card. The workshop card shall be able to store two such records.

5.4. *Control card*

C1.164 5.4.1. CARD IDENTIFICATION

The control card shall be able to store the following card identification data:

— card number,
— issuing Member State, issuing authority name, issue date,
— card beginning of validity date, card expiry date (if any).

5.4.2. CARD HOLDER IDENTIFICATION

The control card shall be able to store the following card holder identification data:

— control body name,
— control body address,
— surname of the holder,
— first name(s) of the holder,
— preferred language.

5.4.3. CONTROL ACTIVITY DATA

The control card shall be able to store the following control activity data:

— date and time of the control,
— type of the control (displaying and/or printing and/or VU downloading and/or card downloading),

— period downloaded (if any),

— VRN and Member State registering authority of the controlled vehicle,

— card number and card issuing Member State of the driver card controlled.

The control card shall be able to hold at least 230 such records.

5.5. *Company card*

5.5.1. CARD IDENTIFICATION

C1.165

The company card shall be able to store the following card identification data:

— card number,

— issuing Member State, issuing authority name, issue date,

— card beginning of validity date, card expiry date (if any).

5.5.2. CARD HOLDER IDENTIFICATION

The company card shall be able to store the following card holder identification data:

— company name,

— company address.

5.5.3. COMPANY ACTIVITY DATA

The company card shall be able to store the following company activity data:

— date and time of the activity,

— type of the activity (VU locking in and/or out, and/or VU downloading and/or card downloading),

— period downloaded (if any),

— VRN and Member State registering authority of vehicle,

— card number and card issuing Member State (in case of card downloading).

The company card shall be able to hold at least 230 such records.

[Paragraph 5 of Chap.IV to Annex 1B is printed as amended by Regulation **C1.166**
(EC) 432/2004 art.1(2).]

V   Installation of Recording Equipment

1. Installation

New recording equipment shall be delivered non-activated to fitters or vehicle   **C1.167**
manufacturers, with all calibration parameters, as listed in Chapter III(20), set to appropriate and valid default values. Where no particular value is appropriate, literal parameters shall be set to strings of "?" and numeric parameters shall be set to "0". [Delivery of security relevant parts of the recording equipment can be restricted if required during security certification.]

Before its activation, the recording equipment shall give access to the calibration function even if not in calibration mode.

Before its activation, the recording equipment shall neither record nor store data referred by points III.12.3. to III.12.9. and III.12.12 to III.12.14. inclusive.

During installation, vehicle manufacturers shall pre-set all known parameters.

[Vehicle manufacturers or fitters shall activate the installed recording equipment at the latest before the vehicle is used in scope of Regulation (EC) No.561/2006.]

The activation of the recording equipment shall be triggered automatically by the first insertion of a workshop card in either of its card interface devices.

Specific pairing operations required between the motion sensor and the vehicle unit, if any, shall take place automatically before or during activation.

After its activation, the recording equipment shall fully enforce functions and data access rights.

The recording and storing functions of the recording equipment shall be fully operational after its activation.

[Installation shall be followed by a calibration. The first calibration may not necessarily include entry of the vehicle registration number (VRN), when it is not known by the approved workshop having to undertake this calibration. In these circumstances, it shall be possible, for the vehicle owner, and at this time only, to enter the VRN using his Company Card prior to using the vehicle in scope of Regulation (EC) No.561/2006 (e.g by using commands through an appropriate menu structure of the vehicle unit's man-machine interface.) Any update or confirmation of this entry shall only be possible using a Workshop Card.]

The recording equipment must be positioned in the vehicle in such a way as to allow the driver to access the necessary functions from his seat.

2. Installation plaque

C1.168

[After the recording equipment has been checked on installation, an installation plaque which is clearly visible and easily accessible shall be affixed onto the recording equipment. In cases where this is not possible, the plaque shall be affixed to the vehicle's "B" pillar so that it is clearly visible. For vehicles that do not have a "B" pillar, the installation plaque should be affixed to the doorframe on the driver's side of the vehicle and be clearly visible in all cases.

After every inspection by an approved fitter or workshop, a new plaque shall be affixed in place of the previous one.]

[The plaque shall bear at least the following details:

— name, address or trade name of the approved fitter or workshop,
— characteristic coefficient of the vehicle, in the form "w = ... imp/km",
— constant of the recording equipment, in the form "k = ... imp/km",
— effective circumference of the wheel tyres in the form "l = ... mm",
— tyre size,
[— the date on which the characteristic coefficient of the vehicle and the effective circumference of the wheel tyres were measured,]
— the vehicle identification number,
— the part of the vehicle where the adaptor, if any, is installed,
— the part of the vehicle where the motion sensor is installed, if not connected to the gear-box or an adaptor is not being used,
— a description of the colour of the cable between the adaptor and that part of the vehicle providing its incoming impulses,
— the serial number of the embedded motion sensor of the adaptor.]

[For M1 and N1 vehicles only, and which are fitted with an adaptor in conformity with Regulation (EC) No.68/2009, and where it is not possible to include all the information necessary, as described in Requirement 250 [*Annex IB, Chap.V, para.2, second sub-paragraph*], a second, additional, plaque may be used. In such cases, this additional plaque shall contain at least the last four indents described in Requirement 250 [*Annex IB, Chap.V, para.2, second sub-paragraph above*].

This second, additional plaque, if used, shall be affixed next to or beside the first primary plaque described in Requirement 250 [*Annex IB, Chap.V, para.2, second sub-paragraph*], and shall have the same protection level. Furthermore the secondary plaque shall also bear the name, address or trade name of the approved fitter or workshop that carried out the installation, and the date of installation.]

[— Installation plaques for vehicles equipped with adaptors, or for vehicles where the motion sensor is not connected to the gear-box shall be fitted at the time of installation. For all other vehicles, installation plaques bearing the new information shall be fitted at the time of inspection following the installation.]

3. Sealing

The following part shall be sealed:

C1.169

— any connection which, if disconnected, would cause undetectable alterations to be made or undetectable data loss,

— the installation plaque, unless it is attached in such a way that it cannot be removed without the markings thereon being destroyed.

The seals mentioned above may be removed:

— in case of emergency,

— to install, to adjust or to repair a speed limitation device or any other device contributing to road safety, provided that the recording equipment continues to function reliably and correctly and is resealed by an approved fitter or workshop (in accordance with Chapter VI) immediately after fitting the speed limitation device or any other device contributing to road safety or within seven days in other cases.

On each occasion that these seals are broken a written statement giving the reasons for such action shall be prepared and made available to the competent authority.

[*Chapter V to Annex 1B is printed as amended by Regulation (EC) 68/2009;* **C1.170** *Regulation (EU) 1266/2009.*]

VI Checks, Inspections and Repairs

Requirements on the circumstances in which seals may be removed, as referred to in Article 12.5 of Regulation (EEC) No. 3821/85 as last amended by Regulation (EC) No. 2135/98, are defined in Chapter V(3) of this annex.

C1.171

1. Approval of fitters or workshops

The Member States will approve, regularly control and certify the bodies to carry out:

C1.172

— installations,

— checks,

— inspections,

— repairs.

In the framework of Article 12(1) of this Regulation, workshop cards will be issued only to fitters and/or workshops approved for the activation and/or the calibration of recording equipment in conformity with this annex and, unless duly justified:

— who are not eligible for a company card,

— and whose other professional activities do not present a potential compromise of the overall security of the system as defined in Appendix 10 [*not reproduced in this work*].

2. Check of new or repaired instruments

Every individual device, whether new or repaired, shall be checked in respect of its proper operation and the accuracy of its reading and recordings, within the limits laid down in Chapter III.2.1. and III.2.2 by means of sealing in accordance with Chapter V.3. and calibration.

C1.173

3. Installation inspection

When being fitted to a vehicle, the whole installation (including the recording equipment) shall comply with the provisions relating to maximum tolerances laid down in Chapter III.2.1 and III.2.2.

C1.174

4. Periodic inspections

Periodic inspections of the equipment fitted to the vehicles shall take place after any

C1.175

repair of the equipment, or after any alteration of the characteristic coefficient of the vehicle or of the effective circumference of the tyres, or after equipment UTC time is wrong by more than 20 minutes, or when the VRN has changed, and at least once within two years (24 months) of the last inspection.

These inspections shall include the following checks:

— that the recording equipment is working properly, including the data storage in tachograph cards function,

— that compliance with the provisions of Chapter III.2.1 and III.2.2 on the maximum tolerances on installation is ensured,

— that the recording equipment carries the type approval mark,

[— that the installation plaque, as defined by Requirement 250 [*Annex IB, Chap.V, para.2, second sub-paragraph*], and the descriptive plaque, as defined by Requirement 169 [*Annex IB, Chap.III, para.24, second sub-paragraph*], are affixed,]

[— that there are no manipulation devices attached to the equipment,]

— that the seals on the equipment and on the other parts of the installation are intact,

— the tyre size and the actual circumference of the wheel tyres.

[If one of the events listed in Chapter III Section 9 (Detection of Events and/or Faults) is found to have occurred since the last inspection and is considered by tachograph manufacturers and/or national authorities as potentially putting the security of the equipment at risk, the workshop shall:

(a) make a comparison between the motion sensor identification data of the motion sensor plugged into the gearbox with that of the paired motion sensor registered in the vehicle unit;

(b) check if the information recorded on the installation plaque matches with the information contained within the vehicle unit record;

(c) by checking if the motion sensor serial number and approval number, if printed on the body of the motion sensor, matches the information contained within the vehicle unit record.]

[Workshops shall keep traces in their inspection reports of any findings concerning broken seals or manipulations devices. These reports shall be kept by workshops for at least two years and made available to the Competent Authority whenever requested to do so.]

These inspections shall include a calibration.

5. Measurement of errors

C1.176   The measurement of errors on installation and during use shall be carried out under the following conditions, which are to be regarded as constituting standard test conditions:

— vehicle unladen, in normal running order,

— tyre pressures in accordance with the manufacturer's instructions,

— tyre wear, within the limits allowed by national law,

— vehicle movement:

— the vehicle shall advance under its own engine power in a straight line on level ground and at a speed of 50 ± 5 km/h. The measuring distance shall be at least 1 000 m,

— provided that it is of comparable accuracy, alternative methods, such as a suitable test bench, may also be used for the test.

6. Repairs

C1.177   Workshops shall be able to download data from the recording equipment to give the data back to the appropriate transport company.

Approved workshops shall issue to transport companies a certificate of data un-downloadability where the malfunction of the recording equipment prevents previously recorded data to be downloaded, even after repair by this workshop. The workshops will keep a copy of each issued certificate for at least one year.

[Chapter VI to Annex IB is printed as amended by Regulation (EU) 1266/ **C1.178**
2009.]

VII   Card Issuing

The card issuing processes set-up by the Member States shall conform to the following: **C1.179**

The card number of the first issue of a tachograph card to an applicant shall have a con-secutive index (if applicable) and a replacement index and a renewal index set to "0".

The card numbers of all non-personal tachograph cards issued to a single control body or a single workshop or a single transport company shall have the same first 13 digits, and shall all have a different consecutive index.

A tachograph card issued in replacement of an existing tachograph card shall have the same card number as the replaced one except the replacement index which shall be raised by "1" (in the order 0,..., 9, A,..., Z).

A tachograph card issued in replacement of an existing tachograph card shall have the same card expiry date as the replaced one.

A tachograph card issued in renewal of an existing tachograph card shall have the same card number as the renewed one except the replacement index which shall be reset to "0" and the renewal index which shall be raised by "1" (in the order 0,..., 9, A,..., Z).

The exchange of an existing tachograph card, in order to modify administrative data, shall follow the rules of the renewal if within the same Member State, or the rules of a first issue if performed by another Member State.

The "card holder surname" for non-personal workshop or control cards shall be filled with workshop or control body name.

[Member States shall exchange data electronically in order to ensure the uniqueness of the tachograph Driver Card that they issue.

The competent authorities of Member States may also exchange data electronically when carrying out checks of driver cards at the roadside or at company premises in order to verify the uniqueness and status of the cards.]

VIII   Type Approval of Recording Equipment and Tachograph Cards

1.   General points

For the purpose of this chapter, the words *"recording equipment"* mean "recording   **C1.180**
equipment or its components". No type approval is required for the cable(s) linking the motion sensor to the VU. The paper, for use by the recording equipment, shall be considered as a component of the recording equipment. [Any vehicle unit manufacturer may ask for type approval of its component with any type of motion sensor, and vice versa, provided each component complies with Requirement 001a [*Annex IB, Chap.II, para.1, third sub-paragraph*].

Recording equipment shall be submitted for approval complete with any integrated ad-ditional devices.

Type approval of recording equipment and of tachograph cards shall include security re-lated tests, functional tests and interoperability tests. Positive results to each of these tests are stated by an appropriate certificate.

Member States type approval authorities will not grant a type approval certificate in ac-cordance with Article 5 of this Regulation, as long as they do not hold:

— a security certificate,

— a functional certificate,

— and an interoperability certificate,

for the recording equipment or the tachograph card, subject of the request for type approval.

Any modification in software or hardware of the equipment or in the nature of materials used for its manufacture shall, before being used, be notified to the authority which granted type approval for the equipment. This authority shall confirm to the manufacturer the extension of the type approval, or may require an update or a confirmation of the relevant functional, security and/or interoperability certificates.

Procedures to upgrade in situ recording equipment software shall be approved by the authority which granted type approval for the recording equipment. Software upgrade must not alter nor delete any driver activity data stored in the recording equipment. Software may be upgraded only under the responsibility of the equipment manufacturer.

2. Security certificate

C1.181   The security certificate is delivered in accordance with the provisions of Appendix 10 [*not reproduced in this work*] to this Annex.

[In the exceptional circumstance that the security certification authorities refuse to certify new equipment on the grounds of obsolescence of the security mechanisms, type approval shall continue to be granted only in this specific and exceptional circumstance, and when no alternative solution, compliant with the Regulation, exists.]

[In this circumstance the Member State concerned shall, without delay, inform the European Commission, which shall, within twelve calendar months of the grant of type approval, launch a procedure to ensure that the level of security is restored to its original levels.]

3. Functional certificate

C1.182   Each candidate for type approval shall provide the Member State's type approval authority with all the material and documentation that the authority deems necessary.

[Manufacturers shall provide the relevant samples of type approved products and associated documentation required by laboratories appointed to perform functional tests, and within one month of the request being made. Any costs resulting from this request shall be borne by the requesting entity. Laboratories shall treat all commercially sensitive information in confidence.]

A functional certificate shall be delivered to the manufacturer only after all functional tests specified in Appendix 9 [*not reproduced in this work*], at least, have been successfully passed.

The type approval authority delivers the functional certificate. This certificate shall indicate, in addition to the name of its beneficiary and the identification of the model, a detailed list of the tests performed and the results obtained.

[The functional certificate of any recording equipment component shall also indicate the type approval numbers of all other type approved compatible recording equipment components.]

4. Interoperability certificate

C1.183   Interoperability tests are carried out by a single laboratory under the authority and responsibility of the European Commission.

The laboratory shall register interoperability test requests introduced by manufacturers in the chronological order of their arrival.

Requests will be officially registered only when the laboratory is in possession of:

— the entire set of material and documents necessary for such interoperability tests,

— the corresponding security certificate,

— the corresponding functional certificate,

The date of the registration of the request shall be notified to the manufacturer.

[No interoperability tests shall be carried out by the laboratory for recording equipment or tachograph cards that have not been granted a security certificate and a functionality certificate, except in the exceptional circumstances described in Requirement 274a [*Annex IB, Chap.VIII, para.2, second sub-paragraph*].]

Any manufacturer requesting interoperability tests shall commit to leave to the laboratory in charge of these tests the entire set of material and documents which he provided to carry out the tests.

The interoperability tests shall be carried out, in accordance with the provisions of paragraph 5 of Appendix 9 [*not reproduced in this work*] of this Annex, with respectively all the types of recording equipment or tachograph cards:

— for which type approval is still valid, or

— for which type approval is pending and that have a valid interoperability certificate.

The interoperability certificate shall be delivered by the laboratory to the manufacturer only after all required interoperability tests have been successfully passed.

If the interoperability tests are not successful with one or more of the recording equipment or tachograph card(s), as requested by requirement 283, the interoperability certificate shall not be delivered, until the requesting manufacturer has realised the necessary modifications and has succeeded with the interoperability tests. The laboratory shall identify the cause of the problem with the help of the manufacturers concerned by this interoperability fault and shall attempt to help the requesting manufacturer in finding a technical solution. In the case where the manufacturer has modified its product, it is the manufacturer's responsibility to ascertain from the relevant authorities that the security certificate and the functional certificates are still valid.

The interoperability certificate is valid for six months. It is revoked at the end of this period if the manufacturer has not received a corresponding type approval certificate. It is forwarded by the manufacturer to the type approval authority of the Member State who has delivered the functional certificate.

Any element that could be at the origin of an interoperability fault shall not be used for profit or to lead to a dominant position.

5. Type approval certificate

The type approval authority of the Member State may deliver the type approval certificate as soon as it holds the three required certificates.   **C1.184**

The type approval certificate shall be copied by the type approval authority to the laboratory in charge of the interoperability tests at the time of deliverance to the manufacturer.

The laboratory competent for interoperability tests shall run a public website on which will be updated the list of recording equipment or tachograph cards models:

— for which a request for interoperability tests has been registered,

— having received an interoperability certificate (even provisional),

— having received a type approval certificate.

6. Exceptional procedure: first interoperability certificates

Until four months after a first couple of recording equipment and tachograph cards (driver, workshop, control and company cards) have been certified to be interoperable, any interoperability certificate delivered (including this very first one), regarding requests registered during this period, shall be considered provisional.   **C1.185**

If at the end of this period, all products concerned are mutually interoperable, all corresponding interoperability certificates shall become definitive.

If during this period, interoperability faults are found, the laboratory in charge of interoperability tests shall identify the causes of the problems with the help of all manufacturers involved and shall invite them to realise the necessary modifications.

If at the end of this period, interoperability problems still remain, the laboratory in charge of interoperability tests, with the collaboration of the manufacturers concerned and with the type approval authorities who delivered the corresponding functional certificates shall find out the causes of the interoperability faults and establish which modifications should be made by each of the manufacturers concerned. The search for technical solutions shall last for a maximum of two months, after which, if no common solution is found, the Commission, after having consulted the laboratory in charge of interoperability tests, shall decide which equipment(s) and cards get a definitive interoperability certificate and state the reasons why.

Any request for interoperability tests, registered by the laboratory between the end of the four-month period after the first provisional interoperability certificate has been delivered and the date of the decision by the Commission referred to in requirement 294, shall be postponed until the initial interoperability problems have been solved. Those requests are then processed in the chronological order of their registration.

C1.186   *[Chapter VIII to Annex IB is printed as amended by Regulation (EU) 1266/ 2009.]*

C1.187
Appendix 1.	Data dictionary *[Omitted.]*
Appendix 2.	Tachograph cards specification *[Omitted.]*
Appendix 3.	Pictograms *[Omitted.]*
Appendix 4.	Printouts *[Omitted.]*
Appendix 5.	Display *[Omitted.]*
Appendix 6.	External interface *[Omitted.]*
Appendix 7.	Data downloading protocol *[Omitted.]*
Appendix 8.	Calibration protocol *[Omitted.]*
Appendix 9.	Type approval—List of minimum required targets *[Omitted.]*
Appendix 10.	Generic security targets *[Omitted.]*
Appendix 11.	Common security mechanisms *[Omitted.]*]
[Appendix 12.	Adaptor for M1 and N1 category vehicles *[Omitted.]*]

C1.188   *[Annex 1B was inserted by Regulation (EC) 1360/2002.]*

ANNEX II

Approval Mark and Certificate

I   Approval Mark

C1.189   1. The approval mark shall be made up of:

— a rectangle, within which shall be placed the letter "e" followed by a distinguishing number or letter for the country which has issued the approval in accordance with the following conventional signs:

[Belgium	6,
[Bulgaria	34]
Czech Republic	8,
Denmark	18,
Germany	1,
Estonia	29,
Greece	23,

Spain	9,
France	2,
Ireland	24,
Italy	3,
Cyprus	CY,
Latvia	32,
Lithuania	36,
Luxembourg	13,
Hungary	7,
Malta	MT,
Netherlands	4,
Austria	12,
Poland	20,
Portugal	21,
[Romania	19]
Slovenia	26,
Slovakia	27,
Finland	17,
Sweden	5,
United Kingdom	11,]

and

— an approval number corresponding to the number of the approval certificate drawn up for prototype of the recording equipment or the record sheet [or of a tachograph card], placed at any point within the immediate proximity of this rectangle.

[Paragraph 1 of Annex II is printed as amended by the Act of Accession **C1.190** *(Austria, Finland, Sweden), Annex I; Regulation (EC) 1360/2002 and by the Act of Accession of the Czech Republic, the Republic of Estonia, the Republic of Cyprus, the Republic of Latvia, the Republic of Lithuania, the Republic of Hungary, the Republic of Malta, the Republic of Poland, the Republic of Slovenia and the Slovak Republic to the European Union, Annex II, with effect from May 12, 2004; Regulation (EC) 1791/2006.]*

2. The approval mark shall be shown on the descriptive plaque of each set of equip-   **C1.191**
ment and on each record sheet [and on each tachograph card]. It must be indelible and must always remain clearly legible.

[Paragraph 2 is printed as amended by Regulation (EC) 1360/2002.]   **C1.192**

3. The dimensions of the approval mark drawn below are expressed in millimetres,   **C1.193**
these dimensions being minima. The ratios between the dimensions must be maintained.

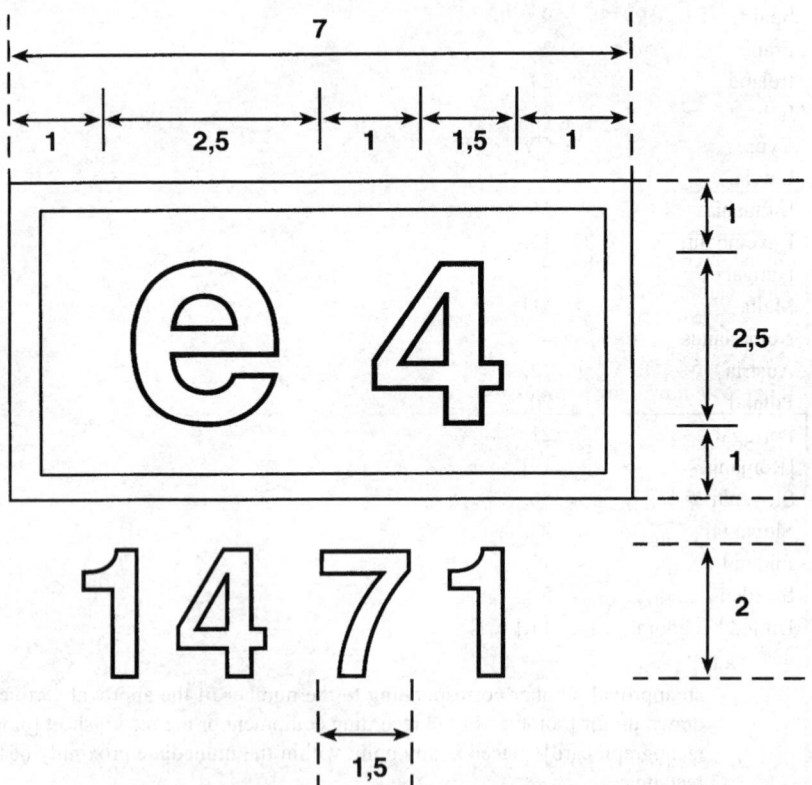

[The characters "e 4" and "1471" are stated to be for guidance only.]

II   Approval Certificate [for Products Compliant with Annex I]

A State having granted approval shall issue the applicant with an approval certificate,   **C1.194**
the model for which is given below. When informing other Member States of approvals issued or, if the occasion should arise, withdrawn, a Member State shall use copies of that
certificate.

APPROVAL CERTIFICATE

Name of competent administration ....
Notification concerning [*the items which are not applicable should be deleted*]:
— approval of a type of recording equipment
— withdrawal of approval of a type of recording equipment
— approval of a model record sheet
— withdrawal of approval of a record sheet

....
                                                    Approval No ....

1.   Trade mark or name ....
2.   Name of type or model..
3.   Name of manufacturer ....
4.   Address of manufacturer ....
      ....
5.   Submitted for approval on ....
6.   Tested at..
7.   Date and number of test report ....
8.   Date of approval...
9.   Date of withdrawal of approval...
10.   Type or types of recording equipment in which sheet is designed to be used
      ....
11.   Place..
12.   Date...
13.   Descriptive documents annexed ....

14.   Remarks..
      ....
                                                    (Signature)

[The heading to Chap.II is printed as amended by Regulation (EC) 1360/   **C1.195**
2002.]

[III   Approval Certificate for Products Compliant with Annex IB

C1.196   A State, having granted approval, shall issue the applicant with an approval certificate, the model of which is given below. When informing other Member States of approvals issued or, if the occasion should arise, withdrawn, a Member State shall use copies of that certificate.

APPROVAL CERTIFICATE FOR PRODUCTS COMPLIANT WITH ANNEX I B

Name of competent administration ....

Notification concerning (3):

☐ approval of

☐ withdrawal of approval of

☐ recording equipment model

☐ recording equipment component (4) ....

☐ a driver's card

☐ a workshop card

☐ a company card

☐ a controller's card

Approval No ....

1. Manufacturing brand or trademark ....

2. Name of model ....

3. Name of manufacturer ....

4. Address of manufacturer ....

5. Submitted for approval for ....

6. Laboratory(ies) ....

7. Date and number of the test(s) ....

8. Date of approval ....

9. Date of withdrawal of approval ....

10. Model of recording equipment component(s) with which the component is designed to be used

11. Place ....

12. Date ....

13. Descriptive documents annexed ....

---

14. Remarks (including the position of seals if applicable)

....
(signature)

---

(3) Tick the relevant boxes.
(4) Specify the component dealt with in the notification.'

C1.197   *[Chapter III to Annex II was inserted by Regulation (EC) 1360/2002.]*

Directive 91/439/EEC of July 29, 1991 on driving licences

[Only selected provisions of this Directive (which have been incorporated into **C2.01**
the provisions of the Convention on driving disqualifications below) are
reproduced. The full text of the Directive (as originally adopted) is reproduced at
O.J. No.L237, August 24, 1991, pp.1–24.

Directive 91/439/EEC will be repealed with effect from January 19, 2013 by
Directive 2006/126/EC (O.J. No.L403, December 30, 2006, pp.18–60). For
selected provisions of the 2006 Directive, § C11.01 below.]

*   *   *

ARTICLE 3

1. ...   **C2.02**

2. *[Omitted.]*

3. ...

— *"Motor vehicle"* means any power-driven vehicle, other than a motorcycle, which is normally used for carrying persons or goods by road or for drawing, on the road, vehicles used for the carriage of persons or goods. This term shall include trolleybuses, i.e. vehicles connected to an electric conductor and not rail-borne. It shall not include agricultural or forestry tractors;

...

*   *   *

ARTICLE 9

For the purpose of this Directive, *"normal"* residence means the place where a **C2.03** person usually lives, that is for at least 185 days in each calendar year, because of personal and occupational ties, or, in the case of a person with no occupational ties, because of personal ties which show close links between that person and the place where he is living.

However, the normal residence of a person whose occupational ties are in a different place from his personal ties and who consequently lives in turn in different places situated in two or more Member States shall be regarded as being the place of his personal ties, provided that such person returns there regularly. This last condition need not be met where the person is living in a Member State in order to carry out a task of a definite duration. Attendance at a university or school shall not imply transfer of normal residence.

Directive 92/6/EEC of February 10, 1992 on the installation and use of speed limitation devices for certain categories of motor vehicles in the Community

C3.01 *THE COUNCIL OF THE EUROPEAN COMMUNITIES,*

Having regard to the Treaty establishing the European Economic Community, and in particular [Article 71] thereof,

Having regard to the proposal from the Commission,

Having regard to the opinion of the European Parliament,

Having regard to the opinion of the Economic and Social Committee,

Whereas one of the objectives of a common transport policy is to lay down common rules applicable to international transport within the Community and to facilitate the circulation of vehicles;

Whereas the growth of road traffic and the resulting increase in danger and nuisance present all Member States with road safety and environmental problems of a serious nature;

Whereas the available engine power for heavy goods vehicles and buses needed for climbing slopes enables them to be driven on level roads at excessive speeds that are not compatible with the specifications of other components of those vehicles such as brakes and tyres; whereas, for that reason and for reasons of environmental protection in certain Member States, speed limitation devices were made compulsory for certain categories of motor vehicles;

Whereas the beneficial effects of speed limitation devices with regard to protection of the environment and energy consumption, the wear and tear of the motor and tyres and road safety will be increased if such devices are in general use;

Whereas the use of speed limitation devices serves no purpose unless the appliances are of a degree of technical perfection such as will provide an adequate guarantee that no fraud is possible;

Whereas, as a first step, requirements should be introduced in the case only of the heaviest categories of motor vehicles which are most involved in international transport and thereafter, depending on technical possibilities and experiences in Member States, could be extended to lighter categories of motor vehicles;

Whereas, in certain Member States, vehicles intended exclusively for the carriage of dangerous goods must be equipped with speed limitation devices set at maximum speeds lower than those provided for by this Directive; whereas, in this specific case, the Member States in question should be allowed to maintain such regulations for vehicles registered within their territory because they enhance road safety and civil protection of the public, in accordance with the objectives of this Directive;

Whereas the installation of speed limitation devices on category M3 and N3 vehicles covered by this Directive, registered before it is brought into effect and intended exclusively for national transport operations could entail excessive costs in certain Member States; whereas it should therefore be made possible for those Member States to postpone the application of Articles 2 and 3 of this Directive to the vehicles concerned;

Whereas this Directive does not affect Member States' prerogatives as regards speed restriction provisions for traffic,

[The preamble is printed as amended by the Treaty of Amsterdam art.12(1)   **C3.02**
and (3).]

HAS ADOPTED THIS DIRECTIVE:

[This Directive is implemented by reg.36B of the Road Vehicles (Construction   **C3.03**
and Use) Regulations 1986 (SI 1986/1078), q.v. For the purposes of reg.36B, the term "set" in relation to a speed limiter has the meaning attributed to it in this Directive and the references in reg.36B to the speed at which a speed limiter is set are construed accordingly (reg.36B(15)).

The text of this Directive is printed as amended by:
    Directive 2002/85/EC of the European Parliament and of the Council (O.J. No.L327, December 4, 2002, p.8) (December 4, 2002).
The amending Directive is referred to in the notes to the principal Directive only by its reference number. The date referred to above is the date on which the amending Directive came into force.]

[ARTICLE 1

For the purpose of this Directive, *"motor vehicle"* means any power-driven   **C3.04**
vehicle falling within category M2, M3, N2 or N3, intended for use on the road and having at least four wheels and a maximum design speed exceeding 25 km/h.

Categories M2, M3, N2 and N3 shall be understood to be those defined in Annex II to Directive 70/156/EEC [*O.J. No.L42, February 23, 1970, p.1, as amended*]].

[Article 1 is printed as substituted by Directive 2002/85/EC.   **C3.05**
With effect from April 29, 2009, Directive 70/156/EEC (O.J. No.L42, February 23, 1970, p.1) referred to above was repealed by Directive 2007/46/EC (O.J. No.L263, October 9, 2007, p.1). The categories of vehicle are now set out in Annex II of the 2007 Directive.]

[ARTICLE 2

Member States shall take the necessary measures to ensure that motor vehicles   **C3.06**
of categories M2 and M3 referred to in Article 1 1 may be used on the road only if equipped with a speed limitation device set in such a way that their speed cannot exceed 100 kilometres per hour.

Category M3 vehicles registered before 1 January 2005 with a maximum mass exceeding 10 tonnes may continue to be equipped with devices on which the maximum speed is set at 100 kilometres per hour.]

[Article 2 is printed as substituted by Directive 2002/85/EC.]   **C3.07**

[ARTICLE 3

C3.08
1. Member States shall take the necessary measures to ensure that motor vehicles of categories N2 and N3 may be used on the road only if equipped with a speed limitation device set in such a way that their speed cannot exceed 90 kilometres per hour.

2. Member States shall be authorised to require that the speed limitation device in vehicles registered in their territory and used exclusively for the transport of dangerous goods is set in such a way that those vehicles cannot exceed a maximum speed of less than 90 kilometres per hour.]

C3.09   *[Article 3 is printed as substituted by Directive 2002/85/EC.]*

[ARTICLE 4

C3.10
1. For motor vehicles of category M3 having a maximum mass of more than 10 tonnes and motor vehicles of category N3, Articles 2 and 3 shall be applied:

   (a) to vehicles registered as from 1 January 1994, from 1 January 1994;

   (b) to vehicles registered between 1 January 1988 and 1 January 1994:

      (i) from 1 January 1995, in the case of vehicles used for both national and international transport;

      (ii) from 1 January 1996, in the case of vehicles used exclusively for national transport.

2. For motor vehicles of category M2, vehicles of category M3 having a maximum mass of more than 5 tonnes but not exceeding 10 tonnes and vehicles of category N2, Articles 2 and 3 shall apply at the latest:

   (a) to vehicles registered as from 1 January 2005;

   (b) to vehicles complying with the limit values set out in Directive 88/77/EEC [*O.J. No.L36, February 9, 1988, p.33, as amended*] registered between 1 October 2001 and 1 January 2005:

      (i) from 1 January 2006 in the case of vehicles used for both national and international transport operations;

      (ii) from 1 January 2007 in the case of vehicles used solely for national transport operations.

3. For a period of no more than three years from 1 January 2005, any Member State may exempt from the provisions of Articles 2 and 3 category M2 vehicles and category N2 vehicles with a maximum mass of more than 3,5 tonnes but not exceeding 7,5 tonnes, registered in the national register and not travelling on the territory of another Member State.]

C3.11   *[Article 4 is printed as substituted by Directive 2002/85/EC.]*

[ARTICLE 5

C3.12
1. The speed limitation devices referred to in Articles 2 and 3 must satisfy the technical requirements laid down in the Annex to Directive 92/24/EEC [*O.J. No.L129, May 14, 1992, p.154*]. However, all vehicles covered by this Directive and registered before 1 January 2005 may continue to be equipped with speed limitation devices which satisfy the technical requirements laid down by the competent national authorities.

2. Speed limitation devices shall be installed by workshops or bodies approved by the Member States.]

[Article 5 is printed as substituted by Directive 2002/85/EC.]   **C3.13**

ARTICLE 6

The requirements of Articles 2 and 3 do not apply to motor vehicles used by   **C3.14**
armed forces, civil defence, fire and other emergency services and forces
responsible for maintaining public order.

The same shall apply for motor vehicles which:

— by their construction, cannot drive faster than the limits provided for in
Articles 2 and 3,
— are used for scientific tests on roads,
— are used only for public services in urban areas.

[ARTICLE 6A

As part of the road safety action programme for the period 2002 to 2010, the   **C3.15**
Commission shall assess the road safety and road traffic implications of adjusting
the speed limitation devices used by category M2 vehicles and by category N2
vehicles with a maximum mass of 7,5 tonnes or less to the speeds laid down by
this Directive.

If necessary, the Commission shall submit appropriate proposals.]

[Article 6A was inserted by Directive 2002/85/EC.]   **C3.16**

ARTICLE 7

1. Member States shall bring into force the laws, regulations and administra-   **C3.17**
   tive provisions necessary to comply with this Directive before 1 October
   1993. They shall immediately inform the Commission thereof.

   When these provisions are adopted by Member States, they shall contain
   a reference to this Directive or shall be accompanied by such reference at
   the time of their official publication. The procedure for making such reference shall be adopted by Member States.

2. Member States shall communicate to the Commission the text of the provisions of national law which they adopt in the field covered by this Directive.

ARTICLE 8

This Directive is addressed to the Member States.   **C3.18**

Council Directive 96/53/EC of July 25, 1996 laying down for certain road vehicles circulating within the Community the maximum authorised dimensions in national and international traffic and the maximum authorised weights in international traffic

C4.01   *THE COUNCIL OF THE EUROPEAN UNION,*

Having regard to the Treaty establishing the European Community, and in particular [Article 71] thereof,

Having regard to the proposal from the Commission,

Having regard to the opinion of the Economic and Social Committee,

Acting in accordance with the procedure laid down in [Article 252] of the Treaty,

(1) Whereas Council Directive 85/3/EEC of 19 December 1984 on the weights, dimensions and certain other technical characteristics of certain road vehicles [O.J. No.L2, January 3, 1985, p.14] established, in the framework of the common transport policy, common standards permitting improved use of road vehicles in traffic between Member States;

(2) Whereas Directive 85/3/EEC has been significantly amended on many occasions; whereas on the occasion of its further amendment it should for reasons of clarity and rationality be recast in a single text together with Council Directive 86/364/EEC of 24 July 1986 [O.J. No.L221, August 7, 1986, p.48] relating to proof of compliance of vehicles with Directive 85/3/EEC;

(3) Whereas differences between standards in force in the Member States with regard to the weights and dimensions of commercial road vehicles could have an adverse effect on the conditions of competition and constitute an obstacle to traffic between Member States;

(4) Whereas, under the principle of subsidiarity, action should be taken at Community level in order to remove this obstacle;

(5) Whereas the above-mentioned standards reflect a balance between the rational and economical use of commercial road vehicles and the requirements of infrastructure maintenance, road safety and the protection of the environment and the fabric of life;

(6) Whereas common standards on the dimensions of vehicles intended for the carriage of goods should remain stable in the long term;

(7) Whereas additional technical requirements related to the weights and dimensions of vehicles may apply to commercial vehicles registered or put into circulation in a Member State; whereas these requirements must not constitute an obstacle to the circulation of commercial vehicles between Member States;

(8) Whereas the definition of "thick-walled refrigerated vehicle" in Article 2 of Directive 85/3/EEC, as amended by Directive 89/388/EEC [O.J. No.L142,

May 25, 1989, p.3] , should be broadened in order to permit Member States to allow refrigerated vehicles no longer meeting the insulation requirements defined in that Article to circulate in their territory;

(9) Whereas its is necessary to clarify the concept of "indivisible load" in order to ensure uniform application of this Directive in respect of permits for vehicles or vehicle combinations carrying such loads;

(10) Whereas the tonne is universally used and understood as the unit of measurement for vehicle weight and is, therefore, applied in this Directive whilst recognising that the formal unit of weight is the newton;

(11) Whereas, in implementation of the internal market, the scope of this Directive should be extended to national transport insofar as it concerns characteristics that significantly affect the conditions of competition in the transport sector and in particular the values relating to the maximum authorised length and width of vehicles and vehicle combinations intended for the carriage of goods;

(12) Whereas, for the other vehicle characteristics, Member States are authorised to apply in their territory different values from those laid down in this Directive only to vehicles used in national traffic;

(13) Whereas road trains using extensible coupling systems in practice attain a maximum length of 18,75m when fully extended; whereas the same maximum length should be authorised for road trains using fixed coupling systems;

(14) Whereas they maximum authorised width of 2,50m for vehicles intended for the carriage of goods can leave insufficient internal space for the efficient loading of pallets, which has given rise to the application of different tolerances beyond that level in the legislation of the Member States concerning domestic traffic; whereas a general adaptation to the current situation is therefore necessary in order to provide for clarity in technical requirements, bearing in mind the road safety aspects of these characteristics;

(15) Whereas if the maximum width of vehicles intended for the carriage of goods is increased to 2,55m, that standard should also be applied to buses; whereas, in respect of buses, it is however necessary to provide for a transitional period to allow the manufacturers concerned to adapt industrial plant;

(16) Whereas, to prevent excessive road damage and to ensure manoeuvrability, when authorising and using vehicles preference should be given to pneumatic or equivalent suspension rather than mechanical suspension; whereas certain maximum axle loads should not be exceeded, and the vehicle must be capable of turning though 360° within certain limit values for the path followed;

(17) Whereas Member States should be permitted, in national goods transport, to allow vehicles or vehicle combinations with dimensions deviating from those laid down in this Directive to circulate in their territory if the transport operations carried out by such vehicles are defined by this Directive as not significantly affecting international competition in the transport sector, i.e. operations carried out by specialised vehicles and operations carried out according to a modular concept;

(18) Whereas, in the case of modular concept operations, there should be

provision for a transitional period to enable a Member State to adapt its road infrastructure;

(19) Whereas vehicles or vehicle combinations constructed applying new technologies or new concepts, according to standards which deviate from those laid down by this Directive, should be allowed to carry out local transport operations for a trial period to enable profit to be drawn from technical progress;

(20) Whereas vehicles which entered into service before the date of implementation of this Directive and which do not comply with the dimension characteristics laid down in this Directive, owing to previously differing national provisions or methods of measurement, should be allowed for a transitional period to continue to provide transport services within the Member State in which the vehicle is registered or put into circulation;

(21) Whereas progress has been made towards adopting Type-Approval Directives for vehicle combinations with five or six axles; whereas, the requirements regarding conformity with characteristics other than weights and dimensions as laid down in Annex II of Directive 85/3/EEC should therefore be deleted;

(22) Whereas such a modification is also necessary in order to avoid rules conflicting with international conventions on road traffic and circulation;

(23) Whereas in order to facilitate the monitoring of compliance with this Directive, it is necessary to ensure that vehicles carry proof of such compliance;

(24) Whereas this Directive does not affect the obligations of the Member States concerning the deadlines for transposition into national law and for application of the Directives which this Directive replaces,

C4.02   *[The preamble is printed as amended by the Treaty of Amsterdam art.12(1) and (3).]*

HAS ADOPTED THIS DIRECTIVE:

C4.03   *[The provisions of Directive 96/53/EC are incorporated into various provisions of English law, e.g. the Road Vehicles (Construction and Use) Regulations 1986 (SI 1986/1078) reg.70B and Sch.11A, para.8A.*

The text of this Directive has been amended by:
     Directive 2002/7/EC of the European Parliament and the Council (O.J. No.L67, March 9, 2002, p.47) (March 9, 2002).

The amending Directive is referred to in the notes to the principal Directive only by its reference number. The date referred to above is the date on which the amending Directive came into force.]

ARTICLE 1

C4.04   1. This Directive applies to:

     [(a) the dimensions of motor vehicles in categories M2 and M3 and their trailers in category 0 and motor vehicles in categories N2 and N3 and their trailers in categories 03 and 04, as defined in Annex II to Council Directive 70/156/EEC of 6 February 1970 on the approximation of the laws of the Member States relating to the type approval of motor vehicles and their trailers;]

(b) the weights and certain other characteristics of the vehicles defined in (a) and specified in Annex I (2) to this Directive.

2. All the values of weights indicated in Annex I are valid as circulation standards and thus refer to loading conditions, not production standards, which will be defined in a later Directive.

[3. This Directive shall not apply to articulated buses comprising more than one articulated section.]

[Article 1 is printed as amended by Directive 2002/7/EC.   **C4.05**

With effect from April 29, 2009, Directive 70/156/EEC (O.J. No.L42, February 23, 1970, p.1) referred to in para.(a) above was repealed by Directive 2007/46/EC (O.J. No.L263, October 9, 2007, p.1). The categories of vehicle are now set out in Annex II of the 2007 Directive.]

<h2 style="text-align:center">ARTICLE 2</h2>

For the purposes of this Directive: **C4.06**

"motor vehicle" shall mean any power-driven vehicle which travels on the road by its own means,

"trailer" shall mean any vehicle intended to be coupled to a motor vehicle excluding semi-trailers, and constructed and equipped for the carriage of goods,

"semi-trailer" shall mean any vehicle intended to be coupled to a motor vehicle in such a way that part of it rests on the motor vehicle with a substantial part of its weight and of the weight of its load being borne by the motor vehicle, and constructed and equipped for the carriage of goods,

"vehicle combination" shall mean either:

— a road train consisting of a motor vehicle coupled to a trailer; or

— an articulated vehicle consisting of a motor vehicle coupled to a semi-trailer,

"conditioned vehicle" shall mean any vehicle whose fixed or movable superstructures are specially equipped for the carriage of goods at controlled temperatures and whose side walls, inclusive of insulation, are each at least 45mm thick,

"bus" shall mean a vehicle with more than nine seats including the driver's seat, constructed and equipped to carry passengers and their luggage. It may have one or two decks and may also draw a luggage trailer,

"articulated bus" shall mean a bus consisting or two rigid sections connected to each other by an articulated section. On this type of vehicle the passenger compartments in each of the two rigid sections shall be intercommunicating. The articulated section shall permit the free movement of travellers between the rigid sections. Connection and disconnection of the two sections shall be possible only in a workshop,

"maximum authorised dimensions" shall mean the maximum dimensions for use of a vehicle, as laid down in Annex I to this Directive,

"maximum authorised weight" shall mean the maximum weight for use of a laden vehicle in international traffic,

"maximum authorised axle weight" shall mean the maximum weight for use in international traffic of a laden axle or group of axles,

"indivisible load" shall mean a load that cannot, for the purposes of carriage by road, be divided into two or more loads without undue expense or risk of damage and which owing to its dimensions or mass cannot be carried by a motor vehicle complying with this Directive in all respects,

"tonne" shall mean the weight executed by the mass of a tonne and shall correspond to 9,8 kilonewtons (kN),

All maximum authorised dimensions specified in Annex I shall be measured in accordance with Annex I to Directive 70/156/EEC, with no positive tolerances.

ARTICLE 3

C4.07

1. A Member State may not reject or prohibit the use in its territory:

— in international traffic, of vehicles registered or put into circulation in any other Member State for reasons relating to their weights and dimensions,

[— in national traffic, of vehicles registered or put into circulation in any other Member State for reasons relating to their dimensions;]

provided that such vehicles comply with the limit values specified in Annex I.

This provision shall apply notwithstanding the fact that:

(a) the said vehicles are not in conformity with the requirements of that Member State with regard to certain weight and dimension characteristics not covered by Annex I;

(b) the competent authority of the Member State in which the vehicles are registered or put into circulation has authorised limits not referred to in Article 4(1) exceeding those laid down in Annex I.

2. However, paragraph 1(a) shall not affect the right of Member States, with due regard to Community law, to require vehicles registered or put into circulation in their own territory to be in conformity with their national requirements on weight and dimension characteristics not covered by Annex I.

3. Member States may require conditioned vehicles to carry an ATP certificate or ATP certification plate provided for in the Agreement of 1 September 1970 on the international carriage of perishable foodstuffs and on the special equipment to be used for such carriage.

C4.08   *[Article 3 is printed as amended by Directive 2002/7/EC.]*

ARTICLE 4

C4.09

[1. Member States shall not authorise the normal circulation within their territories:

(a) of vehicles or vehicle combinations for the national transport of goods which are not in conformity with the characteristics set out in points 1.1, 1.2, 1.4, 1.5, 1.6, 1.7, 1.8, 4.2 and 4.4 of Annex I;

(b) of vehicles for national passenger transport, which are not in conformity with the characteristics set out in points 1.1, 1.2, 1.4a, 1.5 and 1.5a of Annex I.

2. Member States may nonetheless authorise the circulation within their territories:

   (a) of vehicles or vehicle combinations for the national transport of goods which are not in conformity with the characteristics set out in points 1.3, 2, 3, 4.1 and 4.3 of Annex I;

   (b) of vehicles for national passenger transport, which are not in conformity with the characteristics set out in points 1.3, 2, 3, 4.1 and 4.3 of Annex I.]

3. Vehicles or vehicle combinations which exceed the maximum dimensions may only be allowed to circulate on the basis of special permits issued without discrimination by the competent authorities, or on the basis of similar non-discriminatory arrangements agreed on a case-by-case basis with those authorities, where these vehicles or vehicle combinations carry or are intended to carry indivisible loads.

4. Member States may allow [vehicles or vehicle combinations used for transport which] carry out certain national transport operations that do not significantly affect international competition in the transport sector to circulate in their territory with dimensions deviating from those laid down in points 1.1, 1.2, 1.4 to 1.8, 4.2 and 4.4 of Annex I.

   Transport operations shall be considered not significantly to affect international competition in the transport sector if one of the conditions under (a) and (b) is fulfilled:

   (a) the transport operations are carried out in a Member State's territory by specialised vehicles or specialised vehicle combinations in circumstances in which they are not normally carried out by vehicles from other Member States, *e.g.* operations linked to logging and the forestry industry;

   (b) the Member State which permits transport operations to be carried out in its territory by vehicles or vehicle combinations with dimensions deviating from those laid down in Annex I also permits motor vehicles, trailers and semi-trailers which comply with the dimensions laid down in Annex I to be used in such combinations as to achieve at least the loading length authorised in that Member State, so that every operator may benefit from equal conditions of competition (modular concept).

   The Member State concerned which has to adapt its road infrastructure in order to be able to fulfil the condition under (b) may nevertheless prohibit, until 31 December 2003 at the latest, [the circulation in its territory, in national transport operations, of vehicles] or vehicle combinations which exceed current national standards on dimensions, provided that national legislation continues to apply to all Community carriers in a non-discriminatory manner.

   The Member States shall inform the Commission of the measures taken pursuant to this paragraph.

5. Member States may allow vehicles or vehicle combinations incorporating new technologies or new concepts which cannot comply with one or more

requirements of this Directive to carry out certain local transport operations for a trial period. Member States shall inform the Commission thereof.

6. Member States may allow vehicles or vehicle combinations used for goods transport and registered or put into circulation before the implementation of this Directive to circulate in their territory until 31 December 2006 with dimensions exceeding those laid down in points 1.1, 1.2, 1.4 to 1.8, 4.2 and 4.4 of Annex I by virtue of differing national provisions or methods of measurement.

[7. Until 31 December 2020 Member States may authorise buses that were registered or put into circulation before the implementation of this Directive but the dimensions of which exceed those laid down in points 1.1, 1.2, 1.5 and 1.5 *a* of Annex I to circulate within their territories.]

C4.10 *[Article 4 is printed as amended by Directive 2002/7/EC.]*

ARTICLE 5

C4.11 Without prejudice to Article 4(6):

(a) articulated vehicles put into circulation before 1 January 1991 which do not comply with the specifications contained in points 1.6 and 4.4 of Annex I shall be deemed to comply with such specifications for the purposes of Article 3 if they do not exceed a total length of 15,50m;

(b) road trains, the motor vehicle of which was put into circulation before 31 December 1991 and which do not comply with the specifications contained in points 1.7 and 1.8 of Annex I, shall until 31 December 1998 be deemed to comply with such specifications for the purposes of Article 3 if they do not exceed a total length of 18,00m.

ARTICLE 6

C4.12 1. Member States shall take the necessary measures to ensure that Article 1 vehicles referred to in Article 1 and complying with this Directive carry one of the proofs referred to in (a), (b) and (c):

(a) a combination of the following two plates:
— the "manufacturer's plate" established and attached in accordance with Directive 76/114/EEC [*O.J. No.L24, January 30, 1976, p.1, as amended by Directive 78/507/EEC, O.J. No.L155, June 13, 1978, p.31*],
— the plate relating to dimensions, in accordance with Annex III, established and attached in accordance with Directive 76/114/EEC;

(b) a single plate established and attached in accordance with Directive 76/114/EEC and containing the information on the two plates referred to in (a);

(c) a single document issued by the competent authorities of the Member State in which the vehicle is registered or put into circulation. Such document shall bear the same headings and information as the plates referred to in (a). It shall be kept in a place easily accessible to inspection and shall be adequately protected.

2. If the characteristics of the vehicle no longer correspond to those indicated on the proof of compliance, the Member State in which the vehicle is registered shall take the necessary steps to ensure that the proof of compliance is altered.

3. The plates and documents referred to in paragraph 1 shall be recognised by

the Member States as the proof of vehicle compliance provided for in this Directive.

4. Vehicles carrying proof of compliance may be subject:
   — as regards common standards on weights, to random checks,
   — as regards common standards on dimensions, only to checks where there is a suspicion of non-compliance with this Directive.

5. The middle column of the proof of compliance relating to weights shall contain, where appropriate, the Community weight standards applicable to the vehicle in question. As regards vehicles referred to in point 2.2.2(c) of Annex I, the entry "44 tonnes" shall be included in brackets under the maximum authorised weight of the vehicle combination.

6. Each Member State may decide, in respect of any vehicle registered or put into circulation in its territory, that the maximum weights authorised by its national legislation shall be indicated in the proof of compliance in the left-hand column and the technically permissible weights in the right-hand column.

[ARTICLE 7

This Directive shall not preclude the application of road traffic provisions in force in each Member State which permit the weight and/or dimensions of vehicles on certain roads or civil engineering structures to be limited, irrespective of the State of registration of such vehicles or the State where such vehicles were put into circulation.   **C4.13**

This includes the possibility to impose local restrictions on maximum authorised dimensions and/or weights of vehicles that may be used in specified areas or on specified roads, where the infrastructure is not suitable for long and heavy vehicles, such as city centres, small villages or places of special natural interest.]

[Article 7 is printed as substituted by Directive 2002/7/EC.]   **C4.14**

ARTICLE 8

Article 3 shall not apply in Ireland and the United Kingdom until 31 December 1998:   **C4.15**

  (a) as regards the standards referred to in points 2.2, 2.3.1, 2.3.3, 2.4 and 3.3.2 of Annex I:
    — with the exception of the articulated vehicles referred to in point 2.2.2 where:
     (i) the total laden weight does not exceed 38 tonnes;
     (ii) the weight on any tri-axle at the spacing specified in point 3.3.2 does not exceed 22,5 tonnes,
    — with the exception of the vehicles referred to in points 2.2.3, 2.2.4, 2.3 and 2.4, where the total laden weight does not exceed:
     (i) 35 tonnes for the vehicles referred to in points 2.2.3 and 2.2.4;
     (ii) 17 tonnes for the vehicles referred to in point 2.3.1;
     (iii) 30 tonnes for the vehicles referred to in point 2.3.3, subject to compliance with the conditions specified in that point and in point 4.3;
     (iv) 27 tonnes for the vehicles referred to in point 2.4,
  (b) as regards the standard referred to in point 3.4 of Annex I, with the exception of the vehicles referred to in point 2.2, 2.3 and 2.4, where the weight per driving axle does not exceed 10,5 tonnes.

[ARTICLE 8A]

C4.16 Portugal and the United Kingdom may refuse or prohibit the use on their territory until 9 March 2005 of the buses referred to in point 1.1 of Annex I unless they satisfy the following manoeuvrability criteria:

— when the bus is stationary and has its steered wheels so directed that if the vehicle moved, its outermost forward point would describe a circle of 12,50m in radius, a vertical plane tangential to the side of the vehicle which faces outwards from the circle must be established by marking a line on the ground. In the case of an articulated bus the two rigid portions must be aligned with the plane,

— when the bus moves forward on either side following the circle of 12,50m in radius, no part of it may move outside the vertical plane by more than 0,80m in the case of a rigid bus of up to 12m in length or by more than 1,20m in the case of either a rigid bus of over 12m in length or an articulated bus.]

C4.17 *[Article 8A was inserted by Directive 2002/7/EC.]*

ARTICLE 9

C4.18 As regards the standard referred to in point 1.2(a) of Annex I, a Member State may reject or prohibit the use in its territory, until 31 December 1999, of buses with a width exceeding 2,5m.

Member States shall inform the Commission of the measures taken pursuant to this Article. The Commission shall inform the other Member States thereof.

ARTICLE 10

C4.19 *[Omitted.]*

[ARTICLE 10A]

C4.20 With regard to Annex I, point 1.5 *a*, the Commission shall, by 9 March 2005 at the latest, present a report on the feasibility of reducing the value of 0,60m referred to in the second subparagraph of this point to improve the safety conditions related to the manoeuvrability of long buses. If appropriate, the report shall be accompanied by a legislative proposal to amend this Directive accordingly.]

C4.21 *[Article 10A was inserted by Directive 2002/7/EC.]*

ARTICLE 11

C4.22 1. Member States shall bring into force the laws, regulations and administrative provisions necessary to comply with this Directive by 17 September 1997. They shall forthwith inform the Commission thereof.

When Member States adopt these measures, they shall contain a reference to this Directive or shall be accompanied by such reference on the occasion of their official publication. The methods of making such reference shall be laid down by Member States.

2. Member States shall communicate to the Commission the text of the main provisions of domestic law which they adopt in the field covered by this Directive.

ARTICLE 12

C4.23 This Directive shall enter into force on the day of its publication in the *Official Journal of the European Communities*.

[This Directive was published at O.J. No.L235, September 17, 1996, pp.59–   **C4.24**
75.]

ARTICLE 13

This Directive is addressed to the Member States.   **C4.25**

ANNEX I

Maximum Weights and Dimensions and Related Characteristics of Vehicles

1. *Maximum authorised dimensions for the vehicles referred to in Article 1(1)(a)*

[1.1	*Maximum length:*		**C4.26**
	— motor vehicle other than a bus	12,00m	
	— trailer	12,00m	
	— articulated vehicle	16,50m	
	— road train	18,75m	
	— articulated bus	18,75m	
	— bus with two axles	13,50m	
	— bus with more than two axles	15,00m	
	— bus + trailer	18,75m]	

1.2   *Maximum width:*

     (a)   all vehicles   2,55m

     (b)   superstructures of conditioned   2,60m
          vehicles

1.3   *Maximum height (any vehicle)*   4,00m

1.4   Removable superstructures and standardised freight items such as containers are included in the dimensions specified in points 1.1, 1.2, 1.3, 1.6, 1.7, 1.8 and 4.4

[1.4 *a*   If any removable attachments such as ski-boxes are fitted to a bus, its length, including the attachments, must not exceed the maximum length laid down in point 1.1]

1.5   Any motor vehicle or vehicle combination which is in motion must be able to turn within a swept circle having an outer radius of 12,50m and an inner radius of 5,30m

[1.5 *a*   *Additional requirements for buses*

     With the vehicle stationary, a vertical plane tangential to the side of the vehicle and facing outwards from the circle shall be established by marking a line on the ground. In the case of an articulated vehicle, the two rigid portions shall be aligned with the plane.
     When the vehicle moves from a straight line approach into the circular area described in point 1.5, no part of it shall move outside of that vertical plane by more than 0,60m.]

1.6	Maximum distance between the axis of the fifth-wheel king-pin and the rear of a semi-trailer	12,00m
1.7	Maximum distance measured parallel to the longitudinal axis of the road train from the foremost external point of the loading area behind the cabin to the rearmost external point of the trailer of the combination, minus the distance between the rear of the drawing vehicle and the front of the trailer	15,65m
1.8	Maximum distance measured parallel to the longitudinal axis of the road train from the foremost external point of the loading area behind the cabin to the rearmost external point of the trailer of the combination	16,40m

2. Maximum authorised vehicle weight (in tonnes)

C4.27

2.1	*Vehicles forming part of a vehicle combination*	
2.1.1	Two-axle trailer	18 tonnes
2.1.2	Three-axle trailer	24 tonnes
2.2	*Vehicle combinations*	
2.2.1	Road trains with five or six axles	
(a)	two-axle motor vehicle with three-axle trailer	40 tonnes
(b)	three-axle motor vehicle with two or three-axle trailer	40 tonnes
2.2.2	Articulated vehicles with five or six axles	
(a)	two-axle motor vehicle with three-axle semi-trailer	40 tonnes
(b)	three-axle motor vehicle with two or three-axle semi-trailer	40 tonnes
(c)	three-axle motor vehicle with two or three-axle semi-trailer carrying a 40-foot ISO container as a combined transport operation	44 tonnes
2.2.3	Road trains with four axles consisting of a two-axle motor vehicle and a two-axle trailer	36 tonnes
2.2.4	Articulated vehicles with four axles consisting of a two-axle motor vehicle and a two-axle semi-trailer, if the distance between the axles of the semi-trailer:	
2.2.4.1	is 1,3m or greater but not more than 1,8m	36 tonnes
2.2.4.2	is greater than 1,8m	36 tonnes

		+2 tonnes margin when the maximum authorised weight (MAW) of the motor vehicle (18 tonnes) and the MAW of the tandem axle of the semi-trailer (20 tonnes) are respected and the driving axle is fitted with twin tyres and air suspension or suspension recognised as being equivalent within the Community as defined in Annex II
2.3	*Motor vehicles*	
2.3.1	Two-axle motor vehicles	18 tonnes
2.3.2	Three-axle motor vehicles	— 25 tonnes
		— 26 tonnes
		where the driving axle is fitted with twin tyres and air suspension or suspension recognised as being equivalent within the Community as defined in Annex II, or where each driving axle is fitted with twin tyres and the maximum weight of each axle does not exceed 9,5 tonnes
2.3.3	Four-axle motor vehicles with two steering axles	— 32 tonnes
		where the driving axle is fitted with twin tyres and air suspension or suspension recognised as being equivalent within the Community as defined in Annex II, or where each driving axle is fitted with twin tyres and the maximum weight of each axle does not exceed 9,5 tonnes
2.4	*Three-axle articulated buses*	28 tonnes

3. *Maximum authorised axle weight of the vehicles referred to in Article 1(1)(b) (in tonnes)*

C4.28

3.1	*Single axles*	
	Single non-driving axle	10 tonnes
3.2	*Tandem axles of trailers and semi-trailers*	
	The sum of the axle weights per tandem axle must not exceed, if the distance (d) between the axles is:	
3.2.1	less than 1m (d < 1,0)	11 tonnes
3.2.2	between 1,0m and less than 1,3m (1,0 ≤ d < 1,3	16 tonnes

3.2.3	between 1,3m and less than 1,8m (1,3 $\leq$ d < 1,8)	18 tonnes
3.2.4	1,8m or more (1,8 $\leq$ d)	20 tonnes
3.3	*Tri-axles of trailers and semi-trailers*	
	The sum of the axle weights per tri-axle must not exceed, if the distance (d) between the axles is:	
3.3.1	1,3m or less (d $\leq$ 1,3)	21 tonnes
3.3.2	over 1,3m and up to 1,4m (1,3 < d $\leq$ 1,4)	24 tonnes
3.4	*Driving axle*	
3.4.1	Driving axle of the vehicles referred to in 2.2.1 and 2.2.2	11,5 tonnes
3.4.2	Driving axle of the vehicles referred to in points 2.2.3, 2.2.4, 2.3 and 2.4	11,5 tonnes
3.5	*Tandem axles of motor vehicles*	
	The sum of the axle weights per tandem axle must not exceed, if the distance (d) between the axles is:	
3.5.1	less than 1m (d < 1,0)	11,5 tonnes
3.5.2	1,0m or greater but less than 1,3m (1,0 $\leq$ d < 1,3)	16 tonnes
3.5.3	1,3m or greater but less than 1,8m (1,3 $\leq$ d < 1,8)	— 18 tonnes — 19 tonnes

where the driving axle is fitted with twin tyres and air suspension or suspension recognised as being equivalent within the Community as defined in Annex II, or where each driving axle is fitted with twin tyres and where the maximum weight for each axle does not exceed 9,5 tonnes

4. *Related characteristics of the vehicles referred to in Article 1(1)(b)*

C4.29   4.1   *All vehicles*

The weight borne by the driving axle or driving axles of a vehicle or vehicle combination must not be less than 25% of the total laden weight of the vehicle or vehicle combination, when used in international traffic

4.2   *Road trains*

The distance between the rear axle of a motor vehicle and the front axle of a trailer must not be less than 3,00m.

4.3   *Maximum authorised weight depending on the wheelbase*

The maximum authorised weight in tonnes of a four-axle motor vehicle may not exceed five times the distance in metres between the axles and the foremost and rearmost axles of the vehicle

4.4   *Semi-trailers*

The distance measured horizontally between the axis of the fifth-wheel king-pin and any point at the front of the semi-trailer must not exceed 2,04m

C4.30   *[Annex I is printed as amended by Directive 2002/7/EC.]*

ANNEX II

Conditions Relating to Equivalence between Certain Non-Air Suspension Systems and Air Suspension for Vehicle Driving Axle(s)

1. *Definition of Air Suspension*

A suspension system is considered to be air suspended if at least 75% of the spring effect is caused by the air-spring.   **C4.31**

2. *Equivalence to Air Suspension*

A suspension recognised as being equivalent to air suspension must conform to the following: **C4.32**

2.1. during free transient low frequency oscillation of the sprung mass above the driving axle or bogie, the measured frequency and damping with the suspension carrying its maximum load must fall within the limits defined in points 2.2 to 2.5;

2.2. each axle must be fitted with hydraulic dampers. On tandem axle bogies, the dampers must be positioned to minimise the oscillation of the bogies;

2.3. the mean damping ratio D must be more than 20% of critical damping for the suspension in its normal conditions with hydraulic dampers in place and operating;

2.4. the damping ratio D of the suspension with all hydraulic dampers removed or anticipated must be not more than 50% of D;

2.5. the frequency of the sprung mass above the driving axle or bogie in a free transient vertical oscillation must not be higher than 2,0 Hz;

2.6. the frequency and damping of the suspension are given in paragraph 3. The test procedures for measuring the frequency and damping are laid down in paragraph 4.

3. *Definition of Frequency and Damping*

In this definition a sprung mass M (kg) above a driving axle or bogie is considered. The   **C4.33**
axle or bogie has a total vertical stiffness between the road surface and the sprung mass of K Newtons/metre (N/m) and a total damping coefficient of C Newtons per metre per second (N.s/m). The vertical displacement of the sprung mass is Z. The equation of motion for free oscillation of the spring mass is:

$$M\frac{d^2Z}{dt^2} + C\frac{dZ}{dt} + kZ = 0$$

The frequency of oscillation of the sprung mass F (rad/sec) is:

$$F = \sqrt{\frac{K}{M} - \frac{C^2}{4M^2}}$$

The damping is critical when $C = C_o$,
where

$$C_o = 2\sqrt{KM}$$

The damping ratio as a fraction of critical damping is C/C_o.
During free transient oscillation of the sprung mass the vertical motion of the mass will

follow a damped sinusoidal path (Figure 2). The frequency can be estimated by measuring the time for as many cycles of oscillation as can be observed. The damping can be estimated by measuring the heights of successive peaks of the oscillation in the same direction. If the peak amplitudes of the first and second cycles of the oscillation are A_1 and A_2, then the damping ratio D is:

$$D = \frac{C}{C_o} = \frac{1}{2\pi} \ln \frac{A_1}{A_2}$$

"In" being the natural logarithm of the amplitude ratio.

4. Test Procedure

C4.34   To establish by test the damping ratio D, the damping ratio with hydraulic dampers removed, and the frequency F of the suspension, the loaded vehicle should either:

(a) be driven at low speed (5 km/hr ± 1 km/hr) over an 80mm step with the profile shown in Figure 1. The transient oscillation to be analysed for frequency and damping occurs after the wheels on the driving axle have left the step;

or

(b) be pulled down by its chassis so that the driving axle load is 1,5 times its maximum static value. The vehicle held down is suddenly released and subsequent oscillation analysed;

or

(c) be pulled up by its chassis so that the sprung mass is lifted by 80mm above the driving axle. The vehicle held up is suddenly dropped and the subsequent oscillation analysed;

or

(d) be subjected to other procedures insofar as it has been proved by the manufacturer, to the satisfaction of the technical department, that they are equivalent.

The vehicle should be instrumented with a vertical displacement transducer between driving axle and chassis, directly above the driving axle. From the trace, the time interval between the first and second compression peaks can be measured to find the frequency F and the amplitude ratio to obtain the damping. For twin-drive bogies, vertical displacement transducers should be fitted between each driving axle and the chassis directly above it.

FIGURE 1

STEP FOR SUSPENSION TESTS

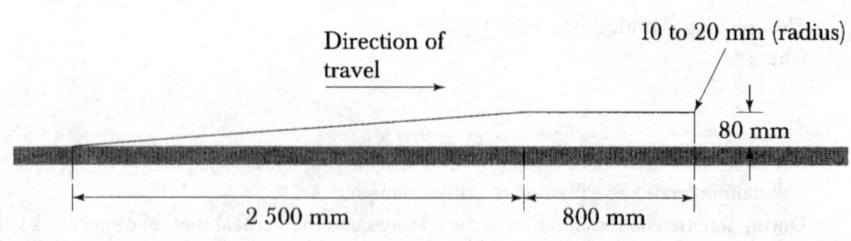

FIGURE 2

A DAMPED TRANSIENT RESPONSE

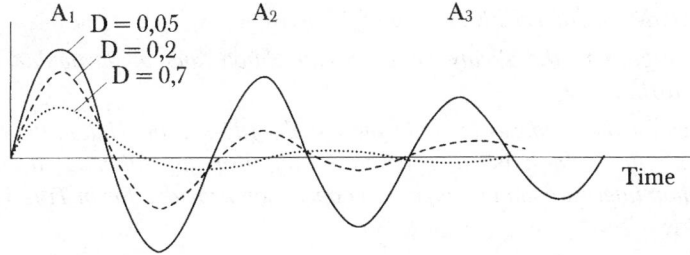

ANNEX III

Plate Relating to Dimensions Referred to in Article 6(1)(a)

I. The plate relating to dimensions, as far as possible affixed next to the plate referred to **C4.35**
in Directive 76/114/EEC, must contain the following data:

1. name of the manufacturer[1];
2. vehicle identification number[2];
3. length of the motor vehicle, trailer or semi-trailer (L);
4. width of the motor vehicle, trailer or semi-trailer (W);
5. data for the measurement of the length of vehicle combinations:
   — the distance (a) between the front of the motor vehicle and the centre of the coupling device (coupling hook or fifth wheel); in the case of a fifth wheel with several coupling points, the minimum and maximum values must be given (a_{min} and a_{max}),
   — the distance (b) between the centre of the coupling device of the trailer (fifth wheel ring) or of the semi-trailer (king-pin) and the rear of the semi-trailer, in the case of a device with several coupling points, the minimum and maximum values must be given (b_{min} and b_{max}).

The length of vehicle combinations is the length of the motor vehicle and trailer or semi-trailer placed in a straight line behind each other.

II. The values given on the proof of compliance shall reproduce exactly the measure- **C4.36**
ments carried out directly on that vehicle.

*   *   *

---

[1] This information need not be repeated where the vehicle carries a single plate containing data on both weights and dimensions.
[2] This information need not be repeated where the vehicle carries a single plate containing data on both weights and dimensions.

Council Act of June 17, 1998 drawing up the Convention on Driving Disqualifications

C5.01 *THE COUNCIL OF THE EUROPEAN UNION,*

Having regard to the Treaty on European Union, and in particular [Article 34(2)(d)] thereof,

Whereas, for the purposes of achieving the objectives of the Union, the Member States regard the giving of effect to driving disqualifications as a matter of common interest coming under the cooperation provided for in Title VI of the Treaty;

HAS DECIDED

that the Convention, the text of which is set out in the Annex and which is signed today by the Representatives of the Governments of the Member States of the Union, is hereby drawn up;

RECOMMENDS

that it be adopted by the Member States in accordance with their respective constitutional rules.

C5.02 *[The text of this Act is printed as amended by the Treaty of Amsterdam art.12(1) and (3).]*

Luxembourg,
17 June 1998.

Convention on Driving Disqualifications

THE HIGH CONTRACTING PARTIES to this Convention, Member States of the European Union,

REFERRING to the Council Act of 17 June 1998 [see previous page],

WHEREAS it is of the utmost importance for road safety within the European Union that a Union-wide effect be given to driving disqualifications by adequate means;

WHEREAS as a result of the free movement of persons and the increasing international road traffic, disqualifications from driving are frequently imposed by a Member State other than that in which the driver normally resides;

WHEREAS having regard to Council Directive 91/439/EEC of 29 July 1991 on driving licences [O.J. No.L237, August 24, 1991, p.1, as amended], national provisions on the withdrawal, suspension and cancellation of driving licences should be applied by the Member State in whose territory the licence holder has his or her normal residence;

WHEREAS drivers disqualified from driving in a Member State other than that of their normal residence ought not to escape the effects of such measure when present in a Member State other than that of the offence;

WHEREAS the Member State of residence of the licence holder should therefore, in respect of offences considered particularly serious and under certain conditions, give effect to driving disqualifications imposed by another Member State by taking measures entailing the withdrawal, suspension or cancellation of his or her driving licence;

WHEREAS the fact that the Member State of residence has given effect to such a disqualification imposed by another Member State, should entail the consequence that the necessary measures are taken to penalise the act of driving a motor vehicle during the period of the disqualification under the laws of any Member State of the European Union in whose territory this may occur,

HAVE AGREED AS FOLLOWS:

ARTICLE 1

For the purposes of this Convention:

    (a) *"driving disqualification"* shall mean any measure related to the commission of a road traffic offence which results in withdrawal or suspension of the right to drive of a driver of a motor vehicle and which is no longer subject to a right of appeal. The measure may continue either a primary, secondary or supplementary penalty or a safety measure and may have been taken either by a judicial authority or by an administrative authority;

    (b) *"State of the offence"* shall mean the Member State within the territory of which the road traffic offence that has given rise to a driving disqualification was committed;

(c) *"State of residence"* shall mean the Member State within the territory of which the person who has been disqualified from driving is normally resident within the meaning of Article 9 of Directive 91/439/EEC;

(d) *"motor vehicle"* shall mean any vehicle covered by the definition in Article 3(3) of Directive 91/439/EEC.

ARTICLE 2

C6.03   The Member States hereby undertake to co-operate, in accordance with the provisions of this Convention, with the objective that drivers who are disqualified from driving in a Member State other than that in which they normally reside should not escape the effects of their disqualification when they leave the State of the offence.

ARTICLE 3

C6.04
1. The State of the offence shall without delay notify the State of residence of any driving disqualification imposed for an offence arising from conduct referred to in the Annex.

2. Each Member State may agree with other Member States that notification to it pursuant to paragraph 1 shall not take place in certain cases in which Article 6(2)(a) would apply.

ARTICLE 4

C6.05
1. Subject to Article 6, the State of residence which has been notified pursuant to Article 3 shall without delay give effect to the decision imposing disqualification from driving taken in the State of the offence in one of the following ways:

   (a) by directly executing the decision imposing disqualification from driving, while taking into account any part of the period of disqualification imposed by the State of the offence which has already been served in the latter; or

   (b) by executing the decision imposing disqualification from driving via a judicial or administrative decision in accordance with the conditions laid down in paragraph 2; or

   (c) by converting the decision imposing disqualification from driving into a judicial or administrative decision of its own, thus, without prejudice to Article 11, substituting for the decision by the State of the offence a new decision in accordance with the conditions laid down in paragraph 3.

2. If it applies the procedure laid down in paragraph 1(b) the State of residence:

   (a) shall take into account any part of the period of the driving disqualification imposed by the State of the offence which has already been served in that State;

   (b) may reduce the duration of the driving disqualification but only to the maximum term provided for acts of the same kind under its national law;

   (c) shall not extend the duration of the driving disqualification imposed by the State of the offence.

3. If it applies the procedure laid down in paragraph 1(c) the State of residence:

    (a) shall be bound by the facts as established insofar as they are stated explicitly or implicitly in the decision imposing disqualification from driving in the State of the offence;

    (b) shall take into account any part of the period of the driving disqualification imposed by the State of the offence which has already been served in that State;

    (c) may reduce the duration of the driving disqualification to align it to the duration which according to its national law would have been applied for the case in question;

    (d) shall not extend the duration of the driving disqualification imposed by the State of the offence;

    (e) may not replace the driving disqualification by a fine or any other measure.

4. When giving effect to a driving disqualification under this Article, the State of residence shall, where necessary, determine a date from which it will enforce the driving disqualification.

5. When giving notification referred to in Article 15(2), each Member State shall indicate in a declaration which of the procedures described in paragraph 1 it intends to apply in its capacity as a State of residence. The declaration made may be replaced by a new declaration at any time.

ARTICLE 5

Giving effect to a driving disqualification pursuant to Article 4 shall be without prejudice to any additional road safety measures that the State of residence may take under its own legislation.   **C6.06**

ARTICLE 6

1. The State of residence shall refuse to give effect to the driving disqualification where: **C6.07**

    (a) the driving disqualification has already been fully enforced in the State of the offence;

    (b) the offender has already had a driving disqualification imposed on him in the State of residence for the same acts and that disqualification has been or is being enforced;

    (c) the offender would have benefited from a general pardon or amnesty in the State of residence if the acts had been committed within the territory of that State;

    (d) the period of limitation for the measure would have expired under its own legislation;

    (e) in the circumstances of the particular case, after receiving any information supplied under Article 8, it considers that the person concerned has not had an adequate opportunity to defend himself.

2. The State of residence may refuse to give effect to the driving disqualification if:

    (a) the conduct for which the driving disqualification has been imposed in the State of the offence does not constitute an offence under the law of the State of residence;

    (b) the remaining period of disqualification which could be enforced in the State of residence is less than one month;

(c) driving disqualification is not a measure available under the legislation of the State of residence for the acts giving rise to the driving disqualification imposed by the State of the offence.

3. When giving the notification referred to in Article 15(2) or at any other time, any Member State may declare that it will always apply paragraph 2 of this Article in part or in full. When such a declaration has been made, the other Member State shall not be obliged to communicate driving disqualifications such as referred to in that declaration pursuant to Article 3 to the Member State that has made the declaration. Any Member State may withdraw its declaration at any time.

Article 7

C6.08

1. The competent authority of the State of the offence shall forward the notification referred to in Article 3 to the central authority of the State of residence.

2. For the purposes of paragraph 1, when giving the notification referred to in Article 15(2), each Member State shall indicate:

   (a) the central authority or central authorities which it designates;
   (b) the competent authorities responsible for submitting the notifications referred to in Article 3.

Article 8

C6.09

1. The notification referred to in Article 3 shall be accompanied by:
   — details serving to locate the person disqualified from driving,
   — the original or a certified copy of the decision imposing a driving disqualification,
   — a brief statement of the circumstances and a reference to the legal provisions in the State of the offence on the basis of which the driving disqualification was imposed, if these are not given in the decision,
   — an attestation that it is final,
   — information regarding the enforcement of the driving disqualification in the State of the offence, including the length of the disqualification and, where known, the dates on which the disqualification starts and expires,
   — the driving licence, if it has been seized.

2. Where the person on whom the driving disqualification has been imposed did not appear personally or was not represented at the proceedings, notifications pursuant to Article 3 must be accompanied by evidence that the person has been duly notified of the proceedings in accordance with the law of the State of the offence.

3. If the information communicated in accordance with paragraphs 1 and 2 is found to be insufficient to allow a decision to be taken pursuant to this Convention, in particular where, in the circumstances of the particular case, there is doubt whether the person concerned has had an adequate opportunity to defend himself, the competent authorities of the State of residence shall request the competent authorities of the State of the offence to provide the necessary supplementary information without delay.

Article 9

C6.10

1. Subject to paragraphs 2 and 3, no translation of the notifications referred to

in Article 3 or of the accompanying material referred to in Article 8 or of any other documents relating to the application of this Convention shall be required.

2. Any Member State may, when giving the notification referred to in Article 15(2), declare that the documents referred to in paragraph 1 forwarded to it by the State of the offence must be accompanied by a translation into one of the official languages of the institutions of the European Communities indicated in its declaration.

3. Except for the document referred to in the second indent of Article 8(1) the documents referred to in paragraph 1 of this Article need not be certified.

ARTICLE 10

The State of residence shall inform the State of the offence of any decision taken in respect of a notification given pursuant to Article 3 and in respect of enforcement and, where it refuses to give effect to a driving disqualification pursuant of Article 6, of the reasons for its refusal. **C6.11**

ARTICLE 11

1. The right of the State of the offence to execute in its territory the full period of the driving disqualification determined by the State of the offence shall not be affected by the decision of the State of residence. **C6.12**

2. When giving the notification referred to in Article 15(2), any Member State may indicate that it will not apply paragraph 1 of this Article in its capacity as the State of the offence.

3. The State of the offence and the State of residence shall exercise their responsibilities under the Convention in such a way as to ensure that the total period of disqualification, taking into account any period of disqualification which is served for the offence concerned in the State of residence, does not exceed the period of disqualification originally determined by the State of the offence.

4. When notifying the person concerned of the decision to disqualify, a State of the offence which proposes to apply paragraph 1 shall at the same time inform the person of this fact, and shall confirm in the notification given in accordance with Article 3 to the State of residence that it has done so.

ARTICLE 12

Each Member State shall adopt the measures necessary to enable it to penalise the driving of a motor vehicle in its territory when the driver is disqualified from driving by the State of residence in implementation of this Convention. **C6.13**

ARTICLE 13

Costs incurred in implementing this Convention shall be borne in the Member State in which they occur. **C6.14**

ARTICLE 14

1. The Court of Justice of the European Communities shall have jurisdiction to rule on any dispute between Member States regarding the interpretation or the application of this Convention whenever such dispute cannot be settled by the Council within six months of its being referred to the Council by one of its members. The Court shall also have jurisdiction to rule on any dispute **C6.15**

between Member States and Commission regarding the interpretation or application of this Convention.

2. Any Member State shall be able to accept, through a declaration made when giving the notification referred to in Article 15(2) or at any later date, the jurisdiction of the Court of Justice to give preliminary rulings on the interpretation of this Convention.

3. A Member State making a declaration pursuant to paragraph 2 shall specify that either:

   (a) any court or tribunal of that State against whose decisions there is no judicial remedy under national law may request the Court of Justice to give a preliminary ruling on a question raised in a case pending before it and concerning the interpretation of this Convention if that court or tribunal considers that a decision on the question is necessary to enable it to give judgment, or

   (b) any court or tribunal of that State may request the Court of Justice to give a preliminary ruling on a question raised in a case pending before it and concerning the interpretation of this Convention if that court or tribunal considers that a decision on the question is necessary to enable it to give judgment.

4. The Statute of the Court of Justice of the European Community and its Rules of Procedure shall apply. Any Member State, whether or not it has made a declaration pursuant to paragraph 2, shall be entitled to submit statements of case or written observations to the Court in cases which arise under paragraph 3.

ARTICLE 15

C6.16

1. This Convention shall be subject to adoption by the Member States in accordance with their respective constitutional requirements.

2. Member States shall notify the Secretary-General of the Council of the European Union of the completion of their constitutional requirements for adopting this Convention.

3. This Convention shall enter into force 90 days after the notification referred to in paragraph 2 by the Member State which, being a Member of the European Union on the date of the adoption by the Council of the Act drawing up this Convention [*q.v.*], is the last to fulfil this formality.

4. Until this Convention enters into force, any Member State may, when giving the notification referred to in paragraph 2 or at any later date, declare that with respect to itself the Convention, except Article 14, shall apply to its relations with Member States that have made the same declaration. Such declarations shall apply as from 90 days after the date of their deposit.

5. This Convention and declarations made in respect of it shall be applicable only to offences committed after the entry into force of the Convention or from the date on which the Convention has become applicable between the Member States concerned.

ARTICLE 16

C6.17

1. This Convention shall be open to accession by any State that becomes a member of the European Union.

2. The text of this Convention in the language of the acceding State, drawn up by the Council of the European Union, shall be authentic.

3. Instruments of accession shall be deposited with the Secretary-General of the Council of the European Union.

4. This Convention shall enter into force with respect to any State that accedes to it 90 days after the deposit of its instrument of accession or on the date of entry into force of the Convention if it has not already entered into force at the time of expiry of those 90 days.

5. Article 15(4) shall apply to acceding Member States.

ARTICLE 17

No reservation may be entered in respect of this Convention.   **C6.18**

ARTICLE 18

As regards the United Kingdom, the provisions of this Convention shall apply   **C6.19**
only to the United Kingdom of Great Britain and Northern Ireland.

ARTICLE 19

[Deposits of instruments of accession, etc.]   **C6.20**

ANNEX

Conduct Covered by Article 3 of the Convention

1. Reckless or dangerous driving (whether or not resulting in death, injury or serious   **C6.21**
risk).

2. Wilful failure to carry out the obligations placed on drivers after being involved in road accidents (hit-and-run driving).

3. Driving a vehicle while under the influence of alcohol or other substances affecting or diminishing the mental and physical abilities of a driver.

Refusal to submit to alcohol and drug tests.

4. Driving a vehicle faster than the permitted speed.   **C6.22**

5. Driving a vehicle whilst disqualified.

6. Other conduct constituting an offence for which a driving disqualification has been imposed by the State of the offence:

    — of a duration of six months or more,
    — of a duration of less than six months where that has been agreed bilaterally between the Member States concerned.

Regulation (EC) 2135/98 of September 24, 1998 amending Regulation (EEC) 3821/85 on recording equipment in road transport and Directive 88/599/EEC concerning the application of Regulations (EEC) 3820/85 and (EEC) 3821/85

C7.01 *THE COUNCIL OF THE EUROPEAN UNION,*

Having regard to the Treaty establishing the European Community, and in particular [Article 71(1)(c) and (d)] thereof,

Having regard to the proposal from the Commission,

Having regard to the opinion of the Economic and Social Committee,

Acting in accordance with the procedure laid down in [Article 252] of the Treaty,

(1) Whereas Council Regulation (EEC) No.3821/85 of 20 December 1985 on recording equipment in road transport [q.v.] lays down the provisions concerning the construction, installation, use and testing of recording equipment in road transport;

(2) Whereas experience has shown that the economic pressures and competition in road transport have led some drivers employed by road haulage companies to flout certain rules, particularly those concerning the driving and rest times laid down in Council Regulation (EEC) No.3820/85 of 20 December 1985 on the harmonisation of certain social legislation relating to road transport [q.v.];

(3) Whereas blatant infringements and fraud present a road safety hazard and are unacceptable for reasons of competition for the individual driver who does not respect the rules;

(4) Whereas road safety would be improved by the automatic recording and regular monitoring, both by the undertaking and by the competent authorities, of details of the driver's performance and behaviour and of the vehicle's journey, such as speed and distance covered;

(5) Whereas Community social regulations contain certain requirements for limits on the daily driving and rest time and also for the total driving and rest time, for up to two weeks; whereas it is difficult to monitor compliance with these requirements given that data are recorded on several daily record sheets, out of which the record sheets for the current week and the last day of the previous week are to be stored in the cab;

(6) Whereas, to put an end to the most common abuses of the present system, it is therefore necessary to introduce new advanced equipment such as recording equipment fitted with an electronic device for storing relevant information and a personal driver card, so ensuring that the data recorded are retrievable, intelligible when printed out, and reliable, and that they provide an indisputable record of the work done by both the driver over the last few days and by the vehicle over a period of several months;

(7) Whereas the total security of the system and its components is essential if recording equipment is to function efficiently;

(8) Whereas provisions need to be established to govern the conditions under which the memory cards provided for in Annex IB may be issued and used;

(9) Whereas the data on drivers' activities must be verifiable by the drivers themselves, by the companies that employ them and by the competent authorities of the Member States; whereas, however, only data relevant to their respective activities should be accessible to the driver and his company;

(10) Whereas the recording equipment provided for in this Regulation must be installed on vehicles put into service for the first time after the publication in the Official Journal of the European Communities of the technical specifications some of which are defined by the Commission in accordance with the committee procedure referred to in Article 18 of Regulation (EEC) No.3821/85; whereas a transitional period is needed to allow new recording equipment to be manufactured in accordance with those technical specifications and granted EC component type-approval;

(11) Whereas it is desirable that recording equipment complying with Annex IB should also offer the possibility of low-cost expansion of its functions for fleet management;

(12) Whereas, in accordance with the principle of subsidiarity, Community action is necessary to amend Regulation (EEC) No.3821/85 in order to ensure that recording equipment complying with Annex IB is compatible with driver cards and that the data produced by recording equipment complying with Annexes I and IB are consistent;

(13) Whereas technical progress necessitates the prompt adoption of the technical requirements laid down in the Annexes to the Regulation; whereas, in order to facilitate the implementation of the measures needed for this purpose, provision should be made for technical adaptations of those Annexes to be approved by the Commission, acting in accordance with the committee procedure as set out in Council Decision 87/373/EEC of 13 July 1987 laying down the procedures for the exercise of implementing powers conferred on the Commission [O.J. No.L197, July 18, 1987, p.33];

(14) Whereas the introduction of new recording equipment means that certain provisions of Directive 88/599/EEC [O.J. No.L325, November 29, 1988, p.55] concerning the application of Regulations (EEC) No.3820/85 and (EEC) No.3821/85 need to be amended,

[The preamble is printed as amended by the Treaty of Amsterdam art.12(1) **C7.02** *and (3).*

With effect from May 1, 2006, Directive 88/599/EC referred to in para.14 of the preamble was repealed by Directive 2006/22/EC (O.J. No.L102, April 11, 2006, p.35) art.17.

With effect from April 11, 2007, Regulation (EEC) 3820/85 was repealed by Regulation (EC) 561/2006 (O.J. No.L102, April 11, 2006) art.28.]

HAS ADOPTED THIS REGULATION:

C7.03   *[The text of this Regulation is printed as amended by:*

             Corrigendum at O.J. No.L49, February 25, 1999, p.46; and

             European Parliament and Council Regulation (EC) 561/2006 (O.J. No.L102, April 11, 2006, p.1) (May 1, 2006).

The amending Regulation is referred to in the notes to the principal Regulation only by its reference number. The date referred to above is the date on which the amending Regulation came into force.

The corrigendum noted above affected only the title to the Regulation.]

ARTICLE 1

C7.04   *[Amends Regulation (EEC) 3821/85, q.v.]*

ARTICLE 2

C7.05   [1.(a)   From the 20th day following the day of publication of Regulation (EC) No.561/2006 of the European Parliament and of the Council of 15 March 2006 on the harmonisation of certain social legislation relating to road transport and amending Council Regulations (EEC) No.3821/85 and (EC) No.2135/98 [*O.J. No.L102, April 11, 2006, p.1*] vehicles put into service for the first time shall be fitted with recording equipment in accordance with the requirements of Annex IB to Regulation (EEC) No.3821/85.]

         (b)   As from the date of entry in to force of the provisions of sub-paragraph (a), vehicles used for the carriage of persons containing more than eight seats apart from the driver's seat and having a maximum weight exceeding 10 tonnes, and also vehicles used for the carriage of goods having a maximum weight exceeding 12 tonnes, registered for the first time as from 1 January 1996, shall in so far as the transmission of signals to the recording equipment with which they are fitted is exclusively electrical, satisfy the requirements of Annex IB to Regulation (EEC) No.3821/85 when the equipment in question is replaced.

     [2.   Member States shall take the necessary measures to ensure that they are able to issue driver cards at the latest on the 20th day following the day of publication of Regulation (EC) No.561/2006.]

     3.   In the event that 12 months after the date of publication of the act referred to in paragraph 1, EC type-approval has not been granted to any item of recording equipment which conforms to the requirements of Annex IB to Regulation (EEC) No.3821/85, the Commission shall submit a proposal to the Council for an extension of the deadline laid down in paragraphs 1 and 2.

     4.   Drivers who, before the date laid down in paragraph 2, drive vehicles fitted with recording equipment conforming to the requirements of Annex IB to Regulation (EEC) No.3821/85 for which the competent authorities have not yet been able to issue a driver card shall at the end of their daily work period print out the information concerning the various periods of time recorded by the recording equipment and shall indicate their identification details on the print-out (name and driving licence number), and sign it.

C7.06   *[Article 2 is printed as amended by Regulation (EC) 561/2006.]*

ARTICLE 3

C7.07   *[Amends Directive 88/599/EEC (not reproduced).]*

ARTICLE 4

[Commencement.] **C7.08**

[This Regulation was published in O.J. No.L274, October 9, 1998, p.1.] **C7.09**

This Regulation shall be binding in its entirety and directly applicable in all Member States.

ANNEX
[Text of Annex IB to Regulation (EEC) 3821/85 before substitution by Regulation (EC) **C7.10**
1360/2002]

Regulation (EC) 2411/98 of November 3, 1998 on the recognition of intra-Community traffic of the distinguishing sign of the Member State in which motor vehicles and their trailers are registered

C8.01   *THE COUNCIL OF THE EUROPEAN UNION,*

Having regard to the Treaty establishing the European Community, and in particular [Article 71(1)(d)] thereof,

Having regard to the proposal from the Commission,

Having regard to the opinion of the Economic and Social Committee,

Acting in accordance with the procedure laid down in [Article 248] of the Treaty,

(1) Whereas the Community has adopted a certain number of measures that are intended to ensure the smooth functioning of an internal market comprising an area without frontiers in which the free movement of goods, persons, services and capital is ensured in accordance with the provisions of the Treaty;

(2) Whereas several Member States are contracting parties to the Vienna Convention of 1968 on road traffic hereinafter referred to as the "Convention", Article 37 of which provides that every motor vehicle in international traffic shall display at the rear, in addition to its registration number, a distinguishing sign of the State in which it is registered;

(3) Whereas the Community is not a contracting party to the Convention and whereas some of its Member States which are parties to it have recourse to the provisions of Article 37 of the Convention; whereas those Member States thus require vehicles from other Member States to display the distinguishing sign provided for by Annex 3 to the Convention; whereas some of those Member States do not recognise other distinguishing signs such as those displayed on registration plates which, while indicating the Member State in which the vehicle is registered, do not conform to Annex 3 to the Convention;

(4) Whereas several Member States have introduced a model registration plate which, on the extreme left, displays a blue zone containing the 12 yellow stars representing the European flag plus the distinguishing sign of the Member State of registration; whereas for the purpose of intra-Community transport this distinguishing sign meets the objective of identifying the State of registration as provided for in Article 37 of the Convention;

(5) Whereas Member States requiring vehicles from other Member States to display the distinguishing sign of the State of registration should also recognise the sign as provided for in the Annex to this Regulation,

C8.02   *[The preamble is printed as amended by the Treaty of Amsterdam art.12(1) and 3.]*

HAS ADOPTED THIS REGULATION:

[As to the Agreement on the European Economic Area generally, see the **C8.03**
introductory note to Section C above.

*For the purposes of that agreement, Regulation (EC) 2411/98 has been
adapted by ibid. Annex XIII, Chap.II para. 24b, as inserted by Decision 85/1999
of the EEA Joint Committee (O.J. No.L296, November 23, 2000, p.45).]*

ARTICLE 1

This Regulation shall apply to vehicles registered in the Member States that   **C8.04**
are driven within the Community.

ARTICLE 2

For the purposes of this Regulation: **C8.05**

1. *"distinguishing sign of the Member State of registration"* shall mean a set
   composed of one to three letters in Latin capitals indicating the Member
   State in which the vehicle is registered;

2. *"vehicle"* shall mean any motor vehicle and its trailer as defined in:
   — Council Directive 70/156/EEC of 6 February 1970 on the approxima-
     tion of the laws of the Member States relating to the type-approval of
     motor vehicles and their trailers [*O.J. No.L42, February 23, 1970, p.1*],
   — Council Directive 92/61/EEC of 30 June 1992 relating to the type-
     approval of two or three-wheel motor vehicles [*O.J. No.L225 August 10,
     1992, p.72.*].

[Directive 92/61/EEC (to which reference is made in art.2(2) in the definition   **C8.06**
*of "vehicle") was repealed by art.19 of Directive 2002/24/EC (O.J. No.L124,
May 9, 2002, pp.1, 8) with effect from November 9, 2003, and references to the
1992 Directive should be construed from that date as references to the 2002
Directive.*

*With effect from April 29, 2009, Directive 70/156/EEC (O.J. No.L42, Febru-
ary 23, 1970, p.1) also referred to in the definition of "vehicle" above was repealed by Directive 2007/46/EC (O.J. No.L263, October 9, 2007, p.1). References to the 1970 Directive should be construed as references to the 2007
Directive.]*

ARTICLE 3

Member States requiring vehicles registered in another Member State to   **C8.07**
display a distinguishing registration sign when they are being driven on their territory shall recognise the distinguishing sign of the Member State of registration
displayed on the extreme left of the registration plate in accordance with the Annex to this Regulation as being equivalent to any other distinguishing sign that
they recognise for the purpose of identifying the State in which the vehicle is
registered.

ARTICLE 4

This Regulation shall enter into force on the day following its publication in   **C8.08**
the *Official Journal of the European Communities*.

[This Regulation was published at O.J. No.L299, November 10, 1998, pp.1–3.]

This Regulation shall be binding in its entirety and directly applicable in all Member States.

SPECIFICATIONS FOR THE DISTINGUISHING SIGN OF THE MEMBER STATE OF REGISTRATION TO BE AFFIXED AT THE EXTREME LEFT OF THE REGISTRATION PLATE

MODEL 1 (example)

MODEL 2 (example)

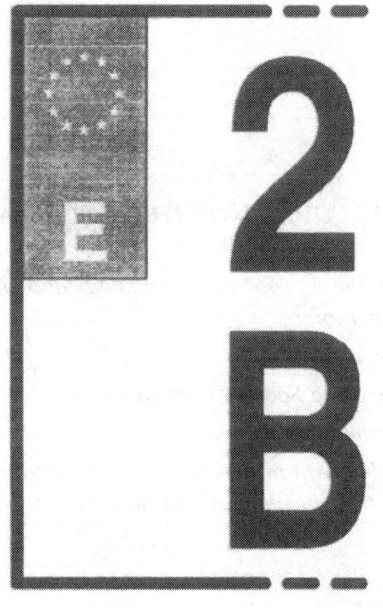

Colours:

1. Retro-reflecting blue background (Munsell reference 5,9 pb 3,4/15,1)

2. 12 retro-reflecting yellow stars

3. Retro-reflecting distinguishing sign of the Member State of registration, of a white or yellow colour

Composition and dimensions:

1. Blue background:

   height = minimum 98 mm

   width = minimum 40 mm, maximum 50 mm

2. The centres of the 12 stars to be arranged in a 15 mm radius circle; distance between two opposing peaks of any star = 4 to 5 mm

3. Distinguishing sign of the Member State of registration:

   height = minimum 20 mm

   width of character stroke = 4 to 5 mm

Where the dimensions of the blue background have been reduced for registration plates taking up two lines (see model 2) and/or for registration plates intended for two or three-wheel motor vehicles, the dimensions of the stars and of the distinguishing sign of the Member State of registration may be proportionately reduced.

Directive 2002/15/EC of March 11, 2002 on the organisation of the working time of persons performing mobile road transport activities

C9.01 *[The Arrangement of Articles set out below has been added editorially and does not form part of the text of the Directive.]*

C9.02 *THE EUROPEAN PARLIAMENT AND THE COUNCIL OF THE EUROPEAN UNION,*

Having regard to the Treaty establishing the European Community, and in particular Article 71 and Article 137(2) thereof,

Having regard to the proposal from the Commission

Having regard to the opinion of the Economic and Social Committee,

Following consultation of the Committee of the Regions,

Acting in accordance with the procedure laid down in Article 251 of the Treaty, and in the light of the joint text approved by the Conciliation Committee on 16 January 2002,

Whereas:

(1) Council Regulation (EEC) No.3820/85 of 20 December 1985 on the harmonisation of certain social legislation relating to road transport laid down common rules on driving times and rest periods for drivers; that Regulation does not cover other aspects of working time for road transport.

(2) Council Directive 93/104/EC of 23 November 1993 concerning certain aspects of the organisation of working time [O.J. No.L307, December 13,

1993, p.18, as amended; not reproduced in this work] makes it possible to adopt more specific requirements for the organisation of working time. Bearing in mind the sectoral nature of this Directive, the provisions thereof take precedence over Directive 93/104/EC by virtue of Article 14 thereof.

(3) Despite intensive negotiations between the social partners, it has not been possible to reach agreement on the subject of mobile workers in road transport.

(4) It is therefore necessary to lay down a series of more specific provisions concerning hours of work in road transport intended to ensure the safety of the transport and the health and safety of the persons involved.

(5) Since the objectives of the proposed actions cannot be sufficiently achieved by the Member States and can therefore, by reason of the scale and effects of the proposed action, be better achieved at Community level, the Community may adopt measures, in accordance with the principle of subsidiarity as set out in Article 5 of the Treaty. In accordance with the principle of proportionality, as set out in that Article, this Directive does not go beyond what is necessary in order to achieve those objectives.

(6) The scope of this Directive covers only mobile workers employed by transport undertakings established in a Member State participating in mobile road transport activities covered by Regulation (EEC) No.3820/85 or, failing that, by the European agreement concerning the work of crews of vehicles engaged in international road transport (AETR).

(7) It should be made clear that mobile workers excluded from the scope of this Directive, other than self-employed drivers, benefit from the basic protection provided for in Directive 93/104/EC. That basic protection includes the existing rules on adequate rest, the maximum average working week, annual leave and certain basic provisions for night workers including health assessment.

(8) As self-employed drivers are included within the scope of Regulation (EEC) No.3820/85 but excluded from that of Directive 93/104/EC, they should be excluded temporarily from the scope of this Directive in accordance with this provisions of Article 2(1).

(9) The definitions used in this Directive are not to constitute a precedent for other Community regulations on working time.

(10) In order to improve road safety, prevent the distortion of competition and guarantee the safety and health of the mobile workers covered by this Directive, the latter should know exactly which periods devoted to road transport activities constitute working time and which do not and are thus deemed to be break times, rest times or periods of availability. These workers should be granted minimum daily and weekly periods of rest, and adequate breaks. It is also necessary to place a maximum limit on the number of weekly working hours.

(11) Research has shown that the human body is more sensitive at night to environmental disturbances and also to certain burdensome forms of organisation and that long periods of night work can be detrimental to the health of workers and can endanger their safety and also road safety in general

(12) As a consequence, there is a need to limit the duration of periods of night work and to provide that professional drivers who work at night should receive appropriate compensation for their activity and should not be disadvantaged as regards training opportunities.

(13) Employers should keep records of instances when the maximum average working week applicable to mobile workers is exceeded.

(14) The provisions of Regulation (EEC) No.3820/85 on driving time in international and national passenger transport, other than regular services, should continue to apply.

(15) The Commission should monitor the implementation of this Directive and developments in this field in the Member States and submit to the European Parliament, the Council, the Economic and Social Committee and the Committee of the Regions a report on the application of the rules and the consequences of the provisions on night work.

(16) It is necessary to provide that certain provisions may be subject to derogations adopted, according to the circumstances, by the Member States or the two sides of industry. As a general rule, in the event of a derogation, the workers concerned must be given compensatory rest periods,

C9.03 *[Directive 93/104/EC of November 23, 1993, as amended (O.J. No.L307, December 13, 1993, p.18) referred to in para.(2) was repealed by Directive 2003/88/EC (O.J. No.L299, November 18, 2003, p.9) art.27 and Annex I, with effect from August 2, 2004. For the repeal of Regulation (EEC) 3820/85, see Regulation (EC) 561/2006 below.*

Directive 2002/15/EC was incorporated into the Agreement on the European Economic Area with effect from May 17, 2003 (see Decision 50/2003 of the EEA Joint Committee (O.J. No.L193, July 31, 2003, p.24)).]

HAVE ADOPTED THIS DIRECTIVE:

ARTICLE 1—PURPOSE

C9.04 The purpose of this Directive shall be to establish minimum requirements in relation to the organisation of working time in order to improve the health and safety protection of persons performing mobile road transport activities and to improve road safety and align conditions of competition.

ARTICLE 2—SCOPE

C9.05 1. This Directive shall apply to mobile workers employed by undertakings established in a Member State, participating in road transport activities covered by regulation (EEC) No.3820/85 or, failing that, by the AETR Agreement.

Without prejudice to the provisions of following sub-paragraph, this Directive shall apply to self-employed drivers from 23 March 2009.

At the latest two years before this date, the Commission shall present a report to the European Parliament and the Council. This report shall analyse the consequences of the exclusion of self-employed drivers from the scope of the Directive in respect of road safety, conditions of competition, the structure of the profession as well as social aspects. The circumstances in each Member State relating to the structure of the transport industry and to the working environment of the road transport profession shall be taken into account. On the basis of this report, the Commission shall submit a proposal, the aim of which may be either, as appropriate

— to set out the modalities for the inclusion of the self-employed drivers within the scope of the Directive in respect of certain self-employed drivers who are not participating in road transport activities in other Member States and who are subject to local constraints for objective reasons, such as peripheral location, long internal distances and a particular competitive environment, or

— not to include self-employed drivers within the scope of the Directive.

2. The provisions of Directive 93/104/EC shall apply to mobile workers excluded from the scope of this Directive.

3. In so far as this Directive contains more specific provisions as regards mobile workers performing road transport activities it shall, pursuant to Article 14 of Directive 93/104/EC, take precedence over the relevant provisions of that Directive.

4. This Directive shall supplement the provisions of Regulation (EEC) No.3820/85 and, where necessary, of the AETR Agreement, which take precedence over the provisions of this Directive.

ARTICLE 3 — DEFINITIONS

For the purposes of this Directive: **C9.06**

(a) *"working time"* shall mean:

1. in the case of mobile workers: the time from the beginning to the end of work, during which the mobile worker is at his workstation, at the disposal of the employer and exercising his functions or activities, that is to say:

— the time devoted to all road transport activities: These activities are, in particular, the following:

(i) driving;

(ii) loading and unloading;

(iii) assisting passengers boarding and disembarking from the vehicle;

(iv) cleaning and technical maintenance;

(v) all other work intended to ensure the safety of the vehicle, its cargo and passengers or to fulfil the legal or regulatory obligations directly linked to the specific transport operation under way, including monitoring of loading and unloading, administrative formalities with police, customs, immigration officers etc.,

— the times during which he cannot dispose freely of his time and is required to be at his workstation, ready to take up normal work, with certain tasks associated with being on duty, in particular during periods of awaiting loading or unloading where their foreseeable duration is not known in advance, that is to say either before departure or just before the actual start of the period in question, or under the general conditions negotiated between the social partners and/or under the terms of the legislation of the Member States;

2. in the case of self-employed drivers, the same definition shall apply to the time from the beginning to the end of work, during which the self-employed driver is at his workstation, at the disposal of the client and exercising his functions or activities other than general administrative work that is not directly linked to the specific transport under way.

The break times referred to in Article 5, the rest times referred to in Article 6 and, without prejudice to the legislation of Member States or agreements between the social partners providing that such periods should be compensated or limited, the periods of availability referred to in (b) of this Article, shall be excluded from working time;

(b) *"periods of availability"* shall mean:

— periods other than those relating to break times and rest times during which the mobile worker is not required to remain at his workstation, but must be available to answer any calls to start or resume driving or to carry out other work. In particular such periods of availability shall include periods during which the mobile worker is accompanying a vehicle being transported by ferryboat or by train as well as periods of waiting at frontiers and those due to traffic prohibitions.

— These periods and their foreseeable duration shall be known in advance by the mobile worker, that is to say either before departure or just before the actual start of the period in question, or under the general conditions negotiated between the social partners and/or under the terms of the legislation of the Member States,

— for mobile workers driving in a team, the time spent sitting next to the driver or on the couchette while the vehicle is in motion;

(c) *"workstation"* shall mean:

— the location of the main place of business of the undertaking for which the person performing mobile road transport activities carries out duties, together with its various subsidiary places of business, regardless of whether they are located in the same place as its head office or main place of business,

— the vehicle which the person performing mobile road transport activities uses when he carries out duties, and

— any other place in which activities connected with transportation are carried out;

(d) *"mobile worker"* shall mean any worker forming part of the travelling staff, including trainees and apprentices, who is in the service of an undertaking which operates transport services for passengers or goods by road for hire or reward or on its own account;

(e) *"self-employed driver"* shall mean anyone whose main occupation is to transport passengers or goods by road for hire or reward within the meaning of Community legislation under cover of a Community licence or any other professional authorisation to carry out the aforementioned transport, who is entitled to work for himself and who is not tied to an employer by an employment contract or by any other type of working hierarchical relationship, who is free to organise the relevant working activities, whose income depends directly on the profits made and who has the freedom to, individually or through co-operation between self-employed drivers, have commercial relations with several customers.

For the purposes of this Directive, those drivers who do not satisfy these criteria shall be subject to the same obligations and benefit from the same rights as those provided for mobile workers by this Directive;

(f) *"person performing mobile road transport activities"* shall mean any mobile worker or self-employed driver who performs such activities;

(g) *"week"* shall mean the period between 00.00 hours on Monday and 24.00 hours on Sunday;

(h) *"night time"* shall mean a period of at least four hours, as defined by national law, between 00.00 hours and 07.00 hours;

(i) *"night work"* shall mean any work performed during night time.

ARTICLE 4—MAXIMUM WEEKLY WORKING TIME

Member States shall take the measures necessary to ensure that: **C9.07**

(a) the average weekly working time may not exceed 48 hours. The maximum weekly working time may be extended to 60 hours only if, over four months, an average of 48 hours a week is not exceeded. The fourth and fifth sub-paragraphs of Article 6(1) of Regulation (EEC) No.3820/85 or, where necessary, the fourth sub-paragraph of Article 6(1) of the AETR Agreement shall take precedence over this Directive, in so far as the drivers concerned do not exceed an average working time of 48 hours a week over four months;

(b) working time for different employers is the sum of the working hours. The employer shall ask the mobile worker concerned in writing for an account of time worked for another employer. The mobile worker shall provide such information in writing.

ARTICLE 5—BREAKS

1. Member States shall take the measures necessary to ensure that, without **C9.08** prejudice to the level of protection provided by Regulation (EEC) No.3820/85 or, failing that, by the AETR Agreement, persons performing mobile road transport activities, without prejudice to Article 2(1), in no circumstances work for more than six consecutive hours without a break. Working time shall be interrupted by a break of at least 30 minutes, if working hours total between six and nine hours, and of at least 45 minutes, if working hours total more than nine hours.

2. Breaks may be subdivided into periods of at least 15 minutes each.

ARTICLE 6—REST PERIODS

For the purposes of this Directive, apprentices and trainees shall be covered by **C9.09** the same provisions on rest time as other mobile workers in pursuance of Regulation (EEC) No.3820/85 or, failing that, of the AETR Agreement.

ARTICLE 7—NIGHT WORK

1. Member States shall take the measures necessary to ensure that: **C9.10**

— if night work is performed the daily working time does not exceed ten hours in each 24 period,

— compensation for night work is given in accordance with national legislative measures, collective agreements, agreements between the two sides of industry and/or national practice, on condition that such compensation is not liable to endanger road safety.

2. By 23 March 2007, the Commission shall, within the framework of the report which it draws up in accordance with Article 13(2), assess the consequences of the provisions laid down in paragraph 1 above. The Commission shall, if necessary, submit appropriate proposals along with that report.

3. The Commission shall present a proposal for a Directive containing provisions relating to the training of professional drivers, including those who perform night work, and laying down the general principles of such training.

ARTICLE 8 — DEROGATIONS

C9.11

1. Derogations from Articles 4 and 7 may, for objective or technical reasons or reasons concerning the organisation of work, be adopted by means of collective agreements, agreements between the social partners, or if this is not possible, by laws, regulations or administrative provisions provided there is consultation of the representatives of the employers and workers concerned and efforts are made to encourage all relevant forms of social dialogue.

2. The option to derogate from Article 4 may not result in the establishment of a reference period exceeding six months, for calculation of the average maximum weekly working time of forty-eight hours.

ARTICLE 9 — INFORMATION AND RECORDS

C9.12   Member States shall ensure that:

(a) mobile workers are informed of the relevant national requirements, the internal rules of the undertaking and agreements between the two sides of industry, in particular collective agreements and any company agreements, reached on the basis of this Directive, without prejudice to Council Directive 91/533/EEC of 14 October 1991 on an employer's obligation to inform employees of the conditions applicable to the contract or employment relationship [*O.J. No.L288, October 18, 1991, p.32; not reproduced in this work*];

(b) without prejudice to Article 2(1), the working time of persons performing mobile road transport activities is recorded. Records shall be kept for at least two years after the end of the period covered. Employers shall be responsible for recording the working time of mobile workers. Employers shall upon request provide mobile workers with copies of the records of hours worked.

ARTICLE 10 — MORE FAVOURABLE PROVISIONS

C9.13   This Directive shall not affect Member States' right to apply or introduce laws, regulations or administrative provisions more favourable to the protection of the health and safety of persons performing mobile road transport activities, or their right to facilitate or permit the application of collective agreements or other agreements concluded between the two sides of industry which are more favourable to the protection of the health and safety of mobile workers. Implementation of this Directive shall not constitute valid grounds for reducing the general level of protection afforded to workers referred to in Article 2(1).

ARTICLE 11—PENALTIES

Member States shall lay down a system of penalties for breaches of the national **C9.14** provisions adopted pursuant to this Directive and shall take all the measures necessary to ensure that these penalties are applied. The penalties thus provided for shall be effective, proportional and dissuasive.

ARTICLE 12—NEGOTIATIONS WITH THIRD COUNTRIES

Once this Directive has entered into force, the Community shall begin negotia- **C9.15** tions with the relevant third countries with a view to the application of rules equivalent to those laid down in this Directive to mobile workers employed by undertakings established in a third country.

ARTICLE 13—REPORTS

1. Member States shall report to the Commission every two years on the **C9.16** implementation of this Directive, indicating the views of the two sides of industry. The report must reach the Commission no later than 30 September following the date on which the two-year period covered by the report expires. The two-year period shall be the same as that referred to in Article 16(2) of Regulation (EEC) No.3820/85.

2. The Commission shall produce a report every two years on the implementation of this Directive by Member States and developments in the field in question. The Commission shall forward this report to the European Parliament, the Council, the Economic and Social Committee and the Committee of the Regions.

ARTICLE 14—FINAL PROVISIONS

1. Member States shall adopt the laws, regulations and administrative provi- **C9.17** sions necessary to comply with this Directive by 23 March 2005 or shall ensure by that date that the two sides of industry have established the necessary measures by agreement, the Member States being obliged to take any steps to allow them to be able at any time to guarantee the results required by this Directive.

   When Member States adopt the measures referred to in the first subparagraph, they shall contain a reference to this Directive or shall be accompanied by such reference on the occasion of their official publication. The methods of making such reference shall be laid down by Member States.

2. Member States shall communicate to the Commission the provisions of national law which they have already adopted or which they adopt in the field covered by this Directive.

3. Member States shall take care that consignors, freight forwarders, prime contractors, sub-contractors and enterprises which employ mobile workers comply with the relevant provisions of this Directive.

ARTICLE 15—ENTRY INTO FORCE

This Directive shall enter into force on the day of its publication in the *Official* **C9.18** *Journal of the European Communities.*

[The Directive was published in O.J. No.L80, March 23, 2002, pp.35–39.]

ARTICLE 16—ADDRESSES

This Directive is addressed to the Member States. **C9.19**

Regulation (EC) 561/2006 of the European Parliament and of the Council of 15 March 2006 on the harmonisation of certain social legislation relating to road transport and amending Council Regulations (EEC) 3821/85 and (EC) 2135/98 and repealing Council Regulation (EEC) 3820/85

C10.01 THE EUROPEAN PARLIAMENT AND THE COUNCIL OF THE EUROPEAN UNION,

Having regard to the Treaty establishing the European Community, and in particular Article 71 thereof,

Having regard to the proposal from the Commission [O.J. No.C51 E, February 26, 2002, p.234],

Having regard to the opinion of the European Economic and Social Committee [O.J. No.C221, September 17, 2002, p.19],

After consulting the Committee of the Regions,

Acting in accordance with the procedure laid down in Article 251 of the Treaty [Opinion of the European Parliament of January 14, 2003 (O.J. No.C38 E, February 12, 2004, p.152), Council Common Position of December 9, 2004 (O.J. No.C63 E, March 15, 2005, p.11) and Position of the European Parliament of April 13, 2005 (O.J. No.C33 E, February 9, 2006, p.425). Legislative resolution of the European Parliament of February 2, 2006 and Decision of the Council of February 2, 2006], in the light of the joint text approved by the Conciliation Committee on 8 December 2005,

WHEREAS:

(1) In the field of road transport, Council Regulation (EEC) No.3820/85 of December 20, 1985 on the harmonisation of certain social legislation relating to road transport [O.J. No.L370, December 31, 1985, p.1] sought to harmonise the conditions of competition between modes of inland transport, especially with regard to the road transport sector, and to improve working conditions and road safety. Progress in these areas should be safeguarded and extended.

(2) Directive 2002/15/EC of the European Parliament and of the Council of March 11, 2002 on the organisation of the working time of persons performing mobile road transport activities [O.J. No.L80, March 23, 2002, p.35, q.v.] requires Member States to adopt measures which limit the maximum weekly working time of mobile workers.

(3) Difficulties have been experienced in interpreting, applying, enforcing and monitoring certain provisions of Regulation (EEC) No.3820/85 relating to driving time, break and rest period rules for drivers engaged in national and international road transport within the Community in a uniform manner in all Member States, because of the broad terms in which they are drafted.

(4) Effective and uniform enforcement of those provisions is desirable if their

objectives are to be achieved and the application of the rules is not to be brought into disrepute. Therefore, a clearer and simpler set of rules is needed, which will be more easily understood, interpreted and applied by the road transport industry and the enforcement authorities.

(5) Measures provided for in this Regulation regarding working conditions should not prejudice the right of the two sides of industry to lay down, by collective bargaining or otherwise, provisions more favourable to workers.

(6) It is desirable to define clearly the scope of this Regulation by specifying the main categories of vehicle which it covers.

(7) This Regulation should apply to carriage by road undertaken either exclusively within the Community or between the Community, Switzerland and the countries party to the Agreement on the European Economic Area.

(8) The European Agreement concerning the Work of Crews of Vehicles engaged in International Road Transport of July 1, 1970 (the AETR), as amended, should continue to apply to the carriage by road of goods and passengers by vehicles registered in any Member State or any country which is a contracting party to the AETR, for the whole of the journey where that journey is between the Community and a third country other than Switzerland and the countries which are contracting parties to the Agreement on the European Economic Area or through such a country. It is essential to modify the AETR as soon as possible, ideally within two years of the entry into force of this Regulation, in order to align its provisions with this Regulation.

(9) In the case of carriage by road using vehicles registered in a third country which is not a contracting party to the AETR, the provisions of the AETR should apply to that part of the journey effected within the Community or within countries which are contracting parties to the AETR.

(10) Since the subject matter of the AETR falls within the scope of this Regulation, the power to negotiate and conclude the Agreement lies with the Community.

(11) If an amendment to the internal Community rules in the field in question necessitates a corresponding amendment to the AETR, Member States should act together to bring about such an amendment to the AETR as soon as possible, in accordance with the procedure laid down therein.

(12) The list of exemptions should be updated to reflect developments in the road transport sector over the past 19 years.

(13) Full definitions of all key terms should be given in order to render interpretation easier and ensure that this Regulation is applied in a uniform manner. In addition, efforts should be made to ensure uniform interpretation and application of this Regulation by national supervisory authorities. The definition of "week" provided in this Regulation should not prevent drivers from starting their working week on any day of the week.

(14) To guarantee effective enforcement, it is essential that the competent authorities, when carrying out roadside checks, and after a transitional period, should be able to ascertain that driving times and rest periods have been properly observed on the day of the check and over the preceding 28 days.

(15) The basic rules on driving times need to be clarified and simplified to allow

effective and uniform enforcement by means of the digital tachograph, as provided for in Council Regulation (EEC) No.3821/85 of December 20, 1985 on recording equipment in road transport [O.J. No.L370, December 31, 1985, p.8. Regulation as last amended by Commission Regulation (EC) 432/2004 (O.J. L71, March 10, 2004, p.3)] and this Regulation. In addition, through a standing committee, Member State enforcement authorities should strive to reach a common understanding of the implementation of this Regulation.

(16) It has proved possible under the rules of Regulation (EEC) No.3820/85 to schedule daily driving periods and breaks to enable a driver to drive for too long without a full break, leading to reduced road safety and a deterioration in the driver's working conditions. It is therefore appropriate to ensure that split breaks are so ordered as to prevent abuse.

(17) This Regulation aims to improve social conditions for employees who are covered by it, as well as to improve general road safety. It does so mainly by means of the provisions pertaining to maximum driving times per day, per week and per period of two consecutive weeks, the provision which obliges drivers to take a regular weekly rest period at least once per two consecutive weeks and the provisions which prescribe that under no circumstances should a daily rest period be less than an uninterrupted period of nine hours. Since those provisions guarantee adequate rest, and also taking into account experience with enforcement practices during the past years, a system of compensation for reduced daily rest periods is no longer necessary.

(18) Many road transport operations within the Community involve transport by ferry or by rail for part of the journey. Clear, appropriate provisions regarding daily rest periods and breaks should therefore be laid down for such operations.

(19) In view of the increase in the cross-border carriage of goods and passengers, it is desirable, in the interests of road safety and enhanced enforcement, for roadside checks and checks at the premises of undertakings to cover driving times, rest periods and breaks undertaken within other Member States or third countries and to determine whether the relevant rules have been fully and properly observed.

(20) The liability of transport undertakings should extend at least to transport undertakings that are legal or natural persons, and should not exclude proceedings against natural persons who are perpetrators, or instigators of, or accessories to, infringements of this Regulation.

(21) It is necessary for drivers working for several transport undertakings to supply each of them with adequate information to enable it to fulfil its responsibilities under this Regulation.

(22) In order to promote social progress and improve road safety, each Member State should retain the right to adopt certain appropriate measures.

(23) National derogations should reflect changes in the road transport sector and be restricted to those elements not now subject to competitive pressures.

(24) The Member States should lay down rules for vehicles used for the carriage of passengers on regular services where the route covered does not exceed 50 km. Those rules should provide adequate protection in terms of permitted driving times and mandatory breaks and rest periods.

(25) It is desirable, in the interests of effective enforcement, that all regular national and international passenger transport services be checked using a standard recording device.

(26) The Member States should lay down rules on penalties applicable to infringements of this Regulation and ensure that they are implemented. Those penalties must be effective, proportionate, dissuasive and non-discriminatory. The possibility of immobilising the vehicle where serious infringements are detected should also be included within the common range of measures open to Member States. The provisions contained in this Regulation pertaining to penalties or proceedings should not affect national rules concerning the burden of proof.

(27) It is desirable in the interests of clear and effective enforcement to ensure uniform provisions on the liability of transport undertakings and drivers for infringements of this Regulation. This liability may result in penal, civil or administrative penalties as may be the case in the Member States.

(28) Since the objective of this Regulation, namely the establishment of clear, common rules on driving times, breaks and rest periods cannot be sufficiently achieved by the Member States and can therefore, by reason of the need for coordinated action, be better achieved at Community level, the Community may adopt measures, in accordance with the principle of subsidiarity as set out in Article 5 of the Treaty. In accordance with the principle of proportionality, as set out in that Article, this Regulation does not go beyond what is necessary in order to achieve that objective.

(29) The measures necessary for the implementation of this Regulation should be adopted in accordance with Council Decision 1999/468/EC of June 28, 1999 laying down the procedures for the exercise of implementing powers conferred on the Commission [O.J. No.L184, July 17, 1999, p.23].

(30) Since provisions concerning the minimum ages of drivers have been laid down in Directive 2003/59/EC [Directive 2003/59/EC of the European Parliament and of the Council of July 15, 2003 on the initial qualification and periodic training of drivers of certain road vehicles for the carriage of goods or passengers, amending Council Regulation (EEC) 3820/85 and Council Directive 91/439/EEC and repealing Council Directive 76/914/EEC (O.J. No.L226, September 10, 2003, p.4). Directive as amended by Council Directive 2004/66/EC (O.J. No.L168, May 1, 2004, p.35)] and must be transposed by 2009, only transitional provisions concerning the minimum age of crews are required in this Regulation.

(31) Regulation (EEC) No.3821/85 should be amended to clarify specific obligations on transport undertakings and drivers as well as to promote legal certainty and to facilitate enforcement of driving time and rest period limits during roadside checks.

(32) Regulation (EEC) No.3821/85 should also be amended to ensure legal certainty as regards the new dates for the introduction of the digital tachograph and for the availability of driver cards.

(33) The introduction of recording equipment pursuant to Regulation (EC) No.2135/98, enabling the activities of a driver over a 28-day period to be recorded electronically on his driver card and electronic records of vehicle

operations to cover a 365-day period, will in future make for more rapid and comprehensive roadside checks.

(34) Under Directive 88/599/EEC [Council Directive 88/599/EEC of November 23, 1988 on standard checking procedures for the implementation of Regulation (EEC) 3820/85 on harmonisation of certain social legislation relating to road transport and Regulation (EEC) 3821/85 on recording equipment in road transport (O.J. No.L325, November 29, 1988, p.55)] roadside checks are confined to daily driving time, daily rest periods, and breaks. When digital recording equipment is introduced driver and vehicle data will be stored electronically and data will be able to be evaluated electronically on the spot. This should, over time, enable simple checks to be carried out on regular and reduced daily rest periods and on regular and reduced weekly rest periods and compensatory rest.

(35) Experience indicates that compliance with the provisions of this Regulation, in particular the specified maximum driving time over a two-week period, cannot be enforced unless proper and effective supervision is brought to bear in roadside checks in relation to the whole of that period.

(36) The application of the legal provisions regarding digital tachographs should be in line with this Regulation in order to achieve optimal effectiveness in monitoring and enforcing certain social provisions in road transport.

(37) For reasons of clarity and rationalisation, Regulation (EEC) No.3820/85 should be repealed and replaced by this Regulation,

HAS ADOPTED THIS REGULATION:

C10.02   *[The text of this Regulation is amended by:*

European Parliament and Council Regulation (EC) 1073/2009 (O.J. No.L300/88, November 14, 2009, p.88) (December 4, 2009).

The amending Regulation is referred to only by its year and number. The date referred to above is the date on which the amending Regulation entered into force; different dates apply for the application of the provisions.]

CHAPTER I

INTRODUCTORY PROVISIONS
ARTICLE 1

C10.03   This Regulation lays down rules on driving times, breaks and rest periods for drivers engaged in the carriage of goods and passengers by road in order to harmonise the conditions of competition between modes of inland transport, especially with regard to the road sector, and to improve working conditions and road safety. This Regulation also aims to promote improved monitoring and enforcement practices by Member States and improved working practices in the road transport industry.

ARTICLE 2

C10.04   1. This Regulation shall apply to the carriage by road:

(a) of goods where the maximum permissible mass of the vehicle, including any trailer, or semi-trailer, exceeds 3,5 tonnes, or

(b) of passengers by vehicles which are constructed or permanently adapted for carrying more than nine persons including the driver, and are intended for that purpose.

2. This Regulation shall apply, irrespective of the country of registration of the vehicle, to carriage by road undertaken:

(a) exclusively within the Community; or

(b) between the Community, Switzerland and the countries party to the Agreement on the European Economic Area.

3. The AETR shall apply, instead of this Regulation, to international road transport operations undertaken in part outside the areas mentioned in paragraph 2, to:

(a) vehicles registered in the Community or in countries which are contracting parties to the AETR, for the whole journey;

(b) vehicles registered in a third country which is not a contracting party to the AETR, only for the part of the journey on the territory of the Community or of countries which are contracting parties to the AETR.

The provisions of the AETR should be aligned with those of this Regulation, so that the main provisions in this Regulation apply, through the AETR, to such vehicles for any part of the journey made within the Community.

ARTICLE 3

This Regulation shall not apply to carriage by road by: **C10.05**

(a) vehicles used for the carriage of passengers on regular services where the route covered by the service in question does not exceed 50 kilometres;

(b) vehicles with a maximum authorised speed not exceeding 40 kilometres per hour;

(c) vehicles owned or hired without a driver by the armed services, civil defence services, fire services, and forces responsible for maintaining public order when the carriage is undertaken as a consequence of the tasks assigned to these services and is under their control;

(d) vehicles, including vehicles used in the non-commercial transport of humanitarian aid, used in emergencies or rescue operations;

(e) specialised vehicles used for medical purposes;

(f) specialised breakdown vehicles operating within a 100 km radius of their base;

(g) vehicles undergoing road tests for technical development, repair or maintenance purposes, and new or rebuilt vehicles which have not yet been put into service;

(h) vehicles or combinations of vehicles with a maximum permissible mass not exceeding 7,5 tonnes used for the non-commercial carriage of goods;

(i) commercial vehicles, which have a historic status according to the legislation of the Member State in which they are being driven and which are used for the non-commercial carriage of passengers or goods.

ARTICLE 4

For the purposes of this Regulation the following definitions shall apply: **C10.06**

(a) *"carriage by road"* means any journey made entirely or in part on roads open to the public by a vehicle, whether laden or not, used for the carriage of passengers or goods;

(b) *"vehicle"* means a motor vehicle, tractor, trailer or semi-trailer or a combination of these vehicles, defined as follows:

— *"motor vehicle"*: any self-propelled vehicle travelling on the road, other than a vehicle permanently running on rails, and normally used for carrying passengers or goods,

— *"tractor"*: any self-propelled vehicle travelling on the road, other than a vehicle permanently running on rails, and specially designed to pull, push or move trailers, semi-trailers, implements or machines,

— *"trailer"*: any vehicle designed to be coupled to a motor vehicle or tractor,

— *"semi-trailer"*: a trailer without a front axle coupled in such a way that a substantial part of its weight and of the weight of its load is borne by the tractor or motor vehicle;

(c) *"driver"* means any person who drives the vehicle even for a short period, or who is carried in a vehicle as part of his duties to be available for driving if necessary;

(d) *"break"* means any period during which a driver may not carry out any driving or any other work and which is used exclusively for recuperation;

(e) *"other work"* means all activities which are defined as working time in Article 3(a) of Directive 2002/15/EC except "driving", including any work for the same or another employer, within or outside of the transport sector;

(f) *"rest"* means any uninterrupted period during which a driver may freely dispose of his time;

(g) *"daily rest period"* means the daily period during which a driver may freely dispose of his time and covers a "regular daily rest period" and a "reduced daily rest period":

— *"regular daily rest period"* means any period of rest of at least 11 hours. Alternatively, this regular daily rest period may be taken in two periods, the first of which must be an uninterrupted period of at least 3 hours and the second an uninterrupted period of at least nine hours,

— *"reduced daily rest period"* means any period of rest of at least nine hours but less than 11 hours;

(h) *"weekly rest period"* means the weekly period during which a driver may freely dispose of his time and covers a "regular weekly rest period" and a "reduced weekly rest period":

— *"regular weekly rest period"* means any period of rest of at least 45 hours,

— *"reduced weekly rest period* means any period of rest of less than 45 hours, which may, subject to the conditions laid down in Article 8(6), be shortened to a minimum of 24 consecutive hours;

(i) *"a week"* means the period of time between 00.00 on Monday and 24.00 on Sunday;

(j) *"driving time"* means the duration of driving activity recorded:

— automatically or semi-automatically by the recording equipment as defined in Annex I and Annex IB of Regulation (EEC) No.3821/85, or

— manually as required by Article 16(2) of Regulation (EEC) No.3821/85;

(k) *"daily driving time"* means the total accumulated driving time between the end of one daily rest period and the beginning of the following daily rest period or between a daily rest period and a weekly rest period;

(l) *"weekly driving time"* means the total accumulated driving time during a week;

(m) *"maximum permissible mass"* means the maximum authorised operating mass of a vehicle when fully laden;

(n) *"regular passenger services"* means national and international services as defined in Article 2 of Council Regulation (EEC) No.684/92 of 16 March 1992 on common rules for the international carriage of passengers by coach and bus [*O.J. No.L74, March 20, 1992, p.1. Regulation as last amended by the 2003 Act of Accession*];

(o) *"multi-manning"* means the situation where, during each period of driving between any two consecutive daily rest periods, or between a daily rest period and a weekly rest period, there are at least two drivers in the vehicle to do the driving. For the first hour of multi-manning the presence of another driver or drivers is optional but for the remainder of the period it is compulsory;

(p) *"transport undertaking"* means any natural person, any legal person, any association or group of persons without legal personality, whether profit-making or not, or any official body, whether having its own legal personality or being dependent upon an authority having such a personality, which engages in carriage by road, whether for hire or reward or for own account;

(q) *"driving period"* means the accumulated driving time from when a driver commences driving following a rest period or a break until he takes a rest period or a break. The driving period may be continuous or broken.

CHAPTER II

CREWS, DRIVING TIMES, BREAKS AND REST PERIODS

ARTICLE 5

1. The minimum age for conductors shall be 18 years.   **C10.07**

2. The minimum age for drivers' mates shall be 18 years. However, Member States may reduce the minimum age for drivers' mates to 16 years, provided that:

(a) the carriage by road is carried out within one Member State within a 50 kilometre radius of the place where the vehicle is based, including local administrative areas the centre of which is situated within that radius;

(b) the reduction is for the purposes of vocational training; and

(c) there is compliance with the limits imposed by the Member State's national rules on employment matters.

ARTICLE 6

C10.08

1. The daily driving time shall not exceed nine hours.

   However, the daily driving time may be extended to at most 10 hours not more than twice during the week.

2. The weekly driving time shall not exceed 56 hours and shall not result in the maximum weekly working time laid down in Directive 2002/15/EC being exceeded.

3. The total accumulated driving time during any two consecutive weeks shall not exceed 90 hours.

4. Daily and weekly driving times shall include all driving time on the territory of the Community or of a third country.

5. A driver shall record as other work any time spent as described in Article 4(e) as well as any time spent driving a vehicle used for commercial operations not falling within the scope of this Regulation, and shall record any periods of availability, as defined in Article 15(3)(c) of Regulation (EEC) No.3821/85, since his last daily or weekly rest period. This record shall be entered either manually on a record sheet, a printout or by use of manual input facilities on recording equipment.

ARTICLE 7

C10.09

After a driving period of four and a half hours a driver shall take an uninterrupted break of not less than 45 minutes, unless he takes a rest period.

This break may be replaced by a break of at least 15 minutes followed by a break of at least 30 minutes each distributed over the period in such a way as to comply with the provisions of the first paragraph.

ARTICLE 8

C10.10

1. A driver shall take daily and weekly rest periods.

2. Within each period of 24 hours after the end of the previous daily rest period or weekly rest period a driver shall have taken a new daily rest period.

   If the portion of the daily rest period which falls within that 24-hour period is at least nine hours but less than 11 hours, then the daily rest period in question shall be regarded as a reduced daily rest period.

3. A daily rest period may be extended to make a regular weekly rest period or a reduced weekly rest period.

4. A driver may have at most three reduced daily rest periods between any two weekly rest periods.

5. By way of derogation from paragraph 2, within 30 hours of the end of a daily or weekly rest period, a driver engaged in multi-manning must have taken a new daily rest period of at least nine hours.

6. In any two consecutive weeks a driver shall take at least:
   — two regular weekly rest periods, or
   — one regular weekly rest period and one reduced weekly rest period of at least 24 hours. However, the reduction shall be compensated by an equivalent period of rest taken en bloc before the end of the third week following the week in question.

   A weekly rest period shall start no later than at the end of six 24-hour periods from the end of the previous weekly rest period.

[6A. By way of derogation from paragraph 6, a driver engaged in a single occasional service of international carriage of passengers, as defined in Regulation (EC) No.1073/2009 of the European Parliament and of the Council of 21 October 2009 on common rules for access to the international market for coach and bus services [*O.J. No.L300, November 14, 2009, p.88, q.v.*], may postpone the weekly rest period for up to 12 consecutive 24-hour periods following a previous regular weekly rest period, provided that:

(a) the service lasts at least 24 consecutive hours in a Member State or a third country to which this Regulation applies other than the one in which the service started;

(b) the driver takes after the use of the derogation:

(i) either two regular weekly rest periods; or

(ii) one regular weekly rest period and one reduced weekly rest period of at least 24 hours. However, the reduction shall be compensated by an equivalent period of rest taken en bloc before the end of the third week following the end of the derogation period;

(c) after 1 January 2014, the vehicle is equipped with recording equipment in accordance with the requirements of Annex IB to Regulation (EEC) No.3821/85; and

(d) after 1 January 2014, if driving during the period from 22.00 to 06.00, the vehicle is multi-manned or the driving period referred to in Article 7 is reduced to three hours.

The Commission shall monitor closely the use made of this derogation in order to ensure the preservation of road safety under very strict conditions, in particular by checking that the total accumulated driving time during the period covered by the derogation is not excessive. By 4 December 2012, the Commission shall draw up a report assessing the consequences of the derogation in respect of road safety as well as social aspects. If it deems it appropriate, the Commission shall propose amendments to this Regulation in this respect.]

7. Any rest taken as compensation for a reduced weekly rest period shall be attached to another rest period of at least nine hours.

8. Where a driver chooses to do this, daily rest periods and reduced weekly rest periods away from base may be taken in a vehicle, as long as it has suitable sleeping facilities for each driver and the vehicle is stationary.

9. A weekly rest period that falls in two weeks may be counted in either week, but not in both.

[Article 8 is printed as amended by Regulation (EC) 1073/2009.]   **C10.11**

ARTICLE 9

1. By way of derogation from Article 8, where a driver accompanies a vehicle   **C10.12**
which is transported by ferry or train, and takes a regular daily rest period, that period may be interrupted not more than twice by other activities not exceeding one hour in total. During that regular daily rest period the driver shall have access to a bunk or couchette.

2. Any time spent travelling to a location to take charge of a vehicle falling within the scope of this Regulation, or to return from that location, when the vehicle is neither at the driver's home nor at the employer's operational cen-

tre where the driver is normally based, shall not be counted as a rest or break unless the driver is on a ferry or train and has access to a bunk or couchette.

3. Any time spent by a driver driving a vehicle which falls outside the scope of this Regulation to or from a vehicle which falls within the scope of this Regulation, which is not at the driver's home or at the employer's operational centre where the driver is normally based, shall count as other work.

CHAPTER III

LIABILITY OF TRANSPORT UNDERTAKINGS

ARTICLE 10

C10.13

1. A transport undertaking shall not give drivers it employs or who are put at its disposal any payment, even in the form of a bonus or wage supplement, related to distances travelled and/or the amount of goods carried if that payment is of such a kind as to endanger road safety and/or encourages infringement of this Regulation.

2. A transport undertaking shall organise the work of drivers referred to in paragraph 1 in such a way that the drivers are able to comply with Regulation (EEC) No.3821/85 and Chapter II of this Regulation. The transport undertaking shall properly instruct the driver and shall make regular checks to ensure that Regulation (EEC) No.3821/85 and Chapter II of this Regulation are complied with.

3. A transport undertaking shall be liable for infringements committed by drivers of the undertaking, even if the infringement was committed on the territory of another Member State or a third country.

   Without prejudice to the right of Member States to hold transport undertakings fully liable, Member States may make this liability conditional on the undertaking's infringement of paragraphs 1 and 2. Member States may consider any evidence that the transport undertaking cannot reasonably be held responsible for the infringement committed.

4. Undertakings, consignors, freight forwarders, tour operators, principal contractors, subcontractors and driver employment agencies shall ensure that contractually agreed transport time schedules respect this Regulation.

5. (a) A transport undertaking which uses vehicles that are fitted with recording equipment complying with Annex IB of Regulation (EEC) No.3821/85 and that fall within the scope of this Regulation, shall:

   (i) ensure that all data are downloaded from the vehicle unit and driver card as regularly as is stipulated by the Member State and that relevant data are downloaded more frequently so as to ensure that all data concerning activities undertaken by or for that undertaking are downloaded;

   (ii) ensure that all data downloaded from both the vehicle unit and driver card are kept for at least 12 months following recording and, should an inspecting officer request it, such data are accessible, either directly or remotely, from the premises of the undertaking;

   (b) for the purposes of this paragraph "downloaded" shall be interpreted in accordance with the definition laid down in Annex IB, Chapter I, point (s) of Regulation (EEC) No.3821/85;

(c) the maximum period within which the relevant data shall be downloaded under (a)(i) shall be decided by the Commission in accordance with the procedure referred to in Article 24(2).

CHAPTER IV

EXCEPTIONS

ARTICLE 11

A Member State may provide for longer minimum breaks and rest periods or shorter maximum driving times than those laid down in Articles 6 to 9 in the case of carriage by road undertaken wholly within its territory. In so doing, Member States shall take account of relevant collective or other agreements between the social partners. Nevertheless, this Regulation shall remain applicable to drivers engaged in international transport operations.   **C10.14**

ARTICLE 12

Provided that road safety is not thereby jeopardised and to enable the vehicle to reach a suitable stopping place, the driver may depart from Articles 6 to 9 to the extent necessary to ensure the safety of persons, of the vehicle or its load. The driver shall indicate the reason for such departure manually on the record sheet of the recording equipment or on a printout from the recording equipment or in the duty roster, at the latest on arrival at the suitable stopping place.   **C10.15**

ARTICLE 13

1. Provided the objectives set out in Article 1 are not prejudiced, each Member State may grant exceptions from Articles 5 to 9 and make such exceptions subject to individual conditions on its own territory or, with the agreement of the States concerned, on the territory of another Member State, applicable to carriage by the following: **C10.16**

   (a) vehicles owned or hired, without a driver, by public authorities to undertake carriage by road which do not compete with private transport undertakings;

   (b) vehicles used or hired, without a driver, by agricultural, horticultural, forestry, farming or fishery undertakings for carrying goods as part of their own entrepreneurial activity within a radius of up to 100 km from the base of the undertaking;

   (c) agricultural tractors and forestry tractors used for agricultural or forestry activities, within a radius of up to 100 km from the base of the undertaking which owns, hires or leases the vehicle;

   (d) vehicles or combinations of vehicles with a maximum permissible mass not exceeding 7,5 tonnes used:

   — by universal service providers as defined in Article 2(13) of Directive 97/67/EC of the European Parliament and of the Council of 15 December 1997 on common rules for the development of the internal market of Community postal services and the improvement of quality of service [*O.J. No.L15, January 21, 1998, p.14. Directive as last amended by Regulation (EC) No.1882/2003 (OJ No.L284, October 31, 2003, p.1)*] to deliver items as part of the universal service, or

— for carrying materials, equipment or machinery for the driver's use in the course of his work.

These vehicles shall be used only within a 50 kilometre radius from the base of the undertaking, and on condition that driving the vehicles does not constitute the driver's main activity;

(e) vehicles operating exclusively on islands not exceeding 2300 square kilometres in area which are not linked to the rest of the national territory by a bridge, ford or tunnel open for use by motor vehicles;

(f) vehicles used for the carriage of goods within a 50 km radius from the base of the undertaking and propelled by means of natural or liquefied gas or electricity, the maximum permissible mass of which, including the mass of a trailer or semi-trailer, does not exceed 7,5 tonnes;

(g) vehicles used for driving instruction and examination with a view to obtaining a driving licence or a certificate of professional competence, provided that they are not being used for the commercial carriage of goods or passengers;

(h) vehicles used in connection with sewerage, flood protection, water, gas and electricity maintenance services, road maintenance and control, door-to-door household refuse collection and disposal, telegraph and telephone services, radio and television broadcasting, and the detection of radio or television transmitters or receivers;

(i) vehicles with between 10 and 17 seats used exclusively for the non-commercial carriage of passengers;

(j) specialised vehicles transporting circus and funfair equipment;

(k) specially fitted mobile project vehicles, the primary purpose of which is use as an educational facility when stationary;

(l) vehicles used for milk collection from farms and the return to farms of milk containers or milk products intended for animal feed;

(m) specialised vehicles transporting money and/or valuables;

(n) vehicles used for carrying animal waste or carcasses which are not intended for human consumption;

(o) vehicles used exclusively on roads inside hub facilities such as ports, interports and railway terminals;

(p) vehicles used for the carriage of live animals from farms to local markets and vice versa or from markets to local slaughterhouses within a radius of up to 50 km.

2. Member States shall inform the Commission of the exceptions granted under paragraph 1 and the Commission shall inform the other Member States thereof.

3. Provided that the objectives set out in Article 1 are not prejudiced and adequate protection for drivers is provided, a Member State may, after approval by the Commission, grant on its own territory minor exemptions from this Regulation for vehicles used in predefined areas with a population density of less than five persons per square kilometre, in the following cases:

— regular domestic passenger services, where their schedule is confirmed by the authorities (in which case only exemptions relating to breaks may be permitted), and

— domestic road haulage operations for own account or for hire or reward, which have no impact on the single market and are needed to maintain certain sectors of industry in the territory concerned and where the exempting provisions of this Regulation impose a limiting radius of up to 100 km.

Carriage by road under this exemption may include a journey to an area with a population density of five persons or more per square kilometre only in order to end or start the journey. Any such measures shall be proportionate in nature and scope.

ARTICLE 14

1. Provided that the objectives set out in Article 1 are not prejudiced, Member States may, after authorisation by the Commission, grant exceptions from the application of Articles 6 to 9 to transport operations carried out in exceptional circumstances.   **C10.17**

2. In urgent cases Member States may grant a temporary exception for a period not exceeding 30 days, which shall be notified immediately to the Commission.

3. The Commission shall inform the other Member States of any exception granted pursuant to this Article.

ARTICLE 15

Member States shall ensure that drivers of vehicles referred to in Article 3(a) are governed by national rules which provide adequate protection in terms of permitted driving times and mandatory breaks and rest periods.   **C10.18**

CHAPTER V

CONTROL PROCEDURES AND SANCTIONS

ARTICLE 16

1. Where no recording equipment has been fitted to the vehicle in accordance with Regulation (EEC) No.3821/85, paragraphs 2 and 3 of this Article shall apply to: **C10.19**

   (a) regular national passenger services, and

   (b) regular international passenger services whose route terminals are located within a distance of 50 km as the crow flies from a border between two Member States and whose route length does not exceed 100 km.

2. A service timetable and a duty roster shall be drawn up by the transport undertaking and shall show, in respect of each driver, the name, place where he is based and the schedule laid down in advance for various periods of driving, other work, breaks and availability.

   Each driver assigned to a service referred to in paragraph 1 shall carry an extract from the duty roster and a copy of the service timetable.

3. The duty roster shall:

   (a) include all the particulars specified in paragraph 2 for a minimum period covering the previous 28 days; these particulars must be updated on regular intervals, the duration of which may not exceed one month;

    (b) be signed by the head of the transport undertaking or by a person autho-
        rised to represent him;

    (c) be kept by the transport undertaking for one year after expiry of the pe-
        riod covered by it. The transport undertaking shall give an extract from
        the roster to the drivers concerned upon request; and

    (d) be produced and handed over at the request of an authorised inspecting
        officer.

ARTICLE 17

C10.20　　1. Member States, using the standard form set out in Decision 93/173/EEC
[*O.J. No.L72, March 25, 1993, p.33*], shall communicate the necessary information to the Commission to enable it to draw up every two years a report
on the application of this Regulation and Regulation (EEC) No.3821/85 and
developments in the fields in question.

2. This information shall be communicated to the Commission not later than
30 September of the year following the end of the two-year period concerned.

3. The report shall state what use has been made of the exceptions provided for
in Article 13.

4. The Commission shall forward the report to the European Parliament and to
the Council within 13 months of the end of the two-year period concerned.

ARTICLE 18

C10.21　　Member States shall adopt such measures as may be necessary for the
implementation of this Regulation.

ARTICLE 19

C10.22　　1. Member States shall lay down rules on penalties applicable to infringements
of this Regulation and Regulation (EEC) No.3821/85 and shall take all
measures necessary to ensure that they are implemented. Those penalties
shall be effective, proportionate, dissuasive and non-discriminatory. No infringement of this Regulation and Regulation (EEC) No.3821/85 shall be
subjected to more than one penalty or procedure. The Member States shall
notify the Commission of these measures and the rules on penalties by the
date specified in the second subparagraph of Article 29. The Commission
shall inform Member States accordingly.

2. A Member State shall enable the competent authorities to impose a penalty
on an undertaking and/or a driver for an infringement of this Regulation
detected on its territory and for which a penalty has not already been
imposed, even where that infringement has been committed on the territory
of another Member State or of a third country.

    By way of exception, where an infringement is detected:

    — which was not committed on the territory of the Member State
      concerned, and

    — which has been committed by an undertaking which is established in,
      or a driver whose place of employment is, in another Member State or
      a third country,

    a Member State may, until 1 January 2009, instead of imposing a penalty,
notify the facts of the infringement to the competent authority in the Member
State or the third country where the undertaking is established or where the
driver has his place of employment.

3. Whenever a Member State initiates proceedings or imposes a penalty for a particular infringement, it shall provide the driver with due evidence of this in writing.

4. Member States shall ensure that a system of proportionate penalties, which may include financial penalties, is in force for infringements of this Regulation or Regulation (EEC) No.3821/85 on the part of undertakings, or associated consignors, freight forwarders, tour operators, principal contractors, subcontractors and driver employment agencies.

ARTICLE 20

1. The driver shall keep any evidence provided by a Member State concerning penalties imposed or the initiation of proceedings until such time as the same infringement of this Regulation can no longer lead to a second proceeding or penalty pursuant to this Regulation.   **C10.23**

2. The driver shall produce the evidence referred to in paragraph 1 upon request.

3. A driver who is employed or at the disposal of more than one transport undertaking shall provide sufficient information to each undertaking to enable it to comply with Chapter II.

ARTICLE 21

To address cases where a Member State considers that there has been an infringement of this Regulation which is of a kind that is clearly liable to endanger road safety, it shall empower the relevant competent authority to proceed with immobilisation of the vehicle concerned until such time as the cause of the infringement has been rectified. Member States may compel the driver to take a daily rest period. Member States shall, where appropriate also withdraw, suspend or restrict an undertaking's licence, if the undertaking is established in that Member State, or withdraw, suspend or restrict a driver's driving licence. The Commission, acting in accordance with the procedure in Article 24(2) shall develop guidelines with a view to promoting a harmonised application of this Article.   **C10.24**

ARTICLE 22

1. Member States shall assist each other in applying this Regulation and in checking compliance herewith.   **C10.25**

2. The competent authorities of the Member States shall regularly exchange all available information concerning:

    (a) infringements of the rules set out in Chapter II committed by non-residents and any penalties imposed for such infringements;

    (b) penalties imposed by a Member State on its residents for such infringements committed in other Member States.

3. The Member States shall regularly send relevant information concerning the national interpretation and application of this Regulation to the Commission, which will make this information available in electronic form to other Member States.

4. The Commission shall support dialogue between Member States concerning national interpretation and application of this Regulation through the Committee referred to in Article 24(1).

ARTICLE 23

C10.26   The Community shall enter into any negotiations with third countries which may prove necessary for the purpose of implementing this Regulation.

ARTICLE 24

C10.27   1. The Commission shall be assisted by the Committee set up under Article 18(1) of Regulation (EEC) No.3821/85.

2. Where reference is made to this paragraph, Articles 3 and 7 of Decision 1999/468/EC shall apply, having regard to the provisions of Article 8 thereof.

3. The Committee shall adopt its rules of procedure.

ARTICLE 25

C10.28   1. At the request of a Member State, or on its own initiative, the Commission shall:

     (a) examine cases where differences in the application and enforcement of any of the provisions of this Regulation arise and particularly concerning driving times, breaks and rest periods;

     (b) clarify the provisions of this Regulation, with a view to promoting a common approach.

2. In the cases referred to in paragraph 1 the Commission shall take a decision on a recommended approach in accordance with the procedure referred to in Article 24(2). The Commission shall communicate its decision to the European Parliament, the Council and to the Member States.

CHAPTER VI

FINAL PROVISIONS

ARTICLE 26

C10.29   *[Amends Regulation (EEC) 3821/85, q.v. (not reproduced).]*

ARTICLE 27

C10.30   *[Amends Regulation (EC) 2135/98, q.v. (not reproduced).]*

ARTICLE 28

C10.31   Regulation (EEC) No.3820/85 is hereby repealed and replaced by this Regulation. Notwithstanding, paragraphs 1, 2 and 4 of Article 5 of Regulation (EEC) No.3820/85 shall continue to apply until the dates set out in Article 15(1) of Directive 2003/59/EC.

ARTICLE 29

C10.32   This Regulation shall enter into force on 11 April 2007, with the exception of Articles 10(5), 26(3) and (4) and 27, which shall enter into force on 1 May 2006.

This Regulation shall be binding in its entirety and directly applicable in all Member States.

[The Regulation was published in O.J. No.L102, April 11, 2006, pp.1–14.]

Directive 2006/126/EC of December 20, 2006 on driving licences (Recast)

[This Directive (O.J. No.L403, December 30, 2006, pp.18–60) (generally in force January 19, 2007) repeals Directive 91/439/EEC (O.J. No.L237, August 24, 1991, pp.1–24, see § C2.01 above) with effect from January 19, 2013. Selected provisions are reproduced below.] **C11.01**

*   *   *

ARTICLE 1—CATEGORIES, DEFINITIONS AND MINIMUM AGES

1. *[Omitted.]* **C11.02**
2. *[Omitted.]*
3. *[Omitted.]*
4. motor vehicles:
   — *"motor vehicle"* means any power-driven vehicle, which is normally used for carrying persons or goods by road or for drawing, on the road, vehicles used for the carriage of persons or goods. This terms shall include trolleybuses, i.e. vehicles connected to an electric conductor and rail-borne. It shall not include agricultural or forestry tractors.

   ...

*   *   *

ARTICLE 12—NORMAL RESIDENCE

For the purposes of this Directive, *"normal residence"* means the place where **C11.03** a person usually lives, that is for at least 185 days in each calendar year, because of personal and occupational ties, or, in the case of a person with no occupational ties, because of personal ties which show close links between that person and the place where he is living.

However, the normal residence of a person whose occupational ties are in a different place from his personal ties and who consequently lives in turn in different places situated in two or more Member States shall be regarded as being the place of his personal ties, provided that such person returns there regularly. This last condition need not be met where the person is living in a Member State in order to carry out a task of a definite duration. Attendance at a university or school shall not imply transfer of normal residence.

[Article 12 applies from January 19, 2009.] **C11.04**

Regulation (EC) 1072/2009 of October 21, 2009 on common rules for access to the international road haulage market

C12.01   *THE EUROPEAN PARLIAMENT AND THE COUNCIL OF THE EUROPEAN UNION,*

Having regard to the Treaty establishing the European Community, and in particular Article 71 thereof,

Having regard to the proposal from the Commission,

Having regard to the opinion of the European Economic and Social Committee,

After consulting the Committee of the Regions,

Acting in accordance with the procedure laid down in Article 251 of the Treaty,

WHEREAS:

(1) A number of substantial changes are to be made to Council Regulation (EEC) No 881/92 of 26 March 1992 on access to the market in the carriage of goods by road within the Community to or from the territory of a Member State or passing across the territory of one or more Member States [O.J. No.L95, April 9, 1992, p.1], to Council Regulation (EEC) No 3118/93 of 25 October 1993 laying down the conditions under which non-resident carriers may operate national road haulage services within a Member State [O.J. No.L279, November 12, 1993, p.1], and to Directive 2006/94/EC of the European Parliament and of the Council of 12 December 2006 on the establishment of common rules for certain types of carriage of goods by road [O.J. No.L374, December 27, 2006, p.5]. In the interests of clarity and simplification, those legal acts should be recast and incorporated into one single regulation.

(2) The establishment of a common transport policy entails, inter alia, laying down common rules applicable to access to the market in the international carriage of goods by road within the territory of the Community, as well as laying down the conditions under which non-resident hauliers may operate transport services within a Member State. Those rules must be laid down in such a way as to contribute to the smooth operation of the internal transport market.

(3) To ensure a coherent framework for international road haulage throughout the Community, this Regulation should apply to all international carriage on Community territory. Carriage from Member States to third countries is still largely covered by bilateral agreements between the Member States and those third countries. Therefore, this Regulation should not apply to that part of the journey within the territory of the Member State of loading or unloading as long as the necessary agreements between the Community and the third countries concerned have not been concluded. It should, however, apply to the territory of a Member State crossed in transit.

(4) The establishment of a common transport policy implies the removal of all restrictions against the person providing transport services on the grounds of

nationality or the fact that he is established in a different Member State from the one in which the services are to be provided.

(5) The establishment of a common transport policy implies the removal of all restrictions against the person providing transport services on the grounds of nationality or the fact that he is established in a different Member State from the one in which the services are to be provided.

(6) The gradual completion of the single European market should lead to the elimination of restrictions on access to the domestic markets of Member States. Nevertheless, this should take into account the effectiveness of controls and the evolution of employment conditions in the profession, the harmonisation of the rules in the fields of, inter alia, enforcement and road user charges, and social and safety legislation. The Commission should closely monitor the market situation as well as the harmonisation mentioned above and propose, if appropriate, the further opening of domestic road transport markets, including cabotage.

(7) Under Directive 2006/94/EC, a certain number of types of carriage are exempt from Community authorisation and from any other carriage authorisation. Within the framework of the organisation of the market provided for by this Regulation, a system of exemption from the Community licence and from any other carriage authorisation should be maintained for some of those types of carriage, because of their special nature.

(8) Under Directive 2006/94/EC, the carriage of goods with vehicles of a maximum laden weight of between 3.5 tonnes and 6 tonnes was exempt from the requirement for a Community licence. Community rules in the field of road transport of goods, however, apply in general to vehicles with a maximum laden mass of more than 3.5 tonnes. Thus, the provisions of this Regulation should be aligned with the general scope of application of Community road transport rules and should only provide for an exemption for vehicles with a maximum laden mass of up to 3.5 tonnes.

(9) The international carriage of goods by road should be conditional on the possession of a Community licence. Hauliers should be required to carry a certified true copy of the Community licence aboard each of their vehicles in order to facilitate effective controls by enforcement authorities, especially those outside the Member State in which the haulier is established. To this end, it is necessary to lay down more detailed specifications as regards the layout and other features of the Community licence and the certified copies.

(10) Roadside checks should be carried out without direct or indirect discrimination on grounds of the nationality of the road transport operator or the country of establishment of the road transport operator or of registration of the vehicle.

(11) The conditions governing the issue and withdrawal of Community licences and the types of carriage to which they apply, their periods of validity and the detailed rules for their use should be determined.

(12) A driver attestation should also be established in order to allow Member States to check effectively whether drivers from third countries are lawfully employed or at the disposal of the haulier responsible for a given transport operation.

(13) Hauliers who are holders of Community licences provided for in this Regulation and hauliers authorised to operate certain categories of international haulage service should be permitted to carry out national transport services within a Member State on a temporary basis in conformity with this Regulation, without having a registered office or other establishment therein. When such cabotage operations are performed, they should be subject to Community legislation such as Regulation (EC) No 561/2006 of the European Parliament and of the Council of 15 March 2006 on the harmonisation of certain social legislation relating to road transport [O.J. No.L102, April 11, 2006, p.1] and to national law in force in specified areas in the host Member State.

(14) Provisions should be adopted to allow action to be taken in the event of serious disturbance of the transport markets affected. For that purpose it is necessary to introduce a suitable decision-making procedure and for the required statistical data to be collected.

(15) Without prejudice to the provisions of the Treaty on the right of establishment, cabotage operations consist of the provision of services by hauliers within a Member State in which they are not established and should not be prohibited as long as they are not carried out in a way that creates a permanent or continuous activity within that Member State. To assist the enforcement of this requirement, the frequency of cabotage operations and the period in which they can be performed should be more clearly defined. In the past, such national transport services were permitted on a temporary basis. In practice, it has been difficult to ascertain which services are permitted. Clear and easily enforceable rules are thus needed.

(16) This Regulation is without prejudice to the provisions concerning the incoming or outgoing carriage of goods by road as one leg of a combined transport journey as laid down in Council Directive 92/106/EEC of 7 December 1992 on the establishment of common rules for certain types of combined transport of goods between Member States [O.J. No.L368, December 17, 1992, p.38]. National journeys by road within a host Member State which are not part of a combined transport operation as laid down in Directive 92/106/EEC fall within the definition of cabotage operations and should accordingly be subject to the requirements of this Regulation.

(17) The provisions of Directive 96/71/EC of the European Parliament and of the Council of 16 December 1996 concerning the posting of workers in the framework of the provision of services [O.J. No.L18, January 21, 1997, p.1] apply to transport undertakings performing a cabotage operation.

(18) In order to perform efficient controls of cabotage operations, the enforcement authorities of the host Member States should, at least, have access to data from consignment notes and from recording equipment, in accordance with Council Regulation (EEC) No 3821/85 of 20 December 1985 on recording equipment in road transport [O.J. No.L370, December 31, 1985, p.8].

(19) Member States should grant each other mutual assistance with a view to the sound application of this Regulation.

(20) Administrative formalities should be reduced as far as possible without abandoning the controls and penalties that guarantee the correct application

and effective enforcement of this Regulation. To this end, the existing rules on the withdrawal of the Community licence should be clarified and strengthened. The current rules should be adapted to allow the effective sanctioning of serious infringements committed in a host Member State. Penalties should be non-discriminatory and proportionate to the seriousness of the infringements. It should be possible to lodge an appeal in respect of any penalties imposed.

(21) Member States should enter in their national electronic register of road transport undertakings all serious infringements committed by hauliers which have led to the imposition of a penalty.

(22) In order to facilitate and strengthen the exchange of information between national authorities, Member States should exchange the relevant information through the national contact points set up pursuant to Regulation (EC) No 1071/2009 of the European Parliament and of the Council of 21 October 2009 establishing common rules concerning the conditions to be complied with to pursue the occupation of road transport operator [O.J. No.L300, November 14, 2009, p.51].

(23) The measures necessary for the implementation of this Regulation should be adopted in accordance with Council Decision 1999/468/EC of 28 June 1999 laying down the procedures for the exercise of implementing powers conferred on the Commission [O.J. No.L184, July 17, 1999, p.23].

(24) In particular, the Commission should be empowered to adapt Annexes I, II and III to this Regulation to technical progress. Since those measures are of general scope and are designed to amend non-essential elements of this Regulation, they must be adopted in accordance with the regulatory procedure with scrutiny provided for in Article 5a of Decision 1999/468/EC.

(25) Member States should take the necessary measures to implement this Regulation, in particular as regards effective, proportionate and dissuasive penalties.

(26) Since the objective of this Regulation, namely to ensure a coherent framework for international road haulage throughout the Community, cannot be sufficiently achieved by the Member States and can therefore, by reason of its scale and effects, be better achieved at Community level, the Community may adopt measures, in accordance with the principle of subsidiarity as set out in Article 5 of the Treaty. In accordance with the principle of proportionality, as set out in that Article, this Regulation does not go beyond what is necessary in order to achieve that objective,

HAVE ADOPTED THIS REGULATION: **C12.02**

CHAPTER I

GENERAL PROVISIONS
ARTICLE 1

Scope

1. This Regulation shall apply to the international carriage of goods by road for hire or reward for journeys carried out within the territory of the Community.

2. In the event of carriage from a Member State to a third country and vice versa, this Regulation shall apply to the part of the journey on the territory of any Member State crossed in transit. It shall not apply to that part of the journey on the territory of the Member State of loading or unloading, as long as the necessary agreement between the Community and the third country concerned has not been concluded.

3. Pending the conclusion of the agreements referred to in paragraph 2, this Regulation shall not affect:

    (a) provisions relating to the carriage from a Member State to a third country and vice versa included in bilateral agreements concluded by Member States with those third countries;

    (b) provisions relating to the carriage from a Member State to a third country and vice versa included in bilateral agreements concluded between Member States which, under either bilateral authorisations or liberalisation arrangements, allow loading and unloading in a Member State by hauliers not established in that Member State.

4. This Regulation shall apply to the national carriage of goods by road undertaken on a temporary basis by a non-resident haulier as provided for in Chapter III.

5. The following types of carriage and unladen journeys made in conjunction with such carriage shall not require a Community licence and shall be exempt from any carriage authorisation:

    (a) carriage of mail as a universal service;

    (b) carriage of vehicles which have suffered damage or breakdown;

    (c) carriage of goods in motor vehicles the permissible laden mass of which, including that of trailers, does not exceed 3,5 tonnes;

    (d) carriage of goods in motor vehicles provided the following conditions are fulfilled:

       (i) the goods carried are the property of the undertaking or have been sold, bought, let out on hire or hired, produced, extracted, processed or repaired by the undertaking;

       (ii) the purpose of the journey is to carry the goods to or from the undertaking or to move them, either inside or outside the undertaking for its own requirements;

       (iii) motor vehicles used for such carriage are driven by personnel employed by, or put at the disposal of, the undertaking under a contractual obligation;

       (iv) the vehicles carrying the goods are owned by the undertaking, have been bought by it on deferred terms or have been hired provided that in the latter case they meet the conditions of Directive 2006/1/EC of the European Parliament and of the Council of 18 January 2006 on the use of vehicles hired without drivers for the carriage of goods by road [*O.J. No.L33, February 4, 2006, p.82*]; and

       (v) such carriage is no more than ancillary to the overall activities of the undertaking;

    (e) carriage of medicinal products, appliances, equipment and other articles required for medical care in emergency relief, in particular for natural disasters.

Point (d)(iv) of the first subparagraph shall not apply to the use of a replacement vehicle during a short breakdown of the vehicle normally used.

6. The provisions of paragraph 5 shall not affect the conditions under which a Member State authorises its nationals to engage in the activities referred to in that paragraph.

ARTICLE 2

Definitions

For the purposes of this Regulation: **C12.03**

1. *"vehicle"* means a motor vehicle registered in a Member State, or a coupled combination of vehicles the motor vehicle of which at least is registered in a Member State, used exclusively for the carriage of goods;

2. *"international carriage"* means:

   (a) a laden journey undertaken by a vehicle the point of departure and the point of arrival of which are in two different Member States, with or without transit through one or more Member States or third countries;

   (b) a laden journey undertaken by a vehicle from a Member State to a third country or vice versa, with or without transit through one or more Member States or third countries;

   (c) a laden journey undertaken by a vehicle between third countries, with transit through the territory of one or more Member States; or

   (d) an unladen journey in conjunction with the carriage referred to in points (a), (b) and (c);

3. *"host Member State"* means a Member State in which a haulier operates other than the haulier's Member State of establishment;

4. *"non-resident haulier"* means a road haulage undertaking which operates in a host Member State;

5. *"driver"* means any person who drives the vehicle even for a short period, or who is carried in a vehicle as part of his duties to be available for driving if necessary;

6. *"cabotage operations"* means national carriage for hire or reward carried out on a temporary basis in a host Member State, in conformity with this Regulation;

7. *"serious infringement of Community road transport legislation"* means an infringement which may lead to the loss of good repute in accordance with Article 6(1) and (2) of Regulation (EC) No 1071/2009 and/or to the temporary or permanent withdrawal of a Community licence.

CHAPTER II

INTERNATIONAL CARRIAGE

ARTICLE 3

General Principle

International carriage shall be carried out subject to possession of a Com-   **C12.04** munity licence and, if the driver is a national of a third country, in conjunction with a driver attestation.

ARTICLE 4

Community Licence

C12.05
1. The Community licence shall be issued by a Member State, in accordance with this Regulation, to any haulier carrying goods by road for hire or reward who:

(a) is established in that Member State in accordance with Community legislation and the national legislation of that Member State; and

(b) is entitled in the Member State of establishment, in accordance with Community legislation and the national legislation of that Member State concerning admission to the occupation of road haulage operator, to carry out the international carriage of goods by road.

2. The Community licence shall be issued by the competent authorities of the Member State of establishment for renewable periods of up to 10 years.

Community licences and certified copies issued before the date of application of this Regulation shall remain valid until their date of expiry.

The Commission shall adapt the period of validity of the Community licence to technical progress, in particular the national electronic registers of road transport undertakings as provided for in Article 16 of Regulation (EC) No 1071/2009. Those measures, designed to amend non-essential elements of this Regulation, shall be adopted in accordance with the regulatory procedure with scrutiny referred to in Article 15(2).

3. The Member State of establishment shall issue the holder with the original of the Community licence, which shall be kept by the haulier, and the number of certified true copies corresponding to the number of vehicles at the disposal of the holder of the Community licence, whether those vehicles are wholly owned or, for example, held under a hire purchase, hire or leasing contract.

4. The Community licence and the certified true copies shall correspond to the model set out in Annex II, which also lays down the conditions governing its use. They shall contain at least two of the security features listed in Annex I.

The Commission shall adapt Annexes I and II to technical progress. Those measures, designed to amend non-essential elements of this Regulation, shall be adopted in accordance with the regulatory procedure with scrutiny referred to in Article 15(2).

5. The Community licence and the certified true copies thereof shall bear the seal of the issuing authority as well as a signature and a serial number. The serial numbers of the Community licence and of the certified true copies shall be recorded in the national electronic register of road transport undertakings as part of the data relating to the haulier.

6. The Community licence shall be issued in the name of the haulier and shall be non-transferable. A certified true copy of the Community licence shall be

kept in each of the haulier's vehicles and shall be presented at the request of any authorised inspecting officer.

In the case of a coupled combination of vehicles, the certified true copy shall accompany the motor vehicle. It shall cover the coupled combination of vehicles even where the trailer or semi-trailer is not registered or authorised to use the roads in the name of the licence holder or where it is registered or authorised to use the roads in another State.

ARTICLE 5

Driver Attestation

1. A driver attestation shall be issued by a Member State, in accordance with this Regulation, to any haulier who: **C12.06**
    - (a) is the holder of a Community licence; and
    - (b) in that Member State, either lawfully employs a driver who is neither a national of a Member State nor a long-term resident within the meaning of Council Directive 2003/109/EC of 25 November 2003 concerning the status of third-country nationals who are long-term residents [*O.J. No.L16, January 23, 2004, p.44*], or lawfully uses a driver who is neither a national of a Member State nor a long-term resident within the meaning of that Directive and who is put at the disposal of that haulier in accordance with the conditions of employment and of vocational training laid down in that Member State:
        - (i) by laws, regulations or administrative provisions; and, as appropriate;
        - (ii) by collective agreements, in accordance with the rules applicable in that Member State.

2. The driver attestation shall be issued by the competent authorities of the Member State of establishment of the haulier, at the request of the holder of the Community licence, for each driver who is neither a national of a Member State nor a long-term resident within the meaning of Directive 2003/109/EC whom that haulier lawfully employs, or for each driver who is neither a national of a Member State nor a long-term resident within the meaning of that Directive and who is put at the disposal of the haulier. Each driver attestation shall certify that the driver named therein is employed in accordance with the conditions laid down in paragraph 1.

3. The driver attestation shall correspond to the model set out in Annex III. It shall contain at least two of the security features listed in Annex I.

4. The Commission shall adapt Annex III to technical progress. Those measures, designed to amend non-essential elements of this Regulation, shall be adopted in accordance with the regulatory procedure with scrutiny referred to in Article 15(2).

5. The driver attestation shall bear the seal of the issuing authority as well as a signature and a serial number. The serial number of the driver attestation may be recorded in the national electronic register of road transport undertakings as part of the data relating to the haulier who puts it at the disposal of the driver designated therein.

6. The driver attestation shall belong to the haulier, who puts it at the disposal of the driver designated therein when that driver drives a vehicle using a Community licence issued to that haulier. A certified true copy of the driver attestation issued by the competent authorities of the haulier's Member State of establishment shall be kept at the haulier's premises. The driver attestation shall be presented at the request of any authorised inspecting officer.

7. A driver attestation shall be issued for a period to be determined by the issuing Member State, subject to a maximum validity of 5 years. Driver attestations issued before the date of application of this Regulation shall remain valid until their date of expiry.

The driver attestation shall be valid only as long as the conditions under which it was issued are satisfied. Member States shall take appropriate measures to ensure that if those conditions are no longer met, the haulier returns the attestation immediately to the issuing authorities.

Article 6

Verification of Conditions

C12.07

1. Whenever an application for a Community licence or an application for renewal of a Community licence in accordance with Article 4(2) is lodged, the competent authorities of the Member State of establishment shall verify whether the haulier satisfies or continues to satisfy the conditions laid down in Article 4(1).

2. The competent authorities of the Member State of establishment shall regularly verify, by carrying out checks each year covering at least 20% of the valid driver attestations issued in that Member State, whether the conditions, referred to in Article 5(1), under which a driver attestation has been issued are still satisfied.

Article 7

Refusal to Issue and Withdrawal of Community Licence and Driver Attestation

C12.08

1. If the conditions laid down in Article 4(1) or those referred to in Article 5(1) are not satisfied, the competent authorities of the Member State of establishment shall reject an application for the issue or renewal of a Community licence or the issue of a driver attestation, by means of a reasoned decision.

2. The competent authorities shall withdraw a Community licence or a driver attestation where the holder:

   (a) no longer satisfies the conditions laid down in Article 4(1) or those referred to in Article 5(1); or

   (b) has supplied incorrect information in relation to an application for a Community licence or for a driver attestation.

Chapter III

Cabotage

Article 8

Cabotage

C12.09

1. Any haulier for hire or reward who is a holder of a Community licence and

whose driver, if he is a national of a third country, holds a driver attestation, shall be entitled, under the conditions laid down in this Chapter, to carry out cabotage operations.

2. Once the goods carried in the course of an incoming international carriage have been delivered, hauliers referred to in paragraph 1 shall be permitted to carry out, with the same vehicle, or, in the case of a coupled combination, the motor vehicle of that same vehicle, up to three cabotage operations following the international carriage from another Member State or from a third country to the host Member State. The last unloading in the course of a cabotage operation before leaving the host Member State shall take place within 7 days from the last unloading in the host Member State in the course of the incoming international carriage.

   Within the time limit referred to in the first subparagraph, hauliers may carry out some or all of the cabotage operations permitted under that subparagraph in any Member State under the condition that they are limited to one cabotage operation per Member State within 3 days of the unladen entry into the territory of that Member State.

3. National road haulage services carried out in the host Member State by a non-resident haulier shall only be deemed to conform with this Regulation if the haulier can produce clear evidence of the incoming international carriage and of each consecutive cabotage operation carried out.

   Evidence referred to in the first subparagraph shall comprise the following details for each operation:
   (a) the name, address and signature of the sender;
   (b) the name, address and signature of the haulier;
   (c) the name and address of the consignee as well as his signature and the date of delivery once the goods have been delivered;
   (d) the place and the date of taking over of the goods and the place designated for delivery;
   (e) the description in common use of the nature of the goods and the method of packing, and, in the case of dangerous goods, their generally recognised description, as well as the number of packages and their special marks and numbers;
   (f) the gross mass of the goods or their quantity otherwise expressed;
   (g) the number plates of the motor vehicle and trailer.

4. No additional document shall be required in order to prove that the conditions laid down in this Article have been met.

5. Any haulier entitled in the Member State of establishment, in accordance with that Member State's legislation, to carry out the road haulage operations for hire or reward specified in Article 1(5)(a), (b) and (c) shall be permitted, under the conditions set out in this Chapter, to carry out, as the case may be, cabotage operations of the same kind or cabotage operations with vehicles in the same category.

6. Permission to carry out cabotage operations, within the framework of the types of carriage referred to in Article 1(5)(d) and (e), shall be unrestricted.

ARTICLE 9

Rules Applicable to Cabotage Operations

1. The performance of cabotage operations shall be subject, save as otherwise   **C12.10**

provided in Community legislation, to the laws, regulations and administrative provisions in force in the host Member State with regard to the following:

    (a) the conditions governing the transport contract;

    (b) the weights and dimensions of road vehicles;

    (c) the requirements relating to the carriage of certain categories of goods, in particular dangerous goods, perishable foodstuffs and live animals;

    (d) the driving time and rest periods;

    (e) the value added tax (VAT) on transport services.

The weights and dimensions referred to in point (b) of the first subparagraph may, where appropriate, exceed those applicable in the haulier's Member State of establishment, but they may under no circumstances exceed the limits set by the host Member State for national traffic or the technical characteristics mentioned in the proofs referred to in Article 6(1) of Council Directive 96/53/EC of 25 July 1996 laying down for certain road vehicles circulating within the Community the maximum authorised dimensions in national and international traffic and the maximum authorised weights in international traffic [*O.J. No.L235, September 17, 1996, p.59*].

2. The laws, regulations and administrative provisions referred to in paragraph 1 shall be applied to non-resident hauliers under the same conditions as those imposed on hauliers established in the host Member State, so as to prevent any discrimination on grounds of nationality or place of establishment.

ARTICLE 10

Safeguard Procedure

C12.11

1. In the event of serious disturbance of the national transport market in a given geographical area due to, or aggravated by, cabotage, any Member State may refer the matter to the Commission with a view to the adoption of safeguard measures and shall provide the Commission with the necessary information and notify it of the measures it intends to take as regards resident hauliers.

2. For the purposes of paragraph 1:

"serious disturbance of the national transport market in a given geographical area" means the existence on the market of problems specific to it, such that there is a serious and potentially enduring excess of supply over demand, implying a threat to the financial stability and survival of a significant number of hauliers,

"geographical area" means an area covering all or part of the territory of a Member State or extending to all or part of the territory of other Member States.

3. The Commission shall examine the situation on the basis in particular of the relevant data and, after consulting the committee referred to in Article 15(1), shall decide within 1 month of receipt of the Member State's request whether or not safeguard measures are necessary and shall adopt them if they are necessary.

Such measures may involve the temporary exclusion of the area concerned from the scope of this Regulation.

Measures adopted in accordance with this Article shall remain in force for a period not exceeding 6 months, renewable once within the same limits of validity.

The Commission shall without delay notify the Member States and the Council of any decision taken pursuant to this paragraph.

4. If the Commission decides to adopt safeguard measures concerning one or more Member States, the competent authorities of the Member States involved shall be required to take measures of equivalent scope in respect of resident hauliers and shall inform the Commission thereof. Those measures shall be applied at the latest as from the same date as the safeguard measures adopted by the Commission.

5. Any Member State may refer to the Council a decision taken by the Commission pursuant to paragraph 3 within 30 days of its notification. The Council, acting by a qualified majority may, within 30 days of that referral, or, if there are referrals by several Member States, of the first referral, take a different decision.

The limits of validity laid down in the third subparagraph of paragraph 3 shall apply to the Council's decision. The competent authorities of the Member States concerned shall be required to take measures of equivalent scope in respect of resident hauliers, and shall inform the Commission thereof. If the Council takes no decision within the period referred to in the first subparagraph, the Commission decision shall become final.

6. Where the Commission considers that the measures referred to in paragraph 3 need to be prolonged, it shall submit a proposal to the Council, which shall take a decision by qualified majority.

CHAPTER IV

MUTUAL ASSISTANCE AND PENALTIES

ARTICLE 11

Mutual Assistance

Member States shall assist one another in ensuring the application and monitoring of this Regulation. They shall exchange information via the national contact points established pursuant to Article 18 of Regulation (EC) No 1071/2009.   C12.12

ARTICLE 12

Sanctioning of Infringements by the Member State of Establishment

1. In the event of a serious infringement of Community road transport legislation committed or ascertained in any Member State, the competent authorities of the Member State of establishment of the haulier who has committed such infringement shall take the appropriate action which may include a warning, if provided for by national law, to pursue the matter which may lead, inter alia, to the imposition of the following administrative penalties: C12.13

    (a) temporary or permanent withdrawal of some or all of the certified true copies of the Community licence;

(b) temporary or permanent withdrawal of the Community licence.

These penalties may be determined after the final decision on the matter has been taken and shall have regard to the seriousness of the infringement committed by the holder of the Community licence and to the total number of certified true copies of that licence that he holds in respect of international traffic.

2. In the event of a serious infringement regarding any misuse whatsoever of driver attestations, the competent authorities of the Member State of establishment of the haulier who committed such infringement shall impose appropriate penalties, such as:

    (a) suspending the issue of driver attestations;

    (b) withdrawing driver attestations;

    (c) making the issue of driver attestations subject to additional conditions in order to prevent misuse;

    (d) withdrawing, temporarily or permanently, some or all of the certified true copies of the Community licence;

    (e) withdrawing, temporarily or permanently, the Community licence.

These penalties may be determined after the final decision on the matter has been taken and shall have regard to the seriousness of the infringement committed by the holder of the Community licence.

3. The competent authorities of the Member State of establishment shall communicate to the competent authorities of the Member State in which the infringement was ascertained, as soon as possible and at the latest within 6 weeks of their final decision on the matter, which, if any, of the penalties provided for in paragraphs 1 and 2 have been imposed.

If such penalties are not imposed, the competent authorities of the Member State of establishment shall state the reasons therefor.

4. The competent authorities shall ensure that the penalties imposed on the haulier concerned are, as a whole, proportionate to the infringement or infringements which gave rise to such penalties, taking into account any penalty for the same infringement imposed in the Member State in which the infringement was ascertained.

5. The competent authorities of the haulier's Member State of establishment may also, pursuant to national law, bring proceedings against the haulier before a competent national court or tribunal. They shall inform the competent authority of the host Member State of any decisions taken to this effect.

6. Member States shall ensure that hauliers have the right to appeal against any administrative penalty imposed on them pursuant to this Article.

Article 13

Sanctioning of Infringements by the Host Member State

C12.14

1. Where the competent authorities of a Member State are aware of a serious infringement of this Regulation or of Community road transport legislation attributable to a non-resident haulier, the Member State within the territory of which the infringement is ascertained shall transmit to the competent authorities of the haulier's Member State of establishment, as soon as pos-

sible and at the latest within 6 weeks of their final decision on the matter, the following information:

- (a) a description of the infringement and the date and time when it was committed;
- (b) the category, type and seriousness of the infringement; and
- (c) the penalties imposed and the penalties executed.

The competent authorities of the host Member State may request the competent authorities of the Member State of establishment to impose administrative penalties in accordance with Article 12.

2. Without prejudice to any criminal prosecution, the competent authorities of the host Member State shall be empowered to impose penalties on a non-resident haulier who has committed infringements of this Regulation or of national or Community road transport legislation in their territory during a cabotage operation. They shall impose such penalties on a non-discriminatory basis. These penalties may, inter alia, consist of a warning, or, in the event of a serious infringement, a temporary ban on cabotage operations on the territory of the host Member State where the infringement was committed.

3. Member States shall ensure that hauliers have the right to appeal against any administrative penalty imposed on them pursuant to this Article.

ARTICLE 14

Entry in the National Electronic Registers

Member States shall ensure that serious infringements of Community road **C12.15** transport legislation committed by hauliers established in their territory, which have led to the imposition of a penalty by any Member State, as well as any temporary or permanent withdrawal of the Community licence or of the certified true copy thereof, are recorded in the national electronic register of road transport undertakings. Entries in the register which concern a temporary or permanent withdrawal of a Community licence shall remain in the database for 2 years from the time of the expiry of the period of withdrawal, in the case of temporary withdrawal, or from the date of withdrawal, in the case of permanent withdrawal.

CHAPTER V

IMPLEMENTATION

ARTICLE 15

Committee Procedure

1. The Commission shall be assisted by the committee established by Article **C12.16** 18(1) of Regulation (EEC) No 3821/85.

2. Where reference is made to this paragraph, Article 5a(1) to (4) and Article 7 of Decision 1999/468/EC shall apply, having regard to the provisions of Article 8 thereof.

ARTICLE 16

Penalties

Member States shall lay down the rules on penalties applicable to infringe- **C12.17** ments of the provisions of this Regulation, and shall take all the measures necessary to ensure that they are implemented. The penalties provided for must be effective, proportionate and dissuasive. Member States shall notify those provisions to the Commission by 4 December 2011, and shall notify it without delay of any subsequent amendment affecting them.

Member States shall ensure that all such measures are taken without discrimination as to the nationality or place of establishment of the haulier.

ARTICLE 17

Reporting

C12.18

1. Every 2 years Member States shall inform the Commission of the number of hauliers possessing Community licences on 31 December of the previous year and of the number of certified true copies corresponding to the vehicles in circulation at that date.

2. Member States shall also inform the Commission of the number of driver attestations issued in the previous calendar year as well as the number of driver attestations in circulation on 31 December of that same year.

3. The Commission shall draw up a report on the state of the Community road transport market by the end of 2013. The report shall contain an analysis of the market situation, including an evaluation of the effectiveness of controls and the evolution of employment conditions in the profession, as well as an assessment as to whether harmonisation of the rules in the fields, inter alia, of enforcement and road user charges, as well as social and safety legislation, has progressed to such an extent that the further opening of domestic road transport markets, including cabotage, could be envisaged.

CHAPTER VI

FINAL PROVISIONS

ARTICLE 18

Repeals

C12.19   Regulations (EEC) No 881/92 and (EEC) No 3118/93 and Directive 2006/94/EC are hereby repealed.

References to the repealed Regulations and Directive shall be construed as references to this Regulation and shall be read in accordance with the correlation table set out in Annex IV.

ARTICLE 19

Entry into Force

C12.20   This Regulation shall enter into force on the 20th day following its publication in the Official Journal of the European Union.

It shall apply from 4 December 2011, with the exception of Articles 8 and 9, which shall apply from 14 May 2010.

This Regulation shall be binding in its entirety and directly applicable in all Member States.

C12.21   *[This Regulation was published in O.J. No.L300, November 14, 2009, pp.72–87.*

Regulation (EEC) 881/92 and Regulation (EEC) 3118/93, which are repealed with effect from December 4, 2011 by art.18 of this Regulation, are set out in the twenty-fourth edition of this work.]

ANNEX I

Security features of the Community licence and the driver attestation

C12.22   The Community licence and the driver attestation must have at least two of the following security features:

— a hologram,

— special fibres in the paper which become visible under UV-light,

— at least one microprint line (printing visible only with a magnifying glass and not reproduced by photocopying machines),

— tactile characters, symbols or patterns,

— double numbering: serial number of the Community licence, of the certified copy thereof or of the driver attestation as well as, in each case, the issue number,

— a security design background with fine guilloche patterns and rainbow printing.

ANNEX II

Community licence model

EUROPEAN COMMUNITY

(a)   **C12.23**

(Colour Pantone light blue, format DIN A4 cellulose paper 100 g/m2 or more)
(First page of the licence)
(Text in (one of) the official language(s) of the Member State issuing the licence)

Distinguishing sign of the Member State (¹) issuing the licence	Name of the competent authority or body

LICENCE No ...

(or)

CERTIFIED TRUE COPY No

for the international carriage of goods by road for hire or reward

This licence entitles (²) ....
....
....

to engage in the international carriage of goods by road for hire or reward by any route, for journeys or parts of journeys carried out for hire or reward within the territory of the Community, as laid down in Regulation (EC) No 1072/2009 of the European Parliament and of the Council of 21 October 2009 on common rules for access to the international road haulage market and in accordance with the general provisions of this licence.

Particular remarks:	
This licence shall be valid from	to ....
Issued in ....,	on ....
.... (³)	

(¹) The distinguishing signs of the Member States are: (B) Belgium, (BG) Bulgaria, (CZ) Czech Republic, (DK) Denmark, (D) Germany, (EST) Estonia, (IRL) Ireland, (GR) Greece, (E) Spain, (F) France, (I) Italy, (CY) Cyprus, (LV) Latvia, (LT) Lithuania, (L) Luxembourg, (H) Hungary, (MT) Malta, (NL) Netherlands, (A) Austria, (PL) Poland, (P) Portugal, (RO) Romania, (SLO) Slovenia, (SK) Slovakia, (FIN) Finland, (S) Sweden, (UK) United Kingdom.
(²) Name or business name and full address of the haulier.
(³) Signature and seal of the issuing competent authority or body.

(b)

(Second page of the licence)
(Text in (one of) the official language(s) of the Member State issuing the licence)

GENERAL PROVISIONS

This licence is issued under Regulation (EC) No 1072/2009.

It entitles the holder to engage in the international carriage of goods by road for hire or reward by any route for journeys or parts of journeys carried out within the territory of the Community and, where appropriate, subject to the conditions laid down herein:

— where the point of departure and the point of arrival are situated in two different Member States, with or without transit through one or more Member States or third countries,

— from a Member State to a third country or vice versa, with or without transit through one or more Member States or third countries,

— between third countries with transit through the territory of one or more Member States,

and unladen journeys in connection with such carriage.

In the case of carriage from a Member State to a third country or vice versa, this licence is valid for that part of the journey carried out within the territory of the Community. It shall be valid in the Member State of loading or unloading only after the conclusion of the necessary agreement between the Community and the third country in question in accordance with Regulation (EC) No 1072/2009.

The licence is personal to the holder and is non-transferable.

It may be withdrawn by the competent authority of the Member State which issued it, notably where the holder has:

— not complied with all the conditions for using the licence,

— supplied incorrect information with regard to the data needed for the issue or extension of the licence.

The original of the licence must be kept by the haulage undertaking.

A certified copy of the licence must be kept in the vehicle.[1] In the case of a coupled combination of vehicles it must accompany the motor vehicle. It covers the coupled combination of vehicles even if the trailer or semi-trailer is not registered or authorised to use the roads in the name of the licence holder or if it is registered or authorised to use the roads in another State.

The licence must be presented at the request of any authorised inspecting officer.

Within the territory of each Member State, the holder must comply with the laws, regulations and administrative provisions in force in that State, in particular with regard to transport and traffic.

---

[1] "Vehicle" means a motor vehicle registered in a Member State, or a coupled combination of vehicles the motor vehicle of which at least is registered in a Member State, used exclusively for the carriage of goods.

ANNEX III

Driver attestation model

EUROPEAN COMMUNITY

(a)   **C12.24**

(Colour Pantone pink, format DIN A4 cellulose paper 100g/m2 or more)
(First page of the attestation)
(Text in (one of) the official language(s) of the Member State issuing the attestation)

Distinguishing sign of the Member State (¹) issuing the attestation	Name of the competent authority or body

DRIVER ATTESTATION No ...

for the carriage of goods by road for hire or reward under a Community licence

(Regulation (EC) No 1072/2009 of the European Parliament and of the Council of 21 October 2009 on common rules for access to the international road haulage market)

This attestation certifies that on the basis of the documents presented by:
....
....(²)

the following driver:

Name and forename	
Date and place of birth	Nationality ....
Type and reference number of identity paper	
Date of issue	Place of issue ....
Driving licence number	
Date of issue	Place of issue ....
Social security number	

is employed, in accordance with the laws, regulations or administrative provisions and, as appropriate, the collective agreements, in accordance with the rules applicable in the following Member State, on the conditions of employment and of vocational training of drivers applicable in that Member State to carry out road transport operations in that State:
....(³)

Particular remarks ....
....

This attestation shall be valid from	to ....
Issued in	on ....
.... (⁴)	

(¹) The distinguishing signs of the Member States are: (B) Belgium, (BG) Bulgaria, (CZ) Czech Republic,(DK) Denmark, (D) Germany, (EST) Estonia, (IRL) Ireland, (GR) Greece, (E) Spain, (F) France, (I) Italy, (CY) Cyprus, (LV) Latvia, (LT) Lithuania, (L) Luxembourg, (H) Hungary, (MT) Malta, (NL) Netherlands, (A) Austria, (PL) Poland, (P) Portugal, (RO) Romania, (SLO) Slovenia, (SK) Slovakia, (FIN) Finland, (S) Sweden, (UK) United Kingdom.
(²) Name or business name and full address of the haulier.
(³) Name of the haulier's Member State of establishment.
(⁴) Signature and seal of the issuing competent authority or body.

(b)

(Second page of the attestation)
(Text in (one of) the official language(s) of the Member State issuing the attestation)

GENERAL PROVISIONS

This attestation is issued under Regulation (EC) No 1072/2009.

It certifies that the driver named therein is employed, in accordance with the laws, regulations or administrative provisions and, as appropriate, the collective agreements, in accordance with the rules applicable in the Member State mentioned on the attestation, on the conditions of employment and of vocational training of drivers applicable in that Member State to carry out road operations in that State.

The driver attestation shall belong to the haulier, who puts it at the disposal of the driver designated therein when that driver drives a vehicle[1] engaged in carriage using a Community licence issued to that haulier. The driver attestation is not transferable. The driver attestation shall be valid only as long as the conditions under which it was issued are still satisfied and must be returned immediately by the haulier to the issuing authorities if these conditions are no longer met.

It may be withdrawn by the competent authority of the Member State which issued it, in particular where the holder has:

— not complied with all the conditions for using the attestation,

— supplied incorrect information with regard to the data needed for the issue or extension of the attestation.

A certified true copy of the attestation must be kept by the haulage undertaking.

An original attestation must be kept in the vehicle and must be presented by the driver at the request of any authorised inspecting officer.

---

[1] "Vehicle" means a motor vehicle registered in a Member State, or a coupled combination of vehicles the motor vehicle of which at least is registered in a Member State, used exclusively for the carriage of goods.

ANNEX IV

Correlation Table

[Omitted.]   **C12.25**

Regulation (EC) 1073/2009 of October 21, 2009 on common rules for access to the international market for coach and bus services, and amending Regulation (EC) 561/2006

C13.01 *THE EUROPEAN PARLIAMENT AND THE COUNCIL OF THE EUROPEAN UNION,*

Having regard to the Treaty establishing the European Community, and in particular Article 71 thereof,

Having regard to the proposal from the Commission,

Having regard to the opinion of the European Economic and Social Committee,

After consulting the Committee of the Regions,

Acting in accordance with the procedure laid down in Article 251 of the Treaty,

WHEREAS:

(1) A number of substantial changes are to be made to Council Regulation (EEC) No 684/92 of 16 March 1992 on common rules for the international carriage of passengers by coach and bus [O.J. No.L74, March 20, 1992, p.1]] and to Council Regulation (EC) No 12/98 of 11 December 1997 laying down the conditions under which non-resident carriers may operate national road passenger transport services within a Member State [O.J. No.L4, January 8, 1998, p.10]]. In the interests of clarity and simplification, those Regulations should be recast and incorporated into one single regulation.

(2) The establishment of a common transport policy entails, inter alia, laying down common rules applicable to the international carriage of passengers by road as well as the conditions under which non-resident carriers may operate national transport services within a Member State.

(3) To ensure a coherent framework for the international carriage of passengers by coach and bus throughout the Community, this Regulation should apply to all international carriage on Community territory. Carriage from Member States to third countries is still largely covered by bilateral agreements between the Member States and those third countries. Therefore, this Regulation should not apply to that part of the journey within the territory of the Member State of picking up or setting down, as long as the necessary agreements between the Community and the third countries concerned have not been concluded. It should, however, apply to the territory of a Member State crossed in transit.

(4) Freedom to provide services constitutes a basic principle of the common transport policy and requires that carriers from all Member States be guaranteed access to international transport markets without discrimination on grounds of nationality or place of establishment.

(5) The international carriage of passengers by coach and bus should be conditional on the possession of a Community licence. Carriers should be required to carry a certified true copy of the Community licence aboard each

of their vehicles, in order to facilitate effective controls by enforcement authorities, especially those outside the Member State in which the carrier is established. The conditions governing the issue and withdrawal of Community licences, their periods of validity and the detailed rules for their use should be determined. It is also necessary to lay down detailed specifications as regards the layout and other features of the Community licence and the certified copies thereof.

(6) Roadside checks should be carried out without direct or indirect discrimination on grounds of the nationality of the road transport operator or the country of establishment of the road transport operator or of registration of the vehicle.

(7) There should be provision for flexible arrangements subject to certain conditions for special regular services and certain occasional services, in order to satisfy market demand.

(8) While maintaining authorisation arrangements for regular services, certain rules should be amended, particularly as regards authorisation procedures.

(9) The authorisation for regular services should henceforth be granted subsequent to an authorisation procedure, unless there are clearly specified grounds for refusal attributable to the applicant. The grounds for refusal relating to the relevant market should be either that the service applied for would seriously affect the viability of a comparable service operated under one or more public service contracts on the direct sections concerned or that the principal purpose of the service is not to carry passengers between stops located in different Member States.

(10) Non-resident carriers should be allowed to operate national road passenger services, but regard should be had to the specific characteristics of each form of service. When such cabotage operations are performed, they should be subject to Community legislation such as Regulation (EC) No 561/2006 of the European Parliament and of the Council of 15 March 2006 on the harmonisation of certain social legislation relating to road transport [O.J. No.L102, April 11, 2006, p.1] and to national law in force in specified areas in the host Member State.

(11) The provisions of Directive 96/71/EC of the European Parliament and of the Council of 16 December 1996 concerning the posting of workers in the framework of the provision of services [O.J. No.L18, January 21, 1997, p.1] apply to transport undertakings performing a cabotage operation.

(12) Where regular services are concerned, only regular services provided as part of a regular international service, excluding urban and suburban services, should be opened up to non-resident carriers, subject to certain conditions, and in particular to the legislation in force in the host Member State.

(13) Member States should grant each other mutual assistance with a view to the sound application of this Regulation.

(14) Administrative formalities should be reduced as far as possible without abandoning the controls and penalties that guarantee the correct application and effective enforcement of this Regulation. To this end, the existing rules on the withdrawal of the Community licence should be clarified and

strengthened. The current rules should be adapted to allow the effective sanctioning of serious infringements committed in a Member State other than the Member State of establishment. Penalties should be non-discriminatory and proportionate to the seriousness of the infringements. It should be possible to lodge an appeal in respect of any penalties imposed.

(15) Member States should enter in their national electronic register of road transport undertakings all serious infringements attributable to carriers which have led to the imposition of a penalty.

(16) In order to facilitate and strengthen the exchange of information between national authorities, Member States should exchange the relevant information through the national contact points set up pursuant to Regulation (EC) No 1071/2009 of the European Parliament and of the Council of 21 October 2009 establishing common rules concerning the conditions to be complied with to pursue the occupation of road transport operator [O.J. No.L300, November 14, 2009, p.51].

(17) The measures necessary for the implementation of this Regulation should be adopted in accordance with Council Decision 1999/468/EC of 28 June 1999 laying down the procedures for the exercise of implementing powers conferred on the Commission [O.J. No.L184, July 17, 1999, p.23].

(18) In particular, the Commission should be empowered to establish the format of certain documents to be used for the application of this Regulation and to adapt Annexes I and II of this Regulation to technical progress. Since those measures are of general scope and are designed to amend non-essential elements of this Regulation by supplementing it with new non-essential elements, they must be adopted in accordance with the regulatory procedure with scrutiny provided for in Article 5a of Decision 1999/468/EC.

(19) Member States should take the necessary measures to implement this Regulation, in particular as regards effective, proportionate and dissuasive penalties.

(20) In order to encourage tourism and the use of environmentally friendly means of transport, Regulation (EC) No 561/2006 should be amended to allow drivers engaged in a single occasional service providing international carriage of passengers to postpone their weekly rest period for up to 12 consecutive 24-hour periods if they are involved in passenger transport activities that typically do not include continuous and long driving hours. Such a postponement should only be allowed under very strict conditions which preserve road safety and take into account the working conditions of drivers, inter alia, the obligation to take weekly rest periods immediately before and after the service. The Commission should monitor closely the use of this derogation. If the factual situation which justifies the use of this derogation changes substantially and the derogation results in a deterioration of road safety, the Commission should take appropriate measures.

(21) Since the objective of this Regulation, namely to ensure a coherent framework for the international carriage of passengers by coach and bus throughout the Community, cannot be sufficiently achieved by the Member States and can therefore, by reason of its scale and effects, be better achieved at Community level, the Community may adopt measures, in accordance with the principle of subsidiarity as set out in Article 5 of the Treaty. In

accordance with the principle of proportionality, as set out in that Article, this Regulation does not go beyond what is necessary in order to achieve that objective.

HAVE ADOPTED THIS REGULATION: **C13.02**

CHAPTER I

GENERAL PROVISIONS
ARTICLE 1

Scope

1. This Regulation shall apply to the international carriage of passengers by coach and bus within the territory of the Community by carriers for hire or reward or by own-account carriers established in a Member State in accordance with its law, using vehicles which are registered in that Member State and are suitable and intended, by virtue of their construction and equipment, to carry more than nine persons, including the driver, and to the movement of such vehicles when empty in connection with such carriage.

   A change of vehicle or an interruption of carriage to enable part of a journey to be made by another means of transport shall not affect the application of this Regulation.

2. In the event of carriage from a Member State to a third country and vice versa, this Regulation shall apply to the part of the journey on the territory of any Member State crossed in transit. It shall not apply to that part of the journey within the territory of the Member State of picking up or setting down, as long as the necessary agreement between the Community and the third country concerned has not been concluded.

3. Pending the conclusion of the agreements referred to in paragraph 2, this Regulation shall not affect provisions relating to the carriage from a Member State to a third country and vice-versa contained in bilateral agreements concluded between Member States and those third countries.

4. This Regulation shall apply to national road passenger services for hire or reward operated on a temporary basis by a non-resident carrier as provided for in Chapter V.

ARTICLE 2

Definitions

For the purposes of this Regulation, the following definitions shall apply: **C13.03**

1. *"international carriage"* means:
   (a) a journey undertaken by a vehicle the point of departure and the point of arrival of which are in two different Member States, with or without transit through one or more Member States or third countries;
   (b) a journey undertaken by a vehicle of which the point of departure and the point of arrival are in the same Member State, while the picking up or setting down of passengers is in another Member State or in a third country;
   (c) a journey undertaken by a vehicle from a Member State to a third

country or vice versa, with or without transit through one or more Member States or third countries; or

(d) a journey undertaken by a vehicle between third countries, with transit through the territory of one or more Member States;

2. *"regular services"* means services which provide for the carriage of passengers at specified intervals along specified routes, passengers being picked up and set down at predetermined stopping points;

3. *"special regular services"* means regular services, by whomsoever organised, which provide for the carriage of specified categories of passengers to the exclusion of other passengers;

4. *"occasional services"* means services which do not fall within the definition of regular services, including special regular services, and the main characteristic of which is the carriage of groups of passengers constituted on the initiative of the customer or the carrier himself;

5. *"own-account transport operations"* means operations carried out for non-commercial and non-profit-making purposes by a natural or legal person, whereby:

— the transport activity is only an ancillary activity for that natural or legal person, and

— the vehicles used are the property of that natural or legal person or have been obtained by that person on deferred terms or have been the subject of a long-term leasing contract and are driven by a member of the staff of the natural or legal person or by the natural person himself or by personnel employed by, or put at the disposal of, the undertaking under a contractual obligation;

6. *"host Member State"* means a Member State in which a carrier operates other than the carrier's Member State of establishment;

7. *"cabotage operations"* means either:

— national road passenger services for hire and reward carried out on a temporary basis by a carrier in a host Member State, or

— the picking up and setting down of passengers within the same Member State, in the course of a regular international service, in compliance with the provisions of this Regulation, provided that it is not the principal purpose of the service;

8. *"serious infringement of Community road transport legislation"* means an infringement which may lead to the loss of good repute in accordance with Article 6(1) and (2) of Regulation (EC) No 1071/2009, and/or to the temporary or permanent withdrawal of a Community licence.

ARTICLE 3

Freedom to Provide Services

C13.04   1. Any carrier for hire or reward referred to in Article 1 shall be permitted in accordance with this Regulation to carry out regular services, including special regular services and occasional services by coach and bus, without discrimination on grounds of nationality or place of establishment if he:

(a) is authorised in the Member State of establishment to undertake carriage by means of regular services, including special regular services, or occasional services by coach and bus, in accordance with the market access conditions laid down by national legislation;

(b) satisfies the conditions laid down in accordance with Community rules on admission to the occupation of road passenger transport operator in national and international transport operations; and

(c) meets legal requirements regarding the standards for drivers and vehicles as laid down, in particular, in Council Directive 92/6/EEC of 10 February 1992 on the installation and use of speed limitation devices for certain categories of motor vehicles in the Community [*O.J. No.L57, March 2, 1992, p.27*], Council Directive 96/53/EC of 25 July 1996 laying down for certain road vehicles circulating within the Community the maximum authorised dimensions in national and international traffic and the maximum authorised weights in international traffic [*O.J. No.L235, September 17, 1996, p.59*] and Directive 2003/59/EC of the European Parliament and of the Council of 15 July 2003 on the initial qualification and periodic training of drivers of certain road vehicles for the carriage of goods or passengers [*O.J. No.L226, September 10, 2003, p.4*].

2. Any own-account carrier referred to in Article 1 shall be permitted to carry out the transport services pursuant to Article 5(5) without discrimination on grounds of nationality or place of establishment if he:

(a) is authorised in the Member State of establishment to undertake carriage by coach and bus in accordance with the market-access conditions laid down in national legislation; and

(b) meets legal requirements regarding the standards for drivers and vehicles as laid down, in particular, in Directives 92/6/EEC, 96/53/EC and 2003/59/EC.

CHAPTER II

COMMUNITY LICENCE AND MARKET ACCESS

ARTICLE 4

Community Licence

1. International carriage of passengers by coach and bus shall be carried out   **C13.05** subject to possession of a Community licence issued by the competent authorities of the Member State of establishment.

2. The competent authorities of the Member State of establishment shall issue the holder with the original of the Community licence, which shall be kept by the carrier, and the number of certified true copies thereof corresponding to the number of vehicles used for the international carriage of passengers at the disposal of the holder of the Community licence, whether those vehicles are wholly owned, or held in another form, particularly under an instalment-purchase, hire or leasing contract.

The Community licence and the certified true copies thereof shall correspond to the model set out in Annex II. They shall contain at least two of the security features listed in Annex I.

The Commission shall adapt Annexes I and II to technical progress. Those measures, designed to amend non-essential elements of this Regulation, shall be adopted in accordance with the regulatory procedure with scrutiny referred to in Article 26(2).

The Community licence and the certified true copies thereof shall bear the seal of the issuing authority as well as a signature and a serial number. The serial numbers of the Community licence and the certified true copies thereof shall be recorded in the national electronic register of road transport undertakings provided for in Article 16 of Regulation (EC) No 1071/2009 as part of the data relating to the carrier.

3. The Community licence shall be issued in the name of the carrier and shall be non-transferable. A certified true copy of the Community licence shall be kept in each of the carrier's vehicles and shall be presented at the request of any authorised inspecting officer.

4. The Community licence shall be issued for renewable periods of up to 10 years. Community licences and certified true copies thereof issued before the date of application of this Regulation shall remain valid until their date of expiry.

5. Whenever an application for a Community licence is lodged, or a Community licence is renewed in accordance with paragraph 4 of this Article, the competent authorities of the Member State of establishment shall verify whether the carrier satisfies or continues to satisfy the conditions laid down in Article 3(1).

6. Where the conditions referred to in Article 3(1) are not satisfied, the competent authorities of the Member State of establishment shall refuse to issue or renew or shall withdraw a Community licence by means of a reasoned decision.

7. Member States shall guarantee the right of the applicant for, or holder of, a Community licence to appeal against a decision by the competent authorities of the Member State of establishment to refuse or withdraw this licence.

8. Member States may decide that the Community licence shall also be valid for national transport operations.

Article 5

Access to the Market

C13.06   1. Regular services shall be open to all, subject, where appropriate, to compulsory reservation.

Such services shall be subject to authorisation in accordance with the provisions of Chapter III.

Regular services from a Member State to a third country and vice versa shall be subject to authorisation in accordance with the bilateral agreement between the Member State and the third country and, where appropriate, the transited Member State, as long as the necessary agreement between the Community and the third country concerned has not been concluded.

The regular nature of the service shall not be affected by any adjustment to the service operating conditions.

The organisation of parallel or temporary services, serving the same public as existing regular services, the non-serving of certain stops and the serving of additional stops on existing regular services shall be governed by the same rules as those applicable to existing regular services.

2. Special regular services shall include:

   (a) the carriage of workers between home and work;

   (b) the carriage of school pupils and students to and from the educational institution.

   The fact that a special service may be varied according to the needs of users shall not affect its classification as a regular service.

   Special regular services shall not be subject to authorisation in accordance with Chapter III where they are covered by a contract concluded between the organiser and the carrier.

3. Occasional services shall not require authorisation in accordance with Chapter III.

   However, the organisation of parallel or temporary services comparable to existing regular services and serving the same public as the latter shall be subject to authorisation in accordance with the procedure laid down in Chapter III.

   Occasional services shall not cease to be occasional services solely on the grounds that they are provided at certain intervals.

   Occasional services may be provided by a group of carriers acting on behalf of the same contractor, and travellers may catch a connection en route, with a different carrier of the same group, on the territory of a Member State.

   The Commission shall establish the procedures for the names of such carriers and the connection points en route to be communicated to the competent authorities of the Member States concerned. Those measures, designed to amend non-essential elements of this Regulation by supplementing it, shall be adopted in accordance with the regulatory procedure with scrutiny referred to in Article 26(2).

4. Empty journeys by vehicles in connection with the transport operations referred to in the third subparagraph of paragraph 2, and in the first subparagraph of paragraph 3, shall likewise not require authorisation.

5. Own-account transport operations shall be exempt from any system of authorisation but shall be subject to a system of certificates.

   The certificates shall be issued by the competent authorities of the Member State in which the vehicle is registered and shall be valid for the entire journey including transit.

   The Commission shall establish the format of the certificates. Those measures, designed to amend non-essential elements of this Regulation by supplementing it, shall be adopted in accordance with the regulatory procedure with scrutiny referred to in Article 26(2).

CHAPTER III

REGULAR SERVICES SUBJECT TO AUTHORISATION

ARTICLE 6

Nature of Authorisation

1. Authorisations shall be issued in the name of the carrier and shall be non-   **C13.07**

transferable. However, a carrier who has received an authorisation may, with the consent of the competent authority of the Member State in whose territory the point of departure is situated, hereinafter referred to as the "*authorising authority*", operate the service through a subcontractor. In this case, the name of the subcontractor and its role shall be indicated in the authorisation. The subcontractor shall satisfy the conditions laid down in Article 3(1). For the purposes of this paragraph, the point of departure shall mean "*one of the termini of the service*".

In the case of undertakings associated for the purpose of operating a regular service, the authorisation shall be issued in the names of all the undertakings and shall state the names of all the operators. It shall be given to the undertaking that manages the operation and copies shall be given to the other undertakings.

2. The period of validity of an authorisation shall not exceed 5 years. It may be set at less either at the request of the applicant or by mutual consent of the competent authorities of the Member States on whose territory passengers are picked up or set down.

3. Authorisations shall specify the following:
   (a) the type of service;
   (b) the route of the service, giving in particular the point of departure and the point of arrival;
   (c) the period of validity of the authorisation;
   (d) the stops and the timetable.

4. The Commission shall establish the format of the authorisations. Those measures, designed to amend non-essential elements of this Regulation by supplementing it, shall be adopted in accordance with the regulatory procedure with scrutiny referred to in Article 26(2).

5. Authorisations shall entitle their holder(s) to operate regular services in the territories of all Member States over which the routes of the service pass.

6. The operator of a regular service may use additional vehicles to deal with temporary and exceptional situations. Such additional vehicles may be used only under the same conditions as set out in the authorisation referred to in paragraph 3.

In this case, the carrier shall ensure that the following documents are carried on the vehicle:
   (a) a copy of the authorisation of the regular service;
   (b) a copy of the contract between the operator of the regular service and the undertaking providing the additional vehicles or an equivalent document;
   (c) a certified true copy of the Community licence issued to the operator providing the additional vehicles for the service.

Article 7

Submission of Application for Authorisation

C13.08
1. Applications for authorisation of regular services shall be submitted to the authorising authority.
2. The Commission shall establish the format of the applications. Those

measures, designed to amend non-essential elements of this Regulation by supplementing it, shall be adopted in accordance with the regulatory procedure with scrutiny referred to in Article 26(2).

3. Persons applying for authorisation shall provide any further information which they consider relevant or which is requested by the authorising authority, in particular a driving schedule making it possible to monitor compliance with Community legislation on driving and rest periods and a copy of the Community licence.

ARTICLE 8

Authorising Procedure

1. Authorisations shall be issued in agreement with the authorities of all the Member States in whose territories passengers are picked up or set down. The authorising authority shall forward to such authorities, as well as to the competent authorities of Member States whose territories are crossed without passengers being picked up or set down, a copy of the application, together with copies of any other relevant documentation, and its assessment. **C13.09**

2. The competent authorities of the Member States whose agreement has been requested shall notify the authorising authority of their decision on the application within 2 months. This time limit shall be calculated from the date of receipt of the request for agreement which is shown in the acknowledgement of receipt. If the decision received from the competent authorities of the Member States whose agreement has been requested is negative, it shall contain a proper statement of reasons. If the authorising authority does not receive a reply within 2 months, the authorities consulted shall be deemed to have given their agreement and the authorising authority may grant the authorisation.

   The authorities of the Member States whose territories are crossed without passengers being picked up or set down may notify the authorising authority of their comments within the time limit laid down in the first subparagraph.

3. The authorising authority shall take a decision on the application within 4 months of the date of submission of the application by the carrier.

4. Authorisation shall be granted unless:

   (a) the applicant is unable to provide the service which is the subject of the application with equipment directly available to him;

   (b) the applicant has not complied with national or international legislation on road transport, and in particular the conditions and requirements relating to authorisations for international road passenger services, or has committed serious infringements of Community road transport legislation in particular with regard to the rules applicable to vehicles and driving and rest periods for drivers;

   (c) in the case of an application for renewal of authorisation, the conditions of authorisation have not been complied with;

   (d) a Member State decides on the basis of a detailed analysis that the service concerned would seriously affect the viability of a comparable service covered by one or more public service contracts conforming to Community law on the direct sections concerned. In such a case, the

Member State shall set up criteria, on a non-discriminatory basis, for determining whether the service applied for would seriously affect the viability of the abovementioned comparable service and shall communicate them to the Commission, upon its request;

(e) a Member State decides on the basis of a detailed analysis that the principal purpose of the service is not to carry passengers between stops located in different Member States.

In the event that an existing international coach and bus service is seriously affecting the viability of a comparable service covered by one or more public service contracts conforming to Community law on the direct sections concerned, due to exceptional reasons which could not have been foreseen at the time of granting the authorisation, a Member State may, with the agreement of the Commission, suspend or withdraw the authorisation to run the international coach and bus service after having given 6 months' notice to the carrier.

The fact that a carrier offers lower prices than those offered by other road carriers or the fact that the link in question is already operated by other road carriers shall not in itself constitute justification for rejecting the application.

5. The authorising authority and the competent authorities of all the Member States involved in the procedure to reach the agreement provided for in paragraph 1 may refuse applications only on the basis of reasons provided for in this Regulation.

6. Having completed the procedure laid down in paragraphs 1 to 5, the authorising authority shall grant the authorisation or formally refuse the application.

Decisions refusing an application shall state the reasons on which they are based. Member States shall ensure that transport undertakings are given the opportunity to make representations in the event of their application being refused.

The authorising authority shall inform all the authorities referred to in paragraph 1 of its decision, sending them a copy of any authorisation.

7. If the procedure for reaching the agreement referred to in paragraph 1 does not enable the authorising authority to decide on an application, the matter may be referred to the Commission within the time limit of 2 months calculated from the date of communication of a negative decision by one or more of the Member States consulted pursuant to paragraph 1.

8. After having consulted the Member States concerned, the Commission shall, within 4 months from receipt of the communication from the authorising authority, take a decision which shall take effect 30 days after the notification to the Member States concerned.

9. The Commission decision shall continue to apply until an agreement is reached between the Member States concerned.

ARTICLE 9

Renewal and Alteration of Authorisation

C13.10   Article 8 shall apply, mutatis mutandis, to applications for the renewal of authorisations or for alteration of the conditions under which the services subject to authorisation must be carried out.

In the event of a minor alteration to the operating conditions, in particular adjustment of intervals, fares and timetables, the authorising authority need only supply the other Member States concerned with information relating to the alteration.

The Member States concerned may agree that the authorising authority alone shall decide on alterations to the conditions under which a service is operated.

ARTICLE 10

Lapse of an Authorisation

1. Without prejudice to the provisions of Regulation (EC) No 1370/2007 of the   **C13.11**
   European Parliament and of the Council of 23 October 2007 on public passenger transport services by rail and by road [*O.J. No.L315, December 3,
   2007, p.1*], an authorisation for a regular service shall lapse at the end of its
   period of validity or 3 months after the authorising authority has received
   notice from its holder of his intention to withdraw the service. Such notice
   shall contain a proper statement of reasons.

2. Where demand for a service has ceased to exist, the period of notice provided
   for in paragraph 1 shall be of 1 month.

3. The authorising authority shall inform the competent authorities of the other
   Member States concerned that the authorisation has lapsed.

4. The holder of the authorisation shall notify users of the service concerned of
   its withdrawal 1 month in advance by means of appropriate publicity.

ARTICLE 11

Obligations of Carriers

1. Save in the event of force majeure, the operator of a regular service shall,   **C13.12**
   until the authorisation expires, take all measures to guarantee a transport
   service that fulfils the standards of continuity, regularity and capacity and
   complies with the other conditions laid down by the competent authority in
   accordance with Article 6(3).

2. The carrier shall display the route of the service, the bus stops, the timetable,
   the fares and the conditions of carriage in such a way as to ensure that such
   information is readily available to all users.

3. Without prejudice to Regulation (EC) No 1370/2007, it shall be possible for
   the Member States concerned, by common agreement and in agreement
   with the holder of the authorisation, to make changes to the operating conditions governing a regular service.

CHAPTER IV

OCCASIONAL SERVICES AND OTHER SERVICES EXEMPT FROM AUTHORISATION

ARTICLE 12

Control Documents

1. Occasional services shall be carried out under cover of a journey form with   **C13.13**
   the exception of the services referred to in the second subparagraph of
   Article 5(3).

2. A carrier operating occasional services shall fill out a journey form before each journey.

3. The journey form shall contain at least the following information:

   (a) the type of service;

   (b) the main itinerary;

   (c) the carrier(s) involved.

4. The books of journey forms shall be supplied by the competent authorities of the Member State where the carrier is established or by bodies appointed by those authorities.

5. The Commission shall establish the format of the journey form, the book of journey forms and the way in which they are used. Those measures, designed to amend non-essential elements of this Regulation by supplementing it, shall be adopted in accordance with the regulatory procedure with scrutiny referred to in Article 26(2).

6. In the case of the special regular services referred to in the third subparagraph of Article 5(2), the contract or a certified true copy thereof shall serve as the control document.

ARTICLE 13

Local Excursions

C13.14   Within the framework of an international occasional service, a carrier may carry out occasional services (local excursions) in a Member State other than that in which it is established.

Such services shall be intended for non-resident passengers previously carried by the same carrier on one of the international services mentioned in the first paragraph and shall be carried out with the same vehicle or another vehicle from the same carrier or group of carriers.

CHAPTER V

CABOTAGE

ARTICLE 14

General Practice

C13.15   Any carrier who operates road passenger transport services for hire or reward and who holds a Community licence shall be permitted, under the conditions laid down in this Chapter and without discrimination on grounds of the carrier's nationality or place of establishment, to operate the cabotage operations as specified in Article 15.

ARTICLE 15

Authorised Cabotage Operations

C13.16   Cabotage operations shall be authorised for the following services:

   (a) special regular services provided that they are covered by a contract concluded between the organiser and the carrier;

   (b) occasional services;

(c) regular services, performed by a carrier not resident in the host Member State in the course of a regular international service in accordance with this Regulation with the exception of transport services meeting the needs of an urban centre or conurbation, or transport needs between it and the surrounding areas. Cabotage operations shall not be performed independently of such international service.

ARTICLE 16

Rules Applicable to Cabotage Operations

1. The performance of the cabotage operations shall be subject, save as otherwise provided in Community legislation, to the laws, regulations and administrative provisions in force in the host Member State with regard to the following: **C13.17**
   (a) the conditions governing the transport contract;
   (b) the weights and dimensions of road vehicles;
   (c) the requirements relating to the carriage of certain categories of passengers, namely schoolchildren, children and persons with reduced mobility;
   (d) the driving time and rest periods;
   (e) the value added tax (VAT) on transport services.

   The weights and dimensions referred to in point (b) of the first subparagraph may, where appropriate, exceed those applicable in the carrier's Member State of establishment, but they may under no circumstances exceed the limits set by the host Member State for national traffic or the technical characteristics mentioned in the proofs referred to in Article 6(1) of Directive 96/53/EC.

2. Save as otherwise provided in Community legislation, cabotage operations which form part of the transport services provided for in Article 15(c) shall be subject to the laws, regulations and administrative provisions in force in the host Member State regarding authorisations, tendering procedures, the routes to be operated and the regularity, continuity and frequency of services as well as itineraries.

3. The technical standards of construction and equipment which must be met by vehicles used to carry out cabotage operations shall be those laid down for vehicles put into circulation in international transport.

4. The national laws, regulations and administrative provisions referred to in paragraphs 1 and 2 shall be applied to non-resident carriers under the same conditions as those imposed on carriers established in the host Member State, so as to prevent any discrimination on grounds of nationality or place of establishment.

ARTICLE 17

Control Documents for Cabotage Operations

1. Cabotage operations in the form of occasional services shall be carried out under cover of a journey form as referred to in Article 12 which shall be kept on board the vehicle and be presented at the request of any authorised inspecting officer. **C13.18**

2. The following information shall be entered in the journey form:

(a) the points of departure and arrival of the service;

(b) the date of departure and the date on which the service ends.

3. The journey forms shall be supplied in books as referred to in Article 12 certified by the competent authority or body in the Member State of establishment.

4. In the case of special regular services, the contract concluded between the carrier and the transport organiser, or a certified true copy thereof, shall serve as the control document.

   However, a journey form shall be filled out in the form of a monthly statement.

5. The journey forms used shall be returned to the competent authority or body in the Member State of establishment in accordance with procedures to be laid down by that authority or body.

CHAPTER VI

CONTROLS AND PENALTIES

ARTICLE 18

Transporting Tickets

C13.19

1. Carriers operating a regular service, excluding special regular services, shall issue either individual or collective transport tickets indicating:

(a) the points of departure and arrival and, where appropriate, the return journey;

(b) the period of validity of the ticket;

(c) the fare of transport.

2. The transport ticket provided for in paragraph 1 shall be presented at the request of any authorised inspecting officer.

ARTICLE 19

Inspections on the Road and in Undertakings

C13.20

1. The authorisation or control document shall be carried on the vehicle and shall be presented at the request of any authorised inspecting officer.

2. Carriers operating international carriage of passengers by coach and bus shall allow all inspections intended to ensure that operations are being conducted correctly, in particular as regards driving and rest periods. In the context of the implementation of this Regulation, authorised inspecting officers shall be empowered to:

(a) check the books and other documentation relating to the operation of the transport undertaking;

(b) make copies of, or take extracts from, the books and documentation on the premises;

(c) have access to all the transport undertaking's premises, sites and vehicles;

(d) require the production of any information contained in books, documentation or data bases.

ARTICLE 20

Mutual Assistance

Member States shall assist one another in ensuring the application and moni-   **C13.21**
toring of this Regulation. They shall exchange information via the national
contact points established pursuant to Article 18 of Regulation (EC) No 1071/
2009.

ARTICLE 21

Withdrawal of Community Licences and Authorisations

1. The competent authorities of the Member State where the carrier is   **C13.22**
   established shall withdraw the Community licence where the holder:

   (a) no longer satisfies the conditions laid down in Article 3(1); or

   (b) has supplied inaccurate information concerning the data which were
       required for the issue of the Community licence.

2. The authorising authority shall withdraw an authorisation where the holder
   no longer fulfils the conditions on the basis of which the authorisation was
   issued under this Regulation, in particular where the Member State in which
   the carrier is established so requests. That authority shall immediately
   inform the competent authorities of the Member State concerned.

ARTICLE 22

Sanctioning of Infringements by the Member State of Establishment

1. In the event of a serious infringement of Community road transport legisla-   **C13.23**
   tion committed or ascertained in any Member State, in particular with regard
   to the rules applicable to vehicles, driving and rest periods for drivers and
   the provision without authorisation of parallel or temporary services, as
   referred to in the fifth subparagraph of Article 5(1), the competent authorities of the Member State of establishment of the carrier who committed the
   infringement shall take appropriate action, which may include a warning if
   provided for by national law, to pursue the matter. This may lead, inter alia,
   to the imposition of the following administrative penalties:

   (a) the temporary or permanent withdrawal of some or all of the certi-
       fied true copies of the Community licence;

   (b) the temporary or permanent withdrawal of the Community licence.

   These penalties may be determined after the final decision on the matter
   has been taken and shall have regard to the seriousness of the infringement
   committed by the holder of the Community licence and to the total number
   of certified true copies of that licence held in respect of international traffic.

2. The competent authorities of the Member State of establishment shall communicate to the competent authorities of the Member State in which the
   infringements were ascertained, as soon as possible and at the latest within 6
   weeks of their final decision on the matter, which, if any, of the penalties
   provided for in paragraph 1 have been imposed.

   If such penalties are not imposed, the competent authorities of the
   Member State of establishment shall state the reasons therefor.

3. The competent authorities shall ensure that the penalties imposed on the car-

rier concerned are, as a whole, proportionate to the infringement or infringements which gave rise to such penalties, taking into account any penalty for the same infringement imposed in the Member State in which the infringement was ascertained.

4. This Article is without prejudice to the possibility of the competent authorities of the Member State of establishment of the carrier instituting proceedings before a national court or tribunal. In the event that such proceedings are brought, the competent authority in question shall inform the competent authorities of the Member States in which the infringements were ascertained thereof.

5. Member States shall ensure that carriers have the right to appeal against any administrative penalty imposed on them pursuant to this Article.

Article 23

Sanctioning of Infringements by the Host Member State

C13.24

1. Where the competent authorities of a Member State are aware of a serious infringement of this Regulation or of Community road transport legislation attributable to a non-resident carrier, the Member State within the territory of which the infringement is ascertained shall transmit to the competent authorities of the carrier's Member State of establishment, as soon as possible and at the latest within 6 weeks of their final decision, the following information:

    (a) a description of the infringement and the date and time when it was committed;

    (b) the category, type and seriousness of the infringement; and

    (c) the penalties imposed and the penalties executed.

    The competent authorities of the host Member State may request that the competent authorities of the Member State of establishment impose administrative penalties in accordance with Article 22.

2. Without prejudice to criminal prosecution, the competent authorities of the host Member State may impose penalties on non-resident carriers who have committed infringements of this Regulation or of national or Community road transport legislation in their territory on the occasion of a cabotage operation. The penalties shall be imposed on a non-discriminatory basis and may, inter alia, consist of a warning, or, in the event of a serious infringement, a temporary ban on cabotage operations within the territory of the host Member State where the infringement was committed.

3. Member States shall ensure that carriers have the right to appeal against any administrative penalty imposed on them pursuant to this Article.

Article 24

Entry in the National Electronic Registers

C13.25

Member States shall ensure that serious infringements of Community road transport legislation attributable to carriers established in their territory, which have led to the imposition of a penalty by any Member State, as well as any temporary or permanent withdrawal of the Community licence or of the certified true copy thereof are recorded in the national electronic register of road transport undertakings. Entries in the register which concern a temporary or permanent withdrawal of a Community licence shall remain in the database for at least 2 years from the time of the expiry of the period of withdrawal, in the case of temporary withdrawal, or from the date of withdrawal, in the case of permanent withdrawal.

CHAPTER VII

IMPLEMENTATION

ARTICLE 25

Agreements between Member States

1. Member States may conclude bilateral and multilateral agreements on the further liberalisation of the services covered by this Regulation, in particular as regards the authorisation system and the simplification or abolition of control documents, especially in border regions.   C13.26

2. Member States shall inform the Commission of any agreements concluded under paragraph 1.

ARTICLE 26

Committee Procedure

1. The Commission shall be assisted by the committee established by Article 18(1) of Council Regulation (EEC) No 3821/85 of 20 December 1985 on recording equipment in road transport [*O.J. No.L370, December 31, 1985, p.8*].   C13.27

2. Where reference is made to this paragraph, Article 5a(1) to (4) and (5)(b), and Article 7 of Decision 1999/468/EC shall apply, having regard to the provisions of Article 8 thereof.

ARTICLE 27

Penalties

Member States shall lay down the rules on penalties applicable to infringements of the provisions of this Regulation and shall take all measures necessary to ensure that they are implemented. The penalties provided for must be effective, proportionate and dissuasive. Member States shall notify those provisions to the Commission by 4 December 2011 and shall notify it without delay of any subsequent amendment affecting them.   C13.28

Member States shall ensure that all such measures are taken without discrimination as to the nationality or place of establishment of the carrier.

ARTICLE 28

Reporting

1. Every 2 years Member States shall communicate to the Commission the number of authorisations for regular services issued the previous year and the total number of authorisations for regular services valid at the end of that reporting period. This information shall be given separately for each country of destination of the regular service. Member States shall also communicate to the Commission the data concerning cabotage operations, in the form of   C13.29

    special regular services and occasional services, carried out during the reporting period by resident carriers.

2. Every 2 years the competent authorities in the host Member State shall send the Commission statistics on the number of authorisations issued for cabotage operations in the form of the regular services referred to in Article 15(c).

3. The Commission shall establish the format of the table to be used for the communication of the statistics referred to in paragraph 2. Those measures, designed to amend non-essential elements of this Regulation by supplementing it, shall be adopted in accordance with the regulatory procedure with scrutiny referred to in Article 26(2).

4. Member States shall inform the Commission no later than 31 January of every year of the number of carriers holding a Community licence as at 31 December of the previous year and of the number of certified true copies corresponding to the number of vehicles in circulation on that date.

ARTICLE 29

Amendment to Regulation (EC) No 561/2006

C13.30 *[Omitted.]*

CHAPTER VIII

FINAL PROVISIONS

ARTICLE 30

Repeals

C13.31   Regulations (EEC) No 684/92 and (EC) No 12/98 are hereby repealed.

    References to the repealed Regulations shall be construed as references to this Regulation and shall be read in accordance with the correlation table set out in Annex III.

ARTICLE 31

Entry into Force

C13.32   This Regulation shall enter into force on the 20th day following its publication in the Official Journal of the European Union.

    It shall apply from 4 December 2011, with the exception of Article 29, which shall apply from 4 June 2010.

    This Regulation shall be binding in its entirety and directly applicable in all Member States.

C13.33   *[This Regulation was published in O.J. L300, November 14, 2009, pp.88–105.*

    Regulation (EEC) 684/92 and Regulation (EC) 12/98, which are repealed with effect from December 4, 2011 by art.30 of this Regulation, are set out in the twenty-fourth edition of this work.]

ANNEX I

Security features of the Community licence and the driver attestation

The Community licence and the driver attestation must have at least two of the following security features: **C13.34**

— a hologram,

— special fibres in the paper which become visible under UV-light,

— at least one microprint line (printing visible only with a magnifying glass and not reproduced by photocopying machines),

— tactile characters, symbols or patterns,

— double numbering: serial number of the Community licence, of the certified copy thereof or of the driver attestation as well as, in each case, the issue number,

— a security design background with fine guilloche patterns and rainbow printing.

ANNEX II

Community licence model

EUROPEAN COMMUNITY

C13.35

(a)

(Colour Pantone light blue, format DIN A4 cellulose paper, 100 g/m2 or more)
(First page of the licence)
(Text in the official language(s) or one of the official languages of the Member State issuing the licence)

Distinguishing sign of the Member State (¹) issuing the licence	Name of the competent authority or body

LICENCE No ...

(or)

CERTIFIED TRUE COPY No

for the international carriage of passengers by coach and bus for hire or reward

The holder of this licence (²) ....
....
....

is authorised to carry out international carriage of passengers by road for hire or reward in the territory of the Community pursuant to the conditions laid down by Regulation (EC) No 1073/2009 of the European Parliament and of the Council of 21 October 2009 on common rules for access to the international market for coach and bus service and in accordance with the general provisions of this licence.

Comments:	
This licence is valid from	To ....
Issued in	On ....
.... (³)	

(¹) The distinguishing signs of the Member States are: (B) Belgium, (BG) Bulgaria, (CZ) Czech Republic, (DK) Denmark, (D) Germany, (EST) Estonia, (IRL) Ireland, (GR) Greece, (E) Spain, (F) France, (I) Italy, (CY) Cyprus, (LV) Latvia, (LT) Lithuania, (L) Luxembourg, (H) Hungary, (MT) Malta, (NL) Netherlands, (A) Austria, (PL) Poland, (P) Portugal, (RO) Romania, (SLO) Slovenia, (SK) Slovakia, (FIN) Finland, (S) Sweden, (UK) United Kingdom.
(²) Full name or business name and full address of the carrier.
(³) Signature and seal of the competent authority or body issuing the licence.

(b)

(Second page of the licence)
(Text in the official language(s) or one of the official languages of the Member State issuing the licence)

GENERAL PROVISIONS

1. This licence is issued pursuant to Regulation (EC) No 1073/2009.

2. This licence is issued by the competent authorities of the Member State of establishment of the carrier for hire or reward who:

   (a) is authorised in the Member State of establishment to undertake carriage by means of regular services, including special regular services, or occasional services by coach and bus;

   (b) satisfies the conditions laid down in accordance with Community rules on admission to the occupation of road passenger transport operator in national and international transport operations;

   (c) meets legal requirements regarding the standards for drivers and vehicles.

3. This licence permits the international carriage of passengers by coach and bus for hire or reward on all transport links for journeys carried out in the territory of the Community:

   (a) where the point of departure and point of arrival are situated in two different Member States, with or without transit through one or more Member States or third countries;

   (b) where the point of departure and the point of arrival are in the same Member State, while the picking up or setting down of passengers is in another Member State or in a third country;

   (c) from a Member State to a third country and vice versa, with or without transit through one or more Member States or third countries;

   (d) between third countries crossing the territory of one or more Member States in transit; and empty journeys in connection with transport operations under the conditions laid down by Regulation (EC) No 1073/2009.

   In the case of a transport operation from a Member State to a third country and vice versa, Regulation (EC) No 1073/2009 is applicable, for the part of the journey on the territory of Member States crossed in transit. It does not apply to that part of the journey within the territory of the Member State of picking up or setting down, as long as the necessary agreement between the Community and the third country concerned has not been concluded.

4. This licence is personal and non-transferable.

5. This licence may be withdrawn by the competent authority of the Member State of issue in particular where the carrier:

   (a) no longer satisfies the conditions laid down in Article 3(1) of Regulation (EC) No 1073/2009;

   (b) has supplied inaccurate information regarding the data required for the issue or renewal of the licence;

   (c) has committed a serious infringement or infringements of Community road transport legislation in any Member State, in particular with regard to the rules applicable to vehicles, driving and rest periods for drivers and the provision, without authorisation, of parallel or temporary services as referred to in the fifth subparagraph of Article 5(1) of Regulation (EC) No 1073/2009. The competent authorities of the Member State of establishment of the carrier who committed the infringement may, inter alia, withdraw the Community licence or make temporary or permanent withdrawals of some or all of the certified true copies of the Community licence.

These penalties are determined in accordance with the seriousness of the breach committed by the holder of the Community licence and with the total number of certified true copies that he possesses in respect of his international transport services.

6. The original of the licence must be kept by the carrier. A certified true copy of the licence must be carried on the vehicle carrying out an international transport operation.

7. This licence must be presented at the request of any authorised inspecting officer.

8. The holder must, on the territory of each Member State, comply with the laws, regulations and administrative measures in force in that State, particularly with regard to transport and traffic.

9. *"Regular services"* means services which provide for the carriage of passengers at specified intervals along specified routes, passengers being taken up and set down at predetermined stopping points, and which are open to all, subject, where appropriate, to compulsory reservation.

The regular nature of the service shall not be affected by any adjustment to the service operating conditions.

Regular services require authorisation.

"Special regular services" means regular services, by whomsoever organised, which provide for the carriage of specified categories of passengers, to the exclusion of other passengers, at specified intervals along specified routes, passengers being taken up and set down at predetermined stopping points.

Special regular services shall include:

(a) the carriage of workers between home and work;

(b) carriage of school pupils and students to and from the educational institution.

The fact that a special service may be varied according to the needs of users shall not affect its classification as a regular service.

Special regular services do not require authorisation if they are covered by a contract between the organiser and the carrier.

The organisation of parallel or temporary services, serving the same public as existing regular services, requires authorisation.

"Occasional services" means services which do not fall within the definition of regular services, including special regular services, and whose main characteristic is that they carry groups constituted on the initiative of a customer or of the carrier himself. The organisation of parallel or temporary services comparable to existing regular services and serving the same public as the latter shall be subject to authorisation in accordance with the procedure laid down in Chapter III of Regulation (EC) No 1073/2009. These services shall not cease to be occasional services solely on the grounds that they are provided at certain intervals.

Occasional services do not require authorisation.

ANNEX III

Correlation Table

[Omitted.]   **C13.36**

Section D

International Agreements

European Agreement concerning the Work of Crews of Vehicles engaged in International Road Transport (AETR) (Cmnd. 7401)

ARRANGEMENT OF ARTICLES

VI.   Checks and inspections

*   *   *

Appendix 2. Approval Mark and Certificate
I.   Approval mark

*   *   *

THE CONTRACTING PARTIES,   **D1.02**

Being desirous of promoting the development and improvement of the
international transport of passengers and goods by road,

Convinced of the need to increase the safety of the road traffic, to make regulations governing certain conditions of employment in international road transport
in accordance with the principles of the International Labour Organisation, and
jointly to adopt certain measures to ensure the observance of those regulations,

HAVE AGREED AS FOLLOWS,

[The text of this agreement has been amended as follows: **D1.03**
    Cmnd. 9037 (August 3, 1983);
    Cm. 3042 (April 24, 1992);
    Cm. 3135 (February 28, 1995);
    UNECE Working Party on Road Transport TRANS/SC.1/375/Add.1
    (Amendment 5) (June 16, 2006); and
    UNECE Working Party on Road Transport ECE/TRANS/SC.1/386/
    Add.1 (Amendment 6) (September 20, 2010).

*The amending provisions are referred to in the notes to the agreement by ref-
erence to the appropriate command paper or UNECE amendment. The dates
referred to above are the dates on which the amendments came into force.*

The UNECE amending documents are available at http://www.unece.org/
trans/main/sc1/sc1rep.html *[accessed January 14, 2011].*]

Article 1: Definitions

For the purposes of this Agreement   **D1.04**

   (a) *"vehicle"* means any motor vehicle or trailer; this term includes any
      combination of vehicles;

   (b) *"motor vehicle"* means any self-propelled road vehicle which is
      normally used for carrying persons or goods by road or for drawing, on
      the road, vehicles used for the carriage of persons or goods; this term
      does not include agricultural tractors;

   (c) *"trailer"* means any vehicle designed to be drawn by a motor vehicle
      and includes semi-trailers;

   (d) *"semi-trailer"* means any trailer designed to be coupled to a motor ve-
      hicle in such a way that part of it rests on the motor vehicle and that a
      substantial part of its weight and of the weight of its load is borne by the
      motor vehicle;

   (e) *"combination of vehicles"* means coupled vehicles which travel on the
      road as a unit;

[(f) *"permissible maximum mass"* means the maximum mass of the laden vehicle declared permissible by the competent authority of the State in which the vehicle is registered;]

[(g) *"carriage by road"* means any journey made entirely or in part on roads open to the public of a vehicle, whether laden or not, used for the carriage of passengers or goods;]

(h) *"international road transport"* [*"international carriage by road"*] means road transport which involves the crossing of at least one frontier;

[(i) *"regular services"* means services which provide for the carriage of passengers at specified intervals along specified routes, passengers being taken up and set down at predetermined stopping points.

Rules governing the operations of services or documents taking the place thereof, approved by the competent authorities of Contracting Parties and published by the carrier before coming into operation, shall specify the conditions of carriage and in particular the frequency of services, timetables, faretables and the obligation to accept passengers for carriage, in so far as such conditions are not prescribed by any law or regulation.

Services by whomsoever organised, which provide for the carriage of specified categories of passengers to the exclusion of other passengers, in so far as such services are operated under the conditions specified in the first sub-paragraph of this definition, shall be deemed to be regular services. Such services, in particular those providing for the carriage of workers to and from their place of work or of schoolchildren to and from school, are hereinafter called *"special regular services"*;]

[(j) *"driver"* means any person, whether wage-earning or not, who drives the vehicle even for a short period, or who is carried on a vehicle as part of his duties in order to be available for driving if necessary;]

(k) *"crew member"* means the driver or either of the following, whether wage-earning or not

   (i) a driver's mate, i.e. any person accompanying the driver in order to assist him in certain manoeuvres and habitually taking an effective part in the transport operations, though not a driver in the sense of paragraph (j) of this article;

   (ii) a conductor, i.e. any person who accompanies the driver of a vehicle engaged in the carriage of passengers and is responsible in particular for the issue or checking of tickets or other documents entitling passengers to travel on the vehicle;

[(l) *"week"* means the period between 0000 hours on Monday and 2400 hours on Sunday;]

[(m) *"rest"* means any uninterrupted period during which the driver may freely dispose of his time.]

[(n) *"Break"* means any period during which a driver may not carry out any driving or any other work and which is used exclusively for recuperation;

(o) *"Daily rest period"* means the daily period during which a driver may freely dispose of his time and covers a "regular daily rest period" and a "reduced daily rest period":

   (i) *"Regular daily rest period"* means any period of rest of at least 11 hours. Alternatively, this regular daily rest period may be taken in two periods, the first of which must be an uninterrupted period of at least 3 hours and the second an uninterrupted period of at least 9 hours;

   (ii) *"Reduced daily rest period"* means any period of rest of at least 9 hours but less than 11 hours;

(p) *"Weekly rest period"* means the weekly period during which a driver may freely dispose of his time and covers a "regular weekly rest period" and a "reduced weekly rest period":

   (i) *"Regular weekly rest period"* means any period of rest of at least 45 hours;

   (ii) *"Reduced weekly rest period"* means any period of rest of less than 45 hours, which may, subject to the conditions laid down in article 8, paragraph (6), of the Agreement be shortened to a minimum of 24 consecutive hours;

(q) *"Other work"* means all working activities except driving, including any work for the same or another employer, within or outside of the transport sector. It does not include waiting time and time not devoted to driving spent in a vehicle in motion, a ferryboat or a train;

(r) *"Driving time"* means the duration of driving activity recorded automatically or semi automatically or manually in the conditions defined in this Agreement;

(s) *"Daily driving time"* means the total accumulated driving time between the end of one daily rest period and the beginning of the following daily rest period or between a daily rest period and a weekly rest period;

(t) *"Weekly driving time"* means the total accumulated driving time during a week;

(u) *"Driving period"* means the accumulated driving time from when a driver commences driving following a rest period or a break until he takes a rest period or a break. The driving period may be continuous or broken;

(v) *"Multi-manning"* means the situation where, during each period of driving between any two consecutive daily rest periods, or between a daily rest period and a weekly rest period, there are at least two drivers in the vehicle to do the driving. For the first hour of multi-manning the presence of another driver or drivers is optional, but for the remainder of the period it is compulsory;

(w) *"Transport undertaking"* means any natural person, any legal person, any association or group of persons without legal personality, whether profit-making or not, or any official body, whether having its own legal personality or being dependent upon an authority having such a personality, which engages in carriage by road, whether for hire or reward or for own account.]

[Article 1 is printed as amended by Cm. 3042; TRANS/SC.1/386/Add.1.   **D1.05**

In art.1, the square brackets used in the definition of "international road transport" occur in the text of the agreement and (unlike the use of square brackets elsewhere in this work) do not denote amendments to the text.

On depositing their instruments of accession to or ratification of this agreement, the governments of Belgium, Denmark, France, Luxembourg, the Netherlands and the United Kingdom each made the following declaration: "Transport operations between Member States of the European Economic Community shall be regarded as national transport operations within the meaning of the AETR in so far as such operations do not pass in transit through the territory of a third State which is a contracting party to the AETR " (cf. art.2(2) of Council Regulation (EEC) 2829/77).]

[Article 2: Scope

D1.06   1. This Agreement shall apply in the territory of each Contracting Party to all international road transport performed by any vehicle registered in the territory of the said Contracting Party or in the territory of any other Contracting Party.

2. Nevertheless, unless the Contracting Parties whose territory is used agree otherwise, this Agreement shall not apply to international road transport performed by:

(a) Vehicles used for the carriage of goods where the permissible maximum mass of the vehicle, including any trailer or semi-trailer, does not exceed 3.5 tonnes;

(b) Vehicles used for the carriage of passengers which, by virtue of their construction and equipment, are suitable for carrying not more than nine persons, including the driver, and are intended for that purpose;

(c) Vehicles used for the carriage of passengers on regular services where the route covered by the service in question does not exceed 50 kilometres;

(d) Vehicles with a maximum authorized speed not exceeding 40 kilometres per hour;

(e) Vehicles owned or hired without a driver by the armed services, civil defence services, fire services, and forces responsible for maintaining public order when the carriage is undertaken as a consequence of the tasks assigned to these services and is under their control;

(f) Vehicles used in emergencies or rescue operations, including the non-commercial transport of humanitarian aid;

(g) Specialized vehicles used for medical purposes;

(h) Specialized breakdown vehicles operating within 100 kilometres of their base;

(i) Specialized breakdown vehicles operating within 100 kilometres of their base;

(j) Vehicles with a maximum permissible mass not exceeding 7.5 tonnes used for non-commercial carriage of goods;

(k) Commercial vehicles which have a historical status according to the legislation of the Contracting Party in which they are being driven and which are used for the non-commercial carriage of passengers or goods.]

D1.07   *[Article 2 is printed as substituted by TRANS/SC.1/386/Add.1.]*

[Article 3: Application of some provisions of the Agreement to road transport performed by vehicles registered in the territories of non-Contracting States

1. Each Contracting Party shall apply in its territory, in respect of international **D1.08** road transport performed by any vehicle registered in the territory of a State which is not a Contracting Party to this Agreement, provisions not less strict than those laid down in articles 5, 6, 7, 8, 9 and 10 of this Agreement.

[2.(a) However, it shall be open to any Contracting Party, in the case of a vehicle registered in a State which is not a Contracting Party to this Agreement, merely to require, in lieu of a control device conforming to the specifications in the Annex to this Agreement, daily record sheets completed manually by each crew member for the period of time from the moment of entry into the territory of the first Contracting Party.

(b) For this purpose, each crew member shall write on his record sheet the information concerning his professional activities and rest periods, using the appropriate graphic symbols as defined in article 12 of the Annex to this Agreement.]

[Article 3 is printed as substituted by Cm. 3042 and as amended by TRANS/ **D1.09** *SC.1/386/Add.1.]*

[Article 4: General principles

Each Contracting Party may apply higher minima or lower maxima than those **D1.10** laid down in articles 5 to 8 inclusive. Nevertheless, the provisions of this Agreement shall remain applicable to drivers, engaged in international road transport operations on vehicles registered in another Contracting or non-Contracting State.]

[Article 4 is printed as substituted by Cm. 3042.] **D1.11**

[Article 5: Crews

1. The minimum ages for drivers engaged in the carriage of goods shall be as **D1.12** follows:

(a) for vehicles, including, where appropriate, trailers or semi-trailers, having a permissible maximum weight of not more than 7.5 tonnes, 18 years;

(b) for other vehicles:

21 years, or

18 years provided that the person concerned holds a certificate of professional competence recognised by one of the Contracting Parties confirming that he has completed a training course for drivers of vehicles intended for the carriage of goods by road. Contracting Parties shall inform one another of the prevailing national minimum training levels and other relevant conditions relating to drivers engaged in international carriage of goods under this Agreement.

2. Any driver engaged in the carriage of passengers shall have reached the age of 21 years.

Any driver engaged in the carriage of passengers on journeys beyond a 50 kilometre radius from the place where the vehicle is normally based must also fulfil one of the following conditions:

(a) he must have worked for at least one year in the carriage of goods as a driver of vehicles with a permissible maximum weight exceeding 3.5 tonnes;

     (b) he must have worked for at least one year as a driver of vehicles used to provide passenger services on journeys within a 50 kilometre radius from the place where the vehicle is normally based, or other types of passenger services not subject to this Agreement provided the competent authority considers that he has by so doing acquired the necessary experience;

     (c) he must hold a certificate of professional competence recognised by one of the Contracting Parties confirming that he has completed a training course for drivers of vehicles intended for the carriage of passengers by road.]

D1.13   *[Article 5 is printed as substituted by Cm. 3042.]*

[Article 6: Driving periods

D1.14   1. The daily driving time, as defined in article 1, paragraph (s), of this Agreement, shall not exceed 9 hours. It may be extended to at most 10 hours not more than twice during the week.

    2. The weekly driving time, as defined in article 1, paragraph (t), of this Agreement, shall not exceed 56 hours.

    3. The total accumulated driving time during any two consecutive weeks shall not exceed 90 hours.

    4. Driving periods shall include all driving in the territory of Contracting and non-Contracting Parties.

    5. A driver shall record as other work any time spent as described in article 1, paragraph (q), as well as any time spent driving a vehicle used for commercial operations not falling within the scope of this Agreement, and shall record any periods of availability, as set out in article 12, paragraph 3 (c), of the Annex to this Agreement. This record shall be entered either manually on a record sheet or printout or by use of the manual input facilities of the recording equipment.]

D1.15   *[Article 6 is printed as substituted by Cm. 3042 and as amended by TRANS/ SC.1/386/Add.1.]*

[Article 6bis: Interruption of the daily rest period in the course of combined transport operations

D1.16   […]

    [Repealed by Cm. 3042.]

[Article 7: Breaks

D1.17   1. After a driving period of four and a half hours, a driver shall take an uninterrupted break of not less than 45 minutes, unless he begins a rest period.

    2. This break, as defined in article 1, paragraph (n), of this Agreement, may be replaced by a break of at least 15 minutes followed by a break of at least 30 minutes each distributed over the driving period or immediately after this period in such a way as to comply with the provisions of paragraph 1.

    3. For the purposes of this article, the waiting time and time not devoted to driving spent in a vehicle in motion, a ferryboat or a train shall not be regarded as "other work", as defined in article 1, paragraph (q), of this Agreement, and will be able to be qualified as a "break".]

D1.18   *[Article 7 is printed as substituted by Cm. 3042 and as amended by TRANS/ SC.1/386/Add.1.]*

[Article 8: Rest periods

  1. A driver shall take daily and weekly rest periods as defined in article 1,   **D1.19** paragraphs (o) and (p).

  2. Within each period of 24 hours after the end of the previous daily rest period or weekly rest period, a driver shall have taken a new daily rest period.

If the portion of the daily rest period which falls within that 24-hour period is at least 9 hours but less than 11 hours, then the daily rest period in question shall be regarded as a reduced daily rest period.

  3. By way of derogation from paragraph 2, within 30 hours of the end of a daily or weekly rest period, a driver engaged in multi-manning must have taken a new daily rest period of at least 9 hours.

  4. A daily rest period may be extended to make a regular weekly rest period or a reduced weekly rest period.

  5. A driver may have at most three reduced daily rest periods between any two weekly rest periods.

  6. (a) In any two consecutive weeks, a driver shall take at least:

    (i) Two regular weekly rest periods; or

    (ii) One regular weekly rest period and one reduced weekly rest period of at least 24 hours. However, the reduction shall be compensated by an equivalent period of rest taken *en bloc* before the end of the third week following the week in question.

    A weekly rest period shall start no later than at the end of six 24-hour periods from the end of the previous weekly rest period.

  (b) By way of derogation from paragraph 6 (a), a driver engaged in a single service of international carriage of passengers, other than a regular service, may postpone the weekly rest period for up to twelve consecutive 24-hour periods following a previous regular weekly rest period, provided that:

    (i) the service lasts at least 24 consecutive hours in a Contracting Party or a third country other than the one in which the service started, and

    (ii) the driver takes after the use of the derogation:

      a. either two regular weekly rest periods, or

      b. one regular weekly rest period and one reduced weekly rest period of at least 24 hours. However, the reduction shall be compensated by an equivalent period of rest taken *en bloc* before the end of the third week following the end of the derogation period,

    and

    (iii) four years after the country of registration has implemented the digital tachograph, the vehicle is equipped with recording equipment in accordance with the requirements of Appendix 1B of the Annex, and

    (iv) after 1 January 2014, in case of driving during the period from 22:00 to 06:00, the vehicle is multi-manned or the driving period referred to in Article 7 is reduced to three hours.

  (c) By way of derogation from paragraph 6 (a), drivers who are engaged in multi manning shall take each week a regular weekly rest period of at least 45 hours. This period may be reduced to a minimum of 24 hours (reduced weekly rest period). However, each reduction shall be compensated by an equivalent period of rest taken *en bloc* before the end of the third week following the week in question.

A weekly rest period shall start no later than at the end of six 24-hour periods from the end of the previous weekly rest period.

7. Any rest taken as compensation for a reduced weekly rest period shall be attached to another rest period of at least 9 hours.

8. Where a driver chooses to do this, daily rest periods and reduced weekly rest periods taken away from base may be taken in a vehicle, as long as it has specially fitted sleeping facilities for each driver as foreseen by the constructor's design, and it is stationary.

9. A weekly rest period that falls in two weeks may be counted in either week, but not in both.]

D1.20 *[Article 8 is printed as substituted by TRANS/SC.1/386/Add.1.]*

[Article 8 bis: Derogations from article 8

D1.21 1. By way of derogation from article 8, where a driver accompanies a vehicle which is transported by ferryboat or train and takes a regular daily rest period, that period may be interrupted not more than twice by other activities provided the following conditions are fulfilled:

(a) That part of the daily rest period spent on land must be able to be taken before or after the portion of the daily rest period taken on board the ferryboat or the train;

(b) The period between the portions of the daily rest period must be as short as possible and may on no account exceed a total of one hour before embarkation or after disembarkation, customs formalities being included in the embarkation or disembarkation operations.

During all the portions of the daily rest period, the driver shall have access to a bunk or couchette.

2. Any time spent travelling to a location to take charge of a vehicle falling within the scope of this Agreement, or to return from that location, when the vehicle is neither at the driver's home nor at the employer's operational centre where the driver is normally based, shall not be counted as a rest or break unless the driver is in a ferryboat or train and has access to suitable sleeping facilities.

3. Any time spent by a driver driving a vehicle which falls outside the scope of this Agreement to or from a vehicle which falls within the scope of this Agreement and which is not at the driver's home or at the employer's operational centre where the driver is normally based shall count as "other work".]

D1.22 *[Article 8 bis is printed as inserted by TRANS/SC.1/386/Add.1.]*

[Article 9: Exceptions

D1.23 Provided that road safety is not thereby jeopardised and to enable him to reach a suitable stopping place, the driver may depart from the provisions of this Agreement to the extent necessary to ensure the safety of persons, of the vehicle or of its load. [The driver shall indicate the nature of and reason for his departure from those provisions on the record sheet or on a printout of the control device or in his duty roster, at the latest on arrival at a suitable stopping place.]]

D1.24 *[Article 9 is printed as substituted (for the original art.11) by Cm. 3042 and as amended by TRANS/SC.1/386/Add.1.]*

[Article 10: Control device

1. The Contracting Parties shall prescribe the installation and use on vehicles **D1.25** registered in their territory of a control device according to the requirements of this Agreement and the Annex and Appendices thereto.

2. The control device within the sense of this Agreement shall, as regards construction, installation, use and testing, comply with the requirements of this Agreement and the Annex and Appendices thereto.

3. A control device conforming to Council Regulation (EEC) No.3821/85 of 20 December 1985 as regards construction, installation, use and testing shall be considered as conforming to the requirements of this Agreement and the Annex and Appendices thereto.]

[Article 10 is printed as substituted by TRANS/Sc.1/375/Add.1.] **D1.26**

Articles 11–25

[Omitted.] **D1.27**

*   *   *

<h2 align="center">SIGNATURES</h2>

[The following states have signed and ratified the Agreement: **D1.28**
    Austria
    Belgium
    Federal Republic of Germany
    France
    Italy
    Luxembourg
    the Netherlands
    Norway
    Poland
    Portugal
    Sweden
    Switzerland, and
    the United Kingdom (including the Isle of Man).

The Agreement came into operation, in accordance with the original art.16, para.4, on January 5, 1976; it came into operation in the United Kingdom on August 18, 1978.

On signature of the Agreement, the Contracting States agreed the following declaration which was set out in the Protocol of Signature to the agreement: "The Contracting Parties declare that this Agreement is without prejudice to such provisions as may, if appropriate, subsequently be drawn up in the matter of the duration and spread-over of work."]

<h2 align="center">ACCESSIONS</h2>

[The following countries have also acceded or succeeded to the Agreement: **D1.29**

Albania	*Liechtenstein*
Andorra	*Lithuania*

Armenia	*Macedonia (former Yugoslav Republic)*
Azerbaijan	*Malta*
Belarus	*Moldova*
Bosnia and Herzegovina	*Monaco*
Bulgaria	*Romania*
Croatia	*Russian Federation*
Cyprus	*San Marino*
Czech Republic	*Serbia*
Denmark	*Slovakia*
Estonia	*Slovenia*
Finland	*Spain*
Greece	*Turkey*
Hungary	*Turkmenistan*
Ireland	*Ukraine*
Kazakhstan	*Uzbekistan]*
Latvia	

[ANNEX

CONTROL DEVICE

GENERAL PROVISIONS

I. TYPE APPROVAL

Article 1

D1.30   For the purposes of this Chapter, the words "*control device*" shall mean "*control device or its components*".

Applications for the approval of a type of control device or of a model record sheet or memory card shall be submitted, accompanied by the appropriate specifications, by the manufacturer or his agent to a Contracting Party. No application in respect of any one type of control device or of any one model record sheet or memory card may be submitted to more than one Contracting Party.

Article 2

D1.31   A Contracting Party shall grant its type approval to any type of control device, to any model record sheet or memory card which conforms to the requirements laid down in Appendix 1 or 1B to this Annex, provided that the Contracting Party is in a position to check that production models conform to the approved prototype.

The control device referred to in Appendix 1B may not be granted type approval until the whole system (the control device itself, driver card and electrical gearbox connections) has demonstrated its capacity to resist attempts to tamper with or alter the data on driving times. The tests necessary to establish this shall be carried out by experts familiar with up-to-date tampering techniques.

Any modifications or additions to an approved model must receive additional type approval from the Contracting Party which granted the original type approval.

Article 3

D1.32   Contracting Parties shall issue to the applicant an approval mark, which shall conform to the model shown in Appendix 2, for each type of control device or model record sheet or memory card which they approve pursuant to article 2.

Article 4

The competent authorities of the Contracting Party to which the application for **D1.33**
type approval has been submitted shall, in respect of each type of control device or model record sheet or memory card which they approve or refuse to approve, either send within one month to the authorities of the other Contracting Parties a copy of the approval certificate accompanied by copies of the relevant specifications, or, if such is the case, notify those authorities that approval has been refused; in cases of refusal they shall communicate the reasons for their decision.

Article 5

1. If a Contracting Party which has granted type approval as provided for in **D1.34**
article 2 finds that a certain control device or record sheet or memory card bearing the type approval mark which it has issued does not conform to the prototype which it has approved, it shall take the necessary measures to ensure that production models conform to the approved prototype. The measures taken may, if necessary, extend to withdrawal of the type approval.

2. A Contracting Party which has granted type approval shall withdraw such approval if the control device or record sheet or memory card which has been approved is not in conformity with this Annex or its Appendices or displays in use any general defect which makes it unsuitable for the purpose for which it is intended.

3. If a Contracting Party which has granted type approval is notified by another Contracting Party of one of the cases referred to in paragraphs 1 and 2, it shall also, after consulting the latter Contracting Party, take the steps laid down in those paragraphs, subject to paragraph 5.

4. A Contracting Party which ascertains that one of the cases referred to in paragraph 2 has arisen may forbid until further notice the placing on the market and putting into service of the control device or record sheets or memory card. The same applies in the cases mentioned in paragraph 1 with respect to control devices or record sheets or memory cards which have been exempted from the initial verification, if the manufacturer, after due warning, does not bring the equipment into line with the approved model or with the requirements of this Annex.

In any event, the competent authorities of the Contracting Parties shall notify one another within one month, of any withdrawal of type approval or of any other measures taken pursuant to paragraphs 1, 2 and 3 and shall specify the reasons for such action.

5. If a Contracting Party which has granted type approval disputes the existence of any of the cases specified in paragraphs 1 or 2 notified to it, the Contracting Parties concerned shall endeavour to settle the dispute.

Article 6

1. An applicant for type approval of a model record sheet shall state on his ap- **D1.35**
plication the type or types of control device on which the sheet in question is designed to be used and shall provide a suitable device of such type or types for the purpose of testing the sheet.

2. The competent authorities of each Contracting Party shall indicate on the approval certificate for the model record sheet the type or types of control device on which that model sheet may be used.

Article 7

D1.36   No Contracting Party may refuse to register any vehicle fitted with a control device, or prohibit the entry into service or use of such vehicle for any reason connected with the fact that the vehicle is fitted with such device, if the control device bears the approval mark referred to in article 3 and the installation plaque referred to in article 9.

Article 8

D1.37   All decisions pursuant to this Annex refusing or withdrawing approval of a type of control device or model record sheet or memory card shall specify in detail the reasons on which they are based. A decision shall be communicated to the party concerned, who shall at the same time be informed of the remedies available to him under the laws of the Contracting Party and of the time limits for the exercise of such remedies.

II. INSTALLATION AND INSPECTION

Article 9

D1.38   1. The control device may be installed or repaired only by fitters or workshops approved by the competent authorities of Contracting Parties for that purpose after the latter, should they so desire, have heard the views of the manufacturers concerned.

The period of administrative validity of approved workshop and fitter cards shall not exceed one year.

If a card issued to an approved workshop or fitter is to be extended, is damaged, malfunctions, is lost or stolen, the authority shall supply a replacement card within five working days of receiving a detailed request to that effect.

Where a new card is issued to replace an old one, the new card shall bear the same "workshop" information number, but the index shall be increased by one. The authority issuing the card shall maintain a register of lost, stolen or defective cards.

Contracting Parties shall take any measure necessary to prevent the cards distributed to approved fitters and workshops from being falsified.

2. The approved fitter or workshop shall place a special mark on the seals which it affixes and, in addition, shall enter for a control device in conformity with Appendix 1B, the electronic security data for carrying out, in particular, the authentication checks. The competent authorities of each Contracting Party shall maintain a register of the marks and electronic security data used and of approved workshop and fitter cards issued.

3. The competent authorities of the Contracting Parties shall send each other their lists of approved fitters and workshops and the cards issued to them and also copies of the marks and of the necessary information relating to the electronic security data used.

4. For the purpose of certifying that installation of the control device took place in accordance with the requirements of this Annex an installation plaque affixed as provided in Appendix 1 or 1B shall be used.

5. Seals may be removed by fitters or workshops approved by the competent authorities in accordance with the provisions of paragraph 1 of this article or in the circumstances described in Appendix 1 or 1B of this Annex.

III. USE OF EQUIPMENT

Article 10

The employer and drivers shall ensure the correct functioning and proper use **D1.39** of, on the one hand, the control device and, on the other, the driver card where a driver is required to drive a vehicle fitted with a control device in conformity with Appendix 1B.

Article 11

1. The employer shall issue a sufficient number of record sheets to drivers of **D1.40** vehicles fitted with the control device in conformity with Appendix 1, bearing in mind the fact that these sheets are personal in character, the length of the period of service, and the possible obligation to replace sheets which are damaged, or have been taken by an authorized inspecting officer. The employer shall issue to drivers only sheets of an approved model suitable for use in the control device installed in the vehicle.

Where the vehicle is fitted with a control device in conformity with Appendix 1B, the employer and the driver shall ensure that, taking into account the length of the period of service, the printing on request referred to in Appendix 1B can be carried out correctly in the event of an inspection.

[2.(a) The undertaking shall keep record sheets and printouts, whenever printouts have been made to comply with article 12, paragraph 1, in chronological order and in a legible form for at least a year after their use and shall give copies to the drivers concerned who request them. The undertaking shall also give copies of downloaded data from the driver cards to the drivers concerned who request them and the printed papers of these copies. The record sheets, printouts and downloaded data shall be produced or handed over at the request of any authorized inspecting officer.

(b) An undertaking which uses vehicles that are fitted with a control device complying with Appendix 1B of the present Annex and that fall within the scope of this Agreement shall:

(i) Ensure that all data are downloaded from the vehicle unit and driver card as regularly as is stipulated by the Contracting Party and that relevant data are downloaded more frequently so as to ensure that all data concerning activities undertaken by or for that undertaking are downloaded;

(ii) Ensure that all data downloaded from both the vehicle unit and driver card are kept for at least 12 months following recording and, should an inspecting officer request it, such data are accessible, either directly or remotely, from the premises of the undertaking.

For the purposes of this subparagraph, "downloaded" shall be interpreted in accordance with the definition laid down in Appendix 1B, Chapter I, point (s).]

3. The driver card as defined in Appendix 1B shall be issued, at the request of

the driver, by the competent authority of the Contracting Party where the driver has his normal residence.

A Contracting Party may require any driver subject to the provisions of the Agreement and normally resident on its territory to hold a driver card.

(a) For the purposes of this Agreement "*normal residence*" means the place where a person usually lives, that is for at least 185 days in each calendar year, because of personal and occupational ties, or, in the case of a person with no occupational ties, because of personal ties which show close links between that person and the place where he is living.

However, the normal residence of a person whose occupational ties are in a different place from his personal ties and who consequently lives in turn in different places situated in two or more Contracting Parties shall be regarded as being the place of his personal ties, provided that such person returns there regularly. This last condition need not be met where the person is living in a Contracting Party in order to carry out a fixed-term assignment.

(b) Drivers shall give proof of their place of normal residence by any appropriate means, such as their identity card or any other valid document.

(c) Where the competent authorities of the Contracting Party issuing the driver card have doubts as to the validity of a statement as to normal residence made in accordance with point (b), or for the purpose of certain specific controls, they may request any additional information or evidence.

(d) The competent authority of the issuing Contracting Party shall, as far as this can be done, ensure that the applicant does not already hold a valid driver card.

4.(a) The competent authority of the Contracting Party shall personalize the driver card in accordance with the provisions of Appendix 1B.

The period of administrative validity of the driver card shall not exceed five years.

The driver may hold one valid driver card only. The driver is authorized to use only his own personalized driver card. The driver shall not use a driver card which is defective or which has expired.

When a driver card is issued replacing an old one, the new card shall bear the same driver card issue number but the index shall be increased by one. The issuing authority shall keep records of issued, stolen, lost or defective driver cards for a period at least equivalent to their period of validity.

If the driver card is damaged, malfunctions or is lost or stolen, the authority shall supply a replacement card within five working days of receiving a detailed request to that effect.

In the event of a request for the renewal of a card whose expiry date is approaching, the authority shall supply a new card before the expiry date provided that the request was sent to it within the time limits laid down in the fourth subparagraph of article 12(1).

(b) Driver cards shall be issued only to applicants who are subject to the provisions of the Agreement.

(c) The driver card shall be personal. It may not, during its official period of validity, be withdrawn or suspended for whatever reason unless the competent authority of a Contracting Party finds that the card has been falsified, or the driver is using a card of which he is not the holder, or that the card held has been obtained on the basis of false declarations and/or forged documents. If such suspension or withdrawal measures are taken by a Contracting Party other than the Contracting Party of issue, the former shall return the card to the authorities of the Contracting Party which issued it and shall indicate the reasons for returning it.

(d) Driver cards issued by Contracting Parties shall be mutually recognized.

Where the holder of a valid driver card issued by a Contracting Party has established his normal place of residence in another Contracting Party, he may ask for his card to be exchanged for an equivalent driver card; it shall be the responsibility of the Contracting Party which carries out the exchange to verify if necessary whether the card produced is actually still valid.

Contracting Parties carrying out an exchange shall return the old card to the authorities of the Contracting Party of issue and indicate the reasons for so doing.

(e) Where a Contracting Party replaces or exchanges a driver card, the replacement or exchange, and any subsequent replacement or renewal, shall be registered in that Contracting Party.

(f) Contracting Parties shall take all the necessary measures to prevent any possibility of driver cards being falsified.

5. Contracting Parties shall ensure that data needed to monitor compliance with the present Agreement which are recorded and stored by the control device in conformity with Appendix 1B to this Annex can be stored for 365 days after the date of their recording and that they can be made available under conditions that guarantee the security and accuracy of the data.

Contracting Parties shall take any measures necessary to ensure that the resale or decommissioning of a control device cannot detract, in particular, from the satisfactory application of this paragraph.

Article 12

1. Drivers shall not use dirty or damaged record sheets or driver card. The   **D1.41**
sheets or driver card shall be adequately protected on this account.

In case of damage to a sheet or driver card bearing recordings, drivers shall attach the damaged sheet or driver card to a spare sheet or a [appropriate] sheet used to replace it.

If the driver card is damaged, malfunctions or is lost or stolen, the driver shall apply within seven calendar days for its replacement to the competent authorities of the Contracting Party in which he has his normal residence.

Where a driver wishes to renew his driver card, he shall apply to the competent authorities of the Contracting Party in which he has his normal residence not later than 15 working days before the expiry date of the card.

[2.(a) Drivers shall use the record sheets or driver card every day on which they are driving, starting from the moment they take over the vehicle. The record sheet or driver card shall not be withdrawn before the end of the daily working period unless its withdrawal is otherwise authorized. No record sheet or driver card may be used to cover a period longer than that for which it is intended.

When there is more than one driver on board a vehicle fitted with a control device in conformity with Appendix 1B, each driver shall ensure that this driver card is inserted in the correct slot in the tachograph.

(b) When, as a result of being away from the vehicle, a driver is unable to use the control device fitted to the vehicle, the periods of time indicated in paragraph 3, second indent, (b), (c) and (d), below shall:

    (i) If the vehicle is fitted with a control device in conformity with Appendix 1, be entered on the record sheet, either manually, by automatic recording or other means, legibly and without dirtying the sheet; or

    (ii) If the vehicle is fitted with a control device in conformity with Appendix 1B, be entered on the driver card using the manual entry facility provided in the recording equipment.

(c) Drivers shall amend the record sheets as necessary should there be more than one driver on board the vehicle, so that the information referred to in paragraph 3, second indent, (b), (c) and (d), below is recorded on the record sheet of the driver who is actually driving.]

3. Drivers shall:

    — ensure that the time recorded on the sheet agrees with the official time in the country of registration of the vehicle,

    — operate the switch mechanisms enabling the following periods of time to be recorded separately and distinctly:

(a) under the sign

or

driving time;

(b) under the sign

or

all other periods of work;

(c) under the sign

or

other periods of availability, namely:

— waiting time, i.e. the period during which drivers need remain at their posts only for the purpose of answering any calls to start or resume driving or to carry out other work,

— time spent beside the driver while the vehicle is in motion,

— time spent on a bunk while the vehicle is in motion;

(d) under the sign

or

breaks in work and daily rest periods.

4. Each Contracting Party may permit all the periods referred to in paragraph 3, second indent (b) and (c) to be recorded under the sign

on the record sheets used on vehicles registered in its territory.

5. Each crew member concerned shall enter the following information on his record sheet:

(a) on beginning to use the sheet—his surname and first name;

(b) the date and place where use of the sheet begins and the date and place where such use ends;

(c) the registration number of each vehicle to which he is assigned, both at the start of the first journey recorded on the sheet and then, in the event of a change of vehicle, during use of the sheet;

(d) the odometer reading:

— at the start of the first journey recorded on the sheet,

— at the end of the last journey recorded on the sheet,

— in the event of a change of vehicle during a working day (reading on the vehicle to which he was assigned and reading on the vehicle to which he is assigned);

(e) if relevant, the time of any change of vehicle.

5. *bis.* The driver shall enter in the control device in conformity with Appendix 1B the symbols of the countries in which he begins and ends his daily work period.

The above data entries shall be activated by the driver, and may be entirely manual or automatic if the control device is linked to a satellite tracking system.

6. The control device defined in Appendix 1 shall be so designed that it is possible for an authorized inspecting officer, if necessary after opening the equipment, to read the recordings relating to the nine hours preceding the time of the check without permanently deforming, damaging or soiling the sheet.

The device shall, furthermore, be so designed that it is possible, without opening the case, to verify that recordings are being made.

[7.(a) Where the driver drives a vehicle fitted with a control device in conformity with Appendix 1, he must be able to produce, whenever an inspecting officer so requests:

   (i) The record sheets for the current week and those used by the driver in the previous 15 calendar days;

  (ii) The driver card, if he holds one; and

 (iii) Any manual record and printout made during the current week and the previous 15 calendar days, as required under this Agreement.

From the date of application defined in article 13 bis of this Agreement, the time periods referred to under (i) and (iii) shall cover the current day and the previous 28 calendar days.

(b) Where the driver drives a vehicle fitted with a control device in conformity with Appendix 1B, he must be able to produce, whenever an inspecting officer so requests:

   (i) The driver card of which he is holder;

  (ii) Any manual record and printout made during the current week and the previous 15 calendar days, as required under this Agreement;

 (iii) The record sheets corresponding to the same period as the one referred to in the previous subparagraph during which he drove a vehicle fitted with a control device in conformity with Appendix 1.

From the date of application defined in article 13 bis of this Agreement, the time periods referred to under (ii) shall cover the current day and the previous 28 calendar days.]

(c) An authorized inspecting officer may check compliance with the Agreement by analysis of the record sheets, of the displayed or printed data which have been recorded by the control device or by the driver card or, failing this, by analysis of any other supporting document that justifies non-compliance with a provision, such as those laid down in article 13(2) and (3).

8. It shall be forbidden to falsify, suppress or destroy data recorded on the record sheet, stored in the control device or on the driver card, or print-outs from the control device as defined in Appendix 1B. The same applies to any manipulation of the control device, record sheet or driver card which may result in data and/or printed information being falsified, suppressed or destroyed. No device which could be used to carry out the manipulations mentioned shall be present on the vehicle.

Article 13

D1.42   1. In the event of breakdown or faulty operation of the control device, the employer shall have it repaired by an approved fitter or workshop, as soon as circumstances permit.

If the vehicle is unable to return to the premises within a period of one week calculated from the day of the breakdown or of the discovery of defective operation, the repair shall be carried out en route.

Measures taken by the Contracting Parties may give the competent authorities power to prohibit the use of the vehicle in cases where breakdown or faulty operation has not been put right as provided in the foregoing subparagraphs.

[2.(a) While the device is unserviceable or malfunctioning, the driver shall mark on the record sheet or sheets, or on an appropriate sheet to be attached to the record sheet or to the driver card, on which he shall enter data enabling him to be identified (name and number of his driving licence or name and number of his driver card), including his signature, all information for the various periods of time which are no longer recorded or printed out correctly by the control device.

(b) Where a driver card is damaged, malfunctions, is lost or stolen, or is not in the possession of the driver, the driver shall:

(i) At the start of his journey, print out the details of the vehicle he is driving, and enter onto that printout:

— Details that enable the driver to be identified (name and number of his driving licence or name and number of his driver card), including his signature;

— The periods referred to in article 12, paragraph 3, second indent, points (b), (c) and (d);

(ii) At the end of his journey, print out the information relating to periods of time recorded by the control device, record any periods of other work, availability and rest undertaken since the printout that was made at the start of the journey, where not recorded by the tachograph, and mark on that document details that enable the driver to be identified (name and number of his driving licence or name and number of his driver card), including his signature.]

3. If a driver card is damaged or if it malfunctions, the driver shall return it to the competent authority of the Contracting Party in which he has his normal residence. Theft of the driver card shall be the subject of a formal declaration to the competent authorities of the State where the theft occurred.

Loss of the driver card must be reported in a formal declaration to the competent authorities of the Contracting Party that issued it and to the competent authorities of the Contracting Party of normal residence where they are different.

The driver may continue to drive without a driver card for a maximum period of 15 calendar days or for a longer period if this is necessary for the vehicle to return to its premises, provided he can prove the impossibility of producing or using the card during this period.

Where the authorities of the Contracting Party in which the driver has his normal residence are different from those which issued his card and where the latter are requested to renew, replace or exchange the driver card, they shall inform the authorities which issued the old card of the precise reasons for its renewal, replacement or exchange.

Article 14

1. Pursuant to article 13, paragraph 2 (b) of the Agreement, drivers who are **D1.43** driving a vehicle registered in a Contracting Party and to whom the competent authorities have not yet been able to issue the driver cards and who, during the transitional period referred to in paragraph 1 of this article, drive in international traffic with a vehicle fitted with a digital control device in accordance with Appendix 1B to the Annex, must be able to produce, whenever an inspecting officer so requests, the printouts and/or the record sheets for the current week and, in any event, the printout and/or record sheet for the last day on which he drove during the previous week.

2. Paragraph 1 does not apply to drivers of vehicles registered in a country where it is obligatory to use a driver card. However, drivers shall produce printouts whenever an inspecting officer so requests.

3. The printouts referred to in paragraph 1 shall be marked with the details that enable the drivers to be identified (name and number of the driving licence), including their signature.]

D1.44   *[Chapters I to III to the Annex are printed as substituted by TRANS/SC.1/375/ Add.1 and as amended by TRANS/SC.1/386/Add.1.]*

APPENDIX 1

REQUIREMENTS FOR CONSTRUCTION, TESTING, INSTALLATION AND INSPECTION

I. DEFINITIONS

D1.45   In this appendix

(a) *"control device"* means equipment intended for installation in road vehicles to show and record automatically or semi-automatically details of the movement of those vehicles and of certain working periods of their drivers;

(b) *"record sheet"* means a sheet designed to accept and retain recorded data, to be placed in the control device and on which the marking devices of the latter inscribe a continuous record of the information to be recorded;

(c) *"constant of the control device"* means the numerical characteristic giving the value of the input signal required to show and record a distance travelled of 1 kilometre; this constant must be expressed either in revolutions per kilometre ($k=$ ... rev/km), or in impulses per kilometre ($k=$ ... imp/km);

(d) *"characteristic coefficient of the vehicle"* means the numerical characteristic giving the value of the output signal emitted by the part of the vehicle linking it with the control device (gearbox output shaft or axle) while the vehicle travels a distance of one measured kilometre under normal test conditions (see Chapter VI, paragraph 4 of this appendix) . The characteristic coefficient is expressed either in revolutions per kilometre ($W =$ rev/km) or in impulses per kilometre ($W =$ ... imp/km);

(e) *"effective circumference of wheel tyres"* means the average of the distances travelled by the several wheels moving the vehicle (driving wheels) in the course of one complete rotation. The measurement of these distances must be made under normal test conditions (see Chapter VI, paragraph 4 of this appendix) and is expressed in the form: $1 =$ ... mm.

II. GENERAL CHARACTERISTICS AND FUNCTIONS OF CONTROL DEVICE

D1.46   The control device must be able to record the following:

1. distance travelled by the vehicle;
2. speed of the vehicle;
3. driving time;
4. other periods of work or of availability;
5. breaks from work and daily rest periods;
6. opening of the case containing the record sheet;
7. for electronic control device which is device operating by signals

transmitted electrically from the distance and speed sensor, any interruption exceeding 100 milliseconds in the power supply of the recording equipment (except lighting), in the power supply of the distance and speed sensor and any interruption in the signal lead to the distance and speed sensor.

For vehicles used by two drivers the control device must be capable of recording simultaneously but distinctly and on two separate sheets details of the periods listed under 3, 4 and 5.

III. CONSTRUCTION REQUIREMENTS FOR CONTROL DEVICE

A. GENERAL POINTS

1. Control device shall include the following: **D1.47**

   (a) Visual instruments showing:

   distance travelled (distance recorder),

   speed (speedometer),

   time (clock).

   (b) Recording instruments comprising:

   a recorder of the distance travelled,

   a speed recorder,

   one or more time recorders satisfying the requirements laid down in Chapter III C 4.

   (c) A means of marking showing on the record sheet individually:

   each opening of the case containing that sheet,

   for electronic control device, as defined in point 7 of Chapter II, any interruption exceeding 100 milliseconds in the power supply of the control device (except lighting), not later than at switching-on the power supply again,

   for electronic control device, as defined in point 7 of Chapter II, any interruption exceeding 100 milliseconds in the power supply of the distance and speed sensor and any interruption in the signal lead to the distance and speed sensor.

2. Any inclusion in the equipment of devices additional to those listed above must not interfere with the proper operation of the mandatory devices or with the reading of them.

The control device must be submitted for approval complete with any such additional devices.

3. Materials

   (a) All the constituent parts of the control device must be made of materials with sufficient stability and mechanical strength and stable electrical and magnetic characteristics.

   (b) Any modification in a constituent part of the control device or in the nature of the materials used for its manufacture must, before being applied in manufacture, be submitted for approval to the authority which granted type-approval for the control device.

4. Measurement of distance travelled

The distances travelled may be measured and recorded either:

so as to include both forward and reverse movement, or

so as to include only forward movement.

Any recording of reversing movements must on no account affect the clarity and accuracy of the other recordings.

5. Measurement of speed

   (a) The range of speed measurement shall be as stated in the type-approval certificate.

   (b) The natural frequency and the damping of the measuring device must be such that the instruments showing and recording the speed can, within the range of measurement, follow acceleration changes of up to 2m/section 2, within the limits of accepted tolerances.

6. Measurement of time (clock)

   (a) The control of the mechanism for resetting the clock must be located inside a case containing the record sheet; each opening of that case must be automatically recorded on the record sheet.

   (b) If the forward movement mechanism of the record sheet is controlled by the clock, the period during which the latter will run correctly after being fully wound must be greater by at least 10 per cent than the recording period corresponding to the maximum sheet-load of the equipment.

7. Lighting and protection

   (a) The visual instruments of the control device must be provided with adequate non-dazzling lighting.

   (b) For normal conditions of use, all the internal parts of the control must be protected against damp and dust. In addition they must be made proof against tampering by means of casings capable of being sealed.

B. VISUAL INSTRUMENTS

D1.48   1. Distance travelled indicator (distance recorder)

   (a) The value of the smallest grading on the control device showing distance travelled must be 0.1 kilometres. Figures showing hectometres must be clearly distinguishable from those showing whole kilometres.

   (b) The figures on the distance recorder must be clearly legible and must have an apparent height of at least 4mm.

   (c) The distance recorder must be capable of reading up to at least 99,999.9 kilometres.

2. Speed indicators (speedometer)

   (a) Within the range of measurement, the speed scale must be uniformly graduated by 1, 2, 5 or 10 kilometres per hour. The value of a speed graduation (space between two successive marks) must not exceed 10 per cent of the maximum speed shown on the scale.

   (b) The range indicated beyond that measured need not be marked by figures.

   (c) The length of each space on the scale representing a speed difference of 10 kilometres per hour must not be less than 10 millimetres.

   (d) On an indicator with a needle, the distance between the needle and the control device face must not exceed 3 millimetres.

3. Time indicator (clock)

The time indicator must be visible from outside the control device and give a clear, plain and unambiguous reading.

C. RECORDING INSTRUMENTS

1. General points   **D1.49**

   (a) All equipment, whatever the form of the record sheet (strip or disc) must be provided with a mark enabling the record sheet to be inserted correctly, in such a way as to ensure that the time shown by the clock and the time-marking on the sheet correspond.

   (b) The mechanism moving the record sheet must be such as to ensure that the latter moves without play and can be freely inserted and removed.

   (c) For record sheets in disc form, the forward movement device must be controlled by the clock mechanism. In this case, the rotating movement of the sheet must be continuous and uniform, with a minimum speed of 7 millimetres per hour measured at the inner border of the ring marking the edge of the speed recording area.

   In equipment of the strip type, where the forward movement device of the sheets is controlled by the clock mechanism the speed of rectilinear forward movement must be at least 10 millimetres per hour.

   (d) Recording of the distance travelled, of the speed of the vehicle and of any opening of the case containing the record sheet or sheets must be automatic.

2. Recording distance travelled

   (a) Every kilometre of distance travelled must be represented on the record by a variation of at least 1 millimetre on the corresponding co-ordinate.

   (b) Even at speeds reaching the upper limit of the range of measurement, the record of distances must still be clearly legible.

3. Recording speed

   (a) Whatever the form of the record sheet, the speed recording stylus must normally move in a straight line and at right angles to the direction of travel of the record sheet.

However, the movement of the stylus may be curvilinear, provided the following conditions are satisfied:

   the trace drawn by the stylus must be perpendicular to the average circumference (in the case of sheets in disc form) or to the axis (in the case of sheets in strip form) of the area reserved for speed recording,

   the ratio between the radius of curvature of the trace drawn by the stylus and the width of the area reserved for speed recording must be not less than 2.4 to 1 whatever the form of the record sheet,

   the markings on the time-scale must cross the recording area in a curve of the same radius as the trace drawn by the stylus. The spaces between the markings on the time-scale must represent a period not exceeding 1 hour.

   (b) Each variation in speed of 10 kilometres per hour must be represented on the record by a variation of at least 1.5 millimetres on the corresponding co-ordinate.

4. Recording time

(a) Control device must be so constructed that the period of driving time is always recorded automatically and that it is possible, through the operation where necessary of a switch device to record separately the other periods of time as follows:

(i) under the sign

driving time;

(ii) under the sign

all other periods of work;

(iii) under the sign

other periods of availability, namely:

waiting time, i.e. the period during which drivers need remain at their posts only for the purpose of answering any calls to start or resume driving or to carry out other work,

time spent beside the driver while the vehicle is in motion,

time spent on a bunk while the vehicle is in motion;

(iv) under the sign

breaks in work and daily rest periods.

Each contracting party may permit all the periods referred to in sub-paragraphs (ii) and (iii) above to be recorded under the sign

on the record sheets used on vehicles registered in its territory.

(b) It must be possible, from the characteristics of the traces, their relative positions and if necessary the signs laid down in paragraph 4(a) to distinguish clearly between the various periods of time.

The various periods of time should be differentiated from one another on the record by differences in the thickness of the relevant traces, or by any other system of at least equal effectiveness from the point of view of legibility and ease of interpretation of the record.

(c) In the case of vehicles with a crew consisting of more than one driver, the recordings provided for in paragraph 4(a) must be made on two separate sheets, each sheet being allocated to one driver. In this case, the forward movement of the separate sheets must be effected either by a single mechanism or by separate synchronised mechanisms.

D. CLOSING DEVICE

1. The case containing the record sheet or sheets and the control of the mecha- **D1.50**
nism for resetting the clock must be provided with a lock.

2. Each opening of the case containing the record sheet or sheets and the
control of the mechanism for resetting the clock must be automatically recorded
on the sheet or sheets.

E. MARKINGS

1. The following markings must appear on the instrument face of the control **D1.51**
device:

> close to the figure shown by the distance recorder, the unit of measure-
> ment of distance, indicated by the abbreviation "km",
>
> near the speed scale, the marking "km/h",
>
> the measurement range of the speedometer in the form "Vmin … km/h,
> Vmax … km/h". This marking is not necessary if it is shown on the
> descriptive plaque of the equipment.

However, these requirements shall not apply to control devices approved
before 10 August 1970.

2. The descriptive plaque must be built into the equipment and must show the
following markings, which must be visible on the control device when installed:

> name and address of the manufacturer of the equipment,
>
> manufacturer's number and year of construction,
>
> approval mark for the control device type,
>
> the constant of the equipment in the form "k = … rev/km" or "k = … imp/
> km",
>
> optionally, the range of speed measurement, in the form indicated in point
> 1,
>
> should the sensitivity of the instrument to the angle of inclination be
> capable of affecting the readings given by the equipment beyond the
> permitted tolerances, the permissible angle expressed as:

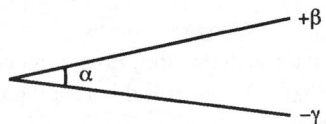

> where α is the angle measured from the horizontal position of the front
> face (fitted the right way up) of the equipment for which the instrument
> is calibrated, while β and δ represent respectively the maximum
> permissible upward and downward deviations from the angle of
> calibration α.

F. MAXIMUM TOLERANCES (VISUAL AND RECORDING INSTRUMENTS)

1. On the test bench before installation: **D1.52**

> (a) distance travelled:
>> 1 per cent more or less than the real distance, where the distance is at
>> least 1 kilometre;
>
> (b) speed:

> 3 km/h more or less than the real speed;

(c) time:

> ± two minutes per day with a maximum of 10 minutes per 7 days in cases where the running period of the clock after rewinding is not less than that period.

2. On installation:

(a) distance travelled:

> 2 per cent more or less than the real distance, where that distance is at least 1 kilometre;

(b) speed

> 4 km/h more or less than real speed;

(c) time

> ± two minutes per day, or
>
> ± 10 minutes per seven days.

3. In use:

(a) distance travelled:

> 4 per cent more or less than the real distance, where that distance is at least 1 kilometre;

(b) speed

> 6 km/h more or less than the real speed;

(c) time:

> ± two minutes per day, or
>
> ± 10 minutes per seven days.

4. The maximum tolerances set out in paragraphs 1, 2 and 3 are valid for temperatures between 0° and 40°C, temperatures being taken in close proximity to the equipment.

5. Measurement of the maximum tolerances set out in paragraphs 2 and 3 shall take place under the conditions laid down in Chapter VI.

IV. RECORD SHEETS

A. GENERAL POINTS

D1.53   1. The record sheets must be such that they do not impede the normal functioning of the instrument and that the records which they contain are indelible and easily legible and identifiable.

The record sheets must retain their dimensions and any records made on them under normal conditions of humidity and temperature.

In addition it must be possible by each crew member to enter on the sheets, without damaging them and without affecting the legibility of the recordings, the following information:

(a) on beginning to use the sheet—his surname and first name;

(b) the date and place where use of the sheet begins and the date and place where such use ends;

(c) the registration number of each vehicle to which he is assigned, both at the start of the first journey recorded on the sheet and then, in the event of a change of vehicle, during use of the sheet;

(d) the odometer reading:

at the start of the first journey recorded on the sheet,

at the end of the last journey recorded on the sheet,

in the event of a change of vehicle during a working day (reading on the vehicle to which he was assigned and reading on the vehicle to which he is to be assigned);

(e) the time of any change of vehicle.

Under normal conditions of storage, the recordings must remain clearly legible for at least one year.

2. The minimum recording capacity of the sheets, whatever their form, must be 24 hours.

If several discs are linked together to increase the continuous recording capacity which can be achieved without intervention by staff, the links between the various discs must be made in such a way that there are no breaks in or overlapping of recordings at the point of transfer from one disc to another.

B. RECORDING AREAS AND THEIR GRADUATION

1. The record sheets shall include the following recording areas: **D1.54**

an area exclusively reserved for data relating to speed,

an area exclusively reserved for data relating to distance travelled,

one or more areas for data relating to driving time, to other periods of work and availability to breaks from work and to rest periods for drivers.

2. The area for recording speed must be scaled off in divisions of 20 kilometres per hour or less. The speed corresponding to each marking on the scale must be shown in figures against that marking. The symbol "km/h" must be shown at least once within the area. The last marking on the scale must coincide with the upper limit of the range of measurement.

3. The area for recording distance travelled must be set out in such a way that the number of kilometres travelled may be read without difficulty.

4. The area or areas reserved for recording the periods referred to in point 1 must be so marked that it is possible to distinguish clearly between the various periods of time.

C. INFORMATION TO BE PRINTED ON THE RECORD SHEETS

Each sheet must bear, in printed form, the following information: **D1.55**

name and address or trade name of the manufacturer,

approval mark for the model of the sheet,

approval mark for the type or types of control devices in which the sheet may be used,

upper limit of the speed measurement range, printed in kilometres per hour.

By way of minimal additional requirements, each sheet must bear, in printed form a time-scale graduated in such a way that the time may be read directly at intervals of 15 minutes while each 5-minute interval may be determined without difficulty.

D. FREE SPACE FOR HAND-WRITTEN INSERTIONS

A free space must be provided on the sheets such that drivers may as a minimum write in the following details: **D1.56** surname and first name of the driver,

date and place where use of the sheet begins and date and place where such use ends,

the registration number or numbers of the vehicle or vehicles to which the driver is assigned during the use of the sheet,

odometer readings from the vehicle or vehicles to which the driver is assigned during the use of the sheet,

the time at which any change of vehicle takes place.

V. INSTALLATION OF CONTROL DEVICE

A. GENERAL POINTS

D1.57   1. Control device must be positioned in the vehicle in such a way that the driver has a clear view from his seat of speedometer, distance recorder and clock while at the same time all parts of those instruments, including driving parts, are protected against accidental damage.

2. It must be possible to adapt the constant of the control device to the characteristic coefficient of the vehicle by means of a suitable device, to be known as an adaptor.

Vehicles with two or more axle ratios must be fitted with a switch device whereby these various ratios may be automatically brought into line with the ratio for which the control device has been adapted to the vehicle

3. After the control device has been checked on installation, an installation plaque shall be affixed to the vehicle beside the device or in the device itself and in such a way as to be clearly visible. After every inspection by an approved fitter or workshop requiring a change in the setting of the installation itself, a new plaque must be affixed in place of the previous one.

The plaque must show at least the following details:

name, address or trade name of the approved fitter or workshop,

characteristic coefficient of the vehicle, in the form "w = ... rev/km" or "w = ... imp/km",

effective circumference of the wheel tyres in the form "l = ... mm",

the dates on which the characteristic coefficient of the vehicle was determined and the effective measured circumference of the wheel tyres.

B. SEALING

D1.58   The following parts must be sealed:

(a) the installation plaque, unless it is attached in such a way that it cannot be removed without the markings thereon being destroyed;

(b) the two ends of the link between the control device proper and the vehicle;

(c) the adaptor itself and the point of its insertion into the circuit;

(d) the switch mechanism for vehicles with two or more axle ratios;

(e) the links joining the adaptor and the switch mechanism to the rest of the control device;

(f) the casings required under Chapter III A 7(b).

In particular cases, further seals may be required on approval of the control device type and a note of the positioning of these seals must be made on the approval certificate.

Only the seals mentioned in (b), (c) and (e) may be removed in cases of emergency; for each occasion that these seals are broken a written statement giving the reasons for such action must be prepared and made available to the competent authority.

VI. CHECKS AND INSPECTIONS

The Contracting Party shall nominate the bodies which shall carry out the **D1.59** checks and inspections.

1. Certification of new or repaired instruments

Every individual device, whether new or repaired, shall be certified in respect of its correct operation and the accuracy of its readings and recordings, within the limits laid down in Chapter III F 1, by means of sealing in accordance with Chapter V B (f).

For this purpose the Contracting Party may stipulate an initial verification, consisting of a check on and confirmation of the conformity of a new or repaired device with the type-approved model and/or with the requirements of this annex and its appendices or may delegate the power to certify to the manufacturers or to their authorised agents.

2. Installation

When being fitted to a vehicle, the control device and the whole installation must comply with the provisions relating to maximum tolerances laid down in Chapter III F 2.

The inspection tests shall be carried out by the approved fitter or workshop on his or its responsibility.

3. Periodic inspections

(a) Periodic inspections of the control device fitted to vehicles shall take place at least every two years and may be carried out in conjunction with roadworthiness tests of vehicles.

These inspections shall include the following checks:

that the control device is working correctly,

that the control device carries the type-approval mark,

that the installation plaque is affixed,

that the seals on the control device on the other parts of the installation are intact,

the actual circumference of the tyres.

(b) An inspection to ensure compliance with the provision of Chapter III F 3 on the maximum tolerances in use shall be carried out at least once every six years, although each Contracting Party may stipulate a shorter interval or such inspection in respect of vehicles registered in its territory. Such inspections must include replacement of the installation plaque.

4. Measurement of errors

The measurement of errors on installation and during use shall be carried out under the following conditions, which are to be regarded as constituting standard test conditions:

vehicle unladen, in normal running order,

tyre pressures in accordance with the manufacturer's instructions.

tyre wear within the limits allowed by law,

movement of the vehicle: the vehicle must proceed, driven by its own engine, in a straight line and on a level surface, at a speed of 50±5 km/h; provided that it is of comparable accuracy, the test may also be carried out on an appropriate test bench.

[APPENDIX 1B

REQUIREMENTS FOR THE CONSTRUCTION, TESTING, INSTALLATION AND INSPECTION OF THE DIGITAL CONTROL DEVICE USED IN ROAD TRANSPORT]

D1.60   *[Omitted.]*

[Appendix 1B was inserted by TRANS/SC.1/375/Add.1.]

APPENDIX 2

APPROVAL MARK AND CERTIFICATE

I. APPROVAL MARK

D1.61   [1. The approval mark shall be made up of:

A rectangle, within which shall be placed the letter "e" followed by a distinguishing number for the country which has issued the approval in accordance with the following conventional signs:

[Germany	1	Estonia	29
France	2	Moldova	30
Italy	3	Bosnia-Herzegovina	31
Netherlands	4	Latvia	32
Sweden	5	Liechtenstein	33
Belgium	6	Bulgaria	34
Hungary	7	Kazakhstan	35
Czech Republic	8	Lithuania	36
Spain	9	Turkey	37
Serbia	10	Turkmenistan	38
United Kingdom	11	Azerbaijan	39
Austria	12	The former Yugoslav	40
Luxembourg	13	Republic of Macedonia	
Switzerland	14	Andorra	41
Norway	16	Uzbekistan	44
Finland	17	Ukraine	46
Denmark	18	[Malta	50]
Romania	19	Albania	54
Poland	20	Armenia	55

Portugal	21	Montenegro	56
Russian Federation	22	San Marino	57
Greece	23	Monaco	59]
Ireland	24		
Croatia	25		
Slovenia	26		
Slovakia	27		
Belarus	28		

Subsequent numbers shall be assigned:

(i) To countries Contracting Parties to the 1958 Agreement Concerning the Adoption of Uniform Conditions of Approval and Reciprocal Recognition of Approval for Motor Vehicle Equipment and Parts [*Cmnd. 2535; not reproduced in this work*] the same numbers as assigned to those countries by that Agreement;

(ii) To countries non-Contracting Parties to the 1958 Agreement —in the chronological order in which they ratify or accede to this Agreement;

and

An approval number corresponding to the number of the approval certificate drawn up for the prototype of the control device or the record sheet, placed at any point within the immediate proximity of this rectangle.

Note: In order to ensure in the future conformity between conventional signs in the 1958 Agreement and those set up in the AETR Agreement new Contracting Parties should be allocated the same number in both Agreements.]

2. The approval mark shall be shown on the descriptive plaque of each set of control device and on each record sheet. It must be indelible and must always remain clearly legible.

3. The dimensions of the approval mark drawn below are expressed in millimetres, these dimensions being minima. The ratios between the dimensions must be maintained.

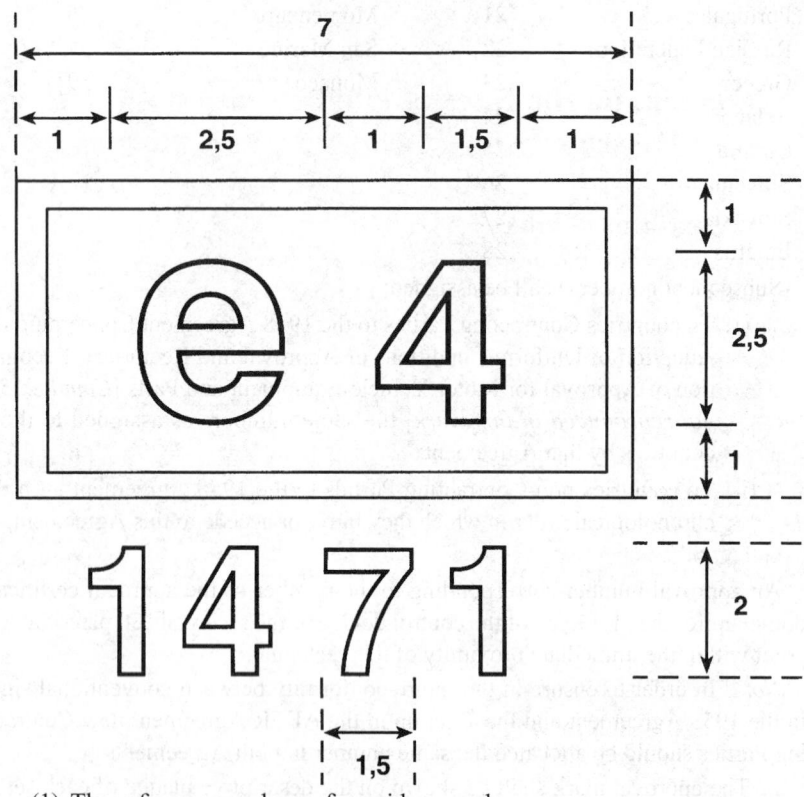

(1) These figures are shown for guidance only.

[II. APPROVAL CERTIFICATE FOR PRODUCTS IN ACCORDANCE WITH APPENDIX 1]

D1.62   *[Omitted.]*

[APPENDIX 3

MODEL FORMS]

D1.64   *[Omitted.]*

[Appendix 3 was inserted by TRANS/SC.1/386/Add.1.]

[III. APPROVAL CERTIFICATE FOR PRODUCTS IN ACCORDANCE WITH APPENDIX 1B]

D1.65   *[Omitted.]*

[The Annex is printed as substituted by Cm. 3042 and as subsequently amended by Cm. 3135; TRANS/SC.1/375/Add.1; TRANS/SC.1/386/Add.1.

The "Note" at the end of para.1 of Chap.I (approval mark) of Appendix 2 to the Annex is part of the text of that paragraph and not an editorial comment.]

D1.66   PROTOCOL OF SIGNATURE

Agreement on the International Occasional Carriage of Passengers by Coach and Bus (Interbus Agreement)

THE CONTRACTING PARTIES: **D2.01**

Having regard to the desire to promote the development of international transport in Europe and especially to facilitate the organisation and operation thereof,

Having regard to the desire to facilitate tourism and cultural exchange between the Contracting Parties,

Whereas:

The Agreement on the international carriage of passengers by road by means of occasional coach and bus services (ASOR), signed in Dublin on 26 May 1982 [*O.J. No.L230, August 5, 1982, pp.39–56*] does not provide for any scope for the accession of new Parties.

The experience and the liberalisation achieved by this latter Agreement should be maintained.

It is desirable to provide for harmonised liberalisation of certain international occasional services by coach and bus and the transit operations thereof.

It is desirable to provide for certain harmonised rules of procedure for non-liberalised international occasional services, that are thus still subject to authorisation.

It is necessary to provide for a high degree of harmonisation of the technical conditions applying to buses and coaches carrying out international occasional services between Contracting Parties in order to improve road safety and protection of the environment.

It is necessary that Contracting Parties should apply uniform measures concerning the work of the crews of buses and coaches engaged in international road transport.

It is desirable to provide for harmonisation of the conditions for access to the occupation of road passenger transport operator.

The principle of non-discrimination on grounds of nationality or the place of establishment of the transport operator, and of the origin or destination of the bus or coach, should be considered to be a basic condition applying to the provision of international transport services.

It is necessary to provide for uniform models for transport documents such as the control document for liberalised occasional services and also the authorisation and the application form for non-liberalised services in order to facilitate and simplify inspection procedures.

It is necessary to provide for certain harmonised measures on the enforcement of the Agreement, especially as far as control procedures, penalties and mutual assistance are concerned.

It is appropriate to establish certain procedures for the management of the Agreement in order to ensure proper enforcement and to permit some technical adaptation of the Annexes.

The Agreement should be open for accession to future members of the European Conference of Ministers of Transport and to certain other European countries,

HAVE DECIDED to establish uniform rules for the international occasional carriage of passengers by coach and bus, and

HAVE AGREED AS FOLLOWS:

SECTION I

Scope and Definitions

Article 1: Scope

D2.02   1. This Agreement shall apply:

(a) to the international carriage of passengers, of any nationality, by road by means of occasional services:

— between the territories of two Contracting Parties, or starting and finishing on the territory of the same Contracting Party and, should the need arise during such services, in transit through the territory of another Contracting Party or through the territory of a non-Contracting State,

— carried out by transport operators for hire or reward established in a Contracting Party in accordance with its law and holding a licence to undertake carriage by means of international occasional services by coach and bus,

— using buses and coaches registered in the Contracting Party where the transport operator is established;

(b) to unladen journeys of the buses and coaches concerned with these services.

2. None of the provisions of this Agreement may be interpreted as providing the possibility of operating national occasional services in the territory of a Contracting Party by operators established in another Contracting Party.

3. The use of buses and coaches designed to carry passengers for the transport of goods for commercial purposes shall be excluded from the scope of this Agreement.

4. This Agreement does not concern own-account occasional services.

Article 2: Non-discrimination

D2.03   Contracting Parties shall ensure that the principle of non-discrimination on the grounds of the nationality or the place of establishment of the transport operator, and of the origin or destination of the bus or coach, is applied, in particular with regard to fiscal provisions as established in section VI, as well as control and penalties as established in section IX.

Article 3: Definitions

D2.04   For the purposes of this Agreement, the following definitions shall apply:

1. *"buses and coaches"* are vehicles which, by virtue of their construction and their equipment, are suitable for carrying more than nine persons, including the driver, and are intended for that purpose;

2. *"international occasional services"* are services between the territory of at

least two Contracting Parties falling within neither the definition of regular services or special regular services nor the definition of a shuttle service. Such services may be operated with some degree of frequency without thereby ceasing to be occasional services;

3. *"regular services"* are services which provide for the carriage of passengers according to a specified frequency and along specified routes, whereby passengers may be taken up or set down at predetermined stopping points. Regular services can be subject to the obligation to respect previously established timetables and tariffs;

4. *"special regular services"* are services, by whomsoever organised, which provide for the carriage of specified categories of passengers to the exclusion of other passengers, in so far as such services are operated under the conditions specified in point 3. Special regular services shall include:
— the carriage of workers between home and work,
— the carriage of school pupils and students to and from the educational institution.

The fact that a special regular service may be varied according to the needs of users shall not affect its classification as a regular service;

1. *"shuttle services"* are services whereby, by means of repeated outward and return journeys, previously formed groups of passengers are carried from a single place of departure to a single destination. Each group, consisting of the passengers who made the outward journey, shall be carried back to the place of departure on a later journey by the same transport operator.

   Place of departure and destination shall mean, respectively, the place where the journey begins and the place where the journey ends, together with, in each case, the surrounding localities within a radius of 50 km;
2. in the course of shuttle services, no passenger may be taken up or set down during the journey;
3. the first return journey and the last outward journey in a series of shuttles shall be made unladen;
4. however, the classification of a transport operation as a shuttle service shall not be affected by the fact that, with the agreement of the competent authorities in the Contracting Party or Parties concerned:
   — passengers, notwithstanding the provisions of subparagraph 1, make the return journey with another group or another transport operator,
   — passengers, notwithstanding the provisions of subparagraph 2, are taken up or set down along the way,
   — the first outward journey and the last return journey of the series of shuttles are, notwithstanding the provisions of subparagraph 3, made unladen;

6. *"Contracting Parties"* are those signatories that have consented to be bound by this Agreement and for which this Agreement is in force.

This Agreement applies to those territories where the Treaty establishing the European Community is applied and under the conditions laid down in that Treaty and to BOSNIA AND HERZEGOVINA, BULGARIA, CROATIA, THE CZECH REPUBLIC, ESTONIA, HUNGARY, LATVIA, LITHUANIA, MOLDOVA, POLAND, ROMANIA, SLOVAKIA, SLOVENIA and TURKEY, as far as they have concluded this Agreement;

7. *"competent authorities"* are those authorities designated by the Member States of the Community and by the other Contracting Parties to carry out the tasks set out in sections V, VI, VII, VIII and IX of this Agreement;

8. *"transit"* means the part of a transport operation through the territory of a Contracting Party without passengers being picked up or set down.

SECTION II

CONDITIONS APPLYING TO ROAD PASSENGER TRANSPORT OPERATORS

Article 4

D2.05   1. Contracting Parties which have not yet done so shall apply provisions equivalent to those established by the European Community Directive referred to in Annex 1.

2. *[Omitted.]*

SECTION III

TECHNICAL CONDITIONS APPLYING TO VEHICLES

Article 5

D2.06   The buses and coaches used to carry out the international occasional services covered by this Agreement shall comply with the technical standards laid down in Annex 2.

SECTION IV

ACCESS TO THE MARKET

Article 6: Liberalised occasional services

D2.07   The following occasional services shall be exempted from authorisation on the territory of any Contracting Party other than that in which the transport operator is established:

1. closed-door tours, that is to say services whereby the same bus or coach is used to carry the same group of passengers throughout the journey and to bring them back to the place of departure. The place of departure is in the territory of the Contracting Party in which the transport operator is established;

2. services which make the outward journey laden and the return journey unladen. The place of departure is in the territory of the Contracting Party in which the transport operator is established;

3. services during which the outward journey is made unladen and all the passengers are taken up in the same place, provided that one of the following conditions is met:

    (a) passengers constitute groups, on the territory of a non-Contracting Party or of a Contracting Party other than that in which the transport operator is established or that where the passengers are taken up, that have been formed under contracts of carriage made before their arrival in the territory of the latter Contracting Party. Passengers are carried on the territory of the Contracting Party in which the transport operator is established;

(b) passengers have been previously brought, by the same transport operator in the circumstances provided for under point 2, into the territory of
the Contracting Party where they are taken up again and carried into the
territory of the Contracting Party in which the transport operator is
established;

(c) passengers have been invited to travel into the territory of another
Contracting Party, the cost of transport being borne by the person issuing the invitation. Such passengers must constitute a homogeneous
group, which has not been formed solely with a view to undertaking that
particular journey and which is brought into the territory of the Contracting Party in which the transport operator is established.

The following shall also be exempted from authorisation:

4. transit operations through the territory of Contracting Parties in conjunction
with occasional services that are exempted from authorisation;

5. unladen buses and coaches to be used exclusively for the replacement of a
bus or a coach damaged or broken down, while performing an international service covered by this Agreement.

For services provided by transport operators established within the European
Community, the points of departure and/or destination of the services can be in
any Member State of the European Community, independently of the Member
State in which the bus or coach is registered or the Member State in which the
transport operator is established.

Article 7: Non-liberalised occasional services

1. Occasional services other than those referred to in Article 6 shall be subject   **D2.08**
to authorisation in accordance with Article 15.

2. For services provided by transport operators established within the
European Community, the points of departure and/or destination of the services
can be in any Member State of the European Community, independently of the
Member State in which the bus or coach is registered or the Member State in
which the transport operator is established.

SECTION V

SOCIAL PROVISIONS

Article 8

The Contracting Parties to this Agreement which have not yet done so shall ac-   **D2.09**
cede to the European Agreement concerning the work of crews of vehicles
engaged in international road transport (AETR) of 1 July 1970, as subsequently
amended, or shall apply Community Regulations (EEC) No 3820/85 and (EEC)
No 3821/85 as in force at the entry into force of this Agreement.

SECTION VI

CUSTOM AND FISCAL PROVISIONS

Article 9

[Omitted.]   **D2.10**

SECTION VII

CONTROL DOCUMENTS FOR OCCASIONAL SERVICES EXEMPTED FROM AUTHORISATION

Article 10

D2.11   The provision of services referred to in Article 6 shall be carried out under cover of a control document issued by the competent authorities or by any duly authorised agency of the Contracting Party in which the transport operator is established.

Article 11

D2.12   1. The control document shall consist of detachable passenger waybills in duplicate in books of 25. The control document shall conform to the model shown in Annex 3 to this Agreement.

2. Each book and its component passenger waybills shall bear a number. The passenger waybills shall also be numbered consecutively, running from 1 to 25.

3. The wording on the cover of the book and that on the passenger waybills shall be printed in the official language or several official languages of the Contracting Party in which the transport operator is established.

Article 12

D2.13   1. The book referred to in Article 11 shall be made out in the name of the transport operator; it shall not be transferable.

2. The top copy of the passenger waybill shall be kept on the bus or coach throughout the journey to which it refers.

3. The transport operator shall be responsible for seeing that passenger waybills are duly and correctly completed.

Article 13

D2.14   1. The passenger waybill shall be completed in duplicate by the transport operator for each journey before the start of the journey.

2. For the purpose of providing the names of passengers, the transport operator may use a previously completed list on a separate sheet, which shall be annexed to the passenger waybill. The transport operator's stamp or, where appropriate, the transport operator's signature or that of the driver of the bus or coach shall be placed both on the list and on the passenger waybill.

3. For the services involving an outward unladen journey referred to in Article 6(3), the list of passengers may be completed as provided for in paragraph 2 at the time when the passengers are taken up.

Article 14

D2.15   The competent authorities of two or more Contracting Parties may agree that the list of passengers need not be drawn up. In that case, the number of passengers must be shown on the control document.

The Joint Committee established in Article 23 shall be informed of these agreements.

SECTION VIII

AUTHORISATION FOR NON-LIBERALISED OCCASIONAL SERVICES

Article 15

D2.16   1. An authorisation for each occasional service which has not been liberalised under the provisions of Article 6 shall be issued, in mutual agreement by the competent authorities of the Contracting Parties where passengers are picked up or set down as well as by the competent authorities of the Contracting Parties crossed in transit. When the point of departure or destination is situated in a Member State of the European Community, the transit through other Member States of the Community will not be subject to authorisation.

2. The authorisation shall conform to the model laid down in Annex 5.

Article 16: Application for authorisation

1. The application for authorisation shall be submitted by the transport opera- **D2.17** tor to the competent authorities of the Contracting Party on whose territory the point of departure is situated.

Applications shall conform to the model laid down in Annex 4.

2. Transport operators shall fill in the application form and attach evidence that the applicant is licensed to perform carriage by means of international occasional services by coach and bus referred to in Article 1(1)(a), second indent.

3. The competent authorities of the Contracting Party in whose territory the place of departure is situated shall examine the application for authorisation of the service concerned and, in the case of its approval, shall forward it to the competent authorities of the Contracting Party(ies) of destination as well as the competent authorities of the Contracting Parties in transit.

4. As a derogation from Article 15(1), Contracting Parties whose territories are crossed in transit may decide that their agreement is no longer necessary for services envisaged in this section. In this case, the Joint Committee established in Article 23 shall be informed of this decision.

5. The competent authorities of the Contracting Party(ies) whose agreement has been requested shall issue the authorisation within one month, without discrimination as to the nationality or place of establishment of the transport operator. If these authorities do not agree on the terms of the authorisation they shall inform the competent authorities of the Contracting Party(ies) concerned of the relevant reasons.

Article 17

The competent authorities of two or more Contracting Parties may agree to **D2.18** simplify the authorisation procedure, the model of application for authorisation and the model of authorisation for the occasional services carried out between these Contracting Parties. The Joint Committee established in Article 23 shall be informed of these agreements.

SECTION IX

CONTROLS, PENALTIES AND MUTUAL ASSISTANCE

Article 18

The control documents referred to in Article 10 and the authorisations referred **D2.19** to in Article 15 shall be carried on the bus or coach and shall be presented at the request of any authorised inspecting officer.

Article 19

The competent authorities in the Contracting Parties shall ensure that transport **D2.20** operators comply with the provisions of this Agreement.

Article 20

D2.21   A certified true copy of the licence to perform carriage by means of international occasional services by bus and coach referred to in Article 1(1)(a), second indent, shall be kept on the bus or coach and shall be presented at the request of any authorised inspecting officer.

The Joint Committee established in Article 23 shall be informed about the models of such a document issued by the competent authorities of the Contracting Parties.

Article 21

D2.22   The competent authorities of the Contracting Parties shall lay down a system of penalties for breaching this Agreement. The penalties thus provided for shall be effective, proportionate and dissuasive.

Article 22

D2.23   1. Where serious or repeated infringements of regulations concerning road transport, especially those concerning driving and resting time and road safety, have been committed by non-resident transport operators and might lead to withdrawal of the licence to practise as a road passenger transport operator, the competent authorities of the Contracting Party concerned shall provide the competent authorities of the Contracting Party in which such a transport operator is established with all of the information in their possession concerning those infringements and the penalties that they have imposed.

2. The competent authorities of the Contracting Party in whose territory the serious or repeated infringement of regulations concerning road transport, especially those concerning driving and resting time and road safety have occurred, may temporarily deny access for the transport operator concerned to the territory of this contracting party.

As far as the European Community is concerned, the competent authority of a Member State may only temporarily deny access to the territory of that Member State. Competent authorities of the Contracting Party of establishment of the transport operator and the Joint Committee established in Article 23 shall be informed of such measures.

3. Where serious or repeated infringements of regulations concerning road transport, especially those concerning driving and resting time and road safety, have been committed by a transport operator, the competent authorities of the Contracting Parties where the transport operator is established shall take the appropriate measures to avoid repetition of those infringements; these measures may include the suspension or the withdrawal of the licence to practise as a road passenger transport operator. The Joint Committee established in Article 23 shall be informed of such measures.

4. Contracting Parties shall guarantee the right of the transport operator to appeal against the sanctions imposed.

SECTION X

THE JOINT COMMITTEE

Articles 23, 24

D2.24   *[Omitted.]*

SECTION XI

GENERAL AND FINAL PROVISIONS

Articles 25–27

[Omitted.]   **D2.25**

Article 28: Entry into force

1. This Agreement shall enter into force for the Contracting Parties that have **D2.26** approved or ratified it, when four Contracting Parties including the European Community have approved or ratified it, on the first day of the third month following the date on which the fourth instrument of approval or ratification is deposited, or even on the first day of the sixth month, under condition in the latter case that a corresponding declaration be made at the time of the ratification of the Agreement.

2. This Agreement shall enter into force, for each Contracting Party that approves or ratifies it after the entry into force provided for in paragraph 1, on the first day of the third month following the date on which the Contracting Party concerned has deposited its instrument of approval or ratification.

Articles 29–34

[Omitted.]   **D2.27**

SIGNATURES

[The Interbus Agreement was signed on behalf of the European Community on **D2.28** *June 22, 2001 and by Bosnia and Herzegovina, Bulgaria, Croatia, the Czech Republic, Hungary, Latvia, Lithuania, Moldova, Poland, Romania, Slovakia, Slovenia and Turkey on June 30, 2001. It was approved on behalf of the European Community by Decision 2002/917/EC (O.J. No.L321, November 26, 2002, p.11) and entered into force on January 1, 2003.*

The contracting parties, which have signed and ratified the Interbus Agreement are as follows:

    Albania
    Bosnia and Herzegovina
    Bulgaria
    Croatia
    the Czech Republic
    the European Community
    Hungary
    Lithuania
    Latvia
    Macedonia
    Moldova
    Montenegro
    Poland
    Romania
    Slovenia, and
    Turkey.

The Agreement provides for future accession.]

ANNEX

ANNEX 1 THE CONDITIONS APPLYING TO ROAD PASSENGER TRANSPORT OPERATORS

D2.29   The European Community Directive referred to in Article 4 is the following:

Council Directive 96/26/EC of 29 April 1996 on admission to the occupation of road haulage operator and road passenger transport operator and mutual recognition of diplomas, certificates and other evidence of formal qualification intended to facilitate for these operators the right to freedom of establishment in national and international transport operations (*Official Journal of the European Communities* L 124, 23.5.1996, p. 1), as last amended by Council Directive 98/76/EC of 1 October 1998 (*Official Journal of the European Communities* L 277, 14.10.1998, p. 17).

ANNEX 2 TECHNICAL STANDARDS APPLYING TO BUSES AND COACHES

ARTICLE 1

D2.30   As from the date of entry into force for each Contracting Party of the Interbus Agreement, buses and coaches carrying out international occasional carriage of passengers shall comply with the rules established in the following legal texts:

(a) Council Directive 96/96/EC of 20 December 1996 on the approximation of the laws of the Member States relating to roadworthiness tests for motor vehicles and their trailers (*Official Journal of the European Communities* L 46, 17.2.1997, p. 1);

(b) Council Directive 92/6/EEC of 10 February 1992 on the installation and use of speed limitation devices for certain categories of motor vehicles in the Community (*Official Journal of the European Communities* L 57, 2.3.1992, p. 27);

(c) Council Directive 96/53/EC of 25 July 1996 laying down for certain road vehicles circulating within the Community the maximum authorised dimensions in national and international traffic and the maximum authorised weights in international traffic (*Official Journal of the European Communities* L 235, 17.9.1996, p. 59);

(d) Council Regulation (EEC) No 3821/85 of 20 December 1985 on recording equipment in road transport (*Official Journal of the European Communities* L 370 of 31.12.1985, p. 8), as last amended by Commission Regulation (EC) No 2135/98 of 24.9.1998 (*Official Journal of the European Communities* L 274, 9.10.1998, p. 1) or equivalent rules established by the AETR Agreement including its Protocols.

ARTICLE 2

D2.31   As from the date of entry into force of the Interbus Agreement for each Contracting Party, Contracting Parties other than the European Community shall comply, for buses and coaches carrying out international occasional carriage of passengers, with the technical requirements of the following Community Directives or equivalent UN-ECE Regulations on uniform provisions concerning the type-approval for new vehicles and their equipment.

Item	UN-ECE Regulation/last amendment	EC Directive (original — latest)	Date of implementation within the EU
Exhaust emission	49/01 49/02, approval A 49/02, approval B	88/77 91/542 step 1 91/542 step 2 96/1	1.10.1993 1.10.1996
Smoke	24/03	72/306	2.8.1972
Noise emission	51/02	70/157 84/424 92/97	1.10.1989 1.10.1996
Brake system	13/09	71/320 88/194 91/422 98/12	1.10.1991 1.10.1994
Tyres	54	92/23	1.1.1993
Light installation	48/01	76/756 91/663 97/28	1.1.1994

ARTICLE 3

The buses and coaches carrying out the following services: **D2.32**

(a) services from any Member State of the Community (except Greece) to any Contracting Party of Interbus;

(b) services from any Contracting Party of Interbus to any Member State of the Community (except Greece);

(c) services from any Contracting Party of Interbus to Greece in transit through any other Member State of the Community carried out by transport operators established in any Contracting Party of Interbus;

shall be subject to the following rules.

1. Buses and coaches first registered before 1 January 1980 cannot be used for the occasional services covered by the Interbus Agreement.

2. Buses and coaches first registered between 1 January 1980 and 31 December 1981 can be used only until 31 December 2000.

3. Buses and coaches first registered between 1 January 1982 and 31 December 1983 can be used only until 31 December 2001.

4. Buses and coaches first registered between 1 January 1984 and 31 December 1985 can be used only until 31 December 2002.

5. Buses and coaches first registered between 1 January 1986 and 31 December 1987 can be used only until 31 December 2003.

6. Buses and coaches first registered between 1 January 1988 and 31 December 1989 can be used only until 31.12.2004.

7. Only buses and coaches first registered as from 1 January 1990 (EURO 0) can be used from 1 January 2005.

8. Only buses and coaches first registered as from 1 October 1993 (EURO 1) can be used from 1 January 2007.

ARTICLE 4

Buses and coaches carrying out the following services: **D2.33**

(a) services from Greece to Contracting Parties of Interbus;

(b) services from Contracting Parties of Interbus to Greece;

shall be subject to the following rules:

1. Buses and coaches first registered before 1 January 1980 cannot be used for the occasional services covered by the Interbus Agreement.

2. Buses and coaches first registered between 1 January 1980 and 31 December 1981 can be used only until 31 December 2000.

3. Buses and coaches first registered between 1 January 1982 and 31 December 1983 can be used only until 31 December 2001.

4. Buses and coaches first registered between 1 January 1984 and 31 December 1985 can be used only until 31 December 2003.

5. Buses and coaches first registered between 1 January 1986 and 31 December 1987 can be used only until 31 December 2005.

6. Buses and coaches first registered between 1 January 1988 and 31 December 1989 can be used only until 31 December 2007.

7. Only buses and coaches first registered as from 1 January 1990 (EURO 0) can be used from 1 January 2008.

8. Only buses and coaches first registered as from 1 January 1993 (EURO 1) can be used from 1 January 2010.

ARTICLE 5

D2.34   Community buses and coaches used in bilateral traffic between Greece and other Member States of the Community in transit through Contracting Parties of the Interbus Agreement are not covered by present rules on technical standards, but are subject to European Community rules.

ARTICLE 6

D2.35   1. The rules on technical standards included in bilateral agreements or arrangements between Member States of the Community and Contracting Parties of the Interbus Agreement, concerning bilateral traffic and transit, which are stricter than the rules established in this Agreement may be applied until 31 December 2006.

2. Member States of the Community and Contracting Parties of the Interbus Agreement concerned shall inform the Joint Committee established in Article 23 of the Agreement on the contents of such bilateral agreements or arrangements.

ARTICLE 7

D2.36   1. A document proving the date of the vehicle's first registration shall be kept on board and shall be presented at the request of any authorised inspecting officer. For the purpose of this Annex, the terms "date of vehicle's first registration" shall refer to the first registration of the vehicle after its manufacture. When this date of registration is not available, it will be referred to as the date of construction.

2. Where the original bus engine has been replaced by a new engine, the document referred to in paragraph 1 of this Article shall be substituted by a document proving the compliance of the new engine with the relevant type-approval rules mentioned in Article 3.

ARTICLE 8

D2.37   1. Notwithstanding the provision referred to in paragraph (a) of Article 1 of this Annex, Contracting Parties may establish random inspections in order to control that the buses and coaches concerned comply with the provisions of Directive 96/96/EC. For the purpose of this Annex "random inspections" shall mean an unscheduled and therefore unexpected inspection of a bus or coach circulating on the territory of a Contracting Party carried out by the authorities at the roadside.

2. In order to carry out the roadside inspection provided for in this Annex, competent authorities of Contracting Parties shall use the checklist included in Annex IIa and IIb. A copy of this checklist drawn up by the authority which carried it out shall be given to the driver of the bus or coach and presented on request in order to simplify or avoid, where possible, subsequent inspections within a short and unreasonable period.

3. If the vehicle examiner considers that the deficiency in the maintenance of the bus or coach justifies further examination, the bus or coach may be subjected to a roadworthiness test at an approved testing centre in accordance with Article 2 of Directive 96/96/EC.

4. Without prejudice to other penalties which may be imposed, if the consequence of the random inspection is that the bus or coach does not comply with the provisions of Directive 96/96/EC and therefore is considered to present a serious risk to its occupants or other road users, the bus or coach may be banned immediately from use on public roads.

5. Roadside checks shall be carried out without discrimination on the grounds of nationality, residence or registration of buses and coaches and drivers respectively.

ANNEX IIA

CHECKLIST

1. Place of check:.......... 2. Date:.......... 3. Time: **D2.38**

4. Vehicle nationality mark and registration number:...........................

5. Class of vehicle

☐ Coach ([1])

6. Name and address of transport operator carrying out transport:

....

7. Nationality: ....

8. Driver: ....

9. Consignor, address, place of loading: ....

10. Consignee, address, place of unloading:.....................................

11. Gross mass of unit: ....

12. Reason for failure:
    — braking system and components
    — steering linkages
    — lamps, lighting and signalling devices
    — wheels/hubs/tyres

---

[1] Motor vehicle with at least four wheels used for the carriage of passengers, comprising more than eight seats in addition o the driver's seat (categories M2, M3).

— exhaust system
— smoke opacity (diesel)
— gaseous emissions (petrol).

13. Miscellaneous/remarks

14. Authority/officer having carried out the inspection:

15. Result of inspection:
— pass
— passed with minor defects
— serious defects
— immediate prohibition.

Signature of testing inspector/Authorisation

ANNEX IIB

TECHNICAL STANDARDS OF THE ROADSIDE CHECK

D2.39   Buses and coaches as defined in Article 3 of this Agreement shall be maintained in such a condition that they can be deemed as roadworthy by the inspection authorities.

The items that shall be inspected will include those that are considered to be important for the safe and clean operation of the bus or coach. As well as simple functional checks (lighting, signalling, tyre condition, etc.), specific tests and/or inspections shall be carried out on the vehicle's brakes and the motor vehicle's emissions in the following manner:

1. Brakes

Every part of the braking system and its means of operation shall be maintained in good and efficient working order and be properly adjusted.

The bus or coach's brakes shall be capable of performing the following three braking functions:

(a) for buses and coaches and their trailers and semi-trailers, a service brake capable of slowing down the vehicle and of stopping it safely, rapidly and efficiently, whatever its conditions of loading and whatever the upward or downward gradient of the road on which it is moving;

(b) for buses and coaches and their trailers and semi-trailers, a parking brake capable of holding the bus or coach stationary, whatever its condition of loading, on a noticeable upward or downward gradient, the operative surfaces of the brake being held in the braking position by a device whose action is purely mechanical;

(c) for buses and coaches, a secondary (emergency) brake capable of slowing down and stopping the bus or coach, whatever its condition of loading, within a reasonable distance, even in the event of failure of the service brake.

Where the maintenance condition of the bus or coach is in doubt, the inspection authorities may test the bus' or coach's braking performance in accordance with some or all of the provisions of Directive 96/96/EC Annex II(I).

2. Exhaust emissions

D2.40   2.1. Exhaust emission

2.1.1. *Buses and coaches equipped with positive-ignition (petrol) engines*

(a) Where the exhaust emissions are not controlled by an advanced emission control system such as a three-way catalytic converter which is lambda-probe controlled:

1. visual inspection of the exhaust system in order to check that there is no leakage;

2. if appropriate, visual inspection of the emission control system in order to check that the required equipment has been fitted.

After a reasonable period of engine conditioning (taking account of the bus or coach manufacturer's recommendations) the carbon monoxide (CO) content of the exhaust gases is measured when the engine is idling (no load).

The maximum permissible CO content in the exhaust gases is that stated by the bus or coach manufacturer. Where this information is not available or where Member States' competent authorities decide not to use it as a reference value, the CO content must not exceed the following:

— for buses and coaches registered or put into service for the first time between the date from which Contracting Parties required the buses and coaches to comply with Directive 70/220/EEC[2] and 1 October 1986: CO—4,5% vol,

— for buses and coaches registered or put into service for the first time after 1 October 1986: CO—3,5% vol.

(b) Where the exhaust emissions are controlled by an advanced emission control system such as a three-way catalytic converter which is lambda-probe controlled:

1. visual inspection of the exhaust system in order to check that there are no leakages and that all parts are complete;

2. visual inspection of the emission control system in order to check that the required equipment has been fitted;

3. determination of the efficiency of the bus or coach's emission control system by measuring the lambda value and the CO content of the exhaust gases in accordance with Section 4 or with the procedures proposed by the manufacturers and approved at the time of type-approval. For each of the tests, the engine is conditioned in accordance with the bus or coach manufacturer's recommendations;

4. exhaust pipe emissions—limit values:

measurement at engine idling speed:

the maximum permissible CO content in the exhaust gases is that stated by the bus or coach manufacturer. Where this information is not available, the maximum CO content must not exceed 0,5% vol

Measurement at high idle speed, engine speed to be at least 2000 min[-1]:

CO content: maximum 0,3% vol

[2] Council Directive 70/220/EEC of 20 March 1970 on the approximation of the laws of the Member States relating to measures to be taken against air pollution by emissions from motor vehicles (OJ L 76, 6.4.1970, p. 1) and corrigendum (OJ L 81, 11.4.1970, p. 15), as last amended by Directive 94/12/EC of the European Parliament and of the Council (OJ L 100, 19.4.1994, p. 42).

lambda: $1 \pm 0{,}03$ in accordance with the manufacturer's specifications.

2.1.2. *Buses and coaches equipped with compression ignition (diesel) engines*

Measurement of exhaust gas opacity with free acceleration (no load from idling up to cut-off speed). The level of concentration must not exceed the level recorded on the plate pursuant to Directive 72/306/EEC.[3] Where this information is not available or where Contracting Parties' competent authorities decide not to use it as a reference, the limit values of the coefficient of absorption are as follows:

maximum coefficient of absorption for:

— naturally aspirated diesel engines = $2{,}5 \ \mathrm{m^{-1}}$,

— turbo-charged diesel engines = $3{,}0 \ \mathrm{m^{-1}}$

or equivalent values where use is made of equipment of a type different from that used for EC type-approval.

2.1.3. *Test equipment*

Buses' and coaches' emissions are tested using equipment designed to establish accurately whether the limit values prescribed or indicated by the manufacturer have been complied with.

2.2. Where appropriate, a check on the correct functioning of the on-board diagnostic (OBD) emission monitoring system.

---

[3] Council Directive 72/306/EEC of 2 August 1972 on the approximation of the laws of the Member States relating to the measures to be taken against the emission of pollutants from diesel engines for use in vehicles (OJ L 190, 20.8.1972, p. 1); Directive as last amended by Commission Directive 89/491/EEC (OJ L 238, 15.8.1989, p. 43).

ANNEX 3

MODEL OF CONTROL DOCUMENT FOR OCCASIONAL SERVICES EXEMPTED FROM AUTHORISATION

D2.41

ANNEX 3

Model of control document for occasional services exempted from authorisation

(green-coloured paper: DIN A4 = 29,7 cm x 21 cm)

(Front cover — recto)

> (To be worded in the official language(s) or one of the official languages of the Contracting Party where the transport operator is established)

State in which the control document is issued
— Distinguishing sign of the country (¹)

Competent authority or duly authorised agency

Book No ....

INTERBUS

BOOK OF PASSENGER WAYBILLS

For the international carriage of passengers by road by means of occasional coach and bus services established pursuant to:

— Articles 6 and 10 of the Agreement on the international occasional carriage of passengers by coach and bus - Interbus Agreement.

Name or trade name of the transport operator: ....

....

Address: ....

....

....
(Place and issue of book)   (Signature and stamp of the authority issuing the book)

(¹) Belgium (B), Denmark (DK), Germany (D), Greece (GR), Spain (E), France (F), Ireland (IRL), Italy (I), Luxembourg (L), Netherlands (NL), Portugal (P), United Kingdom (UK), Finland (FIN), Austria (A), Sweden (S), Bulgaria (BG), Czech Republic (CZ), Estonia (EST), Hungary (H), Lithuania (LT), Latvia (LV), Poland (PL), Romania (RO), Slovak Republic (SK), Slovenia (SLO) to be completed.

(green-coloured paper: DIN A4 = 29,7 cm × 21 cm)

(Flyleaf of the book of waybills — recto)

> (To be worded in the official language(s) or one of the official languages of the Contracting Party where the transport operator is established)

IMPORTANT NOTICE

1. Services covered by the Interbus Agreement are the following.

1. International carriage of passengers of any nationality, by road by means of occasional services:

   — between the territories of two Contracting Parties, or starting and finishing in the territory of the same Contracting Party, and should the need arise during such service, in transit through the territory of another Contracting Party or through the territory of a non-Contracting State,

   — carried out by transport operators for hire or reward established in a Contracting Party in accordance with its law and holding a licence to undertake carriage by means of international occasional services by coach and bus,

   — using buses and coaches registered in the territory of the Contracting Party where the transport operator is established which by virtue of their construction and their equipment, are suitable for carrying more than nine persons, including the driver, and are intended for that purpose.

2. Unladen journeys of the buses and coaches concerned with these services.

3. For the purposes of the Interbus Agreement, the term 'territory of a Contracting Party' covers, as far as the European Community is concerned, those territories where the Treaty establishing that Community is applied and under the conditions laid down in that Treaty.

4. The possibility of operating national occasional services in a Contracting Party by operators established in another Contracting Party is excluded from the scope of the Interbus Agreement.

5. The use of buses and coaches designed to carry passengers, for the transport of goods for commercial purposes is excluded from the scope of this Agreement.

6. The Interbus Agreement does not concern own-account occasional services.

2. International occasional services exempted from authorisation on the territory of any Contracting Party other than that in which the transport operator is established under the terms of Article 6 of the Interbus Agreement are the following:

1. Closed-door tours, that is to say services whereby the same bus or coach is used to carry the same group of passengers throughout the journey and to bring them back to the place of departure. The place of departure is in the territory of the Contracting Party in which the transport operator is established.

2. Services which make the outward journey laden and the return journey unladen. The place of departure is in the territory of the Contracting Party in which the transport operator is established.

3. Services during which the outward journey is made unladen and all the passengers are taken up in the same place, provided that one of the following conditions is met:

   a) passengers constitute groups, on the territory of a non-Contracting Party or a Contracting Party other than that in which the transport operator is established or that where the passengers are taken up, that have been formed under contracts of carriage made before their arrival in the territory of the latter Contracting Party. Passengers are carried on the territory of the Contracting Party in which the transport operator is established;

   b) passengers have been previously brought, by the same transport operator in the circumstances provided for under point 2, into the territory of the Contracting Party where they are taken up again and carried into the territory of the Contracting Party in which the transport operator is established;

   c) passengers have been invited to travel into the territory of another Contracting Party, the cost of transport being borne by the person issuing the invitation. Such passengers must constitute a homogeneous group, which has not been formed solely with a view to undertaking that particular journey and which is brought into the territory of the Contracting Party in which the transport operator is established.

4. Transit operations through Contracting Parties in conjonction with occasional services that are exempted from authorisation shall also be exempted from authorisation.

5. Unladen buses and coaches to be used exclusively for the replacement of a damaged or broken-down bus or coach, performing an international service covered by this Agreement shall also be exempted from authorisation.

For services provided by transport operators established within the European Community, the points of departure and/or destination of the services can be in any Member State of the European Community, independently of the Member State in which the bus or coach is registered or the Contracting Party in which the transport operator is established.

3. Conditions applicable to buses and coaches

Buses and coaches used to carry out international occasional services covered by the Interbus Agreement shall comply with the technical standards according to Article 5 and Annex 2 of such Agreement.

4. Information concerning the completion of the waybill

1. For each journey carried out as an occasional service the transport operator must complete a passenger waybill in duplicate, before the start of the journey.

   For the purpose of providing the names of passengers, the transport operator may use a list previously completed on a separate sheet, which shall be annexed to the passenger waybill. The transport operator's stamp or, where appropriate, the transport operator's signature or that of the driver of the vehicle must be placed both on the list and on the passenger waybill.

   For services where the outward journey is made laden, the list of passengers may be completed as provided above at the time when the passengers are taken up.

   The top copy of the passenger waybill must be kept on board the bus or coach throughout the journey and be produced whenever required by any authorised inspecting officer.

2. For services where the outward journey is made unladen, referred to in point 4C of the waybill, the transport operator must attach the following supporting documents to the passenger control document:

   — in cases mentioned under 4C1: the copy of the contract of carriage in so far as some countries require it, or any other equivalent document which establishes the essential data of this contract (especially place, country and date of conclusion, place, country and date when passengers are taken up, place and country of destination),

   — in the case of services falling within 4C2: the passenger waybill which accompanied the bus or coach during the corresponding journey made by the transport operator outward laden/return unladen in order to bring the passengers into the territory of the Contracting Party where they are taken up again,

   — in the case of services falling within 4C3: the letter of invitation from the person issuing the invitation or a photocopy thereof.

3. In the course of occasional services, no passenger may be taken up or set down during the journey, save for exemption authorised by the competent authorities. In that case an authorisation is needed.

4. The transport operator is responsible for seeing that passenger waybills are duly and correctly completed. They shall be completed in block letters and in indelible ink.

5. The book of waybills is not transferable.

INTERBUS   (PASSENGER WAYBILL — RECTO)   (Green coloured paper: DIN A4 = 29,7 cm × 21 cm)

(To be worded in the official language(s) or one of the official languages of the Contracting Party where the transport operator is established

Book No ....
Waybill No ....

(State in which the document is issued)
— Distinguishing sign of the country

	Vehicle registration No	Number of passenger seats available
2	Name or trade name of transport operator	....
3	Name of driver or drivers	1. .... 2. .... 3. ....

Type of service (put a cross in the appropriate box and add the required supplementary information)

A	Closed-door tours (kørsel uden optagning eller afsætning af passagerer undervejs)	B Outward journey laden/ return journey unladen ○ Locality where passengers are set down and distinguishing sign of the country ....

C   Outward journey unladen and all the passengers are taken up in the same place and transported to the country in which the transport operator is established
○ Locality where passengers are picked up and distinguishing sign of the country ....
....

4		

C1	(a) The passengers were grouped together, under a contract of carriage made on .... (Date)
	with .... (travel agency, association, etc.)
	(b) The passengers were grouped together on the territory of:
	   (a) non-contracting Party .... (Country)
	   (b) Contracting Party other than that in which the transport operator is established .... (Country)
	(c) Place and Contracting Party where the passengers have been taken up .... (Country)
	(d) To be carried to the Contracting Party of establishment of the transport Operator .... (Country)
	□ Copy of the contract of carriage or equivalent document is attached (cf. Important notice, point 4).	

C2	Passengers have previously been brought by the same transport operator on a service referred to in B, to the contracting Party in which they are to be taken up again and carried out into the territory of the Contracting Party in which the transport operator is established □ The passenger waybill for the previous outward laden journey and unladen return journey is attached.	
C3	Passengers have been invited to travel to .... (Place and country) Cost of transport being borne by the person issuing the invitation and the passengers constitute a homogeneous group which has not been formed solely with a view to undertaking that particular journey. The letter of invitation (or a photocopy thereof) is attached. The group is brought into the territory of the Contracting Party where the transport operator is established.	

D2.44

(Passenger waybill — verso)

Itinerary		Daily Stages				
Dates	From locality/country	To locality/country	Km laden	Km unladen	Border-crossing points	

5

List of passengers

1		22		43	
2		23		44	
3		24		45	
4		25		46	
5		26		47	
6		27		48	
7		28		49	
8		29		50	
9		30		51	
10		31		52	
11		32		53	
12		33		54	
13		34		55	
14		35		56	
15		36		57	
16		37		58	
17		38		59	
18		39		60	
19		40		61	
20		41		62	
21		42		63	

6 (list of passengers)

7 Date of completion of waybill: Signature of the transport operator:

8 Unforeseen changes:

9 Control stamps if any

(Item 6, if necessary, can be completed on a separate sheet that will be firmly affixed to this document.)

ANNEX 4

MODEL OF APPLICATION FOR AN AUTHORISATION FOR AN INTERNATIONAL OCCASIONAL SERVICE

ANNEX 4   **D2.45**

Model of application for an authorisation for an international occasional service

(White paper — A4)

> To be worded in the official language(s) or one of the official languages of the Contracting Parties where the request is made

APPLICATION FOR AN AUTHORISATION TO START AN INTERNATIONAL OCCASIONAL SERVICE

carried out by coach or bus between Contracting Parties in accordance with Article 7 of the Agreement on the international occasional carriage of passengers by coach or bus

(Interbus Agreement)

....
(Competent authority of the Contracting Party from which the service departs, namely, the first pick-up point for passengers)

1. Information concerning the applicant for authorisation:

   Name or trade name: ....

   Address: ....

   Country: ....

   Tel.: ....

   Fax: ....

D2.46

(Second page of the application)

2. Purpose, reasons and description of the occasional service:

....

....

....

....

3. Information concerning the route:

(a) Place of departure of service: .... Country: ....

(b) Place of destination of service: .... Land: ....

Principal route of service and border crossing points:

....

....

....

....

Countries whose territory is crossed without passengers being picked up or set down:

....

....

....

....

4. Date of carrying out of service: ....

5. Registration No of bus(es) or coach (es): ....

....

....

6. Any additional information:

....

....

....

....

7.

....
(Place and date)   (Signature of applicant)

(Third page of the application)

IMPORTANT NOTICE

1. Transport operators shall fill in the application form and attach evidence that the applicant has a licence to undertake carriage by means of international occasional services by coach and bus referred to in Article 1(1)(a), second indent, of the Interbus Agreement.

2. Occasional services other than those referred to in Article 6 of the Interbus Agreement shall be subject to authorisation namely, services other than the following:

   1. **closed-door tours,** that is to say services whereby the same bus or coach is used to carry the same group of passengers throughout the journey and to bring them back to the place of departure. The place of departure is in the territory of the Contracting Party in which the transport operator is established;

   2. **services which make the outward journey laden and the return journey unladen.** The place of departure is in the territory of the Contracting Party in which the transport operator is established;

   3. **services during which the outward journey is made unladen** and all the passengers are taken up in the same place, provided that one of the following conditions is met:.

      (a) passengers constitute groups, on the territory of a non-Contracting Party or of a Contracting Party other than that in which the transport operator is established or that where the passengers are taken up, that have been formed under contracts of carriage made before their arrival in the territory of the latter Contracting Party. Passengers are carried on the territory of the Contracting Party in which the transport operator is established;

      (b) passengers have been previously brought, by the same transport operator in the circumstances provided for under point 2, into the territory of the Contracting Party where they are taken up again and carried into the territory of the Contracting Party in which the transport operator is established;

      (c) passengers have been invited to travel into the territory of another Contracting Party, the cost of transport being borne by the person issuing the invitation. Such passengers must constitute a homogeneous group, which has not been formed solely with a view to undertaking that particular journey and which is brought into the territory of the Contracting Party in which the transport operator is established;

   4. **transit operations** through Contracting Parties in conjunction with occasional services that are exempted from authorisation shall also be exempted from authorisation;

   5. **unladen buses and coaches** to be used exclusively for the replacement of a bus or coach damaged or broken down while performing an international service covered by this Agreement shall also be exempted from authorisation.

   For services provided by transport operators established within the European Community, the points of departure and/or destination of the services can be in any Member State of the European Community, independently of the Member State in which the bus or coach is registered or the Member State in which the transport operator is established.

3. The application shall be made to the competent authority of the Contracting Party in which the service departs, namely, the first pick-up point for passengers.

4. The buses and coaches to be used shall be registered on the territory of the Contracting Party of establishment of the transport operator.

5. The buses and coaches used to carry out international occasional services covered by the Interbus Agreement shall comply with the technical standards laid down in Annex 2 to that agreement.

ANNEX 5

MODEL OF AUTHORISATION FOR NON-LIBERATED OCCASIONAL SERVICE

D2.48

ANNEX 5

Model of authorisation for non-liberalised occasional services

(First page of authorisation)

(Pink paper — A4)

> To be worded in the official language(s) or one of the official languages of the Contracting Parties issuing the authorisation

ISSUING CONTRACTING PARTY

— International distinguishing sign (¹)

COMPETENT AUTHORITY

(Stamp)

AUTHORISATION No ...

for an international occasional service carried out by coach or bus between Contracting Parties in accordance with Article 7 of the Agreement on the international occasional carriage of passengers by coach and bus

(Interbus Agreement)

to: ....
(Surname, first name or trade name of transport operator)

Address: ....

Country: ....

Tel. ....

Fax ....

....
(Place and date of issue)

....
(Signature and stamp of issuing authority)

(¹) Belgium (B), Denmark (DK), Germany (D), Greece (GR), Spain (E), France (F), Ireland (IRL), Italy (I), Luxembourg (L), Netherlands (NL), Portugal (P), United Kingdom (UK), Finland (FIN), Austria (A), Sweden (S), Bulgaria (BG), Czech Republic (CZ), Estonia (EST), Hungary (H), Lithuania (LT), Latvia (LV), Poland (PL), Romania (RO), Slovak Republic (SK), Slovenia (SLO) to be completed.

(Second page of authorisation)

1. Purpose, reasons and description of the occasional service:

....

....

....

....

2. Information concerning the route:

   (a) place of departure of service: .... country: ....

   (b) place of destination of service: .... country: ....

   Principal route of service and border crossing points:

....

....

....

3. Date of provision of the service: ....

4. Registration No of the bus(es) or coach(es): ....

....

5. Other conditions:

....

....

6. Passenger list attached

....
(Stamp of authority issuing authorisation)

D2.50

> To be worded in the official language(s) or one of the official languages of the Contracting Parties issuing the authorisation

IMPORTANT NOTICE

1. The authorisation is valid for the entire journey. It may only be used by a transport operator whose name and registration number of the bus or coach is indicated thereon.

2. The authorisation shall be kept on the bus or coach for the duration of the journey and shall be presented whenever enforcement officials so request.

3. The list of passengers is to be annexed to this authorisation.

Model of declaration to be made by Interbus Contracting Parties concerning Article 4 and Annex 1

Conditions applying to road passenger transport operators

DECLARATION BY .... (Name of the Contracting Party)

CONCERNING ARTICLE 4 AND ANNEX 1

1. The three conditions established in Title I of Council Directive 96/26/EC of 29 April 1996 on admission to the occupation of road haulage operator and road passenger transport operator and mutual recognition of diplomas, certificates and other evidence of formal qualification intended to facilitate for these operators the right to freedom of establishment in national and international transport operations (*Official Journal of the European Communities* L 124 of 23.5.1996, p. 1), as last amended by Council Directive 98/76/EC of 1 October 1998, (*Official Journal of the European Community* L 277 of 14.1.1998. p.17):

    (a) have been introduced in the national legislation by

    .... (reference to the Law);

    (b) will be introduced in the national legislation

    .... (date).

2. As far as the condition concerning the 'appropriate financial standing' is concerned, the existing legislation establishes that the transport operator must have available capital and reserves of at least:

    — EUR .... (or equivalent in national currency) per vehicle used or

    — EUR .... (or equivalent in national currency) per seat of the passenger transport buses or coaches used by the transport operator.

It is envisaged that the amount of the 'appropriate financial standing' will be adapted to the requirements of Directive 96/26/EC on .... (date, or no later than 1.1.2005).

[This Agreement is the copyright of the EC Commission and is reproduced from O.J. No.L321, November 26, 2002, pp.13–43.]

INDEX

FROM SWEET & MAXWELL

This index has been prepared using Sweet and Maxwell's Legal Taxonomy. Main index entries conform to keywords provided by the Legal Taxonomy except where references to specific documents or non-standard terms (denoted by quotation marks) have been included. These keywords provide a means of identifying similar concepts in other Sweet & Maxwell publications and online services to which keywords from the Legal Taxonomy have been applied. Readers may find some minor differences between terms used in the text and those which appear in the index. Suggestions to *sweetandmaxwell.taxonomy@thomson.com*

All entries are to paragraph number.

INDEX

Driving when unfit
see also Preliminary tests
causing death when under the influence, A18.16 – A18.17
detention until fit to drive, A18.42 – A18.43
exemption from licensing offences, A19.10
generally, A18.18 – A18.19
interpretation provisions, A18.44 – A18.45
tramcars, A18.451 – A18.452
Driving while disqualified
causing death by driving while disqualified, A18.14 – A18.15
generally, A18.263 – A18.264
Driving while over the limit
see also Breath tests
detention until fit to drive, A18.42 – A18.43
exemption from licensing offences, A19.10
generally, A18.20 – A18.21
interpretation provisions, A18.44 – A18.45
Driving with uncorrected defective eyesight
generally, A18.233
Driving without a licence
see also Driving licences
causing death by driving while unlicensed, A18.14 – A18.15
generally, A18.214 – A18.215
seizure of unlicensed vehicles
generally, A18.406 – A18.407
removal, retention and disposal of seized vehicles, A18.408 – A18.409
Driving without insurance
causing death by driving while uninsured, A18.14 – A18.15
generally, A18.358 – A18.359
seizure of uninsured vehicles
generally, A18.406 – A18.407
removal, retention and disposal of seized vehicles, A18.408 – A18.409
Drug driving
see Driving when unfit
Drug testing
preliminary tests, A18.28 – A18.29
"Dual carriageways"
HGV parking on central reservations, A18.66 – A18.69
speed limits, A13.73 – A13.74
traffic signs and signals
backing and mounting, B57.193
light signals, B57.46 – B57.48, B57.100 – B57.101
matrix signs, B57.57 – B57.58, B57.98 – B57.99
placing, B57.197 – B57.199
warning signals, B57.56
Dual-purpose vehicles
driving licences
competence to drive, B46.13
generally, B46.59
Duty to provide information
see Provision of information
EC law
see EU law
ECE conspicuity requirements
see Marking
Either way offences
Crown Court powers in relation to summary offences on committal, A17.08 – A17.09
penalties on summary conviction, A9.10 – A9.11
Electric vehicles
electrically assisted pedal cycles

Electric vehicles—*cont.*
age limits, A18.94 – A18.95
exclusion from definition of motor vehicles, A18.443 – A18.444
vehicle excise duty, A24.190 – A24.191, B55.06
vehicle registration, B55.06
vehicle excise duty, A24.221
Emergencies
see also Emergency vehicles
motorways
excluded traffic, B10.22
hard shoulders, B10.14
pedestrians, B10.22
passenger vehicle drivers' hours, B1.03 – B1.08
Emergency exits
see also Doors
passenger vehicles
exceptions, B9.55 – B9.62
generally, B9.25
minibuses, B15.322
obstruction, B9.39
width of gangways, B9.27 – B9.28
Emergency vehicles
blue warning beacons, B23.32
drivers' hours, A4.48 – A4.49
insurance, A18.360 – A18.361
lifeboat vehicles
RNLI track-laying vehicles, B59.55
vehicle excise duty, A24.205
motorways, B10.23
speed limits, A13.79 – A13.80
vehicle excise duty
ambulances and health service vehicles, A24.198 – A24.203
fire and rescue vehicles, A24.194 – A24.197
lifeboat vehicles, A24.205
mine rescue vehicles, A24.204
police vehicles, A24.193
Emissions
compression ignition engines, B15.390 – B15.393
end of series exemptions, B15.152 – B15.153, B15.337 – B15.363
Minister's approval certificates, B15.262 – B15.267
smoke, vapour, gases, oils, etc., B15.144 – B15.149
spark-ignition engines, B15.374 – B15.389
vehicle excise duty
light passenger vehicles with low CO_2 emissions, A24.233 – A24.234
reduced pollution certificates, A24.132 – A24.133
Endangering road users
see Causing danger to road users
Endorsements
Community licence holders, A19.222 – A19.223
deception, A19.121
discharge, combination with, A19.115 – A19.118
driver training courses
approval of courses, A19.60 – A19.61
certificates of completion, A19.58 – A19.59
reduction of penalty points, A19.56 – A19.57
supplementary provisions, A19.62 –

Identification—*cont.*
A19.245
statutory statements, A19.159 – A19.160,
A19.253 – A19.254
Ignition interlock programme orders
see Alcohol ignition interlock programme orders
Illegally obtained evidence
see Unfair evidence
Immobilisation of vehicles
see also Removal of vehicles
generally, A13.96 – A13.97
goods vehicles used without operators' licences
application of proceeds of sale, B53.28 – B53.29
applications to traffic commissioners, B53.17 – B53.18
disposal of vehicle contents, B53.27
disposal of vehicles, B53.24 – B53.25
extensions of time, B53.34 – B53.35
generally, A26.06 – A26.07, A26.88, B53.05
immobilisation, B53.08 – B53.09
interference with/removal of immobilisation notices or devices, B53.10 – B53.11
interpretation provisions, A26.89, B53.03 – B53.04
notification of detention of vehicles or property, B53.15 – B53.16
obstruction of authorised persons, A26.93, B53.31
offences (immobilisation), B53.08
offences (securing possession), A26.94 – A26.95, B53.32
release of detained vehicles, B53.06 – B53.07
release of immobilised vehicles, B53.12 – B53.13
removal and delivery of detained property, B53.14
return of detained vehicles, B53.22 – B53.23
return of vehicle contents, B53.26
invalid carriages, A13.98 – A13.99
London, A13.101 – A13.102
passenger vehicles used without operators' licences
custody of property, B69.20
detention of property, passengers and personal effects, A11.86 – A11.87
detention of vehicles and contents, B69.04
disposal of contents and personal effects, B69.18 – B69.19
disposal of vehicles, B69.17
generally, A11.18 – A11.19
immobilisation of vehicles, A11.88 – A11.89, B69.06 – B69.07
informing people of detention of property, B69.10
interpretation provisions, A11.85, B69.03
obstruction of authorised persons, A11.96, B69.23
offences relating to return of vehicles, A11.97, B69.24
passengers, B69.05
removal and delivery of property into custody of nominated custodian, B69.09
return of contents and personal effects,

Immobilisation of vehicles—*cont.*
B69.08, B69.18
return of vehicles, B69.11 – B69.12
sale or destruction of vehicles, B69.17
sale proceeds, B69.21
prohibition of driving
application of immobilisation powers, B67.04
application of RTOA 1988, A33.14, B67.20
authorised persons, A33.13
disputes, A33.12, B67.19
immobilisation of vehicles, A33.08, B67.05
interpretation provisions, A33.15 – A33.19, B67.03
offences (failure to move vehicles), B67.06
offences (immobilisation), A33.09, B67.07 – B67.08
offences (securing possession), A33.11, B67.09
relevant cases, A33.07
removal and disposal of vehicles, A33.10, B67.10 – B67.18
uninsured vehicles
application of RTOA 1988, A18.491
authorised persons, A18.490
disputes, A18.489
generally, A18.368 – A18.369, A18.485
interpretation provisions, A18.492 – A18.494
offences (immobilisation), A18.486
offences (securing possession), A18.488
removal and disposal of vehicles, A18.487
unlicensed vehicles
application of provisions, A24.253 – A24.254
authorised persons, A24.251 – A24.252, B38.06
disapplication of regulations, B38.07 – B38.08
disposal, A24.239 – A24.240, B38.14 – B38.23
disputes, A24.249 – A24.250, B38.26 – B38.27
generally, A24.69 – A24.70
immobilisation, A24.235 – A24.236, B38.09 – B38.10
interference with/removal of immobilisation notices or devices, B38.13
interpretation provisions, A24.255 – A24.260, B38.04 – B38.05
offences (immobilisation), A24.237 – A24.238, B38.13 – B38.15
offences (securing possession), A24.241 – A24.242, B38.22
offences (vouchers), A24.245 – A24.246, B38.25
payment of sums where licence not produced, A24.243 – A24.244, B38.24 – B38.25
release, B38.11 – B38.12
removal, A24.239 – A24.240, B38.14 – B38.23
vouchers, A24.247 – A24.248, B38.24 – B38.25
Impairment tests
preliminary tests, A18.26 – A18.27
Impersonation
vehicle examiners, A18.429, A24.94 – A24.95

Light rail—*cont.*
  tramcars, B25.03 – B25.04, B25.07 –
      B25.08
  transitional provisions, B25.13 – B25.18
  trolley vehicles, B25.05 – B25.06,
      B25.09 – B25.10
  road traffic regulation, A13.138 – A13.139
  signs, B57.78
  traffic signals, B57.51 – B57.52
  vehicle excise duty, A24.189
Light signals
  see Traffic signals
Lights
  amber warning beacons
    generally, B23.33, B23.51, B23.105
    mobile cranes, B59.110
    recovery vehicles, B59.163, B59.170
  Approval Regulations, vehicles approved
      under, B23.20 – B23.21
  bicycles, B23.57
  blue warning beacons, B23.32
  brake lights, B23.98 – B23.99
  colour, B23.23 – B23.24
  dim-dip devices, B23.69 – B23.74
  dipped-beam headlights, B23.76 – B23.77,
      B23.135
  direction indicators, B23.81 – B23.87
  electrical connections, B23.31
  end-outline marker lights, B23.48 – B23.49,
      B23.100 – B23.101
  equivalent standards, B23.08 – B23.09
  European approval marks, B23.01
  exemptions
    generally, B23.10
    hand-drawn/hand-propelled vehicles,
        B23.17
    invalid carriages, B23.16
    military vehicles, B23.15
    temporarily imported vehicles, B23.13
    towing/towed vehicles, B23.14
    tramcars, B23.18 – B23.19
    vehicle examiners, B23.11 – B23.12
    vehicles proceeding to port for export,
        B23.13
  filament lights, B23.29 – B23.30
  fog lights
    front fog lights, B23.50, B23.80
    rear fog lights, B23.95 – B23.97
  front position lights
    dim-dip devices and running lights, B23.69
        – B23.74
    requirements, B23.48 – B23.49, B23.63 –
        B23.68
  hand-drawn/hand-propelled vehicles
    exemptions, B23.17
    obligatory lights, reflectors, rear markings
        and devices, B23.59
  hazard warning lights, B23.88
  headlights
    dipped-beam headlights, B23.76 – B23.77,
        B23.135
    generally, B23.50
    main-beam headlights, B23.78 – B23.79
  horse-drawn vehicles, B23.58
  indicators, B23.81 – B23.87
  inspection, B23.54
  interpretation provisions, B23.06 – B23.07
  invalid carriages
    exemptions, B23.16
    requirements, B22.09 – B22.10
  main-beam headlights, B23.78 – B23.79

Lights—*cont.*
  maintenance, B23.46 – B23.47
  military vehicles, B23.15
  minibus steps, B15.331
  motorcycles, B23.56
  movement, B23.25 – B23.26
  number plate lights, B23.48 – B23.49,
      B23.104, B50.12
  obligatory lights, reflectors, rear markings
      and devices
    amber warning beacons, B23.33, B23.51,
        B23.105
    bicycles, B23.57
    generally, B23.36 – B23.37
    hand-drawn/hand-propelled vehicles,
        B23.59
    horse-drawn vehicles, B23.58
    motor vehicles, B23.55
    motorcycles, B23.56
    obscuration, B23.38
    pedestrian-controlled vehicles, B23.58
    track-laying vehicles, B23.58
    trailers drawn by bicycles, B23.61
    trailers drawn by motor vehicles, B23.60
  obscuration, B23.38
  optional lights, reflectors, rear markings and
      devices, B23.39 – B23.40
  overhanging loads or equipment, B23.43 –
      B23.44
  passenger vehicles
    generally, B9.42
    internal lighting, B9.17
  pedestrian-controlled vehicles, B23.58
  prohibited uses, B23.52 – B23.53
  projecting trailers, loads or equipment,
      B23.43 – B23.44
  rear fog lights, B23.95 – B23.97
  rear markings
    maintenance, B23.46 – B23.47
    obligatory markings, B23.36 – B23.37
    optional markings, B23.39 – B23.40
    requirements, B23.113 – B23.126
  rear position lights
    generally, B23.48 – B23.49, B23.91 –
        B23.94
    sale of non-compliant lights, A18.206 –
        A18.207
  rear registration plate lights, B23.48 –
      B23.49, B23.104, B50.12
  reflectors
    front retro reflectors, B23.129 – B23.131
    maintenance, B23.46 – B23.47
    obligatory reflectors, B23.36 – B23.37
    obscuration, B23.38
    optional reflectors, B23.39 – B23.40
    pedal retro reflectors, B23.127 – B23.128
    rear retro reflectors, B23.109 – B23.112
    sale of non-compliant reflectors, A18.206 –
        A18.207
    side retro reflectors, B23.106 – B23.108
  reversing lights, B23.102 – B23.103
  road marking illumination, B57.38 – B57.39
  road sign illumination, B57.23 – B57.26,
      B57.125 – B57.126
  running lights, B23.69 – B23.74
  sale of non-compliant tail lights, A18.206 –
      A18.207
  school bus signs, B23.34 – B23.35,
      B23.132 – B23.133
  seriously reduced visibility, B23.48 – B23.49
  side marker lights

Test certificates
see MoT certificates
Test vehicles
authorisation requirements, B59.38
carriage of loads, B59.211 – B59.213
conditions of use, B59.214 – B59.216
interpretation provisions, B59.207
length requirements, B59.39
passenger vehicles, A11.15
recognised categories, B59.37
restrictions on use, B59.208 – B59.210
weight requirements, B59.41
width requirements, B59.40
Testing
see Vehicle tests
Theft Act offences
aggravated vehicle-taking, A3.04 – A3.05
going equipped to steal, A3.06 – A3.07
taking vehicles without consent, A3.01 –
A3.03
Time limits
commencement of proceedings
generally, A19.11 – A19.12
specified offences, A19.228 – A19.245
detention without charge, A14.39 – A14.40
Toilets
see Sanitary conveniences
Toucan crossings
see Pedestrian crossings
Towing
see also Trailers
holding or getting on to vehicles to be towed
or carried, A18.82 – A18.83
lights, B23.14
recovery vehicles, B59.165 – B59.169
Track-laying vehicles
see also Engineering plant; Special vehicles
agricultural vehicles, B59.27 – B59.28
authorisation requirements, B59.43
lights, B23.58
recognised categories, B59.42
restrictions on use, B59.44
RNLI vehicles, B59.55
road authority consent, B59.45
speed limits, A13.150 – A13.152
tracks, B15.66
Tractive units
see Articulated vehicles
Tractors
see Agricultural vehicles
Trade licences
see also Vehicle licences
change of name or address, B55.33 – B55.34
conditions, B55.60, B55.100 – B55.106
issue, A24.19 – A24.20
motor traders, definition of, B55.58
multiple licences, A24.23
offences, A24.73 – A24.74
permitted use of vehicles
generally, A24.21, B55.61
interpretation provisions, B55.107 –
B55.108
manufacturers keeping vehicles for
research and development, B55.113
motor traders, B55.109 – B55.112
vehicle testers, B55.114
registration marks
assignment, B55.62
display, B55.66 – B55.67
surrender, A24.23
trade plates

Trade licences—*cont.*
issue, B55.63 – B55.64
replacements, B55.65
Traffic authorities
see Highway authorities
Traffic commissioners
conduct of goods/passenger vehicle licence
holders
grant of licences, A18.284 – A18.285
revocation/suspension of licences,
A18.292 – A18.293
goods vehicle driving licences, A18.280 –
A18.281
notifications by goods vehicle operators,
A26.33 – A26.34
passenger vehicle operators
disclosure of convictions, A11.28 –
A11.29, B33.24, B33.32 – B33.34
provision of information on vehicles,
A11.30 – A11.31
Traffic cones
see Traffic signs (temporary obstructions)
Traffic cylinders
see Traffic signs (temporary obstructions)
Traffic directions
motorways, B10.23
pedestrians, A18.103 – A18.104
vehicles, A18.99 – A18.100
Traffic lights
see Traffic signals
Traffic management
see also Traffic directions
events held on roads, A13.23 – A13.28
experimental traffic schemes, A13.11 –
A13.14
special roads, A13.29 – A13.31
temporary prohibitions or restrictions on
roads
events held on roads, A13.23 – A13.28
generally, A13.18 – A13.22
traffic directions
motorways, B10.23
pedestrians, A18.103 – A18.104
vehicles, A18.99 – A18.100
Traffic officers
production of passenger/goods vehicle documents, A18.410 – A18.411
removal and disposal of vehicles
abandoned vehicles on land adjoining relevant roads, B66.08
interpretation provisions, B66.02
method of removal, B66.11
notice to occupiers of land, B66.09
objections by occupiers of land, B66.10
relevant roads, B66.03 – B66.04
restrictions on exercise of powers, B66.07
roads other than relevant roads, B66.05 –
B66.06
waiting restrictions, B66.13 – B66.15
traffic directions
motorways, B10.23
pedestrians, A18.103 – A18.104
vehicles, A18.99 – A18.100
Traffic orders
contravention, A13.03 – A13.04
experimental traffic orders, A13.11 – A13.14
Greater London, A13.05 – A13.10
Traffic pyramids
see Traffic signs (temporary obstructions)
Traffic regulation orders
see Traffic orders

Working time—*cont.*
    generally, B61.21
    offences due to fault of others, B61.22
  penalties, C9.14
  periods of availability, B61.09
  prohibition notices
    appeals, B61.33
    generally, B61.31
    supplementary provisions, B61.32
  prosecutions
    consent to prosecute, B61.24
    inspectors, B61.25

Working time—*cont.*
  records, B61.13 – B61.16, C9.12
  reference periods, B61.07
  rest periods, B61.11, C9.09
Works services
  see International passenger transport
Works trucks
  number plates, B50.11
Workshop cards
  see Tachographs
Zebra crossings
  see Pedestrian crossings